ISBN 978-0-260-69969-5
PIBN 10964974

FB &c Ltd, Dalton House, 60 Windsor Avenue, London, SW19 2RR.
Company number 08720141. Registered in England and Wales.

For support please visit www.forgottenbooks.com

THE

ACTS AND RESOLVES,

PUBLIC AND PRIVATE,

OF THE

PROVINCE OF THE MASSACHUSETTS BAY:

PRESENTED BY

The Commonwealth of Massachusetts

TO Uriel H. Crocker.

HENRY B. PEIRCE,
Secretary of the Commonwealth.

ELLIS AMES,
A. C. GOODELL,
Commissioners.

(UNDER RESOLVE 1870, CHAP. 20.)

VOLUME III.

THE

ACTS AND RESOLVES,

PUBLIC AND PRIVATE,

OF THE

PROVINCE OF THE MASSACHUSETTS BAY:

TO WHICH ARE PREFIXED

THE CHARTERS OF THE PROVINCE.

WITH

HISTORICAL AND EXPLANATORY NOTES, AND AN APPENDIX.

PUBLISHED UNDER CHAPTER 87 OF THE RESOLVES OF THE GENERAL COURT
OF THE COMMONWEALTH FOR THE YEAR 1867.

VOLUME III.

BOSTON:
PRINTED FOR THE COMMONWEALTH, BY ALBERT J. WRIGHT,
CORNER OF MILK AND FEDERAL STREETS.
1878.

ACTS,

PASSED 1742–43.

ACTS

PASSED AT THE SESSION BEGUN AND HELD AT BOSTON, ON THE TWENTY-SIXTH DAY OF MAY, A. D. 1742.

CHAPTER 1.

AN ACT FOR GRANTING THE SUM OF TWO THOUSAND THREE HUNDRED AND FIFTY POUNDS FOR THE SUPPORT OF HIS MAJESTY'S GOVERNOUR.

Preamble.

WHEREAS there have been sundry grants made for his excellency's support, which alth[ô][*ough*] pass['][*e*]d both houses, have not been consented to by him, nor has his excellency received any thing for his support, since the arrival of the royal commission to him,—

*Be it enacted by the Governour, Council and House of Representatives,**

£2,350 granted to the governor.

That the sum of two thousand three hundred and fifty pounds in bills of credit, equal to those of the last emission, be and hereby is granted unto his most excellent majesty to be paid out of the publick treasury to his excellency, William Shirley, Esq[r]., captain-general and governour-in-ch[ei][*ie*]f in and over this his majesty's province of the Massachusetts Bay, for his past services since his taking upon himself the administration of the government; and further to enable him to go on in managing the publick affairs. [*Passed June 4.*

* The eleventh article of instructions issued to Governor Dudley, March 5, 1701-2, is as follows: "Art. 11. The style of enacting laws to be 'by the Governor, Council and Assembly' and no other."

This instruction, in substance, was renewed to every succeeding governor. It was the eleventh of Burgess's and Shute's instructions, the seventh of Burnet's and Shirley's, the eighth of Belcher's, the fifth of Bernard's, and the sixth of Pownal's, Hutchinson's and Gage's. In Belcher's, and his successors', however, the word "Assembly" was dropped, and "House of Representatives" substituted therefor.

The objectionable words, "*and by the authority of the same,*" by which, in the enacting clause of the first act under the charter, the colonists had appeared to assert their autonomy, were from this time omitted, as a concession to Governor Shirley, who, accordingly, in a letter dated November 11, 1742, reported to the Duke of Newcastle his success in securing this compliance with the royal instructions.

This change, it will be observed, was first made towards the close of the last session of the previous year (1741-42, chapters 18, 20, 23 and 24); but, except in chapter 20, the objectionable words, though omitted before the leading enacting clause, were retained before certain sections of those acts.

CHAPTER 2.

AN ACT FOR ALLOWING NECESSARY SUPPLIES TO THE EASTERN AND WESTERN INDIANS, AND FOR REGULATING TRADE W[I]TH THEM.

Preamble. 1737-38, chap. 7. 1740-41, chap. 11.

WHEREAS the Indians in the eastern and western parts of this province have many years since acknowledged their subjection and obedience to the crown of Great Britain, and have their dependance on this government for supplies of cloathing and other necessaries; to the intent, therefore, that they may be furnished with the same at such easy rates and prices as may oblige them to a firm adherence to his maj[es]ty's interest, several truck-houses having been erected and set up for that purpose,—

Be it enacted by the Governour, Council and House of Represent-[ati]ves,

Clothing, provisions, &c., to be prepared for the trade with the Indians.

[SECT. 1.] That provisions, cloathing and other supplies suitable for a trade with the said Indians be procured with the several sums that have been, now are, or shall be hereafter granted for that purpose by the general court, and the produce thereof applied, from time to time, for the supplying the said Indians as aforesaid, by such person or persons as shall annually be chosen by this court, who shall proceed according to the instructions they shall receive from this court, or from the governour and council on any emergency in the recess of this court: *provided*, such instructions and directions be consistent with the instructions they receive from the general court; which person or persons so chosen shall annually lay before this court fair accounts of his or their proceedings herein; and all supplies of cloathing, provisions and other things shall be lodged at such places, to the eastward and elsewhere, as the general court have heretofore ordered, or as they shall from time to time order and appoint.

Accounts of the trade to be annually laid before the General Court.

And be it further enacted,

Truck-masters to be appointed by the General Court.

[SECT. 2.] That a suitable person be appointed by this court for each of the places where any of the goods aforesaid are lodged, as a truck-master, to have the care and management of the trade with the Indians, the said truck-masters to draw commissions for their service at the rate of five per cent only, both for sales and returns, on the goods they shall trade with; which truck-masters shall be under oath, and shall give sufficient security for the faithful discharge of that trust, and attending such instructions as shall be from time to time given them by this court, and, in the recess of the court, by the governo[u]r and council as aforesaid; and the said truck-masters shall keep fair acco[un]ts of their trade and dealing with the s[ai]d Indians, and shall return the same, together with the produce thereof, from time to time, to the person or persons who shall be appointed to supply them with the goods as afores[ai]d, the said accounts to be laid before the court. And neither the truck-master, nor any officer or soldier residing at any of the truck-houses, either on account of themselves, or any other person or persons, shall be suffered to trade with or barter for any goods, wares or merchandize, or other thing whatsoever, with any Indian or Indians, upon pain that every truck-master, officer or soldier so offending, shall, on conviction thereof, forfeit and pay the sum of twenty-five pounds for each offence, to be recovered by bill, plaint or information in any of his majesty's courts of record[s] within this province; and any officer or truck-master so offending, is hereby disqualified and declared uncapable of serving as an officer or truck-master in the pay and service of this province ever after such offence; and in case of the death of any truck-master, or mismanagem[en]t in that trust, during the recess of the

To be allowed five per cent for their service.

Truck-masters not to trade on their own account.

court, another shall be put in his place by the governo[*u*]r, w[*i*]th the advice of the council, until[l] the next session of the general court.

And be it further enacted,

[Sect. 3.] That the said truck-masters shall sell the goods to the Indians at the price set in the invoice sent them from time to time, without any advance thereon, and shall allow the Indians for their fur[r]s and other goods as the market shall be in Boston, according to the latest advices they shall receive from the person or persons that shall supply them for the same commodities of equal goodness; and that the truck-masters do supply the Indians with rum in moderate quantities, as they shall in prudence judge convenient and necessary, at the rate as charged in the invoices from time to time. Goods to be sold according to invoice.

[Sect. 4.] And in case any of the said truck-masters shall presume to sell any goods at higher rates than they are set at by the government, or shall charge to the governm[*en*]t more for any furrs or other goods than they allowed the Indians for the same, such truck-master, being convicted thereof, shall forfeit and pay the sum of fifty pounds; and the more effectually to prevent such fraud, and also all private trading with said Indians, each and every truck-master, when and so often as he shall settle and adjust his account with the officer appointed by this court for supplying the Indians, shall make oath before the s[*ai*]d officer, who is hereby authorized and required to administer the same in manner following:—

You, A. B., do swear that the goods committed to you for the supply of the Indians, have been sold at no higher rates than they were set at by the government, and that you have charged for the furrs and other goods you have made returns of, no more than you paid the Indians for the same; and that you have not, directly [n]or indirectly, been concerned in any trade with said Indians on your private or particular acco[*un*]t, and have not countenanced or connived at any such trade managed or transacted by any person under you. So help you God. Oath.

And be it further enacted,

[Sect. 5.] That from and after the publication of this act, no person or persons whatsoever, other than the truck-masters that shall be appointed in manner as is before provided, shall or may presume, by themselves or any other for them, directly or indirectly, to sell, give, truck, barter or exchange to any of the aforesaid Indians, any strong beer, ale, cyder, perry, wine, rum, brandy, or any other strong liquor, by what name or names soever called or known, on penalty of forfeiting the sum of twenty-five pounds for each offence; and in case any rum or strong liquor shall be sold or traded with on board any vessel, or transported into those parts for sale, the person or persons so trading with the Indians in rum and other strong liquors, shall forfeit [*and pay*] the sum of one hundred pounds for each offence; and the offences aforesaid shall be tried at any of his majesty's courts of record within this province; and the justices of the said courts are accordingly impow[e]red and directed to hear and determine thereon, the plaintiff or complainant filing his information at least fourteen days before the sitting of the court, in the clerk's office of said court before whom the matter is to be heard and tried; and the plaintiff shall also summon or notify the defendant thereof according to law: one moiety of all fines and forfeitures arising by virtue of this act, to be laid out in procuring supplies for carrying on the trade with the Indians, the other moiety to him or them that shall inform and sue for the same in any of the courts aforesaid. Private persons not to sell strong drink to the Indians. Penalty.

[Sect. 6.] This act to continue and be in force till the end of the session of the general assembly in May, one thousand seven hundred and forty-three, and no longer. [*Passed July* 1. Limitation.

CHAPTER 3.

AN ACT FOR SUPPLYING THE TREASURY WITH THE SUM OF FIFTEEN THOUSAND POUNDS, FOR DISCHARGING THE PUBLICK DEBTS, &c[A], AND FOR DRAWING IN THE SAID BILLS INTO THE TREASURY AGAIN, AND FOR STATING THEIR VALUE IN DISCHARGING OF PUBLICK AND PRIVATE DEBTS.

Be it enacted by the Governour, Council and House of Representatives,

£15,000 in bills of credit to be emitted.

[SECT. 1.] That there be forthwith imprinted a certain number of bills of credit of this province of the same tenor and form with the bills last emitted by this court at their sessions in November last, and to be always valued and taken in all publick payments as those of the last emission by law are or shall be, which in the whole shall amount to the sum of fifteen thousand pounds and no more; the said bills to be signed by the committee already appointed by this court for that purpose; and the said committee are hereby directed and impowered to take care and make effectual provision, so soon as may be, to imprint the said bills, and to sign and deliver the same to the treasurer, taking his receipt for the same; and the said committee shall be under oath for the faithful performance of the trust by this act reposed in them.

And be it further enacted,

Appropriations of this emission.

[SECT. 2.] That the treasurer be and hereby is impowered to issue forth and emit the said sum of fifteen thousand pounds for the necessary support and defence of the government, and the protection and preservation of the inhabitants thereof; viz[t]., the sum of five thousand six hundred and fifty pounds, part of the aforesaid sum of fifteen thousand pounds, shall be applied for the payment of the wages that now are or that hereafter may be due by virtue of the establishment of Castle William, Richmond Fort, George's Truck-House, Saco Truck-House, Brunswick Fort, the block-house above Northfield, the sloop in the country's service, and the province snow, and the treasurer's usual disbursements; the sum of two thousand six hundred and fifty pounds, part of the aforesaid sum of fifteen thousand pounds, shall be applied for the payment of a grant made to his excellency, William Shirley, Esq[r]., captain-general and governour-in-chief, and to pay the members of his majesty's council; the sum of three thousand and two hundred pounds, part of the aforesaid sum of fifteen thousand pounds, shall be applied for the payment of such other grants as are or shall be made by this court, and for the payment of stipends, bounties and premiums established by law, and for the payment of all other matters and things which this court have or shall, either by law or orders, provide for the payment of, out of the publick treasury, and for no other purpose whatsoever; the sum of twelve hundred pounds, part of the aforesaid sum of fifteen thousand pounds, shall be applied for the discharge of other debts owing from this province to persons who have served or shall serve them, by order of this court, in such matters [and] [*or*] things where there is no establishment, nor any certain sum assigned for such service; and for paper, printing and writing for this court, the expences of committees of council, or of the house, or of both houses, entertainment of Indians, and presents made them by this court, the surgeon of Castle William, and wooding of said castle; and the sum of eighteen hundred pounds, part of the aforesaid sum of fifteen thousand pounds, shall be applied to the payment of the members of the house of representatives serving in the general court, during their several sessions this present year until May next.

£5,650 for wages of officers, soldiers, and seamen, and the treasurer's disbursements.

£2,650 for the governor and council.

£3,200 for grants, &c.

£1,200 for debts, where there is no establishment.

£1,800 for the representatives.

And whereas, there are, sometimes, publick entertainments, and, from time to time, contingent and unforeseen charges that demand prompt payment,—

Be it further enacted,

[Sect. 3.] That the sum of five hundred pounds, the remaining part of the aforesaid sum of fifteen thousand pounds, be applied to defrey and pay such entertainments and contingent charges, and for no other use whatsoever. £500 for contingent charges.

And be it enacted,

[Sect. 4.] That if there be a surplusage in any sum appropriated, such surplusage shall lie in the treasury for the further order of this court. Surplusage to lie in the treasury.

And be it further enacted,

[Sect. 5.] That each and every warrant for drawing money out of the treasury shall direct the treasurer to take the same out of such sums as are respectively appropriated for the payment of such publick debts as the draughts are made to discharge; and the treasurer is hereby directed and ordered to pay such money out of such appropriations as directed to, and no other, upon pain of refunding all such sum or sums as he shall otherwise pay, and to keep exact and distinct accompts of all payments made out of such appropriated sums; and that the secretary to whom it belongs to keep the muster rolls and accompts of charge, shall lay before the house, when they shall direct, all such muster rolls and accompts after payment thereof. Warrants to express the appropriations.

And as a fund and security for drawing the said sum of fifteen thousand pounds into the treasury again,—

Be it further enacted,

[Sect. 6.] That there be and hereby is granted unto his most excellent majesty, for the ends and uses aforesaid, a tax of three thousand seven hundred and fifty pounds, to be levied on polls, and estates both real and personal, within this province, according to such rules and in such proportions on the several towns and districts within the same, as shall be agreed upon and ordered by this court in their present session, and paid into the treasury on or before the last day of December next. £3,750 to be brought in, in the year 1742.

And as a further fund and security for drawing the remaining part of the said sum of fifteen thousand pounds into the treasury again,—

Be it further enacted,

[Sect. 7.] That there be and hereby is granted unto his most excellent majesty, for the ends and uses aforesaid, a tax of three thousand seven hundred and fifty pounds, to be levied on polls, and estates both real and personal, within this province, according to such rules and in such proportion on the several towns and districts within the same, as shall be agreed upon and ordered by this court at their session in May, one thousand seven hundred and forty-three, and paid into the publick treasury on or before the last day of December then next after. £3,750 in 1743.

And as a further fund and security for drawing the remaining part of the said sum of fifteen thousand pounds into the treasury again,—

Be it further enacted,

[Sect. 8.] That there be and hereby is granted unto his most excellent majesty, for the ends and uses aforesaid, a tax of three thousand seven hundred and fifty pounds, to be levied on polls, and estates both real and personal, within this province, according to such rules and in such proportion on the several towns and districts within the same, as shall be agreed upon and ordered by the great and general court or assembly at their session in May, one thousand seven hundred and forty-four, and paid into the publick treasury again on or before the last day of December then next after. £3,750 in 1744.

And as a further fund and security for drawing the remaining part of the said sum of fifteen thousand pounds into the treasury again,—

Be it enacted,

£1,950 in 1745. [SECT. 9.] That there be and hereby is granted unto his most excellent majesty for the ends and uses aforesaid, a tax of one thousand nine hundred and fifty pounds, to be levied on polls, and estates both real and personal, within this province, according to such rules and in such proportion on the several towns and districts within the same, as shall be agreed upon and ordered by the great and general court or assembly at their session in May, one thousand seven hundred and forty-five, and paid into the public[*k*] treasury again on or before the last day of December then next after.

And as a fund and security for drawing in such sum or sums as shall be paid out to the representatives of the several towns,—

Be it enacted,

Tax to be made for what is paid to the representatives. [SECT. 10.] That there be and hereby is granted unto his most excellent majesty a tax of such sum or sums as shall be paid to the several representatives as aforesaid, to be levied and assessed on the polls and estates of the inhabitants of the several towns according to what their respective representatives shall so receive, which sums shall be set on the said towns in the next province tax. And the assessors of the said towns shall make their assessment for this tax, and apportion the same according to the rule that shall be prescribed by act of the general assembly, for assessing the next province tax; and the constables in their respective districts shall pay in the same when they pay in the province tax for the next year: of which the treasurer is hereby directed to keep a distinct and sep[e][*a*]rate account; and if there be any surplusage, the same shall l[y][*i*]e in the hands of the treasurer for the further order of this court.

And be it further enacted,

Tax for the money hereby emitted to be made according to the preceding tax act, in case. [SECT. 11.] That in case the general court shall not in their present sessions, and at their respective sessions in May, one thousand seven hundred and forty-three, one thousand seven hundred and forty-four, and one thousand seven hundred and forty-five, agree and conclude upon an act apportioning the several sums which by this act is engaged shall be in each of these several years apportioned, assessed and levied, that then and in such case each town and district within this province shall pay (by a tax to be levied on the polls and estates, both real and personal, within their districts) the same part and proportion of the said sums as the said towns or districts shall have been taxed by the general court in the tax act then next preceding; and the province treasurer is hereby fully impowered and directed, some time in the present session, and some time in the month of June in each of these years, one thousand seven hundred and forty-three, one thousand seven hundred and forty-four, and one thousand seven hundred and forty-five, to issue and send forth his warrants, directed to the selectmen or assessors of each town and district within this province, in manner as aforementioned in this act, requiring them to assess the polls, and estates both real and personal, within their respective towns or districts for their respective part and proportion of the several sums before directed and engaged to be assess[*e*]'d by this act, and the assessors, as also persons assess[*e*]'d, shall observe, be governed by, and subject to, all such rules and directions as shall have been given in the said next preceeding tax act.

And be it further enacted,

Taxes to be paid in the several species herein enumerated. [SECT. 12.] That the inhabitants of this province shall have liberty, if they see fit, to pay the several sums for which they respectively may, in pursuance of this act, be assess[*e*]'d, in bills of credit hereby emitted, according to their several denominations; or in coined silver, at six shillings and eightpence per ounce, troy weight, and of sterling alloy, or in coined gold, proportionably; or in merchantable hemp, flax, winter and Isle-of-Sable codfish, refin[*e*]'d bar-iron, bloomery-iron, h[o][*a*]llow iron-ware, Indian corn, rye, wheat, barley, pork, beef, duck or canvas, whalebone, cordage, train-oyl, beeswax, baberry-wax, tallow, pease, sheepswool, or tann[*e*]'d sole-leather (the aforesaid commodities being of the produce or manufactures of this province), at such moderate rates and prices as the respective general assemblies of the present year and of the years one thousand seven hundred and forty-three, one thousand seven hundred and forty-four, and one thousand seven hundred and forty-five, shall set them at; the several persons paying their taxes in any of the commodities aforementioned, to run the risque and pay the charge of transporting the said commodities to the province treasury; but if the aforesaid general assemblies shall not, at their respective sessions in May, some time before the twentieth day of June, agree upon and set the aforesaid species or commodities at some certain prices, that then the eldest councello[u]r, for the time being, of each of those count[y][*ie*]s in the province, of which any one of the council is an inhabitant, together with the province treasurer, or the major part of them, be a committee, who hereby are directed and fully authorized and impower[*e*]d to do it; and in their setting of the prices and rating the value of those commodit[y][*ie*]s, to state so much of them, respectively, at six shillings and eightpence as an ounce of silver will purchase at that time in the town of Boston, and so *pro ratâ*. And the treasurer is hereby directed to insert in the several warrants by him sent to the collectors of the taxes in those years, respectively, with the names of the afore-recited commodities, the several prices or rates which shall be set on them, either by the general assembly or the committee aforesaid, and direct the aforesaid collectors to receive them so.

How the commodities brought into the treasury are to be rated.

[Sect. 13.] And the aforesaid commodities so brought into the treasury, shall, as soon as conveniently may be, be disposed of by the treasurer to the best advantage for so much as it will fetch in bills of credit hereby to be emitted, or for silver or gold; which silver and gold shall be delivered to the possessor of said bills in exchange for them; that is to say, one ounce of silver coin, and so gold in proportion, for six shillings and eightpence, and *pro ratâ* for a greater or less sum. And if any loss shall happen by the sale of the aforesaid species, or by any unforeseen accident, such deficiency shall be made good by a tax of the year next following, so as fully and effectually to call in the whole sum of fifteen thousand pounds in said bills hereby ordered to be emitted; and if there be a surplusage it shall remain a stock in the treasury.

Treasurer to sell the said commodities.

And be it further enacted,

[Sect. 14.] That any debt contracted before the thirty-first day of October last, which might have been paid and discharged in and by province bills of the old tenor, and also any debt contracted between the said thirty-first day of October and the first day of April last (where the contracting parties have not expressly otherwise agreed) may be discharged by the bills by this act to be emitted, in proportion as one to four; that is to say, that a debt of twenty-six shillings and eightpence, dischargeable or contracted as aforesaid, may be discharged by six shillings and eightpence in bills by this act to be emitted, or by one ounce of silver, and so in proportion for a greater or less sum. [*Passed July* 1.

Rules for paying private debts.

CHAPTER 4.

AN ACT IN ADDITION TO AND FOR REND[E]RING MORE EFFECTUAL AN ACT FOR REGULATING THE ASSIZE OF CASK, AND PREVENTING DECEIT IN PACKING OF FISH, BEEF AND PORK, FOR SALE, MADE IN THE FOURTH YEAR OF THE REIGN OF KING WILLIAM AND QUEEN MARY; AND ALSO FOR THE PREVENTING FRAUD AND INJUSTICE IN THE MEASURING OF GRAIN.

Preamble. 1692-3, chap. 17. 1718-19, chap. 16. 1722-23, chap. 4. 1730-31, chap. 5. 1737-38, chap. 12.

WHEREAS there does daily appear great fraud and deceit in the packing of beef and pork and other provisions, the produce of other colonies vended or consumed in this province; and whereas the act or law already made for preventing such fraud and deceit hath been found ineffectual for that purpose, so that a further provision is necessary to be made,—

Be it therefore enacted by the Governo[u]r, Council and House of Repres[entati]ves,

Pork, beef, and fish to be repacked and pickled.

[SECT. 1.] That from and after the first day of October next, all barrels and other casks of pork, beef, fish or other provision imported into this province shall be repacked and pickled before the same shall be sold or exposed to sale to any person whatsoever; which repacking and pickling shall be performed and done by fit persons appointed for that purpose, for every town where such provisions are usually brought for sale, or from whence they are exported for a foreign market. And the justices of the peace in the several counties are hereby impowered and directed, at their first general quarter-sessions to be holden in each respective county in this province, yearly, to appoint a suitable number of persons for each town as aforesaid, and to swear them to the due and faithful[l] execution of their office; and any such person so appointed refusing to officiate, shall be liable and subject as in and by the act of the fourth of King William and Queen Mary.

Packer to be chosen and sworn. 1692-3, chap. 17.

And be it further enacted,

Assize of cask and quantity of meat, &c.

[SECT. 2.] That all cask used for packing fish, beef, pork or any other commodity imported as afores[ai]d within this province, being of the full assize required in the aforesaid act, and as free of sap as may be, each and every barrel of merchantable pork imported here, when exposed to sale in any town or place within this province where such officers or packers shall have been appointed as aforesaid, after being repacked and pickled as afores[ai]d, shall contain at least two hundred and twenty pounds of pork; and there shall not be pack'd in any barrel more than four legs, four shoulders and four half-heads, and every half-barrel and greater or lesser cask shall be in proportion; and each and every barrel of merchantable beef shall contain no more than three legs or shins; and the packer shall be allowed sixpence per barrel for every barrel repack'd as afores[ai]d, and in proportion for larger cask.

And be it further enacted,

Cask to be marked after repacking.

[SECT. 3.] That every packer to be appointed as afores[ai]d, after repacking and pickling any beef, pork, fish or other commodities, shall set a brand or mark with the first letters of his Christian and sirname, and the town where he dwells at length, on all such cask, barrels or half-barrels, wherein he hath repack['][e]d and pickled any beef, pork, fish or other provisions. And in case any such packer, appointed and sworn as aforesaid, shall be guilty of any fraud or deceit in packing or repacking any beef, pork, fish, or other provision, or any cask used for packing or repacking the same, contrary to the true intent and meaning of this act, shall forfeit and pay the sum of forty shillings for every cask or barrel of provision so deceitfully packed or repacked: one half to the

Penalty for packers not doing their duty.

informer, who shall sue for the same in any of his majesty's courts of record within this province proper to try the same, the other half to the poor of the town where such offence is committed.

And for rend[*e*]ring the said act more effectual,—

Be it further enacted,

[Sect. 4.] That whosoever shall sell or expose to sale any barrels or other casks of beef, pork or any other provisions imported into any town within this province where such packers shall be appointed as afores[*ai*]d, before the same shall be repack[']['e]d and pickled and branded by the packer thereof as afores[*ai*]d, shall forfeit and pay the sum of twenty shillings per barrel for every offence: one half to the informer, who shall sue for the same before any of his majesty's courts of record proper to try the same, the other half to the poor of the town where such offence is committed. Penalty for selling provisions not repacked.

And be it further enacted,

[Sect. 5.] That there be a suitable number of measurers of corn, and all sort of grain, in every seaport town within this province, to be appointed as aforesaid, wh[o*] being likewise sworn for the faithful[l] discharge of that office, at the request of the purchaser, shall measu[re*] all corn and grain that shall be imported and sold out of any ship or other vessel, and shall have and receive of him one farthing per bushel for every bushel of corn or grain by him so measured, when the quantity measured exceeds ten bushels, and one halfpenny per bushel when the quantity be less than ten bushels. Measurers of corn, their duty and fee.

And be it further enacted,

[Sect. 6.] That whosoever shall expose to sale within the said province any corn or other grain, and shall refuse to suffer the same to be measured as aforesaid, being requested thereto by the purchaser, shall forfeit and pay forty shillings to such person or persons as shall make proof thereof to any of his majesty's justices of the peace. Penalty for refusing to have grain measured as above.

And be it further enacted,

[Sect. 7.] That every such measurer of corn and grain as afores[*ai*]d, shall, at the expence of the respective towns they belong to, be provided each with two half-bushels, Winchester measure, which shall on the top thereof have two strips of iron, each crossing the same on a level, to prevent any deceit in striking the s[*ai*]d measure when full of grain; and in case any such measurer of grain shall be guilty of any fraud or deceit in measuring any sort of grain, he shall forfeit and pay the sum of five pounds; and in case of his refusal to attend the afores[*ai*]d service when he shall be thereto requested, he shall forfeit and pay the sum of five shillings for each and every offence, to be recovered and disposed of as afores[*ai*]d. Winchester measure to be used for grain. Penalty on the measurers. Neglect of their duty.

[Sect. 8.] This act to continue and be in force for the space of three years from the publication thereof, and no longer. [*Passed July 1; published July 5.* Limitation.

CHAPTER 5.

AN ACT FOR ESTABLISHING AND BETTER REGULATING FEES WITHIN THIS PROVINCE.

Whereas some services of a publick nature have no fees stated by law, and others which have been established by two acts, made in the Preamble. 1692-3, chap. 37. 1701-2, chap. 7.

* Parchment injured, and these letters cut off.

fourth and thirteenth years of King William and Queen Mary, by reason of the alteration of circumstances, are become unequal,—

Be it therefore enacted by the Governour, Council and House of Representatives,

Rates of fees for officers.

[SECT. 1.] That from and after the publication of this act, the following fees, in bills of credit, emitted for the supply of the treasury the last year, or in other province bills, or gold [or] [*and*] silver in proportion (at the choice of the payer), may be taken for the future; viz[t].,—

JUSTICE'S FEES.

	£	s.	d.
For granting original summons or attachment, sixpence,	£0	0s.	6d.
Subpœna for each witness, one penny,	0	0	1
Entring an action, one shilling and sixpence,	0	1	6
Writ of execution, one shilling,	0	1	0
Filing papers, each one penny,	0	0	1
Taxing a bill of cost, threepence,	0	0	3
Entring up judgment, ninepence,	0	0	9
Bond for appeal, sixpence,	0	0	6
Copy of evidences, each threepence,	0	0	3
Copy of judgment, threepence,	0	0	3
Copy of a writ or summons, fourpence,	0	0	4
Each recognizance, one shilling,	0	1	0
Confessing judgment, sixpence,	0	0	6
Affidavit out of court in order to the tr[i][*y*]al of any cause, sixpence,—	0	0	6
in other causes, together with certificate and entry, sixpence,	0	0	6
Acknowledging an instrument with one or more seals, provided it be done at one and the same time, one shilling,	0	1	0
A warrant, sixpence,	0	0	6
Each day's attendance at the sessions, to be paid out of the fines, two shillings,	0	2	0

CORONER'S FEES.

	£	s.	d.
For serving a writ or summons, and travel[*l*]ing fees, the same as sheriffs.			
Taking an inquisition, to be paid out of the deceas[*e*]d's estate, six shillings and eightpence,—	0	6	8
if no estate, then to be paid by the county treasurer, three shill[*ing*]'s and fourpence,	0	3	4
For travelling and expences for taking an inquisition, each day, six shill[*ings*],	0	6	0
The foreman of the jury, three shillings,	0	3	0
Every other juror, two shillings and sixpence,	0	2	6

JUDGE OF PROBATE'S FEES.

	£	s.	d.
For granting administration or guardianship, bonds, and letters of administration or guardianship;—			
to the judge, two shillings,	0	2	0
to the register, one shilling and ninepence,	0	1	9
Proving a will, three shillings; whereof one shilling and ninepence to the judge, and one shilling and threepence to the register,	0	3	0
Recording a will or inventory of one page, and filing the same, one shilling and threepence,—	0	1	3
for every page more, of twenty-eight lines, of eight words in a line, sixpence,	0	0	6

	£	s.	d.
For copy of a will or inventory, each page of twenty-eight lines, sixpence, ...	£0	0s.	6d.
Allowing accompts, sètling and dividing of intestate estates, two shillings and sixpence, ...	0	2	6
Every citation, sixpence, ...	0	0	6
Every *quietus*, to the judge one shilling, to the register one shilling, ...	0	2	0
Warrant for appriz[e]ing or dividing estates, one shilling,	0	1	0
Making out commission to receive and examine the claims of creditors in insolvent estates, and registring the same, two shillings, ...	0	2	0
Registring the commissioner's report, each page of twenty-eight lines, sixpence, ...	0	0	6
Making out and entring an order upon the administrat[ors][*ion*] to pay out the estate [to] [*of*] the several creditors, in proportion returned by the commissioners, ninepence, ...	0	0	9

IN THE SUPERIOUR COURT.

JUSTICES' FEES.

	£	s.	d.
Entring every action, six shillings,—	0	6	0
out of which, to the clerk, one shilling, ...	0	1	0
Taking every special bail, one shilling, ...	0	1	0
Allowing a writ of error, one shilling and sixpence, . .	0	1	6
Allowing a *habeas corpus*, one shilling, ...	0	1	0
Confessing judgment, one shilling, ...	0	1	0
Acknowledging satisfaction of a judgment on record, sixpence, ...	0	0	6
In all criminal cases where a fine is set, three shillings, .	0	3	0
Taxing a bill of cost, sixpence, ...	0	0	6
Attorney's fee, to be allowed in the bill of cost taxed, six shillings, ...	0	6	0

CLERK'S FEES.

	£	s.	d.
Every writ of *scire facias*, one shilling and sixpence; every writ of review, two shillings and sixpence, . . .	0	4	0
Every rule of court, threepence, ...	0	0	3
Filing a declaration, sixpence, ...	0	0	6
Entring appearance, threepence, ...	0	0	3
Signing a judgment by default, sixpence, ...	0	0	6
Receiving and recording a verdict, sixpence, ...	0	0	6
Copies of all records, each page of twenty-eight lines, eight words in a line, sixpence,—	0	0	6
if less than one page, sixpence, ...	0	0	6
Every action withdrawn or nonsuit, sixpence, ...	0	0	6
Every petition read, sixpence,—	0	0	6
order thereon, sixpence, ...	0	0	6
Filing the papers of each cause, one penny per paper, .	0	0	1
Every execution, one shilling, ...	0	1	0

In Criminal Cases.

	£	s.	d.
Drawing and engrossing an indictment or information, one shill[*ing*], ...	0	1	0
Every appearance, threepence, ...	0	0	3
Discharge of any person upon bail for the peace or good behaviour, and warrant thereon, sixpence, . . .	0	0	6
For awarding and making forth process against the def[*endan*]t on information, sixpence, ...	0	0	6
Every warrant for the peace or good behaviour, sixpence, .	0	0	6

IN THE INFERIOUR COURT.

JUSTICES' FEES.

	£	s.	d.
Entry of every action, five shillings,—	£0	5s.	0d.
of which, to the clerk, one shilling, ...	0	1	0
Taking special bail, one shilling, ...	0	1	0
Confessing judgment or default, sixpence,— . . .	0	0	6
of which the clerk to have fourpence, ...	0	0	4
Acknowledging satisfaction of judgment on record, sixpenee, ...	0	0	6
Taxing a bill of cost, sixpence; threepence whereof to the clerk, ...	0	0	6
Attorney's fee, to be allowed in the bill of cost tax[e]d, five shillings, ...	0	5	0
Appeal, sixpence; recognizance, one shilling; whereof half to the clerk, ...	0	1	6

CLERKS' FEES.

Every writ and seal, sixpence, ...	0	0	6
Every appearance, threepence, ...	0	0	3
Entring and recording a verdict, sixpence, . . .	0	0	6
Making up record, sixpence, ...	0	0	6
Copies of all records, each as before, sixpence, . . .	0	0	6
Every action withdrawn or nonsuit, sixpence, . . .	0	0	6
Every execution, one shilling, ...	0	1	0

CLERK OF THE SESSIONS' FEES.

Entring a complaint or indictment, one shilling, . .	0	1	0
Discharging a recognizance, sixpence, ...	0	0	6
Each warrant against criminals, sixpence, ...	0	0	6
Every summons or subpœna, twopence, ...	0	0	2
Every recognizance for the peace or good behaviour, sixpence, ...	0	0	6
Every l[y][*i*]cence for publick entertainment or retailing, two shillings,—	0	2	0
whereof to the clerk, one shilling, ...	0	1	0

SHERIFF'S OR CONSTABLE'S FEES.

For serving an original summons, sixpence; every *capias* or attachment in civil, or warrants in criminal, cases for trial, one shilling,—	0	1	6
and for travel from the place whence the writ issues to the defendant's place of abode, one penny half-penny per mile, and no more, ...	0	0	1½
Bail bond, sixpence, ...	0	0	6
Serving execution in every personal action, if twenty pounds or under, sixpence per pound; for all others not exceeding forty pounds, threepence per pound; for all others not exceeding one hundred pounds, twopence per pound; all others above one hundred pounds, one penny per pound; for travel to return the execution, twopence per mile.			
For giving livery and seizen of real estates, seven shillings and sixpence; travel as before, ...	0	7	6
Every trial, sixpence, ...	0	0	6
Every precept for the choice of representatives, one shilling, to be paid out of the county treasuries respectively,	0	1	0
Each constable, for attending the grand jury, each day, one shilling and sixpence, ...	0	1	6

CRYER'S FEES.

Calling the jury, threepence, ...	£0	0s.	3d.
Every nonsuit, sixpence, ...	0	0	6
Every verdict, sixpence, ...	0	0	6

GOALER'S FEES.

For turning the key on each prisoner committed, two shillings and sixpence; viz[t]., one shilling and threepence in, and one shilling and threepence out,	0	2	6
For dieting each person, two shillings and sixpence per week, ...	0	2	6

MESSENGER OF THE HOUSE OF REPRESENTATIVES FEES.

For serving every warrant from the house of representatives, which they may grant for arresting, imprisoning or taking into custody any person, one shilling and sixpence, ...	0	1	6
For travel, each mile out, one penny halfpenny per mile, .	0	0	1½
For keeping and providing food for such person each day, two shillings and sixpence, ...	0	2	6
For his discharge or dismission, one shilling and sixpence, to be paid as by law already provided, . . .	0	1	6

GRAND JUROR'S FEES.

Foreman, each day, one shilling and sixpence, . . .	0	1	6
Each other, one shilling and threepence, ...	0	1	3
Allowance to the party for whom cost shall be taxed in the respective courts before mentioned in this act, one shilling per diem, ...	0	1	0
Allowance for witnesses in civil causes, one shilling and sixpence per diem, ...	0	1	6

PETIT JUROR'S FEES.

To the foreman, in every case at the superiour court, one shilling and threepence, ...	0	1	3
To every other juror, one shilling, ...	0	1	0
To the foreman, in every case at the inferiour court, or sessions, one shilling, ...	0	1	0
To every other juror, ninepence, ...	0	0	9

FOR MARRIAGES.

For each marriage, two shillings and sixpence; whereof to be paid to the town clerk, sixpence, ...	0	2	6
To the town clerk, for every publishment of the banns of matrimony and entring thereof, one shilling, . .	0	1	0
Every certificate of such publishment, ninepence, . .	0	0	9
Recording births and deaths, each, fourpence, . . .	0	0	4
For a certificate of the birth or death of any person, threepence, ...	0	0	3
For every search of record, when no copy is required, threepence, ...	0	0	3

COUNTY REGISTER'S FEES.

For entring or recording any deed, conveyance or mortgage, for the first page, ninepence,—	0	0	9

and sixpence a page for so many pages more as it shall contain, a[c]counting after the rate of twenty-eight lines, of eight words to a line to each page, and proportionably for so much more as shall be under a page,— . . . . £0 0s. 6d.
and threepence for his attestation on the original, of the time, book and folio where it is recorded,— . . . 0 0 3
and for discharge of a mortgage as aforesaid, sixpence, and no more, ... 0 0 6

And be it further enacted,

Penalty for taking other fees. [SECT. 2.] That whosoever shall demand and take any greater or other fees for the matters before mentioned, or any of them, than are allowed to be demanded and taken by this act, and shall be thereof convict, shall forfeit and pay for each offence, the sum of ten pounds, to be applied the one moiety to his majesty for and towards the support of this government, and the other moiety to him or them that shall sue for the same; to be recovered by action, bill, plaint or information, in any court of record proper to try the same. Penalty for not serving warrants, &c. And all officers to whom any warrant, summons, *capias* or attachment shall be committed, and who shall receive fees for the service thereof, are hereby required, without unnecessary delay, to serve and execute the same, on forfeiture of ten pounds, to be recovered and applied as aforesaid, beside making Proviso. good such damage as the party may sustain by such delay: *provided*, in civil causes, the fees for travel and service be first tender[e]d and paid if required by such officer.

Continuance of this act. 1692-3, chap. 37. 1701-2, chap. 7. [SECT. 3.] This act to continue and be in force for the space of one year from the publication thereof, and no longer; the act made in the fourth year of the reign of King William and Queen Mary, for regulating fees, as also an act made in the thirteenth year of the reign of King William the Third, relating to attorneys, or any other act respecting the establishment of fees, notwithstanding. [*Passed July* 1.

CHAPTER 6.

AN ACT FOR GRANTING UNTO HIS MAJESTY AN EXCISE UPON WINES, LIQUORS AND OTHER STRONG DRINK SOLD BY RETAIL, AND UPON LEMMONS AND LIMES.

Preamble. WE, his majesty's most loyal and dutiful subjects, the representatives of the province of the Massachusetts Bay, in general court assembled, being desirous to lessen the present debt of the province, by drawing in a number of the bills of credit in pursuance of several grants of this court heretofore made, have chearfully and unanimously granted, and do hereby give and grant unto his most excellent majesty for the ends and uses above mentioned, and for no other uses, an excise upon all brandy, rum and other spirit[t]s distilled, and upon all wines whatsoever sold by retail, and upon lemmons and limes taken in or used in making of punch or other liquors mixed for sale, or otherwise consumed in taverns or other licensed houses within this province, to be raised, levied, collected and paid by and upon every taverner, innholder, common victualler and retailer within each respective county, in manner following,—

And be it accordingly enacted by the Governour, Council and Representatives in General Court assembled, and by the authority of the same,

Time of this act's continuance. [SECT. 1.] That from and after the twenty-ninth day of June, one thousand seven hundred and forty-two, for the space of three years, every person licensed for retailing brandy, rum or other spirits, or wine, shall pay the duties following; viz[t].,—

For every gallon of brandy, rum and spirits distilled, threepence. Rates of excise.

For every gallon of wine of every sort, threepence.

—a pipe of wine to be accounted one hundred gallons.

For every hundred of lemmons, two shillings and one penny.

For every hundred of limes, ninepence.

And so proportionably for any other quantity or number.

And be it further enacted,

[Sect. 2.] That there be one or more collectors in each county annually appointed by the general court, or by the court of general sessions of the peace where it shall happen that such collectors refuse to accept said office, or be removed by death or for mismanagement, to take charge of this duty of excise, who shall have power to inspect the houses of all such as are licensed, and of such as are suspected to sell without license, which collectors shall be upon oath to take care of the execution of this law, and to prosecute the breakers of it, and have power to appoint under-officers upon oath; and the said collectors shall carefully examine the accompts of every licensed person in their respective counties, and demand, sue for and receive the several sums due from them by this act, and shall give in an account, under their hands, of the particular sums they receive, together with the names of the persons of whom received, unto the treasurer, upon oath, which oath the treasurer is hereby impowered and directed to administer, in the words following; viz[t].,— Collectors to be appointed. To give account upon oath.

You, A. B., do swear this is a just and true accompt of the excise upon all liquors by you received in the county of , and that the persons of whom you received the same were also upon oath. So help you God. Form of the oath.

[Sect. 3.] And at the time of receiving any money, the said collector shall give two receipts of the same tenor and date, mentioning what sum or sums they have received from any taverner, innholder, common victualler or retailer, one of which receipts to be by the said taverner, innholder, common victualler or retailer returned to the court of general sessions of the peace within their respective counties at the next session of such court, and the clerks of the said court[s] shall, within twenty days after receipt thereof, transmit the same to the treasurer or receiver-general; and such collectors shall pay into the publick treasury of this province all such sums as they shall receive, within six months from the date of their commission, and so from time to time within the space of six months, as long as they shall continue in such office, on pain of forfeiting the reward given such collectors by this act, who shall be allowed five per cent on all money by them collected and paid into the treasury as aforesaid; each collector before he enter into the said office to give bond for double the sum that is usually received for excise annually in said county, to the treasurer of this province for the time being, and his successo[u]rs in said office, with sufficient sureties, for the faithful[l] discharge of his duty, and that he will duly pay in the money that he shall collect to the treasurer of the province for the time being; which bond shall be executed before the court of general sessions of the peace in the respective counties where the said collectors live, and be transmitted to the treasurer of the province, by the clerk of the peace within such county, within three months after the bond is executed. And the said treasurer shall put in suit the bonds of all such collectors who shall neglect to make due payment within sixty days after the expiration of the year. Five per cent for collecting.

And be it further enacted by the authority aforesaid,

Account to be taken.

[SECT. 4.] That every taverner, innholder, common victualler and retailer shall, after the twenty-ninth day of June, one thousand seven and forty-two, take an exact account of all rum, brandy and other distilled spirits and wine, then by him, and give an account of the same unto the said collector upon oath; and such other persons as shall be licensed during the continuance of the said act shall also give an account as aforesaid, upon oath, of what rum, brandy and other distill[e][']d spirits and wine he or they shall have by him or them at the time of his or their license; which oath the collector shall have power to administer in the words following; viz[t].,—

You, A. B., do swear, that the account exhibited by you is a true and just account of all the rum, brandy and distilled spirits, and wine, now by you. So help you God.

And be it further enacted,

Within six months, accounts to be delivered.

[SECT. 5.] That every taverner, innholder, common victualler, and retailer, shall make a fair entry in a book of all such rum, brandy, and other distilled spirits, and wine, as he or they or any for him or them shall buy, distill, or take in for sale after such account taken, and at the end of every six months deliver the same in writing, under his or their hands, to the collector, who is to administer an oath to him or them, that the said account is, *bonâ fide*, just and true, and that he or they do not know of any rum, brandy, or distilled spirits, or wine, sold directly or indirectly by him or them, or any under him or them, or by his or their privity or consent, but what is contained in the account now exhibited, and shall pay him the duty thereof, excepting such part as the collector shall find is still remaining by him or them: twenty per cent to be allowed for leakage and other waste, for which no duty is to be paid.

Twenty per cent allowed for leakage.

Penalty on collectors not administering the oath.

[SECT. 6.] And every collector who shall neglect or refuse to administer such oath in manner as aforesaid, being thereof convict by due course of law, shall forfeit and pay the sum of twenty pounds, for the use of the province, to be recovered in manner as by this act is provided, and so *toties quoties*.

General sessions to take recognizance.

[SECT. 7.] And the justices in their general sessions of the peace shall take recognizances with sufficient sureties, of all persons by them licen[s][c]ed, both as to their keeping good rule and order, and duly observing the laws relating to persons so licen[s][c]ed, as also for their duly and truly rendering an account in writing under their hands as aforesaid, and paying their excise in manner as aforesaid; which recognizance shall be taken within the space of thirty days after the granting such licen[c][*s*]es, otherwise the person licensed shall lose the benefit of his or her said licence; nor shall any person be licen[s][*c*]ed by said justices that hath not accounted with the collector of excise, and produced his receipt in full at the time for such licen[s][c]e.

And be it further enacted,

Penalty on giving a false account.

[SECT. 8.] That every taverner, innholder, common victualler, or retailer, who shall be found to give a false acco[mp][*un*]t of any brandy, distilled spirits, or wine, by him or her at the time of his or her taken licence, or bought, distilled or taken in for sale afterwards, or refuse to give in an account on oath as aforesaid, shall be rendered incapable of having a licence afterwards, and be prosecuted by the collector for his or her neglect, and ordered by the general sessions of the peace to pay such sum of money as they may conclude that the excise of liquors, &c[a]. by him or her sold within such time, would have amounted to, to be paid to the collector for the use of the province.

Provided alwa[ie][*y*]*s*,—

And it is the true intent and meaning of this act,

[Sect. 9.] That if any taverner, retailer, or common victualler, shall buy of another taverner, or retailer, such small quantities of liquors as the law obliges him to account to the collector for and pay the excise, the taverner, retailer, or common victualler shall, notwithstanding, be accountable and pay the excise, as if none had been paid by the person he bought the same of. **Proviso.**

And whereas notwithstanding the laws made against selling strong drink without licence, many persons not regarding the penalties and forfeitures in the said act, do receive and entertain persons in their houses, and sell great quantities of spirits and other strong drink without licence so to do first had and obtained, by reason whereof great debaucheries are committed and kept secret, the end of this law in a great measure frustrated, and such as take licen[s][c]es and pay the excise greatly wronged and injured. **Preamble.**

Be it therefore further enacted,

[Sect. 10.] That whosoever after the twenty-ninth day of June, one thousand seven hundred and forty-two, shall presume to sell any brandy, rum, or other distilled spirits, wine, beer, cyder, perry, or any other strong drink in any smaller quantity than a quarter-cask (twenty gallons to be accounted a quarter-cask), without licence first had and obtained from the general sessions of the peace, and recognizing in manner as aforesaid, shall forfeit the sum of three pounds, one half whereof to be for the use and benefit of the poor of the town where the offence shall be committed, and the other half to him who shall inform and sue for the same, and costs of prosecution; and all such as shall refuse or neglect to pay the fine aforesaid, shall stand closely and strictly committed in the common goal of the county for forty days at least, and not to have the liberty of the goaler's house or yard; and any goaler giving any person liberty contrary to this act, shall forfeit and pay three pounds, to be employed in manner as aforesaid, and pay costs of prosecution as aforesaid. And if any person or persons not liceu[s][c]ed as aforesaid, shall order, allow, permit, or connive at the selling of any strong drink contrary to the true intent and meaning of this law, by his or her child or children, servant or servants, or any other person or persons belonging to, or in his or her house or family, and be thereof convict, he, she or they shall be reputed the offender or offenders, and shall suffer the same penalties as if he, she or they had sold such drink themselves, unless such person or persons will, *bonâ fide*, swear that he, she or they did not order, allow or permit thereof, or connive thereat. **Forfeiture of £3 for selling without license.**

And be it further enacted,

[Sect. 11.] That two credible persons declaring upon oath what they know of any facts that may be judged to be against this law forbidding unlicen[s][c]ed persons to sell strong drink, shall be sufficient to convict such person or persons thereof, altho[*ugh*] their testimony be to two different facts.: *provided*, there be not more than the space of twenty days between the facts concerning which they declare. **Two persons' evidence sufficient.**

And be it further enacted,

[Sect. 12.] That all fines, forfeitures and penalties arising by this act, shall and may be recovered by presentment of the grand jury, at the court of sessions, or by bill, plaint or information before any three of his majesty's justices of the peace, *quorum unus*, in the respective counties where such offence shall be committed, which said three justices are hereby impowered to try and determine the same: *saving always*, to any person or persons who shall think him, her or themselves aggrieved by the sentence or determination of the said three justices as aforesaid, **How fines shall be recovered.**

liberty of appeal therefrom to the next court of general sessions of the peace to be holden in and for said county, at which court such offence shall be finally determined: *provided*, that in said appeal the same rules be observed as are already by law required in appeals from one or more justices to the court of general sessions of the peace.

And be it further enacted,

Evidence, if before three justices, to be in writing.

[SECT. 13.] That all evidences relating to the aforesaid offence of selling strong drink without licence, when the trial shall be before three justices of the peace as aforesaid, shall be taken in writing; and in case the witnesses cannot be had and obtained to appear on appeal before the court of sessions, that then and in such case the s[*ai*]d written evidence shall be deem'd as valid, to all intents and purposes, by the said court of sessions, as if the said witnesses had appeared, and there given in their evidence *viva voce*. And the said justices shall make a fair entry or record of all such their proceedings, such record to be lodged with the justice who is of the quorum.

And be it further enacted,

Houses not licensed.

[SECT. 14.] That when and so often as it shall be observed that there is a resort of persons to houses suspected to sell strong drink without licence, any justice of the peace shall have full power to convene such persons before him, and examine them upon oath touching the person suspected of selling or retailing strong drink in such houses, and [*up*]on just grounds of suspicion, such justice shall call to his assistance two other justices, qualified as aforesaid, who shall proceed to hear and adjudge said offence agreeable to such rules and directions as are in this act before provided, and if upon such examination had, any person shall be convicted of such offence, the whole of the penalty of three pounds in this act before provided for selling strong drink without licence, shall be to and for the use of the poor of the town where such offence shall be committed.

And be it further enacted,

Penalty on persons refusing to give evidence.

[SECT. 15.] That if any person or persons shall be summoned to appear before the grand jury to give evidence relating to any person's selling strong drink without licence, or to appear before the court of general sessions of the peace, or three justices as aforesaid, to give evidence on the trial of any person informed against, presented, or indicted for the selling strong drink without licen[s][*c*]e, and shall neglect or refuse to appear or to give evidence in that behalf, every person so offending shall forfeit and pay the sum of three pounds, for the use of the county where the offence shall be committed.

And be it further enacted,

[SECT. 16.] That all the rates, fines and forfeitures heretofore mentioned, shall be in the bills of the last emission, or other bills equivalent thereto. [*Passed July* 1; *published July* 5.

CHAPTER 7.

AN ACT FOR GRANTING A SUM FOR THE PAY OF THE MEMBERS OF THE COUNCIL AND HOUSE OF REPRESENTATIVES IN GENERAL COURT ASSEMBLED, AND FOR ESTABLISHING THE WAGES, &c., OF SUNDRY PERSONS IN THE SERVICE OF THE PROVINCE.

Be it enacted by the Governour, Council and House of Representatives,

Councillors' pay for attendance in the General Court.

[SECT. 1.] That from the beginning of the present session of the general court unto the end of their several sessions till May next, each member of the council shall be [e][*i*]ntitled to four shillings and sixpence per diem, to be paid out of the publick treasury by warrant according to the direction of the royal charter, upon certificate given by the secretary of the number of days of such member's attendance and travel to and from the court; twenty miles to be accounted a day's travel.

And be it further enacted,

[Sect. 2.] That each member of the house of represen[*tati*]ves serving the time aforesaid, shall be paid three shillings per diem upon certificate given by the clerk of the house of represent[*ati*]ves of the number of days of such member's attendance and travel to and from the court, twenty miles to be accounted a day's travel. Representatives' pay.

And be it further enacted,

[Sect. 3.] That the wages of the captain of Castle William shall be after the rate of sixty pounds per annum, from the twenty-first of May, one thousand seven hundred and forty-two, to the twentieth of May, one thousand seven hundred and forty-three; of the lieutenant for that term, thirty-five pounds fifteen shillings; of the chaplain, thirty pounds; of the gunner, fifty pounds; of the gunner's mate, thirty-four shillings and threepence per month; of two serjeants, each twenty-three shillings per month; of six quarter-gunners, each twenty-three shillings per month; of three corporals, each twenty-one shillings and ninepence per month; of two drummers, each twenty-one shillings and ninepence per month; of one armourer, thirty-four shillings and threepence per month; of forty centinels, each twenty shillings per month: for their subsistence, six shillings and threepence per week per man. Wages of the garrison at Castle William.

And be it further enacted,

[Sect. 4.] That the wages of the captain of Richmond Fort, from May the twenty-first, one thousand seven and forty-two, to May the twentieth, one thousand seven hundred and forty-three, shall be at the rate of twenty shillings per month; and of ten centinels, each ten shillings per month; of one interpreter, thirty shillings per month; of one armourer, thirty shillings per month; and for the chaplain, twenty-five pounds per annum. Richmond Fort.

And be it further enacted,

[Sect. 5.] That the wages of the captain of the truck-house on George's River, from May the twenty-first, one thousand seven hundred and forty-two, to the twentieth of May, one thousand seven hundred and forty-three, shall be at the rate of twenty shillings per month; of one lieutenant, thirteen shillings and sixpence per month; of one serjeant, thirteen shillings and sixpence per month; of two corporals, each twelve shillings per month; of thirteen centinels, each ten shillings per month; of one armourer, thirty shillings per month; of one interpreter, thirty shillings per month; and to the chaplain there, twenty-five pounds per annum. Truck-house at George's River.

And be it further enacted,

[Sect. 6.] That the wages of the commanding officer of the fort at Brunswick, from May the twenty-first, one thousand seven hundred and forty-two, to the twentieth of May, one thousand seven hundred and forty-three, shall be at the rate of thirteen shillings and sixpence per month; of six centinels, each ten shillings per month. Brunswick Fort.

And be it further enacted by the authority afores[ai]d,

[Sect. 7.] That the wages of the captain of the truck-house above Northfield, from the twenty-first of May, one thousand seven hundred and forty-two, to May the twentieth, one thousand seven hundred and forty-three, shall be at the rate of twenty shillings per month; of one lieutenant, thirteen shillings and sixpence per month; of one serjeant, thirteen shillings and sixpence per month; of one corporal, twelve shillings per month; of sixteen centinels, each ten shillings per month; Truck-house above Northfield.

of one interpreter, thirty shillings per month; of the chaplain there, twenty-five pounds per year; and that there be allowed for the subsist[a][e]nce of each man, two shillings and sixpence per week.

And be it further enacted,

Truck-house at Saco River. [SECT. 8.] That the wages of the captain of the truck-house at Saco, from the twenty-first of May, one thousand seven hundred and forty-two, to the twentieth of May, one thousand seven hundred and forty-three, shall be at the rate of twenty shillings per month; of one lieutenant, thirteen shillings and sixpence per month; of one corporal, twelve shillings per month; of thirteen centinels, each ten shillings per month; of one armourer, thirty shill[*in*]gs per month; of one interpreter, thirty shillings per month.

And be it further enacted by the authority afores[ai]d,

Frederick Fort. [SECT. 9.] That the wages of the commanding officer of Frederick Fort, from the twenty-first of May, one thousand seven hundred and forty-two, to the twentieth of May, one thousand seven hundred and forty-three, shall be at the rate of thirteen shillings and sixpence per month; of six centinels, each ten shillings per month.

And be it further enacted by the authority aforesaid,

Country's sloop. [SECT. 10.] That the wages of the captain of the sloop in the country's service, from the twenty-first of May, one thousand seven hundred and forty-two, to the twentieth day of May, one thousand seven hundred and forty-three, shall be at the rate of fifty shillings per month; of the mate, thirty shillings per month; of three sailors, twenty-five shillings each per month; for the sloop, seven pounds ten shillings per month.

And be it further enacted,

Province snow. [SECT. 11.] That the wages of the captain of the province snow, from May the twenty-first, one thousand seven hundred and forty-two, to the twentieth of May, one thousand seven hundred and forty-three, shall be at the rate of five pounds per month; the lieutenant, three pounds ten shillings per month; the master, three pounds per month; the doctor, three pounds per month; the chaplain, three pounds per month; the gunner, fifty shillings per month; the boatswain, forty-five shillings per month; the mate, forty shillings per month; the steward, thirty-five shillings per month; the cook, thirty-five shillings per month; the gunner's mate, thirty-five shillings per month; the pilot, fifty shillings per month; the boatswain's mate, thirty-five shillings per month; the carpenter, forty-five shillings per month; the cooper, thirty-five shillings per month; the armourer, thirty-five shillings per month; the coxswain, thirty-five shillings per month; two quartermasters, each thirty-five shillings per month; the carpenter's mate, thirty-five shillings per month; seventy sailors or foremast men, thirty shillings per month.

And be it further enacted,

Oath to be made to the muster-roll. [SECT. 12.] That before payment of any muster-roll be allowed, oath be made by the officer or person presenting such roll, that the officers and soldiers born on such roll have been in actual service for the whole time they stand entred thereon.

And be it further enacted,

Grants and wages aforesaid to be paid out of the supply bill now before this court, or equivalent. [SECT. 13.] That the several grants and wages made and established in this act shall be paid out of the fifteen thousand pounds ordered to be emitted by the bill for the supply of the treasury now before this court, out of the respective appropriations therein made for that purpose, or equivalent thereto in such monies as shall be raised and put into the treasury by the next act that shall be made for the supply of the same. [*Passed July 1; published July 5.*

CHAPTER 8.

AN ACT IN ADDITION TO THE SEVERAL ACTS OR LAWS OF THIS PROVINCE FOR THE SETTLEMENT AND SUPPORT OF MINISTERS.

Preamble.

1692-3, chaps. 26 and 46. 1695-6, chap. 8. 1702, chap. 10. 1706, chap. 9. 1715-16, chap. 17. 1723-4, chap. 14. 1728-9, chap. 4. 1731-2, chap. 11. 1734-5, chap. 6. 1737-8, chap. 6. 1740-41, chap. 6.

Whereas the professed members of the Church of England have complained that they are unreasonably taxed for the support of divine worship in the manner established by the laws of this province, while they and their families constantly attend the worship of God according to the usage and order of the Church of England, either within their own or some neighbouring town, parish or precinct,—

Be it enacted by the Governour, Council and House of Representatives,

Tax of persons attending at the Church of England, to be paid their own minister.

[Sect. 1.] That the members of the Church of England and their estates shall be taxed to the support of the publick worship of God with the other estates and inhabitants within the bounds of any town, parish or precinct, according to the laws of this province. And the treasurer of such town, parish or precinct, as he receiveth any such tax, shall deliver the taxes collected of every profess[t][*'d*] member of the Church of England unto the minister of the said church with whom he usually and frequently attends the publick worship of God on the Lord's days, which minister shall have power to receive, and if need be to recover the same in the law, to support him in the place whereunto he is duly designed and sent; and if by that means any deficiency happeneth in the salary of any minister setled by the laws of this province, such town, parish or precinct, within two months after such deficiency appeareth, shall make good the same: *provided, nevertheless*, that all such professed members of the Church of England shall be [e][*i*]ntirely excused from paying any taxes toward[s] the settlement of any minister or building any meeting-house pursuant and according to the direction and orders of the laws of this province, and utterly debarred from voting any ways concerning such ministers or meeting-houses.

Deficiency provided for.

Members of the Church of England excused from charges towards the settlement of ministers, &c.

Provided, also,

Proviso.

[Sect. 2.] That no person shall be exempted, or his tax paid over to any minister of the Church of England, unless such minister and his church-wardens shall first certify to the treasurer of such town or parish where he lives that such person is a member of the Church of England, and usually and frequently attends the publick worship of God with them on the Lord's days as aforesaid. [*Passed July* 1.

CHAPTER 9.

AN ACT FOR HOLDING A COURT OF OYER AND TERMINER IN AND FOR THE ISLAND OF NANTUCKET.

Preamble.

Whereas there now stands committed in his majesty's goal in the island of Nantucket one Harry Jude, an Indian man, charged with the murther of Mercy Moab, an Indian woman, who ought, as the law now stands, to be tried by a special court of assize and general goal delivery; but forasmuch as the judges of the court of assize and general goal delivery cannot attend that service, the summer months being taken up with the several superio[*u*]r courts of judicature, courts of assize and [goal] general [*goal*] delivery, as they are now established, besides the great charge and trouble of the judges' repairing thither, and a court of oyer and terminer (noticed in the royal charter) have and can exercise the same jurisdiction and authority in all capital offences,—

Be it therefore enacted by the Governo[u]r, Council and House of Represent[ati]ves, for the reasons above mentioned, and that speedy justice may be done,—

Special court to be held at Nantucket for the trial of Harry Jude, &c.

That the inquiry, hearing and tryal of the said Harry Jude for the murther of the said Mercy Moab, and any other capital offences upon the said island of Nantucket already committed, may, with all convenient speed, be had at Nantucket aforesaid, by special commissioners of oyer and terminer, to be appointed by his excellency the governo[u]r, with the advice and consent of the council; any law, usage or custom to the contrary thereof notwithstanding. [*Passed July* 1.

CHAPTER 10.

AN ACT FOR ALTERING THE TIME FOR HOLDING THE INFERIO[*U*]R COURT OF COMMON PLEAS IN THE COUNTY OF SUFFOLK, AND ALSO THE COURT OF GENERAL SESSIONS OF THE PEACE AND INFERIOR COURT OF COMMON PLEAS IN THE COUNTY OF HAMPSHIRE.

Preamble.

WHEREAS by law the time appointed for holding the inferio[*u*]r court of common pleas for the county of Suffolk on the third Tuesday of March, annually, and also the court of general sessions of the peace and inferio[*u*]r court[*s*] of common pleas for the county of Hampshire on the first Tuesdays of March and December, annually, is found on many accounts very inconvenient,—

Be it therefore enacted by the Governour, Council and House of Representatives,

Courts in Suffolk and Hampshire altered. 1740-41, chap. 13. 1699-1700, chap. 2, § 2.

That the inferio[*u*]r court of common pleas held at Boston for the county of Suffolk on the third Tuesday of March annually, shall be henceforth held and kept at Boston aforesaid, on the first Tuesday of April yearly, and also that the court of general sessions of the peace and inferio[*u*]r court of common pleas holden at Northampton for the county of Hampshire on the first Tuesdays of March and December, annually, shall be henceforth held and kept at Northampton on the second Tuesdays of February and November yearly. [*Passed July* 1.

CHAPTER 11.

AN ACT TO PREVENT DAM[*M*]AGE BEING DONE UNTO BILLINGSGATE BAY IN THE TOWN OF EASTHAM, BY CATTLE AND HORSE-KIND AND SHEEP FEEDING ON THE BEACH AND ISLANDS ADJOINING THERETO.

Preamble.

WHEREAS many persons frequently drive numbers of neat cattle, horse-kind and sheep to feed upon the beach and islands adjoining to Billingsgate Bay, whereby the ground is much broken and damnified, and the sand blown into the bay, to the great dam[*m*]age not only of private persons in their employment of getting oysters, but also to the publick, by filling up said bay, which is often used by seamen in stress of weather,—

Be it therefore enacted by the Governo[u]r, Council and House of Representatives,

[SECT. 1.] That from and after the publication of this act, no person or persons shall presume to turn or drive any neat cattle, or horse-kind, or sheep, to or upon the islands or beach lying westerly of Billingsgate Bay and south of Griffin's Island (so called) in the town of Eastham, to feed thereon, upon the penalty of ten shillings a head for all neat cattle, and for every horse or mare, and two shillings and sixpence for each sheep that shall be turned or found feeding on said islands and beach which l[y][*ie*] south of Griffin's Island; which penalty shall be recovered by the selectmen or treasurer of the said town of Eastham, or any other person that shall inform and sue for the same, the one half of the said forfeiture to him or them who shall inform and sue for the same, the other half to be to and for the use of the poor of the said town.

Horses, cattle, and sheep not to feed on Billingsgate Beach, &c.

Penalty.

And be it further enacted,

[SECT. 2.] That if any neat cattle, or horse-kind, or sheep, shall at any time hereafter be found feeding on the said islands and beach south of Griffin's Island, that it shall and may be lawful for any person to impound the same, immediately giving notice to the owners, if known, otherwise to give publick notice thereof in the said town of Eastham and the two next adjoining towns; and the impounder shall relieve the said creatures with suitable meat and water while impounded; and if the owner thereof appear, he shall pay the sum of two shillings and sixpence to the impounders for each neat beast and horse-kind, and eightpence for each sheep, and the reasonable cost of relieving them, besides the pound-keeper's fees. And if no owner appear within the space of six days to redeem the said cattle or horse-kind or sheep so impounded, and to pay the dam[*m*]ages and costs occasioned by impounding the same, then and in every such case, the person or persons impounding such cattle, or horse-kind, or sheep, shall cause the same to be sold at publick vendue, to pay the cost and charges arising about the same (publick notice of the time and place of such sale to be given in the said town of Eastham and in the town of Truro forty-eight hours beforehand); and the overplus, if any there be, arising by such sale, to be returned to the owner of such cattle, or horse-kind, or sheep at any time within twelve months next after, upon his demanding the same; but if no owner appear within the said twelve months, then the said overplus shall be, one half to the party impounding, and the other half to the use of the poor of the said town of Eastham.

Cattle to be impounded if found feeding on the beach, &c.

Rules referring to such impounded cattle.

And be it further enacted,

[SECT. 3.] That the said town of Eastham, at their meeting in March, annually, for the choice of town officers, be authorized and impow[e]red to chuse one or more meet person or persons, whose duty it [shall be*] to see [that*] this act be observed, and prosecute the breakers thereof, who shall be sworn to the faithful discharge of their office; and in case any person so chosen shall refuse to be sworn, he shall forfeit and pay ten shillings to the poor of the said town of Eastham, and the said town of Eastham, at a town meeting warned for that purpose, may at any time before March next chuse such officers, who shall continue until their annual meeting in March next.

Officers may be chosen to put this act in execution.

[SECT. 4.] This act to continue and be in force for the space of five years from the publication thereof, and no longer. [*Passed July* 1; *published July* 5.

Limitation.

* These words cut out from the parchment.

ACTS

PASSED AT THE SESSION BEGUN AND HELD AT BOSTON, ON THE EIGHTEENTH DAY OF NOVEMBER, A. D. 1742.

CHAPTER 12.

AN ACT TO PREVENT INCUMBRANCES ABOUT THE DOORS OF THE COURT-HOUSE IN BOSTON.

Preamble.

WHEREAS the doors of the court-house in the town of Boston, are often incumbred by teams and other ways, so as very much to obstruct the members of the general court in their passage to and from the said house,—

Be it therefore enacted by the Governour, Council and House of Represent[ati]ves,

Penalty for encumbering the doors of the court-house.

[SECT. 1.] That no person or persons whatsoever shall presume to incumber the said house by stopping, or suffering to stand, any coach, chaise, chair, team, cart, sled, truck or wheelbarrow, or by laying any lumber, stones, mud, dirt or other incumbrance whatsoever within the distance of twenty-four feet from the west end, thirty feet from the bottom of the steps at the east end, and ten feet from either side of the said house, upon pain of forfeiting five shillings unto the doorkeeper to the general court for the time being, and by him to be recovered before a justice of the peace.

Penalty for offending, after warning by the doorkeeper.

[SECT. 2.] And in case any person or persons offending in either of the particulars before mentioned, after being thereto required by the doorkeeper, shall not forthwith remove any such incumbrance, he or they shall forfeit the sum of twenty shillings, to be recovered in like manner as aforesaid.

Provided nevertheless,

Proviso.

[SECT. 3.] That this act shall not be construed so as to hinder any coach, chariot, chaise, or chair from standing within the limits aforesaid, which shall be used by the governour, lieutenant-governo[*u*]r, or any of the members of the general court for the time being. [*Passed and published January* 6, 1742–43.

CHAPTER 13.

AN ACT FOR PREVENTING UNNECESSARY EXPENSE IN THE ATTENDANCE OF PETIT JURORS ON THE SEVERAL COURTS OF JUSTICE WITHIN THIS PROVINCE.

Preamble. 1738-9, chap. 4.

WHEREAS petit jurors are oftentimes detained at the tr[y][*i*]al and hearing of causes which are not committed to them by reason of the agreement of parties, abatement of the writ, or discontinuance; whereby the plaintiff becomes nonsuit, and frequently (especially in the inferiour court of common pleas) judgment is entred up against the defendant by default, whereby great part of the jury's time is taken up, without their being allowed any benefit by law, notwithstanding their being obliged to give their constant attendance during the time of the courts' sitting, until[l] all the actions depending there are finished; wherefore,—

Be it enacted by the Governour, Council and House of Repres[entati]ves,

[SECT. 1.] That petit jurors, in the court of general sessions of the peace and inferio[*u*]r court of common pleas to be held within and for the county of Suffolk, shall not be obliged to give their attendance until[l] the second Tuesday of said courts' sitting; and at the said courts that are to be held within all other counties within this province, on the second day of the said courts' sitting; to the end that the said courts may proceed upon and determine all pleas in bar and abatem[*en*]t of writ[*t*]s and all other matters and things that relate to such actions as are not committed to the jury; so that their time and attendance be not unnecessarily taken up and delayed. And the clerks of the respective courts afores[*ai*]d are hereby ordered and directed, in making out writs of *venire facias* for the choice of petit jurors, to give directions accordingly. The time of attendance of petit jurors stated.

And be it further enacted,

[SECT. 2.] That no action be entred in any of the courts aforesaid after the first day of their sitting; and all pleas in bar of the action or abatem[*en*]t of the writ be either entred thereon or filed with the clerk of the said court before the jury be [e][*i*]mpanneled; and if the defendant in any action suffer default and comes into court and moves for a re-entry of his action, after the jury be [e][*i*]mpanneled, on paying the pla[*i*]ntiff or his attorney such legal cost as shall then have arose, and half fees to the petit jury, to whom the same shall be ordered by said court, he shall be admitted to a re-entry of his action, and to all such privileges as by law he was [e][*i*]ntitled to on his first entry. [*Passed January* 15, 1742-43. No action to be entered after the first day of the courts' sitting, &c.

CHAPTER 14.

AN ACT FOR SUPPLYING THE TREASURY WITH THE SUM OF TWELVE THOUSAND POUNDS, FOR DISCHARGING THE PUBLICK DEBTS, &c., AND FOR DRAWING IN THE SAID BILLS INTO THE TREASURY AGAIN, AND FOR STATING THEIR VALUE IN DISCHARGING OF PUBLICK AND PRIVATE DEBTS.

Be it enacted by the Governour, Council and House of Representatives,

[SECT. 1.] That there be forthwith imprinted a certain number of bills of credit of this province of the same tenor and form with the bills emitted by this court at their sessions in November, one thousand seven hundred and forty-one, and at their sessions in May last, and to be always valued and taken in all publick payments as the aforesaid bills of the same form and tenor already extant, are or shall be valued and taken, which in the whole shall amount to the sum of twelve thousand pounds and no more; the said bills to be signed by such committee as shall be chosen by this court for that purpose; and the said committee are £12,000, in bills of credit, to be emitted.

hereby directed and impowered to take care and make effectual provision, so soon as may be, to imprint the said bills, and to sign and deliver the same to the treasurer, taking his receipt for the same; and the said committee shall be under oath for the faithful[l] performance of the trust by this act reposed in them.

And be it further enacted,

Appropriations of this emission.

[SECT. 2.] That the treasurer be and hereby is impowered to issue forth and emit the said sum of twelve thousand pounds for the necessary support and defence of the government, and the protection and preservation of the inhabitants thereof; viz[t]., the sum of four thousand pounds, part of the aforesaid sum of twelve thousand pounds, shall be applied for the payment of the wages that now are or that hereafter may be due by virtue of the establishment of Castle William, Richmond Fort, George's Truck-house, Saco Truck-house, Brunswick Fort, the block-house above Northfield, the sloop in the country's service, and the province snow, and the treasurer's usual disbursements; and the sum of eleven hundred pounds, part of the aforesaid sum of twelve thousand pounds, shall be appl[y][*i*]ed towards the compleating the repairs and works begun and carried on at Castle William, pursuant to such grants as or shall be made by this court; and the sum of four thousand five hundred pounds, part of the aforesaid sum of twelve thousand pounds, shall be applied for the payment of such other grants as are or shall be made by this court, and for the payment of stipends, bount[y][*ie*]s and premiums established by law, and for the payment of all other matters and things which this court have or shall either by law or orders provide for the payment of, out of the publick treasury, and for no other purpose whatsoever: the sum of sixteen hundred pounds, part of the aforesaid sum of twelve thousand pounds, shall be applied for the discharge of other debts owing from this province to persons who have served or shall serve them by order of this court in such matters and things where there is no establishment, nor any certain sum assigned for such service; and for paper, printing and writing for this court, the expences of committees of council, or of the house, or of both houses, entertainment of Indians and presents made them by this court, the surgeon of Castle William, and wooding of said castle; and the sum of eight hundred pounds, the remaining part of the aforesaid sum of twelve thousand pounds, shall be applied for the payment of the members of the house of representatives serving in the general court, during their several sessions this present year and until November next.

£4,000 for wages of officers, soldiers, and seamen, and the treasurer's disbursements.

£1,100 for repairs, &c., at Castle William.

£4,500 for grants, &c.

£1,600 for debts where there is no establishment.

£800 for the representatives.

And be it enacted,

Surplusage to lie in the treasury.

[SECT. 3.] That if there be a surplusage in any sum appropriated, such surplusage shall l[y][*i*]e in the treasury for the further order of this court.

And be it further enacted,

Warrants to express the appropriations.

[SECT. 4.] That each and every warrant for drawing money out of the treasury shall direct the treasurer to take the same out of such sums as are respectively appropriated for the payment of such publick debts as the draughts are made to discharge; and the treasurer is hereby directed and ordered to pay such money out of such appropriations as directed to, and no other, upon pain of refunding all such sum or sums as he shall otherwise pay, and to keep exact and distinct acco[un][*mp*]ts of all payments made out of such appropriated sums; and that the secretary to whom it belongs to keep the muster rolls and accompts of charge, shall lay before the house, when they direct, all such muster rolls and accompts after payment thereof.

And as a fund and security for drawing the said sum of twelve thousand pounds into the treasury again,—

Be it further enacted,

[SECT. 5.] That there be and hereby is granted unto his most excellent majesty, for the ends and uses aforesaid, a tax of seven thousand five hundred pounds, to be levied on polls, and estates both real and personal, within this province, according to such rules and in such proportions on the several towns and districts within the same, as shall be agreed upon and ordered by this court at their session in May, one thousand seven hundred and forty-three, and paid into the publick treasury on or before the last day of December then next after. £7,500 to be brought in, in the year 1743.

And as a further fund and security for drawing the remaining part of the said sum of twelve thousand pounds into the treasury again,—

Be it further enacted,

[SECT. 6.] That there be and hereby is granted unto his most excellent majesty, for the ends and uses aforesaid, a tax of three thousand five hundred pounds, to be levied on polls, and estates both real and personal, within this province, according to such rules and in such proportions on the several towns and districts within the same, as shall be agreed upon and ordered by the great and general court or assembly at their session in May, one thousand seven hundred and forty-four, and paid into the publick treasury again on or before the last day of December then next after. £3,500 in 1744.

And as a fund and security for drawing in such sum or sums as shall be paid out to the representatives of the several towns,—

Be it enacted,

[SECT. 7.] That there be and hereby is granted unto his most excellent majesty, a tax of such sum or sums as shall be paid to the several representatives as aforesaid, to be levied and assessed on the polls and estates of the inhabitants of the several towns, according to what their respective representatives shall so receive; which sums shall be set on the said towns in the next province tax. And the assessors of the said towns shall make their assessment for this tax, and apportion the same according to the rule that shall be prescribed by act of the general assembly for assessing the next province tax, and the constables, in their respective districts, shall pay in the same when they pay in the province tax for the next year, of which the treasurer is hereby directed to keep a distinct and separate account; and if there be any surplusage, the same shall l[y][*i*]e in the hands of the treasurer for the further order of this court. Tax to be made for what is paid to the representatives.

And be it further enacted,

[SECT. 8.] That in case the general court shall not at their respective sessions in May, one thousand seven hundred and forty-three, and one thousand seven hundred and forty-four, agree and conclude upon an act apportioning the several sums which by this act is engaged shall be, in each of these several years, apportioned, assessed and levied, that then and in such case each town and district within this province, shall pay (by a tax to be levied on the polls, and estates both real and personal, within their districts) the same part and proportion of the said sums as the said towns and districts shall have been taxed by the general court in the tax act then next preceding; and the province treasurer is hereby fully impowered and directed some time in the month of June in each of these years, one thousand seven hundred and forty-three, and one thousand seven hundred and forty-four, to issue and send forth his warrants, directed to the selectmen or assessors of each town and district within this province, in manner as aforementioned in this act, requiring them to assess the polls, and estates both real and personal, within their respective towns [or] [*and*] districts, for their respective part and proportion of the several sums before directed and engaged to be assessed by this act; and the assessors, as also persons Tax for the money hereby emitted, to be made according to the preceding tax act, in case.

assessed, shall observe, be governed by and subject to all such rules and directions as shall have been given in the said next preceding tax act.

And be it further enacted,

Taxes to be paid in the several species herein enumerated.

[SECT. 9.] That the inhabitants of this province shall have liberty, if they see fit, to pay the several sums for which they respectively may, in pursuance of this act, be assessed, in bills of credit of the form and tenor by this act emitted, or in bills of the middle tenor, according to their several denominations, or in bills of the old tenor, accounting four for one; or in coined silver, at six shillings and eightpence per ounce, troy weight, and of sterling alloy, or in gold coin, proportionably; or in merchantable hemp, flax, winter and Isle-of-Sable codfish, refined bar-iron, bloomery-iron, hallow iron-ware, Indian corn, rye, wheat, barley, pork, beef, duck or canvas, whalebone, cordage, train oyl, beeswax, baberry-wax, tallow, pease, sheepswool, or tann'[e]d sole-leather (the aforesaid commodities being of the produce or manufactures of this province), at such moderate rates and prices as the respective general assembl[y][*ie*]s of the years one thousand seven hundred and forty-three, and one thousand seven hundred and forty-four, shall set them at; the several persons paying their taxes in any of the commodities aforementioned, to run the risque and pay the charge of transporting the said commodities to the province treasury; but if the aforesaid general assembl[y][*ie*]s shall not, at their respective sessions in May, some time before the twentieth day of June, agree upon and set the aforesaid species or commodities at some certain prices, that then the eldest councello[u]r, for the time being, of each of those count[y][*ie*]s in the province, of which any one of the council is an inhabitant, together with the province treasurer, or the major part of them, be a committee, who hereby are directed and fully authorized and impowered to do it; and in their setting of the prices and rating the value of those commodities, to state so much of them, respectively, at six shillings and eightpence as an ounce of silver will purchase at that time in the town of Boston, and so *pro ratâ*. And the treasurer is hereby directed to insert in the several warrants by him sent to the collectors of the taxes in those years, respectively, with the names of the afore-recited commodities, the several prices or rates which shall be set on them, either by the general assembly or the committee aforesaid, and direct the aforesaid collectors to receive them so.

How the commodities brought into the treasury are to be rated.

Treasurer to sell the said commodities.

[SECT. 10.] And the aforesaid commodities so brought into the treasury, shall, as soon as conveniently may be, be disposed of by the treasurer to the best advantage for so much as it will fetch in bills of credit hereby to be emitted, or for silver or gold, which silver and gold shall be delivered to the possessor of said bills in exchange for them; that is to say, one ounce of silver coin, and so gold in proportion, for six shillings and eightpence, and *pro ratâ* for a greater or less sum; and if any loss shall happen by the sale of the aforesaid species, or by any unforeseen accident, such deficiency shall be made good by a tax of the year next following, so as fully and effectually to call in the whole sum of twelve thousand pounds in said bills hereby ordered to be emitted; and if there be a surplusage it shall remain a stock in the treasury.

And be it further enacted,

Rule for paying private debts.

[SECT. 11.] That any debt contracted before the thirty-first day of October, one thousand seven hundred and forty-one, which might have been paid and discharged in and by province bills of the old tenor, and also any debt contracted between the said thirty-first day of October and the first day of April last (where the contracting part[y][*ie*]s have not expresly otherwise agreed) may be discharged by the bills by this act to be emitted, in proportion as one to four; that is to say, that a debt of twenty-six shillings and eightpence, dischargeable or contracted as aforesaid, may be discharged by six shillings and eightpence in bills by this act to be emitted, or by one ounce of silver, and so in proportion for a greater or less sum. [*Passed January* 12; *published January* 17, 1742-43.

CHAPTER 15.

AN ACT FOR APPORTIONING AND ASSESSING A TAX OF EIGHT THOUSAND POUNDS IN BILLS OF THE TENOR AND FORM LAST EMITTED.

WHEREAS the general court or assembly of the province of the Massachusetts Bay have in their present sessions ordered the province treasurer, impost officer, the several constables and collectors in all publick payments, to receive twenty shillings in bills of the first new tenor in discharge of twenty shillings tax or duty in bills of the form and tenor last emitted by the said court, aud so in proportion for a greater or less sum, and hereby a deficiency is occasioned in the funds for drawing in the publick bills of credit. Wherefore, to preserve and maintain the credit of the bills of this province, and effectually to draw in such sum or sums as may be deficient as aforesaid, we, his majesty's most loyal and dutiful subjects, the representatives of the province of the Massachusetts Bay, pray that it may be enacted. Preamble.

And be it accordingly enacted by the Governour, Council and House of Representatives,

[SECT. 1.] That there be and hereby is granted unto his most excellent majesty for the ends aforesaid, and for no other purpose whatsoever, a tax of eight thousand pounds to be levied on polls, and estates both real and personal, within this province, according to such rules and in such proportion on the several towns and districts within the same, as shall be agreed on and ordered by this court at their sessions in May, one thousand seven hundred and forty-six, to be paid into the publick treasury on or before the last day of December next after. £8,000 to be paid the last of December, 1746.

And be it further enacted,

[SECT. 2.] That in case the general court shall not, at their session in May, one thousand seven hundred and forty-six, agree and conclude upon an act apportioning the sum of eight thousand pounds, which by this act is engaged shall be in said year apportioned, assessed, and lev[y][*i*]ed, that each town and district within this province, shall pay, by a tax to be lev[y][*i*]ed on the polls, and estates real and personal, within their respective districts, the same part and proportion of said sum as the said towns or districts shall have been taxed by the general court in the tax act then next prece[*e*]ding; and the province treasurer is hereby fully impowered and required, some time in the month of June, in the year one thousand seven hundred and forty-six, to issue [*out*] and send forth his warrants, directed to the selectmen or assessors of each town and district within this province, requiring them to assess the polls, and estates real and personal, within their respective towns and districts, for their respective part and proportion of the said sum of eight thousand pounds, as before directed by this act; and the assessors and all persons assessed, shall observe, be governed by, and subject to all such rules and directions as shall have been given in the said next preceeding tax act. [*Passed January* 15; *published January* 17, 1742-43. To be levied by the last tax act. Warrants to issue for it in June.

CHAPTER 16.

AN ACT FOR MAKING MORE EFFECTUAL AN ACT [E][*I*]NTITLED, "AN ACT FOR REGULATING THE MILITIA."

Preamble. 1693-94, chap 3.

WHEREAS the several penalties set or ordered to be imposed by the said act [e][*i*]ntitled, "An Act for regulating the militia," made and pass[*e*]d in the fifth year of the reign of King William and Queen Mary, do not answer the good design proposed in said act; for remedy whereof,—

Be it enacted by the Governour, Council and House of Represent-[ati]ves,

Clerks may distrain or sue for fines.

[SECT. 1.] That the clerk of each respective [troop or] company may, *ex officio*, distrain for any fine or penalty, for breach of any of the clauses or paragraphs in the aforesaid act, for breach of which he might have distrained by force of said act, or may recover the same by action of debt before a justice of the peace, or any court of record proper to try the same; all the said forfeitures to be applied to the uses mentioned in said act.

And for preventing the misapplication of the money to be levied and collected for breach of said act,—

Be it further enacted,

Shall keep fair accounts.

[SECT. 2.] That the clerk of each troop or company shall make and fairly enter in a book, to be kept for that purpose, a particular account of the several fines and forfeitures collected and recovered as aforesaid; and of the mon[ey][*ie*]s so collected, he shall lay out and improve so much as shall be necessary (his own fees, as by law established, being first deducted) for purchasing of drums, colours, halberds, and other necessaries for the use of the troop or company whereunto he belongs, as from time to time he shall receive orders from the captain or chief officer, in writing, under his hand; and every such clerk shall likewise make a fair entry of his several disbursem[*en*]ts of the money by him collected, setting forth the use to which the same has been applied, and, some time in the month of March, yearly, if required, deliver to the captain, and to such others as are or may be concerned in ordering the disposition of any part of the mon[ey][*ie*]s so collected, an attested copy of such account of his receipts and disbursem[*en*]ts, and shall receive, for his trouble therein (to be paid out of the fines), such recompence as the commission officers of such company shall judge reasonable; and the overplus, if any be, on ballance of such account shall, in the month of March, annually, render to the treasurer of the town where such company is, to be improved for the purchasing of arms, powder, bullets, and such other ammunition for a town stock, as by said act is required; and every military clerk shall be under oath, to be administred to him by a justice of the peace for the same county, for the faithful[l] discharge of his duty and trust in every of the particulars before mentioned; and upon conviction, before the court of general sessions of the peace (upon complaint made), of neglect therein, shall forfeit and pay the sum of five pounds, to be laid out and improved for the purposes aforesaid.

Purchase drums, &c., by the captain's order.

Account to the captain, &c., in March annually;—

and render the overplus to the town treasurer;—

and be sworn to faithfulness in his office.

And be it further enacted,

Succeeding clerk to recover what is not accounted for.

[SECT. 3.] That upon the death or removal of any military clerk, his successor in the said office shall have power, and is hereby authorized to demand, sue for, and recover of such clerk, if living, and of the executors or administrators of any clerk deceased, such sum or sums of money, collected as aforesaid, as remained in his hands at the time of his death or removal, and not applied to the use of such company, according to the directions of the law.

And be it further enacted,

[SECT. 4.] That when any servant, apprentice or other person, under the age of twenty-one years, liable by law to train, and, having been duly warned (not less than four day's notice beforehand to be accounted sufficient, unless in case of an alarm or other extraordinary occasion), shall not attend on military exercises on training days, or on military watches, the master, parent or other person who hath the immediate care and governm[*en*]t of such delinquent, shall be answerable for such neglect, and be obliged to satisfy and pay the fine by law imposed for such delinquency, and shall be liable to a suit for the same, as above provided.

Masters and parents shall answer the fines of minors.

And be it further enacted,

[SECT. 5.] That every person listed and orderly admitted into any company, shall so continue and attend his duty there, unless such person, by name, be dismiss'd, by writing, under the hand of the chief officer of the company or regiment to which he belongs, or of the captain-general or commander-in-chief of the province, or be removed out of the town or precinct, on pain of incurring, for each offence or neglect, the penalty by law already provided in case of non-appearance on training days.

How soldiers of any company may be dismissed.

[SECT. 6.] This act to continue and be in force for the term of seven years from the publication thereof, and no longer. [*Passed January* 15; *published January* 17, 1742-43.

Limitation.

CHAPTER 17.

AN ACT TO PREVENT THE SPREADING OF THE SMALL-POX AND OTHER INFECTIOUS SICKNESS, AND TO PREVENT THE CONCEALING OF THE SAME.

WHEREAS the inhabitants of sundry towns in this province are often exposed to the infection of the small-pox and other malignant, contagious distempers, by persons coming from the neighbouring governments visited with such infectious sickness, and by goods transported hither that carry infection with them,—

Preamble. 1739-40, chap. 1.

Be it therefore enacted by the Governour, Council and House of Represent[*ati*]*ves,*

[SECT. 1.] That any person or persons, coming from any place, in either of the neighbouring colonies or provinces, where the small-pox or other malignant, infectious distemper is prevailing, into any town within this province, who shall not, within the space of two hours from their first coming, or from the time they shall first be informed of their duty by law in this particular, give notice to one or more of the selectmen or town clerk of such town, of their coming thither, and of the place from whence they came, shall forfeit and pay the sum of twenty pounds; and if any person or persons, coming into any town of this province from any such place visited with the small-pox or other infectious sickness, shall not, within the space of two hours (after warning given him or them for that purpose by the selectmen of such town), depart out of this province, in such case it shall and may be lawful[1] for any justice of the peace of such county, by warrant, directed to a constable or other proper officer, to cause such person or persons to be removed, with any their goods that may probably give infection, unto the colony or

Within two hours, to give notice of their coming, on pain of £20.

To depart in two hours, on pain of £20.

government from whence they came; and any person removed by warrant as aforesaid, who, during the prevalency of such distemper, shall presume to return into any town of this province without liberty first obtained from such justice, or from the selectmen of such town, shall forfeit and pay the sum of one hundred pounds.

And be it further enacted,

He that entertains him shall forfeit £20.

[SECT. 2.] That any inhabitant of this province who shall entert[a]in in his house any person warned to depart as aforesaid, by the space of two hours after notice given him or her by one or more of the selectmen, of such warning, shall forfeit and pay the sum of twenty pounds.

And be it further enacted,

Persons to be appointed to examine travellers, &c., and stay them from travelling, on pain of £20.

[SECT. 3.] That it shall and may be lawful[l] for the selectmen of any town or towns near to or bordering on either of the neighbouring governments, to appoint, by writing, under their hands, some meet person or persons to attend at ferries or other places by or over which passengers and travellers, coming from such infected places, may pass or be transported; which person or persons so appointed, shall have power to examine such passengers and travellers as they may suspect to bring infection with them, and, if need be, to hinder and restrain them from travelling, 'till licen[s][c]ed thereto by a justice of the peace within such county, or by the selectmen of the town into which such person or persons shall come; and any passenger who, coming from such infected place, shall, without licence as aforesaid, presume to travel or abide in this province after they shall have been cautioned and admonished, by the person or persons appointed as aforesaid, to depart, shall forfeit and pay the sum of twenty pounds, and be removed thence by warrant as aforesaid.

Use of the fines.

[SECT. 4.] The several forfeitures arising by virtue of this act, to be, one moiety to and for the use of the town where the offence shall be committed, the other moiety to him or them who shall inform and sue for the same in any of his majesty's courts of record within this province.

And be it further enacted,

A pole and red cloth to be hung out of an infected house, on pain of £50.

[SECT. 5.] That from and after the publication of this act, when any person is visited with the small-pox in any town of this province, immediately, upon knowledge thereof, the head of the family in which such person is sick, shall acquaint the selectmen of the town therewith, and also hang out, on a pole at least six feet in length, a red cloth not under one yard long and half a yard wide, from the most publick part of the infected house, the said sign thus to continue 'till the house, in the judgm[*en*]t of the selectmen, is thoroughly aired and cleansed, upon penalty of forfeiting and paying the sum of fifty pounds for each offence, one half for the informer, and the other half for the use of the poor of the town where such offence shall be committed, to be sued for and recovered by the treasurer of the town, or the informer, by action, bill, plaint or information, in any of his majesty's courts of record; and if the party be unable, or refuses to pay such fine, then to be punished by whipping, not exceeding thirty stripes.

And be it further enacted,

To inform the selectmen of symptoms, on penalty of £50.

[SECT. 6.] That when the small-pox is in any town of this province, and any person in said town (not having had the same) shall then be taken sick, and any pestulous eruptions appear, the head of that family wherein such person is, shall immediately acquaint one or more of the selectmen of the town therewith, that so the said selectmen may give directions therein, upon penalty of forfeiting the sum of fifty pounds, to be recovered and applied for the uses aforesaid, the whole charge to be born by the person thus visited, if able to defr[a][*e*]y the same; but if, in the judgm[*en*]t of the selectmen of the town, such person is indigent and unable, then the said charge to be born by the town whereto he or she belongs.

Provided, always,—

[SECT. 7.] That this act shall not be understood to extend to persons in any town where more than twenty families are known to be visited with the small-pox at one and the same time.

Limitation.

[SECT. 8.] This act to continue and be in force for the space of seven years, and no longer. [*Passed January* 15; *published January* 17, 1742–43.

CHAPTER 18.

AN ACT IN ADDITION TO THE SEVERAL LAWS OF THIS PROVINCE RELATING TO THE SUPPORT OF POOR AND INDIGENT PERSONS.

Preamble. 1692-93, chap. 28, § 9. 1699-1700, ch. 8. 1735-36, chap. 4. 1740-41, chap. 20.

WHEREAS it has sometimes so happened, and may hereafter happen, that persons that are poor and unable to support themselves, have and may greatly suffer by reason of the neglect of the selectmen or overseers of the poor of the town which, by law, is chargeable with their support, by reason of doubts and disputes touching what town or persons are, by law, liable to be at charge for their support, or on supposition or pretence that the condition and circumstances of such poor persons are not so necessitous as to require rel[ei][*ie*]f from the town, or to render them a proper town charge; for remedy whereof for the future,—

Be it enacted by the Governour, Council and House of Represent[*ati*]*ves,*

The justices to determine who are the poor of a town.

[SECT. 1.] That every such doubt, controversy or dispute, as aforementioned, shall be determined by the justices of the court of general sessions of the peace, in the county to which such poor person doth belong; and the said justices are hereby fully authorized and impowered fully to determine the same, upon application to them made for that purpose.

And be it further enacted,

The overseers of the poor shall conform, on penalty of 40s.

[SECT. 2.] That in case the selectmen or overseers of the poor in any town, where there are such chosen and specially appointed for that purpose, shall refuse or neglect to take the care of, and afford the necessary rel[ei][*ie*]f to any poor and indigent person or persons that shall have been deemed and adjudged (by the justices in sessions) to stand in need of such rel[ei][*ie*]f, and to be the proper charge of the town to which such selectmen or overseers do belong, every such delinquent selectman or overseer shall, on each conviction, before the justices of the court aforesaid, of such refusal or neglect, be by them amerced in a sum not exceeding forty shillings, at the discretion of the court, regard being had to the circumstances extenuating or aggravating the offence; such sum to be levied by distress and sale of such offenders' goods, and to be applied for the support of the poor of the town where such delinquent selectmen or overseers dwell.

And be it further enacted,

The justices may assess the town, on their neglect.

[SECT. 3.] That when any town shall refuse or neglect to defr[a][*e*]y the charges heretofore arisen, or that shall arise and accrue for the support of such indigent person or persons as ought to be supported at such town's proper charge; in such case the said justices are hereby impowered to assess the inhabitants of such town therefor, and to cause the same to be added to such town's proportion of the county tax, and therewith to be collected and paid into the county treasury, and to be disposed of, by order of said justices, for defr[a][e]ying the charges incurred for the support of such indigent person or persons as aforementioned.

And be it further enacted,

Such as have been at charge shall be refunded by the town.

[SECT. 4.] That whosoever hath been, or hereafter shall be at charge for the rel[ei][*ie*]f of such necessitous and indigent person or persons, who ought to be rel[ei][*ie*]ved and supported by the town or towns to which they respectively belong, during the time or part of the time that the selectmen or overseers of the poor have or shall neglect their duty in that behalf, the person or persons that have been or shall be at charge for their rel[ei][*ie*]f shall be refunded by such town or towns by order of the justices as afores[*ai*]d, and the same shall be assessed and collected in manner as before-mentioned.

Limitation.

[SECT. 5.] This act to continue and be in force for the term of three years, and no longer. [*Passed January* 15; *published January* 17, 1742-43.

CHAPTER 19.

AN ACT TO PREVENT UNNECESSARY LAWSUITS.

Preamble. 1734-35, chap. 4. 7 Mass. 143.

WHEREAS it frequently happens in controversies upon book-debts or single contracts, that when the action comes upon trial the defendant pleads and urges payment, and, as an evidence, produces his acco[un][*mp*]t; *and whereas* the common practice is to give judgm[*en*]t without admitting any account in favour of the defendant, whereby he is necessitated to bring forward a suit himself, which occasions a further cost, and sometimes exposeth him to the loss of his debt, by reason of the original plaintiff's poverty or absconding,—

Be it therefore enacted by the Governour, Council and House of Representatives in General Court assembled,

The defendant on single contract may give his account in evidence to ballance the demand and prove it, as the plaintiff may his.

[SECT. 1.] That when and so often as any person is or shall be served with an original process in any action or plea, either of debt or of the case, for any sum of money due upon single contract between the parties for any goods sold or service done, due by account, whether such account be open or a ballance thereof be made and sign'd by the parties, to appear before any justice of the peace or inferio[*u*]r court of common pleas, before whom such case is cognizable, he shall be allowed by the court either to plead specially, or upon the general issue give his account in evidence by way of ballance to the plaintiff's demand, and be admitted to all such method and course of proving his account as any plaintiff upon his suit might; and the court or justice before whom such trial shall be, are hereby directed and impowered to compare and ballance the accounts of plaintiff and defendant, and to give judgm[*en*]t for so much only as shall appear upon such ballance due to the plaintiff; and if nothing appear due to the plaintiff on such ballance, to give judgment for costs to the defendant.

And to the intent the plaintiff may have sufficient opportunity to examine and make all just objections to the defendant's account,—

Be it further enacted,

And shall therefore file his account beforehand.

[SECT. 2.] That no defendant shall be admitted to produce or give his account in evidence upon any suit or trial as above, in a cause triable before a justice of the peace, unless he shall have left a copy of such account four days at least before the day of trial with the justice before whom the same is to be tried; and if the cause be before the inferio[*u*]r court of common pleas, then a copy of his account as above shall be left with the clerk of the court at least seven days before the day of the court's sitting; and the justice of the peace and clerk of the court, respectively, are hereby directed and required, at the desire of the plaintiff or his attorney, to grant a copy of such account.

[SECT. 3.] This act to continue and be in force for the space of seven years from the publication thereof, and from thence to the end of the next session of the gen[*era*]l court, and no longer. [*Passed January* 15; *published January* 17, 1742-43. Limitation.

CHAPTER 20.

AN ACT IN ADDITION TO THE SEVERAL ACTS FOR REGULATING THE ASSIZE OF CASKS, AND PREVENTING DECEIT IN THE PACKING OF FISH, BEEF AND PORK FOR SALE.

WHEREAS it is required in and by the several acts for regulating the assize of cask, and preventing deceit in the packing of fish, beef and pork for sale, that the cask used for packing provisions should be made free of sap; which may occasion some difficulty to the packers, who may apprehend themselves obliged to refuse some cask which may be every way sufficient, tho' not exactly conformable to the words of the law as it now stands,— Preamble. 1742-43, chap. 4.

Be it therefore enacted by the Governour, Council and House of Representatives,

[SECT. 1.] That from and after the publication of this act, the packers of fish, beef and pork be and hereby are allowed to pass as merchantable and according to law any cask used in packing the commodities aforesaid which they in their best judgment shall think sufficient to hold pickle without danger of leaking, altho' the staves of which the said cask are made may not be intirely free from sap. The packers to allow cask.

And as the allowance by law to the packers is found insufficient,—

Be it further enacted,

[SECT. 2.] That for packing or repacking and pickling each barrel[l] of pork, beef or fish, the packer shall be allowed twelvepence, and in proportion for greater or less cask, except where the buyer and seller shall agree that the pork, beef or fish shall not be pickled (as not being for exportation) in which case the allowance shall be ninepence only, and the packer shall be paid by the person selling the commodities aforesaid. Allowed 12*d*. or 9*d*.

[SECT. 3.] This act to continue and be in force until[l] the fifth day of July, one thousand seven hundred and forty-five, and no longer. [*Passed January* 15; *published January* 17, 1742-43. Limitation.

CHAPTER 21.

AN ACT TO ENABLE THE PROPRIETORS OF HASSANAMISCO LANDS IN THE TOWNSHIP OF GRAFTON TO RAISE MON[EY][*IE*]S FOR SUPPORTING THE MINISTRY, AND DEFRAYING THE OTHER CHARGES ARISEN AND ARISING THERE.

WHEREAS the proprietors of Hassanamisco lands in the township of Grafton, by an act of this governm[*en*]t pass'd in the first year of his Preamble. 1727-28, chap. 14. 1734-35, chap. 20.

present majesty's reign, are obliged to erect a meeting-house and school-house, and to support a minister and schoolmaster there, and four-fifths of the charge thereby arising was by said act ordered to be defr[a][e]yed by forty persons, to whom liberty was granted to purchase said lands, the other fifth part by nine families before that time set[t]led there, and that the afores[ai]d proportion of charges, together with the method then assigned for raising and collecting mon[ey][ie]s to defr[a][e]y the same should continue and be observed until[l] those lands should be made a township; *and whereas* said lands have since been erected into a township, and that before the whole of the charges so incurred were collected in pursuance of said act; wherefore, to enable said proprietors to collect the same,—

Be it enacted by the Governour, Council and House of Represent-[ati]ves,

Manner of the assessment.

That the assessors of the propriety of Grafton, *alias* Hassanamisco, be and hereby are enabled to assess the several proprietors of the said tract of land purchased by said forty persons, and set[t]led or possessed by said nine families, for all charges which may still be behind and unpaid, and which arose or were occasioned by the compliance of said proprietors with the duties required of them by the aforesaid act; four-fifths thereof to be apportioned upon the present proprietors of the lands petitioned for and purchased by the aforesaid forty persons, the other fifth on the present proprietors of the lands which were possessed by said nine English persons or families before the said act. And the collector or collectors of the said proprietors of Grafton, *alias* Hassanamisco, are hereby enabled and impowered to gather and collect such taxes as shall be committed to him or them by the assessors as aforesaid, and upon the refusal of any of the proprietors who shall be assessed as aforesaid, to pay such sum or sums as shall be set upon and required of them, the collector or collectors to whom the said tax is committed are hereby impowered and directed to make sale to the highest bidder of so much of the said proprietor's land, who shall so refuse to pay, as shall satisfy his part of said assessm[en]t, the overplus, if any there be, to be returned to the said proprietor; and the said collector or collectors shall post up a notification in some publick place in said Hassanamisco, and also give notice of the intended sale in one or more of the publick newspapers at least thirty days before the time appointed for said sale. [*Passed January* 15; *published January* 17, 1742-43.

Collectors to sell the lands of such as pay not their tax.

CHAPTER 22.

AN ACT TO PREVENT FIRING THE WOODS.

Preamble.

WHEREAS it is found by experience that the burning of the woods does greatly impoverish the lands, prevent the growth of wood, and destroys much fence, to the great detriment of the owners; for prevention whereof for the future,—

Be it enacted by the Governour, Council and House of Represent-[ati]ves,

None to fire the woods lying in common, without leave, on pain of 40s., and answer the damage to the proprietors.

[SECT. 1.] That from and after the publication of this act, no person or persons shall wittingly and willingly set fire in any woods or land lying in common within the bounds of any town, without leave first had from the town or proprietors, respectively, owners of such land lying in common, by a major vote, at a meeting for that purpose appointed, under the penalty of forty shillings, to be recovered by action or information, before any justice of the peace in the county where the offence is committed, such penalty to be for the use of the person or persons who shall prosecute or sue for the same; and the party offending shall be further liable to the action of the town, proprietors or particular persons damnified by such fire; and in case such fire shall be set or kindled by any person under age, such penalty shall be recovered of the parent or master, respectively, of such person under age, unless it shall appear such person under age was employed or directed by some person other than the parent or master, in which case the person so employing or directing shall be liable thereunto.

In case of infants.

And be it further enacted,

[SECT. 2.] That it shall and may be lawful[l] for any town or proprietors of any such lands as afores[*ai*]d, to give order for the setting fire in the lands to them respectively belonging, and to ch[oo][*u*]se two or more persons for that service, who shall appoint times for that purpose, and give seasonable notice thereof in the town where such lands l[y][*i*]e, and to the selectmen of such adjacent town, near the borders whereof the woods may be that are to be set on fire as aforesaid.

The town or proprietors may give leave, first giving public notice to such as may be affected by it.

And inasmuch as it is ofttimes impossible to prove such facts by direct testimonies,—

Be it further enacted,

[SECT. 3.] That upon process brought for setting fire as aforesaid, where proof cannot be made in the ordinary method and course of the law, if the plaintiff, complainant or other credible person, shall swear that fire has been kindled as is declared in the writ, and there does appear such circumstances as shall render it highly probable, in the judgm[*en*]t of the court or justice before whom the tr[y][*i*]al is, that the fire was kindled by the defendant, his child or servant, or by some other child or person under the age of fourteen years, directed or employed by the defendant for that purpose, then, and in such case, unless the person charged (being of the age of fourteen years or upwards) will acquit himself, upon oath administred to him by the court or justice before whom the tr[y][*i*]al is, the plaintiff or complainant shall recover against the defendant, the penalty by this act imposed, and costs; but if the defendant shall acquit himself upon oath as afores[*ai*]d, judgment shall be entred up for the defendant, his costs ag[*ain*]st the plaintiff.

Manner of conviction.

[SECT. 4.] This act to continue and be in force for the space of three years from the publication thereof, and no longer. [*Passed January* 15; *published January* 17, 1742-43.

Limitation.

CHAPTER 23.

AN ACT FOR GRANTING TO THOMAS SYMMES, GENTLEMAN, AND GRACE PARKER, WIDOW, BOTH OF CHARLESTOWN, IN THE COUNTY OF MIDDLESEX, THE SOLE PRIVILE[*D*]GE OF MAKING STONE-WARE.

WHEREAS Thomas Symmes, gent[*lema*]n, and Grace Parker, widow, both of Charlestown, in the county of Middlesex, have represented to this court, that, having procured a person well skilled in the art or m[i][*y*]stery of making stone-ware, and engaged him to instruct them therein, they are willing to undertake the making that kind of ware within this province, and have thereupon prayed that they may enjoy the sole privile[*d*]ge of making the same for such term of time as this govern[*men*]t, in consideration of the expensiveness and risque of the

Preamble.

undertaking, shall judge reasonable; and this court, being willing to give due encouragem[*en*]t to undertakings likely to prove beneficial to the publick; therefore,—

Be it enacted by the Governour, Council and House of Represent-[ati]ves,

Term of the privilege, fifteen years.

[SECT. 1.] That the sole right, privile[*d*]ge, and advantage of making the kind of ware commonly called stone-ware, be and hereby is granted to the said Thomas Symmes and Grace Parker, and to their respective heirs and assigns, to have and to hold to their only use, benefit, and behoof, for and during the full space and term of fifteen years, to commence on and from the publication of this act.

And be it further enacted,

Prohibition to others: penalty, £20.

[SECT. 2.] That all and every other person and persons whosoever, be and hereby are strictly forbidden to make the said ware within this province at any time or times during the term aforesaid; and every person offending against this act shall, on each conviction, forfeit and pay the sum of twenty pounds, to be recovered by the said Thomas Symmes and Grace Parker, their heirs or assigns, by action, bill, plaint or information, in any of his majesty's courts of record in the county where the offence shall be committed.

And be it further enacted,

And their buildings for that purpose a common nuisance.

[SECT. 3.] That every kiln, house or other edifice that shall be used in the making or burning any ware of the kind aforementioned, within the term aforesaid, whether the same be already erected, or shall hereafter be erected (unless by allowance and permission of the said Thomas Symmes and Grace Parker, or their heirs, or by special order of this governm[*en*]t, to be made in case of the said grantees failing to carry on the aforesaid business with effect during the term aforementioned), shall be deemed a common nusance, and the court of general sessions of the peace in the county where such nusance may be, shall cause the same to be demolished, and the charge of so doing to be answered and paid by disposing of so much of the materials as shall be necessary to satisfy the same. [*Passed January* 15; *published January* 17, 1742-43.

CHAPTER 24.

AN ACT FOR THE MORE EASY PARTITION OF LANDS.

Preamble.

WHEREAS the partition of lands is often delayed by reason that the parties concerned therein are very numerous, and live remote from each other, and sometimes in parts beyond the seas, and are, as to some of them, unknown, to the hind[e]rance and retarding of improvem[*en*]t and settlements of lands in this province; for remedy whereof,—

Be it enacted by the Governour, Council and House of Represent-[ati]ves,

Any partner may petition the superior court, and have a partition by five freeholders.

[SECT. 1.] That from and after the publication of this act, any person or persons interested with any others in any lot or grant of land, or other real estate, making application, either by themselves or their lawful[l] agents, attorneys or guardians, to the superio[*u*]r court of judicature, holden for and within the respective counties of this province where such lot, grant or estate lies, the said court is hereby authorized and impowered to cause partition of such estate to be made, and the share or shares of the party or parties applying for the same, to be set off and divided from the rest, such petition to be made upon oath by five freeholders, or the major part of them, to be appointed by said court, and a return of such partition to be made to the clerk's office of said court; and the partition or division so made, being accepted by the said court, and there recorded, shall be valid and effectual to all intents and purposes.

Provided, nevertheless,—

[SECT. 2.] That before such partition be made, where any infants or persons under age, or *non compos*, are interested, guardians shall be appointed for all such persons, according to law. And if any person interested in any such estate, happen, at the time when such application shall be made, to be beyond sea, or out of the province, and has no sufficient attorney within the same, that then, and in such cases, the justices of said court shall appoint some discreet and indifferent person as agent for such absent party, and, on his or her behalf, to be advising in the making of such partition. Guardians shall first be appointed to any infant or *non compos*, interested, and agents for persons out of the province.

Provided, also,—

[SECT. 3.] That before such partition be made, due notice, by special order of said court, be given to all concerned that are known and within this province, that so they may be present, if they see meet, at the time of making the same. Notice to persons absent, before the partition is made.

Provided, also,—

[SECT. 4.] That if any partners should have a larger share set off than what is such partners' true and real interest, or if any share set off should be more than equal in value to the proportion it was set off for, then, and in every such case, upon complaint made within three years next after such partition, by any aggrieved partner or partners, who, at the time of making such partition, were out of the province, and not notified thereof as aforesaid, a partition as afores[ai]d shall be made *de novo;* and in such new partition, every partner shall be allowed for all the improvements he or they shall have made on any of their respective parts, and so much, and no more, taken off from any share, as such share shall be adjudged more than the proportion of the whole it was designed for, estimating all the lands, or other real estate, as in its original state, or in the state wherein it was when first divided. If more is set off to any one than is his due, a new partition may be made upon complaint thereof within three years, allowing for improvements made.

[SECT. 5.] This act to continue and be in force for the space of three years from the publication thereof, and no longer. [*Passed January* 14; *published January* 17, 1742-43. Limitation.

CHAPTER 25.

AN ACT TO PREVENT THE MULTIPLICITY OF LAWSUITS.

WHEREAS of late it hath been the practice of some of the sheriffs, undersheriffs, or their deputies, within this province, to receive from some of the justices of the peace, and the clerks of the courts within the respective counties, blank writs, and then fill them up and serve them, and sometimes appear, by virtue of a power of attorney, to pursue the same; which practice has a tendency very much to increase the number of lawsuits, and to a partial administration of justice; for remedy whereof,— Preamble.

Be it enacted by the Governour, Council and House of Representatives,

[SECT. 1.] That no sheriff, undersheriff, or deputy sheriff within this province, from and after the publication of this act, shall presume to draw or fill up any writ[t] for any matter or thing whatsoever, triable before any of his majesty's justices of the peace or courts of record Sheriffs not to fill up writs.

within this province, or be any ways of advice or assistance therein, unless in cases where he or they are concerned as plaintiff; and in case it appears to the justice or court to whom such writ[t] is returned, that any writ[t] was so drawn or fill'd up as aforesaid, such justice or court shall dismiss the same, and allow costs for the defendant.

And be it further enacted,

Nor appear by power of attorney, &c.

[SECT. 2.] That no appearance of any sheriff, his undersheriff, or deputy, before any justice of the peace or court of record, by virtue of a power of attorney, shall be allowed good to any intent or purpose whatsoever, in the county where he is an officer, except where the party giving the power lives out of the province, and in this case his appearance shall not be allowed if he filled the writ.

Limitation.

[SECT. 3.] This act to continue and be in force for the space of seven years from the publication thereof, and no longer. [*Passed January* 15; *published January* 17, 1742–43.

CHAPTER 26.

AN ACT FOR INLISTING THE INHABITANTS OF DORCHESTER INTO HIS MAJESTY'S SERVICE FOR THE DEFENCE OF CASTLE WILLIAM, AS OCCASION SHALL REQUIRE.

Preamble.

WHEREAS the safety of this province in a great measure depends on the strength of his majesty's Castle William, and it being necessary that a good number of men skilful[l] in the management of the great artillery, should be always ready there,—

Be it enacted by the Governour, Council and House of Represent-[ati]ves,

The militia of Dorchester to be enlisted for the castle.

[SECT. 1.] That the inhabitants of the town of Dorchester, who are by law subject to common musters and military exercises there, not exceeding fifty years of age, shall be [e][*i*]nlisted under the present captains or other officers as the captain-general shall commissionate, who shall repair to Dorchester Neck, and be transported over to Castle William eight days in each year, in such months as the captain-general shall order, and shall on the said days be, by the gunner and quarter-gunners, exercised in the mounting, dismounting, level[*l*]ing, traversing and firing the great guns, and shall be obliged hereunto, and the observance of such orders as shall be given them in this exercise, under the like pains and penalties that soldiers are under to obey their officers in said castle in time of service.

And be it further enacted,

Fine on the delinquents, 5s.

[SECT. 2.] That if any of the men in the town of Dorchester [e][*i*]nlisted as aforesaid shall neglect, absent, or refuse to attend at time and place for the exercise of the great artillery as aforesaid, being thereof notified and warned to appear, for every such day's neglect such soldier shall pay to the clerk of the company for the use thereof the sum of five shillings.

And whereas the soldiers of the militia in this province are obliged to train but four days in a year, extraordinary musters excepted,—

Be it therefore enacted,

Those that attend shall be paid for it, &c.,—

[SECT. 3.] That the officers and soldiers that shall appear the eight days at Castle William, as is provided for in this act, shall be paid for four of the said days after the rates following: the captain, five shillings; lieutenant, four shillings; ensign, three shillings and sixpence; serjeants and clerks, three shillings; drummers and corporals, two shillings and ninepence: private centinels, two shillings and sixpence per diem each, out of the province treasury: and that such officers and soldiers be allowed subsistence, as the other officers and soldiers have, during their service at said castle.

And for the further encouragement of the said men enlisted and exercised as aforesaid, and that they may be expert in the management of the great artillery,—

Be it further enacted,

[SECT. 4.] That all and every man shall be excused from all other military service, and from all impresses into other service that other soldiers by law are liable to. And be exempted from other duties.

And be it further enacted,

[SECT. 5.] That upon any alarm at Castle William, every man, able of body, as well those [e][*i*]nlisted by virtue of this act, as others, within the town of Dorchester, except such persons as are by law obliged to attend upon the governo[*u*]r for the time being, shall forthwith appear compleat with their arms and ammunition according to law, at the said Castle William, there to attend and follow such commands as shall be given for his majesty's service, and that on the penalty of paying five pounds to the clerk of the said company; the said fines to be recovered before any justice of peace or court proper to hear and try the same. Upon an alarm at Castle William, they shall attend, upon pain of £5.

[SECT. 6.] This act to continue and be in force for the space of three years. [*Passed January* 15; *published January* 17, 1742-43. Limitation.

CHAPTER 27.

AN ACT TO PREVENT GAMING FOR MONEY OR OTHER GAIN.

WHEREAS games and exercises, although lawful, should not be otherwise used than as innocent and moderate recreations, and not as trades or callings to gain a living, or make unlawful[l] advantage thereby,— Preamble. 1736-37, chap. 17.

Be it therefore enacted by the Governour, Council and House of Represent[ati]ves,—

[SECT. 1.] That from and after the twenty-fifth day of March, which will be in the year of our Lord one thousand seven hundred and forty-three, all notes, bills, bonds, judgments, mortgages, or other securities or conveyances whatsoever given, granted, drawn, or enter'd into, or executed by any person or persons whatsoever, where the whole or any part of the consideration of such conveyances or securities shall be for any money or other valuable thing whatsoever, won by gaming, or playing at cards, dice, tables, tennis, bowles, or other game or games whatsoever; or by betting on the side or hands of such as do game at any of the games afores[*ai*]d, or for the reimbursing or repaying any money knowingly lent or advanced for such gaming or betting as aforesaid, or lent or advanced at the time and place of such play to any person or persons so gaming or betting as aforesaid; or that shall during such play, so play or bett, shall be utterly void, frustrate, and of none effect, to all intents and purposes whatsoever; and that where such mortgages, securities, or other conveyances shall be of lands, tenements, or hereditaments, or shall be such as incumber or affect the same, such mortgages, securities, or other conveyances shall enure and be to and for the sole use and benefit of and shall devolve upon such person or persons as should or might have or be [e][*i*]ntitled to such lands, tenements, or hereditam[*en*]ts in case the said grantor or grantors thereof, or the person or persons so incumbring the same, had been All security for money won at gaming, or betting upon games, shall be void. 1 Allen, 566. 116 Mass. 273. To whom the estate shall then come.

naturally dead; and as if such mortgages, securities, or other conveyances had been made to such person or persons so to be [e][*i*]ntitled after the decease of the person or persons so incumbring the same; and that all grants or conveyances to be made for the preventing of such lands, tenements, or hereditaments from coming to or devolving upon such person or persons hereby intended to enjoy the same as afores[*ai*]d, shall be deemed fraudulent and void and of none effect, to all intents and purposes whatsoever.

And be it further enacted,

The loser, after payment, may recover it back.

[SECT. 2.] That from and after the said twenty-fifth day of March, any person or persons whatsoever who shall at any time, or sitting, by playing at cards, dice, tables, or other game or games whatsoever, or by betting on the sides or hands of such as do play at any game or games as aforesaid, lose to any one or more person or persons so playing or betting, any sum or sums of money, or any other valuable thing [or things] whatsoever, and shall pay or deliver the same or any part thereof, the person or persons so losing and paying or delivering the same shall be at liberty, within three months then next after, to sue for and recover the money or goods so lost and paid, or delivered, or any part thereof, from the respective winner or winners thereof, with costs of suit, by action of debt founded on this act, to be prosecuted in any of his maj[*es*]ty's courts of record, in w[*hi*]ch actions or suits no essoign, protection, wager of law, or more than one imparlance, shall be allowed; in w[*hi*]ch actions it shall be sufficient for the plaintiff to alledge that the defendant or defendants are indebted to the plaintiff, or received to the plaintiff's use, the mon[ey][*ie*]s so lost and paid, or converted the goods won of the plaintiffs to the defendant's use, whereby the plaintiff's action accrued to him according to the form of this act, without setting forth the special matter. And in case the person or persons who shall lose such money or other thing as aforesaid, shall not within the time afores[*ai*]d really and *bonâ fide*, and without coven or collusion sue, and with effect prosecute, for the money or other thing so by him or them lost and paid, or delivered as afores[*ai*]d, it shall and may be lawful[l] to and for any person or persons, by any such action or suit as aforesaid, to sue for and recover the same and treble the value thereof, with costs of suit, against such winner or winners as afores[*ai*]d; the one moiety thereof to the use of the person or persons that will sue for the same, and the other moiety to the use of the poor of the town where the offence shall be committed.

In default thereof, any other person may sue and recover treble the value, of the winner.

And for the better discovery of the mon[ey][*ie*]s or other thing so won, and to be sued for and recovered as aforesaid,—

It is hereby further enacted,

The winner shall discover upon oath the sum or thing so won.

[SECT. 3.] That all and every the person or persons, who by virtue of this present act shall and may be liable to be sued for the same, shall be obliged and compellable to answer upon oath such bill or bills as shall be preferred against him or them in any of the courts of record within this province, for discovering the sum and sums of money or other thing so won at play as afores[*ai*]d.

Provided always,—

And be it, nevertheless, enacted,

And such repayment shall excuse the winner from any other penalty.

[SECT. 4.] That upon the discovery and repaym[*en*]t of the money or other thing to be so discovered and repaid as afores[*ai*]d, the person or persons who shall so discover and repay the same as aforesaid, shall be acquitted, indemnified, and discharged from any other or further punishm[*en*]t, forfeiture, or penalty, which he or they may have incurred by the playing for or winning such money or other thing so discovered and repaid as aforesaid; anything in this present act contained to the contrary thereof in any wise notwithstanding.

[SECT. 5.] This act to continue and be in force for the space of seven years from the publication thereof, and no longer. [*Passed January* 15; *published January* 17, 1742-43. Limitation.

CHAPTER 28.

AN ACT IN FURTHER ADDITION TO AND EXPLANATION OF [THE] [*AN*] ACT [E][*I*]NTITLED AN "ACT FOR REGULATING TOWNSHIPS, CHOICE OF TOWN OFFICERS," &c.

WHEREAS in and by an act made in the fourth year of the reign of King William and Queen Mary, [e][*i*]ntitled "An Act for regulating of townships, choice of town officers, and setting forth their power," the freeholders and inhabitants of each town who are rateable at twenty pounds estate to one single rate besides the poll, are impow[e]red to assemble and to give their votes in choice of town officers in the month of March annually, but no rule of valuation is therein prescribed, whereby such estate, qualifying to vote as aforesaid, shall be estimated, nor is it declared whether the like estate shall qualify a voter in other town affairs; and there being no law of this province expresly setting forth and ascertaining the qualification of voters in precincts and parishes, by reason of which many doubts and controversies have arisen; for preventing whereof for the future,— Preamble. 1692-93, chap. 28. 1693-94, chap. 20, § 18. 1699-1700, chaps. 12, 26. 1710-11, chap. 7, § 1. 1713-14, chap. 16, § 1.

Be it enacted by the Governo[*u*]*r, Council and House of Represent*-[*ati*]*ves*,

[SECT. 1.] That henceforward no person shall be deemed duly qualified or be admitted to vote in the choice of officers, or in the other affairs to be transacted at any meeting of the town, precinct or parish where he dwells, but such only who are personally present at such meeting, and have a rateable estate in such town or district, besides the poll, amounting to the value of twenty pounds, by the following method of estimation; viz[t]., real estate to be set at so much only as the rents or income thereof for the space of six years would amount to were it let at a reasonable rate; and personal estate and faculty to be estimated according to the rule of valuation prescribed in the act from time to time made for apportioning and assessing publick taxes. All voters to be inhabitants present of a certain ratable estate, &c.

And be it further enacted,

[SECT. 2.] That when any dispute shall arise respecting the qualifications of any person offering his vote in any such publick meeting, the same shall be determined by the moderator of such meeting according to the list and valuation of estates and faculties of persons, in such town or district, last made by assessors under oath; and if it thereby appear that such person is not qualified as by this act is provided, his vote shall not be received: *provided*, that the value of lands leased shall not be reckoned to qualify the ter-tenant, but to qualify the lessor if he be an inhabitant in such town, precinct or parish. Determinable by the moderator by the last list. The rate of lands in lease, whom to qualify.

Provided also,—

[SECT. 3.] That when such dispute shall happen to arise in any town, precinct or parish meeting, before a moderator shall be chosen, in such case the major part of the selectmen then present, or of the precinct or parish committee, shall, respectively, determine the same in manner as aforesaid; and the assessors of each town and district are hereby required to lodge with the clerk of their respective towns and districts an attested copy of such their list and valuation from year to year, which he shall produce for the purpose afores[*ai*]d as there shall be occasion; and every assessor, bel)nging to such town or precinct Such dispute may be determined by the selectmen, in case. Assessors shall lodge a copy of the list yearly with the clerk.

where the inhabitants are not usually doomed, neglecting his duty herein, shall forfeit and pay the sum of forty shillings, to be recovered before any of his majesty's justices of the peace of the same county.

And be it further enacted,

The moderator permitting a person unqualified to vote, forfeits,—

and he that puts in more than one vote, forfeits.

[SECT. 4.] That if the moderator of any such meeting shall countenance and permit any person not qualified as aforesaid, whose qualification for voting has been called in question, to give his voice in any such meeting, he shall forfeit and pay the sum of five pounds; and whosoever shall presume to put in more than one vote at a time shall forfeit and pay the sum of five pounds; one moiety of the said forfeitures to be for the use of the poor of the town where the offence shall be committed, and the other moiety to him or them that shall inform or sue for the same in any of his majesty's courts of record.

And whereas several towns of the province do not give in an exact account of their rateable estate, and so the assessors are obliged to doom the inhabitants according to the best of their skill and judgment, whereby the qualification of voters in such places may be more difficult to come at; wherefore,—

Be it enacted,

The qualification of voters.

[SECT. 5.] That where a full invoice and valuation of the rateable estates in any town or district is not taken, and the assessors, on oath, do doom the inhabitants, those persons only shall be allowed to vote who are rated two-third parts so much for their estates and faculties as for one single poll, in the last tax of such town or district, respectively.

Provided always,—

Saving the voters for representatives.

[SECT. 6.] That nothing in this act shall be interpreted to exclude any person[s] from the privilege of voting in the choice of representatives, who are duly qualified therefor according to the royal charter.

Limitation.

[SECT. 7.] This act to continue for the space of four years, and no longer. [*Passed January* 15; *published January* 17, 1742-43.

CHAPTER 29.

AN ACT FOR THE MORE EASY PARTITION OF LANDS OR OTHER REAL ESTATE GIVEN BY WILL, AND HELD IN COMMON AND UNDIVIDED AMONG THE DEVISEES.

Preamble.

WHEREAS it is usual for persons by their last wills to devise their real estates to sundry of their children or others, to be divided to and amongst them in some certain proportion, a division whereof cannot be obtained by the act of the parties, by reason of their disagreem[*en*]t or some legal incapacity that some of them are under, and other methods for obtaining such partition are attended with charge, delay and other inconveniences, to the prejudice of such estate; for remedy whereof,—

Be it enacted by the Governo[*u*]*r, Council and House of Represent*[*ati*]*ves,*

The judge of probates to order a division of lands, &c., devised.

[SECT. 1.] That when and so often as any devisee, or his guardian, who holds any real estate in partnership with any other person or persons by force of any last will and testament, shall make application to the judge of probate of wills, &c., in the county where such estates lie[s], for a division thereof, it shall and may be lawful[l] for such judge of probate to order the whole of the real estate so devised (or that part of it the partition whereof is requested) to be divided to and amongst the devisees in proportion according to the will of the testator, by five good and discreet freeholders of the same county, to be appointed by the judge of probate, and to be sworn to the due performance of that service by the said judge, or by a justice of the peace of the same county, in case the estate to be divided be not within ten miles from the town where the judge himself dwells, notice being first given to all parties concerned to be present at the making such partition, if they see cause; which partition or division being returned into the probate office and approved by the judge, and there recorded, shall be valid in the law to all intents and purposes, unless upon the appeal of any party aggr[ei][*ie*]ved at the partition so made, the same should be reversed or altered by the governour and council.

Notice to be given to all parties.

An appeal.

Provided,

[SECT. 2.] That no partition of such estate shall be made where the proportion belonging to the devisees or any of them shall appear by the tenor of the devise[*e*] to be disputable and uncertain.

Except the proportion of the devisees be doubtful.

Provided also,

[SECT. 3.] That where any of the devisees are minors or out of this province, guardians be first appointed for such minors according to law, and some discreet and indifferent person be appointed by said judge to represent and act for such absent party, who shall be allowed six months after his return into the province to appeal to the gov[*ernou*]r and council from such judgm[*en*]t.

Guardians shall be first appointed, &c.

[SECT. 4.] This act to continue and be in force for the term of three years, and no longer. [*Passed January* 15; *published January* 17, 1742-43.

Limitation.

CHAPTER 30.

AN ACT FOR ERECTING A TRACT OF LAND COMMONLY CALLED NEW LISBORN, LYING IN THE COUNTY OF HAMPSHIRE, INTO A TOWNSHIP BY THE NAME OF PELHAM.

WHEREAS there are a considerable number of families setled on a tract of land commonly called New Lisburn, lying in the county of Hampshire, who have represented to this court that they labour under great difficulties, by reason of their not being incorporated into a township,—

Be it therefore enacted by the Governour, Council and House of Represent^ves,

That the lands afores^d be and hereby are erected into a seperate and distinct township, by the name of Pelham, the bounds whereof to be as follows; vizt., bounding easterly on a tract of land commonly called Quabin, granted to a number of Canada and Narraganset soldiers; southerly, on a lot of equivalent land, so called, belonging to the Reverend M^r. Edwards and Mrs. Rebecca Hanley; westerly, on the east bounds of the town of Hadley; and northerly, partly on a new township commonly called Road Town, and partly on a new township commonly called New Salem; and that the inhabitants on the land afores^d be and hereby are vested with all the powers, privileges and immunities which the inhabitants of other towns within this province are, or, by law, ought to be vested with. [*Passed January* 15, 1742-43.

CHAPTER 31.

AN ACT FOR APPORTIONING AND ASSESSING A TAX OF TWENTY THOUSAND POUNDS IN BILLS OF CREDIT OF THE TENOR AND FORM LAST EMITTED; AND ALSO FOR APPORTIONING AND ASSESSING A FURTHER TAX OF ONE THOUSAND SIX HUNDRED AND THIRTY-EIGHT POUNDS AND THREEPENCE ONE FARTHING, IN BILLS OF CREDIT OF SAID TENOR AND FORM PAID THE REPRESENTATIVES FOR THEIR SERVICE AND ATTENDANCE IN GENERAL COURT, AND TRAVEL.

WHEREAS the great and general court or assembly of the province of the Massachusetts Bay did, at their session in November, one thousand seven hundred and forty-one, pass an act for the levying a tax of seven thousand five hundred pounds in bills by the said act emitted, and for the levying a tax of twenty thousand pounds in bills before current in the province, said twenty thousand pounds being equal to five thousand pounds of the bills emitted by said act; and said sums of seven thousand five hundred pounds, and three thousand seven hundred and fifty pounds,* were ordered by said act to be assessed this present year; and, at their session in May, one thousand seven hundred and forty-two, did pass an act for the levying a tax of three thousand seven hundred and fifty pounds in bills emitted by said act, to be assessed this present year; and also a tax of three thousand seven hundred and fifty pounds, to be assessed in the year one thousand seven hundred and forty-three, the whole of the several sums aforesaid amounting to the sum of twenty thousand pounds: and by the several aforesaid acts, provision was made, that the general court might, in the several years, apportion the several sums on the several towns in the province, if they thought fit; and the assembly aforesaid have likewise ordered that the sum of one thousand six hundred and thirty-eight pounds and threepence farthing, being the one half of such sums or sums as were paid the representatives in the years one thousand seven hundred and thirty-nine, and one thousand seven hundred and forty, should be levied and assessed on the polls and estates of the inhabitants of the several towns, according to what their respective representatives have received; wherefore, for the ordering, directing and effectual drawing in the sum of sixteen thousand two hundred and fifty pounds, pursuant to the funds and grants aforesaid, and for removing or bringing forward the fund for three thousand seven hundred and fifty pounds laid on the year one thousand seven hundred and forty-three as aforesaid, and laying the same on this present year, and drawing the said sum into the treasury according to the apportionment now agreed to by this court; and also for drawing in the sum of one thousand six hundred and thirty-eight pounds and threepence one farthing, paid the representatives as aforesaid; all which is unanimously approved, ratified and confirmed; we, his majesty's most loyal and dutiful subjects, the representatives in general court assembled, pray that it may be enacted,—

1741-42, chap. 11, § 15. 1741-42, chap. 11, § 26. 1742-43, chap. 3, § 6. 1742-43, chap. 3, § 7. 1741-42, chap. 11, § 29.

And be it accordingly enacted by the Governour, Council and House of Representatives,

[SECT. 1.] That each town and district within this province be assessed and pay as such town's and district's proportion of the sum of twenty thousand pounds in bills of the tenor last emitted, as also for the fines laid on them, and their representatives' pay, the several sums following; that is to say,—

* *Sic.* £5,000?—See 1741-42, chap. 11, §§ 5 and 11.

IN THE COUNTY OF SUFFOLK.

	REPRESENTATIVES' PAY.		PROVINCE TAX.		SUM TOTAL.
Boston, . .	Fifty-seven pounds nineteen shillings and threepence, ...	£57 19s. 3d.	Three thousand six hundred pounds, ...	£3,600 0s. 0d.	£3,657 19s. 3d.
Roxbury, . .	Eleven pounds fourteen shillings and seven-pence halfpenny, ...	11 14 7½	One hundred eighty-six pounds three shillings and four-pence, ...	186 3 4	197 17 11½
Dorchester, .	Fifteen pounds three shillings and sixpence,	15 3 6	One hundred seventy-six pounds eight shillings and fourpence, ...	176 8 4	191 11 10
Milton, . .	Fourteen pounds five shillings and seven-pence farthing, ...	14 5 7¼*	Eighty-one pounds eleven shillings and eightpence, .	81 11 8	95 17 3½*
Brantrey, . .	Eighteen pounds one shilling and a half-penny, ...	18 1 0½	One hundred and ninety-five pounds, ...	195 0 0	213 1 0½
Weymouth, .	Seventeen pounds seven shillings and six-pence, ...	17 7 6	One hundred and twelve pounds sixteen shillings and eightpence, ...	112 16 8	130 4 2
Hingham, . .	Fourteen pounds two shillings and nine-pence, ...	14 2 9	Two hundred and ten pounds eleven shillings and eight pence, ...	210 11 8	224 14 5
Dedham, . .	Sixteen pounds eight shillings and two-pence halfpenny, ...	16 8 2¼*	One hundred thirty-eight pounds and fifteen shillings, .	138 15 0	155 3 2¼*
Medfield, . .	Thirteen pounds eleven shillings and six-pence, ...	13 11 6	Eighty-four pounds and fifteen shillings, . . .	84 15 0	98 6 6
Wrentham, .	Fourteen pounds eleven shillings and ten-pence halfpenny, ...	14 11 10½	One hundred and five pounds eighteen shillings and fourpence, ...	105 18 4	120 10 2½
Medway, . .	Six pounds eight shillings and a penny half-penny, ...	6 8 1½	Fifty-five pounds eighteen shillings and fourpence, .	55 18 4	62 6 5½
Stoughton, .	Eighteen pounds and three farthings, . .	18 0 0¾	One hundred and two pounds eleven shillings and eight-pence, ...	102 11 8	120 11 8¾
Hull, . . .	. . . .	0 0 0	Forty-four pounds thirteen shillings and fourpence, .	44 13 4	44 13 4
Brookline, .	Six pounds ten shillings, ...	6 10 0	Sixty-six pounds eleven shillings and eightpence, . .	66 11 8	73 1 8
Needham, . .	Fifteen pounds fifteen shillings and three farthings, ...	15 15 0¾	Fifty-nine pounds eleven shillings and eightpence, .	59 11 8	75 6 8¾
Bellingham, .	. . . .	0 0 0	Twenty-two pounds eight shillings and fourpence, .	22 8 4	22 8 4
Walpole, . .	. . . .	0 0 0	Thirty-four pounds and fifteen shillings, ...	34 15 0	34 15 0
Chelsea, . .	Eleven pounds sixteen shillings and seven-pence halfpenny, ...	11 16 7½	Eighty-seven pounds three shillings and fourpence, .	87 3 4	98 14 11½
		£251 15s. 8½d.		£5,365 13s. 4d.	£5,617 9s. 0½d.

* *Sic.*

IN THE COUNTY OF ESSEX.

	REPRESENTATIVES' PAY.		PROVINCE TAX.		SUM TOTAL.
Salem, . .	Thirty-two pounds eleven shillings and ninepence, ...	£32 11s. 9d.	Six hundred pounds, ...	£600 0s. 0d.	£632 11s. 9d.
Ipswich, . .	Thirty-six pounds and eleven shillings, .	36 11 0	Five hundred fifty-two pounds eight shillings and fourpence, ...	552 8 4	588 19 4
Newbury, . .	Eighteen pounds nine shillings and ninepence, ...	18 9 9	Five hundred and twelve pounds five shillings, . .	512 5 0	530 14 9
Marblehead, .	Seventeen pounds eighteen shillings and threepence, ...	17 18 3	Three hundred eighty-nine pounds six shillings and eightpence, ...	389 6 8	407 4 11
Lyn, . .	Eighteen pounds and eightpence farthing,	18 0 8¼*	Two hundred and ten pounds six shillings and eightpence, ...	210 6 8	228 7 4¼
Andover, . .	Sixteen pounds ten shillings and ninepence,	16 10 9	Two hundred and forty-one pounds thirteen shillings and fourp., ...	241 13 4	258 4 1
Beverly, . .	Eighteen pounds five shillings and sevenpence three farthings, ...	18 5 7¾*	One hundred fifty-four pounds and ten shillings, . .	154 10 0	172 15 7¾
Rowley, . .	Eighteen pounds seventeen shillings and ninepence, ...	18 17 9	One hundred and fifty pounds fifteen shillings, . .	150 15 0	169 12 9
Salisbury, . .	Fifteen pounds seven shillings and fourpence halfpenny, ...	15 7 4½	One hundred and thirty-three pounds six shillings and eightpence, ...	133 6 8	148 8 0½
Haverhill, . .	Seventeen pounds and [illegible], . .	17 0 9	One hundred and thirty-five pounds eleven shillings and eightpen., ...	135 11 8	152 11 5
[illegible]r, . .	Sixteen pounds [illegible] shillings and sixpence,	16 15 6	Two hundred and fifty pounds fifteen shillings, . .	250 15 0	267 10 6
Topsfield, . .	Seventeen pounds sixteen shillings and sixpence, ...	17 16 6	Seventy-six pounds eleven shillings and eightpence, .	76 11 8	94 7 2
Boxford, . .	Seventeen pounds [illegible] shillings and six[illegible], ...	17 15 6	Ninety-six pounds one shilling and eightpence, . .	96 1 8	113 17 2
Almsbury, .	Sixteen pounds eighteen shillings and ninepence, ...	16 18 9	One hundred and eleven pounds three shillings and fourpence, ...	111 3 4	128 2 1
Bradford, . .	Sixteen pounds eight shillings and tenpence halfpenny, ...	16 8 10½	Eighty-three pounds fifteen shillings, ...	83 15 0	100 3 10½
[illegible]n, . .	Sixteen pounds [illegible] shillings and sixpence, ...	16 19 6	Sixty-nine pounds eighteen shillings and fourpence, .	69 18 4	86 17 10
Manchester, .	. . . .	0 0 0	Sixty-three pounds one shilling and eightpence, . .	63 1 8	63 1 8
[illegible]n, . .	. . . .	0 0 0	Thirty pounds sixteen shillings and eightpence, . .	30 16 8	30 16 8
[illegible]n, .	Nine pounds seven shillings and sevenpence halfpenny, ...	9 7 7½	Fifty-nine pounds fifteen shillings, ...	59 15 0	69 2 7½
Rumford, . .	. . . .	0 0 0	. . . .	0 0 0	0 0 0
		£321 9s. 11½d.		£3,922 1s. 8d.	£4,243 11s. 7½d.

IN THE COUNTY OF MIDDLESEX.

Cambridge,	Seven pounds ten shillings,	£7 10s. 0d.	One hundred thirty-two pounds,	£132 0s. 0d.	£139 10s. 0d.
Charlstown,	Fourteen pounds and sixteen shillings,	14 16 0	Two hundred and seventy pounds six shillings and eightpence,	270 6 8	285 2 8
Watertown,	Sixteen p[illegible]ds and sevenpence halfpenny,	16 0 7½	Eighty-seven pounds eleven shillings and eightpence,	87 11 8	103 12 3½
Concord,	Seventeen pounds eighteen shillings and [illegible]e,	17 18 3	One hundred sixty-four pounds eighteen shillings and fourpence,	164 18 4	182 16 7
Weston,	Thirteen pounds ten shillings and ninepence,	13 10 9	Seventy-seven pounds thirteen shillings and fourpence,	77 13 4	91 4 1
Woburn,	Seventeen pounds [illegible]en shillings and a penny halfpenny,	17 13 1½	One hundred and twenty-eight pounds fifteen shillings,	128 15 0	146 8 1½
Reading,	Sixteen pounds eighteen shillings and a penny halfpenny,	16 18 1½	One hundred forty-one pounds six shillings and eightpence,	141 6 8	158 4 9½
Sudbury,	Sixteen pounds seventeen [illegible]llings and [illegible]e,	16 17 3	One hundred and forty-seven pounds,	147 0 0	163 17 3
Marlborough,	Seventeen [illegible]ds [illegible]en shillings and [illegible]nepence,	17 11 9	One hundred and fifty-one pounds fifteen shillings,	151 15 0	169 6 9
Lexington,	Seventeen pounds and thirteen shillings,	17 13 0	Ninety-one pounds and five shillings,	91 5 0	108 18 0
Newton,	Sixteen pounds nine shillings and fourpence halfpenny,	16 9 4½	One hundred and forty-two pounds three shillings and fourpence,	142 3 4	158 12 8½
Malden,	Fifteen pounds and one shilling,	15 1 0	One hundred and eighteen pounds six shillings and eightpence,	118 6 8	133 7 8
Chelmsford,	Ten pounds five shillings and threepence,	10 5 3	Eighty-one pounds thirteen shillings and fourpence,	81 13 4	91 18 7
Billerica,	Sixteen pounds fourteen shillings and sixpence,	16 14 6	Eighty-four pounds and five shillings,	84 5 0	100 19 6
Sherbourn,	Fifteen pounds ten shillings and elevenpence halfpenny,	15 10 11½	Fifty-three pounds one shilling and eightpence,	53 1 8	68 12 7½
Holliston,	. . . .	0 0 0	Thirty-seven pounds sixteen shillings and eightpence,	37 16 8	37 16 8
Groton,	Sixteen pounds eleven shillings and ninepence,	16 11 9	One hundred and thirty pounds one shilling and eightpence,	130 1 8	146 13 5
Framingham,	Sixteen pounds two shillings and sixpence,	16 2 6	One hundred and seven pounds eleven shillings and eightpence,	107 11 8	123 14 2
Medford,	Fifteen pounds seven shillings and threepence,	15 7 3	Sixty-three pounds eleven shillings and eightpence,	63 11 8	78 18 11
Stow,	. . . .	0 0 0	Forty-nine pounds thirteen shillings and fourpence,	49 13 4	49 13 4
Dunstable,	Six pounds eleven shillings and sixpence,	6 11 6	Forty pounds,	40 0 0	46 11 6
Dracut,	. . . .	0 0 0	Thirty-three pounds three shillings and fourpence,	33 3 4	33 3 4

* Sic.

IN THE COUNTY OF MIDDLESEX—*Continued.*

	REPRESENTATIVES' PAY.		PROVINCE TAX.		SUM TOTAL.
Stoneham,	. . . .	£0 0*s.* 0*d.*	Forty-two pounds eleven shillings and eightpence,	£42 11*s.* 8*d.*	£42 11*s.* 8*d.*
Littleton,	Two pounds three shillings and ninepence,	2 3 9	Forty-nine pounds eighteen shillings and fourpence,	49 18 4	52 2 1
Hopkinton,	Fifteen pounds seven shillings and tenpence halfpenny,	15 7 10½	Forty-one pounds thirteen shillings and fourpence,	41 13 4	57 1 2½
Bedford,	. . . .	0 0 0	Forty pounds fifteen shillings,	40 15 0	40 15 0
Westford,	Fourteen pounds twelve shillings and sixpence,	14 12 6	Fifty-three pounds thirteen shillings and fourpence,	53 13 4	68 5 10
Wilmington,	. . . .	0 0 0	Thirty-eight pounds and five shillings,	38 5 0	38 5 0
Tewksbury,	. . . .	0 0 0	Thirty-five pounds and five shillings,	35 5 0	35 5 0
[illegible]n,	. . . .	0 0 0	Twenty-six pounds and fifteen shillings,	26 15 0	26 15 0
Waltham,	Seventeen pounds fourteen shillings and fourpence halfpenny,	17 14 4½	Seventy-one pounds sixteen shillings and eightpence,	71 16 8	89 11 0½
[illegible]d,	Nine pounds one shilling and a penny halfpenny,	9 1 1½	Twenty pounds,	20 0 0	29 1 1½
		£344 2*s.* 7*d.*		£2,754 3*s.* 4*d.*	£3,098 15*s.* 11*d.*

IN THE COUNTY OF HAMPSHIRE.

Springfield,	Fifteen pounds seven shillings and ninepence,	£15 7*s.* 9*d.*	Two hundred and nineteen pounds three shillings and fourpence,	£219 3*s.* 4*d.*	£234 11*s.* 1*d.*
Northampton,	Sixteen pounds ten shillings and sixpence,	16 10 6	One hundred forty-four pounds one shilling and eightpence,	144 1 8	160 12 2
Hadley,	Ten pounds and four shillings,	10 4 0	One hundred and three pounds one shilling and eightpence,	103 1 8	113 5 8
Hatfield,	Ten pounds one shilling and sixpence,	10 1 6	Sixty-six pounds three shillings and fourpence,	66 3 4	76 4 10
Westfield,	Eleven pounds eight shillings and ninepence,	11 8 9	Eighty-four pounds eleven shillings and eightpence,	84 11 8	96 0 5
Suffield,	Six pounds five shillings and threepence,	6 5 3	One hundred and ten pounds one shilling and eightpence,	110 1 8	116 6 11
Enfield,	Fifteen pounds seven shillings and fourpence halfpenny,	15 7 4½	Sixty-five pounds six shillings and eightpence,	65 6 8	80 14 0½
Deerfield,	Five pounds sixteen shillings and threepence,	5 16 3	Sixty-six pounds and fifteen shillings,	66 15 0	72 11 3
Sunderland,	. . . .	0 0 0	Thirty-four pounds,	34 0 0	34 0 0

Northfield,	. . . .	£0 0s. 0d.	Twenty-nine pounds sixteen shillings and eightpence,	£29 16s. 8d.	£29 16s. 8d.
Brimfield,	Four pounds three shillings and ninepence,	4 3 9	Fifty-eight pounds eleven shillings and eightpence,	58 11 8	62 15 5
Somers,	. . . .	0 0 0	Thirty-five pounds eighteen shillings and fourpence,	35 18 4	35 18 4
Sheffield,	. . . .	0 0 0	Thirty-five pounds,	35 0 0	35 0 0
Elbows,	. . . .	0 0 0	Twenty pounds,	20 0 0	20 0 0
		£95 5s. 1½d.		£1,072 11s. 8d.	£1,167 16s. 9½d.

IN THE COUNTY OF WORCESTER.

[illegible]r,	Ten pounds fourteen shillings and fourpence halfpenny,	£10 14s. 4½d.	Sixty-eight pounds eight shillings and fourpence,	£68 8s. 4d.	£79 2s. 8½d.
Lancaster,	Eighteen pounds eighteen shillings and sixpence,	18 18 6	One hundred and thirteen pounds six shillings and eightpence,	113 6 8	132 5 2
[illegible]n,	Fifteen pounds ten shillings and elevenpence farthing,	15 10 11¼	One hundred and sixteen pounds eight shillings and fourpence,	116 8 4	131 19 3¼
Woodstock,	Fifteen pounds and fifteen shillings,	15 15 0	One hundred and two pounds eighteen shillings and fourpence,	102 18 4	118 13 4
Brookfield,	Fifteen pounds twelve shillings and sevenpence halfpenny,	15 12 7½	Sixty-nine pounds eleven shillings and eightpence,	69 11 8	85 4 3½
Southborough,	Nine pounds ten shillings and threepence,	9 10 3	Forty-five pounds three shillings and fourpence,	45 3 4	54 13 7
[illegible]r,	Nine pounds two shillings and fourpence halfpenny,	9 2 4½	Sixty-three pounds thirteen shillings and fourpence,	63 13 4	72 15 8½
Rutland,	. . . .	0 0 0	Forty-one pounds and five shillings,	41 5 0	41 5 0
Lunenburg,	Eight pounds six shillings and a penny halfpenny,	8 6 1½	Fifty-one pounds,	51 0 0	59 6 1½
Westborough,	. . . .	0 0 0	Seventy pounds sixteen shillings and eightpence,	70 16 8	70 16 8
Shrewsbury,	Five pounds three shillings and tenpence halfpenny,	5 3 10½	Sixty-two pounds thirteen shillings and fourpence,	62 13 4	67 17 2½
Oxford,	. . . .	0 0 0	Forty-seven pounds eighteen shillings and fourpence,	47 18 4	47 18 4
Sutton,	Fifteen pounds and ninepence,	15 0 9	Seventy-five pounds thirteen shillings and fourpence,	75 13 4	90 14 1
Uxbridge,	Ten pounds fourteen shillings and fivepence farthing,	10 14 5¼	Fifty-three pounds eighteen shillings and fourpence,	53 18 4	64 12 9¼
Harvard,	Eight pounds one shilling and tenpence halfpenny,	8 1 10½	Forty-six pounds three shillings and fourpence,	46 3 4	54 5 2½
Grafton,	. . . .	0 0 0	Thirty-nine pounds three shillings and fourpence,	39 3 4	39 3 4
Upton,	Eight pounds one shilling and threepence,	8 1 3	Fifteen pounds eighteen shillings and fourpence,	15 18 4	23 19 7
Dudley,	. . . .	0 0 0	Thirty-three pounds thirteen shillings and fourpence,	33 13 4	33 13 4

IN THE COUNTY OF WORCESTER—*Continued.*

	REPRESENTATIVES' PAY.		PROVINCE TAX.		SUM TOTAL.
Bolton,	. . . .	£0 0*s.* 0*d.*	Forty-four pounds eighteen shillings and fourpence,	£44 18*s.* 4*d.*	£44 18*s.* 4*d.*
Sturbridge,	. . . .	0 0 0	Seventeen pounds,	17 0 0	17 0 0
Leominster,	. . . .	0 0 0	Fourteen pounds,	14 0 0	14 0 0
Western,	. . . .	0 0 0	Thirteen pounds and five shillings,	13 5 0	13 5 0
		£150 12*s.* 4½*d.*		£1,206 16*s.* 8*d.*	£1,357 9*s.* 0½*d.*

IN THE COUNTY OF PLYMOUTH.

	REPRESENTATIVES' PAY.		PROVINCE TAX.		SUM TOTAL.
Plymouth,	Twelve pounds fourteen shillings and fourpence halfpenny,	£12 14*s.* 4½*d.*	One hundred eighty-seven pounds eight shillings and fourpence,	£187 8*s.* 4*d.*	£200 2*s.* 8½*d.*
Plimpton,	Thirteen pounds and ten shillings,	13 10 0	Ninety-nine pounds eight shillings and fourpence,	99 8 4	112 18 4
Scituate,	Eighteen pounds ten shillings and [illegible] pe[illegible] [illegible]ny,	18 10 10½	Two hundred eighty-seven pounds eleven shillings and eightp.,	287 11 8	306 2 6½
Bridgwater,	Seventeen pounds five [illegible]ings and sevenpence halfpenny,	17 5 7½	Two hundred twenty-eight pounds one shilling and eightpence,	228 1 8	245 7 3½
[illegible]d,	Eleven pounds one shilling and [illegible]pe[illegible] three farthings,	11 1 9¾	One hundred and forty-two pounds,	142 0 0	153 1 9¾
Pembrook,	Fifteen pounds three shillings and sixpence,	15 3 6	Seventy-six pounds six shillings and eightpence,	76 6 8	91 10 2
[illegible]y,	Two [illegible]nds seventeen shillings and sixpence,	2 17 6	Sixty-six pounds sixteen shillings and eightpence,	66 16 8	69 14 2
[illegible]rough,	Ten pounds one shilling and sixpence,	10 1 6	One hundred sixty-eight pounds eight shillings and fourpence,	168 8 4	178 9 10
Rochester,	Sixteen pounds eight shillings and sixpence,	16 8 6	One hundred and seven pounds six shillings and eightpence,	107 6 8	123 15 2
Abbington,	. . . .	0 0 0	Forty-seven pounds eighteen shillings and fourpence,	47 18 4	47 18 4
Kingston,	Five pounds fourteen shillings and fourpence halfpenny,	5 14 4½	Fifty-two pounds eight shillings and fourpence,	52 8 4	58 2 8½
Hanover,	. . . .	0 0 0	Sixty-one pounds and fifteen shillings,	61 15 0	61 15 0
Halifax,	. . . .	0 0 0	Forty pounds,	40 0 0	40 0 0
Warham,	. . . .	0 0 0	Twenty pounds,	20 0 0	20 0 0
		£123 8*s.* 0¾*d.*		£1,585 10*s.* 0*d.*	£1,708 18*s.* 0¾*d.*

IN THE COUNTY OF BARNSTABLE.

Barnstable,	Twelve pounds sixteen shillings and sixpence,	£12 16s. 6d.	Two hundred pounds fifteen shillings,	£200 15s. 0d.	£213 11s. 6d.
Yarmouth,	Fourteen pounds five shillings and threepence,	14 5 3	One hundred twenty-three pounds sixteen shillings and eightp.,	123 16 8	138 1 11
Sandwich,	Eleven pounds seventeen shillings and ninepence,	11 17 9	One hundred and eight pounds three shillings and fourpence,	108 3 4	120 1 1
Eastham,	Fourteen pounds one shilling and ninepence,	14 1 9	One hundred forty-nine pounds six shillings and eightpence,	149 6 8	163 8 5
Truro,	. . . .	0 0 0	Nineteen pounds eleven shillings and eightpence,	19 11 8	19 11 8
Harwich,	Fourteen pounds eight shillings and ninepence,	14 8 9	One hundred and three pounds ten shillings,	103 10 0	117 18 9
Falmouth,	Twelve pounds nineteen shillings and a penny halfpenny,	12 19 1½	Seventy-three pounds six shillings and eightpence,	73 6 8	86 5 9½
Chatham,	. . . .	0 0 0	Sixty pounds eighteen shillings and fourpence,	60 18 4	60 18 4
Provincetown,	. . . .	0 0 0	. . . .	0 0 0	0 0 0
		£80 9s. 1½d.		£839 8s. 4d.	£919 17s. 5½d.

IN THE COUNTY OF BRISTOL.

Bristol,	Sixteen pounds three shillings and ninepence,	£16 3s. 9d.	One hundred thirty-one pounds thirteen shillings and fourpence,	£131 13s. 4d.	£147 17s. 1d.
Taunton,	Sixteen pounds and fourpence halfpenny,	16 0 4½	Two hundred pounds three shillings and fourpence,	200 3 4	216 3 8½
Norton,	Fourteen pounds thirteen shillings and a penny halfpenny,	14 13 1½	One hundred pounds and ten shillings,	100 10 0	115 3 1½
Easton,	. . . .	0 0 0	Thirty-nine pounds six shillings and eightpence,	39 6 8	39 6 8
Dartmouth,	Ten pounds fifteen shillings and fourpence halfpenny,	10 15 4½	Three hundred and ten pounds one shilling and eightpence,	310 1 8	320 17 0½
Dighton,	Sixteen pounds fourteen shillings and sixpence,	16 14 6	Seventy pounds fifteen shillings,	70 15 0	87 9 6
Rehoboth,	Fifteen pounds nine shillings and sevenpence halfpenny,	15 9 7½	Two hundred forty-seven pounds one shilling and eightpence,	247 1 8	262 11 3½
Little Compton,	Sixteen pounds thirteen shillings and a penny halfpenny,	16 13 1½	One hundred forty-one pounds thirteen shillings and fourpence,	141 13 4	158 6 5½

IN THE COUNTY OF BRISTOL—*Continued.*

	REPRESENTATIVES' PAY.		PROVINCE TAX.		SUM TOTAL.
Swanzey with Shawamet,	Fifteen pounds three shillings and threepence,	£15 3s. 3d.	One hundred ninety-eight pounds thirteen shillings and fourpen.,	£198 13s. 4d.	£213 16s. 7d.
Tiverton,	Sixteen pounds one shilling and a penny farthing,	16 1 $1\frac{1}{4}$	One hundred and sixty pounds,	160 0 0	176 1 $1\frac{1}{4}$
Freetown,	. . . . . .	0 0 0	Sixty-five pounds fifteen shillings,	65 15 0	65 15 0
Attleborough,	Fourteen pounds eighteen shillings,	14 18 0	One hundred pounds ten shillings,	100 10 0	115 8 0
Barrington,	. . . . . .	0 0 0	Fifty-seven pounds eight shillings and fourpence,	57 8 4	57 8 4
Raynham,	. . . . . .	0 0 0	Forty-five pounds eleven shillings and eightpence,	45 11 8	45 11 8
Berkley,	. . . . . .	0 0 0	Forty-three pounds one shilling and eightpence,	43 1 8	43 1 8
		£152 12s. $2\frac{3}{4}$d.		£1,912 5s. 0d.	£2,064 17s. $2\frac{3}{4}$d.

IN THE COUNTY OF YORK.

Y[illegible]k,	Nineteen pounds three shillings and tenpence halfpenny,	£19 3s. $10\frac{1}{2}$d.	One hundred eighty-three pounds one shilling and eightpence,	£183 1s. 8d.	£202 5s. $6\frac{1}{2}$d.
K[illegible]ry,	Fourteen pounds sixteen shillings and threepence,	14 16 3	Two hundred fifty-two pounds one shilling and eightpence,	252 1 8	266 17 11
Berwick,	Thirteen pounds fifteen shillings,	13 15 0	One hundred and twelve pounds one shilling and eightpence,	112 1 8	125 16 8
Wells,	Fourteen pounds three shillings,	14 3 0	Eighty-eight pounds five shillings,	88 5 0	102 8 0
Falmouth,	Fifteen pounds one shilling and sixpence,	15 1 6	One hundred fifty-three pounds sixteen shillings and eightpen.,	153 16 8	168 18 2
Biddeford,	Sixteen pounds fifteen shillings and fourpence halfpenny,	16 15 $4\frac{1}{2}$	Sixty pounds fifteen shillings,	60 15 0	77 10 $4\frac{1}{2}$
Arundel,	. . . . . .	0 0 0	Thirty-nine pounds eleven shillings and eightpence,	39 11 8	39 11 8
Scarborough,	Four pounds eighteen shillings and ninepence,	4 18 9	Sixty-nine pounds eighteen shillings and fourpence,	69 18 4	74 17 1
North Yarmouth,	. . . . . .	0 0 0	Thirty-nine pounds,	39 0 0	39 0 0
[illegible]n,	. . . . . .	0 0 0	Forty pounds,	40 0 0	40 0 0
Brunswick,	. . . . . .	0 0 0	Eighteen pounds ten shillings,	18 10 0	18 10 0
		£98 13s. 9d.		£1,057 1s. 8d.	£1,155 15s. 5d.

IN THE COUNTY DUKES COUNTY.

Edgartown, .	Twelve pounds seventeen shillings and sevenpence halfpenny, ...	£12 17s. 7½d.	Forty-nine pounds sixteen shillings and eightpence, .	£49 16s. 8d.	£62 14s. 3½d.
Chilmark, .	. . . .	0 0 0	Sixty-three pounds three shillings and fourpence, .	63 3 4	63 3 4
Tisbury, .	. . . .	0 0 0	Thirty-nine pounds one shilling and eightpence, .	39 1 8	39 1 8
		£12 17s. 7½d.		£152 1s. 8d.	£164 19s. 3½d.

IN NANTUCKET COUNTY.

Sherbourn, .	Six pounds thirteen shillings and ninepence, ...	£6 13s. 9d.	One hundred thirty-one pounds sixteen shillings and eightpence, ...	£131 16s. 8d.	£138 10s. 5d.

	REPRESENTATIVES' PAY.		[illegible] TAX.		SUM TOTAL.
SUFFOLK, .	Two hundred and fifty-one [illegible] fifteen shillings and eightpence farthing, . .	£251 15s. 8¼d.	Five thousand three hundred [illegible] five pounds thirteen shillings and [illegible], ...	£5,365 13s. 4d.	£5,617 9s. 0¼d.
ESSEX, .	Three hundred twenty-one [illegible] [illegible] shillings and elevenpence halfpenny, .	321 9 11½	Three thousand [illegible] hundred twenty-two pounds one shilling and eightpence, ...	3,922 1 8	4,243 11 7½
MIDDLESEX, .	Three hundred forty-four pounds two shillings and sevenpence, ...	344 2 7	Two [illegible] seven hundred fifty-four [illegible] thirteen shillings and fourpence, ...	2,754 13 4	3,098 15 11
HAMPSHIRE, .	Ninety-five pounds five shillings and a penny [illegible], ...	95 5 1½	One thousand and seventy-two pounds [illegible] shillings and eightpence, ...	1,072 11 8	1,167 16 9½
WORCESTER, .	One hundred fifty [illegible] twelve shillings and fourpence [illegible], ...	150 12 4½	One thousand two hundred and six pounds sixteen shillings and eightpence, ...	1,206 16 8	1,357 9 0½
PLYMOUTH, .	One hundred and twenty-three pounds and eight shillings three farthings, . . .	123 8 0¾	One thousand five [illegible] and eighty-five pounds [illegible] shillings, ...	1,585 10 0	1,708 18 0¾
BARNSTABLE, .	Eighty pounds nine shillings and a penny [illegible], ...	80 9 1½	Eight hundred and thirty-nine pounds eight shillings and fourpence, ...	839 8 4	919 17 5½
BRISTOL, .	One [illegible] fifty-two pounds [illegible] shillings and twopence three farthings, . .	152 12 2¾	One thousand [illegible] hundred and twelve [illegible] and five shillings, ...	1,912 5 0	2,064 17 2¾

	REPRESENTATIVES' PAY.		PROVINCE TAX.		SUM TOTAL.
YORK, . .	Ninety-eight pounds thirteen shillings and ninepence, ...	£98 13s. 9d.	One thousand fifty-seven pounds one shilling and eightpence, ...	£1,057 1s. 8d.	£1,155 15s. 5d.
DUKES COUNTY,	Twelve pounds seventeen shillings and sevenpence halfpenny, ...	12 17 7½	One hundred fifty-two pounds one shilling and eightpence, ...	152 1 8	164 19 3½
NANTUCKET, .	Six pounds thirteen shillings and ninepence, ...	6 13 9	One hundred thirty-one pounds sixteen shillings and eightpence, ...	131 16 8	138 10 5
		£1,638 0s. 3¼d.		£20,000 0s. 0d.	

And be it further enacted,

[SECT. 2.] That the treasurer do forthwith send out his warrants directed to the selectmen or assessors of each town or district within this province, requiring them, respectively, to assess the sum hereby set upon such town or district in manner following; that is to say, to assess all rateable male polls above the age of sixteen years at four shillings and twopence per poll, and proportionably in assessing the fines mentioned in this act, and the additional sum receiv'd out of the treasury, for the payment of the representatives (except the governour, lieutenant-governour and their families, the president, fellows and students of Harvard College, setled ministers and grammar schoolmasters who are hereby exempted, as well from being taxed for their polls as for their estates, being in their own hands and under their actual management and improvement); and other persons, if such there be, who, thro' age, infirmity, or extream poverty, in the judgment of the assessors, are not capable to pay towards publick charges, they may exempt their polls and so much of their estates as in their prudence they shall think fit and judge meet.

[SECT. 3.] And the justices in the general sessions, in the respective counties assembled, in granting a county tax or assessment, are hereby ordered and directed to apportion the same on the several towns in such county in proportion to their province rate, exclusive of what has been paid out of the publick treasury to the representative of such town for his service; and the assessors of each town in the province are also directed in making an assessment to govern themselves by the same rule; and all estates, both real and personal, lying within the limits of such town or district, or next unto the same, not paying elsewhere, in whose hands, tenure, occupation, or possession soever the same is or shall be found, and also the incomes or profits, which any person or persons, except as before excepted, do or shall receive from any trade, faculty, business, or employment whatsoever, and all profits that shall or may arise by money or other estate not particularly otherwise assessed, or commissions of profit in their improvement, according to their understanding and cunning, at one penny on the pound, and to abate or multiply the same, if need be, so as to make up the sum set and ordered hereby for such town or district to pay; and in making their assessments to estimate houses and lands at six years' income of the yearly rents, in the bills last emitted, whereat the same may be reasonably set or let for in the place where they lye: *saving* all contracts between landlord and tenant, and where no contract is, the landlord to reimburse one half of the tax set upon such houses and lands; and to estimate Indian, negro and molatto servants proportionably as other personal estate, according to their sound judgment and discretion; as also to estimate every ox of four years old and upwards at forty shillings in bills of the last emission; every cow of three years old and upwards, at thirty shillings; every horse and mare of three years old and upwards, at forty shillings; every swine of one year old and upwards, at eight shillings; every goat and sheep of one year old and upwards, at three shillings: likewise requiring the assessors to make a fair list of the said assessment, setting forth in distinct columns, against each particular person's name, how much he or she is assessed at for polls, and how much for houses and lands, and how much for personal estate and income by trade or faculty; and the list or lists so perfected and signed by them, or the major part of them, to commit to the collectors, constable or constables of such town or district, and to return a certificate of the name or names of such collectors, constable or constables, together with the sum total to each of them committed, unto himself, sometime before the last day of January.

[SECT. 4.] And the treasurer for the time being, upon the receipt of such certificate, is hereby impowered and ordered to issue forth his warrants to the collector, constable or constables of such town or district, requiring him or them, respectively, to collect the whole of each respective sum assessed on each particular person, before the last day of May next; and of the inhabitants of the town of Boston, sometime in the month of March next; and to pay in their collection, and issue the accompts of the whole, at or before the last day of June, which will be in the year of our Lord one thousand seven hundred and forty-three.

And be it further enacted,

[SECT. 5.] That the assessors of each town and district, respectively, in convenient time before their making the assessment, shall give seasonable warning to the inhabitants, in a town meeting, or by posting up notifications in some place or places in such town or district, or notify the inhabitants to give or bring into the assessors true and perfect lists of their polls, rateable estate, and income by trade or faculty. And if any person or persons shall neglect or refuse so to do, or bring in a false list, it shall be lawful to and for the assessors to assess such person or persons, according to their known ability in such town, in their sound judgment and discretion, their due proportion to this tax, as near as they can, agreable to the rules herein given, under the penalty of twenty shillings for each person that shall be convicted by legal proof, in the judgment of the said assessors, of bringing in a false list; the said fines to be for the use of the poor of such town or district where the delinquent lives, to be levied by warrant from the assessors, directed to the collector or constables, in manner as is directed for gathering town assessments, and to be paid in to the town treasurer or selectmen for the use aforesaid: *saving*, to the party aggrieved at the judgment of the assessors in setting forth such fine, liberty of appeal therefrom to the court of general sessions of the peace within the county, for relief, as in case of being overrated. And if any person or persons shall not bring in a list of their estate as aforesaid to the assessors, he or they so neglecting shall not be admitted to make application to the court of sessions for any abatement of the assessment laid on him.

[SECT. 6.] And if the party be not convicted of any falseness in the list, by him presented, of polls, rateable estate, or income by any trade or faculty, business or employment, which he doth or shall exercise, or in gain by money at interest or otherwise, or other estate not particularly assess'd; such list shall be a rule for such person's proportion to the tax, which the assessors may not exceed.

Preamble. *And forasmuch* as ofttimes sundry persons, not belonging to this province, bring considerable trade and merchandize, and by reason that the tax or rate of the town where they come to trade and traffick is finished and deliver'd to the constable or collector, and before the next year's assessment are gone out of the province, and so pay nothing towards the support of the government, tho', in the time of their residing there, they reap'd considerable gain by trade, and had the protection of the government,—

Be it further enacted,

Transient traders to be rated. [SECT. 7.] That when any such person or persons shall come and reside in any town of this province, and bring any merchandize, and trade and deal therewith, the assessors of such town are hereby impowred to rate and assess all such persons according to their circumstances, pursuant to the rules and directions in this act providen, tho' the former rate may have been finished, and the new one not perfected as aforesaid.

And be it further enacted,

[SECT. 8.] That when any merchant, trader or factor, inhabitant of some one town within this province, shall transact or carry on trade and business in some other town in the province, the assessors of such town where such trade and business shall be carried on as aforesaid, be and hereby are impowered to rate and assess all such merchants, traders and factors, their goods or merchandize, for carrying on such trade and exercising their faculty in such town, pursuant to the rules and directions in this act.

[SECT. 9.] And the constables or collectors are hereby enjoyned to levy and collect all such sums committed to them, and assess'd on persons who are not of this province, or are inhabitants of any other town as aforesaid, and pay the same into the town treasury.

And be it further enacted,

[SECT. 10.] That the inhabitants of this province shall have liberty, if they see fit, to pay the several sums for which they may respectively be assess'd at, as their proportion of the aforesaid sum of twenty thousand pounds, in bills of credit of the last emission, or in bills of credit of the middle tenor, so called, according to their denominations, or in bills of the old tenor, accounting four for one; or in coined silver, at the rate of six shillings and eightpence per ounce, troy weight; or in gold coin, at the rate of four pounds eighteen shillings per ounce; or in good, merchantable hemp, at fourpence per pound; or merchantable flax, at fivepence per pound; or in good, merchantable, winter, Isle-of-Sable codfish, at ten shillings per quintal; or in good, refined bar-iron, at fifteen pounds per ton; or bloomery-iron, at twelve pounds per ton; or in good, hollow iron-ware, at twelve pounds per ton; or in good Indian corn, at two shillings and threepence per bushel; or good winter rye, at two shillings and sixpence per bushel; or good winter wheat, at three shillings per bushel; or in good barley, at two shillings per bushel; or good barrel pork, at two pounds per barrel; or in barrel beef, at one pound five shillings per barrel; or in duck or canvas, at two pounds ten shillings per bolt, each bolt to weigh forty-three pounds; or in long whalebone, at two shillings and threepence per pound; or merchantable cordage, at one pound five shillings per hundred; or in good train-oyl, at one pound ten shillings per barrel; or in good bees-wax, at tenpence per pound; or in bayberry-wax, at sixpence per pound; or in tryed tallow, at fourpence per pound; or in good pease, at three shillings per bushel; or in good sheepswool, at ninepence per pound; or good, tann'd sole-leather, at fourpence per pound: all which aforesaid commodities shall be of the produce of this province, and, as soon as conveniently may, be disposed of by the treasurer to the best advantage, for so much as they will fetch in bills of credit, or for silver and gold; and the several persons who pay their taxes in any of the commodities before mentioned, shall run the risque and pay the charge of transporting the same to the province treasury.

Tax may be paid in other species, besides the bills emitted.

[SECT. 11.] And if any loss shall happen by the sale of any of the aforesaid species, it shall be made good by a tax the next year; and if there be a surplusage, it shall remain a stock in treasury. [*Passed January* 6, 1742-43.

ACTS

PASSED AT THE SESSION BEGUN AND HELD AT BOSTON, ON THE THIRTY-FIRST DAY OF MARCH, A. D. 1743.

CHAPTER 32.

AN ACT FOR FIXING THE TIMES FOR HOLDING THE SUPERIO[*U*]R COURTS OF JUDICATURE, COURTS OF ASSIZE AND GENERAL GOAL DELIVERY, AND COURTS OF GENERAL SESSIONS OF THE PEACE, AND INFERIO[*U*]R COURTS OF COMMON PLEAS, WITHIN THE SEVERAL COUNTIES IN THIS PROVINCE.

Be it enacted by the Governo[u]r, Council and House of Representatives,

The times and places of holding inferior courts and courts of general sessions of the peace.

1699-1700, ch. 1. 1704-1705, ch. 1. 1708-1709, ch. 9. 1711-12, chap. 3, § 6. 1712-13, chap. 5. 1715-16, chap. 2. 1719-20, chaps. 4, 5. 1722-23, chap. 13. 1725-26, chap. 6. 1727-28, chap. 16. 1728-29, chap. 19. 1735-36, chap. 3. 1736-37, chap. 21. 1740-41, chap. 5. 1742-43, chap. 10.

[SECT. 1.] That the times and places for holding and keeping the courts of general sessions of the peace, and inferio[*u*]r courts of common pleas within the respective counties in this province, for the future, shall be as followeth; that is to say, for the county of Suffolk, at Boston on the first Tuesday of July, October, January and April; for the county of Essex, at Salem on the second Tuesday in July and last Tuesday in December, at Newbury on the last Tuesday in September, at Ipswich on the last Tuesday in March; for the county of Middlesex, at Cambridge on the third Tuesday in May, at Charlestown on the second Tuesday in December and March, at Concord on the last Tuesday in August; for the county of Hampshire, at Springfield on the third Tuesday in May and last Tuesday in August, at Northampton on the second Tuesday in February and November; for the county of Worcester, at Worcester on the first Tuesday in November and February, the second Tuesday in May, and the third Tuesday in August; for the county of Plymouth, at Plymouth on the first Tuesday in March, on the third Tuesday in May, September and December; for the county of Barnstable, at Barnstable on the last Tuesday in June, and on the third Tuesday of March, October and January; for the county of Bristol, at Bristol on the second Tuesday in March, June, September and December; for the county of York, at York on the first Tuesday of April, July and January, at Falmouth on the first Tuesday in October; for Dukes County, at Edgartown on the first Tuesday in March and last Tuesday in October; for the county of Nantucket, at Sherburn on the last Tuesday in March and first Tuesday in October, yearly, and in every year, from time to time.

And be it further enacted,

Times and places of holding the superior courts, &c.

1699-1700, ch. 3. 1703-1704, ch. 8. 1711-12, chap. 3. 1714, chap. 9, § 6. 1715-16, chap. 20. 1717-18, chap. 8.

[SECT. 2.] That the times and places for holding and keeping the superio[*u*]r court of judicature, court of assize, and general goal delivery shall, for the future, be as followeth; that is to say, within and for the county of Suffolk, at Boston on the third Tuesday in August and February; within and for the county of Essex, at Salem on the second Tuesday in November, at Ipswich on the second Tuesday in May; within and for the county of Middlesex, at Cambridge on the first

Tuesday in August, at Charlestown on the last Tuesday in January; within and for the county of Hampshire, at Springfield on the fourth Tuesday in September; within and for the county of Worcester, at Worcester on the third Tuesday in September; within and for the county of Plymouth, at Plymouth on the second Tuesday of July; within and for the county of Barnstable and Dukes County, at Barnstable on the third Tuesday in July; within and for the county of Bristol, at Bristol on the fourth Wednesday in October; within and for the county of York, at York on the third Wednesday in June, yearly, and in every year, from time to time, until this court shall order otherwise. [*Passed April* 23, 1743.

1720-21, chaps. 1, 13. 1721, chap. 3. 1724-25, chap. 11. 1727-28, chap. 16. 1733-34, chap. 9. 1735-36, chap. 24. 1736-37, chap. 21. 1740-41, chap. 13. 1741-42, chap. 19.

CHAPTER 33.

AN ACT IN ADDITION TO THE SEVERAL ACTS FOR REGULATING FENCES.

WHEREAS the several laws already made are ineffectual for obliging persons to make and maintain partition-fences between their lands under improvement, whereby the aggrieved parties are put to great expence and charge in forcing a compliance by the rules of the law,—

Preamble. 1693-94, chap. 7. 1698, chap. 12. 1718-19, chap. 3. 1727-28, chap. 13. 1740-41, chap. 19.

Be it enacted by the Governour, Council and House of Representatives,

[SECT. 1.] That from and after the first day of May next, that the respective proprietors of all lands enclosed with fence, shall keep up and maintain partition-fences between their and the next adjoining enclosures, in equal halves according to law, so long as both parties continue to improve the same, and in case either party lay his enclosure common, the party improving shall allow for his half of said partition-fence what the same shall be judged worth, in the estimation of two or more of the fence-viewers of such town; and if any person shall enclose such land afterwards, or, by joining fences with another, enclose his lands before lying common, he shall thereupon pay to the person who owns the partition-fence the value of one half of the same, in the judgment of the fence-viewers as aforesaid; and all partition-fences hereafter to be made, shall be in like manner done and maintained by the improving parties in equal halves; and in case either party refuse, after six days' notice, to make up his half thereof, the aggrieved party shall forthwith apply himself to two or more of the fence-viewers of such town, who hereby are impowered and enabled to make up the same according to law, and upon such person's refusal, who ought to pay for the same, with their costs and charges thereon, to prosecute and sue for it in any court of law proper to try the same.

Rules for the charge of partition fences.

And in case any dispute shall arise about the respective owner's right to any part of such fence, and his or their obligation to maintain the same, upon application made to two or more of the fence-viewers of such town where the land lies, they are hereby impowered to assign to each party his share thereof; and such settlement being recorded in the town-clerk's office, shall be binding upon such persons, and they obliged always thereafter to maintain their part of said fence as aforesaid; and in case any of the parties aforesaid refuse or neglect, after six days' notice given, to erect, keep up and maintain the partition-fences as is by this act prescribed, upon application made to two or more of the fence-viewers aforesaid, they shall do or cause the same to be done at the cost of the person neglecting his duty, who, in case of refusal, shall be liable to the suit of such fence-viewers for the recovery

Methods for determining disputes about the charge of partition fences thereof, in manner as aforesaid, who shall be allowed double for all their charge and expence in procuring materials, and doing the workmanship thereof: *saving, always*, to every person and persons, any particular agreement touching the making and maintaining partition-fences between their lands. [*Passed April* 23, 1743.

CHAPTER 34.

AN ACT TO ENABLE THE TOWN OF WEYMOUTH TO REGULATE AND ORDER THE TAKING AND DISPOSING OF THE FISH CALLED SHADD AND ALEWIVES, WITHIN THE LIMITS OF THAT TOWN.

Preamble.

WHEREAS the town of Weymouth, in the county of Suffolk, have been at considerable expence and charge in purchasing and opening a water passage for the fish called shadd and alewives from the sea into a pond called Whitman's Pond and Great Pond, being wholly within the bounds of said town, it seems reasonable and but just that the sole ordering the taking of said fish, and the disposition of them when taken, should be wholly vested in said town of Weymouth; to w[*hi*]ch purpose,—

Be it enacted by the Governour, Council and House of Represent-[*ati*]*ves,*

Town of Weymouth to regulate the fishing at Whitman's Pond.

[SECT. 1.] That from and after the publication of this act, it shall and may be lawful[l] for the inhabitants of the said town of Weymouth, at a meeting regularly assembled for that purpose, from time to time during the continuance of this act, to determine and order how, in what manner, by whom and what place or places, time or times in the year, the said fish may be taken within the town aforesaid, and shall cause a copy of such order, attested by the town clerk, to be posted up in some publick place in s[*ai*]d town of Weymouth, whereunto all persons shall conform with respect to the taking and disposing of said fish, on penalty that the offender against the same shall forfeit and pay the sum of ten shillings for each offence, to be recovered before any justice of the peace, by the treas[*ure*]r of the town of Weymouth, and applied, the one moiety to the poor of the town of Weymouth, and the other to him or them that may sue for the same.

Provided,

Proviso for the neighboring towns.

[SECT. 2.] The said town of Weymouth do, for the benefit of the neighbouring towns, appoint one or more meet person or persons to fish for their supply during the usual season, and give publick notice on or before the twentieth of this instant April, and, for the future, on or before the first day of April annually, of time, place, person or persons by which they are to be supplied, and for such fish so supplied and delivered, that the said town of Weymouth, or those employed by them, shall demand or receive no more than fourpence per hundred for alewives, and six shillings per hundred for shadd, and so in proportion for a greater or lesser quantity.

And provided, also,

Justices to appoint persons for the neighboring towns.

[SECT. 3.] That if the person or persons appointed by the s[*ai*]d town of Weymouth for the purpose afores[*ai*]d, shall neglect or refuse that service, upon application of any two or more persons aggr[ei][*ie*]ved to the two next justices in the neighbouring towns, they may appoint one or more meet person or persons, which shall be subject to the general orders of said town respecting the fishery aforesaid, and who shall give sufficient security, to the acceptance of the afores[*ai*]d justices, to render and pay to the treasurer of the said town of Weymouth the full produce of his or their fishing, at the rates aforesaid, after a reasonable deduction being made at the discretion of the justices aforesaid for the said person or persons' time and labour therein; *saving, always*, to the Indians the right of fishing in the ponds afores[*ai*]d, and the water-passages leading thereto.

[SECT. 4.] This act to continue and be in force for the space of three years from the publication thereof, and no longer. [*Passed April* 23; *published April* 30, 1743.

NOTES.—There were four sessions of the General Court this year; but no acts were passed at the second session, which began September 2, and ended September 10.

The engrossments of all the acts of this year are preserved, except of chapters 31 and 33, and all the public acts were printed, except chapter 30.

The following is the title of the only private act passed this year:—

"An Act to take off the Entail from certain Lands in Ipswich in the County of Essex, late the Estate of John Wainwright, Esqr, Deceased, & to enable Christain Wainwright, his Relict, Widow, to sell the same." [*Passed June* 18.

This was disallowed by the Privy Council.

The acts of the first session, and also chapter 31, were delivered by Mr. Kilby, the agent of the province, to the clerk of the Privy Council, in waiting, July 8, 1743. The acts of the first session had been duly certified for transmission, at Boston, on the 13th of October, 1742, and chapter 31 was certified, in like manner, January 25, 1742-43. They were laid before the lords justices four days after their reception, and immediately referred to a committee, upon whose report they were submitted to the Board of Trade, July 24, 1743. The Board of Trade, in turn, referred them to Mr. Fane for his opinion in point of law, who, February 29, 1743-44, reported them back as unobjectionable. From time to time, during the month of November, 1745, they were discussed by the Board of Trade. The Board agreed upon a report, April 10, 1746, a draught of which was prepared and signed seven days later.

In this report, chapters 1, 4, 5, 6, and 7 are declared to have expired, and the purposes for which chapters 2, 3, and 31 were enacted are declared to have been completed. With regard to chapters 8, 9, 10, and 11, "relating to the Oeconomy of the Province," the Board say, they "are enacted for the private convenience" of the Province, "and we see no reason why His Majesty may not be graciously pleased to confirm them."

The acts of the third session were filed with the clerk of the Privy Council, August 24, 1743, read, and referred to a committee, September 8, 1743, and, seven days later, read in committee, and referred to the Board of Trade, by whom they were submitted, in regular course, to Mr. Fane. Mr. Fane reported, on the second day of February following, that, as these acts "relate to the Affairs of the Province, and seem calculated for the well ordering and governing the same, I have no objection to any of them."

The Board of Trade reported, April 30, 1746, that chapters 14, 18, 20, 21, 22, 24, 26, and 29 "were for a temporary service and are either expired or the purposes for which they were enacted have been completed," that chapters 12, 13, 15, 16, 17, 19, 23, 25, 27, and 28, "relating to the private Oeconomy of the Province, are enacted for the better convenience thereof, and We see no reason why His Majesty may not be graciously pleased to confirm them" Chapter 30 was specially reported upon, as shown in the note to that chapter, *post*.

In accordance with this report, the Privy Council passed an order, May 28, 1746, confirming chapters 8, 9, 10, 11, 15, 16, 17, 19, 23, 25, 27, and 30.

No record of any action of the Home Government, on the acts of the fourth session, has been discovered. The Lords of Trade, in their report, June 4, 1752, on chapter 16 of the acts of 1749-50, reviving chapter 34 of the acts of 1742-43, represented that the latter act did not appear to them "to have been ever laid before His Majesty." It is important to observe, however, that, in the records of the Board of Trade, a similar representation is minuted against chapters 18 and 22, which were revived and continued by chapter 17 of the acts of 1745-46—the act then under consideration—notwithstanding those chapters had, unquestionably, been laid before the Privy Council, and formally acted upon by them, as stated above.

Chap. 5. "April 13, 1742, An Ordinance for the present Regulation of Fees:—Having been read Three several times in the House of Representatives and by them Pass'd to be an Ordinance of this Court and to be held valid for and during the time limited therein and no longer. In Council: Read Three times & Pass'd a concurrence."—*Council Records, vol. XVII., b.* 3, *p.* 335.

"June 23, 1743. In council Whereas the Act entitled an Act for establishing and better regulating Fees within this Province, passed in the Sixteenth Year of this present Majestys Reign, will expire the fifth day of July next; and it is apprehended the Court will speedily rise so that there will not be opportunity to revive the said Act or make the provision which is necessary in that case until the next Session of this Court: Therefore

Ordered that the several Officers in said Act mentioned be and hereby are directed to take no other Fees than what is directed to in said Act, for the respective services therein mentioned.

In the House of Represent^{ves}; Read and concur'd"—*Ibid., b.* 4, *p.* 108.

Chap. 7. "June 30, 1742, In the House of Represent^{ves}; Ordered that the Treasurer be directed and impowered to pay the Members of the General Court for their Travel and Attendance the present Session out of the surplusage for the £6500 Appropriation for

repairing Forts and Garrisons &c and that as soon as the Committee shall have struck off and signed the Bills ordered to be emitted by the present Supply, he refund the same out of the money thereby appropriated for those purposes respectively.
In Council; Read and Concur'd: Consented to, W. SHIRLEY."
—*Council Records, vol. XVII., b. 3, p.* 449.

Chap. 9. "April 15, 1743 A Petition of Edward Winslow and Timothy Ruggles praying for an allowance from this Court for their time and expence in attending a Court of Oyer and Terminer held at Nantucket in August last for the trial of one Harry Jude (an Indian) for murther, the first of the Petitioners as Clerk of the said Court, and the other as Attorney or Counsel for the King.
In the House of Representves; Read and Ordered that the sum of Eight Pounds be allowed and granted to be paid out of the publick Treasury to the Petitioners, in full consideration for their services herein mentioned. In Council; Read and Concur'd.
Consented to, W. SHIRLEY."
—*Ibid., p.* 667.

Chaps 3 *and* 14. "Jany 14: 1742. In the House of Representves Voted that the Committee for Signing the Publick Bills be directed to cause the following Alterations to be made in the Plates, vizt—in the Middle Plate, the Four Shilling Bill to be altered to Half a Crown, and the Three Shilling Bill to fifteen pence; and that in the lowest Plate, the Two Shilling Bill to be altered to Nine Pence, and the Eight Peny Bill to three pence; and that one half of the sum in Bills to be struck off, be from the first Plate, one thousand pounds from the lowest Plate, and the remainder from the Middle Plate.
In Council; Read and Concur'd, Consented to. W: SHIRLEY."
—*Council Records, vol. XVII., b. 3, p.* 609.
"June 8 1743. In the House of Representves; Whereas it appears to this court that from the Year One Thousand seven hundred and twelve to the Year One Thousand seven Hundred and forty two, it has been the uninterrupted practice of the Executive courts within this Province, in chanceiing penalties upon all Bonds and Mortgages, the condition of which has been the payment of Bills of credit or lawful Money, to make up Judgment for the nominal sum express'd in the condition of such Bonds, with the addition of Interest due thereon; and executions awarded on said Judgments have been levied by the Sheriff for the value of the nominal sum, in Bills of credit of the Old Tenor; and said sum in said Bills have been continually accepted by the creditor in satisfaction of his Debt:
And whereas it further appears, that the Intent and Expectation of those persons who have from time to time borrowed and lent any sum or sums of Bills of credit on penal Bonds and Mortgages (except where the value of the Bills of credit has been fixed and ascertained) has been to pay and be paid the same nominal sum in Bills of credit again, and to run the risque of their rising and falling in value: and the aforesaid practice of the courts, and the said Intent and Expectation of the Parties, have had an influence upon all trade and dealing throughout the Province:
And whereas the aforesaid practice of the Executive courts in making up Judgments on such Bonds & Mortgages being known to be established as aforesaid, this court did in and by two several acts made & passed in the Fifteenth and Sixteenth years of His present Majesty, the first of which is entitled an Act for supplying the Treasury with the sum of Fifteen Thousand Pounds &c and the other an Act for supplying the Treasury with the sum of Twelve Thousand Pounds &c enact and declare that any Debt contracted before the thirty first day of October 1741 which might have been paid and discharged by Province Bills of the Old Tenor, and also any Debt contracted between the said thirty first of October 1741 and the first of April 1742, where the contracting parties have not expressly otherwise agreed, may be discharged by Bills by the said Acts emitted, in proportion of one to four.
And whereas the Judges of some of the Inferior Courts of Common Pleas and of His Majestys Superior Court of Judicature have of late, in making up Judgments for debts upon such Bonds and Mortgages, made an allowance to the creditor for the depreciating of the Bills of credit mentioned in the condition or Proviso of such Bonds or Mortgages from the value they were of at the time of contracting the debt, contrary to the common construction of such Bonds and Mortgages and course of judicial proceedings as aforesaid.—
And whereas it appears that the alteration thus made by the courts of Judicature in their practice in chancering the forfeitures of Bonds and Mortgages, conditioned as aforesaid, and their departure from that which they have heretofore judged to be the most equal rule for chancering the just debt and damage upon such Bonds, will, if pursued, be attended with manifest Injustice and Oppression: Therefore
Resolved that it be and hereby is recommended to the Justices of His Majestys Superior Court of Judicature and they are hereby enabled and impowered at their next Term in their respective Counties, to reconsider such Judgments as they have already given for debts due upon Bonds and Mortgages, conditioned as aforesaid, since the second Tuesday of August last and execution on all such Judgments is staid in the mean time. And it is further recommended to the Justices of the several courts afore mentioned to govern themselves in the future chancering of the penalties of all such Bonds and Mortgages entered into and made before the last day of October, One Thousand seven Hundred and Forty one, by the Intent of the Parties according to the construction thereof which has heretofore been settled and established in the Superior Court, as well as in the Inferior Courts within this Province. In council; Read and Concur'd Consented to WM SHIRLEY."
—*Ibid., b.* 4, *p.* 45.
"June 17. 1743. In the House of Representves; Ordered that the Printer be directed to print the Resolve lately passed this Court relating to the equitable Payment of Debts, and deliver a Duplicate to each Member of the General Court, one for himself, the other for the Town he represents. In council; Read and Concur'd,
Consented to W. SHIRLEY."
—*Ibid., p.* 84.

Chap. 23. "Septem: 10. 1742. A Petition of Isaac Parker of Charlestown, Potter, shewing that he has with great expence learned the art of making Stone Ware, which may be much for the benefit of the Province; but as he has not a stock to carry on the said trade; therefore Praying that this Court would lend him One hundred and twenty five pounds in Bills of the new Emission, without Interest, for carrying on the said business, he giving good security for paying in the money at the time assigned, and that the Petitioner may have the sole privilege of the said manufacture.—

In the House of Representatives; Read and in answer hereto

Ordered that the Petitioner be allowed to receive out of the Appropriation for Premiums now in the Province Treasury, for his encouragement in making Stone Ware, the sum of One hundred and twenty five Pounds, he giving Land Security to the value of Two Hundred Pounds for the Payment of Three Hundred seventy five ounces of Silver into the said Treasury in liew thereof with lawful Interest of the same, at or before the last Day of December 1746; provided nevertheless that if the money be improved for the purposes aforesaid no Interest shall be taken; Provided also that if he pay in the Bills within the time limited therefor, they shall be received in full discharge of his mortgage instead of the Silver; Provided further that the repayment of the whole sum be made within one year from this time, in case the Petitioner does not proceed in the work aforesaid; the Security to be to the satisfaction of the Treasurer. In Council: Read and Concur'd.

Consented to, W: SHIRLEY."

—*Council Records, vol. XVII., b.* 3, *p.* 485.

"Decem[r] 1. 1742. A Petition of Grace Parker and Thomas Symmes both of Charlestown, Shewing that whereas this Court were pleased to give encouragement to Isaac Parker late husband to the said Grace, to carry on the manufacture of Stone Ware, the said Isaac died soon after, the said Grace in partnership with the other Petitioner has undertaken that business, her husband having been at great expence in his life time in providing materials for it; And therefore Praying that the Petitioners may have leave to bring in a bill for granting them the sole privilege of making the said Stone Ware for the term of Fifteen Years

In the House of Represent[ves]; Read and Ordered that the prayer of the Petition be granted, and the Petitioners are allowed to bring in a Bill accordingly. In Council; Read and Concur'd"

—*Ibid., p.* 514.

"March 10. 1747. A Petition of Grace Parker widow of Isaac Parker of Charlestown Potter Dec[d] showing that he met with great Disapointment in carrying on the said Trade, as she hath done since his Decease And therefore praying that she may be allow'd to pay in the Money lent him out of the public Treasury in the present Bills of Credit by five several Annual Payments.

In the House of Represent[ves] Read & Ordered that the Prayer of the Petition be so far granted as that the Time for replacing the sum mentioned of one Hundred & Twenty five Pounds be further lengthn[d] to the last of December 1751. the said Grace giving security to the Province Treasurer for the due Performance thereof & in the mean Time she have the Liberty of paying in the same by three several Annual Payments or sooner if she finds it for her Advantage & without Interest provided the money be improved for the purpose on which it was first granted. In Council Read & Concured.—*Ibid., vol. XVIII., p.* 305.

"January 1. 1749.—On the petition of Grace Parker, and the Order of the two Houses thereon pass'd the 10th of March 1747

In Council, the foregoing petition being read, it was thereupon Ordered that the same be revived, and that the Petitioner be allowed to pay into the publick Treasury, the before mentioned one hundred and twenty-five pounds, in time & manner as set forth in the above written Vote of both Houses, she giving security as therein directed—In the House of Representatives Read & Concur'd—Consented to by the Lieu[t] Governor."—*Ibid., vol. XIX., p.* 110.

"March 9th 1756. A Petition of John & Daniel Parker for themselves and other the Heirs of Isaac Parker of Charlestown deceased, Shewing that the said Isaac divers Years since had the Favour of the Loan of £500. Old Tenor from the Government to Encourage his Carrying on the Manufacture of Stone Ware, that Four hundred of the £500. has been returned into the publick Treasury; But forasmuch as by means of the Death of the said Isaac & other Misfortunes not only the whole of the said loan but a great part of the said Isaac's Estate has been swallowed up, therefore Praying his remaining Debt to the Province may be remitted—

In the House of Representatives; read & Whereas the making of Stone Ware might have been of great advantage to the Publick had the Petitioners Father lived & Succeeded in that Business as well as to himself & his Heirs; but notwithstanding the great Cost & Charge they have been at in their Attempts all their Schemes have in a great measure failed and proved unsuccessful, by means whereof the Petitioners said Fathers Estate has been greatly Injured—Therefore

Ordered that the Prayer of this Petition be granted; And the Sum mentioned of Three hundred Pounds Old tenor said to be due to the Province be & hereby is remitted, and no Demand hereafter shall be made of the said sum or any part thereof In Council; Read & Concur'd."—*Ibid., vol. XXI., p.* 125.

Chap. 30. "In our Report to your Lordships dated the 8th of June 1743, We gave our opinion against this method of erecting & setling Townships since which His Majesty has been pleased to send an Instruction to His Governor of the Massachusets Bay directing him not to give his Assent for the future to any Bill for erecting a new Town or dividing an old one, without a suspending Clause be inserted therein, However as His Majesty's pleasure in this case could not be known at the time when this Act passed, and as there is reason to believe the same may have been carried into execution and that a Precept or Writ may have been issued to the Town thereby erected to send Representatives to the

Assembly, We would submit it to your Lordships, whether His Majesty may not be advised to confirm the said Act.

We are My Lords, Your Lordships most obedient and most humble Servants

MONSON.
R. PLUMER.
I. PITT.
B. LEVESON GOWER.

Whitehall. April 30th 1746."—*Report of Lords of Trade, "Mass. Bay; B. T.," vol. 84, p. 166.*

(*Duplicate*) *Origl not recd this 10th Feby* 1742–3.

"Boston, N. Engld Octr 18th 1742.

My Lords, The Secretary having laid before me at the last Session of the General Court three Ingross'd Bills for the dividing three old Townships and erecting three new ones out of 'em ["*A bill for erecting the northerly part of Shrewsbury, &c., into a township named——*"; "*A bill for erecting the easterly part of Attleboro', &c., into a township named——*"; "*A bill for erecting New Lisborn into a township named——*"] whereby the number of Representatives for those Towns in the Genl Court would be doubled; I was led upon this occasion to examine what increase of new Towns and consequently of Representatives had arisen from this Practise since the date of the present Charter in 1692; And find that since that time thirty three new Towns have been erected by this means, each of which that consist of 120 Voters are by the Province Law intitled to send two Representatives, and all under that number of voters, tho' they should not even exceed 20 are entitled to send one: This practice of splitting one Town into two and sometimes three, has been of late so frequent that sixteen of the thirty three towns were made during Mr Belcher's Administration and the three abovementioned Bills for the like purpose were laid before me for my consent in the first year of my Government; But as this method of multiplying Towns and dividing 'em is entirely unnecessary, since all the inconveniences arising from the large extent of the old ones might as well have been remedyed by dividing 'em into different Precincts and Parishes (which is the case of the old Towns here) as by dividing 'em into several Towns; I have refused my Consent to the three above mention'd Bills, and propose to put an end to this way of increasing the number of Representatives, which seems to promise no good effect for his Majesty's service And as I find by the transactions of the General Court for several years past that the present number of the House of Representatives hath been sufficient to embarrass his Majtys Governt here in some points, tho' the most reasonable for them to comply with, and recommended to 'em in the strongest manner from his Majesty, I would submit it to the consideration of your Lordships whether it might not be for His Majtys service that his Governours in this Province shd for the future use due means to prevent that House from increasing and particularly by the practice of splitting Townships. The expediency of confining the number of Representatives I am apt to think, may further appear to your Lordships from considering the constitution of the Province Charter, whereby another Branch of the Legislative (the Counsellors or Assistants, the number of which is limited to twenty eight) are annually chosen by the General Court in which case, notwithstanding the Governour has a Negative Voice in the Election, the Counsellors who it is possible may all be chosen out of the House and entirely by the Members of the House, who are a great Majority of the General Court, may be reasonably supposed from their Dependency upon their electors to have some check, if not a wrong Byass upon 'em in Disputes between the House and the Governour to the prejudice of his Majesty's Government—If your Lordships upon such consideration should think it would be for His Majesty's service to prevent the further increase of Representatives which may arise not only from the practice of splitting the old Townships but from erecting any Plantations of new Settlers into Townships I would submit it to Your Lordships whether that might not be effected by erecting such new Plantations into Precincts, Parishes or Villages with all the Officers and Privileges of a Township except that of sending Representatives which I apprehend would not be attended with the least inconvenience or discouragement to the propagating of new Settlements, since all the new Towns at present seem to think the maintenance of a Representative a burthen to 'em

As your Lordships may possibly apprehend from what I have said that all the Towns actually use their privilege of sending one or more Represenves to the General Court according to their number of voters, it will be necessary for me to observe that tho' there are at present 160 Towns, most of which are qualifyed to send two Representatives, yet they do not generally send more than from 109 (the number of the present House) to 120 at most which arises from hence, that none of those Towns which are entitled to send two Representatives ever send above one, except the Towns of Boston, Salem, Ipswich & Newbury and very few or none of the new Towns ever send any; But still they have it in their power upon an extraordinary Emergency to double and almost treble their numbers, which they would not fail to do, if they should be desirous of disputing any point with his Majesty's Governour, which they might suspect their ordinary Members would not carry against his Influence in the House.

To apprize your Lordships fully of this affair I have inclosed a particular state of the Constitution of the Province with regard to its number of Representatives and if the House can be led into any act which may limit the number of 'em to what the Towns have usually sent, I shall not fail to embrace the opportunity of doing it; and should be glad of the Honour of knowing your Lordships sentiments upon this matter for the better regulation of my conduct in it.

I am, with the highest respect, My Lords, Your most obedt & most humble Servt

W. SHIRLEY."

(Indorsed) "Recd Febry 10th Read Do 17th 1742-3"—*Governor Shirley to the Lords of Trade, Mass. Bay: B. T., vol. 70, E. e., 70.*

Inclosure above referred to:

"State of the Province of the Massachusetts Bay, as to it's Number of Representatives.

By the Province Charter granted by their late Majesties K. William and Q. Mary in 1692 (pa. 6.) It is ordain'd that there shall be twenty eight Assistants or Counsellors to be advising and assisting to the Governor of the Province for the time being; which Counsellors (pa. 7) are to be elected yearly by the Great and General Court or Assembly, And (pa. 10) the Govr has a negative in such Elections.

Pa. 7. It is ordain'd that a Great & General Court or Assembly shall be conven'd and held by the Govr for the time being, upon every last Wednesday in the Month of May and at such other times as the Govr shall think fit and appoint, which Court is to consist of the Govr and twenty eight Counsellors for the time being and of such Freeholders of the Province, as shall be from time to time elected by the major part of the freeholders and other inhabitants of the respective Towns or other places who shall be present at such Elections; each of said Towns and places being thereby impowered to elect two persons and no more to serve for and represent them in said Great and General Court, To which Court, to be held as aforesaid, power and authority is given from time to time to direct, appoint and declare what number each County, Town and Place shall elect to serve for and represent them in said Court: Provided that no Freeholder or other person shall have a vote in the election of Members to serve in said Court, who at the time of such Election shall not have an estate of Freehold in Land within the Province to the value of forty shillings per annum at least, or other estate to the value of fifty pounds sterling.

By the Province Law pass'd in 1693 pa. 32 of the Law Book, It is enacted that thenceforth every Town within this Province consisting of the number of forty freeholders and other Inhabitants qualify'd by Charter to elect, shall and hereby are enjoined to choose and send one Freeholder as their Representative, and every Town consisting of the number of one hundred and twenty freeholders and other Inhabitants qualifyed as aforesd or upwards, may send two such Representatives; and each Town of the number of thirty freeholders and other Inhabitants qualify'd as aforesaid or upwards under forty, are at liberty to send one or not, but may choose and send one Representative, if they think fit, to serve for and represent them respectively in every Session of the Great and General Court or Assembly from time to time: And all Towns under thirty freeholders may send one Representative, or join with the next Town in the choice of their Representatives, they paying a proportionable part of the Charge: And no Town shall at any time send more than two Representatives, except Boston who are hereby granted to choose and send four.

At the time of passing this Law there were 113 Towns within the Province and by virtue of it the Town of Boston has *constantly* sent four Representatives to the General Court and the Towns of Salem, Ipswich and Newbury two apiece and none of the other Towns above one apiece tho' much the greatest part of 'em duely qualify'd to send two.

By the Province Law pass'd in 1694 (pa. 54 of the Law Book) no persons are qualifyed to be chosen Representative of any Town unless they are Freeholders and Residents in the Town where they are chosen.

By the Province Law pass'd in 1726 (pa. 351, 352 of the Province Law Book) the clause in the Act of 4th W & M. obliging every Town consisting of forty families, to send a Representative to the General Court is repeal'd and no Town under the number of sixty families shall be obliged (unless they think fit) to send a Representative—This Act to continue for three years."—*Ibid.*

"At the Council Chamber Whitehall the 30th day of June 1743.

Present

Their Excellencys the Lords Justices in Council

Whereas there was this day read at the Board a REPORT from the Right Honble the Lords of the Committee of Council upon several Laws past in the Province of the Massachusets Bay, Wherein it was proposed amongst other things, that an Instruction should be sent to William Shirley, Esqre, Govr of the Province of the Massachusets Bay not to give his assent for the future to any Bill for erecting a new Town or dividing an old One without a Clause be inserted therein deferring and suspending the execution thereof until His Majesty's pleasure shall be known—Their Excelcys the Lords Justices taking the same into consideration were pleased with the advice of His Majtys Privy Council to approve thereof, and to Order as it is hereby Ordered, that the Lords Commissrs for Trade & Plantations do prepare the Draught of an Instruction for the Govr or Commander in Chief of the Province of the Massachusets Bay, agreeable to what is above proposed, and lay the same before their Excelcys at this Board. W. SHARPE"

[Indorsed:] "Recd July 15th Read—21st 1743."—"*Mass. Bay: B. T.,*" *vol.* 71, *F. f.* 1, *in Public Record Office.*

Lords of Trade to Govr Shirley 6 July 1743.

"To William Shirley Esq. Governor of the Massachusets Bay

Sir,

* * * * * * * * * * * * *

We agree with you in opinion in what you have represented in your letter of the 18th of Octr 1742, concerning the practice of increasing the number of Townships which may in time prove inconvenient, We have therefore in a late Report to the Lords of the Committee of His Majtys most Honble Privy Council, upon An Act for dividing the Towns of Rochester & Plymouth & erecting a new Town by the name of Wareham, humbly proposed that for the future you should be instructed not to give your assent to any Bill of that kind without a suspending clause."—*Ibid., vol.* 84, *p.* 103.

Province Laws, 1739-40, chap. 7; and see note Vol. II., pp. 1006 and 1007. See also 1740-41, chap. 7, note, and 1741-42, chap. 17, note.

* * * * * * * * * * * * *

"Thursday July 21st 1743.
[Present]
Lord Monson

Mr Plumer. Mr Keene.

Read an Order of Council dated 30th June 1743 Directing this Board to prepare the Draught of an Instruction for Mr Shirley Governor of the Massachusets Bay not to give his assent for the future to any Bill for erecting a new Town or dividing an old one without a Clause inserted therein for suspending the execution thereof until His Majesty's pleasure shall be known.

Ordered that the said Draught be prepared accordingly."—"*Trade Papers," vol.* 45, *p.* 85, *in Public Record Office.*

* * * * * * * * * * *

"Wednesday July 27th 1743

* * * * * * * * * * *

The Draught of an Instruction to Mr Shirley Governor of the Massachusets Bay (ordered to be prepared by the Minutes of the 21st Instant) was laid before the Board and agreed to, and a Representation to the Lords Justices for inclosing the same, was also laid before the Board, agreed to and signed."—*Ibid., p.* 94.

* * * * * * * * * * *

"Representation to the Lords Justices 27 July 1743

To their Excellencies the Lord Justices May it please your Excellencies,

In obedience to your Excellencies commands, signified to us by your Order of the 30th of June last, We have prepared the Draught of an Additional Instruction to William Shirley Esqr Governor of the Massachusets Bay, directing him not to give his assent for the future to any Bill for erecting a new Town or dividing an old one without a Clause be inserted therein, suspending the execution thereof 'till His Majesty's pleasure thereupon shall be known; and humbly take leave to lay the same before Your Excellencies

Which is most humbly submitted

MONSON
M. BLADEN
R. PLUMER
JA: BRUDENELL

Whitehall July 27th 1743."—"*Mass. Bay: B. T.," vol.* 84, *p.* 108, *in Public Record Office.*

"ADDITIONAL INSTRUCTION to William Shirley Esqre His Majesty's Captain General & Governor in Chief in and over the Province and Territory of the Massachusets Bay in New England in America. Given

WHEREAS the number of Townships in your Government is of late years very much encreased and may in time prove inconvenient in case the present method of splitting and dividing old Towns & of erecting new Ones should continue. And whereas any future Settlements may be erected into Precincts, Parishes or Villages with all the Officers and Privileges necessary for their good Government & security without the liberty of sending Representatives to the General Assembly, It is His Majesty's Will & Pleasure that you do not give your assent for the future, to any Bill for erecting a new Town or dividing an old one without a Clause be inserted therein deferring & suspending the execution thereof until His Majesty's pleasure shall be known thereupon."

"Order in Council dated 11 August 1743 Approving above Draught of Additional Instruction and Ordering that Andrew Stone and Edward Weston Secretaries to the Lords Justices do prepare the same for their Excellency's signing."

Indorsed: "Received March 16th 1743-4 Read April 26th 1744."—*Mass. Bay: B. T., vol.* 71, *F.f.* 25, *in Public Record Office.*

ACTS,

PASSED 1743–44.

ACTS

Passed at the Session begun and held at Boston, on the Twenty-fifth day of May, A. D. 1743.

CHAPTER 1.

AN ACT FOR GRANTING THE SUM OF THIRTEEN HUNDRED AND FIFTY POUNDS FOR THE SUPPORT OF HIS MAJESTY'S GOVERNOUR.

Be it enacted by the Governour, Council and House of Representatives, That the sum of thirteen hundred and fifty pounds in bills of publick credit of this province, of the newest form and tenor, be and hereby is granted unto his most excellent majesty, to be paid out of the publick treasury to his excellency William Shirley, Esq[r]., captain-general and governour-in-chief in and over his majesty's province of the Massachusetts Bay, in consideration of his past services, and further to enable him to go on in managing the publick affairs. [*Passed June* 10; *published June* 27.

CHAPTER 2.

AN ACT FOR ESTABLISHING THE WAGES, &c[A], OF SUNDRY PERSONS IN THE SERVICE OF THE PROVINCE.

Be it enacted by the Governour, Council and House of Representatives,

Wages of the garrison at Castle William.

[Sect. 1.] That the wages of the captain of Castle William shall be after the rate of sixty pounds per annum from the twenty-first day of May, one thousand seven hundred and forty-three, to the twentieth day of May, one thousand seven hundred and forty-four; of the lieutenant for that term, thirty-five pounds fifteen shillings; of the chaplain, thirty pounds; of the gunner, fifty pounds; of the gunner's mate, thirty-four shillings and threepence per month; of two sergeants, each twenty-three shillings per month; of six quarter-gunners, each three shillings per month; of three corporals, each twenty-one shillings and ninepence per month; of two drummers, each twenty-one shillings and ninepence per month; of one armourer, thirty-four shillings and threepence per month; of forty centinels, each twenty shillings per month: for their subsistence, six shillings and threepence per week per man.

And be it further enacted,

Richmond Fort.

[Sect. 2.] That the wages of the captain of Richmond Fort, from the twenty-first of May, one thousand seven hundred and forty-three, to the twentieth of May, one thousand seven hundred and forty-four, shall be at the rate of twenty shillings per month; and of ten centinels, each ten shillings per month; of one interpreter, thirty shillings per month; of one armourer, thirty shillings per month; and for the chaplain, twenty-five pounds per annum.

And be it further enacted,

Truck-house at George's River. [SECT. 3.] That the wages of the captain of the truck-house on George's River, from the twenty-first of May, one thousand seven hundred and forty-three, to the twentieth of May, one thousand seven hundred and forty-four, shall be at the rate of twenty shillings per month; of one lieutenant, thirteen shillings and sixpence per month; of one sergeant, thirteen shillings and sixpence per month; of two corporals, each twelve shillings per month; of thirteen centinels, each ten shillings per month; of one armourer, thirty shillings per month; of one interpreter, thirty shillings per month; and to the chaplain there, twenty-five pounds per annum.

And be it further enacted,

Brunswick Fort. [SECT. 4.] That the wages of the commanding officer of the fort at Brunswick, from the twenty-first of May, one thousand seven hundred and forty-three, to the twentieth of May, one thousand seven hundred and forty-four, shall be at the rate of twenty shillings per month; of six centinels, each ten shillings per month.

And be it further enacted,

Truck-house above Northfield. [SECT. 5.] That the wages of the captain of the truck-house above Northf[ei][*ie*]ld, from the twenty-first of May, one thousand seven hundred and forty-three, to the twentieth of May, one thousand seven hundred and forty-four, shall be at the rate of twenty shillings per month; of one lieutenant, thirteen shillings and sixpence per month; of one sergeant, thirteen shillings and sixpence per month; of one corporal, twelve shillings per month; of sixteen centinels, each ten shillings per month; of one interpreter, thirty shillings per month; of the chaplain there, twenty-five pounds per annum, and that there be allowed for the subsist[a][*e*]nce of each man two shillings and sixpence per week.

And be it further enacted,

Truck-house at Saco River. [SECT. 6.] That the wages of the captain of the truck-house at Saco, from the twenty-first of May, one thousand seven hundred and forty-three, to the twentieth of May, one thousand seven hundred and forty-four, shall be at the rate of twenty shillings per month; of one lieutenant, thirteen shillings and sixpence per month; of one corporal, twelve shillings per month; of thirteen centinels, each ten shillings per month; of one armourer, thirty shillings per month; of one interpreter, thirty shillings per month.

And be it further enacted,

Frederick Fort. [SECT. 7.] That the wages of the commanding officer of Frederick Fort, from the twenty-first of May, one thousand seven hundred and forty-three, to the twentieth of May, one thousand seven hundred and forty-four, shall be at the rate of twenty shillings per month; of ten centinels, each ten shillings per month; and of the chaplain there, fifteen pounds per annum.

And be it further enacted,

Country's sloop. [SECT. 8.] That the wages of the captain of the sloop in the country's service, from the twenty-first of May, one thousand seven hundred and forty three, to the twentieth of May, one thousand seven hundred and forty-four, shall be at the rate of fifty shillings per month; of the mate, thirty shillings per month; of three sailors, each twenty-five shillings per month; for the sloop, seven pounds ten shillings per month.

And be it further enacted,

[Sect. 9.] That the wages of the captain of the province snow, from the twenty-first of May, one thousand seven hundred and forty-three, to the twentieth of May, one thousand seven hundred and forty-four, shall be at the rate of five pounds ten shillings per month; the lieutenant, three pounds ten shillings per month; the master, three pounds per month; the doctor, three pounds per month; the chaplain, three pounds per month; the gunner, fifty shillings per month; the boatswain, forty-five shillings per month; the mate, forty shillings per month; the steward, thirty-five shillings per month; the cook, thirty-five shillings per month; the gunner's mate, thirty-five shillings per month; the pilot, fifty shillings per month; the boatswain mate, thirty-five shillings per month; the carpenter, forty-five shillings per month; the cooper, thirty-five shillings per month; the armourer, thirty-five shillings per month; the coxswain, thirty-five shillings per month; two quartermasters, each thirty-five shillings per month; seventy sailors, or for[*e*]mast men, forty shillings per month. Province snow.

And be it further enacted,

[Sect. 10.] That before payment of any muster-roll be allowed, oath be made by the officer or person presenting such roll that the officers and soldiers born on such roll have been in actual service for the whole time they stand entred thereon. [*Passed June* 25; *published June* 27. Oath to be made to the muster-roll.

CHAPTER 3.

AN ACT TO ENABLE THE SURVIVING TRUSTEES, OF THE SEVERAL TOWNS WITHIN THIS PROVINCE, OF THE SIXTY THOUSAND POUNDS' LOAN, WHO HAVE PAID THEIR TOWNS' PROPORTION THEREOF INTO THE PROVINCE TREASURY, WHERE THERE IS NOT A MAJORITY OF THEM LIVING, TO COLLECT THE SEVERAL SUMS DUE FROM PARTICULAR PERSONS TO SUCH [TRUSTEES.] [*TOWNS.*]

Whereas in and by an act made in the first year of his present majesty [e][*i*]ntitled an act for raising and set[*t*]ling a publick revenue, &c., by an emission of sixty thousand pounds in bills of credit on this province, it is provided that the several towns within the province should appoint three or five freeholders as trustees, with power as in said act is at large set forth, and the several towns were also impow[e]red, from time to time, upon the death or removal of any such trustees, to appoint others in their room until[l] the respective sums of the several towns were compleatly paid into the province treasury; but no provision is made where the town's proportion is paid into the treasury, either for the towns to chuse new trustees in case of the death and removal of any such, or for such as survive to recover of particular persons the sums respectively due from them to such trustees, whereby many inconvenienc[*i*]es arise; for remedy whereof,— Preamble.

Be it enacted by the Governour, Council and House of Representatives,

That the surviving trustee or trustees of the sixty thousand pounds' loan which [have] [*has*] been appointed in any town in this province in consequence of the act for emitting said loan be and hereby are fully authorized and impowered to sue for, recover and receive all such sums of the loan aforesaid as are due from any person or persons whatsoever. [*Passed June* 17; *published June* 27. Surviving trustees of the £60,000 loan, their power.

CHAPTER 4.

AN ACT FOR HOLDING A COURT OF OYER AND TERMINER IN AND FOR THE ISLAND OF NANTUCKET.

Preamble.

WHEREAS there now stands committed in his majesty's goal in the island of Nantucket, one Simon Hew, an Indian man, charged with the murder of Margaret, an Indian woman, who ought as the law now stands to be tried by a special court of assize and general goal delivery; but forasmuch as the judges of the court of assize and general goal delivery cannot attend that service, the summer months being taken up with the several superiour courts of judicature, courts of assize and general goal delivery as they are now established, besides the great charge and trouble of the judges repairing thither, and a court of oyer and terminer (noticed in the royal charter) have and can exercise the same jurisdiction and authority in all capital offences,—

Be it therefore enacted by the Governour, Council and House of Representatives, for the reasons above mentioned, and that speedy justice may be done,

Court of Oyer and Terminer to be held at Nantucket.

That the inquiry, hearing and tr[y][*i*]al of the said Simon Hew for the murder of the said Margaret, and any other capital offences upon the said island of Nantucket already committed, may with all convenient speed be had at Nantucket aforesaid, by special commissioners of oyer and terminer, to be appointed by his excellency the governour, with the advice and consent of the council, any law, usage or custom to the contrary notwithstanding. [*Passed June* 17; *published June* 27.

CHAPTER 5.

AN ACT FOR IMPOWERING THE TOWN OF BOSTON TO IMPOSE AND COLLECT A TAX OR DUTY ON COACHES, CHAISES, &c[A], FOR THE USE AND SERVICE OF SAID TOWN.

Preamble.

WHEREAS the town of Boston are at great charge in keeping the highway upon the neck at the entrance into said town in good repair, and it is most equal that the said charge should be born by such persons as principally receive the benefit of said repairs,—

Be it therefore enacted by the Governour, Council and House of Repres[entati]ves,

Town of Boston empowered to lay a tax on coaches, &c.

[SECT. 1.] That the inhabitants of the town of Boston be and hereby are enabled and impowered, at a publick town meeting duly warned for that purpose, to lay such tax or duty on each coach, chariot, chaise, calash or chair used and improved by the inhabitants of said town as shall be judg'd convenient, not exceeding ten shillings per annum for any coach, chariot or four-wheel'd chaise, or five shillings per annum for any two-wheel'd chaise, calash or chair; and the said inhabitants are further impowered, at their meeting in March, annually, for and during the term of five years, to renew the said tax or discontinue the same as they shall judge proper.

And be it further enacted,

Coaches, chaises, &c., to be entered with the town treasurer.

[SECT. 2.] That (publick notice being given to the inhabitants of said town of such tax or duty as afores[*ai*]d) every person improving any coach, chariot, chaise, calash or chair shall, some time in the month of July next after, cause the same to be entred with the town treas-

[*ure*]r and shall pay the rates imposed thereon by vote of said town and by virtue of this act, on pain of forfeiting twenty shillings for each neglect, to be recovered by said treas[*ure*][r], who is hereby authorized and impowered to sue for the same.

And be it further enacted,

Tax on coaches, chaises, &c., to be for repairing Boston Neck, &c.

[Sect. 3.] That the whole of such sums as shall be paid into the town treasury as a tax or duty as afores[*ai*][d], or shall be recovered as fines as aforesaid, shall be and remain as a stock in said treasury for the use of said town, to be drawn out by order of the selectmen for the service of said town in maintaining or repairing the road or highway on Boston Neck, at the entrance into said town; and in case there shall be more than sufficient for that purpose, the overplus shall be applied to the repairing the other highways and streets in said town.

Provided always,

Proviso.

[Sect. 4.] That the coach, chariot and other carriages of his excellency, the governour, and of the set[*t*]led ministers in said town be exempt and free from any such tax or duty, anything contained in this act to the contrary notwithstanding. [*Passed June* 25; *published June* 27.

CHAPTER 6.

AN ACT FOR PREVENTING MISCH[EI][*IE*]F BY UNRULY DOGS ON THE ISLAND OF NANTUCKET.

Preamble. 100 Mass., 141.

Whereas much dam[*m*]age has been done by unruly and misch[ei][*ie*]vous dogs in worrying, wounding, and killing sheep and lambs on the island of Nantucket, by reason of great numbers of such dogs being kept by Indians, as well as English inhabitants there,—

Be it therefore enacted by the Governour, Council and House of Representatives,

Dogs may be killed in Nantucket.

[Sect. 1.] That from and after the publication of this act, it shall and may be lawful[l] for any person or persons within the county of Nantucket, to kill any dog or bitch whatsoever that shall at any time be found there.

And be it further enacted,

Fine for keeping dogs.

[Sect. 2.] That whosoever shall presume to keep any dog or bitch on the said island of Nantucket after the publication of this act, shall forfeit and pay the sum of one pound, to be sued for and recovered by the major part of the selectmen of the town of Sherborn for the time being, before any of his majesty's justices of the peace there; one half to the selectmen that shall sue for the same, and the other half to the poor of said county.

And be it further enacted,

No action to lie against any person that kills a dog.

[Sect. 3.] That no action shall l[y][*i*]e, be heard or tried at any court within this province against such person as shall kill or destroy any such dog or bitch found as afores[*ai*][d], but shall be utterly bar'd by virtue of this act.

Limitation.

[Sect. 4.] This act to continue and be in force for the space of three years from the publication thereof, and no longer. [*Passed June* 25; *published June* 27.

CHAPTER 7.

AN ACT IN ADDITION TO, AND IN EXPLANATION OF SUNDRY CLAUSES OF, AN ACT, [E][*I*]NTIT[*U*]LED "AN ACT TO ASCERTAIN THE VALUE OF MONEY, AND OF THE BILLS OF PUBLICK CREDIT OF THIS PROVINCE," &c[A], MADE AND PASS'D IN THE FIFTEENTH YEAR OF HIS MAJESTY'S REIGN.

Preamble. 1741-42, chap. 12, § 3.

WHEREAS in the law for ascertaining the value of money, and of the bills of publick credit of this province, passed in the fifteenth year of his majesty's reign, it is enacted, that all debts contracted after the last day of March, A. D. 1742, specialties and express contracts excepted, should be deemed equal to lawful[l] money, and every debt of six shillings and eightpence value so contracted, should or might be discharged by one ounce of silver, or six shillings and eightpence of the bills of publick credit emitted that year, or that should thereafter be emitted, equal in value to an ounce of silver: *provided, nevertheless*, that in case such bills should be depreciated below the value they were stated at by said act, that an addition should be made of so much more as would make them equal to the then fixed value afores[*ai*]d. And the judges of the superio[*u*]r court, agreable to the directions of the afores[*ai*]d law, have made inquiry by a committee for that purpose appointed, who have certified into the secretary's office that seven shillings and twopence of the bills of credit, of the last form and teno[u]r, is equal to one ounce of silver; in consequence whereof, judgments have been made up in several courts on debts contracted since the last [*day*] of March afores[*ai*]d at that rate, whereby an addition of sixpence is made to the creditor on every debt of six shillings and eightpence value; *and whereas*, by s[*ai*]d certificate, compared with the rates of bills of exchange in March afores[*ai*]d, it is manifest that the said bills are not depreciated below the value they passed at when first emitted, inasmuch as six shill[*in*]gs and eightpence in said bills will now go as far, in purchasing bills of exchange, as when said act was made, and the aforesaid loss has happened to the debtor from his not strictly attending the direction of said law, whereby every debt of six shillings and eightpence is deemed equal to an ounce of silver (specialties and express contracts excepted), and should have been considered by the debtor, at the time of contracting such debt, as if the same had been payable in lawful[l] money; *and whereas* the bills of publick credit currant in this province, are at present the only medium of the common trade and business within it, there will be continual danger of the debtor's computing his debt according to the depreciated value of such bills, whilst it is deemed by said law to be contracted for lawful[l] money; and thereby great damage may ensue to debtors, contrary to the true intent and meaning of the said law; wherefore,—

Be it enacted by the Governour, Council and House of Represent-[ati]ves,

All debts to be deemed according to value of the bills when contracted.

That all debts contracted since the last of March, A. D. one thousand seven hundred and forty-two, or that shall hereafter be contracted (specialties and express contracts excepted), shall be deemed and adjudged equal to the real value only such bills have passed or shall pass at when such debt was or shall be contracted; and every debt of twenty shillings contracted as afores[*ai*]d, shall or may be always hereafter discharged by twenty shillings in said bills, and so *pro ratâ* for a greater or less sum, unless such bills [shall] have already or should hereafter

Saving an allowance for bills depreciating.

be depreciated below the value they passed at when such debt was or shall be contracted; and in such case, so much shall always be allowed by the respective courts in this province, as shall make said bills equal in value to such debt when contracted, anything contained in the aforesaid law to the contrary notwithstanding. [*Passed June* 25; *published June* 27.

CHAPTER 8.

AN ACT FOR GRANTING UNTO HIS MAJESTY SEVERAL RATES AND DUTYS OF IMPOST AND TUNNAGE OF SHIPPING.

We, his majesty's most loyal and dutifull subjects, the representatives of his majesty's province of the Massachusetts Bay, in New England, being desirous of a collateral fund and security for drawing in the bills of credit on this province, have chearfully and unanimously given and granted and do hereby give and grant unto his most excellent majesty to the end and use aforesaid, and for no other use, the several dutys of impost upon wines, liquors, goods, wares and merchandize that shall be imported into this province, and tunnage of shipping hereafter mentioned; and pray that it may be enacted,—

And be it accordingly enacted by the Governour, Council and House of Representatives,

[Sect. 1.] That from and after the last day of the present session, there shall be paid by the importer of all wines, liquors, goods, wares and merchandize that shall be imported into this province from the place of their growth (salt, cotton wool, provisions, and every other thing of the growth and produce of New England excepted), the several rates or dutys of impost following; vizt.,—

For every pipe of wine of the Western Islands, eight shillings.

For every pipe of Canary, twelve shillings.

For every pipe of Madeira, nine shillings and sixpence.

For every pipe of other sorts not mentioned, nine shillings and sixpence.

For every hogshead of rum, containing one hundred gallons, eight shillings.

For every hogshead of sugar, sevenpence.

For every hogshead of molasses, fourpence.

For every hogshead of tobacco, four shillings and sixpence.

For every ton of logwood, ninepence.

—And so, proportionably, for greater or lesser quantitys.

And all other commodities, goods or merchandize not mentioned or excepted, fourpence for every twenty shillings value: all goods imported from Great Britain excepted.

[Sect. 2.] And for any of the above wines, liquors, goods, wares, merchandize, &c^{a}., that shall be imported into this province, &c^{a}., frō any other port than the places of their growth and produce there shall be paid by the importer double the value of impost appointed by this act to be received for every species abovementioned, unless they do, *bonâ fide*, belong to the inhabitants of this province and came upon their risque from the port of their growth and produce.

And be it further enacted,

[Sect. 3.] That all the aforesaid impost rates and dutys shall be paid in current money or bills of credit of this province of the last emission by the importer of any wines, liquors, goods or merchandize unto the commissioner to be appointed as is hereinafter to be directed for entering and receiving the same, at or before the landing of any wines, liquors, goods or merchandize: only the commissioner or receiver is hereby allowed to give credit to such person or persons where his or their duty of impost in one ship or vessell doth exceed the sum of three pounds; and in case where the commissioner or receiver shall give credit, he shall settle and ballance his accompts with every person on or before the last day of April, so that the same accompts may be ready to be presented to this court in May next. And all entries where the impost or duty to be paid doth not exceed three shillings, shall be made without charge to the importer, and not more than sixpence to be demanded for any other single entry to what value soever.

And be it further enacted,

[SECT. 4.] That all masters of ships or other vessells coming into any harbour or port within this province from beyond sea, or from any other province or colony, before bulk be broken and within twenty-four hours after his arrival at such harbour or port, shall make a report to the commissioner or receiver of the impost, to be appointed as is hereinafter mentioned, of the contents of the lading of such ship or vessell, without any charge or fee to be demanded or paid for the same; which report said master shall give into the commissioner or receiver, under his hand, and shall therein sett down and express the quantities and species of the wines, liquors, goods and merchandize laden on board such ship or vessell, with the marks and numbers thereof, and to whom the same is consigned; and also make oath that the said report or manifest of the contents of his lading, so to be by him given in under his hand as afores[d], contains a just and true accompt, to the best of his knowledge, of the whole lading taken on board and imported in the s[d] vessell from the port or ports such vessell came from, and that he hath not broken bulk nor delivered any of the wines, rum or other distilled liquors or merchandize laden on board the said ship or vessell, directly or indirectly; and if he shall know of any more wines, liquors, goods or merchandize to be imported therein, before the landing thereof he will cause it to be added to his manifest; which manifest shall be agreeable to a printed form made for that purpose, which is to be fill'd up by the s[d] commissioner or receiver according to each particular person's entry; which oath the commissioner or receiver is hereby impowered to administer: after which such master may unload, and not before, on pain of five hundred pounds, to be forfeited and paid by each master that shall neglect his duty on this behalf.

And be it further enacted,

[SECT. 5.] That all merchants, factors and other persons, importers, being owners of or having any of the wines, liquors, goods or merchandize consign'd to them, that by this act are liable to pay impost or duty, shall, by themselves or order, make entry thereof in writing under their hands, with the said commissioner or receiver, and produce unto him an invoice of all such goods as pay *ad valorem*, and make oath thereto in maner following:—

You, A. B., do swear that the entry of the goods and merchandize by you now made, exhibit the present price of said goods at this market, and that, *bonâ fide*, according to your best skill and judgment, it is not less than the real value thereof. So help you God.

—which above oath the commissioner or receiver is hereby impower'd to administer; and they shall pay the duty and impost by this act required, before such wines, liquors, goods, wares or merchandize be landed or taken out of the vessell in which the same shall be imported, on pain of forfieting all such wines, liquors, goods, wares or merchandize so landed or taken out of the vessell in which the same shall be imported.

[Sect. 6.] And no wines, liquors, goods, wares or merchandize that by this act are liable to pay impost or duty, shall be landed on any wharf, or into any warehouse or other place, but in the daytime only, and that after sunrise and before sunsett, unless in the presence and with the consent of the commissioner or receiver, on pain of forfeiting all such wines, liquors, goods, wares and merchandize and the lighter, boat and vessell out of which the same shall be landed or put into any warehouse or other place.

[Sect. 7.] And if any person or persons shall not have and produce an invoice of the quantities of rum or liquors to him or them consign'd, then the cask wherein the same is shall be gaged at the charge of the importer, that the quantities thereof may be known.

And be it further enacted,

[Sect. 8.] That every merchant or other person importing any wines into this province shall be allowed twelve per cent for leakage: *provided*, such wines have not been filled up on board; and that every hogshead, but or pipe of wine that hath two parts thereof leak'd out, shall be accounted for outs, and the merchant or importer to pay no duty or impost for the same. And no master of any ship or vessell shall suffer any wines to be fill'd up on board without giving a certificate of the quantity so filled up, under his hand, before the landing thereof, to the commissioner or receiver of impost for such port, on pain of forfeiting the sum of one hundred pounds.

[Sect. 9.] And if it be made to appear that any wines imported in any ship or vessell be decay'd at the time of unlading thereof, or in twenty days afterwards, oath being made before the commissioner or receiver that the same hath not been landed above that time, the dutys and impost paid for such wine shall be repaid unto the importer thereof.

And be it further enacted,

[Sect. 10.] That the master of any ship or vessell importing any wines, liquors, goods, wares or merchandize shall be liable to and shall pay the impost for such and so much thereof contained in his manifest as shall not be duly enter'd, nor the duty paid for the same by the person or persons to whom such wines, liquors, goods, wares or merchandize are or shall be consigned. And it shall and may be lawfull to and for the master of every ship or other vessell to secure and detain in his hands, at the owner's risque, all such wines, liquors, goods, wares or merchandize imported in any ship or vessell, untill he shall receive a certificate from the commissioner or receiver of the impost that the duty for the same is paid and untill he be repaid his necessary charges in securing the same; or such master may deliver such wines, liquors, goods, wares or merchandize as are not entred unto the commissioner or receiver of the impost in such port or his order, who is hereby impowered and directed to receive and keep the same, at the owner's risque, untill the impost thereof, with the charge, be paid; and then to deliver such wines, liquors, goods, wares or merchandize as such master shall direct.

And be it further enacted,

[Sect. 11.] That the commissioner or receiver of the impost in each port shall be and hereby is impower'd to sue the master of any ship or vessell for the impost or duty for so much of the lading of any wines, liquors, goods, wares or merchandize imported therein, according to the manifest to be by him given upon oath, as aforesaid, as shall remain not entred and the duty of impost thereof not paid. And where any goods, wares or merchandize are such as that the value thereof is not known, whereby the impost to be recovered of the master for the same cannot be ascertained, the owner or person to whom such goods, wares or merchandize are or shall be consign'd, shall be summoned to appear as an evidence at the court where such suit for the impost and duty thereof shall be brought, and be there required to make oath to the value of such goods, wares or merchandize.

And be it further enacted,

[SECT. 12.] That the ship or vessell, with her tackle, apparel and furniture, the master of which shall make default in anything by this act required to be performed by him, shall be lyable to answer and make good the sum or sums forfeited by such master according to this act, for any such default, as also to make good the impost or duty for any wines, liquors, goods, wares and merchandize not entered as aforesaid; and, upon judgment recovered against such master, the said ship or vessell, with so much of the tackle or appurtenances thereof as shall be sufficient to satisfy said judgment, may be taken in execution for the same; and the commissioner or receiver of the impost is hereby impowered to make seizure of such ship or vessell, and detain the same under seizure untill judgement be given in any suit to be commenced and prosecuted for any of the said forfeitures or impost; to the intent that if judgement be rendered for the prosecutor or informer, such ship or vessell and appurtenances may be exposed to sale for satisfaction thereof as is before provided: *unless* the owners, or some on their behalf, for the releasing such ship or vessell from under seizure or restraint, shall give sufficient security unto the commissioner or receiver of impost that seized the same, to respond and satisfy the sum or value of the forfeiture and dutys, with charges, that shall be recovered against the master thereof, upon suit to be brought for the same, as aforesaid; and the master occasioning such loss and damage unto his owners, through his default or neglect, shall be liable unto their action for the same.

And be it further enacted,

[SECT. 13.] That the naval officer within any of the ports of this province shall not clear or give passes to any master of any ship or other vessell, outward bound, untill he shall be certified, by the commissioner or receiver of the impost, that the dutys and impost for the goods last imported in such ship or vessell are paid or secured to be paid.

[SECT. 14.] And the commissioner or receiver of the impost is hereby impower'd to allow bills of store to the master of any ship or vessell importing any wines or liquors, for such private adventurers as shall belong to the master or seamen of such ship or other vessell, at the discretion of the commissioner or receiver, not exceeding three per cent of the lading; and the duties payable by this act for such wines or liquors, in such bills of store mentioned and express'd, shall be abated.

And whereas, many persons have heretofore caused to be imported, from the neighbouring government, into this province, by land carriage, large quantities of wine, rum and other merchandize, subjected to duty by this act, but have made no report thereof to the officer of impost, or any of his deputies, nor have paid any duty therefor, contrary to the true intent and meaning of this act.

Be it therefore further enacted,

[SECT. 15.] That whensoever any rum, wine or other merchandize, by this act subjected to any duty, shall be hereafter imported from any of the neighbouring governments, by land, into any town of this province, the owner thereof, or person importing the same, shall make report thereof to the s[d] officer, or some one of his deputies, and pay the duties hereby required therefor, on pain and penalty of forfeiting the same.

And be it further enacted,

[SECT. 16.] That all penaltys, fines and forfeitures accrewing and arising by virtue of this act, shall be one half to his majesty for the uses and intents for which the aforementioned duties of impost are granted, and the other half to him or them that shall seize, inform and sue for the same, by action, bill, plaint or information, in any of his majesty's courts of record, wherein no essoign, protection or wager of law shall be allowed: the whole charge of the prosecution to be taken out of the half belonging to the informer.

And be it further enacted,

[Sect. 17.] That there shall be paid, by the master of every ship or other vessell, coming into any port or ports in this province to trade or traffick, whereof all the owners are not belonging to this province (except such vessells as belong to Great Britain, the provinces or colonies of Pensilvania, West and East Jersey, New York, Connecticut, New Hampshire and Rhode Island), every voyage such ship or vessell does make, the sum of two shillings per ton, or one pound of good pistol-powder for every ton such ship or vessell is in burthen: *saving* for that part which is owned in Great Britain, this province, or any of the aforesaid governments, which are hereby exempted; to be paid unto the commissioner or receiver of the duties of impost, and to be employed for the ends and uses aforesaid.

[Sect. 18.] And the said commissioner is hereby impowered to appoint a meet and suitable person, to repair unto and on board any ship or vessell, to take the exact measure or tunnage thereof, in case he shall suspect that the register of such ship or vessell doth not express and sett forth the full burthen of the same; the charge thereof to be paid by the master or owner of such ship or vessell, before she be clear'd, in case she shall appear to be of greater burthen: otherwise, to be paid by the commissioner out of the money received by him for impost, and shall be allowed him accordingly, by the treasurer, in his accompts. And the naval officer shall not clear any vessell, untill he be also certified, by the said commissioner, that the duty of tunnage for the same is paid, or that it is such a vessell for which none is payable according to this act.

And be it further enacted,

[Sect. 19.] That there be one fit person, and no more, nominated and appointed by this court, as a commissioner and receiver of the afores[d] dutys of impost and tunnage of shipping, and for the inspection, care and management of the said office, and whatsoever relates thereto, to receive commission for the same from the governour or commander-in-chief for the time being, with authority to substitute and appoint a deputy receiver in each port, and other places besides that wherein he resides, and to grant warrants to such deputy receivers for the s[d] place, and to collect and receive the impost and tunnage of shipping aforesaid that shall become due within such port, and to render the account thereof, and pay in the same, to the said commissioner and receiver: which said commissioner and receiver shall keep fair books of all entries and duties arising by virtue of this act; also, a particular account of every vessell, so that the dutys of impost and tunnage arising on the said vessell may appear; and the same to lye open, at all seasonable times, to the view and perusal of the treasurer and receiver-general of this province (or any other person or persons whom this court shall appoint), with whom he shall account for all collections and payments, and pay all such moneys as shall be in his hands, as the treasurer or receiver-general shall demand it. And the said commissioner or receiver and his deputy or deputies, before their entering upon the execution of their office, shall be sworn to deal truly and faithfully therein, and shall attend in the said office from nine to twelve of the clock in the forenoon, and from two to five of the clock in the afternoon.

[SECT. 20.] And the s[d] commissioner and receiver, for his labour, care and expences in the said office, shall have and receive, out of the province treasury, the sum of twenty-five pounds, the present emission, per annum; and his deputy or deputies to be paid for their service such sum or sums as the said commissioner and receiver, with the treasurer, shall agree upon, not exceeding seven pounds ten shillings each. And the treasurer is hereby ordered, in passing and receiving the said commissioner's accompts, accordingly, to allow the payment of such salary or sallarys, as aforesaid, to himself and his deputy or deputys.

Provided,

[SECT. 21.] That this act shall be and continue in force from the last day of the present session untill the thirty-first day of May, which will be in the year of our Lord one thousand seven hundred and forty-four, and to the end of the next session of the general court, and no longer. [*Passed June 25.*

CHAPTER 9.

AN ACT FOR APPORTIONING AND ASSESSING A TAX OF TWENTY THOUSAND POUNDS, IN BILLS OF CREDIT OF THE TENO[U]R AND FORM LAST EMITTED; AND ALSO FOR APPORTIONING AND ASSESSING A FURTHER TAX OF THREE THOUSAND SEVEN HUNDRED AND THIRTY-EIGHT POUNDS FOUR SHILLINGS AND NINEPENCE THREE FARTHINGS, IN BILLS OF CREDIT OF SAID TENOR AND FORM, PAID THE REPRESENTATIVES FOR THEIR SERVICE AND ATTENDANCE IN GENERAL COURT, AND TRAVEL, AND TO DISCHARGE A FINE LAID THIS PRESENT YEAR ON THE TOWNS OF MEDFIELD, TIVERTON AND FREETOWN, FOR NOT SENDING A REPRESENTATIVE.

1741-42, chap. 11, § 27. WHEREAS the great and general court or assembly of the province of the Massachuset[t]s Bay, did, at their session in November, one thousand seven hundred and forty-one, pass an act for the levying a tax of fifty thousand pounds, in bills before current in the province (said fifty thousand pounds being equal to twelve thousand five hundred pounds of the bills emitted by said act), and, at their sessions in November, one 1742-43, chap. 14, § 5. thousand seven hundred and forty-two, did pass an act for the levying a tax of seven thousand five hundred pounds, in bills emitted by said act, to be assess'd this present year,—the whole of the two sums aforesaid amounting to the sum of twenty thousand pounds; and by the aforesaid acts, provision was made that the general court might, in the several years, apportion the several sums on the several towns in the province, if they thought fit: and the assembly aforesaid have likewise 1741-42, chap. 11, § 29. ordered that the sum of one thousand six hundred and thirty-eight pounds and threepence farthing, being the one half of such sum or sums as were paid the representatives in the years one thousand seven hundred and thirty-nine, and one thousand seven hundred and forty, and also the sum of twenty-one hundred pounds four shillings and sixpence halfpenny, paid the representatives the last year, and laid as a fine on several towns—the said two sums amounting to three thousand seven hundred and thirty-eight pounds four shillings and ninepence three farthings—should be levied and assess'd, on this present year, on the polls and estates of the inhabitants of the several towns, according to what their respective representatives have received; *wherefore*, for the ordering, directing, and effectual drawing in the sum of twenty thousand pounds, pursuant to the funds and grants aforesaid, and drawing the said sum into the treasury, according to the appointment now agreed to by this court; and also for drawing in the sum of three thousand seven hundred and thirty-eight pounds four shillings and ninepence three farthings, paid the representatives, and laid as a fine on the several towns, as aforesaid; all which is unanimously approved, ratif[y][*i*]ed, and confirmed; we, his majesty's most loyal and dutiful subjects, the representatives in general court assembled, pray that it may be enacted,—

And be it accordingly enacted by the Governour, Council and House of Representatives,

[Sect. 1.] That each town and district within this province be assess[*e*]'d and pay, as such town's and district's proportion of the sum of twenty thousand pounds, in bills of the tenor last emitted, as also for the fines laid on them, and their representatives' pay, the several sums following; that is to say,—

IN THE COUNTY OF SUFFOLK.

	REPRESENTATIVES' PAY AND FINES.			PROVINCE TAX.	SUM TOTAL.
Boston,	One hundred twenty-four pounds fifteen shill[ing]s and [3d] [threepence],	£124 15s. 3d.	Three thousand six hundred pounds,	£3,600 0s. 0d.	£3,724 15s. 3d.
Roxbury,	Twenty eight pounds thirteen shillings and spce [½] [halfpenny],	28 13 7½	One hundred eighty-six pounds three shill[ing]s and fourpence,	186 3 4	214 16 11½
Dorchester,	Thirty-two pounds two shillings and sixpence,	32 2 6	One hundred seventy-six pounds eight shill[ing]s and fourpence,	176 8 4	208 10 10
Milton,	four pounds seven shill[ing]s and sevenpence fing,	34 7 7¼	Eighty-one pounds eleven shillings and eightpence,	81 11 8	115 19 3¼
Brantrey,	-nine upds ten shill[ing]s and sixpence halfpenny,	29 10 6½	One hundred and ninety-five pounds,	195 0 0	224 10 6½
Weymouth,	fifty-seven upds fifteen shillings and sixpence,	37 15 6	One hundred and twelve pounds sixteen shill[ing]s and eightpence,	112 16 8	150 12 2
Hingham,	Thirty-two pounds five shillings and ninepence,	32 5 9	Two hundred and ten pounds eleven shillings and eightpence,	210 11 8	242 17 5
Dedham,	Thirty-six pounds sixteen shill[ing]s and twopence halfpenny,	36 16 2½	One hundred thirty-eight pounds and fifteen shillings,	138 15 0	175 11 2½
Medfield,	Thirty-two pounds eighteen shillings and sixpence; and fifteen pounds fine,	47 18 6	Eighty-four pounds and fifteen shillings,	84 15 0	132 13 6
Wrentham,	Thirty-three pounds nine shillings and tenepce ha'[lf]penny,	33 9 10½	One hundred and five pounds eighteen shillings and fourpence,	105 18 4	139 8 2½
[Medway],*	Six pounds eight shillings and one penny ha'[lf] pny,	6 8 1½	Fifty-five pounds eighteen shillings and fourpence,	55 18 4	62 6 5½
Stoughton,	Thirty- ight pounds nine shillings and sixpence three farth'[in]gs,	38 9 6¾	One hundred and two pounds eleven shillings and eightpence,	102 11 8	141 1 2¾
Hull,	. . . .	0 0 0	Forty-four pounds thirteen shillings and fourpence,	44 13 4	44 13 4
Brooklyn,	Twenty-three pounds nine shillings,	23 9 0	Sixty-six pounds eleven shillings and eightpence,	66 11 8	90 0 3
Needham,	Fifteen pounds fifteen shillings and three farthings,	15 15 0¾	Fifty-nine pounds eleven shillings and eightpence,	59 11 8	75 6 8¾
Bellingham,	. . . .	0 0 0	Twenty-two pounds eight shillings and fourpence,	22 8 4	22 8 4
Walpole,	. . . .	0 0 0	Thirty-four pounds and fifteen shillings,	34 15 0	34 15 0
Chelsea,	Eleven pounds sixteen shillings and sevenpence ha'[lf]penny,	11 16 7½	Eighty-seven pounds three shillings and fourpence,	87 3 4	98 19 11½
		£533 13s. 8¾d.		£5,365 13s. 4d.	£5,899 7s. 0¾d.

IN THE COUNTY OF ESSEX.

Salem,	Seventy-three pounds nineteen shill[ing]s and ninepence,	£73 19s. 9d.	Six hundred pounds,	£600 0s. 0d.	£673 19s. 9d.
Ipswich,	Sixty-six pounds five shillings,	66 5 0	Five hundred fifty-two pounds eight shill[ing]s and fourpence,	552 8 4	618 13 4
[illegible]y,	Forty pounds seven shillings and ninepence,	40 7 9	Five hundred and twelve pounds five shillings,	512 5 0	552 12 9
Marblehead,	Thirty-eight pounds twelve shillings and [illegible]e,	38 12 3	Three hundred eighty-nine pounds six shill[ing]s and eightpence,	389 6 8	427 18 11
Lynn,	Thirty-eight pounds eight shillings and eightpence farth[ing],	38 8 8¼	Two hundred and [illegible]ten pounds six shill[ing]s and eightpence,	210 6 8	248 15 4¼
[illegible]r,	Thirty-seven [illegible]ds sixteen shillings and ninepence,	37 16 9	Two hundred and forty-one pounds thirteen shill[ing]s and fourpence,	241 13 4	279 10 1
Beverly,	Thirty-eight pounds four shill[ing]s and sevenpence three farthings,	38 4 7¾	One hundred fifty-four pounds and ten shillings,	154 10 0	192 14 7¾
Rowley,	Thirty-nine [illegible]ls [illegible]en shillings and ninepence,	39 17 9	One hundred and fifty pounds fifteen shillings,	150 15 0	190 12 9
Salisbury,	Thirty-three pounds sixteen shillings and [illegible]ce ha' [lf]penny,	33 16 4½	One hundred and thirty-three pounds six shill[ing]s and eightpence,	133 6 8	167 3 0½
Haverhill,	Thirty-eight pounds eighteen shillings and [illegible]e,	38 18 9	One hundred and thirty-five pounds eleven shill[ing]s and eightpence,	135 11 8	174 10 5
Glocester,	Thirty-eight pounds nineteen shillings and [illegible]e,	38 19 6	Two hundred and fifty pounds fifteen shillings,	250 15 0	289 14 6
Topsfield,	Thirty-nine pounds two shillings and sixpence,	39 2 6	Seventy-six pounds eleven shillings and eightpence,	76 11 8	115 14 2
Boxford,	Thirty-nine pounds one shilling and sixpence,	39 1 6	Ninety-six pounds one shilling and eightpence,	96 1 8	135 3 2
[illegible]y,	Thirty-nine pounds eight shillings and ninepence,	39 8 9	One hundred and eleven pounds three shillings and fourpence,	111 3 4	150 12 1
Bradford,	Thirty-five pounds t[w]elve shill[ing]s and tenpence ha'[lf]penny,	35 12 10½	Eighty-three pounds fifteen shillings,	83 15 0	119 7 10½
Wenham,	Sixteen pounds nineteen shillings and sixpence,	16 19 6	Sixty-nine pounds eighteen shillings and fourpence,	69 18 4	86 17 10
Manchester,	. . . .	0 0 0	Sixty-three pounds one shilling and eightpence,	63 1 8	63 1 8
Methuen,	. . . .	0 0 0	Thirty pounds sixteen shillings and eightpence,	30 16 8	30 16 8
Middleton,	Nine pounds seven shillings and sevenpence ha'[lf]penny,	9 7 7½	Fifty-nine pounds fifteen shillings,	59 15 0	69 2 7½
		£664 19s. 11½d.		£3,922 1s. 8d.	£4,587 1s. 7½d.

* Parchment mutilated by mice.

IN THE COUNTY OF MIDDLESEX.

	REPRESENTATIVES' PAY AND FINES.			PROVINCE TAX.	SUM TOTAL.
Cambridge,	Twenty-four pounds and nine shillings,	£24 9s. 0d.	One hundred and thirty-two pounds,	£132 0s. 0d.	£156 9s. 0d.
Charlestown,	Thirty-one pounds nine shillings,	31 9 0	Two hundred and seventy pounds six shill[ing]s and eightpence,	270 6 8	301 15 8
Watertown,	[illegible]y-six pounds two shillings and [illegible]en-pence ha'[lf]penny,	36 2 7½	Eighty-seven pounds eleven shill[ing]s and eightpence,	87 11 8	123 14 3½
Concord,	Thirty-eight [illegible]unds twelve shillings and [illegible]ce,	38 12 3	One hundred sixty-four pounds eighteen shill[ing]s and fourp[en]ce,	164 18 4	203 10 7
[illegible]n,	Thirty-four pounds four shillings and nine-pence,	34 4 9	Seventy-seven pounds thirteen shill[ing]s and fourpence,	77 13 4	111 18 1
Woburn,	Thirty-seven pounds fifteen shill[ing]s and one penny ha'[lf [illegible]ny,	37 15 1½	One hundred and twenty-eight pounds fifteen shill[ing]s,	128 15 0	166 10 1½
Reading,	Thirty-six pounds eleven shill[ing]s and one penny ha'[lf] [illegible]ny,	36 11 1½	One hundred forty-one pounds six shill[ing]s and eight-pence,	141 6 8	177 17 9½
Sudbury,	Thirty-seven pounds eleven shillings and threepence,	37 11 3	One hundred and forty-seven pounds,	147 0 0	184 11 3
Marlboro[ugh],	Thirty-eight [illegible] five shillings and nine-pence,	38 5 9	One hundred [and] fifty-one pounds fifteen shillings,	151 15 0	190 0 9
[illegible]n,	Thirty-seven pounds [illegible]en shillings,	37 15 0	Ninety-one pounds and five shillings,	91 5 0	129 0 0
[illegible]to[w]n,	Twenty-two [illegible] six shill[ing]s and [illegible]pce ha'[lf]penny,	22 6 4½	One hundred and forty-two pounds three shill[ing]s and fourp[en]ce,	142 3 4	164 9 8½
Malden,	Thirty-two pounds,	32 0 0	One hundred and eighteen pounds six shill[ing]s and eightp[en]ce,	118 6 8	150 6 8
Chelmsford,	Twenty-eight [illegible] [illegible] shillings and threepence,	28 17 3	Eighty-one pounds thirteen shill[ing]s and fourpence,	81 13 4	110 10 7
Billerica,	Thirty-seven pounds eight shillings and six-pence,	37 8 6	Eighty-four [pounds] and five shillings,	84 5 0	121 13 6
[illegible]rn,	Thirty-five pounds eighteen shill[ing]s and elevenpence ha'[lf] [illegible]ny,	35 18 11½	Fifty-three pounds one shilling and eightpence,	53 1 8	89 0 7½
Holliston,	Seventeen pounds eight shillings,	17 8 0	Thirty-seven pounds sixteen shill[ing]s and eightpence,	37 16 8	55 4 8
[illegible]n,	Thirty-six pounds one shilling and nine-pence,	36 1 9	One hundred and thirty pounds one shilling and eight-pence,	130 1 8	166 3 5
Framingham,	Thirty-five [illegible]u[illegible]ds fifteen shillings and six-p[illegible]n[illegible]e,	35 15 6	One hundred and seven pounds eleven shill[ing]s and eightp[en]ce,	107 11 8	143 7 2
Medford,	Thirty-two [illegible]u[illegible]ds six shillings and three-pence,	32 6 3	Sixty-three pounds eleven shill[ing]s and eightpence,	63 11 8	95 17 11
Stow,	[illegible]-one pounds six shillings,	21 6 0	Forty-nine pounds thirteen shill[ing]s and fourpence,	49 13 4	70 19 4
Dunstable,	Six pounds eleven shillings and sixpence,	6 11 6	Forty pounds,	40 0 0	46 11 6
[illegible]t,	. . . .	0 0 0	Thirty-three pounds three shillings and fourpence,	33 3 4	33 3 4
Stoneham,	. . . .	0 0 0	Forty-two pounds eleven shill[ing]s and eightpence,	42 11 8	42 11 8

Littleton,	Twenty-one pounds one shilling and ninepence,	£21 1s. 9d.	Forty-nine pounds eighteen shill[ing]s and fourpence,	£49 18s. 4d.	£71 0s. 1d.
Hopkinton,	Thirty-six pounds seven shill[ing]s and tenpence ha'[lf]penny,	36 7 10½	Forty-one pounds thirteen shill[ing]s and fourpence,	41 13 4	78 1 2½
Bedford,	. . . .	0 0 0	Forty pounds fifteen shillings,	40 15 0	40 15 0
Westford,	Fourteen pounds twelve shillings and sixpence,	14 12 6	Fifty-three pounds thirteen shill[ing]s and fourpence,	53 13 4	68 5 10
Wilmington,	. . . .	0 0 0	Thirty-eight pounds and five shillings,	38 5 0	38 5 0
Tewksbury,	. . . .	0 0 0	Thirty-five pounds and five shillings,	35 5 0	35 5 0
[illegible]n,	. . . .	0 0 0	Twenty-six pounds and fifteen shillings,	26 15 0	26 15 0
[illegible]im,	Thirty-seven pounds sixteen [shill]s fourpence ha'[lf]penny,	37 16 4½	Seventy-one pounds sixteen shill[ing]s and eightpence,	71 16 8	109 13 0½
[Townshen]d,*	Nine pounds one shilling and a penny halfpenny,	9 1 1½	Twenty pounds,	20 0 0	29 1 1½
		£777 15 7		£2,754 13s. 4d.	£3,532 8s. 11d.

IN THE COUNTY OF HAMPSHIRE.

Springfield,	Thirty-one pounds five shillings and ninepence,	£31 5s. 9d.	Two hundred nineteen pounds three shill[ing]s and fourpence,	£219 3s. 4d.	£250 9s. 1d.
Northampton,	Thirty-two pounds fourteen shillings and sixpence,	32 14 6	One hundred and forty-four pounds one shilling and eightp[en]ce,	144 1 8	176 16 2
Hadley,	[illegible]ve pounds sixteen shillings,	25 16 0	One hundred and three pounds one shilling and eightp[en]ce,	103 1 8	128 17 8
Hatfield,	Twenty-six pounds five shillings and sixpence,	26 5 6	Sixty-six pounds three shillings and fourpence,	66 3 4	92 8 10
Westfield,	Thirty-three pounds fifteen shillings and ninepence,	33 15 9	Eighty-four pounds eleven shill[ing]s and eightpence,	84 11 8	118 7 5
[illegible]ld,	[illegible]ty-five pounds [illegible] shillings and [illegible]e,	25 3 3	One hundred and ten pounds one shilling and eightp[en]ce,	110 1 8	135 4 11
Enfield,	Fifteen pounds seven shillings and fourpence halfpenny,	15 7 4½	Sixty-five pounds six shillings and eightpence,	65 6 8	80 14 0½
Deerfield,	Seventeen pounds ten shillings and threepence,	17 10 3	Sixty-six pounds and fifteen shillings,	66 15 0	84 5 3
Sunderland,	. . . .	0 0 0	Thirty-four pounds,	34 0 0	34 0 0
Northfield,	. . . .	0 0 0	Twenty-nine pounds sixteen shill[ing]s and eightpence,	29 16 8	29 16 8

* Parchment mutilated by mice.

IN THE COUNTY OF HAMPSHIRE—*Continued.*

	REPRESENTATIVES' PAY AND FINES.			PROVINCE TAX.	SUM TOTAL.
Brimfield, . .	Four pounds three shillings and ninepence,	4 3 9	Fifty-eight pounds eleven shill[*ing*]s and eightpence, .	58 11 8	62 15 5
Somers, . .	. . . .	0 0 0	Thirty-five pounds eighteen shill[*ing*]s and fourpence, .	35 18 4	35 18 4
Sheffield, . .	. . . .	0 0 0	Thirty-five pounds, ...	35 0 0	35 0 0
Elbows, . .	. . . .	0 0 0	Twenty pounds, ...	20 0 0	20 0 0
		£212 2*s.* 1½*d.*	.	£1,072 11*s.* 8*d.*	£1,284 13*s.* 9½*d.*

IN THE COUNTY OF WORCESTER.

Worcester, .	Thirty-one pounds fourteen shill[*ing*]s and fourpence ha'[*lf*]penny, ...	£31 14*s.* 4½*d.*	Sixty-eight pounds eight shill[*ing*]s and fourpence, .	£68 8*s.* 4*d.*	£100 2*s.* 8½*d.*
Lancastor, . .	Thirty-nine pounds eighteen shill[*ing*]s and sixpence, ...	39 18 6	One hundred and thirteen pounds six shill[*ing*]s and eightpence, ...	113 6 8	153 5 2
Mendon, . .	Thirty-six pounds and elevenpence farthing,	36 0 11¼	One hundred and sixteen pounds eight shill[*ing*]s and fourpence, ...	116 8 4	152 9 3¼
[illegible]lstock, .	Thirty-six pounds fifteen shillings, . .	36 15 0	One hundred and two pounds eighteen shill[*ing*]s and fourpence, ...	102 18 4	139 13 4
[illegible]ld, .	Thirty-eight pounds eleven shill[*ing*]s and sevenpence ha'[*lf*]penny, ...	38 11 7½	Sixty-nine pounds eleven shill[*ing*]s and eightpence, .	69 11 8	108 3 3½
Southborough, .	Thirty pounds sixteen shill[*ing*]s and threepence, ...	30 16 3	Forty-five pounds three shillings and fourp[*en*]ce, . .	45 3 4	75 19 7
L[ei][*ie*]cester,	Nine pounds two shill[*ing*]s and fourpence ha'[*lf*]penny, ...	9 2 4½	Sixty-three pounds thirteen shill[*ing*]s and fourpence, .	63 13 4	72 15 8½
Rutland, . .	. . . .	0 0 0	Forty-one pounds and five shillings, ...	41 5 0	41 5 0
Lunenburgh, .	Eight pounds six shill[*ing*]s and one penny ha'[*lf*]penny, ...	8 6 1½	Fifty-one pounds, ...	51 0 0	59 6 1½
Westborough, .	. . . .	0 0 0	Seventy pounds sixteen shill[*ing*]s and eightpence, .	70 16 8	70 16 8
Shrewsbury, .	Twenty-four pounds sixteen shill[*ing*]s and tenp[*en*]ce ha'[*lf*]penny, ...	24 16 10½	Sixty-two pounds thirteen shill[*ing*]s and fourpence, .	62 13 4	87 10 2½
Oxford, . .	Fourteen pounds seventeen shillings, . .	14 17 0	Forty-seven pounds eighteen shill[*ing*]s and fourpence,	47 18 4	62 15 4
Sutton, . .	Thirty-four pounds ten shill[*ing*]s and ninepence, ...	34 10 9	Seventy-five pounds thirteen shill[*ing*]s and fourpence,	75 13 4	110 4 1
Uxbridge,	Thirty-two pounds nine shill[*ing*]s and elevenpence farthing, ...	32 9 11¼	Fifty-three pounds eighteen shill[*ing*]s and fourpence, .	53 18 4	86 8 3¼
Harvard, . .	Eight pounds one shilling and tenpence ha'[*lf*]penny, ...	8 1 10½	Forty-six pounds three shill[*ing*]s and fourpence, . .	46 3 4	54 5 2½

Grafton, . .	. . . .	£0 0s. 0d.	Thirty-nine pounds three shill[ing]s and fourpence, .	£39 3s. 4d.	£39 3s. 4d.
Upton, . .	Eight pounds one shilling and threepence,	8 1 3	Fifteen pounds eighteen shill[ing]s and fourpence, .	15 18 4	23 19 7
Dudley, . .	. . . .	0 0 0	Thirty-three pounds thirteen shill[ing]s and fourpence,	33 13 4	33 13 4
Bolton, . .	. . . .	0 0 0	Forty-four pounds eighteen shill[ing]s and fourpence, .	44 18 4	44 18 4
Sturbridge, .	. . . .	0 0 0	Seventeen pounds, ...	17 0 0	17 0 0
Leominster, .	. . . .	0 0 0	Fourteen pounds, ...	14 0 0	14 0 0
Western, . .	. . . .	0 0 0	Thirteen pounds and five shillings, ...	13 5 0	13 5 0
		£354 2s. 10½d.		£1,206 16s. 8d.	£1,560 19s. 6½d.

IN THE COUNTY OF PL[I][Y]MOUTH.

Pl[i][y]mouth,	Thirty-two pounds four shill[ing]s and fourpence ha' [illegible]y, ...	£32 4s. 4½d.	One hundred eighty-seven pounds eight shill[ing]s and fourp[en]ce, ...	£187 8s. 4d.	£219 12s. 8½d.
Plympton, .	Thirty-four pounds four shillings, . .	34 4 0	Ninety-nine pounds eight shillings and fourpence, .	99 8 4	133 12 4
Scituate, . .	Thirty-nine pounds four shill[ing]s and tenpence ha'[lf] [illegible]y, ...	39 4 10½	Two hundred eighty-seven pounds eleven shill[ing]s and eightp[ce], ...	287 11 8	326 16 6½
Bridgwater, .	Thirty-two pounds eleven shill[ing]s and sevenpence ha'[lf]pen[n]y, . . .	32 11 7½	Two hundred twenty-eight pounds one shilling and eightp[en]ce, ...	228 1 8	260 13 3½
Marshfield, .	Thirty-one pounds and ninepence three farthings, ...	31 0 9¾	One hundred and forty-two pounds, ...	142 0 0	173 0 9¾
Pembrook, .	Thirty pounds twelve shillings and sixpence, ...	30 12 6	Seventy-six pounds six shillings and eightpence, . .	76 6 8	106 19 2
Duxburough, .	Twenty five pounds four shillings and sixpence, ...	25 4 6	Sixty-six pounds sixteen shillings and eightpence, .	66 16 8	92 1 2
Middleborô[ugh], . .	[illegible]ty-seven pounds twelve shill[ing]s and sixpence, ...	27 12 6	One hundred sixty-eight pounds eight shill[ing]s and fourpence, ...	168 8 4	196 0 10
Rochester, .	Thirty-five pounds eighteen shillings and sixpence, ...	35 18 6	One hundred and seven pounds six shill[ing]s and eightpence, ...	107 6 8	143 5 2
Abbington, .	. . . .	0 0 0	Forty-seven pounds eighteen shillings and fourpence, .	47 18 4	47 18 4
Kingston, . .	Five pounds fourteen shill[ing]s and fourpence ha'[lf]penny, ...	5 14 4½	Fifty-two pounds eight shillings and fourpence, . .	52 8 4	58 2 8½
Han[n]over, .	Twenty-one pounds six shillings, . . .	21 6 0	Sixty-one pounds and fifteen shillings, ...	61 15 0	83 1 0
Halifax, . .	. . . .	0 0 0	Forty pounds, ...	40 0 0	40 0 0
Warham, . .	. . . .	0 0 0	Twenty pounds, ...	20 0 0	20 0 0
		£315 14s. 0¾d.		£1,585 10s. 0d.	£1,901 4s. 0¾d.

IN THE COUNTY OF BARNSTABLE.

	REPRESENTATIVES' PAY AND FINES.			PROVINCE TAX.	SUM TOTAL.
Barnstable,	Thirty-five pounds twelve shill[ing]s and sixpence,	£35 12s. 6d.	Two hundred pounds fifteen shillings,	£200 15s. 0d.	£236 7s. 6d.
Yarmouth,	Thirty-one pounds four shill[ing]s and threepence,	31 4 3	One hundred twenty-three pounds sixteen shill[ing]s and eightp[en]ce,	123 16 8	155 0 11
Sandwich,	Thirty pounds fifteen shill[ing]s and ninepence,	30 15 9	One hundred and eight pounds three shill[ing]s and fourpence,	108 3 4	138 19 1
Eastham,	Thirty-two pounds seven shill[ing]s and ninepence,	32 7 9	One hundred forty-nine pounds six shill[ing]s and eightpence,	149 6 8	181 14 5
[Truro,*]	. . . .	0 0 0	Nineteen pounds eleven shillings and eightpence,	19 11 8	19 11 8
[Harwich,	tw*]enty-six pounds fourteen shill[ing]s and ninepence,	26 14 9	One hundred and three pounds ten shillings,	103 10 0	130 4 9
Falmouth,	Twelve pounds nineteen shill[ing]s and a penny halfpenny,	12 19 1½	Seventy-three pounds six shillings and eightpence,	73 6 8	86 5 9½
Chatham,	. . . .	0 0 0	Sixty pounds eighteen shillings and fourpence,	60 18 4	60 18 4
Provincetown,	. . . .	0 0 0	. . . .	0 0 0	0 0 0
		£169 14s. 1½d.		£839 8s. 4d.	£1,009 3s. 5½d.

IN THE COUNTY OF BRISTOL.

Bristol,	Thirty-eight pounds seven shill[ing]s and ninepence,	£38 7s. 9d.	One hundred thirty-one pounds thirteen shill[ing]s and fourpence,	£131 13s. 4d.	£170 1s. 1d.
Taunton,	Thirty-four pounds eighteen shill[ing]s and fourp[en]ce ha'[lf]penny,	34 18 4½	Two hundred pounds three shill[ing]s and fourpence,	200 3 4	235 1 8½
Norton,	Thirty-three pounds two shill[ing]s and a penny ha'[lf]penny,	33 2 1½	One hundred pounds and ten shillings,	100 10 0	133 12 1½
Easton,	. . . .	0 0 0	Thirty-nine pounds six shillings and eightpence,	39 6 8	39 6 8
Dartmouth,	Twenty-seven pounds eight shill[ing]s and fourp[en]ce ha'[lf]penny,	27 8 4½	Three hundred and ten pounds one shilling and eightp[en]ce,	310 1 8	337 10 0½
Dighton,	Thirty-six pounds one shilling and sixpence,	36 1 6	Seventy pounds [and] fifteen shillings,	70 15 0	106 16 6
Rehoboth,	Thirty-six pounds eighteen shill[ing]s and sevenpence ha'[lf]penny,	36 18 7½	Two hundred forty-seven pounds one shilling and eightp[en]ce,	247 1 8	284 0 3½
Little Compton,	Thirty-four pounds ten shill[ing]s and one penny ha'[lf]penny,	34 10 1½	One hundred forty-one pounds thirteen shill[ing]s and fourp[en]ce,	141 13 4	176 3 5½

Swansey,	Thirty pounds eighteen shillings and threepence,	£30 18s. 3d.	One hundred ninety-eight pounds thirteen shill[ing]s and fourp[en][ce],	£198 13s. 4d.	£229 11s. 7d.
Tiverton,	Sixteen pounds one shilling and a penny, and twenty pounds fine,	36 1 1¼†	One hundred and sixty pounds,	160 0 0	196 1 1¼
Freetown,	Fifteen pounds fine,	15 0 0	Sixty-five pounds fifteen shillings,	65 15 0	80 15 0
Attleborough,	Thirty-four pounds two shillings,	34 2 0	One hundred pounds ten shillings,	100 10 0	134 12 0
Barrington,	. . . . .	0 0 0	Fifty-seven pounds eight shillings and fourpence,	57 8 4	57 8 4
Raynham,	. . . . .	0 0 0	Forty-five pounds eleven shillings and eightpence,	45 11 8	45 11 8
Berkley,	. . . . .	0 0 0	Forty-three pounds one shilling[s] and eightpence,	43 1 8	43 1 8
		£357 8s. 2¾d.		£1,912 5s. 0d.	£2,269 13s. 2¾d.

IN THE COUNTY OF YORK.

[illegible]k,	Forty-three pounds nine shillings and tenp[en]ce ha'[lf]penny,	£43 9s. 10½d.	One hundred eighty-three pounds one shill[ing] and eightp[en]ce,	£183 1s. 8d.	£226 1s. 6½d.
Kittery,	Thirty-seven pounds twelve shillings and threepence,	37 12 3	Two hundred fifty-two pounds one shilling and eightpence,	252 1 8	289 13 11
Berwick,	Thirty-three pounds two shillings,	33 2 0	One hundred and twelve pounds one shilling and eightpence,	112 1 8	145 3 8
Wells,	Thirty-five pounds twelve shillings,	35 12 0	Eighty-eight pounds five shillings,	88 5 0	123 17 0
Falmouth,	Thirty-six pounds one shilling and sixpence,	36 1 6	One hundred fifty-three pounds sixteen shill[ing]s and eightpence,	153 16 8	189 18 2
Biddeford,	Sixteen pounds fifteen shill[ing]s and fourpence ha'[lf]penny,	16 15 4½	Sixty pounds fifteen shillings,	60 15 0	77 10 4½
[illegible]l,	. . . . .	0 0 0	Thirty-nine pounds eleven shill[ing]s and eightpence,	39 11 8	39 11 8
Scarborough,	Fifteen pounds five shillings and ninepence,	15 5 9	Sixty-nine pounds eighteen shill[ing]s and fourpence,	69 18 4	85 4 1
North [illegible]r[illegible]th,	Nineteen pounds sixteen shillings,	19 16 0	Thirty-nine pounds,	39 0 0	58 16 0
[illegible]n,	. . . . .	0 0 0	Forty pounds,	40 0 0	40 0 0
Brunswick,	Eight pounds fourteen shillings,	8 14 0	Eighteen pounds ten shillings,	18 10 0	27 4 0
		£246 8s. 9d.		£1,057 1s. 8d.	£1,303 10s. 5d.

* Parchment mutilated by mice.

† Sic.

IN THE COUNTY OF DUKES COUNTY.

	REPRESENTATIVES' PAY AND FINES.			PROVINCE TAX.	SUM TOTAL.
Edgartown, .	Thirty-nine pounds fourteen shill[ing]s and sevenp[en]ce ha'[lf]penny, . . .	£39 14s. 7½d.	Forty-nine pounds sixteen shill[ing]s and eightpence, .	£49 16s. 8d.	£89 11s. 3½d.
Chilmark, . .	Twenty-two pounds ten shillings, . . .	22 10 0	Sixty-three pounds three shill[ing]s and fourpence, .	63 3 4	85 13 4
Tisbury, . .	Fifteen pounds three shillings, . . .	15 3 0	Thirty-nine pounds one shilling and eightpence, . .	39 1 8	54 4 8
		£77 7s. 7½d.		£152 1s. 8d.	£229 9s. 3½d.

IN NANTUCKET COUNTY.

Sherb[o]urn, .	Twenty-eight pounds seventeen shill[ing]s and ninepence, ...	£28 17s. 9d.	One hundred thirty-one pounds sixteen shill[ing]s and eightp[en]ce, ...	£131 16s. 8d.	£160 14s. 5d.

	REPRESENTATIVES' PAY AND FINES.			PROVINCE TAX.	SUM TOTAL.
SUFFOLK, . .	Five [illegible] [illegible] pounds [illegible]teen shill[ing]s and eightp[en]ce [3 farthings] [¾], ...	£533 13s. 8¾d.	Five thousand three hundred sixty-five pounds thirteen shill[ing]s and 4[d] [pence], ...	£5,365 13s. 4d.	£5,899 7s. 0¾d.
ESSEX, . .	Six hundred sixty-four [illegible] [illegible] shill[ing]s and elevenp[en]ce ha'[lf]-[illegible], ...	664 19 11½	[illegible] [illegible] [illegible] hundred twenty-two pounds one [illegible] and 8[d] [eightpence], ...	3,922 1 8	4,587 1 7½
MIDDLESEX, .	Seven [illegible] [illegible] [illegible] [illegible] fifteen shillings [illegible] [illegible], . . .	777 15 7	[illegible] [illegible] [illegible] hundred fifty-four [illegible] thirteen shill[ing]s and [4d] [fourpence], ...	2,754 13 4	3,532 8 11
HAMPSHIRE, .	[illegible] [illegible] and twelve [illegible] two shill[ing]s and [illegible] [illegible] ha'[lf] [illegible], .	212 2 1½	One [illegible] and [illegible] [illegible] [illegible] shill[ing]s and [illegible], ...	1,072 11 8	1,284 13 9½
WORCESTER, .	[illegible] [illegible] [illegible] fifty-four [illegible] two [illegible]s and [illegible] ha'[lf] [illegible], .	354 2 10½	One [illegible] two hundred and six [illegible] sixteen shill[ing]s and [illegible], ...	1,206 16 8	1,560 19 6½
PL[I][y]MOUTH,	[illegible] hundred and [illegible] pounds fourteen shillings and three farthings, . . .	315 14 0¾	One [illegible] five hundred and [illegible]-five [illegible] ten shillings, ...	1,585 10 0	1,901 4 0¾
BARNSTABLE, .	One hundred [illegible] pounds fourteen shill[ing]s and a penny ha'[lf]penny, .	169 14 1½	Eight [illegible] [illegible] and thirty-nine [illegible] eight shill[ing]s and fourpence, ...	839 8 4	1,009 2 5½
BRISTOL, . .	Three hundred fifty-seven [illegible] eight shillings [illegible] [illegible] three farth[ings],	357 8 2¾	One [illegible] nine hundred and [illegible] [illegible] and five shill[ing]s, ...	1,912 5 0	2,269 13 2¾

York,	Two hundred forty-six pounds eight shillings and ninepence,	£246 8s. 9d.	One thousand fifty-seven pounds one shilling and eightpence,	£1,057 1s. 8d.	£1,303 10. 5d.
Dukes County,	Seventy-seven pounds seven shill[ing]s and sevenpence ha'[lf]penny,	77 7 7½	One hundred fifty-two pounds one shilling and eightpence,	152 1 8	229 9 3½
Nantucket,	Twenty-eight pounds seventeen shillings and ninepence,	28 17 9	One hundred thirty-one pounds sixteen shill[ing]s and eightpence,	131 16 8	160 14 5
		£3,738 4s. 9¾d.		£20,000 0s. 0d.	£23,738 4s. 9¾d.

And be it further enacted,

[SECT. 2.] That the treasurer do forthwith send out his warrants, directed to the selectmen or assessors of each town or district within this province, requiring them, respectively, to assess the sum hereby set upon such town or district, in manner following; that is to say, to assess all rateable male polls above the age of sixteen years, at four shillings and twopence per poll, and proportionably in assessing the fines mentioned in this act, and the additional sum receiv'd out of the treasury for the payment of the representatives (except the governour, lieutenant-governour and their families, the president, fellows and students of Harvard College, setled ministers and grammar school-masters, who are hereby exempted as well from being tax[*e*]d for their polls, [*as for**] their estates being in their own hands and under their actual manag[*e*]ment and improvement) ; and [*other persons, if**] such there be, who, through age, infirmity or extream poverty, in the judgment of the assessors, are not capable to pay towards publick charges, they may exempt their polls, and so much of their estates as in their prudence they shall think fit and judge meet.

[SECT. 3.] And the justices in the general sessions, in the respective counties assembled, in granting a county tax or assessment, are hereby ordered and directed to apportion the same on the several towns in such county in proportion to their province rate, exclusive of what has been paid out of the publick treasury to the representative of such town for his service; and the assessors of each town in the province are also directed, in making an assessment, to govern themselves by the same rule; and all estates, both real and personal, lying within the limits of such town or district, or next unto the same, not paying elsewhere, in whose hands, tenure, occupation or possession soever the same is or shall be found, and also the incomes or profits which any person or persons (except as before excepted) do or shall receive from any trade, faculty, business or employment whatsoever, and all profits that shall or may arise by money or other estate not particularly otherwise assess'd, or commissions of profit in their improvement, according to their understanding and cunning, at one penny on the pound, and to abate or multiply the same, if need be, so as to make up the sum set and ordered hereby for such town or district to pay; and, in making their assessments, to estimate houses and lands at six years' income of the yearly rents, in the bills last emitted, whereat the same may be reasonably set or let for in the place where they lye: *saving* all contracts between landlord and tenant, and where no contract is, the landlord to reimburse one-half of the tax set upon such houses and lands; and to estimate Indian, negro and molatto servants proportionably as other personal estate, according to their sound judgment and discretion; as also to estimate every ox of four years old and upwards, at forty shillings in bills of the last emission; every cow of three years old and upwards, at thirty shillings; every horse and mare of three years old and upwards, at forty shillings; every swine of one year old and upwards, at eight shillings; every goat and sheep of one year old and upwards, at three shillings: likewise requiring the assessors to make a fair list of the said assessment, set[*t*]ing forth, in distinct columns, against each particular person's name, how much he or she is assess[*e*]'d at for polls, and how much for houses and lands, and how much for personal estate and income by trade or faculty; and the list or lists, so perfected and signed by them, or the major part of them, to commit[t] to the collectors, constable or constables of such town or district, and to return a certificate of the name or names of such collectors, constable or

* Parchment mutilated by mice.

constables, together with the sum total to each of them committed, unto himself, some time before the last day of January.

[Sect. 4.] And the treasurer for the time being, upon the receipt of such certificate, is hereby impowered and ordered to issue forth his warrants to the collector, constable or constables of such town or district, requiring him or them, respectively, to collect the whole of each respective sum assess[*e*]'d on each particular person, before the last day of March next; and of the inhabitants of the town of Boston, some time in the month of January next; and to pay in their collection, and issue the accompts of the whole, at or before the last day of March, which will be in the year of our Lord one thousand seven hundred and forty-four.

And be it further enacted,

[Sect. 5.] That the assessors of each town and district, respectively, in convenient time before their making the assessment, shall give seasonable warning to the inhabitants, in a town meeting, or by posting up notifications in some place or places in such town or district, or notify the inhabitants to give or bring in to the assessors true and perfect lists of their polls, rateable estate, and income by trade or faculty, and gain by money at interest. And if any person or persons shall neglect or refuse so to do, or bring in a false list, it shall be lawful to and for the assessors to assess such person or persons, according to their known ability in such town, in their sound judgment and discretion, their due proportion to this tax, as near as they can, agre[e]able to the rules herein given, under the penalty of twenty shillings for each person that shall be convicted by legal proof, in the judgment of the said assessors, of bringing in a false list; the said fines to be for the use of the poor of such town or district where the delinquent lives, to be levied by warrant from the assessors, directed to the collector or constables, in manner as is directed for gathering town assessments, and to be paid in to the town treasurer or selectmen for the use aforesaid: *saving*, to the party aggriev'd at the judgment of the assessors in set[t]ing forth such fine, liberty of appeal therefrom to the court of general sessions of the peace within the county, for rel[ei][*ie*]f, as in case of being over-rated. And if any person or persons shall not bring in a list of their estate as aforesaid to the assessors, he or they so neglecting shall not be admitted to make application to the court of sessions for any abatement of the assessment laid on him.

[Sect. 6.] And if the party be not convicted of any falseness in the list, by him presented, of polls, rateable estate, or income by any trade or faculty, business or employment, which he doth or shall exercise, or in gain by money at interest or otherwise, or other estate not particularly assess'd, such list shall be a rule for such person's proportion to the tax, which the assessors may not exceed.

And forasmuch as ofttimes sundry persons, not belonging to this province, bring considerable [*trade**] and merchandize, and by reason that the tax or rate of the town where they come to [*trade and tra**]ffick is finished and delivered to the constable or collector, and, before the next [*year's assess**]ment, are gone out of the province, and so pay nothing towards the support of the government, tho', in the time of their residing there, they reap'd considerable gain by trade, and had the protection of the government,— Preamble.

Be it further enacted,

[Sect. 7.] That when any such person or persons shall come and reside in any town of this province, and bring any merchandize, and trade and deal therewith, the assessors of such town are hereby impow- Transient traders to be rated.

* Parchment mutilated by mice.

ered to rate and assess all such persons according to their circumstances, pursuant to the rules and directions in this act provided, thou[gh] the former rate may have been finished, and the new one not perfected, as aforesaid.

And be it further enacted,

[SECT. 8.] That when any merchant, trader or factor, inhabitant of some one town within this province, shall transact or carry on trade and business in some other town in the province, the assessors of such town where such trade and business shall be carried on as aforesaid, be and hereby are impowered to rate and assess all such merchants, traders and factors, their goods or merchandize, for carrying on such trade, and exercising their faculty in such town, pursuant to the rules and directions in this act. And the constables or collectors are hereby enjoyned to levy and collect all such sums committed to them, and assess'd on persons who are not of this province, or are inhabitants of any other town as aforesaid, and pay the same into the town treasury.

And be it further enacted,

Tax may be paid in other species besides the bills emitted.

[SECT. 9.] That the inhabitants of this province shall have liberty, if they see fit, to pay the several sums for which they may respectively be assess'd at, as their proportion of the aforesaid sum of twenty-three thousand seven hundred and thirty-eight pounds, four shillings and ninepence three farthings in bills of credit of the last emission, or in bills of credit of the middle tenor, so called, according to their denominations, or in bills of the old tenor, accounting four for one; or in coin[e]'d silver, at the rate of six shillings and eightpence per ounce, troy weight; or in gold coin, at the rate of four pounds eighteen shillings per ounce; or in good merchantable hemp, at fourpence per pound; or merchantable flax, at fivepence per pound; or in good, merchantable, Isle-of-Sable codfish, at ten shillings per quintal; or in good refined bar-iron, at fifteen pounds per ton; or bloomery-iron, at twelve pounds per ton; or in good, hollow iron-ware, at twelve pounds per ton; or in good Indian corn, at two shillings and threepence per bushel; or good winter rye, at two shillings and sixpence per bushel; or good winter wheat, at three shillings per bushel; or in good barley, at two shillings per bushel; or good barrel pork, at two pounds per barrel; or in barrel beef, at one pound five shillings per barrel; or in duck or canvas, at two pounds ten shillings per bolt, each bolt to weigh forty-three pounds; or in long whalebone, at two shillings and threepence per pound; or merchantable cordage, at one pound five shillings per hundred; or in good train-oyl[e], at one pound ten shillings per barrel; or in good beeswax, at tenpence per pound; or in bayber[r]y-wax, at sixpence per pound; or in tried tallow, at fourpence per pound; or in good peas[e], at three shillings per bushel; or in good sheepswool, at ninepence per pound; or good, tann'd sole-leather, at fourpence per pound: all which aforesaid commodities shall be of the produce of this province, and, as soon as conveniently may be, dispos[e]'d of by the treasurer to the best advantage, [and] for so much as they will fetch in bills of credit, or for silver and gold; and the several persons who pay their taxes in any of the commodities before mentioned, shall run the risque and pay the charge of transporting the same to the province treasury.

[SECT. 10.] And if any loss shall happen by the sale of any of the aforesaid species, it shall [be] made good by a tax the next year; and if there be a surplusage, it shall remain a stock in the treasury. [*Passed June* 25.

ACTS

PASSED AT THE SESSION BEGUN AND HELD AT BOSTON, ON THE EIGHTH DAY OF SEPTEMBER, A. D. 1743.

CHAPTER 10.

AN ACT FOR ESTABLISHING AND REGULATING FEES WITHIN THIS PROVINCE.

WHEREAS some services of a publick nature have no fees stated by law, and others which have been established by two acts, made in the fourth and thirteenth years of King William the Third, by reason of the alteration of circumstances, are become unequal,— Preamble. 1692-93, chap. 37. 1742-43, chap. 5.

Be it therefore enacted by the Governour, Council and House of Representatives,

[SECT. 1.] That from and after the publication of this act, the following fees, in bills of credit emitted for the supply of the treasury in the year one thousand seven hundred and forty-one, or in other province bills, or gold or silver in proportion, at the choice of the payer, may be taken for the future; viz[t].,— Rates of fees for officers.

JUSTICE'S FEES.

	£	s.	d.
For granting a writ, summons or original summons, sixpence,	£0	0s.	6d.
Subpœna for each witness, one penny and a halfpenny,	0	0	1½
Entring an action or complaint, one shilling and sixpence,	0	1	6
Writ of execution, one shilling,	0	1	0
Filing papers, each, one penny,	0	0	1
Taxing a bill of cost, threepence,	0	0	3
Entring up judgment in civil or criminal cases, ninepence,	0	0	9
Bond for appeal, sixpence,	0	0	6
Copy of every evidence, original papers or records, sixpence per page for each page of twenty-eight lines, eight words in a line; if less than a page, threepence,	0	0	3
Each recognizance, one shilling,	0	1	0
Confessing judgment, sixpence,	0	0	6
Affidavit out of court in order to the tr[y][i]al of any cause, one shilling,—	0	1	0
in other causes, together with certificate, examining and entry, sixpence,	0	0	6
Acknowledging an instrument with one or more seals, provided it be done at one and the same time, one shilling,	0	1	0
A warrant, sixpence,	0	0	6

	£	s.	d.
Each day's attendance at the sessions, to be paid out of the fines, two shillings, ...	£0	2s.	0d.
Allowance to the party for whom costs shall be taxed, one shilling per day, ten miles' travel to be accounted a day, ...	0	1	0
For witnesses in civil causes, one shilling and sixpence per day, and ten miles' travel to be accounted a day, .	0	1	6
Taking affidavits *in perpetuam*, one shilling to each justice,	0	1	0

CORONER'S FEES.

For serving a writ, summons, or execution, and travel[l]ing-fees, the same as sheriffs.			
Bail bond, sixpence, ...	0	0	6
Every trial, where the sheriff is concerned, ninepence, .	0	0	9
Taking an inquisition, to be paid out of the deceas[e]d's estate, six shillings and eightpence,— . . .	0	6	8
for more than one at the same time, ten shillings,—			
if no estate, then to be paid by the county treasurer, three shillings and fourpence, and for more than one, five shillings, ...	0	3	4
For travel[l]ing and expences for taking an inquisition, each day, six shillings, ...	0	6	0
The foreman of the jury, three shillings; and ten miles accounted a day's travel, one shilling, . . .	0	1	0
Every other juror, two shillings and sixpence,— . .	0	2	6
travel, the same.			

JUDGE OF PROBATE AND REGISTER'S FEES.

For granting administration or guardianship, bonds, and letters of administration or guardianship;—			
to the judge, two shillings, ...	0	2	0
to the register, for writing bond of administration or guardianship, one shilling and ninepence, . .	0	1	9
for writing letter of administration or letters of guardianship, one shilling and sixpence, . .	0	1	6
For granting guardianship of divers minors to the same person and at the same time;—			
to the judge, for each minor, [1s.] [*one shilling*,] . .			
to the register, for each letter of guardianship and bond, one shilling, as before, ...			
Proving a will or codicil; one shilling and ninepence to the judge, and one shilling and threepence to the register, ...	0	3	0
Recording a will, letter of administration or guardianship, inventory or accompt of one page, and filing the same, one shilling and threepence,—	0	1	3
for every page more, of twenty-eight lines, of eight words in a line, ninepence, ...	0	0	9
For copy of a will or inventory, the same for each page, as before.			
Allowing accompts, two shillings and sixpence, . . } Decree for set[t]ling of intestate estates; to the judge, two shillings and sixpence, ... }	0	5	0
To the register, for examining such accompts, one shilling, ...	0	1	0
Every citation; to the register, ninepence, . . .	0	0	9
Every *quietus*; to the judge, one shilling, to the register, one shilling, ...	0	2	0

	£	s.	d.
Warrant or commission for apprizing or dividing estates; one shilling to the judge, one shilling to the register, ...	£0	2s.	0d.
Making out commission to receive and examine the claims of creditors in insolvent estates; to the judge, one shilling, and to the register, one shilling,— . .	0	2	0
for recording the same, one shilling and threepence, .	0	1	3
registering the commissioner's report, each page, ninepence, as above, ...	0	0	9
making out and entring an order upon the administrator to pay out the estate to the several creditors, in proportion returned by the commissioners, one shilling,	0	1	0
for proportioning such estate among the creditors, agreeable to the commissioners' return, when the estate exceeds not fifty pounds; to the register, two shillings,—	0	2	0
and above that sum, three shillings, ...	0	3	0
for recording the same, ninepence per page, as before, .	0	0	9

IN THE SUPERIOUR COURT.

JUSTICE'S FEES.

Entring every action, five shillings, ...	0	5	0
Taking every special bail, one shilling, ...	0	1	0
Allowing a writ of error, one shilling and sixpence, . .	0	1	6
Allowing a *habeas corpus*, one shilling, ...	0	1	0
Taxing a bill of cost, sixpence, ...	0	0	6
Attorney's fee, to be allowed in the bill of cost taxed, six shillings, ...	0	6	0
Granting liberty for the sale of land or estates, testate, two shillings, ...	0	2	0
On receiving each petition, one shilling, ...	0	1	0

CLERK'S FEES.

On entring every action, one shilling, ...	0	1	0
Every writ of *scire facias*, one shilling and sixpence, .	0	1	6
Every writ of review, two shillings and sixpence,— . .	0	2	6
if more than one page, sixpence per page, as before, .	0	0	6
Entring of every rule of court, sixpence, ...	0	0	6
Filing a declaration, ...	0	0	6
Entring appearance, threepence, ...	0	0	3
Signing a judgment by default, sixpence, . . .	0	0	6
Receiving and recording a verdict, sixpence, . . .	0	0	6
Copies of all records, each page of twenty-eight lines, eight words in a line, sixpence,—	0	0	6
if less than one page, sixpence, ...	0	0	6
Every action withdrawn or nonsuit, sixpence, . . .	0	0	6
Every petition read, sixpence,—	0	0	6
order thereon, sixpence, ...	0	0	6
Filing the papers of each cause, one penny per paper, .	0	0	1
Every execution, one shilling, ...	0	1	0
Writ of *habeas corpus*, two shillings, ...	0	2	0
Drawing bail bond, one shilling, ...	0	1	0
Confessing judgment, one shilling, ...	0	1	0
Acknowledging satisfaction of a judgment on record, sixpence, ...	0	0	6
Examining each bill of cost, sixpence, ...	0	0	6

Continuing each cause, and entring the next term, sixpence,	£0	0s.	6d.
Entring up judgment and copying the same, one shilling,	0	1	0
To each *venire*, to be paid out of the county treasuries, respectively, by order from any three of the justices of said court, threepence,	0	0	3

IN THE INFERIOUR COURT OF COMMON PLEAS, AND COURT OF GENERAL SESSIONS.

JUSTICE'S FEES.

Entry of every action, four shillings,	0	4	0
Taxing a bill of cost, sixpence,	0	0	6
Attorney's fee, to be allow'd in the bill of cost taxed, five shillings,	0	5	0
Taking the recognizance on appeals, sixpence,	0	0	6
Each recognizance in granting licences, one shilling,	0	1	0
Proving each deed, two shillings,	0	2	0
Granting every licen[s][c]e for publick entertainment or retailing, one shilling,	0	1	0

CLERK'S FEES.

Every action entred, one shilling,	0	1	0
Every writ and seal, sixpence,	0	0	6
Every appearance, threepence,	0	0	3
Entring and [recording] [*rendring*] a verdict, sixpence,	0	0	6
Recording a judgment, one shilling,	0	1	0
Copies of all records, each page, as before, sixpence,	0	0	6
Every action withdrawn or nonsuit, sixpence,	0	0	6
Every execution, one shilling,	0	1	0
Taking special bail, one shilling; confessing judgment or default, sixpence,	0	1	6
Acknowledging satisfaction of a judgment on record, sixpence,	0	0	6
Writ of *habeas corpus*, two shillings; continuing each cause, and entry at the next court, sixpence,	0	2	6
Entring up judgment and copying, one shilling,	0	1	0
Examining each bill of cost, sixpence; each recognizance, one shilling,	0	1	6
Each *venire*, to be paid out of the county treasuries, respectively, by order of court, threepence,	0	0	3
Writ of *facias habere possessionem*, two shillings,	0	2	0
Filing each paper, a penny,	0	0	1

CLERK OF THE SESSIONS' FEES.

Entring a complaint or indictment, one shilling,	0	1	0
Discharging a recognizance, sixpence,	0	0	6
Each warrant against criminals, sixpence,	0	0	6
Every summons or subpœna, twopence,	0	0	2
Every recognizance for the peace or good behaviour, one shilling,	0	1	0
Granting every licence for publick entertainment or retailing, one shilling,	0	1	0
For each recognizance, one shilling,	0	1	0
Entring up judgment, or entring satisfaction of judgment on record, and copying, one shilling,	0	1	0
Each warrant for county tax, sixpence,	0	0	6

Recording each marriage, to be paid by the town clerks respectively, threepence, ...	£0	0s.	3d.
For minuting the receipt of each petition and order thereon, and recording, ninepence per page, as before, .	0	0	9
Examining and casting the grand jury's acco[*un*]t yearly, and order thereon, to be paid by the county treasurer by order of the court of sessions, one shilling and sixpence, ...	0	1	6
For copies of all original papers or records, ninepence per page, as before, ...	0	0	9
For filing each paper [a penny], ...	0	0	1

SHERIFF'S OR CONSTABLE'S FEES.

For serving an original summons, one shilling, ...	0	1	0
Every *capias* or attachment in civil, or warrants in criminal, cases for trial, one shilling,—	0	1	0
and for travel out and to return the writ (the travel to be certified on the back of the writ or original summons), one penny halfpenny per mile, ...	0	0	1½
Bail bond, sixpence, ...	0	0	6
Serving execution in every personal action, if twenty pounds or under, one shilling per pound; for all others not exceeding forty pounds, sixpence per pound; for all others not exceeding one hundred pounds, fourpence per pound; all others above one hundred pounds, twopence per pound; the fees to be in the same money that the execution is extended for.			
For travel out and to return the execution, twopence per mile, the travel to be accounted from the court-house in each shire town in each county, . . .	0	0	2
For giving livery and seizen of real estates, seven shillings and sixpence,—	0	7	6
travel as before, if of different parcels of land, five shillings each, ...	0	5	0
Every trial, sixpence, ...	0	0	6
Every default, threepence, ...	0	0	3
Every precept for the choice of representatives, one shilling, to be paid out of the county treasur[y][*ie*]s respectively, ...	0	1	0
To the officer attending the grand jury, each day, one shilling and sixpence, ...	0	1	6

CRYER'S FEES.

Calling the jury, threepence, ...	0	0	3
Every default or nonsuit, sixpence, ...	0	0	6
Every verdict, sixpence, ...	0	0	6
Every judgment affirmed on a complaint, sixpence, . .	0	0	6

GOALER'S FEES.

For turning the key on each prisoner committed, two shillings and sixpence; viz[t]., one shilling and threepence in, and one shilling and threepence out, .	0	2	6
For dieting each person, three shillings per week, . .	0	3	0

MESSENGER OF THE HOUSE OF REPRESENTATIVES' FEES.

For serving every warrant from the house of representatives, which they may grant for arresting, imprisoning, or taking into custody any person, one shilling and sixpence,—	£0	1s.	6d.
for travel, each mile out, twopence per mile,—	0	0	2
for keeping and providing food for such person, each day, two shillings and sixpence,—	0	2	6
for his discharge or dismission, one shilling and sixpence, to be paid as by law already provided,	0	1	6

GRAND JUROR'S FEES.

Foreman, each day, two shillings,—	0	2	0
each other, one shilling and sixpence,	0	1	6

PETIT JUROR'S FEES.

To the foreman, in every case at the superiour court, one shilling and threepence,—	0	1	3
to every other juror, one shilling,	0	1	0
To the foreman, in every case at the inferiour court or sessions, one shilling,—	0	1	0
to every other juror, ninepence,	0	0	9

FOR MARRIAGES.

For each marriage, two shillings and sixpence; out of which to be paid to the town clerk for recording, threepence, and to the clerk of the sessions for recording, threepence,	0	2	6
To the town clerk, for every publishment of the banns of matrimony and entring thereof, one shilling,	0	1	0
Every certificate of such publishment, ninepence,	0	0	9
Recording births and deaths, each, fourpence,	0	0	4
For a certificate of the birth or death of any person, threepence,	0	0	3
For every search of record, when no copy is required, threepence,	0	0	3

COUNTY REGISTER'S FEES.

For entring or recording any deed, conveyance or mortgage, for the first page, ninepence,—	0	0	9
and sixpence a page for so many pages more as it shall contain, accounting after the rate of twenty-eight lines, of eight words to a line, to each page, and proportionably for so much more as shall be under a page,—	0	0	6
and threepence for his attestation on the original, of the time, book and folio where it is recorded,—	0	0	3
and for discharge of a mortgage, as aforesaid, sixpence,	0	0	6

GOVERNOUR AND SECRETARY'S FEES.

To the governour, five shillings for registers,	0	5	0
To the secretary, two shillings and sixpence,	0	2	6
For certificates under the province seal; to the governour, five shillings,—	0	5	0
to the secretary, two shillings and sixpence,	0	2	6
For warrants of apprizement, survey, &c[a].; to the governour, three shillings,—	0	3	0
to the secretary, three shillings,	0	3	0

To the governour, for a pass to the castle for each vessel, one shilling and threepence; wood sloops and other coasting vessels, for which passes have not been usually required, excepted, ... £0 1s. 3d.
For a certificate of naval stores, in the whole, five shillings, 0 5 0

And be it further enacted,

[SECT. 2.] That if any of the officers aforesaid shall demand and take any greater or other fees for the matters before mentioned, or any of them, than are allowed to be demanded and taken by this act, and shall be thereof convict, they shall forf[ie][*ei*]t and pay for each offence the sum of ten pounds, to be applied, the one moiety thereof for and towards the support of this government, and the other moiety to him or them that shall sue for the same; to be recovered by action, bill, plaint or information, in any court of record proper to try the same. And all officers to whom any warrant, summons, capias or attachment shall be committed, and who shall receive fees for the service thereof, are hereby required, without unnecessary delay, to serve and execute the same, on forf[ie][*ei*]ture of ten pounds, to be recovered and applied as aforesaid, besides making good such dam[*m*]age as the party may sustain by such delay: *provided*, in civil causes, the fees for travel and service be first tendred and paid if required by such officers.

[SECT. 3.] This act to continue and be in force for the space of one year from the publication thereof, and from thence to the end of the next session of the general court, and no longer. [*Passed and published September* 15. Limitation.

CHAPTER 11.

AN ACT FOR SECURING THE SEASONABLE PAYMENT OF TOWN AND PRECINCT RATES OR ASSESSMENTS.

WHEREAS the method directed to by law, and heretofore practiced by the receivers [or] [*of*] treasurers of towns and precincts, hath been to sue for and recover town and precinct rates and assessments, or the arrears thereof, by mean process against the constable[s] or collectors to whom they were committed to be gathered, who neglected their duty therein, whereby the payments of such rates or assessments into the respective town or precinct treasuries hath been greatly delayed, to the greivous dam[*m*]age of many places; to prevent which for the future,— 1736-37, chap. 15.

Be it enacted by the Governour, Council and House of Represent-[*ati*]ves,

[SECT. 1.] That from and after the publication of this act, if the constable or collector of any town or precinct within this province (to whom any town or precinct rates or assessments have been committed to collect), shall be remiss in his duty by law required, and neglect to collect such rates and assessments as have been committed to him to collect, and to pay in the same to the treasurer or receiver of such town or precinct by the time fixed in the warrant to him directed, or within one month next after the expiration thereof, such treasurer or receiver is hereby impowered, by warrant, under his hand and seal, directed to the sheriff of the county or his deputy (who are hereby respectively directed and impowered to execute the same), to cause such sum or sums of money as such constable or collector hath not paid in, to be levied by distress and sale of his estate, real or personal, returning the overplus, if any there be, and for want of such estate, to take the body of such constable or collector, and to imprison him until[l] he pay the same: *provided*,—

[SECT. 2.] This act shall continue and be in force for the space of ten years from and after the publication thereof, and from thence to the end of the then next session of the general court, and no longer. [*Passed September* 15; *published September* 19.

CHAPTER 12.

AN ACT FOR ERECTING OF WORKHOUSES FOR THE RECEPTION AND EMPLOYMENT OF THE IDLE AND INDIGENT.

Preamble. 1699-1700, chap. 3. 1703-4, chap. 14. 1710-11, chap. 6. 1730-31, chap. 3. 1740-41, chap. 20.

WHEREAS the erecting of houses for the entertainment and employment of idle and slothful[l] persons who refuse to exercise any lawful[l] calling or business, whereby to support themselves and famil[y][*ie*]s, and of the poor and indigent that want means to employ themselves, may be of great advantage to the publick, and more especially to the towns that shall be concern'd in such an undertaking,—

Be it therefore enacted by the Governour, Council and House of Representatives,

Any single town may erect a workhouse, appoint overseers, &c.

[SECT. 1.] That whensoever any town within [the] [*this*] province shall see meet to erect or provide an house for the purpose before mentioned, such town shall be and hereby is authorized and impower[*e*]d so to do; as also, at their publick meetings for the choice of town officers, in the month of March, annually, to ch[oo][*u*]se five, seven or nine overseers of said house, who shall have the inspection, ordering, and government thereof, with power of appointing a master and needful[l] assistants for the more immediate care and oversight of the persons received into, or employed in said house; which overseers, once in every month, and at other times as occasion shall require, shall assemble together to consider and determine of the most proper methods for the discharge of their office, and at their stated monthly meetings, shall have power to make needful[l] orders for the regulation of such house, which orders shall be binding till the next publick meeting of the inhabitants of such town, to whom such orders shall be presented for approbation, and when by them approved, shall be obligatory until[l] revoked by said town.

Overseers may make needful orders for regulating such house.

And be it further enacted,

Two or more towns may erect a workhouse.

[SECT. 2.] That when any number of towns shall agree, at their joint charge and for their common benefit, to erect or provide a workhouse for the employment of persons residing in such towns, that are indigent or idle, or to purchase land whereon to erect such house, and for the accommodation of it, they shall be and hereby are vested with authority so to do; and the regulation, inspection, and government of such house, when erected, ordering the needful[l] repairs of it—with power of appointing a master and other assistants, and him or them, in case of any irregular behaviour, incapacity or other just cause, to remove from their respective offices or trusts—shall be in the hands of the overseers, to be from year to year specially appointed or chosen by the several towns concerned, at their anniversary publick meetings in the month of March; each town to choose five, unless all the towns engaged in the undertaking shall agree upon any other number or proportions: and in case of the death of any overseer, or his removal out of the town for which he was appointed, the vacancy thereby made may be supply'd by such town at any other publick meeting; and if any

May appoint overseers to inspect the house, and order the affairs of it.

town or towns concern[*e*]d, shall neglect to ch[oo][*u*]se such overseers, in such case, the person or persons chosen by the other towns, may proceed in all affairs of said house, any such neglect or refusal notwithstanding.

And be it further enacted,

[SECT. 3.] That there be stated quarterly meetings of all the overseers, on the first Tuesday of the months of April, July, October, and January, from year to year, to be held at the workhouse, in order to inspect the management thereof, and for the ordering the affairs of said house; and besides these stated meetings, intermediate meetings, to be held at the workhouse, may be called, when need requires, by the overseers of any town concern[*e*]d, due notice of the time and occasion thereof being given to the rest in such way and manner as shall be agreed on by the overseers at any general stated meeting.

Overseers to hold quarterly meetings.

And be it further enacted,

[SECT. 4.] That the overseers, when duly assembled, may ch[oo][*u*]se a moderator to regulate the business of the meeting, who shall have a voice in matters voted or transacted by the overseers, in case only of an equi-vote; and, at their first gen[*era*]l meeting in every year, shall likewise cho[o]se a clerk to enter and record all votes and orders that from time to time shall be made and passed by the overseers, who shall be sworn to the faithful[l] discharge of his trust.

May choose a moderator, clerk, &c.

And be it further enacted,

[SECT. 5.] That the overseers for the time being, at a general quarterly meeting, whereat one-half at least of the whole number of overseers shall be present, shall have power to make needful[l] and reasonable orders and by-laws, not repu[n]gnant to the laws of this province, for the better and more decent regulating the said house, and well-ordering the affairs of it; which orders shall be binding until[l] the expiration of the year for which such overseers shall be chosen, or until[l] they shall be by them revoked; and at such meeting may likewise agree with the master or other assistants, and order meet allowance, for their care and service during the term for which such overseers shall be chosen, or such further term as the towns concern[*e*]d shall agree: all other matters of less importance relating to the said house, may be transacted at any other meetings duly warned, when but seven of the overseers are present; subject, nevertheless, to be altered or reversed at any general stated meeting.

May make orders and by-laws.

May order a meet allowance to the master and assistants.

And be it further enacted,

[SECT. 6.] That the yearly stipend or allowance to the master and assistants, over and above what is provided for by this act for their care and trouble, together with the charge of keeping the house in repair, shall be paid by the several towns concerned, in proportion as they are set or rated in the province tax at the time when such repairs shall be made, or such allowance stated by the overseers, or in such other proportion as all the towns concern[*e*]d shall agree; and the town or towns refusing or neglecting to advance their respective proportion of such allowance, or other charges before mentioned, after they shall have been stated and adjusted by the overseers, the same may be recovered of such delinquent town or towns, in any court proper to try the same, by action to be brought by the person or persons whom the overseers may appoint for that purpose.

By whom, and in what proportion, the allowance to the master and charge of repairing the house shall be defrayed.

And be it further enacted,

[SECT. 7.] That any three or more of the overseers in any town already provided with such a house, and of the overseers in any town that (either by themselves or in conjunction with other towns) shall hereafter erect a workhouse, be and they are hereby directed and impowered to commit[t] to such house, by writing under the hands

Overseers of each town concerned empowered to commit persons to the workhouse.

of the s[*ai*]d overseers, to be employ[*e*]d and governed according to the rules and orders of the house, any person or persons, residing in such town, that hereafter in this act are declared liable to be sent thither: *provided*, that no greater number of persons belonging to any town be received into the house than such towns proportion of said house (to be allotted them) can accommodate, when the receiving them will exclude or incom[*m*]od[ate][*e*] such as belong to other towns.

And be it further enacted,

Qualification of persons liable to be sent thither.

[SECT. 8.] That the persons who shall be liable to be sent to, employed, and governed in any workhouse erected or to be erected by one or more towns, pursuant to this or any former act, are all poor and indigent persons, that are maintained by or receive alms from the town; also all persons able of body to work, and not having estate or means otherways to maintain themselves, who refuse or neglect so to do, live a dissolute or vagrant life, and exercise no ordinary or lawful[l] business or calling whereby to gain an honest livelihood; and all such as, having some rat[*e*]able estate, but not enough to qualify [*th*]em to vote in town affairs, do neglect the due care and improvement of it, and, by consuming their time and money in publick houses to the neglect of their proper business, or by other ways mispending what they earn, to the impoverishment of themselves or famil[y][*ie*]s, are likely to become chargeable to the town.

And it is hereby further provided and enacted,

Towns neglecting to provide their proportion of materials, &c., deprived of the privilege of sending persons thither.

[SECT. 9.] That if any town shall refuse or neglect to provide their proportion of the needful[l] furniture for such house, or of the materials, implements, and other necessaries for carrying on the work there to be performed, according to their agreement, or as shall be ordered by the overseers, such town shall be deprived of the priviledge of sending any person thither until[l] such time as they shall comply with such order or agreement.

And be it further enacted,

The master to keep the materials sent by each town apart from those sent by other towns.

[SECT. 10.] That besides the afores[*ai*]d proportion of materials, &c[a]., to be found by the towns concerned, each town may likewise provide such materials, implements, and tools for work as the overseers for such town shall judge any person by them committed to said house can be employed about, with most profit and advantage, during his or her abode there; and the master of the house shall receive such materials, and keep them sep[a][*e*]rate and apart from those that shall be sent by any other town, and shall be accountable to the overseers of each town concerned, as well for the prime stock as for all profits and earnings that shall be made by the labour of those, belonging to such town, under his care; and shall keep a register of the names of the persons committed to such workhouse, with the time of their being received into and discharged from it, and of their earnings by their labour, that so the same may appear to any of the overseers whensoever they shall see cause to inspect them; and all controversies between the master or keeper of such house and the overseers of any town touching his acco[mp][*un*]ts or other affairs whatsoever, may be determined by the overseers of the house at a general meeting.

To be accountable for the prime stock and earnings.

To keep a register, &c.

Controversies betwixt the master and overseers of any town, how to be determined.

And be it further enacted,

Each town to bear the charge of supporting such as they commit to the house.

[SECT. 11.] That no town shall be at charge for the support or relief of any person committed to said house, who was not sent thither by the overseers belonging to such town; nor any person orderly committed to it shall be discharged from it but by the overseers by whom he was committed, or by the overseers, at a general meeting, or otherwise by the justices of the court of general sessions of the peace, in the same county, upon application to them made for that purpose; and every person so committed, if fit and able to work, shall be held and kept

How persons committed may be discharged.

Persons committed to be kept to labor.

stric[k]tly and dil[l]igently [i][*e*]mployed in labour during his or her abode there; and in case they be idle, and shall not duly perform such task or stint as shall be reasonably assign'd them, or shall be stubborn and disorderly, shall be punish[*e*]d according to the orders that shall be made for the ruling, governing, and punishing of the persons there to be committed, not repugnant to the laws of this province.

In case they be idle or disorderly, to be punished.

And be it further enacted,

[SECT. 12.] That one-third part of the profits or earnings of the work done by the persons detained in such house, shall be to the master for and towards his support, over and above such further annual stipend as the overseers see meet to order and allow him as before mentioned for his care and service.

The master to have one-third of the earnings.

And be it further enacted,

[SECT. 13.] That the prime stock, together with the other two-thirds of the profits or incomes of the labour of the persons [i][*e*]mployed there, shall be disposed of by the overseers of the respective towns to whom it belongs, either to the master in satisfaction for his service, care, and expence about the persons by them committed to him, and at such rate as the said overseers and master shall agree, or for the support of the famil[y][*ie*]s of the persons there detained, if any such they have, or otherwise for the use of such town as occasion shall require.

How the other two-thirds of the earnings and the prime stock shall be disposed of.

And be it further enacted,

[SECT. 14.] That any workhouse erected as aforesaid may be discontinued or appl[y][*i*]ed to any other use whensoever the town or towns concerned shall find or judge their circumstances require it, and shall agree so to do.

Any workhouse may be discontinued, in case.

Provided, nevertheless,—

[SECT. 15.] That nothing herein contained shall be construed or understood to abridge the town of Boston, or the overseers of the poor thereof, any priviledge or power, with relation to a workhouse, already granted them by a late law of this province for that purpose made and provided. [*Passed September* 17.

1735-36, chap. 4.

ACTS

PASSED AT THE SESSION BEGUN AND HELD AT BOSTON, ON THE TWENTIETH DAY OF OCTOBER, A. D. 1743.

CHAPTER 13.

AN ACT FOR SUPPLYING THE TREASURY WITH THE SUM OF TWENTY THOUSAND POUNDS FOR PUT[T]ING THE PROVINCE IN A BETTER POSTURE OF DEFENCE, FOR DISCHARGING THE PUBLICK DEBTS, &c., AND FOR DRAWING IN THE SAID BILLS INTO THE TREASURY AGAIN, AND FOR STATING THEIR VALUE IN DISCHARGING PUBLICK AND PRIVATE DEBTS.

Be it enacted by the Governour, Council and House of Representatives,

£20,000 in bills of credit to be emitted.

[SECT. 1.] That the treasurer be and hereby is impowered and ordered to emit and issue forth the sum of twenty thousand pounds in bills of credit of the newest form and tenor now lying in his hands and received for taxes, impost and excise, or, if there shall not be a sufficiency, in new bills of the same form and tenor, which this court may hereafter order, to be always valued and taken as the bills of credit of the last emission are or shall be valued and taken; and the said sum of twenty thousand pounds shall be issued out of the treasury in manner and for the purposes following; viz[t]., the sum of eight thousand one hundred and thirty-one pounds fourteen shillings and threepence, part of the aforesaid sum of twenty thousand pounds, to be applied for the payment of wages that now are or that hereafter may be due by virtue of the establishment of Castle William, Richmond Fort, George's Truck-house, Saco Truck-house, Brunswick Fort, the block-house above Northfield, the sloop in the countr[e]y's service, the province snow, and the treasurer's usual disbursements; and the sum of seven thousand pounds, part of the aforesaid sum of twenty thousand pounds, shall be applied for put[t]ing the province into a better posture of defence, for compleating the repairs of Castle William and other forts and garrisons within this province, pursuant to such grants as are or shall be made by this court for those purposes, and two thousand eight hundred pounds for the payment of such other grants as are or shall be made by this court, and for the payment of stipends, bounties and premiums established by law, and for the payment of all other matters and things which this court have or shall, either by law or orders, provide for the payment of out of the publick treasury, and for no other purpose whatsoever: the sum of one thousand pounds, part of the aforesaid sum of twenty thousand pounds, shall be applied for the discharge of other debts owing from this province to persons who have served or shall serve them by order of this court in such matters and things where there is no establishment nor any certain sum assigned

Appropriation of this emission.

£7,000 for putting the province into better posture of defence.

£2,800 for grants, &c.

£1,000 for debts where is no establishment.

for such service, and for paper, printing and writing for this court, the expences of committees of council, or of the house, or of both houses, entertainment of Indians, and presents made them by this court, the surgeon of Castle William, and wooding of said castle; and the sum of eight hundred pounds, part of the aforesaid sum of twenty thousand pounds, shall be applied for the payment of the members of the house of representatives serving in the general court, during their several sessions this present year and until November next. £800 for the representatives.

And whereas there are sometimes publick entertainments, and, from time to time, contingent and unforeseen charges that demand prompt payment,—

Be it further enacted,

[SECT. 2.] That the sum of two hundred and sixty-eight pounds five shillings and ninepence, the remaining part of the aforesaid sum of twenty thousand pounds, be applied to defray and pay such entertainments and contingent charges, and for no other use whatsoever. £268 5s. 9d. for entertainments, &c.

And be it enacted,

[SECT. 3.] That if there be a surplusage in any sum appropriated, such surplusage shall l[y][*ie*] in the treasury for the further order of this court. Surplusage to lie in the treasury.

And be it further enacted,

[SECT. 4.] That each and every warrant for drawing money out of the treasury, shall direct the treasurer to take the same out of such sums as are respectively appropriated for the payment of such publick debts as the draughts are made to discharge; and the treasurer is hereby directed and ordered to pay such money out of such appropriations as directed to, and no other, upon pain of refunding all such sum or sums as he shall otherwise pay, and to keep exact and distinct accompts of all payments made out of such appropriated sums; and the secretary to whom it belongs to keep the muster-rolls and accompts of charge, shall lay before the house, when they direct, all such muster-rolls and accompts after payment thereof. Warrants to express the appropriations.

And as a fund and security for drawing the said sum of twenty thousand pounds into the treasury again,—

Be it further enacted,

[SECT. 5.] That there be and hereby is granted unto his most excellent majesty, for the ends and uses aforesaid, a tax of eight thousand and eighty-three pounds six shillings and eightpence, to be levied on polls, and estates both real and personal, within this province, according to such rules and in such proportions on the several towns and districts within the same, as shall be agreed upon and ordered by this court at their session in May, one thousand seven hundred and forty-four, and paid into the publick treasury on or before the last day of December then next after. £8,083 6s. 8d. in 1744.

And as a further fund and security for drawing the said sum of twenty thousand pounds into the treasury again,—

Be it further enacted,

[SECT. 6.] That there be and hereby is granted unto his most excellent majesty, for the ends and uses aforesaid, a tax of eight thousand five hundred and eighty-three pounds six shillings and eightpence, to be levied on polls, and estates both real and personal, within this province, according to such rules and in such proportions on the several towns and districts within the same, as shall be agreed upon and ordered by this court at their session in May, one thousand seven hundred and forty-five, and paid into the publick treasury on or before the last day of December then next after. £8,583 6s. 8d. in 1745.

And, as a fund and security for drawing the remaining part of the said sum of twenty thousand pounds into the treasury again,—

Be it further enacted,

£2,533 6s. 8d. in 1746.

[SECT. 7.] That there be and hereby is granted unto his most excellent majesty, for the ends and uses aforesaid, a tax of two thousand five hundred and thirty-three pounds six shillings and eightpence, to be levied on polls, and estates both real and personal, within this province, according to such rules and in such proportions on the several towns and districts within the same, as shall be agreed upon and ordered by the great and general court or assembly at their session in May, one thousand seven hundred and forty-six, and paid into the publick treasury again on or before the last day of December then next after.

And, as a fund and security for drawing in such sum or sums as shall be paid out to the representatives of the several towns,—

Be it enacted,

Tax to be made for what is paid to the representatives.

[SECT. 8.] That there be and hereby is granted unto his most excellent majesty a tax of such sum or sums as shall be paid to the several representatives as aforesaid, to be levied and assessed on the polls and estates of the inhabitants of the several towns, according to what their representatives shall so receive; which sums shall be set on the said towns in the next province tax. And the assessors of the said towns shall make their assessment for this tax, and apportion the same according to the rule that shall be prescribed by act of the general assembly for assessing the next province tax, and the constables, in their respective districts, shall pay in the same when they pay in the province tax for the next year, of which the treasurer is hereby directed to keep a distinct and separate accompt; and if there be any surplusage, the same shall l[y][*ie*] in the hands of the treasurer for the further order of this court.

And be it further enacted,

Tax for the money hereby emitted to be made according to the preceding tax act, in case.

[SECT. 9.] That in case the general court shall not at their sessions in May, one thousand seven hundred and forty-four, one thousand seven hundred and forty-five, and one thousand seven hundred and forty-six, agree and conclude upon an act apportioning the several sums, which by this act is engaged shall be, in each of these several years, apportioned, assessed and levied, that then and in such case each town and district within this province shall pay (by a tax to be levied on the polls, and estates both real and personal, within their districts) the same proportion of the said sums as the said towns and districts shall have been taxed by the general court in the tax act then next preceding; and the province treasurer is hereby fully impowered and directed, some time in the month of June in each of these years, one thousand seven hundred and forty-four, one thousand seven hundred and forty-five, and one thousand seven hundred and forty-six, to issue and send forth his warrants, directed to the selectmen or assessors of each town and district within this province, [in manner as aforementioned in this act*] requiring them to assess the polls, and estates both real and personal, within their several towns and districts, for their respective part and proportion of the several sums before directed and engaged to be assessed by this act; and the assessors, as also persons assessed, shall observe, be govern[e]d by and subject to all such rules and directions as shall have been given in the next preceding tax act.

And be it further enacted,

Taxes to be paid in the several species herein enumerated.

[SECT. 10.] That the inhabitants of this province shall have liberty, if they see fit, to pay the several sums for which they respectively may, in pursuance of this act, be assessed, in bills of credit of the form and tenor by this act emitted, or in bills of the middle tenor, according to their several denominations, or in bills of the old tenor, accounting

* This clause, which does not appear in the printed act, is underscored in the engrossment.

four for one; or in coined silver, at six shillings and eightpence per ounce, troy weight, and of sterling alloy, or in gold coin, proportionably; or in merchantable hemp, flax, winter and Isle-of-Sable codfish, refined bar-iron, bloomery-iron, h[a][o]llow iron-ware, Indian corn, rye, wheat, barley, pork, beef, duck or canvas, whalebone, cordage, train-oyl, bees-wax, bayberry-wax, tallow, peas, sheepswool, or tann'd sole-leather (the aforesaid commodities being of the produce or manufactures of this province), at such moderate rates and prices as the respective general assemblies of the years one thousand seven hundred and forty-four, one thousand seven hundred and forty-five, and one thousand seven hundred and forty six shall set[t] them at; the several persons paying their taxes in any of the commodities aforementioned, to run the risque and pay the charge of transporting the said commodities to the province treasury; but if the aforesaid general assemblies shall not, at their respective sessions in May, some time before the twentieth day of June, agree upon and set[t] the aforesaid species or commodities at some certain prices, that then the eldest councellor, for the time being, of each of those counties in the province, of which any one of the council is an inhabitant, together with the province treasurer, or the major part of them, be a committee, who hereby are directed and fully authorized and impowered to do it; and in their set[t]ling the prices and rat[e]-ing the value of those commodities, to state so much of them, respectively, at six shillings and eightpence as an ounce of silver will purchase at that time in the town of Boston, and so *pro ratâ*. And the treasurer is hereby directed to insert in the several warrants by him sent to the collectors of the taxes in those years, respectively, with the names of the afore-recited commodities, the several prices or rates which shall be set on them, either by the general assembly or the committee aforesaid, and direct the aforesaid collectors to receive them so.

How the commodities brought into the treasury are to be rated.

[SECT. 11.] And the aforesaid commodities, so brought into the treasury, shall, as soon as may be, be disposed of by the treasurer to the best advantage for so much as it will fetch in bills of credit hereby to be emitted, or for silver or gold, which silver and gold shall be delivered to the possessor of said bills, in exchange for them; that is to say, one ounce of silver coin, and so gold in proportion, for six shillings and eightpence, and *pro ratâ* for a greater or less sum; and if any loss shall happen by the sale of the aforesaid species, or by any unforeseen accident, such deficiency shall be made good by a tax of the year next following, so as fully and effectually to call in the whole sum of twenty thousand pounds in said bills hereby ordered to be emitted; and if there be a surplusage, it shall remain a stock in the treasury.

Treasurer to sell the said commodities.

And be it further enacted,

[SECT. 12.] That any debt contracted before the thirty-first day of October, one thousand seven hundred and forty-one, which might have been paid and discharged in and by province bills of the old tenor, and also any debt contracted between the said thirty-first day of October and the first day of April, one thousand seven hundred and forty-two (where the contracting parties have not expressly otherwise agreed), may be discharged by the bills by this act to be emitted, in proportion as one to four; that is to say, that a debt of twenty-six shillings and eightpence, dischargeable or contracted as aforesaid, may be discharged by six shillings and eightpence in bills by this act to be emitted, or by one ounce of silver, and so in proportion for a greater or less sum. [*Passed and published November* 12.

Rule for paying private debts.

CHAPTER 14.

AN ACT FOR PREVENTING THE DESTRUCTION OF WHITE-PINE TREES WITHIN THIS PROVINCE, AND FOR ENCOURAGING THE PRESERVATION OF THEM FOR THE USE OF THE ROYAL NAVY.

Preamble.

WHEREAS their late majesties, King William and Queen Mary, in and by their royal charter granted to this province, bearing date the seventh day of October in the third year of their reign, did, for the better providing and furnishing of masts for the royal navy, reserve to themselves, their heirs [and] successors "all trees of the diameter of twenty-four inches, and upwards, of twelve inches from the ground, growing upon any soil or tract of land within" the said province or territory before that not granted to any private persons, and also thereby did restrain and forbid "all persons whatsoever from felling, cutting or destroying any such trees without the royal licence" of them, their heirs and successors, first had and obtained; *and whereas* the white-pine trees are more especially fit for masting the royal navy; therefore, to render the afores[*ai*]d reservation more effectual to the good purposes intended [t]hereby,—

Be it enacted by the Governour, Council and House of Representatives,

Offence of cutting off pine-trees fit for masts, to be tried in his majesty's courts, if the prosecutor see cause.

[SECT. 1.] That no person shall, at any time after the publication of this act, presume to cut, fell or destroy any white-pine trees which are or shall, at the time of felling the same, be of the diameter of twenty-four inches, or upwards, of* twelve inches from the ground, growing or standing in any soil or tract of land within this province not granted to any private person or persons before the date of the aforesaid charter (without his majesty's royal licence for so doing first had and obtained) or to be aiding or assisting therein, or in drawing away the said pine trees after the same shall have been so cut, felled or destroyed, on pain of being prosecuted as well in any of his majesty's courts of record within this province, for the penalty already by law inflicted for such offence, as by law they already may in the court of vice-admiralty, at the election of the prosecutor, but not in both: *provided*, such prosecution be commenced within six months from the time when the offence shall be committed; which penalty, when recovered, shall be applied in such manner as by law is already provided.

Preamble.

And whereas the hind[*e*]ring and obstructing the workmen who may be employed by virtue of his maj[*es*]ty's royal licence to fell such trees as is aforesaid, growing upon any such tract of land as is before mentioned, for the use of the royal navy, or vexing them with groundless suits for what they shall do in that business, will be very prejudicial to his majesty's aforesaid service by discouraging workmen from being concerned therein; now, for prevention thereof,—

Be it enacted,

Provision against causeless actions brought against those that cut white pines by the king's license.

[SECT. 2.] That, from and after the publication of this act, no person or persons shall presume to hinder or obstruct any workmen or workman, employed in the afores[*ai*]d service upon any soil or tract of land within this province not granted to any private person or persons before the date of the afores[*ai*]d charter. And in case any workman employ[e]d in the afores[*ai*]d service shall be sued, in any action, in any of his maj[*es*]tys. courts of judicature, for felling or haling away any such tree or trees, growing or being upon any soil or tract of land not granted to any private person or persons before the date afores[*ai*]d, and being of the diameter of twenty-four inches, and upwards, of* twelve inches

* This word is underscored in the engrossment.

from the ground, at the time of felling the same, the defendant in such action shall be admitted to plead the general issue, and to give the special matter in evidence; and in case, after issue joined, judgm[*en*]t shall be given against the plaintiff or plaintiffs in such action, then the justices of the court where the action shall be brought shall allow to the defendant double costs of suit, to be taxed at the same court.

[SECT. 3.] This act to continue and be in force from the publication thereof three years, and no longer. [*Passed November* 11; *published November* 12. Limitation.

CHAPTER 15.

AN ACT TO ENABLE THE PROPRIETORS OF PRIVATE WAYS TO REPAIR THEM IN AN EQUAL MANNER.

WHEREAS there are many private ways in this province, which are seldom used but by the purchasers or proprietors of them, or the owners of the lands to which such ways lead, and are therefore not repaired by the towns in which they respectively l[y][*i*]e, nor have the proprietors or rightful[l] occupants of such ways any power, by the laws of this province, to compel their being repaired by or among themselves; to prevent, therefore, the inconvenienc[*i*]es w[*hi*]ch do or may thence arise,— Preamble.

Be it enacted by the Governour, Council and House of Representatives,

[SECT. 1.] That one-fourth part of the proprietors and rightful[l] occupants of any private way (where there are four or more of them) may at any time, when they shall apprehend there is occasion therefor, call a meeting of all the proprietors and rightful[l] occupants, by posting up a notification in some publick place or places in the town or towns where such way is, seven days before the time appointed for such meeting, signifying the time, place, and business of such meeting; and the major part of the proprietors and rightful[l] occupants so assembled, shall have full power to choose a clerk, a committee to call meetings, and a surveyor who shall be sworn to the faithful[l] discharge of his trust, as town officers are, and have the same power with respect to such ways as the surveyors of other ways are by law invested with, and shall be governed by the same rules as are prescribed by law for their direction; each proprietor's and occupant's proportion of labour to be determined by a major vote of those present at such meeting; and in case of the default of any proprietor or occupant in attending said work, by himself, or other sufficient person in his stead, to be subject to the same fines and penalties as in case of highways, and be recovered in the same manner, and applied to the like uses. Proprietors of private ways empowered to order their being repaired in an equal manner.

[SECT. 2.] This act to continue and be in force for the space of three years from and after the publication thereof, and no longer. [*Passed November* 11; *published November* 12. Limitation.

CHAPTER 16.

AN ACT IN ADDITION TO AND FOR RENDRING MORE EFFECTUAL AN ACT MADE IN THE FOURTEENTH YEAR OF HIS PRESENT MAJESTY'S REIGN, [E][*I*]NTITLED "AN ACT TO PREVENT DAM[*M*]AGE BEING DONE TO THE HARBOUR OF CAPE COD BY CATTLE AND HORSEKIND FEEDING ON PROVINCETOWN LAND."

WHEREAS it is represented, that, since the making of the act pass'd in the fourteenth year of his present majesty's reign, [e][*i*]ntitled "An Preamble. 1740-41, chap. 15.

Act to prevent dam[m]age being done to the harbour of Cape Cod by cattle and horsekind feeding on Provincetown land," so many of the inhabitants of said town have withdrawn from thence as to leave a number there insufficient to transact affairs as a town, whereby the good intention of said act for preserving the said important harbour may be frustrated.

Be it therefore enacted by the Governour, Council and House of Representatives,

The present inhabitants of Provincetown enabled to act for preventing damage to the harbor of Cape Cod.

That the present inhabitants of the aforesaid town be and hereby are enabled to choose officers and transact all other matters, whatsoever, necessary for the executing the said act, according to the true design and meaning thereof, as fully, to all intents and purposes, as thô[ugh] none of the said inhabitants had withdrawn; and William Rotch, one of the principal inhabitants of said town, is appointed to call a meeting of said inhabitants for the purposes aforesaid. [*Passed November* 11; *published November* 13.

CHAPTER 17.

AN ACT FOR THE MORE SPEEDY FINISHING OF THE LAND-BANK OR MANUFACTORY SCHEME.

Preamble.

WHEREAS notwithstanding the directors and partners of the late Land-bank Company have, in general, publickly renounced their scheme, and great numbers of them have redeemed their just proportions of the said late company's bills, and delivered them up to be consumed; yet many of the partners still neglect to do it, by means whereof those who have paid a due obedience to the law, in this regard, still remain exposed to the actions of the possessors of the said late company's bills, commouly called the manufactory bills, which are now outstanding, and many of them have suffered great loss thro[ugh] the default of their partners, who contemptuously refuse to redeem their due proportions of the said bills; now, for the more speedy finishing of the said scheme in as equitable a manner as may be, and preventing such of the directors and partners as have compl[y][i]ed with the law, from suffering ruin or damage thro[ugh] the obstinacy or neglect of their delinquent partners,—

Be it enacted by the Governour, Council and House of Representatives,

Commissioners for finishing the land bank scheme.

[SECT. 1.] That John Jeffries, Samuel Danforth, and John Chandler, Esqrs., be commissioners to receive commission for the purposes hereafter mentioned from the governour; and the said commissioners, or any two of them, shall, by virtue of this act, have full power effectually to order and adjust all the affairs and business necessary for the just and equal finishing of the said Land-bank and Manufactory Scheme: which commissioners, before their entring upon the execution of the said trust, shall take the following oath; viz[t].,—

Their power.

Commissioners' oath.

I, A. B., do swear, that I will faithfully, honestly, and impartially manage and discharge the trust reposed in me by the commission for ordering and adjusting all the affairs necessary for the finishing of the Land-bank Scheme, without favour or affection, prejudice or malice, to the best of my skill. So help me God.

[SECT. 2.] And the said commissioners, or any two of them, shall have full power to call before them and examine upon oath any persons whomsoever, touching the affairs and trade of the said late company, and to order all the effects, books, papers, and writings, relating to the said scheme and trade, to be delivered up to them, that they may discover all the debts and credits of the said late company, and the quantity of their bills emitted; how many of them are redeemed and consumed, or lying ready to be consumed, and by whom they were redeemed; how many are still outstanding; what loss and charge hath already incurred upon them; and what is the proportion of every director and partner of the said late company for the redemption of the outstanding bills.

For preventing fraudulent conveyances.

And, for preventing any fraudulent alienations or conveyances of the estates of such of the aforesaid late directors and partners who have not redeemed their just proportions of the said bills, in order to defraud the said late company's creditors, and avoid the effect of this act,—

Be it further enacted,

Commissioners' power.

[SECT. 3.] That, from and after the publication of this act, the estate of each and every such director and partner shall be thereby bound and subjected to the payment of such sum or sums of money as shall be assessed upon him by the said commissioners, or any two of them, with the approbation and allowance of the great and general court of this province (as is hereinafter mentioned) for the redemption of their respective proportions of the bills of the said late company, and their equitable part and share of all loss and charges arising by the said scheme, in such manner as the same or any part of it would be bound and subjected by the actual service of process of attachment upon it at the suit of any creditor, according to the ordinary course of the law and the usage within this province; and the said commissioners, or any two of them, are hereby enabled in their own names to demand and receive such sums of money as shall be so assessed upon any of the delinquent directors or partners, and allowed by the general court as aforesaid, and also to raise the same by mortgaging, in their own names, that part of any delinquent director's or partner's estate which he had mortgaged to the said late company for performance of his covenants and agreements with them; or, if need be, in their own names to sue for and recover the aforesaid sums, or any part thereof, in any of his majesty's courts within the county of Suffolk, by such actions as the nature of the case shall require.

[SECT. 4.] And the said commissioners, or any two of them, are hereby likewise enabled, in their own names, to demand and receive of and from any person or persons whatsoever, any money, goods or effects, whatsoever, due or owing from them to the said late Land-bank Company, and if need be in their own names to sue for and recover the same in any of his majesty's courts within the county of Suffolk, by such action as the nature of the case shall require; and shall apply all such sums of money, goods, and effects as they shall receive and recover of and from the said delinquent directors and partners, and the debtors of the said late company, or any of them, together with such sums of money as they shall raise by mortgaging the aforesaid estates of the said delinquent directors and partners, or any of them, towards the redemption of the outstanding bills of the said late company, and shall from time to time give publick notice in the "Boston Gazette" of what sums of money they shall so receive, that the possessors of the said bills may bring the same in to them to be redeemed.

[SECT. 5.] And the said commissioners, or any two of them, are hereby enabled equitably to apportion whatsoever loss shall finally appear to arise by the said scheme or trade to the said late company in general, or to any of the said directors or partners in particular, either thro' the insolvency of any of the said late directors and partners, or by means of the charge attending the said late Manufactory

Scheme, or otherwise, howsoever, among the said late directors and partners in general, as the justice of the case shall require; so as that each of them may bear, as near as may be, his equitable proportion of the loss and burthen arising by their said late scheme or trade; and are hereby enabled, in their own names, to demand, sue for, and recover, in any of his majesty's courts within the county of Suffolk, in such manner as is aforesaid, of and from each and every of the said late directors and partners, such sum and sums of money as shall be so assessed upon any of them with the approbation and allowance of the great and general court, for their respective shares of the aforesaid loss and burthen, from time to time, till the aforesaid scheme shall be finished, and thereupon all the said manufactory bills which shall be received by the said commissioners shall be burnt, and the plates of the said late company, from whence they were struck, be defaced and broken; and all the securities given by any of the said late directors and partners, to the said late company, shall be cancelled by the said commissioners, or any two of them, in their own names.

Provided always,—

Directors and partners liable to the suits of the possessors of the bills, and others.

[SECT. 6.] That this act shall not be adjudged or construed to be intended to hinder the possessors of any of the manufactory bills from making the same demands upon any of the late directors and partners of the said late manufactory company, for the redemption of the said bills, as they might have made upon them before the publication of this act; and that the estates of the said directors and partners shall be as liable to be attach'[*e*]d at such suits of the possessors of the said bills, or of any other just creditor, as they were before the making of this act, anything herein contained to the contrary thereof in any wise notwithstanding.

Provided, also,—

Provision for an appeal to the governor and council.

[SECT. 7.] That the said commissioners shall make a report of their proceedings, in the execution of their aforesaid trust, to the great and general court, at their session which will begin and be held in May next, for their approbation and allowance or disallowance thereof, either in whole or in part; and that any of the said late directors and partners who shall think himself aggrieved by such proceedings of the said commissioners, may file his appeal, from their determination to the said court at their aforesaid session, in the secretary's office, at any time before the said session of the said court; and in case the receipt of any sum in the said manufactory bills, charged upon any of the said late directors and partners by the said commissioners, shall be denied in such appeal, or the redemption of any of the said bills, or the payment of any sum of money to the said late company, for which no allowance has been made by the commissioners, shall be insisted upon in such appeal, or any person upon whom the commissioners shall assess any sum of money to be paid, shall deny, in such appeal, that he was either a partner or director, or anyways concerned in the said late manufactory scheme, and the appellant, in any of these cases, pray that a feigned issue at law may be directed to be tr[y][*i*]ed for the determination of any of the said matters of fact, in one of his majesty's courts of judicature, then the great and general court shall, upon the appellant's depositing ten pounds, lawful money, in the secretary's office, as caution money for the payment of costs, if the verdict upon the tr[y][*i*]al of such issue shall be found against him, direct an issue at law, accordingly, to be tr[y][*i*]ed at the superiour court of judicature to be held, for the county of Suffolk, next after such order made; which tr[y][*i*]al shall be a final determination of such matter: and in case the verdict in the same shall be for the appellant, then his aforesaid caution money, deposited in the secretary's office, shall be returned to him; and the

Matters to be tried in the superior court.

Caution to be given in the secretary's office.

clerk of the superiour court of judicature is hereby directed to return a copy of the record of such tr[y][*i*]al into the secretary's office as soon as may be, for the information of the great and general court therein, which shall thereupon proceed to the determination of the appeal.

And be it further enacted,

[SECT. 8.] That all mortgages of any lands or tenements of any of the said late directors or partners, made by the said commissioners, or any two of them as aforesaid, shall be good and effectual to all intents and purposes in the law; and the former mortgages thereof made by the owners to the said late company, shall be thereupon cancelled and discharged by the said commissioners, or any two of them, in their own names.

Mortgages to be made by the commissioners, to be good.

And whereas several parcels of the said manufactory bills may be lodged in some or other of his majesty's courts of judicature within this province, upon judgments obtained there by some of the possessors of such bills against some of the directors or partners of the late Land-bank Company; for the redemption of the said bills,—

Preamble.

Be it further enacted,

[SECT. 9.] That the justices of such courts shall, within thirty days after the publication of this act, cause such bills to be delivered up to the aforesaid commissioners, with a certificate of the names of the possessors who lodged the said bills in court, and of the directors or partners of the said late company against whom judgment was obtained for the redemption of the said bills.

Bills lodged in the courts to be delivered to the commissioners.

[SECT. 10.] And the said commissioners shall be allowed each ten shillings for every day of their attendance upon the execution of their said trust, and no more, to be paid by the late directors and partners of the aforesaid scheme, as also all other necessary charges which they may be at in prosecuting the affair aforesaid, out of the effects of the said late company, and shall render an account of their proceedings to the great and general court, when and so often as thereunto required, and shall sit three days at least in a week for the dispatch of said business, until the same shall be finished.

Allowance to the commissioners.

And be it further enacted,

[SECT. 11.] That in case of the death or refusal of any of the commissioners aforesaid, such vacancy shall be supply'[e]d by the great and general court. [*Passed November* 10; *published November* 11.

Provision in case of a vacancy.

ACTS

PASSED AT THE SESSION BEGUN AND HELD AT BOSTON, ON THE EIGHTH DAY OF FEBRUARY, A. D. 1743–44.

CHAPTER 18.

AN ACT TO PREVENT THE GREAT INJURY AND INJUSTICE ARISING TO THE INHABITANTS OF THIS PROVINCE BY THE FREQUENT AND VERY LARGE EMISSIONS OF BILLS OF PUBLIC CREDIT IN THE NEIGHBOURING GOVERNMENTS.

Preamble. 1738-39, chap. 14, § 1.

WHEREAS the bills of this and the neighbouring governments are and have been the principal medium of trade and commerce in this province, and some of those governments, more especially that of Rhode Island, have frequently made extravagant emissions of their bills, which, by as frequent experience, have been found a great means of depreciating all the bills of public credit current among us, whereby great injustice hath been introduced; and should the same practice be continued, it would be greatly injurious to the inhabitants of this province, and ruinous to many,—

Be it therefore enacted by the Governour, Council and House of Representatives,

Penalty for paying or receiving bills of Rhode Island government issued since 1742, and bills of other neighboring governments hereafter issued.

[SECT. 1.] That no person or persons whosoever shall within this province, wittingly and wilfully utter, offer to put off, take or receive any bill or bills of credit of the colony of Rhode Island, emitted since the year one thousand seven hundred and forty-two, or of that or any other of the neighbouring governments, that shall hereafter be emitted, in payment of any debt, for purchase of any goods, or for any valuable consideration whatsoever, on pain of forfeiting for each bill so uttered, offered or received, the sum of three pounds, and of being ever after disabled from bearing any office of honour or profit under this government.

And be it further enacted,

Penalty for officers' passing or receiving such bills.

[SECT. 2.] That any person in this government bearing any office or offices of profit or honour, that shall be convicted of having wilfully and wittingly uttered, offered to put off, taken or received any such bill or bills in payment of any debt, or for purchase of any goods, or for any valuable consideration whatsoever, shall for such offence be *ipso facto* discharged from such his office or offices, and shall be thereby utterly disabled to have or hold any office of profit or honour within this province, and shall likewise forfeit for each such bill by him uttered, offered or received, the sum of ten pounds.

And be it further enacted,

Penalty to innholders, &c., for such offence.

[SECT. 3.] That any innholder, retailer or common victualler, who after the publication of this act shall wittingly and wilfully utter, offer to put off, taken or received any such bill or bills in payment of any debt, or for purchase of any goods, or for any victuals or liquors bought or sold, or to be bought or sold, or for any entertainment given or to be given, or for any other valuable consideration whatsoever, such innholder, retailer or common victualler, beside his being liable to the fine first beforementioned, shall forfeit his licence, and be disabled from holding or using any such employment for the future.

And be it further enacted,

[SECT. 4.] That every mortgage, bill, bond, other assurance or instrument in writing, whatever, that hereafter shall be executed, for the consideration whereof, in whole or in part, such bills shall be received or paid, and legal proof hereof be made, such mortgage, bill, bond, assurance or instrument in writing, whatever, shall be deemed a fraudulent bargain, and shall be utterly void in law.

Bonds and mortgages for such bills to be void.

And be it further enacted,

[SECT. 5.] That any person that shall receive or pay any such bill or bills, and shall first inform against and prosecute the other party concerned with him or her therein, so that he or she be convict of receiving or paying such bill or bills for any valuable consideration whatever, such prosecutor shall be indemnified from the penalty in this act, and shall likewise be intitled to one half of the forfeiture aforesaid.

Witnesses to be indemnified, and have one-half of the forfeiture.

And be it further enacted,

[SECT. 6.] That every merchant, shopkeeper or trader shall be answerable for every offence against this act, committed either by him or herself, or any of his or her houshold or family that are under his or her immediate care and government, and be obliged to satisfy and pay the sum of ten pounds for every such offence; unless such merchant, shopkeeper or trader shall make oath, *bonâ fide*, that such an offence was committed without his or her privity, countenance or connivance.

Penalty to merchants and traders.

And be it further enacted,

[SECT. 7.] That any justice of the peace shall have power, and is hereby authorized, upon information or complaint to him made of any breach of this act, to convene before him the person or persons so complained of, and to grant summons for witnesses to appear before him to be examined on oath as to their knowledge touching the fact or facts refer'd to in such complaint, and, upon just ground, to bind over the person or persons complained of or informed against, and to require sufficient security for his or her appearance at the next court of general sessions of the peace in the county where the offence is alledged to be committed, to answer such complaint; and any person refusing to give evidence at the tryal of such as may be sued, presented, indicted or complained of for any violation of this act, shall be liable to the same penalty as the person presented or complained of is liable to in case he shall be convict; but shall not be subject to any damage by any discovery he might make by his oath, in case he should take it.

Justices to proceed against offenders by binding them over, &c.

And be it further enacted,

[SECT. 8.] That the courts of general sessions of the peace, in the respective counties, be and they hereby are impowered and directed, at their next term for sitting, and so, from time to time, during the continuance of this act, to appoint five meet persons in each town within their respective counties, to inform against and prosecute the violaters of this act; and, in the town of Boston, the number of persons to be appointed to that office and duty, shall be fifteen, which officers shall have and enjoy the same benefit and advantage as other informers; and if any person so appointed shall refuse or neglect, after due notice given him for that purpose, to take his oath (to be administred to him by such court, or a justice of the peace), and to serve in said office, he shall forfeit and pay the sum of five pounds.

Persons to be appointed to inform against the breach of this act.

And be it further enacted,

Penalty of officers' neglecting their duty.

[SECT. 9.] That if any justice of the peace, grand juror or other officer, shall wilfully and wittingly omit the performance of his duty in the execution of this act, such officer shall forfeit and pay the sum of twenty pounds.

Forfeitures, how to be disposed of.

[SECT. 10.] The several forfeitures before mentioned to be applied, the one moiety thereof to the use of the poor of the town where the offence shall be committed, the other moiety to him or them who shall inform or sue for the same (and in case there be no informer that shall prosecute such offender, in such case the whole of the forfeiture shall be applied to the use first mentioned), and may be recovered by action, bill, plaint or information, in any of his majesty's courts of record within the same county, or by presentment of the grand jury, who are hereby strictly enjoined to present all breaches of this act; and no essoign, priviledge, protection or wager of law, shall be allowed in any such suit or prosecution as aforesaid.

How to be recovered.

Provided nevertheless,

Proviso.

[SECT. 11.] That all suits or prosecutions for the breach of this act, shall commence within twelve months from the time of committing the offence.

And be it further enacted,

This act to be publicly read in the courts, and grand jurors to be charged.

[SECT. 12.] That the justices of the respective courts of general sessions of the peace within this province, shall cause this act to be publickly read at opening their courts, from time to time, and shall give in charge to the grand jury duly to enquire after, and make presentment of, all persons that shall presume to offend in violation of this act; and the selectmen of each town within this province, are alike required to cause this act to be publickly read at their several town meetings in May next, for the choice of representatives.

Limitation.

[SECT. 13.] This act to continue and be in force for the space of two years from the publication hereof, and to the end of the May session then next after, and no longer. [*Passed and published March* 17, 1743-44.

CHAPTER 19.

AN ACT FOR REGULATING THE HOSPITAL ON RAINSFORD['S] ISLAND, AND FURTHER PROVIDING IN CASE OF SICKNESS.

Preamble. 1738-39, chap. 8.

WHEREAS a good and convenient house hath been provided at the charge of the province, on the island called Rainsford's Island, for the reception of such persons as shall be visited with any contagious sickness,—

Be it therefore enacted by the Governour, Council and House of Represent[ati]ves,

Masters of infected vessels to be notified where to come to anchor.

[SECT. 1.] That the commanding officer at Castle William, and the keeper of the lighthouse, shall notify and direct the masters of all vessels coming near them, wherein any infectious sickness is or hath lately been, at their coming in, to come to anchor as near the beforementioned house as may be, that the sick persons, and everything else on board said ship that may give infection (proper to be put into the said house), may be removed into it with the greater ease and safety.

And be it further enacted,

Leave to be had of the selectmen for landing passengers or goods.

[SECT. 2.] That upon application made by said master or commander, to the selectmen of the town of Boston, the said selectmen are hereby impowered to permit such passengers, goods or lading as they shall judge free from infection, to come on shore, or be taken out and disposed of as the owners shall see meet; and such passengers and goods as shall not be permitted as afore[*ai*]d, shall remain on board, or be put into the said hospital.

[SECT. 3.] And if any master or immediate commander of any such vessel for the time being, shall come on shore, or suffer any of his people or passengers to come on shore, or any boats to come on board, or suffer any goods to be taken out of his vessel, unless permitted as aforesaid, or shall come up with his vessel, until[l], by a certificate, under the hands of the selectmen as aforesaid, it shall appear to the captain-general that the said vessel, company and goods are clear of infection, and the orders for stopping and detaining the same be removed and taken off, he shall, for every such offence, forfeit the sum of fifty pounds; and in case he be not able to pay that sum, he shall suffer six months' impriso[*n*]ment. And if any sailors or passengers, coming in said vessel, shall, without the knowledge or consent of the master, presume to come on shore, or up above the said castle, or if any person from town or country presume to go on board such vessel, or to go to the aforesaid house or hospital in time of infection there, without leave from the authority afores[*ai*]d; or if any person, put sick into the said house, or sent there on suspicion of being infected, shall presume to go off the island without leave as aforesaid; every person offending in any of the above mentioned particulars, shall forfeit the sum of ten pounds; and in case any person be not able to pay the said sum, he shall suffer two months' imprisonm[*en*]t.

Forfeiture for contempt by the master.

Penalty for sick or suspected persons offending against this act.

And be it further enacted,

[SECT. 4.] That when and so often as any ship or other vessel, wherein any infection or infectious sickness hath lately been, shall come to any port or harbour within this province; or when and so often as any person or persons belonging to, or that may, either by sea or land, come into, any town or place near the publick hospital within this province, shall be visited, or who lately before may have been visited, with any infectious sickness, two of the justices of the peace, and selectmen of such place, be impowered immediately to order the said vessel and sick persons to the province hospital or house afores[*ai*]d, there to be taken care of according to the direction of this act; and where any such ship, vessel or persons cannot, without any great inconvenience and dam[*m*]age, be ordered to the afores[*ai*]d house or hospital, in every such case the rules and directions are to be observed, which are already made in and by the act pass'd in the thirteenth year of the reign of his late majesty King William the Third, [e][*i*]ntitled, "An act providing in case of sickness." 1701-2, chap. 9.

Two justices and selectmen to order sick persons to the hospital.

And be it further enacted,

[SECT. 5.] That if any master, seaman or passenger belonging to any ship on board which any infection is or hath lately been, or is suspected to have lately been, or coming from any port where any infectious mortal distemper prevails, shall refuse to make answer upon oath to such questions as may be asked by the selectmen of the town to which such ship shall come, relating to such infection, such master, seaman or passenger shall forfeit the sum of fifty pounds; and in case he be not able to pay said sum, he shall suffer six months' imprisonment; all the above mentioned fines to be sued for and recovered by the province treasurer for the time being; one third of the fines to be to his majesty, for the use of this governm[*en*]t, one third to the informer, and one third to the province treasurer for the time being. And where any person shall be convicted of any offence against this act, and suffer the pains of imprisonment, and shall be unable to pay the costs of prosecution, such costs shall be allowed and paid out of the province treasury.

Penalty for not answering on examination.

Selectmen of Boston to provide nurses, &c. [SECT. 6.] And the selectmen of Boston are directed and impowered to provide nurses, assistance and other necessaries for the comfort and rel[ei][*ie*]f of such sick persons sent to said hospital as aforesaid, the charge thereof to be born by the said persons themselves if able, or if poor and indigent, then at the immediate charge of the province.

Limitation. [SECT. 7.] This act to continue in force five years from the publication thereof, and to the end of the session of the general court next after, and no longer. [*Passed and published March* 5, 1743-44.

CHAPTER 20.

AN ACT PROVIDING THAT THE SOLEMN AFFIRMATION OF THE PEOPLE CALLED QUAKERS SHALL, IN CERTAIN CASES, BE ACCEPTED INSTEAD OF AN OATH IN THE USUAL FORM; AND FOR PREVENTING INCONVENIENC[*I*]ES BY MEANS OF THEIR HAVING HERETOFORE ACTED IN SOME TOWN OFFICES WITHOUT TAKING THE OATHS BY LAW REQUIRED FOR SUCH OFFICES.

Preamble. 1719-20, chap. 11. WHEREAS the people called Quakers profess to be in their consciences scrupulous of taking an oath in the form by law required,—

Be it therefore enacted by the Governour, Council and House of Represent[ati]ves,

[SECT. 1.] That, from and after the publication of this act, every Quaker within this province who shall be required upon any lawful[l] occasion to take an oath where, by law, an oath is required, shall, instead of the usual form, be permitted to make his, or her, solemn affirmation or declaration in the words following; viz[t].,—

Form of the affirmation to be taken by Quakers. I, A. B., do solemnly and sincerely affirm and declare under the pains and penalties of perjury.

—which said solemn affirmation or declaration shall be adjudged and taken,—

And it is hereby enacted and declared,

[SECT. 2.] To be of the same force and effect to all intents and purposes in all courts of justice and other places where by law an oath is required within this province, as if such Quaker had taken an oath in the usual form.

And be it further enacted,

Quakers' acting contrary to the said affirmation to be deemed wilful and corrupt perjury. [SECT. 3.] That if any Quaker making such solemn affirmation or declaration shall be lawfully convicted, wilfully, falsly, and corruptly, to have affirmed or declared any matter or thing which, if the same had been in the usual form, would have amounted to wilful[l] and corrupt perjury, every such Quaker so offending shall incur the same penalties and forfeitures as, by the laws of this province, are enacted against persons convicted of wilful and corrupt perjury.

Provided always, and be it enacted,

Proviso. [SECT. 4.] That no Quaker or reputed Quaker shall by virtue of this act be qualified or permitted to give evidence in any criminal causes, or serve on any juries in any of the courts within this province (without taking the oath by law required, except in civil causes only; and in such causes such person shall be liable to serve as a juror on taking the affirmation aforementioned, and on refusing to take the same, shall be subjected to the same fine that others are by law subjected to for not serving as jurors), nor bear any office in this governm[*en*]t where an oath is by law required to qualify a person for the discharge of such office, except in town offices only, and in such case not to serve as an assessor or collector for any rate or tax to be made for the support of the minister or ministers in any town, or for building or repairing of any house for the publick worship of God within the same.

And it is therefore further provided and enacted,

[SECT. 5.] That where one half or more of the assessors or collectors of any town shall be of the people called Quakers, such of the inhabitants of s[*ai*]d town who are not Quakers may and shall at the same meeting, at which such assessors or collectors, being Quakers, are chosen, proceed to the choice of an equal number of other persons who are not Quakers; and such assessors and collectors so chosen shall be as fully qualified by themselves, where the whole number of the first-chosen assessors are Quakers, or together with the other assessors who are not Quakers, when any such there be, to make rates and taxes for the settlem[*en*]t and support of the ministry, and for building and repairing any house or houses for the publick worship of God within such town, and for no other purposes; and such collector shall be as fully impowered to collect the same as they, the s[*ai*]d assessors and collectors, would have been had no other assessors or collectors been before chosen: and any assessor or collector so chosen shall be liable to the same penalty for refusing to serve in their respective office as he would have been had he been chosen and refused to serve as assessor or collector of all the rates and taxes in s[*ai*]d town. Provision made where one-half or more of the assessors or collectors are Quakers.

And whereas in sundry towns within this province the town clerk and other town officers, being of the people called Quakers, have neglected or refused to qualify themselves by taking the oaths to the execution of such office by law annexed, and yet have continued to serve in said offices, and should the consequent proceedings of such town be called in question as illegal and so set aside, many and great inconvenienc[*i*]es and much confusion would arise,— Preamble.

Be it therefore further enacted,

[SECT. 6.] That all the acts and proceedings of any town within this province, where all or any of the officers, being Quakers, have neglected or refused to take the oaths to such offices by law annexed, and yet have continued in the execution of their respective offices, be and hereby are as fully established and confirmed as such acts and proceedings would have been had such officers been under oath as by law required. Proceedings of Quakers made valid.

[SECT. 7.] This act to continue and be in force for the space of three years from the publication thereof, and from thence to the end of the then next session of the general court, and no longer. [*Passed March* 1; *published March* 5, 1743-44.* Limitation.

CHAPTER 21.

AN ACT TO REGULATE THE EXPENCE OF PRIVATE BRIDGES.

WHEREAS it sometimes happens that some particular person or persons, for his or their own private advantage, build and erect a bridge or bridges across some river or stream, and, after, neglect or refuse to keep such bridge or bridges in repair, by means whereof the town or towns in which such bridge or bridges are erected have been presented, Preamble.

* No date is affixed to the governor's signature on the engrossment of this act, but, according to Secretary Willard's report, it was signed March 5. In the records, however, the date of passage is given as above.

and suffered loss and dam[*m*]age, althô such town was not consenting to the building thereof, nor receive general and common advantage thereby; wherefore,—

Be it enacted by the Governour, Council and House of Representatives,

Court of general sessions to determine as to private bridges.

[SECT. 1.] That from and after the publication of this act, upon application made to the court of general sessions of the peace by any person or persons, setting forth that any bridge or bridges that have already been erected, or that may hereafter, be erected by any partienlar person or persons for his or their private advantage, either in or adjacent to the town where such person or persons live, or any other town, for the building of which there was not the especial consent of the town or towns where such bridge or bridges l[y][*i*]e, or to which they are adjacent, nor the order of the s[*ai*]d court for building the same, nor any order nor special agreement for keeping such bridge or bridges in repair, that such bridge or bridges are neglected and not kept in due repair; in every such case, upon application made as aforesaid, it shall and may be lawful[l] for the said court either to discontinue such bridge or bridges (if the person or persons erecting them shall neglect to keep them in due repair), or otherwise finally to determine how, in what manner, and by whom such bridge or bridges shall be repaired and maintained, whether at the charge of the person or persons that built the same, their heirs, or such other person or persons as live near and reap the principal advantage of such bridge or bridges, as the said court shall judge most reasonable, and make out such orders and assessments on any particular person, persons or towns as shall be found necessary for effecting such repairs from time to time, and, if need be, to award execution thereon in such manner as the circumstances of the case may require; to which orders, assessments and executions all proper officers and other persons are hereby directed to conform.

Limitation.

[SECT. 2.] This act to continue and be in force for the space of three years, and no longer. [*Passed March* 21; *published March* 24, 1743-44.*

CHAPTER 22.

AN ACT FOR RENDRING MORE EFFECTUAL THE LAWS ALREADY IN BEING RELATING TO THE ADMEASUREMENT OF BOARDS, PLANK AND TIMBER, AND FOR PREVENTING FRAUD AND ABUSE IN SHINGLES, BEEF AND PORK EXPORTED FROM THIS PROVINCE, AND ALSO FOR REGULATING THE ASSIZE OF STAVES AND HOOPS.

Preamble. 1695-6, chap. 5. 1710-11, chap. 7. 1727, chap. 7.

WHEREAS, in and by an act pass'd in the ninth year of her late majesty, Queen Ann[*e*], [e][*i*]ntitled, "An Act for the admeasurement of boards, plank and timber, and regulating the tale of shingles," it is declared, "That in each maritime town within this province where boards, plank, timber and slit-work are usually imported or brought to sale, or exported beyond sea, there be two or more honest, skilful[l] persons annually elected by such town, at the time of their anniversary choice of town officers, to be surveyors and measurers of boards, plank, timber and slit-work and surveyors of shingles, who shall be sworn in manner as other town officers to the faithful[l] performance of the duty of their office"; but no provision is made for the admeasurement and

* The date of publication of this and the two following chapters is given in the printed acts as March 22, but the date followed in the text is taken from the engrossed act, and is more likely correct.

view thereof in the places where such boards, plank, timber and slit-work are usually cut or brought to the water-side where the same may be ship[t][*d*], rafted or floated off, which by experience has been found very inconvenient; for remedy whereof,—

Be it enacted by the Governour, Council and House of Representatives,

[SECT. 1.] That in each and every town within this province where boards, plank and timber are rafted off or brought for sale by land- or water-carriage, from whence the same may be rafted or floated, there shall be one or more honest, skilful person or persons, elected by such town sometime before the tenth of June next, and at the time of the choice of other town officers, annually, to be surveyors and measurers of timber, who shall be sworn, in manner as other town officers, to the faithful[l] performance of the duty of his or their office.

Persons to be annually elected surveyors and measurers of timber, &c.

[SECT. 2.] And all boards, plank, timber and slit-work imported or brought by land- or water-carriage for sale, before their delivery upon sale or their being rafted or floated off, shall be viewed, surveyed and measured by one of the said officers, having consideration for drying and shrinking, and also marked anew to the just contents, making reasonable allowance for rots, splits and wains, and each end of each piece of timber shall be marked with the brand of the town where such timber is measured as aforesaid; the buyer to pay the officer three-pence per t[u][*o*]n for viewing, measuring and marking, and so *pro ratâ* for a greater or less quantity.

And be it further enacted,

[SECT. 3.] That if any person or persons shall presume to ship, raft or float off any boards, plank or timber, unless the same shall first have been viewed, surveyed, measured and marked by a sworn surveyor as afores[*ai*]d, he or they shall forfeit the value thereof; two-thirds of the same to the use of the poor of the town where the offence is committed, and the other third to the surveyor or any other person or persons who shall sue for the same, which he or they are hereby enabled to do by action, bill, plaint or information, in any court proper to try the same.

Penalty for shipping of boards, plank, and timber not surveyed.

[SECT. 4.] *And whereas* great fraud and abuse is practi[c][s]ed in making and packing of shingles and hoops, and also in making and cutting of staves exported from this province; for preventing the same for the future,—

Preamble.

Be it further enacted,

[SECT. 5.] That, from and after the tenth day of June next, no shingles, staves nor hoops shall be exported to a foreign market from any town in this province, that shall be under the following assize; viz[t]., each shingle to bear eighteen inches or fifteen inches in length (according to which of those lengths they are sold for), and not less than three inches broad exclusive of sap, except cedar shingles only, w[*hi*][ch] shall be of the afores[*ai*][d] breadth, the sap included, and half an inch thick at the thick end, and well shaved and free from winding; and every bundle of shingles shall hold out, one with another, at least four inches in breadth; and all pipe-staves shall be at least four feet eight inches in length, three inches broad clear of sap, at least half an inch thick on the heart or thinnest edge and every part thereof; and all white oak hogshead staves shall be three feet and four inches in length, three inches broad clear of sap, and at least half an inch thick on the heart or thinnest edge and every part thereof; and all red-oak hogshead staves shall be three feet and an half in length, three inches broad, and at least half an inch thick on the heart or thinnest edge and every part thereof; and all barrel staves shall be thirty inches in length, three inches broad, clear of sap, and at least half an inch thick on the heart or thinnest edge and every part thereof, and all well and propor-

Assize of shingles, staves and hoops.

tionably split; and all hogshead hoops that are exported beyond sea from any town w[i]th in this province shall be made of white-oak or walnut, and from twelve to fourteen feet in length, and of good and sufficient substance, and well shaved, and one-half, at least, of the hoops in each bundle shall be fourteen feet long.

And be it further enacted,

Shingles to be surveyed in the towns where they are made, &c.

[SECT. 6.] That each town where shingles are made or sold may and shall chuse one or more surveyors of shingles, to be under oath, who shall be allowed by the buyer twopence per thousand for his service in surveying and telling. And before any shingles are sent from the town where they are made, or at the place of first sale, before their delivery they shall be viewed, surveyed and measured by a sworn surveyor, and the town brand set upon the hoop of the bundle; and all shingles offer'd to sale without being surveyed and marked as aforesaid shall be forfeited.

Cullers of staves and hoops to be chosen in the maritime towns.

[SECT. 7.] And in each maritime town, within this province, from whence staves or hoops are usually exported beyond sea, there shall be two or more suitable persons chosen by such towns sometime before the tenth of June next, and at their meeting in March, annually, to be viewers and cullers of staves and hoops, who shall be under oath faithfully to discharge their office, and shall be allowed for their time and service therein as follows; viz[t]., for pipe staves, one shill[in]g and threepence per thous[an]d; for hogsh[ea]d staves, one shill[in]g per thousand; and for barrel staves, ninepence per thous[an]d, as well refuse, as merchantable; the merchantable to be paid by the person buying the same and the refuse by the seller; and for surveying hoops, one penny halfpenny per hundred, to be paid by the buyer.

And be it further enacted,

Staves and hoops to be surveyed before shipped.

[SECT. 8.] That from and after the tenth day of June next, all staves that shall be exported from this province beyond sea shall be first culled, and all hoops first viewed and surveyed by one of the officers afores[ai]d, and certificate given by the culler or surveyor to the master or comm[ande]r of the ship or vessel on board which they are laden of the quantity by him so culled or surveyed; and the wyths or hoops with which the bundles of hoops are packed shall be sealed w[i]th the brand of the town from whence they are exported; and that all shingles that shall be exported beyond sea shall likewise be certified, by one of the survey[o]rs already required by law to be chosen in the maritime towns of the province, to have been by him surveyed or viewed and approved, and the number or quantity thereof; who shall be allowed by the shipper twopence per thousand for surveying and certifying as afores[ai]d.

Preamble.

And whereas, notwithstanding the laws already in being, great quantities of pork and beef are exported beyond sea, w[hi]ch have not been packed or repacked by the officers by law required to be chosen for that purpose,—

Be it further enacted,

Pork and beef to be packed by the sworn packer.

[SECT. 9.] That from and after the tenth day of June aforesaid, no pork or beef of the produce of this province or any other of his majesty's American plantations, shall be exported beyond sea that shall not first have been certified by the packer to have been by him packed or repacked according to law.

And [be] *it further enacted,*

Certificate of staves, hoops, shingles, beef and pork, to be given in to the impost office.

[SECT. 10.] That from and after the said tenth day of June, all vessels having any staves, hoops or shingles aboard for their cargo, and also any pork or beef, whether for their cargo or provision for their voyage, before any such vessel shall be cleared at the impost office, the master or comm[ande]r of such vessel shall deliver into the impost officer a certificate of such staves, hoops, shingles, beef and pork's having been culled, surveyed or packed as afores[*ai*][d]; and shall likewise make oath, before the said impost officer, who is hereby impowered and required to administer the same, that the staves, hoops, shingles, beef and pork on board his vessel are, *bonâ fide*, the same staves, hoops, shingles, beef and pork certified to have been culled, surveyed or packed as afores[*ai*]d. And the impost officer, for the service afores[*ai*][d], shall be allowed one shilling for each vessel[l].

Limitation.

[SECT. 11.] This act to continue and be in force until[l] the tenth day of June, one thous[*an*]d seven hund[*re*]d and forty-seven, and to the end of the session of the gen[*era*][l] court then next after. [*Passed March* 22; *published March* 24, 1743-44.*

CHAPTER 23.

AN ACT TO PREVENT UNNECESSARY EXPENCE IN SUITS AT LAW.

Preamble.

WHEREAS divers promisory notes, bills or other obligations for payment of mon[ey][*ie*]s [or] [*and*] other things therein specified, when they are executed by the same party, and made payable to one and the same person, and the possessor or obligee has put them in suit at the same time, hav[e][*ing*] usually been included in one writ[t], and may ordinarily be so (where the promises or obligations are of the same kind) without dam[*m*]age or inconvenience to the plaintiff, and with much less cost and expence than what would be incurred by so many several and distinct suits; notwithstanding which some ill-disposed persons, for the recovery of what was due to them on such several notes or other obligations, have purchased as many distinct writ[t]s, and thereby multiplied their suits at the same court with intent only to burthen the defendant with great and unnecessary cost and charge; therefore, to discourage and prevent such practices for the future,—

Be it enacted by the Governour, Council and House of Represent[*ati*][ves],

When divers actions are brought on several notes or bonds from the same persons, costs to be given only for one, in case.

[SECT. 1.] That where several actions shall hereafter be brought in any court of record within this province against the same person or persons jointly, and at the same term, on several instruments of the same kind, whether notes, bills or bonds, that might conveniently have been included in one and the same writ[t], in such case if it shall be suggested or appear to the court probable that such actions were severed and multiplied with intent only to vex the defendant or defendants, or to put him or them to needless cost and charge, unless the plaintiff or plaintiffs shall shew forth such reasonable cause for bringing such several and distinct suits as to the justices of such court shall be satisfactory, the plaintiff or plaintiffs recovering judgm[*en*][t] thereon shall be allowed costs in one of such actions only.

Limitation.

[SECT. 2.] This act to continue and be in force for the space of three years from the publication thereof, and no longer. [*Passed March* 22; *published March* 24, 1743-44.*

* See note to chap. 21, *ante*.

CHAPTER 24.

AN ACT TO IMPOWER JUSTICES OF THE PEACE TO SUMMON WITNESSES.

Preamble.

WHEREAS it often happens that when disputes of a civil nature arise between parties, the matter is submitted to the arbitrament and determination of persons mutually chosen between them, or, where actions are commenced, the parties enter into a rule of court, whereby much cost and long contentions in the law are prevented, but for want of proper authority to summon witnesses before the arbitrators and referees, such submissions, references and peaceable settlements of disputes are not so easy as otherwise they might be; wherefore,—

Be it enacted by the Governour, Council and House of Represent-[ati]ves,

Justices empowered to summon witnesses in arbitrations, references, &c.

[SECT. 1.] That, when any such dispute or difference arising between parties, shall, by them, be submitted to the arbitrament and determination of persons mutually chosen between them, or where actions are commenced, and the parties have entred into a rule of court, it shall and may be lawful[l] for any one of his majesty's justices of the peace within this province, in the respective counties, on application of either of the parties, or of the persons arbitrating, to grant subpœnas to summon and cause to appear, before the arbitrators or referees, such person or persons as shall be named, for evidences in the premises, as fully and in the same manner as, by law, he might in cases depending before himself; and every person so summoned that shall refuse or neglect to appear and make oath before a justice of the peace, in the presence of the arbitrators or referees, as aforesaid, having first been paid as in civil causes is allowed to witnesses, shall be subject to the same forfeiture and damage as, by law, he might be were he summoned to appear before any court of record, and should refuse or neglect obedience thereto.

Penalty for witnesses refusing to give evidence.

And be it further enacted,

How witnesses going abroad are to be sworn.

[SECT. 2.] That when any witness may be going to sea, or lives more than thirty miles from the place of the sitting of the referees or arbitrators, or, by reason of age, sickness or other bodily infirmities, is uncapable of travelling and appearing in person, then any justice of the peace, to whom application may, in such case, be made, is hereby impowered and directed to proceed in taking such person's evidence according to the law made for taking affidavits out of court. [*Passed March* 22; *published March* 24, 1743-44.

CHAPTER 25.

AN ACT FOR THE PRESERVATION OF AND TO PROMOTE THE GROWTH OF A CERTAIN PARCEL OF WOOD AND TIMBER IN THE TOWNSHIP OF IPSWICH, IN THE COUNTY OF ESSEX.

Preamble.

WHEREAS there is a large tract or parcel of wood land lying in the said township of Ipswich, commonly known by the name of Chebacco Woods, situate more particularly between Chebacco Ponds and Manchester town line; which wood land is lotted, laid out and owned by a considerable number of persons: and whereas it would be of great advantage to said town, as well as to the particular owners of the said wood and timber, that the growth thereof should be preserved from the feeding and browsing of cattle and sheep, which are frequently turn'd and kept there in considerable numbers; and the laws already in force for imbodying proprietors of common fields, not reaching this case, there needs a further provision; wherefore,—

Be it enacted by the Governour, Council and House of Representatives,

[SECT. 1.] That, after the publication of this act, it shall and may be lawful for any five of the proprietors of said woodland to apply to a justice of the peace within the same county, setting forth in writing the intended bounds by which they would limit their proposed propriety, together with their intention for imbodying for that purpose, with the time and place of their intended meeting, on which application the justice shall make out his warrant to one of the principal proprietors so applying, to notify the said owners and proprietors to assemble and meet, by posting up a notification for that end, on one publick house in each of the parishes in said town, twenty day[s] at least before the time of such meeting, at which time and place it shall be lawful for the said proprietors to meet to choose a moderator and clerk; and if two-thirds of the whole proprietors, to be reckoned by interest, shall see meet, they may by a vote imbody themselves into a society, in which society the whole proprietors owning lands within the proposed limits shall be concluded, and may at said meeting agree upon some proper methods for calling proprietors' meetings for the future; and the said proprietors so imbodyed shall have and enjoy all the powers and privile[d]ges for the ordering and managing the affairs of the said wood, and for the preservation and increase thereof, as fully and amply to all intents and purposes, as any proprietors of common or general fields already imbodyed, do or may enjoy by laws of this province already in force respecting any improvements.

Method for calling a meeting of the proprietors of Chebacco Woods.

Power of the said proprietors in their meeting.

Provided nevertheless,—

[SECT. 2.] That if any one of the said proprietors shall think himself aggrieved by their imbodying as aforesaid, and shall then enter his dissent with the clerk of said meeting, he may apply for relief to the court of general sessions of the peace next to be holden within the said county; and the said court may thereupon appoint three persons indifferent and disinterested to hear the part[y][*ie*]s, duly weigh and consider the circumstances, and report their opinion to the said court what may be reasonable to be done between the said part[y][*ie*]s; which report being returned, the court shall enter up judgm[*en*]t thereon, and such judgm[*en*]t shall be binding, anything herein contained notwithstanding. And the said proprietors shall observe the same rules and methods in ordering and managing their whole affairs, in all respects, as the laws have provided in cases of common or general fields. [*Passed March* 22; *published March* 24, 1743-44.

Aggrieved persons may apply to the general sessions of the peace.

CHAPTER 26.

AN ACT IN ADDITION TO AN ACT MADE IN THE FIFTEENTH YEAR OF HIS PRESENT MAJESTY'S REIGN, INTITULED "AN ACT IN ADDITION TO AN ACT MADE TO PREVENT THE DESTRUCTION OF THE FISH CALLED ALEWIVES, AND OTHER FISH."

WHEREAS in and by an act made in the fifteenth year of his present majesty's reign, intituled "An Act in addition to an act made to prevent the destruction of alewives and other fish," it is provided, that all persons that should thereafter build any mill-dam or dams, or that had,

Preamble.

1741-42, chap. 16.

before the time of the passing of the same, built any such dam across any river or stream where the salmon, shad, alewives or other fish usually pass up into the natural ponds to cast their spawn, shall make or open a sufficient passage-way for the fish to pass up such river or stream through or round such dam, and shall keep it open for the free passage of the fish, from the first day of April to the last day of May, annually; and also, that a sufficient water-passage round, through or over such dams, should be made for the passage of such fish, or their young spawn, in the season of their going down such river or stream, on penalty of fifty pounds for every offence; but, by reason that no direction is therein given with respect to the sufficiency of the sluice or passage so to be made or left open, there arises great difficulty to the owner or occupant of such dams in complying therewith: *and, whereas,* by reason that in some streams and rivers the said fish pass sooner, and, in others, later, in the year than the time prescribed in said additional act, as well as that the time of their passing up and down is, in some streams and rivers, longer, and, in some, shorter, so that it is found by experience that the general rule, in the aforesaid cases, by law provided, does not only fail of the good ends proposed thereby, but also exposes the owners and occupants of such dams to trouble and damage not necessary to answer the good purposes of said additional act; wherefore,—

Be it enacted by the Governour, Council and House of Representatives,

Owners or occupants of dams may apply to the sessions to order the passages for fish, and the circumstances thereof.

[SECT. 1.] That it shall and may be lawful for any owner or occupant of any such dam or dams already built, or that may hereafter be built, and who are or may be obliged by said additional act, to open or leave open such passage as aforesaid, to apply to the next court of general sessions of the peace, to be holden in and for the county where such mill-dam is; and the justices of the court respectively, on such application, are impowered and directed to appoint a committee of three sufficient, and, as much as may be, disinterested, persons, under oath to repair to the dam where the passage is proposed to be opened, and carefully view the same, and, in the best manner they are able, to inform themselves of the most proper place for the passage of such fish up and down stream, of what dimensions the same shall be made, or appointed to be, and what part of each year, and how long the same shall be kept open, and return the same, under their hands, or the hands of the major part of them, to the said court for their acceptance; which return, so made and accepted, shall be deemed and adjudged the lawful rule of proceeding in making and keeping open the passage and passages for the fish in passing up and down the rivers and streams for the future, anything contained to the contrary in said addititional act notwithstanding.

Provided, nevertheless,

Parties aggrieved by such order to apply to the sessions for relief.

[SECT. 2.] That if, at any time after such determination, either party shall think themselves aggrieved by such determination, it shall and may be lawful for the owner or owners, occupant or occupants, of such mill-dam or dams, or any other five persons of the other party, who may expect benefit by said fish passing up such rivers or streams, once more to apply to the said court for a new view and report on the premises in manner aforesaid, which, being by said court accepted, shall be final;

Charge, how to be borne.

the charge of such application to be born by the persons applying, in case no material alteration on the first return is made, but, otherways, be born by the owners of the dam, in proportion to their interest, to be first stated and allowed by the said court of general sessions, and may be recovered by action or actions of debt in any court proper to try the same. [*Passed February* 27, 1743-44.

CHAPTER 27.

AN ACT TO CONFIRM SEVERAL VOTES OF THE PROPRIETORS OF THE WESTERLY HALF OF LEICESTER.

WHEREAS the proprietors of the westerly half of the town of Leicester, at their meeting on the second of November last, voted that their lands be subjected to a tax of twopence, old tenor, per acre, for the year 1744, and a further tax of twopence, old tenor, per acre, yearly, for the four next years, for and towards the support of a learned, orthodox minister in that part of the said town; and also that their said lands shall be subjected to a further tax of a penny, old tenor, per acre, for the first year; viz[t]., the year 1744, to pay contingent charges; and that the said proprietors, at their meeting on the fifteenth of this instant February, chose Mr. Samuel Hunt their treasurer, and voted that the lands shall be subjected to a further tax of a penny, new tenor, per acre, towards the set[t]lement of a minister: *provided, always*, that those of the proprietors and setlers that have subscribed a writing, dated the 27th of December last, for that purpose, shall pay to Mr. Treasurer Hunt the several sums therein set against their names, amounting together to the sum of a hundred and seven pounds, old tenor; and at both the meetings aforesaid, the said proprietors voted, that Mess[*ieu*]rs James Wilson, John Stebbins, and Moses Smith, inhabitants of the westerly half of Leicester, be assessors of the monies voted as aforesaid, and that Mess[*ieu*]rs John Cunningham, Samuel Bemus, Jun[r]., and Joshua Barton be collectors to collect the monies that shall be assess[*e*]d on the said proprietors by the said assessors; and also that the clerk be desired to make application to the great and general court to confirm the votes aforesaid: *and whereas* Samuel Tyley, Jun[r]., clerk of the said proprietors, hath prefer'd his humble petition in behalf of the said proprietors to the great and general court now sit[*t*]ing, praying them to pass an act or law for confirming the votes aforesaid, and enabling the said assessors to assess, and the said collectors to collect, and the said treasurer to receive the monies aforesaid; therefore,— Preamble. 1723-24, chap. 17.

Be it enacted by the Governour, Council and House of Representatives,

That the votes aforesaid, made by the said proprietors in manner as aforesaid, be and hereby are confirmed, and that the said assessors, or any two of them, and the said collectors, after they have been duly sworn for those purposes, be and hereby are impowered and enabled to assess the said inhabitants, and collect and receive the mone[ie][*y*]s aforesaid, in the same manner as other towns or precincts have heretofore assess[*e*]d and collected their rates and taxes; and that the said treasurer, or his successors, be and hereby is enabled to receive the same: which the said collectors are to pay to the said treasurer accordingly. [*Passed February* 25; *published March* 17, 1743-44. Votes of the proprietors of the west part of Leicester confirmed.

CHAPTER 28.

AN ACT TO EXPLAIN A PARAGRAPH IN AN ACT OF THIS PROVINCE, MADE IN THE PRESENT YEAR OF HIS MAJESTY'S REIGN, FOR THE MORE SPEEDY FINISHING THE LAND-BANK OR MANUFACTORY SCHEME.

WHEREAS in and by an act made and pass'd at the session of this court, held the twentieth day of October last, [e][*i*]ntit[*u*]led "An Act Preamble. 1743-44, chap. 17.

for the more speedy finishing the land-bank or manufactory scheme," it is, among other things, provided that the said act "shall not be adjudged or construed to be intended to hinder the possessors of any of the manufactory bills from making the same demands upon any of the late directors and partners of the said late manufactory company for the redemption of the said bills, as they might have made upon them before the publication of the said act, and that the estates of the said directors and partners shall be as liable to be attached at such suits of the possessors of the said bills, or of any other just creditor, as they were before the making of the said act, anything therein contained to the contrary therefore in anywise notwithstanding"; and in and by another clause of the said act, it is enacted, "that whereas several parcels of the said manufactory bills may be lodged in some or other of his majesty's courts of judicature within this province, upon judgments obtained there, by some of the possessors of such bills, against some of the directors or partners of the late land-bank company, for the redemption of the said bills; the justices of the said courts shall, within thirty days after the publication of that act, cause such bills to be delivered up to the afores[*ai*]d commissioners, with a certificate of the names of the possessors who lodged the said bills in court, and of the directors or partners of the said late company, against whom judgment was obtained for the redemption of the said bills"; *and whereas* it may have happened that some of the possessors of the said manufactory bills, who had, before the making of the afores[*ai*]d act, obtained judgments in some or other of his majesty's courts of judicature within this province, against some of the directors or partners of the said late manufactory company, for the value of some of the said bills and interest due thereon, pursuant to the act of parliament in that case made and provided, and had thereupon lodged such bills in the court where they had obtained such judgments, but had not then, nor have yet received satisfaction upon those judgments; *and whereas* some doubt has arisen whether the justices of his majesty's courts of judicature, where any of the s[*ai*]d manufactory bills are lodged as aforesaid, are not directed and bound by the last-recited clause of the afores[*ai*]d act of this court, to deliver up all the same without exception to the afores[*ai*]d commiss[*ione*]rs, as well in cases where the late possessors of the said bills, who have obtained judgm[*en*]t in their court for the value of the same, and interest due thereon, with cost[s] of suit[*s*], have not received full satisfaction upon such judgments, as in cases where they have received satisfaction upon the same, which construction of the said clause is contrary to, and inconsistent with, the plain sense of the hereinbefore first-recited clause of the same act, and to the intent and meaning of the said act in general; now, for removing the said doubt, and preventing any misconstruction of the said act in the case before mentioned,—

Be it enacted and declared by the Governour, Council and House of Representatives,

Manufactory bills, for which value has been received, only, to be delivered to the commissioners.

That the true intent and meaning of the hereinbefore recited clauses of the afores[*ai*]d act for the more speedy finishing of the land-bank or manufactory scheme, was, at the time of passing the said act, and shall be, adjudged, construed and taken to be, that such only of the said manufactory bills, for the value of which judgments as afores[*ai*]d have been obtained, and the late possessors have received full satisfaction, according to such judgments (and it so appears by the records of the said courts), shall be delivered out of any of the said courts of judicature, to the afores[*ai*]d commissioners, anything in the afore-recited act to the contrary notwithstanding. [*Passed and published February* 28, 1743–44.

CHAPTER 29.

AN ACT TO ENABLE JUSTICES OF THE PEACE AND TOWN CLERKS TO ADMINISTER AN OATH TO SEALERS OF WEIGHTS AND MEASURES, &c[A]., AND TO ESTABLISH THEIR FEES.

WHEREAS by law it is provided that sealers of weights and measures when chosen shall be presented to the court of general sessions of the peace to be sworn, which by reason of the distance of many towns in this province from any such court, often occasions great delay and unnecessary trouble; for preventing of which for the future,— Preamble. 1692-93, chap. 30, § 1.

Be it enacted by the Governour, Council and House of Representatives,

[SECT. 1.] That from and after the publication of this act, it shall and may be lawful[1] for any one of his majesty's justices of the peace in the respective counties to administer an oath to any sealer of weights and measures that may be chosen (as by law already provided) in any town within the county where such justice lives, or the town clerk in such towns where no justice dwells, and such sealer so chosen and sworn shall be deemed legally qualified for his trust. Justices of peace and town clerks to administer the oath to sealers of weights and measures.

And whereas, in the late law for establishing fees, no provision is made for such offices, and by the alteration of the value of money the former fees are become unequal,—

Be it enacted,

[SECT. 2.] That for the future the fees for the first sealing any weight, measure, scale or beam shall be one penny halfpenny, and for each after-sealing any such weight, measure, scale or beam, one penny, which the sealer may demand and take, and no more; any law, usage or custom to the contrary notwithstanding. [*Passed March* 5; *published March* 17, 1743-44. Fees for sealers fixed.

NOTES.—There were four sessions of the General Court this year. The second session was held, by adjournment, September 8, and continued ten days. No proclamation of prorogation, during this year, has been discovered, although Mr. Secretary Willard certified that the second session was prorogued to October 20; and it clearly appears that the General Court sat again from February 8, to March 22, 1743-44. The fourth session was adjourned to April 4, 1744. On the next day it was adjourned to April 18, and again, on that day, to April 24, and was dissolved April 28.

The engrossments of all the acts of this year are preserved, except of chapters 18 and 26; and all were printed with the sessions acts, except chapters 8 and 9.

Chapter 7 was transmitted to the Lords of Trade, by Governor Shirley, in July of this year; chapter 17 was forwarded, in like manner, on the 7th of November following, and chapter 14 a week later. The action of the Home Government upon those acts will be found in the notes to the respective chapters, *post*.

With the exception of chapter 7, no trace has been found of the reception of the acts of the first session. The acts of the last three sessions were regularly certified to the Lords of Trade, by Secretary Willard, August 9, 1744, and were received October 26, and read on the 14th of November following. They were referred to Mr. Fane for his opinion, in point of law, but, excepting chapters 14 and 17, have not been traced further in the records of the Lords of Trade or of the Privy Council.

The approval of these last-named acts was certified to Governor Shirley by the Lords of Trade in a letter bearing date August 9, 1744.

Chap. 7. "Wednesday, October 26th, 1743. [Present] Col. Bladen, Mr. Plumer, Mr. Keene.

* * * * * * * * * * * * *

Rece[d] another letter from M[r] Shirley dated at Boston July 1743, transmitting an *Act to explain the Act to ascertain the value of money & of the bills of Credit passed in June last* and containing his reasons for passing it."—*Trade-papers, vol.* 45, *p.* 108, *in Public-Record Office.*

* * * * * * * * * * * * *

An Act in addition to and in explanation of sundry Clauses of an Act entitled an Act to ascertain the value of Money and of the Bills of Publick Credit of this Province &[c]

To which Acts I have no objection, as they entirely relate to the affairs of this Province and seem intended for the well ordering & governing the same. I am, My Lord,

Your Lordships most obed[t] Ser[t].

4 Feb[y]. 1743. FRAN. FANE."

—*Mass. Bay, B. T., vol.* 71, *F. f.* 18, *in Public-Record Office.*

Chap. 13. "Sept. 10, 1743. In the House of Represent^ves; Whereas the Appropriation for grants in the late Act for supplying the Treasury is exhausted, and sundry grants have been made by this court which are not yet paid, & other grants necessary for the service of the Province may hereafter be made, and the attendance of the Members of the Court at this season of the year, in order to prepare and pass a Bill for the supply of the Treasury, will be extreamly prejudicial to their affairs: And whereas part of several other appropriations remains in the Treasury, which may not be necessary to be drawn out till the Court shall sit again:

It is therefore Ordered that the sum of Forty three pounds five shillings and seven pence three farthings, being the surplus of the Five Thousand Pounds—appropriation for the service of His Majesty in the late Expedition to the West Indies, and the sum of Four Hundred and eighty pounds ten shillings and ten pence remaining of the Seven Hundred Pounds formerly taken from the Five Thousand Pounds—appropriation aforesaid, and the sum of Three Hundred pounds part of the Five Hundred Pounds appropriation for payment of contingent charges, and the sum of Eleven Hundred and Ninety two pounds sixteen shillings and nine pence half peny, being the surplus of the Four Thousand Pounds—appropriation for payment of Forts and Garrisons &c the whole of the several sums aforesaid amounting to Two Thousand and sixteen pounds thirteen shillings and three pence one farthing be taken from the several Appropriations to which they respectively belong and applied or appropriated for the payment of such Grants as are or shall be made by this Court the several sums, taken as aforesaid, to be restored or made good to their respective appropriations by the next act for supply of the Treasury that shall pass this court. In Council; Read and Concur'd.

Consented to W. SHIRLEY."

Council Records, Vol. XVII., b. 4, p. 134.

Chap. 14. This was one of the acts included in Mr. Fane's report of February 4, 1743-4, quoted in *note* to chap. 7, *ante*. It was submitted to him by the Board of Trade on the 27th of the previous month; and on the 24th of February a draught of a representation for the King's assent thereto was prepared and signed by the Board.

"*Order in Council confirming an Act passed in Nov.* 1743.

At the Court at St. James's the 9th day of May 1744 Present The King's most Excellent Majesty in Council

Whereas by Commission under the Great Seal of Great Britain the Governor, Council and Assembly of the Province of the Massachusetts Bay in New England are authorized and empowered to constitute and ordain Laws which are to continue and be in force unless His Maj^ty's pleasure be signifyed to the contrary—And whereas in pursuance of the said Commission an Act was past in the said Province in November 1743 in the Words following Viz^t:

An Act for preventing the destruction of White Pine Trees within this Province and for encouraging the preservation of them for the use of the Royal Navy.

(Mem^d. Here the Act was inserted at length.)

Which said Law having been under the consideration of the Lords Commissioners for Trade and Plantations and also of a Committee of the Lords of His Majesty's most Honourable Privy Council, the said Lords of the Committee this day presented the said Law to His Majesty at this Board with their opinion that the same was proper to be approved— His Majesty taking the same into consideration was pleased with the advice of His Privy Council to declare his approbation of the said Law And pursuant to His Majesty's Royal Pleasure thereupon expressed the said Law is hereby confirmed finally enacted and ratifyed accordingly Whereof the Governor or Commander in Chief of the said Province for the time being and all others whom it may concern are to take notice and govern themselves accordingly. A true Copy W. SHARPE."

—*Mass. Bay, B. T., vol.* 71, *F. f.* 37, *in Public-Record Office.*

Chap. 17. "Nov. 5, 1714. A Projection or Scheme for Establishing a Fund or Bank of Credit upon a Land Security; which may give the Bills issued therefrom a general Currency. Sent up from the Represent^ves with an Order pass'd thereon; viz. Ordered that no private Company or Partnership proceed to the Making or Emitting of any Bills of Credit, as a Medium of Exchange in Trade, without the Allowance & Approbation of this Court:

Read & Concur'd:— Consented to. J. DUDLEY."

—*Council Records, vol. IX., p.* 436.

* * * * * * * * * * * * * *

I now transmit to your Lordships an Act of an Equitable nature, which I believe will be effectual for the purposes design'd by the late Bill (if it shall have his Maj^ty's Royal Approbation) and which is so framed as that I hope it may appear to your Lordships, as it does to me, to stand clear of all the Objections against that Bill.

The extraordinary powers given by the late Bill to the Commissioners were a power by their Warrant to the Sheriff to break open doors, chests &c^a in order to seize the effects, books & papers of the late Directors; an absolute power to assess any sum upon any of the Delinquent Directors or Partners without liberty of appealing from their determination in case of any grievance as also to apportion the general Loss among 'em without any appeal, likewise to sell that part of any Delinquent Directors or Partners Estate which had been before mortgaged to the Company at their discretion for payment of the sums assess'd upon 'em and those Delinquent Partners & Directors were made incapable of alienating such part of their Estates from and after the Publication of the Act without special leave from the Governour and Council and all the Acts of the Commissioners in general were to be final except that they were to be accountable to the General Court for their Receipts and Payments—Whereas this Act has no other effect for binding and subjecting the Estates of the Delinquent Directors and Partners from and after the Publication of it to the payment of such sums as shall be assess'd upon 'em by the Commissioners with the allowance of the General Court, than the actual service of an ordinary Writ of Attachment at the suit of any Creditor would have upon their Estates for subjecting 'em to the payment of any common Debt, according to the common course of the Law—and usage within the Province: The Commissioners have no power to break open Locks, no absolute power to assess any sums of money upon any Partner or Director, but they are oblig'd to make a Report of their Assessments and all their other Acts to the General Court which must give a sanction to 'em before they are binding and may disallow 'em: And such Partners or Directors who think themselves aggrieved by any of their Determinations, may appeal from 'em to the General Court; and if they choose to have any material facts not agreed between them and the Commissioners try'd in a Court of Law upon an issue to be directed by the Gen[l] Court such issue is to be directed for the Trial of 'em by a jury in his Maj[tys] Superior Court of Judicature; so that no party can lose the benefit of a Trial at Law, if he desires it; And the Commissioners have no power to make sale of that part of any Delinquent Partner's or Director's Estate, which was before mortgag'd to the Company, as was before given 'em by the late Bill, but only to mortgage it; And it is expressly provided by the Act that notwithstanding anything contained in it, or done in pursuance of it, the persons and estates of the Partners and Directors shall be liable to the same Demands and Attachments of the Possessors of the Bills as they were before the making of the Act; So that this Act of the General Court does not in the least interfere with the Act of Parliament by taking away the Remedy which that gave the Possessors of the Bills against the Partners or Directors, and substituting another in lieu of it, unless the Possessors choose to bring in their bills to the Commissioners to be redeem'd by them, which is in their favour; nor does it in the least clash with the Act of Parliament by declaring or supposing any of the Agreements or Covenants between the Partners and Directors in forming and executing their late scheme to be good in Law, which the Act of Parliament declares to be illegal and void; but is manifestly calculated to carry the Act of Parliament into Execution according to its full intent, which I suppose was to punish and burthen the whole Company and not that such of 'em, who should pay a due obedience to the Act, should be ruin'd in their Estates and Families, and those who were dishonest and refractory should avoid their part of the Loss and Burthen by their obstinacy, which among so great a number as eight hundred, of which the Company consisted, must have been the fate of some if this Act had not been made; besides their being subjected to the Oppression of such persons as buying up the Bills of some ignorant possessors at a great discount, either out of avarice in pique against particular persons, harrass 'em with demands in order to exact sums of money from 'em to let their suits drop and contribute to keep such of the Bills as are now outstanding in a Circulation—And it seems to me upon the whole that this Act of the General Court is so well guarded and that it is framed in such manner, as that, if any Act effectual to answer the ends design'd by this and consistent with the Act of Parliam[t] can be devis'd, this is such a one.

And your Lordships perceive that this Act provides that in case of the Death or refusal of any of the Commissioners, such Vacancy is not to be filled up by the Governor and Council, as was provided by the former Bill, and which I understand was excepted to by your Lordships, but is to be supply'd by the General Court.

And I would particularly observe to your Lordships that I have taken care that the Commissioners shall only proceed to audit the accounts of the Company and make report of their proceedings to the Gen[l] Court (at their next May Sessions) which must give sanction to all that they do, so that I have it absolutely in my power to hinder the Act from being carried into execution, 'till I know his Maj[tys] pleasure upon it, and I shall accordingly suspend the execution of it till then; and I hope that the steps, which the Commissioners will take in the meantime in auditing and settling the affairs of the Company and in apportioning the loss which will arise from the whole scheme, in order to be lay'd before the General Court, may tend to check several mischievous practises, one of which is an endeavour to influence some Members of the Assembly, who have been lately active in his Maj[tys] service by intimidating 'em with Demands of large sums of Manufactory Bills, in order to make 'em oppose the measures of the Government for the sake of getting rid of such demands; for which special purpose some sums of those Bills have been purchased of the Possessors, which is a vile abuse of the Act of Parliament.

As it appears to me that this Act would be for the service of his Maj[tys] Govern[t] here, as well as very much for that of the Country and correct several abuses of the Act of Parliament, I hope your Lordships will not find anything so exceptionable in it as to hinder his Majesty's approbation of it; And if your Lordships would be pleased to signify to me his Maj[tys] pleasure upon it as early as may be consistent with your conveniency, so that I may know how to act upon it by the beginning of next June I should esteem it a singular mark of your Goodness & Favour to me.

I shall observe your Commands relating to the Lands between Nova Scotia and the River of Sagadehock, and an account of the state of the Paper Currency and all other matters in your last letter not answer'd here, and am with the highest respect

My Lords

Your obedient and

most humble Servant

W. SHIRLEY.

—*Letter to the Lords of Trade*, 7 *Nov.*, 1743; *Mass. Bay, B. T., vol.* 71, *F. f.* 16, *in Public-Record Office.*

This act was sent to Mr. Fane with chapter 14; and was included in his report of February 4, 1743–44, above quoted, and also in the representation of the Board of Trade referred to in the *note* to chapter 14, *ante*.

Order in Council confirming an Act passed in Nov. 1743.

At the Court at St. James' the 9th day of May 1744. Present, The King's most Excellent Majesty in Council.

Whereas by Commission under the Great Seal of Great Britain the Governor Council and Assembly of the Province of the Massachusetts Bay in New England are authorized and empowered to constitute and ordain Laws which are to continue and be in force unless His Majesty's pleasure be signifyed to the contrary—And whereas in pursuance of the said Commission an Act was past in the said Province in November 1743 in the Words following, Viz[t]:

An Act for the more speedy finishing of the Land Bank or Manufactory Scheme (Mem[d] Here the Act was inserted at length)

Which said Law having been under the consideration of the Lords Commissioners for Trade and Plantations and also of a Committee of the Lords of His Maj[tys] most honourable Privy Council, the said Lords of the Committee this day presented the said Law to His Majesty at this Board with their opinion that the same was proper to be approved—His Majesty taking the same into consideration was pleased with the advice of His Privy Council to declare his approbation of the said Law— And pursuant to His Majesty's Royal Pleasure thereupon expressed the said Law is hereby confirmed, finally enacted and ratifyed accordingly—Whereof the Governor or Commander in Chief of the said Province for the time being and all others whom it may concern are to take notice and govern themselves accordingly.

A true Copy. W. SHARPE.

—*Ibid., F. f.* 38.

Chap. 26. "June 24, 1742. A petition of Timothy Sprague of Malden, Shewing that he has for many years past been in controversies in the law, respecting a Mill and Mill Dam at a place called Spot Pond, which he and his Ancestors have been in possession of, for about an hundred years past; that he is threatened by his adversaries to be sued for the penalty of an Act lately pass'd, entitled An Act in Addition to An Act made to prevent the destruction of the Fish called Alewives and other Fish; And for as much as in reason and equity he ought not to be subjected to the penalty of the said Act; therefore Praying that this Court would expressly except his Dam from the said Act.

In the House of Represent[ves]; Read and Ordered that the Consideration of this Petition be refer'd to the next Session of this Court; and all proceedings with respect to the Petitioners Mill Dam within mentioned in consequence of the law made the last year, entitled An Act in Addition to An Act to prevent the destruction of Alewives, be suspended in the mean time In Council; Read and Concur'd.

Consented to W. SHIRLEY."

—*Council Records, vol.* XVII., *b.* 3, *p.* 436.

Chap. 27. "February 15, 1713. The following Order pass'd in the House of Represent[ves] read and concur'd; viz.

Upon reading a petition of Joshua Lamb, Richard Draper, Samuel Ruggles, Benjamin Tucker and others, setting forth that upon the twenty-seventh day of January, 1686, for a valuable consideration therefor paid, they purchased of Philip Trays and Monehhue his wife, John Wanscom and Wawonnow his wife and other Indians the heirs of Oarashoe, the original sachem of a place called Towtaid lying near Worcester, a certain tract of land, containing eight miles square, abutting southerly on the land which the Govern[r] lately purchased of the Indians, and westerly the most southerly corner, upon a little pond called Paupogquincog; then to a little hill called Wehapehatonon; and from thence to a little hill called Aspomscok; and so then easterly upon a line untill it come against Worcester bounds, and joins unto their bounds, as may be seen more at large by the Original Deed executed by the said Indians, proprietors, and acknowledged before the Hon[ble] William Stoughton Esq[r] praying a confirmation of the said tract of land to them and their associates; That they may be encouraged to proceed forthwith to settle the same with inhabitants under such directions and reservations as shall be thought meet.

Ordered that the prayer of the petitioners be granted, provided that within seven years time, fifty families settle themselves in as defensible and regular a way as the circumstances of the place will allow, on part of the said land; and that a sufficient quantity thereof be reserved for the use of a Gospel Ministry there and a school; provided also that this interfere with no former grant; and that this grant shall not exceed the quantity of eight miles square; the town to be named Leicester, and to ly to the County of Middlesex.

Consented to, J. DUDLEY."

—*Council Records, vol. IX. p.* 351.

"February 16, 1713. The following Order pass'd the House of Represent[ves] read and concur'd; viz.

Ordered that John Chandler Esq[r] survey[r] be appointed to lay out the tract of land granted this present session to be a township by the name of Leicester, at the charge of the grantees, and lay a plat thereof before this court at their session in May next for confirmation.

Consented to, J. DUDLEY."

—*Ibid.*, p. 353.

ACTS,

Passed 1744–45.

ACTS

PASSED AT THE SESSION BEGUN AND HELD AT BOSTON, ON THE THIRTIETH DAY OF MAY, A. D. 1744.

CHAPTER 1.

AN ACT FOR THE MORE EFFECTUAL GUARDING AND SECURING OUR SEACOASTS, AND FOR THE ENCOURAGEMENT OF SEAMEN TO ENLIST THEMSELVES IN THE PROVINCE SNOW, OR SUCH VESSELS OF WAR AS SHALL BE COMMISSIONED AND FITTED OUT BY THIS OR OTHER OF HIS MAJESTY'S GOVERNMENTS DURING THIS PRESENT WAR WITH FRANCE.

Be it enacted by the Governour, Council and House of Representatives,

[SECT. 1.] That the officers and ship's company of the province snow, or such vessels of war as shall be commissioned and fitted out by this government during the present war, shall have the sole interest and property of and in all and every ship, vessel, goods, and merchandize, as they or either of them, since the first day of June instant, have seized or taken, or shall hereafter seize or take, from the French king, his vassals or subjects, during the present war with France.

Vessels and cargo taken from the French allowed to the captors, being in vessels of war commissioned from this Government.

And, as a further encouragement to the officers, seamen, and others aboard said vessels of war, to attack, take, and destroy any ships of war or privateers belonging to the enemy,—

[SECT. 2.] That there shall be paid unto the officer, seamen, and others, that shall have been actually on board such of the before-mentioned vessels of war, in any action where any vessel or vessels of war, or privateers, shall have been taken from the enemy, sunk, burnt or otherwise destroyed, three pounds for every man which was living on board any vessel or vessels so taken, sunk, burnt or otherwise destroyed, at the beginning of the engagement between them; the number of such men to be proved by the oaths of three or more of the chief officers or men which were belonging to the said vessel or vessels of war, or privateer, of the enemy, at the time of her or their being taken as prize, sunk, burnt or otherwise destroyed, before the governour, lieutenant-governour or one or more of his majesty's council of this province, and by either of them certified; the said prizes, with the goods and merchandize on board the same, after having paid the duties of impost, with the premiums aforesaid, shall be divided among the captors as follows: to the captain, two-eighths; to the lieutenant and master, one-eighth; to the warrant-officers, one-eighth; to the petty officers, one-eighth; and to the ship's company, three-eighths: and the captain, officers, and ship's company shall appoint their respective agents for the receiving, management, and distribution of their particular shares accordingly.

£3 allowed for each prisoner and person killed in any vessel of war.

Manner of proof of persons killed, &c.

In what proportion the booty and premium is to be divided.

See note to chap. 16, *post*.

And, for the encouragement of vessels of war commissioned and fitted out by any of his majesty's colonies, and all private vessels of war and trading vessels that have letters of marque or commissions as private vessels of war from this or any of his majesty's aforesaid governments, against the subjects of the French king during this present war, to attack, take, burn, sink or otherwise destroy any ships of force belonging to the enemy,—

Be it further enacted,

Vessels and cargo and premium of £3 for each prisoner, &c., to be allowed to the captors commissioned in the neighboring Governments; and vessels taken within certain limits.

[SECT. 3.] That there shall be paid unto the officers, seamen, and others that shall have been actually on board such of the before-mentioned vessels of war, in any action where any ship or ships of war, or privateer, shall have been taken from the enemy, sunk, burnt or otherwise destroyed on the coast of this province within the following limits; viz., from Nantucket and Seconnet on the south, to Canso on the northeast, three pounds in bills of this province for every man which was living on board any such vessel or vessels so sunk, taken, burnt, or otherwise destroyed, at the beginning of the engagement between them; the number of such men to be proved and certified in manner as before mentioned: the premiums aforesaid to be distributed to such persons, and in such proportions, as prizes respectively taken by the vessels aforesaid are or ought to be distributed; all which premiums shall be duly and seasonably paid out of this province treasury in course as all other payments are made. [*Passed June* 19; *published June* 23.

CHAPTER 2.

AN ACT FOR LEVYING SOLDIERS.

Preamble.

For the more speedy and effectual levying of soldiers for his majesty's service, when and so often as there shall be occasion for the same, for the preservation and defence of his majesty's subjects and interests, and the prosecuting, encountring, repelling or subduing such as shall at any time attempt, in hostile manner, to enterprize the destruction, invasion, detriment or annoyance of this his majesty's province, or any of his majesty's subjects therein; and for the better preventing disappointments, thro' default of any employed in levying of such soldiers, or by the non-appearance of such as shall be levyed,—

Be it enacted by the Governour, Council and House of Representatives,

Duty of the chief officers of the regiments in levying soldiers.

[SECT. 1.] That when and so often as the chief officer of any regiment of militia within this province shall receive orders from the captain-general or commander-in-chief, for the time being, of the said province, for the impressing or causing to be impressed for his majesty's service, out of the regiment under his command, so many soldiers as in such orders shall be mentioned, such chief officer of the regiment shall forthwith thereupon issue forth his warrants to the captains or chief officers of the companies or troops within his regiment, or such of them as he shall think fit, requiring them respectively to impress out of the militia, in the companies or troops under their command, so many able soldiers, furnished and provided as the law directs, and in the whole shall make up the number which by the orders of the captain-general or commander-in-chief he shall be directed to impress, on pain that every chief officer of a regiment that shall neglect or not do his utmost to send forth his warrants seasonably (having orders for the same as above mention'd) shall forfeit and pay a fine of fifty pounds.

Penalty for not doing his duty.

Duty of the chief officer of a company or troop.

[SECT. 2.] And every captain or other chief officer of any company or troop that shall receive any warrant from the chief officer of the regiment whereto such company or troop belongs, for the impressing out of the same any soldier or soldiers for his majesty's service, shall thereupon use his utmost endeavour to impress, or cause to be impressed, so many soldiers as by such warrant he shall be required to impress, and to have them at the place of rendezvous in time as therein shall be mentioned, on pain that every captain or chief officer of any company or troop that shall neglect, or not do his utmost, to comply with and perform any warrant to be by him received as aforesaid from the chief officer of the regiment, shall, for such neglect and default, pay a fine of twenty pounds.

[Sect. 3.] And every officer or soldier that shall receive a warrant from his captain, or the chief officer of the company or troop in which he is inlisted, for the impressing of men, shall forthwith attend and perform the same, on pain of paying a fine of five pounds. Penalty for not doing his duty.

[Sect. 4.] And all persons are required to be aiding and assisting to him in the execution of such warrant, on pain of forfeiting the sum of three pounds. Penalty for other persons' neglect.

[Sect. 5.] And if any person, authorized as aforesaid to impress any soldier or soldiers for his majesty's service, shall exact or take any reward to discharge or spare any from said service, he shall forfeit ten pounds for every twenty shillings he shall so exact or take, and so *pro ratâ*. Penalty for taking a reward to discharge soldiers.

[Sect. 6.] All which fines and penalties aforesaid shall be, one moiety thereof unto his majesty, for and towards the support of the government of this province, and the other moiety to him or them that shall inform and sue for the same, by action, bill, plaint or information, in any court of record. Disposition of the fines.

And be it further enacted,

[Sect. 7.] That every person, liable and fit for service, being orderly impressed as aforesaid for his majesty's service, by being commanded in his majesty's name to attend said service, shall, by himself or other meet person in his room (to the acceptance of his captain or chief officer), attend the same at time and place appointed, compleat with arms and ammunition, if such he have, or is able to purchase the same, on pain of suffering six months' imprisonment, without bail or mainprize, to be committed by mittimus from any justice of the peace, or chief officer of the company or troop, where no justice of the peace lives in the town, upon conviction before one of his majesty's justices of the peace of such neglect, unless such person, within the space of twenty-four hours next after being impressed, shall either procure some meet person, or, in default thereof, pay to his captain or chief officer, by whose warrant he shall be impressed, the sum of ten pounds, to be employed for the procuring and fitting out of a suitable person in the stead of him so paying the said sum, for the service for which he was impressed, if such other suitable person be timely to be had, otherwise to be paid to the selectmen of the town to which such impressed person belongs, for and towards procuring of arms for such persons as are unable to purchase the same for themselves, and for which such indigent soldier shall be answerable. Duty of persons impressed. Penalty.

[Sect. 8.] And if the captain or officer to whom the said sum of ten pounds shall be paid as aforesaid by any person impressed, cannot seasonably procure another suitable person to serve in the stead of him that was before impressed, he shall renew his warrants as often as there shall be occasion, until the number sent for from him be compleated. And all persons paying the said sum of ten pounds as before mentioned, shall be esteemed as persons that have served, and be no further or otherwise liable to any after impress than those that actually go forth in that service. In what case impressed persons may be excused.

[Sect. 9.] And all persons lawfully impowered to impress, may pursue any person that absconds from the impress, or makes his escape, Penalty for escaping or absconding from the impress.

and may impress such person in any place within the province; and if any person impressed as aforesaid for his majesty's service, being so duly returned, shall remove or go out of the province, and not attend the service as required, such person, at his return, shall be apprehended, by warrant from any justice of the peace, and be by him committed to prison, unless such person give sufficient security to answer it at the next court of general sessions of the peace; and upon due conviction of the said offence, by the oath of him that impressed him, shall suffer six months' imprisonment, or pay a fine of fifteen pounds, to be paid to the selectmen of the town where such person belonged at the time of his being impress'd, for purchasing arms.

[SECT. 10.] And if any person, directly or indirectly, by counsel or otherwise, shall prevent the impressing, conceal any person impressed, or, knowingly, further his escape, such person shall pay as a fine, three pounds.

And be it further enacted,

When the pay of soldiers is to begin.

[SECT. 11.] That all soldiers shall be in pay from the time of their being impressed, till they be orderly discharged, and have reasonable time allowed them to repair to their usual places of abode.

Penalty for officers exchanging soldiers for gain.

[SECT. 12.] And if any captain or other chief officer shall dismiss any soldier retained in his majesty's service, and assume another, for gain, such captain or other chief officer shall forfeit the sum of ten pounds for every twenty shillings he shall so exact, to be recovered and disposed of in manner as is before provided for the fine or penalty on officers neglecting to execute warrants for impressing of soldiers.

[SECT. 13.] And every person who hath or shall impress any soldiers for his majesty's service, shall transmit a list of them to the chief officer of the regiment or troop, particularly mentioning servants, if any such there be, and to whom they belong, that so their masters may receive their wages, who are hereby impowered so to do.

And be it further enacted,

Maimed soldiers and seamen to be relieved by the public.

[SECT. 14.] That all such soldiers and seamen that, from the commencement of the present war, have been, or, during the continuance thereof, may be, wounded in his majesty's service within this province, and are thereby maimed or otherwise disabled, shall be relieved out of the publick treasury, as the great and general court or assembly shall order.

And be it further enacted,

Soldiers to be furnished with arms.

[SECT. 15.] That any impress'd man or men appearing at the place of rendezvous, being actually destitute of arms and ammunition of his own, and unable to purchase the same, he or they shall be furnished out of the town stock, if any there be, otherwise it shall be in the power of the captain or chief officer of the company or troop by whom he is impress'd, to impress arms and ammunition for him or them, the value of which shall be paid out of the publick treasury, as the great and general court shall order. And every soldier thus furnished with arms, shall allow, out of his wages, fourpence per week for the same, and return such arms, or otherwise pay for the same. And if any soldier shall lose his arms in his majesty's service, not through his own neglect or default, such loss shall be born by the province.

To allow 4*d.* per week for province arms.

Provided,

Limitation.

[SECT. 16.] That this act shall continue in force unto the end of the sessions of the general assembly, to be begun and held on the last Wednesday in May, which will be in the year of our Lord, one thousand seven hundred and forty-six, and no longer. [*Passed June* 18; *published June* 23.

CHAPTER 3.

AN ACT TO PREVENT SOLDIERS AND SEAMEN IN HIS MAJESTY'S SERVICE BEING ARRESTED FOR DEBT.

Be it enacted by the Governour, Council and House of Representatives,

[Sect. 1.] That if any person whatsoever, other than the commissary, shall trust or give credit to any soldier, mariner, or sailor, during his being actually in his majesty's service, for cloathing or other things whatsoever, no process shall be granted or served on such soldier for any debt so contracted until he be dismiss'd the service; and every writ or process granted or served contrary hereto shall be deemed and adjudged, *ipso facto*, void. And any justice of the peace within the county, where any such soldier or mariner is committed or restrained, upon process granted for debt or pretention of debt contracted as aforesaid, shall, upon certificate given to him from the captain or chief officer under whose command such soldier or mariner is, setting forth that at the time of such debt contracted he then was and still continues a soldier or mariner in his majesty's pay, forthwith order his release from confinement and return to his duty. Soldier, mariner, or sailor, not to be trusted by any, except the commissary.

And be it further enacted,

[Sect. 2.] That no person who is or shall be impressed, hired, or voluntarily inlisted into his majesty's service either by sea or land, shall, during his continuance therein, be liable to be taken out of his majesty's service by any process or execution, unless for some criminal matter, for any sum under the value of twenty pounds bills of credit of the last emission, nor for any greater sum, until oath shall be made by the plaintiff or plaintiffs, before one of the justices of the court out of which the execution or process shall issue, or before two justices of the peace, *quorum unus*, in the county where the plaintiff may happen to be, that to his or their knowledge there is, *bona fide*, due from such person as the process or execution is desired to issue against, twenty pounds of the currency aforesaid at least. No person impressed, hired, or enlisted to be arrested for less than £20, unless for criminal matters.

And be it further enacted,

[Sect. 3.] That no person in his majesty's service shall pawn, truck, barter, or sell his arms, ammunition, or cloathing, on penalty of being punished by riding the wooden horse, running the gantlet, or other like military punishment; and the person accepting or receiving the same shall be compelled to restore and make good the same without price or redemption, and shall further (if in his majesty's service) suffer military punishment as aforesaid. Persons in his majesty's service not to sell their arms.

And be it further enacted,

[Sect. 4.] That all debts contracted for strong or spirituous liquors by any soldier or mariner while in his majesty's service shall be void, and the creditor forever debarred from any process or benefit of the law for recovery of the same. Soldier or mariner not to be trusted for strong liquors.

[Sect. 5.] This act to be in force for the space of two years: *provided* the present war with the French king, his allies and vassals, continue so long, and not otherwise, and no longer. [*Passed and published June 23.*] Limitation.

CHAPTER 4.

AN ACT FOR GRANTING THE SUM OF FOURTEEN HUNDRED AND FORTY POUNDS FOR THE SUPPORT OF HIS MAJESTY'S GOVERNOUR.

Be it enacted by the Governour, Council and House of Representatives, That the sum of fourteen hundred and forty pounds in bills of credit of the last emission, or other bills equivalent, be and hereby is granted unto his most excellent majesty, to be paid out of the publick treasury to his excellency William Shirley, Esq., captain-general and governour-in-chief in and over his majesty's province of the Massachusetts Bay, for his past services, and further to enable him to manage the publick affairs of this province. The aforesaid sum of fourteen hundred and forty pounds, in bills of the last emission, or other bills of credit equivalent, shall be paid out of the next general supply bill that shall be hereafter agreed on and passed by this court. [*Passed June* 18; *published June* 23.

CHAPTER 5.

AN ACT FOR SUPPLYING THE TREASURY WITH THE SUM OF TWENTY-SIX THOUSAND AND THIRTY-SEVEN POUNDS TEN SHILLINGS IN BILLS OF CREDIT, FOR PUTTING THE PROVINCE IN A BETTER POSTURE OF DEFENCE, FOR DISCHARGING THE PUBLICK DEBTS, &c., AND FOR DRAWING IN THE SAID BILLS INTO THE TREASURY AGAIN, AND FOR STATING THEIR VALUE IN DISCHARGING PUBLICK DEBTS.

Be it enacted by the Governour, Council and House of Representatives,

£2,637 10*s.* bills of credit to be emitted.

[SECT. 1.] That there be forthwith imprinted a certain number of bills of credit on this province of the following denominations; viz., forty shillings, thirty shillings, twenty shillings, and fifteen shillings, which in the whole shall amount to the sum of twenty-six thousand and thirty-seven pounds ten shillings; which bills shall be signed by a committee to be appointed by this court, and shall be of the following form:—

No. ( ) Twenty Shillings.

Form of the bills.

This bill of Twenty Shillings, due to the possessor thereof from the province of the Massachusetts Bay, shall be equal to two ounces thirteen pennyweight and eight grains of coin'd silver, troy weight, of sterling alloy, or gold coin at the rate of five pounds ten shillings and threepence per ounce, and shall be so accepted in all payments in the treasury, agreeable to act of assembly 1744.

By order of the General Court or Assembly.

} *Committee.*

—and so, *mutatis mutandis*, for a greater or less sum.

[SECT. 2.] And the said committee are hereby impowered and directed to take care and make effectual provision, so soon as may be, to imprint the aforesaid sum of twenty-six thousand and thirty-seven pounds ten shillings, and to sign and deliver the said sum to the treasurer, taking his receipt for the same; and the said committee shall be under oath for the faithful performance of the trust by this act reposed in them.

£6,000 for wages at Castle William and other

[SECT. 3.] And the said sum of twenty-six thousand and thirty-seven pounds ten shillings shall be issued out of the treasury in manner and for the purposes following; viz., the sum of six thousand pounds, part of the aforesaid sum of twenty-six thousand and thirty-seven pounds ten shillings, shall be applied for the payment of wages that now are, or that hereafter may be, due by virtue of the establishment of Castle William, Richmond Fort, George's Truck-house, Saco Truck-house, Brunswick Fort, the province snow, and other vessels in the country's service, and the treasurer's usual disbursements; and the sum of twelve thousand pounds, part of the aforesaid sum of twenty-six thousand and thirty-seven pounds ten shillings, shall be applied for putting the province into a better posture of defence, for subsisting and paying of the officers and soldiers who are or may be employed in the service of the province, according to the several establishments, for purchasing all needful warlike stores, and for compleating the repairs of Castle William, and other forts and garrisons within this province, pursuant to such grants as are or shall be made by this court: the sum of five thousand seven hundred pounds, part of the aforesaid sum of twenty-six thousand thirty-seven pounds ten shillings, shall be applied for the payment of such other grants as are or shall be made by this court, for the payment of his majesty's council, for the payment of stipends, bounties and premiums established by law, and for the payment of all other things which this court have or shall, either by law or orders, provide for the payment of out of the publick treasury, and for no other purpose whatsoever; the sum of one thousand pounds, part of the aforesaid sum of twenty-six thousand and thirty-seven pounds ten shillings, shall be applied for the discharge of other debts owing, from this province, to persons who have served or shall serve them by order of this court, in such matters and things where there is no establishment, nor any certain sum assigned for such service; and for paper, printing and writing for this court; the expences of committees of council, or of the house, or of both houses; entertainments of Indians, or presents made them by this court; the surgeon of Castle William, and wooding of said castle; and the sum of one thousand thirty-seven pounds ten shillings, part of the aforesaid sum of twenty-six thousand and thirty-seven pounds ten shillings, shall be applied for the payment of the members of the house of representatives serving in the general court during their several sessions this present year.

garrisons, &c., the province snow, &c.

£12,000 for putting the province into a better posture of defence, &c.

£5,700 for payment of grants, &c.

£1,000 for debts where is no establishment.

£1,037 10s. for the representatives.

And whereas there are sometimes publick entertainments, and, from time to time, contingent and unforeseen charges that demand prompt payment,—

Be it further enacted,

[Sect. 4.] That the sum of three hundred pounds, the remaining part of the aforesaid sum of twenty-six thousand and thirty-seven pounds ten shillings, be applied to defrey and pay such entertainments and contingent charges, and for no other use whatsoever.

£300 for entertainments, &c.

And be it enacted,

[Sect. 5.] That if there be a surplusage in any sum appropriated, such surplusage shall lie in the treasury for the further order of this court.

Surplusage to lie in the treasury.

And be it further enacted,

[Sect. 6.] That each and every warrant for drawing money out of the treasury, shall direct the treasurer to take the same out of such sums as are respectively appropriated for the payment of such publick debt as the draughts are made to discharge; and the treasurer is hereby directed and ordered to pay such money out of such appropriations as directed to, and no other, upon pain of refunding all such sum and sums as he shall otherwise pay, and to keep exact and distinct accounts of all payments made out of such appropriated sums; and the secretary, to whom it belongs to keep the muster rolls and accounts of charge, shall lay

Warrants to express the appropriations.

before the house, when they direct, all such muster rolls and accounts, after payment thereof.

And as a fund and security for drawing the said sum of twenty-six thousand and thirty-seven pounds ten shillings into the treasury again,—

Be it further enacted,

£4,966 13s. 4d. in 1744. [SECT. 7.] That there be and hereby is granted unto his most excellent majesty, for the ends and uses aforesaid, a tax of four thousand nine hundred sixty-six pounds thirteen shillings and fourpence, to be levied on polls, and estates both real and personal, within this province, according to such rules, and in such proportions, on the several towns and districts within the same, as shall be agreed upon and ordered by this court, at their present session, and paid into the publick treasury on or before the last day of December then next after.

And as a further fund and security for drawing the said sum of twenty-six thousand and thirty-seven pounds ten shillings into the treasury again,—

Be it further enacted,

£10,266 13s. 4d. in 1745. [SECT. 8.] That there be and hereby is granted unto his most excellent majesty, for the ends and uses aforesaid, a tax of ten thousand two hundred and sixty-six pounds thirteen shillings and fourpence, to be levied on polls, and estates both real and personal, within this province, according to such rules, and in such proportions, on the several towns and districts within the same, as shall be agreed upon and ordered by this court, at their session in May, one thousand seven hundred and forty-five, and paid into the publick treasury on or before the last day of December then next after.

And as a further fund and security for drawing the said sum of twenty-six thousand and thirty-seven pounds ten shillings into the treasury again,—

Be it further enacted,

£9,766 13s. 4d. in 1746. [SECT. 9.] That there be and hereby is granted unto his most excellent majesty, for the ends and uses aforesaid, a tax of nine thousand seven hundred and sixty-six pounds thirteen shillings and fourpence, to be levied on polls, and estates both real and personal, within this province, according to such rules, and in such proportions, on the several towns and districts within the same, as shall be agreed upon and ordered by the great and general court or assembly, at their session in May, one thousand seven hundred and forty-six, and paid into the publick treasury again on or before the last day of December then next after.

And as a fund and security for drawing in such sum or sums as shall be paid out to the representatives of the several towns,—

Be it enacted,

Tax to be made for what is paid to the representatives. [SECT. 10.] That there be and hereby is granted unto his most excellent majesty, a tax of such sum or sums as shall be paid to the several representatives as aforesaid, to be levied and assessed on the polls and estates of the inhabitants of the several towns, according to what their representatives shall so receive; which sums shall be set on the towns in the next province tax. And the assessors of the said towns shall make their assessment for this tax, and apportion the same according to the rule that shall be prescribed by act of the general assembly, for assessing the next province tax, and the constables, in their respective districts, shall pay in the same when they pay in the province tax for the next year, of which the treasurer is hereby directed to keep a distinct and seperate account; and if there be any surplusage, the same shall lie in the hands of the treasurer for the further order of this court.

And be it further enacted,

[Sect. 11.] That in case the general court shall not at their sessions in May, in the years one thousand seven hundred and forty-four, one thousand seven hundred and forty-five, and one thousand seven hundred and forty-six, agree and conclude upon an act apportioning the several sums which by this act is engaged shall be in each of these several years apportioned, assessed and levied, that then and in such case each town and district within this province shall pay, by a tax to be levied on the polls, and estates both real and personal, within their districts, the same proportion of the said sums as the said towns and districts shall have been taxed by the general court in the tax act then next preceeding; and the province treasurer is hereby fully impowred and directed, some time in the month of June in each of these years, one thousand seven hundred and forty-four, one thousand seven hundred and forty-five, and one thousand seven hundred and forty-six, to issue and send forth his warrants, directed to the selectmen or assessors of each town and district within this province, requiring them to assess the polls, and estates both real and personal, within their several towns and districts, for their respective part and proportion of the several sums before directed and engaged to be assessed by this act, and the assessors, as also persons assessed, shall observe, be governed by and subject to all rules and directions as shall have been given in the next preceeding tax act.

Tax for the money hereby emitted to be made according to the preceding tax act, in case.

And be it further enacted,

[Sect. 12.] That the inhabitants of this province shall have liberty, if they see fit, to pay the several sums for which they respectively may, in pursuance of this act, be assessed, in bills of credit of the form and tenor by this act emitted, or in bills of the last emission, or in bills of the middle tenor, according to their several denominations, or in bills of the old tenor, accounting four for one; or in coin'd silver, at seven shillings and sixpence per ounce, troy weight, and of sterling alloy, or in gold coin, proportionably; or in merchantable hemp, flax, winter and Isle-of-Sable codfish, refined bar-iron, bloomery-iron, hollow iron-ware, Indian corn, rye, wheat, barley, pork, beef, duck or canvas, whalebone, cordage, train-oil, beeswax, bayberry-wax, tallow, pease, sheepswool, or tann'd sole-leather (the aforesaid commodities being of the produce or manufactures of this province), at such moderate rates and prizes as the respective general assemblies of the years one thousand seven hundred and forty-four, one thousand seven hundred and forty-five, and one thousand seven hundred and forty-six shall set them at; the several persons paying their taxes in any of the commodities aforementioned, to run the risque and pay the charge of transporting the said commodities to the province treasury; but if the aforesaid general assemblies shall not, at their respective sessions in May, some time before the last day of June, agree upon and set the aforesaid species or commodities at some certain prizes, that then the eldest councellor, for the time being, of each of those counties in the province, of which any one of the council is an inhabitant, together with the province treasurer, or the major part of them, be a committee, who hereby are directed and fully authorized and impowered to do it; and in their settling the prizes and rating the value of those commodities, to state so much of them, respectively, at seven shillings and sixpence as an ounce of silver will purchase at that time in the town of Boston, and so *pro ratâ*. And the treasurer is hereby directed to insert in the several warrants by him sent to the collectors of the taxes in those years, respectively, with the names of the afore-recited commodities, the several prizes and rates which shall be set on them, either by the general assembly or the committee aforesaid, and direct the aforesaid collectors to receive them so.

Taxes to be paid in the several species herein enumerated.

How the commodities brought into the treasury are to be rated.

Treasurer to sell the said commodities.

[SECT. 13.] And the aforesaid commodities so brought into the treasury shall, as soon as may be, be disposed of by the treasurer to the best advantage for so much as they will fetch in bills of credit hereby to be emitted, or for silver and gold, which silver and gold shall be delivered to the possessor of said bills in exchange for them; that is to say, one ounce of silver coin, and so gold in proportion, for seven shillings and sixpence, and *pro ratâ* for a greater or less sum; and if any loss shall happen by the sale of the aforesaid species, or by any unforeseen accident, such deficiency shall be made good by a tax of the next year following, so as fully and effectually to call in the whole sum of twenty-six thousand thirty-seven pounds ten shillings in said bills hereby ordered to be emitted; and if there be a surplusage, it shall remain a stock in the treasury. [*Passed June* 20; *published June* 23.

CHAPTER 6.

AN ACT TO PREVENT ALL TRAITEROUS CORRESPONDENCE WITH HIS MAJESTY'S ENEMIES.

FOR preventing all traiterons correspondence with the French king or his subjects, or such of the Indians who are or shall be in alliance with him, and supplying them with warlike or other stores,—

Be it enacted by the Governour, Council and House of Representatives,

Correspondence with his majesty's enemies, by letters or otherwise, forbidden on pain of death. 1706.7, chap. 8.

[SECT. 1.] That if at any time after the publication of this act any person or persons shall hold a correspondence with any of his majesty's enemies, by letters or otherwise, whereby they shall give them intelligence tending to their aid and comfort in carrying on the war against his majesty, and to the damage of his majesty's subjects or interests, or to the benefit or advantage of the enemy; or shall send or load, or transport or deliver, or cause to be sent or loaded, or transported or delivered unto or for the use of the said French king, or any of his subjects residing within his dominions, or any town or territory in his possession, or into or for any port or place within his said dominions, or within this province, or any of the neighbouring provinces or colonies, or on the seas adjoining thereto, unto or for the use of such of the Indians who are or shall be in alliance with him, or enemies to his majesty and the government of this his majesty's province, inhabiting or being in any of the places aforesaid, any arms, ordnance, powder, bullets, shot, lead, pitch, tar, hemp, masts, cordage, iron, steel, brass, pewter (wrought or unwrought), saltpetre, or any sort of provisions, or cloathing of any kind, or any other supplies, every person or persons offending as aforesaid, and being thereof convicted or attainted by due course of law, shall be deemed, declared and adjudged to be a traitor or traitors, and suffer the pains of death, and also lose and forfeit as in cases of high treason.

And be it further enacted,

Persons not to depart out of the province with intent to reside among the king's enemies, on pain of death.

[SECT. 2.] That if any of his majesty's subjects within this province shall, from and after the publication of this act, without licence from his majesty's governour or commander-in-chief of this his majesty's province, for the time being, by and with the consent of the council, voluntarily go, repair or embark in any vessel or vessels, with an intent to go into, reside or inhabit in any of the dominions or territories of the said French king, or amongst any of the Indians who are or shall be in alliance with him, or enemies as aforesaid, and be upon full proof convicted thereof, every person or persons so offending shall be taken, deemed and adjudged to be a felon, and suffer the pains of death.

And be it further enacted,

[Sect. 3.] That where any of the offences against this act shall be committed out of this province, or without the body of any county within the province, where the judges of assize and general goal delivery are directed by law to sit, every such offence may and shall be alledged and laid to be perpetrated and done in any place and county within the same, and shall be accordingly inquired of and tried in such county. Offences done out of the province to be laid as done in some county in the province.

And be it further enacted,

[Sect. 4.] That all and every person or persons who shall hereafter be accused, indicted or prosecuted for anything made or declared treason by this act, shall be intitled to the benefit of the act of parliament made in the seventh year of the reign of King William the Third, intitled "An Act for regulating trials in cases of treason and misprision of treason." Act of parliament of the 7th of King William III. may be pleaded. 7 W. III., chap. 3.

Provided, always,—

[Sect. 5.] That nothing in this act contained shall be construed, intended, deemed or taken to extend to bar the necessary relief and supply of any French prisoners of war, or of any flag of truce, or to the supply of the English prisoners in French or Indian hands; or for secret services made or done at all times by direction of the governor or commander-in-chief for the time being, with the advice of the council; or to bar a present charitable relief to any of the enemy that by adversity may be cast on shoar upon this coast, for the necessary preservation of life, intelligence thereof to be forthwith dispatch'd to the governour.

[Sect. 6.] This act to continue and be in force for the space of two years, if the war with the French king continue so long, and no longer. [*Passed June 26; published June 27.*

CHAPTER 7.

AN ACT FOR ESTABLISHING THE WAGES, &c., OF SUNDRY PERSONS IN THE SERVICE OF THE PROVINCE.

Be it enacted by the Governour, Council and House of Representatives,

[Sect. 1.] That the wages of the captain of Castle William shall be after the rate of sixty pounds per annum, from the twentieth day of May, one thousand seven hundred and forty-four, to the nineteenth day of November, one thousand seven hundred and forty-four; of the lieutenant for that term, forty pounds; of the chaplain, forty pounds; of the gunner, fifty pounds; of the gunner's mate, forty shillings per month; of four serjeants, each thirty shillings per month; of six quarter-gunners, each thirty shillings per month; of six corporals, each twenty-six shillings and sixpence per month; of two drummers, each twenty-six shillings and sixpence per month; of one armourer, forty shillings per month; of ninety-six centinels, each twenty-two shillings and sixpence per month; for their subsistence, six shillings and threepence per week per man. Wages of the garrison at Castle William.

And be it further enacted,

[Sect. 2.] That the wages of the captain of Richmond Fort from the twentieth day of May, one thousand seven hundred and forty-four, to the nineteenth day of November, one thousand seven hundred and forty-four, shall be at the rate of forty shillings per month; of one ser- Richmond Fort.

jeant, twenty-five shillings per month; of one corporal, twenty-four shillings per month; of one armourer, thirty shillings per month; and for the chaplain, twenty-five pounds per annum; of one interpreter, fifteen shillings per month, being a centinel; and of twenty centinels, twenty-two shillings and sixpence per month.

And be it further enacted,

Truck-house at George's River. [SECT. 3.] That the wages of the captain of the truck-house on George's River, from the twentieth day of May, one thousand seven hundred and forty-four, to the nineteenth day of November, one thousand seven hundred and forty-four, shall be at the rate of forty shillings per month; of one lieutenant, twenty-six shillings per month; of one serjeant, twenty-five shillings per month; of two corporals, each twenty-four shillings per month; of thirty-three centinels, each twenty-two shillings and sixpence per month; of one armourer, fourteen shillings per month, he being lieutenant; of one interpreter, thirty shillings per month; and to the chaplain there, twenty-five pounds per annum.

And be it further enacted,

Brunswick Fort. [SECT. 4.] That the wages of the commanding officer of the fort at Brunswick, from the twentieth day of May, one thousand seven hundred and forty-four, to the nineteenth day of November, one thousand seven hundred and forty-four, shall be at the rate of forty shillings per month; of eleven centinels, each twenty-two shillings and sixpence per month; one serjeant, at twenty-five shillings per month.

And be it further enacted,

Truck-house at Saco River. [SECT. 5.] That the wages of the captain of the truck-house at Saco, from the twentieth day of May, one thousand seven hundred and forty-four, to the nineteenth day of November, one thousand seven hundred and forty-four, shall be at the rate of forty shillings per month; of one lieutenant, twenty-six shillings per month; of one corporal, twenty-four shillings per month; of one serjeant, twenty-five shillings per month; of twenty centinels, each twenty-two shillings and sixpence per month; of one armourer, thirty shillings per month; of one interpreter, being captain, ten shillings per month.

And be it further enacted,

Frederick Fort. [SECT. 6.] That the wages of the commanding officer at Frederick Fort, from the twentieth day of May, one thousand seven hundred and forty-four, to the nineteenth day of November, one thousand seven hundred and forty-four, shall be at the rate of forty shillings per month; of twenty-one centinels, each twenty-two shillings and sixpence per month; and of the chaplain there, fifteen pounds per annum.

And be it further enacted,

Country's sloop. [SECT. 7.] That the wages of the captain of the sloop in the country's service, from the twentieth day of May, one thousand seven hundred and forty-four, to the nineteenth day of November, one thousand seven hundred and forty-four, shall be at the rate of fifty shillings per month; of the mate, thirty shillings per month; of eight sailors, each twenty-five shillings per month; for the sloop, seven pounds ten shillings per month.

And be it further enacted,

Province snow. [SECT. 8.] That the wages of the captain of the province snow, from the twentieth day of May, one thousand seven hundred and forty-four, to the twentieth day of November, one thousand seven hundred and forty-four, shall be at the rate of five pounds ten shillings per month; the lieutenant, three pounds twelve shillings per month; the master, three pounds two shillings per month; the doctor, three pounds two shillings per month; the chaplain, three pounds two shillings per month; the gunner, two pounds eighteen shillings per month; the boatswain, two pounds fifteen shillings per month; the mate, two pounds ten shillings per month; the steward, two pounds five shillings per month; the cook, two pounds five shillings per month; the gunner's mate, two pounds five shillings per month; the pilot, two pounds eighteen shillings per month; the boatswain's mate, two pounds five shillings per month; the carpenter, two pounds fifteen shillings per month; the cooper, two pounds five shillings per month; the armourer, two pounds five shillings per month; the coxswain, two pounds five shillings per month; two quartermasters, each two pounds five shillings per month; eighty sailors, or foremast men, each forty shillings per month.

And be it further enacted,

[Sect. 9.] That the wages of the captain of the brigantine, "Boston Packet," now in the service of the province, from the first day of July, one thousand seven hundred and forty-four, to the nineteenth day of November, one thousand seven hundred and forty-four, shall be at the rate of five pounds ten shillings per month; the lieutenant, three pounds twelve shillings per month; the master, three pounds two shillings per month; the doctor, three pounds two shillings per month; the gunner, two pounds eighteen shillings per month; the boatswain, two pounds fifteen shillings per month; the mate, two pounds ten shillings per month; the steward, two pounds five shillings per month; the cook, two pounds five shillings per month; the gunner's mate, two pounds five shillings per month; the pilot, two pounds eighteen shillings per month; the boatswain's mate, two pounds five shillings per month; the carpenter, two pounds fifteen shillings per month; the cooper, two pounds five shillings per month; the armourer, two pounds five shillings per month; the coxswain, two pounds five shillings per month; two quartermasters, each two pounds five shillings per month; and eighty sailors, or foremast men, forty shillings each per month. The "Boston Packet."

And be it further enacted,

[Sect. 10.] That the wages of the captain of the sloop, "Orphan Techao," now in the service of the province, from the eleventh day of June, one thousand seven hundred and forty-four, to the nineteenth day of November, one thousand seven hundred and forty-four, shall be at the rate of five pounds ten shillings per month; the lieutenant, three pounds twelve shillings per month; the master, three pounds two shillings per month; the doctor, three pounds two shillings per month; the gunner, two pounds eighteen shillings per month; the boatswain, two pounds fifteen shillings per month; the mate, two pounds ten shillings per month; the steward, two pounds five shillings per month; the cook, two pounds five shillings per month; the gunner's mate, two pounds five shillings per month; the pilot, two pounds eighteen shillings per month; the boatswain's mate, two pounds five shillings per month; the carpenter, two pounds fifteen shillings per month; the cooper, two pounds five shillings per month; the armourer, two pounds five shillings per month; the coxswain, two pounds five shillings per month; two quartermasters, each two pounds five shillings per month: eighty sailors, or foremast men, at forty shillings each per month. Sloop "Orphan Techao."

And be it further enacted,

[Sect. 11.] That before payment of any muster-roll be allowed, oath be made by the officer or person presenting such roll, that the officers and soldiers born on such roll have been in actual service for the whole time they stand entred thereon. [*Passed June 30; published July 5.* Oath to be made before muster-rolls be allowed.

CHAPTER 8.

AN ACT TO REMOVE THE TRIAL OF JEREMY JUDE, SO CALLED, FROM THE COUNTY OF NANTUCKET TO THE COUNTY OF BARNSTABLE.

Preamble.

WHEREAS one Jeremy Jude, so called, stands committed to his majesty's goal in Edgartown, in Dukes County, for murdering one Simon Aaron at Sherbourn, in the island and county of Nantucket, in the month of January last; *and whereas* the appointing a special court of assize, to be held by the justices of that court on said island, in this time of war and danger, may be very prejudicial to the interest of this government,—

Be it enacted by the Governour, Council and House of Representatives,

That the trial of the said Jeremy Jude for the offence aforesaid, or any other capital offence he may have been guilty of, be had at Barnstable, in the county of Barnstable, at the next court of assize to be held there in the month of July next; and the justices of said court are hereby impowred to issue out all processes necessary thereto; and that six grand jurors, and four petty jurors for the said trial, be of the inhabitants of Nantucket. [*Passed June* 30; *published July* 5.

CHAPTER 9.

AN ACT FOR APPORTIONING AND ASSESSING A TAX OF TWENTY-FIVE THOUSAND POUNDS, IN BILLS OF CREDIT; AND ALSO FOR APPORTIONING AND ASSESSING A FURTHER TAX OF EIGHTEEN HUNDRED AND SEVENTY-ONE POUNDS FOURTEEN SHILLINGS AND EIGHTPENCE, IN BILLS OF CREDIT, PAID THE REPRESENTATIVES FOR THEIR SERVICE AND ATTENDANCE IN GENERAL COURT, AND TRAVEL; AS ALSO THE SUM OF ONE HUNDRED AND THIRTY POUNDS, FINES LAID UPON SEVERAL TOWNS FOR NOT SENDING A REPRESENTATIVE.

1741-42, chap. 11, § 16. 1742-43, chap. 3, § 8. 1742-43, chap. 14, § 5. 1743-44, chap. 13, § 5. 1744-45, chap. 5, § 7. 1744-45, chap. 5, § 10.

WHEREAS the great and general court or assembly of the province of the Massachusetts Bay, did, at their session in May, one thousand seven hundred and forty-one, pass an act for the levying a tax of six thousand six hundred and sixty-six pounds thirteen shillings and fourpence, in bills emitted by said act; and, at their sessions in May, one thousand seven hundred and forty-two, did pass an act for the levying a tax of three thousand seven hundred and fifty pounds, in bills emitted by said act; and, at their session in November, one thousand seven hundred and forty-two, did pass an act for the levying a tax of three thousand five hundred pounds, in bills emitted by said act; and, at their sessions in May, one thousand seven hundred and forty-three, did pass an act for levying a tax of eight thousand and thirty-three pounds * six shillings and eightpence, in bills emitted by said act; and have this present session pass'd an act for the levving a tax of four thousand nine hundred sixty-six pounds thirteen shillings and fourpence, in bills emitted by said act; each of the several sums aforesaid to be assessed this present year,—amounting in the whole to twenty-six thousand nine hundred and sixteen pounds thirteen shillings and fourpence; and by the aforesaid acts, provision was made that the general court might, in the several years, apportion the several sums on the several towns in the province, if they thought fit: and the assembly aforesaid have likewise ordered that the sum of one hundred and thirty pounds, fines on

* This apparently an error, the amount of bills to be recalled being £8083, 6*s*. 8*d*.

several towns, and the sum of eighteen hundred seventy-one pounds fourteen shillings and eightpence, paid the representatives the last year, should be levyed and assessed, on this present year, on the polls and estates of the inhabitants of the several towns, according to what their respective representatives have received; *wherefore*, for the ordering, directing, and effectual drawing in the sum of twenty-five thousand pounds, pursuant to the funds and grants aforesaid, and drawing the said sum into the treasury, according to the appointment now agreed to by this court, which, with the sum of seventeen hundred eighty-six pounds thirteen shillings and fourpence, arising by the duties of impost, tunnage of shipping and excise, and the sum of one hundred and thirty pounds, fines laid on the several towns in and by this act mentioned, will make the sum of twenty-six thousand nine hundred and sixteen pounds thirteen shillings and fourpence, and also for drawing in the sum of eighteen hundred and seventy-one pounds fourteen shillings and eightpence, paid the representatives; all which is unanimously approved, ratified, and confirmed; we, his majesty's most loyal and dutiful subjects, the representatives in general court assembled, pray that it may be enacted,—

And be it accordingly enacted by the Governour, Council and House of Representatives,

[Sect. 1.] That each town and district within this province be assessed and pay, as such town's and district's proportion of the sum of twenty-five thousand pounds, in bills of credit, as also for the fines laid on them, and their representatives' pay, the several sums following; that is to say,—

IN THE COUNTY OF SUFFOLK.

	REPRESENTATIVES' PAY, AND FINES.			PROVINCE TAX.	SUM TOTAL.
Boston,	Sixty-two pounds eight shillings,	£62 8s. 0d.	Four thousand five hundred pounds,	£4,500 0s. 0d.	£4,562 8s. 0d.
Roxbury,	Fifteen pounds twelve shillings,	15 12 0	Two hundred thirty-two pounds fourteen shillings and twopence,	232 14 2	248 6 2
Dorchester,	Fifteen pounds twelve shillings,	15 12 0	Two hundred and twenty pounds ten shillings and fivepence,	220 10 5	236 2 5
Milton,	Eighteen pounds six shillings,	18 6 0	One hundred and one pounds nineteen shillings and sevenpence,	101 19 7	120 5 7
Brantrey,	Eighteen pounds three shillings,	18 3 0	Two hundred forty-three pounds fifteen shillings,	243 15 0	261 18 0
Weymouth,	Nineteen pounds eight shillings and sixpence,	19 8 6	One hundred forty-one pounds and tenpence,	141 0 10	160 9 4
Hingham,	Nineteen pounds nineteen shillings,	19 19 0	Two hundred sixty three pounds four shillings and sevenpence,	263 4 7	283 3 7
Dedham,	Nineteen pounds eight shillings and sixpence,	19 8 6	One hundred seventy-three pounds eight shillings and ninepence,	173 8 9	192 17 3
Medfield,	. . . .	0 0 0	One hundred and five pounds eighteen shillings and ninepence,	105 18 9	105 18 9
Wrentham,	Nineteen pounds nineteen shillings,	19 19 0	One hundred thirty two pounds seven shillings and elevenpence,	132 7 11	152 6 11
Medway,	Fine, twelve pounds ten shillings,	12 10 0	Sixty-nine pounds seventeen shillings and elevenpence,	69 17 11	82 7 11
Stoughton,	Nineteen pounds eight shillings and sixpence,	19 8 6	One hundred twenty-eight pounds four shillings and sevenpence,	128 4 7	147 13 1
Hull,	. . . .	0 0 0	Fifty-five pounds sixteen shillings and eightpence,	55 16 8	55 16 8
Brookline,	Fifteen pounds eleven shillings,	15 11 0	Eighty-three pounds four shillings and sevenpence,	83 4 7	98 15 7
Needham,	. . . .	0 0 0	Seventy-four pounds nine shillings and sevenpence,	74 9 7	74 9 7
Bellingham,	. . . .	0 0 0	Twenty-eight pounds and fivepence,	28 0 5	28 0 5
Walpole,	. . . .	0 0 0	Forty-three pounds eight shillings and ninepence,	43 8 9	43 8 9
Chelsea,	. . . .	0 0 0	One hundred and eight pounds nineteen shillings and twopence,	108 19 2	108 19 2
		£256 5s. 6d.		£6,707 1s. 8d.	

IN THE COUNTY OF ESSEX.

Salem,	Thirty-nine pounds eighteen shillings,	£39 18s. 0d.	Seven hundred and fifty pounds,	£750 0s. 0d.	£789 18s. 0d.
Ipswich,	Thirty-eight pounds five shillings,	38 5 0	Six hundred and ninety pounds ten shillings and five-pence,	690 10 5	728 15 5
Newbury,	Forty pounds four shillings,	40 4 0	Six hundred ard forty pounds six shillings and three-[illegible]pe,	640 6 3	680 10 3
Marblehead,	Seventeen pounds seventeen shillings,	17 17 0	Four hundred and eighty-six pounds thirteen shillings and fourpence,	486 13 4	504 10 4
Lynn,	Nineteen pounds eight shillings and six-pence,	19 8 6	Two [illegible]red and sixty-two pounds eighteen shillings and [illegible]pe,	262 18 4	282 6 10
Andover,	Twenty-one pounds,	21 0 0	Three hundred and two pounds one shilling and eight-pence,	302 1 8	323 1 8
Beverly,	Nineteen pounds four shillings,	19 4 0	One hundred and ninety-three pounds two shillings and [illegible]pe,	193 2 6	212 6 6
Rowley,	Twenty-one pounds,	21 0 0	One [illegible]d and eighty [illegible]ght pounds eight shillings and ninepence,	188 8 9	209 8 9
Salisbury,	Sixteen pounds thirteen shillings,	16 13 0	One hundred and sixty-six pounds thirteen shillings and fourpence,	166 13 4	183 6 4
Haverhill,	Seventeen pounds eleven shillings,	17 11 0	One hundred and sixty-nine pounds nine shillings and sevenpence,	169 9 7	187 0 7
Glocester,	Twenty-one pounds twelve shillings,	21 12 0	[illegible]ee hundred and thirteen pounds eight shillings and ninepence,	313 8 9	335 0 9
Topsfield,	Nineteen pounds one shilling,	19 1 0	Ninety-five pounds fourteen shillings and sevenpence,	95 14 7	114 15 7
Boxford,	Twenty-two pounds ten shillings,	22 10 0	One [illegible]red and twenty pounds two shillings and one penny,	120 2 1	142 12 1
[illegible]y,	Twenty-one pounds eighteen shillings,	21 18 0	One hundred and thirty-eight pounds [illegible]en shillings twop.,	138 19 2	160 17 2
Bradford,	Nineteen pounds,	19 0 0	One [illegible]red and four pounds thirteen shillings and [illegible]pence,	104 13 9	123 13 9
Wenham,	Twenty pounds and twopence,	20 0 2	Eighty-seven pounds seven shillings and elevenpence,	87 7 11	107 8 1
[illegible]r,	. . . .	0 0 0	Seventy-two pounds twelve shillings and one penny,	72 12 1	72 12 1
[illegible]en,	. . . .	0 0 0	Thirty-eight pounds ten shillings and ten [illegible]pence,	38 10 10	38 10 10
[illegible]n,	Six pounds sixteen shillings and sixpence,	6 16 6	Sev[illegible]ty-four pounds thirteen shillings and [illegible]pe,	74 13 9	81 10 3
Rumford,	. . . .	0 0 0	. . . .	0 0 0	0 0 0
		£381 18s. 2d.		£4,896 7s. 1d.	

IN THE COUNTY OF MIDDLESEX.

	REPRESENTATIVES' PAY, AND FINES.			PROVINCE TAX.	SUM TOTAL.
Cambridge,	Fifteen pounds twelve shillings,	£15 12s. 0d.	One hundred and sixty-five pounds,	£165 0s. 0d.	£180 12s. 0d.
Charlestown,	Thirty pounds eighteen shillings,	30 18 0	Three hundred and thirty-seven pounds eighteen shillings and fourp.,	337 18 4	368 16 4
Watertown,	Eighteen pounds eighteen shillings,	18 18 0	One hundred and three pounds four shillings and sevenpence,	103 4 7	122 2 7
Concord,	Eighteen pounds one shilling,	18 1 0	Two hundred and six pounds two shillings and elevenpence,	206 2 11	224 3 11
Weston,	Nineteen pounds nineteen shillings,	19 19 0	Ninety-seven pounds one shilling and eightpence,	97 1 8	117 0 8
Woburn,	Eighteen pounds eighteen shillings,	18 18 0	One hundred and sixty pounds eighteen shillings and ninepence,	160 18 9	179 16 9
Reading,	Eighteen pounds,	18 0 0	One hundred and seventy-six pounds thirteen shillings and fourp.,	176 13 4	194 13 4
Sudbury,	Nineteen pounds ten shillings,	19 10 0	One hundred and eighty-three pounds fifteen shillings,	183 15 0	203 5 0
Marlborough,	Twenty-one pounds,	21 0 0	One hundred and eighty-nine pounds thirteen shillings and ninep.,	189 13 9	210 13 9
Lexington,	Seventeen pounds seventeen shillings,	17 17 0	One hundred and fourteen pounds one shilling and threepence,	114 1 3	131 18 3
Newton,	Eighteen pounds eighteen shillings,	18 18 0	One hundred and seventy-seven pounds fourteen shillings,	177 14 0	196 12 0
Malden,	Fifteen pounds twelve shillings,	15 12 0	One hundred and forty-seven pounds eighteen shillings and fourp.,	147 18 4	163 10 4
Chelmsford,	Twenty pounds five shillings,	20 5 0	One hundred and two pounds one shilling and eightpence,	102 1 8	122 6 8
Billerica,	Sixteen pounds sixteen shillings,	16 16 0	One hundred and five pounds six shillings and threepence,	105 6 3	122 2 3
Sherburn,	{ Eighteen pounds nineteen shillings and sixpence,	18 19 6	} Sixty-six pounds seven shillings and a penny,	66 7 1	97 16 7
	{ Twelve pounds ten shillings, fine,	12 10 0	}		
Holliston,		0 0 0	Forty-seven pounds five shillings and tenpence,	47 5 10	47 5 10
Groton,	Twenty pounds fourteen shillings,	20 14 0	One hundred and sixty-two pounds twelve shillings and one penny,	162 12 1	183 6 1
Framingham,	Eighteen pounds three shillings,	18 3 0	One hundred and thirty-four pounds nine shillings and sevenpence,	134 9 7	152 12 7
Medford,	Fifteen pounds twelve shillings,	15 12 0	Seventy-nine pounds nine shillings and sevenpence,	79 9 7	95 1 7
Stow,	Twenty pounds eight shillings,	20 8 0	Sixty-two pounds one shilling and eightpence,	62 1 8	82 9 8
Dunstable and Nottingham,		0 0 0	Thirty-seven pounds ten shillings,	37 10 0	37 10 0
Dracut,		0 0 0	Forty-one pounds nine shillings and twopence,	41 9 2	41 9 2
Stoneham,		0 0 0	Fifty-three pounds four shillings and sevenpence,	53 4 7	53 4 7

Littleton,	Eighteen pounds six shillings,	£18 6s. 0d.	Seventy-four pounds seventeen shillings and elevenpence,	£74 17s. 11d.	£93 3s. 11d.
Hopkinton,	Twenty pounds two shillings,	20 2 5	Fifty-two pounds one shilling and eightpence,	52 1 8	72 3 8
Bedford,	. . . .	0 0 0	Forty-nine pounds three shillings and fourpence,	49 3 4	49 3 4
Westford,	Eighteen pounds eighteen shillings,	18 18 0	Sixty-seven pounds one, and eightpence,	67 1 8	85 19 8
Wilmington,	. . . .	0 0 0	Forty-seven pounds sixteen shillings and threepence,	47 16 3	47 16 3
Tewksbury,	. . . .	0 0 0	Forty-four pounds one shilling and threepence,	44 1 3	44 1 3
[illegible]n,	. . . .	0 0 0	Thirty-three pounds eight shillings and ninepence,	33 8 9	33 8 9
Waltham,	Eighteen pounds eighteen shillings,	18 18 0	Ninety-one pounds eleven shillings and fivepence,	91 11 5	110 9 5
[illegible]d,	. . . .	0 0 0	Eighteen pounds fifteen shillings one penny,	18 15 1	18 15 1
English Inhabitants of Natick,	. . . .	0 0 0	Twenty-five pounds,	25 0 0	25 0 0
		£452 14s. 6d.		£3,455 16s. 9d.	

IN THE COUNTY OF HAMPSHIRE.

Springfield,	Twenty-one pounds nine shillings,	£21 9s. 0d.	[illegible]o hundred seventy-three p[illegible]s [illegible]teen shillings and twop.,	£273 19s. 2d.	£295 8s. 2d.
Northampton,	Twelve pounds four shillings,	12 4 0	One hundred and eighty p[illegible]s two shillings and one p[illegible]y,	180 2 1	192 6 1
Hadley,	Twelve pounds four shillings,	12 4 0	One hundred and twenty-eight pounds [illegible]teen shillings and one pen.,	128 17 1	141 1 1
Hatfield,	Eleven pounds eight shillings,	11 8 0	Eighty-two pounds [illegible]teen shillings and [illegible]ce,	82 14 2	94 2 2
Westfield,	Seventeen pounds eight shillings,	17 8 0	One hundred and five p[illegible]ds fourteen shillings and [illegible]pe,	105 14 7	123 2 7
Suffield,	Sixteen pounds four shillings,	16 4 0	One hundred thirty [illegible]en pounds twelve shillings and one p[illegible]y,	137 12 1	153 16 1
Enfield,	Seventeen pounds five shillings, and twelve pounds ten shillings fine,	29 15 0	Eighty-one pounds thirteen shillings and fourpence,	81 13 4	111 8 4
Deerfield,	Eleven pounds seventeen shillings,	11 17 0	Eighty-three pounds eight shillings and ninepence,	83 8 9	95 5 9
Sunderland,	. . . .	0 0 0	Forty-two pounds ten shillings,	42 10 0	42 10 0
Northfield,	. . . .	0 0 0	Thirty-seven * five shillings and tenpence,	37 5 10	37 5 10
Brimfield,	. . . .	0 0 0	Seventy-three pounds four shillings and sevenpence,	73 4 7	73 4 7
Somers,	. . . .	0 0 0	Forty-four pounds seventeen shillings and elevenpence,	44 17 11	44 17 11
Sheffield,	. . . .	0 0 0	Forty-three pounds fifteen shillings,	43 15 0	43 15 0
Elbows,	. . . .	0 0 0	Twenty-five pounds,	25 0 0	25 0 0
		£132 9s. 0d.		£1,340 14s. 7d.	

* Sic.

IN THE COUNTY OF WORCESTER.

	REPRESENTATIVES' PAY, AND FINES.			PROVINCE TAX.	SUM TOTAL.
[illegible]r,	Nineteen pounds nineteen shillings,	£19 19s. 0d.	[illegible]-five [illegible] ten shillings and [illegible],	£85 10s. 5d.	£105 9s. 5d.
Lancaster,	Twenty pounds two shillings,	20 2 0	One [illegible] forty-one pounds thirteen shillings and [illegible],	141 13 4	161 15 4
[illegible]n,	Twenty pounds five shillings,	20 5 0	One hundred forty-five pounds ten shillings and fourpence,	145 10 4	165 15 4
Woodstock,	Seven pounds ten shillings,	7 10 0	One hundred twenty-eight pounds [illegible] shillings and [illegible].,	128 12 11	136 2 11
Brookfield,	Twenty-two pounds sixteen shillings,	22 16 0	Eighty-six pounds nineteen shillings and [illegible],	86 19 7	109 15 7
Southborough,	Twenty-one pounds,	21 0 0	Fifty-six pounds nine shillings and twopence,	56 9 2	77 9 2
Leicester,	Fine, twelve pounds ten shillings,	12 10 0	[illegible]-nine pounds eleven shillings and eightpence,	79 11 8	92 1 8
Rutland,	. . . .	0 0 0	Fifty-one pounds eleven shillings and [illegible],	51 11 3	51 11 3
Lunenburg,	. . . .	0 0 0	Sixty-three [illegible] fifteen shillings,	63 15 0	63 15 0
Westborough,	Twenty-two pounds one shilling,	22 1 0	Eighty- [illegible] [illegible] ten shillings and [illegible],	88 10 10	110 11 10
Shrewsbury,	Nineteen pounds four shillings,	19 4 0	[illegible]- [illegible] [illegible] six shillings and eightpence,	78 6 8	97 10 8
Oxford,	Thirteen pounds four shillings,	13 4 0	Fifty-nine pounds seventeen shillings and elevenpence,	59 17 11	73 1 11
Sutton,	Twelve pounds three shillings,	12 3 0	[illegible]-four [illegible] eleven shillings and [illegible],	94 11 8	106 14 8
Uxbridge,	. . . .	0 0 0	Sixty- [illegible] pounds seven shillings and elevenpence,	67 7 11	67 7 11
Harvard,	. . . .	0 0 0	Fifty-seven [illegible] fourteen shillings and twopence,	57 14 2	57 14 2
Grafton,	. . . .	0 0 0	Forty-eight pounds [illegible] shillings and [illegible],	48 19 2	48 19 2
Upton,	. . . .	0 0 0	Nineteen [illegible] [illegible] shillings and elevenpence,	19 17 11	19 17 11
[illegible]y,	. . . .	0 0 0	Forty-two pounds one shilling and eightpence,	42 1 8	42 1 8
Bon,	. . . .	0 0 0	Fifty-six pounds two shillings and elevenpence,	56 2 11	56 2 11
Sturbridge,	. . . .	0 0 0	Twenty-one pounds five shillings,	21 5 0	21 5 0
Leominster,	. . . .	0 0 0	Seventeen pounds ten shillings,	17 10 0	17 10 0
Western,	. . . .	0 0 0	Sixteen [illegible] eleven shillings and [illegible],	16 11 3	16 11 3
		£190 14s. 0d.		£1,508 10s. 9d.	

IN THE COUNTY OF PLYMOUTH.

Plymouth,	Seventeen pounds eight shillings,	£17 8s. 0d.	Two hundred thirty-four pounds five shillings and fivepence,	£234 5s. 5d.	£251 13s. 5d.
Plimpton,	Seventeen pounds seventeen shillings,	17 17 0	One hundred twenty-four pounds five shillings and fivepence,	124 5 5	142 2 5
Scituate,	Twenty-one pounds,	21 0 0	Three hundred fifty-nine pounds nine shillings and sevenpence,	359 9 7	389 9 7

Bridgwater,	Twenty-one pounds,	£21 0s. 0d.	Two hundred eighty-five pounds two shillings and one penny,	£285 2s. 1d.	£306 2s. 1d.
Marshfield,	Twenty-one pounds eleven shillings and six-pence,	21 11 6	One hundred seventy-seven [illegible] ten shillings,	177 10 0	199 1 6
Pembroke,	. . . .	0 0 0	Ninety-five pounds eight shillings and [illegible],	95 8 4	95 8 4
Duxbury,	Twenty-one pounds nine shillings,	21 9 0	Eighty-three pounds ten shillings and [illegible],	83 10 10	104 19 10
Middleborough,	Six pounds eighteen shillings,	6 18 0	[illegible]o hundred and ten pounds ten shillings and [illegible]-pence,	210 10 5	217 8 5
Rochester,	Fifteen pounds six shillings,	15 6 0	One hundred thirty-four pounds three shillings and fourpence,	134 3 4	149 9 4
Abbington,	. . . .	0 0 0	Fifty-nine [illegible] [illegible]en shillings and elevenpence,	59 17 4*	59 17 11
Kingston,	. . . .	0 0 0	Sixty-five pounds ten shillings and fivepence,	65 10 5	65 10 5
Hanover,	. . . .	0 0 0	Seventy-seven [illegible] three shillings and ninepence,	77 3 9	77 3 9
Hallifax,	. . . .	0 0 0	Fifty pounds,	50 0 0	50 0 0
Warham,	. . . .	0 0 0	Twenty-five pounds,	25 0 0	25 0 0
		£142 9s. 6d.		£1,981 17s. 6d.	

IN THE COUNTY OF BARNSTABLE.

Barnstable,	Seventeen pounds two shillings,	£17 2s. 0d.	[illegible]o [illegible] fifty pounds eighteen shillings [illegible] nine-pence,	£250 18s. 9d.	£268 0s. 9d.
[illegible]th,	Sixteen pounds nineteen shillings, Twelve pounds ten shillings fine,	16 19 0 12 10 0	One [illegible] fifty-four [illegible] fifteen shillings and ten-[illegible],	154 15 10	184 4 10
Sandwich,	Twelve pounds six shillings,	12 6 0	One hundred thirty-five [illegible] four shillings and [illegible],	135 4 2	147 10 2
Eastham,	Nineteen pounds four shillings,	19 4 0	One hundred eighty-six [illegible] thirteen shillings [illegible] fourpen.,	186 13 4	205 17 4
Truro,	. . . .	0 0 0	Twenty-four pounds nine shillings and [illegible],	24 9 7	24 9 7
Harwich,	Nine pounds three shillings,	9 3 0	One hundred [illegible] [illegible] seven shillings and [illegible],	129 7 6	138 10 6
Falmouth,	Twelve pounds ten shillings fine,	12 10 0	Ninety-one [illegible] thirteen shillings and [illegible],	91 13 4	104 3 4
th[illegible]m,	. . . .	0 0 0	Seventy-six [illegible] two shillings and elevenpence,	76 2 11	76 2 11
Provincetown,	. . . .	0 0 0	. . . .	0 0 0	0 0 0
		£99 14s. 0d.		£1,049 5s. 5d.	

* Sic.

IN THE COUNTY OF BRISTOL.

	REPRESENTATIVES' PAY, AND FINES.			PROVINCE TAX.	SUM TOTAL.
Bristol,	Twenty pounds eleven shillings,	£20 11s. 0d.	[illegible] hundred sixty-four [illegible] eleven shillings and eightpence,	£164 11s. 8d.	£185 2s. 8d.
[illegible],	Twenty-one pounds,	21 0 0	[illegible] hundred fifty [illegible] four shillings and [illegible]pence,	250 4 2	271 4 2
Norton,	Sixteen pounds seven shillings,	16 7 0	[illegible] hundred twenty-five pounds twelve shillings and [illegible],	125 12 6	141 19 6
[illegible],	. . . .	0 0 0	Forty-nine [illegible] [illegible] [illegible] [illegible] fourpence,	49 3 4	49 3 4
Dartmouth,	Fifteen pounds twelve shillings,	15 12 0	Three hundred eighty-[illegible] [illegible] twelve shillings [illegible] [illegible] pen.,	387 12 1	403 4 1
Dighton,	Seven pounds thirteen shillings,	7 13 0	Eighty-eight [illegible] [illegible] shillings [illegible] [illegible],	88 8 9	96 1 9
[illegible],	Twenty pounds seventeen shillings,	20 17 0	Three hundred [illegible] eight [illegible] [illegible] shillings and one [illegible],	308 17 1	329 14 1
[illegible] [illegible],	Fifteen pounds nine shillings,	15 9 0	[illegible] [illegible] [illegible]-[illegible] pounds one shilling and eightpence,	177 1 8	192 10 8
Swansey with Shawamet,	Twenty-three pounds thirteen shillings, Twenty pounds fine,	23 13 0 / 20 0 0	[illegible] [illegible] [illegible] six [illegible] [illegible] eightpence,	248 6 8	291 19 8
Tiverton,	Twenty pounds fine,	20 0 0	[illegible] [illegible] pounds,	200 0 0	220 0 0
Freetown,	Fifteen pounds fine,	15 0 0	Eighty-two [illegible] three shillings and [illegible],	82 3 9	97 3 9
[illegible],	Nineteen pounds four shillings,	19 4 0	One hundred twenty-five [illegible] [illegible] [illegible] and [illegible],	125 12 6	144 16 6
Barrington,	. . . .	0 0 0	[illegible] [illegible] [illegible] fifteen [illegible] and [illegible],	71 15 5	71 15 5
Raynham,	. . . .	0 0 0	Fifty-six [illegible] [illegible] shillings [illegible] [illegible],	56 19 7	56 19 7
Berkley,	. . . .	0 0 0	[illegible] [illegible] [illegible] [illegible] [illegible] [illegible] penny,	53 17 1	53 17 1
		£215 6s. 0d.		£2,390 6s. 3d.	

IN THE COUNTY OF YORK.

York,	Seventeen pounds five shillings,	£17 5s. 0d.	Two hundred twenty-eight pounds seventeen shillings and one p.,	£228 17s. 1d.	£246 2s. 1d.
Kittery,	Eighteen pounds six shillings,	18 6 0	Three hundred and fifteen pounds two shillings and one penny,	315 2 1	333 8 1
Berwick,	Nineteen pounds seven shillings,	19 7 0	One hundred thirty-three pounds seventeen shillings and one pen.,	133 17 1	153 4 1
Wells,	Twenty-five pounds four shillings,	25 4 0	One hundred and ten pounds six shillings and threepence,	110 6 3	135 10 3
Falmouth,	Fourteen pounds eight shillings,	14 8 0	One hundred ninety-two pounds five shillings and tenpence,	192 5 10	206 13 10

Biddeford,	. . . .	£0 0s. 0d.	Seventy-five pounds eighteen shillings and ninepence,	£75 18s. 9d.	£75 18s. 9d.
Arundel,	. . . .	0 0 0	Forty-nine pounds nine shillings and sevenpence,	49 9 7	49 9 7
Scarborough,	. . . .	0 0 0	Ninety-nine pounds seventeen shillings and elevenpence,	99 17 11	99 17 11
North Yarmouth,	Twenty-three pounds eleven shillings,	23 11 0	Forty-two pounds ten shillings,	42 10 0	66 1 0
Georgetown,	. . . .	0 0 0	Fifty pounds,	50 0 0	50 0 0
Brunswick,	Five pounds eight shillings,	5 8 0	Sixteen pounds seventeen shillings and sixpence,	16 17 6	22 5 6
		£123 9s. 0d.		£1,315 2s. 1d.	

IN THE COUNTY OF DUKES COUNTY.

Edgartown,	. . . .	£0 0s. 0d.	Sixty-two pounds five shillings and tenpence,	£62 5s. 10d.	£62 5s. 10d.
Chilmark,	. . . .	0 0 0	Seventy-eight pounds nineteen shillings and twopence,	78 19 2	78 19 2
Tisbury,	. . . .	0 0 0	Forty-eight pounds seventeen shillings and one penny,	48 17 1	48 17 1
		£0 0s. 0d.		£190 2s. 1d.	

IN NANTUCKET COUNTY.

Sherburne,	Six pounds fifteen shillings,	£6 15s. 0d.	One hundred sixty-four pounds fifteen shillings and tenpence,	£164 15s. 10d.	£171 10s. 10d.

	REPRESENTATIVES' PAY, AND FINES.	PROVINCE TAX.	SUM TOTAL.
Suffolk, ...	£256 5*s.* 6*d.*	£6,707 1*s.* 8*d.*	£6,963 7*s.* 2*d.*
Essex, ...	381 18 2	4,896 7 1	5,278 5 3
Middlesex, ...	452 14 6	3,455 16 9	3,908 11 3
Hampshire, ...	132 9 0	1,340 14 7	1,473 3 7
Worcester, ...	190 14 0	1,508 10 9	1,699 4 9
Plymouth, ...	142 9 6	1,981 17 6	2,124 7 0
Bristol, ...	215 6 0	2,390 6 3	2,605 12 3
Barnstable, ...	99 14 0	1,049 5 5	1,148 19 5
York, ...	123 9 0	1,315 2 1	1,438 11 1
Dukes County, ...	0 0 0	190 2 1	190 2 1
Nantucket, ...	6 15 0	164 15 10	171 10 10
	£2,001 14*s.* 8*d.*	£25,000 0*s.* 0*d.*	£27,001 14*s.* 8*d.*

And be it further enacted,

[SECT. 2.] That the treasurer do forthwith send out his warrants, directed to the selectmen or assessors of each town or district within this province, requiring them, respectively, to assess the sum hereby set upon such town or district, in manner following; that is to say, to assess all rateable male polls above the age of sixteen years, at five shillings and threepence per poll, and proportionably in assessing the fines mentioned in this act, and the additional sum received out of the treasury for the payment of the representatives (except the governour, lieutenant-governour and their families, the president, fellows and students of Harvard College, setled ministers and grammar school-masters, who are hereby exempted as well from being taxed for their polls, as for their estates being in their own hands and under their actual management and improvement); and other persons, if such there be, who, thro' age, infirmity or extream poverty, in the judgment of the assessors, are not capable to pay towards publick charges, they may exempt their polls, and so much of their estates as in their prudence they shall think fit and judge meet.

[SECT. 3.] And the justices in the general sessions, in the respective counties assembled, in granting a county tax or assessment, are hereby ordered and directed to apportion the same on the several towns in such county in proportion to their province rate, exclusive of what has been paid out of the publick treasury to the representative of such town for his service; and the assessors of each town in the province are also directed, in making an assessment, to govern themselves by the same rule; and all estates, both real and personal, lying within the limits of such town or district, or next unto the same, not paying elsewhere, in whose hands, tenure, occupation or possession soever the same is or shall be found, and also the incomes or profits which any person or persons, except as before excepted, do or shall receive from any trade, faculty, business or employment whatsoever, and all profits that shall or may arise by money or other estate not particularly otherwise assessed, or commissions of profit in their improvement, according to their understanding and cunning, at one penny on the pound; and to abate or multiply the same, if need be, so as to make up the sum set and ordered hereby for such town or district to pay; and, in making their assessments, to estimate houses and lands at six years' income of the yearly rents, in the bills last emitted, whereat the same may be reasonably set or let for in the place where they lye: *saving* all contracts between landlord and tenant, and where no contract is, the landlord to reimburse one-half of the tax set upon such houses and lands; and to estimate Indian, negro and molatto servants proportionably as other personal estate, according to their sound judgment and discretion: as also to estimate every ox of four years old and upwards, at forty shillings in bills of the last emission; every cow of three years old and upwards, at thirty shillings; every horse and mare of three years old and upwards, at forty shillings; every swine of one year old and upwards, at eight shillings; every goat and sheep of one year old and upwards, at three shillings: likewise requiring the assessors to make a fair list of the said assessment, setting forth, in distinct columns, against each particular person's name, how much he or she is assessed at for polls, and how much for houses and lands, and how much for personal estate, and income by trade or faculty; and the list or lists, so perfected and signed by them, or the major part of them, to commit to the collectors, constable or constables of such town or district, and to return a certificate of the name or names of such collectors, constable or constables, together with the sum total to each of them committed, unto himself, some time before the last day of October.

[Sect. 4.] And the treasurer for the time being, upon the receipt of such certificate, is hereby impowered and ordered to issue forth his warrants to the collector, constable or constables of such town or district, requiring him or them, respectively, to collect the whole of each respective sum assessed on each particular person, before the last day of May next; and of the inhabitants of the town of Boston, some time in the month of March next; and to pay in their collection, and issue the accompts of the whole, at or before the last day of June, which will be in the year of our Lord one thousand seven hundred and forty-five.

And be it further enacted,

[Sect. 5.] That the assessors of each town and district, respectively, in convenient time before their making the assessment, shall give seasonable warning to the inhabitants, in a town meeting, or by posting up notifications in some place or places in such town or district, or notify the inhabitants to give or bring in to the assessors true and perfect lists of their polls, and rateable estate, and income by trade or faculty, and gain by money at interest; and if any person or persons shall neglect or refuse so to do, or bring in a false list, it shall be lawful to and for the assessors to assess such person or persons, according to their known ability in such town, in their sound judgment and discretion, their due proportion to this tax, as near as they can, agreeable to the rules herein given, under the penalty of twenty shillings for each person that shall be convicted by legal proof, in the judgment of the said assessors, of bringing in a false list; the said fines to be for the use of the poor of such town or district where the delinquent lives, to be levied by warrant from the assessors, directed to the collector or constables, in manner as is directed for gathering town assessments, and to be paid in to the town treasurer or selectmen for the use aforesaid: *saving* to the party aggrieved at the judgment of the assessors in setting forth such fine, liberty of appeal therefrom to the court of general sessions of the peace within the county, for relief, as in case of being overrated. And if any person or persons shall not bring in a list of their estate as aforesaid to the assessors, he or they so neglecting shall not be admitted to make application to the court of sessions for any abatement of the assessment laid on him.

[Sect. 6.] And if the party be not convicted of any falseness in the list, by him presented, of polls, rateable estate, or income by any trade or faculty, business or employment, which he doth or shall exercise, or in gain by money at interest or otherwise, or other estate not particularly assess'd, such list shall be a rule for such person's proportion to the tax, which the assessors may not exceed.

And whereas there are number of English inhabitants in the plantation of Natick, in the county of Middlesex, who have not been heretofore assessed towards the payment of the province tax,—

Be it therefore enacted,

The assessors of Sherburn to assess £25 upon the English inhabitants of Natick.

[SECT. 7.] That the sum of twenty-five pounds, part of the said sum of twenty-five thousand pounds, be assessed upon the said inhabitants, and the assessors of the town of Sherbourn are hereby impowered and required to make the said assessment upon them, after giving seasonable warning to the inhabitants of said plantation, in some one method prescribed in this act, and to follow the other directions herein; and the said inhabitants are hereby also required to conform to the rules prescribed by this act, and subjected to the penalties of it: *saving* to them liberty of appeal, as to other inhabitants of the province; and the constables or collectors of the town of Sherbourn are hereby enjoyned to levy or collect all such sums committed to them and assessed upon the said inhabitants, and pay the same into the province treasury.

How to be collected and paid.

And forasmuch as ofttimes sundry persons, not belonging to this province, bring considerable trade and merchandize, and by reason that the tax or rate of the town where they come to trade and traffick is finished and delivered to the constable or collector, and, before the next year's assessment, are gone out of the province, and so pay nothing towards the support of the government, tho', in the time of their residing there, they reap'd considerable gain by trade, and had the protection of the government,—

Be it further enacted,

Transient traders to be rated.

[SECT. 8.] That when any such person or persons shall come and reside in any town of this province, and bring any merchandize, and trade and deal therewith, the assessors of such town are hereby impowered to rate and assess all such persons according to their circumstances, pursuant to the rules and directions in this act provided, tho' the former rate may have been finished, and the new one not perfected, as aforesaid.

And be it further enacted,

[SECT. 9.] That when any merchant, trader or factor, inhabitant of some one town within this province, shall transact or carry on trade and business in some other town in the province, the assessors of such town where such trade and business shall be carried on as aforesaid, be and hereby are impowered to rate and assess all such merchants, traders and factors, their goods and merchandize, for carrying on such trade, and exercising their faculty in such town, pursuant to the rules and directions of this act.

[SECT. 10.] And the constables or collectors are hereby enjoyned to levy and collect all such sums committed to them, and assess'd on persons who are not of this province, or are inhabitants of any other town as aforesaid, and pay the same into the town treasury.

And be it further enacted,

Tax may be paid in other species besides the bills emitted.

[SECT. 11.] That the inhabitants of this province shall have liberty, if they see fit, to pay the several sums for which they may respectively be assess'd at, as their proportion of the aforesaid sum of twenty-five thousand pounds, one-fifth part thereof, and no more, in bills of the last emission, or the whole in bills of credit emitted in the years one thousand seven hundred and forty-one, one thousand seven hundred and forty-two, and one thousand seven hundred and forty-three, or in coined silver, at the rate of six shillings and eightpence per ounce, troy weight; or in gold coin, at the rate of four pounds eighteen shillings per ounce; or in bills of credit of the middle tenor, so called, according to their denominations; or in bills of the old tenor, accounting four for one; or in good merchantable hemp, at fourpence per pound; or merchantable flax, at fivepence per pound; or in good, merchantable,

Isle-of-Sable codfish, at ten shillings per quintal; or in good refined bar-iron, at fifteen pounds per ton; or bloomery-iron, at twelve pounds per ton; or in good, hollow iron-ware, at twelve pounds per ton; or in good Indian corn, at two shillings and threepence per bushel; or good winter rye, at two shillings and sixpence per bushel; or good winter wheat, at three shillings per bushel; or in good barley, at two shillings per bushel; or in good barrel pork, at two pounds per barrel; or in barrel beef, at one pound five shillings per barrel; or in duck or canvas, at two pounds ten shillings per bolt, each bolt to weigh forty-three pounds; or in long whalebone, at two shillings and threepence per pound; or merchantable cordage, at one pound five shillings per hundred; or in good train-oyl, at one pound ten shillings per barrel; or in good beeswax, at tenpence per pound; or in bayberry-wax, at sixpence per pound; or in tryed tallow, at fourpence per pound; or in good pease, at three shillings per bushel; or in good sheepswool, at ninepence per pound; or in good, tann'd sole-leather, at fourpence per pound: all which aforesaid commodities shall be of the produce of this province, and, as soon as conveniently may be, disposed of by the treasurer to the best advantage, for so much as they will fetch in bills of credit, or for silver and gold; and the several persons who pay their taxes in any of the commodities before mentioned, shall run the risque and pay the charge of transporting the same to the province treasury.

[Sect. 12.] And if any loss shall happen by the sale of any of the aforesaid species, it shall be made good by a tax of the next year; and if there be a surplusage, it shall remain a stock in the treasury. [*Passed June* 30.

ACTS,

PASSED AT THE SESSION BEGUN AND HELD AT BOSTON, ON THE NINTH DAY OF AUGUST, A. D. 1744.

CHAPTER 10.

AN ACT FOR ENLISTING INTO HIS MAJESTY'S SERVICE A NUMBER OF THE INHABITANTS OF THE TOWNS OF WEYMOUTH AND CHARLESTOWN, SO AS TO MAKE TWO INDEPENDENT COMPANIES OF SIXTY MEN EACH, EXCLUSIVE OF OFFICERS, FOR THE DEFENCE OF CASTLE WILLIAM, AS OCCASION SHALL REQUIRE.

Preamble.

WHEREAS the safety of this province in a great measure depends on the strength of his majesty's Castle William, and it being necessary that a sufficient number of men skilful in the management of the great artillery, should be always ready there,—

Be it therefore enacted by the Governour, Council and House of Representatives,

Two companies for Castle William to be taken out of the towns of Weymouth and Charlestown.

[SECT. 1.] That such of the inhabitants of the said towns of Weymouth and Charlestown, who are by law subject to common musters and military exercises there, not exceeding fifty years of age, as are willing to be enlisted into the service aforesaid, shall be enlisted, not exceeding the number of one hundred and twenty in the whole, under such officers as the captain-general shall commissionate, who shall repair to Castle William eight days in each year, in such months as the captain-general shall order, and shall on the said days be, by the gunner and quarter-gunners, exercised in the mounting, dismounting, levelling, traversing and firing the great guns, and shall be obliged hereunto, and the observance of such orders as shall be given them in this exercise, under the like pains and penalties that soldiers are under to obey their officers in said castle in time of service.

And be it further enacted,

Fine for non-attendance.

[SECT. 2.] That if any of the men enlisted as aforesaid shall neglect, absent, or refuse to attend at time and place for the exercise of the great artillery as aforesaid, being thereof notified and warned to appear, for every such day's neglect such soldier shall pay to the clerk of the company, for the use thereof, the sum of five shillings.

And be it further enacted,

Subsistence to be allowed during attendance.

[SECT. 3.] That such officers and soldiers be allowed subsistence, as the officers and soldiers have, during their service at said castle.

And for the encouragement of the said men enlisted and exercised as aforesaid, and that they may be expert in the management of the great artillery,—

Be it further enacted,

[SECT. 4.] That all and every man shall be excused from all other military service, and from all impresses into other service that other soldiers by law are liable to. Soldiers to be exempt from other duties.

And be it further enacted,

[SECT. 5.] That upon any alarm at Castle William, all the men enlisted by virtue of this act shall forthwith appear compleat with their arms and ammunition according to law, at the said Castle William, there to attend and follow such commands as shall be given for his majesty's service, and that on the penalty of paying five pounds each man, for non-attendance as aforesaid, to the clerk of the said company for the use thereof; the said fines to be recovered before any justice of the peace or court proper to hear and try the same. Penalty for not appearing at alarms.

[SECT. 6.] This act to continue and be in force until January seventeenth, one thousand seven hundred and forty-five, and no longer. Limitation.

[*Passed and published August* 18.

CHAPTER 11.

AN ACT FOR PUNISHING OF OFFICERS OR SOLDIERS WHO SHALL MUTINY, OR DESERT HIS MAJESTY'S SERVICE.

WHEREAS the raising and levying of forces is necessary in time of actual war, or common danger by insurrection or rebellion, for the safety and defence of this province, and of his majesty's subjects and interests therein, and in the neighbouring provinces or colonies; *and whereas* no man may be forejudged of life or limb, or subjected to any kind of punishment by martial law, or in any other manner than by the judgment of his peers, and according to the known and established laws of the province; yet, nevertheless, it being requisite for retaining such forces as shall be raised for his majesty's service, on occasion as before mentioned, in their duty, that an exact discipline be observed, and that soldiers who shall mutiny or stir up sedition, or shall desert his majesty's service, be brought to a more exemplary and speedy punishment than the usual forms of law will allow,— Preamble.

Be it therefore enacted by the Governour, Council and House of Representatives,

[SECT. 1.] That every person that shall be in his majesty's service, being mustered and in pay as an officer or soldier, who shall at any time during the continuance of this act, excite, cause or join in any mutiny or sedition in the army, company, fortress or garrison whereto such officer or soldier belongs, or shall desert his majesty's service in the army, company, fortress or garrison, shall suffer death or such other punishment as by a court-martial shall be inflicted. Punishment for mutiny and desertion.

And be it further enacted,

[SECT. 2.] That the captain-general or commander-in-chief of this province, for the time being, may, by virtue of this act, and during the continuance thereof, have full power and authority, by and with the advice and consent of the council, to grant commission to any colonel or other field-officer in his majesty's service and under pay, from time to time, to call and assemble courts-martial for punishing such offences as aforesaid. Courts-martial to be called.

And be it further enacted,

[SECT. 3.] That no court-martial, which shall have power to inflict any punishment, by virtue of this act, for any of the offences aforesaid, Constitution of the said court.

shall consist of fewer than eleven, whereof none to be under the degree of a commission-officer, and the president of such court-martial not to be under the degree of a field-officer, or the then commander-in-chief of the forces under pay, where the offender is to be tried; and that such court-martial shall have power and authority to summon evidences, and to administer an oath to any witness, in order to the examination or trial of the offences aforesaid.

And be it further enacted,

Method of the court's proceedings.

[SECT. 4.] That in all trials of offenders by courts-martial, to be held by virtue of this act, where the offence may be punished by death, every officer present at such trial, before any proceeding be had thereupon, shall take an oath before the court, and a justice of the peace, if any such be there present; otherwise the president of such court, being first sworn by two of the other members thereof, shall administer the oath unto the others; and the president of such court, and any two other members thereof, are hereby respectively authorized to administer the same in these words; that is to say,—

You shall well and truly try and determine, according to your evidence, the matter now before you, between our sovereign lord the king, and the prisoner to be tried. So help you God.

[SECT. 5.] And no sentence of death shall be given against any offender in such case by any court-martial, unless nine of the eleven officers present shall concur therein; and if there be a greater number of officers present, then the judgment shall pass by the concurrence of the greater part of them so sworn, provided such major part shall not be less than nine; nor shall any sentence of death pass'd by courts-martial, by virtue of this act, upon any offender, be put in execution, until report be made of the whole matter, by the president of such court, unto the captain-general or commander-in-chief of this province, for the time being, in order to receive his directions therein; and the prisoner shall be kept in safe custody in the mean time, and the provost-marshal shall have a warrant, signed by the president of the court, to cause execution to be done according to sentence, before the same be executed.

Provided always,—

Proviso.

[SECT. 6.] That nothing in this act contained shall extend, or be construed, to exempt any officer or soldier whatsoever from the ordinary process of law.

Limitation.

[SECT. 7.] This act to continue and be in force for the space of two years from the publication thereof, in case the war with France continue so long, or otherwise to the end of the said war, and no longer. [*Passed August* 18; *published August* 30.

CHAPTER 12.

AN ACT IN FURTHER ADDITION TO AND EXPLANATION OF THE ACT FOR THE MORE SPEEDY FINISHING OF THE LAND-BANK OR MANUFACTORY SCHEME.

Preamble. 1743-44, chap. 17.

WHEREAS in and by an act passed in the seventeenth year of his present majesty's reign, intituled "An Act for the more speedy finishing of the Land-bank or Manufactory Scheme," it is provided that the commissioners therein named should make a report of their proceedings, in the execution of their trust, to this court at their present session, for their approbation and allowance or disallowance thereof, either in whole or in part, and that any of the late directors and partners of the late Land-bank or Manufactory Company who should think himself aggrieved by the proceedings of the said commissioners, might file his appeal from their determination to the court, in the secretary's office, at any time before the present session thereof; *and whereas* the affairs of the said late company have been since found to be so circumstanced that an assessment on all the late directors and partners for their respective proportions of the whole of the charge and loss that has arisen on said scheme and trade could not be made before the present session of this court; but the said commissioners have, during the present session thereof, assessed such of the delinquent partners in said scheme as have paid no part of what is due from them to the said late company, nor have otherwise redeemed any part of the bills which they borrowed and received of the said late company in divers sums of money, consisting of the principal sums by the said delinquent partners respectively received from the said late company in Land-bank or Manufactory bills, and the interest due thereon, together with the further sums of six pounds on every hundred of the original sum drawn out of the said late company's stock, or borrowed out of the same by such of the said assessed partners as were concerned in trade, and three pounds on the hundred as the proportion of the other assessed partners, and *pro ratâ* for any greater or less sum; and have made a report of their said proceedings to this court, which report is dated sixteenth of August, one thousand seven hundred and forty-four; *but inasmuch* as the parties so assessed have had no opportunity, in case they should think themselves aggrieved by the said proceedings, of filing their appeal from the aforesaid determination of the said commissioners to this court, at their present session, as in and by the before, in part, recited act it is provided they should have liberty to do,—

Be it therefore enacted by the Governour, Council and House of Representatives,

Appeal allowed to the partners of the Land-bank to the general court, from the commissioners' determination.

[Sect. 1.] That the said partners of the said late Manufactory Company, who have been assessed by the said commissioners in manner aforesaid, and every of them, shall have liberty, in case they or any of them shall think themselves aggrieved by the beforementioned determination and assessment, to appeal from the same to this court at their next session, provided they shall file such appeal or appeals in the secretary's office on or before the seventh day of September next ensuing; and such appeals, and the matters arising thereon, shall be wholly governed, tried and determined by the rules prescribed touching appeals by the said, in part, recited act. And the aforesaid proceedings of the said commissioners, and every part thereof, are hereby declared to be allowed and approved of by this court against such of the partners assessed as aforesaid, who shall not file their appeals from the same as aforesaid within the term herein before limited for that purpose; and such of the said partners shall be chargeable to pay to the said commissioners the respective sum or sums assessed upon them; and on neglect of payment thereof, the said commissioners may, in their own names, raise, sue for, and recover the same in such manner as in and by the said former act is provided.

Provided nevertheless,

Commissioners to give notice of their assessments in the Boston newspapers.

[Sect. 2.] That the said commissioners shall give notice to the late partners of the late Manufactory Company by them assessed as aforesaid, of the several beforemention'd assessments, by causing a list or schedule of the same, together with a copy of this act, to be inserted in the four weekly prints, called, the "Boston Weekly Postboy," the "Boston Evening Post," the "Boston Gazette, or Weekly Journal," and the

"Boston Weekly News-Letter," which shall be next published after the publication of this act.

Preamble.

And whereas the affairs of the said late company are under such circumstances that the same cannot be adjusted and finished in an equitable manner by one single assessment, but divers assessments by the said commissioners on the late directors and partners of the said late company, and divers reports of their proceedings to this court, are requisite for that purpose,—

Be it further enacted,

Commissioners to make divers assessments if they judge fit.

[SECT. 3.] That the said commissioners, or any two of them, shall and may, from time to time, until the affairs of the said late company be wholly settled and finished, as often as there shall be occasion, make such assessments on any of the said late directors and partners as they shall judge necessary for finishing the said Land-bank or Manufactory Scheme in the most equitable manner, pursuant to the directions of the said, in part, recited act; and upon every such assessment's being made, the said commissioners shall give the parties thereby assessed, notice thereof, by causing lists or schedules of such assessments to be inserted in the beforemention'd weekly prints, which shall be next published after the making the said assessment; and that any of the said late directors or partners, who shall think himself aggrieved by any such determination and assessment, to be made by the said commissioners, may, at any time within fourteen days next after, notice thereof being published in the four beforemention'd weekly prints, file his appeal from the same to this court, in the secretary's office; and all such appeals, and the matters arising thereon, shall be wholly governed, tried and determined by the rules prescribed touching appeals by the said, in part, recited act.

Appeal to be allowed from them.

And be it further enacted,

Assessment to be lodged in the commissioners' chamber.

[SECT. 4.] That every further assessment made by the said commissioners, shall remain in the chamber of the court-house in Boston, wherein the said commissioners usually meet for the execution of their trust, until the expiration of the said fourteen days hereinbefore limited for the filing of appeals, ready for the inspection of such of the parties therein assessed as shall desire the same, and copies thereof, attested by the clerk of the said commissioners, shall be delivered to them upon their request, and at their proper charge; and that the said commissioners shall make report of their proceedings in every such assessment, to this court, as soon afterwards as may be, for their approbation and allowance or disallowance thereof, in whole or in part; and each and every of the said late directors and partners shall be chargeable to pay to the said commissioners the sum or sums in which he or they shall be from time to time assessed by the said commissioners, with the approbation of this court; and on neglect of payment thereof, the said commissioners may, in their own names, raise, sue for, and recover the same in such manner as by the said former act is provided.

Directors and partners chargeable to pay the sums assessed.

Commissioners empowered to sue.

And be it further enacted,

Copies of assessments to be delivered out of the secretary's office.

[SECT. 5.] That attested copies of the assessment hereinbefore mentioned to be already made by the said commissioners, shall be delivered out of the secretary's office to any of the parties therein assessed, upon their request, and at their proper charge.

Preamble.

And whereas in and by the before-mentioned act, the said commissioners are obliged to sit three days in a week for the dispatch of the affairs of said scheme, until the same shall be finished; *and whereas* their attendance for so great a part of the week may not be necessary after they shall have made their next assessment, and reported the same,—

Be it therefore enacted,

[SECT. 6.] That the said commissioners shall not be obliged, after they shall have presented their next assessment on the aforesaid Manufactory Company to this court, for their allowance, to sit more than one day in a week, unless when they shall judge that the affairs of said company shall require more frequent attendance. [*Passed August* 18.

Commissioners not obliged to sit more than one day in the week.

ACTS

PASSED AT THE SESSION BEGUN AND HELD AT BOSTON, ON THE TENTH DAY OF OCTOBER, A. D. 1744.

CHAPTER 13.

AN ACT FOR ESTABLISHING AND REGULATING FEES WITHIN THIS PROVINCE.

Preamble. 1692-93, chap. 37. 1701-2, chap. 7. 1742-43, chap. 5.

WHEREAS some services of a public nature have no fees stated by law, and others which have been established by two acts, made in the fourth and thirteenth years of King William the Third, by reason of the alteration of circumstances, are become unequal,—

Be it therefore enacted by the Governour, Council and House of Representatives,

Rates of fees for officers.

[SECT. 1.] That from and after the publication of this act, the following fees in bills of credit emitted for the supply of the treasury in the year one thousand seven hundred and forty-one, or in other province bills, or gold or silver in proportion, at the choice of the payer, may be taken for the future; viz.,—

JUSTICE'S FEES.

For granting a writ, summons or original summons, sixpence.
Subpœna, for each witness, one penny halfpenny.
Entring an action or complaint, one shilling and sixpence.
Writ of execution, one shilling.
Filing papers, each, one penny.
Taxing a bill of cost, threepence.
Entring up judgment in civil or criminal cases, ninepence.
Bond for appeal, sixpence.
Copy of every evidence, original papers or records, sixpence per page for each page of twenty-eight lines, eight words in a line: if less than a page, threepence.
Each recognizance, one shilling.
Confessing judgment, sixpence.
Taking affidavits out of their own courts in order to the trial of any cause, one shilling,—
in other cases, together with certificate, examining and entry, sixpence,—
in perpetuam, to each justice, one shilling.
Acknowledging an instrument with one or more seals, provided it be done at one and the same time, one shilling.
A warrant, sixpence.
Each day's attendance at the sessions, to be paid out of the fines, two shillings.
Allowance to the party for whom costs shall be taxed, one shilling per day, ten miles' travel to be accounted one day.

For witnesses in civil causes, one shilling and sixpence per day, and ten miles' travel to be accounted a day.

For granting a warrant, swearing apprizers relating to strays, and entring the same, one shilling and sixpence.

CORONER'S FEES.

For serving a writ, summons or execution, and travelling fees, the same as by this act is hereafter allowed to sheriffs.

Bail bond, sixpence.

Every trial where the sheriff is concerned, ninepence.

Taking an inquisition, to be paid out of the deceased's estate, six shillings and eightpence; if for more than one at the same time, ten shillings in the whole; if no estate, then to be paid by the county treasurer, three shillings and fourpence,—and for more than one, five shillings.

For travelling and expences for taking an inquisition, each day, six shillings.

The foreman of the jury, three shillings; and, ten miles accounted a day's travel, one shilling per day;—

every other juror, two shillings and sixpence, and travel the same as the foreman.

JUDGE OF PROBATE AND REGISTER'S FEES.

For granting administration or guardianship, bonds, and letters of administration or guardianship,—

to the judge, two shillings.

To the register for writing bond of administration or guardianship, one shilling and ninepence.

for writing letters of administration or letters of guardianship, one shilling and sixpence.

For granting guardianship of divers minors to the same person and at the same time: to the judge, for each minor, one shilling; to the register, for each letter of guardianship and bond, as before.

Proving a will or codicil; one shilling and ninepence to the judge, and one shilling and threepence to the register.

Recording a will, letter of administration or guardianship, inventory or account, of one page, and filing the same, one shilling and threepence.

for every page more, of twenty-eight lines, of eight words in a line, ninepence.

For a copy of a will or inventory, the same for each page, as before.

Allowing accounts, two shillings and sixpence; decree for settling of intestate estates: to the judge, two shillings and sixpence,—

to the register, for examining such accounts, one shilling.

A citation: to the register, ninepence.

A *quietus:* to the judge, one shilling; to the register, one shilling.

Warrant or commission for apprizing or dividing estates; one shilling to the judge, one shilling to the register.

Making out commission to receive and examine the claims of creditors to insolvent estates; to the judge, one shilling, and to the register, one shilling: for recording the same, one shilling and threepence.

Registring the commissioner's report, each page, ninepence, as above.

Making out and entring an order among the administrators for the distribution of the estate, one shilling.

For proportioning such estate upon the creditors, agreable to the commissioners' return, when the estate exceeds not fifty pounds; to the register, two shillings, and above that sum, three shillings.

For recording the same, ninepence per page, as before.

IN THE SUPERIOUR COURT.

JUSTICE'S FEES.

Entring an action, five shillings.
Taking special bail, one shilling.
Allowing a writ of error, one shilling and sixpence.
Allowing an *habeas corpus*, one shilling.
Taxing a bill of cost, sixpence.
Attorney's fee, to be allowed in the bill of cost taxed, six shillings.
Granting liberty for the sale or partition of real estates, two shillings.
On receiving each petition, one shilling.

CLERK'S FEES.

On entring an action, one shilling.
A writ of *scire facias*, one shilling and sixpence.
A writ of review, two shillings and sixpence;—
if more than one page, ninepence per page, as before.
Entring a rule of court, sixpence.
Filing a declaration, sixpence.
Entring appearance, threepence.
Signing a judgment by default, sixpence.
Receiving and recording a verdict, sixpence.
Copies of all records, each page, of twenty-eight lines, eight words in a line, ninepence;—
if less than one page, sixpence.
Every action withdrawn or nonsuit, sixpence.
Every petition read, sixpence;—
order thereon, sixpence.
Filing the papers of each cause, one penny per paper.
Every execution, one shilling.
Writ of *habeas corpus*, two shillings.
Drawing bail bond, one shilling.
Confessing judgment, one shilling.
Acknowledging satisfaction of a judgment on record, sixpence.
Examining each bill of cost, sixpence.
Continuing each cause, and entring the next term, sixpence.
Entring up judgment and copying the same, one shilling.
To each *venire*, to be paid out of the county treasuries, respectively, by order from any three of the justices of said court, threepence.

IN THE INFERIOUR COURT OF COMMON PLEAS, AND COURT OF GENERAL SESSIONS.

JUSTICE'S FEES.

Entry of every action, four shillings.
Taxing a bill of cost, sixpence.
Attorney's fee, to be allowed in the bill of cost taxed, five shillings.
Taking the recognizance on appeals, sixpence.
Each recognizance in granting licences, one shilling.
Proving each deed, two shillings.
Granting every licence for publick entertainment or retailing, one shilling.

CLERK'S FEES.

Every action entred, one shilling.
Every writ and seal, sixpence.
Every appearance, threepence.
Entring and rendring a verdict, sixpence.

Recording a judgment, one shilling.
Copies of all records, each page, as before, ninepence.
Every action withdrawn or nonsuit, sixpence.
Every execution, one shilling.
Taking special bail, one shilling; confessing judgment, or default, sixpence.
Acknowledging satisfaction of a judgment on record, sixpence.
Writ of *habeas corpus*, two shillings.
Continuing each cause and entry at the next court, sixpence.
Entring up judgment, and copying, one shilling.
Examining each bill of cost, sixpence.
Each recognizance, one shilling.
Each *venire*, to be paid out of the county treasuries, respectively, by order of court, threepence.
Writ of *facias habere possessionem*, two shillings.
Filing each paper, one penny.

CLERK OF THE SESSIONS' FEES.

Entring a complaint or indictment, one shilling.
Discharging a recognizance, sixpence.
Each warrant against criminals, sixpence.
Every summons or subpœna, twopence.
Every recognizance for the peace or good behaviour, one shilling.
Granting every licence for publick entertainment or retailing, one shilling.
For each recognizance, one shilling.
Entring up judgment, or entring satisfaction of judgment on record, and copying, one shilling.
Warrant for county tax, sixpence.
For minuting the receipt of each petition and order thereon, and recording, ninepence per page, as before.
Examining and casting the grand jury's account yearly, and order thereon, to be paid by the county treasurer by order of the court of sessions, one shilling and sixpence.
For copies of all original papers or records, ninepence per page, as before.
For filing each paper, one penny.

SHERIFF'S OR CONSTABLE'S FEES.

For serving an original summons, one shilling.
Every *capias* or attachment in civil, or warrants in criminal, cases for trial, one shilling; and for travel out and to return the writ (the travel to be certified on the back of the writ or original summons), one penny halfpenny per mile.
Serving execution in personal action, if twenty pounds or under, one shilling per pound; for all others not exceeding forty pounds, twelvepence per pound for twenty pounds thereof, and sixpence per pound for the remaining part; for all others not exceeding one hundred pounds, for forty pounds thereof, as for an execution not exceeding forty pounds, and for the remaining part, fourpence per pound; and all others above one hundred pounds, for one hundred pounds thereof, as for an execution not exceeding one hundred pounds, and for the remaining part, twopence per pound.
For travel out, and to return the execution, twopence per mile; all travel to be accounted from the court-house in each shire town in each county, except for justices' writs, the travel for which to be accounted from the place from whence the writ issues.

For giving livery and seizin of real estates, seven shillings and sixpence, travel as before: if of different parcels of land, five shillings each.
Every trial, sixpence.
Every default, threepence.
A bail bond, sixpence.
Every precept for the choice of representatives, one shilling, to be paid out of the county treasuries, respectively.
To the officer attending the grand jury, each day, one shilling and sixpence.

CRYER'S FEES.

Calling the jury, threepence.
A default or nonsuit, sixpence.
A verdict, sixpence.
A judgment affirmed on a complaint, sixpence.

GOALER'S FEES.

For turning the key on each prisoner committed, two shillings and sixpence; viz., one shilling and threepence in, and one shilling and threepence out.
For dieting each person, three shillings per week.

MESSENGER OF THE HOUSE OF REPRESENTATIVES' FEES.

For serving every warrant from the house of representatives, which they may grant for arresting, imprisoning, or taking into custody any person, one shilling and sixpence.
For travel, each mile out, twopence per mile.
For keeping and providing food for such person, each day, two shillings and sixpence.
For his discharge or dismission, one shilling and sixpence, to be paid as by law already provided.

GRAND JUROR'S FEES.

Foreman, per day, two shillings.
Each other juror, one shilling and sixpence.

PETIT JUROR'S FEES.

To the foreman, in every case at the superiour court, one shilling and threepence.
To every other juror, one shilling.
To the foreman, in every case at the inferiour court or sessions, one shilling.
To every other juror, ninepence.

FOR MARRIAGES.

For each marriage, to the minister or justice officiating, two shillings and sixpence.
For recording it; to the town clerk, to be paid by the justice or minister, sixpence; and to the clerk of the sessions, to be paid by the town clerk, threepence.
To the town clerk, for every publishment of the banns of matrimony, and entring thereof, one shilling.
Every certificate of such publishment, ninepence.
Recording births and deaths, each, fourpence.
For a certificate of the birth or death of any person, threepence.
For every search of record, when no copy is required, threepence.

COUNTY REGISTER'S FEES.

For entring or recording any deed, conveyance or mortgage, for the first page, ninepence; and sixpence a page for so many pages more as it shall contain, accounting after the rate of twenty-eight lines, of eight words to a line, to each page, and proportionably for so much more as shall be under a page, and threepence for his attestation on the original, of the time, book and folio where it is recorded. and for [a] discharge of a mortgage, as aforesaid, sixpence.

GOVERNOUR'S AND SECRETARY'S FEES.

For registers: to the governour, five shillings; to the secretary, two shillings and sixpence.
For certificates under the province seal: to the governour, five shillings; to the secretary, two shillings and sixpence.
For warrants of apprizement, survey, &c.: to the governour, three shillings; to the secretary, three shillings.
To the governour, for a pass to the castle, for each vessel, one shilling and threepence: wood-sloops and other coasting vessels for which passes have not been usually required, excepted.
For a certificate of naval stores, in the whole, five shillings.

And be it further enacted,

[SECT. 2.] That if any of the officers aforesaid shall demand and take any greater or other fees for the matters before mentioned, or any of them, than are allowed to be demanded and taken by this act, and shall be thereof convict, they shall forfeit and pay for each offence the sum of ten pounds, to be applied, the one moiety thereof for and towards the support of this government, and the other moiety to him or them that shall sue for the same; to be recovered by action, bill, plaint or information, in any court of record proper to try the same. And all officers to whom any warrant, summons, capias or attachment shall be committed, and who shall receive fees for the service thereof, are hereby required, without unnecessary delay, to serve and execute the same, on forfeiture of ten pounds, to be recovered and applied as aforesaid, besides making good such dammage as the party may sustain by such delay: *provided*, in civil causes, the fees for travel and service be first tendred and paid if required by such officers. Penalty for taking excessive fees.

[SECT. 3.] This act to continue and be in force for the space of one year from the publication thereof, and from thence to the end of the next session of the general court, and no longer. [*Passed October* 26; *published October* 31. Limitation.

CHAPTER 14.

AN ACT FOR REVIVING AND CONTINUING SUNDRY LAWS OF THIS PROVINCE IN THIS ACT MENTIONED, EXPIRED OR NEAR EXPIRING.

WHEREAS an act was made and pass'd in the twelfth year of his present majesty's reign, [e][*i*]ntitled "An Act to prevent the unnecessary journeying of the members of the general court"; and also an act was made and pass'd in the thirteenth year of his said majesty, [e][*i*]ntitled "An Act in addition to an act [e][*i*]ntitled 'An Act for the better preservation and increase of deer within this province'"; and also another act was made and pass'd in the same year, [e][*i*]ntitled "An Act for the effectual preventing of horses, neat cattle, sheep and swine from running at large or feeding upon a certain island called Preamble. 1738-39, chap. 25. 1739-40, chap. 3. 1739-40, chap. 8.

1739-40, chap. 12. Plumb Island, lying in Ipswich Bay, in the county of Essex"; and another act was made and pass'd in the same year, [e][*i*]ntitled "An Act in addition to the several laws of this province relating to common 1741-42, chap. 6. roads and private ways"; and another act was made and pass'd in the fifteenth year of his present majesty, [e][*i*]ntitled "An Act for the rel[ci][*ie*]f of poor prisoners for debt"; all which several laws are expir[e]d, or will expire at the end of the present session of the general court; *and whereas* the afores[*ai*][d] laws have by experience been found beneficial and necessary for the several purposes for which they were pass'd,—

Be it therefore enacted by the Governour, Council and House of Representatives,

Several acts continued or revived. That all and every of the aforesaid acts, and every matter and clause therein contained, be and hereby are revived, and shall continue and remain in full force until[l] the last day of October, which will be in the year one thousand seven hundred and fifty-one, and to the end of the session of the general court then next after. *Passed October* 26; *published October* 31.

CHAPTER 15.

AN ACT FOR APPROPRIATING A PART OF THE ISLAND CALLED GOVERNOUR'S ISLAND, IN THE HARBOUR OF BOSTON, TO THE PUBLIC USE OF THIS GOVERNMENT.

Preamble. WHEREAS it has been represented by the captain-general, and it appears to this court, that it is of great importance to the safety of this his majesty's province, that two batteries, with a suitable number of cannon to be planted thereon, be, without delay, built and erected on the island called Governour's Island, situate and lying in Boston harbour, and easterly of his majesty's Castle William, which island is now the property and in the possession of Mrs. Anne Winthrop, of said Boston, in the county of Suffolk, widow, and after her decease is, by the indenture of Adam Winthrop, of Boston, merchant, of the one part, and John Wainwright, of Ipswich, Esq., on the other part, bearing date the twenty-seventh day of December, one thousand seven hundred, to descend to the use and behoof of the heirs begotten of the bodies of Adam Winthrop, late of said Boston, Esq., deceased, and the said Anne Winthrop, forever; and in default of such heirs, to the use and behoof of the next and right heirs of him, the said Adam Winthrop, forever, and to no other use, intent or purpose whatsoever; *and whereas*, by reason of said indenture it is found impracticable to obtain a sufficient deed of conveyance of a suitable part of said island, from the said Anne Winthrop or any other person, whereon to erect and build the said batteries, and, consequently, for the captain-general to proceed in erecting and building the same without the interposition of this court, altho' it is judged by them of absolute necessity for the publick safety; therefore,—

Be it enacted by the Governour, Council and House of Representatives, and it is hereby enacted,

Sheriff of Suffolk to lay out land for the province, on Governor's Island, and take possession of it. [SECT. 1.] That it shall and may be lawful for the captain-general and governour-in-chief in and over his majesty's province of the Massachusetts Bay, to issue his order, directed to the high sheriff of the county of Suffolk, requiring him forthwith to repair to the said island, and in the name and behalf of this government, to bound out in such place thereof and in such form as the captain-general shall direct, the full quantity of three acres and an half thereof, and in the name and for the use of this government to take possession of the said three acres and an half he shall so bound out, with the flatts before the same; and the said sheriff shall certify his proceedings herein, with the bounds of the said three acres and an half laid out as aforesaid, into the secretary's office, by him to be recorded in the book of records of this province.

And be it further enacted,

[SECT. 2.] That the said three acres and an half of said island so bounded out, possession thereof being taken, and return and record thereof being made as aforesaid, and also the flatts before the same, shall thenceforward, by virtue and force of this act, be adjudged and deemed the lawful right and property of this government, and shall be and remain to their use for the building and improving the said batteries, and for other defensible preparations, forever hereafter.

Said land to be appropriated for building batteries thereon.

Be it further enacted,

[SECT. 3.] That if any action or actions, of what name or nature soever, shall at any time hereafter be brought by any person or persons for the recovery of the said three acres and an half of the said island, and the flatts, out of the hands of this government, or for dammages for the improvement of the same, or against any particular person or persons, such action or actions tending to defeat or in anywise to interrupt or impede the plain and necessary intent and design of this act, or against the said sheriff for any matter or thing he shall do in consequence hereof, this act may be pleaded in bar to all and every such action or actions respectively, and the same shall be bar'd and made void accordingly.

Any action to be brought for recovery of the said land, or against the sheriff, to be barred by this act.

And to the intent that full satisfaction may be made by this government to the said Anne and the heirs before mentioned,—

Be it further enacted,

[SECT. 4.] That six prudent and sufficient persons shall be appointed, three thereof by the secretary of this province, and three by the said Anne Winthrop, or in case of her neglect or refusal, by his majesty's justices of the superiour court, or any three of them; and in case the major part of said appraizers shall not agree, they shall have power to chuse a seventh, and said appraizers shall be under oath to estimate and apprize the said three acres and an half of land, and the flatts aforesaid, in lawful money; and the appraizement and value so made and taken by them, or the major part of them, shall be returned to the said secretary, and shall by him be recorded in the aforesaid book, for the benefit and behoof of the said Anne Winthrop and heirs aforesaid, in manner following; viz., the lawful interest of the whole sum shall be annually paid by the treasurer of this province, for the time being, out of the appropriations that are or may be made for satisfying of grants, to the said Anne Winthrop during her natural life, and at her decease the principal shall be paid to the said heirs in such proportion as the remaining part of said island shall be lawfully distributed and settled on them in consequence of the indenture aforesaid. [*Passed October* 26.

Persons to be appointed for appraising the said land.

Satisfaction to be made to the proprietor out of the public treasury.

CHAPTER 16.

AN ACT FOR GRANTING UNTO HIS MAJESTY SEVERAL RATES AND DUTIES OF IMPOST AND TUNNAGE OF SHIPPING.

WE, his majesty's most loyal and dutiful subjects, the representatives of his majesty's province of the Massachusetts Bay, in New England, being desirous of a collateral fund and security for drawing in the bills of credit on this province, have cheatfully and unanimously given and granted and do hereby give and grant unto his most excellent majesty to the end and use aforesaid, and for no other use, the several duties of impost upon wines, liquors, goods, wares and merchandize that shall be imported into this province, and tunnage of shipping hereafter mentioned; and pray that it may be enacted,—

And be it accordingly enacted by the Governour, Council and House of Representatives,

[SECT. 1.] That from and after the last day of the present session, there shall be paid by the importer of all wines, liquors, goods, wares and merchandize that shall be imported into this province from the place of their growth (salt, cotton-wool, provisions, and every other thing of the growth and produce of New England, and also all prize goods condemned in any port of this province excepted), the several rates or duties of impost following; vizt.,—

For every pipe of wine of the Western Islands, eight shillings.

For every pipe of Madera, nine shillings and sixpence.

For every pipe of other sorts not mentioned, nine shillings and sixpence.

For every hogshead of rum, containing one hundred gallons, eight shillings.

For every hogshead of sugar, sevenpence.

For every hogshead of molasses, fourpence.

For every hogshead of tobacco, four shillings and sixpence.

For every ton of logwood, ninepence.

—And so, proportionably, for greater or lesser quantities.

And all other commodities, goods or merchandize not mentioned or excepted, fourpence for every twenty shillings value: all goods imported from Great Britain excepted.

[SECT. 2.] And for any of the above wines, liquors, goods, wares, merchandize, &c., that shall be imported into this province, &c., from any other port than the places of their growth and produce, there shall be paid by the importer double the value of impost appointed by this act to be received for every species above mentioned, unless they do, *bonâ fide*, belong to the inhabitants of this province and came upon their risque from the port of their growth and produce.

And be it further enacted,

[SECT. 3.] That all the aforesaid impost rates and duties shall be paid in current money or bills of credit of this province of the last emission by the importer of any wines, goods, liquors or merchandize unto the commissioner to be appointed as is hereinafter to be directed for entring and receiving the same, at or before the landing of any wines, liquors, goods or merchandize: only the commissioner or receiver is hereby allowed to give credit to such person or persons where his or their duty of impost in one ship or vessel doth exceed the sum of three pounds; and in case where the commissioner or receiver shall give credit, he shall settle and ballance his accompts with every person on or before the last day of April, so that the same accompts may be ready to be presented to this court in May next. And all entries where the impost or duty doth not exceed three shillings, shall be made without charge to the importer, and not more than sixpence to be demanded for any other single entry to what value soever.

And be it further enacted,

[SECT. 4.] That all masters of ships or other vessels coming into any harbour or port within this province from beyond sea, or from any other province or colony, before bulk be broken and within twenty-four hours after his arrival at such harbour or port, shall make a report to the commissioner or receiver of the impost, to be appointed as hereinafter mentioned, of the contents of the lading of such ship or vessel, without any charge or fee to be demanded or paid for the same; which report said master shall give in to the commissioner or receiver, under his hand, and shall therein set down and express the quantities and species of the wines, liquors, goods, and merchandize laden on board such ship or vessel, with the marks and numbers thereof, and to whom the same is consign'd; and also make oath that the said report or manifest of the contents of his lading, so to be by him given in under his hand as aforesaid, contains a just and true account, to the best of his knowledge, of the whole lading taken on board and imported in the said vessel from the port or ports such vessel came from, and that he hath not broken bulk nor delivered any of the wines, rum or other distilled liquors or merchandize laden on board the said ship or vessel, directly or indirectly; and if he shall know of any more wines, liquors, goods or merchandize to be imported therein, before the landing thereof he will cause it to be added to his manifest; which manifest shall be agreable to a printed form made for that purpose, which is to be filled up by the said commissioner or receiver according to each particular person's entry; which oath the commissioner or receiver is hereby impowered to administer: after which s'd master may unload, and not before, on pain of five hundred pounds, to be forfeited and paid by each master that shall neglect his duty in this behalf.

And be it further enacted,

[SECT. 5.] That all merchants, factors and other persons, importers, being owners thereof, or having any of the wines, liquors, goods or merchandize consigned to them, that by this act are liable to pay impost or duty, shall, by themselves or order, make entry thereof in writing, under their hands, with the said commissioner or receiver, and produce unto him an invoice of all such goods as pay *ad valorem*, and make oath thereto in manner following:—

You, A. B., do swear that the entry of the goods and merchandize by you now made, exhibit the present price of said goods at this market, and that, *bonâ fide*, according to your best skill and judgment, it is not less than the real value thereof. So help you God.

—which above oath the commissioner or receiver is hereby impowered to administer; and they shall pay the duty and impost by this act required, before such wines, liquors, goods, wares or merchandize be landed or taken out of the vessel in which the same shall be imported, on pain of forfeiting all such wines, liquors, goods, wares or merchandize so landed and taken out of the vessel in which the same shall be imported.

[SECT. 6.] And no wines, liquors, goods, wares or merchandize that by this act are liable to pay impost or duty, shall be landed on any wharff, or into any warehouse or other place, but in the daytime only, and that after sunrise or before sunset, unless in the presence and with the consent of the commissioner or receiver, on pain of forfeiting all such wines, liquors, goods, wares and merchandize, and the lighter, boat or vessel out of which the same shall be landed or put into any warehouse or other place.

[SECT. 7.] And if any person or persons shall not have and produce an invoice of the quantities of rum or liquors to him or them consigned, then the cask wherein the same is shall be gaged at the charge of the importer, that the quantities thereof may be known.

And be it further enacted,

[SECT. 8.] That every merchant or other person importing any wines into this province shall be allowed twelve per cent for leakage: *provided*, such wines have not been filled up on board; and that every hogshead, butt or pipe of wine that hath two parts thereof leaked out, shall be accounted for outs, and the merchant or importer to pay no duty or impost for the same. And no master of any ship or vessel shall suffer any wines to be filled up on board without giving a certificate of the quantity so filled up, under his own hand, before the landing thereof, to the commissioner or receiver of impost for such port, on pain of forfeiting the sum of one hundred pounds.

[SECT. 9.] And if it may be made to appear that any wines imported in any ship or vessel be decayed at the time of unlading thereof, or in twenty days afterwards, oath being made before the commissioner or receiver that the same hath not been landed above that time, the duties and impost paid for such wines shall be repayed unto the importer thereof.

And be it further enacted,

[SECT. 10.] That the master of every ship or vessel importing any wines, liquors, goods, wares or merchandizes, shall be liable to and shall pay the impost for such and so much thereof, contained in his manifest, as shall not be duly entred, nor the duty paid for the same by the person or persons by whom such wines, liquors, goods, wares or merchandize are or shall be consigned. And it shall and may be lawful, to and for the master of every ship or other vessel, to secure and detain in his hands, at the owner's risque, all such wines, liquors, goods, wares or merchandize imported in any ship or vessel, until he shall receive a certificate, from the commissioner or receiver of the impost, that the duty for the same is paid, and until he be repaid his necessary charges in securing the same; or such master may deliver such wines, liquors, goods, wares or merchandizes as are not entred, unto the commissioner or receiver of the impost in such port or his order, who is hereby impowered and directed to receive and keep the same, at the owner's risque, until the impost thereof, with the charges, be paid; and then to deliver such wines, liquors, goods, wares or merchandize as the master shall direct.

And be it further enacted,

[SECT. 11.] That the commissioner or receiver of the impost in each port, shall be and hereby is impowered to sue the master of any ship or vessel, for the impost or duty for so much of the lading of any wines, liquors, goods, wares or merchandize imported therein, according to the manifest to be by him given upon oath, as aforesaid, as shall remain not entred and the duty of impost thereof not paid. And where any goods, wares or merchandize are such as that the value thereof is not known, whereby the impost to be recovered of the master, for the same, cannot be ascertained, the owner or person to whom such goods, wares or merchandize are or shall be consigned, shall be summoned to appear as an evidence at the court where such suit for the impost and the duty thereof shall be brought, and be there required to make oath to the value of such goods, wares or merchandize.

And be it further enacted,

[SECT. 12.] That the ship or vessel, with her tackle, apparel and furniture, the master of which shall make default in anything by this act required to be performed by him, shall be liable to answer and make good the sum or sums forfeited by such master, according to this act, for any such default, as also to make good the impost or duty for any wines, liquors, goods, wares and merchandize not entred as aforesaid; and, upon judgment recovered against such master, the said ship or vessel, with so much of the tackle or appurtenances thereof as shall be sufficient to satisfy said judgment, may be taken in execution for the same; and the commissioner or receiver of the impost is hereby impowered to make seizure of such ship or vessel, and detain the same under seizure until judgment be given in any suit to be commenced and prosecuted for any of the said forfeitures or impost; to the intent that if judgment be rendred for the prosecutor or informer, such ship or vessel and appurtenances may be exposed to sale, for satisfaction thereof, as is before provided: *unless* the owners, or some on their behalf, for releasing such ship or vessel from under seizure or restraint, shall give sufficient security unto the commissioner or receiver of impost that seized the same, to respond and satisfy the sum or value of the forfeiture and duties, with the charges, that shall be recovered against the master thereof, upon suit to be brought for the same, as aforesaid; and the master occasioning such loss and damage unto his owners, through his default or neglect, shall be liable unto their action for the same.

And be it further enacted,

[SECT. 13.] That the naval officer within any of the ports of this province shall not clear or give passes unto any master of any ship or other vessel, outward bound, until he shall be certified, by the commissioner or receiver of the impost, that the duties and impost for the goods last imported in such ship or vessel are paid or secured to be paid.

[SECT. 14.] And the commissioner or receiver of impost is hereby impowered to allow bills of store to the master of any ship or vessel importing any wines or liquors, for such private adventures as shall belong to the master or seamen of such ship or other vessel, at the discretion of the commissioner or receiver, not exceeding three per cent of the lading; and the duties payable by this act for such wines or liquors, in the bills of store mentioned and expressed, shall be abated.

And whereas, many persons have heretofore caused to be imported, from the neighbouring governments, into this province, by land-carriage, large quantities of wine, rum and other merchandize, subjected to duty by this act, but have made no report thereof to the officer of impost, or any of his deputies, nor have paid any duty therefor, contrary to the true intent and meaning of this act,—

Be it therefore enacted,

[SECT. 15.] That whensoever any rum, wine or other merchandize, by this act subjected to any duty, shall be hereafter imported from any of the neighbouring governments, by land, into any town of this province, the owner thereof, or person importing the same, shall make report thereof to the said officer, or some one of his deputies, hereby required therefor, on pain and penalty of forfeiting the same.

And be it further enacted,

[SECT. 16.] That all penalties, fines and forfeitures accruing and arising by virtue of this act, shall be one half to his majesty for the uses and intents for which the aforementioned duties of impost are granted, and the other half to him or them that shall seize, inform and sue for the same, by action, bill, plaint or information, in any of his majesty's courts of record, wherein no essoign, protection or wager of law shall be allowed: the whole charge of the prosecution to be taken out of the half belonging to the informer.

And be it further enacted,

[SECT. 17.] That there shall be paid, by the master of every ship or other vessel, coming into any port or ports in this province to trade and traffick, whereof all the owners are not belonging to this province (except such vessels as belong to Great Britain, the provinces or colonies of Pensylvania, West and East Jersey, New York, Connecticutt, New Hampshire and Rhode Island), every voyage such ship or vessel does make, one pound of good pistol-powder for every ton such ship or vessel is in burthen: *saving* for that part which is owned in Great Britain, this province, or any of the aforesaid governments, which are hereby exempted; to be paid unto the commissioner or receiver of the duties of impost, and to be employed for the ends and uses aforesaid.

[SECT. 18.] And the said commissioner is hereby impowered to appoint a meet and sutable person, to repair unto and on board any ship or vessel, to take the exact measure and tonnage thereof, in case he shall suspect that the register of such ship or vessel doth not express and set forth the full burthen of the same; the charge thereof to be paid by the master or owner of such ship or vessel, before she be cleared, in case she shall appear to be of greater burthen: otherwise, to be paid by the commissioner out of the money received by him for impost, and shall be allowed him accordingly, by the treasurer, in his accompts. And the naval officer shall not clear any vessel, until he be also certified, by the said commissioner, that the duty of tunnage for the same is paid, or that it is such a vessel for which none is payable according to this act.

And be it further enacted,

[SECT. 19.] That there be one fit person, and no more, nominated and appointed by this court, as a commissioner and receiver of the aforesaid duties of impost and tunnage of shipping, and for the inspection, care and management of the said office, and whatsoever relates thereto, to receive commission for the same from the governour or commander-in-chief for the time being, with authority to substitute and appoint a deputy receiver in each port, and other places besides that wherein he resides, and to grant warrants to such deputy receivers for the said place, and to collect and receive the impost and tunnage of shipping aforesaid that shall become due within such port, and to render the accompt thereof, and pay in the same, to the said commissioner and receiver: which said commissioner and receiver shall keep fair books of all entries and duties arising by virtue of this act; also, a particular account of every vessel, so that the duties of impost and tunnage arising on the said vessel may appear; and the same to lye open, at all seasonable times, to the view and perusal of the treasurer and receiver-general of this province, (or any other person or persons whom this court shall appoint,) with whom he shall accompt for all collections and payments; and pay all such monies as shall be in his hands, as the treasurer or receiver-general may demand it. And the said commissioner or receiver and his deputy or deputies, before their entring upon the execution of their office, shall be sworn to deal truly and faithfully therein, and shall attend in the said office from nine to twelve of the clock in the forenoon, and from two to five a-clock in the afternoon.

[SECT. 20.] And the said commissioner and receiver, for his labour, care and expences in the said office, shall have and receive, out of the province treasury, the sum of twenty-five pounds, the present emission, per annum; and his deputy or deputies to be paid for their service such sum or sums as the said commissioner and receiver, with the treasurer, shall agree upon, not exceeding seven pounds ten shillings each. And the treasurer is hereby ordered, in passing and receiving the said commissioner's accompts, accordingly, to allow the payment of such salary or salaries, as aforesaid, to himself and his deputy or deputies.

Provided,

[SECT. 21.] That this act shall be and continue in force one year from the last day of the present session, and from thence to the end of the session of the general court then next after, and no longer. [*Passed October* 26.

ACTS

PASSED AT THE SESSION BEGUN AND HELD AT BOSTON, ON THE TWENTY-EIGHTH DAY OF NOVEMBER, A. D. 1744.

CHAPTER 17.

AN ACT FOR THE SUPPLYING THE TREASURY WITH THE SUM OF TEN THOUSAND POUNDS, FOR DISCHARGING THE PUBLIC[K] DEBTS, &C[A]., AND FOR DRAWING IN THE SAID BILLS INTO THE TREASURY AGAIN.

Be it enacted by the Governour, Council and House of Representatives,

£10,000 bills of credit to be emitted.

[SECT. 1.] That the treasurer be and hereby is impowered and ordered to emit and issue forth the sum of ten thousand pounds in bills of credit of the last tenor and date, now lying in his hands and received in for taxes, impost and excise, which shall pass in all public[k] payments equal to other new tenor bills emitted since one thousand seven hundred and forty; or, if there shall not be a sufficiency of such bills, that then the committee appointed by this court for signing bills, are hereby directed and impowered to take care and make effectual provision, so soon as may be, to imprint the said bills, or so many as may be needed to compleat the said sum, and to sign and deliver the same to the treasurer, taking his receipt for the same; and the said committee shall be under oath for the faithful[l] performance of the trust by this act reposed in them; and the said sum of ten thousand pounds shall be issued out of the treasury in manner and for the purposes following; viz[t]., the sum of four thousand and sixty-five pounds seventeen shillings and threepence, part of the aforesaid sum of ten thousand pounds, to be applied for the payment of wages that now are or that hereafter may be due by virtue of the establishment of Castle William, Frederick Fort, Richmond Fort, George's Truck-house, Saco Truck-house, Brunswick Fort, the sloop in the countr[e]y's service, the province snow, the brigantine "Boston Packet," and the sloop "Orphan of Techao," and the treasurer's usual disbursements; and the sum of three thousand three hundred pounds, part of the aforesaid sum of ten thousand pounds, shall be applied for put[t]ing the province into a better posture of defence, for compleating the repairs of Castle William and other forts, for paying of such officers and soldiers as have done service for the province, whose wages are now due, which officers and soldiers shall be paid out of this appropriation preferable to any other service; and for such officers and soldiers as are or may be in the province service, according to the several establishments for that purpose, for purchasing all needful[l] warlike stores for the several forts and garrisons within this province, pursuant to such grants as are or shall be made by this court for those purposes; and the sum of twelve hundred pounds, part of the said sum of ten thousand pounds, for the payment of his majesty's council, and such other grants

£4,065 17*s*. 3*d*. for wages at Castle William and other garrisons, &c.

The province snow, &c.

£3,300 for putting the province into a better posture of defence, &c.

£1,200 for payment of grants, &c.

as are or shall be made by this court, and for the payment of stipends, bounties and premiums established by law; and for the payment of all other matters and things which this court have or shall, either by law or orders, provide for the payment of out of the publick treasury, and for no other purpose whatsoever; the sum of five hundred pounds, part of the aforesaid sum of ten thousand pounds, shall be applied for the discharge of other debts owing from this province to persons that have served or that shall serve them by order of this court in such matters and things where there is no establishment nor any certain sum assigned for such service, and for paper, printing and writing for this court, the expences of committees of council, or of the house, or of both houses, the surgeon of Castle William, and wooding of said castle; and the sum of eight hundred pounds, part of the aforesaid sum of ten thousand pounds, shall be applied for the payment of the house of representatives serving in the general court during their several sessions this present year. £500 for debts where is no establishment. £800 for the representatives.

And whereas there are sometimes publick entertainments, and, from time to time, contingent and unforeseen charges that demand prompt payment,—

Be it further enacted,

[SECT. 2.] That the sum of one hundred and thirty-four pounds two shillings and ninepence, the remaining part of the aforesaid sum of ten thousand pounds, be applied to defrey and pay such entertainments and contingent charges, and for no other use whatsoever. £134 2*s*. 9*d*. for entertainments, &c.

And be it enacted,

[SECT. 3.] That if there be a surplusage in any sum appropriated, such surplusage shall l[y][*i*]e in the treasury for the further order of this court. Surplusage to lie in the treasury.

And be it further enacted,

[SECT. 4.] That each and every warrant for drawing money out of the treasury, shall direct the treasurer to take the same out of such sums as are respectively appropriated for the payment of such public[k] debts as the draughts are made to discharge; and the treasurer is hereby directed and ordered to pay such money out of such appropriations as directed to, and no other, upon pain of refunding all such sum or sums as he shall otherwise pay, and to keep exact and distinct accompts of all payments made out of such appropriated sums; and the secretary, to whom it belongs to keep the muster-roll and accompts of charge, shall lay before the house, when they direct, all such muster-rolls and accompts after payment thereof. Warrants to express the appropriations.

And as a fund and security for drawing the said sum of ten thousand pounds into the treasury again,—

Be it further enacted,

[SECT. 5.] That there be and hereby is granted unto his most excellent majesty, for the ends and uses aforesaid, a tax of five thousand two hundred pounds, to be levied on polls, and estates both real and personal, within this province, according to such rules and in such proportions on the several towns and districts within the same, as shall be agreed upon and ordered by this court at their session in May, one thousand seven hundred and forty-five, and paid into the public[k] treasury on or before the last day of December then next after. £5,200 in 1745.

And as a further fund and security for drawing in the said sum of ten thousand pounds into the treasury again,—

Be it further enacted,

[SECT. 6.] That there be and hereby is granted unto his most excellent majesty, for the ends ahd uses aforesaid, a tax of four thousand pounds, to be levied on polls, and estates both real and personal, within this province, according to such rules and in such proportions £4,000 in 1746.

on the several towns and districts within the same, as shall be agreed upon and ordered by this court at their session in May, one thousand seven hundred and forty-six, and paid into the publick treasury on or before the last day of December then next after.

And as a fund and security for drawing in such sum or sums as shall be paid out to the representatives of the several towns,—

Be it enacted,

Tax to be made for what is paid the representatives.

[SECT. 7.] That there be and hereby is granted unto his most excellent majesty a tax of such sum or sums as shall be paid to the several representatives as aforesaid, to be levied and assess[*e*]'d on the polls and estates of the inhabitants of the several towns, according to what their several representatives shall so receive; which sums shall be set on the towns in the next province tax. And the assessors of the said towns shall make their assessment for this tax, and apportion the same according to the rules that shall be prescribed by the act of the general assembly for assessing the next province tax, and the constables, in their respective districts, shall pay in the same when they pay in the province tax for the next year, of which the treasurer is hereby directed to keep a distinct and seperate accompt; and if there be any surplusage, the same shall l[y][*i*]e in the hands of the treasurer for the further order of this court.

And be it further enacted,

Tax for the money hereby emitted to be made according to the preceding tax act, in case.

[SECT. 8.] That in case the general court shall not at their sessions in May, one thousand seven hundred and forty-five, and one thousand seven hundred and forty-six, agree and conclude upon an act apportioning the sum, which by this act is engaged shall be, in those years, apportioned, assess[*e*]'d and levied, that then and in such case each town and district within this province shall pay, by a tax to be levied on the polls, and estates both real and personal, within their districts, the same proportion of the said sums as the said towns and districts shall have been taxed by the general court in the tax act then next preceding; and the province treasurer is hereby fully impowered and directed, some time in the month of June, in the year one thousand seven hundred and forty-five, and one thousand seven hundred and forty-six, to issue and send forth his warrants, directed to the selectmen or assessors of each town and district within this province, requiring them to assess the polls, and estates both real and personal, within their several towns and districts, for their respective part and proportion of the sum before directed and engaged to be assess[*e*]'d by this act; and the assessors, as also persons assessed, shall observe, be governed by and subject to all such rules and directions as shall have been given in the next preceding tax act.

And be it further enacted,

Taxes to be paid in the several species herein enumerated.

[SECT. 9.] That the inhabitants of this province shall have liberty, if they see fit, to pay the several sums for which they respectively may, in pursuance of this act, be assessed, in bills of credit of the form and teno[u]r by this act emitted, or in other new-tenor bills, or in bills of the middle tenor, according to their several denominations, or in bills of the old tenor, accounting four for one; or in coined silver, at seven shillings and sixpence per ounce, troy weight, and of sterling alloy, or in gold coin, proportionably; or in merchantable hemp, flax, winter and Isle-of-Sable codfish, refined bar-iron, bloomery-iron, hollow iron-ware, Indian corn, rye, wheat, barley, pork, beef, duck or canvas, whalebone, cordage, train-oil, beeswax, bayberry-wax, tallow, peas, sheepswool, or tann'd sole-leather (the aforesaid commodities being of the produce or manufactures of this province), at such moderate rates and prices as the general assembly of the year one thousand seven hundred and forty-five, and one thousand seven hundred and forty-six, shall set them at; the several persons paying their taxes in any of the commodities aforementioned, to run the risque and pay the charge of transporting the said commodities to the province treasury; but if the aforesaid general assembly shall not, at their sessions in May, some time before the twentieth day of June, in each year, agree upon and set[t] the aforesaid species and commodities at some certain price[s], that then the eldest councello[u]r[*s*], for the time being, of each of those counties in the province, of which any one of the council is an inhabitant, together with the province treasurer, or the major part of them, be a committee, who hereby are directed and fully authorized and impowered to do it; and in their set[*t*]ling the prices and rat[c]ing the value of those commodities, to state so much of them, respectively, at seven shillings and sixpence as an ounce of silver will purchase at that time in the town of Boston, and so *pro ratâ*. And the treasurer is hereby directed to insert in the several warrants by him sent to the several collectors of the taxes in each year, with the names of the afore-recited commodities, the several prices or rates which shall be set on them, either by the general assembly or the committee aforesaid, and direct the aforesaid collectors to receive them so.

How the commodities brought into the treasury are to be rated.

[SECT. 10.] And the aforesaid commodities so brought into the treasury shall, as soon as may be, be disposed of by the treasurer to the best advantage for so much as they will fetch in bills of credit hereby to be emitted, or for silver or gold, which silver and gold shall be delivered to the possessor of said bills in exchange for them; that is to say, one ounce of silver coin, and so gold in proportion, for seven shillings and sixpence, and so *pro ratâ* for a greater or less sum; and if any loss shall happen by the sale of the aforesaid species, or by any unforeseen accident, such deficiency shall be made good by a tax of the year next following, so as fully and effectually to call in the whole sum of ten thousand pounds in said bills hereby ordered to be emitted; and if there be a surplusage, it shall remain a stock in the treasury. [*Passed and published January* 9, 1744-45.

Treasurer to sell the said commodities.

CHAPTER 18.

AN ACT IN ADDITION TO AN ACT [E][*I*]NTITLED "AN ACT FOR THE REL[EI][*IE*]F OF POOR PRISONERS FOR DEBT."

Preamble.

WHEREAS in and by an act made and pass[*e*]'d in the fifteenth year of his present majesty's reign, [c][*i*]ntitled "An Act for the rel[ci][*ie*]f of poor prisoners for debt," it is provided that, upon security being given to the goaler or prison-keeper for the payment of eight shillings per week for and towards the support of any prisoner after such prisoner's having made oath that he has not any estate sufficient to support himself in prison or pay prison charges, "the goaler or keeper shall detain and keep in close custody such prisoner so long as said sum shall be paid, but upon failure of payment thereof" he shall be set at liberty; *and whereas* the aforesaid act was in and by an act made and pass[*e*]'d at the last session of this court revived and continued until[l] the last day of October, one thousand seven hundred and fifty-one, and until[l] the end of the session of the general court next after; *and whereas* in and by an act [e][*i*]ntitled "An Act for ascertaining the value of money," the lawful money of this province has been set[*t*]led at a different rate from the nominal value of the bills of credit current at the time of passing the first aforementioned act, and should the aforesaid

1741-42, chap. 6.

1744-45, chap. 14.

1741-42, chap. 12.

allowance of eight shillings per week be now understood and construed to intend eight shillings lawful money, it would prove unequal and injurious,—

Be it therefore enacted by the Governour, Council and House of Representatives,

Prisoners, how to be detained, and when released.

[SECT. 1.] That upon any prisoner's having taken the oath, and certificate having been made thereof as by the aforesaid act for the rel[ei][*ie*]f of poor prisoners for debt is provided, and the creditor or creditors, their agent or attorney, executor or administrator, having given security to the goaler or keeper of the prison where such prisoner now is or hereafter may be, for the payment of two shillings and sixpence per week in lawful money or bills of credit of this province equivalent thereto, for and towards the support of such prisoner while he or she shall be detained in prison, the said goaler or keeper shall detain and keep in close custody such prisoner so long as said sum shall be paid, but upon failure of payment thereof shall set him or her at liberty; and the several goalers or prison-keepers in this province are required to govern themselves accordingly.

Limitation.

[SECT. 2.] This act to continue and be in force for and during the term of the continuance of the aforementioned act for the rel[ei][*ie*]f of poor prisoners for debt. [*Passed December* 26, 1744; *published January* 9, 1744-45.

CHAPTER 19.

AN ACT TO ENCOURAGE THE [E][*I*]NLISTING SOLDIERS INTO HIS MAJESTY'S SERVICE, IN THE INTENDED EXPEDITION AGAINST CAPE BRETON.

Be it enacted by the Governour, Council and House of Representatives,

Volunteers in his majesty's service, not to be arrested, &c.

[SECT. 1.] That whoever has entred or shall enter or [e][*i*]nlist into his majesty's service as a voluntier in the intended expedition against the French settlements [of] [*at*] Cape Breton, shall not be liable to be taken out of his majesty's service aforesaid by any process or execution, unless for some criminal matter, for any sum whatsoever; and every soldier whose body shall be arrested by mean process or execution after his [e][*i*]nlistment into said service, may and shall be set at liberty by two justices of the peace, *quorum unus*, in the county where such soldier is taken, upon application made [by] him or his superio[*u*]r officer, upon proof made of his [e][*i*]nlistment into the service afores[*ai*]d.

Proviso.

Provided, always,—

[SECT. 2.] This act shall not be construed to stay the process of any creditor of such [e][*i*]nlisted soldier, after his return from the said expedition, or his dismission from the s[*ai*]d service; nor at all to stay any process or execution against a deficient constable or collector, for any taxes committed to him to collect. [*Passed January* 30; *published February* 4, 1744-45.

CHAPTER 20.

AN ACT FOR RAISING, BY A LOTTERY, THE SUM OF SEVEN THOUSAND FIVE HUNDRED POUNDS, FOR THE SERVICE OF THIS PROVINCE IN THE PRESENT YEAR.

WHEREAS his majesty's subjects in this province have been at great charges in the year current, not only for the protection of the seacoast, but for the defence of the frontier of New England, and also for the protection of his majesty's province of Nova Scotia, and the inhabitants having already been subjected to a heavy tax on polls and estates the present year, and a debt still remaining which the representatives of the said province are desirous should be provided for in a manner the least burthensome to the inhabitants,— Preamble.

Be it therefore enacted by the Governo[u]r, Council and House of Representatives,

[SECT. 1.] That it shall and may be lawful for any person or persons, inhabitants of this province, or any other of his majesty's subjects, or for[r]eigners, to adventure, advance and pay to the managers or directors hereinafter appointed, the sum of thirty shillings, or divers entire sums of thirty shillings, one-fifth thereof in bills of credit of this province, of the new teno[u]r, so called, or in the old teno[u]r bills, accounting four for one; the other four-fifths either in like bills, or in bills of credit of the other governments of New England, the currency of which are not prohibited by law. And every such adventurer, for every such sum of thirty shillings which he, she or they shall so advance, shall have such right, interest and lot in the lottery by this act allowed and established, as is hereinafter mentioned. Persons allowed to take out tickets.

And be it further enacted,

[SECT. 2.] That Samuel Watts, John Quincy, James Bowdoin, Robert Hale and Thomas Hutchinson, esq[ui]r[e]s, or any three of them, shall be managers or directors for preparing and delivering out tickets, and to oversee the drawing of lots, and to order, do and perform such other matters and things as are hereafter, in and by this act, directed and appointed by such managers or directors to be done and performed; and that such managers and directors shall meet together, from time to time, for the execution of the powers and trusts in them reposed by this act; and they shall cause books to be prepared, in which every leaf shall be divided into three columns, and upon the innermost of said three columns, there shall be printed twenty-five thousand tickets, number[e]'d one, two, three, and so on, progressively, till they arrive to the number of twenty-five thousand; and upon the middle column, in every of the said books, shall be printed twenty-five thousand tickets, of the same breadth and form, and number[e]'d in like manner; and in the extreme column of the said books, there shall be printed a third rank or series of tickets, of the same number of those of the other two columns: which tickets shall severally be of an oblong figure, and, in the said books, shall be joined with oblique lines, flourishes or devices, in such manner as the said managers and directors, or the major part of them, shall think most safe and convenient, and that every ticket in the third or extreme column of the said books, shall have written or printed thereupon, besides the number of such ticket and the present year of our Lord, these words, "MASSACHUSETTS GOVERNMENT LOTTERY.". Names of the managers or directors. Number of tickets, and form.

And it is further enacted,

[SECT. 3.] That the said managers and directors shall, upon payment of thirty shillings, as aforesaid, for a ticket, from any person or How tickets are to be delivered.

persons adventuring in this lottery, cut out of the said book or books, so as to be put into his or their custody, through the said oblique lines, flourishes or devices, indentwise, one of the tickets in the said extreme columns, which shall be signed by one of the said managers or directors; and the ticket so cut off shall be delivered to such adventurer as afores[ai]d.

And be it further enacted,

Tickets to be indented, rolled up, and put in boxes, &c.

[SECT. 4.] That the said managers and directors, or the major part of them, shall, in the presence of such of the adventurers as may attend, cause all the tickets in the middle column of the books aforesaid, to be cut off, indentwise, thrô[*ugh*] the said oblique lines, flourishes or devices, and to be carefully roll'd up, and made fast with thread or silk, and to be put into a box to be prepared for that purpose, and to be mark[*e*]d with the letter "A," which is presently to be put into another strong box, and to be locked up with five different locks and keys,—one to be kept by each of the said managers and directors,—and sealed with their seals, until[l] the said tickets are to be drawn as is hereinafter mentioned; and that the tickets in the first or innermost columns of the said books, shall remain still in the books for discovering any mistake or fraud, if any should happen to be committed contrary to the true meaning of this act.

And be it further enacted,

Books to be prepared, and tickets printed therein.

[SECT. 5.] That the said managers, or the major part of them, shall also prepare, or cause to be prepared, other books, in which every leaf shall be divided or distinguished into two colums, and upon the innermost of those two colums there shall be printed twenty-five thousand tickets, and upon the outermost of the said two colums there shall be printed twenty-five thousand tickets, all which shall be of equal length and breadth, as near as may be,—which two columns in the said books shall be joined with some flourish or device through which the outermost ticket may be cut off indentwise; and that five thousand four hundred and twenty-two tickets, part of those to be contained in the outermost columns of the books last mentioned, shall be and be called the "benefit tickets," to which extraordinary benefits shall belong, as hereinafter mentioned. And the said managers and directors shall cause the said benefit tickets to be written upon or otherwise expressed, as well in figures as in words at length, in manner following; that is to say, upon two of them, one thousand two hundred and fifty pounds; upon four of them severally, six hundred and twenty-five pounds; upon six of them severally, three hundred and seventy-five pounds; upon eight of them severally, two hundred and fifty pounds; upon sixteen of them severally, one hundred and twenty-five pounds; upon every one of thirty-six of them severally, sixty-two pounds ten shillings; upon every one of one hundred and fifty of them severally, thirty pounds; upon every one of five thousand two hundred, three pounds fifteen shillings; which several sums make, in the whole, the sum of thirty-seven thousand five hundred pounds. And the said managers shall cause all the said tickets contained in the outermost column of the last-mentioned books to be, in the presence of such of the said adventurers as may be there, to be * carefully cut out, indentwise, through the said flourish or device, and carefully roll[*e*]'d up, and fastened with thread or silk, and to be put into another box to be prepared for that purpose, and to be mark[*e*]'d with the letter "B," which box shall be presently put into another strong box, and locked up with five different locks and keys,—one key to be kept by each of said managers, and to be sealed up with their seals, until[l] these tickets shall also be drawn in the manner and form hereinafter mentioned. And the whole business of cutting off and rolling up, and putting into the said boxes, shall be performed by the

The number and sum of the benefit tickets.

Benefit tickets to be rolled up and put into a separate box.

* *Sic.*

said managers and directors, within six days, at the least, before the drawing of the said lottery shall begin.

And be it further enacted,

[SECT. 6.] That on or before the ninth day of April, one thousand seven hundred and forty-five (notice of the time being given in the publick prints at least fourteen days before), the said managers and directors shall cause the said several boxes, with all the tickets therein, to be brought into Faneuil Hall, or such other convenient place in the town of Boston, as shall be agreed upon by the major part of the directors, by nine of the clock in the forenoon of the same day, and placed on a table, there for that purpose, and shall then and there severally attend this service, and cause the two boxes containing the tickets to be severally taken out of the other two boxes in which they shall have been locked up, and the tickets or lots in the respective innermost boxes being, in the presence of such adventurers as will be there for the satisfaction of themselves, well shaken and mingled in each box distinctly; and some one fit person, to be appointed and directed by the managers aforesaid, or the major part of them, shall take out and draw one ticket from the box where the said number[e]'d tickets shall be put as aforesaid, and one other indifferent and fit person, to be appointed and directed in like manner, shall presently take out a ticket or lot from the box where the said five thousand four hundred and twenty-two benefit, and nineteen thousand five hundred and seventy-eight blank, tickets shall be promiscuously put as aforesaid, and immediately both the tickets so drawn shall be opened, and the number of the benefit, as well as blank, tickets, shall be named aloud; and if the ticket taken or drawn from the box containing the benefit, and blank, lots, shall appear to be a blank, then the numbered ticket so drawn with the said blank at the same time, shall both be put on one file; and if the ticket so drawn or taken from the box containing the benefit, and blank, lots, shall appear to be one of the benefit tickets, then the principal sum written upon such benefit ticket[s], whatever it be, shall be entred, by such clerk or clerks as the said managers, or the major part of them, shall employ and oversee for this purpose, being first sworn to a faithful discharge of his or their office, into a book to be kept for entring the numbers coming up with the said benefit tickets; and the said benefit, and numbered, tickets so drawn together shall be put upon another file; and so the said drawing of the tickets shall continue, by taking one ticket at a time out of each box, and with opening, naming aloud and filing the same, and by entring the benefit lots in such method as is before mentioned, until[l] the whole number be compleatly drawn; and if the same cannot be performed in one day's time, the said managers shall cause the boxes to be locked up and sealed in manner as aforesaid, and adjourn till next day, and so from day to day, and every day, except on the Lord's day; and then open the same and proceed as above, till the said whole number shall be drawn as aforesaid; and afterwards the said numbered tickets so drawn, with the benefit tickets drawn against the same, shall be and remain in a strong box, locked up as aforesaid, and under the custody of the said managers, until[l] they shall take them out to examine, adjust and set[t]le the property thereof. And, as soon as conveniently may be after the drawing is over, the said managers are required to cause to be printed and published, the number of the ticket drawn against each benefit ticket, and the principal sum written on the same, and if any contention or dispute shall arise in adjusting the property of the said benefit tickets, the major part of the said managers agre[e]ing therein, shall determine to whom it doth or ought to belong.

Time and place of drawing tickets.

Benefit tickets to be entered by the managers' clerk or clerks.

Managers may adjourn from day to day until all are drawn.

[SECT. 7.] And if any person shall forge or counterfeit any ticket or tickets to be made forth on this act, or alter any of the numbers thereof,

Penalty for persons who forge or counterfeit tickets, &c.

or utter, vend, barter or dispose of, or offer to dispose of, any false, altered, forged or counterfeit ticket or tickets, or bring any forged or counterfeit ticket or tickets, the number whereof is altered, knowing the same to be altered, to the said managers, or any of them, or to any other person, to the intent to defraud this province, or any adventurer upon this act, that then every such person or persons, being thereof convicted in due form of law, shall suffer such pains and penalties as is by law provided in cases of forgery.

The managers to commit such to prison.

[SECT. 8.] And the said managers or directors, or any two of them, are hereby authorized, required and impowered to cause any person or persons bringing or uttering such forged or counterfeit ticket or tickets as aforesaid, to be apprehended and committed to close goal, to be proceeded against according to law.

Provided always,—

And it is hereby enacted,

[SECT. 9.] That each manager and director for putting this act in execution, before his acting in such commission, shall take the following oath; viz[t].,

Directors' oath.

I, A. B., do swear that I will faithfully execute the trust reposed in me, and that I will not use any indirect act or means to obtain a prize or benefit lot for myself or any other person whatsoever, and that I will do the utmost of my endeavour to prevent any undue or sinister practice to be done by any person whatsoever, and that I will, to the best of my judgment, declare to whom any prize, lot or ticket does of right belong, according to the true intent and meaning of the act of this province, made in the eighteenth year of his majesty's reign in that behalf. So help me God.

—which shall and may be administred by any two or more of the other managers and directors.

And be it further enacted,

Four-fifths of the benefit tickets to be paid the owners or proprietors.

[SECT. 10.] That from each benefit ticket there shall be deducted twenty per cent, or one-fifth part, to and for the use and service of this government; and the managers or directors as aforesaid, shall, within forty days after the drawing of said lottery is finished, pay to each owner or proprietor of the said benefit tickets, the remaining four-fifths of the full sum wrote or expressed as aforesaid on the said tickets, which will make, in the whole, the sum of thirty thousand pounds; and the remaining sum of seven thousand five hundred pounds, after deducting such necessary charges as shall be allowed by the governour and council (any allowance to the directors and managers for their service excepted), shall be paid in to the province treasury in bills of this province, there to remain until[l] the further order of this court.

And be it further enacted,

Undisposed tickets to remain as the interest, share and lot of the province.

[SECT. 11.] That if any of the aforesaid number[*e*]'d tickets shall remain in the hands of the directors or managers, undispos[*e*]'d of when the time set by this act for drawing said lottery shall be arrived, that then, and in such case, all and every such ticket shall be and remain as the interest, share and lot of this province, and the number of the said remaining undispos[*e*]'d tickets shall be, by the directors or managers, given out to the province treasurer, in order to be drawn for the province.

Provided, notwithstanding,—

Proviso.

[SECT. 12.] That if there shall not be at least twenty thousand tickets disposed of at the time appointed for drawing the lottery, the managers and directors aforesaid shall wholly desist from any further proceedings until[l] they shall receive further orders from the general court, anything in this act to the contrary notwithstanding.

And be it further enacted,

[SECT. 13.] That the directors or managers by this act appointed, shall have such allowance[*s*] for their services as the general court shall hereafter o[*rder**], and in case of the death, refusal or incapacity of attendance of any one or more of said managers, the vacancy shall be fill[*e*]'d up by the governour and council. [*Passed January* 9; *published February* 4, 1744-45. Directors' allowances to be made by the general court.

CHAPTER 21.

AN ACT FOR SUPPLYING THE TREASURY WITH THE SUM OF FIFTY THOUSAND POUNDS FOR PUTTING THE PROVINCE IN A BETTER POSTURE OF DEFENCE, FOR DISCHARGING THE PUBLIC DEBTS, &c., AND FOR DRAWING IN THE SAID BILLS INTO THE TREASURY AGAIN.

Be it enacted by the Governour, Council and House of Representatives,

[SECT. 1.] That the treasurer be and hereby is impowered and ordered to emit and issue forth the sum of fifty thousand pounds in bills of credit of the last tenor and date, now lying in his hands and received in for taxes, impost and excise, which shall pass in all public payments equal to other new tenor bills emitted since one thousand seven hundred and forty; or if there be not a sufficiency of such bills, that then the committee appointed by this court for signing bills are hereby directed and impowered to take care and make effectual provision so soon as may be, to imprint the said bills, or so many as may be needed to compleat the said sum, and to sign and deliver the same to the treasurer, taking his receipt for the same, and the said committee shall be under oath for the faithful performance of the trust by this act reposed in them; and the said sum of fifty thousand pounds shall be issued out of the treasury in manner and for the purposes following; viz., the sum of thirty thousand pounds, part of the aforesaid sum of fifty thousand pounds, shall be applied for the payment of officers and soldiers, transports and wages of seamen, and for purchasing provisions and all needful warlike stores for the carrying on an expedition against Cape Breton, pursuant to such grants as this court shall hereafter make for that purpose; or in case the expedition should be prevented, that then the remaining part of the said thirty thousand pounds shall be applied for payment of grants made by this court; and the sum of eight thousand pounds, part of the aforesaid sum of fifty thousand pounds, shall be applied for purchasing of a ship of force for the preservation and defence of the trade of this province, as this court in their present sessions shall agree upon; the sum of ten thousand pounds, part of the aforesaid sum of fifty thousand pounds, shall be applied for the payment of such other grants as are and shall be made by this court, and for the payment of stipends, bounties, premiums established by law, and for the payment of all other matters and things which this court have, or shall, either by law or orders, provide for the payment of out of the publick treasury, and for no other purpose whatsoever; and the sum of one thousand and four hundred pounds, part of the aforesaid sum of fifty thousand pounds, shall be applied for the discharge of other debts owing from this province to persons who have served or shall serve them by order of this court in such matters and things where there is no establishment, nor any certain sum assigned

£50,000 in bills of credit, to be emitted.

Appropriation of this emission.

£8,000 for purchasing a ship of force.

£10,000 for grants, &c.

£1,400 for debts where is no establishment.

* Parchment injured.

for such service, and for paper, printing, and writing for this court, and the expences of committees; and the sum of six hundred pounds, the remaining part of the aforesaid sum of fifty thousand pounds, shall be applied for the payment of the members of the house of representatives serving in the general court the several sessions during this year.

£600 for representatives.

And be it enacted,

Surplusage to lie in the treasury.

[SECT. 2.] That if there be a surplusage in any sum appropriated, such surplusage shall lie in the treasury for the further order of this court.

And be it further enacted,

Warrants to express the appropriations.

[SECT. 3.] That each and every warrant for drawing money out of the treasury, shall direct the treasurer to take the same out of such sums as are respectively appropriated for payment of such publick debts as the draughts are made to discharge; and the treasurer is hereby directed and ordered to pay such money out of such appropriations as directed to, and no other, upon pain of refunding all such sum or sums as he shall otherwise pay, and to keep exact and distinct accompts of all payments made out of such appropriated sums; and the secretary, to whom it belongs to keep the muster-rolls and accompts of charge, shall lay before the house, when they direct, all such muster-rolls and accompts after payment thereof.

And as a fund and security for drawing the said sum of fifty thousand pounds into the treasury again,—

Be it further enacted,

£20,700 in 1747.

[SECT. 4.] That there be and hereby is granted to his most excellent majesty, for the ends and uses aforesaid, a sum of twenty thousand and seven hundred pounds, to be levied on polls, and estates both real and personal, within this province, according to such rules and in such proportions on the several towns and districts within the same, as shall be agreed upon and ordered by this court at their session in May, one thousand seven hundred and forty-seven, and paid into the publick treasury on or before the last day of December then next after.

And as a further fund and security for drawing the said sum of fifty thousand pounds into the treasury again,—

Be it further enacted,

£20,700 in 1748.

[SECT. 5.] That there be and hereby is granted unto his most excellent majesty, for the ends and uses aforesaid, a tax of twenty thousand and seven hundred pounds, to be levied on polls, and estates both real and personal, within this province, according to such rules and in such proportions on the several towns and districts within the same, as shall be agreed upon and ordered by this court at their session in May, one thousand seven hundred and forty-eight, and paid into the publick treasury on or before the last day of December then next after.

And as a fund and security for drawing in the sum of eight thousand pounds, appropriated in this act for the purchasing a ship of force for the preservation and defence of the trade of this province (being the remaining part of the said sum of fifty thousand pounds), into the treasury again,—

Be it enacted,

£8,000 on ships and other vessels.

1744-45, chap. 22.

[SECT. 6.] That the tax or duty laid upon ships and other vessels in and by an act made and passed by this court at their present sessions, intitled "An Act for granting to his majesty a duty on tonnage," shall be the fund and security for sinking and effectually drawing in said sum of eight thousand pounds, and for no other purpose whatsoever.

And as a fund and security for drawing in such sum or sums as shall be paid out to the representatives of the several towns,—

Be it enacted,

Tax to be made for what is paid the representatives.

[SECT. 7.] That there be and hereby is granted unto his most excellent majesty a tax of such sum or sums as shall be paid the representatives aforesaid, to be levied and assessed on the polls and estates of the inhabitants of the several towns, according to what their representatives shall so receive; which sums shall be set on the towns in the province tax, in the years one thousand seven hundred and forty-seven, and one thousand seven hundred and forty-eight; and the assessors of the said towns shall make their assessment for this tax and apportion the same according to the rule that shall be prescribed by act of the general assembly for assessing the province tax in the years abovesaid; and the constables in their respective districts shall pay in the same when they pay in the province tax for the years aforesaid, of which the treasurer is hereby directed to keep a distinct and separate account; and if there be any surplusage, the same shall lie in the hands of the treasurer for the further order of this court.

And be it further enacted,

[SECT. 8.] That in case the general court shall not, at their sessions in May, one thousand seven hundred and forty-seven, and one thousand seven hundred and forty-eight, agree and conclude upon an act apportioning the several sums which by this act is engaged shall be in each of these several years apportioned, assessed and levied, that then and in such case each town and district within this province shall pay, by a tax to be levied on the polls, and estates both real and personal, within their districts, the same proportion of the said sums as the said towns and districts shall have been taxed by the general court in the tax act then next preceding; and the province treasurer is hereby fully impowered and directed, some time in the month of June in each of these years one thousand seven hundred and forty-seven and one thousand seven hundred and forty-eight, to issue and send forth his warrants, directed to the selectmen or assessors of each town and district within this province, requiring them to assess the polls, and estates both real and personal, within their several towns and districts, for their respective part and proportion of the several sums before directed and engaged to be assessed by this act; and the assessors, as also persons assessed, shall observe, be governed by and subject to all such rules and directions as shall have been given in the next preceding tax act.

Tax for the money hereby emitted, to be made according to the preceding tax act.

And be it further enacted,

[SECT. 9.] That the inhabitants of this province shall have liberty, if they see fit, to pay the several sums for which they respectively may, in pursuance of this act, be assessed, in bills of credit of the form and tenor by this act emitted, or in other new-tenor bills, or in bills of the middle tenor, according to their several denominations, or in bills of the old tenor, accounting four for one; or in coined silver, at seven shillings and sixpence per ounce, troy weight, and of sterling alloy, or in gold coin, proportionably; or in merchantable hemp, flax, winter and Isle-of-Sable codfish, refined bar-iron, bloomery-iron, hollow iron-ware, Indian corn, rye, wheat, barley, pork, beef, duck or canvas, whalebone, cordage, train-oil, beeswax, bayberry-wax, tallow, peas, sheepswool, or tann'd sole-leather (the aforesaid commodities being of the produce or manufactures of this province), at such moderate rates and prices as the respective general assemblies of the years one thousand seven hundred and forty-seven, and one thousand seven hundred and forty-eight, shall set them at; the several persons paying their taxes in any of the commodities aforementioned, to run the risque and pay the charge of transporting the said commodities to the province treasury; but if the aforesaid general assemblies shall not, at their respective sessions in May, some time before the twentieth day of June, agree upon and set the aforesaid species or commodities at some certain prices, that then the eldest councellor, for the time being, of each of those counties in the province, of which any one of the council is an inhabitant, together

Taxes to be paid in the several species herein enumerated.

with the province treasurer, or the major part of them, be a committee, who hereby are directed and fully authorized and impowered to do it; and in their settling the prices and rating the value of those commodities, to state so much of them, respectively, at seven shillings and sixpence as an ounce of silver will purchase at that time in the town of Boston, and so *pro ratâ*. And the treasurer is hereby directed to insert in the several warrants by him sent to the collectors of the taxes in those years, respectively, with the names of the afore-recited commodities, the several rates or prices which shall be set on them, either by the general assembly or the committee aforesaid, and direct the aforesaid collectors to receive them so.

Commodities brought into the treasury, how to be rated.

Treasurer to sell the said commodities.

[SECT. 10.] And the aforesaid commodities, so brought into the treasury, shall, as soon as may be, be disposed of by the treasurer to the best advantage for so much as it will fetch in bills of credit hereby to be emitted, or any of the bills of credit aforementioned, or for silver or gold, which silver and gold shall be delivered to the possessor of said bills in exchange for them; that is to say, one ounce of silver coin, and so gold in proportion, for seven shillings and sixpence, and so *pro ratâ* for a greater or less sum; and if any loss shall happen by the sale of the aforesaid species, or by any unforeseen accident, such deficiency shall be made good by a tax of the year next following, so as fully and effectually to call in the sum of forty-two thousand pounds in said bills hereby ordered to be emitted, and for which a tax on polls and estates is in this act laid as a fund; and if there be a surplusage, it shall remain a stock in the treasury. [*Passed February* 5; *published February* 9, 1744–45.

CHAPTER 22.

AN ACT FOR GRANTING TO HIS MAJESTY A DUTY OF TONNAGE ON SHIPPING.

Preamble.

WHEREAS it appears necessary for his majesty's service, and for the preservation and defence of the trade of this province, that a ship of force, mounting twenty carriage-guns, be provided and made for that purpose as soon as possible, and that in order to purchasing such a ship, the treasury be forthwith supplied with the sum of eight thousand pounds in bills of the last emission, which sum, considering the heavy burthen of publick taxes the province now lays under, and the increase thereof that will be occasioned by the yearly support and maintenance of said ship, over and above the usual charge, also that the advantage of such a ship will chiefly accrue to the trade, it appears but equal and just that the same should be repaid into the treasury by a tax or duty on shipping; wherefore,—

Be it enacted by the Governour, Council and House of Representatives,

£8,000 to be paid on vessels entering into port or harbor within this province, &c.

[SECT. 1.] That from and after the publication of this act, until the end of seven years, and as much longer as the war shall continue, there be and hereby is granted to his most excellent majesty, for the drawing in and sinking the said sum of eight thousand pounds, as also towards the charge of maintaining such a ship during the war (if it should continue after the said sum of eight thousand pounds is paid) the sum of sixpence a ton in silver money, at six shillings and eightpence per ounce, or in lieu thereof, equivalent in bills of credit of this province, on all ships and other vessels (excepting common coasters and fishing vessels) entring into port or harbour within this province, other than such as shall clear out of some other port or harbour within the same; and on all coasters trading from harbour to harbour within this province, and fishing vessels, the like sum of sixpence per ton a year.

And to render this act effectual,—

Be it further enacted,

[SECT. 2.] That the tonnage of all vessels, except fishing and coasting vessels, shall be measured and taken in manner as is directed in the act for building the lighthouse, passed in the first year of King George the First, chapter the third; and the commissioner of impost, or his deputy, is hereby directed and impowered, before he enters any ship or vessel that is by law required to enter, to demand and receive the duty by this act intended to be paid, and shall certify the same to the naval officer, and the said naval officer is hereby strictly forbidden to clear out any ship or other vessel until the master or owner of such ship or vessel shall produce a certificate that he has paid the duty by this act designed to be paid; and in case the master of any ship or vessel refuse to enter at the custom-house office as by law obliged, or to pay the duty by this act provided, any such delinquent or refusing master, over and above the penalty by law already provided, shall be liable to the action or actions of the impost-officer for the time being, for the recovery of the duty by this act imposed, in any of his majesty's courts of record, or before any justice of the peace, as the nature of the case shall require; to prosecute which action or actions the said impost-officer or officers are hereby respectively impowered.

Tonnage of vessels to be measured

1715-16, chap. 4.

Vessels not to be cleared until the duty is paid.

Be it further enacted,

[SECT. 3.] That the selectmen or assessors of every town within this province, where any fishing and coasting vessels may belong, are hereby impowered and directed to assess and tax the vessels aforesaid, according to the direction of this act hereinbefore expressed; the measure of the vessel, in case of doubt, to be taken at the cost of the respective owners or masters, by the said assessors, unless the account of their measure first given in, be just and true (in which cases the charge to be born by the respective towns); and the said assessment and tax, when made, to commit to the constable or collectors of their towns respectively, who are hereby impowered and obliged to collect the same of the master or other person having the principal care thereof, and pay it into the province treasury; and the said assessors are further required and directed to transmit to the province treasurer, yearly, a list of every vessel by them, according to the tenor of this act, assessed and taxed, together with a certificate of the name or names of the constable or collectors to whom the said assessment shall have been by them committed to collect: and the province treasurer is hereby impowered and directed to issue out his warrants for the recovery of the said duty or tax assessed as aforesaid on any coasting and fishing vessels against any delinquent constables or collectors as is by law in other cases made and provided.

Selectmen or assessors empowered to tax coasting vessels.

Provided, nevertheless,

[SECT. 4.] This act shall not be construed to exempt any vessel aforesaid from being taxed as vessels heretofore. [*Passed April* 5; *published April* 6, 1745.

Proviso.

CHAPTER 23.

AN ACT FOR SUPPLYING THE TREASURY WITH THE SUM OF FIFTY THOUSAND POUNDS, FOR DISCHARGING THE PUBLIC[K] DEBTS, &c., AND FOR DRAWING IN THE SAID BILLS INTO THE TREASURY AGAIN.

Be it enacted by the Governour, Council and House of Representatives,

£50,000 in bills of credit, to be emitted.

[SECT. 1.] That the treasurer be and hereby is impowered and ordered to emit and issue forth the sum of fifty thousand pounds in bills of credit of the last tenor and date, now lying in his hands, and received for taxes, impost and excise, which shall pass in all public[k] payments, equal to other new-tenor bills emitted since one thousand seven hundred and forty, or if there be not a sufficiency of such bills, that then the committee appointed by this court for signing bills are hereby directed and impowered to take care and make effectual provision, as soon as may be, to imprint the said bills, or so many as may be needed to compleat the said sum, and to sign and deliver the same to the treasurer, taking his receipt for the same; and the said committee shall be under oath for the faithful performance of the trust by this act reposed in them. And the said sum of fifty thousand pounds shall be issued out of the public[k] treasury in [the] manner and for the purposes following; viz[t]., for the payment of officers and soldiers, transports and wages of seamen, and for purchasing provisions and all needful warlike stores for the carrying on an expedition against Cape Breton, pursuant to such grants as this court hath or shall hereafter make for that purpose, or in case the expedition should be prevented, that then the remaining part of the said sum of fifty thousand pounds shall be applied for the payment of grants made by this court.

Appropriation of this emission.

And be it enacted,

Surplusage to lie in the treasury.

[SECT. 2.] That if there be a surplusage in any of this sum appropriated, such surplusage shall l[y][*ie*]e in the treasury for the further order of this court.

And be it further enacted,

Warrants to express the appropriations.

[SECT. 3.] That each and every warrant for drawing this money out of the treasury, shall direct the treasurer to take the same out of the aforesaid sum as is directed, and no other, upon pain of refunding all such sum or sums as he shall otherwise pay, and to keep exact and distinct accompts of all payments made out of the aforesaid sum. And the secretary, to whom it belongs to keep the muster-rolls and accompts of charge, shall lay before the house, when they direct, all such muster-rolls and accompts, after payment thereof.

And as a fund and security for drawing the aforesaid sum of fifty thousand pounds into the treasury again,—

Be it further enacted,

£25,000 in 1749.

[SECT. 4.] That there be and hereby is granted [un]to his most excellent majesty, for the ends and uses aforesaid, a tax of twenty-five thousand pounds, to be levied on polls, and estates both real and personal, within this province, according to such rules and in such proportions on the several towns and districts within the same, as shall be agreed upon and ordered by this court at their session in May, one thousand seven hundred and forty-nine, and paid into the publick treasury on or before the last day of December then next after.

And as a further fund and security for drawing the aforesaid sum of fifty thousand pounds into the treasury again,—

Be it further enacted,

£25,000 in 1750.

[SECT. 5.] That there be and hereby is granted unto his most excellent majesty, for the ends and uses aforesaid, a tax of twenty-five thousand

sand pounds, to be levied on polls, and estates both real and personal, within this province, according to such rules and in such proportions, on the several towns and districts within the same, as shall be agreed upon and ordered by this court at their session in May, one thousand seven hundred and fifty, and paid into the publick treasury on or before the last day of December then next after.

And be it further enacted,

[SECT. 6.] That in case the general court shall not, at their sessions in May, one thousand seven hundred and forty-nine, and one thousand seven hundred and fifty, agree and conclude upon an act apportioning the several sums which by this act is engaged shall be, in each of these several years, apportioned, assessed and levied, that then and in such case each town and district within this province shall pay, by a tax to be levied on the polls, and estates both real and personal, within their districts, the same proportion of the said sums as the said towns and districts shall have been taxed by the general court in the tax act then next preceeding. And the province treasurer is hereby fully impowered and directed, some time in the month of June in each of these years, one thousand seven hundred and forty-nine, and one thousand seven hundred and fifty, to issue and send forth his warrants, directed to the selectmen or assessors of each town and district within this province, requiring them to assess the polls, and estates both real and personal, within their several towns and districts, for their respective part and proportion of the several sums before directed and engaged to be assessed by this act; and the assessors, as also persons assessed, shall observe, be governed by, and subject to all such rules and directions as shall have been given in the next preceding tax act.

Tax for the money hereby emitted, to be made according to the preceding tax act.

And be it further enacted,

[SECT. 7.] That the inhabitants of this province shall have liberty, if they see fit, to pay the several sums for which they respectively may, in pursuance of this act, be assessed, in bills of credit of the form and tenor by this act emitted, or in other new-tenor bills, or in bills of the middle tenor, according to their several denominations, or in bills of the old tenor, accounting four for one; or in coined silver, at seven shillings and sixpence per ounce, troy weight, of sterling alloy, or in gold coin proportionably; or in merchantable hemp, flax, winter and Isle-of-Sable codfish, refined bar-iron, bloomery-iron, hollow iron-ware, Indian corn, rye, wheat, barley, pork, beef, duck or canvas, whalebone, cordage, train-oil, beeswax, bayberry-wax, tallow, peas[e], sheepswool, or tan[*n*]'d sole-leather (the aforesaid commodities being of the produce or manufactories of this province), at such moderate rates and prices as the respective general assemblys of the years one thousand seven hundred and forty-nine, and one thousand seven hundred and fifty, shall set them at; the several persons paying their taxes in and of the commodities aforementioned, to run the risque and pay the charge of transporting the said commodities to the province treasury; but if the aforesaid general assembl[y][*ie*]s shall not, at their respective sessions in May, some time before the twent[y][*i*]eth day of June, agree upon and set the aforesaid species or commodities at some certain prices, that then the eldest councellor, for the time being, in each of those counties of the province, of which any one of the council is an inhabitant, together with the province treasurer, or the major part of them, be a committee, who [are] hereby [*are*] directed and fully authorized and impowered to do it; and in [*their*] setting the prices and rating the value of those commodities, to state so much of them, respectively, at seven shillings and sixpence as an ounce of silver will purchase at that time in the town of Boston, and so *pro ratâ*. And the treasurer is hereby directed to insert in the several warrants by him sent to the col-

Taxes to be paid in the several species herein enumerated.

Commodities brought into the treasury, how to be rated.

lectors of the taxes in those years, respectively, with the names of the afore-recited commodities, the several rates or prices which shall be set on them either by the general assembly, or the committee aforesaid, and direct the aforesaid collectors to receive them so.

Treasurer to sell the said commodities.

[SECT. 8.] And the aforesaid commodities so brought into the treasury, shall, as soon as may be, be disposed of by the treasurer to the best advantage for so much as it will fetch in bills of credit hereby to be emitted, or any of the bills of credit aforementioned, or for silver or gold, which silver and gold shall be delivered to the possessor of said bills in exchange for them; that is to say, one ounce of silver coin, and so gold in proportion, for seven shillings and sixpence, and so *pro ratâ* for a greater or less sum; and if any loss shall happen by the sale of the aforesaid species, or by any unforeseen accident, such deficiency shall be made good by a tax of the year next following, so as fully and effectually to call in the sum of fifty thousand pounds in said bills hereby ordered to be emitted, and for which a tax on polls and estates is in this act laid as a fund; and if there be a surplusage, it shall remain a stock in the treasury. [*Passed March* 9, 1744–45; *published April* 6, 1745.

CHAPTER 24.

AN ACT FOR GRANTING A SUM FOR THE PAY OF THE MEMBERS OF THE COUNCIL AND HOUSE OF REPRESENTATIVES, IN GENERAL COURT ASSEMBLED, AND FOR ESTABLISHING THE WAGES, &c[A]., OF SUNDRY PERSONS IN THE SERVICE OF THE PROVINCE.

Be it enacted by the Governour, Council and House of Represent-[ati]ves,

Pay of the members of the council.

[SECT. 1.] That from the beginning of the present session of the general court, unto the end of their several sessions, 'till May next, each member of the council shall be entitled to four shillings and sixpence per diem, to be paid out of the public[k] treasury, by warrant, according to the direction of the royal charter, upon certificate given by the secretary of the number of days of such member's attendance, and travel to and from the court, twenty miles to be accounted a day's travel.

And be it further enacted,

Pay of the representatives.

[SECT. 2.] That each member of the house of represent[*ati*]ves serving the time afores[*ai*]d, shall be paid three shillings per diem, upon certificate given by the clerk of the house of represent[*ati*]ves of the number of days of such member's attendance, and travel to and from the court, twenty miles to be accounted a day's travel.

And be it further enacted,

Pay of the officers and soldiers at Castle William.

[SECT. 3.] That the wages of the captain of Castle William shall be after the rate of sixty pounds per annum, from the nineteenth day of November, one thousand seven hundred and forty-four, to the twentieth day of March, one thousand seven hundred and forty-four; of the lieutenant, for that term, forty pounds; of the chaplain, forty pounds; of the gunner, fifty pounds; of the gunner's mate, forty shillings per month; of four ser[g][*j*]eants, each thirty shillings per month; of six quarter-gunners, each thirty shillings per month; of six corporals, each twenty-six shillings and sixpence per month; two drummers, each twenty-six shillings and sixpence per month; of one armourer, forty shillings per month; of forty centinels, each twenty-two shillings and sixpence per month: for their subsistence, six shillings and threepence per week per man.

And be it further enacted,

[SECT. 4.] That the wages of the captain of Richmond Fort, from the nineteenth day of Nov[*embe*]r, one thousand seven hundred and forty-four, to the twentieth day of March, one thousand seven hundred and forty-four, shall be at the rate of forty shillings per month; of one ser[g][*j*]eant, twenty-five shillings per month; of one corporal, twenty-four shillings per month; of one armourer, thirty shillings per month; and for the chaplain, twenty-five pounds per annum; of one interpreter, fifteen shillings per month, being a centinel; and of twelve centinels, twenty-two shillings and sixpence per month. Richmond Fort.

And be it further enacted,

[SECT. 5.] That the wages of the captain of the truck-house on George's River, from the nineteenth day of Novem[*be*]r, one thousand seven hundred and forty-four, to the twentieth day of March, one thousand seven hundred and forty-four, shall be at the rate of forty shillings per month; of one lieutenant, twenty-six shillings per month; of one ser[g][*j*]eant, twenty-five shillings per month; of two corporals, each twenty-four shillings per month; of thirty-three centinels, each twenty-two shillings and sixpence per month; of one armourer, fourteen shill[*in*]gs per month, he being lieutenant; of one interpreter, thirty shillings per month; and of the chaplain there, twenty-five pounds per annum. George's River.

And be it further enacted,

[SECT. 6.] That the wages of the commanding officer of the fort at Brunswick, from the nineteenth day of Novem[*be*]r, one thousand seven hundred and forty-four, to the twentieth day of March, one thousand seven hundred and forty-four, shall be at the rate of forty shillings per month; of seven centinels, each twenty-two shillings and sixpence per month; one ser[g][*j*]eant, at twenty-five shillings per month. Brunswick Fort.

And be it further enacted,

[SECT. 7.] That the wages of one ser[g][*j*]eant at the truck-house at Saco, from the nineteenth day of Novem[*be*]r, one thousand seven hundred and forty-four, to the twentieth day of March, one thousand seven hundred and forty-four, shall be at the rate of thirty shillings per month; of one corporal, twenty-four shillings per month; of eight centinels, each twenty-two shill[*in*]gs and sixpence per month. Saco truck-house.

And be it further enacted,

[SECT. 8.] That the wages of the commanding officer at Frederick Fort, from the nineteenth day of Nov[*embe*]r, one thousand seven hundred and forty-four, to the twentieth day of March, one thousand seven hundred and forty-four, shall be at the rate of forty shillings per month; and of the chaplain there, fifteen pounds per annum; and of twenty-one centinels, each at twenty-two shillings and sixpence per month. Frederick Fort.

And be it further enacted,

[SECT. 9.] That the wages of the captain of the sloop in the country's service, from the nineteenth day of Nov[*embe*]r, one thousand seven hundred and forty-four, to the twentieth day of March, one thousand seven hundred and forty-four, shall be at the rate of fifty shillings per month; of the mate, thirty shillings per month; of eight sailors, each twenty-five shillings per month; for the sloop, seven pounds ten shillings per month. Country's sloop.

And be it further enacted,

[SECT. 10.] That the wages of the captain of the province snow, from the twentieth day of November, one thousand seven hundred and forty-four, to the twentieth day of March, one thousand seven hundred and forty-four, shall be at the rate of five pounds ten shillings per month; the lieutenant, three pounds ten shillings per month; the gunner, two pounds eighteen shillings per month; the boatswain, two Province snow.

pounds fifteen shillings per month; two sailors or foremast men, each forty shillings per month.

And be it further enacted,

Oath to be made, &c.

[SECT. 11.] That before payment of any muster-roll be allowed, oath be made by the officer or person presenting such roll, that the officers and soldiers born on such roll, have been in actual service for the whole time they stand entred thereon. [*Passed April* 5; *published April* 6, 1745.

CHAPTER 25.

AN ACT TO PREVENT MISCHIEF BEING DONE BY UNRULY DOGS.

Preamble. 1737-38, chap. 10.

WHEREAS much dam[*m*]age has been done by unruly dogs in worrying, wounding, and killing neat cattle, sheep and lambs within this province, to the great loss of many persons, the owners of such creatures; for the preventing whereof,—

Be it enacted by the Governour, Council and House of Representatives,

Dog or bitch to be killed when found out of the inspection of the owner.

[SECT. 1.] That from and after the publication of this act, it shall and may be lawful to and for any person or persons within this province, to kill and destroy any dog or bitch whatsoever that shall be found, out of the immediate care and inspection of its owner or keeper, within or crossing over any common land, field or inclosure (excepting the land of the owner of such dog or bitch), in the day-time; or that shall be found, between sunset[t] and sunrise, anywhere out of the care and inspection of its owners as aforesaid; and if the owner of such dog or bitch, being known and informed, within eight hours next after, of his or her dog or bitch's being seen out of the care and inspection as aforesaid, and oath made thereof before some one justice of the peace (or town clerk, who is hereby impowered to administer and certify the same), and shall refuse to kill, or cause to be kill[*e*]d, his dog or bitch forthwith, shall forfeit and pay the sum of forty shillings to the person who shall inform and sue for the same by bill, plaint or information, before any of his majesty's justices of the peace in the county where the owner of such dog or bitch dwells.

And be it further enacted,

Owners of any dog or bitch to pay damages.

[SECT. 2.] That the owner of any dog or bitch that shall tear or kill any calves or neat cattle, sheep or lambs, shall be liable to pay treble dam[*m*]ages to the person or persons injured, to be heard and tried before any of his majesty's justices of the peace in the county where the owner of such misch[ei][*ie*]vous dog or bitch dwells, if the dam[*m*]age exceeds not forty shillings; and where the dam[*m*]age exceeds that sum, before any of his majesty's courts of record in the county where the owner dwells as aforesaid, upon bill, plaint, writ[t] or information as aforesaid.

And be it further enacted,

Action not to be brought, &c.

[SECT. 3.] That no action shall l[y][*i*]e, be heard or tried at any court within this province against such person who shall or may kill or destroy any dog or bitch found as aforesaid; but shall be utterly barred by virtue of this act.

Provided, nevertheless,

Proviso.

[SECT. 4.] That this act shall not extend to or be in force in any town in the county of York, anything before therein contained to the contrary notwithstanding.

Limitation.

[SECT. 5.] This act to continue and be in force for the space of ten years from the publication thereof, and thence to the end of the then next session of the general court, and no longer. [*Passed April* 5; *published April* 6, 1745.

CHAPTER 26.

AN ACT TO PREVENT NEAT CATTLE AND HORSES RUNNING AT LARGE AND FEEDING ON THE BEACHES ADJOINING TO EASTERN-HARBOUR MEADOWS, IN THE TOWN OF TRURO.*

WHEREAS there are certain meadow-lands within the township of Truro, in the county of Barnstable, called Eastern-Harbour Meadows, on which many of the inhabitants of said town depend for their hay, and the said meadow-land lies adjoining to two long, sandy beaches, on which no fence can well be made to stand, and by reason of cattle and horses trampling and feeding there the beach grass, which was wont to prevent the driving of the sand from the beaches to the meadows, is destroyed, and a great part of the meadows already covered with sand, and become useless for grass, and the whole in danger of being buried with the sands, if not timely prevented,— Preamble. 1738-39, chap. 16.

Be it therefore enacted by the Governour, Council and House of Representatives,

[SECT. 1.] That from and after the publication of this act, no person shall presume to turn or drive any neat cattle or horses upon the said beaches or meadows to feed, or leave them at large there, on the penalty of ten shillings a head for all neat cattle and for every horse-kind so turn[e]d upon any of the said beaches or meadows to feed, or that shall be found at large there; which penalty may be recovered by any of the proprietors of said beaches or meadows, one moiety thereof to be to the informer that shall sue for the same, and the other moiety to be to and for the use of the poor of the town of Truro. Penalty for leaving cattle or horse-kind to feed at large on the meadows in Truro.

And be it further enacted,

[SECT. 2.] That it shall be lawful for any owner or proprietor of the said meadows or beaches, or other person, finding any cattle or horse-kind feeding or going at large upon the beaches or meadows afores[ai]d, or any of them, to impound the same; and the person or persons impounding them shall give public[k] notice thereof in the town of Truro and in the two next adjoining towns; and shall rel[ei][ie]ve said creatures whilst impounded, with suitable meat and water; and the owner thereof appearing, he shall pay to the impounder two shillings and sixpence dam[m]ages for each head of neat cattle or horse-kind so impounded, and costs of impounding them; and if the owner do not appear within the space of six days and pay the dam[m]age and costs occasioned by impounding the same, then and in every such case, the person or persons impounding such cattle or horse-kind shall cause them to be sold at publick vendue for paying such dam[m]ages and costs, and the charge arising by such sale (public[k] notice of the time and place of such sale being given forty-eight hours beforehand) and the overplus, if any be, to be returned to the owner of such cattle or horse-kind, on his demand, at any time within twelve months next after the sale; and if no owner shall appear within the said twelve months, then one moiety of the overplus shall be to the party impounding, and the other moiety thereof to the use of the poor of the town of Truro. Cattle, &c., to be impounded, if found feeding at large. To be sold if no owner appears.

And be it further enacted,

[SECT. 3.] That the proprietors of the said meadows and beaches, and the proprietors of the lotted land on the Cape, shall make and Proprietors of the meadows, &c., to make

* See note to chapter 27, *post*.

and maintain fences. maintain a sufficient fence, in equal proportion betwixt them, or otherwise prevent their cattle from passing to the eastward of the westerly part of Strout's Meadow, so called, and the proprietors of the afores[*ai*]d meadows, with the proprietors of Truro, not having right in said meadows, that turn horses or cattle on the commons there, be likewise obliged to erect and maintain a fence that shall prevent horses and cattle from passing to the westward of the east end of Eastern-Harbour Meadows, or otherwise to restrain them from feeding or going at large there, on pain of incurring the penalty afores[*ai*]d for each head of cattle or horse-kind that shall be found there, and of having them impounded and otherwise proceeded with in manner as before mentioned.

Limitation. [SECT. 4.] This act to continue in force five years from the publication thereof, and from thence to the end of the next session of the general court, and no longer. [*Passed April* 5; *published April* 6, 1745.

CHAPTER 27.

AN ACT IN ADDITION TO THE ACT FOR PREVENTING DAM[*M*]AGE TO THE HARBOUR OF CAPE COD, BY CATTLE AND HORSE-KIND FEEDING ON PROVINCETOWN LANDS.

Preamble. 1740-41, chap. 15. WHEREAS the provision made in and by the act [e][*i*]ntitled "An Act to prevent dam[*m*]age being done to the harbour of Cape Cod," made and pass[*e*]d in the fourteenth year of his present majesty's reign, has been found ineffectual for that end,—

Be it therefore enacted by the Governour, Council and House of Represent[*ati*]*ves*,

Pound to be kept and maintained by the selectmen of Provincetown. [SECT. 1.] That a sufficient pound be kept and maintained by the selectmen of Provincetown, in such part of said town as they shall judge most commodious for the inhabitants, for impounding of creatures that shall be suffered to feed on the lands there, whether upland, meadow or beach, contrary to the afores[*ai*]d act; and that the reasonable charge of the erecting and maintaining the same be repaid them out of the publick treasury by warrant from the governour, with the advice and consent of the council.

And be it further enacted,

Constable to make search for horses, &c. [SECT. 2.] That the constable of Provincetown for the time being shall, and he is hereby strictly required to, take effectual care that the afores[*ai*]d act be put in execution for preventing dam[*m*]age to the harbour aforesaid; as also one day in every week, from the first of April to the last of Octo[*be*]r, to make diligent search for horses and cattle on Provincetown lands, and to cause such of them to be impounded as by this act are not allowed to feed there; and such constable, for every day he shall faithfully attend said service and make oath thereof before a justice of the peace, shall be allowed one shilling and threepence, to be paid out of the publick treasury.

What cattle may feed on the lands. [SECT. 3.] And the inhabitants of said Provincetown are hereby allowed to keep and to suffer to feed on the lands there, one bull and three yoke of oxen amongst the inhabitants in general, as also one horse and one cow for each family, and no more; save that such person as shall have licence to keep an house of publick entertainment, shall have liberty to keep two cows during the continuance of such his licence.

And be it further enacted,

Forfeiture for cutting or carrying off brush. [SECT. 4.] That whosoever, after the publication of this act, shall presume to cut down or carry off any trees, poles or brush from any part of the land within the bounds of Provincetown or Cape Cod, standing or growing there within one hundred and sixty pole from high-water mark, shall forfeit and pay the sum of five shillings for every tree or pole, and one shilling for every bush so cut or carried off; the one-half of said forfeiture to be to him or them that shall inform and sue for the same, and the other half to be to and for the use of the poor of the said town of Provincetown, to be recovered before a justice of the peace of the same county.

[SECT. 5.] This act to continue and be in force one year from the publication thereof, and from thence to the end of the next session of the general court, and no longer. [*Passed April* 5; *published April* 6, 1745. Limitation.

CHAPTER 28.

AN ACT TO REGULATE THE PAY OF SOLDIERS AND MARINERS, AND TO PREVENT FRAUD THEREIN.

WHEREAS no direction is given in the law how soldiers and mariners, serving his majesty in the pay of this province, shall receive their wages,— Preamble. 1744-45, chap. 7.

Be it enacted by the Governour, Council and House of Represent[*ati*]*ves*,

[SECT. 1.] That during the next two years after the publication of this act, when any muster-roll for the wages of the soldiers and mariners serving this province is pass[*e*]'d and allowed, and a warrant granted for the payment thereof, the province treasurer shall pay to the soldiers and mariners born thereon the sums respectively due to them, either to him or them in person, or to his or their express order in writing, and not otherwise. How soldiers' and mariners' wages are to be paid.

And to prevent the said treasurer being imposed on by counterfeit orders, or by persons who may pretend to have been in the publick service when they have not,—

Be it further enacted,

[SECT. 2.] That no soldier or mariner appearing in person, or sending his order as afores[*ai*]d, shall be allowed to receive his wages until[l] he produce a certificate either from under the hand of the captain or chief commanding officer that impressed, or inlisted and sent him out, or under the hand of one or other of the commission officers under whom he served, setting forth that he was impressed, or inlisted and sent out, or that he did actually serve his majesty as aforesaid, which certificate shall be given by the afores[*ai*]d officers without fee or demand. Certificate to be produced before payment.

And to enable parents, guardians, and masters to receive the wages due for their sons under age, wards or servants, as also to prevent such sons, wards or servants from receiving or mispending the same,—

Be it further enacted,

[SECT. 3.] That when and so often as any son under age, ward or servant, consequent on the captain-general's order, during the time afores[*ai*]d, shall be impress[*e*]'d, or inlisted and sent out, the commanding officer or officers, out of whose regiment or company they shall be taken, shall certify in writing, and cause to be transmitted to the chief commanding officer or officers to whom they are sent, by him or them to be transferred to the officer or officers under whom they are to serve, not only the names of such sons, wards or servants, but that they are sons, wards or servants, and what towns or places their fathers, guar- Commanding officers to be certified who are sons, wards, or servants.

dians or masters then live in; and the commanding officer or officers under whom they serve shall, from time to time, specify the same on the muster-roll when it is presented for allowance; and every father, guardian or master of any such son, ward or servant may demand and receive the same, either in person or by his order, in manner as aforesaid; and no such son, ward or servant, employed as afores[*ai*]d, shall be allowed to receive, either in person or by his order, any part of his wages of s[*ai*]d treasurer without express allowance, in writing, from his parent, guardian or master for that purpose.

Provided, nevertheless,—

Proviso. [SECT. 4.] That any captain or chief commanding officer, under whom such son under age, ward or servant shall serve, may, if he sees it needful[l], allow him or them to receive and take up, of him or some other person, things necessary for his comfortable subsistence, in cloathing, &c[a]., at reasonable prices, the one-half of his wages as they shall become due from time to time. [*Passed April* 5; *published April* 6, 1745.

CHAPTER 29.

AN ACT IN FURTHER ADDITION TO AN ACT ASCERTAINING THE VALUE OF MONEY, AND OF THE BILLS OF PUBLIC[K] CREDIT OF THIS PROVINCE.

Preamble. 1741-42, chap. 12. WHEREAS notwithstanding the provision that is made in and by an act pass'd in the fifteenth year of his present majesty's reign, [e][*i*]ntitled "An Act to ascertain the value of money, and of the bills of publick credit of this province, granted this present year for the supply of the treasury, and for securing the credit of said bills," for securing to any creditor or creditors what the bills of credit might sink or depreciate in their value between the time of contracting the debt and the payment thereof, it has been a frequent practice for creditors to exact and take of their debtors, for the loan of any sum or sums of money lent, and for forbearance of their debts, more than six per cent, by which practice some of the good and wholesome laws of this province, and the equitable intent and designs of them, are eluded, and great oppression and injustice introduced, to the reproach of this government; now, for the prevention thereof for the future,—

Be it enacted by the Governour, Council and House of Represent-[*ati*]*ves,*

No allowance to be made for the depreciating of the bills where anything has been allowed already for it. [SECT. 1.] That in all actions hereafter to be brought for the recovering any debt or sum due upon bond, or otherwise contracted and payable in bills of credit since the thirty-first day of March, one thousand seven hundred and forty-two, or that may be contracted within five years of that date, if the debtor will tender his oath in court that the creditor has received anything for the loan or forbearance of such debt, either in money, bills, goods, or by any new bond, bill, note of hand, order, or under colour of being paid for any service or thing, or by keeping back any part of the sum specified to be paid in the condition of any bond or other specialty, or by any other way or means whatsoever, either directly or indirectly, more than six pounds for the loan or forbearance of one hundred pounds for a year, and so after that rate for a greater or less sum, or for a longer or shorter time, then and in such case, unless the [creditor] [*owner*] will make oath to the contrary, judgment shall be made up only for the exact nominal sum received by or due from the debtor, with lawful[l] interest for the same, if it be payable with interest, but if the creditor will tender and actually give his oath as afores[*ai*]d, then judgment shall be entred up for the full value of said debt, as it was at the time of contracting the same.

And whereas there may be debts and sums payable in bills of credit or lawful money yet due and owing from man to man, that were contracted before the s[*ai*]d [31st] [*thirty-first*] day of March, one thousand seven hundred and forty-two, and no provision made in the law for making good to the creditors what the bills, in which such debts or sums might be discharged, have depreciated or fallen; *and inasmuch* as it appears just and equal that the loss and dam[*m*]age arising to such creditors by the falling and depreciating of the bills of credit since the s[*ai*]d thirty-first day of March, should be made good,— Preamble.

Be it further enacted,

[SECT. 2.] That in all such cases it shall be in the power of the justices of the several courts within this province, to make up judgm[*en*]t for such additional sum or sums as the s[*ai*]d bills shall be found to have depreciated from the s[*ai*]d [31st] [*thirty-first*] day of March, until[l] the time of making up such judgm[*en*]t, but not for any other or longer time; in w[*hi*]ch judgment the same rule shall be observed as in case of debts contracted after the said thirty-first day of March, as in this act is before provided: *saving always* to the debtor the same rel[ei][*ie*]f in case he has in any manner or way, directly or indirectly, paid or allowed more than six per cent as afores[*ai*]d, as is provided for him in this act respecting any debt or sum that was contracted or agreed upon after the said thirty-first day of March. Provision for making good the value of the debts before March 31, 1742.

And whereas many of his majesty's subjects in this province, from an apprehension that the bills of credit of the new tenor were to be valued, taken and esteemed as lawful money, from wh[*ic*]h apprehensions many persons have obliged themselves, by their bonds and otherways, to pay lawful money where nothing but s[*ai*]d bills were received, or goods for w[*hi*]ch the creditor would have received bills in payment, nor was anything else intended or expected by either party at the time of contracting the debt; notwithstanding which, some of the executive courts of this province have, contrary to the expectation and intention of the parties as afores[*ai*]d, made up their judgments on said debts for lawful money only, and construed the same not to be payable in said bills, whereby the debtor has been capable of discharging or satisfying the execution only with silver, the extream scarcity of which renders it almost impracticable to satisfy the debt without paying such additional sum to the creditor as he will be pleased to take in said bills, much to the debtor's oppression, which this government ought to prevent; wherefore,— Preamble.

Be it enacted,

[SECT. 3.] That when any sum or sums of money, due or contracted for since the first emission of the said new-tenor bills, in the year one thousand seven hundred and forty-one, or that shall be contracted for within the space of five years from that date, on bond, bill, note, or otherwise, whether with interest or without, if the debtor will tender his oath that he received of the creditor no silver on which said debt or sum then sued for arose, or that it was not agreed by the parties that silver should be paid in discharge of such debt or sum due, that then and in every such case, unless the creditor will, *bonâ fide*, make oath that silver was received or agreed for, and understood, and intended to be paid by the parties at the time of contracting the s[*ai*]d debt or agreem[*en*]t for the sum sued for, the judgm[*en*]t shall be given for bills of credit or lawful money at the debtor's election, allowing in such judgm[*en*]t for what the s[*ai*]d bills may have depreciated from Judgment to be given only for bills where silver was not lent or received.

the [31st] [*thirty-first*] day of March, one thousand seven hundred and forty-two, to the time the judgm[*en*]t is made up: *saving always* to the debtor the same rel[ei][*ie*]f in cases of this nature which is by this act already provided for him where more than six per cent has been paid for the loan or forbearance of any sum as aforesaid. [*Passed January* 9, 1744-45.

Saving.

CHAPTER 30.

AN ACT FOR THE MORE SPEEDY EXTINGUISHMENT OF FIRE, AND PRESERVING GOODS [E][*I*]NDANGERED BY IT.

Preamble. 1711-12, chap. 5.

WHEREAS the contiguity or nearness of houses in many towns in this province makes it difficult, when they accidentally take fire, to preserve them, and prevent its spreading, by reason of the inhabitants being terrified by so grievous a calamity, and the want of proper persons appointed to direct such as may be ready to assist; and moreover ill-minded persons take the advantage of the hurry and confusion attending such accidents to plunder, and to embezzle the goods of their distressed neighbours; wherefore,—

Be it enacted by the Governour, Council, and House of Represent-[*ati*]*ves*,

All towns empowered to choose fire-wards.

[SECT. 1.] That the several towns within this province may, if they see fit, at their anniversary meeting in March, annually appoint a suitable number of persons, not exceeding ten, who shall be denominated fire-wards, and have each, for a distinguishing badge of the office, a staff of five feet long, painted red, and headed with a bright brass spire six inches long.

Their duty.

[SECT. 2.] And the fire-wards aforementioned are hereby required, upon notice of the breaking forth of fire, taking with them their badges respectively, immediately to repair to the place, and vigo[u]rously exert themselves in requiring and procuring assistance to extinguish and prevent the spreading of the fire, and for the pulling down or blowing up any houses, or any other service relating thereto, as they may be directed by two or three of the chief civil or military officers of the town, to put a stop to the fire, and in removing hous[e]hold stuff, goods, and merchandizes out of any dwelling-houses, storehouses or other buildings actually on fire, or in danger thereof, in appointing guards to secure and take care of the same, and to suppress all tumults and disorders; and due obedience is required to be yielded to them, and each of them accordingly, for that service.

Penalty for refusing to assist them in extinguishing of fire.

[SECT. 3.] And all disobedience, neglect or refusal in any shall be inform[*e*]d of to some of his majesty's justices of the peace within two days next after, and the offenders therein, upon conviction thereof before any two justices, *quorum unus*, shall forfeit and pay the sum of forty shillings each, to be levied and distributed by the discretion of the selectmen among the poor, most distressed by the fire; and in case the offender or offenders are unable to satisfy the fine, then to suffer ten days' imprisonment.

And be it further enacted,

Penalty for persons' purloining or concealing goods saved from the fire.

[SECT. 4.] That if any evil-minded persons shall take advantage of such calamity to rob, plunder, purloin, [i][*e*]mbez[*z*]le, convey away or conceal any goods, merchandizes or effects of the distressed inhabitants, whose houses are on fire, or endangered thereby, and put upon removing their goods, and shall not restore and give notice thereof to the owner or owners, if known, or bring them into such publick place as shall be appointed and assigned by the governour and council, within the space of two days next after proclamation made for that purpose, the person or persons so offending, and being thereof convicted, shall be deemed th[ei][*ie*]ves, and suffer the utmost severities of the pains and penalties by law provided against such. [*Passed April* 5; *published April* 6.

CHAPTER 31.

AN ACT FOR ASCERTAINING THE BOUNDS OF THE TOWN OF DIGHTON, AND FOR THE CONFIRMATION OF THEIR POWERS AND PRIVILEGES.

WHEREAS in the year one thousand seven hundred and twelve the South Precinct in Taunton was erected into a township by the name of Dighton, but the bounds thereof were not fully ascertained, and by reason thereof of late there have some disputes arisen, and application hath been made to this court to ascertain the bounds,— Preamble. 1734-35, chap. 19.

Be it enacted by the Governour, Council and House of Representatives,

[SECT. 1.] That the bounds of the said town of Dighton shall be as follows; viz[t]., beginning at a heap of stones by a rock near the water-side on the westerly side of Broad Cove, and from thence running westerly to a heap of stones near Bristol old path; and from thence westerly to a heap of stones near two miles from said Broad Cove, and then running northerly about two miles to a stump of an ash tree; thence west and by north, to Rehoboth ancient line, to a stake and stones about it, being the north corner of the town of Swanzey, and the southwest corner of the said town of Dighton; thence northerly on a straight line to a marked tree, commonly called the "Horseshoe"; thence easterly by marked trees down to the Three-Mile River, so called; then with said river to Taunton Great River; then down Taunton Great River 'till it comes to the bounds first mentioned, together with Assonet[t] Neck, so far northerly as to come to the northerly bound of the land that was Mr. Edward Shove's; and that the land included within the bounds aforesaid shall always hereafter be deemed a township by the name of Dighton as aforesaid, and that the inhabitants thereof be invested with the powers, privileges, and immunities that the inhabitants of any of the towns within this province by law are or ought to be invested with, any law, order or custom to the contrary notwithstanding. Bounds of the town of Dighton stated. Inhabitants vested with the powers of a town.

[SECT. 2.] And all former acts and proceedings of the inhabitants of the said town of Dighton are hereby declared, to all intents and purposes, as valid, and of as full effect as if the said town had by an act of this court been incorporated and invested with the powers and privileges of a township at the time of their being taken off from Taunton, or sep[e][*a*]rated as aforesaid. Former acts of the said town confirmed.

Provided always,—

[SECTION 3.] That property shall not be affected by this act, any construction thereof, or of any part thereof, to the contrary notwithstanding. [*Passed January* 8, 1744-45. Proviso.

NOTES.—There were four sessions of the General Court this year, at each of which acts were passed. The engrossments of all the acts of the first and second sessions, and also of chapters 13, 15, 16, 21, and 22, are lost; but all these were, fortunately, printed, with the other acts of the sessions, except chapter 16, which is here printed from a MS record of acts, in the Secretary's office. The chapters not mentioned above were also printed

The acts of the first three sessions were transmitted to the Board of Trade by Governor Shirley, and were laid before the Board, Nov. 1, 1745. The acts of the fourth session were forwarded by Secretary Willard, July 30, 1745, and were received by the Board of Trade September 17, following, and read before them October 24.

Chapters 1 and 6 were duly certified to the Privy Council, by the Governor's order, July 7, 1744, and were received, and referred to a committee, on the ninth of August following. They were reported back, October 5, read again, October 10, and immediately referred to the Board of Trade. From the Board they went, in the usual course, the same day, to Mr. Fane, who reported, two days later, that he had "no objection" to them "in point of law." Some difficulties arising in the course of the consideration of these acts by the Board, chapter 1 was again referred to Mr. Fane, whose report, as well as other proceedings relating to that act, will be found in the note to chapter 1, *post*.

Chap. 1. "June 2, 1744. His Majesty's Declaration of War against the French King was published about Five o'clock this afternoon out of the Balcony of the Council Chamber, the Governor, Council, and House of Representatives, His Majesty's Justices of the Peace and other officers attending the same; the Regiment of Militia of the Town of Boston being under arms. At the same time His Majesty's Proclamation for encouraging the prosecution of the War by his Majesty's Ships of War, Privateers, &c was also published." —*Council Records, vol. XVII., b. 4, p.* 391.

"To Francis Fane, Esqre

Sir, I am directed by my Lords Commissrs for Trade & Plantations to send you back and to desire you to reconsider the first of the two inclosed Acts passed in the Province of the Massachusetts Bay in June last, on which you lately made your Report, Entitd "An Act for the more effectual guarding and securing our Sea Coasts &c." and to compare the same with the several Acts of Parliament passed here, since the commencement of the War with Spain and France for the better encouragement of Seamen in His Majty's service, as likewise with His Majesty's Declaration & Proclamation for the distribution of Prizes & give the Board your opinion whether the Province Snow & the other Vessels mentioned in the said Act to be equip'd by other Governments are to be deem'd ships of War or Privateers & whether in either case they are entituled to the Bounties given by the said British Acts.

I am, Sir,
Your most humble Servant
THO. HILL.

WHITEHALL
Nov.* 29th, 1744."

—*Mass. Bay, B. T., Vol.* 84, *p.* 138, *in Public-Record Office.*

"To the Right Honble the Lords Comissrs for Trade and Plantations.

My Lords, In obedience to Your Lordsps commands signified to me by Mr Hill desiring me to reconsider an Act passed in the Province of the Massachusetts Bay in June last Entituled *An Act for the more effectual guarding and securing our Sea Coasts, &c* and to compare the same with the several Acts of Parliament passed here since the commencement of the Warr with Spain and France, for the better encouragement of Sea Men in His Majesty's service, as likewise with His Majesty's Declaration and Proclamation for the distribution of Prizes and to give Your Lordships my opinion whether the Province Snow and the other Vessells mentioned in the said Act to be equiped by other Governments are to be deemed Ships of Warr or Privateers and whether in either case they are entitled to the Bountys given by the said British Acts—I beg leave to acquaint your Lordships, that I have reconsidered the said Massachusets Act, and the several Acts and the Declaration and Proclamation referred too, and I find the Acts of Parliament, the Declaration and Proclamation, to be conceiv'd in such general Terms and Words, that I apprehend they will be construed as intended for the benefit of all His Majesty's Subjects, under the particular descriptions in any his Dominions either at home or abroad and therefore I think the Province Snow and the other Vessels mentioned in the said Massachusets Act will be Entitled to the Bountys given by the said British Acts, as they must be considered as Ships of Warr or Privateers, But rather as Privateers, because they are not in His Majesty's Pay.—As to the Massachusets Act itself, if it continues in force, the Ships which are there described will also be entitled to the Bounty of three pounds a man given by this Act as well as to the British Bountys, whether that is reasonable or not I must submit to your Lordships consideration; But I must observe that I think the Legislature of this Province have gone a little too far in disposing of His Majesty's right to the Prizes taken from the Enemy, solely by their own authority.

Which is humbly submitted by
My Lords
Your Lordships
most obedient Servant
FRAN: FANE.

7th November, 1744."—*Ibid*

"Thursday, November 8th, 1744. Col. Bladen—Mr Plumer Mr Keene. Sr Cha: Gilmour

The Board having reconsidered the Order of the Lords of the Committee of Council referring to this Board two Acts pass'd in the Massachusets Bay August 29, 1744, and Mr Fane's Report upon one of them Entituled *An Act for the more effectual guarding & securing their Sea Coasts.*

Ordered that the Secretary acquaint Mr Fane, Council to the Board & Mr Kilby, Agent for the Province of the Massachusets Bay, that the Board desires their attendance this day sen'night, in order to have some discourse with them on the subject of the aforesaid Act."

* * * * * * * * * * *

—*Trade Papers (Journals), vol.* 46, *p.* 132, *in Public-Record Office.*

"Thursday November 15th 1744 Col. Bladen. Mr Plumer Mr Keene. Sir Cha: Gilmour

Mr Fane & Mr Kilby attending as appointed by the Minutes of the 8th Inst: the Board after some discourse had with them on the subject of the *Act* of the Massachusets *for*

* *Sic*,— a mistake for October.

the more effectual guarding & securing their Sea Coasts, deferred the further consideration thereof to another opportunity. M. BLADEN."

—*Ibid., p.* 135.

"Thursday, January 24th 1744–5. [Present] Lord Monson Col. Bladen. Mr Plumer. Sr John Philips. Mr Pitt.

* * * * * * * * * * *

The Board at the same time took again into consideration the *Act for the more effectual guarding and securing our Sea Coasts &c* mentioned in the Minutes of the 15th of Novr last, & having had some Discourse with Mr Kilby thereupon, agreed that the said Act should lye by, till he should write a letter to Mr Shirley for an Explanation of certain Clauses in the same Act and receive an answer thereto."

* * * * * * * * * * *

—[*Journals*] *Trade Papers, vol.* 47, *p.* 15, *ibid.*

"Tuesday, April 28th 1747. [Present] Lord Monson Mr Plumer. Lord Dupplin. Mr Pitt. Mr Fane.

* * * * * * * * * * *

The Draught of a Report to the Lords of the Committee of Council upon two Acts passed in the Province of the Massachusets Bay in June 1744 referred to this Board by Order of Council the 29th of August following, was laid before the Board, agreed to & order'd to be trans-crib'd.

* * * * * * * * * * *

—*Ibid., vol.* 49, *p.* 77. MONSON."

"Wednesday, April 29th 1747. [Present] Lord Monson. Mr Pitt. Mr Leveson Gower Mr Fane.

* * * * * * * * * * *

The Report to the Lords of the Committee of Council upon two Acts passed in the Massachusets Bay in June 1744, ordered to be trans-cribed by the Minutes of Yesterday, was laid before the Board and signed. MONSON."

—*Ibid., p.* 79.

"Report of Lords of Trade on Acts passed in June 1744.

To the Right Honoble the Lords of the Committee of His Majty's most Honoble Privy Council.

My Lords, We have had under our consideration two Acts passed in the Province of the Massachusetts Bay in June 1744 referr'ed to us by your Lordships Order of the 29th of August 1744.

We have also consulted Mr Fane one of His Majesty's Counsel at Law upon the said Acts who has no objection thereto in point of Law, Whereupon We take leave to acquaint your Lordships

That the first of these Acts relates to the public service & security of the said Province and therefore We see no reason why His Majesty may not be graciously pleased to confirm the same, Vizt:

An Act for the more effectual guarding & securing our Sea Coasts & for the encouragement of Seamen to enlist themselves in the Province Snow—or such Vessels of War as shall be commissioned & fitted out by this or other of His Majesty's Governments during the present War with France.

The following Act was enacted for a temporary service & expired in June 1746. Vizt:—

An Act to prevent all Traiterous Correspondence with His Majesty's Enemies.

We are, My Lords, Your Lordships most obedt & most humble Servts

MONSON.
I. PITT.
B. LEVESON GOWER
FRAN: FANE
R. PLUMER.

WHITEHALL
April 29th, 1747."

—*Mass. Bay, B. T., vol.* 84, *p.* 198, *in Public-Record Office.*

"*Order in Council confirming an Act passed in June* 1744.

At the Court at Kensington the 3rd of June 1747 Present The King's most Excellent Majesty in Council.

Whereas by Commission under the Great Seal of Great Britain, the Govr, Council and Assembly of the Province of the Massachusets Bay in New England, are authorized and empowered to constitute and ordain Laws, which are to continue and be in force, unless His Majesty's pleasure be signified to the contrary:—And whereas in pursuance of the said Commission, An Act was passed in the said Province in June 1744, Entituled as follows—Vizt.

"An Act for the more effectual guarding and securing our Sea Coasts and for the encouragement of Seamen to enlist themselves in the Province Snow—or such Vessels of War as shall be commissioned and fitted out by this or other of His Majesty's Governments during the present War with France. Which said Law, having been under the consideration of the Lords Commissrs for Trade and Plantations, and also of a Committee of the Lords of His Majtys most Honourable Privy Council, the said Lords of the Committee this day presented the said Law to His Majesty at this Board with their opinion that the same was proper to be approved—His Majesty taking the same into consideration, was pleased with the advice of His Privy Council to declare his approbation of the said Law, and pursuant to His Majesty's Royal Pleasure thereupon expressed, the said Law is hereby confirmed, finally Enacted and ratified accordingly—Whereof the Governor or Commander in Chief of the said Province for the time being, and all others whom it may concern are to take notice and govern themselves accordingly.

A true Copy W. SHARPE."

—*Ibid., vol.* 72, *F. f.* 101.

Chap. 2. "October 23, 1744. In the House of Represent^{ves}; Voted that the Wages of the Officers appointed for the Defence of the Frontiers be as follows, vizt.
That the wages of the Captains be Forty Shillings each per month.
One Lieutenant to each Company, Thirty shillings per month.
Two Sergeants to every forty men, Twenty seven shillings and six pence per month.
One Clerk to each Company, Twenty Seven shillings and six pence per month.
Two Corporals to every forty men, Twenty Six shillings per month each.
In Council; Read and Concur'd. Consented to W. SHIRLEY."
—*Council Records, vol. XVII., b. 4, p.* 533.

"October 25, 1744. In the House of Represent^{ves}; Voted that there be and hereby is granted to be paid out of the publick Treasury, to any company, party, or person singly, of His Majesty's subjects; belonging or residing within this Province, who shall voluntarily and at their own proper cost and charge, go out and kill a male Indian of the age of twelve years or upwards of the Tribe of St Johns or Cape Sables, after this time and before the last day of June, Anno Dom. 1745, or for such part of that Term as the war shall continue in any place to the Eastward of a line to be fixed by His Excellency the Governor and His Majestys Council, some where to the Eastward of Penobscot, and produce his Scalp in evidence of his death, the sum of One Hundred Pounds in Bills of Credit of this Province of the new Tenour, and the sum of One Hundred and Five Pounds in said Bills for any male of like age, who shall be taken captive and delivered to the Order of the Captain General, to be at the disposal and for the use of the Government. And the sum of Fifty Pounds in said Bills for Women and the like sum for Children under the age of Twelve years, killed in fight, and Fifty five Pounds for such when taken prisoners, and the plunder. Provided that no payment be made as aforesaid for killing or Captivating any of said Indians, until proof Thereof be made to the acceptance of the Governor and Council. And that the Captain General be desired forthwith to give notice to the several Tribes of the Eastern Indians who are still in amity with us, of the Boundary Line aforesaid, and that this Government have determined to treat as enemies all such Indians as live beyond it and that he also be desired, as soon as may be, to demand of the said Eastern Tribes their Quota of men stipulated by Govr Dummers Treaty to join with ours in any War enterd into by us with the other Tribes for their breach of the Articles of said Treaty.
In Council; Read and Concur'd Consented to W. SHIRLEY."
—*Ibid., p.* 539.

Chap. 12. "Aug. 18, 1744. In the House of Represent^{ves} Forasmuch as this Court are informed that there have been paid into the late Directors of the Manufactory Company (so called) by the late Partners in the Land Bank or Manufactory Scheme, and are now in the hands of Samuel Adams Esqr considerable quantities of said Companies Bills remaining unconsumed; and the Commissioners appointed by law to order and adjust the affairs of said Scheme have received and from time to time may receive further sums in said Bills; the receiving of which till said Scheme shall be finished will be attended with great risque and other inconveniences; Therefore
Ordered that said Commissioners be authorized to take into their own hands the afore mentioned Bills received by said late Directors, and to cause them, with such other of said Bills as have been or shall be paid in to themselves by the delinquent Partners in said Scheme, to be consumed and burnt to ashes from time to time as they shall receive them.
In Council; Read and Concur'd. Consented to W. SHIRLEY."
—*Ibid.*, p. 494.

Chap. 16. "October 13, 1744. A Petition of Thomas Hutchinson, Esqr Agent for the Officers and Company of the Brigantine Hawk Privateer fitted out by divers Inhabitants of this Province. Shewing that they have brought in several French Prizes, in which they have brought in divers goods which are subject to pay duties of Impost; praying that the said duties may be taken off.
In the House of Represent^{ves} Read and Ordered that the Prayer of the Petition be granted, and that the said liquors and other goods be freed from the duties of Impost and that the Comm^{r} of Impost govern himself accordingly. And it is further Ordered that all Prize Goods which shall be brought in and condemned within this Province during the present war with France and Spain, shall be exempt from all Duties which such goods are or would be liable to by any Law of this Province, had they been imported for merchandize or in the ordinary way of Trade and Commerce.
In Council; Read and Concur'd. Consented to W. SHIRLEY."
—*Ibid., p.* 506.

Chap. 19. "Feb. 8 1744. In the House of Represent^{ves}; Voted the following Wages for four months, if the Expedition continue so long, vizt:
That the Wages of a Brigadier General, be Fifteen Pounds per month.
A Colonel, Twelve Pounds.
A Lieutenant Colonel, Ten Pounds.
A Major Eight Pounds ten shillings.
Adjutant General, Four Pounds ten shillings.
Captain of Fifty men Four Pounds ten shillings.
A Lieutenant Three Pounds.
A Second Lieutenant, or Ensign, Two Pounds.
A Sergeant, One Pound twelve shillings.
A Corporal, One Pound eight shillings.
A Clerk, One Pound twelve shillings.
A Quarter Master General, Four Pounds—
A Surgeon General, Five Pounds —
Two Surgeons to each Regiment, each Four Pounds ten shillings

One Drum Major, One Pound twelve shillings
A common Drummer One Pound eight shillings
One Chaplain to each Regiment, each Four Pounds ten shillings
One Armourer for each Regiment One Pound twelve shillings, of which the principal to be allowed Three Pounds per month.
One Captain of the Artillery, Nine Pounds.
One Lietenant, Four Pounds ten shillings.
Sixteen Gunners, each Two Pounds.
Two Bombardiers, each Eight Pounds ten shillings.
Two Assistants, each Two Pounds.
Two Clerks, for the service of the General, each Two Pounds ten shillings per month.
In Council; Read and Concur'd Consented to W. SHIRLEY."
—*Ibid.*, *p.* 682.

Chap. 20. "January 9 1744. The two Houses proceeded this day according to Order, to the choice of Managers of the Publick Lottery, and the following persons were chosen by the major Vote of the Council & House of Represent^ves^ vizt. James Bowdoin, Samuel Watts, John Quincy, Robert Hale, and Thomas Hutchinson Esq^rs^
To which Elections His Excellency signed his Consent."
—*Ibid.*, *p.* 631.
"Jany 10 1744. In Council; Ordered that the Managers of the Lottery appointed by this Court be and hereby are directed to prepare a proper abstract of the Act lately pass'd relating to the said Lottery that so His Majesty's subjects of this Province & the neighbouring Provinces and Colonies may be duly and seasonably advertised of the substance of the said Act; and that the Managers take care that the said Abstract be forthwith published in all the Weekly News papers in the town of Boston;—
In the House of Represent^ves^; Read and Concur'd Consented to W. SHIRLEY."
—*Ibid.*, *p.* 632.
"Feb. 2 1744. In Council, Whereas the liberty of adventuring in the Government Lottery erected by a late Act of this Province is granted to all persons without discrimination; and whereas the permitting of Indians, Negroes, or Molattoes to purchase tickets or draw any Lot or Lots might prove of mischievous consequence in many respects;—
It is therefore hereby Ordered that the Managers of said Lottery do not deliver any Ticket to any Indian Negroe or Molattoe, or to others on their behalf, or in partnership with them; & no Indian, Negroe or Molattoe, or their partners so adventuring shall be entitled to any benefit, Lot or Lots whatsoever, and the said Managers be & hereby are impowered to examine any person who applies to them for any of said Tickets, on Oath, about their being any ways concerned with any Indian Negro or Molatto, in any such Tickets as well at the time of purchasing the same, as when any Benefit, Lot or Lots shall be claimed as having been drawn in consequence or by vertue of any Ticket purchased as aforesaid.
In the House of Represent^ves^; Read and Concur'd Consented to W. SHIRLEY."
—*Ibid.*, *p.* 674.

Chap. 27. "Feb 24 1743, A Petition of James Bowdoin and a great number of others Merchants in the Town of Boston setting forth the great importance of the Harbour of Cape Cod to the navigation of this Province; and praying that this Court would take proper measures to preserve it.
In Council; Read and Refer'd to a Committee to whom was refer'd the consideration of the Petition of Jonathan Payne and others
In the House of Represent^ves^; Read and Concur'd."
—*Ibid.*, *p.* 278.
"March 20, 1743. John Cushing Esqr; from the Committee on the Petitions relating to Cape Cod Harbour &^c^ gave in the following Report vizt.
The Committee to whom this Petition was refer'd, as also the Petition of James Bowdoin Esqr, & others merchants, relating to Cape Cod Harbour, are of Opinion that for the better understanding the Facts alleged in the Petitions a Committee be appointed to repair to Cape Cod, view the Harbour, consider the Facts alleged in the Petition, and report their Opinion thereon at the next Session of this Court. All which is humbly submitted.
By JOHN CUSHING per Order.
In Council; Read and Accepted, and Ordered that Thomas Berry Esqr with such as the Honble House shall join, be a committee for the purposes in the Report mentioned.
In the House of Represent^ves^; Read and Concur'd, and Coll Miller and Mr Skinner are joined in the affair. And the Committee are directed to repair to Cape Cod on or before the tenth of May and to give notice to the Inhabitants of Truro that they do not drive any Cattle on the Beach to the Northward of Eastern Harbour Meadows in the mean time. In Council; Read and Concur'd Consented to W. SHIRLEY."
—*Ibid.*, *pp.* 340, 341.
"Aug. 17 1744 Thomas Berry Esqr from the Committee on the affair of Cape Cod Harbour and Eastern Harbour Meadows gave in the following Report, vizt—
The Committee appointed on this Petition, after having notified the Town of Truro, repaired to said Town and Province Town, and thence proceeded to view the Beaches, Sands and Harbour of Cape Cod; and upon the best information find that little or no alteration hath been made in the Harbour for the last thirty or forty years, accepting the Western Creek or Cove, which is nigh filled up. We find the Wood all gone from the Wood End, so called, and a very long flat Beach which lies much exposed and hath nothing to keep the Sands from blowing, unless the Beach Grass be allowed to grow, the only thing that can prevent those sands from driving into the Harbour. We learn that the sands to the Northward of Race Point are greatly blown in upon the Upland, and that it is of the greatest consequence to the Province that all possible care be taken to prevent the Woods being cut off on the back of Province Town, and that nothing be allowed to be done that may any ways tend to prevent the Beach Grass growing on the Sand Banks, the only thing

that can be thought of to prevent the Sands blowing, and thereby the Harbour secured from all apprehended danger—We have also viewed the Eastern Harbour Meadows and Beach, and find a large quantity of good Salt Meadow covered and destroyed with the Sand which blew from the Beach. We also observe that where the Beach Grass is permitted to grow it prevents the sand from blowing; and where Cattle and Horses have been kept off, the Beach Grass comes in, in most places. We further observed that at the Head of Strouts Creek Northward the Sand is blown in a great way among the Trees and lies very high, and may in a little while blow over into said Creek. We also find that in the lotted Lands to the North Westward of Strouts Creek, belonging to Truro, there is little else than Cranberry Swamps, nothing to induce any person to turn any creatures there, were it not for a prospect from the Province Town Lands. Wherefore the Committee are of Opinion that the Constable of Province Town be strictly enjoined to put in execution the Act to prevent damage being done to the Harbour of Cape Cod by Cattle &c and that a Pound be built there at the Province Charge, & that the Constable be obliged one day every week from the first of March to the last of October to search Province Town Woods and Beaches for Cattle and Horses, and impound all others but what belongs to the Inhabitants of said Town, and that said Inhabitants be allowed one Cow to a family and one Bull to go with said Cows, and that said Constable be allowed one shilling and three pence for every day he shall faithfully attend said service, and make Oath thereof before one of His Majesty's Justices of the Peace in the County of Barnstable; and that an act be made (exclusive of the lotted Lands) of the same tenour with the late act made for preventing Cattle and Horses feeding on Eastern Harbour Meadows, and of the lotted Lands making and keeping up a sufficient fence in equal proportion or watching the Cattle and preventing them from passing to the Westward of Strouts Creek. And the Proprietors of the aforesaid Meadow with the Proprietors of Truro (not having right in said Meadows, and that turn cattle or horses on the common) be obliged to make and maintain a fence or keep the cattle from going West of the East end of Eastern Harbour Meadow. All which is humbly submitted.

By Order of the Committee. THO BERRY.

In Council; Read and Ordered that the Report be accepted, and that Samuel Danforth Esq[r] with such as the Hon[ble] House of Representatives shall join, be a Committee to prepare a Bill or Bills accordingly.

In the House of Represent[ves] Read and Concur'd and M[r] Prout and Major Cushing are joined in the affair."—*Ibid.*, *p.* 487.

Chap. 31. "May 30, 1712. "Upon Reading a Petition of Cpt. Jared Talbot Agent for the South Precinct in Taunton, Praying in the name and Behalf of the Inhabitants of said precinct that they may be made a Town, as prayed for in a Former Petition:

Ordered that the Prayer of the Petition be granted for a Township; The town to be named Dighton: There having been a Hearing betwixt the Petitioner and the Agents for the Town of Taunton before this Court in a former Session some Time since, And that upon the Application of the Selectmen of Taunton or of Dighton, the former Committee assigned to survey or propose a Line for the Precinct be desired and impowered to perfect, describe, and fully ascertain the Line throughout, and Report the same to this Court not including any Lands but what is properly within the Township of Taunton; Saving the determining the Charge of the Building and Repairing of Bridges upon a Hearing at any Time before this Court, As also a Proportion of all Arreareges or Town Charges accruing, whilst Taunton Township remained entire before division; And that a Plat of this Township be presented.

Concur'd by the Representatives. Consented to, J DUDLEY."
—*Ibid.*, *vol. IX.*, *p.* 195.

"March 2, 1743. John Cushing Esq[r]; from the Committee of both Houses on the Petition of the Town of Dighton, gave in the following Report, viz[t],

The Committee to whom was refer'd the Petition of Sylvester Richmond Esq[r] in behalf of the Town of Dighton, have repaired to Dighton, heard the parties, considered their Original Grants and Purchases, viewed the said Township, and have taken a Plat thereof, which is herewith humbly presented; and thereupon beg leave to say; First that the Red Lines on the said Plat delineated, set forth the contents of the four miles square from the River belonging to the Town of Dighton by their Indian Deed; secondly, the pricked Lines in the said Plat describe the Southerly and Westerly extent of what is contained in Governor Hickleys Deed of Confirmation, with allowance of eight Degrees for Variation of the Compass: Thirdly, the Black Lines describe the Town of Dighton according to their Perambulations with Swanzey, Rehoboth, & Taunton, under the hands of the Select men of each Town at divers times since the Year 1700. By which it appears that the Black Lines aforesaid contain Two Thousand six hundred and eighty four acres more than the Contents of four miles square, and five hundred and fifty acres less than what is contained in Governor Hinckleys Confirmation Deed. Wherefore upon the whole the Committee are of Opinion that the lands contained within the Black Lines aforesaid, which are agreeable to their Perambulation for many years past, be at all times accounted to be within the Jurisdiction of the Town of Dighton, but not to effect the property thereof on any account whatsoever. All which is humbly submitted.

By JOHN CUSHING Per Order.

In Council; Read and Ordered that this Report be accepted, and that the Accompt of the Committes time and expence, amounting to the sum of Twenty eight Pounds eighteen shillings and two pence, be paid by the parties, viz[t]: One half by the Town of Dighton, and the other half by Charles Church Esq[r]; and others the Respondents. In the House of Represent[ves]; Read and Concur'd Consented to W. SHIRLEY."
—*Ibid.*, *vol. XVII.*, *b.* 4, *p.* 306.

ACTS,

PASSED 1745–46.

ACTS

Passed at the Session begun and held at Boston, on the Twenty-ninth day of May, A. D. 1745.

CHAPTER 1.

AN ACT FOR APPORTIONING AND ASSESSING A TAX OF THIRTY THOUSAND POUNDS, IN BILLS OF CREDIT; AND ALSO FOR APPORTIONING AND ASSESSING A FURTHER TAX OF TWO THOUSAND FOUR HUNDRED AND TWENTY-ONE POUNDS EIGHT SHILLINGS AND SIXPENCE, IN BILLS OF CREDIT, PAID THE REPRESENTATIVES FOR THEIR SERVICE AND ATTENDANCE IN GENERAL COURT, AND TRAVEL; AND ALSO THE SUM OF TWO HUNDRED AND THIRTY-FIVE POUNDS, FINES LAID UPON SEVERAL TOWNS FOR NOT SENDING A REPRESENTATIVE.

Whereas the great and general court or assembly of the province of the Massachusetts Bay, did, at their session in May, one thousand seven hundred and forty-one, pass an act for the levying a tax of six thousand six hundred and sixty-six pounds thirteen shillings and fourpence, in bills emitted by said act; and, at their session in May, one thousand seven hundred and forty-two, did pass an act for the levying a tax of one thousand nine hundred and fifty pounds, in bills emitted by said act; and, at their session in May, one thousand seven hundred and forty-three, did pass an act for the levying a tax of eight thousand and eighty-three pounds six shillings and eightpence,* in bills emitted by said act; and at their session in May, one thousand seven hundred and forty-four, did pass an act for the levying a tax of ten thousand two hundred and sixty-six pounds thirteen shillings and fourpence, in bills emitted by said act; and at their session in November, one thousand seven hundred and forty-four, did pass an act for the levying a tax of five thousand two hundred pounds, in bills emitted by said act; each of the several sums aforesaid to be assess[e]d this present year,—amounting in the whole to thirty-two thousand one hundred and sixty-six pounds thirteen shillings and fourpence; and by the aforesaid acts, provision was made that the general court might, in the present year, apportion the several sums on the several towns in the province, if they thought fit: and the assembly aforesaid have likewise ordered that the sum of two hundred thirty-five pounds, fines on several towns, and the sum of two thousand four hundred and twenty-one pounds eight shillings and sixpence, paid the representatives the last year, should be levyed and assessed, on this present year, on the polls and estates of the inhabitants of the several towns, according to what their respective representatives have received; *wherefore*, for the ordering, directing and effectual drawing in the sum of thirty thousand

1741-42, chap. 11, § 17.

1742-43, chap. 3, § 9.

1743-44, chap. 13, § 6.

1744-45, chap. 5, § 8.

1744-45, chap. 17, § 5.

* This is, apparently, an error; the amount of bills to be recalled being £8,583 6*s*. 8*d*. The mistake was first made in the marginal note to the supply-bill.—See 1743-44, chap. 13, § 6.

pounds, pursuant to the funds and grants aforesaid, and drawing the said sum into the treasury, according to the appointment now agreed to by this court; which, with the sum of two thousand four hundred sixty-seven pounds five shillings and tenpence, arising by the duties of impost, tun[n]age of shipping and excise, and the sum of two hundred and thirty-five pounds, fines laid on the several towns in and by this act mentioned, will make the sum of thirty-two thousand one hundred and sixty-six pounds thirteen shillings and fourpence; and also for drawing in the sum of two thousand four hundred and twenty-one pounds eight shillings and sixpence, paid the representatives; all which is unanimously approved, rat[y][i]fied, and confirmed; we, his majesty's most loyal and dutiful subjects, the representatives in general court assembled, pray that it may be enacted,—

And be it accordingly enacted by the Governour, Council and House of Representatives,

[SECT. 1.] That each town and district within this province be assessed and pay, as such town's and district's proportion of the sum of thirty thousand pounds, in bills of credit, as also for the fines laid on them, and their representatives' pay, the several sums following; that is to say,—

IN THE COUNTY OF SUFFOLK.

	Representatives' pay, and fines.	Province tax.	Sum total.	
Boston,	£63 0s. 0d.	£5,400 0s. 0d.	Five thousand four hundred and sixty-three pounds,	£5,463 0s. 0d.
Roxbury,	20 8 0	279 5 0	Two hundred ninety-nine pounds thirteen shillings,	299 13 0
Dorchester,	20 8 0	264 12 6	Two hundred eighty-five pounds and sixpence,	285 0 6
Milton,	22 4 0	122 7 6	One hundred forty-four pounds eleven shillings and [6d] [*sixpence*],	144 11 6
Bra[i]ntre[e][*y*],	25 7 0	292 10 0	Three hundred seventeen pounds seventeen shillings,	317 17 0
[illegible]h,	25 10 0	169 5 0	One hundred ninety-four pounds fifteen shillings,	194 15 0
Hingham,	22 7 0	315 17 6	Three hundred thirty-eight pounds four shillings and sixpence,	338 4 6
[illegible]a,	22 7 0	208 2 6	Two hundred thirty pounds nine shillings and sixpence,	230 9 6
f[illegible]d,	23 11 0	127 2 6	One hundred and sixty-five pounds thirteen shillings and sixpence,	165 13 6
" fine,	15 0 0			
Wrentham,	24 12 0	158 17 6	One hundred and eighty-three pounds nine shillings and sixpence,	183 9 6
[illegible]May['s] fine,	15 0 0	83 17 6	Ninety-eight pounds seventeen shillings and sixpence,	98 17 6
Stoughton,	24 1 6	153 17 6	One hundred seventy-seven pounds nineteen shillings,	177 19 0
Hull,	0 0 0	67 0 0	Sixty-seven pounds,	67 0 0
Brookline,	20 8 0	99 17 6	One hundred and twenty pounds five shillings and sixpence,	120 5 6
Needham,	0 0 0	89 7 6	Eighty-nine pounds seven shillings and sixpence,	89 7 6
Bellingham,	0 0 0	33 12 6	Thirty-three pounds twelve shillings and sixpence,	33 12 6
[illegible]e,	0 0 0	52 2 6	Fifty-two pounds two shillings and sixpence,	52 2 6
[illegible]a,	0 0 0	130 15 0	One hundred and thirty pounds fifteen shillings,	130 15 0
	£344 3s. 6d.	£8,048 10s. 0d.	Eight thousand three hundred ninety-two pounds, thirteen shillings and [6d] [*sixp.*],	£8,392 13s. 6d.

IN THE COUNTY OF ESSEX.

	Representatives' pay, and fines.	Province tax.	Sum total.	
Salem,	£26 2s. 0d.	£900 0s. 0d.	Nine hundred and twenty-six pounds two shillings,	£926 2s. 0d.
Ipswich,	54 12 0	828 12 6	Eight hundred and eighty-three pounds four shillings and sixpence,	883 4 6
Newbury,	55 13 0	768 7 6	Eight hundred and twenty-four pounds and sixpence,	824 0 6
Marblehead,	26 0 6	584 0 0	Six hundred and ten pounds and sixpence,	610 0 6
Lynn,	25 11 6	315 10 0	Three hundred and forty-one pounds one shilling and sixpence,	341 1 6
Andover,	27 6 0	362 10 0	Three hundred and eighty-nine pounds sixteen shillings,	389 16 0
Beverly,	24 15 0	231 15 0	Two hundred and fifty-six pounds ten shillings,	256 10 0
Rowley,	27 9 0	226 2 6	Two hundred and fifty-three pounds eleven shillings and sixpence,	253 11 6
Salisbury,	24 3 0	200 0 0	Two hundred and twenty-four pounds three shillings,	224 3 0

IN THE COUNTY OF ESSEX—*Continued.*

	REPRESENTATIVES' PAY, AND FINES.	PROVINCE TAX.	SUM TOTAL.	
Haverhill,	£29 8s. 0d.	£203 7s. 6d.	Two hundred and thirty-two pounds fifteen shillings and sixpence,	£232 15s. 6d.
Glocester,	27 0 0	376 2 6	Four hundred and three pounds two shillings and sixpence,	403 2 6
Topsfield,	25 16 0	114 17 6	One hundred and forty pounds [illegible] shillings and [illegible]pence,	140 13 6
Boxford,	28 10 0	144 2 6	One hundred and seventy-two pounds twelve shillings and sixpence,	172 12 8
Almsbury,	29 14 0	166 15 0	One hundred and ninety-six pounds nine shillings,	196 9 0
Bradford,	26 6 0	125 12 6	One hundred and fifty-one pounds [illegible]teen shillings and [6d] [*sixpence*],	151 18 6
Wenham,	26 4 0	104 17 6	One hundred and thirty-one pounds one shilling and sixpence,	131 1 6
Manchester,	0 0 0	87 2 6	Eighty-seven pounds two shillings and [six]pence,	87 2 6
Methuen,	0 0 0	46 5 0	Forty-six pounds five shillings,	46 5 0
Middleton,	8 3 6	89 12 6	Ninety-seven pounds sixteen shillings,	97 16 0
Rumford,	0 0 0	0 0 0	. . . .	0 0 0
	£492 13s. 6d.	£5,875 12s. 6d.	Six thousand three hundred and sixty-eight pounds, six shillings,	£6,368 6s. 0d.

IN THE COUNTY OF MIDDLESEX.

Cambridge,	£20 8s. 0d.	£198 0s. 0d.	Two hundred and eighteen pounds eight shillings,	£218 8s. 0d.
Charlestown,	38 17 0	405 10 0	Four hundred and forty-four pounds seven shillings,	444 7 0
Watertown,	24 9 0	123 17 6	One hundred [and] forty-eight pounds six shillings [illegible] [6d] [*sixpence*],	148 6 6
[illegible]n,	26 2 0	247 7 6	Two hundred and [illegible]-three pounds nine shillings and [illegible]pence,	273 9 6
Concord,	26 2 0	116 10 0	One hundred and forty-two pounds [illegible] shillings,	142 12 0
Woburn,	24 18 0	193 2 6	Two hundred and [illegible]teen pounds and sixpence,	218 0 6
Reading,	24 18 0	212 0 0	Two hundred and thirty-six pounds [illegible] shillings,	236 18 0
[illegible]y,	26 2 0	220 10 0	Two hundred and forty-six pounds [illegible] shillings,	246 12 0
Marlborough,	27 6 0	227 12 6	Two hundred and fifty-four pounds [illegible] shillings and [illegible]pence,	254 18 6
Lexington,	24 18 0	136 17 6	One hundred and sixty-one pounds [illegible]teen shillings and sixpence,	161 15 6
Newton,	24 18 0	213 5 0	Two hundred and thirty-eight pounds three shillings,	238 3 0
[illegible]n,	20 8 0	177 10 0	One hundred and ninety-seven pounds eighteen shillings,	197 18 0
Chelmsford,	16 13 0	122 10 0	One hundred and thirty-nine pounds three shillings,	139 3 0
Billerica,	14 5 0	126 7 6	One hundred a[nd] forty pounds [illegible] shillings and sixpence,	140 12 6
Sherburn, fine,	12 10 0	79 12 6	Ninety-two pounds two shillings and sixpence,	92 2 6
Holliston,	0 0 0	56 15 0	Fifty-six pounds [illegible]teen shillings,	56 15 0
[illegible]n,	26 2 0	195 2 6	Two hundred and [illegible]-one pounds, four shillings and sixpence,	221 4 6

Framingham,	£24 18s. 0d.	£161 7s. 6d.	One hundred [and] eighty-six pounds five shillings and sixpence,	£186 5s. 6d.
Medford,	20 8 0	95 7 6	One hundred and fifteen pounds fifteen shillings and sixpence,	115 15 6
Stow,	27 6 0	74 10 0	One hundred and sixteen pounds sixteen shillings,	116 16 0
" [illegible],	15 0 0			
Dunstable [illegible] [illegible],	0 0 0	45 0 0	Forty-five pounds,	45 0 0
[illegible]t],	0 0 0	49 15 0	Forty-nine pounds fifteen shillings,	49 15 0
[illegible]n,	0 0 0	63 17 6	Sixty-three pounds seventeen shillings and sixpence,	63 17 6
[illegible]n,	21 15 0	89 17 6	One hundred and eleven pounds twelve shillings and sixpence,	111 12 6
[illegible]n,	25 4 0	62 10 0	Eighty-seven pounds fourteen shillings,	87 14 0
Bedford, fine,	10 0 0	59 0 0	Sixty-nine pounds,	69 0 0
Westford,	23 11 0	80 10 0	One hundred and fourteen pounds one shilling,	114 1 0
" fine,	10 0 0			
[illegible]n,	0 0 0	57 7 6	Fifty-seven pounds seven shillings and sixpence,	57 7 6
Tewksb[er][u]ry,	0 0 0	52 17 6	Fifty-two pounds seventeen shillings and sixpence,	52 17 6
[illegible],	0 0 0	40 2 6	Forty pounds two shillings and sixpence,	40 2 6
Waltham,	24 18 0	109 17 6	One hundred and thirty-four pounds fifteen shillings and [6d] [*sixpence*],	134 15 6
Townshend,	15 9 0	22 10 0	Thirty-seven pounds nineteen shillings,	37 19 0
English Inhabitants of Natick,	0 0 0	30 0 0	Thirty pounds,	30 0 0
	£597 5s. 0d.	£4,147 0s. 0d.	Four thousand seven hundred and forty-four pounds, five shillings,	£4,744 5s. 0d.

IN THE COUNTY OF HAMPSHIRE.

Springfield,	£21 6s. 0d.	£328 15s. 0d.	Three hundred and fifty pounds one shilling,	£350 1s. 0d.
Nor[illegible]n,	19 10 0	216 2 6	Two [illegible] and [illegible]-five pounds [illegible] shillings and [6d] [*sixpence*],	235 12 6
Hadley,	12 12 0	154 12 6	One hundred and [illegible] pounds four shillings and [illegible],	167 4 6
[illegible]d,	11 11 0	99 5 0	One [illegible] and ten pounds sixteen shillings,	110 16 0
[illegible]d,	21 7 6	126 17 6	One hundred and forty-eight pounds five shillings,	148 5 0
[illegible]d,	25 8 6	65 2 6	One hundred and ninety [illegible] shillings,	190 11 0
Enfield,	0 0 0	98 0 0	[illegible],	98 0 0
Deerfield,	14 2 0	100 2 6	One hundred and fourteen pounds four shillings and [illegible],	114 4 6
[illegible]d,	0 0 0	51 0 0	Fifty-one pounds,	51 0 0
Northfield,	0 0 0	44 15 0	Forty-four [illegible] fifteen shillings,	44 15 0
[illegible]d, fine,	15 0 0	87 17 6	One [illegible] and two pounds seventeen shillings and sixpence,	102 17 6
Somers,	0 0 0	53 17 6	Fifty-three [illegible] seventeen shillings and sixpence,	53 17 6
[illegible]d,	0 0 0	52 10 0	Fifty-two [illegible] ten shillings,	52 10 0

IN THE COUNTY OF HAMPSHIRE—*Continued.*

	REPRESENTATIVES' PAY, AND FINES.	PROVINCE TAX.	SUM TOTAL.	
Elbows,	£0 0s. 0d.	£30 0s. 0d.	Thirty pounds,	£30 0s. 0d.
Stockbridge,	6 6 0	0 0 0	Six pounds six shillings,	6 6 0
	£147 3s. 0d.	£1,608 17s. 6d.	One thousand seven hundred and fifty-six pounds and sixpence,	£1,756 0s. 6d.

IN THE COUNTY OF WORCESTER.

[illegible]r,	£25 1s. 0d.	£102 12s. 6d.	One hundred and twenty-seven pounds thirteen shillings and sixpence,	£127 13s. 6d.
[illegible]r,	27 15 0	170 0 0	One hundred and ninety-seven pounds fifteen shillings,	197 15 0
[illegible]n,	25 16 0	174 12 6	Two hundred and fifteen pounds eight shillings and sixpence,	215 8 6
" i[illegible]e,	15 0 0			
[illegible]k,	25 19 0	154 7 6	One hundred and eighty pounds six shillings and sixpence,	180 6 6
Brookfield,	21 0 0	104 7 6	One hundred and twenty-five pounds seven shillings and sixpence,	125 7 6
Southborough,	27 6 0	67 15 0	One hundred and seven pounds eleven shillings,	107 11 0
" [*fine*],	12 10 0			
L[ei] [illegible]er,	0 0 0	95 10 0	Ninety-five pounds ten shillings,	95 10 0
[illegible]d, fine,	10 0 0	61 17 6	Seventy-one pounds seventeen shillings and sixpence,	71 17 6
Lunenburg,	0 0 0	76 10 0	Seventy-six pounds ten shillings,	76 10 0
Westborough,	26 8 0	106 5 0	One hundred and thirty-seven pounds thirteen shillings,	137 13 0
" fine,	5 0 0			
Shrewsbury,	22 13 0	94 0 0	One hundred and thirty-six pounds thirteen shillings,	136 13 0
" fine,	20 0 0			
Oxford,	0 0 0	71 17 6	Seventy-one pounds seventeen shillings and sixpence,	71 17 6
Sutton, fine,	10 0 0	113 10 0	One hundred and twenty-three pounds ten shillings,	123 10 0
Uxbridge,	0 0 0	80 17 6	Eighty pounds seventeen shillings and sixpence,	80 17 6
Harvard, [illegible],	5 0 0	69 5 0	Seventy-four pounds five shillings,	74 h 0
[illegible]n, fine,	10 0 0	58 15 0	Sixty-eight pounds fifteen shillings,	68 15 0
Upton,	0 0 0	23 17 6	Twenty-three pounds seventeen shillings and sixpence,	23 17 6
[illegible]y,	0 0 0	50 10 0	Fifty pounds ten shillings,	50 10 0
Bolton, fine,	5 0 0	67 7 6	Seventy-two pounds seven shillings and sixpence,	72 7 6
Sturbridge,	0 0 0	25 10 0	Twenty-five pounds ten shillings,	25 10 0

Leominster,	£0 0s. 0d.	£21 0s. 0d.	Twenty-one pounds,	£21 0s. 0d.
Western,	0 0 0	19 17 6	Nineteen pounds seventeen shillings and sixpence,	19 17 6
	£294 8s. 0d.	£1,810 5s. 0d.		£2,104 13s. 0d.

IN THE COUNTY OF PLYMOUTH.

[illegible]th,	£22 12s. 0d.	£281 2s. 6d.	Three hundred [illegible] three [illegible] fourteen shillings and [illegible],	£303 14s. 6d.
Plympton,	17 5 0	149 2 6	One hundred and sixty-six [illegible] seven [illegible] and sixpence,	166 7 0
[illegible]e,	23 14 0	431 7 6	Four hundred and fif[illegible] [illegible] one shilling [illegible] [illegible],	45 1 0
Bridgwater,	27 6 0	342 2 6	[illegible] hundred [illegible] sixty-nine [illegible] [illegible]ight shillings and [illegible],	369 8 0
[illegible]d,	22 14 0	213 0 0	[illegible]o hundred and [illegible]-five [illegible] fourteen shillings and [illegible],	235 14 0
r[illegible]e],	15 9 0	114 10 0	One [illegible] and [illegible]-nine [illegible] [illegible] shillings,	129 19 0
Duxbury,	24 18 0	100 5 0	One hundred and [illegible]-five [illegible] [illegible] shillings,	125 3 0
[illegible]h,	22 1 0	252 12 6	Two [illegible] [illegible] seventy-four [illegible] [illegible] shillings and [6d] [*sixpence*],	274 13 6
[illegible]r,	21 3 0	161 0 0	One [illegible] and [illegible]-two [illegible] three shillings,	182 3 0
[[illegible]n,	0 0 0	71 17 6	Seventy-one pounds seventeen [illegible] and [illegible],	71 17 6
Kingston,	0 0 0	78 12 6	Seventy-eight [illegible] twelve shi[*lli*]ngs and sixpence,	78 12 6
Han[n]over,	0 0 0	92 12 6	[illegible] [illegible] twelve [illegible] and sixpence,	92 12 6
Hal[l]ifax,	0 0 0	60 0 0	Sixty [illegible],	60 0 0
Warh[illegible]m,	0 0 0	30 0 0	Thirty [illegible],	30 0 0
	£197 2s. 6d.	£2,378 5s. 0d.	Two thousand five hundred and seventy-five pounds seven shillings and [6d] [*sixpen.*],	£2,575 7s. 6d.

IN THE COUNTY OF BARNSTABLE.

Barnstable,	£24 6s. 0d.	£301 2s. 6d.	Three hundred and twenty-five pounds eight shill[*in*]gs and [6d] [*sixpence*],	£325 8s. 6d.
Yarmouth,	0 0 0	185 15 0	One hundred and eighty-five pounds fifteen shillings,	185 15 0
Sandwich,	20 14 0	162 5 0	One hundred and eighty-two pounds nineteen shillings,	182 19 0
Eastham,	21 15 0	224 0 0	Two hundred and forty-five pounds fifteen shillings,	245 15 0
Truro,	11 11 0	29 7 6	Forty pounds eighteen shillings and sixpence,	40 18 6
Harwich,	25 19 0	155 5 0	One hundred and eighty-one pounds four shillings,	181 4 0
Falmouth,	0 0 0	110 0 0	One hundred and ten pounds,	110 0 0

IN THE COUNTY OF BARNSTABLE—*Continued.*

	REPRESENTATIVES' PAY, AND FINES.	PROVINCE TAX.	SUM TOTAL.	
Chatham,	£0 0*s.* 0*d.*	£91 7*s.* 6*d.*	Ninety-one pounds seven shillings and sixpence,	£91 7*s.* 6*d.*
Provincetown,	0 0 0	0 0 0	. . . .	0 0 0
	£104 5*s.* 0*d.*	£1,259 2*s.* 6*d.*	One thousand three hundred and sixty-three pounds, seven shill[*in*]gs and sixpence,	£1,363 7*s.* 6*d.*

IN THE COUNTY OF BRISTOL.

Bristol,	£24 2 0*d.*	£197 10*s.* 0*d.*	Two hundred and twenty-two pounds two shillings,	£22 2 0*d.*
Taunton,	27 150	300 5 0	Three hundred and twenty-eight [illegible] pds,	80
Norton,	24 90	150 15 0	One hundred and seventy-five pounds four shillings,	40
Easton,	0 0 0	59 0 0	Fifty-nine pounds,	60
Dartmouth,	30	465 2 6	Four [illegible] and [illegible]-ine pls [illegible]en shillings and [6d] [*sixpence*],	86 1
Dighton,	70 1	106 2 6	One hundred and twenty-three pnls [illegible]en shillings and six-pence,	06 1
Rehoboth,	27 6 0	370 12 6	Three hundred and [illegible] [illegible]en pnls eighteen shill[*in*]gs and [6d] [*sixpence*],	397 18 6
Little Compton,	20 9 0	212 10 0	Two hundred and thirty-two pounds [illegible]en shillings,	232 19 0
Swanzey with Shawamett,	0 0 0	298 0 0	Two hundred and ninety-eight pds,	298 0 0
Tiverton, fine,	30 0 0	240 0 0	Two hundred and seventy nds,	270 0 0
Freetown, fine,	20 0 0	98 12 6	One hundred and [illegible]en pounds [illegible]e shillings and sixpence,	118 12 6
Attleborough,	24 9 0	150 15 0	One [illegible]d and [illegible]-five pls four shillings,	175 4 0
Barrington,	0 0 0	86 2 6	Eighty-six pounds two shillings and sixpence,	86 2 6
Raynham,	0 0 0	68 7 6	Sixty-eight pnls seven [illegible]gs and [illegible]e,	68 7 6
Berkley,	0 0 0	64 12 6	Sixty-four pnls twelve [illegible]gs and sixpence,	64 12 6
	£241 9*s.* 0*d.*	£2,868 7*s.* 6*d.*	Three thousand one hundred and nine pounds sixteen shill[*in*]gs and [6d] [*sixpence*],	£3,109 16*s.* 6*d.*

IN THE COUNTY OF YORK.

York,	£28 10s. 0d.	£274 12s. 6d.	Three dred and three pds two lligs and ipe,	£303 2s. 6d.
Kittery,	26 14 0	378 2 6	Four dred and four pds ssin lligs and ipe,	04 16 6
Berwick,	25 16 0	160 12 6	One dred and tly-six pds eght sligs and pe,	186 8 6
Wells,	24 0 0	132 7 6	One dred and fifty-six pds sen lligs and spe,	156 7 6
dRth,	32 17 0	230 15 0	Two-hundred and ty-htee pds twelve llgs,	263 12 0
ddl,	11 8 0	91 2 6	One hundred and two pds ten shillings and ipe,	102 10 6
Al,	16 1 0	59 7 6	Sy-ive pds ight shillings and spe,	75 8 6
Scarborough,	13 10 0	119 17 6	One dred and ty-htee pds een shillings and [6d] [sixpence],	133 7 6
North Yarmouth,	33 6 0	51 0 0	Eighty-four pds six shillings,	84 6 0
dn,	0 0 0	60 0 0	Sixty pds,	60 0 0
Brunswick,	0 0 0	20 5 0	Fity pds five shillings,	20 5 0
	£212 2s. 0d.	£1,578 2s. 6d.	One thousand seven hundred and ninety pounds, four shillings and sixpence,	£1,790 4s. 6d.

IN THE COUNTY OF DUKES COUNTY.

Edgartown,	£12 13s. 0d.	£74 15s. 0d.	Eighty-seven pounds eight shillings,	£87 8s. 0d.
Chilmark,	0 0 0	94 15 0	Ninety-four pounds fifteen shillings,	94 15 0
Tisbury,	0 0 0	58 12 6	Fifty-eight pounds twelve shillings and sixpence,	58 12 6
	£12 13s. 0d.	£228 2s. 6d.	Two hundred and forty pounds, fifteen shillings and sixpence,	£240 15 6d.

IN NANTUCKET[T] COUNTY.

Sherburn,	£13 4s. 0d.	£197 15s. 0d.	Two hundred and ten pounds nineteen shillings,	£210 19s. 0d.

	REPRESENTATIVES' PAY, AND FINES.	PROVINCE TAX.	SUM TOTAL.	
Suffolk,	£344 3s. 6d.	£8,048 10s. 0d.	Eight [illegible] three hundred [illegible] [illegible]-two pds thirteen shil[illegible] [illegible] [illegible] [illegible]],	£8,392 13s. 6d.
Essex,	492 13 6	5,875 12 6	Six [illegible] three hundred [illegible] [illegible] [illegible] [illegible] [illegible] shilli[illegible],	6,368 6 0
Middlesex,	597 5 0	4,147 0 0	Four [illegible] seven hundred [illegible] fo[illegible] [illegible] [illegible] five [illegible]lings,	4,744 5 0
Hampshire,	147 3 0	1,608 17 6	[illegible] [illegible] [illegible] hundred [illegible] [illegible] [illegible] [illegible] [illegible] [illegible],	1,756 0 6
Worcester,	294 8 0	1,810 5 0	Two [illegible] [illegible] [illegible] [illegible] four [illegible] [illegible] [illegible],	[illegible]4 13 0
Plymouth,	197 2 6	2,378 5 0	Two [illegible] [illegible] [illegible] [illegible] [illegible] [illegible] [illegible] [illegible] [illegible] sixp[ence],	2,575 7 6
Bristol,	241 9 0	2,868 7 6	Three [illegible] [illegible] [illegible] [illegible] [illegible] [illegible] [illegible] [illegible] [illegible] [illegible],	3,109 16 6
Barnstable,	104 5 0	1,259 2 6	[illegible] [illegible] three hundred [illegible] [illegible] [illegible] [illegible] [illegible] [illegible]li[illegible][s] and [6d] [illegible]],	1,363 7 6
York,	212 2 0	1,578 2 6	[illegible] [illegible] [illegible] [illegible] [illegible]ty pds four [illegible] [illegible] [illegible],	1,790 4 6
Dukes County,	12 13 0	228 2 6	Two [illegible] [illegible] [illegible] [illegible] fifteen [illegible] [illegible] [illegible],	[illegible] 15 6
Nantucket,	13 4 0	197 15 0	[illegible] hundred [illegible] [illegible] [illegible] [illegible] [illegible],	20 19 0
	£2,656 8s. 6d.	£30,000 0s. 0d.	Thirty-two thousand six hundred [and] fifty-six pounds, eight shillings and sixp[ence],	£32,656 8s. 6d.

And be it further enacted,

[Sect. 2.] That the treasurer do forthwith send out his warrants, directed to the selectmen or assessors of each town or district within this province, requiring them, respectively, to assess the sum hereby set upon such town or district, in manner following; that is to say, to assess all rateable male polls above the age of sixteen years, within their respective towns or [districts] [*districts*], or next adjoining to them, belonging to no other town, at six shillings and threepence per poll, and proportionably in assessing the fines mentioned in this act, and the additional sum receiv[e]'d out of the treasury for the payment of the representatives (except the governour, lieutenant-governo[u]r and their famil[y][*ie*]s, the president, fellows and students of Harvard College, setled ministers and grammar school-masters, who are hereby exempted as well from being taxed for their polls, as for their estates being in their own hands and under their actual management and improvement); and other persons, if such there be, who, thro' age, infirmity or extream poverty, in the judgment of the assessors, are not capable to pay towards publick charges, they may exempt their polls, and so much of their estates as in their prudence they shall think fit[t] and judge meet.

[Sect. 3.] And the justices in the general sessions, in the respective counties assembled, in granting a county tax or assessment, are hereby ordered and directed to apportion the same on the several towns in such county in proportion to their province rate, exclusive of what has been paid out of the publick treasury to the representative of such town for his service; and the assessors of each town in the province are also directed, in making an assessment, to govern themselves by the same rule; and all estates, both real and personal, lying within the limits of such town or district, or next unto the same, not paying elsewhere, in whose hands, tenure, occupation or possession soever the same is or shall be found, and also the incomes [and] [*or*] profits which any person or persons, except as before excepted, do or shall receive from any trade, faculty, business or employment whatsoever, and all profits that shall or may arise by money or other estate not particularly otherwise assessed, or commissions of profit in their improvement, according to their understanding and cunning, at one penny on the pound; and to abate or multiply the same, if need be, so as to make up the sum set and ordered hereby for such town or district to pay; and, in making their assessments, to estimate houses and lands at six years' income of the yearly rents, in the bills last emitted, whereat the same may be reasonably set or let for in the place where they lye: *saving* all contracts between landlord and tenant, and where no contract is, the landlord to reimburse one-half of the tax set[t] upon such houses and lands; and to estimate Indian, negro and molatto servants proportionably as other personal estate, according to their sound judgment and discretion; as also to estimate every ox of four years old and upwards, at forty shillings in bills of the last emission; every cow of three years old and upwards, at thirty shillings; every horse and mare of three years old and upwards, at forty shillings; every swine of one year old and upwards, at eight shillings; every goat and sheep of one year old and upwards, at three shillings: likewise requiring the assessors to make a fair list of the said assessment, setting forth, in distinct col[l]um[*n*]s, against each particular person's name, how much he or she is assessed at for polls, and how much for houses and lands, and how much for personal estate, and income by trade or faculty; and the list or lists, so perfected and signed by them, or the major part of them, to commit to the collectors, constable or constables of such town or district, and to return a certificate of the name or names of such collectors, constable or

30

constables, together with the sum total to each of them committed, unto himself, some time before the last day of October.

[SECT. 4.] And the treasurer for the time being, upon the receipt of such certificate, is hereby impowered and ordered to issue forth his warrants to the collector, constable or constables of such town or district, requiring him or them, respectively, to collect the whole of each respective sum assessed on each particular person, before the last day of May next; and of the inhabitants of the town of Boston, some time in the month of March next; and to pay in their collection, and issue the accompts of the whole, at or before the last day of June, which will be in the year of our Lord one thousand seven hundred and forty-six.

And be it further enacted,

[SECT. 5.] That the assessors of each town and district, respectively, in convenient time before their making the assessment, shall give seasonable warning to the inhabitants, in a town meeting, or by posting up notifications in some place or places in such town or district, or notify the inhabitants to give or bring in to the assessors true and perfect lists of their polls, and rateable estate, and income by trade or faculty, and gain by money at interest; and if any person or persons shall neglect or refuse so to do, or bring in a false list, it shall be lawful to and for the assessors to assess such person or persons, according to their known ability in such town, in their sound judgment and discretion, their due proportion to this tax, as near as they can, agreeable to the rules herein given, under the penalty of twenty shillings for each person that shall be convicted by legal proof, in the judgment of the said assessors, of bringing in a false list; the said fines to be for the use of the poor of such town or district where the delinquent lives, to be lev[y][*i*]ed by warrant from the assessors, directed to the collector or constables, in manner as is directed for gathering town assessments, and to be paid in to the town treasurer or selectmen for the use aforesaid: *saving* to the party aggrieved at the judgment of the assessors in setting forth such fine, liberty of appeal therefrom to the court of general sessions of the peace within the county for relief, as in case of being overrated. And if any person or persons shall not bring in a list of their estate as aforesaid to the assessors, he or they so neglecting shall not be admitted to make application to the court of sessions for any abatement of the assessment laid him.

[SECT. 6.] And if the party be not convicted of any falseness in the list, by him presented, of polls, rateable estate, or income by any trade or faculty, business or employment, which he doth or shall exercise, or in gain by money at interest or otherwise, or other estate not particularly assess[e]'d, such list shall be a rule for such person's proportion to the tax, which the assessors may not exceed.

And whereas there are a number of English inhabitants in the plantation of Natick, in the county of Middlesex, belonging to no particular town,—

Be it further enacted,

[SECT. 7.] That the sum of thirty pounds, part of the said sum of thirty thousand pounds, be assessed upon the said inhabitants, and the assessors of the town of Sherb[*o*]urn are hereby impowered and required to make the said assessment upon them, after giving seasonable warning to the inhabitants of [the] said plantation, in some one method prescribed in this act, and to follow the other directions herein; and the said inhabitants are hereby also required to conform to the rules prescribed in this act, and subjected to the penalties of it: *saving* to them liberty of appeal, as to other inhabitants of the province. And the constables or collectors of the town of Sherb[*o*]urn are hereby enjoyned to levy or collect all such sums committed to them and assessed upon the said inhabitants, and pay the same into the province treasury.

And forasmuch as, ofttimes, sundry persons, not belonging to this province, bring considerable trade and merchandize, and by reason that the tax or rate of the town where they come to trade is finished and delivered to the constable or collector, and, before the next year's assessment, are gone out of the province, and so pay nothing towards the support of the government, tho', in the time of their residing there, they reap[c]'d considerable gain by trade, and had the protection of the government,—

Be it further enacted,

[Sect. 8.] That when any such person or persons shall come and reside in any town of this province, and bring any merchandize, and trade and deal therewith, the assessors of such town are hereby impowered to rate and assess all such persons according to their circumstances, pursuant to the rules and directions in this act provided, tho' the former rate may have been finished, and the new one not perfected, as aforesaid.

And be it further enacted,

[Sect. 9.] That when any merchant, trader or factor, inhabitant of some one town within this province, shall transact or carry on trade and business in some other town in the province, the assessors of such town where such trade and business shall be carried on as aforesaid, be and hereby are impowered to rate and assess all such merchants, traders and factors, their goods and merchandize, for carrying on such trade, and exercising their faculty in such town, pursuant to the rules and directions of this act.

[Sect. 10.] And the constables or collectors are hereby enjoyned to levy and collect all such sums committed to them, and assess[e]'d on persons who are not of this province, or are inhabitants of any other town as aforesaid, and pay the same into the town treasury.

And be it further enacted,

[Sect. 11.] That the inhabitants of this province [shall] have liberty, if they see fit[*t*], to pay the several sums for which they may respectively be assess[e]'d at, as their proportion of the aforesaid sum of thirty thousand pounds in bills of the last emission, or the bills of credit emitted in the years one thousand seven hundred and forty-one, one thousand seven hundred and forty-two, and one thousand seven hundred and forty-three, or in coined silver, at the rate of six shillings and eightpence per ounce, troy weight; or in gold coin, at the rate of four pounds eighteen shillings per ounce; or in bills of credit of the middle tenor, so called, according to their denominations; or in bills of the old tenor, accounting four for one; or in good merchantable hemp, at fourpence per pound; or merchantable flax, at fivepence per pound; or in good, merchantable, Isle-of-Sable[s] codfish, at ten shillings per quintal; or in good refined bar-iron, at fifteen pounds per ton; or bloomery-iron, at twelve pounds per ton; or in good, hollow iron-ware, at twelve pounds per ton; or in good Indian corn, at two shillings and threepence per bushel; or good winter rye, at two shillings and sixpence per bushel; or good winter wheat, at three shillings per bushel; or in good barley, at two shillings per bushel; or [*in*] good barrel pork, at two pounds per barrel; or in barrel beef, at one pound five shillings per barrel; or in duck or canvas, at two pounds ten shillings per bolt, each bolt to weigh forty-three pounds; or in long whalebone, at two shillings and threepence per pound; or merchantable cordage, at one pound five shillings per hundred; or in good train-o[i][*y*]l, at one pound ten shillings per barrel; or in good beeswax, at tenpence per pound; or in bayberry-wax, at sixpence per pound; or in try[e]d tallow, at fourpence per pound; or in good pease, at three shillings per bushel; or in good sheepswool, at ninepence per pound; or in good, tann'd sole-leather, at fourpence per pound: all which aforesaid commodities shall be of the produce of this province, and, as soon as conveniently may, be disposed of by the treasurer to the best advantage, for so much as they will fetch in bills of credit, or for silver and gold; and the several persons who pay their taxes in any of the commodities before mentioned, shall run the risque and pay the charge of transporting the same to the province treasury.

[SECT. 12.] And if any loss shall happen by the sale of any of the aforesaid species, it shall be made good by a tax of the next year; and if there be a surplusage, it shall remain a stock in the treasury. [*Passed June* 28; *published July* 9.

CHAPTER 2.

AN ACT FOR GRANTING UNTO HIS MAJESTY AN EXCISE UPON WINES AND SPIRITS DISTILLED, SOLD BY RETAIL, AND UPON LIMES AND LEMMONS.

Preamble.

WE, his majesty's most loyal and dutiful subjects, the representatives of the province of the Massachusetts Bay, in general court assembled, being desirous to lessen the present debt of the province, by drawing in a number of the bills of credit, have chearfully and unanimously granted, and do hereby give and grant unto his most excellent majesty, for the ends and uses above mentioned, and for no other uses, an excise upon all brandy, rum and other spirits distilled, and upon all wines whatsoever sold by retail, and upon lemmons and limes taken in and used in making of punch or other liquors mixed for sale, or otherwise consumed,in taverns, or other licensed houses within this province, to be raised, lev[y][i]ed, collected and paid by and upon every taverner, innholder, common victualler and retailer within each respective county, in manner following:—

And be it accordingly enacted by the Governour, Council and House of Representatives,

Excise granted for three years.

[SECT. 1.] That from and after the twenty-ninth day of June, one thousand seven hundred and forty-five, for the space of three years, every person licensed for retailing brandy, rum or other spirits, or wine, shall pay the dut[y][ie]s following:—

Rates of excise.

For every gallon of brandy, rum and spirits distilled, threepence.
For every gallon of wine of every sort, threepence.
For every hundred of lemmons, two shillings and a penny.
For every hundred of limes, ninepence.
And so proportionably for any other quantity or number.

And be it further enacted,

Taverners, &c., to take an account of liquors, &c., and give an account thereof to the farmers to be appointed.

[SECT. 2.] That every taverner, innholder, common victualler and retailer, shall, upon the said twenty-ninth day of June, take an exact account of all brandy, rum and other distilled spirits, and wine, and of all lemmons and limes then by him or her, and give an account of the same, upon oath, if required, unto the person or persons to whom the dut[y][ie]s of excise in the respective count[y][ie]s shall be lett or farmed, as in and by this act is hereafter directed; and such other person as shall be licensed during the continuance of this act, shall also give an account, upon oath, as aforesaid, of what brandy, rum and other distilled spirits, and wine, and of what lemmons or limes he or they shall have by him or them at the time of his or their licen[s][c]e; which oath the person or persons farming the dut[y][*ie*]s aforesaid shall have power to administer in the words following; viz[t].,—

You, A. B., do swear that the account exhibited by you is a true and just account of all brandy, rum and other distilled spirits, and wine, lemmons and limes you had by you on the twenty-ninth day of June last. So help you God. Oath.

And where such person shall not have been licen[s][c]ed on said twenty-ninth day of June, the form of the oath shall be so far var[y][*i*]ed, as that instead of those words, "on the twenty-ninth day of June last," these words shall be inserted and used; "at the time of taking your liceu[s][c]e."

And be it further enacted,

[Sect. 3.] That every taverner, innholder, common victualler and retailer, shall make a fair entry in a book, of all such rum, brandy and other distilled spirit, and wine, as he or they, or any for him or them, shall buy, distil[l], or take in for sale after such account taken, and of all lemmons and limes taken in and consumed or used as aforesaid, and at the end of every six months, deliver the same, in writing, under their hands, to the farmer or farmers of the dut[y][*ie*]s aforesaid, who are impowered to administer an oath to him or them, that the said account is *bonâ fide*, just and true, and that he or they do not know of any brandy, rum or other distilled spirits, or wine, sold, directly or indirectly, or of any lemmons or limes used in punch or otherwise, by him or them, or any under him or them, or by his or their privity or consent, but what is contained in the account now exhibited, and shall pay him the duty thereof, excepting such part as the farmer shall find is still remaining by him or them; twenty per cent to be allowed on the liquors aforementioned for leakage and other wast[*e*], for which no duty is to be paid. Within six months accounts to be delivered. Twenty per cent allowed for leakage.

Provided always, and it is the true intent and meaning of this act,—

[Sect. 4.] That if any taverner, retailer or common victualler, shall buy of another taverner or retailer such small quantity of liquors as this act obliges him to account for to the farmer, and pay the excise, the taverner, retailer or common victualler shall, notwithstanding, be accountable and pay the excise, as if none had been paid by the person he bought the same of. Proviso.

And be it further enacted,

[Sect. 5.] That every taverner, innholder, common victualler or retailer, who shall be found to give a false account of any brandy, distilled spirits, wine, or other the commodities aforesaid, by him or her on the said twenty-ninth of June, or at the time of his or her taking licence, or bought, distilled or taken in for sale afterwards, or used as aforesaid, or refuse to give in an account, on oath, as aforesaid, shall be rendered incapable of having a licence afterwards, and shall be prosecuted by the farmer of the excise in the same county, for his or her neglect, and ordered by the general sessions of the peace to pay double the sum of money as they may judge that the excise of liquors, &c[a]., by him or her sold within such time, would have amounted to, to be paid to the said farmer. Penalty on giving a false account.

And be it further enacted,

[Sect. 6.] That the justices in their general sessions of the peace shall take recognizances, with sufficient sureties, of all persons by them licen[s][c]ed, both as to their keeping good rule and order, and duly observing the laws relating to persons so licen[s][c]ed, and for their duly and truly rendering an account in writing under their hands as aforesaid, and paying their excise in manner as aforesaid; as also that General sessions to take recognizance.

they shall not use their liceu[s][*c*]e in any house besides that wherein they dwell; which recognizance shall be taken within the space of thirty days after the granting of such licence, otherwise the persons licen[s][*c*]ed shall l[o]ose the benefit of his or her said licence; and no person shall be licen[s][*c*]ed by the said justices that hath not accounted with the farmer, and paid him the excise due to him from such person at the time of his asking for such licen[s][*c*]e.

Preamble. *And whereas*, notwithstanding the laws made against selling strong drink without licence, many persons not regarding the penalt[y][*ie*]s and forfeitures in the said act, do receive and entertain persons in their houses, and sell great quantit[y][*ie*]s of spirits and other strong drink, without licence so to do first had and obtained, by reason whereof great debaucheries are committed and kept secret, the end of this law in a great measure frustrated, and such as take licences and pay the excise greatly wrong[*e*]d and injured,—

Be it therefore further enacted,

Forfeiture of £3 for selling without license. [SECT. 7.] That whosoever, after the said twenty-ninth day of June, one thousand seven hundred and forty-five, shall presume, directly or indirectly, to sell any brandy, rum or other distilled spirits, wine, beer, cyder, perry or any other strong drink, in any smaller quantity than a quarter cask (twenty gallons to be accounted a quarter cask, and all delivered to one person without drawing any part of it off), without licence first had and obtained from the court of general sessions of the peace, and recognizing in manner as aforesaid, shall forfeit and pay for each offence, the sum of three pounds to the farmer, and costs of prosecution; and all such as shall refuse or neglect to pay the fine aforesaid, shall stand closely and strictly committed in the common goal of the county for three months at least, and not to have the liberty of the goaler's house or yard; and any goaler giving any person liberty contrary to this act, shall forfeit and pay three pounds, and pay costs of prosecution as aforesaid; and if any person or persons, not licenced as aforesaid, shall order, allow, permit or connive at the selling of any strong drink, contrary to the true intent or meaning of this act, by his or her child or children, servant or servants, or any other person or persons belonging to or in his or her house or family, and be thereof convict, he, she or they shall be reputed the offender or offenders, and shall suffer the same penalt[y][*ie*]s as if he, she or they had sold such drink themselves.

And be it further enacted,

One evidence sufficient. [SECT. 8.] That when any person shall be complained of for selling any strong drink without licence, one witness produced to one such fact, and another produced to another, shall be sufficient conviction, provided there be not more than the space of forty days between the facts concerning which such witnesses declare. And when and so often as it shall be observed that there is a resort of persons to houses suspected to sell strong drink without licence, any justice of the peace shall have full power to convene such persons before him, and examine them upon oath concerning the person suspected of selling or retailing strong drink in such houses, outhouses or other dependencies thereof, and on just ground to bind over the person suspected, and the witnesses, to the next court of general sessions of the peace for the county where such person shall dwell.

And be it further enacted,

Penalty on persons refusing to give evidence. [SECT. 9.] That if any person or persons shall be summoned to appear before a justice of the peace, or the grand jury, to give evidence relating to any person's selling strong drink without licence, or to appear before the court of general sessions of the peace, or other courts proper to try the same, to give evidence on the tr[y][*i*]al of any person informed against, presented or indicted for the selling strong drink without licence, and shall neglect or refuse to appear, or to give evidence in that behalf, every person so offending shall forfeit the sum of twenty pounds; the one half to be for his majesty, the other half to and for the use of him or them who shall sue for the same as aforesaid. And when it shall so happen that witnesses are bound to sea before the sitting of the court where any person or persons informed against for selling strong drink without licence is or are to be prosecuted for the same, in every such case, the deposition of any witness or witnesses in writing, taken before any two of his majesty's justices of the peace, *quorum unus*, and sealed up and delivered into court, the adverse party having first had a notification in writing sent to him or her of the time and place of caption, shall be esteemed as sufficient evidence in the law to convict any person or persons offending against this act, as if such witness or witnesses had been present at the time of trial, and given his, her or their deposition *viva voce;* and every person or persons who shall be summoned to give evidence before two justices of the peace in manner as aforesaid, and shall neglect or refuse to appear or to give evidence relating to the facts he or she shall be [e][*i*]nquired of, shall be liable and subject to the same penalty as he or she would have been by virtue of this act, for not appearing, or neglecting or refusing to give his or her evidence before the grand jury or court as aforesaid.

And be it further enacted,

[SECT. 10.] That all fines, forfeitures, and penalt[y][*ie*]s arising by this act shall and may be recovered by presentment of the grand jury at the court of sessions, or by bill, plaint, complaint or information, where the sum forfeited does not exceed three pounds, before any one of his majesty's justices of the peace in the respective count[y][*ie*]s where such offence shall be committed; which said justice is hereby impow[e]red to try and determine the same. And such justice shall make a fair entry or record of all such his proceedings: *saving always* to any person or persons who shall think him, her or themselves aggrieved by the sentence or determination of the said justice as aforesaid, liberty of appeal therefrom to the next court of general sessions of the peace to be holden in and for said county, at which court such offence shall be finally determined: *provided* that in said appeal the same rules be observed as are already by law required in appeal from justices to the court of general sessions of the peace.

How fines shall be recovered.

And to the end the revenue arising from the aforesaid dut[y][*ie*]s of excise may be advanced for the greater benefit and advantage of the publick,—

Be it further enacted,

[SECT. 11.] That one or more persons to be nominated and appointed by the general court for and within the several counties within this province, timely publick notice being first given of the time, place, and occasion of their meeting, shall have power, and are hereby authorized, from time to time, to contract and agree with any person for or concerning the farming the dut[y][*ie*]s in this act mentioned, upon brandy, rum, or other the liquors and commodities aforesaid, in the respective count[y][*ie*]s for which they shall be appointed, as may be for the greatest profit and advantage of the publick, so as the same exceed not the term of three years after the commencement of this act; and every person to whom the dut[y][*ie*]s of excise in any county shall be let[t] or farmed, shall have power to inspect the houses of all such as are licen[s][*c*]ed, and of such as are suspected to sell without licence, and to demand, sue for, and recover the excise due from licen[s][*c*]ed persons by virtue of this act.

Persons chosen by the general court have power to farm out the excise.

And be it further enacted,

Farmers to give bond with sureties, to the province treasurer.

[SECT. 12.] That the farmer shall give bond with two sufficient suret[y][*ie*]s, to the province treasurer for the time being, and his successors in said office, in double the sum of money that shall be contracted for, with condition that the sum agreed be paid into the province treasury for the use of the province, at the expiration of one year from the date of such bond, which bond the person or persons to be appointed as aforesaid a committee for such county are to take, and the same to lodge with the treasurer aforesaid, within twenty days after such bond is executed, and the said treasurer, upon failure or neglect of payment at the time therein limit[*t*]ed, shall and hereby is impow[e]red and directed to put such bond in suit, and to receive the money due thereon for the use aforementioned; and the said committees shall render an account of their proceedings touching the farming this duty on rum, wine, and other the liquors and species aforesaid in their respective count[y][*ie*]s to the general court in the first week of their fall sessions, and shall receive such sum or sums for their trouble and expences in said affair as said court shall think fit[t] to allow them.

Farmers may constitute deputies.

[SECT. 13.] And every person farming the excise in any county may substitute and appoint one or more deput[y][*ie*]s under him, upon oath, to collect and receive the excise aforesaid, which shall become due in such county, and pay in the same to the farmer; which deputy or deput[y][*ie*]s shall have, use and exercise all such powers and authorit[y][*ie*]s as in and by this act is given or committed to the farmers for the better collecting the dut[y][*ie*]s aforesaid, or prosecuting of offenders against this act.

And be it further enacted, anything hereinbefore contained to the contrary notwithstanding,

Farmers may compound and agree with retailers or innholders for their whole excise by the year.

[SECT. 14.] That it shall and may be lawful to and for the said farmers, and every of them, to compound and agree with any retailer or innholder within their respective divisions, from time to time, for his or her excise for the whole year in one entire sum, as they in their discretion shall think fit[t] to agree for, without making any entry thereof, as is before directed; and all and every person or persons, to whom the said excise or any part thereof shall be let[t] or farmed by themselves or their lawful substitutes, may and hereby are impow[e]red to sue for and recover in any of his majesty's courts of record, or before a justice of the peace where the matter is not above his cognizance, any sum or sums that shall grow due from any of the aforesaid duties of excise, where the party or part[y][*ie*]s for whom the same is or shall become due shall refuse or neglect to pay the same.

And be it further enacted,

Penalty for farmer's conniving at persons not licensed selling strong drink.

[SECT. 15.] That in case any person farming the excise as aforesaid, or his deputy, shall at any time during their continuance in said office, wittingly and willingly connive at, or allow, any person or persons within their respective divisions, not licenced by the court of general sessions of the peace, their selling any brandy, wine, rum, or other liquors by this act forbidden, such farmer or deputy, for every such offence, shall forfeit the sum of fifty pounds, one half whereof shall be to his majesty for the use of the province, the other half to him or them that shall inform or sue for the same, and shall thenceforward be forever disabled from serving in said office. [*Passed June* 29; *published July* 9.

CHAPTER 3.

AN ACT FOR GRANTING THE SUM OF FIFTEEN HUNDRED POUNDS FOR THE SUPPORT OF HIS MAJESTY'S GOVERNOUR.

Be it enacted by the Governour, Council and House of Representatives,

[Sect. 1.] That the sum of fifteen hundred pounds, in bills of credit of the last emission, be and hereby is granted unto his most excellent majesty, to be paid out of the publick treasury to his excellency William Shirley, Esq., captain-general and governour-in-chief in and over his majesty's province of the Massachusetts Bay, for his past services, and further to enable him to manage the publick affairs of the province.

[Sect. 2.] The aforesaid sum of fifteen hundred pounds shall be paid out of the next general supply bill that shall be hereafter agreed on and pass'd by this court. [*Passed June* 25; *published July* 9.

CHAPTER 4.

AN ACT FOR GRANTING A SUM FOR THE PAY OF THE MEMBERS OF THE COUNCIL AND HOUSE OF REPRESENTATIVES IN GENERAL COURT ASSEMBLED, AND FOR ESTABLISHING THE WAGES, &c[A]., OF SUNDRY PERSONS IN THE SERVICE OF THE PROVINCE.

Be it enacted by the Governour, Council and House of Representatives,

Pay of the members of the council.

[Sect. 1.] That from the beginning of the present session of the general court unto the end of their several sessions till May next, each member of the council shall be [e][*i*]ntitled to four shillings and sixpence per diem, to be paid out of the publick treasury, by warrant according to the direction of the royal charter, upon certificate given of the number of days of such member's attendance, and travel to and from the court, twenty miles to be accounted a day's travel.

And be it further enacted,

Pay of the representatives.

[Sect. 2.] That each member of the house of representatives serving the time afores[*ai*]d shall be paid three shillings per diem, upon certificate given by the clerk of the house of represent[*ati*]ves of the number of days of such member's attendance, and travel to and from the court, twenty miles to be accounted a day's travel.

And be it further enacted,

Pay of the officers and soldiers at Castle William.

[Sect. 3.] That the wages of the captain of Castle William shall be after the rate of sixty pounds per annum, from the twentieth day of March, one thousand seven hundred and forty-four, to the twentieth day of November, one thousand seven hundred and forty-five; of the lieutenant, for that term, forty pounds; of the chaplain, forty pounds; of the gunner, fifty pounds; of the gunner's mate, forty shillings per month; of four ser[g][*j*]eants, each thirty shillings per month; and of six quarter-gunners, each thirty shillings per month; of six corporals, each twenty-six shillings and sixpence per month; two drummers, each twenty-six shillings and sixpence per month; of one armourer, forty shillings per month; of forty centinels, each twenty-two shillings and sixpence per month: for their subsistence, six shillings and threepence per week per man.

And be it further enacted,

Richmond Fort.

[Sect. 4.] That the wages of the captain of Richmond Fort, from the twentieth day of March, one thousand seven hundred and forty-four, to the twentieth day of November, one thousand seven hundred and forty-five, shall be at the rate of forty shillings per month; of one ser[g][j]eant, twenty-five shillings per month; of one corporal, twenty-four shillings per month; of one armourer, thirty shillings per month; and for the chaplain, twenty-five pounds per annum; of one interpreter, fifteen shillings per month, being a centinel; and of twenty centinels, twenty-two shillings and sixpence per month.

And be it further enacted,

George's River. [SECT. 5.] That the wages of the captain of the truck-house on George's River, from the twentieth day of March, one thousand seven hundred and forty-four, to the twentieth day of November, one thousand seven hundred and forty-five, shall be at the rate of forty shillings per month; of one lieutenant, twenty-six shillings per month; of one ser[g][j]eant, twenty-five shillings per month; of two corporals, each twenty-four shillings per month; of thirty-three centinels, each twenty-two shillings and sixpence per month; of one armourer, fourteen shillings per month, he being lieutenant; of one interpreter, thirty shillings per month; and of the chaplain there, twenty-five pounds per annum.

And be it further enacted,

Brunswick Fort. [SECT. 6.] That the wages of the commanding officer at Fort Brunswick, from the twentieth day of March, one thousand seven hundred and forty-four, to the twentieth day of November, one thousand seven hundred and forty-five, shall be at the rate of forty shillings per month; of eleven centinels, each twenty-two shillings and sixpence per month; one ser[g][j]eant, at twenty-five shillings per month.

And be it further enacted,

Saco truck-house. [SECT. 7.] That the wages of one ser[g][j]eant at the truck-house at Saco, from the twentieth day of March, one thousand seven hundred and forty-four, to the twentieth day of November, one thousand seven hundred and forty-five, shall be at the rate of thirty shillings per month; and of one corporal, twenty-four shillings per month; of twelve centinels, each twenty-two shillings and sixpence per month.

And be it further enacted,

Frederick Fort. [SECT. 8.] That the wages of the commanding officer at Frederick Fort, from the twentieth day of March, one thousand seven hundred and forty-four, to the twentieth day of November, one thousand seven hundred and forty-five, be at the rate of forty shillings per month; and of the chaplain there, fifteen pounds per annum; and of twenty-one centinels, each twenty-two shillings and sixpence per month.

And be it further enacted,

Country's sloop. [SECT. 9.] That the wages of the captain of the sloop in [the*] countr[e]y's service, from the twentieth day of March, one thousand seven hundred and forty-four, to the twentieth day of November, one thousand seven hundred and forty-five, shall be at the rate of fifty shillings per month; of the mate, thirty shillings per month; of eight sailors, each twenty-five shillings per month; for the sloop, seven pounds ten shillings per month.

And be it further enacted,

Oath to be made, &c. [SECT. 10.] That before payment of any muster-roll be allowed, oath be made by the officer or person presenting such roll, that the officers and soldiers born on such roll have been in actual service for the whole time they stand ent[e]red thereon. [*Passed June* 27; *published July* 9.

* The engrossment is mutilated here.

CHAPTER 5.

AN ACT FOR ENCOURAGING THE KILLING OF WOLVES, BEARS, WILDCAT[T]S AND CATTAMOUNTS, WITHIN THIS PROVINCE.

Be it enacted by the Governour, Council and House of Representatives,

[Sect. 1.] That whosoev[*er**] hath, since the twenty-fourth of April last, or shall from and after the publication of this act, kill any grown wolf, bear, wildcat[t] or cattamount, or any wolf's, wildcat or cattamount's whelps, or bear's cubbs, under one year old, and other than such as shall be taken out of the belly of any female bear, wolf[e], wildcat[t] or cattamount within this province, and bring the whole head thereof unto the const[*able**] of the town in which such wolf[e], bear, wildcat[t] or cattamount, or wolf's, wildcat[t]'s or cattamount's whelp[*s*], or bear's cubb, shall be [*killed**], or to the constable of the town next adjacent unto the place where the same was killed without the bounds of any township, th[*e**] constable, in the presence of one or more of the selectmen, shall cut[t] both the ears off the same. Premium allowed for killing wolves, bears, wildcats and catamounts. 1741-42, chap. 23.

[Sect. 2.] And such selectman or me[*n and**] constable, shall give the party a receipt for the said head, expressing whether it be, in their judgment, a grown wolf[e], bear, [*wild**]cat or cat[t]amount, or wolf[e]'s, wildcat[t] or cattamount's whelp, or bear's cubb, and upon producing such receipt, the party sh[*all**] be paid and allowed by the selectmen or treasurer of such town, out of the town stock for the same, the following pr[*emiums**], and no other; viz[t]., the sum of forty shillings in the bills last emitted by this court, or other bills of this province equ[*ivalent**] thereto, for a wolf[e]; and for a wolf[e]'s whelp, the sum of thirteen shillings and fourpence; for a cattamount, fifty shil[*lings**]; for a cattamount's whelp, twenty-five shillings; and for every bear that shall be killed from the first of April to [*the**] last of August, yearly, ten shillings; for every bear's cub[*b*] killed during that season, five shillings; for a wildcat[t], the s[*um**] of six shillings; and the sum of three shillings for every wildcat[t]'s whelp.

[Sect. 3.] And all such payments so made, shall be allowed [*by**] the treasurer and receiver-general of this province, upon his receiving a certificate, under the hands of a major part of the selectmen in such town, and town treasurer, where any such be, or town clerk, expressing the same, which certificate shall be in the following form; viz[t].,—

Mr. Treasurer,

This may certify that there hath been paid out of the town stock of A., for grown wol[f][*v*]es, bears, wildcat[t]s or cattamounts, and wolves', wildcat[t]s' or cattamounts' whelps, or bears' cubs, killed in or near this town since the day of last past, and the heads thereof brought unto our constable or constables, and the ears cut[t] off in the presence of some of ourselves, as the law directs, and so certif[y][*i*]ed unto us; in the whole, the sum of pounds; which sum we desire you to allow to our town by paying the same unto , our town treasurer. Dated in aforesaid, the day of , anno domini, 17 . Form of the certificate.

} *Selectmen, town treasurer, or town clerk.*

And be it further enacted,

[Sect. 4.] That the treasurer do cause a competent number of blank certificates in the form aforesaid, to be printed at the publick Province treasurer to provide certificates.

* The parchment is mutilated.

charge, and affix his own seal thereto, and is hereby ordered to deliver so many unto the selectmen of each town or place respectively, or some one of them, as shall be necessary for the use of such town or place.

And be it further enacted,

Inhabitants to be assessed for the premiums.

[SECT. 5.] That the selectmen of each town respectively shall be and hereby are sufficiently authorized and impow[e]red to assess the inhabitants of [*their**] town yearly, in due proportion as near as they can, such sum and sums as they shall judge necessary to answer the payments to [*be**] made out of the town stock as aforesaid, together with the other charges of the town, and to cause the same to be collected in manner as [*is**] by law directed for the gathering of town rates.

And for preventing any persons receiving a premium for any grown or you[*ng**] wolf, bear, wildcat[t] or cat[t]amount, killed without the bounds of this province,—

Be it enacted,

Oath to be made that the creatures were killed within the province.

[SECT. 6.] That when and so often as any person shall bring the head of any grown or young wolf[e], bear, wildcat[t] or cattamount, to the constable of any town or distr[*ict**] within this province, and it be suspected that it was not killed within the same, such person shall not be [e][*i*]ntitled to the reward in [*this**] act provided, until he makes oath before one of his majesty's justices of the peace, or selectmen of the town, in such town where [*no**] justice of the peace dwells, who are hereby impow[e]red to administer the same, that such wolf[e], bear, wildcat[t] or cattamount, [*was**] *bonâ fide* killed within this province.

And be it further enacted,

Indians to be entitled to the premiums.

[SECT. 7.] That if any Indian shall kill any wolf, bear, [*wild**]cat or cattamount, or wol[f][*ve*]s' wildcat[t]s', or cattamounts' whelp[*s*] or bear's cub[b] within this province, he shall be [e][*i*]ntitled to the [*same**] reward in this act provided for killing thereof, in case such Indian bring the head of such wolf, bear, wildcat[t] or cattamo[*unt**], or wolf[e]'s, wildcat[t]'s or cattamount's whelp, or bear's cubb to a constable, and satisfy the selectmen of the town where the sa[*me**] is brought, that it was killed within this province.

Limitation.

[SECT. 8.] This act to continue and be in force for the space of five years from the publication thereof, and no longer. [*Passed June* 29; *published July* 9.

CHAPTER 6.

AN ACT FOR SUPPLYING THE TREASURY WITH THE SUM OF SEVENTY THOUSAND POUNDS, FOR DISCHARGING THE PUBLIC DEBTS, &c[A]., AND FOR DRAWING IN THE SAID BILLS INTO THE TREASURY AGAIN.

Be it enacted by the Governour, Council, and House of Representatives,

£70,000 bills of credit to be emitted.

[SECT. 1.] That the treasurer be and hereby is impow[e]red and ordered to emit and issue forth the sum of seventy thousand pounds in bills of credit of the last tenor and date, now lying in his hands, and receiv[e]'d in for taxes, impost, and excise, which shall pass in all publick payments equal to other new-tenor bills, emitted since one thousand seven hundred and forty; or, if there shall not be a sufficiency of such bills, that then the committee appointed by this court for signing bills are hereby directed and impow[e]red to take care and make effect-

* The parchment is mutilated.

ual provision, [so] [*as*] soon as may be, to imprint the said bills, or so many as may be needed to compleat the said sum, and to sign and deliver the same to the treasurer, taking his receipt for the same; and the said committee shall be under oath for the faithful[l] performance of the trust by this act reposed in them. And the said sum of seventy thousand pounds shall be issued out of the treasury in manner and for the purposes following; viz[t]., the sum of five thousand pounds, part of the aforesaid sum of seventy thousand pounds, be appl[y][*i*]ed for the payment of wages that now are, or that hereafter may be, due by virtue of the establishment of Castle William, Frederick Fort, Richmond Fort, George's Truck-house, Saco Truck-house, Brunswick Fort, the sloop in the countr[e]y's service, and the treasurer's usual disbursements; and the sum of six thousand pounds, part of the aforesaid sum of seventy thousand pounds, shall be appl[y][*i*]ed for putting the province into a better posture of defence, for compleating the repairs of Castle William and other forts, for paying of such officers and soldiers as have done service for the province, whose wages are now due, which officers and soldiers shall be paid out of this appropriation preferable to any other service; and for such officers and soldiers as are and may be in the province service, according to the several establishments for that purpose, for purchasing all needful[l] warlike stores for the several forts and garrisons within this province, pursuant to such grants as are or shall be made by this court for those purposes; and the sum of eleven thousand five hundred pounds, part of the aforesaid sum of seventy thousand pounds for the payment of his majesty's council, and such other grants as are or shall be made by this court; and for the payment of stipends, bounties, and premiums established by law; and for the payment of all other matters and things which this court have or shall, either by law or orders, provide for the payment of out of the publick treasury, and for no other purpose whatsoever: the sum of one thousand pounds, part of the aforesaid sum of seventy thousand pounds, shall be applied for the discharge of other debts owing from this province to persons that have served or shall serve them by order of this court in such matters and things where there is no establishment, nor any certain sum assigned for such service, and for paper, printing, and writing for this court, the expences of the committees of council, or of the house, or of both houses, the surgeon of Castle William, and wooding of said castle; and the sum of two thousand four hundred pounds, part of the aforesaid sum of seventy thousand pounds, shall be appl[y][*i*]ed for the payment of the house of representatives serving in the general court during their several sessions this present year; and the sum of forty-three thousand eight hundred pounds, part of the aforesaid sum of seventy thousand pounds, shall be applied to defr[e][*a*]y the charges of the expedition against his majesty's enem[y][*ie*]s at Cape Breton and parts adjacent.

£5,000 for wages at Castle William and other garrisons, &c.

£6,000 for putting the province into a better posture of defence, &c.

£11,500 for payment of his majesty's council, and other grants, &c.

£1,000 for debts where there is no establishment.

£2,400 for the pay of the representatives.

£43,800 for the charges of the expedition against Cape Breton.

And whereas there are sometimes publick entertainments, and, from time to time, contingent and unforeseen charges that demand prompt payment,—

Be it further enacted,

[Sect. 2.] That the sum of three hundred pounds, the remaining part of the aforesaid sum of seventy thousand pounds, be applied to defrey and pay such entertainments and contingent charges, and for no other use whatsoever.

£300 for entertainments, &c.

And be it enacted,

[Sect. 3.] That if there be a surplusage in any sum appropriated, such surplusage shall l[y][*i*]e in the treasury for the further order of this court.

Surplusage to lie in the treasury.

And be it further enacted,

Warrants to express the appropriations. [SECT. 4.] That each and every warrant for drawing money out of the treasury shall direct the treasurer to take the same out of such sums as are respectively appropriated for the payment of such publick debts as the draughts are made to discharge; and the treasurer is hereby directed and ordered to pay such money out of such appropriation as directed to, and no other, upon pain of refunding all such sum or sums as he shall otherwise pay, and to keep exact and distinct accompts of all payments made out of such appropriated sums; and the secretary, to whom it belongs to keep the muster-rolls and accompts of charge, shall lay before the house, when they direct, all such muster-rolls and accompts after payment thereof.

And as a fund and security for drawing the said sum of seventy thousand pounds into the treasury again,—

Be it further enacted,

£33,800 in 1751. [SECT. 5.] That there be and hereby is granted unto his most excellent majesty, for the ends and uses aforesaid, a tax of thirty-three thousand eight hundred pounds, to be levyed on polls, and estates both real and personal, within this province, according to such rules and in such proportion[s] on the several towns and districts within the same, as shall be agreed upon and ordered by this court at their session in May, one thousand seven hundred and fifty-one, and paid into the publick treasury on or before the last day of December then next after.

And as a further fund and security for drawing in the said sum of seventy thousand pounds into the treasury again,—

Be it further enacted,

£33,800 in 1752. [SECT. 6.] That there be and hereby is granted unto his most excellent majesty, for the ends and uses aforesaid, a tax of thirty-three thousand eight hundred pounds, to be levyed on polls, and estates both real and personal, within this province, according to such rules and in such proportion[s] on the several towns and districts within the same, as shall be agreed upon and ordered by this court at their session in May, one thousand seven hundred and fifty-two, and paid into the publick treasury on or before the last day of December then next after.

And as a fund and security for drawing in such sum or sums as shall be paid out to the representatives of the several towns,—

Be it enacted,

Tax to be made for what is paid the representatives. [SECT. 7.] That there be and hereby is granted unto his most excellent majesty a tax of such sum or sums as shall be paid to the several representatives as aforesaid, to be lev[y][*i*]ed and assessed on the polls and estates of the inhabitants of the several towns, according to what their several representatives shall so receive, which sums shall be set[t] on the towns in the next province tax; and the assessors of the said town shall make their assessment for this tax, and apportion the same according to the rules that shall be prescribed by the act of the general assembly for assessing the next province tax; and the constables in their respective districts shall pay in the same when they pay in the province tax for the next year, of which the treasurer is hereby directed to keep a distinct and seperate account; and if there be any surplusage, the same shall l[y][*i*]e in the hands of the treasurer for the further order of this court.

And be it further enacted,

Tax for the money hereby emitted to be made according to the preceding tax act, in case. [SECT. 8.] That in case the general court shall not at their session in May, one thousand seven hundred and fifty-one, and one thousand seven hundred and fifty-two, agree and conclude upon an act apportioning the sum which by this act is engaged shall be in those years apportioned, assessed and lev[y][*i*]ed, that then and in such case each town and district within this province shall pay, by a tax to be lev[y][*i*]ed on the polls, and estates both real and personal, within their districts, the same proportions of the said sums as the said towns and districts shall have been taxed by the general court in the tax act then next preceeding; and the province treasurer is hereby fully impow[e]red and directed, some time in the month of June, in the year one thousand seven hundred and fifty-one, and one thousand seven hundred and fifty-two, to issue and send forth his warrants, directed to the selectmen or assessors of each town and district within this province, requiring them to assess the polls, and estates both real and personal, within their several towns and districts, for their respective part and proportion of the sum before direc[*ted* *] and engaged to be assessed by this act; and the assessors, as also persons assessed, shall observe, be govern[*ed by* *], and subject to all such rules and directions as shall have been given in the next preceedin[*g* *] tax act.

And be it further enacted,

[Sect. 9.] That the inhabitants of this province shall [*have**] liberty, if [*they see fit, to pay the s* *]everal sums for which they respectively may, in pursuance of th[*is act,**] be assessed [*in bills of credit of the form a* *]nd tenor by this act emitted, or in other new-tenor bills, [*or in**] bills of the middle tenor, according to their several denominations, or in bills of the old tenor, accounting four for one; or in coined silver, at seven shillings and sixpence per ounce, troy weight, and [*of**] sterling alloy, or in gold coin, proportionably; or in merchantable hemp, flax, winter and Isle-of-Sab[*le**] codfish, refined bar-iron, bloomery-iron, hollow iron-ware, Indian corn, rye, wheat, barley, pork, beef, duck or canvas, whalebone, cordage, train-oil, beeswax, bayberry-wax, tallow, peas[e], sheepswo[*o*]l[l], or tan[*n*]'d sole-leather (the aforesaid commodities being of the produce or manufactures of this province), at such moderate rates and prices as the general assembly of the year[*s*] one thousand seven hundred and fifty-one, and one thousand seven hundred and fifty-two, shall set[t] them at; the several persons paying their taxes in any of the commodities aforementioned, to run the risque and pay the charge of transporting the said commodities to the province treasury; but if the aforesaid general assembly shall not, at their sessions in May, some time before the twentieth day of June in each year, agree upon and set the aforesaid species and commodities at some certai[*n* *] price, that then the eldest councellors, for the time being, of each of those count[y][*ie*]s in the province, of which any one of the council is an inhabitant, together with the province treasurer, or the major part of them, be a committee, who hereby are directed and fully authorized and impowered to do it; and in their set[*t*]ling the p[*rices* *] and rating the value of those commodities, to state so much of them, respectively, at seven shillings and sixpen[*ce* *] as an ounce of silver will purchase at that time in the town of Boston, and so *pro ratâ*. And the treasurer is hereby directed to insert in the several warrants by him sent to the several collectors of [*the*] taxes in each y[*ear**], with the names of the afore-recited commodities, the several prices or rates which shall be set[t] on them, either by the general assembly or the committee aforesaid, and direct the aforesaid collectors to receive them so.

Taxes to be paid in the several species herein enumerated.

How the commodities brought into the treasury are to be rated.

[Sect. 10.] And the aforesaid commodities, so brought into the treasury, shall, as soon as may be, be disposed of by the treasurer to the best advantage for so much as they will fetch in bills of credit hereby to be emitted, or for silver or gold, which silver and gold shall be delivered to the possessor of said bills in exchange for them; that is to say, one ounce of silver coin, and so gold in proportion, for seven shillings and

Treasurer to sell the said commodities.

* The parchment is mutilated.

sixpence, and so *pro ratâ* for a greater or less sum; and if any loss shall happen by the sale of the aforesaid species, or by any unforeseen accident, such deficiency shall be made good by a tax of the year next following, so as fully and effectually to call in the whole sum of seventy thousand pounds in said bills hereby ordered to be emitted; and if there be a surplusage, it shall remain a stock in the treasury. [*Passed July* 2; *published July* 9.

CHAPTER 7.

AN ACT TO PREVENT UNNECESSARY COST BEING A[*LLOWED**] TO PARTIES AND WITNESSES IN THE SEVERAL COURTS OF JUSTICE WITHIN THIS PROVINCE.

Preamble.

WHEREAS oftentimes there are several plaintiffs or defendants in one and the same action, brought either to the superio[*u*]r court, or the inferio[*u*]r court of common pleas within the respective counties, and in taxing the bills of cost arising on said actions, all the plantiffs or defendants mentioned in the writ so brought are allowed for their attendance, altho' it frequently happens that only one of the plantiffs or defendants do actually attend, and sometimes neither of them; and inasmuch as an allowance is sometimes made for witnesses not summoned, or when summoned for much longer time than such witnesses have actually attended the court, by which means bills of cost are exorbitantly enhanced; for the prevention whereof for the future,—

Be it enacted by the Governour, Council and House of Representatives,

Justices of the several courts to allow cost but for one person as plaintiff or defendant, except.

[SECT. 1.] That from and after the publication of this act, neither the justices of the superio[*u*]r court, nor the justices of the inferio[*u*]r court of common pleas in the respective counties within this province, shall, in taxing any bills of cost, allow for the attendance of more than one person as plantiff or defendant, altho' there are more plantiffs or defendants than one, in any suit or action, and appear by themselves or by their attorney or attorneys, except where the defendants plead severally; and in case of the actual attendance of either plantiff or defendant, they shall be allowed in the bill of cost for no longer time than they make evident to the court the number of miles they travel, and time of their attendance as aforesaid.

And be it further enacted,

No person filing a complaint to be allowed for more than three days' attendance.

[SECT. 2.] That no person filing a complaint in the superio[*u*]r court or inferio[*u*]r court respectively for the affirmation of a former judgment, shall be allowed at any time more than three days' attendance in the bills of costs to be taxed by said courts.

And be it further enacted,

No witness, not served with a *subpœna*, to be allowed more than one day's attendance, &c.

[SECT. 3.] That no witness giving his or her deposition in any case, who shall not be served with a subpœna, shall be allowed in the bill of cost[*s*] any more than one day's attendance, nor shall any witness summoned to appear be allowed for more days than such witness shall actually attend and make it evident to the court where the action shall be commenced, by their certifying on the subpœna the number of miles of their travel, and time that he or she has actually attended.

[SECT. 4.] This act to continue and be in force for the space of five years from the publication hereof, and no longer. [*Passed June* 29; *published July* 11.

* The parchment is mutilated.

ACTS

PASSED AT THE SESSION BEGUN AND HELD AT BOSTON, ON THE SEVENTEENTH DAY OF JULY, A. D. 1745.

CHAPTER 8.

AN ACT FOR SUPPLYING THE TREASURY WITH THE SUM OF SEVENTY THOUSAND POUNDS FOR THE USE AND SERVICE OF HIS MAJESTY'S GARRISON AT LOUISBOURG, AND FOR REPAIRING THE FORTRESSES AND OTHER BUILDINGS THERE, AND FOR DRAWING IN THE SAID BILLS INTO THE TREASURY AGAIN.

Be it enacted by the Governour, Council and House of Representatives,

[SECT. 1.] That the treasurer be and hereby is impowred and ordered to emit and issue forth the sum of seventy thousand pounds in bills of credit of the last tenor and date now lying in his hands, and receiv'd for taxes, impost and excise, which shall pass in all publick payments equal to the other new-tenor bills, emitted since one thousand seven hundred and forty; or if there be not a sufficiency of such bills, that then the committee for signing bills are hereby directed and impowred to take care and make effectual provision, as soon as may be, to imprint the said bills, or so many as may be needed to compleat the said sum, and to sign and deliver the same to the treasurer, taking his receipt for the same; and the said committee shall be under oath for the faithful performance of the trust by this act reposed in them; and the said sum of seventy thousand pounds shall be issued out of the publick treasury for the purpose following; viz., for the use and service of his majesty's garrison at Louisbourg, and for repairing the fortresses and other buildings there. £70,000 bills of credit to be emitted.

And be it enacted,

[SECT. 2.] That if there be a surplusage in the sum appropriated as aforesaid, such surplusage shall lie in the treasury for the further order of this court. Surplusage to lie in the treasury.

And as a fund or security for drawing the aforesaid sum of seventy thousand pounds into the treasury again,—

Be it further enacted,

[SECT. 3.] That there be and hereby is granted unto his most excellent majesty, for the ends and uses aforesaid, a tax of thirty-five thousand pounds, to be levyed on polls, and estates both real and personal, within this province, according to such rules and in such proportions on the several towns and districts within the same, as shall be agreed upon and ordered by this court at their session in May, one thousand seven hundred and fifty-three, and paid into the publick treasury on or before the last day of December then next after. £35,000 in 1753.

And as a further fund and security for drawing in the aforesaid sum of seventy thousand pounds into the treasury again,—

Be it further enacted,

£35,000 in 1754. [SECT. 4.] That there be and hereby is granted unto his most excellent majesty, for the ends and uses aforesaid, a tax of thirty-five thousand pounds, to be levyed on polls, and estates both real and personal, within this province, according to such rules and in such proportions on the several towns and districts within the same, as shall be agreed upon and ordered by this court at their session in May, one thousand seven hundred and fifty-four, and paid into the publick treasury on or before the last day of December then next after.

And be it further enacted,

Tax for the money hereby emitted to be made according to the preceding tax act, in case. [SECT. 5.] That in case the general court shall not at their sessions in May, one thousand seven hundred and fifty-three, and one thousand seven hundred and fifty-four, agree and conclude upon an act apportioning the several sums which by this act is engaged shall be in each of those years apportioned, assessed and levied, that then and in such case each town and district within this province shall pay, by a tax to be levied on the polls, and estates both real and personal, within their districts, the same proportion of the said sums as the said towns and districts shall have been taxed by the general court in the tax act then next preceeding; and the province treasurer is hereby fully impowred and directed, some time in the month of June in each of those years, one thousand seven hundred and fifty-three and one thousand seven hundred and fifty-four, to issue and send forth his warrants, directed to the selectmen or assessors of each town and district within this province, requiring them to assess the polls, and estates both real and personal, within their several towns and districts, for their respective part and proportion of the sums before directed and engaged by this act to be assessed; and the assessors, as also persons assessed, shall observe, be governed by and subject to all such rules and directions as shall have been given in the next preceeding tax act.

And be it further enacted,

Taxes to be paid in the several species herein enumerated. [SECT. 6.] That the inhabitants of this province shall have liberty, if they see fit, to pay the several sums for which they respectively may, in pursuance of this act, be assessed, in bills of credit of the form and tenor by this act emitted, or in any other new-tenor bills, or in bills of the middle tenor, according to their several denominations, or in bills of the old tenor, accounting four for one; or in coined silver at seven shillings and sixpence per ounce, troy weight, of sterling alloy, or in gold coin, proportionably; or in merchantable hemp, flax, winter and Isle-of-Sable codfish, refined bar-iron, bloomery-iron, hollow iron-ware, Indian corn, rye, wheat, barley, pork, beef, duck or canvas, whalebone, cordage, train-oil, beeswax, bayberry-wax, tallow, peas[e], sheepswool, or tann'd sole-leather (the aforesaid commodities being of the produce or manufactories of this province), at such moderate rates and prices as the respective general assemblys of the years one thousand seven hundred and fifty-three and one thousand seven hundred and fifty-four shall set them at; the several persons paying their taxes in any of the commodities aforementioned, to run the risque and pay the charge of transporting the said commodities to the province treasury; but if the aforesaid general assemblys shall not, at their respective sessions in May, some time before the twentieth day of June, agree upon and set the aforesaid species and commodities at some certain price, that then the eldest councellor, for the time being, in each of those counties in the province, of which any one of the council is an inhabitant, together with the province treasurer, or the major part of them, be a committee, who are hereby directed and fully authorized and impowered to do it; and in their setting the prices and rating the value of those commodities, to state so much of

How the commodities brought into the treasury are to be rated.

them, respectively, at seven shillings and sixpence as an ounce of silver will purchase at that time in the town of Boston, and so *pro ratâ*. And the treasurer is hereby directed to insert in the several warrants by him sent to the collectors of the taxes in those years, respectively, with the names of the afore-recited commodities, the several rates or prices which shall be set on them, either by the general assembly or the committee aforesaid, and direct the aforesaid collectors to receive them so.

[SECT. 7.] And the aforesaid commodities so brought into the treasury shall, as soon as may be, be disposed of by the treasurer to the best advantage for so much as they will fetch in bills of credit aforementioned, or for silver or gold, which silver and gold shall be delivered to the possessor of said bills in exchange for them; that is to say, one ounce of silver coin, and so gold in proportion, for seven shillings and sixpence, and so *pro ratâ* for a greater or less sum; and if any loss shall happen by the sale of the aforesaid species, by any unforeseen accident, such deficiency shall be made good by a tax of the year next following, so as fully and effectually to call in the whole sum of seventy thousand pounds in said bills hereby ordered to be emitted, and for which a tax on polls and estates is in this act laid as a fund; and if there be a surplusage, it shall remain a stock in the treasury. *Treasurer to sell the said commodities.*

[*Passed August* 2; *published August* 7.

CHAPTER 9.

AN ACT TO SUBJECT THE UNIMPROVED LANDS WITHIN THIS PROVINCE TO BE SOLD FOR PAYMENT OF TAXES ASSESSED ON THEM BY ORDER OF THE GREAT AND GENERAL COURT AND VOTES AND AGREEMENTS OF THE PROPRIETORS THEREOF.

Preamble.

WHEREAS it frequently happens that the proprietors of unimproved lands within the several towns, precincts, new plantations and propriet[ie][*or*]s within this province, neglect or delay to pay their proportions of the sums from time to time assessed on such lands by order of the great and general court, and according to their own agreements, towards defr[a][*e*]ying the publick charges arising within such towns, precincts, new plantations and proprieties,—

Be it therefore enacted by the Governour, Council and House of Representatives,

Assessors of taxes on unimproved lands, their power.

Unimproved lands to be sold for paying charges, in case the owners refuse or neglect to pay the sums laid on them by assessors appointed for that purpose.

[SECT. 1.] That if the assessors of any of the towns, precincts, new plantations or proprieties within this province, have, or at any time to come shall, pursuant to the direction or orders of the general court, levy or assess a tax upon the unimproved lands of the proprietors, situate in any of the towns within this province, for defraying the publick charges arising in the said towns, precincts, new plantations or proprieties, or if the assessors chosen by the proprietors of the common and undivided land in any of the towns or new plantations within this province, pursuant to the votes and agreements of such propriety, have or shall levy or assess a tax upon such proprietors by them thought necessary to carry on and prosecute any actions or suits that may be brought by or against them, or for the carrying on and managing of any other publick affair relating to such proprietors, or performance of the conditions of their grant respectively; and such proprietors shall neglect or delay to pay to the collector or collectors the sums from time to time levied or assessed upon their lands as aforesaid, for sixty days after such assessment is made, and published by posting up the same in the town or precinct where such land lies, and in the shire town of the county, that then and in such case it shall and may be lawful for such assessors respectively to post up, in some publick place or places in the town or precinct where the lands lie, notifications of the intended sale of so much, and no more, of such delinquent proprietor's land or common rights as they shall judge necessary to pay and satisfy such rates and taxes, and other necessary intervening charges, three months before the same be sold; and also the assessors shall be obliged, for the notification of the non-resident proprietors, to adverti[z][*s*]e in the publick prints, three several weeks, the intended sale, at least three months before the land be sold: and if any delinquent proprietors do not by that time pay such rates or assessm[*en*]ts and charges, then and in such case, it shall and may be lawful for the assessors, at a publick vendue, to sell and execute absolute deeds in the law for the conveyance of such lands of the proprietors to the person or persons who will give most for the same; which deeds shall be good and valid to all intents and purposes in the law, for conveying such estates to the grantees, their heirs and assigns for ever; and if the said lands be sold for more, then the overplus, after all charges arising about the same are subducted, to be paid to such delinquent proprietors or their order; the money which the said lands shall be sold for, to be lodged in the hands of the treasurers of the respective towns, precincts or proprieties, who are hereby directed to attend the orders of the assessors of such towns, precincts or proprieties, for payment of the same, pursuant to the true intent and meaning of this act, reserving to such non-resident proprietors as are not inhabitants of this province, their heirs or assigns, a liberty for redemption of their lands so sold, they paying to the grantees, or their heirs respectively, within one year afterwards, the sums for which the said lands were sold, with double dam[*m*]ages, until[l] the same be redeemed.

Notifications of the sale of lands to be inserted in the public prints.

Overplus of money to be lodged with the town treasurers.

Limitation.

[SECT. 2.] This act to continue and be in force for the space of seven years from the publication thereof, and no longer. [*Passed July 26; published August 7.*

ACT

PASSED AT THE SESSION BEGUN AND HELD AT BOSTON, ON THE THIRTIETH DAY OF OCTOBER, A. D. 1745.

CHAPTER 10.

AN ACT FOR REVIVING AN ACT, [E][*I*]NTITLED "AN ACT FOR ESTABLISHING AND REGULATING FEES WITHIN THIS PROVINCE," MADE AND PASS'D IN THE EIGHTEENTH YEAR OF HIS PRESENT MAJESTY'S REIGN.

WHEREAS an act was made and pass'd in the eighteenth year of his present majesty's reign, [e][*i*]ntitled "An Act for establishing and regulating fees within this province," which hath been found beneficial, and is judged necessary, but is now expired,— **Preamble.** **1744-45, chap. 13.**

Be it therefore enacted by the Lieutenant-Governo[*u*]*r, Council and House of Representatives,*

That the aforesaid act for establishing and regulating fees, and every matter and clause therein contained, be and hereby is revived, and shall continue and remain in full force until[l] the last day of November, which will be in the year one thousand seven hundred and forty-six, and to the end of the session of the general court then next after. **Act for regulating fees, revived for one year.**

[*Passed November* 30; *published December* 2.

ACTS

PASSED AT THE SESSION BEGUN AND HELD AT BOSTON, ON THE ELEVENTH DAY OF DECEMBER, A. D. 1745.

CHAPTER 11.

AN ACT FOR THE SUPPLYING THE TREASURY WITH THE SUM OF FIFTY THOUSAND POUNDS, FOR DISCHARGING THE PUBLICK DEBTS, &c., AND FOR DRAWING IN THE SAID BILLS INTO THE TREASURY AGAIN.

Be it enacted by the Governour, Council and House of Representatives,

£50,000 bills of credit to be emitted.

[SECT. 1.] That the treasurer be and hereby is impowered and ordered to emit and issue forth the sum of fifty thousand pounds in bills of credit of the last tenor and date, now lying in his hands and received in for taxes, impost and excise, which shall pass in all publick payments equal to other new-tenor bills emitted since one thousand seven hundred and forty; or, if there shall not be a sufficiency of such bills, that then the committee appointed by this court for signing bills, are hereby directed and impowered to take care and make effectual provision, as soon as may be, to imprint so many as may be needed to compleat the said sum, and to sign and deliver the same to the treasurer, taking his receipt for the same; and the said committee shall be under oath for the faithful performance of the trust by this act reposed in them; and the said sum of fifty thousand pounds shall be issued out of the treasury in manner and for the purposes following; viz., the sum of five thousand seven hundred and ninety pounds, part of the aforesaid sum of fifty thousand pounds, shall be applied for the payment of wages that now are or that hereafter may be due by virtue of the establishment of Castle William, Frederick Fort, Richmond Fort, George's Truck-house, Saco Truck-house, Brunswick Fort, and the sloop in the country's service; and the sum of sixteen thousand pounds, part of the aforesaid sum of fifty thousand pounds, shall be applied for putting the province into a better posture of defence, for compleating the repairs at Castle William and other forts, for paying of such officers and soldiers as have done service for the province, whose wages are now due, which officers and soldiers shall be paid out of this appropriation preferable to any other service; and for such officers and soldiers as are or may be in the province service, according to the several establishments for that purpose, for purchasing all needful warlike stores, and for the commissary's necessary disbursements for the service of the several forts and garrisons and other forces within this province, pursuant to such grants as are or shall be made by this court for those purposes; and the sum of two thousand pounds, part of the aforesaid sum of fifty thousand pounds, shall be applied for the payment of his majesty's council, and such other grants as are or shall be made by this court, and for the payment of stipends, bounties, and premiums established by law; and for the payment of all other matters and things which this court have

£5,790 for wages at Castle William and other garrisons.

£16,000 for putting the province into a better posture of defence, &c.

£2,000 for payment of his majesty's council, and other grants, etc.

or shall, either by law or orders, provide for the payment of out of the publick treasury, and for no other purpose whatsoever; and the sum of one thousand two hundred and ten pounds, part of the aforesaid sum of fifty thousand pounds, shall be applied for the discharging of other debts owing from this province to persons that have served or that shall serve them by order of this court in such matters and things where there is no establishment nor any certain sum assigned for such service, and for paper, printing and writing for this court, the surgeon of Castle William, and wooding of said castle; and the remaining sum of twenty-five thousand pounds, part of the aforesaid sum of fifty thousand pounds, shall be applied to defrey the charge of the late expedition against his majesty's enemies at Cape Breton and parts adjacent, and for making further necessary provision for the service of his majesty's works and and forces there. £1,210 for debts where there is no establishment. £25,000 for the charges of the expedition against Cape Breton.

And be it further enacted,

[SECT. 2.] That if there be a surplusage in any sum appropriated, such surplusage shall lie in the treasury for the further order of this court. Surplusage to lie in the treasury.

And be it further enacted,

[SECT. 3.] That each and every warrant for drawing money out of the treasury, shall direct the treasurer to take the same out of such sums as are respectively appropriated for the payment of such publick debts as the draughts are made to discharge; and the treasurer is hereby directed and ordered to pay such money out of such appropriation as directed to, and no other, upon pain of refunding all such sum or sums as he shall otherwise pay, and to keep exact and distinct accompts of all payments made out of such appropriated sums; and the secretary, to whom it belongs to keep the muster-roll and accompts of charge, shall lay before the house, when they direct, all such muster-rolls and accompts after payment thereof. Warrants to express the appropriations.

And as a fund and security for drawing the said sum of fifty thousand pounds into the treasury again,—

Be it further enacted,

[SECT. 4.] That there be and hereby is granted unto his most excellent majesty, for the ends and uses aforesaid, a tax of twenty-five thousand pounds, to be levied on polls, and estates both real and personal, within this province, according to such rules and in such proportions on the several towns and districts within the same, as shall be agreed upon and ordered by this court at their session in May, one thousand seven hundred and fifty-five, and paid into the publick treasury on or before the last day of December then next after. £25,000 in 1755.

And as a further fund and security for drawing in the said sum of fifty thousand pounds into the treasury again,—

Be it further enacted,

[SECT. 5.] That there be and hereby is granted unto his most excellent majesty, for the ends and uses aforesaid, a tax of twenty-five thousand pounds, to be levied on polls, and estates both real and personal, within this province, according to such rules and in such proportions on the several towns and districts within the same, as shall be agreed upon and ordered by this court at their session in May, one thousand seven hundred and fifty-six, and paid into the publick treasury on or before the last day of December then next after. £25,000 in 1756.

And be it further enacted,

[SECT. 6.] That in case the general court shall not at their session in May, one thousand seven hundred and fifty-five, and one thousand seven hundred and fifty-six, agree and conclude upon an act apportioning the sum which by this act is engaged shall be, in those years, apportioned, assessed and levied, that then and in such case each Tax for the money hereby emitted to be made according to the preceding tax act, in case.

town and district within this province shall pay, by a tax to be levied on the polls, and estates both real and personal, within their districts, the same proportions of the said sums as the said towns and districts shall have been taxed by the general court in the tax act then next preceeding; and the province treasurer is hereby fully impowered and directed, some time in the month of June, in the year one thousand seven hundred and fifty-five, and one thousand seven hundred and fifty-six, to issue and send forth his warrants, directed to the selectmen or assessors of each town and district within this province, requiring them to assess the polls, and estates both real and personal, within their several towns and districts, for their respective part and proportion of the sum before directed and engaged to be assessed by this act; and the assessors, as also persons assessed, shall observe, be governed by and subject to all such rules and directions as shall have been given in the next preceeding tax act.

And be it further enacted,

Taxes to be paid in the several species herein enumerated.

[SECT. 7.] That the inhabitants of this province shall have liberty, if they see fit, to pay the several sums for which they respectively may, in pursuance of this act, be assessed, in bills of credit of the form and tenor by this act emitted, or in other new-tenor bills, or in bills of the middle tenor, according to their several denominations, or in bills of the old tenor, accounting four for one; or in coined silver, at seven shillings and sixpence per ounce, troy weight, and of sterling alloy, or in gold coin, proportionably; or in merchantable hemp, flax, winter and Isle-of-Sable codfish, refined bar-iron, bloomery-iron, hallow iron-ware, Indian corn, rye, wheat, barley, pork, beef, duck or canvas, whalebone, cordage, train-oil, beeswax, bayberry-wax, tallow, peas, sheepswool, or tann'd sole-leather (the aforesaid commodities being of the produce or manufactures of this province), at such moderate rates and prices as the general assembly of the years one thousand seven hundred and fifty-five, and one thousand seven hundred and fifty-six, shall set them at; the several persons paying their taxes in any of the commodities aforementioned, to run the risque and pay the charge of transporting the said commodities to the province treasury; but if the aforesaid general assembly shall not, at their sessions in May, some time before the twentieth day of June, in each year, agree upon and set the aforesaid species and commodities at some certain price, that then the eldest councellor, for the time being, of each of those counties in the province, of which any one of the council is an inhabitant, together with the province treasurer, or the major part of them, be a committee, who hereby are directed and fully authorized and impowered to do it; and in their settling the prices and rating the value of those commodities, to state so much of them, respectively, at seven shillings and sixpence as an ounce of silver will purchase at that time in the town of Boston, and so *pro ratâ*. And the treasurer is hereby directed to insert in the several warrants by him sent to the several collectors of the taxes in each year, with the names of the afore-recited commodities, the several prices or rates which shall be set on them, either by the general assembly or the committee aforesaid, and direct the aforesaid collectors to receive them so.

How the commodities brought into the treasury are to be rated.

Treasurer to sell the said commodities.

[SECT. 8.] And the aforesaid commodities, so brought into the treasury, shall, as soon as may be, be disposed of by the treasurer to the best advantage for so much as they will fetch in bills of credit hereby to be emitted, or for silver or gold, which silver and gold shall be delivered to the possessors of said bills in exchange for them; that is to say, one ounce of silver coin, and so gold in proportion, for seven shillings and sixpence, and so *pro ratâ* for a greater or less sum; and if any loss shall happen by the sale of the aforesaid species, or by any unforeseen accident, such deficiency shall be made good by a tax of the year next following, so as fully and effectually to call in the whole sum of fifty thousand pounds in said bills hereby ordered to be emitted; and if there be a surplusage, it shall remain a stock in the treasury. [*Passed January* 10; *published February* 3, 1745-46.

CHAPTER 12.

AN ACT IN ADDITION TO AN ACT MADE AND PASS'D IN THE EIGHTEENTH AND NINETEENTH YEAR OF HIS PRESENT MAJESTY, [E][*I*]NTITLED "AN ACT FOR GRANTING UNTO HIS MAJESTY AN EXCISE UPON WINES AND SPIRITS DISTILLED, SOLD BY RETAIL, AND UPON LIMES AND LEMMONS."

Preamble. 1745-46, chap. 2.

WHEREAS notwithstanding the provision made in and by an act made and pass'd in the eighteenth and nineteenth year of his present majesty, [e][*i*]ntitled "An Act for granting unto his majesty an excise upon wines and spirits distilled, sold by retail, and upon limes and lemmons," many persons, in violation of said act, do, in a private and clandestine manner, sell without licence, wines and spirituous liquors by retail, and in order to prevent the means of detection and conviction, Indian, negro and molatto slaves, children and others under age of discretion, are employed and sent to receive such wines and spirituous liquors, and by this and other means the good intent of the afores[*ai*]d law has, in a great measure, been frustrated; for the more effectual prevention of all offences against s[*ai*]d act for the future,—

Be it therefore enacted by the Governour, Council and House of Represent[ati]ves,

Penalty for selling strong drink to any Indian, negro, &c.

[SECT. 1.] That when and so often as any person shall be complained of for selling any strong drink without licence to any Indian, negro or molatto slave, or to any child or other person under the age of discretion, and upon the declaration of any such Indian, negro or molatto slaves, child or other person under the age of discretion, and other circumstances concurring, it shall appear to be highly probable, in the judgment of the court or justice before whom the trial shall be, that the person complained of is guilty, then and in every such case, unless the defendant shall acquit him- or herself upon oath, to be administred to him or her by the court or justice that shall try the cause, such defendant shall forfeit and pay three pounds to the farmer of excise, and costs of prosecution; but if the defendant shall acquit him- or herself upon oath as afores[*ai*]d, the court or justice may and shall enter up judgment for the defendant to recover costs.

Recitation of a former act.

And whereas in and by the afores[*ai*]d act it is provided, that "when and so often as it shall be observed that there is a resort of persons to houses suspected to sell strong drink without licence, any justice of the peace shall have full power to convene such persons before him, and examine them upon oath concerning the person suspected of selling or retailing strong drink in such houses, out-houses or other dependenc[*i*]es thereof, and on just grounds to bind over the person suspected, and the witnesses, to the next court of general sessions of the peace in the county where such person shall dwell,"—and the afores[*ai*]d clause has been construed and understood to restrain such justice from proceeding to trial, and giving judgment in the case of such suspected person,—

Be it further enacted,

Justice's power to make up judgment against suspected persons.

[SECT. 2.] That if, upon such examination of such witnesses, and hearing the defence of such suspected person, it shall appear to the justice there is sufficient proof of the violation of the afores[*ai*]d act by selling strong drink without licence, judgm[*en*]t shall thereupon be made up against such person, and he shall forfeit and pay in like manner as if process had been commenced, by bill, plaint or information before the s[*ai*]d justice.

And be it further enacted,

Offending persons to enter into bonds after first conviction.

[SECT. 3.] That after any person shall have been once convicted of selling strong liquors without licence, contrary to said act, or to this additional act, he shall, upon every such offence after such first conviction, be obliged to enter into bonds, with one or more sureties, in the penalty of twenty pounds, to his majesty, for the use of this governm[*en*]t, that he will not in like manner offend or be guilty of any breach of the said acts; and upon refusal to give such bond, he shall be committed to prison until[l] he shall comply therewith.

And in order to discourage and prevent any groundless or vexatious suits that may be brought against the farmer of excise,—

Be it enacted,

Farmer's liberty to plead the general issue.

[SECT. 4.] That in all actions that may be brought against the farmer of excise for any breach or neglect of his duty in the execution of his office and trust, he shall have liberty to plead the general issue, and thereupon give any special matter in evidence; and in case judgm[*en*]t shall be for the defendant, he shall recover treble costs.

And whereas sowre oranges are frequently used in punch and other mixt liquors, as well as lem[*m*]ons [or] [*and*] limes,—

Be it therefore enacted,

Duty on sour oranges.

[SECT. 5.] That every person who shall, after the publication of this act, be licen[c][*s*]ed, or shall renew their licen[s][*c*]e as a taverner or retailer, shall pay as a duty, for every hundred of sowre oranges, two shillings and a penny, and so *pro ratâ* for any less or greater number, to be recovered in like manner as is provided for the recovering the duty laid on lemmons and limes.

And be it further enacted,

Provision in case of the death of any farmer.

[SECT. 6.] That in case of the death of the farmer of excise in any county, the executors or administ[*rato*]rs of such farmer shall, upon their taking such trust of executor or admin[*istrato*]r upon them, have and enjoy all the powers, and be subject to all the duties the farmer had or might enjoy, or was subject to, by force of the act afore ment[*ione*]d or of this additional act.

Limitation.

[SECT. 7.] This act to continue and be in force until[l] the twenty-ninth day of June, one thousand seven hundred and forty-eight, and no longer. [*Passed January* 31; *published February* 3, 1745–46.

CHAPTER 13.

AN ACT FOR [E][*I*]NLISTING THE INHABITANTS OF DORCHESTER, WEYMOUTH AND CHARLESTOWN INTO HIS MAJESTY'S SERVICE FOR THE DEFENCE OF CASTLE WILLIAM, AS OCCASION SHALL REQUIRE.

Preamble. 1742-43, chap. 26.

WHEREAS the safety of this province in a great measure depends on the strength of his maj[*es*]ty's Castle William, and it is necessary that a great number of men, skilful in the managem[*en*]t of the great artillery, should be always ready to attend there,—

Be it enacted by the Governour, Council and House of Represent-[ati]ves,

[SECT. 1.] That all the inhabitants of the town of Dorchester who are by law subject to common musters and military exercises, not exceeding fifty years of age, and such of the inhabitants of the towns of Weymouth and Charlestown as are willing to be [e][*i*]nlisted, not exceeding one hundred and twenty in the whole from the two last towns, shall be [e][*i*]nlisted under the present captains or such other officers as the captain-general shall commissionate, who shall repair to Dorchester Neck and be transported over to Castle William four days in each year, in such months as the captain-general shall order, and shall on the said days be, by the gunner and quarter-gunners, exercised in the mounting, dismounting, levelling, traversing and firing the great guns, and shall be obliged hereunto, and to the observance of such orders as shall be given them in this exercise, under the like pains and penalties that soldiers are under to obey their officers in said castle in time of service. Enlisted inhabitants of Dorchester, Weymouth, and Charlestown to appear at Castle William on occasion.

And be it further enacted,

[SECT. 2.] That if any of the men [e][*i*]nlisted as aforesaid shall not duly attend at time and place for the exercise of the great artillery as aforesaid, being thereof notified and warned to appear, for every such day's neglect of attendance, such soldier shall pay to the clerk of the company, for the use thereof, five shillings. Penalty for not attending.

And for the encouragement of the said men that shall be [e][*i*]nlisted and exercised as aforesaid,—

Be it further enacted,

[SECT. 3.] That every person so inlisted shall be excused from all other military service, and from all impresses into other service that other soldiers by law are liable to. Enlisted persons excused other military service, &c.

And be it further enacted,

[SECT. 4.] That upon any alarm at Castle William every man able of body, as well those [e][*i*]nlisted by virtue of this act, as also all others within the town of Dorchester, except such persons as are by law obliged to attend upon the governour for the time being, shall forthwith appear, compleat with their arms and ammunition according to law, at the said Castle William, there to attend and follow such commands as shall be given for his majesty's service, and that on the penalty of paying five pounds to the clerk of the said company for the use of the province; the aforesaid fines to be recovered before any justice of the peace or court proper to hear and try the same. Inhabitants of Dorchester to appear at Castle William upon an alarm.

[SECT. 5.] This act to continue and be in force unto the end of the sessions of the general assembly to be begun and held on the last Wednesday in May, which will be in the year one thousand seven hundred and forty-eight, and no longer. [*Passed January* 25; *published March* 11, 1745-46. Limitation.

CHAPTER 14.

AN ACT FOR PREVENTING THE UNNECESSARY DESTRUCTION OF ALEWIVES IN THE TOWN OF SANDWICH.

WHEREAS the laws already provided against the destruction of the fish called alewives, do not in divers circumstances reach the case of Herring River, in the town of Sandwich, so that nevertheless great waste is made of them by ill-minded persons, to the great dam[*m*]age of the publick; to prevent which,— Preamble. 1743-44, chap. 26.

Be it enacted by the Governour, Council and House of Represent-[ati]ves,

No person to set or draw any seine, net, &c., for catching alewives in Herring River in Sandwich, without obtaining license.

[SECT. 1.] That from and after the publication of this act, no person or persons whomsoever shall, on any pretence, presume to stretch, set or draw any seine or drag-net, or set up any wares or other fishing engines in any part of the river known by the name of Herring River, in the town of Sandwich, or use any other instrument for the catching alewives but dip-nets or scoop-nets, without first obtaining special licence therefor by a vote of the inhabitants of said Sandwich legally assembled at their anniversary meeting in March, nor in any manner whatever, at any time or times, place or places thereof, but such as shall be determined and appointed at such meeting, on penalty of a fine of five pounds for each offence; to be paid by every person concerned in taking said fish in either of the ways forbidden by this act, or in any other place than such as shall be assigned by the said town as afores[ai]d, and be recovered by action, bill, plaint or information in any court proper to try the same: all fines and forfeitures arising by this act to be disposed of, one half for the benefit of the poor of said town, the other to him or them who shall inform and sue for the same.

Penalty for offence.

Preamble.

And whereas a considerable part of the banks of said river is covered with thick woods, and thereby so obscured as that persons may frequently offend against this act without being discovered, and thereby the good design of it be defeated, unless special provision be made therefor,—

Be it therefore enacted by the authority aforesaid,

Method of conviction, &c.
1726-27, chap. 3.

[SECT. 2.] That the manner, rules and methods of conviction of offenders against this act be the same as are directed and provided in and by an act [e][*i*]ntitled "An Act in addition to and for rendring more effectual an act made in the tenth year of the reign of King William the Third, [e][*i*]ntitled 'An Act for preventing of trespasses,'" made in the twelfth year of the reign of his late majesty, King George.

Limitation.

[SECT. 3.] This act to continue and be in force for the space of three years from the publication thereof, and no longer. [*Passed January* 29; *published March* 11, 1745–46.

CHAPTER 15.

AN ACT FOR SUPPLYING THE TREASURY WITH THE SUM OF TWENTY THOUSAND POUNDS.

Preamble.

WHEREAS the large sums with which the treasury has already been suppl[y][*i*]ed for defreying the expence of the expedition against Cape Breton, and the necessary charges consequent thereupon, have been found insufficient for those purposes, and a considerable sum still remains due from this province,—

Be it therefore enacted by the Governour, Council and House of Representatives,

£20,000 bills of credit to be emitted.

[SECT. 1.] That the treasurer be and hereby is impowered and ordered to emit and issue forth the sum of twenty thousand pounds in bills of credit of the last tenor and date, now lying in his hands and received for taxes, impost and excise, which shall pass in all publick payments equal to other new-tenor bills emitted since one thousand seven hundred and forty; or, if there [*shall not*] be [not] a sufficiency of such bills, that then the committee appointed by this court for signing bills, are hereby directed and impowered to take care and make effectual provision, as soon as may be, to imprint the said bills, or so many as may be needed to compleat the said sum, and to sign and deliver the same to the treasurer, taking his receipt for the same; and the said committee shall be under oath for the faithful performance of the trust by this act reposed in them; and the said sum of twenty thousand pounds shall be issued out of the publick treasury pursuant to such grants as this court hath or shall hereafter make, for discharging such debts as are or may be due from this province in consequence of the late expedition against Cape Breton.

And be it enacted,

[SECT. 2.] That if there be a surplusage in any of this sum appropriated, such surplusage shall l[y][*i*]e in the treasury for the further order of this court. Surplusage to lie in the treasury.

And be it further enacted,

[SECT. 3.] That each and every warrant for drawing this money out of the treasury, shall direct the treasurer to take the same out of the aforesaid sum as is directed, and no other, upon pain of refunding all such sum or sums as he shall otherwise pay, and to keep exact and distinct acco[un][*mp*]ts of all payments made out of the aforesaid sum; and the secretary, to whom it belongs to keep the muster-rolls and accompts of charge, shall lay before the house, when they shall direct, all such muster-rolls and accompts after payment thereof. Warrants to express the appropriations.

And as a fund and security for drawing the aforesaid sum of twenty thousand pounds into the treasury again,—

Be it further enacted,

[SECT. 4.] That there be and hereby is granted [*un*]to his most excellent majesty for the ends and uses aforesaid, a tax of ten thousand pounds, to be lev[y][*i*]ed on polls, and estates both real and personal, within this province, according to such rules and in such proportions on the several towns and districts within the same as shall be agreed upon and ordered by this court at their session in May, one thousand seven hundred and fifty-five, and paid into the publick treasury on or before the last day of December then next after. £10,000 in 1755.

And as a further fund and security for drawing the aforesaid sum of twenty thousand pounds into the treasury again,—

Be it further enacted,

[SECT. 5.] That there be and hereby is granted unto his most excellent majesty, for the ends and uses aforesaid, a tax of ten thousand pounds, to be lev[y][*i*]ed on polls, and estates both real and personal, within this province, according to such rules and in such proportions on the several towns and districts within the same, as shall be agreed upon and ordered by this court at their session in May, one thousand seven hundred and fifty-six, and paid into the publick treasury on or before the last day of December then next after. £10,000 in 1756.

And be it further enacted,

[SECT. 6.] That in case the general court shall not, at their session in May, one thousand seven hundred and fifty-five, and one thousand seven hundred and fifty-six, agree and conclude upon an act apportioning the several sums which, by this act, is engaged shall be in each of these several years apportioned, assessed, and lev[y][*i*]ed, that then and in such case each town and district within this province shall pay, by a tax to be lev[y][*i*]ed on the polls, and estates both real and personal, within their districts, the same proportion of the said sums as the said towns and districts shall have been taxed by the general court in the tax act then next preceeding; and the province treasurer is hereby fully impowered and directed, some time in the month of June, in each of these years, one thousand seven hundred and fifty-five, and Tax for the money hereby emitted to be made according to the preceding tax act, in case.

one thousand seven hundred and fifty-six, to issue and send forth his warrants directed to the selectmen or assessors of each town and district within this province, requiring them to assess the polls, and estate[s] both real and personal, within their several towns and districts, for their respective part and proportion of the several sums before directed and engaged to be assessed by this act; and the assessors, as also persons assessed, shall observe, be governed by, and subject to all such rules and directions as shall have been given in the next prec[e]eding tax act.

And be it further enacted,

Taxes to be paid in the several species herein enumerated.

[SECT. 7.] That the inhabitants of this province shall have liberty, if they see fit, to pay the several sums for which they respectively may, in pursuance of this act, be assessed, in bills of credit of the form and tenor by this act emitted, or in other new-tenor bills, or in bills of the middle tenor, according to their several denominations, or in bills of the old tenor, accounting four for one; or in coined silver, at seven shillings and sixpence per ounce, troy weight, of sterling alloy, or in gold coin, proportionably; or in merchantable hemp, flax, winter and Isle-of-Sable codfish, refined bar-iron, bloomery-iron, hallow iron-ware, Indian corn, rye, wheat, barley, pork, beef, duck or canvas, whalebone, cordage, train-oil, beeswax, bayberry-wax, tallow, peas[e], sheepswool, or tann'd sole-leather (the aforesaid commodities being of the produce or manufactures of this province), at such moderate rates and prices as the respective general assembl[y][*ie*]s of the years one thousand seven hundred and fifty-five, and one thousand seven hundred and fifty-six, shall set them at; the several persons paying their taxes in any of the commodities aforementioned, to run the risque and pay the charge of transporting the said commodities to the province treasury; but if the aforesaid general assembl[y][*ie*]s shall not, at their sessions in May, some time before the twentieth day of June, agree upon and set[t] the aforesaid species or commodities at some certain prices, that then the eldest councellor, for the time being, in each of those counties of the province, of which any one of the council is an inhabitant, together with the province treasurer, or the major part of them, be a committee, who hereby are directed and fully authorized and impowered to do it; and in their setting the prices and rating the value of those commodities, to state so much of them, respectively, at seven shillings and sixpence as an ounce of silver at that time will purchase in the town of Boston, and so *pro ratâ*. And the treasurer is hereby directed to insert in the several warrants by him sent to the collectors of the taxes in those years, respectively, with the names of the afore-recited commodities, the several rates or prices which shall be set on them, either by the general assembly, or the committee aforesaid, and direct the aforesaid collectors to receive them so.

How the commodities brought into the treasury are to be rated.

Treasurer to sell the said commodities.

[SECT. 8.] And the aforesaid commodities so brought into the treasury, shall, as soon as may be, be disposed of by the treasurer to the best advantage for the most it will fetch in bills of credit hereby to be emitted, or any of the bills of credit aforementioned, or for silver or gold, which silver and gold shall be delivered to the possessor of said bills in exchange for them; that is to say, one ounce of silver coin, and so gold in proportion, for seven shillings and sixpence, and so *pro ratâ* for a greater or less sum; and if any loss shall happen by the sale of the aforesaid species, or by any unforeseen accident, such deficiency shall be made good by a tax of the year next following, so as fully and effectually to call in the aforesaid sum of twenty thousand pounds in said bills hereby ordered to be emitted, and for which a tax on polls and estates is in this act laid as a fund; and if there be a surplusage, it shall remain a stock in the treasury. [*Passed February* 8; *published March* 11, 1745-46.

CHAPTER 16.

AN ACT IN ADDITION TO THE ACT, [E][*I*]NTITLED "AN ACT FOR APPOINTING COMMISSIONERS OF SEWERS."

WHEREAS the water in some rivers or streams is raised and kept at such heighth, by mill-dams erected across the same, that it has been found difficult to discover, and impracticable to remove, the obstructions that occasion the overflowing of meadows, whilst the owners of such dams have refused to empty their mill-ponds by opening the flood-gates or other sufficient passage for the water, that had been raised by such dams, to flow out, by means whereof commissioners of sewers have been much hindred in the execution of their trust, and the owners of such meadows have thereby, in great measure, lost the benefit intended by said act; [w*][*t*]herefore, for preventing the like inconvenience for the future,— Preamble. 1702, chap. 11.

Be it enacted by the Governour, Council and House of Represent-[ati]ves,

[SECT. 1.] That when and so often as commissioners of sewers shall judge it necessary, in order to the well executing their trust in discovering or removing the natural obstructions in rivers or streams over which any mill-dam is erected, that the water, which had thereby been stopt and raised above its usual heighth, should flow out; in such case it shall be lawful, and such commissioners are hereby impowered, to open, or cause to be opened, the flood-gates, and to cause to be made and opened other needful sluices or passages in or about such dam or dams, and such passages to keep open whilst they are using the proper means for discovering or removing such obstructions; as also for the more speedy draining of meadows in time of great floods; and in such manner as that the owner or owners of such mill-dam or dams may suffer as little inconvenience or dam[*m*]age thereby as may be. Commissioners of sewers empowered to open flood-gates, &c.

And be it further enacted,

[SECT. 2.] That if the owner of such mill-dam shall suffer dam[*m*]age by the opening or keeping open such sluices or passages as afores[*ai*]d, the s[*ai*]d commissioners shall order him reasonable satisfaction, by their estimation, for such dam[*m*]age, and shall assess the same on the proprietors of the overflowed lands or meadows, at whose request and for whose benefit such commissioners were appointed, and to cause the same to be collected in manner as in and by the s[*ai*]d act is provided for collecting of other charges. Owners of mill-dams opened, to be allowed damages.

And be it further enacted,

[SECT. 3.] That the owner or owners of any dam or dams, or other person whosoever, that directly or indirectly shall molest or hinder any such commissioners, or others employed by them, in the execution of the power or trust reposed in them by this or any former act, by shutting up or stopping any passage made or opened by them or by their order for any the purposes afores[*ai*]d, shall, for each offence, forfeit and pay, as a fine to his majesty, for the use of this governm[*en*]t, the sum of twenty pounds; to be recovered by bill, plaint or information, in any court proper to try the same, after the manner of conviction, and by the same rules and methods as are provided and directed to in an act [e][*i*]ntitled "An Act in addition to and for rendring more effectual an act made in the tenth year of the reign of King William the Third, [e][*i*]ntitled 'An Act for preventing of trespasses.'" Penalty for owners of mill-dams who shall molest or hinder commissioners in the execution of their power. 1726-27, chap. 3.

And whereas it has been found necessary, in order to remove the Preamble.

* "t" is overwritten in a later hand.

natural obstructions in rivers and streams, that the course of the water there be stopt, by dams erected for that purpose, during the time that workmen are employed in removing them,—

Be it therefore further enacted,

Commissioners empowered to erect dams, provided, &c.

[SECT. 4.] That it shall be lawful for commissioners of sewers, when and so often as they shall find it needful, to erect or cause to be erected, any dam or dams upon or across any river or stream wherein such obstructions are found, for the greater ease and dispatch in removing them; *provided* such dam or dams be taken down as soon as conveniently may be after the work is finished, and meet recompence be made, in manner as aforesaid, for any dam[*m*]ages that may thereby accrue to the owner or owners of the land against or over which such dam or dams shall abutt or be erected, or which, by occasion of such dam, may happen for a time to be overflowed with water: *saving always*, the liberty of appeal from any orders or determinations of the said commissioners, to the governour and council, as by the afore-mentioned act in that behalf is provided.

Saving.

Limitation.

[SECT. 5.] This act to continue and be in force for the space of five years from the publication thereof, and no longer. [*Passed February* 6, 1745-46; *published March* 27, 1746.

CHAPTER 17.

AN ACT FOR REVIVING AND CONTINUING SUNDRY LAWS OF THIS PROVINCE IN THIS ACT MENTIONED, EXPIRED, OR NEAR EXPIRING.

Preamble. 1740-41, chap. 19. 1742-43, chap. 18. 1742-43, chap. 22. 1742-43, chap. 29.

WHEREAS an act was made and pass[*e*]d in the fourteenth year of his present majesty's reign, [e][*i*]ntitled "An Act in further addition to an act for regulating of fences, &c[a].;" and another act was made and pass[*e*]d in the sixteenth year of his present majesty, [e][*i*]ntitled "An Act in addition to the several laws of this province relating to the supporting of poor and indigent persons;" and another act was made and pass[*e*]d in the same year, [e][*i*]ntitled "An Act to prevent firing the woods;" and another act was made and pass'd in the same year, [e][*i*]ntitled "An Act for the more easy partition of lands or other real estate given by will, and held in common and undivided among the devisees;"—all which several laws are expired or near expiring: *and whereas* the afores[*ai*]d laws have, by experience, been found beneficial and necessary for the several purposes for which they were pass[*e*]d,—

Be it therefore enacted by the Governour, Council and House of Representatives,

Limitation of sundry laws.

That all and every of the afores[*ai*]d acts, and every matter and clause therein contained, be and hereby are revived, and shall continue and remain in force until[l] the last day of December, which will be in the year one thousand seven hundred and fifty-two, and to the end of the session of the general court then next after. [*Passed January* 29, 1745-46; *published March* 27, 1746.

CHAPTER 18.

AN ACT IMPOWERING THE SUPERIO[*U*]R COURT OF JUDICATURE, COURT OF ASSIZE AND GENERAL GOAL DELIVERY, AT THEIR PRESENT TERM, TO PROCEED TO THE TRIAL OF SUNDRY PRISONERS NOW IN HIS MAJESTY'S GOAL IN THE COUNTY OF SUFFOLK.

WHEREAS there are divers persons now in goal in the county of Suffolk, who were committed on suspicion of murders, felonies, or other high crimes and misdemeanors perpetrated within the body of that county, whereof if due inquiry be not speedily made, great Inconvenienc[*i*]es may arise; *and whereas* the grand jury impanel[*le*]d and sworn at the sup[*eriou*]r court of judicature, court of assize and general goal delivery, holden at Boston for and within the county of Suffolk, on the third Tuesday of February last, is, by the said court, dismiss[*e*]d, but the said court is not yet adjourned without day,— Preamble.

Be it therefore enacted by the Governour, Council and House of Represent[ati]ves,

That the said court may and shall without delay, cause the usual process to be made out for choosing and summoning a suitable number of good and lawful men of such of the towns in the said county of Suffolk as have been accustomed to send grand jurors to the said court, or of such towns as the s[*ai*]d court shall think most proper to send their *venires* unto, to serve as grand jurors at the said court now holden at Boston afores[*ai*]d; and every person duly chosen and return[*e*]d on such *venire*, shall be and hereby is obliged to give his immediate attendance accordingly, under the penalty by law already provided in case of grand jurors upon their default of attendance: and the s[*ai*]d court shall impanel, swear and charge them to inquire of, and present all murders and other felonies, high crimes and misdemeanours, committed or done within the said county, and may proceed to the trial of any person or persons that shall by such grand jury be presented or indicted of or for any murder or other felony, high crime or misdemeanour, and give judgm[*en*]t, and award execution thereupon, according to the usual course of the law. [*Passed April.* 24; *published April* 26, 1746. Court's power to proceed to the trial of sundry criminals.

CHAPTER 19.

AN ACT IN ADDITION TO AN ACT, [E][*I*]NTITLED "AN ACT DIRECTING HOW RATES AND TAXES TO BE GRANTED BY THE GENERAL ASSEMBLY, AS ALSO COUNTY, TOWN, AND PRECINCT RATES; SHALL BE ASSESSED AND COLLECTED," MADE AND PASS'D IN THE FOURTH YEAR OF HIS PRESENT MAJESTY'S REIGN.

WHEREAS no provision is made, in the act [e][*i*]ntitled "An Act directing how rates and taxes granted by the general assembly, as also county, town, and precinct rates, shall be assessed and collected," for appointing collectors or constables, where towns neglect to choose them; whereby, unless there be some remedy, the good design of said act, to secure the payment of the taxes granted by the general assembly, will be frustrated,— Preamble. 1730, chap. 1. 1743-44, chap. 11.

Be it therefore enacted by the Governour, Council and House of Representatives,

[SECT. 1.] That where any town or towns have neglected or shall neglect to choose constables or collectors to gather the rates or taxes Sheriff empowered to collect rates or taxes in towns that have or shall neglect to choose constables or collectors.

granted by the general court, that in such case the sheriff of the county shall be and hereby is impow[e]red and directed to collect such rates or taxes, having received an assessment made of the proportion of the several persons rateable in such town, together with a warrant under the hands of such assessors as shall be appointed by the court of general sessions of the peace in the county where such deficient town l[y][*i*]es, according to the aforesaid act of the fourth year of his present majesty's reign; and the said assessors are hereby directed, where any town has for divers[e] years past, or shall for several years together hereafter, neglect to choose assessors or constables and collectors, to add together the several sums annually due, as also the several fines of twenty pounds due for each year's neglect, and their own allowance by law establish[t][*ed*], to be proportioned among the several inhabitants and others rateable in such town according to their best judgment.

And be it further enacted by the authority aforesaid,

Sheriff to post up copy of assessment and warrant.

[SECT. 2.] That the sheriff, upon receiving the aforesaid assessment, and warrant for collecting it, shall forthwith post up in some publick place of the town assessed, an attested copy of such assessment and warrant, and shall make no distress for any of the sums so assessed till after thirty days from his posting it up; and any person or persons paying the sum or sums respectively assessed on him or them, to the sheriff before the expiration of the aforesaid thirty days, shall pay at the rate of five per cent over and above, to the sheriff for his fees, and no more; but all such as shall neglect to pay the sum or sums assessed for the space of thirty days or longer from the aforesaid posting up the copy of the assessment, shall be proceeded against by the sheriff in way of distress, as collectors by law are impowred, and may require suitable aid for that purpose; and they shall each one pay the fees for the sheriff's service and travel, as in other cases where distraint is made.

And to the intent the courts of general sessions of the peace, in the several counties where such deficient towns shall respectively belong, may, from time to time, seasonably appoint assessors as needful[l],—

Be it enacted by the authority aforesaid,

Treasurer to send a certificate to the clerk of the court of general sessions of the county where deficient towns belong.

[SECT. 3.] That the province treasurer, for the time being, shall, as soon as may be, after he hath issued his warrants to the assessors of the several towns, for assessing and collecting the rates and taxes granted by the general assembly, for the space of sixty days, without any account of such town's choice of collectors or constables, whether it be a town that hath neglected to make such choice, or that hereafter shall neglect so to do, in every such case the said treasurer shall send a certificate to the clerk of the court of general sessions of the peace for the county whereto the deficient town belongs, of such their deficiency, who shall lay it before said court of sessions at their next sitting; whereupon the said court shall forthwith proceed to appoint assessors to assess and proportion the rates and taxes granted as aforesaid; and the assessors so appointed, shall, as soon as may be, take an oath to the faithful[l] discharge of their trust, before the said court or some one or more of the justices by the court of sessions to be appointed for that purpose; and if any person appointed an assessor as aforesaid shall refuse to serve, he shall forfeit the sum of twenty pounds to his majesty for the use of the province; and the court of sessions shall immediately proceed to appoint others. [*Passed February* 8, 1745–46.

CHAPTER 20.

AN ACT IN ADDITION TO, AND FOR RENDRING MORE EFFECTUAL, THE LAWS ALREADY IN BEING FOR PREVENTING THE DESTRUCTION OF THE FISH CALLED ALEWIVES, AND OTHER FISH.

WHEREAS in and by an act made in the fifteenth year of his present majesty's reign, [e][*i*]ntitled "An Act in addition to an act made to prevent the destruction of alewives, and other fish," it is provided, that all persons that should hereafter build any mill-dam or dams, or that had, before the time of passing the same, built any dam across any such river or stream where the salmon, shadd, alewives, or other fish, usually pass up into the natural ponds to cast their spawn, shall make or open "a sufficient passage-way for the fish to pass up such river or stream through or round such dam, and shall keep it open for the free passage of the fish, from the first day of April to the last day of May, annually," and also, that a sufficient water-passage round, thro[*ugh*] or over such dam, should be made for the passage of such fish, or their young spawn, in the season of their going down such river or stream, on penalty of fifty pounds for every offence; and in and by an act made in the seventeenth year of his present majesty's reign, [e][*i*]ntitled "An Act in addition to an act made in the fifteenth year of his present majesty's reign, [e][*i*]ntitled 'An Act in addition to an act made to prevent the destruction of the fish called alewives, and other fish,'" it is provided, "That it shall and may be lawful for any owner or occupant of any such dam or dams already built, or that may hereafter be built, and who are or may be obliged by said additional act to open or leave open such passage as afores[*ai*]d, to apply to the next court of general sessions of the peace to be holden in and for the county where such mill-dam is; and the justices of the court respectively, on such application, are impowered and directed to appoint a committee of three sufficient, and, as much as may be, disinterested, persons, under oath to repair to the dam where such passage is proposed to be opened, and carefully view the same, and in the best manner they are able, to inform themselves of the most proper place for the passage of such fish up and down stream, of what dimensions the same shall be, or be appointed to be made, and what part of each year, and how long the same shall be kept open, and return the same, under their hands, or the hands of the major part of them, to the said court for their acceptance; which return so made and accepted, shall be deemed and adjudged the lawful rule of proceeding in making and keeping open the passage and passages for the fish in passing up and down the rivers and streams for the future, anything contained to the contrary in s[*ai*]d additional act notwithstanding,"—

Preamble.
1741-42, chap. 16, § 1.
1743-44, chap. 26, § 1.

And whereas it may happen that in some rivers or streams, across which dams are built, it may be doubtful whether the fish may be said usually to pass or cast their spawn, and so as to render it necessary that a way should be left open in such dams for their free passage, and many inconvenienc[*i*]es may arise from such doubt or uncertainty,—

Be it therefore enacted by the Governour, Council and House of Represent[ati]ves,

[SECT. 1.] That when and so often as application shall be made to the court of sessions, by the owner or occupant of any mill-dam or dams, either of such dams as have no passage-way, or of such dams thro[*ugh*] which a passage-way has already been made, and a committee shall thereupon be appointed by such court, pursuant to the last-recited act, and such committee shall repair to any dam or dams, and it shall appear

Court of general sessions to determine the expediency of dams, &c., upon the report of a committee.

to them, upon inquiry, that the fish do not, or in case of a passage being made or kept open, would not, usually pass up the river or stream, across which such dam is or shall be built, in such numbers as that it is necessary a passage-way thro[*ugh*] such dam should be made or kept open, or that the passing of the fish up such river will not be of greater general benefit than the leaving open of passage-ways in such dams will be of dam[*m*]age to the owners of the mills, and other persons, then and in either of such cases, said committee shall be impowered to make a report that such passage-way is not necessary, and such report, being accepted by the court of sessions, the owner or occupant of such dam shall thereupon be freed from all obligation to make or keep open any passage, anything in the aforementioned acts to the contrary notwithstanding; and the charge of the application that shall be made by the owner or occupant of any mill-dam or dams, and all proceedings of the court thereupon, pursuant to this act, or to the said last-recited act, shall be born and paid by such owner or occupant.

Provided always,—

Proviso. [SECT. 2.] That if, at any time after such determination, any person, apprehending it necessary that a passage-way should be opened in such dam, shall thereupon make application to the court of sessions, said court shall be impowered to appoint a new committee, who shall have the same power the first committee by law had, or might have had; and upon such committee's reporting that a passage-way is necessary in such dam or dams, and the dimensions thereof, and the time it shall be kept open, and upon such report being accepted by the court of sessions, the owner or occupant of such mill or dam shall be as fully obliged to keep open such passage as if the former report had never been made and accepted, anything in this act to the contrary notwithstanding; the charge of such application, and all proceedings thereupon, to be paid by the person or persons making the same, or by the owner or occupant of such dam, as the court of sessions shall order.

Preamble. *And whereas* in some counties within this province, the justices of the court of sessions have refused to admit any application from the owner or occupant of any mill or mill-dam, by reason that such application has not been made at the court next immediately following the publication of the last-recited act,—

Be it further enacted,

Further power of the court of sessions. [SECT. 3.] That the several courts of sessions within this province be and hereby are impowered and directed to admit, proceed and determine upon any such application at any court at any time held for the county; and all such proceedings shall be deemed as valid to all intents and purposes as if they had been acted upon at the court next immediately following the publication of said act.

Preamble. *And whereas* in many rivers or streams within this province, neither shad, salmon nor alewives usually swim, or would pass up such river or stream, although a passage-way was made and kept open through the several dams built across such rivers or streams, and the advantage of other fish that pass up such rivers or streams is not equal to the dam[*m*]age that may arise by keeping open a passage-way thro[*ugh*] such dams,—

Be it therefore enacted,

In what case mill-dam or dams are to be kept open. [SECT. 4.] That no owner or occupant of any mill-dam or dams built or to be built within this province, shall be liable to any penalty for not making or keeping open a passage-way through such dam or dams, except those dams only which are built across those rivers or streams where either of the aforementioned fish; viz[*t*]., shad, salmon or alewives, usually swim or pass; any former law, usage or custom to the contrary notwithstanding.

Provided always,

[SECT. 5.] That it shall be in the power of any person at any time to make application to the court of sessions, setting forth that the passage of other fish up such rivers or streams is of such advantage as to render a passage-way through any dam or dams necessary, and the justices of the court of sessions are impowered on such application to appoint a committee to repair to such dam or dams, and upon such committee's reporting that a passage-way or ways for the fish is necessary, the dimensions thereof, and the time for keeping it open, and upon such report's being accepted, the owner or occupant of such dam or dams shall be as fully obliged to make and keep open such passage-way or ways as if shad, salmon or alewives usually pass[e]d up such river or stream. Application may be made to the court of sessions relating to dams, &c.

And whereas the mill-dam in the town of Watertown, refer[re]d to in the afores[ai]d act of the [15th] [*fifteenth*] of his present majesty, has not been subjected in like manner with the other mill-dams within this province,— Preamble.

Be it therefore enacted,

[SECT. 6.] That if any person or persons whatsoever shall cause the dam of said mill to be raised, so as to prevent the passage of the fish over the same at any time between the breaking up of the ice in the winter or spring and the first day of May annually, and in any year hereafter, without the express leave or consent of the selectmen of the towns of Watertown and Newtown, every person so offending shall forfeit and pay the sum of five pounds for each offence, to be recovered in any court of record proper to try the same, and for the use of him or them that shall inform and sue therefor. [*Passed March* 22, 1745-46. Mill-dam in Watertown not to be raised in a certain time, except, &c.

CHAPTER 21.

AN ACT FOR ALTERING THE TIMES FOR HOLDING THE SUPERIOUR COURT OF JUDICATURE, COURT OF ASSIZE, AND GENERAL GOAL DELIVERY WITHIN THE COUNTIES OF ESSEX AND YORK.

WHEREAS the time by law appointed for holding the superiour courts for the counties of Essex and York is found on some accounts inconvenient,— Preamble.

Be it therefore enacted by the Governour, Council and House of Representatives,

[SECT. 1.] That the superiour court of judicature, court of assize, and general goal delivery, that was by law to be holden at Ipswich, for the county of Essex, on the second Tuesday of May yearly, shall be held at Ipswich aforesaid, for said county of Essex, on the first Tuesday of June yearly; and the superiour court of judicature, court of assize, and general goal delivery, that was by law to have been holden within and for the county of York, at York, on the third Wednesday in June yearly, shall be held at York aforesaid, for the said county of York, on the second Tuesday of June yearly. Alteration of the time for holding the superior court in the counties of Essex and York. 1742-43, chap. 32, § 2.

And be it further enacted,

[SECT. 2.] That all appeals, reviews, recognizances, warrants or other processes, already issued, taken, and filed, which were to be heard and tried at either of the courts aforesaid, shall not fail or be discontinued, but be obligatory, continued over, held good and valid to all intents and purposes in the law, and may be pleaded, heard, and proceeded on, at the next respective courts appointed by this act to be held All appeals already issued not to be discontinued, but proceeded upon.

in the several counties aforesaid; and all officers and other persons concerned therein are to conform themselves accordingly.

Provided, also,

[SECT. 3.] That all executions, returnable to the respective courts formerly established, be returned at the times therein mentioned, the alterations aforesaid notwithstanding. [*Passed April* 26, 1746.

CHAPTER 22.

AN ACT FOR THE EXPLANATION AND FURTHER ENFORCEM[*EN*]T OF THE LAWS MADE FOR THE OBSERVATION OF THE LORD'S DAY.

Preamble. 1741-42, chap. 7.

WHEREAS in and by an act made and pass'd in the fifteenth year of his present majesty's reign, [e][*i*]ntitled "An Act in further addition to the several acts for the observation and keeping of the Lord's Day," it is enacted, that his majesty's justices of the peace shall bind over the offenders against that act to appear before "the next court of general sessions of the peace for the county where the offence shall be committed," &c.; *and whereas* it so happens that divers such offenders are strangers, and not inhabitants in the town where the offence is committed, nor of any other town in this province, and persons so mean and obscure that they cannot afterwards be found, so that without a speedy way of proceeding against them, they will have an advantage to avoid justice, and with respect to such person[*s*] the good intent of the said law may be thereby wholly frustrated and defeated; *and whereas* a doubt has arisen in divers persons, who are enjoined by law to put in execution the laws made for the due observation of the Lord's Day, whether the act above mentioned does not repeal some clauses in an act made in the
1692-3, chap. 22. fourth year of King William and Queen Mary, for the better observation and keeping of the Lord's Day, and other subsequent acts made for the same good purposes; and thro[*ugh*] these means there have been great neglects of prosecuting and punishing persons guilty of the prophanation of the Sab[*b*]ath; now, to prevent the evil consequences of such wrong constructions of the laws in that case made and provided,—

It is hereby declared by the Governour, Council and House of Represent[ati]ves,

Precedent laws relating to the Lord's day not repealed, but remain in full force and virtue.

[SECT. 1.] That it is not the true intent and meaning of the first-mention[*e*]d act, made in the fifteenth year of his present majesty's reign, to repeal any of the precedent laws made for the observation of the Lord's Day, or any paragraphs or clauses thereof, but that the same ought to remain in full force and virtue.

And it is hereby accordingly enacted,

[SECT. 2.] That the s[*ai*]d precedent laws do and shall remain in full force and virtue, as if the s[*ai*]d act of the fifteenth year of his present majesty's reign had never been made: *saving* that by the s[*ai*]d act his majesty's justices of the peace have liberty given them to prosecute the offences therein mentioned in the manner as is therein directed, if they judge it will best answer the general intention of the laws for the better observation of the Lord's Day. [*Passed April* 24, 1746.

CHAPTER 23.

AN ACT FOR GRANTING UNTO HIS MAJESTY SEVERAL RATES AND DUTIES OF IMPOST AND TUNNAGE OF SHIPPING.

WE, his majesty's most loyal and dutiful subjects, the representatives of the province of the Massachusetts Bay, in New England, being desirous of a collateral fund and security for drawing in the bills of credit on this province, have chearfully and unanimously given and granted and do hereby give and grant unto his most excellent majesty to the end and use aforesaid, and for no other use, the several duties of impost upon wines, liquors, goods, wares and merchandize that shall be imported into this province, and tonnage of shipping hereafter mentioned; and pray that it may be enacted,—

And be it accordingly enacted by the Governour, Council and House of Representatives,

[SECT. 1.] That from and after the last day of the last session of this court, and during the space of one year, and from thence to the end of the then next session of the general court, there shall be paid by the importer of all wines, liquors, goods, wares and merchandize that shall be imported into this province from the place of their growth (salt, cotton-wool, provisions, and every other thing of the growth and produce of New England, and and* also all prize goods condemned in any port of this province, excepted), the several rates or duties of impost following; viz[t].,—

For every pipe of wine of the Western Islands, eight shillings.

For every pipe of Madeira, nine shillings and sixpence.

For every pipe of other sorts not mentioned, nine shillings and sixpence.

For every hogshead of rum, containing one hundred gallons, eight shillings.

For every hogshead of sugar, sevenpence.

For every hogshead of molasses, fourpence.

For every hogshead of tobacco, four shillings and sixpence.

For every ton of logwood, ninepence.

—And so, proportionably, for greater or lesser quantities.

And all other commodities, goods or merchandize not mentioned or excepted, fourpence for every twenty shillings value: all goods imported from Great Britain excepted.

[SECT. 2.] And for any of the above wines, liquors, goods, wares, merchandize, &c[a]., that shall be imported into this province, &c[a]., from any other port than the places of their growth and produce, their shall be paid by the importer double the value of impost appointed by this act to be received for every species above mentioned, unless they do, *bonâ fide*, belong to the inhabitants of this province and came upon their risque from the port of their growth and produce.

And be it further enacted,

[SECT. 3.] That all the aforesaid impost rates and duties shall be paid in current money or bills of credit of this province of the last emission, by the importer of any wines, liquors, goods or merchandize, unto the commissioner to be appointed as is hereinafter to be directed for entring and receiving the same, at or before the landing ôf any wines, liqùors, goods or merchandize: only the commissioner or receiver is hereby allowed to give credit to such person or persons where his or their duty of impost, in one ship or vessel, doth exceed the sum of

* *Sic.*

three pounds; and in cases where the commissioner or receiver shall give credit, he shall setle and ballance his accounts with every person on or before the last day of April, so that the same accounts may be ready to be presented to this court in May next after. And all entries where the impost or duty to be paid doth not exceed three shillings, shall be made without charge to the importer, and not more than sixpence to be demanded for any other single entry to what value soever.

And be it further enacted,

[SECT. 4.] That all masters of ships or other vessels coming into any harbour or port within this province from beyond sea, or from any other province or colony, before bulk be broken and within twenty-four hours after his arrival at such harbour or port, shall make a report to the commissioner or receiver of the impost, to be appointed as is hereinafter mentioned, of the contents of the lading of such ship or vessel, without any charge or fee to be demanded or paid for the same; which report said master shall give in to the commissioner or receiver, under his hand, and shall therein set down and express the quantities and species of the wines, liquors, goods and merchandize laden on board such ship or vessel, with the marks and numbers thereof, and to whom the same is consigned; and also make oath that the said report or manifest of the contents of his lading, so to be by him given in under his hand as afores'd, contains a just and true account, to the best of his knowledge, of the whole lading taken on board and imported in the said vessel from the port or ports such vessel came from, and that he hath not broken bulk, nor delivered any of the wines, rum or other distilled liquors or merchandize laden on board the said ship or vessel, directly or indirectly; and if he shall know of any more wines, liquors, goods or merchandize to be imported therein, before the landing thereof he will cause it to be added to his manifest; which manifest shall be agreable to a printed form for that purpose, which is to be filled up by the said commissioner or receiver according to each particular person's entry; which oath the commissioner or receiver is hereby impowered to administer: after which said master may unload, and not before, on pain of five hundred pounds, to be forfeited and paid by each master that shall neglect his duty in this behalf.

And be it further enacted,

[SECT. 5.] That all merchants, factors and other persons, importers, being owners thereof, or having any of the wines, liquors, goods or merchandize consigned to them, that by this act are liable to pay impost or duty, shall, by themselves or order, make entry thereof in writing, under their hands, with the said commissioner or receiver, and produce unto him an invoice of all such goods as pay *ad valorem*, and make oath thereto in manner following:—

You, A. B., do swear that the entry of the goods and merchandize by you now made, exhibits the present price of said goods at this market, and that, *bonâ fide*, according to your best skill and judgment, it is not less than the real value thereof. So help you God.

—which above oath the commissioner or receiver is hereby impowered to administer; and they shall pay the duty and impost by this act required, before such wines, liquors, goods, wares or merchandize be landed or taken out of the vessel in which the same shall be imported.

[SECT. 6.] And no wines, liquors, goods, wares or merchandize that by this act are liable to pay impost or duty, shall be landed on any wharff, or into any warehouse or other place, but in the daytime only, and that after sunrise and before sunset, unless in the presence and with the consent of the commissioner or receiver, on pain of forfeiting all such wines, liquors, goods, wares and merchandize, and the lighter, boat or vessel out of which the same shall be landed or put into any warehouse or other place.

[SECT. 7.] And if any person or persons shall not have and produce an invoice of the quantities of rum or liquors to him or them consigned, then the cask wherein the same is shall be gaged at the charge of the importer, that the quantities thereof may be known.

And be it further enacted,

[SECT. 8.] That every merchant or other person importing any wines into this province shall be allowed twelve per cent for leakage: *provided*, such wines shall not have been filled up on board; and that every hogshead, butt or pipe of wine that hath two parts thereof leaked out, shall be accounted for outs, and the merchant or importer to pay no duty for the same. And no master of any ship or vessel shall suffer any wines to be filled up on board without giving a certificate of the quantity so filled up, under his hand, before the landing thereof, to the commissioner or receiver of impost for such port, on pain of forfeiting the sum of one hundred pounds.

[SECT. 9.] And if it be made to appear that any wines imported in any ship or vessel be decayed at the time of unlading thereof, or in twenty days afterwards, oath being made before the commissioner or receiver that the same hath not been landed above that time, the duties and impost paid for such wines shall be repaid unto the importer thereof.

And be it further enacted,

[SECT. 10.] That the master of every ship or vessel importing any liquors, goods, wares or merchandizes, shall be liable to and shall pay the impost for such and so much thereof contained in his manifest, as shall not be duly entred, nor the duty paid for the same by the person or persons to whom such wines, liquors, goods, wares or merchandize are or shall be consigned. And it shall and may be lawful, to and for the master of every ship or other vessel, to secure and detain in his hands, at the owner's risque, all such wines, liquors, goods, wares or merchandize imported in any ship or vessel, untill he shall receive a certificate, from the commissioner or receiver of the impost, that the duty for the same is paid, and untill he be repaid his necessary charges in securing the same; or such master may deliver such wines, liquors, goods, wares or merchandize as are not entred, unto the commissioner or receiver of the impost in such port, or his order, who is hereby impowered and directed to receive and keep the same, at the owner's risque, untill the impost thereof, with the charges, be paid; and then to deliver such wines, liquors, goods, wares or merchandize as such master shall direct.

And be it further enacted,

[SECT. 11.] That the commissioner or the receiver of the impost in each port, shall be and hereby is impowered to sue the master of any ship or vessel, for the impost or duty for so much of the lading of any wines, liquors, goods, wares or merchandize imported therein, according to the manifest to be by him given upon oath, as aforesaid, as shall remain not entred and the duty of impost thereof not paid. And where any goods, wares or merchandize are such as that the value thereof is not known, whereby the impost to be recovered of the master, for the same, cannot be ascertained, the owner or person to whom such goods, wares or merchandize are or shall be consigned, shall be summoned to appear as an evidence at the court where such suit for the Dmpost* and the duty thereof shall be brought, and be there required to make oath to the value of such goods, wares or merchandize.

* *Sic.*

And be it further enacted,

[SECT. 12.] That the ship or vessel, with her tackle, apparel and furniture, the master of which shall make default in anything by this act required to be performed by him, shall be liable to answer and make good the sum or sums forfeited by such master, according to this act, for any such default, as also to make good the impost or duty for any wines, liquors, goods, wares and merchandize not entred as aforesaid; and, upon judgment recovered against such master, the said ship or vessel, with so much of the tackle or appurtenances thereof as shall be sufficient to satisfy said judgment, may be taken in execution for the same; and the commissioner or receiver of the impost is hereby impowered to make seizure of such ship or vessel, and detain the same under seizure untill judgment be given in any suit to be commenced and prosecuted for any of the said forfeitures or impost; to the intent that, if judgment be rendred for the prosecutor or informer, such ship or vessel and appurtenances may be exposed to sale, for satisfaction thereof, as is before provided: *unless* the owners, or some on their behalf, for the releasing such ship or vessel from under seizure or restraint, shall give sufficient security unto the commissioner or receiver of impost that seized the same, to respond and satisfy the sum or value of the forfeiture and duties, with charges, that shall be recovered against the master thereof, upon suit to be brought for the same, as aforesaid; and the master occasioning such loss or damage unto his owners, thrô his default or neglect, shall be liable unto their action for the same.

And be it further enacted,

[SECT. 13.] That the naval officer within any of the ports of this province shall not clear or give passes unto any master of any ship or other vessel, outward bound, untill he shall be certified, by the commissioner or receiver of the impost, that the duties and impost for the goods last imported in such ship or vessel are paid or secured to be paid.

[SECT. 14.] And the commissioner or receiver of the impost is hereby impowered to allow bills of store to the master of any ship or vessel importing any wines or liquors, for such private adventures as shall belong to the master or seamen of such ship or vessel, at the discretion of the commissioner or receiver, not exceeding three per cent of the lading; and the duties payable by this act for such wines or liquors, in such bills of stores mentioned and expressed, shall be abated.

And whereas, many persons heretofore have caused to be imported, from the neighbouring governments, into this province, by land-carriage, large quantities of wine, rum and other merchandize, subjected to duty by this act, but have made no report thereof to the officer of impost, or any of his deputies, nor have paid any duty therefor, contrary to the true intent and meaning of this act,—

Be it therefore enacted,

[SECT. 15.] That, whensoever any rum, wine or other merchandize, by this act subjected to any duty, shall be hereafter imported from any of the neighbouring governments, by land, into any town of this province, the owner thereof, or person importing the same, shall make report thereof to the said officer, or some one of his deputies, and pay the duties hereby required therefor, on pain and penalty of forfeiting the same.

And be it further enacted,

[SECT. 16.] That all penalties, fines and forfeitures accruing and arising by virtue of this act, shall be one half to his majesty for the uses and intents for which the aforementioned duties of impost are granted, and the other half to him or them that shall seize, inform and sue for the same, by action, bill, plaint or information, in any of his majesty's courts of record, wherein no essoign, protection or wager of law shall be allowed: the whole charge of the prosecution to be taken out of the half belonging to the informer.

And be it further enacted,

[SECT. 17.] That there shall be paid, by the master of every ship or other vessel, coming into any port or ports in this province, to trade or traffick, whereof all the owners are not belonging to this province (except such vessels as belong to Great Britain, the provinces or colonies of Pensilvania, West and East Jersey, New York, Connecticut, New Hampshire and Rhode Island), every voyage such ship or vessel does make, one pound of good pistol-powder for every ton such ship or vessel is in burthen: *saving* for that part which is owned in Great Britain, this province, or any of the aforesaid governments, which are hereby exempted; to be paid unto the commissioner or receiver of the duties of impost, and to be employed for the ends and uses aforesaid.

[SECT. 18.] And the said commissioner is hereby impowered to appoint a meet and suitable person, to repair unto and on board any ship or vessel, to take the exact measure or tonnage thereof, in case he shall suspect that the register of such ship or vessel doth not express and set forth the full burthen of the same; the charge thereof to be paid by the master or owner of such ship or vessel, before she be cleared, and in case she shall appear to be of greater burthen: otherwise, to be paid by the commissioner out of the money received by him for impost, and shall be allowed him, accordingly, by the treasurer, in his accounts. And the naval officer shall not clear any vessel, untill he be also certified, by the commissioner, that the duty of tonnage for the same is paid, or that it is such a vessel for which none is payable according to this act.

And be it further enacted,

[SECT. 19.] That there be one fit person, and no more, nominated and appointed by this court, as a commissioner and receiver of the afore^{sd} duties of impost and tonnage of shipping, and for the inspection, care and managem^t of the said office, and whatsoever relates thereto, to receive commission for the same from the governor or commander-in-chief for the time being, with authority to substitute and appoint a deputy receiver in each port, and other places besides that wherein he resides, and to grant warrants to such deputy receivers for the s^d place, and to collect and receive the impost and tunnage of shipping afores^d that shall become due within such port, and to render the account thereof, and to pay in the same, to the said commissioner and receiver: which said commissioner and receiver shall keep fair books of all entries and duties arising by virtue of this act; also, a particular account of every vessel, so that the duties of impost and tonnage arising on the said vessell may appear; and the same to lye open, at all seasonable times, to the view and perusal of the treasurer and receiver-general of this province (or any other person or persons whom this court shall appoint), with whom he shall account for all collections and payments, and pay all such moneys as shall be in his hands, as the treasurer or receiver-general shall demand it. And the s^d commissioner or receiver and his deputy or deputies, before their entring upon the execution of their office, shall be sworn to deal truly and faithfully therein, and shall attend in the said office from nine to twelve of the clock in the forenoon, and from two to five a-clock in the afternoon.

[SECT. 20.] And the s'd commissioner and receiver, for his labour, care and expences in the said office, shall have and receive, out of the province treasury, the sum of twenty-five pounds, per annum; and his deputy or deputies to be paid for their service such sum or sums as the said commissioner and receiver, with the treasurer, shall agree upon, not exceeding seven pounds ten shillings each. And the treasurer is hereby ordered, in passing and receiving the said commissioner's accounts, accordingly, to allow the payment of such salary or salaries, as aforesaid, to himself and his deputy or deputies. [*Passed January* 10, 1745–46.

NOTES.—There were five sessions of the General Court this year; but no acts were passed at the third session. The engrossments of chapters 3, 8, and 11 are not in the Secretary's office, and are supposed to have been destroyed in the great fire of 1747. All the acts of this year were printed with the sessions-acts, except chapters 1 and 23, which, being a tax-act and impost-act, respectively, were printed separately.

All the acts of this year were duly certified to the Privy Council, by Governor Shirley, under the province seal, September 30, 1746. They were laid before the Council by Mr. Kilby, the agent of the province, January 1, 1746–47, and on the 27th of the same month, were referred to the Board of Trade. By the Board of Trade they were next submitted to Matthew Lamb, the successor of Mr. Fane, "for his opinion thereon in point of law." The letter from Thomas Hill, Secretary of the Board of Trade, transmitting the acts to Mr. Lamb, is dated June 18, 1747; and Mr. Lamb's report on these acts bears date from "Lincolnes Inn, 14th November, 1747."

In this report, "no objection" is made to chapters 2, 3, 4, 5, 7, 9, 10, 12, 13, 14, 16, 17, 18, 19, 20, 21, 22, 23; and the list is indorsed "No objection. With observations on some." These observations are given hereunder in notes to the respective chapters.

The acts again came up for consideration in the Board of Trade, upon the report of Mr. Lamb, on different days during the month of November, 1749; and on the 27th of that month, the Board agreed upon a report, in which chapters 1, 2, 3, 4, 6, 8, 10, 11, 12, 13, 14, 15, 18, and 23 are declared to have been "for a Temporary Service and are either expired, or the purposes for which they were enacted have been completed"; and chapters 5, 7, 9, 16, 19, 20, 21, and 22 are declared to "relate to the Œconomy of the Province and are enacted for their private convenience, and We see no reason why His Majesty may not be graciously pleased to confirm them." The report concludes with comments on chapter 17, which are given in the note to that chapter, *post.*—See, also, note to 1746–47, chapter 8, *post.*

On the 14th of December, 1749, an order in Council was passed confirming chapters 5, 7, 9, 16, 19, 20, 21, 22.

Chap. 1. "This Act is for raiseing of money which was granted by severall former Acts therein mentioned."—*Report of Mr. Lamb, to the Board of Trade, Mass. Bay, B. T., vol.* 72, *F. f.* 102, *in Public-Record office.*

Chap. 6. "The method of raiseing Money in the manner mentioned in this Act is in a very extraordinary way but is such as has been usuall in this Province as appears by the Act No. 1."—*Ibid.*

Chap. 8. "This Act of the like extraordinary nature as the Act No 6."—*Ibid.*

Chap. 11. "This Act of the like extraordinary nature as the Acts Nos 6 & 8."—*Ibid.*

Chap. 15. "This Act of like extraordinary nature as the Acts Nos 6. 8. & 11."—*Ibid.*

Chap. 17. "We must acquaint your Lordships that all the several Laws thereby revived have been confirmed by His Majesty except that for preventing mischief by unruly dogs in the island of Nantucket which Act does not appear to us to have been ever laid before His Majesty as it ought to have been pursuant to the directions of the Charter of the said Province granted by King William and Queen Mary.

1743.44, chap. 6.

As it appears however from the annexed printed Copy of the said Act transmitted to us by the Secretary of the said Province that it was enacted only for their private convenience, We see no reason why His Majesty may not be graciously pleased to confirm the above mentioned two Acts. We are

My Lords
Your Lordships
most obedient and
most humble Servants

DUNK HALIFAX
I. PITT
I. GRENVILLE
DUPPLIN

Whitehall November 27th 1749."—*Report of Lords of Trade, to the Privy Council, ibid., vol.* 84, *p.* 244.

This report was on the above chapter, and chapter 8, of the acts of 1746–47. The *act to prevent mischief by unruly dogs, &c.*, was revived by the latter act, and hence it follows that the Lords of Trade were satisfied, at the date of the above report, that all the acts revived by the act of this year, had been confirmed by the Crown; yet, as late as 1754, a minute appears in the files of the Board of Trade, to the effect that, chapter 19 of the acts of 1740–41, and chapter 18, of the acts of 1742–43, had never been laid before the King in Council.

Chap. 21. See note to 1747–48, chap. 15.

ACTS,

PASSED 1746–47.

ACTS

Passed at the Session begun and held at Boston, on the Twenty-eighth day of May, A. D. 1746.

CHAPTER 1.

AN ACT FOR APPORTIONING AND ASSESSING A TAX OF TWENTY-EIGHT THOUSAND FOUR HUNDRED AND NINETY-NINE POUNDS SEVEN SHILLINGS AND SIXPENCE, IN BILLS OF CREDIT; AND ALSO FOR APPORTIONING AND ASSESSING A FURTHER TAX OF TWO THOUSAND FOUR HUNDRED AND FORTY-TWO POUNDS THREE SHILLINGS AND NINEPENCE, IN BILLS OF CREDIT, PAID THE REPRESENTATIVES FOR THEIR SERVICE AND ATTENDANCE IN THE GENERAL COURT, AND TRAVEL; AND ALSO THE SUM OF ONE HUNDRED AND TWENTY-SEVEN POUNDS TEN SHILLINGS, FINES LAID UPON SEVERAL TOWNS FOR NOT SENDING A REPRESENTATIVE.

Whereas the great and general court or assembly of the province of the Massachusetts Bay, did, at their session in May,* one thousand seven hundred and forty-one, pass an act for levying a tax of six thousand six hundred and sixty-six pounds thirteen shillings and fourpence, in bills of credit by said act emitted; and, at their session in May,* one thousand seven hundred and forty-two, did pass an act for levying a tax of eight thousand pounds, in bills of credit emitted by said act; and, at their session in May,† one thousand seven hundred and forty-three, did pass an act for the levying a tax of two thousand five hundred and thirty-three pounds six shillings and eightpence, in bills of credit emitted by said act; and, at their session in May,‡ in the same year, did pass an act for levying a tax of four thousand pounds, in bills of credit emitted by said act; each of the several sums aforesaid to be assessed this present year,—amounting in the whole to the sum of thirty thousand nine hundred and sixty-six pounds thirteen shillings and fourpence; and by the aforesaid acts provision was made that the general court might, this present year, apportion the same on the several towns in this province, if they thought fit: and the assembly aforesaid have likewise ordered that the sum of one hundred and twenty-seven pounds ten shillings, fines laid on several towns, and the sum of two thousand four hundred and forty-two pounds three shillings and sixpence, paid the representatives the last year, should be levyed and assessed, this present year, on the polls and estates of the inhabitants of the several towns, according to what their representatives have respectively received; *wherefore*, for the ordering, directing, and effectual drawing

1741-42, chap. 11, § 18.

1742-43, chap. 15, § 1.

1743-44, chap. 13, § 7.

1744-45, chap. 17, § 6.

* *Sic.*—November. † October. ‡ November, 1744.

The sum of the taxes levied in the acts referred to above, falls short of the total sum apportioned in this act, by £9,766 13*s*. 4*d*., which is the amount of the tax granted by chapter 5 of the acts of 1744-45, § 9,—a reference omitted in the above preamble, undoubtedly, by mistake.

the sum of thirty-three thousand five hundred and thirty-six pounds six shillings and tenpence, pursuant to the funds and grants aforesaid, into the treasury, according to the apportion now agreed to by this court, the sum of two thousand four hundred sixty-seven pounds five shillings and tenpence, arising by the duties of impost, tunnage of shipping and excise, first deducted, there remains the sum of thirty-one thousand and sixty-nine pounds one shilling, to be drawn into the treasury in the following manner; viz., twenty-eight thousand four hundred and ninety-nine pounds seven shillings and sixpence, by a tax on polls and estates on the several towns, and two thousand four hundred and forty-two pounds three shillings and sixpence, paid the representatives the last year; and the further sum of one hundred and twenty-seven pounds ten shillings, fines laid on several towns for not sending a representative, by this act, amounting in the whole to thirty-one thousand and sixty-nine pounds one shilling: all which is unanimously approved, ratified, and confirmed; we, his majesty's most loyal and dutiful subjects, the representatives in general court assembled, pray that it may be enacted,—

And be it accordingly enacted by the Governour, Council and House of Representatives,

[SECT. 1.] That each town and district within this province be assessed and pay, as such town's and district's proportion of the sum of thirty-one thousand and sixty-nine pounds one shilling, in bills of credit, as also for the fines laid on them, and their representatives' pay, the several sums following; that is to say,—

IN THE COUNTY OF SUFFOLK.

	Representatives' Pay, and Fines.	Province Tax.	Sum Total.	
Boston,	£79 18s. 0d.	£5,129 18s. 0d.	Five thousand two hundred and nine pounds sixteen shillings,	£5,209 16s. 0d.
Roxbury,	23 14 0	265 5 7	Two hundred and eighty-eight pounds nineteen shillings and seven-pence,	288 19 7
Dorchester,	20 14 0	251 8 0	Two hundred and seventy-two pounds two shillings,	272 2 0
Milton,	18 13 0	116 5 2	One hundred and thirty-four pounds eighteen shillings and two-pence,	134 18 2
Braintree,	26 17 6	277 17 6	Three hundred and four pounds fifteen shillings,	304 15 0
Weymouth,	26 17 0	160 15 9	One hundred and eighty-seven pounds twelve shillings and nine-pence,	187 12 9
Hingham,	27 12 0	300 1 8	Three hundred and twenty-seven pounds thirteen shillings and eight-pence,	327 13 8
Dedham,	25 8 6	197 13 1	Two hundred and twenty-three pounds one shilling and sevenpence,	223 1 7
[illegible],	1 16 0	120 15 5	One hundred and twenty-two pounds eleven shillings and fivepence,	122 11 5
[illegible],	27 12 0	151 18 8	One hundred and seventy-nine pounds ten shillings and eightpence,	179 10 8
[illegible],	15 0 0	79 13 8	Ninety-four pounds thirteen shillings and eightpence,	94 13 8
Stoughton,	26 17 0	146 3 8	One hundred and seventy-three pounds and eightpence,	173 0 8
Hull,	0 0 0	63 13 0	Sixty-three pounds thirteen shillings,	63 13 0
Brookline,	18 0 0	94 17 8	One hundred and twelve pounds seventeen shillings and eightpence,	112 17 8
[illegible],	15 0 0	84 18 1	Ninety-nine pounds eighteen shillings and one penny,	99 18 1
Bellingham,	0 0 0	31 18 11	Thirty-one pounds eighteen shillings and elevenpence,	31 18 11
[illegible],	0 0 0	49 10 5	Forty-nine pounds ten shillings and fivepence,	49 10 5
[illegible],	20 11 0	123 3 3	One hundred and forty-three pounds fourteen shillings and three-pence,	143 14 3
	£374 10s. 0d.	£7,645 17s. 6d.		£8,020 7s. 6d.

IN THE COUNTY OF ESSEX.

	Representatives' Pay, and Fines.	Province Tax.	Sum Total.	
Salem,	£27 12s. 0d.	£854 18s. 0d.	Eight hundred and eighty-two pounds ten shillings,	£882 10s. 0d.
Ipswich,	41 12 0	787 3 1	Eight hundred and twenty-eight pounds fifteen shillings and a penny,	828 15 1
Newbury,	29 5 0	729 19 2	Seven hundred and fifty-nine pounds four shillings and twopence,	759 4 2
Marblehead,	27 12 0	554 16 0	Five hundred and eighty-two pounds eight shillings,	582 8 0

IN THE COUNTY OF ESSEX—*Continued.*

	[illegible]	PROVINCE TAX.	SUM TOTAL.	
Lynn,	£25 19s. [illegible]	£299 14s. 6d.	Three hundred [illegible] twenty-five [illegible] thirteen shillings [illegible]	£325 13s. [illegible]
[illegible],	29 2 0	344 7 6	Three [illegible] sixpence,	373 9 6
Beverly,	16 8 6	220 3 3	Two [illegible]	236 11 9
[illegible],	28 19 0	214 16 5	[illegible] forty-three [illegible]	243 15 5
Salisbury,	27 13 0	190 0 0	[illegible] shillings,	217 13 0
Haverhill,	27 0 0	193 4 2	[illegible] four [illegible]	220 4 2
[illegible],	25 4 0	357 6 5	Three [illegible]	382 10 5
[illegible],	25 1 0	109 2 8	[illegible] three [illegible]	134 3 8
Boxford,	30 2 0	136 18 5	[illegible]	167 0 5
[illegible],	29 8 0	158 8 3	[illegible] three-pence,	187 16 3
Bradford,	25 19 0	119 6 11	One [illegible] forty-five [illegible] five [illegible]	145 5 11
[illegible],	22 19 0	99 12 8	[illegible] shillings [illegible]	122 11 8
[illegible],	0 0 0	82 15 5	Eighty-two [illegible]	82 15 5
[illegible],	0 0 0	43 18 9	Forty-three [illegible] eighteen shillings [illegible]	43 18 9
[illegible],	12 12 0	85 2 11	Ninety-[illegible] fourteen [illegible]	97 14 11
Rumford,	0 0 0	0 0 0	. . . . . .	0 0 0
	£452 7s. 6d.	£5,581 14s. 6d.		£6,034 2s. 0d.

IN THE COUNTY OF MIDDLESEX.

[illegible],	£20 14s. [illegible]	£188 1s. 4d.	Two [illegible] fifteen [illegible] fourpence,	£208 15s. 4d.
[illegible],	41 8 0	385 3 6	[illegible]	426 11 6
[illegible],	26 2 0	117 13 8	[illegible] forty-three [illegible] fifteen [illegible]	143 15 8
[illegible],	27 12 0	234 19 2	Two [illegible]	262 11 2
[illegible],	27 3 0	110 13 6	[illegible]	137 16 6
Woburn,	26 2 0	183 9 5	[illegible] pounds eleven [illegible]	209 11 5
Reading,	25 1 0	201 8 0	Two [illegible]	226 9 0
[illegible],	27 12 0	209 9 6	Two [illegible]	237 1 6
Marlborough,	26 8 0	216 4 11	[illegible] forty-[illegible]	242 12 11
[illegible],	25 4 0	130 0 8	[illegible] fifty-five [illegible]	155 4 8

Newton,	£26 2s. 0d.	£202 11s. 9d.	Two hundred and [illegible]eight pounds [illegible]teen shillings and nine-p[illegible]ce,	£228 13s. 9d.
Malden,	20 14 0	168 12 6	One [illegible] and eighty-nine pounds six [illegible] and [illegible]pence,	189 6 6
Chelmsford,	22 19 0	116 7 6	One hundred and thirty-nine pounds six shillings and sixpence,	139 6 6
Billerica,	27 3 0	120 1 2	One [illegible]dred and forty-seven pounds four shillings and [illegible]pence,	147 4 2
Sherburn,	0 0 0	75 12 11	Seventy-five pounds twelve shillings and elevenpence,	75 12 11
Holliston,	28 10 0	53 18 3	Eighty-two pounds eight shillings and [illegible]pence,	82 8 3
[illegible]on,	26 11 0	185 7 5	[T]wo hundred and eleven pounds eighteen shillings and fivepence,	211 18 5
Framingham,	26 8 0	153 6 2	One hundred and seventy-nine pounds fourteen [illegible] and two-p[illegible],	179 14 2
[illegible]ford,	20 14 0	90 12 2	One hundred and [illegible]en pounds six shillings and twopence,	111 6 2
Stow,	18 2 0	70 15 6	Eighty-eight [illegible] [illegible]teen shillings and [illegible],	88 17 6
Dunstable and Nottingham,	0 0 0	42 15 0	Forty-two pounds fifteen shillings,	42 15 0
Dracut,	0 0 0	47 5 3	Forty-seven pounds five [illegible] and [illegible]pence,	47 5 3
Stoneham,	0 0 0	60 13 8	Sixty pounds thirteen shillings and eightpence,	60 13 8
[illegible]ton,	26 8 0	85 7 8	One hundred and [illegible]en pounds fifteen shillings and [illegible]pence,	111 15 8
Hopkinton,	26 5 0	59 7 6	Eighty-five pounds [illegible] shillings and sixpence,	85 12 6
Bedford,	10 0 0	56 1 0	[Si]xty-six pounds one [illegible],	66 1 0
Westford,	0 12 0	76 9 6	[Se]venty-seven pounds one shilling and sixpence,	77 1 6
Wilmington,	0 0 0	54 10 2	Fifty-four pounds ten shillings and [illegible]pence,	54 10 2
[illegible]y,	0 0 0	50 4 8	Fifty pounds four [illegible] and eightpence,	50 4 8
[illegible]ton,	0 0 0	38 2 5	Thirty-eight pounds two shillings and fivepence,	38 2 5
[illegible],	26 2 0	104 7 8	One [illegible] and thirty pounds nine shillings and [illegible]pence,	130 9 8
[illegible]field,	10 13 0	21 7 6	Thirty-two pounds and [illegible]pence,	32 0 6
[illegible] [illegible] of Natick,	0 0 0	28 10 0	Twenty-eight pounds ten [illegible],	28 10 0
	£590 9s. 0d.	£3,939 11s. 0d.		£4,530 0s. 0d.

IN THE COUNTY OF HAMPSHIRE.

Springfield,	£20 2s. 0d.	£312 6s. 0d.	Three hundred and thirty-two pounds eight shillings,	£332 8s. 0d.
Northampton,	14 8 0	205 6 3	Two hundred and nineteen pounds fourteen shillings and threepence,	219 14 3
Hadley,	1 9 0	146 17 6	One hundred and forty-eight pounds six shillings and sixpence,	148 6 6
Hatfield,	20 11 0	94 5 8	One hundred and fourteen pounds sixteen shillings and eightpence,	114 16 8
Westfield,	17 5 0	120 10 8	One hundred and thirty-seven pounds fifteen shillings and eightpence,	137 15 8
Suffield,	16 12 0	156 17 5	One hundred and seventy-three pounds nine shillings and fivepence,	173 9 5
Enfield,	26 11 0	93 2 0	One hundred and nineteen pounds thirteen shillings,	119 13 0
Deerfield,	11 17 0	95 2 5	One hundred and six pounds nineteen shillings and fivepence,	106 19 5
Sunderland,	0 0 0	48 9 0	Forty-eight pounds nine shillings,	48 9 0

IN THE COUNTY OF HAMPSHIRE—*Continued.*

	REPRESENTATIVES' PAY, AND FINES.	PROVINCE TAX.	SUM TOTAL.	
Northfield,	£0 0*s.* 0*d.*	£42 10*s.* 3*d.*	Forty-two pounds ten shillings and threepence,	£42 10*s.* 3*d.*
Brimfield,	0 0 0	83 9 8	Eighty-three pounds nine shillings and eightpence,	83 9 8
Somers,	0 0 0	51 3 8	Fifty-one pounds three shillings and eightpence,	51 3 8
Sheffield,	0 0 0	49 17 6	Forty-nine pounds seventeen shillings and sixpence,	49 17 6
Elbows,	0 0 0	28 10 0	Twenty-eight pounds ten shillings,	28 10 0
Stockbridge,	0 0 0	0 0 0	. . . .	0 0 0
	£128 15*s.* 0*d.*	£1,528 8*s.* 0*d.*		£1,657 3*s.* 0*d.*

IN THE COUNTY OF WORCESTER.

Worcester,	£24 11*s.* 0*d.*	£97 9*s.* 11*d.*	One hundred and [illegible]-two pounds and elevenpence,	£122 0*s.* 11*d.*
Lancaster,	26 7 0	161 10 0	One hundred and eighty-seven pounds [illegible]teen shillings,	187 17 0
[illegible]n,	1 4 0	165 17 9	One [illegible] and sixty-seven pounds one shilling and ninepence,	167 1 9
[illegible]k,	25 7 0	146 13 2	One hundred and seventy-two [illegible] and twopence,	172 0 2
Brookfield,	27 3 0	99 3 2	One hundred and twenty-six pounds six shillings and [illegible],	126 6 2
Southborough,	0 12 0	64 7 3	Sixty-four [illegible] [illegible]teen [illegible] and threepence,	64 19 3
[illegible]r,	23 9 6	90 14 6	One hundred and fourteen pounds four shillings,	114 4 0
Rutland,	0 0 0	58 15 8	Fifty-eight pounds fifteen shillings and eightpence,	58 15 8
Lunenburgh,	12 0 0	72 13 6	Eighty four pounds thirteen shillings and sixpence,	84 13 6
[illegible]h,	0 15 0	100 18 9	One hundred and one pounds thirteen shillings and [illegible],	101 13 9
Shrewsbury,	0 0 0	89 6 0	Eighty-nine pounds six shillings,	89 6 0
Oxford,	10 0 0	68 5 8	Seventy-eight pounds five shillings and eightpence,	78 5 8
Sutton,	15 0 0	107 16 6	One [illegible] and twenty-two [illegible] [illegible]teen shillings and sixpence,	122 16 6
Uxbridge,	0 0 0	76 16 8	Seventy-six pounds sixteen shillings and eightpenee,	76 16 8
Harvard,	10 0 0	65 15 9	Seventy-five [illegible] fifteen shillings and ninepence,	75 15 9
Grafton,	0 0 0	55 16 3	[illegible]-five pounds sixteen shillings and threepence,	55 16 3
[illegible]n,	0 0 0	22 13 8	Twenty-two pounds thirteen shillings and eightpence,	22 13 8
Dudley,	0 0 0	47 19 6	Forty-[illegible] [illegible]teen shillings and sixpence,	47 19 6
Bolton,	0 0 0	64 0 2	[illegible]-four pounds and twopence,	64 0 2
Sturbridge,	0 0 0	24 4 6	[illegible]-four [illegible] four shillings and sixpence,	24 4 6
Leominster,	0 0 0	19 19 0	Nineteen pounds nineteen [illegible],	19 19 0
Western,	0 0 0	18 17 8	Eighteen pounds seventeen shillings and eightpence,	18 17 8
	£176 8*s.* 6*d.*	£1,719 15*s.* 0*d.*		£1,896 3*s.* 6*d.*

IN THE COUNTY OF PLYMOUTH.

[illegible],	£24 0s. 0d.	£267 0s. 5d.	Two [illegible] and [illegible]-one pounds and [illegible],	£291 0s. 5d.
Plympton,	21 3 0	141 13 5	One [illegible] and [illegible]-two pounds sixteen shillings and [illegible],	162 16 5
[illegible],	26 2 0	409 16 1	Four [illegible] and [illegible]-five pounds [illegible]en shillings and a [illegible],	435 18 1
Bridgewater,	29 2 0	325 0 5	Three hundred and fifty-four pounds two shillings and [illegible],	354 2 5
Marshfield,	22 18 6	202 7 0	[illegible]o hundred and [illegible] pounds five shillings and sixpence,	225 5 6
Pembrook,	39 2 0	108 15 6	One [illegible] and forty-seven pounds [illegible]en shillings and six-[illegible],	147 17 6
Duxbury,	29 14 0	95 4 9	One [illegible] and twenty-four pounds eighteen shillings and nine-pence,	124 18 9
Middleborough,	24 6 0	239 19 5	Two [illegible] and [illegible]-four pounds five shillings and [illegible],	264 5 5
Rochester,	24 15 0	152 19 0	One hundred and [illegible]en pounds fourteen shillings,	177 14 0
[illegible],	0 0 0	68 5 8	Sixty-eight pounds five shillings and eightpence,	68 5 8
Kingston,	0 0 0	74 13 11	[illegible]four pounds thirteen shillings and [illegible],	74 13 11
[illegible],	0 0 0	87 19 11	[illegible]en pounds [illegible]en shillings and el[illegible],	87 19 11
Halifax,	0 0 0	57 0 0	Fifty-seven pounds,	57 0 0
[illegible],	0 0 0	28 0 0	Twenty-eight pounds ten shillings,	28 10 0
	£241 2s. 6d.	£2,259 5s. 6d.		£2,500 8s. 0d.

IN THE COUNTY OF BARNSTABLE.

Barnstable,	£25 1s. 0d.	£286 0s. 5d.	Three [illegible] and eleven pounds one shilling and fivepence,	£311 1s. 5d.
Yarmouth,	19 10 0	176 9 3	One [illegible] and [illegible]-five pounds [illegible]en shillings and [illegible]pence,	195 19 3
Sandwich,	23 14 0	154 2 9	One [illegible] and [illegible]en pounds [illegible] shillings and nine-pence,	177 16 9
Eastham,	23 7 0	212 16 0	Two [illegible] and thirty-six pounds three shillings,	236 3 0
Truro,	3 12 0	27 18 3	[illegible]-one pounds ten shillings and [illegible],	31 10 3
Harwich,	9 3 0	147 9 9	One [illegible] and [illegible]-six pounds [illegible] shillings and [illegible],	156 12 9
Falmouth,	30 6 0	104 10 0	One [illegible] and [illegible]-four pounds [illegible]en [illegible],	134 16 0
Chatham,	0 0 0	86 16 2	[illegible]six pounds [illegible]en shillings and [illegible],	86 16 2
	£134 13s. 0d.	£1,196 2s. 7d.		£1,330 15s. 7d.

IN THE COUNTY OF BRISTOL.

	REPRESENTATIVES' PAY, AND FINES.	PROVINCE TAX.	SUM TOTAL.	
Bristol,	£27 12s. 0d.	£187 12s. 6d.	Two [illegible] and fifteen pounds four shillings and sixpence,	£215 4s. 6d.
[illegible],	29 17 0	285 4 9	Three [illegible] and fifteen pounds one shilling and ninepence,	315 1 9
Norton,	25 10 0	143 4 3	One [illegible] and sixty-eight pounds fourteen shillings and three-pence,	168 14 3
Easton,	0 0 0	56 1 0	Fifty-six [illegible] one shilling,	56 1 0
Dartmouth,	22 1 0	441 16 4	Four hundred and sixty-three [illegible] seventeen shillings and four-pence,	463 17 4
Dighton,	28 10 0	100 16 5	One hundred and twenty-nine [illegible] six [illegible] and [illegible],	129 6 5
Rehoboth,	26 11 0	352 1 11	Three hundred and seventy-eight pounds twelve shillings and elevenpence,	378 12 11
[illegible] Compton,	24 0 0	201 17 6	Two hundred and twenty-five pounds seventeen shillings and six-pence,	225 17 6
Swansey with Shawamett,	26 5 0	283 2 0	Three hundred and nine [illegible] seven shillings,	309 7 0
[illegible],	0 0 0	227 19 0	[illegible] hundred and twenty-seven pounds nineteen shillings,	227 19 0
Freetown,	0 0 0	93 13 11	[illegible] the pounds thirteen shillings and [illegible],	93 13 11
Attleborough,	23 5 0	143 4 3	One hundred and sixty-six pounds nine shillings and [illegible],	166 9 3
Barrington,	0 0 0	81 16 5	Eighty-one [illegible] sixteen [illegible] and fivepence,	81 16 5
Raynham,	0 0 0	64 19 2	Sixty-four pounds [illegible] [illegible] and twopence,	64 19 2
Berkley,	0 0 0	61 7 11	Sixty-one pounds, seven shillings and elevenpence,	61 7 11
	£233 11s. 0d.	£2,724 17s. 4d.		£2,958 8s. 4d.

IN THE COUNTY OF YORK.

York,	£33 18s. 0d.	£260 17s. 11d.	[illegible] hundred and ninety-four [illegible] [illegible] shillings and [illegible],	£294 15s. 11d.
Kittery,	23 5 0	359 4 2	Three [illegible] and [illegible]-two [illegible] [illegible] shillings and [illegible],	382 9 2
Wells,	20 11 0	152 11 11	One [illegible] and seventy-[illegible] [illegible] two shillings and [illegible]pence,	173 2 11
Berwick,	24 12 0	125 15 2	One [illegible] and fifty pounds [illegible] shillings and [illegible],	150 7 2
Falmouth,	39 9 0	219 4 3	Two [illegible] and fifty-eight [illegible] [illegible] shillings and [illegible]pence,	258 13 3
Biddeford,	22 6 0	86 11 5	One [illegible] and eight [illegible] [illegible] shillings and [illegible],	108 17 5
Arundel,	1 13 0	56 8 2	[illegible] [illegible] one shilling and [illegible],	58 1 2
Scarborough,	0 0 0	113 17 8	One [illegible] and [illegible] [illegible] [illegible] shillings and eight-pence,	113 17 8

North Yarmouth,	£33 15s. 0d.	£48 9s. 0d.	Eighty-two pounds and four shillings,	£82 4s. 0d.
Georgetown,	0 0 0	57 0 0	Fifty-seven pounds,	57 0 0
Brunswick,	0 0 0	19 4 9	Nineteen pounds four shillings and ninepence,	19 4 9
	£199 9s. 0d.	£1,499 4s. 5d.		£1,698 13s. 5d.

IN THE COUNTY OF DUKES COUNTY.

Edgartown,	£17 2s. 0d.	£71 0s. 3d.	Eighty-eight pounds two shillings and threepence,	£88 2s. 3d.
Chilmark,	0 0 0	90 0 3	Ninety pounds and threepence,	90 0 3
Tisbury,	0 0 0	55 13 11	Fifty-five pounds thirteen shillings and elevenpence,	55 13 11
	£17 2s. 0d.	£216 14s. 5d.		£233 16s. 5d.

IN NANTUCKET COUNTY.

Sherburn,	£21 6s. 0d.	£187 17s. 3d.	Two hundred and nine pounds three shillings and threepence,	£209 3s. 3d.

Suffolk,	£374 10s. 0d.	£7,645 17s. 6d.	Eight thousand and twenty pounds seven shillings and sixpence,	£8,020 7s. 6d.
Essex,	452 7 6	5,581 14 6	Six thousand and thirty-four pounds two shillings,	6,034 2 0
Middlesex,	590 9 0	3,939 11 0	Four thousand five hundred and thirty pounds,	4,530 0 0
Hampshire,	128 15 0	1,528 8 0	One thousand six hundred and fifty-seven pounds three shillings,	1,657 3 0
Worcester,	176 3 8	1,719 15 0	One thousand eight hundred and ninety-six pounds three shillings and sixpence,	1,896 3 6
Plymouth,	241 2 6	2,259 5 6	Two thousand and five hundred pounds eight shillings,	2,500 8 0
Bristol,	233 11 0	2,724 17 4	Two thousand nine hundred and fifty-eight pounds eight shillings and fourpence,	2,958 8 4
Barnstable,	134 13 0	1,196 2 7	One thousand three hundred and thirty pounds fifteen shillings and sevenpence,	1,330 15 7
York,	199 9 0	1,499 4 5	One thousand six hundred and ninety-eight pounds thirteen shillings and fivepence,	1,698 13 5
Dukes County,	17 2 0	216 14 5	Two hundred and thirty-three pounds sixteen shillings and fivepence,	233 16 5
Nantucket,	21 6 0	187 17 3	Two hundred and nine pounds three shillings and threepence,	209 3 3
	£2,569 13s. 6d.	£28,499 7s. 6d.		£31,069 1s. 0d.

And be it further enacted,

[SECT. 2.] That the treasurer do forthwith send out his warrants, directed to the selectmen or assessors of each town or district within this province, requiring them, respectively, to assess the sum hereby set upon such town or district, in manner following; that is to say, to assess all rateable male polls above the age of sixteen years, within their respective towns or districts, or next adjoining to them, belonging to no other town, at six shillings and threepence per poll, and proportionably in assessing the fines mentioned in this act, and the additional sum received out of the treasury for the payment of the representatives (except the governour, lieutenant-governor and their families, the president, fellows and students of Harvard College, setled ministers and grammar-school masters, who are hereby exempted as well from being taxed for their polls, as for their estates being in their own hands and under their actual management and improvement); and other persons, if such there be, who, thro' age, infirmity or extream poverty, in the judgment of the assessors, are not capable to pay towards publick charges, they may exempt their polls, and so much of their estates as in their prudence they shall think fit and judge meet.

[SECT. 3.] And the justices in the general sessions, in the respective counties assembled, in granting a county tax or assessment, are hereby ordered and directed to apportion the same on the several towns in such county in proportion to their province rate, exclusive of what has been paid out of the publick treasury to the representative of such town for his service; and the assessors of each town in the province are also directed, in making an assessment, to govern themselves by the same rule; and all estates, both real and personal, lying within the limits of such town or district, or next unto the same, not paying elsewhere, in whose hands, tenure, occupation or possession soever the same is or shall be found, and also the incomes or profits which any person or persons, except as before excepted, do or shall receive from any trade, faculty, business or employment whatsoever, and all profits that shall or may arise by money or other estate not particularly otherwise assessed, or commissions of profit in their improvement, according to their understanding and cunning, at one penny on the pound; and to abate or multiply the same, if need be, so as to make up the sum set and ordered hereby for such town or district to pay; and, in making their assessments, to estimate houses and lands at six years' income of the yearly rents, in the bills last emitted, whereat the same may be reasonably set or let for in the place where they lye: *saving* all contracts between landlord and tenant, and where no contract is, the landlord to reimburse one-half of the tax set upon such houses and lands; and to estimate negro, Indian and molatto servants proportionably as other personal estate, according to their sound judgment and discretion; as also to estimate every ox of four years old and upwards, at forty shillings in bills of the last emission; every cow of three years old and upwards, at thirty shillings; every horse and mare of three years old and upwards, at forty shillings; every swine of one year old and upwards, at eight shillings; every goat and sheep of one year old and upwards, at three shillings: likewise requiring the said assessors to make a fair list of the said assessment, setting forth, in distinct columns, against each particular person's name, how much he or she is assessed at for polls, and how much for houses and lands, and how much for personal estate, and income by trade or faculty; and if as guardian, or for any estate in his or her improvement in trust, to be distinctly express'd; and the list or lists, so perfected and signed by them, or the major part of them, to commit to the collectors, constable or constables of such town or district, and to return a certificate of the name or names of such collectors, constable or constables, together with the sum total to each of them committed, unto himself, some time before the last day of October.

[Sect. 4.] And the treasurer for the time being, upon receipt of such certificate, is hereby impowered and ordered to issue forth his warrants to the collector, constable or constables of such town or district, requiring him or them, respectively, to collect the whole of each respective sum assessed on each particular person, before the last day of May next; and of the inhabitants of the town of Boston, some time in March next; and to pay in their collection, and issue the accompts of the whole, at or before the last day of June, which will be in the year of our Lord one thousand seven hundred and forty-seven.

And be it further enacted,

[Sect. 5.] That the assessors of each town and district, respectively, in convenient time before their making the assessment, shall give seasonable warning to the inhabitants, in a town meeting, or by posting up notifications in some place or places in such town or district, or notify the inhabitants to give or bring in to the assessors true and perfect lists of their polls, and rateable estate, and income by trade or faculty, and gain by money at interest; and if any person or persons shall neglect or refuse so to do, or bring in a false list, it shall be lawful to and for the assessors to assess such person or persons, according to their known ability in such town, in their sound judgment and discretion, their due proportion of this tax, as near as they can, agreeable to the rules herein given, under the penalty of twenty shillings for each person that shall be convicted by legal proof, in the judgment of the said assessors, of bringing in a false list; the said fines to be for the use of the poor of such town or district where the delinquent lives, to be levied by warrant from the assessors, directed to the collector or constables, in manner as is directed for gathering town assessments, and to be paid in to the town treasurer or selectmen for the use aforesaid: *saving* to the party aggrieved at the judgment of the assessors in setting forth such fine, liberty of appeal therefrom to the court of general sessions of the peace within the county, for relief, as in case of being overrated. And if any person or persons shall not bring in a list of their estate, as aforesaid, to the assessors, he or they so neglecting shall not be admitted to make application to the court of sessions for any abatement of the assessment laid on him.

[Sect. 6.] And if the party be not convicted of any falseness in the list, by him presented, of polls, rateable estate, or income by any trade or faculty, business or employment, which he doth or shall exercise, or in gain by money at interest or otherwise, or other estate not particularly assessed, such list shall be a rule for such person's proportion to the tax, which the assessors may not exceed.

And forasmuch as, ofttimes, sundry persons, not belonging to this province, bring considerable trade and merchandize, and by reason that the tax or rate of the town where they come to trade is finished and delivered to the constable or collector, and, before the next year's assessment, are gone out of the province, and so pay nothing towards the support of the government, though, in the time of their residing here, they reaped considerable gain by trade, and had the protection of the government,—

Be it further enacted,

[Sect. 7.] That when any such person or persons shall come and reside in any town within this province, and bring any merchandize, and trade, to deal therewith, the assessors of such town are hereby impowered to rate and assess all such persons according to their circumstances, pursuant to the rules and directions in this act provided, though the former rate may have been finished, and the new one not perfected, as aforesaid.

[SECT. 8.] And the constables or collectors are hereby enjoyned to levy and collect all such sums committed to them, and assessed on persons who are not of this province, and pay the same into the town treasury.

And be it further enacted,

[SECT. 9.] That the inhabitants of this province have liberty, if they see fit, to pay the several sums for which they may respectively be assess'd at, as their proportion of the aforesaid sum of thirty-one thousand and sixty-nine pounds one shilling, in bills of credit emitted in and since the year one thousand seven hundred and forty-one, according to their denominations; or in coined silver at the rate of six shillings and eightpence per ounce, troy weight; or in gold coin, at the rate of four pounds eighteen shillings per ounce; or in bills of credit of the middle tenor, so called, according to their denominations; or in bills of the old tenor, accounting four for one; or in good merchantable hemp, at fourpence per pound; or in good, merchantable, Isle-of-Sable codfish, at ten shillings per quintal; or in good refined bar-iron, at fifteen pounds per ton; or in bloomery-iron, at twelve pounds per ton; or in hollow iron-ware, at twelve pounds per ton; or in good Indian corn, at two shillings and three-pence per bushel; or in good winter rye, at two shillings and six-pence per bushel; or in good winter wheat, at three shillings per bushel; or in good barley, at two shillings per bushel; or in good barrel pork, at two pounds per barrel; or in barrel beef, at one pound five shillings per barrel; or in duck or canvas, at two pounds ten shillings per bolt, each bolt to weigh forty-three pounds; or in long whalebone, at two shillings and threepence per pound; or in merchantable cordage, at one pound five shillings per hundred; or in good train-oyl, at one pound ten shillings per barrel; or in good beeswax, at tenpence per pound; or in bayberry-wax, at sixpence per pound; or in tryed tallow, at fourpence per pound; or in good pease, at three shillings per bushel; or in good sheepswool, at nine-pence per pound; or in good, tann'd sole-leather, at fourpence per pound: all which aforesaid commodities shall be of the produce of this province, and, as soon as conveniently may, be disposed of by the treasurer to the best advantage, for so much as they will fetch in bills of credit, or for silver and gold; and the several persons that pay their taxes in any of the commodities afore mentioned, to run the risque and pay the charge of transporting the same to the province treasury.

[SECT. 10.] And if any loss shall happen by the sale of the aforesaid species, it shall be made good by a tax of the next year; and if there be a surplusage, it shall remain a stock in the treasury. [*Passed June* 26; *published July* 1.

CHAPTER 2.

AN ACT TO PREVENT SOLDIERS AND SEAMEN IN HIS MAJESTY'S SERVICE FROM BEING ARRESTED FOR DEBT.

Be it enacted by the Governour, Council and House of Representatives,

No person, except the commissary, to trust or give credit to any soldier,

[SECT. 1.] That if any person whatsoever, other than the commissary, shall trust or give credit to any soldier, mariner or sailor, during his being actually in his majesty's service, for cloathing or other things whatsoever, no process shall be granted or served on such soldier for any debt so contracted until he be dismiss'd the service, and every writ or process granted or served contrary hereto shall be deemed and adjudged, *ipso facto*, void; and any justices of the peace within the county where any such soldier or mariner is committed or restrained upon process granted for debt or pretension of debt contracted as aforesaid, shall, upon certificate given to him from the captain or chief officer under whose command such soldier or mariner is, setting forth that at the time of such debt contracted, he then was and still continues a soldier or mariner in his majesty's pay, forthwith order his release from confinement and return to his duty.

mariner, or sailor, during their being in the service.

1744-45, chap. 3.

And be it further enacted,

[Sect. 2.] That no person who is or shall be impressed, hired or voluntarily inlisted into his majesty's service, either by sea or land, shall, during his continuance therein, be liable to be taken out of his majesty's service by any process or execution, unless for some criminal matter, for any sum under the value of twenty pounds, bills of credit of the last emission, nor for any greater sum until oath shall be made by the plaintiff or plaintiffs, before one of the justices of the court out of which the execution or process shall issue, or before two justices of the peace, *quorum unus*, in the county where the plaintiff may happen to be, that to his or their knowledge there is, *bonâ fide*, due from such person as the process or execution is desired to issue against, twenty pounds of the currency aforesaid at least. And every soldier whose body shall contrary to the intent of this act be arrested by mean process or execution after his inlistment into said service, may and shall be set at liberty by two justices of the peace, *quorum unus*, in the county where such soldier is taken, upon application made by him or his superior officer, and proof of his being entred into the service aforesaid.

Persons impressed, hired, or enlisted, either by sea or land, not to be taken out of the service, unless.

And be it further enacted,

[Sect. 3.] That no person in his majesty's service shall pawn, truck, barter or sell his arms, ammunition or cloathing, on penalty of being punished by riding the wooden horse, running the gantlet, or other like military punishment, and the person accepting or receiving the same shall be compel'd to restore and make good the same without price or redemption, and shall further, if in his majesty's service, suffer military punishment as aforesaid.

No person in the service to pawn or sell his arms, &c., on penalty, &c.

And be it further enacted,

[Sect. 4.] That all debts contracted for strong or spirituous liquors, by any soldier or mariner while in his majesty's service, shall be void, and the creditor forever debarred from any process or benefit of the law for recovery of the same.

Debts contracted for strong drink forfeited.

Provided always,

[Sect. 5.] That this act shall not be construed to stay the process of any creditor of such soldier or sailor as aforesaid, after his dismission from the said service, nor at all to stay any process or execution against a defective constable or collector, for any tax or taxes committed to him to collect.

Process not to be stayed after dismission from service, &c.

[Sect. 6.] This act to be in force for the space of two years from the publication thereof, and no longer. [*Passed June* 28; *published July* 1.

Limitation.

CHAPTER 3.

AN ACT FOR SUPPLYING THE TREASURY WITH THE SUM OF EIGHTY-TWO THOUSAND POUNDS, FOR CARRYING ON THE EXPEDITION PROPOSED AGAINST CANADA, AND FOR DISCHARGING THE PUBLICK DEBTS, &c., AND FOR DRAWING IN THE SAID BILLS INTO THE TREASURY AGAIN.

Be it enacted by the Governour, Council and House of Representatives,

£82,000 bills of credit to be emitted.

[SECT. 1.] That the treasurer be and hereby is impowered and ordered to emit and issue forth the sum of eighty-two thousand pounds, in bills of credit of the last tenor and date, now lying in his hands and received in for taxes, impost and excise, which shall pass in all publick payments equal to other new-tenor bills emitted since one thousand seven hundred and forty, or if there shall not be a sufficiency of such bills, that then the committee to be appointed by this court for signing bills are hereby directed and impowered to take care and make effectual provision, as soon as may be to imprint so many as may be needed to compleat the said sum, and to sign and deliver the same to the treasurer, taking his receipt for the same; and the said committee shall be under oath for the faithful performance of the trust by this act reposed in them; and the said sum of eighty-two thousand pounds shall be issued out of the publick treasury in manner and for the purposes following; viz., the sum of five thousand seven hundred and ninety pounds, part of the aforesaid sum of eighty-two thousand pounds, shall be applied for the payment of wages that now are or that hereafter may be due by virtue of the establishment of Castle William, Frederick Fort, Richmond Fort, George's Truck-house, Saco Truck-house, Brunswick Fort, and the sloop in the country's service; and the sum of sixteen thousand pounds, part of the aforesaid sum of eighty-two thousand pounds, shall be applied for putting the province into a better posture of defence, for compleatting the repairs at Castle William and other forts, for paying such officers and soldiers as have done service for the province whose wages are now due; which officers and soldiers shall be paid out of this appropriation preferable to any other service, and for such officers and soldiers as are or may be in the province service according to the several establishments for that purpose, for purchasing all needful warlike stores, and for the commissary's necessary disbursements for the service of the several forts and garrisons and other forts within this province, pursuant to such grants as are or shall be made by this court for those purposes; and the sum of twelve thousand pounds, part of the aforesaid sum of eighty-two thousand pounds, shall be applied for the payment of his majesty's council and such other grants as are or shall be made by this court, and for the payment of stipends, bounties and præmiums established by law, and for the payment of all other matters and things which this court have or shall, either by law or orders, provide for the payment of out of the publick treasury, and for no other purpose whatsoever; and the sum of twelve hundred and ten pounds, part of the aforesaid sum of eighty-two thousand pounds, shall be applied for the discharge of other debts owing from this province to persons that have served or shall serve them by order of this court in such matters and things where there is no establishment, nor any certain sum assigned for such service, and for paper, printing and writing for this court, the surgeon of Castle William, and wooding of the said castle; and the sum of twenty-five thousand pounds, part of the aforesaid sum of eighty-two thousand pounds, shall be applied to pay the bounty and procure blankets and beds given

£5,790 for wages at Castle William and other garrisons, &c.

£16,000 for putting the province into a better posture of defence, &c.

£12,000 for payment of his majesty's council, &c.

£1,210 for debts where there is no establishment.

£25,000 for the charges of the intended expedition against Canada.

by this court to encourage men to enlist into his majesty's service for the intended expedition against Canada; and the sum of twenty thousand pounds, part of the aforesaid sum of eighty-two thousand pounds, shall be applied towards defreying the charge of the late expedition against his majesty's enemies at Cape Breton; and the remaining sum of two thousand pounds, part of the aforesaid sum of eighty-two thousand pounds, shall be applied for the payment of the house of representatives, serving in the general court during their several sessions this present year.

£20,000 for the late expedition against Cape Breton.

£2,000 for the pay of the representatives.

And be it further enacted,

[Sect. 2.] That if there be a surplusage in any sum appropriated, such surplusage shall lie in the treasury for the further order of this court.

Surplusage to lie in the treasury.

And be it further enacted,

[Sect. 3.] That each and every warrant for drawing money out of the treasury, shall direct the treasurer to take the same out of such sums as are respectively appropriated for the payment of such publick debts as the draughts are made to discharge; and the treasurer is hereby directed and ordered to pay such money out of such appropriations as directed to, and no other, upon pain of refunding all such sum or sums as he shall otherways pay, and to keep exact and distinct accounts of all payments made out of such appropriated sums; and the secretary, to whom it belongs to keep the muster-rolls and accompts of charge, shall lay before the house, when they direct, all such muster-rolls and accompts, after payment thereof.

Warrants to express the appropriations.

And as a fund and security for drawing the said sum of eighty-two thousand pounds into the treasury again,—

Be it further enacted,

[Sect. 4.] That there be and hereby is granted unto his most excellent majesty, for the ends and uses aforesaid, a tax of twenty thousand pounds, to be levyed on polls, and estates both real and personal, within this province, according to such rules and in such proportions on the several towns and districts within the same, as shall be agreed upon and ordered by this court at their session in May, one thousand seven hundred and fifty-seven, and paid into the publick treasury on or before the last day of December then next after.

£20,000 in 1757.

And as a further fund and security for drawing the said sum of eighty-two thousand pounds into the treasury again,—

Be it further enacted,

[Sect. 5.] That there be and hereby is granted unto his most excellent majesty, for the ends and uses aforesaid, a tax of twenty thousand pounds, to be levyed on polls, and estates both real and personal, within this province, according to such rules and in such proportions on the several towns and districts within the same, as shall be agreed upon and ordered by this court at their session in May, one thousand seven hundred and fifty-eight, and paid into the publick treasury on or before the last day of December then next after.

£20,000 in 1758.

And as a further fund and security for drawing the said sum of eighty-two thousand pounds into the treasury again,—

Be it further enacted,

[Sect. 6.] That there be and hereby is granted unto his most excellent majesty, for the ends and uses aforesaid, a tax of twenty thousand pounds, to be levyed on polls, and estates both real and personal, within this province, according to such rules and in such proportions on the several towns and districts within the same, as shall be agreed upon and ordered by this court at their session in May, one thousand seven hundred and fifty-nine, and paid into the publick treasury on or before the last day of December then next after.

£20,000 in 1759.

And as a further fund and security for drawing the said sum of eighty-two thousand pounds into the treasury again,—

Be it further enacted,

£20,000 in 1760.

[SECT. 7.] That there be and hereby is granted unto his most excellent majesty, for the ends and uses aforesaid, a tax of twenty thousand pounds, to be levied on polls, and estates both real and personal, within this province, according to such rules and in such proportions on the several towns and districts within the same, as shall be agreed upon and ordered by this court at their session in May, one thousand seven hundred and sixty, and paid into the publick treasury on or before the last day of December then next after.

And as a fund and security for drawing in such sum or sums as shall be paid out to the representatives of the several towns,—

Be it enacted,

Tax to be made for what is paid the representatives.

[SECT. 8.] That there be and hereby is granted unto his most excellent majesty, a tax of such sum or sums as shall be paid to the several representatives as aforesaid, to be levied and assessed on the polls and estates of the inhabitants of the several towns, according to what their several representatives shall so receive, which sums shall be set on the towns in the next province tax; and the assessors of the said towns shall make their assessment for this tax, and apportion the same according to the rules that shall be prescribed by the act of the general court for assessing the next province tax, and the constables in their respective districts shall pay in the same when they pay in the province tax for the next year, of which the treasurer is hereby directed to keep a distinct and seperate account; and if there be any surplusage, the same shall lie in the hands of the treasurer for the further order of this court.

And be it further enacted,

Tax for the money hereby emitted, to be made according to the preceding tax act, in case.

[SECT. 9.] That in case the general court shall not, at their session in May, one thousand seven hundred and fifty-seven, one thousand seven hundred and fifty-eight, one thousand seven hundred and fifty-nine, and one thousand seven hundred and sixty, agree and conclude upon an act apportioning the sum which by this act is engaged shall be, in those years, apportioned, assessed and levied, that then and in such case, each town and district within this province shall pay, by a tax to be levied on polls, and estates both real and personal, within their districts, the same proportion of the said sums as the said towns and districts shall have been taxed by the general court in the tax act then next preceeding; and the province treasurer is hereby fully impowred and directed, some time in the month of June, one thousand seven hundred and fifty-seven, one thousand seven hundred and fifty-eight, one thousand seven hundred and fifty-nine, and one thousand seven hundred and sixty, to issue and send forth his warrants, directed to the assessors or selectmen of each town and district within this province, requiring them to assess the polls, and estates both real and personal, within their several towns and districts, for their respective part and proportion of the sum before directed and engaged to be assessed by this act; and the assessors, as also persons assessed, shall observe, be governed by, and subject to all such rules and directions as shall have been given in the next preceeding tax act.

And be it further enacted,

Taxes to be paid in the several species herein enumerated.

[SECT. 10.] That the inhabitants of this province shall have liberty, if they see fit, to pay the several sums for which they respectively may, in pursuance of this act, be assessed, in bills of credit of the form and tenor by this act emitted, or in other new-tenor bills, or in bills of the middle tenor, according to their several denominations, or in bills of the old tenor, accounting four for one; or in coined silver, at seven shillings and sixpence per ounce, troy weight, of sterling alloy, or in gold coin proportionably; or in merchantable hemp, flax, winter and Isle-of-Sable codfish, refined bar-iron, bloomery-iron, hollow iron-ware, Indian corn, rye, wheat, barley, pork, beef, duck or canvas, whalebone, cordage, train-oil, beeswax, bayberry-wax, tallow, peas, sheepswool, or tann'd sole-leather (the aforesaid commodities being of the produce or manufactures of this province), at such moderate rates and prizes as the general assemblies of the years one thousand seven hundred and fifty-seven, one thousand seven hundred and fifty-eight, one thousand seven hundred and fifty-nine, and one thousand seven hundred and sixty shall set them at; the several persons paying their taxes in any of the commodities aforementioned, to run the risque and pay the charge of transporting the said commodities to the province treasury; but if the aforesaid general assemblies shall not, at their session in May, some time before the twentieth day of June in each year, agree upon and set the aforesaid species and commodities at some certain price, that then the eldest councellor, for the time being of each of those counties in the province, of which any one of the councellors is an inhabitant, together with the province treasurer, or the major part of them, be a committee, who hereby are directed and fully authorized and impowred to do it; and in their settling the prizes and rating the value of those commodities, to state so much of them, respectively, at seven shillings and sixpence as an ounce of silver will purchase at that time in the town of Boston, and so *pro ratâ*. And the treasurer is hereby directed to insert in the several warrants by him sent to the several collectors of the taxes in each year, with the names of the afore-recited commodities and the several prizes or rates which shall be set on them, either by the general assembly or the committee aforesaid, and direct the aforesaid collectors to receive them so.

How the commodities brought into the treasury are to be rated.

[Sect. 11.] And the aforesaid commodities, so brought into the treasury, shall, as soon as may be, be disposed of by the treasurer to the best advantage, for so much as they will fetch in bills of credit hereby to be emitted, or for silver or gold, which silver and gold shall be delivered to the possessors of said bills in exchange for them; that is to say, one ounce of silver coin, and so gold in proportion, for seven shillings and sixpence, and so *pro ratâ* for a greater or less sum; and if any loss shall happen by the sale of the aforesaid species, or by any unforeseen accident, such deficiency shall be made good by a tax of the year next following, so as fully and effectually to call in the whole sum of eighty-two thousand pounds in said bills hereby ordered to be emitted; and if there be a surplusage, it shall remain a stock in the treasury. [*Passed June* 10; *published July* 1.

Treasurer to sell the said commodities.

CHAPTER 4.

AN ACT FOR GRANTING A SUM FOR THE PAY OF THE MEMBERS OF THE COUNCIL AND HOUSE OF REPRESENTATIVES, IN GENERAL COURT ASSEMBLED, AND FOR THE ESTABLISHING THE WAGES, &c., OF SUNDRY PERSONS IN THE SERVICE OF THE PROVINCE.

Be it enacted by the Governour, Council and House of Representatives,

[Sect. 1.] That from the beginning of the present session of the general court, unto the end of their several sessions, till May next, each member of the council shall be intitled to four shillings and sixpence per diem, to be paid out of the publick treasury by warrant, ac-

Pay of the members of the council.

cording to the direction of the royal charter, upon certificate given by the secretary of the number of days of such member's attendance and travel to and from the court, twenty miles to be accounted a day's travel.

And be it further enacted,

Pay of the representatives.

[SECT. 2.] That each member of the house of representatives serving the time aforesaid, shall be paid three shillings per diem, upon certificate given by the clerk of the house of representatives of the number of days of such member's attendance and travel to and from the court, twenty miles to be accounted a day's travel.

And be it further enacted,

Pay of the officers and soldiers at Castle William.

[SECT. 3.] That the wages of the captain of Castle William shall be after the rate of sixty pounds per annum, from the nineteenth day of November, one thousand seven hundred and forty-five, to the twentieth day of November, one thousand seven hundred and forty-six; of the lieutenant, for that term, forty pounds; of the chaplain, forty pounds; of the gunner, thirty-two pounds ten shillings; of the gunner's mate, forty shillings per month; of four serjeants, each thirty shillings per month; six quarter-gunners, each thirty shillings per month; of six corporals, each twenty-six shillings and sixpence per month; two drummers, each twenty-six shillings and sixpence per month; of one armourer, forty shillings per month; of one hundred centinels until the first day of September, and forty centinels only from said first day of September until the twentieth of November next, each twenty-two shillings and sixpence per month: for their subsistence, six shillings and threepence per week per man.

And be it further enacted,

Richmond Fort.

[SECT. 4.] That the wages of the captain of Richmond Fort, from the nineteenth day of November, one thousand seven hundred and forty-five, to the twentieth day of November, one thousand seven hundred and forty-six, shall be at the rate of forty shillings per month; of one serjeant, twenty-five shillings per month; of one corporal, twenty-four shillings per month; of one armourer, thirty shillings per month; and for the chaplain, twenty-five pounds per annum; of one interpreter, fifteen shillings per month, being a centinel; and twelve centinels, twenty-two shillings and sixpence per month.

And be it further enacted,

Truck-house at George's River.

[SECT. 5.] That the wages of the captain of the truck-house on George's River, from the nineteenth day of November, one thousand seven hundred and forty-five, to the twentieth day of November, one thousand seven hundred and forty-six, shall be at the rate of forty shillings per month; of one lieutenant, twenty-six shillings per month; of one serjeant, twenty-five shillings per month; of two corporals, each twenty-four shillings per month; of thirty-three centinels, each twenty-two shillings and sixpence per month; of one armourer, fourteen shillings per month, he being lieutenant; of one interpreter, thirty shillings per month; and of the chaplain there, twenty-five pounds per annum.

And be it further enacted,

Brunswick Fort.

[SECT. 6.] That the wages of the commanding officer of the fort at Brunswick, from the nineteenth day of November, one thousand seven hundred and forty-five, to the twentieth day of November, one thousand seven hundred and forty-six, shall be at the rate of forty shillings per month; of eleven centinels, each twenty-two shillings and sixpence per month; one serjeant, at twenty-five shillings per month.

And be it further enacted,

Truck-house at Saco River.

[SECT. 7.] That the wages of one serjeant at the truck-house at Saco, from the nineteenth day of November, one thousand seven hundred and forty-five, to the twentieth day of November, one thousand seven hundred and forty-six, shall be at the rate of thirty shillings per month; of one corporal, twenty-four shillings per month; of twelve centinels, each twenty-two shillings and sixpence per month.

And be it further enacted,

[Sect. 8.] That the wages of the commanding officer of Frederick Fort, from the nineteenth day of November, one thousand seven hundred and forty-five, to the twentieth day of November, one thousand seven hundred and forty-six, shall be at the rate of forty shillings per month; of the chaplain there, fifteen pounds per annum; and of twenty-one centinels, each at twenty-two shillings and sixpence per month. Frederick Fort.

And be it further enacted,

[Sect. 9.] That the wages of the captain of the sloop in the country's service, from the nineteenth day of November, one thousand seven hundred and forty-five, to the twentieth day of November, one thousand seven hundred and forty-six, shall be at the rate of four pounds per month; of the mate, three pounds ten shillings per month; of eight sailors, each forty shillings per month; for the sloop, three shillings and ninepence per ton per month. Country's sloop.

And be it further enacted,

[Sect. 10.] That before payment of any muster-roll be allowed, oath be made by the officer or person presenting such roll, that the officers and soldiers born on such roll have been in actual service for the whole time they stand entred thereon. [*Passed June* 28; *published July* 1. Oath to be made, &c.

CHAPTER 5.

AN ACT FOR SUPPLYING THE TREASURY WITH THE SUM OF TWENTY-FIVE THOUSAND POUNDS FOR THE EXPEDITION AGAINST CANADA, AND FOR DRAWING IN THE SAID BILLS INTO THE TREASURY AGAIN.

Be it enacted by the Governour, Council and House of Representatives,

[Sect. 1.] That the treasurer be and hereby is impowred and ordered to emit and issue forth the sum of twenty-five thousand pounds, in bills of credit of the last tenor and date, now lying in his hands, and received for taxes, impost, and excise, which shall pass in all publick payments equal to other new-tenor bills emitted since one thousand seven hundred and forty; or, if there be not a sufficiency of such bills, that then the committee to be appointed for signing bills are hereby directed and impowred to take care and make effectual provision, as soon as may be, to imprint the said bills, or so many as may be needed to compleat the said sum, and to sign and deliver the same to the treasurer, taking his receipt for the same; and the said committee shall be under oath for the faithful performance of the trust by this act reposed in them; and the said sum of twenty-five thousand pounds shall be issued out of the publick treasury for the purpose following; viz., for purchasing provisions, fitting transports, and paying advance wages of sailors in the expedition intended against Canada, and for no other use and purpose whatsoever. £25,000 bills of credit to be emitted. £25,000 for purchasing provisions, fitting transports, paying advance wages, &c., for the intended expedition against Canada.

And be it enacted,

[Sect. 2.] That if there be any surplusage in the sum appropriated as aforesaid, such surplusage shall lie in the treasury for the further order of this court. Surplusage to lie in the treasury.

And as a fund and security for drawing the said sum of twenty-five thousand pounds into the treasury again,—

Be it further enacted,

£6,250 in 1757.

[SECT. 3.] That there be and hereby is granted unto his most excellent majesty, for the ends and uses aforesaid, a tax of six thousand two hundred and fifty pounds, to be levyed on polls, and estates both real and personal, within this province, according to such rules and in such proportions on the several towns and districts within the same, as shall be agreed upon and ordered by this court at their session in May, one thousand seven hundred and fifty-seven, and paid into the publick treasury on or before the last day of December then next after.

And as a further fund and security for drawing in the said sum of twenty-five thousand pounds into the treasury again,—

Be it further enacted,

£6,250 in 1758.

[SECT. 4.] That there be and hereby is granted unto his most excellent majesty, for the ends and uses aforesaid, a tax of six thousand two hundred and fifty pounds, to be levyed on polls, and estates both real and personal within this province, according to such rules and in such proportions on the several towns and districts within the same, as shall be agreed upon and ordered by this court at their session in May, one thousand seven hundred and fifty-eight, and paid into the publick treasury on or before the last day of December then next after.

And as a further fund and security for drawing the said sum of twenty-five thousand pounds into the treasury again,—

Be it further enacted,

£6,250 in 1759.

[SECT. 5.] That there be and hereby is granted unto his most excellent majesty, for the ends and uses aforesaid, a tax of six thousand two hundred and fifty pounds, to be levyed on polls, and estates both real and personal, within this province, according to such rules and in such proportions on the several towns and districts within the same, as shall be agreed upon and ordered by this court at their session in May, one thousand seven hundred and fifty-nine, and paid into the publick treasury on or before the last day of December then next after.

And as a further fund and security for drawing in the said sum of twenty-five thousand pounds into the treasury again,—

Be it further enacted,

£6,250 in 1760.

[SECT. 6.] That there be and hereby is granted unto his most excellent majesty, for the ends and uses aforesaid, a tax of six thousand two hundred and fifty pounds, to be levied on polls, and estates both real and personal, within this province, according to such rules and in such proportions on the several towns and districts within the same, as shall be agreed upon and ordered by this court at their session in May, one thousand seven hundred and sixty, and paid into the publick treasury on or before the last day of December then next after.

And be it further enacted,

Tax for the money hereby emitted, to be made according to the preceding tax act, in case.

[SECT. 7.] That in case the general court shall not, at their sessions in May, one thousand seven hundred and fifty-seven, one thousand seven hundred and fifty-eight, one thousand seven hundred and fifty-nine, and one thousand seven hundred and sixty, agree and conclude upon an act apportioning the several sums which by this act is engaged shall be, in each of those years, apportioned, assessed and levyed, that then and in such case, each town and district within this province shall pay, by a tax to be levyed on the polls, and estates both real and personal, within their districts the same proportion of the said sums as the said towns and districts shall have been taxed by the general court in the next tax act then next preceeding; and the province treasurer is hereby fully impowred and directed, sometime in the month of June in each of those years, one thousand seven hundred and fifty-seven, one thousand seven hundred and fifty-eight, one thousand seven hundred and fifty-nine, and one thousand seven hundred and sixty, to issue and send forth his warrants, directed to the selectmen or assessors of each town and district within this province, requiring them to assess the polls, and estates both real and personal, within their several towns and districts, for their respective part and proportion of the sums before directed and engaged by this act to be assessed; and the assessors, as also persons assessed, shall observe, be governed by, and subject to all such rules and directions as shall have been given in the next preceeding tax act.

And be it further enacted,

[Sect. 8.] That the inhabitants of this province shall have liberty, if they see fit, to pay the several sums for which they respectively may, in pursuance of this act, be assessed, in bills of credit of the form and tenor by this act emitted, or in other new-tenor bills, or in bills of the middle tenor, according to their several denominations, or in bills of the old tenor, accounting four for one; or in coined silver, at seven shillings and sixpence per ounce, troy weight, of sterling alloy, or in gold coin, proportionably; or merchantable hemp, flax, winter and Isle-of-Sable codfish, refined bar-iron, bloomery-iron, hollow iron-ware, Indian corn, rye, wheat, barley, pork, beef, duck or canvas, whalebone, cordage, train-oil, beeswax, bayberry-wax, tallow, peas, sheepswool, or tann'd sole-leather (the aforesaid commodities being of the produce or manufactures of this province), at such moderate rates and prizes as the respective general assemblies of the years one thousand seven hundred and fifty-seven, one thousand seven hundred and fifty-eight, one thousand seven hundred and fifty-nine, and one thousand seven hundred and sixty, shall set them at; the several persons paying their taxes in any of the commodities aforementioned, to run the risque and pay the charge of transporting the said commodities to the province treasury; but if the aforesaid general assemblies shall not, at their respective sessions in May, some time before the twentieth day of June, agree upon and set the aforesaid species and commodities at some certain price, that then the eldest councellor, for the time being of each of those counties in the province, of which any one of the council is an inhabitant, together with the province treasurer, or the major part of them, be a committee, who are hereby directed and fully authorized and impowred to do it; and in their settling the prizes and rating the value of those commodities, to state so much of them, respectively, at seven shillings and sixpence as an ounce of silver will purchase at that time in the town of Boston, and so *pro ratâ*. And the treasurer is hereby directed to insert in the several warrants by him sent to the collectors of the taxes in those years, respectively, with the names of the afore-recited commodities, the several rates or prices which shall be set on them by the general assembly or the committee aforesaid, and direct the aforesaid collectors to receive them so.

Taxes to be paid in the several species herein enumerated.

How the commodities brought into the treasury are to be rated.

[Sect. 9.] And the aforesaid commodities, so brought into the treasury, shall, as soon as may be, be dispos'd of by the treasurer to the best advantage for so much as they will fetch in bills of credit afore mentioned, or for silver and gold, which silver and gold shall be delivered to the possessor of said bills in exchange for them; that is to say, one ounce of silver coin, and so gold in proportion, for seven shillings and sixpence, and so *pro ratâ* for a greater or less sum; and if any loss shall happen by the sale of the aforesaid species, by any unforeseen accident, such deficiency shall be made good by a tax of the year next following, so as fully and effectually to call in the whole sum of twenty-five thousand pounds in said bills hereby ordered to be emitted, and for which a tax on polls and estates is in this act laid as a fund;

and if there be a surplusage, it shall remain a stock in the treasury. [*Passed June* 13; *published July* 1.

CHAPTER 6.

AN ACT RELATING TO VIEWS BY A JURY, IN CIVIL ACTIONS.

Be it enacted by the Governour, Council and House of Representatives,

Courts may allow jurors to have the view of messuages, lands, &c., in question, and to be tried.

[SECT. 1.] That from and after the publication of this act, in all actions brought in any of his majesty's courts of record, within this province, where it shall appear to the court in which such actions are depending, that it will be proper and necessary that the jurors who are to try the issues in any such actions should have the view of the messuages, lands or place in question, in order to their better understanding the evidence that will be given upon the trial of such issues; in every such case, the respective courts in which such actions shall be depending may order the jury to the place in question, who, then and there, shall have the matters in question shewn them by two persons to be appointed by the court, and the special cost of all such views as allowed by the court shall, before the trial, be paid by the party who moved for the view (the adverse party not consenting thereto), and shall, at the taxation of the bill of cost, have the same allowed him upon his recovering judgment on such trial; and upon all views, with the consent of parties, ordered by the court, the costs thereof as allowed by the court, shall, before trial, be equally paid by the said parties; and in the taxation of the bill of costs, the party recovering judgment shall have the sum by him paid allowed to him; any law, usage or custom to the contrary notwithstanding.

By whom cost of view is to be paid.

Limitation.

[SECT. 2.] This act to continue and be in force for the space of five years from the publication thereof, and to the end of the session of the general court next after, and no longer. [*Passed June* 28; *published July* 1.

CHAPTER 7.

AN ACT FOR HOLDING A COURT OF OYER AND TERMINER, IN AND FOR THE ISLAND OF NANTUCKET.

Preamble.

WHEREAS one Jeremy Jude, an Indian man, now stands committed to his majesty's goal in the island of Nantucket, charged with the murther of Simon Aaron, an Indian man, who ought, as the law now stands, to be tried by a special court of assize and general goal delivery, but forasmuch as the judges of the said court of assize and general goal delivery cannot attend that service, the summer months being taken up with the several superiour courts of judicature, courts of assize and general goal delivery, as they are now established, beside the great charge and trouble of the judges repairing thither, and a court of oyer and terminer have and can exercise the same jurisdiction and authority in all capital offences,—

Be it therefore enacted by the Governour, Council and House of Representatives,

Trial of Jeremy Jude, &c., by five commissioners.

For the reasons above mentioned, and that speedy justice may be done, that the inquiry, hearing and trial of the said Jeremy Jude for the murther of the said Simon Aaron, and any other capital offences upon the said island of Nantucket already committed, may, with all convenient speed, be had at Nantucket aforesaid, by five special commissioners of oyer and terminer, to be appointed by his excellency the governour, with the advice and consent of the council, three of whom to be a quorum; any law, usage or custom to the contrary notwithstanding. [*Passed June* 28; *published July* 1.

CHAPTER 8.

AN ACT FOR REVIVING AND CONTINUING THE LAWS OF THIS PROVINCE IN THIS ACT MENTIONED, EXPIRED OR NEAR EXPIRING.

Preamble.

Whereas an act was made and pass'd in the seventeenth year of his present majesty's reign, intitled "An Act for preventing mischief by unruly dogs on the island of Nantucket"; and another act was made and pass'd in the eighteenth year of his present majesty's reign, intitled "An Act to prevent all traiterous correspondence with his majesty's enemies," which laws are expired or near expiring; *and whereas* the afores[*ai*]d laws have been, by experience, found beneficial and necessary for the purposes for which they were passed,—

1743-44, chap. 6.

1744-45, chap. 6.

Be it therefore enacted by the Governour, Council and House of Representatives,

Revival of sundry laws.

That all and every of the aforesaid acts, and every matter and clause therein contained, be and hereby are revived, and shall continue and remain in force until[l] the twentieth day of May, which will be in the year one thousand seven hundred and fifty-three, and to the end of the session of the general court then next after. [*Passed July* 25; *published July* 28.

ACTS

PASSED AT THE SESSION BEGUN AND HELD AT BOSTON, ON THE FOURTH DAY OF AUGUST, A. D. 1746.

CHAPTER 9.

AN ACT FOR SUPPLYING THE TREASURY WITH THE SUM OF TWENTY THOUSAND POUNDS FOR THE EXPEDITION AGAINST CANADA, AND FOR DRAWING IN THE SAID BILLS INTO THE TREASURY AGAIN.

Be it enacted by the Governour, Council and House of Representatives,

£20,000 bills of credit to be emitted, for billeting soldiers, purchasing provisions, &c., for the intended expedition against Canada.

[SECT. 1.] That the treasurer be and hereby is impowered and ordered to emit[t] and issue forth the sum of twenty thousand pounds, in bills of credit of the last tenor and date, now lying in his hands and received for taxes, impost, and excise, which shall pass in all publick payments equal to other new-tenor bills emitted since one thousand seven hundred and forty; or, if there be not a sufficiency of such bills, that then the committee already appointed for signing bills, are hereby directed and impowered to take care and make effectual provision, as soon as may be, to imprint the said bills, or so many as may be needed to compleat the said sum, and to sign and deliver the same to the treasurer, taking his receipt for the same, and the committee shall be under oath for the faithful[l] performance of the trust by this act reposed in them; and the said sum of twenty thousand pounds shall be issued out of the publick treasury for the purpose[*s*] following; viz[t]., for billeting the soldiers, purchasing provisions, fitting the transports, and paying advance wages of sailors in the expedition intended against Canada, and for no other use or purpose whatsoever.

And be it further enacted,

Surplusage to lie in the treasury.

[SECT. 2.] That if there be a surplusage in the sum appropriated as aforesaid, such surplusage shall l[y][*i*]e in the hands of the treasurer for the further order of this court.

And as a fund and security for drawing the said sum of twenty thousand pounds into the treasury again,—

Be it further enacted,

£10,000 in 1749.

[SECT. 3.] That there be and hereby is granted unto his most excellent majesty, for the ends and uses aforesaid, a tax of ten thousand pounds, to be levied on polls, and estates both real and personal, within this province, according to such rules and in such proportions on the several towns and districts within the same, as shall be agreed upon and ordered by this court at their session in May, one thousand seven hundred and forty-nine, and paid into the publick treasury on or before the last day of December then next after.

And as a further fund and security for drawing the said sum of twenty thousand pounds into the treasury again,—

Be it further enacted.

£10,000 in 1750.

[SECT. 4.] That there be and hereby is granted unto his most excellent majesty, for the ends and uses aforesaid, a tax of ten thousand pounds, to be levied on polls, and estates both real and personal, within this province, according to such rules and in such proportions on the several towns and districts within the same, as shall be agreed upon and ordered by this court at their session in May, one thousand seven hundred and fifty, and paid into the publick treasury on or before the last day of December then next after.

And be it further enacted,

[SECT. 5.] That in case the general court shall not, at their sessions in May, one thousand seven hundred and forty-nine, and one thousand seven hundred and fifty, agree and conclude upon an act apportioning the several sums which by this act is engaged, shall be in each of those years apportioned, assessed, and levied, that then and in such case each town and district within this province shall pay by a tax to be levied on polls, and estates both real and personal, within their districts, the same proportion of the said sums as the said towns and districts shall have been taxed by the general court in the tax act then next preceeding; and the province treasurer is hereby directed and fully impowered, some time in the month of June in each of those years, one thousand seven hundred and forty-nine, and one thousand seven hundred and fifty, to issue and send forth his warrants, directed to the selectmen or assessors of each town and district within this province, requiring them to assess the polls, and estates both real and personal, within their several towns and districts, for their respective part and proportion of the sums before directed and engaged by this act to be assessed; and the assessors, as also persons assessed, shall observe, be governed by, and subject to all such rules and directions as shall have been given in the next preceeding tax act.

Tax for the money hereby emitted to be made according to the preceding tax in case.

And be it further enacted,

[SECT. 6.] That the inhabitants of this province shall have liberty, if they see fit, to pay the several sums for which they respectively may, in pursuance of this act, be assessed, in bills of credit of the form and tenor by this act emitted, or in other new-tenor bills, or in bills of the middle tenor, according to their several denominations, or in bills of the old tenor, accounting four for one; or in coined silver, at seven shillings and sixpence per ounce, troy weight, of sterling alloy, or in gold coin, proportionably; or in merchantable hemp, flax, winter and Isle-of-Sable codfish, refined bar-iron, bloomery-iron, hollow iron-ware, Indian corn, rye, wheat, barley, pork, beef, duck or canvas, whalebone, cordage, train-oil, beeswax, bayberry-wax, tallow, pease, sheepswool, or tann'd sole-leather (the aforesaid commodities being of the produce or manufactures of this province), at such moderate rates and prices as the respective general assemblies of the years one thousand seven hundred and forty-nine, [*and*] one thousand seven hundred and fifty, shall set[t] them at; the several persons paying their taxes in any of the commodities afore mentioned, to run the risque and pay the charge of transporting the said commodities to the province treasury; but if the aforesaid general assemblies shall not, at their respective sessions in May, some time before the twentieth day of June, agree upon and set[t] the aforesaid species and commodities at some certain price, that then the eldest counc[i][e]ll[e][*o*]r, for the time being, in each of those counties in the province, of which any one of the council is an inhabitant, together with the province treasurer, or the major part of them, be a committee, who are hereby directed and fully impowered and authorized to do it; and in their set[*t*]ling the prices and rating the value of those commodities, to state so much of them, respectively, at seven shillings and sixpence as an ounce of silver will purchase at the time in the town of Boston, and so *pro ratâ*. And the treasurer is hereby directed to insert in the several warrants by him sent to the

Taxes to be paid in the several species herein enumerated.

How the commodities brought into the treasury are to be rated.

collectors of the taxes in those years, respectively, with the names of the afore-recited commodities, the several rates or prices which shall be set on them, either by the general assembly or the committee aforesaid, and direct the aforesaid collectors to receive them so.

[SECT. 7.] And the aforesaid commodities, so brought into the treasury, shall, as soon as may be, be disposed of by the treasurer to the best advantage for so much as they will fetch in bills of credit afore mentioned, or for silver or gold, which silver and gold shall be delivered to the possessor of said bills in exchange for them; that is to say, one ounce of silver coin, and so gold in proportion, for seven shillings and sixpence, and so *pro ratâ* for a greater or less sum; and if any loss shall happen by the sale of the aforesaid species, or by any unforeseen accident, such d[i][e][f]fic[i]ency shall be made good by a tax of the year next following, so as fully and effectually to call in the whole sum of twenty thousand pounds in said bills hereby ordered to be emitted, and for which a tax on polls and estates is in the act laid as a fund; and if there be a surplusage, it shall remain a stock in the treasury. [*Passed August* 15; *published August* 19.

ACTS

PASSED AT THE SESSION BEGUN AND HELD AT BOSTON, ON THE TWENTY-SEVENTH DAY OF AUGUST, A. D. 1746.

CHAPTER 10.

AN ACT IN FURTHER ADDITION TO AN ACT INTITLED "AN ACT FOR HIGHWAYS."

WHEREAS in and by an act made in the twelfth year of the reign of her late majesty, Queen Ann, intitled "An Act in addition to the law of this province, intitled 'An Act for highways,' made in the fifth year of the reign of the late King William and Queen Mary," provision is made for the laying out particular private ways between any inhabitants or proprietors within their respective towns to or for any original lot, but no power or liberty is therein given for the laying out any such way to any tract of land that is not an original lot, which is oftentimes equally necessary; wherefore,— Preamble. 1713-14, chap. 8.

Be it enacted by the Governour, Council and House of Representatives,

[SECT. 1.] That the selectmen of each town respectively, and in case of their delay or refusal, his majesty's justices of the peace within the several counties of this province, at any of their general sessions, be and hereby are fully authorized and impowered, by themselves or others, to lay out, or cause to be laid out, particular or private ways as shall be thought necessary, to or for any tract of land not an original lot, as they are by said act of Queen Ann[*e*], for an original lot; under the same regulations and restrictions, and observing the same rules as are therein specified, directed and provided. Selectmen, and in case of their refusal, the justices, empowered to lay out highways.

[SECT. 2.] This act to continue in force for the space of three years from the publication thereof, and from thence to the end of the next session of the general court, and no longer. [*Passed and published September* 13.* Limitation.

CHAPTER 11.

AN ACT TO PREVENT THE FIRING OF GUNS CHARGED WITH SHOT[T] OR BALL IN THE TOWN OF BOSTON.

WHEREAS by the indiscreet firing of guns laden with shot[t] and ball within the town and harbour of Boston, the lives and limbs of many persons have been lost, and others have been in great danger, as well as other dammage has been sustained; for the prevention thereof for the future,— Preamble. 1713-14, chap. 6.

* The bill was passed to be enacted, by both branches, August 12, but was signed by the Governor as above, and was printed with the acts of this session.

Be it enacted by the Governour, Council and House of Representatives,

Penalty for firing off loaded cannon.

[SECT. 1.] That no person or persons, from and after the publication of this act, shall presume to discharge or fire off any cannon laden with shot[t], from any wharf[*f*]e or vessel in that part of the harbour of said town which is above the castle, on pain of forfeiting the sum of fifteen pounds for each gun so fired or discharged; one moiety of said penalty to be to and for the use of the poor of said town of Boston, and the other moiety to him or them who shall inform, complain and sue for the same, to be recovered by action, bill, plaint or information, before any of his majesty's courts of record within the county of Suffolk; and upon refusal thereof, such person shall suffer three months' imprisonm[*en*]t without bail or mainprize.

And be it further enacted,

Penalty for discharging guns or pistols loaded with shot or ball.

[SECT. 2.] That no person shall, from and after the publication of this act, discharge any gun or pistol, charged with shot[t] or ball, in the town of Boston (the islands thereto belonging excepted), or in any part of the harbour between the castle and said town, on pain of forfeiting forty shillings [for] each gun or pistol so fired or discharged, to be recovered before one or more of his majesty's justices of the peace for the county of Suffolk, and disposed of in manner as aforesaid; or shall suffer ten days' imprisonment. And for the more effectual conviction of any person or persons so offending, it shall be lawful for any person to seize and take into custody any gun so fired off, and deliver the same to one of the next justices of the peace in said town of Boston, in order to its being produced at time of trial.

Provided, nevertheless,—

Proviso.

[SECT. 3.] That this law shall not be so construed or understood as to prevent soldiers, in their common-training days, with the leave and by order of the commission officers of the company to which they belong, or other persons, at other times, with the leave of one or more of the field-officers of the regiment in Boston, from firing at a mark or target[t], for the exercise of their skill and judgment, provided it be done at the lower end of the common; nor from firing at a mark, from the several batteries in the town of Boston, with the leave of the captain-general, and nowhere else.

Limitation.

[SECT. 4.] This law to continue and be in force for the space of three years, and no longer. [*Passed and published September* 13.

CHAPTER 12.

AN ACT IN ADDITION TO THE SEVERAL ACTS FOR THE BETTER REGULATING THE INDIANS.

Preamble.

WHEREAS the several laws already in force are insufficient for the well regulating of the Indian natives of this province in their several plantations,—

Be it enacted by the Governour, Council, and House of Representatives,

Three proper persons to be appointed as guardians to the Indians in their respective plantations.

[SECT. 1.] That there be three proper persons appointed, for the future, by this court, near to every Indian plantation in this province, guardians to the said Indians in their respective plantations, who are hereby impowered to take into their hands the said Indians' lands, and allot to the several Indians of the several plantations such parts of the said lands and meadows as shall be sufficient for their particular improvement, from time to time, during the continuance of this act; and the remainder, if any there be, shall be let out by the guardians of the said respective plantations to suitable persons for a term not exceeding the continuance of this act; and such part of the income thereof as is necessary shall be applied for the support of such of the proprietors, in their respective plantations, as may be sick or unable to support themselves, and the surplusage thereof, if any there be, shall be distributed amongst them, according to their respective rights or interest, for providing necessaries for themselves and families and for the payment of their just debts, at the discretion of their said guardians; and that the respective guardians aforesaid be hereby impowered and enabled, in their own names and in their capacities as guardians, to bring forward and maintain any action or actions for any trespass or trespasses that may be committed on the said Indian land, and that any liberty, or pretended liberty, obtained from any Indian or Indians, for cutting off any timber, wood, hay, milking pine-trees, carrying off any o[a]r[e], or planting of, or improving, said lands, shall not be any bar to said guardians in their said action or actions: *provided* that nothing in this act shall be understood to bar any person or persons from letting creatures run upon the said Indians' unimprov'd lands that lye common and contiguous to other towns or proprietors. Proviso.

And it is also further provided,

[SECT. 2.] That nothing in this act shall be understood to bar any Indian or Indians from selling their lands, where there is any former patent or court grant for the same. Further proviso.

And be it further enacted,

[SECT. 3.] That no action shall be brought against any of the said Indians for any debt hereafter to be by them contracted with any English persons, for any sum exceeding ten shillings, except the same be first examined and allowed by the court of general sessions of the peace for the county where such Indian or Indians live, or the respective guardians of such plantations where such Indian or Indians live, except specialties, approbated according to the law of this province made in the fourth and fifth year of the reign of his majesty King George the First, intitled "An Act in addition to the act for preventing abuses to the Indians, made in the twelfth year of King William." No action to be brought against any Indian for more than ten shillings, except. 1718-19, chap. 9.

And be it further enacted,

[SECT. 4.] That the several guardians aforesaid shall keep a fair account of their proceedings in the abovesaid affair, to be by them laid before the general court from year to year, by said court to be adjusted and allowed of. Guardians to keep a fair account, &c.

[SECT. 5.] This act to continue and be in force for the space of seven years from the publication thereof, and from thence to the end of the next session of the general court, and no longer. [*Passed and published September* 13. Limitation.

CHAPTER 13.

AN ACT TO PREVENT THE GREAT INJURY AND INJUSTICE ARISING TO THE INHABITANTS OF THIS PROVINCE BY THE FREQUENT AND VERY LARGE EMISSIONS OF BILLS OF PUBLICK CREDIT IN THE GOVERNMENT OF RHODE ISLAND.

WHEREAS the bills of this and the neighbouring governments are, and have been, the principal medium of trade and commerce in this province, and some of those governments, more especially that of Rhode Island, have frequently made extravagant emissions of their bills, Preamble. 1743-44, chap. 18.

which by as frequent experience have been found a great means of depreciating all the bills of publick credit current among us, whereby great injustice hath been introduced; and, should the same practice be continued, it would be greatly injurious to the inhabitants of this province, and ruinous to many,—

Be it therefore enacted by the Governour, Council and House of Represent[ati]ves,

Penalty for paying or receiving bills of Rhode Island government, issued since 1742, or hereafter emitted.

[SECT. 1.] That no person or persons whosoever shall, within this province, wittingly and wilfully utter, offer to put off, take or receive any bill or bills of credit of the colony of Rhode Island, emitted since the year one thous[*an*]d seven hundred and forty-two, or that shall hereafter be emitted, in payment of any debt, for purchase of any goods, or for any valuable consideration whatsoever, on pain of forfeiting, for each bill so uttered, offered or receiv[*e*]d, the sum of three pounds, and of being ever after disabled from bearing any office of honour or pro[f]fit under this governm[*en*]t.

And be it further enacted,

Penalty for officers passing or receiving such bills.

[SECT. 2.] That any person in this governm[*en*]t, bearing any office or offices of profit or honour, that shall be convicted of having wilfully and wittingly uttered, offered to put off, taken or received any such bill or bills, in payment of any debt, or for purchase of any goods, or for any valuable consideration whatsoever, shall for such offence be, *ipso facto*, discharged from such his office or offices, and shall be thereby utterly disabled to have or hold any office of pro[f]fit or honour within this province, and shall likewise forfeit for each such bill by him utter[*e*]d, offer[*e*]d or receiv[*e*]d, the sum of ten pounds.

And be it further enacted,

Penalty to innholders, &c., for such offence.

[SECT. 3.] That any in[*n*]holder, retailer or common victualer, who, after the publication of this act, shall wittingly and wilfully utter, offer to put off, take or receive any such bill or bills, in paym[*en*]t of any debt, or for purchase of any goods, or for any victuals or liquors bought or sold, or to be bought or sold, or for any entertainm[*en*]t given or to be given, or for any other valuable consideration whatsoever, such in[*n*]-holder, retailer or common victualer, beside his being liable to the fine first before ment[*ione*]d, shall forfeit his licen[s][c]e, and be disabled from holding or using any such employm[*en*]t for the future.

And be it further enacted,

Bonds and mortgages for such bills, to be void.

[SECT. 4.] That every mortgage, bill, bond, instrument of insurance, or other instrument in writing whatsoever, that shall hereafter be executed, for the consideration whereof, in whole or in part, such bills shall be received or paid, and legal proof hereof be made, such mortgage, bill, bond, assurance or instrument in writing, whatsoever, shall be deemed a fraudulent bargain, and utterly void in law.

And be it further enacted,

Witnesses to be indemnified, &c.

[SECT. 5.] That any person that shall receive or pay any such bill or bills, and shall first inform against and prosecute the other party concerned with him or her therein, so that he or she be convicted of receiving or paying such bill or bills, for any valuable consideration whatever, such prosecutor shall be indemnifyed from the penalty in this act, and shall likewise be intitled to one-half the forfeiture aforesaid.

And be it further enacted,

Penalty to merchants and traders.

[SECT. 6.] That every merchant, shopkeeper or trader shall be answerable for every offence against this act committed either by him or herself, or any of his or her houshold or family that are under his or her im[*m*]ediate care or government, and be obliged to satisfy and pay the sum of ten pounds for every such offence, unless such merchant, shopkeeper or trader shall make oath, *bonâ fide*, that such offence was committed without his or her privity, countenance or connivance.

And be it further enacted,

[SECT. 7.] That any justice of the peace shall have power, and is hereby authorized, upon information or complaint to him made of any breach of this act, to convene before him the person or persons so complained of, and to grant summons for witnesses to appear before him to be examined upon oath as to their knowledge touching the fact or facts referr[e]d to in such complaint, and upon just ground to bind over the person or persons complained of or informed against, and to require sufficient security for his or her appearance at the next court of general sessions of the peace in the county where the offence is alledged to be committed, to answer such complaint; and any person refusing to give evidence at the trial of such as may be sued, presented, indicted or complained of for any violation of this act, shall be liable to the same penalty as the person presented or complained of is liable to in case he shall be convict, but shall not be subject to any dam[m]age by any discovery he might make by his oath, in case he should take it. Justices to proceed against offenders by binding them over, &c.

And be it further enacted,

[SECT. 8.] That the courts of general sessions of the peace in the respective counties be, and they hereby are, directed and impowered, at their next term for sitting, and so from time to time, annually, during the continuance of this act, to appoint five meet persons in each town within their respective counties to inform against and prosecute the violators of this act (and in the town of Boston the number of persons to be appointed to that office and duty shall be fifteen), which officers shall have and enjoy the same benefit and advantage as other informers; and if any person so appointed shall refuse or neglect, after due notice given him for that purpose, to take his oath (to be administred to him by such court or a justice of the peace), and to serve in that office, he shall forfeit and pay the sum of five pounds. Persons to be appointed to inform against the breach of this act.

And be it further enacted,

[SECT. 9.] That if any justice of the peace, grand juror or other officer shall wilfully and wittingly omit the performance of his duty in the execution of this act, such officer shall forfeit and pay the sum of twenty pounds. Penalty of officers neglecting their duty.

[SECT. 10.] The several forfeitures afore mentioned to be applied, the one moiety thereof to the use of the poor of the town where the offence shall be committed, the other moiety to him or them that shall inform and sue for the same (and in case there be no informer that shall prosecute such offender, then the whole of the forfeiture shall be applied to the use first mentioned), and may be recovered by action, bill, plaint or information, in any of his majesty's courts of record within the same county, or by presentment of the grand jury, who are hereby strictly enjoined to present all breaches of this act; and no essoign, priviledge, protection or wager of law shall be allowed in any such suit or prosecution as aforesaid. Forfeitures, how to be disposed of. How to be recovered.

Provided, nevertheless,—

[SECT. 11.] That all suits or prosecutions for the breach of this act shall commence within twelve months from the time of committing the offence. Proviso.

And be it further enacted,

[SECT. 12.] That the justices of the respective courts of general sessions of the peace, within this province, shall cause this act to be publickly read at opening their courts, from time to time, and shall give in charge to the grand jury duly to enquire after, and make presentment of, all persons that shall presume to offend in violation of this act; and the selectmen of each town within this province are alike required to cause this act to be publickly read at their several town meetings in March, annually, during the continuance of this act. This act to be publicly read in the courts, and grand jurors to be charged.

Limitation.

[SECT. 13.] This act to continue and be in force for the space of three years, and no longer. [*Passed and published September* 13.

CHAPTER 14.

AN ACT FOR SUPPLYING THE TREASURY WITH THE SUM OF TEN THOUSAND POUNDS FOR THE EXPEDITION AGAINST CANADA, AND FOR DRAWING IN THE SAID BILLS INTO THE TREASURY AGAIN.

Be it enacted by the Governour, Council and House of Representatives,

£10,000 in bills of credit to be emitted for the intended expedition to Canada.

[SECT. 1.] That the treasurer be and hereby is impowered and ordered to emit and issue forth the sum of ten thousand pounds in bills of credit of the last tenor and date, now lying in his hands and received for taxes, impost and excise, which shall pass in all publick payments equal to other new-tenor bills emitted since one thousand seven hundred and forty; or, if there be not a sufficiency of such bills, that then the committee already appointed for signing bills, are hereby directed and impowered to take care and make effectual provision, as soon as may be, to imprint the said bills, or so many as may be needed to compleat the said sum, and to sign and deliver the same to the treasurer, taking his receipt for the same; and the committee shall be under oath for the faithful performance of the trust by this act reposed in them; and the said sum of ten thousand pounds shall be issued out of the publick treasury for the necessary service of the intended expedition to Canada, pursuant to such grants as are or shall be made for that purpose.

And be it further enacted,

Surplusage to lie in the treasury.

[SECT. 2.] That if there be a surplusage in the sum appropriated as aforesaid, such surplusage shall l[y][*i*]e in the hands of the treasurer for the further order of this court.

And as a fund and security for drawing the said sum of ten thousand pounds into the treasury again,—

Be it further enacted,

£5,000 in 1747.

[SECT. 3.] That there be and hereby is granted unto his most excellent majesty, for the ends and uses aforesaid, a tax of five thousand pounds, to be lev[y][*i*]ed on polls, and estates both real and personal, within this province, according to such rules, and in such proportions on the several towns and districts within the same, as shall be agreed upon and ordered by this court at their session in May, one thousand seven hundred and forty-seven, and paid into the publick treasury on or before the last day of December then next after.

And as a further fund and security for drawing the said sum of ten thousand pounds into the treasury again,—

Be it further enacted,

£5,000 in 1748.

[SECT. 4.] That there be and hereby is granted unto his most excellent majesty, for the ends and uses aforesaid, a tax of five thousand pounds, to be lev[y][*i*]ed on polls, and estates both real and personal, within this province, according to such rules, and in such proportions on the several towns and districts within the same, as shall be agreed upon and ordered by this court at their session in May, one thousand seven hundred and forty-eight, and paid into the publick treasury on or before the last day of December then next after.

And be it further enacted,

Tax for the money hereby emitted to be made according to the preceding tax act, in case.

[SECT. 5.] That in case the general court shall not, at their sessions in May, one thousand seven hundred and forty-seven, and one thousand seven hundred and forty-eight, agree and conclude upon an act apportioning the several sums, which by this act is engaged shall be, in each of those years, apportioned, assessed and lev[y][*i*]ed, that then and in such case each town and district within this province shall pay, by a tax to be levied on polls, and estates both real and personal, within their districts, the same proportion of the said sums as the said towns and districts shall have been taxed by the general court in the tax act then next preceeding; and the province treasurer is hereby directed and fully impowered, some time in the month of June in each of those years, one thousand seven hundred and forty-seven, and one thousand seven hundred and forty-eight, to issue and send forth his warrants, directed to the selectmen or assessors of each town and district within this province, requiring them to assess the polls, and estates both real and personal, within their several towns and districts, for their respective part and proportion of the sums before directed and engaged by this act to be assessed; and that the assessors, as also persons assessed, shall observe, be governed by, and subject to all such rules and directions as shall have been given in the next preceeding tax act.

And be it further enacted,

[SECT. 6.] That the inhabitants of this province shall have liberty, if they see cause, to pay the several sums for which they respectively may, in pursuance of this act, be assessed, in bills of credit of the form and tenor by this act emitted, or in other new-tenor bills, or in bills of the middle tenor, according to their several denominations, or in bills of the old tenor, accounting four for one; or in coined silver, at seven shillings and sixpence per ounce, troy weight, of sterling alloy, or in gold coin, proportionably; or in merchantable hemp, flax, winter and Isle-of-Sable codfish, refined bar-iron, bloomery-iron, hollow iron-ware, Indian corn, rye, wheat, barley, pork, beef, duck or canvas, whalebone, cordage, train-oil, beeswax, bayberry-wax, tallow, pease, sheepswool, or tann'd sole-leather (the aforesaid commodities being of the produce or manufactures of this province), at such moderate rates and prices as the respective general assemblies of the years one thousand seven hundred and forty-seven, and one thousand seven hundred and forty-eight, shall set[t] them at; the several persons paying their taxes in any of the commodities afore mentioned, to run the risque and pay the charge of transporting the said commodities to the province treasury; but if the aforesaid general assemblies shall not, at their respective sessions in May, some time before the twentieth day of June, agree upon and set the aforesaid species and commodities at some certain price, that then the eldest councell[e][*o*]r, for the time being, in each of those counties in the province, of which any one of the council is an inhabitant, together with the province treasurer, or the major part of them, be a committee, who are hereby directed and fully impowered and authorized to do it; and in their set[*t*]ling the prices and rating the value of those commodities, to state so much of them, respectively, at seven shillings and sixpence as an ounce of silver will purchase at that time in the town of Boston, and so *pro ratâ*. And the treasurer is hereby directed to insert in the several warrants by him sent to the collectors of the taxes in those years, respectively, with the names of the afore-recited commodities, the several rates or prices which shall be set on them, either by the general assembly or the committee aforesaid, and direct the aforesaid collectors to receive them so.

Taxes to be paid in the several species herein enumerated.

How the commodities brought into the treasury are to be rated.

[SECT. 7.] And the aforesaid commodities, so brought into the treasury, shall, as soon as may be, be disposed of by the treasurer to the best advantage for so much as they will fetch in bills of credit afore mentioned, or for silver or gold, which silver and gold shall be delivered to the possessor of said bills in exchange for them; that is to say, one ounce of silver coin, and so gold in proportion, for seven shillings and sixpence, and so *pro ratâ* for a greater or less sum; and if any loss shall happen by the sale of the aforesaid species, or by any unforeseen accident, such d[i][*e*]f[f]iciency shall be made good by a tax of the year next following, so as fully and effectually to call in the whole sum of ten thousand pounds in said bills hereby ordered to be emitted, and for which a tax on polls and estates is in this act laid as a fund; and if there be a surplusage, it shall remain a stock in the treasury. [*Passed and published September* 13.

ACTS

PASSED AT THE SESSION BEGUN AND HELD AT BOSTON, ON THE SIXTH DAY OF NOVEMBER, A. D. 1746.

CHAPTER 15.

AN ACT FOR MAKING THE TOWN OF TAUNTON THE SHIRE OR COUNTY TOWN OF THE COUNTY OF BRISTOL, INSTEAD OF THE TOWN OF BRISTOL, AND FOR REMOVING THE BOOKS OF RECORDS, AND PAPERS, OF THE COUNTY OF BRISTOL, THAT ARE IN THE TOWN OF BRISTOL, TO THE SAID TOWN OF TAUNTON.

Be it enacted by the Governour, Council and House of Representatives,

[SECT. 1.] That from and after the thirteenth day of November, in the year of our Lord one thousand seven hundred and forty-six, the town of Taunton shall be and hereby is made and established the county or shire town of the county of Bristol, instead of the town of Bristol, and that the superiour court of judicature, court of assize and general goal delivery, and the court of general sessions of the peace, and inferiour court of common pleas, which by law were heretofore to be held and kept at the said town of Bristol for the said county, shall forever hereafter be held and kept at the said town of Taunton, within and for said county, on such days respectively, from time to time, as are now by law established for said county, and for the same respective ends and purposes, and with the same authority, respectively, as, heretofore, the said courts were held and kept in the town of Bristol; and all causes, suits and actions depending and to have been heard in the several courts in said town of Bristol, for said county, shall be heard and tr[y][*i*]ed at Taunton, by the said courts respectively, on the same days on which they should have been heard and tried at Bristol before the passing of this act.

Taunton made and established the shire town in the county of Bristol.

Courts to be hereafter kept at Taunton.

Actions depending to be heard and tried at Taunton.

[SECT. 2.] And all writs, whether original or of execution, informations, presentments, *venires* for jurymen, and all other writings and instruments that by law were returnable to the several courts or offices in Bristol, shall be and hereby are made returnable to the same courts and offices, respectively, in the town of Taunton.

Writs, &c., made returnable to Taunton.

[SECT. 3.] And all the records and papers of the court of general sessions of the peace, inferiour court of common pleas, court of probate of wills and for granting letters of administration, and of the register of deeds, now in the said town of Bristol, shall be forthwith delivered to George Leonard, Esq[r]., Mr. Thomas Foster and John Shephard, Esq[r]., or the major part of them, who shall cause them immediately to be conveyed to the said town of Taunton, and there safely deposited under the care of the same persons as heretofore, or others, as the said committee shall judge best, who shall serve in these offices with full power, and shall give the same obligations and be under the like penalties as they or others had or were under heretofore, until this court shall further order, or others shall be duly appointed in their stead.

Records, &c., to be delivered to a committee and conveyed to Taunton.

40

[SECT. 4.] And the said committee are also directed to demand and receive of the treasurer of said county, now living in the town of Bristol, all money, records and papers to said county belonging, which they are also directed to remove and deposit at Taunton, in the same manner as is before directed concerning the records and papers to the said courts belonging; and the several clerks, treasurer, register, and all other persons who are possessed of any records, books, papers, money or other things belonging to said county (such person or persons living now in said town of Bristol), are hereby impowered and required to deliver them forthwith to the said committee.

Sheriff directed to convey prisoners to Taunton.

[SECT. 5.] And the sheriff of the said county is hereby directed to cause all prisoners now in his majesty's goal in the county of Bristol, to be conveyed to said town of Taunton, and there put under safe custody, in some proper place to be kept for that purpose, 'till said county shall provide a proper goal in said town of Taunton, or 'till they shall be delivered by due course of law. [*Passed November* 13; *published November* 14.

CHAPTER 16.

AN ACT FOR SUPPLYING THE TREASURY WITH THE SUM OF TWENTY THOUSAND TWO HUNDRED POUNDS, FOR DISCHARGING THE PUBLICK DEBTS, &c[A]., AND FOR DRAWING IN THE SAID BILLS INTO THE TREASURY AGAIN.

Be it enacted by the Governour, Council and House of Representatives,

£22,200 bills of credit to be emitted.

[SECT. 1.] That the treasurer be and hereby is impowered and ordered to emit and issue forth the sum of twenty thousand two hundred pounds in bills of credit of the last tenor and date, now lying in his hands, and received in for taxes, impost, and excise, which shall pass in all publick payments, equal to other new-tenor bills emitted since one thousand seven hundred and forty; or, if there shall not be a sufficiency of such bills, that then the committee appointed by this court for signing bills are hereby directed and impowered to take care and make effectual provision, as soon as may be, to imprint the said bills, or so many as may be needed to compleat the said sum, and to sign and deliver the same to the treasurer, taking his receipt for the same; and the said committee shall be under oath for the faithful[l] performance of the trust by this act reposed in them. And the said sum of twenty thousand two hundred pounds shall be issued out of the treasury in manner and for the purposes following; viz[t]., the sum of five thousand pounds, part of the aforesaid sum of twenty thousand two hundred pounds, shall be applied for the payment of wages that now are, or hereafter may be, due by virtue of the establishment of Castle William, Frederick Fort, Richmond Fort, George's Truck-house, Saco Truck-house, Brunswick Fort, the sloop in the country's service, and the commissary's usual disbursements; and the sum of twelve thousand pounds, part of the aforesaid sum of twenty thousand two hundred pounds, shall be applied for putting the province into a better posture of defence, for compleating the repairs at Castle William and other forts, for paying off such officers and soldiers as have done service for the province, whose wages are now due, and for such officers and soldiers as are or may be in the province service, according to the several establishments for that purpose, for purchasing all needful[l] warlike stores for the several forts and garrisons within this province, pursuant to such grants

£5,000 for wages at Castle William and other garrisons, &c.

£12,000 for putting the province into a better posture of defence, &c.

as are or shall be made by this court for those purposes; and the sum of three thousand pounds, part of the aforesaid sum of twenty thousand two hundred pounds, shall be applied for the discharge of other debts owing from this province to persons that have served or shall serve them by order of this court in such matters and things where there is no establishment nor any certain sum assigned for such service, and for paper, printing and writing for this court, the expences of the committees of council, or of the house, or of both houses, the surgeon of Castle William, and wooding of the said castle. £3,000 for debts where there is no establishment.

And whereas there are sometimes publick entertainments, and, from time to time, contingent and unforeseen charges that demand prompt payment,—

Be it further enacted,

[SECT. 2.] That the sum of two hundred pounds, the remaining part of the aforesaid sum of twenty thousand two hundred pounds, be applied to defrey and pay such entertainments and contingent charges, and for no other use whatsoever. £200 for entertainments, &c.

And be it further enacted,

[SECT. 3.] That if there be a surplusage in any sum appropriated, such surplusage shall l[y][*i*]e in the treasury for the further order of this court. Surplusage to lie in the treasury.

And be it further enacted,

[SECT. 4.] That each and every warrant for drawing money out of the treasury shall direct the treasurer to take the same out of such sums as are respectively appropriated for the payment of such publick debts as the drafts are made to discharge; and the treasurer is hereby directed and ordered to pay such money out of such appropriation as directed to, and no other, upon pain of refunding all such sum or sums as he shall otherwise pay, and to keep exact and distinct acco[un][*mp*]ts of all payments made out of such appropriated sums; and the secretary, to whom it belongs to keep the muster-rolls and acco[un][*mp*]ts of charge, shall lay before the house, when they direct, all such muster-rolls and acco[un][*mp*]ts after payment thereof. Warrants to express the appropriations.

And as a fund and security for drawing the said sum of twenty thousand two hundred pounds into the treasury again,—

Be it further enacted,

[SECT. 5.] That there be and hereby is granted unto his most excellent majesty, for the ends and uses aforesaid, a tax of five thousand and fifty pounds, to be levied on polls, and estates both real and personal, within this province, according to such rules and in such proportions on the several towns and districts within the same, as shall be agreed upon and ordered by this court at their session in May, one thousand seven hundred and fifty-seven, and paid into the publick treasury on or before the last day of December then next after. £5,050 in 1757.

And as a further fund and security for drawing in the said sum of twenty thousand two hundred pounds into the treasury again,—

Be it further enacted,

[SECT. 6.] That there be and hereby is granted unto his most excellent majesty, for the ends and uses aforesaid, a tax of five thousand and fifty pounds, to be levied on polls, and estates both real and personal, within this province, according to such rules and in such proportions on the several towns and districts within the same, as shall be agreed upon and ordered by this court at their session in May, one thousand seven hundred and fifty-eight, and paid into the publick treasury on or before the last day of December then next after. £5,050 in 1758.

And as a further fund and security for drawing in the said sum of twenty thousand two hundred pounds into the treasury again,—

Be it further enacted,

£5,050 in 1759.

[SECT. 7.] That there be and hereby is granted unto his most excellent majesty, for the ends and uses aforesaid, a tax of five thousand and fifty pounds, to be levied on polls, and estates both real and personal, within this province, according to such rules and in such proportions on the several towns and districts within the same, as shall be agreed upon and ordered by this court at their session in May, one thousand seven hundred and fifty-nine, and paid into the publick treasury on or before the last day of December then next after.

And as a further fund and security for drawing in the said sum of twenty thousand two hundred pounds into the treasury again,—

Be it further enacted,

£5,050 in 1760.

[SECT. 8.] That there be and hereby is granted unto his most excellent majesty, for the ends and uses aforesaid, a tax of five thousand and fifty pounds, to be levied on polls, and estates both real and personal, within this province, according to such rules and in such proportions on the several towns and districts within the same, as shall be agreed upon and ordered by this court at their session in May, one thousand seven hundred and sixty, and paid into the publick treasury on or before the last day of December then next after.

And be it further enacted,

Tax for the money hereby emitted to be made according to the preceding tax act, in case.

[SECT. 9.] That in case the general court shall not at their session in May, one thousand seven hundred and fifty-seven, and one thousand seven hundred and fifty-eight, and one thousand seven hundred and fifty-nine, and one thousand seven hundred and sixty, agree and conclude upon an act apportioning the sum which by this act is engaged shall be in those years apportioned, assessed and lev[y][*i*]ed, that then and in such case each town and district within this province shall pay, by a tax to be lev[y][*i*]ed on the polls, and estates both real and personal, within their districts, the same proportion of the said sums as the said towns and districts shall have been taxed by the general court in the tax act then next preceeding; and the province treasurer is hereby fully impowered and directed, some time in the month of June, in the year one thousand seven hundred and fifty-seven, and one thousand seven hundred and fifty-eight, and one thousand seven hundred and fifty-nine, and one thousand seven hundred and sixty, to issue and send forth his warrants, directed to the selectmen or assessors of each town and district within this province, requiring them to assess the polls, and estates both real and personal, within their several towns and districts, for their respective part and proportion of the sum before directed and engaged to be assessed by this act; and the assessors, as also persons assessed, shall observe, be governed by, and subject to all such rules and directions as shall have been given in the next preceeding tax act.

And be it further enacted,

Taxes to be paid in the several species herein enumerated.

[SECT. 10.] That the inhabitants of this province shall have liberty, if they see fit, to pay the several sums for which they respectively may, in pursuance of this act, be assess[*e*][']d, in bills of credit of the form and tenor by this act emitted, or in other new-tenor bills, or in bills of the middle tenor, according to their several denominations, or in bills of the old tenor, accounting four for one; or in coined silver, at seven shillings and sixpence per ounce, troy weight, and of sterling alloy, or in gold coin, proportionably; or in merchantable hemp, flax, winter and Isle-of-Sable codfish, refined bar-iron, bloomery-iron, hollow iron-ware, Indian corn, rye, wheat, barley, pork, beef, duck or canvas, whalebone, cordage, train-oil, beeswax, bayberry-wax, tallow, pease, sheepswool, or tan[*n*]'d sole-leather (the aforesaid commodities being of the produce or manufactures of this province), at such moderate rates and prices as the general assembl[y][*ie*]s of the years one thousand seven hundred and fifty-seven, and one thousand seven hundred and fifty-eight, and one thousand seven hundred and fifty-nine, and one thousand seven hundred and sixty, shall set them at; the several persons paying their taxes in any of the commodities aforementioned, to run the risque and pay the charge of transporting the said commodities to the province treasury; but if the aforesaid general assembl[y][*ies*] shall not, at their session in May, some time before the twentieth day of June in each year, agree upon and set the aforesaid species and commodities at some certain price, that then the eldest councellor, for the time being, of each of those counties in the province, of which any one of the council is an inhabitant, together with the province treasurer, or the major part of them, be a committee, who are hereby directed and fully authorized and impowered to do it; and in their set[*t*]ling the prices and rating the value of those commodities, to state so much of them, respectively, at seven shillings and sixpence as an ounce of silver will purchase at that time in the town of Boston, and so *pro ratâ*. And the treasurer is hereby directed to insert in the several warrants by him sent to the several collectors of the taxes in each year, with the names of the afore-recited commodities, the several prices or rates which shall be set on them, either by the general assembly or the committee aforesaid, and direct the aforesaid collectors to receive them so.

How the commodities brought into the treasury are to be rated.

[SECT. 11.] And the aforesaid commodities so brought into the treasury, shall, as soon as may be, be disposed of by the treasurer to the best advantage for so much as they will fetch in bills of credit hereby to be emitted, or for silver or gold, which silver and gold shall be delivered to the possessor of said bills in exchange for them; that is to say, one ounce of silver coin, and so gold in proportion, for seven shillings and sixpence, and so *pro ratâ* for a greater or less sum; and if any loss shall happen by the sale of the aforesaid species, or by any unforeseen accident, such deficiency shall be made good by a tax of the year next following, so as fully and effectually to call in the whole sum of twenty thousand two hundred pounds in said bills hereby ordered to be emitted; and if there be a surplusage, it shall remain a stock in the treasury. [*Passed November* 15.

ACTS

PASSED AT THE SESSION BEGUN AND HELD AT BOSTON, ON THE TWENTY-FOURTH DAY OF DECEMBER, A. D. 1746.

CHAPTER 17.

AN ACT MORE EFFECTUALLY TO PREVENT PROFANE CURSING AND SWEARING.

Preamble.

FORASMUCH as the horrible, impious and execrable vices of profane cursing and swearing, so highly displeasing to Almighty God, and offensive to every Christian, are become so frequent and notorious, that unless speedily and effectually punished, they may justly provoke the divine vengeance to increase the many calamities this people now labour under. And whereas the laws now in being for punishing those crimes have not answered the good intentions for which they were designed,—

Be it therefore enacted by the Governour, Council and House of Representatives,

Penalty for profane cursing or swearing.

[SECT. 1.] That from and after the twentieth day of February, instant, if any person or persons that have arrived at discretion, in the judgment of the justice before whom the conviction may be, shall profanely curse or swear in the hearing of any justice of the peace, or, being charged therewith, shall confess such offence, or be otherwise convicted thereof on the oath of any sheriff, deputy-sheriff, coroner, constable, grand juror or tythingman, where such evidence shall be satisfactory to the justice that shall take cognizance of the offence, or on the oath of any one or more witness or witnesses, where the evidence shall be satisfactory as aforesaid, every person so offending, shall forfeit and pay, for the use of the poor of the town where such offence is committed, a sum not exceeding eight shillings, nor less than four, according to the aggravations of the offence and the quality and circumstances of the offender, in the judgment of the justice or court before whom the conviction is; and in case the same person or persons shall, after conviction, offend a second time, such offender or offenders shall forfeit and pay double, and if a third time, treble the sum forfeited on the first conviction, and the like sum on every conviction afterwards. And if, on any trial and conviction, proof shall be made that more than one profane oath or curse were uttered by the same person at the same time, and in the presence or hearing of the same witness or witnesses, the person so offending, for every profane oath or curse so uttered, after the first, shall forfeit and pay a sum not under one shilling, nor exceeding two shillings. And in case any person convicted of profane cursing or swearing, shall not immediately pay the sum or sums so forfeited, he shall be committed to the common goal or house of correction, there to remain not exceeding ten days, nor less than five days.

Provided always,—

And it is hereby enacted,

[SECT. 2.] That in case any common soldier in his majesty's service, or any common sailer or seamen belonging to any ship or vessel, shall be convicted of profane cursing or swearing as aforesaid, and shall not immediately pay down the penalty by him forfeited, such common soldier or seaman, instead of being committed as aforesaid, shall, by the said justice of the peace, be ordered to be publickly set in the stocks or cage, for the first offence not exceeding three hours, and for the second or any after offence, shall be publickly whipt, not exceeding twenty nor less than ten stripes. And if any Indian, negro or molatto slave, shall be convicted of profane swearing and cursing, and the fine is not immediately paid, such slave shall be publickly whipt by order of such justice, not exceeding twenty stripes, nor less than ten. Proviso.

And be it further enacted,

[SECT. 3.] That if any person or persons shall profanely swear or curse in the hearing of any sheriff, deputy-sheriff or constable, they and each of them are hereby authorized and required to apprehend and secure such offender or offenders, being unknown to them, and to require suitable aid therein, and him or them forthwith to carry before some justice of the peace for the same county, that so such offender or offenders may be convicted and punished for the said offence. And in case any person profanely swearing or cursing in the hearing of any sheriff, deputy-sheriff, coroner, constable, grand juror or tythingman, shall be known to any or either of them, such sheriff, under-sheriff, coroner, constable, grand juror or tythingman, shall and is hereby required forthwith to give information thereof to some justice of the peace of the same county, in order that the offender or offenders may be convicted and punished for the same in manner and form as in and by this act is directed. Sheriff, &c., to apprehend and secure offenders against this act.

And be it further enacted,

[SECT. 4.] That every justice of the peace before whom any person or persons shall be convicted of profane cursing or swearing, shall cause the conviction to be drawn up in the form following:—

Suffolk ss. BE IT REMEMBERED, that on the day of , in the year of his majesty's reign, A. B. was convicted before me, one of his majesty's justices of the peace for the county of , of swearing one [or more] profane oath [or oaths], or of uttering one [or more] profane curse or curses [as the case shall be]. Given under my hand and seal the day and year aforesaid. Form of conviction.

—which said form and conviction shall be deemed and taken to be final to all intents and purposes, saving as herein after is expressed; and the said justice before whom such conviction shall be, shall cause the same to be fairly wrote over, and returned to the then next court of general sessions of the peace for the county where the offence is committed, there to be read in open court, and to be filed by the clerk of the peace, and remain and be kept amongst the records of said court.

Saving always,—

And it is hereby provided and enacted,

[SECT. 5.] That when any person shall be convicted before a justice of the peace of profane cursing or swearing, if the defendant shall confess the words alledged to have been uttered, and shall plead specially that the words spoken do not amount to or import a profane oath or curse within the meaning and intention of this act, in such case it shall and may be lawful for such defendant to appeal from the sentence of the justice before whom he was convicted, to the justices of the same Saving.

county in their then next general sessions of the peace, who shall hear and finally determine the same, the appellant claiming his appeal at the time of declaring the said sentence, and recognizing with sureties in a reasonable sum, not exceeding five pounds, to prosecute his appeal with effect, and to perform the order of the said court thereon.

And be it further enacted,

Penalty for justices' neglecting their duty.

[SECT. 6.] That if any justice of the peace, upon due information and complaint made against any person or persons for profane cursing or swearing, shall wittingly and wilfully omit the performance of his duty in the execution of this act, he shall forfeit and pay the sum of five pounds; one moiety thereof to the informer that shall sue for the same, and the other moiety to the use of the poor of the town where he resides, to be recovered by action or information in any of his majesty's courts of record within the respective counties where such offence is committed; and no essoin, protection or wager of law shall be allowed, or more than one imparlance.

And be it further enacted,

Penalty for constables, &c., omitting their duty.

[SECT. 7.] That if any constable, grand juror, tythingman, or other officer enjoined by this act to inform against the violaters of it, shall wittingly and willingly omit the performance of his duty in the execution of this act, and be thereof duly convicted before any justice of the peace for the county where such offence is committed, he shall forfeit and pay the sum of forty shillings, to be levied and recovered by distress and sale of the offender's goods and chattels by virtue of a warrant, under the hand and seal of such justice, to be disposed of, one moiety thereof to the informer, the other moiety to the use of the poor of the town where the offence is committed; and in case such offender shall not have sufficient goods and chattels whereon to levy the said penalty, it shall and may be lawful for such justice of the peace to commit the offender to goal for the space of six days, there to remain without bail or mainprize.

And be it further enacted,

Penalty for such who shall neglect to give aid, &c.

[SECT. 8.] That if any person being required to give aid to any sheriff, deputy-sheriff or constable, as by this act is provided, shall neglect or refuse the same, and be thereof convict before any justice of the peace, by the oath of any such sheriff, deputy-sheriff or constable, or other legal witness or witnesses to the satisfaction of such justice, such person so refusing shall forfeit and pay the sum of forty shillings; the one-half to the informer, and the other half to the poor of the town where the offence is committed; and every person giving aid, as before is provided in this act, shall receive the same allowance therefor as is by law made to witnesses in civil causes.

Provided always,—

And it is hereby enacted,

Proviso.

[SECT. 9.] That no person shall be prosecuted or troubled for any offence against this law, unless the same be proved or prosecuted within twenty days next after the offence is committed.

And, that no person may plead ignorance of this law, but that it may be generally known,—

Be it further enacted,

This act recommended to be read, &c.

[SECT. 10.] That immediately after the publication of it from the court-house in Boston, a printed copy of this act shall be transmitted to every minister within the government, to whom it is hereby recommended to read, or cause the same to be publickly read, before their several congregations immediately on his receiving the same; and also on the Lord's Day next succeeding the choice of town officers, yearly during the continuance of this act.

And be it further enacted,

[SECT. 11.] That the justices of the court of assize and general goal delivery, and the justices of the peace for the several counties within this province at their general sessions, shall cause this act to be publickly read at the opening of their respective courts from time to time. This act to be read at the opening of the courts.

[SECT. 12.] This act to continue and be in force for the term of three years from the publication thereof, and to the end of the then next session of the general court, and no longer. [*Passed February* 10; *published February* 13, 1746-47. Limitation.

CHAPTER 18.

AN ACT TO ENABLE THE PROPRIETORS OF PRIVATE WAYS TO REPAIR THEM IN AN EQUAL MANNER.

WHEREAS there are many private ways in this province which are seldom used but by the purchasers or proprietors of them, or the owners of the lands to which such ways lead, and are therefore not repaired by the towns in which they respectively lie; nor have the proprietors or rightful occupants of such ways any power by the laws of this province to compel their being repaired by or among themselves; to prevent, therefore, the inconvenienc[i]es which do or may thence arise,— Preamble.

Be it enacted by the Governour, Council and House of Representatives,

[SECT. 1.] That when and so often as any number of the proprietors and rightful occupants of any private way, where there are more than four of them, shall judge a proprietors' meeting necessary, three of them applying to a justice of the peace in the county where said way lies, such justice is hereby impowered to grant a warrant for calling the same, or otherwise one-fourth part of the said proprietors may of themselves call such meeting; in either case to be done by warrant under the hand of said justice or fourth part respectively, posted up in some publick place or places in the town or towns where such way is, seven days before the time appointed for such meeting, signifying the time, place, and business thereof; and the major part of the proprietors and rightful occupants so assembled shall have full power to agree on any other way of calling future meetings, to choose a clerk and a surveyor, who shall be sworn to the faithful discharge of their respective trusts as town officers are; and such surveyor shall have the same power with respect to such ways as the surveyors of highways are by law invested with, and shall be governed by the same rules as are prescribed by law for their direction; each proprietor's and occupant's proportion of labour to be determined by a major vote of those present at such meeting. And in case of the default of any proprietor or occupant in attending said work by himself or other sufficient person in his stead, to be subject to the same fines and penalties as in case of highways, and be recovered in the same manner, and applied to the same uses. Proprietors and occupants of private ways may apply for a meeting, &c. Major part may agree for calling future meetings. Penalty for not attending.

[SECT. 2.] This act to continue and be in force for the space of three years from and after the publication thereof, and no longer. [*Passed February* 13; *published March* 2, 1746-47. Limitation.

CHAPTER 19.

AN ACT FOR GRANTING THE SUM OF NINETEEN HUNDRED POUNDS FOR THE SUPPORT OF HIS MAJESTY'S GOVERNOUR.

Be it enacted by the Governour, Council and House of Representatives, That the sum of nineteen hundred pounds in bills of credit of the last emission, be and hereby is granted unto his most excellent majesty, to be paid out of the publick treasury unto his excellency William Shirley, Esq[r]., captain-general and governour-in-chief in and over his majesty's province of the Massachusetts Bay, for his past services, and further to enable him to manage the publick affairs of the province. [*Passed January* 29; *published March* 2, 1746-47.

CHAPTER 20.

AN ACT FOR SUPPLYING THE TREASURY WITH THE SUM OF EIGHT THOUSAND TWO HUNDRED POUNDS, FOR DEFREYING THE CHARGE OF THE LATE INTENDED EXPEDITION AGAINST CANADA, AND FOR DISCHARGING THE PUBLICK DEBTS, &c[a]., AND FOR DRAWING IN THE SAID BILLS INTO THE TREASURY AGAIN.

Be it enacted by the Governour, Council and House of Representatives,

£8,200 to be emitted.

[SECT. 1.] That the treasurer be and hereby is impowered and ordered to issue forth the sum of eight thousand two hundred pounds in bills of credit of the last tenor and date, now lying in his hands, and received in for taxes, impost and excise, which shall pass, in all publick payments, equal to other new-tenor bills issued since one thousand seven hundred and forty, or, if there be not a sufficiency of such bills, that then the committee appointed by this court for signing bills are hereby directed and impow[e]red to take care and make effectual provision, as soon as may be, to imprint so many as may be needed to compleat the said sum, and to sign and deliver the same to the treasurer, taking his receipt for the same; and the said committee shall be under oath for the faithful[l] performance of the trust by this act reposed in them. And the said sum of eight thousand two hundred pounds shall be issued out of the publick treasury for the purposes and in manner following; viz[t]., the sum of five thousand pounds, part of the aforesaid sum of eight thousand and two hundred pounds, shall be appl[y][*i*]ed for discharging what is due for putting the province into a better state of defence, for paying off such officers and soldiers as are or may be in the province service, according to the several establishments for that purpose, for purchasing needful[l] warlike stores for the several forts and garrisons within this province, pursuant to such grants as are or shall be made by this court for those purposes; and the sum of three thousand pounds, part of the aforesaid sum of eight thousand two hundred pounds, shall be appl[y][*i*]ed for defreying the charge of the late intended expedition against Canada.

And whereas there are sometimes publick entertainments, and, from time to time, contingent and unforeseen charges that demand prompt payment,—

Be it further enacted,

£200 for entertainments, &c.

[SECT. 2.] That the sum of two hundred pounds, the remaining part of the aforesaid sum of eight thousand two hundred pounds, shall be appl[y][*i*]ed to defrey and pay such entertainments and contingent charges, and for no other use whatsoever.

And be it further enacted,

[SECT. 3.] That if there be a surplusage in any sum appropriated, such surplusage shall l[y][*i*]e in the hands of the treasurer for the further order of this court.

Surplusage to lie in the treasury.

And be it further enacted,

[SECT. 4.] That each and every warrant for drawing money out of the treasury, shall direct the treasurer to take the same out of such sums as are respectively appropriated for the payment of such publick debts as the drafts are made to discharge; and the treasurer is hereby directed and ordered to pay such money out of such appropriation as directed to, and no other, upon pain of refunding all such sum or sums as he shall otherwise pay, and to keep exact and distinct accompts of all payments made out of such appropriated sums; and the secretary to whom it belongs to keep the muster-rolls and accompts of charge, shall lay before the house, when they direct, all such muster-rolls and accompts after payment thereof.

Warrants to express the appropriations.

And as a fund and security for drawing the said sum of eight thousand two hundred pounds into the treasury again,—

Be it enacted,

[SECT. 5.] That there be and hereby is granted unto his most excellent majesty, for the ends and uses aforesaid, a tax of eight thousand two hundred pounds, to be levied on polls, and estates both real and personal, within this province, according to such rules and in such proportions on the several towns and districts within the same as shall be agreed upon and ordered by this court at their session in May, one thousand seven hundred and forty-seven, and paid into the publick treasury on or before the last day of December then next after.

£8,200 in 1747.

And be it further enacted,

[SECT. 6.] That in case the general court shall not at their session in May, one thousand seven hundred and forty-seven, agree and conclude upon an act apportioning the sum which by this act is engaged shall be in that year apportioned, assessed and levied, that then and in such case each town and district within this province shall pay, by a tax to be levied on the polls, and estates both real and personal, within their districts, the same proportion of the said sum as the said towns and districts shall have been taxed by the general court in the tax act then next preceeding; and the province treasurer is hereby fully impowered and directed, some time in the month of June, in the year one thousand seven hundred and forty-seven, to issue and send forth his warrants, directed to the selectmen or assessors of each town and district within this province, requiring them to assess the polls, and estates both real and personal, within their several towns and districts, for their respective part and proportion of the sum before directed and engaged to be assessed by this act; and the assessors, as also persons assessed, shall observe, be governed by and subject to all such rules and directions as shall have been given in the next preceeding tax act.

Tax for the money hereby emitted to be made according to the preceding tax act, in case.

And be it further enacted,

[SECT. 7.] That the inhabitants of this province shall have liberty, if they see fit[t], to pay the several sums for which they respectively may, in pursuance of this act, be assessed, in bills of credit of the form and tenor by this act emitted, or in other new-tenor bills, or in bills of the middle tenor, according to their several denominations, or in bills of the old tenor, accounting four for one; or in coined silver, at seven shillings and sixpence per ounce, troy weight, and of sterling alloy, or in gold coin, proportionably; or in merchantable hemp, flax, winter and Isle-of-Sable codfish, refined bar-iron, bloomery-iron, hollow iron-ware,

Taxes to be paid in the several species herein enumerated.

Indian corn, rye, wheat, barley, [pork], beef, [*pork*], duck or canvas, whalebone, cordage, train-oil, beeswax, bayberry-wax, tallow, peas[*e*], sheepswool, or tann'd sole-leather (the aforesaid commodities being of the produce or manufactures of this province), at such moderate rates and prices as the general assembly of the year one thousand seven hundred and forty-seven, shall set[t] them at; the several persons paying their taxes in any of the commodities before mentioned, to run the risque and pay the charge of transporting the said commodities to the province treasury; but if the aforesaid general assembly shall not, at their session in May, some time before the twentieth day of June, in said year, agree upon and set[t] the aforesaid species and commodities at some certain price, that then the eldest counc[i][*e*]ll[e][*o*]r, for the time being, in each of those counties in the province, of which any one of the council is an inhabitant, together with the province treasurer, or the major part of them, be a committee, who are hearby directed and fully authorized and impowered to do it; and in their set[*t*]ling the prices and rating the value of those commodities, to state so much of them, respectively, at seven shillings and sixpence as an ounce of silver will purchase at that time in the town of Boston, and so *pro ratâ*. And the treasurer is hereby directed to insert in the several warrants by him sent to the several collectors of [*the*] taxes in said year, with the names of the afore-recited commodities, the several rates or prices which shall be set on them, either by the general assembly or the committee aforesaid, and direct the aforesaid collectors to receive them so.

How the commodities brought into the treasury are to be rated.

[SECT. 8.] And the aforesaid commodities so brought into the treasury, shall, as soon as may be, be disposed of by the treasur[er][*y*] to the best advantage for so much as they will fetch in bills of credit hereby to be emitted, or for silver or gold, which silver and gold shall be delivered to the possessor of said bills in exchange for them; that is to say, one ounce of silver coin, and so gold in proportion, for seven shillings and sixpence, and so *pro ratâ* for a greater or less sum; and if any loss shall happen by the sale of the aforesaid species, or by any unforeseen accident, such deficiency shall be made good by a tax of the year next following, so as fully and effectually to call in the whole sum of eight thousand two hundred pounds in said bills hereby ordered to be issued; and if there be a surplusage, it shall remain a stock in the treasury. [*Passed January* 29; *published March* 2, 1746-47.

CHAPTER 21.

AN ACT TO REVIVE AND AMEND AN ACT MADE IN THE EIGHTEENTH YEAR OF HIS PRESENT MAJESTY'S REIGN, INTITLED "AN ACT FOR LEVYING SOLDIERS."

Preamble. 1744-45, chap. 2.

WHEREAS an act made in the eighteenth year of his present majesty's reign, entitled "An Act for levying soldiers," which was to continue in force from the publication thereof to the end of the session of the general court in May, 1746, is near expiring,—

Be it therefore enacted by the Governour, Council and House of Representatives,

All matters and things in the former law for levying soldiers revived, saving.

[SECT. 1.] That the said act, and all the matters and things therein contained, shall be and are [herein and] hereby enacted, declared and appointed to be and continue in full force, power and virtue until[l] the first day of June, which will be in the year of our Lord one thousand seven hundred and forty-eight, and from thence to the end of the session of the general court then next after: *provided* the war with the French king, his allies and vassals, shall continue so long; save in such particulars as by this present act is or are hereinafter altered or amended.

And whereas in and by a clause in the afores[*ai*]d act, it is enacted and declared, "That every person liable and fit for service, being orderly impressed as aforesaid for his majesty's service, by being commanded, in his majesty's name, to attend said service, shall, by himself or other meet person in his room, to the acceptance of his captain or chief officer, attend the same at time and place appointed, compleat with arms and ammunition, if such he have, or is able to purchase the same, on pain of suffering six months' imprisonment without bail or mainprize, or * be committed by mittimus from any justice of the peace, or chief officer of the company or troop, where no justice of the peace lives in the town, upon conviction, before one of his majesty's justices of the peace, of such neglect, unless such person, within the space of twenty-four hours next after being impressed, shall either procure some meet person, or, in default thereof, pay to his captain or chief officer, by whose warrant he shall be impressed, the sum of ten pounds, to be employed for the procuring and fitting out of a suitable person in the stead of him so paying the said sum, for the service for which he was impressed, if such other suitable person be timely to be had, otherwise to be paid to the selectmen of the town to which such impressed person belongs, for and towards procuring of arms for such person[s] as are unable to purchase the same for themselves, and for which such indigent soldiers shall be answerable,"— Clause in the former act recited and enacted. 1744-45, chap. 2, § 7.

Be it enacted and declared,

[SECT. 2.] That the aforesaid clause be and hereby is so far altered and amended, as that the said penalty of imprisonment shall be for the term of twelve months; and all sums that shall be paid, by any person impressed, to the chief officer of any companies, and which shall not be employed for procuring and fitting out a suitable person in the stead of him so paying, shall, by such officer, be paid into the town treasury sometime before the annual meeting of such town in March in each and every year, for the use of such town; and such officer shall give in to the treasurer of said town an attested account of the sums by him received and paid; and upon such officer's neglecting to render such account and pay such sum as shall be due, the said town treasurer is hereby impowered to demand and sue therefor accordingly; anything in the said recited act to the contrary notwithstanding.

And whereas in and by another clause in the aforesaid act it is provided, "That all persons lawfully impowered to impress, may pursue any person that absconds from the impress, or makes his escape, and may impress such person in any place within the province; and if any person impressed as aforesaid for his majesty's service, being so duly returned, shall remove or go out of the province, and not attend the service as required, such person, at his return, shall be apprehended by warrant from any justice of the peace,† and upon due conviction of the said offence by the oath of him that impressed him, shall suffer six months' imprisonment, or pay a fine of fifteen pounds,"— Clause in the former act recited and enacted. 1744-45, chap. 2, § 9.

Be it enacted,

[SECT. 3.] That during the continuance of this act, the said penalty of imprisonment shall be for and during the term of twelve months, and the said fine shall be twenty pounds; anything in the said recited clause to the contrary notwithstanding.

* "to," in the former act, omitted here.

† "and be by him committed to prison unless such person give sufficient security to answer it at the next court of general sessions of the peace" omitted here.

Clause in the former act recited and enacted.

1744-45, chap. 2, § 13.

And whereas in and by another clause in said act it is provided and declared, "That every person who hath or shall impress any soldiers for his majesty's service, shall transmit a list of them to the chief officer of the regiment or troop[*s*], particularly mentioning servants, if any such there be, and to whom they belong, that so their masters may receive their wages, who are hereby impowered so to do,"—

Be it further enacted,

[SECT. 4.] That in any and every such list there shall likewise be particularly mentioned all such as are sons under age, that so their parents may receive such wages as may be due for their service. [*Passed February* 13; *published March* 2, 1746-47.*

CHAPTER 22.

AN ACT FOR REVIVING AND CONTINUING SUNDRY LAWS OF THIS PROVINCE EXPIRED OR NEAR EXPIRING.

Preamble.

1736-37, chap. 4.

1740-41, chap. 15.

1743-44, chap. 16. 1744-45, chap. 27.

1742-43, chap. 28.

1742-43, chap. 11.

1743-44, chap. 14.

1743-44, chap. 21.

WHEREAS an act was made and pass'd in the ninth and tenth year of his present majesty's reign, intitled "An Act to enable the overseers of the poor, and selectmen, to take care of idle and disorderly persons"; and another act was made and pass'd in the fourteenth year of his said majesty's reign, intitled "An Act to prevent dam[*m*]age being done to the harbour of Cape Cod by cattle and horse-kind feeding on Provincetown lands"; in addition whereto, and for rendring the said act more effectual, there were two other acts pass'd, one in the seventeenth and the other in the eighteenth year of his said majesty's reign; and another act was made and pass'd in the sixteenth year of his said majesty's reign, intitled "An Act in further addition to and explanation of an act for regulating townships, choice of town officers, &c."; and another act was made and passed in the same year, intitled "An Act to prevent dam[*m*]age being done to Billingsgate Bay, in the town of Eastham, by cattle, horse-kind, and sheep feeding on the beach and islands adjoining thereto"; and another act was made and pass'd in the seventeenth year of his said majesty's reign, intitled "An Act to prevent the destruction of white-pine trees within this province, and to encourage the preservation of the same for the use of the royal navy"; and another act was made and pass'd in the same year, intitled "An Act to regulate the expence of private bridges": which laws are expired or near expiring; *and whereas* the aforesaid laws have by experiecne been found beneficial and necessary for the several purposes for which they were pass'd,—

Be it therefore enacted by the Governour, Council and House of Representatives,

The foregoing laws revived enacted.

That all and every of the aforesaid acts, and every matter and clause therein contained, be, and hereby are, revived, and shall continue and remain in force until[l] the last day of January, whi[ll][*ch*] will be in the year of our Lord one thousand seven hundred and fifty-six, and to the end of the session of the general court then next after. [*Passed February* 5; *published March* 2, 1746-47.

* The bill was passed to be enacted, by both branches, September 5, but was signed by the Governor as above, and was printed with the acts of this session.

CHAPTER 23.

AN ACT FOR REVIVING AND CONTINUING A LAW OF THIS PROVINCE, INTITLED "AN ACT FOR PUNISHING OF OFFICERS OR SOLDIERS WHO SHALL MUTINY OR DESERT HIS MAJESTY'S SERVICE."

WHEREAS an act was made and pass'd in the eighteenth year of his present majesty's reign, intitled "An Act for punishing of officers or soldiers who shall mutiny or desert his majesty's service," which law hath been found beneficial, and is judged necessary, but is now expired,— Preamble. 1744-45, chap. 11.

Be it therefore enacted by the Governour, Council and House of Representatives,

That the said act, and every matter and clause therein contained, be and hereby is revived, and shall continue and remain in full force for the space of three years from the publication hereof, in case the war with France continue so long, or otherwise to the end of the said war, and no longer. [*Passed February* 10; *published March* 2, 1746–47. Act against mutiny and desertion revived and enacted.

ACTS

PASSED AT THE SESSION BEGUN AND HELD AT BOSTON, ON THE SIXTEENTH DAY OF APRIL, A. D. 1747.

CHAPTER 24.

AN ACT FOR ESTABLISHING AND REGULATING FEES WITHIN THIS PROVINCE.

Preamble. 1692-93, chap. 37. 1701-2, chap. 7. 1744-45, chap. 13. 1745-46, chap. 10.

WHEREAS some services of a publick nature have no fees stated by law, and others, which have been established by two acts, made in the fourth and thirteenth years of King William the Third, by reason of the alteration of circumstances are become unequal,—

Be it therefore enacted by the Governour, Council and House of Representatives,

Rates of fees for officers.

[SECT. 1.] That from and after the publication of this act, the following fees, in bills of credit emitted for the supply of the treasury in the year one thousand seven hundred and forty-one, or in other province bills of the last form and tenor, at the choice of the payer, may be taken for the future; viz[t].,—

JUSTICE'S FEES.

For granting a writ, summons or original summons, sixpence.
Subpœna, for each witness, threepence.
Entring an action or complaint, one shilling and sixpence.
Writ of execution, one shilling.
Filing papers, each one penny.
Taxing a bill of cost, threepence.
Entring up judgment in civil or criminal cases, ninepence.
Bond for appeal, sixpence.
Copy of every evidence, original papers or records, sixpence per page for each page of twenty-eight lines, eight words in a line: if less th[a][*e*]n a page, threepence.
Each recognizance, one shilling.
Confessing judgment, sixpence.
Taking affidavits out of their own courts in order to the trial of any cause, one shilling,—
in other cases, together with certificate, examining and entry, sixpence,—
in perpetuam, to each justice, one shilling.
Acknowledging an instrument with one or more seals, provided it be done at one and the same time, one shilling.
A warrant, sixpence.
Each day's attendance at the session, to be paid out of the fines, two shillings.
Allowance to the party for whom costs shall be taxed, one shilling per day, ten miles' travel to be accounted one day.

For witnesses in civil causes, one shilling and sixpence per day, and ten miles' travel to be accounted one day.

For granting a warrant, swearing apprizers relating to strays, and entring the same, one shilling and sixpence.

CORONER'S FEES.

For serving a writ, summons or execution, and travelling fees, the same as by this act is hereafter allowed to sheriffs.

Bail bond, sixpence.

Every trial where the sheriff is concerned, ninepence.

Taking an inquisition, to be paid out of the deceased's estate, six shillings and eightpence; if more than one at the same time, ten shillings in the whole; if no estate, then, to be paid by the county treasurer, three shillings and fourpence,—and for more th[a][*e*]n one, five shillings.

For travelling and expences for taking an inquisition, each day, six shillings.

The foreman of the jury, three shillings; and, ten miles accounted a day's trav[i][*e*]l, one shilling per day;—

every other juror, two shillings and sixpence, and trav[i][*e*]l the same as [*the*] foreman.

JUDGE OF PROBATE AND REGISTER'S FEES.

For granting administration or guardianship, bonds, and letters of administration and guardianship,—

to the judge, two shillings.

To the register, for writing bond of administration or guardianship, one shilling and ninepence.

for writing letters of administration or letters of guardianship, one shilling and sixpence.

For granting guardianship of divers[e] minors to the same person at the same time: to the judge, for each minor, one shilling; to the register, for each letter of guardianship and bond, as before.

Proving a will or codicil; one shilling and ninepence to the judge, and one shilling and threepence to the register.

Recording a will, letter of administration or guardianship, inventory or account, of one page, and filing the same, one shilling and threepence.

for every page more, of twenty-eight lines, of eight words in a line, ninepence.

For copy of a will or inventory, the same for each page, as before.

Allowing accounts, two shillings and sixpence; decre[*e*] for set[*t*]ling of intestate estates: to the judge, two shillings and sixpence,—

to the register, for examining such accounts, one shilling.

A citation: to the register, ninepence.

A *quietus:* to the judge, one shilling; to the register, one shilling.

Warrant or commission for appri[s][*z*]ing or dividing estates; one shilling to the judge, one shilling to the register.

Making out commission to receive and examine the claims of creditors to insolvent estates; to the judge, one shilling, to the register, one shilling: for recording the same, one shilling and sixpence.

Registring the commissioner's report, each page, ninepence, as above.

Making out and entring an order upon the administrators for the distribution of the estate, one shilling.

For proportioning such estate among the creditors, agre[e]able to the commissioner's return, when the estate exceeds not fifty pounds; to the register, two shillings, and, above that sum, three shillings.
For recording the same, ninepence per page, as before.

IN THE SUPERIOUR COURT.

JUSTICE'S FEES.

Entring an action, five shillings.
Taking a special bail, one shilling.
Allowing a writ of error, one shilling and sixpence.
Allowing an *habeas corpus*, one shilling.
Taxing a bill of cost, sixpence.
Attorney's fee, to be allowed in the bill of cost taxed, six shillings.
Granting liberty for the sale or partition of real estates, two shillings.
On receiving each petition, one shilling.

CLERK'S FEES.

On entring an action, one shilling.
A writ of *scire facias*, one shilling and sixpence.
A writ of review, two shillings and sixpence;—
if more than one page, ninepence per page, as before.
Entring a rule of court, sixpence.
Filing a declaration, sixpence.
Entring an appearance, threepence.
Signing a judgment by default, sixpence.
Receiving and recording a verdict, sixpence.
Copies of all records, each page, of twenty-eight lines, eight words in a line, ninepence;—
if less than one page, sixpence.
Every action withdrawn or nonsuit, sixpence.
Every petition read, sixpence; order thereon, sixpence.
Filing the papers of each cause, one penny per paper.
Every execution, one shilling.
Writ of *habeas corpus*, two shillings.
Drawing bail bond, one shilling.
Confessing judgment, one shilling.
Acknowledging satisfaction of a judgment, on record, sixpence.
Examining each bill of cost, sixpence.
Continuing each cause, and entring the next term, sixpence.
Entring up judgment and copying the same, one shilling,
To each *venire*, to be paid out of the county treasuries, respectively, by order from any three of the justices of said court, threepence.

IN THE INFERIO[U]R COURT OF COMMON PLEAS, AND COURT OF GENERAL SESSIONS.

JUSTICE'S FEES.

Entry of every action, four shillings.
Taxing a bill of cost, sixpence.
Attorney's fee, to be allowed in the bill of cost taxed, five shillings.
Taking recognizance on appeals, sixpence.
Each recognizance in granting licences, one shilling.
Proving each deed, two shillings.
Granting every licence for publick entertainment, one shilling.

CLERK'S FEES.

Every action entred, one shilling.
Every writ and seal, sixpence.
Every appearance, sixpence.
Entring and recording a verdict, sixpence.
Recording a judgment, one shilling.
Copies of all records, each page, as before, ninepence.
Every action withdrawn or nonsuit, sixpence.
Every execution, one shilling.
Taking special bail, one shilling; confessing judgment, or default, sixpence.
Acknowledging satisfaction of a judgment on record, sixpence.
Writ of *habe*[u][*a*]*s corpus*, two shillings.
Continuing each cause, and entry at the next court, sixpence.
Entring up judgment, and copying, one shilling.
Examining each bill of cost, sixpence.
Each recognizance, one shilling.
Each *venire*, to be paid out of the county treasuries, respectively, by order of court, threepence.
Writ of *facias habere possessionem*, two shillings.
Filing each paper, one penny.

CLERKS OF THE SESSIONS' FEES.

Entring a complaint or indictment, one shilling.
Discharging a recognizance, sixpence.
Each warrant against criminals, sixpence.
Each summons or subpœna, threepence.
Every recognizance for the peace or good behaviour, one shilling.
Granting every licence for publick entertainment or retailing, one shilling.
For each recognizance, one shilling.
Entring up judgment, or entring satisfaction of judgment, on record, and copying, one shilling.
Warrant for county tax, sixpence.
For min[i]uting the receipt of each petition, and order thereon, and recording, ninepence per page, as before.
Examining and casting the grand jur[or][*y*]'s account, yearly, and order thereon, to be paid by the county treasurer by order of the court of sessions, one shilling and sixpence.
For cop[y][*ie*]s of all original papers or records, ninepence per page, as before.
For filing each paper, one penny.

SHERIFF'S OR CONSTABLE'S FEES.

For serving an original summons, one shilling.
Every *capeas* or attachment in civil, or warrants in criminal, cases for trial, one shilling; and for travel out and to return the writ (the travel to be certified on the back of the writ or orginal summons), one penny halfpenny per mile.
Serving execution in personal action, if twenty pounds or under, one shilling per pound; for all others, not exceeding forty pounds, twelvepence per pound [for] [*of*] twenty pounds thereof, and sixpence per pound for the remaining; for all others, not exceeding one hundred pounds, for forty pounds thereof, as for an execution not exceeding forty pounds, and for the remaining part, fourpence per pound; and all others, above one hundred pounds,

for one hundred pounds thereof, as for an execution not exceeding one hundred pounds, and for the remaining part, twopence per pound.

For travel out, and to return the execution, twopence per mile; all travel to be accounted from the court-house in each shire town in each county: except for justices' writs, the travel[l] for which to be accounted from the place from whence the writ issues.

For serving an execution upon a judgment of court for partition of real estate, to the sheriff, seven shillings and sixpence per day; and for travel and expences, fourpence halfpenny per mile out from the place of his abode; and to each juror, three shillings and ninepence per day; and for travel[l] and expences, fourpence halfpenny per mile.

For giving livery and seizin of real estates, seven shillings and sixpence; travel as before: or if different parcels of land, five shillings each.

Every trial, sixpence.

Every default, threepence.

A ba[i]l[e] bond, sixpence.

Every precept for the choice of representatives, one shilling; to be paid out of the county treasuries, respectively.

To the officer attending the grand jury, each day, one shilling and sixpence.

CRYER'S FEES.

Calling the jury, threepence.

A nonsuit or default, sixpence.

A verdict, sixpence.

A judgment affirmed on a complaint, sixpence.

GOALER'S FEES.

For turning the key on each person committed, two shillings and sixpence; viz[t]., one shilling and threepence in, and one shilling and threepence out.

For dieting each person, three shillings and ninepence per week.

MESSENGER OF THE HOUSE OF REPRESENTATIVES' FEES.

For serving every warrant from the house of representatives, which they may grant for arresting, imprisoning, or taking into custody any person, one shilling and sixpence.

For travel, each mile out, twopence per mile.

For keeping and providing food for such person, each day, two shillings and sixpence.

For his discharge or dismission, one shilling and sixpence, to be paid as by law already provided.

GRAND JUROR'S FEES.

Foreman, per day, two shillings and sixpence.

Each other juror, two shillings.

PETIT JUROR'S FEES.

To the foreman, in every case at the superiour court, one shilling and ninepence; for every other juror, one shilling and sixpence.

To the foreman, in every case at the inferiour court or sessions, one shilling and threepence; to every other juror, one shilling.

FOR MARRIAGES.

For each marriage, to the minister or justice officiating, two shillings and sixpence.

For recording it; to the town clerk, to be paid by the justice or minister, sixpence; and to the clerk of the session[s], to be paid by the town clerk, threepence.

To the town clerk, for every publishment of the banns of matrimony, and entring thereof, one shilling.

Every certificate of such publishment, ninepence.

Recording births and deaths, each, fourpence.

For every certificate of the birth or death of any person, threepence.

For every search of record, when no copy is required, threepence.

COUNTY REGISTER'S FEES.

For entring or recording any deed, conveyance or mortgage, for the first page, ninepence; and sixpence per page for so many pages more as it shall contain, accounting after the rate of twenty-eight lines, of eight words to a line, to each page, and proportionably for so much more as shall be under a page; and threepence for his attestation on the original, of the time, book and folio where it is recorded;—

and for a discharge of a mortgage, as aforesaid, sixpence.

GOVERNOUR'S AND SECRETARY'S FEES.

For registers: to the governour, five shillings; to the secretary, two shillings and sixpence.

For certificates under the province seal: to the governour, five shillings; to the secretary, two shillings and sixpence.

For warrants of appri[s][*z*]ement[*s*], survey, &c.: to the governour, three shillings; to the secretary, three shillings.

To the governour, for a pass to the castle, for each vessel[l], one shilling and threepence: wood-sloops and other coasting vessel[l]s, for which passes have not been usually required, excepted.

For a certificate of naval stores, in the whole, five shillings.

Be it further enacted,

[SECT. 2.] That if any of the officers aforesaid shall demand and take any greater or other fees for the matters before mentioned, or any of them, than are allowed to be demanded and taken by this act, and shall be thereof convict, they shall forfeit and pay for each offence the sum of ten pounds, to be appl[y][*i*]ed, the one moiety thereof for and towards the support of this government, and the other moiety to him or them that shall sue for the same; to be recovered by action, bill, plaint or information, in any court of record proper to try the same. And all officers to whom any warrant, summons, capias or attachment shall be committed, and who shall receive fees for the service thereof, are hereby required, without unnecessary delay, to serve and execute the same, on forfeiture of ten pounds, to be recovered and applied as aforesaid, besides making good such dam[*m*]ages as the party may sustain by such delay: *provided*, in civil causes, the fees for trav[i][*e*]l and service be first tend[e]red and paid if required by such officers. **Penalty for taking excessive fees.**

[SECT. 3.] This act to continue and be in force one year from the publication thereof, and no longer. [*Passed April* 25; *published April* 27, 1747. **Limitation.**

CHAPTER 25.

AN ACT FOR SUPPLYING THE TREASURY WITH THE SUM OF TWENTY THOUSAND POUNDS, IN BILLS OF CREDIT, FOR DISCHARGING THE PUBLICK DEBTS, AND FOR DRAWING THE SAID BILLS INTO THE TREASURY AGAIN.

Be it enacted by the Governour, Council and House of Representatives,

£20,000 bills of credit, to be emitted.

[SECT. 1.] That the treasurer be and hereby is impowered and ordered to issue forth the sum of twenty thousand pounds in bills of credit of the last tenor and date, now lying in his hands and received in for taxes, impost and excise, which shall pass in all publick and private payments equal to other new-tenor bills issued since one thousand seven hundred and forty; or, if there be not a sufficiency of such bills, that then the committee appointed by this court for signing bills, are hereby directed and impow[e]red to take care and make effectual provision, as soon as may be, to imprint so many as may be needed to compleat the said sum, and to sign and deliver the same to the treasurer, taking his receipt for the same; and the said committee shall be under oath for the faithful[l] performance of the trust by this act reposed in them; and the said sum of twenty thousand pounds shall be issued out of the publick treasury for the purposes and in manner following; viz[t]., the sum of twelve thousand pounds, part of the aforesaid sum of twenty thousand pounds, shall be applied for discharging such debts as are or may be due for putting the province into a better posture of defence, compleating the repairs at Castle William and other fortifications, and for paying the officers and soldiers employ[e]'d for the defence of the province, pursuant to such grants as are or shall be made by this court; and the sum of one thousand pounds, part of the aforesaid sum of twenty thousand pounds, shall be apply[e]'d for the discharge of debts owing from this province to persons that have served or shall serve them by order of this court, in such matters and things where there is no establishment, nor any certain sum assigned for such services; and the sum of three thousand pounds, part of the aforesaid sum of twenty thousand pounds, shall be applied for defr[e][*a*]ying the charge of the late intended expedition against Canada; and the sum of three thousand five hundred pounds, part of the aforesaid sum of twenty thousand pounds, shall be applied for the payment of grants made or to be made by this court, and any other matters and things which this court have or shall by law or order provide for the payment of out of the publick treasury, and for no other service whatsoever; and the sum of five hundred pounds, the remainder of the said sum of twenty thousand pounds, shall be applied for the payment of the members of the house of representatives, during the present year.

And be it further enacted,

Surplusage to lie in the treasury.

[SECT. 2.] That if there be a surplusage in any sum appropriated, such surplusage shall l[y][*i*]e in the treasury for the further order of this court.

And be it further enacted,

Warrants to express the appropriations.

[SECT. 3.] That each and every warrant for drawing money out of the treasury, shall direct the treasurer to take the same out of such sums as are respectively appropriated for the payment of such publick debts as the drafts are made to discharge; and the treasurer is hereby directed and ordered to pay such money out of such appropriations as directed to, and no other, upon pain of refunding all such sum or sums as he shall otherwise pay, and to keep exact and distinct accompts of all payments made out of such appropriated sums; and the secretary, to whom it belongs to keep the muster-rolls and accompts of charge, shall lay before the house, when they direct, all such muster-rolls and accompts after payment thereof.

And as a fund and security for drawing the said sum of twenty thousand pounds into the treasury again,—

Be it enacted,

[SECT. 4.] That there be and hereby is granted unto his most excellent majesty for the ends and uses aforesaid, a tax of nine thousand seven hundred and fifty pounds, to be levied on polls, and estates both real and personal, within this province, according to such rules and in such proportion on the several towns and districts within the same, as shall be agreed upon and ordered by this court at their session in May, one thousand seven hundred and forty-seven, and paid into the publick treasury on or before the last day of December then next after. £9,750 in 1747.

And as a further fund and security for drawing the said sum of twenty thousand pounds into the treasury again,—

Be it enacted,

[SECT. 5.] That there be and hereby is granted unto his most excellent majesty, for the ends and uses aforesaid, a tax of nine thousand seven hundred and fifty pounds, to be levied on polls, and estates both real and personal, within this province, according to such rules and in such proportions on the several towns and districts within the same, as shall be agreed upon and ordered by this court at their session in May, one thousand seven hundred and forty-eight, and paid into the publick treasury on or before the last day of December then next after. £9,750 in 1748.

And as a fund and security for drawing in such sum or sums as shall be paid out to the representatives of the several towns,—

Be it enacted,

[SECT. 6.] That there be and hereby is granted unto his most excellent majesty, a tax of such sum or sums as shall be paid to the several representatives as aforesaid, to be levied and assessed on the polls and estates of the inhabitants of the several towns, according to what their several representatives shall receive; which sums shall be set on the towns in the next province tax, and the assessors of the said towns shall make their assessment for this tax, and apportion the same according to the rules that shall be prescribed by the act of the general court for assessing the next province tax; and the constables in their respective districts shall pay in the same when they pay in the province tax for the next year, of which the treasurer is hereby directed to keep a distinct and seperate account; and if there be any surplusage, the same shall l[y][*i*]e in the hands of the treasurer for the further order of this court. Tax for the sum paid the representatives.

And be it further enacted,

[SECT. 7.] That in case the general court shall not, at their session in May, one thousand seven hundred and forty-seven, and one thousand seven hundred and forty-eight, agree and conclude upon an act apportioning the sum which, by this act, is engaged shall be in those years apportioned, assessed, and levied, that then and in such case each town and district within this province shall pay, by a tax to be levied on polls, and estates both real and personal, within their districts, the same proportion of the said sums as the said towns and districts shall have been taxed by the general court in the tax act then next preceeding; and the province treasurer is hereby fully impowered and directed, some time in the month of June, in the years one thousand seven hundred and forty-seven, and one thousand seven hundred and forty-eight, to issue and send forth his warrant, directed to the selectmen or assessors of each town and district within this province, requiring them to assess the Tax for the money hereby emitted, to be made according to the preceding tax act, in case.

polls, and estates both real and personal, within their several towns and districts, for their respective part and proportion of the sum before directed and engaged to be assessed by this act; and the assessors, as also persons assessed, shall observe, be governed by, and subject to all such rules and directions as shall have been given in the next preceeding tax act.

And be it further enacted,

Taxes to be paid in the several species herein enumerated.

[SECT. 8.] That the inhabitants of this province shall have liberty, if they see fit, to pay the several sums for which they respectively may, in pursuance of this act, be assessed, in bills of credit of the form and tenor by this act emitted, or in other new-tenor bills, or in bills of the middle tenor, according to their several denominations, or in bills of the old tenor, accounting four for one; or in coined silver, at seven shillings and sixpence per ounce, troy weight, and of sterling alloy, or in gold coin, proportionably; or in merchantable hemp, flax, winter and Isle-of-Sable codfish, refined bar-iron, bloomery-iron, hollow iron-ware, Indian corn, rye, wheat, barley, pork, beef, duck or canvis, whalebone, cordage, train-oil, beeswax, bayberry-wax, tallow, pease, sheepswool, or tann'd sole-leather (the aforesaid commodities being of the produce or manufactures of this province), at such moderate rates and prices as the general assembl[ie][*y*]s of the years one thousand seven hundred and forty-seven, and one thousand seven hundred and forty-eight shall set them at; the several persons paying their taxes in any of the commodities before mentioned, to run the risque and pay the charge of transporting the said commodities to the province treasury; but if the aforesaid general assembl[ies][*y*] shall not, at their sessions in May, some time before the twentieth day of June, in each year, agree upon and set[t] the aforesaid species and commodities at some certain price, that then the eldest councellor, for the time being, of each of those counties in the province, of which any one of the councellors is an inhabitant, together with the province treasurer, or the major part of them, be a committee, who hereby are directed and fully authorized and impowered to do it; and in their set[*t*]ling the prices and rating the value of those commodities, to state so much of them, respectively, at seven shillings and sixpence as an ounce of silver will purchase at that time in the town of Boston, and so *pro ratâ*. And the treasurer is hereby directed to insert in the several warrants by him sent to the several collectors of the taxes in each year, with the names of the afore-recited commodities, and the several prices or rates which shall be set on them, either by the general assembly or the committee aforesaid, and direct the aforesaid collectors to receive them so.

How the commodities brought into the treasury are to be rated.

[SECT. 9.] And the aforesaid commodities, so brought into the treasury, shall, as soon as may be, be disposed of by the treasurer to the best advantage for so much as they will fetch in bills of credit hereby to be emitted, or for silver or gold, which silver and gold shall be delivered to the possessor of said bills in exchange for them; that is to say, one ounce of silver coin, and so gold in proportion, for seven shillings and sixpence, and so *pro ratâ* for a greater or less sum; and if any loss shall happen by the sale of the aforesaid species, or by any unforeseen accident, such d[if][*e*]ficiency shall be made good by a tax of the year next following, so as fully and effectually to call in the whole sum of twenty thousand pounds in said bills hereby ordered to be emitted; and if there be a surplusage, it shall remain a stock in the treasury. [*Passed April* 7*; *published April* 27, 1747.

* This date is according to the record, but the date of signing, according to the engrossment, is April 8.

CHAPTER 26.

AN ACT FOR THE BETTER REGULATING SWINE.

Be it enacted by the Governour, Council and House of Represent-[ati]ves,

[SECT. 1.] That from and after the publication of this act, no swine shall be suffered to go at large, or be out of the inclosure of the owner thereof, under the penalty of one shilling for each swine, for the first offence, and two shillings for each offence after the first, together with costs of prosecution, to be forfeited and paid by the owner of such swine found going at large, as aforesaid; which fine or forfeiture, together with the charge of prosecution, may be recovered by the proper hogreeves or any other person, by bill, plaint or information, before any one of his majesty's justices of the peace in such county where such forfeiture shall arise, or by impounding such swine, and proceeding with them as the law hath directed in case of impounding. Swine not to go at large, on penalty. 1736-37, chap. 22.

And whereas it may so happen that the owner of such swine as go at large may not be known,—

[SECT. 2.] In such case the party that finds any swine going at large shall have power to impound them; and if no owner appear within forty-eight hours, or appearing, do neglect or refuse to pay the forfeiture, together with the charges, that then the party impounding them shall cause them to be cried or posted up in the town where they are impounded, and in the [two] towns next adjoining; and shall likewise cause the marks of the swine to be entred with the town clerk, and shall rel[ei][*ie*]ve such swine with necessary food during the time they are in pound; and if no owner appear, and pay the said penalty and charges, within ten days after such impounding, then such swine shall be sold at an outcry to the highest bidder, by two suitable persons, to be appointed and sworn to the faithful discharge of their trust by the next justice of the peace, or town clerk where no justice dwells; which sellers shall give publick notice of the time and place of such sale twenty-four hours before hand; and out of the proceeds of such sale shall pay unto the party the said forfeiture and costs, as by bill allowed by said justice or town clerk, and the surplusage thereof he shall deliver to the treasurer of such town, to be kept for the unknown owner; and if no owner do appear within the space of one year, then the town treasurer shall deliver the one half of the surplusage to the prosecutor, and the other half to the overseers of the poor, for the use of the poor of such town: *provided, nevertheless*, that it shall be in the power of any town, in a town meeting for that purpose appointed, from time to time, by a vote, to give liberty for swine going at large within the bounds of such town; and in such case it shall be lawful for any and every person or persons to suffer his or their swine to go at large, anything in this act contained to the contrary notwithstanding: *provided, always*, that every person suffering his swine to go at large by virtue of such town vote, shall, before he suffer his swine to go at large, as afores[*ai*]d, cause each of them to be well and sufficiently ringed in the nose and yoked, and constantly kept so ringed and yoked; otherwise he shall be liable to, and shall pay, the forfeiture and cost, as is by this act before mentioned and provided; *saving*, that they may go unyoked from the last day of October to the first day of April. Swine to be impounded and sold, if no owner appear. Proviso. Swine going at large to be yoked.

And to the intent all persons may know what a sufficient yoking doth mean,—

It is hereby declared,

[SECT. 3.] That no yoke shall be accounted sufficient, which is not Sufficient yoke.

the full depth of the swine's neck above the neck, and half so much below the neck, and the soal or bottom of the yoke three times as long as the breadth or thickness of the swine's neck.

And for the rendring this act more effectual,—

Be it further enacted,

Hog-reeves to be annually chosen.

[SECT. 4.] That every town within the province, at their annual meeting in March, for the choice of town officers, shall chuse two or more hogreeves, but not the same persons more than once in four years; and in case any town shall at any time hereafter neglect to ch[u][*oo*]se hogreeves at such meeting, that in every such case the selectmen of the town are impow[e]red and [re][*in*]quired to appoint hogreeves, until[l] a suitable number do accept and are sworn, whose duty it shall be, upon complaints to them or either of them made, to take due care that this act be duly observed, and to prosecute the breakers thereof; which hogreeves shall be sworn to the faithful and impartial discharge of their office; and if any person so chosen or appointed shall refuse or neglect forthwith to be sworn as afores[*ai*]d, or neglect his duty in s[*ai*]d office, he shall forfeit and pay twenty shillings to the use of the poor of such town; and upon his refusal, another shall be forthwith appointed in his room by the selectmen, to be under the like penalty, and so 'till others will accept the s[*ai*]d office; w[*hi*]ch penalty shall be recovered by a prosecution before one of his majesty's justices of the peace in the county where such person dwells. And if, upon neglect of any town to chuse according as by this act they are required, the selectmen of such town shall fail of appointing hogreeves, as they are by this act directed, they shall forfeit and pay the sum of twenty pounds for such neglect; the one half to his majesty, for and towards the support of the governm[*en*]t, the other half to him or them that shall prosecute for such neglect in any of his maj[*es*]ty's courts of record within this province; and if it shall appear that any of the selectmen were ready and willing to do their duty required by this act, the penalty or forfeiture shall be laid on those only who shall be negligent of their duty by this act required.

Penalty for neglect or refusal.

Provided,

Limitation.

[SECT. 5.] That this act continue and be in force for the space of ten years from the publication thereof, and to the end of the then next sitting of the general court, and no longer. [*Passed April* 25; *published April* 27, 1747.

CHAPTER 27.

AN ACT TO PREVENT DAMMAGE BEING DONE UNTO NOSSETT MEADOW, BY CATTLE AND HORSE-KIND FEEDING ON THE BEACH ADJOINING THERETO.

Preamble.

WHEREAS many persons frequently drive numbers of neat-cattle and horse-kind to feed upon the beach called Nossett Beach, adjoining to Nossett Meadow, in Eastham, whereby the ground is much broken, and the sand blown away, so that the said beach is in great danger of being totally broke away, and by that means the meadow adjoining will be greatly damnified, if not wholly lost,—

Be it therefore enacted by the Governour, Council and House of Representatives,

Proprietors empowered to erect and maintain a fence.

[SECT. 1.] That the proprietors of the meadow and beach, called Nossett Beach and Meadow, are hereby impowered, at their own cost and charge, according to each one's interest, to erect and maintain a fence, such a one as they shall agree upon, from the enclosed land of Joseph Mayo to the southerly end of the land called the Table-land at the seaside, for the preservation of said beach and meadow.

And it is further enacted,

[SECT. 2.] That from and after the publication of this act, no person or persons shall presume to turn or drive any neat cattle or horse-kind upon said meadow or beach between the first of March and the last of November annually, upon the penalty of ten shillings a head for all neat cattle and horse-kind that shall be turned or found feeding on said beach and meadow between the said first of March and last day of November aforesaid; which penalty shall be recovered by the selectmen or treasurer of the said town of Eastham, or any other person that shall inform and sue for the same, the one-half of the said forfeiture to him or them who shall inform and sue for the same, the other half to be to and for the use of the poor of said town. **Penalty for turning or driving cattle to feed on Nossett Meadow, &c.**

And be it further enacted,

[SECT. 3.] That if any ne[e][*a*]t cattle or horse-kind shall, at any time hereafter, be found feeding on the said beach or meadow, between the first of March and last of November as aforesaid, that it shall and may be lawful for any person to impound the same, and to proceed in every other respect agre[e]able to an act made in the sixteenth year of his present majesty's reign, entitled "An Act to prevent dammage being done unto Billingsgate Bay, in the town of Eastham, by cattle and horse-kind and sheep feeding on the beach and islands adjoining thereto"; and also said town to proceed in the method mentioned in the aforesaid act in their choice of officers, to look after said Nossett Meadow and Beach. **Cattle found feeding contrary to this act, to be impounded, &c.** **1742-43, chap. 11.**

[SECT. 4.] This act to continue and be in force for the space of five years from the publication thereof, and no longer. *Passed April* 25; *published April* 27, 1747.

CHAPTER 28.

AN ACT TO PREVENT THE DESTRUCTION OF THE MEADOW[S] CALLED SANDY-NECK MEADOW, IN BARNSTABLE, AND FOR THE BETTER PRESERVATION OF THE HARBOUR THERE.

WHEREAS there is a certain parcel[l] of salt meadow call[*e*]'d Sandy-Neck Meadow, in the township of Barnstable, on which many of the inhabitants of that and other towns, greatly depend for their hay, and the said meadow lies adjoining to a sandy beach near six miles in length, on which no fence can be made to stand; and by reason of neat cattle and horses being turned thereon to feed, the beach grass is destroyed, and the said beach trod loose, by reason whereof in high winds and storms the sand blows upon said meadow, and into said harbour, and the whole of said meadows are in great danger of being covered with sand, and also said harbour in great danger of being spoiled, by the sand's blowing therein, if not timely prevented,— **Preamble.**

Be it therefore enacted by the Governour, Council and House of Represent[ati]ves,

[SECT. 1.] That from and after the publication of this act, no person or persons shall presume to turn or drive any neat cattle or horse-kind, to or upon said Sandy Neck, any where to the eastward of Sandwich line, to feed thereon, upon the penalty of ten shillings a head for **No person to turn or drive cattle, &c., on Sandy Neck, on penalty.**

all neat cattle and horse-kind that shall be turned or found feeding on s[*ai*]d neck or meadow adjoining, which penalty shall be recovered by the selectmen or treasurer of said town of Barnstable, or any other person that shall inform and sue for the same; the one half of the said forfeiture to him or them who shall inform and sue for the same, the other half to be to and for the use of the poor of the said town.

And be it further enacted,

Cattle, &c., found feeding contrary to this act, to be impounded, &c.

[SECT. 2.] That if any neat cattle or horse-kind shall, at any time hereafter, be found feeding on the s[*ai*]d Sandy Neck and meadows adjoining east of Sandwich line as afores[*ai*]d, that it shall and may be lawful for any person to impound the same, immediately giving notice to the owners, if known, otherwise to give publick notice thereof in the s[*ai*]d town of Barnstable, and the two next adjoining towns; and the impounder shall rel[ei][*ie*]ve the said creatures with suitable meat and water while impounded; and if the owner thereof appear, he shall pay the sum of two shillings and sixpence to the impounder for each neat-beast and horse-kind, and the reasonable cost of rel[ei][*ie*]ving them, besides the pound-keeper's fees; and if no owner appear within the space of six days to redeem the said cattle or horse-kind so impounded, and to pay the dam[*m*]ages and costs occasioned by impounding the same, then and in every such case, the person or persons impounding such cattle or horse-kind, shall cause the same to be sold at publick vendue, to pay the costs and charges arising about the same, publick notice of the time and place of such sale to be given in s[*ai*]d town of Barnstable and in the town of Sandwich, forty-eight hours beforehand, and the overplus, if any there be, arising by such sale, to be returned to the owner of such cattle or horse-kind, at any time within twelve months next after, upon his demanding the same; but if no owner appear within said twelve months, then the overplus shall be one half to the party impounding, and the other half to the use of the poor of the s[*ai*]d town of Barnstable.

And be it further enacted,

Officers to be annually chosen.

[SECT. 3.] That the s[*ai*]d town of Barnstable, at their meeting in March, annually, for the choice of town officers, be authorized and impow[e]red to ch[u][*oo*]se one or more meet person or persons, whose duty it shall be to see that this act be observed, and prosecute the breakers thereof; who shall be sworn to the faithful discharge of their office: and in case any person so chosen shall refuse to be sworn, he shall forfeit and pay ten shillings to the poor of s[*ai*]d town of Barnstable, and said town to proceed to ch[u][*oo*]se others in their room; and the said town of Barnstable, at a town meeting, warned for that purpose, may, at any time before March next, ch[u][*oo*]se such officers, who shall continue [untill] [*to*] their annual meeting in March next.

Penalty for refusing.

Limitation.

[SECT. 4.] This act to continue and be in force for the space of five years from the publication thereof, and no longer. [*Passed April* 25; *published April* 27, 1747.

NOTES.—There were eight sittings of the General Court this year; but at the fourth and seventh no acts were passed. The May session was adjourned from June 28 to July 15; but this adjournment seems not to have been regarded as terminating the session, since chapter 8, which was passed July 25, was printed as the last act of the first session. The acts passed after July were printed under distinct captions; and the periods between the recesses of the Assembly are not distinguishable from other and regular sessions, except that, in each, the Assembly met after an adjournment, and not after a prorogation. According to the rule followed in this edition of the laws, these different periods of the Assembly's sitting are to be regarded as separate sessions.

The engrossments of all the acts of this year, except of the first seven chapters, are preserved; and all were printed with the sessions-acts, except chapter 1, which, being a tax-act, was printed separately.

The acts of the first three sessions were duly certified to the Privy Council, November 1, 1746. On the 27th of January they were referred to the Lords of Trade, and on the 18th of June, 1747, they were sent, by the latter, to Mr. Lamb, for his opinion thereon in point of law. This opinion was given in a report dated November 14, 1747, which is indorsed, "No objection. With observations on some." The report of the Lords of Trade is dated November 27, 1749, and sets forth that chapters 1, 2, 3, 4, 5, 7, 9, 10, 11, 13, and 14 "were for a Temporary service and are either expired, or the purposes for which they were enacted have been completed"; that chapters 6 and 12 "relate to the Œconomy of the Province and are enacted for their private Convenience and We see no reason why His Majesty may not be graciously pleased to confirm them." Chapter 8 was included with chapter 7 of the acts of 1745-46, in a special report, which has been printed in the note to that chapter, *ante*.

In accordance with the recommendations of the Lords of Trade, an order in Council was passed 14 December, 1749, confirming chapters 6, 8, and 12.

The five acts of the last session were enclosed, with a letter from Secretary Willard, to Secretary Hill, November 1, 1748. The minutes of the Privy Council show that these acts were received January 5, 1748-49. They reached the Board of Trade by the 8th of the next month. There, an order was passed that they be sent to Mr. Lamb. No further trace of these acts has been discovered in the Public-Record Office, and, as late as 1753, the records of the Board of Trade contain a memorandum that chapters 27 and 28 had "not been laid before the Crown."

As to the acts of the intervening sessions, it may be inferred that they were received by the Lords of Trade, from the following statement of Secretary Willard, in his letter of November 1, 1748, transmitting the acts of the 8th session: "The Minutes of the Assembly and the Laws are a continuation of what were sent you home by His Majesty's ship the Mermaid in the Summer 1747 without any interruption, the General Court Book for that time being accidentally saved out of the fire when the Court House was burnt," &c.

Chap. 1. "October 4th 1746. In the House of Representves Voted that the Parish Assessors of the Plantation of Natick be & hereby are impowred & directed to assess & the Parish Collectors, to collect, such sum as shall be set on the said plantation as their proportion of the Province & County Tax, And the Province Treasurer & the Treasurer of the County of Middlesex, are impowred & required from time to time to issue their Warrants accordingly. In Council Read & Concur'd Consented to by the Govern'r."—*Council Records, vol. XVIII., p.* 6.

"June 11. 1747. A Petition of the Town of Pembroke, praying to have the fine laid upon them the last year for not sending a Representative remitted to them in consideration of the small number of their Inhabitants and their poverty.

In the House of Represent.ves Read & Ordered that the sum of five pounds be allowed the Town of Pembroke out of the publick Treasury in consideration of the fine imposed upon them the last year as above mentioned.

In Council Read & Concur'd Consented to by the Governor."—*Ibid.*, p. 151.

Chap. 12. "Jany 3, 1746. In the House of Representvs. Voted that this Court proceed to the Choice of Guardians to the Indians in the Several Plantations on Tuesday next at three o'clock in the Afternoon, for the Care of the following places, vizt. Three for Natick, Three for Stoughton, Three for Grafton & Dudley, Three for Yarmoth, Harwitch, & Eastham, Three for Marchpec, Barnstable, Sandwich & Falmouth, Three for Plymouth, Pembroke, & Middleboro'. Three for Marthas Vineyard, & Three for Nantucket, Agreeable to the Act made the present Year entitled an Act in addition to the Several Acts for the better regulating the Indians.

In Council Read & Concur'd."—*Ibid., p.* 35.

"Jany 6, 1746. This Day being appointed for electing Guardians to the Indians in their several Plantations, the two Houses proceeded to the said Choice. And the following Persons were duly chosen by the Major Vote of the Council & House of Representvs vizt.

For Natick, Samuel Danforth, Joseph Richards, & John Jones Esqrs. For Stoughton, Andrew Oliver, Samuel Miller Esqs & Capt John Shepherd For Grafton & Dudley, John Chandler Edward Baker, & Saml Liscomb Esqs For Yarmoth, Harwich & Eastham, Mr. Samuel Knowles, Mr. Jos. Freeman, & Mr. Miller. For Marshpee, Barnstable, Sandwich & Falmouth, Sylvanus Bourn, Jas Otis, & David Crocker Esqs. For Plymouth Pembroke & Middleboro', John Cushing & James Warren Esqs & Capt. Josiah Edson junr. For Marthas Vineyard, Zaccheus Mahew, John Sumner Esqs & Mr. Hunt. For Nantucket, Messrs Abijah Folger, Daniel Bunker & Jonathan Coffin."—*Ibid., p.* 38.

"Jany 9, 1746. In Council Ordered that Capt. Thomas Wiswall be Guardian of the Indians at Stoughton, in the room of Andrew Oliver Esqr who desires to be excused from that service.

In the House of Representvs Read & Concur'd."—*Ibid., p.* 42.

"January 26, 1749. In the House of Representves Voted that Mr John Winslow, Samuel White Esqr & Stephen Chase be the Guardians over the Indians that are Proprietors of Lands within the Town of Freetown & that the said Guardians be fully impowered to take care of said Lands and suffer no person to cutt off any Timber on said lands unless it be by their consent & Allowance. And that the produce of their said lands or what their timber may sell for, be improved for the support of the said Indians as they may stand in need thereof, the said Guardians to render an Account of their procedings to this Court, once in two years, during their continuance in said Trust. In Council, Read & Concur'd—Consented to by the Lieut Governor."—*Ibid., vol. XIX., p.* 141.

Chap. 15. "June 5, 1747. A Petition of Eser Brown Nathaniel Sole, Daniel Barny, John Winslow & Sylvester Richmond Representves of the Towns of Swanzey Dartmouth Rehoboth Freetown & Dighton in the County of Bristol setting forth the inconveniencies of having Taunton the Shire Town of said County & the more convenient situation of Dighton and therefore praying that for the future the said Town of Dighton may be the County or Shire Town. In the House of Representves Read & Ordered that the Petitioners serve the several Towns in the County of Bristol who have not joined in this Petition with copies thereof respectively that they show cause if any they have on the first Tuesday of the next Sitting of this Court why the prayer of the Petition should not be granted. In Council Read & Concurd."—*Ibid., vol. XVIII., p.* 144.

"August 14, 1747 On the petition of divers Represent^ves of Towns in the County of Bristol praying that Dighton may be made the shire Town of said County In Council Read again together with the Answers of the several Towns Ordered by this Court to be notified hereof & the matter being fully considered Unanimously Ordered that this petition be dismiss'd In the House of Represent^ves Read & Concur'd"—*Ibid., p.* 188.

Chap. 17. "Novr 12, 1746. In the House of Represent^vs. Upon a motion made & seconded, Voted that Mr. Hubbard, Coll. Miller, & Mr. Foster, with such as the Honble Board shall appoint be a Committee to prepare the Draught of a Bill in addition to the several acts of the Province for preventing prophane Cursing & Swearing.

In Council Read & Concur'd, & Francis Foxcraft, Josiah Willard, & Andrew Oliver Esq^s are joined in the affair."—*Ibid., p.* 19.

Chap. 20. "April 23, 1747. In the House of Represent^ves Whereas the Encouragement already given for scouting the Woods after the Indian Enemy has been found ineffectual Therefore voted that there be & hereby is granted to be paid out of the Province Treasury the sum of two hundred & fifty pounds for each Indian killed & the Scalp produced to the Governor & Council as Evidence & for every Indian Captive taken westward of Nova Scotia within six months from this time by any Scouting Party of the Inhabitants of this Province that shall go with permission or Warrant for that purpose as Voluntiers on that service the money to be equally divided among the Persons concerned without respect to office that they be allowed one pound of powder three pounds of bulletts & six flints to each man at their first setting out & also to be subsisted while scouting such Partys to keep a correct Journal of their Marches and Procedings——Voted also that the sum of one hundred pounds be allowed to any Soldier or Party of Soldiers in the pay of this Province who shall within that time Captivate or kill any Indian producing the Scalp as aforesaid or to any other person or persons who shall do the same in his own defence or in the Defence of any of his Majestys Subjects in this Province and all former Grants of this nature heretofore passed by this Court excepting that on the twenty-eighth day of January last are hereby superceded & set aside.

In Council Read & Concurr'd

Consented to by the Governor."—*Ibid., p.* 119.

Chap. 24. "February 14, 1746. The Secretary delivered the following Message from his Excellency to both Houses——Gentlemen of the Council & House of Represent^ves

When I first entered upon the Administration of the Government I found the Province overwhelmed with Law suits occasioned principally by the cheapness of the Law the pernicious mischiefs of which to the whole Community I pointed out to the two Houses in my Speech of the 2^d April 1742 to which I must referr you and thereupon induced them to pass an Act for stating the fees of the Courts of Judicature at double the value they were then of: which has had the Effect to reduce the number of Law Suits in the Province to considerably less than one half of what they amounted to before as you will perceive by the difference between the Entries in the Inferior Court of the County of Suffolk in the year 1740 & in the years 1745 & 1746 which will serve to shew you the decrease of them in the other Counties where I am informed the number of Actions is proportionably lessened. And I am sorry Gentlemen that the Province should so suddenly relapse into the same Evil with it's eyes open; as it will do if the Value of the fees of the Courts of Judicature is suffered to sink as low as it was in the year 1740 & 1741 which they are in a fair way of doing by the Depretiation of the bills of credit and perhaps lower by the end of three years—For these Reasons Gentlemen I think it would be wrong for me to consent to the Engros't Bill now lying before entitled an Act for reviving an Act for the establishing & regulating Fees within this Province, made & pass'd in the eighteenth year of his present Majesty's Reign; and hope you will agree with me that this matter deserves your farther consideration at your next Meeting—There are also some other things in the last Law for stating the fees which will require an Amendment and which I shall point out to you at your next Session."—*Ibid., p.* 76.

ACTS,

PASSED 1747–48.

ACTS

Passed at the Session begun and held at Boston, on the Twenty-seventh day of May, A. D. 1747.

CHAPTER 1.

AN ACT FOR APPORTIONING AND ASSESSING A TAX OF THIRTY-NINE THOUSAND ONE HUNDRED AND THREE POUNDS THIRTEEN SHILLINGS AND SEVENPENCE; AND ALSO FOR APPORTIONING AND ASSESSING A FURTHER TAX OF TWO THOUSAND EIGHT HUNDRED AND SEVENTY-EIGHT POUNDS ELEVEN SHILLINGS AND SIXPENCE, PAID THE REPRESENTATIVES FOR THEIR SERVICE AND ATTENDANCE IN THE GENERAL COURT, AND TRAVEL; AMOUNTING IN THE WHOLE TO FORTY-ONE THOUSAND NINE HUNDRED AND EIGHTY-TWO POUNDS FIVE SHILLINGS AND [A] [*ONE*] PENNY.

Whereas the great and general court or assembly of the province of the Massachusetts Bay, did, at their session in February, one thousand seven hundred and forty-four, pass an act for levying a tax of twenty thousand [*and*] seven hundred pounds, in bills of credit by said act emitted, and, at their session in September,* one thousand seven hundred and forty-six, did pass an act for levying a tax of five thousand pounds, in bills of credit emitted by said act; and, at their session in March,† the same year, did pass an act for levying a tax of eight thousand two hundred pounds, in bills of credit emitted by said act; and, at their session in April, one thousand seven hundred and forty-seven, did pass an act for levying a tax of nine thousand seven hundred and fifty pounds, in bills of credit emitted by said act;—each of the several sums aforesaid to be assessed this present year,—amounting in the whole to the sum of forty-three thousand six hundred and fifty pounds; and by the aforesaid acts, provision was made that the general court might, this present year, apportion the same on the several towns in this province, if they thought fit: and the assembly aforesaid have likewise ordered the sum of two thousand eight hundred and seventy-eight pounds eleven shillings and sixpence, paid the representatives the last year, should be levied and assessed, this present year, on the polls and estates of the inhabitants of the several towns, according to what their representatives have respectively received; *wherefore*, for the ordering, directing and effectual drawing the sum of forty-six thousand five hundred and twenty-eight pounds eleven shillings and sixpence, pursuant to the funds and grants aforesaid, into the treasury, according to the apportion now agreed to by this court; the sum of four thousand four hundred and four pounds twelve shillings and eightpence, arising by the

1744-45, chap. 21, § 4.

1746-47, chap. 14, § 5.

1746-47, chap. 20, § 5.

1746-47, chap. 25, § 4.

1746-47, chap. 4, § 2.

* The session began August 14.

† This act was passed January 29, 1746-47, at the session which began December 24, 1746, and ended February 14, 1746-47. The act was published March 2, 1746-47.

duties of impost, tunnage of shipping and excise, with the sum of one hundred and forty-one pounds thirteen shillings and ninepence, fines, which sums being first deducted, there remains the sum of forty-one thousand nine hundred and eighty-two pounds five shillings and a penny to be drawn into the treasury in the following manner; viz[t]., thirty-nine thousand one hundred and three pounds thirteen shillings and sevenpence by a tax on polls and estates in the several towns, and two thousand eight hundred seventy [and] eight pounds eleven shillings and sixpence, paid the representatives the last year; which sums amount to forty-one thousand nine hundred and eighty-two pounds five shillings and a penny; all which is unanimously approved, ratified and confirmed; we, his majesty's most loyal and dutiful subjects, the representatives in general court assembled, pray that it may be enacted,—

And be it accordingly enacted by the Governour, Council and House of Representatives,

[SECT. 1.] That each town and district within this province be assessed and pay, as such town's and district's proportion of the sum of thirty-nine thousand one hundred and three pounds thirteen shillings and sevenpence, in bills of credit, and their representatives' pay, two thousand eight hundred and seventy [and] eight pounds eleven shillings and sixpence; viz[t]., the several sums following; that is to say,—

IN THE COUNTY OF SUFFOLK.

	Representatives' pay and fines.	Province tax.	Sum total.	
Boston,	£99 9s. 0d.	£7,050 15s. 8d.	Seven thousand one hundred and fifty pounds four shillings and eightpence,	£7,150 4s. 8d.
Roxbury,	25 16 0	363 7 0	Three hundred and eighty-nine pounds three shillings,	389 3 0
Dorchester,	25 16 0	343 8 0	Three hundred and sixty-nine pounds four shillings,	369 4 0
Milton,	30 9 0	158 10 0	One hundred and eighty-eight pounds nineteen shillings,	188 19 0
Braintree,	31 2 0	380 5 0	Four hundred and eleven pounds seven shillings,	411 7 0
Weymouth,	31 2 0	220 7 0	Two hundred and fifty-one pounds nine shillings,	251 9 0
Hingham,	30 18 0	411 4 0	Four hundred and forty-two pounds two shillings,	442 2 0
Dedham,	26 14 0	270 6 0	Two hundred and ninety-seven pounds,	297 0 0
Medfield,	15 9 0	165 14 0	One hundred and eighty one pounds three shillings,	181 3 0
Wrentham,	32 11 0	215 19 9	Two hundred and forty-eight pounds ten shillings and ninepence,	248 10 9
Medway,	0 0 0	100 2 3	One hundred pounds two shillings and threepence,	100 2 3
Stoughton,	31 2 6	200 11 0	Two hundred and thirty-one pounds thirteen shillings and sixpence,	231 13 6
Hull,	0 0 0	86 19 0	Eighty-six pounds nineteen shillings,	86 19 0
Brookline,	0 0 0	129 16 0	One hundred and twenty-nine pounds sixteen shillings,	129 16 0
Needham,	0 0 0	108 3 0	One hundred and eight pounds three shillings,	108 3 0
Bellingham,	0 0 0	44 16 0	Forty-four pounds sixteen shillings,	44 16 0
[illegible]	0 0 0	67 7 0	Sixty-seven pounds seven shillings,	67 7 0
[illegible]	23 11 0	169 12 0	One hundred and ninety-three pounds three shillings,	193 3 0
	£403 19s. 6d.	£10,487 2s. 8d.	Ten thousand eight hundred [*and*] ninety-one pounds two shillings and twopence,	£10,891 2s. 2d.

IN THE COUNTY OF ESSEX.

	Representatives' pay and fines.	Province tax.	Sum total.	
Salem,	£30 1s. 0d.	£1,174 11s. 6d.	One thousand two hundred and four pounds twelve shillings and sixpence,	£1,204 12s. 6d.
Ipswich,	51 18 0	1,081 12 0	One thousand one hundred and thirty-three pounds ten shillings,	1,133 10 0
Newbury,	32 14 0	1,003 7 0	One thousand and thirty-six pounds one shilling,	1,036 1 0
Marblehead,	21 18 0	761 19 0	Seven hundred and eighty-three pounds seventeen shillings,	783 17 0
Lynn,	29 3 6	410 8 0	Four hundred and thirty-nine pounds eleven shillings and sixpence,	439 11 6
Andover,	33 3 0	474 12 0	Five hundred and seven pounds fifteen shillings,	507 15 0
Beverly,	17 6 6	302 14 0	Three hundred and twenty pounds and sixpence,	320 0 6
Rowley,	30 6 0	294 13 0	Three hundred and twenty-four pounds nineteen shillings,	324 19 0

IN THE COUNTY OF ESSEX—*Continued.*

	REPRESENTATIVES' PAY AND FINES.	PROVINCE TAX.	SUM TOTAL.	
Salisbury,	£29 5s. [illegible]	£260 17s. 0d.	[illegible]o hundred and [illegible]nty pounds two [illegible]s,	£290 2s. 0d.
Haverhill,	29 17 0	265 9 0	Two hundred and [illegible]-five [illegible]nds six [illegible]s,	295 6 0
Gloucester,	32 11 0	491 8 0	Five hundred and twenty-three pounds [illegible] shillings,	523 19 0
Topsfield,	0 6 0	149 4 0	One hundred and forty-nine pounds ten shillings,	149 10 0
Boxford,	34 10 0	187 7 0	[illegible]o hundred and twenty-one pounds seventeen shillings,	221 17 0
[illegible]y,	27 15 0	216 3 0	Two hundred and forty-three [illegible] [illegible]en shillings,	243 18 0
Bradford,	28 1 0	163 8 0	One hundred [illegible] [illegible] pounds [illegible] [illegible]s,	[illegible]1 9 0
Wenham,	32 14 0	135 1 0	One hundred and sixty-seven [illegible] [illegible] shillings,	167 15 0
[illegible]r,	0 0 0	112 9 0	One hundred and [illegible] pounds [illegible] shillings,	112 9 0
[illegible]n,	0 0 0	58 18 0	Fifty-eight pounds eighteen shillings,	58 18 0
[illegible]n,	0 6 0	116 8 0	One [illegible] and sixteen [illegible] fourteen [illegible]llings,	116 14 0
Rumford,	0 0 0	0 0 0	. . . .	0 0 0
	£461 15s. 0d.	£7,660 8s. 6d.		£8,122 3s. 6d.

IN THE COUNTY OF MIDDLESEX.

Cambridge,	£25 16s. [illegible]	£258 8s. 0d.	Two hundred and [illegible] [illegible]our pounds [illegible]our [illegible]s,	£284 4s. 0d.
Charlestown,	51 3 0	529 5 0	Five hundred and eighty pounds eight [illegible]s,	580 8 0
Watertown,	30 9 0	160 7 0	One hundred and [illegible]nty pounds [illegible] [illegible]s,	190 16 0
Concord,	31 1 0	321 2 0	Three [illegible] and [illegible]-two pounds three shillings,	352 3 0
[illegible]n,	30 3 0	[illegible]0 8 0	One [illegible] and eighty pounds eleven shillings,	180 11 0
[illegible]n,	29 8 0	251 9 0	Two [illegible] and eighty pounds seventeen shillings,	280 17 0
Reading,	28 10 0	278 10 0	Three [illegible] and seven [illegible]s,	307 0 0
[illegible]y,	31 16 0	287 5 0	Three [illegible] and [illegible] pounds one shilling,	319 1 0
Marlborough,	31 4 0	298 6 0	Three [illegible] and twenty-nine pounds [illegible] shillings,	329 10 0
Lexington,	30 3 0	178 1 0	Two hundred and eight pounds four [illegible],	208 4 0
[illegible]n,	30 9 0	278 2 0	[illegible] [illegible] and eight pounds [illegible] shillings,	308 11 0
[illegible]n,	25 16 0	231 5 0	[illegible]o [illegible] and fifty-seven pounds one shilling[s],	257 1 0
[illegible]ford,	24 10 0	160 1 0	One hundred and eighty-four pounds eleven [illegible],	184 11 0
[illegible]a,	31 16 0	168 1 0	One hundred and [illegible]-nine [illegible] seventeen shillings,	199 17 0
[illegible]n,	29 5 0	103 2 0	One hundred and [illegible]-two pounds seven [illegible]s,	132 7 0
Holl[c][i]ston,	0 6 0	73 2 0	[illegible] [illegible]s eight shillings,	73 8 0
Groton,	29 8 0	248 6 0	Two hundred and seventy-seven pounds fourteen shillings,	277 14 0
Framing[ton][*ham*],	24 6 0	214 1 0	Two [illegible] and thirty-eight pounds seven [illegible]s,	238 7 0

Medford,	£25 1s. 0d.	£123 1s. 0d.	One hundred and forty-eight pounds two shillings,	£148 2s. 0d.
Stow,	0 0 0	96 10 0	Ninety-six pounds ten shillings,	96 10 0
Dunstable and Nottingham,	0 0 0	63 18 0	Sixty-three pounds eighteen shillings,	63 18 0
Dracut[t],	0 0 0	63 6 0	Sixty-three [illegible] six shillings,	63 6 0
Stoneham,	0 0 0	83 15 0	Eighty-three [illegible] fifteen shillings,	83 15 0
Littleton,	27 15 0	116 5 0	One hundred and forty-four pounds,	144 0 0
Hopkin[s]ton,	24 18 0	80 7 0	One [illegible] and five pounds five shillings,	105 5 0
Bedford,	15 0 0	77 5 0	Ninety-two [illegible] five shillings,	92 5 0
Westford,	31 1 0	106 4 0	One hundred and thirty-seven pounds five shillings,	137 5 0
Wilmington,	0 0 0	73 3 0	Seventy-three pounds three shillings,	73 3 0
Tewk[e]sbury,	0 0 0	69 10 0	Sixty-nine [illegible] ten shillings,	69 10 0
Acton,	0 0 0	52 1 0	Fifty-two pounds one [illegible],	52 1 0
Waltham,	30 9 0	144 0 0	One hundred and seventy-four pounds nine shillings,	174 9 0
Townshend,	11 17 0	29 10 0	Forty-one pounds seven [illegible],	41 7 0
English inhab[*itan*]ts of Natick,	0 0 0	45 10 0	Fo[illegible] pounds ten shillings,	45 10 0
	£681 10s. 0d.	£5,413 6s. 0d.		£6,094 16s. 0d.

IN THE COUNTY OF HAMPSHIRE.

Springfield,	£27 9s. 0d.	£429 12s. 7d.	Four hundred and fifty-seven [illegible] one [illegible] and [illegible],	£457 1s. 7d.
[illegible]on,	14 8 0	281 5 0	[illegible] hundred and [illegible]-five pounds thirteen shillings,	295 13 0
H[illegible]ey,	12 9 0	202 8 0	Two hundred and fourteen pounds [illegible] [illegible],	214 17 0
Hatfield,	19 19 0	129 1 0	One [illegible] and forty-nine pounds,	149 0 0
[illegible]d,	28 19 0	168 3 0	One hundred and [illegible] pounds two shillings,	197 2 0
[illegible]d,	29 11 0	214 3 0	Two hundred and forty-three [illegible] fourteen shillings,	243 14 0
[illegible]d,	15 15 0	127 9 0	One hundred and forty-three pounds four shillings,	143 4 0
[illegible]d,	25 7 0	129 2 0	One hundred and fifty-four pounds [illegible] shillings,	154 9 0
Sunderland,	0 0 0	66 4 0	Sixty-six pounds four shillings,	66 4 0
Northfield,	0 0 0	57 10 0	Fifty-seven [illegible] ten shillings,	57 10 0
Brimfield,	18 6 0	114 3 0	One [illegible] and [illegible]-two [illegible] nine shillings,	132 9 0
Somers,	0 0 0	70 2 0	Seventy [illegible] two shillings,	70 2 0
[illegible]d,	0 0 0	68 0 0	Sixty-eight pounds,	68 0 0
[illegible],	0 0 0	38 5 0	Thirty-[illegible] [illegible] five shillings,	38 5 0
Stockbridge,	0 0 0	0 0 0		0 0 0
	£192 3s. 0d.	£2,095 7s. 7d.		£2,287 10s. 7d.

IN THE COUNTY OF WORCESTER.

	REPRESENTATIVES' PAY, AND FINES.	PROVINCE TAX.	SUM TOTAL.	
Worcester,	£20 17s. 0d.	£133 13s. 0d.	One hundred and fifty-four pounds ten shillings,	£154 10s. 0d.
Lancaster,	29 17 0	221 9 0	Two hundred and fifty-one pounds six shillings,	251 6 0
Mendon,	32 5 0	228 8 0	Two hundred and sixty pounds thirteen shillings,	260 13 0
Woodstock,	26 5 0	200 5 0	Two hundred and twenty-six pounds ten shillings,	226 10 0
Brookfield,	24 15 0	137 4 0	One hundred and sixty-one pounds nineteen shillings,	161 19 0
Southborough,	47 17 0	88 14 0	One hundred and thirty-six pounds eleven shillings,	136 11 0
Leicester,	21 19 6	123 10 0	One hundred and forty-five pounds nine shill[in]gs and sixpence,	145 9 6
Rutland,	0 0 0	80 9 0	Eighty pounds nine shillings,	80 9 0
Lunenburg,	14 5 0	99 7 0	One hundred and thirteen pounds twelve shillings,	113 12 0
Westborough,	31 1 0	137 14 0	One hundred and sixty-eight pounds fifteen shillings,	168 15 0
Shrewsbury,	27 6 0	122 11 0	One hundred and forty-nine pounds seventeen shillings,	149 17 0
Oxford,	0 0 0	93 9 0	Ninety-three pounds nine shillings,	93 9 0
Sutton,	0 0 0	147 10 0	One hundred and forty-seven pounds ten shillings,	147 10 0
Uxbridge,	26 18 0	104 9 0	One hundred and thirty-one pounds seven shillings,	131 7 0
Har[w][v]ard,	0 0 0	90 11 0	Ninety pounds eleven shillings,	90 11 0
Grafton,	0 0 0	76 5 0	Seventy-six pounds five shillings,	76 5 0
Upton,	0 0 0	30 8 0	Thirty pounds eight shillings,	30 8 0
Dudley,	0 0 0	65 5 0	Sixty-five pounds five shillings,	65 5 0
Bolton,	0 0 0	88 6 0	Eighty-eight pounds six shillings,	88 6 0
Sturbridge,	0 0 0	33 3 0	Thirty-three pounds three shillings,	33 3 0
Leomin[i]ster,	0 0 0	27 5 0	Twenty-seven pounds five shillings,	27 5 0
Western,	0 0 0	26 3 0	Twenty-six pounds three shillings,	26 3 0
	£303 5s. 6d.	£2,355 18s. 0d.		£2,659 3s. 6d.

IN THE COUNTY OF PLYMOUTH.

Plymouth,	£24 12s. 0d.	£366 2s. 5d.	Three hundred and ninety pounds fourteen shill[in]gs and [5d] [*five-pence*],	£390 14s. 5d.
Plympton,	28 1 0	194 17 0	Two hundred and twenty-two pounds eighteen shillings,	222 18 0
Scituate,	33 3 0	560 19 0	Five hundred and ninety-four pounds two shillings,	594 2 0
Bridgwater,	33 3 0	44 15 0	Four hundred and seventy-seven pounds eighteen shillings,	477 18 0
Marshfield,	26 18 6	275 19 0	Three hundred and two pounds seventeen shillings and sixpence,	302 17 6
Pembro[o]k[e],	0 6 0	148 10 0	One hundred and forty-eight pounds sixteen shillings,	148 16 0
Duxbury,	31 19 0	130 9 0	One hundred and sixty-two pounds eight shillings,	162 8 0

Middleborough,	£31 4s. 0d.	£327 11s. 0d.	Three hundred and fifty-eight pounds fifteen shillings,	£358 15s. 0d.
Rochester,	23 5 0	210 15 0	Two hundred and thirty-four pounds,	234 0 0
Ab[b]ington,	0 0 0	94 18 0	Ninety-four pounds eighteen shillings,	94 18 0
Kingston,	0 0 0	102 17 0	One hundred and two pounds seventeen shillings,	102 17 0
Hanover,	0 0 0	121 15 0	One hundred and twenty-one pounds fifteen shillings,	121 15 0
Halifax,	0 0 0	78 12 0	Seventy-eight pounds twelve shillings,	78 12 0
Warham,	0 0 0	39 10 0	Thirty-nine pounds ten shillings,	39 10 0
	£232 11s. 6d.	£3,097 9s. 5d.		£3,330 0s. 11d.

IN THE COUNTY OF BARNSTABLE.

Barnstable,	£27 4s. 0d.	£392 12s. 9d.	Four hundred and nineteen pounds sixteen shillings and 9 pence,	£419 16s. 9d.
Sandwich,	21 9 0	211 4 0	Two hundred and thirty-two pounds thirteen shillings,	232 13 0
Yarmouth,	25 19 0	242 15 0	Two hundred and sixty-eight pounds fourteen shillings,	268 14 0
Eastham,	29 11 0	291 11 0	Three hundred and twenty-one pounds two shillings,	321 2 0
Truro,	0 0 0	52 18 0	Fifty-two pounds eighteen shillings,	52 18 0
Harwich,	27 6 0	187 17 0	Two hundred and fi[ve][f]teen pounds three shillings,	215 3 0
Falmouth,	18 6 0	142 3 0	One hundred and sixty pounds nine shillings,	160 9 0
Chatham,	0 0 0	119 12 0	One hundred and nineteen pounds twelve shillings,	119 12 0
	£149 15s. 0d.	£1,640 12s. 9d.		£1,790 7s. 9d.

IN THE COUNTY OF BRISTOL.

Bristol,	£15 15s. 0d.	£258 9s. 8d.	Two [illegible] and [illegible]-four [illegible] four shillings and 8 pence,	£274 4s. 8d.
[illegible]n,	34 10 0	690 5 0	Four [illegible]red and twenty-four pounds fifteen [illegible],	424 15 0
[illegible]n,	26 5 0	197 4 0	Two [illegible] and twenty-three [illegible] [illegible]ine shillings,	223 9 0
[illegible]n,	28 1 0	77 10 0	One [illegible] and five pounds [illegible] [illegible],	105 11 0
Dartmouth,	23 17 0	605 13 0	Six hundred and [illegible]-[illegible]ine pounds ten shillings,	629 10 0
Dighton,	34 1 0	138 8 0	One hundred and seventy-two [illegible] [illegible]ine shillings,	172 9 0
Rehoboth,	31 13 0	484 4 0	Five [illegible]red and fifteen [illegible] [illegible]een shillings,	515 17 0
Little [illegible],	14 14 0	276 5 0	[illegible]o hundred and [illegible]ty pounds [illegible]een [illegible],	290 19 0
[illegible]ey w[i]th Shawamett,	31 4 0	388 1 0	Four hundred and [illegible]een pounds five shillings,	419 5 0
Tiverton,	12 0 0	313 6 0	[illegible] hundred and [illegible]-five [illegible] six shillings,	325 6 0
[illegible]n,	26 11 0	128 3 0	One hundred and fifty-four [illegible] [illegible]een shillings,	154 14 0
[illegible]gh,	18 18 0	196 1 0	Two hundred and [illegible]een [illegible] [illegible] [illegible],	214 19 0

IN THE COUNTY OF BRISTOL—*Continued.*

	REPRESENTATIVES' PAY, AND FINES.	PROVINCE TAX.	SUM TOTAL.	
Barrington,	£0 0*s.* 0*d.*	£112 10*s.* 0*d.*	One hundred and twelve pounds ten shillings,	£112 10*s.* 0*d.*
Raynham,	0 0 0	89 15 0	Eighty-nine pounds fifteen shillings,	89 15 0
Berkley,	0 0 0	83 15 0	Eighty-three pounds fifteen shillings,	83 15 0
	£297 9*s.* 0*d.*	£3,739 9*s.* 8*d.*		£4,036 18*s.* 8*d.*

IN THE COUNTY OF YORK.

[illegible]k,	£25 16*s.* 0*d.*	£358 5*s.* 0*d.*	Three [illegible] and eighty-four pounds one shilling,	£384 1*s.* 0*d.*
Kittery,	12 18 0	492 10 0	Five hundred and five pounds eight shillings,	505 8 0
Berwick,	12 18 0	232 10 9	Two hundred [illegible] forty-five pounds eight [illegible] and [9^d] [*nine-pence*],	245 8 9
Wells,	13 1 0	151 1 3	One [illegible] sixty-four [illegible] two shillings and [3^d] [*three-pence*],	164 2 3
Falmouth,	35 17 0	300 18 0	Three hundred and thirty-six [illegible] [illegible] shillings,	336 15 0
[illegible]d,	5 6 0	118 19 0	One hundred and [illegible] pounds five [illegible],	119 5 0
Arundel,	14 8 0	77 11 0	[illegible]-one [illegible] [illegible]en shillings,	91 19 0
Scarborough,	0 0 0	155 14 0	One hundred and fifty-five pounds fourteen shillings,	155 14 0
North [illegible]h,	30 15 0	66 6 0	Ninety- [illegible] pounds one [illegible],	97 1 0
[illegible]n,	0 0 0	78 5 0	Seventy-eight pounds five [illegible],	78 5 0
Brunswick,	0 0 0	26 15 0	Twenty-six pounds [illegible] shillings,	26 15 0
	£145 19*s.* 0*d.*	£2,058 15*s.* 0*d.*		£2,204 14*s.* 0*d.*

IN THE COUNTY OF DUKES COUNTY.

Edgartown,	£0 0*s.* 0*d.*	£97 10*s.* 0*d.*	Ninety-seven pounds ten shillings,	£97 10*s.* 0*d.*
Chilmark,	0 0 0	123 10 0	One hundred and twenty-three pounds ten shillings,	123 10 0
Tisbury,	0 0 0	77 1 0	Seventy-seven pounds one shilling,	77 1 0
	£0 0*s.* 0*d.*	£298 1*s.* 0*d.*		£298 1*s.* 0*d.*

IN NANTUCKET COUNTY.

Sherburn,	£10 4s. 0d.	£257 3s. 0d.	Two hundred and sixty-seven pounds seven shillings,	£267 7s. 0d.
Suffolk,	£403 19s. 6d.	£10,487 2s. 8d.	Ten thousand eight hundred and ninety-one pounds two shill[in]gs and twopence,	£10,891 2s. 2d.
Essex,	461 15 0	7,660 8 6	Eight thousand one hundred and twenty-two pounds three shill[in]gs and sixpence,	8,122 3 6
Middlesex,	681 10 0	5,413 6 0	Six thousand and ninety-four pounds sixteen shillings,	6,094 16 0
Hampshire,	192 3 0	2,095 7 7	Two thousand two hundred and eighty-seven pounds ten shillings and sevenpence,	2,287 10 7
Worcester,	303 5 6	2,355 18 0	Two thousand six hundred and fifty-nine pounds three shillings and sixpence,	2,659 3 6
Plymouth,	232 11 6	3,097 9 5	Three thousand three hundred and thirty pounds and elevenpence,	3,330 0 11
Barnstable,	149 15 0	1,640 12 9	One thousand seven hundred and ninety pounds seven shill[in]gs and ninepence,	1,790 7 9
Bristol,	297 9 0	3,739 9 8	Four thousand and thirty-six pounds eighteen shillings and eightpence,	4,036 18 8
York,	145 19 0	2,058 15 0	Two thousand two hundred and four pounds fourteen shillings,	2,204 14 0
Dukes County,	0 0 0	298 1 0	Two hundred and ninety-eight pounds one shilling,	298 1 0
Nantucket,	10 4 0	257 3 0	Two hundred and sixty-seven pounds seven shillings,	267 7 0
	£2,878 11s. 6d.	£39,103 13s. 7d.	Forty-one thousand nine hundred and eighty-two pounds five shil-l[in]gs and a pen[ny],	£41,982 5s. 1d.

And be it further enacted,

[SECT. 2.] That the treasurer do forthwith send out his warrants, directed to the selectmen or assessors of each town or district within this province, requiring them, respectively, to assess the sum hereby set on such town or district, in manner following; that is to say, to assess all rateable male polls above the age of sixteen years, within their respective towns or districts, or next adjoyning to them, belonging to no other town, at eight shillings and fourpence per poll, and proportionably in assessing the fines mentioned in this act, and the additional sum received out of the treasury for the payment of the representatives (except the governour, lieutenant-governour and their famil[y][*ie*]s, the president, fellows and students of Harvard Colle[d]ge, set[*t*]led ministers and gramm[e][*a*]r-school masters, who are hereby exempted as well from being taxed for their polls, as for their estates being in their own hands and under their actual management and improvement); and other persons, if such there be, who, thrô age, infirmity or extream poverty, in the judgment of the assessors, are not capable to pay towards publick charges, they may exempt their polls, and so much of their estate as in their prudence they shall think fit and judge meet.

[SECT. 3.] And the justices in the general sessions, in the respective counties assembled, in granting a county tax or assessment, are hereby ordered and directed to apportion the same on the several towns in such county in proportion to their province rate, exclusive of what has been [paid] out of the publick treasury to the representative of such town for his service; and the assessors of each town in the province are also directed, in making an assessment, to govern themselves by the same rule; and all estates, both real and personal, lying within the limits of such town or district, or next unto the same, not paying elsewhere, in whose hands, tenure, occupation or possession soever the same is or shall be found, and also the incomes or profits which any person or persons, except as before excepted, do or shall receive from any trade, faculty, business or employment whatsoever, and all profits that shall or may arise by money or other estate not particularly otherwise assessed, or commissions of profit in their improvement, according to their understanding and cunning, at one penny on the pound; and to abate or multiply the same, if need be, so as to make up the sum set and ordered hereby for such town or district to pay; and, in making their assessment, to estimate houses and lands at six years' income of the yearly rents, in the bills last emitted, whereat the same may be reasonably set or let for in the place where they lye: *saving* all contracts between landlord and tenant, and where no contract is, the landlord to reimburse one-half of the tax set upon such houses and lands; and to estimate negro, Indian and molatto servants proportionably as other personal estate, according to their sound judgment and discretion; as also to estimate every ox of four years old and upwards, at forty shillings in bills of the last emission; every cow of three years old and upwards, at thirty shillings; every horse and mare at three years old and upwards, at forty shillings; every swine of one year old and upwards, at eight shillings; every goat and sheep of one year old and upwards, at three shillings: likewise requiring the said assessors to make a fair list of the said assessment, setting forth, in distinct colum[*n*]s, against each particular person's name, how much he or she is assessed at for polls, and how much for houses and lands, and how much for personal estate, and income by trade or faculty, and if as guardian, or for any estate in his or her improvement, in trust, to be distinctly expres[*se*]d; and the list or lists, so perfected and signed by them, or the major part of them, to commit to the collectors, constable or constables of such town or district, and to return a certificate of the name or names of such collectors, constable or constables, together with the sum total to each of them committed, unto himself, some time before the last day of October.

[Sect. 4.] And the treasurer for the time being, upon receipt of such certificate, is hereby impowered and ordered to issue forth his warrants to the collector, constable or constables of such town or district, requiring him or them, respectively, to collect the whole of each respective sum assessed on each particular person, before the last day of May next; and of the inhabitants of the town of Boston, some time in March next; and to pay in their collection, and issue the acco[un][*mp*]ts of the whole, at or before the last day of June, which will be in the year of our Lord one thousand seven hundred and forty-eight.

And be it further enacted,

[Sect. 5.] That the assessors of each town and district, respectively, in convenient time before their making the assessment, shall give seasonable warning to the inhabitants, in a town meeting, or by posting up notifications in some place or places in such town or district, or notify the inhabitants to give or bring in to the assessors true and perfect lists of their polls, and rateable estate, and income by trade or faculty, and gain by money at interest; and if any person or persons shall neglect or refuse so to do, or bring in a false list, it shall be lawful to and for the assessors to assess such person or persons, according to their known ability in such town, in their sound judgment and discretion, their due proportion of this tax, as near as they can, agreeable to the rules herein given, under the penalty of twenty shillings for each person that shall be convicted by legal proof, in the judgment of the said assessors, of bringing in a false list; the said fines to be for the use of the poor of such town or district where the delinquent lives, to be levied by warrant from the assessors, directed to the collector or constables, in manner as is directed for gathering town assessments, and to be paid in to the town treasurer or selectmen for the use aforesaid: *saving* to the party aggrieved at the judgment of the assessors in setting forth such fine, liberty of appeal therefrom to the court of general sessions of the peace within the county for relief, as in case of being overrated. And if any person or persons shall not bring in a list of their estate as aforesaid to the assessors, he or they so neglecting shall not be admitted to make application to the court of sessions for any abatement of the assessment laid on him.

[Sect. 6.] And if the party be not convicted of any falseness in the list, by him presented, of the polls, rateable estate, or income by trade or faculty, business or employment, which he doth or shall exercise, or in gain by money at interest or otherwise, or other estate not particularly assessed, such list shall be a rule for such person's proportion to the tax, which the assessors may not exceed.

And forasmuch as, ofttimes, sundry persons, not belonging to this province, bring considerable trade and merchandize, and by reason that the tax or rate of the town where they come to trade is finished and delivered to the constable or collector, and, before the next year's assessment, are gone out of the province, and so pay nothing towards the support of the government, tho[ugh], in the time of their residing here, they reap[e]'d considerable gain by trade, and had the protection of the government,—

Be it further enacted,

[Sect. 7.] That when any such person or persons shall come and reside in any town within this province, and bring any merchandize, and trade, to deal therewith, the assessors of such town are hereby impowered to rate and assess all such persons according to their circumstances, pursuant to the rules and directions in this act provided, tho the former rate may have been finished, and the new one not perfected, as aforesaid; and the constable[s] or collectors are hereby enjoyned to levy and collect all such sums committed to them and assessed on persons who are not of this province, and pay the same into the town treasury.

And be it further enacted,

[SECT. 8.] That the inhabitants of this province have liberty, if they see fit, to pay the several sums for which they respectively may be assessed at, as their proportion of the aforesaid sum of thirty-nine thousand one hundred and three pounds thirteen shillings and sevenpence, in bills of credit emitted in and since the year one thousand seven hundred and forty-one, according to their denominations; or in coined silver, at the rate of seven shillings and sixpence per ounce, troy weight, or in gold coin in proportion; or in bills of credit of the middle tenor, so called, according to their several denominations; or in bills of the old tenor, accounting four for one; or in good merchantable hemp, at fourpence per pound; or in good merchantable Isle-of-Sable codfish, at ten shillings per quintal; or in good refined bar-iron, at fifteen pounds per ton; or in bloomery-iron, at twelve pounds per ton; or in hollow iron-ware, at twelve pounds per ton; or in good Indian corn, at two shillings and sixpence per bushel[l]; or in good winter rye, at two shillings and sixpence per bushel[l]; or in good winter wheat, at three shillings per bushel[l]; or in good barley, at two shillings per bushel[l]; or in good barrel[l] pork, at two pounds per barrel[l]; or in barrel[l] beef, at one pound five shillings per barrel[l]; or in duck or canvas, at two pounds ten shillings per bolt, each bolt to weigh forty-three pounds; or in long whalebone, at two shillings and threepence per pound; or in merchantable cordage, at one pound five shillings per hundred; in good train-o[y][*i*]l, at one pound ten shillings per barrel[*l*]; or in good beeswax, at tenpence per pound; or in good bayberry-wax, at sixpence per pound; or in try[e]'d tallow, at fourpence per pound; or in good pease, at three shillings per bushel[l]; or in [*good*] sheepswool, at ninepence per pound; or in good tann'd sole-leather, at fourpence per pound: all which aforesaid commodities shall be of the produce of this province, and, as soon as conveniently may, be disposed of by the treasurer to the best advantage, for so much as they will fetch in bills of credit, or for silver and gold; and the several persons paying their taxes in any of the commodities afore mentioned, to run the risque and pay the charge of transporting the said commodities to the province treasurer.

[SECT. 9.] And if any loss shall happen by the sale of the aforesaid species, it shall be made good by a tax of the next year; and if there be a surplusage, it shall remain a stock in the treasury.

And whereas by the late determination and order of his majesty in council, the town of Bristol falls within the colony of Rhode Island, and part of the town[s] of Little Compton, Swan[s][*z*]ey, Tiverton and Barrington, by said determination, likewise fall[s] within said colony; and altho[*ugh*] it be just and equitable that a proportion of the debts contracted by this government while the said towns were under the jurisdiction of it, should be paid by the inhabitants and estates of that part of said towns which falls within the colony of Rhode Island, yet, inasmuch as no provision is made by the aforesaid order of his majesty for raising and assessing the same,—

Be it therefore further enacted,

[SECT. 10.] That the treasurer be and hereby is discharged from any part of the tax laid on said town of Bristol, and on that part of the said towns of Little Compton, Swan[s][*z*]ey, Tiverton and Barrington, which now falls within the colony of Rhode Island, apportioned in this tax-act, until his majesty's pleasure shall be signified thereupon.

And it is further enacted,

[Sect. 11.] That all proceedings with respect to the tax on that part of the said towns of Little Compton, Swan[s][*z*]ey, Tiverton and Barrington, which remains within this province, be regulated agreeable to such orders as have pass[*e*]'d or shall hereafter pass this court, anything in this act to the contrary notwithstanding. [*Passed June* 29.

CHAPTER 2.

AN ACT FOR SUPPLYING THE TREASURY WITH THE SUM OF EIGHT THOUSAND POUNDS FOR DEFR[E][*A*]YING THE CHARGE OF THE LATE INTENDED EXPEDITION AGAINST CANADA, AND FOR DISCHARGING THE PUBLICK DEBTS, &c., AND FOR DRAWING IN THE SAID BILLS INTO THE TREASURY AGAIN.

Be it enacted by the Governour, Council and House of Representatives,

[Sect. 1.] That the treasurer be and hereby is impowered and ordered to issue forth the sum of eight thousand pounds in bills of credit of the last tenor and date, now lying in his hands, and received in for taxes, impost and excise, which shall pass in all publick payments equal to other new-tenor bills, issued since one thousand seven hundred and forty; or, if there be not a sufficiency of such bills, that then the committee appointed by this court for signing bills are hereby directed and impow[e]red to take care and make effectual provision, as soon as may be, to imprint so many as may be needed to compleat the said sum, and to sign and deliver the same to the treasurer, taking his receipt for the same; and the said committee shall be under oath for the [f]faithful[l] performance of the trust by this act reposed in them; and the said sum of eight thousand pounds shall be issued out of the publick treasury for the purposes and in manner following; viz[t]., the sum of five thousand pounds, part of the aforesaid sum of eight thousand pounds, shall be appl[y][*ie*]d for discharging what is due for putting the province into a better state of defence, for paying off such officers and soldiers as are or may be in the province service, according to the several establishments for that purpose, for purchas[e]ing needful[l] warlike stores, pursuant to such grants as are or shall be made by this court for those purposes: the sum of three thousand pounds, part of the aforesaid sum of eight thousand pounds, shall be applyed for discharging and paying such grants that are or may be made by this court.

£8,000 bills of credit to be emitted.

And be it further enacted,

[Sect. 2.] That each and every warrant for drawing money out of the treasury, shall direct the treasurer to take the same out of such sums as are respectiv[*e*]ly appropriated for the payment of such publick debts as the drafts are made to discharge; and the treasurer is hereby directed and ordered to pay such money out of such appropriation as directed to, and no other, upon pain of refunding all such sum or sums as he shall otherwise pay, and to keep exact and distinct accompts of all payments made out of such appropriated sums; and the secretary, to whom it belongs to keep the muster-rolls and accompts of charge, shall lay before the house, when they direct, all such muster-rolls and acco[mp][*un*]ts after payment thereof.

Warrants to express the appropriations.

And as a fund and security for drawing the said sum of eight thousand pounds into the treasury again,—

Be it enacted,

£8,000 in 1748.

[SECT. 3.] That there be and hereby is granted unto his most excellent majesty, to the ends and uses aforesaid, a tax of eight thousand pounds, to be levied on polls, and estates both real and personal, within this province, according to such rules and in such proportions on the several towns and districts within the same, as shall be agreed upon and ordered by this court at their session in May, one thousand seven hundred and forty-eight, and paid into the publick treasury on or before the last day of December then next after.

And be it further enacted,

Tax for the money hereby emitted, to be made according to the preceding tax act, in case.

[SECT. 4.] That in case the general court shall not at their session in May, one thousand seven hundred and forty-eight, agree and conclude upon an act apportioning the sum which by this act is engaged shall be in that year apportioned, assessed and levied, that then and in such case each town and district within this province shall pay, by a tax to be levied on polls, and estates both real and personal, within their districts, the same proportion of the said sum as the said towns and districts shall have been taxed by the general court in the tax act then next preceeding; and the province treasurer is hereby fully impower[*e*]d and directed, some time in the month of June, in the year one thousand seven hundred and forty-eight, to issue and send forth his warrants, directed to the selectmen or assessors of each town and district within this province, requir[e]ing them to assess the polls, and estates both real[l] and personal, within their several towns and districts, for their respective part and proportion of the sum before directed and engaged to be assessed by this act; and the assessors, as also persons assessed, shall observe, be govern[*e*]d by and subject to all such rules and directions as shall have been given in the next preceeding tax act.

And be it further enacted,

Taxes to be paid in the several species herein enumerated.

[SECT. 5.] That the inhabitants of this province shall have liberty, if they see fit, to pay the several sums for which they respectiv[*e*]ly may, in pursuance of this act, be assessed, in bills of credit of the form and tenor by this act emitted, or in other new-tenor bills, or in bills of the middle tenor, according to their several denominations, or in bills of the old tenor, accounting four for one; or in coined silver, at seven shillings and sixpence per ounce, troy weight, sterling alloy, or in gold coin, proportionably; or in merchantable hemp, flax, winter and Isle-of-Sable codfish, refined bar-iron, bloomery-iron, h[a][*o*]llow iron-ware, Indian corn, rye, wheat, barley, beef, pork, duck or canv[a][*i*]s, whalebone, cordage, train-oil, beeswax, bayberry-wax, tallow, pease, sheepswool[*l*], or tann'd sole-leather (the aforesaid commodities being of the produce or manufact[u][*o*]r[e]s of this province), at such moderate rates and prices as the general assembly of the year one thousand seven hundred and forty-eight shall set[*t*] them at[t]; the several persons paying their taxes in any of the commodities afore mentioned, to run the risque and pay the charge of transporting the said commodities to the province treasury; but if the aforesaid general assembly shall not, at their session in May, some time before the twentieth day of June, in said year, agree upon and set the aforesaid species and commodities at some certain price, that then the eldest councellor, for the time being, in each of those count[y][*ie*]s in the province, of which any one of the council is an inhabitant, together with the province treasurer, or the major part of them, be a committee, who are hereby authorized and fully impow[*e*]red to do it; and in their set[l][*t*]ing the prices and rating the value of those commodities, to state so much

How the commodities brought into the treasury are to be rated.

of them, respectiv[e]ly, at seven shillings and sixpence as an ounce of silver will purchase at that time in the town of Boston, and so *pro ratâ*. And the treasurer is hereby directed to insert in the several warrants by him sent to the several collectors of the taxes in said year, with the names of the afore-recited commodities, the several rates or prices which shall be set on them, either by the general assembly or the committee aforesaid, and direct the aforesaid collectors to receive them so.

[Sect. 6.] And the aforesaid commodities, so brought into the treasury, shall, as soon as may be, be disposed of by the treasurer to the best advantage for so much as they will fetch in bills of credit hereby to be emitted, or for silver or gold, which silver and gold shall be delivered to the possessor of said bills in exchange for them; that is to say, one ounce of silver coin[e], and so gold in proportion, for seven shillings and sixpence, and so *pro ratâ* for a greater or less[or] sum; and if any loss shall happen by the sale of the aforesaid species, or by any unforeseen accident, such deficiency shall be made good by a tax of the year next following, so as fully and effectually to call in the whole sum of eight thousand pounds in said bills hereby ordered to be issued; and if there be a surplusage, it shall remain a stock in the treasury. [*Passed June* 29; *published July* 2.

CHAPTER 3.

AN ACT TO PREVENT THE DESTRUCTION OF WILD FOWL.

Preamble. 1737-38, chap. 16.

Whereas the water-fowl of divers[e] kinds which were wont in former years, in great numbers, to frequent the mar[i][*a*]time towns of this province, were of great service and benefit to the inhabitants, both for meat and feathers, but are now in great measure affrighted and driven away by many persons, who have made use of floats, or rafts, therein to go off as well by night as by day, to shoot them at a distance from the shoar upon the flat[t]s and feeding-grounds, and from the land, by night; which practices, if continued, are likely to have the ill-effect to cause the fowl wholly to desert and disuse the said towns; for prevention whereof,—

Be it enacted by the Governour, Council and House of Representatives,

Penalty for using floats trimmed or dressed.

[Sect. 1.] That if any person or persons shall at any time after one month from the publication of this act, make use of any float, raft, or canoe, any ways trim'd or dress'd up, wherewith, by night or by day, to approach and shoot at any water-fowl in any part of this province, or shoot at any such fowl by night, from the land, or from out of any boat, canoe, float or other vessel[l], he or they so offending shall each of them forfeit and pay for the first offence the sum of twenty shillings to the informer, to be recovered before one of his majesty's justices of the peace for the county where the fact shall be committed, and forty-five shillings for every offence afterwards, to be recovered before the justices of the court of general sessions of the peace, by bill, plaint or information; the one-half to the informer and the other half for the use of the poor of the town where the fact shall be committed.

Limitation.

[Sect. 2.] This act to continue and be in force for the space of five years from the publication thereof, and no longer. [*Passed June* 29; *published July* 2.

CHAPTER 4.

AN ACT TO PREVENT THE DISTURBANCE GIVEN THE GENERAL COURT, BY COACHES, CHAISES, CHAIRS, CARTS, TRUCKS, AND OTHER CARRIAGES, PASSING BY THE PROVINCE COURT-HOUSE IN THE TIME OF THEIR SITTING.

Preamble. 1742-43, chap. 12.

FORASMUCH as the passing of coaches, chaises, chairs, carts, trucks and other carriages, on the south and north side of the court-house in Boston, gives great interruption to the debates and proceedings of the general court in the time of their sitting; for preventing of which,—

Be it enacted by the Governour, Council and House of Representatives,

Penalty for coaches, &c., passing by either side of the court-house, in the time of the sitting of the general court.

[SECT. 1.] That after five days from the publication of this act, any person or persons presuming to drive or pass any coach, chaise, chair, cart, truck, or other carriage, by one or more horses or cattle (sleds and slays only excepted), in King['s] Street, either on the south side or on the north side of the province court-house in Boston, during any sitting of the general court, between the hours of nine in the morning and one in the afternoon, or between the hours of three and seven in the afternoon (either house then actually sitting), shall, for every such offence, forfeit and pay, as a fine, for the use of the doorkeeper for the time being, the sum of five shillings, to be immediately paid him by the offender or offenders; and in case of refusal, it shall be in the power of the doorkeeper to require sufficient assistance to arrest and seize the offender or offenders, and him or them to carry before a justice of the peace, who is hereby impowered and directed, on proof of the offence, to commit the offender or offenders to prison, until he or they shall pay the said fine, and cost arising thereon; and in case the doorkeeper shall not arrest and seize the refusing offender as aforesaid, he, the said doorkeeper, may recover the fine by warrant from any one of his majesty's justices of the peace.

Provided,

[SECT. 2.] That this act shall not be construed or understood to relate to any coach, chariot, chaise or chair, belonging to his excellency the governour, the lieutenant-governour, or any of the members of the general court.

Provided, also,

[SECT. 3.] That nothing in this act shall be understood or construed to restrain any of the hous[e]holders, or inhabitants living in King['s] Street in Boston, on either side of the court-house, or any person improving any of the cellars under the court-house, from causing any coach, chaise, chair, cart or trucks, in the service of such hous[e]holder or inhabitant, or person improving as aforesaid, to be brought to or carried from their respective dwellings, or the said cellars, during the sitting of the general court.

Limitation.

[SECT. 4.] This act to continue and be in force for one year from the publication thereof, and no longer. [*Passed June 29; published July 2.*

CHAPTER 5.

AN ACT TO PREVENT DAM[M]AGE BEING DONE ON THE MEADOWS AND BEACHES LYING IN THE TOWNSHIP OF BARNSTABLE, ON THE SOUTH SIDE OF THE HARBOUR, CONTIGUOUS TO THE [LATE] COMMON FIELDS IN SAID TOWN.

Whereas many persons frequently drive numbers of neat cattle, horses, sheep and swine, to feed upon the beaches, meadows and shoars adjoining to the late common fields in said Barnstable, between said fields and the harbour, whereby the ground is much broken and damnified and the sand blown on said meadows and uplands adjoining, to the great dam[m]age not only of private persons in their property, but also to the said town in general, so far as relates to said town's meadow appropriated to maintain a pound,— Preamble.

Be it enacted by the Governour, Council and House of Representatives,

[Sect. 1.] That from and after the publication of this act, no person or persons shall presume to turn or drive any ne[e][a]t cattle, or horse-kind, or sheep, or swine, to or upon any of the beaches, meadows or shoars that lye between the late common fields in said Barnstable, anywhere from Calves'-Pasture Point, to Yarmouth line, round as the shoar goes, upon the penalty of ten shillings a head for ne[e][a]t cattle, horses or mares, and two shillings and sixpence for each sheep and swine, that shall be turned and found on said beaches, meadows or shoars, within the limits aforesaid; which penalty shall be recovered by the selectmen or treasurer of the said town of Barnstable, or any other person that shall inform and sue for the same: the one half of the said forfeiture to him or them that shall inform and sue for the same, the other half to be to and for the use of the poor of the said town. No person to turn or drive any cattle, &c., on the beaches, &c., of Barnstable.

And be it further enacted,

[Sect. 2.] That if any neat cattle, or horse-kind, or sheep, or swine, shall, at any time hereafter, be found feeding on the said beaches, meadows or shoars, that l[y][i]e between the late common fields and the harbour, in said Barnstable, any where from Calves'-Pasture Point to Yarmouth line, [b][r]ound as the shoar goes, that it shall and may be lawful for any person to impound the same, immediately giving notice to the owners, if known, otherwise to give publick notice thereof in the said town of Barnstable, and the two next adjoining towns; and the impounder shall rel[ei][ie]ve the said creatures with suitable meat and water while impounded; and if the owner thereof appear, he shall pay the sum of two shillings and sixpence to the impounder, for each neat beast and horse-kind, and eight pence for each sheep and swine, and the re[a]sonable cost of relieving them, besides the pound-keeper's fees. And if no owner appear within the space of six days to redeem the said cattle or horse-kind, sheep or swine so impounded, and to pay the costs and dam[m]ages occasioned by impounding the same, then and in every such case the person or persons impounding such cattle or horse-kind, sheep or swine, shall cause the same to be sold at publick vendue, and pay the cost and charges arising about the same (publick notice of the time and place of such sale, to be given in the said town of Barnstable and in the town of Yarmouth, forty-eight hours before hand), and the overplus, if any there be, arising by such sale, to be returned to the owner of such cattle or horse-kind, sheep or swine, at any time within twelve months next after, upon his demanding the same; but if no owner appear within the said twelve months, then the said overplus shall be one half to the party impounding, and the other half to the use of the poor of the said town of Barnstable. Cattle found feeding on the beaches aforesaid, to be impounded, &c.

And be it further enacted,

Persons to be annually chosen to see this act observed. [SECT. 3.] That the said town of Barnstable, at their meeting in March, annually, for the choice of town officers, be authorized and impowered to chuse one or more meet person or persons whose duty it shall be to see this act observed, and to prosecute the breakers thereof, and who shall be sworn to the faithful[l] discharge of their office; and in case any person so chosen shall refuse to be sworn, he shall forfeit and pay ten shillings for the use of the poor of the said town of Barnstable; and upon such refusal, said town from time to time to proceed to a new choice of such officer or officers: and the said town of Barnstable, at a town-meeting warned for that purpose, may, at any time before March next, chuse such officers, who shall continue until their annual meeting in March next.

Limitation. [SECT. 4.] This act to continue and be in force for the space of five years from the publication thereof, and no longer. [*Passed June* 29; *published July* 2.

CHAPTER 6.

AN ACT FOR REVIVING AND CONTINUING SUNDRY LAWS OF THIS PROVINCE, EXPIRED OR NEAR EXPIRING.

Preamble. WHEREAS an act was made and pass'd in the tenth and eleventh years
1737-38, chap. 6. of his present majesty's reign, entitled "An Act further to exempt persons commonly called Quakers, within this province, from being
1737-38, chap. 8. taxed for and towards the support of ministers"; and another act made and pass'd in the same year, [i][e]ntitled "An Act in further addition to an act made and pass'd in the first year of his present majesty's reign, entitled 'An Act to prevent coparceners, joint tenants and tenants in common, from committing strip and waste upon lands by them
1740-41, chap. 6. held in common and undivided'"; and another act made and pass'd in the thirteenth and fourteenth year of his present majesty's reign, entitled "An Act further to exempt persons commonly called Annabaptists, within this province, from being taxed for and towards the support
1743-44, chap. 20. of ministers"; and another act made and pass'd in the seventeenth year of his present majesty's reign, entitled "An Act for providing that the solemn affirmation of the people called Quakers, shall in certain cases be accepted instead of an oath in the usual form, and for preventing inconvenienc[i]es by means of their having heretofore acted in some town offices, without taking the oaths by law required for such offices";
1743-44, chap. 22. and another act made and pass'd in the same year, entitled "An Act for rendering more effectual the laws already in being relating to the admeasurement[s] of boards, plank, and timber, and for preventing fraud and abuse in shingles, beef and pork, exported from this province, and also for regulating the assize of staves and hoops";—all which several laws are expired or near expiring: *and whereas* the aforesaid laws have, by experience, been found beneficial and necessary for the several purposes for which they were passed,—

Be it therefore enacted by the Governour, Council and House of Representatives,

Reviving of several acts. That all and every of the aforesaid acts, and every matter and clause therein contained, be and hereby are continued and revived, and shall continue and remain in full force ten years from the publication of this act, and no longer. [*Passed June* 29; *published July* 2.

CHAPTER 7.

AN ACT TO PREVENT DECEIT IN THE GAGE OF CASK.

Whereas his majesty's good subjects within this province, are greatly damaged in the make and measure of their cask, and particularly those of rum and molasses, inasmuch as the hogsheads and other cask, which ought to answer the gage by the rod, have been proved, and upon trial in their drawing off, there hath been wanting seven or eight gallons, and sometimes more, in a hogshead; which persons are obliged to pay for more than they really receive; for remedy whereof,— Preamble. 1737-38, chap. 12.

Be it enacted by the Governour, Council and House of Represent[ati]ves,

[Sect. 1.] That all rum and molasses in casks of all sorts, from a barrel and upwards, that shall be exposed to sale, be mathematically gaged by Gunter-scale, and the quantity said cask can contain, being full, to be set and marked on one head by the gager with a marking-iron; and the said gager shall demand and receive of the owner or owners of such rum or molasses threepence for every cask by him gaged as afores[ai]d, and no more. Rum and molasses to be mathematically gauged.

And be it further enacted,

[Sect. 2.] That the justices of the peace, at their first general sessions in each respective county of this province, from the publication of this act, and afterwards yearly, shall in every town where there shall be occasion, chuse and appoint a fit person or persons to be a gager or gagers, who shall be sworn to the due execution of their office by one of his majesty's justices of the peace within the same county, in the words following; viz[t].,— Justices in their sessions yearly to appoint a gauger or gaugers.

You, A. B., being appointed a gager, according to law, do swear that you will, from time to time, diligently and faithfully discharge and execute the office of a gager, within the limits whereto you are appointed, for the ensuing year and until[l] another be chosen and sworn in your place; and that by and in all the particulars mentioned in the law whereto your office hath relation and you will do therein impartially without fear or favour. So help you God. Gauger's oath.

[Sect. 3.] And every person or persons who shall presume to sell any rum or molasses without being gaged as this act directs, and having the gager's mark upon it, shall forfeit and pay for every cask by him or them sold contrary to the true intent and meaning of this act, the sum of five pounds; one half to the poor of the town where the offence is committed, and the other half to the informer, who shall inform and sue for the same in any of his majesty's courts of record within this province. Penalty for selling without the gauger's mark.

[Sect. 4.] This act to continue and be in force for the space of ten years from the publication thereof, and no longer. [*Passed June* 29; *published July* 2. Limitation.

CHAPTER 8.

AN ACT FOR GRANTING UNTO HIS MAJESTY SEVERAL RATES AND DUTIES OF IMPOST AND TONNAGE OF SHIPPING.

We, his majesty's most loyal and dutiful subjects, the representatives of the province of the Massachusetts Bay, in New England, being desirous of a colateral fund and security for drawing in the bills of credit on this province, have chearfully and unanimously given and granted and do hereby give and grant unto his most excellent majesty to the end and use aforesaid, and for no other use, the several duties of impost upon wines, liquors, goods, wares and merchandize that shall be imported into this province, and tunnage of shipping hereafter mentioned; and pray that it may be enacted,—

And be it accordingly enacted by the Governour, Council and House of Representatives,

[SECT. 1.] That from and after the publication of this act, and during the space of one year, there shall be paid by the importer of all wines, liquors, goods, wares and merchandizes that shall be imported into this province from the place of their growth (salt, cotton-wool, provisions, and every other thing of the growth and produce of New England, and also all prize goods condemned in any part of this province, excepted), the several rates or duties of impost following; viz[t].,—

For every pipe of wine of the Western Islands, one pound.

For every pipe of Madera, one pound five shillings.

For every pipe of other sorts not mentioned, one pound five shillings.

For every hogshead of rum, containing one hundred gallons, one pound.

For every hogshead of sugar, sevenpence.

For every hogshead of molasses, fourpence.

For every hogshead of tobacco, four shillings and sixpence.

For every ton of logwood, ninepence.

—And so, proportionably, for greater or lesser quantities.

And all other commodities, goods or merchandize not mentioned or excepted, fourpence for every twenty shillings value: all goods imported from Great Britain excepted.

[SECT. 2.] And for any of the above wines, liquors, goods, wares and merchandize, &c., that shall be imported into this province from any other port than the places of their growth and produce, there shall be paid by the importer double the value of impost appointed by this act to be received for every species above mentioned, unless they do, *bonâ fide*, belong to the inhabitants of this province and came upon their risque from the port of their growth and produce.

And be it further enacted,

[SECT. 3.] That all the aforesaid impost rates and duties shall be paid in current money or bills of credit of this province of the last emission, by the importer of any wines, liquors, goods or merchandize, unto the commissioners to be appointed as is hereinafter to be directed for entring and receiving the same, at or before the landing of any wines, liquors, goods or merchandize: only the commissioner or receiver is hereby allowed to give credit to such person or persons where his or their duty of impost, in one ship or vessel, doth exceed the sum of three pounds; and in case where the commissioner or receiver shall give credit, he shall settle and ballance his accompts with every person on or before the last day of April, so that the same accounts may be ready to be presented to this court in May next after. And all entries where the impost or duty to be paid doth not exceed three shillings, shall be made without charge to the importer, and not more than sixpence to be demanded for any other single entry to what value soever.

And be it further enacted,

[SECT. 4.] That all masters of ships or other vessells coming into any harbour or port within the province from beyond sea, or from any other province or colony, before bulk be broken and within twenty-four hours after his arrival at such harbour or port, shall make a report to the commissioner or receiver of the impost, to be appointed as is hereinafter mentioned, of the contents of the lading of such ship or vessell, without any charge or fee to be demanded or paid for the same; which report said master shall give in to the commissioner or receiver, under his hand, and shall therein set down and express the quantities and species of the wines, liquors, goods and merchandize laden on board such ship or vessell, with the marks and numbers thereof; and to whom the same is consigned; and also make oath that the said report or manifest of the contents of his lading, so to be by him given in, under his hand as aforesaid, contains a just and true accompt, to the best of his knowledge, of the whole lading taken on board and imported in the said vessell from the port or ports such vessell came from, and that he hath not broken bulk, nor delivered any of the wines, rum or other distill'd liquors or merchandize laden on board the said ship or vessell, directly or indirectly; and if he shall know of any more wines, liquors, goods or merchandize to be imported therein, before the landing thereof he will cause it to be added to his manifest; which manifest shall be agreeable to a printed form for that purpose, which is to be filled up by the said commissioner or receiver according to each particular person's entry; which oath the commissioner or receiver is hereby impowered to administer: after which said master may unload, and not before, on pain of five hundred pounds, to be forfeited and paid by each master that shall neglect his duty in this behalf.

And be it further enacted,

[Sect. 5.] That all merchants, factors and other persons, importers, being owners thereof, or having any of the wines, liquors, goods or merchandize consigned to them, that by this act are lyable to pay impost or duty, shall, by themselves or order, make entry thereof in writing, under their hands, with the said commissioner or receiver, and produce unto him an invoice of all such goods as pay *ad valorem*, and make oath thereto in manner following:—

> You, A. B., do swear that the entry of the goods and merchandize by you now made, exhibits the present price of said goods at this market, and that, *bonâ fide*, according to your best skill and judgment, it is not less than the real value thereof. So help you God.

—which above oath the commissioner or receiver is hereby impowered to administer; and they shall pay the duty and impost by this act required, before such wines, liquors, goods, wares or merchandize be landed or taken out of the vessell in which the same shall be imported.

[Sect. 6.] And no wines, liquors, goods, wares or merchandize that by this act are liable to pay impost or duty, shall be landed on any wharffe, or into any warehouse or other place, but in the daytime only, and that after sunrise and before sunsett, unless in the presence and with the consent of the commissioner or receiver, on pain of forfeiting all such wines, liquors, goods, wares and merchandize, and the lighter, boat or vessell out of which the same shall be landed or put into any warehouse or other place.

[Sect. 7.] And if any person or persons shall not have and produce an invoice of the quantities of rum or liquors to him or them consigned, then the cask wherein the same is shall be gaged at the charge of the importer, that the quantities thereof may be known.

And be it further enacted,

[Sect. 8.] That every merchant or other person importing any wines into this province shall be allowed twelve per cent for leakage: *provided*, such wines shall not have been filled up on board; and that every hogshead, butt or pipe of wine that hath two parts thereof leaked out, shall be accounted for outs, and the merchant or importer to pay no duty for the same. And no master of any ship or vessell shall suffer any wines to be filled up on board without giving a certificate of the quantity so filled up, under his hand, before the landing thereof, to the commissioner or receiver of impost for such port, on pain of forfeiting the sum of one hundred pounds.

[SECT. 9.] And if it be made to appear that any wines imported in any ship or vessell be decayed at the time of unlading thereof, or in twenty days afterwards, oath being made before the commissioner or receiver that the same hath not been landed above that time, the duties and impost paid for such wines shall be repaid unto the importer thereof.

And be it further enacted,

[SECT. 10.] That the master of every ship or vessell importing any liquors, goods, wares or merchandizes, shall be liable to and shall pay the impost for such and so much thereof, contained in his manifest, as shall not be duly entred, nor the duty paid for the same by the person or persons to whom such wines, liquors, goods, wares or merchandize are or shall be consigned. And it shall and may be lawfull, to and for the master of every ship or other vessell, to secure and detain in his hands, at the owner's risque, all such wines, liquors, goods, wares or merchandize imported in any ship or vessell, until he shall receive a certificate, from the commissioner or receiver of the impost, that the duty for the same is paid, and until he be repaid his necessary charges in securing the same; or such master may deliver such wines, liquors, goods, wares or merchandize as are not entred, unto the commissioner or receiver of the impost in such port, or his order, who is hereby impowered and directed to receive and keep the same, at the owner's risque, until the impost thereof, with the charges, be paid; and then to deliver such wines, liquors, goods, wares or merchandize as such master shall direct.

And be it further enacted,

[SECT. 11.] That the commissioner or the receiver of the impost in each port, shall be and hereby is impowered to sue the master of any ship or vessell, for the impost or duty for so much of the lading of any wines, liquors, goods, wares or merchandize imported therein, according to the manifest to be by him given upon oath, as aforesaid, as shall remain not entred and the duty of impost thereof not paid. And where any goods, wares or merchandize are such as that the value thereof are not known, whereby the impost to be recovered of the master, for the same, cannot be ascertained, the owner or person to whom such goods, wares or merchandize are or shall be consigned, shall be summoned to appear as an evidence at the court where such suit for the impost and the duty thereof shall be brought, and be there required to make oath to the value of such goods, wares or merchandize.

And be it further enacted,

[SECT. 12.] That the ship or vessell, with her tackle, apparrell and funiture, the master of which shall make default in anything by this act required to be performed by him, shall be liable to answer and make good the sum or sums forfeited by such master, according to this act, for any such default, as also to make good the impost or duty for any wines, liquors, goods, wares and merchandize not entred as aforesaid; and, upon judgment recovered against such master, the said ship or vessell, with so much of the tackle or appurces thereof as shall be sufficient to satisfy said judgment, may be taken in execution for the same; and the commissioner or receiver of the impost is hereby impowered to make seizure of such ship or vessell, and detain the same under seizure until judgment be given in any suit to be commenced and prosecuted for any of the said forfeitures or impost; to the intent that, if judgment be rendered for the prosecutor or informer, such ship or vessell and appurces may be exposed to sale, for satisfaction thereof, as is before provided: *unless* the owners, or some on their behalf, for the releasing such ship or vessell from under seizure or restraint, shall give sufficient security unto the commissioner or receiver of impost that seized the same, to respond and satisfy the sum or value of the forfeiture and duties, with charges, that shall be recovered against the master thereof, upon suit to be brought for the same, as aforesaid; and the master occasioning such loss and damage unto his owners, thro his default or neglect, shall be liable unto their action for the same.

And be it further enacted,

[Sect. 13.] That the naval officer within any of the ports of this province shall not clear or give passes unto any master of any ship or other vessell, outward bound, until he shall be certified, by the commissioner or receiver of the impost, that the duties and impost for the goods last imported in such ship or vessell are paid or secured to be paid.

[Sect. 14.] And the commissioner or receiver of the impost is hereby impowered to allow bills of store to the master of any ship or vessell importing any wines or liquors, for such private adventures as shall belong to the master or seamen of such ship or vessell, at the discretion of the commissioner or receiver, not exceeding three per cent of the lading; and the duties payable by this act for such wines or liquors, in such bills of stores mentioned and expressed, shall be abated.

And whereas, many persons heretofore have caused to be imported, from the neighbouring governments, into this province, by land-carriage, large quantities of wine, rum and other merchandize, subjected to duty by this act, but have made no report thereof to the officer of impost, or any of his deputies, nor have paid any duty therefor, contrary to the true intent and meaning of this act,—

Be it therefore enacted,

[Sect. 15.] That, whensoever any rum, wine or other merchandize, by this act subjected to any duties, shall be hereafter imported from any of the neighbouring governments, by land, into any town of this province, the owner thereof, or person importing the same, shall make report thereof to the said officer, or some one of his deputies, and pay the duties hereby required therefor, on pain and penalty of forfeiting the same.

And be it further enacted,

[Sect. 16.] That all penalties, fines and forfeitures accruing and arising by virtue of this act, shall be one half to his majesty for the uses and intents for which the aforementioned duties of impost are granted, and the other half to him or them that shall seize, inform and sue for the same, by action, bill, plaint or information, in any of his majesty's courts of record, wherein no essoign, protection or wager of law shall be allowed: the whole charge of prosecution to be taken out of the half belonging to the informer.

And be it further enacted,

[Sect. 17.] That there shall be paid, by the master of every ship or other vessell, coming into any port or ports into this province, to trade or traffick, whereof all the owners are not belonging to this province (except such vessells as belong to Great Britain, the provinces or colonies of Pensilvania, West and East Jersy, New York, Connecticut, New Hampshire and Rhode Island), every voyage such ship or vessell does make, one pound of good pistol-powder for every ton such ship or vessell is in burthen: *saving* for that part which is owned in Great Britain, this province, or any of the aforesaid governments, which are hereby exempted; to be paid unto the commissioner or receiver of the duties of impost, and to be employed for the ends and uses aforesaid.

[SECT. 18.] And the said commissioner is hereby impowered to appoint a meet and suitable person, to repair unto and on board any ship or vessell, to take the exact measure or tonnage thereof, in case he shall suspect that the register of such ship or vessell doth not express and set forth the full burthen of the same; the charge thereof to be paid by the master or owner of such ship or vessell, before she be cleared, and in case she shall appear to be of greater burthen: otherwise, to be paid by the commissioner out of the money received by him for impost, and shall be allowed him, accordingly, by the treasurer, in his accompts. And the naval officer shall not clear any vessell, until he be also certified, by the commissioner, that the duty of tonnage for the same is paid, or that it is such a vessell for which none is payable according to this act.

And be it further enacted,

[SECT. 19.] That when and so often as any wine or rum imported into this province, the duty of impost upon which shall have been paid agreeable to this act, shall be reship'd and exported from this government to any other part of the world (the governments of New Hampshire, Connecticutt and Rhode Island excepted) that then, and in every such case, if the exporter of such wine or rum shall make oath, at the time of shipping, before the receiver of impost, or his deputy, that the whole of the wine or rum so ship'd has, *bonâ fide*, had the aforesaid duty of impost paid on the same, and shall afterwards produce a certificate, from some officer of the customs, that the same has been landed out of this government,—or otherwise, in case such rum or wines be exported to any place where there is no officer of the customs, or to any foreign port, the master of the vessell in which the same shall be exported shall make oath that the same has been landed out of the government, and the exporter shall, upon producing such certificate, or upon such oath of the master, make oath that he verily believes no part of said wine or rum has been relanded in this province,—such exporter shall be allowed to draw back from the receiver of impost as follows; vizt.,—

For every pipe of Western Island wine, fifteen shillings.

For every pipe of Madeira and other sorts, eighteen shillings.

And for every hogshead of rum, fifteen shillings.

And be it further enacted,

[SECT. 20.] That there be one fit person, and no more, nominated and appointed by this court, as a commissioner and receiver of the aforesaid duties of impost and tunnage of shipping, and for the inspection, care and management of the said office, and whatsoever relates thereto, to receive commission for the same from the governour or commander-in-chief for the time being, with authority to substitute and appoint a deputy receiver in each port, and other places besides that wherein he resides, and to grant warrants to such deputy receivers for the said place, and to collect and receive the impost and tonnage of shipping as aforesaid that shall become due within such port, and to render the account thereof, and to pay in the same, to the said commissioner and receiver: which said commissioner and receiver shall keep fair books of all entrys and duties arising by virtue of this act; also, a particular account of every vessell, so that the duties of impost and tonnage arising on the said vessell may appear; and the same to lye open, at all seasonable times, to the view and perusal of the treasurer and receiver-general of this province (or any other person or persons whom this court shall appoint), with whom he shall accompt for all collections and payments, and pay all such moneys as shall be in his hands, as the treasurer or receiver-general shall demand it. And the said commissioner or receiver and his deputy or deputies, before their entring upon the execution of their office, shall be sworn to deal truly and faithfully therein, and shall attend in the said office from nine to twelve of the clock in the forenoon, and from two to five a'clock in the afternoon.

[Sect. 21.] And the said commissioner and receiver, for his labour, care and expences in the said office, shall have and receive, out of the province treasury, the sum of twenty-five pounds, per annum; and his deputy or deputies to be paid for their service such sum or sums as the said commissioner and receiver, with the treasurer, shall agree upon, not exceeding seven pounds ten shillings each. And the treasurer is hereby ordered, in passing and receiving the said commissioner's accompts, accordingly, to allow the payment of such salary or salarys, as aforesaid, to himself and his deputies.

Provided,

[Sect. 22.] That no duties of impost shall be demanded for any goods imported after the publication of this act, by vertue of any former act for granting unto his majesty any rates, duties of impost, &c. [*Passed June* 29; *published July* 2.

ACTS

PASSED AT THE SESSION BEGUN AND HELD AT BOSTON, ON THE TWELFTH DAY OF AUGUST, A. D. 1747.

CHAPTER 9.

AN ACT FOR GRANTING A SUM FOR THE PAY OF THE MEMBERS OF THE COUNCIL AND HOUSE OF REPRESENTATIVES, IN GENERAL COURT ASSEMBLED, AND FOR THE ESTABLISHING THE WAGES, &c., OF SUNDRY PERSONS IN THE SERVICE OF THE PROVINCE.

Be it enacted by the Governour, Council and House of Representatives,

Pay of the members of the council.

[SECT. 1.] That from the beginning of the present session of the general court, unto the end of their several sessions, till May next, each member of the council shall be entitled to seven shillings and sixpence per diem, to be paid out of the publick treasury, by warrant, according to the direction of the royal charter, upon certificate, given by the secretary, of the number of days of such member's attendance, and travel to and from the court; twenty miles to be accounted a day's travel.

And be it further enacted,

Pay of the representatives.

[SECT. 2.] That each member of the house of representatives serving the time aforesaid, shall be paid five shillings per diem, upon certificate, given by the clerk of the house of representatives, of the number of days of such member's attendance, and travel to and from the court; twenty miles to be accounted a day's travel.

And be it further enacted,

Pay of the officers and soldiers at Castle William.

[SECT. 3.] That the wages of the captain of Castle William shall be after the rate of seventy-five pounds per annum, from the nineteenth day of November, one thousand seven hundred and forty-six, to the nineteenth day of November, one thousand seven hundred and forty-seven; of the lieutenant, for that term, fifty pounds; of the chaplain, fifty pounds; of the gunner, forty pounds twelve shillings and sixpence; of the gunner's mate, fifty shillings per month; of four serjeants, each thirty-seven shillings and sixpence per month; six quarter-gunners, each thirty-seven shillings and sixpence per month; six corporals, thirty-three shillings each per month; two drummers, each thirty-three shillings per month; one armourer, fifty shillings per month; of forty-five centinels, each twenty-eight shillings per month: for their subsistence, seven shilling and sixpence per week, per man.

And be it further enacted,

Richmond Fort.

[SECT. 4.] That the wages of the captain of Richmond Fort, from the twentieth day of November, one thousand seven hundred and forty-six, to the twentieth day of November, one thousand seven hundred and forty-seven, shall be at the rate of fifty shillings per month; of one serjeant, thirty-one shillings and threepence per month; of one corporal, thirty shillings per month; of one armourer, thirty-seven shillings and sixpence per month; and for the chaplain, thirty-one pound five shillings per annum; of one interpreter, eighteen shillings and ninepence per month, being a centinel; and twelve centinels, twenty-eight shillings and twopence per month.

And be it further enacted,

[SECT. 5.] That the wages of the captain of the truck-house [on] [*of*] George's River, from the twentieth day of November, one thousand seven hundred and forty-six, to the twentieth day of November, one thousand seven hundred and forty-seven, shall be at the rate of fifty shillings per month; of one lieutenant, thirty-two shillings and sixpence per month; of one serjeant, thirty-one shillings and threepence per month; of two corporals, each thirty shillings per month; of thirty-three centinels, each twenty-eight shillings and twopence per month; of an armourer, seventeen shillings and sixpence per month; he being lieutenant; of one interpreter, thirty-seven shillings and sixpence per month; and of the chaplain there, thirty-one pounds five shillings per annum. Truck-house on George's River.

And be it further enacted,

[SECT. 6.] That the wages of the commanding officer of the fort at Brunswick, from the twentieth day of November, one thousand seven hundred and forty-six, to the twentieth day of November, one thousand seven hundred and forty-seven, shall be at the rate of fifty shillings per month; of eleven centinels, each twenty-eight shillings and twopence per month; one serjeant, thirty-one shillings and threepence per month. Brunswick Fort.

And be it further enacted,

[SECT. 7.] That the wages of one serjeant at the truck-house at Saco, from the twentieth day of November, one thousand seven hundred and forty-six, to the twentieth day of November, one thousand seven hundred and forty-seven, shall be at the rate of thirty-seven shillings and sixpence per month; of one corporal, thirty shillings per month; of twelve centinels, each twenty-eight shillings and twopence per month. Truck-house on Saco River.

And be it further enacted,

[SECT. 8.] That the wages of the commanding officer at Frederick Fort, from the twentieth day of November, one thousand seven hundred and forty-six, to the twentieth day of November, one thousand seven hundred and forty-seven, shall be at the rate of fifty shillings per month; of the chaplain there, eighteen pounds fifteen shillings per annum; and twenty-one centinels, each at twenty-eight shillings and twopence per month. Frederick Fort.

And be it further enacted,

[SECT. 9.] That before payment of any muster-rolls be allowed, oath be made by the officer or person presenting such roll, that the officers and soldiers born on such roll have been in actual service for the whole time they stand entered thereon. [*Passed September* 8*; *published September* 14. Oath to be made, &c.

CHAPTER 10.

AN ACT FOR GRANTING THE SUM OF NINETEEN HUNDRED POUNDS, FOR THE SUPPORT OF HIS MAJESTY'S GOVERNOUR.

Be it enacted by the Governour, Council and House of Representatives,

That the sum of nineteen hundred pounds, in bills of credit of the form and tenor last emitted, be and hereby is granted unto his most excellent majesty, to be paid out of the publick treasury to his excellency William Shirley, Esq[r]., captain-general and governour-in-chief in and over his majesty's province of the Massachusetts-Bay, for his

* So according to the record; the date of signing is September 5, on the engrossment.

past services, and further to enable him to manage the publick affairs of the province. [*Passed August* 12 *; *published September* 14.

CHAPTER 11.

AN ACT TO ENABLE THE PROPRIETORS OF SUNCOOK TO RAISE MONEY FOR THE SUPPORT OF THEIR PRESENT MINISTER.

Preamble.

WHEREAS the proprietors of Suncook are under a special covenant to support the Rev[d]. Mr. Whittemore, the present pastor of the church there, but by reason of the late order of his majesty in council respecting the northern boundary of this province, a difficulty has arisen in assessing and collecting money for the purposes aforesaid, whereby considerable inconvenience[s] has arisen, for the removal of which the aid of this court is necessary,—

Be it therefore enacted by the Governour, Council and House of Representatives,

Suncook proprietors empowered to assemble and meet to choose officers, &c.

[SECT. 1.] That it shall be in the power of said proprietors of Suncook to assemble and meet at the dwelling-house of Henry Abbot[t] of Andover, in the county of Essex, in[*n*]holder, on the third Tuesday of October next, at two a'clock in the afternoon, to choose a moderator and clerk, and raise money on said proprietors, necessary to enable them to fulfil[l] the said covenant, and to defrey the charge of the lawsuit that has already been brought by the said minister against the said proprietors, and the necessary expence of assessing and collecting the same; also, to choose assessors, collectors, and a treasurer, for assessing, collecting and receiving the sum and sums so raised; and to choose a committee to call the said proprietors together in March yearly, and at such other times as shall be found necessary for raising money to enable them, from time to time, to fulfill the covenant aforesaid, and to defrey other necessary ministerial charges for the future; and to choose other officers, as occasion may require: the said officers to observe the same rules, in assessing and collecting the respective sums that may be granted to be raised as aforesaid, as the parish assessors and collectors are by law obliged to observe, and to be vested with the same power.

And to the intent the said meeting in October next may be seasonably known,—

Ordered,

[SECT. 2.] That Benjamin Johnson of Woburn be directed to give notice thereof in the "Boston Weekly Gazette[e]," on each of the four weeks that shall next succeed the publication of this act, setting forth the time, place and business of their said meeting.

[SECT. 3.] This act to continue and be in force for the space of five years from the publication thereof, and no longer. [*Passed September* 8 †; *published September* 14.

* This bill was passed to be enacted at the first session, but was not signed by the Governor until the above date. According to the record the date of signing was September 8.

† So according to the record; but according to the engrossment the Governor signed the bill September 5.

CHAPTER 12.

AN ACT IN FURTHER ADDITION TO AND FOR EXPLANATION OF CERTAIN CLAUSES IN THREE SEVERAL ACTS HEREINAFTER MENTION'D, MADE AND PASS'D IN THE [SIXTEENTH] [*FIFTEENTH*] SEVENTEENTH AND EIGHTEENTH YEARS OF HIS PRESENT MAJESTY'S REIGN, FOR ASCERTAINING THE VALUE OF MONEY, AND OF THE BILLS OF PUBLICK CREDIT OF THIS PROVINCE.

WHEREAS in and by an act made and pass'd in the fifteenth year of his present majesty's reign, [e][*i*]ntit[*u*]led "An Act to ascertain the value of money, and of the bills of publick credit of this province, granted this present year for the supply of the treasury, and for securing the credit of said bills," the several courts of judicature are directed, in making up judgments for debts that should be contracted within the term of five years therein limit[*t*]ed, except as therein excepted, in case the province bills by said act emitted, or that should thereafter be emitted, should be depreciated below the value they were set at by said act, to allow the creditor so much in said bills as should make amends for their depreciation below their then stated value, or the value at which such other bills should be stated; *and whereas* in the rule by said act prescribed for determining the value of such bills, from time to time, for the purpose afores[*ai*]d, only silver and bills of exchange are made the standard whereby said bills are to be estimated in order to the paym[*en*]t of private debts to be contracted within the time afores[*ai*]d; which rule, by experience, has been found to be unequal, and not to answer the good intention of the said act, inasmuch as the bills of credit, being the only medium of trade and commerce in this and the other governm[*en*]ts in New England, their value cannot be truly estimated by the prices of any one or two particular commodities or merchandizes, such as bills of exchange and silver now are, and have for several years past been, within this and the afores[*ai*]d other colonies, and the prices of which in bills of publick credit have been found liable to be very suddenly and immoderately increased by a few persons for the sake of serving their own particular trade or interest, whereby the bills of credit have often been, to the great gr[ei][*ie*]vance of debtors, much depreciated with respect to bills of exchange and silver, tho', at the same time, they have kept their value with respect to all other commodities and merchandizes in this province: now, for preventing any future inconvenience which may arise to the debtor from estimating the value of bills of credit by comparing them with the prices of bills of exchange, and silver, alone,— Preamble. 1741-42, chap. 12.

Be it enacted by the Governour, Council and House of Represent-[*ati*]*ves,*

[SECT. 1.] That when any valuation shall be made of the bills of publick credit on this province, in pursuance of said act and for the purposes therein mentioned, regard shall be had not only to silver and bills of exchange, but to the prices of provisions and other necessaries of life, and to the difference that may arise from the plenty or scarcity of them, or other circumstances which may casually occasion the rise or fall of them, at the respective seasons wherein such valuation shall be made as aforesaid. Price of provisions, &c., to be considered in the valuation of the bills.

And whereas the aforemention'd act directs that the valuation of the bills of publick credit as aforesaid, for the purposes afores[*ai*]d, shall be made once in every six months by the general assembly, and in want thereof by a com[*mit*]tee consisting of the eldest councello[u]r for the time being, in each of those counties where any member of his majesty's council is an inhabitant; *and whereas* the said act doth not expressly declare that the determination made by any number of the said committee short of the whole, shall be accounted valid for the purposes afores[*ai*]d, and doubts and disputes have thereupon arisen; for prevention whereof for the future,—

Be it enacted by the Governour, Council and House of Represent-[*ati*]*ves,*

Five councillors to be a quorum for valuing the bills.

[SECT. 2.] That any five of the said councellors shall be a quorum; and every valuation of the bills of publick credit to be made by the whole number of the said councellors, or the major part of such of them as shall convene and be present at the time of making the same (provided the number present be not less than five, and that due notice has been previously given to the rest that shall then be within this province, of the time, place and occasion of their meeting), shall be deemed and counted valid in the law for the purposes in said act mention'd.

And whereas, altho' the method of making up judgm[*en*]t on private debts, with allowance for the sinking of the value of the province bills, as prescribed in the aforesaid act and in another act made and pass'd in the eighteenth year of his present majesty's reign, [e][*i*]ntit[*u*]led "An Act in further addition to an act for ascertaining the value of money, and of the bills of publick credit of this province," is limit-[*t*]ed to debts contracted within or before certain periods mentioned in said acts, respectively, and is not extended to debts thereafter to be contracted; yet unless some certain term of time be limit[*t*]ed for calling in such debts, and for the continuance of the afores[*ai*]d method of making up judgm[*en*]t thereupon, many of said debts may be long outstanding, and, in consequence thereof, it will be requisite, for a rule to the executive courts in their proceedings, that a valuation of said bills be, from time to time, made either by the general assembly or such others as by law are appointed for that service, 'till every of those debts shall be discharged, how long soever that time may be protracted, to the hindrance and interruption of the publick affairs of the province, or to the great trouble, expence and loss of time to those concerned therein; for prevention of which and other inconvenienc[*i*]es,—

1744-45, chap. 29.

Be it enacted by the Governo[*u*]*r, Council and House of Represent-*[*ati*]*ves,*

Limitation of the time for bringing actions on this act.

[SECT. 3.] That in all and every action and actions which shall be brought from and after the last day of September, w[*hi*]ch will be in the year of our Lord one thousand seven hundred and forty-nine, the aforementioned method of making up judgments in the several executive courts of this province, on all debts and dues contracted before the last day of March, one thousand seven hundred and forty-seven, by virtue or in consequence of the power and directions given in the acts afores[*ai*]d, or either of them, shall cease and determine, and no allowance shall be made in making up such judgments for any depreciation of the bills of credit, unless the debt on which such action shall arise did not become payable 'till after the last day of September, *Anno Domini* one thousand seven hundred and forty-nine, or unless the creditor now be and shall continue out of this province 'till after the expiration of the said term, and have no lawful[l] agent or attorney therein, or be a person *non compos mentis,* and have no lawful[l] guardian, or be under some other legal incapacity of bringing his action for the recovery of such debt within the term hereinbefore limit[*t*]ed for that purpose; and if after that term suit shall be brought for any such debts, judgments shall be made up according to the last valuation that shall have been then made.

Saving.

Preamble.

And whereas in and by an act made and pass'd in the seventeenth year of his present majesty's reign, entitled "An Act in addition to and in explanation of sundry clauses of an act, entitled 'An Act to ascertain the value of money, and of the bills of publick credit of this province,'" made and pass'd in the [15th] [*fifteenth*] year of his maj[*es*]ty's reign, it is enacted "That all debts contracted since the last of March, one thousand seven hundred and forty-two, or that shall thereafter be contracted, specialties and express contracts excepted, shall be deemed and adjudged equal to the real value only such bills have passed, or shall pass, at when such debt was or shall be contracted; and every debt of twenty shillings, contracted as aforesaid, shall or may be always hereafter discharged by twenty shillings in said bills; and so *pro ratâ* for a greater or less sum, unless such bills have already, or should hereafter be, depreciated below the value they passed at when such debt was or shall be contracted; and in such case so much shall always be allowed by the respective courts in this province as shall make said bills equal in value to such debt when contracted." 1743-44, chap. 7.

And whereas the debts referred to in the said act appear, by the purview thereof, to be such only as then had been or should be contracted within five years from the last day of March, one thousand seven hundred and forty-two, yet as the said act has by some been construed to extend to debts to be contracted after the expiration of said term, and in consequence of such construction, if admitted, many inconveniencies may arise; wherefore, for prevention thereof, and for removing any doubts or disputes touching the meaning of said act in the case before mentioned,—

Be it enacted and declared by the Governour, Council and House of Representatives,

[SECT. 4.] That the debts referred to and intended in the last herein-before-recited act are such only as had been or should be contracted within the before-mentioned term of five years, from the last day of March one thousand seven hundred and forty-two; and that the rule therein given to the courts of judicature, respecting the allowance to be made for the depreciation of the bills of publick credit, was intended and shall be adjudged, construed and taken to be restrained to debts contracted within the term aforesaid, and not to extend to any other whatsoever. [*Passed September* 12.]

Time for contracting debts, that are to have benefit upon depreciation of the bills, stated

ACT

PASSED AT THE SESSION BEGUN AND HELD AT BOSTON, ON THE SEVENTEENTH DAY OF NOVEMBER, A. D. 1747.

CHAPTER 13.

AN ACT FOR SUPPLYING THE TREASURY WITH THE SUM OF THIRTY-FOUR THOUSAND POUNDS, FOR DISCHARGING THE PUBLICK DEBTS, &c., AND FOR DRAWING THE SAID BILLS INTO THE TREASURY AGAIN.

Be it enacted by the Governour, Council and House of Representatives,

£34,000 bills of credit to be emitted.

[SECT. 1.] That the treasurer be and is hereby impow[e]red and ordered to issue forth the sum of thirty-four thousand pounds in bills of credit of the last tenor and date, now lying in his hands, and received in for taxes, impost and excise, which shall pass in all publick payments, equal to other new-tenor bills emitted since one thousand seven hundred and forty, or if there be not a sufficiency of such bills, that then the committee appointed by this court for signing bills be hereby directed and impowered to take care and make effectual provision to imprint the said bills, or so many as may be needed to compleat the said sum, and to sign and deliver the same to the treasurer, taking his receipt for the same; and the said committee shall be under oath for the faithful performance of the trust by this act reposed in them. And the said sum of thirty-four thousand pounds shall be issued out of the [*publick*] treasury for the purposes and in the manner following; viz[t]., the sum of fourteen thousand pounds, part of the aforesaid sum of thirty-four thousand pounds, shall be applied for the payment of wages that now are or hereafter may be due by virtue of the establishment of Castle William, Frederick Fort, Richmond Fort, George's Truck-house, Saco Truck-house, Brunswick Fort, the ship "Massachusetts Frigate," brigantine "Boston Packet," the sloop in the countr[e]y's service, and the commissary's usual disbursements; and the sum of eleven thousand pounds, part of the aforesaid sum of thirty-four thousand pounds, shall be applied for putting the province into a better posture of defence, for paying off the officers and soldiers in the province service according to the several establishments for that purpose, for purchasing all needful warlike stores for the several forts and garrisons within this province, pursuant to such grants as are or shall be made by this court for those purposes; and the sum of five thousand eight hundred pounds, part of the aforesaid sum of thirty-four thousand pounds, shall be applied for the payment of his majesty's council, and for the payment of all other matters and things for which any grant has been or shall be made by this court, and for all [*other*] stipends, bount[y][*ie*]s and premiums, established by law, or order of court, and for no other purpose whatever.

£14,000 for wages at Castle William and other garrisons, &c.

£11,000 for putting the province into a better posture of defence, &c.

£5,800 for payment of his majesty's council, &c.

And whereas there are sometimes publick entertainments, and, from time to time, contingent and unforeseen charges that demand prompt payment,—

Be it further enacted,

[SECT. 2.] That the sum of two hundred pounds, part of the said sum of thirty-four thousand pounds, shall be applied to defray and pay such entertainments and contingent charges that demand prompt payment; and the sum of three thousand pounds, part of the aforesaid sum of thirty-four thousand pounds, shall be applied for the payment of the house of representatives in the general court during their several sessions this present year.

£200 contingent charges, &c.

£3,000 for the pay of the representatives.

And be it further enacted,

[SECT. 3.] That if there be a surplusage in any sum appropriated, such surplusage shall lye in the treasury for the further order of this court.

Surplusage to lie in the treasury.

And be it further enacted,

[SECT. 4.] That each and every warrant for drawing money out of the treasury, shall direct the treasurer to take the same out of such sums as are respectively appropriated for the payment of such publick debts as the drafts are made to discharge; and the treasurer is hereby directed to pay such money out of such appropriations as directed to, and no other, upon pain of refunding all such sum or sums as he shall otherwise pay, and to keep exact and distinct accompts of all payments made out of such appropriated sums; and the secretary, to whom it belongs to keep the muster-rolls and accompts of charge, shall lay before the house, when they direct, all such muster-rolls and accompts after payment thereof.

Warrants to express the appropriations.

And as a fund and security for drawing the said sum of thirty-four thousand pounds into the treasury again,—

Be it enacted,

[SECT. 5.] That there be and hereby is granted unto his most excellent majesty, for the ends and uses aforesaid, a tax of twenty-one thousand pounds, to be levied on polls, and estates both real and personal, within this province, according to such rules and in such proportions on the several towns and districts within the same, as shall be agreed upon and ordered by this court at their session in May, one thousand seven hundred and forty-eight, and paid into the publick treasury on or before the last day of December then next after.

£21,000 in 1748.

And as a further fund and security for drawing in the said sum of thirty-four thousand pounds,—

Be it enacted,

[SECT. 6.] That the sum of ten thousand pounds, part of the aforesaid sum of thirty-four thousand pounds, be brought in by impost and excise in the year one thousand seven hundred and forty-eight.

£10,000 in 1748.

And as a fund and security for drawing in such sum or sums as shall be paid out to the representatives of the several towns,—

Be it enacted,

[SECT. 7.] That there be and hereby is granted unto his most excellent majesty a tax of such sum or sums as shall be paid to the representatives aforesaid, to be levied and assessed on the polls and estates of the inhabitants of the several towns, according to what their several representatives shall so receive; which sums shall be set on the towns in the next province tax. And the assessors of the said towns shall make their assessment for this tax, and apportion the same according to the rules that shall be prescribed by the act of the general court for assessing the next province tax, and the constables, in their respective districts, shall pay in the same when they pay in the next province tax for the next year, of which the treasurer is hereby directed to keep a distinct and separate accompt; and if there be any surplusage, the

Tax to be made for what is paid the representatives.

same shall lye in the hands of the treasurer for the further order of this court.

And be it further enacted,

Tax for the money hereby emitted, to be made according to the preceding tax act, in case.

[SECT. 8.] That in case the general court shall not at their session in May, one thousand seven hundred and forty-eight, agree and conclude upon an act for raising the aforesaid sum of ten thousand pounds, by impost and excise, in the year one thousand seven hundred and forty-eight, and also upon an act apportioning the aforesaid sum of twenty-one thousand pounds, which by this act is engaged shall be, in said year, apportioned, assessed and levied, that then and in such case each town and district within this province shall pay, by a tax to be levied on polls, and estates both real and personal, within their districts, the same proportion of the said sums of ten thousand pounds and twenty-one thousand pounds as the said towns and districts shall have been taxed by the general court in the tax act then next preceeding; and the province treasurer is hereby directed and fully impowered, some time in the month of June, in the year one thousand seven hundred and forty-eight, to issue and send forth his warrants, directed to the selectmen or assessors of each town and district within this province, requiring them to assess the polls, and estates both real and personal, within their several towns and districts, for their respective part and proportion of the said sums of ten thousand pounds and twenty-one thousand pounds before directed and engaged to be raised and assessed by this act; and the assessors, as also persons assessed, shall observe, be governed by and subject to all such rules and directions as shall have been given in the next preceeding tax act.

And be it further enacted,

Taxes to be paid in the several species herein enumerated.

[SECT. 9.] That the inhabitants of this province shall have liberty, if they see fit, to pay the several sums for which they respectively may, in pursuance of this act, be assessed, in bills of credit of the form and tenor by this act emitted, or in other new-tenor bills, or in bills of the middle tenor, according to their several denominations, or in bills of the old tenor, accounting four for one; or in coined silver, at seven shillings and sixpence per ounce, troy weight, and of sterling alloy, or in gold coin, proportionably; or in merchantable hemp, flax, winter and I[s][*l*]le-of-Sable codfish, refined bar-iron, bloomery-iron, hollow iron-ware, Indian corn, rye, wheat, barley, beef, pork, duck or canvas, whalebone, cordage, train-oil, beeswax, tallow, peas[e], sheepswool, or tann'd sole-leather (the aforesaid commodities being of the produce or manufactures of this province), at such moderate rates and pri[c][*z*]es as the aforesaid general assembly of the year one thousand seven hundred and forty-eight shall set them at; the several persons paying their taxes in any of the commodities afore mentioned, to run the risque and pay the charge of transporting the said commodities to the province treasury; but if the aforesaid general assembly shall not, at their session in May, some time before the twentieth day of June, in said year, agree upon and set the aforesaid species and commodities at some certain price, that then the eldest councello[u]r, for the time being, in each of those counties in the province, of which any one of the council is an inhabitant, together with the province treasurer, or the major part of them, be a committee, who are hereby directed and fully authorized and impow[e]red to do it; and in their settling the prizes and rating the value of those commodities, to state so much of them, respectively, at seven shillings and sixpence as an ounce of silver will purchase at that time in the town of Boston, and so *pro ratâ*. And the treasurer is hereby directed to insert in the several warrants by him sent to the several collectors of the taxes in said year, with the names of the afore-recited commodities, the several rates

How the commodities brought into the treasury are to be rated.

or prices which shall be set on them, either by the general assembly or the committee aforesaid, and direct the aforesaid collectors to receive them so.

Treasurer to sell the said commodities.

[SECT. 10.] And the aforesaid commodities so brought into the treasury shall, as soon as may be, be disposed of by the treasurer to the best advantage for so much as they will fetch in bills of credit hereby to be emitted, or for silver or gold, which silver or gold shall be delivered to the possessor of said bills in exchange for them; that is to say, one ounce of silver coin, and so gold in proportion, for seven shillings and sixpence, and so *pro ratâ* for a greater or lesser sum; and if any loss shall happen by the sale of the aforesaid species, or by any unforeseen accident, such deficiency shall be made good by a tax of the year next following, so as fully and effectually to call in the whole sum of thirty-four thousand pounds in said bills hereby ordered to be issued; and if there be a surplusage, it shall remain a stock in the treasury. [*Passed December* 12.*

* This bill was passed to be enacted at the third session, but was not signed by the Governor until the above date.

ACTS

PASSED AT THE SESSION BEGUN AND HELD AT BOSTON, ON THE THIRD DAY OF FEBRUARY, A. D. 1747–48.

CHAPTER 14.

AN ACT FOR SUPPLYING THE TREASURY WITH THE SUM OF TWENTY-FIVE THOUSAND POUNDS FOR DISCHARGING THE PUBLICK DEBTS, &c[A]., AND FOR DRAWING THE SAID BILLS INTO THE TREASURY AGAIN.

Be it enacted by the Governour, Council and House of Representatives,

£25,000 bills of credit to be emitted.

[SECT. 1.] That the treasurer be and hereby is impow[e]red and ordered to emit and issue forth the sum of twenty-five thousand pounds in bills of credit of the last tenor and date, now lying in his hands, and received in for taxes, impost and excise, which shall pass in all publick and private payments, equal to other new-tenor bills emitted since one thousand seven hundred and forty, or if there shall not be a sufficiency of such bills, that then the committee appointed by this court for signing bills are hereby directed and impow[e]red to take care and make effectual provision, as soon as may be, to imprint so many as may be needed to compleat the said sum, and to sign and deliver the same to the treasurer, taking his receipt for the same; and the said committee shall be under oath for the faithful performance of the trust by this act reposed in them. And the said sum of twenty-five thousand pounds shall be issued out of the treasury in manner and for the purposes following;

£21,563 for paying officers and soldiers.

viz[t]., the sum of twenty-one thousand five hundred and sixty-three pounds, part of the aforesaid sum of twenty-five thousand pounds, shall be appl[y][i]ed for paying of such officers and soldiers as have done service for the province, whose wages are now due, according to the several establishments for that purpose, for purchasing all needful warlike stores and for the commissary's necessary disbursements for the service of the several forts and garrisons, and other forces within this province, pursuant to such grants as are or shall be made by this court for those

£3,237 for payment of other debts, &c.

purposes; and the sum of three thousand two hundred and thirty-seven pounds, part of the aforesaid sum of twenty-five thousand pounds, shall be appl[y][i]ed for the discharging of other debts owing from this province to persons that have served or shall serve them by order of this court in such matters and things where there is no establishment nor any certain sum assigned for such service, and for paper, printing and writing for this court, and the surgeon of Castle William, and

£200 for public entertainments, &c.

wooding of said castle; and the remaining sum of two hundred pounds shall be appl[y][i]ed to defrey the charge of any publick entertainments, or any contingent unforeseen charges that demand prompt payment, and for no other use whatsoever.

And be it further enacted,

[SECT. 2.] That if there be a surplusage in any sum appropriated, such surplusage shall l[y][*i*]e in the treasury for the further order of this court.

Surplusage to lie in the treasury.

And be it further enacted,

[SECT. 3.] That each and every warrant for drawing money out of the treasury, shall direct the treasurer to take the same out of such sums as are respectively appropriated for the payment of such publick debts as the drafts are made to discharge; and the treasurer is hereby directed and ordered to pay such money out of such appropriation as directed to, and no other, upon pain of refunding all such sum or sums as he shall otherwise pay, and to keep exact and distinct accompt[s] of all payments made out of such appropriated sums; and the secretary, to whom it belongs to keep the muster-rolls and accompts of charge, shall lay before the house, when they direct, all such muster-rolls and accompts after payment thereof.

Warrants to express the appropriations.

And as a fund and security for drawing the said sum of twenty-five thousand pounds into the treasury again,—

Be it further enacted,

[SECT. 4.] That there be and hereby is granted unto his most excellent majesty, for the ends and uses aforesaid, a tax of twenty-five thousand pounds, to be levied on polls, and estates both real and personal, within this province, according to such rules and in such proportions, on the several towns and districts within the same, as shall be agreed upon and ordered by this court at their session in May, one thousand seven hundred and forty-eight, and paid into the public[*k*] treasury on or before the last day of December then next after.

£25,000 in 1748.

And be it further enacted,

[SECT. 5.] That in case the general court shall not at their session in May, one thousand seven hundred and forty-eight, agree and conclude upon an act apportioning the sum, which by this act is engaged shall be, in that year, apportioned, assessed and levied, that then and in such case each town and district within this province shall pay, by a tax to be levied on polls, and estates both real and personal, within their districts, the same proportions of the said sum as the said towns and districts shall have been taxed by the great and general court in the tax act then next preceeding; and the province treasurer is hereby fully impow[e]red and directed, some time in the month of June, in the year one thousand seven hundred and forty-eight, to issue and send forth his warrants, directed to the selectmen or assessors of each town and district within this province, requiring them to assess the polls, and estates both real and personal, within their several towns and districts, for their respective part and proportion of the sum before directed and engaged to be assessed by this act; and the assessors, as also persons assessed, shall observe, be governed by and subject to all such rules and directions as shall have been given in the next preceeding tax act.

Tax for the money hereby emitted, to be made according to the preceding tax act, in case.

And be it further enacted,

[SECT. 6.] That the inhabitants of this province shall have liberty, if they see fit, to pay the several sums for which they respectively may, in pursuance of this act, be assessed, in bills of credit of the form and tenor by this act emitted, or in other new-tenor bills, or in bills of the middle tenor, according to their several denominations, or in bills of the old tenor, accounting four for one; or in coined silver, at seven shillings and sixpence an ounce, troy weight, of sterling alloy, or in gold coin, proportionably; or in merchantable hemp, flax, winter and Isle-of-Sable codfish, refined bar-iron, bloomery-iron, hollow iron-ware, Indian corn, rye, wheat, barley, pork, beef, duck or canvas, whalebone, cordage, train-oil, beeswax, tallow, peas[e], sheepswool, or

Taxes to be paid in the several species herein enumerated.

tann'd sole-leather (the aforesaid commodities being of the produce or manufactures of this province), at such moderate rates and pri[c][z]es as the general assembly of the year one thousand seven hundred and forty-eight shall set them at; the several persons paying their taxes in any of the commodities aforementioned, to run the risque and pay the charge of transporting the said commodities to the province treasury; but if the aforesaid general assembly shall not, at their session in May, some time before the twent[y][*i*]eth day of June, in said year, agree upon and set the aforesaid species and commodities at some certain rates and prices, that then the eldest counc[i][*e*]ll[e][*o*]r, for the time being, of each of those counties in the province, of which any one of the council is an inhabitant, together with the province treasurer, or the major part of them, be a committee, who are hereby authorized and fully impow[e]red to do it; and in their set[*t*]ling the pri[c][*z*]es and rating the value of those commodities, to set so much of them, respectively, at seven shillings and sixpence as an ounce of silver will purchase at that time in the town of Boston, and so *pro ratâ*. And the treasurer is hereby directed to insert in the several warrants by him sent to the several collectors of the taxes in said year, with the names of the afore-recited commodities, the several rates or prices which shall be set on them, either by the general assembly or the committee aforesaid, and direct the aforesaid collectors to receive them so.

How the commodities brought into treasury are to be rated.

Treasurer to sell the said commodities.

[SECT. 7.] And the aforesaid commodities so brought into the treasury shall, as soon as may be, be disposed of by the treasurer to the best advantage for so much as they will fetch in bills of credit hereby to be emitted, or for silver and gold, which silver and gold shall be delivered to the possessor of said bills in exchange for them; that is to say, one ounce of silver coin, and so gold in proportion, for seven shillings and sixpence, and so *pro ratâ* for a greater or less sum; and if any loss shall happen by the sale of the aforesaid species, or by any unforeseen accident, such d[i][*e*][f]ficiency shall be made good by a tax of the year next following, so as fully and effectually to call in the whole sum of twenty-five thousand pounds in said bills hereby ordered to be emitted; and if there be a surplusage, it shall remain a stock in the treasury. [*Passed February* 24, 1747-48; *published March* 31, 1748.

CHAPTER 15.

AN ACT FOR ALTERING THE TIMES APPOINTED FOR HOLDING THE SUPERIOUR COURT OF JUDICATURE, COURT OF ASSIZE AND GENERAL GOAL DELIVERY, WITHIN AND FOR THE COUNTIES OF ESSEX AND BRISTOL.

Preamble. 1699-1700, chap. 3, § 2. 1742-43, chap. 32, § 2. 1745-46, chap. 21. 1746-47, chap. 15.

WHEREAS the times by law appointed for holding the superiour court of judicature, court of assize and general goal delivery at Salem, within and for the county of Essex, and at Taunton, within and for the county of Bristol, are found to be inconvenient,—

Be it therefore enacted by the Governour, Council and House of Representatives,

Alteration of courts at Salem and Taunton.

[SECT. 1.] That the time for holding the said superiour court of judicature, court of assize and general goal delivery at Salem, for the county of Essex, shall henceforth be the third Tuesday in October annually; and the time for holding the said court at Taunton, for the county of Bristol, shall henceforth be the second Tuesday in May annually; and all officers and other persons concerned are required to conform themselves accordingly.

And be it further enacted,

[SECT. 2.] That all appeals, writs of rev[ei][*ie*]w, recognizances, warrants and other process already issued, taken or depending in the said county of Bristol, which were to have been returned or proceeded on at the time heretofore appointed by law for holding the said court at Taunton, shall be valid and stand good, to all intents and purposes in the law, and shall be returned and proceeded on at the time appointed by this act for holding the same. [*Passed February* 23, 1747–48; *published March* 31, 1748.

CHAPTER 16.

AN ACT FOR EXPLAINING AN ACT, [E][*I*]NTIT[*U*]LED "AN ACT TO PREVENT AND MAKE VOID CLANDESTINE AND ILLEGAL PURCHASES OF LANDS FROM [*THE*] INDIANS," SO FAR AS RELATES TO THE DEVI[C][S]E OR BEQUEST OF ANY REAL ESTATE BY THE LAST WILL AND TESTAMENT OF ANY INDIANS.

WHEREAS doubts have arisen, whether the act pass'd in the thirteenth **Preamble.**
year of King William the Third, [e][*i*]ntit[*u*]led "An Act to prevent **1701-2, chap. 11.**
and make void clandestine and illegal purchases of lands from the Indians," doth extend to any device or bequest of real estate made by the last will and testament of any Indian,—

Be it therefore declared and enacted by the Governour, Council and House of Represent[*ati*]*ves*,

That the said act was intended to extend, and did, doth and ought to be understood to extend, to all devises of real estates made by the last wills and testaments of any of the said Indians; and all such devises of lands or other real estate, whatsoever, by any last will and testament from any Indian or Indians inhabiting within this province, to any English person or persons, that have been heretofore made and have not been approved by the general court, and also all such as shall hereafter be madė, unless the approbation of the general court shall be obtained, are hereby declared utterly void and of no effect. [*Passed March* 3, 1747-48; *published March* 31, 1748. **Explanation of an act relating to Indians' selling lands.**

NOTES.—There were six sessions of the General Court this year; but no acts were passed at the third and sixth sessions.

The engrossments of all the acts of this year are preserved, and all were printed with the sessions-acts, except chapters 1 and 8, which being, respectively, the tax act and impost act, were printed separately.

Secretary Willard enclosed all the acts of this year with his letter to Secretary Hill, dated November 1, 1748. On the 8th of February, following, these acts were referred by the Board of Trade to Mr. Lamb for his opinion thereon in point of law, but no evidence has been discovered that they were ever laid before the Privy Council. As late as June, 1754, a memorandum in the records of the Board of Trade states that chapters 3 and 5 were never laid before the Crown.

On the morning of the 9th of December, O. S., this year, the court-house in Boston was destroyed by fire, and with it a large part of the records of the Province. The following is the record of the course taken by the Assembly to replace the lost records:—

"Decr 9, 1747. In the House of Represent^{ves} Ordered that Mr Frost, Capt Partridge & Col^{o} Otis with such as the Honble Board shall appoint be a Committee to enquire after and secure any Books Records & Papers that may have been preserv'd from the Flames which consum'd the Court House this morning—In Council, Read and Concur'd—& Josiah Willard, Sam^{ll} Welles and Andrew Oliver Esq^{rs} are joined in the affair.

In the House of Represent^{ves} The House taking into further Consideration the Awfull Providence of God in the Destruction of the Court House & great Part of the Public Records by Fire.

Ordered that Mr Speaker Col^{o} Stoddard, Col^{o} Heath, Col^{o} Choate, Mr Frost Capt Partridge & Col^{o} Otis with such as the Honble Board shall join be a Committee to consider and

Report what is necessary to be done by the Court at this juncture—In Council, Read & concur'd & Josiah Willard, Sam[ll] Welles, John Cushing, John Chandler & Andrew Oliver Esq[rs] are joined in the affair."—*Council Records, vol. XVIII, p.* 261.

"Decem[r] 11, 1747. Josiah Willard Esq[r] from the Committee of both Houses appointed to Consider the Circumstances of the Province in Relation to the Desolation of the Court House—gave in the following Report, viz.

The Committee appointed to Consider what may be proper for this Court to do with respect to the Circumstances the public affairs of the Province are brought into by the late Burning of the Court House &c. Report as their Opinion that the Secretary be directed forthwith to get the Duplicate of the General Court Books, now in his Hands fairly transcrib'd & when finished that they be kept in a Seperate place from the said Duplicate: That forasmuch as the said Duplicate reaches no further than the fifth of July 1737, The Agents of this Province in London be directed to procure if possible from the Lords Commissioners of Trade and Plantations, the Copies of the said Generall Court Books from the said fifth of July 1737, to the fourteenth of February last, now lying in their Office, the said Agents leaving Copys thereof in the said office, to be drawn in the Cheapest manner they can, by employing some other Persons than the Clerks of that office, if that may be allow'd; But if the said Copies now laying in that Office cannot be obtained, that then the Copys taken from them, as above, being first examin'd and attested by the said Agents be bound up in three Volumes, leaving in each Book a number of Leaves for a Table & transmitted here as soon as may be——That the Agents be also directed to enquire into the state of the minutes of Council of this Province from the Year 1692 to the End of February last, (suppos'd to ly in the said Plantation Office) whether they are compleat, and if so at what expence they may be procur'd? and inform this Court as soon as may be——That the Secretary record in his Office the first or Old Charter of this Province And the Charter of King William & Queen Mary with the Commiss[s] of the Governour Lieut. Governour Justices of the Superiour Court & his Own.

That the Clerks of the Peace be directed to send into the Secretary's Office, perfect Lists of the Justices of the Peace (distinguishing those that are in the Quorum) & the Justices of the Inferiour Court & Common Pleas in their respective Countys. In the name of the Committee—J. Willard

In the House of Represent[ves] Read & Ordered that this Report be accepted.

In Council; Read & Concur'd, and Consented to by the Governour."—*Ibid., p.* 262.

"Dec[r] 11, 1747. In the House of Represent[ves] Ordered that the Secretary be directed to improve as many Clerks as he shall judge Necessary for drawing Duplicates of the Records of the Generall Court of the Province. In Council Read and concur'd——Consented to by the Governour."—*Ibid., p.* 263.

"Decem[r] 1st, 1749. In the House of Represent[ves] Ordered that the Secretary be directed to employ some proper Persons, at the Charge of the Province, to put all the Papers which were saved from the Flames in the late Fire which consumed the Town House, upon File in proper Order. In Council; Read & Concur'd Consented to by the Lieu[t] Govern[r]."—*Ibid., vol. XIX., p.* 76.

Chap. 4. "June 13, 1746. In the House of Represent[ves] Voted that all Persons be strictly forbidden to beat any Drums within ten rods of the Court House during the Sitting of either House, upon pain of the displeasure of this Court, unless by order of the Governor and Council.

In Council Read and Concur'd. Consented to by the Governor."—*Ibid., vol. XVII., b.* 5, *p.* 52.

Chap. 11. "April 24. 1747. A Petition of William Lovejoy & others Inhabitants of a place called Suncook, setting forth their difficulties by reason of their being taken within the boundaries of New Hampshire, upon running of the Northern line & the Government of New Hampshire casting of all care of them; shewing also that their late Minister has recoverd Judgment against them at the Quarter Sessions held at Charlestown in this Province for nine years Arrearage of Salary and inasmuch as the Petitioners had no opportunity to defend themselves against this action having no knowledge of it till Judgment was pass'd, therefore praying for Relief from this Court, as to this Judgment & Execution & the claims of New Hampshire men to their lands.

In the House of Represent[ves] Read & Ordered that the consideration of this Petition be refer'd till the next May Session, and Execution within mentioned is stayed in the mean time.

In Council Read & Concur'd. Concented to by the Governor."—*Ibid., vol. XVIII., p.* 123.

"May 30. 1747. On the petition of William Lovejoy & others of Suncook, praying as enter'd the 23[d] of April last.

In Council, Read & Order'd that Samuel Welles, Joseph Wilder, & John Chandler Esq[rs] with such as the Honb[le] House shall join be a Committee to take this petition under consideration & report what they judge proper for this Court to do thereon.

In the House of Represent[ves] Read & Concurr'd, and Mr. Hubbard, Mr Lee Cpt. Gardner & Coll. Gerrish are joined in the affair."—*Ibid., p.* 138.

"June 3. 1747. Samuel Welles Esq[r] from the Committee of both Houses on the petition of William Lovejoy & others of Suncook gave in their Report.

In the House of Represent[ves] Read & Ordered that this Petition be recommitted: & the Committee are directed to hear the Parties; or any person who shall appear on their behalf; & report as soon as may be what they judge proper for this Court to do thereon.

In Council, Read & Concurr'd."—*Ibid., p.* 140.

"August 25. 1747. John Hill Esq[r] from the Committee on Suncook Affair reported as follows,

The Committee to whom was referr'd the petition of the Proprietors of a place called Suncook, report that the said Proprietors be impower'd to collect the Assessment already made, for the payment of the Arrearages of the Minister's Salary, also to raise, Assess &

collect, such sums of money as may be needfull to enable them for the future to fullfill their Contract with him & to pay the charges of the suit mentioned in the petition; and that the petitioners have leave to bring in a bill accordingly.

In Council, Read & Accepted.

In the House of Representves Read & Concurr'd.—*Ibid*, *p*. 201.

Chap. 15. "October 11, 1746. In the House of Representvs. Whereas the time for holding the Superior Court of Judicature Court of Assize & General Goal Delivery at Bristol is by Law established to be on the fourth Wednesday of October & the time for holding the Court of general Sessions of the peace & Inferior Court of Common Pleas at Barnstable within & for the County of Barnstable is by Law established to be on the third Tuesday of October, which this year happens to be on the day immediately before the said fourth Wednesday & many persons being obliged to give their attendance at the said Superior Court of Judicature & Court of Assize as also at said Court of General Sessions of the peace & Inferior Court of common pleas which renders it impracticable to have all the before mentioned Courts to sit on the Days aforesaid.

Therefore Ordered that the said Court of General Sessions of the Peace & Inferior Court of Common Pleas be adjourn'd to the first Tuesday of November next & all officers & persons, concern'd in said Courts are ordered to confine themselves to that time & all Writs, Pleas & Processes, whatsoever are to be hear'd adjudged & determined at that time as fully to all Intents & purposes as if said Court sat on the third Tuesday of October.

In Council Read & Concur'd. Consented to by the Governr."—*Ibid*., *p*. 10.

ACTS,

PASSED 1748–49.

ACTS

PASSED AT THE SESSION BEGUN AND HELD AT BOSTON, ON THE TWENTY-FIFTH DAY OF MAY, A. D. 1748.

CHAPTER 1.

AN ACT FOR APPORTIONING AND ASSESSING A TAX OF NINETY-ONE THOUSAND POUNDS; AND ALSO FOR APPORTIONING AND ASSESSING A FURTHER TAX OF FOUR THOUSAND FOUR HUNDRED AND EIGHTEEN POUNDS FIVE SHILLINGS, PAID THE REPRESENTATIVES FOR THEIR SERVICE AND ATTENDANCE IN THE GENERAL COURT, AND TRAVEL; AND NINETY POUNDS, SUNDRY FINES IMPOSED ON TOWNS FOR NOT SENDING REPRESENTATIVES; AMOUNTING IN THE WHOLE TO NINETY-FIVE THOUSAND FIVE HUNDRED AND EIGHT POUNDS FIVE SHILLINGS.

WHEREAS the great and general court or assembly of the province of
the Massachusetts Bay, did, at their session* in February, one thousand 1744-45, chap. 21,
seven hundred and forty-four, pass an act for levying a tax of twenty § 5.
thousand and seven hundred pounds, in bills of credit by said act
emitted; and, at their session in September,† one thousand seven hundred and forty-six, did pass an act for levying a tax of five thousand 1746-47, chap. 14,
pounds, in bills of credit emitted by said act; and, at their session in § 4.
March, one thousand seven hundred and forty-six, did pass an act for
levying a tax of nine thousand seven hundred and fifty pounds, in
bills of credit emitted by said act; and, at their session in May, one
thousand seven hundred and forty-seven, did pass an act for levying a 1747-48, chap. 2,
tax of eight thousand pounds, in bills of credit emitted by said act; § 3.
and, at their session in October,‡ the same year, did pass an act for 1747-48, chap. 13,
levying a tax of twenty-one thousand pounds, in bills of credit emitted § 5.
by said act; and, at their session in February, the same year, did pass
an act for levying a tax of twenty-five thousand pounds, in bills of 1747-48, chap. 14,
credit emitted by said act; each of the several sums aforesaid to be § 4.
assessed the present year,—amounting in the whole to eighty-nine thousand four hundred and fifty pounds; and [by] [*in*] the aforesaid acts
provision was made that the general court might, this present year,
apportion the same on the several towns in this province, if they thought
fit: and the assembly aforesaid have likewise ordered the sum of four 1747-48, chap. 13,
thousand four hundred and eighteen pounds five shillings, paid the § 7.
representatives the last year, should be levied and assessed, this present
year, on the polls and estates of the several towns, according to what
their several representatives have respectively received; and the assembly aforesaid have also ordered that the sum of ten thousand pounds be 1747-48, chap. 13,
brought into the treasury by impost and excise, or otherwise, by a tax § 6.

* This session began November 28, 1744, and, after several short recesses, was dissolved April 25, 1745.

† This session began August 27.

‡ This session began November 17.

on polls and estates this present year, all which sums amount to one hundred and three thousand eight hundred and sixty-eight pounds five shillings; *wherefore*, for the ordering, directing and effectual drawing in the sum of one hundred and three thousand eight hundred and sixty-eight pounds five shillings, pursuant to the funds and grants aforesaid, into the treasury, according to the apportionment now agreed to by this court; the sum of eight thousand three hundred and seventy pounds, arising by the duties of impost, tunnage of shipping and excise, with the sum of ninety pounds, fines, being first deducted, there remains the sum of ninety-five thousand four hundred and eight[*een*]* pounds five shillings to be drawn into the treasury in the following manner; viz[t]., ninety-one thousand† pounds by a tax on the polls and estates of the several towns, and four thousand four hundred and eighteen pounds five shillings, paid the representatives the last year; we, his majesty's most loyal and dutiful subjects, the representatives in general court assembled, pray that it may be enacted,—

And be it accordingly enacted by the Governour, Council and House of Representatives,

[SECT. 1.] That each town and district within this province be assessed and pay, as such town's and district's proportion of the sum of ninety-one thousand pounds, in bills of credit, and their representatives' pay, and fines, four thousand five hundred and eight pounds five shillings, the several sums following; that is to say,—

* £95,408.

† £90,990.

IN THE COUNTY OF SUFFOLK.

	Representatives' Pay, and Fines.	Province Tax.	Sum Total.	
Boston,	£130 10s. 0d.	£16,380 0s. 0d.	Sixteen [illegible] [illegible] five [illegible] [illegible] and ten pounds ten shillings,	£16,510 10s. 0d.
Roxbury,	37 15 0	847 1 2	Eight [illegible] [illegible] [and] [illegible] four pounds [illegible] shillings and two-pence,	884 16 2
Dorchester,	37 15 0	802 13 11	Eight [illegible] [illegible] and forty [illegible] pounds eight [illegible] and [illegible],	840 8 11
Milton,	17 15 0	371 4 1	Three [illegible] [illegible] and eighty-eight [illegible] [illegible] shillings and [a] [one] penny,	388 19 1
Braintree,	45 15 0	887 5 0	Nine [illegible] [illegible] and [illegible] three [illegible],	933 0 0
[illegible],	45 17 6	513 7 10	Five hundred and fifty-nine [illegible] five shillings and [illegible],	559 5 4
[illegible],	39 10 0	958 3 1	Nine [illegible] [illegible] and ninety-seven pounds thirteen shillings and [a] [one] penny,	997 13 1
[illegible],	45 17 6	631 6 3	Six [illegible] [illegible] and [illegible] pounds three shillings and nine-pence,	677 3 9
[illegible],	40 5 0	385 12 3	Four [illegible] [illegible] and twenty-five pounds [illegible] shillings and three-pence,	425 17 3
[illegible],	41 5 0	508 6 2	Five hundred and [illegible] nine pounds [illegible] shillings and [illegible],	549 11 2
[illegible],	32 2 6	228 0 10	Two hundred and sixty pounds three shillings and [illegible],	260 3 4
[illegible],	45 17 6	466 15 1	Five [illegible] [illegible] and [illegible] pounds [illegible] shillings and [illegible],	512 12 7
[illegible],	0 0 0	203 4 8	Two [illegible] [illegible] and three [illegible] pounds four [illegible] and [illegible],	203 4 8
[illegible],	37 15 0	302 19 1	Three [illegible] [illegible] and forty pounds fourteen [illegible] and [a] [one] penny,	340 14 1
[illegible],	25 0 0	271 2 1	Two [illegible] and [illegible] pounds two shillings and [a] [one] [illegible],	296 2 1
Bellingham,	0 0 0	101 19 11	One [illegible] [illegible] and [illegible] pounds [illegible] shillings and [illegible],	101 19 11
[illegible],	0 0 0	158 2 3	One [illegible] [illegible] and fifty-eight pounds two shillings and [illegible],	158 2 3
[illegible],	34 15 0	351 2 2	Three [illegible] [illegible] and eighty-five pounds [illegible] [illegible] and two-pence,	385 17 2
	£657 15s. 0d.	£24,368 5s. 8d.	[Twenty-five thousand and twenty-six pounds and eightpence],	£25,026 0s. 8d.

IN THE COUNTY OF ESSEX.

Salem,	£39 10s. 0d.	£2,730 0s. 0d.	Two thousand seven hundred and sixty-nine pounds ten shillings,	£2,769 10s. 0d.
Ipswich,	47 10 0	2,513 9 11	Two thousand five hundred and sixty pounds nineteen shill[in]gs and elevenpence,	2,560 19 11

IN THE COUNTY OF ESSEX—*Continued.*

	[illegible]es' [illegible], [illegible]d fines.	Province tax.	Sum total.	
[illegible],	£50 5s. 0d.	£2,330 14s. 9d.	Two [illegible] [illegible] [illegible] and eighty [illegible]ds [illegible] shill[*in*]gs and [9d] [*ninepence*],	£2,380 19s. 9d.
Marblehead,	33 0 0	1,771 9 4	[illegible] [illegible] eight hundred and four [illegible] [illegible] shill[*in*]gs and [illegible],	1,804 9 4
Lynn,	45 17 6	957 0 4	[illegible] [illegible] and two [illegible]ds [illegible] shillings and [illegible],	1,002 17 10
[illegible]r,	44 5 0	1,099 11 8	[illegible] [illegible] [illegible] and [illegible] [illegible]ds [illegible] [illegible] and [8d] [*eightp.*],	1,143 16 8
Beverl[e]y,	32 5 0	702 19 6	Seven [illegible] and [illegible] pounds four [illegible] and [illegible],	735 4 6
Rowley,	44 0 0	685 18 3	Seven [illegible] and [illegible] [illegible]ds [illegible] shill[*in*]gs and [3d] [*threepence*],	729 18 3
Salisbury,	44 10 0	606 13 4	Six hundred and fifty-one [illegible]ds three shillings and [illegible],	651 3 4
Haverhill,	41 10 0	616 18 1	Six [illegible] and fifty-eight [illegible]ds eight shillings and [a] [*one*] [illegible]y,	658 8 1
G[illegible]]cester,	42 5 0	1,140 18 3	[illegible] [illegible] one hundred and [illegible] [illegible]ds [illegible] shill[*in*]gs and [3] [*threep.*],	1,183 3 3
[illegible]d,	38 0 0	348 9 1	Three hundred and eighty-six [illegible], [illegible] shillings and [a] [*one*] [illegible]y,	386 9 1
Boxford,	42 5 0	437 3 7	Four [illegible] and seventy-nine [illegible]ds eight shillings and seven-p[illegible]e,	479 8 7
[illegible]y,	46 15 0	505 16 2	Five hundred and [illegible]-two pounds [illegible]n shillings and [illegible]e,	52 11 2
Bradford,	44 15 0	381 1 3	Four [illegible] and twenty-five [illegible]ds [illegible] shillings and three-p[illegible],	425 16 3
W[illegible],	47 0 0	318 2 5	Three [illegible] and sixty-five [illegible]ds two [illegible] and [illegible]e,	365 2 5
[illegible]r,	0 0 0	264 5 7	Two [illegible] and sixty-four [illegible] five [illegible] and [illegible]e,	264 5 7
[illegible]n,	0 0 0	140 5 10	[illegible] [illegible] and [illegible] [illegible]ds [illegible] shillings and [illegible]e,	140 5 10
[illegible]n,	14 10 0	271 17 3	Two [illegible] and [illegible]x [illegible] [illegible] [illegible] and [illegible],	286 7 3
Rumford,	0 0 0	0 0 0		0 0 0
	£698 2s. 6d.	£17,822 14s. 7d.		£18,520 17s. 1d.

IN THE COUNTY OF MIDDLESEX.

Cambridge,	£60 0s. 0d.	£600 12s. 0d.	Six hundred and sixty pounds twelve shillings,	£660 12s. 0d.
Charlestown,	66 10 0	1,230 0 4	Twelve hundred and ninety-six pounds ten shillings and fourpence,	1,296 10 4
Watertown,	45 0 0	375 15 1	Four hundred and twenty pounds fifteen shillings and a penny,	420 15 1

[illegible],	£46 15s. 0d.	[illegible]50 7s. 5d.	Seven [illegible] and [illegible]-seven [illegible] two shillings and [illegible] [fivepence],	£797 2s. 5d.
[illegible],	43 10 0	353 7 8	Three [illegible] and [illegible] [illegible] [illegible] seventeen shillings and [8d] [eightpence],	396 17 8
Woburn,	45 0 0	585 16 3	Six hundred [illegible] thirty pounds [illegible] shillings and [illegible],	630 16 3
Reading,	45 0 0	643 1 4	Six [illegible] and [illegible]-eight pounds one shilling and fourpence,	688 1 4
[illegible],	46 15 0	668 17 0	Seven [illegible] and fifteen [illegible] twelve [illegible],	715 12 0
[illegible],	37 15 0	538 8 4	Five [illegible] and seventy-six [illegible] three [illegible] and [4d] [fourpence],	576 3 4
Marlborough,	39 10 0	690 9 3	Seven hundred and [illegible] [illegible] [illegible] shill[in]gs [3d] [threepence],	729 19 3
Lexington,	43 5 0	[illegible] 3 9	Four hundred and fifty-eight [illegible] eight shill[in]gs and [9d] [ninepence],	458 8 9
[illegible],	45 0 0	[illegible]6 17 2	Six [illegible] and ninety [illegible] pounds [illegible] shill[in]gs and [2d] [[illegible]pence],	691 17 2
[illegible],	40 15 0	371 11 8	[illegible] [illegible] and [illegible] pounds six shill[in]gs and [illegible],	412 6 8
Billerica,	43 15 0	383 6 9	[illegible] [illegible] and [illegible] [illegible] pounds [illegible] [illegible] and [9d] [ninepence],	427 1 9
[illegible],	37 5 0	241 10 7	Two [illegible] and [illegible]-eight pounds [illegible] shill[in]gs and [7d] [sevenpence],	278 15 7
[illegible] [illegible],	0 0 0	172 2 10	[illegible] [illegible] and [illegible]-two [illegible] two shill[in]gs and [illegible],	172 2 10
Groton,	48 15 0	591 17 7	Six [illegible] and forty [illegible] [illegible] [illegible] and [illegible],	640 12 7
Framingham,	29 15 0	489 10 1	Five [illegible] and [illegible] pounds five [illegible] and [1d] [[illegible]penny],	519 5 1
[illegible],	37 15 0	289 6 1	Three [illegible] and [illegible]-seven [illegible] one [illegible] and a [illegible],	327 1 1
Stow,	46 0 0	225 19 8	Two hundred and seventy-one pounds [illegible] shill[in]gs and [8d] [eightpence],	271 19 8
Dunstable and Nottingham,	0 0 0	136 10 0	[illegible] [illegible] and thirty-six [illegible] ten shillings,	136 10 0
Dracut[t],	0 0 0	150 18 2	[illegible] [illegible] and fifty [illegible] eighteen shillings and twopence,	150 18 2
Stoneham,	0 0 0	193 15 1	[illegible] hundred and [illegible] [illegible] fifteen shillings and [a] [one] [illegible],	193 15 1
Littleton,	44 15 0	272 12 5	Three [illegible] and [illegible] [illegible] seven [illegible] and fivepence,	317 7 5
Hopkin[s]ton,	41 10 0	189 11 8	Two [illegible] and [illegible] [illegible] one shilling and eightpence,	231 1 8
Bedford,	0 0 0	178 19 4	[illegible] [illegible] and [illegible]-eight [illegible] [illegible] shill[in]gs and fourpence,	178 19 4
Westford,	0 0 0	244 3 8	Two hundred and forty-four pounds three shill[in]gs and eightpence,	244 3 8
Wilmington,	0 0 0	174 0 9	One hundred and seventy-four pounds and ninepence,	174 0 9
Tewk[e]sbury,	0 0 0	160 7 9	One hundred and sixty pounds seven shillings and ninepence,	160 7 9
Acton,	0 0 0	121 14 3	One hundred and twenty-one pounds fourteen shill[in]gs and threepence,	121 14 3
Waltham,	31 15 0	333 5 9	Three hundred and sixty-five pounds and ninepence,	365 0 9

IN THE COUNTY OF MIDDLESEX—*Continued.*

	REPRESENTATIVES' PAY, AND FINES.	PROVINCE TAX.	SUM TOTAL.	
Townshend,	£0 0*s.* 0*d.*	£68 5*s.* 0*d.*	Sixty-eight pounds five shillings,	£68 5*s.* 0*d.*
English inhab[*itan*]ts of Natick,	0 0 0	91 0 0	Ninety-one pounds,	91 0 0
	£966 0*s.* 0*d.*	£12,579 4*s.* 8*d.*		£13,545 4*s.* 8*d.*

IN THE COUNTY OF HAMPSHIRE.

Springfield,	£44 15*s.* 0*d.*	£997 4*s.* 2*d.*	One thousand and forty-one pounds [illegible] shillings and [illegible],	£1,041 19*s.* 2*d.*
Northampton,	12 0 0	655 11 7	Six hundred and sixty-seven pounds [illegible] shillings and sevenp[illegible]e,	667 11 7
Hadley,	40 5 0	469 0 7	Five hundred and nine pounds five shillings and sevenpence,	509 5 7
Hatfield,	42 5 0	301 1 2	Three hundred and forty-three pounds six shillings and [illegible],	343 6 2
Westfield,	36 0	384 17 1	Four hundred and twenty pounds seventeen shillings and a penny,	420 17 1
Suffield,	35 5 0	500 17 7	Five hundred and thirty-six [illegible] two shill[*in*]gs and sevenpence,	536 2 7
Enfield,	47 5 0	297 5 4	Three hundred and forty-four pounds ten shillings and fourpence,	344 10 4
[illegible]d,	40 15 0	303 14 3	Three [illegible] and forty-four pounds nine shillings and threepence,	344 9 3
Sunderland,	0	154 14 0	One hundred and fifty-four pounds [illegible] shillings,	154 14 0
[illegible]d,	0 0 0	135 14 10	One hundred and thirty-five pounds fourteen shill[*in*]gs and tenpee,	135 14 10
[illegible]d,	31 5 0	266 11 1	Two [illegible] and ninety-seven [illegible] sixteen shillings and a penny,	297 16 1
Somers,	0 0 0	163 8 5	One [illegible] and sixty-three pounds eight shillings and [illegible],	163 8 5
[illegible]d,	0 0 0	159 5 0	One hundred and fifty-nine pounds five shillings,	159 5 0
Elbows,	0 0 0	91 0 0	[illegible] [illegible],	91 0 0
	£329 15*s.* 0*d.*	£4,880 5*s.* 1*d.*		£5,210 0*s.* 1*d.*

IN THE COUNTY OF WORCESTER.

Worcester,	£36 2*s.* 6*d.*	£311 5*s.* 11*d.*	Three hundred and forty-seven pounds eight shillings and fivepence,	£347 8*s.* 5*d.*
Lancaster,	46 10 0	515 13 4	Five hundred [and] sixty-two pounds three shillings and fourpence,	562 3 4
Mendon,	43 0 0	529 13 11	Five hundred [*and*] seventy-two pounds thirteen shillings and elevenpence,	572 13 11
Woodstock, £40 fine,	78 15 0	468 5 5	Five hundred and forty-seven pounds and fivepence,	547 0 5

Brookfield,	£42 15s. 0d.	£316 12s. 1d.	Three [illegible] [and] [illegible]-nine [illegible] [illegible] shill[in]gs and a penny,	£359 7s. 1d.
Southborough,	0 0 0	205 10 2	[illegible]o hundred and five pounds ten shillings and [illegible],	205 10 2
L[ei][ie] [illegible], £25 fine,	62 7 6	289 13 8	Three hundred and [illegible]o pounds one shilling and [illegible],	352 1 2
Rutland,	0 0 0	187 13 9	One [illegible] and [illegible]- seven pounds thirteen [illegible] and nine-pence,	187 13 9
Lunenb[o]urg[h],	44 10 0	232 1 0	Two hundred and [illegible]-six pounds [and] [illegible] shillings,	276 11 0
Westborough,	41 0 0	322 5 10	Three hundred [illegible] [illegible]- three pounds five [illegible] and [illegible],	363 5 10
Shrewsbury,	39 5 0	285 2 8	[illegible] [illegible] and [illegible]-four [illegible] seven shillings and eight-pence,	324 7 8
Oxford,	41 10 0	218 0 5	[illegible]o hundred [and] fifty-nine pounds ten shillings and [illegible],	259 10 5
[illegible],	37 15 0	344 5 8	Three [illegible] [illegible] [illegible]wo pounds and [illegible],	382 0 8
Uxbridge,	0 0 0	245 6 5	[illegible]o hundred and [illegible] [illegible] six shillings and [illegible],	245 6 5
[illegible],	50 5 0	210 1 2	[illegible]o hundred and [illegible] pounds six [illegible] and [illegible],	260 6 2
Grafton,	0 0 0	178 4 2	One hundred and [illegible]- ight pounds four shillings and [illegible],	178 4 2
Upton,	0 0 0	72 8 5	Seventy-two pounds ight shillings and [illegible],	72 8 5
[illegible],	0 0 0	153 3 8	One hundred and fifty-three [illegible] three shillings and [illegible]ence,	153 3 8
Bolton,	15 15 0	204 7 5	Two hundred and [illegible] pounds two shillings and [illegible],	220 2 5
Sturbridge,	0 0 0	77 7 0	[illegible]- [illegible] [illegible] [illegible] seven shillings,	77 7 0
[illegible],	0 0 0	63 14 0	[illegible]- three pounds [illegible] fourteen shillings,	63 14 0
[illegible],	0 0 0	60 5 9	[illegible]ty pounds five shillings and [illegible],	60 5 9
Hardwick,	0 0 0	45 10 0	Forty-five [illegible] [illegible] ten [illegible],	45 10 0
	£579 10s. 0d.	£5,536 11s. 10d.		£6,116 1s. 10d.

IN THE COUNTY OF PLYMOUTH.

Plymouth,	£42 10s. 0d.	£852 14s. 11d.	Eight [illegible] and [illegible]-five [illegible] four shillings and [illegible]-[illegible],	£895 4s. 11d.
Plym[p]ton,	45 10 0	452 6 11	Four hundred and ninety-seven pounds [illegible] shillings and [illegible]-pence,	497 16 11
Scituate,	48 10 0	[illegible]08 10 1	[illegible] [one thousand [illegible]] [illegible] and fifty-seven pounds and one [illegible],	1,357 0 1
[illegible],	38 5 0	1,037 15 7	Ten hundred [one thousand] and seventy-six [illegible] and [illegible]-pence,	1,076 0 7
[illegible],	40 2 6	646 2 0	Six hundred and eighty-six [illegible] four shillings and sixpence,	686 4 6
Pembroke,	48 10 0	347 6 4	Three [illegible] and [illegible]-five pounds sixteen [illegible] and four-pence,	395 16 4
Duxbury,	45 0 0	304 1 10	Three hundred and forty-nine [illegible] one [illegible] and [illegible],	349 1 10

IN THE COUNTY OF PLYMOUTH—*Continued.*

	REPRESENTATIVES' PAY, AND FINES.	PROVINCE TAX.	SUM TOTAL.	
Middleborough,	£50 5s. 0d.	£766 5s. 11d.	Eight hundred and sixteen pounds ten shillings and elevenpence,	£816 10s. 11d.
Rochester,	35 5 0	488 7 4	Five hundred and twenty-three pounds twelve shillings and fourpence,	523 12 4
Abington,	0 0 0	218 0 5	Two hundred and eighteen pounds and fivepence,	218 0 5
Kingston,	0 0 0	238 9 11	Two hundred and thirty-eight pounds nine shillings and elevenpence,	238 9 11
Han[n]over,	0 0 0	280 19 3	Two hundred and eighty pounds nineteen shillings and threepence,	280 19 3
Halifax,	0 0 0	182 0 0	One hundred and eighty-two pounds,	182 0 0
Warham,	0 0 0	91 0 0	Ninety-one pounds,	91 0 0
	£393 17s. 6d.	£7,214 0s. 6d.		£7,607 18s. 0d.

IN THE COUNTY OF BARNSTABLE.

	REPRESENTATIVES' PAY, AND FINES.	PROVINCE TAX.	SUM TOTAL.	
Barnstable,	£55 0s. 0d.	£913 8s. 3d.	Nine hundred and sixty-eight [illegible] pounds eight shillings and [illegible]pence,	£968 8s. 3d.
Sandwich,	41 15 0	492 3 2	Five hundred and thirty-three pounds eighteen shillings and twopence,	533 18 2
[illegible]h,	32 0 0	563 8 10	Five hundred and [illegible]-five pounds eight shillings and [illegible]pence,	595 8 10
Eastham,	43 10 0	679 9 4	Seven hundred and twenty-two pounds [illegible]teen shillings and fourpence,	722 19 4
Truro,	0 0 0	89 2 1	Eighty-nine pounds two shillings and a penny,	89 2 1
Harwich,	43 10 0	470 18 6	Five hundred and fourteen pounds eight shillings and sixpence,	514 8 6
Falmouth,	38 10 0	333 13 4	Three hundred and seventy-two pounds three shillings and fourpence,	372 3 4
Chatham,	0 0 0	277 3 5	Two hundred and seventy-seven pounds three shillings and fivepence,	277 3 5
	£254 5s. 0d.	£3,819 6s. 11d.		£4,073 11s. 11d.

IN THE COUNTY OF BRISTOL.

Bristol,	£0 0s. 0d.	£599 1s. 8d.	Five [illegible]d ad ninety-nine [illegible]ds one [illegible]g ad [illegible]e,	£599 1s. 8d.
Taunton,	44 5 0	910 15 2	Nine hundred and fifty-five [illegible]ds ad t[illegible]e,	[9]55 0 2
Norton,	23 15 0	457 5 6	Four [illegible]d ad th- one u[illegible]ds ad [illegible]e,	481 0 6
Easton,	0 0 0	178 19 4	[illegible] [illegible]d and [illegible]ght [illegible]ds [illegible]n shillings ad f[illegible]r-p,	178 19 4
Dartmouth,	45 15 0	1,410 17 7	[illegible] [illegible]d ad fifty-six [illegible]ds [illegible]e shilli[illegible]s ad seven-p,	1,456 12 7
Dighton,	25 15 0	321 18 3	Three [illegible]d ad forty-[illegible]en [illegible]ds thirteen shillings ad three-pe,	347 13 3
Rehoboth,	39 0 0	1,124 4 7	E[illegible]n [illegible]e [illegible] [illegible]d *one*] [illegible]d ad sixty-three [illegible]ds four shillings ad [illegible]e,	1,163 4 7
Little Compton,	0 0 0	644 11 8	Six [illegible]d and forty-four [illegible]ds eleven shilli[illegible]s ad [illegible],	644 11 8
Swan[z][s]ey with Shawamet,	37 5 0	903 18 8	[illegible]e [illegible]d ad forty-one [illegible]ds three shillings ad eightpence,	[9]41 3 8
Tiverton,	0 0 0	728 0 0	Seven hundred ad t[illegible]ght [illegible]ds,	728 0 0
Freetown,	28 10 0	299 3 3	Three [illegible]d [*d*] [illegible] t[illegible]-[illegible]en [illegible]ds [illegible]n shillings ad [illegible]e,	327 13 3
Attleborough,	36 5 0	457 5 6	F[illegible]r [illegible]d ad t[illegible]-three [illegible]ds [illegible]n [illegible]s ad [illegible]e,	493 10 6
Barrington,	0 0 0	261 4 11	Two [illegible]d ad t[illegible]e [illegible]ds f[illegible]r [illegible]s ad [illegible]e,	261 4 11
Raynham,	0 0 0	207 8 1	Two [illegible]d ad seven [illegible]ds eight [illegible]s ad [ne] [*a*] [illegible]ny,	207 8 1
Berkley,	0 0 0	196 0 7	[illegible]e hundred ad [illegible] [illegible]ix [illegible]ds ad e[illegible]e,	196 0 7
	£280 10s. 0d.	£8,700 14s. 9d.		£8,981 4s. 9d.

IN THE COUNTY OF YORK.

York,	£38 0s. [illegible]	£[illegible]33 0s. 7d.	Eight hundred and seventy-one pounds and sevenpence,	£871 [illegible] 7d.
Kittery,	36 10 0	1,146 19 7	Eleven [*one thousand one*] hundred and eighty-three pounds nine shillings and sevenpen[ce],	1,183 9 7
Berwick,	27 10 0	487 4 7	Five hundred and fourteen pounds fourteen shillings and seven-pence,	514 14 7
Wells,	18 10 0	[illegible]1 10 9	Four hundred and twenty pounds and ninepence,	420 0 9
Falmouth,	39 0 0	699 18 10	Seven hundred and thirty-eight pounds eighteen shillings and [seven] [*ten*] pence,	738 18 10
Biddeford,	30 0 0	276 8 3	Three hundred and six pounds eight shillings and threepence,	306 8 3
Arund[l]e[*l*],	0 0 0	180 2 1	One hundred and eighty pounds two shillings and one penny,	180 2 1

IN THE COUNTY OF YORK—*Continued.*

	REPRESENTATIVES' PAY, AND FINES.	PROVINCE TAX.	SUM TOTAL.	
Scarborough,	£30 10*s.* 0*d.*	£363 12*s.* 5*d.*	Three hundred and ninety-four pounds two shillings and fivepence,	£394 2*s.* 5*d.*
North Yarmouth,	54 0 0	154 14 0	Two hundred and eight pounds [*and*] fourteen shillings,	208 14 0
Georgetown,	30 0 0	182 0 0	Two hundred and twelve pounds,	212 0 0
Brunswick,	23 5 0	61 8 6	Eighty-four pounds thirteen shillings and sixpence,	84 13 6
	£327 5*s.** 0*d.*	£4,786 19*s.* 7*d.*		£5,114 4*s.* 7*d.*

IN THE COUNTY OF DUKES COUNTY.

Edgartown,	£0 0*s.* 0*d.*	£226 14*s.* 10*d.*	Two hundred and twenty-six pounds fourteen shillings and tenpence,	£226 14*s.* 10*d.*
Chilmark,	0 0 0	287 8 2	Two hundred and eighty-seven pounds eight shillings and twopence,	287 8 2
Ti[l]sbury,	0 0 0	177 16 7	One hundred and seventy-seven pounds sixteen shillings and sevenpence,	177 16 7
	£0 0*s.* 0*d.*	£691 19*s.* 7*d.*		£691 19*s.* 7*d.*

IN NANTUCKET COUNTY.

Sherburn[e],	£21 5*s.* 0*d.*	£599 16*s.* 10*d.*	Six hundred and twenty-one pounds one shilling and tenpence,	£621 1*s.* 10*d.*

* In the printed act this is incorrectly given as 12*s.*

RECAPITULATION.

County			Sum in words	Total
Suffolk,	£657 15s. 0d.	£24,368 5s. 8d.	Twenty-five [illegible] and twenty-six [illegible] and eightpence,	£25,026 0s. 8d.
Essex,	698 2 6	17,822 14 7	[illegible] [illegible] five hundred and [illegible] [illegible] [illegible] shil-l[ings] and a [illegible],	18,520 17 1
[illegible]ex,	966 0 0	12,579 4 8	[illegible] [illegible] five [illegible] and forty-five [illegible] four shil-[illegible] and [illegible][ce],	13,545 4 8
[illegible]e,	329 15 0	4,880 5 1	Fifty- [*five* [illegible]] two [illegible] and [illegible] [illegible] and [a] [*one*] penny,	5,210 0 1
W[illegible]r,	579 10 0	5,536 11 10	Six [illegible] one hundred and [illegible] [illegible] one shilling and [illegible]-[illegible],	6,116 1 10
[illegible]h,	393 17 6	7,214 0 6	[illegible] [illegible] six hundred and seven [illegible] [*and*] [illegible] shil-lings,	7,607 18 0
[illegible]e,	254 5 0	3,819 6 11	F[illegible] [illegible] and [illegible] [illegible] [illegible] shilli[n]gs and eleven-[illegible],	4,073 11 11
Bristol,	280 10 0	8,700 14 9	Eight [illegible] [illegible] [illegible] and [illegible] [illegible] four shil-l[ings] and [illegible],	8,981 4 9
York,	327 5 0	4,786 19 7	Fifty- [*[illegible]* [illegible]] one [illegible] and [illegible] [illegible] four shil-[illegible] and [illegible],	5,114 4 7
Dukes County,	0 0 0	691 19 7	S[illegible] hundred and [illegible] [illegible] [illegible] [illegible] and seven-pence,	691 19 7
Nantucket,	21 5 0	599 16 10	S[illegible] hundred and [illegible]-one [illegible] one shilling[s] and [illegible]pence,	621 1 10
	£4,508 5s. 0d.	£91,000 0s. 0d.	[*Ninety-five thousand five hundred and eight pounds and five shil-lings*],	£95,508 5s. 0d.

And be it further enacted,

[SECT. 2.] That the treasurer do forthwith send out his warrants, directed to the selectmen or assessors of each town or district within this province, requiring them, respectively, to assess the sum hereby set on such town or district, in manner following; that is to say, to assess all rateable male polls above the age of sixteen years, within their respective towns or districts, or next adjoyning to them, belonging to no other town, at nineteen shillings and sixpence per pol[e][*l*], and proportionably in assessing the fines mentioned in this act, and the additional sum received out of the treasury for the payment of the representatives (except the governour, lieutenant-governour and their families, the president, fellows and students of Harvard College, set[*t*]led ministers and gramm[e][*a*]r-school masters, who are hereby exempted as well from being taxed for their polls, as for their estates being in their own hands and under their actual management and improvement); and other persons, if such there be, who, thro'[*ugh*] age, infirmity or extre[a]m[*e*] poverty, in the judgment of the assessors, are not cap[e]-able to pay towards publick charges, they may exempt their polls, and so much of their estates as in their prudence they shall think fit and judge meet.

[SECT. 3.] And the justices in the general sessions, in the respective count[y][*ie*]s assembled, in granting a county tax or assessment, are hereby ordered and directed to apportion the same on the several towns in such county in proportion to their province rate, exclusive of what has been paid out of the publick treasury to the representative of such town for his service; and the assessors of each town in the province are also directed, in making an assessment, to govern themselves by the same rule; and all estates, both real and personal, lying within the limits of such town or district, or next unto the same, not paying elsewhere, in whose hands, tenure, occupation or possession soever the same is or shall be found, and also the incomes or profits which any person or persons, except as before excepted, do or shall receive from any trade, faculty, business or [i][*e*]mployment whatsoever, and all profits that shall or may arise by money or other estate not particularly otherwise assessed, or commissions of profit in their improvement, according to their understanding and cunning, at one penny on the pound; and to abate or multiply the same, if need be, so as to make up the sum set and ordered hereby for such town or district to pay; and, in making their assessments, to estimate houses and lands at six years' income of the yearly rents, in the bills last emitted, whereat the same may be reasonably set or let for in the place where they lye: *saving* all contracts between landlord and tenant, and where no contract is, the landlord to reimburse one-half of the tax set upon such houses and lands; and [*to*] estimate negro, Indian and molatto servants proportionably as other personal estate, according to their sound judgment and discretion; as also to estimate every ox of four years old and upwards, at forty shillings in bills of the last emission; every cow of three years old and upwards, at thirty shillings; every horse and mare of three years old and upwards, at forty shillings; every swine of one year old and upwards, at eight shillings; every g[r]oat and sheep of one year old and upwards, at three shillings: likewise requiring the said assessors to make a fair list of the said assessment, setting forth, in distinct columns, against each particular person's name, how much he or she is assessed at for polls, and how much for houses and lands, and how much for personal estate, and income by trade or faculty; and if as guardian, or for any estate, in his or her improvement, in trust, to be distinctly express[e]d; and the list or lists, so perfected and signed by them, or the major part of them, to commit to the collectors or constables of such town or district, and to return a certificate of the name or names of such collectors, constable or constables, together with the sum total to each of them committed, unto himself, some time before the last day of October.

[Sect. 4.] And the treasurer for the time being, upon receipt of such certificate, is hereby impowered and ordered to issue forth his warrants to the collector, constable or constables of such town or district, requiring him or them, respectively, to collect the whole of each respective sum assessed on each particular person, before the last day of May next; and of the inhabitants of the town of Boston, some time in March next; and to pay in their collection, and issue the accompts of the whole, at or before the last day of June, which will be in the year of our Lord one thousand seven hundred and forty-nine.

And be it further enacted,

[Sect. 5.] That the assessors of each town and district, respectively, in convenient time before their making the assessment, shall give seasonable warning to the inhabitants, in a town meeting, or by posting up notifications in some place or places in such town or district, or notify the inhabitants to give or bring in to the assessors true and perfect lists of their polls, and rateable estate[s], and income by trade or faculty, and gain by money at interest; and if any person or persons shall neglect or refuse so to do, or bring in a false list, it shall be lawful to and for the assessors to assess such person or persons, according to their known ability in such town, in their sound judgment and discretion, their due proportion of this tax, as near as they can, agreeable to the rules herein given, under the penalty of twenty shillings for each person that shall be convicted by legal proof, in the judgment of the said assessors, of bringing in a false list; the said fines to be for the use of the poor of such town or district where the delinquent lives, to be lev[y][*i*]ed by warrant from the assessors, directed to the collector or constable, in manner as is directed for gathering town assessments, and to be paid in to the town treasury or selectmen for the use aforesaid: *saving* to the party ag[*g*]rieved at the judgment of the assessors in setting forth such fine, liberty of appeal therefrom to the court of general sessions of the peace within the county, for relief, as in case of being overrated. And if any person or persons shall not bring in a list of their estate, as aforesaid, to the assessors, he or they so neglecting shall not be admitted to make application to the court of sessions for any abatement of the assessment laid on him.

[Sect. 6.] And if the party be not convicted of any falseness in the list, by him presented, of the polls, rateable estate, or income by trade or faculty, business or employment, which he doth or shall exercise, or in gain by money at interest or otherwise, or other estate not particularly assessed, such list shall be a rule for such person's proportion to the tax, which the assessors may not exceed.

And forasmuch as, oftentimes, sundry persons, not belonging to this province, bring considerable trade and merchandize, and by reason that the tax or rate of the town where they come to trade is finished and delivered to the constable or collector, and, before the next year's assessment, are gone out of the province, and so pay nothing towards the support of the government, tho'[*ugh*], in the time of their residing there, they reaped considerable gain by trade, and had the protection of the government,—

Be it further enacted,

[Sect. 7.] That when any such person or persons shall come and reside in any town within this province, and bring any merchandize, and trade, to deal therewith, the assessors of such town are hereby impowered to rate and assess all such persons according to their circumstances, pursuant to the rule and directions in this act provided, tho' the former rate may have been finished, and the new one not perfected, as aforesaid; and the constables or collectors are hereby enjoyned to levy and collect all such sums committed to them, and assessed on persons who are not of this province, and pay the same in to the town treasury.

And be it further enacted,

[SECT. 8.] That the inhabitants of this province have liberty, if they see fit, to pay the several sums for which they respectively may be assessed at, as their proportion of the aforesaid sum of ninety-four thousand five hundred and eight pounds five shillings, in bills of credit emitted in and since the year one thousand seven hundred and forty-one, according to their denominations; or in coined silver, at seven shillings and sixpence per ounce, troy weight, or in gold coin in proportion; or in bills of credit of the middle tenor, so called, according to their several denominations; or in bills of the old tenor, accounting four for one; or in good merchantable hemp, at fourpence per pound; or in good, merchantable, Isle-of-Sable codfish, at ten shillings per quintal; or in good refined bar[r]-iron, at fifteen pounds per ton; or in bloomery-iron, at twelve pounds per ton; or in h[a][*o*]llow iron-ware, at twelve pounds per ton; or in good Indian corn, at two shillings and threepence per bushel[l]; or in good winter rye, at two shillings and sixpence per bushel[l]; or in good winter wheat, at three shillings per bushel[l]; or in good barley, at two shillings per bushel[l]; or in good barrel[l] pork, at two pounds per barrel[l]; or in barrel[l] beef, at one pound five shillings per barrel[l]; or in duck or canvas, at two pounds ten shillings per bolt, each bolt to weigh forty-three pounds; or in long whalebone, at two shillings and threepence per pound; or in merchantable cordage, at one pound five shillings per hundred; or in good train-o[i][*y*]l, at one pound ten shillings per barrel[l]; or in good be[a][*e*]swax, at tenpence per pound; or in good bayberry-wax, at sixpence per pound; or in good tryed tallow, at fourpence per pound; or in good pease, at three shillings per bushel[l]; or in good sheepswool, at ninepence per pound; or in good, tann[e]d sole-leather, at fourpence per pound: all which aforesaid commodities shall be of the produce of this province, and, as soon as conveniently may, be disposed of by the treasurer to the best advantage, for so much as they will fetch in bills of credit, or for silver and gold; and the several persons paying their taxes in any of the commodities afore mentioned, to run the risque and pay the charge of transporting the said commodities to the province treasury.

[SECT. 9.] And if any loss shall happen by the sale of the aforesaid species, it shall be made good by a tax of the next year; and if there be a surplusage, it shall remain a stock in the treasury.

And whereas by the late determination and order of his majesty in council, the town of Bristol falls within the colony of Rhode Island; and part of the towns of Little Compton, Swan[s][*z*]ey, Tiverton and Barrington, by said determination, likewise falls within said colony; and altho it be just and equitable that a proportion of the debts contracted by this government while the said towns were under the jurisdiction of it, should be paid by the inhabitants and estates of that part of said towns which falls within the colony of Rhode Island, [and] [*yet*], inasmuch as no provision is made, by the aforesaid order of his majesty, for raising and assessing the same,—

Be it further enacted,

[SECT. 10.] That the treasurer be and hereby is discharged from any part of the tax on said town of Bristol, and that part of the said town[s] of Little Compton, Swanzey, Tiverton and Barrington, which now falls within the colony of Rhode Island, apportioned [in] this tax-act, until his majesty's pleasure shall be signif[y][*i*]ed thereupon.

And be it further enacted,

[SECT. 11.] That all proceedings with respect to the tax on that part of the said towns of Little Compton, Swan[s][*z*]ey, Tiverton and Barrington, which remains within this province, be regulated agreeable to such orders as have passed or shall hereafter pass this court, anything in this act to the contrary notwithstanding. [*Passed June* 23; *published June* 27.

CHAPTER 2.

AN ACT FOR GRANTING UNTO HIS MAJESTY SEVERAL RATES AND DUTIES OF IMPOST AND TUNNAGE OF SHIPPING.

WE, his majesty's most loyal and dutiful subjects, the representatives of the province of the Massachusetts Bay, in New England, being desirous of a colateral fund and security for drawing in the bills of credit on this province, have chearfully and unanimously given and granted, and do hereby give and grant, unto his most excellent majesty, to the end and use aforesaid, and for no other use, the several duties of impost upon wines, liquors, goods, wares and merchandizes that shall be imported into this province, and tonnage of shipping, hereafter mentioned; and pray that it may be enacted,—

And be it accordingly enacted by the Governour, Council and House of Representatives,

[SECT. 1.] That from and after the publication of of* this act, and during the space of one year, there shall be paid by the importer of all wines, liquors, goods, wares and merchandize that shall be imported into this province from the place of their growth (salt, cotton-wool, provisions, and every other thing of the growth and produce of New England, and also all prize goods condemned in any part of this province, excepted), the several rates or duties of impost following; viz[t]., —

For every pipe of wine of the Western Island, one pound.

For every pipe of Maderia, one pound five shillings.

For every pipe of other sorts not mentioned, one pound five shillings.

For every hogshead of rum, containing one hundred gallons, one pound.

For every hogshead of sugar, sixpence.

For every hogshead of molasses, fourpence.

For every hogshead of tobacco, ten shillings.

For every ton of logwood, ninepence.

—And so, proportionably, for greater or lesser quantitys.

And all other commodities, goods or merchandize not mentioned or excepted, fourpence for every twenty shillings value: all goods imported from Great Britain excepted.

[SECT. 2.] And for any of the above wines, liquors, goods, wares and merchandize, &c[a]., that shall be imported into this province from any other port than the places of their growth and produce, there shall be paid by the importer double the value of impost appointed by this act to be received for every species above mentioned, unless they do, *bonâ fide*, belong to the inhabitants of this province and came upon their risque from the port of their growth and produce.

And be it further enacted,

[SECT. 3.] That all the aforesaid impost rates and duties shall be paid in current money or bills of credit of this province of the last emission, by the importer of any wines, liquors, goods or merchandize, unto

* *Sic.*

the commissioner to be appointed, as is hereinafter to be directed, for entring and receiving the same, at or before the landing of any wines, liquors, goods or merchandize: only the commissioner or receiver is hereby allowed to give credit to such person or persons, where his or their duty of impost, in one ship or vessell, doth exceed the sum of three pounds; and in cases where the commissioner or receiver shall give credit, he shall settle and ballance his accounts with every person, on or before the last day of April, so that the same accounts may be ready to be presented to this court in May next after. And all entrys, where the impost or duty to be paid doth not exceed three shillings, shall be made without charge to the importer; and not more than sixpence to be demanded for any other single entry, to what value soever.

And be it further enacted,

[SECT. 4.] That all masters of ships or other vessells, coming into any harbour or port within this province, from beyond sea, or from any other province or colony, before bulk be broken, and within twenty-four hours after his arrival at such harbour or port, shall make a report, to the commissioner or receiver of the impost, to be appointed as is hereinafter mentioned, of the contents of the lading of such ship or vessell, without any charge or fee to be demanded or paid for the same; which report said master shall give in to the commissioner or receiver, under his hand, and shall therein set down and express the quantities and species of the wines, liquors, goods and merchandize laden on board such ship or vessell, with the marks and numbers thereof, and to whom the same is consigned; and also make oath that the said report or manifest of the contents of his lading, so to be by him given in under his hand, as aforesaid, contains a just and true account, to the best of his knowledge, of the whole lading taken on board and imported in the said vessell from the port or ports such vessell came from, and that he hath not broken bulk, nor delivered any of the wines, rum or other distilled liquors or merchandize, laden on board the said ship or vessell, directly or indirectly; and if he shall know of any more wines, liquors, goods or merchandize to be imported therein, before the landing thereof he will cause it to be added to his manifest; which manifest shall be agreeable to a printed form for that purpose, which is to be filled up by the said commissioner or receiver according to each particular person's entry; which oath the commissioner or receiver is hereby impowered to administer: after which said master may unload, and not before, on pain of five hundred pounds, to be forfeited and paid by each master that shall neglect his duty in that behalf.

And be it further enacted,

[SECT. 5.] That all merchants, factors and other persons, importers, being owners thereof, or having any of the wines, liquors, goods or merchandize consigned to them, that by this act are liable to pay impost or duty, shall, by themselves or order, make entry thereof in writing, under their hands, with the commissioner or receiver, and produce unto him an invoice of all such goods as pay *ad valorum*,* and make oath thereto in manner following:—

You, A. B., do swear that the entry of the goods and merchandize by you now made, exhibits the present price of said goods at this market, and that, *bonâ fide*, according to your best skill and judgment, is not less than the real value thereof. So help you God.

—which above oath the commissioner or receiver is hereby impowered to administer; and they shall pay the duty or impost by this act required, before such wines, liquors, goods, wares or merchandize be landed or taken out of the vessell in which the same shall be imported.

* *Sic.*

[Sect. 6.] And no wines, liquors, goods, wares or merchandize that by this act are liable to pay impost or duty, shall be landed on any wharffe, or into any warehouse or other place, but in the daytime only, and that after sunrise and before sunset, unless in the presence and with the consent of the commissioner or receiver, on pain of forfeiting all such wines, liquors, goods, wares and merchandize, and the lighter, boat or vessell out of which the same shall be landed or put into any warehouse or other place.

[Sect. 7.] And if any person or persons shall not have and produce an invoice of the quantities of rum or liquors to him or them consigned, then the cask wherein the same is, shall be gaig'd at the charge of the importer, that the quantities thereof may be known.

And be it further enacted,

[Sect. 8.] That every merchant or other person importing any wines into this province, shall be allowed twelve per cent for leakage: *provided* such wines shall not have been filled up on board; and that every hogshead, butt or pipe of wine that hath two third parts thereof leaked out, shall be accounted for outs, and the merchant or importer to pay no duty for the same. And no master of any ship or vessell that shall suffer any wines to be filled up on board without giving a certificate of the quantity so filled up, under his hand, before the landing thereof, to the commissioner or receiver of impost for such port, on pain of forfeiting the sum of one hundred pounds.

[Sect. 9.] And if it may be made to appear that any wines imported in any ship or vessell be decayed at the time of unlading thereof, or in twenty days afterwards, oath being made before the commissioner or receiver that the same hath not been landed above that time, the duties and impost paid for such wines shall be repaid unto the importer thereof.

And be it further enacted,

[Sect. 10.] That the master of every ship or vessell importing any liquors, goods, wares or merchandizes, shall be liable to and shall pay the impost for such and so much thereof, contained in his manifest, as shall not be duly entered, nor the duty paid for the same by the person or persons to whom such wines, liquors, goods, wares or merchandizes are or shall be consigned. And it shall and may be lawful, to and for the master of every ship or other vessell, to secure and detain in his hands, at the owner's risque, all such wines, liquors, goods, wares or merchandize imported in any ship or vessell, until he shall receive a certificate, from the commissioner or receiver of the impost, that the duty for the same is paid, and until he be repaid his necessary charges in securing the same; or such master may deliver such wines, liquors, goods, wares or merchandize as are not entred, unto the commissioner or receiver of the impost in such port, or his order, who is hereby impowered and directed to receive and keep the same, at the owner's risque, until the impost thereof, with the charges, be paid; and then to deliver such wines, liquors, goods, wares or merchandize as such master shall direct.

And be it further enacted,

[Sect. 11.] That the commissioner or receiver of the impost in each port, shall be and hereby is impowered to sue the master of any ship or vessell, for the impost or duty for so much of the lading of any wines, liquors, goods, wares or merchandizes imported therein, according to the manifest to be by him given upon oath, as aforesaid, as shall remain not entred and the duty of impost therefor not paid. And where any goods, wares or merchandize are such as that the value thereof is not known, whereby the impost to be recovered of the master, for the same, cannot be ascertained, the owner or person to whom such goods, wares or merchandize are or shall be consigned, shall be summoned to appear as an evidence at the court where such suit for the impost and the duty thereof shall be brought, and be there required to make oath to the value of such goods, wares or merchandize.

And be it further enacted,

[SECT. 12.] That the ship or vessell, with her tackle, apparrell and furniture, the master of which shall make default in anything by this act required to be performed by him, shall be liable to answer and make good the sum or sums forfeited by such master, according to this act, for any such default, as also to make good the impost or duty for any wines, liquors, goods, wares and merchandize not entred as aforesaid; and, upon judgment recovered against such master, the said ship or vessell, with so much of the tackle or appurtenances thereof as shall be sufficient to satisfy said judgment, may be taken in execution for the same; and the commissioner or receiver of the impost is hereby impowered to make seizure of the said ship or vessell, and detain the same under seizure till judgment be given in any suit to be commenced and prosecuted for any of the said forfeitures or impost; to the intent that, if judgment be rendered for the prosecutor or informer, such ship or vessell and appurtenances may be exposed to sale, for satisfaction thereof, as is before provided: *unless* the owners, or some on their behalf, for the releasing of such ship or vessell from under seizure or restraint, shall give sufficient security unto the commissioner or receiver of impost that seized the same, to respond and satisfy the sum or value of the forfeiture and duties, with charges, that shall be recovered against the master thereof, upon suit to be brought for the same, as aforesaid; and the master occasioning such loss or damage unto his owners, thro his default or neglect, shall be liable to their action for the same.

And be it further enacted,

[SECT. 13.] That the naval officer within any of the ports of this province shall not clear or give passes to any master of any ship or other vessel, outward bound, until he shall be certified, by the commissioner or receiver of the impost, that the duty and impost for the goods last imported in said ship or vessel are paid or secured to be paid.

[SECT. 14.] And the commissioner or receiver of the impost is hereby impowered to allow bills of store to the master of any ship or vessel importing any wines or liquors, for such private adventures as shall belong to the master or seamen of such ship or vessel, at the discretion of the commissioner or receiver, not exceeding three per cent of the lading; and the duties payable by this act for such wines or liquors, in such bills of stores mentioned and expressed, shall be abated.

And for the more effectually preventing any wines, rum or other distilled spirits being brought into this province from the neighbouring governments, by land, or in small boats and vessells, or any other way, and also to prevent wines, rum and other distilled spirits being first sent out of this province, to save the duty of impost, and afterwards brought into this government again,—

Be it enacted,

[SECT. 15.] That the commissioner and receiver of the aforesaid dutys of impost shall, and he is hereby impowered and injoyned to, appoint some suitable person or persons as his deputy or deputys, in all such places in this province where it is likely that wine, rum and other distilled spirits will be brought out of other governments into this; which officers shall have power to seize the same, unless the owner shall make it appear that the duty of impost has been paid therefor since their being brought into or relanded in this government; and such officer or officers are also impowered to search, in all suspected places, for such wines, rum and distilled spirits brought or relanded in this government, where the duty is not paid as aforesaid, and to seize and secure the same for the ends and uses as in this act is hereafter provided.

And be it further enacted,

[Sect. 16.] That all penalties, fines and forfeitures accruing and arising by virtue of this act shall be one half to his majesty for the uses and intents for which the aforementioned dutys of impost are granted, and the other half to him or them that shall seize, inform and sue for the same, by action, bill, plaint or information, in any of his majesty's courts of record, wherein no essoign, protection or wager of law shall be allowed; the whole charge of prosecution to be taken out of the half belonging to the informer.

And be it further enacted,

[Sect. 17.] That there shall be paid, by the master of every ship or other vessel, coming into any port or ports of this province, to trade or traffick, whereof all the owners are not belonging to this province (except such vessels as belong to Great Britain, the provinces or colonies of Pensylvania, West and East Jersey, New York, Connecticut, New Hampshire and Rhode Island), every voyage such ship or vessel does make, one pound of good pistol-powder for every ton such ship or vessel is in burthen: *saving* for that part which is owned in Great Britain, this province, or any of the aforesaid governments, which are hereby exempted; to be paid unto the commissioner or receiver of the dutys of impost, and to be employed for the ends and uses aforesaid.

[Sect. 18.] And the said commissioner is hereby impowered to appoint a meet and suitable person, to repair unto and on board any ship or vessel, to take the exact measure or tunnage thereof, in case he shall suspect that the register of such ship or vessel doth not express and set forth the full burthen of the same; the charge thereof to be paid by the master or owner of such ship or vessel, before she shall be cleared, in case she shall appear to be of greater burthen: otherwise, to be paid by the commissioner out of the money received by him for impost, and shall be allowed him, accordingly, by the treasurer, in his accompts. And the naval officer shall not clear any vessel, until he be also certified, by the commissioner, that the duty of tonnage for the same is paid, or that it is such a vessel for which none is payable according to this act.

And be it further enacted,

[Sect. 19.] That when and so often as any wine or rum imported into this province, the duty of impost upon which shall have been paid agreeable to this act, shall be reshipped and exported from this government to any other part of the world, that then, and in every such case, the exporter of such wine or rum shall make oath, at the time of shipping, before the receiver of impost, or his deputy, that the whole of the wine or rum so shipped has, *bonâ fide*, had the aforesaid duty of impost paid on the same, and shall afterwards produce a certificate, from some officer of the customs, that the same has been landed out of this government,—or otherwise, in case such rum or wines shall be exported to any place where there is no officer of the customs, or to any foreign port, the master of the vessel in which the same shall be exported shall make oath that the same has been landed out of the government, and the exporter shall, upon producing such certificate, or upon such oath of the master, make oath that he verily believes no part of said wines or rum has been relanded in this province,—such exporter shall be allowed to draw back from the receiver of impost as follows; vizt.:—

For every pipe of Western-Island wine, fifteen shillings.

For every pipe of Madeira and other sorts, eighteen shillings.

And for every hogshead of rum, fifteen shillings.

And be it further enacted,

[SECT. 20.] That there be one fit person, and no more, nominated and appointed by this court, as a commissioner and receiver of the aforesaid dutys of impost and tunnage of shipping, and for the inspection, care and management of the said office, and whatsoever relates ther. to, to receive commission for the same from the governour and commander-in-chief for the time being, with authority to substitute and appoint a deputy receiver in each port, and other places besides that wherein he resides, and to grant warrants to such deputy receivers for the said place, and to collect and receive the impost and tunnage of shipping as aforesaid that shall become due within such port, and to render the accompt thereof, and to pay in the same, to the said commissioner and receiver: which said commissioner and receiver shall keep fair books of all entrys and dutys arising by virtue of this act; also, a particular account of every vessel, so that the dutys of impost and tunnage arising on the said vessel may appear; and the same to lye open, at all seasonable times, to the view and perusal of the treasurer and receiver-general of this province (or any other person or persons whom this court shall appoint), with whom he shall account for all collections and payments, and pay all such monys as shall be in his hands, as the treasurer or receiver-general shall demand it. And the said commissioner or receiver and his deputy or deputys, before their entering upon the execution of their office, shall be sworn to deal truly and faithfully therein, and shall attend in the said office from ten of the clock in the forenoon, until one in the afternoon.

[SECT. 21.] And the said commissioner and receiver, for his labour, care and expences in the said office, shall have and receive, out of the province treasury, the sum of fifty pounds per annum; and his deputy or deputys to be paid for their service such sum or sums as the said commissioner and receiver, with the treasurer, shall agree upon, not exceeding ten pounds, per annum, each; and the treasurer is hereby ordered, in passing and receiving the said commissioner's accompts, accordingly, to allow the payment of such salary or salarys, as aforesaid, to himself and his deputys.

Provided,

[SECT. 22.] That no dutys of impost shall be demanded for any goods imported after the publication of this act, by virtue of any former act for granting unto his majesty any rates and duties of impost, &c[a]. [*Passed June* 23; *published June* 27.

CHAPTER 3.

AN ACT FOR SUPPLYING THE TREASURY WITH THE SUM OF ONE HUNDRED THOUSAND POUNDS, FOR DISCHARGING THE PUBLICK DEBTS, &c[A]., AND FOR DRAWING THE SAID BILLS INTO THE TREASURY AGAIN.

Be it enacted by the Governour, Council and House of Representatives,

£100,000 bills of credit to be emitted.

[SECT. 1.] That the treasurer be and hereby is impow[e]red and ordered to emit and issue forth the sum of one hundred thousand pounds, in bills of credit of the last tenor and date, now lying in his hands and received in for taxes, impost and excise, which shall pass in all publick and private payments equal to other new-tenor bills emitted since one thousand seven hundred and forty; and the said sum of one hundred thousand pounds shall be issued out of the treasury in [*the*] manner and for the purposes following; viz[t]., the sum of forty thousand pounds, part of the aforesaid sum of one hundred thousand pounds, shall be appl[y][*i*]ed for the payment of wages that now are or that hereafter may be due by virtue of the establishment of Castle William, Frederick Fort, Richmond Fort, George's Truck-house, Saco Truck-house, Brunswick Fort, and the sloop in the country's service, and the forces upon the eastern and western frontiers; and the sum of thirty-four thousand pounds, part of the aforesaid sum of one hundred thousand pounds, shall be appl[y][*i*]ed for purchasing all needful warlike stores, and for the commissary's necessary disbursements for the service of the several forts and garrisons and other forces within this province, pursuant to such grants as are or shall be made by this court for those purposes; and the sum of eighteen thousand pounds, part of the aforesaid sum of one hundred thousand pounds, shall be appl[y][*i*]ed for the payment of his majesty's council and such other grants as are or shall be made by this court, and for the payment of stipends, bounties and premiums established by law, and for the payment of all other matters and things which this court have or shall, either by law or orders, provide for the payment of out of the publick treasury, and for no other purpose whatsoever; and the sum of three thousand pounds, part of the aforesaid sum of one hundred thousand pounds, shall be appl[y][*i*]ed for the discharge of other debts owing from this province to persons that have served or shall serve them by order of this court in such matters and things where there is no establishment, nor any certain sum assigned for such service, and for paper, printing and writing for this court, the surgeon of Castle William, and wooding of said castle; and the sum of five hundred pounds, part of the aforesaid sum of one hundred thousand pounds, shall be appl[y][*i*]ed to defrey any contingent unforeseen charges that may demand prompt payment, and for no other use whatsoever; and the sum of four thousand five hundred pounds, the remaining part of the aforesaid sum of one hundred thousand pounds, shall be appl[y][*i*]ed for the payment of the members of the house of representatives serving in the general court during their several sessions this present year.

£40,000 for Castle William and other forts, &c.

£34,000 for purchasing warlike stores, &c.

£18,000 for the payment of the council, grants, &c.

£3,000 for payment of debts, &c.

£500 for contingent charges, &c.

£4,500 for the representatives.

And be it further enacted,

[Sect. 2.] That if there be a surplusage in any sum appropriated, such surplusage shall l[y][*i*]e in the treasury for the further order of this court.

Surplusage to lie in the treasury.

And be it further enacted,

[Sect. 3.] That each and every warrant for drawing money out of the treasury, shall direct the treasurer to take the same out of such sums as are respectively appropriated for the payment of such publick debts as the draughts are made to discharge; and the treasurer is hereby directed and ordered to pay such money out of such appropriation[*s*] as directed to, and no other, upon pain of refunding all such sum or sums as he shall otherwise pay, and to keep exact and distinct accounts of all payments made out of such appropriated sums; and the secretary, to whom it belongs to keep the muster-rolls and accounts of charge, shall lay before the house, when they direct, all such muster-rolls and acco[mp][*un*]ts, after payment thereof.

Warrants to express the appropriations.

And as a fund and security for drawing the said sum of one hundred thousand pounds into the treasury again,—

Be it further enacted,

[Sect. 4.] That there be and hereby is granted unto his most excellent majesty, for the ends and uses aforesaid, a tax of ninety-five thousand five hundred pounds, to be levied on polls, and estates both real and personal, within this province, according to such rules and in such proportions on the several towns and districts within the same, as shall

£95,500 in 1749.

be agreed upon and ordered by this court at their session in May, one thousand seven hundred and forty-nine, and paid into the publick treasury on or before the last day of December then next after.

And as a fund and security for drawing in such sum or sums as shall be paid out to the representatives of the several towns,—

Be it enacted,

Tax for the sum paid the representatives.

[SECT. 5.] That there be and hereby is granted unto his most excellent majesty, a tax of such sum or sums as shall be paid to the several representatives as aforesaid, to be levied and assessed on the polls and estates of the inhabitants of the several towns, according to what their representatives shall so receive, which sums shall be set on the said towns in the next province tax; and the assessors of the said towns shall make their assessment for this tax, and apportion the same according to the rule that shall be prescribed by act of the general assembly for assessing the next province tax, and the constables in their respective districts shall pay in the same when they pay in the province tax for the next year, of which the treasurer is hereby directed to keep a distinct and seperate account; and if there be any surplusage, the same shall l[y][*i*]e in the hands of the treasurer for the further order of this court.

And be it further enacted,

Tax for the money hereby emitted to be made according to the preceding tax act, in case.

[SECT. 6.] That in case the general court shall not, at their session in May, one thousand seven hundred and forty-nine, agree and conclude upon an act apportioning the sum which by this act is engaged shall be, in this year, apportioned, assessed and levied, that then and in such case, each town and district within this province shall pay, by a tax to be levied on polls, and estates both real and personal, within their districts, the same proportion of the said sums as the towns and districts aforesaid shall have been taxed by the general court in the tax act then next preceeding; and the province treasurer is hereby fully impow[e]red and directed, some time in the month of June, in the year one thousand seven hundred and forty-nine, to issue and send forth his warrants, directed to the selectmen or assessors of each town and district within this province, requiring them to assess the polls, and estates both real and personal, within their several towns and districts, for their respective part and proportion of the sum before directed and engaged to be assessed by this act; and the assessors, as also all persons assessed, shall observe, be governed by, and subject to all such rules and directions as shall have been given in the next preceeding tax act.

And be it further enacted,

Taxes to be paid in the several species herein enumerated.

[SECT. 7.] That the inhabitants of this province shall have liberty, if they see fit, to pay the several sums for which they respectively may, in pursuance of this act, be assessed, in bills of credit of the form and tenor by this act emitted, or in other new-tenor bills, or in bills of the middle tenor, according to their several denominations, or in bills of the old tenor, accounting four for one; or in coin'd silver, at seven shillings and sixpence per ounce, troy weight, and of sterling alloy, or in gold coin proportionably; or in merchantable hemp, flax, winter and Isle-of-Sable codfish, refin'd bar-iron, bloomery-iron, hollow iron-ware, Indian corn, rye, wheat, barley, pork, beef, duck or canvas, whalebone, cordage, train-oil, beeswax, bayberry-wax, tallow, peas[e], sheepswool, or tann'd sole-leather (the aforesaid commodities being of the produce or manufactures of this province), at such moderate rates and prices as the general assembly of the year one thousand seven hundred and forty-nine shall set them at; the several persons paying their taxes in any of the commodities aforemention'd, to run the risque and pay the charge of transporting the said commodities to the province treasury; but if the aforesaid general assembly shall not, at their session in

How the commodities brought into the treasury are to be rated.

May, some time before the twentieth day of June in the said year, agree upon and set the aforesaid species and commodities at some certain price, that then the eldest councell[e][o]r, for the time being of each of those counties in the province, of which any one of the council is an inhabitant, together with the province treasurer, or the major part of them, be a committee, who hereby are directed and fully authorized and impow[e]red to do it; and in their set[t]ling the prices and rating the value of those commodities, to state so much of them, respectively, at seven shillings and sixpence as an ounce of silver will purchase at that time in the town of Boston, and so *pro ratâ*. And the treasurer is hereby directed to insert in the several warrants by him sent to the several collectors of the taxes of such year, with the names of the afore-recited commodities, the several prices or rates which shall be set on them, either by the general assembly or the committee aforesaid, and direct the aforesaid collectors to receive them so.

[Sect. 8.] And the aforesaid commodities, so brought into the treasury, shall, as soon as may be, be disposed of by the treasurer to the best advantage, for so much as they will fetch in bills of credit hereby to be emitted, or for silver and gold, which silver and gold shall be delivered to the possessors of said bills in exchange for them; that is to say, one ounce of silver coin, and so gold in proportion, for seven shillings and sixpence, and so *pro ratâ* for a greater or less sum; and if any loss shall happen by the sale of the aforesaid species, or by any unforeseen accident, such d[i][e]f[f]iciency shall be made good by a tax of the year next following, so as fully and effectually to call in the whole sum of one hundred thousand pounds in said bills hereby ordered to be emitted; and if there be a surplusage, it shall remain a stock in the treasury. [*Passed June* 23; *published June* 27.

Treasurer to sell the said commodities.

CHAPTER 4.

AN ACT FOR GRANTING UNTO HIS MAJESTY AN EXCISE UPON WINES AND SPIRITS DISTILLED, SOLD BY RETAIL, AND UPON LIMES, LEMMONS AND ORANGES.

Preamble.

We, his majesty's most loyal and dutiful subjects, the representatives of the province of the Massachusetts Bay, in general court assembled, being desirous to lessen the present debt of the province, by drawing in a number of the bills of credit, have chearfully and unanimously granted, and do hereby give and grant unto his most excellent majesty, for the ends and uses above mentioned, and for no other uses, an excise upon all brandy, rum and other spirits distilled, and upon all wines whatsoever sold by retail, and upon lemmons, limes and oranges taken in and used in making of punch or other liquors mixed for sale, or otherwise consumed, in taverns or other licen[s][c]ed houses within this province, to be raised, levied, collected and paid by and upon every taverner, in[n]holder, common victualler and retailer within each respective county, in manner following:—

And be it accordingly enacted by the Governour, Council and House of Representatives,

[Sect. 1.] That from and after the twenty-ninth day of June, one thousand seven hundred and forty-eight, for the space of three years, every person licen[s][c]ed for retailing rum, brandy or other spirits, or wine, shall pay the duties following:—

Time of this act's continuance.

For every gallon of brandy, rum and spirits distilled, sixpence.

Rates of excise.

For every gallon of wine of every sort, sixpence.
For every hundred of lemmons or oranges, five shillings.
For every hundred of limes, two shillings.
—And so proportionably for any other quantity or number.

And be it further enacted,

Account to be taken.

[SECT. 2.] That every taverner, in[n]holder, common victual[l]er and retailer, shall, upon the said twenty-ninth day of June, take an exact account of all brandy, rum and other distilled spirits, and wine, and of all lemmons, oranges and limes then by him or her, and give an account of the same, upon oath, if required, unto the person or persons to whom the duties of excise in the respective counties shall be let or farmed, as in and by this act is hereafter directed; and such other person[s] as shall be licen[s][c]ed during the continuance of this act, shall also give an account, as aforesaid, upon what brandy, rum or other distilled spirits, and wine, and of what lemmons, oranges or limes he or they shall have by him or them at the time of his or their licen[s][c]e; which oath the person or persons farming the duties aforesaid shall have power to administer in the words following; viz.,—

Form of oath.

You, A. B., do swear that the account exhibited by you is a just and true account of all brandy, rum and other distilled spirits, and wine, lemmons, oranges and limes you had by you on the twenty-ninth day of June last. So help you God.

And where such person shall not have been licen[s][c]ed on said twenty-ninth day of June, the form of the oath shall be so varied as that instead of those words, "on the twenty-ninth day of June last," these words shall be inserted and used, "at the time of taking your licence."

And be it further enacted,

Within six months, accounts to be delivered.

[SECT. 3.] That every taverner, in[n]holder, common victual[l]er and retailer shall make a fair entry in a book, of all such rum, brandy and other distilled spirits, and wine, as he or they, or any for him or them, shall buy, distill and take in for sale after such account taken, and of all lemmons, oranges and limes taken in, consumed or used as aforesaid, and at the end of every six months, deliver the same, in writing, under their hands, to the farmer or farmers of the duties aforesaid; who are impow[e]red to administer an oath to him or them, that the said account is, *bonâ fide*, just and true, and that he or they do not know of any rum, brandy or other distilled spirits, or wine, sold, directly or indirectly, or of any lemmons, oranges or limes used in punch or otherwise, by him or them, or any under him or them, or by his or their privity or consent, but what is contained in the account now exhibited, and shall pay him the duty thereof, excepting such part as the fa[rmer*] shall find is still remaining by him or them; twenty per cent to be allowed on the liquors aforemention[e]'d for leakage and other waste, for which no duty is to be paid.

Twenty per cent. allowed for leakage.

Provided always, and it is the true intent and meaning of this act,—

Proviso.

[SECT. 4.] That if any taverner, retailer or common victualler, shall buy of another taverner or retailer such small quantity of liquors as this act obliges him to account for to the farmer, and pay the excise, the taverner, retailer or common victual[l]er shall, notwithstanding, be accountable and pay the excise, as if none had been paid by the person he bought the same of.

And be it further enacted,

Penalty on giving a false account.

[SECT. 5.] That every taverner, in[n]holder, common victual[l]er or retailer, who shall be found to give a false account of any brandy,

* The parchment is injured here.

distilled spirits, wine, or other the commodities aforesaid, by him or her on the said twenty-ninth of June, or at the time of his or her taking licen[s][c]e, or bought, distilled, or taken in for sale afterwards, or used as aforesaid, or refuse to give in an acco[mp][*un*]t, on oath, as aforesaid, shall be rendered incapable of having a licen[s][*c*]e afterwards, and shall be prosecuted by the farmer of the excise in the same county, for his or her neglect, and ordered by the general sessions of the peace to pay double the sum of money as they may judge that the excise of liquors, &c[a]., by him or her sold within such time, would have amounted to, to be paid to the said farmer.

And be it further enacted,

[Sect. 6.] That the justices in their general sessions of the peace shall take recognizances, with sufficient sureties, of all persons by them licen[s][*c*]ed, both as to their keeping good rule and order, and duly observing the laws relating to persons so licen[s][*c*]ed, and for their duly and truly rendering an account in writing under their hands as aforesaid, and paying their excise in manner as afores[*ai*]d; as also that they shall not use their licen[s][*c*]e in any house besides that wherein they dwell; which recognizance shall be taken within the space of thirty days after the granting of such licen[s][*c*]e, otherways the persons licen[s][*c*]ed shall lose the benefit of his or her said licen[s][*c*]e; and no persons shall be licen[s][*c*]ed by the said justices that hath not accounted with the farmer, and paid him the excise due to him from such person at the time of his asking for such licen[s][*c*]e.

General sessions to take recognizance.

And whereas, notwithstanding the laws made against selling strong drink without licen[s][*c*]e, many persons not regarding the penalties and forfeitures in the said act, do receive and entertain persons in their houses, and sell great quantities of spirits and other strong drink, without licen[s][*c*]e so to do first had and obtained, by reason whereof great debaucheries are committed and kept secret, the end of this law in a great measure frustrated, and such as take licen[s][*c*]es and pay the excise greatly wronged and injured,—

Preamble.

Be it therefore further enacted,

[Sect. 7.] That whosoever, after the said twenty-ninth day of June, one thousand seven hundred and forty-eight, shall presume, directly or indirectly, to sell any brandy, rum or other distilled spirits, wine, beer, cyder, perry or any other strong drink, in any smaller quantity than a quarter cask (twenty gallons to be accounted a quarter cask, and all delivered to one person without drawing any part of it off), without licen[s][*c*]e first had and obtained from the court of general sessions of the peace, and recognizing in manner as aforesaid, shall forfeit and pay for each offence, the sum of three pounds to the farmer, and costs of prosecution; and all such as shall refuse or neglect to pay the fine afores[*ai*]d, shall stand closely and strictly committed in the common goal of the county for three months at least, and not to have the liberty of the goaler's house or yard; and any goaler giving any person liberty contrary to this act, shall forfeit and pay three pounds, and pay costs of prosecution as aforesaid: and if any person or persons, not licen[s][*c*]ed as aforesaid, shall order, allow, permit or connive at the selling of any strong drink, contrary to the true intent or meaning of this act, by his or her child or children, servant or servants, or any other person or persons belonging to or in his or her house or family, and be thereof convict, he, she or they shall be reputed the offender or offenders, and shall suffer the same penalties as if he, she or they had sold such drink themselves.

Forfeiture of £3 for selling without license, &c.

And be it further enacted,

[Sect. 8.] That when any person shall be complained of for selling any strong drink without licen[s][*c*]e, one witness produced to one

One witness sufficient for conviction.

such fact, and another produced to another, shall be sufficient conviction, provided that there be not more than the space of forty days between the facts concerning which such witnesses declare. And when and so often as it shall be observed that there is a resort of persons to houses suspected to sell strong drink without licen[s][c]e, any justice of the peace shall have full power to convene such persons before him, and examine them upon oath concerning the person suspected of selling or retailing strong drink in such houses, out-houses or other dependencies thereof; and if upon examination of such witnesses, and hearing the defence of such suspected person, it shall appear to the justice there is sufficient proof of the violation of this act by selling strong drink without licence, judgment may thereupon be made up against such person, and he shall forfeit and pay in like manner as if process had been commenced by bill, plaint or information before the said justice, or otherwise said justice may bind over the person suspected and the witnesses, to the next court of general sessions of the peace for the county where such person shall dwell.

And be it further enacted,

Penalty for selling strong drink to negroes, mulattoes, &c.

[SECT. 9.] That when and so often as any person shall be complained of for selling any strong drink without licence to any Indian, negro or molatto slave, or to any child or other person under the age of discretion, and upon the declaration of any such Indian, negro or molatto slaves, child or other person under the age of discretion, and other circumstances concurring, it shall appear to be highly probable in the judgm[*en*]t of the court or justice before whom the trial shall be, that the person complained of is guilty, then, and in every such case, unless the defendent shall acquit him- or herself upon oath (to be administred to him or her by the court or justice that shall try the cause), such defendant shall forf[ie][*ei*]t and pay three pounds to the farmer of excise and costs of prosecution; but if the defendant shall acquit him- or herself upon oath as afores[*ai*]d, the court or justice may and shall enter up judgment for the defend[*an*]t to recover costs.

And be it further enacted,

Persons after first conviction to enter into bonds.

[SECT. 10.] That after any person shall have been once convicted of selling strong liquors without licence, contrary to this act, he shall, upon every offence after such first conviction, be obliged to enter into bonds, with one or more sureties, in the penalty of twenty pounds, to his majesty, for the use of this governm[*en*]t, that he will not, in like manner, offend or be guilty of any breach of this act; and upon refusal to give such bond, he shall be committed to prison until[l] he shall comply therewith.

And be it further enacted,

Penalty on persons refusing to give evidence.

[SECT. 11.] That if any person or persons shall be summoned to appear before a justice of the peace, or the grand jury, to give evidence relating to any person's selling strong drink without licence, or to appear before the court of general sessions of the peace, or other court proper to try the same, to give evidence on the tr[y][*i*]al of any person informed against, presented or indicted for the selling strong drink without licence, and shall neglect or refuse to appear, or to give evidence in that behalf, every person so offending shall forfeit the sum of twenty pounds; the one half to be for his majesty, the other half to and for the use of him or them who shall sue for the same as afores[*ai*]d. And when it shall so happen that witnesses are bound to sea before the sitting of the court where any person or persons informed against, for selling strong drink without licence, is or are to be prosecuted for the same, in every such case, the deposition of any witness or witnesses in writing, taken before any two of his majesty's justices of the peace, *quorum unus*, and sealed up and delivered into court, the adverse party having first had a notification in writing sent to him or her of the time and place of caption, shall be esteemed as sufficient evidence, in the law, to convict any person or persons offending against this act, as if such witness or witnesses had been present at the time of tr[y][*i*]al, and given his, her or their deposition *vivâ voce;* and every person or persons who shall be summoned to give evidence before two justices of the peace, in manner as aforesaid, and shall neglect or refuse to appear, or to give evidence relating to the facts he or she shall be inquired of, shall be liable and subject to the same penalty as he or she would have been by virtue of this act, for not appearing, or neglecting or refusing to give his or her evidence before the grand jury or court as aforesaid.

And be it further enacted,

[Sect. 12.] That all fines, forfeitures and penalties arising by this act shall and may be recovered by action, bill, plaint or information, before any court of record proper to try the same; and where the sum forfeited does not exceed three pounds, by action or complaint before any one of his majesty's justices of the peace in the respective counties where such offence shall be committed; which said justice is hereby impow[e]red to try and determine the same. And such justice shall make a fair entry or record of all such his proceeding: *saving always* to any person or persons who shall think him-, her- or themselves aggr[ei][*ie*]ved by the sentence or determination of the said justice, as aforesaid, liberty of appeal therefrom to the next court of general sessions of the peace to be holden in and for said county, at which court such offence shall be finally determined: *provided* that in said appeal the same rules be observed as are already by law required in appeals from justices to the court of general sessions of the peace. How fines are to be recovered.

And to the end the revenue arising from the aforesaid duties of excise may be advanced for the greater benefit and advantage of the publick,—

Be it further enacted,

[Sect. 13.] That one or more persons, to be nominated and appointed by the general court, for and within the several counties within this province, publick notice being first given of the time and place and occasion of their meeting, shall have power, and are hereby authorized, from time to time, to contract and agree with any person for or concerning the farming the duties in this act mentioned, upon brandy, rum, or other the liquors and commodities aforesaid, in the respective counties for which they shall be appointed, as may be for the greatest prof[f]it and advantage of the publick, so as the same exceed not the term of three years after the commencement of this act; and every person to whom the duties of excise in any county shall be let or farmed, shall have power to inspect the houses of all such as are licen[s][*c*]ed, and of such as are suspected to sell without licence, and to demand, sue for, and recover the excise due from licen[s][*c*]ed persons by virtue of this act. Persons empowered to farm out the excise.

And be it further enacted,

[Sect. 14.] That the farmer shall give bond with two sufficient sureties, to the province treasurer for the time being, and his successors in said office, in double the sum of money that shall be contracted for, with condition that the sum agreed be paid into the province treasury, for the use of the province, at the expiration of one year from the date of such bond; which bond the person or persons to be appointed a committee of such county are to take, and the same to lodge with the treasurer as aforesaid, within twenty days after such bond is executed. And the said treasurer, upon failure or neglect of payment at the time therein limit[*t*]ed, shall and hereby is impow[e]red and directed to put such bond in suit, and to receive the money due thereon for the use Farmer to give bond that the sum agreed for be paid into the public treasury.

afore mentioned; and the said committee shall render an account of their proceedings touching the farming this duty on rum, wine and other the liquors and species afore mentioned, in their respective counties, to the general court in the first week of their fall sessions, and shall receive such sum or sums for their trouble and expences in said affair as said court shall think fit to allow them.

[SECT. 15.] And every person farming the excise in any county may substitute and appoint one or more deputies under him, upon oath, to collect and receive the excise aforesaid, which shall become due in such county, and pay in the same to the farmer; which deputy or deputies shall have, use and exercise all such powers and authorities as in and by this act are given or committed to the farmers for the better collecting the duties aforesaid, or prosecuting of offenders against this act.

And be it further enacted, anything hereinbefore contained to the contrary notwithstanding,

Farmers may compound with any retailer or innholder.

[SECT. 16.] That it shall and may be lawful to and for the said farmers, and every of them, to compound and agree with any retailer or innholder within their respective divisions, from time to time, for his or her excise for the whole year, in one entire sum, as they in their discretion shall think fit to agree for, without making any entry thereof as is before directed; and all and every person or persons, to whom the said excise or any part thereof shall be let or farmed, by themselves or their lawful substitutes, may and hereby are impow[e]red to sue for and recover, in any of his majesty's courts of record (or before a justice of the peace where the matter is not above his cognizance), any sum or sums that shall grow due from any of the aforesaid duties of excise, where the party or parties for whom the same is or shall become due shall refuse or neglect to pay the same.

And be it further enacted,

Penalty for farmers or their deputies offending.

[SECT. 17.] That in case any person farming the excise as afores[*ai*]d, or his deputy, shall, at any time during their continuance in said office, wittingly and willingly connive at, or allow, any person or persons within their respective divisions, not licen[s][*c*]ed by the court of general sessions of the peace, their selling any brandy, wine, rum or other liquors by this act forbidden, such farmer or deputy, for every such offence, shall forfeit the sum of fifty pounds; one half [w][*t*]hereof shall be to his majesty for the use of the province, the other half to him or them that shall inform or sue for the same, and shall thenceforward be forever disabled from serving in said office.

And in order to discourage and prevent any groundless or vexatious suits that may be brought against the farmer of excise,—

Be it enacted,

Farmer's liberty to plead, &c.

[SECT. 18.] That in all actions that may be brought against the farmer of excise for any breach or neglect of his duty in the execution of his office and trust, he shall have liberty to plead the general issue, and thereupon give any special matter in evidence; and in case judgment shall be for the defendant he shall recover treble costs.

And be it further enacted,

Provision in case of death, &c.

[SECT. 19.] That in case of the death of the farmers of excise in any county the executors or administrators of such farmer shall, upon their taking such trust of executor or administrator upon them, have and enjoy all the powers, and be subject to all the duties, the farmer had or might enjoy or was subject to by force of this act. [*Passed June* 23; *published June* 27.

CHAPTER 5.

AN ACT FOR LEVYING SOLDIERS.

For the more speedy and effectual levying of soldiers for his majesty's service, when and so often as there shall be occasion for the same, for the preservation and defence of his majesty's subjects and interests, and the prosecuting, encountring, repelling or subduing such as shall at any time attempt, in hostile manner, to enterprize the destruction, invasion, detriment or annoyance of this his majesty's province, or any of his majesty's subjects therein; and for the better preventing disappointments, thro' the default of any employed in levying such soldiers, or by the non-appearance of such as shall be levyed,— Preamble. 1744-45, chap. 2. 1746-47, chap. 21.

Be it enacted by the Governour, Council and House of Representatives,

[Sect. 1.] That when and so often as any chief officer of any regiment of militia within this province shall receive orders from the captain-general or commander-in-chief, for the time being, of the said province, for the [im]pressing or causing to be impressed for his majesty's service, out of the regiment under his command, so many soldiers as in such orders shall be mentioned, such chief officer of the regiment shall forthwith thereupon issue forth his warrants to the captains or chief officers of the companies or troops within his regiment, or such of them as he shall think fit, requiring them respectively to impress out of the militia, in the companies or troops under their command, so many able soldiers, furnished and provided as the law directs, and in the whole shall make up the number which by the orders of the captain-general or commander-in-chief he shall be directed to impress, on pain that every chief officer of a regiment that shall neglect or not do his utmost to send forth his warrants seasonably (having orders for the same as above mentioned), shall forfeit and pay a fine of fifty pounds. Duty of chief officers in levying soldiers. Penalty for not doing duty.

[Sect. 2.] And every captain or other chief officer of any company or troop that shall receive any warrant from the chief officer of the regiment whereto such company or troops belongs, for the impressing out of the same any soldier or soldiers for his majesty's service, shall thereupon use his utmost endeavour to impress, or cause to be impressed, so many soldiers as by such warrant he shall be required to impress, and to have them at the place of rendezvous in time as therein shall be mentioned, on pain that every captain or chief officer of any company or troop that shall neglect, or not do his utmost, to comply with and perform any warrant to be by him received as aforesaid from the chief officer of the regiment, shall, for such neglect and default, pay a fine of twenty pounds. Duty of the chief officer of a company or troop. Penalty for not doing his duty.

[Sect. 3.] And every officer or soldier that shall receive a warrant from his captain, or the chief officer of the company or troop in which he is inlisted, for the impressing of men, shall forthwith attend and perform the same, on [pain of] paying a fine of five pounds.

[Sect. 4.] And all persons are required to be aiding and assisting to him in the execution of such warrant, on pain of forfeiting the sum of three pounds. Penalty for other persons' neglect.

[Sect. 5.] And if any person, authorized as aforesaid to impress any soldier or soldiers for his majesty's service, shall exact or take any reward to discharge or spare any from said service, he shall forfeit ten pounds for every twenty shillings he shall so exact or take, and so *pro ratâ*. Penalty for taking a reward to discharge soldiers.

[Sect. 6.] All which fines and penalties aforesaid shall be, one moiety thereof unto his majesty, for and towards the support of the government of this province, and the other moiety to him or them that Disposition of fines.

shall inform and sue for the same, by action, bill, plaint or information, in any court of record.

And be it further enacted,

Duty of persons impressed.

[SECT. 7.] That every person, liable and fit for service, being orderly impressed as aforesaid for his majesty's service, by being commanded in his majesty's name to attend the said service, shall, by himself or other meet person in his room (to the acceptance of his captain or chief officer), attend the same at time and place appointed, compleat with arms and ammunition, if such he have, or is able to purchase the same, on pain of forfeiting and paying to his captain or chief officer, by whose warrant he was impressed, within twenty-four hours next after such impressment, the sum of ten pounds, who, on payment thereof, shall give a receipt therefor; and in default of such payment, or of procuring some meet person in his stead, to the acceptance of said officer, the said sum shall be lev[i][*y*]ed by distress and sale of the goods or chattles of such offender, or of the goods and chattles of his parent or master, in case such impressed person be a son under age or a servant; and the officer, by whose warrant he was impressed, shall be and hereby is fully impowered and required to levy and collect the said sum in such manner as constables of towns within this province are impowered to levy the publick taxes; and for want of goods or chattles whereon to make distress, such offender shall suffer six months' imprisonment, without bail or mainprize, to be committed by mittimus from any justice of the peace of the same county, upon due conviction of such neglect.

Fines to be levied on goods and chattels, &c.

[SECT. 8.] And of the mon[*i*]e[y]s to be so lev[i][*y*]ed or collected, such captain or chief officer shall lay out and improve so much as shall be necessary for the procuring and fitting out of one or more suitable person or persons, as there may be occasion, to perform the service for which any soldier or soldiers, forfeiting as aforesaid, shall have been impressed, the overplus of such mon[*i*]e[y]s to be paid into the town treasury, some time before the annual meeting of such town in March, in each and every year, for the use of such town; and such officer shall give in to the treasurer of said town an attested accompt of the sums by him received and paid; and upon such officer's neglecting to render such accompt and pay such sum as shall be due, the said town treasurer is hereby impowered to demand and sue therefor accordingly.

In what case impressed persons may be excused.

[SECT. 9.] And if the captain or officer to whom the said sum of ten pounds shall be paid as aforesaid by any person impressed, cannot seasonably procure another suitable person to serve in the stead of him that was before impressed, or if any person impressed shall suffer imprisonment or shall make his escape, in each and every such case the said captain or officer shall renew his warrants as often as there shall be occasion, until the number sent for from him be compleated; and all persons paying the said sum of ten pounds as before mentioned, shall be esteemed as persons that have served, and be no further or otherwise liable to any after impress than those that actually go forth in that service.

Penalty for escaping or absconding from the impress.

[SECT. 10.] And all persons lawfully impow[e]red to impress, may pursue any person that absconds from the impress, or makes his escape, and may impress such person in any place within the province; and if any person impressed as aforesaid for his majesty's service [being so duly returned, shall remove or go out of the province, and not attend the service] as required, such person, at his return, shall be apprehended, by warrant from any justice of the peace, and be by him committed to prison, unless such person give sufficient security to answer it at the next court of general sessions of the peace; and upon due conviction of the said offence, by the oath of him that impressed him, shall suffer twelve months' imprisonment, or pay a fine of twenty pounds, to be paid to the selectmen of the town where such person belonged to at the time of his being impressed, for purchasing arms.

[Sect. 11.] And if any person, directly or indirectly, by coun-[ci][*se*]l or otherwise, shall prevent the impressing, conceal any person impressed, or, knowingly, further his escape, such person shall pay, as a fine, three pounds.

And be it further enacted,

[Sect. 12.] That all soldiers shall be in pay from the time of their being impressed, till they be orderly discharged, and have reasonable time allowed them to repair to their usual places of abode. **When the pay of soldiers is to begin.**

[Sect. 13.] And if any captain or other chief officer shall dismiss any soldier retained in his majesty's service, and assume another, for gain, such captain or other chief officer shall forfeit the sum of ten pounds for every twenty shillings he shall so exact, to be recovered and disposed of in manner as is before provided for the fine or penalty on officers neglecting to execute warrants for impressing of soldiers.

[Sect. 14.] And every person who shall impress any soldiers for his majesty's service, shall transmit a list of them to the chief officer of the regiment or troop, particularly mentioning sons under age, or servants, if any such there be, and to whom they belong, that so their fathers or masters may receive their wages, who are hereby impowered so to do.

And be it further enacted,

[Sect. 15.] That all such soldiers and seamen that, from the commencement of the present war, have been, or, during the continuance thereof, may be, wounded in his majesty's service within this province, and are thereby maimed or otherwise disabled, shall be relieved out of the publick treasury, as the great and general court or assembly shall order. **Maimed soldiers and seamen to be relieved.**

And be it further enacted,

[Sect. 16.] That any impressed man or men appearing at the place of rendezvous, being actually destitute of arms and ammunition of his own, and unable to purchase the same, he or they shall be furnished out of the town stock, if any there be, otherwise it shall be in the power of the captain or chief officer of the company or troop by whom he is impressed, to impress arms and ammunition for him or them, the value of which shall be paid out of his wages, fourpence per week for the same, and return such arms, or otherwise pay for the same. And if any soldier shall loose his arms in his majesty's service, not thro' his own neglect or default, such loss shall be born by the province. **Soldiers to be furnished with arms.**

Provided,—

[Sect. 17.] That this act shall continue in force unto the end of the sessions of the general assembly, to be begun and holden on the last Wednesday in May, which will be in the year of our Lord, one thousand seven hundred and fifty, and no longer. [*Passed June* 24; *published June* 27. **Limitation.**

CHAPTER 6.

AN ACT FOR CONTINUING SUNDRY LAWS OF THIS PROVINCE, EXPIRED OR NEAR EXPIRING.

Whereas an act was made and pass'd in the tenth and eleventh year of his present majesty's reign, entitled "An Act in further addition to an act entitled 'An Act for the relief of idiots and distracted persons'"; and an act made in the twelfth year of his [present] majesty's **Act about idiots, &c. 1737-38, chap. 9.**

Absconding debtors. 1738-39, chap. 15. Sheep and goats. 1740-41, chap. 23. Porters. 1741-42, chap. 5.

reign, entitled "An Act to enable creditors to receive their just debts out of the effects of their absent or absconding debtors"; another act made in the fourteenth year of his present majesty's reign, entitled "An Act to encourage the increase of sheep and goats"; and an act made in the fifteenth year of his present majesty's reign, entitled "An Act for the better regulating of porters employed within the town of Boston";—all which laws are expired or near expiring: *and whereas* the afores[*ai*]d laws have, by experience, been found beneficial, and necessary for the several purposes for which they were pass[e]d,—

Be it therefore enacted by the Governour, Council and House of Representatives,

Limitation.

That all and every of the aforesaid acts, and every matter and clause therein contained, be and hereby are continued and revived, and shall continue and remain in full force ten years from the publication of this act, and no longer. [*Passed June 23; published June 27.*

CHAPTER 7.

AN ACT FOR ENLISTING THE INHABITANTS OF DORCHESTER, WEYMOUTH AND CHARLESTOWN INTO HIS MAJESTY'S SERVICE FOR THE DEFENCE OF CASTLE WILLIAM, AS OCCASION SHALL REQUIRE.

Preamble.

WHEREAS the safety of this province in a great measure depends on the strength of his majesty's Castle William, and it is necessary that a great number of men skilful in the management of the great artillery should be always ready to attend there,—

Be it enacted by the Governour, Council, and House of Representatives,

Enlisted inhabitants of Dorchester, Weymouth, and Charlestown, to appear at Castle William, on occasion.

[SECT. 1.] That all the inhabitants of the town of Dorchester who are by law subject to common musters and military exercises, not exceeding fifty years of age, and such of the inhabitants of the towns of Weymouth and Charlestown as are willing to be enlisted, not exceeding one hundred and twenty in the whole from the two last towns, shall be enlisted under the present captains, or such other officers as the captain-general shall commissionate, who shall repair to Dorchester Neck, and be transported over to Castle William, four days in each year, in such months as the captain-general shall order; and shall on the said days be, by the gunner and quarter-gunners, exercised in the mounting, dismounting, levelling, traversing and firing the great guns, and shall be obliged hereunto, and to the observance of such orders as shall be given them in this exercise, under the like pains and penalties that soldiers are under to obey their officers in said castle in time of service.

And be it further enacted,

Penalty for not attending.

[SECT. 2.] That if any of the men enlisted as aforesaid shall not duly attend at time and place for the exercise of the great artillery, as afores[*ai*]d, being thereof notified and warned to appear, for every such day's neglect of attendance such soldier shall pay to the clerk of the company, for the use thereof, ten shillings.

And for the encouragem[*en*]t of the said men that shall be enlisted and exercised as aforesaid,—

Be it further enacted,

Enlisted persons excused other military service, &c.

[SECT. 3.] That every person so [e][*i*]nlisted shall be excused from all other military service, and from all impresses into other service that other soldiers by law are liable to.

And be it further enacted,

Inhabitants of Dorchester to appear at Castle

[SECT. 4.] That upon any alarm at Castle William, every man able of body, as well those enlisted by virtue of this act as also all others within the town of Dorchester, except such persons as are by law obliged to attend upon the governour for the time being, shall forthwith appear, compleat with their arms and ammunition according to law, at the said Castle William, there to attend and follow such commands as shall be given for his majesty's service, and that on the penalty of paying five pounds to the clerk of the said company, for the use of the province; the afores[ai]d fines to be recovered before any justice of the peace or court proper to hear and try the same. William upon an alarm.

[Sect. 5.] This act to continue and be in force for five years, provided the war continue[s] with the French king and his vassals for that time, and no longer. [*Passed June* 23; *published June* 27. Limitation.

ACTS

PASSED AT THE SESSION BEGUN AND HELD AT BOSTON, ON THE TWENTY-SIXTH DAY OF OCTOBER, A. D. 1748.

CHAPTER 8.

AN ACT FOR GRANTING THE SUM OF TWENTY-FOUR HUNDRED POUNDS, FOR THE SUPPORT OF HIS MAJESTY'S GOVERNOUR.

Grant to the Governor.

Be it enacted by the Governour, Council and House of Representatives, That the sum of twenty-four hundred pounds, in bills of credit of the form and tenor last emitted, be and hereby is granted to his most excellent majesty, to be paid out of the publick treasury to his excellency William Shirley, Esq., captain-general and governour-in-chief in and over his majesty's province of the Massachusetts-Bay, for his past services and further to enable him to manage the publick affairs of the province. [*Passed November* 18; *published November* 28.

CHAPTER 9.

AN ACT FOR THE EASE OF PRISONERS FOR DEBT.

Preamble. 1740-41, chap. 22.

FORASMUCH as, in divers counties within this province, the prisons are so small, that, when there are any numbers of prisoners, there are not rooms or apartments sufficient for the receiving and securing of them, without lodging felons and other criminals and prisoners for debt together in one and the same room; which is very inconvenient,—

Be it therefore enacted by the Governour, Council and House of Representatives,

Prisons to be made with convenient apartments.

[SECT. 1.] That, in the several counties within this province, the prisons that are or shall be erected within the said counties, shall be made so large as that there may be sufficient and convenient apartments for the receiving and lodging of prisoners for debt, seperate and distinct from felons and other criminals.

And be it further enacted,

Debtors to have separate apartments.

[SECT. 2.] That any person imprisoned for debt, either upon mean process or execution, shall be permitted and allowed to have a chamber and lodging in any of the houses or apartments belonging to such prisons, and liberty of the yard within the same in the daytime, but not to pass without the limits of the prison, upon reasonable payment to be made for chamber room, not exceeding one shilling and sixpence per week; such prisoner giving bond to the sheriff, with two sufficient sureties, being freeholders, bound jointly and severally, in double the sum for which he is imprisoned, with the condition under-written in form following; viz.,—

"That, if the above-bounden A. B., now prisoner in his majesty's goal in B., within the county of S., at the suit of C. D., do and shall from henceforth continue and be a true prisoner in the custody, guard and safe keeping of J S., keeper of the same prison, and in the custody, guard and safe keeping of his deputy, officers and servants, or some one of them, within the limits of the said prison, until he shall be lawfully discharged, without committing any manner of escape or escapes during the time of his restraint, then this obligation to be void, or else to abide in full force and virtue." Form of the bond to be given.

[SECT. 3.] And in case of any escape, the whole penalty of such bond shall be to and for the use of the creditor, and such bond shall be transferred and assigned over to the creditor by the sheriff, with full power to enable him to put the same in suit; and the creditor shall recover the whole sum therein expressed, and the court shall make up judgment accordingly; and the sheriff delivering up such bond to the creditor, so assigned as aforesaid, shall not be liable to any action of escape for any prisoner enlarged upon security given in manner as aforesaid. Forfeitures for the creditors.

Provided always,

[SECT. 4.] That the sureties be approved as sufficient by the justices of that court before whom the cause upon such commitment is to be tried, or from whence execution issued, or any two of them being together, or by two justices of the county, *quorum unus*, as aforesaid, where the debtor is imprisoned, and no other surety to be accepted. Proviso.

[SECT. 5.] This act shall continue and be in force for the space of ten years from the publication thereof, and from thence to the end of the session of the general court then next after, and no longer. [*Passed November* 11; *published November* 28. Limitation.

CHAPTER 10.

AN ACT APPOINTING WILLIAM COFFIN, FARMER OF EXCISE FOR THE COUNTY OF SUFFOLK, IN THE ROOM OF JEFFRY BEDGOOD.

WHEREAS the committee appointed to farm out the excise on wines and distilled spirits sold by retail, and on limes, lemmons and oranges, for the county of Suffolk, on the twenty-fourth day of June last, let the same to farm for the term of three years, commencing from the twenty-ninth of June last, for two thousand five hundred pounds, new tenor, per annum, to Mr. Jeffry Bedgood; and whereas the said Jeffry Bedgood and William Coffin have, by their several petitions, represented that the said Bedgood appeared to hire the same only for the said Coffin, and not for himself, and prayed that the said Bedgood might be discharged of and from said undertaking, and his bonds be cancelled, and that the said Coffin might be put in his place, with all the benefits, powers and trusts of said office of farmer of excise, and give his own bonds, with security, to be accepted in lieu of those given by the said Bedgood,— Preamble. 1748-49, chap. 4, § 13.

Be it therefore enacted by the Governour, Council and House of Representatives,

[SECT. 1.] That Jacob Wendell, James Allen and Adam Cushing, Esqrs., be directed and impowred to take bonds of the said William Coffin, with security, for the same sum and of the same tenor with the bonds, aforesaid, given by the said Jeffry Bedgood, in lieu of those given by said Bedgood; and thereupon to deliver to the said Bedgood his aforesaid bonds or cause the same to be discharged and cancelled. William Coffin to give bond as farmer of excise, &c.

And be it further enacted,

[SECT. 2.] That upon the said William Coffin's giving bonds as aforesaid, the said William Coffin shall be vested with all the rights, benefits, Vested with the rights and powers of said office.

priviledges and powers, of a farmer of said excise for said county, that have and shall accrue to the farmer of the excise aforesaid, for said county, from the twenty-ninth day of June last until three years, commencing therefrom, shall be compleat and ended, and with the same power and right of prosecuting in his own name, as farmer of said excise, any offenders against any laws relating to such excise, or any branch thereof, and the same benefit in, and share of, the forfeitures such offenders shall incur, whether such offences were committed before or after the making of this act, so that it be within the three years commencing from the twenty-ninth day of June last; and likewise to demand an account of, and receive, excise, from said twenty-ninth day of June last, of any person or persons from whom the same, by law, is or shall become due within the county and term aforesaid; and to sue any such persons for the penalty for not accounting to him therefor, in the same manner as the said Jeffry Bedgood might have done had he continued to be farmer of said excise; and enabled and impowered to transact any and everything relating to the duty or interest of a farmer of said excise, to all intents and purposes, as fully, and in the same manner, as he could or might have done had he, and not the said Jeffry Bedgood, been made farmer of said excise on the said twenty-fourth day of June last, anything in any other law to the contrary notwithstanding. [*Passed November* 18; *published November* 28.

ACTS

PASSED AT THE SESSION BEGUN AND HELD AT BOSTON, ON THE TWENTY-FIRST DAY OF DECEMBER, A. D. 1748.

CHAPTER 11.

AN ACT FOR INQUIRING INTO THE RATEABLE ESTATE OF THE PROVINCE.

WHEREAS the rateable estate of the several towns in this province may be very much altered since the last valuation taken by this court,— Preamble. 1741-42, chap. 9.

Be it enacted by the Governour, Council and House of Representatives,

[SECT. 1.] That the assessors of each town within this province, who shall be chosen for the year one thousand seven hundred and forty-nine, shall, on oath, take and lodge in the secretary's office, by the last Wednesday of May, one thousand seven hundred and forty-nine, a true and perfect list, according to their best skill and understanding, and conformable to a list settled and agreed on by the general court, and to be recorded in the secretary's office, a printed copy thereof to be sent by the treasurer to the clerk of each town and district which has heretofore been assessed to the province tax, therein to set forth an account of all male polls of sixteen years old and upwards, whether at home or abroad, distinguishing such as are exempt from rates through age or otherwise, and of all rateable estates, both real and personal, within their respective towns, and to whom the same belongs, and of all Indian, negro and molatto servants, whether for life or for a term of years, and of all farms or parcels of land lying adjacent to and rated in such town; and an account of what any farm or house within the town, that is improved by hire, rents for by the year, and who was the occupant thereof in the year one thousand seven hundred and forty-eight; also, what number of vessels, and of what burthen, have sailed from their respective ports to any other, except those in New England, in the year one thousand seven hundred and forty-eight; and the said assessors, in taking such valuation, shall distinguish the different improvements of the real estate into the following parts; viz., houses, pasture and tillage-land, salt, fresh and English mowing-land, with the number of acres of orchard, and what stock the pasture ordinarily is capable of feeding, and what quantity of produce the said tillage-, mowing- and orchard-land yearly affords, one year with another: *excepting* the governour, lieutenant-governour, president, fellows and tutors of Harvard College, settled ministers and grammar-school masters, with their families, who, for their polls and estates in their own actual improvement, shall be exempted out of this act. And the said assessors, before they enter on this work, shall take the following oath; viz.,—

List of polls and estates to be lodged in the secretary's office.

Printed form thereof to be recorded.

Direction to the assessors in the valuation.

Form of the assessors' oath.

You, A. B., being chosen assessors for the town of B. for the year one thousand seven hundred and forty-nine, do severally swear that you will faithfully and impartially, according to your best skill and judgment, do and perform the whole duty of an assessor, as directed and enjoined by an act of this province of the present year, intitled "An Act for inquiring into the rateable estate of the province," without favour or prejudice. So help you God.

—Which oath, in such town where no justice dwells, shall be administred by the town clerk.

Penalty for refusing the oath, or neglect of duty.

[SECT. 2.] And every assessor who is chosen by any town in the year one thousand seven hundred and forty-nine, accepting such choice, that shall refuse to take the said oath, or, taking the same, shall neglect or refuse to take the list aforesaid, or shall any way prevaricate therein, shall, for each of those offences, forfeit and pay a fine not exceeding forty pounds. And every person refusing or neglecting to give such assessor or assessors a true account of his rateable estate, improvements or rent, agreable to the true intent of this act, shall, for each offence, forfeit and pay the sum of five pounds.

Penalty for giving a false account of polls and estate.

[SECT. 3.] And in case any account given by any person, in pursuance of this act, shall be, by the assessor or assessors taking the same, suspected of falshood, it shall be in the power of either of such assessors to administer an oath to the truth of said account; and if such suspected person shall refuse to swear to the truth of such account, according to his best judgment, when thereto required by any one of the assessors, such refusal shall be deem'd a refusal to give an account of his rateable estate, and the person so refusing, shall be subject to the fine in that case by this act provided, without further or other evidence for his conviction on trial. And every assessor shall be allowed out of the treasury of his respective town, the sum of five shillings for every day he shall be necessarily employed in taking the lists afore mentioned.

Assessors' pay.

And be it further enacted,

Assessors to give into the secretary's office a list for the year 1748.

[SECT. 4.] That the assessors of each town within this province for the year one thousand seven hundred and forty-eight, shall, by the said last Wednesday in May, one thousand seven hundred and forty-nine, on oath, transmit to the secretary's office true and perfect copies of their province tax-lists for the year one thousand seven hundred and forty-eight, on penalty that each assessor neglecting his duty therein, shall forfeit and pay the sum of twenty pounds: *provided,* that the town of Boston, if they find it impracticable to form such a list of valuation, and so represent it to this court at the session in May next, shall be excused from the penalty for such omission, at the same time laying before the court copies of their tax-lists for the year one thousand seven hundred and forty-eight.

Town of Boston to be excepted, in case.

Fines, how to be recovered and applied.

[SECT. 5.] All fines and forfeitures arising by this act may be recovered by bill, plaint or information, or by action of debt, in any of his majesty's courts within this province proper to try the same, and shall be applied, two thirds to him or them that shall inform or sue for the same, and the other third to his majesty, to and for the use of this government. [*Passed January* 28; *published February* 2, 1748-49.

CHAPTER 12.

AN ACT FOR THE MORE EASY PARTITION OF LANDS.

Preamble. 1742-43, chap. 24. 9 Mass., 374.

WHEREAS the partition of lands is often delayed by reason that the parties concerned therein are very numerous, and live remote from each other, and sometimes in parts beyond the seas, and are some of them, unknown, to the hindrance and retarding of the improvement and settlement of lands in this province; for remedy whereof,—

Be it enacted by the Governour, Council and House of Representatives,

[SECT. 1.] That from and after the publication of this act, any person or persons interested with any others in any lot or grant of land, making application, either by themselves or their lawful agents, attorneys or guardians, to the superiour court of judicature, the said court, whether then holden in the county where such lands lie, or in any other county within this province, is hereby authorized and impowred to cause partition to be made of such lands, with the buildings thereon, if any such there be, and the share or shares of the party or parties applying for the same, to be set off and divided from the rest, such partition to be made by five freeholders, under oath, or the major part of them, to be appointed by said court, and a return of such partition to be made into the clerk's office of said court; and the partition or division so made, being accepted by the said court, and there recorded, and also recorded in the registry of deeds in the county where such estate lies, shall be valid and effectual to all intents and purposes. Superior court upon application to make partition of lands.

Provided, nevertheless,—

[SECT. 2.] That before such partition be made, where any infants or persons under age, or *non compos mentis*, are interested, guardians shall be appointed for all such persons, according to law, if they live within this province. And if any person or persons interested in any such estate, happen, at the time when such application shall be made, to have been beyond sea or out of this province for the space of one year, and not expected to return into the same within the space of six months more, and have no sufficient attorney within the same, that then, and in such cases, the justices of said court shall appoint some discreet and indifferent person or persons as agent or agents for such absent party or parties, and on his, her or their behalf to be advising in making such partition; and due notice to all concerned, that are known and within this province, shall be given before such partition be made, that so they may be present, if they see meet, at the time of making the same. Exception where any persons are *non compos* or out of the province.

Provided also,—

[SECT. 3.] That no partition be made where any partner shall be beyond sea, and shall not have been absent twelve months, or shall be expected to return within six months; anything in this act to the contrary notwithstanding. Proviso.

Provided also,—

[SECT. 4.] That if any partner should have a larger share set off than is such partner's true and real interest, or if any share set off should be more than equal in value to the proportion it was set off for, then, and in every such case, upon complaint to the court which caused said partition to be made, within three years of the making thereof, by any aggrieved partner or partners, who, at the time of making such partition, were out of the province, and not notified thereof as aforesaid in time for them to be present at the same, the said court shall cause a partition thereof to be made *de novo*. Case where the partition may be made *de novo*.

[SECT. 5.] And in such new partition, so much and no more shall be taken off from any share, as such share shall be adjudg'd more than the proportion of the whole it was design'd for, estimating such lands as in their original state, or the state they were in when first divided; and in case any improvements shall have been made on the part that may by such new partition be taken off as aforesaid, the partner who made such improvements shall have reasonable satisfaction made them by the partner or partners to whose share the same shall be added, by the estimation of the freeholders employ'd in making such new partition, or the major part of them.

Limitation.

[SECT. 6.] This act to continue and be in force for the space of seven years from the publication thereof, and no longer. [*Passed February* 1; *published February* 2, 1748-49.

CHAPTER 13.

AN ACT TO PREVENT DAMAGE BEING DONE ON THE BEACH AND MEADOWS IN PLYMOUTH, ADJOINING TO SAID BEACH, COMMONLY KNOWN BY THE NAME OF PLYMOUTH BEACH.

Preamble.

WHEREAS persons frequently drive numbers of neat cattle, horses and sheep, to feed upon Plymouth Beach and the meadows adjoining to said beach, whereby the said beach is much broken, and the sea breaks over it and carries the sand into the harbour and upon the meadows; and there is great danger, if such practices are not prevented, that the harbours in said town will be intirely ruined, and the meadows within said beach utterly spoiled, to the great damage of the owners thereof,—

Be it enacted by the Governour, Council and House of Representatives,

No neat cattle, horses, or sheep to be turned on Plymouth beach or meadows. Penalty.

[SECT. 1.] That from and after the publication of this act, no person or persons shall presume to turn or drive on any neat cattle, horse-kind or sheep, upon the beach called Plymouth Beach, or upon the meadows adjoining, upon the penalty of ten shillings a head for neat cattle or horses, and three shillings for each sheep, that shall be turned or found on said beach or meadows; which penalty shall be recovered by the selectmen or town treasurer of said town of Plymouth, or any other person that shall inform or sue for the same: the one half of said forfeiture to him or them that shall inform or sue for the same, the other half to be to and for the use of the poor of said town of Plymouth.

And be it further enacted,

Creatures turned on said beach, &c., to be impounded.

[SECT. 2.] That if any neat cattle, horse-kind or sheep shall, at any time, be found feeding on said beach, meadows or shores adjoining to said beach, that it shall and may be lawful for any person to impound the same, immediately giving notice to the owner or owners of the same, if known, otherwise to give publick notice thereof in said town of Plymouth; and the impounder shall relieve said creatures with suitable meat and water while impounded; and if the owner thereof appear, he shall pay two shillings and sixpence for each neat beast or horse-kind, and eightpence for each sheep, and the reasonable cost of relieving them, besides the pound-keeper's fees. And if no owner appear within the space of three days to redeem the said cattle, horse-kind or sheep so impounded, and to pay the cost and damage occasioned by impounding the same, then and in every such case the person or persons impounding such cattle, horse-kind or sheep, shall cause the same to be sold at publick vendue, and pay the cost and charges arising about the same (publick notice of the time and place of such sale being given in the said town of Plymouth and the two neighbouring towns, forty-eight hours beforehand), and the overplus, if any there be, arising by such sale, to be returned to the owner or owners of such cattle, horse-kind or sheep, at any time within two months next after such sale, upon his demanding the same; but if no owner appears within said two months, then the said overplus shall be one half to the person impounding, and the other half to be returned to the town treasurer of said town of Plymouth, for the use of the poor of said town.

Owners thereof to pay a fine and cost of relieving.

Creatures to be sold, in case.

Provided,—

[SECT. 3.] That nothing in this act shall be construed to prevent any of the owner or owners of said beach or meadows, or any improving under them, from turning on their horses they ride, or cattle improved in their teams, to feed on said beach or meadows, while they are cutting or carting their hay off said beach or meadows adjoining. Proviso.

And be it further enacted,

[SECT. 4.] That the said town of Plymouth, at their meeting in March, annually, for the choice of town officers, be authorized and impowered to chose one or more meet person or persons whose duty it shall be to see this act observed, and to prosecute the breakers thereof, who shall be sworn to the faithful discharge of their office; and in case any person so chosen shall refuse to be sworn, he shall forfeit and pay the sum of twenty shillings for the use of the poor of the town of Plymouth; and upon said refusal, said town may, from time to time, proceed to a new choice of such officer or officers: and said town of Plymouth, at a town meeting warned for that purpose, may at any time choose such officers, who shall continue 'till their annual meeting in March next. Officers to be chosen to see this act executed. Penalty for refusing the oath.

[SECT. 5.] This act to continue and be in force for the space of seven years from the publication thereof, and no longer. [*Passed January* 24; *published February* 2, 1748-49. Limitation.

CHAPTER 14.

AN ACT TO PREVENT DAMAGE BY FIRE IN THE TOWNS OF BOSTON AND CHARLESTOWN.

WHEREAS great damage has many times arisen from fires which have begun in sailmakers' and riggers' lofts, and spread to the buildings adjacent,— Preamble.

Be it enacted by the Governour, Council and House of Representatives,

[SECT. 1.] That from and after the first day of September, which shall be in the year of our Lord one thousand seven hundred and forty-nine, it shall not be lawful for any person to occupy or improve any tenement or building whatsoever, in any part of the towns of Boston or Charlestown, for the business or employment of a sailmaker or rigger, save only in such parts of the town as the selectmen of the said towns, respectively, or the major part of them, shall determine convenient,—such determination to be certified under the hand of the town clerk. Sailmakers' lofts in Boston and Charlestown to be allowed of by the selectmen.

[SECT. 2.] And if any person shall offend against this act, he shall forfeit and pay the sum of twenty pounds for every six months, and so in proportion for a greater or less time, he shall so occupy or improve any tenement or building that shall not be licensed or allowed as aforesaid; one half thereof to and for the use of the poor of the town of Boston or Charlestown, respectively, the other half to him or them that shall inform and sue for the same,—to be recovered before the court of general sessions of the peace for the county where the offence shall be committed. Penalty for offending.

[SECT. 3.] This act to continue and be in force until the first day of September, one thousand seven hundred and fifty-two, and no longer. [*Passed January* 31; *published February* 2, 1748-49. Limitation.

CHAPTER 15.

AN ACT FOR DRAWING IN THE BILLS OF CREDIT OF THE SEVERAL DENOMINATIONS WHICH HAVE AT ANY TIME BEEN ISSUED BY THIS GOVERNMENT AND ARE STILL OUTSTANDING, AND FOR ASCERTAINING THE RATE OF COIN'D SILVER IN THIS PROVINCE FOR THE FUTURE.

Preamble.

WHEREAS the sum of one hundred and eighty-three thousand six hundred and forty-nine pounds two shillings and sevenpence halfpenny, sterling money, has been granted by the parliament of Great Britain, for reimbursing to this province their expences in taking and securing Cape Breton,—

Be it enacted by the Governour, Council and House of Representatives,

Persons empowered to act for the province in taking care of the money granted by parliament for the charge at Cape Breton.

[SECT. 1.] That the Honourable Sir Peter Warren, Knight of the Bath, William Bollan, Esq., agent for this province, and Eliakim Palmer, Esq., of London, merchant, they or two of them,—the said William Bollan, agent, as aforesaid, except in case of his death, always to be one,—be and are hereby authorized and impowred to give a full discharge to the right honourable the lords commissioners of the treasury, for the sum granted as aforesaid, whensoever the same shall have been issued; or to the Bank of England, in case the same shall have been there deposited; or to any person or persons in whose possession or custody soever the same is or shall be; to prefer the humble address of the general court of this province to the king's most excellent majesty, that he would be graciously pleased to order the said sum to be transported to this government in foreign coin'd silver, on board some one or more of his majesty's ships; and to pursue such instructions as the said general court shall judge necessary concerning the transportation of the said granted sum to this province.

And be it further enacted,

The province treasurer empowered to receive said money on its arrival.

[SECT. 2.] That the treasurer of the province for the time being, be and hereby is fully authorized and impowred to demand and receive the whole and every part of the money aforesaid from the commander of any vessel or vessels on board of which the same shall be ship'd, upon the arrival thereof within this government.

And be it further enacted,

The said money to be exchanged for bills of credit.

[SECT. 3.] That from and after the thirty-first day of March, which shall be in the year of our Lord one thousand seven hundred and fifty, the possessor and possessors of each and every of the bills of credit of this province which shall then be outstanding, upon bringing such bill or bills to the treasurer aforesaid, shall be intitled to and receive, in exchange for every such bill or bills, silver at the rate following; viz., for every forty-five shillings in bills commonly known and understood by bills of the old form and tenor, one piece of eight; and for every eleven shillings and threepence in bills of the new form and tenor, and also of the middle form and tenor, one piece of eight; and so proportionably for a greater or less sum in the bills of each and any of the forms and tenors aforesaid: *provided, nevertheless,* that if the possessors aforesaid shall not offer such bills in exchange within one year from and after the said thirty-first day of March, one thousand seven hundred and fifty, all right or claim to the redemption or exchange thereof shall determine and cease.

Provided always,—

Proviso respecting bills of the neighboring governments.

[SECT. 4.] That such of the bills of credit of this province as shall be the property of the inhabitants of Connecticut, New Hampshire and

Rhode Island, may and shall be redeemed or exchanged by the bills of credit of each of those governments, respectively, that may be in the hands of the inhabitants of this government; anything in this act to the contrary notwithstanding.

And whereas all debts, dues, demands, bargains and contracts whatsoever, unless otherwise specially agreed or contracted, are now understood to be payable and may be discharged by the publick bills of credit of this province; and upon any action or actions being brought in the courts of judicature within this province, and judgment being made upon such action, and execution issued, such execution may be now satisfied and discharged by the publick bills of credit as aforesaid, with the addition of a greater or less sum according to the time when such debts were contracted,— Preamble.

Be it enacted,

[SECT. 5.] That from and after the thirty-first day of March, which shall be in the year of our Lord one thousand seven hundred and fifty, all debts, dues, demands, bargains and contracts payable in bills of credit as aforesaid, shall be understood to be payable in coin'd silver only; and all executions in consequence of any judgment of court in all actions heretofore brought or that may at any time hereafter be brought for the recovery of such debts, dues, demands, bargains and contracts made and contracted as aforesaid, shall and may be then discharged by silver at the rate following; viz., every forty-five shillings of such debts, dues or demands which were payable or might be discharged by bills of the old tenor, shall and may be discharged by one mill'd piece-of-eight; and every eleven shillings and threepence of such debts, dues or demands which were payable or might be discharged by bills of the middle tenor, or by bills of the new tenor, shall and may be discharged by one mill'd piece-of-eight, with such addition, according to the time of contracting, as the laws of this province do or shall require; and so proportionably of any debt or demand of greater or less value. Contracts after March 31, 1750, to be understood to be in silver money.

And whereas in and by the several acts of this government for issuing the publick bills of credit, provision has been made for drawing said bills into the publick treasury again by certain taxes which it is provided by said acts shall be laid on the several towns in this government in each of the several years from this present year until the year one thousand seven hundred and sixty,—

Be it further enacted,

[SECT. 6.] That the several clauses in the acts aforesaid, providing for the bringing into the province treasury, by taxes, the several sums, in bills of credit issued by virtue of such acts, be and hereby are repealed, and declared null and void. Repeal of the clauses in divers acts for taxes.

And whereas the sum granted by parliament as aforesaid, may prove insufficient to redeem or exchange the whole sum which is now outstanding in said bills of credit, at the rates aforesaid,—

Be it further enacted,

[SECT. 7.] That there be and hereby is granted unto his most excellent majesty, a tax of seventy-five thousand pounds, to be levied on polls, and estates both real and personal, within this province, according to such rules and in such proportions on the several towns and districts within the same, as shall be agreed upon and ordered by this court at their session in May, one thousand seven hundred and forty-nine, to be paid into the publick treasury on or before the last of December then next ensuing; and the tax aforesaid is hereby declared to be payable in bills of credit of the new form and tenor, or of the middle form and tenor, according to their respective denominations, or in bills of the old Tax for £75,000 to be levied in 1749.

tenor, accounting four for one, or in Spanish mill'd dollars, at the rate of eleven shillings and threepence each.

And be it further enacted,

Treasurer to issue his warrants in case there be no act for apportioning said tax.

[SECT. 8.] That in case the general court shall not, at their sessions in May, and before the twentieth day of June, one thousand seven hundred and forty-nine, agree and conclude upon an act apportioning the sum which by this act is engaged shall be in said year apportioned, assessed and levied, that then and in such case, each town and district within this province shall pay, by a tax to be levied on the polls, and estates both real and personal, within their districts, the same proportion of the said sum as the said towns and districts shall have been taxed by the general court in the tax-act then last preceeding; and the province treasurer is hereby fully impowred and directed, some time in the month of June in the year one thousand seven hundred and forty-nine, to issue and send forth his warrants, directed to the selectmen or assessors of each town and district within this province, requiring them to assess the polls, and estates both real and personal, within their several towns and districts for their respective part and proportion of the sum before directed and engaged to be assessed;* and the assessors, as

* So much of this chapter as authorized the apportionment of this tax, was printed, together with the apportionment, in pamphlet form, and distributed by the authority of the General Assembly. Copies of this pamphlet are still in existence, but are extremely rare; and, as the act is important, it has been deemed proper to subjoin the apportionment, in the margin, omitting the extracts from the act.

No act having been agreed upon and passed, during the May session of the year 1749, for apportioning the tax, the Treasurer issued his warrants to the selectmen or assessors of the several towns and districts, in conformity with the provisions of this chapter, having calculated the apportionment upon the basis of the tax-act of the year 1748-49. In these warrants, however, he inadvertently exceeded the rate of poll-tax prescribed by law, which was the cause of much difficulty and delay in collecting. To provide a remedy in this emergency, the following resolve was passed:—

"Decem[r] 14. 1749. In the House of Represent[ves] Whereas the Province Treasurer in Consequence of the Law of this Province, made & pass'd by the Great & General Court, at their Session, & Session, begun & held at Boston, upon Wednesday the 25th of May 1748, & Continued by Prorogation & Adjournm[ts] to Wednesday the 21st day of December following & then met, Entitled An Act for drawing in the Bills of Credit of the several Denominations which have at any Time been issued by this Governm[t] & are still Out standing, & for Ascertaining the Rate of coined Silver in this Province for the future. did in June last issue his Warrants directed to the several Selectmen or Assessors of the several Towns in this Province requiring them to Assess the Polls & Estates of the Inhabitants of the said Town, as he apprehended agreable to the Rules & Directions of the said Act; But being afterwards sensible of the Mistake in the Sums by said Warrants directed to be levied upon the Polls, did on the first day of Aug[st] last under his hand notify most or all of the said Assessors of the said Mistake & therein direct that the Sum to be levied on each Poll towards the said Tax should be sixteen Shillings & one penny, which Sum was agreable to the said Act & true Intent thereof. Therefore Resolved that the Select Men or Assessors of the several Towns in this Province, who have not made their Assessments conformable to the said Direction of the said Treasurer, that they forthwith make their respective Assessments, & that they therein conform themselves to the said Warrants & Direction in Explanation thereof; And all Persons are hereby enjoined to conform themselves thereto, as thô the said Warrants had been originally issued according to the true Intent of the Law; And where such Assessments have been made by any of the Select Men or Assessors of the Towns of this Province, agreable to the said Warrants & After Directions in Explanation thereof, It is hereby Ordered that the same be held good & valid; And all persons are enjoined to conform themselves accordingly. In Council, Read & Concur'd. Consented to by the Lieu[t] Governour."—*Council Records, vol. XIX., p.* 89.

Other difficulties were encountered in the assessment and collection of this tax, the most notable instances of which occurred in the town of Salem, where the assessors through "a misapprehension of the law" assessed not only all stock in trade, and the principal of money loaned, but also the profits of the former, and lawful interest on the latter.

On the petition of Benjamin Lynde, the younger, afterwards chief justice of the Superior Court of Judicature, and others, this assessment was set aside by the General Assembly: the money collected was ordered to be paid into the town treasury, and provision was made for correcting all inequalities, by allowing to the parties who had already overpaid to the collectors, credits in the settlement of their taxes for the next year.

Efforts were made to have the assessment ratified and confirmed by a resolve of the general court; but these proved unavailing. New embarrassments arose in subsequent attempts to comply with the order of the General Court. To avoid these, agreements were made among the tax-payers, in town-meeting, with the understanding that they were to be ratified by the general court.

The case was still further complicated by the act, which was passed before the tax had been collected, erecting a part of the town of Salem into the district of Danvers; and also persons assessed, shall observe, be governed by, and subject to all such rules and directions as shall have been given in the last preceeding tax-act; and if there be any surplusage, it shall remain a stock in the treasury.

Preamble.

And whereas it is provided by this act that the whole sum now outstanding in bills of credit, which have been the medium and instrument of trade and commerce for many years past, shall be sunk, partly by a tax, and partly by being exchanged for the sum granted by parliament as aforesaid,—which sum may prove sufficient to serve as a medium instead of said bills,—and it being of great importance that all possible means should be us'd for establishing an invariable silver currency for the future,—

Be it enacted,

Contracts and debts to be paid after March 31, 1750, in silver money.

[SECT. 9.] That all bargains and contracts, debts and dues whatsoever which shall be agreed, contracted or made after the thirty-first day of March, one thousand seven hundred and fifty, shall be understood

again the authority of the Legislature had to be invoked to determine the proportion of tax to be paid by the town of Salem, and the new district, respectively.

The full records relating to this matter are reserved for publication in the Appendix, with other resolves and orders of the General Court, of a declaratory nature.

The apportionment above referred to, is as follows:—

N.B. The part, or proportion, agreable to the last preceeding tax-act, which each town or district within this province is to be assessed, and pay, of the abovesaid seventy-five thousand pounds in bills of credit, this present year, one thousand seven hundred and forty-nine, as also their representatives pay, three thousand five hundred and seventy-two pounds, seventeen shillings and six pence, is the several sums following; that is to say,—

IN THE COUNTY OF SUFFOLK.

	Representatives' Pay and Fines.	Province Tax.	Sum Total.	
Boston, . .	£109 12s. 6d.	£13,500 0s. 0d.	Thirteen thousand six hundred & nine pounds twelve shill. & sixpen., ...	£13,609 12s. 6d.
Roxbury, .	32 17 6	698 0 0	Seven hundred and thirty pounds seventeen shillings and sixpence,	730 17 6
Dorchester, .	32 17 6	661 5 0	Six hundred and ninety-four pounds two shillings and sixpence, ...	694 2 6
Milton, . .	39 2 6	305 15 0	Three hundred ,and forty-four pounds seventeen shillings and sixpence, ...	344 17 6
Braintree, .	39 2 6	731 0 0	Seven hundred and seventy pounds two shillings and sixpence, . .	770 2 6
Weymouth, .	39 15 0	423 1 0	Four hundred and sixty-two pounds and sixteen shillings, .	462 16 0
Hingham, .	31 7 6	789 11 0	Eight hundred and twenty pounds eighteen shillings and sixpence, .	820 18 6
Dedham, .	35 15 0	520 10 0	Five hundred and fifty-six pounds and five shillings, ...	556 5 0
Medfield, .	35 7 6	317 6 0	Three hundred and fifty-two pounds thirteen shillings and sixpence, ...	352 13 6
Wrentham, .	39 17 6	419 3 0	Four hundred and fifty-nine pounds and sixpence, ...	459 0 6
Medway, .	35 2 6	187 18 0	Two hundred and twenty three pounds and sixpence, ...	223 0 6
Stoughton, .	39 15 0	385 0 0	Four hundred and twenty-four pounds and fifteen shillings, .	424 15 0
Hull, . .	00 0 0	167 6 0	One hundred and sixty-seven pounds and six shillings, . .	167 6 0
Brookline, .	00 0 0	250 1 0	Two hundred and fifty pounds and one shilling, ...	250 1 0
Needham, .	00 0 0	223 6 0	Two hundred and twenty-three pounds and six shillings, . .	223 6 0
Bellingham, .	00 0 0	84 10 0	Eighty-four pounds and ten shillings, ...	84 10 0
Walpole, .	00 0 0	130 12 0	One hundred and thirty pounds and twelve shillings, ...	130 12 0
Chelsea, . .	32 17 6	289 6 0	Three hundred and twenty-two pounds three shillings and sixpence, ...	322 3 6
	£643 10s. 0d.	£20,083 10s. 0d.		£20,627 0s. 0d.

Rates of Spanish money.

Penalty to those who receive or pay silver money at any higher rate.

and are hereby declared to be in silver, at six shillings and eightpence per ounce; and all Spanish mill'd pieces of eight, of full weight, shall be accounted, taken and paid at the rate of six shillings per piece, for the discharge of any contracts or bargains to be made after the said thirty-first day of March, one thousand seven hundred and fifty: the half's, quarters and other less pieces of the same coin to be accounted, received, taken or paid in the same proportion; and if any person shall, for the discharge of any such contracts or bargains, account, receive, take or pay any silver coin, or any of the said pieces at any greater or higher rate than that at which the same is hereby regulated and allowed, every such person so accounting, receiving, taking or paying the same, shall forfeit the sum of fifty pounds for every offence, one moiety thereof to his majesty, his heirs and successors, to and for the use of this government, the other moiety to him or them that shall sue for the same; to be recovered, with full costs of suit, by action of debt, bill, plaint or information, in any of his majesty's courts of record within this province, or by presentment of the grand jury; and all persons whatsoever are hereby required to conform their books and accounts according to the regulation aforesaid, any former usage to the contrary notwithstanding; and any books and accounts which shall not be made to conform to the said regulation, shall not be admitted or allowed to be produced in evidence for the recovery of any debt in any of his majesty's courts within this province.

IN THE COUNTY OF ESSEX.

	Representatives' Pay and Fines.	Province Tax.	Sum Total.	
Salem,	£53 15s. 0d.	£2,250 0s. 0d.	Two thousand three hundred and three pounds and fifteen shillings,	£2,303 15s. 0d.
Ipswich,	38 12 6	2,071 13 0	Two thousand one hundred and ten pounds five shillings and sixpence,	2,110 5 6
Newbury,	77 2 6	1,921 5 0	One thous. nine hundred & ninety-eight pounds seven shillings & sixp.,	1,998 7 6
Marblehead,	40 7 6	1,459 15 0	One thousand five hundred pounds two shillings and sixpence,	1,500 2 6
Lynn,	39 15 0	788 18 0	Eight hundred and twenty-eight pounds and thirteen shillings,	828 13 0
Andover,	33 0 0	906 0 0	Nine hundred and thirty-nine pounds,	939 0 0
Beverly,	30 7 6	579 15 0	Six hundred and ten pounds two shillings and sixpence,	610 2 6
Rowley,	41 2 6	565 11 0	Six hundred and six pounds thirteen shillings and sixpence,	606 13 6
Salisbury,	22 12 6	499 19 0	Five hundred and twenty-two pounds eleven shillings and sixpence,	522 11 6
Haverhill,	31 17 6	508 11 0	Five hundred and forty pounds eight shillings and sixpence,	540 8 6
Gloucester,	34 10 0	940 9 0	Nine hundred and seventy-four pounds and nineteen shillings,	974 19 0
Topsfield,	36 15 0	286 17 0	Three hundred and twenty-three pounds and twelve shillings,	323 12 0
Boxford,	42 17 6	360 5 0	Four hundred and three pounds two shillings and sixpence,	403 2 6
Almsbury,	44 2 6	417 1 0	Four hundred and sixty-one pounds three shillings and sixpence,	461 3 6
Bradford,	38 17 6	314 8 0	Three hundred and fifty-three pounds five shillings and sixpence,	353 5 6
Wenham,	00 0 0	262 2 0	Two hundred and sixty [two?] pounds and two shillings,	262 2 0
Manchester,	00 0 0	217 11 0	Two hundred and seventeen pounds and eleven shillings,	217 11 0
Methuen,	00 0 0	115 7 0	One hundred and fifteen pounds and seven shillings,	115 7 0
Middleton,	33 10 0	224 3 0	Two hundred and fifty-seven pounds and thirteen shillings,	257 13 0
Rumford,	00 0 0	00 0 0		0 0 0
	£639 5s. 0d.	£14,689 10s. 0d.		£15,328 15s. 0d.

And whereas bills of credit have been the only medium of trade within this government for many years past, and the bills of Connecticut, New Hampshire and Rhode Island, have passed promiscuously with the bills of this government, and the inhabitants of this government will be liable to greater evils than they have ever yet suffered if the bills of those governments continue current within this province,— Preamble.

IN THE COUNTY OF MIDDLESEX.

	Representatives' Pay and Fines.	Province Tax.	Sum Total.	
Cambridge,	£31 2*s.* 6*d.*	£494 10*s.* 0*d.*	Five hundred and twenty-five pounds twelve shillings and sixpence,	£525 12*s.* 6*d.*
Charlestown,	37 15 0	1,013 14 0	One thousand and fifty-one pounds and nine shillings,	1,051 9 0
Watertown,	39 2 6	309 16 0	Three hundred and forty-eight pounds eighteen shillings and sixpence,	348 18 6
Concord,	38 12 6	618 0 0	Six hundred and fifty-six pounds twelve shillings and sixpence,	656 12 6
Weston,	40 7 6	290 18 0	Three hundred and thirty-one pounds five shillings and sixpence,	331 5 6
Woburn,	39 2 6	483 0 0	Five hundred and twenty-two pounds two shillings and sixpence,	522 2 6
Reading,	39 2 6	530 0 0	Five hundred and sixty-nine pounds two shillings and sixpence,	569 2 6
Sudbury,	40 7 6	550 7 0	Five hundred and ninety pounds fourteen shillings and sixpence,	590 14 6
Malden,	32 17 6	443 15 0	Four hundred and seventy-six pounds twelve shillings and sixpence,	476 12 6
Marlborough,	36 12 6	568 15 0	Six hundred and five pounds seven shillings and sixpence,	605 7 6
Lexington,	39 2 6	343 7 0	Three hundred and eighty-two pounds nine shillings and sixpence,	382 9 6
Newton,	39 2 6	533 5 0	Five hundred and seventy-two pounds seven shillings and sixpence,	572 7 6
Chelmsford,	39 7 6	305 15 0	Three hundred and forty-five pounds two shillings and sixpence,	345 2 6
Billerica,	40 7 6	315 15 0	Three hundred and fifty-six pounds two shillings and sixpence,	356 2 6
Sherbourne,	33 10 0	198 15 0	Two hundred and thirty-two pounds and five shillings,	232 5 0
Holliston,	38 17 6	141 18 0	One hundred and eighty pounds fifteen shillings and sixpence,	180 15 6
Groton,	32 17 6	474 12 0	Five hundred and seven pounds nine shillings and sixpence,	507 9 6
Framingham,	37 5 0	403 16 0	Four hundred and forty-one pounds and one shilling,	441 1 0
Medford,	31 2 6	238 5 0	Two hundred and sixty-nine pounds seven shillings and sixpence,	269 7 6
Stow,	41 12 6	186 10 0	Two hundred and twenty-eight pounds two shillings and sixpence,	228 2 6
Dunstable & Nottingham,	00 0 0	125 19 0	One hundred and twenty-five pounds nineteen shillings,	125 19 0
Dracut,	28 7 6	124 15 0	One hundred and fifty-three pounds two shillings and sixpence,	153 2 6
Stoneham,	00 0 0	159 19 0	One hundred and fifty-nine pounds and nineteen shillings,	159 19 0
Littleton,	39 17 6	224 5 0	Two hundred and sixty-four pounds two shillings and sixpence,	264 2 6
Hopkinston,	00 0 0	155 15 0	One hundred and fifty-five pounds and fifteen shillings,	155 15 0
Bedford,	00 0 0	147 10 0	One hundred and forty-seven pounds and ten shillings,	147 10 0
Westford,	39 17 6	203 1 0	Two hundred and forty-two pounds eighteen shillings and sixpence,	242 18 6
Wilmington,	00 0 0	143 7 0	One hundred and forty-three pounds and seven shillings,	143 7 0
Tewksbury,	00 0 0	132 17 0	One hundred and thirty-two pounds and seventeen shillings,	132 17 0
Acton,	00 0 0	100 10 0	One hundred pounds and ten shillings,	100 10 0

Be it further enacted,

Penalty for receiving or passing bills of the neighboring governments.

[SECT. 10.] That if any person, from and after the thirty-first day of March, one thousand seven hundred and fifty, shall account, receive, take or pay any bill or bills of credit of either of the governments of Connecticut, New Hampshire or Rhode Island, in discharge of any contract or bargain, or for any valuable consideration whatsoever, every such person so accounting, receiving, taking or paying the same, shall forfeit the sum of fifty pounds for every offence, to be recovered and applied in like manner with the forfeiture or penalty for receiving or paying silver coin at any higher rate than is regulated by this act.

And be it further enacted,

Oath to be taken by persons chosen to office that they have not received or paid said bills.

[SECT. 11.] That from and after the last day of March, which shall be in the year of our Lord one thousand seven hundred and fifty, until the last day of March, which shall be in the year of our Lord one thousand seven hundred and fifty-four, every person who shall be chosen to serve in any office in any of the towns of this province, shall, before his entrance upon said office, take the following oath, to be administred by a justice of the peace, or where no justice of the peace shall be present, by the town clerk, who is hereby impowred to administer the same; viz. :—

Form of oath.

You, A. B., do, in the presence of God, solemnly declare, that you have not, since the last day of March, 1750, wittingly and willingly, directly or indi-

IN THE COUNTY OF MIDDLESEX—*Continued.*

	Representatives' Pay and Fines.	Province Tax.	Sum Total.	
Waltham, .	£32 7s. 6d.	£274 14s. 0d.	Three hundred and seven pounds and one shilling and sixpence, .	£307 1s. 6d.
Townshend, .	21 10 0	56 0 0	Seventy-seven pounds and ten shillings, ...	77 10 0
English inhabitants of Natick, .	00 0 0	75 0 0	Seventy-five pounds, . . .	75 0 0
	£910 7s. 6d.	£10,368 5s. 0d.		£11,278 12s. 6d.

IN THE COUNTY OF HAMPSHIRE.

Springfield, .	£28 15s. 0d.	£821 16s. 0d.	Eight hundred fifty pounds and eleven shillings, ...	£850 11s. 0d.
Northampton,	28 15 0	539 16 0	Five hundred and sixty-eight pounds and eleven shillings, .	568 11 0
Hadley, . .	27 0 0	386 15 0	Four hundred and thirteen pounds and fifteen shillings, . . .	413 15 0
Hatfield, .	27 0 0	248 3 0	Two hundred and seventy-five pounds and three shillings, . .	275 3 0
Westfield, .	28 17 6	317 15 0	Three hundred and forty-six pounds twelve shillings and sixpence, ...	346 12 6
Suffield, . .	14 0 0	413 5 0	Four hundred and twenty-seven pounds and five shillings, . .	427 5 0
Enfield, . .	23 12 6	244 15 0	Two hundred and sixty-eight pounds seven shillings and sixpence, ...	268 7 6
Deerfield, .	10 0 0	250 13 0	Two hundred and sixty pounds and thirteen shillings, . . .	260 13 0
Sunderland, .	00 0 0	127 15 0	One hundred and twenty-seven pounds and fifteen shillings, .	127 15 0
Northfield, .	00 0 0	112 6 0	One hundred and twelve pounds and six shillings, ...	112 6 0
Brimfield, .	33 5 0	219 4 0	Two hundred and fifty-two pounds and nine shillings, . . .	252 9 0
Somers, . .	00 0 0	134 7 0	One hundred and thirty-four pounds and seven shillings, .	134 7 0
Sheffield, .	00 0 0	131 0 0	One hundred and thirty-one pounds, ...	131 0 0
Elbows, . .	00 0 0	75 0 0	Seventy-five pounds, . . .	75 0 0
	£221 5s. 0d.	£4,022 10s. 0d.		£4,243 15s. 0d.

rectly, either by yourself or any for or under you, been concerned in receiving or paying, within this government, any bill or bills of credit of either of the governments of Connecticut, New Hampshire or Rhode Island. So help you God.

Penalty in case of refusal to take said oath.

[SECT. 12.] And where any person chosen as aforesaid, shall refuse or neglect to take the oath aforesaid on tendering the same, the town shall proceed to the choice of another person in his room; and where any person shall be elected during the term aforesaid, by any town into any office, to the non-acceptance or refusal whereof a penalty is by law annexed, such person neglecting or refusing to take the oath aforesaid, shall be liable to the same penalty as is by law provided for the non-acceptance or refusal of such office.

And be it further enacted,

Persons chosen representatives to take the said oath.

[SECT. 13.] That when any person, during the term aforesaid, shall be chosen to represent any town within this province, in the general court or assembly, such person so chosen shall take the oath aforesaid, and return shall be made by the selectmen upon the back of the precept, that the person so chosen has taken the oath required in the act made and passed in the twenty-second year of his majesty King George the Second, intitled "An act for drawing in the bills of credit of the several denominations which have at any time been issued by this government, and are still outstanding, and for ascertaining the rate of coin'd silver in this province for the future;" and if any person so chosen shall refuse or neglect to take the oath aforesaid, such refusal or neglect shall

IN THE COUNTY OF WORCESTER.

	Representatives' Pay and Fines.	Province Tax.	Sum Total.	
Worcester,	£33 0*s.* 0*d.*	£256 6*s.* 0*d.*	Two hundred and eighty-nine pounds and six shillings,	£289 6*s.* 0*d.*
Lancaster,	40 2 6	425 12 0	Four hundred and sixty-five pounds fourteen shillings and sixpence,	465 14 6
Mendon,	41 2 6	436 16 0	Four hundred and seventy-seven pounds eighteen shillings and sixpence,	477 18 6
Woodstock,	00 0 0	385 14 0	Three hundred and eighty-five pounds and fourteen shillings,	385 14 0
Brookfield,	13 17 6	260 8 0	Two hundred and seventy-four pounds five shillings and sixpence,	274 5 6
Southborough,	00 0 0	169 0 0	One hundred and sixty-nine pounds,	169 0 0
Leicester,	00 0 0	239 0 0	Two hundred and thirty-nine pounds,	239 0 0
Rutland,	00 0 0	154 18 0	One hundred and fifty-four pounds and eighteen shillings,	154 18 0
Lunenburgh,	00 0 0	191 5 0	One hundred and ninety-one pounds and five shillings,	191 5 0
Westborough,	00 0 0	265 6 0	Two hundred and sixty-five pounds and six shillings,	265 6 0
Shrewsbury,	34 15 0	234 17 0	Two hundred and sixty-nine pounds and twelve shillings,	269 12 0
Oxford,	00 0 0	179 13 0	One hundred and seventy-nine pounds and thirteen shillings,	179 13 0
Sutton,	00 0 0	283 10 0	Two hundred and eighty-three pounds and ten shillings,	283 10 0
Uxbridge,	00 0 0	201 18 0	Two hundred and one pounds and eighteen shillings,	201 18 0
Harvard,	00 0 0	173 10 0	One hundred and seventy-three pounds and ten shillings,	173 10 0
Grafton,	00 0 0	147 16 0	One hundred and forty-seven pounds and sixteen shillings,	147 16 0
Upton,	00 0 0	59 6 0	Fifty-nine pounds and six shillings,	59 6 0
Dudley,	00 0 0	126 10 0	One hundred and twenty-six pounds and ten shillings,	126 10 0
Bolton,	00 0 0	168 6 0	One hundred and sixty-eight pounds and six shillings,	168 6 0
Sturbridge,	00 0 0	63 10 0	Sixty-three pounds and ten shillings,	63 10 0
Leominster,	00 0 0	52 15 0	Fifty-two pounds and fifteen shillings,	52 15 0

be deem'd a refusal to serve as a representative, and the town shall proceed to the choice of another person in his room.

And be it further enacted,

Councillors to take said oath; [SECT. 14.] That the oath aforesaid shall be administred to each of the members of his majesty's council every year during the term aforesaid, at the same time when the usual oaths required to be taken by the said members of his majesty's council shall be administred; and all officers, civil and military, within this government, who shall be nominated or appointed during the term aforesaid, shall, before they receive their respective commissions, take the oath aforesaid, and their respective —as also officers chosen by the general court, commissions shall otherwise be void; and all persons elected into any office during the term aforesaid, by the general assembly, shall be deem'd not qualified to enter upon the execution of their respective offices until —and all other officers civil and military. they have taken the oath aforesaid; and all officers, civil and military, appointed by this government, who shall be in commission in the month of June, one thousand seven hundred and fifty-three, shall, some time in said month, take the oath aforesaid; and in case of neglect thereof, their respective commissions shall become and are hereby declared to be void.

And be it further enacted,

The said oath to be taken upon issuing executions on judgments of courts. [SECT. 15.] That no execution shall be issued, during the term aforesaid, from the office of any clerk of any of the inferiour courts of common pleas, or of the superiour courts of judicature, for any sum whatsoever, unless the plaintiff or plaintiffs, suing in his or their own right, and

IN THE COUNTY OF WORCESTER—*Continued.*

	Representatives' Pay and Fines.	Province Tax.	Sum Total.	
Western, .	£00 0s. 0d.	£49 10s. 0d.	Forty-nine pounds and ten shillings, ...	£49 10s. 0d.
Hardwick, .	00 0 0	37 4 0	Thirty-seven pounds and four shillings, ...	37 4 0
	£162 17s. 6d.	£4,562 10s. 0d.		£4,725 7s. 6d.

IN THE COUNTY OF PLYMOUTH.

Plymouth, .	£39 2s. 6d.	£703 10s. 0d.	Seven hundred and forty-two pounds twelve shillings and sixpence, ...	£742 12s. 6d.
Plympton, .	37 5 0	372 15 0	Four hundred and ten pounds, .	410 0 0
Scituate, .	16 7 6	1,078 12 0	One thousand and ninety-four pounds nineteen shillings and sixpence, ...	1,094 19 6
Bridgwater, .	40 15 0	855 10 0	Eight hundred and ninety-six pounds and five shillings, . .	896 5 0
Marshfield, .	35 10 0	532 5 0	Five hundred and sixty-seven pounds and fifteen shillings, .	567 15 0
Pembroke, .	40 17 6	286 10 0	Three hundred and twenty-seven pounds seven shillings and sixpence, ...	327 7 6
Duxbury, .	42 2 6	250 10 0	Two hundred and ninety-two pounds twelve shillings and sixpence, ...	292 12 6
Middleborough, .	40 7 6	631 15 0	Six hundred and seventy-two pounds two shillings and sixpence, ...	672 2 6
Rochester, .	00 0 0	402 10 0	Four hundred and two pounds and ten shillings, ...	402 10 0
Abbington, .	00 0 0	179 13 0	One hundred and seventy-nine pounds and thirteen shillings, .	179 13 0
Kingston, .	00 0 0	196 10 0	One hundred and ninety-six pounds and ten shillings, ...	196 10 0
Hanover, .	00 0 0	231 10 0	Two hundred and thirty-one pounds and ten shillings, . .	231 10 0
Halifax, .	00 0 0	150 0 0	One hundred and fifty pounds, .	150 0 0
Warham, .	00 0 0	75 0 0	Seventy-five pounds, . . .	75 0 0
	£292 7s. 6d.	£5,946 10s. 0d.		£6,238 17s. 6d.

dwelling within this province, shall first take the oath aforesaid, and certificate thereof shall be made on such execution ; and if any execution shall issue or go forth during the term aforesaid without such certificate, the same shall be and is hereby declared to be void.

Taverners, innholders, and retailers to take said oath.

[SECT. 16.] And no licence shall be granted to, nor any recognizance taken from, any taverner, innholder or retailer, by the justices of any of the courts of sessions within this province during the term aforesaid, until such taverner, innholder or retailer shall have taken said oath in presence of the court, or certificate of his having so done, from a justice of peace, shall be presented to the court.

Provided always,—

Proviso in case persons are possessed of the bills of the other governments.

[SECT. 17.] That when any inhabitant of this province shall be sued or have his person or estate taken by mean process, or in execution, for any debt contracted before the thirty-first day of March, one thousand seven hundred and fifty, with any of the inhabitants of either of the

IN THE COUNTY OF BARNSTABLE.

	Representatives' Pay and Fines.	Province Tax.	Sum Total.	
Barnstable, .	£46 15s. 0d.	£752 10s. 0d.	SeVen hundred and ninety-nine pounds and five shillings, . .	£799 5s. 0d.
Sandwich, .	35 2 6	405 10 0	Four hundred and forty pounds twelve shillings and sixpence, .	440 12 6
Yarmouth, .	38 0 0	464 1 0	FiVe hundred and two pounds and one shilling, ...	502 1 0
Eastham, .	50 7 6	559 14 0	Six hundred and ten pounds one shilling and sixpence, . . .	610 1 6
Truro, . .	00 0 0	73 12 0	SeVenty-three pounds and twelVe shillings, ...	73 12 0
Harwich, .	47 15 0	388 4 0	Four hundred and thirty-five pounds and nineteen shillings, .	435 19 0
Falmouth, .	37 12 6	275 13 0	Three hundred and thirteen pounds five shillings and sixpence, . .	313 5 6
Chatham, .	00 0 0	228 6 0	Two hundred and twenty-eight pounds and six shillings, . .	228 6 0
	£255 12s. 6d.	£3,147 10s. 0d.		£3,403 2s. 6d.

IN THE COUNTY OF BRISTOL.

	Representatives' Pay and Fines.	Province Tax.	Sum Total.	
Bristol, . .	£00 0s. 0d.	£493 13s. 0d.	Four hundred and ninety-three pounds and thirteen shillings, .	£493 13s. 0d.
Taunton, .	31 12 6	750 16 0	SeVen hundred and eighty-two pounds eight shillings and sixpence, ...	782 8 6
Norton, . .	34 15 0	376 13 0	Four hundred and eleVen pounds and eight shillings, ...	411 8 0
Easton, . .	00 0 0	147 10 0	One hundred and forty-seVen pounds and ten shillings, . . .	147 10 0
Dartmouth, .	47 17 6	1,162 18 0	One thousand two hundred & ten pounds fifteen shillings & sixpence, ...	1,210 15 6
Dighton, .	31 5 0	265 12 0	Two hundred and ninety-six pounds and seVenteen shillings, .	296 17 0
Rehoboth, .	41 17 6	926 10 0	Nine hundred and sixty-eight pounds seVen shillings and sixpence, ...	968 7 6
Little Compton, . .	00 0 0	530 16 0	FiVe hundred and thirty pounds and sixteen shillings, ...	530 16 0
Swansey with Shawamet, .	19 0 0	745 5 0	SeVen hundred and sixty-four pounds and five shillings, . .	764 5 0
TiVerton, .	00 0 0	600 8 0	Six hundred pounds and eight shillings, ...	600 8 0
Freetown, .	23 17 6	246 9 0	Two hundred and seVenty pounds six shillings and sixpence, . .	270 6 6
Attleborough,	38 5 0	376 12 0	Four hundred and fourteen pounds and seVenteen shillings, . .	414 17 0
Barrington, .	00 0 0	215 0 0	Two hundred and fifteen pounds, .	215 0 0
Raynham, .	00 0 0	170 13 0	One hundred and seventy pounds and thirteen shillings, . . .	170 13 0
Berkley, .	00 0 0	161 10 0	One hundred and sixty-one pounds and ten shillings, ...	161 10 0
	£268 10s. 0d.	£7,170 5s. 0d.		£7,438 15s. 0d.

governments aforesaid, upon making oath that he was possess'd of any sum in bills of credit of the government to which his creditor belongs, before the said thirty-first day of March, one thousand seven hundred and fifty, and has continu'd to be so possess'd, he shall have liberty to tender the same; and the creditor shall be oblig'd to accept the same towards payment or discharge of such debt, in like manner as if this act had never pass'd.

Provided also, and it is accordingly to be understood,—

Proviso in case the bills of other governments should be sunk.

[SECT. 18.] That if the bills of credit of said governments of Connecticut, New Hampshire and Rhode Island, shall be drawn in and sunk, and the paper currency of said governments shall be brought to an end, and cease, at any time before the said thirty-first day of March, one thousand seven hundred and fifty-four, then, and in such case, the three last preceeding enacting clauses of this act shall become void and have no further effect.

Preamble.

And whereas the sum of one hundred and eighty-three thousand six hundred and forty-nine pounds two shillings and sevenpence halfpenny, sterling, granted by parliament as aforesaid, and the further sum of seventy-five thousand pounds, now granted to be assess'd in bills of credit in the year one thousand seven hundred and forty-nine, on the polls and estates of the inhabitants of this province, are by this act become the sole fund and security for the whole sum in bills of credit outstanding, and in case the said sterling sum, granted as aforesaid, be not imported into this province before the said thirty-first day of March, one thousand seven hundred and fifty, the exchanging the bills of credit as is above intended will be rendered impracticable, and, the former funds or securities being made void, there will remain a fund for seventy-five

IN THE COUNTY OF YORK.

	Representatives' Pay and Fines.	Province Tax.	Sum Total.	
York,	£26 5*s*. 0*d*.	£686 10*s*. 0*d*.	Seven hundred and twelve pounds and fifteen shillings,	£712 15*s*. 0*d*.
Kittery,	37 5 0	945 14 0	Nine hundred and eighty-two pounds and nineteen shillings,	982 19 0
Berwick,	37 10 0	401 12 0	Four hundred and thirty-nine pounds and two shillings,	439 2 0
Wells,	46 17 6	330 10 0	Three hundred and seventy-seven pounds seven shillings and sixpence,	377 7 6
Falmouth,	38 17 6	576 18 0	Six hundred and fifteen pounds fifteen shillings and sixpence,	615 15 6
Biddeford,	00 0 0	227 10 0	Two hundred and twenty-seven pounds and ten shillings,	227 10 0
Arundel,	00 0 0	148 12 0	One hundred and forty-eight pounds and twelve shillings,	148 12 0
Scarborough,	00 0 0	299 9 0	Two hundred and ninety-nine pounds and nine shillings,	299 9 0
Nor. Yarmouth,	51 7 6	127 10 0	One hundred and seventy-eight pounds seventeen shillings & sixpence,	178 17 6
Georgetown,	11 0 0	150 0 0	One hundred and sixty-one pounds,	161 0 0
Brunswick,	00 0 0	50 5 0	Fifty pounds and five shillings,	50 5 0
	£249 2*s*. 6*d*.	£3,944 10*s*. 0*d*.		£4,193 12*s*. 6*d*.

IN THE COUNTY OF DUKES COUNTY.

Edgartown,	£00 0*s*. 0*d*.	£187 8*s*. 0*d*.	One hundred and eighty-seven pounds and eight shillings,	£187 8*s*. 0*d*.
Chilmark,	00 0 0	236 10 0	Two hundred and thirty-six pounds and ten shillings,	236 10 0
Tisbury,	00 0 0	146 12 0	One hundred and forty-six pounds and twelve shillings,	146 12 0
	£00 0*s*. 0*d*.	£570 10*s*. 0*d*.		£570 10*s*. 0*d*.

thousand pounds only, and the remainder of the said bills of credit will become of no value to the possessors,—

Be it therefore provided,—

[SECT. 19.] And it is accordingly hereby enacted, that if the sum granted by parliament as aforesaid shall not be received within this government on or before the thirty-first day of March, one thousand seven hundred and fifty, then, and in such case, the several acts of this province for drawing in the said bills, and all and every part of said acts, shall be and continue in full force, anything in this act to the contrary notwithstanding, and all and every part of this act shall be void and have no further effect. **Acts for drawing in the bills, to be in force in case the silver money should not arrive in the province before the 31st of March, 1750.**

Saving always, that whereas the sum of one hundred and thirty thousand five hundred pounds in said bills of credit. is engaged by said acts to be drawn in by a tax in the year one thousand seven hundred and forty-nine, and by this act provision is made for drawing seventy-five thousand pounds, part of said sum only, in said year, which part of this act may have had its effect, and the time will be elapsed for drawing in the remaining part of said one hundred and thirty thousand five hundred pounds,—

It is therefore hereby enacted and declared,

[SECT. 20.] That in such case the sum of fifty-five thousand five hundred pounds, the remaining part of said sum of one hundred and thirty thousand five hundred pounds, shall be and hereby is added to the tax of thirty-five thousand pounds, engag'd to be assess'd in the year one thousand seven hundred and fifty; and the inhabitants of this province shall be assess'd for said sum at the same time and in like manner and proportion as is by law provided that they shall be assess'd for said thirty-five thousand pounds; and the treasurer is hereby required to issue his warrants accordingly. [*Passed January* 26, 1748–49. **Saving £55,500, which is to be added to the tax in 1750.**

IN THE COUNTY OF NANTUCKET.

	Representatives' Pay and Fines.	Province Tax.	Sum Total.	
Sherburne, .	£30 0*s*. 0*d*.	£494 10*s*. 0*d*.	Five hundred and twenty-four pounds and ten shillings, . .	£524 10*s*. 0*d*.
Suffolk, . .	£543 10*s*. 0*d*.	£20,083 10*s*. 0*d*.	Twenty thousand six hundred and twenty-seven pounds, . . .	£20,627 0*s*. 0*d*.
Essex, . .	639 5 0	14,689 10 0	Fifteen thousand three hundred and twenty-eight pounds & fifteen shill., ...	15,328 15 0
Middlesex, .	910 7 6	10,368 5 0	Eleven thous. two hundred & seventy-eight pounds twelve shill. & sixp., ...	11,278 12 6
Hampshire, .	221 5 0	4,022 10 0	Four thousand two hundred and forty-three pounds and fifteen shillings, ...	4,243 15 0
Worcester, .	162 17 6	4,562 10 0	Four thousand seven hundred and twenty-five pounds seven shillings & sixpen., ...	4,725 7 6
Plymouth, .	292 7 6	5,946 10 0	Six thous. two hundred and thirty-eight pounds seventeen shill. & sixp., ...	6,238 17 6
Barnstable, .	255 12 6	3,147 10 0	Three thousand four hundred & three pounds two shillings & sixpence, ...	3,403 2 6
Bristol, . .	268 10 0	7,170 5 0	Seven thousand four hundred & thirty-eight pounds & fifteen shillings, ...	7,438 15 0
York, . .	249 2 6	3,944 10 0	Four thousand one hundred & ninety-three pounds twelve shill. & sixp., ...	4,193 12 6
Dukes County,	00 0 0	570 10 0	Five hundred and seventy pounds and ten shillings, ...	570 10 0
Nantucket, .	30 0 0	494 10 0	Five hundred and twenty-four pounds and ten shillings, . .	524 10 0
	3,572 17*s*. 6*d*.	£75,000 0*s*. 0*d*.		£78,572 17*s*. 6*d*.

CHAPTER 16.

AN ACT IN FURTHER ADDITION TO AN ACT ENTITLED "AN ACT FOR THE MORE SPEEDY FINISHING THE LAND-BANK OR MANUFACTORY SCHEME."

Preamble. 1744-45, chap. 12.

IT appearing to this court, notwithstanding the provision made for the speedy finishing the Land-bank or Manufactory Scheme, in the act of the seventeenth year of his present majesty's reign, intitled "An Act for the more speedy finishing the Land-bank or Manufactory Scheme," that there are great difficulties in the way of the commissioners, by said act appointed to finish said scheme without the further aid of this court, more especially occasioned by the destruction of the books and papers of the said late Land-bank Company, and of the said commissioners, in the late burning of the court-house in Boston,—

Be it therefore enacted by the Governour, Council and Representatives,

Commissioners empowered and directed to assess persons according to the list.

[SECT. 1.] That the said commissioners, or a major part of them, be directed and impowered, and hereby they are directed and impowered, as soon as may be, to make an assessment on those persons mentioned in a list printed in the supplement of the "Boston Gazette," 1745; which list is hereby declared to contain a true and exact account of the partners in said late Land-bank Scheme; and the said assessment shall be made for the full sum in said list, printed in said "Gazette," and such further sum as said commissioners shall judge necessary to redeem all the outstanding bills of said company, principal and interest, make good deficiencies by the failing of any partners, and to defrey the just incidental charges; and every receipt from said commissioners, or other satisfactory evidence, of payment on the aforesaid assessment lately printed in the "Boston Gazette," shall be taken and received by said commissioners as payment for the sum or sums they amount to, in the assessment now directed to; upon and according to which assessment now ordered (being first approved by the general court, after being inserted in all the weekly newspapers printed in Boston, sixty days before its presentation to the general court, that all concerned may object if they see cause) the said commissioners shall issue their warrants of distress against such partners as shall neglect to pay for sixty days after the general court's approbation: which warrant of distress shall be in the form following; viz.,—

Warrants of distress to be issued.

PROVINCE OF THE MASSACHUSETTS BAY.

Form thereof.

JOHN JEFFRIES, SAMUEL DANFORTH, JOHN CHANDLER, Esqrs., Commissioners for the more speedy finishing the Land-bank or Manufactory Scheme,—

[L. S.]

To the Sheriff of the County of A, his undersheriff or deputy, or either of the constables of B.,—Greeting:

By vertue of an act of the great and general court or assembly of said province, made at their session begun and held at Boston, upon Wednesday, the twenty-sixth day of October, 1748, entitled "An Act in further addition to an act entitled 'An Act for the more speedy finishing the Land-bank or Manufactory Scheme,'" there was an assessment made on the late directors and partners in said scheme, for the drawing in the remainder of the outstanding bills emitted on said scheme, which assessment has been duly published in all the publick newspapers in Boston, agreable to said act, and passed the approbation of the general court; since which more than sixty days are passed: in which assessment A. B., of C., in the county of E., a late partner in said scheme, was assessed the sum of , in lawful money or Manufactory bills, as his part or proportion; and altho' publick notice has been given of said assessment, as aforesaid, yet the said A. B. hitherto neglects to pay in the same, as is by said act required:—

Wherefore, by virtue of the authority to us given in and by the aforesaid act, these are, in his majesty's name, to require you to levy by distress and sale of the estate, real and personal, of the said A. B., the above sum of , lawful money, and bring the same to us, at our office in Boston, forthwith, returning the overplus, if any be, to the said A. B.; and if there cannot be found in your precinct estate sufficient to discharge the same, then you are to commit the said A. B., if to be found in your precinct, to the common goal of the county of E., there to remain until he has paid the said sum of , lawful money, and charges; for all which this shall be your sufficient warrant: save, only, that if you shall take the real estate of the said A. B., that then the said A. B., his heirs, executors, administrators or assigns, shall have liberty, for three months thereafter, to redeem the same, and if the same shall not be redeemed within three months as aforesaid, by paying said sum of , and charges, then you are required to sell the same as aforesaid, and return this warrant, and your doings thereon, into the office of the register of deeds for the county of E., there to be recorded.

Given, under our hands and seals, at Boston, the day of , 174 , in the year of our Sovereign Lord, , by the Grace of God King of Great Britain, &c.

J. J.
S. D.
J. C.

[SECT. 2.] And all sheriffs, their undersheriffs and deputies, and, where they are interested, all coroners, and, where the sum exceeds not ten pounds, all constables, are impowred and required to execute them on the persons whose names are contained in said list, or their estates, real or personal. Direction to the sheriffs, coroners and constables, for executing the warrants.

And as some of said partners are or may be deceased, or out of the province, before such warrants of distress shall be issued,—

[SECT. 3.] The said sheriffs, coroners and constables are hereby impowred and directed to take such estate as they may find belonged to such deceased person, or was by law liable to be taken if such deceased person or persons were then living, and in the province; the estate taken, whether real or personal, to be sold, and the overplus, if any, to be returned as by law required in ordinary cases of execution or distress: save only that the liberty of redeeming the real estate shall extend to three months only, after being taken; upon the expiration of which term of three months, if the same be not redeemed, the sheriff or other officer who took the same, shall return the warrant of distress, with his doings thereon, into the office of the register of deeds, in the county where the lands lie, there to be recorded.

[SECT. 4.] And if there shall be a surplus in the hands of the commissioners, after redeeming said bills and paying the necessary charges, the said commissioners shall divide and pay the same equitably to and among the said late partners, said division being first approved by the general court. Surplus, how to be disposed of.

And to the intent all possessors of said Land-bank bills may more readily and easily receive such sum or sums as may be due upon or for their bills,—

Be it further enacted,

[SECT. 5.] That the said commissioners, or a major part of them, shall, as soon as they are enabled to redeem them, give publick notice in all the said weekly newspapers, of the time or times, and place or places in the town of Boston, when and where they will attend to redeem them; which publick notice, being inserted six weeks successively in all the weekly newspapers printed in Boston, hereby is made and declared to be a legal tender to all and every possessor and possessors of said bills. Time and place of the commissioners' meeting for redeeming the bills to be publicly notified.

And forasmuch as, by the said burning, many papers and evidences were lost, whereby said commissioners may be much embarrass'd, which might be eased by papers, books or receipts in other persons' hands,—

Be it enacted and declared,

Commissioners empowered to demand papers.

[SECT. 6.] That said commissioners be and hereby they are authorized and impowred to demand and receive of the late directors, treasurer, endorser, partners and clerks of the said late company, any and all papers they shall judge needful, giving receipt for them, and to examine the said persons on oath touching the affairs of said late company. And the said commissioners, or a major part of them, are directed to meet, for the first four weeks after the publication of this act, two days in each week, and for the next four weeks, one day in each week, and after that, one day each alternate or every other week, 'till the scheme be finished, and no oftener, unless, on a representation made to the governour and council, they shall direct the commissioners to meet more frequently. [*Passed January* 3, 1748-49.

CHAPTER 17.

AN ACT IN ADDITION TO, AND FOR EXPLANATION OF, AN ACT ENTITLED "AN ACT FOR LIMITATION OF ACTIONS, AND FOR AVOIDING SUITS AT LAW, WHERE THE MATTER IS OF LONG STANDING."

Preamble. 1740-41, chap. 4, § 1.

WHEREAS, in and by an act made in the thirteenth year of his present majesty's reign, entitled "An Act for limitation of actions, and for avoiding suits in law where the matter is of long standing," it is, among other things, enacted, "That all actions for arrearages of rent, or grounded on any lending or contract, without specialty, should be brought within four years next after the cause of such action, in cases where the cause of action should arise after the publication of the said act, and, in those cases where the cause of action had arisen before, within four years after the publication thereof, and not afterwards"; *and whereas* the latter part of the said clause was, at the time of making the said act, generally understood to be meant and intended only of such actions grounded on lending or contract, without specialty, as are express'd in the act of parliament, which was pass'd in the twenty-first year of the reign of King James the First, entituled "An Act for limitation of actions and avoiding suits at law"; from which act the before-recited law of this province is, with respect to the actions therein mentioned, in a great measure copied; but yet the same, construed in it's utmost latitude, may be understood to include actions of the case upon bill or note of hand, and has lately been so adjudged by some of the courts of judicature within this province; and by the like construction may be deem'd to extend to all actions of account and upon the case, whatsoever, not excepting such accounts as concern the trade of merchandize between merchant and merchant, their factors or servants;—by which construction, in the courts of judicature, very many creditors have been greatly surprized and injured, who, upon the aforesaid general understanding of the said clause of the aforesaid provincial act, and thro' lenity to their debtors, have foreborn to bring actions for the recovery of debts due to them by promissary note, or otherwise howsoever, upon simple contract, within the time limitted in the aforesaid law of this province for bringing actions grounded upon lending or contract, without specialty, and will thereby, upon the aforesaid construction of the latter part of said recited clause, be barr'd from bringing actions for the recovery of the same, and great mischief and inconvenience may arise in the trade of merchandize, and dealings between merchant and merchant, and other traders within this province: now, for remedying and preventing the same,—

Be it declared and enacted by the Governour, Council and House of Representatives,

[SECT. 1.] That all actions of account, or upon the case, grounded on any lending or contract or otherwise howsoever, in which the cause of action has arisen before the publication of this act, and which have not yet been commenced or prosecuted to effect, may be brought and prosecuted at any time within four years after the publication hereof; and in cases where such actions have been commenced, and judgment hath been given upon plea in bar, or on tryal, for the defendant, the plaintiff or plaintiffs in such action, their executors or administrators, may bring and prosecute a writ of review of the said action in such court where the same was tried,—within three years after the making up such judgments,—for the reversing the same, and recovering of their debt, anything in the aforesaid act contain'd to the contrary notwithstanding; and shall have the like advantage for recovering the same, as if the said act had never been made: and that all actions of account, and upon the case, other than such accounts as concern the trade of merchandize between merchant and merchant, their factors or servants (the cause whereof shall arise after the publication of this act), shall be brought within the term of four years next after the cause of such actions, and not afterwards; and that all actions of account, which concern the trade of merchandize between merchant and merchant, their factors or servants, as aforesaid, may be brought and prosecuted at any time after the cause of such action, at the pleasure of such persons as may be concerned; anything in the aforesaid act to the contrary in anywise notwithstanding.

Further time allowed for bringing actions of account and on the case.

Time limited for bringing actions of account and on the case.

Provided always, and be it further enacted,

[SECT. 2.] That this act shall not be understood to bar any infant, feme-covert, person imprisoned, beyond the seas, or *non compos mentis*, from bringing either of the actions before mentioned within the term before set and limitted for bringing such actions, reckoning from the time that such impediment shall be removed.

Proviso.

And whereas it may happen that some debtors may be out of this province during the whole or some considerable part of the term of time by this act allowed and limitted for bringing such actions as aforesaid, and the creditors in such case not have like advantage with other creditors for recovering their debts,—

Preamble.

It is therefore hereby further provided and enacted,

[SECT. 3.] That if any debtor shall continue out of this province more than twelve months within the aforesaid term, in such case the creditor shall be allowed such further time for bringing his action and recovering his debt as shall appear, to the satisfaction of the court in which such action shall be brought, that the debtor had continued out of the province within the four years before mentioned. [*Passed February* 1, 1748-49.

Proviso where debtor continues out of the province.

ACTS

PASSED AT THE SESSION BEGUN AND HELD AT BOSTON, ON THE FIFTH DAY OF APRIL, A. D. 1749.

CHAPTER 18.

AN ACT TO PREVENT DAMAGE BEING DONE ON THE BEACH IN BIDDEFORD, AND MEADOWS ADJOINING TO SAID BEACH, COMMONLY KNOWN BY THE NAME OF WINTER HARBOUR-BEACH.

Preamble.

WHEREAS by the frequent numbers of neat cattle, horses and sheep feeding upon said beach and the meadows adjoining thereto, the said beach is much broken, and the sea breaks over it and carries the sand into the harbour and upon the meadows; and there is great danger, if such practices are not prevented, that the harbour in said town will be intirely ruined, and the meadows within said beach utterly spoiled, to the great damage of the owners thereof,—

Be it enacted by the Governour, Council and House of Representatives,

No neat cattle, horses or sheep to be turned on Winter-Harbor Beach or meadows.

Penalty.

[SECT. 1.] That from and after the publication of this act, no person or persons shall presume to turn or drive any neat cattle, horse-kind or sheep, upon the beach called Winter Habour Beach, in Biddeford, or upon the meadows adjoining, upon the penalty of ten shillings a head for neat cattle or horses, and three shillings for each sheep, that shall be turned or found on said beach or meadows: the one half of said forfeiture to be to the informer, and the other half to and for the use of the poor of said town of Biddeford.

And be it further enacted,

Creatures turned on said beach, &c., to be impounded.

Owners to pay a fine, and cost of relieving.

Creatures to be sold, in case.

[SECT. 2.] That if any neat cattle, horse-kind or sheep, shall, at any time, be found feeding on said beach, meadows or shores adjoining to said beach, it shall and may be lawful for any person to impound them, immediately giving notice to the owner or owners of the same, if known, otherwise to give publick notice thereof in said town of Biddeford; and the impounder shall relieve said creatures with suitable meat and water while impounded; and if the owner thereof appear, he shall pay two shillings for each neat beast or horse-kind, and eightpence for each sheep, and the reasonable cost of relieving them, besides the pound-keeper's fees. And if no owner appear within the space of three days to redeem the said cattle, horse-kind or sheep so impounded, and to pay the cost and damage occasioned by impounding the same, then and in every such case the person or persons impounding such cattle, horse-kind or sheep, shall cause the same to be sold at publick vendue, and pay the cost and charges about the same (publick notice of the time and place of such sale being given in the said town of Biddeford and the two neighbouring towns, forty-eight hours before hand), and the overplus, if any there be, arising by such sale, to be returned to the owner or owners of such cattle, horse-kind or sheep, at any time within two months next after such sale, upon his demanding the same; but if no owner appears within said two months, then the said overplus shall be one half to the persons impounding, and the other half to be returned to the town treasurer of said town of Biddeford, for the use of the poor of said town.

And be it further enacted,

[SECT. 3.] That the inhabitants of the said town of Biddeford shall and may, from time to time, have liberty of setting up two fences in the most convenient places across the country road, in order the more effectually to prevent cattle, horses and sheep going and feeding on said beach: *provided* a gate be made in each fence sufficient for the passage of carts and other carriages. Fences may be erected.

And be it further enacted,

[SECT. 4.] That the said town of Biddeford, at their meeting in March, annually, for the choice of town officers, be authorized and impowred to chuse one or more meet person or persons whose duty it shall be to see this act observed, and to prosecute the breakers thereof, who shall be sworn to the faithful discharge of their office; and in case any person so chosen shall refuse to be sworn, he shall forfeit and pay the sum of twenty shillings for the use of the poor of the town of Biddeford; and upon said refusal, said town may from time to time proceed to a new choice of such officer or officers: and said town of Biddeford, at a town-meeting warned for that purpose, may, at any time, chuse such officers, who shall continue 'till their annual meeting in March next. Officers to be chosen to see this act executed.

[SECT. 5.] This act to continue and be in force for the space of three years from the publication thereof, and no longer. [*Passed April* 22; *published April* 27, 1749. Limitation.

CHAPTER 19.

AN ACT FOR CONTINUING TWO LAWS OF THIS PROVINCE, IN THIS ACT MENTIONED, WHICH ARE NEAR EXPIRING.

WHEREAS an act was made and pass'd in the fifteenth year of his present majesty's reign, intitled "An Act for the better regulating the choice of petit jurors"; and another act was made and pass'd in the nineteenth year of his present majesty's reign, intitled "An Act for preventing the unnecessary destruction of alewives in the town of Sandwich," both which laws are near expiring; and the said laws have by experience been found beneficial and necessary for the several purposes for which they were passed,— Revival of two laws. 1741-42, chap. 18. Choice of petit jurors. 1745-46, chap. 14. Destruction of alewives in Sandwich.

Be it therefore enacted by the Governour, Council and House of Representatives,

That each of the afore-recited acts, and every matter and clause therein contained, be and hereby are continued and revived, and shall continue and remain in full force five years from the publication of this act, and no longer. [*Passed April* 22; *published April* 27; 1749.

NOTES.—There were four sessions of the General Court this year, at all of which acts were passed. The engrossments of the acts of the first session, only, are preserved. All the acts, however, were printed as of the sessions in which they were, respectively, enacted except chapters 1 and 2, which were printed separately.

The acts of the first session were received by the clerk of the Privy Council, in waiting, June 28, 1749, having been regularly certified for forwarding, on the 7th of October previous. On the 29th of June they were referred to the Lords of Trade, by whom they were received on the 6th of July, and sent the next day to Mr. Lamb, for his opinion thereon. Mr. Lamb's report to the Board is dated December 6, 1751, and concludes as follows: "Upon perusall & consideration of the aforement[d] Acts I have no objection to make thereto in point of Law."

The acts of the last three sessions were despatched from Boston under date of September 8, 1749, and had reached the Privy Council by the 4th of December following, when they were referred to a committee. By this committee they were ordered to be sent to the Lords of Trade, December 8; and were received by the Board, January 17, 1749-50. On the 3d of April, 1750, they were sent to Mr. Lamb, in the usual course, and were reported back by him December 6, 1751. In this report, "no objection" is entered against chapters 8, 9, 10, 11, 12, 13, 14, 18 and 19; but special comments are made on chapters 15, 16 and 17, which are hereunder given, in full, in the notes to those chapters, respectively. Mr. Lamb concludes his report in the same language used by him at the close of his report, of the same date, on the acts of the first session.

On the 4th of June, 1752, the Lords of Trade signed their report to the Privy Council. In this report, chapters 1, 2, 3, 4, 5, 7, 8 and 10 are represented as "for a temporary service, and are either expired or the purposes for which they were granted have been completed." Chapters 9, 11, 12, 13, 14, 16, 17 and 18 are represented as appearing "to have been enacted for the particular convenience and benefit of the Province, and," the report continues, "as Mr. Lamb has no objection to any of them in point of Law, We see no reason why His Majesty may not be graciously pleased to confirm them"; and chapters 6, 15 and 19 are commented upon in the language given hereunder in notes to those chapters.

Upon this report an order in Council was passed, June 30, 1752, confirming chapters 9, 11, 12, 13, 14, 16, 17, 18 and 19.

Chapter 15 was separately acted upon by the Home Government, and confirmed, by an order in Council, June 28, 1749, the particulars of which are given in the note to that chapter, *post*.

In the list certified by Secretary Willard, and acted upon by the Lords of Trade and the Privy Council, the acts, after chapter 7, are treated as of one session, and chapters 18 and 19, which were passed at the session held, by adjournment, April 5, 1749, are placed before chapters 15, 16 and 17, which were passed at the session held, by adjournment, December 21, 1748. There seems to be no good reason for this grouping of the acts, unless the convening of the Assembly in October, after a prorogation, was considered the proper commencement of a session that could only be terminated by another prorogation, or dissolution. As records of many, if not most, of the prorogations have not been preserved, it would be impracticable to adopt this rule in dividing the sessions at this day; and even if such a division could be strictly made, it would be far more convenient, for historical purposes, at least, to group the acts according to the several sittings during which they were passed. See, also, preface, pp. xx. and xxi.

Chap. 3. "As to the Bill for the Supply of the Treasury, tho' I am still of the mind that it would have been much more, for the General Good of the Province to have Stop'd your Hands as to Issuing more Paper Money, & to have gone into some Safer Way for the supply of the Treasury, Yet considering the present Exigency, And the great Hardships that some Persons might be put to by delaying the Supply, I have thought proper to sign my Consent to the Bill"—*Message of Governor Shirley to the Assembly, June* 23, 1748: *Council Records, vol. XVIII., pp.* 369-70.

Chap. 4. "June 24. 1748. In the House of Represent[ves] Voted that James Allen & Adam Cushing Esq[rs] with such as the Hon[ble] Board, shall join, be, and hereby are appointed a Comm[tee] to Lett to Farm the Excise in the County of Suffolk Pursuant to an act for granting an Excise &c as passed this Court in the present Session—That Thomas Rowell & James Collins Esq[r] with such as the Hon[ble] Board shall join be a Comm[tee] for the purpose aforesaid in the County of Essex—Andrew Boardman Esq[r] & Mr James Russell, with such as the Hon[ble] Board shall join in the County of Middlesex.—John Worthington Esq[r] & Mr Phineas Lyman with such as the Hon[ble] Board shall join, in the County of Hampshire—Nahum Ward Esq[r] & Capt Will[m] Richardson with such as the Hon[ble] Board shall join, in the County of Worcester,—Isaac Little & Thomas Foster Esq[rs] with such as the Hon[ble] Board shall join in the County of Plymouth —James Otis & Joseph Thatcher Esq[rs] with such as the Hon[ble] Board shall join in the County of Barnstable—Capt. Sam[ll] Tyler & James Williams Esq[r] with such as the Hon[ble] Board shall join in the County of Bristol—John Storer & Simon Frost Esq[rs] with such as the Hon[ble] Board shall join, in the County of York—Mr John Sumner & Mr John Norton with such as the Hon[ble] Board shall join in Dukes County.—Mr Abisha Folger & Mr Josiah Coffin with such as the Hon[ble] Board shall join in the County of Nantuckett.

In Council, Read & Concurred & Jacob Wendell Esq[r] is joined to the said Comm[tee] to Farm the Excise in the County of Suffolk—Thomas Berry Esq[r] in the County of Essex.—Ezekiel Cheever Esq[r] in the County of Middlesex—Joseph Pynchon Esq[r] in the County of Hampshire.—John Chandler Esq[r] in the County of Worcester.—John Cushing Esq[r] in the County of Plymouth—John Otis Esq[r] in the County of Barnstable—George Leonard Esq[r] in the County of Bristol.—Jeremiah Moulton Esq[r] in the County of York —Zaccheus Mahew Esq[r] in the County of Dukes County & John Bunker Esqr. in the County of Nantuckett. Consented to by the Governour"—*Ibid*, *p.* 371.

"Nov[r] 3[d] 1748. Jacob Wendell Esq[r] from the Commtee for letting out to Farm the Excise on Strong Liquors for the County of Suffolk. Reported as follows, viz. The Comm[tee] appointed the 24th of June last to farm out the Excise on Strong Liquors &c in the County of Suffolk have attended that Service & sold the same to the highest Bidder Capt. Jeffry Bedgood for Two Thousand five Hundred Pounds Bills of the last Tenor pr Annum for Three Years Commencing the 29 of June last & have taken Three Bonds, executed by said Bedgood, William Coffin & Thomas Green for the Payment of the same to the Province Treasurer, to whom we have delivered said Bonds—Jacob Wendell pr Order. In Council Read & Accepted—In the House of Represent[ves] Read and Concured—Consented to by the Governour"—*Ibid*., *p.* 380.

"November 5 1748 George Leonard Esqr from the Comm^tee appointed to let to Farm the Excise on Wines Liquors &c in the County of Bristol. Reported that they had Farmed the same for three years from the 29th of June last unto Samuel White of Taunton Esqr for one hundred & Twenty Eight Pounds, in Bills of the last Emission pr. Year & had taken Bonds with suretys for the Payment thereof and delivered them into the Hands of the Province Treasurer—In Council: Read & accepted—In the House of Represent^ves Read & Concured. Consented to by the Governour."—*Ibid., p.* 384.

"Novr 8. 1748. Thos Berry Esqr from the Comm^tee appointed to farm out the Excise on Wines Liquors &c in the County of Essex. Reported that they had let out the said Excise to Benj^a Prescott jun^r of Salem for three years from the 29th of June last for seven Hundred & seventy six Pounds five shillings p^r annum & had taken Bonds of him with suretys to the Province Treasurer for the Payment thereof & delivered them to the Treasurer—In Council Read & Accepted—

In the House of Represent^ves Read & Concur'd—Consented to by ye Govr"—*Ibid., p.* 385.

John Otis Esqr from the Comm^tee for farming out the Excise on strong Liquors &c in the County of Barnstable reported that they had let out said Excise to David Gorham Esqr for three years from the 29th of June last at the Rate of one Hundred & fifty four Pounds ten shillings per Annum & taken his Bond with Sureties and lodged them with the Treasurer—In Council Read & Accepted—In the House of Represent^ves Read & Concured Consented to by the Governour."—*Ibid., p.* 389.

"Nov 11. 1748. John Chandler Esqr from the Comm^tee for farming out the excise in Worcester County on Wines Liquors &c reported that they had let out said Excise to John Chandler Junr for three years at the Rate of One Hundred & fifty seven Pounds pr Annum & have taken Bonds with Suretys which they have lodged with the Province Treasurer.—In Council Read & accepted—In the House of Represent^ves Read & Concured—Consented to by the Governour."—*Ibid., p.* 391.

"February 1. 1748, The Report of the Committee for letting out the Excise in the County of Nantucket was Accepted by both Houses & Consented to by the Governour"—*Ibid., p.* 443.

"February 1. 1748. The Report of the Comm^tee for letting out the Excise in the County of Middlesex was Accepted by both Houses & Consented to by the Governour"—*Ibid., p.* 443.

"June 28. 1750. In the House of Represent^ves Whereas in the Act made & pass'd in the twenty first Year of His present Majesty's Reign intitled an Act for granting unto his Majesty an Excise upon Wine & Spirits distilled, sold by Retail & upon Limes Lemmons & Oranges, mention is made of certain Sums, to be paid for the Duties of Excise on Brandy Rum & other Commodities therein mentioned, as also of certain Sums to be forfeited & paid for the Violation or Non Observance of said Act; But no Discrimination is therein made betwixt lawful Money & Bills of publick Credit. nor is it declared whether those Sums shall be paid (according to their Nominal Value) in the one or in the other determinately; By reason whereof some Doubts & Disputes have arisen, & may arise unless prevented by this Court.

Therefore. Resolved that by the several Sums in said Act mentioned (either as a Duty of Excise or as a Penalty) were intended so much in Bills of publick Credit then last Emitted or Value there of, & no more, And the said Act, ought so to be understood & Construed & put in Execution accordingly. In Council; Read & Concur'd—Consented to by the Lieut-Govern^r."—*Ibid., vol. XIX., p* 224.

Chap. 6. "Upon the three following Acts entituled:—

An Act for continuing sundry Laws of this Province expired or near expiring. 1748-49, chap. 19.

An Act for continuing two Laws of this Province in this Act mentioned which are near expiring. 1747-50, chap. 16.

An Act for reviving and continuing of sundry Laws that are expired or near expiring 1742-43, chap. 34.

We beg leave to acquaint Your Lordships that all the several Laws, thereby revived or continued have been confirmed by His Majesty except the *Act to enable the Town of Weymouth to regulate and order the taking and disposing of the fish called Shadd and Alewives within the limits of that Town,* and the *Act to enable Creditors to receive their just debts out of the effects of their absent or absconding Debtors,* which acts do not appear to us to have been ever laid before His Majesty as they ought to have been pursuant to the directions of the Charter of the said Province granted by King William & Queen Mary. 1738-39, chap. 15.

As it appears however from the annex'd Copies of the said Acts, transmitted to us by the Secretary of the said Province that they were enacted only for their private convenience, We see no reason why His Majesty may not be graciously pleased to confirm the above-mentioned three Acts."—*Report of the Lords of Trade: "Mass. Bay, B. T." vol.* 84. *p.* 262, *in Public-Record Office.*

By referring to the notes at the end of the year 1738-39, it will be seen that the above-named act of that year reached the Board of Trade, and was submitted to, and reported upon by, Mr. Fane. Nothing further, however, has been discovered tending to show that this act, or the acts of the fourth session of the year 1742-43, including chapter 34 above mentioned, were ever formally laid before the Privy Council.

Chap. 7. "April 21. 1749. His Excellency sent the following Message to both Houses by the Secretary.

Gentlemen of the Council & House of Representatives One of the Members of his Majesty's Council has laid before me a villanous Paper importing a wicked Conspiracy for robbing him of part of his Estate, by extorting a sum of Money from him, & threatning him with the burning of his House, Warehouses and Vessells & the murthering of his Person in case of his refusal to comply with their Demands.

Gentlemen, This being the first Instance of this Kind of execrable Villany attempted in this Province, it highly imports this Legislature to make Provision for Preventing & punishing the same Attempts for the future; Wherefore I desire you would immediately take the matter into Consideration & do what you judge Necessary before you Rise.

In the House of Representves Read together with the Paper referred to, and Ordered that Mr. Speaker, Colo. Heath, Colo Otis, Colo Dwight, & Colo Buckminster, with such as the Honble Board shall join be a Committee to consider this Message & Paper referred to, & report what they judge proper for this Court to do thereon; the Committee to sit forthwith In Council Read & Concured; And Samuel Welles, Samll Danforth, Andrew Oliver and John Otis Esqrs are joined in the affair."—*Council Records, vol. XVIII., p.* 467.

"April 22d 1749. Samuel Welles, Esqr from the Committee on his Excellency's Message referring to the threatning Letter sent to one of his Majesty's Council gave in the following Report

The Committee appointed to Consider of his Excellency's Message of this Day are of Opinion, that all possible means should be used to detect & punish the horrid Crimes his Excellency refers to, & to prevent such heinous & detestable Practices for the future; And therefore they humbly Apprehend it to be proper for the two Houses to desire & advise his Excellency to issue a Proclamation promising a Reward of two hundred Pounds, Bills of the last Emission to any Person or Persons who shall inform or discover one or more concerned in this Wicked Conspiracy so that he or they may be Convicted; And if the Informer shall have been an Accomplice or engaged in said Crime, he shall be forgiven, And to the End the greater Horrour & Detestation may be raised in the minds of his Majesty's good Subjects with respect to this atrocious & execrable Design: The Committee humbly report as their Opinion that the two Houses desire his Excellency to insert in the Proclamation, the sum & substance of the Anonymous Letter refered to in the Message & Some of the impious, insolent inhuman Message verbatim that thereby all his Majesty's good Subjects may see how reasonble & necessary it is that they join Universally in their Endeavours to bring forward to Exemplary Punishment the profligate & abandon'd Wretches concerned in this Wicked & impudent Combination: The Committee would propose that some Gentlemen of each House be appointed to prepare the Draught of a Bill for the more easy & effectual preventing or detecting such Abominable & dangerous Crimes hereafter to be laid before this Court at the begginning of their Session in May next

April 21. 1749. by Order of the Committee Samll Welles.

In the House of Representves Read & Accepted & Mr. Speaker, Mr Hubbard, with such as the Honble Board shall join are a Committee to prepare the Draught of a Bill Accordingly In Council; Read & Concured.

Consented to by the Governour."—*Ibid., p.* 470.

Chap. 8. On the 10th of June, a bill appropriating £1900 for the support of the Governor was passed to be enacted by both branches of the Assembly, and on the 14th the Governor sent the following message to both branches:—

"The Secretary has laid before me, for my signing, an Engross'd Bill (pass'd to be Enacted by both houses) for granting the sum of Nineteen Hundred Pounds for my Support. I am very sorry I have this Occasion to continue, or, rather, revive the Dispute between his Majesty & this Province, concerning the support of his Governour, after his Majesty's gracious Condescention Manifested in his Instruction to me on that Head, at my Entrance upon the Goverment. By this Instruction I was commanded first to recommend it to the Assembly in the most pressing & effectual manner, to pass an act for the settlement of one Thousand Pounds Sterling pr Annum on my self & my Successors in the Goverment or at least upon my self, during the whole Time of my Goverment. But in case the assembly should not readily comply, with this his Majesty's reasonable Recommendation I was Impowred in the Mean Time, for the Support of my Dignity, as his Majesty's Governour to give my Consent to such Bill as should be annually pass'd for paying me a Salary of one Thousand Pounds Sterling, or the Value thereof in Money of this Province until his Majesty's Royal Pleasure should be signified to the Contrary &c. Provided such Act be the first that shall be pass'd by the Assembly of the Province before they proceed upon the other Business of that Session.

By Vertue of the Indulgence given me in the latter part of this Instruction I have from Time to Time, accepted the Grants made for my support by former assemblys (all wch excepting the last were about the Value of one Thousand Pounds Sterling) without engaging in any considerable disputes; which would have been Extreemly contrary to my Disposition. As to the Grant wch was made me last Year, tho' it was considerably short of the sum which his Majesty insists upon, yet as I was loth at so Critical a Juncture as that was to enter into Any Controversy with the last assembly, least it should have had a bad Effect upon our affairs depending in great Britain, by giving a Disgust to the Goverment there, I acquies'd in it not doubting but the succeeding assemblys would have a proper Consideration of what I should suffer by my acceptance of that Grant.

But now Gentlemen, that you should still proceed to make a Defalcation from my Salary of at least one quarter part of the sum which his Majesty expects should be allowed for the Support of his Governour, & that at a Time when the Cares & Burthens of Goverment are so great in this Province, as in no degree to be parralled in Any other of his Majesty's Plantations, & wn the Extravagant Prices of all necessaries of Life in this Province do so much Exceed even the Ordinary Exchange between Great Britain & this Place, I am perswaded must be highly displeasing to his Majesty & looked upon by him as an Instance of yr Ingratitude to him for his late favour in promoting yr Reimburstment for the Expences of the Late Expedition against Cape Breton, wch there can be no doubt now of their being secured to you.

Upon these Considerations, Gentlemen of the House of Representves, I must desire you would reconsider the Bill for my support & make such Alterations therein as may make me some Amends for the Deficiency in the last Year's Grant, & put it into my Power to sign my Consent to it consistently with his Majesty's Instructions"—*Ibid., pp.* 357-8.

Four days later the House of Representatives sent to the Governor the following message in reply:—

"May it please yr Excellency—The House having taken under their mature Consideration yr message to both Houses of the 14th Instant, moving the House to reconsider & make some Alterations in the Bill which has pass'd both Houses this Session for your Excy's Support beg Leave thereupon humbly to say, that it is with Pleasure the House observes yr Excy's expresses a Reluctancy at Reviving a Dispute Relating to fixing a salary on the Governour for any certain Time; A Dispute which in some former Administrations, has been attended with the most uncomfortable Consequences, & which if Revived, might Endanger the peace & Harmony, that has hitherto subsisted in the present, & which this House most earnestly desire, may still continue, & can assure your Excellency that we should be very loth to give your Excellency the least ground of uneasiness by witholding such an Ample & honorable support as is agreable to the Dignity of your Station, & the Ability of the People we represent, which we think ought to be the Rule of our Proceeding in this Affair. On these Principles former Assemblys (as this House apprehend) have proceeded in the several Grants they have from Time to Time made for your Excellency's Support; which tho' not always the same in Value, you have been pleased to accept; and it appears Evident to this House, that it was on the Assurance formerly given to his Majesty, that future assemblys would make the Dignity of the Governour's Station & the Ability of the People considered together, the Rule of their Proceedings in this affair that the controversy about fixing the salary was discontinued, & Leave given to receive the same Accordingly.

The Grant of Nineteen Hundred Pounds for your Excellency's Support now under Consideration on the most carefull Survey of the Circumstances of the People; we can't but apprehend equal to Any ever yet made to yr Excellency for that Purpose; And if Sr there be Any Difference in its real Value (of which the House are not convinced) yet that difference is abundantly more than Ballanced by the different Circumstances of disadvantage that this People Labour under. True it is & we Acknowledged it with hearts full of Gratitude to our most Gracious Sovereign, his Parliment & Ministry that there is now a hopefull Prospect, if not a Certainty of a Great Part of that Load of Debt arising by the Reduction of Cape Breton &c. being paid from Home; but then your Excellency will please to Consider that this is but a partial Deliverance & Freedom from Total Ruin & Despair only; & that notwithstanding this, we are under very heavy & distressing Circumstances not only in Comparison of other Goverments on the Continent, to whom we are a Cover in this Time of War but also (and which we take to be more directly to our purpose) if compared with our selves a few Years past, which appears evident from the following Instances

First, A Yearly Expence of abt Four Hundred Thousand Pounds Old Tenor is occasioned by the War, & this Sum laid as a Tax on this People this present Year,—Secondly, A great Number of our valuable Towns & Inhabitants in our Northern & Southern Boundarys, have been taken from us & annexed to other Goverments,—Thirdly many Thousands of our Rateable Inhabitants have been carried from us by the Expedition against Louisbourg the forming & Recruiting the two American Regiments there, the Protection of Nova Scotia, the manning of the King's Ships, & the Defence of our Frontiers, besides considerable Numbers, who from the Peculiar Distresses of this Province are daily removing into other Goverments. by which both our Trade & Husbandry are very much Stagnated & discouraged:—These things greatly Lessen our Ability & render the present Grant to yr Excellency, more in proportion thereto, than any other heretofore made:—And on these Accounts the House have Voted to make no Alteration there.

The House therefore most Earnestly pray yr Excellency to Accept the same (which was chearfully made you) as equall to the present Ability of this People; In whose Burthens & Distresses your Excellency can have no Delight."—*Ibid*, *pp.* 364-5.

On the 22d of June the Governor sent back the following message:—

"Gentlemen of the House of Representves—Yesterday your Committee delivered me your Message in Answer to mine of the 14th Instant to both Houses, concerning the Bill lately pass'd for my support, wherein you express your earnest Desire that I would accept the Grant that you have therein made me,—As to the reasons set forth in your Message why you have Voted not to make any alterations in your present Grant, I shall not now make any further Answer to them, than by saying, I don't think them sufficient to Justify me in Accepting it. I would only observe upon what you mention of my acceptance from Time to Time of the several former Grants made me as not being all of them the same in Value; That the Difference between Any of them in Value except the last, was so trifling, that I did not think fit to Enter into any Dispute about it, & that all of them the last only excepted were of about the Value of one Thousand Pounds Sterling each. And as to the last Grant, Gentlemen, I have before told you That I declined Entering into Any Dispute concerning it, because such a Dispute on your Part would have been disagreeable to his Majesty, & might have had a very Ill Effect upon the Interests of the Province then depending, for the Consideration of Parliament, which I don't think should be urged as an Argument for my accepting this present Grant likewise, the case being now much altered in that respect.

Upon the whole Gentlemen I look upon my self restrained by his Majesty's Instructions from Accepting yr Grant, & am therefore determined not to sign my Consent to the Bill."—*Ibid.*, *p.* 368.

On the 11th of November, following, a new bill was passed to be enacted by both branches of the Assembly granting the Governor the sum of £2,000 for his support. To this bill the Governor expressed his objections in the following message to both branches:—

"The Secretary has laid before me a Bill pass'd to be Enacted by both Houses for granting the sum of Two Thousand Pounds for my Support. I was in Hopes that upon further Consideration of my Refusal of the Grant of Nineteen Hundred Pounds pass'd the last Session, your present Grant would have been so Much Increased as to have made it unnecessary for me (Gentlemen of the House of Representves) to make reply to your Message of the 18th of June, wherein you assign your Reasons for not then Enlarging your Grant of Nineteen Hundred Pounds; But since the Addition, you have made to that sum in your Present Grant, is so Small that it Still falls greatly Short of a Support for me Suitable to my Station. I shall Enter upon the Consideration of your Message.

You then say Gentlemen you should be very loth to give me the least ground of Uneasiness by with'olding such An Ample & honorable Support as is Agreable to the Dignity of My Station & the Ability of the People you represent, which you think ought to be the Rule of your Proceeding in this Affair: That you Apprehend former Assemblys have Proceeded on these Principles in their Several Grants. And that it appears Evident to this House that it was on the Assurance formerly given to his Majesty that future Assemblys would make the Dignity of the Governour's Station & the Ability of the People considered together the Rule of their Proceeding in this Affair, that the Controversy About fixing the Salary was discontinued & Leave given to receive the same Accordingly. I shall therefore Gentlemen consider the Matter in Dispute between us in the same Light with you, so that the Question will be, whether you have in y^r present Grant, for my Support conformed to what you say ought to be the Rule of your Proceedings, to the Principles upon which former Assemblys have Acted, & to the Assurance they have given to his Majesty in this case & wch we apprehend to have been his Majesty's Inducement for discontinuing his Demand of a fixed Salary for his Governour. The Resolving of this Gentlemen will depend upon the determination of two Points viz. what sum may be deemed under the present Circumstances of the Country An Ample & honorable Support for his Majesty's Governour of this Province, suitable to the Dignity of his Station, and the Abilitys of the People, & whether the Sum you have granted for my Support is of that Value.

As to the first of these points; upon tracing the Disputes concerning a fixed Salary back to Mr Burnet's Administration in 1728. it appears that Three Thousand Pounds in the Province Bills of the old Tenor according to their real Value of that Year in the Judgment of the Assembly who gave his Majesty the Assurance referred to in your Message, viz, that succeeding Assemblys according to the Ability of the Province, would Grant his Governour As Ample a Support, as the Grant then made by them thought no more than what was requisite for the Governour's Support & what the Ability of the Province could then Afford. Now Gentlemen, if the Three Thousand Pounds in Bills of Credit then Granted Govern^or Burnet, Compared with the Prices of Provisions & other Necessarys of Life, was at that Time equall to Three Thousand Pounds in Bills of Credit of the last Emission, Compared with the present Prices of Provisions & Necessarys of Life as is the Case, supposing the Prices of them Computed in Bills of the Old Tenor to be only four Times as much now as they were in the Year 1728. which is a Computation of their Rise, & of that of the Price of Labour too Moderate to Admit of Any reasonable Doubt; then it undeniably follows, upon the Assurance that was given to his Majesty by former Assemblys & induced him to discontinue his Demand of a fixed Salary for his Governour, and the Principles you Acknowledge other Assemblys have Acted upon, as also the Rule which you Profess you are bound to *are bound to* govern yourselves by, that Three Thousand Pounds in Bills of the last Emission is the Sum which ought to be granted for my Support, if the Circumstances of your Constituents can afford it.

As to the Computation I have made of the Proportion between the Value of Three Thousand Pounds in Bills of Credit of the Old Tenor 1728, & of Three Thousand Pounds in Bills of the last Emission at this Time it will appear to be a very Moderate one, if the present Bills are compared with the Price of Silver as well as that of Provisions; The Price of which former is known to be at the Rate of 5s Sterl^g ℔ ounce in Bills of Credit of the Old Tenor, & of the latter compared with the present Price of Silver to be one quarter part at the least more than what the Price of Provisions in 1728, Compared likewise with the current Price of Silver, at that Time was, which would make the Value of Three Thousand Pounds in Bills of the Old Tenor to have been in 1728, equal to the present Value of Three Thousand one Hundred & twenty five Pounds in Bills of the last Emission; To this Computation of the Value of the Bills of Credit now Compared with the Present Price of Silver, your own & that of the former Assemblys in the Bill & Letter transmitted to your Agents in England agrees· But if this Computation of the Value of Bills of Credit is Compared with their present Settled Value in private Bills of Exchange then it will appear to be still more Moderate.

As to the Abilitys of the People, Gentlemen, you say that evidently Appears that your Constituents are under distressing Circumstances if Compared with themselves a few Years past from the following perticulars, viz, 1.st The Public Debt. 2dly The great Number of your valuable Towns & Inhabitants in your Northern & Southern Boundarys which have been taken from you & annexed to other Goverments, 3dly The many Thousand of your Rateable Inhabitants which have been carried off from you by the Expedition against the Spanish Settlements in the West Indies & Cape Breton; by the forming & recruiting the two American Regiments there; the Protection of Nova Scotia; The Manning the Kings Ships, & the Defence of our own Territorys, besides Considerable Numbers who are dayly removing into other Goverments by which your Trade & Husbandry are very much Stagnated & Diminished.

Now Gentlemen, as to your present Number of Rateable Polls Compared with the Number of them in 1728. It appears by the Several Valuations begun in the Year 1727, 1735 & 1741. & ended 1728, 1736 & 1742, that in the Year 1728 the Rateable Polls did not exceed—30.000. That in 1736 they were increased to—34 000. & in 1742 to—41 000. & if the same proportionable Increase is allowed between the Year 1742 & the present Time as was in the preceeding six Years without Any Deduction for the Losses you Mention, then they would Amount now to 48.000 at least out of which if you Deduct for the rateble Polls carried off from you with the Towns that have been Anexed to other Goverments a 1000, for those taken off in the two Expeditions, 1900, (as to those which were last sent to Annapolis which were about 270, they will return this winter) for those lost in the protection of Nova Scotia 150, for those lost in the Defence of your own Frontiers 100, & for those taken from you by Removals into the Other Colonies 100 more, which are I apprehend Sufficient Allowances for these Deductions & Amount in the whole to 3250, then your Increase of rateable Polls since the Year 1728. will remain 14750, or near one half of what the Number within the Province then was.

What Number of Inhabitants may have been taken off from you in forming & Recruiting the Two American Regiments is uncertain but with respect to the forming & Recruiting my own I can say, that I have raised in the whole upwards of a 1000 men, about 170 of which were enlisted at Louisburg out of the New England Soldiers employed in the Defence of the Place, & what Number of these belonged to this Province I can't say, but I don't reckon that I have Enlisted 250 out of this Prov^{ce}, & as to recruiting within it I have wholy Abstain'd from that, & none have been Enlisted for my Regiment within it since the Beggnning of the Expedition against Canada, except a few Scattering Men who have voluntarily offered themselves to one or other of my officers; what Number of Men you may likewise have lost by Manning the Kings Ships I can't Say, the Burthen of that I know Gentlemen has lain very hard upon this Province, and tho. I belive the Kings Ships have left many Deserters here yet I am sensible that the Trade & Privateers of other Colonies have had the Benefit of their Service. But for the Two last Articles, I dare say 750 Men will be a large Allowance for your Loss of Inhabitants this way, during the late War, which will leave your Increase of Rateable Polls, within these last 20 years 14000. And in this Calculation I have Omitted to make many Deductions out of the Men taken from you in the two Expeditions, & for the Protection of Nova Scotia, & by forming & Recruiting the two American Regiments, for transient Persons not setled Among you, idle Vagrants better Spared than Kept in a Community. And such a Number of the Men as might probably According to the common Course of Mortality in the Country have died at home.

As to the Quantity of improved Lands or Rateable Estate taken from the Province in the Controverted Towns in the Nothern & Southern Boundaries which have been adjudged to Belong & have been Anexed to other Goverments, it appears by the Act for Apportioning the Tax, when these Towns remained with the Province, that the Proportion of the Tax assessed upon them was not one fortieth Part of the Whole, from which Proportion I would Observe to you I collected the aforementioned Number of Rateable Polls then within them: And as to what the Increase of that & other Improvements within the Province has been since the Year 1728. I will not take upon me to determine, but doubtless Gentlemen, it has been very considerable. In the Year 1728. you had 128 Towns capable of sending Represent^{ves} & in the present Year 153, which is An Increase of 25 Towns, most of which were Erected out of New Plantations & the rest branched out of other Towns, I am informed there are other Plantations will be rated the next Valuation. It may be difficult to make an Exact Valuation of the Increase of Rateable Estates within the 153 Townships now remaning with the Province, but as I have before Observed, it is doubless Gentlemen very Considerable

As to the Present Public Debt, Gentlemen, the Sum Granted by Parliament, for the reimbursment of your Charges in the Expedition against Cape Breton, which is £183.000 Ster^{g}. will upon the Scheme of Redeeming the Outstanding Bills (for drawing in which the Treasurer has now issued his Warrants) at the Rate of £10 in the Bills for one Pound Sterling, sink the whole Debt, except about £50.000 in Bills of the last Emission, which making An Allowance for the Difference between the Value of the Bills of Credit in the Year 1744, at the Commencement of the War with France, & their present Value does not exceed one sixth part of what the Province's Debt was at That Time, & holds no Proportion with the Debt of the Succeding Years; Notwithstanding which & the Lopping off the Controverted Towns & loss of Inhabitants, which you Observe in your Message, former Assemblys Never pleaded the Inability of their Constituents against Continuing to make the same Grants for my Support which were made before the Rupture with France, And as to the public Debt in the Year 1728, it is well known that it was much heavier than the present one will be, when reduced by the Reimburstment, I have Mentioned, wch may now be certainly depended upon.

It therefore seems most evident, Gentlemen, upon the whole, that the Ability of the People is not less'ned, but considerably encreased Since the Year 1728 in which Case according to the Assurance then given to his Majesty that succeding Assemblys should Grant his Governour "as Ample a Support in Proportion to the Ability of the Province as that Assembly had done then" which is the Rule you Acknowledge you ought to be governed by, that is in your own Words "that the Dignity of the Governour's Station & the Ability of the People, considered together, ought to be the Rule of your Proceeding in this Affair" it plainly follows, that my Support ought to be enlarged in Proportion to the increace of the Province's Ability, instead of being Lessned in the Same Proportion; which is done by your last Grant if the Intrinsecal Value of it not the Nominal Sum only is Considered.

This being the State of the Case Gentlemen, & when the Grants to the Other Officers of the Governments are raised on Account of the Dearness of Provisions & the Depreciation of the Bills of Credit & for Extraordinary Services; as is also the Pay of your own House from 3 *s*. in Bills of the last Emission ℔ Diem at which it was Settled in 1742 to 5 *s*. in Bills of the same Tenor in 1747, all which has been done since Any Considerable nominal Addition has been made to my Salary; How you can reasonably deny to do me the like Justice I cant discover.—You Complain Gentlemen of the Burden & Distress of the Province, & that the Reimburstment granted by the Parliament is but a partial deliverance from total Ruin" —War is a Calamity greater or less whenever it befalls a Country; but has not the late Wars been Attended likewise with unparrallald Sucesses & most Signal Deliverances to this Province, & was it ever known that at the End of a War was less in Debt than when it entered into it, which will be this Province's Case upon the Remittance of the Reimburstment, which will besides put An End to the paper Currency, a great Evil in the Time of Peace & an unsupportable one in the Time of War; And at the same Time at once introduce into the Province Such a Medium of Commerce as will lay a Lasting Foundation for its future Prosperity; & do you call this Gentlemen a partial Deliverance only from total Ruin: What had been the State of the Province if instead of the Acquisition of Cape Breton & the Preservation of Nova Scotia the Enemy had held Possession of the first during the War And his Majesty had lost the latter to them? You might then Gentlemen have more justly looked upon the Province as under distressed Circumstances & total Ruin.

And if you duly Consider the Part I have Acted in this Affair, as Candidly as former Assemblys have done, you will I'm perswaded think, I have had my full Share of the Burthen of the War & that you have no reason to insinuate in your Message that I take Delight in the Burdens & Distresses of the People, because I refuse a Grant of a diminishd Value, which is not a bare Subsistance for my Family much less An Ample & Honorable Support, suitable to the Dignity of my Station & the Ability of your Constituents which you agree ought to be the measure of my Salary.

Gentlemen, I have forbore Entring into a Dispute with you for Some Time out of a Tenderness to the Interests of the Province that have been lately depending in England which I hope will not be looked upon by you in a different Light; & it is now with regret that I enter into it, I could have told you in a very few Words that my determined Resolution is not to Accept of your Grant but I thought it more proper to reason the Matter with you in your own way of Considering it. I have only to add that tho His Majesty's Instructions are not binding upon you they are upon me; And I can't but think your own Assurances given his Majesty are Obligatory upon you, tho' his Majesty's Instructions to me are not so; And if any disagreable Consequences should happen from a Dispute of this Kind with him to your Constituents, be this Message a Standing Witness between me & your House to which of us this People and their Posterity are to impute such consequences.—*Ibid.*, *pp.* 392-396.

On the 17th of November, the bill granting £2,400 for the support of the Governor was passed to be engrossed in both branches, and, on the next day, it was passed to be enacted by the Council and House of Representatives.

Chap. 10. See note to chapter 4, *ante.*

Chap. 15. The interest excited by this act, and by the important events which led to its passage,—an interest which will continue to be felt, in some degree, until the unanimity of the public, on questions involved in the issuing and redemption of paper currency, leaves no ground for debate,—seems to justify the following very full publication of records of the progress of this act both in the Assembly, and in England, where it was carefully considered by the ministers of the Crown, upon whose representation it was confirmed:—

"March 6. 1746. In Council Ordered that John Osborne Josiah Willard & Andw Oliver Esqrs with such as the Honble House shall join be a Committee to prepare the Draft of an humble Memorial to his Majesty further to represent to him the distressed circumstances occasioned by the present war & the vast expences arising therefrom especially in relation to the late Expedition against Cape Breton & the designed Expedition against Canada, & earnestly to request his Majesty's favr for our Relief. In the House of Represent.ves Read & Nonconcurr'd"—*Council Records, vol. XVIII.*, *p* 83.

"February 16, 1747-8 A Memorial of Thos Hutchinson of Boston Esqr offering proposals to the Consideration of the Court Referring to the Medium of Trade within this Province. In the House of Representves Read & Ordered that Mr Speaker Colo Choate Colo Hale Mr Hubbard & Colo Heath with such as the Honble Board shall appoint be a Committee to take this Memorial under Consideration & Report what they judge proper for this Court to do thereon In Council Read & Concur'd & Jacob Wendell, Samel Welles William Foye Samuel Watts and Andrew Oliver Esqrs are Joined in the affair"—*Ibid.*, *p.* 275.

"Febr'y 26 1747 The Committee appointed to take under Consideration the Memorial of Thos. Hutchinson Esqr and to make Report have maturely considered the same & are unanimously of Opinion that the Proposals in the Memorial may prove very salutory to this Province; & the Committee have prepar'd a Bill wch is herewith humbly offer'd: a Copy whereof they are of Opinion should be sent to the Goverments of Connetticut New Hampshire & Rhode Island & that it should be propos'd to each of these Goverments to appoint Commissioners to meet in this Province the 12th of Aprill next or as soon after as may be to treat with such Commissioners as shall be appointed by this Goverment in Order to the bringing to a Period the Bills of all these several Goverments in like manner as is propos'd for the Bills of this & also to settle the Rates & Value of Money in the several Goverments for the future—JACOB WENDELL by Order

In the House of Representves Read & Ordered that this Report be accepted. In Council; Read & Concur'd Consented to by the Governour."—*Ibid.*, *p.* 288.

The following is the only record during this session relating to the passage of this bill; yet it will be observed that Governor Shirley distinctly states in his speech at the beginning of the October session that it has "passed both Houses":—

"Febry 26, 1747. A Bill intituled, an Act for calling in & Exchanging the Bills of Credit of the several Denominations which have at any Time been Issued by this Government & are still outstanding & for Ascertaining the Rate of Coin'd Silver in this Province for the future. Read in both Houses."—*Ibid.*

"Febry 27. 1747. In the House of Representves Voted that Mr Speaker & John Choate Esqr with such as the Honble Board shall appoint be a Committee to treat with such Gentlemen as shall be appointed by the other Goverments, pursuant to the Vote of this Court of acceptance of the Report of both Houses upon the Memorial of Thomas Hutchinson Esqr. In Council Read & Concur'd & Samll Watts Esqr is join'd in the Affair Consented to by the Governour."—*Ibid.*, *p.* 289.

"March 5. 1747. A Draught of a letter to the Neighbouring Goverments on the Subject of the Bills for sinking the Bills of Credit, reported by the Committee on that affair was accepted by both Houses & signed by the Governour."—*Ibid.*, *p.* 298.

"June 20, 1748. The Secretary laid before the Board a Letter he had Recd from Mr Agent Kilbey dated March 6, 1747 relating to the proceedings of the House of Commons referring to the Charge of the Expedition against Cape Breton—Which was read & sent down to the House."—*Ibid.*, *p.* 366.

"Octor 27. 1748. The Secretary went down on a Message from his Excellency to the House of Representves to inform them that as the Council Chamber was not sufficient to receive them, He should deliver his Speech to the Court in Faneuil Hall, & therefore desired that their House might be so dispos'd as to recive him & the Council. Which being done his Excellency & the Council went & seated themselves in the Hall, And there his Excellency delivered the following Speech to both Houses.

Gentlemen of the Council & House of Represent^{ves} I have given the General Court as long a Recess for the Conveniency of the Members attending their own affairs in the Country as the public Business would admitt of; But there being Matters of Moment which require your immediate Consideration, I have thought Proper to meet you without further Delay.—By the Advices I have received from Great Britain, I have reason to think that the Bill transmitted to your Agents, containing a Scheme for sinking the whole Paper Currency of this Province by means of the late Reimburstment voted by Parliament & which pass'd both Houses of the last Assembly have induced his Majesty's Ministers, to whose Consideration the manner of paying the Money Voted for the Benefit of the Colonies concern'd is referred, to determine it shall be paid in such manner as will put an End to the Paper Currency in New England; so that That seems to be [no longer ?] a matter of Doubt. And as various Schemes have been formed by Gentlemen in England, & offered to the Goverment upon the Subject of the Reimburstment, many of which have a Manifest Tendency to Lessen the Benefit of it to the Province; It is doubtless a Matter of the utmost Importance that the General Assembly should be very speedy in persuing those Measures which they have Entered into in Order to prevent Any bad Schemes taking Effect, & which would also be acceptable to the Goverment, And might speed the remittance of the money. For Compassing all which, if you are of Opinion that anything can be added to the Scheme already propos'd, for the manner of the Reimburstment being made wherein my concurrence is necessary, I shall most readily join with you in doing what may be proper & for the Benefit of the Province, and as it's probable the Parliament will meet early in the Winter no Time should be lost for sending our Dispatches Home upon this weighty affair.

The perticular Project I refer to, you will be informed of from the Letter of one of your Agents to the two Houses, & you will find by the Extract of a letter from your other Agent to me dated Agust 9th. which I have Ordered the Secretary to Lay before you, that the Injustice of most of them with regard to the Province has been duly remark'd & oppos'd by him, that there is a good Prospect of his defeating them, & that the Reimburstment will be made in the most Beneficial Manner for the Colonies, which encourages me in Another Letter of the 27th of August, to hope he shall be able to write to the Two Houses upon by the next Ships to their Satisfaction; In the mean Time has desired me to let you know the Reasons of his not doing it by these Last Ships, which you will find express'd by himself in the Extract of a Letter."—*Ibid., pp.* 373, 374.

"Novr 2^{d} 1748. John Osborn from the Comm^{tee} of both Houses on the Affair of the Reimburstment of the Charges at Cape Breton reported as follows, viz.

The Committee apointed to Consider that part of his Excellencys Speech which relates to the Money granted by Parliament, for Reimbursting, the Expence of Taking & Keeping Cape Breton, having attended that Service, report as their Opinion, That Messengers be forthwith dispatch'd to the Goverments of Conneticutt New Hampshire & Rhode Island, again desiring them to Appoint Commissioners to meet the last Wednesday of this Month, or as soon after as may be at Boston to treat with Commissioners from this Court upon the best Method of applying the Money granted by Parliament, to the Redemption of the Bills of Credit, & upon ways & means effectually to regulate the Currencies of these Goverments for the future. And that a proper Letter be prepared to be sent home by the first Ship signifying the Courts Continuing in their Resolution, to apply the Grant of Parliament to the Redemption of the Bills, so far as it shall be sufficient for that purpose, & to sink the Remainder of the Bills at the same Time in the Manner proposed by the Bill sent from this Court or in other such effectual Way as shall be agreed on. In the House of Represent^{ves} Read & Accepted, & the Committee are directed to prepare a Letter Accordingly. In Council Read & Concured—Consented to by the Governour."—*Ibid., p.* 379.

"November 5. 1748. John Osborn Esqr from the Comm^{tee} of both Houses appointed to prepare a Letter to be sent Home on the Affair of the Reimburstment of the charges in taking & Keeping Cape Breton Reported a Draught thereof—In the House of Represent^{ves} Read & Accepted & Ordered that the Secretary be directed to sign the same in the Name of this Court & forward the same to Willm Bollan & Christopher Kilby Esq^{rs}."—*Ibid., p.* 383.

"Novr 17 1748. In the House of Represent^{ves} Voted, that Christopher Kilby Esqr one of the Agents of this Province at the Court of Great Britain be dismissed from said Agency, And his power to appear for & in behalf of the Province is hereby vacated & declared to determine & cease In Council Read & Concured. Consented to by the Governour. —*Ibid., p.* 400.

"Novr 17. 1748. In the House of Represent^{ves} Voted that the Secretary be directed forthwith to Cause the Letter Ordered by this Court in their present Session to be sent to William Bollan & Christopher Kilby Esq^{s} (then joint Agents of this Province, to be Copied & sent by Express to Portsmouth in Order to its being forwarded to Great Britain by the Mast Fleet, & that said Letter & such Copies as may be necessary, be now directed to William Bollan Esqr. & that the first Letter or Copies directed jointly as aforesaid be Stayed from going forward.

In Council. Read & Concured. Consented to by the Governour."—*Ibid.*

"Novr 17 1748. In the House of Represent^{ves} Ordered that the Secretary be directed to inclose to Christopher Kilby Esqr a Copy of the Vote of the Court for dismissing him from the Agency of this Province: In Council Read & Concured. Consented to by the Governour."—*Ibid.*

"Novr 18th 1748. The Comm^{tee} to whom was referred the Consideration of the Letter to Mr Agent Bollan reported the Draught of a Petition from the General Court to the Right Honble the Lords Commissioners Respecting the payment of the money granted by Parliament to this Province, to reimburse their Charge in the Reduction of Cape Breton. In the House of Represent^{ves} Read & Accepted & Ordered that the Speaker be directed to sign the same in Name of this House.—In Council Read & Concured & Ordered that the Secretary sign the same in the name of the Council. Consented to by the Governour." —*Ibid*, *p*. 403.

"November 21st 1748. The Secretary laid before the Council divers Letters he had just now recd from Willm Bollan Esqr & Christopher Kilby Esqr with several Papers Accompanying them which were read. Letters of the same Tenor directed to the Speaker were brought up from the House of Representatives with the following Vote. In the House of Represent'es Ordered that the Committee of Both Houses appointed to write to Mr Agent Bollan, take the Letters & Papers recd from said Agent & a Letter from Christopher Kilby Esqr under Consideration & report thereon; and Colo Heath, Mr Tyng, Mr. Jeffry, are Added to the Committee. In Council Read & Concured."—*Ibid*., *p*. 408.

"Novembr 22d 1748. Sr. Willm Pepperell from the Committee of both Houses for considering the last Letters from Wm Bollan & Christopher Kilbey Esqrs. reported the Draft of a Petition to the Right Honble the Lords Commissioners of his Majesty's Treasury referring to the Grant of Parliament for Reimbursing the charges on Cape Breton to be sent by this Court. Which was accepted by both Houses & Consented to by the Governour."—*Ibid*., *p*. 409.

"Novembr 22d 1748. In the House of Representves Voted that William Bollan Esqr Agent for the Province at the Court of Great Britain be & the said William Bollan Esqr is hereby Authorized & impowred to give a full And Ample Discharge to the Right Honble the Lords Commiss1s. of his Majesty's Treasury for the sum granted by Parliament in Order to Reimburse the Expence the Province have been at in taking and Securing Cape Breton, upon such sums being Deposited in the Bank of England for the use & Order of the Province.—In Council Read & Concured. Consented to by the Governour."—*Ibid*.

"Decr 22d 1748. His Excellency sent the following Message to both Houses by the Secretary. vizt.

Gentlemen of the Council & House of Representatives As the Principal End of your Meeting at this Time is to take under Consideration what is further Necessary to be done by this Court for Redeeming our Bills of Credit and bringing to a Period the Paper Currency of this Province, & for Applying to those Purposes in the best Manner, the Grant made by Parliament for Reimbursing the Expence of taking and keeping Cape Breton, I hope you will apply your selves to this weighty Affair; upon the Sucess of which the well being of this Province does depend with all diligence & not suffer yourselves to be diverted from it by any Business Whatsoever, the Matter requiring the utmost Dispatch, lest thro' your Delay Any Measures should be taken that may not be so well Calculated for the Interest of the Province as the Provision of an Act of Assembly would be. The Proposal which we made to the Neighbouring Goverments to join with us in consulting upon this important Affair, And our Appointment of a meeting of Commissrs for that End made this short Delay Necessary. But there being now no Prospect of having Any Assistance from them, no Time should be lost for your Proceeding on this Business. And I am perswaded if we now take Effectual Care (according to our repeated Professions) that this money when received shall be applied for putting a Period to the Paper Currency of this Province by Enacting a Law for that Purpose, all Obstacles to our receiving it may be wholy removed."—*Ibid*., *p*. 415.

"Decr 22d 1748. In Council Ordered that Samll Welles, Joseph Wilder, & Benja Lynde Esqrs with such as the Honble House shall join, be a Committee to take under Consideration that part of his Excellency's Message of the 21st of Novr last, which Relates to Rules proper to be given to the Courts of Judicature in Making up Judgments, & as soon as may be report what they judge proper for this Court to do thereon. In the House of Repre-sent'es Read & Concured. & Major Cushing, Colo Ward, Capt. Little & Capt. Powell, are joined in the Affair."—*Ibid*., *pp*. 415, 416.

"Decr 22d 1748. On His Excellency's Message to both Houses on the Affair of the Reimbursment of the Charges at Cape Breton, Entered this Day, In the House of Represent'es Ordered that Mr Speaker, Mr. Hubbard, Colo Heath, Colo Miller, Major Lawrence, Capt. Little, Mr. Tyng, Capt Spurr, & Mr. Russell, with such as the Honble Board shall join be a Committee to take the Subject Matter thereof under Consideration & report what they judge proper for this Court to do thereon. In Council Read & Concured; And John Osborn Ezekiel Lewis, Samuel Welles, Joseph Wilder, Benja Lynde, John Quincy & Andrew Oliver Esqrs are joined in the Affair"—*Ibid*., *p*. 416.

"January 6th 1748. The Committee appointed to Consider his Excellency's Message to both Houses of the Twenty first of last Month referring to the Money allowed by Parliament &c gave in their Report. To which both Houses Voted a Non Acceptance."—*Ibid*., *p*. 424.

"January 6th 1748. In the House of Representves Ordered, that Mr. Speaker, Mr. Tyng, Colo Choate, Colo Otis, Capt. Little, Mr Hall, Mr. Hubbard, Mr. Foster, & Colo Heath, with such as the Honble Board shall join, be a Committee further to Consider what may be necessary to be done for Applying the sum granted by Parliament towards the Redemption of the Paper Medium & for Substituting a Silver Medium in the place thereof. The Committee to sit forthwith & report as soon as may be. In Council Read & Concured & John Osborn, Jacob Wendell, Samll Welles, Willm Foye, Samll Watts, John Chandler, Sylvanus Bourn, & Andrew Oliver Esqrs are joined in the Affair."—*Ibid*.

"January 18th 1748. A Bill entitled An Act for drawing in the Bills of Credit, of the several Denominations which have at any Time been issued by this Goverment & are still out standing, & for ascertaining the Rate of coined Silver in this Province for the future. (Reported by the Committee of both Houses) Having been Read three Times in the House of Representves & there pass'd to be Engross'd. In Council Read a first Time." —*Ibid*, *p* 432.

"January 19. 1748. The Bill entitled An Act for drawing in the Bills of Credit of several Denominations which have at any Time been issued by this Goverment & are still outstanding & for ascertaining the Rate of Coined Silver in this Province for the Future. In Council, Read a Second time & passed a Concurrence to be Engross'd."—*Ibid*.

"Janu[r] 21. 1748. In the House of Represent[ves] Voted, that the Engross'd Bill entitled An Act for drawing in the Bills of Credit of the several Denominations which have at any Time been issued by this Goverment, & are still Out standing & for ascertaining the Rate of Coined Silver in the Province for the future be forthwith Printed, & that a Copy thereof be delivered to each Member of the Court, & a Copy sent to the Selectmen of Every Town in this Province, who are hereby required to lay the same before their respective Towns at the Anniversary Meeting in March for their Opinion thereon, if they see Cause & to give Notice thereof in the Warrant, for such meeting, & to make a Return to this Court the next Sitting After.

In Council Read & Non Concured."—*Ibid., p.* 433.

"Jan[y] 26. 1748. An Engross'd Bill Entitled An Act for drawing in the Bills of Credit of the Several Denominations, which have at Any Time been issued by this Goverment, & are still outstanding & for ascertaining the Rate of Coined Silver in this Province for the future. Having been Read three several Times in the House of Represent[ves] & in Council. Passed to be Enacted by both Houses & signed by the Governour."—*Ibid., p.* 435.

"Jan[y] 26. 1748. In the House of Represent[ves] Ordered that the Committee appointed to prepare Instructions to the Agents be directed to sit forthwith on that Affair & Also that they prepare the Form of An Address to his Majesty to accompany the same. In Council Read & Concured."—*Ibid., p.* 436.

"Jan[y] 27. 1748. John Osborn Esq[r] from the Committee appointed to prepare a Draught of an Address to his Majesty referring to the Reimburstment: Reported the same, Which was Read & accepted by both Houses."—*Ibid.*

"Jan[y]. 27. 1748. In Council Ordered that the Comm[tee] appointed to draw up an Address to his Majesty, & the Instructions to the Agents be likewise directed to prepare a Letter to be sent to the three Goverments of Conneticutt, Rhode Island & New Hampshire, respecting the Act for drawing in the Bills of Credit of this Province & ascertaining the Rate of Coined Silver & report the same as soon as may be.—In the House of Represent[ves] Read & Concured."—*Ibid.*

"January 28. 1748. John Osborn Esq[r] from the Comm[tee] appointed to prepare instructions to the Agents, gave in the Draught of two Letters of Instruction to all the Agents on the affair of the Grant of Parliament for the Charges of Cape Breton. As also two seperate Letters to S[r] Peter Warren & Eliakim Palmer Esq[rs] All which Letters were accepted by the whole Court.

The said Comm[tee] likewise reported the Draught of a Circular Letter to be sent to the Goverments of Conneticutt New Hampshire & Rhode Island. which was also accepted by the whole Court."—*Ibid., p.* 437.

"January 28. 1748. In Council Voted, that the Secretary take Care that the Act lately passed this Court for drawing in the Bills of Credit &c be forthwith printed seperately: and that a Number of the Copies be taken off. Sufficient to furnish every Member of this Court with one for each Town in the Goverment —In the House of Represent[ves] Read & Concurred. Consented to by the Governour."—*Ibid.*

"January 31. 1748. The Secretary was Ordered to sign the Address to his Majesty referring to the Reimbursment of the Charge at Cape Breton, in the name of the Council." —*Ibid, p.* 440.

"April 21. 1749. In the House of Represent[ves] Voted, that his Excellency William Shirley Esq[r] the Governour, Josiah Willard, Esq[r] the Secretary of the Province & Tho[s] Hutchinson, Esq[r] the Speaker of this House be impowred in the Name & behalf of the Province, to sign & deliver a proper. Deed or Instrument, with the Seal of the Province thereto affixed authorizing & Impowring, the Hon[ble] S[r] Peter Warren Knight of the Bath, William Bollan Esq[r] Agent for this Province, at the Court of Great Brittain & Eliakim Palmer, Esq[r]. of London, Merchant, them or two of them (the said Will[m] Bollan, Esq[r] except in the case of his Death alwas to be one) to receive the whole any & every Part of the Hundred & Eighty three thousand six hundred & forty nine Pounds two shillings & seven pence Sterling granted by Parliament to reimburse the Province their Expences in taking & securing for his Majesty the Island of Cape Breton and its dependances & to give a full discharge for the same. In Council Read & Concured. Consented to by the Governour." —*Ibid., p.* 466.

"Novem[r] 23[d] 1749. I congratulate you, Gentlemen, upon the favour of Divine Providence in the safe Arrival of the Money allowed by the Parliament of Great Britain for our Expence in reducing Cape Breton, whereby we are enabled in a good Measure to pay off the great Debt contracted by the Charge of the late War, & now lying upon this Province; And We by the Blessing of God upon Our wise & faithful Management of this Advantage, deliver this Province from the Evils & Mischiefs (particularly the Injustice & Oppression) arising from the uncertain & sinking value of the Paper Medium."—*Extract from the Speech of Lieutenant-Governor Phips: Ibid., vol. XIX., p.* 67.

"Monday. January 23rd 1748-9

[Present]

Earl of Halifax

M[r] Grenville Lord Dupplin

M[r] Fane

The Board being informed that a Bill had been prepared in and passed through the Council and Assembly of His Majesty's Province of the Massachusetts Bay relative to the Paper Currency of the said Province, and that the said Bill had been transmitted to M[r] Bollan, Agent for the said Province, their Lordships ordered the Secretary to write to M[r] Bollan to desire his attendance at the Board tomorrow morning at eleven o'clock"

* * * *

—"*Trade Papers" (Journals) vol.* 51, *in Public Record Office.*

"Tuesday. January 24th 1748-9.
Earl of Halifax
Mr Pitt. Mr Leveson Gower
Mr Grenville. Lord Dupplin
Mr Fane

Mr Bollan, Agent for the Province of the Massachusetts Bay, attending as had been desired, their Lordships acquainted him that Mr Shirley Governor of the said Province having in a Speech lately made by him to the Council and Assembly thereof informed them that a Bill, which they had prepared and had passed through both Houses and had been transmitted to him the Agent relating to the calling in and sinking the Bills of Credit, had induced the Govern' here to determine upon the method of reimbursing to the said Province their Expences in the Louisbourg Expedition, and no such Bill having been laid before this Board or as they were informed before any other of His Majesty's Ministers who had the direction of these matters, they thought proper to require of him some information with respect to the said Bill and to acquaint him with the mischiefs and difficulties that might arise from the Government's not being informed of the sense of the Province upon an Affair, the determination of which was now under consideration; Whereupon Mr Bollan informed their Lordships, that the Province of the Massachusets Bay, having in February last come into measures with respect to the application of the Money granted to them by Parliament, and the Speaker of the Assembly having drawn up a Memorial with proposals to reduce the outstanding Bills by this Money and other sums to be borrowed for that purpose the General Assembly appointed a Committee of both Houses to consider thereof, who reported that these Proposals were beneficial to the Province and a Bill agreeable thereto was accordingly ordered to be drawn, and persons were appointed to join with the other Provinces who had engaged in the Expedition, to consider in what manner to take up the whole Paper Credit, that he believed Commissioners were sent for this purpose, but that some or one of the Governments declined it—That this Bill was sent to him, with Instructions containing (as he understood them) discretionary power of either laying or not laying it before the Government, as he should judge proper, that he not thinking the Bill compleat and finding there was likely to be great difficulty in borrowing the money proposed thereby, did not care to lay the same before the Government, but transmitted a state of the Paper Credit to the Province and desired positive orders about it, but the orders he has received in consequence thereof, do still leave it to his discretion. That as to what Mr Shirley had asserted in his Speech, he was mistaken and he believes, never did receive such information as he mentioned, but might have been induced to go so far as he did in order to strengthen and give credit to the Proposals & thereby engage persons (disinclined) to come into them—That this was a matter wherein Property was greatly concerned and if the Transactions of the Province thereupon were made publick advantages might be made thereof by particular persons, prejudicial to the interests of the Province and therefore he did not think proper to lay them before the Board, but was very willing to communicate them to any Member of the Board or to any other of His Majesty's Ministers who had the direction of these matters.

* * * *

—*Ibid.*

"At the Council Chamber Whitehall. the 13th of April 1749.
By the Right Honourable the Lords of the Committee of Council for Plantation Affairs

WHEREAS the Agent of the Province of the Massachusetts Bay did deliver into the Hands of the Clerk of the Council in Waiting an Act passed in that Province in January last Entituled "An Act for drawing in the Bills of Credit of the several denominations "which have at any time been issued by this Governm' and are still outstanding and for "ascertaining the rate of Coined Silver in this Province for the future" And whereas His Majesty was pleased on the 16th of last month to refer the said Act to this Committee —Their Lordships this day took the same into their consideration and are hereby pleased to referr the said Act (which is hereunto annexed) to the Lords Commissioners for Trade and Plantations to examine into the same and report their opinion thereupon to this Committee with all convenient speed."—"*Mass. Bay, B. T.*" *vol.* 73, *G. g.* 113, *in Public Record Office.*

[L. S.] "By his Excellency William Shirley Esqre Captain General and Governour in Chief in and over his Majesty's Province of the Massachusetts Bay in New England.

I do hereby Certify that the Great and General Court or Assembly of the Province of the Massachusetts Bay aforesaid at their Session held at Boston the 21st day of December 1748 made and passed an Act entitled, An Act for drawing in the Bills of Credit of the several denominations which have at any time been issued by this Governm' and are still outstanding and for ascertaining the rate of coin'd silver in this Province for the future— Pass'd in the House of Representatives Jany 24. 1748—And that the Papers hereunto annexed contain a true and authentick copy of the said Act.

In Testimony whereof I have caused the publick seal of the said Province to be hereunto affixed; Dated at Boston the thirty first day of January 1748 in the twenty second year of his Majesty's Reign.

W. SHIRLEY

By his Excellency's command
J. WILLARD,
Secretary."

—*Ibid.*

"*John Pownall to Matthew Lamb Esq.* 18 *April* 1749.

To,
Matthew Lamb Esqre

Sir,

I am directed by my Lords Commissioners for Trade and Plantations to send you the inclosed Act passed in the Province of the Massachusetts Bay in January last, Entituled

An Act for drawing in the Bills of Credit of the several denominations which have at any time been issued by this Government and are still outstanding, and for ascertaining the rate of coined silver in this Province for the future.

And to desire your opinion thereupon in point of Law, with all possible dispatch, it being necessary that the said Act should be laid before his Majesty as soon as conveniently can be.

I am, Sir,

Your most humble Servant
JOHN POWNALL

Whitehall
April 18th 1749" }—*Ibid., vol.* 84, *p.* 215.

"*Report of Mat. Lamb on an Act passed in January* 1749.

To the Right Honorable the Lords Commissioners for Trade and Plantations.

My Lords,

In pursuance of your Lordships Comands signifyed to me by Mr Pownall's letter, wherein you are pleased to desire my opinion in point of Law upon the following Act passed in the Province of the Massachusets Bay in January 1748 I have perused and considered the same (viz.)

An Act for drawing in the Bills of Credit of the severall denominations which have at any time been issued by this Government and are still outstanding And for ascertaining the rate of coined silver in this Province for the future.

This Act is imperfectly worded concerning the receipt of the money which has been granted by Parliament for the use of this Province, for there are no expresse words that authorize Sir Peter Warren and the others to receive the money, but they are authorized and impowered to give a full discharge for it *whensoever the same shall have been issued* without mentioning to whom it is to be issued. They are also authorized to address his Majesty to order the money to be transported in *Foreign Coined Silver* on board His Majesty's ships, And to pursue such Instructions as the Generall Court of the said Province shall think necessary concerning the transporting the said Money. *Since this Act has been before me, in order to have the same explained,* I have applied for the Instructions given to Sir Peter Warren &c And find thereby that the Act was thus worded with a design to have the money transported by his Majesty's Order according to the Address rather then to be received by Sir Peter Warren &c to save the charges of freight and insurance and the risque of the money being transported And in case they do not succeed in getting the Money transported that way, Then Sir Peter Warren &c are directed by their Instructs to receive the money themselves, and transport the same in such manner as is therein directed. I thought it proper to make this observation to your Lordships to explain the reasons for the Act being so worded, But I make no objection thereto as it will be the concern of the Treasury to settle this matter when the Money is paid.

This Act settles the rate of Spanish Coin which has been heretofore settled by the Act of the sixth of Queen Anne But this Act goes further by setting a value upon *Silver* which may be done by a new Law if thought to be necessary.

I have no objection to make to this Act in point of Law and am

My Lords
Your Lordships
most obedient
humble Servant
MAT LAMB.

Lincolnes Inne
25 April 1749." }—*Ibid., vol.* 84, *G. g.*, 14.

Thursday May 4th 1749
[Present]
Earl of Halifax

Mr Pitt. Mr Leveson Gower
Mr Grenville. Lord Dupplin
Mr Fane. Sir Thos. Robinson.

Read Mr Lamb's Report upon an Act passed at Boston in Jany 1748-9, containing several observations thereupon dated 25th April 1749

Agreed that the Order of the Lords of the Committee of Council referring the above mentioned Act, mentioned in the Minutes of the 18th of last Month be taken into consideration tomorrow morning and that Mr Bollan Agent for the Province of the Massachusetts Bay have notice to attend.

—*Trade Papers (Journals) vol.* 51, *in Public Record Office.*

Monday May 8th 1749
Earl of Halifax

Mr Pitt. Mr Grenville. Lord Dupplin.

* * * *

Mr Bollan Agent for the Province of the Massachusetts Bay attending moved their Lordships for their favourable Report upon an Act passed in that Province for drawing in the Bills of Credit by means of the money voted in Parliament for reimbursing to the said Province their expences in the Louisbourg Expedition

Ordered that the Draught of a Report to the Lords of the Committee of Council be prepared proposing the confirmation of the said Act

* * * *

—*Ibid.*

Wednesday May 10th 1749.
Earl of Halifax

Mr Pitt. Mr Grenville
Lord Dupplin. Mr Fane
Sir Thos. Robinson

The Draught of a Report to the Lords of the Committee of Council upon the Act passed in the Province of the Massachusetts Bay relating to the Bills of Credit having been prepared pursuant to the preceding Minutes was laid before the Board agreed to and ordered to be transcribed

* * * *

—*Ibid.*

Thursday. May 11th 1749.

Mr Pitt. Lord Dupplin
Mr Fane. Sir Thos. Robinson

The Draught of the Report to the Lords of the Committee of Council ordered to be transcribed by the preceding Minutes was laid before the Board and signed.

* * * *

—*Ibid.*

"*Report of Lords of Trade on Act passed in January* 1749.

To the Right Honorable the Lords of the Committee of His Majesty's most honorable Privy Council.

My Lords,

Pursuant to your Lordships Order of the 13th Ult. We have had under our consideration An Act passed in His Majty's Province of the Massachusets Bay in January last, Entitled

An Act for drawing in the Bills of Credit of the several denominations, which have at any time been issued by this Government, and are still outstanding and for ascertaining the rates of Coined Silver in this Province for the Future

We have also consulted Mr Lamb, one of His Majesty's Counsel at Law upon this Act, who has reported to us "that the said Act is imperfectly worded concerning the receipt of "the money which has been granted by Parliament for the use of this Province for there "are no express words that authorize Sir Peter Warren and the others to receive the "money, but they are authorized and empowered to give a full discharge for it, whenso- "ever the same shall have been issued, without mentioning to whom it is to be issued, "they are also authorized to address his Majesty to order the Money to be transported in "Foreign coined silver on board.His Majesty's ships and to pursue such Instructions as "the General Court of the said Province shall think necessary concerning the transporting "the said Money and that he had applied for the Instructions given to Sir Peter Warren "&c and found thereby that the Act was thus worded, with a design to have the Money "transported by his Majesty's Order according to the Address rather then to be received "by Sir Peter Warren &c to save the charges of Freight & Insurance and the risque of the "Money being transported And in case they do not succeed in getting the money trans- "ported that way, then Sir Peter Warren &ca are directed by their Instructions to receive "the Money themselves and transport the same in such manner as is therein directed." But that he has no objection thereto in point of Law; However we shall take leave to lay before your Lordships Our Observations upon such other parts of the said Act as appear to us to deserve your Lordships consideration

The two great objects of this Act are;

1st Entirely to sink and abolish all the paper Bills of Credit at present outstanding in the said Province; And

2ndly By means of the Money granted by Parliament for reimbursing to the said Province their Expences in taking & securing to the Crown of Great Britain the Island of Cape Breton and its Dependencies to substitute in lieu of the Bills of Credit an invariable silver currency for the future.

The Legislature of the said Province in order to carry the beneficial purposes of this Act into execution in a manner as effectual and as equitable as the circumstances of their situation will admit, have thought it necessary to exchange their outstanding Bills for silver at the rate of ten Pounds in Bills of what is called the old Tenor, for one Pound sterling (which is less than half the nominal value affixed to the said Bills by the several Acts for creating them) at which rate the whole Paper Currency will be sunk except the sum of seventy five thousand pounds new Tenor, for the sinking of which, provision is made by a tax to be levied in the present year, so that the whole will be entirely abolished within the year 1750, provided the Money granted by Parliament arrives in the Province within that time.

But as the alteration made by this Act in the nominal value so set upon the said Bills of Credit, may appear to your Lordships at the first view to be in some degree a breach of the public faith of the Province and an injustice to the Possessors of the said Bills, We think proper to observe to your Lordships, that the said Bills of Credit have by frequent and large emissions of them, both before and since the breaking out of the late War, as well as by many other concurrent circumstances, been from time to time greatly depreciated, and that it is represented to us, that by far the greatest part thereof have passed from Hand to Hand, and been received by the present Possessors at even a lower rate than is set upon them by this Act, therefore should they be redeemed at their nominal value (which at the very time of their Emission they never really bore) as the first possessors never did or could receive near that nominal value, so it would be unreasonable that the present Possessors should avail themselves of a Benefit which they have never purchased, and cannot in equity be entitled to; If to these are added the following considerations—the exhausted condition of this Province; the great scarcity or rather total want of silver there;—the excessive quantity of Bills now current;—the distance of the periods for calling them in by Taxes;—the little Expectations the Possessors of the Bills could entertain and indeed the absolute improbability of their being exchanged for silver by any other means than the application of the money granted by Parliament to that purpose, this must seem to us to be the most equal rate that could be fixed between the Debtor and Creditor, as also between the Possessors of the Bills and the Government, and so it is represented to us by Mr Shirley the Governor of that Province.

In order to establish a silver currency for the future in lieu of the said Bills of Credit, there is a Clause in the Act which declares that all Bargains, Contracts, Debts, Dues &ca which shall be made or agreed after the 31st of March 1750 shall be in silver at six shillings and eight pence per ounce, and that all Spanish milled Pieces of Eight of full weight shall be accounted taken and paid at the rate of six shillings per piece for the discharge of every contract or bargain after the said 31st of March 1750, and the halves, quarters and other lesser pieces of the same coin to be taken or paid in the same proportion, with a penalty of fifty Pounds upon any person taking or paying them at a higher rate, which said Rates are agreeable to the Act of the 6th of Queen Anne for ascertaining the rates of Foreign Coins in the Plantations in America.

We must likewise acquaint your Lordships that Provision is made by this Act to prevent the Bills of Credit of the Neighbouring Governors of Rhode Island Connecticut and New Hampshire, who have not yet taken any steps to abolish them, from passing current in the Massachusetts Bay, and tho' the Oaths and penalties imposed to prevent the same, may appear of an extraordinary nature, yet as the Governor of that Province has represented to us, that all pecuniary penalties alone, tho' imposed in the strictest manner, have been found by experience to have had no effect in this case, several Penal Laws for that purpose having proved ineffectual and that there seems to be a necessity for having recourse to other provisions which may be effectual and that the Provisions of this Act are no more than what the nature of the case requires, in order to suppress an evil which prevails so strongly and the continuation of which will defeat the good intentions of this Province in sinking their own Bills; We hope they will appear to your Lordships to be necessary for the effectual executions of this Act, and your Lordships will likewise observe that these provisions are only temporary from March 1750 to March 1754.

We must further observe to your Lordships that this Act repeals several Clauses in former Acts, which have been confirmed by His Majesty, whereby these Bills of Credit were to have been called in by Taxes to be levied in certain years, without having a clause inserted therein suspending the execution of it untill His Majesty's pleasure be known, but as that Repeal is only conditional in case the money granted by Parliament arrives within the time limited, in which case the whole end and intended operation of those Clauses will be performed in a more beneficial manner, and if that condition should not happen, then those Clauses will continue in force and the outstanding Bills of Credit will be drawn into the Treasury and sunk by the Taxes laid on the several years till 1760, in the same manner as if this Act had not been made; We submit it to Your Lordships judgment whether the not having such a Clause inserted therein may not be dispensed with, and the rather as His Majesty's Governor of the said Province has represented to us, that a Dispute with the Assembly on that subject would have prevented the passing of this Act so advantageous to the welfare of that Province and so necessary for the commerce of this Kingdom.

Upon the whole, We are of opinion that it may be adviseable for your Lordships to lay the said Act before His Majesty for His Royal Confirmation

We are
My Lords
Your Lordships
most obedient and
most humble Servants
I. PITT.
DUPPLIN.
FRANCIS FANE
T. ROBINSON

Whitehall
May 11th 1749" } —*Ibid., vol.* 84, *p.* 266.

"At the Court at Kensington. the 28th day of June 1749.
Present
The King's most Excellent Majesty in Council

WHEREAS by Commission under the Great Seal of Great Britain, the Governor Council and Assembly of the Province of the Massachusets Bay in New England are authorized and empowered to make constitute and ordain Laws which are to continue and be in force unless His Majesty's pleasure be signified to the contrary—And Whereas in pursuance of the said Commission An Act was passed in the said Province in January last in the Words following—Vizt

"An Act for drawing in the Bills of Credit of the several Denominations which have "at any time been issued by this Government and are still outstanding and for as- "certaining the rate of coined Silver in this Province for the future"

Memd Here the Act was inserted at length

Which said Law having been under the consideration of the Lords Commissrs for Trade and Plantations and also of a Committee of His Majesty's most Honorable Privy Council, the said Lords of the Committee this day presented the said Law to His Majesty at this Board, with their Opinion, that the same was proper to be approved. His Majesty taking the same into consideration was pleased with the advice of His Privy Council, to declare his approbation of the said Law. And pursuant to His Majesty's Royal pleasure thereupon expressed, the said Law is hereby confirmed finally enacted and ratifyed accordingly. Whereof the Governor or Commander in Chief of the said Province for the time being and all others whom it may concern, are to take notice and govern themselves accordingly.

A true Copy
W. SHARPE"

—*Ibid.*, "*B. T., vol.* 73, *G. g.*," 30.

"The provision made by this act for the exchange of the bills and for establishing a silver currency was altogether conditional, and depended upon a grant of Parliament for reimbursement of the charge of the Cape Breton expedition. This being at a distance and not absolutely certain, the act had no sudden effect upon the minds of the people, but when the news of the grant arrived the discontent appeared more visible, and upon the arrival of the money there were some beginnings of tumults, and the authors and promoters of the measure were threatned. The government passed an act with a severe penalty against riots, and appeared determined to carry the other act for exchanging the [1749-50, chap. 7.]

bills into execution. The apprehension of a *shock* to trade proved groundless; the bills being dispersed through every part of the province, the silver took place instead of them, a good currency was insensibly substituted in the room of a bad one, and every branch of business was carried on to greater advantage than before. The other governments, especially Connecticut and Rhode Island, who refused, upon being invited, to conform their currency to the Massachusetts, felt a *shock* in their trade which they have not yet recovered. The latter had been the importers, for the Massachusets, of West India goods for many years, which ceased at once. New Hampshire, after some years, revived its business, and increased their trade in English goods, which formerly they had been supplied with from the Massachusets. Perhaps they have rather exceeded."—*Hutchinson's Hist. Mass. (Ed. 1767) vol. II., p.* 440.—See, also, note to 1750-51, chapter 17, *post.*

Chap. 16. "This Act is in addition to an Act passed in this Province the 17th of His present Majesty which has been confirmed and I must submitt the propriety of this Act to your Lordships."—*Opinion of Mr. Lamb: "Mass. Bay, B. T., vol.* 73, *G. g.*, 43," *in Public Record Office.*

Chap. 17. "This Act is in addition to and explanation of a former Act passed in this Province the 13th year of His present Majesty which has been confirmed And the propriety of this Act I must also submitt to your Lordships"—*Ibid.*

Chap. 19. See note to chapter 6, *ante.*

ACTS,

PASSED 1749–50.

ACTS

Passed at the Session begun and held at Boston, on the Thirty-first day of May, A. D. 1749.

CHAPTER 1.

AN ACT FOR GRANTING THE SUM OF TWENTY-TWO HUNDRED POUNDS, FOR THE SUPPORT OF HIS MAJESTY'S GOVERNOUR.

Be it enacted by the Governour, Council and House of Represent-[*ati*]*ves*,

That the sum of twenty-two hundred pounds, in bills of credit of the form and teno[u]r last emitted, be and hereby is granted to his most excellent majesty, to be paid out of the publick treasury to his excellency William Shirley, Esq[r]., captain-general and governour-in-chief in and over his majesty's province of the Massachusetts Bay, out of the next supply-bill, for his past services, and further to enable him to manage the publick affairs of the province. [*Passed June* 23 *; *published July* 1.

Grant to the governor.

CHAPTER 2.

AN ACT IN ADDITION TO THE SEVERAL LAWS OF THIS PROVINCE MADE FOR REGULATING OF THE FERRIES BETWIXT BOSTON AND CHARLESTOWN, AND BETWIXT BOSTON AND WINNISIMET.

For the more speedy transportation of passengers over Charlestown and Win[*n*]isimet ferries,—

Be it enacted by the Governour, Council and House of Represent-[*ati*]*ves*,

[Sect. 1.] That from and after the first day of October next, there be six sufficient boats, with able, sober persons to row in them, kept and maintained for the transportation of persons and horses over the ferry between Boston and Charlestown; three of said boats to be assigned and used only for the transportation of passengers and such vessels as are used for carrying milk to market,—the other three for conveying of horses, chaise and other luggage, and all such passengers who desire to pass in them; that two boats; viz[t]., one for passengers, and one for horses and other luggage,—be always passing on the water, from side to side, when they may with safety, and, as either of said boats shall strike the shoar, on either side, the other boat there, assigned to the same use, shall immediately put off.

Six boats appointed for Charlestown Ferry.

1710-11, chap. 1.
1718-19, chap. 6.
1739-40, chap. 1.

Different use of the boats.

* June 24 is given, on the engrossment, as the date of the Governor's signature; but on the record it appears as stated above.

And be it further enacted,

Rates of ferriage.

[SECT. 2.] That it shall and may be lawful for the ferrymen to demand and receive for each passenger over said ferry an halfpenny, sterling; for a man and horse, fourpence halfpenny, in bills of the last emission; for an horse and chaise or chair, fifteen pence, in like bills; and for other luggage of fifty pounds' weight or upward, the fare or price for carriage to be at the rate of an halfpenny, sterling, for every hundred weight, and no more.

And for the greater convenience of passing to and from the boats,—
Be it enacted,

Ferry-ways to be enlarged.

[SECT. 3.] That the ways for landing on either side of the said ferry be inlarged or widened to double their present w[i][*e*]dth; and that until[l] such inlargement be made, and the afore[mentioned] [*said*] number of boats provided, nothing more be demanded for ferrage than heretofore has been usual.

And whereas the number of boats by law heretofore assigned for the ferry betwixt Boston and Winnisimet is found insufficient,—
Be it further enacted,

Four boats to be at Winnisimmet Ferry, two with sails, and two row-boats.

[SECT. 4.] That from and after the first day of October next, there be four sufficient boats provided and maintained for the more speedy transportation of passengers over said ferry, with two sober, able-bodied men (one whereof to be a white man) constantly to attend each boat; two of the said boats to be equip[t]['*d*] with good sails and two good oars, the other two to be row[e]-boats or barges, and furnished with four oars each.

And be it further enacted,

Time for passing.

[SECT. 5.] That two of the said boats (whereof one to be a row[e]-boat) shall be constantly passing on the water, from side to side, in such seasons wherein they may with safety, from sunrise until[l] nine of the clock at night, from the first day of April until[l] the first day of November, annually; and from eight o'clock in the morning [*un*]til[l] eight o'clock at night during the remainder of the year. And when any one of the said boats shall land on either shoar, the other boat on the same side shall immediately put off; and one or more of the ferrymen shall, within the hours before mentioned, constantly abide at or near each boat, to keep them from grounding, and to attend on passengers.

And be it further enacted,

Penalty for ferrymen's neglect of duty.

[SECT. 6.] That every ferryman or other person or persons [i][*e*]mployed to attend either of the said ferries, who shall neglect his duty, in violation of this act, in either of the particulars herein mentioned, he shall forfeit and pay the sum of ten shillings; one half whereof to be to the informer, and the other half to and for the use of the poor of the town, either of Boston, Charlestown or Chelsea, respectively, in whichsoever the offender shall dwell.

And be it further enacted,

Rates of ferriage.

[SECT. 7.] That the fare of said ferry, from and after the said first day of October next, be as follows; viz[t]., for each passenger in one of the said row[e]-boats, ninepence; for a horse, eighteen pence; for a horse and chaise or chair, with two wheels, three shillings; for other luggage, exceeding fifty pounds' weight, at the rate of fourpence halfpenny per hund[*re*]d, in bills of publick credit of the last emission, and no more; and for each passenger in one of the [sd] sail-boats, sixpence; for a horse, eighteen pence; for an horse and chaise or chair, with two wheels, three shill[*in*]gs; for other luggage, exceeding [50'] [*fifty pounds'*] weight, at the rate of threepence per hund[*re*]d, in bills of publick credit of the last emission, and no more.

Limitation.

[SECT. 8.] This act to continue and be in force for the space of three years from the publication thereof, and no longer. [*Passed June* 29; *published July* 1.

CHAPTER 3.

AN ACT TO PREVENT THE DISTURBANCE GIVEN THE GENERAL COURT BY THE PASSING OF COACHES, CHAISES, CARTS, TRUCKS AND OTHER CARRIAGES BY THE PROVINCE COURT-HOUSE.

Forasmuch as the noise occasioned by the passing of coaches, chaises, carts, trucks and other carriages on the south and north side of the court-house, in King Street in Boston, gives great interruption to the debates and proceedings of the general court in the time of their sitting; for preventing of which for the future,— Preamble. 1747-48, chap. 4.

Be it enacted by the Governour, Council and House of Represent-[*ati*]*ves*,

[Sect. 1.] That an iron chain be properly fix[t]['*d*] to a post to be set in the ground within six feet of the south-west corner of the house late in the possession of Samuel Rand, deceased, on the north side of the said court-house, and that the said chain be extended across the street, at four feet distance from the pavements in the nighest place, and fast[e]ned by a lock, to a post to be set in the ground within six feet of the north-west corner of the said court-house; and that one other iron chain be in like manner fix[t]['*d*] to a post to be set in the ground within six feet of the south-west corner of the said court-house; and that the said chain be extended across the street at four feet in heighth from the pavement, at least, and fast[e]ned by a lock to another post to be set in the ground within six feet of the buildings opposite to the said south-west corner; and that the doorkeeper of this court be and hereby is directed, from day to day, during the sitting of this court, to extend and fix the said chains across the said street, there to be continued until[l] the adjournment of the same from time to time; and upon the adjournment, the said doorkeeper is directed to take away the said chain. Chains to be set up to prevent the general court's being disturbed by coaches, carts, &c.

[Sect. 2.] This act to continue and be in force for the space of one year from the publication, and no longer. [*Passed June* 23; *published July* 1.

CHAPTER 4.

AN ACT FOR GRANTING UNTO HIS MAJESTY SEVERAL RATES AND DUTYS OF IMPOST AND TUNNAGE OF SHIPPING.

We, his majesty's most loyall and dutifull subjects, the representatives of the province of the Massachusetts Bay, in New England, being desirous of a colateral fund and security for drawing in the bills of credit on this province, have chearfully and unanimously given and granted and do hereby give and grant unto his most excellent majesty to the end and use aforesaid, and for no other use, the several dutys of impost upon wines, liquors, goods, wares and merchandizes that shall be imported into this province, and tunnage of shipping hereafter mentioned; and pray that it may be enacted,—

And be it accordingly enacted by the Governour, Council and House of Representatives,

[Sect. 1.] That from and after the publication of this act, and during the space of one year, there shall be paid by the importer of all wines, liquors, goods, wares and merchandize that shall be imported into this province from the place of their growth (salt, cotton-wool, provisions, and every other thing of the growth and produce of New England, and also all prize goods condemned in any part of this province, excepted), the several rates or dutys of impost following; viz[t]., —

For every pipe of wine of the Western Islands, one pound.

For every pipe of Madeira, one pound five shillings.

For every pipe of other sorts not mentioned, one pound five shillings.

For every hogshead of rum, containing one hundred gallons, one pound.

For every hogshead of sugar, sixpence.

For every hogshead of molasses, fourpence.

For every hogshead of tobacco, ten shillings.

For every tun of logwood, ninepence.

—And so, proportionably, for greater or lesser quantitys.

And all other commoditys, goods or merchandize not mentioned or excepted, fourpence for every twenty shillings value: all goods imported from Great Britain, and hogshead and barrell staves and heads from any of his majesty's colonies and provinces on this continent excepted.

[SECT. 2.] And for any of the above wines, liquors, goods, wares and merchandize, &c[a]., that shall be imported into this province from any other port than the places of their growth and produce, there shall be paid by the importer double the value of impost appointed by this act to be received for every species above mentioned, unless they do, *bonâ fide*, belong to the inhabitants of this province and come upon their risque from the port of their growth and produce.

And be it further enacted,

[SECT. 3.] That all the aforesaid impost rates and dutys shall be paid in currant money or bills of credit of the last emission, by the importer of any wines, liquors, goods or merchandize, unto the commissioner to be appointed as is hereinafter to be directed for entring and receiving the same, at or before the landing of any wines, liquors, goods or merchandize: only the commissioner or receiver is hereby allowed to give credit to such person or persons where his or their duty of impost, in one ship or vessell, doth exceed the sum of three pounds; and in cases where the commissioner or receiver shall give credit, he shall settle and ballance his accompts with every person on or before the last day of April, so that the same accompts may be ready to be presented to this court in May next after. And all entries where the impost or duty to be paid doth not exceed three shillings, shall be made without charge to the importer, and not more than sixpence to be demanded for any other single entry to what value soever.

And be it further enacted,

[SECT. 4.] That all masters of ships or other vessells coming into any harbour or port within this province from beyond sea, or from any other province or colony, before bulk be broken and within twenty-four hours after his arrival at such harbour or port, shall make a report to the commissioner or receiver of the impost, to be appointed as is hereinafter mentioned, of the contents of the lading of such ship or vessell, without any charge or fee to be demanded or paid for the same; which report said master shall give in to the commissioner or receiver, under his hand, and shall therein set down and express the quantitys and species of the wines, liquors, goods and merchandize laden on board such ship or vessell, with the marks and numbers thereof, and to whom the same is consigned; and also make oath that the said report or manifest of the contents of his lading, so to be by him given in, under his hand as aforesaid, contains a just and true account, to the best of his knowledge, of the whole lading taken on board and imported in the said vessell from the port or ports such vessell came from, and that he hath not broken bulk, nor delivered any of the wines, rum or other distilled liquors or merchandize laden on board the said ship or vessell, directly or indirectly; and if he shall know of any more wines, liquors, goods or merchandize to be imported therein, before the landing thereof he will cause it to be added to his manifest; which manifest shall be agreeable to a printed form for that purpose, which is to be filled up by the said commissioner or receiver according to each particular person's entry; which oath the commissioner or receiver is hereby impowred to administer: after which said master may unload, and not before, on pain of five hundred pounds, to be forfeited and paid by each master that shall neglect his duty in that behalf.

And be it further enacted,

[Sect. 5.] That all merchants, factors and other persons, importers, being owners thereof, or having any of the wines, liquors, goods or merchandizes consigned to them, that by this act are liable to pay impost or duty, shall, by themselves or order, make entry thereof in writing, under their hands, with the commissioner or receiver, and produce unto him an invoice of all such goods as pay *ad valorem*, and make oath thereto in manner following:—

You, A. B., do swear that the entry of the goods and merchandize by you now made, exhibits the present price of said goods at this markett, and that, *bonâ fide*, according to your best skill and judgment, is not less than the real value thereof. So help you God.

—which above oath the commissioner or receiver is hereby impowred to administer; [and they sh*]all pay the duty or impost by this act required, before such wines, liquors, goods, wares or merchandize be [landed or take*]n out of the vessell in which the same shall be imported.

[Sect. 6.] And no wines, liquors, goods, wares or merchandize that [by this act a*]re liable to pay impost or duty, shall be landed on any wharff, or into any warehouse or other place, but in the day [time only,*] and that after sunrise and before sunsett, unless in the presence and with the consent of the commissioner or [receiver*], on pain of forfeiting all such wines, liquors, goods, wares and merchandize, and the lighter, boat or vessell out of [which*] the same shall be landed or put into any warehouse or other place.

[Sect. 7.] And if any person or persons shall not have and [pr*]oduce an invoice of the quantitys of rum or liquors to him or them consigned, then the cask wherein the same is shall be [g*]aged at the charge of the importer, that the quantitys thereof may be known.

And be it further enacted,

[Sect. 8.] That every merchant or other person importing any wines into this province [sh*]all be allowed twelve per cent for leakage: *provided*, such wines shall not have been filled up on board; and that every [hogs*]head, butt or pipe of wine that hath two third parts thereof leaked out, shall be accounted for outs, and the merchant or [imp*]orter to pay no duty for the same. And no master of any ship or vessell shall suffer any wines to be filled up on board without [givin*]g a certificate of the quantity so filled up, under his hand, before the landing thereof, to the commissioner or receiver of [imp*]ost for such port, on pain of forfeiting the sum of one hundred pounds.

[Sect. 9.] And if it may be made to appear that any wines [im*]ported in any ship or vessell be decayed at the time of unlading thereof, or in twenty days afterwards, oath being made [be*]fore the commissioner or receiver that the same hath not been landed above that time,

* The parchment is mutilated here.

the dutys and impost paid for such wines shall be repaid unto the importer thereof.

And be it further enacted,

[SECT. 10.] That the master of every ship or vessell importing any liquors, goods, wares or merchandize, shall be liable to and shall pay the impost for such and so much thereof, contained in his manifest, as shall not be duly entred, nor the duty paid for the same by the person or persons to whom such wines, liquors, goods, wares or merchandize are or shall be consigned. And it shall and may be lawfull, to and for the master of every ship or other vessell, to secure and detain in his hands, at the owner's risque, all such wines, liquors, goods, wares or merchandize imported in any ship or vessell, untill he shall receive a certificate, from the commissioner or receiver of the impost, that the duty for the same is paid, and untill he be repaid his necessary charges in securing the same; or such master may deliver such wines, liquors, goods, wares or merchandize as are not entred, unto the commissioner or receiver of the impost in such port, or his order, who is hereby impowred and directed to receive and keep the same, at the owner's risque, untill the impost thereof, with the charges, be paid; and then to deliver such wines, liquors, goods, wares or merchandizes as such master shall direct.

And be it further enacted,

[SECT. 11.] That the commissioner or receiver of the impost in each port, shall be and is hereby impowred to sue the master of any ship or vessell, for the impost or duty for so much of the lading of any wines, liquors, goods, wares or merchandize imported therein, according to the manifest to be by him given upon oath, as aforesaid, as shall remain not entred and the duty of impost therefor not paid. And where any goods, wares or merchandize are such as that the value thereof is not known, whereby the impost to be recovered of the master, for the same, cannot be ascertained, the owner or person to whom such goods, wares or merchandize are or shall be consigned, shall be summoned to appear as an evidence at the court where such suit for the impost and the duty thereof shall be brought, and be there required to make oath to the value of such goods, wares or merchandize.

And be it further enacted,

[SECT. 12.] That the ship or vessell, with her tackle, apparrell and furniture, the master of which shall make default in anything by this act required to be performed by him, shall be liable to answer and make good the sum or sums forfeited by such master, according to this act, for any such default, as also to make good the impost or duty for any wines, liquors, goods, wares and merchandize not entred as aforesaid; and, upon judgment recovered against such master, the said ship or vessell, with so much of the tackle or appurces thereof as shall be sufficient to satisfie said judgment, may be taken in execution for the same; and the commissioner or receiver of the impost is hereby impowred to make seizure of the said ship or vessell, and detain the same under seizure untill judgment be given in any suit to be commenced and prosecuted for any of the said forfeitures or imposts; to the intent that, if judgment be rendred for the prosecutor or informer, such ship or vessell and appurces may be exposed to sale, for satisfaction thereof, as is before provided: *unless* the owners, or some on their behalf, for the releasing of such ship or vessell from under seizure or restraint, shall give sufficient security unto the commissioner or receiver of impost that seized the same, to respond and satisfy the sum or value of the forfeiture and dutys, with charges, that shall be recovered against the master thereof, upon suit to be brought for the same, as aforesaid; and the master occasioning such loss or damage unto his owners, through his default or neglect, shall be liable unto their action for the same.

And be it further enacted,

[Sect. 13.] That the naval officer within any of the ports of this province shall not clear or give passes unto any master of any ship or other vessell, outward bound, untill he shall be certified, by the commissioner or receiver of the impost, that the duty and impost for the goods last imported in said ship or vessell are paid or secured to be paid.

[Sect. 14.] And the commissioner or receiver of the impost is hereby impowred to allow bills of store to the master of any ship or vessell importing any wines or liquors, for such private adventures as shall belong to the master or seamen of such ship or vessell, at the discretion of the commissioner or receiver, not exceeding three per cent of the lading; and the dutys payable by this act for such wines or liquors, in such bills of stores mentioned and expressed, shall be abated.

And for the more effectually preventing any wines, rum or other distilled spirits being brought into this province from the neighbouring governments, by land, or in small boats and vessells, or any other way, and also to prevent wines, rum and other distilled spirits being first sent out of this province, to save the duty of impost, and afterwards brought into this government again,—

Be it enacted,

[Sect. 15.] That the commissioner and receiver of the aforesaid dutys of impost shall and he is hereby impowred and enjoyned to appoint some suitable person or persons as his deputy or deputys in all such places in this province where it is likely that wine, rum, and other distilled spirits will be brought out of other governments into this, which officers shall have power to seize the same, unless the owner shall make it appear that the duty of impost has been paid therefor since their being brought into or relanded in this government; and such officer or officers are also impowred to search in all suspected places for such wines, rum and distilled spirits brought or relanded in this government, where the duty is not paid as aforesaid, and to seize and secure the same for the ends and uses as is in this act hereafter provided.

And be it further enacted,

[Sect. 16.] That all penaltys, fines and forfeitures accruing and arising by virtue of this act, shall be one half to his majesty for the uses and intents for which the aforementioned duties of impost are granted, and the other half to him or them that shall seize, inform and sue for the same, by action, bill, plaint or information, in any of his majesty's courts of record, wherein no essoign, protection or wager of law shall be allowed: the whole charge [of the*] prosecution to be taken out of the half belonging to the informer.

[*An**]*d be it further enacted,*

[Sect. 17.] That there shall be paid, by the master of every ship or other vessell, coming [into any p*]ort or ports of this province, to trade or traffick, whereof all the owners are not belonging to this province (except such [vessells as*] belong to Great Britain, the provinces or colonys of Pensylvania, West and East Jersey, New York, Connecticutt, [New H*]ampshire and Rhode Island), every voyage such ship or vessell does make, one pound of good pistol-powder for every [ton su*]ch ship or vessell is in burthen: *saving* for that part which is owned in Great Britain, this province, or any of the aforesaid [g*]overnments, which are hereby exempted; to be paid unto the commissioner or receiver of the dutys of impost, and to be employed for the ends and uses aforesaid.

[Sect. 18.] And the said commissioner is hereby impowred to appoint a meet and suitable person, to repair unto and on board any ship or vessell, to take the exact measure or tunnage thereof, in case he shall

* The parchment is mutilated here.

suspect that the register of such ship or vessell doth not express and sett forth the full burthen of the same; the charge thereof to be paid by the master or owner of such ship or vessell, before she shall be cleared, in case she shall appear to be of greater burthen: otherwise, to [be*] paid by the commissioner out of the money received by him for impost, and shall be allowed him, accordingly, by the treasurer, in [h*]is accompts. And the naval officer shall not clear any vessell, untill he be also certified, by the commissioner, that the duty of [tu*]nnage for the same is paid, or that it is such a vessell for which none is payable according to this act.

And be it further enacted,

[SECT. 19.] That when and so often as any wine or rum imported into this province, the duty of impost on which shall have been paid agreeable to this act, shall be reshipped and exported from this government to any other part of the world, that then and in every such case, the exporter of such wine or rum shall make oath, at the time of shipping, before the receiver of impost, or his deputy, that the whole of the wine or rum so shipped has, *bonâ fide*, had the aforesaid duty of impost paid on the same, and shall afterwards produce a certificate, from some officer of the customs, that the same has been landed out of this government,—or otherwise, in case such rum or wines shall be exported to any place where there is no officer of the customs, or to any foreign port, the master of the vessell in which the same shall be exported shall make oath that the same has been landed out of the government, and the exporter shall, upon producing such certificate, or upon such oath of the master, make oath that he verily believes no part of said wines or rum has been relanded in this province,—such exporter shall be allowed to draw back from the receiver of impost as follows; viz[t].,—

For every pipe of Western Island wine, fifteen shillings.

For every pipe of Madeira and other sorts, eighteen shillings.

And for an hogshead of rum, fifteen shillings.

And be it further enacted,

[SECT. 20.] That there be one fit person, and no more, nominated and appointed by this court, as a commissioner and receiver of the aforesaid dutys of impost and tunnage of shipping, and for the inspection, care and managment of the said office, and whatsoever thereto relates, to receive commission for the same from the governour and commander-in-chief for the time being, with authority to substitute and appoint a deputy receiver in each port, and other places besides that wherein he resides, and to grant warrants to such deputy receivers for the said place, and to collect and receive the impost and tunnage of shipping as aforesaid that shall become due within such port, and to render the account thereof, and to pay in the same, to the said commissioner and receiver: which said commissioner and receiver shall keep fair books of all entrys and dutys arising by virtue of this act; also, a particular account of every vessell, so that the dutys of impost and tunnage arising on the said vessell may appear; and the same to lye open, at all seasonable times, to the view and perusal of the treasurer and receiver-general of this province (or any other person or persons whom this court shall appoint); with whom he shall account for all collections and payments, and pay all such moneys as shall be in his hands, as the treasurer or receiver-general shall demand it. And the said commissioner or receiver and his deputy or deputys, before their entring upon the execution of their office, shall be sworn to deal truly and faithfully therein, and shall attend in the said office from ten of the clock in the forenoon, untill one in the afternoon.

[SECT. 21.] And the said commissioner and receiver, for his labour,

* The parchment is mutilated here.

care and expences in the said office, shall have and receive, out of the province treasury, the sum of fifty pounds, per annum; and his deputy or deputys to be paid for their service such sum or sums as the said commissioner and receiver, with the treasurer, shall agree upon, not exceeding ten pounds per annum each. And the treasurer is hereby ordered, in passing and receiving the said commissioner's accounts, accordingly, to allow the payment of such salary or salaries, as aforesaid, to himself and his deputys.

Provided,

[Sect. 22.] That no dutys of impost shall be demanded for any goods imported after the publication of this act, by virtue of any former act for granting unto his majesty any rates and dutys of impost, &c[a]. [*Passed June* 23*; *published July* 1.

* On the engrossment this act appears to have been signed by the Governor, June 24; but the record has been followed above.

ACTS

PASSED AT THE SESSION BEGUN AND HELD AT BOSTON, ON THE SECOND DAY OF AUGUST, A. D. 1749.

CHAPTER 5.

AN ACT FOR THE BETTER REGULATING THE CHOICE OF PETIT JURORS.

Be it enacted by the Governour, Council and House of Representatives,

Lists of persons liable to serve on juries, to be taken by the selectmen.

[SECT. 1.] That the selectmen of each town within this province shall, within their respective [*to**]wns, some time before the first day of December, take a list of the persons liable by law, and which they shall judge able and well qualified, to serve on the [*pet**]it juries, and lay the same before the town at a meeting to be immediately called for that purpose, and the towns shall, respectively, at such meeting select out of [*t**]he list one-quarter of the number so laid before them, such as they judge most suitable to serve as jurors at the superiour court of judicature, court of assize and general goal delivery, and put their names, written on seperate p[ei][*ie*]ces of paper, in one box, and the remainder of such of them as the town shall think suitable, in the same manner into another box, to serve as jurors in the inferiour court of common pleas and court of general sessions of the peace, to be provided by the selectmen for that purpose, and deliver the same to the town clerk, to be by him kept under lock and key.

Persons to be distinguished for the superior and inferior courts, and their names put into separate boxes.

And be it further enacted,

Names to be drawn, and such persons to serve on the juries.

[SECT. 2.] That when at any time after the first of December next, during the continuance of this act, any *venire facias* shall issue forth for the choice of petit jurors, and the inhabitants of each town shall be assembled for that purpose, the town clerk, or one or more of the selectmen in case of his absence or sickness, shall carry into the meeting the box wherein the names of those persons are put who are designed to serve at the court from whence the *venire facias* issued, which shall be unlock'd in the meeting, and the major part of the selectmen, who are hereby enjo[y][*i*]ned to be present, and the constable who shall warn said meeting shall particularly notify them and the town clerk for that purpose; and the town clerk, or in his absence one or more of the selectmen, shall draw out so many tickets as there are jurors required by the *venire*, who shall be the persons that shall be returned to serve as jurors: *saving*, that if any whose names are so drawn are sick or otherwise unable to serve at that time, in the judgment of the town, their names shall be returned into the box, and others drawn in their stead.

Persons to serve on juries but once in three years.

[SECT. 3.] And to the intent the same persons may not serve too often, the clerk or selectmen who shall draw the ticket or name of any

* The parchment is mutilated here.

person returned to serve as aforesaid, shall enter on the back thereof the date of such draft, and return the same into the box again, and said person or persons shall not be obliged, altho' drawn at any time, to serve as jurors oftener than once in three years, and no person who has served as a petit juror within two years past shall be obliged to serve again until three years be compleated from the time of his last serving, notwithstanding his name's being drawn as aforesaid.

[SECT. 4.] And the selectmen shall, in the same manner, once in every year during the continuance of this act, take a new list of such other persons as may become suitable and qualified, and lay the same before the town, whose names being first by them allowed, shall be put into their respective boxes in manner as aforesaid. And as well that all may do duty, as that the deficiency that may have happened by death or otherwise may be supplied at such time, the town may, if they think fit, make a new regulation of the list before received, and transfer the names from one box to another, as they judge needful[l].

And whereas it often happens that the persons returned to serve as petit jurors [o][*a*]bscond, and the respective constables are put to great difficulty, and frequently prevented from notifying them,— Preamble.

Be it further enacted,

[SECT. 5.] That from and after the first of December next, and during the continuance of this act, the clerks of the respective courts in this province, shall and hereby are obliged to issue out their *venires* from their respective offices thirty days at least before the return day; and the respective constables, upon receipt of the said *venires*, are hereby obliged to notify their towns thereof, so that the several meetings may be held six days at least before the sitting of the court from whence the *venire*[s] issue[s], and the constables are hereby directed, in case they cannot personally notify those who are so drawn, upon their leaving a certificate of their being drawn as aforesaid, with the time and place of their respective courts sitting, at the usual place of such person's abode, four days before the sitting thereof; and it shall be deemed a sufficient notification. Rules for notification and issuing *venire*s.

[SECT. 6.] And if any person drawn and notified as aforesaid, shall neglect to attend and serve accordingly, unless reasonable excuse be made to the justices of the respective courts, he shall be fined in a sum not exceeding forty shillings of the last emission; and if such jurors belong to the town of Boston, they shall be fined in a sum not exceeding twenty pounds of the same emission for the superiour court only, to be divided between the petit jurors drawn as aforesaid and serving at such court. Penalty for persons not attending as jurors.

And be it further enacted,

[SECT. 7.] That the justices of the respective courts aforesaid are hereby directed, upon motion from either party in any cause that shall be tried after the first of December next, and during the continuance of this act, to put any juror to answer upon oath, whether returned as aforesaid or a talisman "whether he doth[e] expect to gain or loose by the issue of the cause then depending; whether he is any way[s] related to either party; and whether he hath been of council to either party; or directly or indirectly given his opinion, or is sensible of any prejudice in the cause"? And if it shall then appear to said court that such juror does not stand indifferent in said cause, he shall be set aside from the trial of that cause, and another appointed in his stead. Method for preventing partial jurors.

And whereas it frequently happens that many of the jurors so chosen to serve in the several courts of judicature within this province fail of attendance, and by reason of challenges made by parties to several of said jurors, the number of returned jurors are too few to serve at said courts; for remedy whereof,— Preamble.

Be it enacted,

New *venires* to be issued, in case.

[SECT. 8.] That from and after the first of December next, and during the continuance of this act, it shall and may be lawful for the justices of the courts aforesaid, when sitting, and as they shall judge there is occasion, to cause new writs of *venire facias* to be forthwith issued out and directed to the constables of the several towns in the county in which said court is held, for the appointment and return of so many good and lawful men to serve upon the jury at said court as shall be directed in the writ, which jurors shall be forthwith appointed, and being notified and returned to the said court, shall be and hereby are obliged to give their immediate attendance accordingly, under the penalty by this act provided for non-appearance of jurors.

And be it further enacted,

Jurors' fees.

[SECT. 9.] That the fees for the petit jurors in the county of Suffolk, at the superiour court, shall be twenty-six shillings a case, the foreman to have four shillings and the other jurors two shillings each.

And be it further enacted,

The act of the 15th of his present majesty, relating to jurors, revived. 1741-42, chap. 18.

[SECT. 10.] That the law made and passed in the fifteenth year of his present majesty's reign, [e][*i*]ntit[u]led "An Act for the better regulating the choice of petit jurors, be and hereby is revived, and all and every part thereof declared to be and continue in full force and virtue, until the first day of December next, and no longer: *saving* only, that whereas, in and by said act it is provided that when any person shall neglect to attend and serve as a juror, being drawn and notified, unless reasonable excuse be made to the justices of the respective courts, he shall be fined in a sum not exceeding forty shillings,—it is hereby provided, enacted and declared that when any juror, being an inhabitant of the town of Boston, altho' such juror may already have been drawn for and notified to serve at the superiour court, shall neglect to attend and serve accordingly, unless reasonable excuse be made as aforesaid, he shall be fined in a sum not exceeding twenty pounds, to be divided between the petit jurors drawn as aforesaid, serving at [*said**] court.

Limitation.

[SECT. 11.] [*This**] act to continue and be in force until the first of September, which shall be in the year of our Lord one thousand seven hundred and fifty-six, and [*to the e**]nd of the session of the general court next after, and no longer. [*Passed August* 12; *published August* 22.

CHAPTER 6.

AN ACT FOR REGULATING THE HOSPITAL ON RAINSFORD ISLAND, AND FURTHER PROVIDING IN CASE OF SICKNESS.

Preamble. 1743-44, chap. 19.

WHEREAS a good and convenient house hath been provided, at the charge of the province, on the island called Rainsford's Island, for the reception of such persons as shall be visited with any contagious sickness,—

Be it therefore enacted by the Governour, Council and House of Representatives,

Inquiry to be made at the castle respecting infectious vessels.

[SECT. 1.] That inquiry shall be made by the officer or other person on duty at Castle William, of every vessel coming from sea and passing by said castle, whether they are all well on board, and also whether any

* The parchment is mutilated here.

infectious sickness has been on board since they left the port from whence they last came; and if any vessel inquired of as aforesaid shall have any sickness on board, and upon further inquiry the same shall appear to be the plague, small-pox or any other malignant, infectious distemper, in such case order shall be given to the master or commander of such vessel forthwith to go down with his vessel, and anchor as near the hospital at Rainsford's Island as conveniently may be; or if any vessel inquired of as aforesaid shall have had any infectious sickness on board since they left the port from whence they last came, in such case orders shall be given to the master or commander of such vessel immediately to anchor, and to remain at anchor until[l] a certificate shall be obtained from the major part of the selectmen of the town of Boston, that they are of opinion such vessel may come up to town without danger to the inhabitants, or until[l] the said master shall receive orders from the said selectmen to go with his vessel and anchor near the hospital aforesaid; and in case any master or commander shall, by himself or people on board, make false answer when hail'd by the castle, or, after orders given as aforesaid, shall neglect or refuse to anchor near the castle as aforesaid, or come on shoar, or suffer any passengers or persons belonging to the vessel to come on shoar, or any goods to be taken out before the vessel shall have anchor'd, or without liberty from the selectmen as aforesaid, or in case any master or commander, ordered to anchor near the hospital aforesaid, shall neglect or refuse so to do, in every such case every master or commander so offending shall forfeit and pay the sum of one hundred pounds, or suffer six months' imprisonment.

Selectmen to certify the safety of Vessels coming into the harbor.

Penalty for the master's offence.

And be it further enacted,

[SECT. 2.] That upon application made to the selectmen of the town of Boston by any master or commander of any vessel at anchor near the hospital aforesaid, the said selectmen are hereby impow[e]red to permit such passengers, goods or lading, as they shall judge free from infection, to come on shoar, or be taken out and disposed of as the owners shall see meet; and such passengers and goods as shall not be permitted as aforesaid, shall remain on board, or be landed on said island.

Leave to be had of the selectmen for landing passengers or goods.

[SECT. 3.] And if any master or immediate commander of any such vessel, for the time being, shall come on shoar, or suffer any of his people or passengers to come on shoar, or any boats to come on board, or suffer any goods to be taken out of his vessel, unless permitted as aforesaid, or shall come up with his vessel, until[l], by a certificate under the hands of the selectmen or major part of them as aforesaid, it shall appear to the captain-general that the said vessel, company and goods are clear of infection, and the orders for stopping and detaining the same be removed and taken off, he shall for every such offence forf[ie][*ei*]t the sum of fifty pounds; and in case he be not able to pay that sum, he shall suffer three months' imprisonment: and if any sailors or passengers coming in said vessel shall, without the knowle[d]ge or consent of the master, presume to come on shoar, or up above the said castle, or if any person from town or country shall, knowingly, presume to go on board such vessel, or go to the aforesaid house or island in time of infection there, without leave as aforesaid; or if any person put sick into the said house, or sent there on suspicion of being infected, shall presume to go off the island, without leave as aforesaid,—every person offending in any of the particulars above mentioned, shall forfeit the sum of forty pounds; and in case any person be not able to pay the said sum, he shall suffer two months' imprisonment: all the before-mentioned fines to be sued for and recovered by the selectmen of the town of Boston, for the time being; one moiety

Forfeiture for contempt by the master and others.

thereof to be to his majesty for the use of this governm[*en*]t, the other moiety to the informer.

And be it further enacted,

Justices of the peace to order infectious vessels or persons to the hospital.

[SECT. 4.] That when and so often as any ship or other vessel, wherein any infection or infectious sickness hath lately been, shall come to any port or harbour within this province; or when and so often as any person or persons belonging to, or that may either by sea or land come into, any town or place near the publick hospital within this province, shall be visited, or who lately before may have been visited with any infectious sickness, two of the justices of the peace or selectmen of such place be and hereby are impow[e]red immediately to order the said vessel and sick persons to the province hospital or house aforesaid, there to be taken care of according to the direction of this act; and where any such ship, vessel or persons cannot, without great inconvenience and damage, be ordered to the aforesaid house or hospital, in every such case the rules and directions are to be observed which are already made in and by the act pass'd in the thirteenth year of the reign of his late majesty King William the Third, [e][*i*]ntit[u]led

1701-2, chap. 9.

"An Act providing in case of sickness."

And be it further enacted,

Penalty for not answering, on oath, referring to infection.

[SECT. 5.] That if any master, seaman or passenger belonging to any ship, on board which any infection is or hath lately been, or is suspected to have lately been, or coming from any port where any infectious, mortal distemper prevails, shall refuse to make answer upon oath to such questions as may be asked by the selectmen of the town, who are hereby impow[e]red to administer the same, to which such ship shall come, relating to such infection, such master, seaman or passenger shall forfeit the sum of fifty pounds; and in case he be not able to pay said sum, he shall suffer six months' imprisonment; the above-mention[*e*]d fine to be sued for and recovered by the selectmen of the respective towns where the offence shall be committed: one moiety thereof to be to his majesty for the use of this government, and the other moiety to the informer. And where any person shall be convicted of any offence against this act, and suffer the pains of imprisonment, and shall be unable to pay the costs of prosecution, such costs shall be paid by the several towns to which such persons respectively belong; or, if not inhabitants, shall be allowed and paid out of the province treasury.

[SECT. 6.] And the selectmen of Boston are directed and impow[e]red to provide nurses, assistance and other necessaries for the comfort and rel[ei][*ie*]f of such sick persons sent to said hospital as aforesaid; the charge thereof to be born by the said persons themselves, if able; or, if poor and indigent, by the towns to which they respectively belong; or, if not inhabitants, then at the immediate charge of the province.

Continuance of the act.

[SECT. 7.] This act to be and continue in force until[l] the first day of September, which shall be in the year of our Lord one thous[*an*]d seven hundred and fifty-six, and to the end of the session of the general court next after, and no longer. [*Passed August* 12; *published August* 26.*

* In the printed acts the date of publication is given as August 22; but the memorandum on the engrossment has been followed above.

CHAPTER 7.

AN ACT FOR THE PUNISHING SUCH OFFENDERS AS SHALL BE ANY WAYS CONCERNED IN CONTRIVING, WRITING OR SENDING ANY INCENDIARY OR MENACING LETTERS IN ORDER TO EXTORT SUMS OF MONEY OR OTHER THINGS OF VALUE FROM ANY OF HIS MAJESTY'S GOOD SUBJECTS.

WHEREAS there has been, of late, divers letters without a name, sent to several of his majesty's good subjects of this and some of the neighbouring governments by abandoned vil[*l*]ains, demanding from them large sums of money, and threatning ruin and destruction to their persons and estates, in case they should fail of a compliance with their demands; therefore, for the deterring and punishing such offenders and their accomplices,— Preamble.

Be it enacted by the Governour, Council and House of Represent-[ati]ves,

[SECT. 1.] That if any person or persons shall send any such letter or letters without a name subscribed, or signed with a fictitious or counterfeit name, requiring or demanding any sum or sums of money, or any other valuable thing, knowing the purport thereof, or that shall counsel, advise or contrive any such letter as afores[*ai*]d, or that shall indite or write the same, and be convicted thereof, such person or persons shall be punished by sitting on the gallows for the space of one hour, with a rope about his, her or their neck, and afterwards shall be set upon the pillory, and there have one of his, her or their ears cut off, and be further punished by imprisonm[*en*]t for the space of three years, during all which time such person or persons shall be kept to hard work, and shall, every three months from the commitment, be brought out and whipt twenty stripes on the naked back, at the publick whipping-post. Penalty for sending threatening letters to extort money.

And be it further enacted,

[SECT. 2.] That if any person shall be knowing to the contriving any such letter as aforesaid, or to the writing, carrying or sending the same, tho' not concerned therein, and shall not immediately discover the same to some lawful authority, such person shall be deemed guilty of an high misdemeanour. Penalty for contriving, writing, &c., such letters.

And be it further enacted,

[SECT. 3.] That this act shall be publickly read by the town clerk in each town through this province, at their meetings in March, annually. Act to be read in town meetings.

[SECT. 4.] This act to continue and be in force for the space of three years from the publication thereof, and no longer. [*Passed August* 18*; *published August* 22. Limitation.

* This is according to the record; but the engrossment gives the date August 19.

ACTS

PASSED AT THE SESSION BEGUN AND HELD AT BOSTON, ON THE TWENTY-SECOND DAY OF NOVEMBER, A. D. 1749.

CHAPTER 8.

AN ACT IN ADDITION TO, AND RENDRING MORE EFFECTUAL, AN ACT INTITLED "AN ACT FOR DRAWING IN THE BILLS OF CREDIT OF THE SEVERAL DENOMINATIONS WHICH HAVE AT ANY TIME BEEN ISSUED BY THIS GOVERNMENT, AND ARE STILL OUTSTANDING, AND FOR ASCERTAINING THE RATE OF COINED SILVER IN THIS PROVINCE FOR THE FUTURE," MADE IN THE TWENTY-SECOND YEAR OF HIS PRESENT MAJESTY'S REIGN.

Preamble. 1748-49, chap. 15.

WHEREAS it is declared and provided in said act in the words following: "And whereas the sum of one hundred and eighty-three thousand six hundred and forty-nine pounds two shillings and sevenpence halfpenny, sterling, granted by parliament as aforesaid; and the further sum of seventy-five thousand pounds, now granted to be assessed in bills of credit in the year [1749] [*one thousand seven hundred and forty-nine*], on the polls and estates of the inhabitants of this province, are by this act become the sole fund and security for the whole sum in bills of credit outstanding, and in case the said sterling sum, granted as aforesaid, be not imported into this province before the said thirty-first day of March, [1750] [*one thousand seven hundred and fifty*], the exchanging the bills of credit, as is above intended, will be rendred impracticable, and, the former funds and securities being made void, there will remain a fund for seventy-five thousand pounds only, and the remainder of said bills of credit will become of no value to the possessors: *Be it therefore provided, and it is accordingly hereby enacted*, that if the sum granted by parliament as aforesaid, shall not be received within this government on or before the thirty-first day of March, [1750] [*one thousand seven hundred and fifty*], then and in such case, the several acts of this province for drawing in the said bills, and all and every part of said acts, shall be and continue in full force, anything in this act to the contrary notwithstanding; and all and every part of this act shall be void, and have no further effect,"—

And whereas certain deductions and stoppages have been made from the aforesaid sum of one hundred and eighty-three thousand six hundred and forty-nine pounds two shillings and sevenpence halfpenny, sterling, by means whereof the whole and every part of said sum has not yet been, and cannot be, received within this government before the said thirty-first of March, [1750] [*one thousand seven hundred and fifty*], which has occasioned doubts and uncertainty in the minds of some, whether the said act is not or may not thereby become void and of no effect,—

Be it therefore enacted by the Lieutenant-Governour, Council and House of Representatives,

That the said act be and hereby is declared to be in as full force, and shall have the same effect, to all intents and purposes, as if the exact sum of one hundred eighty-three thousand six hundred and forty-nine pounds two shillings and sevenpence halfpenny, sterling, had been received within this government without any deductions or stoppages made as aforesaid; any construction that has been or may be put on the aforesaid paragraph to the contrary notwithstanding. [*Passed January* 18; *published January* 22, 1749-50.

Act for drawing in the bills of credit, &c., confirmed.

CHAPTER 9.

AN ACT TO PREVENT VEXATIOUS LAWSUITS.

WHEREAS it is the practice of divers persons in this government to vex their neighbours, and put them to excessive costs, by suing them to some distant court in some county of the province where neither plaintiff nor defendant is an inhabitant; and such suits are frequently sustained, notwithstanding the law of this province enables the several inferiour courts of common pleas, and the superiour court of judicature, to try matters only that happen and arise within the county where the court is held, by reason whereof many inconvenc[*i*]es have arisen: for prevention whereof,—

Preamble.

Be it enacted by the Lieutenant-Governour, Council and House of Representatives,

That from and after the publication of this act, no personal action or suit shall be brought by any plaintiff or plaintiffs, that are inhabitants of this government, to any inferiour court of common pleas in any of the counties within this province, where neither the plaintiff nor plaintiffs by whom such suit is brought, nor the defendant nor defendants against whom such suit is brought, shall be an inhabitant within such county where such suit is brought as aforesaid, but all such actions or suits shall be barred, and the defendant or defendants so sued, shall recover double costs of the suit; *saving* where such defendant or defendants against whom such suit is brought are not inhabitants of this province, in such case such action or suit may be brought in any of the counties within this province: *provided, nevertheless,* in cases of trespass *vi et armis,* and debts due by bond that by the face of said bond are made local, those actions may be tried where the trespass shall have been committed, or where said bonds [shall] have been given. [*Passed December* 29, 1749; *published January* 9, 1749-50.

No personal action to be tried at the inferior court, &c., in any county where neither party is an inhabitant.

Saving.

Proviso.

CHAPTER 10.

AN ACT IN ADDITION TO THE ACT TO ENABLE TWO JUSTICES TO ADJOURN A COURT UPON SPECIAL OCCASIONS.

WHEREAS in and by an act made in the seventh year of the reign of King William the Third, intitled* "An Act to enable two justices to

Preamble.

1694-95, chap. 21, § 2.

* The title of the act is incorrectly given in this preamble. See the act referred to, Vol. I., p. 190.

adjourn a court upon special occasions," any two of his majesty's justices of the superiour court of judicature, &c[a]., and inferiour court of common pleas, respectively, whenever such courts, by any providential, necessary and unavoidable let or hindrance of their attendance, cannot be held and kept on the day by law appointed for holding the same, are impow[e]red, by writ under their hands and seals, directed to the sheriff of the county, to adjourn such court unto a further day; but no provision is made in and by said act for any further adjournment, which may be found necessary for the same reasons,—

Be it therefore enacted by the Lieutenant-Governour, Council and House of Representatives,

Two justices empowered to adjourn a court after a first adjournment, in case.

[SECT. 1.] That when and so often as it shall happen that either of the said courts cannot, for any of the reasons mentioned in the said act, be held and kept on the day to which, by virtue of the aforesaid act, the same may have been adjourned, or on any day to which the justices of the respective courts, at their session, may have adjourned the same, or on any day to which the same may be adjourned by the general court, it shall and may be lawful for any two of the justices of such court, in like manner as in the said act is mentioned, to adjourn the same to some further day; and the sheriff, upon receipt of such justice's writ for that purpose, shall conform himself to the directions of the former law.

And be it further enacted,

Manner of notifying such adjournments.

[SECT. 2.] That whenever, by reason of any extraordinary let or hindrance, such two justices cannot, without extream difficulty, transmit any writ for the adjournment of such court, to the sheriff, they may cause a notification of such adjournm[*en*]t or adjournments to be posted up on the house where the court was to have been held, and at such other publick places as they may judge most suitable to give speedy notice thereof to the county; and such adjournment shall be adjudged good to all intents and purposes. [*Passed January* 22; *published February* 26, 1749–50.

CHAPTER 11.

AN ACT TO ALLOW THE TOWN OF SWANZEY, IN THE COUNTY OF BRISTOL, TO SET UP AND CARRY ON A LOTTERY FOR THE REBUILDING AND KEEPING IN REPAIR MILES' BRIDGE, IN SAID TOWN.

Preamble.

1719-20, chap. 8.

1732-33, chap. 14.

WHEREAS by a law of this province made in the sixth year of the reign of his late majesty King George the First, intitled "An Act to suppress lotteries"; and another law made in the sixth year of his present majesty's reign, in addition to the aforesaid act, the setting up or carrying on lotteries are suppressed, unless allowed by act of parliament or law of this province; *and whereas* the said town of Swanzey have represented their inability of rebuilding and keeping in repair the great bridge and causeway in said town, called Miles' Bridge, by reason great part of said town is taken off to Rhode Island by the late settlement of the boundary-line betwixt the two governments, and pray the allowance of setting up and carrying on a lottery in said town for that purpose,—

Be it therefore enacted by the Lieutenant-Governour, Council and House of Representatives,

Town of Swanzey empowered to have a lottery for repairing Miles' Bridge.

[SECT. 1.] That the said town of Swanzey be and hereby is allowed and authorized to set up and carry on a lottery within said town, for the use and purpose aforesaid, of the amount of twenty-five thousand pounds, old tenor, drawing out of each prize ten per cent., and said town be impow[e]red to make rules for the regular and practicable proceeding in said affair, and to appoint times and places, and meet persons for managers therein, who shall be sworn to the faithful discharge of their trust.

And in order to prevent any bubble or cheat's happening to the purchasers or drawers of the tickets,—

Be it further enacted,

[SECT. 2.] That said Swanzey shall be answerable to the purchasers or drawers of the tickets for any deficiency or misconduct of the managers, according to the true intent of lotteries. [*Passed December* 11, 1749; *published January* 9, 1749–50. Town of Swanzey to be answerable for any deficiency or mismanagement.

CHAPTER 12.

AN ACT TO PREVENT THE UNNECESSARY DESTRUCTION OF ALEWIVES IN THE TOWN OF MIDDLEBOROUGH.

WHEREAS there are great quantities of the fish called alewives, that pass up the rivers and brooks in the town of Middleborough to cast their spawn; and notwithstanding the penalties annexed to the many good and wholesome laws of this province already made to prevent the destruction of alewives, yet many ill-minded and disorderly persons are not deterred therefrom,— Preamble. 1745-46, chap. 20.

Be it therefore enacted by the Lieutenant-Governour, Council and House of Representatives,

[SECT. 1.] That whoever shall presume to take any of the said fish in the afores[*ai*]d rivers or brooks, or any part thereof, by any ways or means whatever, at any other place than at the old Stone Ware, so called, in Namasket River in said town, and at such place in the brook called Assawampset[*t*] Brook, in said town, as the inhabitants thereof shall vote and order, such person shall forfeit the sum of forty shillings; and the scoop-net or other instruments with which such person may take the said fish, shall be forfeited. Places where the fish are to be taken.

And whereas some persons who may disguise themselves, and others who may be unknown, may take or attempt to take the said fish at other places than at the aforesaid Stone Ware and Assawampsett Brook, and may refuse to discover their names, places of abode and occupations, by which means the prosecution of such offenders may be prevented, and the good design of this act be defeated; and there being some passages of said rivers and brooks that are much narrower than others, and by reason thereof the course of the said fish may be more easily stopped by canoes and other obstructions,— Preamble.

Be it therefore further enacted,

[SECT. 2.] That if any person or persons, who may be unknown, shall take or attempt to take any of the aforesaid fish in any other part of said rivers and brooks than those before mentioned, it shall be in the power of any of his majesty's justices of the peace of the county of Pl[i][*y*]mouth, on his own view, to examine such person or persons concerning their names, places of abode and occupations; or in case no justice of the peace may be present, then it shall be lawful for any sheriff or deputy sheriff of said county, or constable of the aforesaid town, or two or more persons who may be present at their so taking or attempting to take the said fish, to convey such offender immediately before any of his majesty's justices of the peace for the said county, to be examined as aforesaid; and on such offender's refusal to give an Penalty for taking fish in other places.

account of his or their names, places of abode and occupations, such justice may commit him or them to his majesty's goal in said county, until[l] they give such account, unless such offenders will forthwith pay the aforesaid penalty of forty shillings. And whoever shall presume to fasten or keep any canoe or canoes or other obstructions within or nigh any narrow passage, or the middle of said river[s] or brooks, so that it may be reasonably thought that the course of the said fish may be thereby obstructed, such person or persons shall forfeit the sum of ten shillings for every hour such obstruction shall continue; and in case it doth not appear how it might have been made, then it shall be in the power of any justice of the peace of said county to order it to be removed.

Penalty for giving obstructions to the fish.

And be it further enacted,

Inhabitants may be witnesses.

[SECT. 3.] That no person shall be disqualified as a witness in order to any conviction upon this act, by reason of his or her being an inhabitant of said town.

And be it further enacted,

Penalty for servants and children offending.

[SECT. 4.] That when any children or servants shall offend against this act, or any part thereof, they shall be punished by whipping, not exceeding five stripes, setting in the stocks not exceeding two hours, or imprisonment not exceeding twenty-four hours, at the discretion of the court or justices before whom the conviction may be, unless such offenders, by themselves, their parents or masters, or others on their behalf, shall forthwith pay the forfeiture aforesaid: such parents or masters being notified of such conviction forty-eight hours before said punishment be inflicted.

Disposition of forfeitures.

[SECT. 5.] All the penalties and forfeitures in this act mentioned to be disposed of, one moiety to the use of the poor of the said town, and the other moiety to the informer, to be recovered on information or complaint before any justice of the peace of the afores[*ai*]d county, where the penalty may not exceed forty shillings. And such justice is hereby impow[e]red to issue his warrant for apprehending such offender or offenders, and upon conviction, to restrain or commit the offender or offenders to his majesty's goal aforesaid, until[l] the fine imposed for such offence be satisfied, or cause the same to be levied by distress and sale of the offender's goods, returning the overplus, if any there be. And where the penalty may exceed the sum of forty shillings, then it may be recovered by action, bill, plaint or information, in any court proper to try the same.

And be it further enacted,

Rule of conviction.

[SECT. 6.] That the manner, rules and methods of conviction of offenders against this act, may be the same as are directed and provided in and by an act made in the twelfth year of the reign of his late majesty King George, [e][*i*]ntitled "An Act in addition to and for rendring more effectual an act made in the tenth year of the reign of King William the Third, [e][*i*]ntitled 'An Act for preventing of trespasses.'"

1723-24, chap. 10.

Limitation.

[SECT. 7.] This act to continue in force for the space of three years from its publication, and no longer. [*Passed December* 23,* 1749; *published January* 9, 1749-50.

* The record has been followed here; but on the engrossment the date of the Governor's assent is December 27.

CHAPTER 13.

AN ACT TO PREVENT ANY PERSON'S OBSTRUCTING THE FISH IN THEIR PASSING UP INTO MONATIQUOT RIVER, WITHIN THE TOWN OF BRAINTRE[Y][*E*].

WHEREAS the act made and passed in the fourteenth year of his present majesty's reign, intitled "An Act to prevent any person's obstructing the fish in their passing up into Monatiquot River, within the town of Braintre[y][*e*], hath been found beneficial to the said town and towns adjacent, but is now expired,— Preamble.

Be it enacted by the Lieut[enan]t-Governour, Council and House of Representatives,

[SECT. 1.] That no person or persons whosoever, from the first day February next, to the last day of May, yearly, during the continuance of this act, shall presume to take, kill or hale ashoar any fish with seines or drag-nets in the said river Monatiquot, or in any part of the river between the town of Weymouth and said town of Braintre[y][*e*], through which they pass into the same, upon pain of forfeiting for each and every offence, on due conviction thereof, the sum of ten pounds, to be recovered by action, bill, plaint or information in any of his majesty's courts of record proper to try the same; the one half of the said forfeitures to be to and for the use of the towns of Weymouth and Braintre[y][*e*] in equal proportion, the other half to him or them who shall inform and sue for the same. Season for taking fish, limited. Penalty for breach of this act.

[SECT. 2.] This act to continue and be in force for the space of three years from the first day of February next, and no longer. [*Passed December* 12, 1749; *published January* 9, 1749–50. Limitation.

CHAPTER 14.

AN ACT TO PREVENT DAMAGE BEING DONE ON THE BEACH, HUMOCKS AND MEADOWS BELONGING TO THE TOWN OF SCITUATE, LYING BETWEEN THE SOUTHERLY END OF THE "THIRD CLIFF," SO CALLED, AND THE MOUTH OF THE NORTH RIVER.

WHEREAS persons frequently drive numbers of neat cattle and horses, and sometimes sheep, and may also drive goats, if not restrained, to feed on the beach, humocks and meadows in Scituate, lying between the Third Cliff and the mouth of the North River, and oftentimes cut down trees and shrubs in said humocks, and carry them away, whereby said beach is broken, and the land made loose, and by the winds and storms is drove on the said meadow and flat[t]s or sedge-ground; and there is great danger, if such practices are not prevented, that the said meadows and sedge ground will be utterly ruined, and the river greatly damnified,— Preamble.

Be it therefore enacted by the Lieutenant-Governo[u]r, Council and House of Represent[ati]ves,

[SECT. 1.] That from and after the publication of this act, no person or persons shall presume to turn or drive any neat cattle, horsekind, sheep or goats, upon said beach, humocks or sedge-ground adjoining to said beach, to feed thereon, upon the penalty of ten shillings a head for all neat cattle and for every horse-kind, and two shillings for every sheep or goat, that shall be turned or found feeding on said beach, Cattle, horses, &c., not to be driven on the beach.

humocks or sedge-ground adjoining to said beach; which penalty shall be recovered from him or them that shall so drive said cattle, horse-kind, sheep or goats, or from the owner or owners of said cattle, horse-kind, sheep or goats, that shall so order them to be driven, by the selectmen or treasurer of the town of Scituate, or any other person that shall inform or sue for the same: the one half of the said forfeiture to him or them who shall inform or sue for the same, the other half to be to and for the use of the poor of the said town.

And be it further enacted,

Cattle, &c., to be impounded.

[SECT. 2.] That if any neat cattle, horse-kind, sheep or goats shall be found feeding on said beach, humocks or sedge ground adjoining to said beach, it shall and may be lawful for any person to impound the same, forthwith giving notice to the owner or owners, if known, otherwise to give publick notice thereof by posting up notifications in some publick place in said town of Scituate; and the impounder shall rel[ei][*ie*]ve said creatures with suitable meat and water while impounded; and if the owner thereof appear, he shall pay the reasonable cost for rel[ei][*ie*]ving them, besides the lawful fees to the pound-keeper. And if no owner appear within three days to redeem the said creatures so impounded, and pay as aforesaid, then and in every such case the person or persons impounding such creatures, shall cause the same to be sold at publick vendue, and pay the penalty as afores[*ai*]d, with all other cost and charges arising about the same (publick notice of the time and place of such sale being first given in the said town of Scituate and the two next adjacent towns three several days beforehand), and the overplus, if any there be, arising by such sale, to be returned to the owner or owners of such creatures, if he or they appear within two months next after such sale, upon his demanding the same; but if no owner appears within said two months to demand the same, then the said overplus shall be one half to the person impounding, and the other half to be returned to the town treasurer for the use of the poor of the said town of Scituate.

Impounded, to be sold, in case.

And be it further enacted,

Penalty for cutting down trees or shrubs.

[SECT. 3.] That if any person or persons shall presume to cut down any tree or shrub standing or growing on said beach or humocks, without leave or licence first had and obtained of said town of Scituate, he or they so offending shall forfeit and pay to the use of the said town the sum of twenty shillings for each tree or shrub so cut down; and all such methods of proof shall be allowed in any action to be brought by said town therefor, as is provided in an act made in the twelfth year of King George the First, in addition to an act made for preventing of trespasses.

1726-27, chap. 3.

Limitation.

[SECT. 4.] This act to be in force for the space of five years from the publication thereof, and no longer. [*Passed December* 13, 1749; *published January* 9, 1749–50.

CHAPTER 15.

AN ACT TO PREVENT DAMAGE BEING DONE ON THE MEADOWS LYING IN THE TOWNSHIP OF YARMOUTH, CALLED NOBSCUSSET MEADOW.

Preamble.

WHEREAS many persons frequently drive numbers of neat cattle, horses, sheep and swine, to feed upon the beaches and shoars adjoining to said Nobscusset meadows in said Yarmouth, between said meadow and the harbour, whereby the ground is much broken and damnified, and the sand blown on said meadows, and [s][*l*]ands adjoining, to the great damage not only of private persons in their property, but also to the said town in general, so far as relates to said meadow, harbour and the lands adjoining,—

Be it enacted by the Lieutenant-Governour, Council and House of Representatives,

[SECT. 1.] That from and after the publication of this act, no person or persons shall presume to turn or drive any neat cattle, or horse-kind, or sheep, or swine, to or upon any of the beaches, meadows or sho[*a*]r[e]s at said Nobscusset, south-west of a place called "Black Earth," in said Yarmouth, from the first day of March to the last [*day*] of November, annually, upon the penalty of ten shillings a head for neat cattle, horses or mares, and one shilling for each sheep and swine, that shall be turned and found on said beaches, meadows or sho[*a*]r[e]s, within the time and limits aforesaid; which penalty shall be recovered by the selectmen or treasurer of the said town of Yarmouth, or any other person that shall inform and sue for the same: the one half of the said forfeiture to him or them that shall inform and sue for the same, the other half to be to and for the use of the poor of the said town. Persons forbidden to drive cattle, &c., on Nobscusset Meadow. Penalty.

And be it further enacted,

[SECT. 2.] That if any neat cattle, or horse-kind, or sheep, or swine, shall, at any time hereafter, be found feeding on the said beaches, meadows or sho[a]r[*e*]s, south-west of Black Earth afores[*ai*]d, within the times afores[*ai*]d, that it shall and may be lawful for any person to impound the same, immediately giving notice to the owners, if known, otherwise to give publick notice thereof in the said town of Yarmouth, and the two next adjoining towns; and the impounder shall rel[ei][*ie*]ve the said creatures with suitable meat and water while impounded; and if the owner thereof appear, he shall pay the sum of two shillings and sixpence to the impounder, for each neat beast and horse-kind, and sixpence for each sheep and swine, and the reasonable cost of rel[ei][*ie*]ving them, besides the pound-keeper's fees. And if no owner appear within the space of six days to redeem the said cattle or horse-kind, sheep or swine so impounded, and to pay the costs and damages occasioned by impounding the same, then and in every such case the person or persons impounding such cattle or horse-kind, sheep or swine, shall cause the same to be sold at publick vendue, and to pay the cost and charges arising about the same (publick notice of the time and place of such sale, to be given in the said town of Yarmouth, forty-eight hours beforehand), and the overplus, if any there be, arising by such sale, to be returned to the owner of such cattle or horse-kind, sheep or swine, at any time within twelve months next after, upon his demanding the same; but if no owner appear within the said twelve months, then the said overplus shall be one half to the party impounding, and the other half to the use of the poor of the said town of Yarmouth. Cattle to be impounded, in case. Cattle to be sold, in case.

And be it further enacted,

[SECT. 3.] That the said town of Yarmouth, at their meeting in March, annually, for the choice of town officers, be authorized and impow[e]red to choose one or more meet person or persons whose duty it shall be to see this act observed, and to prosecute the breakers thereof, and who shall be sworn to the faithful discharge of their office: and in case any person so chosen shall refuse to be sworn, he shall forfeit and pay, for the use of the poor of the said town of Yarmouth, the sum of forty shillings; and upon such refusal, said town from time to time to proceed to a new choice of such officer or officers. Officers to be chosen to put th's act 'n execution. Penalty for not serving.

Provided nevertheless, and it is hereby declared,—

[SECT. 4.] That this act shall not be construed so as to restrain any person or persons on the whaling or fishing business, from turning their Proviso.

horses on the p[ei][*ie*]ce of common near s[*ai*]d meadows, in case they confine such horses to the s[*ai*]d common.

Limitation. [SECT. 5.] This act to continue and be in force for the space of five years from the publication thereof, and no longer. [*Passed January* 2; *published January* 9, 1749-50.

CHAPTER 16.

AN ACT FOR REVIVING AND CONTINUING OF SUNDRY LAWS THAT ARE EXPIRED OR NEAR EXPIRING.

Laws expired. Referring to the poor. 1740-41, chap. 20. Petitions to the general court. 1741-42, chap. 1. Poor. 1741-42, chap. 4. Expense at funerals. 1741-42, chap. 14. Weymouth, fishing. 1742-43, chap. 34. Expense in lawsuits. 1743-44, chap. 23. Firing guns with shot, in Boston. 1746-47, chap. 11. Militia. 1742-43, chap. 16. Assize of cask, &c. Measuring grain. 1742-43, chap. 4. Assize of cask, &c. 1742-43, chap. 20.

WHEREAS an act was made in the fourteenth year of his present majesty's reign, intitled "An Act for explanation of and supplement to the act referring to the poor"; and three other acts in the fifteenth year of his said majesty's reign; namely, an act intitled "An Act to prevent unnecessary petitions to the great and general court," one other act intitled "An Act in addition to an act intitled 'An Act for explanation of and supplement to an act referring to the poor,'" and another act intitled "An Act to retrench the extraordinary expence at funerals"; and one other act in the sixteenth year of the said reign, intitled "An Act to enable the town of Weymouth to regulate and order the taking and disposing of the fish called shadd and alewives within the limits of that town"; and two other acts in the seventeenth year of the aforesaid reign; namely, an act intitled "An Act to prevent unnecessary expence in suits at law," and one other act intitled "An Act to prevent the firing of guns charged with shot or ball, in the town of Boston"; and one other act made in the sixteenth year of his present majesty's reign, intitled "An Act for making more effectual an act intitled 'An Act for regulating the militia'"; and one other act made in the sixteenth year of his present majesty's reign, intitled "An Act in addition to and for rendring more effectual an act for regulating the assize of cask, and preventing deceit in packing of fish, beef and pork for sale, made in the fourth year of the reign of King William and Queen Mary, and also for the preventing of fraud and injustice in the measuring of grain,"—which act took place the first of October, 1742; also another act made in the sixteenth year of his present majesty's reign, intitled "An Act in addition to the several acts for regulating the assize of casks, and preventing deceit in packing of fish, beef and pork for sale";—all which laws are expired, and, having been found beneficial, and necessary for the several purposes for which they were passed,—

Be it therefore enacted by the Lieutenant-Governour, Council and House of Representatives,

Said laws renewed. [SECT. 1.] That all and every of the said acts, and every matter and clause therein contained, be and hereby are revived, and shall continue in force from the publication of this act until[1] the twenty-fifth day of March, one thousand seven hundred and sixty, and from thence to the end of the then next session of the general court.

Laws near expiring. Unnecessary lawsuits. 1742-43, chap. 19. 1742-43, chap. 25. Gaming. 1742-43, chap. 27. Highways. 1746-47, chap. 10. Cursing and swearing. 1746-47, chap. 17.

And whereas three several acts were passed in the sixteenth year of his aforesaid majesty's reign; namely, an act intitled "An Act to prevent unnecessary lawsuits," [another act intitled "An Act to prevent the multiplicity of lawsuits," and] another act intitled "An Act to prevent gaming for money or other gain"; and three other acts in the twentieth year of the same reign; namely, an act intitled "An Act in further addition to an act intitled 'An Act for highways'"; one other act intitled "An Act more effectually to prevent profane cursing and swearing"; and another act intitled "An Act to enable the proprietors of private ways to repair them in equal manner";—all which laws are near expiring; and having also been found beneficial for the several purposes for which they were made,— Private ways. 1746-47, chap. 18.

Be it therefore enacted,

[SECT. 2.] That all and every the said acts, and every matter and clause therein contained, shall be and they hereby are continued, and to remain in force from the time in them severally limit[t]ed for their expiration, unto the beforementioned twenty-fifth day of March, 1760, and from thence to the end of the then next session of the general court, and no longer. [*Passed January* 11; *published January* 22,* 1749-50. Said laws continued.

CHAPTER 17.

AN ACT FOR SUPPLYING THE TREASURY WITH THE SUM OF EIGHTEEN THOUSAND FOUR HUNDRED POUNDS, LAWFUL MONEY, FOR DISCHARGING THE PUBLICK DEBTS, &c[A].

Be it enacted by the Lieutenant-Governour, Council and House of Representatives, in General Court assembled,

[SECT. 1.] That the treasurer be and hereby is impow[e]red and ordered to emit and issue forth, at such time and in such manner as is hereinafter directed, the sum of eighteen thousand four hundred pounds, lawful money, now lying in his hands; and the said sum of eighteen thousand four hundred pounds, lawful money, shall be issued out of the treasury in the manner and for the purposes following; viz[t]., the sum of seven thousand pounds, part of the aforesaid sum of eighteen thousand four hundred pounds, shall be appl[y][i]ed for the payment of wages that now are or that hereafter may be due by virtue of the establishment of Castle William, Frederick Fort, Richmond Fort, George's Truck-house, Saco Truck-house, and the sloop in the country's service, and the forces that are and have been upon the eastern and western frontiers; and the sum of three thousand five hundred pounds, part of the aforesaid sum of eighteen thousand four hundred pounds, shall be appl[y][i]ed for purchasing provisions, and for the commissary's other necessary disbursements for the service of the several forts and garrisons and other forces within this province, pursuant to such grants as are or shall be made by this court for those purposes; and the sum of five thousand five hundred and ten pounds, part of the aforesaid sum of eighteen thousand four hundred pounds, shall be appl[y][i]ed for the payment of his majesty's council, and such other grants as are or shall be made by this court, and for the payment of stipends, bounties and premiums, established by law, and for the payment of all other matters and things which this court have or shall, either by law or orders, provide for the payment of out of the publick treasury, and for no other purpose whatsoever; and the sum of two hundred and ten pounds, part of the aforesaid sum of eighteen thousand four hundred pounds, shall be appl[y][i]ed to the discharge of other debts owing from this province to persons that have served or that shall serve them by order of this court in such matters and things where there is no establishment nor any certain sum assigned for such service; and for paper, printing and writing for this court, the surgeon of Castle William, and wooding of said castle; and the sum of two

Treasury supplied with £18,400.

£7,000 for Castle William and other forts, forces, &c.

£3,500 for purchasing provisions, &c.

£5,510 for councillors' pay, grants, &c.

£210 for debts where there is no establishment.

£280 for contingent charges.

* This date is taken from the engrossment; on the printed act it appears January 23.

hundred and eighty pounds, part of the aforesaid sum of eighteen thousand four hundred pounds, shall be appl[y][i]ed to defr[a][e]y any contingent unforeseen charges that may demand prompt payment, and for no other use whatsoever; and the sum of nineteen hundred pounds, the remaining part of the aforesaid sum of eighteen thousand four hundred pounds, shall be appl[y][i]ed for the payment of the members of the house of representatives serving in the general court during their several sessions this present year.

£1,900 for representatives' pay.

And be it further enacted,

Surplusage to lie in the treasury.

[SECT. 2.] That if there [be] a surplusage in any sum appropriated, such surplusage shall l[y][i]e in the treasury for the further order of this court.

And be it further enacted,

Money to be paid out of the proper appropriations.

[SECT. 3.] That each and every warrant for drawing money out of the treasury, shall direct the treasurer to take the same out of such sums as are respectively appropriated for the payment of such publick debts as the drafts are made to discharge; and the treasurer is hereby directed and ordered to pay the same out of such appropriations as directed to, and no other, upon pain of refunding all such sum or sums as he shall otherwise pay, and to keep exact and distinct accompts of all payments made out of such appropriated sums; and the secretary, to whom it belongs to keep the muster-rolls and accompts of charge, shall lay before the house of representatives, when they direct, [all] [*lay*] such muster-rolls and accompts after payment thereof.

And whereas divers grants have been made by this court payable in bills of the last emission, and the debts due and owing from this province have been understood to be payable in the same,—

Be it further enacted,

Proportion between bills of the last emission and lawful money.

[SECT. 4.] That every debt of eleven shillings and threepence in bills aforesaid, that is now due and owing, or that may become due from this province before the thirty-first day of March, one thousand seven hundred and fifty, shall and may be discharged by one milled dollar, and so *pro ratâ* for any greater or less sum; and the treasurer is hereby directed and required to pay all such drafts as are or shall be made pursuant to law upon the treasury, payable in bills of the last emission accordingly: *provided always*, and it is accordingly to be understood, that no part of the sum of eighteen thousand four hundred pounds aforesaid, shall be issued out of the publick treasury in silver before the thirty-first day of March next, anything in this act to the contrary notwithstanding.

No silver to be issued until after the 31st of March next.

Provided also, that it shall and may be lawful for the treasurer, at any time between the publication of this act and the thirty-first day of March aforesaid, to issue forth bills of credit that may be lying in his hands, and were received in for taxes, impost and excise, in discharge of any warrants that shall have been drawn on him and made payable out of any of the appropriations in this act, to such person or persons as shall declare their desire to receive such bills of credit according to their nominal value in discharge of such warrant.

Bills of credit to be paid, where they are desired.

And be it further enacted,

Provision in case of deficiency of silver.

[SECT. 5.] That if by means of issuing the aforesaid sum of eighteen thousand four hundred pounds, lawful money, for the payment of the debts of this province or members of the house of representatives, there should not be a sufficient quantity of lawful silver money in the treasury, together with the other provision that is or shall by law be made for the exchanging and drawing in the outstanding bills of this province, that then the treasurer of this province be and hereby is authorized, impow[e]red and required, in the name and behalf of this government, forthwith upon such deficiency appearing, to borrow the aforesaid sum of eighteen thousand and four hundred pounds, or such part thereof as shall be necessary to supply such deficiency occasioned in manner aforesaid, which sum to be made payable from this government on or before the last day of December, one thousand seven hundred and fifty-one, allowing an interest therefor not exceeding six per cent per annum; which sum so borrowed shall be employed by the treasurer for the exchanging and drawing in the outstanding bills of this province, and no otherwise.

And as a fund and security for drawing in and for the payment of such sum as the treasurer shall and may borrow as aforesaid, and the interest arising thereon,—

Be it enacted,

[SECT. 6.] That there be and hereby is granted unto his most excellent majesty, a tax of sixteen thousand five hundred pounds, with the interest thereof, or such part of the aforesaid sum of sixteen thousand five hundred pounds, and the interest thereof, as the treasurer, pursuant to this act, shall and may borrow as aforesaid, to be levied on polls, and estates both real and personal, within this province, according to such rules, and in such proportions on the several towns and districts within the same, as shall be agreed on and ordered by this court at their session in May, one thousand seven hundred and fifty-one, and paid into the publick treasury on or before the last day of December then next after. £16,500, &c., in 1751.

And as a fund and security for drawing in and for the payment of such sum or sums as shall be paid out to the representatives of the several towns,—

Be it further enacted,

[SECT. 7.] That there be and hereby is granted unto his most excellent majesty, a tax of such sum or sums as shall be paid to the several representatives as aforesaid, to be levied and assessed on the polls and estates of the inhabitants of the several towns, according to what their representatives shall so rec[ie][*ei*]ve; which sums, together with the interest (if any such) that may be due thereon, shall be set on the said towns in the next province tax. And the assessors of the said towns shall make their assessment for this tax, and apportion the same according to the rule that shall be prescribed by the general assembly for the assessing the next province tax, and the constables, in their respective districts, shall pay in the same when they pay in the province tax for the year one thousand seven hundred and fifty-one, of which the treasurer is hereby directed to keep a distinct and seperate accompt; and if there be any surplusage, the same shall l[y][*i*]e in the hands of the treasurer for the further order of this court. Tax to be made for what is paid the representatives.

Be it further enacted,

[SECT. 8.] That in case the general court shall not at their session in May, one thousand seven hundred and fifty-one, agree and conclude upon an act ap[p]ortioning the sums which by this act are engaged shall be, in the year one thousand seven hundred and fifty-one, appor[ti]oned, assessed and levied, that then and in such case each town and district within this province shall pay, by a tax to be levied on polls, and estates both real and personal, within their districts, the same proportion of the said sums as the said towns and districts shall have been taxed by the general court in the tax act then preceeding; and the province treasurer is hereby fully impow[e]red and directed, sometime in the month of June, in the year one thousand seven hundred and fifty-one, to issue and send forth his warrants, directed to the selectmen or assessors of each town and district within this province, requiring them to assess the polls, and estates both real and personal, within their several towns and districts, for their respective part and Tax for the money hereby emitted, to be made according to the preceding tax act, in case.

proportion of the sums engaged by this act to be assessed; and the assessors, as also persons assessed, shall observe, be governed by and subject to all such rules and directions as shall have been given in the next preceeding tax act.

And be it further enacted,

Taxes to be paid in the several species herein enumerated.

[SECT. 9.] That the inhabitants of this province shall have liberty, if they see fit, to pay the several sums for which they respectively may, in pursuance of this act, be assessed, in silver, at six shillings and eight pence per ounce, troy weight, and of sterling alloy, or in gold coin, proportionably; or in merchantable hemp, flax, winter and Isle-of-Sable codfish, refined bar[r]-iron, bloomary-iron, hollow iron-ware, Indian corn, rye, wheat, barley, pork, beef, duck or canvis, whalebone, cordage, train-oil, beeswax, bayberry-wax, tallow, pease, sheepswool, or tan[n]'d soal-leather (the aforesaid commodities being of the produce or manufacture of this province), at such moderate rates and prices as the general assembly of the year one thousand seven hundred and fifty-one shall set them at; the several persons paying their taxes in any of the commodities afore mentioned, to run the risque and pay the charge of transporting the said commodities to the province treasury; but if the aforesaid general assembly shall not, at their session in May, sometime before the twentieth day of June, in the said year, agree upon and set the aforesaid species and commodities at some certain prices, that then the eldest councellors, for the time being, of each of those counties in the province, of which any one of the council is an inhabitant, together with the province treasurer, or the major part of them, be a committee, who are hereby directed and fully authorized and impow[e]red to do it; and in set[*t*]ling their prices and rating the value of those commodities, to state so much of them, respectively, as an ounce of silver will purchase at that time in the town of Boston, and so *pro ratâ.* And the treasurer is hereby directed to insert in the several warrants by him sent to the several collectors of taxes for that year, with the names of the afore-recited commodities, the several prices or rates which shall be set on them, either by the general assembly or the committee aforesaid, and direct the aforesaid collectors to receive them so.

How the commodities brought into the treasury are to be rated.

Treasurer to sell the said commodities.

[SECT. 10.] And the aforesaid commodities so brought into the treasury shall, as soon as may be, be disposed of by the treasurer to the best advantage for so much as they will fetch in silver at six shillings and eight pence per ounce, or gold coin proportionably; and if any loss shall happen by the sale of the aforesaid species, or by any unforeseen accident, such deficiency shall be made good by a tax of the year next following, so as fully and effectually to pay in the full sum that may be borrowed as aforesaid; and if there be a surplusage, it shall remain a stock in the treasury. [*Passed January* 22; *published January* 23, 1749.

ACTS

PASSED AT THE SESSION BEGUN AND HELD AT BOSTON, ON THE TWENTY-SECOND DAY OF MARCH, A. D. 1749-50.

CHAPTER 18.

AN ACT IN ADDITION TO AN ACT MADE AND PASS[*E*]'D IN THE TWENTY-SECOND YEAR OF HIS MAJ[*ES*]TY'S REIGN, INTIT[U]LED "AN ACT FOR DRAWING IN THE BILLS OF CREDIT OF THE SEVERAL DENOMINATIONS WHICH HAVE AT ANY TIME BEEN ISSUED BY THIS GOVERNM[*EN*]T AND ARE STILL OUTSTANDING, AND FOR ASCERTAINING THE RATE OF COINED SILVER IN THIS PROVINCE FOR THE FUTURE."

WHEREAS in and by an act made and pass[*e*]'d in the twenty-second year of his present majesty's reign, intit[u]led "An act for drawing in the bills of credit of the several denominations which have at any time been issued by this government and are still outstanding, and for ascertaining the rate of coined silver in this province for the future," it is, among other things, enacted and declared in the words following; viz[t]., "That no execution shall be issued during the term aforesaid from the office of any clerk of any of the inferiour courts of common pleas, or of the superiour courts of judicature, for any sum whatsoever, unless the plaintiff or plaintiffs, suing in his or their own right, shall first take the oath aforesaid; and certificate thereof shall be made on such execution"; *and whereas* such clerk, *ex officio*, is not impow[e]red to administer such oath, and by means thereof great delay may be occasioned to many plaintiffs, and loss and damage thereby arise,— Preamble. 1748-49, chap. 15. 1749-50, chap. 8.

Be it therefore enacted,

[SECT. 1.] That the clerks of the superiour court of judicature, and the several clerks of the inferiour courts of common pleas, within this province be, and hereby are, impow[e]red to administer such oath, when it hath not already been done before a justice of peace and certified to the clerk, to any plaintiff or plaintiffs whatsoever, suing in his or their right, and dwelling within this province; and certificate may, and shall be, made thereof accordingly. And for administring the oath as aforesaid, such clerk shall be allow[*e*]'d threepence, and no more. Clerks of the courts empowered to administer oaths upon taking out executions.

And be it further enacted,

[SECT. 2.] That for each certificate on an execution, the clerk of the court signing the same shall be allowed threepence, lawful money, and no more; and the cost and charge of such oath and certificate shall be added to the sum in the execution required to be levied accordingly. [*Passed April* 12; *published April* 21, 1750. Fee for administering the oath and for certifying it.

CHAPTER 19.

AN ACT FOR ASCERTAINING THE RATES AT WHICH COINED SILVER AND GOLD, AND ENGLISH HALFPENCE AND FARTHINGS, MAY PASS WITHIN THIS GOVERNMENT.

Preamble. 1748-49, chap. 15, § 9.

WHEREAS in and by an act made and pass[e]'d in the twenty-second year of his present majesty's reign, intitled "An act for drawing in the bills of credit of the several denominations which have at any time been issued by this governm[en]t and are still outstanding, and for ascertaining the rate of coin'd silver in this province for the future," it is enacted in the words following; viz[t]., "That all bargains and contracts, debts and dues whatsoever, which shall be agreed, contracted or made after the thirty-first day of March, 1750, shall be understood, and are hereby declared, to be in silver, at six shillings and eightpence per ounce; and all Spanish mill'd pieces-of-eight, of full weight, shall be accounted, taken and paid at the rate of six shillings per p[ei][*ie*]ce for the discharge of any contracts or bargains to be made after the said thirty-first day of March, 1750; the halves, quarters and other less p[ei][*ie*]ces of the same coin to be accounted, received, taken or paid in the same proportion"; *and whereas*, there is great reason to apprehend that many and great inconvenc[*i*]es may arise, in case any coin'd silver or gold, or English halfpence and farthings, should pass at any higher rate than in a just proportion to Spanish p[ei][*ie*]ces-of-eight, or coin'd silver, at the rates aforesaid,—

Be it therefore enacted by the Lieutenant-Governour, Council and House of Representatives,

Rates of coins stated.

[SECT. 1.] That it shall not be lawful for any person within this government, from and after the thirty-first day of March, one thousand seven hund[*re*]d and fifty, to receive, take or pay any of the following coin at any greater or higher rate than is allowed by this act; viz[t]., a guinea, at twenty-eight shillings; an English crown, at six shillings and eight pence; an half-crown, at three shillings and fourpence; an English shilling, at one shilling and fourpence; an English sixpence, at eightpence; a double Johannes, or gold coin of Portugal, of the value of three pounds twelve shillings sterling, at four pounds sixteen shillings; a single Johannes, of the value of thirty-six shillings sterling, at forty-eight shillings; a mo[y][*i*]dore, at thirty-six shillings; a pistole of full weight, at twenty-two shillings; three English farthings for one penny; and English halfpence in greater or less numbers in proportion.

And be it further enacted,

Penalty for giving more for any the said coins than according to establishment.

[SECT. 2.] That if any person within this government shall, after the thirty-first day of March, one thousand seven hundred and fifty, for the discharge of any contract or bargain, account, receive, take or pay any of the several species of coins before mentioned at any greater or higher rate than at which the same is hereby regulated, set[*t*]led and allowed to be accounted, received, taken or paid, every person so accounting, receiving, taking or paying the same contrary to the directions herein contained, shall forfeit the sum of fifty pounds for every such offence, one moiety thereof to his majesty for the use of this government, the other moiety to such person or persons as shall sue for the same; to be recovered with full costs of suit, by action of debt, bill, plaint or information, in any of his majesty's courts within this province.

Provided always, and it is hereby declared,—

Proviso relating to bargains, &c., made before March 31, 1750.

[SECT. 3.] That nothing in this act shall be understood to restrain any person or persons from accounting, receiving, taking or paying any of the abovementioned species or coins in discharge of any debts, contracts or bargains made before the thirty-first day of March, one thous[*an*]d seven hund[*re*]d and fifty, at the following rates; viz[t]., for any debt contracted before the said thirty-first day of March, and understood to be payable in bills of the old teno[u]r, in such proportion higher or greater than the rates set at in this act as forty-five shillings is to six shillings; and for any debt contracted before the said thirty-first day of March, and understood to be payable in bills of the middle tenor or bills of the new tenor, in such proportion higher or greater than the rates set at in this act as eleven shillings and threepence is to six shillings; anything in this act to the contrary notwithstanding. [*Passed March* 31; *published April* 2, 1749–50.

CHAPTER 20.

AN ACT IN FURTHER ADDITION TO THE SEVERAL ACTS OF THIS PROVINCE MADE FOR THE DISTRIBUTION AND SETTLEMENT OF THE ESTATES OF INTESTATES.

Preamble. 1692-93, chap. 14, § 1. 1700-1701, chap. 4. 1710-11, chap. 2. 1719-20, chap. 10, §§ 3 and 4. 1723-24, chap. 3, § 2. 1730-31, chap. 2. 1733-34, chap. 5. 1734-35, chap. 16.

WHEREAS by the laws of this province made for the distribution and settlement of the estates of intestates, it is provided that such real estates as cannot, without prejudice to or spoiling them, be divided among all the children of any person dying intestate and leaving children, may be setled on one or so many of them as the estate will conveniently accommodate; but no provision by law has as yet been made for the like settlement of estates, uncapable of a division among all the heirs, where the intestate dies without issue,—

Be it therefore enacted by the Lieutenant-Governour, Council and House of Representatives,

Settlement of intestate estates where there is no issue.

That where the real estate of any person dying intestate and not leaving issue, cannot be divided among all the heirs, without great prejudice to or spoiling the whole, the judge of the probate of wills in the county in which such intestate person last dwelt, shall have power, and he is hereby authorized to order and assign the same to one or so many of the next of kin to such intestate, in equal degree, or their legal representatives, as such estate will conveniently accommodate without prejudice to or spoiling the whole (preference being given to the male heirs among such as are of kin in equal degree), in manner as the same might by law have been set[*t*]led on the children of the intestate in case he or she had left issue. [*Passed April* 12; *published April* 21, 1750.

CHAPTER 21.

AN ACT FOR GRANTING UNTO HIS MAJESTY AN EXCISE UPON SUNDRY ARTICLES HEREAFTER ENUMERATED, FOR AND TOWARDS THE SUPPORT OF HIS MAJESTY'S GOVERNM[*EN*]T, OF THIS PROVINCE.

Disallowed by the Privy Council, June 30, 1752.*

Preamble.

WE, your majesty's most loyal and dutiful subjects, the representatives of the province of the Massachusetts Bay, in general court assembled, have chearfully and unanimously granted and do hereby give and

* For reasons for disallowance, see the note to this chapter, *post.*

grant unto his most excellent majesty, to be applied to the support of his majesty's government of this province, according to such acts, votes or orders of the general court, as shall hereafter be made for that purpose, an excise upon the several articles hereafter named; and,—

Be it accordingly enacted by the Lieutenant-Governour, Council, and House of Representatives,

Duty to be paid for tea, coffee, arrack, snuff, and china-ware.

[SECT. 1.] That there shall be paid for all tea, coffee, arrack, snuff, and china-ware, the sundry duties following, viz[t].,—

For every pound of tea, twelvepence.

For every pound of coffee, twopence.

For every gallon of arrack, two shillings and sixpence.

For every pound of snuff, sixpence.

For all china-ware, five per cent *ad valorem*, at the retail price.

And be it further enacted,

No person to sell the things enumerated without license.

[SECT. 2.] That from and after the first day of August next, and during the continuance of this act, no person or persons whatsoever, other than such as shall obtain licence from the justices in general sessions to sell tea, coffee, arrack, snuff and china-ware, shall or may presume to sell the same; and every person so licensed shall give bond, with sufficient sureties, for their well and truly paying the duties laid on those articles he or they shall be licensed to sell, and that he or they will use his or their licen[s][*c*]e in such house or houses as shall be therein named, and no other; and that he or they will render to the collector or collectors, on oath, a just and true accompt of all the said commodities by him or them sold, from time to time, and pay unto the said collector or collectors, at the end of every half-year, the sum or sums of excise that may arise pursuant to this law.

Bond to be given.

And be it further enacted,

License not to be renewed unless the duty for the time past be paid.

[SECT. 3.] That the said licen[s][*c*]e be renewed yearly, and bond given as aforesaid; and that the said licen[s][*c*]es be renewed to no persons whatsoever, unless he or they, before their receiving the same, produce certificate, under the hand of the collector, of his or their having paid the full of the excise due from them as aforesaid.

And be it further enacted,

Penalty for selling without license.

[SECT. 4.] That if any person or persons not licensed as afores[*ai*]d, unless as hereafter is provided, shall, from and after the first day of Aug[*us*]t next, presume, directly or indirectly, by themselves, or any under them, to sell any tea, coffee, arrack, snuff, or china-ware, by any quantity, weight, number or measure, he, she or they shall, for every such offence, on due conviction, forfeit and pay a sum not exceeding ten pounds, nor under two pounds, at the discretion of the court before whom the conviction may be; one half to the informer, and the other half to his majesty for and towards the support of this government, and to be paid into the prov[s][*ince*] treasury accordingly: the manner of conviction to be the same as of persons selling strong liquors without licen[s][*c*]e, as is by law already provided.

1748-49, chap. 4, § 8.

And be it further enacted,

Collectors of this duty to be appointed.

[SECT. 5.] That there be one or more collectors in each county annually appointed by the general court; and, in case of death or refusal, the court of gen[*era*]l sessions of the peace are hereby impow[e]red to take charge of the aforesaid duty of excise; and each of the said collectors shall give bond with sureties, before he enter into said office, to the treasurer of the province, in such sum as the court of general sessions of the peace shall order, not exceeding one thousand pounds, conditioned for his faithful performance of his duty and paying into the treasury all such sums as he shall collect by virtue of this act; and said collectors, respectively, shall also be under oath to see to the observation of this law, and to prosecute the breakers of it, and may

To give bond.

To be under oath.

and are hereby authorized and impow[e]red to appoint one or more officers under them, who shall also be under oath, to inquire after and prosecute the breakers of this law; and the said collectors are hereby impow[e]red and required, every half year, carefully to examine on oath the accompts of every person licensed to sell any or either of the before-mentioned articles in their respective counties, and demand and receive the several sums due from them by virtue of this act; and shall give in a particular accompt, under their hands, of the particular sums they received, together with the names of the persons of whom received, and pay in the same unto the province treasurer upon oath, which oath the said treasurer is hereby directed and impow[e]red to administer, and each collector shall be allowed five per cent for all monies received by him as afores[*ai*]d and paid into the province treasury.

Collectors to examine licensed persons on oath.

To render an account to the treasurer on oath.

Allowed five per cent.

And be it further enacted,

[SECT. 6.] That if any person licensed as aforesaid, shall not, within the space of one month next after the time limited by law for their paying the duties aforesaid, account with and pay the collectors the sums due from them for the excise aforesaid, in manner as aforesaid, that then the said collectors are hereby impow[e]red and required to put such deficient or delinquent person's bond in suit; and upon his recovering and receiving the money due thereon, he shall pay in the same to the province treasury, and shall be allowed two and an half per cent for doing the same.

Collectors to put delinquent's bonds in suit.

Provided, nevertheless,

[SECT. 7.] It shall and may be lawful, anything in this act contained to the contrary notwithstanding, for all and every person or persons that shall import any of the before-enumerated articles, or that at the time of the publication of this act may be possessed of any of the same, to sell or export the same out of this province, or sell and dispose of the same within this province, to such as are licensed to sell and retail the same, and to no other person[s] whomsoever, without being subject to the penalty by this act imposed on those that shall transgress the same.

Proviso.

And be it further enacted,

[SECT. 8.] That the justices in the several counties be and hereby are impow[e]red, at their several sessions during the continuance of this act, to grant licen[s][c]es for the selling and retailing any of the afores[*ai*]d articles to all such fit and proper persons as shall apply to them for the same; and all persons desiring licen[s][c]es are hereby directed to apply to the justices in sessions for said licen[s][c]e accordingly; and the person receiving such licen[s][c]e shall pay no other or greater fee than four shillings in the whole (two shillings to the court, and two shillings to the clerk), for his or her liceu[s][c]e and bond aforesaid.

General sessions to grant licenses.

Fee for license.

And be it further enacted,

[SECT. 9.] That every person residing within this province, excepting the governour-in-chief, the lieutenant-governour, the set[t]led ministers, and president of Harvard College, for the time being, that are or shall be the owners of any coach, chariot, chaise, calash, or chair, shall certify the same to the collector of excise in the county in which they reside, on or before the first day of July, annually, and pay the sums herein respectively set on said coaches, chariots, chaises, calashes and chairs, by the first of September; viz[t]., for every coach, ten shilling; for every chariot, five shillings; for every chaise, three shillings; for every calash, two shillings; for every chair, two shillings; upon pain of forfeiting the sum of twenty shillings for such coach, chariot, chaise, calash or chair, which shall not be certified, and for which the duty shall not be paid as afores[*ai*]d, to be recovered by the said col-

Duty to be paid for coaches, chariots, chaises, calashes, and chairs.

Duty to be recovered by the collectors. lectors, who are impow[e]red and required to demand and sue for said excise, and for all such forfeitures as may arise by the neglect of any person or persons as aforesaid. And the said collectors are hereby further required to pay into the province treasury, all such sum or sums as they shall so receive, on or before the first day of October, annually, during the continuance of this act; and shall be allowed five per cent for all money so received by them and paid into the province treasury as aforesaid.

Provided, nevertheless,

Proviso. [SECT. 10.] That if any such coach, chariot, chaise, calash, or chair shall not, at any time in either of the years during the continuance of this act, be actually used or improved, the same shall be exempted from the tax hereby laid thereon, for such year in which the same shall not be used or improved as aforesaid.

Limitation. [SECT. 11.] This act to continue and be in force until[l] the first day of August, which shall be in the year of our Lord one thousand seven hundred and fifty-three, and no longer. [*Passed April* 20; *published April* 21, 1750.

CHAPTER 22.

AN ACT AGAINST DIMINISHING [AND] [*OR*] COUNTERFEITING MONEY.

Be it enacted by the Lieutenant-Governour, Council and House of Represent[ati]ves,

Punishment for counterfeiting, clipping, or diminishing any coin, &c. 1700-1701, chap. 17. 1702-3, chap. 2. Or uttering such coin. [SECT. 1.] That if any person or persons, after the publication of this act, shall forge or counterfeit money or coin, the currency of which is established or regulated by the laws of this province, or shall forge or counterfeit any money or coin that is or shall be current in this province, or shall for gain, wash, clip, round, file, impair, falsify, scale, lighten, or diminish any or either of the monies or coins aforesaid, or that shall utter any such false, forged, counterfeit, washed, clipped, rounded, filed, impaired, scaled, lightned, or diminished money or coin, knowing the same to be false, forged, counterfeited, washed, clipped, rounded, filed, impaired, scaled, lightned, or diminished, and be thereof convicted at the superiour court of judicature, court of assize and general goal delivery, every such person shall be fined at the discretion of the said court, and also be set in the pillory for the space of one hour, and then have one of his, her or their ears cut off, and from thence shall be drawn to the gallows and set thereon with a rope about his or their necks for the space of an hour, and shall then be publickly whipped not exceeding twenty stripes, and shall then be committed to the house of correction (but not receive the usual punishment at his, her or their first entrance), and be kept to hard labour for the space of three years.

Provided, nevertheless,—

Proviso. Punishment on a second conviction. [SECT. 2.] That the justices of said court may and shall, at their discretion, abate any part of the pains and penalties aforesaid, according to the circumstance of the offence; and upon a second conviction of any or either of the offences aforesaid, such offender or offenders shall be committed to the house of correction, and there kept to hard labour for the space of twenty years.

Saving always,—

Saving. [SECT. 3.] That nothing in this act mentioned shall be construed so as to prevent any goldsmith or other person from melting into bull-ion or working into plate any of the mon[i]e[y]s aforesaid, except his majesty's coins.

Provided, also,—

[SECT. 4.] That the making use of the copper halfpence and farthings, for the making or mending any vessel, shall not be construed a breach of this act. Proviso.

And be it further enacted,

[SECT. 5.] That whoever shall inform of any of the foregoing offences, so as the offender or offenders may be convicted of the same, such informer shall receive out of the treasury of this province the sum of twenty-five pounds. Reward to the informer.

And be it further enacted,

[SECT. 6.] That whoever shall buy or receive any clippings, scalings or filings of any of the aforesaid coins, knowing them to be clippings, scalings or filings of the same, shall be imprisoned for the space of one year, and pay a fine of fifty pounds, one moiety whereof shall be to his majesty for and towards the use of the government within this province, and the other moiety to him or them that shall inform of said offence, so as the offender or offenders may be convicted of the same. Penalty for buying clippings of coin, &c.

[SECT. 7.] This act to continue and be in force for the space of five years from and after the publication of it, and no longer. [*Passed April* 18; *published April* 21, 1750. Limitation.

CHAPTER 23.

AN ACT IN ADDITION TO AND FOR RENDRING MORE EFFECTUAL AN ACT FOR THE RESTRAINING THE TAKING EXCESSIVE USURY.

WHEREAS in and by an act made and pass'd in the fifth year of the reign of King William and Queen Mary, intitled "An Act for the restraining the taking excessive usury," it is enacted, "That no person or persons whatsoever, from and after the first day of August, in the year of our Lord one thousand six hundred ninety-three, upon any contract to be made after that time, shall take, directly or indirectly, for loan of any mon[i]e[y]s, wares, merchandize or other commodities whatsoever, above the value of six pounds for the forbearance of one hundred pounds for a year, and so after that rate for a greater or lesser sum, or for a longer or shorter time"; notwithstanding which, many persons do presume to take and reserve much more for interest than the rate aforesaid,—to the discouragement of industry, trade and commerce in this province,—the discovery and detecting whereof is difficult, and the provision by the law already made has prov[e]'d in many cases ineffectual; for preventing whereof for the future,— Preamble. 1693, chap. 1.

Be it enacted by the Lieutenant-Governour, Council and House of Representatives,

[SECT. 1.] That when and so often as any person or persons are or shall be sued on any bond, contract, mortgage or assurances whatsoever, made after the tenth day of April, *Anno Domini* one thousand seven hundred and fifty, for the payment of any moneys, wares or merchandize, or other commodities whatsoever, whereby or wherein any sum is given, secured or taken for the forbearing or giving day of payment for a longer or shorter time, then and in such case, the creditor being alive, if the debtor or debtors shall come into court where the said cause is to be tried, and shall offer to make oath, and, if required Penalty for taking more than six per cent for interest. Proof to be made by the debtor's oath,—

by the court, actually swear to the same, that there is taken, reserv[e]'d or secured by such bond, contract, mortgage or assurance, above the rate of six pounds in the hundred for the forbearance of the same,—whether it be money or other things,—for one year, and so after that rate for any greater or lesser sum, or for a longer or shorter time; or that the creditor or creditors have received more than at the rate of six pounds in the hundred for the loan of the money or other things sued for, such bond, contract, mortgage or assurance shall be utterly void, and the debtor fully and absolutely discharged from the payment of any moneys, goods or other things lent, exchanged, bargained, sold or agreed for as aforesaid, unless the creditor or creditors will, *bonâ fide*, swear that he, she or they have not, directly or indirectly, wittingly taken or received more than after the rate of six per cent for forbearance or giving day of payment, and that by such bond, contract, mortgage or assurance there is not reserv[e]'d, secur[e]'d or taken more than after the rate of six per cent for forbearance or giving day of payment for the goods, moneys or other things sued for or demanded; any law, usage or custom to the contrary notwithstanding.

—unless the creditor will discharge himself upon oath.

Provided,—

Proviso.

[SECT. 2.] Nothing in this act shall extend to the letting of cattle, or other usages of like nature in practice amongst farmers, or maritime contracts amongst merchants; as bottomry, insurance or course of exchange, as hath been heretofore accustomed.

Limitation.

[SECT. 3.] This act to continue and be in force for the space of five years from the publication thereof, and no longer. [*Passed April* 11; *published April* 21, 1750.

CHAPTER 24.

AN ACT FOR PREVENTING STAGE-PLAYS AND OTHER THEATRICAL ENTERTAINMENTS.

Preamble.

FOR preventing and avoiding the many and great mischiefs which arise from publick stage-plays, interludes and other theatrical entertainments, which not only occasion great and unnecessary expences, and discourage industry and frugality, but likewise tend generally to increase immorality, impiety and a contempt of religion,—

Be it enacted by the Lieutenant-Governour, Council and House of Representatives,

Penalty for letting any house for stage-plays, &c.

[SECT. 1.] That from and after the publication of this act, no person or persons, whosoever, shall or may, for his or their gain or for any price or valuable consideration, let[t] or suffer to be used and improv[e]'d any house, room or place whatsoever, for acting or carrying on any stage-plays, interludes or other theatrical entertainments, on pain of forfeiting and paying, for each and every day or time such house, room or place shall be let[t], used or improved contrary to this act, twenty pounds.

And be it further enacted,

Penalty to actors and spectators.

[SECT. 2.] That if at any time or times whatsoever, from and after the publication of this act, any person or persons shall be present, as an actor in, or spectator of, any stage-play, interlude or theatrical entertainment, in any house, room or place where a greater number of persons than twenty shall be assembled together, every such person shall forfeit and pay, for every time he or they shall be present as aforesaid, five pounds.

[SECT. 3.] The forfeitures and penalties aforesaid to be one half to his majesty for the use of the government, the other half to him or them that shall inform and sue for the same. And the aforesaid forfeitures and penalties may likewise be recovered by presentment of the grand jury; in which case the whole of the forfeiture shall be to his majesty for the use of this government. Disposal and manner of recovering the penalties.

[SECT. 4.] This act to be in force and continue five years from the publication hereof, and no longer. [*Passed April* 11; *published April* 21, 1750. Limitation.

CHAPTER 25.

AN ACT IN ADDITION TO THE ACT, INTIT[U]LED "AN ACT TO PREVENT DAMAGE BEING DONE UNTO BILLINGSGATE BAY, IN THE TOWN OF EASTHAM, BY CATTLE AND HORSE-KIND, AND SHEEP, FEEDING ON THE BEACH AND ISLANDS ADJOINING THERETO."

WHEREAS Samuel Smith, Esq[r]., for himself and the proprietors of the islands and beach lying westerly of Billingsgate Bay, and south of Griffin's Island, have represented to this court, that the good end proposed by the act made in the sixteenth year of his present majesty's reign, intit[u]led "An Act to prevent damage being done unto Billingsgate Bay, in the town of Eastham, by cattle and horse-kind, and sheep, feeding on the beach and islands adjoining thereto," will be wholly frustrated, unless further provision be made for that purpose, and therefore have proposed, at their own cost, to build a fence across the north part of the great island, and so into the sea, as also a house on said island, and set[t]le and continue a family therein to secure the same, in case they may be allowed the privilege of feeding a number of cattle thereon at certain seasons of the year,— Preamble. 1742-43, chap. 11.

Be it therefore enacted by the Lieutenant-Governour, Council and House of Representatives,

[SECT. 1.] That for and during the term of seven years, accounting from the first of March, one thousand seven hundred and forty-nine, it shall and may be lawful for the said Samuel Smith, and the proprietors aforesaid, and their heirs, executors and administrators, to feed, on the beach and islands aforesaid, five cattle, from the first of March to the first of May, and twenty-five head of cattle, from the first of October until[l] the last of November, annually; and one cow, for the use of the family that may be setled on said island, for and during the whole of the term before mentioned, anything in the aforesaid act to the contrary notwithstanding,— Proprietors of Billingsgate Beach and islands allowed to feed a number of cattle thereon.

Provided,—

[SECT. 2.] That he the said Samuel Smith, and the proprietors aforesaid, their heirs, executors or administrators, shall and do make and maintain a good and sufficient fence across the north part of the said island, and into the sea; also build a house on said island, and set[t]le and keep a family therein during the term aforesaid. [*Passed April* 17; *published April* 21, 1750. Proviso.

CHAPTER 26.

AN ACT TO PREVENT DAMAGE BEING DONE ON THE MEADOWS AND BEACHES LYING IN AND ADJOINING ON THE NORTH SIDE OF THE TOWN OF HARWICH, BETWEEN SKEKET-HARBOUR, ON THE EAST, AND SETUCKET-HARBOUR, ON THE WEST.

Preamble.

WHEREAS many persons frequently drive numbers of neat cattle, horses, sheep and swine, to feed upon the beaches, meadows and shores adjo[y][*i*]ning to the north side of Harwich, lying between Skeket-harbour, on the east, and Setucket-harbour, on the west, whereby the ground is much broken and damnified and the sand blown on said adjo[y][*i*]ning meadows and uplands, to the great damage not only of sundry private persons in their property, but also to the inhabitants of said town in general,—

Be it enacted by the Lieutenant-Governour, Council and House of Represent[*ati*]*ves*,

Penalty for horses and sheep or swine feeding on Harwich beaches and meadows.

[SECT. 1.] That from and after the publication of this act, no person or persons shall presume to turn any neat cattle, horse-kind, sheep or swine, to or upon any of the beaches, meadows or shores that l[y][*i*]e on the north side of the town of Harwich, between Skeket-harbour, on the east, and Setu[c]ket-harbour, on the west, at any time between the first of April and the last of October yearly, during the continuance of this act, on penalty of paying for each offence five shillings a head for neat cattle, horses or mares of one year old or upwards, and one shilling and sixpence a head for each sheep or swine, that shall be turned or found on said beaches, meadows or shores, within the limits aforesaid; which penalty shall be recovered by the selectmen or treasurer of the said town of Harwich, or any other person that shall inform of and sue for the same: the one half of said forfeiture to him or them that shall inform of and sue for the same, the other half to be to and for the use of the poor of said town: *provided* the said town of Harwich, in conjunction with the town of Eastham, or proprietors of said beach or sedge ground, keep up a two-rail fence during said time, on or near the place, as usual, on the east side of great Skeket-harbour, beginning at the land of Nathan[i][*a*]el Freeman, Esq[r]., thence extending north-westerly on said flatts or sedge ground, near half a mile as usual.

How to be recovered and disposed of.

Proviso.

And be it further enacted,

Cattle found feeding on said meadows, &c., to be impounded.

[SECT. 2.] That if any neat cattle, horse-kind, sheep or swine, shall, at any time hereafter, be found feeding on the said beaches, meadows or shores that l[y][*i*]e between said Skeket-harbour and said Setu[c]ket-harbour, in said Harwich, it shall and may be lawful for any person to impound the same, immediately giving notice thereof to the owners, if known, otherwise to give publick notice thereof by posting the same up in some publick place in said town, and the two next adjoining towns; and the impounder shall rel[ei][*ie*]ve the said creatures with suitable meat and water while impounded; and if the owner thereof appear to redeem his impounded creatures, he shall pay one shilling and sixpence to the impounder, for each neat beast and horse-kind, and sixpence for each sheep and swine, and the reasonable costs of rel[ei][*ie*]ving, besides the pound-keeper's fees as by law appointed for such creatures. And if no owner appear within the space of six days to redeem the said cattle, horse-kind, sheep or swine so impounded, and to pay the cost[s] and damage occasioned by impounding the same, then and in every such case the person impounding such cattle or horse-kind, sheep or swine, shall cause the same to be sold at publick vendue, and pay the cost[s] and charges arising about the same (pub-

To be sold, where the owner doth not appear.

lick notice of the time and place of such sale, to be given in the said town of Harwich and in the towns of Eastham and Yarmouth, forty-eight hours beforehand), and the overplus, if any there be, arising by such sale, to be returned to the owner of such cattle or horse-kind, sheep or swine, at any time within twelve months next after, upon his demanding the same; but if no owner appear within the said twelve months, then the said overplus shall be one half to the party impounding such cattle, horse-kind, sheep or swine, and the other half to the use of the poor of said town of Harwich.

Disposal of the produce.

And be it further enacted,

[SECT. 3.] That the said town of Harwich, at a meeting of said town called for that purpose, or at their meeting in March, annually, for the choice of town officers, be authorized and impow[e]red to chuse one or more meet person or persons whose duty it shall be to see to the due observance of this act, and to prosecute the breakers thereof, and who shall be sworn to the faithful discharge of their office; and in case any person so chosen shall refuse to be sworn, he shall forfeit and pay ten shillings for the use of the poor of said town of Harwich; and upon such refusal, said town, from time to time, to proceed to a new choice of such officer or officers, until[l] one or more person or persons will serve therein.

Persons to be chosen to see to the observance of this act.

Provided,—

[SECT. 4.] That nothing in this act shall be construed to prevent the owner or owners of said beach or meadows, or any improving under them, from turning on their horses they ride, or cattle they improve in their teams, to feed on said beach or meadows while they are cutting or carting their hay off said beach or meadows adjo[y][*i*]ning.

Proviso.

[SECT. 5.] This act to continue and be in force for the space of five years from the publication thereof, and no longer. [*Passed April* 18; *published April* 21, 1750.

Limitation.

CHAPTER 27.

AN ACT IN ADDITION TO THE ACT, INTIT[U]LED "AN ACT TO ENCOURAGE THE INCREASE OF SHEEP AND GOATS."

WHEREAS in and by an act made in the fourteenth year of his present majesty's reign, intit[u]led "An Act to [i][e]ncourage the increase of sheep and goats," it is enacted, "That from and after the publication of the said act, no rams or he-goats shall be suffered to go at large, or be out of the inclosure of the owner thereof, from the tenth day of August 'till after the fifteenth day of November, annually, under the penalty of fifteen shillings"; which has been found inconvenient in some towns in this province, inasmuch as, by a strict adherence to the said act, the lambs and kids will annually come too late for prof[f]it; wherefore,—

Preamble. 1740-41, chap. 23.

Be it enacted by the Lieutenant-Governour, Council and House of Representatives,

That it shall be in the power of any town, at a town meeting for that purpose appointed, by a vote, to give liberty for rams or he-goats to go at large, within the bounds of such town, at any other times than those limited in said act, or to restrain them, as the several towns at such meeting shall think proper; and in such case it shall be lawful for any and every person or persons to suffer his or their rams and he-goats to go at large, anything in the before-recited act to the contrary notwithstanding. [*Passed April* 12; *published April* 21, 1750.

Towns may give liberty for sheep and goats to go at large, &c.

NOTES.—There were but four sessions of the General Court this year.

The engrossments of all the acts of this year are preserved, and all were printed with the sessions-acts, except chapter 4, which, being an impost-act, was separately printed and distributed.

By command of Lieutenant-Governor Phips, all the acts of the year were duly certified for transmission to the Privy Council, May 28, 1750; and on the 27th of September, following, they were delivered to the clerk of the Privy Council, in waiting, by the Agent of the Province. On the 4th of October they were referred to a Committee of the Council, which, in turn, referred them to the Lords Commissioners for Trade, etc., November 15, 1750.

On the 29th of November, the Board for Trade ordered them to be sent to Mr. Lamb, for his opinion, etc., and Mr Lamb's report is dated January 3, 1752.

The report of the Board of Trade was prepared and ordered to be transcribed, May 26, 1752, and on the 4th of June was signed.

In this report, chapters 1, 4, and 17 are declared to have been "for a temporary service, and are either expired, or the purposes for which they were granted have been completed." Chapters 2, 3, 5, 6, 7, 9, 10, 11, 12, 13, 14, 15, 19, 20, 22, 23, 24, 25, 26, and 27 are declared to "appear to have been enacted for the particular convenience and benefit of the Province and as Mr. Lamb"—the report continues—"has no objection to any of them in point of Law, We see no reason why His Majesty may not be graciously pleased to confirm them"; and on chapters 8, 18, and 19, which the report describes as containing "certain Regulations for the more effectual carrying into execution & supplying some defects in the Provisions of" the act of 1748–49, chapter 15, "confirmed by His Majesty," the following representation is made: "and as the last of them is not contrary but as near as may be agreeable to the Act of the 6th of Queen Anne *for ascertaining the Rates of Foreign Coins in the Plantations in America.* We beg leave to lay the said Acts before your Lordships as proper to be confirmed." Chapter 16 is represented as reviving an act (1742–43, chap. 34) which did not appear to the Board to have been laid before the King in Council; but the report recommends that this chapter be confirmed, nevertheless, "as it appears" * * * "from the annex'd copies of the said Acts, transmitted to us by the Secretary of the said Province that they were enacted only for their private convenience." The report concludes with special comments on chapter 21, and recommends that it be disallowed. These comments are given in full in the note to that chapter, *post.*

Two orders in council were passed June 30, 1752; one of them expressly confirming and ratifying chapters 2, 3, 5, 6, 7, 8, 9, 10, 11, 12, 13, 14, 15, 16, 18, 19, 20, 22, 23, 24, 25, 26, and 27, and the other disallowing chapter 21. The latter is given in full in the note to the chapter last named, *post.*

Chap. 1. "June 24. 1749. The Secretary has laid before me your Engross'd Bill for granting me the Sum of Twenty two hundred Pounds for my Support.

I think (Gentlemen of the House of Represent^ves) I might have expected a larger Grant from You; But as I understand the Reason of your not granting me the same nominal Sum you did last Year, was the melancholy Prospect now before you, of having the Fruits of the Earth cut off by a threatning Drought; thô I believe I shall have a double Share of the Distress which may arise to the Province on that Account; yet as I hope my Acceptance of the Sum now granted me for the before mentioned Reason, will be regarded by You as a proof that I am not desirous to decline bearing my part in any publick Calamity of the People within my Governm^t, I readily accept it."—*Governor Shirley's Message to the Assembly: Council Records, vol. XIX., p.* 28.

Chap. 2. "Jany. 20. 1746. A Petition of the President & Fellows of Harward Colledge in Cambridge, Shewing how much the Revenue of the said Colledge (upon which the Support of their Officers does depend) is deminish'd by the low Rates of the Ferriage over Charles River; which Ferry is the Estate of the said Colledge, & therefore Praying that the said Ferriage may be set at the Rates they were at, when first established by the General Court. In the House of Represent^ves Read & Ordered that Major Appleton, Mr Hall, Mr Russell, Capt Read, Mr Foster, Dr Pynchon, & Coll. Choat, with such as the Honble Board shall appoint be a Committee to take this Petition under Consideration & report what they judge proper for this Court to do thereon. In Council Read & Concur'd & Jacob Wendell"—*Ibid., vol. XVIII., p.* 53.

"February 13. 1746. Jacob Wendell Esqr from the Committee appointed to consider the Petition of the President and Fellows of Harvard College gave in their Report. In Council Read & Ordered that the Consideration of this Report be Refer'd to the next Sitting of the Court, & that the Committee in the mean time, consider of some proper method for regulating the said Ferry & make report at the said Sitting. In the House of Represent^ves Read & Concurr'd. Consented to by the Governor."—*Ibid., p.* 73.

"June 2. 1747. In the House of Represent^ves Ordered that Major Lawrence & Capt Wilder be added to the Committee of both Houses, upon the petition of the President & Fellows of Harvard College, respecting the Regulation of the Ferry over Charles River in the room of Joseph Pynchon & Daniel Appleton Esq^rs who are not of the House this present year, the Committee to sit forthwith, & report as soon as may be. In Council, Read & Concur'd."—*Ibid., p.* 139.

Chap. 7. "March 21. 1746. The Secretary laid before the Court an Anonimous Letter directed to the Governor & Council containing Scandalous Reflections upon the conduct of the Government, particularly respecting the billeting of the Soldiers.

In the House of Represent^ves Voted that Mr. Welles, Coll. Choate & Mr. Goldsbury, with such as the Honble Board shall join, be a Committee to take said letter under consideration & report as soon as may be what they judge proper to do thereon. In Council Read & Concurr'd & Joseph Dwight & James Minot Esq^rs are added in the said affair."—*Ibid., p.* 96.

"April 21, 1749. His Excellency sent the following Message to both Houses by the Secretary.

Gentlemen of the Council & House of Representatives,

One of the Members of his Majesty's Council has laid before me a villanous Paper importing a wicked Conspiracy for robbing him of part of his Estate, by extorting a Sum of Money from him, & threatning him with the burning of his House Warehouses and Vessells & the murthering of his Person in Case of his refusal to comply with their Demands.

Gentlemen. This being the first Instance of this Kind of execrable Villany attempted in this Province, it highly imports this Legislature to make Provision for Preventing & punishing the same Attempts for the future; Wherefore I desire you would immediately take the matter into Consideration & do what you judge Necessary before you Rise.

In the House of Represent^{ves} Read together with the Paper referred to, and Ordered that Mr Speaker Colo Heath, Colo. Otis, Col^{o} Dwight, & Col^{o} Buckminster with such as the Honble Board shall join be a Committee to consider this Message & Paper referred to & report what they judge proper for this Court to do thereon: the Committee to sit forthwith.

In Council Read & Concured, And Samuel Welles, Sam^{ll} Danforth, Andrew Oliver, and John Otis Esq.^{rs} are joined in the affair."—*Ibid., p.* 467.

"April 22^{d} 1749. Samuel Welles Esqr from the Committee on his Excellency's Message referring to the threatning Letter sent to one of his Majesty's Council, gave in the following Report, The Committee appointed to Consider of his Excellency's Message of this Day are of Opinion, that all possible means should be used to detect & punish the horrid Crimes his Excellency referrs to & to prevent such heinous & detestable Practices for the future; And therefore they humbly Apprehend it to be proper for the two Houses to desire & advise his Excellency to issue a Proclamation promissing a Reward of two hundred Pounds, Bills of the last Emission to any Person or Persons who shall inform or discover one or more concerned in this Wicked Conspiracy so that he or they may be Convicted; And if the Informer shall have been an Accomplice or engaged in said Crime, he shall be forgiven: And to the End the greater Horrour & Detestation may be raised in the minds of his Majestys good Subjects with respect to this Atrocious & execrable Design; The Committee humbly report as their Opinion, that the two Houses desire his Excellency to insert in the Proclamation, the Sum & substance of the Anonymous Letter refered to in the Message & some of the impious, insolent, inhuman Message verbatim; that thereby all his Majesty's good Subjects may see how reasonble & necessary it is that they join Universally in their Endeavours to bring forward to Exemplary Punishment the profligate & abandon'd Wretches concerned in this Wicked & impudent Combination. The Committee would propose that some Gentlemen of each House be appointed to prepare the Draught of a Bill for the more easy & effectual preventing or detecting such Abominable & dangerous Crimes hereafter to be laid before this Court at the begging of their Session in May next.

April 21. 1749. by Order of the Committee Sam^{ll} Welles. In the House of Represent^{ves} Read & Accepted & Mr. Speaker, Mr Hubbard, with such as the Honble Board shall join are a Committee to prepare the Draught of a Bill accordingly. In Council Read & Concured.

Consented to by the Governour"—*Ibid., p.* 470.

"June 1st 1749. Gentlemen I must inform you of a new & flagrant Instance of the same kind of audacious Villany, which was begun to be practiced a little before the Dissolution of the last Court in an Anonymous Letter being sent to me by one or more of the abandon'd Offenders concerned in this Criminal Practice, to demand my laying a Sum of Money for them in a secret Place, & in Case of my Refusal.—threatning to burn the Province House & my own House in the Country, & in their Letter treating the Proclamation I issued at the Desire of both Houses for Apprehending the Persons concerned in these Attempts with the utmost Indignity. The Letter I shall order to be laid before you & desire you will without Delay prepare a Bill for suppressing this Kind of Wickedness & punishing the Authors as they justly deserve. * * * *

I must earnestly recommend to you to proceed in the Affairs that may ly before you with the greatest Harmony & Unanimity which will prove one of the most effectual methods to dispirit those lawless Villains that are Enemies to all Governm^{t} & therefore would rejoice in every thing they may apprehend will tend to weaken the hands of it, for ordaining & inflicting on them a just Punish[ment] for their crimes"—*Ibid., vol. XIX., pp.* 5 *and* 6.

"August 3 1749. Gentlemen of the Council & House of Represent^{ves} I now lay before you a new Instance (which I have had the Information of from New Hampshire) of the same kind of Villany that was twice lately practiced in this Province for extorting money by threatning Gentlemen of Substance with the Destruction of their Estates & Persons in Case of Refusal to comply with the Demands of these Miscreants.

I am sorry that this Court has not yet pass'd any Act for the preventing & punishing this pernicious Practice, thô I recommended it to the last Court in their last Session. I must therefore desire that there may be no further Delay to provide for the Safety of his Majesty's Subjects of this Province & their Interests in this Case, & for the Punishment of such Offenders."—*Ibid., p.* 43.

"Augst 4th 1749. In the House of Repres.^{ves}. This House having taken into Consideration his Excellency's Message of Yesterday relating to the Atrocious Crimes that Some Villains, as yet unknown, have been guilty of, for extorting Money, by threatning Gentlemen of Substance, with the Destruction of their Estates & Persons, in case of Refusal to comply with the Demands of these Miscreants. Voted that James Otis, Israel Williams & James Allen Esq^{rs} with such as the hon^{ble} Board shall Join be a Committee to prepare, & bring in a Bill for preventing & punishing such pernicious Practices for the future. In Council, Read & Concur'd; and Andrew Oliver & Joseph Pynchon Esq^{rs} are Joined in the Affair."—*Ibid.*

Chap. 8. "March 31. 1750. In the House of Represent^ves It appearing to this House that in the exchangeing our present Currency, it will give great dispatch, as well as tend much to the ease of the Subjects, if six persons be appointed a Committee (three of whom to be a Quorum) to assist in s^d Affair, Therefore Voted that James Allen Esqr Andrew Boardman Esqr Mr James Russell & Thomas Foster Esq^s with such whom the Honb^le Board shall join, be a Committee (who shall be under oath for the faithfull discharge of their Trust & accountable to this Court, & for which Service they shall each receive five shillings a day) in order to receive from the Possessors of the bills of this Province, exclusive of the inhabitants of Connecticut Rhode Island & New Hampshire, what bills may be brought to exchange, agreable to the Act for drawing in the bills of credit, made in the 22^d year of his Majesty's Reign; which Committee shall attend each day in the week except Lord's days & Saturdays from nine to one, & from three to seven a clock of each day, until the further Order of this Court; and for each sum or sums in such bills they may so receive (after they have been counted & told by two persons at least of said Committee) they are impowered & directed to give Orders on the Treasurer, to the persons of whom they may receive such bills, & also to keep a list of such Orders, which list shall be transmitted by them to the Treasurer, under their hands or the hands of the Major part of them, from time to time, as they may give said Orders; & shall from day to day consume to Ashes what bills they may so receive, keeping an Accompt of what sums may be so consumed; and if among the bills which shall be offered in Exchange, there appear to be any that are Counterfeit, or suspected to be so, said Committee are to stop the same, & take the names of the persons of whom they receive them for the further Examination & Order of this Court; And the Treasurer in exchanging the said money, agreable to the afores^d Act, is hereby impowered & directed to pay three pence of the Copper half pence & farthings that are now in the Treasury, in every twenty shillings he shall so exchange, & so in proportion for a greater sum; & shall also in each Exchange, deliver Pillar'd money & milled money, according to the respective proportion & value of the same that may be in the Treasury, & shall be at liberty to pay unto any person (that may desire the same) three pence in every twenty shillings that may be exchanged in the bills that are proposed to be emitted for the convenience of small change, & so in proportion for a greater sum; And the Treasurer is further impowerd & directed to appoint a sufficient number of persons to assist him in exchanging the aforesaid Silver & Copper (for whose Conduct he shall be accountable in such exchange) And they together with the Treasurer shall attend said business at the same times at which the before mentioned Committee are obliged to attend. And it is further Ordered that the Committee chosen as aforesaid be impowered & directed to receive of the Inhabitants of this Governm^t any sum or sums of the bills of Connecticut, Rhode Island or New Hampshire & give Receipts & make fair Entries of the same, & from whom received; they making oath before the s^d Committee, or a Justice of the peace or Town Clerk (where no Justice dwells) that the bills by them tendered, are their own property, & that they were actually possessed of the same before the first day of April 1750, and said Committee are also directed & impowered to examine all persons bringing any sums of the bills of this Province to exchange for Silver, whether the same be their own property, or the property of their Neighbours Inhabitants of this Province, & whether they have, & whether they have not received such bills for Silver sold directly or indirectly to any Inhabitant, or Resident in the aforesaid Governments of Connecticut Rhode Island or New Hampshire since the 30th of March 1750, & to administer on Oath to such persons as they shall judge proper, to answer to all such questions, as shall be asked them respecting the said bills; and upon refusal to swear they shall not have their bills exchanged; And upon the said Committees discovering the said bills so tendered, to be the property of the Inhabitants of any of the aforesaid Governments, that in such case, the bills of the respective Governm^ts in the hands of said Committee shall be given in exchange for the bills of this Province; and said bills or Silver shall be given to the persons who have lodged the Bills of the aforesaid Governments in the hands of said Committee, in proportion to the sum or sums so lodged, at the end of every two months; And in case there be not a sufficiency to redeem all the bills of the other Governments in the hands of said Committee, the Committee to deliver the said bills to the Owners of the same when they please to call for them In Council; Read & Concur'd and Samuel Watt, John Quincy & Ezekiel Cheever Esq^rs are joined in the affair. Consented to by the Lieut: Governor"—*Ibid., p.* 157.

"March 31. 1750. In Council; In order to disperse the Silver now in the Treasury in the speediest & most general manner amongst the Inhabitants of the Province Voted that upon Monday & Tuesday the second & third of April next the Treasurer be directed to pay no higher or greater sum than fifty dollars or the value thereof to any one person & that in every payment he deliver three pence in copper half pence or farthings for each twenty shillings of such payment, or such greater proportion of Copper as the person exchanging shall desire, and that he deliver a proportion of hammer'd money to the milled according to the quantity of each now in the Treasury & such proportion of the bills ordered to be Emitted as any person shall desire. In the House of Represent^ves Read & Non Concur'd"—*Ibid.*

Chap. 17. "January 4. 1749. The House of Represent^ves having sent a Message to enquire whether the Board had proceded on the Bill for supplying the Treasury and being answered that it was Nonconcurr'd, desired that it might be sent down and it was sent down accordingly: And then A Message was brought up from the House of Represent^ves by Joseph Buckminster Esqr and others, with the Supply Bill, & for moving the Board to reconsider their Vote of Nonconcurrence thereon And the Board accordingly appointed to consider the said Message tomorrow at eleven o'clock in the forenoon."—*Ibid., p* 116.

"January 5. 1749. The Board in compliance with the Message sent up from the House yesterday. Voted to reconsider their Vote of Nonconcurrence on the Supply Bill, and after further debate had on the said Bill, again Nonconcur'd the Vote for Engrossing the same, and thereupon Voted to send down to the House the following Message viz,

The Board in compliance with the desire of the House, have voted a Reconsideration, of the Vote of Nonconcurrence on the Supply Bill, and after a further debate on said Bill, have again Nonconcur'd the Vote of the Honble House for Engrossing the same. But inasmuch as the Board differ from the House, on that part of the Bill only, which respects the issueing any part of the Silver in the Treasury before the time appointed by Law for issuing the whole; and being desirous of preserving that Harmony which has always subsisted between the two Houses do therefore propose a free Conference on the Subject aforesaid by Committees, if the Honble House think proper or otherwise between the two Houses

A Message was thereupon brought up from the House by Cpt John Tyng, that they agree to the above proposal of a Conference between both Houses on the Supply Bill & move that it may be had this Afternoon— Voted that Jacob Wendell, Benjamin Lynde, John Quincy, Andrew Oliver & Thomas Hutchinson Esqrs be Managers for the Board at said Conference——The House of Representves coming up to the Council Chamber, the two Houses attended the said Conference; and one of the Managers for the Board opening the Subject matter thereof, the Managers for the House disagreed to it; and after some debate thereon, Mr Speaker & the House return'd to their Chamber."—*Ibid., p.* 117.

"January 18. 1749. The following Message was sent down to the House of Representves by Josiah Willard Esqr & others viz, The Board observe with some concern the great Earnestness with which the Honble House have urged a Concurrence on the Bill for Supply of the Treasury; And altho it appears unusual & Unparliamentary thus repeatedly to send up the same Bill in the same Session, yet the Board to prevent as much as may be all Misunderstanding between the two Houses, have again taken the Bill into consideration, but have Voted a Non Concurrence thereon: The Board would by no means retard any Supply of the Treasury that may be Salutary for the Province; And had not the Bill required the Treasurer to issue the Silver before the thirty first of March next, no Exception had been taken to any other parts thereof"—*Ibid., p.* 131.

"January 20. 1749. An Engross'd Bill entitled An Act for supplying the Treasury with the sum of eighteen thousand four hundred pounds lawfull money for discharging the publick debts &c Having been read three several times in the House of Representves and in Council Pass'd to be Enacted by both Houses."—*Ibid., p.* 133.

"January 22. 1749. His Honor the Lieut. Governor sign'd the Engrost Bill for Supplying the Treasury with the sum of eighteen thousand four hundred pounds &c."—*Ibid., p.* 134.

Chap. 19. "Novemr 23d 1749. And as I can make no doubt but that the Act of this Province for drawing in Our Bills (upon the Faith of which we seem to be distinguished from the other Colonies of New England, respecting the timely Payment of Our Charges in the late Expedition) will be kept inviolate; So I would recommend to you to make such other Provision, as the Exigency of the Case may require, for rendring that Act more effectual for the good Ends designed thereby, especially for preventing the Silver Money going out of the Province, & for encouraging the Growth & Produce of this Province, so as to render us less dependent on the other Colonies for the Necessaries of Life."—*Extract from the Speech of Lieutenant-Governor Phips: Ibid., p.* 67.

"January 6. 1749. In Council, Voted that Samuel Danforth, Andrew Oliver & Thomas Hutchinson Esqrs with such as the Honble House shall join be a Committee to prepare a Bill, for restraining the Currency of English half pence & farthings; and also of all coined Silver & Gold which may probably be Currant after the thirty first of March next, at any higher rate than in proportion to milled dollars at six shillings; & for determining said proportion, the said Committee are also to consider & report some method for providing small money to serve for Change In the House of Representves Read & Concur'd, and Peter Oliver Esqr Coll. Choat, Mr Hubbard, & Coll Appleton are joined in the Affair." —*Ibid., p.* 118.

"January 27. 1749. Samuel Danforth Esqr from the Committee referring to the Copper money & for providing Change &c gave in the following Report.

The Committee appointed to prepare a Bill for restraining the Currency of half pence & farthings & coined Silver & Gold at any higher rate than in proportion to milled Dollars at six shillings, & to consider some method for providing change, having attended the service so far as the other business of the Court would admit, & being apprehensive that the latter part of their Commission is of most immediate necessity, with respect to that humbly report, that a Committee be appointed by this Court; & impowered & directed forthwith to cause to be struck off & signed as soon as may be small bills of the Form & Denominations following viz. *One Quarter Dollar, eighteen pence lawfull money of Massachusetts Bay. A B. Committee* And that there be likewise the several Denominations of one eighth of a dollar or nine pence, one twelfth of a dollar or six pence, one sixteenth of a dollar or four pence half penny, one twenty fourth of a dollar or three pence, one seventy second of a dollar or one penny; and that there be such a proportion of each Denomination as the Committee think best; and that the whole sum amount to & do not exceed three thousand pounds lawfull money; and that the same be delivered to the Treasurer, and that he pay the same out of the Treasury in exchange for the bills of credit now outstanding, or in discharge of any Warrants drawn on him, to such persons as are willing to receive the same at par with lawfull money, and that he likewise pay out the same in exchange for Milled Dollars to such persons as are desirous thereof. The Committee further report, that in order effectually to establish the value of said Bills, the Treasurer be directed to reserve in his hand the sum of three thousand pounds in milled dollars at six shillings pr dollar, to be & remain as a Fund & Security for the Bills aforesaid, & when soever any possessor of the said bills shall bring to the Treasurer any sums that shall be equal to one two or any other number of Dollars, he shall be obliged forthwith to exchange the said bills with dollars according to their Denomination. The Committee ask leave to sit again, & prepare a Bill agreable to the first part of their Commission; and report the same at the next Sitting of the Court; which is humbly submitted

By order of the Committee Saml Danforth In the House of Representatives. Read and Accepted. In Council Read & Concur'd Consented to by the Lieut Govern^r"—*Ibid., p.* 142.

"From an aversion to a silver currency, the body of the people changed in a few months and took an aversion to paper, though it had silver as a fund to secure the value of it. A sufficient quantity of small silver for change could not be procured in England, when the grant made by parliament was sent to America. The assembly, therefore, ordered a deposit to remain in the treasury, of three thousand pounds in dollars, and issued small paper bills of different denominations, from one penny to eighteen pence; and every person, possessed of them to the amount of one dollar or any larger sum, might exchange the bills at the treasury for silver upon demand. The whole sum was prepared, but a small part only was issued, and scarcely any person would receive them in payment, choosing rather a base coin imported from Spain, called pistorines, at 20 per cent, more than the intrinsic value."—*Hutchinson's Hist. Mass., vol.* 3, *p.* 9.

"March 29. 1750 A petition of Rogers & Fowle of Boston Printers, shewing that they have procured & printed an exact Original Table, for stating the rate & proportion of the bills of credit in lawfull Silver money, & in other Silver & Gold coin, praying for the sole privilege of vending said Table for one year In the House of Represent^ves Read & Committed to the Gentlemen appointed to consider the stating of the Currencies &c In Council, Read & Non Concur'd."—*Council Records, vol. XIX., p.* 152.

"March 29. 1750. A petition of Samuel Kneeland of Boston, printer, praying that the petition of Rogers & Fowle for the sole privilege of printing their money Table may not be granted, or if the Court should think fit to grant it that the petitioner may have the sole privilege of printing a Table which he has procured to be made called the Countryman's Table &c In the House of Represent^ves Read & Ordered that this petition be committed to the Gentlemen appointed to consider the Stating of the Currencies and report thereon In Council, Read & Non Concur'd.—*Ibid., pp.* 152 *and* 153.

"January 30 1751 In the House of Represent^ves; Ordered that the Treasurer be directed in paying the Silver out of the Treasury to pay the Halves & Quarter & Eighths & Sixteenths of Dollars in Proportion to the Silver that is still left in the Treasury. In Council; Read & Concur'd——Consented to by the Lieu^t Govr"—*Ibid., p.* 289.

"This taxes the rate of Money more fully than in the Act of the 22nd of his present Majesty therein referred to or by the Act of the 6th of Queen Anne which must be submitted to Your Lordships."—*Report of Mr. Lamb, to the Board of Trade:* "*Mass. Bay, B. T., vol.* 73, *G. g.* 44," *in Public Record Office.*

Chap. 20. "This Act which relates to the reall Estates of Intestates is agreeable to the Law at present subsisting in this and some other Provinces, tho' not to the Law of England."—*Ibid.*

Chap. 21. "June 6 1749. In the House of Repres^ves. Ordered that Mr Speaker; Coll Heath Col^o Choate, Mr Hubbard, Mr Hall, Cpt Allen. Mr Frost Capt^t Little & Capt White with such as the Honble Board shall join be a committee to consider of some proper Encouragement for improving of the natural advantages of the Soil & Climate & better improving the Fishery & employing the Inhabitants of this Province to the best Advantage, & for having a proper Duty upon Commodities imported unnecessary to the Inhabitants of the Province

In Council; Read and Concur'd; and Sir Wm Pepperell, Jeremiah Moulton Samuel Watts John Quincy John Chandler Ezekiel Cheever, Andrew Oliver Joseph Punchon & Thomas Hutchinson Esq^rs are joined in the affair"—*Council Records, vol. XIX., p.* 7.

"Novem^r 24 1749. In Council; Ordered that Joseph Wilder & James Minot Esq^rs be upon the Committee of both Houses appointed to consider of some proper Encouragement for Improving the natural Advantages of the Soil & Climate of this Province &^c in the room of Sir William Pepperell, who is gone to England, & Jeremiah Moulton Esqr who probably will not be here this Session, & that the said Committee meet as soon as may be, & report thereon,—

In the House of Represent^ves; Read & Concur'd"—*Ibid., p.* 69.

"Decem^r 20. 1749. In the House of Represent^ves Ordered that Mr Speaker, Col^o Storer, Capt. Pierson, Col^o Willard, & Mr Hubbard, with such as the Honble Board shall Join be a Committee to consider & project what Duty will be proper to be laid upon the unnecessary Commodities imported & consumed within this Province:—In Council; Read & Concur'd, And Jacob Wendell, Samuel Watts John Chandler & Andrew Oliver Esq^rs are Joined in the Affair."—*Ibid., p.* 94.

"This Act lays a duty by way of excise upon severall Comodities therein mentioned which seems to be intended to be laid upon and to be paid by the Retailer—As there is a provisoe that all and every persons that shall import any of the Comodities may sell and dispose of the same within this Province to such as are licensed to sell & retail the same *and no other person* without being subject to the penalty of this Act, But tho' the Importer may sell the same *to the Retailer,* without being subject to the penalty, Yet as he is restrained from selling *to any other person* And as this Restraint may be a prejudice to the Importer in this respect, as well as to the price of his goods that he sells to the Retailer, who is afterwards to pay an excise upon them, And therefore lessens the value of the goods imported, I must submitt it to your Lordships if this excise will not affect the trade of this Kingdom and fall within the meaning of the 16th Article of the Governour's Instructions."—*Report of Mr. Lamb, to the Board of Trade:* "*Mass. Bay, B. T., vol.* 73, *G. g.* 44," *in Public Record Office.*

"With respect to the following Act * * * * * * We must observe to Your Lordships that Mr Lambe has reported to us [here follows the above report] By the 16th Article of His Majestys Instructions to His Governor of the Massachusetts Bay, referr'd to by Mr.

Lamb, the said Governor is required "not to pass or give his Assent to any Bill of un-"usual or extraordinary nature and importance whereby His Majesty's Prerogative or "the property of His subjects may be prejudiced, or the trade or shipping of this King-"dom any ways affected untill he shall have transmitted to His Majesty the draught of "such Bill or Bills and shall have received His Royal Pleasure thereupon unless he shall "take care in the passing of any Bill of such nature as before mentioned that there be a "Clause inserted therein suspending and deferring the execution thereof until His Majes-"ty's pleasure shall be known concerning the same" And it is also further expressly declared "that no Duty shall be laid upon British Shipping or upon the Products or "Manufactures of Great Britain" And as this Law lays a Duty upon several Commodities imported from this Kingdom whereby the Trade thereof will be manifestly prejudiced and affected, contrary to the Tenor of the said Instruction, We submit to Your Lordships whether this Act should not receive His Majesty's Disapprobation.

We are My Lords Your Lordships most obedient and most humble Servants.

DUNK HALIFAX
I. PITT.
J. GRENVILLE."

Whitehall June 4th 1752.

—*Report of Lords of Trade: Ibid., vol.* 84, *p.* 262.

"At the Council Chamber, Whitehall the 30th day of June 1752

Present

Their Excellencys the Lords Justices in Council.

Whereas by Commission under the Great Seal of Great Britain, the Governor Council and Assembly of the Province of Massachusets Bay in New England in America, are authorized and empowered to constitute and ordain Laws which are to continue and be in force unless His Majesty's pleasure be signified to the contrary—And whereas in pursuance of the said Commission a Law was passed in the said Province in April 1750 Entituled as follows. viz[t]:—

"An Act for granting unto His Majesty an Excise upon sundry Articles hereafter "enumerated for and towards the support of His Majesty's Government of this Province"

Which said Law having been under the consideration of the Lords Commissrs for Trade and Plantations and also of a Committee of the Lords of His Majesty's most Honourable Privy Council, The said Lords of the Committee this day presented the said Law to their Excellencys at this Board with their Opinion, that the same out to be Repealed. Their Excellencys the Lords Justices taking the same into consideration were pleased with the advice of His Majesty's Privy Council, to declare their disallowance of the said Law. And pursuant to their Excellency's Pleasure thereupon expressed the said Law is hereby repealed, declared void and of none effect. Whereby the Governor or Commander in Chief of the said Province for the time being and all others whom it may concern are to take notice and govern themselves accordingly

A true copy W SHARPE."—*Ibid., vol.* 73, *G. g.* 46.

Chap. 24. "A tragedy* was performed at the British coffee house in Boston by two young Englishmen, assisted by some comrades from the town. The novelty of the exhibition attracted great numbers of people into King Street, where, in a pressure for admittance, disturbances arose, which rendered the affair notorious. The legislature, at its next session, for the preservation of the system of economy and purity, which had been thus far transmitted from the forefathers, made a law, prohibiting theatrical entertainments. The reasons, assigned in the preamble to the act, are: 'to prevent and avoid the 'many great mischiefs which arise from public stage plays, interludes, and other theatrical 'entertainments, which not only occasion great and unnecessary expences, and discourage 'industry and frugality, but likewise tend greatly to increase impiety and a contempt for 'religion.'"—*Holmes's Annals, vol.* 2, *p.* 184.

* Otway's "Orphan, or Unhappy Marriage."

ACTS,

PASSED 1750–51.

ACTS

Passed at the Session begun and held at Boston, on the Thirtieth day of May, A. D. 1750.

CHAPTER 1.

AN ACT FOR IMPOWERING THE PROVINCE TREASURER TO BORROW THE SUM OF FIVE THOUSAND POUNDS, FOR APPLYING THE SAME TO DISCHARGE THE DEBTS OF THE PROVINCE AND DEFREY THE CHARGES OF GOVERNMENT, AND FOR MAKING PROVISION FOR THE REPAYMENT OF THE SUM SO BORROWED.

Be it enacted by the Lieutenant-Governour, Council and House of Representatives,

[Sect. 1.] That the treasurer of this province be and hereby is impowered to borrow from such person or persons as shall appear ready to lend the same, a sum not exceeding five thousand pounds in Spanish mill'd dollars; and the sum so borrowed shall be a stock in the treasury, to be applyed for defreying the charges of this government in manner as in this act is after directed, and for every sum so borrowed, the treasurer shall give a receipt of the form following; viz.,— Treasurer empowered to borrow £5,000 for the province.

Province of the Massachusetts Bay, day of 17 , received from the sum of pounds, for the use and service of the Province of the Massachusetts Bay; and in behalf of said Province, I do hereby promise and oblige myself and my successors in the office of treasurer, to repay the said , his heirs or assigns, on or before the tenth day of June, one thousand seven hundred and fifty-two, the aforesaid sum of pounds, with interest for the same, at and after the rate of six per cent per annum. Witness my hand, , Treasurer. Form of his receipt for said money.

—and no receipt shall be given for any sum less than fifty pounds; and the treasurer is hereby directed to use his discretion in borrowing said sum at such times as that he may be enabled to comply with the draughts that may be made on the treasury in pursuance of this act.

And be it further enacted,

[Sect. 2.] That the aforesaid sum of five thousand pounds shall be issued out of the treasury in manner and for the purposes following; viz., the sum of seventeen hundred and fifty pounds, part of the aforesaid sum of five thousand pounds, shall be applyed for the service of the several forts and garrisons within this province, pursuant to such orders and grants as are or shall be made by this court for those purposes; and the further sum of one thousand pounds, part of the aforesaid sum of five thousand pounds, shall be applyed for the purchasing provisions and the commissary's necessary disbursements for the service of the several forts and garrisons within this province, pursuant to such grants £1,750 appropriated for forts and garrisons. £1,000 for commissary's stores.

as are or shall be made by this court for those purposes; and the further sum of six hundred pounds, part of the aforesaid sum of five thousand pounds, shall be applyed for the payment of such premiums and grants that now are, or hereafter may be made by this court; and the further sum of nine hundred pounds, part of the aforesaid sum of five thousand pounds, shall be applyed for the discharging other debts owing from this province to persons that have served or shall serve them by order of this court, in such matters and things where there is no establishment nor any certain sum assign'd for such service, and for paper, writing and printing for this court; and the sum of six hundred pounds, part of the aforesaid sum of five thousand pounds, shall be applyed for the payment of his majesty's council and house of representatives, serving in the general court during the several sessions for this present year.

£600 for premiums and grants.

£900 for debts where there is no establishment.

£600 for the members of the court.

And whereas there are sometimes contingent and unforeseen charges that demand prompt pay,—

Be it further enacted,

£150 for contingent charges.

[SECT. 3.] That the sum of one hundred and fifty pounds, being the remaining part of the aforesaid sum of five thousand pounds, be applyed to pay such contingent charges, and for no other purpose whatever.

And in order to enable the treasurer effectually to discharge the receipts and obligations by him given in pursuance of this act,—

Be it enacted,

Duty of impost and excise made a fund for repayment of said £5,000.

[SECT. 4.] That the duty of impost and excise for the year one thousand seven hundred and fifty-one, shall be applyed for the payment and discharge of the principle and interest that shall be due on said receipts and obligations, and to no other purpose whatever.

And as a further fund and security for drawing the said sum of five thousand pounds into the treasury again,—

Be it further enacted,

Tax of £5,000, for further security, to be levied in the year 1751.

[SECT. 5.] That there be and hereby is granted unto his most excellent majesty, a tax of five thousand pounds, to be levied on polls, and estates real and personal, within this province, according to such rules and in such proportion on the several towns and districts within the same, as shall be agreed on and ordered by the general court of this province at their session in May, one thousand seven hundred and fifty-one, which sum shall be paid into the treasury on or before the tenth day of February next after.

Be it further enacted,

Tax for the money hereby emitted, to be made according to the preceding tax act, in case.

[SECT. 6.] That in case the general court shall not, at their session in May, and before the twentieth day of June, one thousand seven hundred and fifty-one, agree and conclude upon an act apportioning the sum which by this act is engaged shall be, in said year, apportioned, assess'd and levied, that then and in such case, each town and district within this province shall pay, by a tax to be levied on the polls, and estates both real and personal, within their districts, the same proportion of the said sum as the said towns and districts shall have been taxed by the general court in the tax act then last preceeding: *saving* what relates to the pay of the representatives, which shall be assess'd on the several towns they represent; and the province treasurer is hereby fully impowered and directed, some time in the month of June, in the year one thousand seven hundred and fifty-one, to issue and send forth his warrants, directed to the selectmen or assessors of each town and district within this province, requiring them to assess the polls, and estates both real and personal, within their several towns and districts, for their respective part and proportion of the sum before directed and engaged to be assess'd, and also for the fines upon the several towns that have not sent a representative; and the assessors, as also the persons assessed, shall observe, be governed by, and subject to all such rules and directions as shall have been given in the last preceeding tax act.

Provided always,—

[Sect. 7.] That the remainder of the sum which shall be brought into the treasury by the duties of impost and excise for the year one thousand seven hundred and fifty-one, and the tax of five thousand pounds ordered by this act to be assess'd and levied, over and above what shall be sufficient to discharge the receipts and obligations aforesaid, shall be and remain as a stock in the treasury, to be applyed as the general court of this province shall hereafter order, and to no other purpose whatsoever, anything in this act to the contrary notwithstanding. Remainder to be and remain as a stock in the treasury.

And be it further enacted,

[Sect. 8.] That the treasurer is hereby directed and ordered to pay the sum of five thousand pounds, borrowed as aforesaid, out of such appropriations as shall be directed to by warrant, and no other, upon pain of refunding all such sum or sums as he shall otherwise pay; and the secretary to whom it belongs to keep the muster-rolls and accompts of charge, shall lay before the house of representatives, when they direct, such muster-rolls and accompts after payment thereof. [*Passed June* 21; *published June* 30. Money to be paid out of the proper appropriations.

CHAPTER 2.

AN ACT FOR GRANTING THE SUM OF THREE HUNDRED POUNDS FOR THE SUPPORT OF HIS HONOUR THE LIEUTENANT-GOVERNOUR AND COMMANDER-IN-CHIEF.

Be it enacted by the Lieutenant-Governour, Council and House of Representatives,

That the sum of three hundred pounds, be and hereby is granted unto his most excellent majesty, to be paid out of the publick treasury to his honour Spencer Phips, Esq[r]., lieutenant-governour and commander-in-chief in and over his majesty's province of the Massachusetts Bay, for his past services, and further to enable him to manage the publick affairs of the province. [*Passed June* 29*; *published June* 30. Grant to the governor.

CHAPTER 3.

AN ACT IN EXPLANATION OF AN ACT MADE AND PASSED IN THE EIGHTEENTH YEAR OF HIS PRESENT MAJESTY'S REIGN, ENTITULED "AN ACT FOR GRANTING TO HIS MAJESTY A DUTY OF TONNAGE ON SHIPPING."

Whereas in and by an act made and pass'd in the eighteenth year of his present majesty's reign, entitled "An Act for granting to his majesty a duty of tonnage on shipping," the treasury of this province was supplied with the sum of eight thousand pounds, in bills of credit, for building and maintaining a ship of twenty guns; and in consideration of the advantage of such a ship to the trade of the province, certain Preamble. 1744-45, chap. 22.

* From the record: the date given in the parchment is June 30.

rates and duties on shipping were by said act granted to be paid for the term of seven years, and as much longer as the war should continue, in order to draw into the treasury the said sum of eight thousand pounds, and to maintain said ship during the war. *And whereas*, a peace was concluded before the expiration of said term of seven years, and the sum that has already been rais'd by the duty aforesaid, together with the sum said ship may be sold for, will be sufficient to draw into the treasury the said sum of eight thousand pounds; and it appears to be contrary to the true intent and design of the act aforesaid, that a burthen should be continued on the trade for any longer term than during said ship's being advantageous to it,—

Be it therefore enacted by the Lieutenant-Governour, Council and House of Representatives,

Act for tonnage on shipping to expire upon the publication of this act.

That from and after the publication of this act, each and every of the rates and duties imposed on shipping by the act made and pass'd in the eighteenth year of his present majesty's reign as aforesaid, shall determine and cease, altho' the term of seven years from the publication of the said act be not expired; any construction that may be put on said act, or any part thereof, to the contrary notwithstanding. [*Passed June* 14; *published June* 30.

CHAPTER 4.

AN ACT FOR CONTINUING SEVERAL LAWS OF THIS PROVINCE, IN THIS [*ACT**] MENTIONED, WHICH ARE NEAR EXPIRING.

Preamble.

1749-50, chap. 3.

1745-46, chap. 7.

1745-46, chap. 5.

1744-45, chap. 26.

WHEREAS an act was made and pass'd in the twenty-third year of his present majesty's reign, intitled "An Act to prevent the disturbance given the general court by the passing of coaches, chaises, carts, trucks and othe[*r**] carriages by the province court-house"; and another act was made and pass'd in the eighteenth and nineteenth years of his present majesty's reign, [i][*e*]ntitled "An Act to prevent unnecessary cost being allowed to parties and witnesses in the several courts of justice within this province"; and another act was made and pass'd in the eighteenth and nineteenth years of his present majesty's reign, [i][*e*]ntitled "An Act for encouraging the killing of wolves, bears, wildcats and catamounts within this province"; and another act was made and pass'd in the eighteenth year of his present majesty's reign, [i][*e*]ntitled "An Act to prevent neat cattle and horses running at large and feeding on the beaches adjoining to Eastern harbour meadows in the town of Truro";—which several laws ar[*e**] near expiring; and the said laws have by experience been found beneficial, and necessary for the several purposes for which they were passed,—

Be it therefore enacted by the Lieutenant-Governour, Council and House of Represent[*ati*]*ves*,

Said laws continued.

Saving.

That each of the afore-recited acts, and every matter and clause therein contained (saving that the several penalties in said acts mentioned, which were payable in bills of the last emission, shall be understood in this act to be a sum in lawful money equal to said sum in last emission bills), be and hereby are continued and to remain in force for the space of five years from the time in them severally limited for their expiration, and from thence to the end of the then next session of the general court and no longer. [*Passed June* 28; *published June* 30.

* These letters are missing from the parchment, which is mutilated.

CHAPTER 5.

AN ACT IN ADDITION TO THE ACT FOR THE BETTE[*R**] REGULATING SWINE.

Whereas in and by an act made and pass'd in the twentieth year of [*his**] present majesty's reign, entitled "An Act for the better regulating swine," it is, [*am**]ong other things, enacted, "That from and after the publication thereof, no swine shall be suffered to go at large, or be out of the inclosure of the owner thereof," under certain penalties in said act mentioned; "*Provided nevertheless*, That it shall be in the power of any town, in a town-meeting for that purpose appointed, from time to time, by a vote, to give liberty for swine going at large within the bounds of such town; and in such case, it shall be lawful for any and every person and persons to suffer his or their swine to go at large"; *and whereas* the power therein granted to the several towns of assembling for giving liberty for swine to go at large is not restrained to any particular time of the year; by reason whereof some towns have been, sundry times, called together for that purpose in different, and sometimes in busy, seasons of the year, whereby their private affairs and business have been interrupted, and much time needles[s]ly expended, and contentions raised among the inhabitants; for the prevention whereof for the future,— Preamble. 1746-47, chap. 26, § 1. 1746-47, chap. 26, § 2.

Be it enacted by the Lieuten[*an*]*t-Governo*[*u*]*r, Council and House of Represent*[*ati*]*ves,*

[Sect. 1.] That from and after the publication of this act, the power of the several towns of granting liberty for swine to go at large, be and the same is hereby restrained to the month of March, in the several years during which the said act is to continue in force, and to the anniversary meeting for the choice of town-officers in the same month, at which time it shall be lawful[l] for any town to give liberty for swine to go at large during the whole or such part of the year as shall be judged most for the benefit of the inhabitants. Power of towns, for granting liberty for swine to go at large, limited.

And whereas the situation and circumstances of the different parts of some towns may be such, as that it may be convenient that swine go at large in one part, and not so in another part of the same town,— Preamble.

Be it therefore further enacted,

[Sect. 2.] That when the inhabitants of any tow[*n**] within this province shall judge it most convenient for swine to go at large in so[*me**] certain part or parts only of the town, such town is hereby impowered (under t[*he**] aforementioned restriction as to time) to grant liberty for swine to go at lar[*ge**] within such limits as shall be assigned for that purpose by the town; and if any swine shall be found going at large without such limits, either of place or time, as shall be so assigned, the owner or owners thereof shall incur the penalties by [*the**] act aforesaid in such case already provided. Limits for swine going at large.

[Sect. 3.] This act to continue in force until the end of the sitting of the general court in May, [*An**]*no Domini*, one thousand seven hundred and fifty-seven, and no longer. [*Passed and published June* 30. Limitation.

* These letters are missing from the parchment, which is mutilated.

CHAPTER 6.

AN ACT FOR GRANTING TO HIS MAJESTY SEVERAL RATES AND DUTIES OF IMPOST AND TONNAGE OF SHIPPING.

WE, his majesty's most loyal and dutiful subjects, the representatives of the province of the Massachusetts Bay, in New England, being desirous of a colateral fund and security for drawing in part of a tax of eighteen thousand four hundred pounds granted the last year, have chearfully and unanimously given and granted, and do hereby give and grant, to his most excellent majesty, to the end and use aforesaid, and to no other use, the several duties of impost upon wines, liquors, goods, wares and merchandize that shall be imported into this province, and tunnage of shipping, hereafter mentioned; and pray that it may be enacted,—

And be it accordingly enacted by the Lieutenant-Governour, Council and House of Representatives,

[SECT. 1.] That from and after the publication of this act, and during the space of one year, there shall be paid by the importer of all wines, liquors, goods, wares and merchandize that shall be imported into this province from the place of their growth (salt, cotton-wool, pig-iron, provisions, and every other thing of the growth and produce of New England, and also all prize goods condemned in any part of this province, excepted), the several rates or duties of impost following; viz[t].,—

For every pipe of wine of the Western Islands, ten shillings and eightpence.

For every pipe of Medara, twelve shillings.

For every pipe of other sorts not mentioned, twelve shillings.

For every hogshead of rum, containing one hundred gallons, nine shillings.

For every hogshead of sugar, threepence.

For every hogshead of molasses, twopence.

For every hogshead of tobacco, five shillings and sixpence.

For every ton of logwood, fourpence.

—And so, proportionably, for greater or lesser quantities.

And all other commodities, goods or merchandize not mentioned or excepted, fourpence for every twenty shillings value: all goods imported from Great Britain, and hogshead and barrell-staves and heads from any of his majesty's colonies and provinces on this continent, excepted.

[SECT. 2.] And for any of the above wines, liquors, goods, wares and merchandize, et[a]., that shall be imported into this province from the port of their growth and produce, by any of the inhabitants of the other provinces or colonies on this continent, or the English West-India Islands, or in any ship or vessell to them belonging, on the proper account of any of the said inhabitants of the other provinces or colonies on this continent, or of the inhabitants of any of the English West-Indea Islands, there shall be paid by the importer double the impost appointed by this act to be received for every species above mentioned; and for all rum, sugar and molasses imported and brought into this province in any ship or vessell, or by land-carriage, from any of the colonies of Connecticutt, New Hampshire or Rhode Island, shall be paid by the importer, the rates and duties following:—

For every hogshead of rum, containing one hundred gallons, twenty shillings.

For every hogshead of molasses, containing one hundred gallons, eightpence.

For every hogshead of sugar, containing one thousand weight, one shilling.

—And in that proportion for more or less thereof: *provided always*, that all European goods, and for all other goods, wares and merchandize, eightpence for every twenty shillings value; all hogshead and barrell-staves and heading from any of his majesty's provinces or colonies, all provisions and other things that are the growth of New England, all salt, cotton-wool and pig-iron are and shall be exempted from every the rates and duties aforesaid.

[Sect. 3.] Impost rates and duties shall be paid in current lawful money, by the importer of any wines, liquors, goods or merchandize, unto the commissioner to be appointed, as is hereinafter to be directed, for entring and recieving the same, at or before the landing of any wines, liquors, goods or merchandize: only the commissioner or reciever is hereby allowed to give credit to such person or persons, where his or their duty of impost, in one ship or vessell, doth exceed the sum of three pounds; and in cases where the commissioner or reciever shall give credit, he shall ballance and settle his accounts with every person on or before the last day of April, so that the same accounts may be ready to be produced in court in May next after. And all entries, where the impost or duties to be paid doth not exceed three shillings, shall be made without charge to the importer; and not more than sixpence to be demanded for any other single entry to what value soever.

And be it further enacted,

[Sect. 4.] That the master of every ship or vessell coming into this province from any other place, shall, within twenty-four hours after his arrival in any port or harbour, and before bulk is broken, make report and deliver a manifest, in writing, under his hand, to the commissioner aforesaid, of the contents of the loading of such ship or vessell, therein particularly expressing the species, kind and quantities of all the wines, liquors, goods, wares and merchandize imported in such ship or vessell, with the marks and numbers thereof, and to whom the same are consigned; and make oath before the said commissioner that the same manifest contains a just and true account of all the load taken on board and imported in such ship or vessell, and so far as he knows or believes; and that if he knows of any more wines, liquors, goods, wares or merchandize loaden on board such ship or vessell, and imported therein, he will forthwith make report thereof to the commissioner aforesaid, and cause the same to be added to his manifest.

And be it further enacted,

[Sect. 5.] That if the master of any such ship or vessell shall break bulk, or suffer any of the wines, liquors, goods, wares and merchandize imported in such ship or vessell to be unloaden before report and entry thereof be made as aforesaid, he shall forfeit the sum of one hundred pounds.

And be it further enacted by the authority aforesaid,

[Sect. 6.] That all merchants and other persons, being owners of any wines, liquors, goods, wares and merchandize imported into this province, for which any of the rates or duties aforesaid are payable, or having consigned to them, shall make a like entry thereof with the commissioner aforesaid, and produce an invoice of all such goods as pay *ad valorem*, and make oath before him in form following; vizt.,—

You, A. B., do swear that the entry of the goods and merchandize by you now made, exhibits the present price of said goods at this market, and that, *bonâ fide*, according to your best skill and judgment, is not less than the real value thereof. So help you God.

—which oath the commissioner or reciever is hereby impowered to administer; and they shall pay the duty or impost by this act required, before such wines, liquors, goods, wares or merchandize be landed or taken out of the vessell in which the same shall be imported.

[SECT. 7.] And no wines, liquors, goods, wares or merchandize that by this act are liable to pay impost or duty, shall be landed on any wharffe, or into any warehouse or other place, but in the daytime only, and that after sunrize and before sunset, unless in the presence and with the consent of the commissioner or reciever, on pain of forfeiting all such wines, liquors, goods, wares and merchandize, and the lighter, boat or vessell out of which the same shall be landed or put into any warehouse or other place.

[SECT. 8.] And if any person or persons shall not have and produce an invoice of the quantities of rum or liquors to him or them consigned, then the cask wherein the same is, shall be gaged at the charge of the importer, that the contents thereof may be known.

And be it further enacted,

[SECT. 9.] That the importer of all wines, liquors, goods, wares and merchandize, within one year after the publication of this act, by land-carriage, or in small vessells or boats, shall make report and deliver a manifest thereof to the commissioner aforesaid or his deputy, therein particularly expressing the species, kind and quantity of all such wines, liquors, goods, wares and merchandize so imported, with the marks and numbers thereof, when, how and by whom brought; and shall make oath, before the said commissioner or his deputy, to the truth of such report and manifest, and shall also pay the several duties aforesaid by this act charged and chargeable upon such wines, liquors, goods, wares and merchandize, before the same are landed, housed or put into any store or place whatever.

And be it further enacted,

[SECT. 10.] That every merchant or other person importing any wines into this province, shall be allowed twelve per cent for leakage: *provided,* such wines shall not have been filled up on board; and that every hogshead, but or pipe of wine that hath two-thirds thereof leaked out, shall be accounted for outs, and the merchant or importer to pay no duty for the same. And no master of any ship or vessell shall suffer any wines to be filled up on board without giving a certificate of the quantity so filled up, under his hand, before the landing thereof, to the commissioner or reciever of impost for such port, on pain of forfeiting the sum of one hundred pounds.

[SECT. 11.] And if it may be made to appear that any wines imported in any ship or vessell be decayed at the time of unlading thereof, or in twenty days afterwards, oath being made before the commissioner or reciever that the same hath not been landed above that time, the duties and impost paid for such wines shall be repaid unto the importer thereof.

And be it further enacted,

[SECT. 12.] That the master of every ship or vessell importing any wines, liquors, goods, wares or merchandize, shall be liable to and shall pay the impost for such and so much thereof, contained in his manifest, as shall not be duly entered, nor the duty paid for the same by the person or persons to whom such wines, liquors, goods, wares or merchandize are or shall be consigned. And it shall and may be lawful, to and for the master of every ship or other vessell, to secure and detain in his hands, at the owner's risque, all such wines, liquors, goods, wares and merchandize imported in any ship or vessell, until he receives a certificate, from the commissioner or reciever of the impost, that the duty for the same is paid, and until he be repaid his necessary charges in securing the same; or such master may deliver such wines, liquors, goods, wares or merchandize as are not entred, in to the commissioner or reciever of the impost in such port, or his order, who is hereby impowered and directed to recieve and keep the same, at the owner's risque, until the impost thereof, with the charges, be paid; and then to deliver such wines, liquors, goods, wares or merchandize as such master shall direct.

And be it further enacted,

[Sect. 13.] That the commissioner or reciever of the impost in each port, shall be and hereby is impowered to sue the master of any ship or vessell, for the impost or duty of so much of the lading of any wines, liquors, goods, wares or merchandize imported therein, according to the manifest to be by him given upon oath, as aforesaid, as shall remain not entered and the duty of impost therefor not paid. And where any goods, wares or merchandize are such as that the value thereof is not known, whereby the impost to be recovered of the master, for the same, cannot be ascertained, the owner or person to whom such goods, wares or merchandize are or shall be consigned, shall be summoned to appear as an evidence at the court where such suit for the impost and the duty thereof shall be brought, and be there required to make oath to the value of such goods, wares or merchandize.

And be it further enacted,

[Sect. 14.] That the ship or vessell, with her tackle, apparrell and furniture, the master of which shall make default in anything by this act required to be performed by him, shall be liable to answer and make good the sum or sums forfeited by such master, according to this act, for any such default, as also to make good the impost or duty for any such wines, liquors, goods, wares or merchandize not entred as aforesaid; and, upon judgment recovered against such master, the said ship or vessell, and so much of the tackle or appurtenances thereof as shall be sufficient to satisfy said judgment, may be taken into execution for the same; and the commissioner or reciever of the impost is hereby impowered to make seizure of the said ship or vessell, and detain the same under seizure until judgment be given in any suit to be commenced and prosecuted for any of the said forfeitures or impost; to the intent that, if judgment be rendered for the prosecutor or informer, such ship or vessell and appurtenances may be exposed to sale, for satisfaction thereof, as is before provided: *unless* the owners, or some on their behalf, for the releasing of such ship or vessell from under seizure or restraint, shall give sufficient security unto the commissioner or reciever of impost that seized the same, to respond and satisfy the sum or value of the forfeiture and duties, with charges, that shall be recovered against the master thereof, upon such suit to be brought for the same, as aforesaid; and the master occasioning such loss or damage unto his owners, through his default or neglect, shall be liable unto their action for the same.

And be it further enacted,

[Sect. 15.] That the naval officer within any of the ports of this province shall not clear or give passes to any master of any ship or other vessell, outward bound, until he shall be certified, by the commissioner or reciever of the impost, that the duty and impost for the goods last imported in such ship or vessell are paid or secured to be paid.

[Sect. 16.] And the commissioner or reciever of the impost is hereby impowered to allow bills of store to the master of any ship or vessell importing any wines or liquors, for such private adventures as shall belong to the master or seamen of such ship or vessell, at the discretion of the commissioner or reciever, not exceeding three per cent of the lading; and duties payable by this act for such wines and liquors, in such bills of stores mentioned and expressed, shall be abated.

And for the more effectual preventing any wines, rum or other distill'd spirits being brought into the province from the neighbouring governments, by land, or in small boats or vessells, or any other way, and also to prevent wines, rum or other distill'd spirits being first sent out of this province, to save the duty of impost, and afterwards brought into the government again,—

Be it enacted,

[SECT. 17.] That the commissioner and reciever of the aforesaid duties of impost shall, and he is hereby impowered and enjoyned to, appoint one suitable person or persons as his deputy or deputys, in all such places in this province where it is likely that wine, rum or other distilled spirits will be brought out of other governments into this; which officers shall have power to seize the same, unless the owner can make it appear that the duty of impost has been paid therefor since their being brought into or relanded in this government; and such officer or officers are also impowered to search, in all suspected places, for such wines, rum and distilled spirits brought or relanded in this government, where the duty is not paid as aforesaid, and to seize and secure the same for the ends and uses as in this act is hereafter provided.

And be it further enacted,

[SECT. 18.] That the commissioner or his deputys shall have full power to administer the several oaths aforesaid, and to search in all suspected places for all such wines, rum, liquors, goods, wares and merchandize as are brought into this province, and landed contrary to the true intent and meaning of this act, and to seize the same for the uses hereinafter mentioned.

And be it further enacted,

[SECT. 19.] That there shall be paid, by the master of every ship or other vessell, coming into any port or ports of this province, to trade or traffick, whereof all the owners are not belonging to this province (except such vessells as belong to Great Britain, the provinces or colonies of Pensilvania, West and East Jersey, Connecticutt, New York, New Hampshire and Rhode Island), every voyage such ship or vessell does make, one pound of good pistol-powder for every ton such ship or vessell is in burthen: *saving* for that part which is owned in Great Britain, this province, or any of the aforesaid governments, which are hereby exempted; to be paid unto the commissioner or reciever of the duties of impost, and to be employed for the ends and uses aforesaid.

[SECT. 20.] And the said commissioner is hereby impowered to appoint a meet and suitable person, to repair unto and on board any ship or vessell, to take the exact measure or tonnage thereof, in case he shall suspect that the register of such ship or vessell doth not express and set forth the full burthen of the same; the charge thereof to be paid by the master or owner of such ship or vessell, before she shall be cleared, in case she shall appear to be of a greater burthen: otherwise, to be paid by the commissioner out of the money received by him for impost, and shall be allowed him, accordingly, by the treasurer, in his accompts. And the naval officer shall not clear any vessell, until he be also certified, by the commissioner, that the duty of tonnage for the same is paid, or that it is such a vessell for which none is payable according to this act.

And be it further enacted,

[SECT. 21.] That when and so often as any wine or rum imported into this province, the duty of impost upon which shall have been paid agreeable to this act, shall be reshipped and exported from this government to any other part of the world, that then, and in every such case, the exporter of such wine or rum shall make oath, at the time of shipping, before the reciever of impost, or his deputy, that the whole of the wine or rum so shipped has, *bonâ fide*, had the aforesaid duties of impost paid on the same, and shall afterwards produce a certificate, from some officer of the customs, that the same has been landed out of this government,—or otherwise, in case such rum or wines shall be exported to any place where there is no officer of the customs, or to any foreign port, the master of the vessell in which the same shall be exported shall make oath that the same has been landed out of the government, and the exporter shall, upon producing such certificate, or upon such oath of the master, make oath that he verily believes no part of said wines or rum has been relanded in this province,—such exporter shall be allowed to draw back from the reciever of impost as follows; vizt.,—

For every pipe of Western-Island wine, eight shillings.

For every pipe of Medara and other sorts, nine shillings.

For an hogshead of rum, eight shillings.

Provided always,—

[Sect. 22.] That if, after reshipping any such rum or wine to be exported as aforesaid, and giving security as aforesaid, in order to obtain the drawback aforesaid, the wine or rum so shipped to be exported, or any part thereof, shall be relanded in this province, or brought into the same from any other province or colony, that then and over and above the penalty of the bond aforesaid, which shall be levyed and recovered to his majesty's use, for the ends the duties aforesaid, are granted, all such rum and wine so relanded and brought again into this province shall be forfeited, and may be seized by the commissioner aforesaid, or his deputy.

And be it further enacted,

[Sect. 23.] That there be one fitt person, and no more, nominated and appointed by this court, as a commissioner and reciever of the aforesaid duties of impost and tunnage of shipping, and for the inspection, care and management of the said office, and whatsoever thereto relates, to recieve commission for the same from the governour or commander-in-chief for the time being, with authority to substitute and appoint a deputy reciever in each port, and other places besides that wherein he resides, and to grant warrants to such deputy recievers for the said place, and to collect and recieve the impost and tunnage of shipping as aforesaid that shall become due within such port, and to render the account thereof, and to pay in the same, to the said commissioner and reciever: which said commissioner and reciever shall keep fair books of all entries and duties arising by virtue of this act; also, a particular account of every vessell, so that the duties of impost and tunnage arising on the said vessell may appear; and the same to lye open, at all seasonable times, to the view and perusal of the treasurer or reciever-general of this province (or any other person or persons whom this court shall appoint), with whom he shall accqunt for all collections and payments, and pay all such monies as shall be in his hands, as the treasurer or reciever-general shall demand it. And the said commissioner or reciever and his deputy or deputys, before their entring upon the execution of their office, shall be sworn to deal truly and faithfully therein, and shall attend in the said office from ten of the clock in the forenoon, until one in the afternoon.

[Sect. 24.] And the said commissioner and reciever, for his labour, care and expences in the said office, shall have and recieve, out of the province treasury, the sum of forty-five pounds per annum; and his deputy or deputys to be paid for their service such sum or sums as the said commissioner and reciever, with the treasurer, shall agree upon, not exceeding five pounds per annum, each; and the treasurer is hereby ordered, in passing and recieving the said commissioner's accounts, accordingly, to allow the payment of such salary or salarys, as aforesaid, to himself and his deputys.

And be it further enacted by the authority aforesaid,

[SECT. 25.] That no duty of impost shall be demanded for any goods imported after the publication of this act, by virtue of any former act for granting unto his majesty any rates and duties of impost, and that all penalties, fines and forfeitures accruing and arising by virtue of any breach of this act, shall be one half to his majesty for the uses and intents for which the abovementioned duties of impost are granted, and the other half to him or them that shall seize, inform and sue for the same, by action, bill, plaint or information, in any of his majesty's courts of record, wherein no essoign, protection or wager of law shall be allowed: the whole charge of the prosecution to be taken out of the half belonging to the informer. [*Passed and published June* 30.

ACTS

PASSED AT THE SESSION BEGUN AND HELD AT BOSTON, ON THE TWENTY-SIXTH DAY OF SEPTEMBER, A. D. 1750.

CHAPTER 7.

AN ACT IN EXPLANATION OF AN ACT MADE IN THE REIGN OF KING WILLIAM THE THIRD, INTITLED "AN ACT FOR REVIEW IN CIVIL CAUSES."

WHEREAS some doubt has arisen, and may arise, whether the act made in the thirteenth year of the reign of King William the Third, intitled "An Act for review in civil causes," extends to judgments given on informations filed by impost officers or their deputies, for the declaration of the forfeiture of goods by them seized,— Preamble. 1701-1702, ch. 6.

Be it therefore enacted by the Lieutenant-Governour, Council and House of Represent[ati]ves,

That the said act doth not, nor ever did, neither ought to be construed to extend to judgments given on such informations. [*Passed October* 6; *published October* 12. Explanation of an act on reviews.

CHAPTER 8.

AN ACT FOR ESTABLISHING AND REGULATING FEES OF THE SEVERAL OFFICERS, WITHIN THIS PROVINCE, AS ARE HEREAFTER MENTIONED.

Be it enacted by the Lieutenant-Governour, Council and House of Representatives, in General Court assembled,

[SECT. 1.] That from and after the publication of this act, the establishment of the fees belonging to the several officers hereafter mentioned, in this province, be as followeth; viz[t].,— Fees established. 1746-47, chap. 24.

JUSTICE'S FEES.

For granting a writ and summons or original summons, one shilling. Justice's fees.
Subp[e][œ]na, for each witness, one penny halfpenny.
Entring an action or complaint, two shillings.
Writ of execution, sixteenpence.
Filing papers, each, one penny halfpenny.
Taxing a bill of cost, threepence.
Entring up judgment in civil or criminal cases, ninepence.
Copy of every evidence, original papers or records, eightpence per page for each page of twenty-eight lines, eight words in a line: if less than a page, fourpence.
Each recognizance or bond of appeal, one shilling.

Taking affidavits out of their own courts in order for the tr[y][*i*]al of any cause, one shilling,—
in other cases, together with certificate, examining and entring, sixpence,—
in perpetuam, to each justice, one shilling.
Acknowledging an instrument with one or more seals, provided it be done at one and the same time, one shilling.
A warrant, one shilling.
For granting a warrant, swearing apprizers relating to strays, and entring the same, one shilling and sixpence.

CORONER'S FEES.

Coroner's fees. For serving a writ, summons or execution, and travelling fees, the same as by this act is hereafter allowed to sheriffs.
Bail bond, one shilling.
Every tryal where the sheriff is concerned, eightpence.
Taking an inquisition, to be paid out of the deceased's estate, eight shillings; if more than one at the same time, twelve shillings in the whole; if no estate, then, to be paid out of the county treasury, five shillings.
For travelling and expences for taking an inquisition, each day, four shillings.
The foreman of the jury, three shillings; and, ten miles accounted a day's travel, one shilling per day;—
every other juror, two shillings and sixpence, and travel the same as the foreman.

JUDGE OF PROBATE'S AND REGISTER'S FEES.

Judge of probate's and register's fees. For granting administration or guardianship,—
to the judge, three shillings.
To the register, for writing letter and bond of administration or guardianship, two shillings and sixpence.
For granting guardianship of divers minors to the same person and at the same time: to the judge, for each minor, one shilling and sixpence; to the register, for each letter of guardianship and bond, as before.
Proving a will or codicil; three shillings and sixpence to the judge, and two shillings and sixpence to the register.
Recording a will, letter of administration or guardianship, inventory or account, of one page, and filing the same, one shilling and threepence;—
for every page more, of twenty-eight lines, of eight words in a line, eightpence.
For copy of a will or inventory, the same for each page, as before.
Allowing accounts; three shillings to the judge. Decree for settling of intestate estates: to the judge, three shillings;—
for examining such accounts, one shilling.
A citation, ninepence.
A *quietus:* to the judge, one shilling; to the register, one shilling.
Warrant or commission for apprizing or dividing estates; one shilling and sixpence to the judge, to the register, one shilling.
Making out commission to rec[ie][*ei*]ve and examine the claims of creditors to insolvent estates; to the judge, one shilling, to the register, one shilling: for recording the same, as before.
Registring the commissioner's report, each page, eightpence.
Making out and entring an order upon the administrators for the distribution of the estate; to the judge, one shilling and sixpence, to the register, one shilling.

For proportioning such estate among the creditors, agre[e]able to the commissioner's return, when the estate exceeds not fifty pounds, three shillings; and, above that sum, four shillings.
For recording the same, eightpence per page.

IN THE SUPERIOUR COURT.

JUSTICE'S FEES.

Justices of the superior court, fees.

Entring an action, six shillings and eightpence.
Taking special bail, one shilling and sixpence.
Allowing a writ of error, two shillings.
Allowing a[n] *habeas corpus*, sixteenpence.
Taxing a bill of cost, eightpence.
Attorney's fee, to be allowed in the bill of cost taxed, seven shillings.
Granting liberty for the sale or partition of real estates, one shilling.
On rec[ie][*ei*]ving each petition, one shilling.
Allowance to the party for whom costs shall be taxed, and to witnesses in civil and criminal causes, one shilling and sixpence per day, ten miles' travel to be accounted a day; and the same allowance to be made to parties as to witnesses at the inferiour courts, courts of sessions and before a justice of the peace.

CLERK'S FEES.

Clerk's fees.

On entring an action, one shilling and fourpence.
A writ of *scire facias*, two shillings.
A writ of review, two shillings and sixpence.
Entring a rule of court, sixpence.
Filing a declaration, eightpence.
Entring appearance, fourpence.
Signing a judgment by default, eightpence.
Rec[ie][*ei*]ving and recording a verdict, eightpence.
Cop[y][*ie*]s of all records, each page, of twenty-eight lines, eight words in a line, eightpence per page;—
if less than one page, sixpence.
Every action withdrawn or nonsuit, eightpence.
Every petition read, eightpence; order thereon, eightpence.
Filing the papers of each cause, one penny per paper.
Every execution, one shilling and fourpence.
A writ of *habeas corpus*, two shillings.
Confessing judgment or default, one shilling.
Acknowledging satisfaction of a judgment, on record, eightpence.
Examining each bill of cost, sixpence.
Continuing each cause, and entring the next term, one shilling.
Entring up judgment and copying the same, two shillings.
To each *venire*, to be paid out of the county treasur[y][*ie*]s, respectively, by order from any three of the justices of said court, threepence.
Each recognizance, one shilling.

IN THE INFERIOUR COURT OF COMMON PLEAS.

[*JUSTICE'S FEES.*]

Justices of the inferior court, fees.

Entry of every action, five shillings and fourpence.
Taxing a bill of cost, sixpence.
Ta[k][*x*]ing a recognizance on appeals, one shilling.
Proving a deed, one shilling.
Attorney's fee, to be allowed in the bill of cost taxed, six shillings.

IN THE COURT OF GENERAL SESSIONS OF THE PEACE.

Court of general sessions of the peace.

Each day's attendance at the sessions, to be paid out of the fines, two shillings and eightpence.
Granting every licence to innholders and retail[e][*o*]rs, one shilling.
And taking their recognizances, one shilling.
Each recognizance in criminal causes, one shilling.

CLERK'S FEES.

Clerk's fees.

Every action entred, one shilling and fourpence.
Every writ and seal, sixpence.
Every appearance, fourpence.
Entring and recording a verdict, eightpence.
Recording a judgment, one shilling.
Cop[y][*ie*]s of all records, each page, of twenty-eight lines, eight words in a line, eightpence.
Every action withdrawn or nonsuit, eightpence.
Every execution, one shilling and fourpence.
Confessing judgment or default, eightpence.
Acknowledging satisfaction of a judgment on record, eightpence.
A writ of *habeas corpus*, two shillings.
Continuing each cause, and entring at the next term, eightpence.
Each recognizance, one shilling.
Examining each bill of cost, sixpence.
Each *venire*, to be paid out of the county treasur[y][*ie*]s, respectively, by order of court, threepence.
Writ of *facias habere possessionem*, two shillings.
Filing each paper, one penny.

GOVERNOUR AND SECRETARY'S FEES.

Governor and secretary's fees.

For registers: to the governour, three shillings; to the secretary, two shillings.
For certificates under the province seal: to the governour, three shillings; to the secretary, two shillings.
For warrants of appr[ais][*iz*]ements, s[u][*e*]rvey, &c.: to the governour, three shillings; to the secretary, three shillings.
To the governour, for a pass to the castle, for each vessel[l], one shilling: wood-sloops and other coasting vessel[l]s, for which passes have not been usually required, excepted.
For a certificate of naval stores, in the whole, three shillings.

SECRETARY'S FEES.

Secretary's fees.

For engrossing the acts or laws of the general assembly, six shillings each, to be paid out of the publick revenue.
Every commission for the justices of each county, and commission of oyer and terminer, six shillings and eightpence, to be paid out of the publick revenue.
Special warrant or mittimus by order of the governour and council, each, two shillings and sixpence.
Every commission under the great seal, for places of profit, five shillings, to be paid by the person commissionated.
[Eve*]ry bond, three shillings.
[Ev*]ery order of council to the benefit of particular persons, two shillings.

* These letters are missing from the parchment, which is mutilated.

Every writ for electing of assemblymen, directed to the sheriff or marshal[l] under the province seal, five shillings, to be paid out of the publick revenue.

For transcribing the acts or laws passed by the general assembly into a book, eightpence per page,—each page to contain twenty-eight lines, eight words in a line, and so proportionably,—to be paid out of the publick revenue.

Every commission for military officers, to be paid out of the public treasury, two shillings.

CLERK OF THE SESSIONS' FEES.

Clerk of the sessions' fees.

Entring a complaint or indictment, one shilling and fourpence.

Discharging a recognizance, eightpence.

Each warrant for criminals, one shilling.

Every summons or subp[e][*œ*]na, twopence.

Every recognizance for the peace or good behaviour, one shilling.

For every recognizance, one shilling.

Entring up judgment; or entring satisfaction of judgment, on record, and copying, one shilling.

Warrant for county tax, one shilling.

For minuting the receipt of each petition, and order thereon, and recording, eightpence per page, as before.

Examining and casting the grand jur[ors'][*y's*] account, yearly, and order thereon, to be paid by the county treasurer by order of the court of sessions, one shilling and sixpence.

For cop[y][*ie*]s of all records or original papers, eightpence per page, as before.

For filing each paper, one penny.

SHERIFF'S OR CONSTABLE'S FEES.

Sheriffs' or constables' fees.

For serving an original summons, one shilling.

Every cap[i][*e*]as or attachment in civil, or warrants in criminal, cases for tr[y][*i*]al, sixteenpence; and for travel out, one penny halfpenny per mile; and for the return of the writ (the travel to be inserted on the back of the writ or orginal summons), one penny halfpenny per mile.

Levying execution in personal actions, for the first twenty pounds or under, ninepence per pound; above that, not exceeding forty pounds, fourpence per pound; above that, not exceeding one hundred pounds, twopence per pound; for whatsoever it exceeds one hundred pounds, one penny per pound.

For travel out, one penny halfpenny per mile, and for the return of the execution, one penny halfpenny per mile; all travel in serving writs and executions, to be accounted from the officer's house who does the service, to the place of service, and from thence to the court-house or place of tr[y][*i*]al.

For giving livery and seizin of real estates, six shillings, travel as before: if of different parcels of land, four shillings each.

For serving an execution upon a judgment of court for partition of real estates, to the sheriff, five shillings per day; and for travel and expences, threepence per mile out from the place of his abode; and to each juror, two shillings per day; and for travel and expences, threepence per mile.

Every tr[y][*i*]al, eightpence.

Every default, fourpence.

A bail bond, eightpence.

Every precept for the choice of representatives, and returning it, sixteenpence; to be paid out of the county treasur[y][*ie*]s, respectively.

To the officer attending the grand jury, each day, two shillings.

To the officer attending the petit jury, one shilling every cause.

For dispersing *venires* from the clerk of the superiour court, and the province treas[*ure*]r's warrants, fourpence each.

For dispersing proclamations, sixpence each,

For the encouragement unto the sheriff to take and use all possible care and diligence for the safe keeping of the prisoners that shall be committed to his custody, he shall have such sal[l]ary allowed him for the same as the justices of the court of gen[*era*]l sessions of the peace within the same county shall think fit and order, not exceeding ten pounds per annum for the county of Suffolk, and not exceeding five pounds per annum ap[ei][*ie*]ce for the count[ie][*y*]s of Essex and Middlesex, and not exceeding three pounds per annum ap[ei][*ie*]ce in each of the other counties within the province, to be paid out of the treasury of such county.

CRYER'S FEES.

Crier's fees. Calling the jury, fourpence.

A default or nonsuit, eightpence.

A verdict, eightpence.

A judgm[*en*]t affirmed on a complaint, eightpence.

GOALER'S FEES.

Jailer's fees. For turning the key on each prisoner committed, three shillings; viz[t]., one shilling and sixpence in, and one shilling and sixpence out.

For dieting each person, for a week, three shillings.

MESSENGER OF THE HOUSE OF REPRESENTATIVES' FEES.

Messenger of the house of representatives' fees. For serving every warrant from the house of representatives, which they may grant for arresting, imprisoning, or taking into custody any person, one shilling and sixpence.

For travel, each mile out, twopence per mile.

For keeping and providing food for such person, each day, one shilling and sixpence.

For his discharge or dismission, one shilling and sixpence.

GRAND JUROR'S FEES.

Grand jurors' fees. Foreman, per day, two shillings and sixpence.

Each other juror, two shillings.

PETIT JUROR'S FEES.

Petit jurors' fees. To the foreman, in every case at the superiour court, two shillings; to every other juror, one shilling and sixpence.

To the foreman, in every cause at the inferiour court or sessions, one shilling; to every other juror, tenpence.

1749-50, chap. 5. Except the county of Suffolk, which is to be regulated by the law relating to jurors pass'd the last year.

FOR MARRIAGES.

Fees for marriages. For each marriage, to the minister or justice officiating, four shillings.

For recording it: to the town clerk, to be paid by the justice or minister, fourpence; and to the clerk of the sessions, to be paid by the town clerk, twopence.

To the town clerk, for every publishment of the banns of matrimony, and entring thereof, one shilling.

Every certificate of such publishment, sixpence.

Recording births and deaths, each, twopence.

For a certificate of the birth or death of any person, threepence.

For every search of record, where no copy is required, twopence.

COUNTY REGISTER'S FEES.

For entring or recording or copying any deed, conveyance or mortgage, for the first page, ninepence; and eightpence per page for so many pages more as it shall contain, accounting after the rate of twenty-eight lines, of eight words in a line, to each page, and proportionably for so much more as shall be under a page; and threepence for his attestation on the original, of the time, book and folio where it is recorded;— County register's fees.

and for a discharge of a mortgage, eightpence.

And be it further enacted,

[SECT. 2.] That if any person or persons shall demand or take any greater fee or fees for any of the services aforesaid, than is by this law provided, he or they shall forfeit and pay to the person or persons injured, the sum of ten pounds for every offence, to be recovered in any court proper to hear and determine the same. Penalty for taking excessive fees.

[SECT. 3.] This act to be in force for the space of two years from the publication thereof, and from thence to the end of the then next session of the general court, and no longer. [*Passed October* 9; *published October* 12. Limitation.

CHAPTER 9.

AN ACT FOR IMPOWERING THE PROVINCE TREASURER TO BORROW THE SUM OF FOUR THOUSAND POUNDS, FOR APPLYING THE SAME TO DISCHARGE THE DEBTS OF THE PROVINCE, AND DEFREY THE CHARGES OF GOVERNMENT, AND FOR MAKING PROVISION FOR THE REPAYMENT OF THE SUM SO BORROWED.

Be it enacted by the Lieutenant-Governour, Council and House of Representatives,

[SECT. 1.] That the treasurer of this province be and hereby is impowred to borrow, from such person or persons as shall appear ready to lend the same, a sum not exceeding four thousand pounds, in Spanish mill'd dollars; and the sum so borrowed, shall be a stock in the treasury, to be applied for defreying the charges of this government, in manner as in this act is after directed; and for every sum so borrowed, the treasurer shall give a receipt of the form following; viz.,— Treasurer empowered to borrow £4,000 for the province.

Province of the Massachusetts Bay, day of , 175 , borrowed and received of A. B., Spanish mill'd dollars, of full weight, for the use of this province; and as their treasurer do promise to pay the same number of like dollars to the said A. B., or order, by the tenth day of June, 1752, with lawful interest for the same, annually, 'till paid. Form of his receipt for said money.

W—— F——, Treasurer.

—and no receipt shall be given for any sum less than five pounds: and the treasurer is hereby directed to use his discretion in borrowing said sum, at such times as that he may be enabled to comply with the draughts that may be made on the treasury in pursuance of this act.

And be it further enacted,

[SECT. 2.] That the aforesaid sum of four thousand pounds shall be issued out of the treasury in manner and for the purposes following; viz., the sum of twelve hundred and eighty pounds, part of the aforesaid sum of four thousand pounds, shall be applied for the service of the several forts and garrisons within this province, pursuant to such orders £1,280 appropriated for forts and garrisons.

and grants as are or shall be made by this court for those purposes; and the further sum of eight hundred pounds, part of the aforesaid sum of four thousand pounds, shall be applied for the purchasing provisions, and the commissary's necessary disbursements for the service of the several forts and garrisons within this province, pursuant to such grants as are or shall be made by this court for those purposes; and the further sum of five hundred and twenty pounds, part of the aforesaid sum of four thousand pounds, shall be applied for the payment of such premiums and grants that now are or hereafter may be made by this court; and the further sum of seven hundred and sixty pounds, part of the aforesaid sum of four thousand pounds, shall be applied for the discharging other debts owing from this province to persons that have served or shall serve them by order of this court in such matters and things where there is no establishment, nor any certain sum assigned for such service, and for paper, writing and printing for this court; and the sum of five hundred and twenty pounds, part of the aforesaid sum of four thousand pounds, shall be applied for the payment of his majesty's council and house of representatives serving in the general court during the several sessions for this present year.

£800 for commissary's stores, &c.

£520 for premiums and grants.

£760 for debts where there is no establishment.

£520 for the members of the court.

And whereas there are sometimes contingent and unforeseen charges that demand prompt payment,—

Be it further enacted,

£120 for contingent charges.

[SECT. 3.] That the sum of one hundred and twenty pounds, being the remaining part of the aforesaid sum of four thousand pounds, be applied to pay such contingent charges, and for no other purpose whatsoever.

And in order to enable the treasurer effectually to discharge the receipts and obligations by him given in pursuance of this act,—

Be it enacted,

Duty of impost and excise made a fund for repayment of said £4,000.

[SECT. 4.] That the duty of impost and excise for part of the years one thousand seven hundred and fifty and fifty-one, and ending in the year one thousand seven hundred and fifty-one, shall be applied for the payment and discharge of the principal and interest that shall be due on said receipts and obligations, and to no other purpose whatever.

And as a further fund and security for drawing the said sum of four thousand pounds into the treasury again,—

Be it further enacted,

Tax of £400 for further security, to be levied in the year 1752.

[SECT. 5.] That there be and hereby is granted unto his most excellent majesty, a tax of four thousand pounds, to be levied on polls, and estates real and personal, within this province, according to such rules and in such proportion on the several towns and districts within the same, as shall be agreed on and ordered by the general court of this province at their session in May, one thousand seven hundred and fifty-one, which sum shall be paid into the treasury on or before the tenth day of February next after.

Be it further enacted,

Tax for the money hereby emitted, to be made according to the preceding tax act, in case.

[SECT. 6.] That in case the general court shall not, at their session in May, and before the twentieth day of June, one thousand seven hundred and fifty-one, agree and conclude upon an act apportioning the sum which by this act is engaged shall be, in said year, apportioned, assessed and levied, that then, and in such case, each town and district within this province shall pay, by a tax to be levied on the polls, and estates both real and personal, within their districts, the same proportion of the said sum as the said towns and districts should have been taxed by the general court in the tax act then last preceeding: *saving* what relates to the pay of the representatives, which shall be assess'd on the several towns they represent; and the province treasurer is hereby fully impowred and directed, some time in the month of June, in the year one thousand seven hundred and fifty-one, to issue and send forth his warrants, directed to the selectmen or assessors of each town and district within this province, requiring them to assess the polls, and estates both real and personal, within their several towns and districts, for their respective part and proportion of the sum before directed and engaged to be assessed; and also for the fines upon the several towns that have not sent a representative: and the assessors, as also persons assessed, shall observe, be governed by, and subject to all such rules and directions as have been given in the last preceeding tax act.

Provided always,—

[SECT. 7.] That the remainder of the sum which shall be brought into the treasury, by the duties of impost and excise for the years one thousand seven hundred and fifty and fifty-one aforesaid, and the tax of four thousand pounds ordered by this act to be assessed and levied, over and above what shall be sufficient to discharge the receipts and obligations aforesaid, shall be and remain as a stock in the treasury, to be applied as the general court of this province shall hereafter order, and to no other purpose whatsoever; anything in this act to the contrary notwithstanding. Remainder to be and remain as a stock in the treasury.

And be it further enacted,

[SECT. 8.] That the treasurer is hereby directed and ordered to pay the sum of four thousand pounds, borrowed as aforesaid, out of such appropriations as shall be directed to by warrant, and no other, upon pain of refunding all such sum or sums as he shall otherways pay; and the secretary, to whom it belongs to keep the muster-rolls and accompts of charge, shall lay before the house of representatives, when they direct, such muster-rolls and accompts after payment thereof. [*Passed October* 10; *published October* 12. Money to be paid out of the proper appropriations.

CHAPTER 10.

AN ACT IN FURTHER ADDITION TO AN ACT, INTITLED "AN ACT FOR RENDRING MORE EFFECTUAL THE LAWS ALREADY IN BEING, RELATING TO THE ADMEASUREMENT OF BOARDS, &c., AND FOR PREVENTING FRAUD AND ABUSE IN SHINGLES, &c."

WHEREAS the laws now in force for regulating the assize of shingles and the admeasurement of boards are insufficient to answer the good and salutary ends proposed by them,— Preamble. 1743-44, chap. 22.

Be it enacted by the Lieutenant-Governour, Council and House of Representatives,

[SECT. 1.] That all shingles that are exposed to public sale in this province shall be at least, one with another, four inches in breadth, fifteen inches in length, one third of an inch thick at the butt end of the shingle,—neither of them to be under three inches in width; and that all shingles, before they are ship'd off from any of the maritime towns in said province, shall be culled by a sworn culler, who is hereby fully authorized and required to condemn all those shingles that shall be short of the dimensions aforesaid; and in case there shall be above five shingles that are under two inches in width or twelve inches in length, in a bundle of two hundred and fifty, and so in proportion to a larger or smaller bundle, the bundle in which such shingles are contained shall be forfeited; and the surveyor or culler is hereby required and fully authorized to condemn all such shingles, notice being first given to the owner or owners of said shingles to be present, if he or they see cause: Rules for the dimensions of shingles. Penalty for not conforming thereto,—

—to be for the use of the poor. which shingles shall be delivered to the selectmen or overseers of the poor in the town where such shingles are condemned, for the benefit of the poor of said town, first deducting therefrom the charge of culling or surveying.

And be it further enacted,

Penalty for the cullers' neglect of duty. [SECT. 2.] That if any sworn culler or surveyor shall neglect or refuse to do his duty in condemning all such shingles aforesaid, he shall, upon conviction in any of his majesty's courts, forfeit the sum of ten pounds; one half for the informer, and the other moiety for the poor of the town where such offence is committed: to be recovered by bill, plaint or information.

And be it further enacted,

Shingles not surveyed, to be forfeited. [SECT. 3.] That all shingles in each town where they are made, or at the place of first sale, before their delivery, shall be surveyed by a sworn surveyor, and the town-brand set upon the hoop of the bundle; and all shingles offered to sale, without being surveyed and marked as aforesaid, shall be forfeited: and the surveyor is hereby impowered and directed to condemn all such shingles for the use of the poor of the town where such shingles are condemned; and in case the surveyor shall refuse or neglect to do his duty, he shall forfeit the sum of ten pounds; one half for the poor of the town, the other moiety for him that shall inform or sue for the same, to be recovered by bill, plaint or information in any of his majesty's courts.

Preamble. *And whereas* there is often great fraud and deceit in the admeasurement of boards, by reason that the surveyors are not by law obliged to have any regard to the thickness of the boards, by which means great wrong and injury is done to the purchaser who imports them to foreign markets,—

Be it therefore enacted,

Regulation of the thickness of boards. [SECT. 4.] That all boards that are brought to market shall be full one inch thick, and of a square edge, to be reckoned merchantable; and that the surveyor or surveyors upon oath are hereby authorized and required to make proper allowance to the purchaser, in their admeasurement, for those boards that are short of an inch in thickness, and that are not square-edged, as well as for those that are split and knotty.

Limitation. [SECT. 5.] This act to continue and be in force for the space of five years from the publication thereof, and no longer. [*Passed October* 10; *published October* 12.

CHAPTER 11.

AN ACT IN ADDITION TO AND EXPLANATION OF AN ACT MADE THIS PRESENT YEAR, INTITLED "AN ACT FOR GRANTING UNTO HIS MAJESTY SEVERAL RATES AND DUTIES OF IMPOST AND TONNAGE OF SHIPPING."

Preamble. 1750-51, chap. 6. WHEREAS in and by an act made and pass'd this present year, intitled "An Act for granting unto his majesty several rates and duties of impost and tonnage of shipping," it is provided, "That all penalties, fines and forfeitures ac[c]ruing and arising by virtue" of the said act, "shall be one half to his majesty, for the uses and intents for which the" duties of impost therein mentioned "are granted, and the other half to him or them that shall seize, inform and sue for the same, by action, bill, plaint or information, in any of his majesty's courts of record, wherein no essoign, protection or wager of law shall be allowed; the whole charge of prosecution to be taken out of the half belonging to the informer,"—

Be it enacted by the Lieut[enan]t-Governour, Council and House of Representatives,

That from and after the publication of this act, in all cases where any claimer shall appear, and shall not m[*a*]ke good the claim, the charges of prosecution shall be born and paid by the said claimer, and not by the informer; anything in the afores[*ai*]d act, or any part thereof, to the contrary notwithstanding. [*Passed October* 6; *published October* 12.

Claimer of goods seized by the impost-officer, not making good his claim, to pay charges.

ACTS

PASSED AT THE SESSION BEGUN AND HELD AT BOSTON, ON THE TENTH DAY OF JANUARY, A. D. 1750–51.

CHAPTER 12.

AN ACT TO REGULATE THE IMPORTATION OF GERMANS AND OTHER PASSENGERS COMING TO SETTLE IN THIS PROVINCE.

Preamble.

WHEREAS Germans and other persons may be imported in so great numbers in one vessel, that through want of necessary room and accommodations, they may often contract mortal and contagious distempers, and thereby occasion not only the death of great numbers of them in their passage, but also by such means on their arrival in this province, those who may survive, may be so infected as to spread the contagion, and be the cause of the death of many others; to the end, therefore, that such an evil practice may be prevented, and inconveniencies thence arising avoided as much as may be,—

Be it enacted by the Lieutenant-Governour, Council and House of Representatives,

Sufficient room and provisions to be allowed to passengers coming in any vessel to settle in this province.

[SECT. 1.] That from and after the publication of this act, no master or commander of any ship, or other vessel whatsoever, bound to the port of Boston, or elsewhere within this province, shall import into said port of Boston, or into any other port within this province, any greater number of passengers, in any one ship or other vessel, than such only as shall be well provided with good and wholesome meat, drink and other necessaries for passengers and others, during the whole voyage; and shall have room therein to contain, for single freight or passengers of the age of fourteen years or upwards, at least six feet in length, and one foot and six inches in breadth, and if under the age aforesaid, to contain the same length and breadth for every two such passengers.

Penalty to any delinquent master.

[SECT. 2.] And if any master or commander of any ship or other vessel, against the tenor of this act, shall import into this province any one or greater number of passengers not accommodated or provided during his voyage with good and wholesome meat, drink, room and other necessaries as aforesaid, such master or commander shall forfeit and pay, for every passenger so imported into this province, the sum of five pounds; to be recovered by action of debt, with full costs of suit, in any court of record within this province: the one half of said forfeiture to any one who will sue for the same to effect, and the other half to the province treasurer, to be applied towards payment of the charges and expences of this province: *provided*, such action shall be commenced within the space of forty days next after any such offence shall be committed; or such delinquent may be indicted for the same in the next court of general sessions of the peace for the county where the offence shall be committed, and, on due conviction, be fined, at the discretion of the court, not exceeding five pounds for each passenger exceeding the number by this act allowed to be imported as aforesaid.

And to the end this act and the provisions herein made may be more particularly observed,—

Be it further enacted,

[SECT. 3.] That the commissioner of impost for the time being, or his lawful deputies, in going on board any ship or other vessel importing passengers, either by his or their view, or otherwise, shall, and is hereby required to, inform himself of the condition and circumstances of the passengers on board, and whether they have been provided for, and accommodated with the provisions, room and other necessaries herein directed; and where at any time a deficiency shall appear to him or any of them, he or they shall forthwith give notice of the same to some one or more of the justices of the peace for the county where the offence is committed, to the end the person or persons delinquent may be sent for, or bound over, to the next court of general sessions of the peace, then and there to answer for such offence.

The impost-officer and his deputies empowered to make inquiry referring to the observation of this act.

And be it further enacted,

[SECT. 4.] That every master or commander of any ship or other vessel importing any passenger or passengers to be landed within this province, who, in their passage hither, or soon after their arrival, may happen to die, leaving goods, chattles, money or other effects on board such ship or other vessel, or in the hands or custody of any such master or commander, every such master or commander, within the space of twenty days next after his arrival, or after the decease of every such passenger, shall exhibit to the register of the judge of probate of wills and granting administration, for the county where such goods and effects shall be, a true and perfect inventory, upon oath, of all such goods, chattles, money or other effects, to the end that after payment of all just demands which shall be due to the said master or commander, or to his or their owner or owners, the remainder of such goods and effects may be committed to the custody of some proper person or persons for the benefit of the wife and children, or other kindred, or creditors of the deceased, as the case may require, and the law in such case shall direct.

Provision for saving the money, goods, &c., of any passengers that may die on the passage.

And be it further enacted,

[SECT. 5.] That if any such master or commander of any such ship or other vessel shall neglect or refuse to exhibit such an inventory of the goods and effects of any such passenger or passengers so dying as aforesaid, every such master or commander shall forfeit and pay the sum of two hundred pounds, to be recovered and applied as aforesaid. [*Passed February* 6, 1750-51.

Penalty for any master's neglect of exhibiting an inventory of such goods, &c.

CHAPTER 13.

AN ACT FOR HOLDING A SUPERIOUR COURT OF JUDICATURE, COURT OF ASSIZE AND GENERAL GOAL DELIVERY AT OTHER TIMES THAN THOSE ALREADY APPOINTED BY LAW.

WHEREAS the time by law appointed for holding the superiour court of judicature, court of assize and general goal delivery is but once in six months in any county, and but once a year in many counties, by reason whereof felons, by making their escape, or by the death of witnesses, may avoid justice, or great charges may arise by keeping such offenders in goal, as well as damages accrue to witnesses by being detained until[1] the time by law appointed for holding the court where

Preamble. 1747-48, chap. 15.

such offenders are triable; and as there is not by the laws of this province, sufficient provision made for remedying the inconvenienc[*i*]es aforesaid,—

Be it enacted by the Lieutenant-Governour, Council and House of Representatives,

Governor and council empowered to call a special court of assize, &c.

[SECT. 1.] That the governour or commander-in-chief, for the time being, by and with the advice and consent of the council, may, upon such occasions, by precept, directed to the justices of the superiour court of judicature, court of assize and general goal delivery, order and appoint them to hold a superiour court of judicature, court of assize and general goal delivery for inquiring of, hearing and determining all such felonies, on certain days and places by them to be appointed in the county where such offence by law is triable; and that the justices aforesaid, upon the receipt of such precept, shall cause process to issue for summoning grand jurors and petit jurors out of the several towns,—as is usual for the stated courts,—to attend such special court at the time and place appointed by the justices thereof for holding the same, and make out all other necessary process; and do whatever else is or may be requisite to be done for the holding such court, inquiring of such felonies, hearing and determining the same, giving judgment and awarding execution thereon, as fully as the superiour court of judicature, court of assize and general goal delivery might or could do at a time by law appointed for holding such court.

And be it further enacted,

How the court may be adjourned.

[SECT. 2.] That if any such special court can't be held on the day appointed therefor, any one of the justices thereof may adjourn the same from time to time until[l] such court can be held. [*Passed February* 11*; *published February* 16, 1750–51.

CHAPTER 14.

AN ACT FOR RAISING THE SUM OF TWELVE HUNDRED POUNDS BY LOTTERY, FOR BUILDING AND MAINTAINING A BRIDGE OVER THE RIVER PARKER, IN THE TOWN OF NEWBURY, AT THE PLACE CALLED OLDTOWN FERRY.

Preamble.

WHEREAS the building a bridge over the river Parker, in the town of Newbury, in the county of Essex, at the place called Oldtown Ferry, will be of publick service; *and whereas* the town of Newbury have, by Mr. Daniel Farn[a][*u*]m, their agent, applied to this court for liberty to raise the sum of twelve hundred pounds, by lottery, for building and maintaining a bridge over the said river, at the ferry-place aforesaid, under the direction of persons to be appointed by this government,—

Be it therefore enacted by the Lieutenant-Governour, Council and House of Representatives,

A lottery to be set up in Newbury for building a bridge over the river Parker.

That Thomas Berry, John Greenleaf, Joseph Gerrish and Joseph Atkins, Esquires, and the said Daniel Farn[a][*u*]m, or any three of them, be and hereby are allowed and impow[e]red to set up and carry on a lottery, within the said town of Newbury, amounting to such a sum as, by drawing ten per cent out of each prize, they may thereby raise the sum of twelve hundred pounds; to be applied, by them or any three of them, towards building and maintaining a good and sufficient bridge at the place aforesaid, and for defraying the necessary charges of the lottery aforesaid; and that the said Thomas Berry, John Green-

* According to the memorandum on the engrossment, the bill was signed February 9; but the record has been followed above.

leaf, Joseph Gerrish, Joseph Atkins and Daniel Farn[a][u]m, or any three of them, be and hereby are impow[e]red to make all necessary rules for the regular proceeding therein, and shall be sworn to the faithful discharge of their trust aforesaid, and be answerable to the purchasers and drawers of the ticket[t]s for any deficiency or misconduct; and that the money so raised shall be applied to the uses and purposes aforesaid. [*Passed January* 29; *published February* 16, 1750–51.

CHAPTER 15.

AN ACT FOR SUPPLYING THE TREASURY WITH TWENTY-SIX THOUSAND SEVEN HUNDRED MILL'D DOLLARS.

Preamble.

WHEREAS the payment of the publick debts of this government requires a speedy and further supply of the treasury; and as the circumstances of the several towns in the province are so alter'd since the last valuation was taken, as that a just and equal tax can't be levied; therefore,—

Be it enacted by the Lieutenant-Governour, Council and House of Representatives,

Persons allowed to take out tickets.

[SECT. 1.] That any person or persons may adventure, advance and pay to the managers or directors hereinafter named, three mill'd dollars, and as many times that number of such dollars as they please; and that every adventurer, for every three such dollars so advanced, shall have such right and interest in the lottery hereby established as is hereafter provided.

And be it further enacted,

Names of the managers or directors.

[SECT. 2.] That Samuel Watts, Esq., Thomas Hutchinson, Esq., Joseph Richards, Esq., Mr. Harrison Gray and Mr. James Russel, or any three of them, shall be managers or directors for preparing and delivering out tickets, and to oversee the drawing of lots, and to order, do and perform such other matters and things as are hereafter, in and by this act, directed and appointed by such managers or directors to be done and performed; and that such managers and directors shall meet together, from time to time, for the execution of the powers and trusts in them reposed by this act; and they shall cause books to be prepared, in which every leaf shall be divided into three columns, and upon the innermost of said three columns, there shall be printed eight thousand nine hundred tickets, numbered one, two, three, and so on, progressively, 'till they arrive to the number of eight thousand nine hundred; and upon the middle column, in every of the said books, shall be printed eight thousand nine hundred tickets, of the same breadth and form, and numbered in like manner; and in the extreme column of the said books, there shall be printed a third rank of* series of tickets, of the same number of those of the other two columns: which tickets shall severally be of an oblong figure, and, in the said books, shall be joined with oblique lines, flourishes or devices, in such manner as the said managers and directors, or the major part of them, shall think most safe and convenient, and that every ticket in the third or extreme column of the said books, shall have written or printed thereupon, besides the number of such ticket and the present year of our Lord, these words, "MASSACHUSETTS GOVERNMENT LOTTERY."

Number of tickets and form.

And it is further enacted,

How tickets are to be delivered.

[SECT. 3.] That the said managers and directors shall, upon payment of three dollars, as aforesaid, for a ticket, from any person or

* *Sic*, or ?

persons adventuring in this lottery, cut out of the said book or books, so as to put into his or their custody, through the said oblique lines, flourishes or devices, indentwise, one of the tickets in the said extreme columns, which shall be signed by one of the said managers or directors; and the ticket so cut off shall be delivered to such adventurer as aforesaid.

And be it further enacted,

Tickets to be indented, rolled up, and put into boxes, &c.

[SECT. 4.] That the said managers and directors, or the major part of them, shall, in the presence of such of the adventurers as may attend, cause all the tickets in the middle column of the books aforesaid, to be cut off, indentwise, through the said oblique lines, flourishes or devices, and to be carefully roll'd up, and made fast with thread or silk, and to be put into a box to be prepared for that purpose, and to be marked with the letter "A," which is presently to be put into another strong box, and to be locked up with five different locks and keys,—one to be kept by each of the said managers and directors,—and sealed with their seals, until the said tickets are to be drawn as is hereinafter mentioned; and that the tickets in the first or innermost columns of the said books, shall remain still in the books, for discovering any mistake or fraud, if any should happen to be committed contrary to the true meaning of this act.

And be it further enacted,

Books to be prepared, and tickets printed therein.

[SECT. 5.] That the said managers, or the major part of them, shall also prepare, or cause to be prepared, other books, in which every leaf shall be divided or distinguished into two columns, and upon the innermost of those two columns there shall be printed eight thousand nine hundred tickets, and upon the outermost of said two columns there shall be printed eight thousand nine hundred tickets,—all which shall be of equal length and breadth, as near as may be,—which two columns in the said books shall be joined with some flourish or device through which the outermost ticket may be cut off indentwise; and that two thousand two hundred and twenty-five tickets, part of those to be contained in the outermost columns of the books last mentioned, shall be and be called the "benefit tickets," to which extraordinary benefits shall belong, as hereinafter mentioned. And the said managers and directors shall cause the said benefit tickets to be written upon or otherwise expressed, as well in figures as in words at length, in manner following; that is to say, upon one of them, one thousand dollars; upon another of them, six hundred dollars; upon another of them, four hundred and fifteen dollars; upon two of them severally, three hundred dollars; upon three of them severally, two hundred dollars; upon four of them severally, one hundred and fifty dollars; upon eight of them severally, one hundred dollars; upon ten of them severally, seventy-five dollars; upon twenty of them severally, fifty dollars; upon seventy of them severally, forty dollars; upon one hundred of them severally, thirty dollars; upon two thousand and five of them severally, seven dollars. And the said managers shall cause all the said tickets contained in the outermost column of the last-mentioned books to be, in the presence of such of the said adventurers as may be there, to be carefully cut out, indentwise, through the said flourish or device, and carefully rolled up, and fastened with thread or silk, and to be put into another box to be prepared for that purpose, and to be marked with the letter "B"; which box shall be presently put into another strong box, and locked up with five different locks and keys,—one key to be kept by each of said managers,—and to be sealed up with their seals, until these tickets shall also be drawn in the manner and form hereinafter mentioned. And the whole business of cutting off and rolling up, and putting into the said boxes, shall be performed by the said managers

The number and sum of the benefit tickets.

Benefit tickets to be rolled up and put into a separate box.

and directors, within six days, at least, before the drawing of the said lottery shall begin.

And be it further enacted,

Time and place of drawing the tickets.

[SECT. 6.] That on or before the eighteenth day of April next (notice of the time being given in the publick prints at least fourteen days before), the said managers and directors shall cause the said several boxes, with all the tickets therein, to be brought into Faneuil Hall, or such other convenient place in the town of Boston, as shall be agreed upon by the major part of the directors, by nine of the clock in the forenoon of the same day, and placed on a table, there for that purpose, and shall then and there severally attend this service, and cause the two boxes containing the tickets to be severally taken out of the other two boxes in which they shall have been locked up, and the tickets or lots in the respective innermost boxes being, in the presence of such adventurers as will be there for the satisfaction of themselves, well shaken and mingled in each box distinctly; and some one fit person, to be appointed and directed by the managers aforesaid, or the major part of them, shall take out and draw one ticket from the box where the said numbered tickets shall be put as aforesaid, and one other indifferent and fit person, to be appointed and directed in like manner, shall presently take out a ticket or lot from the box where the said two thousand two hundred and twenty-five benefit, and six thousand six hundred and seventy-five blank, tickets shall be promiscuously put as aforesaid, and immediately both the tickets so drawn shall be opened, and the number of the benefit, as well as the blank, tickets, shall be named aloud; and if the ticket taken or drawn from the box containing the benefit, and blank, lots, shall appear to be a blank, then the numbered ticket so drawn with the said blank at the same time, shall both be put on one file; and if the ticket so drawn or taken from the box containing the benefit, and blank, lots, shall appear to be one of the benefit tickets, then the number of dollars written upon such benefit tickets, whatever it be, shall be entred, by such clerk or clerks as the said managers, or the major part of them, shall employ and oversee for this purpose, being first sworn to a faithful discharge of his or their office, into a book to be kept for entring the numbers coming up with the said benefit tickets; and the said benefit, and numbered, tickets so drawn together shall be put upon another file; and so the said drawing of the tickets shall continue, by taking one ticket at a time out of each box, and with opening, naming aloud and filing the same, and by entring the benefit lots in such method as is before mentioned, until the whole number be compleatly drawn; and if the same cannot be performed in one day's time, the said managers shall cause the boxes to be locked up and sealed in manner as aforesaid, and adjourn 'till next day, and so from day to day, and every day, except on the Lord's day; and then open the same and proceed as above, 'till the said whole number shall be drawn as aforesaid; and afterwards the said numbered tickets so drawn, with the benefit tickets drawn against the same, shall be and remain in a strong box, locked up as aforesaid, and under the custody of the said managers, until they shall take them out to examine, adjust and settle the property thereof. And, as soon as conveniently may be after the drawing is over, the said managers are required to cause to be printed and published, the number of the ticket drawn against each benefit ticket, and the number of dollars written on the same, and if any contention or dispute shall arise in adjusting the property of the said benefit tickets, the major part of the said managers agreeing therein, shall determine to whom it doth or ought to belong.

Benefit tickets to be entered by the clerk or clerks.

Managers may adjourn from day to day till all are drawn.

Penalty for persons who forge or counterfeit tickets, &c.

[SECT. 7.] And if any person shall forge or counterfeit any ticket or tickets to be made forth on this act, or alter any of the numbers, certificate or certificates thereof, or utter, vend, barter or dispose of, or offer to dispose of, any false, altered, forged or counterfeit ticket or tickets, or bring any forged or counterfeit ticket or tickets, the number whereof is altered, knowing the same to be altered, to the said managers, or any of them, or to any other person, to the intent to defraud this province, or any adventurer upon this act, that then every such person or persons, being thereof convicted in due form of law, shall suffer such pains and penalties as is by law provided in cases of forgery.

The managers to commit such to prison.

[SECT. 8.] And the said managers or directors, or any two of them, are hereby authorized, required and impowered to cause any person or persons bringing or uttering such forged or counterfeit ticket or tickets as aforesaid, to be apprehended and committed to close goal, to be proceeded against according to law.

Provided always,—

And it is hereby enacted,

[SECT. 9.] That each manager and director for putting this act in execution, before his acting in such commission, shall take the following oath; viz.,—

Director's oath.

I, A. B., do swear that I will faithfully execute the trust reposed in me, and that I will not use any indirect act or means to obtain a prize or benefit lot for myself or any other person whatsoever, and that I will do the utmost of my endeavour to prevent any undue or sinister practice to be done by any person whatsoever, and that I will, to the best of my judgment, declare to whom any prize, lot or ticket does of right belong, according to the true intent and meaning of the act of this province, made in the twenty-fourth year of his majesty's reign in that behalf. So help me God.

—which shall and may be administred by any two or more of the other managers and directors.

Be it further enacted,

—dollars to be lodged with the treasury before the time of drawing.

[SECT. 10.] That the managers or directors of said lottery, shall pay into the hands of the treasury all such number of dollars as they shall receive for the sale of the tickets, before they proceed to draw said lottery. And one or more of the managers or directors aforesaid, after the drawing of said lottery is compleated, are hereby ordered and directed to certify upon each benefit ticket the number of dollars it drew in said lottery; and the treasurer of the province for the time being, is hereby impowred and directed to pay off all such benefit tickets to the possessor or possessors thereof, in one year from the drawing of said lottery, with three per cent for the same until paid, without any deduction; which will make in the whole twenty-six thousand two hundred dollars.

And be it further enacted,

Tickets not taken up to be for the province.

[SECT. 11.] That if any of the aforesaid numbered tickets shall remain in the hands of the directors or managers, undispos'd of when the time set by this act for drawing said lottery shall be arriv'd, that then, and in such case, all and every such ticket shall be and remain as the interest, share and lot of this province, and the number of the said remaining undispos'd tickets shall be, by the directors or managers, given out to the province treasurer, in order to be drawn for the province.

Provided, notwithstanding,—

Proviso.

[SECT. 12.] That if there should not be at least five thousand tickets disposed of at the time appointed for drawing the lottery, the managers and directors aforesaid shall wholly desist from any further proceedings until they shall receive further orders from the general court, anything in this act to the contrary notwithstanding.

And as a fund and security for paying off the benefit tickets,—

Be it further enacted,

[SECT. 13.] That there be and hereby is granted unto his most excellent majesty, a tax of eight thousand and ten pounds, to be levied on polls, and estates real and personal, within this province, according to such rules and in such proportion on the several towns and districts within the same, as shall be agreed on and ordered by the general court of this province at their session in May, one thousand seven hundred and fifty-one, which sum shall be paid into the treasury on or before the first day of February next after.

Tax on polls and estates for paying benefit tickets.

Be it further enacted,

[SECT. 14.] That in case the general court shall not, at their session in May next, and before the twentieth day of June, one thousand seven hundred and fifty-one, agree and conclude upon an act apportioning the sum which by this act is engaged shall be, in said year, apportioned, assessed and levied, that then, and in such case, each town and district within this province shall pay, by a tax to be levied on the polls, and estates both real and personal, within their districts, the same proportion of the said sum as the said towns and districts should have been taxed by the general court in the tax act then last preceeding: *saving* what relates to the pay of the representatives, which shall be assess'd on the several towns they represent; and the province treasurer is hereby fully impowred and directed, some time in the month of June, in the year one thousand seven hundred and fifty-one, to issue and send forth his warrants, directed to the selectmen or assessors of each town and district within this province, requiring them to assess the polls, and estates both real and personal, within their several towns and districts, for their respective part and proportion of the sum before directed and engaged to be assess'd, and also for the fines upon the several towns that have not sent a representative; and the assessors, as also persons assessed, shall observe, be govern'd by, and subject to all such rules and directions as have been given in the last preceeding tax act.

Tax to be made according to the preceding tax act, in case.

And be it further enacted,

[SECT. 15.] That the sum of seven thousand eight hundred and sixty pounds shall be issued out of the treasury, in manner and for the purposes following; viz., the sum of two thousand five hundred and sixty pounds, part of the aforesaid sum of seven thousand eight hundred and sixty pounds, shall be applied for the service of the several forts and garrisons within this province, pursuant to such orders and grants as are or shall be made by this court for those purposes; and the further sum of sixteen hundred pounds, part of the aforesaid sum of seven thousand eight hundred and sixty pounds, shall be applied for the purchasing provisions and the commissarie's necessary disbursements for the service of the several forts and garrisons within this province, pursuant to such grants as are or shall be made by this court for those purposes; and the further sum of one thousand and forty pounds, part of the aforesaid sum of seven thousand eight hundred and sixty pounds, shall be applied for the payment of such præmiums and grants that now are, or hereafter may be made by this court; and the further sum of one thousand five hundred and twenty pounds, part of the aforesaid sum of seven thousand eight hundred and sixty pounds, shall be applied for the discharging other debts owing from this province to persons that have served or shall serve them, by order of this court, in such matters and things where there is no establishment nor any certain sum assign'd for such service, and for paper, writing and printing for this court; and the sum of one thousand and forty pounds, part of the aforesaid sum of seven thousand eight hundred and sixty pounds, shall be applied for the payment of his majesty's council and house of representatives, serving in the general court during the several sessions for this present year.

£2,560 for forts and garrisons.

£1,600 for purchasing provisions, &c.

£1,040 for præmiums and grants.

£1,520 for debts where there is no establishment.

£1,040 for the members of the court.

And whereas there are sometimes contingent and unforeseen charges that demand prompt payment,—

Be it further enacted, .

£100 for contingent charges.

[SECT. 16.] That the sum of one hundred pounds, being the remaining part of the aforesaid sum of seven thousand eight hundred and sixty pounds, be applied to pay such contingent charges, and for no other purpose whatsoever.

Provided always,—

Remainder to be and remain as a stock in the treasury.

[SECT. 17.] That the remainder of the sum which shall be brought into the treasury by the tax aforesaid, over and above what shall be sufficient to pay off the benefit tickets as aforesaid, shall be and remain as a stock in the treasury, to be applied as the general court of this province shall hereafter order, and to no other purpose whatsoever; any thing in this act to the contrary notwithstanding.

And be it further enacted,

Money to be paid out of the proper appropriations.

[SECT. 18.] That the treasurer is hereby directed and ordered to pay the sum of eight thousand and ten pounds, as aforesaid, out of such appropriations as shall be directed to by warrant, and no other, upon pain of refunding all such sum or sums as he shall otherwise pay; and the secretary to whom it belongs to keep the muster-rolls and accompts of charge, shall lay before the house of representatives, when they direct, such muster-rolls and accompts after payment thereof.

And be it further enacted,

Directors' allowance to be made by the general court.

[SECT. 19.] That the directors or managers by this act appointed, shall have such allowances for their services as the general court shall hereafter order, and in case of the death, refusal or incapacity of attendance of any one or more of said managers, the vacancy shall be fill'd up by the governour and council. [*Passed February* 8; *published February* 16, 1750-51.

CHAPTER 16.

AN ACT FOR GRANTING THE SUM OF THREE HUNDRED POUNDS, FOR THE SUPPORT OF HIS HONOUR THE LIEUTENANT-GOVERNOUR AND COMMANDER-IN-CHIEF.

Be it enacted by the Lieutenant-Governour, Council and House of Representatives,

Governor's grant.

That the sum of three hundred pounds be and hereby is granted unto his most excellent majesty, to be paid out of the publick treasury to his honour Spencer Phips, Esq[r]., lieutenant-governour and commander-in-chief in and over his majesty's province of the Massachusetts Bay, for his past services, and further to enable him to manage the publick affairs of the province. [*Passed February* 15;* *published February* 16, 1750-51.

CHAPTER 17.

AN ACT FOR PREVENTING AND SUPPRESSING OF RIOTS, ROUTS AND UNLAWFUL ASSEMBLIES.

Preamble.

WHEREAS the provision already made by law has been found insufficient to prevent routs, riots and tumultuous assemblies, and the evil consequences thereof; wherefore,—

* See the note to this chapter, *post*.

Be it enacted by the Lieutenant-Governour, Council and House of Representatives,

[SECT. 1.] That from and after the publication of this act, if any persons, to the number of twelve or more, being arm'd with clubs or other weapons, or if any number of persons, consisting of fifty or upwards, whether armed or not, shall be unlawfully, riotously or tumultuously assembled, any justice of the peace, field officer or captain of the militia, sheriff of the county or undersheriff, or any constable of the town, shall, among the rioters, or as near to them as he can safely come, command silence while proclamation is making, and shall openly make proclamation in these or the like words:— Officers to make proclamation when persons are riotously assembled.

Our sovereign lord the king chargeth and commandeth all persons being assembled, immediately to disperse themselves, and peaceably to depart to their habitations, or to their lawful business; upon the pains contained in the act of this province made in the twenty-fourth year of his majesty King George the Second, for preventing and suppressing of riots, routs and unlawful assemblies. God save the King. Form of the proclamation.

And if such persons so unlawfully assembled, shall, after proclamation made, not disperse themselves within one hour, it shall be lawful for every such officer or officers, and for such other persons as he or they shall command to be assisting, to seize such persons, and carry them before a justice of the peace; and if such person shall be killed or hurt by reason of their resisting the persons so dispersing or seizing them, the said officer or officers and their assistants shall be indemnified and held guiltless.

[SECT. 2.] And all persons who, for the space of one hour after proclamation made as aforesaid,—or to whom proclamation ought to have been made, if the same had not been hindred,—shall unlawfully, routously, riotously and tumultuously continue together, or shall wilfully let or hinder any such officer, who shall be known, or shall openly declare himself to be such, from making the said proclamation, shall forfeit all their lands and tenements, goods and chattles, to his majesty (or such a part thereof as shall be adjudged by the justices before whom such offence shall be tried), to be applied towards the support of the government of this province; and shall be whipt thirty-nine stripes on the naked back at the publick whipping-post, and suffer one year's imprisonment, and once every three months during said imprisonment receive the same number of stripes on the naked back at the publick whipping-post as aforesaid. Penalty for disobedience.

[SECT. 3.] And if any such person or persons, so riotously assembled, shall demolish or pull down, or begin to demolish or pull down, any dwelling-house or other house parcel thereof, any house built for publick uses, any barn, mill, malt-house, store-house, shop or ship, he or they shall suffer the same pains and penalties as are before provided in this act.

And be it further enacted,

[SECT. 4.] That this act shall be read at every general sessions of the peace, and at the anniversary meeting of each town, within this province, annually; and no person shall be prosecuted for any offence contrary to this act, unless prosecution be commenced within twelve months after the offence committed. This act to be read at the anniversary meeting of the towns and general sessions of the peace.

Provided always,—

[SECT. 5.] That where there shall appear any circumstances to mitigate or alleviate any of the offences against this act, in the judgment of the court before which such offence shall be tried, it shall and may be lawful for the judges of such court to abate the whole of the pun- Judges empowered to abate the punishment of whipping, in case.

ishment of whipping, or such part thereof as they shall judge proper; anything in this act to the contrary notwithstanding.

Continuance of the act.

[SECT. 6.] This act to continue and be in force for the space of three years from the publication thereof, and no longer. [*Passed and published February* 14, 1750–51.

CHAPTER 18.

AN ACT IN ADDITION TO AN ACT, INTITLED "AN ACT TO PREVENT DAMAGE BEING DONE ON THE BEACH, HUMOCKS AND MEADOWS BELONGING TO THE TOWN OF SCITUATE, LYING BETWEEN THE SOUTHERLY END OF THE 'THIRD CLIFT,' SO CALLED, AND THE MOUTH OF THE NORTH RIVER."

Preamble.
1749-50, chap. 14.

WHEREAS in and by an act made and passed in the twenty-third year of his present majesty's reign, intitled "An Act to prevent damage being done on the beach, humocks and meadows belonging to the town of Scituate, lying between the southerly end of the 'Third Clift,' so called, and the mouth of the North River," the penalt[y][*ie*]s for turning or driving neat cattle, horse-kind, sheep or goats upon such beach, humocks or sedge-ground adjo[y][*i*]ning to said beach, to feed thereon, are to be recovered from him or them that shall so drive said cattle, horse-kind, sheep or goats, or from the owner or owners of them that shall so order them to be driven; and it is found, by experience, that proof thereof can seldom be obtained, whereby the good end and design of said act in a great measure is defeated,—

Be it therefore enacted by the Lieutenant-Governour, Council and House of Representatives,

Neat cattle and other creatures to be impounded if found feeding on the meadows, &c.

[SECT. 1.] That if any neat cattle, horse-kind, sheep or goats shall be found feeding on said beach, humocks, meadows or sedge-ground adjoyning to said beach, it shall and may be lawful for any person to impound the same, such person to observe the rules and directions in the said act prescribed in case of impounding; and the owner or owners of them shall forfeit and pay to the impounder one shilling a head for all neat cattle and horse-kind, and twopence for every sheep or goat; and the said penalt[y][*ie*]s or forfeitures shall be paid, before the creatures, which shall or may be impounded by virtue of this act, be discharged or released by the pound-keeper.

Provided, nevertheless,—

Rates to be paid for such impounded creatures.

[SECT. 2.] The owner or owners of the creatures so impounded may, if they think fit, replevie such creatures, on condition they give sufficient bond, with one or more suret[y][*ie*]s, to prosecute such replevin to effect before some justice of the peace in the same county, within fifteen days from the date of such replevin, and to pay all such forfeitures and costs as shall be awarded or adjudged against them. [*Passed February* 8; *published February* 16, 1750–51.

CHAPTER 19.

AN ACT FOR GRANTING UNTO BENJAMIN CRABB THE SOLE PRIVILE[*D*]GE OF MAKING CANDLES OF COARSE SPERMACÆTI OYL.

Preamble.

WHEREAS Benjamin Crabb, of Rehoboth, in the county of Bristol, has represented to this court that he, and no other person in the province, has the art of pressing, fluxing and chrystalizing of spermacæti and coarse spermacæti oyl, and of making candles of the same so prepared, and has been at great expence in providing himself with proper implements therefor, and is willing, on due encouragement, to undertake and carry on that business here, and to teach and instruct five of the inhabitants of this province his art aforesaid: this court being willing to encourage an undertaking so likely to prove beneficial to the province; therefore,—

Be it enacted by the Lieutenant-Governour, Council and House of Representatives,

[SECT. 1.] That the said Benjamin Crabb, and his heirs, shall and may have and enjoy the sole use, exercise and benefit of making candles of coarse spermacæti oyl so prepared, until[l] the thirty-first day of May, which shall be in the year of our Lord one thousand seven hundred and sixty-one: *provided*, that he do forthwith [i][*e*]ngage in and carry on the business aforesaid, within this province, and shall, some time before the thirty-first day of May, one thousand seven hundred and fifty-two, remove to some place within seven miles of the town of Boston, and there set up works suitable for carrying on the said business, and shall then and there manufacture all such quantities of oyl as can be procured fit for the purpose; and shall likewise, within five years from the publication of this act, well and fully instruct five of the inhabitants of this province, two of whom shall be appointed by the general court if they see cause, in the art aforesaid.

Benj. Crabb to have the sole privilege of making candles of coarse spermaceti-oil.

Proviso.

And be it further enacted,

[SECT. 2.] That no person or persons, saving such only as shall have first obtained the consent of s[*ai*]d Crabb or his heirs, signified under his or their hand, in writing, shall sell within this province, or export out of it, any candles made of the oyl prepared as aforesaid, during the time the said Crabb and his heirs are intit[u]led to the privile[*d*]ge aforesaid, other than such as are made by the said Crabb, his heirs or assigns, on pain of forfeiting [ten*] pounds for each offence. [*Passed February* 20; *published February* 23, 1750–51.

Penalty for others selling the said candles without his consent.

* This word is gone from the parchment, which is mutilated.

ACTS

PASSED AT THE SESSION BEGUN AND HELD AT BOSTON, ON THE TWENTY-SEVENTH DAY OF MARCH, A. D. 1751.

CHAPTER 20.

AN ACT IN ADDITION TO AN ACT INTITLED "AN ACT FOR SUPPLYING THE TREASURY WITH TWENTY-SIX THOUSAND SEVEN HUNDRED MILL'D DOLLARS."

Preamble. 1750-51, chap. 15, § 6.

WHEREAS by the act aforesaid, for the supply of the treasury, it is enacted that it shall be done by a lottery, and the drawing of said lottery is fix'd upon the eighteenth of April, provided five thousand tickets should then be disposed of; *and whereas* there is no prospect of that number being sold by that time,—

Be it enacted by the Lieutenant-Governour, Council and House of Representatives,

Lottery to be drawn the 5th of June next, in case.

[SECT. 1.] That the time for drawing said lottery be and hereby is put off to the fifth day of June next, at which time the managers and directors are ordered and impowered to proceed to drawing of said lottery, if the aforesaid number of five thousand tickets shall then have been disposed of.

And for the encouragement of said lottery,—

Be it further enacted,

Province bills and orders on the treasury to be received for tickets.

[SECT. 2.] That the managers or directors be and are hereby impowered and directed to receive province bills, as well as silver, for said tickets, as also warrants on the treasury for any demands that the money received by virtue of this lottery is appropriated to discharge. And the said directors or managers are hereby enjoined to deliver to the province treasurer all such sums of money as they have already received, and such sums as from time to time they shall receive, for tickets that have or may be disposed of; and the said treasurer is directed to receive the same, and give his receipts therefor, as also to receive, as equal to money, such warrants as shall be delivered to said directors in exchange for the tickets. And the directors or managers shall give publick notice in the newspapers at least ten days before the drawing of the lottery, that so the adventurers may be present, if they see fit.

Preamble.

And whereas, in and by said act, it is provided that the benefit tickets shall be paid within one year from the time of drawing said lottery, at the rate of three per cent interest per annum; now if it should so happen that there should be any deficiency in the treasury, that the whole of such benefit tickets cannot be paid according to the true intent of said act,—

Be it further enacted,

Six per cent per annum allowed for

[SECT. 3.] That all and every owner and possessor of such benefit tickets as shall not be paid off within one year as aforesaid by reason of such deficiency, shall draw an interest, after the rate of six per cent per annum, during the time of such deficiency in the treasury: *provided*, demand be made of payment within twenty days after the year is expired. [*Passed April* 18; *published April* 27, 1751. tickets not paid in time.

CHAPTER 21.

AN ACT PROVIDING FOR THE SUPPORT OF MINISTERS IN NEW PLANTATIONS.

WHEREAS the power by law granted to the courts of general sessions of the peace within this province to afford relief to ministers who shall not be suitably supported, is so restrained as not to extend to the relief of such ministers as are or may be settled in new plantations not erected into towns or districts; and it being necessary that provision be made by law for the encouragement and maintenance of such,— Preamble. 1715-16, chap. 17.

Be it therefore enacted by the Lieutenant-Governour, Council and House of Representatives,

[SECT. 1.] That in case of neglect in the proprietors or occupants of any new plantation, within this province, in fulfilling their contract or agreement with the minister or ministers of such plantation, qualified as the law directs, respecting his or their settlement or support, the court of general sessions of the peace within and for the county wherein such plantation is, are hereby impowred and directed, upon application to them made for that purpose, to provide for the relief of such minister or ministers; and in case the assessors for such new plantation do or shall neglect duly to assess and apportion the full sum voted or agreed on for the settlement or support of such minister or ministers, according to the true intent of the contract, the said court are hereby impowred and directed to appoint three or more sufficient freeholders within the same county, to assess the occupants or proprietors who are parties to such contract, such sum as, at the time of making such application, shall be judged by said court to be due to such minister or ministers by virtue of such contract, together with such further sum, in case payment has been long and unreasonably delayed, as said court shall judge sufficient, to afford to such minister or ministers meet recompence for any damage[s] sustained by such neglect: such assessment to be made on the occupants or proprietors, in such proportion as they may have agreed among themselves, or, if no such agreement shall appear, as said court shall judge most just and equitable. Ministers of new plantations, their salaries to be assessed by the court of general sessions of the peace.

[SECT. 2.] And said court shall make out and affix to a list of such assessment a warrant, in like form, *mutatis mutandis*, as is by law prescribed for levying and collecting of town rates or assessments; which warrant shall be signed by the clerk of such court, and directed to the collector or collectors of taxes in such plantation, if any there be, or to such person or persons as said court shall appoint for that purpose, requiring him or them to collect and levy the sum total of the said list, and to pay in the same unto such minister or ministers, or to such person or persons as said court shall appoint to receive the same for his or their use; and such collector or collectors, or other person or persons to whom such warrant shall be directed, are hereby fully authorized to execute the same, and to collect such assessment of the persons named in such list, wheresoever they may be found within this province. Warrant in usual form to be directed to the collectors, to collect said assessment.

And be it further enacted,

[SECT. 3.] That when and so often as timely payment of his or their dues shall be withheld from the minister or ministers of such new plan- Delinquent assessors and collectors to be conVented before the court.

tation, the justices of the said court of general sessions of the peace are hereby impowred and directed to convent before them the assessors, collector or collectors, or such others as have been or may be specially appointed by the occupants or proprietors of such plantation, to take care in that matter; and, upon conviction of neglect therein, to impose a fine on each delinquent not exceeding forty shillings for the first offence, and upon every after conviction of such neglect, to impose a fine of four pounds, to be levied by distress and sale of the offender's goods, and to be applied for the making of meet satisfaction unto the assessors or collectors that may have been appointed and employed by said court in the service aforesaid; the remainder, if any be, to be paid to the county treasurer, for defreying the necessary charges of the county.

Fine to be imposed.

Limitation.

[SECT. 4.] This act to continue and be in force for the space of five years from the publication thereof, and no longer. [*Published* April* 27, 1751.

CHAPTER 22.

AN ACT IN ADDITION TO AN ACT FOR REGULATING FENCES, CATTLE, &c.

Preamble.

1693-4, chap. 7, § 9.

WHEREAS in and by an act made and pass'd in the fifth year of the reign of King William and Queen Mary, intitled "An Act for regulating fences, cattle, &c.," it is enacted, "That for every sheep in every town, going on the commons without being under the hand of a shepherd, from the first of May to the last of October in every year, the owner or keeper of the said sheep shall pay the sum of threepence for every sheep at any time so found running on the common, not under the hand of a shepherd or keeper, betwixt the first of May and last of October yearly"; and it being found by experience that great damage is often done by sheep in the month of April, especially among English grain; therefore to prevent such inconveniencies for the future,—

Be it enacted by the Lieutenant-Governour, Council and House of Representatives,

Fine for sheep going at large without a shepherd, between the 15th of March and the last of October, yearly, unless allowed by the town.

[SECT. 1.] That for every sheep in any town within this province, going on the commons or ways, without being under the immediate care and inspection of a shepherd or keeper, from the fifteenth of March to the last day of October in every year, the owner or keeper of such sheep shall pay threepence for each and every sheep so found running on the commons or ways, without a shepherd or keeper, at any time from the fifteenth day of March to the last of October.

Provided, nevertheless,—

Proviso.

[SECT. 2.] That it shall be in the power of any town, at their annual meeting in March, by a vote, to give liberty for sheep to go at large, the whole or any part of the time, between the said fifteenth day of March and the first day of May; and in such case, it shall be lawful for the sheep in such town to go at large during such time as shall be so voted; anything in this or the before-recited act to the contrary notwithstanding.

Limitation.

[SECT. 3.] This act to continue and be in force for five years from the publication thereof, and no longer. [*Passed April* 26; *published April* 27, 1751.

* The date of the passage of this act has not been ascertained, owing to the imperfection of the records and the loss of the engrossment. The bill took its first reading, in the Council, March 29, 1751.

CHAPTER 23.

AN ACT IN ADDITION TO THE SEVERAL LAWS ALREADY IN BEING FOR THE MORE SPEEDY FINISHING THE LAND-BANK OR MANUFACTORY SCHEME.

WHEREAS an assessment was made by the commissioners appointed by the act of this province, pass'd in the seventeenth year of his present majesty's reign, intitled "An Act for the more speedy finishing the Land-bank or Manufactory Scheme," on certain delinquent partners, so called, and said assessment was published in the "Boston Gazette, or Weekly Journal," of the 21st of August, 1744; and another assessment was made by said commissioners on other delinquent partners, so called, and published in the "Boston Gazette, or Weekly Journal," of the 13th of November, 1744; and a further assessment was made by said commissioners on the late directors and partners of said company, and published in the supplement to the "Boston Evening Post" of the 27th of December, 1745: all which assessments have been received in part only; *and whereas*, by reason of the burning of the court-house in Boston, and the papers that were therein relating to the Land-bank or Manufactory Scheme, it is now become impossible to ascertain the exact sum which has been paid by said director* and partners in consequence of said assessments, otherwise than from the books, papers or other evidence which may be produced by said directors and partners themselves,— Preamble. 1743-44, chap. 17.

Be it therefore enacted by the Lieutenant-Governour, Council and House of Representatives,

[SECT. 1.] That each and every one of said late directors and partners assessed by said commissioners, whose names are published in the aforesaid "Gazettes or Journals" of the 21st of August, 1744, and of the 13th of November, 1744, and the supplement to the "Boston Evening Post" of the 27th of September, 1745, and their estates, shall be held and are hereby declared to be liable to the payment of the sums affixed to their names, respectively, saving such part thereof only which said directors and partners, or their representatives, shall make appear, by receipts or other evidence which shall be satisfactory to the commissioners, has already been paid in discharge of said assessments; and each and every of the said directors and partners in the several assessments aforesaid, and their estates, shall likewise be held and are hereby declared to be liable to the payment of interest on the whole or such part of their respective assessments as they shall not make appear to have been discharged, at and after the rate of six per cent per annum, to be computed from the time such assessment, or such part thereof, respectively, as shall remain unpaid, became payable or due, until the time of payment; and each and every of the delinquent partners whose names were published in the "Gazettes" of 21st August and 13th November, 1744, and their estates as aforesaid, are held and hereby declared to be liable to the payment of the further sum of ten per cent; and each and every of the directors and partners whose names were published in the supplement to the "Boston Evening Post" of the 27th December, 1745, and their estates, are held and hereby declared to be liable to the payment of five per cent on the sums respectively due and unpaid, over and above the interest aforesaid, in consideration of the charges which have been caused by their nonpayment of their respective parts of the assessments aforesaid.

Directors and partners to be held to the payment of the sum affixed to their names in the "Boston Gazette," &c.

Saving what is already paid.

Six per cent added as interest.

Ten per cent added.

Five per cent added for charges.

* *Sic.*

Preamble.

And whereas there appears to be a balance due from several of said directors, agreable to a report of a committee of the general court, signed, John Wheelwright, per order, and dated April 17th, 1751, and the vote or order of the general court accepting said report, amounting, in the whole, to seven hundred and forty-eight pounds three shillings and threepence, Land-bank money, so called; *and whereas* it is reasonable that each and every of the directors of said company should pay the sum of forty pounds, Land-bank money, as their proportion to what the partners have already been assessed for the charge and loss sustained by said Land-bank or Manufactory Company, over and above the sum of twenty pounds, lawful money, which has heretofore been assessed on each of said directors,—

Be it therefore enacted,

Directors to pay the balances in the committee's report.

[SECT. 2.] That the several directors still surviving and mentioned in said report, and their estates, and also the estates of such of said directors as are deceased, be and hereby are declared to be held and made liable to the payment of the aforesaid balances as are respectively declared by said report to be due from them to said company; and also, to the further sum of forty pounds, Land-bank money, each, as aforesaid, such payments to be made in Land-bank money, or lawful money equivalent.

And be it further enacted,

Warrants to be issued against the directors and partners.

[SECT. 3.] That if either of the late directors and partners, or their heirs, executors or administrators, shall not have paid the sums which, by this act, they, the said directors and partners, or their estates, are held and made liable to the payment of, on or before the first day of August, 1751, then, and in such case, the said commissiners* be and hereby are impowred and required, any judgments of court heretofore obtained and unsatisfied notwithstanding, forthwith to issue their warrants of distress against the persons or estates of each surviving director and partner, and the estates of each director and partner deceased, from whom any part of the sum required by this act to be paid as aforesaid, shall then remain due; which warrant shall be in the form following:—

Form of the warrants of distress.

To the Sheriff of the County of A., his undersheriff or deputy,—Greeting:

By virtue of the authority given to us in and by an act made and pass'd in the twenty-fourth year of his majesty King George the Second, intitled "An Act in addition to the several laws already in being for the more speedy finishing the Land-bank or Manufactory Scheme," these are in his majesty's name to require you to levy, by distress and sale of the estate of A. B., of C., in the county of E., the sum of , lawful money, and bring the same to us at our office in Boston forthwith, returning the overplus, if any be, to the said A. B.; and if there cannot be found in your precinct estate sufficient to discharge the same, then you are to commit the said A. B., if to be found in your precinct, to the common goal of the county of E., there to remain until he has paid the said sum of , lawful money, and charges; for all which this shall be your sufficient warrant: *save*, only, that if you shall take the real estate of the said A. B., that then the said A. B., his heirs, executors, administrators or assigns, shall have liberty, for three months thereafter, to redeem the same, and if the same shall not be not redeemed within three months as aforesaid, by paying said sum of , and charges, then you are required to sell the same as aforesaid, and return this warrant, and your doings thereon, into the office of the register of deeds for the county of E., there to be recorded.

Given under our hands and seals, at Boston, the day of , 175 , in the year of our Sovereign Lord, , by the Grace of God King of Great Britain, &c.

J. J.
S. D.
J. C.

* *Sic.*

[SECT. 4.] And all sheriffs, their undersheriffs and deputies, are impowred and required to execute the said warrant on the persons whose names shall be inserted therein, or their estates, real or personal; and where the sheriff, his undersheriff or deputy is concerned, such warrant may be directed to the coroner of the county of A., or his deputy, and be executed by either of them; and as some of said persons are or may be deceased, or out of the province, before such warrant or warrants of distress shall be issued, the said sheriffs and coroners are hereby impowred and directed to take such estate as they may find belonged to such deceased person, or was by law liable to be taken, if such deceased person or persons were then living, and in the province; the estate taken, whether real or personal, to be sold, and the overplus, if any, to be returned, as by law required in ordinary cases of execution or distress: *save*, only, that the liberty of redeeming the real estate shall extend to three months only after being taken; upon the expiration of which term of three months, if the same be not redeemed, the sheriff, or other officer who took the same, shall return the warrant of distress, with his doings thereon, into the office of register of deeds in the county where the lands lie, there to be recorded.

Officers empowered to execute said warrants.

Three months allowed to redeem real estates.

And whereas it may happen that a further sum may be still necessary to be raised in order to finish the affairs of the said Land-bank or Manufactory Company,—

Preamble.

Be it further enacted,

[SECT. 5.] That if the whole sum which shall be due, and which shall be recovered on or before the first day of December, 1751, on the several assessments aforesaid, and from the several directors for what is by this act declared to be due from them, shall not be sufficient to exchange the whole of the bills of said company that are now outstanding, and to pay the charges that have arisen or may arise therein, then, and in such case, the commissioners aforesaid be and hereby are impowred and required to make a further assessment on directors and partners in proportion to the sum which shall appear to the satisfaction of the commissioners to have been originally received or taken out by each person: *saving*, only, that each director shall be assessed in proportion as if he had received or taken out two hundred and fifty pounds, altho' the certain sum by such director received or taken out shall not appear.

Commissioners empowered to make further assessments.

[SECT. 6.] And said commissioners shall cause such assessment to be published in the "Boston Gazette or Weekly Journal," and each of the persons who may be so assessed, and their estates, shall be held and are hereby declared to be liable and obliged to the payment of the respective sums on them asssessed, in like manner as those directors and partners who have not paid the former assessments are by this act declared to be liable and obliged to the payment thereof; and if either of the directors or partners so assessed, or their executors or administrators, shall not, within sixty days after the publication of such assessment, pay to said commissioners the sum on such director or partner assess'd, the said commissioners are hereby required and impowred, unless such assessment shall be set aside or disannulled by the general court, forthwith to issue their warrants of distress against the persons or estates of each surviving director and partner, and the estates of each director and partner deceased, respectively; which warrants shall be in the form before prescribed by this act: and all sheriffs, undersheriffs and their deputies, and, where they are interested, all coroners, are impowred and required to execute such warrants in like manner, and observe the same rules as prescribed for the executing warrants for any of the former assessments mentioned in this act.

Assessments to be published.

Warrants to be issued on such assessments.

And whereas in and by the afore-recited act, intitled "An Act for the

Preamble.

more speedy finishing the Land-bank or Manufactory Scheme," it is enacted in the words following: "That from and after the publication of this act, the estate of each and every such director and partner shall be thereby bound and subjected to the payment of such sum or sums of money as shall be assessed upon him by the said commissioners, or any two of them, with the approbation and allowance of the great and general court of this province, as is hereinafter mentioned, for the redemption of their respective proportions of the bills of the said late company, and their equitable part and share of all losses and charges arising by the said scheme, in such manner as the same would be bound and subjected by the actual service of process of attachment upon it at the suit of any creditor according to the ordinary course of the law and the usage within this province,"—

1743-44, chap. 17, § 3.

Be it further enacted,

Real estates subjected to satisfy the same.

[SECT. 7.] That all and every part of the lands and tenements of each and every director and partner, which were bound and subjected by the said last-recited clause, in whose possession soever the same now is or hereafter may be, be and hereby is declared to continue to be held subjected and liable to the payment or discharge of the sums declared by this act, respectively, to be due from or required to be assessed upon such director and partner, as well those who shall be deceased as those who shall have survived; and shall be liable to be taken by distress, as if then in the actual possession of such director or partner.

And be it further enacted,

Notice to be given by commissioners of their redeeming the Land-bank notes.

[SECT. 8.] That as soon as the commissioners shall have received a sufficient sum, in their judgment, to redeem the Land-bank bills, so called, which may be outstanding, they shall give publick notice thereof, in all the weekly newspapers published in the town of Boston, three weeks successively, of the time or times, and place or places, in said town, when and where they will attend to redeem said bills; which publick notice hereby is made and declared to be a legal tender to all and every possessor and possessors of said bills. [*Passed and published April* 24, 1751.

CHAPTER 24.

AN ACT IN FURTHER ADDITION TO AN ACT MADE AND PASS'D IN THE TWENTY-SECOND YEAR OF HIS PRESENT MAJESTY'S REIGN, INTITLED "AN ACT FOR DRAWING IN THE BILLS OF CREDIT OF THE SEVERAL DENOMINATIONS WHICH HAVE AT ANY TIME BEEN ISSUED BY THE GOVERNMENT AND ARE STILL OUTSTANDING, AND FOR ASCERTAINING THE RATE OF COINED SILVER IN THIS PROVINCE FOR THE FUTURE."

Preamble.
1748-49, chap. 15.

WHEREAS, notwithstanding the provision made for enforcing the payment of the publick taxes into the treasury, many of the constables and collectors of the towns within this province have neglected or delayed to pay in the sums committed to them to collect, and other unforeseen accidents have happened, by means whereof a larger sum in bills of credit is now outstanding than there is silver in the treasury sufficient to redeem or exchange, and the possessors of said bills will be injured, unless relieved by the government, and the paper currency of the province cannot be brought to a full period by the time proposed; in order therefore that the possessors of the bills which still remain outstanding, and the possessors of the orders given by the committee of the general court for bills brought in and burnt, may have justice done them,—

Be it enacted by the Lieutenant-Governour, Council and House of Representatives,

[SECT. 1.] That the possessors of the bills of credit of this province, which are now outstanding, who shall bring in the same by the third of June next, shall be entitled to the immediate exchange of one-eighth part thereof in silver, at the like rate with those which have been redeemed or exchanged already; and the remaining seven-eighths shall be redeemed or exchanged with silver at the like rate, on or before the thirty-first day of December, one thousand seven hundred and fifty-one, with the addition of a premium of one per cent, and interest from the thirty-first day of March last, until paid, at the rate of six per cent per year: and each and every of the orders which shall have been given before the thirty-first of March, one thousand seven hundred and fifty-one, by the committee aforesaid, shall be redeemed and paid off with silver, at the same time, and at the like rate, with interest as aforesaid, from the date of said order, until paid.

Possessors of the bills entitled to one-eighth in silver.

The remainder to be paid by the 31st of December, 1751.

Interest to be allowed.

And be it further enacted,

[SECT. 2.] That the committee appointed by the general court, for receiving from the possessors the bills of credit of this province, may and shall continue to sit until the third day of June next, and no longer; and whensoever any of the said possessors shall bring any of the said bills to the committee, such possessor shall receive therefor two orders for every sum, each order to be signed by three of the committee at least; viz., one, for one-eighth part of the principal sum, which the treasurer shall cause immediately to be discharged and paid out of the silver now remaining in the treasury, or that may hereafter be bro't in for taxes, and the other, for seven-eighths of said sum, which order shall be accepted by the treasurer, and shall be in the form following; viz.,—

Committee for exchanging the bills to sit till June 3, 1751.

To give two orders for each sum received.

To the treasurer of the province of the Massachusetts Bay,

SIR: Pay to A. B. or bearer, in lawful silver money, at six shillings and eightpence per ounce, or Spanish mill'd dollars, at six shillings apiece, by the thirty-first of December next, with a premium of one per cent, and lawful interest for said sum, from thirty-first March past, 'till paid, being for in bills of credit this province, of the old tenor, received of the said A. B. this day of , 1751.

Form of the order for seven-eighths.

And be it further enacted,

[SECT. 3.] That the orders given as aforesaid, shall and may be received by the several constables and collectors for all taxes that are already due, accounting the principal sum only, without any allowance for interest or premium, and the treasurer shall receive them from, and give discharge to, the said collector or constables accordingly; and in case any of the said orders shall remain outstanding after the warrants, for the tax for eighteen thousand four hundred pounds, lawful money, conditionally engaged to be assessed in the year one thousand seven hundred and fifty-one, shall go forth, said orders shall be received in discharge of said tax, accounting both the principal sum, interest and premium due on said orders, provided the same be paid before the thirty-first of December next.

Which may be received by the collectors of taxes.

And be it further enacted,

[SECT. 4.] That the committee of the general court shall, from day to day, transmit to the province treasurer, an exact list of all the orders by them given, and such persons as shall first bring their bills to be exchanged, and shall first take orders therefor, shall be entitled to have such orders first paid off and discharged; and immediately upon the treasurer's being possessed of a sum not less than three thousand

Committee to transmit lists of their orders to the treasurer.

Public notice to be given when

the treasury is in cash.

pounds, lawful money, in silver, he shall give publick notice in all the newspapers, that so as many of the first-dated orders as shall amount to the sum of three thousand pounds, may then be paid off and discharged; and the like publick notice shall be given, from time to time, when and so often as there shall be a stock of three thousand pounds for the purpose aforesaid: and if any orders shall not be tendered within thirty days after such publick notice given, the interest and also the premium which would be otherwise due on such orders, shall then determine and cease. [*Passed April* 26, 1751.*

NOTES.—The foregoing were the only sessions of the General Court this year. The engrossments of chapters 2, 4, 5, 6, 7, 8, 11, 13, 14, 16, 18, and 19, only, are preserved. The acts of each session were printed together, except chapter 6, which, being an impost act, was printed by itself for separate distribution.

No evidence has been discovered that the acts of the first session ever reached the Privy Council, or that they were considered by the Board of Trade.

The acts of the last three sessions were formally certified for transmission to the Privy Council, September 25, 1751. They were duly received and laid before the Council, March 11, 1752, and were immediately referred to a committee. From this committee they went, in regular course, to the Lords Commissioners for Trade and Plantations, where the letter from Secretary Willard, transmitting them, was read, March 19, 1752, and they were ordered to be sent to Mr. Lamb, for his opinion thereon in point of law.

Mr. Lamb's report is dated January 12, 1755, and sets forth that he has "perused and considered these acts," and that he has no objection to offer against any of them except chapters 17 and 23. His comments on the two acts last named are given in the notes to those chapters, *post*.

On the 29th of January, Mr. Lamb's report was considered in the Board of Trade, and a draught of a representation was ordered "to be prepared proposing the confirmation of such of" these acts "as have not expired by their own limitation or have not had their full effect." On the 4th of February this draught had been prepared, and was agreed to at the Board, and ordered to be transcribed; and on the next day it was signed.

This report represents that chapters 8, 9, 11, 14, 15, 16, 17, 20, and 24 "were for temporary services and are either expired or the purposes for which they were passed have been completed"; and that chapters 7, 10, 12, 13, 18, 19, 21, 22, and 23 "appear to have been enacted for the particular Convenience and relate to the present Œconomy of the Province, and"—to further quote the language of the report—"as Mr. Lamb, one of his Majesty's Counsel at Law, whose opinion has been taken upon these Acts, has no objection to any of them in point of Law; We see no reason why His Majesty may not be graciously pleased to confirm them."

Accordingly, on the 11th of March, 1755, an order was passed, in Council, confirming chapters 7, 10, 12, 13, 18, 19, 21, 22, and 23.

Chap. 1. "From the first introduction of paper money, it had been the practice of government to issue bills for public charges, and to make a tax for the payment of the sum issued, in future years, into the treasury again. The bills being all exchanged by the silver imported from England, and provision made by law, that no bills of credit should ever after pass as money, there was a difficulty in providing money for the immediate service of government, until it could be raised by a tax. Few people were, at first, inclined to lend to the province, though they were assured of payment in a short time with interest. The treasurer, therefore, was ordered to make payment to the creditors of government in promissory notes, payable to the bearer in silver in two or three years, with lawful interest. This was really better than any private security; but the people, who had seen so much of the bad effects of their former paper money, from its depreciation, could not consider this as without danger, and the notes were sold for silver at discount, which continued until it was found that the promise made by government was punctually performed. From that time, the public security was preferred to private, and the treasurer's notes were more sought for than those of any other person whomsoever. This was the era of public credit in Massachusetts Bay."—*Hutchinson's History of Mass., vol.* 3, *pp.* 9 *and* 10.

Chap. 2. "April 6. 1750. His Honor the Lieutennant Governor sent down the following Message to the House by the Secretary, viz, Gentlemen of the House of Represent^ves The Secretary has laid before me the vote of the two Houses granting the sum of two hundred pounds to the Lieutennant Governor & Commander in cheif in consideration of his past Services in that important Station I cannot but observe to you, that it is more than six months since the Administration of the Government has devolved upon me, that my whole time is spent in the publick Service & consequently that I have good reason to expect from you a Sum sufficient for my support; such a sum as shall be equal to the common Expence of a Family (which many of you must be sensible, the sum now granted is not) besides some further Allowance for the honor of the Station his Majesty has been pleased to place me in I am desirous of preserving a perfect Harmony & good Understanding between the several Branches of the Legislature, so far as shall consist with the Honor of his Majesty's Commission; but this I shall always endeavor to maintain; And in order to enable me to do it more effectually, I must desire you to send for your Vote, and to make such Addition to the Grant, as shall render it agreable to the Assurances given by a former Assembly to his Majesty, that they would support his Governor suitable to the dignity of his Station, on

* See note to this chapter, *post*.

failure whereof, they acknowledged his Majesty would have just reason to show his Displeasure"—*Council Records, vol. XIX., p.* 164.

"April 7th. 1750 In the House of Representves Voted that two hundred Pounds be granted & allowed to be paid out of the publick Treasury to the Honble Spencer Phips Esqr Lieut. Governour & Commander in Chief in Consideration of his past Services in that Important Station In Council; Read & Concur'd.—Consented to by the Lieut Governr."—*Ibid., p.* 169.

Chaps. 4, 5, *and* 6. The Governor's signature to the engrossment of each of these acts is not dated.

Chap. 8. "October 9th 1750 The Secretary having by Order of his Honour the Lieut. Governour proposed to both Houses, that in the Engross'd Bill entitled "an Act for establishing & regulating the Fees of the several Officers within this Province as are hereafter "mentioned" The Term of the Continuance of the said Act should be reduc'd to two Years, the two Houses agreed thereto, And Amendmt being made thereon accordingly His Honour signed his Consent to the said Act"—*Ibid., p.* 251.

Chap. 12. "Novemr 23d 1749. * * * * The Mention whereof leads me to observe, that as a more general Cultivation of Our Lands, & thereby the Increase of the Produce of this Province, as well as the carrying on the Manufactures in it, is greatly impeded by reason of the Scarcity of Labourers, may it not therefore deserve your Consideration whether Something may not be done to encourage industrious & well disposed Protestant Foreigners to Settle among us, & whether some of Our Acts which require Security to be given to such as shall bring them hither have not eventually (tho' beside the Intention of the Legislature) discouraged & prevented the Importation of many such, & whether the said Acts may not be altered & amended, & such Provision by Law, be made, as for the future may prevent so manifest & extensive an Inconvenience."—*Extract from the speech of Lieutenant-Governor Phips: ibid., p.* 67.

See also note to 1749-50, chapter 21, *ante*, under date of June 6, and November 24, 1749.

"January 26 1749. A Petition of Joshua Winslow Esqr & others Merchants in Boston proposing to this Court in case they may have the use of the Ship Massachusetts Frigate upon terms particularly mentioned in their petition to employ her in a Voyage to Ireland for transporting Protestants of that Country into this Province, and praying that they may be allowed the use of the said Ship for that purpose accordingly—

In the House of Representves; Read & Voted that the Ship Massachusetts Frigate with the Tackling & furniture as they ly (warlike stores & Artillery with such other Stores as the Committee of this Court shall judge unnecessary for the Voyage excepted) shall be Apprized by three Judicious men upon Oath; for which Apprized value the Petitioners shall give Security to the Province Treasurer to pay in case of loss, & for the performance of the several Articles in this Vote After which they shall at their own cost & expense fit the said Ship for the Seas; & order some skilfull person (giving the preference to Cpt Moses Bennet, provided they can agree with him on like terms as with another) to proceed with her to the North part of Ireland, from whence they shall cause to be brought in said Ship not less than three hundred nor more than five hundred & fifty Foreign Protestants (of which number there shall be at least thirty Families) and shall land the same in some part of this Province (the danger of the seas & Mortality excepted) and shall within thirty days after her arrival at Boston deliver up said Ship to the Treasurer, or any Committee that shall be appointed by this Court to receive her together with all her Tackle, Stores & Appurtenances, agreable to an Inventory which shall be taken by the Master of said Ship, after she is fitted & before she sails from Boston, & shall be lodged with the Treasurer (Ordinary wear & tear excepted) Provided nevertheless that in case the Ship should during the Voyage (which shall be limited to twelve months from this time) meet with any loss or extraordinary damage, the said Petitioners shall make good the same to the Province & shall give Security to the Treasurer accordingly—

In Council; Read & Concur'd—Consented to by the Lieut Governor."—*Council Records, vol. XIX., p.* 140.

"January 27 1749. In the House of Representves; Ordered that the Committee heretofore appointed to dispose of the Ship Massachusetts Frigate be impowered to carry the Vote of the Court into Execution pass'd this Session respecting the said Ship; and that Mr Tyng be of the Committee in the room of of Thomas Foster Esqr who declines that Service.

In Council Read & Concur'd—Consented to by the Lieut Govern."—*Ibid., p.* 142.

"June 29th 1750. In the House of Representves; Read & it appearing that by reason of unforeseen & unavoidable accidents, the intended Voyage within mentioned cannot be performed in the twelve month limited for performing the same; Therefore Ordered that a further Time be allowed the Petitioners for performing the Voyage aforesaid in, & that the same be extended to the first of October 1751, upon the Conditions of the former Order mentioned; Provided the Petitioners shall continue to bear all charges upon the Ship that it be necessary to preserve her in good Repair, & shall continue to keep a sufficient Number of hands in Pay to look after her. & shall execute their Contract with the General Courts Committee within ten days from this Time

In Council; Read & Concur'd—Consented to by the Lieut Governr."—*Ibid., p.* 227.

"October 11th 1750. Jacob Wendell Esqr. from the Committee appointed to take Care of the Ship Massachusetts Frigate gave in the following Report; vizt The Committee appointed the 27th of January last, to carry the Vote of the Court respecting the Ship Massachusetts Frigate into Execution, do report, viz, That on the Application of Mr Samuel Wentworth for himself & the other Petitioners, the Committee allowed them to take the Ship into their Possession; And the Petitioners gave Orders for the Ship being removed from Mr Hutchinson's Wharff to the graving Yard & from thence to Clark's Wharff.—That the Committee applied to Mr. Secretary for a Warrant of Apprizement to be made out to Richard Bill Esqr. Mr. Jeffrey Bedgood & Mr Stephen Boutineau, for apprizing the Ship, & acquainted Mr Samuel Wentworth of it, who well approved of said Gentlemen, & as soon as the Warrant was obtained, it was given to Richard Bill Esq[r] & he with the other Gentlemen desired to proceed thereon, as soon as possibly they could & make Return into the Secretary's office;—The Committee in the mean time employed a scrivener to draw a proper Instrument for the Petitioners to execute to the Treasurer of the Province, agreable to the General Courts Direction; And when it was done was given to Mr Wentworth for himself & the others concerned with him, to look over, who in some days after returned the same, & said they approved of it & were ready to sign it, when it was drawn fair; And the Committee sent to Mess[rs] Winslow, Wentworth & Gunter to come to the Court House & execute said Bond; which they did but some of the Committee was just then so engaged in the publick Affairs, that they could not go down immediately, when notice was given that they were attending, but did as soon as possibly they could go down to them, when M[r] Gunter was gone, & Mr Winslow & Mr Wentworth said if we would give them the Bond, they & Mr Gunter would execute it, & return it to Jacob Wendell Esq[r] & they were asked for it by him, but never returned it according to their Promise, but some time in May told him, they design'd to petition the General Court for granting a further Time to perform the Voyage into Ireland, accordingly they did put in their Petition the 7th of June, & it pass'd the Court & was granted the 29th—The Committee some days after got a Copy of the Court's further Grant to them, which was sent to them; And thereon they gave their Answer in Writing the 24th of July, that they did not accept thereof; But they have had Possession of the Ship ever since they first gave Capt. Bennet Directions to remove her from Mr. Hutchinson's Wharff until the 27th of August, when the Lieut. Governour & Council gave Directions to the Committee to take Care that she be caulked. Jacob Wendell ℘ order. In the House of Represent[ves] Read & Accepted. In Council Read & Concur'd.—Consented to by the Lieut. Govern[r]."—*Ibid., p.* 260.

"April 3 1752. In the House of Representatives, Voted That the Committee appointed to take Care of the Massachusets Frigate be directed to make Sale of the same & Appurtenances, for the best Advantage of the Province, as soon as may be Excepting Warlike Stores: In Council Read and Concurred Consented to by the Lieutenant Governor."—*Ibid., p.* 442.

"A society was formed in Boston for promoting industry and frugality. The government of the colony, to forward this laudable design, purchased the factory in Boston. It also granted four townships of land for the use of foreign protestants, and permitted the provincial frigate to be employed in their transportation."—*Holmes Annals, vol.* 2, *p.* 180.

"January 11. 1749. In the House of Represent[ves] Ordered that the Committee appointed by both Houses, to consider of some proper Encouragement for improving the natural Advantages of the Soil &c be directed to prepare the draught of a Bill, to Supesede or explain any Act or Acts that have in any measure, a tendency to discourage the Importation of Foreign Protestants & report thereon—In Council, Read & Concur'd."—*Ibid., p.* 122.

"January 26. 1749. In the House of Represent[ves] Voted that there be four Townships allowed for Foreign Protestants to settle in, viz. two in the Western & two in the Eastern parts of this Province, that each Township shall be settled with one hundred & twenty Settlers, such Settlers to be so many distinct Families, Single men of the Age of twenty one years who shall actually settle to be accounted as part of the number. The two western Townships to be the Eastermost Township lately laid out at or near Fort Massachusetts & the other to ly East thereof, & to contain the quantity of seven miles square; This Township to extend East & West from Charlemont to the Township aforesaid; and North & South to make up the quantity of seven miles square as aforesaid. The Eastern Townships to contain six miles square each & in Order for their being laid out, that a Survey be made from Sabago pond to the head of Berwick; & that these two Townships be laid out contiguous to some Township already laid out there; and that there be a Reserve of two hundred acres in each of said four Townships; which is hereby granted to Mr Joseph Crellius, on condition, that he import, or cause to be imported & settled in each of s[d] Townships, in three years from this time one hundred & twenty Protestant Settlers as aforesaid: Also that there be reserved two hundred acres for the use of the Government where Fort Massachusetts stands: And that all the remainder of said four Townships be granted to one hundred & twenty Settlers in a Township; provided that they make one hundred & twenty three Shares in a Township viz one for the first settled Minister, one for the Ministry & one for a School, provided also that they settle in each Town a learned Protestant Minister in five years from this time; always provided that the said four Townships be severally settled with one hundred & twenty such settlers in three years from such time; provided further that each settler by himself, or some other family shall remain on his Settlem[t] for the space of Seven years, or his Share shall revert to the Province & may by the Government be disposed of to some other person. In Council, Read & Concur'd—Consented to by the Lieut. Govern[r]."—*Ibid., p.* 138.

"May 31st 1750 And now I am speaking on these Heads, I must acquaint you that M[r] Crellius a German Gentleman (with whom the last Assembly treated about the transporting of Protestant Families of that Nation into this Province) is now come to attend upon this Affair in Person & has delivered to me some further & more particular Proposals he has to make, for effecting this Design; w[ch] I shall lay before you: And by what I can learn of the Character & Disposition of that People, I apprehend it to be of great Importance to encourage their Settlement among us; For together with other Benefits likely to accrue from it, It is probable they will introduce many useful Manufactures & teach us by their Example those most necessary & excellent Arts for increasing our Wealth, I mean Frugality & Diligence in which we are at present exceedingly defective"—*Extract from a speech of Lieutenant-Governor Phips to the Assembly: ibid., p.* 194.

"June 1. 1750. In the House of Represen[ves] Ordered that Judge Russell, Col[o] Otis, Mr, Allen, Mr. Hall, & M[r] Tyng, with such as the Honble. Board shall join be a Committee to take the two first Paragraphs of His Honour's Speech of Yesterday under Consideration (together with the Papers refer'd to) & report what they Judge proper for the Court to do thereon: In Council; Read & Concur'd, And Jacob Wendell Joseph Wilder, John Chandler & Andrew Oliver Esq[rs.] are joined in the Affair"—*Council Records, ibid., p.* 196.

"June 12th 1750 A memorial of Joseph Crellius, proposing to engage a Number of Substantial Trades men from Germany to Settle within this Province in Case they might have a Tract of Land of about two hundred Acres within some Town in the Province, & that they may have the Priviledges of a Town within themselves; Praying the Consideration of this Court thereon. In the House of Representves Read & Ordered that Mr Tyng, Mr. Pomroy & Mr Stockbridge with such as the Honble Board shall join be a Committee to take this Memorial under Consideration & report what they Judge proper for this Court to do thereon;—In Council; Read & Concur'd, and Jacob Wendell & Andrew Oliver Esqrs are joined in the Affair."—*Ibid., p.* 204.

"Decemr 27. 1751. Since your last Session a Number of Families are arrived here from Germany with a Design to settle on some of the unimproved Lands of the Province; They are not sufficient to fill up a Township; But there is Encouragement that a greater Number will follow them the next Year; I shall order to be laid before you some Letters I have received from a Gentleman of Character on this Subject & you will consider what is proper to be done by you in relation to it"—*Extract from a speech of Lieutenant-Governor Phips, to the Assembly: ibid., p.* 401.

"Decemr 28. 1751. In the House of Representves Ordered that Mr Speaker, Judge Russell, Mr. Tyng, Mr Gray, & Mr. Trowbridge with such as the honble Board shall Join be a Committee to take His Honours Speech & the Letters therein refer'd to under consideration & report what they Judge proper for this Court to do thereon—In Council; Read & Concur'd." "On the Vote of the House for a Committee on the Lieutt Governour's Speech, Enter'd this Day,—In Council; Read & Concur'd; And Jacob Wendell Samuel Watts Andrew Oliver & Thomas Hutchinson Esqrs are joined in the Affair."—*Council Records, ibid., p.* 402-3.

"Decemr 31. 1751 Jacob Wendell Esqr from the Committeé of both Houses on the Lieut. Governour's Speech; gave in the following Report; vizt * * * * * * * The Committee have made some Inquiry from Persons acquainted therewith, into the Circumstances of the German Families lately imported, & it appears that some of them are in Danger of suffering during the Winter Season; And therefore the Committee are of Opinion that a more particular Inquiry be made into this Affair, that so such of the said Germans as are incapable of supporting themselves may receive such Relief as may be thought proper. * * * * * * Jacob Wendell ℔ order. In Council; Read & Ordered that this Report be accepted. In the House of Representves Read & Concur'd—Consented to by the Lieut Governr."—*Ibid., p.* 403.

"Jany 1. 1752. In the House of Representves Voted that the Commissary General be directed to Supply Mr. Etter with Blankets & Beds, now in his hands, not exceeding ten each for the use of the poor Germans, who are now suffering by reason of the Severity of the Season; The Blankets & Beds to be returned when the Germans have done with them; And in Case the Commissary has not a sufficient Number, he is then directed to purchase, so many as shall be wanting to enable him to comply with this Order. In Council Read & Concur'd.—Consented to by the Lieut Governr."—*Ibid., p.* 405.

"June 6th 1753 A Memorial of Jacob Hatterick and others German Protestants, Shewing that by Incouragement offered by this Government they have been induced to Transport themselves & Families into this Province to settle upon such Lands as shall be alloted to them, Praying for the Direction of this Government; and that they be allowed to settle in the Western Parts of the Province In the House of Representatives; Read and it appearing that in the year 1749 this Court granted four Townships in Order to encourage Foreign Protestants to come and settle in this Government and granted a Farm of Land in each of said Townships to Mr Joseph Crellius, in Case he caused to be settled in each of said Townships One hundred and twenty Families, by the Time limited in said Grants; But it appearing also that the said Mr Crellius has failed of bringing forward said Settlements; And that the Poor Petrs are left without any Aid; Therefore—Voted that Colo Patridge and Colo Wothington with such as the Honble Board shall join be a Committee to lay out Thirty one House Lots not Exceeding Ten Acres each, Contiguous to each other in the German Township so called at Fort Massachusets; and also so much of the Intervail Lands in said Township to each of said House Lots as shall make up an 123rd part thereof considered with Relation to Quantity and Quality; And that the Petrs have Liberty to settle upon and improve said Lands, agreeable to the Original Grant of the Court and further that said Committee lay out in said Township, Forty eight House Lots more not exceeding Ten Acres each, one for the first Protestant Minister, one for the Ministry and one for the School and also to divide the remainder of the Intervale Lands into forty eight equal Shares or Rights considered as aforesaid with Relation to Quantity and Quality; One of which shall be for the first settled Minister, and one for the Ministry and one for the School—And Inasmuch as the Petitioners have Signified their Desires that some English Families may be admitted as Settlers with them, on the same Lands; That therefore the said Committee admit Forty five Settlers in Addition to the Petitioners, Each of which Forty five Settlers shall pay to the said Committee, for the use of the Government, the Sum of Six Pounds thirteen Shillings and four pence; & give Bond in the Sum of Fifty Pounds to said Committee to perform the like Conditions of Settlement from this Time forward, as were enjoined in the Original Grant of the Township; And that in all after Divisions of Land in the said Town the Petitioners shall each of them have an 123rd Part thereof, And the remainder of the Township shall be divided to and among the other admitted Settlers with the publick Rights afore mentioned, each an equal Part; And that the Original Grant made in said Township to Mr Joseph Crellius is hereby declared void and forfeited to the Government he not having complied with the Conditions thereof, The aforesaid Committee to be accountable. In Council; Read and Concur'd and John Chandler Esqr is joined in the Affair. Consented to by the Lieutenant Governor"—*Ibid., vol. XX., p.* 37.

"June 14. 1753 In the House of Representatives; Whereas a Number of Germans appear desirous to join in Settling the Township at Fort Massachusets lattely granted to Thirty one German Petitioners, with a Number of English, who shall appear to purchase

Rights in Order to a Settlement, And there appearing several of the said Petitioners willing to resign their Interest in s^d Grant & that others may be admitt^d in their Stead;—Voted that the Committee appointed by this Court to admitt Settlers &c in said Township be impowered and directed to admit others of the said Germans into the said Township on the Conditions of the aforesaid Grant in the Room & Stead of such of the said Petitioners as shall appear willing within one Month to resign their Interest in said Grant; Provided that they do not give anything to the first Grantees in Consideration of their being admitted in their room. In Council; Read and Concur'd—Consented to by the Lieutenant Governor."—*Ibid., p.* 53.

"January 30. 1752. In the House of Representatives Voted that Mr Speaker, Mr Allen & Mr Tyng with such as the Honble Board shall join be a Committee take under Consideration the Letter this Court has received from Mr Luther of Germany, and prepare an Answer thereto in the Recess of the Court, & Report thereon at the next Sitting of this Court, In Council Read & Concurred; and Jacob Wendell, Samuel Danforth & John Quincy Esq^rs are joined in the Affair."—*Ibid., vol. XIX., p.* 441.

"June 3. 1752 In Council Ordered that Jacob Wendell, Samuel Danforth, and Thomas Hutchinson Esq^rs with such as shall be joined by the Honble House of Representves be a Committee to take under Consideration the Letter this Court has received from Mr. Luther of Germany and prepare an answer thereto. In the House of Representatives Read & Concurred, & Mr Allen, Mr Tyng Col^o Otis, & Capt. Williams are joined in the Affair." —*Ibid., p.* 471.

"December 14. 1752 In Council Voted that John Quincy Esqr be of the Committee for preparing the Draught of a Letter to Mr Councellor Luther in the room of Samuel Danforth Esqr who is not able to attend that Affair, The Committee to set forthwith. In the House of Representatives Read and Concur'd "—*Ibid., p.* 513.

"December 21. 1752 Jacob Wendell Esqr from the Committee of both Houses appointed to prepare the Draught of a Letter to Mr Councellor Luther, Reported the same In Council Read and accepted & Ordered, that the Secretary prepare & sign a fair Draught of this Letter & forward it accordingly;—In the House of Representatives Read & Concur'd —Consented to by the Lieu^t Governor."—*Ibid , p.* 519.

"April 2. 1753 The Secretary laid before the Court a Letter he had received from Samuel Waldo Esqr of London, and therewith a Packet directed to the General Court from Mr Luther of Frankfort, relating to the German Protestants transportation hither." —*Ibid., vol. XX., p.* 5.

"April 3. 1753. On the Letter from Mr Councell^r Luther & Brigadier Waldo mentioned Yesterday, In the House of Representatives; Read & Ordered that Judge Russell, Mr. Allen, & Col^o Otis, with such as the Honble Board shall appoint be a Committee to take the said Letters and Papers accompanying them, under Consideration, and report what they Judge Proper for this Court to do thereon:—In Council; Read and Concur'd; And Andrew Oliver and Thomas Hutchinson Esq^rs are joined in this Affair."—*Ibid., p.* 6.

"December 4. 1754. A Letter directed to this Court from Mr. Luther of Frankfort in Germany. In the House of Representatives, Ordered that Mr Welles, Judge Russell, & Col^o Otis together with such as the Honble Board shall join, be a Committee to take under Consideration a Letter from Mr Luther, dated Frankfort June 28. 1754, and report what they think proper for this Court to do thereon,—In Council, Read & Concurd; And Andrew Oliver & Thomas Hutchinson Esq^rs are joined in the Affair."—*Ibid , p.* 341.

"An attempt was made to settle a manufacturing German town, a few miles from Boston, within the limits of the township of Braintree; but it never flourished. The private undertakers grew discouraged; the emigrants complained of being disappointed and deserted; the assembly first slackened their correspondence with Mr. Luther, and, after a year or two, ceased answering his frequent letters, which were filled with complaint of neglect, and hard usage. Mr. Phipps, the lieutenant-governor, was concerned for the honour of the government, and repeatedly recommended to the assembly a proper notice of Mr. Luther, and a consideration of his service and expense, but without any effect. The house had been brought into the correspondence, by the influence of a few persons who deserted the cause, and were under no apparent concern at the reproaches upon government. Some of the members, both of the council and of the house, earnestly endeavoured to persuade the general assembly to do as a collective body, that, which every individual would in honour have been bound, and, perhaps by law might have been compelled to do; but they could not prevail."—*Hutchinson's History of Mass., vol.* 3, *p.* 12.

See also 1756, chap. 41, *post.*

Chap. 14. "April 9th 1750. A Petition of Daniel Farnum in behalf of the Town of Newbury setting forth the Publick Benefit of having a Bridge built at the Place called Old Town Ferry & praying that a Lottery may be set up to defrey the Charge of it. In the House of Representves Read & Ordered that the further Consideration of this Petition be refer'd till May Session. In Council; Read & Concur'd—Consented to by the Lieu^t Govern.^r"—*Council Records, vol. XIX., p.* 172.

Chap. 16. "His Honour the Lieut: Governor sent the following Message to both Houses by the Secretary; Viz^t

Gentlemen of the Council & House of Representatives.

The Secretary has laid before me a Bill, granting the sum of Three Hundred Pounds towards my Support: When you granted the like Sum in May Session, I was very much in Doubt whether I ought to accept it; Thó I flattered myself that in your Winter Session you would agree upon a Grant which should make up for what the former was Deficient; But I am very much Disappointed. These Grants are considerably short of the Proportion in which former Assemblies have paid the Lieutenant Governor of the Province, in the Absence of the Governor; And yet I cannot Charge my Self with want of Application to & constant Attendance upon the Affairs of the Government. And you must be sensible,

I am put to greater Inconvenience & Expence than if my Residence was in Boston; Which has been the Case with the former Lieutenant Governor.

When you are doing Honour to the Province by making Additions to the Allowances of several of the Officers of the Government, I am sorry you should distinguish the Commander in Chief by granting him a lesser Allowance than has been usual.

I must therefore desire you to take this Affair again into your Consideration; and add such further Sum to your present Grant as that I may be able with Honour to accept the Same."—*Dated February* 7, 1750-51: *ibid., p.* 299.

This act was signed by the Lieutenant-Governor, February 8, according to the memorandum on the engrossment; but the record shows that it was signed February 15, immediately after the following grant has been passed:—

"In the House of Represent:ves Ordered that there be granted, & allowed to be paid out of the publick Treasury to His Honour the Lieuten' Governor and Commander in Chief the Sum of Eighty Pounds, over & above the Grant made His Honour the fifth Currant, in Consideration of his past Services, and further to enable him to manage the publick Affairs of the Province.

In Council; Read & Concur'd:—Consented to by the Lieut: Govern' "—*Ibid., p.* 311.

Chap. 17. "The aversion, in the common people, to a silver and gold currency, had occasioned several tumultuous assemblies in and near the town of Boston. The paper, they said, was not worth hoarding, but silver and gold would all fall to the share of men of wealth, and would either be exported or hoarded up, and no part of it would go to the labourer, or the lower class of people, who must take their pay in goods, or go without. In a short time experience taught them, that it was as easy for a frugal industrious person to obtain silver, as it had been to obtain paper; and the prejudice in the town of Boston was so much abated, that when a large number of people from Abingdon, and other towns near to it, came to Boston, expecting to be joined by the like people there, they were hooted at, and insulted by the boys and servants, and obliged to return home disappointed.

The assembly being then sitting, it was thought proper to pass an act for preventing riots, upon the plan of the act of parliament known by the name of the Riot Act, except that the penalty is changed from death, to other severe and infamous punishment.

This was a temporary act, but was not suffered to expire; and continued in force until riots took place to prevent the execution of acts of parliament which were deemed grievous, and then it was discontinued."—*Hutchinson's Hist. Mass., vol.* 3, *p* 8.

"This Act is agreeable to the Act passed here the first of King George the First called the Riot Act with a difference in the Penalty which in the Riot Act here is made Felony." —*Report of Mr. Lamb, to the Board of Trade:* "*Mass. Bay, B. T., vol.* 74, *H. h.*, 38," *in Public Record Office.*

Chap. 21. "February 3. 1747. Gentlemen of the Council & House of Representatives. I have heard so much of the Difficultys which many of the Ministers of the Gospell within this Province are brought under, thro; the great Depreciation of the Bills of Credit, in Which their Salarys are paid, & the little care taken by their People to make them proper allowances for it, that it seems probable many of them will soon be necessitated to quit the Ministry & betake themselves to Secular Employments for a Livelyhood; In which case there will be great Danger of the Pulpit's being fill'd with Ignorant & Illiterate Men, And of all manner of foolish & hurtfull Errors being thereby propogated; wherefore as I esteem it the indispensable Duty of the Legislature, to do everything in their Power for the Support & Advancement of the Christian Religion; I must earnestly Recomend it to you to take Care that the Ministers of the Gospel be properly Supported, & that you would Make Enquiry into this Grievance which I have Mentioned, & if you find their Case as is Represented that you would provide a sutable Redress"—*Council Records, vol. XVIII., p.* 269.

"Feb. 4. 1747. In the House of Represent.ves Ordered; that Col° Choat, Mr Foster, Mr Hubbard, Mr Witt, Mr Royall, Coll. Otis, & Col° Richmond, with such as the Honble Board shall Appoint be a Committee, to take under Consideration & report upon that Paragraph of his Ex'cy's Speech Relating to the Support of the Ministers of the Gospel thro' the Province as also what is Necessary to be done for the Relief of the Widows & Orphans, with Respect to the Depreciation of Bills of Credit.

In Council Read & Concurd. & Jacob Wendell, John Cushing & Samll. Danforth Samll Watts, James Minot & Andrew Oliver Esqrs. are joined in the Affair."—*Ibid., p.* 270.

"March. 1. 1747. The Committee on the affair of the Ministers Suppoit, reported a Bill for that purpose, viz. A Bill entitled an Act for the more effectual Support of Ministers. In Council Read & Sent down"—*Ibid , p.* 290.

"March 2d 1747. In the House of Representves. Voted, that it be & it hereby is Strongly recommended to the Several Churches & Congregations within this Province to make an Honorable provision for the Support of their Ministers proportionable to the great Rise of the Necessaries of Life since their Settlement. Also, Voted that the Clerks of the several Towns within the Province which have not been divided into Parishes, & also the Clerks of Every Parish & Precinct within the Province be required to lodge in the Secretary's Office some time before the sitting of the Court in May next an attested Copy of the Contract made with the Minister of such Parish or Precinct at his Settlement, & also an Attested Copy from the Record of the Salary granted or paid to such Minister the present Year & also of the Salary granted for the Year 1748 where such Grant shall have been made; & further Ordered that this Vote be forthwith printed, & that the Sherriff of the Several Countys of the Province take effectual Care that the Clerks of each Town & Precinct be furnished with a Copy hereof, & to be by them laid before their respective Towns & Precincts as soon as may be. In Council; Read & Concured Consented to by the Governour"—*Ibid., p.* 292.

Chap. 23. "This Act I must referr to Your Lordships for your approbation to do what is agreeable to the Act of the seventeenth of the present King which I have not seen."—*Report of Mr. Lamb, to the Board of Trade: "Mass. Bay, B. T., vol.* 74, *H. h.,* 38," *in Public Record Office.*

Chap. 24. "April 24th 1751. The Secretary delivered the following Message from the Lieut Governour to both Houses;—

Gentlemen of the Council & House of Representves The Secretary has laid before me an Engross'd Bill entitled an Act in further Addition to an Act made & pass'd in the twenty second year of his present Majesty's Reign, entitled an Act for drawing in the Bills of Credit of the several Denominations which have at any time been issued by the Government, & are still outstanding & for Ascertaining the rate of Coined Silver in the Province for the future. By this Bill, Gentlemen you make certain Receipts or Certificates given by a Commitee of the General Court, to be a Tender in Law, in discharge of all private Debts & Contracts whatsoever; And thus you repeal or enervate the Act (to which you call this Bill an Addition) in one of the most Material Parts of it, whereby coined Silver at six shillings & eight pence ℔ ounce or mill'd Dollars at six shillings each, are declared to be the only Tender for discharging of Debts, This is directly against his Majesty's Instructions to me, & I think besides that, it would prove of fatal consequence to the Country; Therefore I cannot give my Consent to it & at the same time, I am desirous that Justice should be done to the Possessors of the Outstanding Bills; And I earnestly recommend to you the making Provision therefor, in such a Way & manner as that I may concur with you in it."—*Council Records, vol. XIX., p.* 350.

This bill, in its original form, was passed to be enacted, by the House, April 18, but was rejected by the Council. After some modification it was passed to be enacted by both branches, April 24, and vetoed by the Governor as shown in his speech, above. On the 25th, the bill, in a new draught, was passed to be engrossed, in both branches, and, on the next day, was enacted and signed.

ACTS,

Passed 1751–52.

ACTS

PASSED AT THE SESSION BEGUN AND HELD AT BOSTON, ON THE TWENTY-NINTH DAY OF MAY, A. D. 1751.

CHAPTER 1.

AN ACT TO ENABLE AND IMPOWER THE INHABITANTS OF NEW PLANTATIONS WITHIN THIS PROVINCE, ENJO[Y][*I*]NED AND SUBJECTED BY LAW, OR THAT MAY HEREAFTER BE ENJO[Y][*I*]NED AND SUBJECTED, TO PAY PROVINCE AND COUNTY TAXES, TO ASSESS, LEVY AND COLLECT THE SAME.

Preamble.

WHEREAS there are sundry new plantations within this province by law enjo[y][*i*]ned to pay province and county taxes, that are not impowered to choose the proper officers to assess, levy and collect the said taxes,—

Be it enacted by the Lieutenant-Governour, Council and House of Represent[ati]ves,

Freeholders of new plantations to have a meeting in August next, to choose officers.

[SECT. 1.] That the freeholders of every such new plantation be and are hereby impow[e]red and required to assemble together on the first Monday of August next, at the usual places for holding their publick meetings, and, being so assembled, shall choose a moderator and clerk for said meeting; which clerk shall be immediately sworn, truly to enter and record all such votes as shall be passed at said meeting,—by a justice of the peace, if any be present; otherwise, by the moderator of said meeting,—and shall then proceed to choose three assessors to make a valuation of estates and faculties of persons in such plantations, agreable to law, and to assess such province and county taxes as are or shall be set on the inhabitants of such new plantation, to be paid this or any former year; as also a collector to levy and collect the same: which assessors and collectors shall be sworn to the faithful discharge of the duty of their respective offices, before a justice of the peace for the county within which such new plantation lies, if present; otherwise, by the clerk for said meeting,

And be it further enacted,

Inhabitants of new plantations to meet in March, annually.

[SECT. 2.] That the inhabitants of the abovesaid plantations, qualified as by law is required of voters in town affairs, are hereby impow[e]red and enjo[y][*i*]ned, some time in the month of March, annually, to assemble together, upon due notice given by the collector or collectors then in office, pursuant to warrant, under the hands of the assessors, or the major part of them, who shall have been last chosen,—and who are hereby impow[e]red and required to issue such warrant,—at such time and place as shall be, by said assessors, appointed; and shall then and there choose a clerk for said meeting, who shall be sworn in manner as is before prescribed for the swearing the clerk for the first meeting, and three assessors, and one or more collectors, to assess and

Duty of assessors and collectors of taxes.

levy such province and county taxes on said inhabitants as they shall, from time to time, be enjo[y][*i*]ned by law to pay; and said assessors and collectors, as well those that shall be chosen on the said first Monday of August, as those who shall, by virtue of this act, be hereafter annually chosen in said new plantations, shall be liable to all such penalties, in case they or any of them shall refuse to be sworn and serve in said offices, or in case of any default therein, as the assessors of province and county taxes for towns are by law liable or may be subjected to; and said assessors are hereby impowered and required to make out such warrants, *mutatis mutandis*, as assessors of county taxes for towns are by law impowered to make out, and to direct the same to said collector or collectors; and the said collector or collectors are hereby impowered to levy, collect and [i][*e*]nforce the payment of all the afores[*ai*]d taxes in all such ways, and by all such means, as constables and collectors of province and county taxes are by law impowered to do, of the inhabitants of the towns within this province.

Duty of the clerks.

[SECT. 3.] And the clerk at said annual meeting, shall, immediately on the election of said assessors and collectors, make and give out to the collector or collectors for the then last preceeding year, a list of the names of those persons who shall be chosen assessors and collectors at said meeting for the ensuing year; which collector or collectors shall forthwith thereupon summon each of said assessors and collectors for the then ensuing year, to appear at a certain time and place, within the space of seven days from the time of their election, before a justice of the peace, if any dwell in such new plantation; or otherwise, before the clerk chosen at said meeting,—to take the oath, *mutatis mutandis*, which assessors and collectors of publick taxes for towns are, by law, enjo[y][*i*]ned to take; w[*hi*]ch oath said clerk, in such case, is hereby impowered to administer.

And to the intent that the inhabitants of said new plantations may have due notice and warning given them of the meeting which they are before in this act impowered and required to hold on the first Monday of August next, and of the ends and purposes thereof,—

Be it enacted,

Clerk of the peace in the county to notify the meeting in August next.

[SECT. 4.] That each clerk of the court of general sessions of the peace, for the several counties within this province wherein any of the afores[*ai*]d new plantations l[y][*ie*], shall, in some convenient time before the s[*ai*]d first Monday of August next, make and cause to be delivered a warrant, under his hand, directed to some principal inhabitant in each of s[*ai*]d new plantations within their respective counties, therein expressing the time, place and purposes for holding said meetings, and requiring such inhabitant[*s*] to notify all the inhabitants of said new plantation, qualified as in this act is provided, of said meeting, and the time, place and purposes thereof, three days at the least before the time set in this act for holding the same; which warrant the inhabitant to whom said warrant shall be directed, is hereby enjo[y][*i*]ned and required to execute, and make return of, under his hand, into said meeting, under the penalty of forty shillings, to be recovered by complaint, information or action of debt, before any of his maj[*es*]ty's justices of the peace for the county wherein said inhabitant, making default in the premis[*s*]es, shall dwell; said forty shillings to be for the use and benefit of the person or persons who shall inform or sue for the same. [*Passed June* 21; *published June* 25.

CHAPTER 2.

AN ACT IN ADDITION TO AN ACT MADE AND PASS[*E*]'D IN THE FIRST YEAR OF THE REIGN OF HIS MAJESTY KING GEORGE THE FIRST, INTITLED "AN ACT FOR BUILDING AND MAINTAINING A LIGHT-HOUSE UPON THE GREAT BREWSTER (CALLED 'BEACON-ISLAND'), AT THE ENTRANCE OF THE HARBOUR OF BOSTON."

Whereas the lighthouse at the entrance of the harbour of Boston hath been greatly damaged by fire, and it hath been ordered by this court that it should be repaired; and it being reasonable that the charge of such repairs should be born by those who receive the immediate benefit thereof,— Preamble.

Be it therefore enacted by the Lieut[enan]t-Governo[u]r, Council and House of Represent[ati]ves,

That the commissioner of impost be and hereby is directed, by himself and his several deputies, to demand and receive of the master of every vessel (which, within the space of two years from the publication of this act, shall clear out from any port within this province, being bound to any port without this province), over and above what is already by law provided, the following rates at each time of clearance; viz[t]., for every vessel of less than one hundred tons, two shillings; for every vessel of above one hundred tons, and not exceeding two hundred tons, three shillings; and for every vessel of above two hundred tons, four shillings: the tonnage to be computed according to what such vessels may measure in carpenter's tonnage, and not according to the register of such vessel: and the said commiss[*ione*]r of impost shall once in every quarter of the year pay such sums as he or his deputies shall receive for the afores[*ai*]d duties, to the province treasurer, to be applied to the uses aforesaid. [*Passed June* 22; *published June* 25. New duty for the lighthouse. 1715-16, chap. 4.

CHAPTER 3.

AN ACT FOR ALTERING THE TIME APPOINTED FOR HOLDING THE COURT OF GENERAL SESSIONS OF THE PEACE AND INFERIOUR COURT OF COMMON PLEAS, AT CONCORD, WITHIN AND FOR THE COUNTY OF MIDDLESEX.

Whereas the time appointed by law for holding the court of general sessions of the peace and inferiour court of common pleas, at Concord, within and for the county of Middlesex, is found to be inconvenient,— Preamble.

Be it therefore enacted by the Lieutenant-Governour, Council and House of Represent[ati]ves,

[Sect. 1.] That the time for holding the said court of general sessions of the peace and inferiour court of common pleas at Concord, for the county of Middlesex, shall henceforth be on the first Tuesday of September annually; and all officers and other persons concerned, are required to conform themselves accordingly. Time for holding the courts at Concord, altered. 1742-43, chap. 32, § 1.

And be it further enacted,

[Sect. 2.] That all writ[t]s, suits, plaints, processes, appeals, reviews, recognizances, warrants, or other matters or things, whatsoever, which now are, or at any time before the said first Tuesday of September shall be, issued, taken or depending in the said county of Middlesex, which were to have been returned or proceeded on at the time Processes to remain good.

heretofore appointed by law for holding the said courts at Concord, shall be valid, and stand good to all intents and purposes in the law, and shall be returned and proceeded on at the time appointed by this act for holding the same. [*Passed June* 20; *published June* 25.

CHAPTER 4.

AN ACT FOR ALTERING THE TIME FOR HOLDING THE COURT OF GENERAL SESSIONS OF THE PEACE AND THE INFERIOUR COURT OF COMMON PLEAS FOR THE COUNTY OF NANTUCKET.

Preamble. WHEREAS the time by law appointed for holding the court of general sessions of the peace and inferiour court of common pleas for the county of Nantucket, on the last Tuesday of March, annually, is found on divers accounts inconvenient,—

Be it therefore enacted by the Lieutenant-Governo[u]r, Council, and House of Representatives,

Time for holding Nantucket courts altered. 1742-43 chap. 32, § 1. That the said court of general sessions of the peace and inferiour court of common pleas, appointed to be holden for the county of Nantucket, upon the last Tuesday of March, shall hereafter be holden and kept upon the first Tuesday of March, annually. [*Passed and published June* 18.

CHAPTER 5.

AN ACT FOR GRANTING UNTO HIS MAJESTY AN EXCISE UPON WINES AND SPIRITS DISTILL[*E*]'D, SOLD BY RETAIL, AND UPON LIMES, LEMMONS AND ORANGES.

Preamble. WE, his majesty's most loyal and dutiful subjects, the representatives of the province of the Massachusetts Bay, in general court assembled, being desirous to lessen the present debt of the province, have chearfully and unanimously granted, and do hereby give and grant unto his most excellent majesty, for the ends and uses above mentioned, and for no other uses, an excise upon all brandy, rum and other spirits distill[e]'d, and upon all wines whatsoever sold by retail, and upon lemmons, limes and oranges taken in and used in making of punch or other liquors mix[e]'d for sale, or otherw[ays][*ise*] consum[e]'d, in taverns or other licens[e]'d houses within this province, to be rais[e]'d, levied, collected and paid by and upon every taverner, innholder, common victualler and retailer within each respective county, in manner following:—

And be it accordingly enacted by the Lieutenant-Governour, Council and House of Representatives,

Time of this act's continuance. [SECT. 1.] That from and after the twenty-ninth day of June, one thousand seven hundred and fifty-one, for the space of one year, every person licens[e]'d for retailing rum, brandy or other spirits, or wine, shall pay the duties following:—

Rates of excise. For every gallon of brandy, rum and spirits distill'd, fourpence.
For every gallon of wine of every sort, sixpence.
For every hundred of lemmons or oranges, four shillings.
For every hundred of limes, one shilling and sixpence.
—And so proportionably for any other quantity or number.

And be it further enacted,

[Sect. 2.] That every taverner, innholder, common victualler and retailer, shall, upon the said twenty-ninth day of June, take an exact account of all brandy, rum and other distill[*e*]'d spirits, and wine, and of all lemmons, oranges and limes then by him or her, and give an account of the same, upon oath, if required, unto the person or persons to whom the duties of excise in the respective count[y][*ie*]s shall be let or farm[*e*]'d, as in and by this act is hereafter directed; and such other persons as shall be licens[*e*]'d during the continuance of this act, shall also give an account, as aforesaid, upon what brandy, rum or other distill[*e*]'d spirits, and wine, and of what lemmons, oranges or limes he or they shall have by him or them at the time of his or their licen[s][c]e; which oath the person or persons farming the duties aforesaid shall have power to administer in the words following; viz[t].,— Account to be taken.

You, A. B., do swear that the account exhibited by you is a just and true account of all brandy, rum and other distill[*e*]'d spirits, and wine, lemmons, oranges and limes you had by you on the twenty-ninth day of June last. So help you God. Form of an oath.

And where such person shall not have been licens[*e*]'d on said twenty-ninth day of June, the form of the oath shall be so varied, as that instead of those words, "on the twenty-ninth day of June last," these words shall be inserted and used, "at the time of taking your licen[s][c]e."

And be it further enacted,

[Sect. 3.] That every taverner, innholder, common victualler and retailer, shall make a fair entry in a book, of all such rum, brandy and other distill[*e*]'d spirits, and wine, as he or they, or any for him or them, shall buy, distill and take in for sale after such account taken, and of lemmons, oranges and limes taken in, consum[*e*]'d or used as aforesaid, and at the end of every six months, deliver the same, in writing, under their hands, to the farmer or farmers of the duties aforesaid, who are impow[e]red to administer an oath to him or them, that the said account is, *bonâ fide*, just and true, and that he or they do not know of any rum, brandy or other distill[*e*]'d spirits, or wine, sold, directly or indirectly, or of any lemmons, oranges or limes used in punch or otherwise, by him or them, or any under him or them, or by his or their privity or consent, but what is contain[*e*]'d in the account now exhibited, and shall pay him the duty thereof, excepting such part as the farmer shall find is still remaining by him or them: twenty per cent to be allowed on the liquors aforemention[e]'d for leakage and other waste, for which no duty is to be paid. Within six months, accounts to be delivered. Twenty per cent allowed for leakage.

Provided always, and it is the true intent and meaning of this act,— Proviso.

[Sect. 4.] That if any taverner, retailer or common victualler, shall buy of another taverner or retailer such small quantity of liquors as this act obliges him to account for to the farmer, and pay the excise, such taverner, retailer or common victualler shall be exempted and excus[*e*]'d from accounting or paying any excise therefor, inasmuch as the same is accounted for, and the excise therefor to be paid, by the taverner or retailer of whom he bought the same.

And be it further enacted,

[Sect. 5.] That every taverner, innholder, common victualler or retailer, who shall be found to give a false account of any brandy, distill[*e*]'d spirits, wine, or other the commodities aforesaid, by him or her on the said twenty-ninth day of June, or at the time of his or her taking liceu[s][*c*]e, or bought, distill[*e*]'d, or taken in for sale afterwards, or used as aforesaid, or refuse to give in an account, on oath, as afore- Penalty on giving a false account.

said, shall be render[e]'d incapable of having a licen[s][c]e afterwards, and shall be prosecuted by the farmer of excise in the same county, for his or her neglect, and ordered by the general sessions of the peace to pay double the sum of money as they may judge that the excise of liquors, &c., by him or her sold within such time, would have amounted to, to be paid to the said farmer.

And be it further enacted,

General sessions to take recognizance.

[SECT. 6.] That the justices in their general sessions of the peace shall take recognizances, with sufficient suret[y][ie]s, of all persons by them licens[e]'d, both as to their keeping good rule and order, and duly observing the laws relating to persons so licens[e]'d, and for their duly and truly rendering an account in writing under their hands as aforesaid, and paying their excise in manner as aforesaid; as also that they shall not use their licen[s][c]e in any house besides that wherein they dwell; which recognizance[s] shall be taken within the space of thirty days after the granting of such licen[s][c]e, otherw[ays][ise] the persons licens[e]'d shall lo[o]se the benefit of his or her said licen[s][c]e; and no person shall be licens[e]'d by the said justices that hath not accounted with the farmer, and paid him the excise due to him from such person at the time of his asking for such licen[s][c]e.

Preamble.

And whereas, notwithstanding the laws made against selling strong drink without licen[s][c]e, many persons not regarding the penalties and forfeitures in the said act, do receive and entertain persons in their houses, and sell great quantit[y][ie]s of spirits and other strong drink, without licen[s][c]e so to do first had and obtained; by reason whereof great debaucheries are committed and kept secret, the end of this law in a great measure frustrated, and such as take licen[s][c]es and pay the excise greatly wrong[e]'d and injured,—

Be it therefore further enacted,

Forfeiture of £2 for selling without license, &c.

[SECT. 7.] That whosoever, after the said twenty-ninth day of June, one thousand seven hundred and fifty-one, shall presume, directly or indirectly, to sell any brandy, rum or other distill[e]'d spirits, wine, beer, cyder, perry or any other strong drink, in any smaller quantity than a barrel[l] (thirty gallons to be accounted a barrel[l], and all delivered to one person, without drawing any part of it off), without liceu[s][c]e first had and obtained from the court of general sessions of the peace, and recognizing in manner as aforesaid, shall forfeit and pay for each offence, the sum of two pounds to the farmer, and costs of prosecution; and all such as shall refuse or neglect to pay the fine aforesaid, shall stand closely and strictly committed in the common goal of the county for three months at least, and not to have the liberty of the goaler's house or yard; and any goaler giving any person liberty contrary to this act, shall forfeit and pay two pounds, and pay costs of prosecution as aforesaid. And if any person or persons, not licens[e]'d as aforesaid, shall order, allow, permit or connive at the selling of any strong drink, contrary to the true intent or meaning of this act, by his or her child or children, servant or servants, or any other person or persons belonging to or in his or her house or family, and be thereof convict, he, she or they shall be reputed the offender or offenders, and shall suffer the same penalties as if he, she or they had sold such drink themselves.

And be it further enacted,

One witness sufficient for conviction.

[SECT. 8.] That when any person shall be complained of for selling any strong drink without licen[s][c]e, one witness produced to one such fact, and another produced to another, shall be sufficient conviction, provided that there be not more than the space of forty days between the facts concerning which such witnesses declare. And when and so often as it shall be observed that there is a resort of persons to houses suspected to sell strong drink without licen[s][*c*]e, any justice of the peace shall have full power to convene such persons before him, and examine them upon oath concerning the person suspected of selling or retailing strong drink in such houses, outhouses or other dependencies thereof; and if upon examination of such witnesses, and hearing the defence of such suspected person, it shall appear to the justice there is sufficient proof of the violation of this act by selling strong drink without licen[s][*c*]e, judgment may thereupon be made up against such person, and he shall forfeit and pay in like manner as if process had been commenced by bill, plaint or information before the said justice; or otherwise said justice may bind over the person suspected, and the witnesses, to the next court of general sessions of the peace for the county where such person shall dwell.

And be it further enacted,

[Sect. 9.] That when and so often as any person shall be complained of for selling any strong drink without licen[s][*c*]e to any negro, Indian or molatto slave, or to any child or other person under the age of discretion, and upon the declaration of any such Indian, negro or molatto slaves, child or other person under the age of discretion, and other circumstances concurring, it shall appear to be highly probable in the judgment of the court or justice before whom the trial shall be, that the person complained of is guilty, then, and in every such case, unless the defendant shall acquit him- or herself upon oath (to be administ[e]r[*e*]'d to him or her by the court or justice that shall try the cause), such defendant shall forfeit and pay two pounds to the farmer of excise, and costs of prosecution; but if the defendant shall acquit him- or herself upon oath as aforesaid, the court or justice may and shall enter up judgment for the defendant to recover costs. Penalty for selling strong drink to negroes, mulattoes, &c.

And be it further enacted,

[Sect. 10.] That after any person shall have been once convicted of selling strong liquors without licen[s][*c*]e, contrary to this act, he shall, upon every offence after such first conviction, be obliged to enter into bonds, with one or more suret[y][*ie*]s, in the penalty of twenty pounds, to his majesty, for the use of this government, that he will not, in like manner, offend or be guilty of any breach of this act; and upon refusal to give such bond, he shall be committed to prison until he comply therewith. Persons after first conviction to enter into bonds.

And be it further enacted,

[Sect. 11.] That if any person or persons shall be summoned to appear before a justice of the peace, or the grand jury, to give evidence relating to any persons selling strong drink without licen[s][*c*]e, or to appear before the court of general sessions of the peace, or other court proper to try the same, to give evidence on the trial of any person informed against, presented or indicted for the selling strong drink without licen[s][*c*]e, and shall neglect or refuse to appear, or to give evidence in that behalf, every person so offending shall forfeit the sum of twenty pounds and cost of prosecution; the one half of the penalty aforesaid to be to his majesty for the use of the province, the other half to and for the use of him or them who shall sue for the same as aforesaid. And when it shall so happen that witnesses are bound to sea before the s[e][*i*]tting of the court where any person or persons informed against, for selling strong drink without licen[s][*c*]e, is or are to be prosecuted for the same, in every such case, the deposition of any witness or witnesses, in writing, taken before any two of his majesty's justices of the peace, *quorum unus*, and sealed up and delivered into court, the adverse party having first had a notification in writing sent to him or her of the time and place of caption, shall be esteem[*e*]'d as sufficient evidence, in the law, to convict any person or persons offending against this act, as Penalty on persons refusing to give evidence.

if such witness or witnesses had been present at the time of trial, and given his, her or their deposition *viva voce;* and every person or persons who shall be summoned to give evidence before two justices of the peace, in manner as aforesaid, and shall neglect or refuse to appear, or to give evidence relating to the facts he or she shall be inquired of, shall be liable and subject to the same penalty as he or she would have been by virtue of this act, for not appearing, or neglecting or refusing to give his or her evidence before the grand jury or court [*as*] aforesaid.

And be it further enacted,

How fines are to be recovered.

[SECT. 12.] That all fines, forfeitures and penalties arising by this act shall and may be recovered by action, bill, plaint or information, before any court of record proper to try the same; and where the sum forfeited does not exceed two pounds, by action or complaint before any one of his majesty's justices of the peace in the respective count[y][*ie*]s where such offence shall be committed; which said justice is hereby impower[*e*]'d to try and determine the same. And such justice shall make a fair entry or record of all such his proceedings: *saving always* to any person or persons who shall think him-, her- or themselves aggr[*i*]ev[i]ed by the sent[a][*e*]nce or determination of the said justice as aforesaid, liberty of appeal therefrom to the next court of general sessions of the peace to be holden in and for said county, at which court such offence shall be finally determined: *provided* that in said appeal the same rules be observed as are already, by law, required in appeals from justices to the court of general sessions of the peace.

And to the end the revenue arising from the aforesaid duties of excise may be advanced for the greater benefit and advantage of the publick,—

Be it further enacted,

Persons empowered to farm out the excise.

[SECT. 13.] That one or more persons, to be nominated and appointed by the general court, for and within the several count[y][*ie*]s within this province, publick notice being first given of the time and place and occasion of their meeting, shall have power, and are hereby authorized, from time to time, to contract and agree with any person for or concerning the farming the duties in this act mentioned, upon brandy, rum, or other the liquors and commodities aforesaid, in the respective counties for which they shall be appointed, as may be for the greatest profit and advantage of the publick, so as the same exceed not the term of one year after the commencement of this act; and every person to whom the duties of excise in any county shall be let or farm[*e*]'d, shall have power to inspect the houses of all such as are licens[*e*]'d, and of such as are suspected to sell without licen[s][*c*]e, and to demand, sue for, and recover the excise due from licens[*e*]'d persons by virtue of this act.

And be it further enacted,

Farmer to give bond that the sum agreed for be paid into the public treasury.

[SECT. 14.] That the farmer shall give bond with two sufficient suret[y][*ie*]s, to the province treasurer for the time being, and his successors in said office, in double the sum of money that shall be contracted for, with condition that the sum agreed be paid into the province treasury, for the use of the province, at the expiration of one year from the date of such bond; which bond the person or persons to be appointed a committee of such county are to take, and the same to lodge with the treasurer as aforesaid, within twenty days after such bond is executed; and the said treasurer, upon failure or neglect of payment at the time therein limit[*t*]ed, shall and is hereby impow[e]red and directed to put such bond in suit, and to receive the money due thereon for the use afore mentioned; and the said committee shall render an account of their proceedings touching the farming this duty on rum, wine and other the liquors and species afore mentioned, in their respective count[y][*ie*]s, to the general court in the first week of their fall sessions, and shall receive such sum or sums for their trouble and expences in said affair as said court shall think fit[t] to allow them.

[Sect. 15.] And every person farming the excise in any county may substitute and appoint one or more deputy or deput[y][*ie*]s under him, upon oath, to collect and receive the excise aforesaid, which shall become due in such county, and pay in the same to the farmer; which deputy or deput[y][*ie*]s shall have, use and exercise all such powers and authorit[y][*ie*]s as in and by this act are given or committed to the farmers for the better collecting the duties aforesaid, or prosecuting of offenders against this act.

And be it further enacted, anything hereinbefore contained to the contrary notwithstanding,

[Sect. 16.] That it shall and may be lawful to and for the said farmers, and every of them, to compound and agree with any retailer or innholder within their respective divisions, from time to time, for his or her excise for the whole year, in one entire sum, as they in their discretion shall think fit[t] to agree for, without making any entry thereof as is before directed; and all and every person or persons, to whom the said excise or any part thereof shall be let or farmed, by themselves or their lawful substitutes, may and are hereby impowered to sue for and recover, in any of his majesty's courts of record (or before a justice of the peace where the matter is not above his cognizance), any sum or sums that shall grow due from any of the aforesaid duties of excise, where the party or part[y][*ie*]s for whom the same is or shall become due shall refuse or neglect to pay the same. Farmers may compound with any retailer or innholder.

And be it further enacted,

[Sect. 17.] That in case any person farming the excise as aforesaid, or his deputy, shall, at any time during their continuance in said office, wittingly and willingly connive at, or allow, any person or persons within their respective divisions, not licens[e]'d by the court of general sessions of the peace, their selling any brandy, wine[*s*], rum or other liquors by this act forbidden, such farmer or deputy, for every such offence, shall forfeit the sum of fifty pounds and cost of prosecution; one half of the penalty aforesaid to be to his majesty for the use of the province, the other half to him or them that shall inform [or] [*and*] sue for the same, and shall thenceforward be forever disabl[e]d from serving in said office. Penalty for farmers or their deputies offending.

And be it further enacted,

[Sect. 18.] That in case of the death of the farmers of excise in any county, the ex[*e*]c[*ut*]ors or adm[*inistrat*]ors of such farmer shall, upon their taking such trust of ex[*e*]c[*ut*]or or adm[*inistrat*]or upon them, have and enjoy all the powers, and be subject to all the duties, the farmer had or might enjoy or was subject to by force of this act. [*Passed and published June* 18. Provision in case of death, &c.

CHAPTER 6.

AN ACT FOR GRANTING THE SUM OF THREE HUNDRED POUNDS FOR THE SUPPORT OF HIS HONOUR THE LIEUTENANT-GOVERNOUR AND COMMANDER-IN-CHIEF.

Be it enacted by the Lieutenant-Governour, Council and House of Representatives,

That the sum of three hundred pounds be and hereby is granted unto his most excellent majesty, to be paid out of the publick treasury, and Governor's grant.

to be taken out of the next supply, to his honour Spencer Phips. Esqr., lieutenant-governour and commander-in-chief in and over his majesty's province of the Massachusetts Bay, for his past services, and further to enable him to manage the publick affairs of the province. [*Passed June* 21; *published June* 25.

CHAPTER 7.

AN ACT FOR REVIVING AND CONTINUING SUNDRY LAWS OF THIS PROVINCE, THAT ARE EXPIRED [AND] [*OR*] NEAR EXPIRING.

Preamble. Unnecessary journeying of members. 1738-39, chap. 25. Preservation of deer. 1739-40, chap. 3. To prevent horses, &c., feeding on Ipswich Beach. 1739-40, chap. 8. Private ways. 1739-40, chap. 12. Relief of poor prisoners for debt. 1741-42, chap. 6. To prevent spreading the small-pox. 1742-43, chap. 17. Multiplicity of lawsuits. 1742-43, chap. 25. Regulating the hospital on Rainsford Island. 1743-44, chap. 19. Commissioners of sewers. 1745-46, chap. 16. Views by a jury. 1746-47, chap. 6. Firing of guns in Boston. 1746-47, chap. 11.

WHEREAS an act was made and pass'd in the twelfth year of his present majesty's reign, intitled "An Act to prevent the unnecessary journeying of the members of the general court"; and also an act was made and pass[*e*]'d in the thirteenth year of his present majesty's reign, intitled "An Act in addition to an act intitled 'An Act for the better preservation and increase of deer within this province'"; and also another act was made and pass[*e*]'d in the thirteenth year of his present majesty's reign, intitled "An Act for the effectual preventing of horses, neat cattle, sheep and swine from running at large or feeding upon a certain island, called Plumb Island, lying in Ipswich Bay, in the county of Essex"; and another act was made and pass[*e*]'d in the thirteenth year of his present majesty's reign, intitled "An Act in addition to the several laws of this province relating to common roads and private ways"; and also another act was made and pass[*e*]'d in the fifteenth year of his present majesty's reign, intitled "An Act for the rel[ei][*ie*]f of poor prisoners for debt"; and also another act was made and pass[*e*]'d in the sixteenth year of his present majesty's reign, intitled "An Act to prevent the spreading of the small-pox and other infectious sickness, and to prevent the concealing of the same"; and also another act was made and pass[*e*]'d in the same year, intitled "An Act to prevent the multiplicity of lawsuits"; and also another act was made and pass[*e*]'d in the seventeenth year of his present majesty's reign, intitled "An Act for regulating the hospital on Rainsford's Island, and further providing in case of sickness"; and also another act was made and pass[*e*]'d in the nineteenth year of his present majesty's reign, intitled "An Act in addition to the act intitled 'An Act for appointing commissioners of sewers'"; and also an act was made and pass[*e*]'d in the twentieth year of his present maj[*es*]ty's reign, intitled "An Act relating to views by a jury in civil actions"; and another act was made and pass[*e*]'d in the same year, intitled "An Act to prevent the firing of guns charged with shot or ball, in the town of Boston";—all which laws are expired or near expiring: *and whereas* the afores[*ai*]d laws have, by experience, been found beneficial for the several purposes for which they were made and pass[*e*]'d,—

Be it therefore enacted by the Lieut[*enan*]*t-Governour, Council and House of Repres*[*entati*]*ves,*

Said laws continued.

That all and every of the afores[*ai*]d acts, and every matter and clause therein contained, be and hereby are continued and revived, and shall continue and remain in full force for the space of three years from the first day of July next, and no longer. [*Passed June* 22; *published June* 25.

CHAPTER 8.

AN ACT FOR CONTINUING THE TIME FOR DRAWING THE LOTTERY ESTABLISHED BY AN ACT PASS[*E*]'D IN THE TWENTY-FOURTH YEAR OF HIS PRESENT MAJESTY, INTIT[U]LED "AN ACT FOR SUPPLYING THE TREASURY WITH TWENTY-SIX THOUSAND SEVEN HUNDRED MILL'D DOLLARS, AND FOR MAKING FURTHER PROVISION RELATING TO SAID LOTTERY."

Whereas an act intit[u]led "An Act for supplying the treasury with twenty-six thousand seven hundred mill'd dollars," pass[*e*]'d the great and general court of this province, begun and held at Boston upon Wednesday, the thirtieth day of May, 1750, and continued by prorogation to Thursday, the tenth day of January following; by which act a lottery was established for the end and purpose of supplying the treasury as abovesaid, and the eighteenth day of April last was therein prefix[*e*]'d and appointed as the time for drawing said lottery; *and whereas* by one other act or law of his majesty's province, made in addition to the abovesaid act, the time of drawing said lottery was put off to the fifth day of June instant, at which time the managers and directors were ordered and impowered to proceed to the drawing of said lottery, if the number of five thousand tickets should then have been disposed of; and the days aforesaid set for drawing said lottery being now lapsed, and by reason thereof the end propos[*e*]'d in said lottery cannot be answered and obtained without some further act of this court respecting said lottery; *and whereas* it is apprehended that the time for drawing said lottery having been h[eretofore][*itherto*] made pendant on the sale of a certain number of tickets by the certain days above mentioned, has proved a great discouragement and obstruction to the disposal of said tickets, and that if a perem[*p*]tory day was set for the drawing said lottery, it would very much promote the sale of said tickets,— Preamble. 1750-51, chap. 15. 1750-51, chap. 20.

Be it therefore enacted and declared by the Lieutenant-Governour, Council and House of Representatives.

[Sect. 1.] That the said lottery shall be revived, and is accordingly hereby revived, and all the proposals, engagements and declarations contained and made in the aboves[*ai*]d acts, by and on the part of this province to be kept and performed, and all the paragraphs therein contained, investing any persons with power to act and transact any matters in and about said lottery, are hereby revived, and shall be and remain of the same force and effect as they were before, or would have been if the said days therein prefix'd for drawing said lottery had not lapsed and expired. Former laws relating to this lottery, revived.

And be it further enacted,

[Sect. 2.] That the sixth day of August next shall be the time for drawing said lottery; at which time the managers and directors of said lottery are ordered and impowered to proceed to the drawing thereof. Time for the drawing the lottery fixed.

And be it further enacted,

[Sect. 3.] That if any of the tickets mentioned in the said act, whereby said lottery was established, shall remain in the hands of the directors or managers, undisposed of when the time set by this act for drawing said lottery shall come, that then and in such case all and every such ticket shall be and remain as the interest, share and lot of this province. Undisposed tickets to be the property of the province.

Provided, nevertheless,—

[Sect. 4.] That the managers or directors may, if they see cause, next after the first or second day's drawing, adjourn the further draw- Proviso.

ing for seven days, and in the meantime dispose of all or any of the tickets that may then remain unsold, valuing the same at a rate proportionable to the blanks and prizes which shall be then undrawn; and at the expiration of said seven days, the tickets which shall have been drawn as the property of the province, together with the remaining undisposed tickets, shall be, by the directors and managers, delivered to the treasurer as the lot of the province. [*Passed and published June* 13.

CHAPTER 9.

AN ACT FOR GRANTING TO HIS MAJESTY SEVERAL RATES AND DUTIES OF IMPOST AND TUNNAGE OF SHIPPING.

WHEREAS, in and by an act of this province, pass'd in the twenty-third and twenty-fourth year of his majesty's reign, the treasurer was impowered to borrow the sum of five thousand pounds for the supply of the treasury; and, in order to enable him to discharge the receipts and obligations that should by him be given for said sum in pursuance of the aforementioned act, it was therein provided that the dutys of impost and excise, for the year one thousand seven hundred and fifty-one, should be applied to that and to no other use whatever,—

WE, his majesty's most loyal and dutiful subjects, the representatives of the province of the Massachusetts Bay, in New England, being desirous of enabling the said treasurer to discharge the receipts and obligations as aforesaid, have chearfully and unanimously given and granted and do hereby give and grant to his most excellent majesty to the end and use aforesaid, and to no other use, the several duties of impost upon wines, liquors, goods, wares and merchandize that shall be imported into this province, and tunnage of shipping hereafter mentioned; and pray that it may be enacted,—

And be it accordingly enacted by the Lieutenant-Governour, Council and House of Representatives,

[SECT. 1.] That from and after the publication of this act, and during the space of one year, there shall be paid by the importer of all wines, liquors, goods, wares and merchandize that shall be imported into this province from the place of their growth (salt, cotton-wool, pig-iron, provisions, and every other thing of the growth and produce of New England, and also all prize goods condemn'd in any part of this province, excepted), the several rates or duties of impost following; vizt.,—

For every pipe of wine of the Western Islands, eighteen shillings.

For every pipe of Medara, twenty shillings.

For every pipe of other sorts not mention'd, eighteen shillings.

For every hogshead of rhum, containing one hundred gallons, fifteen shillings.

For every hogshead of sugar, fourpence.

For every hogshead of molasses, fourpence.

For every hogshead of tobacco, six shillings.

For every ton of logwood, fourpence.

—And so, proportionably, for greater or lesser quantities.

And all other commodities, goods or merchandize not mentioned or excepted, fourpence for every twenty shilling value: all goods imported from Great Britain, and hogshead- and barrell-staves and heads from any of his majesty's colonys and provinces on this continent, excepted.

[Sect. 2.] And for any of the above wines, liquors, goods, wares and merchandize, &c^{ra}., that shall be imported into this province from the port of their growth and produce, by any of the inhabitants of the other provinces or colonies on this continent, or the English West-India Islands, or in any ship or vessell to them belonging, on the proper account of any of the said inhabitants of the other provinces or colonys on this continent, or of the inhabitants of any of the English West-India Islands, there shall be paid by the importers double the impost appointed by this act to be received for every species above mentioned; and for all rum, sugar and molasses, imported and brought into this province in any ship or vessel, or by land-carriage from any of the colonies of Connecticut, New Hampshire or Rhode Island, shall be paid by the importer the rates and duties following:—

For every hogshead of rum, containing one hundred gallons, thirty-three shillings.

For every hogshead of molasses, containing one hundred gallons, one shilling and sixpence.

For every hogshead of sugar, containing one thousand weight, two shillings.

—And in that proportion for more or less thereof; and for all European goods, and for all other goods, wares or merchandize, eightpence for every twenty shillings value: *provided always*, that all hogshead and barrel-staves and hedding from any of his majesty's provinces or colonies, all provisions and other things that are the growth of New England, all salt, cotton-wool and pig-iron, are and shall be exempted from every the rates and duties aforesaid.

And be it further enacted,

[Sect. 3.] That the impost rates and duties aforesaid shall be paid in current lawful money by the importer of any wines, liquors, goods or merchandize, unto the commissioner to be appointed as is hereinafter to be directed for entering and receiving the same, at or before the landing of any wines, liquors, goods or merchandize: only the commissioner or receiver is hereby allowed to give credit to such person or persons where his or their duty of impost, in one ship or vessel, doth exceed the sum of six pounds; and in cases where the commissioner or receiver shall give credit, he shall ballance and settle his accompts with every person on or before the last day of April, so that the same accompts may be ready to be produced in court in May next after. And all entrys where the impost or duties to be paid doth not exceed three shillings, shall be made without charge to the importer, and not more than sixpence to be demanded for any other single entry to what value soever.

And be it further enacted,

[Sect. 4.] That the master of every ship or vessel coming into this province from any other place, shall, within twenty-four hours after his arrival in any port or harbour, and before bulk is broken, make report and deliver a manifest, in writing, under his hand, to the commissioner aforesaid, of the contents of the loading of such ship or vessell, therein particularly expressing the species, kind and quantitys of all the wines, liquors, goods, wares and merchandize imported in such ship or vessel, with the marks and numbers thereof, and to whom the same are consign'd; and make oath before the said commissioner that the same manifest contains a just and true account of all the lading taken on board and imported in such ship or vessel, so far as he knows or believes; and that if he knows of any more wines, liquors, goods, wares or merchandize laden on board such ship or vessel, and imported therein, he will forthwith make report thereof to the commissioner aforesaid, and cause the same to be added to his manifest.

And be it further enacted,

[SECT. 5.] That if the master of any such ship or vessel shall break bulk, or suffer any of the wines, liquors, goods, wares and merchandize imported in such ship or vessel to be unloaden before report and entry thereof be made as aforesaid, he shall forfeit the sum of one hundred pounds.

And be it further enacted,

[SECT. 6.] That all merchants, and other persons, being owners of any wines, liquors, goods, wares or merchandize imported into this province (for which any of the rates or duties aforesaid are payable), or having the same consign'd to them, shall make a like entry thereof with the commissioner aforesaid, and produce an invoice of all such goods as pay *ad valorem*, and make oath before him in form following; vizt.,—

You, A. B., do swear that the entry of the goods and merchandize by you now made, exhibits the present price of said goods at this market, and that, *bonâ fide*, according to your best skill and judgment, it is not less than the real value thereof. So help you God.

—which oath the commissioner or receiver is hereby impowered to administer; and the owners aforesaid shall pay the duty or impost by this act required, before such wines, liquors, goods, wares or merchandize be landed or taken out of the vessel in which the same shall be imported.

[SECT. 7.] And no wines, liquors, goods, wares or merchandize that by this act are liable to pay impost or duty, shall be landed on any wharffe, or into any warehouse or other place, but in the day time only, and that after sunrise and before sunset, unless in the presence and with the consent of the commissioner or receiver, on pain of forfeiting all such wines, liquors, goods, wares and merchandize, and the lighter, boat or vessel out of which the same shall be landed or put into any warehouse or other place.

[SECT. 8.] And if any person or persons shall not have and produce an invoice of the quantitys of rum or liquors to him or them consign'd, then the cask wherein the same is shall be gaged at the charge of the importer, that the contents thereof may be known.

And be it further enacted,

[SECT. 9.] That the importer of all wines, liquors, goods, wares and merchandize, within one year from and after the publication of this act, by land-carriage, or in small vessells or boats, shall make report, and deliver a manifest thereof, to the commissioner aforesaid or his deputy, therein particularly expressing the species, kind and quantity of all such wines, liquors, goods, wares and merchandize so imported, with the marks and numbers thereof, when, how and by whom brought; and shall make oath before the said commissioner or his deputy, to the truth of such report and manifest, and shall also pay the several dutys aforesaid, by this act charg'd and chargeable upon such wines, liquors, goods, wares and merchandize, before the same are landed, hous'd or put into any store or place whatever.

And be it further enacted,

[SECT. 10.] That every merchant or other person importing any wines into this province shall be allow'd twelve per cent for leakage: *provided*, such wines shall not have been fill'd up on board; and that every hogshead, butt or pipe of wine that hath two-thirds thereof leaked out, shall be accounted for outs, and the merchant or importer to pay no duty for the same. And no master of any ship or vessell shall suffer any wines to be fill'd up on board without giving a certificate of the quantity so fill'd up, under his hand, before the landing thereof, to the commissioner or receiver of impost for such port, on pain of forfeiting the sum of one hundred pounds.

[Sect. 11.] And if it may be made to appear that any wines imported in any ship or vessel be decay'd at the time of unloading thereof, or in twenty days afterwards, oath being made before the commissioner or receiver that the same hath not been landed above that time, the duties and impost paid for such wines shall be repaid unto the importer thereof.

And be it further enacted,

[Sect. 12.] That the master of every ship or vessel importing any wines, liquors, goods, wares or merchandize, shall be liable to and shall pay the impost for such and so much thereof, contain'd in his manifest, as shall not be duly enter'd, nor the duty paid for the same by the person or persons to whom such wines, liquors, goods, wares or merchandize are or shall be consign'd. And it shall and may be lawful, to and for the master of every ship or other vessell, to secure and detain in his hands, at the owner's risque, all such wines, liquors, goods, wares and merchandize imported in any ship or vessel, until he receives a certificate, from the commissioner or receiver of the impost, that the duty for the same is paid, and until he be repaid his necessary charges in securing the same; or such master may deliver such wines, liquors, goods, wares or merchandize as are not enter'd, unto the commissioner or receiver of the impost in such port, or his order, who is hereby impowered and directed to receive and keep the same, at the owner's risque, until the impost thereof, with the charges, be paid; and then to deliver such wines, liquors, goods, wares or merchandize as such master shall direct.

And be it further enacted,

[Sect. 13.] That the commissioner or receiver of the impost in each port, shall be and hereby is impowered to sue the master of any ship or vessel, for the impost or duty of so much of the lading of any wines, liquors, goods, wares or merchandize imported therein, according to the manifest to be by him given upon oath, as aforesaid, as shall remain not enter'd and the duty of impost therefor not paid. And where any goods, wares or merchandize are such as that the value thereof is not known, whereby the impost to be recovered of the master, for the same, cannot be ascertain'd, the owner or person to whom such goods, wares or merchandize are or shall be consign'd, shall be summoned to appear as an evidence at the court where such suit for the impost and the duty thereof shall be brought, and be there required to make oath to the value of such goods, wares or merchandize.

And be it further enacted,

[Sect. 14.] That the ship or vessel, with her tackle, apparrell and furniture, the master of which shall make default in anything by this act required to be performed by him, shall be liable to answer and make good the sum or sums forfeited by such master, according to this act, for any such default, as also to make good the impost or duty for any such wines, liquors, goods, wares and merchandize not enter'd as aforesaid; and, upon judgment recovered against such master, the said ship or vessel, with so much of the tackle and appurces thereof as shall be sufficient to satisfy said judgments, may be taken into execution for the same; and the commissioner or receiver of the impost is hereby impowered to make seizure of the said ship or vessel, and detain the same under seizure until judgment be given in any suit to be commenced and prosecuted for any of the said forfeitures of impost; to the intent that, if judgment be rendered for the prosecutor or informer, such ship or vessel and appurces may be exposed to sale, for satisfaction thereof, as is before provided: *unless* the owners, or some on their behalf, for the releasing of such ship or vessell from under seizure or restraint, shall give sufficient security unto the commissioner or receiver of impost that seized the same, to respond and satisfy the sum or value of the forfeitures and duties, with charges, that shall be recovered against the master thereof, upon such suit to be brought for the same, as aforesaid; and the master occasioning such loss or damage unto his owners, through his default or neglect, shall be liable unto their action for the same.

And be it further enacted,

[SECT. 15.] That the naval officer within any of the ports of this province shall not clear or give passes to any master of any ship or other vessel, outward bound, until he shall be certified, by the commissioner or receiver of the impost, that the duty and impost for the goods last imported in such ship or vessel are paid or secured to be paid.

[SECT. 16.] And the commissioner or receiver of the impost is hereby impowered to allow bills of store to the master of any ship or vessel importing any wines or liquors, for such private adventures as shall belong to the master or seaman of such ship or vessel, at the discretion of the commissioner or receiver, not exceeding three per cent of the lading; and the duties payable by this act for such wines and liquors, in such bills of stores mentioned and expressed, shall be abated.

And for the more effectual preventing any wines, rum or other distill'd spirits being brought into the province from the neighbouring governments, by land, or in small boats or vessells, or any other way, and also to prevent wines, rum, or other distill'd spirits, being first sent out of this province, to save the duty of impost, and afterwards brought into this government again,—

Be it enacted,

[SECT. 17.] That the commissioner and receiver of the aforesaid duties of impost shall, and he is hereby impower'd and enjoyn'd to, appoint one suitable person or persons as his deputy or deputys, in all such places in this province where it is likely that wine, rum, or other distill'd spirits will be brought ought of other governments into this; which officers shall have power to seize the same, unless the owners shall make it appear that the duty of impost has been paid therefor since their being brought into or relanded in this government; and such officer or officers are also impowered to search, in all suspected places, for such wines, rum and distill'd spirits brought or relanded in this government, where the duty is not paid as aforesaid, and to seize and secure the same for the ends and uses as in this act is hereafter provided.

And be it further enacted,

[SECT. 18.] That the commissioner or his deputys shall have full power to administer the several oaths aforesaid, and to search in all suspected places for all such wines, rum, liquors, goods, wares and merchandize as are brought into this province, and landed contrary to the true intent and meaning of this act, and to seize the same for the uses hereinafter mentioned.

And be it further enacted,

[SECT. 19.] That there shall be paid, by the master of every ship or other vessel, coming into any port or ports of this province, to trade or traffick, whereof all the owners are not belonging to this province (except such vessells as belong to Great Britain, the provinces or colonies of Pensylvania, West and East Jersey, Connecticut, New York, New Hampshire and Rhode Island), every voyage such ship or vessel does make, one pound of good pistol-powder for every ton such ship or vessell is in burthen: *saving* for that part which is owned in Great Britain, this province, or any of the aforesaid governments, which are hereby exempted; to be paid unto the commissioner or receiver of the dutys of impost, and to be employ'd for the ends and uses aforesaid.

[Sect. 20.] And the said commissioner is hereby impowered to appoint a meet and suitable person, to repair unto and on board any ship or vessel, to take the exact measure or tonnage thereof, in case he shall suspect that the register of such ship or vessel doth not express and set forth the full burthen of the same; the charge thereof to be paid by the master or owner of such ship or vessel, before she shall be cleared, in case she shall appear to be of a greater burthen: otherwise, to be paid by the commissioner out of the money received by him for impost, and shall be allowed him, accordingly, by the treasurer, in his accompts. And the naval officer shall not clear any vessel, until he be certified also, by the commissioner, that the duty of tonnage for the same is paid, or that it is such a vessel for which none is payable according to this act.

And be it further enacted,

[Sect. 21.] That when and so often as any wine or rum imported into this province, the duty of impost upon which shall have been paid agreeable to this act, shall be reshipp'd and exported from this government to any other part of the world, that then, and in every such case, the exporter of such wine or rum shall make oath, at the time of shipping, before the receiver of impost, or his deputy, that the whole of the wine or rum so shipp'd has, *bonâ fide*, had the aforesaid duty of impost paid on the same, and shall afterwards produce a certificate, from some officer of the customs, that the same has been landed out of this government,—or otherwise, in case such rum or wines shall be exported to any place where there is no officer of the customs, or to any foreign port, the master of the vessel in which the same shall be exported shall make oath that the same has been landed out of the government, and the exporter shall, upon producing such certificate, or upon such oath of the master, make oath that he verily believes no part of said wines or rum has been relanded in this province,—such exporter shall be allowed to draw back from the receiver of impost as follows; viz[t].,—

For every pipe of Western-Island wine, fifteen shillings.

For every pipe of Medara and other sorts, seventeen shillings.

For every hogshead of rum, thirteen shillings.

Provided, always,—

[Sect. 22.] That if, after the shipping any such rum or wine to be exported as aforesaid, giving security as aforesaid, in order to obtain the draw-back aforesaid, the wine or rum so shipp'd to be exported, or any part thereof, shall be relanded in this province, or brought into the same from any other province or colony, that then all such rum and wine so relanded and brought again into this province, shall be forfeited and may be seized by the commissioner aforesaid, or his deputy.

And be it further enacted,

[Sect. 23.] That there be one fitt person, and no more, nominated and appointed by this court, as a commissioner and receiver of the aforesaid duties of impost and tunnage of shipping, and for the inspection, care and management of the said office, and whatsoever thereto relates, to receive commission for the same from the governour and commander-in-chief, for the time being, with authority to substitute and appoint a deputy receiver in each port, or other places besides that wherein he resides, and to grant warrants to such deputy receivers for the said place, and to collect and receive the impost and tunnage of shipping as aforesaid that shall become due within such port, and to render the account thereof, and to pay in the same, to the said commissioner and receiver: which said commissioner and receiver shall keep fair books of all entrys and duties arising by virtue of this act; also, a particular account of every vessel, so that the duties of impost and tunnage arising on the said vessel may appear; and the same to lie open, at all seasonable times, to the view and perusal of the treasurer or receiver-general of this province (or any other person or persons whom this court shall appoint), with whom he shall account for all collections and payments, and pay all such moneys as shall be in his hands, as the treasurer or receiver-general shall demand it. And the said commissioner or receiver and his deputy or deputys, before their entring upon the execution of their office, shall be sworn to deal truly and faithfully therein, and shall attend in the said office from ten of the clock in the forenoon, until one in the afternoon.

[SECT. 24.] And the said commissioner and receiver, for his labour, care and expences in the said office, shall have and receive, out of the province treasury, the sum of forty pounds, per annum; and his deputy or deputys to be paid for their service such sum or sums as the said commissioner and receiver, with the treasurer, shall agree upon, not exceeding four pounds, per annum, each. And the treasurer is hereby ordered, in passing and receiving the said commissioner's accounts, accordingly, to allow the payment of such salary or salarys, as aforesaid, to himself and his deputys.

And be it further enacted by the authority aforesaid,

[SECT. 25.] That no duty of impost shall be demanded for any goods imported after the publication of this act, by virtue of any former act for granting unto his majesty any rates and duties of impost, and that all penaltys, fines and forfeitures accruing and arising by virtue of any breach of this act, shall be one half to his majesty for the uses and intents for which the afore-mentioned duties of impost are granted, and the other half to him or them that shall seize, inform and sue for the same by action, bill, plaint or information, in any of his majesty's courts of record, wherein no essoign, protection or wager of law shall be allowed: the whole charge of prosecution to be taken out of the half belonging to the informer.

And be it further enacted,

[SECT. 26.] That from and after the publication of this act, in all causes where any claimer shall appear, and shall not make good the claim, the charges of prosecution shall be born and paid by the said claimer, and not by the informer. [*Passed and published June* 18.

CHAPTER 10.

AN ACT FOR APPORTIONING AND ASSESSING A TAX OF THIRTY THOUSAND THREE HUNDRED AND NINETY-FOUR POUNDS, EIGHT SHILLINGS AND EIGHTPENCE; AND ALSO FOR APPORTIONING AND ASSESSING A FURTHER TAX OF FIVE THOUSAND TWO HUNDRED AND NINETY POUNDS, ELEVEN SHILLINGS AND FOURPENCE, PAID THE REPRESENTATIVES FOR THEIR SERVICE AND ATTENDANCE IN THE GENERAL COURT, AND TRAVEL[L], AND FOR FINES LAID ON SEVERAL TOWNS FOR NOT SENDING A REPRESENTATIVE; AMOUNTING IN THE WHOLE TO THIRTY-FIVE THOUSAND SIX HUNDRED AND EIGHTY-FIVE POUNDS.

WHEREAS the great and general court or assembly of the province of
1749-50, chap. 17. the Massachusetts Bay, did, at their session in November, one thousand
seven hundred and forty-nine, pass an act for levying a tax of eighteen
1750-51, chap. 1, § 5. thousand four hundred pounds; and, at their session in May, one
thousand seven hundred and fifty, did pass an act for levying a tax of
1750-51, chap. 9, § 5. five thousand pounds; and, at their session in September, one thousand
seven hundred and fifty, did pass an act for levying a tax of four thou-

sand pounds; and, at their session in January, one thousand seven 1750-51, chap. 15. hundred and fifty, did pass an act for levying a tax of eight thousand and ten pounds;—each of the several sums aforesaid to be levyed and assessed this present year,—amounting in the whole to the sum of thirty-five thousand six hundred and eighty-five pounds; and by the aforesaid acts, provision was made that the general court might, this present sitting, apportion the same on the several towns and districts within this province, if they thought fit: wherefore, for the ordering, directing and effectual drawing in the sum of thirty-five thousand six hundred and eighty-five pounds, pursuant to the funds and grants aforesaid, into the treasury, according to the apportion now agreed to by this court; all which is unanimously approved, ratified and confirmed; we, his majesty's most loyal[1] and dutiful[1] subjects, the representatives in general court assembled, pray that it may be enacted,—

And be it accordingly enacted by the Lieutenant-Governour, Council and House of Representatives,

[Sect. 1.] That each town and district within this province be assessed and pay, as such town and district's proportion of the sum of thirty thousand three hundred and ninety-four pounds, eight shillings and eightpence, and their representatives' pay, and fines laid on several towns, the sum of five thousand two hundred and ninety pounds, eleven shillings and fourpence; viz[t]., the several sums following; that is to say,—

IN THE COUNTY OF SUFFOLK.

	REPRESENTATIVES' PAY, AND FINES.	PROVINCE TAX.	SUM TOTAL.	
Boston,	£173 8s. 0d.	£5,170 8s. 0d.	Five [illegible] and [illegible] hundred and forty-three pounds sixteen shillings,	£5,343 16s. 0d.
Roxbury,	47 16 0	281 10 0	Three hundred and [illegible]-nine pounds six shillings,	329 6 0
Dorchester,	44 8 0	279 6 0	Three hundred and [illegible] pounds fourteen shillings,	323 14 0
Milton,	29 12 0	148 17 0	One hundred and [illegible]-[illegible] pounds [illegible] shillings,	178 9 0
Bra[i][illegible],	54 16 0	322 10 0	Three hundred and seventy-seven pounds six shillings,	377 6 0
[illegible],	56 0 0	189 15 0	Two hundred and [illegible]-five pounds fifteen [illegible],	245 15 0
Hingham,	55 12 0	333 15 0	Three hundred and eighty-[illegible] pounds seven shillings,	389 7 0
[illegible],	54 16 0	221 15 0	Two hundred and [illegible] pounds eleven shillings,	276 11 0
Medfield,	37 16 0	137 15 0	One [illegible] and [illegible] pounds [illegible] shillings,	175 11 0
[illegible],	25 4 0	222 10 0	Two [illegible] and [illegible]-[illegible] pounds fourteen shillings,	247 14 5
Medway,	10 0 0	114 12 0	One hundred and [illegible] pounds twelve shillings,	124 12 0
[illegible],	51 2 0	214 15 0	Two hundred and sixty-five pounds [illegible] shillings,	265 17 0
Hull,	0 0 0	51 15 0	Fifty-one pounds fifteen shillings,	51 15 0
Brookline,	47 8 0	86 14 0	One hundred and [illegible]-four pounds two shillings,	134 2 0
[illegible],	10 0 0	113 17 0	One hundred and [illegible] pounds [illegible] shillings,	123 17 0
Bellingham,	0 0 0	42 10 0	Forty-two pounds ten shillings,	42 10 0
[illegible],	0 0 0	74 17 0	Seventy-four pounds seventeen shillings,	74 17 5
[illegible],	47 16 0	116 3 0	One hundred and sixty-three pounds [illegible] shillings,	163 19 0
	£745 14s. 0d.	£8,123 4s. 0d.		£8,868 18s. 0d.

IN THE COUNTY OF ESSEX.

Salem,	£81 0s. 0d.	£800 12s. 0d.	Eight hundred and eighty-one pounds [illegible] shillings,	£881 12s. 0d.
Ipswich,	81 8 0	682 5 0	Seven hundred and [illegible] pounds [illegible] shillings,	763 13 0
Newbury,	60 4 0	880 15 0	Nine hundred and forty pounds [illegible] shillings,	940 19 0
[illegible],	57 12 0	522 0 0	Five hundred and [illegible] pounds [illegible] shillings,	579 19 0
Lynn,	57 0 0	281 5 0	Three hundred and thirty-eight pounds five shillings,	338 5 0
Andover,	55 8 0	383 10 0	Four hundred and [illegible]-[illegible] pounds eighteen shillings,	438 18 0
Beverly,	52 16 0	184 5 0	[illegible]wo hundred and thirty-seven pounds, [illegible],	237 1 0
Rowley,	42 12 0	242 17 0	Two hundred and [illegible] pounds [illegible] shillings,	285 9 0
Salisbury,	58 0 0	186 4 0	Two hundred and forty-four pounds four shillings,	244 4 0
Haverhill,	50 8 0	223 2 0	Two hundred and [illegible]-[illegible] pounds [illegible] shillings,	273 10 0
Gl[illegible]ter,	42 0 0	396 10 0	Four hundred and [illegible]-[illegible] pounds [illegible] shillings,	438 10 0

Towns				Sums total
Topsfield,	£16 12s. 0d.	£107 3s. 0d.	One hundred and twenty-three pounds fifteen shillings,	£123 15s. 0d.
Boxford,	58 0 0	140 5 0	One hundred and ninety-eight pounds five shillings,	198 5 0
Almsbury,	58 16 0	176 15 0	Two hundred and thirty-five pounds eleven shillings,	235 11 0
Bradford,	26 8 0	157 5 0	One hundred and eighty-three pounds thirteen shillings,	183 13 0
Wenham,	0 0 0	89 5 0	Eighty-nine pounds five shillings,	89 5 0
Manchester,	0 0 0	64 5 0	Sixty-four pounds five shillings,	64 5 0
Methuen,	5 0 0	102 5 0	One hundred and seven pounds five shillings,	107 5 0
Middleton,	10 0 0	79 8 0	Eighty-nine pounds eight shillings,	89 8 0
Rumford,	0 0 0	0 0 0		0 0 0
	£813 4s. 0d.	£5,700 3s. 0d.		£6,513 7s. 0d.

IN THE COUNTY OF MIDDLESEX.

Towns				Sums total
Cambridge,	£31 8s. 0d.	£203 5s. 0d.	[illegible] and [illegible] pounds [illegible] shillings,	£234 13s. 0d.
[illegible]n,	89 8 0	319 5 0	Four [illegible] and [illegible] pounds thirteen shillings,	408 13 0
[illegible]n,	56 0 0	121 4 0	[illegible] hundred and seventy-seven pounds [illegible] shillings,	177 4 0
Concord,	64 12 0	242 17 0	[illegible] and seven pounds [illegible] shillings,	307 9 0
[illegible]n,	57 8 0	118 10 0	[illegible] hundred and seventy-five pounds [illegible] shillings,	175 18 0
[illegible]n,	44 12 0	197 5 0	Two hundred and forty-[illegible] pounds [illegible] shillings,	241 17 0
Reading,	56 0 0	201 16 0	Two [illegible] and [illegible] pounds [illegible] shillings,	257 16 0
[illegible]y,	57 12 0	215 10 0	[illegible] hundred and [illegible] pounds [illegible] shillings,	273 2 0
Marlborough,	58 16 0	214 15 0	Two hundred and seventy-[illegible] pounds eleven shillings,	273 11 0
Lexington,	54 16 0	136 5 0	[illegible] and [illegible] pounds [illegible] shilling,	191 1 0
[illegible]n,	56 0 0	197 15 0	Two hundred and fifty-three pounds [illegible] shillings,	253 15 0
[illegible]n,	46 16 0	159 6 0	Two [illegible] and six pounds two shillings,	206 2 0
Chelmsford,	52 0 0	121 8 0	[illegible] hundred and [illegible] pounds [illegible] shillings,	173 8 0
Billerica,	54 4 0	125 1 0	[illegible] hundred and [illegible] pounds five [illegible],	179 5 0
Sherburn,	10 0 0	83 17 0	[illegible] pounds [illegible] shillings,	93 17 0
Holliston,	5 0 0	68 5 0	Seventy-three pounds five shillings,	73 5 0
Groton,	45 0 0	222 13 0	Two hundred and sixty-seven pounds [illegible] shillings,	267 13 0
Framingham,	54 16 0	162 3 0	Two hundred and [illegible] pounds [illegible] shillings,	216 19 0
Medford,	26 12 0	109 11 0	[illegible] and thirty-six pounds three shillings,	136 3 0
Stow,	59 0 0	74 7 0	[illegible] hundred and [illegible]-three pounds seven [illegible],	133 7 0
Dunstable [illegible] Nottingham inhabitants,	0 0 0	51 7 2	[illegible] pounds seven [illegible] and [illegible],	51[1]7 2
Dracut[t],	0 0 0	58 8 0	Fifty-eight pounds eight [illegible],	58 8 0
[illegible]n,	0 0 0	52 7 0	Fifty-two pounds seven shillings,	52 7 0

IN THE COUNTY OF MIDDLESEX—*Continued.*

	REPRESENTATIVES' PAY AND FINES.	PROVINCE TAX.	SUM TOTAL.	
Littleton,	£55 8s. 0d.	£85 8s. 0d.	One hundred and forty pounds sixteen shillings,	£140 16s. 0d.
Hopkinston,	26 8 0	74 10 0	One hundred pounds eighteen shillings,	100 18 0
Bedford,	0 0 0	70 3 0	Seventy pounds three shillings,	70 3 0
Westford,	22 16 0	82 7 0	One hundred and five pounds three shillings,	105 3 0
Wilmington,	0 0 0	60 14 0	Sixty pounds fourteen shillings,	60 14 0
Tewksbury,	0 0 0	59 16 0	Fifty-nine pounds sixteen shillings,	59 16 0
Acton,	0 0 0	44 8 0	Forty-four pounds eight shillings,	44 8 0
Waltham,	38 4 0	104 4 0	One hundred and forty-two pounds eight shillings,	142 8 0
Townshend,	0 0 0	45 7 0	Forty-five pounds seven shillings,	45 7 0
English inhab[*itan*]ts of Natick,	0 0 0	41 4 0	Forty-one pounds four shillings,	41 4 0
	£1,122 16s. 0d.	£4,125 1s. 2d.		£5,247 17s. 2d.

IN THE COUNTY OF HAMPSHIRE.

Springfield,	£56 16s. 0d.	£296 7s. 0d.	Three [illegible] and [illegible] pounds three shillings,	£353 3s. 0d.
Northampton,	58 16 0	196 12 0	Two hundred and fifty-five pounds [illegible] shillings,	255 8 0
[illegible],	59 16 0	156 1 0	Two [illegible] and [illegible] pounds [illegible] shillings,	215 17 0
[illegible],	36 0 0	91 10 0	One hundred and [illegible] pounds ten shillings,	127 10 0
[illegible],	56 12 0	118 19 0	One hundred and seventy-five pounds eleven shillings,	175 11 0
Suffield,	10 0 0	163 3 0	One hundred and [illegible] pounds three shillings,	173 3 0
Enfield,	13 6 8	88 9 0	One hundred and one pounds fifteen shillings and [illegible],	101 15 8
Deerfield,	45 4 0	88 19 0	One hundred and thirty-[illegible] pounds [illegible] shillings,	134 3 0
Sunderland,	15 8 0	51 17 0	Sixty-[illegible] pounds five shillings,	67 5 0
[illegible],	0 0 0	32 5 0	Thirty-two [illegible], five shillings,	32 5 0
Brimfield,	10 0 0	100 13 0	One hundred and ten [illegible], [illegible] shillings,	110 13 0
Somers,	0 0 0	62 10 0	[illegible] pounds ten shillings,	62 10 0
Sheffield,	24 8 0	101 8 0	One [illegible] and [illegible] pounds sixteen shillings,	125 16 0
[illegible]s or Kingston,	0 0 0	36 7 0	Thirty-six pounds seven shillings,	36 7 0
Stockbridge,	0 0 0	0 0 0		0 0 0
[illegible],	0 0 0	31 10 0	Thirty-one pounds ten shillings,	31 10 0
Bedford,	0 0 0	21 7 0	Twenty-one pounds seven shillings,	21 7 0
Coldspring,	0 0 0	21 7 0	Twenty-one pounds seven shillings,	21 7 0
Quab[*b*]in,	0 0 0	23 5 0	Twenty-three pounds five shillings,	23 5 0
[illegible],	0 0 0	13 4 0	Thirteen pounds four shillings,	13 4 0

New Marlborô or No. 2,	£0 0s. 0d.	£22 17s. 0d.	Twenty-two pounds seventeen shillings,	£22 17s. 0d.
Parish at Ware River,	0 0 0	31 10 0	Thirty-one pounds ten shillings,	31 10 0
	£386 6s. 8d.	£1,750 0s. 0d.		£2,136 6s. 8d.

IN THE COUNTY OF WORCESTER.

[illegible]r,	£45 2s. [illegible]	£160 15s. 0d.	[illegible] [illegible] ad five [illegible] [illegible] [illegible],	£[illegible]5 17s. 0d.
Lan[illegible],	44 4 0	182 2 0	Two [illegible] ad [illegible] [illegible] [illegible],	226 6 0
[illegible],	60 12 0	173 8 0	Two [illegible] ad thirty- [illegible] [illegible],	234 0 0
[illegible]k,	18 13 4	196 12 0	Two hundred ad [illegible] [illegible] i[illegible]e [illegible] ad [illegible],	215 5 4
[illegible]d,	56 0 0	142 15 0	[illegible]e [illegible] ad [illegible] [illegible] [illegible] [illegible],	[illegible] 15 0
Southborough,	34 16 0	78 13 0	[illegible]e [illegible] ad [illegible] [illegible] [illegible] [illegible],	13 9 0
[illegible]i] [illegible]r,	62 6 0	142 15 0	Two [illegible] ad [illegible] [illegible] [illegible] [illegible],	205 1 0
[illegible]d,	10 0 0	100 4 0	[illegible]e [illegible] ad [illegible] [illegible] four [illegible],	10 4 0
[illegible]g[h],	10 0 0	106 5 0	[illegible]e [illegible] ad [illegible] [illegible] five [illegible],	16 5 0
[illegible]h,	37 0 0	109 5 0	[illegible]e hundred ad [illegible] [illegible] [illegible] five [illegible],	46 5 0
[illegible],	37 0 0	127 15 0	[illegible]e [illegible] ad [illegible] [illegible] fifteen [illegible],	[illegible]4 15 0
Oxford,	38 12 0	97 5 0	[illegible]e hundred ad [illegible] [illegible] [illegible] [illegible] [illegible]llings,	[illegible]5 17 0
S[illegible]n,	53 4 0	139 10 0	[illegible]e hundred ad [illegible] [illegible] [illegible] [illegible]llings,	192 14 0
[illegible]e,	19 18 0	96 8 0	[illegible]e [illegible] ad [illegible] [illegible] [illegible] [illegible],	16 6 0
[illegible]d,	36 12 0	87 10 0	[illegible]e [illegible] ad [illegible] [illegible] [illegible]o shillings,	124 2 0
Grafton,	0 0 0	71 8 0	[illegible]e [illegible] eight [illegible],	71 8 0
Upton,	18 16 0	47 8 0	[illegible] [illegible] four [illegible],	66 4 0
Dudley,	0 0 0	56 10 0	[illegible]x [illegible] [illegible] [illegible],	56 10 0
Bolton,	35 16 0	87 5 0	[illegible]e [illegible] ad [illegible]e punds one shilling,	123 1 0
[illegible]e,	0 0 0	36 16 0	[illegible] [illegible] [illegible]n shillin g,	36 16 0
Leominster,	0 0 0	44 10 0	Forty-four [illegible] [illegible] [illegible],	44 10 0
[illegible],	0 0 0	43 5 0	[illegible]e [illegible] five [illegible],	43 5 0
[illegible]k,	0 0 0	55 8 0	Fifty- [illegible] [illegible] [illegible] [illegible],	55 8 0
Holden,	0 0 0	27 18 0	[illegible]n [illegible] [illegible]n shilli g,	27 18 0
[illegible]g,	0 0 0	32 4 0	[illegible]o [illegible] [illegible] [illegible],	32 4 0
[illegible]s,	0 0 0	24 6 2	[illegible]r [illegible] [illegible] [illegible] ad [illegible] [illegible]e,	24 6 2
	£618 11s. 4d.	£2,468 0s. 2d.		£3,086 11s. 6d.

IN THE COUNTY OF PLYMOUTH.

	[illegible] PAY, AND FI[illegible]	PROVINCE TAX.	SUM TOTAL.	
Pl[illegible]outh,	£51 [illegible]s. [illegible]	£242 17s. 0d.	[illegible] hundred and nine[illegible] pounds [illegible] shillings,	£294 9. [illegible]
Pl[illegible]pton,	52 8 0	142 3 0	[illegible] hundred and ninety-four pounds eleven shillings,	94 11 0
[illegible]c,	58 0 0	333 10 0	Three hundred and n[illegible] pounds [illegible]n shillings,	31 10 0
[illegible]r,	58 8 0	393 16 0	[illegible] hundred and [illegible] pounds four [illegible]s,	52 4 0
[illegible]l,	42 2 0	227 3 0	[illegible] hundred and sixty-nine pounds five shillings,	29 5 0
[illegible]c,	58 16 0	121 8 0	[illegible] hundred and eighty pounds [illegible] shillings,	30 4 0
Duxbury,	28 8 0	110 15 0	One hundred and thirty-nine pounds three [illegible]s,	39 3 0
[illegible]h,	45 8 0	276 5 0	Three hundred and [illegible] pounds thirteen shillings,	31 13 0
[illegible] s[illegible]r,	49 12 0	167 5 0	Two [illegible] and sixteen pounds [illegible]n shillings,	26 17 0
[illegible]n,	8 0 0	114 14 0	[illegible] [illegible] and [illegible]y-two pounds [illegible]n shillings,	22 14 0
[illegible]n,	5 0 0	82 5 0	[illegible] pounds five [illegible],	87 5 0
[illegible]n[n]over,	56 16 0	107 7 0	[illegible] [illegible] and [illegible]y-four pounds three shillings,	64 3 0
[illegible]x,	0 0 0	68 9 0	Sixty-[illegible] pounds nine [illegible]s,	68 9 0
Wa[illegible]h,	0 0 0	70 3 2	[illegible]y pounds [illegible] shillings and [illegible],	70 3 2
	£514 10s. 0d.	£2,458 0s. 2d.		£2,972 10s. 2d.

IN THE COUNTY OF BARNSTABLE.

Barnstable,	£62 2s. 8d.	£214 15s. 0d.	Two hundred and seventy-six pounds seventeen shillings and eight-pence,	£276 17s. 8d.
Sandwich,	42 16 0	152 7 0	One hundred and ninety-five pounds three shillings,	95 3 0
Yarmouth,	34 2 8	140 15 0	One hundred and seventy-four pounds seventeen shillings and eight-pence,	74 17 8
Eastham,	56 4 0	173 10 0	Two hundred and twenty-nine pounds fourteen shillings,	29 14 0
Truro,	0 0 0	81 10 0	Eighty-one pounds ten shillings,	81 10 0
Harwich,	61 12 0	135 3 0	One hundred and ninety-six pounds fifteen shillings,	96 15 0
Falmouth,	27 0 0	95 8 0	One hundred and twenty-two pounds eight shillings,	22 8 0
Chatham,	0 0 0	76 12 0	Seventy-six pounds twelve shillings,	76 12 0
	£283 17s. 4d.	£1,070 0s. 0d.		£1,353 17s. 4d.

IN THE COUNTY OF BRISTOL[L].

Taunton,	£53 8s. 0d.	£295 5s. 0d.	Three hundred and forty-eight pounds thirteen shillings,	£348 13s. 0d.
Norton,	55 0 0	188 3 0	Two hundred and forty-three pounds three shillings,	213 3 0
Easton,	0 0 0	89 3 0	Eighty-nine pounds three shillings,	89 3 0
Dartmouth,	63 4 0	546 5 0	Six hundred and nine pounds nine shillings,	609 9 0
Dighton,	26 12 0	130 5 0	One hundred fifty-six pounds seventeen shillings,	156 17 0
Rehoboth,	47 0 0	418 12 0	Four hundred and sixty-five pounds twelve shillings,	465 12 0
[illegible],	0 0 0	0 0 0	. . . .	0 0 0
Swanzey with Shawam[m]et[t],	55 0 0	186 10 0	Two hundred and forty-one pounds ten shillings,	241 10 0
Freetown,	51 8 0	120 2 0	One hundred and seventy-one pounds ten shillings,	171 10 0
Attleborough,	51 12 0	199 6 0	Two hundred and fifty pounds eighteen shillings,	250 18 0
Barrington,	0 0 0	0 0 0	. . . .	0 0 0
Raynham,	0 0 0	77 5 0	Seventy-seven pounds five shillings,	77 5 0
Berkley,	0 0 0	69 4 2	Sixty-nine pounds four shillings and twopence,	69 4 2
	£403 4s. 0d.	£2,320 0s. 2d.		£2,723 4s. 2d.

IN THE COUNTY OF YORK.

York,	£57 0s. 0d.	£295 2s. 0d.	Three hundred and fifty-two pounds two shillings,	£352 2s. 0d.
[illegible]ry,	52 16 0	348 4 0	Four hundred and one [illegible],	401 0 0
Berwick,	43 16 0	182 2 0	Two hund[illegible] and twenty-five pounds eighteen shillings,	225 18 0
Wells,	61 12 0	134 5 0	One hundred and [illegible]-five pounds seventeen shillings,	195 17 0
Falmouth,	63 12 0	287 12 0	Three hundred and fifty-one pounds four shillings,	351 4 0
Biddeford,	5 0 0	122 13 0	One hundred and twenty-seven pounds [illegible] shillings,	127 13 0
Arundel,	0 0 0	68 15 0	Sixty-eight pounds fifteen shillings,	68 15 0
Scarborough,	0 0 0	104 12 0	One hundred and four pounds [illegible] shillings,	104 12 0
North Yarmouth,	34 0 0	44 10 0	Seventy-eight pounds ten shillings,	78 10 0
[illegible]n,	0 0 0	48 5 0	Forty-eight pounds five shillings,	48 5 0
Brunswick,	0 0 0	43 10 0	Forty-three pounds ten shillings,	43 10 0
Sheepscut[t],	0 0 0	30 10 0	Thirty pounds ten shillings,	30 10 0
	£317 16s. 0d.	£1,710 0s. 0d.		£2,027 16s. 0d.

IN THE COUNTY OF DUKES COUNTY.

	Representatives' Pay, and Fines.	Province Tax.	Sum Total.	
Edgartown,	£27 4s. 0d.	£116 15s. 0d.	One hundred and forty-three pounds nineteen shillings,	£143 19s. 0d.
Chilmark,	25 8 0	105 15 0		131 3 0
Tisbury,	0 0 0	67 10 0		67 10 0
	£52 12s. 0d.	£290 0s. 0d.		£342 12s. 0d.

IN NANTUCKET[T] COUNTY.

Sherburn,	£32 0s. 0d.	£380 0s. 0d.	Four hundred and twelve pounds,	£412 0s. 0d.

RECAPITULATION.

	Representatives' pay, and [illegible]es.	Province tax.	Sum total.	
Suffolk,	£745 14s. 0d.	£8,123 4s. 0d.	Eight [illegible] eight [illegible] [and] sixty-eight [illegible] eighteen [illegible],	£8,868 18s. 0d.
Essex,	813 4 0	5,700 3 0	Six [illegible] five hundred [illegible] [illegible] seven shillings,	6,513 7 0
[illegible]x,	1,122 16 0	4,125 1 2	Five [illegible] two hundred & forty- [illegible] [illegible] seventeen shil-l[in]gs & [illegible]e],	5,247 17 2
Hampshire,	386 6 8	1,750 0 0	[illegible] [illegible] one [illegible] and thirty-six [illegible] six shillings and [illegible]],	2,136 6 8
Worcester,	618 11 4	2,468 0 2	[illegible] thousand and eighty-six pounds [illegible] shillings and six-[illegible],	3,086 11 6
[illegible]h,	514 10 0	2,458 0 2	[illegible] [illegible] nine hundred & seventy-two [illegible] ten [illegible] & [illegible]],	2,972 10 2
[illegible]e,	283 17 4	1,070 0 0	[Thirteen] [*one thousand three*] hundred & fifty-three [illegible] seven-teen shillings & fourpen[ce],	1353 17 4
Bristol,	403 4 0	2,320 0 2	[illegible] thousand [illegible] [illegible] & [illegible] [illegible] four shillings & [illegible]pen[ce],	2,723 4 2
York,	317 16 0	1,710 0 0	Two [illegible] and [illegible] pounds sixteen shillings,	2,027 16 0
[illegible] [illegible]y,	52 12 0	290 0 0	Three [illegible] and forty-two pounds [illegible] [illegible],	342 12 0
[illegible][t],	32 0 0	380 0 0	Four [illegible] and [illegible] pounds,	412 0 0
	£5,290 11s. 4d.	£30,394 8s. 8d.		£35,685 0s. 0d.

And be it further enacted,

[SECT. 2.] That the treasurer do forthwith send out his warrants, directed to the selectmen or assessors of each town or district within this province, requiring them, respectively, to assess the sum hereby set upon such town or district, in manner following; that is to say, to assess all rateable male pol[e][*l*]s above the age of sixteen years, within their respective towns or districts, or next adjo[y][*i*]ning to them, belonging to no other town, five shillings per poll, and proportionably in assessing the fines mentioned in this act, and the additional sum received out of the treasury for the payment of the representatives (except the governour, the lieutenant-governour and their famil[y][*ie*]s, the president, fellows and students of Harvard Colle[d]ge, settled ministers and grammar-school masters, who are hereby exempted as well from being taxed for their polls, as for their estates being in their own hands and under their actual management and improvement); and other persons, if such the[*i*]r[e] be, who, thrô[*ugh*] age, infirmity or extream poverty, in the judgment of the assessors, are not capable to pay towards publick charges, they may exempt their polls, and so much of their estates as in their prudence they shall think fit and judge meet.

[SECT. 3.] And the justices in their general sessions, in the respective count[y][*ie*]s assembled, in granting a county tax or assessment, are hereby ordered and directed to apportion the same on the several towns in such county in proportion to their province rate, exclusive of what has been paid out of the publick treasury to the representative of each town for his service; and the assessors of each town in the province are also directed, in making an assessment, to govern themselves by the same rule; and all estates, both real and personal, lying within the limits of such town or district, or next unto the same, not paying elsewhere, in whose hands, tenure, occupation or possession soever the same is or shall be found, and also the incomes or profits which any person or persons, except as before excepted, do or shall receive from any trade, faculty, business or employment whatsoever, and all profits that shall or may arise by money or other estate not particularly otherwise assessed, or commissions of profit in their improvement, according to their understanding and cun[*n*]ing, at one penny on the pound; and to abate or multiply the same, if need be, so as to make up the sum set[t] and ordered hereby for such town or d[e][*i*]strict to pay; and, in making their assessment, to estimate houses and lands at six years' income of the yearly rents, whereat the same may be reasonably set or let[t] for in the place where they lye: *saving* all contracts between landlord and tenant, and where no contract is, the landlord to reimburse one-half of the tax set upon such houses and lands; and to estimate negro, Indian and molatto servants proportionably as other personal estate, according to their sound judgment and discretion; as also to estimate every ox of four years old and upwards, at forty shillings; every cow of three years old and upwards, at thirty shillings; every horse and mare of three years old and upwards, at fo[u]rty shillings; every swine of one year old and upwards, at eight shillings; goats and sheep of one year old, three shillings each: likewise requiring the said assessors to make a fair list of the said assessment, setting forth, in d[e][*i*]stinct columns, against each particular person's name, how much he or she is assessed at for polls, and how much for houses and lands, and how much for personal estate, and income by trade or faculty, and if as guardian, or for any estate in his or her improvement, in trust, to be d[e][*i*]stinctly expressed; and the list or lists, so perfected and signed by them, or the major part of them, to commit to the collectors, constable or constables of such town or d[e][*i*]strict, and to return a certificate of the name or names of such collectors, constable or constables, together with the sum total to each of them committed, unto himself, some time before the last day of October next.

[Sect. 4.] And the treasurer for the time being, upon receipt of such certificate, is hereby impow[*e*]red and ordered to issue forth his warrants to the collector, constable or constables of such town or d[e][*i*]strict, requiring him or them, respectively, to collect the whole of each respective sum assessed on each particular person, before the last day of December next; and to pay in their collection, and issue the accompts of the whole, at or before the last day of March, which will be in the year of our Lord one thousand seven hundred and fifty-two.

And be it further enacted,

[Sect. 5.] That the assessors of each town and d[e][*i*]strict, respectiv[*e*]ly, in convenient time before their making the assessment, shall give seasonable warning to the inhabitants, in a town meeting, or by posting up notifications in some place or places in such town or d[e][*i*]strict, or notify the inhabitants some other way, to give or bring in to the assessors true and perfect lists of their polls, and rat[*e*]able estate, and income by trade or faculty, and gain by money at interest; and if any person or persons shall neglect or refuse so to do, or bring in a false list, it shall be lawful[l] to and for the assessors to assess such person or persons, according to their known ability in such town, in their sound judgment and discretion, their due proportion of this tax, as near as they can, agreeable to the rules herein given, under the penalty of twenty shillings for each person that shall be convicted by legal proof, in the judgment of the said assessors, of bringing in a false list; the said fines to be for the use of the poor of such town or d[e][*i*]strict where the delinquent lives, to be lev[y][*i*]ed by warrant from the assessors, directed to the collector or constables, in manner as is directed for gathering town assessments, and to be paid in to the town treasurer or selectmen for the use aforesaid: *saving* to the party ag[*g*]r[ei][*ie*]ved at the judgment of the assessors in setting forth such fine, liberty of appeal therefrom to the court of general sessions of the peace within the county, for relief, as in case of being overrated. And if any person or persons shall not bring in a list of their estate, as aforesaid, to the assessors, he or they so neglecting shall not be admitted to make application to the court of sessions for any abatement of the assessment laid on him.

[Sect. 6.] And if the party be not convicted of any fals[*e*]ness in the list, by him presented, of the polls, rat[*e*]able estate, or income by trade or faculty, business or employment, which he doth or shall exercise, or in gain by money at interest or otherwise, or other estate not particularly assessed, such list shall be a rule for such person's proportion to the tax, which the assessors may not exceed.

And forasmuch as, ofttimes, sundry persons, not belonging to this province, bring considerable trade and merchandize, and by reason that the tax or rate of the town where they come to trade is finished and delivered to the constable or collector, and, before the next year's assessment, are gone out of the province, and so pay nothing towards the support of the government, thô[*ugh*], in the time of their residing here, they reaped considerable gain by trade, and had the protection of the government,—

Be it further enacted,

[Sect. 7.] That when any such person or persons shall come and reside in any town within this province, and bring any merchandize, and trade, to deal therewith, the assessors of such town are hereby impow[*e*]red to rate and assess all such persons according to their circumstances, pursuant to the rules and directions in this act provided, thô the former rate may have been finished, and the new one not perfected, as aforesaid; and the constables or col[*l*]ectors are hereby enjoyned to levy and collect all such sums committed to them, and assessed on persons who are not of this province, and pay the same in to the town treasury.

And be it further enacted,

[SECT. 8.] That the inhabitants of this province have liberty, if they see fit, to pay the several sums for which they may respectively be assessed, as their proportion of the aforesaid sum of thirty thousand three hundred and ninety-four pounds eight shillings and eightpence, in good merchantable hemp, or in good, merchantable, Isle-of-Sable codfish, or in good refined bar-iron, or in bloomery-iron, or in hollow iron-ware, or in good Indian corn, or in good winter rye, or in good winter wheat, or in good barley, or in good barrell pork, or in barrell beef, or in duck or canvas, or in long whalebone, or in merchantable cordage, or in good train oyl, or in good beeswax, or in good bayberry-wax, or in tryed tallow, or in good pease, or in good sheepswool, or in good tanned sole-leather; and that the eldest councellors, for the time being, of each of those countys in the province, of which any one of the councellers is an inhabitant, together with the province treasurer, or the major part of them, be a committee, who are hereby directed and fully authorized and impowred, once in every month, if need be, to agree and sett the several species and commoditys aforesaid, at some certain price, at which they shall be received towards the payment of the sums aforesaid: all which aforesaid commoditys shall be of the produce of this province, and, as soon as conveniently may, be disposed of by the treasurer to the best advantage, for so much as they will fetch in money; and the several persons paying their taxes in any of the commoditys afore mentioned, to run the risque and pay the charge of transporting the said commodit[y][*ie*]s to the province treasury.

[SECT. 9.] And if any loss shall happen by the sale of the aforesaid species, it shall be made good by a tax of the next year; and if there be a surplusage, it shall remain a stock in the treasury.

And be it further enacted,

[SECT. 10.] That the inhabitants of this province shall have full liberty to pay in the several sums which they shall respectively be assessed in pursuance of this act, in bills of credit on this province: *provided*, they pay the bills aforesaid to the collectors of said assessments, on or before the last day of December next. [*Passed June* 21; *published June* 25.

ACT

PASSED AT THE SESSION BEGUN AND HELD AT BOSTON, ON THE SECOND DAY OF OCTOBER, A. D. 1751.

CHAPTER 11.

AN ACT FOR SUPPLYING THE TREASURY WITH THE SUM OF FOUR THOUSAND FIVE HUNDRED AND FORTY-FIVE POUNDS.

WHEREAS in the late proposed supply of the treasury with twenty-six thousand seven hundred milled dollars, there happens a deficiency of four thousand five hundred and forty-five pounds, so that the debts of the government which require a speedy payment, cannot be discharged until the treasury is farther supplyed with that sum; therefore,— Preamble. 1750-51, chap. 15.

Be it enacted by the Lieutenant-Governour, Council and House of Representatives,

[SECT. 1.] That the province treasurer be and hereby is ordered to borrow and take up, on lawful interest, the sum of four thousand five hundred and forty-five pounds, for the use of this government; and that he give to such persons as shall lend the same, his promissory notes for the payment of the sums by them respectively lent, to them or the bearer of such notes, within six months, with lawful interest for the same, until paid. Treasurer to borrow £4,545 on his notes.

And be it further enacted,

[SECT. 2.] That the province treasurer apply the sum so borrowed towards the payment of such of the government's debts as were to have been discharged by the said twenty-six thousand seven hundred mill'd dollars, and that the province treasurer pay off and discharge the notes aforesaid, as they shall become due, out of the monies that shall come into the treasury by force of the last act made for supplying the same. Said money to be applied to discharge the debts of the government.

[*Passed October* 9; *published October* 12.

ACTS

PASSED AT THE SESSION BEGUN AND HELD AT BOSTON, ON THE TWENTY-SEVENTH DAY OF DECEMBER, A. D. 1751.

CHAPTER 12.

AN ACT IN ADDITION TO AN ACT MADE AND PASS[*E*]'D IN THE THIRTEENTH YEAR OF KING WILLIAM THE THIRD, INTITLED "AN ACT PROVIDING IN CASE OF SICKNESS."

Be it enacted by the Lieutenant-Governour, Council and House of Representatives,

Clothing and other goods suspected to be infected, to be liable to be stopped and secured.

1701-2, chap. 9.

[SECT. 1.] That when and as often as there shall be brought into any town within this province, whether it shall be from any other town within the province, or from parts without the province, any baggage, cloathing or goods of any kind soever, and it shall be made to appear by the selectmen of the town, or major part of them, to which such baggage, cloathing or other goods shall be brought, to the satisfaction of any one of his majesty's justices of the peace, that there is just cause to suspect such baggage, cloathing or other goods to be infected with the plague, small-pox, pestilential fever, or other malignant, contagious distemper, it shall and may be lawful for such justice of the peace, and he is hereby required, in such case, by warrant, under his hand and seal, directed to the sheriff or his deputy, or any constable of the town in which such baggage, cloathing or other goods shall be, requiring him to impress so many men as said justice shall judge necessary, to secure such baggage, cloathing or other goods to be secured, and said men to set and post as a guard and watch over the house or houses, or other place or places where such baggage, cloathing or other goods shall be lodged; which guard and watch are hereby required to take effectual care to prevent such baggage, cloathing or other goods being removed or intermedled with by any persons whatever, until[l] due inquiry be made into the circumstances thereof; and in case it shall appear to the said justice highly probable that such baggage, cloathing or other goods are infected with the plague, small-pox, pestilential fever, or other malignant, contagious distemper, said justice is hereby impowered and directed to issue a warrant, under his hand and seal, directed to the sheriff or his deputy, or the constable of the town where such goods, cloathing or baggage shall be, requiring said sheriff, deputy or constable to remove said baggage, cloathing or other goods, to some convenient house or place from whence there shall be the least danger of the infection's spreading, or being conveyed, there to remain until[l] such baggage, cloathing or other goods shall be sufficiently aired, and until[l] it shall appear to the satisfaction of the selectmen of the town where such baggage, cloathing or other goods shall be, that they be free from all infection; and said sheriff, deputy sheriff or constable, in the execution of

Manner of proceeding therein.

said warrant, are impow[e]red and directed, if need be, to break up any house, warehouse, shop or other place or places, particularly mentioned in such warrant, where such baggage, cloathing or other goods shall be; and in case of opposition or resistance, to require such aid and assistance as shall be necessary to effect the removal of such baggage, cloathing or other goods, and repel the force and resistance which shall or may be made thereto.

Penalty for not assisting the officer.

[SECT. 2.] And all persons are hereby required, at the commandment of either of the said officers having such warrant, under the penalty of forty shillings, to be recovered before the justice granting the same, to assist said officer in the removing said baggage, cloathing or other goods, unless they make an excuse to the satisfaction of such justice; and the charges of securing such baggage, cloathing and other goods, transporting and airing the same, shall be born and paid by the owners thereof, at such rates and prizes as shall be set and appointed by the selectmen of the town where such baggage, cloathing or other goods shall be; and in case of refusal, to be recovered by suit at law by all and every person and persons concerned and employed in and about the business of securing, removing and airing said baggage, cloathing or other goods.

Charges to be borne by the owner of the goods, &c.

And be it further enacted,

Warrants to be made out to take up convenient housing.

[SECT. 3.] That if need so require, any justice of the peace may, and is hereby impow[e]red, on application to him made by the selectmen of the town in which such infected baggage, cloathing or other goods shall be, to make out a warrant to the sheriff of the county or his deputy, or constable of the town where such baggage, cloathing or other goods shall be, requiring said officer, with the advice and direction of the selectmen of said town, to impress and take up convenient housing or stores, for the receiving, lodging and safe keeping thereof, until[l] the same shall be sufficiently aired, as aforesaid. [*Passed January* 30; *published January* 31, 1752.

CHAPTER 13.

AN ACT IN FURTHER ADDITION TO THE ACT INTITLED "AN ACT FOR REVIEW IN CIVIL CAUSES."

Preamble. 1701-2, chap. 6. 1720-21, chap. 11. 1732-33, chap. 13. 1734-35, chap. 5. 1750-51, chap. 7.

WHEREAS the defendant in any personal action may, by force of the act made in addition to the act [e][*i*]ntitled "An Act for review in civil causes," have execution of the judgm[*en*]t of the superiour court of judicature, court of assize and general goal delivery, given on the trial of the appeal, stayed six months in some counties, and a year in others, only by giving bond, with security, approved of by that court at the time of entring such judgment, conditioned to prosecute a writ of review of such action, with effect, at the next superiour court of judicature, court of assize and general goal delivery to be holden in and for the county where such judgment is given, and to answer and pay the original plaintiff double interest for the debt recovered, and double additional costs in case the judgment be affirmed, although the estate attach'd by force of the original writ is not thereby held or subjected to satisfy the plaintiff's demand for more than thirty days after the judgment given on the appeal; and in all cases where bail is given to the action, the sureties cannot be compelled either to satisfy the judgment, or deliver up the principal: wherefore, for preventing creditors being defrauded of their just debts by executions being so stayed,—

Be it enacted by the Lieutenant-Governour, Council and House of Represent[ati]ves,

Bond to be given for prosecuting reviews where execution is stayed, in double the sum recovered, and costs.

[SECT. 1.] That execution of the judgment of the superiour court of judicature, court of assize and general goal delivery, given on the trial of the appeal in any suit, shall not be stayed, unless the original defendant, his executors or administrators, give bond at the time of entring such judgment, to the party or parties that obtained the same, with sufficient sureties, to be approved of by the court, in double the sums recovered, to review the action at the next superiour court of judicature, court of assize and general goal delivery to be holden in and for that county, and to pay to the party or parties that obtained the judgment upon the tr[i][*y*]al of the appeal the sum so recovered, with interest therefor, after the rate of twelve per cent per annum, and double the costs arising on such review, if the judgment be not thereon reversed, in whole or in part, or otherwise satisfied; and if reversed in part only, then to pay him or them that obtained the judgment on the trial of the appeal what remains due by force thereof, and is not reversed by the judgm[*en*]t of said court given on such review, or otherwise satisfied, together with interest therefor, after the rate of six per cent per annum.

Provided always,—

Proviso.

[SECT. 2.] That nothing in this act shall extend to any suit already commenced, wherein, upon the mean process, bail was given or estate attach[*e*]'d. [*Passed January* 30; *published January* 31, 1752.

CHAPTER 14.

AN ACT FOR ERECTING THE VILLAGE PARISH, AND MIDDLE PARISH, SO CALLED, IN THE TOWN OF SALEM, INTO A DISTINCT AND SEPERATE DISTRICT BY THE NAME OF DANVERS.

Preamble.

WHEREAS the town of Salem is very large, and the inhabitants of the Village and Middle parishes, so called, within the same (many of them, at least), live at a great distance from that part of the first parish in Salem where the publick affairs of the town are transacted, and also from the grammar school which is kept in the said first parish; *and whereas* most of the inhabitants of the said first parish are either merchants, traders or mechanicks, and those of the said Village and Middle parishes are chiefly husbandmen, by means whereof many disputes and difficulties have arisen, and may hereafter arise in the managing their publick affairs together, and especially touching the apportioning of their publick taxes; for preventing of which inconvenienc[*i*]es for the future,—

Be it enacted by the Lieutenant-Governour, Council and House of Repres[entati]ves,

Village, and Middle Precinct in Salem erected into a precinct.

[SECT. 1.] That the part of the said town of Salem which now constitutes the Village and Middle parishes in said town, according to their boundaries, and the inhabitants thereon, be erected into a seperate and distinct district by the name of Danvers; and that said inhabitants shall do the duties that are required and enjo[y][*i*]ned on other towns, and enjoy all the powers, privile[*d*]ges and immunities that towns in this province by law enjoy, except that of seperately chusing and sending one or more representatives to represent them at the general assembly; in lieu whereof,—

Be it further enacted,

[SECT. 2.] That the said inhabitants of said parishes shall, from time to time, have full power and liberty to join with the said town of Salem in the choice of one or more represent[*ati*]ves to represent them and the said town at the general assembly, and also of being chosen for that purpose, as if this act had not been made; and the said town of Salem are required to notify said inhabitants of the said Middle and Village parishes, of all meetings that shall be called for the choice of represent[*ati*]ves as aforesaid, as by law they have heretofore been obliged to do.

Inhabitants of said district to join with the inhabitants of Salem in the choice of representatives.

And be it further enacted,

[SECT. 3.] That the said town of Salem, and the inhabitants by this act erected into a seperate district, shall, respectively, be held to fulfil[*l*] the agreement entred into on the twenty-third day of October last, in like manner as if the said inhabitants had been by this act erected into a seperate and distinct township. [*Passed January* 28; *published January* 31, 1752.

Salem to fulfil their agreement with the inhabitants of this district.

CHAPTER 15.

AN ACT FOR ERECTING THE PLANTATION CALLED THE ELBOWS, INTO A DISTRICT BY THE NAME OF PALMER.

WHEREAS it hath been represented to this court that the inhabitants of the plantation, in the county of Hampshire, called the Elbows, labour under difficulties, by reason of their not being incorporated into a district,—

Preamble.

Be it enacted by the Lieutenant-Governo[u]r, Council and House of Represent[ati]ves,

[SECT. 1.] That the plantation aforesaid be and hereby is erected into a district by the name of Palmer, bounding as follows; viz., easterly on the town of Western; northerly, partly on the plantation called Cold Spring, and partly on Ware-River Precinct, called Roads Farm; southerly and westerly on the town of Brimfield; and that the inhabitants thereof be and are hereby invested with all the powers, privile[*d*]ge[*s*] and immuni[ni]ties that the inhabitants of towns within this province are or by law ought to be vested with: *saving* only in the choice of a representative; which, it is represented, said inhabitants are not at present desirous of.

The plantation called the Elbows, erected into a district.

Bounds thereof.

Be it further enacted,

[SECT. 2.] That all rates and taxes heretofore assessed or ordered to be assessed, pursuant to the laws and orders of this court, upon the inhabitants of said Elbows Plantation, shall be levied, collected and fully compleated, agreable to the laws or orders by which they were assessed. [*Passed January* 30; *published January* 31, 1752.

Rates and taxes heretofore ordered to be assessed shall be collected.

CHAPTER 16.

AN ACT FOR SUPPLYING THE TREASURY WITH THE SUM OF EIGHTEEN THOUSAND SIX HUNDRED POUNDS, TO BE APPLIED TO DISCHARGE THE DEBTS OF THE PROVINCE, AND DEFREY THE CHARGES OF THE GOVERNMENT.

Be it enacted by the Lieutenant-Governour, Council and House of Represent[ati]ves,

Committee of the general court empowered to borrow for the government £18,600.

[SECT. 1.] That Andrew Oliver, Thomas Hubbard, Esquires, and Mr. Harrison Gray, be a committee, who are hereby impowered to borrow, for a term not exceeding two years, from such person or persons as shall appear ready to lend the same, a sum not exceeding eighteen thousand six hundred pounds in Spanish mill'd dollars or lawful money, at six shillings and eightpence per ounce; or gold at five pounds one shilling and sevenpence per ounce; or governm[en]t securities which became due the thirty-first day of Decem[be]r past, or that shall become due the tenth day of June next; also in warrants on the treasury; and shall give security to the lenders of the money so borrowed, and shall pay the same to the treasurer, he giving his receipt therefor; and the sum so borrowed shall be applied in manner as in this act is after directed; and for every sum so borrowed the committee aforesaid shall give a note of the form following, viz[t].,—

Form of the committee's note to the lenders.

Province of the Massachusetts Bay, day of , 175 , borrowed and received of A. B. the value of Spanish mill'd dollars, of full weight, for the use of this province; and, as their committee, do promise to pay the same number of like dollars, or the value in lawful money, at six shillings and eightpence per ounce, or in gold at the rate of five pounds one shilling and sevenpence per ounce, to the said A. B., or order, by the day of , 175 , with lawful interest for the same annually 'till paid.

} Committee.

No note to be given under £6.

—and no note shall be given for any sum less than six pounds: and the comm[itt]ee is hereby directed to use their discretion in borrowing said sum at such times as that the treasurer may be enabled to comply with the draughts that may be made on the treasury in pursuance of this act.

And be it further enacted,

[SECT. 2.] That the afores[ai]d sum of eighteen thousand six hundred pounds shall be issued out of the treasury in manner and for the purposes following; viz[t]., the sum of seven thousand one hundred pounds, part of the afores[ai]d sum of eighteen thousand six hundred pounds, shall be applied for the service of the several forts and garrisons within this province, pursuant to such orders and grants as are or shall be made by this court for those purposes; and the further sum of eighteen hundred pounds, part of the afores[ai]d sum of eighteen thousand six hundred pounds, shall be applied for the purchasing provisions and the commissary's necessary disburs[e]ments for the service of the several forts and garrisons within this province, pursuant to such grants as are or shall be made by this court for those purposes; and the further sum of six thousand pounds, part of the afores[ai]d sum of eighteen thousand six hundred pounds, shall be appl[i][y]ed for the paym[en]t of such premiums and grants that now are, or hereafter may be, made by this court: and the further sum of fifteen hundred pounds, part of the afores[ai]d sum of eighteen thousand six hundred pounds, shall be applied for the discharge of other debts owing from this province to persons that have served, or shall serve them, by order of this court, in such matters and things where there is no establishm[en]t, nor any

£7,100 to be issued for forts and garrisons, &c.

£1,800 for provisions, commissary's disbursements, &c.

£6,000 for grants, &c.

£1,500 for debts where there is no establishment, &c.

certain sum assigned for that purpose; and for paper, writing and printing for this court: and the sum of two thousand one hundred pounds, part of the afores[*ai*]d sum of eighteen thousand six hundred pounds, shall be applied for the paym[*en*]t of his maj[*es*]ty's council, and house of repres[*entati*]ves, serving in the general court during the several sessions for this present year. £2,100 for councillors' and representatives' attendance.

And whereas there are sometimes contingent and unforeseen charges that demand prompt paym[*en*]t,—

Be it further enacted,

[SECT. 3.] That the sum of one hundred pounds, being the remaining part of the afores[*ai*]d sum of eighteen thousand six hundred pounds, be applied to pay such contingent charges, and for no other purpose whatsoever. £100 for contingent charges.

And in order to enable the treasurer effectually to discharge the notes and obligations so given by the said committee in pursuance of this act,—

Be it enacted,

[SECT. 4.] That the duty of impost and excise for two years from the twenty-ninth of June, one thousand seven hundred and fifty-two, shall be applied for the paym[*en*]t and discharge of the principal and interest that shall be due on said notes and obligations, and to no other purpose whatever. Duties of impost and excise a security to discharge the committee's notes.

And as a further fund and security for drawing in the said sum of eighteen thousand six hundred pounds to the treasury again,—

Be it further enacted,

[SECT. 5.] That there be, and hereby is, granted unto his most excellent majesty a tax of eighteen thousand six hundred pounds, to be levied on the polls, and estates real and personal, within this province, according to such rules, and in such proportion on the several towns and districts within the same, as shall be agreed on and ordered by the general court of this province at their sessions in May, one thousand seven hundred and fifty-two, which sum shall be paid into the treasury on or before the thirty-first day of Decem[*be*]r next after. Tax of £18,600 granted, —to be paid by the 31st of December, 1752.

Be it further enacted,

[SECT. 6.] That in case the general court shall not at their session in May, and before the twentieth day of June, one thousand seven hund[*re*]d and fifty-two, agree and conclude upon an act apportioning the sum which, by this act, is engaged to be in said year apportioned, assessed and levied, that then, and in such case, each town and district within this province shall pay a tax, to be levied on the polls, and estates both real and personal, within their districts, the same proportion of the said sum as the said towns and districts should have been taxed by the gen[*era*]l court in the tax act then last prece[*e*]ding: *saving* what relates to the pay of the represent[*ati*]ves, which shall be assessed on the several towns they represent. And the province-treasurer is hereby fully impowered and directed, some time in the month of June, one thous[*an*]d seven hundred and fifty-two, to issue and send forth his warrants, directed to the selectmen or assessors of each town and district within this province, requiring them to assess the polls, and estates both real and personal, within their several towns and districts, for their respective part and proportion of the sum before directed and engaged to be assessed, and also for the fines upon the several towns for not sending a represent[*ati*]ve; and the assessors, as also persons assessed, shall observe, be govern[*e*]'d by, and subject to all such rules and directions as have been given in the last prece[*e*]ding tax act. Tax to be apportioned according to the last tax act, in case.

Provided always,—

Any surplusage of money to lie in the treasury for further order.

[SECT. 7.] That the remainder of the sum which shall be brought into the treasury by the duties of impost and excise for two years next ensuing the twenty-ninth day of June, one thousand seven hund[re]d and fifty-two, and the tax of eighteen thousand and six hundred pounds ordered by this act to be assessed and levied, over and above what shall be sufficient to discharge the notes and obligations afores[ai]d, shall be and remain as a stock in the treasury, to be applied as the gen[era]l court of this province shall hereafter order, and to no other purpose whatsoever; anything in this act to the contrary notwithstanding.

And be it further enacted,

The treasurer to conform to the appropriations.

[SECT. 8.] That the treasurer is hereby directed and ordered to pay the sum of eighteen thous[an]d six hundred pounds, borrowed as afores[ai]d, out of such appropriations as shall be directed to by warrant, and no other; and the secretary to whom it belongs to keep the muster-rolls and accompts of charge, shall lay before the house of repres[entati]ves, when they direct, such muster-rolls and accompts, after paym[en]t thereof.

Be it further enacted,

Taxes may be paid in government notes.

[SECT. 9.] That any person who may be assessed by virtue of this act, shall have liberty, if he sees fit, to pay his tax in governm[en]t notes as afores[ai]d; and the collectors are hereby impow[e]red and directed to receive the same, and pay them into the treasury accordingly.

And be it further enacted,

Treasurer to pay principal and interest as it becomes due.

[SECT. 10.] That the treasurer pay the principal and interest, as the same shall respectively become due, on all the notes given by the comm[itt]ee aforesaid, for all such sums as they shall so borrow for the governm[en]t, and deposit in the treasury.

And *whereas* the borrowing or taking up the government's notes or securities, in manner as in and by this act is provided, will so far lessen the provision intended for defr[a][e]ying the charges of the governm[en]t, and supplying the several appropriations in this act; and a sufficient fund having been laid by former tax acts for the payment of the said governm[en]t's notes or securities,—

Be it therefore enacted,

Committee to demand money of the treasurer.

[SECT. 11.] That the committee by this act appointed be and hereby are directed to demand and receive from the treasurer the sums expressed in such notes or securities, as the same shall respectively become due and he shall be able to pay the same, and to replace the same in the treasury, in order to the said sums being applied to the purposes intended by this act, and to compleat the several appropriations therein.

And be it further enacted,

Former warrants on exhausted appropriations, to be paid.

[SECT. 12.] That any warrants which may have been given by the governour and council, and were payable out of any exhausted appropriations in any former acts for supplying the treasury, shall become due, and accordingly be paid, respectively, out of the appropriations for the like purposes in this act.

And *whereas* it may so happen that some of the persons who have done service for this governm[en]t, and for the payment of which the sum raised by this act is intended, may be willing to lend the sum due to them, on interest, and to take notes therefor from the committee by this act appointed,—

Be it therefore enacted,

Committee to give notes on the treasurer's certificates of money borrowed on warrants, &c.

[SECT. 13.] That when and so often as any person or persons who shall have warrant on the treasury, payable out of any of the appropriations in this act mentioned, shall bring such warrant to the treasurer, he shall thereupon give his certificate to the committee, expressing the sum such person or persons shall be willing to lend; and the same committee shall give out notes therefor, in like manner as if the same sum had been brought to them in silver or gold; and the treasurer shall give credit to the com[*mit*]tee for the sum expressed in such certificate, and shall charge the respective appropriations with the payment thereof, until[l] such appropriation shall be exhausted. [*Passed January* 23; *published January* 31, 1752.

CHAPTER 17.

AN ACT FOR THE BETTER REGULATION OF THE COURSE OF JUDICIAL PROCEEDINGS.

WHEREAS by an act made and passed in the second year of the reign of Queen Ann, it is provided that "all pleas in bar or abatement shall be made originally in the inferio[*u*]r courts, in suits there brought; and that when a writ shall, by jud[*g*]ment of court, be barred or abated, and the plaintiff or demandant appeals from such judgment to the superio[*u*]r court of judicature, if, upon hearing the appeal, the superio[*u*]r court, notwithstanding the pleas in bar or abatement, adjudge the writ to be good and well brought, they shall reverse the judg[e]ment of the inferio[*u*]r court, and award to the appellant his full costs of both courts; and the next session of the inferio[*u*]r court, holden for the same county, shall proceed to tr[y][*i*]al of the merits of the cause upon the same writ without any delay, a new entry thereof being made; and that the same rule and method of proceeding be observed in appeals to be made from the judgment, in bar or abatement, given by any justice of the peace, to the inferio[*u*]r court of commoh pleas"; in which course of proceeding, suits are not only frequently unreasonably delayed, but the parties are therein put to needless expence: to the end therefore that justice may more speedily, and with less expence, be done,— Preamble. 1703-4, chap. 13, § 1.

Be it enacted by the Lieutenant-Governo[*u*]*r, Council and House of Representatives,*

[SECT. 1.] That when the superio[*u*]r court of judicature, court of assize and general goal delivery shall reverse a judgment given by any inferio[*u*]r court of common pleas for abating a writ; and when any inferio[*u*]r court of common pleas shall reverse a like judgment given by a justice of the peace, the respective courts that reverse the judgment shall proceed to try the cause, give judgment therein and award execution thereon. Upon reversing judgment in abatement of writs, the court to proceed to try the cause on the merits.

[SECT. 2.] This act to continue and be in force for the space of three years from the publication thereof, and no longer. [*Passed January* 30*; *published January* 31, 1752. Limitation.

* The records make this date January 24; but it is clearly entered as above on the engrossment, in the handwriting of the secretary.

CHAPTER 18.

AN ACT FOR GRANTING THE SUM OF THREE HUNDRED POUNDS FOR THE SUPPORT OF HIS HONOUR THE LIEUTENANT-GOVERNO[U]R AND COMMANDER-IN-CHIEF.

Be it enacted by the Lieutenant-Governo[u]r, Council and House of Representatives,

Grant to the lieutenant-governor.

That the sum of three hundred pounds be and hereby is granted unto his most excellent majesty, to be paid out of the publick treasury to his honour Spencer Phips, Esq[r]., lieutenant-governo[u]r and commander-in-chief in and over his majesty's province of the Massachuset[t]s Bay, for his past services, and further to enable him to manage the publick affairs of the province. [*Passed January* 30 *; *published January* 31, 1752.

CHAPTER 19.

AN ACT TO IMPOWER THE PROPRIETORS OF THE MEETING-HOUSE IN THE FIRST PARISH IN SALEM, WHERE THE REVEREND MR. JOHN SPARHAWK NOW OFFICIATES, AND ALSO THE PROPRIETORS OF THE MEETING-HOUSE IN THE THIRD PARISH IN NEWBURY, WHERE THE REVEREND MR. JOHN LOWELL OFFICIATES, TO RAISE MONEY FOR DEFR[A][E]YING MINISTERIAL AND OTHER NECESSARY CHARGES.

Preamble.

WHEREAS it is found inconvenient to raise money for defr[a][e]ying ministerial charges in the first parish in Salem, and third parish in Newbury, by an assessment or tax on polls and estates in said parishes,—

Be it therefore enacted by the Lieutenant-Governour, Council and House of Representatives,

Proprietors of the meeting-houses in the First Parish in Salem, and the Third Parish in Newbury, empowered to assess pews, &c., to pay ministerial charges, &c.

[SECT. 1.] That the proprietors of the meeting-house in said first parish in Salem, in which the Reverend Mr. John Sparhawk officiates, and the proprietors of the meeting-house in the third parish in Newbury, in which Mr. John Lowell officiates, be and hereby are allowed and impowered to raise, by an assessment or tax on the pews in the respective meeting-houses afore mentioned, such sum or sums as shall be agreed upon by the proprietors, or the major part of such of them as shall be assembled at any legal meeting called for that purpose, for defr[a][e]ying the ministerial and other incidental charges; the first meeting of such proprietors to be called agreable to the direction of the act made and pass[e]'d in the eighth and ninth years of his present majesty's reign, [i][e]ntitled "An Act directing how meetings of proprietors in wharves, or other real estate, may be called."

1735-6, chap. 5, § 1.

And to the intent that such tax or assessment may be equitably made and duly collected,—

Be it further enacted,

Manner of proceeding in raising such tax.

[SECT. 2.] That the proprietors of the respective meeting-houses afore mentioned be and hereby are impowered to cause the pews in each of the afores[ai]d meeting-houses to be valued according to the convenience of said pews, and the s[c]ituation thereof, and to put a new estimate upon the pews, from time to time, as shall be found necessary,

* This date is taken from the engrossment, apparently written in by the lieutenant-governor when he signed it. The date given in the record is January 29.

and to determine how much each pew, or part of a pew, shall pay towards defr[a][*e*]ying the charges aforesaid, and the time and manner in which the same shall be paid; and appoint a collector or collectors to collect the sum or sums so agreed to be raised, who shall be sworn to the faithful discharge of his said trust. And if any proprietor or owner of a pew in either of the aforementioned houses shall neglect or refuse to pay the sum or sums assessed thereon, after having twenty days' notice thereof given him by the collector, the proprietors of the respective meeting-houses shall be, and hereby are, impowered by themselves, or by their committee, to sell or dispose of the pew of such delinquent according to the valuation thereof, as afores[*ai*]d, and with the money raised by such sale to pay the assessm[*en*]t or tax on said pew remaining unpaid, together with the charges arising on the sale; the overplus, if any there be, to be returned to the owner thereof.

Provided, nevertheless,—

[SECT. 3.] That when the owner of any pew shall make a tender of the same to the proprietors, or to their comm[*itt*]ee, at the valuation afores[*ai*]d, and they shall refuse or neglect to accept the same, no sum shall be deducted out of the sale of said pew but such only as shall have become due before the making of said tender. **Proviso.**

And whereas application hath been made to this court to enable the proprietors of the meeting-house in said third parish in Newbury to raise part of the sum that may be necessary for defr[a][*e*]ying ministerial charges, on the persons and estates of such as occupy pews or seats in said meeting-house, and usually attend the publick worship of God, in said house, over and above what may be raised on the pews,— **Preamble.**

Be it therefore enacted,

[SECT. 4.] That the proprietors of said house be and hereby are impow[e]red to tax or assess the several persons occupying or possessing pews or seats, or parts of pews and seats, who usually attend the publick worship in said house, according to their several abilities and circumstances, in order to raise money sufficient, together with what may be assessed on the pews, to defr[a][*e*]y their ministerial and other incidental charges; and the said assessm[*en*]t or tax shall be made and collected by such rules as parish taxes are made and collected; and thereupon all other persons, and their estates in said parish, not usually attending the publick worship in said house, as well as those who do, shall be freed from all parish taxes during their continuing to raise money as aforesaid. **The whole ministerial charge to be raised on the proprietors at Newbury.** **Other persons to be freed.**

[SECT. 5.] This act to continue and be in force for the space of three years from the publication of the same, and no longer. [*Passed January* 29; *published January* 31, 1752. **Limitation.**

NOTES.—There were four sessions of the General Court this year; but at the fourth session, which was held at Harvard College on account of the prevalence of small-pox in Boston, no acts were passed,—the Lieutenant-Governor refusing his assent to the only bill that was passed to be enacted.

The engrossments of all the acts of this year, except chapter 11, are preserved, and all were printed with the other acts of the respective sessions, except chapters 9 and 10, which were separately printed for distribution among the several assessors and officers of impost.

The acts of the first session were duly certified for transmission, September 25, 1751, and were forwarded, with a letter from Secretary Willard, November 1, following. They were delivered by the agent of the Province, to the clerk of the Privy Council, in waiting, March 11, 1752, and immediately referred to a committee. By this committee they were referred to the Lords of Trade, on the nineteenth of March, and were received and read at the Board the same day, and again, April 15, when they were referred to Mr. Lamb, for his opinion thereon in point of law. Mr. Lamb's report bears date January 12, 1755, and is to the effect that he has no objection to offer to any of the acts submitted to him. This report was read at the Board, January 29, 1755, and the draught of a representation was ordered to be prepared, proposing the confirmation of such of these acts "as have not expired by their own limitation, or have not had their full effect." This draught, having been prepared, was ordered to be transcribed, February 4, and was signed February 5, 1755.

The report of the Lords of Trade represents that chapters 2, 5, 6, 7, 8, 9, and 10 "were for temporary services and are either expired, or the purposes for which they were passed have been completed," and that chapters 1, 3, and 4 "appear to have been enacted for the particular convenience, and relate to the present Œconomy of the Province," &c., and concludes, "We see no reason why His Majesty may not be graciously pleased to confirm them."

Accordingly, an order passed the Privy Council, March 11, 1755, confirming chapters 1, 3, and 4.

The acts of the second and third sessions were transmitted by Secretary Willard, with a letter dated November 30, 1752. This letter was read at the Board of Trade, February 2, 1753, and the accompanying acts were ordered to "be sent to Mr. Lamb for his opinion thereupon in point of Law." No record of further action by the Home Government on these acts has been discovered.

Chap. 10. "January 3. 1752. In the House of Representves Whereas by an Act apportioning & assessing a Tax of £30394. 8. 8. & also for Apportioning a further Tax of £5290. 11. 4. paid the Representves for their Service & Attendance in the General Court & Travel, & for Fines laid on Several Towns for not sending a Representve Amounting in the whole to £35,685, among other things It is Enacted, that the Inhabitants of this Province shall have full Liberty to pay in the several Sums, which they shall respectively be assessed in pursuance of that Act, in Bills of Credit on this Province; Provided they pay the Bills aforesaid to the Collectors of said Assessment on or before the last Day of December 1751; And whereas by a Resolve of this Court, the fifth of October last, the Treasurer is directed to receive of the Collectors of Taxes, any of the Government Notes, which are payable on or before the 31st of December 1751, for the Payment of their respective Collections; Accounting Principal & Interest & Premium due thereon, provided the said Notes were brought into the Treasury on or before the said 31st of December 1751; And whereas said Term is elapsed, & the whole of the said Tax is not yet paid in, to the Collectors impowered to collect the Same, by reason that the Warrants for collecting came to them so late, that it has been impracticable fully to effect the same; And as by the Act aforesaid the Collectors have Time allowed them to the 31st of March next, to Settle their Accounts with the Province Treasurer,

Therefore Voted that the Inhabitants of the Province have full Liberty to pay the several Sums, which they are respectively Assessed in Bills of Credit aforesaid, or in Government Notes, that were payable the 31st of December last, accounting Principal & Premium, as also the Interest due thereon until the 31st day of Decemr last & no longer.

In Council; Read & Concur'd Consented to by the Lieut Governr."—*Council Records, vol. XIX., p.* 407.

Chap. 12. "June 5. 1752. A Petition of the Town of Boston Setting forth the distressed State of the said Town by the Prevailing of the small Pox among them the great Increase of the Poor, Decay of their Trade, & the Removal of many of their Inhabitants to other Towns, with Other Misfortunes; Praying for the Compassion of this Court either by granting them a Sum of Money out of the publick Treasury, or in such other way as shall appear best to the Wisdom of the Court.

In the House of Representatives Read & the following Vote Pass'd; vizt.—

Whereas by reason of the Small Pox so generally prevailing in the Town of Boston, many Persons are reduced to very great Streights & necessitous Circumstances, who otherwise would have been in a Capacity to have Subsisted their Familys in comfortable Circumstances

Resolved that the Sum of Six hundred Pounds be allowed & paid out of the publick Treasury to the Overseers of the Poor of the Town of Boston, to be distributed among such Persons as they shall judge to stand in need of Releif for the Reasons aforesaid.

In Council Read & Concur'd Consented to by the Lieutenant Governor."—*Ibid., p.* 481.

Chap. 14. "January 22 1752. A Memorial of Samuel Flynt, Daniel Epes junr Esqr & others in behalf of the Village & Middle Precincts in Salem, Setting forth the many Inconveniences they labour under in their present Circumstances, & Praying that they may be set off from the said Town, & incorporated into a District In Council, Read & Ordered that the Memorialists serve the Town of Salem with a Copy of this Petition, that so they may shew cause, if any they have on the first Wednesday of the next Sitting of the General Court why the Prayer thereof should not be granted.——In the House of Repres.ves Read & Non-concur'd."—*Ibid., p.* 425.

ACTS,

PASSED 1752–53.

ACTS

Passed at the Session begun and held at Concord, on the Twenty-seventh day of May, A. D. 1752.

CHAPTER 1.

AN ACT IN FURTHER ADDITION TO THE ACT FOR LIMITATION OF ACTIONS, AND FOR AVOIDING SUITS AT LAW, WHERE THE MATTER IS OF LONG STANDING.

WHEREAS in a late law of this province, entitled "An Act in addition to and for [an] explanation of an act, entitled 'An Act for limitation of actions, and avoiding suits at law, where the matter is of long standing,'" made and pass[e]d in the twenty-second year of his present majesty's reign, the time limited for commencing of all actions of accompt, and upon the case, excepting as therein is excepted, will expire in September next; *and whereas* the difficulties arisen by the exchange of the medium of trade in this province, and the prevalency of the small-pox in Boston and sundry other towns in this gover[n]ment, render it almost impracticable to have such accompts and actions of the case set[t]led within the time by said act limit[t]ed for that purpose,— Preamble. 1748-49, chap. 17.

Be it therefore enacted by the Lie[v][*utenan*]*t-Governour, Council and House of Representativ*[*e*]*s*,

That the time for commencing of actions of accompts, and of the case, by said act limited as aforesaid, be and the same is hereby extended to the first day of September, which will be in the year of our Lord one thousand seven hundred and fifty-fo[w][*u*]r; and no suit hereafter to be brought in such cases shall be barred, if commenced before the expiration of said term. [*Passed June* 5; *published June* 16. Act continued till September, 1754.

CHAPTER 2.

AN ACT IN ADDITION TO AN ACT FOR THE MORE SPEEDY EXTINGUISHMENT OF FIRE, AND PRESERVING GOODS ENDANGERED BY IT.

WHEREAS in and by an act made and passed in the eighteenth year of his present majesty's reign, entitled "An Act for the more speedy extinguishment of fire, and preserving goods enda[n]gered by it," it is enacted that the several towns within this province may, if they see fit, at their anniversary meeting in March, annually, appoint a suitable number of persons, not exceeding ten, who shall be denominated firewards, whose particular business shall be to take care and govern at fires, which, from time to time, may break out, as in and by said act they Preamble. 1744-45, chap. 30, § 1.

are directed and impowered to do; *and whereas*, by experience, the fire-wards, who have been annually chosen by the town of Boston, have been found to be of great use and service to the said town at times of fires, and it is apprehended it would greatly serve the said town if their numbers were increased,—

Be it therefore enacted by the Lieutenant-Governour, Council and House of Representatives,

Town of Boston empowered to choose twelve fire-wards.

That it shall and may be lawful[l] for the town of Boston, who at present have ten fire-wards, at any town meeting warned for that purpose, to el[l]ect and appoint two more meet persons as fire-wards, who shall serve in that office till their anniversary meeting in March next; and from thenceforward, as they shall see cause, to chuse twelve persons for that purpose, annually, who shall do the duty and be invested with the like powers and priviledges as fire-wards in and by the said act are invested withal. [*Passed June* 4; *published June* 16.

CHAPTER 3.

AN ACT FOR GRANTING UNTO HIS MAJESTY AN EXCISE UPON WINES AND SPIRITS DISTILLED, SOLD BY RETAIL, AND UPON LIMES, LEM-[*M*]ONS AND ORANGES.

WE, his majesty's most loyal and dutiful subjects, the representatives of the province of the Massachuset[*t*]s Bay, in general court assembled, being desirous to lessen the present debt of the province, have chearfully and unanimously granted, and do hereby give and grant unto his most excellent majesty, for the ends and uses above mentioned, and for no other uses, an excise upon all brandy, rum and other spirits distilled, and upon all wines whatsoever sold by retail, and upon lemmons, limes and oranges taken in and used in making of punch or other liquors mixed for sale, or otherwise consumed, in taverns or other licensed houses within this province, to be raised, levied, collected and paid by and upon every taverner, innholder, common victual[*l*]er and retailer within each respective county, in manner following:—

And be it accordingly enacted by the Lieutenant-Governour, Council and House of Representatives,

Time of this act's continuance.

[SECT. 1.] That from and after the twenty-ninth day of June, one thousand seven hundred and fifty-two, for the space of one year, every person licensed for retailing rum, brandy or other spirits, or wine, shall pay the duties following:—

Rate of excise.

For every gallon of brandy, rum and spirits distill[*e*]'d, fourpence.
For every gallon of wine of every sort, sixpence.
For every hundred of lem[*m*]ons or oranges, four shillings.
For every hundred of limes, one shilling and sixpence.
—And so proportionably for any other quantity or number.

And be it further enacted,

Account to be taken.

[SECT. 2.] That every taverner, innholder, common victual[*l*]er and retailer, shall, upon the said twenty-ninth day of June, take an exact acco[mp][*un*]t of all brandy, rum and other distilled spirits, and wine, and of all lem[*m*]ons, oranges and limes then by him or her, and give an account of the same, upon oath, if required, unto the person or persons to whom the duties of excise in the respective counties shall be let[t] or farmed, as in and by this act is hereafter directed; and such other persons as shall be licensed during the continuance of this act, shall also give an account, as aforesaid, upon oath, what brandy, rum or other distilled spirits, and wine, and of what lem[*m*]ons, oranges or limes he or they shall have by him or them at the time of his or their licence; which oath the person or persons farming the duties aforesaid shall have power to administer in the words following; viz[t].,—

You, A. B., do swear that the acco[mp][*un*]t exhibited by you is a just and true acco[mp][*un*]t of all brandy, rum and other distilled spirits, and wine, lem[*m*]ons, oranges and limes you had by you on the twenty-ninth day of June last. So help you God. **Form of an oath.**

And where such person shall not have been licens[c]ed on said twenty-ninth day of June, the form of the oath shall be so varied as that instead of those words, "on the twenty-ninth day of June last," these words shall be inserted and used, "at the time of your taking your licence."

And be it further enacted,

[Sect. 3.] That every taverner, innholder, common victual[*l*]er and retailer shall make a fair entry in a book, of all such rum, brandy and other distilled spirits, and wine, as he or they, or any for him or them, shall buy, distill and take in for sale after such acco[mp][*un*]t taken, and of lem[*m*]ons, oranges and limes taken in, consumed or used as aforesaid, and at the end of every six months, deliver the same, in writ[t]ing, under their hand, to the farmer or farmers of the duties aforesaid, who are impow[e]red to administer an oath to him or them, that the said acco[mp][*un*]t is, *bonâ fide*, just and true, and that he or they do not know of any rum, brandy or other distilled spirits, or wine, sold, directly or indirectly, or of any lem[*m*]ons, oranges or limes used in punch or otherwise, by him or them, or any under him or them, or by his or their privity or consent, but what is contained in the acco[mp][*un*]t now exhibited, and shall pay him the duty thereof, excepting such part as the farmer shall find is still remaining by him or them; twenty per cent to be allowed on the liquo[u]rs afore mentioned for leakage and other waste, for which no duty is to be paid. **Within six months, accounts to be delivered.** **Twenty per cent allowed for leakage.**

Provided always, and it is the true intent and meaning of this act,—

[Sect. 4.] That if any taverner, retailer or common victual[*l*]er, shall buy of any other taverner or retailer such small quantity of liquo[u]rs as this act obliges him to acco[mp][*un*]t for to the farmer, and pay the excise, such taverner, retailer or common victual[*l*]er shall be exempted and excused from acco[mp][*un*]ting or paying any excise therefor, inasmuch as the same is acco[mp][*un*]ted for, and the excise therefor to be paid, by the taverner or retailer of whom he bought the same. **Proviso.**

And be it further enacted,

[Sect. 5.] That every taverner, innholder, common victual[*l*]er or retailer, who shall be found to give a false acco[mp][*un*]t of any brandy, distilled spirits, or wine, or other the commodit[y][*ie*]s aforesaid, by him or her on the said twenty-ninth day of June, or at the time of his or her taking licen[s][c]e, or bought, distilled, or taken in for sale afterwards, or used as aforesaid, or refuse to give in an acco[mp][*un*]t, on oath, as aforesaid, shall be rendered incapable of having a licence afterwards, and shall be prosecuted by the farmer of excise in the same county, for his or her neglect, and ordered by the general sessions of the peace to pay double the sum of money as they may judge that the excise of liquo[u]rs, &c., by him or her sold within such time, would have amounted to, to be paid to the said farmer. **Penalty on giving a false account.**

And be it further enacted,

[Sect. 6.] That the justices in their general sessions of the peace shall take recognizances, with sufficient sureties, of all persons by them **General sessions to take recognizance.**

licensed, both as to their keeping good rule and order, and duly observing the laws relating to persons so licensed, and for their du[e]ly and tru[e]ly rendering an acco[mp][*un*]t in writ[t]ing under their hands as aforesaid, and paying their excise in manner as aforesaid; as also that they shall not use their licence in any house besides that wherein they dwell; which recognizance shall be taken within the space of thirty days after the granting of such licence, otherwise the persons licensed shall lose the benefit of his or her said licence; and no person shall be licensed by the said justices that hath not acco[mp][*un*]ted with the farmer, and paid him the excise due to him from such person at the time of his asking for such licence.

Preamble.

And whereas, notwithstanding the laws made against selling strong drink without licence, many persons not regarding the penalties and forfeitures in the said act, do receive and entertain persons in their houses, and sell great quantit[y][*ie*]s of spirits and other strong drink, without licence so to do first had and obtained, by reason whereof great debaucheries are committe[e]d and kept secret, the end of this law in a great measure frustrated, and such as take licences and pay the excise greatly wronged and injured,—

Be it therefore enacted,

Forfeiture of £4 for selling without license, &c.

[SECT. 7.] That whosoever, after the said twenty-ninth day of June, one thousand seven hundred and fifty-two, shall presume, either directly or indirectly, to sell any brandy, rum or other distilled spirits, wine, beer, cyder, perry or any other strong drink, in any smaller quantity than a barrel (thirty gallons to be accounted a barrel, and all delivered to one person without drawing any part of it off), without licence first had and obtained from the court of general sessions of the peace, and recognizing in manner as aforesaid, shall forfeit and pay for each offence, the sum of four pounds and costs of prosecution; the one half to the farmer, and the other half to the informer: and all such as shall refuse or neglect to pay the fine aforesaid, shall stand closely and strictly committed in the common goal of the county for three months at least, and not to have the liberty of the goaler's house or yard; and any goaler giving any person liberty contrary to this act, shall forfeit and pay two pounds, and pay costs of prosecution as aforesaid: and if any person or persons, not licensed as aforesaid, shall order, allow, permit[t] or connive at the selling of any strong drink, contrary to the true intent or meaning of this act, by his or her child or children, servant or servants, or any other person or persons belonging to or in his or her house or family, and be thereof convict, he, she or they shall be reputed the offender or offenders, and shall suffer the same penalties as if he, she or they had sold such drink themselves.

And be it further enacted,

One witness sufficient for conviction.

[SECT. 8.] That when any person shall be complained of for selling any strong drink without licence, one witness produced to one such fact, and another produced to another, shall be sufficient conviction, provided that there be not more than the space of six months between the facts concerning which such witnesses declare. And when and so often as it shall be observed that there is a resort of persons to houses suspected to sell strong drink without licence, any justice of the peace shall have full power to convene such persons before him, and examine them upon oath concerning the person suspected of selling or retailing strong drink in such houses, outhouses or other depend[a][*e*]ncies thereof; and if upon examination of such witnesses, and hearing the defence of such suspected person, it shall appear to the justice there is sufficient proof of the violation of this act by selling strong drink without licence, judg[e]ment may thereupon be made up against such person, and he shall forfeit and pay in like manner as if process had been commenced by bill, plaint or information before the said justice, or otherw[ays][*ise*] may bind over the person suspected and the witnesses, to the next court of general sessions of the peace for the county where such person shall dwell.

And be it further enacted,

[Sect. 9.] That when and so often as any person shall be complained of for selling any strong drink without licence to any negro, Indian or molatto slave, or to any child or other person under the age of discretion, and upon the declaration of any such Indian, negro or molatto slaves, child or other person under the age of discretion, and other circumstances concurring, it shall appear to be highly probable in the judgment of the court or justice before whom the trial shall be, that the person complained of is guilty, then, and in every such case, unless the defendant shall acquit him- or herself upon oath (to be administ[e]red to him or her by the court or justice that shall try the cause), such defendant shall forfeit and pay two pounds to the farmer of excise and costs of prosecution; but if the defendant shall acquit him- or herself upon oath as aforesaid, the court or justice may and shall enter up judgment for the defend[a][*e*]nt to recover costs. Penalty for selling strong drink to negroes, mulattoes, &c.

And be it further enacted,

[Sect. 10.] That after any person shall have been once convicted of selling strong liquo[u]rs without licence, contrary to this act, he shall, upon every offence after such first conviction, be obliged to enter into bonds, with one or more sureties, in the penalty of twenty pounds, to his majesty, for the use of this government, that he will not, in like manner, offend or be guilty of any breach of this act; and upon refusal to give such bond, he shall be committed to prison until[l] he comply therewith. Persons after first conviction to enter into bonds.

And be it further enacted,

[Sect. 11.] That if any person or persons shall be summoned to appear before a justice of the peace, or the grand jury, to give evidence relating to any person's selling strong drink without licence, or to appear before the court of general sessions of the peace, or other court proper to try the same, to give evidence on the trial of any person informed against, presented or indicted for the selling strong drink without licence, and shall neglect or refuse to appear, or to give evidence in that behalf, every person so offending shall forfeit the sum of twenty pounds and cost of prosecution; the one half of the penalty aforesaid to be to his majesty for the use of the province, the other half to and for the use of him or them who shall sue for the same as aforesaid. And when it shall so happen that witnesses are bound to sea before the sitting of the court where any person or persons informed against, for selling strong drink without licence, is or are to be prosecuted for the same, in every such case, the deposition of any witness or witnesses in writ[t]ing, taken before any two of his majesty's justices of the peace, *quorum unus*, and sealed up and delivered into court, the adverse party having first had a notification in writing sent to him or her of the time and place of caption, shall be esteemed as sufficient evidence, in the law, to convict any person or persons offending against this act, as if such witness or witnesses had been present at the time of trial, and given his, her or their deposition *viva voce;* and every person or persons who shall be summoned to give evidence before two justices of the peace, in manner as aforesaid, and shall neglect or refuse to appear, or to give evidence relating to the facts he or she shall be inquired of, shall be liable and subject to the same penalty as he or she would have been by virtue of this act, for not appearing, or neglecting or refusing to give his or her evidence before the grand jury or court as aforesaid. Penalty on persons refusing to give evidence.

And be it further enacted,

How fines are to be recovered.

[SECT. 12.] That all fines, forfeitures and penalties arising by this act shall and may be recovered by action, bill, plaint or information, before any court of record proper to try the same; and where the sum forfeited does not exceed four pounds, by action or complaint before any two of his majesty's justices of the peace, *quorum unus*, in the respective counties where such offence shall be committe[e]d; which said justices are impowered to try and determine the same. And such justices shall make a fair entry or record of all such their proceedings: *saving always* to any person or persons who shall think him-, her- or themselves aggr[ei][*ie*]ved by the sentence or determination of the said justices, liberty of appeal therefrom to the next court of general sessions of the peace to be holden in and for said county, at which court such offence shall be finally determined: *provided* that in said appeal the same rules be observed as are already, by law, required in appeals from justices to the court of general sessions of the peace.

And to the end the revenue a[r]rising from the aforesaid duties of excise may be advanced for the greater benefit and advantage of the publick,—

Be it further enacted,

Persons empowered to farm out the excise.

[SECT. 13.] That one or more persons, to be nominated and appointed by the general court, for and within the several counties within this province, publick notice being first given of the time and place and occasion of their meeting, shall have full power, and are hereby authorized, from time to time, to contract and agree with any person for or concerning the farming the duties in this act mentioned, upon brandy, rum, or other the liquo[u]rs and commodities aforesaid, in the respective counties for which they shall be appointed, as may be for the greatest profit and advantage of the publick, so as the same exceed not the term of one year after the commencement of this act; and every person to whom the duties of excise in any county shall be let[t] or farmed, shall have power to inspect the houses of all such as are licensed, and of such as are suspected of selling without licence, and to demand, sue for, and recover the excise due from licensed persons by virtue of this act.

And be it further enacted,

Farmer to give bond that the sum agreed for be paid into the public treasury.

[SECT. 14.] That the farmer shall give bond with two sufficient sureties, to the province treasurer for the time being, and his successors in said office, in double the sum of mon[*e*]y that shall be contracted for, with condition that the sum agreed be paid into the province treasury, for the use of the province, at the expiration of one year from the date of such bond; which bond the person or persons to be appointed a committee of such county are to take, and the same to lodge with the treasurer as aforesaid, within twenty days after such bond is executed. And the said treasurer, upon failure or neglect of payment at the time therein limitted, shall and is hereby impow[e]red and directed to issue out his execution, returnable in sixty days, against such farmers of excise and their sureties, or either of them, for the full sum expressed in the condition of their bonds, as they shall respectively become due, in the same manner as he is enabled by law to issue out his executions against defective constables; and the said committee shall render an account of their proceedings touching the farming this duty on rum, wine and other the liquo[u]rs and species afore mentioned, in their respective counties, to the general court in the first week of their fall sessions, and shall receive such sum or sums for their trouble and expence in said affair as said court shall think fit to allow them.

[SECT. 15.] And every person farming the excise in any county may substitute and appoint one or more deputy or deputies under him, upon oath, to collect and receive the excise aforesaid, which shall become due in such county, and pay in the same to such farmer; which deputy or deputies shall have, use and exercise all such powers and authorities as in and by this act are given or committed to the farmers for the better collecting the duties aforesaid, or prosecuting of offenders against this act.

And be it further enacted, anything hereinbefore contained to the contrary notwithstanding,

[Sect. 16.] That it shall and may be lawful[l] to and for the said farmers, and every of them, to compound and agree with any retailer or innholder within their respective divisions, from time to time, for his or her excise for the whole year, in one entire sum, as they in their discretion shall think fit to agree for, without making any entry thereof as is before directed; and all and every person or persons, to whom the said excise or any part thereof shall be let or farmed, by themselves or their lawful substitutes, may and hereby are impow[e]red to sue for and recover, in any of his majesty's courts of record (or before a justice of the peace where the matter is not above his cognizance), any sum or sums that shall grow due f[rom][*or*] any of the aforesaid duties of excise, where the party or parties f[or][*rom*] whom the same is or [or] shall become due shall refuse or neglect to pay the same.

Farmers may compound with any retailer or innholder.

And be it further enacted,

[Sect. 17.] That in case any person farming the excise as aforesaid, or his deputy, shall, at any time during their continuance in said office, wittingly and willingly connive at, or allow, any person or persons within their respective divisions, not licensed by the court of general sessions of the peace, their selling any brandy, wines, rum or other liquo[u]rs by this act forbidden, such farmer or deputy, for every such offence, shall forfeit the sum of fifty pounds and cost[s] of prosecution; one half of the penalty aforesaid to be to his majesty for the use of the province, the other half to him or them that shall inform and sue for the same, and shall thenceforward be forever disabled from serving in said office.

Penalty for farmers or their deputies offending.

And be it further enacted,

[Sect. 18.] That in case of the death of the farmers of excise in any county, the executors or administrators of such farmer shall, upon their taking such trust of executor or administrator upon them, have and enjoy all the powers, and be subject to all the duties, the farmer had or might enjoy or was subject to by force of this act. [*Passed June* 4*; *published June* 16.

Provision in case of death, &c.

CHAPTER 4.

AN ACT FOR GRANTING THE SUM OF THREE HUNDRED POUNDS FOR THE SUPPORT OF HIS HONOUR THE LIEUTENANT-GOVERNOUR AND COMMANDER-IN-CHIEF.

Be it enacted by the Lieutenant-Governour, Council and House of Representatives,

That the sum of three hundred pounds be and hereby is granted unto his most excell[*en*]t majesty, to be paid out of the publick treasury to his honour Spencer Phib[p]s, Esq[r]., lieutenant-governour and commander-

Governor's grant.

* So entered on the engrossment; but on the record it appears to have been signed June 3.

mander-in-chief in and over his majesty's province of Massachuset[*t*]s Bay, for his past services, and further to enable him to manage the publick affairs of the province. [*Passed June* 4; *published June* 16.

CHAPTER 5.

AN ACT FOR ALTERING THE TIMES FOR HOLDING THE SUPERIOUR COURT OF JUDICATURE, COURT OF ASSIZE AND GENERAL GOAL DELIVERY, NEXT TO BE HOLDEN WITHIN AND FOR THE COUNT[Y][*IE*]S OF WORCESTER AND HAM[*P*]SHIRE.

Preamble.

WHEREAS by reason of there being but nineteen days in the month of September next, the superiour court of judicature, court of assize and general goal delivery, cannot this year be held in and for the county of Ham[*p*]shire, at the time by law appointed for holding the same, nor can the said court this year be holden in and for the county of Worcester at the time by law appointed for holding the same, without great inconvenience to the justices thereof,—

Be it therefore enacted by the Lieutenant-Governour, Council and House of Representatives,

Alteration of the times for holding the superior court in the counties of Worcester and Hampshire. 1742-43, chap. 32, § 2.

That the superiour court of judicature, court of assize and general goal delivery, which by law was appointed to be holden yearly at Worcester, in and for the county of Worcester, on the third Tuesday of September, and at Springfield in and for the county of Ham[*p*]shire, on the fourth Tuesday of the same month, shall this year be holden at Worcester, in and for the county of Worcester, on the second Tuesday of September next, and at Springfield, in and for the county of Ham[*p*]shire, on the third Tuesday of the same month; and all appeals made, and all writ[t]s, recognizances, and process returnable to the said court at either of the times heretofore by law appointed for holding the same, shall be returned to, and heard and tryed by the said court at the respective times by this act appointed for holding the same; and all persons bound by recognizance, or otherwise, to appear at the said court, at either of the times by law heretofore appointed for holding said court, shall in like manner be held and obliged to appear at the said court, at the respective times by this act appointed for holding the same, and abide by and perform the judgment that shall be then given by the said court thereon. [*Passed June* 5; *published June* 16.

CHAPTER 6.

AN ACT ENABLING THE ASSESSORS OF THE TOWN OF STOUGHTON, FOR THE YEAR 1751, AS ALSO THE ASSESSORS OF THE FIRST AND THIRD PARISHES IN SAID TOWN, TO ASSESS THE INHABITANTS OF SAID TOWN AND PARISHES FOR THE SEVERAL TAXES FOR SAID YEAR; AS ALSO THE CONSTABLES OR COLLECTORS FOR SAID YEAR, TO COLLECT THE SAME.

Preamble.

WHEREAS the assessors of the town of Stoughton, for the year [1751] [*one thousand seven hundred fifty-one*], in making their assessments for said year, assessed the po[e][*l*]s at five shillings only, without proportioning the additional sum paid the representative on the pol[c][*l*]s, and also from a misapprehension of the law, taxed the principal sum of the money at interest, and not the interest of the money only, which they ought to have done, whereby great inequality arises to many persons in said town,—

Be it therefore enacted by the L[eiv][*ieutenan*]*t-Governour, Council and House of Representatives*,

[Sect. 1.] That the said assessment be and hereby is declared unlawful[l] and void; and the constables or collectors to whom warrants have been given for collecting the same, are hereby forbidden to proceed any further in collecting said assessments; and they are hereby required forthwith to pay in to the treasurer of said town of Stoughton all such mon[*i*]e[y]s as they have received in consequence of such warrants, whether of province, town or county taxes, and to deliver up to the said treasurer the respective rate-lists, with credit to each man's name of what he has paid.

Stoughton assessments made by the assessors for the year 1751 declared void.

And be it further enacted,

[Sect. 2.] That the assessors of said town of Stoughton, for the year [1751] [*one thousand seven hundred fifty-one*], be and hereby are directed forthwith to make the said assessment anew, and to assess the said town of Stoughton for the whole sum of province, town and county charges, that they were to be assessed in said year [1751] [*one thousand seven hundred fifty-one*], excepting those families set off to the town of Walpole as to ministerial and school charges; and in making said assessment shall only tax the lawful[l] interest of money; and all other estate to be assessed as the law directs: and in their taxing the pol[e][*l*]s in said town, shall, over and above the five shillings which a pol[e][*l*] is set at, also proportion the additional sum paid the representative on pol[e][*l*]s and estate, and shall commit the lists of their s[*ai*]d assessments to the constables or collectors of said town for the year [1751] [*one thousand seven hundred fifty-one*].

The same assessors to make the said assessments anew.

Rules for their proceedings therein.

[Sect. 3.] And the province treasurer is hereby impowered and directed to send out his warrants to the constables or collectors of the said town of Stoughton for the year [1751] [*one thousand seven hundred fifty-one*], requiring them to collect the said province tax, and the said assessors for [1751] [*one thousand seven hundred fifty-one*], as also the clerk of the peace for the county of Suffolk, are alike impowered and directed to issue their respective warrants to the said constables or collectors, requiring them to collect the town and county taxes that are to be assessed as aforesaid.

Province treasurer to send out his warrants.

As also the clerk of the peace for the county of Suffolk.

[Sect. 4.] And each of the said collectors or constables are required in collecting said assessments to give credit to any person so much as appears he paid of the said assessment upon the former rate-lists; and if any person paid more than what he shall be assessed in the new assessment to the province, town and county charges, he shall be refunded the overplus by the said town treasurer; and in case the sums either of the persons paid upon the former rate-lists be not sufficient to discharge the sums in the new assessment, they are hereby subjected to pay to the said collectors or constables such further sums as shall make up the whole they are assessed in the new assessment.

Rules for the collectors to observe.

And be it further enacted,

[Sect. 5.] That the inhabitants of the first and third parishes in said town, as also the assessors and collectors of said parishes for said year [1751] [*one thousand seven hundred fifty-one*], are hereby subjected to conform to the aforesaid rule with regard to their parish assessments.

First and third parishes in Stoughton to conform to the same rule.

And be it further enacted,

[Sect. 6.] That the respective constables or collectors of said town for the year [1751] [*one thousand seven hundred fifty-one*], as also the

As also their assessors and collectors.

collectors of the first and third parishes in said town, are hereby impowered and directed to collect said assessments, and to pay in the same as they shall be directed and required by their respective warrants. [*Passed June* 5; *published June* 16.

CHAPTER 7.

AN ACT FOR GRANTING TO HIS MAJESTY SEVERAL RATES AND DUTIES OF IMPOST AND TUNNAGE OF SHIPPING.

1751-52, chap. 16. WHEREAS in and by an act of this province, passed in the present year of his majesty's reign, Andrew Oliver, Thomas Hubbard, Esqrs., and Mr. Harrison Gray, were impowered to borrow, for a term not exceeding two years, a sum not exceeding eighteen thousand six hundred pounds, in Spanish mill'd dollars, or lawfull mony at six shillings and eightpence per ounce, or gold at five pounds one shilling and sevenpence per ounce, or government's securities, which became due the thirty-first day of December past, or shall become due the tenth of this instant June, also in warrants on the treasury; and [should *] give security to the lenders of the mony so borrowed, and should pay the same into the treasury, for the supply thereof; and by the said act it was further ordered that the treasurer should pay the principle and interest as the same should respectively become due, on all the notes given by the committee aforesaid, for all such sums as they should so borrow for the government, and deposit in the treasury; and in order to enable the treasurer to discharge the notes and obligations that should by the committee be given for said sum, in pursuance of the afore-mentioned act, it was therein provided, that the duty of impost for two years, from the twenty-ninth day of June, 1752, should be applyed for the payment and discharge of the principle and interest that should become due on said notes and obligations, and to no other purpose whatever,—

We, his majesty's most loyal and dutiful subjects, the representatives of the province of Massachusetts Bay, in New England, being desirous of enabling the treasurer to discharge the notes and obligations as aforesaid, have chearfully and unanimously given and granted, and do hereby give and grant, to his most excellent majesty, to the end and use aforesaid, and to no other use, the several duties of impost upon wines, liquors, goods, wares and merchandizes that shall be imported into this province, and tunnage of shipping, hereafter mentioned; and pray that it may be enacted,—

And be it accordingly enacted by the Lieutenant-Governour, Council and House of Representatives,

[SECT. 1.] That from and after the publication of this act, and during the space of one year, there shall be paid by the importer of all wines, liquors, goods, wares and merchandize that shall be imported into this province from the place of their growth (salt, cotton-wool, pig-iron, provisions, and every other thing of the growth and produce of New England, and also all prize goods condemned in any part of this province, excepted), the several rates or duties of impost following; vizt.,—

For every pipe of wine of the Western Islands, eighteen shillings.

For every pipe of Madeira, twenty shillings.

For every pipe of other sorts not mentioned, eighteen shillings.

* This word is imperfectly written in the engrossment.

For every hogshead of rum, containing one hundred gallons, fifteen shillings.

For every hogshead of sugar, fourpence.

For every hogshead of molasses, fourpence.

For every hogshead of tobacco, six shillings.

For every ton of logwood, fourpence.

—And so, proportionably, for greater or lesser quantities.

And all other commodities, goods or merchandize not mentioned or excepted, fourpence for every twenty shillings value: all goods imported from Great Britain, and hogshead and barrel-staves and heading from any of his majesty's colonies and provinces on this continent, excepted.

[Sect. 2.] And for any of the above wines, liquors, goods, wares and merchandize, &c[a]., that shall be imported into this province from the port of their growth and produce, by any of the inhabitants of the other provinces or colonies on this continent, or the English West-India Islands, or in any ship or vessel to them belonging, on the proper account of any of the said inhabitants of the other provinces or colonies on this continent, or of the inhabitants of any of the English West-India Islands, there shall be paid by the importers double the impost appointed by this act to be received for every species above mentioned; and for all rum, sugâr and molasses imported and brought into this province in any ship or vessel, or by land-carriage, from any of the colonies of Connecticut, New Hampshire or Rhode Island, shall be paid by the importer, the rates and duties following:—

For every hogshead of rum, containing one hundred gallons, thirty-three shillings.

For every hogshead of molasses, containing one hundred gallons, one shilling and sixpence.

For every hogshead of sugar, containing one thousand weight, two shillings.

—And in that proportion for more or less thereof.

And for all European goods, and for all other goods, wares or merchandize, eightpence for every twenty shillings value: *provided always*, that all hogshead and barrel-staves and heading from any of his majesty's provinces or colonies, all provisions and other things that are the growth of New England, all salt, cotton-wool and pig-iron are and shall be exempted from every the rates and duties aforesaid.

And be it further enacted,

[Sect. 3.] That the impost rates and duties afores[d] shall be paid in current lawful money, by the importer of any wines, liquors, goods or merchandize, unto the commissioner to be appointed, as is hereinafter to be directed, for entring and receiving the same, at or before the landing of any wines, liquors, goods or merchandize: only the commissioner or receiver is hereby allowed to give credit to such person or persons, where his or their duty of impost, in one ship or vessel, doth exceed the sum of six pounds; and in cases where the commissioner or receiver shall give credit, he shall ballance and settle his accompts with every person on or before the last day of April, so that the same accompts may be ready to be produced in court in May next after. And all entries, where the impost or duties to be paid doth not exceed three shillings, shall be made without charge to the importer; and not more than sixpence to be demanded for any other single entry to what value soever.

And be it further enacted,

[Sect. 4.] That the master of every ship or vessel coming into this province from any other place, shall, within twenty-four hours after his arrival in any port or harbour, and before bulk is broken, make report and deliver a manifest, in writing, under his hand, to the commissioner afores[d], of the contents of the loading of such ship or vessel, therein particularly expressing the species, kind and quantities of all the wines, liquors, goods, wares and merchandize imported in such ship or vessel, with the marks and numbers thereof, and to whom the same are consigned; and make oath before the said commissioner that the same manifest contains a just and true accompt of all the lading taken on board and imported in such ship or vessel, so far as he knows or beleives; and that if he knows of any more wines, liquors, goods, wares or merchandize laden on board such ship or vessel, and imported therein, he will forthwith make report thereof to the commissioner aforesaid, and cause the same to be added to his manifest.

And be it further enacted,

[SECT. 5.] That if the master of any such ship or vessel shall break bulk, or suffer any of the wines, liquors, goods, wares and merchandize imported in such ship or vessel to be unloaden before report and entry thereof be made as aforesaid, he shall forfeit the sum of one hundred pounds.

And be it further enacted,

[SECT. 6.] That all merchants and other persons, being owners of any wines, liquors, goods, wares or merchandize imported into this province, for which any of the rates or duties afores[d] are payable, or having the same consigned to them, shall make a like entry thereof with the commissioner afores[d], and produce an invoice of all such goods as pay *ad valorem*, and make oath before him in form following; viz[t].,—

You, A. B., do swear that the entry of the goods and merchandize by you now made, exhibits the present price of said goods at this market, and that, *bonâ fide*, according to your best skill and judgment, it is not less than the real value thereof. So help you God.

—which oath the commissioner or receiver is hereby impowered and derected to administer; and the owners aforesaid shall pay the duty of impost by this act required, before such wines, liquors, goods, wares or merchandize be landed or taken out of the vessel in which the same shall be imported.

[SECT. 7.] And no wines, liquors, goods, wares or merchandize that by this act are liable to pay impost or duty, shall be landed on any wharfe, or into any warehouse or other place, but in the daytime only, and that after sunrise and before sunset, unless in the presence and with the consent of the commiss[r] or receiver, on pain of forfeiting all such wines, liquors, goods, wares and merchandize, and the lighter, boat or vessel out of which the same shall be landed or put into any warehouse or other place.

[SECT. 8.] And if any person or persons shall not have and produce an invoice of the quantities of rum or liquors to him or them consigned, then the cask wherein the same is, shall be gauged at the charge of the importer, that the contents thereof may be known.

And be it further enacted,

[SECT. 9.] That the importer of all wines, liquors, goods, wares and merchandize, within one year from and after the publication of this act, by land-carriage, or in small vessels or boats, shall make report and deliver a manifest thereof to the commissioner aforesaid or his deputy, therein particularly expressing the species, kind and quantity of all such wines, liquors, goods, wares and merchandize so imported, with the marks and numbers thereof, when, how and by whom brought; and shall make oath, before the said commissioner or his deputy, to the truth of such report and manifest, and shall also pay the several duties aforesaid by this act charged and chargeable upon such wines, liquors, goods, wares and merchandize, before the same are landed, housed or put into any store or place whatever.

And be it further enacted,

[SECT. 10.] That every merchant or other person importing any wines into this province, shall be allowed twelve per cent for leakage: *provided*, such wines shall not have been filled up on board; and that every hogshead, butt or pipe of wine that hath two-thirds thereof leaked out, shall be accounted for outs, and the merchant or importer to pay no duty for the same. And no master of any ship or vessel shall suffer any wines to be filled up on board without giving a certificate of the quantity so filled up, under his hand, before the landing thereof, to the commissioner or receiver of impost for such port, on pain of forfeiting the sum of one hundred pounds.

[SECT. 11.] And if it may be made to appear that any wines imported in any ship or vessel be decayed at the time of unloading thereof, or in twenty days afterwards, oath being made before the commiss[r] or receiver that the same hath not been landed above that time, the duties and impost paid for such wines shall be repayed unto the importer thereof.

And be it further enacted,

[SECT. 12.] That the master of every ship or vessel importing any wines, liquors, goods, wares or merchandize, shall be liable to and shall pay the impost for such and so much thereof, contained in his manifest, as shall not be duly entred, nor the duty paid for the same by the person or persons to whom such wines, liquors, goods, wares or merchandize are or shall be consigned. And it shall and may be lawful, to and for the master of every ship or other vessel, to secure and detain in his hands, at the owner's risque, all such wines, liquors, goods, wares and merchandize imported in any ship or vessel, untill he receives a certificate, from the commissioner or receiver of the impost, that the duty for the same is paid, and untill he be repaid his necessary charges in securing the same; or such master may deliver such wines, liquors, goods, wares or merchandize as are not entred, unto the commissioner or receiver of the impost in such port, or his order, who is hereby impowered and directed to receive and keep the same, at the owner's risque, untill the impost thereof, with the charges, be paid; and then to deliver such wines, liquors, goods, wares or merchandize as such master shall direct.

And be it further enacted,

[SECT. 13.] That the commissioner or receiver of the impost in each port, shall be and hereby is impowered to sue the master of any ship or vessel, for the impost or duty of so much of the lading of any wines, liquors, goods, wares or merchandize imported therein, according to the manifest to be by him given upon oath, as aforesaid, as shall remain not entered and the duty of impost therefor not paid. And where any goods, wares or merchandize are such as that the value thereof is not known, whereby the impost to be recovered of the master, for the same, cannot be ascertained, the owner or person to whom such goods, wares or merchandize are or shall be consigned, shall be summoned to appear as an evidence at the court where such suit for the impost and the duty thereof shall be brought, and be there required to make oath to the value of such goods, wares or merchandize.

And be it further enacted,

[SECT. 14.] That the ship or vessel, with her tackle, apparel and furniture, the master of which shall make default in anything by this act required to be performed by him, shall be liable to answer and make good the sum or sums forfeited by such master, according to this act, for any such default, as also to make good the impost or duty for any such wines, liquors, goods, wares and merchandize not entred as aforesaid; and, upon judgment recovered against such master, the said ship or vessel, with so much of the tackle or appurtenances thereof as shall be sufficient to satisfy said judgment, may be taken into execution for the same; and the commissioner or receiver of the impost is hereby impowered to make seizure of the said ship or vessel, and detain the same under seizure untill judgment be given in any suit to be commenced and prosecuted for any of the said forfeitures of impost; to the intent that, if judgment be rendred for the prosecutor or informer, such ship or vessel and appurtenances may be exposed to sale, for satisfaction thereof, as is before provided: *unless* the owners, or some on their behalf, for the releasing of such ship or vessel from under seizure or restraint, shall give sufficient security unto the commissioner or receiver of impost that seized the same, to respond and satisfy the sum or value of the forfeitures and duties, with charges, that shall be recovered against the master thereof, upon such suit to be brought for the same, as aforesaid; and the master occasioning such loss or damage unto his owners, through his default or neglect, shall be liable unto their action for the same.

And be it further enacted,

[SECT. 15.] That the naval officer within any of the ports of this province shall not clear or give passes to any master of any ship or other vessel, outward bound, untill he shall be certified, by the commissioner or receiver of the impost, that the duty and impost for the goods last imported in such ship or vessel are paid or secured to be paid.

[SECT. 16.] And the commiss[r] or receiver of the impost is hereby impowered to allow bills of store to the master of any ship or vessel importing any wines or liquors, for such private adventures as shall belong to the master or seamen of such ship or vessel, at the discretion of the commissioner or receiver, not exceeding three per cent of the lading; and the duties payable by this act for such wines and liquors, in such bills of stores mentioned and expressed, shall be abated.

And for the more effectual preventing any wines, rum or other distilled spirits being brought into the province from the neighbouring governments, by land, or in small boats or vessels, or any other way, and also to prevent wines, rum or other distilled spirits being first sent out of this province to save the duty of impost, and afterwards brought into the governm[t] again,—

Be it enacted,

[SECT. 17.] That the commissioner and receiver of the afores[d] duties of impost shall, and he is hereby impowered and enjoyned to, appoint one suitable person or persons as his deputy or deputies, in all such places in this province where it is likely that wine, rum or other distilled spirits will be brought out of other governments into this; which officers shall have power to seize the same, unless the owner shall make it appear that the duty of impost has been paid therefor since there being brought into or relanded in this government; and such officer or officers are also impowered to search, in all suspected places, for such wines, rum and distilled spirits brought or relanded in this government, where the duty is not paid as aforesaid, and to seize and secure the same for the ends and uses as in this act is hereafter provided.

And be it further enacted,

[SECT. 18.] That the commissioner or his deputies shall have full power to administer the several oaths afores[d], and to search in all suspected places for all such wines, rum, liquors, goods, wares and merchandize as are brought into this province, and landed contrary to the true intent and meaning of this act, and to seize the same for the uses hereinafter mentioned.

And be it further enacted,

[Sect. 19.] That there shall be paid, by the master of every ship or other vessel, coming into any port or ports of this province, to trade or traffick, whereof all the owners are not belonging to this province (except such vessels as belong to Great Britain, the provinces or colonies of Pensilvania, West and East Jersey, Connecticut, New York, New Hampshire and Rhode Island), every voyage such ship or vessel does make, one pound of good pistol-powder for every ton such ship or vessel is in burden: *saving* for that part which is owned in Great Britain, this province, or any of the afores[d] governments, which are hereby exempted; to be paid unto the commiss[r] or receiver of the duties of impost, and to be employed for the ends and uses aforesaid.

[Sect. 20.] And the said commiss[r] is hereby impowered to appoint a meet and suitable person, to repair unto and on board any ship or vessel, to take the exact measure or tunnage thereof, in case he shall suspect that the register of such ship or vessel doth not express and set forth the full burthen of the same; the charge thereof to be paid by the master or owner of such ship or vessel, before she shall be cleared, in case she shall appear to be of a greater burthen: otherwise, to be paid by the commiss[r] out of the money received by him for impost, and shall be allowed him, accordingly, by the treasurer, in his accompts. And the naval officer shall not clear any vessel, untill he be certified, also, by the commiss[r], that the duty of tunnage for the same is paid, or that it is such a vessel for which none is payable according to this act.

And be it further enacted,

[Sect. 21.] That when and so often as any wine or rum imported into this province, the duty of impost upon which shall have been paid agreeable to this act, shall be reshipped and exported from this government to any other part of the world, that then, and in every such case, the exporter of such wine or rum shall make oath, at the time of shipping, before the receiver of impost, or his deputy, that the whole of the wine or rum so shipped has, *bonâ fide*, had the aforesaid duty of impost paid on the same, and shall afterwards produce a certificate, from some officer of the customs, that the same has been landed out of this government,—or otherwise, in case such rum or wines shall be exported to any place where there is no officer of the customs, or to any foreign port, the master of the vessel in which the same shall be exported shall make oath that the same has been landed out of the government, and the exporter shall, uppon producing such certificate, or uppon such oath of the master, make oath that he verily beleives no part of said wines or rum has been relanded in this province,—such exporter shall be allowed to draw back from the receiver of impost as follows; viz[t].,—

For every pipe of Western-Island wine, fifteen shillings.

For every pipe of Madeira and other sorts, seventeen shillings.

And for every hogshead of rum, thirteen shillings.

Provided always,—

[Sect. 22.] That if, after the shipping any such wine or rum to be exported as aforesaid, and giving security as aforesaid, in order to obtain the drawback aforesaid, the wine or rum so shipped to be exported, or any part thereof, shall be relanded in this province, or brought into the same from any other province or colony, that then all such rum and wine so relanded and brought again into this province shall be forfeited, and may be seized by the commissioner aforesaid, or his deputy.

And be it further enacted,

[Sect. 23.] That there be one fit person, and no more, nominated and appointed by this court, as a commissioner and receiver of the aforesaid duties of impost and tonnage of shipping, and for the inspection, care and management of the said office, and whatsoever thereto relates, to receive commission for the same from the governour or commander-in-chief for the time being, with authority to substitute and appoint a deputy receiver in each port, and other places besides that wherein he resides, and to grant warrants to such deputy receivers for the said place, and to collect and receive the impost and tonnage of shipping as aforesaid that shall become due within such port, and to render the accompt thereof, and to pay in the same, to the said commissioner and receiver: which said commissioner and receiver shall keep fair books of all entries and duties arrising by virtue of this act; also, a particular accompt of every vessel, so that the duties of impost and tonnage arrising on the said vessel may appear; and the same to lye open, at all seasonable times, to the view and perusal of the treasurer or receiver-general of this province (or any other person or persons whom this court shall appoint), with whom he shall accompt for all collections and payments, and pay all such monies as shall be in his hands, as the treasurer or receiver-general shall demand it. And the said commissioner or receiver and his deputy or deputies, before their entering upon the execution of their office, shall be sworn to deal truely and faithfully therein, and shall attend in the said office from ten of the clock in the forenoon, untill one in the afternoon.

[SECT. 24.] And the said commissioner and receiver, for his labour, care and expences in the said office, shall have and receive, out of the province treasury, the sum of sixty pounds per annum; and his deputy or deputies to be paid for their service such sum or sums as the said commissioner and receiver, with the treasurer, shall agree upon, not exceeding four pounds per annum, each; and the treasurer is hereby ordered, in passing and receiving the said commissioner's accompts, accordingly, to allow the payment of such salary or salaries, as aforesaid, to himself and his deputies.

And be it further enacted,

[SECT. 25.] That no duty of impost shall be demanded for any goods imported after the publication of this act, by virtue of any former act for granting unto his majesty any rates and duties of impost, and that all penalties, fines and forfeitures accruing and arrising by virtue of any breach of this act, shall be one half to his majesty for the uses and intents for which the aforementioned duties of impost are granted, and the other half to him or them that shall seize, inform and sue for the same, by action, bill, plaint or information, in any of his majesty's courts of record, wherein no essoign, protection or wager of law shall be allowed: the whole charge of the prosecution to be taken out of the half belonging to the informer.

And be it further enacted,

[SECT. 26.] That from and after the publication of this act, in all causes where any claimer shall appear, and shall not make good the claim, the charges of prosecution shall be born and paid by the said claimer, and not by the informer. [*Passed June* 4; *published June* 16.

CHAPTER 8.

AN ACT FOR THE SUPPLY OF THE TREASURY WITH EIGHT THOUSAND ONE HUNDRED AND FORTY-TWO POUNDS FOUR SHILLINGS, AND FOR DRAWING THE SAME AGAIN INTO THE TREASURY; ALSO FOR APPORTIONING AND ASSESSING A TAX OF TWENTY-FIVE THOUSAND POUNDS; AND ALSO FOR APPORTIONING AND ASSESSING A FURTHER TAX OF ONE THOUSAND SEVEN HUNDRED AND FORTY-TWO POUNDS FOUR SHILLINGS, PAID THE REPRESENTATIVES FOR THEIR SERVICE AND ATTENDANCE IN THE GENERAL COURT, AND TRAVEL, AND FOR FINES LAID ON SEVERAL TOWNS FOR NOT SENDING A REPRESENTATIVE: AMOUNTING IN THE WHOLE TO TWENTY-SIX THOUSAND SEVEN HUNDRED FORTY-TWO POUNDS FOUR SHILLINGS.

Whereas the great and general court or assembly of the province of the Massachusetts Bay, did, at their session in December, one thousand seven hundred and fifty-one, pass an act for levying a tax of eighteen thousand six hundred pounds; and by the said act provision was made that the general court might, this present sitting, apportion the same on the several towns and districts within this province, if they thought fit; *and whereas* the treasurer is, in and by this act, directed to issue out of the treasury, the sum of eight thousand one hundred forty-two pounds four shillings, for the ends and purposes as is hereinafter mentioned; wherefore, for the ordering, directing, and effectual drawing in the sum of twenty-six thousand seven hundred and forty-two pounds four shillings, pursuant to the funds and grants aforesaid, into the treasury, according to the last apportion agreed to by this court: all which is unanimously approved, ratified, and confirmed; we, his majesty's most loyal and dutiful subjects, the representatives in general court assembled, pray that it may be enacted,— 1751-52, chap.16.

And be it accordingly enacted by the Lieutenant-Governour, Council and House of Representatives,

[Sect. 1.] That each town and district within this province be assessed and pay, as such town and district's proportion of the sum of twenty-five thousand pounds, and their representatives' pay, and fines laid on several towns, the sum of one thousand seven hundred and forty-two pounds four shillings; viz., the several sums following; that is to say,—

IN THE COUNTY OF SUFFOLK.

	[illegible]es' Pay [illegible] Fines.	Province Tax.	Sum Total.	
Boston,	£48 16s. 0d.	£4,250 0s. 0d.	Four [illegible] two [illegible] ninety-eight [illegible] sixteen shillings,	£4,298 16s. 0d.
[illegible]y,	12 4 0	231 5 0	Two [illegible] [illegible] [illegible] nine shillings,	243 9 0
Dorchester,	12 4 0	228 17 1	Two [illegible] forty-one [illegible] one shilling and one penny,	241 1 1
M[illegible]on,	0 0 0	121 11 3	One [illegible] [illegible]-one pounds eleven shillings and [illegible],	121 11 3
[illegible]e,	14 12 0	263 17 1	Two [illegible] [illegible]ht pounds nine shillings and one [illegible],	278 9 1
[illegible]h,	0 0 0	155 10 5	One [illegible] [illegible] [illegible] ten shillings and [illegible],	155 10 5
Hingham,	14 12 0	273 15 0	Two [illegible] [illegible]-eight [illegible] [illegible]en shillings,	288 7 0
Dedham,	14 18 0	181 17 6	One [illegible] [illegible]-six [illegible] fifteen [illegible] and [illegible],	196 15 6
Medfield,	12 16 0	112 10 0	One [illegible] [illegible]-five pounds six [illegible],	125 6 0
Wrentham,	13 8 0	181 5 0	One [illegible] [illegible]-four [illegible] [illegible] [illegible],	194 13 0
Brook[illegible],	0 0 0	70 0 0	Seventy [illegible],	70 0 0
[illegible],	12 18 0	92 5 10	One [illegible] and five pounds [illegible] shillings and tenpence,	105 3 10
[illegible]n,	29 6 0	175 0 0	Two [illegible] and four [illegible] six shillings,	204 6 0
[illegible]y,	10 0 0	92 5 10	[illegible] [illegible] and two pounds five shillings and [illegible],	102 5 10
Bellingham,	0 0 0	35 16 8	[illegible] pounds sixteen shillings and [illegible],	35 16 8
Hull,	0 0 0	42 16 3	Forty-two [illegible] sixteen shillings and [illegible],	42 16 3
[illegible]e,	0 0 0	61 13 4	Sixty-one pounds thirteen shillings and fourpence,	61 13 4
Chelsea,	0 0 0	95 10 5	Ninety-five [illegible] ten shillings and [illegible],	95 10 5
	£195 14s. 0d.	£6,665 16s. 8d.		£6,861 10s. 8d.

IN THE COUNTY OF ESSEX.

Salem and Danvers,	£89 12s. 0d.	£656 9s. 2d.	Seven [illegible] [illegible]six [illegible] one [illegible] and [illegible],	£746 1s. 2d.
Ipswich,	15 0 0	561 17 6	Five [illegible] [illegible]ix [illegible] seventeen shillings and sixpence,	576 17 6
Newbury,	13 0 0	723 4 7	Seven [illegible] [illegible] [illegible] four [illegible] and sevenpence,	736 4 7
[illegible]d,	51 16 0	429 1 3	[illegible] [illegible] and [illegible] [illegible] [illegible] shillings and [illegible],	480 17 3
Lyn[illegible],	18 0 0	231 2 11	Two [illegible] forty-nine [illegible] two shillings and elevenpence,	249 2 11
[illegible]r,	15 16 0	317 3 9	[illegible] [illegible] [illegible]-two pounds nineteen [illegible] and [illegible],	332 19 9
Beverly,	11 14 0	152 16 3	One [illegible] [illegible] [illegible] ten shillings and [illegible],	164 10 3
Rowley,	14 4 0	200 0 0	Two [illegible] and [illegible] [illegible] four [illegible],	214 4 0
[illegible]y,	15 12 0	157 5 10	One [illegible] [illegible]-two pounds seventeen shillings and tenpence,	172 17 10
Haverhill,	5 16 0	184 13 9	One hundred and ninety [illegible] [illegible]ine shillings and [illegible],	190 9 9
[illegible]r,	14 4 0	326 19 7	[illegible] [illegible] [illegible]-one [illegible] three shillings and sevenpence,	341 3 7
[illegible]ld,	24 16 0	87 10 0	One [illegible] and twelve [illegible] six [illegible],	112 6 0
Boxford,	28 8 0	115 14 7	One [illegible] [illegible] [illegible] two shillings and sevenpence,	144 2 7
[illegible]y,	17 0 0	[illegible]5 0 0	One [illegible] and sixty-two [illegible],	162 0 0

Bradford, ...	£11 0s. [illegible]	£129 15s. 10d.	One hundred and forty pounds fifteen shillings and tenpence, . .	£140 [illegible] 10d.
Wenham, ...	0 0 0	73 10 10	Seventy-three pounds ten shillings and tenpence, ...	73 10 10
Middleton, ...	10 0 0	65 6 3	Seventy-five pounds six shillings and threepence, ...	75 6 3
Manchester, ...	0 0 0	52 12 1	Fifty-two pounds twelve shillings and one penny, ...	52 12 1
Methuen, ...	0 0 0	83 15 0	Eighty-three pounds fifteen shillings, ...	83 15 0
Rumford, ...	0 0 0	0 0 0	. . . .	0 0 0
	£355 18s. 0d.	£4,693 19s. 2d.		£5,049 17s. 2d.

IN THE COUNTY OF MIDDLESEX.

Cambridge, ...	£0 0s. 0d.	£168 2s. 6d.	One hundred sixty-eight [illegible] two shillings and [illegible], . .	£168 2s. 6d.
[illegible], ...	12 4 0	262 10 0	Two hundred [illegible] four [illegible] fourteen shillings, ...	274 14 0
Watertown, ...	14 12 0	99 1 3	One [illegible] thirteen pounds thir[illegible] shillings and threepence, .	113 13 3
[illegible], ...	12 4 0	162 10 0	One hundred seventy-four [illegible] fourteen [illegible], ...	174 14 0
[illegible], ...	5 8 0	200 0 0	Two hundred and five [illegible] eight shillings, ...	205 8 0
[illegible], ...	14 12 0	162 10 0	One hundred seventy-[illegible] two shillings, ...	177 2 7*
Sudbury, ...	15 4 0	175 14 7	One hundred and [illegible] shillings and sevenpence, .	190 18 0*
Marlborough, ...	15 16 0	175 0 0	One [illegible] ninety [illegible], ...	190 16 0
[illegible], ...	11 4 0	102 10 0	One hundred and thirteen pounds fourteen shillings, ...	13 14 0
Framingham, ...	15 16 0	133 15 0	One [illegible] eleven shillings, ...	149 11 0
Lexington, ...	14 12 0	112 10 0	One hundred [illegible] two shillings, ...	127 2 0
[illegible], ...	14 16 0	100 0 0	One [illegible] fourteen [illegible] shillings, ...	114 16 0
[illegible], ...	10 0 0	69 1 3	[illegible] pounds one shilling and [illegible], ...	79 1 3
Reading, ...	14 12 0	165 0 0	One hundred seventy-nine [illegible] twelve shillings, ...	179 12 0
Malden, ...	12 4 0	31 13 4	One hundred forty-three pounds seventeen shillings [illegible] fourpence, .	43 17 4
[illegible], ...	15 0 0	97 1 8	One hundred and twelve [illegible] one shilling and [illegible], . .	112 1 8
Medford, ...	22 4 0	90 2 1	One hundred and twelve [illegible] six shillings and one [illegible], . .	112 6 1
[illegible], ...	17 0 0	70 4 2	Eighty-seven [illegible] four shillings and [illegible], ...	87 4 2
[illegible], ...	8 0 0	61 5 0	[illegible] five shillings, ...	69 5 0
Westford, ...	9 0 0	67 10 0	Seventy-six [illegible] ten shillings, ...	76 10 0
[illegible], ...	13 4 0	86 9 2	[illegible] thirteen shillings and [illegible], ...	99 13 2
[illegible], ...	0 0 0	38 4 7	[illegible] four shillings and [illegible], ...	38 4 7
Stow, ...	8 0 0	[illegible] 5 0	Sixty-nine pounds five shillings, ...	69 5 0
[illegible], ...	0 0 0	43 17 1	Forty-three [illegible] shillings and one penny, . . .	43 17 1
Groton, ...	14 12 0	184 3 4	One [illegible] ninety-eight [illegible] fifteen shillings [illegible], .	198 15 4

* Sic.

IN THE COUNTY OF MIDDLESEX—*Continued.*

	REPRESENTATIVES' PAY AND FINES.	PROVINCE TAX.	SUM TOTAL.	
Wilmington,	£0 0*s*. 0*d*.	£50 0*s*. 0*d*.	Fifty pounds,	£50 0*s*. 0*d*.
English inhabitants of Natick,	0 0 0	34 15 10	Thirty-four pounds fifteen shillings and tenpence,	34 15 10
Dracut,	0 0 0	49 3 4	Forty-nine pounds three shillings and fourpence,	49 3 4
Bedford,	0 0 0	57 7 11	Fifty-seven pounds seven shillings and elevenpence,	57 7 11
Holliston,	7 0 0	55 14 7	Sixty-two pounds fourteen shillings and sevenpence,	62 14 7
Tewksbury,	0 0 0	49 3 4	Forty-nine pounds three shillings and fourpence,	49 3 4
Acton,	0 0 0	36 5 0	Thirty-six pounds five shillings,	36 5 0
Dunstable and Nottingham inhabitants,	0 0 0	42 10 0	Forty-two pounds ten shillings,	42 10 0
	£297 4*s*. 0*d*.	£3,395 0*s*. 0*d*.		£3,692 4*s*. 0*d*.

IN THE COUNTY OF HAMPSHIRE.

Springfield,	£19 16*s*. 0*d*.	£243 6*s*. 8*d*.	Two [illegible] sixty-three pounds two shillings and eightpence,	£263 2*s*. 8*d*.
Northampton,	18 8 0	161 2 11	One hundred seventy-[illegible] pounds [illegible] shillings and elevenpence,	179 10 11
Hatfield,	26 0 0	74 17 11	One hundred pounds seventeen shillings and elevenpence,	100 17 11
[illegible]ld,	28 4 0	97 7 11	One hundred and twenty five pounds [illegible] shillings and elevenpence,	125 11 11
Enfield,	0 0 0	72 7 11	Seven[illegible]two pounds seven shillings and elevenpence,	72 7 11
Deerfield,	10 0 0	72 14 2	[illegible] pounds [illegible] shillings and twopence,	82 14 2
Sheffield,	14 16 0	83 0 5	Ni[illegible] pounds [illegible] shillings and fivepence,	97 16 5
Northfield,	0 0 0	26 2 11	Twenty-six pounds two shillings and elevenpence,	26 2 11
Hadley,	19 12 0	128 15 0	One hundred forty-[illegible] pounds seven shillings,	148 7 0
Suffield,	0 0 0	134 7 6	One hundred thirty-four [illegible] seven shillings and sixpence,	134 7 6
Sunderland,	0 0 0	42 18 4	Forty-two [illegible] shillings and fourpence,	42 18 4
Brimfield,	22 14 0	82 5 10	One hundred and four [illegible] shillings and tenpence,	104 19 10
Somers,	0 0 0	51 13 4	[illegible]-one [illegible] shillings and fourpence,	51 13 4
[illegible], or Kingston,	0 0 0	30 16 8	[illegible] pounds [illegible] shillings and eightpence,	30 16 8
Pelham,	0 0 0	26 5 0	[illegible]-six pounds five shillings,	26 5 0
Bedford,	0 0 0	17 10 0	Seventeen pounds [illegible],	17 10 0
Coldspring,	0 0 0	17 10 0	Seventeen pounds [illegible] shillings,	17 10 0
[illegible]in,	0 0 0	19 11 8	Ni[illegible] eleven shillings and eightpence,	19 11 8
Blandford,	0 0 0	11 0 10	Eleven pounds and tenpence,	11 0 10
New Marlborough, or No. 2,	0 0 0	18 15 0	Eighteen [illegible] shillings,	18 15 0

Parish at Ware River,	£0 0s. 0d.	£25 0s. 0d.	Twenty-five pounds,	£25 0s. 0d.
Stockbridge,	0 0 0	0 0 0	. . . .	0 0 0
	£159 10s. 0d.	£1,437 10s. 0d.		£1,597 0s. 0d.

IN THE COUNTY OF WORCESTER.

[illegible]r,	£0 0s. 0d.	£131 17s. 6d.	One hundred thirty-one [illegible] [illegible] [illegible]llings and sixpence,	£131 1 7. 6.
Lancaster,	16 8 0	150 0 0	One hundred sixty-six pounds [illegible]ight shillings,	166 8 0
Mendon,	12 0 0	143 15 0	One hundred fifty-five pounds [illegible]n shillings,	155 15 0
Woodstock,	0 0 0	161 13 4	One hundred sixty-one pounds [illegible] shillings and fourpence,	161 13 4
[illegible] [illegible]d,	26 8 0	118 0 5	One hundred forty-four pounds [illegible]ight shillings and [illegible],	144 8 5
Oxford,	14 4 0	79 15 10	Ninety-three pounds [illegible] [illegible]ngs and tenpence,	93 19 10
[illegible]n,	10 0 0	114 13 9	One [illegible] [illegible] twenty-four [illegible] thirteen shillings and [illegible],	124 13 9
Rutland,	17 12 0	82 14 2	One hundred [illegible] six [illegible]ngs and twopence,	100 6 2
Leicester,	15 2 0	117 14 2	One hundred [illegible]-two [illegible] sixteen [illegible] and twopence,	132 16 2
Southborough,	8 0 0	64 9 7	Seventy-two pounds [illegible]ine shillings and [illegible],	72 9 7
Westborough,	0 0 0	90 2 1	Ninety pounds two shillings and one [illegible],	90 2 1
Shrewsbury,	10 12 0	105 0 0	One hundred [illegible] [illegible] and [illegible] shillings,	115 12 0
[illegible]gh,	17 0 0	88 0 5	One hundred and five pounds and [illegible],	105 0 5
Uxbridge,	16 0 0	79 13 9	Ninety-five pounds [illegible] shillings and ninepence,	95 13 9
Harvard,	14 12 0	72 5 10	Eighty-six pounds seventeen [illegible]ngs and tenpence,	86 17 10
Dudley,	0 0 0	47 10 0	Forty-seven pounds and ten shillings,	47 10 0
Bolton,	13 2 0	72 1 8	Eighty-five pounds three [illegible] and eightpence,	85 3 8
Upton,	0 0 0	39 15 10	Thirty-nine pounds [illegible] shillings and [illegible],	39 15 10
Sturbridge,	14 16 0	31 2 11	Forty-five pounds [illegible] [illegible] and [illegible],	45 18 11
[illegible]r,	0 0 0	37 10 0	[illegible]-[illegible] pounds and ten shillings,	37 10 0
Hardwick,	8 0 0	46 5 0	[illegible]-four pounds and five [illegible],	54 5 0
[illegible]n,	0 0 0	23 15 0	[illegible]-three pounds and [illegible] shillings,	23 15 0
Western,	0 0 0	36 5 0	[illegible]-six pounds and five shillings,	36 5 0
[illegible]n,	15 0 0	60 16 8	Seventy-five pounds [illegible] shillings and eightpence,	75 16 8
[illegible]g,	0 0 0	27 1 8	[illegible]-[illegible] [illegible] one shilling and eightpence,	27 1 8
[illegible]ss,	0 0 0	20 16 8	Twenty pounds [illegible] shillings and eightpence,	20 16 8
	£228 16s. 0d.	£2,042 16s. 3d.		£2,271 12s. 3d.

IN THE COUNTY OF PLYMOUTH.

	[illegible]s' pay, [illegible] fines.	Province tax.	Sum total.	
[illegible],	£13 12s. [illegible]	£200 0s. 0d.	Two hundred [illegible] pounds and [illegible] shillings,	£213 12s. [illegible]
[illegible],	13 16 0	275 0 0	[illegible] hundred [illegible] pounds and [illegible] shillings,	288 16 0
[illegible],	16 8 0	90 12 6	One hundred and seven pounds and sixpence,	107 0 6
[illegible],	11 18 0	186 17 6	One hundred and [illegible] pounds [illegible] shillings and sixpence,	198 15 6
Bridgwater,	15 0 0	324 11 8	Three hundred [illegible] pounds eleven [illegible] and [illegible],	339 11 8
[illegible],	29 4 0	228 4 7	[illegible] hundred and fifty-seven pounds [illegible] shillings and sevenpence,	257 8 7
Rochester,	16 16 0	137 12 1	One hundred fifty-four pounds eight shillings and one [illegible],	154 8 1
[illegible],	27 8 0	116 9 2	One hundred [illegible]-three pounds seventeen shillings and twopence,	143 17 2
[illegible],	13 12 0	100 0 0	One hundred and [illegible] pounds [illegible] [illegible],	113 12 0
Kingston,	22 10 0	67 5 10	[illegible] pounds [illegible] shillings and [illegible],	89 15 10
Hanover,	15 16 0	87 10 0	[illegible] hundred and [illegible] pounds six shillings,	103 6 0
[illegible],	18 0 0	94 1 3	One [illegible] and [illegible] pounds one shilling and threepence,	112 1 3
Hallifax,	0 0 0	55 8 4	[illegible]-five pounds eight [illegible] and [illegible],	55 8 4
Warham,	0 0 0	57 10 0	[illegible] pounds ten shillings,	57 10 0
	£214 0s. 0d.	£2,021 2s. 11d.		£2,235 2s. 11d.

IN THE COUNTY OF BARNSTABLE.

Barnstable,	£9 [illegible] 0d.	£175 0s. 0d.	One hundred eighty-four pounds,	£184 0s. 0d.
Yarmouth,	15 0 0	114 11 8	One hundred twenty-nine pounds eleven shillings and eightpence,	129 11 8
Sandwich,	15 12 0	125 0 0	One hundred and forty pounds twelve shillings,	140 12 0
Eastham,	17 4 0	142 10 0	One hundred fifty-nine pounds fourteen shillings,	159 14 0
Harwich,	0 0 0	110 12 6	One hundred and ten pounds twelve shillings and sixpence,	110 12 6
Chatham,	0 0 0	62 16 3	Sixty-two pounds sixteen shillings and threepence,	62 16 3
Truro,	0 0 0	67 7 11	Sixty-seven pounds seven shillings and elevenpence,	67 7 11
Falmouth,	0 0 0	77 10 0	Seventy-seven pounds ten shillings,	77 10 0
	£56 16s. 0d.	£875 8s. 4d.		£932 [illegible] 4d.

IN THE COUNTY OF BRISTOL.

Taunton,	£14 2s. [illegible]	£241 7s. 1d.	Two [illegible] fifty-five [illegible] [illegible] shillings and one penny,	£255 [illegible] d.
Rehoboth,	7 12 0	345 18 9	Three hundred [illegible]-three pounds [illegible] shillings and ninepence,	33 10 9
[illegible]ey with Shawamet,	13 4 0	153 10 10	One [illegible] [illegible] [illegible] [illegible] [illegible] and tenpence,	[illegible]6 14 10
Dartmouth,	16 8 0	450 0 0	Four hundred [illegible]-six [illegible] and [illegible] [illegible],	[illegible]6 8 0
[illegible]	13 0 0	150 18 9	One hundred sixty-three [illegible] [illegible] [illegible] and [illegible],	[illegible]3 18 9
[illegible]h,	16 2 0	164 15 10	One hundred [illegible] [illegible] [illegible] [illegible] and tenpence,	[illegible]0 17 10
Dighton,	11 0 0	106 9 2	One hundred and seventeen [illegible] [illegible] shillings and [illegible],	117 9 2
Freetown,	8 0 0	98 6 8	One hundred and six [illegible] six [illegible] and eightpence,	[illegible]6 6 8
Raynham,	0 0 0	63 10 10	[illegible] [illegible] [illegible] [illegible] and tenpence,	63 10 10
Easton,	8 0 0	73 0 5	[illegible] [illegible] and fivepence,	81 0 5
Berkley,	0 0 0	56 15 5	[illegible] [illegible] [illegible] shillings and [illegible],	56 15 5
Barrington,	0 0 0	0 0 0		0 0 0
	£107 18s. 0d.	£1,904 13s. 9d.		£2,012 11s. 9d.

IN THE COUNTY OF YORK.

York,	£11 1 [illegible] [illegible]	£244 15s. 10d.	[illegible] [illegible] fifty-six [illegible] seven [illegible] [illegible] tenpence,	£256 7s. 10d.
[illegible]y,	16 4 0	287 10 0	Three hundred [illegible] three [illegible] fourteen [illegible],	[illegible]3 14 0
Wells,	17 4 0	110 0 0	[illegible] hundred [illegible] [illegible] [illegible] four [illegible],	127 4 0
[illegible],	12 0 0	150 0 0	One hundred sixty-two [illegible],	162 0 0
Falmouth,	18 12 0	237 10 0	[illegible] [illegible] [illegible] [illegible] two [illegible],	[illegible]6 2 0
Biddeford,	10 0 0	100 16 8	[illegible] hundred and ten [illegible] [illegible] [illegible] [illegible] [illegible],	110 16 8
[illegible]l,	0 0 0	56 0 10	[illegible] [illegible] [illegible] and tenpence,	56 0 10
Scarborough,	8 0 0	85 18 9	Ninety-three [illegible] [illegible] shillings and [illegible],	93 18 9
North [illegible]h,	17 4 0	37 7 11	Fifty-four [illegible] eleven [illegible] [illegible] [illegible],	54 11 11
[illegible]n,	0 0 0	39 13 9	[illegible] pounds thirteen [illegible] [illegible] [illegible],	39 13 9
Brunswick,	0 0 0	35 14 7	Thirty-five [illegible] fourteen shillings [illegible] [illegible],	35 14 7
Sheepscut,	0 0 0	25 0 0	[illegible]-five [illegible],	25 0 0
	£110 16s. 0d.	£1,410 8s. 4d.		£1,521 4s. 4d.

IN THE COUNTY OF DUKES COUNTY.

	Representatives' pay, and fines.	Province tax.	Sum total.	
Edgartown,	£8 0s. 0d.	£96 13s. 4d.	One hundred and four pounds thirteen shillings and fourpence,	£104 13s. 4d.
Chilmark,	0 0 0	86 15 5	Eighty-six pounds fifteen shillings and fivepence,	86 15 5
Tisbury,	0 0 0	55 8 4	Fifty-five pounds eight shillings and fourpence,	55 8 4
	£8 0s. 0d.	£238 17s. 1d.		£246 17s. 1d.

IN NANTUCKET COUNTY.

Sherburne,	£7 12s. 0d.	£314 7s. 6d.	Three hundred twenty-one pounds nineteen shillings and sixpence,	£321 19s. 6d.

	Representatives' pay, and fines.	Province tax.	Sum total.	
Suffolk,	£195 14s. 0d.	£6,665 16s. 8d.	Six [illegible] [illegible]ght hundred sixty-one [illegible] [illegible] shillings and eight-[illegible]pe,	£6,861 10s. 8d.
Essex,	355 18 0	4,693 19 2	Five [illegible] and forty-nine [illegible] [illegible] shillings and two-pence,	5,049 17 2
Middlesex,	297 4 0	3,395 0 0	Three [illegible] six hundred ninety-two [illegible] four shillings,	3,692 4 0
Hampshire,	159 10 0	1,437 10 0	One [illegible] five [illegible] [illegible] [illegible],	1,597 0 0
Worcester,	228 16 0	2,042 16 3	Two thousand two hundred [illegible]-one [illegible] twelve shillings & [illegible]pe,	2,271 12 3
Plymouth,	214 0 0	2,021 2 11	Two [illegible] two hundred [illegible]-five [illegible] two shillings & [illegible]e,	2,235 2 11
Barnstable,	56 16 0	875 8 4	[illegible] hundred thirty-two pounds four [illegible] [illegible] fourpence,	932 4 4
Bristol,	107 18 0	1,904 13 9	Two [illegible] [illegible] twelve pounds [illegible] shillings and [illegible]pe,	2,012 11 9
York,	110 16 0	1,410 8 4	One [illegible] five hundred [illegible] [illegible] [illegible] [illegible] and fourpence,	1,521 4 4
Dukes County,	8 0 0	238 17 1	Two [illegible] forty-six [illegible] [illegible] shillings [illegible] one [illegible],	246 17 1
Nantucket,	7 12 0	314 7 6	Three hundred twenty-one [illegible] [illegible] [illegible] [illegible] sixpence,	321 19 6
	£1,742 4s. 0d.	£25,000 0s. 0d.		£26,742 4s. 0d.

And be it further enacted,

[Sect. 2.] That the treasurer do forthwith send out his warrants, directed to the selectmen or assessors of each town or district within this province, requiring them, respectively, to assess the sum hereby set upon such town or district, in manner following; that is to say, to assess all rateable male polls above the age of sixteen years, within their respective towns or districts, or next adjoining to them, belonging to no other town, four shillings and twopence per poll, and proportionably in assessing the fines mentioned in this act, and the additional sum received out of the treasury for the payment of the representatives (except the governour, the lieutenant-governour and their families, the president, fellows and students of Harvard College, settled ministers and grammar-school masters, who are hereby exempted as well from being taxed for their polls, as for their estates being in their own hands and under their actual management and improvement); and other persons, if such their be, who, through age, infirmity or extream poverty, in the judgment of the assessors, are not capable to pay towards publick charges, they may exempt their polls, and so much of their estate as in their prudence they shall think fit and judge meet.

[Sect. 3.] And the justices in their general sessions, in the respective counties assembled, in granting a county tax or assessment, are hereby ordered and directed to apportion the same on the several towns in such county in proportion to their province rate, exclusive of what has been paid out of the publick treasury to the representative of each town for his service; and the assessors of each town in the province are also directed, in making an assessment, to govern themselves by the same rule; and all estates, both real and personal, lying within the limits of such town or district, or next unto the same, not paying elsewhere, in whose hands, tenure, occupation or possession soever the same is or shall be found, and also the incomes or profits which any person or persons, except as before excepted, do or shall receive from any trade, faculty, business or employment whatsoever, and all profits that shall or may arise by money or other estate not particularly otherwise assessed, or commissions of profit in their improvement, according to their understanding or cunning, at one penny on the pound; and to abate or multiply the same, if need be, so as to make up the sum set and ordered hereby for such town or district to pay; and, in making their assessment, to estimate houses and lands at six years' income of the yearly rents whereat the same may be reasonably set or let for in the place where they lye: *saving* all contracts between landlord and tenant, and where no contract is, the landlord to reimburse one-half of the tax set upon such houses and lands; and to estimate negro, Indian and molatto servants proportionably as other personal estate, according to their sound judgment and discretion; as also to estimate every ox of four years old and upwards, at forty shillings; every cow of three years old and upwards, at thirty shillings; every horse and mare of three years old and upwards, at forty shillings; every swine of one year old and upwards, at eight shillings; goats and sheep of one year old, three shillings each: likewise requiring the said assessors to make a fair list of the said assessment, setting forth, in distinct columns, against each particular person's name, how much he or she is assessed at for polls, and how much for houses and lands, and how much for personal estate, and income by trade or faculty, and if as guardian, or for any estate in his or her improvement, in trust, to be distinctly expressed; and the list or lists, so perfected and signed by them, or the major part of them, to commit to the collectors, constable or constables of such town or district, and to return a certificate of the name or names of such collectors, constable or constables, together with the sum total to each of them committed, unto himself, some time before the last day of October next.

[SECT. 4.] And the treasurer for the time being, upon receipt of such certificate, is hereby impowered and ordered to issue forth his warrants to the collector, or constable or constables of such town or district, requiring him or them, respectively, to collect the whole of each respective sum assessed on each particular person, before the last day of December next; and to pay in their collection, and issue the accompts of the whole, at or before the last day of March, which will be in the year of our Lord one thousand seven hundred and fifty-three.

And be it further enacted,

[SECT. 5.] That the assessors of each town and district, respectively, in convenient time before their making the assessment, shall give seasonable warning to the inhabitants, in a town meeting, or by posting up notifications in some place or places in such town or district, or notify the inhabitants some other way to give or bring in to the assessors true and perfect lists of their polls, and rateable estate, and income by trade or faculty, and gain by money at interest; and if any person or persons shall neglect or refuse so to do, or bring in a false list, it shall be lawful to and for the assessors to assess such person or persons, according to their known ability in such town, in their sound judgment and discretion, their due proportion of this tax, as near as they can, agreeable to the rules herein given, under the penalty of twenty shillings for each person that shall be convicted by legal proof, in the judgment of the said assessors, of bringing in a false list; the said fines to be for the use of the poor of such town or district where the delinquent lives, to be levied by warrant from the assessors, directed to the collector or constables, in manner as is directed for gathering town assessments, and to be paid into the town treasurer or selectmen for the use aforesaid: *saving* to the party aggrieved at the judgment of the assessors in setting forth such fine, liberty of appeal therefrom to the court of general sessions of the peace within the county for relief, as in case of being overrated. And if any person or persons shall not bring in a list of their estate as aforesaid to the assessors, he or they so neglecting shall not be admitted to make application to the court of sessions for any abatement of the assessment laid on him.

[SECT. 6.] And if the party be not convicted of any falseness in the list, by him presented, of the polls, rateable estate, or income by trade or faculty, business or employment, which he doth or shall exercise, or in gain by money at interest or otherwise, or other estate not particularly assessed, such list shall be a rule for such person's proportion to the tax, which the assessors may not exceed.

And forasmuch as, ofttimes, sundry persons, not belonging to this province, bring considerable trade and merchandize, and by reason that the tax or rate of the town where they come to trade is finished and delivered to the constable or collector, and, before the next year's assessment, are gone out of the province, and so pay nothing towards the support of the government, though, in the time of their residing here, they reaped considerable gain by trade, and had the protection of the government,—

Be it further enacted,

[SECT. 7.] That when any such person or persons shall come and reside in any town within this province, and bring any merchandize, and trade, to deal therewith, the assessors of such town are hereby impowered to rate and assess all such persons according to their circumstances, pursuant to the rules and directions in this act provided, tho' the former rate may have been finished, and the new one not perfected, as aforesaid; and the constables or collectors are hereby enjoyned to levy and collect all such sums committed to them and assessed on persons who are not of this province, and pay the same into the town treasury.

And be it further enacted,

[Sect. 8.] That the inhabitants of this province have liberty, if they see fit, to pay the several sums for which they may be respectively assessed, as their proportion of the aforesaid sum of twenty-six thousand seven hundred and forty-two pounds four shillings, in good merchantable hemp, or in good, merchantable, Isle-of-Sable codfish, or in good refined bar-iron, or in bloomery-iron, or in hollow iron-ware, or in good Indian corn, or in good winter rye, or in good winter wheat, or in good barley, or in good barrel pork, or in barrel beef, or in duck or canvas, or in long whalebone, or in merchantable cordage, or in good train-oyl, or in good beeswax, or in good bayberry-wax, or in tryed tallow, or in good pease, or in good sheepswool[1], or in good tanned sole-leather; and that the eldest councellors, for the time being, of each of those counties in the province, of which any one of the councellors is an inhabitant, together with the province treasurer, or the major part of them, be a committee, who are hereby directed and fully authorized and impowered, once in every month, if need be, to agree and sétt the several species and commodities aforesaid at some certain price, at which they shall be received towards the payment of the sums aforesaid; all which aforesaid commodities shall be of the produce of this province, and, as soon as conveniently may, be disposed of by the treasurer to the best advantage for so much as they will fetch in money; and the several persons paying their taxes in any of the commodities afore mentioned to run the risque and pay the charge of transporting the said commodities to the province treasury.

[Sect. 9.] And if any loss shall happen by the sale of the aforesaid species, it shall be made good by a tax of the next year; and if there be a surplusage, it shall remain a stock in the treasury.

And be it further enacted,

[Sect. 10.] That the inhabitants of this province shall have full liberty to pay in the several sums, which they shall respectively be assessed in pursuance of this act, in bills of credit on this province; also in government securities, signed by Andrew Oliver, Thomas Hubbard, Esqrs., and Mr. Harrison Gray, with the interest that may become due thereon: *provided,* they pay the bills aforesaid to the collectors of said assessments on or before the last day of December next.

And whereas, eight thousand one hundred and forty-two pounds four shillings, part of the above tax, has not been appropriated in any supply-bill for the payment of the publick debts,—

Be it further enacted,

[Sect. 11.] That the said sum of eight thousand one hundred forty-two pounds four shillings, shall be issued out of the treasury, when received of the constables and collectors, in manner and for the purposes following; that is to say, the sum of two thousand five hundred pounds, part of the aforesaid sum of eight thousand one hundred forty-two pounds four shillings, shall be applyed for the service of the several forts and garrisons within this province, pursuant to such orders and grants as are or shall be made by this court for those purposes; and the further sum of seven hundred pounds, part of the aforesaid sum of eight thousand one hundred forty-two pounds four shillings, shall be applyed for the purchasing provisions, the commissary's necessary disbursements for the service of the several forts and garrisons within this province, pursuant to such grants as are or shall be made by this court for those purposes; and the further sum of three thousand five hundred pounds, part of the aforesaid sum of eight thousand one hundred forty-two pounds four shillings, shall be applyed for the payment of such premiums and grants that now are or hereafter may be made by this court; and the further sum of five hundred pounds, part of the aforesaid sum of eight thousand one hundred forty-two pounds four shillings, shall be applied for the discharge of other debts owing from this province to persons that have served, or shall serve them, by order of this court, in such matters and things where there is no establishment nor any certain sum assigned for that purpose, and for paper, writing and printing for this court; and the further sum of eight hundred ninety-two pounds, part of the aforesaid sum of eight thousand one hundred forty-two pounds four shillings, shall be applyed for the payment of his majesty's council and house of representatives, serving in the general court during the several sessions for this present year.

And whereas there are sometimes contingent and unforeseen charges that demand prompt pay,—

Be it further enacted,

[SECT. 12.] That the sum of fifty pounds four shillings, part of the aforesaid sum of eight thousand one hundred forty-two pounds four shillings, be applied to pay such contingent charges, and for no other purpose whatsoever.

And be it further enacted,

[SECT. 13.] That the treasurer is hereby directed and ordered to pay the sum of eight thousand one hundred forty-two pounds four shillings, brought in by taxes as aforesaid, out of such appropriations as shall be directed to by warrant, and no other; and the secretary, to whom it belongs to keep the muster-rolls and accompts of the charge, shall lay before the house of representatives, when they direct, such muster-rolls and accompts after payment thereof. [*Passed June 5.*

ACTS

PASSED AT THE SESSION BEGUN AND HELD AT CAMBRIDGE,* ON THE TWENTY-SECOND DAY OF NOVEMBER, A. D. 1752.

CHAPTER 9.

AN ACT FOR DIVIDING THE TOWN OF GROTON, AND MAKING A DISTRICT BY THE NAME OF SHIRLEY.

WHEREAS the inhabitants of the southwest[ward][*er*]ly part of the town of Groton, by reason of the difficulties they labour under, being remote from the place of the publick worship of God, have addressed this court to be set off a seperate district, whereunto the inhabitants of said town have manifested their consent,— Preamble.

Be it therefore enacted by the Lieutenant-Governour, Council and House of Representatives,

[SECT. 1.] That the southwestwardly part of the town of Groton, comprehended within the following boundaries; viz[t]., beginning at the mouth of Squanacook River, where it runs into Lancaster River; from thence up said Lancaster [River], till it comes to land belonging to the township of Stow; thence westwardly, bounding southwardly, to said Stow land, till it comes to the southwest corner of the township of Groton; thence northwardlv, bounding westwardly, to Lunenburgh and Townsend, to Squanacook River aforesaid; thence down said river, and jo[y][*i*]ning thereto, to the mouth thereof; being the first bound,—be and hereby is set off from the said town of Groton, and erected into a separate and distinct district, by the name of Shirley; and that the inhabitants thereof be and hereby are vested with all the powers, privile[*d*]ges and immunities which the inhabitants of any town within this province do, or, by law, ought to enjoy: *excepting* only the privile[*d*]ge of chosing a representative to represent them in the great and general court, in chusing of whom the inhabitants of said district shall jo[y][*i*]n with the inhabitants of the town of Groton, as heretofore has been usual, and also in paying said representative. Southwardly part of Groton made a district, by the name of Shirley. Bounds thereof. Privileges granted said district.

Provided, nevertheless,—

[SECT. 2.] The said district shall pay their proportionable part of all such town, county, parish and province charges as are already assessed upon the town of Groton, in like manner as though this act had never been made. Proviso.

And be it further enacted,

[SECT. 3.] That Mr. John Whitney be and hereby is impowered to issue his warrant, directed to some principal inhabitant in said district, requiring him to notify and warn the inhabitants of said district qualified by law to vote in town affairs, to meet at such time and place as Mr. John Whitney empowered to call the first meeting.

* Adjourned, the next day, to Boston, where the remainder of the session was held.

shall be therein set forth, to chuse all such officers as shall be necessary to manage the affairs of said district. [*Passed January* 5; *published January* 6, 1753.

CHAPTER 10.

AN ACT FOR ERECTING THE SECOND PRECINCT IN THE TOWN OF NORTHAMPTON, INTO A SEPERATE DISTRICT, BY THE NAME OF SOUTHAMPTON.

Be it enacted by the Lieutenant-Governour, Council and House of Represent[*ati*]*ves*,

Second precinct in Northampton made a separate district. Bounds thereof.

[SECT. 1.] That the said second precinct in Northampton, bounding north on the Long Division, so called, of common lands in said Northampton; easterly, on the country road, until[l] it comes to the south end of the Mountain Division of Commons; then east on that division, until[l] it comes to Springfield North Line; then on Springfield North Line aforesaid, until[l] it comes to the southeast corner of Northampton bounds; and south on the town of Westfield, and west on the lands, some time since country land, now belonging to David Ingersol[*e*], Esq[r]., of Sheffield's Equivalent Land, so called,—be and hereby is erected into a seperate and distinct district, by the name of Southampton; and that the said district be invested with all the powers, privile[*d*]ges and immunities that towns in this province, by law, do or may enjoy, that of sending a representative to the general assembly only excepted; and that the said district shall have full liberty and right, from time to time, to join with the town of Northampton in chosing a representative to represent them at the general assembly; and that the district shall, from time to time, be at their proportionable part of the expence of such representative; and that the town of Northampton, as often as they shall call a meeting for the choice of representatives, shall, from time to time, give seasonable notice to the clerk of said district for the time being, of the time and place of holding said meeting, to the end that said district may jo[y][*i*]n them therein; and the clerk of said district shall set up, in some publick place in said district, a notification thereof accordingly.

Privileges, &c., granted said district.

Provided, nevertheless,—

And be it further enacted,

Proviso.

[SECT. 2.] That the said district shall pay their proportion of all town, county and province taxes, already set on, or granted to be raised by, said town, as if this act had not been made.

And be it further enacted,

Joseph Hawley, Esq., empowered to call the first meeting.

[SECT. 3.] That Joseph Hawley, Esq[r]., be and hereby is impowered to issue his warrant, directed to some principal inhabitant in said district, requiring him to notify and warn the inhabitants of said district, qualified by law to vote in town affairs, to meet at such time and place as shall be therein set forth, to ch[o][*u*]se all such officers as shall be necessary to manage the affairs of said district. [*Passed January* 5; *published January* 6, 1753.

CHAPTER 11.

AN ACT FOR GRANTING THE SUM OF THREE HUNDRED AND FIFTY POUNDS, FOR THE SUPPORT OF HIS HONOUR THE LIEUTENANT-GOVERN[*OU*]R AND COMMANDER-IN-CHIEF.

Be it enacted by the Lieutenant-Governour, Council and House of Represent[*ati*]*ves*,

THAT the sum of three hundred and fifty pounds be and hereby is granted to his most excellent majesty, to be paid out of the publick treasury to his honour Spencer Phips, Esq[r]., lieutenant-governour and commander-in-chief in and over his majesty's province of the Massachusetts Bay, for his past services, and further to enable him to manage the publick affairs of the province. [*Passed January* 5; *published January* 6, 1753.

Governor's support.

CHAPTER 12.

AN ACT FOR FURTHER REGULATING THE PROCEEDINGS OF THE COURTS OF PROBATE WITHIN THIS PROVINCE.

Be it enacted by the Lieutenant-Governour, Council and House of Repres[*entati*]*ves*,

[SECT. 1.] That every person named or to be named executor in any last will and testament duly proved and approved, and who hath or shall accept of that trust, shall stand accountable to the judge of probate, for the time being, of the county where such last testam[*en*]t was or shall be so approved, for and concerning the estate of the testator, in his or her hands or possession, and touching his or her proceedings in discharge of said trust, when thereunto lawfully required; and every such executor who, not having fully administred the estate of the testator, and paid his debts and legacies, shall refuse or neglect to account as afores[*ai*]d, on oath, at such reasonable time as the said judge shall assign, being duly cited thereunto by such judge, upon application to him made for that purpose by any heir, legatee or creditor, shall stand charged in the same manner, and incur the same penalties and forfeitures, to be alike recovered and applied, as, upon their refusal to exhibit an inventory, executors are liable to by force of the act made in the twelfth year of his present majesty's reign, intitled "An Act for the more effectual obliging of executors to inventory the estates of their testators."

Executors of wills to account with the Judge of Probate.
1692.3, chap. 46, § 2.
1703-4, chap. 12.
1719-20, chap. 10.
Penalty.
1738.39, chap. 23.

Provided always,—

[SECT. 2.] That nothing in this act foregoing shall be understood to extend to any executor who is or may be the residuary legatee to any last will and testament, and who may or shall have given bond for the payment of debts and legac[y][*ie*]s in manner as is by law already provided.

Proviso in case the executor be a residuary legatee.

And be it further enacted,

[SECT. 3.] That every commissioner for receiving the claims of the creditors to any estate represented insolvent shall be under oath faithfully to discharge the trust reposed in him, such oath to be administred by the judge of probate in all cases where the commiss[*ione*]rs shall live within ten miles of such judge's dwelling-house, otherwise, either by the said judge, or by any justice of the peace for the county.

And be it further enacted,

Judge of probate to issue warrants upon embezzlement.

[SECT. 4.] That when and so often as any person suspected of concealing or embezzleing any part of the estate of any person deceased, shall have been cited pursuant to law, and shall refuse to appear before the judge of probate, the said judge is hereby impow[e]red, by warrant under his hand and seal, directed to any sheriff, his deputy or constable, or any of them, to cause such suspected person to be apprehended and brought before such judge, in order to his being examined and proceeded with as the law in such case doth direct.

And be it further enacted,

Persons that have been intrusted or have any part of the estate in their hands, to be proceeded with in case of concealment.

[SECT. 5.] That the several judges of probate be, and they are hereby impow[e]red, by warrant as afores[*ai*]d, to convene before them any person that has been or may be intrusted by any executor or administrator with any part of the estate of the testator or intestate, and to be assisting to such executor or administrator in the execution of their trust, and shall refuse, upon due citation issued from the judge of probate for that purpose, to appear before him, and render a full account upon oath of any money, goods or chattels, and of any bonds, accounts or other papers left by the testator or intestate which he shall have taken into his hands or custody, and of his proceedings for and on behalf of such executor or administrator in his capacity as such. And if such person shall refuse to render account as afores[*ai*]d, such judge may proceed against him, as judges of probate are by law authorized to proceed against any person or persons suspected of concealment, who refuse to acquit themselves on oath.

And be it further enacted,

The judge to appoint guardians of minors above fourteen, in case.

[SECT. 6.] That when any minor above the age of fourteen years shall be cited by the judge of probate to choose a guardian, and such minor shall refuse or neglect to appear, or when any minor above the age of fourteen years, after appearing, shall refuse to ch[u][*oo*]se a guardian, or any guardian chosen by such minor shall be unable to give sufficient security, or when any minor above the age of fourteen years shall be out of this province; in every such case, the judge of probate shall have the same power to appoint a guardian as such judge by law would have in case such minor were under the age of fourteen years.

Provided, nevertheless,—

Proviso in case a minor lives more than ten miles from the judge.

[SECT. 7.] That when any minor above the age of fourteen years, living more than ten miles from the judge's dwelling-house, shall choose a guardian, such minor may have that choice certified to the judge by any justice of the peace in the same county, or by the town clerk, if no justice shall dwell in such town, which choice shall be deemed as good and valid in the law, as if done in said judge's presence.

And be it further enacted,

Judge to cite witnesses.

[SECT. 8.] That when any person shall be cited to appear as a witness before any judge of probate in any cause or hearing, and such person shall refuse to appear or to give evidence, he shall be liable to the like penalty or damage as he would be liable to for refusing to appear or give evidence in any of his maj[*es*]ty's courts within this province: and all sheriffs, deputy-sheriffs and constables, are hereby required duly to serve all legal warrants or summons to them directed by any judge of probate; and all contempt of authority in any cause or hearing before any judge of probate, shall and may be punished in like manner as such contempt of authority in any of his maj[*es*]ty's courts within this province might or could by law be punished.

How to proceed in case of contempt.

Limitation.

[SECT. 9.] This act to continue and be in force for the space of three years from the publication thereof, and no longer. [*Passed January* 5; *published January* 6, **1753.**

CHAPTER 13.

AN ACT FOR THE MORE EASY PARTITION OF LANDS OR OTHER REAL ESTATE, GIVEN BY WILL, AND HELD IN COMMON AND UNDIVIDED AMONG THE DEVISEES.

Preamble.

Whereas it is usual for persons by their last wills to devise their real estates to sundry of their children or others, to be divided to and amongst them in some certain proportion, a division whereof cannot be obtained by the act of the parties, by reason of their disagreem[*en*]t or some legal incapacity that some of them are under, and other methods for obtaining such partition are attended with charge, delay, and other inconvenienc[*i*]es, to the prejudice of such estate; for remedy whereof,—

Be it enacted by the Lieutenant-Governour, Council and House of Represent[*ati*]*ves*,

The judge of probate empowered to divide real estates given by will.

1692-3, chap. 14. 1703-4, chap. 12. 1719-20, chap. 10.

[Sect. 1.] That when and so often as any devisee, or his guardian, who holds any real estate in partnership with any other person or persons by force of any last will and testament, shall make application to the judge of probate of wills, &c[a]., in the county where such estates lie, for a division thereof, it shall and may be lawful for such judge of probate to order the whole of the real estate so devised, or that part of it the partition whereof is requested, to be divided to and amongst the devisees in proportion according to the will of the testator, by five good and discreet freeholders of the same county, to be appointed by the judge of probate, and to be sworn to the due performance of that service by the said judge; or by a justice of the peace of the same county, in case the estate to be divided be not within ten miles from the dwelling-house of the said judge: notice being first given to all parties concerned to be present at the making of such partition, if they see cause; which partition or division being return[*e*]'d into the probate office, and approved by the judge, and there recorded, shall be valid in the law to all intents and purposes, unless upon the appeal of any party aggr[ei][*ie*]ved at the partition so made, the same should be reversed or altered by the governour and council.

Preamble.

And whereas it sometimes happens that real estates devised by will lie in common and undivided with other real estate, and in order to a just and more convenient partition or division of the real estate so devised, it may be deem[*e*]'d necessary that partition or division should be first made between the estate so devised, and the other estate lying in common therewith,—

Be it further enacted,

Division to be made where lands lie in common.

[Sect. 2.] That in every such case it shall and may be lawful for the judge of probate of wills, &c[a]., in the county where such estate lies, to impower the five freeholders appointed as aforesaid, first to make partition or division between the lands or other real estate given by will, and any other lands or real estate lying in common therewith, notice being first given to all parties as above directed; and the charge of the division of any estate by virtue of this act, such charge being first set[*t*]led and allowed by the judge, shall be born by the several persons interested, in proportion to their respective interests therein.

Provided,—

Proviso in disputable cases.

[Sect. 3.] That no partition shall be made where the proportion belonging to the devisees, or any of them, shall appear by the tenor of the device to be disputable and uncertain.

Provided also,—

Guardians to be appointed for minors out of the province.

[Sect. 4.] That where any of the persons interested are minors, or out of the province, guardians be first appointed for such minors according to law, and some discreet and indifferent person be appointed by said judge, to represent and act for such absent party, who shall be allowed twelve months to appeal to the governour and council from such judgment.

Limitation. [SECT. 5.] This act to continue and be in force for the term of ten years, and no longer. [*Passed January* 5; *published January* 6, 1753.

CHAPTER 14.

AN ACT FOR ALLOWING NECESSARY SUPPLIES TO THE EASTERN INDIANS, AND FOR REGULATING TRADE WITH THEM, PREVENTING ABUSES THEREIN, AND FOR THE PREVENTING PERSONS HUNTING ON THE LAND TO THE EASTWARD OF SACO RIVER, OR TRADING WITH THEM, OTHER THAN THE TRUCK-MASTERS CHOSEN BY THE GENERAL COURT.

Preamble. 1742-43, chap. 2. WHEREAS the Indians in the eastern parts of this province, have many years since recognized their subjection and obedience to the crown of Great Britain, and have this year renewed the same, and have their depend[e][*a*]nce on this government for supplies of cloathing, provisions, and other necessaries; to the intent therefore that they may be furnished with the same at such easy rates as may engage them to a firm adherence to his majesty's interest,—

Be it enacted by the Lieutenant-Governour, Council and House of Represent[*ati*]*ves*,

Supplies to be sent to the eastern Indians. [SECT. 1.] That provisions, cloathing and other suitable supplies for a trade with the Indians, be procured with the several sums that have been, now are, or shall hereafter be granted for that purpose by the general court, and applied, from time to time, for supplying the said Indians as aforesaid, by such person or persons as shall annually be chosen by this court, who shall proceed according to the instructions they shall receive from this court, or from the commander-in-chief for the time being, by and with the advice of the council, on any emergency in the recess of this court; *provided* such instructions and directions be consistent with such instructions as are or may be given by the general court; and all supplies of cloathing, provisions and other necessaries shall be lodged at such places in the eastern parts of this province, and elsewhere, as the general court have or hereafter may order.

The governor and council to direct upon emergency in the recess of the court.

And be it further enacted,

Truck-masters to be appointed by the court. [SECT. 2.] That a suitable person be appointed by this court for each of the places where any of the goods aforesaid are lodged, as truck-masters for the managem[*en*]t of the trade with the Indians; and to be paid for his service such sum or sums as this court shall judge reasonable for his allowance in said capacity; and in case of the death or removal of any one or more of said truck-masters by mismanagem[*en*]t in said trust, during the recess of the court, another shall be put in his room by the commander-in-chief, with the advice of the council; which truck-masters shall be under oath, and give sufficient security to the province treasurer for the faithful discharge of their office, and shall observe the instructions which, from time to time, shall be given them, and shall not trade for themselves, only in the capacity of a truck-master, with the Indians, or any other person or persons; neither may any officer or soldier, residing at or within any of the truck-houses, or any other persons in the pay of this governm[*en*]t, either on account of themselves, or any other person or persons, presume to trade with the Indians, on board any ship or vessel or transport, in those parts, for any of the aforementioned goods; nor shall it be lawful for any other per-

By the governor and council, in case.

To give security.

Not to trade on their own account.

All other persons forbidden to trade with them.

son or persons to sell, truck, barter or exchange with any Indian or Indians, any strong beer, cyder, wine, rum, brandy, or any other strong liquor, cloathing, or any other thing whatsoever the Indians may want, on penalty of forty shillings, or six months' imprisonm[en]t for each and every offence above mentioned.

And be it further enacted,

[SECT. 3.] That the said truck-masters shall sell the goods to the Indians at the prizes set in the invoices sent them from time to time by the commissary, which shall be the same which he gave for the goods in the town of Boston, without any advance thereon; and shall allow the Indians, for their furrs and other peltry, as the market shall be at Boston, according to their several qualities, by the latest advices that they shall receive from the said officer, who shall send the prices to the several truck-masters at least twice in a year; viz[t]., every spring and fall; and the truck-masters may supply the Indians with rum in moderate quantities, as they shall, in prudence, judge convenient and necessary.

Rules for regulating the truck trade.

[SECT. 4.] And in case any of the truck-masters shall presume to sell any goods at higher rates than they are set at by the governm[en]t, or shall charge to the governm[en]t more for any furrs or other goods than they allowed the Indians therefor, such truck-masters, being convicted thereof, shall forfeit and pay the sum of one hundred pounds, and shall thenceforth be altogether disabled to hold or exercise any office within this governm[en]t; and the more effectually to prevent or detect any such pernicious practices, each and every truck-master, when and so often as he shall settle and adjust his account with the said officer appointed by this court for supplying the Indians, shall make oath before the said officer, who is hereby authorized and appointed to administer the same, in manner following; viz[t].,—

Penalty for not observing them.

You, A. B., do swear that the goods committed to you for the supply of the Indians, have been sold at no higher rates than they were set at by the government, and that you have charged for the furrs and goods you have made returns of, no more than you have paid the Indians for. So help you God.

Truck-masters to render account on oath.

And for the better discovery of such ill-disposed persons, who, thro[ugh] greediness of filthy lucre, and regardless of the publick good, shall privately sell or deliver any sort of strong drink to any Indian or Indians, of which it is difficult to obtain positive evidence, other than the accusation of such Indian or Indians,—

Be it further enacted,

[SECT. 5.] That the accusation and affirmation of any Indian or Indians, the accuser and accused being brought face to face at the time of trial, shall be accounted and held to be a legal conviction of the persons accused of giving, selling, or delivering wine, rum or any other strong drink or liquors to such Indian or Indians, unless the persons accused shall acquit himself, upon oath, which the court, in all such cases, are hereby impow[e]red to administer in the form following; viz[t].,—

Manner of proof of selling strong drink to the Indians by the Indians' accusation.

You, A. B., do swear that neither yourself, [n]or any other by your order, general or particular assent, privity, knowledge or allowance, directly or indirectly, did give, sell or deliver any wine, cyder, rum or other strong liquors or drink, by what name or names soever called or known, unto the Indian by whom and whereof you are now accused. So help you God.

Persons may purge themselves by oath.

And be it further enacted,

[SECT. 6.] That upon the complaint or information of any other person for the breach of this law, there being such circumstances as render

Manner of proceeding in case

of other person's complaint.

it highly probable, in the judgment of the justice before whom the trial is, that the person complained of is guilty of the breach of the said act; then, and in every such case, unless the defendant shall acquit himself upon oath, as aforesaid, to be administred to him by the justice before whom the trial shall be, the same shall be accounted a legal conviction of the defendant's giving, selling, or delivering of wine or other strong liquors, of which he or they shall be accused, and he or they shall pay and suffer the penalty already by this act provided; but in case the defendant shall acquit himself upon oath, to be administred to him as aforesaid, that then he shall recover against the complainant double his cost occasioned by such prosecution.

And be it further enacted,

Proceeding in case of complaint made to a justice of the peace.

[SECT. 7.] That upon the accusation of an Indian, or complaint of any other person, to any of his maj[*es*]ty's justices of the peace within this province, against any person for selling, giving or delivering any wine, rum or other strong liquors, to any Indian, contrary to the true intent and meaning of this act, the justice may tender to the person accused or complained of, the afores[*ai*]d oath, unless there be such other circumstances concurring as render it highly probable, in the opinion of the justice, that the person accused is guilty, which, if he refuses to take, he shall bind him in a bond of recognizance, not exceeding one hundred pounds, with sureties, to answer the same at the court of general sessions of the peace next to be held in the county where the offence is committed; but if the person accused shall acquit himself upon oath, as afores[*ai*]d, the justice shall dismiss the person, and allow him double his cost, ag[*ain*]st the complainant, occasioned by such prosecution.

And be it further enacted,

Penalty for false swearing.

[SECT. 8.] That if any person or persons shall hereafter be convicted of false swearing in any case in this act mentioned, he or they shall be liable to the same pains and penalties as is already by law provided ag[*ain*]st wilful perjury.

And be it further enacted,

Hunting in the eastern parts prohibited under penalty.

[SECT. 9.] That whoever shall hunt after or take any bever or other furrs, on land lying to the northw[*ar*]d of any English settlem[*en*]ts, and eastw[*ar*]d of Saco Truck-house, and be thereof convicted before a justice of the peace, shall forfeit and pay the sum of forty shillings, to be disposed of, one half to the informer, the other half to be paid to the truckmaster-general for the relief of the widows and children of such of the tribes of Indians as have usually traded at the truck-houses, as this court shall order and direct.

Continuance of this act.

[SECT. 10.] This act to continue and be in force for three years from the publication thereof, and no longer. [*Passed January* 5; *published January* 6, 1753.

CHAPTER 15.

AN ACT IN ADDITION TO AN ACT PASS'D THE THIRTEENTH YEAR OF HIS PRESENT MAJESTY'S REIGN, [E][*I*]NTIT[U]LED "AN ACT FURTHER TO EXEMPT PERSONS COMMONLY CALLED A[N]NABAPTISTS WITHIN THIS PROVINCE FROM BEING TAXED FOR AND TOWARDS THE SUPPORT OF MINISTERS."

1740-41, chap. 6.

WHEREAS, notwithstanding the provision already made by an act made and pass'd in the thirteenth year of his present majesty's reign, intit[u]led, "An Act further to exempt persons commonly called

A[n]nabaptists within this province from being taxed for and towards the support of ministers," in order to ascertain and make known what persons are of that perswasion which denominates them A[n]nabaptists, and who shall enjoy the privile[*d*]ges, and be esteemed as intit[u]led to the exemption from taxes, &c[a]., in said act mentioned, many doubts have already arisen thereon, and, in many cases, the said exemption has been extended to many persons to whom the same was never designed to extend; for preventing whereof for the future, and in order to ascertain more effectually what persons shall be esteemed and accounted as A[n]nabaptists, and to whom the said exemption[*s*] shall be hereafter extended,—

Be it enacted by the Lieutenant-Governour, Council and House of Represent[ati]ves,

[SECT. 1.] That no person for the future shall be so esteemed to be an A[n]nabaptist as to have his pol[e][*l*] or pol[e][*l*]s and estate exempted from paying a proportionable part of the taxes that shall be raised in the town or place where he or they belong, but such whose names shall be contained in the lists taken by the assessors, as in said act provided, or such as shall produce a certificate, under the hands of the minister and of two principal members of such church, setting forth that they consciencionsly believe such person or persons to be of their perswasion, and that he or they usually and frequently attend the publick worship in such church on Lord's days. Rule for denominating person, Anabaptists in the sense of the law.

And be it further enacted,

[SECT. 2.] That no minister, nor the members of any A[n]nabaptist church as aforesaid, shall be esteemed qualified to give such certificate as aforesaid other than such as shall have obtained from three other churches commonly called Annabaptists, in this or the neighbouring provinces, a certificate from each respectively, that they esteem such church to be one of their denomination, and that they conscien[t][*c*]iously believe them to be Annabaptists; the several certificates afores[*ai*]d to be lodged with the town clerk, where the Annabaptist, desiring such exemption, dwells, some time betwixt the raising or granting of the tax and the assessment of the same on the inhabitants. Rule for denominating Anabaptist ministers.

[SECT. 3.] This act to continue and be in force for five years from the publication thereof, and no longer. [*Passed January* 5; *published January* 6, 1753. Limitation.

CHAPTER 16.

AN ACT TO PREVENT THE BREAKING OR DAMNIFYING OF LAMPS SET UP IN OR NEAR STREETS, FOR ENLIGHTNING THE SAME.

WHEREAS the enlight[*e*]ning streets by lamps set up in or near the same, is not only ornamental, but very advantag[i][*e*]ous to those that pass and repass in and thro' the same in the night-time on their lawful business,— Preamble.

Be it enacted by the Lieutenant-Governour, Council and House of Represent[ati]ves,

[SECT. 1.] That if any person or persons shall wilfully break, remove or damnify any lamp or lamps set up or placed in or near any street for enlightning the same; or shall, between the s[i][*e*]tting of the sun and the rising thereof, extinguish the light of any such lamp, or be aiding and assisting therein, and be thereof convict, by the confession of the party or parties, or the oath of one or more credible witness before two justices of the peace, *quorum unus*, who are Damnifying and extinguishing of lamps set up in streets, &c., prohibited.

hereby impowered to hear and determine the same, he or they so offending, shall, for every such offence, pay a fine not exceeding five pounds, at the discretion of the court or justices before whom the conviction shall be, and costs of prosecution; and if any person or persons so convicted shall afterwards presume so to break, remove or damnify any such lamp or lamps, or extinguish the light thereof, and be thereof convicted as aforesaid, he or they so offending, shall, for every such offence, pay a fine not exceeding ten pounds, at the discretion of the justices or court before whom the conviction shall be, and costs of prosecution; and where any such offender shall not pay the fine within six hours after sentence given therefor, the offender shall be punished for such offence by being imprisoned not exceeding six months: and in case the person committing the offence afores[*ai*]d be a negro, Indian or molatto servant, such serv[*an*]t, instead of his being imprisoned, may, upon the first conviction, be publickly whipped, not exceeding ten stripes, and upon a [2d] [*second*] or any after conviction, not exceeding twenty stripes.

Penalty for the first offence;— for the second offence:— In case of negroes, Indians, or mulattoes.

[SECT. 2.] And all such fines shall be applied in this manner;. namely, out of the same the owner or owners of such lamp or lamps shall be paid the damages he or they have sustained by their lamps being so broken, removed or damnified; and the residue shall be to him or them that shall inform of any breach of this act, and prosecute the same to effect.

Application of fines.

Provided always,—

[SECT. 3.] That the owners of any lamps placed or set up as aforesaid, may at any time take down or remove the same, or extinguish the light thereof, anything in this act notwithstanding.

Proviso.

[SECT. 4.] This act to continue and be in force five years from the publication thereof, and no longer. [*Passed January* 5; *published January* 6, 1753.

Limitation.

CHAPTER 17.

AN ACT FOR REVIVING AND CONTINUING OF SUNDRY LAWS THAT ARE EXPIRED OR NEAR EXPIRING.

WHEREAS the several acts hereinafter mentioned, which are now expired, have been found useful and beneficial; namely, an act made in the nineteenth year of his present majesty's reign, intitled "An Act to subject the unimprov[*e*]'d lands within this province to be sold for payment of taxes, assessed on them by order of the great and general court, and votes and agreements of the proprietors thereof," and two other acts made in the twentieth year of said reign, one intitled "An Act to prevent damage being done unto Nosset Meadow by cattle and horse-kind feeding on the beach adjoining thereto," the other intitled "An Act to prevent the destruction of the meadow called Sandy-Neck Meadow in Barnstable, and for the better preservation of the harbour there"; and one other act made in the twenty-first year of the said reign, intitled "An Act to prevent the destruction of wild fowl"; and two other acts made in the twenty-second year of said reign, one an act intitled "An Act to prevent damage by fire in the towns of Boston and Charlestown," the other intitled "An Act to prevent damage being done on the beach in Biddeford and meadows adjoining to said beach, commonly known by the name of Winter-Harbour Beach"; and one other act, made in the twenty-third year of the aforesaid reign, intitled

Expired acts revived. Taxing of unimproved lands. 1745-46, chap. 9. Nosset meadow. 1746-47, chap. 27. Barnstable meadow. 1746-47, chap. 28. Wild fowl. 1747-48, chap. 3. Damage by fire. 1748-49, chap. 14. Biddeford meadows. 1748-49, chap. 18.

"An Act for the punishing such offenders as shall be anyways concerned in contriving, writing or sending any incendiary or menacing letters in order to extort sums of money or other things of value from any of his majesty's good subjects,"— Menacing letters. 1749-50, chap. 7.

Be it therefore enacted by the Lieutenant-Governour, Council and House of Repres[entati]ves,

[SECT. 1.] That the said recited acts and all and every article, clause, matter and thing therein respectively contained, be and they hereby are revived, and shall be in force from the publication of this act until the twenty-fifth day of March, which will be in the year of our Lord one thousand seven hundred and sixty-one, and from thence to the end of the then next session of the gen[*era*]l court. All revived.

And whereas the several acts hereafter mentioned, which are near expiring, have also been found useful and beneficial; namely, three acts made in the nineteenth* year of his present majesty's reign, one intitled "An Act in further addition to an act for regulating of fences, &c[a]"; another intitled "An Act in addition to the several laws of this province relating to the supporting of poor and indigent persons"; the other intitled "An Act to prevent firing the woods"; and two other acts made in the twenty-third year of the said reign, the one intitled "An Act to prevent the unnecessary destruction of alewives in the town of Middleborough," the other intitled "An Act to prevent any persons obstructing the fish in their passing up into Monatiquot River within the town of Braintre[y][*e*]." Acts near expiring continued. Fences, &c. 1740-41, chap. 19. Poor persons, 1742-43, chap. 18. 1742-43, chap. 22. Alewives in Middleborough. 1749-50, chap. 12. Fish in Monatiquot River. 1749-50, chap. 13.

Be it therefore further enacted,

[SECT. 2.] That the said last-recited acts, and all and every matter and thing therein respectively contained, shall be and hereby are continued from the time limit[*t*]ed for their expiration unto the twenty-fifth of March afores[*ai*]d, and from thence to the end of the next session of the general court, and no longer. [*Passed January* 5; *published January* 6, 1753. All continued.

CHAPTER 18.

AN ACT FOR FURTHER PREVENTING ALL RIOTOUS, TUMULTUOUS AND DISORDERLY ASSEMBLIES OR COMPANIES OF PERSONS, AND FOR PREVENTING BONFIRES IN ANY OF THE STREETS OR LANES WITHIN ANY OF THE TOWNS OF THIS PROVINCE.

WHEREAS many and great disorders have of late years been committed by tumultuous companies of men, children and negroes, carrying about with them pageants and other shews through the streets and lanes of the town of Boston, and other towns within this province, abusing and insulting the inhabitants, and demanding and exacting money by menaces and abusive language; and besides the horrid profaneness, impiety and other gross immoralities usually found in such companies, a person has lately been killed when orderly walking in the streets of the town of Boston, by one or more belonging to such tumultuous company; and the aforesaid practices have been found by experience to encourage and cultivate a mobbish temper and spirit in many of the inhabitants, and an opposition to all government and order,— Preamble.

* These acts were only revived and continued by 1745-46, chap. 17; but they were passed as in the margin.

Be it therefore enacted by the Lieutenant-Governour, Council and House of Representatives,

Persons disguised to go about with pageants and armed with any weapons, exacting money, &c.,—

[SECT. 1.] That if any persons, being more than three in number, and being arm'd all or any of them with sticks, clubs or any kind of weapons, or disguised with vizards, so called, or painted or disco[u]lour[e]d faces, or being in any other manner disguis[e]'d, shall assemble together, having any kind of imagery or pageantry with them, as a publick shew, in any of the streets or lanes of the town of Boston or any other town within this province, or if any person or persons being of or belonging to any company having any imagery or pageantry for a publick shew, shall, by menaces or otherwise, exact, require, demand or ask any money or other thing of value from any of the inhabitants or other persons, in the streets, lanes or houses of any town within this province, every person being of or assembled with such company, shall for each offence forfeit and pay the sum of forty shillings, or suffer imprisonm[en]t not exceeding one month; or if the offender shall be a negro servant, in lieu of the imprisonm[en]t, he may be whip['t][*ped*] not exceeding ten stripes, at the discretion of the justice before whom the trial shall be.

to be punished by fine or imprisonment.

Negroes, &c., may be punished by whipping.

And be it further enacted,

Persons carrying pageants, &c., in the night, though unarmed, to be punished.

[SECT. 2.] That if any persons to the number of three or more, between sun-setting and sun-rising, being assembled together in any of the streets or lanes of any town within this province, shall have any kind of imagery or pageantry for a publick shew, althô none of the company so assembled shall be arm'd or disguis[e]'d, or exact, demand or ask any money or thing of value, every person being of such company shall forfeit and pay the sum of forty shillings, or suffer imprisonment not exceeding one month, or if the offender shall be a negro servant, in lieu of the imprisonment he may be whip'[t][*d*] not exceeding ten stripes, at the discretion of the justice before whom the trial shall be.

And whereas bonfires have been sometimes kindled in the streets, lanes and other parts of several of the towns of this province, to the endangering of the lives and estates of the inhabitants,—

Be it further enacted,

Bonfires in streets or lanes forbidden.

[SECT. 3.] That if any person or persons shall set fire to any pile, or any combustible stuff, or be anyways concern[e]'d in causing or making a bonfire in any street or lane, or any other part of any town within this province, such bonfire being within ten rods of any house or building, every person so offending shall for each offence forfeit the sum of forty shillings or suffer imprisonment not exceeding one month, or if the offender shall be a negro servant, in lieu of the imprisonment, he may be whip'[t][*d*] not exceeding ten stripes, at the discretion of the justice before whom the trial shall be: the several fines in this act to be applied, when recovered, one half to the poor of the town where the offence shall be committed, and the other half to him or them that shall inform and sue for the same; and all masters are hereby made liable to the payment of the several fines as afores[*ai*]d, for the offences of their servants, and all parents for the offences of their children under age, not being servants.

Penalty.

Masters and parents liable for their servants and children.

Limitation.

[SECT. 4.] This act to continue and be in force for three years from the publication thereof, and to the end of the session of this court then next after, and no longer. [*Passed January* 5; *published January* 6, 1753.

CHAPTER 19.

AN ACT FOR CONFIRMING THE PROCEEDINGS OF WILLIAM FOYE, ESQ[r]., TREASURER OF THIS PROVINCE, DANIEL RUSSELL, ESQ[r]., COMMISSIONER OF IMPOST, AND JOHN WHEELWRIGHT, ESQ[r]., COMMISSARY-GENERAL, IN THEIR RESPECTIVE CAPACITIES.

WHEREAS William Foye, Esqr., having been elected and appointed treasurer of this province, Daniel Russell, Esqr., commissioner of impost, and John Wheelwright, Esqr., commissary-general, did, thrô inadvertency, enter upon the execution of their respective offices aforesaid, and do and transact sundry things therein before they had taken all the oaths by law required to be by them taken, whereby many inconvenienc[*i*]es may arise, notwithstanding their having since taken the oaths, unless the things by them so done and transacted be confirmed,— Preamble.

Be it therefore enacted by the Lieutenant-Governour, Council and House of Represent[*ati*]*ves*,

That all things done and transacted by William Foye, Esq[r]., as treasurer of this province; Daniel Russell, Esq[r]., as commissioner of impost; and John Wheelwright, Esq[r]., as commissary-general, in the execution of their respective offices aforesaid; and all and every the doings and transactions of any person or persons in the name and behalf of the said William Foye, Daniel Russell, and John Wheelwright, Esqrs., or either of them, in their respective capacities as afores[*ai*]d, or by v[i][*e*]rtue of any power or authority from them, or either of them, at any time before their, or either of their, taking the oaths by law required to be, by each of them, respectively taken, which would have been good and valid had they, before the doing thereof, taken such oaths, shall be and hereby are confirmed and made valid, their omission aforesaid notwithstanding. [*Passed January* 5; *published January* 6, 1753. Treasurer, commissioner-of-impost officer, and commissary-general, their doings in their offices, before their taking the oaths, confirmed.

CHAPTER 20.

AN ACT FOR PREVENTING DAMAGE BY HORSES GOING AT LARGE.

Be it enacted by the Lieutenant-Governour, Council and House of Representatives,

[SECT. 1.] That all horses and horse-kind, of one year old and upwards, that shall be suffered to go at large, shall be constantly fetter'd, with a sufficient pair of fetters, from the first day of April to the last day of November; and the owner of any such horse or horse-kind that shall be found going at large on the commons or ways in any town within this province, not being sufficiently fetter'd, shall forfeit and pay the sum of three shillings, to be recovered by action before a justice of the peace in the same county, and to be applied, one moiety thereof to the use of the poor of the town where such owner dwells, the other moiety to him or them that shall sue for the same. Horse-kind not to go at large without fetters. Penalty.

Provided, nevertheless,—

[SECT. 2.] That it shall be in the power of any town, legally assembled for that purpose, to give liberty for horses going at large without fetters, within the bounds of such town, or within such part or division of the town, from the first day of April to the last day of November, as shall be agreed on by the inhabitants at such meeting. Proviso.

And be it further enacted,

When such horses are to be impounded.

[SECT. 3.] That when the owner of any horse-kind going at large without being fetter'd as by this act is required, is unknown, in such case the party finding such horse or horse-kind may impound them, and otherwise proceed with them as the law directs in case of strays.

Limitation.

[SECT. 4.] This act to continue and be in force for the space of five years from the publication thereof, and no longer. [*Passed January* 5; *published January* 6, 1753.

ACTS

PASSED AT THE SESSION BEGUN AND HELD AT BOSTON, ON THE TWENTY-EIGHTH DAY OF MARCH, A. D. 1753.

CHAPTER 21.

AN ACT FOR ALTERING THE TIMES FOR HOLDING THE SUPERIOUR COURT OF JUDICATURE, COURT OF ASSIZE AND GENERAL GOAL DELIVERY, WITHIN THE COUNTIES OF PL[I][Y]MOUTH, BARNSTABLE AND BRISTOL.

WHEREAS the holding of the superiour court of judicature, court of assize and general goal delivery, at Taunton, within and for the county of Bristol, at the time appointed by law, being the second Tuesday in May yearly, would, as the style of the year is now altered, be, in many respects, inconvenient; *and whereas* the time for holding the same cannot be conveniently altered without altering likewise the times for holding the said court in the counties of Pl[i][*y*]mouth and Barnstable,— Preamble. 1742-43, chap. 32, § 2. 1746-47, chap. 15. 1747-48, chap 15.

Be it therefore enacted by the Lieutenant-Governour, Council and House of Repres[entati]ves,

[SECT. 1.] That the time for holding the sup[*eriou*]r court of judicature, court of assize and general goal delivery, at Taunton, within and for the county of Bristol, shall for the future be the second Tuesday of July yearly; and that the time for holding the said court at Pl[i][*y*]mouth, within and for the county of Pl[i][*y*]mouth, shall hereafter be the third Tuesday of July yearly; and that the time for holding the said court at Barnstable, for the counties of Barnstable and Dukes-county, shall hereafter be the fourth Tuesday of July yearly. Time of the superior court's sitting in Plymouth, Barnstable, and Bristol counties, altered.

And be it further enacted,

[SECT. 2.] That all writ[t]s and other process already issued, and all appeals, reviews, recognizances and other matters whatsoever taken, filed, continued or any ways depending, which were to be heard, tried or proceeded on in the said court, at the respective towns of Taunton, for the county of Bristol, Pl[i][*y*]mouth, for the county of Pl[i][*y*]mouth, Barnstable, for the counties of Barnstable and Dukes-county, according to the respective times or days already appointed by law, shall not fail or be discontinued, but be valid, and stand good to all intents and purposes in the law, and be heard, tried and determined at the respective times and days set and appointed by this act; and all officers and other persons concerned are required to conform themselves accordingly. [*Passed April* 12; *published April* 14, 1753. All matters depending in said courts, continued.

CHAPTER 22.

AN ACT IN ADDITION TO THE SEVERAL ACTS OR LAWS FOR THE SUPPRESSING OF LOTTERIES.

Preamble. 1719-20, chap. 8. 1732-33, chap. 14.

WHEREAS divers good and wholesome laws have been made and pass'd by this governm[*en*]t for suppressing of lotteries, and thereby preventing a vain and foolish expence, tending to the impoverishment of unwary people; which laws are in a great measure rendred ineffectual by the lotteries which are frequently set up in the neighbouring governm[*en*]ts, and by the sale of such lottery tickets to the inhabitants of this province,—

Be it therefore enacted by the Lieutenant-Governour, Council and House of Representatives,

Penalty for publishing lottery tickets of other governments.

[SECT. 1.] That if any person or persons, after the tenth day of May next, shall, within this province, be aiding or assisting in any lottery, by printing, writing, or any other ways publishing an account of the sale of such lottery ticket or tickets, such person or persons shall for such offence forf[ie][*ei*]t a sum not exceeding twenty pounds, to be recovered by information, plaint, bill or action at law, in any of his majesty's courts of record within this province; the one half thereof to his majesty, to be applied towards the support of this governm[*en*]t, and the other half to him or them that shall inform and sue for the same.

And be it further enacted,

Penalty for selling lottery tickets.

[SECT. 2.] That if any person or persons shall within this province give, sell, or otherwise dispose of, or shall therein offer or expose to sale any ticket or tickets in any lottery, excepting such as shall be established by act of parliament, or by act of this governm[*en*]t, such person or persons so offending, shall forfeit a sum not exceeding forty pounds for each ticket so given, sold or disposed of, or so exposed to sale, to be recovered in manner and for the use aforesaid.

And be it further enacted,

Penalty for buying lottery tickets.

[SECT. 3.] That if any person or persons within this province, shall receive or purchase any such lottery ticket or tickets, such person or persons shall likewise forfeit a sum not exceeding forty pounds for each ticket so received, or purchased by him or them, to be likewise recovered and applied as in manner aforesaid.

Provided, nevertheless,—

Person informing, to be freed.

[SECT. 4.] That if such receiver or publisher shall inform against or prosecute the person or persons who gave, sold or disposed of the same, so as that he or they shall be convicted of said offence, such receiver or purchaser shall not in that case be liable to the penalty aforesaid, but shall be wholly freed and exempted therefrom. [*Passed April* 12; *published April* 14, 1753.

CHAPTER 23.

AN ACT FOR ERECTING THE SECOND PRECINCT IN THE TOWN OF GROTON INTO A SEPERATE DISTRICT.

Be it enacted by the Lieutenant-Governour, Council and House of Represent[ati]ves,

Second precinct in Groton made

[SECT. 1.] That the Second Precinct in Groton, bounding southerly on the old country road leading to Townshend, west[er][*ward*]ly on

Townshend line, northerly on the line last run by the governm[*en*]t of New Hampshire, as the boundary betwixt that province and this, easterly to the middle of the river called Lancaster River, from where the s[*ai*]d boundary line crosses said river, so up the middle of the said river to where the bridge did stand, called Kemp's Bridge, to the road first mentioned, be and hereby is erected into a seperate district by the name of Pepperrell; and that the said district be and hereby is invested with all the privileges, powers and immunities that towns in this province by law do or may enjoy, that of sending a representative to the gen[*era*]l assembly only excepted; and that the inhabitants of said district shall have full power and right, from time to time, to jo[y][*i*]n with the said town of Groton in the choice of a representative or representatives, in which choice they shall enjoy all the privileges w[*hi*]ch by law they would have been [e][*i*]ntitled to if this act had not been made; and that the said district shall, from time to time, pay their proportionable part of the expence of such representative or representatives, according to their respective proportions of the province tax; and that the said town of Groton, as often as they shall call a meeting for the choice of a representative, shall give seasonable notice to the clerk of said district, for the time being, of the time and place of holding such meeting, to the end that said district may jo[y][*i*]n them therein; and the clerk of said district shall set up in some publick place in s[*ai*]d district a notification thereof accordingly, or otherwise give seasonable notice, as the district shall determine.

a district by the name of Pepperell.

Bounds thereof.

Privileges respecting a representative.

Provided, nevertheless, and be it further enacted,

[SECT. 2.] That the s[*ai*]d district shall pay their proportion of all town, county and province taxes, already set on or granted to be raised by said town, as if this act had not been made; and also be at one half the charge in building and repairing the two bridges on Lancaster River aforesaid in said district.

The inhabitants to pay their proportion of taxes already granted in Groton.

Provided also, and be it further enacted,

[SECT. 3.] That no poor person residing in said district, and who have been warned by the selectmen of said Groton to depart said town, shall be understood as hereby exempted from any process they would have been exposed to if this act had not been made.

Proviso about the poor.

And be it further enacted,

[SECT. 4.] That William Lawrence, Esq[r]., be and hereby is impowered to issue his warrant, directed to some principal inhabitant in s[*ai*]d district, requiring him to notify the inhabitants of said district to meet at such time and place as he shall appoint, to chuse all such officers as by law they are impowered to chuse for conducting the affairs of said district. [*Passed April* 12; *published April* 14, 1753.

Meeting to be called.

CHAPTER 24.

AN ACT FOR ERECTING THE SECOND PRECINCT IN THE TOWN OF LEICESTER INTO A SEPERATE DISTRICT.

Be it enacted by the Lieutenant-Governour, Council and House of Representatives,

[SECT. 1.] That the said Second Precinct in Leicester, bounding north on the town of Rutland, easterly on the First Parish in Leicester, southerly on land called the Country Gore, westerly on the town of Brookfield, be and hereby is erected into a seperate and distinct district by the name of Spencer; and that the said district be invested with all

A new district made in Leicester.

Bounds thereof.

Privileges.

the powers, privileges and immunities that towns in this province by law do or may enjoy, that of sending a [a] representative to the general assembly only excepted; and that the said district shall have full liberty and right, from time to time, to join with the town of Leicester in choosing a representative to represent them at the general assembly; and that the district shall, from time to time, be at their proportionable part of the expence of such representative; and that the town of Leicester, as often as they shall call a meeting for the choice of representatives, shall, from time to time, give seasonable notice to the clerk of said district for the time being, of the time and place of holding of said meeting, to the end that said district may join therein; and the clerk of said district shall set up in some publick place in said district a notification thereof accordingly.

Provided, nevertheless,—

And be it further enacted,

Taxes already made in Leicester to be good.

[SECT. 2.] That the said district shall pay their proportion of all town, county and province taxes already set on or granted to be raised by said town, as if this act had not been made.

And be it further enacted,

Meeting to be called.

[SECT. 3.] That Thomas Steel[e], Esq[r]., be and hereby is impowered to issue his warrant, directed to some principal inhabitant in said district, requiring him to notify and warn the inhabitants of said district, qualified by law to vote in town affairs, to meet at such time and place as shall be therein set forth, to choose all such officers as shall be necessary to manage the affairs of said district. [*Passed April* 12; *published April* 14, 1753.

CHAPTER 25.

AN ACT FOR ERECTING THE NORTHWESTERLY PART OF THE TOWN OF RUTLAND INTO A SEP[A][*E*]RATE DISTRICT.

Be it enacted by His Honour the Lieut[enan]t-Governour, Council and House of Represent[ati]ves,

A new district made in Rutland.

[SECT. 1.] That the northwesterly part of the township of Rutland, as delineated and described in a plan presented to the gen[*era*]l assembly in April [1749] [*one thousand seven hundred and forty-nine*], on file in the secretary's office, be and hereby is erected into a seperate district by the name of Rutland District; and that the s[*ai*]d district be and hereby is invested with all the powers and privile[*d*]ges that towns in this province by law do or may enjoy, that of sending a representative to the gen[*era*]l assembly only excepted; and that the inhabitants of said district shall have full power, from time to time, to join with the said town of Rutland in the choice of a representative, or of being chosen, in which choice they shall enjoy all the privileges w[*hi*]ch by law they would have been entitled to if this act had not been made, and shall pay their proportionable share or part of the expence of such representative; and that the said town of Rutland, as often as they call a meeting of such town for the choice of a representative, shall give seasonable notice to the clerk of said district, for the time being, of the time and place of holding such meeting, to the end that said district may join with them therein; and the clerk of s[*ai*]d district shall forthwith give direction to the constable or constables of said district, to notify as usual in other town meetings; and that such meeting[*s*], from time to time, shall be regulated by the selectmen of said town and district jo[y][i]ntly, or such of them as shall be present and take upon them the s[ai]d trust.

And be it further enacted,

[SECT. 2.] That all the acts done by the inhab[itan]ts of said district, as such, and by virtue of an order of the general assembly pass'd the fourteenth day of April, [1749] [*one thousand seven hundred and forty-nine*], which were otherwise according to law, shall be held good and valid to all intents and purposes; and all officers then chosen, and now in office, shall be esteemed proper officers, and invested with the same power and authority as if the said inhabitants had been erected into a seperate district by a law of this province, instead of said order.

Acts of the inhabitants of the said district since April, 1749, confirmed.

[*Passed April* 12; *published April* 14, 1753.

CHAPTER 26.

AN ACT FOR ERECTING THE SECOND PRECINCT IN THE TOWN OF HADLEY, INTO A SEPERATE DISTRICT.

Be it enacted by the Lieutenant-Governour, Council and House of Represent[ati]ves,

[SECT. 1.] That the said second precinct in Hadl[e]y, bounding westerly on Connecticut River, southerly on the north line of the town of Springfield, and easterly on the westerly line of the precinct or plantation called Cold Spring, and northerly on the highest part of the mountain called Mount Holyoke, so far as that extends, and from the Mountain Gate at the west end of said mountain, by the meadow fence, to Connecticut River, and from the east end of said mountain on an east line; from thence to Cold-Spring west line aforesaid,—be and hereby is erected into a seperate district by the name of South Hadley; and that the said district be and hereby is invested with all the privileges, powers and immunities that towns in this province, by law, do or may enjoy, that of sending a representative to the general assembly only excepted; and that the inhabitants of said district shall have full power and right, from time to time, to join with the said town of Hadl[e]y in the choice of a representative, in which choice they shall enjoy all the privileges which by law they would have been entitled to if this act had not been made; and that the said district shall, from time to time, pay their proportionable part of the expence of such representative, according to their respective proportions of the province tax; and that the said town of Hadl[e]y, as often as they shall call a meeting for the choice of a representative, shall give seasonable notice to the clerk of said district, for the time being, of the time and place of holding such meeting, to the end that said district may join them therein; and the clerk of said district shall set up, in some publick place in said district, a notification thereof accordingly.

Second precinct in Hadley made a district by the name of South Hadley.

Bounds thereof.

Privileges respecting a representative.

Provided, nevertheless,—

And be it further enacted,

[SECT. 2.] That the said district shall pay their proportion of all town, county and province taxes already set on or granted to be raised by said town, as if this act had not been made.

The inhabitants to pay their proportion of taxes already granted in Hadley,

Provided, also,—

[SECT. 3.] That the inhabitants of said district shall retain and enjoy the same right and share in all common and undivided land, and in

—and enjoy their part of the land;

all school lands in said township of Hadl[e]y, if any such there be, as they would have had if this act had not been made.

Provided, also,—

And be it further enacted,

—as also of moneys, &c.

[SECT. 4.] That of all monies or other personal estate, belonging to said town, if any such they have, the inhabitants of the said district shall have and enjoy a proportion thereof, equal to the proportion they paid of the charges of said town, according to their last town tax.

Provided, also,—

And be it further enacted,

Proviso about the poor.

[SECT. 5.] That no poor persons residing in s[*ai*]d district, and who have been warned by the selectmen of said Hadl[*e*]y to depart said town, shall be understood as hereby exempted from any process they would have been exposed to if this act had not been made.

And be it further enacted,

Meeting to be called.

[SECT. 6.] That Eleazer Porter, Esq[r]., be and hereby is impowered to issue his warrant, directed to some principal inhabitant in s[*ai*]d district, requiring him to notify the inhab[*itan*]ts of s[*ai*]d district to meet at such time and place as he shall appoint, to chuse all such officers as by law they are impow[e]red to chuse for conducting the affairs of said district. [*Passed April* 12; *published April* 14, 1753.

CHAPTER 27.

AN ACT FOR ANNEXING CERTAIN LANDS WITHIN THIS PROVINCE, TO THE COUNTIES OF HAMPSHIRE, WORCESTER AND YORK.

Be it enacted by the Lieutenant-Governour, Council and House of Representatives,

Province lands to be annexed to the county of Hampshire.

[SECT. 1.] That all the lands within this province not belonging to any particular county, and lying westward of Connecticut River, and from said river to the utmost western bounds of the province, be and hereby are annexed to the county of Hampshire.

And be it further enacted,

To the county of Worcester. 1730-31, chap. 8.

[SECT. 2.] That all the lands within this province adjo[y][*i*]ning to the county of Worcester, and not laid to any other county, be and hereby are annexed to the county of Worcester.

And be it further enacted,

To the county of York.

[SECT. 3.] That all the lands within this province lying eastward of the province of New Hampshire, be and hereby are annexed to the county of York. [*Passed April* 12; *published April* 14, 1753.

CHAPTER 28.

AN ACT FOR ESTABLISHING AND REGULATING FEES OF THE SEVERAL OFFICERS, WITHIN THIS PROVINCE, HEREAFTER MENTIONED.

Be it enacted by the Lieutenant-Governour, Council and House of Representatives, in General Court assembled,

Fees established. 1750-51, chap. 8.

[SECT. 1.] That from and after the publication of this act, the establishment of the fees belonging to the several officers hereafter mentioned, in this province, be as followeth; viz[t].,—

JUSTICE'S FEES.

For granting a writ[t] and summons, or original summons, one shilling. Justice's fees.
Subpœna, for each witness, one penny halfpenny.
Entring an action or complaint, two shillings.
Writ[t] of execution, sixteen pence.
Filing papers, each, one penny halfpenny.
Taxing a bill of cost, threepence.
Entring up judgment in civil or criminal cases, ninepence.
Copy of every evidence, original papers or records, eightpence per page for each page of twenty-eight lines, eight words in a line: if less than a page, fourpence.
Each recognizance or bond of appeal, one shilling.
Taking affidavits out of their own courts in order for the trial of any cause, one shilling, and eighteen pence for his travel every ten miles, and so in proportion;—
in other cases, together with certificate, examining and entring, sixpence;—
in perpetuam, to each justice, one shilling.
Acknowledging an instrum[*en*]t with one or more seals, provided it be done at one and the same time, one shilling.
A warrant, one shilling.
For granting a warrant, swearing apprizers relating to strays, and entring the same, one shilling and sixpence.

CORONER'S FEES.

For serving a writ[t], summons or execution, and travelling fees, the same as by this act is hereafter allowed to sheriffs. Coroner's fees.
Bail bond, one shilling.
Every trial where the sheriff is concern[*e*]'d, eightpence.
Taking an inquisition, to be paid out of the deceased's estate, eight shillings; if more than one at the same time, twelve shillings in the whole; if no estate, then, to be paid out of the county treasury, five shillings.
For travelling and expences for taking an inquisition, each day, four shillings.
The foreman of the jury, three shillings; and, ten miles accounted a day's travel, one shilling per day;—
every other juror, two shillings and sixpence, and travel the same as the foreman.
The constable, for his expences, summoning the jury and attendance, four shillings per diem.

JUDGE OF PROBATE'S AND REGISTER'S FEES.

For granting administration or guardianship,—
to the judge, three shillings.
To the register, for writing letter and bond of administration or guardianship, two shillings and sixpence. Judge of probate's and register's fees.
For granting guardianship of divers[e] minors to the same person and at the same time: to the judge, for each minor, one shilling and sixpence; to the register, for each letter of guardianship and bond, as before.
Proving a will or codicil[l]; three shillings and sixpence to the judge, and two shillings and sixpence to the register.
Recording a will, letter of administration or guardianship, inventory or acco[mp][*un*]t, of one page, and filing the same, one shilling and threepence;—
for every page more, of twenty-eight lines, of eight words in a line, eightpence.

For copy of a will and inventory, for each page, eightpence.
Allowing acco[mp][*un*]ts, three shillings to the judge.
Decree for set[*t*]ling of intestate estates: to the judge, three shillings;—for examining such acco[mp][*un*]ts, one shilling.
A citation, ninepence.
A *quietus:* to the judge, one shilling, to the register, one shilling.
Warrant or commission for apprizing or dividing estates; one shilling and sixpence to the judge; to the register, one shilling.
Making out commission to receive and examine the claims of creditors to insolvent estates; to the judge, one shilling, to the register, one shilling: for recording, eightpence each page.
Registring the commissioner's report, each page, eightpence.
Making out and entring an order upon the administrators for the distribution of the estate; to the judge, one shilling and sixpence, to the register, one shilling.
For proportioning such estate among the creditors, agreable to the commissioner's return, when the estate exceeds not fifty pounds, three shillings; and, above that sum, four shillings.
For recording the same, eightpence per page.

IN THE SUPERIOUR COURT.

JUSTICE'S FEES.

Justices of the superior court, fees.

Entring an action, six shillings and eightpence.
Taking special bail, one shilling and sixpence.
Allowing a writ[t] of error, two shillings.
Allowing a *habeas corpus*, sixteen pence.
Taxing a bill of cost, eightpence.
Attorney's fee, to be allowed in the bill of cost taxed, where the case is tried by a jury, twelve shillings; where it is otherw[ays][*ise*], six shillings.
Granting liberty for the sale or partition of real estates, one shilling.
On receiving each petition, one shilling.
Allowance to the party for whom costs shall be taxed, and to witness[es] in civil and criminal causes, one shilling and sixpence per day, ten miles' travel to be accounted a day; and the same allowance to be made to parties, as to witnesses at the inferiour courts, courts of sessions and before a justice of the peace.

CLERK'S FEES.

Clerk's fees.

A writ[t] of review, three shillings.
A writ[t] of *scire facias*, two shillings.
A writ[t] of execution, one shilling and sixpence.
A writ[t] of *facias habere possessionem*, two shillings and sixpence.
A writ[t] of *habeas corpus*, two shillings.
Copies of all records, each page, of twenty-eight lines, eight words in a line, ninepence; less than a page, sixpence.
Entring each action for trial, four shillings.
Entring each complaint, two shillings.
Each petition entred and read, one shilling.
Order on each petition granted, one shilling.
Receiving and recording a verdict, one shilling.
Entring a rule of court, ninepence.
Confessing judgm[*en*]t or default, one shilling.
Every action withdrawn or nonsuit, one shilling.
Entring an appearance, sixpence.
Acknowledging satisfaction of a judgment, on record, eightpence.
Examining each bill of cost, eightpence.

Continuing each cause, and entring the same next term, one shilling.
Filing each paper in each cause, one penny halfpenny.
Proving a deed in court, and certifying the same, one shilling.
Entring up judgm[*en*]t and recording the same at large, two shillings.
For each *venire*, to be paid out of the county treasuries, respectively, on the justice's certificate[*s*], threepence.
Every writ[t] and seal other than before mentioned, two shill[*in*]gs.
Every subpœna, one penny halfpenny.
Each recognizance, one shilling.

IN THE INFERIOUR COURT OF COMMON PLEAS.

JUSTICE'S FEES.

Justices of the inferior court, fees.

Entr[ing][*y*] of every action, five shillings and fourpence.
Taxing a bill of cost, sixpence.
Taxing a recognizance on appeals, one shilling.
Proving a deed, one shilling.
Attorney's fee, to be allowed in the bill of cost taxed, six shillings.

IN THE COURT OF GENERAL SESSIONS OF THE PEACE.

Court of general sessions of the peace.

Each day's attendance at the sessions, to be paid out of the fines, two shill[*in*]gs and eightpence.
Granting every licen[s][*c*]e to innholders and retailers, one shilling,—and taking their recognizances, one shilling.
Each recognizance in criminal causes, one shilling.

CLERK'S FEES.

Clerk's fees.

Every action entred, one shilling and fourpence.
Every writ[t] and seal, sixpence.
Every appearance, fourpence.
Entring and recording a verdict, eightpence.
Recording a judgm[*en*]t, one shilling.
Copies of all records, each page, of twenty-eight lines, eight words in a line, eightpence.
Every action withdrawn or nonsuit, eightpence.
Every execution, one shill[*in*]g and fourpence.
Confessing judgm[*en*]t or default, eightpence.
Acknowledging satisfaction of a judgm[*en*]t on record, eightpence.
A writ of *habeas corpus*, two shillings.
Continuing each cause, and entring at the next term, eightpence.
Each recognizance, one shilling.
Examining each bill of cost, sixpence.
Each *venire*, to be paid out of the county treasuries, respectively, by order of court, threepence.
Writ[t] of *facias habere possessionem*, two shillings.
Filing each paper, one penny.

GOVERNOUR AND SECRETARY'S FEES.

Governor and secretary's fees.

For registers: to the governour, three shillings; to the secretary, two shillings.
For certificates under the province seal: to the governour, three shil-l[*in*]gs; to the secretary, two shill[*in*]gs.
For warrants of apprizements, survey, &c[a].: to the govern[*ou*]r, three shill[*in*]gs; to the secretary, three shill[*in*]gs.

To the governo[*u*]r, for a pass to the castle, for each vessel, one shilling: wood-sloops and other coasting vessels, for which passes have not been usually required, excepted.

For a certificate of naval stores, in the whole, three shillings.

SECRETARY'S FEES.

Secretary's fees.

For engrossing the acts or laws of the general assembly, six shill[*in*]gs each, to be paid out of the publick revenue.

Every commission for the justices of each county, and comm[*issio*]n of oyer and terminer, six shillings and eightpence, to be paid out of the publick revenue.

Special warrant or mittimus by order of the govern[*ou*]r and council, each, two shillings and sixpence.

Every commission under the great seal, for places of profit, six shil[*in*]gs and eightpence, to be paid by the person commissionated.

Every bond, three shillings.

Every order of council to the benefit of particular persons, two shillings.

Every writ[t] for electing of assemblymen, directed to the sheriff or marshal under the province seal, five shill[*in*]gs, to be paid out of the publick revenue.

For transcribing the acts or laws passed by the gen[*era*]l assembly into a book, eightpence per page,—each page to contain twenty-eight lines, eight words in a line, and so proportionably,—to be paid out of the publick revenue.

Every commission for military officers, to be paid out of the public treasury, two shillings.

CLERK-OF-THE-SESSIONS' FEES.

Clerk-of-the-sessions' fees.

Entring a complaint or indictm[*en*]t, one shill[*in*]g and fourpence.

Discharging a recognizance, eightpence.

Each warrant for criminals, one shilling.

Every summons or subpœna, twopence.

Every recognizance for the peace or good behaviour, one shilling.

For every recognizance, one shilling.

Entring up judgm[*en*]t, or entring satisfaction of judgm[*en*]t, o[r][*n*] record, and copying, one shilling.

Warrant for county tax, one shilling.

For minuting the receipt of each petition, and order thereon, and recording, eightpence per page, as before.

Examining and casting the grand jury's acco[mp][*un*]ts, yearly, and order thereon, to be paid by the county treasurer by order of the court of sessions, one shill[*in*]g and sixpence.

For copies of all records or original papers, eightpence per page, as before.

For filing each paper, one penny.

For transmitting to the selectmen of every town in the county a list of the names of the persons in such town licensed the year before, sixpence, to be paid by each person licensed, and no more.

SHERIFF'S OR CONSTABLE'S FEES.

Sheriff's or constable's fees.

For serving an original summons, one shilling.

Every cap[i][*e*]as or attachm[*en*]t in civil, or warrants in criminal, cases for trial, sixteen pence; and for travel out, one penny half penny per mile; and for the return of the writ[t] (the travel to be inserted on the back of the writ[t] or orginal summons), one penny halfpenny per mile.

Levying executions in personal actions, for the first twenty pounds or under, ninepence per pound; above that, not exceeding forty pounds, fourpence per pound; above that, not exceeding one hundred pounds, twopence per pound; for whatsoever it exceeds one hundred pounds, one penny per pound.

For travel out, one penny halfpenny per mile, and for the return of the execution, one penny halfpenny per mile; all travel in serving writ[t]s and executions, to be accounted from the officer's house who does the service, to the place of service, and from thence to the court-house or place of trial.

For giving livery and seizin of real estates, six shillings, travel as before: if of different parcels of land, four shillings each.

For serving an execution upon a judgm[*en*]t of court for partition of real estates, to the sheriff, five shillings per day; and for travel and expences, threepence per mile out from the place of his abode: and to each juror, two shillings per day; and for travel and expences, threepence per mile.

Every trial, eightpence.

Every default, fourpence.

A bail bond, eightpence.

For making out every precept for the choice of represent[*ati*]ves, sending the same to the several towns, and returning it to the secretary's office, sixteen pence; to be paid out of the county treasuries, respectively.

To the officer attending the grand jury, each day, two shillings.

To the officer attending the petit jury, one shilling every cause.

For dispersing *venires* from the clerk of the sup[*eriou*]r court, and the province treasurer's warrants, fourpence each.

For dispersing proclamations, sixpence each,

For the encouragem[*en*]t unto the sheriff to take and use all possible care and diligence for the safe keeping of the prisoners that shall be committed to his custody, he shall have such salary allowed him for the same as the justices of the court of gen[*era*]l sessions of the peace within the same county shall think fit and order; not exceeding ten pounds per annum for the county of Suffolk, and not exceeding five pounds per annum ap[ei][*ie*]ce for the countys of Essex and Middlesex, and not exceeding three pounds per annum ap[ei][*ie*]ce in each of the other counties within the province: to be paid out of the treasury of such county.

CRYER'S FEES.

Calling the jury, fourpence. Crier's fees.

A default or nonsuit, eightpence.

A judgment affirmed on a complaint, eightpence.

A verdict, eightpence.

TO THE CAPTAIN OF CASTLE WILLIAM.

For every pass from the govern[*ou*]r for outward-bound vessels (coasters, fishing and wood vessels excepted), one shilling. Captain-of-the-castle's fees

GOALER'S FEES.

For turning the key on each prisoner committed, three shillings; viz[t]., one shilling and sixpence in, and one shilling and sixpence out. Jailer's fees.

For dieting each person, for a week, three shill[*in*]gs.

MESSENGER-OF-THE-HOUSE-OF-REPRES[ENTATI]VES' FEES.

For serving every warrant from the house of repres[*entati*]ves, wh[*ic*]h they may grant for arresting, imprisoning, or taking into custody any person, one shilling and sixpence. Messenger-of-the-house-of-representatives' fees.

For travel, each mile out, twopence per mile.

For keeping and providing food for such person, each day, one shill[*in*]g and sixpence.

For his discharge or dismission, one shill[*in*]g and sixpence.

GRAND JURORS' FEES.

Grand jurors' fees.

Foreman, per day, two shillings and sixpence.

Each other juror, two shillings.

PETIT JURORS' FEES.

Petit jurors' fees.

To the foreman, in every cause at the sup[*eriou*]r court, two shill[*in*]gs; to every other juror, one shill[*in*]g and sixpence.

To the foreman, in every cause at the inferio[*u*]r court, or sessions, one shilling; to every other juror, tenpence.

Except the county of Suffolk, which is to be regulated by the law relating to jurors, which pass'd *Anno* one thousand seven hundred and forty-nine.

FOR MARRIAGES.

Fees for marriages.

For each marriage, to the minister or justice officiating, four shill[*in*]gs.

For recording it: to the town clerk, to be paid by the justice or minister, fourpence; and to the clerk of the sessions, to be paid by the town clerk, twopence.

To the town clerk, for every publishm[*en*]t of the banns of matrimony, and entring thereof, one shilling.

Every certificate of such publishm[*en*]t, sixpence.

Recording births and deaths, each, twopence.

For a certificate of the birth or death of any person, threepence.

COUNTY REGISTER'S FEES.

County register's fees.

For entring or recording or copying any deed, conveyance or mortgage, for the first page, ninepence; and eightpence per page for so many pages more as it shall contain, accounting after the rate of twenty-eight lines, of eight words in a line, to each page; and proportionably for so much more as shall be under a page; and threepence for his attestation on the original, of the time, book and folio where it is recorded: the fees to be paid at the offering the instrument;—

and for a discharge of a mort[g]age, eightpence.

And be it further enacted,

Penalty for taking excessive fees.

[SECT. 2.] That if any person or persons shall demand or take any greater fee or fees, for any of the services afores[*ai*]d, than is by this law provided, he or they shall forfeit and pay to the person or persons injured, the sum of ten pounds for every offence, to be recovered in any court proper to hear and determine the same.

Limitation.

[SECT. 3.] This act to continue and be in force for the space of three years from the publication thereof, and from thence to the end of the next session of the gen[*era*]l court, and no longer. [*Passed April* 12; *published April* 14, 1753.

NOTES.—There were but three sessions of the General Court this year. The first session was held at Concord, on account of the small-pox which then prevailed in Boston. On the fifth of June the Assembly was prorogued to September 27th (16th, Old Style), but was again prorogued, by proclamation, August 28th, to meet at Harvard College on the twenty-second of November, following. The second day of this session, at the request of the House of Representatives, the Lieutenant-Governor ordered an adjournment to the court-house at Boston, where the remainder of this, and the third, session were held.

The adoption of the Gregorian Calendar took effect this year: the day following the 31st of December was called January 1, 1752; and eleven days were struck out after the third day of September, which was reckoned the fourteenth. The act of parliament referred to in the following order, is reserved for the Appendix:—

"January 22, 1752. In Council, Ordered that the Act of Parliam[t] pass'd in the twenty fourth year of his present Majesty's Reign, entitled, An Act for regulating the Commencem[t] of the Year, & for correcting the Calender now in Use, be printed & bound up with the Laws of this Province, for the better Information of the Inhabitants thereof, & that it be recorded in the Secretary's Office in the Book of Laws.——In the House of Repres.[ves] Read & concur'd.——

Consented to by the Lieut[t] Governor."—*Council Records, vol. XIX., p.* 424.

No further trace has been found of the proceedings of the Home Government respecting the acts of the first session, than a memorandum, in the minutes of the Lords Commissioners for Trade and Plantations, that they were received by the Board, February 2, 1753, and were, by them, sent to Mr. Lamb. The date of the letter of Secretary Willard, transmitting them, is November 30, 1752.

The acts of the second and third sessions were certified for transmission, December 30, 1753, and received by the Privy Council, from Mr. Bollan, the Agent of the Province, May 15, 1754. On the 29th of May they were referred to a committee, who, in turn, referred them to the Lords of Trade, June 14.

The Board of Trade ordered them to be sent to Mr. Lamb, for his opinion, thereupon, in point of law, July 23, 1754. The report of Sir Matthew Lamb—which was, that "upon perusal and consideration of these Acts I have no objection thereto in point of law."—was read at the Board, March 24 and 25, 1756, and, on the latter day, the draught of a report was ordered to be prepared, which, having been completed, was signed on the 6th of April.

This report of the Lords of Trade is dated April 13, 1756, and represents that chapters 11, 12, 14, 18, and 28 "were for temporary services and are either expired by their own Limitation or the purposes for which they were enacted have been completed," and that chapters 9, 10, 13, 15, 16, 17, 19, 20, 21, 22, 23, 24, 25, 26, and 27 "relate to the internal œconomy of the Province and appear to have been enacted for its private Convenience, and" —the report continues—" We see no reason why His Majesty may not be graciously pleased to confirm them."

An order was, accordingly, passed in the Privy Council, dated July 7, 1756, confirming chapters 9, 10, 13, 15, 16, 17, 19, 20, 21, 22, 23, 24, 25, 26, and 27.

Chap. 2. An engrossed bill, with this same title, was passed to be enacted by both houses at the April session of 1751–52, but did not receive the Lieutenant-Governor's signature. It is referred to in the margin of the record thus: "Engross'd Bill ab[t] Fire Wards pass[d] by both Houses"—*Council Records, vol. XIX., p.* 445.

Chap. 3. "June 4, 1752. In the House of Representatives Voted that M[r] Speaker & M[r] Allen with such as the Hon[ble] Board shall join, be a Committee to farm out the Excise for the County of Suffolk——In Council Read & Concur'd & Jacob Wendell Esq[r] is joined in the Affair——Consented to by the Lieutenant Governor."

On the same day the following persons were chosen committees to farm out the excise for the respective counties hereafter named; viz.,—

Capt. Davis and Mr. Newhall on the part of the House, and Benjamin Lynde, Esq., on the part of the Council, for the county of Essex;—

Maj. Lawrence and Mr. Trowbridge on the part of the House, and Ezekiel Chever, Esq., on the part of the Council, for the county of Middlesex;—

Col. Porter and Maj. Worthington on the part of the House, and Oliver Partridge, Esq., on the part of the Council, for the county of Hampshire;—

Capt. Wilder and Mr. Steel on the part of the House, and John Chandler, Esq., on the part of the Council, for the county of Worcester;—

Col. Bradford and Mr. Winslow on the part of the House, and John Cushing, Esq., on the part of the Council, for the county of Plymouth;—

Col. Otis and Mr. Freeman on the part of the House, and John Otis, Esq., on the part of the Council, for the county of Barnstable;—

Col. Leonard and Capt. White on the part of the House, and George Leonard, Esq., on the part of the Council, for the county of Bristol;—

Maj. Cutt and Capt. Plaistead on the part of the House, and John Hill, Esq., on the part of the Council, for the county of York;—

Col. Mayhew and Capt. Norton on the part of the House, and Payne Mayhew, Esq., on the part of the Council, for the county of Dukes county;—

Mr. Folger and Mr. Richard Coffin on the part of the House, and Josiah Coffin, Esq., on the part of the Council, for the county of Nantucket.—*Council Records, vol. XIX., p.* 473.

"November 29th 1752. A Report of the Committee appointed by this Court to Let out to Farm the Excise on Wine Liquours &c for the County of Worcester, shewing that they have let out the same for one Year to Mr Ezra Taylour of Southborrô for the sum of £75. 6. 8. Lawfull Mony and have taken Bonds and delivered them to the Treasurer; Their Accompt of Time and Expence Amounting to £2. 9. 4 ——In the House of Repre[tves] Read & Accepted; And the within mentioned Sum is allowed accordingly In Council Read & Concur'd—— Consented to by the Lieutenant Govern[r]

A Report of the Committee appointed to let out to Farm the Excise upon Wine, Liquours &c for the County of Middlesex, shewing that they have let out the same for one Year to M[r] John Hunt of Watertown for the sum of £722. 13. 4 and have taken Bonds and lodged them with the Treasurer, their Accompt of Time and Expence, Amounts to £2. 14. 2—— In the House of Represent[ves] Read & Accepted, & Ordered that the within Accompt be allowed——In Council Read & Concur'd Consented to by the Lieutenant Governor

A Report of the Committee appointed to let out to Farm the Excise on Wine Rum &c for the County of York in the present Year, shewing that they have let out the same to Jeremiah Moulton jun[r] of York for £66. 12——& have taken Bond & Lodged it with the Treasurer; Their Accompt of Time & Expence being £2. 10. 5. In the House of Representatives, Read & Accept[d] & Order[d] that this Accompt be allowed In Council Read & Concur'd——Consented to by the Lieu[t] Governor."—*Ibid., pp.* 490, 491, 492.

The above reports from the committees appointed to farm out the excise for Worcester, Middlesex and York counties were followed by reports from the committees for the other counties; and the dates of their reports, with the names of the farmers of excise appointed by them respectively, are as follows:—

December 12, 1752. Hampshire county; to Noah Ashly Esqr for £15s —*Ibid.*, *p.* 509.

December 27, 1752. Plymouth county; to Mr. Benjamin White of Boston, for £243. 6. 8. —*Ibid.*, *p.* 525.

December 27, 1752. Bristol county; to Mr Benjamin White of Boston, for £94.—*Ibid.*, *p.* 526.

December 28, 1752. Suffolk county; to William Story of Boston, for £2138. 13s.—*Ibid.*, *p.* 527.

April 6, 1753. Barnstable county; to David Freeman Esqr for £142. 8.—*Ibid.*, *vol.* XX., *p.* 10.

April 7, 1753. Dukes county; to Gershom Cethcart for £17.—*Ibid.*, *p.* 15.

April 12, 1753. Essex county; to Mr. Timothy Fuller of Middleton, for £647. 6. 8.—*Ibid.*, *p.* 20.

Chap. 18. "November 27. 1752. In Council; Whereas, under Pretence of Commemorating the Preservation of the King and Parliament from the Traterous Conspiracy commonly known by the name of the Gun Powder Plot, many grievous Disorders for divers years past have been committed in the Town of Boston on the Evening of the fifth of November, & the Pageants or Shows generally made use of on that Occasion, have of late years been greatly multiplied, the Disorders have proportionably Increased; And on the Evening of the seventeenth of November this present year according to the late alteration of the Calender, the day before which answers to the fifth, having been set apart by this Government to be observed in a religious Manner, a Person was killed in the Street of the said Town, by a disorderly riotous Crew of People; And furthermore, it is evident that instead of encouraging an Abhorrence of Popery & Forming a Spirit of Loyalty in the Youth of the Town, the aforesaid Practices have been attended with horrible Profaness, & other the greatest Immoralities, & have raised a Mobbish tulmultous Spirit in Children and Youth & has a direct Tendency to promote a Contempt of Government & Order; Therefore,——Voted that Jacob Wendell Andrew Oliver & Thomas Hutchinson Esq^rs with such as the hon^ble House shall join be a Committee to prepare & bring in a Bill for the effectual preventing the like Disorders for the future;——In the House of Representatives Read & Concur'd. & Mr Speaker Mr Gray Col^o Otis & Mr Tyng are joined in the affair."—*Council Records*, *vol.* XIX., *p.* 487.

Chap. 19. "January 4. 1753. Report of the Committee on the Affair of the Treasurers not being Sworn.

The Committee appointed for the within mentioned Purpose Having met & Considered the Affair, are humbly of Opinion that Mr Foye's neglecting to take the Oath required by Law respecting the Bills of the other Governments, renders it necessary that an Act should be pass'd, to confirm all the otherwise legal Acts and doings of the said Mr Foye as Province Treasurer, and that a Bill be brought in accordingly Benj^a Lynde per Order.

Which Report was accepted by both Houses with the following Additions & Amendments, viz, That this Committee prepare the Draught of a Bill accordingly, That the Bill provide also that the past Proceedings of Daniel Russell and John Wheelwright Esq^rs be made good and Valid thô they have not been qualifyed according to Law. And that Mr Treasurer Foye be directed, if he see fit, to take the Oath aforesaid, in Order to qualify him to Act for the future in his Office as Mr Russell & Mr Wheelwright have done ——And that the Treasurer be enjoined to perfect his Particular Accompt of the State of the Treasury to the first day of February next agreeable to the Vote of the House entered the 4th of June last and that he lay the said Account before the Committee of both Houses appointed for that Purpose on the thirtieth of Novr last within six weeks from this time, On Pain of the Displeasure of this Court. Consented to by the Lieutenant Governor."—*Ibid.*, *p.* 534.

Chap. 21. "December 1st 1752. In the House of Representatives; Whereas by Law the Court of General Sessions of the Peace and Inferiour Court of Common Pleas for the County of Bristol, are to be held at Taunton on the second Tuesday of December Instant, & Many Concerned in the s^d Court are Members of the General Court, Which it is probable will be Sitting at that Time;

Therefore Ordered that the said Court of General Sessions of the Peace & Inferiour Court of Common Pleas be and they hereby are Adjourned to the last Tuesday of Jan^ry next; And all Officers & others concerned in said Courts are to conform themselves accordingly, & that all Processes, & other Matters and things depending in said Courts & which are by Law to be heard tried & proceeded upon at said Term shall be heard tried and proceeded on the said last Tuesday of January next & the Justices of the said Courts are hereby required to conform themselves accordingly In Council Read & Concur'd——Consented to by the Lieutenant Govern^r."—*Ibid.*, *p.* 494.

Chap. 24. Novem^r. 24. 1742. A Petition of John Ormes in behalf of the Settlers of the Westerly part of the Town of Leicester, shewing that the said Westerly half was reserved to themselves by the Proprietors when they granted the other part to those that should settle thereon; that the Petitioners are so far distant from the body of the Town as that they cannot attend their duty there without great difficulty, and that they can have little or no benefit from the School; and forasmuch as the said Town have Voted their Consent to their being a separate Township, and they are daily increasing and like to be a competent number if they had the Privileges of a Town; therefore praying that this Court would erect them, according to the bounds set forth in their Petition, into a Township. In the House of Represent^ves. Read and Ordered that the prayer of the Petition be granted, and

the Petitioner is allowed to bring in a Bill accordingly. In Council: Read and Concur'd."
—*Ibid., vol XVII., b. 3, p.* 501.

"Novem. 30. 1742. A Bill entitled An Act to erect the Westerly part of Leicester into a separate and distinct Township:—Having been read Three several times in the House of Representves, and there Pass'd to be Engross'd. In Council; Read a First time."—*Ibid., p.* 512.

"Decemr 2. 1742. The Bill entitled An Act for erecting the Westerly Part of the Town of Leicester in the County of Worcester into a Township by the Name of——; In Council; Read a Second time, and Pass'd a Concurrence to be Engross'd."—*Ibid , p.* 516.

"Decem. 4. 1742. An Engross'd Bill entitled An Act for erecting the Westerly half of the town of Leicester into a Township by the name of——; Having been read Three several times in the House of Representatives and in Council:—Pass'd to be Enacted by both Houses."—*Ibid., p.* 524.

"April 2. 1743. A Petition of John Ormes in behalf of the Proprietors and Settlers of the Westerly part of Leicester, Shewing that notwithstanding they have built a Meeting house and had preaching among them for some years pass'd, yet the Town have taxed them for the support of the Minister in the other part; and therefore Praying that what money they have already paid for the Ministry in the other part since they have had preaching among them, may be returned, and that they may be exempted from that charge for the future. In Council; Read and Ordered that the Prayer of the Petition be so far granted as that the Petitioners be freed from paying any part of the charge that has arisen in the year 1742, for the support of the Ministry at Leicester, as also any charge that may arise for the future towards the support of the Ministry in the East half of said Town, in case the Petitioners be constantly provided with an able learned and orthodox Minister and of good conversation to dispence the Word of God to them. In the House of Representves; Read and Concur'd. Consented to W: SHIRLEY.—*Ibid., p.* 629.

"Septemr 14. 1743. A Petition of Jonathan Witt and John How, & divers other Inhabitants of the Easterly part of Leicester and Southerly part of Rutland, setting forth their great difficulties in attending the publick Worship of God in their respective Towns, that they have petitioned them for their Consent to their being set off a separate Precinct, which they refused to grant; and therefore praying that this Court would make them a distinct Precinct by the Bounds particularly described in this Petition. In the House of Representves; Read and Ordered that the Petitioners serve the Towns of Leicester and Rutland with Copies of this Petition, that they shew cause if any they have, on the first Tuesday of the next Sitting of this Court why the prayer thereof should not be granted. In Council; Read and Concur'd. Consented to W: SHIRLEY."—*Ibid., b.* 4, *p.* 148.

"March 22 1743. On the Petition of Jonathan Witt, John How, and others, Inhabitants of the Towns of Leicester & Rutland, Praying as enter'd Septemr. 14. 1743. In Council; Ordered that the consideration of this Petition be further refer'd to the next May Sessions, that so the Petitioners may have an opportunity to notify the Towns of Leicester & Rutland of this Order; which they have hitherto failed of doing. In the House of Representves; Read and Concur'd. Consented to *J: BELCHER*.*—*Ibid., p.* 350.

"June 19. 1744. A Petition of Matthias How in behalf of divers Inhabitants of the Towns of Leicester and Rutland, praying for a new Precinct, showing that by reason of divers accidents and occurrences the said Petition which was entered the 14th of September last, has never yet been fully considered and determined but is now discontinued; and therefore praying that the said Petition may be revived and determined upon. In Council; Read and Ordered that the Petition within refer'd to, be and hereby is revived, and the consideration thereof further refer'd to the second Tuesday of the next Sitting of this Court; and that the Memorialist serve the Towns of Leicester & Rutland with copies of this Memorial and the before mentioned petition, that so they may shew cause, at the day aforesaid, if any they have, why the Prayer thereof should not be granted. In Council; Read and Concur'd. Consented to W: SHIRLEY."—*Ibid., p.* 425.

"July 18. 1744. A Petition of John Ormes in behalf of the Proprietors of the Westerly part of the Town of Leicester, praying they may be erected into a separate Precinct, and the Inhabitants enjoy the Privileges of Inhabitants of other Precincts. In the House of Representves; Read and Voted that the Inhabitants and Estates in the Westerly half of the Town of Leicester bounding Easterly on the Settlers part, so called, to the ancient Divisional Line formerly established between the Proprietors and Settlers Northerly and Southerly on the North and South Bounds of said Town, and West on Brookfield East Bounds, be and hereby are created into a separate and distinct Parish or Precinct and invested with all the privileges and powers which other Parishes do by law enjoy. In Council; Read and Concur'd. Consented to W: SHIRLEY."—*Ibid., p.* 457.

"Aug. 17. 1744. On the Petition of divers Inhabitants of Leicester and Rutland, praying to be made a separate Precinct In Council; Read again together with the answers, and the matter being fully considered; Ordered that this Petition be dismiss'd. In the House of Representves. Read & Non Concur'd, & Ordered that the consideration of this Petition be refer'd till the next Sitting of the Court. In Council; Read and Non Concur'd."—*Ibid., p.* 490.

"Decemr 22. 1749. The Secretary delivered the following Message from the Lieutt Governour to both Houses, vizt

Gentlemen of the Council & House of Representves,

The Secretary has laid before me for my Signing an Engross'd Bill pass'd both Houses for incorporating the West or Second Precinct in the Township of Leicester into a distinct & Separate Township &c. Whereupon I must Acquaint you that I am restrained from giving my Consent to this Bill, unless Provision be made that the Number of Representves be not thereby increased, or a clause for suspending the Execution of the Act until his Majesty's Pleasure shall be known thereupon, be inserted in the said Bill."—*Ibid., vol. XIX , p.* 96.

* This is evidently an error of the recording clerk, and is underscored in the original.

"January 4, 1749. The following Message to his Honor the Lieuten[t] Governor, was brought up from the House of Represent[ves] by James Allen Esq[r] & others viz

May it please your Honor.

The House taking into consideration your Honor's Message of the 22[d] of December, wherein you are pleased to inform the two Houses, that you are restrained from your giving your consent to an Engross'd Bill, pass'd both Houses, for incorporating the west or second Precinct into a distinct Township, unless Provision be made that the number of Represent[ves] be not thereby increased, or a Clause for suspending the Execution of the Act, until his Majesty's pleasure should be known thereupon, be inserted in said Bill; beg leave to say, they are at a loss to know, why your Honor apprehends yourself restrained from giving your consent to the bill, unless provision be made that the number be not thereby increased, or a Clause for suspending the Execution of the Act, until his Majesty's pleasure should be known thereupon, be inserted in the said Bill; but must suppose your Honor induced so to judge, either from the Reason & Nature of the thing, or from some Restraint, in their late Maj[ties] Charter to this Province; which are the only Rules of Government, in this His Majestys Province, in neither of which can the House find any Restraint, in which Opinion the House are the more confirmed, from the Fate of a late Bill in the Honb[le] House of Commons of which your Honor is well knowing.

The House apprehend the forming that part of Leicester, into a distinct Township, will be for the prosperity of his Majestys Subjects, in which his Majesty always takes pleasure; the end of Government being his Majesty's Honor & the happiness of his Subjects, & that the people be fully represented is for his Majesty's Honor & the happiness of his Subjects, & is agreable to his Majestys Charter, & the Laws of this Province, is the Opinion of this House; But were it not so, the number of Represent[ves] the Town of Leicester by Charter & The Laws of this Province are now entitled to, are not enlarged by this Bill; And therefore the House flatter themselves. your Honor will give your Consent."—*Ibid.*, *p* 114.

The profession, in the above message from the House, of ignorance as to why the Lieutenant-Governor should suppose himself restrained from assenting to this bill, without a suspending clause, will, in the face of the royal instructions on that subject, seem disingenuous, if it is not borne in mind that those instructions were issued to the Governor, and not, expressly, to the Lieutenant-Governor; who, it was claimed, should be guided solely by the terms of the charter, and a consideration of the welfare of the people. This point, it must be admitted, is extremely fine, but not smaller than many objections gravely entertained by the Ministry in their dealings with the Province.

Chap. 25. "June 6. 1754. A Petition of the Inhabitants of Rutland District, setting forth their Difficulties in supporting the publick Charges of the said District, without the Assistance on the Non Resident Proprietors, Praying that they may be impowered by this Court to lay a Tax of Three farthings ℔ Acre ℔ Annum on all the Lands there, for the Space of Five Years for defraying the Ministerial & other publick Charges there. In the House of Representatives, Read & Ordered that the Petition[rs] serve the Proprietors of said District, by inserting the Substance of this Petition in one or more of the publick News Papers, three Weeks successively, so that they shew Cause, if any they have, on the second Fryday of the next sitting of this Court, why the Prayer thereof should not be granted:—In Council Read & Concur'd."—*Council Records, vol.* XX, *p.* 255.

"October 26. 1754. On the Petition of John Chaldwell Agent for the Inhabitants of Rutland District, as Enter'd the 6th of June last. In Council; Read again together with the Answer of Jonas Clark Esq[r] Proprietors Clerk; And Ordered that Benjamin Lynde & Eleazer Porter Esq[rs] with such as the Hon[ble] House shall join, be a Com[tee] to hear the Parties, consider the Petition and Answer, and report what the judge proper for this Court to do thereon:——In the House of Representatives Read & Concur'd, & Col[o] Brattle, Capt. Mercy and M[r] Gibbs of Newtown are joined in the Affair."—*Ibid.*, *p.* 295.

"November 2. 1754. Report on the Petition of the District of Rutland; viz[t],

The Committee on the Petition of John Caldwell, for and in behalf of the District of Rutland, having considered the said Petition with the Answer made to the same, and heard such of the Parties as were pleased to attend; have agreed to and humbly report it as their Opinion, That on the Treasurer of said Districts lodging in the Hands of the Proprietors Clerk, an Account of the Sums collected on the Tax ordered by the General Court in the Year 1749, with an Account, how and in what Manner the same has been expended, the Assessors of the District of Rutland should be impowered to assess the Proprietors Lands in said District, and all other Lands in the same, excepting those granted to the Minister or Ministry, at the Rate of an Half-penny per Standard Acre, for the three Years next ensuing; the Sum arising thereby to be employed for the finishing the Meeting House, Maintaining a Minister, clearing of Roads or other publick Services; and that the Collectors for the time being be impowered agreable to the Law, to collect the same, and pay it unto the Treasurer of the said District, who shall be appointed to receive the same; Which is submitted In the Name and by Order of the Committee, Benjamin Lynde.

In Council; Read & Accepted & Ordered that the Assessors of the said District be and hereby are impowered to assess the said Lands, at the Rate of one half penny per Standard Acre for three Years next ensuing and the Collectors to collect & pay in the same, and that the Sum arising thereby be disposed of accordingly. In the House of Representatives Read & Concur'd—Consented to by the Governour."—*Ibid.*, *p.* 306.

ACTS,

PASSED 1753–54.

ACTS

PASSED AT THE SESSION BEGUN AND HELD AT BOSTON, ON THE THIRTIETH DAY OF MAY, A. D. 1753.

CHAPTER 1.

AN ACT IN ADDITION TO AN ACT, INTITLED "AN ACT DIRECTING HOW MEETINGS OF PROPRIETORS OF LANDS LYING IN COMMON MAY BE CALLED."

WHEREAS there are sundry tracts of common and undivided lands in this province, lying within no township or precinct, which are owned by considerable numbers of proprietors, and no effectual provision has as yet been made by law, either for calling meetings of the proprietors of such lands, or for the raising and collecting moneys granted for the common good and service of such proprietors; whereby the settlement and improvement of such lands have been much obstructed and delayed,— Preamble. 13 Allen, 543.

Be it therefore enacted by the Lieutenant-Govern[ou]r, Council and House of Represent[ati]ves,

[SECT. 1.] That whensoever five, where there are so many, or the major part of the owners or proprietors of such common lands, where the number shall be less, shall judge it expedient to have a meeting of the proprietors thereof, and shall thereupon, by writing, apply, by petition, to any justice of the peace for the county wherein such their lands as aforesaid l[y][*i*]e, or to a justice of the peace thro' this province, to call a meeting of any such proprietors as aforesaid, to be had at such time and place, and on such occasions as shall be expressed in such petition, such justice so applied unto, is hereby authorized and directed to grant and issue out his warrant, directed to one of the proprietors desiring such meeting, or to the clerk of such propriety, if there be one, requiring him to notify and warn the other proprietors of such common lands to meet and assemble together at the time and place appointed therefor, as aforesaid; which notice and warning shall be given by advertising the same, with the time, place and occasions of meeting, in the several Boston weekly newspapers, forty days at least before the day appointed for such meeting; and such proprietors may, by themselves or their lawful attorneys, at such meeting, appoint such a method for calling their meetings, for the future, as they shall judge most convenient, which shall always be under the same regulations as all other proprietary meetings are; and may chuse a clerk and such other officers as are usually chosen by other proprieties, then, and from time to time, as their occasions shall require; and may transact and pass upon any other matters and affairs for the benefit of such propriety, which the proprietors of new townships or plantations granted by this govern-m[*en*]t are by law enabled to do: *provided*, such matters be mentioned in the notifications for such meetings; and such clerk, being du[e]ly

Method of calling proprietors' meeting.

Powers of the said proprietors in their meetings.

sworn as the clerks of other proprieties, by law, ought to be, shall have the like power with them.

And be it further enacted,

To raise moneys for the use of the propriety.
11 Mass., 175.

[SECT. 2.] That such proprietors, at any of their meetings, pursuant to this act, may, by themselves or their lawful attorneys, grant and order any suitable sum or sums of money to be raised and levied upon their several rights in such lands equally and rateably, according to their respective interests and shares therein, for bringing forward and compleating the settlem[*en*]t of such common lands, and for the prosecution or defending any lawsuits for or against such proprietors, and for carrying on and managing any other affairs for the common good of such proprieties; and every such proprietor as shall neglect to pay to the collector or treasurer or committee of such propriety, such sum or sums of money as shall, from time to time, be duly granted and voted to be raised and levied upon his right and share in such lands, for the space of six months to those who live in the province, and twelve months to those who live out of the province, after such grant, and his proportion thereof, shall be published in the several publick prints, as afores[*ai*]d, then the committee of the proprietors of such common lands, or the major part of such comm[*itt*]ee, may and are hereby fully impowered, from time to time, at a publick vendue, to sell and convey away so much of such delinquent proprietor's right or share in said common lands, as will be sufficient to pay and satisfy his tax or proportion of such grant, and all reasonable charges attending such sale, to any person that will give most for the same; notice of such sale being given in the said prints forty days at least beforehand, and may accordingly execute and give a good deed or deeds of conveyance of the lands so sold, unto the purchaser thereof, to hold in fee simple: *provided, nevertheless*, that the proprietor or proprietors whose right or share in such lands shall be so sold, shall have liberty to redeem the same in twelve months after said sale, by paying the sum the land sold for, and charges, together with the further sum of twelve pounds for each hundred pounds produced by such sale; and so *pro ratâ* for any less or greater sum. [*Passed June* 19; *published June* 23.

And to make sale of the lands of the delinquents.

Proviso.

CHAPTER 2.

AN ACT FOR ERECTING THE TOWNSHIP OF NEW SALEM, SO CALLED, IN THE COUNTY OF HAMPSHIRE, INTO A DISTRICT.

Be it enacted by the Lieut[*enan*]*t-Governour, Council and House of Repres*[*entati*]*ves,*

New Salem constituted a district.

[SECT. 1.] That the s[*ai*]d township of New Salem, with the additional grant made to s[*ai*]d township, be and hereby is erected into a district by the name of New Salem; and that the said district be and hereby is invested with all the privileges, powers and immunities that towns in this province, by law, do or may enjoy, that of sending a representative to the gen[*era*]l assembly only excepted; and the inhabitants of said district shall have full power and right, from time to time, until[l] the further order of this court, to jo[y][*i*]n with the town of Sunderland in the choice of a representative; and that the said district shall, from time to time, pay their proportionable part of the expence of such representative, according to their respective proportions of the province tax; and that the s[*ai*]d town of Sunderland, as often as they shall call a meeting for the choice of a representative, shall give season-

Powers thereof.

To join with Sunderland in choice of a representative.

able notice to the clerk of said district for the time being, of the time and place of holding such meeting, to the end that said district may join them therein; and the clerk of said district shall set up, in some publick place in s[*ai*]d district, a notification thereof accordingly.

And be it further enacted,

[Sect. 2.] That all the lands in s[*ai*]d district be taxed one penny per acre for the space of three years; and that the monies thereby raised shall be employed in finishing the meeting-house, repairing roads, and for defi[a][*e*]ying other publick charges in said district. Lands to be taxed there.

Provided, nevertheless,—

[Sect. 3.] That nothing contained in this act shall be understood to supersce[e]d[*e*] the order of this court in April last, respecting the province, their taking possession of all forfeited grants after the time limit[*t*]ed in said order. Proviso.

And be it further enacted,

[Sect. 4.] That Eleazer Porter, Esq[r]., be and hereby is impowered to issue his warrant directed to some principal inhabitant in said district, requiring him to notify the inhabitants of said district to meet at such time and place as he shall appoint, to chuse all such officers as by law they are impow[e]red to chuse for conducting the affairs of said district. [*Passed June* 15; *published June* 23. Meeting to be called.

CHAPTER 3.

AN ACT FOR ERECTING THE NORTHEASTERLY PART OF THE TOWN OF DEERFIELD INTO A SEPERATE DISTRICT.

Be it enacted by the Lieutenant-Governour, Council and House of Representatives,

[Sect. 1.] That the northeasterly part of the town of Deerfield, bounding south by the line called the Eight-thousand-acre Line, to run from Connecticut river west to the west end of the first tier of lots, which l[y][*ie*] west of the Seven-mile Line, so called, from thence north nineteen degrees east to the north side of the town bounds, thence east on the town line to Connectiver river, thence on said river to the first mentioned bounds; be and hereby is erected into a seperate district by the name of Greenfield; and that the said district be and hereby is invested with all the privileges, powers and immunities that towns in this province do or may enjoy, that of sending a representative to the general court only excepted; and that the inhabitants of said district shall have full power and right, from time to time, to join with the said town of Deerfield in the choice of a representative or representatives (who may be chosen either in the town or district), in which choice they shall enjoy all the privileges which by law they would have been [*i*][e]ntitled to, if this act had not been made; and that the said district shall, from time to time, pay their proportionable part of the expence of such repres[*entati*]ve or repres[*entati*]ves, according to their respective proportions of the province tax, and that the said town of Deerfield, as often as they shall call a meeting for the choice of a representative, shall give seasonable notice to the clerk of said district for the time being, of the time and place of holding such meeting, to the end that said district may join them therein; and the clerk of said district shall set up in some publick place, in said district, a notification thereof accordingly, or otherwise give seasonable notice as the district shall determine. Bounds of the district of Greenfield. Powers thereof. To join with Deerfield in sending a representative.

Provided, nevertheless,—

And be it further enacted,

Proviso. [SECT. 2.] That the said district shall pay their proportion of all town, county, and province taxes already set on, or granted to be raised by, said town, as if this act had not been made.

And be it further enacted,

Cheapside land. [SECT. 3.] That the lands in a certain interval or meadow called Cheapside, which do now belong to Timothy Childs, jun[r]., and David Wells, shall pay their taxes to said district, so long as they are owned by any persons living within said district.

Provided, also,—

And be it further enacted,

Place of the meeting-house. [SECT. 4.] That the first meeting-house in said district shall be set up at a place called the Trap Plain, where the committee of the town of Deerfield have fixed a white-oak stake.

Provided, also,—

And be it further enacted,

Unimproved lands to be taxed for the ministry, &c. [SECT. 5.] That a tax of one penny farthing per acre be levied upon the unimproved allotted lands in s[*ai*]d district so soon as the frame of a meeting-house is erected at the afores[*ai*]d place; and also a further tax of one penny farthing per acre upon said unimproved lands, so soon as a minister is settled within said district, which taxes are to be employed for building said meeting-house, and settling and supporting a minister.

Provided, nevertheless,—

And be it further enacted,

Proviso. [SECT. 6.] That the non-resident proprietors of lands in said district shall be allowed to vote in the meetings of said district with regard to building a meeting-house, and also with regard to the salary and settlem[*en*]t that shall be given to a minister.

Provided, also,—

Proviso. [SECT. 7.] That the said district shall have the improvement of one half of the sequestred lands on the north side of Deerfield river, until there shall be another district or parish made out of the said town of Deerfield.

Provided, also,—

And be it further enacted,

Proportion of province and county tax. [SECT. 8.] That the said district shall hereafter pay the same proportionable part of all county and province taxes that shall be laid on the town of Deerfield, as there was levied on the polls and rateable estate within the limits of said district for the last tax until[l] this court shall otherw[ays][*ise*] order, or set out their proportions.

Provided, also,—

And be it further enacted,

Proviso about poor, warned to depart. [SECT. 9.] That no poor person or persons residing in said district, and who have been warned by the selectmen of said Deerfield to depart said town, shall be understood as hereby exempted from any process they would have been expos'd to if this act had not been made.

And be it further enacted,

District meeting to be called. [SECT. 10.] That Elijah Williams, Esq[r]., be and hereby is impow[e]red to issue his warrant, directed to some principal inhabitant of said district, to meet at such time and place as he shall appoint, to choose all such officers as by law they are impowered to choose for conducting the affairs of said district. [*Passed June* 9; *published June* 23.

CHAPTER 4.

AN ACT FOR ERECTING A PLACE CALLED SHEEPSCOT, IN THE COUNTY OF YORK, INTO A DISTRICT BY THE NAME OF NEWCASTLE.

Whereas it hath been represented to this court that the inhabitants of Sheepscot aforesaid labour under difficulties by reason of their not being incorporated into a district,— Preamble.

Be it enacted by the Lieut[enan]t-Governour, Council and House of Representatives,

[Sect. 1.] That the said place or plantation called Sheepscot, with the inhabitants thereon, be and hereby is erected into a district by the name of Newcastle, bounding as follow[eth][*ing*]: beginning at the narrows called Sheepscot Narrows, at the upper end of Wiscasset[t] Bay, and so extending from the narrows up the said river eight miles; from thence southeast to Damariscotta River, and to extend down said river eight miles; and from thence to run to Sheepscot River, at the place first mentioned; and that the said district be and hereby is invested with all the privileges, powers and immunities that towns in this province by law do or may enjoy, that of sending a representative to the general assembly only excepted. Newcastle constituted a district. Powers thereof

And be it further enacted,

[Sect. 2.] That the assessment made by the selectmen chosen by the said inhabitants for the year one thousand seven hundred and fifty-one, be confirmed, and that the constable or collector chosen for the same year by said inhabitants, who have collected some part of said assessm[*en*]t, be and hereby are impowered and directed to finish their collection, and pay it according to the direction of their warrant, and that the selectmen who shall be chosen by said inhabitants for the year one thousand seven hundred and fifty-three, be and hereby are directed and impow[e]red forthwith to assess on the said inhabitants and their estates the sum set upon them in the province tax *Anno Domini* one thousand seven hundred and fifty-two, and that the constable or constables or collectors who shall be chosen for the year one thousand seven hundred and fifty-three, be and hereby are impow[e]red and directed to collect the same, and pay it into the province treasury as soon as may be. Assessment for 1751, confirmed. Inhabitants to be taxed.

And be it further enacted,

[Sect. 3.] That Mr. James Cargill be and hereby is impow[e]red to notify and warn the inhabitants of said district qualified by law to vote in town affairs, to meet at such time and place as he shall appoint, to chuse all such officers as shall be necessary to manage the affairs of said district. [*Passed June* 19; *published June* 23. Meeting to be called.

CHAPTER 5.

AN ACT FOR GRANTING UNTO HIS MAJESTY AN EXCISE UPON WINES AND SPIRITS DISTILL[E]'D, SOLD BY RETAIL, AND UPON LIMES, LEMMONS AND ORANGES.

We, his majesty's most loyal and dutiful subjects, the representatives of the province of the Massachusetts Bay, in general court assembled, being desirous to lessen the present debt of the province, have che[c][*a*]rfully and unanimously granted and do hereby give and grant unto his Preamble.

most excellent majesty for the ends and uses above mentioned, and for no other uses, an excise upon all brandy, rum and other spirits distill[e]'d, and upon all wines whatsoever sold by retail, and upon lemmons, limes and oranges taken in and used in making of punch or other liquors mixed for sale, or otherwise consum[e]'d, in taverns or other licensed houses within this province, to be raised, levied, collected and paid by and upon every taverner, innholder, common victualler and retailer within each respective county, in manner following:—

And be it accordingly enacted by the Lieutenant-Governo[u]r, Council and House of Representatives,

Time of this act's continuance.

[SECT. 1.] That from and after the ninth day of July, one thousand seven hundred and fifty-three, for the space of one year, every person licens[e]'d for retailing rum, brandy or other spirits, or wine, shall pay the dut[y][ie]s following:—

For every gallon of brandy, rum and spirits distill'd, fourpence.

For every gallon of wine of every sort, sixpence.

For every hundred of lemmons or oranges, four shillings.

For every hundred of limes, one shilling and sixpence.

—And so proportionably for any other quantity or number.

And be it further enacted,

Account to be taken.

[SECT. 2.] That every taverner, innholder, common victualler and retailer, shall, upon the said ninth day of July, take an exact account of all brandy, rum and other distill[e]'d spirits, and wine, and of all lemmons, oranges and limes then by him or her, and give an account of the same, upon oath, if required, unto the person or persons to whom the dut[y][ie]s of excise in the respective count[y][ie]s shall be let or farmed, as in and by this act is hereafter directed; and such other persons as shall be licens[e]'d during the continuance of this act, shall also give an account, as aforesaid, upon oath, what brandy, rum or other distill[e]'d spirits, and wine, and of what lemmons, oranges or limes he or they shall have by him or them at the time of his or their licen[s][c]e; which oath the person or persons farming the dut[y][ie]s aforesaid shall have power to administer in the words following; viz[t].,—

Form of the oath.

You, A. B., do swear that the account exhibited by you is a just and true account of all brandy, rum and other distill[e]'d spirits, and wine, lemmons, oranges and limes you had by you on the ninth day of July last. So help you God.

And where such person or persons shall not have been licens[e]'d on said ninth day of July, the form of the oath shall be so varied, as that instead of those words, "on the ninth day of July," these words shall be inserted and used, "at the time of taking your licen[s][c]e."

And be it further enacted,

Within six months, accounts to be delivered.

[SECT. 3.] That every taverner, innholder, common victualler and retailer, shall make a fair entry in a book, of all such rum, brandy and other distill[e]'d spirits, and wine, as he or they, or any for him or them, shall buy, distill and take in for sale after such account taken, and of lemmons, oranges and limes taken in, consum[e]'d or used as aforesaid, and at the end of every six months, deliver the same, in writing, under their hand, to the farmer or farmers of the dut[y][ie]s aforesaid, who are impow[e]red to administer an oath to him or them, that the said account is, *bonâ fide*, just and true, and that he or they do not know of any rum, brandy or other distill[e]'d spirits, or wine, sold, directly or indirectly, or of any lemmons, oranges or limes used in punch or otherwise, by him or them, or any under him or them, or by his or their privity or consent, but what is contained in the account now exhibited, and shall pay him the duty thereof, excepting such part as the farmer shall find is still remaining by him or them: twenty per cent to be allowed on the liquors afore mentioned for leakage, usage and other waste, for which no duty is to be paid. Twenty per cent allowed for leakage.

Provided always, and it is the true intent and meaning of this act,—

[Sect. 4.] That if any taverner, retailer or common victualler, shall buy of another taverner or retailer such small quantity of liquors as this act obliges him to account for to the farmer, and pay the excise, such taverner, retailer or common victualler shall be exempted and excused from accounting or paying any excise therefor, inasmuch as the same is accounted for, and the excise therefor to be paid, by the taverner or retailer of whom he bought the same. Proviso.

And be it further enacted,

[Sect. 5.] That every taverner, innholder, common victualler or retailer, who shall be found to give a false acco[mp][*un*]t of any brandy, distill[*e*]'d spirits, or wine, or other the commodities aforesaid, by him or her on the said ninth day of July, or at the time of his or her taking licen[s][*c*]e, or bought, distill[*e*]'d, or taken in for sale afterwards, or used as aforesaid, or neglect or refuse to give in an account, on oath, as aforesaid, shall be rendered incapable of having a licen[s][*c*]e afterwards, and shall be prosecuted by the farmer of excise in the same county, for his or her neglect, and ordered by the general sessions of the peace to pay double the sum of money as they may judge that the excise of liquors, &c., by him or her sold within such time, would have amounted to, to be paid to the said farmer. Penalty on giving a false account.

And be it further enacted,

[Sect. 6.] That the justices in their general sessions of the peace shall take recognizances, with sufficient suret[y][*ie*]s, of all persons by them licens[*e*]'d, both as to their keeping good rule and order, and duly observing the laws relating to persons so licens[*e*]'d, and for their duly and truly rend[e]ring an account in writing under their hands as aforesaid, and paying their excise in manner as aforesaid; as also that they shall not use their licen[s][*c*]e in any house besides that wherein they dwell; which recognizance shall be taken within the space of thirty days after the granting of such licen[s][*c*]e, otherwise the persons licens[*e*]'d shall lose the benefit of his or her said licen[s][*c*]e; and no person shall be licens[*e*]'d by the said justices that hath not accounted with the farmer, and paid him the excise due to him from such person at the time of his or her asking for such licen[s][*c*]e. General sessions to take recognizance.

And whereas, notwithstanding the laws made against selling strong drink without licen[s][*c*]e, many persons not regarding the penalt[y][*ie*]s and forfeitures in the said act, do receive and entertain persons in their houses, and sell great quantit[y][*ie*]s of spirits and other strong drink, without licen[s][*c*]e so to do first had and obtained; by reason whereof great debaucheries are committed and kept secret, the end thereby and design of this law is in a great measure frustrated, and such as take licen[s][*c*]es and pay the excise greatly wronged and injured,— Preamble.

Be it therefore enacted,

[Sect. 7.] That whosoever, after the said ninth day of July, one thousand seven hundred and fifty-three, shall presume, either directly or indirectly, to sell any brandy, rum or other distill[*e*]'d spirits or wine, (in any less quantity than thirty gallons, and all delivered to one person, at one time, without drawing any part of it off), or any beer, cyder, perry, or other strong drink, in less quantity than ten gallons, without licen[s][*c*]e first had and obtained from the court of general sessions of the peace, and recognizing in manner as aforesaid, shall forfeit and pay for each offence, the sum of four pounds, and costs of prosecution; one half to the farmer, and the other half to the informer; and all such Forfeiture of £4 for selling without license, &c.

as shall refuse or neglect to pay the fine aforesaid, shall stand closely and strictly committed in the common goal of the county for three months at least, and not to have the liberty of the goaler's house or yard; and any goaler giving any person liberty contrary to this act, shall forfeit and pay two pounds, and pay costs of prosecution as aforesaid. And if any person or persons, not licensed as aforesaid, shall order, allow, permit or connive at the selling of any strong drink, contrary to the true intent or meaning of this act, by his or her child or children, servant or servants, or any other person or persons belonging to or in his or her house or family, and be thereof convicted, he, she or they shall be reputed the offender or offenders, and shall suffer the same penalt[y][*ie*]s as if he, she or they had sold such drink themselves.

And be it further enacted,

One witness sufficient for conviction.

[SECT. 8.] That when any person shall be complained of for selling any strong drink without licen[s][*c*]e, one witness produced to the satisfaction of the justice or court before whom such complaint shall be tried, shall be deem[*e*]'d sufficient for conviction. And when and so often as it shall be observed that there is a resort of persons to houses suspected to sell strong drink without licen[s][*c*]e, any justice of the peace shall have full power to convene such persons before him, and examine them upon oath concerning the person suspected of selling or retailing strong drink in such houses, outhouses or other dependencies thereof; and if upon examination of such witnesses, and hearing the defence of such suspected person, it shall appear to the justice there is sufficient proof of the violation of this act by selling strong drink without licen[s][*c*]e, judgment may thereupon be made up against such person, and he shall forfeit and pay in like manner as if process had been commenced by bill, plaint or information before the said justice; or otherwise may bind over the person suspected, and the witnesses, to the next court of general sessions of the peace for the county where such person shall dwell.

And be it further enacted,

Penalty for selling strong drink to negroes, mulattoes, &c.

[SECT. 9.] That when and so often as any person shall be complained of for selling any strong drink without licen[s][*c*]e to any negro, Indian or molatto slave, or to any child or other person under the age of discretion, and upon the declaration of any such Indian, negro or molatto slaves, child or other person under the age of discretion, and other circumstances concurring, it shall appear to be highly probable in the judgment of the court or justice before whom the trial shall be, that the person complained of is guilty, then, and in every such case, unless the defendant shall acquit him- or herself upon oath (to be administred to him or her by the court or justice that shall try the cause), such defendant shall forfeit and pay two pounds to the farmer of excise, and costs of prosecution; but if the defendant shall acquit him- or herself upon oath as aforesaid, the court or justice may and shall enter up judgment for the defendant to recover costs.

And be it further enacted,

Persons after first conviction to enter into bonds.

[SECT. 10.] That after any person shall have been once convicted of selling strong liquors without licen[s][*c*]e, contrary to this act, he shall, upon every offence after such first conviction, be obliged to enter into bonds, with one or more suret[y][*ie*]s, in the penalty of twenty pounds, to his majesty, for the use of this government, that he will not, in like manner, offend or be guilty of any breach of this act; and upon refusal to give such bond, he shall be committed to prison until he comply therewith.

And be it further enacted,

Penalty on persons refusing to give evidence.

[SECT. 11.] That if any person or persons shall be summoned to appear before a justice of the peace, or the grand jury, to give evidence relating to any persons selling strong drink without licen[s][*c*]e, or to appear before the court of general sessions of the peace, or other court proper to try the same, to give evidence on the trial of any person informed against, presented or indicted for the selling strong drink without licen[s][*c*]e, and shall neglect or refuse to appear, or to give evidence in that behalf, every person so offending shall forfeit the sum of twenty pounds and cost of prosecution; the one half of the penalty aforesaid to be to his majesty for the use of the province, the other half to and for the use of him or them who shall sue for the same as aforesaid. And when it shall so happen that witnesses are bound to sea before the sitting of the court where any person or persons informed against, for selling strong drink without licen[s][*c*]e, is or are to be prosecuted for the same, in every such case, the deposition of any witness or witnesses, in writing, taken before any two of his majesty's justices of the peace, *quorum unus*, and sealed up and delivered into court, the adverse party having first had a notification in writing sent to him or her of the time and place of caption, shall be esteem[*e*]'d as sufficient evidence, in the law, to convict any person or persons offending against this act, as if such witness or witnesses had been present at the time of trial, and given his, her or their deposition, *viva voce;* and every person or persons who shall be summoned to give evidence before two justices of the peace, in manner as aforesaid, and shall neglect or refuse to appear, or to give evidence relating to the facts he or she shall be inquired of, shall be liable and subject to the same penalty as he or she would have been by virtue of this act, for not appearing, or neglecting or refusing to give his or her evidence, before the grand jury or court as aforesaid.

And be it further enacted,

[SECT. 12.] That all fines, forfeitures and penalt[y][*ie*]s arising by this act shall and may be recovered by action, bill, plaint or information, before any court of record proper to try the same; and where the sum forfeited does not exceed four pounds, by action or complaint before any one of his majesty's justices of the peace in the respective count[y][*ie*]s where such offence shall be committed; which said justice is hereby impow[e]red to try and determine the same; and such justice shall make a fair entry or record of all such proceedings: *saving always* to any person or persons who shall think him-, her- or themselves aggr[ei][*ie*]ved by the sentence or determination of the said justice, liberty of appeal therefrom to the next court of general sessions of the peace to be holden in and for said county, at which court such offence shall be finally determin[*e*]'d: *provided*, that in said appeal the same rules be observed as are already, by law, required in appeals from justices to the court of general sessions of the peace. How fines are to be recovered.

And to the end the revenue arising from the aforesaid dut[y][*ie*]s of excise may be advanced for the greater benefit and advantage of the publick,—

Be it further enacted,

[SECT. 13.] That one or more persons, to be nominated and appointed by the general court, for and within the several count[y][*ie*]s within this province, publick notice being first given of the time and place and occasion of their meeting, shall have full power, and are hereby authorized, from time to time, to contract and agree with any person for or concerning the farming the dut[y][*ie*]s in this act mentioned, upon brandy, rum, or other the liquors and commodities aforesaid, in the respective count[y][*ie*]s for which they shall be appointed, as may be for the greatest profit and advantage of the publick, so as the same exceed not the term of one year after the commencement of this act; and every person to whom the duties of excise in any county shall be let or farmed, shall have power to inspect the houses of all such as are li- Persons empowered to farm out the excise.

cens[*e*]'d, and of such as are suspected of selling without licen[s][c]e, and to demand, sue for, and recover the excise due from licens[*e*]'d persons by virtue of this act.

And be it further enacted,

Farmer to give bond that the sum agreed for be paid into the public treasury.

[SECT. 14.] That the farmer shall give bond with two sufficient suret[y][*ie*]s, to the province treasurer for the time being, and his successors in said office, in double the sum of money that shall be contracted for, with condition that the sum agreed be paid into the province treasury, for the use of the province, at the expiration of one year from the date of such bond; which bond the person or persons to be appointed a committee of such county are to take, and the same to lodge with the treasurer as aforesaid, within twenty days after such bond is executed; and the said treasurer, upon failure or neglect of payment at the time therein limit[*t*]ed, shall and is hereby impow[e]red and directed to issue out his execution (returnable in sixty days) against such farmers of excise and their suret[y][*ie*]s, or either of them, for the full sum express[*e*]'d in the condition of their bonds, as they shall respectively become due, in the same manner as he is enabled by law to issue out his executions against defective constables; and the said committee shall render an account of their proceedings touching the farming this duty on rum, wine and other the liquors and species afore mentioned, in their respective count[y][*ie*]s, to the general court in the first week of their fall sessions, and shall receive such sum or sums for their trouble and expence in said affair as said court shall think fit to allow them.

[SECT. 15.] And every person farming the excise in any county may substitute and appoint one or more deputy or deput[y][*ie*]s under him, upon oath, to collect and receive the excise aforesaid, which shall become due in such county, and pay in the same to such farmer; which deputy or deput[y][*ie*]s shall have, use and exercise all such powers and authorit[y][*ie*]s as in and by this act are given or committed to the farmers for the better collecting the dut[y][*ie*]s aforesaid, or prosecuting of offenders against this act.

And be it further enacted, anything hereinbefore contain[e]'d to the contrary notwithstanding,

Farmers may compound with any retailer or innholder.

[SECT. 16.] That it shall and may be lawful to and for the said farmers, and every of them, to compound and agree with any retailer or innholder within their respective divisions, from time to time, for his or her excise for the whole year, in one entire sum, as they in their discretion shall think fit to agree for, without making any entry thereof as is before directed; and all and every person or persons, to whom the said excise or any part thereof shall be let or farmed, by themselves or their lawful substitutes, may and hereby are impow[e]red to sue for and recover, in any of his majesty's courts of record (or before a justice of the peace where the matter is not above his cognizance), any sum or sums that shall grow due for any of the aforesaid dut[y][*ie*]s of excise, where the party or part[y][*ie*]s from whom the same is or shall become due shall refuse or neglect to pay the same.

And be it further enacted,

Penalty for farmers or their deputies, offending.

[SECT. 17.] That in case any person farming the excise as aforesaid, or his deputy, shall, at any time during their continuance in said office, wittingly and willingly connive at, or allow, any person or persons within their respective divisions, not licens[*e*]'d by the court of general sessions of the peace, their selling any brandy, wines, rum or other liquors by this act forbidden, such farmer or deputy, for every such offence, shall forfeit the sum of fifty pounds and cost of prosecution; one half of the penalty aforesaid to be to his majesty for the use of the province, the other half to him or them that shall inform and sue for the same, and shall thenceforward be forever disabled from serving in said office.

And be it further enacted,

[Sect. 18.] That in case of the death of the farmers of excise in any county, the executors or administrators of such farmer shall, upon their taking [of] such trust of executor or administrator upon them, have and enjoy all the powers, and be subject to all the duties, the farmer had or might enjoy or was subject to by force of this act. [*Passed June* 15*; *published June* 23. Provision in case of death, &c.

CHAPTER 6.

AN ACT FOR REVIVING AND CONTINUING SUNDRY LAWS OF THIS PROVINCE, EXPIRED OR NEAR EXPIRING.

Whereas an act was made and pass[*e*]'d in the sixteenth and seventeenth year of his present majesty's reign, intitled "An Act for securing the seasonable payment of town and precinct rates or assessments"; and another act was made and pass[*e*]'d in the seventeenth year of his said majesty's reign, intitled "An Act for preventing mischief by unruly dogs on the Island of Nantucket"; and another act was made and pass'd in the twentieth year of his s[*ai*]d majesty's reign, intitled "An Act in addition to the several acts for the better regulating the Indians"; and another act was made and pass'd in the twenty-first year of his said majesty's reign, intitled "An Act to enable the proprietors of Suncook to raise money for the support of their present minister"; and another act was made and pass'd in the twenty-fourth year of his said majesty's reign, intitled "An Act for preventing and suppressing of riots, routs and unlawful assemblies";—all which several laws are expired or near expiring: *and whereas* the afores[*ai*]d laws have, by experience, been found beneficial and necessary for the several purposes for which they were pass'd,— Expired and expiring laws revived. Town and precinct rates. 1743-44, chap. 11. Mischief by unruly dogs. 1743-44, chap. 6. Regulation of Indians. 1746-47, chap. 12. Proprietors of Suncook. 1747-48, chap. 11. Suppressing of riots, &c. 1750-51, chap. 17.

Be it therefore enacted by the Lieutenant-Govern[ou]r, Council and House of Repres[entati]ves,

That all and every of the aforesaid acts, and every matter and clause therein contained, be and hereby are continued and revived, and shall continue and remain in full force for the space of five years from the publication hereof, and no longer. [*Passed June* 15*; *published June* 23.

CHAPTER 7.

AN ACT FOR GRANTING THE SUM OF THREE HUNDRED AND FORTY POUNDS, FOR THE SUPPORT OF HIS HONOUR THE LIEUTENANT-GOVERN[*OU*]R AND COMMANDER-IN-CHIEF.

Be it enacted by the Lieut[enan]t-Governour, Council and House of Representatives,

That the sum of three hundred and forty pounds be and hereby is granted to his most excellent majesty, to be paid out of the publick treasury to his honour Spencer Phips, Esq[r]., lieutenant-governour and commander-in-chief in and over his majesty's province of the Massa- Governor's grant.

* According to the record this act was passed June 19.

chusetts Bay, for his past services, and further to enable him to manage the publick affairs of the province. [*Passed June* 11*; *published June* 23.

CHAPTER 8.

AN ACT FOR GRANTING THE SUM OF FIFTEEN HUNDRED POUNDS TO ENCOURAGE THE MANUFACT[ORY][*URE*] OF LINNEN.

Preamble. WHEREAS, through the great decay of trade and business, the number of poor is greatly increased, and the burthen of supporting them lies heavy on many of the towns within this province, and many persons, especially women and children, are destitute of employment, and in danger of becoming a publick charge; *and whereas* divers well-disposed persons have contributed, and continue to contribute, sums of money to encourage setting the poor to work in the several branches of the linnen manufacture, which sums of money have been, and continue to be, paid into the hands of Andrew Oliver, Esq[r]., Mr. Thomas Greene, Thomas Hubbard, Esq[r]., Mr. John Franklin, Mr. Middlecot Cooke, Mr. Thomas Gunter, Mr. William Clarke, Mr. Sylvester Gardiner, Mr. William Bowdoin, and Mr. Isaac Winslow, in order to be by them applied to the purposes aforesaid; therefore, further to encourage the laudable design of the several contributors as aforesaid,—

Be it enacted by the Lieut[enan]t-Governour, Council and House of Repres[entati]ves,

Duty to be laid upon coaches, chaises, &c. [SECT. 1.] That there be and hereby is granted a tax or duty on every coach, chariot, chaise, calash and chair, within this province, to be paid by the owner thereof, annually, during the term of five years, to commence the first of August next, excepting the governour, lieut[enan]t-governour, the president of Harvard College, and the settled ministers thro'[ugh] the province; viz[t]., on every coach, ten shillings; on every chariot, five shillings; on every chaise, three shillings; on every calash, two shillings; and on every chair, two shillings; *provided always*, that if any coach, chariot, chaise, calash or chair, shall not at any time in any year during the continuance of this act be actually used or improved, the tax for such year shall not be required or accounted due.

Proviso.

And be it further enacted,

Owners of coaches, chaises, &c., to give in an account to the town treasurer. [SECT. 2.] That every person, inhabitant of or resident within this province, who now is, or during the term of five years afores[ai]d, shall be owner of any one or more coach, chariot, chaise, calash or chair, be and hereby is required, every year during their being owners of such coach, [chariot], chaise, calash or chair, and sometime before the first of October in each year, to exhibit and give in to the treasurer of the town or district of which he shall be at such time an inhabitant or resident, or where there shall be no treasurer, to the selectmen, a true account or list of every such coach, chariot, chaise, calash or chair, and pay to said treasurer, or where there shall be no treasurer, to the selectmen, the tax or duty by this act assessed or laid thereon, on pain of forfeiting double the sum so assessed or laid, for each neglect; such forfeiture to be recovered by the afores[ai]d Andrew Oliver, Thomas Greene, Thomas Hubbard, John Franklin, Middlecot Cooke, Thomas Gunter, William Clarke, Sylvester Gardiner, William Bowdoin and Isaac Winslow, or the major part of them, before any justice of the

Penalty for not giving account.

* Passed June 8, according to the record.

peace in the county where any person or persons so neglecting shall dwell or reside.

And be it further enacted,

[Sect. 3.] That the several town treasurers within this province, or where there shall be no treasurer, the selectmen, be and hereby are required to render an account to the afores[*ai*]d Andrew Oliver, Thomas Greene, Thomas Hubbard, John Franklin, Middlecot Cooke, Thomas Gunter, William Clarke, Sylvester Gardiner, William Bowdoin and Isaac Winslow, or the major part of them, of the sums which shall by such town treas[*ure*]rs or selectmen be received by v[i][*e*]rtue of this act, and the names of the several persons who have paid the same, and shall accordingly pay such sums annually on or before the first of November every year, to the said And[*re*]w Oliver, Thomas Greene, Tho[*ma*]s Hubbard, John Franklin, Middlecot Cooke, Tho[*ma*]s Gunter, William Clarke, Sylvester Gardiner, Will[*ia*]m Bowdoin and Isaac Winslow, or the major part of them, or to such person or persons as shall be from time to time by them or the major part of them deputed or appointed: the said town treasurers or selectmen first deducting five per cent for receiving and paying the same; and the several matters and things required by this act to be performed and done by the several town treasurers are hereby declared to be part of the office and trust of a town treasurer, or where there shall be no treas[*ure*]r, of the selectmen, to the faithful discharge whereof they are by law required annually to be under oath.

Town treasurers, &c., to render account to the managers of the linen manufacture.

And be it further enacted,

[Sect. 4.] That the several sums from time to time received by the said Andrew Oliver, Tho[*ma*]s Greene, Tho[*ma*]s Hubbard, John Franklin, Middlecot Cooke, Tho[*ma*]s Gunter, Will[*ia*]m Clarke, Sylvester Gardiner, Will[*ia*]m Bowdoin and Isaac Winslow, by virtue of this act, shall by them be applied to the purchasing a p[ei][*ie*]ce of land, and building or purchasing a convenient house within the town of Boston, for carrying on the business of spinning, weaving and other necessary parts of the linnen manufacture, and to no other purpose whatsoever; and the said And[*re*]w Oliver, Tho[*ma*]s Greene, Tho[*ma*]s Hubbard, John Franklin, Middlecot[t] Cooke, Tho[*ma*]s Gunter, Will[*ia*]m Clarke, Sylvester Gardiner, Will[*ia*]m Bowdoin and Isaac Winslow, shall annually every year lay before the general court or assembly of this province at their sessions in May, an account of the sums received by virtue of this act, and how the same have been disburs[*e*]'d or applied; and they shall be held at all times during their improvem[*en*]t of the afores[*ai*]d house and land, to cause to be instructed in the manufacture afores[*ai*]d, free of any expence for such instruction, at least one person from every town in this province which shall see cause to send one for that purpose; and the said house and land shall be employed for the purposes afores[*ai*]d during the pleasure of the general court aforesaid, and no longer.

The money raised, to be applied for providing a house and land for the linen manufacture.

Managers to account therefor to the general court.

Provided always, and it is accordingly to be understood,—

[Sect. 5.] That if at the expiration of any year before the fifth year the tax or duty by this act laid, shall have amounted to the sum of fifteen hundred pounds, the said tax or duty shall thenceforward determine and cease; and in case there shall at any time have been received by the said And[*re*]w Oliver, Tho[*ma*]s Greene, Tho[*ma*]s Hubbard, John Franklin, Middlecot[t] Cooke, Tho[*ma*]s Gunter, Will[*ia*]m Clarke, Sylvester Gardiner, Will[*ia*]m Bowdoin and Isaac Winslow, a greater sum than fifteen hundred pounds, the overplus shall by them be paid into the publick treasury.

Proviso.

And be it further enacted,

[Sect. 6.] That if it shall appear, at the expiration of the five years

Further provision in case of deficiency.

in this act mentioned, that the afores[*ai*]d tax or duty shall not have amounted to the sum of fifteen hundred pounds, further provision shall be made by the general court for compleating the said sum of fifteen hundred pounds, and applying it to the purposes aforesaid. [*Passed June* 15; *published June* 23.

CHAPTER 9.

AN ACT TO PREVENT FIRING THE WOODS.

Preamble. 1742-43, chap. 22. 1745-46, chap. 17.

WHEREAS it is found by experience, that the burning of the woods does greatly impoverish lands, prevent the growth of wood. and destroy much fence, to the great detrim[*en*]t of the owners; for the prevention whereof for the future,—

Be it enacted by the Lieut[*enan*]*t-Governo*[*u*]*r, Council and House of Represent*[*ati*]*ves*,

Penalty for firing woods.

[SECT. 1.] That from and after the publication of this act, no person or persons shall wittingly and willingly set fire in any woods or land lying in common within the bounds of any town, without leave first had from the town or proprietors, respectively, owners of such land lying in common, by a major vote, at a meeting for that purpose appointed, under the penalty of forty shillings, to be recovered by action or information before any justice of the peace in the county where the offence is committed, such penalty to be for the use of the person or persons who shall prosecute or sue for the same; and the party offending shall be further liable to the action of the town, proprietors or particular persons damnified by such fire. And in case such fire shall be set or kindled by any person under age, such penalty shall be recovered of the parent or master, respectively, of such person under age, unless it shall appear such person under age was employed or directed by some person other than the parent or master, in which case, the person so employing or directing, shall be liable thereunto.

Method of prosecution.

And be it further enacted,

Lawful for towns or proprietors of lands to set fire to their own lands.

[SECT. 2.] That it shall and may be lawful for any town or proprietors of any such lands as afores[*ai*]d, to give order for the setting fire in the lands to them respectively belonging, and to chuse two or more persons for that service, who shall appoint times for that purpose, and give seasonable notice thereof in the town where such lands l[y][*i*]e, and to the selectmen of such adjacent town near the borders whereof the woods may be that are to be set on fire, as aforesaid.

And inasmuch as it is ofttimes impossible to prove such facts by direct testimonies,—

Be it further enacted,

Method of prosecution when children, &c., fire the woods.

[SECT. 3.] That upon process brought for setting fire, as aforesaid, where proof cannot be made in the ordinary method and course of the law, if the plaintiff, complainant, or other credible person, shall swear that fire has been kindled as is declared in the writ[t], and there does appear such circumstances as shall render it highly probable, in the judgment of the court or justice before whom the trial is, that the fire was kindled by the defendant, his child or servant, or by some other child or person under the age of fourteen years, directed or employed by the defendant for that purpose, then, and in such case, unless the person charged, being of the age of fourteen years or upwards, will acquit himself upon oath, administred to him by the court or justice before whom the trial is, the plaintiff or complainant shall recover against the defendant the penalty by this act imposed, and costs; but if the defendant shall acquit himself upon oath, as aforesaid, judgm[*en*]t shall be entred up for the defendant his costs against the plantiff.

And be it further enacted,

[Sect. 4.] That from and after the publication of this act, every person who shall wittingly and willingly set on fire any woodlands lying in common within the bounds of any new plantation in this province, or any woodlands brought into severalty, other than his own, lying either in the bounds of any town or new plantation, open and uninclos[*e*]'d, or any woodlands belonging to any particular person or persons, not within the bounds of any town or new plantation, or any part of the unappropriated woodlands belonging to and within the bounds of this province, without leave first had and obtained from those who have right to give the same, shall forfeit the sum of forty shillings, to be recovered with full costs of suit, by any person who shall sue for the same, in the same manner, and to the same use, and the same method of proof shall be allowed as is provided in this act. Penalty for firing lands lying in common.

And be it further enacted,

[Sect. 5.] That the penalty given by this act against firing woods, shall be likewise recovered by presentment of the grand jury; and on the trial of any presentm[*en*]t of any offence against this act, the same proof and evidence shall be sufficient to convict the person presented, as is made sufficient in case of private suit for the penalty. And all forfeitures and penalties that shall be recovered by presentm[*en*]t of the grand jury by virtue of this act, shall be to his majesty, his heirs and successors, to and for the use of this government. Penalty may be recovered by grand jury, and shall be to the province.

Provided always,—

[Sect. 6.] That no person shall be obliged to pay any of the abovesaid forfeitures or penalties for the same offence, on presentm[*en*]t of the grand jury, and on private and personal action both; but one recovery in either of said methods shall be a final bar[r] to any after-charge or prosecution in the other, for the same penalty. One recovery of a forfeiture shall bar any after trial.

And be it further enacted,

[Sect. 7.] That in all personal actions brought for the recovery of damages sustained by any person or persons, by means of setting on fire any wood[s] or woodlands, to whomsoever the same may belong, whether it lie in common or severalty, inclos'd or not inclos'd, the abovementioned evidence and method of proof shall be allowed and adjudged sufficient for the plantiff to maintain his action and recover his damages upon [or] against the defendant. Method of evidence.

[Sect. 8.] This act to continue and be in force for the space of ten years from the publication thereof, and no longer. [*Passed June* 19; *published June* 23. Limitation.

CHAPTER 10.

AN ACT FOR THE SUPPLY OF THE TREASURY WITH NINE THOUSAND POUNDS, AND FOR APPORTIONING THE SAME, AND FOR DRAWING IT INTO THE TREASURY; AND ALSO FOR ASSESSING A FURTHER TAX OF ONE THOUSAND FIVE HUNDRED AND TWENTY-THREE POUNDS SIX SHILLINGS, PAID THE REPRESENTATIVES FOR THEIR SERVICE AND ATTENDANCE IN THE GENERAL COURT, AND TRAVEL, AND FOR FINES LAID ON SEVERAL TOWNS FOR NOT SENDING A REPRESENTATIVE; AND THE FURTHER SUMS HEREAFTER MENTIONED, ON THE TOWNS HEREAFTER NAMED, IN THE COUNTY OF SUFFOLK, FOR THE REPAIRS OF THE TOWN-HOUSE; VIZ[T]., THE TOWN OF BOSTON, FIFTEEN HUNDRED AND SIXTEEN POUNDS EIGHTEEN SHILLINGS AND FOURPENCE; THE TOWN OF BRAINTREE, THIRTY-SIX POUNDS TEN SHILLINGS; THE TOWN OF BROOKLINE, NINE POUNDS FIFTEEN SHILLINGS; AND THE TOWN OF CHELSEA, THIRTEEN POUNDS SIX SHILLINGS: AND ALSO ONE OTHER TAX ON THE TOWNS HEREAFTER NAMED, IN THE PROVINCE, FOR FORMER ARREARS NOW DUE; VIZ[T]., THE TOWN OF BOSTON, TWENTY-TWO POUNDS EIGHTEEN SHILLINGS AND FIVEPENCE; NORTH YARMOUTH, TWENTY-ONE POUNDS TWO SHILLINGS AND NINEPENCE; GEORGETOWN, FIFTEEN POUNDS SIX SHILLINGS AND TENPENCE; KITTERY, THIRTY-FOUR POUNDS ELEVEN SHILLINGS AND SIXPENCE; BERWICK, THIRTEEN SHILLINGS AND SEVENPENCE; HOPKINSTON, FIFTEEN SHILLINGS AND TWOPENCE; CAMBRIDGE, FOURTEEN SHILLINGS AND NINEPENCE; IPSWICH, SIXTY-EIGHT POUNDS FIVE SHILLINGS AND FOURPENCE; MARBLEHEAD, ONE HUNDRED AND EIGHT POUNDS SIXTEEN SHILLINGS AND SEVENPENCE; BOXFORD, THIRTEEN SHILLINGS AND FOURPENCE; LEICESTER, FIVE POUNDS THIRTEEN SHILLINGS AND FOURPENCE; DISTRICT OF SPENCER, TWO POUNDS SIXTEEN SHILLINGS AND EIGHTPENCE; BRIDGWATER, FIFTEEN POUNDS SEVENTEEN SHILLINGS AND FIVEPENCE; CHATHAM, ONE POUND NINETEEN SHILLINGS.—AMOUNTING IN THE WHOLE TO TWELVE THOUSAND FOUR HUNDRED POUNDS.

WE, his majesty's most loyal and dutiful subjects, the representatives in general court assembled, pray it may be enacted,—

And it is accordingly enacted by the Lieutenant-Governo[u]r, and House of Representatives,

[SECT. 1.] That each town and district within this province be assess[e]'d and pay, as such town's and district's proportion of the sum of nine thousand pounds,—and their representatives' pay, and fines laid on several towns,—the sum of one thousand five hundred and twenty-three pounds, six shillings; and the sum of fifteen hundred [*and*] seventy-six pounds nine shillings and fourpence, on sundry towns, remaining due, for the repairs of the town-house; and a further sum of three hundred pounds four shillings and eightpence, being the arrears due to the province from the towns above named, the several sums following; that is to say,—

IN THE COUNTY OF SUFFOLK.

	Representatives' pay, and fines.	Arrears and dues for the repairs of town-house.	Province tax.	Sum total.	
Boston,	£47 0s. 0d.	£1,539 16s. 9d.	£1,487 5s. 0d.	Three t[illegible] and [illegible]-four pounds one shilling and ninepence,	£3,074 1s. 9d.
Roxbury,	13 12 0	0 0 0	83 5 0	Ninety-six pounds seventeen shillings,	96 17 0
Dorchester,	13 14 0	0 0 0	82 7 9	Ninety-six pounds one shilling and ninepence,	96 1 9
M[illegible]n,	15 2 0	0 0 0	43 15 3	Fifty-eight pounds seventeen shillings and threepence,	58 17 3
Braintree,	16 12 0	36 10 0	94 19 9	One [illegible] and forty-eight pounds one shilling and ninep[illegible],	148 1 9
[illegible]h,	0 0 0	0 0 0	55 19 9	Fifty-five pounds [illegible] shillings and [illegible],	55 19 9
Hingham,	12 16 0	0 0 0	98 11 0	One [illegible] and eleven pounds seven shillings,	111 7 0
Dedham,	15 4 0	0 0 0	65 9 6	Eighty pounds thirteen shil[illegible]gs and [illegible],	80 13 6
M[illegible]d,	17 0 0	0 0 0	40 10 0	Fifty-seven [illegible] ten shillings,	57 10 0
Wrentham,	17 16 0	0 0 0	65 5 0	[illegible] pounds one [illegible],	83 1 0
[illegible]e,	0 0 0	9 15 0	25 4 0	Thirty-four pounds [illegible] shillings,	34 19 0
[illegible]m,	16 14 0	0 0 0	33 4 6	Forty-nine pounds eighteen shillings and sixpence,	49 18 6
[illegible]n,	1 10 0	0 0 0	60 10 0	[illegible] pounds,	62 0 0
Medway,	0 0 0	0 0 0	33 4 6	Thirty-three pounds four shillings and sixpence,	33 4 6
Bellingham,	0 0 0	5 0 0	12 18 0	Twelve pounds eighteen shillings,	12 18 0
Hull,	0 0 0	0 0 0	15 8 3	Fifteen pounds eight shillings and [illegible],	15 8 3
[illegible]e,	8 0 0	0 0 0	24 14 0	Thirty-two pounds fourteen shillings,	32 14 0
[illegible]a,	0 0 0	13 6 0	34 7 9	Fo[illegible]y-[illegible] pounds thirteen shillings and [illegible],	47 13 9
	£195 0s. 0d.	£1,599 7s. 9d.	£2,356 19s. 0d.		£4,151 6s. 9d.

IN THE COUNTY OF ESSEX.

Salem and Danvers,	£2 2s. 8d.	Salem,	£157 10s. 0d.	One hundred and fifty-nine pounds twelve shillings and eightpence,	£159 12s. 8d.
	1 1 4	Danvers,	78 16 6	Seventy-nine pounds seventeen shillings and tenpence,	79 17 10
Ipswich,	9 16 0	£68 5s. 4d.	202 5 6	Two hundred and eighty pounds six shillings and tenpence,	280 6 10
Newbury,	12 12 0	0 0 0	260 7 3	Two hundred and seventy-two pounds nineteen shillings and threepence,	272 19 3
Marblehead,	1 12 0	108 16 7	154 9 3	Two hundred and sixty-four pounds seventeen shillings and tenpence,	264 17 10
Lynn,	15 2 0	0 0 0	83 4 3	Ninety-eight pounds six shillings and threepence,	98 6 3
Andover,	13 18 6	0 0 0	114 3 9	One hundred and twenty-eight pounds one shilling and ninepence,	128 1 9

IN THE COUNTY OF ESSEX—*Continued.*

	REPRESENTATIVES' PAY, AND FINES.	ARREARS AND DUES FOR THE REPAIRS OF TOWN-HOUSE.	PROVINCE TAX.	SUM TOTAL.	
Beverly,	£10 0s. 0d.	£0 0s. 0d.	£55 0s. 3d.	Sixty-five pounds and [illegible],	£65 0s. 3d.
Rowley,	17 2 0	0 0 0	72 0 0	Eighty-nine pounds two shillings,	89 2 0
Salisbury,	12 0 0	0 0 0	56 12 6	Sixty-eight pounds twelve shillings and sixpence,	68 12 6
Haverhill,	10 2 0	0 0 0	66 9 9	Seventy-six pounds [illegible] [illegible] and [illegible],	76 11 9
[illegible]r,	14 4 0	0 0 0	117 14 3	One hundred and [illegible]-one pounds [illegible] shillings and threepence,	131 18 3
Topsfield,	2 0 0	0 0 0	31 10 0	Thirty-three pounds ten shillings,	33 10 0
Boxford,	2 0 0	0 13 4	41 13 3	Forty-four [illegible] six shillings and [illegible],	44 6 7
[illegible]bury,	19 6 0	0 0 0	52 4 0	Seventy-one pounds ten shillings,	71 10 0
Bradford,	18 10 0	0 0 0	46 14 6	Sixty-five pounds four shillings and sixpence,	65 4 6
W[illegible]m,	10 0 0	0 0 0	26 9 6	Thirty-six pounds [illegible] shillings and sixpence,	36 9 6
[illegible]n,	0 0 0	0 0 0	23 10 3	[illegible] [illegible] ten shillings and threepence,	23 10 3
M[illegible]r,	0 0 0	0 0 0	18 18 9	Eighteen pounds eighteen shillings and [illegible],	18 18 9
[illegible]n,	0 0 0	0 0 0	30 3 0	Thirty [illegible] three shillings,	30 3 0
	£171 8s. 0d.	£177 15s. 3d.	£1,689 16s. 6d.		£2,038 19s. 9d.

IN THE COUNTY OF MIDDLESEX.

	REPRESENTATIVES' PAY, AND FINES.	ARREARS AND DUES FOR THE REPAIRS OF TOWN-HOUSE.	PROVINCE TAX.	SUM TOTAL.	
[illegible]ge,	£22 8s. 0d.	£0 14s. 9d.	£60 10s. 6d.	Eighty-three pounds thirteen shillings and [illegible]pence,	£83 13s. 3d.
Ch[illegible]n,	11 4 0	0 0 0	94 10 0	One hundred and five pounds fourteen shillings,	105 14 0
[illegible]wn,	16 6 0	0 0 0	35 13 3	Fifty-one pounds [illegible] shillings and threepence,	51 19 3
Woburn,	15 10 0	0 0 0	58 10 0	Seventy-four pounds,	74 0 0
Concord,	25 0 0	0 0 0	72 0 0	Ni[illegible] pounds,	97 0 0
[illegible]n,	16 6 0	0 0 0	58 10 0	Seventy-four pounds sixteen shillings,	74 16 0
Sudbury,	16 2 0	0 0 0	63 5 3	Seventy-nine pounds [illegible] shillings and threepence,	79 7 3
Marlborô[*ugh*],	17 10 0	0 0 0	63 0 0	Eighty pounds ten shillings,	80 10 0
Bil[illegible],	13 16 0	0 0 0	36 18 0	Fifty [illegible] fourteen shillings,	50 14 0
Framingham,	14 4 0	0 0 0	48 3 0	Sixty-two pounds seven shillings,	62 7 0
Lexington,	16 0 0	0 0 0	39 10 0	Fifty-five pounds ten shillings,	55 10 0
Chelmsford,	17 8 0	0 0 0	36 0 0	Fifty-three pounds eight shillings,	53 8 0
Sherburne,	9 8 0	0 0 0	24 17 3	[illegible]-four [illegible] five shillings and threepence,	34 5 3
Reading,	16 8 0	0 0 0	59 8 0	Seventy-five pounds [illegible] shillings,	75 16 0
[illegible]n,	13 10 0	0 0 0	47 8 0	Sixty [illegible] [illegible] shillings,	60 18 0

[illegible]n,	£16 4s. 0d.	£0 0s. 0d.	£34 19s. 0d.	[illegible] pounds three [illegible],	£51 3s. 0d.
Medford,	1 4 0	0 0 0	33 8 9	Thirty-four pounds twelve shillings and [illegible],	34 12 9
[illegible]n,	0 0 0	0 0 0	25 5 6	Twenty-five pounds five shillings and sixpence,	25 h 6
Hopkinston,	0 0 0	0 15 2	22 1 0	[illegible]-two pounds sixteen [illegible] and twopence,	22 16 2
Westford,	22 8 0	0 0 0	24 6 0	Forty-six pounds fourteen shillings,	46 14 0
Waltham,	16 4 0	0 0 0	31 2 6	Forty-seven [illegible] six shillings and [illegible],	47 6 6
Towns[h]end,	0 0 0	0 0 0	13 15 3	[illegible] pounds fifteen shillings and [illegible],	13 15 3
S[illegible],	15 12 0	0 0 0	22 1 0	Thirty-seven pounds thirteen shillings,	37 13 0
Stoneham,	0 0 0	0 0 0	15 15 9	Fifteen pounds fifteen shillings and [illegible],	15 15 9
District of Shirley,	1 11 9	0 0 0	6 3 9	[illegible] pounds [illegible] shillings and sixpence,	7 15 6
Groton,	11 15 5	0 0 0	45 18 3	Fifty-seven pounds thirteen shillings and eightpence,	57 13 8
District of Pepperrell,	3 12 10	0 0 0	14 4 0	Seventeen pounds sixteen shillings and [illegible],	17 16 10
Wilmington,	0 0 0	0 0 0	18 0 0	Eighteen pounds,	18 0 0
English [illegible] of Natick,	0 0 0	0 0 0	12 10 6	Twelve pounds ten shillings and sixpence,	12 10 6
[illegible],	0 0 0	0 0 0	17 14 0	Seventeen pounds fourteen shillings,	17 14 0
Bedford,	0 0 0	0 0 0	20 13 3	Twenty pounds thirteen shillings and threepence,	20 13 3
Holliston,	0 0 0	0 0 0	20 1 3	Twenty pounds one shilling and threepence,	20 1 3
Tewksbury,	0 0 0	0 0 0	17 14 0	Seventeen pounds fourteen shillings,	17 14 0
Acton,	0 0 0	0 0 0	13 1 0	Thirteen pounds one shilling,	13 1 0
Dunstable and Nottingham, inhabitants,	0 0 0	0 0 0	15 6 0	Fifteen pounds six shillings,	15 6 0
	£329 12s. 0d.	£1 9s 11d.	£1,222 4s. 0d.		£1,553 5s. 11d.

IN THE COUNTY OF HAMPSHIRE.

Springfield,	£20 [illegible] 0d.	£0 0s. 0d.	£87 12s. 0d.	One hundred and [illegible] pounds [illegible] shillings,	£107 12s. 0d.
No[rt]l[illegible],	18 0 0	0 0 0	48 5 3	Sixty-four pounds five shillings and threepence,	64 5 3
So[ut]hampton,	3 0 0	0 0 0	9 15 0	Twelve pounds fifteen shillings,	12 15 0
Hatfield,	0 0 0	0 0 0	26 19 3	[illegible] pounds [illegible] shillings and threepence,	26 19 3
[illegible]d,	0 0 0	0 0 0	35 1 3	[illegible] pounds one shilling and threepence,	35 1 3
Enfield,	0 0 0	0 0 0	26 1 3	Twenty-six pounds one shilling and threepence,	26 1 3
Deerfield,	10 12 0	0 0 0	26 3 6	[illegible] pounds [illegible] shillings and sixpence,	36 15 6
Sheffield,	15 18 0	0 0 0	38 17 9	Fifty-four pounds fifteen shillings and [illegible],	54 15 9
Northfield,	0 0 0	0 0 0	9 8 3	[illegible] pounds eight shillings and [illegible],	9 8 3
Hadley,	11 11 4	0 0 0	30 2 8	Forty-one pounds fourteen shillings,	41 14 0
District South-Hadley,	6 4 8	0 0 0	16 4 4	[illegible] pounds nine shillings,	22 9 0

IN THE COUNTY OF HAMPSHIRE—*Continued.*

	REPRESENTATIVES PAY, AND FINES.	ARREARS AND DUES FOR THE REPAIRS OF TOWN-HOUSE.	PROVINCE TAX.	SUM TOTAL.	
Suffield, . . .	£0 0s. 0d.	£0 0s. 0d.	£48 7s. 6d.	Forty-eight pounds seven shillings and sixpence, ...	£48 7s. 6d.
Sunderland, . . .	5 0 0	0 0 0	15 9 0	Twenty pounds nine shillings, ...	20 9 0
Brimfield, . . .	0 0 0	0 0 0	29 12 6	Twenty-nine pounds twelve shillings and sixpence, ...	29 12 6
Somers, . . .	0 0 0	0 0 0	18 12 0	Eighteen pounds twelve shillings, ...	18 12 0
Palmer, Elbows, or Kingston, . . .	0 0 0	0 0 0	11 2 0	Eleven pounds two shillings, ...	11 2 0
Pelham, . . .	0 0 0	0 0 0	9 9 0	Nine pounds nine shillings, ...	9 9 0
Bedford, . . .	0 0 0	0 0 0	6 6 0	Six pounds six shillings, ...	6 6 0
Coldspring, . . .	0 0 0	0 0 0	6 6 0	Six pounds six shillings, ...	6 6 0
Quabbin, . . .	0 0 0	0 0 0	7 1 0	Seven pounds one shilling, ...	7 1 0
Blan[d]ford, . .	0 0 0	0 0 0	3 19 6	Three pounds nineteen shillings and sixpence, ...	3 19 6
New Marlborough, or No. 2, . . .	0 0 0	0 0 0	6 15 0	Six pounds fifteen shillings, ...	6 15 0
Parish at Ware River, .	0 0 0	0 0 0	9 0 0	Nine pounds, ...	9 0 0
Stockbridge, . .	0 0 0	0 0 0	9 0 0	Nine pounds, ...	9 0 0
	£88 6s. 0d.	£0 0s. 0d.	£535 10s. 0d.		£623 16s. 0d.

IN THE COUNTY OF WORCESTER.

	REPRESENTATIVES PAY, AND FINES.	ARREARS AND DUES FOR THE REPAIRS OF TOWN-HOUSE.	PROVINCE TAX.	SUM TOTAL.	
Worcester, . . .	£12 2s. 0d.	£0 0. 0d.	£47 9s. 6d.	Fifty-nine pounds eleven shillings and sixpence, ...	£59 11s. 6d.
[illegible]ir, . . .	17 8 0	0 0 0	54 0 0	Seventy-one pounds eight shillings, ...	71 8 0
Mn, . . .	14 0 0	0 0 0	51 15 0	Sixty-five pounds fifteen shillings, ...	65 15 0
[illegible]k, . .	0 0 0	0 0 0	58 4 0	Fifty-eight pounds four shillings, ...	58 4 0
Brookfield, . . .	0 0 0	0 0 0	42 9 9	Forty-two pounds nine shillings and ninepence, ...	42 9 9
Oxford, . . .	14 10 0	0 0 0	28 14 6	Forty-three pounds four shillings and sixpence, ...	43 4 6
Sutton, . . .	11 8 0	0 0 0	41 5 9	Fifty-two pounds thirteen shillings and ninepence, ...	52 13 9
Rutland, . . .	19 16 0	0 0 0	29 15 6	Forty-nine pounds eleven shillings and sixpence, ...	49 11 6
No.-west District of Rutland, . . .	0 0 0	0 0 0	6 15 0	Six pounds fifteen shillings, ...	6 15 0
Leicester, . . .	6 9 4	5 13 4	28 5 0	Forty pounds seven shillings and eightpence, ...	40 7 8
District of Spencer, .	3 4 8	2 16 8	14 2 6	Twenty pounds three shillings and tenpence, ...	20 3 10
Southborough, . .	15 16 0	0 0 0	23 4 3	Thirty-nine pounds and threepence, ...	39 0 3
Westborough, . .	28 6 0	0 0 0	32 8 9	Sixty pounds fourteen shillings and ninepence, ...	60 14 9

[illegible]ry,	£12 [illegible] 0d.	£0 0s. 0d.	£87 16s. 0d.	[illegible] [illegible]s,	£60 4s. 0d.
[illegible],	18 18 0	0 0 0	31 13 9	Fifty [illegible] [illegible] [illegible] [illegible] and [illegible]pence,	50 11 9
Uxbridge,	0 0 0	0 0 0	28 13 9	[illegible]enty-eight [illegible] [illegible] [illegible] shillings and [illegible]pence,	28 13 9
Harvard,	10 0 0	0 0 0	26 0 6	[illegible] six [illegible] and [illegible]pence,	36 0 6
[illegible]y,	5 0 0	0 0 0	17 2 0	Twenty-two [illegible] [illegible] [illegible]s,	22 2 0
Bolton,	17 14 0	0 0 0	25 19 0	[illegible] [illegible] thirteen [illegible],	43 13 0
Upton,	0 0 0	0 0 0	14 6 6	[illegible] [illegible] six [illegible] and [illegible],	14 6 6
[illegible],	15 0 0	0 0 0	11 4 3	[illegible]ty-[illegible] [illegible] four shillings and [illegible]pence,	26 4 3
Leominster,	0 0 0	0 0 0	13 10 0	[illegible] [illegible] [illegible] [illegible]s,	13 10 0
Hardwick,	0 0 0	0 0 0	16 13 0	Sixteen [illegible] [illegible] [illegible]s,	16 13 0
[illegible]n,	0 0 0	0 0 0	8 11 0	[illegible]s,	8 11 0
[illegible]n,	0 0 0	0 0 0	13 1 0	[illegible] [illegible] one [illegible],	13 1 0
Grafton,	8 0 0	0 0 0	21 18 0	[illegible] [illegible] [illegible] shillings,	29 18 0
[illegible]g,	0 0 0	0 0 0	9 15 0	[illegible]ne [illegible] fifteen shillings,	9 15 0
[illegible]s,	0 0 0	0 0 0	7 10 0	Se[illegible]en [illegible] ten [illegible]s,	7 10 0
	£230 0s. 0d.	£8 10s. 0d.	£742 3s. 3d.		£980 13s. 3d.

IN THE COUNTY OF PLYMOUTH.

[illegible]h,	£43 0s. 0d.	£0 0s. 0d.	£72 0s. 0d.	One [illegible] and [illegible] [illegible],	£115 0s. 0d.
[illegible]e,	14 4 0	0 0 0	99 0 0	One h[illegible] and [illegible] [illegible] [illegible] [illegible],	113 4 0
[illegible]y,	18 4 0	0 0 0	32 12 6	Fifty [illegible] [illegible] [illegible] and [illegible]pence,	50 16 6
[illegible]d,	16 12 0	0 0 0	67 5 6	[illegible] [illegible] [illegible] [illegible] and [illegible],	83 17 6
Bri[illegible]r,	18 4 0	15 17 5	116 17 0	One [illegible] and fifty [illegible] [illegible] shillings and [illegible]pence,	150 18 5
[illegible]h,	0 0 0	0 0 0	82 3 3	[illegible]o [illegible] [illegible] [illegible] and [illegible]pence,	82 3 3
[illegible]r,	35 0 0	0 0 0	49 10 9	[illegible]r [illegible] ten [illegible] and [illegible],	84 10 9
[illegible]n,	0 0 0	0 0 0	41 18 6	[illegible]-one [illegible] [illegible] [illegible] and [illegible]pence,	41 18 6
[illegible][o]k[e],	17 0 0	0 0 0	36 0 0	[illegible]y-three [illegible],	53 0 0
[illegible]n,	0 0 0	0 0 0	24 4 6	[illegible]y-four [illegible] four shillings [illegible] [illegible]pence,	24 4 6
[illegible]r,	18 4 0	0 0 0	31 10 0	[illegible]-nine [illegible] [illegible]en shillings,	49 14 0
[illegible]n,	0 0 0	0 0 0	33 17 3	Thirty-three [illegible] [illegible] [illegible] and [illegible]pence,	33 17 3
[illegible],	7 0 0	0 0 0	19 19 0	[illegible] [illegible] [illegible] shillings,	26 19 0
[illegible]m,	0 0 0	0 0 0	20 14 0	[illegible]y [illegible] [illegible]en shillings,	20 14 0
	£187 8s. 0d.	£15 17s. 5d.	£727 12s. 3d.		£930 17s. [illegible]

IN THE COUNTY OF BARNSTABLE.

	REPRESENTATIVES' PAY, AND FINES.	ARREARS AND DUES FOR THE REPAIRS OF TOWN-HOUSE.	PROVINCE TAX.	SUM TOTAL.	
Barnstable,	£19 8s. 0d.	£0 0s. 0d.	£63 0s. 0d.	Eighty-two pounds eight shillings,	£82 8s. 0d.
Yarmouth,	16 8 0	0 0 0	41 5 0	Fifty-seven pounds thirteen shillings,	57 13 0
Sandwich,	15 16 0	0 0 0	45 0 0	Sixty pounds sixteen shillings,	60 16 0
Eastham,	8 16 0	0 0 0	51 6 0	Sixty pounds two shillings,	60 2 0
Harwich,	0 0 0	0 0 0	39 16 6	Thirty-nine pounds sixteen shillings and sixpence,	39 16 6
Chatham,	0 0 0	1 19 0	22 12 3	Twenty-four pounds eleven shillings and threepence,	24 11 3
Truro,	0 0 0	0 0 0	24 5 3	Twenty-four pounds five shillings and threepence,	24 5 3
Falmouth,	0 0 0	0 0 0	27 18 0	Twenty-seven pounds eighteen shillings,	27 18 0
	£60 8s. 0d.	£1 19s. 0d.	£315 3s. 0d.		£[illegible]7 10s. 0d.

IN THE COUNTY OF BRISTOL.

	REPRESENTATIVES' PAY, AND FINES.	ARREARS AND DUES FOR THE REPAIRS OF TOWN-HOUSE.	PROVINCE TAX.	SUM TOTAL.	
[illegible]n,	£9 0s. 0d.	£0 0s. 0d.	£86 17s. 9d.	One hundred five pounds seventeen shillings and ninepence,	£105 17s. 9d.
[illegible]h,	13 16 0	0 0 0	124 10 9	One hundred and thirty-eight pounds six shillings and ninepence,	138 6 9
[illegible], [illegible]th Shaw-[illegible]t,	12 4 0	0 0 0	55 5 6	Sixty-seven pounds nine shillings and sixpence,	67 9 6
Dartmouth,	22 4 0	0 0 0	162 0 0	One hundred and eighty-four pounds four shillings,	184 4 0
Norton,	34 0 0	0 0 0	54 6 9	Eighty-eight pounds six shillings and ninepence,	88 6 9
[illegible]h,	17 2 0	0 0 0	59 6 6	Seventy-six pounds eight shillings and sixpence,	76 8 6
[illegible]n,	19 16 0	0 0 0	38 6 6	Fifty-eight pounds two shillings and sixpence,	58 2 6
Freetown,	14 0 0	0 0 0	35 8 0	Forty-nine pounds eight shillings,	49 8 0
Raynham,	0 0 0	0 0 0	22 17 6	Twenty-two pounds seventeen shillings and sixpence,	22 17 6
Easton,	10 0 0	0 0 0	26 5 9	Thirty-six pounds five shillings and ninepence,	36 5 9
[illegible]y,	0 0 0	0 0 0	20 8 9	Twenty pounds eight shillings and ninepence,	20 8 9
Barrington,	0 0 0	0 0 0	0 0 0	. . . .	0 0 0
	£162 2s. 0d.	£0 0s. 0d.	£685 13s. 9d.		£847 15s. 9d.

IN THE COUNTY OF YORK.

York,	£5 4s. 0d.	£0 0s. 0d.	£88 2s. 6d.	Ninety-three pounds six shillings and sixpence,	£93 6s. 6d.
Kittery,	17 8 0	34 11 6	103 10 0	One hundred and fifty-five pounds nine shillings and sixpence,	155 9 6
Wells,	12 2 0	0 0 0	39 12 0	Fifty-one pounds fourteen shillings,	51 14 0
Berwick,	16 4 0	0 13 7	54 0 0	Seventy pounds seventeen shillings and sevenpence,	70 17 7
Falmouth,	0 0 0	0 0 0	85 10 0	Eighty-five pounds ten shillings,	85 10 0
Biddeford,	14 0 0	0 0 0	36 6 0	Fifty pounds six shillings,	50 6 0
Arundel[l],	0 0 0	0 0 0	20 3 6	Twenty pounds three shillings and sixpence,	20 3 6
Scarborough,	16 8 0	0 0 0	30 18 9	Forty-seven pounds six shillings and ninepence,	47 6 9
North Yarmouth,	3 16 0	21 2 9	13 9 3	Thirty-eight pounds eight shillings,	38 8 0
Georgetown,	0 0 0	15 8 10	14 5 9	Twenty-nine pounds twelve shillings and sevenpence,	29 12 7
Brunswick,	0 0 0	0 0 0	12 17 3	Twelve pounds seventeen shillings and threepence,	12 17 3
Sheepscut,	0 0 0	0 0 0	9 0 0	Nine pounds,	9 0 0
	£85 2s. 0d.	£71 14s. 8d.	£507 15s. 0d.		£664 11s. 8d.

IN THE COUNTY OF DUKES COUNTY.

Edgartown,	£6 16s. 0d.	£0 0s. 0d.	£34 16s. 0d.	Forty-one pounds twelve shillings,	£41 12s. 0d.
Chilmark,	0 0 0	0 0 0	31 4 9	Thirty-one pounds four shillings and ninepence,	31 4 9
Tisbury,	0 0 0	0 0 0	19 19 0	Nineteen pounds nineteen shillings,	19 19 0
	£6 16s. 0d.	£0 0s. 0d.	£85 19s. 9d.		£92 15s. 9d.

IN NANTUCKET COUNTY.

Sherburne,	£7 4s. 0d.	£0 0s. 0d.	£131 3s. 6d.	One hundred and thirty-eight pounds seven shillings and sixpence,	£138 7s. 6d.

	REP[RESENTATI]VES' PAY, AND FINES.	ARREARS AND REPAIRS OF THE TOWN-HOUSE.	PROVINCE TAX.	SUM TOTAL.	
Suffolk, ...	£195 0s. 0d.	£1,599 7s. 9d.	£2,356 19s. 0d.	Four thousand one hundred & fifty-one pounds six shillings & ninepence, ...	£4,151 6s. 9d.
Essex, ...	171 8 0	177 15 3	1,689 16 6	Two thousand and thirty-eight pounds nineteen shillings and ninepence, ...	2,038 19 9
Middlesex, ...	329 12 0	1 9 11	1,222 4 0	Fifteen hundred and fifty-three pounds five shillings and elevenpence, ...	1,553 5 11
Hampshire, ...	88 6 0	0 0 0	535 10 0	Six hundred and twenty-three pounds sixteen shillings, ...	623 16 0
Worcester, ...	230 0 0	8 10 0	742 3 3	Nine hundred and eighty pounds thirteen shillings and threepence,	980 13 3
Plymouth, ...	187 8 0	15 17 5	727 12 3	Nine hundred and thirty pounds seventeen shillings and eightpence,	930 17 8
Barnstable, ...	60 8 0	1 19 0	315 3 0	Three hundred and seventy-seven pounds ten shillings, ...	377 10 0
Bristol, ...	162 2 0	0 0 0	685 13 9	Eight hundred and forty-seven pounds fifteen shillings and ninepence, ...	847 15 9
York, ...	85 2 0	71 14 8	507 15 0	Six hundred and sixty-four pounds eleven shillings and eightpence,	664 11 8
Dukes County, . . .	0 16 0	0 0 0	85 19 9	Ninety-two pounds fifteen shillings and ninepence, ...	92 15 9
Nantucket, ...	7 4 0	0 0 0	131 3 6	One hundred and thirty-eight pounds seven shillings and sixpence,	138 7 6
	£1,523 6s. 0d.	£1,876 14s. 0d.	£9,000 0s. 0d.		£12,400 0s. 0d.

And be it further enacted,

[Sect. 2.] That the treasurer do forthwith send out his warrants, directed to the selectmen or assessors of each town or district within this province, requiring them, respectively, to assess the sum hereby set upon such town or district, in manner following; that is to say, to assess all rateable male polls above the age of sixteen years, within their respective towns or districts, or next adjo[y][*i*]ning to them, belonging to no other town, one shilling and sixpence per poll, and proportionably in assessing the fines mentioned in this act, and the additional sum received out of the treasury for the payment of the representatives (except the governo[*u*]r, the lieutenant-governo[*u*]r and their families, the president, fellows and students of Harvard College, set[*t*]led ministers and grammar-school masters, who are hereby exempted as well from being taxed for their polls, as for their estates being in their own hands and under their actual management and improvement; as also all the estate pertaining to Harvard College); and other persons, if such the[*i*]r[e] be, who, thrô[*ugh*] age, infirmity or extream poverty, in the judgment of the assessors, are not capable to pay towards publick charges, they may exempt their polls, and so much of their estates as in their prudence they shall think fit and judge meet.

[Sect. 3.] And the justices in their general sessions, in the respective counties assembled, in granting a county tax or assessment, are hereby ordered and directed to apportion the same on the several towns in such county in proportion to their province rate, exclusive of what has been paid out of the publick treasury to the representative of each town for his service; and the assessors of each town in the province are also directed, in making an assessment, to govern themselves by the same rule; and all estates, both real and personal, lying within the limits of such town or district, or next unto the same, not paying elsewhere, in whose hands, tenure, occupation or possession soever the same is or shall be found, and also the incomes or profits which any person or persons, except as before excepted, do or shall receive from any trade, faculty, business or employment whatsoever, and all profits that shall or may arise by money or other estate not particularly otherwise assess[*e*]'d, or commissions of profit in their improvement, according to their understanding or cunning, at a halfpenny on the pound; and to abate or multiply the same, if need be, so as to make up the sum set and ordered hereby for such town or district to pay; and, in making their assessment, to estimate houses and lands at six years' income of the yearly rents whereat the same may be reasonably set or let for in the place where they l[i][*y*]e: *saving* all contracts between landlord and tenant, and where no contract is, the landlord to reimburse one-half of the tax set upon such houses and lands; and to estimate negro, Indian and molatto servants proportionably as other personal estate, according to their sound judgment and discretion; as also to estimate every ox of four years old and upwards, at forty shillings; every cow of three years old and upwards, at thirty shillings; every horse and mare of three years old and upwards, at forty shillings; every swine of one year old and upwards, at eight shillings; goats and sheep of one year old, three shillings each: likewise requiring the said assessors to make a fair list of the said assessment, setting forth, in distinct columns, against each particular person's name, how much he or she is assess[*e*]'d at for polls, and how much for houses and lands, and how much for personal estate, and income by trade or faculty, and if as guardian, or for any estate in his or her improvement, in trust, to be distinctly express[*e*]'d; and the list or lists, so perfected and signed by them, or the major part of them, to commit to the collectors, constable or constables of such town or district, and to return a certificate of the name or names of such collectors, constable or constables, with the sum total to each of them committed, unto himself, some time before the last day of October next.

[SECT. 4.] And the treasurer for the time being, upon receipt of such certificate, is hereby impowered and ordered to issue forth his warrants to the collector, or constable or constables of such town or district, requiring him or them, respectively, to collect the whole of each respective sum assess[*e*]'d on each particular person, before the last day of December next; and to pay in their collection, and issue the accompts of the whole, at or before the last day of March next, which will be in the year of our Lord one thousand seven hundred and fifty-four.

And be it further enacted,

[SECT. 5.] That the assessors of each town or district, respectively, in convenient time, before their making [of] the assessment, shall give seasonable warning to the inhabitants, in a town meeting, or by posting up notifications in some place or places in such town or district, or notify the inhabitants some other way to give or bring in to the assessors true and perfect lists of their polls, rateable estate, and income by trade or faculty, and gain by money at interest; and if any person or persons shall neglect or refuse so to do, or bring in a false list, it shall be lawful to and for the assessors to assess such person or persons, according to their known ability in such town, in their sound judgment and discretion, their due proportion of this tax, as near as they can, agre[e]able to the rules herein given, under the penalty of twenty shillings for each person that shall be convicted by legal proof, in the judgment of the said assessors, in bringing in a false list; the said fines to be for the use of the poor of such town or district where the delinquent lives, to be levied by warrant from the assessors, directed to the collector or constables, in manner as is directed for gathering town assessments, to be paid in to the town treasurer or selectmen for the use aforesaid: *saving* to the party aggr[ei][*ie*]ved at the judgment of the assessors in setting forth such fine, liberty of appeal therefrom to the court of general sessions of the peace within the county for relief as in case of being overrated. And if any person or persons shall not bring in a list of their estate as aforesaid to the assessors, he or they so neglecting shall not be admitted to make application to the court of general sessions for any abatement of the assessment laid on him.

[SECT. 6.] And if the party be not convicted of any falseness in the list, by him presented, of the polls, rateable estate, or income by trade or faculty, business or employment, which he does or shall exercise, or in gain by money at interest or otherwise, or other estate not particularly assess[*e*]'d, such list shall be a rule for such person's proportion to the tax, which the assessors may not exceed.

And forasmuch as, oftentimes, sundry persons, not belonging to this province, bring considerable trade and merchandi[s][*z*]e, and by reason that the tax or rate of the town where they come to trade is finished and delivered to the constable or collectors, and, before the next year's assessment, are gone out of the province, and so pay nothing towards the support of the government, though, in the time of their residing here, they reaped considerable gain by trade, and had the protection of the government,—

Be it further enacted,

[SECT. 7.] That when any such person or persons shall come and reside in any town within this province, and bring any merchandi[s][*z*]e, and trade, to deal therewith, the assessors of such town are hereby impowered to rate and assess all such persons according to their circumstances, pursuant to the rules and directions in this act provided, tho'[ugh] the former rate may have been finished, and the new one not perfected, as aforesaid.

And be it further enacted,

[Sect. 8.] That when any merchant, trader, or factor, inhabitant of some one town within this province, shall traffic, or carry on trade and business, and set up a store in some other town in the province, the assessors of such town where such trade and business shall be carried on as aforesaid, be and hereby are impowered to rate and assess all such merchants, traders, and factors, their goods and merchandi[s][*z*]e, for carrying on such trade and exercising their faculty in such town, pursuant to the rules and directions of this act; and that before any such assessors shall rate such persons as afore mentioned, the selectmen of the town where such trade is carried on shall transmit a list of such persons as they shall judge may be rated within the intent of this act; and the constables or collectors are hereby enjoined to levy and collect all such sums committed to them and assessed on persons who are not of this province, or are residents in other towns than those where they carry on their trade, and pay the same.

And be it further enacted,

[Sect. 9.] That the inhabitants of this province have liberty, if they see fit, to pay the several sums for which they may be respectively assess[*e*]'d, of the aforesaid sum of twelve thousand and four hundred pounds, in good merchantable hemp, or in good, merchantable, Isle-of-Sable codfish, or in good refin[*e*]'d bar[r]-iron, or in bloomery-iron, or in h[a][*o*]llow iron-ware, or in good Indian corn, or in good winter rye, or in good winter wheat, or in good barley, or in good barrel[l] pork, or in barrel[l] beef, or in duck or canvas, or in long whalebone, or in merchantable cordage, or in good train oyl, or in good beeswax, or in good bayberry-wax, or in tr[i][*y*]ed tallow, or in good pe[e][*a*]se, or in good sheepswool[*l*], or in good tann[*e*]'d sole-leather; and that the eldest councellors, for the time being, of each of those count[y][*ie*]s in the province, of which any one of the councellors is an inhabitant, together with the province treasurer, or the major part of them, be a committee, who are hereby directed and fully authorized and impowered, once in every month, if need be, to agree and set the several species and commodities aforesaid at some certain price, at which they shall be received towards the payment of the sums aforesaid: all which aforesaid commodities shall be of the produce of this province, and, as soon as conveniently may, be disposed of by the treasurer to the best advantage for so much as they will fetch in money; and the several persons paying their taxes in any of the commodities afore mentioned to run the risque and pay the charge of transporting the said commodities to the province treasury.

[Sect. 10.] And if any loss shall happen by the sale of the aforesaid species, it shall be made good by a tax of the next year; and if there be a surplusage, it shall remain as a stock in the treasury.

And whereas, the said sum of twelve thousand and four hundred pounds has not been appropriated to any supply bill for the payment of the publick debts,—

Be it enacted,

[Sect. 11.] That the said sum of twelve thousand and four hundred pounds, shall be issued out of the treasury, when received of the constables and collectors, in manner and for the purposes following; that is to say, the sum of two thousand and five hundred pounds, part of the said sum of twelve thousand and four hundred pounds, shall be applied for the service of the several forts and garrisons within this province, pursuant to such orders and grants as are or shall be made by this court for those purposes; and the further sum of seven hundred pounds, part of the aforesaid sum of twelve thousand and four hundred pounds, shall be appl[i][*y*]ed for the purchasing provisions, commissary's necessaries and disbursements for the service of the several forts and garrisons within this province, pursuant to such grants as are or shall be made by this court for that purpose; and the further sum of three thousand five hundred pounds, part of the said sum of twelve thousand and four hundred pounds, shall be applied for the payment of such premiums and grants that now are or hereafter may be made by this court; and the further sum of five hundred pounds, part of the aforesaid sum of twelve thousand and four hundred pounds, shall be applied for the discharge of other debts owing from this province to persons that have served, or shall serve them, by order of this court, in such matters and things where there is no establishment nor any certain sum assign[e]'d them for that purpose, and for paper, writing and printing; and the further sum of nine hundred pounds, part of the aforesaid sum of twelve thousand and four hundred pounds, shall be appl[i][*y*]ed for the payment of his majesty's council and house of representatives, serving in the general court during the several sessions of this present year.

And as there are sometimes contingent and unforeseen charges that demand prompt pay,—

Be it enacted,

[SECT. 12.] That the sum of fifty pounds, part of the aforesaid sum of twelve thousand and four hundred pounds, be applied to pay such contingent charges; and the further sum of four thousand two hundred and fifty pounds, being the remainder of the aforesaid sum of twelve thousand and four hundred pounds, remain in the hands of the treasurer to be drawn out for such uses as this court shall hereafter order, and for no other purpose whatsoever.

And be it further enacted,

[SECT. 13.] That the treasurer is hereby directed and ordered to pay the sum of twelve thousand and four hundred pounds, brought in by taxes as aforesaid, out of such appropriations as shall be directed to by warrant, and no other; and the secretary, to whom it belongs to keep the muster-rolls and acco[un][*mp*]ts of the charge, shall lay before the house of representatives, when they direct, such muster-rolls and acco[un][*mp*]ts, after payment thereof. [*Passed June* 21*; *published June* 23.

CHAPTER 11.

AN ACT FOR GRANTING TO HIS MAJESTY SEVERAL RATES AND DUTIES OF IMPOST AND TUNNAGE OF SHIPPING.

1751-52, chap. 16. WHEREAS, in and by an act of this province, pass'd in the twenty-fifth of his majesty's reign, Andrew Oliver, Thomas Hubbard, Esq[rs]., and Mr. Harrison Gray, were impowered to borrow, for a term not exceeding two years, a sum not exceeding eighteen thousand six hundred pounds, in Spanish mill'd dollars, or lawful money at six shillings and eightpence per ounce, or gold at five pounds one shilling and sevenpence per ounce, or government's securities, which became due the thirty-first day of December, 1751, or that became due the tenth day of June, 1752; also in warrants on the treasury, and should give secu-

* According to the record, this act was signed June 22.

rity to the lenders of the money so borrowed, and should pay the same into the treasury, for the supply thereof; and by the said act it was further ordered that the treasurer should pay the principal and interest as the same should respectively become due, on all the notes given by the committee afores[d], for all such sums as they should so borrow for the government, and deposit in the treasury; and in order to enable the treasurer to discharge the notes and obligations that should by the committee be given for said sum, in pursuance of the afore-mentioned act, it was therein provided, that the duty of impost for two years, from the twenty-ninth day of June, 1752, should be applied for the payment and discharge of the principal and interest that should become due on said notes and obligations, and to no other purpose whatever,—

We, his maj[ty's] most loyal and dutiful subjects, the represent[ves] of the province of the Massachusetts Bay, in New England, being desirous of enabling the treasurer to discharge the notes and obligations as aforesaid, have chearfully and unanimously given and granted and do hereby give and grant, to his most excellent majesty, to the end and use aforesaid, and to no other use, the several duties of impost upon wines, liquors, goods, wares and merchandize that shall be imported into this province, and tunnage of shipping, hereafter mentioned; and pray that it may be enacted,—

And be it accordingly enacted by the Lieutenant-Govern[r], Council and House of Repres[ves],

[Sect. 1.] That from and after the twenty-sixth day of June curr[t], and during the space of one year, there shall be paid by the importer of all wines, liquors, goods, wares and merchandize that shall be imported into this province by any of the inhabitants thereof (salt, cotton-wooll, pig-iron, mehogany, black walnut, lignum-vitæ, red cedar and brazilleto wood, provisions, and every other thing of the growth and produce of New England, and also all prize goods condemn'd in any part of this province, excepted), the several rates and duties of impost following; vizt.,—

For every pipe of wine of the Western Islands, twenty-four shillings.

For every pipe of Madaira, twenty-six shillings and eightpence.

For every pipe of other sorts not mention'd, twenty-four shillings.

For every hogshead of rum, containing one hundred gallons, twenty shillings.

For every hogshead of sugar, fourpence.

For every hogshead of molosses, fourpence.

For every hogshead of tobacco, ten shillings.

For every ton of logwood, fourpence.

—And so, proportionably, for greater or lesser quantitys.

And all other commodities, goods or merchandize not mention'd or excepted, fourpence for every twenty shillings value: all goods imported from Great Britain, and hogshead and barrell-staves and heading from any of his majesty's colonys and provinces on this continent, excepted.

[Sect. 2.] And for any of the above wines, liquors, goods, wares and merchandize, &c., that shall be imported into this province by any of the inhabitants of the other provinces or colonies on this continent, or of the English West-India Islands, or in any ship or vessel to them belonging, on the proper account of any of the said inhabitants of the other provinces or colonies on this continent, or of the inhabitants of any of the West-India Islands, there shall be paid by the importers double the impost appointed by this act to be received for every species above mentioned; and for all rum, sugar and molosses, imported and brought into this province by any ship or vessel, or by land-carriage, from any of the colonies of Connecticut, New Hampshire or Rhode Island, shall be paid by the importer, the rates and duties following:—

For every hogshead of rum, containing one hundred gallons, forty shillings.

For every hogshead of molosses, containing one hundred gallons, eightpence.

For every hogshead of sugar, containing one thousand weight, eightpence.

—And in that proportion for more or less thereof;

And for all European goods, and for all other goods, wares or merchandize, eightpence for every twenty shillings value: *provided always*, that all hogshead and barrel-staves and heading from any of his majesty's provinces or colonies, all provisions and other things that are the growth of New England, all salt, cotton-wool and pig-iron, mehogany, black walnut, lignum-vitæ, red cedar and brazilletto wood, are and shall be exempted from every the rates and duties aforesaid.

And be it further enacted,

[SECT. 3.] That the impost rates and duties aforesaid shall be paid in current lawful money by the importer of any wines, liquors, goods or merchandize, unto the commissioner to be appointed, as is hereinafter to be directed, for entering and receiving the same, at or before the landing of any wines, liquors, goods or merchandize: only the commissioner or receiver is hereby allowed to give credit to such person or persons, where his or their duty of impost, in one ship or vessel, doth exceed the sum of six pounds; and in cases where the commissioner or receiver shall give credit, he shall ballance and settle his accompts with every person on or before the last day of April, so that the same accompts may be ready to be produced in court in May next after. And all entries, where the impost or duties to be paid doth not exceed three shillings, shall be made without charge to the importer; and not more than sixpence to be demanded for any other single entry to what value soever.

And be it further enacted,

[SECT. 4.] That the master of every ship or vessel coming into this province from any other place, shall, within twenty-four hours after his arrival in any port or harbour, and before bulk is broken, make report and deliver a manifest, in writing, under his hand, to the commissioner aforesaid, of the contents of the loading of such ship or vessel, therein particularly expressing the species, kind and quantitys of all the wines, liquors, goods, wares and merchandize imported in such ship or vessel, with the marks and numbers thereof, and to whom the same are consign'd; and make oath before the said commissioner that the same manifest contains a just and true accompt of all the lading taken on board and imported in such ship or vessel, so far as he knows or believes; and that if he knows of any more wines, liquors, goods, wares or merchandize laden on board such ship or vessel, and imported therein, he will forthwith make report thereof to the commissioner aforesaid, and cause the same to be added to his manifest.

And be it further enacted,

[SECT. 5.] That if the master of any ship or vessell shall break bulk, or suffer any of the wines, liquors, goods, wares and merchandize imported in such ship or vessel to be unloaden before report and entry thereof be made as aforesaid, he shall forfeit the sum of one hundred pounds.

And be it further enacted,

[SECT. 6.] That all merchants and other persons, being owners of any wines, liquors, goods, wares or merchandize imported into this province, for which any of the rates or dutys aforesaid are payable, or having the same consign'd to them, shall make a like entry thereof with the commissioner aforesaid, and produce an invoice of all such goods as pay *ad valorem*, and make oath before him in form following; vizt.,—

You, A. B., do swear that the entry of the goods and merchandize by you now made, exhibits the present price of said goods at this market, and that, *bonâ fide*, according to your best skill and judgment, it is not less than the real value thereof. So help you God.

—which oath the commissioner or receiver is hereby impowered and directed to administer; and the owners aforesaid shall pay the duty of impost by this act required, before such wines, liquors, goods, wares or merchandize be landed or taken out of the vessel in which the same shall be imported.

[Sect. 7.] And no wines, liquors, goods, wares or merchandize that by this act are liable to pay impost or duty, shall be landed on any wharffe, or into any warehouse or other place, but in the daytime only, and that after sunrise and before sunset, unless in the presence and with the consent of the commissioner or receiver, on pain of forfeiting all such wines, liquors, goods, wares and merchandize, and the lighter, boat or vessel out of which the same shall be landed or put into any warehouse or other place.

[Sect. 8.] And if any person or persons shall not have and produce an invoice of the quantitys of rum or liquors to him or them consign'd, then the cask wherein the same is, shall be gauged at the charge of the importer, that the contents thereof may be known.

And be it further enacted,

[Sect. 9.] That the importer of all wines, liquors, goods, wares and merchandize, within one year from and after the publication of this act, by land-carriage, or in small vessells or boats, shall make report and deliver a manifest thereof to the commissioner aforesaid or his deputy, therein particularly expressing the species, kind and quantity of all such wines, liquors, goods, wares and merchandize so imported, with the marks and numbers thereof, when, how and by whom brought; and shall make oath, before the said commissioner or his deputy, to the truth of such report and manifest, and shall also pay the several dutys aforesaid by this act charged and chargable upon such wines, liquors, goods, wares and merchandize, before the same are landed, housed or put into any store or place whatever.

And be it further enacted,

[Sect. 10.] That every merchant or other person importing any wines into this province, shall be allowed twelve per cent for leakage: *provided*, such wines shall not have been filled up on board; and that every hogshead, butt or pipe of wine that hath two-thirds thereof leak'd out, shall be accounted for outs, and the merchant or importer to pay no duty for the same. And no master of any ship or vessel shall suffer any wines to be fill'd up on board without giving a certificate of the quantity so filled up, under his hand, before the landing thereof, to the commissioner or receiver of impost for such port, on pain of forfeiting the sum of one hundred pounds.

[Sect. 11.] And if it may be made to appear that any wines imported in any ship or vessel be decayed at the time of unloading thereof, or in twenty days afterwards, oath being made before the commissioner or receiver that the same hath not been landed above that time, the duties and impost paid for such wines shall be repay'd unto the importer thereof.

And be it further enacted,

[Sect. 12.] That the master of every ship or vessel importing any wines, liquors, goods, wares or merchandize, shall be liable to and shall pay the impost for such and so much thereof, contain'd in his manifest, as shall not be duly enter'd, nor the duty paid for the same by the person or persons to whom such wines, liquors, goods, wares or merchandize are or shall be consign'd. And it shall and may be lawful, to and for the master of every ship or other vessel, to secure and detain in his hands, at the owner's risque, all such wines, liquors, goods, wares and merchandize imported in any ship or vessel, until he receives a certificate, from the commissioner or receiver of the impost, that the duty for the same is paid, and until he be repaid his necessary charges in securing the same; or such master may deliver such wines, liquors, goods, wares or merchandize as are not entered, unto the commissioner or receiver of the impost in such port, or his order, who is hereby impowered and directed to receive and keep the same, at the owner's risque, until the impost thereof, with the charges, be paid; and then to deliver such wines, liquors, goods, wares or merchandize as such master shall direct.

And be it further enacted,

[SECT. 13.] That the commissioner or receiver of the impost in each port, shall be and hereby is impowered to sue the master of any ship or vessel, for the impost or duty of so much of the lading of any wines, liquors, goods, wares or merchandize imported therein, according to the manifest to be by him given upon oath, as aforesaid, as shall remain not enter'd and the duty of impost therefor not paid. And where any goods, wares or merchandize are such as that the value thereof is not known, whereby the impost to be recovered of the master, for the same, cannot be ascertain'd, the owner or person to whom such goods, wares or merchandize are or shall be consign'd, shall be summoned to appear as an evidence at the court where such suit for the impost and the duty thereof shall be brought, and be there required to make oath to the value of such goods, wares or merchandize.

And be it further enacted,

[SECT. 14.] That the ship or vessel, with her tackle, apparrell and furniture, the master of which shall make default in anything by this act required to be perform'd by him, shall be liable to answer and make good the sum or sums forfeited by such master, according to this act, for any such default, as also to make good the impost or duty for any such wines, liquors, goods, wares and merchandize not entred as aforesaid; and, upon judgment recovered against such master, the said ship or vessel, with so much of the tackle or appurces thereof as shall be sufficient to satisfy said judgment, may be taken into execution for the same; and the commissioner or receiver of the impost is hereby impowered to make seizure of the said ship or vessel, and detain the same under seizure until judgment be given in any suit to be commenced and prosecuted for any of the said forfeitures of impost; to the intent, if judgment be rendered for the prosecutor or informer, such ship or vessel and appurces may be expos'd to sale, for satisfaction thereof, as is before provided: *unless* the owners, or some on their behalf, for the releasing of such ship or vessel from under seizure or restraint, shall give sufficient security unto the commissioner or receiver of impost that seiz'd the same, to respond and satisfy the sum or value of the forfeitures and duties, with charges, that shall be recover'd against the master thereof, upon such suit to be brought for the same, as aforesaid; and the master occasioning such loss or damage unto his owners, through his default or neglect, shall be liable unto their action for the same.

And be it further enacted,

[SECT. 15.] That the naval officer within any of the ports of this province shall not clear or give passes to any master of any ship or other vessel, outward bound, until he shall be certified, by the commissioner or receiver of the impost, that the duty and impost for the goods last imported in such ship or vessel are paid or secured to be paid.

[Sect. 16.] And the commissioner or receiver of the impost is hereby impowered to allow bills of store to the master of any ship or vessel importing any wines or liquors, for such private adventures as shall belong to the master or seamen of such ship or vessel, at the discretion of the commissioner or receiver, not exceeding three per cent of the lading; and the duties payable by this act for such wines and liquors, in such bills of stores mentioned and expressed, shall be abated.

And for the more effectual preventing any wines, rum or other distill'd spirits being brought into the province from the neighbouring governments, by land, or in small boats or vessells, or any other way, and also to prevent wines, rum or other distill'd spirits being first sent out of this province, to save the duty of impost, and afterwards brought into the government again,—

Be it enacted,

[Sect. 17.] That the commissioner and receiver of the aforesaid duties of impost shall, and he is hereby impowered and enjoyned to, appoint one suitable person or persons as his deputy or deputys, in all such places in this province where it is likely that wine, rum or other distill'd spirits will be brought out of other governments into this; which officers shall have power to seize the same, unless the owner shall make it appear that the duty of impost hath been paid therefor since their being brought into or relanded in this government; and such officer or officers are also impowered to search, in all suspected places, for such wines, rum and distilled spirits brought or relanded in this government, where the duty is not paid as aforesaid, and to seize and secure the same for the ends and uses as in this act is hereafter provided.

And be it further enacted,

[Sect. 18.] That the commissioner or his deputys shall have full power to administer the several oaths aforesaid, and to search in all suspected places for all such wines, rum, liquors, goods, wares and merchandize as are brought into this province, and landed contrary to the true intent and meaning of this act, and to seize the same for the uses hereinafter mentioned.

And be it further enacted,

[Sect. 19.] That there shall be paid, by the master of every ship or other vessel, coming into any port or ports of this province, to trade or traffick, whereof all the owners are not belonging to this province (except such vessels as belong to Great Britain, the provinces or colonies of Pensylvania, West and East Jersey, Connecticut, New York, New Hampshire and Rhode Island), every voyage such ship or vessel doth make, one pound of good pistol-powder for every ton such ship or vessel is in burthen: *saving* for that part which is owned in Great Britain, this province, or any of the aforesaid governments, which are hereby exempted; to be paid unto the commissioner or receiver of the dutys of impost, to be employ'd for the ends and uses aforesaid.

[Sect. 20.] And the said commissioner is hereby impowered to appoint a meet and suitable person, to repair unto and on board any ship or vessel, to take the exact measure or tunnage thereof, in case he shall suspect that the register of such ship or vessel doth not express and set forth the full burthen of the same; the charge thereof to be paid by the master or owner of such ship or vessel, before she shall be cleared, in case she shall appear to be of a greater burthen: otherwise, to be paid by the commissioner out of the money received by him for impost, and shall be allowed him, accordingly, by the treasurer, in his accompts. And the naval officer shall not clear any vessel, until he be certifyed, also, by the commissioner, that the duty of tunnage for the same is paid, or that it is such a vessel for which none is payable according to this act.

And be it further enacted,

[SECT. 21.] That when and so often as any wine or rum imported into this province, the duty of impost upon which shall have been paid agreeable to this act, shall be reshipp'd and exported from this government to any other part of the world, that then, and in every such case, the exporter of such wine or rum shall make oath, at the time of shipping, before the receiver of impost, or his deputy, that the whole of the wine or rum so shipped has, *bonâ fide*, had the aforesaid duty of impost paid on the same, and shall afterwards produce a certificate, from some officer of the customs, that the same has been landed out of this government,—or otherwise, in case such rum or wines shall be exported to any place where there is no officer of the customs, or to any foreign port, the master of the vessell in which the same shall be exported shall make oath that the same has been landed out of the government, and the exporter shall, upon producing such certificate, or upon such oath of the master, make oath that he verily believes no part of said wines or rum has been relanded in this province,—such exporter shall be allowed to draw back from the receiver of impost as follows; viz[t].,—

For every pipe of Western-Island wine, twenty shillings.

For every pipe of Madeira and other sorts, twenty-two shillings.

And for every hogshead of rum, eighteen shillings.

Provided, always,—

[SECT. 22.] That if, after the shipping any such wine or rum to be exported as aforesaid, and giving security as aforesaid, in order to obtain the draw-back aforesaid, the wine or rum so shipped to be exported, or any part thereof, shall be relanded in this province, or brought into the same from any other province or colony, that then all such rum and wine so relanded and brought again into this province, shall be forfeited and may be seized by the commissioner aforesaid, or his deputy.

And be it further enacted,

[SECT. 23.] That there be one fit person, and no more, nominated and appointed by this court, as a commissioner and receiver of the aforesaid dutys of impost and tunnage of shipping, and for the inspection, care and management of the said office, and whatsoever thereto relates, to receive commission for the same from the governor or commander-in-chief for the time being, with authority to substitute and appoint a deputy receiver in each port, or other places besides that wherein he resides, and to grant warrants to such deputy receivers for the said place, and to collect and receive the impost and tunnage of shipping as aforesaid that shall become due within such port, and to render the account thereof, and to pay in the same, to the said commissioner and receiver: which said commissioner and receiver shall keep fair books of all entrys and duties arising by virtue of this act; also, a particular account of every vessel, so that the duties of impost and tunnage arising on the said vessel may appear; and the same to. ly open, at all seasonable times, to the view and perusal of the treasurer or receiver-general of this province (or any other person or persons whom this court shall appoint), with whom he shall account for all collections and payments, and pay all such monies as shall be in his hands, as the treasurer or receiver-general shall demand it. And the said commissioner or receiver and his deputy or deputys, before their entring upon the execution of their office, shall be sworn to deal truly and faithfully therein, and shall attend in said office from ten of the clock in the forenoon, until one in the afternoon.

[SECT. 24.] And the said commissioner and receiver, for his labor, care and expences in the said office, shall have and receive, out of the province treasury, the sum of sixty pounds per annum; and his deputy or deputys to be paid for their service such sum or sums as the said commissioner and receiver, with the treasurer, shall agree upon, not exceeding four pounds per annum, each; and the treasurer is hereby ordered, in passing and receiving the said commissioner's accounts, accordingly, to allow the payment of such salary or salarys, as aforesaid, to himself and his deputys.

And be it further enacted,

[Sect. 25.] That all penaltys, fines and forfeitures accruing and arising by virtue of any breach of this act, shall be one half to his majesty for the uses and intents for which the afore-mentioned dutys of impost are granted, and the other half to him or them that shall seize, inform and sue for the same, by action, bill, plaint or information, in any of his majesty's courts of record, wherein no essoign, protection or wager of law shall be allowed: the whole charge of the prosecution to be taken out of the half belonging to the informer.

And be it further enacted,

[Sect. 26.] That from and after the publication of this act, in all causes where any claimer shall appear, and shall not make good the claim, the charges of prosecution shall be born and paid by the said claimer, and not by the informer. [*Passed June* 15; *published June* 23.

ACTS

PASSED AT THE SESSION BEGUN AND HELD AT BOSTON, ON THE FIFTH DAY OF SEPTEMBER, A. D. 1753.

CHAPTER 12.

AN ACT FOR SETTING OFF THE INHABITANTS, AS ALSO ESTATES OF THE PROPRIETORS, OF THAT PART OF THE PRECINCT OF SALEM AND BEVERLY, SO CALLED, WHICH IS PART OF SALEM, TO THE TOWN OF BEVERLY.

Be it enacted by the Governour, Council and House of Representatives,

Divers inhabitants set off from Salem to Beverly.

[SECT. 1.] That all the inhabitants, with their estates and the estates of the proprietors of that part of said precinct which is part of Salem, by the same bounds as it was heretofore set off to make the precinct of Salem and Beverly, be and hereby are set off and annexed to the town of Beverly, and made part and parcel thereof, to do duty and receive privile[d]ges therein, for the future, with the rest of the inhabitants of the said town of Beverly.

Be it further enacted,

Money to be paid by Salem to Beverly.

[SECT. 2.] That the sum of thirteen pounds six shillings and eightpence, allowed by the town of Salem to the aforesaid inhabitants and proprietors, agreable to the vote of said town on the nineteenth day of March last, shall be paid into the treasury of the town of Beverly for the use and service of said town.

Be it further enacted,

Part of Salem tax set to Beverly.

[SECT 3.] That one-tenth part of the province tax, which, according to the last valuation, was set upon the town of Salem, shall hereafter be taken off from the town of Salem and laid upon the town of Beverly; and the treasurer of the town of Beverly shall pay into the treasury of the town of Salem one-tenth part, likewise, of the sum of the province tax set on the town of Salem the current year; being the said inhabitants' and proprietors' proportion of said tax.

And be it further enacted,

Charge of highways to be borne by Beverly.

[SECT. 4.] That all charges for repairing the highways in Salem part of said precinct, or otherwise, since the nineteenth day of March last, shall be born[e] and paid by the town of Beverly, and assessed on the estates and inhabitants there accordingly; and the inhabitants of that part of said precinct shall be exempted from paying any taxes in the town of Salem, for province, county or town charges, from and after the said nineteenth day of March last. [*Passed in the Council,—with amendments, agreed to, the same day, by the Representatives,—September* 11.*]

* This is the only record that has been discovered respecting the date of passage of this act. The date of publication has not been found.

CHAPTER 13.

AN ACT TO APPOINT COMMISSIONERS TO EXAMINE INTO THE BOUNDARY-LINE OR LINES BETWEEN THIS GOVERNMENT AND NEW YORK, AND TO TREAT WITH THE COMMISSIONERS APPOINTED BY THE COLONY OF NEW YORK RESPECTING THE SAME.

WHEREAS disputes of late have arisen with respect to the right of soil and jurisdiction of the lands which lie west of and near to the towns of Sheffield and Stockbridge, and encroachments have been made upon the lands of this province,— Preamble.

Be it enacted by the Governour, Council and House of Representatives, That Samuel Welles, Esq., John Chandler, Esq., Thomas Hutchinson, Esq., James Otis, Esq., and Oliver Partridge, Esq., be and hereby are appointed commissioners to examine into the boundary lines between this province and New York; and they are hereby authorized and directed to repair to the town of Middleton, in the colony of Connecticut, upon the fifteenth day of November next, then and there to meet with commissioners appointed by the government of New York for the same purpose, or to meet at such other time or at such other place in said colony as shall be mutually agreed upon between the commissioners aforesaid; and the said Samuel Welles, Esq., John Chandler, Esq., Thomas Hutchinson, Esq., James Otis, Esq., and Oliver Partridge, Esq., or the major part of them, are hereby fully authorized and impowred to treat with the said commissioners from New York, and to receive such proposals as they shall make for settling the said boundary-line, as likewise to pursue all such steps and methods, and to make such other proposals to the said commissioners from New York, as to them, the said Samuel Welles, John Chandler, Thomas Hutchinson, James Otis and Oliver Partridge, or the major part of them, shall seem most advisable, in order to procure a speedy and legal settlement of the boundary aforesaid: *provided, always,* that no such proposed settlement shall actually be made by the said commissioners, but the same shall be reported by them to the general assembly of this province. [*Passed September* 13; *published September* 22.

Commissioners appointed to settle the boundary with New York government.

Proviso.

CHAPTER 14.

AN ACT TO IMPOWER THE PROPRIETORS OF THE MEETING-HOUSE IN THE FIRST PARISH IN SALEM, WHERE THE REVEREND MR. DUDLEY LEAVITT NOW OFFICIATES, TO RAISE MONEY TO DEFREY MINISTERIAL AND OTHER NECESSARY CHARGES.

WHEREAS the raising of money for defreying ministerial charges, in the First Parish in Salem, by an assessment or tax on polls and estates in said parish, is, under its present circumstances, attended with many difficulties and inconveniences,— Preamble.

Be it therefore enacted by the Governour, Council and House of Representatives,

[SECT. 1.] That the proprietors of the meeting-house in said First Parish in Salem, in which the Reverend Mr. Dudley Leavitt officiates, be and hereby are allowed and impowred to raise, by an assessment or tax on the pews in said meeting-house, such sum or sums as shall be

Proprietors of Mr. Dudley Leavitt's meeting-house to lay taxes on pews, &c.

agreed upon by the proprietors, or the major part of such of them as shall be assembled at any legal meeting called for that purpose, for the defreying the ministerial and other incidental charges; the first meeting of such proprietors to be called agreable to the direction of the act made and passed in the eighth and ninth years of his present majesty's reign, intitled "An Act directing how meetings of proprietors in wharves or other real estates besides lands may be called."

1735-36, chap. 5, § 1.

And to the intent that such tax or assessment may be equitably made and duly collected,—

Be it further enacted,

Pews to be valued and assessed.

[SECT. 2.] That the proprietors of the said meeting-house be, and hereby are, impowred to cause the pews in the said meeting-house to be valued according to the convenience of said pews and their scituation, and to put a new estimate on the pews, from time to time, as shall be found necessary, and to determine how much each pew, or part of a pew, shall pay towards defreying the charges aforesaid, and the time and manner in which the same shall be paid; and appoint a collector or collectors to collect the sum or sums so agreed to be rais'd, who shall be sworn to the faithful discharge of his or their said trust; and if any proprietor or owner of a pew in the said meeting-house shall neglect or refuse to pay the sum or sums assessed thereon, after having twenty days' notice thereof given him by the collector or collectors, the proprietors of the said meeting-house shall be, and hereby are, impowred, by themselves or by their committee, to sell or dispose of the pew of such delinquent, according to the valuation thereof as aforesaid, and, with the money rais'd by such sale, to pay the assessment or tax on said pew remaining unpaid, together with the charges arising on the sale; the overplus, if any there be, to be returned to the owner thereof.

Collectors to be appointed.

Pews to be sold, in case.

Provided, nevertheless,—

[SECT. 3.] That when the owner of any pew shall make a tender of the same to the proprietors, or to their committee, at the valuation aforesaid, and they shall refuse or neglect to accept the same, no sum shall be deducted out of the sale of said pew but such only as shall have become due before the making of such tender.

Limitation.

[SECT. 4.] This act to continue and be in force for the space of three years from the publication of the same, and no longer. [*Passed September* 14; *published September* 22.

CHAPTER 15.

AN ACT IN ADDITION TO AN ACT INTITLED "AN ACT FOR ENCOURAGING THE KILLING OF WOLVES, BEARS, WILDCATS AND CATAMOUNTS WITHIN THIS PROVINCE."

Preamble.

1745-46, chap. 5. 1750-51, chap. 4.

WHEREAS the number of wolves and other beasts of prey are very much increased in many parts of this province, and the encouragement given by law for destroying them has failed of answering the proposed design,—

Be it therefore enacted by the Governour, Council and House of Representatives,

Premium for killing wolves, catamounts, and wildcats.

[SECT. 1.] That, for the future, whosoever shall, during the continuance of this act, kill any wolves, catamounts or wildcat[*t*]s within this province, they shall be intitled to the following premiums out of the publick treasury; that is to say, for every such grown wolf of one year old, four pounds; for every wolf's whelp, under one year old and not taken out of the belly of a wolf, forty shillings; for every cat[t]amount, four pounds; for every cat[t]amount's whelp, under one year old, not taken out of the belly of a catamount, forty shillings; for every grown wildcat, ten shillings; for every wildcat's whelp, under a year old as aforesaid, five shillings.

And be it further enacted,

[SECT. 2.] That the method of proof of the killing of such beast[s], and the same process for obtaining such premium, shall be had by this act as is appointed by the aforesaid act. Method of proof.

[SECT. 3.] This act to be in force three years from the twentieth day of October, one thousand seven hundred and fifty-three, and no longer. [*Passed to be engrossed September* 11*; *published September* 22. Limitation.

* The engrossment of this act not having been found, the above date, from the records, is the nearest item that could be discovered indicating the date of passage.

ACTS

PASSED AT THE SESSION BEGUN AND HELD AT BOSTON, ON THE FOURTH DAY OF DECEMBER, A. D. 1753.

CHAPTER 16.

AN ACT TO INCORPORATE WILLIAM STARKEY AND OTHERS, BY THE NAME OF THE MARINE SOCIETY.

Preamble.

WHEREAS a considerable number of persons that are or have been masters of vessel[l]s, have for many years past associated themselves in the town of Boston; and the principal ends of said society are to improve the knowledge of this coast, by their several members', upon their arrival from sea, communicating their observations, inwards and outwards, of the variation of the needle, the soundings, courses [*and*] distances, and all other remarkable things about it, in writing, to be lodged with the society; to make the navigation more safe, and to rel[ei][*ie*]ve one another and their families in poverty, or other accidents in life which they are more particularly liable to; and for this end they have rais[*e*]'d a considerable common stock, out of which they have from time to time contributed largely to the aforesaid purposes; and finding themselves under difficulties and discouragements in preserving the designs of their institution[s] without an incorporation, have, by their committee, petitioned to this court to be incorporated for the aforesaid purposes; *and whereas* their intention appears laudable and deserving encouragement,—

Be it therefore enacted by the Governour, Council and House of Representatives,

Names of the members of the Marine Society.

[SECT. 1.] That William Starkey, Edward Cahill, Isaac Freeman, Richard Humphr[e]ys, Edward Fryer, Moses Bennet, Jonathan Clarke, John Cullom, Joseph Prince, John Graham, Abraham Remmick, James Collingwood, John Church, Malachia Salter, John Cowley, John Jones, William Ellery, Adam McNeal[*e*], Thomas Oliver, Joshua Loring, Richard Wait, Nathaniel Howland, Francis Wells, Esq[r]., Abraham Hammett, Francis Ingraham, Samuel Coverly, William Sharrad, Roger Passmore, Mat[*t*]hew West, Thomas Allison, William Orne, James Hodges, Jonathan Bennet, Jonathan Fuller, Jeremiah Rogers, William Hutchinson, Benjamin Hallowell, Jun[r]., Joseph Inches, James Gould, Simon Tufts, Samuel Tufts, Giles Tidmarsh, Lewis Turner, Samuel Wells, William Ward, Daniel McCarty, Job Prince, James Hatch, Waffe Rand, Charles Giles, Peter Oliver, William Rhodes, David Baschard, William Eggleston, George Briggs, John Bradford, John Cathcart, Christopher Gardner, Henry Aitken, James Clarke, Joseph Dummet, Thomas Auston, James Belson, William Gowen, Nehemiah Robbins, Henry Bethune, James Clouston, Jonathan Waldo, William Coffin, Andrew Craige; Samuel Gallop, Nathanael Patten, Richard Mower, Jonathan Snelling, Philip Lewis, William Bathaw, James

Kirkwood, William Gorden, Thomas Mitchell, Thomas Potts, John Phillips, John Simpson, Jun[r]., Abraham Francis, Patrick James, Nathanael Williams, Thomas Adams, John Gaffney, Edward Emerson, Joseph Trout, the members of said society, be incorporated and made a body politick for the aforesaid purposes, by the name of the "Marine Society, at Boston, in New England"; and that they, their associates and successors, have perpetual succession by said name; and have a power of making by-laws, for the preservation and advancement of said body, not repugnant to the laws of the government, with penalties either of disfranchisement from said society, or of a mulct not exceeding twenty shillings, or without penalties, as it shall seem most meet; and have licence to make and appoint their common seal; and be liable to be sued, and enabled to sue, and make purchases, and take donations of real and personal estates, for the purposes aforesaid, not exceeding the sum of five hundred pounds per annum, and to manage and dispose said estate as shall seem fit: and said society shall have a master, deputy master, treasurer and clerk, and other officers they shall think proper. Marine Society in Boston incorporated.

And be it further enacted,

[SECT. 2.] That the said Marine Society shall, on the first, second, third and fourth Tuesdays of February next, assemble to appoint their first master, deputy master, treasurer and clerk, and other officers they shall think proper, and their seal, and make by-laws; and said officers shall continue till the first Tuesday in November next, on which day the said Marine Society shall meet, and annually, afterwards, on said day of the month of November, at Boston, to chuse a master, deputy master, treasurer and clerk, and other officers they shall think proper, and to make, alter and annul their by-laws; and if, by reason of any emergency, the business of said annual assembly cannot be compleated on the said day, they may adjourn, once, to a short day, to finish it, and no more; and said society shall meet at said Boston on the first Tuesday of every month for all other business; and whenever any of the officers of said society shall die, or be disabled or remove out of the government, others shall be appointed or elected in their room at the next meeting: and all instruments which said society shall lawfully make shall, when in the name of said society, and pursuant to the votes thereof, and signed and delivered by the master, deputy master, treasurer and clerk, and such other officers and persons as the said society shall appoint, and sealed with their common seal, bind said society and be valid in law. And the commander-in-chief of this province is hereby authorized to give a charter of incorporation, under the province seal, to the aforenamed persons and their associates accordingly. [*Passed January* 25, 1754. Regulation of their meetings. Matters to be therein transacted. The governor empowered to grant a charter.

CHAPTER 17.

AN ACT IN ADDITION TO AN ACT [I][*E*]NTITLED "AN ACT IMPOWERING JUSTICES OF THE PEACE TO DECIDE DIFFERENCES NOT EXCEEDING FORTY SHILLINGS."

WHEREAS, in and by an act made and passed in the ninth year of his late majesty King William the Third, impowering justices of the peace to decide differences not exceeding forty shillings, it is, among other things, provided, that all justices shall keep fair records of all their proceedings, from time to time; but no provision is therein made, in case of a justice's death, for executing a judgment, given and recorded by him, which remains unsatisfied at the time of his decease,— Preamble. 1697, chap. 8.

Be it therefore enacted by the Governour, Council and House of Representatives,

Writ of *scire facias* to be issued on the judgment of a deceased justice.

[SECT. 1.] That where judgment is or shall be given by a justice of the peace, in any civil action of which by law he had cognizance, and a fair record thereof made by him, if the same remains unsatisfied at the time of his decease it shall and may be lawful[l] for any justice of the peace of the same county, upon application made to him by the party who recovered the judgment, to issue out a writ[t] of *scire facias* thereon, returnable to himself in seven days; and upon the debtor's default of appearance, or not shewing just cause to the contrary, the same justice may award execution of such judgment, returnable to himself in thirty days, and likewise award reasonable costs on the *scire facias*: *provided*, that no writ[t] of *scire facias* shall be granted as aforesaid, unless application be made therefor within twelve months after the decease of the justice before whom the judgment was recovered.

And be it further enacted,

Persons having such judgments in keeping, to deliver an attested copy.

[SECT. 2.] That any person who hath in his or her keeping the records of a deceased justice, being requested by the party who hath a judgment there entered as aforesaid, and being tendered a reasonable sum for his or her time and trouble, shall, without delay, deliver an attested copy of such records to the person requesting the same, which copy, certified on oath, shall be received and accounted as sufficient evidence as if the justice was then living; and if he or she shall neglect it [for] [*by*] the space of three days, he or she shall, for his or her neglect, forf[ie][*ei*]t the sum of three pounds, to the use of the party ag[*g*]r[ei][*ie*]ved, to be by him recovered in an action of debt in any of his majesty's courts of record.

Penalty for neglect or refusal.

And whereas, in and by an act made and passed in the second year of the reign of her late majesty Queen Anne, entitled "An Act relating to executors and administrators," provision is made, in case of waste, for awarding execution against an executor or administrator, of his own proper goods or estate, on a *scire facias*, to be issued out of the clerk's office of the same court where judgment has been recovered against the estate of a testator or intestate; but no provision hath been made in like cases cognizable before a justice of the peace,—

1703-4, chap. 12, § 4.

Be it therefore further enacted,

Justices of the peace empowered to issue such writs of *scire facias*.

[SECT. 3.] That, in all such cases, it shall and may be lawful[l] for a justice of the peace to issue out a writ[t] of *scire facias*, and award execution thereupon, in like manner as may be done in any court of record by vertue of the provision in the act last mentioned. [*Passed January* 25, 1754.

CHAPTER 18.

AN ACT FOR THE MORE EASY RECOVERING THE CHARGES THAT ATTEND THE PARTITION AND SETTLEMENT OF REAL ESTATE[S], AND TO CAUSE THE PERSONS INTERESTED IN SUCH ESTATE[S] TO BE DULY NOTIFIED BEFORE PARTITION BE ORDERED.

WHEREAS it sometimes happens that some of the persons interested in real estates refuse to pay their rateable proportion of the necessary charge which attends the dividing or set[*t*]ling the same,—

Be it therefore enacted by the Governour, Council and House of Representatives,

Warrant of distress to be issued on per-

[SECT. 1.] That when and so often as partition shall be made of any real estate by the rules of the common law, and when and so often as any real estate shall be set[*t*]led or divided agreable to the special provision made by the laws of this province, in any and every such case, when any one or more of the parties interested shall neglect or refuse to pay their just proportion of the charge which may attend such division or settlement, it shall and may be lawful for the court by which such division or settlement shall be made, to issue forth a warrant of distress against any delinquent or delinquents interested as aforesaid: *provided*, an account of such charge be first laid before the said court, and the just proportion of the persons interested setled and allowed, they having been duly notified to be present at such settlement or allowance if they see cause.

sons refusing to pay charges on the division of estates.

Proviso.

And be it further enacted,

[SECT. 2.] That when and so often as any petition shall be prefer[r]'d to the justices of the superiour court to order partition of any real estate held in common and undivided, the said justices shall not proceed to order such partition until[l] it shall be made appear to them that the several persons interested in such estate, and living within this province, or the attorneys of such as are absent and have attorneys residing within this province, have been duly notified of such petition and have had opportunity to make their exception to the granting the same. [*Passed January* 25; *published January* 26, 1754.

Superior court to notify persons concerned before estates be divided.

CHAPTER 19.

AN ACT IN ADDITION TO AN ACT MADE IN THE FIFTH YEAR OF HER LATE MAJESTY QUEEN ANNE, ENTITLED "AN ACT FOR A NEW CHOICE OF TOWN OFFICERS ON SPECIAL OCCASIONS."*

WHEREAS, in and by said act, it is provided that in case of the non-acceptance, death or removal of any person chosen to office in any of the towns in this province at their annual meeting in March, the said towns may, upon due warning given, and notice of the occasion, chuse any officer or officers to fill up such vacancy; but by said act no provision is made respecting precincts, from which inconvenienc[*i*]es have often happened,—

Preamble.

1706-7, chap. 3, § 2.

Be it therefore enacted by the Governour, Council and House of Represent[ati]ves,

That from and after the tenth day of January next, the several precincts within this province shall have and enjoy the same power and privileges in the chusing any officer or officers, where such vacancy happens in them, as towns, by law, are invested with. [*Passed January* 25; *published January* 26, 1754.

Precincts to have the same power in choosing officers, that towns have.

CHAPTER 20.

AN ACT IN ADDITION TO AN ACT [I][*E*]NTITLED "AN ACT AGAINST DIMINISHING OR COUNTERFEITING MONEY."

WHEREAS, in and by an act made and pass[*e*]'d in the twenty-third year of his present majesty's reign, [i][*e*]ntitled "An Act against dimin-

Preamble.

1749-50, chap. 22.

* There was no act bearing this title; the chapter referred to in the margin is undoubtedly the act intended.

ishing or counterfeiting money,' it is, among other things, provided, that when any person shall be convicted, of any of the offences therein mentioned, at the superiour court of judicature, court of assize and general goal delivery, every such person shall be fined at the discretion of the said court; *and whereas* it sometimes happens that such offender is not able to pay the adjudged fine, or so much as the costs of prosecution,—

Be it enacted by the Governour, Council and House of Represent- [*ati*]*ves*,

Persons convicted for counterfeiting or diminishing money to be sold, in case.

That when any person shall be convicted as aforesaid, and thereupon sentenced by the said court to pay a fine, if such offender shall be unable, or shall refuse, to pay the same together with the costs of prosecution, the sheriff of the county where such offender shall have been so convicted, shall be and hereby is impow[e]red to dispose of said offender, in service, to any of his majesty's subjects, for such term as shall be assigned by the court aforesaid, not exceeding the space of ten years; and the sheriff shall pay the money thereby raised, into the publick treasury, having first deducted so much as shall be necessary to pay the cost[s] of prosecution. [*Passed January* 25; *published January* 26, 1754.

CHAPTER 21.

AN ACT FOR INCORPORATING THE PLANTATION CALLED BEDFORD, IN THE COUNTY OF HAMPSHIRE, INTO A SEPERATE DISTRICT BY THE NAME OF GRANVILLE.

Preamble.

WHEREAS it is represented to this court that the inhabitants of said plantation labour under great difficulties and inconvenienc[*i*]es, by reason of their not being invested with the privileges of a district; therefore,—

Be it enacted by the Governour, Council and House of Representatives,

Bounds of Granville District.

[SECT. 1.] That the whole of the tract of land in the county of Hampshire, called Bedford, bounding as follows; viz[t]., beginning at a large heap of stones at the southeast corner of said tract, on the line of the colony of Connecticut, thence running no[*rth*], 10 degrees east, 448 perch, to a pine tree, marked; thence north, 17 degrees west, 90 perch; thence no[*rth*], 160 perch; thence north, 35 degrees east, 123 perch; thence north, 24 degrees east, 210 perch, to a heap of stones over Man's Brook; thence north, 4 degrees east, 200 perch, to a heap of stones with a chestnut staddle, marked; thence north, 11 degrees west, 164 perch, to a large heap of stones; thence north, 200 perch, to the northeast corner of the said tract, being two small chestnut staddles, marked, with stones about them; from thence west, 22 degrees north, 916 perch, on Westfield line, to the southeast corner of Blan[d]ford, being a birch-tree, marked, on the bank of a brook; thence on said Blan[d]ford line, west, 20 degrees no[*rth*], 2,240 perch, to the southwest corner of said Blan[d]ford; thence the same course, 660 perch, to a hemlock tree, marked, with stones about it, on the west branch of Farmington river, and is the northwest corner of said tract; from thence, bounding on said west branch of Farmington river, as the same runs, to a great hemlock tree at the colony line, being the southwest corner of said tract; from thence, on the said colony line, east 9 degrees, south 3,220 perch to the first station; be and hereby is erected into a distinct and seperate district by the name of Granville; and that the inhabitants thereof be and hereby are invested with all the powers, privileges and immunities that towns in this province by law do or may enjoy; that of sending a representative to represent them at this court only excepted. Privileges.

Provided,—

[SECT. 2.] That nothing in this act shall be understood, or so construed, as in any manner to superceed or make void any order or orders of this court now in force, respecting the method of making assessments within said plantation; but that the same shall remain and be as effectual as if this act had not been made. Proviso.

And be it further enacted,

[SECT. 3.] That John Worthington, Esq[r]., be and hereby is impow[e]red to issue his warrant to some principal inhabitant of the said plantation, requiring him in his majesty's name to warn and notify the said inhabitants, qualified by law to vote in town affairs, that they meet together at such time and place, in said plantation, as by said warrant shall be appointed, to chuse such officers as may be necessary to manage the affairs of said district; and the said inhabitants being so met, shall be and hereby are impow[e]red to chuse such officers accordingly. [*Passed January* 25; *published January* 26, 1754. Power for calling a meeting.

CHAPTER 22.

AN ACT FOR ERECTING THE NORTH PARISH, IN THE TOWN OF SUNDERLAND, INTO A SEPERATE DISTRICT, BY THE NAME OF MONTAGUE.

Be it enacted by the Governour, Council and House of Representatives,

[SECT. 1.] That the said north parish in Sunderland, bounding as follows: to begin at Connecticut river, twenty rods north of the mouth of Slate-stone brook, from thence, east, to the east side of the town bounds; thence, on the line of the said town, to the northeast corner of the town bounds, and from thence, north, to Miller's river; from thence, westerly, by Miller's river, to the mouth thereof where it enters into Connecticut river; and from thence, by Connecticut river, unto the first-mentioned bounds;—be, and hereby is, erected into a seperate district by the name of Montague; and that the said district be, and hereby is, invested with all the privile[d]ges, powers and immunities that towns in this province by law do or may enjoy, that of sending a representative to the general assembly only excepted; and that the inhabitants of said district shall have full power and right, from time to time, to join with the said town of Sunderland in the choice of a representative; in which choice they shall enjoy all the privile[d]ges which by law they would have been entitled to if this act had not been made; and that the said district shall, from time to time, pay their proportionable part of the expence of such representative, according to their respective proportions of the province tax; and that the said town of Sunderland, as often as they shall call a meeting for the choice of a representative, shall give seasonable notice to the clerk of said district, for the time being, of the time and place of holding such meeting, to the end that the said district may join them therein; and the clerk of said district shall set up, in some publick place in said district, a notification thereof accordingly. Bounds of Montague District. Privileges.

Provided, nevertheless,—

And be it further enacted,

Proviso.

[SECT. 2.] That the said district shall pay their proportion of all town, county and province taxes already set or granted to be rais[*e*]'d on said town, as if this act had not been made.

And be it further enacted,

Power for calling a meeting.

[SECT. 3.] That Elijah Williams, Esq[r]., be and hereby is impow[e]red to issue his warrant to some principal inhabitant in said district, requiring him to notify and warn the inhabitants of said district, qualified by law to vote in town affairs, to meet, at such time and place as shall be therein set forth, to chuse all such officers as shall be necessary to manage the affairs of said district. [*Passed January* 25, 1754.

CHAPTER 23.

AN ACT FOR THE EFFECTUAL PREVENTING THE CURRENCY OF THE BILLS OF CREDIT OF CONNECTICUT, NEW HAMPSHIRE AND RHODE ISLAND, WITHIN THIS PROVINCE.

Preamble. 1748-49, chap. 15, § 11.

WHEREAS, in and by an act made and pass'd in the twenty-second year of his present majesty's reign, entitled "An Act for drawing in the bills of credit of the several denominations which have at any time been issued by this government, and are still outstanding, and for ascertaining the rate of coined silver in this province for the future," it is, among other things, enacted and declared, that from and after the last day of March, one thousand seven hundred and fifty, until the last day of March, one thousand seven hundred and fifty-four, an oath shall be required of certain persons and in certain cases in said act particularly declared, of the form following:—

Form of the oath.

You, A. B., do, in the presence of God, solemnly declare that you have not, since the last day of March, 1750, wittingly and willingly, directly or indirectly, either by yourself or any other for or under you, been concerned in receiving or paying, within this government, any bill or bills of credit of either of the governments of Connecticut, New Hampshire or Rhode Island. So help you God.

—*and whereas* the said bills of credit still continue current within the governments aforesaid, and have greatly depreciated in their value, and are liable to depreciate still further, and it is of great importance to the interest of the inhabitants of this province, and to the interest of such of his majesty's subjects in Great Britain and elsewhere as have trade and commerce here, that the currency of said bills should be effectually prevented throughout this government,—

Be it therefore enacted by the Governour, Council and House of Representatives,

Persons chosen into any office, to take said oath.

[SECT. 1.] That from and after the thirtieth day of March which shall be in the year of our Lord one thousand seven hundred and fifty-four, every person who shall be chose to serve in any office in any of the towns or districts or precincts of this province, shall, before his entrance upon such office, take the following oath, to be administred by a justice of the peace, or, where no justice of the peace shall be present, by the town, district, or precinct, clerk, who is hereby impowred to administer the same; viz.,—

You, A. B., do, in the presence of God, solemnly declare that you have not, since the thirtieth day of March, 1754, wittingly and willingly, directly or indirectly, either by yourself or any for or under you, been concerned in receiving or paying, within this government, any bill or bills of credit of either of the governments of Connecticut, New Hampshire or Rhode Island. So help you God.

[SECT. 2.] And where any person, chosen as aforesaid, shall refuse or neglect to take the oath aforesaid, on tendring the same, the town, district or precinct shall proceed to the choice of another person in his room; and where any person shall be elected by any town, district or precinct into any office, to the non-acceptance or refusal whereof a penalty is by law annexed, such person neglecting or refusing to take the oath aforesaid shall be liable to the same penalty as is by law provided for the non-acceptance or refusal of such office.

Penalty in case of refusal to take said oath.

And be it further enacted,

[SECT. 3.] That when any person shall be chosen to represent any town within this province in the general court or assembly, such person so chosen shall take the oath aforesaid; and return shall be made by the selectmen, upon the back of the precept, that the person so chosen has taken the oath required in the act made and passed in the twenty-seventh year of his majesty King George the Second, entitled "An Act for the effectual preventing the currency of the bills of credit of Connecticut, New Hampshire and Rhode Island within this province"; and if any person so chosen shall refuse or neglect to take the oath aforesaid, such refusal or neglect shall be deem'd a refusal to serve as a representative; and the town shall proceed to the choice of another person in his room.

Persons chosen representatives, to take the said oath.

1753-54, chap. 23.

And be it further enacted,

[SECT. 4.] That the oath aforesaid shall be administred to each of the members of his majesty's council, every year, at the same time when the usual oaths required to be taken by the said members of his majesty's council shall be administred; and all officers, civil and military, within this government, who shall be nominated or appointed, shall, before they receive their respective commissions, take the oath aforesaid, and their respective commissions shall otherwise be void; and all persons elected into any office by the general assembly shall be deemed not qualified to enter upon the execution of their respective offices until they have taken the oath aforesaid.

Councillors to take said oath,—

and also all officers, civil and military.

And be it further enacted,

[SECT. 5.] That no execution shall be issued from the office of any clerk of any of the inferiour courts of common pleas, or of the superiour courts of judicature, for any sum whatsoever, unless the plaintiff or plaintiffs, suing in his or their own right, and dwelling within this province, shall first take the oath aforesaid, to be administred by a justice of the peace, or by the clerk of the court from which such execution shall issue; and certificate thereof shall be made on such execution; and if any execution shall issue or go forth without such certificate, the same shall be and is hereby declared to be void; and no licence shall be granted to, nor any recognizance taken from, any taverner, innholder or retailer, by the justices of any of the courts of sessions within this province, until such taverner, innholder or retailer shall have taken said oath in presence of the court, or certificate of his having so done, from a justice of the peace, shall be presented to the court.

The said oath to be taken upon issuing executions on judgments of courts.

Taverners, innholders, and retailers to take said oath.

And be it further enacted,

[SECT. 6.] That for every oath administred as aforesaid by the clerk of any court, he shall be allowed threepence, and for every certificate by him signed as aforesaid, threepence, and no more; and the cost and charge of such oath and certificate shall be added to the sum in the execution required to be levied accordingly.

Limitation. [SECT. 7.] This act to continue and be in force until the last day of March which shall be in the year of our Lord one thousand seven hundred and fifty-seven, and no longer. [*Passed December* 27, 1753; *published January* 26, 1754.

CHAPTER 24.

AN ACT FOR SUPPLY OF THE TREASURY WITH TEN THOUSAND POUNDS, AND APPLYING THE SAME FOR THE DISCHARGE OF THE PUBLICK DEBTS.

Preamble. 1753-54, chap. 10, § 11.

WHEREAS, in and by an act made and passed by this court at their session in May last, entitled "An Act for the supply of the treasury, &c.," there was the sum of twelve thousand four hundred pounds ordered to be levied and assessed upon the towns and districts within this province, eight thousand one hundred and fifty pounds of which sum only has been appropriated for the payment of publick debts; so that, when the above-mentioned tax is received into the treasury, there will be a surplusage of four thousand two hundred and fifty pounds; *and whereas* the moneys already in the treasury, received for lands, and what is still due for lands and for the province galley, amount to the sum of three thousand two hundred and forty-one pounds twelve shillings and sixpence, which money is not appropriated for any use whatever, which, with the surplusage arising by the tax aforesaid, make seven thousand four hundred and ninety-one pounds twelve shillings

1751-52, chap. 16. and sixpence; *and whereas*, by the provision made by this court in the year one thousand seven hundred and fifty-two, by a tax of eighteen thousand six hundred pounds, and by the duties of impost and excise, which were mortgaged for two years for the redemption of the government securities redeemable the twentieth of January, one thousand seven hundred and fifty-four, there will be a considerable surplusage in the treasury after said notes are discharged; wherefore,—

Be it enacted by His Excellency the Governour, Council and House of Representatives,

£10,000 to be issued. [SECT. 1.] That the said sum of seven thousand four hundred and ninety-one pounds twelve shillings and sixpence, when received into the treasury, as also the further sum of two thousand five hundred and eight pounds seven shillings and sixpence, part of the surplusage that will be in the treasury after the securities above mentioned are paid off, making in the whole the sum of ten thousand pounds, shall be issued in the manner and for the purposes following; that is to say, the sum

£3,400 for forts and garrisons, &c. of three thousand four hundred pounds, part of the aforesaid sum of ten thousand pounds, shall be applied for the service of the several forts and garrisons within this province, pursuant to such orders and

£700 for provisions and other commissary stores. grants as are or shall be made by this court for those purposes; and the further sum of seven hundred pounds, part of the aforesaid sum of ten thousand pounds, shall be applied for the purchasing of provisions, comissary's necessary disbursements for the service of the several forts and garrisons within this province, pursuant to such grants as

£4,000 for grants, &c. are or shall be made by this court for that purpose; and the further sum of four thousand pounds, part of the aforesaid sum of ten thousand pounds, shall be applied for the payment of such premiums and grants that now are, or hereafter may be made by this court; and the further sum of three hundred pounds, part of the aforesaid sum of ten thousand pounds, shall be applied for the discharge of other debts owing from this province to persons that have served or shall serve them, by order of this court, in such matters and things where there is no establishment nor any certain sum assigned them for that purpose, and for paper, writing and printing for this court; and the further sum of fifteen hundred pounds, part of the aforesaid sum of ten thousand pounds, shall be applied for the payment of his majesty's council and house of representatives, serving in the general court during the several sessions for this present year. £300 for debts where there is no establishment. £1,500 for the pay of the members.

And whereas there are sometimes contingent and unforeseen charges that demand prompt pay,—

Be it further enacted,

[SECT. 2.] That the sum of one hundred pounds, the remaining part of the aforesaid sum of ten thousand pounds, be applied to pay such contingent charges, and for no other purpose whatsoever.

And be it further enacted,

[SECT. 3.] That the treasurer is hereby directed and ordered to pay the sum of ten thousand pounds out of such appropriations as shall be directed to by warrant, and no other; and the secretary, to whom it belongs to keep the muster-rolls and accompts of charge, shall lay before the house of representatives, when they direct, such muster-rolls and accompts, after payment thereof. [*Passed December* 18, 1753; *published January* 26, 1754.

CHAPTER 25.

AN ACT FOR GRANTING THE SUM OF FOURTEEN HUNDRED POUNDS, FOR THE SUPPORT OF HIS MAJESTY'S GOVERNOUR.

Be it enacted by the Governour, Council and House of Representatives,

THAT the sum of fourteen hundred pounds be and hereby is granted unto his most excellent majesty, to be paid out of the publick treasury to his excellency William Shirley, Esq[r]., captain-general and governour-in-chief in and over his majesty's province of the Massachusetts Bay, for his past services, and further to enable him to go on in managing the publick affairs. [*Passed December* 20, 1753; *published January* 26, 1754.

CHAPTER 26.

AN ACT FOR IMPOWERING THE PROVINCE TREASURER TO BORROW THE SUM OF FIVE THOUSAND POUNDS, AND FOR APPLYING THE SAME FOR THE REDEMPTION OF THE BILLS OF CREDIT OF THIS PROVINCE THAT ARE STILL OUTSTANDING, AND FOR MAKING PROVISION FOR THE REPAYMENT OF THE SUM SO BORROWED.

WHEREAS, notwithstanding the provision made by this court to draw in and sink the bills of credit of this government, there is still a considerable quantity outstanding, to the great prejudice of trade and commerce,— Preamble.

Be it enacted by the Governour, Council and House of Representatives,

[SECT. 1.] That the treasurer of this province be and hereby is impowred to borrow from such person or persons as shall appear ready Treasurer empowered to borrow £5,000.

to lend the same, a sum not exceeding five thousand pounds, in mill'd dollars, at six shillings apiece, or silver at six shillings and eightpence per ounce; and the sum so borrowed shall be a stock in the treasury, to be applied for the redemption of said bills of credit, in manner as in this act is after directed; and for every sum so borrowed, the treasurer shall give a receipt in the form following; viz.,—

Form of treasurer's receipt.

Province of the Massachusetts Bay, day of 17 , received from the sum of pounds, for the use and service of the province of the Massachusetts Bay; and in behalf of said province, I do hereby promise and oblige myself and successors in the office of treasurer, to repay the said , his heirs or assigns, on or before the first day of June, one thousand seven hundred and fifty-five, the aforesaid sum of pounds, with interest for the same, at and after the rate of six per cent per annum. Witness my hand, A. B., Treasurer.

—and no receipt shall be given for less than twenty pounds.

And be it further enacted,

Bills of credit to be exchanged from March 1, to June 1, 1754.

[SECT. 2.] That the treasurer of the province be and hereby is impowred and directed, from the first day of March next until the first day of June following, to receive from the possessors the bills of credit of this province; which bills he shall keep seperate from those that he shall receive to the first day of March next, of constables, collectors, sheriffs and excise-masters; and in case he shall suspect any bill or bills to be counterfeit, he is hereby impowred and directed to stop such bill or bills, writing on the said bill or bills the person's name of whom he received it, or them, for the further direction of this court.

Suspected bills to be stopped.

And be it further enacted,

Bills to be exchanged for silver.

[SECT. 3.] That the treasurer of the province, immediately upon his receiving the bills as aforesaid, not suspected by the treasurer to be counterfeit, shall discharge the same in mill'd dollars, at six shillings apiece, or silver at six shillings and eightpence per ounce, out of the money borrowed for that purpose.

And be it further enacted,

Bills to be burned.

[SECT. 4.] That the treasurer shall sort the bills so received by him, in order, for a committee who shall hereafter be appointed by this court to tell and consume the same to ashes; which committee's receipt for the sum so told up and burnt shall be a sufficient discharge to the treasurer.

And be it further enacted,

Right of redeeming to cease after June 1, 1754.

[SECT. 5.] That from and after the first day of June, one thousand seven hundred and fifty-four, all right of redemption of said bills of credit of this province that may be then outstanding shall thenceforward determine and cease; and if any person or persons within this government shall, after the said first day of June, one thousand seven hundred and fifty-four, receive or pay away any of the bills aforesaid, he, she or they so offending, upon conviction thereof before any of his majesty's courts of record, shall forfeit and pay the sum of ten pounds, to be recovered by bill, plaint or information; one half for the use of this government, and the other half to him or them that shall inform or sue for the same: *provided, always*, that if any possessor of said bills shall, within the term hereinbefore limited for that purpose, have tendered the same to the province treasurer to be exchanged, and there shall not be monies sufficient, of the sum to be borrowed as aforesaid, to exchange the same, in such case such possessor shall not be subject to the penalty aforesaid, nor be denied the privilege of having such bills redeemed so soon as the treasurer shall be furnished with monies sufficient for that purpose, if tendered within such term of time as may hereafter be limited for the same.

Penalty for paying or receiving bills after that time.

Proviso.

And in order to enable the treasurer effectually to discharge the receipts and obligations by him given in pursuance of this act,—

Be it enacted,

[SECT. 6.] That there be and hereby is granted unto his most excellent majesty a tax of five thousand pounds, to be levied on polls, and estates real and personal, within this province, according to such rules and in such proportion on the several towns and districts within the same, as shall be agreed on and ordered by the general court of this province at their session in May, one thousand seven hundred and fifty-four; which sum shall be paid into the treasury on or before the thirty-first day of March next after. Tax of £5,000 granted.

And as an additional fund and security for drawing the said sum of five thousand pounds into the treasury again,—

Be it enacted,

[SECT. 7.] That the duty of impost, for the year one thousand seven hundred and fifty-four, shall be applied towards discharging said receipts and obligations. Fund.

And be it further enacted,

[SECT. 8.] That in case the general court shall not at their session in May, and before the twentieth day of June, one thousand seven hundred and fifty-four, agree and conclude upon an act apportioning the sum which by this act is engaged to be, in said year, apportioned, assessed and levied, that then, and in such case, each town and district within this province shall pay, by a tax to be levied on the polls, and estates both real and personal, within their districts, the same proportion of the said sum as the said towns and districts were taxed by the general court in the tax act then last preceeding: *saving* what relates to the pay of the representatives, which shall be assessed on the several towns they represent; and the province treasurer is hereby fully impowred and directed, some time in the month of June, one thousand seven hundred and fifty-four, to issue and send forth his warrants, directed to the selectmen or assessors of each town and district within this province, requiring them to assess the polls, and estates both real and personal, within their several towns and districts, for their respective part and proportion of the sum before directed and engaged to be assessed, and also for the fines upon the several towns for not sending a representative; and the assessors, as also persons assessed, shall observe, be governed by and subject to all such rules and directions as have been given in the last preceeding tax act. [*Passed January* 25; *published January* 26, 1754. Rule for apportioning the tax in case no tax act shall be agreed on.

CHAPTER 27.

AN ACT TO ENABLE THE PROPRIETORS OF STOW, IN THE COUNTY OF MIDDLESEX, SO OFTEN AS IT SHALL BE THOUGHT NECESSARY FOR THEM, TO RAISE MONEY FOR THE USE OF SAID PROPRIETORS; AND TO TAX AND ASSESS THE ORIGINAL PROPRIETORS OF SAID TOWN, AND THEIR HEIRS, IN EQUAL PROPORTION TO THEIR INTEREST WHEN THE FIRST LO[T]TS WERE DIVIDED AND DRAWN.

WHEREAS the proprietors of the town of Stow, in the county of Middlesex, have long since divided almost all the common lands formerly belonging to the said proprietors, into severalty, and looked upon themselves, in a manner, divested of being any longer a propriety; *and whereas,* of late, there hath been a dispute, between the proprietors Preamble.

of Littleton, in the same county, and sundry persons that held lands under and by grants from the proprietors of Stow aforesaid, relating to the boundary line between the said proprietors of Stow and the proprietors of Littleton aforesaid, by reason whereof it is become absolutely necessary for the proprietors of Stow aforesaid to raise money and assess the an[t][c]ient proprietors of Stow,—

Be it therefore enacted by the Governour, Council and House of Represent[ati]ves,

Proprietors of Stow empowered to hold meetings.

[SECT. 1.] That John Whitman, Esq[r]., issue his warrant, directed to any one of the proprietors of Stow aforesaid, requiring him to warn a meeting of the proprietors of Stow aforesaid, to meet at a certain time and place, in said Stow, as shall be therein appointed, in which all such rules and orders as to the warning and posting the same shall be observed as is usual for the warning of any other proprietors' meeting within this province; in which warrant notice shall be given for the chusing a moderator, as usual, a proprietors' clerk, treasurer, assessors, and collectors, for said proprietors, and also for the chusing a committee to call meetings for the said proprietors, for the future, and for the granting and raising such sum and sums as shall, by the major vote of said proprietors, be thought necessary for the use of said proprietors; in which meeting all the original proprietors of Stow afores[ai]d, that drew lot[t]s in the first division of said common lands in Stow aforesaid, or their heirs, shall be allowed to vote according to the interest they respectively had at the time when the first division of said common lands were made; and in making of said assessment of any sum or sums of money for the use of said proprietors, the same shall be assessed on such of the original proprietors of said Stow, their and each of their heirs, in equal proportion, according to the interest they or their predecessors had at the time of the first division of said lot[t]s being made and drawn as aforesaid; and any such tax or assessment being made as aforesaid, and committed to the collector or collectors that shall be then chosen, having duly taken the oaths that such officers are required by the laws of this province to take, shall have full power to levy and collect the same, in as full and ample a manner as the collectors of any town, district or parish in this province have in the gathering and collecting of any town, district or parish taxes.

Officers to be chosen.

Money to be raised by assessment.

Collectors to levy it.

And be it further enacted,

Manner of proceeding in their meeting.

[SECT. 2.] That the clerk of said proprietors that shall be chosen at the meeting aforesaid, from time to time, and at all times, as often as there shall be occasion and he shall receive orders from the committee of said proprietors, or the major part of them, shall issue his warrant to some [one] of the proprietors of Stow aforesaid, requiring him to warn a meeting of the proprietors afores[ai]d, to meet in Stow aforesaid, for the transacting of such business relating to the affairs of said proprietors as shall be thought needful, according to the usual customs of other proprietors within this province; and that they shall have power, from time to time, as they shall see meet, to grant and raise money for the use of the proprietors aforesaid, and to assess the same upon the original proprietors that drew the original lot[t]s in their first division afores[ai]d, if living; and if any of them be dead, then such deceased['s] proprietor's proportion of such moneys shall be assessed on their heirs enjoying any estate from their said ancestors, and that in proportion to their respective shares therein: *saving* only, that if any of said original proprietors shall have conveyed, by deed of release, his share in said propriety to any other person, and so has no interest depending on the afores[ai]d dispute, such proprietor's proportion of such assessment as shall be made by virtue of this act shall be assessed on the present owner of such proprietor's share therein, who shall be

Money to be raised from the original proprietors or heirs.

Saving.

obliged to pay the same to the collector or collectors of said proprietors, who are hereby impow[e]red and required to levy and collect the same.

[SECT. 3.] This act to remain and be in force for the space of five years from the publication thereof, and no longer. [*Passed January* 25; *published January* 26, 1754.

CHAPTER 28.

AN ACT IN ADDITION TO AN ACT ENTITLED "AN ACT TO ENABLE CREDITORS TO RECEIVE THEIR JUST DEBTS OUT OF THE EFFECTS OF THEIR ABSENT OR ABSCONDING DEBTORS."

Preamble. 1738-39, chap. 15. 1748-49, chap. 6.

WHEREAS in and by an act intitled "An Act to enable creditors to receive their just debts out of the effects of their absent or absconding debtors," which act, in the twenty-first year of his present majesty's reign, was revived and continued in force for the term of ten years, provision was intended to be made for the recovery of any sums that may be justly due to any person, out of the goods, effects or credits of any absent or absconding person or persons, that may be in the hands of any attorney, factor, agent or trustee, and not exposed to view; and some doubts have arisen how far the remedy provided by the said act, according to the true intent thereof, does extend, and in what actions and demands plaintiffs or complainants may recover and receive their dues and damages which they are intitled to, from absent or absconding persons in manner as in and by said act is provided,—

Be it enacted by the Governour, Council and House of Representatives,

Species of actions in which creditors may receive their debts out of the estate of absent and absconding debtors.

That the remedy provided in and by said act was intended, and shall be construed and understood, to extend to all actions of debt, detinue, account, and covenant, and to all actions upon the case, in trover, *indebitatis assumpsit*, and express contract; and that all persons intitled to either of said actions against any such absent or absconding person, are creditors within the true intent and meaning of said act, and intitled to any method of relief in and by said act given to creditors. [*Passed January* 25; *published January* 26, 1754.

CHAPTER 29.

AN ACT IN ADDITION TO THE SEVERAL LAWS OF THIS GOVERNMENT MADE FOR THE REGULATING GENERAL FIELDS.

Preamble. 1741-42, chap. 3.

WHEREAS, by law, the fence-viewers chosen in the several towns within this province are obliged to view defective and insufficient fence, in case complaint be made to them, and the person complaining pay them three shillings per diem, and for a less time sixpence an hour, and, upon the fence-viewer's finding the fence defective, he is obliged to notif[ie][*y*] the owner thereof, who hath six days by law allowed him to repair the same; which, if he sufficiently repair within said term, the complainant, who hath paid the fence-viewer[*s*] for viewing the same, cannot recover the money by him so paid; for remedy whereof,—

Be it enacted by the Governour, Council and House of Represent-[*ati*]*ves*,

Complainant not to pay the fence-viewer of fences before he views. Owner of the fence to pay double fees, in case.

[SECT. 1.] That each and every fence-viewer within this province, and that hereafter may be chosen into said office, shall be obliged, upon complaint made to him, to view any insufficient fences without the complainant's first paying him therefor; and in case the owner of such insufficient fence neglect or refuse to pay him the fee allowed by law for viewing such fence, for the space of one month, he shall have and recover of the owner of said fence double the sum allowed by law for that service; but in case the fence complained of appear to the fence-viewer to be sufficient, that then the person complaining shall pay the like fee to the fence-viewer.

Preamble.

And whereas it often happens that horses, cattle and other creatures are found damage-feasant in general fields, which are either clandestinely turned in, or are so unruly as to get in where the fence is sufficient and according to law, and, when impounded, the owners thereof will replieve the same (because there may be some defect in the fence incompassing such general field, tho'[*ugh*] the same may be at a great distance from the place where such creatures actually got into the field), and judgm[*en*]t recovered against the person impounding, w[*hi*]ch may be very unjust and unreasonable; therefore,—

Be it further enacted,

Creatures to be impounded, unless the fence be proved insufficient.

[SECT. 2.] That when and so often as any creatures are taken in any general field, and impounded, and a writ of replevin is taken out to replieve the same, the court or justice before whom the action is brought, shall be and hereby is impowered to give judgment against the owner of said creatures, unless by such owner it be made to appear they got into the field where the fence was insufficient at the time of their getting in, or were put in by some other person.

Preamble.

And whereas it often happens, in fencing general fields, for the conveniency of fencing, considerable quantities of rocky and barren land, not capable of tillage, are taken into such fields, the owners of which are now by law obliged to fence for the same, and also pay taxes equal to the other lands in said field whenever an assessm[*en*]t is made by the proprietors of such field, which is very unjust; therefore,—

Be it further enacted,

Owners of rocky, unimproved lands to pay for no part of the general fence.

[SECT. 3.] That all lands now lying in general fields, or that hereafter may be taken into the same, that are so rocky or barren that the owners thereof have never improved the same, either by mowing, plowing or feeding, said owners shall not be obliged to fence for them any part of the fence incompassing such general fields, nor shall they be taxed for them in any rate raised by the proprietors of such field, until[l] such time as they shall make improvement thereon.

Limitation.

[SECT. 4.] This act to continue and be in force three years from the first day of February next, and no longer. [*Passed January* 25; *published January* 26, 1754.

CHAPTER 30.

AN ACT FOR PREVENTING THE UNNECESSARY DESTRUCTION OF ALEWIVES IN THE TOWN OF SANDWICH.

Preamble.

WHEREAS the laws already provided against the destruction of the fish called alewives, do not, in divers circumstances, reach the case of Herring River, in the town of Sandwich, so that, nevertheless, great waste is made of them by ill-minded persons, to the great damage of the publick; to prevent which,—

Be it enacted by the Governour, Council and House of Representatives,

[SECT. 1.] That from and after the first day of April next, no person or persons whomsoever shall, on any pretence, presume to stretch, set or draw any seine or drag-net, or set up any wares or other fishing-engines in any part of the river known by the name of Herring river, in the town of Sandwich, or ponds adjacent thereto where the fish usually spawn, or use any other instrument for the catching alewives but dip-nets or scoop-nets, without first obtaining special licence therefor by a vote of the inhabitants of said Sandwich legally assembled at their anniversary meeting in March, nor in any manner whatever, at any time or place in said river or pond but such as shall be determined and appointed at such meeting, on penalty of a fine of five pounds for each offence; to be paid by every person concerned in taking said fish, in either of the ways forbidden by this act or in any other place than such as shall be assigned by the said town as aforesaid, and be recovered by action, bill, plaint or information in any court proper to try the same. Regulation of the use of nets for taking of alewives. 1745-46, chap. 14. 1748-49, chap. 19.

And be it further enacted,

[SECT. 2.] That all fish taken in said river or ponds, contrary to the true intent of this act, shall be liable to be forfeited to the overseers appointed by said town. Fish otherwise taken to be forfeit.

And be it further enacted,

[SECT. 3.] That all coasters or boatmen shall give in, upon oath, if required, to the town-clerk of said Sandwich, what quantity of the said alewives they have taken on board, and who were the owners of said fish. Account to be taken of fish transported.

[SECT. 4.] All fines and forfeitures arising by this act to be disposed of, one half for the benefit of the poor of said town, the other to him or them who shall inform and sue for the same. Disposal of fines.

And whereas a considerable part of the banks of said river is covered with thick woods, and thereby so obscured as that persons may frequently offend against this act without being discovered, and thereby the good design of it be defeated, unless special provision be made therefor. Preamble.

Be it therefore enacted,

[SECT. 5.] That the manner, rules and methods of conviction of offenders against this act, be the same as are directed and provided in and by an act, intitled "An Act in addition to and for rendring more effectual an act made in the tenth year of the reign of King William the Third, intitled 'An Act for preventing of trespasses,'" made in the twelfth year of the reign of his late majesty King George the First. Manner of prosecution. 1726-27, chap. 3.

[SECT. 6.] This act to be in force for the space of three years from the first day of April next, and no longer. [*Passed January* 25; *published January* 26, 1754. Limitation.

CHAPTER 31.

AN ACT FOR PREVENTING MISCHIEF BY UNRULY DOGS ON THE ISLANDS OF MARTHA'S VINEYARD, CHEBAQUID[O][*U*]CK, AND ALSO ON THE ISLAND OF NANTUCKET.

WHEREAS much damage has been done by unruly and mischievous dogs, in worrying, wounding and killing sheep and lambs on the island of Martha's Vineyard, and also on the island[s] of Nantucket and Preamble.

Chebaquiduck, by reason of great numbers of such dogs being kept by Indians as well as English inhabitants there,—

Be it therefore enacted by the Governo[u]r, Council and House of Represent[ati]ves,

Dogs on Martha's Vineyard, &c., may be killed after March 1, 1754.

[SECT. 1.] That from and after the first day of March next, it shall and may be lawful for any person or persons living on any part of Martha's Vineyard, or on the islands of Nantucket or Chebaquiduck, to kill any dog or bitch, whatsoever, that shall at any time be found on said Martha's Vineyard, or on said islands of Nantucket or Chebaquiduck.

And be it further enacted,

Penalty for keeping dogs, &c.

[SECT. 2.] That whosoever shall presume to keep any dog or bitch on the island of Martha's Vineyard, or on the island of Nantucket or Chebaquiduck, after the said first day of March next, shall forfeit and pay the sum of twenty shillings, to be sued for and recovered by such person or persons as shall inform against the breaches of this act; one half thereof to the informer, and the other half to the poor of the town where the offence shall be committed.

And be it further enacted,

How actions are to be tried.

[SECT. 3.] That if any action shall be brought or prosecuted either before a justice of peace, or in any court within this province, against such persons as shall kill or destroy any such dog or bitch, found as aforesaid, the defendant shall plead the general issue, and give this act in evidence; and thereupon such justice or court shall bar said action, and allow the defendant his reasonable cost.

Limitation.

[SECT. 4.] This act to continue and be in force for the space of three years from the first day of March next, and no longer. [*Passed January** 11; *published January* 26, 1754.

* According to Secretary Willard's memorandum on the engrossment, this act was signed April 11; but since it appears printed among the acts of the December session, with a memorandum of its publication as above, the memorandum of the secretary is assumed to be erroneous, although there is no indorsement upon the engrossment, of the publication, which might aid in determining the true date.

ACTS

PASSED AT THE SESSION BEGUN AND HELD AT BOSTON, ON THE TWENTY-SEVENTH DAY OF MARCH, A. D. 1754.

CHAPTER 32.

AN ACT FOR ESTABLISHING AND CONFIRMING DIVERS WRIT[T]S AND PROCESSES ISSUED OUT OF THE OFFICE OF THE CLERK OF THE INFERIOUR COURT OF COMMON PLEAS FOR THE COUNTY OF ESSEX, SINCE THE TWENTY-FOURTH DAY OF JANUARY LAST, SO FAR AS RELATES TO THE TESTE WHICH SUCH WRIT[T]S AND PROCESSES BEAR.

Preamble.

WHEREAS, in and by an act pass[*e*]'d in the thirteenth year of King William the Third, [e][*i*]ntitled "An Act prescribing forms of writ[t]s in civil causes," it is, among other things, provided, that all original or judicial processes or writ[t]s issuing out of the clerk's office of the inferiour court of common pleas, shall bear teste of the first justice named in the commission for holding such court, and upon any vacancy by his death or removal, then of the justice next named in the said commission, for the time being; *and whereas*, on the twenty-fifth day of January, 1754, upon the resignation of Timothy Lindall, Esq[r]., first justice of the inferiour court of common pleas for the county of Essex, Henry Gibbs, Esq[r]., was commissioned to be one of the justices of the said court, in the room and stead of the said Timothy Lindal[*l*]; notwithstanding which, divers processes and writ[t]s have issued out of the office of the clerk of the said court, dated on or since the said twenty-fifth day of January, bearing the teste of the said Timothy Lindall, whilst others have bourn the teste of Thomas Berry, Esq[r]., the next eldest justice in the commission for the said court, as by law they ought to do; wherefore for removing all exceptions against the validity of such processes and writ[t]s bearing the teste of Timothy Lindall, so far as relates to the said teste,—

Be it enacted by the Governour, Council and House of Represent-[ati]ves,

Writs, &c., bearing test Timothy Lindall, Esq., in Essex inferior court, confirmed.

That all writ[t]s and processes whatsoever, at any time issued from the office of the clerk of the inferiour court of common pleas for the county of Essex, and dated since the twenty-fourth day of January, 1754, bearing the teste of Timothy Lindall, Esq[r]., late first justice of said court, shall be deemed, and they are hereby declared to be, to all intents and purposes whatsoever, as valid and effectual, in law, as if said writ[t]s and processes had bore the teste of Thomas Berry, Esq[r]., the next justice in commission for said court, as, according to the true intent and meaning of the afores[*ai*]d act of the thirteenth of King William the Third, they should and ought to have done. [*Passed March* 27; *published April* 24, 1754.

CHAPTER 33.

AN ACT FOR ALTERING THE TIMES APPOINTED FOR HOLDING THE SUPERIOUR COURT OF JUDICATURE, COURT OF ASSIZE AND GENERAL GOAL DELIVERY, WITHIN AND FOR THE COUNTIES OF ESSEX AND YORK; AND ALSO FOR ALTERING SOME OF THE COURTS OF GENERAL SESSIONS OF THE PEACE AND INFERIOUR COURTS OF COMMON PLEAS, WITHIN AND FOR THE COUNTIES OF PL[I][Y]MOUTH, BARNSTABLE AND YORK.

Preamble.

WHEREAS the times by law appointed for holding the superiour court of judicature, court of assize and general goal delivery, at Ipswich, within and for the county of Essex; and at York, within and for the county of York; and the holding the courts of general sessions of the peace, and the inferiour court of common pleas, the third Tuesday of September, within and for the county of Plimouth; and the holding the courts of general sessions of the peace, and the inferiour courts of common pleas, on the last Tuesday of June, the third Tuesday of October, and the third Tuesday of January, within and for the county of Barnstable; and the holding the court of general sessions of the peace, and the inferiour court of common pleas, within and for the county of York, on the first Tuesday of July, are found inconvenient,—

Be it therefore enacted by the Governour, Council and House of Representatives,

Superior court in Essex and York counties altered. 1745-46, chap. 21. 1742-43, chap. 32.

[SECT. 1.] That the time for holding the superiour court of judicature, court of assize and general goal delivery at Ipswich, for the county of Essex, shall henceforth be the second Tuesday of June, annually; and the time for holding the said court at York, for the county of York, shall henceforth be the third Tuesday of June, annually; and the time for holding the court of general sessions of the peace, and the inferiour court of common pleas, within and for the county of Pl[i][y]mouth, shall henceforth be the last Tuesday of September, annually; and the times for holding the said courts of general sessions of the peace, and the inferiour courts of common pleas, within and for the said county of Barnstable, shall henceforth be the second Tuesday in May, the third Tuesday in September, and the first Tuesday in December, annually; and the time for holding the court of general sessions of the peace, and the inferiour court of common pleas, within and for the county of York, shall henceforth be the second Tuesday of July, annually: and all officers and other persons concerned, are required to conform themselves accordingly.

And be it further enacted,

Appeals, &c., to the superior court, already taken out for Essex and York, to be returned at the altered time.

[SECT. 2.] That all appeals, writ[t]s of review[s], recognizances, warrants and other processes already issued, taken or depending in the said counties of Essex or York, which were to have been returned or proceeded on at the times heretofore appointed by law for holding the said superiour courts at Ipswich or York, shall be valid and stand good to all intents and purposes in the law, and shall be returned and proceeded on at the times appointed by this act for holding the said superiour courts respectively.

And be it further enacted,

Writs, appeals, &c., already issued for the inferior court for Barnstable, to be proceeded on in the next term.

[SECT. 3.] That all appeals, writ[t]s, recognizances, warrants and other processes, already issued, taken or depending in the said county of Barnstable, which were to have been returned or proceeded upon at the time heretofore appointed by law for holding the said court of general sessions of the peace and inferiour court of common pleas at Barnstable on the last Tuesday of June, shall be valid and stand good to all intents and purposes, in the law, and shall be returned and proceeded on at the time appointed by this act for holding said court of general sessions of the peace and inferiour court of common pleas, on the third Tuesday of September next.

And be it further enacted,

[SECT. 4.] That all appeals, writ[t]s, recognizances, warrants and other processes, already issued, taken or depending in the said county of York, which were to have been returned or proceeded on at the time heretofore appointed by law for holding the said court of gen[*era*]l sessions of the peace and inferiour court of common pleas at York on the first Tuesday of July, shall be valid and stand good to all intents and purposes in the law, and shall be returned and proceeded on at the time appointed by this act for holding said court of gen[*era*]l sessions of the peace and inferiour court of common pleas on the second Tuesday of July next. [*Passed April* 19 ; *published April* 24, 1754. The like for the inferior court in York.

CHAPTER 34.

AN ACT IN FURTHER ADDITION TO THE ACT FOR LIMITATION OF ACTIONS, AND FOR AVOIDING SUITS IN LAW, WHERE THE MATTER IS OF LONG STANDING.

WHEREAS by a law of this province, entit[u]led "An Act in further addition to the act for the limitation of actions and for avoiding suits at law where the matter is of long standing," made and pass[*e*]'d in the twenty-fifth year of his present majesty's reign, the time limit[*t*]ed for commencing all actions of account and upon the case, excepting such as are excepted in another act, entit[u]led "An Act in addition to and for the explanation of an act [e][*i*]ntit[u]led 'An Act for the limitation of actions and avoiding suits at law where the matter is of long standing,'" made and pass[*e*]'d in the twenty-second year of his present majesty's reign, will expire in September next; *and whereas* it is almost impracticable to have such accounts and actions settled within the time now limit[*t*]ed by law for that purpose,— Preamble. 1752-53 chap. 1. 1748-49, chap. 17.

Be it therefore enacted by the Governour, Council and House of Representatives,

[SECT. 1.] That the time for commencing of actions of the case upon notes of hand, or upon book acco[mp][*un*]ts, limit[*t*]ed by the said act of the twenty-second, or by said act made in the twenty-fifth, year of his present majesty's reign, shall be and is hereby extended to the last day of March, which will be in the year of Lord one thousand seven hundred and fifty-six; and no suit hereafter to be brought in such cases shall be barred if commenced before the expiration of said term. Time continued for commencing actions of the case, upon notes of hand and book accounts.

And that this law may be more generally known,—

Be it further enacted,

[SECT. 2.] That the clerk of every town and district within this province shall read, or cause the same to be read, in their respective towns and districts, at their anniversary meetings in March and May, annually; and the justices of the several courts of common pleas within the respective counties, shall cause the same to be publickly read at the opening of their courts, from time to time, after the publication of this act, and until[l] the last day of March, one thousand seven hundred and fifty-six. [*Passed April* 19 ; *published April* 24, 1754. This act to be read in town meetings,— and at the sessions of the peace.

CHAPTER 35.

AN ACT FOR ERECTING A NEW TOWN WITHIN THE COUNTY OF MIDDLESEX, BY THE NAME OF LINCOLN.

Preamble.

WHEREAS the inhabitants of the easterly part of Concord, the southwesterly part of Lexington, and the northerly part of Weston have addressed this court, setting forth the many difficulties they now labour under, which might be effectually remedied if they were constituted a township,—

Be it therefore enacted by the Governour, Council and House of Representatives,

A new town made called Lincoln.

[SECT. 1.] That the easterly part of the said town of Concord, the southwesterly part of the said town of Lexington, and the northerly part of the said town of Weston, as hereafter set forth and described, be and hereby are set[t] off, constituted and erected into a seperate and distinct township by the name of Lincoln, the bounds of the said township to be as follows; viz[t]., to begin at Concord River, where the line goes over said river between Concord and Sudbury, and runs down said river to a brook that runs out of Well Meadow, so called; from thence, to the southeasterly side of Walden Pond, so called; from thence, to the northwesterly corner of a lot of land lately belonging to Daniel Brooks, on the south side of the country road; then running, easterly, with the country road (one-half whereof to belong to and be maintained by each town) until[l] it comes to Joshua Brooks's tan[*n*]-house; and from the northwest corner of said tan[*n*]-house, to the northwest corner of John Wheat's land, adjoining to Benjamin Wheeler's land; and thence, by said Wheeler's land, to Bedford line; and, by Bedford line, to Concord Corner, adjoining to Lexington; and from thence, in a strait line, to a little bridge in the country road, a little westerly of Thomas Nelson's house; thence, to the top of a little hill eastward of Nehemiah Abbot's house; thence, to Waltham northwest corner, including Elisha Cutler's land; from thence, on Waltham line, to the southwest corner of John Be[a]m[u][*i*]s's land; thence, running south, to the southeast corner of Benjamin Brown's land; thence, turning and running westerly, by said Brown's land, to a stake and heap of stones, being the northwest corner of Bra[y]dyl Smith's land; thence, to a rock in the squadron line, a little northwest of the school-house; thence, to the corner of the wall on the north side of Concord road, so called, being upon the division line between Theophilus Mansfield and Josiah Parks; thence, running south, upon the division line between said Mansfield and said Parks, to the squadron line; thence, in the same course, [of] [*to*] the division line between Nathanael Allen and Ephraim Parks; thence, westerly, by the division line between said Allen and said Parks, till it comes to a townway; thence, westerly, in a str[eigh][*ai*]t line, across a corner of said Parks's land, to a heap of stones, being a corner between said Allen and said Parks; thence, westerly, between [the] said Allen and the said Parks, till it comes to Abbot's meadow; thence, in the same course, to Sudbury line, and by said line to the place first mentioned: and that the inhabitants of the said land, as before bounded and described, be and hereby are vested and endowed with the powers, priviledges, and immunities that the inhabitants of any of the towns within this province are or ought by law to be vested or endowed with.

Bounds of said town.

Provided,—

Lincoln inhabitants to pay

[SECT. 2.] That the inhabitants of [*the*] said town of Lincoln shall pay their proportion, agreable to what the inhabitants taken off by the said town of Lincoln from the town of Concord paid in the last tax, of the charges that may hereafter arise in building or repairing [*of*] a bridge or bridges over the great river in the town of Concord and the said town of Lincoln; and also their proportion of the charges of maintaining any poor person or persons that are now out of the town of Concord, but, by reason of their former residence there, may become a charge to the said town of Concord. Their proportion of charges, &c.

Provided also,—

And be it further enacted,

[SECT. 3.] That the said several inhabitants taken from the towns of Concord, Lexington and Weston, by this act, shall pay their proportion of all town, county [and] precinct and province taxes already assessed on said towns or precincts, as if this act had not been made. Proviso.

And be it further enacted,

[SECT. 4.] That James Minot, Esq[r]., be and hereby is directed and impowered to issue his warrant to some principal inhabitant in said town of Lincoln, requiring him to notify and warn the inhabitants of [*the*] said town of Lincoln, qualified by law to vote in town affairs, to meet, at such time and place as shall therein be set forth, to chuse all such officers as towns chuse in the month of March annually; and said officers shall be enjoined to take the oaths now required by law to be taken by town officers. [*Passed April* 19, 1754. Power for calling a meeting.

CHAPTER 36.

AN ACT FOR DIVIDING THE TOWN OF CONCORD, AND MAKING A DISTRICT OF THE NORTHERLY PART THEREOF BY THE NAME OF CARLISLE.

WHEREAS the inhabitants of the northerly part of the town of Concord, by reason of their being remote from the place of the publick worship of God, have petitioned this court to be set off a seperate district,—

Be it enacted by the Governour, Council and House of Representatives,

[SECT. 1.] That the northerly part of the town of Concord within the following bounds; viz[t]., beginning at Concord River, at the mouth of Ralph's Brook, so called, and running, westerly, to a white-oak tree on or by the highway on the easterly side of Hunt's Hill, otherwise called Gravel Hill; thence, still westerly, to a heap of stones by the wall in the highway, about four rods northerly of Daniel Cole's barn, and so, extending on a streight line, to a way a little westerly of Richard Temple's house; and then running northerly, by said way, which leads toward Acton Line, till it comes to Benjamin Temple's land; thence, running to Acton Line, so as to take into the new district the said Benjamin Temple's land; and from thence, bounded on Acton and Billerica, until[l] it comes to Concord River, taking in Blood's Farm, so called; and then, on Concord River, to where the line first began, be and hereby is set off from the said town of Concord, and erected into a separate and distinct district by the name of Carlisle; and that the inhabitants thereof do the duties that are required, and be [*in*]vested with all the powers, priviledges and immunities which the inhabitants of any town within this province do, or by law ought to, enjoy, excepting only the privilege of chusing a representative to represent them in the great and general court; in chusing of whom the inhabitants of said district shall join with the inhabitants of the town of Concord, as they Bounds of Carlisle district.

have heretofore done, and also in paying said representative; and that the town of Concord, as often as they shall call a meeting for the choice of a representative, shall give seasonable notice to the clerk of said district, for the time being, of the time and place of said meeting, to the end that the said district may jo[y][*i*]n them therein; and the clerk of said district shall set up, in some publick place in said district, a notification thereof accordingly: *provided, nevertheless*, the said district shall pay their proportionable part of all such town, county, parish and province charges as are already assessed, in like manner as though this act had never been made.

And be it further enacted,

Carlisle inhabitants to pay their proportion of the great bridge.

Power for calling the first meeting.

[SECT. 2.] That the inhabitants of the said district shall, from time to time, forever, hereafter, pay their proportionable part of the charge of keeping in good repair the great North Bridge, so called, over Concord River; and that James Minot, Esq[r]., is hereby impowered to issue his warrant, directed to some principal inhabitant in said district, requiring him to warn the inhabitants of said district, qualified by law to vote in town affairs, to meet, at such time and place as shall be therein set forth, to chuse all such officers as shall be necessary to manage the affairs of said district. [*Passed April* 19; *published April* 24, 1754.

CHAPTER 37.

AN ACT FOR INCORPORATING THE PLANTATION CALLED QUABIN, IN THE COUNTY OF HAMPSHIRE, INTO A TOWN BY THE NAME OF GREENWICH.

Preamble.

WHEREAS it is represented to this court that the inhabitants of the plantation called Quabin, in the county of Hampshire, labour under great difficulties and inconvenienc[*i*]es by reason of their not being invested with privile[*d*]ges of a town; therefore,—

Be it enacted by the Governour, Council and House of Representatives,

A new town made called Greenwich.

Bounds of said town.

[SECT. 1.] That the whole of that tract of land in the county of Hampshire, called Quabin, bounded as follows; viz[t]., eastwardly on Lamb's Town; southerly on Read's Land; westerly, partly on Equivalent Land, and partly on Salem Town; northerly, partly on Salem Town and partly on White's Town, be and hereby is erected into a distinct and seperate town by the name of Greenwich; and that the inhabitants thereof be and hereby are invested with all the powers, privileges and immunities that towns in this province by law do or may enjoy.

Provided,—

Proviso relating to assessments.

[SECT. 2.] That nothing in this act shall be understood or so construed as in any manner to superse[e]d[*e*] or make void any order or orders of this court now in force respecting the method of making assessments within said plantation, but that the same shall remain and be as effectual as if this act had not been made.

And be it further enacted,

Power for calling the first meeting.

[SECT. 3.] That John Worthington, Esq[r]., be and hereby is impow[e]red to issue his warrant to some principal inhabitant of the said plantation, requiring him, in his majesty's name, to warn and notify the said inhabitants, qualified to vote in town affairs, that they meet together, at such time and place in said plantation as by said warrant shall be appointed, to chuse such officers as may be necessary to manage the affairs of said town; and the inhabitants being so met, shall be and hereby are impow[e]red to chuse such officers accordingly; and the said John Worthington, Esq[r]., is hereby appointed moderator of said meeting, to order and regulate the same. [*Passed April* 20;* *published April* 24, 1754.

CHAPTER 38.

AN ACT FOR ERECTING A TOWN IN THE COUNTY OF WORCESTER, AT A PLANTATION CALLED NICHEWOAG, BY THE NAME OF PETERSHAM.

Preamble.

WHEREAS the plantation commonly called N[i][*e*]chewoag, in the county of Worcester, is compleatly filled with inhabitants, who have built and finished a convenient meeting-house for the publick worship of God, and have settled a learned Protestant minister amongst them, and have addressed this court to be erected into a sep[a][*e*]rate and distinct township, to hold and enjoy equal powers and privileges with the other towns in the province,—

Be it enacted by the Governour, Council and House of Representatives,

A new town called Petersham.

[SECT. 1.] That the plantation of Nichewoag, in the county of Worcester, as the same is hereafter bounded and described, be and hereby is set off and constituted a sep[a][*e*]rate and distinct township by the name of Petersham; the bounds of said township being as follows; viz[t]., begin[*n*]ing at a heap of stones on Rutland-District Northwest line, and run[*n*]ing six miles, from the northerly corner thereof; from thence, run[*n*]ing north, thirty-four degrees west, by the needle, one thousand eight hundred and twenty-four perch, to a beach-tree with stones; from thence, run[*n*]ing west, thirty-five degrees south, two thousand one hundred and twenty-eight perch, to the west angle; from thence, run[*n*]ing south, thirty-six degrees east, one thousand six hundred and fifty perch, to a heap of stones, the westerly corner of said Rutland District; and from thence, on Rutland-District Northwest line to where it began: and that the inhabitants thereof be and hereby are vested and endowed with equal powers, privile[*d*]ges and immunities that the inhabitants of any other towns within this province are or ought by law to be vested or endowed with.

Bounds of said town.

And be it further enacted,

Delinquent proprietors to pay a sixtieth part of all rates.

[SECT. 2.] That such of the grantees as have not fully compl[y][*i*]ed with the conditions of settlement be and hereby are subjected, each one, to pay a sixtieth part of all rates and taxes that shall hereafter be laid on the inhabitants of said town, as well as for the support of the ministry among them, and other town charges, until[l] they have compl[y][*i*]ed with the conditions of settlement. [*Passed April* 20;† *published April* 24, 1754.

* According to the General-Court records, this act was signed April 19, and again April 23; but on the engrossment the date, apparently in the Governor's handwriting, is clearly as given above.

† According to the record, this was signed again April 23.

CHAPTER 39.

AN ACT TO ENABLE THE JUSTICES OF THE COURT OF GENERAL SESSIONS OF THE PEACE, AT THEIR SEVERAL SESSIONS IN THE COUNTY OF DUKES COUNTY, MORE EFFECTUALLY TO REGULATE AND KEEP UP A CONSTANT FERRY FROM DUKES COUNTY TO FALMOUTH, IN THE COUNTY OF BARNSTABLE.

Preamble. 1729-30, chap. 7.

WHEREAS there is provision already made by law for the justices, in their quarter sessions throughout this province, to licence persons to keep ferries, and state the fa[re][*ir*]s or prices of each ferry, both for man and beast, and to take bond of each ferryman, &c[a]., but no provision is made by law to enable the justices, in their sessions, to lay a tax on any county for the upholding and maintaining of ferries, either by building boats, wharves, ways, &c[a]., where no particular person or persons will be at the cost thereof; by means whereof the said county of Dukes County is wholly destitute of a ferry, from said county (which is an island) to the mainland, whereby many inconvenienc[*i*]es daily happen to those that have occasion to go to and from said county,—

Be it therefore enacted by the Governour, Council and House of Representatives,

Quarter-sessions in Dukes County, to assess the inhabitants, for keeping a ferry.

That the justices of the court of general sessions of the peace, at any of their sessions hereafter to be held in and for said county of Dukes County, are hereby enabled and directed to raise monies, and to assess the inhabitants of said county of Dukes County, and their estates, as well for the building of ferryboats, making and maintaining suitable wharves and ways for ferry-ways, for the conveniency of keeping a ferry in said county, in as full and ample a manner as the justices in said quarter sessions are by law already enabled to do for defreying the necessary repairs of bridges, prisons, the maintenance of poor prisoners, and all other proper county charges; and under the same regulations and restrictions. [*Passed April* 19; *published April* 24, 1754.

CHAPTER 40.

AN ACT IMPOWERING THE PROVINCE TREASURER TO BORROW FIVE THOUSAND THREE HUNDRED POUNDS, AND FOR APPLYING THE SAME TO DEFREY THE CHARGE OF BUILDING A FORT ON KENNEBECK RIVER, AND FOR SUNDRY OTHER PURPOSES ORDERED BY THIS COURT.

Preamble.

WHEREAS it is very necessary that a good and defensible fort be soon built on Kennebeck River (the present fort being in a ruinous and irrepa[i]rable state), as also that many other expensive affairs be carried on very speedily, which, in the whole, have been estimated to require the sum of five thousand three hundred pounds; which sum this court have voted and agreed to borrow, the same not being in the treasury,—

Be it therefore enacted by the Governour, Council and House of Representatives,

Treasurer empowered to borrow £5,300.

[SECT. 1.] That the treasurer of this province be and hereby he is impowered to borrow from such person or persons as shall be willing to lend the same, a sum not exceeding five thousand three hundred pounds, in milled dollars, at six shillings each, or other coined silver at six shillings and eightpence per ounce; and the sum so borrowed shall be a stock in the treasury, and applied for building a fort on Kennebeck River, in such place and manner as the captain-general shall think proper; and for defreying the charge of his excellency the governour's proposed voyage to the eastern parts of this province, and of the council and other attendants; for paying the wages of five hundred men, including officers, which his excellency may order eastward, and to pay the bounty ordered at inlistment, as also their subsistence; and to purchase presents proper for the Six Nations, and to defr[a][*e*]y the charge of commissioners attending the General Convention at Albany; and for no other purposes whatsoever: and if there be a surplusage, it shall remain a stock in the treasury; and for every sum so borrowed, the treasurer shall give a receipt and obligation in the form following; viz[t].,—

Province of the Massachusetts Bay, day of , 1754, received of . the sum of pounds, for the use and service of the province of the Massachusetts Bay, and, in behalf of said province, I do hereby promise and oblige myself and successors in the office of treasurer to repay to the said or order, on or before the first day of May, 1755, the aforesaid sum of pounds, with interest at the rate of six per cent per annum. Witness my hand, A. B., Treasurer. Form of treasurer's receipt.

—and no receipt shall be given for less than twenty pounds.

And in order to enable the treasurer effectually to discharge the receipts and obligations by him given in pursuance of this act,—

Be it enacted,

[SECT. 2.] That there be and hereby is granted unto his most excellent majesty a tax of five thousand three hundred pounds, to be levied on polls, and estates real and personal, within this province, according to such rules and in such proportion on the several towns and districts within the same, as shall be agreed on and ordered by the general court of this province at their sessions in May, one thousand seven hundred and fifty-four, which sum shall be paid into the treasury on or before the thirty-first day of March next after. Tax of £5,300 granted.

And as an additional fund and security for drawing the said sum of five thousand three hundred pounds into the treasury again,—

Be it enacted,

[SECT. 3.] That the duty of excise for one year from July, one thousand seven hundred and fifty-four, shall be applied towards discharging said receipts and obligations. Fund.

And be it further enacted,

[SECT. 4.] That in case the general court shall not, at their sessions in May, and before the twentieth day of June, one thousand seven hundred and fifty-four, agree and conclude upon an act apportioning the sum which by this act is engaged to be, in said year, apportioned, assessed and levied, that then, and in such case, each town and district within this province shall pay, by a tax to be levied on the polls, and estates both real and personal, within their limits, the same proportion of the said sum as the said towns and districts were taxed by the gen[*era*]l court in the tax act then last preceeding: *saving* what relates to the pay of the repres[*entati*]ves, which shall be assessed on the several towns they represent; and the province treasurer is hereby fully impowered and directed, some time in the month of June, one thousand seven hundred and fifty-four, to issue and send forth his warrants, directed to the selectmen or assessors of each town and district within this province, requiring them to assess the polls, and estate[s] both real and personal, within their several towns and districts, and for their respective parts and proportion of the sum before directed and engaged Rule for apportioning the tax in case no tax act shall be agreed on.

to be assessed, and also for the fines upon the several towns for not sending a representative.

[SECT. 5.] And the assessors, as also persons assessed, shall observe, be govern[*e*]d by, and subject to all such rules and directions as have been given in the then last preceeding tax act. [*Passed April* 18; *published April* 24, 1754.

CHAPTER 41.

AN ACT FOR LEVYING SOLDIERS, AND TO PREVENT SOLDIERS AND SEAMEN IN HIS MAJESTY'S SERVICE FROM BEING ARRESTED FOR DEBT.

Preamble. 1748-49, chap. 5.

FOR the more speedy and effectual levying of soldiers for his majesty's service, when and so often as there shall be occasion for the same, for the preservation and defence of his majesty's subjects and interests, and the prosecuting, encountring, repelling or subduing such as shall at any time attempt, in hostile manner, to enterprize the destruction, invasion, detriment or annoyance of this his majesty's province, or any of his majesty's subjects therein, and for the better preventing disappointments, thro' the default of any employed in levying such soldiers, or by the non-appearance of such as shall be levyed,—

Be it enacted by the Governour, Council and House of Representatives,

Duty of chief officers in levying soldiers.

[SECT. 1.] That when and so often as any chief officer of any regiment of militia within this province shall receive orders from the captain-general or commander-in-chief, for the time being, of the said province, for the pressing, or causing to be impressed, for his majesty's service, out of the regiment under his command, so many soldiers as in such orders shall be mentioned, such chief officer of the regiment shall forthwith thereupon issue forth his warrants to the captains or chief officers of the companies or troops within his regiment, or such of them as he shall think fit, requiring them, respectively, to impress, out of the militia in the companies or troops under their command, so many able soldiers, furnished and provided as the law directs, and,* in the whole, shall make up the number which, by the orders of the captain-general or commander-in-chief, he shall be directed to impress, on pain that every chief officer of a regiment that shall neglect, or not do his utmost, to send forth his warrants seasonably (having orders for the same as above mentioned), shall forf[ie][*ei*]t and pay a fine of thirty pounds. And every colonel or field-officer of any regiment that shall, directly or indirectly, take or receive anything whatsoever, for the discharging of any soldier that shall be impressed for his majesty's service, except those of his own company or troop, shall forf[ie][*ei*]t and pay a fine of ten pounds, for each and every man by him so discharged for the sake of gain.

Penalty for not doing duty.

Duty of the chief officer of a company or troop.

[SECT. 2.] And every captain or other chief officer of any company or troop, that shall receive any warrant from the chief officer of the regiment, whereto such company or troop belongs, for the impressing out of the same any soldiers for his majesty's service, shall thereupon use his utmost endeavour to impress, or cause to be impressed, so many soldiers as by such warrant he shall be required to impress, and to have them at the place of rendezvous at the time as therein shall be mentioned, on pain that every captain or chief officer of any company or troop, that shall neglect, or not do his utmost, to comply with and perform any warrant to be by him received as aforesaid from the chief

Penalty for not doing his duty.

* *Sic.*

officer of the regiment, shall, for such neglect and default, pay a fine of ten pounds.

[SECT. 3.] And every officer or soldier that shall receive a warrant from his captain, or the chief officer of the company or troop in which he is [e][*i*]nlisted for the impressing of men, shall forthwith attend and perform the same, on paying a fine of three pounds.

Penalty for other persons' neglect.

[SECT. 4.] And all persons are required to be aiding and assisting to him in the execution of such warrant, on pain of forf[ie][*ei*]ting the sum of forty shillings.

Penalty for taking a reward to discharge soldiers.

[SECT. 5.] And if any person authorized as aforesaid to impress any soldier or soldiers for his majesty's service, shall exact or take any reward to discharge or spare any from said service, he shall forf[ie][*ei*]t ten pounds for every twenty shillings he shall so exact or take, and so *pro ratâ*.

Disposition of the fines.

[SECT. 6.] All which fines and penalties aforesaid, shall be, one moiety thereof, unto his majesty for and towards the support of the government of this province, and the other moiety, to him or them that shall inform and sue for the same, by action, bill, plaint or information, in any court of record.

And be it further enacted,

Duty of persons impressed.

[SECT. 7.] That every person liable and fit for the service, being orderly impressed, as aforesaid, for his majesty's service, by being commanded, in his majesty's name, to attend the said service, shall, by himself, or other meet person in his room, to the acceptance of his captain or chief officer, attend the same at time and place appointed, compleat with arms and ammunition, if such he have or is able to purchase the same, on pain of forf[ie][*ei*]ting and paying to his captain or chief officer, by whose warrant he was impressed, within twenty-four hours next after such impressment, the sum of five pounds, who, on payment thereof, shall give a receipt therefor; and in default of such payment, or of procuring some meet person in his stead to the acceptance of said officer, the said sum shall be lev[y][*i*]ed by distress and sale of the goods and chattels of such offender, or of the goods and chatt[e]l[*e*]s of his parent or master, in case such impressed person be a son under age, or a servant; and the officer by whose warrant he was impressed, shall be and is hereby fully impowered and required to levy and collect the said sum in such manner as constables of towns and districts within this province, are impowered to levy the publick taxes; and for want of goods and chatt[e]l[*e*]s whereon to make distress, such offender shall suffer six month's imprisonment, without bail or mainprize, to be committed by mittimus from any justice of the peace of the same county, upon due conviction of such neglect.

Fines to be levied on goods and chattels, &c.

[SECT. 8.] And of the monies to be so levyed or collected, such captain or chief officer shall lay out and improve so much as shall be necessary for the procuring and fitting out of one or more suitable person or persons, as there may be occasion, to perform the service for which any soldier or soldiers forf[ie][*ei*]ting, as aforesaid, shall have been impressed, the overplus of such monies to be paid into the town or district treasury some time before the annual meeting of such town or district in March, in each and every year, for the use and only benefit of such company or troop in said town or district to which such person or persons, impressed as aforesaid, belonged at the time of his or their being impressed; and said town or district treasurer is hereby enjo[y][*i*]ned, under the penalty of five pounds, as aforesaid, to pay the same out from time to time, to any impressed man or men, by order of the captain or chief officer of such company or troop such impressed man or men belonged to; and such officer shall give in to the treasurer of said town or district an attested acco[mp][*un*]t of the sum by him received and paid;

and upon such officer's neglecting to render such acco[mp][*un*]t, and pay[*ing*] such sums as shall be due, such officer, for such neglect, shall forf[ie][*ei*]t and pay to such town or district treasurer, for the use of such town or district, as aforesaid, the sum of forty pounds; and the said town or district treasurer is hereby impowered to demand and sue therefor accordingly.

[SECT. 9.] And if the captain or officer to whom the said sum of five pounds shall be paid, as aforesaid, by any person impressed, cannot seasonably procure another suitable person to serve in the stead of him that was before impressed, or if any person impressed shall suffer imprisonment, or shall make his escape, in each and every such case, the said captain or officer shall renew his warrants as often as there shall be occasion, until[l] the number sent for from him be compleated; and all persons paying the said sum of five pounds, as before mentioned, shall be esteemed as persons that have served, and be no further or otherwise liable to any after-impress than those that actually go forth in that service.

[SECT. 10.] And all persons lawfully impowered to impress may pursue any person that absconds from the impress, or makes his escape, and may impress such person in any place within the province; and if any person impressed, as aforesaid, for his majesty's service as required, such person, at his return, shall be apprehended by warrant from any justice of the peace, and be by him committed to prison, unless such person give sufficient security to answer it at the next court of general sessions of the peace; and upon due conviction of the said offence, by the oath of him that impressed him, shall suffer twelve month's imprisonment, or pay a fine of ten pounds, to be paid to the selectmen of the town or district where such person belonged to at the time of his being impressed, for purchasing arms for the use of the company to which such person belonged.

[SECT. 11.] And if any person, directly or indirectly, by coun[c][*s*]el or otherwise, shall prevent the impressing, conceal any person impressed, or, knowingly, further his escape, such person shall pay, as a fine, three pounds.

And be it further enacted,

When the pay of soldiers is to begin.

[SECT. 12.] That all soldiers shall be in pay from the time of their being impressed till they be orderly discharged, and have reasonable time allowed them to repair to their usual places of abode.

[SECT. 13.] And if any captain or other chief officer shall dismiss any soldier detained in his majesty's service, and assume another for gain, such captain or chief officer shall forf[ie][*ei*]t the sum of ten pounds for every twenty shillings he shall so exact, to be recovered and disposed of in manner as is before provided for the fine or penalty on officers neglecting to execute warrants for impressing of soldiers.

[SECT. 14.] And every person who shall impress any soldiers for his majesty's service, shall transmit a list of them to the chief officer of the regiment or troop, particularly mentioning sons under age, or servants, if any such there be, and to whom they belong, that so their fathers or masters may receive their wages, who are hereby impowered so to do.

And be it further enacted,

Maimed soldiers and seamen to be relieved.

[SECT. 15.] That all such soldiers and seamen that, from the commencement of this act, have been, or, during the continuance thereof, may be, wounded in his majesty's service within this province, and are thereby maimed or otherwise disabled, shall be rel[ei][*ie*]ved out of the publick treasury, as the great and general court or assembly shall order.

And be it further enacted,

[Sect. 16.] That any impressed man or men appearing at the place of rendezvous, being actually destitute of arms and ammunition of his own, and unable to purchase the same, he or they shall be furnished out of the town stock, if any there be; otherwise, it shall be in the power of the captain or chief officer of the company or troop by whom he is impressed, to impress arms and ammunition for him or them, which arms shall be apprized by two suitable persons appointed and sworn for that purpose; and the persons so appointed and sworn, shall give a certificate of the apprized value to the person or persons from whom the said arms are taken, for the use of which arms shall be paid out of his wages one penny per week for the same, and return such arms, or otherwise pay for the same; and if any soldier shall lose his arms in his majesty's service, not thrô his own neglect or default, such loss shall be born[*e*] by the province. Soldiers to be furnished with arms.

And be it further enacted,

[Sect. 17.] That if any person whatsoever, other than the commissary, shall trust or give credit to any soldier, mar[r]iner or sailor, during his being actually in his majesty's service, for cloathing or other things whatsoever, no process shall be granted or served on such soldier for any debt so contracted, until[l] he be dismiss'd the service; and every writ[t] or process granted or served contrary [*t*]hereto, shall be deemed and adjudg[*e*]'d, *ipso facto*, void. No process to be served for clothing, &c., while in the service.

[Sect. 18.] And any justices of the peace within the county where any such soldier or mar[r]iner is committed or restrained, upon process granted for debt, or pretension of debt, contracted as aforesaid, shall, upon certificate given to him from the captain or chief officer under whose command such soldier or mar[r]iner is, setting forth that at the time of such debt contracted he was then and still continues a soldier or mariner in his majesty's pay, forthwith order his release from confinement, and return to his duty.

And be it further enacted,

[Sect. 19.] That no person who is or shall be impressed, hired or voluntarily [e][*i*]nlisted into his majesty's service, either by sea or land, shall, during his continuance therein, be liable to be taken out of his majesty's service by any process or execution, unless for some criminal matter, for any sum under the value of ten pounds; nor for any greater sum until[l] oath shall be made by the plaintiff or plaintiffs, before one of the justices of the court out of which the execution or process shall issue, or before two justices of the peace, *quorum unus*, in the county where the plaintiff may happen to be, that to his or their knowledge there is, *bonâ fide*, due from such person as the process or execution is desired to issue against, ten pounds at least; and every soldier whose body shall, contrary to the intent of this act, be arrested by mean process or execution after his inlistment into said service, may and shall be set at liberty by two justices of the peace, *quorum unus*, in the county where such soldier is taken, upon application made by him or his superiour officer, and proof of his being entered into the service aforesaid. No person impressed, hired, or enlisted to be arrested for less than £10, unless for criminal matters.

And be it further enacted,

[Sect. 20.] That no person in his majesty's service shall pawn, truck, barter or sell his arms, am̄[*m*]unition or cloathing, on penalty of being punished by riding the wooden horse, run[*n*]ing the gantlet or other like military punishment; and the person accepting or receiving the same, shall be compell[*e*]'d to restore and make good the same without price or redemption, and shall, further, if in his majesty's service, suffer military punishment as aforesaid. Persons in his majesty's service not to sell their arms, &c.

And be it further enacted,

Soldier or mariner not to be trusted for strong liquors.

[SECT. 21.] That all debts contracted for strong or spirituous liquors, by any soldier or mar[r]iner while in his majesty's service, shall be void, and the creditor forever debarred from any process or benefit of the law for recovery of the same.

Provided, always,—

Process not to be stayed after dismission from service.

[SECT. 22.] That this act shall not be construed to stay the process of any creditor of such soldier or sailor, as aforesaid, after his dismission from the said service, nor at all to stay any process or execution against a defective constable or collector, for any tax or taxes committed to him to collect.

Provided, also,—

Limitation.

[SECT. 23.] That this act shall continue in force unto the first day of June, which will be in the year of our Lord one thousand seven hundred and fifty-seven, and no longer. [*Passed April* 20;* *published April* 24, 1754.

CHAPTER 42.

AN ACT FOR FURTHER REGULATING THE COURSE OF JUDICIAL PROCEEDINGS.

Preamble.

WHEREAS trials of civil actions, upon appeals and reviews, have been unnecessarily multiplied, to the great charge and gr[ei][*ie*]vance of many of his majesty's subjects within this province,—

Be it therefore enacted by the Governour, Council and House of Represent[ati]ves,

No review allowed at the inferior court but in case, &c.

[SECT. 1.] That no writ of review shall hereafter be brought, to any inferiour court of common pleas, unless the action be already begun; and that whensoever in any action that shall hereafter be brought in any of the courts within this province, the party, whether plaintiff or defendant, which shall have recovered judgment on the first trial, shall likewise recover on a second trial, no review shall be allowed in such action.

No review allowed where either party hath obtained two judgments.

[SECT. 2.] This act to continue and be in force for three years from the twenty-fifth day of January, one thousand seven hundred and fifty-four, and no longer. [*Passed April* 23;† *published April* 24, 1754.

CHAPTER 43.

AN ACT IN ADDITION TO THE ACT MADE AND PASS[*E*]'D IN THE EIGHTH YEAR OF HER LATE MAJESTY QUEEN ANN[*E*], [E][*I*]NTIT[U]LED "AN ACT FOR REGULATING OF DRAINS OR COMMON SHORES."

Preamble.

1709-10, chap. 5, § 3.

WHEREAS, in and by an act made and passed in the eighth year of the reign of her late majesty Queen Ann[*e*], intit[u]led "An Act for regulating of drains and common shores," it is enacted, among other things, "That it shall and may be lawful to and for any one or more of the inhabitants of any town, at his or their own cost and charge, to

* According to the record, this chapter was signed April 19.

† This chapter was passed to be enacted January 24; and, according to the record, it was signed April 17. The engrossment has been followed, as the signature thereon appears to have been dated by the Governor.

make and lay a common shore or main drain for the benefit of themselves and others that shall think fit to jo[y][*i*]n therein; and every person that shall afterwards enter his or her particular drain into such common shore or main drain, or by any more remote means receive benefit thereby, for the draining of their cellars or lands, shall be obliged to pay unto the owner or owners of such common shore or main drain a proportionable part of the charge of making or repairing the same, or so much thereof as shall be below the place where any particular drain enters thereinto, at the judgment of the selectmen of the town, or major part of them"; *and whereas* it frequently happens that the main drains or common shores decay and fill up, and the persons immediately affected thereby are obliged to repair such common shore to prevent damage to themselves and others whose drains enter above as well as below them, and no particular provision is made by said act to compel such persons as dwell above that part where common shores are repaired and have not sustained damage, to pay their proportionable share thereof as shall be adjudged by the selectmen, nor in what manner the same shall be recovered, which has already occasioned many disputes and controversies; wherefore, for preventing the same for the future,—

Be it enacted by the Governour, Council and House of Representatives,

[SECT. 1.] That whensoever it shall hereafter happen, after the first day of June next, that any common shore or main drain is stopped or gone to decay, so that it will be necessary to open such common shore or main drain to remove such stoppage and repair it, not only the person or persons who shall so do, or cause the same to be done, but all others whose drains enter, either above or below, such common shore or main drain, or receive any benefit by said common shore or main drain, shall pay such a proportionable part of the whole expence of opening and repairing the common shore or main drain as shall be adjudged to them by the selectmen of the town, or a major part of them, to be certified under their hands; and if any person or persons, after such certificate is made, shall refuse to pay the same, within ten days, to the person so appointed by the selectmen to receive it, being duly notified thereof, he shall be liable and subject to pay to such person appointed double the sum mentioned in such certificate, and all costs arising upon such refusal; and such person is hereby fully authorized and impowered to bring an action or actions for the same accordingly: *provided, always,* that nothing in this act shall be construed or understood to set aside or make void any covenants or agreements already made, or that hereafter may be made, among the proprietors of such drains or common shores.

Owners of drains, &c., to pay their proportion of the charge for opening of them.

Provided, in case of contract.

[SECT. 2.] This act to continue [to] [*and*] be in force for five years from the first day of June next, and no longer. [*Passed April* 17; *published April* 24, 1754.

Limitation.

CHAPTER 44.

AN ACT TO PREVENT NEAT CATTLE AND HORSES RUNNING AT LARGE AND FEEDING ON THE BEACHES AND MEADOWS BELOW THE BANKS, IN THE TOWN OF TRURO, FROM THE HOUSE OF JOSHUA ATKINS TO BOUND BROOK, AND ALSO ON THE COMMON MEADOW AT AND ABOUT PAMIT HARBOUR AND RIVER, AS FAR UP AS THE WADING-PLACE BY JOHN LUMBART'S.

WHEREAS there are certain meadow-lands within the township of Truro, in the county of Barnstable, called Pamit Meadows, on which

Preamble. 1750-51, chap. 4.

many of the inhabitants of said town depend for their hay, and the said meadow-land lies adjo[y][*i*]ning to sandy beaches, next the sea, on which no fence can well be made to stand, and by reason of cattle and horses trampling and feeding there, the beach-grass, which was wont to prevent the driving of the sand from the beaches to the meadows, is destroyed, and a great part of the meadows already covered with sand and become useless for grass, and the whole in danger of being buried with the sands, if not timely prevented,—

Be it therefore enacted by the Governour, Council and House of Represent[*ati*]*ves*,

No person to turn or drive any cattle on the beaches, &c., of Truro.

[SECT. 1.] That no person shall presume to turn or drive any neat cattle, or horses, upon the said beaches or meadows, to feed, or leave them at large there, on the penalty of five shillings a head for all neat cattle, and for every horse-kind so turned upon any of the said beaches or meadows, to feed, or that shall be found at large there; which penalty may be recovered by any of the proprietors of said beaches or meadows, one moiety thereof to be to the informer that shall sue for the same, and the other moiety to be to and for the use of the poor of the town of Truro.

And be it further enacted,

Cattle found feeding on the beaches aforesaid, to be impounded, &c.

[SECT. 2.] That it shall be lawful for any owner or proprietor of the said meadows or beaches, or other person, finding any cattle or horse-kind feeding or going at large upon the beaches or meadows aforesaid, or any of them, to impound the same; and the person or persons impounding them shall give publick notice thereof in the town of Truro, and in the two next adjo[y][*i*]ning towns, and shall rel[ei][*ie*]ve said creatures whilst impounded, with suitable meat and water; and the owner thereof appearing, he shall pay to the impounder, one shilling and sixpence damages for each head of neat cattle or horse-kind so impounded, and cost[s] of impounding them: and if the owner do not appear within the space of six days, and pay the damage, and costs occasioned by impounding the same, then, and in every such case, the person or persons impounding such cattle or horse-kind shall cause them to be sold at publick vendue, for paying such damages and costs, and the charge arising by such sale (publick notice of the time and place of such sale being given forty-eight hours beforehand); and the overplus, if any be, to be returned to the owner of such cattle or horse-kind, on his demand, at any time within twelve months next after the sale; and if no owner shall appear within the said twelve months, then one moiety of the overplus shall be to the party impounding, and the other moiety thereof to the use of the poor of the town of Truro.

Limitation.

[SECT. 3.] This act to continue and be in force for the space of three years from the first day of June next, and no longer. [*Passed April* 19; *published April* 24, 1754.

NOTES.—There were four sessions of the General Court this year. The first session was prorogued, on the twenty-second day of June, to August 15; but, on the first day of August, it was again prorogued, by proclamation, to September 5. On the tenth of August, Governor Shirley, having returned, issued his proclamation confirming the last prorogation by the Lieutenant-Governor. The second session continued from the fifth to the fourteenth of September, inclusive. There is no record of a prorogation of the Assembly at the end of this session; but, as the third session began December 4, after "several prorogations," it may be inferred that the court was prorogued to the latter date. The third session was interrupted by two recesses between the 22d and 26th of December and the 12th and 16th of January; and was concluded January 25, 1754. The fourth session began March 27, and ended April 23.

All the acts of this year were printed: chapters 10 and 11, separately; and the engrossments are preserved except of chapters 12, 13, 14, 15, 16, 17, 22, 23, 24, 25, 26, 28, 30, and 35.

The acts of the first session were certified for transmission, October 17, 1753; and were delivered, by Mr. Bollan, the agent of the Province, May 15, 1754. They were referred to a committee of the Privy Council, by whom, in turn, they were ordered to be submitted to the Lords of Trade, June 14; and the latter ordered them to be sent to Mr. Lamb, July 23, 1754. The acts of the second and third sessions were certified, in like manner, October 21,

1754, accompanied by a letter from Secretary Willard, dated October 23. They were received by the Board of Trade, in December following, but were not lodged in the Council-office until January 24, 1755. On the 29th of January they were referred to a committee of the Privy Council, and, on the next day, were sent, by this committee, to the Lords of Trade. By the latter they were ordered to be sent to Sir Matthew Lamb, for his opinion, &c., February 4, but were not actually sent until June 19, 1755.

Sir Matthew Lamb's reports to the Lords of Trade, covering all the acts of this year, were read at the Board, March 24, 1756; and were to the effect that upon perusal and consideration of these acts he had no objection thereto, in point of law. The acts having been considered by the Board at this sitting, the draught of a report to the Lords of the committee of the Privy Council, was, next day, ordered to be prepared. On the 6th of April this draught was agreed to and ordered to be transcribed, and on the 13th of April was signed, together with a letter to Governor Shirley, on chapters 8 and 35, which had been prepared at the same time. The substance of this letter is hereafter given in the notes to the chapters above named.

In their above-mentioned report the Lords of Trade represent that chapters 5, 7, 10, 11, 24, 25, 26, and 40 "were passed for temporary services and are either expired by their own Limitation or the purposes for which they were enacted, have been completed"; that chapters 1, 2, 3, 4, 6, 8, 9, 12, 13, 14, 15, 16, 17, 18, 19, 20, 21, 22, 23, 27, 28, 29, 30, 31, 32, 33, 34, 36, 37, 38, 39, 41, 42, 43, and 44 "relate to the internal œconomy of the Province and appear to have been enacted for its private Convenience, and We see no reason why His Majesty may not be graciously pleased to confirm them"; and they conclude with a special report upon chapter 35, which is given at length, hereafter, in the note to that chapter.

In accordance with the representations of the Lords of Trade, an order was passed in Council, July 7, 1756, confirming the thirty-six acts last enumerated, above.

Chap. 4. "April 11, 1753. A Petition of James Cargell in behalf of the Inhabitants of the Plantation called Sheepscot, setting forth the Inconveniences they are under for want of Power to raise Taxes and other matters necessary for the regular Management of their Affairs, Therefore Praying that they may be erected into a District according to the Bounds set forth in the Petition.

In Council; Read and Ordered that the Prayer of the Petition be so far granted as that the Petitioners and the other Inhabitants of Sheepscot with the Lands described and contained within the Bounds mentioned in their Petition to this Court Anno 1751, be set of a District and that they be vested with all the Powers and Priviledges with other Districts; And that the Assessment made by the Select men chosen by the said Inhabitants for the Year 1751 be confirmed; and that the Constables or Collectors so chosen, for the same Year who have collected some part of the said Assessment be impowered and directed to finish their Collection and pay it according to the Directions of their Warrant; and that the Select Men who shall be chosen for the Year 1753 be directed and impowered forthwith to assess on the said Inhabitants and their Estates the Sum set on them in the Province Tax Act 1752 and that the Constable or Constables or Collectors who shall be chosen for the Year 1753 be impowered & directed to collect the same and pay it into the Province Treasury as soon as may be & the Petitioners have leave to bring in a Bill accordingly. In Council; Read and Concur'd.—Consented to by the Lieut Govern^r."—*Council Records, vol.* XX., *p.* 19.

Chap. 5. "June 19, 1753. In the House of Representatives; Voted that Mr Welles and Capt. Spurr wth such as the Honble Board shall join be a Committee to farm out the Excise for the County of Suffolk:—In Council Read and Concur'd & Jacob Wendell Esqr is joined in the Affair—Consented to by the Lieutenant Governor

In the House of Representatives; Voted that Mr Cogswell and Mr Greenleaf with such as the Honble Board shall join be a Committee to Farm out the Excise for the County of Essex—In Council Read & Concur'd; And Benj^a Lynde Esqr is joined in the Affair Consented to by the Lieutenant Governor

In the House of Representatives; Voted that Mr James Russell & Capt Livermore with such as the Honble Board shall join be a Committee to Farm out the Excise for the County of Middlesex—In Council; Read and Concur'd and Ezekiel Chever Esqr is joined in the Affair—Consented to by the Lieut Governor

In the House of Representatives; Voted that Col^o Patridge & Col^o Worthington with such as the Honble Board shall join be a Committee to farm out the Excise for the County of Hampshire In Council; Read and Concur'd; And Eleazer Porter Esqr is joined in the Affair Consented to by the Lieutenant Governor

In the House of Representatives Voted that Col^o Marcy and Capt Ayers with such as the Honble Board shall join be a Committee to farm out the Excise for the County of Worcester. In Council; Read and Concur'd; And John Chandler Esqr is joined in the Affair Consented to by the Lieutenant Governor

In the House of Representatives; Voted that Col^o Winslow & Col^o Bradford with such as the Honble Board shall join, be a Committee to farm out the Excise for the County of Plymouth. In Council; Read and Concur'd; And John Cushing Esqr is joined in the Affair—Consented to by the Lieutenant Governor

In the House of Representatives; Voted that Col^o Cotton & Col^o Otis with such as the Honble Board shall join, be a Committee to farm out the Excise for the County of Barnstable In Council; Read and Concur'd; And John Otis Esqr is joined in the Affair—Consented to by the Lieutenant Governor

In the House of Representatives; Voted that Capt White and Capt Cobb with such as the Honble Board shall join, be a Committee to farm out the Excise for the County of Bristol In Council; Read and Concur'd; And George Leonard Esqr is joined in the Affair Consented to by the Lieutenant Governor

In the House of Representatives; Voted that Mr Welles and Capt Prebble with such as the Honble Board shall join, be a Committee to farm out the Excise for the County of

York In Council; Read and Concur'd; And Jabez Fox Esqr is joined in the Affair Consented to by the Lieutenant Governor

In the House of Representatives; Voted that Col^o Mahew & Capt Norton with such as the Honble Board shall join, be a Committee to Farm out the Excise for the County of Dukes County In Council; Read and Concur'd; And John Allen Esqr is joined in the Affair—Consented to by the Lieut Governor

In the House of Representatives; Voted that Mr Folger & Mr Richard Coffin with such as the Honble Board shall join, be a Committee to Farm out the Excise for the County of Nantucket In Council; Read and Concur'd; And Josiah Coffin Esqr is joined in the Affair Consented to by the Lieutenant Governor "—*Ibid.*, *p.* 60.

"June 19, 1753. In the House of Representatives; Voted that the Committees of the Several Counties through the Province appointed to farm out the Excise (the Counties of Dukes County & Nantucket excepted) Insert in the publick Prints the Time and Place designed for that Purpose; And that the Commencem^t of the Rates for said Excise is on the ninth of July next In Council; Read & Concur'd—Consented to by the Lieutenant Governor."—*Ibid.*, *p.* 61.

"September 13, 1753. The Committee for Letting out to Farm the Excise for the County of Nantucket, for the present Year, reported that they had let out the same to Obed Hussey for Twenty five Pounds seventeen shillings and had lodged his Bond in the Treasury, Their Charge being £2. 4. 1. In the House of Representatives; Read and Accepted and Voted that the Sum of Two Pounds four shillings and one peny be allowed and paid out of the publick Treasury in Discharge of the within Accompt—In Council; Read & Concur'd:—Consented to by the Governor."—*Ibid.*, *p.* 87.

"September 14, 1753. The Committee appointed to let out to Farm the Excise for the County of Hampshire for this present Year; reported that they had let out the same to Noah Ashley Esqr for One hundred and thirty five Pounds and had lodged his Bonds in the Treasury, The Committees Charges in the Affair being £1. 2.—In the House of Representatives; Read and Ordered that the Report be Accepted, and that the Sum of One Pound two shillings be allowed and paid out of the publick Treasury to the Committee in full discharge of the foregoing Acco^t In Council; Read and Concur'd:—Consented to by the Governor.

The Committee appointed to let out to Farm the Excise in the County of Worcester, for this present Year, reported that they had let out the same to John Hunt of Watertown for the Sum of Two hundred and seventy two Pounds and had lodged his Bonds in the Treasury, The Committees Charge being £2. 6. 8. In the House of Representatives; Read and Voted that the above Report be accepted; and that the said Committee be allowed and paid out of the publick Treasury the sum of Two Pounds six shillings and eight pence in full Discharge of their Accompt.—In Council; Read & Concur'd:—Consented to by the Govern.^r."—*Ibid.*, *pp.* 90, 91.

"December 18, 1753. The Committee for letting out to Farm the Excise upon Strong Drink in the County of Bristol; reported that they had let out the same for the present Year for the Sum of One hundred and thirty Pounds to Capt George Morey of Norton, taken his Bond and lodged it with the Treasurer; Their Charge being £2. 9. 8 In the House of Representatives Read and Ordered that the above Report be accepted; And the Sum of Two Pounds nine shillings and eight pence be allowed & paid to the s^d Committee for their Trouble and Expence in Farming the s^d Excise: In Council; Read & Concur'd —Consented to by the Governor."—*Ibid*, *p.* 118.

"December 19, 1753. A Report of the Committee for letting out to Farm the Excise on Strong Drink in the County of Barnstable shewing that they had let it out to David Gorham Esqr for the Sum of One hundred and thirty four Pounds two shillings and eight pence, took Bond and lodged it with the Treasurer their own Acco^t of Time and expence being £1. 18. 8.—In the House of Representatives Read and Ordered that the above Report be Accepted; and that the Sum of One Pound eighteen shillings and eight pence be allowed and paid the said Committee for their Trouble and Expence in Farming said Excise:—In Council; Read and Concur'd—Consented to by the Governor."—*Ibid.*, *p.* 122.

"December 31, 1753. The Committee for letting out to Farm the Excise of Strong Liquors &c in the County of Plymouth for this present Year, reported that they had let out the same to Theophilus Cotton for Two hundred and four Pounds, & had taken Bond and lodged it in the Treasury; Their own Charge being £3. 10.—:—In the House of Representatives Read and Accepted; And thereupon ordered that the Sum of Three Pounds ten shillings be paid out of the Publick Treasury to the Committee in full for their time & Expences in the Sale thereof—In Council; Read & Accepted—Consented to by the Governor"—*Ibid.*, *p.* 134.

"January 9, 1754. The Committee for letting out to Farm the Excise of Strong Liquours in the County of York for this present Year, reported that they had let out the same to Elisha Jones for seven hundred Dollars for this present Year, had taken Bonds and lodged them in the Treasury, Their own Charge being £2. 16. 8 In the House of Representatives Read and Accepted and Ordered that the Sum of Two Pounds sixteen shillings and eight pence be allowed and paid out of the publick Treasury to said Committee for their Time and Expence in farming said Excise In Council Read and Concur'd—Consented to by the Governor."—*Ibid.*, *p.* 147.

"The Committee for letting out to Farm the Excise on Strong Liquors in the County of Essex, for this present Year, reported that they had let it out to Mr Jonathan Porter (who purchased it for Mr John Hunt) for the Sum of One Thousand and two Pounds thirteen shillings and four pence, had taken Bonds and lodged them in the Treasury their own Charge being £6. 10. 9.—In the House of Representatives; Read and Accepted, And Ordered that the Sum of Six Pounds ten shillings and nine pence be allowed & paid out of the publick Treasury to s^d Committee in full for their time and Expence in farming s^d Excise. In Council; Read and Concur'd—Consented to by the Governor."—*Ibid.*

"January 21, 1754. The Committee appointed to let out to Farm the Excise on Strong

Drink in the County of Middlesex reported that they had let out the same to William Story for the Sum of Seven hundred and thirty six Pounds, and have taken Bonds and lodged them in the Treasury; Their own Charge being £2. 8. 2—In the House of Representatives; Read and Accepted and Ordered that the said Committee be allowed and paid out of the publick Treasury the Sum of Two Pounds eight shillings and two pence in full for their Time & Expences in farming said Excise In Council; Read and Concur'd—Consented to by the Governor."—*Ibid., p.* 171.

Chap. 8. "June 2nd 1753. A Memorial of Andrew Oliver Esqr Thomas Hubbard Esqr Mr Thomas Greene and others, Shewing that a Number of Gentlemen of this Province from a View to the Publick Good, have entered into a Voluntary Subscription for raising Monies to promote Industry and employ the Poor, more especially in the Linen Manufacture, and have put their Affairs into the immediate Managemt of the Memorialists, and have directed them to make Application to this Honble Court for their Countenance and Assistance; Therefore Praying for the same more especially that they would provide a publick Building for Carrying on said Manufacture to be under such regulations as the Court shall judge fit.

In the House of Representatives; Read & Ordered that Mr Welles, Colo Winslow, Colo Otis, Colo Buckminster, Colo Patridge & Colo Lawarance with such as the Honble Board shall appoint, be a Committee to take the Subject Matter of this Memorial under Consideration and report what they judge Proper for this Court to do thereon.

In Council; Read and Concur'd; And Benjamin Lynde, John Cushing, Samuel Watts, John Quincy, Sylvanus Bourn, & Eleazer Porter Esqrs are joined in the Affair."—*Ibid., p.* 35.

"June 8, 1753. Samuel Watts Esqr from the Committee of both Houses on the Petition of Andrew Oliver Esqr and others referring to the Linnen Manufacture, reported as follows

The Committee to whom was refer'd the Petition of Andrew Oliver Esqr & others, Having carefully Considered the Contents thereof, & visited the Places where their Manufactures or Business are carried on or transacted; and very particularly inquired into their Designs, Doings and proceedings, are fully of Opinion That their Projection is of great and universal Importance to this Province, & very much deserves the Countenance and Encouragement of the Great and General Court; and accordingly the Committee are humbly of Opinion, That a suitable ps of Land be purchased some where in the Town of Boston, & thereon a House built convenient for carrying on the Linen Manufacture; And that the Petitioners and their Successors in the Care and Oversight of said Manufacture, have the use of the said House and Land Rent free untill this Court shall otherwise Order; and that every Town in this Province have Liberty if they see cause, to send, at least, one Person to said House to be instructed in any or every Branch of the Linen Business Gratis. It is computed that about Fifteen hundred Pounds will be requisite; and for Raising this Sum It is proposed that a Duty be laid on all Coaches, Chariots, Chaises, Calashes & Riding Chairs within the Province and that the Petrs have Leave to bring in a Bill accordingly: All which is humbly Submitted By Order of the Committee Samll Watts

In the House of Representatives Read and Ordered that this Report be Accepted, And that the Petitioners have Liberty to bring in a Bill for the Purposes within mentd

In Council; Read and Concur'd."—*Ibid., p.* 43.

"The anniversary of the Society in Boston for encouraging industry and employing the poor was celebrated with extraordinary attention. In the afternoon, about three hundred young female spinsters, decently dressed, appeared on the common at their spinning wheels. The wheels were placed regularly in three rows, and a female was seated at each wheel. The weavers also appeared, cleanly dressed, in garments of their own weaving. One of them, working at a loom on a stage, was carried on men's shoulders, attended with music. An immense number of spectators was present at this interesting spectacle. Rev. Dr. Cooper preached a discourse, and a collection was made for the benefit of the institution. A Manufactory house, a large and handsome brick building, was erected about this time in Longacre street; and an excise, laid by the general court on carriages and other articles of luxury, was appropriated to it. Its original design was for carrying on manufactures in the town, particularly the linen manufacture; but 'some untoward circumstances taking place,' that manufacture was wholly set aside. The Institution continued but three or four years."—*Holmes's Annals, vol.* 2, *p.* 196, *and note; sub anno*, 1753.

"January 8, 1755. Report of the Trustees for the Encouragement of the Linnen Manufacture;

Pursuant to an Order of the Great & General Court, laying a Tax on certain Wheel Carriages, in order to raise the Sum of Fifteen hundred Pounds, to encourage the Manufacture of Linnen; We the Subscribers, appointed Trustees for that Purpose, humbly offer an Account herewith of what we have received by Virtue of said Act, before the first of October 1754, amounting to £128 19s 3d Lawful Money; out of which we have paid £115. towards purchasing a Pcice of Land, whereon has been erected a House for carrying on said Manufacture;——We beg leave to report that we have been obliged thô very unwillingly, to sue many Persons who have been deficient in their Payments; and fear we shall be obliged to sue many more, who are deficient the Currant Year,

THOMAS GUNTER MIDDLECOT COOK ANDREW OLIVER
WILLIAM BOWDOIN WILLIAM CLARKE THOMAS GREENE.

In the House of Representatives; Read & Accepted: In Council; Read & Concur'd;——Consented to by the Governour."—*Council Records, vol.* XX., *p.* 371.

"The passing of Laws in the Plantations for encouraging Manufactures, which any ways interfere with the manufactures of this Kingdom, has always been thought improper and has ever been discouraged. The great expence which this Country has been and is still at for the defence and protection of the Colonies, while they on the other hand contribute little or nothing to the taxes with which it is burthen'd, gives it a just claim to restrain them in such attempts. And altho' the great importation of foreign Linnens does in some sort take off the objection to a Linnen Manufacture in the Colonys yet as Parliament has lately and particularly this year given great encouragement to this Manufacture here, We desire yo will be cautious of assenting to Laws of this kind for the future."—*Lords of Trade, to Governor Shirley, April 13, 1756; "Mass. Bay, B. T.," vol. 84, p. 327, in Public Record Office.*

Chap. 16. "December 13, 1752. The Bill to incorporate William Starkey & others into a Society by the Name of the Marine Society, was read again & Debated in Council; And then

Voted that the said Bill be refer'd over to the next Session."—*Council Records, vol. XIX., p.* 510.

"December 26, 1753. A Petition of Jonathan Clarke and others a Committee of the Persons commonly called the Marine Society, Praying that their former Petition may be revived, and that they may be allowed to bring in a Bill for their Incorporation

In the House of Representatives Read and Ordered that the Prayer of the Petition be granted; and that the Petitioners have Liberty to bring in a Bill accordingly In Council Read and Concurd."—*Ibid., vol. XX., p.* 127.

Chap. 23. "April 15th 1754. In the House of Representatives Whereas sundry Disputes have arisen whether the Town Officers chosen in the Month of March last, & did not take the Oath relating to the Receiving & Passing the Bills of the other Governments untill this present Month of April, should take the Oath prescribed by the former Law relating to the receiving or passing the said Bills, or the Oath prescribed by the last Law relating thereto; and many Inconveniences being likely to arise therefrom; Therefore Ordered that the several Persons chosen to any Town Office, in any of the Towns within this Province, in the Month of March last, & shall take the Oath prescribed by the last Law relating to the receiving or passing the said Other Government Bills, shall be held & deemed qualified to Serve in said Office, as thô they had taken the Oath prescribed by the said former Law, and likewise those Persons who were chosen to any Town Office in the Month of March last, & have in this present Month of April taken the Oath prescribed by the said last Law shall be deemed & held qualified to serve in the said Town Offices, as tho' they had taken the Oath prescribed in the said former Law:——In Council Read & Concur'd

Consented to by the Governour."—*Ibid., p.* 220.

"October 25, 1754. A Petition of the Selectmen of the Town of Pelham in the County of Hampshire, setting forth the great Difficulties the Inhabitants of said Town are under, by reason of their Assessors & Collectors of Taxes neglecting to take the Oath respecting the Bills of Credit of the Neighbouring Governments, Praying that this Court would give such Order thereon, as also in Respect of the Repairs of their Highways, as may be necessary for the Relief of the said Town.

In the House of Representatives, In order to remedy the Inconveniences and Difficulties, which the Town of Pelham have fallen into, mentioned in the Petition of the Select Men of said Town, exhibited to this Court. Voted & Ordered that the Constables & Collectors of said Town, of all and every the Assessments whether Province, Town or County, who have been chosen and sworne to those Offices in said Town, either in the Month of March 1750, or in any other Year since, before the Month of March last, and who have not finished and perfected their Collections of the Sum total of the several Assessments, which within that time have been made; of any Sums lawfully ordered, set or granted to be assessed on the Inhabitants of said Town, and Assessed by Assessors who had taken the Assessors Oath, be and hereby are impowered to finish & perfect their Collections, of all such Assessments, and to enforce the Payment of all such Sums in which particular Persons are and have been assessed in said Assessments, which remain unpaid by all such Ways and Methods as Constables and Collectors of Taxes, in all respects qualified are impowered to do by Law: And that said Constables and Collectors of Pelham shall be accountable to the Province Treasurer, Treasurer for the County of Hampshire, and Treasurer of the said Town of Pelham for the time being respectively for all the respective Sums which have been or shall be collected on Province, Town & County Assessments, and shall be compelled and obliged to pay in all such Sums to said Treasurers respectively to whom they are due by all such Ways & Means as qualified Constables and Collectors may by Law be obliged to do.

And it is further Ordered that the Surveyors of Ways for said Town in the Year 1750, and in each succeeding Year since; shall render to the Surveyor of Ways for said Town for the time being, a true Account of all those Persons who did not do and perform their proportionable Part of Work, at making and maintaining Ways in said Town, during the time that the Surveyors of Ways for said Town were not qualified, by taking the Oath required by Law, respecting the Bills of Credit of the Neighbouring Governments: And said Surveyors of Ways for the time being, are hereby directed and impowered to order and oblige all such Persons, as in that time neglected to do their Proportion of Work at the Ways, in the first Place to do and perform so much Work at the Ways in said Town, as shall be equal to the whole of each respective Polls Proportion, thro' the whole time aforesaid, which Work such Persons have neglected to perform, before they shall proceed to notify and order the Inhabitants of said Town in general to begin and enter on a Course of Work at the Ways, to be performed in a legal Proportion by all the Inhabitants of said Town, without any respect to former Defects of any of said Inhabitants. In Council; Read & Concur'd;——Consented to by the Governour."—*Ibid., p.* 291.

Also, see 1752-53, chapter 19, and note.

Chap. 33. "January 10, 1749. In Council, Whereas the usual time for holding the Court of General Sessions of the Peace & Inferior Court of Common pleas for the County of Barnstable, will be on the third Tuesday of January Instant, and whereas several of the Justices of the said Court of Sessions & Common pleas are Members of the General Court, & divers important Affairs are now depending—Therefore Ordered that the said Court of General Sessions of the Peace, & Inferior Court of Common pleas for the said County of Barnstable be and hereby are adjourned to the third Tuesday of February next; and all persons whom this Order may concern are to govern themselves accordingly——In the House of Represent^{ves} Read & Concur'd——Consented to by the Lieut Governor."—*Ibid., vol. XIX., p.* 121.

"January 27, 1749. In Council, Whereas the Court of General Sessions of the Peace & Inferior Court of Common pleas for the County of Barnstable, appointed by Law to be held on the third Tuesday of January Instant was by this Court adjourned to the third Tuesday of February next, which happens to be so near to the next Session of the said Courts in s^{d} County that it is Apprehended considerable charge may be saved to s^{d} County if said Court should be further Adjourned to the time of their next Sitting Therefore Ordered that the said Courts of General Sessions of the Peace and Inferior Court of Common pleas, which were by this Court adjourned to the said third Tuesday of February next be & hereby are further Adjourned to the third Tuesday of March next; and all persons whom this Order may concern are to govern themselves accordingly In the House of Represent^{ves} Read & Concur'd.——Consented to by the L$^{t.}$ Governor."—*Ibid., p.* 141.

Chap. 35. "As this Act gives to the new Town all the Privileges of any other Town, of which we apprehend that of sending a Representative to the General Court is one, it ought not to have been passed without a suspending clause, Agreeable to the Addition Instruction given to you in the Year 1743, founded upon the complaint then made of the great increase of the number of the Assembly, by this practice of splitting Towns and erecting new ones; But as the repeal of this Law upon this account might be attended with great inconvenience, We shall content ourselves with desiring that you will for the future be more cautious of assenting to Laws of this sort."—*Lords of Trade, to Governor Shirley, ut supra, cap.* 8, *note.*

"We must beg leave to acquaint Your Lordships that as the Inhabitants of the said new Town are thereby invested with all the powers and privileges that the Inhabitants of any of the Towns within the Province are or ought by law to be vested or endowed with (which words comprehend the privilege of sending a Representative to the Assembly) it ought not to have been passed, without a Clause suspending its execution until His Maj^{tys} pleasure might be known, as required by an additional Instruction which in order to prevent the exorbitant increase of the number of Representatives in Assembly His Majesty was pleased to give to Govr. Shirley in the year 1743; However as the said Act must have been in a great measure carried into execution and sums of money may have been levied on the Inhabitants for the purposes therein mentioned and the Repeal of it may be productive of much confusion and inconvenience We shall not therefore propose to Your Lordships that the said Act may receive His Majesty's disallowance but We shall think it our duty to direct Mr Shirley to take especial care for the future to pay a strict regard and obedience to the said Additional Instruction.

We are, My Lords, Your Lordships most obedient
and most humble Servants

DUNK HALIFAX
SOAME JENYNS
RICH^{D} RIGBY
JAME^{S} OSWALD"

Whitehall
April 13th 1756.

—*Report of Lords of Trade:* "*Mass. Bay, B. T.,*" *vol.* 84, *p.* 330.

Chap. 38. "June 4th 1754. In the House of Representatives; Voted that John Murray Esqr: be & hereby is impowered to issue a Warrant to some Principal Inhabitant of the Town of Petersham, in the County of Worcester, requiring him in his Majesty's Name to warn & notify the said Inhabitants qualified to Vote in Town Affairs, that they meet together at such Time and Place in said Town, as by said Warrant shall be appointed, to chuse such Officers as Towns chuse in the Month of March annually; And said Officers shall be enjoined to take the Oaths now required by Law to be taken by Town Officers, as also to transact such other Matters & Things relating to High Ways, as may be expressed in said Warrant: in Council Read & Concurr'd;——Consented to by the Governour."—*Council Records, vol.* XX., *p.* 251.

Chap. 40. "March 28, 1754. * * * *
I must apprize you likewise that tho' I have sent Orders to Cpt Lithgow for puting Richmond Fort into as good a Posture of Defence as the ruinous State would admit, which the imminent Danger it may be in from a sudden Attack made necessary for me to do, Yet I cann't but think that all Money expended upon the Repairs of it above what the present Emergency makes absolutely necessary, will be an useless Expence to the Province, it being so far decayed as not to be capable of being made Strong by any Repairs whatsoever."—*Extract from Governor Shirley's speech to the Assembly, Council Records, vol.* XX., *p.* 186.

"April 10, 1754. * * * *
We look upon it to be of absolute necessity that the French should at all Events be prevented from making any Settlements whatsoever on the River Kennebeck, or the carrying Place at the head of it,

As Richmond Fort on that River is in a decaying State, We desire your Excellency to order a new Fort to be erected of about one hundred & twenty feet square, as far up the River above Richmond Fort as your Excellency shall think fit, and to cause the Garrison, Artillery & Stores at Richmond to be removed to the new Fort and the old one to be demolished

We pray your Excellency likewise to order a sufficient Force up to the carrying Place to remove any French that may be settling there: But as we apprehend that our Success under Providence will depend very much on your taking this Affair into your immediate Care & Direction: We therefore pray your Excellency to submit to the Inconveniences of a Voyage to the Eastern parts of the Province; and there to give such Orders for the Purposes aforesaid as you shall find necessary. And that your Excellencys Person may be secure against any Attempts of French or Indians; And you may be enabled to effect the Building the Fort aforesaid, and to destroy any French Settlement that may be carrying on, We will make Provision for the Pay & Subsistence of Five hundred Men, Which Number (including the six independent Companies already ordered), We desire you to cause to be inlisted, as you shall think proper,

We will also make ample Provision for your Excellencys Voyage, and for an Interview with the Indians, if you shall find it expedient, We hope by your Excellencys prudent Management, these Indians will be convinc'd that it is their Interest to continue at Peace with Us, and as we are sincerely desirous that every thing may be done, which may tend to perpetuate the same, we will readily defrey the Charge of supporting & educating a considerable Number of the principal Indian Children, If your Excellency can prevail on their Friends to agree to it."—*Extract from an answer of the Assembly to the Governor's speech. Ibid., p.* 210.

"April 11th 1754, In the House of Representatives, Whereas the Fort at Richmond is in a very ruinous Condition, & past Repair, and a more suitable Place may be found further up Kennebeck River whereon to erect a new One; And in Asmuch as it is the earnest Desire of the Two Houses, that His Excellency the Governour would take the Trouble of a Voyage to the Eastern Parts of this Province, to give Directions concerning this Fort, as well as other important Matters; And the two Houses have also concluded to desire his Excellency to give Orders for inlisting five hundred Men, including Officers to attend his Commands Eastward; As also that Commissioners with a Present to the six Nations from this Province shall attend the General Convention at Albany in June next;

Therefore, for carrying on & accomplishing these Purposes & no other The House now grant the Sum of Five Thousand, three hundred Pounds, and for supplying the Treasury direct the Province Treasurer to borrow the said Sum of Five Thousand, three hundred Pounds on lawfull Interest for a Term not exceeding One Year, as soon as may be; and that as a collateral Security, the Excise for the Year 1753, be mortgaged,

And it is also Voted that his Excellency be desired to issue a Proclamation, as soon as he shall think proper for enlisting the Men, as above proposed, for a Time not exceeding three Months, upon the Bounty of Forty shillings at enlistment, & the Wages of Twenty shillings & eight pence per Month; Which this House now Vote shall be given private Centinels; And that the Wages of Officers shall be in proportion, In Council; Read & Concur'd—Consented to by the Governour."—*Ibid., p.* 215.

"June 8th 1754. His Excellency sent to the House, the following Message by the Secrety

Gentlemen of the House of Representatives,

I have this Morning received a Memorial from Collo John Winslow (whom I have appointed the Chief Commander of the Forces raised & to be raised for the Service Eastward) Wherein he signifies to me that upon Mustering the five hundred Men first ordered to be raised, there are only one hundred & ninety seven Men that Come provided with effective Arms, so that there will be wanting three hundred & three Arms for equiping the Men already raised, besides the dificiency that may happen among the Three hundred still to be raised, As you will find upon reading the said Memorial, which I herewith send unto you,

Now, Gentlemen, I know no other way of supplying this great Dificiency, upon this Emergency, than by borrowing so many Arms as will be needfull out of the several Town Stocks, with the Engagement of this Court to restore the same after the Service shall be over, in as good Condition as they were received; or making the whole good both as to Number & Quality: If you can find out any better Way it will be very acceptable to Me; But something must forthwith be effectually done by this Court, Otherwise this important Service will be greatly impeeded if not utterly fustrated."—*Ibid., p.* 258.

"The Massachusetts assembly was influenced by the friends of the governor, to address him to raise a small army, and to order a detachment to this supposed settlement, and, if the rumour should be well founded, to break it up; and, at all events, to secure by forts the passes from Quebec, for New England, by the way of Kennebeck. The assembly also desired him to go into the eastern part of the province, and there to take upon himself the immediate direction of the affair. He accordingly made a voyage from Boston, to Falmouth in Casco Bay, and took with him a quorum of his council, and several principal members of the house, who, having, by their advice, been instrumental in promoting his measures, would think themselves bound, upon their return, to promote a sanction of them in the general assembly.

He first held a treaty or conference with the Indian chiefs at Falmouth, to prevent their being alarmed from fear of hostilities against them; and then ordered the forces which he had raised, consisting of eight hundred men under the command of Mr. John Winslow, who had been a captain in the royal army at the siege of Carthagene, and was on half pay, to the river Kennebeck. There they first built a fort, about three quarters of a mile below Tacomick Falls, and about thirty-seven miles above Richmond fort. This new fort took the name of Halifax, out of respect to the then secretary of state. A number of persons who claimed a tract of land upon this river, under a long dormant, and lately-revived grant from the assembly of the colony of New Plymouth, obtained leave from the governor to erect another fort, eighteen miles below the first, at a place called Cushnock. This he called Fort Western from a gentleman of his acquaintance in Sussex, in England; and in each fort a garrison was placed in the pay of the province.

Five hundred men then marched to what was called the carrying-place, and to a pond which they supposed to be half way over it, without finding any marks of French or Indian settlements, made or intended to be made; and then returned to Casco Bay.

Thus ended this expedition, which was very expensive; and though it was, in every part of it, the project of the governor, yet, as it had the appearance of originating in the assembly, there was no room for complaint."—*Hutchinson's History of Mass., vol.* 3, *pp.* 25 *and* 26.

ACTS,

Passed 1754–55.

ACTS

Passed at the Session begun and held at Boston, on the Twenty-ninth day of May, A. D. 1754.

CHAPTER 1.

AN ACT FOR IMPOWERING THE CORPORATION OF HARVARD COLLEGE, IN CERTAIN CASES, TO ALIENATE LANDS OR OTHER REAL ESTATE, AND TO MAKE SALE OF A FARM IN BILLERICA.

Preamble.

WHEREAS the president and fellows of Harvard College, by virtue of the charter of incorporation granted them by the general court of the late colony of the Massachusetts in the year 1650, are impowered to purchase and acquire to themselves, or take and receive upon free gift or donation, any lands, tenements or hereditaments, not exceeding the value of five hundred pounds per annum; but no power is given them, by the said charter, to alienate any lands or other real estate whatsoever; which in some cases may be necessary for promoting the good ends designed in their incorporation,—

Be it therefore enacted by the Governour, Council and House of Representatives,

President and fellows of Harvard College empowered to make sale of lands.

[SECT. 1.] That where the president and fellows of Harvard College are, or shall become, seized of any lands, tenements or hereditaments, by virtue of a judgment recovered on any mortgage, or by virtue of an execution for the satisfaction of a judgment in any personal action (the time allowed by law for redemption being expired), it may and shall be lawful[1] for the said president and fellows, and they are hereby authorized and impowered, with the advice and consent of the overseers of said college, to make sale of such lands, tenements and hereditaments, or any part thereof, and to execute deeds effectual in law for conveying the same; the monies arising by such sales to be applied to the uses in the said charter mentioned, and to no other use or purpose whatsoever.

And whereas it hath been represented to this court that it would be for the interest of the said college, if sale were made of a certain farm or tract of land, belonging thereto, which is situated in that part of the town of Billerica called Shawshin,—

Be it therefore enacted,

President, &c., to make sale of a farm in Billerica.

[SECT. 2.] That it shall be lawful[1] for the president and fellows of said college to make sale of the said farm or tract of land, and they are hereby authorized to give and execute a good and sufficient deed or deeds of conveyance of the same; the proceeds of such sale to be vested in other real estate, which they may judge will be of greater advantage to that society. [*Passed June* 7; *published June* 20.

CHAPTER 2.

AN ACT TO ENABLE JOHN PAYNE OF BOSTON, GENTLEMAN, TO ATTEST CERTAIN RECORDS IN THE PROBATE OFFICE OF THE COUNTY OF SUFFOLK.

Preamble.

WHEREAS the records in the probate office of the county of Suffolk, from the seventeenth day of February, one thousand seven hundred and forty-three, until[l] the first day of February, one thousand seven hundred and fifty-four, have not been attested by the register of probates for said county; *and whereas* John Payne of Boston, gentleman, for and during the whole term aforesaid, has acted as a clerk in said office, and all original papers registred in the books of said office have, by the said Payne, been compared with the registry or records, before such papers were delivered out of said office,—

Be it therefore enacted by the Governour, Council and House of Represent[*ati*]*ves*,

John Payne, gentleman, empowered to attest records.

That the aforesaid John Payne be, and he hereby is, fully authorized and impowered to attest the books of records of the said probate office, from the seventeenth day of February, one thousand seven hundred and forty-three, until[l] the first day of February, one thousand seven hundred and fifty-four, having been first sworn to the faithful performance of his trust; and all records in said office during the term aforesaid, so attested, shall be, and are hereby declared, to all intents and purposes as valid and effectual as if such attestation had been made by the register of probate for said county, duly appointed by the governour with the advice and consent of the council. [*Passed June* 11;* *published June* 20.

CHAPTER 3.

AN ACT FOR GRANTING UNTO HIS MAJESTY AN EXCISE UPON SUNDRY ARTICLES HEREAFTER ENUMERATED, FOR AND TOWARDS THE SUPPORT OF HIS MAJ[*ES*]TY'S GOVERNM[*EN*]T OF THIS PROVINCE.

Preamble.

WE, your majesty's most loyal and dutiful subjects, the represent[*ati*]ves of the province of the Massachusetts Bay, in general court assembled, have chearfully and unanimously granted and do hereby give and grant unto his most excellent majesty, to be applied to the support of his maj[*es*]ty's governm[*en*]t of this province, according to such acts, votes or orders of the general court as shall hereafter be made for that purpose, an excise upon the several articles hereafter named; and,—

Be it accordingly enacted by the Governour, Council and House of Represent[*ati*]*ves*,

[SECT. 1.] That there shall be paid for all tea, coffee, and East-India ware, called china-ware, the sundry duties following; viz[t].,—

For every pound of tea, fourpence.

For every pound of coffee, one penny.

For all East-India ware, called china-ware, five per cent *ad valorem* at the retail price.

And be it further enacted,

No person to sell tea, coffee,

[SECT. 2.] That from and after the first day of July next, and until the first day of July w[*hi*]ch will be in the year of our Lord one

* June 10, according to the record.

thous[*an*]d seven hundred and fifty-six, no person or persons whatsoever, other than such as shall obtain licen[s][*c*]es from the justices in general sessions to sell tea, coffee and china-ware, unless as is hereinafter provided, shall directly or indirectly, by themselves or any under them, presume to sell the same; and every person so licen[s][*c*]ed shall give bond, with sufficient sureties, for their well and truly paying the duties laid on those articles he or they shall be licen[s][*c*]ed to sell, and that he or they will use his or their licen[s][*c*]e in such house or houses as shall be therein named, and no other; and that he or they will render to the farmer or his deputy, on oath, a just and true account of all commodities by him or them sold, from time to time, and pay unto the said farmer or his deputy, at the end of every half year, the sum or sums of excise that may arise pursuant to this law. and china-ware, without license.

Provided, nevertheless,—

[Sect. 3.] It shall and may be lawful to sell or dispose of any tea or china-ware to any person whatsoever, in case such tea or china-ware be in a chest or package as imported, and not less in value than twenty pounds lawful money; and also to sell or dispose of any coffee to any person whatsoever, in a quantity not less than one hundred weight; and also for any person, at the time of the publication of this act possessed of any of the said commodities, to sell or dispose of the same, in any quantities whatsoever, to such persons as are licen[s][*c*]ed to sell and retail the same, anything in this act to the contrary notwithstanding. Proviso.

Provided, always, and it is the true intent and meaning of this act,—

[Sect. 4.] That if any person licen[s][*c*]ed to sell any of the aforesaid commodities shall purchase them of any other person liceu[s][*c*]ed to sell the same, such purchaser shall not be held to pay an excise on any quantity so purchased. Proviso.

And be it further enacted,

[Sect. 5.] That the said licen[s][*c*]e be renewed yearly, and bond given as afores[*ai*]d; and that the said licen[s][*c*]es be renewed to no persons whatever, unless he or they before their receiving the same produce certificate, under the hand of the farmer or his deputy, of his or their having paid the full of the excise due from them as afores[*ai*]d. Licenses to be renewed yearly.

And be it further enacted,

[Sect. 6.] That if any person or persons not licen[s][*c*]ed as aforesaid, unless as is herein provided, shall, from and after the first day of July next, presume, directly or indirectly, by themselves, or any under them, to sell any tea, coffee or china-ware, by any quantity, weight, number or measure, he, she or they shall, for every such offence, on due conviction, forf[ie][*ei*]t and pay the sum of four pounds, one half to the informer and the other half to the farmer, the manner of conviction to be the same as of persons selling strong liquors without licen[s][*c*]e, as is by law already provided. Fine for selling without license. 1753-54, chap. 5, § 8.

And to the end the revenues arising from the afores[*ai*]d duties of excise may be advanced for the greater benefit and advantage of the publick,—

Be it further enacted,

[Sect. 7.] That one or more persons, to be nominated and appointed by the general court, for and within the several counties within this province (publick notice being first given of the time and place and occasion of their meeting), shall have full power, and are hereby authorized, from time to time, to contract and agree with any person for or concerning the farming the duties in this act mentioned upon tea, coffee and china-ware in the respective counties for which they shall be appointed, as may be for the greatest prof[f]it and advantage of the publick, so as the same exceed not the term of one year after the com- Duties on tea, &c., to be farmed.

Farmer to have power to inspect houses.

mencem[*en*]t of this act. And every person to whom the duties of excise in any county shall be let or farmed shall have power to inspect the houses of all such as are licen[s][*c*]cd, and of such as are suspected of selling without liceu[s][*c*]e, and to demand, sue for and recover the excise due from licen[s][*ce*]d persons by virtue of this act.

And be it further enacted,

Farmer to give bond.

[SECT. 8.] That the farmer shall give bond, with two sufficient sureties, to the province treasurer for the time being, and his successors in said office, in double the sum of money that shall be contracted for, with condition that the sum agreed be paid into the province treasur[y][*er*] for the use of the province, at the expiration of one year from the date of such bond, which bond the person or persons to be appointed a committee of such county are to take, and the same to lodge with the treasurer as afores[*ai*]d within twenty days after such bond is executed. And the said treasurer, upon failure or neglect of paym[*en*]t at the time therein limited, shall and is hereby impow[e]red and directed to issue out his execution, returnable in sixty days, against such farmers of excise and their sureties, or either of them, for the full sum express'd in the condition of their bonds, as they shall respectively become due, in the same manner as he is enabled by law to issue out his executions ag[*ain*]st defective constables; and the said comm[*itt*]ee shall render an acco[*un*]t of their proceedings touching the farming this duty on tea, coffee and china-ware aforementioned in their respective counties, to the gen[*era*]l court in the first week of their fall sessions, and shall receive such sum or sums for their trouble and expence in said affair as said court shall think fit to allow them; and every person farming the excise in any county may substitute and appoint one or more deputy or deputies under him to collect and receive the excise aforesaid which shall become due in such county, and pay in the same to such farmer, which deputy or deputies shall have, use, and exercise all such powers and authorities as in and by this act are given or com[*m*]itted to the farmers for the better collecting the duties afores[*ai*]d, or prosecuting of offenders against this act.

Treasurer to sue out the bonds, in case.

Committee for letting out to farm said duties to be accountable to the general court.

Farmer may appoint deputies,

And be it further enacted, anything hereinbefore contained to the contrary notwithstanding,—

—may compound with licensed persons,

[SECT. 9.] That it shall and may be lawful to and for the said farmers, and every of them, to compound and agree with any person or persons within their respective divisions, from time to time, for his or her excise for the whole year in one entire sum, as they, in their discretion, shall think fit to agree for; and all and every person or persons to whom the said excise, or any part thereof, shall be let or farmed by themselves or their lawful substitutes, may and hereby are impowered to sue for and recover, in any of his majesty's courts of record, or before a justice of the peace, where the matter is not above his cognizance, any sum or sums that shall grow due for any of the aforesaid duties of excise, where the party or parties from whom the same is or shall become due shall refuse or neglect to pay the same.

—and sue for excise.

And be it further enacted,

Farmer's fine, in case of connivance.

[SECT. 10.] That in case any person farming the excise as afores[*ai*]d, or his deputy, shall, at any time during their continuance in said office, wittingly and willingly connive at or allow any person or persons within their respective divisions, not licen[s][*c*]ed by the court of general sessions of the peace, their selling any tea, coffee or china-ware, such farmer or deputy, for every such offence, shall forfeit the sum of fifty pounds, and cost of prosecution, one half of the penalty aforesaid to be to his majesty for the use of the province, the other half to him or them that shall inform and sue for the same, and shall thenceforward be forever disabled from farming the same.

And be it further enacted,

[Sect. 11.] That in case of the death of the farmers of excise in any counties, the executors or administrators of each farmer shall, upon their taking such trust of executor or administrator upon them, have and enjoy all the powers, and be subject to all the duties, the farmer had or might enjoy, or was subject to by force of this act. Executors or administrators of deceased farmers to have their power, &c.

And be it further enacted,

[Sect. 12.] That the justices in the several counties be and hereby are impow[e]red, at their several sessions during the continuance of this act, to grant licen[s][c]es for the selling and retailing any of the afores[*ai*]d articles, to all such fit and proper persons as shall apply to them for the same; and all persons desiring licen[s][c]es, are hereby directed to apply to the justices in sessions for said licen[s][c]e accordingly, they taking bonds, with sufficient sureties, to secure the full value of the excise on tea, coffee and china-ware, which it is probable may be sold by the persons petitioning for such licen[s][c]e; and the person receiving such license, shall pay no other or greater fee than two shillings in the whole, one shilling to the court, and one shilling to the clerk, for his or her licence and bond afores[*ai*]d. Court of sessions to give license.

And be it further enacted,

[Sect. 13.] That in such counties where the courts of general sessions of the peace shall not sit in thirty days after s[*ai*]d first of July next, it shall be in the power of two of his maj[*es*]ty's justices of the peace in such county, *quorum unus*, to grant licen[s][c]es for selling the commodities afores[*ai*]d, to all such persons as shall apply for the same, upon giving the security by this act required; and the justices' granting such licen[s][c]e, and returning a certificate thereof, under their hands, to the next court of general sessions of the peace, shall be adjudged sufficient to entitle the person so licen[s'][*ce*]d, to sell said commodities for one year next after said certificate is so returned. —or two justices, in case.

[*Passed and published June* 16.*

CHAPTER 4.

AN ACT FOR PUNISHING OF OFFICERS OR SOLDIERS WHO SHALL MUTINY, OR DESERT HIS MAJESTY'S SERVICE.

Whereas this governm[*en*]t have judg[*e*]'d it necessary that a number of forces should be raised and levied for the safety and defence of this province, and of his majesty's subjects and interest therein; *and whereas* no man may be forejudg'd of life or limb, or subjected to any kind of punishm[*en*]t by martial law, or in any other manner than by the judgm[*en*]t of his peers, and according to the known and established laws of the province; *yet, nevertheless*, it being requisite for retaining such forces as are or shall be raised for his maj[*es*]ty's service on the present occasion in their duty, that an exact discipline be observed, and that soldiers who shall mutiny or stir up sedition, or shall desert his maj[*es*]ty's service, be brought to a more exemplary and speedy punishm[*en*]t than the usual forms of law will allow,— Preamble.

Be it therefore enacted by the Govern[*ou*]*r, Council and House of Repres*[*entati*]*ves*,

[Sect. 1.] That every person that shall be in his maj[*es*]ty's service, being mustered and in pay as an officer or soldier, who shall, at any time during the continuance of this act, excite, cause or join in any mutiny or sedition in the army, company, fortress or garrison whereto Punishment for mutiny, sedition, &c.

* June 20, according to the date of publishment on the printed act.

95

such officer or soldier belongs, or shall desert his maj[*es*]ty's service in the army, company, fortress or garrison, shall suffer death, or such other punishment as, by a court-mar[ti][*sh*]al, shall be inflicted.

And be it further enacted,

Captain-general may grant commission for calling courts-martial.

[SECT. 2.] That the captain-gen[*era*]l or comm[*ande*]r-in-chief of this province for the time being, may, by virtue of this act, and during the continuance thereof, have full power and authority, by and with the advice and consent of the council, to grant commission to any colonel or other field-officer in his maj[*es*]ty's service, and under pay, from time to time, to call and assemble courts-martial for punishing such offences as aforesaid.

And be it further enacted,

Courts-martial not to consist of less than eleven.

[SECT. 3.] That no court-martial w[*hi*]ch shall have power to inflict any punishm[*en*]t by virtue of this act, for any of the offences aforesaid, shall consist of fewer than eleven, whereof none to be under the degree of a comm[*a*]n[*ding*] officer, and the president of such court-martial not to be under the degree of a field-officer, or the then comm[*ande*]r-in-chief of the forces under pay, where the offender is to be tried, and that such court-martial shall have power and authority to summon witnesses, and to administer an oath to any witness, in order to the examination or trial of the offences afores[*ai*]d.

Their power.

And be it further enacted,

Officers to be sworn.

[SECT. 4.] That in all trials of offenders by courts-martial, to be held by virtue of this act, where the offence may be punished by death, every officer present at such trial, before any proceeding be had thereupon, shall take an oath before the court and a justice of the peace, if any such be there present; otherwise the president of such court, being first sworn by two of the other members thereof, shall administer the oath unto the others; and the president of such court, and any two other members thereof, are hereby respectively authorized to administer the same in these words; that is to say,—

Form of oath.

You shall well and truly try and determine, according to your evidence, the matter now before you, between our sovereign lord the king and the prisoner to be tried. So help you God.

No sentence of death to be given unless nine concur therein.

[SECT. 5.] And no sentence of death shall be given ag[*ain*]st any offender in such case by any court-mar[ti][*sh*]al, unless nine of the eleven officers present shall concur therein; and if there be a greater number of officers present, then the judgment shall pass by the concurrence of the greater part of them so sworn: *provided* such major part shall not be less than nine; nor shall any sentence of death, pass'd by courts-mar[ti][*sh*]al by virtue of this act upon any offender, be put in execution until[l] report be made of the whole matter by the president of such court, unto the captain-gen[*era*]l or comm[*ande*]r-in-chief of this province for the time being, in order to receive his directions therein; and the prisoner shall be kept in safe custody in the mean time: and the provost-marshal shall have a warr[*an*]t signed by the president of the court, to cause execution to be done according to sentence, before the same be executed.

Provided, always,—

Proviso.

[SECT. 6.] That nothing in this act contained shall extend, or be construed, to exempt any officer or soldier whatsoever from the ordinary process of law.

Limitation.

[SECT. 7.] This act to continue and be in force for the space of one year from the publication thereof, provided the said forces shall be so long retained in the service, or until[l] they shall be discharged from the same. [*Passed and published June* 19.*

* June 20, according to the date of publishment on the printed act.

CHAPTER 5.

AN ACT FOR REVIVING AND CONTINUING SUNDRY LAWS OF THIS PROVINCE, THAT ARE EXPIRED OR NEAR EXPIRING.

Whereas an act was made and passed in the twelfth year of his present majesty's reign, intit[u]led "An Act to prevent the unnecessary journeying of the members of the great and general court"; and also another act was made and passed in the thirteenth year of his present majesty's reign, intit[u]led "An Act for the effectual preventing of horses, neat cattle, sheep and swine from running at large or feeding upon a certain island called Plumb Island, lying in Ipswich Bay, in the county of Essex"; and another act was made and passed in the thirteenth year of his present majesty's reign, intitled "An Act in addition to the several laws of this province relating to common roads and private ways"; and also another act was made and passed in the fifteenth year of his present majesty's reign, intitled "An Act for the relief of poor prisoners for debt"; and also another act was made and passed in the sixteenth year of his present majesty's reign, intitled "An Act to prevent the spreading of the small-pox, and other infectious sickness, and to prevent the concealing of the same"; and also another act was made and passed in the same year, intit[u]led "An Act to prevent the multiplicity of law-suits"; and also another act was made and passed in the seventeenth year of his present majesty's reign, intit[u]led "An Act for regulating the hospital on Rainsford Island, and further providing in case of sickness"; and also another act was made and passed in the nineteenth year of his present majesty's reign, intitled "An Act in addition to an act for appointing commissioners of sewers"; and also an act was made and passed in the twentieth year of his present majesty's reign, intitled "An Act relating to views by a jury in civil causes"; and another act was made and passed in the same year, intitled "An Act to prevent the firing of guns charged with shot or ball, in the town of Boston";—all which laws are expired or near expiring: *and whereas* the aforesaid laws have, by experience, been found beneficial for the several purposes for which they were made and passed,—

Preamble. Unnecessary journeying of members. 1738-39, chap. 25. To prevent horses, &c., feeding on Ipswich Beach. 1739-40, chap. 8. Private ways. 1739-40, chap. 12. Relief of poor prisoners for debt. 1741-42, chap. 6. To prevent spreading the small-pox. 1742-43, chap. 17. Multiplicity of lawsuits. 1742-43, chap. 25. Rainsford Island. 1743-44, chap. 19. Commissioners of sewers. 1745-46, chap. 16. Views by a jury. 1746-47, chap. 6. Firing of guns. 1746-47, chap. 11.

Be it therefore enacted by the Governour, Council and House of Representatives,

That all and every of the aforesaid acts, and every matter and clause therein contained, be and hereby are continued and revived, and shall continue and remain in full force for the space of five years from the first day of July next, and no longer. [*Passed June* 16; *published June* 14.*

Said laws continued.

* June 20, according to the date of publishment on the printed act.

CHAPTER 6.

AN ACT FOR GRANTING THE SUM OF THIRTEEN HUNDRED POUNDS, FOR THE SUPPORT OF HIS MAJESTY'S GOVERNO[*U*]R.

Be it enacted by the Governo[u]r, Council and House of Representatives,

That the sum of thirteen hundred pounds be and hereby is granted unto his most excellent majesty, to be paid out of the publick treasury to his excellency William Shirley, Esq[r]., captain-general and governour-in-chief in and over his majesty's province of the Massachuset[*t*]s Bay, for his past services, and further to enable him to go on in managing the publick affairs. [*Passed June* 7; *published June* 20.

CHAPTER 7.

AN ACT FOR FURTHER CONTINUING THE ACT, [E][*I*]NTIT[UT]LED "AN ACT IN ADDITION TO AN ACT, INTITLED 'AN ACT FOR THE BETTER PRESERVATION AND INCREASE OF DEER WITHIN THIS PROVINCE.'"

Preamble. 1739-40, chap. 3.

WHEREAS the act of this province, intitled "An Act in addition to an act, intit[u]led 'An Act for the better preservation and increase of deer within this province,'" made and passed in the thirteenth year of King George the First, and by divers subsequent acts continued in force, will expire the first day of July next; and the said act having, by experience, been found beneficial,—

Be it therefore enacted by the Governo[u]r, Council and House of Representatives,

The above law, &c., continued till July, 1764.

That the aforesaid act, and every matter and clause therein contained, be and hereby is continued and revived, and shall remain in full force until[l] the first day of July, which will be in the year of our Lord one thousand seven hundred and sixty-four: *saving* only that the penalty in said act for killing or possessing the raw flesh or skin of any buck, dow or fawn, from and after the tenth day of December until[l] the first day of August, annually, shall hereafter be understood to extend to such persons as shall kill or possess the raw flesh or skin of any buck, do[e][*w*] or fawn, from and after the twenty-first day of December until[l] the eleventh day of August, annually, and to no others. [*Passed June* 16;* *published June* 20.

CHAPTER 8.

AN ACT TO PREVENT MISCHIEF BEING DONE BY UNRULY DOGS IN THE TOWN OF BEVERLY.

Be it enacted by the Governo[u]r, Council and House of Representatives,

Assessors of Beverly empowered to assess the owners of dogs, &c., in said town.

That the assessors of the town of Beverly, for the time being, are hereby required and [i][*e*]njoined to make diligent and strict enquiry what dogs are kept in said town, and are alike authorized and required to assess the owner or keeper of every dog, bitch or whelp, or the parent, guardian or master of such owner or keeper, the sum of four shillings to every province tax or assessment, and proportionably to every other tax or assessment that shall be made in said town.

This act to continue for the space of three years from and after the first day of July, 1754, and no longer. [*Passed June* 6; *published June* 20.

* This is the date of signature on the engrossment, in the handwriting of the Governor; but according to the record it was signed June 13.

CHAPTER 9.

AN ACT FOR IMPOWERING THE PROVINCE TREASURER TO BORROW THE SUM OF TWENTY-ONE HUNDRED AND FOURTEEN POUNDS, AND APPLYING THE SAME TOWARDS THE EXPENCE OF SENDING THREE HUNDRED MEN EASTWARD.

Whereas the present state of affairs makes it necessary that there should be an addition to the five hundred men already voted to be sent to the eastern parts of this province for the security thereof,— Preamble.

Be it enacted by the Governour, Council and House of Representatives,

[Sect. 1.] That the treasurer of this province be and hereby is impowered to borrow from such person or persons as shall be ready to lend, a sum not exceeding twenty-one hundred and fourteen pounds in Spanish mill'd dollars at six shillings each, or other coined silver at six shillings and eightpence per ounce, to be applyed towards the expence of enlisting, subsisting, transporting, and paying the wages of three hundred men, officers included, for the service aforesaid; and for every sum so borrowed, the treasurer shall give a receipt in manner following:— Treasurer empowered to borrow £2,114.

Province of the Massachusetts Bay, day of . Received of the sum of , for the use and service of the province of the Massachusetts Bay, and, in behalf of said province, I do hereby promise and oblige myself and successors in the office of treasurer, to repay to the said , or order, on or before the first day of May, [1755] [*one thousand seven hundred and fifty-five*], the aforesaid sum of , with interest at the rate of six per cent per annum. Witness my hand. Form of treasurer's receipt.

And whereas the excise on spirituous liquors, beginning in the year 1753, and will end this present year, amounting to four thousand seven hundred eighty-two pounds six shillings and eightpence, was mortgaged as an additional security for the redemption of the governm[*en*]t securities that were payable the twentieth of January last, and a ballance will remain in the treasurer's hands, when said securities are discharged, sufficient for the present exigence,— 1751-52, chap. 16.

Be it enacted,

[Sect. 2.] That said excise upon spirituous liquors shall be further mortgaged as a fund to discharge the said sum of twenty-one hundred and fourteen pounds, and shall be applied towards discharging the treasurer's receipts and obligations for the money which he shall borrow by virtue of this act, accordingly. [*Passed June* 8; *published June* 20. Excise mortgaged for payment of the same.

CHAPTER 10.

AN ACT FOR GRANTING UNTO HIS MAJESTY SEVERAL RATES AND DUTIES OF IMPOST AND TUNNAGE OF SHIPPING.

Whereas in and by an act of this province, pass'd at their session in December, 1753, the province treasurer was impowered to borrow a sum not exceeding five thousand pounds, in mill'd dollars, at six shillings apeice, or silver at six shillings and eightpence per ounce, for the redemption of the bills of credit of this province that were then outstanding; and, by said act, the treasurer was ordered to give his receipts or obligations to the lenders to repay the money so borrowed by the first day of June, 1755; and in order to enable the treasurer to discharge the receipts and obligations that should by him be given for the said sum, in pursuance of the afore-mentioned act, it was therein provided, that the duty of impost for the year one thousand seven hundred and fifty-four, should be applied towards discharging said receipts and obligations,—

We, his majesty's most loyal and dutiful subjects, the representatives of the province of the Massachusetts Bay, in New England, being desirous of enabling the treasurer to discharge the receipts and obligations as aforesaid, have chearfully and unanimously given and granted, and do hereby give and grant, to his most excellent majesty, to the end and use aforesaid, and to no other use, the several duties of impost upon wines, liquors, goods, wares and merchandize that shall be imported into this province, and tunnage of shipping, hereafter mentioned; and pray that it may be enacted,—

And be it accordingly enacted by the Governor, Council and House of Representatives,

[SECT. 1.] That from and after the twenty-sixth day of June current, and during the space of one year, there shall be paid by the importer of all wines, liquors, goods, wares and merchandize that shall be imported into this province by any of the inhabitants thereof (salt, cotton-wool, pig-iron, mehogany, black-walnut, lignum vitæ, red cedar, and brazilleto and logwood, provisions, and every other thing of the growth and produce of New England, tobacco excepted, and also all prize goods condemned in any part of this province, excepted), the several rates and duties of impost following; vizt.,—

For every pipe of wine of the Western Islands, fifteen shillings.

For every pipe of Madeira, one pound six shillings and eightpence.

For every pipe of other sorts not mentioned, fifteen shillings.

For every hogshead of rum, containing one hundred gallons, thirteen shillings and fourpence.

For every hogshead of sugar, fourpence.

For every hogshead of molasses, fourpence.

For every hogshead of tobacco, ten shillings.

—And so, proportionably, for greater or lesser quantitys.

And all other commodities, goods or merchandize not mentioned or excepted, fourpence for every twenty shillings value: all goods the product and manufacture of Great Britain, and hogshead and barrell-staves and headings from any of his majesty's colonies and provinces on this continent, excepted.

[SECT. 2.] And for any of the above wines, liquors, goods, wares and merchandize, &c., that shall be imported into this province by any of the inhabitants of the other provinces or colonies on this continent, or of the English West-India Islands, or in any ship or vessell to them belonging, on the proper account of any of the said inhabitants of the other provinces or colonies on this continent, or of the inhabitants of any of the West-India Islands, there shall be paid by the importers double the impost appointed by this act to be received for every species above mentioned; and for all rum, sugar and molasses imported and brought into this province by any ship or vessell, or by land-carriage, from any of the colonies of Connecticut, New Hampshire or Rhode Island, shall be paid by the importer, the rates and duties following:—

For every hogshead of rum, containing one hundred gallons, thirteen shillings and fourpence.

For every hogshead of molasses, containing one hundred gallons, eightpence.

For every hogshead of sugar, containing one thousand weight, eightpence.

—And in that proportion for more or less thereof.

And for all European goods, and for all other goods, wares or merchandize, eightpence for every twenty shillings value: *provided always*, that all hogshead and barrell-staves and heading from any of his majesty's provinces or colonies, all provisions and other things that are the growth of New England (tobacco excepted), all salt, cotton-wool and pig-iron, mehogony, black-walnut, lignum vitæ, red cedar, logwood and brazilleto wood, are and shall be exēmpted from every the rates and duties aforesaid.

And be it further enacted,

[Sect. 3.] That the impost rates and duties aforesaid shall be paid in current lawful money, by the importer of any wines, liquors, goods or merchandize, unto the commissioner to be appointed, as is hereinafter to be directed, for entring and receiving the same, at or before the landing of any wines, liquors, goods or merchandize: only the commissioner or receiver is hereby allowed to give credit to such person or persons, where his or their duty of impost, in one ship or vessell, doth exceed the sum of six pounds; and in cases where the commissioner or receiver shall give credit, he shall ballance and settle his accounts with every person on or before the last day of April, so that the same accounts may be ready to be produced in court in May next after. And all entries, where the impost or duties to be paid doth not exceed three shillings, shall be made without charge to the importer; and not more than sixpence to be demanded for any other single entry to what value soever.

And be it further enacted,

[Sect. 4.] That the master of every ship or vessell coming into the province from any other place, shall, within twenty-four hours after his arrival in any port or harbour, and before bulk is broken, make report and deliver a manifest, in writing, under his hand, to the commissioner aforesaid, of the contents of the loading of such ship or vessell, therein particularly expressing the species, kind and quantitys of all the wines, liquors, goods, wares and merchandize imported in such ship or vessell, with the marks and numbers thereof, and to whom the same are consigned; and make oath before the commissioner that the same manifest contains a just and true account of all the lading taken on board and imported in such ship or vessell, so far as he knows or beleives; and that if he knows of any more wines, liquors, goods, wares or merchandize laden on board such ship or vessell, and imported therein, he will forthwith make report thereof to the commissioner aforesaid, and cause the same to be added to his manifest.

And be it further enacted,

[Sect. 5.] That if the master of any ship or vessell shall break bulk, or suffer any of the wines, liquors, goods, wares and merchandize imported in such ship or vessell to be unloaden before report and entry thereof be made as aforesaid, he shall forfeit the sum of one hundred pounds.

And be it further enacted,

[Sect. 6.] That all merchants and other persons, being owners of any wines, liquors, goods, wares or merchandize imported into this province, for which any of the rates or duties aforesaid are payable, or having the same consigned to them, shall make a like entry thereof with the commissioner aforesaid, and produce an invoice of all such goods as pay *ad valorem*, and make oath before him in form following; vizt.,—

You, A. B., do swear that the entry of the goods and merchandize by you now made, exhibits the sterling value of said goods, and that, *bonâ fide*, according to your best skill and judgment, it is not less than the then value. So help you God.

—which oath the commissioner or receiver is hereby impowered and directed to administer; and the owners aforesaid shall pay the duty of impost by this act required, before such wines, liquors, goods, wares or merchandize be landed or taken out of the vessell in which the same shall be imported.

[SECT. 7.] And no wines, liquors, goods, wares or merchandize that by this act are liable to pay impost or duty, shall be landed on any wharffe, or into any warehouse or other place, but in the daytime only, and that after sunrise and before sunset, unless in the presence and with the consent of the commissioner or receiver, on pain of forfeiting all such wines, liquors, goods, wares and merchandize, and the lighter, boat or vessell out of which the same shall be landed or put into any warehouse or other place.

[SECT. 8.] And if any person or persons shall not have and produce an invoice of the quantitys of rum or liquors to him or them consigned, then the cask wherein the same is, shall be gauged at the charge of the importer, that the contents thereof may be known.

And be it further enacted,

[SECT. 9.] That the importer of all wines, liquors, goods, wares and merchandize, within one year from and after the publication of this act, by land-carriage, or in small vessells or boats, shall make report and deliver a manifest thereof to the commissioner aforesaid or his deputy, therein particularly expressing the species, kind and quantity of all such wines, liquors, goods, wares and merchandize so imported, with the marks and numbers thereof, when, how and by whom brought; and shall make oath, before the said commissioner or his deputy, to the truth of such report and manifest, and shall also pay the several duties aforesaid by this act charged and chargeable upon such wines, liquors, goods, wares and merchandize, before the same are landed, housed or put into any store or place whatever.

And be it further enacted,

[SECT. 10.] That every merchant or other person importing any wines into this province, shall be allowed twelve per cent for leakage: *provided*, such wines shall not have been filled up on board; and that every hogshead, butt or pipe of wine that hath two-thirds thereof leaked out, shall be accounted for outs, and the merchant or importer to pay no duty for the same. And no master of any ship or vessell shall suffer any wines to be filled up on board without giving a certificate of the quantity so filled up, under his hand, before the landing thereof, to the commissioner or receiver of impost for such port, on pain of forfeiting the sum of one hundred pounds.

[SECT. 11.] And if it may be made to appear that any wines imported in any ship or vessell be decayed at the time of unloading thereof, or in twenty days afterwards, oath being made before the commissioner or receiver that the same hath not been landed above that time, the duties and impost paid for such wines shall be repayed unto the importer thereof.

And be it further enacted,

[SECT. 12.] That the master of every ship or vessell importing any liquors, wines, goods, wares or merchandize, shall be liable to and shall pay the impost for such and so much thereof, contained in his manifest, as shall not be duly entred, nor the duty paid for the same by the person or persons to whom such wines, liquors, goods, wares or merchandize are or shall be consigned. And it shall and may be lawful, to and for the master of every ship or other vessell, to secure and detain in his hands, at the owner's risque, all such wines, liquors, goods, wares and merchandize imported in any ship or vessell, until he receives a certificate, from the commissioner or receiver of the impost, that the duty for the same is paid, and until he be repaid his necessary charges in securing the same; or such master may deliver such wines, liquors, goods, wares or merchandize as are not entered, unto the commissioner or receiver of the impost in such port, or his order, who is hereby impowered and directed to receive and keep the same, at the owner's risque, until the impost thereof, with the charges, be paid; and then to deliver such wines, liquors, goods, wares or merchandize as such master shall direct.

And be it further enacted,

[Sect. 13.] That the commissioner or receiver of the impost in each port, shall be and hereby is impowered to sue the master of any ship or vessell, for the impost or duty of so much of the lading of any wines, liquors, goods, wares or merchandize imported therein, according to the manifest to be by him given upon oath, as aforesaid, as shall remain not entered and the duty of impost thereof not paid. And where any goods, wares or merchandize are such that the value thereof is not known, whereby the impost to be recovered of the master, for the same, cannot be ascertained, the owner or person to whom such goods, wares or merchandize are or shall be consigned, shall be summoned to appear as an evidence at the court where such suit for the impost and the duty thereof shall be brought, and be there required to make oath to the value of such goods, wares or merchandize.

And be it further enacted,

[Sect. 14.] That the ship or vessell, with her tackle, apparrell and furniture, the master of which shall make default in anything by this act required to be performed by him, shall be liable to answer and make good the sum or sums forfeited by such master, according to this act, for any such default, as also to make good the impost or duty for any such wines, liquors, goods, wares and merchandize not entred as aforesaid; and, upon judgment recovered against such master, the said ship or vessell, with so much of the tackle or appurces thereof as shall be sufficient to satisfy said judgment, may be taken into execution for the same; and the commissioner or receiver of the impost is hereby impowered to make seizure of the said ship or vessell, and detain the same under seizure until judgment be given in any suit to be commenced and prosecuted for any of the said forfeitures of impost; to the intent, if judgment be rendered for the prosecutor or informer, such ship or vessell and appurces may be exposed to sale, for satisfaction thereof, as is before provided: *unless* the owners, or some on their behalf, for the releasing of such ship or vessell from under seizure or restraint, shall give sufficient security unto the commissioner or receiver of impost that seized the same, to respond and satisfy the sum or value of the forfeitures and duties, with charges, that shall be recovered against the master thereof, upon such suit to be brought for the same, as aforesaid; and the master occasioning such loss or damage unto his owners, through his default or neglect, shall be liable unto their action for the same.

And be it further enacted,

[Sect. 15.] That the naval officer within any of the ports of this province shall not clear or give passes to any master of any ship or other vessell, outward bound, until he shall be certified, by the commissioner or receiver of the impost, that the duty and impost for the goods last imported in such ship or vessell are paid or secured to be paid.

[SECT. 16.] And the commissioner or receiver of the impost is hereby impowered to allow bills of store to the master of any ship or vessell importing any wines or liquors, for such private adventures as shall belong to the master or seamen of such ship or vessell, at the discretion of the commissioner or receiver, not exceeding three per cent of the lading; and the duties payable by this act for such wines and liquors, in such bills of stores mentioned and expressed, shall be abated.

And for the more effectual preventing any wines, rum or other distill'd spirits being brought into the province from the neighbouring governments, by land, or in small boats or vessells, or any other way, and also to prevent wines, rum or other distill'd spirits being first sent out of this province (to save the duty of impost), and afterwards brought into the government again,—

Be it enacted,

[SECT. 17.] That the commissioner and receiver of the aforesaid duties of impost shall, and he is hereby impowered and enjoyned to, appoint one suitable person or persons as his deputy or deputys, in all such places of this province where it is likely that wine, rum or other distill'd spirits will be brought out of other governments into this; which officers shall have power to seize the same, unless the owner shall make it appear that the duty of impost has been paid therefor since their being brought into or relanded in this government; and such officer or officers are also impowered to search, in all suspected places, for such wines, rum and distill'd spirits brought or relanded in this government, where the duty is not paid as aforesaid, and to seize and secure the same for the ends and uses as in this act is hereafter provided.

And be it further enacted,

[SECT. 18.] That the commissioner or his deputys shall have full power to administer the several oaths aforesaid, and to search in all suspected places for all such wines, rum, liquors, goods, wares and merchandize as are brought into this province, and landed contrary to the true intent and meaning of this act, and to seize the same for the uses hereinafter mentioned.

And be it further enacted,

[SECT. 19.] That there shall be paid, by the master of every ship or other vessell, coming into any port or ports of this province, to trade or traffick, whereof all the owners are not belonging to this province (except such vessells as belong to Great Britain, the provinces or colonies of Pennsylvania, West and East Jersey, Connecticut, New York, New Hampshire and Rhode Island), every voyage such ship or vessell doth make, one pound of good pistol-powder for every ton such ship or vessell is in burthen: *saving* for that part which is owned in Great Britain, this province, or any of the aforesaid governments, which are hereby exempted; to be paid unto the commissioner or receiver of the duties of impost, and to be employed for the ends and uses aforesaid.

[SECT. 20.] And the said commissioner is hereby impowered to appoint a meet and suitable person, to repair unto and on board any ship or vessell, to take the exact measure or tunnage thereof, in case he shall suspect the register of such ship or vessell doth not express and set forth the full burthen of the same; the charge thereof to be paid by the master or owner of such ship or vessell, before she shall be cleared, in case she shall appear to be of a greater burthen: otherwise, to be paid by the commissioner out of the money received by him for impost, and shall be allowed him, accordingly, by the treasurer, in his accompts. And the naval officer shall not clear any vessell, until he be certified, also, by the commissioner, that the duty of tunnage for the same is paid, or that it is such a vessell for which none is payable according to this act.

And be it further enacted,

[Sect. 21.] That when and so often as any wine or rum imported into this province, the duty of impost upon which shall have been paid agreeable to this act, shall be reshipp'd and exported from this government to any other part of the world, that then, and in every such case, the exporter of such wine or rum shall make oath, at the time of shipping, before the receiver of impost, or his deputy, that the whole of the wine or rum so shipped has, *bonâ fide*, had the aforesaid duty of impost paid on the same, and shall afterwards produce a certificate, from some officer of the customs, that the same has been landed out of this government,—or otherwise, in case such rum or wines shall be exported to any place where there is no officer of the customs, or to any foreign port, the master of the vessell in which the same shall be exported shall make oath that the same has been landed out of the government, and the exporter shall, upon producing such certificate, or upon such oath of the master, make oath that he verily believes no part of said wines or rum has been relanded in this province,—such exporter shall be allowed to draw back from the receiver of impost as follows; viz[t].,—

For every pipe of Madaira, twenty-two shillings.

For every pipe of Western-Island wines, and other sorts, ten shillings.

And for every hogshead of rum, twelve shillings.

Provided, always,—

That if, after the shipping any such wine or rum to be exported as aforesaid, and giving security as aforesaid, in order to obtain the drawback aforesaid, the wine or rum so shipped to be exported, or any part thereof, shall be relanded in this province, or brought into the same from any other province or colony, that then all such rum and wine so relanded and brought again into this province shall be forfeited, and may be seized by the commissioner aforesaid, or his deputy.

And be it further enacted,

[Sect. 22.] That there be one fit person, and no more, nominated and appointed by this court, as a commissioner and receiver of the aforesaid duties of impost and tunnage of shipping, and for the inspection, care and management of the said office, and whatsoever thereto relates, to receive commission for the same from the governor or commander-in-chief for the time being, with authority to substitute and appoint a deputy receiver in each port, or other places besides that in which he resides, and to grant warrants to such deputy receivers for the said place, and to collect and receive the impost and tunnage of shipping as aforesaid that shall become due within such port, and to render the account thereof, and to pay in the same, to the said commissioner and receiver: which said commissioner and receiver shall keep fair books of all entries and duties arising by virtue of this act; also, a particular account of every vessell, so that the duties of impost and tunnage arising on the said vessell may appear; and the same to lie open, at all seasonable times, to the view and perusal of the treasurer or receiver-general of this province (or any other person or persons whom this court shall appoint), with whom he shall account for all collections and payments, and pay all such moneys as shall be in his hands, as the treasurer or receiver-general shall demand it. And the said commissioner or receiver and his deputy or deputys, before their entering upon the execution of their office, shall be sworn to deal truly and faithfully therein, and shall attend in the said office from ten of the clock in the forenoon, until one in the afternoon.

[Sect. 23.] And the said commissioner and receiver, for his labour, care and expences in the said office, shall have and receive, out of the province treasury, the sum of sixty pounds per annum; and his deputy or deputys shall receive, for their service, five per cent for whatever sums they shall receive and pay. And the treasurer is hereby ordered, in passing and receiving the said commissioner's accompts, accordingly, to allow the payment of such salary or salarys, as aforesaid, to himself and his deputies.

And be it further enacted,

[SECT. 24.] That all penalties, fines and forfeitures accruing and arising by virtue of any breach of this act, shall be one half to his majesty for the uses and intents for which the aforementioned duties of impost are granted, and the other half to him or them that shall seize, inform and sue for the same, by action, bill, plaint or information, in any of his majesty's courts of record, wherein no essoign, protection or wager of law shall be allowed: the whole charge of the prosecution to be taken out of the half belonging to the informer.

And be it further enacted,

[SECT. 25.] That from and after the publication of this act, in all causes where any claimer shall appear, and shall not make good the claim, the charges of prosecution shall be born and paid by the said claimer, and not by the informer. [*Passed June* 16 ;* *published June* 20.

CHAPTER 11.

AN ACT FOR THE SUPPLY OF THE TREASURY WITH THE SUM OF NINE THOUSAND FOUR HUNDRED FIFTY-SIX POUNDS SEVEN SHILLINGS AND EIGHTPENCE, AND FOR DRAWING THE SAME INTO THE TREASURY AGAIN; ALSO FOR APPORTIONING AND ASSESSING A TAX OF EIGHTEEN THOUSAND POUNDS; AND ALSO FOR APPORTIONING AND ASSESSING A FURTHER TAX OF TWO THOUSAND FOUR HUNDRED AND TWENTY-THREE POUNDS ONE SHILLING, PAID THE REPRESENTATIVES FOR THEIR SERVICE AND ATTENDANCE IN THE GENERAL COURT, AND TRAVEL, AND FOR FINES LAID ON SEVERAL TOWNS FOR NOT SENDING A REPRESENTATIVE: BOTH WHICH SUMS AMOUNT, IN THE WHOLE, TO TWENTY THOUSAND FOUR HUNDRED TWENTY-THREE POUNDS ONE SHILLING.

WHEREAS the great and general court or assembly of the province of the Massachusetts Bay, did, at their session in December, one thousand seven hundred and fifty-three, pass an act for levying a tax of five thousand pounds; and at their session in March, one thousand seven hundred and fifty-four, did pass another act for levying a tax of five thousand three hundred pounds, and by said acts provision was made that the general court might, [*at their*] [this] present sitting, apportion the same on the several towns and districts within this province, if they thought fit; *and whereas* the great and general court of this province, at their session in September, one thousand seven hundred and fifty-three, did pass an order impowering the province treasurer to borrow the sum of six hundred sixty-six pounds thirteen shillings and fourpence, to be by him remitted to Mr. Agent Bollan, which monies the treasurer has borrowed and remitted and given his receipt and obligation for the same; *and whereas*, the treasurer is, in and by this act, directed to issue out of the treasury, the sum of nine thousand four hundred fifty-six pounds seven shillings and eightpence, for the ends and purposes as is hereinafter mentioned; wherefore, for the ordering, directing and effectual drawing in the sum of twenty thousand four hundred twenty-three pounds one shilling, pursuant to the funds and grants aforesaid, unto the treasury, according to the

1753-54, chap. 26, § 6.

1753-54, chap. 40, § 2.

* Signed June 12, according to the record.

last apportion agreed to by this court; all which is unanimously approved, ratified, and confirmed; we, his majesty's most loyall and dutifull subjects, the representatives in general court assembled, pray that it may be enacted,—

And be it accordingly enacted by the Governour, Council and House of Representatives,

[Sect. 1.] That each town and district within this province be assessed and pay, as such town and district's proportion of the sum of eighteen thousand pounds, and their representatives' pay, and fines laid on several towns, the sum of two thousand four hundred twenty-three pounds one shilling, the several sums following; that is to say,—

IN THE COUNTY OF SUFFOLK.

	REPRESENTATIVES' PAY, AND FINES.	PROVINCE TAX.	SUM TOTAL.	
Boston,	£80 16s. 0d.	£2,974 10s. 0d.	Three thousand fifty-five upds six shillings,	£3,055 6s. 0d.
Roxbury,	20 4 0	166 10 0	One hundred eighty-six pounds fourteen shillings,	186 14 0
Dorchester,	20 4 0	164 15 6	One hundred eighty-four pounds nineteen shillings and sixpence,	184 19 6
Milton,	24 0 0	87 10 6	One [illegible] and eleven pounds ten shillings and sixpence,	111 10 6
[illegible]ee,	19 0 0	189 19 6	Two hundred and eight pounds [illegible]teen shillings and sixpence,	208 19 6
Weymouth,	24 4 0	111 19 6	One hundred thirty-six pounds three shillings and sixpence,	136 3 6
Hingham,	24 12 0	197 2 0	[illegible] twenty-one pounds fourteen shillings,	221 14 0
Dedham,	24 8 0	130 19 0	One hundred fifty-five pounds seven shillings,	155 7 0
[illegible]d,	24 16 0	81 0 0	One [illegible] and five pounds sixteen shillings,	105 16 0
Wrentham,	25 0 0	130 10 0	One hundred fifty-five [illegible] ten shillings,	155 10 0
Brookline,	0 0 0	50 8 0	Fifty [illegible] eight shillings,	50 8 0
Needham,	24 8 0	66 9 0	Ninety pounds and seventeen shillings,	90 17 0
Stoughton,	23 12 0	121 0 0	One hundred forty-four pounds twelve shillings,	144 12 0
Medway,	20 12 0	66 9 0	Eighty-seven pounds one shilling,	87 1 0
Bellingham,	0 0 0	25 16 0	Twenty-five pounds sixteen shillings,	25 16 0
Hull,	0 0 0	30 16 6	Thirty pounds sixteen shillings and sixpence,	30 16 6
Walpole,	0 0 0	49 8 0	Forty-nine pounds eight shillings,	49 8 0
[illegible]a,	0 0 0	68 15 6	Sixty-eight pounds fifteen shillings and sixpence,	68 15 6
	£355 16s. 0d.	£4,713 18s. 0d.		£5,069 14s. 0d.

IN THE COUNTY OF ESSEX.

Salem,	£21 14s. 3d.	£283 10s. 0d.	[illegible] and five [illegible] four shillings and threepence.	£305 4s. 3d.
Danverse,	0 0 0	157 13 0	One [illegible] fifty-seven pounds thirteen shillings,	157 13 0
Ipswich,	22 0 0	404 11 0	Four hundred [illegible]-six upds [illegible]leen [illegible],	426 11 0
Newbury,	52 0 0	520 14 6	Five [illegible]-two upds fourteen shillings [illegible],	572 14 6
Marblehead,	23 16 0	308 18 6	[illegible] hundred thirty-two upds fourteen [illegible] and sixpence,	332 14 6
Lynn,	24 8 0	166 8 6	One [illegible] and [illegible]nty [illegible] [illegible]en shillings and [illegible],	190 16 6
[illegible]r,	26 8 0	228 7 6	Two hundred fifty-four upds fifteen shillings and sixpence,	254 15 6
Beverly,	25 14 9	141 10 6	One hundred sixty-seven pounds five [illegible] and [illegible],	167 5 3
Rowley,	26 8 0	144 0 0	One [illegible] and [illegible]nty upds [illegible]ight shillings,	170 8 0
Salisbury,	22 4 0	113 5 0	One hundred thirty-five upds [illegible],	135 9 0
Haverhill,	10 0 0	132 19 6	One hundred [illegible] upds [illegible]teen shillings and sixpence,	142 19 6
Glo[u]cester,	22 4 5	235 8 6	Two hundred [illegible] upds twelve shillings and sixpence,	257 12 6
Topsfeild,	24 4 0	63 0 0	Eighty-seven upds four shillings,	87 4 0

Boxford,	£25 16s. 0d.	£83 6s. 6d.	One hundred and nine pounds two shillings and sixpence,	£109 2s. 6d.
Almsbury,	10 0 0	104 8 0	One hundred and fourteen pounds eight shillings,	114 8 0
Bradford,	25 4 0	93 9 0	One hundred and eighteen pounds thirteen shillings,	118 13 0
Wenham,	0 0 0	52 19 0	Fifty-two pounds nineteen shillings,	52 19 0
Middleton,	0 0 0	47 0 6	Forty-seven pounds and sixpence,	47 0 6
Manchester,	0 0 0	37 17 6	Thirty-seven pounds seventeen shillings and sixpence,	37 17 6
Methuen,	0 0 0	60 6 0	Sixty pounds six shillings,	60 6 0
Rumford,	0 0 0	0 0 0	. . . .	0 0 0
	£362 1s. 0d.	£3,379 13s. 0d.		£3,741 14s. 0d.

IN THE COUNTY OF MIDDLESEX.

Cambridge,	£41 8s. 0d.	£125 14s. 0d.	One hundred sixty-seven pounds two shillings,	£167 2s. 0d.
[illegible]n,	17 6 0	162 13 0	One [illegible]dred seventy-nine pounds nineteen shillings,	179 19 0
Watertown,	22 0 0	66 13 6	Eighty-eight pounds thirteen shillings and sixpence,	88 13 6
[illegible]n,	20 4 0	117 0 0	One hundred thirty-seven [illegible]ds four shillings,	137 4 0
Concord,	12 16 0	74 12 6	Eighty-seven pounds eight shillings and sixpence,	87 8 6
[illegible]n,	24 0 0	117 0 0	One hundred forty-one [illegible]s,	141 0 0
S[illegible]y,	24 16 0	126 10 6	One hundred fifty-one pounds six shillings and sixpence,	151 6 6
Marlborough,	25 0 0	126 0 0	One hundred fifty-one pounds,	151 0 0
Billerica,	21 8 0	73 16 0	Ninety-five pounds four shillings,	95 4 0
Fram[illegible]m,	25 12 0	96 6 0	One hundred [illegible]-one pounds eighteen shillings,	121 18 0
Lexington,	22 4 0	55 18 0	Seventy-eight [illegible]s two shillings,	78 2 0
Chelmsford,	24 16 0	72 0 0	N[illegible]ty-six pounds sixteen shillings,	96 16 0
Sherburne,	19 12 0	49 14 6	Sixty-nine [illegible]s six shillings and sixpence,	69 6 6
Reading,	24 0 0	118 16 0	One hundred and forty-two pounds sixteen shillings,	142 16 0
[illegible]n,	20 4 0	94 16 0	One hundred and fifteen pounds,	115 0 0
[illegible]n,	18 15 0	74 7 4	N[illegible] pounds two shillings and [illegible]e,	93 2 4
Medford,	23 4 0	93 4 6	One [illegible]d and [illegible]en pounds eight shillings and sixpence,	116 8 6
[illegible]n,	25 8 0	50 11 0	Seventy-five pounds nineteen shillings,	75 19 0
Hopkinston,	0 0 0	44 2 0	Forty-four pounds two shillings,	44 2 0
Westford,	0 4 0	48 12 0	Forty-eight [illegible]s sixteen shillings,	48 16 0
District of Shirley,	0 0 0	12 7 6	Twelve pounds seven shillings and sixpence,	12 7 6
[illegible]m,	24 0 0	62 5 0	Eighty-six pounds five shillings,	86 5 0
Townshend,	0 0 0	27 10 6	[illegible]ty-s[illegible] pounds ten shillings and sixpence,	27 10 6
S[illegible]w,	0 4 0	44 2 0	Forty-four pounds six shillings,	44 6 0
Stoneham,	0 0 0	31 11 6	Thirty-one [illegible]ds eleven shillings and sixpence,	31 11 6
Groton,	23 0 0	88 17 0	One hundred and eleven pounds seventeen shillings,	111 17 0

IN THE COUNTY OF MIDDLESEX—*Continued.*

	REPRESENTATIVES' PAY AND FINES.	PROVINCE TAX.	SUM TOTAL.	
Wilmington,	£0 0*s.* 0*d.*	£36 0*s.* 0*d.*	Thirty-six pounds,	£36 0*s.* 0*d.*
Natick,	0 0 0	25 1 0	Twenty-five pounds one [illegible],	25 1 0
Dracutt,	0 0 0	35 8 0	Thirty-five pounds eight shillings,	35 8 0
Bedford,	0 0 0	41 6 6	Forty-one pounds six shillings and sixpence,	41 6 6
Holliston,	15 12 0	40 2 6	Fifty-five [illegible] fourteen shillings and sixpence,	55 14 6
Tewksbury,	0 0 0	35 8 0	Thirty-five [illegible] eight shillings,	35 8 0
Acton,	0 0 0	26 2 0	Twenty-six [illegible] two shillings,	26 2 0
Dunstable,	0 16 0	33 11 6	Thirty-four pounds seven shillings and sixpence,	34 7 6
District of Pepperell,	0 0 0	28 8 0	[illegible]-eight [illegible] eight shillings,	28 8 0
Lincoln,	11 17 0	53 4 2	Sixty-five pounds one shilling and twopence,	65 1 2
Carlisle,	6 0 0	34 16 0	Forty pounds sixteen shillings,	40 16 0
	£494 6*s.* 0*d.*	£2,444 8*s.* 0*d.*		£2,938 14*s.* 0*d.*

IN THE COUNTY OF HAMPSHIRE.

Springfield,	£26 12*s.* 0*d.*	£175 4*s.* 0*d.*	Two [illegible] and one [illegible] [illegible]en shillings,	£201 16*s.* 0*d.*
North[H]ampton,	31 4 0	96 10 6	One [illegible] and [illegible] [illegible] fourteen shillings and sixpence,	127 14 6
H[illegible]ld,	30 12 0	53 18 6	Eighty-four pounds ten shillings and sixpence,	84 10 6
[illegible]d,	22 12 0	70 2 6	[illegible]-two [illegible] fourteen shillings and sixpence,	92 14 6
Enfield,	0 0 0	52 2 6	Fifty-two pounds two shillings and sixpence,	52 2 6
[illegible]d,	14 10 0	36 2 6	Fifty [illegible] [illegible] shillings and [illegible],	50 12 6
[illegible]d,	14 4 0	77 15 6	[illegible]-one pounds [illegible] shillings and [illegible],	91 19 6
Northfield,	0 0 0	18 16 6	Eighteen [illegible] [illegible] shillings and sixpence,	18 16 6
Hadley,	0 4 0	60 5 4	Sixty [illegible] nine shillings and fourpence,	60 9 4
Suffield,	0 0 0	96 15 0	N[illegible] pounds [illegible] shillings,	96 15 0
Sunderland,	31 0 0	17 16 10	Forty-eight pounds [illegible] shillings and [illegible],	48 16 10
Montague District,	0 0 0	13 1 2	Thirteen [illegible] one shilling and [illegible],	13 1 2
Brimfield,	24 4 0	59 5 0	Eighty-three pounds nine shillings,	83 9 0
[illegible],	0 0 0	37 4 0	Thirty-seven [illegible] four shillings,	37 4 0
Southampton,	0 0 0	19 10 0	[illegible] [illegible] ten shillings,	19 10 0
District of South Hadley,	0 0 0	32 8 8	Thirty-two pounds eight shillings and eightpence,	32 8 8
Palmer,	0 0 0	22 4 0	[illegible]-two pounds four shillings,	22 4 0
Pelham,	0 0 0	18 18 0	Eighteen pounds eighteen shillings,	18 18 0

Bedford,	£0 0s. 0d.	£12 12s. 0d.	Twelve pounds twelve shillings,	£12 12s. 0d.
Coldspring,	0 0 0	12 12 0	Twelve pounds twelve shillings,	12 12 0
Greenwich,	0 0 0	14 2 0	Fourteen pounds two shillings,	14 2 0
Blandford,	0 0 0	7 19 0	Seven pounds nineteen shillings,	7 19 0
New Marlborough, or No. 2,	0 0 0	13 10 0	Thirteen pounds ten shillings,	13 10 0
Parish at Ware River,	0 0 0	18 0 0	Eighteen pounds,	18 0 0
Stockbridge,	0 0 0	18 0 0	Eighteen pounds,	18 0 0
Greenfield,	6 10 0	16 4 6	Twenty-two pounds fourteen shillings and sixpence,	22 14 6
	£201 12s. 0d.	£1,071 0s. 0d.		£1,272 12s. 0d.

IN THE COUNTY OF WORCESTER.

Worcester,	£22 10s. 0d.	£94 19s. 0d.	One [illegible] and [illegible] [illegible] nine shillings,	£117 9s. 0d.
Lancaster,	24 0 0	108 0 0	One [illegible] and thirty-two [illegible],	132 0 0
Mendon,	25 8 0	103 10 0	One [illegible] and [illegible] [illegible] eighteen shillings,	128 18 0
Woodstock,	0 0 0	116 8 0	One [illegible] and [illegible] [illegible] eight shillings,	116 8 0
Brookfield,	27 16 0	84 19 6	One hundred and twelve [illegible] [illegible] shillings and [illegible],	112 15 6
Oxford,	14 8 0	57 9 0	Seventy-one [illegible] [illegible] [illegible],	71 17 0
Sutton,	24 16 0	82 11 6	One [illegible] and seven [illegible] [illegible] shillings and sixpence,	107 7 6
[illegible]d,	20 19 2	59 11 0	Eighty [illegible] ten shillings and twopence,	80 10 2
West District of Rutland,	5 4 10	13 10 0	Eighteen [illegible] fourteen [illegible] and [illegible],	18 14 10
Leicester,	14 13 4	56 10 0	Seventy-one [illegible] three shillings and fourpence,	71 3 4
[illegible]ict of Spencer,	7 6 8	28 5 0	[illegible]-five [illegible] [illegible] [illegible] and eightpence,	35 11 8
[illegible],	24 16 0	46 8 6	[illegible]-one [illegible] four shillings and sixpence,	71 4 6
Westborough,	0 4 0	64 17 6	[illegible]-five pounds one shilling and [illegible],	65 1 6
Shrewsbury,	25 0 0	75 12 0	One [illegible] pounds [illegible] shillings,	100 12 0
Lunenburg,	25 8 0	63 7 6	[illegible]-ight pounds [illegible] shillings and [illegible],	88 15 6
Uxbridge,	25 12 0	57 7 6	[illegible] [illegible] [illegible] shillings and sixpence,	82 19 6
Harvard,	25 4 0	52 1 0	[illegible] pounds five [illegible],	77 5 0
Dudley,	0 0 0	34 4 0	Thirty-four pounds four shillings,	34 4 0
Bolton,	17 8 0	51 18 0	[illegible] [illegible] six [illegible],	69 6 0
[illegible],	0 0 0	28 13 0	[illegible]-ight pounds thirteen [illegible],	28 13 0
Sturbridge,	23 8 0	22 8 6	Forty-five pounds sixteen shillings and sixpence,	45 16 6
[illegible],	0 0 0	27 0 0	[illegible] [illegible],	27 0 0
[illegible],	0 0 0	33 6 0	[illegible] [illegible] six shillings,	33 6 0
Holden,	0 0 0	17 2 0	Seventeen [illegible] two shillings,	17 2 0
[illegible],	0 0 0	26 2 0	Twenty-six [illegible] two shillings,	26 2 0

IN THE COUNTY OF WORCESTER—*Continued.*

	REPRESENTATIVES' PAY, AND FINES.	PROVINCE TAX.	SUM TOTAL.	
Grafton,	£0 0*s.* 0*d.*	£43 16*s.* 0*d.*	Forty-three pounds sixteen shillings,	£43 16*s.* 0*d.*
Petersham,	0 0 0	19 10 0	Nineteen pounds ten shillings,	19 10 0
Douglass,	0 0 0	15 0 0	Fifteen pounds,	15 0 0
New-Braintree District,	0 0 0	0 0 0	. . . . . .	0 0 0
	£354 2*s.* 0*d.*	£1,484 6*s.* 6*d.*		£1,838 8*s.* 6*d.*

IN THE COUNTY OF PLYMOUTH.

Plymouth,	£0 4*s.* 0*d.*	£144 0*s.* 0*d.*	One hundred and forty-four pounds four shillings,	£144 4*s.* 0*d.*
Scituate,	24 4 0	198 0 0	Two hundred and twenty-two pounds four shillings,	222 4 0
Duxbury,	26 8 0	65 5 0	Ninety-one pounds thirteen shillings,	91 13 0
Marshfield,	16 0 0	134 11 0	One hundred and fifty pounds eleven shillings,	150 11 0
Bridgwater,	25 12 0	233 14 0	Two hundred and fifty-nine pounds six shillings,	259 6 0
Middleborough,	26 4 0	164 6 6	One hundred and ninety pounds ten shillings and sixpence,	190 10 6
Rochester,	0 4 0	99 1 6	Ninety-nine pounds five shillings and eightpence,	99 5 8
Plympton,	23 8 0	83 17 0	One hundred and seven pounds five shillings,	107 5 0
Pembrook,	25 12 0	72 0 0	Ninety-seven pounds twelve shillings,	97 12 0
Kingston,	11 12 0	48 9 0	Sixty pounds one shilling,	60 1 0
Han[ov]er,	24 12 0	63 0 0	Eighty-seven pounds twelve shillings,	87 12 0
Ab[*b*]ington,	25 0 0	67 14 6	Ninety-two pounds fourteen shillings and sixpence,	92 14 6
Hallifax,	0 0 5	39 18 0	Thirty-nine pounds eighteen shillings,	39 18 0
Warham,	0 0 0	41 8 0	Forty-one pounds eight shillings,	41 8 0
	£229 0*s.* 0*d.*	£1,455 4*s.* 6*d.*		£1,684 4*s.* 6*d.*

IN THE COUNTY OF BARNSTABLE.

Barnstable,	£27 16*s.* 0*d.*	£126 0*s.* 0*d.*	One hundred and fifty-three pounds sixteen shillings,	£153 16*s.* 0*d.*
Yarmouth,	0 4 0	82 10 0	Eighty-two pounds fourteen shillings,	82 14 0
Sandwich,	21 0 0	90 0 0	One hundred and eleven pounds,	111 0 0
Eastham,	17 0 0	102 12 0	One hundred [*and*] nineteen pounds twelve shillings,	119 12 0
Harwic[k][*h*],	0 0 0	79 13 0	Seventy-nine pounds thirteen shillings,	79 13 0

Chatham,	£0 0s. 0d.	£45 4s. 6d.	Forty-five pounds four shillings and sixpence,	£45 4s. 6d.
Truro,	0 0 0	48 10 6	Forty-eight pounds ten shillings and sixpence,	48 10 6
Falmouth,	0 0 0	55 16 0	Fifty-five pounds sixteen shillings,	55 16 0
	£66 0s. 0d.	£630 6s. 0d.		£696 6s. 0d.

IN THE COUNTY OF BRISTOL.

Taunton,	£27 0s. 0d.	£173 15s. 6d.	Two ı dhd pls dn shillings ud sixpence,	£200 15s. 6d.
Rehoboth,	18 16 0	249 1 6	Two hundred sixty-seven pls tan ligs ad pie,	267 17 6
Swanzey with Shawamett,	27 8 0	110 11 0	One ı rid th- sen pds ean shillings,	137 19 0
Dartmouth,	28 16 0	324 0 0	Three ı dhd fi- two pls tin ligs,	352 16 0
Norton,	0 4 0	108 13 6	One dhd and eight puls teen slgs and sixpence,	108 17 6
Attleborough,	25 0 0	118 13 0	One ı rid forty- htee pds thirteen shillings,	143 13 0
Dighton,	26 8 0	76 13 0	One hundred ad three pls ne l lig,	103 1 0
Freetown,	0 0 0	70 16 0	Sety pls tin shillings,	70 16 0
Raynham,	0 0 0	45 15 0	Forty-five upds fifteen shillings,	45 15 0
Easton,	0 0 0	52 11 6	Fifty-two puls edn ligs ad pie,	52 11 6
Berkley,	0 0 0	40 17 6	Forty pls stn sligs ad spe,	40 17 6
	£153 12s. 0d.	£1,371 7s. 6d.		£1,524 19s. 6d.

IN THE COUNTY OF YORK.

York,	£27 12s. 0d.	£176 5s. 0d.	Two hundred and three pounds seventeen shillings,	£203 17s. 0d.
Kittery,	22 4 0	207 0 0	Two hundred twenty-nine pounds four shillings,	229 4 0
Wells,	28 0 0	79 4 0	One hundred and seven pounds four shillings,	107 4 0
Berwick,	21 16 0	108 0 0	One hundred and twenty-nine pounds sixteen shillings,	129 16 0
Falmouth,	32 12 0	171 0 0	Two hundred and three pounds twelve shillings,	203 12 0
Biddeford,	0 0 0	72 12 0	Seventy-two pounds twelve shillings,	72 12 0
Ar[r]undel,	0 0 0	40 7 0	Forty pounds seven shillings,	40 7 0
Scarborough,	25 0 0	61 17 6	Eighty-six pounds seventeen shillings and sixpence,	86 17 6
North Yarmouth,	0 0 0	26 18 6	Twenty-six pounds eighteen shillings and sixpence,	26 18 6
Georgetown,	0 0 0	28 11 6	Twenty-eight pounds eleven shillings and sixpence,	28 11 6

IN THE COUNTY OF YORK—*Continued.*

	REPRESENTATIVES' PAY, AND FINES.	PROVINCE TAX.	SUM TOTAL.	
Brunswick,	£0 0*s.* 0*d.*	£25 14*s.* 6*d.*	Twenty-five pounds fourteen shillings and sixpence,	£25 14*s.* 6*d.*
Sheepscut[t],	0 0 0	18 0 0	Eighteen pounds,	18 0 0
	£157 4*s.* 0*d.*	£1,015 10*s.* 0*d.*		£1,172 14*s.* 0*d.*

IN THE COUNTY OF DUKES COUNTY.

Edgartown,	£24 8*s.* 0*d.*	£69 12*s.* 0*d.*	Ninety-four pounds,	£94 0*s.* 0*d.*
Chilmark,	0 0 0	62 9 6	Sixty-two pounds nine shillings and sixpence,	62 9 6
Tisbury,	0 0 0	39 18 0	Thirty-nine pounds eighteen shillings,	39 18 0
	£24 8*s.* 0*d.*	£171 19*s.* 6*d.*		£196 7*s.* 6*d.*

IN NANTUCKET COUNTY.

Sherburne,	£25 0*s.* 0*d.*	£262 7*s.* 0*d.*	Two hundred eighty-seven pounds seven shillings,	£287 7*s.* 0*d.*

	Representatives' Pay, and Fines.	Province Tax.	Sum Total.	
Suffolk,	£355 16s. 0d.	£4,713 18s. 0d.	Five thousand sixty-nine pounds fourteen shillings,	£5,069 14s. 0d.
Essex,	362 1 0	3,379 13 0	Three thousand seven hundred forty-one pounds fourteen shillings,	3,741 14 0
Middlesex,	494 6 0	2,444 8 0	Two thousand nine hundred thirty-eight pounds fourteen shillings,	2,938 14 0
Hampshire,	201 12 0	1,071 0 0	Twelve hundred seventy-two pounds twelve shillings,	1,272 12 0
Worcester,	354 2 0	1,484 6 6	Eighteen hundred and thirty-eight pounds eight shillings and sixpence,	1,838 8 6
Plymouth,	229 0 0	1,455 4 6	Sixteen hundred eighty-four pounds four shillings and sixpence,	1,684 4 6
Barnstable,	66 0 0	630 6 0	Six hundred ninety-six pounds six shillings,	696 6 0
Bristol,	153 12 0	1,371 7 6	Fifteen hundred twenty-four pounds nineteen shillings and sixpence,	1,524 19 6
York,	157 4 0	1,015 10 0	Eleven hundred seventy-two pounds fourteen shillings,	1,172 14 0
Dukes County,	24 8 0	171 19 6	One hundred ninety-six pounds seven shillings and sixpence,	196 7 6
Nantucket,	25 0 0	262 7 0	Two hundred eighty-seven pounds seven shillings,	287 7 0
	£2,423 1s. 0d.	£18,000 0s. 0d.		£20,423 1s. 0d.

And be it further enacted,

[SECT. 2.] That the treasurer do forthwith send out his warrants, directed to the selectmen or assessors of each town or district within this province, requiring them, respectively, to assess the sum hereby set upon such town or district, in manner following; that is to say, to assess all rateable male polls above the age of sixteen years, within their respective towns or districts, or next adjoining to them, belonging to no other town, three shillings per poll, and proportionably in assessing the fines mentioned in this act, and the additional sum received out of the treasury for the payment of the representatives (except the governour, the lieutenant-governour, and their famil[y][*i*]es, the president, fellows, professors and students of Harvard College, settled ministers and grammar-school masters, who are hereby exempted as well from being taxed for their polls, as for their estates being in their own hands and under their actual management and improvement; as also all the estate pertaining to Harvard College); and other persons, if such the[*i*]r[e] be, who, thrô[*ugh*] age, infirmity or extre[e][*a*]m poverty, in the judgment of the assessors, are not capable to pay towards publick charges, they may exempt their polls, and so much of their estates as in their prudence they shall think fit and judge meet.

[SECT. 3.] And the justices in their general sessions, in the respective count[y][*i*]es assembled, in granting a county tax or assessment, are hereby ordered and directed to apportion the same on the several towns in such county in proportion to their province rate, exclusive of what has been paid out of the publick treasury to the representative[s] of each town for his service; and the assessors of each town in the province are also directed, in making an assessment, to govern themselves by the same rule; and all estates, both real and personal, lying within the limits of such town or district, or next unto the same, not paying elsewhere, in whose hands, tenure, occupation or possession soever the same is or shall be found, and also the incomes or profits which any person or persons, except as before excepted, do or shall receive from any trade, faculty, business or employment whatsoever, and all profits which shall or may arise by money or other estate not particularly otherwise assessed, or commissions of profit in their improvement, according to their understanding or cunning, at one penny on the pound; and to abate or multiply the same, if need be, so as to make up the sum set and ordered hereby for such town or district to pay; and, in making their assessment, to estimate houses and lands at six years' income of the yearly rents whereat the same may be reasonably set or let for in the place where they lye: *saving* all contracts between landlord and tenant, and where no contract is, the landlord to reïmburse one-half of the tax set upon such houses and lands; and to estimate negro, Indian and molatto servants proportionably as other personal estate, according to their sound judgment and discretion; as also to estimate every ox of four years old and upwards, at forty shillings; every cow of three [years] old and upwards, at thirty shillings; every horse and mare of three years old and upwards, at forty shillings; every swine of one year old and upwards, at eight shillings; goats and sheep of one year old, three shillings each: likewise requiring the said assessors to make a fair list of the said assessment, setting forth, in distinct columns, against each particular person's name, how much he or she is assessed at for polls, and how much for houses and lands, and how much for personal estate, and income by trade or faculty; and if as guardian, or for any estate, in his or her improvement, in trust, to be distinctly expressed; and the list or lists, so perfected and signed by them, or the major part of them, to commit to the collectors, constable or constables of such town or district, and to return a certificate of the name or names of such collector, constable or constables, with the sum total to each of them committed, unto himself, some time before the last day of October next.

[Sect. 4.] And the treasurer, for the time being, upon receipt of such certificate, is hereby impow[*e*]red and ordered to issue forth his warrants to the collector, or constable or constables of such town or district, requiring him or them, respectively, to collect the whole of each respective sum assessed on each particular person, before the last day of December next; and to pay in their collection, and issue the accompts of the whole, at or before the last day of March next, which will be in the year of our Lord one thousand seven hundred and fifty-five.

And be it further enacted,

[Sect. 5.] That the assessors of each town and district, respectively, in convenient time before their making the assessment, shall give seasonable warning to the inhabitants, in a town meeting, or by posting up notifications in some place or places in such town or district, or notify the inhabitants some other way to give or bring in to the assessors true and perfect lists of their polls, rateable estate, and income by trade or faculty, and gain by money at interest; and if any person or persons shall neglect or refuse so to do, or bring in a false list, it shall be lawful to and for the assessors to assess such person or persons, according to their known ability in such town, in their sound judgment and discretion, their due proportion of this tax, as near as they can, agre[e]able to the rules herein given, under the penalty of twenty shillings for each person that shall be convicted by legal proof, in the judgment of the said assessors, in bringing in a false list; the said fines to be for the use of the poor of such town or district where the delinquent lives, to be levied by warrant from the assessors, directed to the collector or constables, in manner as is directed for gathering town assessments, and to be paid into the town treasurer or selectmen for the use aforesaid: *saving* to the party aggrieved at the judgment of the assessors in setting forth such fine, liberty of appeal therefrom to the court of general sessions of the peace within the county, for relief, as in case of being overrated. And if any person or persons shall not bring a list of their estate[*s*], as aforesaid, to the assessors, he or they so neglecting shall not be admitted to make application to the court of general sessions for any abatement of the assessment laid on him.

[Sect. 6.] And if the party be not convicted of any falseness in the list, by him presented, of the polls, rateable estate, or income by trade or faculty, business or employment, which he does or shall exercise, or in gain by money at interest or otherwise, or other estate not particularly assessed, such list shall be a rule for such person's proportion to the tax, which the assessors may not exceed.

And forasmuch as, oftentimes, sundry persons, not belonging to this province, bring considerable trade and merchandize, and by reason that the tax or rate of the town where they come to trade is finished and delivered to the constable or collectors, and, before the next year's assessment, are gone out of the province, and so pay nothing towards the support of the government, though, in the time of their residing here, they reaped considerable gain by trade, and had the protection of the government,—

Be it further enacted,

[Sect. 7.] That when any such person or persons shall come and reside in any town within this province, and bring any merchandize, and trade, to deal therewith, the assessors of such town are hereby impowered to rate and assess all such persons according to their circumstances, pursuant to the rules and directions in this act provided, tho' the former rate may have been finished, and the new one not perfected, as aforesaid.

And be it further enacted,

[SECT. 8.] That when any merchant, trader or factor, inhabitant of some one town within this province, or of any other province, shall traffic or carry on trade or business, or set up a store, in some other town in the province, the assessors of such town where such trade and business shall be carried on as aforesaid be and hereby are impowered to rate and assess all such merchants, traders and factors, their goods and merchandize, for carrying on such trade, and exercising their faculty in such town, pursuant to the rules and directions of this act: *provided*, before any such assessors shall rate such persons, as afore mentioned, the selectmen of the town where such trade is carried on, shall transmit a list of such persons as they shall judge may and ought to be rated, within the intent of this act.

[SECT. 9.] And the constables or collectors are hereby enjoyned to levy and collect all such sums committed to them, and assessed on persons who are not of this province, or are residents in other towns than those where they carry on their trade, and pay the same.

And be it further enacted,

[SECT. 10.] That the inhabitants of this province have liberty, if they see fit, to pay the several sums for which they may be respectively assessed, of the aforesaid sum of twenty thousand and four hundred and twenty-three pounds one shilling, in good merchantable hemp, or in good, merchantable, Isle-of-Sable codfish, or in good refined bar-iron, or in bloomery-iron, or in hollow iron-ware, or in good Indian corn, or in good winter rye, or in good winter wheat, or in good barley, or in good barrel pork, or in barrel beef, or in duck or canvas, or in long whalebone, or in merchantable cordage, or in good train-oyl, or in good beeswax, or in good ba[r]berry-wax, or in tryed tallow, or in good pease, or in good sheepswool[*l*], or in good tann[*e*]'d sole-leather; and that the eldest councellors, for the time being, of each of those counties in the province, of which any one of the councellors is an inhabitant, together with the province treasurer, or the major part of them, be a committee, who are hereby directed and fully authorized and impowered, once in every month, if need be, to agree and set the several species and commodities aforesaid at some certain price, at which they shall be received towards the payment of the sums aforesaid; all which aforesaid commodities shall be of the produce of this province, and, as soon as conveniently may, be disposed of by the treasurer to the best advantage and for as much as they will fetch in money; and the several persons paying their taxes in any of the commodities afore mentioned to run the risque and pay the charge of transporting the said commodities to the province treasury.

[SECT. 11.] And if any loss shall happen by the sale of the aforesaid species, it shall be made good by a tax of the next year; and if there be a surplusage, it shall remain as a stock in the treasury.

And whereas, the sum of nine thousand four hundred and fifty-six pounds seven shillings and eightpence, part of the above tax, has not been appropriated in any supply-bill for the payment of the publick debts,—

Be it further enacted,

[SECT. 12.] That the said sum of nine thousand four hundred and fifty-six pounds seven shillings and eightpence, shall be issued out of the treasury, when received of the constables and collectors, in manner and for the purpose[*s*] following; that is to say, the sum of three thousand pounds, part of the aforesaid sum of nine thousand four hundred and fifty-six pounds seven shillings and eightpence, shall be applied for the service the several forts and garrisons within this province, pursuant to such orders and grants as are or shall be made by this court for those purposes; and the further sum of one thousand pounds, part of the aforesaid sum of nine thousand four hundred and fifty-six pounds seven shillings and eightpence, shall be appl[i][*y*]ed for the purchasing provisions, the commissary's necessary disbursements for the service of the several forts and garrisons within this province, pursuant to such grants as are or shall be made by this court for those purposes; and the further sum of three thousand five hundred pounds, part of the aforesaid sum of nine thousand four hundred and fifty-six pounds seven shillings and eightpence, shall be appl[y][*i*]ed for the payment of such premiums and grants that now are or hereafter may be made by this court; and the further sum of eight hundred pounds, part of the aforesaid sum of nine thousand four hundred and fifty-six pounds seven shillings and eightpence, shall be applied for the discharge of other debts owing from this province to persons that have or shall serve them, by order of this court, in such matters and things where there is no establishment nor any certain sum assigned for that purpose, and for paper, writing and printing for this court; and the further sum of one thousand pounds, part of the aforesaid sum of nine thousand four hundred and fifty-six pounds seven shillings and eightpence, shall be appl[i][*y*]ed for the payment of his majesty's council and house of representatives, serving in the general court during the several sessions of this present year.

And whereas there are sometimes contingent and unforeseen charges that demand prompt pay,—

Be it further enacted,

[Sect. 13.] That the sum of one hundred and fifty-six pounds seven shillings and eightpence, the remaining part of the aforesaid sum of nine thousand four hundred [*and*] fifty-six pound[s] seven shillings and eightpence, be applied to pay such contingent charges, and for no other purpose whatsoever.

And be it further enacted,

[Sect. 14.] That the treasurer is hereby directed and ordered to pay the sum of nine thousand four hundred and fifty-six pounds seven shillings and eightpence, brought in by taxes as aforesaid, out of such appropriations as shall be directed to by warrant, and no other; and the secretary, to whom it belongs to keep the muster-rolls and accompts of the charge, shall lay before the house of representatives, when they direct, such muster-rolls and accompts after payment thereof.

And whereas, by this act, but nine thousand four hundred and fifty-six pounds seven shillings and eightpence, part of the sum of twenty thousand four hundred and twenty-three pounds and one shilling, for which a tax is to go forth, is appropriated and applied for the discharge of the debts of the ensuing year,—

Be it enacted,

[Sect. 15.] That the remaining sum of ten thousand nine hundred and sixty-six pounds thirteen shillings and fourpence, be applied for the discharge of the government securit[y][*ie*]s that will become due the first of May and the first of June next; as also to discharge the securit[y][*ie*]s given for six hundred and sixty-six pounds thirteen shillings and fourpence remitted the agent. [*Passed June* 19; *published June* 20.

ACTS

PASSED AT THE SESSION BEGUN AND HELD AT BOSTON, ON THE SEVENTEENTH DAY OF OCTOBER, A. D. 1754.

CHAPTER 12.

AN ACT FOR THE BETTER SECURING AND RENDERING MORE EFFECTUAL GRANTS AND DONATIONS TO PIOUS AND CHARITABLE USES, AND FOR THE BETTER SUPPORT AND MAINTENANCE OF MINISTERS OF THE GOSPEL, AND DEFR[A][*E*]YING OTHER CHARGES RELATING TO THE PUBLICK WORSHIP.

Preamble. 10 Mass. 97. 12 Mass. 545. 14 Mass. 336. 16 Mass. 493, 497, 501, 507. 10 Pick. 189, 451, 453. 12 Met. 255. 3 Gray, 38, 39, 146. 13 Allen, 505.

WHEREAS many grants and donations have heretofore been made by sundry well-disposed persons, in and by such expressions and terms as plainly show it was the intent and expectation of such grantors and donors that their several grants and donations should take effect so as that the estates granted should go in succession; but doubts have arisen in what cases such donations and grants may operate, so as to go in succession; for ascertaining whereof,—

Be it enacted by the Governour, Council and House of Representatives,

Deacons and church-wardens of Protestant churches to take, in succession, grants and donations, &c.

[SECT. 1.] That the deacons of all the several Protestant churches, not being Episcopal churches, and the church-wardens of the several Episcopal churches, are and shall be deemed so far bodies corporate, as to take in succession all grants and donations, whether real or personal, made either to their several churches, the poor of their churches, or to them and their successors, and to sue and defend in all actions touching the same; and wherever the ministers, elders or vestry shall, in such original grants or donations, have been joined with such deacons or church-wardens as donees or grantees in succession, in such cases such officers and their successors, together with the deacons or church-wardens, shall be deemed the corporation for such purposes as aforesaid.

Ministers to take, in succession, parsonage lands, &c.

[SECT. 2.] And the minister or ministers of the several Protestant churches, of whatever denomination, are and shall be deemed capable of taking, in succession, any parsonage land, or lands granted to the minister and his successors, or to the use of the ministers, and of suing and defending all actions touching the same: *saving* that nothing in this act shall be construed to make void any final judgment of any court of common law or judge of probate: *saving* also, that no alienation of any lands belonging to churches, hereafter made by the deacons without the consent of the church, or a committee of the church for that purpose appointed, or by church-wardens without the consent of the vestry, shall be sufficient to pass the same; and that no alienation hereafter made by ministers, of lands by them held in succession, shall be valid any longer than during such alienors continuing ministers, unless such ministers be ministers of particular towns, districts or pre-

No alienation to be made without consent of the church.

cincts, and make such alienation with the consent of such towns, districts or precincts, or unless such ministers so aliening be ministers of Episcopal churches, and the same be done with the consent of the vestry. And the several churches in this province not being Episcopal churches, are hereby impowered to ch[oo][*u*]se a committee to call the deacons or other church-officers to an account, and, if need be, commence and prosecute any suits touching the same, and also to advise and assist such deacons in the administration of the affairs aforesaid.

And be it further enacted,

[SECT. 3.] That the income of the grants made or to be made to any one such body politick for pious and charitable uses, shall not exceed the sum of three hundred pounds per annum; and also that all such donations hereafter made by deed, w[*hi*]ch shall not be recorded in the register's office in the county where the lands l[y][*i*]e three calendary months before the death of the donor, and all such bequests or devises w[*hi*]ch shall not be made before the last sickness of the person making the same, or at least three months before the death of the testator, shall be utterly void and of no effect; anything in this act contained to the contrary notwithstanding.

Limitation of the income of church grants. 10 Allen, 6.

And whereas the several congregations in the town of Boston, and some others under the like circumstances, are not by law enabled by vote to raise money for the support of the ministry and publick worship among them,—

Be it further enacted,

[SECT. 4.] That in every such case, where moneys cannot be raised as aforesaid for the support of [of] the ministry and defr[a][*e*]ying the other charges necessary for the upholding and maintaining of publick worship, and repairs of the house in which the same is performed, by vertue of any provision in the laws already made for that purpose, the proprietors of the pews, or persons to whom they are allotted in the several houses for publick worship, may, if they think fit, at a publick meeting to be called for that purpose by the proprietor's clerk, deacons or church-wardens, and notice thereof, immediately after divine service, given ten days at least before said meeting, cause the several pews in such houses to be valued according to the convenience and situation thereof; and a new estimate to be put upon said pews from time to time, as shall be found necessary, and a tax to be laid upon each pew according to the convenience and situation thereof as afores[*ai*]d: provided, the s[*ai*]d tax shall not exceed two shillings per week on any one pew; the money so raised to be applied towards the support of the ministry and other charges necessary for maintaining publick worship or repairs of the house; and that the s[*ai*]d proprietors may, at a meeting to be called as afores[*ai*]d, ch[oo][*u*]se a clerk and treasurer, and likewise appoint some suitable persons to demand and receive the several sums so assessed of the owners of such pews; and in case of denial on such demand or neglect of paym[*en*]t three months after such demand, to sell the same, and, after deducting such taxes and costs, to return the surplus to the owners.

Pews may be taxed for the charge of the public worship, &c.

Proviso, the tax exceed not 2s. per week.

Proprietors to choose a clerk, treasurer, &c.

Provided, nevertheless,—

[SECT. 5.] That when the owner of any pew shall make a tender of the same to the proprietors, or to their comm[*itt*]ee, at the valuation w[*hi*]ch shall have been last put thereon, and they shall refuse or neglect to accept the same, no sum shall be deducted out of the sale of s[*ai*]d pew, but such only as shall have become due before the making of such tender. [*Passed January* 10; *published January* 13, 1755.

CHAPTER 13.

AN ACT FOR MAKING AN ADDITION TO THE SECOND PRECINCT IN THE TOWN OF BROOKFIELD, IN THE COUNTY OF WORCESTER, AND DIVIDING THE FIRST PRECINCT IN SAID TOWN INTO TWO PRECINCTS.

Preamble.

WHEREAS it is made evident to this court that the annexing some of the inhabitants of the first precinct in the town of Brookfield, with their lands, to the second precinct in said town, and the dividing the remainder of said first precinct into two precincts, would serve very much to remove many difficulties and inconvenienc[*i*]es which divers of the inhabitants of said first precinct at present labour under, and also very much to accomodate the greatest part of the inhabitants of said first precinct,—

Be it therefore enacted by the Governour, Council and House of Represent[ati]ves,

Bounds of the second precinct in Brookfield.

[SECT. 1.] That all the lands in the present first precinct in said town lying northward of a line beginning at the northeast corner of George H[a][*e*]rrington's lands upon Spencer line, and running westward by his the said George's lands to Five-Mile River Bridge at the country road; from thence, westerly, on the most southwardly parts and lines of the lands of Thomas Slayton, Captain Nathaniel Woolcot, Thomas Moor, Ebenezer Jennings, John Jennings, Obadiah Rice, William Parks, Josiah Converse, Francis Dodge, Paul Dealand, the heirs of John Green, deceased, Stephen Green and Joseph Ranger, Junr.; and from said Ranger's southwest corner to the southwest corner of William Ayre's meadow, on Coy's Brook, so called, near the place where the old schoolhouse stood; and from thence, northward, on the most eastward parts and lines of the land of John Tuff and Josiah Gilbert, and on the most westward parts and lines of the land of Jeremiah Woodbury and John Hill, to Abner Tyler's land; and from thence, on the most eastward part and lines of the lands of Jacob Abbot and Joshua Dodge and Joshua Dodge, Junr., to the center line of said town; and from thence, all the lands eastward of that part of said center line which is northward of the place where the above-described line meets with the said center line, to New-Braintr[y][*ee*] District, be and hereby are annexed to the second precinct in said town of Brookfield; and that all those persons that now are or hereafter may be inhabitants on said lands, be and hereby are incorporated with the second precinct, and shall be always hereafter obliged to do all precinct duties, and shall receive all precinct privile[*d*]ges, in the said second precinct.

And be it further enacted,

Remainder of the lands in Brookfield divided into two precincts.

Bounds of the first precinct.

[SECT. 2.] That the remainder of the lands in the said first precinct in said town of Brookfield be divided into two precincts in manner following; viz[t]., the dividing line shall begin at the southeast corner of Paul Dealand's land, and shall run from thence to the country road in said Brookfield, so as to take in and include all John Rich's land, where he dwells, into the West Precinct or division; and from said country road, said dividing line shall run, in the midst of the town road that leads southward from said country road to the river called Quaboag River, to the southeast corner of Ephraim Bartlet's land; and from thence, westward, southward of all Ephraim Bartlet's and Obadiah Wright's land, to Quaboag River; and from thence the said river shall be the dividing line down said river to the mouth of Salmon Brook; and from thence the dividing line shall run str[eigh][*ai*]t to a large white-oak tree standing in the northeast corner of a tract of land called the Mile-

Square; said tree being a boundary between the townships of Brookfield and Western; and that the lands lying in the said town of Brookfield (and not included in the second precinct), westward of the above dividing line, be and hereby are made a precinct by the name of The First Precinct in the Town of Brookfield; and that the inhabitants of said lands westward of the said dividing line above described, be and hereby are invested with all the powers and privile[*d*]ges, and subjected to all the duties, that precincts in this province by law are invested with and subjected to; and that the lands lying in the said town of Brookfield (and not included in the second precinct), eastward of the above dividing line, be and hereby are made a seperate precinct by the name of The Third Precinct in the Town of Brookfield; and that the inhabitants of the said lands eastward of the said dividing line above described, be and hereby are invested with all the powers and privile[*d*]ges, and subjected to all the duties, that precincts in this province by law are invested with and subjected to.

Bounds of the third precinct.

And be it further enacted,

[SECT. 3.] That all the inhabitants of the lands which by this act are made the first precinct, and all the inhabitants of those lands which by this act are annexed to the said second precinct, be and hereby are and shall forever hereafter be exempted from paying or contributing any part towards the charges and debts that have already arisen or may hereafter arise by reason of the building the new meeting-house, which has lately been erected in said town on the lands by this act made the third precinct in said town, any of the votes of the late first precinct notwithstanding; and that all the materials of the old meeting-house, which was lately standing in said town, now taken down, be equally divided between the said three precincts; and that all the ministerial revenues arising from all and any lands lying in any part of the said town of Brookfield heretofore sequestred to the use of the ministry in said town, shall be always hereafter equally divided between the said three precincts; and that the charge of the committee who were appointed by this court in April, one thousand seven hundred and [fifty][*sixty*]-four, to view the said town, be born and paid by the inhabitants of said town. [*Passed November* 8,* 1754; *published January* 23, 1755.

Inhabitants of the first and second precincts exempted from all charges of the new meeting-house lately erected.

CHAPTER 14.

AN ACT FOR SETTING OFF THE INHABITANTS, AS ALSO THE ESTATES, OF THE WESTERLY PART OF OXFORD INTO A SEPERATE DISTRICT, BY THE NAME OF CHARLTON.

Be it enacted by the Governour, Council and House of Representatives,

[SECT. 1.] That the inhabitants, with their lands, on the westerly part of Oxford, beginning on the south side of Oxford, one mile west of the Village line, so called, thence running north, paralel with said Village line to Oxford north line, be and hereby is set off and erected into a seperate district, by the name of Charlton; and that said district be invested with all the powers, priviledges and immunities that towns in this province by law do or may enjoy, that of sending a representative to the general assembly only excepted; and that the inhabitants of said district shall have full power and right, from time to time, to join with the said town of Oxford in the choice of a representative or representatives, who may be chosen either in the town or district, in which choice they shall enjoy all the priviledges which by law they would have been intitled to if this act had not been made.

Bounds of Charlton district.

* November 7, according to the record.

Provided, nevertheless,—
And be it further enacted,

Proviso.

[SECT. 2.] That the said district shall pay their proportion of all town, county and province taxes already set on, or granted to be raised by, said town as if this act had not been made.

And be it further enacted,

Moses Marcy, Esq., to issue his warrants.

[SECT. 3.] That Moses Marcy, Esq., be and hereby is impowered to issue his warrants, directed to some principal inhabitant in said district, requiring him to notify and warn the inhabitants of said district, qualified by law to vote in town affairs, to meet at such time and place as shall be therein set forth, to chuse all such officers as shall be necessary to manage the affairs of said district. [*Passed November* 21.

CHAPTER 15.

AN ACT DECLARING IN WHAT MANNER THE DECREES AND ORDERS OF THE GOVERNOUR AND COUNCIL, IN CONTROVERSIES CONCERNING MARRIAGE AND DIVORCE, SHALL BE CARRIED INTO EXECUTION.

Preamble. 1692-3, chap. 25, § 4.

WHEREAS in and by an act of this province, made and pass'd in the fourth year of the reign of King William and Queen Mary, it is among other things enacted and declared, that all controversies concerning marriage and divorce shall be heard and determined by the governour and council, but no express provision has been made by the laws of this province for carrying the decrees and orders of the governour and council in such cases into execution,—

Be it therefore enacted by the Governour, Council and House of Represent[ati]ves,

Persons refusing to conform to any legal decree of governor and council, liable to be imprisoned.

That if any person shall refuse or neglect to observe and conform to any legal decree or order, whether interlocutory or final, made, or that shall hereafter be made, by the governour and council in any controversy concerning marriage and divorce, every such person shall be and is hereby declared liable to suffer the pains of imprisonment; and it shall and may be lawful for the secretary of the province to issue a warrant, under his hand and seal, by order of the governour and council, directed to any sheriff or his deputy, requiring him forthwith to arrest the body of such person so refusing or neglecting, and him to commit unto his majesty's goal, there to remain without bail or mainprize, until[l] he shall comply with such decree or order made as aforesaid. [*Passed January* 8; *published January* 13, 1755.

CHAPTER 16.

AN ACT FOR GRANTING UNTO HIS MAJESTY AN EXCISE UPON SPIRITS DISTILLED AND WINE, AND UPON LIMES, LEMMONS AND ORANGES.

Preamble.

WE, his majesty's most loyal and dutiful subjects, the representatives of the province of the Massachusetts Bay, in general court assembled, being desirous to lessen the present debt of the province, have chearfully and unanimously granted, and do hereby give and grant unto his most excellent majesty, for the ends and uses above mentioned, and for no other uses, an excise upon all rum and other spirits distilled, and upon all wines whatsoever, and upon lemmons, limes and oranges, to be raised, levied and collected, and paid by and upon every taverner, innholder, common victualler, retailer and private person within each respective county, in manner following:—

And be it accordingly enacted by the Governour, Council and House of Representatives,

[SECT. 1.] That from and after the twenty-sixth day of December, one thousand seven hundred and fifty-four, every person already licenced for retailing rum or other spirits, or wine, shall pay the duties following:— Time of this act's continuance.

For every gallon of rum and spirits distilled, fourpence.

For every gallon of wine of every sort, sixpence.

For every hundred of lemmons or oranges, four shillings.

For every hundred of limes, one shilling and sixpence.

—And so proportionably for any other quantity or number.

And be it further enacted,

[SECT. 2.] That every taverner, innholder, common victualler and retailer, shall, upon the said twenty-sixth day of December, take an exact acco[mp][*un*]t of all rum and other distilled spirits, and wine, and of all lemmons, oranges and limes then by him or her, and give an account of the same, upon oath, if required, unto the person or persons to whom the duties of excise in the respective counties shall be let or farmed, as in and by this act is hereafter directed; and such other persons as shall be licenced during the continuance of this act, shall also give an account, as aforesaid, upon oath, what rum or other distilled spirits, and wine, or of what lemmons, oranges or limes he or they shall have by him or them at the time of his or their licence; which oath the person or persons farming the duties aforesaid shall have power to administer in the words following; viz[t].,— Account to be taken.

You, A. B., do swear that the accompt exhibited by you is a just and true account of all rum and other distilled spirits, [*and*] wine, lemmons, oranges and limes you had by you on the twenty-sixth of December last. So help you God. Form of the oath.

And when such person or persons shall not have been licenced on said twenty-sixth of December, the form of the oath shall be so varied, as that instead of those words, "on the twenty-sixth [day] of December," these words shall be inserted and used, "at the time of taking your licence."

And be it further enacted,

[SECT. 3.] That every taverner, innholder, common victualler and retailer, shall make a fair entry in a book, of such rum and other distilled spirits, and wine, as he or they, or any for him or them, shall buy, distil[l] and take in after such account taken, and of whom bought, and of lemmons, oranges and limes taken in, consumed or used as aforesaid; and at the end of every six months, deliver the same, in writing, under their hands, to the farmer or farmers of the duties aforesaid, who are impowered to administer an oath to him or them, that the said account is, *bonâ fide*, just and true, and that he or they do not know of any rum or other distilled spirits, or wine, sold, directly or indirectly, or of any lemmons, oranges or limes used in punch or otherwise, by him or them, or any under him or them, or by his or their privity or consent, but what is contained in the account now exhibited, and shall pay him the duty thereof, excepting such part as the farmer shall find is still remaining by him or them: ten per cent to be allowed on the liquors aforementioned for leakage and other waste, for which no duty is to be paid. Within six months, accounts to be delivered. Ten per cent allowed for leakage.

And be it further enacted,

Penalty on giving a false account.

[SECT. 4.] That every taverner, innholder, common victualler or retailer, who shall be found to give a false account of any distilled spirits or wine, or other the commodities aforesaid, by him or her on the said twenty-sixth day of December, or at the time of his or her taking licence, or bought, distilled or taken in as aforesaid afterwards, used as aforesaid, or neglect or refuse to give in an account, on oath, as aforesaid, shall be rendered incapable of having a licence afterwards, and shall be prosecuted by the farmer of excise in the same county, for his or her neglect, and ordered by the general sessions of the peace to pay double the sum of money as they may judge that the excise of liquors, &c[a]., by him or her sold within such time, would have amounted to, to be paid to the said farmer.

And be it further enacted,

General sessions to take recognizance.

[SECT. 5.] That the justices in their general sessions of the peace shall take recognizances, with sufficient sureties, of all persons by them licenced, both as to their keeping good rule and order, and duly observing the laws relating to persons so licen[c][*s*]ed, and for their duly and truly rendering an account in writing under their hands as aforesaid, and paying their excise in manner as aforesaid; as also that they shall not use their licence in any house besides that wherein they dwell; which recognizance shall be taken within the space of thirty days after the granting of such licence, otherwise the persons licenced shall lose the benefit of his or her said licence; and no person shall be licenced by the said justices that hath not accounted with the farmer, and paid him the excise due to him from such person at the time of his or her asking for such licence.

Preamble.

And whereas, notwithstanding the laws made against selling strong drink without licence, many persons not regarding the penalties and forf[ie][*ei*]tures in the said act, do receive and entertain persons in their houses, and sell great quantities of spirits and other strong drink, without licence so to do first had and obtained; by reason whereof great debaucheries are committed and kept secret, and thereby the end and design of this law is, in a great measure, frustrated, and such as take licences and pay the excise greatly wronged and injured,—

Be it therefore enacted,

Forfeiture of £4 for selling without license.

[SECT. 6.] That whosoever, after the said twenty-sixth day of December, instant, shall presume, either directly or indirectly, to sell any rum or other distilled spirits, or wine, in any less quant[*it*]y than thirty gallons, and all delivered to one person at one time, without drawing any part of it off, or any beer, ale, cyder, perry or other strong drink, in less quantity than ten gallons, without licence first had and obtained from the court of general sessions of the peace, and recognizing in manner as aforesaid, shall forf[ie][*ei*]t and pay for each offence, the sum of four pounds, and costs of prosecution, one half to the farmer and the other half to the informer; and all such as shall refuse or neglect to pay the fine aforesaid, shall stand closely and strictly committed in the common goal of the county for six months at least, and not to have the liberty of the goaler's house or yard; and any goaler giving any person liberty contrary to this act, shall forf[ie][*ei*]t and pay four pounds, and pay costs of prosecution as aforesaid. And if any person or persons, not licenced as aforesaid, shall order, allow, permit[t] or connive at the selling of any strong drink, contrary to the true intent or meaning of this act, by his or her child or children, servant or servants, or any other person or persons belonging to or in his or her house or family, and be thereof convicted, he, she or they shall be reputed the offender or offenders, and shall suffer the same penalties as if he, she or they had sold such strong drink themselves.

And be it further enacted,

[SECT. 7.] That when any person shall be complained of for selling any strong drink without licence, one witness produced to the satisfaction of the justice or court before whom such complaint shall be tried, shall be deemed sufficient for conviction. And when and so often as it shall be observed that there is a resort of persons to houses suspected to sell strong drink without licence, any justice of the peace shall have full power to convene such persons before him, and examine them upon oath concerning the person suspected of selling or retailing strong drink in such houses, outhouses or other depend[a][*e*]ncies thereof; and if upon examination of such witnesses, and hearing the defence of such suspected person, it shall appear to the justice there is sufficient proof of the violation of this act by selling strong drink without licence, judgment may thereupon be made up against such person, and he shall forf[ie][*ei*]t and pay in like manner as if process had been commenced by bill, plaint or information before the said justice; or otherwise such justice may bind over the person suspected, and the witnesses, to the next court of general sessions of the peace for the county where such person shall dwell.

One witness sufficient for conviction.

And be it further enacted,

[SECT. 8.] That when and so often as any person shall be complained of for selling any strong drink without licence to any negro, Indian or molatto slave, or to any child or other person under the age of discretion, and upon the declaration of any such Indian, negro or mol[l]atto slaves, child or other person under the age of discretion, and other circumstances concurring, it shall appear to be highly probable in the judgment of the court or justice before whom the trial shall be, that the person complained of is guilty, then, and in every such case, unless the defendant shall acquit him- or herself upon oath (to be administred to him or her by the court or justice that shall try the cause), such defendant shall forf[ie][*ei*]t and pay four pounds to the farmer of excise, and costs of prosecution; but if the defendant shall acquit him- or herself upon oath as aforesaid, the court or justice may and shall enter up judgment for the defendant to recover costs.

Penalty for selling strong drink to negroes, mulattoes, &c.

And be it further enacted,

[SECT. 9.] That after any person shall have been once convicted of selling strong liquors without licence, contrary to this act, he shall, upon every offence after such first conviction, be obliged to enter into bonds, with one or more sureties, in the penalty of twenty pounds, to his majesty, for the use of this government, that he will not, in like manner, offend or be guilty of any breach of this act; and upon refusal to give such bond, he shall be committed to prison until[l] he comply therewith.

Persons after first conviction to enter into bonds.

And be it further enacted,

[SECT. 10.] That if any person or persons shall be summoned to appear before a justice of the peace, or the grand jury, to give evidence relating to any person's selling strong drink without licence, or to appear before the court of general sessions of the peace, or other court proper to try the same, to give evidence on the trial of any [any] person informed against, presented or indicted for the selling strong drink without licence, and shall neglect or refuse to appear, or to give evidence in that behalf, every person so offending shall forf[ie][*ei*]t the sum of twenty pounds and cost of prosecution; the one half of the penalty aforesaid to be to his majesty for the use of the province, the other half to and for the use of him or them who shall sue for the same as aforesaid. And when it shall so happen that witnesses are bound to sea before the sitting of the court where any person or persons informed against, for selling strong drink without licence, is or are to be prosecuted for the

Penalty on persons refusing to give evidence.

same, in every such case, the deposition of any witness or witnesses, in writing, taken before any two of his majesty's justices of the peace, *quorum unus*, and sealed up and delivered into court, the adverse party having first had a notification in writing sent to him or her of the time and place of caption, shall be esteemed as sufficient evidence, in the law, to convict any person or persons offending against this act, as if such witness or witnesses had been present at the time of trial, and given his, her or their deposition *viva voce;* and every person or persons who shall be summoned to give evidence before two justices of the peace, in manner as aforesaid, and shall neglect or refuse to appear, or to give evidence relating to the facts he or she shall be enquired of, shall be liable and subject to the same penalty as he or she would have been by virtue of this act, for not appearing, or neglecting or refusing to give his or her evidence before the grand jury or court as aforesaid.

And be it further enacted,

How fines are to be recovered.

[SECT. 11.] That all fines, forf[ie][*ei*]tures and penalties arising by this act shall and may be recovered by bill, plaint or information, before any court of record proper to try the same; and where the sum forf[ie][*ei*]ted doth not exceed four pounds, by bill, plaint or information before any one of his majesty's justices of the peace in the respective counties where such offence shall be committed; which said justice is hereby impowered to try and determine the same. And such justice shall make a fair entry or record of all such proceedings: *saving always* to any person or persons who shall think him-, her- or themselves aggrieved by the sentence or determination of the said justice, liberty of appeal therefrom to the next court of general sessions of the peace to be holden in and for said county, at which court such offence shall be finally determined: *provided* that in said appeal the same rules be observed as are already, by law, required in appeals from justices to the court of general sessions of the peace: *saving only*, that the recognizance for prosecuting the appeal shall be eight pounds: *provided*, every farmer doth, as he is hereby obliged to, settle all accounts relating to said excise in the county where he is farmer, first giving seasonable and publick notice of the time and place or places where said business shall be transacted: *provided, also*, that such place or places be always in one or other of the towns where the court of general sessions of the peace, by law, is appointed to be held.

Be it further enacted,

Persons empowered to farm out the excise.

[SECT. 12.] That one or more persons, to be nominated and appointed by the general court, for and within the several counties within this province, publick notice being first given of the time and place and occasion of their meeting, shall have full power, and are hereby authorized, from time to time, to contract and agree with any person for or concerning the farming the duties in this act mentioned, upon rum or other the liquors and commodities aforesaid, in the respective counties for which they shall be appointed, as may be for the greatest profit and advantage of the publick, so as the same exceed not the term of one year after the commencement of this act; and every person to whom the duties of excise in any county shall be let or farmed, shall have power to inspect the houses of all such as are licenced, and of such as are suspected of selling without licence, and to demand, sue for, and recover the excise due from licenced persons or others by virtue of this act.

And be it further enacted,

Farmer to give bond that the sum agreed for be paid into the public treasury.

[SECT. 13.] That the farmer shall give bond with two sufficient sureties, to the province treasurer for the time being, and his successors in said office, in double the sum of money that shall be contracted for, with condition that the sum agreed be paid into the province treasury, for the use of the province, at the expiration of one year from the date of such bond; which bond the person or persons to be appointed a committee of such county are to take, and the same to lodge with the treasurer as aforesaid, within twenty days after such bond is executed; and the said treasurer, on failure or neglect of payment at the time therein limit[t]ed, shall and is hereby impowered and directed to issue out his execution, returnable in sixty days, against such farmers of excise and their sureties, or either of them, for the full sum expressed in the condition of their bonds, as they shall respectively become due, in the same manner as he is enabled by law to issue out his executions against defective constables; and the said committee shall render an account of their proceedings touching the farming this duty on rum, wine and other the liquors and species afore mentioned, in their respective counties, to the general court in the first week of the next sitting of this court, and shall receive such sum or sums for their trouble and expence in said affair as said court shall think fit to allow them.

[SECT. 14.] And every person farming the excise in any county may substitute and appoint one or more deputy or deputies under him, upon oath, to collect and receive the excise aforesaid, which shall become due in such county, and pay in the same to such farmer; which deputy or deputies shall have, use and exercise all such powers and authorities as in and by this act are given or committed to the farmers for the better collecting the duties aforesaid, or prosecuting offenders against this act.

And be it further enacted, anything hereinbefore contained to the contrary notwithstanding,

[SECT. 15.] That it shall and may be lawful to and for the said farmers, and every of them, to compound and agree with any retailer or innholder within their respective divisions, from time to time, for his or her excise for the whole year, in one [i][e]ntire sum, as they in their discretion shall think fit to agree for, without making any entry thereof as is before directed; and all and every person or persons, to whom the said excise or any part thereof shall be let or farmed, by themselves or their lawful substitutes, may and hereby are impowered to sue for and recover, in any of his majesty's courts of record (or before a justice of the peace where the matter is not above his cognizance), any sum or sums that shall grow due for any of the aforesaid duties of excise, farmed as aforesaid or otherwise, where the party or parties from whom the same is or shall become due shall refuse or neglect to pay the same.

Farmers may compound with any retailer or innholder.

And be it further enacted,

[SECT. 16.] That in case any person farming the excise as aforesaid, or his deputy, shall, at any time during their continuance in said office, wittingly and willingly conniv[e] at, or allow, any person or persons within their respective divisions, not licenced by the court of general sessions of the peace, their selling any wines, rum or other liquors by this act forbidden, such farmer or deputy, for every such offence, shall forf[ie][ei]t the sum of fifty pounds and costs of prosecution; one half of the penalty aforesaid to be to his majesty for the use of the province, the other half to him or them that shall inform and sue for the same, and shall thenceforward be forever disabled from serving in said office.

Penalty for farmers or deputies offending.

And to the end that the revenue arising from the excise upon spirituous liquors may be encreased and rais[e]'d with more equality for the benefit of the publick,—

Be it enacted,

[SECT. 17.] That from and after the twenty-sixth day of December instant, to the twenty-sixth day of December next, every person consuming, using or any way expending in his or her house, family, apart-

Duties to be paid by private persons for what liquors they expend.

ment or business, any rum or other distilled spirits, or wine, except they purchased the same of a taverner, innholder or retailer in this province, and in a quantity less than thirty gallons, shall pay the duties following; viz[t].,—

For every gallon of rum or distilled spirits, fourpence; and for every gallon of wine, sixpence; the same excise or duty to be paid to the farmers of said excise in each respective county, or their respective deputies; ten per cent being first allowed for leakage.

And be it further enacted,

Such persons to give in writing, under their hands, what liquors they consume, &c.

[SECT. 18.] That every person consuming or any ways expending in his or her house, family, apartment or business, any rum or other distilled spirits, or wine, as aforesaid, except they purchased the same of a taverner, innholder or retailer in this province, as aforesaid, shall, at the end of twelve months from and after said twenty-sixth day of December instant, exhibit and give in writing, under their hands, a full account of all such rum or other distilled spirits, or wine, by them so used, consumed or expended, to the town or district clerk where such person or persons dwell, or, in case of the death or removal of the town or district clerk, to the selectmen of said town or district, who are hereby [*impowered and*] directed [and impowered] to receive the several accounts aforesaid, and deliver the same upon demand made to the farmer or his deputy as aforesaid, on pain of said clerk or selectmen's forf[ie][*ei*]ting and paying to and for the use of said farmer, for each neglect or refusal, the sum of ten pounds, to be recovered by said farmer, as by this act is before provided for the like penalty, or to the farmer of the excise, or to his deputy; and if said account is lodged with the said clerk upon demand made by the farmer or his deputy to the clerk, he shall deliver the same to him or them, first taking an account of the amount of such person's account so lodged and delivered; and no person shall be allowed to amend his account after it hath been so transmitted, unless he, upon oath, will declare that the omission was made through ignorance or forgetfulness; and if the farmer of the excise shall suspect any person of having given in a false account, such farmer shall, at his own cost, notify the person suspected to appear before the next justice of the peace in the county to be sworn thereto; and in case of his refusing to appear before the said justice, or to make oath before the farmer or his deputy, who are hereby impowered to administer the same, said farmer may apply, by himself or his deputy, to a justice of the peace in the same county, living nearest to the person so suspected, who is hereby impowered and directed to summon such suspected person to appear before him, said summons to be served seven days at least before he be obliged to answer, and shall administer to him, if required by the farmer, an oath in the words following; viz[t].,—

Form of the oath.

You, A. B., do swear, that the account by you exhibited, is a full account of all rum or other distilled spirits, or wines, by you consumed, used or any ways expended, directly or indirectly, in your house, family, apartment or business, except such liquors be exported and consumed out of this province (fishing voyages excepted), within twelve months from the said twenty-sixth day of December, according to the best of your knowledge, except what you have purchased of a taverner, innholder or retailer within this province, in a quantity less than thirty gallons. So help you God.

Forfeiture in case of neglect.

—the costs of said summons, service and administring the oath, to be paid by the person summoned as aforesaid; and every person refusing or neglecting to lodge such account with the town or district clerk, the farmer or his deputy, or to appeal and make oath to the same as aforesaid if required, or that shall give a false account, or that shall not pay to the farmer or his deputy the duties aforesaid, on such rum or other distilled spirits, or wines, as by this act he is obliged to pay, within twenty days after the expiration of said term, shall forf[ie][*ei*]t and pay, to and for the use of the farmer of said excise, the sum of ten pounds, and costs of prosecution.

[SECT. 19.] And if any person or persons, from and after the twenty-sixth of December next, shall not have exhibited an account, or compounded with the farmer or his deputy, or shall not have paid his excise as aforesaid, it shall and may be lawful for such farmer of excise or his deputy, to demand of such person or persons an account, upon oath, what spirituous liquors he or they have consumed, used or anyways expended in their house, family, or apartment or business, within twelve months from the twenty-sixth of this instant December as aforesaid: and if said suspected person or persons shall refuse to give to the farmer or his deputy an account as aforesaid, within twenty-four hours after demand, made as aforesaid, or will not declare upon oath that he hath not directly or indirectly consumed, used or anyways expended, any spirituous liquors as aforesaid, saving what he purchased of an innholder or retailer in this province, in a quantity less than thirty gallons, he shall forf[ie][*ei*]t and pay to and for the use of said farmer or his deputy, for such neglect or refusal, the sum of ten pounds.

And be it further enacted,

[SECT. 20.] That every innholder or retailer, consuming, using, selling or any way expending in or out of his house, family, apartment or business, any rum or other distilled spirits, or wine, shall pay therefor to the farmer of the duties aforesaid, or his deputy, unless he shall export the same out of the province; in all which cases, he may and shall enjoy the same priviledges, free from any duty or penalty, as he might have done had he not been a licenced person as aforesaid.

Innholders or retailers to pay the farmers.

And be it further enacted,

[SECT. 21.] That it shall and may be lawful for the said farmers, and every of them, respectively, to compound and agree with any and every particular person within their respective districts, from time to time, for his or her excise, during the continuance of this act, in one [i][*e*]ntire sum, as they in their discretion shall think fit to agree for, without said person's making any entry, or rendering any account thereof, as is before directed with respect to innholders and retailers; anything in this act to the contrary notwithstanding.

Farmers may compound with any person.

And be it further enacted,

[SECT. 22.] That in case of the death of the farmer of excise in any county, the executors or administrators of such farmer shall, upon their accepting such trust of executor or administrator upon them, have and enjoy all the powers, and be subject to all the duties, the farmer had or might enjoy or was subject to by force of this act.

Provision in case of death, &c.

Provided, always,—

And it is the true intent and meaning of this act,

[SECT. 23.] That if any taverner or retailer shall sell to any other taverner or retailer any quantity of distilled liquors or wine, such taverner or retailer, selling as aforesaid, shall not be held to pay such duty, but the taverner or retailer who is the purchaser shall pay the same; and the seller as aforesaid, shall and is hereby required to deliver to the farmer of this duty, a true account of such liquors sold as aforesaid.

Proviso.

Provided, also,—

[SECT. 24.] That none of the clauses in this act, respecting persons being obliged to render an account of the spirituous liquors aforesaid, shall extend, or be deemed or construed to extend, to his excellency the governour, lieutenant-governour, president, fellows, professors, tutors

Persons exempted.

and students of Harvard Colle[d]ge, settled ministers and grammar-school masters, within this province. [*Passed December* 19; *published December* 21.

CHAPTER 17.

AN ACT FOR SUPPLYING THE TREASURY WITH THE SUM OF TWENTY-THREE THOUSAND POUNDS FOR DISCHARGING THE PUBLICK DEBTS, AND FOR DRAWING THE SAME INTO THE TREASURY.

Preamble.

WHEREAS the provision made by this court at their last session, by appropriating part of the tax already gone forth, to discharge the debts of the government, will not only be insufficient for that purpose, but the moneys proposed to be rais'd by the tax aforesaid will not be in the treasury until[l] the thirty-first of March next; *and whereas*, there are and will be several demands upon the treasury which do and will require speedy payment; therefore,—

Be it enacted by the Governour, Council and House of Representatives,

Treasurer empowered to borrow £23,000.

[SECT. 1.] That the treasurer of the province be and he hereby is impowered and directed to borrow from such person or persons as shall be willing to lend the same, a sum not exceeding twenty-three thousand pounds in mill'd dollars at six shillings each, or in other silver at six shillings and eightpence per ounce; and the sum so borrowed shall be applied in manner as in this act is after directed: and for every sum so borrowed the treasurer shall give a receipt and obligation in the form following:—

Form of treasurer's receipt.

Province [*of the*] Massachusetts Bay, day of , 1755.
Received of the sum of for the use and service of the province of the Massachusetts Bay; and in behalf of said province, I do hereby promise and oblige myself and successors in the office of treasurer, to repay to the said , or order, the first day of January, [one thousand seven hundred and fifty-seven] [*1757*], the aforesaid sum of , with interest annually at the rate of six per cent per annum.
Witness my hand, A. B., Treasurer.

Treasurer directed in borrowing money.

—and no receipt shall be given for a sum less than six pounds. And the treasurer is hereby directed to use his discretion in borrowing said sum at such times as that he may be enabled to comply with the draughts that may be made on the treasury in pursuance of this act.

And whereas it may so happen that some of the persons who have done service for this government, and for the payment of which the sum raised by this act is intended, may be willing to lend the sum due to them on interest, and take the treasurer's notes for the moneys so lent,—

Be it further enacted,

Treasurer to give notes on warrants, &c.

[SECT. 2.] That when and so often as any person or persons who shall have a warrant on the treasury payable out of any of the appropriations mentioned in this act, and shall bring such warrant to the treasurer, expressing his willingness to lend the sum mentioned in said warrant to the government, the treasurer in such case shall give out his notes therefor in like manner as if the same sum had been brought to him in dollars or other silver, and shall charge the respective appropriations with the payment thereof, until[l] such appropriation shall be exhausted.

And be it further enacted,

Former warrants on exhausted appro-

[SECT. 3.] That any warrants which may have been given by the governour and council, and were payable out of any exhausted appropriations in any former acts for supplying the treasury, shall be paid respectively out of the appropriations for the like purpose in this act. priations, to be paid.

And be it further enacted,

[SECT. 4.] That the aforesaid sum of twenty-three thousand pounds, when received into the treasury, shall be issued out in manner and for the purposes following; that is to say, eight thousand pounds, part of the sum of twenty-three thousand pounds, shall be applied for the service of the several forts and garrisons within this province, pursuant to such grants and orders as are or shall be made by this court for those purposes; and the further sum of five thousand seven hundred pounds, part of the aforesaid sum of twenty-three thousand pounds, shall be applied for the purchasing provisions and the commissary's necessary disburs[t][*e*]ments for the service of the several forts and garrisons within this province, as also for the commissary's disburs[t][*e*]ments in the late expedition, pursuant to such grants as are or shall be made by this court for those purposes; and the further sum of six thousand pounds, part of the aforesaid sum of twenty-three thousand pounds, shall be applied for the payment of such premiums and grants that now are or may hereafter be made by this court; and the further sum of one thousand pounds, part of the aforesaid sum of twenty-three thousand pounds, shall be applied for the discharge of other debts owing from this province to persons that have served or shall serve them, by order of this court, in such matters and things where there is no establishment nor any certain sum assigned for that purpose; and for paper, writing and printing for this court; and the sum of two thousand two hundred pounds, part of the aforesaid sum of twenty-three thousand pounds, shall be applied for the payment of his majesty's council and house of representatives serving in the great and general court during the several sessions for the present year.

£8,000 to be issued for forts and garrisons.

£5,700 for provisions, commissary's disbursements, &c.

£6,000 for grants, &c.

£1,000 for debts where there is no establishment, &c.

£2,200 for councillors' and representatives' attendance.

And whereas there are sometimes contingent and unforeseen charges that demand prompt payment,—

Be it enacted,

[SECT. 5.] That the sum of one hundred pounds, being the remaining part of the aforesaid sum of twenty-three thousand pounds, be applied to pay such contingent charges, and for no other purpose whatsoever. £100 for contingent charges.

And in order to draw the money into the treasury again and enable the treasurer effectually to discharge the receipts and obligations, with the interest that may be due thereon, by him given in pursuance of this act,—

Be it enacted,

[SECT. 6.] That there be and hereby is granted unto his most excellent majesty, a tax of twenty-three thousand pounds, to be levied on polls, and estates real and personal, within this province, according to such rules and in such proportion on the several towns and districts within the same as shall be agreed on and ordered by the general court of this province at their session in May, one thousand seven hundred and fifty-five, which sum shall be paid into the treasury on or before the thirty-first day of March next after. Tax of £23,000 granted.

And as an additional fund to enable the treasurer to discharge the said notes,—

Be it enacted,

[SECT. 7.] That the duties of impost for the year one thousand seven hundred and fifty-five shall be applied for that purpose, and no other purpose whatsoever. Fund.

And as a further fund to enable the treasurer to discharge said receipts and obligations by him given in pursuance of this act,—

Be it enacted,

Further fund. [SECT. 8.] That the duties of excise, or so much of that duty as is not already mortgaged, arising by virtue of an act for granting unto his majesty an excise upon spirits distilled, and wine, and upon limes, lemmons and oranges for the year one thousand seven hundred and fifty-five, shall be applied for the payment and discharge of the principal and interest that shall be due on said notes, and to no other purposes whatsoever.

And as a further fund as aforesaid,—

Be it enacted,

Further fund. [SECT. 9.] That the duties arising by the act for granting to his majesty several duties upon vellum, parchment and paper, for one year, from the commencement of said act, shall be applied for the payment and discharge of the principal and interest that shall be due on said notes, and to no other purpose whatever.

And be it further enacted,

Rule for apportioning the tax, in case no tax act shall be agreed on. [SECT. 10.] That in case the general court shall not, at their session in May, and before the twentieth of June, one thousand seven hundred and fifty-five, agree and conclude upon an act apportioning the sum which by this act is engaged to be in said year apportioned, assessed and levied, that then, and in such case, each town and district within this province shall pay, by a tax to be levied on the polls, and estates both real and personal, within their districts, the same proportion of the said sum as the said towns and districts were taxed by the general court in the tax act then last preceeding, saving what relates to the pay of the representatives, which shall be assessed on the several towns they represent, and the province treasurer is hereby fully impowered and directed, some time in the month of June, one thousand seven hundred and fifty-five, to issue and send forth his warrants, directed to the selectmen or assessors of each town and district within this province, requiring them to assess the polls, and estates both real and personal, within their several towns and districts, for their respective part and proportion of the sum before directed and engaged to be assessed; and the assessors, as also persons assessed, shall observe, be governed by, and subject to all such rules and directions as have been given in the last preceeding tax act.

And be it further enacted,

The treasurer to conform to the appropriations. [SECT. 11.] That the treasurer is hereby directed and ordered to pay the sum of twenty-three thousand pounds out of such appropriations as shall be directed by warrant, and no other; and the secretary, to whom it belongs to keep the muster-rolls and accompts of charge, shall lay before the house of representatives, when they direct, such muster-rolls and accompts, after payment thereof.

Provided, always,—

Proviso. [SECT. 12.] That the remainder of the sum which shall be brought into the treasury by the duties of impost, excise and stamp duties, before mentioned, and the tax of twenty-three thousand pounds ordered by this act to be assessed and levied, over and above what shall be sufficient to discharge the notes and obligations aforesaid, shall be and remain as a stock in the treasury, and to be applied as the general court of this province shall hereafter order, and to no other purpose whatsoever; anything in this act to the contrary notwithstanding. [*Passed January* 8 *; *published January* 13, 1755.

* January 7, according to the record.

CHAPTER 18.

AN ACT FOR GRANTING TO HIS MAJESTY SEVERAL DUTIES UPON VELLUM, PARCHMENT AND PAPER, FOR TWO YEARS, TOWARDS DEFREYING THE CHARGES OF THIS GOVERNMENT.

WE, his majesty's most loyal and dutiful subjects the representatives in general court assembled, from a sense of the many occasions which engage this province in great expences, for the defence of the frontiers, and for the necessary support of the government, pray that it may be enacted,— Preamble.

And be it accordingly enacted by the Governour, Council and House of Representatives,

[SECT. 1.] That from and after the thirtieth day of April next, there shall be, throughout this his majesty's province, raised, collected and paid unto his majesty, his heirs and successors, during the term of two years, and no longer, for the several and respective things hereafter mentioned, which shall be printed, engrossed or written, during the term aforesaid, the several and respective rates, impositions, duties, charges and sums of money hereinafter expressed, in manner and form following; that is to say,— Rates or duties on several articles hereafter expressed.

For every skin or p[ei][*ie*]ce of vellum or parchment, sheet or p[ei][*ie*]ce of paper, upon which any *capias*, original summons, or any writ of review, or any writ of *scire facias*, or any writ of execution, that shall issue out from the clerk's office, or pass the seal of the superiour court of judicature, court of assize, &c[a]., or of any of the inferiour courts of common pleas, within this province, shall be engrossed or written, the sum of threepence.

For every skin or p[ei][*ie*]ce of vellum, parchment, or sheet or p[ei][*ie*]ce of paper, on which any *capias*, original summons, or execution from any justice of the peace, shall be engrossed or written, twopence.

For every skin or p[ei][*ie*]ce of vellum, parchment, or sheet or p[ei][*ie*]ce of paper, upon which any charter-party, policy of assurance or protest, shall be engrossed or written, the sum of fourpence.

For every skin or p[ei][*ie*]ce of vellum or parchment, sheet or p[ei][*ie*]ce of paper, on which any bill of lading, or receipt for money, or any kind of wares or merchandize that shall be laden on board any ship or vessel[l], shall be engrossed or written, fourpence.

For every p[ei][*ie*]ce of vellum or parchment, sheet or p[ei][*ie*]ce of paper, on which any certificate under the province seal, or the seal of any notary-publick, shall be engrossed or written, fourpence.

For every p[ei][*ie*]ce of vellum or parchment, sheet or p[ei][*ie*]ce of paper, on which any register of a ship or other vessel[l] shall be engrossed or written, fourpence.

For every p[ei][*ie*]ce of vellum or parchment, sheet or p[ei][*ie*]ce of paper, on which any warrant, monition or decree of the court of vice-admiralty shall be engrossed or written, fourpence.

For every p[ei][*ie*]cc of vellum or parchment, sheet or p[ei][*ie*]ce of paper, on which any deed or mortgage of any real estate, the consideration whereof shall be twenty pounds or more, shall be engrossed or written, fourpence.

For every p[ei][*ie*]ce of vellum or parchment, sheet or p[ei][*ie*]ce of paper, on which any deed or mortgage of any real estate, the consideration whereof shall be less than twenty pounds. or any bond or obligation, those taken in the probate office excepted, or other sealed instrument, shall be engrossed or written, twopence.

For every p[ei][*ie*]ce of vellum, parchment, sheet or p[ei][*ie*]ce of paper, on which any newspaper shall be printed, one halfpenny.

For every skin or p[ei][*ie*]ce of vellum or parchment, and for every sheet or p[ei][*ie*]ce of paper, upon which any bill of sale for any ship or vessel[l], or any part of one, shall be written, the sum of fourpence.

For every skin or p[ei][*ie*]ce of vellum or parchment, and for every sheet or p[ei][*ie*]ce of paper, upon which any bill for sale for servants of any sort shall be written, threepence.

And be it further enacted,

Commissioner or commissioners to be chosen as other civil officers.

[SECT. 2.] That, for the better and more effectual levying, collecting and paying the several and respective duties hereby granted, there shall be chosen and appointed, in like manner as other civil officers in this government are chosen and appointed, one or more suitable person or persons, to be a commissioner or commissioners of the stamps for this province, who shall keep an office in the town of Boston, and shall receive such allowance for their service as shall be granted by the general court, and shall, by the space of forty days before the said thirtieth day of April next, provide four different marks or stamps; that is to say, one stamp or mark, with which all vellum, parchment or paper hereinbefore charged with the payment of fourpence, shall be marked or stamped; and one other stamp or mark, with which all vellum, parchment and paper hereinbefore charged with the payment of threepence, shall be marked or stamped; and one other stamp or mark, with which all vellum, parchment and paper hereinbefore charged with the payment of twopence, shall be marked or stamped; and one other stamp or mark, with which all vellum, parchment and paper hereinbefore charged with the payment of one halfpenny, shall be marked or stamped; which said several marks and stamps shall be published by proclamation, to be issued by the governo[u]r, with the advice of the council, a convenient time before the said thirtieth day of April next, to the end that all persons may have due notice thereof. And the said commissioner or commissioners, in providing the said marks or stamps, shall take care they be so contrived that the impression thereof may be durable, and so as the same may be least liable to be forged or counterf[ie][*ei*]ted.

Stamp-office to be kept in Boston.

Commissioner or commissioners to provide stamps, &c.

And be it further enacted,

Commissioner or commissioners to be provided with stamped vellum, parchment, and paper.

[SECT. 3.] That the said commissioner or commissioners shall, from time to time, provide, and be sufficiently furnished with, vellum, parchment and paper, stamped or marked as aforesaid, so as his majesty's subjects may have it in their election to buy the same, without any advance made thereon, except the duty aforesaid, or to bring vellum, parchment or paper to be marked or stamped for the use of themselves or others; and all vellum, parchment or paper so brought, shall be marked or stamped without any delay, on payment of the rates or sums charged by this act.

And be it further enacted,

[SECT. 4.] That the said commissioner or commissioners, before he or they shall be deemed qualified for his or their office or offices, shall take the following oath; viz[t].,—

Commissioner's or commissioners' oath.

You, A. B., do swear, that you will faithfully execute the trust reposed in you, pursuant to an act of this province, intitled "An Act for granting to his majesty certain duties on vellum, parchment and paper, for two years, towards defreying the charges of this government," without fraud or concealment, and that you will, from time to time, true account make of your doings therein, according to the directions in said act. So help you God.

Commissioner or commissioners to give bond.

[SECT. 5.] And the said commissioner or commissioners shall also give bond, with sufficient sureties, unto the province treasurer, in the sum of ten thousand pounds, for his or their faithful discharge of his or their trust, and that he or they will pay into the province treasury, on the first Monday of every month, the sums of money he or they have receiv[e]'d by virtue of this act, which bonds shall not be liable to be chancered; and further, in case such officer or officers be convicted of unfaithfulness in his or their office, he or they shall, forever after, be debarr'd of holding any post of honour or profit in this government.

And be it further enacted,

[SECT. 6.] That the said commissioner or commissioners shall, once in every year, and oftner when required, render an account of his or their doings to the general assembly, and shall pay the sum or sums from him or them due into the province treasury. **To render an account.**

And be it further enacted,

[SECT. 7.] That if any person or persons whatsoever, shall, at any time or times hereafter, counterfeit or forge any stamp or mark to resemble any stamp or mark which shall be provided or made in pursuance of this act, or shall, with a fraudulent design, counterf[ie][*ei*]t or resemble the impression of the same, upon any vellum, parchment or paper, or shall utter, vend or sell any vellum, parchment or paper, with mark or impression thereon, knowing the same to be counterfeit, then every such person so offending, and being thereof convicted, in due form of law, at the superiour court of judicature, court of assize and general goal delivery, shall be fined at the discretion of the said court; also, to be set upon the gallows, with a rope about his neck, for the space of an hour, and shall [be] then [*be*] publickly whipped, not exceeding twenty stripes, and shall then be committed to the house of correction, but not to receive the usual punishment at his or her first entrance, and be kept to hard labour for the space of three years. **Penalty for counterfeiting stamps.**

And be it further enacted,

[SECT. 8.] That if any person or persons shall, at any time or times, during the two years aforesaid, [i][*e*]ngross or write, or cause to be [i][*e*]ngrossed or written, on any vellum, parchment or paper, print or sell any of the instruments, newspapers or writings charged by this act, with a fraudulent intent, before such vellum, parchment or paper be duly stamped or marked, according to the direction of this act, every person so offending, and being thereof convicted in due form of law, shall forf[ie][*ei*]t and pay for each offence the sum of five pounds. **Penalty for vending any of the before-recited instruments before their being stamped.**

And be it further enacted,

[SECT. 9.] That the several courts, officers and justices before mentioned, have power to tax in bills of costs, and the officers that levy executions to take, the respective stamp duties hereinbefore charged, as there shall be occasion, from time to time, the fees already by law established notwithstanding, without being subjected to any penalty for taking said stamp duties. **Officers' power to receive the said stamp duties, &c.**

And be it further enacted,

[SECT. 10.] That the several fines mentioned in this act shall be applied, one half to his majesty, to be paid into the publick treasury, for the use of this government, the other half to him or them that shall inform and sue for the same; or otherwise, by presentment of the grand jury, in which case the whole of such fines shall be paid into the treasury aforesaid for the use of the government. **Fines, how to be disposed.**

And be it further enacted,

[SECT. 11.] That none of the several foregoing writings or instruments required by this act to be stamped or marked, and which shall not be stamped or marked, shall be admitted to be good, useful or available in law or equity, nor shall be pleaded or given in evidence in any of his majesty's courts within this province. **The foregoing instruments not good in law unless stamped.**

And whereas some of the foregoing instruments charged by this act may be sometimes printed in whole or part,—

Be it therefore enacted,

Instruments printed in whole or part included in this act.

[SECT. 12.] That any of said instruments that may be printed wholly or in part, shall be deemed to be included, comprehended and charged by this act, to all intents and purposes, as if the same had been [i][*e*]ngrossed or in writing.

And be it further enacted,

This act to be read at March meetings.

[SECT. 13.] That this act [*shall*] be publickly read in the several towns and districts in this province at their ann[e][*i*]versary town, or district, meetings in March next, by their respective clerks. [*Passed January* 8; *published January* 13, 1755.

CHAPTER 19.

AN ACT IN ADDITION TO AN ACT, INTIT[U]LED "AN ACT FOR GRANTING UNTO HIS MAJESTY AN EXCISE UPON SUNDRY ARTICLES HEREAFTER ENUMERATED, FOR AND TOWARDS THE SUPPORT OF HIS MAJESTY'S GOVERNMENT OF THIS PROVINCE."

Preamble. 1754-55, chap. 8. Words in former act recited.

WHEREAS in and by an act, intitled "An Act for granting unto his majesty an excise upon sundry articles hereafter enumerated, for and towards the support of his majesty's government of this province," made and pass'd in the twenty-seventh year of his present majesty's reign, it is provided in the words following; viz[t]., "*provided, nevertheless*, it shall and may be lawful to sell or dispose of any tea or china-ware to any person whatsoever, in case such tea or china-ware be in a chest or package as imported, and not less in value than twenty pounds lawful money, and also to sell and dispose of any coffee to any person whatsoever, in a quantity not less than one hundred weight"; *and whereas* also by said act it is further provided in the words following; viz[t]., "that if any person licen[s][c]ed to sell any of the aforesaid commodities shall purchase them of any other person liceu[s][c]ed to sell the same, such purchaser shall not be held to pay an excise on any quantity so purchased;" *and inasmuch* as divers persons licen[s][c]ed to sell the said commodities have sold said commodities to other persons licen[s][c]ed to sell the same, in and by such large quantities as that, by v[i][*e*]rtue of the said proviso of said act first recited, the seller was exempted from paying any duties or excise for said commodities, and the purchasers of said commodities, purchasing the same by such large quantities, were exempted from paying any excise for all said commodities sold by them, purchased as aboves[*ai*]d, by v[i][*e*]rtue of the abovesaid proviso last recited, it has so happened that the design of the government to raise a revenue by said act has hitherto been in a great measure frustrated, and also for the future may continue to be frustrated, unless provision be made by this court to prevent the same,—

Be it therefore enacted by the Governour, Council and House of Representatives,

Persons licensed, or to be licensed, to render an account to the farmer on oath.

[SECT. 1.] That from and after the tenth day of January next, and during the continuance of the act before mentioned, every person already licen[s][c]ed to sell all or any of the aforesaid commodities, or that may hereafter, during the continuance of said act, be licen[s][c]ed to sell the same, shall be held and obliged to render to the farmer of the before-mentioned excise, or his deputy, a just and true account, on oath, of all tea, coffee and china-ware by him or her sold or consumed after the tenth day of January next, and also to pay to said farmer, or his deputy, the duties by said act set on said commodities so sold or consumed, be the weight or value of what is sold more or less; anything in the first recited proviso of the before-mentioned act notwithstanding. And every person licen[s][c]ed as aforesaid, who shall presume to sell any of the before-mentioned commodities, and shall refuse or neglect to account with the farmer, and pay the duties required by this act, shall be subject for each offence to the penalty as if he or she should sell without licen[s][c]e, and shall be rendered incapable of renewing his or her licen[s][c]e to sell the same for the future; the penalty to be recovered shall be one half to the informer, and the other half to the farmer, and the manner of conviction shall be the same as of persons selling strong liquors without licen[s][c]e. 1754-55, chap. 16, § 6.

Provided, nevertheless,—

[SECT. 2.] That if any licen[s][c]ed person shall have purchased any of the commodities so sold by him or her, of any other licen[s][c]ed person who shall have paid, or secured to pay, the excise thereon, such licen[s][c]ed person so purchasing shall be exempted from paying any further excise thereon, provided he produce a certificate that the excise thereof is paid, or secured to be paid, as aforesaid. Proviso.

And be it further enacted,

[SECT. 3.] That from and after the tenth day of January next, and during the continuance of said act, every person who shall apply to the court of general sessions of the peace in any county for licen[s][c]e to sell all or any of the said commodities, shall, before such licen[s][c]e be granted to him or her, be obliged to give bond, with sufficient sureties, for their well and truly paying the duties by said act set on said commodities, which by this act all licen[s][c]ed persons are obliged to pay. [*Passed January* 2; *published January* 13, 1755. Persons applying for licenses, to give bond.

CHAPTER 20.

AN ACT TO PREVENT DAMAGE TO ENGLISH GRAIN, ARISING FROM BARBERRY-BUSHES.

WHEREAS it has been found, by experience, that the blasting of wheat and other English grain, is often occasioned by barberry-bushes, to the great loss and damage of the inhabitants of this province,— Preamble.

Be it therefore enacted by the Governour, Council and House of Representatives,

[SECT. 1.] That whoever, whether community or private person, hath any barberry-bushes standing or growing in his or their land within any of the towns in this province, he or they shall cause the same to be extirpated or destroyed on or before the tenth day of June, *Anno Domini* one thousand seven hundred and sixty. Barberry-bushes to be extirpated on or before June, 1760.

Be it further enacted,

[SECT. 2.] That if there shall be any barberry-bushes standing or growing, in any land within this province, after the said tenth day of June, it shall be lawful, by virtue of this act, for any person whomsoever, to enter the lands wherein such barberry-bushes are (first giving three months' notice of his intention so to do, to the owner or occupant thereof), and to cut them down, or pull them up by the roots, and then to present a fair account of his labour and charge therein to the owner Liberty after that time for any person to cut them down, provided, &c.

Provision in case owners or occupants neglect, &c.

or occupant of the said land; and if such owner or occupant shall neglect or refuse, by the space of two months next after the presenting said account, to make to such person reasonable payment as aforesaid, then the person who cut down or pulled up such bushes, may bring his action against such owner or occupant, owners or occupants, before any justice of the peace, if under forty shillings; or otherwise, before the inferiour court of common pleas in the county where such bushes grew; who, upon proof of the cutting down or pulling up of such bushes, by the person who brings the action, or such as were employed by him, shall and is hereby, respectively, impowered to enter up judgment for him to recover double the value of the reasonable expence and labour in such service, and award execution accordingly.

Be it further enacted,

Actions may be brought as in cases of the like nature.

[SECT. 3.] That if the lands on which such bushes grow are common and undivided lands, that then an action may be brought, as aforesaid, against any one of the proprietors, in such manner as the laws of this province provide in such cases where proprietors may be sued.

Be it further enacted,

Surveyors of highways empowered to extirpate barberry-bushes standing in highways.

[SECT. 4.] That the surveyors of the highways, whether publick or private, be and hereby are impowered and required, *ex officio*, to destroy and extirpate all such barberry-bushes as are or shall be in the highways in their respective wards or districts; and if any such shall remain after the aforesaid tenth day of June, *Anno Domini* one thousand seven hundred and sixty, that then the town or district in which such bushes are, shall pay a fine of two shillings for every bush standing or growing in such highway, to be recovered by bill, plaint, information, or the presentment of a grand jury, and to be paid, one half to the informer, and the other half to the treasurer of the county in which such bushes grew, for the use of the county.

Penalty, in case.

Be it further enacted,

Provision if such bushes grow in stone wall, or fence.

[SECT. 5.] That if any barberry-bushes stand or grow in any stone wall, or other fence, either fronting the highway, or dividing between one propriety and another, that then an action may be brought, as aforesaid, against the owner of said fence, or the person occupying the land to which such fence belongs; and if the fence in which such bushes grow is a divisional fence between the lands of one person or community and another, and such fence hath not been divided, by which means the particular share of each person or community is not known, then an action may be brought, as aforesaid, against either of the owners or occupants of said land.

Be it further enacted,

Owner or proprietor to pay for pulling up or destroying said bushes.

[SECT. 6.] That where the occupant of any land shall eradicate and destroy any barberry-bushes growing therein, or in any of the fences belonging to the same (which such occupant is hereby authorized to do, and every action to be brought against him for so doing shall be utterly barred), or shall be obliged, pursuant to this act, to pay for pulling them up or cutting them down, that then the owner or proprietor of such land shall pay the said occupant the full value of his labour and cost in destroying them himself, or what he is obliged to pay to others as aforesaid; and if the said owner or owners shall refuse so to do, then it shall be lawful for said occupant or occupants to withhold so much of the rents or income of said land as shall be sufficient to pay or reimburse his cost and charge arising as aforesaid.

Limitation.

[SECT. 7.] This act to continue and be in force until[1] the tenth day of June, one thousand seven hundred and sixty-four. [*Passed December* 26, 1754; *published January* 13, 1755.

CHAPTER 21.

AN ACT FOR THE SECURING THE GROWTH AND INCREASE OF A CERTAIN PARCEL OF WOOD AND TIMBER IN THE TOWNSHIPS OF IPSWICH AND WENHAM, IN THE COUNTY OF ESSEX.

WHEREAS there is a large tract or parcel of woodland lying in the townships of Ipswich and Wenham, commonly known by the name of Wenham Great Swamp, bounded easterly by a brook and a pond known by the name of Pleasant-Pond Brook; southerly on land belonging to adjacent proprietors; westerly on a meadow and some swamp, known by the name of Wenham Great Meadows; northerly on the meadow known by the name of Saltonstall Meadows, to the brook first mentioned; *and whereas* it would be of great advantage to said towns, as well as to the particular owners of said wood and timber, that the growth thereof should be preserved from feeding and browzing of cattle and sheep, which are frequently turn'd and kept there in considerable numbers; and the laws already in force for embodying proprietors of common fields not reaching this case, there needs a further provision,— Preamble.

Be it therefore enacted by the Governour, Council and House of Representatives,

[SECT. 1.] That from and after the fifteenth day of January instant, it shall and may be lawful for any five of the proprietors of said woodland to apply to a justice of the peace within the same county, setting forth in writing, under their hands the intended bounds by which they would circumscribe their proposed propriety, together with their intentions of incorporation for the purpose aforesaid, with the time and place of their intended meeting; on which application the justice shall make out his warrant to one of the principal proprietors so applying, to notify the said owners and proprietors to assemble and meet, by posting up a notification for that end, in one publick place in said Wenham, and also in the Third Parish in said town of Ipswich, twenty days at least before the time of said meeting; at which time and place it shall be lawful for the said proprietors to meet, and ch[oo][*u*]se a moderator and clerk; and if two-thirds of the whole proprietors (to be reckoned by their interest) shall see meet, they may, by vote, incorporate themselves into one body, in which the whole proprietors owning lands within the limits aforesaid shall be included; and may at said meeting agree upon some proper methods for calling proprietors' meetings for the future: and the said proprietors so incorporated, shall have and enjoy all the powers and privileges for the ordering and managing the affairs of said woodland, for the preservation and interest thereof, as fully and amply, to all intents and purposes, as any proprietors of common and general fields already embodyed do or may enjoy by the laws of this province already in force; the said proposed proprietors observing the same rules and methods in ordering and managing their whole affairs in all respects as the laws have provided in cases of common or general fields.

Proprietors of said woodland, on application to a justice, may have a warrant for a meeting, &c.

Rules to be observed by the proprietors.

[SECT. 2.] This act to continue and be in force for the space of ten years from the publication thereof, and no longer. [*Passed January* 9; *published January* 13, 1755. Limitation.

CHAPTER 22.

AN ACT FOR CONTINUING AN ACT OF THIS PROVINCE, INTITLED "AN ACT TO IMPOWER THE PROPRIETORS OF THE MEETING-HOUSE IN THE FIRST PARISH IN SALEM, WHERE THE REV[D]. MR. JOHN SPARHAWK NOW OFFICIATES, AND ALSO THE PROPRIETORS OF THE MEETING-HOUSE IN THE THIRD PARISH IN NEWBURY, WHERE THE REV[D]. MR. JOHN LOWELL OFFICIATES, TO RAISE MONEY FOR DEFREYING MINISTERIAL AND OTHER NECESSARY CHARGES."

Preamble. WHEREAS an act, intitled "An Act to impower the proprietors of the meeting-house in the First Parish in Salem, where the Rev[d]. Mr. John Sparhawk now officiates, and also the proprietors of the meeting-house in the Third Parish in Newbury, where the Rev[d]. Mr. John Lowell officiates, to raise money for defreying ministerial and other necessary charges," was made and passed in the twenty-fourth year of his present majesty's reign, which act is near expiring; and the same having been found beneficial, and necessary for the purposes for which it was passed,—

Be it therefore enacted by the Governour, Council and House of Representatives,

Continuation of this act. That the said act, and every matter and clause therein contained, be and shall continue in force from the first day of February next, until[l] the first day of February, one thousand seven hundred and sixty, and from thence to the end of the then next session of the general court, and no longer. [*Passed January* 10; *published January* 13, 1755.

CHAPTER 23.

AN ACT FOR THE SUPPLY OF THE TREASURY WITH THE SUM OF SIX THOUSAND POUNDS, AND FOR APPLYING THE SAME FOR THE PAYMENT OF THE FORCES RAISED FOR THE LATE EXPEDITION AT KENNEBECK.

Preamble. 1753-54, chap. 40. 1754-55, chap. 9. WHEREAS the provision made by this court at their sessions in April and May last, of seven thousand four hundred and fourteen pounds, for the above purpose, is insufficient to answer the ends proposed, and it being necessary, as well for the honour of the government as for the encouragement of future expeditions, that a further and an immediate supply should be made, that so the officers and private soldiers who have served the province in the said expedition may forthwith receive their pay according to their several[l] establishments,—

Be it enacted by the Governour, Council and House of Representatives.

Treasurer empowered to borrow £6,000. [SECT. 1.] That the treasurer of the province be and he is hereby impow[e]red and directed to borrow, from such person or persons as shall be willing to lend the same, a sum not exceeding six thousand pounds, in mill'd dollars, at six shillings each, or in other silver at six shillings and eightpence per ounce; and the sum so borrowed shall be applied by the treasurer for the payment and discharge of all such draughts as shall, from time to time, be drawn on him by the governour and council, to be paid out of the appropriation for the forces in the late expedition, &c[a].; and for every sum so borrowed, the treasurer shall give a receipt and obligation in the form following:—

Province of the Massachusetts Bay, day of , 175 . Received of the sum of . for the use and service of the province of the Massachusetts Bay, and, in behalf of said province, I do hereby promise and oblige myself and successors in the office of treasurer, to repay to the said or order, on or before the first of December, seventeen hundred and fifty-six, the aforesaid sum of , with interest annually, at the rate of six per cent per annum. Witness my hand, A. B., Treasurer. Form of treasurer's receipt.

And in order to draw the money into the treasury again, and enable the treasurer effectually to discharge the receipts and obligations, with the interest that may be due thereon, by him given in pursuance of this act,—

Be it further enacted,

[SECT. 2.] That there be and hereby is granted unto his most excellent majesty a tax of six thousand pounds, to be levied on polls, and estates real and personal, within this province, according to such rules, and in such proportion on the several towns and districts within the same, as shall be agreed on and ordered by the general court of this province at their session in May, one thousand seven hundred and fifty-five; which sum shall be paid into the treasury on or before the thirty-first day of March next after. Tax of £6,000 in 1755.

And whereas, when all the government securit[y][*ie*]s are re[c]deemed, excepting what are given by v[i][*e*]rtue of this act, and the outstanding taxes, exclusive of the tax for the present year, are paid into the treasury, there will be considerable surplusage; therefore, as an additional fund or security to enable the treasurer to discharge the notes and obligations by him given in pursuance of this act,— Preamble.

Be it further enacted,

[SECT. 3.] That what surplusage shall be in the treasury after said notes are discharged, shall be applied for the payment and discharge of the principal and interest that shall be due on the receipts and obligations given in pursuance of this act, and to no other purpose whatever. Fund.

And be it further enacted,

[SECT. 4.] That in case the general court shall not, at their session in May, and before the twentieth of June, one thousand seven hundred and fifty-five, agree and conclude upon an act apportioning the sum which by this act is engaged to be, in said year, apportioned, assessed and levied, that then, and in such case, each town and district within this province shall pay a tax, to be levied on the polls, and estates both real and personal, within their limits, the same proportion of the said sum as the said towns and districts were taxed by the general court in the tax act then last preceeding: *saving* what relates to the pay of the representatives, which shall be assessed on the several towns they respectively represent; and the province treasurer is hereby fully impow[e]red and directed, some time in the month of June, one thousand seven hundred and fifty-five, to issue and send forth his warrants, directed to the selectmen or assessors of each town and district within this province, requiring them to assess the polls, and estates both real and personal, within their several towns and districts, and for their respective parts and proportions of the sum before directed; and the assessors, as also persons assessed, shall observe, be governed by, and subject to all such rules and directions as have been given in the then last preceeding tax act. [*Passed and published November* 23. Rule for apportioning the tax in case no tax act shall be agreed on.

ACTS

Passed at the Session begun and held at Boston, on the Fifth day of February, A. D. 1755.

CHAPTER 24.

AN ACT IN FURTHER ADDITION TO THE SEVERAL LAWS ALREADY IN BEING FOR THE MORE SPEEDY FINISHING THE LAND-BANK OR MANUFACTORY SCHEME.

Preamble. 1748-49, chap. 16.

Whereas the Land-bank or Manufactory Scheme cannot be equitably finished unless further provision be made by law for the sale of such real estates of delinquents as are or may be taken by execution or warrants of distress,—

Be it therefore enacted by the Governour, Council and House of Representatives,

Sheriffs empowered to make sale of forfeited estates in the Land-bank, in case.

[Sect. 1.] That every sheriff, undersheriff or deputy sheriff, who (upon the receipt of any execution or warrant of distress, issued or to be issued by the commissioners by law appointed to finish the said scheme, against the estates of any of the late directors or partners therein, for any sum or sums of money assessed or that may be assessed on them, or either of them, or which their estates are by law made liable to the payment of) hath or shall have levied such sum or sums on the whole or any part of the real estate of any such director or partner, and shall have obtained from the register of deeds in the county where such lands l[y][*i*]e, a certificate that, upon a careful search made in the registry of deeds there, it doth not appear that any conveyance or alienation of such estate hath been made by such director or partner and ent[e]red or lodged in such registry at any time before the month of October, *Anno Domini* one thousand seven hundred and forty-three (at which time those estates were by law subjected to the payment of what should appear to be due therefrom to the company of partners), such sheriff or undersheriff or deputy, shall be and hereby is authorized and impowered, after the time allowed by law for the redemption of such estates shall be expired, to make sale thereof, and to make, sign and execute, in due form of law, a deed or deeds of conveyance thereof, with warrant[e][*i*]e; which instrument or instruments of conveyance shall make a good title to the purchaser, his heirs and assigns, forever.

Provided, always,—

And be it further enacted,

Proviso, in cases where the estate is in other hands besides the directors and partners.

[Sect. 2.] That any person or persons, other than the director or partner whose estate shall be taken and sold as aforesaid, or his heirs, assigns or devisees, claiming any right in or to such estate, may, anything in this act before mentioned notwithstanding, bring his or their action for the recovery thereof, provided the same be commenced and pursued within one year from the time of making such conveyance;

and every action of trespass, ejectment, or other action against the sheriff, or other officer, for his doings therein, or that shall be brought to evict or in anywise to molest the purchaser, his heirs or assigns, in the peaceable possession of the estate sold him as aforesaid, at any time after the expiration of said term, shall be utterly barr'd: *saving* such action or actions as may be brought by any person or persons who, at the time of such conveyance, shall be and shall continue out of this province 'till after the expiration of said term, or that shall be brought by any person who, during that time, shall be under some legal incapacity of bringing his action; in either of which cases such action may be brought within one year from and after the removal of such impediment, and not afterwards.

And be it further enacted,

[SECT. 3.] That the several surviving directors and partners in said scheme, and their estates, and the estates of such of them as are deceased, shall be and they are hereby subjected and made liable to answer and refund all costs and charges that may arise in consequence of any such conveyance; such charges to be assessed on them by the said commissioners, and to be rais[*e*]'d and collected in manner and proportion as set forth in the act made in the twenty-fourth year of his present majesty's reign, intitled "An Act in addition to the several laws already in being for the more speedy finishing the Land-bank or Manufactory Scheme."

The estates of surviving and deceased directors and partners made liable to answer charges.

1750-51, chap. 23.

And whereas divers of the mortgages given by the partners, at their first entrance on said scheme, to secure the payment of their dues to the company of partners, are not as yet discharged by the commissioners, nor such dues to the company paid; *and whereas* the original mortgages, lodged in the court-house in Boston, were consumed by fire,—

Preamble.

Be it therefore further enacted,

[SECT. 4.] That upon suit brought, or that may be commenced, upon any such mortgage remaining not discharged, an attested copy of the record thereof in the registry of deeds in the county where the estate so mortgaged lies, shall be deemed good and sufficient to all intents and purposes as if the original mortgage was produced in court on the tr[y][*i*]al.

Attested copy of the mortgages to be valid as the original.

Provided,—

[SECT. 5.] That nothing in this or any former act shall be construed or understood to abridge the said commissioners of the power formerly given them, by the laws of this province, by due course of law, in such cases as they shall judge may require it, to recover of any director or partner what became due from him to the company of partners by force of any former assessment, or otherwise, or of making and executing deeds of conveyance of such estates as have been or may be taken by execution in satisfaction of such dues. [*Passed February* 27; *published February* 28.

Proviso that the commissioners' power be not invalidated.

CHAPTER 25.

AN ACT IN ADDITION TO AN ACT MADE AND PASS[*E*]'D THIS PRESENT YEAR OF HIS MAJESTY'S REIGN, INTITLED "AN ACT FOR SUPPLYING THE TREASURY WITH THE SUM OF TWENTY-THREE THOUSAND POUNDS FOR DISCHARGING THE PUBLICK DEBTS, AND FOR DRAWING THE SAME INTO THE TREASURY."

WHEREAS, in and by an act made and pass'd this present year, intitled "An Act for supplying the treasury with the sum of twenty-

Preamble.

1754-55, chap. 17.

three thousand pounds for discharging the publick debts, and for drawing the same into the treasury," the treasurer of this province is impowered to borrow the said sum of twenty-three thousand pounds, and to give his receipts and obligations in manner as is therein expressed; and notwithstanding provision is made by said act that the persons who lend the same should be repaid in mill'd dollars at six shillings each, or in other silver at six shillings and eightpence per ounce, yet, as it does not appear in the face of said receipts or obligations, it may be a discouragement to many persons disposed to lend,—

Be it therefore enacted by the Governour, Council and House of Representatives,

[SECT. 1.] That all receipts or obligations which shall be given for such parts of the aforesaid sum of twenty-three thousand pounds which still remains to be borrowed, shall be in the form following; [*viz.*],—

New form of treasurer's receipts for money to be borrowed.

Province of the Massachusetts Bay, day of 1755. Received of the sum of , for the use and service of the province of the Massachusetts Bay, and, in behalf of said province, I do hereby promise and oblige myself and successors in the office of treasurer, to pay to the said or order, on or before the first day of January, 1757, the said sum of , in coined silver of sterling alloy, at six shillings and eightpence per ounce, or Spanish mill'd dollars of full weight, at six shillings each, with interest annually, at the rate of six per cent per annum.

And be it further enacted,

Former obligations of the treasurer's to be paid at the same rate.

[SECT. 2.] That all such receipts or obligations as have been already issued in consequence of the aforementioned act, shall be and are hereby declared to be payable in coined silver, of sterling alloy, at six shillings and eightpence per ounce, or Spanish mill'd dollars, at six shillings each, altho' the same be not in express terms promised in said receipts or obligations. [*Passed February* 18; *published February* 22, 1755.

CHAPTER 26.

AN ACT FOR APPOINTING ASSAYERS OF POTASH AND PEARLASH.

Preamble.

WHEREAS potash and pearlash, imported into Great Britain from Russia and other foreign parts, are there used in great quantities, for the purchase whereof large sums of money are annually expended, and carried out of the nation and paid to foreigners; *and whereas* it hath been found by experience that those commodities can be made within this province, not inferiour to the best that is manufactured in foreign parts, and if here made in large quantities and in the best manner, fit for transportation, would be of no small advantage as well to our mother country as to the mercantile and landed interest of the province: *provided*, none but what is good and merchantable should be allowed to be shipped off, and such as, from the excellency of its quality, may obtain a free vent; and as the prohibiting the exportation of such of those commodities as are deficient, or wanting in that degree of goodness and perfection, can no way prejudice the persons already engaged in that business who may be less skilful therein, inasmuch as the method of proceedure in making pearl- and potash of the most perfect kind will soon be communicated to the publick, for the instruction of all persons already engaged, or that shall be inclined to engage, in that manufacture; and as such prohibition will be an effectual mean to preserve and secure the credit of our own produce, and to defeat any attempts of persons abroad, whose private interest may induce them to unite their endeavours to discourage that manufacture here, by undervaluing and decrying, in the markets at home, what shall be transported thither from this province,—

Be it therefore enacted by the Governour, Council and House of Represent[ati]ves,

[SECT. 1.] That from and after the first day of July next, no potash or pearlash made within this province, shall be ship[p]'d or exported but such as shall have been assayed and found to be of sufficient strength and purity, and to have those qualities in such degree of perfection as shall be ascertained and fixed by this court (or such fit persons as shall be appointed and authorized for that purpose), as the standard of such potash and pearlash as shall be deemed merchantable and fit for exportation.

No potash or pearlash to be exported until it has passed an assay.

And be it further enacted,

[SECT. 2.] That some skilful and disinterested person or persons, to be appointed by this court, in such seaport towns within this province where there shall be occasion, be assay-masters for the proving and assaying of potash and pearlash, who shall be sworn to the due and impartial execution of their trust; and their duty shall be, when desired, to inspect and assay all potash and pearlash that shall be brought to any such seaport town to be shipped; and every such assay-master is hereby authorized to open the casks or vessels containing those commodities, and to take out so much thereof for tr[y][i]al as may probably discover the condition of the whole, he returning the same to the owner after tr[y][i]al made thereof: and every cask or other vessel of pearl--or potash, which by such assay shall appear to be good and merchantable, according to the rule or standard that shall be established as aforesaid, he shall mark or imprint with some distinguishing mark or brand, to be appointed by the governour and council, to denote that the same has been assayed and approved.

Assay-master to be appointed and sworn.

Their duty.

And be it further enacted,

[SECT. 3.] That if the owner of any pearl- or potash, or other person employed by him, shall presume to lade or put on board any vessel, any potash or pearlash, other than such as shall have been approved by an assay-master, or shall be contained in any cask that shall not have his mark or stamp upon it, or if any master of a ship or other vessel, or other officer or mariner, shall receive on board any such, the offender or offenders shall incur the penalty of five pounds for each cask or other vessel so shipp[e]'d, to be sued for and recovered in any of his maj[es]ty's courts of record within this province; and all such potash and pearlash, laded or received on board as aforesaid, shall be forfeited; one moiety of such penalty and forfeiture to be to his majesty for the use of this province, the other moiety to him or them that shall inform and sue for the same. And it shall be lawful for any justice of the peace, upon information given of any potash or pearlash put on board any vessel, as afores[ai]d, not mark'd as afores[ai]d, to issue his warrant, directed to the water-bailiff, or to the sheriff or his deputy, or constable, requiring them, respectively, to make seizure of any such potash or pearlash ship[p]'d and not mark'd as afores[ai]d, and to secure the same in order to tr[y][i]al; and such officers are hereby respectively impowered and required to execute the same.

Penalty for shipping any potash or pearlash not approved upon assay.

Method of proceeding against such offenders.

And be it further enacted,

[SECT. 4.] That if after any cask or other vessel of potash or pearlash shall have been approv'd and stamp'd with the assay-master's mark or stamp, any cooper or other person shall presume to shift the contents of such cask or other vessel, and to put therein either of those

Penalty for shifting the potash and pearlash out of the marked cask, &c.

commodities that have not been duly assayed and approved as afores[*ai*]d, such cooper or other person offending therein, shall forfeit and pay the sum of ten pounds, to be recovered and applied in manner as aforesaid.

And be it further enacted,

Assay-master's fee, &c.

[SECT. 5.] That the respective assay-masters shall be paid for every cask, or other vessel, of either of the commodities afores[*ai*]d that he shall assay, the sum of two shillings, to be paid by the owner; and if he refuse to satisfy the officer for his fees afore mentioned, it shall be lawful for him to detain so much of the said commodities as will make him satisfaction for his service; and if the owner do not redeem the same within twenty-four hours, he may then expose it to sale, and out of the proceeds may satisfy himself his fees and charges, returning the overplus, if any be, to the owner.

How to be paid.

Limitation.

[SECT. 6.] This act to continue and be in force from the first of July next, until[l] the first day of July, one thousand seven hund[*re*]d and sixty, and no longer. [*Passed February* 21; *published February* 22, 1755.

CHAPTER 27.

AN ACT FOR THE MORE EFFECTUAL CARRYING INTO EXECUTION SUCH ORDERS AS SHALL, AT ANY TIME, BE GIVEN BY HIS MAJESTY'S GOVERNOUR OR COMMANDER-IN-CHIEF, AT THE DESIRE OF THE TWO HOUSES OF ASSEMBLY (OR OF THE COUNCIL, THE GENERAL COURT NOT SITTING), FOR RESTRAINING VESSELS FROM SAILING OUT OF ANY PORTS WITHIN THIS PROVINCE.

Preamble.

WHEREAS it is sometimes necessary, for his majesty's service, that an embargo[c] should be laid upon ships and other vessels within the province,—

Be it therefore enacted by the Governour, Council and House of Representatives,

Penalty for any vessels sailing, in case of an embargo, without license.

[SECT. 1.] That when and so often as his majesty's governour or commander-in-chief shall be desired by the council and house of representatives (or by the council only, the general court not sitting), to issue a proclamation or order prohibiting vessels to sail or depart from the several ports, harbours, and other parts of the province, and a proclamation or order shall accordingly be issued by the governo[*u*]r or commander-in-chief, with the advice of the council, if any vessel, in contempt of such proclamation or order, shall sail or depart to any port or place, the special leave of the governour or commander-in-chief not being first had and obtained, the master of every vessel so departing shall forfeit and pay the sum of one hundred pounds; and the owner or owners of every such vessel shall likewise forfeit and pay the sum of one hundred pounds; and the said last-mentioned forfeiture shall and may be recovered from any or either of the owners of such vessel, where more than one person shall be interested. And the aforesaid penalties may be sued for and recovered by bill, plaint, or information in any of his majesty's courts of record within this province, one half thereof to his majesty, to be paid into the publick treasury for the use of the province, the other half to him or them that shall inform and sue for the same.

Any one owner may be sued.

Limitation.

[SECT. 2.] This act to continue and be in force for the space of one year from the publication thereof, and no longer. [*Passed February* 21; *published February* 22, 1755.

CHAPTER 28.

AN ACT IN ADDITION TO AND FOR REND[E]RING MORE EFFECTUAL AN ACT, [E][I]NTITLED "AN ACT FOR GRANTING UNTO HIS MAJESTY AN EXCISE UPON SPIRITS DISTILLED, AND WINE, AND UPON LIMES, LEMMONS AND ORANGES."

WHEREAS in and by an act made and pass'd in this twenty-eighth year of his majesty's reign, [e][i]ntitled "An Act for granting unto his majesty an excise upon spirits distilled, and wine, and upon limes, lemmons and oranges," among other things it is directed, that, if the farmer requires it, an oath shall be administred in the words following; viz[t].,— Preamble. 1754-55, chap. 16.

"You, A. B., do swear that the account by you exhibited, is a full account of all rum, or other distilled spirits, or wines, by you consumed, used or any ways expended, directly or indirectly, in your house, family, apartm[en]t or business, except such liquor be exported and consumed out of this province, (fishing-voyages excepted), within twelve months from the said twenty-sixth day of December, according to the best of your knowledge, except what you have purchased of a taverner, innholder or retailer within this province, in a quantity less than thirty gallons. So help you God."

—which said recited oath is apprehended to be, in several respects, defective and insufficient for the purposes intended thereby; wherefore,—

Be it enacted by the Governour, Council and House of Represent[ati]ves,

[SECT. 1.] That instead of the form afore recited, the said oath shall be administred in the form following; viz[t].,—

You, A. B., do swear that the account by you now exhibited is, according to the best of your knowledge, a full account of all rum, and other distilled spirits, and wine, consumed, or, any ways, directly or indirectly, used or expended by you or your family, or any other in your business or employm[en]t, within this province, or, in the fishery, out of the province, since the twenty-sixth day of Decem[be]r, *Anno Domini*, 1754, except what hath been purchased of a licen[s][c]ed taverner, innholder or retailer, within this province, since the 26th December last, in a quantity less than thirty gallons. So help you God. New form of the oath to be taken of persons respecting the accounts of excise.

And the farmer or farmers, his or their deputy or deputies, are hereby as fully impowered to require the said oath to be taken and administred in the form by this act provided as aforesaid, as he or they were, or might be presumed to be, impowered, by law, to have required the said oath to have been taken and administred in the form first before recited; and every person concerned, refusing to conform him- or herself hereto, shall be subject and liable to the same pains and penalties as he or she would, by law, have been liable, on refusal to take the said oath in the said recited form, in case this act had not passed.

And be it further enacted,

[SECT. 2.] That no town or district clerk, selectman or selectmen, who, by the act afores[ai]d, are to receive the accounts, as in and by the said act is provided, shall presume to demand or receive any pay or consideration of any person for receiving, filing or delivering out the same. [*Passed February* 22; *published February* 24, 1755. No officer to have any fee for said accounts.

CHAPTER 29.

AN ACT FOR REVIVING A LAW OF THIS PROVINCE, MADE IN THE TWENTY-THIRD YEAR OF HIS PRESENT MAJESTY'S REIGN, INTITLED "AN ACT TO PREVENT DAMAGE BEING DONE ON THE MEADOWS LYING IN THE TOWNSHIP OF YARMOUTH, CALLED NOBSCUSSET MEADOW."

Preamble. 1749-50, chap. 15.

WHEREAS the aforesaid law hath, by experience, been found beneficial for the purposes for which it was made and passed,—

Be it therefore enacted by the Governour, Council and House of Representatives,

Act for preserving Nobscusset meadows, in Yarmouth.

That the aforesaid act, and every matter and clause therein contained, except as hereafter is excepted, be and hereby is revived, and shall continue and remain in full force for the space of five years from the first day of March next, except where it is said in said act, "Southwest of a place called Black Earth"; that these words be inserted, "South of an east and west line from Fox-Hill to the seashore, and so to the extent of the meadows and beaches aforesaid." [*Passed February* 27; *published February* 28, 1755.

CHAPTER 30.

AN ACT IN ADDITION TO AN ACT MADE IN THE TWENTY-SEVENTH YEAR OF HIS PRESENT MAJESTY'S REIGN, [E][*I*]NTITLED "AN ACT FOR LEVYING SOLDIERS, AND TO PREVENT SOLDIERS AND SEAMEN IN HIS MAJESTY'S SERVICE BEING ARRESTED FOR DEBT."

Preamble. 1753-54, chap. 41.

WHEREAS doubts have arisen whether soldiers that have or shall inlist into the service of his majesty are exempted from paying their province tax, and so liable to be taken and imprisoned by the several constables or collectors that have a demand against them for the same,—

Be it therefore enacted by the Governour, Council and House of Representatives,

Soldiers not liable to be distrained on for their taxes, &c.

[SECT. 1.] That any soldier that hath or shall inlist into his majesty's service, since the making of the act afores[*ai*]d, shall not be liable to be taken, or have his body destrained on, by any constable or collector, for his province tax, during the continuance of said act; and where no estate of such soldier can be found, by any constable or collector, to make distress upon for such tax, and the same be made to appear by the oath of said collector or constable, that then, and in every such case, the loss of such tax shall be born[*e*] by the province; and any constable or collector who shall make it appear to the province treasurer that he hath failed of collecting any sum or sums on any soldier or soldiers inlisted as aforesaid, by a certificate from the selectmen or assessors, or the major part of them, that made the tax, that such person or persons are inlisted and in his majesty's service at the time of such certificate's being made, that then, and in every such case, the province treasurer is hereby directed and impowered to abate such sum or sums to the said constable or collector, and charge the province therewith.

Limitation.

[SECT. 2.] This act to continue in force until the first day of June, one thousand seven hundred and fifty-nine. [*Passed February* 27; *published February* 28, 1755.

CHAPTER 31.

AN ACT FOR PREVENTING THE UNNECESSARY DESTRUCTION OF ALEWIVES, AND OTHER FISH, WITHIN THIS PROVINCE.

WHEREAS the laws already provided against the destruction of the fish called alewives, and other fish, do not, in divers circumstances, reach the case of divers rivers and ponds where said fish usually go to cast their spawns, so that, nevertheless, great waste is made of them by ill-minded persons, to the great damage of the publick,— Preamble. 1735-36, chap. 21.

Be it enacted by the Governo[u]r, Council and House of Repres[entati]ves,

[SECT. 1.] That from and after the fifteenth day of March next, no person or persons whosoever, shall, on any pretence, presume to stretch, set or draw any s[ei][*ie*]ne or drag-net, or set up any w[e]ar[*e*]s or other fishing engines, in any part of the rivers within this province, or ponds adjacent thereto (Merrimack and Connecticut River only excepted), where the fish usually spawn, or use any other instrument for the catching alewives but by dip-nets or scoop-nets, on penalty of a fine of five pounds for each offence, to be paid by every person concerned in taken alewives or other fish in either of the ways forbid by this act. No nets but dip- and scoop-nets to be used in rivers, ponds, &c. Except.

And be it further enacted,

[SECT. 2.] That no person or persons whosoever, shall, on any pretence, presume to stretch, set or draw any seine or drag-net, for the catching of fish in any sort in any of the fresh ponds in this province, on penalty of the fine of five pounds for each offence, to be paid by every person concerned in taking fish in said ponds in either of the ways forbidden by this act. Penalty for breach of this act.

And whereas, by an act or law of this province, made in the fifteenth year of his present majesty's reign, intitled "An Act in addition to an act made to prevent the destruction of the fish called alewives, and other fish," it is therein enacted "that it shall be in the power of any town, at their annual meeting in March, to chuse one or more persons whose business it shall be to see that the passage-ways are open, pursuant to said act, and that said fish may not be obstructed in their usual passing up and down stream, and to appoint the proper place or places for the taking such fish with scoop-nets, and to limit the particular times and days for taking the same;" but no provision is made in said act to oblige the persons so chosen to serve in said business, or to do their duty therein, neither is their any limitation as to the quantities of said fish that shall be taken, in each town, for pickelling and barrelling for a market[t], by reason whereof many mischiefs arise,— Preamble. 1741-42, chap. 16, § 5.

Be it therefore enacted,

[SECT. 3.] That when any person or persons shall be chosen in any town, at their annual meeting in March, to see that passage-ways are open, agreable to the afore-recited paragraph of said act, that every such person shall be under oath to the faithful performance of said trust; and any person, chosen as aforesaid, shall, on his refusal, be subject to the penalty of three pounds, and to be proceeded with in order to the recovery thereof in the same way and manner as persons are by law who refuse to serve as constables. Persons chosen, &c., to be under oath, and fine for not serving. 1692-93, chap. 28, § 8.

And be it further enacted,

[SECT. 4.] That where any town, district or propriety that hath any river or stream that lets the alewives into their natural ponds to cast their spawns, have a desire to catch any of said fish to pickle and barrel[l] up for a marke[t], that, in every such case, where said river or Method to be taken where the stream for fish runs through more towns or districts than one.

stream run[s] through or into more towns, districts or proprieties than one, except where the right of taking fish is otherwise vested, the selectmen of the said several towns, districts, and a committee of the propriet[ie][or]s that are or may be affected thereby shall, sometime in the month of March, and before the first day of April, annually, during the continuance of this act, meet together at such time and place as the selectmen of the oldest town shall agree upon, and then determine what quantity of alewives shall be barrelled up from year to year for a market in the several towns, districts or proprieties they belong to, the votes to be collected according to the major part of those that represent the towns, districts and proprieties said streams pass through or run into, and not according to the numbers of voters; and when so done, the selectmen of each town, district or proprietors' committee, are hereby impowered to let out the said privilege for the most it will fetch, for the use of their several towns, districts or proprieties, in such way and manner as they shall judge most beneficial; and where any town, district or propriety have a stream or streams as afores[*ai*]d, that do not run into any other town, district or propriety, that in such case the selectmen or proprietors' committee shall have the sole power, from year to year, during the continuance of this act, to determine what number of barrels shall be caught for a market as afores[*ai*]d, and shall have the same power of letting out and improving the said rivers or streams in the same manner, as before mentioned, where the town, district or propriety jo[y][*i*]n as aforesaid.

Be it further enacted,

Fine for breach of orders of proprietors.

[SECT. 5.] That if any person or persons shall presume to catch any alewives for marketting, contrary to the allowance or order of the selectmen, or s[*ai*]d propriety's com[*mitt*]ee, where proprie-t[y][*ie*]s are concerned, or the selectmen, where no propriety is concerned, or propriety, where they are concerned only, they shall, every of them, be subjected to the penalty of five pounds for each offence.

Preamble.

And whereas some disputes have arisen, or may arise, whether tide-mills that have or shall be set up on and across the mouth of the rivers where the fish afores[*ai*]d usually go up into the natural ponds to cast their spawns, are within the intent of the last-recited act, and ought to be regulated accordingly,—

Be it enacted,

What tide-mills are subject to this act.

[SECT. 6.] That all tide-mills that have been set upon and across any such rivers or streams since the making the afores[*ai*]d act, or that shall hereafter be set up, shall be understood to be comprehended in said act, and the owners and occupants, and all others concerned, shall conform thereto accordingly, and be subject to the same penalties, for their neglect, as if tide-mills had particularly been named in s[*ai*]d act.

And whereas there has been great destruction of the fish that usually pass up Merrimack River, by reason that people made a constant practice of taking fish in s[*ai*]d river with seine and drag-nets.

Be it therefore enacted,

Days stated for catching fish in Merrimack river.

[SECT. 7.] That no person or persons be allowed, from and after the fifteenth day of March next, and so during the continuance of this act, to catch fish of any sort in any part of Merrimack River that lieth in this governm[*en*]t, oftner than three days in the week, the days to be Tuesday, Wednesday and Thursday in every week, and so, successively, until[l] this act expires; and if any person or persons shall presume to catch fish with sein[*e*]s or drag-nets, at any other times than is hereby allowed, every person or persons so offending shall, for each offence, be subject to a fine of five pounds.

[SECT. 8.] And [that] all the aforesaid fines, penalties and forfeitures, arising pursuant to this act, shall be disposed of, the one half for the benefit of the poor of the town where the offence is committed, the other half to him or them who shall inform and sue for the same. Disposal of fines.

And be it further enacted,

[SECT. 9.] That the manner, rules and methods of convicting offenders against this act, be the same as are directed and provided in and by an act made in the twelfth year of the reign of his late majesty King George the First, intitled "An Act in addition to and for rendring more effectual an act made in the tenth year of the reign of King William the Third, [e][*i*]ntitled 'An Act for preventing of trespasses.'" Rule for conviction. 1726-27, chap. 3. 1698, chap 7.

Provided,—

[SECT. 10.] That nothing in this act shall be understood to restrain the catching of fish called munhadens, with seines or drag-nets, after the first day of June, and until[l] the first day of October, annually, or, in Connecticut River, at any time in the year. Proviso for catching menhaden.

Provided, however,—

[SECT. 11.] That the selectmen of the towns of Cambridge, Charlestown and Medford, or the major part of them, being met together, may give liberty for taking fish in Medford River for a limited time in each week, not exceeding two days, with one or two seines, and no more. Proviso for Medford.

[SECT. 12.] This act to continue and be in force until[l] the fifteenth day of March, *Anno Domini* one thousand seven hundred and fifty-eight. [*Passed February* 26; *published February* 28, 1755. Term of the act's continuance.

ACTS

PASSED AT THE SESSION BEGUN AND HELD AT BOSTON, ON THE TWENTY-FIFTH DAY OF MARCH, A. D. 1755.

CHAPTER 32.

AN ACT IMPOWERING THE PROVINCE TREASURER TO BORROW THE SUM OF FIVE THOUSAND POUNDS, AND FOR APPLYING THE SAME TO DEFR[A][*E*]Y THE CHARGES OF THE INTENDED EXPEDITION WESTWARD.

Be it enacted by the Governour, Council and House of Representatives,

Treasurer empowered to borrow £5,000.

[SECT. 1.] That the treasurer of the province be and hereby is impowered and directed to borrow of such persons as shall be willing to lend the same, a sum not exceeding five thousand pounds, in Span[n]ish mill[e]'d dollars, at six shillings each, or in other silver at six shillings and eightpence per ounce; and the sum so borrowed shall be appl[y][*i*]ed by the treasurer for the payment of all such draughts as shall be drawn on him by the governour or com[*m*]ander-in-ch[ei][*ie*]f for the time being, by and with the advice of the council, for the service of the intended expedition westward; and for every sum so borrowed, the treasurer shall give a receipt and obligation in the form following; viz[t].,—

Form of treasurer's receipt.

Province of the Massachusetts Bay, day of 1755. Received of the sum of , for the use and service of the province of the Massachusetts Bay, and, in behalf of said province, I do hereby promise and oblige myself and successors in the office of treasurer to repay to the said or order, on or before the first day of June, one thousand seven hundred and fifty-seven, the aforesaid sum of , in coined silver of sterling alloy, at six shillings and eightpence per ounce, or Spanish mill[e]'d dollars of full weight, at six shillings each, with interest annually, at the rate of six per cent per annum.

Witness my hand, A. B., Treasurer.

And to enable the treasurer to discharge the said obligations,—

Be it further enacted,

Tax of £5,600 granted.

[SECT. 2.] That there be and hereby is granted to his most excellent majesty, a tax of five thousand six hundred pounds, to be levied on the polls and estates within this province, according to such rules as shall be ordered by the general court of this province at their sessions in May, one thousand seven hundred and fifty-six.

And be it further enacted,

Rule for apportioning the tax in case no tax act shall be agreed on.

[SECT. 3.] That in case the general court shall not, at their sessions in May, one thousand seven hundred and fifty-six, agree and conclude upon a tax act to draw into the treasury the aforesaid sum of five thousand six hundred pounds, that then the treasurer of the province for the time being shall issue his warrants, directed to the selectmen or assessors of the several towns and districts in this province, requiring them respectively to assess, levy and pay in their respective proportions of said sum, according to the rates and proportions, rules and directions of the last preceeding tax act. [*Passed March* 29; *published March* 31, 1755.

CHAPTER 33.

AN ACT TO IMPOWER THE AGENT OF THIS PROVINCE AT THE COURT OF GREAT BRITAIN, TO BORROW MONEY FOR THE USE OF THE PROVINCE.

Be it enacted by the Governour, Council and House of Representatives,

[SECT. 1.] That William Bollan, Esq., agent for this province at the court of Great Britain, or the agent for the time being, be and he hereby is authorized and fully impowered to borrow, for the use of this province, in any part of Great Britain, the sum of twenty-three thousand pounds sterling, in Spanish mill'd dollars, at the lowest interest it can be obtained, for the space of six years; and when he shall have borrowed the same, cause it to be ship'd on board some good ship or vessel, and to be insured in some publick office of insurance, and order it to be delivered to the treasurer of this province. Agent empowered to borrow £23,000 sterling in Great Britain.

And in order to encourage persons to lend said money to the province,—

Be it enacted,

[SECT. 2.] That as a fund and security to raise the said twenty-three thousand pounds, and the interest that shall accrue to become due thereon, a tax is hereby granted on the polls and estates within this province, according to such rules and directions and in such proportions upon the several towns and districts within the same, as shall be agreed on and ordered by the great and general court at their sessions in May, *Anno Domini* one thousand seven hundred and fifty-nine, for so much as shall be sufficient to pay one half of the said sum of twenty-three thousand pounds, and the interest which shall be due thereon, and paid into the treasury by the last day of December next after; and also another tax, to be levied in like manner, according to such rules and in such proportions as shall be agreed on by the great and general court at their sessions in May, *Anno Domini* one thousand seven hundred and sixty, for so much as shall be sufficient to pay the other half of the said sum of twenty-three thousand pounds, and the interest which shall be due thereon, and paid into the treasury by the last day of December next after. Fund and security for money so borrowed, by a tax.

[SECT. 3.] And if the general court shall, in either or both of the aforesaid years, fail of making an act to levy the aforesaid taxes, that then the treasurer for the time being shall and he is hereby impowered to issue out his warrants to the selectmen or assessors of the several towns and districts in the province, for such sums as the respective towns' and districts' proportion of the aforesaid sums shall be, according to the rules then last observed in levying the province tax; and such assessors are hereby required, respectively, to assess, and cause to be levied and paid into the province treasury, the several sums for which they shall receive the province treasurer's warrants as aforesaid. Rule for apportioning the tax in case no tax act shall be agreed on.

Provided, nevertheless,—

[SECT. 4.] That if sufficient provision shall be made by this government for the payment of said sums, or any part thereof, before the Proviso.

times herein set for issuing warrants for said taxes, that then such warrants shall not issue, or shall issue for so much only as shall not be provided for as aforesaid.

And it is hereby further enacted and declared,

Provision for the yearly interest of £23,000 sterling.

[SECT. 5.] That sufficient and timely provision shall be made by the general court of this province for the payment of the interest of the said sum of twenty-three thousand pounds sterling, yearly, as the same shall become due; but if the general court shall, in any year, neglect to make such provision, that then the treasurer of the province, for the time being, shall and he is hereby impowered to issue out his warrants to the selectmen and assessors of the respective towns and districts to assess, levy and pay in, each one their share, respectively, of said deficient sum, according to such rules and proportions as shall have been provided in the last tax act. [*Passed March* 29; *published March* 31, 1755.

CHAPTER 34.

AN ACT TO ENCOURAGE AND FACILITATE THE REMOVAL AND PREVENTION OF FRENCH ENCROACHMENTS ON HIS MAJESTY'S NORTH AMERICAN TERRITORIES.

Preamble.

WHEREAS it may be of very ill consequence if the several measures taking by his majesty's good subjects of this and the governments adjacent, to remove or prevent the encroachments of the French, should be, from time to time, made known and exposed to the people in Louisb[*o*]urgh, or other French settlements in North America, before their execution,—

Be it therefore enacted by his excellency the Governour, Council and House of Representatives, and hereby it is enacted and declared,

Prohibition of holding correspondence, &c., with any of the French king's subjects in North America.

That for the space of four months, to be computed from the last day of March, one thousand seven hundred and fifty-five, it shall be unlawful for any of his majesty's subjects of this province, and they are hereby strictly forbidden to hold any correspondence or communication with any inhabitant of Louisb[*o*]urgh, or any other of the French settlements in North America, either by land or water; and if any person or persons belonging to this province shall be so audacious as to go or send to Louisb[*o*]urgh, or any other French settlement in North America, during said four months, the ship, sloop or other vessel employed, with all her tackle and appurtenances, and her cargo, shall be forfeited: one half to his majesty for the use of this province; the other half to him or them who shall inform and sue for the same in any of his majesty's courts within this province proper to try the same; and be further liable, if a ship or [other] vessel, the master to have one ear cut off, and be publickly whip[t][*ped*] thirty-nine lashes, and be render'd forever [u][*i*]ncapable of holding any place of honour or profit under this government; and the owner or owners, and factor or factors of the owner or owners, of such ship or other vessel, shall forfeit and pay, each, five hundred pounds, to be recover[*e*]'d and dispos[*e*]'d of as above, and be also forever disabled to hold any place of honour or profit under this government. [*Passed March* 29; *published March* 31, 1755.

Penalty for breach of this act.

NOTES.—There were five * sessions of the General Court this year; but at the fifth session, which began April 22 and ended April 28, 1755, no acts were passed.

During this last session a precedent adverse to the propriety of prolonging a session beyond the time of issuing writs for a new assembly, was established. On the twenty-fifth of April the Secretary delivered a message from the Lieutenant-Governor, to both branches of the Assembly, requesting their advice upon this point, which was raised by the Governor's intimation of his wish that the Assembly should be kept in session until he could meet them after his return from New York. The Governor's letter conveying this intimation was dated April 6, 1755, but, though already public, the Lieutenant-Governor had not submitted it to the consideration of the Assembly, apparently because of his expectation of the Governor's speedy return. As the time approached when the writs for convening a new assembly must be issued, the subject was laid before the Assembly in the message mentioned above. A committee, consisting of Mr. Tasker, Col. Hale, Judge Russell, Col. Brattle and Col. Otis, of the Representatives, and Benjamin Lynde, Thomas Hutchinson, Ezekiel Chever and Stephen Sewall, esquires, of the Council, was appointed, the same day, to consider and report upon the message; but the next day, without waiting for a report from this committee, the Representatives sent up the following message, by a committee consisting of "Samuel Welles and others":—

"May it please your Honour,

The House of Representatives have with Attention considered your Message of Yesterday; And as the Sitting of the General Court after Writs are issued for calling a new Assembly is contrary to the most Ancient & Uninterrupted Practice in our Mother Country, and the Universal Custom in all his Majesty's Governments in all the Plantations; We cannot but humbly be of Opinion that the Ancient & Constant Practice in this Province of issuing Writs thirty days before the last Wednesday in May & previous to it the dissolving the then General Court, is most for the Peace & good Order of this Province, & most conducive to his Majesty's Interest."—*Council Records, vol. XX., p.* 442.

No further action appears to have been taken on the subject in either branch before the dissolution of the Assembly, which occurred two days later.

All the acts of this year were printed: chapters 10 and 12 separately; and the engrossments of all preserved, except of chapters 9 and 14. The following is the title of the only private act passed this year:—

"An Act to dissolve the Marriage of Mary Clapham with William Clapham, and to allow her to marry again." [*Passed January* 10; *published January* 13, 1755.—See note to chapter 15, *post.*

The acts of the first session were certified for transmission, October 21, and forwarded with a letter from Secretary Willard, dated October 23, 1754. They were delivered to the clerk of the Privy Council, in waiting, January 24, 1755, having been received by the Board of Trade on the ninth of that month. On the 29th of January, they were referred to a committee of the Privy Council; and, on the next day, this committee referred them to the Lords of Trade, by whom they were ordered to be sent to Sir Matthew Lamb for his opinion thereon, February 4th, 1755. Sir Matthew's report was read at the Board, May 25, 1756. It was to the effect that upon perusal and consideration of these acts he had no objection thereto in point of law. The Lords of Trade, on the same day, ordered the draught of a report to be prepared, which was agreed to and ordered to be transcribed April 6, and signed April 13, 1756.

In their report the Lords of Trade represent that chapters 4, 6, 9, 10, and 11 "were passed for temporary services and are either expired by their own Limitation or the purposes for which they were enacted have been completed"; and that chapters 1, 2, 3, 5, 7, and 8 "appear to have been enacted for" the private convenience of the Province, and that "We see no reason why His Majesty may not be graciously pleased to confirm them." Accordingly, the six chapters last enumerated were confirmed by an order in Council, dated July 7, 1756.

Chapter 16 was certified for transmission, January 14, 1755, and forwarded by Governor Shirley, with a letter bearing date two days earlier. The correspondence, and the action of the Home Government relating to this act, are given in full hereafter, in the note to this chapter, *post.*

All the acts of the second, third, and fourth sessions, including the private act, the title of which is given above, and chapter 16, were certified for transmission, June 18, 1755, and were received by the Board of Trade, July 28. They were not laid before the Privy Council, however, until the twelfth of September following. There they remained until September 22, when they were referred to a committee. On the twenty-fourth of September, this committee referred them to the Lords of Trade, and from the Lords of Trade they went, in the usual course, to Sir Matthew Lamb; but at what time, precisely, does not appear. Sir Matthew Lamb's report to the Lords of Trade is dated December 18, 1756, and, after specially commenting upon chapters 12 and 15,—as shown at length in the notes to those chapters, *post,*—and the private act aforesaid, it concludes, "I have no other Observations or Objections to make than are before mentioned."

On the twelfth of May, 1758, these acts, with others, were considered by the Lords of Trade, in consultation with ex-Governor Shirley, who had been invited for that purpose, and the draught of a report thereon was ordered to be prepared. On the 30th of May, this draught was agreed to and ordered to be transcribed, and, on the sixth of June, it

* Although the first session was adjourned from June 19 to Oct. 17, expressly to avoid the effect of a prorogation upon chapter 16, from which the Governor withheld his signature in order that, before its passage, the bill might be submitted, by the Representatives, to their constituents, during the recess, still, the acts passed after the recess were printed as of a new session, and were so certified to the Privy Council. The convening of the Assembly after this recess is, therefore, assumed to be the commencement of the second session.

was signed. After mentioning that chapter 16 had already been confirmed, the report proceeds to represent that chapters 17, 18, 19, 23, 24, 25, 27, 28, 31, 32, and 34 "appear to have been passed for Temporary services and are either expired by their own limitation or the purposes for which they were enacted have been completed"; that whereas chapter 33, "relative to the raising or borrowing monies for defraying the Expences of Military and other public services, has in great measure taken effect, but the execution of several provisions therein contained in which the public faith of the Province is greatly interested remains still to be completed, for this reason and as Sir Matthew Lamb one of His Majestys Counsel at Law, whose opinion has been taken" * * * "has no objection," &c, therefore, that this act be proposed for confirmation; that chapters 12, 13, 14, 15, 20, 21, 22, 26, 29, and 30, "relate to the internal Œconomy of the Province and appear to have been enacted for it's private convenience, and We see no reason why His Majesty may not be graciously pleased to confirm them"; and the report concludes with a representation on the private act, the title of which is given above.

Upon this report an order was passed in Council, June 16, 1758, confirming the eleven acts last-above named.

Chap. 1. "April 19, 1754. A Petition of the President & Fellows of Harvard Colledge setting forth the Inconveniencies of their Proceeding in the usual Forms of Law in selling such Real Estates as may fall into their Hands by Recoveries on Mortgages, or Executions on Debts, Praying that they may be impowered to sell such Estates after the Right of Redemption is expired & to give a good Deed of them.

In Council; Read & Ordered that the Prayer of the Petition be granted & that the President & Fellows of Harvard Colledge be & hereby are authorized & impowered (with the Advice & Consent of the Overseers of the said College) to sell such Real Estates as shall be recovered on Mortgage or taken on Execution for any Debt or Debts due to the said College after the Right of Redemption of such Estate shall be expired, & to give a Good & sufficient Deed or Deeds in Law for the same; And that the Petitioners have Liberty to bring in a Bill accordingly.

In the House of Representatives Read & Concur'd."—*Council Records, vol.* XX., *p.* 230.

Chap. 3. "June 15, 1754. In the House of Representatives Voted that James Allen & Joseph Richards Esq^rs^ with such as the Honble Board shall join, be a Com^tee^ to farm out the Excise on Tea, Coffee & China Ware for the County of Suffolk, In Council; Read & Concur'd; and John Erving Esqr is joined in the Affair;—Consented to by the Governour."

On the same day the following persons were chosen committees to farm out the excise for the respective counties hereafter named; viz.,—

Henry Gibbs and Joseph Gerrish, Esq^s^., on the part of the House, and Thomas Berry, Esq., on the part of the Council, for the county of Essex;—

William Brattle, Esq., and Mr. James Russell, on the part of the House, and Ezekiel Chever, Esq, on the part of the Council, for the county of Middlesex;—

Josiah Hawley, Esq., and Capt. Moses Marsh, on the part of the House, and Eleazer Porter, Esq., on the part of the Council, for the county of Hampshire;—

William Richardson, Esq., and Capt. Nathan Tyler, on the part of the House, and Joseph Wilder, Esq., on the part of the Council, for the county of Worcester;—

Thomas Foster and Gamaliel Bradford, Esq^s^., on the part of the House, and John Cushing, Esq., on the part of the Council, for the county of Plymouth;—

James Otis and David Crocker, Esq^s^., on the part of the House, and John Otis, Esq., on the part of the Council, for the county of Barnstable;—

Ephraim Leonard, Esq., and Mr. Israel Tisdale, on the part of the House, and George Leonard, Esq, on the part of the Council, for the county of Bristol;—

John Storer, Esq, and Mr. Samuel Hill, on the part of the House, and John Hill, Esq., on the part of the Council, for the county of York;—

Col. Mayhew, and Capt. Norton, on the part of the House, and John Sumner, Esq., on the part of the Council, for the county of Dukes county;—

Abishai Folger, Esq., and Mr. Richard Coffin, on the part of the House, and Josiah Coffin, Esq., on the part of the Council, for the county of Nantucket.—*Ibid., p.* 272.

"January 10, 1755. In the House of Representatives; Ordered that James Bowdoin Esqr, be of the Committee to farm out the Excise upon Tea &c^a^ in the County of Suffolk in the Room of Mr Allen deceased; In Council; Read & Concur'd;—Consented to by the Governour."—*Ibid., p.* 379.

"June 17, 1754. In the House of Representatives Voted that the Committees of the several Counties to farm out the Excise on Tea, Coffee & China Ware insert in the publick Prints, the Time & Place designed for that Purpose, and that the Commencement of the Rates for said Excise is on the first of July next, In Council Read & Concur'd;—Consented to by the Govr.—*Ibid., p.* 276.

"November 25, 1754. A Report presented by the Committee for letting out to farm the Excise upon Tea, Coffee &c^a^, in the County of Worcester, that they had duly put up the same, but no Person appeared to farm the said Excise; And praying Allowance for their Time & Expence therein amounting to the Sum of £2. 2. —. In the House of Representatives; Read & Ordered that the Sum of Two Pounds, two shillings be allowed & paid out of the publick Treasury to said Committee in full of their Accompt; In Council; Read & Concur'd;—Consented to by the Governour.

The Committee appointed to let to farm the Excise upon Tea, Coffee &c^a^, in ye County of York, reported that they had agreed for the same with Mr Foxwell Curtis Cutt for Seven Pounds ten shillings, and had taken his Bond for the same, and lodged it with the Province Treasurer, their Accompt of Time and Expence amounting to £2. 3. 8. In the House of Representatives, Read & Ordered that the Report be accepted, and that the said Committee be allowed the sum of Two Pounds, three shillings and eight pence in full of their Accompt, to be paid out of the publick Treasury. In Council, Read & Concur'd; Consented to by the Governour.

The Committee appointed to let out to farm the Excise on Tea &c[a] in the County of Hampshire, reported that they had agreed for the same with David Ingersol Esq[r]; for Six Pounds seven Shillings; and had taken his Bond for the same, & lodged it with the Province Treasurer, their Account of Time & Expence amounts to £— 14. 8. In the House of Representatives, Read & Ordered that the Report be accepted; & that the Committee be allowed the Sum of Fourteen Shillings & Eight pence, in full of their Accompt, and that the Same be paid out of the publick Treasury. In Council; Read & Concur'd;—Consented to by the Governour."—*Ibid., p.* 337.

The above reports from the Committees appointed to farm out the excise for Worcester, York and Hampshire counties, were followed by reports from the committees for the other counties, and the dates of these reports, together with the names of the farmers of excise appointed by them, respectively, are as follows:—

December 17, 1754. Essex county; to Peter Fry, for £35. 6*s.* 8*d.*—*Ibid., p.* 349.

February 22, 1755. Worcester county; to Mr. Nath[l] Green of Worcester, for £4. 1*s.*—*Ibid., p.* 415.

April 26, 1755. Middlesex county; to William Story of Boston, for £30.—*Ibid., p.* 443.

April 28, 1755. Suffolk County; to Elisha Jones of Weston, for £300 —*Ibid., p.* 448.

"August 13, 1755. In the House of Representatives; Voted that Jeremy Gridley & Samuel Miller Esq[rs] with such as the Hon[ble] Board shall join, be a Committee to farm out the Excise on Tea, Coffee & China Ware for the County of Suffolk. In Council; Read & Concur'd; And Samuel Watts Esq[r] is joined in the Affair. Consented to by the Lieuten[t] Governour."—*Ibid., p.* 516.

On the same day the following persons were chosen committees to farm out the excise for the respective counties hereafter named; viz.,—

John Leach and Daniel Epes jun[r], Esqs., on the part of the House, and Benjamin Lynde, Esq., on the part of the Council, for the county of Essex;—

William Lawrence, Esq., and Mr. James Russell, on the part of the House, and James Minot, Esq , on the part of the Council, for the county of Middlesex;—

Joseph Hawley, Esq., and Mr. Eldad Taylor, on the part of the House, and Eleazer Porter, Esq., on the part of the Council, for the county of Hampshire;—

Timothy Payne, Esq., and Mr. David Wilder, on the part of the House, and John Chandler, Esq., on the part of the Council, for the county of Worcester;—

Thomas Foster, Esq., and Mr. John Brewster, on the part of the House, and John Cushing, Esq., on the part of the Council, for the county of Plymouth;—

James Otis and Nath[l] Stone, Esqs., on the part of the House, and John Otis, Esq., on the part of the Council, for the county of Barnstable;—

Mr. Jonathan Barney and Mr. Tho[s]. Moorey,* on the part of the House, and George Leonard, Esq , on the part of the Council, for the county of Bristol;—

Mr. John Bradbury and Mr. Thomas Perkins, on the part of the House, and John Hill, Esq., on the part of the Council, for the county of York;—

Zaccheus Mayhew and John Sumner, Esqs., on the part of the House, and John Allen, Esq., on the part of the Council, for the county of Dukes county;—

Abishai Folger, Esq., and Capt John Roach, on the part of the House, and John Bunker, Esq., on the part of the Council, for the county of Nantucket.—*Ibid.*

"Nov[r] 4th, 1755. The Committee for letting out to farm the Excise on Tea, Coffee &c., for the County of Suffolk, reported that they had let out the same to William Whitwell of Boston, for Five hundred and five pounds, and have taken his Bond, with sureties, which they have lodged in the Treasury, praying to be allowed their charges —In the House of Representatives, Read, and Ordered that this report be accepted, and that there be allowed out of the Public Treasury the sum of Two Pounds fourteen shillings to the said Committee in full discharge of their Acc[t] annexed In Council; Read and Concurred. Consented to by the Lieu[t] Governor."—*Ibid , vol. XXI., p.* 26.

The above report from the committee appointed to farm out the excise for Suffolk county, was followed by reports from the committees for the other counties, and the dates of these reports, together with the names of farmers of excise appointed by them, respectively, are as follows:—

December 23, 1755. Middlesex county; to Mr. Ezekiel Price, for £30.—*Ibid., p.* 40.

January 28, 1756. York county; to Joseph Simpson, jun[r], for £10. 16*s.*—*Ibid., p.* 64.

February 18, 1756. Worcester county; to Col. Moses Marcy, for £4. 4*s.*—*Ibid., p.* 95.

March 2, 1756. Barnstable county; to Solomon Otis, Esq[r]., for £9. 13*s.* 4*d.*—*Ibid., p.* 113.

April 8, 1756. Plymouth county; to John Churchill of Plymouth, for £5. 17*s.* 4*d.*—*Ibid., p.* 149.

April 16, 1756. Essex county; to Capt. Peter Fry, for £32. 10*s.*—*Ibid , p.* 167.

June 1, 1756. Nantucket county; to Obed Hussey, for £11. 1*s.* 4*d.*—*Ibid., p.* 195.

Chap. 8. "April 23[d], 1755. In the House of Representatives; Whereas the Inhabitants of the Town of Beverly, being of Opinion, that the Destruction of their Sheep of late Years, was occasioned, more by Wolves than unruly Dogs, have made Application to this Court that the Operation of the Act pass'd in the last May Session relating to such Dogs might be suspended;——Therefore Voted that the respective Assessors of the Town of Beverly for the Years 1755 & 1756, be & hereby are required in making the Assessment of the said Years respectively to omit taxing any Person in Consequence of the aforesaid Act:

In Council; Read & Concur'd;——Consented to by the Lieu[t] Govern[r]"—*Ibid., vol. XX., p.* 436.

* Morey?

Chap. 9. "* * * I cann't but think, Gentlemen, that it would be a Point of Prudence & what highly deserves your Consideration, that the Number of Five hundred Men at first proposed for the before mentioned Service should be augmented to such an one as may secure it from being defeated. The Additional Expence that this would occasion to the Province will bear no Proportion to the Mischiefs that would ensue from such a Misfortune.

If the Result of your Deliberations, Gentlemen, should be agreable to my Sentiments upon this Emergency, as I hope they will, I must recommend it to you, Gentlemen of the House of Representatives, to lose no Time in making Provision for a suitable Augmentation of our Forces."—*From the Message of Gov. Shirley, to the Assembly, June* 4, 1754: *Council Records, vol.* XX., *p* 253.

"June 5th, 1754. In the House of Representatives June 4th 1754; The House having taken into Consideration His Excellency's Message of this Day to both Houses, respecting the Augmentation of the Forces ordered to attend his Excellency to the Eastern Parts of this Province, & to build a Fort on Kennebeck River &ca,

Voted that His Excellency the Captain General, be desired forthwith to give Orders for the enlistment of Three hundred Men including Officers, in Addition to the Five hundred Men already enlisted, That the Officers & Soldiers be under the same Restrictions & Limitations, have the same Bounty Money, Pay & Subsistence & to continue in the Service for the same Term of Time;——In Council Read & Concurd.

Consented to by the Governour."—*Vote of the Assembly: ibid.*

"June 6th, 1754. His Excellency sent the following Message to the House by the Secrety

Gentlemen of the House of Representatives

I think it necessary that a Quorum of his Majesty's Council should attend me to the Eastward; & I have Ordered suitable accomodation to be made for them, & also for several Gentlemen of your House, whose Company I have desired, & who have signified their readiness to go with me; and if there be any other Gentlemen of the House, who incline to accompany me, Upon its being signified to me I will give further Orders for their Accomodation likewise."—*Ibid*, *p*. 256.

See, also, note to 1753–54, chap. 40, *ante*.

Chap. 11. "Novr 5, 1754. In the House of Representatives, Whereas in the Tax Act made & passed in June last, the whole Pay of the Representatives from the Town of Groton, the Districts of Shirley & Pepperil was set upon said Groton, and also the whole Pay of the Representative of the Town of Northampton, and District of Southampton was set on Northampton only, whereas the said Districts by Law are obliged to pay the same Proportions of their respective Representatives Pay as the Sums of said Districts Province Tax, is to the Sum of the Tax set on said Towns, Therefore

Resolved & Ordered that the Province Treasurer immediately issue his Warrants again to the Assessors of the Towns of Groton & Northampton, and to all the above said Districts, Requiring the Assessors of said Shirley & Pepperil to assess on the respective Districts aforesaid, the respective & lawful Proportions of the Sum Total of their Representatives Pay for the last Year; and also the Assessors of Southampton to assess on said Southampton their lawful Proportion with Northampton of the Pay of their Representative for the last Year, and the Assessors of the said Towns of Groton & Northampton to assess their respective Towns in the respective Sums that shall remain, after the Proportions of their respective Districts that are joined with them are substracted, anything in the Warrants already issued by said Treasurer to the aforesaid Assessors, to the Contrary notwithstanding. The lawful Proportions of the Pay of the Representative of said Groton, & the said Districts joined with it, for the last Year are as follows, vizt

Total £23. 0. 0.	Groton, ...	£15. 15. 3. 3
	Shirley, ...	2.* 3. 11.
	Pepperil, ...	3. 0. 9. 1

The lawful Parts and Proportions of the Pay of the Representative of Northampton & Southampton for the last Year is as follows; vizt

Total £31. 4. 0.	Northampton, ...	£25. 19. 2. 2
	Southampton, ...	5. 4. 9. 2

To which Rates & Proportions said Treasurer is required to conform his Warrants accordingly;—In Council Read & Concur'd:—Consented to by the Governr."—*Ibid.*, *p*. 308.

"November 14, 1754. In the House of Representatives, It appearing by a Certificate from the Province Treasurer, that the Town of Beverly are overcharged in the last Tax Act for their Representatives pay, the Sum of Two Pounds six shillings & nine pence, Ordered that the said Sum be paid by the Province Treasurer to the Treasurer of the Town of Beverly. In Council Read & Concur'd."—*Ibid.*, *p*. 322.

Chap. 12. "This Act must be submitted to your Lordships how far the power of taking Estates Real and Personal under the restrictions therein mentioned for the use of the Episcopal Churches and of the other Congregations in this Colony is proper."—*Report of Sir M. Lamb: "Mass. Bay, B. T.," vol.* 75, *I. i.*, 3., *in Public Record Office.*

Chap. 13. "April 10, 1754. On the Petitions of William Ayers &ca, Jedadiah Foster &ca, & Josiah Converse &ca In Council; Voted that John Cushing & John Quincy Esqrs with such as the Honble House shall join be a Committee to take under Consideration the several Petitions of William Ayers, & others, Josiah Converse & others, and Jedediah Foster & others, hear the Parties & report what they judge proper for this Court to do thereon;—In the House of Representatives Read & Concur'd & Collo Winslow, Collo Otis & Mr Haywood are joined in the Affair."—*Council Records, vol.* XX., *p*. 211.

* *Sic.*

"The Committee to whom was referr'd the Petitions of the first & second Precincts in Brookfield, & the Petition of Josiah Converse & others, Having heard the Parties & Considered thereon are of Opinion that it is necessary a Committee, should go to Brookfield, and view the Situation & Circumstances of the Petitioners & make Report to this Court at their next Session, what said Court ought to do thereon, and that all Proceedings relating to building a new Meeting House in said first Precinct be stayed in the mean time, all which is humbly submitted. per JOHN CUSHING per order.

In Council Read & Accepted & Ordered that Samuel Watts Esq[r] with such as the Hon[ble] House shall join, be a Committee to repair to the Town of Brookfield, & view the Situation & Circumstances of the Petit[rs] & report at their next Session, what they judge proper for this Court to do thereon; the Charge thereof to be born as this Court shall Order, In the House of Representatives Read & Concur'd; and Capt Livermore & M[r] Phineas Haywood are joined in the Affair, Consented to by the Governour."—*Ibid*, *p.* 214.

November 1, 1754. The Committee on the Petitions of the first & second Precincts of Brookfield, and on the Petition of Josiah Converse &c[a], appointed the tenth of April last, have repaired to the Town of Brookfield, and viewed the Situation thereof, heard the Parties, and considered the same: And upon the whole are humbly of Opinion, that the Bounds of the second Precinct be as follows; viz[t] beginning at the North East Corner of George Harringtons Lands upon Spencer Line, & runing Westerly by his Lands set off to Spencer, to a Place called Five Mile River Bridge; from thence Westerly including Thomas Stetsons Land, Capt Nathaniel Wolcots Land, Thomas Moors, Ebenezer Jennings, Obadiah Rice, William Parks, Josiah Converse, Francis Dodge, Paul Deland, the Heirs of John Green dec[d], Stephen Green, & Joseph Ranger Jun[r] with their Lands; And from the said Rangers South West Corner to the South West Corner of William Ayres Meadow, on Coys Brook, so called, near the old School House, thence Northerly (exclusive of John Tufts Land) including John Hill and Jeremiah Woodburys Land, to Abner Taylours Land, and thence (excluding Jacob Abbot, Joshua Dodge and Joshua Dodge jun[r] and their Lands,) to the Center Line of said Town; then, by said Center Line, Northerly to New Braintree District, with the Lands and Interests in the North east Part of the Town, contained within the Bounds not already incorporated in the second Parish in the said Town of Brookfield; And that then the Remainder of said Town be divided into Two Precincts by the following Bounds, viz[t] begining at the South East Corner of Paul Delands Lands, to the Country Road including John Riches Land; thence by the Town Road including Ephraim Bartlets Land to the River, thence Westerly down the River to the Mouth of Salmon Brook, thence a streight Line to a large white Oak Tree, in the North East Corner of a Tract of Land, called the Mile square, said Tree being a Boundary between Brookfield & Western, and that the West Part of the aforesaid Division be called the first Precinct in said Town; and that the said West Division and also the second Parish in said Town be exempted from paying any Charges that have already arisen or may hereafter arise by Reason of the building the New Meeting House, And that the old Meeting House which has been taken down be equally divided between the proposed three Precincts; And also that the Ministerial Revenue belonging to the said Town of Brookfield be equally divided between the three Precincts,——Which is humbly submitted to the Hon[ble] Court,——SAM[L] WATTS per Ord[r]

In Council, Read & Accepted; & Ordered that a Bill be brought in for the Purposes before mentioned; and that the Charge of the Committee in their within mentioned Service, be born by the whole Town of Brookfield.

In the House of Representatives, Read & Unanimously Concur'd."—*Ibid.*, *p.* 304.

Chap. 14. "April 9, 1754. A Petition of William Alton & thirty seven others, Inhabitants of the West Part of Oxford, setting forth their great Distance from the Body of the Town & the Inconveniences attending, praying that they may be set off with their Families & Estates, & erected into a seperate Town or District: In the House of Representatives Read & Ordered that the Pet[rs] serve the Clerk of the Town of Oxford with a Copy of this Petition, that they shew Cause if any they have on the second Thursday of the next May Session, why the Prayer thereof should not be granted: In Council Read & Concur'd."—*Ibid.*, *p.* 206.

"November 8, 1754. The Committee to whom was referr'd the Petition of William Alton and other Inhabitants of the Town of Oxford, having heard the Parties and considered the Petition with the Circumstances of the Town of Oxford, are humbly of Opinion That the Prayer of the Petition be so far granted, as that the Petitioners with their Lands, & others adjoining, be erected into a seperate District by the following Bounds, viz[t] begining at the South Line of Oxford, one Mile West of the Village Line so called; thence, Northerly paralel with said Village to Leicester South Bounds, thence Westerly with Liecester & Spencer South bounds, untill it come within one Mile and a quarter of Sturbridge East bounds, thence runing one Mile and a quarter westwardly to Oxford North West Corner; thence Southerly with Oxford Southwardly Bounds to Dudley North West Corner, thence with Oxford Southwardly Bounds to where it first began; All which is humbly submitted JOHN GREENLEAF.

In Council; Read & Accepted; and the Petitioners are allowed to bring in a Bill accordingly;——In the House of Representatives Read & Concur'd."—*Ibid.*, *pp.* 315, 316.

Chap. 15. The Governor and Council having granted to Mary Clapham of Boston, a divorce from bed and board against her husband, William Clapham, for adultery on his part, she filed her petition to the General Court, December 4, 1754, for a divorce from the bonds of matrimony, asking also for alimony. This petition was referred, and a bill reported, thereupon, which passed to be enacted in both branches, but failed to receive the Governor's signature.

A new bill was then introduced, which was enacted under the title given in the beginning of these notes. The new bill made no provision for alimony,—the Assembly apparently having concluded that this matter was within the exclusive province of the

Governor and Council. But as the Governor and Council were not expressly empowered to enforce their decrees in matters of this nature, this chapter was enacted to meet the case. It was signed by the Governor, January 10, 1755, and, on the 26th of February, the following decree was passed by the Governor and Council:—

"26th of February 1755. Whereas by an Act of this Province Mary Clapham, late Wife of William Clapham of Boston, Gentleman, has been divorced from her said Husband, & their Marriage declared to be dissolved; and the said Mary having made her humble Application to this Board that a reasonable Allowance may be made her out of the Personal Estate of said William for her Maintenance & Support; & having set forth that she is now possessed of Household Furniture & other Personal Estate of the said William to the amount of about One hundred Pounds Lawful Money:

It is therefore Ordered that the said Household Furniture & other Personal Estate of the said William Clapham now in the Hands of the said Mary not exceeding the Value of One hundred Pounds, be & hereby is assigned to the said Mary, as her own seperate Estate by her to be used & disposed of as she shall think fit, and the said William Clapham & all others concerned are to take Notice of this Order & govern themselves accordingly."—*Executive Records of the Council, vol.* 2, *p.* 386.

"This Act must be submitted to your Lordships how far it may be fit to give power of imprisonment without Bail for not complying with the Decrees and Orders of the Governor and Council concerning Marriage and Divorce. The former Act which is recited in this only giving power to the Governor and Council to hear and determine such controversies." —*Report of Sir M. Lamb: "Mass. Bay, B. T.," vol.* 75, *I. i.*, 3, *in Public Record Office.*

Chap. 16. "June 7th 1754. A Bill intitled an Act for granting unto his Majesty an Excise upon Wines, & Spirits distilled Sold by Retail, & upon Limes, Lemons & Oranges, Having been read three times in the House of Representatives, & there passed to be Engrossed;—In Council Read a first Time."—*Council Records, vol. XX., p.* 257.

"June 8th 1754. In Council Read a second time & Non Concur'd."—*Ibid., p.* 259.

"June 11th 1754. A New Draught of a Bill for granting unto his Majesty an Excise upon Wines & Spirits distilled, sold by Retail &ca, being brought up from the House:—In Council Read a first & second time & passed a Concurrence to be engrossed."—*Ibid., p.* 262.

"June 14, 1754. * * being passed to be enacted in the House of Representves; and brought up in Council; Read and after Debate had thereon, the Question was put Whether the Board pass the said Bill to be enacted? And It was Resolved in the Negative."—*Ibid., p.* 271.

"June 15, 1754. The following Message was brought up from the House of Representatives to the Council by Colo William Brattle Esqr & others vizt,

May it please your Honours,—This House hath a most gratefull Sense of the paternal Care of His Excellency, discovered in his last Message to this House, that we might not rise with an Empty Treasury; The House is fully sensible of the Inconveniences that may arise therefrom but at the same time are quite conscious to themselves, that they have done every thing on their part Consistent with the publick Good; to prevent it.

The House, to prevent Poles & Estates being over burthened, projected & passed to be enacted a Salutary Excise Bill, whereby all that consumed Spirituous Liquors, the Rich as well as the Poor, those that consumed them for Luxury, as well as those who consumed the same for Necessity, might pay as Excise therefor, sent the said Bill to the Honble Board for Concurrence; which by the Honble Board was non Concur'd;—The House desirous to preserve an Harmony with the Honble Board, prepared another, altering the same materialy in many Points, apprehending the Honble Board was not against the Spirit of the Bill, as aforesaid, sent it up to the Honble Board, which was by them passed to be Engrossed; but to our great Surprize was not passed by the Honble Board to be enacted, by means whereof the Treasury is in danger of remaining empty, unless the honble Board is pleased to reconsider said Vote and pass said Bill to be enacted, which if done will be an additional Security to those Persons unto whom said Excise is mortgaged as a Collateral Security:—Wherefore the House desires the honble Board would reconsider said Vote of Non Concurrence, and if they please, to pass the same to be enacted.

In Council; The foregoing Message being read & considered. A Motion was made & seconded that the Board would reconsider their Vote for not passing to be enacted the Engrossed Bill, intitled an Act for granting unto his Majesty an Excise upon Wine & Spirits distil'd, sold by Retail & upon Limes, Lemmons & Oranges; And The said Bill was thereupon Voted to be reconsidered, and upon further Debate had thereon, the said Bill was passed to be enacted."—*Ibid., p.* 273.

"June 17, 1754. The Secretary went down on a Message from His Excellency, to direct the House of Representatives to attend him in the Council Chamber,

Mr Speaker and the House being accordingly come up, His Excellency made the following Speech to both Houses: vizt,

Gentlemen of the Council & House of Representatives,

The Secretary hath laid before me your Engrossed Bill, entitled 'An Act for granting unto his Majesty an Excise upon Wines & Spirits distilled, sold by Retail or consumed within this Province, & upon Limes Lemmons & Oranges.' And I find that one of the principal Reasons given in the Message sent up by the House of Representatives to his Majestys Council on Saturday last for passing it, was to prevent the Polls & Estates of his Majesty's Subjects within this Province, being over burthened,

I have already, Gentlemen, in the Course of this Session, given you such an Instance of my real desire to lighten the Tax upon the Polls & Estates of your Constituents by signing my Consent to the Act for extending the Duty of Impost to all Goods imported from Great Britain, (those only of the Produce or Manufacture of it excepted), whereby the Revenue arising from that Branch of Customes to the Province will now probably be greatly augmented, beyond what it hath been during these thirty years past, that I think you can't doubt of my ready Disposition to concur with you, in any proper Measures for further Easing the Subjects in those Taxes.

But I should ill discharge the Trust reposed in me by his Majesty if for the Sake of Lightning them, I should join in imposing a Burthen upon the People, which would be inconsistent with the natural Rights of every Family in the Community: And such an one I doubt it will appear in the Eyes of your Constituents, to be subjected to keep and render an Account of the Quantity of the Excisable Liquors which they shall consume in their private Houses, to Collectors and their Deputies, and that too upon Oath if required by those Officers, or else to pay a Mulct upon their Refusal to do it,

This Method of raising Money is certainly not only of an extraordinary Kind, but altogether unprecedented in the English Governmt and if a Judgment may be formed of the general Reception which a Law of that nature would meet with throughout this Province, from the Dissatisfaction & Murmering which the News of its being passed by the two Houses, seems already to have raised in several parts of it, It will be so far from producing the salutary Effects, which I am fully persuaded every Gentleman who has voted for it, proposes to his Country, by its being passed into a Law, that it is justly to be apprehended a general Discontent thro' the Province, and Dissatisfaction to his Majestys Government would be the Fruits of it, at the same time that the publick would reap but a very inconsiderable Part of the Advantage proposed by it, according to the Method of Collecting the Tax, which is provided in the Bill,

I must further observe to you, Gentlemen, that this Method of raising Taxes is contrary to the true Policy of Government in every Respect; That requires that the People should pay their Taxes in the most imperceptible Manner, and not in such an one as would have a Tendency daily to remind them of their Burthen, tho' never so necessary; much less when it is imposed in a Manner which may be conceived by them to be grievous & unconstitutional.

I can't avoid remarking to you, Gentlemen of the House of Representatives, that the Circumstances of your tacking this unprecedented Tax to your ordinary Excise, at a time when the Excise of this Year is mortgaged, for securing the Payment of part of the last Years publick Debt, and intimating in your Message to His Majesty's Council, that unless they would concur with you in passing the Bill now under Consideration, the Treasury would be in danger of remaining unsupplied, hath a direct Tendency to weaken the Credit of the Government, tho' I am fully persuaded at the same time; and I hope that it is the universal Sense of the People that the Present Members of this House are uncapable of violating the publick Faith, in any Article or Degree whatsoever;

The Informality of passing this Bill to be Enacted, at the Council Board, is another Circumstance Gentlemen, which I can't omit mentioning, It appears by the Bill that on Thursday last it was passed by the House of Representves to be enacted, and by Records of the Council that on Fryday following, It was Non Concur'd by the Board; that on the same day in the Afternoon in Answer to a Message from the House to the Council, desiring to know whether the Board had acted upon the Bill, they let the House know they had Non Concur'd it; On the Saturday following it appears by the Message of the House to the Board, that they moved the Board to reconsider their Vote of Non Concurrence, upon which the Board almost Instanter, proceeded to reconsider it, (four of their Members which had been present at and given their Votes in the Debate, when the Board Non Concur'd the Vote of the House for passing the Bill to be enacted, being absent, and a smaller Number by four present, than what had voted the Day preceeding, when the Bill was rejected); and the Council then without furthur Formality concur'd the Vote of the House for passing the Bill to be enacted,

Some very important Affairs of the Province, which will not admit of Delay, will not allow me to enter into a thorough Consideration, whether under these before mentioned Circumstances of the Boards Re-consideration of the Vote whereby they rejected this Bill upon the third Reading, & their subsequent Vote of Concurrence for passing it to be Enacted, were not absolute Nulities, That this Proceeding was at least irregular & unparliamentary & of Dangerous Consequence to the publick Service seems to me most evident,

Upon the whole Gentlemen I think the least you can do in Justice to your Constituents, upon this Occasion, will be to pursue the Method frequently used by the General Assembly in Cases of the like Nature, by ordering the Bill to be printed, that your Constituents may be fully acquainted with the Contents of it during the Recess of the Court, and yourselves informed of the General Sentiments of the Country, concerning a Matter of this Importance & Difficulty, which so nearly touches the natural Right of every individual Member in his private Family.

In the mean time, I will preserve the Bill in the same State which it is now in, by making an Adjournment, instead of a Prorogation untill its next Meeting; And if at that time I shall find that you continue of the same Opinion, after having informed yourselves fully of the Sentiments of your Constituents upon this Bill, I shall think myself more at Liberty to pass it, and I shall have all due Regard to the general Voice of the People in a Matter which purely concerns their own just Rights.

In this Case, to save the Excise, which would grow due upon the excised Spirits & Liquors after the ninth day of July untill the time of the next Meeting of the Court, from being lost upon the Expiration of the Excise Act, now in force, It seems to me that you may project a short Bill which may effectually answer that Purpose, without prejudicing your Engrossed Bill now under Consideration."—*Ibid., p.* 274.

"On a Motion made and seconded, Ordered, That the several Members of this House be directed to lay before the Select-Men of their respective Towns, that part of the Excise-Bill which relates to the private Consumption of Wines and Spirits distill'd, and acquaint them it is the Desire of this House that they call their several Towns together, that this House may know the Minds of their Constituents with Regard to said Bill, on the Adjournment of this Court; Also

Ordered, That the Printer for this House be directed to send a Number of Gazettes of this Day, containing His Excellency's Speech of Yesterday, that so the several Members may lay the same before the Select-Men of their respective Towns, together with the Excise-Bill, to be communicated to them."—*Journal of the House of Representatives, June* 18, 1754, *p.* 48.

"November 12, 1754. A Bill, intitled, an Act for granting unto his Majesty an Excise upon Rum, Brandy, and other Spirits distilled within this Province, & also an Additional Impost upon Wine, Rum & other distilled Spirits, brought into this Government, together with an Excise upon Wine & Spirits distilled and sold by Retail within this Province, and upon Limes Lemmons & Oranges; Having been read three times in the House of Representatives & there passed to be Engrossed;——In Council Read a first time and committed."—*Ibid., p.* 319.

"Nov[r] 20, 1754. In Council; Read a second time, and after a long Debate, committed." —*Ibid., p.* 331.

"November 21, 1754. In Council; Read a third Time and Non Concur'd.

"A Message was sent up to the House of Representatives by John Choat Esq[r] & others, to desire the Council to reconsider their Vote of Non Concurrence on the Bill, for granting unto his Majesty an Excise upon Wine, Rum &c[a] inasmuch as the House apprehends the Method therein provided to be most salutary for the Province, & that they would give it Dispatch, that so the Court may have a Recess as soon as may be;

And after the Gentlemen were withdrawn, the Question was put whether the Board would reconsider the said Vote? And it pass'd in the Negative:

And thereupon, Samuel Danforth, Samuel Watts, Andrew Oliver, Thomas Hutchinson and Stephen Sewall Esq[rs] were appointed a Committee to prepare a Message to the House of Representatives, for Assigning the Reasons of the Boards Non Concurrence on the Excise Bill."—*Ibid., p.* 332.

"November 22, 1754. The Committee appointed to prepare the Draught of a Message to the House of Representatives, referring to the Excise Bill; reported the same, Which was Accepted, And is as follows; Viz[t],

Ordered, that the following Message be sent down to the Hon[ble] House of Repres[ves] viz[t]:

The Bill for granting an Excise on Rum, Brandy &c[a]; appears to the Board to contain many new Matters, and of an extraordinary Nature, to be unnecessarily burthensome to a Considerable Number of His Majesty's Subjects, and to have a Tendency to discourage the Trade and Manufactures of the Province,

The Board have no Exception to the general Design of the Bill in subjecting all the Liquors that shall be expended in the Province to an equal Duty, Nor to the Changing the Manner of raising the Duty by laying it on the Manufacturer, & Importer instead of the Retailer; but they are apprehensive that if the Duty on the Stills be farmed; the Province is in danger of losing a great Part of its Revenue, There having never any Trial of it been made, the Amount of it must be very uncertain; A Farmer may put many Thousand Pounds in his Pocket, and no Person but himself make no Judgment of it, And this for a Number of Years together, if the Government should pursue this Method, and there is not the same Exception to Collectors in the Way of raising the Duty, as when it is raised from Retailers &c[a], the Distillers being all known, and the Nature of the Business such as it cannot be carried on in Secret; and their Oath faithfully to account will be as obligatory, & have the same Tendency to exact the full Duty from them, when it is paid to a Collector as when it is paid to a Farmer, And althô it may be urged that the Governments Collectors would not be so active in detecting any fraudulent Importation of Liquors into the Province, as a Farmer would be, yet it appears to the Board that if the Excise on Retailers and other Licenced Persons was farmed, and such licenced Persons were obliged to render an Account upon Oath, Whether they imported the Liquors themselves; and if not, from whom they purchased them, and the Retailers be Importers, or otherwise, such Persons of whom they purchased should be obliged when required, to make it appear that the Liquors by them sold, had paid the Duty of Excise due from the Distiller, or Impost due from the Importer, this would in a great Measure prevent any illicit Importation.

The requiring Bond from the Distillers may be a very great Burthen to some of them, and the Board are of Opinion that if their Stills and Utensils were made liable to the Payment of the Duty, in Case of Failure in the Distiller, it would be a less Burthen on them, as effectual for the Security of the Government, and more agreable to the Provision made by Acts of Parliament in Cases of the like Nature,

The Board are also of Opinion, that it would be a further unnecessary Burthen on the Distillers to make them liable to the Duty on Rum exported, where a Certificate is not returned or other Proof made in a limitted Time, of its having been landed or sold out of the Province; And they are further of Opinion That the Oath of the Exporter, that such is actually exported and not intended to be relanded; & if he afterwards knows or suspects its being relanded he will discover it, may be as effectual and less burthensome; It seems likewise an extream Hardship to oblige the Distiller to pay the duty on all the Rum they may have by them, at the Commencement of the Act, but also what shall be left unsold at the Expiration of it; w[ch] must cause them either to put a Stop to their Business for some time before, or expose them to a certain Loss.

The Board are of Opinion that the farming the Impost, and giving the Farmer such power over the Properties and natural Rights of the Subject, as are given by this Act, especially where any Person, (of how bad a Character soever) if he be the highest Bidder, may be the Farmer, is without President in any Part of his Majesty's Dominions, & may prove very oppressive to the Subjects where the Officers of the Government are employed to collect this part of the Revenue, the Board have no Exception to the farming of it, or if it should be thought necessary to give the Powers of Collection to a Farmer; yet some further Provision should be made with Respect to the Qualifications of such Farmers, than meerly his being the highest Bidder, as the Wisdom of the Government at Home has always thought necessary."—*Ibid., p.* 333.

"November 22, 1754. The following Message to the Council from the House of Represent^ves by Samuel Welles Esqr and others; was brought up—vizt,

May it please your Honours;—The House of Representatives apprehend themselves bound in faithfulness to his Majesty's dutiful & loyal Subjects the People of this Province, their Constituents, thus publickly to bear Testimony against the great Breach made, by the Honble Board this Morning, on our undoubted Right of granting Money, and determining on the Way and Manner of raising & levying the same on the People, without any Proposal, Conference or any other Method to hinder the Proceedings of the House in such an Affair, besides barely Non Concurring their Votes or Orders in such Case.

We are very sensible of the great Importance and Necessity of a good Understanding and Harmony between the two Houses, in the present Distress and difficult Circumstances of the Province; And had not we apprehended that our Silence on so apparent an Encroachment, might hereafter be improved as a Preccedent, we had not thought it so much a Duty to make this Declaration or Protestation, against the Conduct of the Honble Board "—*Ibid*, *p*. 335.

"December 17, 1754. The Bill entitled an Act for granting unto his Majesty an Excise upon Spirits distilled, & upon Wine, & Limes Lemons & Oranges In Council, Read a second Time & passed a Concurrence to be Engross'd."—*Ibid*., *p*. 349.

"December 19, 1754 * * * Having been Read three several Times in the House of Representatives & in Council, Passed to be Enacted by both Houses."—*Ibid*., *p*. 351.

"December 26, 1754. In the House of Representatives Voted that Capt Joseph Williams & Robert Spurr Esqr with such as the Honble Board shall join be a Com^tee to farm out the Excise on Spirituous Liquors for the County of Suffolk;—In Council Read & Concur'd; and Joseph Richards Esqr is joined in the Affair, Consented to by the Governour." —*Ibid*., *p*. 356.

On the same day the following persons were chosen committees to farm out the excise for the respective counties hereafter named; viz.,—

Col. Choate and Col. Hale, on the part of the House, and Benjamin Lynde, Esq., on the part of the Council, for the county of Essex;—

Col. Brattle and Mr. James Russell, on the part of the House, and Ezekiel Chever, Esq., on the part of the Council, for the county of Middlesex;—

Timothy Ruggles and Moses Marcy, Esqs, on the part of the House, and William Richardson, Esq., on the part of the Council, for the county of Worcester;—

Oliver Partridge and Josiah Dwight, Esqs., on the part of the House, and Eleazer Porter, Esq., on the part of the Council, for the county of Hampshire;—

Col. Clapp and Mr. Elisha Barrow, on the part of the House, and John Cushing, Esq., on the part of the Council, for the county of Plymouth;—

Capt. John Norton and Col. Zacheus Mayhew, on the part of the House, and Enoch Cushing, Esq, on the part of the Council, for the county of Dukes County;—

James Otis and David Crocker, Esqs., on the part of the House, and John Otis, Esq., on the part of the Council, for the county of Barnstable;—

John Storer, Esq., and Mr. John Bradbury, on the part of the House, and John Hill, Esq, on the part of the Council, for the county of York;—

Ephraim Leonard, Esq., and Mr. Israel Tisdale, on the part of the House, and George Leonard, on the part of the Council, for the county of Bristol:—

Capt. Obed Hussey and Capt. Jonathan Coffin, on the part of the House, and John Bunker, Esq., on the part of the Council, for the county of Nantucket—*Ibid*., *p*. 357.

February 13, 1755. Mr. Phineas Haywood was appointed for the County of Worcester in the room of Capt. Ruggles who desired to be excused—*Ibid*., *p*. 394.

"December 30, 1754. In the House of Representatives Voted that the Com^tees appointed to farm out the Excise on Spirituous Liquors in the several Counties, advertise the same in the publick Prints, one Month at least before the Sale, and also in such Parts of their respective Counties as they judge likely the Prints will not reach; And wherever the Committee suspect a Combination as to the Purchase of the Excise; that they be & hereby are impowered to contract and agree for the same otherwise than by a publick Vendue. In Council; Read & Concur'd;——Consented to by the Governour,

In the House of Representatives, Ordered that the Committees appointed by this Court to farm out the Excise upon Spirituous Liquors in the respective Counties, that are now at Court, meet & agree upon suitable Times for farming the same in the several Counties:— In Council Read & Concur'd;—Consented to by the Governour"—*Ibid*., *p*. 361.

"January 3, 1755. In the House of Representatives; Ordered that Judge Russell, Col^o Choat, & Col^o Brattle with such as the Honble Board shall join, be a Com^tee to prepare a Letter to Mr Agent Bollan, directing him to use his utmost Endeavour that the Act for granting an Excise upon Spirituous Liquors, and also several Acts passed this Session be not disallowed by his Majesty. In Council; Read & Concur'd; and Samuel Danforth and Sylvanus Bourn Esq^rs are joined in the Affair."—*Ibid*., *p*. 367.

"January 8, 1755. The Committees Report of a Letter to the Agent referring to the Excise Act. In Council; Read & Accepted with Amendments, In the House of Representatives, Read & Non Concur'd, & other Amendm^ts voted."—*Ibid*., *p*. 373.

"January 9, 1755. In Council; Ordered that John Cushing, Thomas Hutchinson & Stephen Sewall Esq^rs be a Committee on the Part of the Board, to confer with such Committee as shall be appointed by the Honble House of Representatives on the Matter in Difference between the two Houses respecting the Letter to Mr Agent Bollan, which relates to the Excise Act passed this Session.——In the House of Representatives; Read & Concur'd; And Col^o Choat, Col^o Hale & Judge Russell are joined in the Affair."—*Ibid*., *p*. 376.

"January 10, 1755. The Committee of the Council for Conferring with a Committee of the House on the Matters in Difference in the Letter reported to be sent to the Agent, reporting the Excise Act pass'd this Session, having reported to the Board:——The Council passed their Acceptance of the said Letter with a new Amendment. Which was agreed to by the House of Representatives."—*Ibid*., *p*. 379.

"January 11, 1755. A Message came up from the House of Representatives by Timothy Ruggles Esqr & others to his Excellency, That it was the earnest Desire of the House that he would use his Interest with the Crown that the Act passed this Session for granting to his Majesty an Excise upon Spirituous Liquors &ca may not be disallowed by his Majesty."—*Ibid., p.* 382.

"* * * and will not detain you longer than to acquaint you, Gentlemen of the House of Representatives, that I have complied with your Request to me, in writing to the Right Honble the Lords Commissioners for Trade and Plantations upon the Subject of the Excise Act."—*Gov. Shirley's speech to the Assembly, Feb. 7, 1755. Council Records, vol. XX., p.* 392.

See the Governor's letter at length, *post*, p. 826.

"Febry 22, 1755. The Committee for letting out to farm the Excise upon Spirituous Liquors &ca in the County of Worcester, report that they had let out the same to Major John Chandler of Worcester for £351. and taken Bond of him, with Sureties, & lodged the same in the Treasury; their Accompt of Charge amounting to three Pounds 4s 8d In the House of Representatives; Read & Ordered that this Report be accepted, and that the Sum of Three Pounds four shillings & eight pence be allowed & paid out of the publick Treasury to the said Committee in discharge of their Travel & Expences:——In Council; Read & Concur'd;—Consented to by the Governr."—*Ibid., p.* 415.

The above report from the committee appointed to farm out the excise for Worcester county was followed by reports from the committees of other counties, and the dates of their reports, together with the names of the farmers of excise appointed by them, respectively, are as follows:—

February 27, 1755. Suffolk county; to Elisha Jones, for £2420.—*Ibid., p.* 421.
April 26, 1755. Bristol county; to Capt. Joseph Joslyn of Hanover, for £168.—*Ibid., p.* 442.
April 26, 1755. Barnstable county; to Nathaniel Little, for £200.—*Ibid., p.* 443.
April 26, 1755. Middlesex county; to Elisha Jones of Weston, for £761, 16*s.* 8*d.*—*Ibid.*
April 28, 1755. Essex county; to Mr. William Coffin, for £1214, 13*s.* 4*d.*—*Ibid., p.* 448.
April 28, 1755. York county; to Capt. Ichabod Goodwin of Berwick, for £249.—*Ibid.*
June 5, 1755. Nantucket county; to Thomas Arthur, for £28.—*Ibid., p.* 463.
June 11, 1755. Plymouth county; to Mr. Seth Briant, for £320.—*Ibid., p.* 474.

"At A Meeting of the Freeholders and others Inhabitants of Glocester qualified for Voting on the Fourth day July Anno Domini 1754. * * * *

Whereas an Extract of a Bill that has passed in the Council and House of Representatives Entitled an Act for Granting his Majesty an Excise upon Wines and Spirits distilled sold by Retail or consumed within this Province and upon Limes Lemmons and Oranges has been this Day laid before the Town Meeting (Whereof mention was made in the Warning tho' not in the Warrant for calling this Meeting) One Paragraph of Which Bill Obliges every Person expending any Rum Wine or distilled Spirits to give in upon Oath to the Collector of the Excise or his Deputy if required an exact Account of all Wine Rum or distilled Spirits consumed in his or her House Family Apartment or Business within Twelve Months from the ninth Day of July instant, together with his Excellency the Governour's Speech thereon importing (among other Things) That the said Paragraph is inconsistent the naturall Rights of every private Family; published in the Gazett of June the Eighteenth last, agreeable to a Vote in the House of Representatives June 14

Voted that the said Part or Paragraph of the said Bill is highly disagreeable to the Inhabitants of the said Town and very greivous as being inconsistent with the naturall Rights of Mankind and much more with the Liberties of Englishmen and that Mr William Stevens their Representative be directed to act in That Capacity in Conformity to these Sentiments.

Voted That Daniel Witham Esqr Daniel Gibbs Esqr Mr Edward Paine Mr Timothy Rogers Epes Sargent junr Esqr Mr Philemon Warner & mr Thomas Sanders junr be a Committee to give The Thanks of the Town to his Excellency the Governour for his Care and Concern for their Rights and Liberty as expressed in his Speech of the 17th of June last and in his refusing to Sign the said Bill."—*Gloucester town-records, vol.* 3, *pp.* 15 *and* 16.

"At a Meeting of the Freeholders and other Inhabitants of Glocester held on the fourteenth Day of January Anno Domini 1755

Capt Isaac Eveleth Moderator * * * *

The Meeting proceeded to consider the Petition relating to late Act laying an Excise upon Strong Liquors

Voted nemine contradicente That The said Act is as greivous as when laid before the Town as a Bill by Order of the honourable House of Representatives and the more greivous inasmuch as What was then Voted by this Town appears not to have been received or any Way taken Notice of by the said House ·

Voted to joyn with such other Towns as shall appear against the said Act and petition his Majesty to have the said Act disallowed.

Voted that Daniel Witham Esqr Mr William Parsons and Mr Edward Pain be a Committee to draw up something relating to the said Act to be laid before the Town at the Adjournment of this Meeting"—*Ibid., p.* 18.

"At A meeting of the Freeholders and other Inhabitants of Glocester by Adjournment on the 21st of January Anno Dom 1755. * * * *

Voted unanimously This Town will Joyn with Boston Newbury Marblehead and such other Towns as think themselves aggreived by the late Excise Act in making Application at Home in Order to prevent said Acts obtaining the royall Assent and that an Agent be chosen by the Town to appear in their Behalf at Home in Order to prevent said Act's obtaining the Royal Assent

Voted unanimously That Christopher Kilby of London Esqr be and is hereby appointed Agent for the Town and is hereby authorized and empowered to appear in Behalf the

Town and to use his utmost Endeav[our] to prevent said Act's obtaining the Royal Assent

Voted that Daniel Witham Esqr Mr William Parsons & m^r Edward Payne be a Committee to forward a letter to [Mr ?] Agent Kilby representing the Greivances the Town labours under by Reason of Said Act and to transmit said Agent such Papers as they shall Judge necessary in the Case

Voted that a Letter read at this Meeting (which is upon File) be accepted as the Sentiments of the Town containing the Exceptions taken against the said Excise Act and forwarded by the aforesaid Comittee to Mr Agent Kilby."—*Ibid., p.* 19.

"August 7th 1754. At a Meeting of the Freeholders and other Inhabitants of the Town of Boston, legally qualified and warned in Publick Town Meeting Assembled at Faneuil Hall on Tuesday the 7th day of August A. D. 1754.

* * * * *

That Article in the Warrant, vizt 'To know the minds of the Inhabitants with regard to a Bill now depending in the General Court laying an Excise on the private Consumption of Wines and Spirits distill'd,' was taken into Consideration and the Abstract of said Bill, and Governour Shirleys Speech relating to it, being read a long Debate thereon was had, and It was unanimously Voted

1st That it is the sense of the Town that, that part of the Excise Bill contain'd in the Abstract now read, is contrary to those principles upon which our happy Constitution is founded, as well as destructive of those priviledges which it Warrants and Defends, that it is Vexatious and Oppressive and tends to Weaken the just Authority of an Oath, and to prejudice the Morals of the Community.

2^ly Voted unanimously that Thanks be returned to His Excellency the Governour, for his Paternal Goodness and Wise Conduct in relation to said Bill, & that his Excellency be requested still to continue his Care for Us in this respect.

3^ly. Voted unanimously that the Thanks of the Town be and hereby is given to the Gentlemen the Representatives of the Town, for the strenuous Opposition they made to said Bill, and that they be desired still to Use their utmost Endeavours to prevent said Bills being pass'd into a Law."—*Boston town-records, vol.* 4, *p.* 352.

"Septr 17th, 1754. * * * *

Your Excellency's late seasonable Interposition in favour of the Natural Rights of Englishmen, so greatly, tho' We trust not wilfully, affected by the late Excise Bill, affords us the most convincing proofs of the Rectitude of your Excellency's Sentiments and the Affection of your Patriot heart for that Constitution, which sweetens, improves and Exalts every other blessing of Life.

We cannot feel the decay of Our Commerce, and the many Burdens which this Town labour under, without the most Melancholly Impressions, but these admit of some Alleviations from your Excellency's wise and vigorous Endeavours to preserve Our dearer Liberties neither is it in our power to relish that Relief with regard to the former which must necessarily grow out of those Methods which tend to destroy the Latter.

We would hope that the Honourable Court may upon mature Consideration find reason to alter their Judgment respecting this affair, which if they should renew and insist upon, We humbly apprehend will be attended with the most Mischievous Consequences, unless your Excellency should finally refuse your Sanction to it.

The Noble Pattern your Excellency has in this Affair held up to our View, highten'd by your Situation in Government and Augmented by your Connection with the Prerogative Convinces us of the tender regard you have for the Liberties of this People, and will not we hope be ever forgotten,

And as this particular Instance of your Excellency's Goodness added to our past Experience of your known Abilities has increas'd Our Confidence in your Administration, it shall be our Study to Afford your Excellency all those Demonstrations of Duty and Affection, which Truth and Justice require, and your Excellency's wise & good Conduct will, we doubt not Secure and perpetuate."—*Portion of address of thanks to the Governor from Town of Boston: Boston town-records, vol.* 4, *p.* 355.

"Gentlemen.

I Thank you for this Address; The sense which you there Express of my Attention to His Majesty's Service, and the preservation of the rights and liberties of his People within this Government, give me a solid Satisfaction nor can I pass over in Silence your late Vote for placing my Picture in Faneuil Hall, with which your Selectmen acquainted me, without Acknowledging the pleasure, I feel from that publick mark of your respect for me.

Whenever it may be in my power to contribute towards reviving the decay'd Trade, and easing the Burthens of this Town, which you mention in your Address, I shall gladly Embrace the Opportunity, and you may be assur'd that my Duty to the King, and the Welfare of his good People within this Province, shall ever be the Rule of my Administration. W. SHIRLEY.

Province House Septr 19th 1754."—*Governor's letter to the Town: ibid., p.* 357.

"January 3^d, 1755. At a Meeting of the Freeholders & other Inhabitants of the Town of Boston legally qualified and warned in Publick Town Meeting Assembled, at Faneuil Hall, on Friday the third day of January A. D. 1755.——

* * * *

The Petition of a great Number of Inhabitants for calling this Meeting was read.

The Act of the Province lately pass'd Entitled An Act for granting unto his Majesty an Excise upon Spirits distill'd and Wines; and upon Limes Lemmons and Oranges—was read.

The Town proceeded to take into Consideration the Article in the Warrant for calling this Meeting, Viz^t 'To Consider and Determine what may be proper for the Town to do, in relation to An Act lately pass'd the General Court, Entitled An Act for granting unto his Majesty an Excise upon Spirits distill'd, and Wines, and upon Limes, Lemmons & Oranges.' and after some debate thereon, It was unanimously

Voted that the Town will make Application at Home in order to prevent said Acts obtaining the Royal Assent.

And then It was Voted that an Agent be chose by the Town to appear in their behalf at Home in order to prevent said Acts obtaining the Royal Assent.

Voted unanimously, that Christopher Kilby of London Esqr be and hereby is appointed Agent for the Town, and he is hereby fully Authorized and Impowered to appear on behalf of the Town, and to use his utmost Endeavours to prevent said Acts obtaining the Royal Assent—

Also Voted unanimously that the said Christopher Kilby Esqr be and hereby is appointed Agent for the Town in any other Matters and Affairs that the Town are concerned in or may hereafter have depending in London, said Agent to Conduct himself according to such directions and Instructions as he may from time to time receive from the Town relating to said Affairs.—

Voted that John Phillips Esqr the Moderator of this Meeting, the Gentlemen the Selectmen, Charles Apthorp Richard Dana and Thomas Greene Esq^{rs} Mr William Cooper Mr Royall Tyler and Mr Isaac Walker be and hereby are appointed a Committee forthwith to forward the Letter now read to Mr Agent Kilby, and to make such further Additions thereto as they may judge proper.

Also Voted that said Committee transmit to the Agent, Governour Shirleys Speech made by him the 17th of June last, relating to said Act, and such other papers as they shall judge requisite—*Ibid*, *vol.* 4, *p* 359.

"At a Meeting of ye Inhabitants of ye Town of Salem lawfully qualified to Vote Sepr 9th AD. 1754—

Voted Coll^o Ichabod Plaisted Moderator of this Meeting

That part of the Excise-Bill which relates to ye private consumption of Wines & Distill'd Spirits being laid before the Town together with His Excellency's Speach respecting ye same, agreable to the order of the Honble The House of Representatives of ye 18th of June last and ye same having been duly consider'd. Voted unanimously That it is the Mind of this Town That the Enacting said Bill would be inconsistent with the natural Rights & Liberties as well as the peace & welfare of ye Inhabitants of this Province." —*Salem town-records: minutes*, 1743–1775.

"At a Full meeting of the qualified Inhabitants of this Town Legally Conven'd the Sixteenth day of Septem^r 1754, According to Notification,

Voted, John Tasker Esqr Moderator.

The Bill relating to the Excise on the privat Consumption of Spiritious Liquors together with His Excellencys Speech to both Houses of Assembly in their late Sitting respecting thereto being read.

After Mature deliberation, the question was put whither they Apprehended it for the Publick Good, that Said Bill should pass into an Act. It pass'd in the Negative Unanimously.

And Voted, that the Representative of this Town be and hereby is desired and directed to Use all proper means to prevent the Same."—*Marblehead town-records*, 1721–1764, *p*. 390.

"At a meeting of the qualified Inhabitants of the Town of Marblehead conven'd the thirteenth day of January 1755. * * * *

Voted, there shall be a Comm^{tte} of Five persons chosen, to Petition His Majesty that the Act lately made and lately pass'd the Genl Court Intituled an Act for Granting unto His Majesty an Excise upon Spiritous Liquors, and Wines, and upon Limes, Lemmons & Oranges be disalow'd.

Voted. Robert Hooper Esqr Mr Ebenezer Stacey Coll^o Jacob Fowle Coll^o Jeremiah Lee & Capt Isaac Freeman Comm^{tte}

Voted. That Christopher Kilby Esqr of London, be and hereby is appointed Agent for this Town to Petition His Majesty to disallow the Act aforesaid. Agreeable to such Instructions as he may receive from the Comm^{tte} afforesaid in behalf of this Town."—*Ibid.*, *p*. 392.

"September 19th, 1754. The town taking into consideration the bill entitled an act for granting to his majesty an excise upon wines and spirits distilled and sold by retail or consumed in this province, voted that they are of opinion that that part of said bill, which related to the consumption of distilled spirits in private families (which was referred to the consideration of the towns) *is an infringement on the natural rights of Englishmen* and ought not to pass into a law, and so forth.

January 21st, 1755. Town voted, first, that the town will act on an act lately made relating to an excise on the private consumption of distilled spirits, wines, lemons, limes and oranges.

Second, voted that the petitioners namely captain Michael Dalton and others and any other gentlemen, who are willing to join them should on their own cost and charge apply home in order to prevent said acts obtaining the royal assent."—*Coffin's History of Newbury*, *p*. 221.

"(*Govr Shirley to Lords of Trade*, 12 *January* 1755).

Boston New England Jany 12th 1755.

My Lords,

The Town of Boston having appointed an Agent to sollicit for His Majesty's disallowance of the inclos'd Excise Act and the House of Representatives having by their Message to me in Council of the 10th Inst. desired that I would use my endeavours for the Royal approbation of it, I beg leave to lay before your Lordships the following Account of this Act, with some Remarks upon it, that your Lordships may be thoroughly informd of the merits of the dispute between the Town of Boston and the two Houses of the General Assembly of the Province in this matter.

That part of the Act, my Lords, which is relative to the excis'd Liquors sold by Taverners, Innholders & other Retailers in quantities under 30 Gallons to any person at one time, is conformable to the ordinary Excise Act, constantly pass'd every year and not objected to: That part only is in question which imposes an excise upon Rum and other Spirits & Wine consumed in private families and not bought of any Retailer: This part of the Act is new and the motives which induced the House of Representatives to extend the duty to these Liquors seem to be that they thought it just, that those Members of the Community whose Estates were large enough to enable them to buy these Liquors of the Merchant in quantities not under 30 Gallons, should pay their proportionable part of the duty with those whose circumstances would not afford their purchasing 'em in so large Quantities: this they conceiv'd would make the Tax more equal; that the Duty would produce a larger revenue to his Majesty towards the support of his Government and consequently lighten the burthen of the poorer sort in the other Taxes necessary to be raised in the Province for that purpose.

This point also, my Lords, as far as I could perceive from the publick debates of the Council, whilst the Bill was depending, & private conversation, is universally allowed by those Members who opposed it, to be reasonable & just, as it seems clearly to be.

The single matter in difference is the manner of collecting this part of the Duty as prescrib'd in the Act which subjects every person to Keep an account of the quantity of rum & other spirits and wine consumed in his private family & not purchas'd of a Retailer and to render it to the Town Clerk where he lives once in a year; and in case the farmer of the Excise for that particular County shall think fit to summon him before a Justice of Peace for that purpose, to make oath to the truth of his Account, or in failure thereof to pay £10:—lawfull money, being of the value of £7: 10s.—sterling to his use.

In June last a Bill of the same kind, differing from this in some small Circumstances, was projected and pass'd in the House of Representatives, the Council at first non concurr'd it, but the House made such a point of it, that the Council in the end concurr'd it, and it was pass'd to be enacted by both Houses and laid before me by the Secretary, for my consent.

As I dislik'd the manner propos'd in the Bill for levying the new Duty and it begun to occasion a dissatisfaction in the Inhabitants of the Town of Boston in particular, which had communicated itself from them to other Towns in the Province, I interpos'd in the affair and made a Speech to both Houses, which after urging the exceptions I had to the Bill, in very strong terms (aggravated perhaps beyond what the necessity of the affair required) I concluded by telling them, that 'I thought the least they could do in justice to their Constituents upon this occasion would be to pursue the method frequently us'd by the General Assembly in cases of the like nature, by ordering the Bill to be printed, that their Constituents might be fully acquainted with the contents of it during the recess of the Court & themselves informed of the general sentiments of the country concerning a matter of this importance and difficulty which so nearly touched the natural right of every individual Member in his private family.'

'That in the mean time I would preserve the Bill in the same state, which it was then in, by making an Adjournment instead of a Prorogation of the Court, until it's next meeting and if at that time I should find that they continued of the same opinion after having informed themselves fully of the sentiments of their constituents upon this Bill, I should think myself more at liberty to pass it and should have all due regard to the general voice of the people in a matter which purely concern'd their own rights.'

'And in order to save the duty which would grow due upon the excis'd Spirits & Liquors, after the ninth day of July, until the time of the next meeting of the Court, from being lost, upon the expiration of the Excise Act then in force, I advis'd the House of Representatives to project a short Bill, which might effectually answer that purpose, without prejudicing their engross'd Bill then under consideration.'

I was in hopes, my Lords, if the House of Representatives could have been induced to pass an Excise Bill in the ordinary form that their fondness for the new part of the Bill then depending might have worn off by the time of their next meeting; But they were so much bent upon carrying their point that they refus'd to pass an Excise Bill in any other form and rose without making any supply of the Treasury.

They however complyed with my advice to them so far, as to pass on the 18th of June the two following Orders of the House viz[t] 'that the several Members of that House be directed to lay before the select men of their respective Towns, that part of the Excise Bill which relates to the private consumption of Wines & Spirits distill'd, and acquaint them it is the desire of the House, that they call their several Towns together, that the House might know the minds of their Constituents with regard to said Bill on the adjournm[t] of the Court'

And 'that the House's Printer be directed to send a number of Gazettes of that day, containing the Governor's Speech of the day before that so the several Members might lay the same before the select men of their respective Towns, to be communicated to them together with the Excise Bill'

At the next Meeting of the Court I received Addresses of thanks from some Towns in the Country by their Members, as I had before done from the Town of Boston in particular for the part I had acted in this affair: But as the House did not think fit to call for the Returns of the select men of the several Towns, it did not appear with certainty what the sense of the major part of them was concerning the late Bill; the House however in the beginning of their Session dropped their old Bill and fram'd another for laying a duty upon all distill'd Liquors, at the Still head (as it is called) join'd with an Impost upon Wine, with sundry new Regulations for making them both effectual for collecting the Duty laid upon the private Consumption of the Excis'd Liquors: But upon considering a Petition from the Distillers against the former part of the Bill, and being of opinion that this Scheme in other parts would probably be very injurious to the trade of the Province in many respects, they quitted it and return'd to their first project and after having sat near eight weeks, pass'd the Act now before your Lordships which was concurr'd by his Majesty's Council & laid before me for my Consent.

The Supply of the Treasury, my Lords, for the current year had been now obstructed for six months after the usual time of making it; no Funds rais'd for discharging the growing debts of the Province; many of the Soldiers and all the Officers & Servants of the Government were suffering by being kept out of their pay; Great sums of money were wanting to purchase fire arms and powder, which the Province stood in need of, and every part of His Majesty's service laboured, all occasion'd by the suspending of my consent to the late Excise Bill.

This situation of affairs required the most mature advisement; I considered my Lords, this was a Money Bill, which always originates in the House of Representatives and which they claim a right to pass in their own way; that the Dispute was concerning these two circumstances, viz:—every person's being oblig'd to keep & render an account of what excis'd Liquors, not bought of Retailers he consum'd yearly in his private family, which Imposition they insisted upon laying on themselves & their Constituents; that they stood ready to make a large supply of the Treasury, for carrying on every part of His Majesty's service, provided his Governor would accept it with this new duty upon the People; that the lengths I had already gone in asserting the People's cause in this matter against their representative Body had greatly embarassed his Maj^ty's service; that if I should refuse my consent to the present Bill there was a prospect of still further confusion, at a time when His Majesty's service in an especial manner requir'd the greatest Harmony to be kept up between me & the two Houses.

Besides the Act is to continue but for one year, and the permitting it's operation to be try'd for that time seem'd the most effectual way to bring the House of Representatives to let it drop for the future: At all events as the present House hath but six months longer to sit, the People will have it in their power either to injoin the Members they choose at the next Election to repeal the Act, or not to pass it again, or to choose new Representatives.

For these Reasons, my Lords, I thought it most adviseable finally to give my consent to the Bill; the immediate consequence hath been a large supply of the Treasury and I hope the Assembly will meet again in the beginning of February (to which time I have prorogu'd them) well dispos'd to promote His Majesty's service in the enterprise proposed to me by Colonel Lawrence and which we are now concerting for dispossessing the French of all their Incroachm^ts in Nova Scotia early in the Spring.

I beg leave now to observe to your Lordships, that the effect of His Majesty's disallowance of this Act would be that the Taverners, Innholders & Retailers will sell the excis'd Liquors at their usual Excise prices, so that that part of the People who shall buy their Liquors of them and not of the Merchant and are of the middling and poorer sort will have paid their part of the duty in those rais'd prices which is computed at about £1000 sterling p^r ann: and by the disallowance of the Act before the time on which the Retailers are obliged to pay to the Farmers of the Excise the duty upon the several species of liquors, which they have sold, or on which the Farmers of the Excise are oblig'd to pay the sum, they have contracted for with the publick, which is a year after the Act takes place, the publick will be wholly depriv'd of the benefit of the Tax and it will in such case be sunk in the pockets of either the Taverners, Innholders & Retailers, or of the Farmers of Excise, neither of which have any right to it.

In this Case likewise all the Governm^t's Creditors, who have taken the Treasurer's Notes payable with Interest out of the Duty of Excise (which by the Supply Act the Treasurer is empowered to give) & those who shall lend it any sums of money upon the security of this Fund will lose their Security; and for discharging their debts a new Tax must be laid, of which too those, who paid the Duty of this Excise to the Retailers as is before mention'd in the advanc'd prices of the Liquors, must bear their proportionable part over again.

In Case this Act is disallow'd before it hath had it's full operation, the publick will also lose the whole benefit of that part of the duty, which is laid upon those exciseable liquors which shall be purchas'd of the Merchant or others in larger quantities than 30 Gallons by one person at one time which is reckon'd at about £4000 Sterling value more and will be sunk in the pockets of the richer sort of the people who have no reasonable pretensions to be exempted from paying their part of the Duty and so increase the burthen of the other Taxes upon the poorer sort.

Thus, my Lords, would £5000 sterling of the publick Taxes be sunk in the pockets of those who have not the least right to it, to the great hardship of others, who are the least able in the community to bear such a loss, the weakening of the Government credit & the disappointment of His Maj^ty's service.

But my Lords these are not all the bad consequences which will probably arise to the Province from his Maj^ty's disallowance of the Act.

I am persuaded that a disallowance of this Act would greatly shock the minds of the Representatives and dissolve his Maj^ty's Government, especially at this Crisis: Tho' they have learned to acquiesce in being restrained from passing Acts of Assembly which intrench upon his Majesty's Prerogative, which have a tendency to weaken his Government, affect the foreign trade of Great Britain, burthen or diminish her trade to the Colonies, lessen the consumption of Commodities either of her growth or manufacture within 'em and even from establishing Manufactures among them, which interfere with her's; but to restrain them either by disallowance of their Acts when pass'd, or standing instructions to their Governors from laying a duty upon Liquors, which in all Communities have ever been esteem'd the most proper object of a Tax or Excise, in such manner as to subject every rank of persons to an equal payment of it and to be collected so as to prevent concealments and frauds in those who ought to pay their parts of it and to make the fund produce what it ought towards the support of His Maj^ty's Governm^t I say my Lords to restrain them from exercising such a discretionary power among themselves would, I am satisfied, grieve them very much at this time, and might tend to quench that ready spirit, which they have hitherto exerted for promoting His Majesty's service and the general welfare of his Dominions upon the Continent; & might also disserve his Government in other respects.

But for what ends my Lords, is his Majesty's disallowance of this Act desired? the principal are to ease those, who shall buy any exciseable liquor of the Merchant in quantities not under 30 Gallons at a time for private consumption in their Families, from a new imposition of being oblig'd to keep an account of what they consume this year, and perhaps to gage their casks at the end of the year and afterwards to give publick acco^t of it upon oath, if the Farmer of Excise shall require it. The number of these within the Province from the best accounts I can get, is very small: All such who buy their liquor of the Retailers are out of the question, as to keeping or rendering any account of the quantity of exciseable liquors they consume in their families; the latter circumstance of discovering the quantity of liquor consum'd at a man's private table is certainly a disagreeable one and the imposition of it is new in the English Government; But where is the necessity for having recourse to the remedy which the Town of Boston desires; if the Act is as disagreeable to the several Towns and such an one as they represent it in their Instructions to their Agent, the People will have their remedy in their own hands within seventeen weeks; the present House of Representative will expire in that time. and they may, if they please, choose such Representatives as will pass a Bill for repealing the Act; in which case there is not the least room to doubt, but that the new Council would concurr it and the Governor give his consent to it.

I can't avoid observing to your Lordships, the irregularity of the Town's proceedings in this case: It seems a settled maxim in Governm^t as well as Law that the last remedy ought not to be resorted to, before the intermediate ones are try'd; No person can in the first instance have recourse to the higher Court of Judicature without first bringing his suit in the Inferior Court from whence an Appeal or Writ of Error lies to the Superior one; The Town of Boston ought certainly to have, according to the ordinary course and rule of Government in like cases, petitioned the House of Representat^ves to be heard against the Bill whilst it was depending there; this was what the Distillers did when the Bill for laying the duty upon the Still head was depending in the House and the Bill was upon their representing the mischievous consequences of it, dropp'd as is before mentioned; It does not appear but that the same proceeding in the Town of Boston might have had the same effect, as to the Excise Bill; The Town ought at least to have try'd this remedy, if that had fail'd they would have had a better pretence to have apply'd to your Lordships for this violent remedy from the Crown.

Petitions to his Majesty, my Lords, from the Assemblies in the Colonies against their Governors for invading the rights or priviledges of the people and their appointing Agents to prosecute them are known cases; But a single Town's appointment of a standing Agent (which appears to be the case of the Town of Boston) at the Boards of State, to oppose the Acts of the whole representative body of the people in conjunction with the two other Branches of the Legislature and that in matters which don't touch their particular Franchises and Interests more than it does those of the rest of the community is I believe of the first impression in the King's Government.

I find my Lords in the Town's letter to their Agent, that they have wrote to several other Towns in the Province inviting them to join in this application; It is very possible some of the fishing Towns may: I don't design to trouble your Lordships into an examination of the whole detail of the Votes, which were pass'd at the Town meeting upon the Excise Act in question, But it may be proper for me to make some cursory remarks upon three of them.

One of the hardships pointed out by them in the Act is, that the poor fishermen will suffer by it: I made the same objection my Lords, in private, to some of the Members of the House of Representatives and was answer'd that the Fishermen never purchase their rum for the voyage, but the Owner of the Vessel constantly provides all supplies for it and among other articles sells that of Rum to the crew at the Excise price; that for this Reason the fishermen were never excepted out of the ordinary Excise Acts; that there never was a complaint made of their being burthened by being subjected to the payment of the Duty and that there could be no just pretence for the Owner of the Vessell to charge the fishermen more for his Rum than the Excise price now: But on the other hand that the excepting of rum consum'd in fishing voyages out of this new Act would open a door for frauds, without procuring any benefit to the fishermen.

Another exception pointed out in the Town's Instructions to their Agent is that this Act will increase the number of Excise Officers which may influence Elections; Your Lordships will naturally imagine from this objection that these Officers are appointed by the Governor; But my Lords it is otherwise, the farmers of the Excise are appointed by Committees chosen by a Ballot Vote of the two Houses, to which the Governor signs his consent, so that if there is any force in the objection it makes against them, and as to the fact itself, I can't think that the Farmers of the Excise will be under a necessity of increasing the number of their Deputies much on account of this Act.

Another Objection is their apprehensions that the Excise may in time be extended to the Provisions of private Consumption as well as to Wines and Spirituous Liquors: This Objection holds equally strong against laying an Excise upon the same kinds of liquors consum'd in publick Houses of Taverners, Innholders &^c; But this Excise laid upon them hath been experienc'd many years in the Province and I dare say it never entered into any one's thoughts to extend it to any species of provisions sold and consum'd in those Houses and until that shall be attempted private Families have no pretence to be apprehensive of such an Excise being laid upon their provisions.

I am afraid I have troubled your Lordships too much already with a particular examination of the objections I have taken notice of, and shall not descend to the others mention'd in the Town's Instructions to their Agent and shall only add and that from the best accounts that I can get of what the produce of this new part of the Excise will probably amount to, I have reason my Lords, to think it will fall so short of the expectation of the Assembly, that they will not press the Act another year, at least the disagreeable part of it which is the obliging every person to give an account of his private consumption of Wine and Spirituous liquors not bought of any Retailer.

Upon the whole, my Lords, a new Assembly must according to the Charter be chosen next May, which will I make no question from the experience I have had of them, act in a matter of this nature, agreeable to the general sense of their Constituents which must at this Election be certainly known; If that should be to have the Act repeal'd, the Assembly must at the same time make provision for discharging the Debts for which the present duty of Excise is mortgaged and for the exigencies of his Majesty's service which might otherwise be effected by the Repeal; so that in such case no inconvenience of any kind could attend the repealing it, whereas several most probably would ensue upon his Majesty's disallowance of it.

At all Events if the Assembly is permitted to settle this matter with their Constituents, let it terminate either way, it seems evident that it can't hurt his Majesty's service in the Province but must have a tendency to promote it: and I think I can be answerable to Your Lordships that the Rum consum'd in fishing Voyages shall be exempted from the payment of the duty, if the Act should be passed again another year, and as it would be a great pleasure to me to have the Town of Boston gratified by leaving the Clause out of the Act which subjects every person, but those who are expressly excepted out of it, to render an account of the excis'd liquors (not bought of Retailers) which is consumed in their private Families and which I shall again make a point of, as far as the good of his Majesty's service at this critical conjuncture will allow me, I can't but conceive strong hopes that I shall be able to induce the Assembly to do it.

But if Your Lordships shall be of opinion that at all events I should not consent to passing the Act again with the like Clause in it and will be pleas'd to signify your directions to me upon it in a Letter, I shall pay the strictest obedience to them and would submit it to Your Lordship's consideration whether that might not be at this time as salutary a method of prohibiting it's being passed again as by a standing Instruction from his Majesty.

I am, with the highest respect,
My Lords,
Your Lordships
most humble and
most obedient Servant
W. SHIRLEY

The Rt. Honble Lords Comm^rs^ of Trade and Plantations—*Mass. Bay, B. T., vol. 74, H. h. 45, in Public Record Office.*"

1755 Wednesday April 23rd "At a Meeting of His Maj^ty's^ Commiss^rs^ for Trade and Plantations.

Present
Earl of Halifax.
Mr Grenville. Mr Edgcumbe. Mr Fane.

* * * * *

Read a Letter from Mr Shirley Govr of the Massachusets Bay to the Board, dated Jan^ry^ 12th 1755 with his Observations upon an Excise Act passed there in Decr 1754 and inclosing,

An Act for granting unto His Majesty an Excise upon Spirits distilled and Wine and upon Limes, Lemons and Oranges passed the 19th Decr 1754.

Message from the Assembly to the Governor relative to the Excise Act.

Ordered that the Secretary do deliver the above mention'd Act to the Clerk of His Majesty's Council in waiting, to be laid before His Majesty in Council.

* * * *

DUNK HALIFAX."

—"*Trade Papers (Journals)*," *vol. 57, in Public Record Office.*

"At the Council Chamber Whitehall. the 7th day of May 1755

By the Right Honourable the Lords of the Committee of Council for Plantation Affairs.

WHEREAS the Agent of the Province of the Massachusetts Bay did deliver into the Hands of the Clerk of the Council in waiting, An Act passed in that Province in December 1754 for granting unto His Majesty an Excise upon Spirits distilled and Wine and upon Limes Lemons and Oranges; And Whereas His Majesty was pleased on the 26th of last month to referr the said Act to this Committee——Their Lordships this day took the same into their consideration and are hereby pleased to referr the said Act (which is hereunto annexed) to the Lords Commissioners for Trade and Plantations to examine into the same, and report their opinion thereupon to this Committee

W. SHARPE

[L. S.] By His Excellency William Shirley Esqre Captain General & Governor in Chief in and over His Majesty's Province of the Massachusetts Bay in New England.

I do hereby Certify that the Great and General Court or Assembly for the Province of the Massachusetts Bay aforesaid, at this Session begun and held at Boston the twenty ninth day of May 1754 and continued by adjournment unto Thursday the seventeenth day of October following, made and pass'd the following Act or Law.

An Act for granting unto His Majesty an Excise upon Spirits distilled and Wine and upon Limes, Lemons and Oranges——Pass'd by the Representatives, in Council and signed by the Governor December 19th 1754 and that the Papers hereunto annexed are a true and authentic Copy of the above mentioned Act.

In Testimony whereof I have caused the public Seal of the Province of the Massachusetts Bay aforesaid to be hereunto affixed; Dated at Boston the fourteenth day of January 1755; In the twenty eighth year of His Majesty's Reign.

W. SHIRLEY

By his Excell^cy's^ Command
J. WILLARD Secry

[*Indorsed*]

R 11th April 1755 by the Hands of Mr Bollan Agent for the said Province—26th D^o^ Read

& Referred to a Committee."—"*Mass. Bay, B. T.," vol. 74, H. h. 50, in Public Record Office.*

"At a Meeting of His Majty's Commrs for Trade and Plantations
Present
Earl of Halifax
Mr Oswald. Mr Pelham
Tuesday May 27th 1755.

* * * *

Read an Order of the Lords of the Committee for Plantation Affairs dated the 7th of May 1755 referring to the Board an Act passed in the Province of the Massachusets Bay in Decr 1754, for granting unto His Majesty an Excise upon Spirits distilled and Wine and upon Limes, Lemons and Oranges, and directing the Board to examine the same and report their opinion thereupon.

Ordered that the said Act be taken into consideration on Tuesday the 10th of June and that the Secretary do give notice thereof to Mr Bollan, Agent for the Province and to Mr Kilby, Agent for the Town of Boston.

* * * *

Dunk Halifax

Tuesday June 10th 1755
Present
Earl of Halifax
Mr Grenville. Mr Oswald. Mr Fane.

Read a letter from Mr Bollan Agent for the Province of the Massachusetts Bay dated the 9th of June 1755 acquainting the Board that he is unable to attend their Lordships this day upon the Excise Act on account of sickness, praying their Lordships to postpone the consideration of it to a further day and inclosing

His Observations on the Laws made in this Century to provide that certain Commodities produced in the English Plantations shall be imported into some other English Plantation or into this Kingdom and for that end to put those Commodities under the same Regulations and Restrictions that Sugars, Tobacco and other goods were subjected to by former Statutes.

Mr Kilby, Agent for the Town of Boston, Marblehead &c attending with his Counsel pursuant to the notice given him by their Lordships Orders, was called in and being acquainted with Mr Bollan's request, it was ordered that the Excise Act should be taken into consideration on this day sennight and the Secretary was directed to give Mr Bollan notice thereof.

Their Lordships took into consideration Mr Bollan's Observations upon the Acts of Trade and Navigation and made some progress therein.

Dunk Halifax"

—"*Trade Papers (Journals)," vol. 57, in Public Record Office.*

"At a Meeting of His Majtys Commrs for Trade and Plantations
Tuesday June 17th 1755
Present
Earl of Halifax
Mr Grenville. Mr Oswald. Mr Fane.

Their Lordships took into consideration an Act passed in the Province of the Massachusetts Bay in Decr 1754 for granting to His Majesty an Excise upon Spirits distilled and Wine and upon Limes, Lemons and Oranges; referred to their Lordships by the Lords of the Committee of Council for Plantation Affairs and Mr Bollan, Agent for the Province and Mr Kilby, Agent for the Towns of Boston, Marblehead and Gloucester with Mr Forrester his Counsel attending without, they were called in, and their Lordships heard what they had to offer for and against the Confirmation of the said Act, and then they withdrew.

Dunk Halifax

Wednesday June 18th 1755
(Present as above)

* * * *

Their Lordships took into consideration the Act passed in the Province of the Massachusetts Bay in Decr 1754 for granting an Excise to his Majesty mentioned in the Minutes of yesterday and ordered the Draught of a Report thereupon to the Lords of the Committee of Council to be prepared

* * * *

Tuesday June 24th 1755.
Earl of Halifax
Mr Grenville. Mr Fane.

The Draught of a Report to the Lords of the Comtee of Council upon the Excise Act pass'd in Mass. Bay in Decr 1754, having been prepared pursuant to the Minutes of the 18th Instant was agreed to and ordered to be transcribed.

* * * *

Tuesday July 1st 1755
(Present)
Earl of Halifax.
Mr Grenville. Mr Pelham.

* * * *

The Draught of a Report to the Lords of the Committee of Council upon the Excise Act passed at Boston in Decr 1754, having been transcribed pursuant to the Minutes of the 24th of last Month was signed"—*Ibid.*

"Report of Lords of Trade on an Act passed Dec. 1754.

To the Right Honble the Lords of the Committee of His Majesty's most Honble Privy Council for Plantation Affairs.

My Lords,

Pursuant to Your Lordships Order dated the 7th of May last, We have had under our

Consideration an Act passed in the Province of the Massachusetts Bay in December 1754 Entituled,

An Act for granting unto His Majesty an Excise upon Spirits distilled and Wine and upon Limes, Lemons and Oranges.

And having been attended by Mr Kilby, whom the Towns of Boston, Marblehead and Gloucester within the said Province have appointed their Agent to solicit the Repeal of the said Act, and by Mr Bollan, Agent for the Province in support of it, and heard what each party had to offer, We beg leave to acquaint your Lordships;

That so much of this Act as relates to the Excised Liquors sold by Taverners, Innholders and other Retailers in quantities less than thirty Gallons to any person at one time, is conformable to the Ordinary Excise Act annually past in the said Province: That part of it only is new, which imposes an Excise upon Rum & other Spirits and Wine brought in larger Quantities than thirty Gallons, & consumed in private Families, which, by the method prescribed for collecting this part of the duty, subjects every person to render to the Town Clerk once in a year an Account of the Quantity of Rum, and other Spirits and Wine, consumed in his private Family; and in case the Farmer of the Excise for that particular County shall think fit to summon him before a Justice of the Peace for that purpose, to make oath to the truth of his account, or on failure thereof to pay Ten Pounds, being of the value Seven Pounds ten shillings sterling, to the use of the said Farmer.

On this new part of the Act the objections of the three Towns above mentioned are chiefly founded. It has been urged on their behalf, that the method of collecting the Excise by Farmers or their Deputies is grievous; that by giving them power to administer an Oath to every person in the Community they may harrass and perplex his Maj^ty's Subjects; that the multiplying oaths on trifling occasions has a tendency to lessen the sanctity of an Oath, and contributes to the spreading of perjury That the obliging persons to expose the secrets of their Familys, by rendring an account of their private consumption is inconsistent with the natural rights of mankind unconstitutional and unprecedented in the English Government.

It has abso been objected, that there being no Clause in this Act to exempt the Fishermen from the payment of this Excise for all spirituous liquors they may purchase at Newfoundland, Halifax, or any other port they may put into for supplies, altho' they should have paid an Excise in those Govern^ts, since they cannot take the Oath required by this Act, without giving an account of the Liquors they purchased in those Provinces, and therefore that this Act tends greatly to the discouragement of the Fishery.

On the other hand it has been urged in support of this Act that it is founded on the principle of equality and impartiality, That the motives which induced the House of Representatives to extend the Duty of Excise in the manner above stated were, that it seem'd just that those members of the Community, whose Estates were large enough to enable them to buy the said Liquors of the Merchants in larger quantities than thirty gallons, should pay their proportionate part of the Duty (from which under all former Excise Acts they have been exempt) with those whose circumstances would not afford their purchasing in so large Quantities This they conceived would make the tax more equal, produce a larger revenue towards the support of His Majesty's Government and consequently lighten the burden of the poorer sort in the other Taxes necessary to be raised for that purpose; That with respect to the rendring an account of private Consumption, the Legislature have laid this burthen on themselves equally with the rest of the Community; That it is no great hardship to give once in a year an account to the best of the party's knowledge of Liquors purchased in large quantities, to the truth of which he is not required to make oath, unless on cause of suspicion.

That the Fishermen never purchase their Rum for the Voyage, but the Owner of the Vessell constantly provides all supplies for it, and among other articles, sells that of Rum to the Crew at the Excise Price; that for this Reason the fishermen were never excepted out of the Ordinary Excise Acts, and there never was a complaint of their being burthen'd by being subjected to the payment of the Duty, and that there can be no just pretence for the owner of the Vessel to charge the Fishermen more for his Rum than the Excise price now; But on the other hand that the excepting of Rum consum'd in fishing Voyages out of this new Act would open a door to frauds, without procuring any benefit to the Fishermen.

It has been further alleged that the Act will expire by its own limitation in December next, by which time the new Assembly (chosen in May last) will be fully apprized of its effect and operation and of the sense of their Constituents upon it, and if it shall have been found grievous and burthensome, they will not pass another Act of the like nature but that as it has now been in force for six months and upwards the disallowance of it must produce many bad consequences. For the poorer and middling sort of people who buy liquors of Retailers, have already contributed to this Tax by paying the Excise price for them and whatever sums have so accrued will be sunk either in the pockets of such Retailers or of the Farmers of Excise, who are not obliged to pay the sum they have contracted for with the publick till the end of the year; And thus the Publick will be deprived of the benefit of this part of the Tax; That, if the Act be disallowed before it has had it's full operation, the publick will also lose the whole benefit of that part of the Duty which is laid on Exciseable Liquors purchased in larger quantities than 30 Gallons, which is computed at about four thousand pounds Sterling, That this Sum will be sunk in the pockets of the richer sort of people who have no reasonable pretensions to be exempted from paying their part of the duty and the burthen of other Taxes will be thereby increased upon the poorer sort—That in such case likewise all the Governments' Creditors who have advanc'd any sums of money on the security of this Fund will lose their security, which will not only be of great detriment to the publick, as it will create a necessity of imposing a new Tax, in order to satisfy such Creditors, but must give such a shock to its Credit as may have the most fatal effects upon any future occasion of raising money on emergencies.

Upon the whole, my Lords, as the mode of levying taxes is a matter of Provincial

Œconomy of which the Representves of the People are the Competent Judges; And as the Repeal of this Act would disappoint His Majesty's service, deprive the publick of the benefit of the duty thereby imposed, put that part of it which has already accrued into the private pockets of Retailers and Farmers of Excise and above all as it must necessarily weaken the credit of the Province, which we conceive may, in the present conjuncture, be of fatal consequence, We are humbly of opinion that the said Act should receive His Majesty's Royal Confirmation.

We are,
My Lords,
Your Lordships
most obedient and
most humble Servants
DUNK HALIFAX
T. PELHAM
J. GRENVILLE

Whitehall July 1st 1755."—"*Mass. Bay, B. T.," vol.* 84, *p.* 312, *in Public Record Office.*

"*Lords of Trade to Govr Shirley* 6 *Aug.* 1755.

To William Shirley Esqre
Governor of the Massachusets Bay
Sir,

* * * *

The reasons which you offer in your letter of the 12th of January in support of the Excise Act, convinced us so clearly of the inexpediency of repealing it, that We thought it our duty, after having heard what the Agents for the Province and for the Towns of Boston, Marblehead and Gloucester had to offer upon it, to lay it before the Lords Justices for their approbation, leaving it to the Representatives of the People, who in this case are the best Judges of what may be for their interest & convenience, to determine on the propriety or impropriety of renewing the like Tax, when the present Act shall be expired.

* * * *

So We bid you heartily farewell and are Your very loving Friends
and humble Servants,
DUNK HALIFAX.
J. PITT.
J. GRENVILLE

Whitehall. August 6th 1755"—"*Mass. Bay, B. T.," vol.* 84, *p.* 321, *in Public Record Office.*

"Order in Council confirming an Act passed in December 1754.

At the Council Chamber Whitehall the 12th day of August 1755.
Present
The Lords Justices in Council

Whereas by Commission under the Great Seal of Great Britain, the Governor, Council and Assembly of the Province of the Massachusetts Bay in New England are authorized and empowered to constitute and ordain Laws which are to continue and be in force unless His Majesty's pleasure be signified to the contrary—And whereas in pursuance of the said Commission An Act was passed in the said Province in December 1754 Entituled as follows—Vizt:—

An Act for granting unto His Majesty an Excise upon Spirits distilled and Wine and upon Limes, Lemons & Oranges.

Which said Law having been under the consideration of the Lords Commissioners for Trade and Plantations and also of a Committee of the Lords of His Majesty's most Honourable Privy Council, The said Lords of the Committee this day presented the said Law to the Lords Justices at this Board with their Opinion that the same was proper to be approved—The Lords Justices taking the same into consideration, were pleased with the advice of his Majesty's Privy Council to declare their approbation of the said Law And pursuant to the Lords Justices pleasure thereupon expressed, the said Law is hereby confirmed, finally enacted and ratified accordingly. Whereof the Governor or Commander in Chief of the said Province for the time being and all others whom it may concern are to take notice and govern themselves accordingly.

A true Copy W. SHARPE"

—*Ibid., vol.* 74, *H. h.* 54.

"A bill was brought forward by the legislature of Massachusetts for granting an excise on wines and spirituous liquors; but, meeting with great opposition, it was referred to the consideration of the people in the several towns. The returns discovering great diversity of opinion, the house, not viewing them as conclusive instructions, voted, that they should not be considered; and the bill was finally enacted and approved."—*Holmes's Annals, vol.* 2, *p.* 203, *anno* 1754.

Chap. 17. "December 30, 1754. His Excellency sent the following Message to the House by the Secretary;

Gentlemen of the House of Representatives

The Bill for laying an Excise upon Wines & Strong Liquors, being now passed through the whole Legislature, I suppose I need not put you in Mind, That (how large a Revenue soever this Act may raise for this Government) It can be no present Supply, Unless something furthur be immediately done to procure, upon the Credit of this Fund, such Sums of Money as will discharge the present Debt of the Province, & (as far as the Fund itself will be sufficient) answer the furthur rising Expence for the Support of the Government, and the Defence and Protection of the Inhabitants thereof: It will be a full

Year before one Penny of this Tax will come into the Treasury; and unless more effectual Means than hitherto have been practis'd in like Cases, be used in this, It will be a much longer Time before the Government will have any great Benefit from this Branch of the Revenue.

Besides, Gentlemen, It seems to me to be very ill Policy to have our Treasury never supplied, till great Debts are first contracted, and the poor Soldiers & other Creditors of the Public are necessitated to spend a great Part of what is honestly due to them, in Attendance, for obtaining the Payment thereof, and sometimes to sell their Dues at great Loss: And by these Means the Credit of the Government is much sunk, and the Subjects of it more backward to serve it than they would be, if they could expect to be paid when the Service is performed; Besides, the large Sums which are paid for the Interest of the Money should put us upon more expedite and frugal Ways of raising the Taxes of all Kinds than any which hitherto have been practic'd.

And I would furthur add on this Head, that I think it would be a great Point of Wisdom in this Government, especially in the present Conjuncture of our Affairs, always to have a Surplusage in the Treasury beyond what will fully discharge the Debts already contracted, and the stated Accruing Expence of Government in its Circumstances, as estimated when the Provision is made, that so in the Recess of the Court there may be no Difficulty to draw out such Sum, as may answer any Exigency of Government; lest otherwise irreparable Damage should accrue to the Publick.

And therefore, Gentlemen, I must earnestly desire you would look into the State of the Treasury and get as much Knowledge as you can of the Sum of the Debts owing from the Government, and do your part for making a full & speedy supply for the Payment of the publick Debts, and for the Support of the Government, and the Protection & Defence of the Inhabitants."—*Council Records, vol.* XX., *p.* 361.

Chap. 18. "January 8, 1755. This Day the two Houses proceeded to the Election of a Commissioner over the Duty of the Stamps, agreable to an Act passed this Session for granting unto his Majesty several Duties upon Vellum, Parchment & Paper &c[a], And M[r] James Russell being duly elected by a Major Vote of the Council & House of Representatives, to be Commissioner of the Duties on Stamps upon Vellum Parchment & Paper;—His Excellency signed his Consent to said Election."—*Council Records, vol.* XX., *p.* 372.

"14th of March, 1755. The Secretary having by Order of the Board prepared the Draught of a Proclamation for setting forth the Stamps to be impressed upon the Instruments, Writings, &c[a] taxed by the General Court, in an Act entitled an Act for granting to his Majesty several Duties upon Vellum, Parchment & Paper for four Years towards defreying the Charges of this Government. The said Proclamation was read & approved of, & thereupon Advised that His Excellency issue said Proclamation accordingly."—*Executive Records of the Council, vol.* 2, *p.* 392.

"BY HIS EXCELLENCY WILLIAM SHIRLEY ESQ[R] Capt[n] General & Gov[r] in Chief in & over his Maj[ty's] Province of the Mass[ts] Bay in New England.

A Proclamation.

Whereas the Great & Gen[l] Court or Assembly of the Province afores[d] did at their Session held by Adjournm[t] on the 17th of Octo[r] last, pass an Act, entitled, An Act for granting unto his Majesty sev[l] Duties upon Vellum, Parchm[t] & Paper towards defraying the Charges of this Gov[t]; Wherein (among other things) it is enacted, That the Comm[r] of the Stamps, (an Officer appointed by the Gen[l] Court for receiving the Duties in the s[d] Act granted) shall be provided with Four different Marks or Stamps, which s[d] Marks & Stamps are to be published by Proclamation.

I have therefore thought fit, with the Advice of his Maj[ty's] Council, hereby to inform all Persons, That the Marks or Stamps of the sev[l] things subjected to the Duties in the s[d] Act will be as follows;

For all such Vellum, Parchm[t] or Paper, whereon shall be engross'd or written any Charter Party, Policy of Assurance or Protest, or any Bill of Lading or Receipt for Money or any kind of Wares or Merchandize that shall be laden on board any Ship or Vessel, or any Certificate under the Province Seal, or the Seal of any Notary Publick, or any Register of a Ship or other Vessel, or any Warrant Monition or Decree of the Court of Vice Admiralty, or any Deed of Mortgage of any Real Estate, the Consideration whereof shall be Twenty Pounds or more, or any Bill of Sale of any Ship or Vessel, or any Part of one shall be written (the Duty whereof is four Pence for each Instrum[t] or Paper) the Device of the Stamp will be a Schooner under Sail, and a Motto on the Ring round it, the Words, Steady, Steady, as in the Margin.

For all such Vellum, Parchm[t] or Paper whereon shall be engross'd or written any Capias, Original Summons, or any Writt of Review, or any Writt of Scire Facias, or any Writ of Execution that shall be issued out of the Clerk's Office or pass the Seal of the Sup[r] Court of Jud[r] Court of Assize &c: or any of the Inf[r] Courts of Common Pleas within the Province, or any Bill of Sale for Servants of any Sort (the Duty whereof is Three Pence for each Instrument or Paper) the Divice of the Stamp will be a Pine Tree, & the Motto on the Ring round it, the Words, Province of the Massachusetts, as in the Margin.

For every Peice of Vellum, Parchm[t] or Paper whereon shall be engross'd or written any Capias Original Summons or Execution from any Justice of the Peace, or any Deed or Mortgage of any real Estate, the Consideration whereof shall be less than Twenty Pounds, or any Bond or Obligation (these taken in the Probate Office excepted) or other Sealed Instrum[t] (the Duty whereof is Two Pence for each Instrum[t] or Paper) the Device will be a Cod Fish with a Motto in the Ring in these Words, Staple of the Massachusetts, as in the Margin.

For every Peice of Vellum, Parchm[t] or Paper, on w[ch] any News Paper shall be printed (the Duty whereof is One Half Penny each) the Device will be a Bird, & in the Ring round it, the Words Half Penney, as in the Margin. And all Persons are hereby further informed, that the Commiss[r] of the Stamps will keep his Office in the Town of

Boston, & will be furnished with Vellum, Parchm^t & Paper mark'd or stamp'd for the purposes in said Act mentioned; and that none of the Instrum^ts or Writings, wch by said Act are subjected to any of the Duties therein mentioned, will be deemed good or available in Law after the thirtieth day of April next, wch shall not be mark'd or stamp'd in manner as aforesaid.

Given at the Council chamber in Boston the fourteenth day of March 1755, in the 28th Year of Our Sovereign Lord George the Second by the Grace of God of Great Britain, France & Ireland King, Def^r of the Faith &c^a.

By His Excellency's Command, W. SHIRLEY.
with the Advice of the Council,
J. WILLARD Sec^ry. GOD SAVE THE KING."—*Records of Civil Commissions; in the office of the Secretary of the Commonwealth, vol. 2, p.* 261.

Chap. 20. It will be seen in the following communication to Silliman's Journal, by the distinguished botanist, Dr. Asa Gray of Cambridge, that the sagacity of the promoters of this measure is fully vindicated by the later researches of European cryptogamists.—

"The effect of barberry-bushes in rusting wheat, after having been long accounted a groundless popular superstition, is at length understood and admitted by the cryptogamists. The botanists used to rebut the charges of the farmers by the statement that the rust in the grain-fields and the prevalent fungus of the barberry belonged to very different genera, and that, therefore, the one could not give origin to the other. But De Bary in Germany, and Œrsted in Denmark, following up similar enquiries by Tulasne in France, have concluded that *Uredo*, *Puccinia* and *Æcidium* are to be regarded, not as so many genera, but as three successive forms of fructification of the same fungus, or, in some sort, an alternation of generations. De Bary ascertained that the spores of *Puccinia graminis* do not germinate when sprinkled on the leaves and stalks of the cereal grains, which this rust infests, while they will germinate on the leaves of the barberry, and there give rise to the *Æcidium berberidis*; and the spores of this are equally inert upon the barberry, but will grow, in their turn, upon wheat, and there reproduce first the *Uredo*, or yellow rust, and later the *Puccinia graminis*, or dark rust. Another species of *Puccinia* equally produces its *Æcidium* upon buckthorn; another alternates between the cereal grains and certain boragineous weeds. These results have been practically tested, in the large way, last summer [1869] in France. Long hedges of barberry planted along the Paris and Lyons railway, in a commune in the Côte d'Or, were complained of by the adjacent cultivators, and were cut away at certain places by way of experiment; and an investigation by the railroad company, whose interests were adverse to such a decision, left no doubt of the injurious effects of the barberry on the contiguous wheat-fields."—*American Journal of Science and the Arts, vol.* 49, 1870, *p.* 406 (*No. CXLVII., 2d series*).

The French account referred to is in "*Bulletin de la Société Botanique de France,*" *tom.* 16, *pp.* 331-333.

Chap. 21. "November 6, 1754. A Petition of Thomas Brown, Samuel Porter & others, Proprietors of a Tract of Land situate in the Towns of Ipswich & Wenham, commonly called Wenham great Swamp, Praying that for the promoting of the Growth of the young Wood there, & other Advantages, this Court would order that the Proprietors do enclose & fence in the same, at the Charge of the Propriety within such Bounds, as are particularly mentioned in the Petition

In the House of Representatives; Read & Ordered that the Petitioners serve the whole of the Proprietors of the Lands mentioned in the said Petition by posting up the Substance thereof in some publick Place in the Town of Wenham, and Ipswich Hamlet, that any concerned may show Cause on the nineteenth Instant, if the Court be then sitting; if not, on the first Tuesday of the next sitting of the Court, why the Prayer thereof should not be granted.——

In Council Read & Concur'd."—*Council Records, vol.* XX., *p.* 310.

"November 25, 1754. On the Petition of Thomas Brown & others, Inhabitants of Ipswich & Wenham, Enter'd Nov^m 6.

In Council; Read again and it Appearing that the Proprietors of the Land within mentioned have been notified agreable to Order, but no Answer given in;——Voted that the Prayer of the Petition be granted; And the Petitioners are allowed to bring in a Bill accordingly.——In the House of Representatives, Read & Concur'd;"—*Ibid., p.* 338.

Chap. 23. "November 21, 1754. His Excellency sent the following Message by the Secretary to the House of Representatives,

Gentlemen of the House of Representatives;—It is proper that I should acquaint you that Major General Winslow, to whom I gave the Chief Command in the late Expedition to the Eastward, is so situated in His Majesty's Service, that it would be improper for him to be made up in the Roll of Pay with the Officers of the Regiment; His good Conduct and indefatigable Vigilance in that Post are so well known to you, that I doubt not you will think they claim a suitable Recompence for his Services: I must therefore recommend it to you to make him such an Acknowledgment for them as will at the same time be for the Honour of the Province, and the Encouragement of Gentlemen of Ability to serve it, to enter into its Service upon future Occasions with the same Spirit & Zeal which he did."—*Council Records, vol.* XX., *p.* 332.

"December 5th, 1754. A Petition of John Winslow Esqr Commander in Chief of the Forces lately in the Service of this Province Eastward * * * *

In the House of Representatives, Read & Ordered that the Prayer of the Petition be granted, and that the Blankets, Knapsacks & Bandileers delivered the Officers and Soldiers employed in the late Service at the Eastward under the Command of Major General Winslow, be given to the said Officers & Soldiers gratis: And the Commissary General is hereby directed not to charge the said Articles in their particular accounts; In Council; Read & Concur'd;—Consented to by the Governour."—*Ibid., pp.* 342-3.

"January 8, 1755. In the House of Representatives; The House having taken under Consideration his Excellency's Message of the 21st of November last,

Ordered that there be allowed & paid out of the publick Treasury to Major General Winslow the Sum of One hundred & thirty Pounds in full for his Services as Chief Commander of the Forces sent last Summer up Kennebeck River for building a Fort there;

In Council; Read & Concur'd;—Consented to by the Governour."—*Ibid., p.* 371.

"December 20, 1754. His Excellency sent the following Message to the House by the Secretary,

Gentlemen of the House of Representatives,

Whilst your Attention was closely employed in providing a Supply for the Treasury, I would not divert it from the publick Business by moving any Matters to you which concerned my own private Interest; But I hope it may not now be an improper Time to move you take under your Consideration my late Services upon the River Kennebeck, and in the Eastern Parts of the Province, and to make me an adequate Grant for them."—*Ibid., p.* 352.

"December 21, 1754. In the House of Representatives, Ordered that the Sum of Two hundred & fifty Pounds be granted and paid out of the publick Treasury to His Excellency William Shirley Esqr Captain General and Governour of this Province, in full Consideration of his Services in the Eastern Parts of the Province in the Summer past.

In Council; Read & Concur'd; Consented to by the Governour."—*Ibid., p.* 354.

"Your Excellency is sensible of the very great Difficulties we are under, & that it has not been yet in our Power to borrow Moneys sufficient to pay the great Cost of the late Expedition to Kennebeck: When the Charges of Government exceed what the People are able annually to pay, we know of no other Way of paying the Surplus, but by borrowing Money or Issuing Bills of Credit: The latter Method has been attended with such mischievous Consequences that nothing but the last Extremity can induce Us to agree to it." —*From answer prepared by a committee of both branches, to the Governor's speech, Feb.* 15, 1755: *ibid., p.* 400.

See, also, 1753-54, chap. 40, and 1754-55, chap. 9, *ante*, and notes to those chapters.

Chap. 24. This act is printed, in the old editions, as of the March session; but it clearly appears, both in the record and on the engrossment, to have been signed the last day of the February (third) session.

Chap. 26. "January 19, 1754. A Petition of John Franklyn and others, Shewing that they have been at great Expence for Introducing forreign Protestants and Settling them within this Province, for the Carrying on several Manufactures useful to the Publick and among other things they have at great Charge set up the making of Potash which they apprehend will be of great Service to the Province; Therefore Praying for Encouragement from this Court either by Granting them a Sum of Money, or otherwise as this Court shall judge best

In the House of Representatives; Read and Voted, that there be and hereby is granted to the said John Franklyn and Company Fifteen hundred Acres of Land to be laid out in the Unappropriated Lands of the Province adjoining to some Town or District, in a regular Form, by a Skillful Surveyr and Chainmen on Oath and that they return a Plan thereof to this Court within Three Years for Confirmation, Provided the said Franklin & Company their Heirs and Assigns do carry on the several Manufactures which the said Company are now engaged in at German Town for the space of seven Years at least from this time; Otherwise the said Lands to revert to the Government. And as a further Encouragement to the said Franklin and Company, That the Captain General be desired to exempt twelve of the Work Men, Such as said Company shall chuse, from Military Duties, so long as the said Manufactory shall be carried on, and that the said twelve Men be excused from Serving as Tithing men, Constables, Grand Jurors and Petit Jurors and Working at High Ways, and be freed from all Taxes, except Ministerial, so long as said Manufactories shall be carried on:

In Council; Read and Concur'd;——Consented to by the Governor."—*Ibid., p.* 169.

"November 16, 1754. A Memorial of Thomas Stevens shewing that, upon Encouragement from Great Britain, he has set up the Manufacture of Potash within this Province, which may be of great Benefit to the Province in general, and therefore praying that a Law may be made to prevent any Potash or Pearl Ash from being exported than what is good & Merchantable, and that Assay Masters may be appointed for surveying such Potash &ca;

In Council; Read and Ordered that Samuel Danforth, & Joseph Pynchon Esqrs with such as the Honble House shall join, be a Committee to take this Memorial under Consideration, and report what they judge proper for this Court to do thereon as soon as may be.

In the House of Representatives, Read & Concur'd, and Colo Brattle, Capt Ashley and Judge Russell are joined in the Affair."—*Ibid., p.* 327.

"January 9, 1755. A Petition of John Franklyn & Isaac Winslow & Company, shewing that they have procured the Fifteen hundred Acres of Land granted to them by the General Court for encouraging the Manufacture of Potash, to be laid out, a Plan whereof is herewith presented, including about Sixty four Acres more, which considering their Losses & Disappointments, they pray the whole may be confirmed to them.

Which Land bounds South on the North Line of Sheffield, West on the East Line of Stockbridge partly, & partly on Land formerly belonging to Colo Ephraim Williams Decd North, partly on said Land & partly on Capt. John Larrabees Land, & partly on Province Land, East on Province Lands; The first Bound is the Northwest Corner of Sheffield on Stockbridge Line, Thence North 7D 45M East, One hundred & twenty Rods to said Land, formerly Colo Ephraim William's Decd Thence East 1D 45M South, One hundred & ten Rods, Thence North 44 Deg. East, Four hundred & eighty Rods to said Capt John Larrabees Land; Thence East 7D. 45M. South, Two hundred & forty Rods to the South East

Corner thereof; thence the same Course Fourteen Rods; thence South 7D. 45M. West, Five hundred & ten Rods to Sheffield Line; Thence Seven hundred and four Rods on Sheffield Line to the first Bound. In the House of Representatives; Read & Ordered that the Prayer of the Petition be so far granted, as that the Plan mentioned in the Petition, be & hereby is Accepted, and that the Lands therein delineated & described, Including the Sixty three Acres & forty Rods laid down on the East Side of said Plan, be confirmed to the Petitioners & Company their Heirs & Assigns forever; Provided the whole contain no More than Fifteen hundred & Sixty three Acres & forty Rods, and does not interfere with any former Grant, Provided also that the said Petitioners & Company be at the Charge of obtaining the Indian Title to said Lands; In Council; Read & Concur'd;—Consented to by the Governour."—*Ibid., p.* 375.

Chap. 27. "February 10, 1755. In the House of Representatives; Voted that the Impost Officer and his Deputies for and during the Term of Twelve Weeks, be & hereby are impowered & directed to demand from the Master of any Vessell, which shall clear out from any Port within this Province, an account, upon Oath, of all Provisions & Warlike Stores, laden or intended to be laden, on board such Vessel before her Sailing, And whensoever it shall appear to the said Officer or Deputy, that any Vessell has on board, or that there is intended to be laden on board any Vessell more Provisions or Warlike Stores than is necessary for the victualling and Defence of such Vessell on her proposed Voyage, said Officer shall require the Master of such Vessell to give Bond with Sureties, in the Penalty of One Thousand Pounds Sterling, That all such Provisions & Stores of War shall be landed in some Port within his Majesty's Dominions, & Certificate returned from the Chief Officer of the Customs of such Port, or if it be at a Port where there is no Officer of the Customs, then from the Chief Magistrate, That all such Provisions & Stores of War have been landed accordingly. And His Excellency, the Governr is desired to give Orders that no Vessel having Provisions & Warlike Stores on board as aforesaid be cleared at the Naval Office, untill Bond shall have been given as above directed; And that any Vessell already cleared out and suspected to have any Quantity of Provisions or Warlike Stores on board be detained untill Security be given as aforesaid; And that His Excellency be likewise desired as soon as he shall think proper to acquaint his Majesty's several Governours on the Continent with this Order, and desire that the like Care may be taken within the several Governments. In Council; Read & Concur'd;—Consented to by the Governour."—*Ibid., p.* 392.

"February 12, 1755. In the House of Representatives; Ordered that the Impost Officer, in taking Bonds to prevent the Exportation of Provisions &ca, according to the Resolve of this Court of Saturday last, be directed to exempt Cod Fish, exported to Europe; And it is accordingly Voted that all Persons have free Liberty to export Fish as aforesaid, said Order notwithstanding.

In Council; Read & Concur'd;—Consented to by the Governour."—*Ibid., p.* 394.

"February 15, 1755. In the House of Representatives; Voted that His Excellency the Governour be desired to lay a general Embargo on the Shipping within this Province for the space of one Month, from this Day; And that no Ship, Sloop or other Vessell be permitted to proceed to Sea, unless the Master or Owner fully satisfy His Excellency that there will be no supply made by such Vessel of Provisions, Arms or Ammunition to any of the French Kings Subjects in America, nor any Intelligence given thereby of the present Military Proceedings of this and the adjacent Governments; and also that His Excellency be desired to move the Neighboring Colonies to come into the same Measures.

In Council; Read & Concur'd;——Consented to by the Governour,"—*Ibid., p.* 399.

"February 15, 1755. In the House of Representatives; Voted that His Excellency the Captain General be desired further to extend the Embargo on Fishing Vessells that go to the Banks untill the fifteenth of March next;

In Council; Read & Concur'd;——Consented to by the Governour."—*Ibid.*

"Febry 21, 1755. A Petition of Jacob Fowle and Robert Hooper Esqrs and a great Number of Others, Inhabitants of Marblehead, setting forth the great Inconvenience and Damage to the Fishing Interest there, to have the Embargo extended to the fifteenth of March, praying that, as to the Fishery it may be limitted to the first of March. In the House of Representatives; Read & Thereupon Voted that His Excellency the Captain General be desired to take off the Embargo from Fishing Vessells upon the first of March next. In Council; Read & Concur'd;—Consented to by the Governr."—*Ibid., p.* 414.

"22d of February, 1755. The Secretary having by His Excellency's Order prepared a Draught of a Proclamation for an Embargo for stopping all Ships & other Vessells from sailing out of any of the Harbours of this Province with the Time limitted. The Same being read & considered was approved of; And Advised that His Excellency issue the said Proclamation accordingly."—*Executive Records of the Council, vol.* 2, *p.* 385.

"Proclamation for an Embargo.

BY HIS EXCELLENCY WILLIAM SHIRLEY EsqR Captn General & Govr in Chief in & over his Majtys Province of the Massachusetts Bay in New England.

A Proclamation

It appearing to me to be necessary for his Majestys Service that a Restraint should be laid upon such Vessels as are now outward bound, from the several Ports of this Province,

I do therefore with the Advice of his Majesty's Council, & at the desire of the House of Representves hereby strictly forbid all Owners & Masters of all whaling & other Fishing Vessels that may be outward bound to suffer such Vessels to depart, untill the first day of March next: And all Owners & Masters of All other outward bound Ships or Vessels to suffer such Vessels to sail or depart untill the fifteenth day of March next (Coasting Vessels from one Part of this Province to another excepted) without express Leave by me, granted for that Purpose, upon Pain of incurring the Penalty of One hundred Pounds imposed by Law; as well upon the Owners as Master of each Vessel that shall so sail or depart. And all Persons concerned, are to take Notice hereof, & govern themselves accordingly.

Given at Boston the twenty second day of Feby 1755, in the 28th Year of the Reign of Our Sovereign Lord George the 2d by the Grace of God of Gt. Britain, France & Ireland King, Deft of the Faith &ca

By his Excy's Command W. SHIRLEY.

J. WILLARD SECRY. God save the King."—*Records of Civil Commissions; in Secretary's Office, vol.* 2, *p.* 258.

"March 25, 1755. As the Embargo I laid on the Shipping of this Province at your Desire has been out for some Days I must recommend it to you, to consider what may be further necessary to prevent any Supplies being carried to the French; In doing which you will act the same Part that all the other Governments have done upon this great Occasion."—*Extract from the speech of the Governor to both Houses: Council Records, vol.* XX., *p.* 425.

"March 26, 1755. In the House of Representatives; Voted that His Excellency be desired to write to the Commanders of His Majesty's Ships of War in Newfoundland to refrain, as much as in them lies, the Exportation of any Provisions to the French Settlements in America, and to acquaint them with the Resolutions of this & the Neighbouring Governments on that Head. In Council; Read & Concur'd."—*Ibid., p.* 426.

"April 28, 1755. A Petition of Samuel Hews & Son of Boston Merchants, shewing that they have on board their Vessel bound to Suranam, a Quantity of Provisions, & for as much as the Transporting of Provision thither does not cross the true Design of the Government in restraining the Exportation of Provisions, therefore Praying for Liberty from this Court that their Vessel may sail to Suranam with the said Provisions.

In Council; Read & Ordered that the Prayer of the within Petition be granted, and that the Petitioner have Leave to export the Provisions within mentioned to Surinam, they giving Bond to the Impost Officer to land them there, and to return a Certificate thereof under the hand of the Principal Officer of the Customs at said Surinam;—— In the House of Representatives Read & Concur'd.——Consented to by the Lieutent Governour."—*Ibid., p.* 447.

Chap. 31. "To his Excellency William Shirley Esqr Capt Genl & Comander in chief of his Majestys Province of the Massa Bay &ca The Honble his Majesties Councill & the Honbl House of Representatives, In Genll Court Assembled Aprill 5. 1756.

The Memoriall of the Selectmen of Danvers Humbly Shews—

That whereas there is a Salt River or Cove, in sd Danvers, runing between the Lands of Capt. Samuel Endecott on ye North & the Lands of the North Field (so called) on ye South, in which ye Inhabitants used to Catch Shad, & some few other Sorts of Fish, which was very Convenient and advantagious to them to Eat fresh but now by a Late law of sd Province they are Debar'd from taking any of sd Fish; And also Whereas, there is no fresh water, or pond att ye Head of sd River, for sd fish to Spawn in, Save only a small Brook, which Terminates in about one Hundred Rods from the Salt Water.

Wherefore your Memorialists Humbly Pray that yr Excelly & Honrs would give Liberty to sd Inhabitants to take sd Fish with a Seine or Ware, three or four Days in a month or otherwise as to yr Excellency & Honrs shall seem meet & as in duty bound shall ever pray.

DANIEL EPES Junr
JAMES PRINCE
CORNELIUS TARBELL
DANIEL MARBLE
} Selectmen of Danvers."

—*Mass. State Archives, vol.* 87, *no.* 429.

"April 13, 1756. A Petition of the Inhabitants of the District of Danvers by their Select Men setting forth their great Dependence upon the Fish that might be taken within their Bounds, but they apprehend the late Law referring to the taking Fish in Scins forbids their taking them in the proper Season, Praying for Liberty to take Fish in Scins Three or Four days in a month or be otherwise releived as this Court shall judge meet,—

In the House of Representatives; Read and Whereas it is apprehended by this House that the Cove in the Memorial mentioned is not included in the design of the Law referred to therein—Therefore,

Voted, That the Inhabitants of said District be & hereby are allowed with the Consent of their Select Men to make use of said Cove to their best Advantage.

In Council; read & Concurd—Consented to by the Governour"—*Council Records, vol. XXI., p.* 158.

Chap. 34. "You must be sensible, Gentlemen, How much the success of this Expedition will depend on its being kept secret from the French: It is for this Reason that I have delayed beginning to enlist the Men untill six Weeks before it is proposed they should embark for the Bay of Funda; which I hope may be a sufficient Time for compleating the Levies and all Preparations for their Imbarkation; In the mean Time such Preparations have been making as were consistent with the Privacy requisite in the Case * * * *

It is prudent that as little should transpire of this Design, as is possible; For which Reason, I doubt not but you will take the same Measures for binding your several Members to Secrecy as was done in the Expedition against Louisbourgh."—*From the Governor's speech to both Houses, Feb.* 7, 1755: *Council Records, vol.* XX., *pp.* 391–2.

"February 15, 1755. In the House of Representatives; Voted that His Excellency the Captain General be desired, as soon as may be to give Orders that all the Subjects of the French King within this Province be forthwith confined, and that His Excellency be desired to write to the Neighbouring Governments to do the like within their respective Governments.

In Council; Read & Concur'd;——Consented to by the Governour."—*Ibid., pp.* 398–9.

ACTS,

PASSED 1755–56.

ACTS

Passed at the Session begun and held at Boston, on the Twenty-eighth day of May, A. D. 1755.

CHAPTER 1.

AN ACT FOR GRANTING UNTO HIS MAJESTY SEVERAL RATES AND DUTIES OF IMPOST AND TUNNAGE OF SHIPPING.

Whereas in and by an act of this province, pass'd at their session in October, one thousand seven hundred and fifty-four, the province treasurer was impowered to borrow a sum not exceeding six thousand pounds; and by another act at their session in January, one thousand seven hundred and fifty-five, another sum not exceeding twenty-three thousand pounds, in Spanish mill'd dollars of full weight, at six shillings apeice, or silver at six shillings and eightpence per ounce, for the discharge of the debts of this province; and, by said act, the treasurer was ordered to give his receipts or obligations to the lenders to repay the money so borrowed; and in order to enable the treasurer to discharge the receipts and obligations that should by him be given for the said sum, in pursuance of the afore-mentioned acts, it was therein provided, that the duty of impost for the year one thousand seven hundred and fifty-five, should be applied towards discharging said receipts and obligations,—

We, his majesty's most loyal and dutiful subjects, the representatives of the province of the Massachusetts Bay, in New England, being desirous of enabling the treasurer to discharge the receipts and obligations aforesaid, have chearfully and unanimously given and granted, and do hereby give and grant, to his most excellent majesty, to the end and use aforesaid, and no other use, the several duties of impost upon wines, liquors, goods, wares and merchandize that shall be imported into this province, and tunnage of shipping, hereafter mentioned; and pray that it may be enacted,—

And be it accordingly enacted by the Governour, Council and House of Representatives,

[Sect. 1.] That from and after the twenty-sixth day of June current, and during the space of eight months, there shall be paid by the importers of all wines, liquors, goods, wares and merchandizes that shall be imported into this province by any of the inhabitants thereof (salt, cotton-wool, pig-iron, mehogany, black-walnut, lignum-vitæ, red-cedar, braziletto and logwood, provisions, and every other thing of the growth and produce of his majesty's colonies and provinces upon this continent, tobacco excepted, and also all prize goods condemned in any part of this province, excepted), the several rates and duties of imposts following; vizt.,—

For every pipe of wine of the Western Islands, fifteen shillings.

For every pipe of Maderia, one pound six shillings and eightpence.

For every pipe of other sorts not mentioned, fifteen shillings.

For every hogshead of rum, containing one hundred gallons, thirteen shillings and fourpence.

For every hogshead of sugar, fourpence.

For every hogshead of molasses, fourpence.

For every hogshead of tobacco, ten shillings.

—And so, proportionably, for greater or less quantities.

And all other commodities, goods or merchandize not mentioned or excepted, fourpence for every twenty shillings value: all goods the product or manufacture of Great Britain, also raw hemp and hogshead- and barrell-staves and heading from any of his majesty's colonies and provinces on this continent, excepted.

[SECT. 2.] And for any of the above wines, liquors, goods, wares and merchandize, &c^a^., that shall be imported into this province by any of the inhabitants of the other provinces and colonies on this continent, or of the English West-India Islands, or in any ship or vessell to them belonging, on the proper accompt of any of the said inhabitants of the other provinces or colonies on this continent, or of the inhabitants of any of the West-India Islands, there shall be paid by the importers double the impost appointed by this act to be received for every species above mentioned: *provided always*, that all hogshead- and barrell-staves and heading from any of his majesty's provinces or colonies, all provisions and other things that are the growth of his majesty's colonies and provinces upon this continent (tobacco excepted), all salt, cotton-wool and pig-iron, mohogany, black-walnut, lignum-vitæ, red-cedar, logwood and brazilletto-wood, and hemp, are and shall be exempted from every the rates and duties aforesaid.

And be it further enacted,

[SECT. 3.] That all goods, wares and merchandize, the property of any of the inhabitants of any the neighbouring provinces or colonies on this continent, that shall be imported into this province, and shall have paid, or secured to be paid, the duty of impost, by this act provided to be paid, and afterwards shall be exported and landed in any of the said provinces or colonies on this continent, then, and in such case, the exporter producing a certificate from some officer of his majesty's customs, that the same have been landed in some of the provinces or colonies aforesaid, such exporter shall be allowed a drawback of the whole duty of impost by him paid, or secured to be paid, as by this act provided.

And be it further enacted,

[SECT. 4.] That the impost rates and duties aforesaid shall be paid in current lawfull money by the importer of any wines, liquors, goods or merchandize, unto the commissioner to be appointed, as is hereinafter to be directed, for entring and receiving the same, at or before the landing any wines, liquors, goods or merchandize: only the commissioner or receiver is hereby allowed to give credit to such person or persons, where his or their duty of impost, in one ship or vessell, doth exceed six pounds; and in cases where the commissioner or receiver shall give credit, he shall ballance and settle his accounts with every person on or before the last day of April, so that the same accounts may be ready to be produced in court in May next after. And all entries, where the impost or duty to be paid doth not exceed three shillings, shall be made without charge to the importer; and not more than sixpence to be demanded for every other single entry to what value soever.

And be it further enacted,

[SECT. 5.] That the master of every ship or vessell coming into this province from any other place, shall, within twenty-four hours after his arrival in any port or harbour, and before bulk is broken, make report and deliver a manifest, in writing, under his hand, to the commissioner aforesaid, of the contents of the loading of such ship or vessell, therein particularly expressing the species, kind and quantities of all the wines, liquors, goods, wares and merchandize imported in such ship or vessell, with the marks and numbers thereof, and to whom the same are consigned; and make oath before the commissioner that the same manifest contains a just and true account of all the lading taken on board and imported in such ship or vessell, so far as he knows or beleives; and that if he knows of any more wines, liquors, goods, wares or merchandize laden on board such ship or vessell, and imported therein, he will forthwith make report thereof to the commissioner aforesaid, and cause the same to be added to his manifest.

And be it further enacted,

[Sect. 6.] That if the master of any ship or vessell shall break bulk, or suffer any of the wines, liquors, goods, or wares and merchandize imported in such ship or vessell to be unloaden before report and entry thereof be made as aforesaid, he shall forfiet the sum of one hundred pounds.

And be it further enacted,

[Sect. 7.] That all merchants and other persons, being owners of any wines, liquors, goods, wares or merchandize imported into this province, for which any of the rates or duties aforesaid are payable, or having the same consigned to them, shall make a like entry thereof with the commissioner aforesaid, and produce an invoice of all such goods as pay *ad valorem*, and make oath before him in form following; vizt.,—

You, A. B., do swear that the entry of the goods and merchandize by you now made, exhibits the sterling value of said goods, and that, *bonâ fide*, according to your best skill and judgment, it is not less than that value. So help you God.

—which oath the commissioner or receiver is hereby impowered and directed to administer; and the owners aforesaid shall pay or give security to pay the duty of impost by this act required, before such wines, liquors, goods, wares or merchandize be landed or taken out of the vessell in which the same shall be imported.

[Sect. 8.] And no wines, liquors, goods, wares or merchandize that by this act are liable to pay impost or duty, shall be landed on any wharff, or into any warehouse or other place, but in the daytime only, and that after sunrise and before sunset, unless in the presence or with the consent of the commissioner or receiver, on pain of forfieting all such wines, liquors, goods, wares and merchandize, and the lighter, boat or vessell out of which the same shall be landed or put into any warehouse or other place.

[Sect. 9.] And if any person or persons shall not have and produce an invoice of the quantities of rum or liquors to him or them consigned, then the cask wherein the same is, shall be gauged at the charge of the importer, that the contents thereof may be known.

And be it further enacted,

[Sect. 10.] That the importer of all wines, liquors, goods, wares and merchandize, within eight months from and after the publication of this act, by land-carriage, or in small vessells or boats, shall make report and deliver a manifest thereof to the commissioner aforesaid or his deputy, therein particularly expressing the species, kind and quantity of all such wines, liquors, goods, wares and merchandize so imported, with the marks and numbers thereof, when, how and by whom brought; and shall make oath, before the said commissioner or his deputy, to the truth of such report and manifest, and shall also pay or secure to be paid the several duties aforesaid by this act charged and chargeable upon such wines, liquors, goods, wares and merchandizes, before the same are landed, housed or put into any store or place whatever.

And be it further enacted,

[SECT. 11.] That every merchant or other person importing any wines in this province, shall be allowed twelve per cent for leakage: *provided,* such wines shall not have been filled up on board; and that every hogshead, butt or pipe of wine that hath two-thirds thereof leaked out, shall be accounted for outs, and the merchant or importer to pay no duty for the same. And no master of any ship or vessell shall suffer any wines to be filled up on board without giving a certificate of the quantity so filled up, under his hand, before the landing thereof, to the commissioner or receiver of impost for such port, on pain of forfieting the sum of one hundred pounds.

[SECT. 12.] And if it may be made to appear that any wines imported in any ship or vessell be decayed at the time of unloading thereof, or in twenty days afterwards, oath being made before the commissioner or receiver that the same hath not been landed above that time, the duties and impost paid for such wines shall be repaid unto the importer thereof.

And be it further enacted,

[SECT. 13.] That the master of every ship or vessell importing any liquors, wines, goods, wares or merchandize, shall be liable to and pay the impost for such and so much thereof, contained in his manifest, as shall not be duly entered, nor the duty paid for the same by the person or persons to whom such wines, liquors, goods, wares or merchandize are or shall be consigned. And it shall and may be lawful, to and for the master of every ship or other vessell, to secure and detain in his hands, at the owner's risque, all such wines, liquors, goods, wares and merchandize imported in any ship or vessell, untill he receives a certificate, from the commissioner or the receiver of the impost, that the duty for the same is paid, and untill he be repaid his necessary charges in securing the same; or such master may deliver such wines, liquors, goods, wares and merchandizes as are not entred, unto the commissioner or receiver of the impost in such port, or his order, who is hereby impowered and directed to receive and keep the same, at the owner's risque, untill the impost thereof, with the charges, be paid or secured to be paid; and then to deliver such wines, liquors, goods, wares or merchandize as such master shall direct.

And be it further enacted,

[SECT. 14.] That the commissioner or the receiver of the impost in each port, shall be and hereby is impowered to sue the master of any ship or vessell, for the impost or duty of so much of the lading of any wines, liquors, goods, wares or merchandize imported therein, according to the manifest to be by him given upon oath, as aforesaid, as shall remain not entred and the duty of impost therefor not paid or secured to be paid. And where any goods, wares or merchandize are such that the value thereof is not known, whereby the impost to be recovered of the master, for the same, cannot be ascertained, the owner or person to whom such goods, wares or merchandize are or shall be consigned, shall be summoned to appear as an evidence at the court where such suit for the impost and the duty thereof shall be brought, and be there required to make oath to the value of such goods, wares or merchandize.

And be it further enacted,

[SECT. 15.] That the ship or vessell, with her tackle, apparel and furniture, the master of which shall make default in anything by this act required to be performed by him, shall be liable to answer and make good the sum or sums forfieted by such master, according to this act, for any such default, as also to make good the impost or duty for any such wines, liquors, goods, wares and merchandize not entred as aforesaid; and, upon judgment recovered against such master, the said ship or vessell, with so much of the tackle or appurtenances thereof as shall be sufficient to satisfy said judgment, may be taken into execution for the same; and the commissioner or receiver of the impost is hereby impowered to make seizure of the said ship or vessell, and detain the same under seizure untill judgment be given in any suit to be commenced and prosecuted for any of the said forfietures of impost; to the intent, that if judgment be rendered for the prosecutors or informer, such ship or vessell and appurtenances may be exposed to sale, for satisfaction thereof, as is before provided: *unless* the owner, or some on their behalf, for releasing of such ship or vessell from under seizure or restraint, shall give sufficient security to the commissioner or receiver of impost that seized the same, to respond and satisfy the sum or value of the forfietures and duties, with charges, that shall be recovered against the master thereof, upon such suit to be brôt for the same, as aforesaid; and the master occasioning such loss or damage unto his owners, through his default or neglect, shall be liable unto their action for the same.

And be it further enacted,

[Sect. 16.] That the naval officer within any of the ports of this province shall not clear or give passes to any master of any ship or vessell, outward bound, untill he shall be certified, by the commissioner or receiver of the impost, that the duty and impost for the goods last imported in such ship or vessell are paid or secured to be paid.

[Sect. 17.] And the commissioner or receiver of the impost is hereby impowered to allow bills of store to the master of any ship or vessell importing any wines or liquors, for such private adventures as shall belong to the master or seamen of such ship or vessell, at the discretion of the commissioner or receiver, not exceeding three per cent of the lading; and the duties payable by this act for such wines or liquors, in such bills of stores mentioned and expressed, shall be abated.

And for the more effectual preventing any wines, rum or other distilled spirits being brought into the province from the neighbouring governments, by land, or in small boats or vessells, or any other way, and also to prevent wines, rum or other distilled spirits being first sent out of this province, to save the duty of impost, and afterwards brought into the government again,—

Be it enacted,

[Sect. 18.] That the commissioner and receiver of the aforesaid duties of impost shall, and he is hereby impowered and enjoined to, appoint one suitable person or persons as his deputy or deputies, in all such places of this province where it is likely that wine, rum or other distilled spirits will be brought out of other governments into this; which officers shall have power to seize the same, unless the owner shall make it appear that the duty of impost has been paid therefor since their being brought into or relanded in this government; and such officer or officers are also impowered to search, in all suspected places, for such wines, rum and distilled spirits brought or relanded in this government, where the duty is not paid as aforesaid, and to seize and secure the same for the ends and uses as in the act hereafter provided.

And be it further enacted,

[Sect. 19.] That the commissioner or his deputies shall have full power to administer the several oaths aforesaid, and to search in all suspected places for all such wines, rum, liquors, goods, wares and merchandize as are brought into this province, and landed contrary to the true intent and meaning of this act, and to seize the same for the uses hereinafter mentioned.

And be it further enacted,

[SECT. 20.] That there shall be paid, by the master of every ship or other vessell, coming into any port or ports of this province, to trade or traffick, whereof all the owners are not belonging to this province (except such vessells as belong to Great Britain, the provinces or colonies of Pennsylvania, West and East Jersey, Connecticut, New York, New Hampshire and Rhode Island), every voyage such ship or vessell doth make, one pound of good pistol-powder for every ton such ship or vessell is in burthen: *saving* for that part which is owned in Great Britain, this province, or any of the aforesaid governments, which are hereby exempted; to be paid unto the commissioner or receiver of the duties of impost, and to be employed for the ends and uses aforesaid.

[SECT. 21.] And the said commissioner is hereby impowered to appoint a meet and suitable person, to repair unto and on board any ship or vessell, to take the exact measure and tunnage thereof, in case he shall suspect the register of such ship or vessell doth not express and set forth the full burthen of the same; the charge thereof to be paid by the master or owner of such ship or vessell, before she shall be cleared, in case she shall appear to be of a greater burthen: otherwise, to be paid by the commissioner out of the money received by him for impost, and shall be allowed him, accordingly, by the treasurer, in his accompts. And the naval officer shall not clear any vessell, untill he be certified, also, by the commissioner, that the duty of tunnage for the same is paid, or that it is such a vessell for which none is payable according to this act.

And be it further enacted,

[SECT. 22.] That when and so often as any wine or rum imported into this province, the duty of impost upon which shall have been paid agreeable to this act, shall be reshipped and exported from this government to any other part of the world, that then, and in every such case, the exporter of such wine or rum shall make oath, at the time of shipping, before the receiver of impost, or his deputy, that the whole of the wine or rum so shipp'd has, *bonâ fide*, had the aforesaid duty of impost paid on the same, and shall afterwards produce a certificate, from some officer of the customs, that the same has been landed out of this government,—or otherwise, in case such rum or wines shall be exported to any place where there is no officer of the customs, or to any foreign port, the master of the vessell in which the same shall be exported shall make oath that the same has been landed out of the government, and the exporter shall, upon producing such certificate, or upon such oath of the master, make oath that he verily believes no part of said wines or rum has been relanded in this province,—such exporter shall be allowed a drawback from the receiver of impost as follows; viz[t].,—

For every pipe of Medaria, twenty-two shillings.

For every pipe of the Western-Island wines, and other sorts, ten shillings.

For every hogshead of rum, twelve shillings.

Provided, always,—

[SECT. 23.] That after the shipping of such wine or rum to be exported as aforesaid, and giving security as aforesaid, in order to obtain the drawback aforesaid, the wine or rum so shipp'd to be exported, or any part thereof, shall be relanded in this province, or brought into the same from any other province or colony, that then all such rum and wine so relanded and brought again into this province, shall be forfieted and may be seized by the commissioner aforesaid, or his deputy.

And be it further enacted,

[Sect. 24.] That there be one fit person, and no more, nominated and appointed by this court, as a commissioner and a receiver of the aforesaid duties of impost and tunnage of shipping, and for the inspection, care and management of the said office, and whatsoever thereto relates, to receive commission for the same from the governour or commander-in-chief for the time being, with authority to substitute and appoint a deputy receiver in each port, or other places besides that in which he resides, and to grant warrants to such deputy receivers for the said place, and to collect and receive the impost and tunnage of shipping as aforesaid that shall become due within such port, and to render the account thereof, and to pay in the same, to the said commissioner and receiver: which said commissioner and receiver shall keep fair books of all entries and duties arising by virtue of this act; also, a particular account of every vessell, so that the duties of impost and tunnage arising on said vessell may appear; and the same to lie open, at all seasonable times, to the view and perusal of the treasurer or receiver-general of this province (or any other person or persons whom this court shall appoint), with whom he shall account for all collections and payments, and pay all such monies as shall be in his hands, as the treasurer or receiver-general shall demand it. And the said commissioner or receiver and his deputy or deputies, before their entring upon the execution of their office, shall be sworn to deal truly and faithfully therein, and shall attend in the said office from ten o'clock in the forenoon, untill one in the afternoon.

[Sect. 25.] And the said commissioner and receiver, for his labour, care and expences in said office, shall have and receive, out of the province treasury, at the rate of sixty pounds per annum; and his deputy or deputies shall receive for their service such sums as the said commissioner of impost, together with the province treasurer, shall judge necessary, for whatever sums they shall receive and pay; and the treasurer is hereby ordered, in passing and receiving the said commissioner's accounts, accordingly, to allow the payment of such salary or salaries, as aforesaid, to himself and his deputies.

And be it further enacted,

[Sect. 26.] That all penalties, fines and forfietures accruing and arising by virtue of any breach of this act, shall be one half to his majesty for the uses and intents for which the afore-mentioned duties of impost are granted, and the other half to him or them that shall seize, inform and sue for the same, by action, bill, plaint or information, in any of his majesty's courts of record, wherein no essoign, protection or wager of law shall be allowed: the whole charge of the prosecution to be taken out of the half belonging to the informer.

And be it further enacted,

[Sect. 27.] That from and after the publication of this act, in all causes where any claimer shall appear, and shall not make good the claim, the charges of prosecution shall be born and paid by the said claimer, and not by the informer. [*Passed June* 21; *published June* 27.

CHAPTER 2.

AN ACT FOR THE SUPPLY OF THE TREASURY WITH THE SUM OF TEN THOUSAND ONE HUNDRED AND FIFTEEN POUNDS FOURTEEN SHILLINGS, AND FOR DRAWING THE SAME INTO THE TREASURY AGAIN; ALSO FOR APPORTIONING AND ASSESSING A TAX OF THIRTY-SIX THOUSAND POUNDS; AND ALSO FOR APPORTIONING AND ASSESSING A FURTHER TAX OF THREE THOUSAND ONE HUNDRED AND FIFTEEN POUNDS FOURTEEN SHILLINGS, PAID THE REPRESENTATIVES FOR THEIR SERVICE AND ATTENDANCE IN THE GENERAL COURT, AND TRAVEL, AND FOR FINES LAID UPON TOWNS THAT DID NOT SEND A REPRESENTATIVE: WHICH SUMS AMOUNT, IN THE WHOLE, TO THIRTY-NINE THOUSAND ONE HUNDRED FIFTEEN POUNDS FOURTEEN SHILLINGS.

1754-55, chap. 23, § 2. 1754-55, chap. 17, § 6.

WHEREAS the great and general court or assembly of the province did, at their session in one thousand seven hundred and fifty-four, pass an act for levying a tax of six thousand pounds; and another act for levying a further tax of twenty-three thousand pounds, and by said acts provision was made that the general court, at this present sitting, might apportion the same on the several towns and districts within this province, if they thought fit; *and whereas* the treasurer is, in and by this act, directed to issue out of the treasury, the sum of ten thousand one hundred and fifteen pounds fourteen shillings for the ends and purposes as is hereinafter mentioned; wherefore, for the ordering, directing and effectual drawing in the sum of thirty-nine thousand one hundred and fifteen pounds fourteen shillings, pursuant to the funds and grants aforesaid, into the treasury, according to the last apportion agreed to by this court; all which is unanimously approved, ratified and confirmed; we, his majesty's most loyall and dutiful subjects, the representatives in general court assembled, pray that it may be enacted,—

And be it accordingly enacted by the Governour, Council and House of Representatives,

[SECT. 1.] That each town and district within this province be assessed and pay, as such town and district's proportion of the sum of thirty-six thousand pounds, and their representatives' pay, and fines, the sum of three thousand one hundred and fifteen pounds fourteen shillings, the several sums following; that is to say,—

IN THE COUNTY OF SUFFOLK.

	Representatives' pay, and fines.	Province tax.	Sum total.	
Boston,	£94 16s. 0d.	£5,931 0s. 0d.	Six [illegible] [illegible]-five p[illegible]s sixteen shillings,	£6,025 16s. 0d.
Roxbury,	23 8 0	333 0 0	Three hundred and fifty-six pounds eight shillings,	356 8 0
Dorchester,	22 12 0	329 11 0	Three hundred and fifty-two p[illegible]s three shillings,	352 3 0
Milton,	29 0 0	175 1 0	Two hundred and four pounds one [illegible],	204 1 0
Braintree,	28 12 0	379 19 0	Four hundred and [illegible]ght pounds [illegible] shillings,	408 11 0
[illegible]h,	27 16 0	223 19 0	[illegible]o hundred and fifty-one pounds [illegible] shillings,	251 15 0
Hingham,	28 12 0	394 4 0	Four hundred [illegible] twenty-two pounds sixteen shillings,	422 16 0
Dedham,	46 4 0	261 18 0	Three hundred and eight pounds two [illegible],	308 2 0
[illegible]d,	23 16 0	162 0 0	One hundred [illegible] eighty-five pounds [illegible] shillings,	[illegible]85 16 0
Wrentham,	0 0 0	277 0 0	[illegible]o hundred a[illegible] seventy-seven [illegible],	277 0 0
Brookl[y][i]ne,	0 0 0	100 16 0	One hundred pounds sixteen shillings,	100 16 0
[illegible]n,	29 0 0	132 18 0	One hundred and sixty-one pounds eighteen shillings,	161 18 0
Stoughton,	8 12 0	226 0 0	[illegible]o [illegible]d a[illegible] thirty-four [illegible] [illegible] shillings,	234 12 0
[illegible]y,	30 0 0	132 18 0	One hundred and sixty-two pounds eighteen shillings,	162 18 0
Bellingham,	10 0 0	51 12 0	Sixty-one pounds twelve shillings,	61 12 0
Hull,	0 0 0	61 13 0	Sixty-one p[illegible]s thirteen shillings,	61 13 0
[illegible]e,	0 0 0	98 16 0	Ninety-eight pounds sixteen shillings,	98 16 0
[illegible]a,	0 0 0	137 11 0	One hundred and [illegible]-[illegible]en pounds eleven shillings,	137 11 0
	£402 8s. 0d.	£9,409 16s. 0d.		£9,812 4s. 0d.

107

IN THE COUNTY OF ESSEX.

	Representatives' pay, and fines.	Province tax.	Sum total.	
Salem,	£28 4s. 0d.	£567 0s. 0d.	Five hundred and ninety-five pounds four shillings,	£595 4s. 0d.
Danvers,	29 8 0	315 6 0	Three hundred and forty-four pounds fourteen shillings,	344 14 0
Ipswich,	27 0 0	809 2 0	Eight hundred and thirty-six pounds two shillings,	836 2 0
Newbury,	65 0 0	1,041 9 0	Eleven hundred and six pounds nine shillings,	1,106 9 0
Marblehead,	26 4 0	617 17 0	Six hundred and forty-four pounds one shilling,	644 1 0
Lynn,	29 12 0	332 17 0	Three hundred and sixty-two pounds nine shillings,	362 9 0
Andover,	25 0 0	456 15 0	Four hundred and eighty-one pounds fifteen shillings,	481 15 0
Beverly,	27 0 0	283 1 0	Three hundred and ten pounds one shilling,	310 1 0
Rowley,	32 8 0	288 0 0	Three hundred and twenty pounds eight shillings,	320 8 0
Salisbury,	32 12 0	226 10 0	Two hundred and fifty-nine pounds two shillings,	259 2 0

IN THE COUNTY OF ESSEX—*Continued.*

	REPRESENTATIVES' PAY, AND FINES.	PROVINCE TAX.	SUM TOTAL.	
Haverhill,	£16 6s. 0d.	£265 19s. 0d.	Two hundred and eighty-two pounds fifteen shillings,	£282 15s. 0d.
Glocester,	28 8 0	470 17 0	Four hundred and ninety-nine pounds five shillings,	499 5 0
Topsfield,	44 4 0	126 0 0	One hundred and seventy pounds four shillings,	170 4 0
Boxford,	30 0 0	166 13 0	One hundred and ninety-six pounds thirteen shillings,	196 13 0
Almsbury,	33 16 0	208 16 0	Two hundred and forty-two pounds twelve shillings,	242 12 0
Bradford,	26 10 0	186 18 0	Two hundred and thirteen pounds eight shillings,	213 8 0
Wenham,	45 16 0	105 18 0	One hundred and fifty-one pounds fourteen shillings,	151 14 0
Middleton,	0 0 0	94 1 0	Ninety-four pounds one shilling,	94 1 0
Manchester,	0 0 0	75 15 0	Seventy-five pounds fifteen shillings,	75 15 0
Meth[ewi][ue]n,	5 0 0	120 12 0	One hundred and twenty-five pounds twelve shillings,	125 12 0
	£552 18s. 0d.	£6,759 6s. 0d.		£7,312 4s. 0d.

IN THE COUNTY OF MIDDLESEX.

Cambridge,	£0 0s. 0d.	£251 8s. 0d.	Two [illegible] and fifty-one [illegible] eight shillings,	£251 8s. 0d.
[illegible]n,	22 16 0	325 6 0	Three hundred and forty-eight [illegible] two shillings,	348 2 0
Watertown,	28 16 0	133 7 0	One hundred and sixty-two pounds three shillings,	162 3 0
Woburn,	39 8 0	234 0 0	[illegible]o hundred and seventy-three [illegible] eight shillings,	273 8 0
Concord,	19 0 0	*148 5 0	One hundred and sixty-eight [illegible] five shillings,	168 5 0
[illegible]n,	27 4 0	234 0 0	[illegible]o hundred and sixty-one pounds four shillings,	261 4 0
Sudbury,	27 8 0	253 1 0	[illegible]o hundred and eighty [illegible] ine [illegible],	280 9 0
Marlborough,	30 16 0	252 0 0	[illegible]o hundred and [illegible] [illegible] sixteen shillings,	282 16 0
Billerica,	27 8 0	147 12 0	One [illegible] [illegible] [illegible]ve [illegible],	175 0 0
Framingham,	27 8 0	192 12 0	Two hundred and twenty [illegible],	220 0 0
Lexington,	0 0 0	167 4 0	One hundred and [illegible] [illegible] [illegible] four shillings,	167 4 0
Chelmsford,	53 0 0	144 0 0	One hundred and [illegible] [illegible] [illegible],	197 0 0
Sherburn[e],	12 0 0	99 9 0	One hundred and [illegible] [illegible] ine shillings,	11 9 0
[illegible]g,	28 12 0	237 12 0	[illegible]o hundred and sixty-six [illegible] four shillings,	266 4 0
Malden,	24 0 0	189 12 0	[illegible]o hundred and thirteen pounds twelve shillings,	213 12 0
[illegible]n,	28 16 0	93 6 8	One hundred and [illegible] [illegible]o pounds two shillings and eightpence,	122 2 8
Medford,	24 8 0	186 9 0	[illegible]o hundred and ten pounds [illegible]en shillings,	210 17 0
[illegible]n,	29 4 0	[illegible] 2 0	One [illegible] [illegible] [illegible] thirty pounds six shil[illegible],	130 6 0
[illegible]n,	0 0 0	88 4 0	Eighty-eight pounds [illegible] shillings,	88 4 0
Westford,	44 4 0	97 4 0	One hundred [and] forty one pounds eight shillings,	41 8 0

Shirley,	£2 14s. 0d.	£24 15s. 0d.	Twenty-seven [illegible] nine shillings,	£27 9s. 0d.
Waltham,	29 0 0	124 10 0	One hundred and [illegible] pounds ten shillings,	153 10 0
Towns[*h*]end,	0 0 0	55 1 0	Fifty-five [illegible] one shilling,	55 1 0
Stow,	10 0 0	88 4 0	Ninety-eight [illegible] four shillings,	98 4 0
Stoneham,	0 0 0	63 3 0	Sixty-three [illegible] three shillings,	63 3 0
Groton,	17 11 2	177 14 0	One hundred and ninety-five [illegible] five shillings and twopence,	195 5 2
Wilmington,	10 0 0	72 0 0	Eighty-two [illegible],	82 0 0
Natick,	0 0 0	50 2 0	Fifty pounds two shillings,	50 2 0
Drac[t]ut,	0 0 0	70 16 0	Seventy [illegible] [illegible] shillings,	70 16 0
Bedford,	0 0 0	82 13 0	[illegible] thirteen shillings,	82 13 0
Holliston,	0 0 0	80 5 0	Eighty [illegible] five shillings,	80 5 0
Tewksbury,	0 0 0	70 16 0	Seventy pounds [illegible],	70 16 0
Acton,	0 0 0	52 4 0	Fifty-two pounds [illegible] shillings,	52 4 0
Dunstable,	0 0 0	67 3 0	Sixty-seven [illegible] three shillings,	67 3 0
Pepper[*r*]ell,	6 2 10	56 16 0	[illegible] eighteen shillings and [illegible],	62 18 10
Lincoln,	25 0 0	106 8 4	One hundred and [illegible] eight shillings and [illegible],	131 8 4
Carlisle,	8 0 0	69 12 0	Seventy-seven [illegible] shillings,	77 12 0
	£602 16s. 0d.	£4,888 16s. 0d.		£5,491 12s. 0d.

IN THE COUNTY OF HAMPSHIRE.

Springfield,	£24 12s. 0d.	£350 8s. 0d.	Three hundred and seventy-five pounds,	£375 0s. 0d.
Northampton,	21 12 0	193 1 0	Two [illegible] and fourteen [illegible] thirteen shillings,	214 13 0
H[illegible],	32 12 0	107 17 0	One hundred and forty pounds nine shillings,	140 9 0
[illegible]d,	24 0 0	140 5 0	One hundred and [illegible] five shillings,	164 5 0
Enfield,	0 0 0	104 5 0	One hundred and four pounds five shillings,	104 5 0
Deerfield,	16 14 0	72 5 0	Eighty-eight pounds nineteen shillings,	88 19 0
Sheffield,	30 4 0	155 11 0	One hundred and eighty-five pounds fifteen shil[illegible],	185 15 0
Northfield,	0 0 0	37 13 0	[illegible] thirteen shillings,	37 13 0
[illegible]y,	17 18 0	120 10 8	One [illegible] and thirty-eight pounds eight shillings and eightpence,	138 8 8
Suffield,	0 0 0	193 10 0	One [illegible] and [illegible] pounds ten shillings,	193 10 0
Sunderland,	12 0 0	35 13 8	Forty-seven pounds thirteen shillings and eightpence,	47 13 8
Montague,	8 0 0	26 2 4	Thirty-four pounds two shillings and fourpence,	34 2 4
Brimfield,	36 4 0	118 10 0	One hundred and fifty-four pounds fourteen shillings,	154 14 0
Somers,	0 0 0	74 8 0	Seventy-[illegible] pounds eight shillings,	74 8 0
Southampton,	5 8 0	39 0 0	Forty-four [illegible] eight shillings,	44 8 0
South H[illegible]ey,	8 14 0	64 17 4	Seventy-three [illegible] shillings and fourpence,	73 11 4

£149, in the printed act.

IN THE COUNTY OF HAMPSHIRE—*Continued.*

	REPRESENTATIVES PAY, [illegible] FINES.	PROVINCE TAX.	SUM TOTAL.	
Palmer,	£0 0s. 0d.	£44 8s. 0d.	Forty-four [illegible] eight shillings,	£44 8s. 0d.
[illegible],	0 0 0	37 16 0	[illegible] pounds sixteen shillings,	37 16 0
Bedford,	0 0 0	25 4 0	[illegible]ve pounds four shillings,	25 4 0
Coldspring,	0 0 0	25 4 0	[illegible]ve [illegible] four shillings,	25 4 0
[illegible],	0 0 0	28 4 0	[illegible]-eight [illegible] shillings,	28 4 0
Blandford,	0 0 0	15 18 0	Fifteen [illegible] shillings,	15 18 0
[illegible] Salem,	7 8 0	18 0 0	[illegible] eight [illegible],	25 8 0
[illegible] Marlborough,	0 0 0	27 0 0	Twenty-seven pounds,	27 0 0
No. One (in the line of towns),	0 0 0	18 0 0	Eighteen pounds,	18 0 0
Ware [illegible],	0 0 0	18 0 0	Eighteen [illegible],	18 0 0
Stockbridge,	0 0 0	36 0 0	Thirty-six [illegible],	36 0 0
Roadtown,	0 0 0	15 0 0	Fifteen [illegible],	15 0 0
[illegible],	7 0 0	32 9 0	Thirty-nine [illegible] nine shillings,	39 9 0
	£252 6s. 0d.	£2,175 0s. 0d.		£2,427 6s. 0d.

IN THE COUNTY OF WORCESTER.

[illegible],	£23 [illegible]s. 0d.	£189 18s. 0d.	[illegible] hundred [illegible] thirteen [illegible] fourteen shillings,	£213 14s. 0d.
[illegible],	30 16 0	216 0 0	Two [illegible] forty-six [illegible] sixteen shillings,	246 16 0
[illegible],	28 12 0	207 0 0	Two hundred [illegible]-five [illegible] shillings,	235 12 0
Woodstock,	0 0 0	232 16 0	Two [illegible]-two pounds sixteen shillings,	232 16 0
[illegible],	28 16 0	169 19 0	One [illegible] and ninety-eight pounds fifteen shillings,	198 15 0
Oxford,	10 18 0	91 18 0	One hundred and two pounds sixteen shillings,	102 16 0
Charlton,	2 14 0	23 0 0	Twenty-five pounds [and] fourteen shillings,	25 14 0
[illegible],	30 12 0	165 3 0	One hundred and [illegible] fifteen [illegible],	195 15 0
Rutland,	20 0 0	119 2 0	One hundred and [illegible] two [illegible],	139 2 0
New-Braintree,	0 0 0	10 0 0	Ten [illegible],	10 0 0
[illegible] of Rutland,	5 0 0	17 0 0	Twenty-two [illegible],	22 0 0
[illegible],	8 13 4	113 0 0	[illegible] hundred and [illegible]-one pounds thirteen shillings and fourpence,	121 13 4
District of Spencer,	4 6 8	56 10 0	Sixty [illegible] sixteen shillings and eightpence,	60 16 8
Southboro[a]u[g][illegible],	15 0 0	92 17 0	One [illegible] and seven pounds seventeen shillings,	107 17 0
Westborough,	0 0 0	129 15 0	One hundred and [illegible] pounds fifteen shillings,	129 15 0
Shrewsbury,	27 4 0	151 4 0	One [illegible] and [illegible] pounds eight shillings,	178 8 0

Lunenburg,	£31 16s. 0d.	£126 15s. 0d.	One hu[illegible] and fifty-eight pounds eleven shillings,	£158 11s. 0d.
Uxbridge,	0 0 0	114 15 0	One hu[illegible] and fourteen pounds fifteen shillings,	114 15 0
Harvard,	15 0 0	104 2 0	One hundred and [illegible]en pounds two [illegible]llings,	119 2 0
Dudley,	10 0 0	68 8 0	Seventy-eight pounds [illegible]ght shillings,	78 8 0
Bolton,	25 8 0	103 16 0	One hundred and twenty-nine pounds four shillings,	129 4 0
Upton,	0 0 0	57 6 0	Fifty-seven pounds six shillings,	57 6 0
Sturbridge,	19 16 0	44 17 0	Sixty-four [illegible] [illegible]en shillings,	64 13 0
Leominster,	0 0 0	54 0 0	Fifty-four pounds,	54 0 0
Hardwick,	26 12 0	66 12 0	[illegible] [illegible] pounds four shillings,	93 4 0
Holden,	0 0 0	34 4 0	[illegible]ur pounds four [illegible]s,	34 4 0
Western,	0 0 0	52 4 0	Fifty-two pounds [illegible] shillings,	52 4 0
Douglas[s],	0 0 0	15 0 0	Fifteen pounds,	15 0 0
[illegible]n,	10 0 0	87 12 0	Ninety-seven [illegible]s twelve shillings,	97 12 0
Petersham,	0 0 0	39 0 0	Thirty-nine pounds,	39 0 0
	£375 0s. 0d.	£2,953 13s. 0d.		£3,328 13s. 0d.

IN THE COUNTY OF PLYMOUTH.

Plymouth,	£19 4s. 0d.	£288 0s. 0d.	Three [illegible] and seven pounds four shillings,	£307 4s. 0d.
[illegible]e,	30 0 0	396 0 0	Four hundred and twenty-six [illegible]s,	426 0 0
[illegible]y,	41 12 0	130 10 0	One hundred [illegible] [illegible]-two pounds two shillings,	172 2 0
[illegible]d,	26 6 0	269 2 0	Two hundred and [illegible]-five [illegible] eight [illegible]s,	295 8 0
Bridgwater,	29 16 0	457 16 0	Four [illegible] and [illegible]-[illegible]en pounds twelve shillings,	487 12 0
Middleborough,	32 12 0	328 13 0	Three hundred and sixty-one pounds five shillings,	361 5 0
Rochester,	27 4 0	198 3 0	Two [illegible] and twenty-five [illegible]s seven [illegible]s,	225 7 0
Plympton,	27 16 0	167 14 0	One hundred and [illegible]ve pounds ten shillings,	195 10 0
Pembro[o]k[e],	29 8 0	163 13 0	One [illegible] and ninety-three pounds one [illegible],	193 1 0
Kingston,	22 12 0	96 18 0	One [illegible] and [illegible]en pounds ten shillings,	119 10 0
Hanover,	26 16 0	116 8 0	One hundred and forty-three pounds four shillings,	143 4 0
Abbington,	42 4 0	135 0 0	One [illegible] and seventy-seven pounds four shillings,	177 4 0
Halifax,	0 0 0	79 16 0	[illegible]e pounds [illegible]en shillings,	79 16 0
W[illegible]m,	0 0 0	82 16 0	Eighty-two pounds sixteen shillings,	82 16 0
	£355 10s. 0d.	£2,910 9s. 0d.		£3,265 19s. 0d.

IN THE COUNTY OF BARNSTABLE.

	REPRESENTATIVES' PAY, AND FINES.	PROVINCE TAX.	SUM TOTAL.	
Barnstable,	£31 8s. 0d.	£252 0s. 0d.	Two hundred and eighty-three pounds eight shillings,	£283 8s. 0d.
Yarmouth,	10 0 0	165 0 0	One hundred and seventy-five pounds,	175 0 0
Sandwich,	2 4 0	180 0 0	One hundred and eighty-two pounds four shillings,	182 4 0
Eastham,	0 0 0	205 4 0	Two hundred and five pounds four shillings,	205 4 0
Harwich,	0 0 0	159 6 0	One hundred and fifty-nine pounds six shillings,	159 6 0
Chatham,	0 0 0	90 9 0	Ninety pounds nine shillings,	90 9 0
Truro,	0 0 0	97 1 0	Ninety-seven pounds one shilling,	97 1 0
Falmouth,	8 0 0	111 12 0	One hundred and nineteen pounds twelve shillings,	119 12 0
	£51 12s. 0d.	£1,260 12s. 0d.		£1,312 4s. 0d.

IN THE COUNTY OF BRISTOL.

	REPRESENTATIVES' PAY, AND FINES.	PROVINCE TAX.	SUM TOTAL.	
[illegible]n,	£31 16s. 0d.	£347 11s. 0d.	[illegible] and [illegible] [illegible]pds seven shillings,	£379 7s. 0d.
Rehoboth,	24 0 0	498 3 0	Five hundred and twenty-two [illegible]pds three shillings,	522 3 0
Swan[s][z]ey, with Shawamet,	34 8 0	221 2 0	Two [illegible]d [illegible]nd fifty-five pounds ten shillings,	255 10 0
Dartmouth,	37 12 0	648 0 0	Six [illegible]d [illegible]nd [illegible]-five pounds [illegible] shillings,	685 12 0
Norton,	21 0 0	217 7 0	[illegible]o hundred and thirty-eight pounds seven shillings,	238 7 0
Attleborough,	30 0 0	237 6 0	Two hundred [illegible]nd sixty-seven [illegible]ds six shillings,	267 6 0
Dighton,	45 16 0	153 6 0	One hundred [illegible]nd ninety-nine [illegible]pds two shillings,	199 2 0
Freetown,	46 4 0	141 12 0	One [illegible]d and eighty-seven [illegible]ds sixteen shillings,	187 16 0
Raynham,	0 0 0	91 10 0	[illegible]-one [illegible]ds ten shillings,	91 10 0
Easton,	2 12 0	105 3 0	One hundred [illegible]d seven [illegible]ds [illegible]en shillings,	107 15 0
Berkley,	0 0 0	81 15 0	Eighty-one pounds [illegible]en shillings,	81 15 0
	£273 8s. 0d.	£2,742 15s. 0d.		£3,016 3s. 0d.

IN THE COUNTY OF YORK.

	REPRESENTATIVES' PAY, AND FINES.	PROVINCE TAX.	SUM TOTAL.	
York,	£36 8s. 0d.	£352 10s. 0d.	Three hundred and eighty-eight pounds eighteen shillings,	£388 18s. 0d.
Kittery,	21 4 0	414 0 0	Four hundred and thirty-five pounds four shillings,	435 4 0
Wells,	35 16 0	158 8 0	One hundred and ninety-four pounds four shillings,	194 4 0

Berwick,	£28 0s. 0d.	£216 0s. 0d.	Two hundred and forty-four pounds,	£244 0s. 0d.
Falmouth,	30 16 0	342 0 0	Three hundred and seventy-two pounds sixteen shillings,	372 16 0
Biddeford,	16 4 0	145 4 0	One hundred [and] sixty-one pounds eight shillings,	161 8 0
Arundel[l],	0 0 0	80 14 0	Eighty pounds fourteen shillings,	80 14 0
Scarborough,	19 0 0	123 15 0	One hundred and forty-two pounds fifteen shillings,	142 15 0
North-Yarmouth,	28 0 0	53 17 0	Eighty-one pounds seventeen shillings,	81 17 0
George-Town,	0 0 0	57 3 0	Fifty-seven pounds three shillings,	57 3 0
Brunswick,	21 4 0	51 9 0	Seventy-two pounds thirteen shillings,	72 13 0
Sheepscut[t],	0 0 0	36 0 0	Thirty-six pounds,	36 0 0
	£236 12s. 0d.	£2,031 0s. 0d.		£2,267 12s. 0d.

IN THE COUNTY OF DUKES-COUNTY.

Edgartown,	£0 0s. 0d.	£139 4s. 0d.	One hundred and thirty-nine pounds four shillings,	£139 4s. 0d.
Chilmark,	0 0 0	124 19 0	One hundred and twenty-four pounds nineteen shillings,	124 19 0
Tisbury,	0 0 0	79 16 0	Seventy-nine pounds sixteen shillings,	79 16 0
	£0 0s. 0d.	£343 19s. 0d.		£343 19s. 0d.

IN [THE] [*NANTUCKET*] COUNTY [OF NANTUCKET].

Sherburne,	£13 4s. 0d.	£524 14s. 0d.	Five hundred and thirty-seven pounds eighteen shillings,	£537 18s. 0d.

	REPRESENTATIVES' PAY, AND FINES.	PROVINCE TAX.	SUM TOTAL.	
Suffolk, ...	£402 8s. 0d.	£9,409 16s. 0d.	[illegible] [illegible] eight [illegible] [illegible] and twelve pounds four shillings, .	£9,812 4s. [illegible]
Essex, ...	552 18 0	6,759 6 0	Seven [illegible] three hundred and twelve pounds [illegible] shillings, .	7,312 4 0
[illegible]x, ...	602 16 0	4,888 16 0	Five [illegible] four hundred and [illegible] pounds twelve shillings,	5,491 12 0
Hampshire, ...	252 6 0	2,175 0 0	[illegible] [illegible] four [illegible] [illegible] and [illegible] pounds six shillings,	2,427 6 0
W[illegible], ...	375 0 0	2,953 13 0	Three [illegible] three [illegible] [illegible] and [illegible] ight pounds thirteen shillings, ...	3,328 13 0
Plymouth, ...	355 10 0	2,910 9 0	Three [illegible] two [illegible] [illegible] and [illegible]-five pounds [illegible] shillings, ...	3,265 19 0
Barnstable, ...	51 12 0	1,260 12 0	One thousand three hundred and twelve pounds four shillings, .	1,312 4 0
Bristol, ...	273 8 0	2,742 15 0	Three [illegible] and sixteen pounds three shillings, ...	3,016 3 0
[illegible]k, ...	236 12 0	2,031 0 0	Two [illegible] two hundred and [illegible] pounds twelve shillings,	2,267 12 0
Dukes County, ...	0 0 0	343 19 0	Three [illegible] [illegible] and [illegible]-three pounds [illegible] shillings, . . .	343 19 0
Nantucket, ...	13 4 0	524 14 0	Five [illegible] [illegible] and thirty [illegible] [illegible] eighteen shillings, . . .	537 18 0
	£3,115 14s. 0d.	£36,000 0s. 0d.		£39,115 14s. 0d.

And be it further enacted,

[Sect. 2.] That the treasurer do forthwith send out his warrants, directed to the selectmen or assessors of each town or district within this province, requiring them, respectively, to assess the sum hereby set upon such town or district, in manner following; that is to say, to assess all rateable polls above the age of sixteen years, within their respective towns or districts, or next adjoining to them, belonging to no other town, six shillings per poll, and proportionably in assessing the fines mentioned in this act, and the additional sum received out of the treasury for the payment of the representatives (except the governo[u]r, the lieutenant-governo[u]r and their families, the president, fellows, professors and students of Harvard College, settled ministers and grammar-school masters, who are hereby exempted as well from being taxed for their polls, as for their estates being in their own hands and under their actual management and improvement; as also all the estate pertaining to Harvard Colle[d]ge); and other persons, if such there be, who, through age, infirmity or extre[a]m[*e*] poverty, in the judgment of the assessors, are not able to pay towards publick charges, they may exempt their polls, and so much of their estates as in their prudence they shall think fit and judge meet. Rules for assessment.

[Sect. 3.] And the justices in their general sessions, in the respective counties assembled, in granting a county tax or assessment, are hereby ordered and directed to apportion the same on the several towns in such county in proportion to their province rate, exclusive of what has been paid out of the publick treasury to the representatives of each town for his service; and the assessors of each town in the province are also directed, in making an assessment, to govern themselves by the same rule; and all estates, both real and personal, lying within the limits of such town or district, or next unto the same, not paying elsewhere, in whose hands, tenure, occupation or possession soever the same is or shall be found, and also the incomes or profits which any person or persons, except as before excepted, do or shall receive from any trade, faculty, business or employment whatsoever, and all profits which [shall or] may [*or shall*] arise by money or other estate not particularly otherwise assessed, or commissions of profit in their improvement, according to their understanding or cunning, at one pen[*n*]y on the pound; and to abate or multiply the same, if need be, so as to make up the sum set and ordered hereby for such town or district to pay; and, in making their assessment, to estimate houses and lands at six years' income of the yearly rents whereat the same may be reasonably set or let for in the place where they lye: *saving* all contracts between landlord and tenant, and where no contract is, the landlord to reimburse one-half of the tax set upon such houses and lands; and to estimate negro, Indian and mol[l]atto servants proportionably as other perso[*n*]al[l] estate, according to their sound judgment and discretion; as also to estimate every ox of four years old and upwards, at forty shillings; every cow of three years old and upwards, at thirty shillings; every horse and mare of three years old and upwards, at forty shillings; every swine of one year old and upwards, at eight shillings; goats and sheep of one year old, at three shillings each: likewise requiring the said assessors to make a fair list of the said assessment, setting forth, in distinct colum[*n*]s, against each particular person's name, how much he or she is assessed at for polls, and how much for houses and lands, and how much for personal estate, and income by trade or faculty, and if as guardian, or for any estate, in his or her improvement, in trust, to be distinctly expressed; and the list or lists, so perfected and signed by them, or the major part of them, to commit[t] to the collectors, constable or constables of such town or district, and to return a certificate of the name or names of such collector, constable or constables, with the sum total to each of them committed, unto himself, some time before the last day of October next.

[SECT. 4.] And the treasurer, for the time being, upon receipt of such certificate, is hereby impowered and ordered to issue forth his warrants to the collector, or constable or constables of such town or district, requiring him or them, respectively, to collect the whole of each respective sum assess[*e*]'d on each particular person, before the last day of December next; and to pay in their collection, and issue the accompts of the whole, at or before the last day of March next, which will be in the year of our Lord one thousand seven hundred and fifty-six.

And be it further enacted,

Inhabitants to bring in a true list of their polls, &c.

[SECT. 5.] That the assessors of each town or district, respectively, in convenient time before their making the assessment, shall give seasonable warning to the inhabitants, in a town meeting, or by posting up notifications in some place or places in such town or district, or notify the inhabitants some other way[s] or give or bring in to the assessors true and perfect lists of their polls, rateable estate, and income by trade or faculty, and gain by money at interest, which they are to render to the assessors on oath, if required; and if they refuse to give in an account of the money at interest, on oath, the assessors are impowered to doom them; and if any person or persons shall neglect or refuse so to do, or bring in a false list, it shall be lawful[l] to and for the assessors to assess such person or persons, according to their known ability in such town, in their sound judgment and discretion, their due proportion of this tax, as near as they can, agreable to the rules herein given, under the penalty of twenty shillings for each person that shall be convicted by legal proof, in the judgment of the said assessors, in bringing in a false list; the said fines to be for the use of the poor of such town or district where the delinquent lives, to be levied by warrant from the assessors, directed to the collectors or constables, in manner as is directed for gathering town assessments, to be paid in to the town treasurer or selectmen for the use aforesaid: *saving* to the party aggrieved at the judgment of the assessors in setting forth such fine, liberty of appeal therefrom to the court of general sessions of the peace within the county, for rel[ci][*ie*]f, as in case of being overrated. And if any person or persons shall not bring a list of their estates, as aforesaid, to the assessors, he or they so neglecting shall not be admitted to make application to the court of general sessions for any abatement of the assessment laid on him.

[SECT. 6.] And if the party be not convicted of any falseness in the list, by him presented, of the polls, rateable estate, or income by trade or faculty, business or employment, which he does or shall exercise, or [in] gain by money at interest or otherwise, or other estate not particularly assessed, such list shall be a rule for such person's proportion to the tax, which the assessors may not exceed.

And forasmuch as, oftentimes, sundry persons, not belonging to this province, bring considerable trade and merchandize, and by reason that the tax or rate of the town where they come to trade is finished and delivered to the constable or collectors, and, before the next year's assessment, are gone out of the province, and so pay nothing towards the support of the government, though, in the time of their residing here, they reaped considerable gain by trade, and had the protection of the government,—

Be it further enacted,

Transient traders to be rated.

[SECT. 7.] That when any such person or persons, shall come and reside in any town within this province, and bring any merchandize, and trade, to deal therewith, the assessors of such town are hereby impowered to rate and assess all such persons, according to their circumstances, pursuant to the rules and directions in this act provided, tho'[ugh] the former rate may have been finished, and the new one not perfected, as aforesaid.

And be it further enacted,

[Sect. 8.] That when any merchant, trader or factor, inhabitant of some one town within this province, or of any other province, shall traf[*f*]ic, or carry on trade or business, or set up a store in some other town in the province, the assessors of such town[s] where such trade and business shall be carried on as aforesaid, be and hereby are impowered to rate and assess all such merchants, traders and factors, their goods and merchandize, for carrying on such trade and business and exercising their faculty in such town, pursuant to the rules and directions of this act; *provided* before any such assessors shall rate such persons as afore mentioned, the selectmen of the town where such trade is carried on, shall transmit a list of such persons as they shall judge may and ought to be rated, within the intent of this act; and the constables or collectors are hereby enjo[i][*y*]ned to levy and collect all such sums committed to them, and assessed on persons who are not of this province, or are residents in other towns than those where they carry on their trade, and pay the same.

Merchants, &c., to be rated for carrying on trade in any other town beside where they dwell.

Selectmen to transmit a list of such persons before they are rated.

And be it further enacted,

[Sect. 9.] That the inhabitants of this province have liberty, if they see fit, to pay the several sums for which they may be respectively assessed, of the aforesaid sum of thirty-nine thousand one hundred and fifteen pounds fourteen shillings, in good merchantable hemp, or in good, merchantable, Isle-of-Sable[s] codfish, or in good refined bar-iron, or in bloomery-iron, or in hollow iron-ware, or in good Indian corn, or in good winter rye, or in good winter wheat, or in good barley, or in good barrel[l] pork, or in barrel[l] beef, or in duck [and] [*or*] canvas, or in long whalebone, or in merchantable cordage, or in good train o[i][*y*]l, or in good beeswax, or in good bayberry-wax, or in tryed tallow, or in good pease, or in good sheepswool, or in good tanned sole-leather; and that the eldest councellors, for the time being, of each of those counties in the province, of which any one of the councellors is an inhabitant, together with the province treasurer, or the major part of them, be a committee, who are hereby directed and fully authorized and impowered, once in every month, if need be, to agree and set the several species and commodities aforesaid at some certain price, at which they shall be received towards the payment of the sums aforesaid: all which aforesaid commodities shall be of the produce of this province, and, as soon as conveniently may, be disposed of by the treasurer to the best advantage, and for so much as they will fetch in money; and the several persons paying their taxes in any of the commodities afore mentioned, to run the risque and pay the charge of transporting the said commodities to the province treasury.

Species in which tax may be paid.

[Sect. 10.] And if any loss shall happen by the sale of the aforesaid species, it shall be made good by a tax of the next year; and if there be a surplusage, it shall remain as a stock in the treasury.

And whereas, the sum of ten thousand one hundred and fifteen pounds fourteen shillings, part of the above tax, has not been appropriated in any supply-bill for the payment of the publick debts,—

Be it further enacted,

[Sect. 11.] That the said sum of ten thousand one hundred and fifteen pounds fourteen shillings shall be issued out of the treasury, when received of the constables and collectors, in manner and for the purposes following; that is to say, the sum of four thousand pounds, part of the

£4,000 to be issued for forts and garrisons.

aforesaid sum of ten thousand one hundred and fifteen pounds fourteen shillings, shall be applied for the service of the several forts and garrisons within this province, pursuant to such orders and grants as are or shall be made by this court for those purposes; and the further sum of one thousand pounds, part of the aforesaid sum of ten thousand one hundred and fifteen pounds fourteen shillings shall be applied for the purchasing of provisions and the commissary's necessary disbursements for the service of the several forts and garrisons within this province, pursuant to such grants as are or shall be made by this court for those purposes; and the further sum of three thousand pounds, part of the aforesaid sum of ten thousand one hundred and fifteen pounds fourteen shillings, shall be applied for the payment of such premiums and grants that now are or hereafter may be made by this court; and the further sum of one thousand pounds, part of the aforesaid sum of ten thousand one hundred and fifteen pounds fourteen shillings, shall be applied for the discharge of other debts owing from this province to persons that have or shall serve them by order of this court, in such matters and things where there is no establishment nor any certain sum assigned for that purpose, and for paper, writing and printing for this court; and the further sum of one thousand pounds, part of the aforesaid sum of ten thousand one hundred and fifteen pounds fourteen shillings, shall be appl[i][*y*]ed for the payment of his majesty's council and house of representatives, serving in the general court during the several sessions this present year.

£1,000 for provisions, commissary's disbursements, &c.

£3,000 for grants.

£1,000 for debts where there is no establishment, &c.

£1,000 for councillors' and representatives' attendance.

And whereas there are sometimes contingent and unforeseen charges that demand prompt pay,—

Be it further enacted,

£115 14*s*. for contingent charges.

[SECT. 12.] That the sum of one hundred and fifteen pounds fourteen shillings, the remaining part of the aforesaid sum of ten thousand one hundred and fifteen pounds fourteen shillings, be applied to pay such contingent charges, and for no other purpose whatsoever.

And be it further enacted,

The treasurer to conform to the appropriations.

[SECT. 13.] That the treasurer be and [*is*] hereby [is] directed and ordered to pay the sum of ten thousand one hundred and fifteen pounds fourteen shillings, brought in by taxes as aforesaid, out of such appropriations as shall be directed to by warrant, and no other; and the secretary, to whom it belongs to keep the muster-rolls and accompts of the charge, shall lay before the house of representatives, where they direct, such muster-rolls and accompts, after payment thereof.

And whereas, by this act, but ten thousand one hundred and fifteen pounds fourteen shillings, part of the sum of thirty-nine thousand one hundred and fifteen pounds fourteen shillings, for which a tax is to go forth, is appropriated and applied for the discharge of the debts of the ensuing year.

Be it enacted,

£29,000 to discharge government securities, &c.

[SECT. 14.] That the remaining sum of twenty-nine thousand pounds be applied for the discharge of the government securities that will become due the first of December, one thousand seven hundred and fifty-six, and the first of January, one thousand seven hundred and fifty-seven. [*Passed June* 24; *published June* 27.

CHAPTER 3.

AN ACT TO ENABLE THE PRECINCT OF TETICUT, IN THE COUNTY OF PL[I][Y]MOUTH, TO RAISE A SUM, BY LOTTERY, TOWARDS BUILDING A BRIDGE OVER TETICUT RIVER.

Whereas the precinct of Teticut have represented to this court the necessity of building a bridge over Teticut River, and prayed this court would enable them to raise a sum, by way of lottery, for that purpose,— Preamble.

Be it therefore enacted by the Governour, Council and House of Representatives,

That Samuel White, Esq[r]., of Taunton, Israel Washburn of Raynham, Ephraim Keith and James Keith, both of Bridgewater, and David Alden of Middleborough, or any three of them, be and hereby are allowed and impowered to set up and carry on a lottery, amounting to such a sum, as by drawing ten per cent out of each prize, may raise a sum of two hundred and ninety pounds lawful money, and no more; and that the said sum be by them, or any three of them, applied to the building a good, sufficient bridge over the said river, and paying the charges of said lottery; and that the said Samuel White, Israel Washburn, Ephraim Keith, James Keith and David Alden, or any three of them, be the managers of said lottery, and impowered to make all necessary rules for managing thereof, and shall be sworn to the faithful discharge of their said trust; and as well the said managers as the said precinct shall be and are hereby declared answerable to the owners of the tickets, in case of any deficiency or misconduct; and if the sum raised thereby shall be more than sufficient, after paying [*of*] the charges of the lottery, to build the said bridge, the surplusage shall be lodged in the hands of the treasurer of the said precinct, to be put at interest, and the interest applied towards the repairs of said bridge. [*Passed and published June* 10.

Samuel White, Esq., of Taunton, and others, empowered to have a lottery for building, &c., Teticut bridge.

Said managers, with the precinct of Teticut, to be answerable, &c.

CHAPTER 4.

AN ACT FOR SUPPLYING THE TREASURY WITH THE SUM OF FIFTY THOUSAND POUNDS, FOR DISCHARGING THE PUBLICK DEBTS, AND FOR DRAWING THE SAME INTO THE TREASURY.

Whereas the provision heretofore made by this court is insufficient to discharge the debts of the government; *and whereas* there are and will be several demands upon the treasury, which do and will require speedy payment; therefore,— Preamble.

Be it enacted by the Governour, Council and House of Representatives,

[Sect. 1.] That the treasurer of the province be and hereby is impowered and directed to borrow from such person or persons as shall be willing to lend the same, a sum not exceeding the sum of fifty thousand pounds in mill'd dollars, at six shillings each, or in other silver at six shillings and eightpence per ounce, for a term not exceeding three years; and the sum so borrowed shall be applied in manner as in this act is hereafter directed; and for every sum so borrowed, the treasurer shall give a receipt and obligation in form following:—

Treasurer empowered to borrow £50,000.

Form of treasurer's receipt.

Province of the Massachusetts Bay, day of , 1755. Received of the sum of , for the use and service of the province of the Massachusetts Bay, and, in behalf of said province, I do hereby promise and oblige myself and successors in the office of treasurer to repay the said or order, the day of , 175 , the aforesaid sum of , in coined silver of sterling alloy, at six shillings and eightpence per o[*unce*] [z]., or Spanish mill[e]'d dollars, at six shill[*in*]gs each, with interest annually, at the rate of six per cent per annum. Witness my hand, A. B., Treasurer.

—and no receipt shall be given for a sum less than six pounds.

Treasurer directed in borrowing money.

[SECT. 2.] And the treasurer is hereby directed to use his discretion in borrowing said sum at such times as that he may be enabled to comply with the draughts that may be made on the treasury in pursuance of this act.

And whereas it may happen that some of the persons who have done service for this government, and for the payment of which the sum raised by this act is intended, may be willing to lend the sum due to them, on interest, and take the treasurer's notes for the money so lent,—

Be it further enacted,

Treasurer to give notes on warrants, &c.

[SECT. 3.] That when and so often as any person or persons, who shall have a warrant on the treasury payable out of any of the appropriations mentioned in this act, and shall bring such warrant to the treasurer, expressing his willingness to lend the sum mentioned in said warrant to the government, the treasurer, in such case, shall give out his notes therefor in like manner as if the same sum had been brought to him in dollars or other silver, and shall charge the respective appropriations with the payment thereof, until[l] such appropriations shall be exhausted.

And be it further enacted,

Former warrants on exhausted appropriations, to be paid.

[SECT. 4.] That any warrants which may have been given by the governour and council, and were payable out of any exhausted appropriations in any former acts for supplying the treasury, shall be paid, respectively, out of the appropriations for the like purpose in this act.

And be it further enacted,

£17,350 to be issued for expedition to Crown Point.

£12,500 for forts and garrisons.

£9,500 for provisions, commissary's disbursements, &c.

£7,000 for premiums, &c.

£1,500 for debts where there is no establishment, &c.

£2,000 for pay of councillors' and representatives' attendance.

[SECT. 5.] That the aforesaid sum of fifty thousand pounds, when received into the treasury, shall be issued out in manner and for the purposes following; that is to say, seventeen thousand three hundred and fifty pounds, part of the sum of fifty thousand pounds, shall be applied for the service of the expedition against Crown Po[*i*][u]nt; and the further sum of twelve thousand five hundred pounds, part of the sum of fifty thousand pounds, shall be applied for the service of the several forts and garrisons within this province, pursuant to such grants and orders as are or shall be made by this court for those purposes; and the further sum of nine thousand five hundred pounds, part of the aforesaid sum of fifty thousand pounds, shall be applied for purchasing provisions and the commissary's necessary disburs[e]ments for the service of the several forts and garrisons within this province; and the further sum of seven thousand pounds, part of the aforesaid sum of fifty thousand pounds, shall be applied for the payment of such premiums and grants that now are or may hereafter be made by this court; and the further sum of fifteen hundred pounds, part of the aforesaid sum of fifty thousand pounds, shall be applied for the discharge of other debts owing from this province to persons that have served or [*that*] shall serve them, by order of this court, in such matters and things where there is no establishment nor any certain sum assigned for that purpose; and for paper, writing and printing for this court; and the sum of two thousand pounds, part of the aforesaid sum of fifty thousand pounds, shall be applied for the payment of his majesty's council and house of representatives serving in the great and general court during the several sessions for the present year.

And whereas there are sometimes contingent and unforeseen charges that demand prompt pay,—

Be it enacted,

[Sect. 6.] That the sum of one hundred and fifty pounds, being the remaining part of the aforesaid sum of fifty thousand pounds, be applied to pay such contingent charges, and for no other purpose whatsoever. £150 for contingent charges.

And in order to draw the money into the treasury again, and enable the treasurer effectually to discharge the receipts and obligations (with the interest that may be due thereon), by him given in pursuance of this act,—

Be it enacted,

[Sect. 7.] That there be and hereby is granted to his most excellent majesty a tax of thirty-six thousand pounds, to be levied on polls, and estates real and personal within this province, according to such rules and in such proportion on the several towns and districts within the same as shall be agreed on and ordered by the general court of this province at their session in May, one thousand seven hundred and fifty-six, which sum shall be paid into the treasury on or before the thirty-first day of March next after. Tax of £36,000 granted, in 1756.

[Sect. 8.] And a further sum of fourteen thousand pounds, the remaining part of the afores[*ai*]'d sum of fifty thousand pounds, to be levied on polls, and estates real and personal within this province, according to such rules and in such proportion on the several towns and districts within the same as shall be agreed on and ordered by the general court of this province at their session in May, one thousand seven hundred and fifty-seven, which sum shall be paid into the treasury on or before the thirty-first day of March next after. Tax of £14,000, in 1757.

And as an additional fund to enable the treasurer to discharge the said notes,—

Be it enacted,

[Sect. 9.] That the duties of impost for the year one thousand seven hundred and fifty-six shall be applied for that purpose, and for no other purpose whatsoever. Fund. 1756-57, chap. 19.

And as a further fund to enable the treasurer to discharge said receipts and obligations by him given in pursuance of this act,—

Be it enacted,

[Sect. 10.] That the duties of excise, or so much of that duty as is not already mortgaged, arising by virtue of an act for granting unto his majesty an excise upon spirits distilled, and wine, and upon limes, lemmons and oranges, for the year one thousand seven hundred and fifty-five, shall be applied for the payment and discharge of the principal and interest that shall become due on said notes, and to no other purposes whatsoever. Further fund. 1755-56, chap. 31.

And as a further fund as aforesaid,—

Be it enacted,

[Sect. 11.] That the duties arising by the act for granting to his majesty several duties upon vellum, parchment and paper, the second year from the commencement of said act, shall be applied for the payment and discharge of the principal and interest that shall be due on said notes, and no other purpose whatsoever. Further fund. 1754-55, chap. 18.

And be it further enacted,

[Sect. 12.] That in case the general court shall not at their sessions in May, and before the thirtieth day of June, one thousand seven hundred and fifty-six, and one thousand seven hundred and fifty-seven, agree and conclude upon an act apportioning the sums which by this Rule for apportioning the tax, in case no tax act shall be agreed on.

act are engaged to be, in said years, apportioned, assessed and levied, that then, and in such case, each town and district within this province shall pay, by a tax to be levied on the polls, and estates both real and personal within their districts, the same proportions of the said sums as the said towns and districts were taxed by the general court in the tax act then last preceeding: *saving* what relates to the pay of the representatives, which shall be assessed on the several towns they represent; and the province treasurer is hereby fully impowered and directed, some time in the months of July, one thousand seven hundred and fifty-six, and one thousand seven hundred and fifty-seven, to issue and send forth his warrants, directed to the selectmen or assessors of each town and district within this province, requiring them to assess the polls, and estates both real and personal within their several towns and districts, for their respective part and proportion of the sum before directed and engaged to be assessed, and the assessors, as also persons assessed, shall observe, be governed by and subject to all such rules and directions as have been given in the last preceeding tax act.

And be it further enacted,

The treasurer to conform to the appropriations.

[SECT. 13.] That the treasurer is hereby directed and ordered to pay the sum of fifty thousand pounds out of such appropriations as shall be directed by warrant, and no other; and the secretary to whom it belongs to keep the muster-rolls and accompts of charge, shall lay before the house of representatives, when they direct, such muster-rolls and accompts, after payment thereof: *provided, always,* that the remainder of the sum which shall be brought into the treasury by the duties of impost, excise, and stamp duties before mentioned, and the tax of fifty thousand pounds ordered by this act to be assessed and levied, over and above what shall be sufficient to discharge the notes and obligations aforesaid, shall be and remain as a stock in the treasury, and to be applied as the general court of this province shall hereafter order, and to no other purpose whatsoever; anything in this act to the contrary notwithstanding. [*Passed June* 11; *published June* 12.

Proviso.

CHAPTER 5.

AN ACT FOR GRANTING THE SUM OF THIRTEEN HUNDRED POUNDS, FOR THE SUPPORT OF HIS MAJESTY'S GOVERNOUR.

Be it enacted by the Governour, Council and House of Representatives,

That the sum of thirteen hundred pounds be and hereby is granted unto his most excellent majesty, to be paid out of the publick treasury to his excellency William Shirley, Esq[r]., captain-general and governour-in-chief in and over his majesty's province of the Massachusetts Bay, for his past services, and further to enable him to go on in managing the publick affairs. [*Passed June* 10; *published June* 12.

CHAPTER 6.

AN ACT FOR THE MORE EFFECTUAL PREVENTION OF SUPPLIES OF PROVISIONS AND WARLIKE STORES TO THE FRENCH, FROM ANY PARTS OF THIS PROVINCE.

WHEREAS, notwithstanding the provision already made by the laws of this government, divers evil-minded persons have found means to transport provisions to Louisb[o]urg[h], either direct from this province, or else from this province to some parts of Newfoundland, and from thence to Louisb[o]urg[h]; by means whereof the present measures now engaged in by his majesty's forces for the security of his subjects, and for removing the encroachments made upon his territories may be prejudiced and defeated,— Preamble.

Be it therefore enacted by the Governour, Council and House of Representatives,

[SECT. 1.] That no provisions, except codfish, nor warlike stores, except so much only as shall be necessary for the ordinary victualling and defence of any vessel, during her proposed voyage, shall be exported from any port or part of this province, until[l] bond be first given by the master of such vessel, with sufficient sureties, in the penalty of one thousand pounds sterling, to the officer or commissioner of impost, that all such provisions and warlike stores so laden shall be relanded in some part of this province, or landed in some one of his majesty's colonies to the southward of Newfoundland, or at Annapolis Royal or Hallifax, in Nova Scotia; and that certificate shall be returned, within twelve months, from the officer of the customs in the places where they shall be landed, that the whole of such provisions and warlike stores have been so landed. No provisions nor warlike stores shall be exported before bond given, &c.

[SECT. 2.] And if any person shall presume to export provisions or warlike stores from this province in a clandestine way, and without obtaining a clearance from the naval officer, every person so offending shall be subject and liable to all the penalties provided by an act of this province made and pass'd this present year, intit[u]led "An Act to encourage and facilitate the removal and prevention of French encroachments on his majesty's North-American territories." 1754 55, chap. 34

And be it further enacted,

[SECT. 3.] That the naval officer shall give no clearance for any vessel, until[l] certificate be produced from the commissioner of impost, that the master of such vessel has conformed to the rules prescribed by this act.

And be it further enacted,

[SECT. 4.] That oath shall be made by the master of every vessel clearing out, before the commissioner of impost, as to the whole quantity of provisions and warlike stores laden, or intended to be laden, on board such vessel.

[SECT. 5.] This act to continue and be in force until[l] the twelfth day of September next, and no longer. [*Passed and published June* 14. Limitation.

CHAPTER 7.

AN ACT FOR PREVENTING THE EXPORTATION OF PROVISIONS AND WARLIKE STORES, OUT OF THIS PROVINCE.

Preamble.

WHEREAS the measures already taken for preventing provisions and warlike stores being carried to the French have proved ineffectual for that purpose,—

Be it enacted by the Governour, Council and House of Represent-[ati]ves,

Exportation of warlike stores and provisions prohibited: *Saving.*

[SECT. 1.] That no warlike stores, or provisions of any kind whatsoever, fish only excepted, shall be exported or carried out of any port or harbour in this province, in any vessel whatever, before the twenty-fourth day of July next: *saving* only such provisions and warlike stores as are necessary for the defence of each respective vessel outward bound, and victualling the mariners on board the same, during their intended voyage, and whereof an account, in writing, shall be given by the master of such vessel, on oath, to the impost officer, or his deputy, on pain of one thousand pounds, lawful money, to be forfeited and paid by the master; and the like sum by the owner and owners, factor and factors, of each respective vessel in which any warlike stores or provisions shall be exported or carried out of any port or harbour in this province; one moiety thereof to the use of this governm[*en*]t, and the other moiety to him or them that shall inform or sue for the same.

And be it further enacted,

Governor and council may prolong the time above limited.

[SECT. 2.] That if the governour or commander-in-ch[ei][*ie*]f, for the time being shall see fit, with the advice and consent of the council, to issue a proclamation, prohibiting the exportation of provisions or warlike stores out of this province, for any time after the said twenty-fourth day of July, not exceeding the twenty-fourth day of September, in this present year, the master, and owner and owners, factor and factors, of any vessel or vessels on board of which such provisions or warlike stores shall be exported, contrary to such proclamation, shall be respectively liable to the same penalties as if the same had been exported before the said twenty-fourth day of July, contrary to this act.

Provided, always,—

[SECT. 3.] That it shall and may be lawful for any provisions or warlike stores to be exported for the service of his maj[*es*]ty's sea or land forces, on board any vessel or vessels licen[s][*c*]ed for that purpose by the governor or comm[*ande*]r-in-chief for the time being, with the advice of the council.

Provided, also,—

Proviso for coasting-vessels, &c.

[SECT. 4.] That it shall and may be lawful for provisions and warlike stores to be laden and transported on board any coasting-vessel, or vessels, passing from one port to another within this province, bond being first given, in a thousand pounds, lawful money, with sufficient sureties, to the impost officer or his deputy, to reland the same in some town in this province, and to return a certificate thereof from the deputy impost-officer residing in the town where they are so relanded, or from the town clerk of such towns wherein no deputy impost-officer resides.

Provided, also,—

Proviso, also, in towns where the fishery is carried on.

[SECT. 5.] That in such towns where the fishery is carried on, and neither the impost officer or his deputy dwells, the masters of fishing vessels may render the acco[*un*]t aforesaid, on oath, to a justice of the peace, or the town clerk of the respective towns out of which they sail, who is hereby impowered to take the same; and the account so taken and attested shall be by them transmitted to the impost officer, which shall be as effectual as thô the same were taken by him, or his deputy.

And be it enacted,

[SECT. 6.] That the impost officer shall be allowed one shilling for each bond so taken, and every justice and town clerk the like sum for every such certificate by them respectively transmitted as afores[*ai*]d, to be paid by the master. [*Passed and published June* 25.

Impost officer, his fee.

CHAPTER 8.

AN ACT IN ADDITION TO AN ACT, INTIT[U]LED "AN ACT FOR GRANTING TO HIS MAJESTY SEVERAL DUTIES UPON VELLUM, PARCHMENT AND PAPER, FOR TWO YEARS, TOWARDS DEFRAYING THE CHARGES OF THIS GOVERNMENT."

WHEREAS, in and by an act, intit[u]led "An Act for granting to his majesty several duties upon vellum, parchment and paper, for two years, towards defr[a][*e*]ying the charges of this government," made and pass[*e*]'d in the present year of his majesty's reign, a duty is laid in the words following; viz[t]., "for every p[ei][*ie*]ce of vellum or parchment, sheet or p[ei][*ie*]ce of paper, on which any deed or mortgage of any real estate, the consideration whereof shall be less than twenty pounds, or any bond or obligation, those taken in the probate office excepted, or other sealed instruments, shall be engross[*e*]'d or written, twopence"; and altho' it was fully intended that no wills or other instruments that were to be presented to, or transacted in, the probate office, should be liable to any duty, and that no warrants of any sort should be subjected to any stamp, yet, some doubts have arisen, whether that clause in the aforesaid act, "or other sealed instruments," does not make it necessary that all instruments not particularly mentioned in said act, should be stampt, to render them good and valid; wherefore, for removing such doubts for the future,—

Preamble. 1754-55, chap. 18.

Words in former act recited.

Be it enacted by the Governour, Council and House of Representatives,

[SECT. 1.] That no wills or other instruments that are to be presented to, or that are transacted in, the probate office, and no warrants from any person or persons that are authorized and impowered by law to grant the same, shall be liable to be stamp[t][*ed*], but that the same shall be held good and available in law to all intents and purposes, without being stampt, anything in the afore-mentioned act notwithstanding.

Instruments not liable to be stamped.

And be it further enacted,

[SECT. 2.] That the commissioner or commissioners appointed, or to be appointed, to receive the duties mentioned in the aforesaid act, shall not stamp, or cause to be stampt, any *capias*, original summons, or any writ of review, writ of *scire facias*, or writ of execution, or any other writ[t]s whatsoever, after the same is filled up, nor any deed, bond or other instrument, after the same is signed or sealed. [*Passed June* 25; *published June* 27.

Instruments not to be stamped, after being signed or sealed.

CHAPTER 9.

AN ACT TO PREVENT DAMAGE BEING DONE ON THE BEACH, HUMOCKS AND MEADOWS BELONGING TO THE TOWN OF SCITUATE, LYING BETWEEN THE SOUTHERLY END OF THE "THIRD CLIFF," SO CALLED, AND THE MOUTH OF THE NORTH RIVER.

Preamble. 1749-50, chap. 14.

WHEREAS persons frequently drive numbers of neat cattle and horses, and sometimes sheep, if not restrained, to feed on the beach, humocks and meadows of Scituate, lying between the Third Cliff and the mouth of North River, and oftentimes cut down trees and shrubs in said humocks, and carry them away, whereby said beach is broken, and the land made loose, and, by the winds and storms, is drove on the said meadow and flat[t]s, or sedge-ground; and there is great danger, if such practices are not prevented, that the said meadows and sedge-ground will be utterly ruined, and the river greatly damnified,—

Be it therefore enacted by the Governo[u]r, Council and House of Representatives,

Cattle found feeding on the beaches aforesaid, to be impounded.

[SECT. 1.] That if any neat cattle, horse-kind or sheep, shall, after the first day of July next, be found feeding on said beach, humocks or sedge-ground adjoining to said beach, it shall and may be lawful for any person to impound the same forthwith, giving notice to the owner or owners, if known; otherwise, to give publick notice thereof, by posting up notifications in some publick place in said town of Scituate; and the impounder shall rel[ei][*ie*]ve said creatures with suitable meat and water while impounded; and if the owner thereof appear, he shall pay to the impounder one shilling a head for all neat cattle and horse-kind, and twopence for every sheep, and also the reasonable costs for rel[ei][*ie*]ving them, besides the lawful fees to the pound-keeper. And if no owner appear within three days to redeem the said creatures so impounded, and pay as aforesaid, then, and in every such case, the person or persons impounding such creatures, shall cause the same to be sold at publick vendue, and pay the penalties as aforesaid, with all other costs and charges arising about the same, publick notice of the time and place of such sale being first given in the said town of Scituate, and the two next adjacent towns, three several days beforehand; and the overplus, if any there be, arising by such sale, to be returned to the owner or owners of such creatures, if he or they appear within two months next after such sale, upon his demanding the same; but if no owner appears within said two months to demand the same, then the said overplus shall be one half to the person impounding, and the other half to be returned to the town treasurer, for the use of the poor of the said town of Scituate.

To be sold, where the owner does not appear.

Disposal of the produce.

And be it further enacted,

Penalty for cutting down trees or shrubs.

[SECT. 2.] That if any person or persons shall presume to cut down any tree or shrub standing or growing on said beach or humocks, without leave or licence first had and obtained of said town of Scituate, he or they so offending, shall forfeit and pay to the use of said town the sum of twenty shillings for each tree or shrub so cut down. And all such methods and proof shall be allowed in any action to be brought by said town therefor, as is provided in an act made in the twelfth year of King George the First, in addition to an act made for preventing of trespasses.

1726-27, chap. 3.

Limitation.

[SECT. 3.] This act to be in force for the space of ten years from the first day of July next. [*Passed June* 25;* *published June* 27.

* Signed June 10, according to the record.

CHAPTER 10.

AN ACT FOR REVIVING AND CONTINUING SUNDRY LAWS, THAT ARE EXPIRED AND NEAR EXPIRING.

Whereas the several acts hereinafter mentioned, which are now expired or near expiring, have been found useful and beneficial; namely, two acts made in the eighteenth year of his present majesty's reign; one intit[u]led "An Act to prevent mischief being done by unruly dogs," the other intit[u]led "An Act to prevent neat cattle and horses running at large and feeding on the beaches adjoining to Eastern-Harbour Meadows, in the town of Truro"; and one other act made in the eighteenth and nineteenth years of said reign, intit[u]led "An Act to prevent unnecessary cost being allowed to parties and witnesses in the several courts of justice within this province"; and one act made in the twenty-second year of said reign, intit[u]led "An Act to prevent damage being done on the beach and meadows in Plymouth adjoining to said beach, commonly known by the name of Plymouth Beach"; four acts made in the twenty-third year of said reign, one intit[u]led "An Act against diminishing or counterfeiting money"; one other, intit[u]led "An Act in addition to and for rendering more effectual an act for the restraining the taking excessive usury"; one other, intit[u]led "An Act to prevent stage-plays and other theatrical entertainments"; and the other act, intit[u]led "An Act to prevent damage being done on the meadows and beaches lying in and adjo[y][i]ning on the north side of the town of Harwich, between Skeket harbour on the east, and Setucket harbour on the west"; an act made in the twenty-fourth year of said reign, intit[u]led "An Act for the better regulation of the course of judicial proceedings"; also "An Act to prevent the disturbance given the general court by the passing of coaches, chaises, carts, trucks and other carriages by the province court-house,"—

Preamble.

Sundry laws expired or near expiring, revived and continued.

1744-45, chap. 25.

1744-45, chap. 26.

1745-46, chap. 7.

1748-49, chap. 13.

1749-50, chap. 22.

1749-50, chap. 23.

1749-50, chap. 24.

1749-50, chap. 26.

1751-52, chap. 17.

1747-48, chap. 4.

Be it therefore enacted by the Governour, Council and House of Representatives,

That such of the before-mentioned acts as are expired, with all and every article, clause, matter and thing therein respectively contained, be and they hereby are revived, and such of said acts as are near expiring are continued, and shall be in force from the twentieth day of June current, for the space of five years, and to the end of the then next session of the general court, and no longer. [*Passed June* 25;* *published June* 27.

Their continuation for five years from the 20th of June, 1755.

* Signed June 19, according to the record.

ACT

PASSED AT THE SESSION BEGUN AND HELD AT BOSTON, ON THE SIXTH DAY OF AUGUST, A. D. 1755.

CHAPTER 11.

AN ACT FOR PREVENTING THE EXPORTATION OF PROVISIONS AND WARLIKE STORES, OUT OF THIS PROVINCE.

Be it enacted by the Lieutenant-Governour, Council and House of Representatives,

Exportation of warlike stores and provisions prohibited: *Saving.*

[SECT. 1.] That no warlike stores, or provisions of any kind whatsoever, fish only excepted, shall be exported or carried out of any port or harbour in this province, in any vessel whatever, before the thirtieth day of September next: *saving* only such provisions or warlike stores as are necessary for the defence of each respective vessel outward bound, and victualling the mariners on board the same during their intended voyage, and whereof an account, in writing, shall be given by the master of such vessel[l], on oath, to the impost officer or his deputy, and where there is no impost officer or deputy, then to a justice of the peace or the town clerk, on pain of one thousand pounds lawful money, to be forf[ie][*ei*]ted and paid by the master, and the like sum by the owner and owners, factor and factors of each respective vessel in which any warlike stores or provisions shall be exported or carried out of any port or harbour in this province; one moiety thereof to the use of this government, and the other moiety to him or them that shall inform or sue for the same; and such masters, owners and factors, respectively, upon their being convicted of the offence aforesaid, at the superiour court of judicature, court of assize and general goal delivery, shall be further liable to stand in the pillory, and have one of their ears cut off.

Penalty, &c., for breach of this act.

And be it further enacted,

Governor and council to prolong the time above limited.

[SECT. 2.] That if the governour or commander-in-chief for the time being shall see fit, with the advice and consent of the council, to issue a proclamation, prohibiting the exportation of provisions or warlike stores out of this province, for any time after the said thirtieth day of September next, not exceeding the thirtieth day of November in this present year, the master, and owner and owners, factor and factors of any vessel or vessels on board of which such provisions or warlike stores shall be exported, contrary to such proclamation, shall be, respectively, liable to the same pains and penalties as if the same had been exported before the said thirtieth day of September, contrary to this act.

Provided, always,—

Proviso for land or sea forces.

[SECT. 3.] That it shall and may be lawful for any provisions or warlike stores to be exported for the service of his majesty's sea or land forces, on board any vessel or vessels licen[c][*s*]ed for that purpose by the governour or commander-in-chief for the time being, with the advice of the council.

Provided, also,—

[SECT. 4.] That it shall and may be lawful for provisions and warlike stores to be laden and transported on board any coasting vessel or vessels, passing from one port to another within this province, bond being first given, in a thousand pounds, lawfull money, with sufficient sureties, to the impost officer or his deputy (and where there is no impost officer or deputy, then to a justice of the peace or the town clerk) to reland the same in some town or district in this province, and to return a certificate thereof from the deputy impost officer residing in the town or district where they are so relanded, or from the town or district clerk of such towns or districts where no deputy impost officer resides.

Proviso for coasting-vessels, &c.

Provided, also,—

[SECT. 5.] That in such towns where the fishery is carried on, and out of which vessel[l]s coasting from one port to another, in this province, and wherein neither the impost officer or his deputy dwells, the masters of such fishing, or coasting, vessel[l]s may render the account aforesaid, on oath, to a justice of the peace, or the town clerk of the respective towns out of which they sail, who is hereby impowered to take the same; and the account so taken and attested shall be by them transmitted to the impost officer, which shall be as effectual as tho' the same were taken by him or his deputy.

Proviso, also, in towns where the fishery is carried on.

And be it enacted,

[SECT. 6.] That the impost officer shall be allowed one shilling for each bond so taken, and every justice and town or district clerk the like sum for every such certificate by them respectively transmitted as aforesaid, to be paid by the master.

Impost officer, his fee.

Provided, also,—

[SECT. 7.] That it shall be unlawful for any of his majesty's subjects of this province, and they are hereby strictly forbidden, to hold any correspondence or communication with any inhabitants of Louisbourg[h], or any other of the French settlements in North America, either by land or water; and if any person or persons belonging to this province shall be so audacious as to go or send to Louisbourg[h], or any other French settlement in North America, during the continuance of this act, the ship, sloop or other vessel[l] employed, with all her tackle and appurtenances, and her cargo, shall be forfeited, one half to his majesty for the use of this province, the other half to him or them who shall inform and sue for the same in any of his majesty's courts within this province proper to try the same; and be further liable, if a ship or vessel[l], the master to have one ear cut off, and be publickly whipp[e]'d thirty-nine lashes, and be render[e]'d forever incapable of holding any place of honour or prof[f]it[t] under this government, and the owner or owners, and factor or factors of the owner or owners, of such ship or other vessel[l] shall forfeit and pay, each, five hundred pounds, to be recovered and dispos'd of as above, and also be forever disabled to hold any place of honour or prof[f]it[t] under this government. [*Passed and published August* 16.

Penalty for holding correspondence or communication with inhabitants of Louisbourg, &c.

ACTS

PASSED AT THE SESSION BEGUN AND HELD AT BOSTON, ON THE FIFTH DAY OF SEPTEMBER, A. D. 1755.

CHAPTER 12.

AN ACT FOR THE MORE SPEEDY LEVYING OF SO[U]LDIERS FOR THE EXPEDITION AGAINST CROWN POINT.

Preamble.

WHEREAS this government have judged it necessary that two thousand men be raised, in addition to those who have been already inlisted or ordered to be raised, to reinforce the army under the command of Major-General Johnson, destin[e]'d to Crown Point, and have thereupon desired his honour the commander-in-chief to order the several companics, both of horse and foot, in all the regiments within this province, those in the county of York excepted, to be mustered on the fifteenth of September instant, and in case the number of two thousand men should not then be inlisted, that the aforesaid number be compleated by an impress to be made as soon as may be; wherefore, for the more speedy and effectual raising and levying of soldiers for the service aforesaid,—

Be it enacted by the Lieutenant-Governour, Council and House of Representatives,

Manner of notifying the muster of the several companies of militia, in order to raise volunteers, &c.

[SECT. 1.] That upon due warning given, by order of the commander-in-chief, by one of the ser[g][*je*]ants or corporals of the several troops and companies, to each person belong[*in*][g] to the same, either in person, or, in case of his absence from home, by leaving a notification in writing at the usual place of his abode, for mustering the companies of horse and foot for the purposes before mentioned, every person who by law is obliged to attend military musters, whether belonging to any troop or foot company, shall punctually attend and continue at such muster at the time and place that shall be appointed therefor, on pain of incurring the penalty of twenty pounds, unless it shall appear on tr[y][*i*]al of the offence that his attendance was necessarily and unavoidably prevented; and every person who shall be impressed for the service aforesaid, shall duly attend the same, either by himself, or by some other effective able-bodied person in his stead, on penalty of the sum of ten pounds, unless he shall have had a discharge from such impress, in writ[t]ing, under the hand of the captain or chief officer of such troop or company, or of the commander-in-chief of the province.

Fine for not serving when impressed.

Manner of recovery.

[SECT. 2.] The penalties aforesaid to be imposed and recovered, as is provided in the nineteenth paragraph of an act of this province, made and passed in the fifth year of their late majesties William and Mary, inti[*t*]led "An Act for regulating the militia," except of minors and servants, whose penalties shall be recovered of their parents or masters respectively, and to be disposed of as fines are, for persons impressed not attending the service, by virtue of an act of this province, made and

1693-4, chap. 3.

passed in the twenty-seventh year of his present majesty's reign, [e][i]ntitled "An Act for lev[e]ying of so[u]ldiers, and to prevent so[u]ldiers and seamen in his majesty's service from being arrested for debt." 1753-54, chap. 41.
[*Passed and published September* 8.

CHAPTER 13.

AN ACT FOR SUPPLYING THE TREASURY WITH THE SUM OF SIXTEEN THOUSAND POUNDS, FOR DISCHARGING THE PUBLICK DEBTS, AND FOR DRAWING THE SAME INTO THE TREASURY.

WHEREAS the provision heretofore made by this court is insufficient to discharge the debts that now are or may become due for the expedition against Crown Point; *and whereas* there are and will be several demands upon the treasury which do and will require speedy payment; therefore,— Preamble.

Be it enacted by the Lieutenant-Governour, Council and House of Representatives,

[SECT. 1.] That the treasurer of the province be and hereby is impowered and directed to borrow from such person or persons as shall be willing to lend the same, a sum not exceeding the sum of sixteen thousand pounds in mill'd dollars, at six shillings each, or in other silver at six shillings and eightpence per ounce, for a term not exceeding eight months; and the sum so borrowed shall be applied in manner as in this act is directed: and for every sum so borrowed, the treasurer shall give a receipt and obligation (but for no sum less than six pounds) in form following:— Treasurer empowered to borrow £16,000.

Province of the Massachusetts Bay, day of , 1755. Received of the sum of , for the use and service of the province of the Massachusetts Bay, and, in behalf of said province, I do hereby promise and oblige myself and successors in the office of treasurer to repay the said or order, the day of 1756, the aforesaid sum of , in coined silver of sterling alloy, at six shillings and eightpence per ounce, or Spanish mill'd dollars, at six shillings each, with interest at the rate of six per cent per annum. Form of treasurer's receipt.

Witness my hand, A. B., Treasurer.

And whereas it may happen that some of the persons who have done service for this government, and for the payment of which the sum raised by this act is intended, may be willing to lend the sum due to them, on interest, and take the treasurer's notes for the money so lent,—

Be it further enacted,

[SECT. 2.] That when and so often as any person or persons who shall have a warrant on the treasury payable out of the appropriation mentioned in this act, and shall bring such warrant to the treasurer, expressing his willingness to lend the sum mentioned in said warrant to the government, the treasurer, in such case, shall give out his notes therefor in like manner as if the same sum had been brought to him in dollars or other silver, and shall charge this appropriation with the payment thereof, until[l] such appropriation shall be exhausted. Treasurer to give notes, on warrants.

And be it further enacted,

[SECT. 3.] That any warrants which may have been given by the governour and council, and were payable out of any exhausted appropriations in any former acts for supplying the treasury, shall be paid, respectively, out of the appropriation for the like purpose in this act. Former warrants on exhausted appropriations, to be paid.

And be it further enacted,

Said £16,000 to be applied for Crown-Point expedition.

[SECT. 4.] That the aforesaid sum of sixteen thousand pounds, when received into the treasury, shall be issued out and applied for the service of the expedition against Crown Point, and for no other purpose whatsoever.

And in order to draw the money into the treasury again, and enable the treasurer effectually to discharge the receipts and obligations (with the interest that may be due thereon), by him given in pursuance of this act,—

Be it enacted,

Tax of £18,000 granted on polls and estates.

[SECT. 5.] That there be and hereby is granted to his most excellent majesty a tax of eighteen thousand pounds, to be levied on polls, and estates real and personal, within this province, according to such rules and in such proportion on the several towns and districts within the same as shall be agreed on and ordered by the general court of this province at their present session; which sum shall be paid into the treasury on or before the thirty-first day of March next. [*Passed and published September* 8.

CHAPTER 14.

AN ACT FOR PREVENTING AND PUNISHING THE DESERTION OF SOLDIERS IN THE EXPEDITION AGAINST CROWN POINT, OR IN THE DEFENCE OF THE FRONTIERS OF THIS GOVERNMENT.

Preamble.

WHEREAS soldiers duly inlisted, or to be inlisted or impressed, for the present expedition against Crown Point, or for the defence of the frontiers of this province, do and may afterwards desert, and be found wandering, or otherwise absenting themselves illegally from his majesty's service,—

Be it therefore enacted by the Lieutenant-Governour, Council and House of Representatives,

Sheriffs, &c., their power to apprehend deserters.

[SECT. 1.] That it shall and may be lawful for the sheriff of any county, or either of his deputies, for any constable or tythingman of the town or place (or any other person) where any person who may be reasonably suspected to be such a deserter shall be found, to apprehend, or cause him to be apprehended, and to cause such person to be brought before any justice of the peace living in or near such town or place, who hath, hereby, power to examine such suspected person; and if by his confession, or the testimony of one or more witness or witnesses, upon oath, or by the knowledge of such justice of the peace, or any other proof, it shall appear or be found that such suspected person is a listed or impressed soldier, as is aforesaid, tho' listed or impressed in any other government, and that he ought to be with the troop or company to which he belongs, such justice of the peace shall, forthwith, cause him to be conveyed to the goal of the county or place where he shall be found, and transmit an account thereof to the commander-in-chief or secretary of this province; and such deserter shall be returned to his service by the first opportunity, and the keeper of such goal shall rec[ie][*ei*]ve the full subsistence of such deserter or deserters, during the time that he or they shall continue in his custody, for the maintenance of the said deserter or deserters, but shall not be intitled to any fee or reward on account of the imprisonment of such deserter or deserters.

To be returned, when taken, to their service.

And for the better encouragement of any person or persons to secure or apprehend such deserters,—

Be it further enacted,

[SECT. 2.] That upon the certificate of such justice of the peace, to the province treasurer, there shall be paid by him to such persons as shall apprehend, or cause to be apprehended, any deserter from his majesty's said service, twenty shillings and the costs of prosecution, to be deducted out of his wages, for every deserter that shall be so apprehended and committed. [*Passed and published September* 9. Allowance for apprehending deserters.

CHAPTER 15.

AN ACT FOR APPORTIONING AND ASSESSING A TAX OF EIGHTEEN THOUSAND POUNDS.

WHEREAS, by an act made and passed this session, the treasurer of the province is enabled to borrow a sum, not exceeding sixteen thousand pounds, to be applied towards defreying the charges of the expedition against Crown Point, and to give his receipts and obligation to repay the same, with interest, by the thirty-first of March, one thousand seven hundred and fifty-six; wherefore, for the effectual drawing the sum of sixteen thousand pounds, and interest, into the treasury, so as to enable the treasurer to discharge the notes that may be given in pursuance of said act, we, his majesty's most loyal and dutiful subjects, the representatives in general court assembled, pray that it may be enacted,—

And be it accordingly enacted by the Lieutenant-Governour, Council and House of Representatives,

[SECT. 1.] That each town and district within this province be assessed and pay, as such town and district's proportion of the sum of eighteen thousand pounds, the several sums following; that is to say,—

IN THE COUNTY OF SUFFOLK.

Boston,	£2,965 10s. 0d.	Two thousand nine hundred and sixty-five pounds ten shillings.
Roxbury,	166 10 0	One hundred and sixty-six pounds ten shillings.
Dorchester,	164 15 6	One hundred and sixty-four pounds fifteen shillings and sixpence.
Milton,	87 10 6	Eighty-seven pounds ten shillings and sixpence.
Braintree,	189 19 6	One hundred and eighty-nine pounds nineteen shillings and sixpence.
Weymouth,	111 19 6	One hundred and eleven pounds nineteen shillings and sixpence.
Hingham,	197 2 0	One hundred and ninety-seven pounds two shillings.
Dedham,	130 19 0	One hundred and thirty pounds nineteen shillings.
Medfield,	81 0 0	Eighty-one pounds.
Wrentham,	138 10 0	One hundred and thirty-eight pounds ten shillings.
Brookline,	50 8 0	Fifty pounds eight shillings.
Needham,	66 9 0	Sixty-six pounds nine shillings.
Stoughton,	113 0 0	One hundred and thirteen pounds.
Medway,	66 9 0	Sixty-six pounds nine shillings.
Bellingham,	25 16 0	Twenty-five pounds sixteen shillings.
Hull,	30 16 6	Thirty pounds sixteen shillings and sixpence.
Walpole,	49 8 0	Forty-nine pounds eight shillings.
Chelsea,	68 15 6	Sixty-eight pounds fifteen shillings and sixpence.
	£4,704 18s. 0d.	

IN THE COUNTY OF ESSEX.

Salem,	£283 10s. 0d.	Two hundred and eighty-three pounds ten shillings.
Danvers,	157 13 0	One hundred and fifty-seven pounds thirteen shillings.
Ipswich,	404 11 0	Four hundred and four pounds eleven shillings.
Newbury,	520 14 6	Five hundred and twenty pounds fourteen shillings and sixpence.
Marblehead,	308 18 6	Three hundred and eight pounds eighteen shillings and sixpence.
Lynn,	166 8 6	One hundred and sixty-six pounds eight shillings and sixpence.
Andover,	228 7 6	Two hundred and twenty-eight pounds seven shillings and sixpence.
Beverly,	141 10 6	One hundred and forty-one pounds ten shillings and sixpence.
Rowley,	144 0 0	One hundred and forty-four pounds.
Salisbury,	113 5 0	One hundred and thirteen pounds five shillings.
Haverhill,	132 19 6	One hundred and thirty-two pounds nineteen shillings and sixpence.
Glo[u]cester,	235 8 6	Two hundred and thirty-five pounds eight shillings and sixpence.
Topsfield,	63 0 0	Sixty-three pounds.
Boxford,	83 6 6	Eighty-three pounds six shillings and sixpence.
Almsbury,	104 8 0	One hundred and four pounds eight shillings.
Bradford,	93 9 0	Ninety-three pounds nine shillings.
Wenham,	52 19 0	Fifty-two pounds nineteen shillings.
Middleton,	47 0 6	Forty-seven pounds [and sixpence].
Manchester,	37 17 6	Thirty-seven pounds seventeen shillings and sixpence.
Meth[ewi][ue]n,	60 6 0	Sixty pounds six shillings.
	£3,379 13s. 0d.	

IN THE COUNTY OF MIDDLESEX.

Cambridge,	£125 14s. 0d.	One hundred and twenty-five pounds fourteen shillings.
Charlestown,	162 13 0	One hundred and sixty-two pounds thirteen shillings.
Watertown,	66 13 6	Sixty-six pounds thirteen shillings and sixpence.
Woburn,	117 0 0	One hundred and seventeen pounds.
Concord,	74 12 6	Seventy-four pounds twelve shillings and sixpence.
Newton,	117 0 0	One hundred and seventeen pounds.
Sudbury,	126 10 6	One hundred and twenty-six pounds ten shillings and sixpence.
Marlborough,	126 0 0	One hundred and twenty-six pounds.
Billerica,	73 16 0	Seventy-three pounds sixteen shillings.
Framingham,	96 6 0	Ninety-six pounds six shillings.
Lexington,	74 7 4	Seventy-four pounds seven shillings and fourpence.
Chelmsford,	72 0 0	Seventy-two pounds.
Sherburne,	49 14 6	Forty-nine pounds fourteen shillings and sixpence.
Reading,	118 16 0	One hundred and eighteen pounds sixteen shillings.
Malden,	94 16 0	Ninety-four pounds sixteen shillings.
Weston,	55 18 0	Fifty-five pounds eighteen shillings.
Medford,	93 4 6	Ninety-three pounds four shillings and sixpence.
Littleton,	50 11 0	Fifty pounds eleven shillings.
Hopkinston,	44 2 0	Forty-four pounds two shillings.
Westford,	48 12 0	Forty-eight pounds twelve shillings.
Shirley,	12 7 6	Twelve pounds seven shillings and sixpence.
Waltham,	62 5 0	Sixty-two pounds five shillings.
Townshend,	27 10 6	Twenty-seven pounds ten shillings and sixpence.
Stow,	44 2 0	Forty-four pounds two shillings.
Stoneham,	31 11 6	Thirty-one pounds eleven shillings and sixpence.
Groton,	88 17 0	Eighty-eight pounds seventeen shillings.
Wilmington,	36 0 0	Thirty-six pounds.
Natick,	25 1 0	Twenty-five pounds one shilling.
Dracut,	35 8 0	Thirty-five pounds eight shillings.
Bedford,	41 6 6	Forty-one pounds six shillings and sixpence.
Holliston,	40 2 6	Forty pounds two shillings and sixpence.
Tewksbury,	35 8 0	Thirty-five pounds eight shillings.

IN THE COUNTY OF MIDDLESEX—*Continued.*

Acton, ...	£26 2*s*. 0*d*.	Twenty-six pounds two shillings.
Dunstable, . . .	33 11 6	Thirty-three pounds eleven shillings and sixpence.
Pepper[*r*]ell, . .	28 8 0	Twenty-eight pounds eight shillings.
Lincoln, . . .	53 4 2	Fifty-three pounds four shillings and twopence.
Carlisle, . . .	34 16 0	Thirty-four pounds sixteen shillings.
	£2,444 8*s*. 0*d*.	

IN THE COUNTY OF HAMPSHIRE.

Springfield, . . .	£175 4*s*. 0*d*.	One hundred and seventy-five pounds four shillings.
Northampton, . .	96 10 6	Ninety-six pounds ten shillings and sixpence.
Hatfield, . . .	53 18 6	Fifty-three pounds eighteen shillings and sixpence.
Westfield, . . .	70 2 6	Seventy pounds two shillings and sixpence.
Enfield, . . .	52 2 6	Fifty-two pounds two shillings and sixpence.
Deerfield, . . .	36 2 6	Thirty-six pounds two shillings and sixpence.
Sheffield, . . .	77 15 6	Seventy-seven pounds fifteen shillings and sixpence.
Northfield, . . .	18 16 6	Eighteen pounds sixteen shillings and sixpence.
Hadley, . . .	60 5 4	Sixty pounds five shillings and fourpence.
Sufficld, . . .	96 15 0	Ninety-six pounds fifteen shillings.
Sunderland, . .	17 16 10	Seventeen pounds sixteen shillings and tenpence
Montague, . . .	13 1 2	Thirteen pounds one shilling and twopence.
Brimfield, . . .	59 5 0	Fifty-nine pounds five shillings
Somers, . . .	37 4 0	Thirty-seven pounds four shillings.
Southampton, . .	19 10 0	Nineteen pounds ten shillings.
South Hadley, . .	32 8 8	Thirty-two pounds eight shillings and eightpence.
Palmer, . . .	22 4 0	Twenty-two pounds four shillings.
Pelham, . . .	18 18 0	Eighteen pounds eighteen shillings.
Bedford, . . .	12 12 0	Twelve pounds twelve shillings.
Coldspring, . . .	12 12 0	Twelve pounds twelve shillings.
Greenwich, . . .	14 2 0	Fourteen pounds two shillings.
Blandford, . . .	7 19 0	Seven pounds nineteen shillings.
New Salem, . . .	9 0 0	Nine pounds.
New Marlboro', . .	13 10 0	Thirteen pounds ten shillings.
No. One, in the line of towns, . . .	9 0 0	Nine pounds.
Ware River, . .	9 0 0	Nine pounds.
Stockbridge, . .	18 0 0	Eighteen pounds.
Roadtown, . . .	7 10 0	Seven pounds ten shillings.
Greenfield, . . .	16 4 6	Sixteen pounds four shillings and sixpence.
	£1,087 10*s*. 0*d*.	

IN THE COUNTY OF WORCESTER.

Worcester, . . .	£94 19*s*. 0*d*.	Ninety-four pounds nineteen shillings.
Lancaster, . . .	108 0 0	One hundred and eight pounds.
Mendon, . . .	103 10 0	One hundred and three pounds ten shillings.
Woodstock, . .	116 8 0	One hundred and sixteen pounds eight shillings.
Brookfield, . . .	84 19 6	Eighty-four pounds nineteen shillings and sixpence.
Oxford, . . .	45 19 0	Forty-five pounds nineteen shillings.
Charlton, . . .	11 10 0	Eleven pounds ten shillings.
Sutton, . . .	82 11 6	Eighty-two pounds eleven shillings and sixpence.
Rutland, . . .	59 11 0	Fifty-nine pounds eleven shillings.
New Braintree, . .	5 0 0	Five pounds.
District of Rutland, .	8 10 0	Eight pounds ten shillings.
Leicester, . . .	56 10 0	Fifty-six pounds ten shillings.
District of Spencer, .	28 5 0	Twenty-eight pounds five shillings.
Southborough, . .	46 8 6	Forty-[six] [*eight*] pounds eight shillings and sixpence.
Westborough, . .	64 17 6	Sixty-four pounds seventeen shillings and sixpence.
Shrewsbury, . .	75 12 0	Seventy-five pounds twelve shillings.

IN THE COUNTY OF WORCESTER—*Continued.*

Lunenburg, . . .	£63 7s. 6d.	Sixty-three pounds seven shillings and sixpence.
Uxbridge, . . .	57 7 6	Fifty-seven pounds seven shillings and sixpence.
Harvard, . . .	52 1 0	Fifty-two pounds one shilling.
Dudley, . . .	34 4 0	Thirty-four pounds four shillings.
Bolton, . . .	51 18 0	Fifty-one pounds eighteen shillings.
Upton, . . .	28 13 0	Twenty-eight pounds thirteen shillings.
Sturbridge, . . .	22 8 6	Twenty-two pounds eight shillings and sixpence.
Leominster, . . .	27 0 0	Twenty-seven pounds.
Hardwick, . . .	33 6 0	Thirty-three pounds six shillings.
Holden, . . .	17 2 0	Seventeen pounds two shillings.
Western, . . .	26 2 0	Twenty-six pounds two shillings.
Douglass, . . .	7 10 0	Seven pounds ten shillings.
Grafton, . . .	43 16 0	Forty-three pounds sixteen shillings.
Petersham, . . .	19 10 0	Nineteen pounds ten shillings.
	£1,476 16s. 6d.	

IN THE COUNTY OF PLYMOUTH.

Plymouth, . . .	£144 0s. 0d.	One hundred and forty-four pounds.
Scituate, . . .	198 0 0	One hundred and ninety-eight pounds.
Duxbury, . . .	65 5 0	Sixty-five pounds five shillings.
Marshfield, . . .	134 11 0	One hundred and thirty-four pounds eleven shillings.
Bridgwater, . .	228 18 0	Two hundred and twenty-eight pounds eighteen shillings.
Middleborough, . .	164 6 6	One hundred and sixty-four pounds six shillings and sixpence.
Rochester, . . .	99 1 6	Ninety-nine pounds one shilling and sixpence.
Plympton, . . .	83 17 0	Eighty-three pounds seventeen shillings.
Pembrook, . . .	81 16 6	Eighty-one pounds sixteen shillings and sixpence.
Kingston[e], . .	48 9 0	Forty-eight pounds nine shillings.
Hanover, . . .	58 4 0	Fifty-eight pounds four shillings.
Abbington, . . .	67 10 0	Sixty-seven pounds ten shillings.
Halifax, . . .	39 18 0	Thirty-nine pounds eighteen shillings.
Warham, . . .	41 8 0	Forty-one pounds eight shillings.
	£1,455 4s. 6d.	

IN THE COUNTY OF BARNSTABLE.

Barnstable, . . .	£126 0s. 0d.	One hundred and twenty-six pounds.
Yarmouth, . . .	82 10	Eighty-two pounds ten shillings.
Sandwich, . . .	90 0	Ninety pounds.
Eastham, . . .	102 12	One hundred and two pounds twelve shillings.
Harwich, . . .	79 13	Seventy-nine pounds thirteen shillings.
Chatham, . . .	45 4	Forty-five pounds four shillings and sixpence.
Truro, . . .	48 10 0	Forty-eight pounds ten shillings and sixpence.
Falmouth, . . .	55 16 0	Fifty-five pounds sixteen shillings.
	£630 6s. 0d.	

IN THE COUNTY OF BRISTOL.

Taunton, . . .	£173 15s. 6d.	One hundred and seventy-three pounds fifteen shillings and sixpence.
Rehoboth, . . .	249 1 6	Two hundred and forty-nine pounds one shilling and sixpence.
Swanzey, with Shawamet, . . .	110 11 0	One hundred and ten pounds eleven shillings.
Dartmouth, . . .	324 0 0	Three hundred and twenty-four pounds.
Norton, . . .	108 13 6	One hundred and eight pounds thirteen shillings and sixpence.
Attleborough, . .	118 13 0	One hundred and eighteen pounds thirteen shillings.
Dighton, . . .	76 13 0	Seventy-six pounds thirteen shillings.
Freetown, . . .	70 16 0	Seventy pounds sixteen shillings.

IN THE COUNTY OF BRISTOL—*Continued.*

Raynham, . . .	£45 15s. 0d.	Forty-five pounds fifteen shillings.
Easton, . . .	52 11 6	Fifty-two pounds eleven shillings and sixpence.
Berkley, . . .	40 17 6	Forty pounds seventeen shillings and sixpence.
	£1,371 7s. 6d.	

IN THE COUNTY OF YORK.

York, ...	£176 5s. 0d.	One hundred and seventy-six pounds five shillings.
Kittery, . . .	207 0 0	Two hundred and seven pounds.
Wells, ...	79 4 0	Seventy-nine pounds four shillings.
Berwick, . . .	108 0 0	One hundred and eight pounds.
Falmouth, . . .	171 0 0	One hundred and seventy-one pounds.
Biddeford, . . .	72 12 0	Seventy-two pounds twelve shillings.
Arundel, . . .	40 7 0	Forty pounds seven shillings.
Scarborough, . .	61 17 6	Sixty-one pounds seventeen shillings and sixpence.
North Yarmouth, .	26 18 6	Twenty-six pounds eighteen shillings and sixpence.
Georgetown, . .	28 11 6	Twenty-eight pounds eleven shillings and sixpence.
Brunswick, . . .	25 14 6	Twenty-five pounds fourteen shillings and sixpence.
Sheepscut, . . .	18 0 0	Eighteen pounds.
	£1,015 10s. 0d.	

IN THE COUNTY OF DUKES COUNTY.

Edgartown, . . .	£69 12s. 0d.	Sixty-nine pounds twelve shillings.
Chilmark, . . .	62 9 6	Sixty-two pounds nine shillings and sixpence.
Tisbury, . . .	39 18 0	Thirty-nine pounds eighteen shillings.
	£171 19s. 6d.	

IN THE COUNTY OF NANTUCKET.

Sherburne, . . .	£262 7s. 0d.	Two hundred and sixty-two pounds seven shillings.

Suffolk, ...	£4,704 18s. 0d.	Barnstable, . . .	£630 6s. 0d.
Essex, ...	3,379 13 0	Bristol, ...	1,371 7 6
Middlesex, ...	2,444 8 0	York, ...	1,015 10 0
Hampshire, ...	1,087 10 0	Dukes County, . . .	171 19 6
Worcester, ...	1,476 16 6	Nantucket, . . .	262 7 0
Plymouth, ...	1,455 4 6		
			£18,000 0s. 0d.

And be it further enacted,

[SECT. 2.] That the treasurer do forthwith send out his warrants, directed to the selectmen or assessors of each town or district within this province, requiring them, respectively, to assess the sum hereby set upon such town or district, in manner following; that is to say, to assess all rateable polls above the age of sixteen years, within their respective towns or districts, or next adjoining to them, belonging to no other town, at three shillings per poll, and to observe the same rules, in proportioning the remainder of the tax, hereby granted, on their several towns and districts, as in the last tax act. [*Passed September* 9.

ACTS

PASSED AT THE SESSION BEGUN AND HELD AT BOSTON, ON THE TWENTY-FOURTH DAY OF SEPTEMBER, A. D. 1755.

CHAPTER 16.

AN ACT FOR PREVENTING THE EXPORTATION OF PROVISIONS AND WARLIKE STORES OUT OF THIS PROVINCE.

Be it enacted by the Lieutenant-Governour, Council and House of Representatives,

Exportation of warlike stores, and provisions, prohibited:— *saving.*

[SECT. 1.] That no warlike stores, or provisions of any kind whatsoever, fish only excepted, shall be exported or carried out of any port or harbour in this province, in any vessel whatever, before the first day of December next: *saving* only such provisions or warlike stores as are necessary for the defence of each respective vessel outward bound, and victualling the mariners on board the same, during their intended voyage, and whereof an account, in writing, shall be given by the master of such vessel, on oath, to the impost officer or his deputy, (and where there is no impost officer or deputy, then to a justice of the peace or the town clerk) on pain of one thousand pounds lawful money, to be forfeited and paid by the master, and the like sum by the owner and owners, factor and factors of each respective vessel in which any warlike stores or provisions shall be exported or carried out of any port or harbour in this province; one moiety thereof to the use of this government, and the other moiety to him or them that shall inform or sue for the same; and such masters, owners and factors, respectively, upon their being convicted of the offence aforesaid, at the superio[*u*]r court of judicature, court of assize and general goal delivery, shall be further liable to stand in the pillory, and have one of their ears cut off.

Penalty, &c., for breach of this act.

And be it further enacted,

Governor and council may prolong the time above.

[SECT. 2.] That if the governour or commander-in-ch[ei][*ie*]f for the time being shall see fit, with the advice and consent of the council, to issue a proclamation, prohibiting the exportation of provisions or warlike stores out of this province, for any time after the said first day of December next, not exceeding the first day of March next after, the master, and owner and owners, factor and factors, of any vessel or vessels on board of which such provisions or warlike stores shall be exported contrary to such proclamation, shall be, respectively, liable to the same pains and penalties as if the same had been exported before the said first day of December, contrary to this act.

Provided, always,—

Proviso for sea, or land, forces.

[SECT. 3.] That it shall and may be lawful for any provisions or warlike stores to be exported for the service of his maj[*es*]ty's sea or land forces, on board any vessel or vessels licenced for that purpose by the governour or comm[*ande*]r-in-chief for the time being, with the advice of the council.

Provided, also,—

[SECT. 4.] That it shall and may be lawful for provisions and warlike stores to be laden and transported on board any coasting vessel or vessels passing from one port to another within this province, bond being first given, in a thousand pounds, lawful[l] money, with sufficient sureties, to the impost officer or his deputy (and where there is no impost officer or deputy, then to a justice of the peace or the town clerk) to reland the same in some town or district in this province, and to return a certificate thereof from the deputy impost-officer residing in the town or district where they are so relanded, or from the town or district clerk of such towns or districts where no deputy impost-officer resides.

Proviso for coasting-Vessels, &c.

Provided, also,—

[SECT. 5.] That in such towns where the fishery is carried on, and out of which vessels coasting from one port to another, in this province, and wherein neither the impost officer or his deputy dwells, the masters of such fishing, or coasting, vessels may render the account aforesaid, on oath, to a justice of the peace, or the town clerk of the respective towns out of w[*hi*]ch they sail, who is hereby impowered to take the same; and the account so taken and attested shall be by them transmitted to the impost officer, w[*hi*]ch shall be as effectual as tho' the same were taken by him or his deputy.

Proviso, also, in towns where the fishery is carried on.

And be it enacted,

[SECT. 6.] That the impost officer shall be allowed one shilling for each bond so taken, and every justice and town or district clerk the like sum for every such certificate by them respectively transmitted as afores[*ai*]d, to be paid by the master.

Impost officer, his fee.

And be it further enacted,

[SECT. 7.] That if any of his majesty's subjects of this province, shall hold any correspondence or communication with any inhabitants of Louisbourg, or any other of the French settlem[*en*]ts in North America, either by land or water, or if any person or persons belonging to this province shall go or send to Louisbourg, or any other French settlement in No[*rth*] America, during the continuance of this act, the ship, sloop or other vessel employed, with all her tac[*k*]l[l]e and appurtenances, and her cargo, shall be forfeited, one half to his majesty for the use of this province, the other half to him or them who shall inform and sue for the same in any of his maj[*es*]ty's courts within this province proper to try the same; and the master of any ship or other vessel, so employed, shall be further liable to have one ear cut off, and be publickly whipped thirty-nine lashes, and be rendred forever incapable of holding any place of honour or prof[*f*]it under this gov[*ernmen*]t, and the owner or owners, and factor or factors of the owner or owners, of such ship or other vessel shall forfeit and pay, each, five hund[*re*]d pounds, to be recovered and disposed of as above, and also be forever disabled to hold any place of honour or profit under this government. [*Passed September* 30; *published October* 1.

Penalty for holding correspondence or communication with inhabitants of Louisbourg, &c

CHAPTER 17.

AN ACT FOR CONFIRMING THE PROCEEDINGS OF THE GENERAL ASSEMBLY CONVENED ON THE FIFTH OF SEPTEMBER, *ANNO DOMINI* 1755.

Preamble.

WHEREAS, upon advices of great importance received from the troops gone upon an expedition against Crown Point, his honour the lieutenant-governour and commander-in-chief, and his majesty's council, judged it absolutely necessary that the general assembly, which stood prorogued to the twenty-fourth day of September instant, should be sooner convened, and the same was accordingly convened, by his honour's proclamation, and held on the fifth of the same month, and, from day to day, continued until[l] the ninth instant, during which time, divers matters of publick importance were transacted; *and whereas* some doubt may possibly arise touching the legality of the proceedings of that assembly, held before the time to which the same stood prorogued; therefore, for the preventing or removing all doubts and disputes touching the same,—

Be it enacted by the Lieutenant-Governour, Council and House of Representatives,

All proceedings of the late convention of the general court confirmed.

That all votes, orders, laws and other matters, made, pass[*e*]'d or transacted by the general assembly convened and held on the fifth of this instant September, and which was held until[l] the ninth day of the same, be and they are hereby established and confirmed, and shall, to all intents and purposes, be deemed valid and effectual in the law, as if the great and general court or assembly had stood prorogued to the said fifth day of September, and had been then held, and the same votes, orders, laws and other matters had been pass'd or transacted by the said great and general court during such their session. [*Passed September* 27; * *published October* 1.

* Signed September 29, according to the record.

ACTS

PASSED AT THE SESSION BEGUN AND HELD AT BOSTON, ON THE TWENTY-SECOND DAY OF OCTOBER, A. D. 1755.

CHAPTER 18.

AN ACT IMPOWERING THE PROVINCE TREASURER TO BORROW THE SUM OF FIVE THOUSAND POUNDS, AND FOR APPLYING THE SAME TO DEPREY THE CHARGES OF THE INTENDED EXPEDITION AGAINST CROWN POINT.

Be it enacted by the Lieutenant-Governour, Council and House of Represent[*ati*][ves],

[SECT. 1.] That the treasurer of the province be and hereby is impowered and directed to borrow, of such persons as shall be willing to lend the same, a sum, not exceeding five thousand pounds, in Spanish mill'd dollars, at six shillings each, or in other silver at six shillings and eightpence per ounce; and the sum so borrowed shall be applied by the treasurer for the payment of all such draughts as shall be drawn on him by the governour or commander-in-chief for the time being, by and with the advice of the council, for the service of the intended expedition against Crown Point; and for every sum so borrowed, the treasurer shall give a receipt and obligation in the form following; viz[t].,— Treasurer empowered to borrow £5,000.

Province of the Massachusetts Bay, the day of 1755. Received of the sum of , for the use and service of the province of the Massachusetts Bay, and, in behalf of said province, I do hereby promise and oblige myself and successors in the office of treasurer to repay the said or order, on or before the first day of June, [one thousand seven hundred and fifty-seven] [*1757*], the afores[*ai*]d sum of , in coined silver of sterling alloy, at six shillings and eightpence per ounce, or Spanish mill'd dollars of full weight, at six shillings each, with interest annually, at the rate of six per cent per annum. Form of treasurer's receipt.

Witness my hand, A. B., Treasurer.

And to enable the treasurer to discharge the said obligations,—

Be it further enacted,

[SECT. 2.] That there be and hereby is granted to his most excellent majesty a tax of five thousand six hundred pounds, to be levied on the polls and estates within this province, according to such rules as shall be ordered by the general court of this province at their sessions in May, one thousand seven hundred and fifty-six. Tax of £5,600, in 1756.

And be it further enacted,

[SECT. 3.] That in case the general court shall not, at their sessions in May, one thousand seven hundred and fifty-six, agree and conclude upon a tax act to draw into the treasury the afores[*ai*]d sum of five thousand six hundred pounds, that then the treasurer of the province, for the time being, shall issue his warrants, directed to the selectmen or assessors of Rule for apportioning the tax, if case no tax act shall be agreed on.

the several towns and districts in this province, requiring them respectively to assess, levy and pay in their respective proportions of said sum, according to the rates and proportions, rules and directions of the last preceeding tax act. [*Passed and published November* 5.

CHAPTER 19.

AN ACT FOR GRANTING THE SUM OF THREE HUNDRED POUNDS, FOR THE SUPPORT OF HIS HONOUR THE LIEUTENANT-GOVERNOUR AND COMMANDER-IN-CHIEF.

Be it enacted by the Lieutenant-Governour, Council and House of Representatives,

That the sum of three hundred pounds be and hereby is granted unto his most excellent majesty, to be paid out of the publick treasury, and to be taken out of the next supply, to his honour Spencer Phips, Esq[uire], lieutenant-governour and commander-in-chief in and over his majesty's province of the Massachusetts Bay, for his past services, and further to enable him to manage the publick affairs of the province. [*Passed October* 29; * *published November* 5.

CHAPTER 20.

AN ACT TO PREVENT THE SUBJECTS OF THE FRENCH KING BEING SUPPLYED WITH PROVISIONS.

Preamble.

WHEREAS it hath been represented to this court that a vessel with Frenchmen on board, that had lately clear[e]d out from a port in New England for the West Indies, has been in divers harbours at or near Martha's Vineyard, with intent, as is suspected, to procure provisions for the French inhabitants of Louisbourg[h]; and as other vessels may put into the same or other harbours, with the same intent,—

Be it therefore enacted by the Lieutenant-Governour, Council and House of Representatives,

Persons to be appointed by the commander-in-chief, for seizing French vessels, &c.

[SECT. 1.] That it shall and may be lawful for the commander-in-chief of this province to appoint some meet person in each town or place whereat vessels may probably put in for provisions for the supply of the subjects of the French king, and the several persons so to be appointed be and they are hereby authorized to make seizure of all vessels having the subjects of the French king on board, and to cause the same to be conveyed to such harbour or place within the province as shall be most convenient for securing them, as also to apprehend and confine such Frenchmen as shall be found on board such vessel or vessels; and shall forthwith give notice thereof to the commander-in-chief, for his orders touching the same.

And be it further enacted,

[SECT. 2.] That every person appointed as aforesaid to the service aforesaid, be and they are hereby impowered to demand and take all needful assistance in the execution of their office; and every person neglecting or refusing his assistance, upon demand thereof made in his

* Signed October 28, according to the record.

majesty's name, by any or either of the officers aforesaid, shall forfeit and pay, for the use of this province, a sum not exceeding five pounds, at the discretion of any one or more of his majesty's justices of the peace of the same county, before whom the offender or offenders shall be convicted: and in case of neglect or refusal to pay the same, such offender or offenders shall be punished by imprisonment not exceeding ten days; and every justice of the peace, upon complaint made of such offence committed within the limits of his county, is hereby authorized to hear and determine the same.

Penalty for denying them assistance.

And be it further enacted,

[SECT. 3.] That every person to be appointed by the commander-in-chief for the service aforesaid, shall, before he shall enter upon the execution of his trust, be under oath, to be administred to him by a justice of the peace, for the faithful performance of the same; and a meet allowance shall be made to such officer and his assistants for their time and trouble, as the governour and council shall determine, to be paid out of the seizure, in case any vessel so seized should, by due process in the law, be condemned, or otherwise out of the publick treasury.

Officers to be under oath.

To be allowed for their service.

[SECT. 4.] This act to continue and be in force during the continuance of an act of this government, made and pass'd on the first instant,* intit[u]led "An Act for preventing the exportation of provisions and warlike stores out of this province." [*Passed November* 1; *published November* 5.

Continuance of the act 1755-56, chap. 16.

CHAPTER 21.

AN ACT FOR ESTABLISHING CERTAIN RECOGNIZANCES ENTRED INTO BY PERSONS HERETOFORE LICEN[S][*C*]ED TO BE INNHOLDERS, TAVERNERS AND RETAILERS.

WHEREAS in order to secure the paym[*en*]t of the duties of excise granted upon spirits distilled, and wine, and upon limes, lemmons and oranges, to those who might farm the same, many persons, heretofore licen[s][c]ed to be innholders, taverners and retailers, have recognized, with sureties, in certain sums, to such persons as were or should be farmers of the duties aforesaid, without expressly naming them, or otherwise ascertaining the recognizees, and thereupon have sold wine, and spirits distilled, by retail; *and whereas* a doubt has arisen whether those recognizances are effectual to enable the farmers of the duties aforesaid to recover the sums to them respectively due from the persons so licen[s][c]ed, or were sufficient to justifie them in selling wine, and spirits distilled, by retail; wherefore for removing such doubts, securing to the farmers aforesaid their just dues, and to the persons so licen[s][c]ed the priviledge thereby intended to be granted them,—

Preamble.

Be it enacted by the Lieutenant-Governour, Council and House of Representatives,

That the farmers of the duties aforesaid, and also the persons so licen[s][c]ed to be innholders, taverners or retailers, shall and may avail themselves, respectively, of the recognizances aforesaid, and of all recognizances heretofore entred into in any of the courts of general sessions of the peace in this province, or before one or more justices out of court, in consequence of such licen[s][c]e granted, in like manner, and in all

Recognizances to the farmers of excise, to stand good.

* *Sic:* the bill had passed to be engrossed in the House, and took its first reading in the Council, October 28.

respects, as they might have done, if the persons, respectively, who farmed the duties afores[*ai*]d, had been therein expressly named as recognizees; and the several recognizances are hereby deemed and declared to be valid and effectual for the purposes aforesaid. [*Passed and published November* 7.*

CHAPTER 22.

AN ACT IN FURTHER ADDITION TO THE ACT FOR LIMITATION OF ACTIONS, AND FOR AVOIDING SUITS IN LAW WHERE THE MATTER IS OF LONG STANDING.

Preamble. 1753-54, chap. 34. WHEREAS, by a law of this province, [e][*i*]ntitled "An Act in further addition to the act for the limitation of actions, and for avoiding suits at law where the matter is of long standing," made and pass'd in the twenty-seventh year of his present majesty's reign, the time limited for commencing all actions of account, and upon the case, excepting such as are excepted in another act, [e][*i*]ntitled "An Act in addition to and for the explanation of an act, [e][*i*]ntitled 'An Act for the limitation of actions, and avoiding suits at law where the matter is of long standing,'" made and pass'd in the twenty-second year of his present majesty's reign, will expire the last day of March next; *and whereas* there are great numbers of men now in the publick service who, if debtors, are by law exempted from arrests for any debt less than ten pounds in value, and, if creditors, are, by reason of their absence, under disadvantages for recovering their just dues, and it is thereby become impracticable to have such accounts and actions settled within the time now limited by law for that purpose,— (1748-49, chap. 17.)

Be it therefore enacted by the Lieutenant-Governour, Council and House of Representatives,

Time for bringing actions of the case, to be extended. [SECT. 1.] That the time for commencing of actions of the case, upon notes of hand, or upon book accounts, limited by the said act of the twenty-second, or by said act made in the twenty-seventh, year of his present majesty's reign, shall be and is hereby extended to the last day of March, which will be in the year of our Lord one thousand and seven hundred and fifty-eight; and no suit hereafter to be brought in such cases shall be barred if commenced before the expiration of said term.

And that this law may be more generally known,—

Be it further enacted,

This act to be read in towns and districts. [SECT. 2.] That the clerk of every town and district within this province shall read, or cause the same to be read, in their respective towns and districts, at their anniversary meetings in March and May, annually; and the justices of the several courts of common pleas within the respective counties shall cause the same to be publickly read at the opening of their courts, from time to time, after the publication of this act, and until[l] the last day of March, one thousand seven hundred and fifty-eight. [*Passed October* 31; *published November* 5.

* On the engrossment the date of publication is given as November 5, although the usual memorandum on the face of the act gives the date of passage, in both branches, and the lieutenant-governor's signature, as November 7, herein agreeing with the record. A printed copy also gives the same date of publication. The date on the engrossment, however, appears to have been altered by writing the figure 5, over 7; and as the latter seems the more probable date it has been followed above.

ACT

PASSED AT THE SESSION BEGUN AND HELD AT BOSTON, ON THE ELEVENTH DAY OF DECEMBER, A. D. 1755.

CHAPTER 23.

AN ACT MAKING PROVISION FOR THE INHABITANTS OF NOVA SCOTIA, SENT HITHER FROM THAT GOVERNMENT, AND LATELY ARRIVED IN THIS PROVINCE.

Preamble.

WHEREAS divers of the inhabitants and families of Nova Scotia have been sent, by order of the governour and council of that province, to this government, and, to prevent their suffering, have been permitted to land, and a committee was appointed by the great and general court of this province to dispose of them in such manner as should be least inconvenient to the province, which committee have accordingly disposed of them in divers towns within the same, where they have been supported in a great measure by said towns, it having been found impracticable for many of them to support themselves,—

Be it therefore enacted by the Lieutenant-Governour, Council and House of Representatives,

Sessions', justices' and selectmens' power relating to the inhabitants of Nova Scotia.

[SECT. 1.] That the courts of general sessions of the peace, and the justices of the peace, in the several counties, and the overseers of the poor, or the selectmen, of the several towns, where said inhabitants or families may have been disposed of, as aforesaid, are hereby directed, authorized and impowered to employ, bind out or support said inhabitants of Nova Scotia, in like manner as by law they would have been impowered to do were they the inhabitants of this province.

And be it further enacted,

Selectmen or overseers to take an account of the charges of their support.

[SECT. 2.] That the selectmen or overseers of the poor in the several towns in this government, where they have been disposed of, as aforesaid, shall keep an exact account of the necessary and unavoidable charges they have been or may be at for their support, until[1] the tenth day of April next, and shall transmit the same to the secretary's office for payment, and in order to ascertain the sum advanced by this government for the service and safety of Nova Scotia, as aforesaid. [*Passed December* 24; *published December* 29.

ACTS

PASSED AT THE SESSION BEGUN AND HELD AT BOSTON, ON THE FOURTEENTH DAY OF JANUARY, A. D. 1756.

CHAPTER 24.

AN ACT FOR RAISING A SUM OF MONEY, BY A LOTTERY OR LOTTERIES, FOR THE PAVING AND REPAIRING THE NECK LEADING OUT OF THE TOWN OF BOSTON, CALLED "BOSTON NECK."

Preamble.

WHEREAS the neck leading out of the town of Boston, called "Boston Neck," by reason of the great number of waggons and other heavy carriages passing over it, and the sea sometimes overflowing it, is frequently out of repair, notwithstanding the great cost and expence the town of Boston has been yearly at for repairing the same; *and whereas* the paving of said neck is the most effectual method of repairing and keeping the same in good order and condition, and will require a considerable sum of money to effect it; for the raising whereof,—

Be it enacted by the Lieutenant-Governour, Council and House of Representatives,

Samuel Grant, Thomas Hill, Joshua Henshaw, Joseph Jackson, Tho. Cushing, Sam. Hewes and John Scollay, selectmen of Boston, allowed and empowered to set up and carry on one or more lotteries.

[SECT. 1.] That Mess[*ieu*]rs Samuel Grant, Thomas Hill, Joshua Henshaw, Joseph Jackson, Thomas Cushing, Samuel Hewes and John Scollay, of Boston aforesaid, or any three of them, be and hereby are allowed and impowered to set[t] up and carry on one or more lottery or lotteries, amounting in the whole to such a sum as, by drawing or deducting ten per cent out of the same, or out of each prize or benefit ticket[t], may raise three thousand pounds, and no more; and that the said sum of three thousand pounds, raised by the deduction aforesaid, be, by the persons above named, paid to the town treasurer of Boston aforesaid, within ten days after the sale of the ticket[t]s of said lottery shall be compleated; or, if the persons afores[*ai*]d shall think fit to raise said sum of three thousand pounds by more lotteries than one, then the money raised by each lottery, by the deduction aforesaid, shall, within ten days after the ticket[t]s of each lottery, respectively, are sold, be paid by them to the treasurer aforesaid; which sum of three thousand pounds, or whatever part thereof shall be so raised, shall be applied towards the paving and repairing the neck aforesaid: *saving* so much of said sum as shall be sufficient to defrey the necessary charges of the lottery or lotteries aforesaid; and to no other use whatsoever, except in case of a surplusage, as in this act hereafter mentioned.

How the money raised thereby shall be disposed of.

And be it further enacted,

Any three of them may be managers or directors.

[SECT. 2.] That the persons aforesaid, or any three of them, be, and they are hereby declared to be, the managers or directors of each and every of the said lottery or lotteries, and are hereby impowered to make all necessary rules, and use all necessary methods, to manage and direct the same, till the whole shall be fully compleated and finished.

And be it further enacted,

[SECT. 3.] That the said managers or directors, with all convenient speed, after the sale of the ticket[t]s of said lottery, or of each lottery, respectively, shall make preparation for the drawing the same, and shall give notice in the public[k] prints, of the time and place of drawing, at least ten days before the said drawing begins, that any of the adventurers, if they think fit, may be present at the drawing; and after the said drawing commences, they, the said managers, may adjourn from day to day, till the whole number of ticket[t]s of each lottery, respectively, shall be drawn: *provided,* the drawing of any one of said lotteries continue not longer than fifteen days, exclusive of Lord's Days.

Said managers to dispose of the tickets, make preparation for the drawing, and give public notice of the same.

[SECT. 4.] And the said managers or directors shall make, or cause to be made, a fair entry, in a book provided for that purpose, of all the ticket[t]s so drawn, and of the blanks and prizes drawn, answering to said ticket[t]s, and within ten days after the drawing of each lottery, respectively, shall be finished, they shall cause a list of the benefit-ticket[t]s, expressing the number and the amount of each of them, to be printed in the public[k] newspapers; at the same time, in the said newspapers, notifying the owners of such benefit-ticket[t]s of the time and place when and where they may apply for the paym[*en*]t of such ticket[t]s; and if any contention or dispute shall arise in adjusting the property of any of the said benefit-ticket[t]s, the major part of the managers shall determine to whom it doth or ought to belong.

Managers directed in their proceedings.

And be it further enacted,

[SECT. 5.] That the said benefit-ticket[t]s shall be paid off by the managers aforesaid within twenty days after the drawing of each lottery, respectively, is finished, upon application of the owner or owners of such ticket[t]s, and delivering them up to be cancelled; and to secure the paym[*en*]t of such benefit-ticket[t]s to the owner or owners of them, the said managers or directors, and their estates, are hereby held and subjected to satisfy and make good the same, in like manner as they and their estates are subjected by law to satisfy and make good their own proper debts: *provided,* that if the money in said managers' hands shall be lost by fire, or any other extraordinary or unavoidable accident, the said managers, and their estates, shall not be so held and subjected.

Benefit-tickets to be paid off by the managers within twenty days after drawing.

And be it further enacted,

[SECT. 6.] That if the owner or owners of any benefit-ticket[t] or ticket[t]s shall, for the space of one year after the drawing aforesaid, neglect to apply for the payment of such ticket[t] or ticket[t]s, unless he, she or they shall have been at sea and out of the province for that term of time (and to such person eighteen months shall be allowed to produce their ticket[t]s), he, she or they shall not be entitled to receive the same, but such ticket[t] and ticket[t]s are hereby declared to be cancelled and of no value; and the money in the hands of said directors, which was to have been applied to the paym[*en*]t of such ticket[t]s, shall, after the expiration of the term afores[*ai*]d, be immediately paid to the town treasurer of said Boston for repairing and keeping in repair the neck aforesaid.

Owners of benefit-tickets not applying for their money in one year, in case, shall not be entitled to the same.

And be it further enacted,

[SECT. 7.] That each manager or director afores[*ai*]d, before his acting in the capacity of manager or director, as afores[*ai*]d, shall take the following oath; viz[t].,—

I, A. B., do swear that I will faithfully execute the trust reposed in me, and that I will not use any indirect act or means to obtain a prize or benefit-lot for myself, or any other person whomsoever, and that I will do the utmost of my endeavour to prevent any undue or sinister practice to be done by any person whomsoever, and that I will, to the best of my judgm[*en*]t, declare to whom any prize, lot or ticket[t] does of right belong, according to

Managers' or directors' oath.

the true intent and meaning of the act of this province made in the twenty-ninth year of his maj[*es*]ty's reign, [e][*i*]ntitled "An Act for the raising a sum of money by a lottery or lotteries, for the paving and repairing the neck leading out of the town of Boston, called 'Boston Neck.'" So help me God.

Persons employed about the lottery or lotteries, to be on oath.

—which oath shall be administ[*e*]red by any justice of the peace in the county of Suffolk; and every person employed about the lottery or lotteries afores[*ai*]d, by the directors afores[*ai*]d, shall take an oath for the faithful performance of his trust, to be administred by any one or more of the directors afores[*ai*]d, who are hereby impowered to administer the same.

And be it further enacted,

In case the whole number of tickets in each lottery shall not be sold in six months after publication of the scheme, the town of Boston may take the remainder to their own account: *provided.*

[SECT. 8.] That if the whole number of ticket[t]s of each lottery, respectively, shall not be sold and disposed of by the said directors within six months after the publication of the scheme of each lottery, respectively, it shall and may be lawful for the town of Boston, if they think fit, to take the remainder of said ticket[t]s, undisposed of as afores[*ai*]d, to their own acco[*un*]t; *provided*, that within one month after the public[k] meeting of said town, to be called for that purpose, a sum of money be raised, and paid to the directors afores[*ai*]d, sufficient to purchase the remainder of said ticket[t]s, which shall, in that case, be delivered to such person or persons as the said town shall appoint to receive the same; but if the whole of said ticket[t]s cannot be sold within the term of six months afores[*ai*]d, and the town afores[*ai*]d refuse to take the ticket[t]s remaining unsold as afores[*ai*]d, then the money received by the said directors for the ticket[t]s sold shall be by them returned to the owners of said ticket[t]s, upon their delivering up their ticket[t]s to the said directors, and the charges arisen shall be defr[a][*e*]yed by the said town of Boston; *provided, nevertheless*, that the said managers shall not hereby be prohibited from carrying on said lottery or lotteries at any other time which they may judge suitable and convenient for the same.

And be it further enacted,

In case of a surplusage, how the same shall be disposed of.

[SECT. 9.] That if the sum raised by means of this act shall be more than sufficient to pave and repair the neck afores[*ai*]d, and defr[a][*e*]y the charges of the lottery or lotteries afores[*ai*]d, and pay the managers afores[*ai*]d for their services, as hereinafter expressed, the surplusage shall be applied towards the paving of such street or streets in the town of Boston as the s[*ai*]d town shall direct.

And be it further enacted,

Penalty for persons who forge or counterfeit tickets, &c.

[SECT. 10.] That if any person shall forge or counterfeit any ticket or tickets, to be made in consequence of this act, or alter any of the numbers thereof, or utter, vend, barter or dispose of any false, altered, forged or counterfeit ticket or ticket[t]s, or bring such ticket or tickets, knowing the same to be such, to the said directors, or any of them, or to any other person, with a fraudulent intent, every such person or persons, being thereof convicted, in due form of law, shall suffer such pains and penalties as are by law provided in cases of forgery.

The managers to commit such to prison.

[SECT. 11.] And the said managers or directors, or any two of them, are hereby authorized, required and impowered to cause any person or persons bringing or uttering such false, altered, forged or counterfeit ticket or tickets, as afores[*ai*]d, to be apprehended and committed to close goal, to be proceeded against according to law.

And be it further enacted,

Managers to keep account of the time of their attendance, and exhibit the same to the town.

[SECT. 12.] That the directors or managers aforesaid shall keep a particular acco[*un*]t of the days of their attendance upon the service afores[*ai*]d, and for each day's attendance shall be allowed the sum of six shillings, the same not to be paid out of the monies raised by virtue of this act, unless there be a sufficiency for the purposes afores[*ai*]d, and for the paym[*en*]t of such their allowances; and, in case of a sufficiency, they shall exhibit an acco[*un*]t of their attendance afores[*ai*]d before a publick meeting of the town afores[*ai*]d, which acco[*un*]t, being examined and found just, shall be paid by the town treas[*ure*]r afores[*ai*]d, upon the order of s[*ai*]d town; but in case there shall not be a sufficiency, the town afores[*ai*]d shall make provision for the paym[*en*]t of such managers' allowance afores[*ai*]d; *provided*, that no more than three of the managers afores[*ai*]d shall be entitled to such allowa[*nce*] for one and the same day. Proviso.

And be it further enacted,

[SECT. 13.] That the managers or directors afores[*ai*]d, after the said lottery, or each of the s[*ai*]d lotteries, respectively, is finished, shall receive the acco[*un*]ts of all charges arisen thereon, and, having found them just, shall certify the same upon s[*ai*]d acco[*un*]ts, and direct the town treas[*ure*]r afores[*ai*]d to pay them of and discharge them. Managers to receive accounts of charge and order payment.

And be it further enacted,

[SECT. 14.] That the selectmen of the town of Boston afores[*ai*]d for the time being, shall contract and agree for the paving and repairing the neck afores[*ai*]d, and for the materials and labour necessary to do the same, at money price, and shall draw on the town treas[*ure*]r afores[*ai*]d for the paym[*en*]t thereof; and, when the s[*ai*]d paving and repairs are finish'd, they shall exhibit a particular acco[*un*]t of the cost of the same, and lay it before the town afores[*ai*]d at one of their publick meetings, in order to be put on file with their other papers. [*Passed January* 23; *published January* 24. Selectmen of Boston, for the time being, to contract and agree for the paving said neck, and for materials, &c., and order pay therefor.

CHAPTER 25.

AN ACT FOR CONTINUING AN ACT MADE [*AND PASSED*] IN THE TWENTY-EIGHTH YEAR OF HIS MAJESTY'S REIGN, [E][*I*]NTITLED "AN ACT FOR GRANTING UNTO HIS MAJESTY SEVERAL RATES AND DUTIES OF IMPOST AND T[U][*O*]NNAGE OF SHIPPING."

WHEREAS, by an act of this province made in the twenty-eighth year of his majesty's reign, intitled "An Act for granting unto his majesty several rates and duties of impost and tunnage of shipping," will expire the twenty-sixth day of February, one thousand seven hundred and fifty-six, and it being convenient that said act should be in force for some time longer,— Preamble. 1754-55, chap. 10.

Be it therefore enacted by the Governour, Council and House of Representatives,

That the act afores[*ai*]d, and every matter and thing therein contained, be and hereby is continued and shall be in force from the said twenty-sixth of February, one thousand seven hundred and fifty-six, to the twenty-sixth day of March next following. [*Passed February* 25; *published February* 26. Said act continued.

CHAPTER 26.

AN ACT FOR REGULATING THE GRAMMAR SCHOOL IN IPSWICH, AND FOR INCORPORATING CERTAIN PERSONS TO MANAGE AND DIRECT THE SAME.

WHEREAS divers piously disposed persons in the first settlement of the town of Ipswich, within the county of Essex, granted and conveyed Preamble.

to feoffees in trust, and to such their successors in the same trust as those feoffees should appoint to hold perpetual succession, certain lands, tenements and annuities by them mentioned, for the use of school-learning in said town forever; of which feoffees the honourable Thomas Berry, Esq[r]., Daniel Appleton and Samuel Rogers, Esqrs., with Mr. Benjamin Crocker, are the only survivors; *and whereas* the town of Ipswich did also, in their laudable concern for promoting learning, about the same time, and for the same use, give and grant to certain persons in said grant mentioned, and to such others as the said town should appoint, a large farm, then called a neck of land, situate in Chebacco, in the same town, with some other lands adjoining; all which farm and lands were soon after leased out for the space of one thousand years, the rents to be applied to the uses of learning in said town as aforesaid; but as is apprehended by some, no power was given by the said town to their trustees to appoint successors in that trust for receiving and applying the rents, or of ordering and directing the affairs of the school in said town, as in the first-mentioned case is provided; from which difference in the original constitution of those grants, which were all designed for one and the same use, considerable disputes have already arisen between the said town and the feoffees; and not only so, but some doubts are started whether it is in the power of said town or feoffees to compel the payment of the rents of the farm and adjoining land before mentioned; *and inasmuch* as the said town of Ipswich, by their vote of the twenty-second day of January, one thousand seven hundred and fifty-six, by and with the consent of the aforementioned feoffees, have agreed to apply to this court for aid in the manner in said vote mentioned; wherefore,—

Be it enacted by the Governour, Council and House of Representatives,

Feoffees of Ipswich school appointed.

[SECT. 1.] That from and after the first day of March next, for and during the space of ten years, the aforenamed Thomas Berry, Daniel Appleton and Samuel Rogers, Esqrs., with Mr. Benjamin Crocker, the present surviving feoffees on the part of the private persons granting lands as afores[*ai*]d, together with Francis Choate, Esq[r]., Capt. Nathaniel Tredwell and Mr. John Patch, Junr., three of the present selectmen of said town, shall be and they are hereby incorporated a joint committee or feoffees in trust, with full power and authority by a majority of them to grant necessary leases of any of said land not prejudicial to any lease already made, and not exceeding the term of ten years, to demand and receive the said rents and annuities, and, if need be, to sue for and recover the same; to appoint grammar-school masters from year to year and time to time, and agree for his salary; to apply the rents and annuities for the paym[*en*]t of his salary and other necessary charges arising by said school; to appoint a clerk and treasurer, and if found necessary, to impose some moderate sum and sums of money to be paid by such scholars as may attend said school, for making up and supplying any deficiency that may happen in the yearly income and annuities of said lands; for defr[a][e]ying the necessary charges that may arise by said school, and enforce the payment; to inspect said school and schoolmaster, and in general to transact and order all matters and things relative to such school, so as may best answer the original intent and design thereof.

Their power.

Account of feoffees' proceedings to be laid before the town annually.

[SECT. 2.] And the said committee or feoffees and their successors shall, at the anniversary meeting of said town in March, yearly, during the continuance of this act, lay before said town a fair account of their proceedings relating to said school for the year then last past.

And for the continuance of the succession of the before-named committee or feoffees,—

Be it enacted,

[SECT. 3.] That if either the said Thomas Berry, Daniel Appleton, Samuel Rogers or Benjamin Crocker, shall decease, or remove out of said town of Ipswich, or otherwise become uncapable or unfit to discharge said trust, it shall and may be lawful for the surviving and qualified remainder of those four gentlemen to appoint some other suitable person or persons in his or their room so deceasing, removing or otherwise unqualified, according to the original intention of their first appointm[*en*]t, so as to keep up the same number of four feoffees thus constituted, and no more; and no person to be appointed a feoffee but an inhabitant of the town of Ipswich: and the aforementioned selectmen shall, from year to year, be succeeded by the three oldest in that office of the selectmen of said town for the time being, other than such of them as may be also one of the aforesaid four feoffees; and in case it should at any time happen that there is not three selectmen chosen by said town that may have served the town before in that office, the deficiency shall be supplyed by those first named in the choice of the town. Provision for the succession of said feoffees, &c.

And for rend[*e*]ring the whole more effectual,—

Be it further enacted,

[SECT. 4.] That the afores[*ai*]d committee or feoffees in trust may, in all matters relative to s[*ai*]d grammar school, in which they may by force of this act be concerned, sue or be sued by the name or char[e][*a*]cter of the feoffees of the grammar school of the town of Ipswich, in the county of Essex; and in this power their successors shall be included with respect to the transactions of those that may have preceeded them in said office. Feoffees, or committee, to sue and be sued.

[SECT. 5.] This act to continue and be in force for the space of ten years, and no longer. [*Passed February* 17; *published February* 26.* Limitation.

CHAPTER 27.

AN ACT FOR SUPPLYING THE TREASURY WITH THE SUM OF SIXTY THOUSAND POUNDS.

WHEREAS the great sums with which the treasury has been suppl[i][*y*]ed, for defr[a][*e*]ying the charges of the late expedition against Crown Point, and other charges of the government, have proved insufficient, and the wages of the forces employed in that service still remain unpaid; *and whereas* the general court have determined upon further prosecuting an expedition, this present year, for removing the encroachm[*en*]ts made and making by the French on his majesty's territories at and near the said Crown Point, and a further sum of money will be necessary to encourage the enlistment of the forces, and to make necessary provision for said expedition, and, all other attempts for obtaining a sufficiency of money having proved ineffectual, his excellency the governour has consented to advance a sum not exceeding forty thousand pounds, lawful money, for the purposes aforesaid; and a further sum being necessary to be immediately raised towards defr[a][*e*]ying the charges of the said expedition,— Preamble.

* The date of the Governor's signature to this act, according to the record, is February 16; but the engrossment has been followed above, both as to the date of passage, and to the date of publication, which appears to be March 1, 1756, in the printed act.

Be it therefore enacted by the Governour, Council and House of Represent[ati]ves,

Treasurer empowered to borrow £40,000 from his excellency the governor.

[SECT. 1.] That the treasurer of this province be and he hereby is impowered and directed to borrow and receive from his excellency William Shirley, Esq[r]., the sum of forty thousand pounds, lawful money, in mill'd dollars, at six shillings each, or in coined silver at six shillings and eightpence per ounce, or in coined gold at the rate at which such gold is set, or restrained from exceeding, by an act of this province made and pass[e]'d in the twenty-third year of his present majesty's reign, intitled "An Act for ascertaining the rates at which coined silver and gold, and English halfpence and farthings, may pass within the governm[en]t."

[SECT 2.] And for the sum so borrowed, the said treasurer shall give his receipt for the value of twenty thousand pounds in the form following:—

Form of treasurer's receipt.

Province of the Massachusetts Bay, day of , 1756.
Received from his excellency William Shirley, Esq[r]., the sum of , lawful money of said province, and I do hereby promise the said William Shirley, and oblige myself and successors in the office of treasurer, to repay the said sum of to the said William Shirley, or his order, by the first day of June, 1758. Witness my hand, H. G., Treasurer.

[SECT. 3.] And for the remaining sum of twenty thousand pounds borrowed of his excellency, the treasurer shall give his receipt in the form following:—

Form of treasurer's receipt.

Province of the Massachusetts Bay, day of , 1756.
Received from his excellency William Shirley, Esq[r]., the sum of , lawful money of said province, and I do hereby promise the said William Shirley, and oblige myself and successors in the office of treasurer, to repay the said sum [*of*] to the said William Shirley, or his order, by the first day of June, 1759.

And be it further enacted,

Service in which said money is to be issued.

[SECT. 4.] That the sum so borrowed as afores[*ai*]d shall be a stock in the treasury, and shall be issued by warrant from the governour or commander-in-chief, with advice and consent of the council, for the payment of the wages that are now due to the officers and soldiers who served in the late expedition against Crown Point, and for the payment of the necessary charges that may attend the enlisting such forces as may be raised for the expedition this present year for removing the encroachm[*en*]ts made on his majesty's territories by the French at and near the said Crown Point, and for preparing and enabling such forces to proceed on said expedition, and for no other purpose whatsoever.

And as a fund and security for drawing said sum of forty thousand pounds into the treasury again, so as to enable the treasurer to repay the money borrowed,—

Be it further enacted,

Fund:—

Tax of £20,000, in 1757.

£20,000, in 1758.

[SECT. 5.] That there be and hereby is granted unto his most excellent majesty, for the ends and uses aforesaid, a tax of forty thousand pounds, to be levied on polls, and estates both real and personal within this province, in manner following; that is to say, twenty thousand pounds, part thereof, according to such rules and in such proportion on the several towns and districts within this province as shall be agreed on and ordered by the general court or assembly, at their session in May, [1757] [*one thousand seven hundred and fifty-seven*], and to be paid into the publick treasury on or before the [31st] [*thirty-first*] of March then next after; and twenty thousand pounds, the other part of said sum, according to such rules and in such proportions on the several towns and districts aforesaid as shall be agreed on and ordered by the general court, at their session in May, [1758] [*one thousand seven hundred and fifty-eight*], and to be paid into the publick treasury on or before the [31st] [*thirty-first*] of March then next after.

And be it further enacted,

[SECT. 6.] That if the general court, at their sessions in May, [1757] [*one thousand seven hundred and fifty-seven*], and in May, [1758] [*one thousand seven hundred and fifty-eight*], some time before the twentieth day of June in each year, shall not agree and conclude upon an act apportioning the sums which by this act are engaged to be, in each of said years, apportioned, assessed and levied, that then, and in such case, each town and district within this province shall pay, by a tax to be levied on the polls, and estates both real and personal within their limits, the same proportion of the said sums as the said towns and districts were taxed by the general court in the tax act then last preceeding; and the province treasurer is hereby fully impowered and directed, some time in the month of June, in each of the years afores[*ai*]d, to issue and send forth his warrants, directed to the selectmen or assessors of each town and district within this province, requirirg them to assess the polls, and estates both real and personal within their several towns and districts, and for their respective parts and proportion of the sums before directed and engaged to be assessed, to be paid into the publick treasury at the aforementioned times; and the assessors, as also persons assessed, shall observe, be govern[*e*]'d by and subject to all such rules and directions as have been given in the last preceeding tax act.

Rule for apportioning the tax, in case no tax act shall be agreed on.

And be it further enacted,

[SECT. 7.] That the said sum of forty thousand pounds thus levied and assessed, shall be applied by the province treasurer to the payment of the full sum so borrowed of his excellency the governour by virtue of this act, and to no other purpose whatsoever.

Treasurer to apply the money that may be granted in Great Britain, for discharge of the money borrowed.

Provided, always, anything in this act to the contrary notwithstanding,—

That whereas humble trust and dependance is had by the general assembly on a reimburs[*e*]ment of the charges arising from the expeditions against Crown Point, and mon[*cy*][*ie*]s for that purpose are expected from Great Britain, and it has been agreed and engaged by a vote of the council and house of represent[*ati*]ves that the mon[*ey*][*ie*]s which shall first arrive, or so much as shall be necessary, shall be applied to the payment of the sum advanced by his excellency the govern[*ou*]r for the purposes before mentioned in this act,—

[SECT. 8.] That the treasurer be and hereby is directed and required to apply such mon[ey][*ie*]s, or so much thereof as shall be necessary, as he shall first, from time to time, receive into the treasury for and on account of the reimburs[*e*]m[*en*]t afores[*ai*]d, to the payment of the sums advanced by his excellency the governour for the purposes mentioned in this act, until[l] the whole sum advanced shall be repaid. And in case twenty thousand pounds of the mon[ey][*ie*]s shall arrive from Great Britain, and be lodged in the treasury before the twentieth day of June, [1757] [*one thousand seven hundred and fifty-seven*], the tax, which otherwise by this act is ordered to go forth, is hereby made null and void.

And be it further enacted,

[SECT. 9.] That if the further sum of twenty thousand pounds shall arrive from Great Britain, and be lodged in the treasury before the twentieth day of June, [1758] [*one thousand seven hundred and fifty-eight*], the tax, which otherwise by this act is ordered to go forth, is hereby made null and void.

Taxes not to be made, in case the money be sent from Great Britain.

And be it further enacted,

[SECT. 10.] That the treasurer of the province for the time being, be and he hereby is fully authorized and impowered to demand and

Treasurer to demand and

receive moneys from Great Britain.

receive the whole and every part of the money aforesaid from the commander of any vessel or vessels, on board of which the same shall be shipped, upon the arrival thereof within this government, or from any other trustee of it.

And be it further enacted,

Treasurer to borrow £20,000.

[SECT. 11.] That the treasurer of the province be and hereby is impowered and directed to borrow, from such person or persons as shall be willing to lend the same, a sum not exceeding twenty thousand pounds, in mill'd dollars, at six shillings each, or in other silver at six shillings and eightpence per ounce; and the sum so borrowed shall be applied in manner as is in this act hereafter directed, and for every sum so borrowed the treasurer shall give a receipt and obligation in form following,—

Form of treasurer's receipt.

Province of the Massachusetts Bay, the day of 1756.
Received of the sum of , for the use and service of the province of the Massachusetts Bay, and, in behalf of said province, I do hereby promise and oblige myself and successors in the office of treasurer to repay the said , or order, the second day of June, 1757, the aforesaid sum of , in coined silver at six shillings and eightpence per ounce, or Spanish mill'd dollars, at six shillings each, with interest annually, at the rate of six per cent per annum.
Witness my hand, H. G., Treas[*ure*]r.

And be it further enacted,

[SECT. 12.] That the aforesaid sum of twenty thousand pounds, when received into the treasury, shall be applied for the service of the expedition against Crown Point.

And in order to draw the same money into the treasury, so as to enable the treasurer effectually to discharge the receipts and obligations (with the interest that may be due thereon), by him given in pursuance of this act,—

Be it enacted,

[SECT. 13.] That there be and hereby is granted to his most excellent majesty, a tax of twenty-two thousand pounds, to be levied on polls, and estates both real and personal within this province, in manner following; that is to say, eleven thousand pounds, part thereof, according to such rules and in such proportion on the several towns and districts within the province as shall be agreed on and ordered by the general court or assembly, at their session in May, [1756] [*one thousand seven hundred and fifty-six*], and to be paid into the publick treasury on or before the [31st] [*thirty-first*] of March next after; and the further sum of eleven thousand pounds, according to such rules and in such proportion on the several towns and districts aforesaid as shall be agreed on and ordered by the general court, at their session in May, [1757] [*one thousand seven hundred and fifty-seven*], and to be paid into the publick treasury on or before the [31st] [*thirty-first*] of March then next after.

Tax of £11,000, in 1756.

Tax of £11,000, in 1757.

And be it further enacted,

Rule for apportioning the tax, in case no tax act shall be agreed on.

[SECT. 14.] That if the general court, at their session in May, [1756] [*one thousand seven hundred and fifty-six*], and in May, [1757] [*one thousand seven hundred and fifty-seven*], sometime before the twentieth day of June in each year, shall not agree and conclude upon an act apportioning the sums which by this act are engaged to be, in each of said years, apportioned, assessed and levied, that then, and in such case, each town and district within this province shall pay, by a tax to be levied on the polls, and estates both real and personal within their limits, the same proportion of the said sums as the said towns and districts were taxed by the general court in the tax act then last preceeding; and the province treasurer is hereby fully impowered and directed, some time in the month of June, in each of the years aforesaid, to issue and send forth his warrants, directed to the selectmen or assessors of each town and district within this province, requiring them to assess the polls, and estates both real and personal within their several towns and districts, for their respective parts and proportion[*s*] of the sums before directed and engaged to be assessed, to be paid into the treasury at the beforementioned times; and the assessors, as also persons assessed, shall observe, be govern[*e*]'d by and subject to all such rules and directions as shall have been given in the last preceeding tax act.

And as a further fund to enable the treasurer to discharge said receipts and obligations by him given in pursuance of this act,—

Be it further enacted,

[SECT. 15.] That the mon[ey][*ie*]s that shall be receiv[*e*]'d from Great Britain, over and above forty thousand pounds, lawful money, which by this act is appropriated for the repayment of that sum borrowed of his excellency William Shirley, Esq[r]., shall be applyed by the treasurer, or so much thereof as shall be needful, for the discharging the said notes by him given, with the interest that may be due thereon, in pursuance of this act.

Money that may come from Great Britain, above that borrowed of the Governor, to be a fund.

And be it further enacted,

[SECT. 16.] That the treasurer is hereby directed and ordered to pay the sum of twenty thousand pounds, as shall be directed by warrant from the governour, with the advice of the council; and the secretary, to whom it belongs to keep the muster-rolls and acco[mp][*un*]ts of charge, shall lay before the house of representatives, when they direct, such muster-rolls and acco[mp][*un*]ts, after payment thereof.

Treasurer to issue the said £20,000.

Provided, always, anything in this act to the contrary notwithstanding,—

[SECT. 17.] That in case ten thousand pounds of the mon[ey][*ie*]s arrive from Great Britain, and be received into the publick treasury, over and above the forty thousand pounds appropriated for repayment of the money borrowed of his excellency William Shirley, Esq., on or before the twentieth day of June next, then, and in such case, the tax which otherwise by this act was to go forth in May, [1756], [*one thousand seven hundred fifty-six*], is hereby declared to be null and void. And in case ten thousand pounds more shall arrive from Great Britain, and be received into the publick treasury before the twentieth of June, [1757], [*one thousand seven hundred and fifty-seven*], then, and in such case, the tax of eleven thousand pounds, which otherwise by this act was to go forth, is hereby declared to be null and void.

Treasurer's warrants for levying the tax, not to issue, in case.

Provided, always,—

[SECT. 18.] That the remainder of the sum that shall be brought in by taxes ordered by this act to be assessed and levied, over and above what shall be sufficient to discharge the notes and obligations aforesaid, with the interest that may be due thereon, shall be and remain as a stock in the treasury, and to be appl[i][*y*]ed as the general court of this province shall hereafter order, and to no other purpose whatsoever. [*Passed February* 28;* *published March* 1, 1756.

Proviso.

* Passed March 1, according to the record.

CHAPTER 28.

AN ACT FOR PREVENTING ANY DANGEROUS CONTAGION THAT MAY BE OCCASIONED BY DOGS AND OTHER BRUTE CREATURES, DYING OF THE DISTEMPER PREVALENT AMONG THEM, LYING UNBURIED.

Preamble.

WHEREAS this government have been informed that a distemper prevails among dogs, cat[t]s and other brute animals, by which great numbers of them have dyed in the town of Boston and elsewhere in the province, within a few days; and as there is danger, if effectual care be not taken that they be buried seasonably, that some contagion may thence arise which may prove prejudicial to the inhabitants,—

Be it therefore enacted by the Governour, Council and House of Representatives,

Carcasses of dead dogs to be buried.

[SECT. 1.] That every owner of any dog, cat[t] or other creature of the brute kind, which shall dye of any distemper, between the fifth day of March instant and the last day of October, in the present and next ensuing year, shall, within three hours next after the death of such brute, cause the same to be buried under ground at the depth of two feet at the least, upon pain of forfeiting forty shillings for every wilful neglect herein, to be recovered before any justice of the peace of the same county, upon information or complaint; one moiety thereof to be to the informer or complainant, and the other moiety to the use of the poor of the town wherein such owner dwells.

And be it further enacted,

Selectmen to appoint persons to take care of the execution of this law.

[SECT. 2.] That the selectmen of the several towns within this province, shall appoint one or more suitable persons in their respective towns, to bury, or cause to be buried, in manner as aforesaid, the carcase of any dog or other brute, which they may find unburied within the term aforesaid, and shall order a meet recompence to be made to such person or persons for their trouble, at the charge of the owner of such dogs or other brute, if the owner be known; or otherwise, at the charge of the town where such carcase shall be found.

And be it further enacted,

Their power.

[SECT. 3.] That every person so to be appointed by the selectmen in any town, shall be and is hereby impowered, by due course of law, to recover of the delinquent owner of any dog, cat[t] or other brute that shall dye and be left unburied, contrary to this act, a reasonable recompence for his trouble in burying them, together with costs of prosecution.

Limitation.

[SECT. 4.] This act to be in force from and after the fifth day of March instant, and to continue till the first day of October, *Anno Domini* one thousand seven hundred and fifty-seven. [*Passed March* 3; * *published March* 4, 1756.

CHAPTER 29.

AN ACT FOR THE SUPPLY OF THE TREASURY WITH ELEVEN THOUSAND POUNDS.

Preamble.

WHEREAS the provision already made by this court is insufficient to discharge the publick debts,—

Be it enacted by the Governour, Council and House of Representatives,

[SECT. 1.] That the treasurer of the province be and he is hereby impowered and directed to borrow, of such person or persons as shall be

* Passed March 5, according to the record; but this was one day after the publication, according to both the parchment and the printed act.

willing to lend the same, a sum not exceeding eleven thousand pounds, in mill'd dollars, at six shillings each, or in other silver at six shillings and eightpence per ounce; one half of said sum to be repaid by the thirtieth day of June, one thousand seven hundred and fifty-seven, and the other half by the thirtieth day of June, one thousand seven hundred and fifty-eight; and the sum so borrowed shall be applied by the treasurer for the payment of all such draughts as shall be drawn on him by the governour or commander-in-chief for the time being, with the advice of the council, out of the respective appropriations hereafter mentioned in this act; and for every sum so borrowed, which shall be agreed to be repaid by the thirtieth day of June, one thousand seven hundred and fifty-seven, the treasurer shall give a receipt and obligation in form following:—

Province of the Massachusetts Bay, the day of , 1756. Received of the sum of , for the use and service of the province of the Massachusetts Bay, and, in behalf of said province, I do hereby promise and oblige myself and successors in the office of treasurer to repay the said or order, the thirtieth day of June, 1757, the aforesaid sum of , in coined silver of sterling alloy, at six shillings and eightpence per ounce, or in mill'd dollars, at six shillings each, with interest annually, at the rate of six per cent per annum. Form of treasurer's receipt.

Witness my hand, A. B., Treasurer.

[SECT. 2.] And for every sum borrowed as aforesaid, and which shall be agreed to be repaid by the thirtieth day of June, one thousand seven hundred and fifty-eight, the receipt or obligation aforesaid shall be so varied as that the time of payment expressed therein shall be the thirtieth day of June, one thousand seven hundred and fifty-eight, and no receipt shall be given for a sum less than six pounds; and the treasurer is hereby directed to use his discretion in borrowing said sum at such times as that he may be enabled to comply with the draughts that shall be made on the treasury in pursuance of this act.

And be it further enacted,

[SECT. 3.] That the aforesaid sum of eleven thousand pounds, when received into the treasury, shall be issued out in manner and for the purposes following; that is to say, a sum not exceeding five thousand six hundred pounds, part of the aforesaid sum of eleven thousand pounds, shall be applied for the discharging of debts contracted for firearms and ammunition; and the further sum of four thousand pounds, part of the aforesaid sum of eleven thousand pounds, shall be applied for the service of the several forts and garrisons within this province; and the further sum of one thousand pounds, part of the aforesaid sum of eleven thousand pounds, shall be applied for the payment of his majesty's council and house of representatives serving in the general court during the several sessions for the present year; and the further sum of three hundred pounds, part of the aforesaid sum of eleven thousand pounds, shall be applied for the discharge of other debts owing from this province to persons who have served or shall serve them, by order of this court, in such matters and things where there is no establishment nor any certain sum assigned for that purpose, and for paper, writing and printing for this court.

£5,600 for firearms and ammunition.

£4,000 for forts and garrisons.

£1,000 for pay of councillors' and representatives' attendance.

£300 for debts, where there is no establishment.

And whereas there are sometimes contingent and unforeseen charges that demand prompt payment,—

Be it enacted,

[SECT. 4.] That the sum of one hundred pounds, being the remaining part of the aforesaid sum of eleven thousand pounds, be applied to pay such contingent charges, and for no other purpose whatsoever. £100 for contingent charges.

And in order to draw the money into the treasury again, and to enable the treasurer effectually to discharge the receipts and obligations (with the interest that may be due thereon), by him given for one-half of the aforesaid sum of eleven thousand pounds, and which shall be made payable by the thirtieth day of June, one thousand seven hundred and fifty-seven, in pursuance of this act,—

Be it enacted,

Tax of £6,000, granted in 1756.

[SECT. 5.] That there be and hereby is granted to his most excellent majesty a tax of six thousand pounds, to be levied on the polls and estates within this province, according to such rules and in such proportions as shall be ordered by the general court of this province, at their sessions in May, one thousand seven hundred and fifty-six.

And be it further enacted,

Rule for apportioning the tax, in case no tax act shall be agreed on.

[SECT. 6.] That in case the general court shall not, by the twentieth of June, one thousand seven hundred and fifty-six, agree and conclude upon a tax act to draw into the treasury the aforesaid sum of six thousand pounds by the thirty-first day of March then next following, that then the treasurer of the province, for the time being, sometime in the month of July immediately following the twentieth day of June aforesaid, is hereby fully impowered and directed to issue his warrants, directed to the selectmen or assessors of the several towns and districts in this province, requiring them, respectively, to assess, levy and pay in their respective proportions of said sum according to the rates and proportions, rules and directions of the last preceeding tax act.

And to enable the treasurer effectually to discharge the receipts and obligations by him given for the other half of the aforesaid sum of eleven thousand pounds, and which shall be made payable by the thirtieth day of June, one thousand seven hundred and fifty-eight, with the interest that may be due thereon, in pursuance of this act,—

Be it enacted,

Tax of £6,300, granted in 1757.

[SECT. 7.] That there be and hereby is granted to his most excellent majesty, a tax of six thousand three hundred pounds, to be levied on the polls and estates within this province, according to such rules and in such proportions as shall be ordered by the general court of this province, at their sessions in May, one thousand seven hundred and fifty-seven.

And be it further enacted,

Rule for apportioning the tax, in case no tax act shall be agreed on.

[SECT. 8.] That in case the gen[*eral*][l] court shall not, by the twentieth day of June, one thousand seven hundred and fifty-seven, agree and conclude upon a tax act to draw into the treasury the afores[*ai*]d sum of six thousand three hundred pounds by the thirty-first day of March then next following, that then the treasurer of the province for the time being, some time in the month of July immediately following the twentieth day of June, one thousand seven hundred and fifty-seven, aforesaid, is hereby fully impowered and directed to issue his warrants, directed to the selectmen or assessors of the several towns and districts in this province, requiring them, respectively, to assess, levy and pay in their respective proportions of said sum according to the rates and proportions, rules and directions of the last preceeding tax act. [*Passed March* 10 ;* *published March* 11,† 1756.

* Passed March 9, according to the record; but the date appears as above, on the engrossment, in the Governor's handwriting.

† Published March 8, according to the printed act. The engrossment has been followed, above.

CHAPTER 30.

AN ACT FOR PREVENTING THE EXPORTATION OF PROVISIONS AND WARLIKE STORES, OUT OF THIS PROVINCE.

Be it enacted by the Governour, Council and House of Representatives,

[SECT. 1.] That no warlike stores, or provisions of any kind whatsoever, fish only excepted, shall be exported or carried out of any port or harbour in this province, in any vessel whatever, before the twentieth day of June next: *saving* only such provisions or warlike stores as are necessary for the defence of each respective vessel outward bound, and victualling the mariners on board the same, during their intended voyage, and whereof an account, in writing, shall be given by the master of such vessel, on oath, to the impost officer or his deputy, and where there is no impost officer or deputy, then, to a justice of the peace or town clerk, on pain of one thousand pounds, lawful money, to be forfeited and paid by the master, and the like sum by the owner and owners, factor and factors, of each respective vessel in which any warlike stores or provisions shall be exported or carried out of any port or harbour in this province; one moiety thereof to the use of this government, and the other moiety to him or them that shall inform or sue for the same; and such masters, owners and factors, respectively, upon their being convicted of the offence aforesaid at the superiour court of judicature, court of assize and general goal delivery, shall be further liable to stand on the pillory, and have one of their ears cut off. Exportation of warlike stores, and provisions, prohibited:— saving. Penalty, &c., for breach of this act.

And whereas it has been the practice of some persons to pack beef and pork, and other provisions, in barrels and other casks, and mark on the outside of said cask, mackerell or fish, with intent to elude this act,—

Be it therefore further enacted,

[SECT. 2.] That when any vessel is bound out of this government with pickled fish of any kind on board, the master, freighter or freighters, shall make oath, either before the impost officer or his deputy, or before one of his majesty's justices of the peace in the county where such vessels sail from, or where the freighter or freighters dwell, that every cask that is shipt on board such outward-bound vessel as fish, is, *bonâ fide*, pickled fish, and that there is no more provisions or warlike stores shipt, or intended to be shipt, on board said vessel, than is necessary for defending and victualling such vessel as afores[*ai*]d; and no vessel outward bound, shall be cleared out by the impost officer or his deputy, until[l] such oath be first made. Master or freighter to make oath as to the contents of casks.

And be it further enacted,

[SECT. 3.] That any cooper or other person who shall pack or put up in any cask, any provisions of any kind, in order to be shipt on board any vessel bound out of this governm[*en*]t, as aforesaid, and shall put, or cause to be put, on any fallacious mark, whereby to induce any person to bel[ei][*ie*]ve there is not contained anything in said cask that in fact they do contain, and be thereof convicted as aforesaid, shall suffer the same penalties that the master or owners afores[*ai*]d are liable to, by this act, in case of exporting and carrying provisions and warlike stores out of this province. Penalty for putting a false mark.

And be it further enacted,

[SECT. 4.] That every freighter that shall be convict of shipping on board any outward-bound vessel, or any master that shall, knowingly, take on board any provisions with a false mark thereon, with a design to elude this act, and be thereof convict in the superiour court afore- Penalty for shipping or receiving on board provisions with a false mark.

s[*ai*]d, shall suffer the same penalties as if said provisions had been sent out of this province contrary to this act, as before mentioned.

And be it further enacted,

Governor and council may prolong the time above.

[SECT. 5.] That if the governour or commander-in-chief for the time being shall see fit, with the advice and consent of the council, to issue a proclamation, prohibiting the exportation of provisions or warlike stores out of this province, for any time after the said twentieth day of June next, and not exceeding the twentieth day of November following, in this present year, the master, and owner and owners, factor and factors, of any vessel or vessels, on board of which such provisions or warlike stores shall be exported or shipped, contrary to such proclamation, shall be respectively liable to the same pains and penalties as if the same had been exported before the said twentieth day of June, contrary to this act.

Provided, always,—

Proviso for sea, or land, forces.

[SECT. 6.] That it shall and may be lawful for any provisions or warlike stores to be exported for the service of his majesty's sea or land forces, on board any vessel or vessels licensed for that purpose by the govern[*ou*]r or commander-in-ch[ei][*ie*]f for the time being, with the advice of the council.

Provided, also,—

Proviso for coasting-vessels, &c.

[SECT. 7.] That it shall and may be lawful for provisions and warlike stores to be laden and transported on board any coasting-vessel, or vessels, passing from one port to another within this province, bonds being first given, in a thousand pounds, lawful money, w[*i*]th sufficient sureties, to the impost officer or his deputy, and where there is no impost officer or deputy, then to a justice of the peace or the town clerk, to reland the same in some town or district in this province, and to return a certificate thereof from the deputy impost-officer residing in the town or district where they are so relanded, or from the town or district clerk of such towns or districts where no deputy impost-officer resides.

Provided, also,—

Proviso, also, where the fishery is carried on.

[SECT. 8.] That in such towns where the fishery is carried on, and out of which vessels coasting from one port to another in this province, and wherein neither impost officer or his deputy dwells, the masters of such fishing or coasting vessels may render the account afores[*ai*]d, on oath, to a justice of the peace, or the town or district clerk of the respective towns out of which they sail, who is hereby impowered to take the same; and the account so taken and attested shall be by them transmitted to the impost officer, which shall be as effectual as though the same were taken by him or his deputy.

And be it enacted,

Impost officer's fee.

[SECT. 9.] That the impost officer shall be allow[*e*]'d one shilling for each bond so taken, and every justice and town or district clerk the like sum for every such certificate by them respectively transmitted as afores[*ai*]d, to be paid by the master.

And be it further enacted,

Penalty for holding correspondence or communication with inhabitants of Louisbourg, &c.

[SECT. 10.] That it shall be unlawful for any of his majesty's subjects of this province, and they are hereby strictly forbidden, to hold any correspondence or communication with any inhabitants of Louisbourg, or any other of the French settlements in North America, either by land or water; and if any person or persons belonging to this province shall presume to go or send to Louisbourg, or any other French settlement in North America, during the continuance of this act, the ship, sloop or other vessel employed, with all her tackle and appurtenances, and her cargo, shall be forfeited, one half to his majesty for the use of this province, the other half to him or them who shall inform and sue for the same in any of his majesty's courts within this province proper to try the same; and be further liable, if a ship or vessel, the master to have one ear cut off, and be publickly whipt thirty-nine lashes, and the owner or owners, and factor or factors of the owner or owners, of such ship or other vessel shall forfeit and pay, each, five hundred pounds, to be recovered and disposed of as above, and also be forever disabled to hold any place of honour or prof[f]it under this government. [*Passed February* 27; *published March* 1.

CHAPTER 31.

AN ACT FOR GRANTING UNTO HIS MAJESTY AN EXCISE UPON SPIRITS DISTILLED AND WINE, AND UPON LIMES, LEM[*M*]ONS AND ORANGES.

WE, his majesty's most loyal [1] and dutiful subjects, the representatives of the province of the Massachusetts Bay, in general court assembled, being desirous to lessen the present debt of the province, have chearfully and unanimously granted, and do hereby give and grant unto his most excellent majesty, for the end and use above mentioned, and for no other use, an excise upon all rum and other spirits distilled, and upon all wines whatsoever, and upon lemmons, limes and oranges, to be raised, levied, collected and paid in manner and form following:— Preamble.

And be it accordingly enacted by the Governour, Council and House of Representatives,

[SECT. 1.] That from and after the twenty-sixth day of March, one thousand seven hundred and fifty-six, and until[1] the twenty-sixth of March, one thousand seven hundred and fifty-seven, every person already licenced, or that shall hereafter be licenced, to retail rum or other spirits, or wine, shall pay the duties following:— Time of this act's continuance.

For every gallon of rum and spirits distilled, fourpence.

For every gallon of wine of every sort, sixpence.

For every hundred of lemmons or oranges, four shillings.

For every hundred of limes, one shilling and sixpence.

—And so proportionably for any other quantity or number.

And be it further enacted,

[SECT. 2.] That every retailer of wine, rum or spirits distilled, taverner, innholder and common victualler, shall, on the said twenty-sixth day of March next, take a just and true account, in writing, of all wine, rum and spirits distilled, and of all limes, lemmons and oranges then by him or her, or in his or her possession; and that every person who shall hereafter be licenced to be a taverner, innholder, common victualler or retailer of wine, rum or spirits distilled, shall take a like account of all wine, rum and spirits distilled, and of all limes, lemmons and oranges by him or her, or in his or her possession, at the time of such licence granted; and that every taverner, innholder, and common victualler and retailer of wine, rum or spirits distilled shall make a fair entry, in a book by them respectively to be kept for that purpose, of all such wine, rum or spirits distilled, as he or she, or any person or persons for him or her, shall buy, distill, take in or receive after such first account taken, and when and of whom the same was bought and taken in; and at the expiration of every half year shall take a just and true account how much thereof then remains by them; and shall, in writing, under their hands, render to him or them that shall farm the duties aforesaid the whole of those several accounts, and shall also, if re- Account to be taken.

quested, make oath, in the form following, before such farmer or farmers, who are hereby impowered to administer the same :—

Form of the oath.

You, A. B., do swear that the account by you now rendred is, to the best of your knowledge, a just and true account of all the wine, rum and distilled spirits, limes, lemmons and oranges you had by you, or in your possession, on the twenty-sixth day of March, one thousand seven hundred and fifty-six, and also of all the wine, rum and distilled spirits bought, distilled, taken in or received by you, or by any person or persons for or under you, or by or with your knowledge, allowance, consent or connivance, and that there still remains thereof in your possession unsold, so much as is in this account said to remain by you unsold; and that you do not know or bel[ei] [*ie*]ve that there hath been by you, or by any other person or persons for or under you, or by your or their order, allowance, consent or connivance, either directly or indirectly, sold, used or consumed any wine, or liquor for, or as, wine; any rum or distilled spirits, or liquor for, or as, rum or distilled spirits; or that there hath been any limes, lemmons or oranges by you, or by any person or persons for or under you, or by your order, consent, allowance or connivance, used or consumed in making punch, or otherwise, since the said twenty-sixth day of March, besides what is contained in the account by you now rendered. So help you God.

[SECT. 3.] And for every person that was not licenced on the said twenty-sixth day of March, the form of the oath shall be so varied, as that instead of mentioning that day, the time of their being licenced shall be inserted and used; and for every person rendering an account after the first, the oath shall be so varied, as that instead of expressing the day aforesaid, the time of taking and rendering their last account shall be inserted and used.

Duties to be paid to the farmer.

[SECT. 4.] And every such taverner, innholder, common victualler and retailer shall pay the duties aforesaid to him or them that shall farm the same, [f]or the whole of the several articles mentioned in such account rendered, save only for such part thereof as remains in their hands unsold: *provided, nevertheless*, that for leakage, &c[a]., ten per cent shall be allowed them on all liquors in such account mentioned, besides what remains in their hands unsold.

Ten per cent allowed for leakage.

And be it further enacted,

Taverner, &c., to give bond.

[SECT. 5.] That every person hereafter licenced to be a taverner, innholder, common victualler or retailer of wine, rum or spirits distilled shall, within thirty days after such licence granted, and before he or she sell by vertue of the same, not only become bound to keep good rule, &c[a]., as by law is already required, but shall also become bound, with sufficient sureties, by way of recognizance, to his majesty, for the use of him or them that have farmed or shall farm the duties aforesaid, in a sufficient sum, to be ordered by the court that grants the licence, which sum shall not be less than fifty pounds, conditioned that they shall take, keep and render the accounts aforesaid, and pay the duties aforesaid, as in and by this act is required.

And be it further enacted,

Forfeiture for neglect in keeping and rendering accounts.

[SECT. 6.] That every such taverner, innholder, common victualler and retailer, who shall neglect or refuse to take, keep and render such accounts as by this act is required, or that shall neglect or refuse to take the oath aforesaid, if required, shall forf[ie][*ei*]t and pay, to him or them that shall farm the duties aforesaid, double the sum which the court of general sessions of the peace in that county shall adjudge that the duties of excise upon the liquors, limes, lem[m]ons and oranges by such taverner, innholder, common victualler or retailer, or by any for or under him or them, sold, used or consumed would have amounted to; and no person shall be licenced by the justices of the general sessions of the peace that hath not accounted with the farmer, and paid him the excise aforesaid, due from such person at the time of his or her taking or renewing such licence.

And whereas, notwithstanding the laws made against selling strong drink without licence, many persons not regarding the penalties in said acts, do receive and entertain persons in their houses, and sell great quantities of spirits and other strong drink, without licence; by reason whereof great debaucheries are committed and kept secret, and such as take licences and pay the duties of excise therefor are greatly wronged, and the farmers unjustly deprived of their dues,— Preamble.

Be it therefore enacted,

[SECT. 7.] That if any distiller, importer or any other person whatsoever, after the said [26th] [*twenty-sixth*] day of March, shall presume, directly or indirectly, to sell any rum or other distilled spirits, or wine, in less quantity than twenty-five gallons, or any beer, ale, cyder, perry or other strong drink, in any quantity less than ten gallons, without licence first had and obtained from the court of general sessions of the peace in that county, and recognizing in manner as aforesaid, shall forf[ie][*ei*]t and pay for each offence, the sum of four pounds, lawful money, and costs of prosecution, one half to the farmer of said duties and the other half to the informer; and all such as shall neglect or refuse to pay the fine aforesaid, shall stand closely committed in the common goal of the county, and not have the liberty of the goaler's house or yard, until[l] said sum of four pounds is paid, with costs; and any goaler giving liberty contrary to this act, shall forf[ie][*ei*]t and pay the said sum of four pounds, and cost[s] of prosecution. Forfeiture of £4 for selling without license.

And whereas, in order to elude the design of this act, some persons may join together and buy wine, rum, brandy and other spirits distilled in quantities above twenty-five gallons, and afterwards divide the same among themselves in less quantities,—

Be it therefore enacted,

[SECT. 8.] That where two or more persons, not licenced as aforesaid, shall join together, and purchase wine, rum, brandy or spirits distilled, or shall employ any other person or persons not licenced as aforesaid to do it, and shall afterwards divide the same, or cause it to be divided among themselves, or otherwise, in less quantities than twenty-five gallons, they shall be deemed and taken to be sellers of such wine, rum, brandy and other distilled spirits, and each and every of them shall be subject to the same pains, penalties and forf[ie][*ei*]tures as any person by this act is who shall sell wine, rum or spirits distilled, without licence first had and obtained. Persons not licensed joining together in purchasing liquors and dividing the same, liable to a forfeiture.

And whereas some doubts have arisen whether the lending or delivering wine, rum, brandy or spirits distilled to others, for their use, upon agreement or in confidence of having the like liquors returned again, be a sale thereof; wherefore, for removing all such doubts,—

Be it enacted,

[SECT. 9.] That all wine, rum, brandy and other spirituous liquors, lent or delivered to others for their use, upon such like consideration, is, and shall be deemed and taken to be, an absolute sale thereof. And that every person not licenced as aforesaid, that shall order, allow, permit or connive at the selling wine, rum, brandy or distilled spirits, contrary to the true intent and meaning of this act, by his or their child or children, servant or servants, or any other person or persons in or belonging to his or her house or family, shall be deemed and taken to be the seller of such liquors, and be subject to the aforesaid pains and penalties provided against such offenders, and shall be recovered in like manner: *provided*, that if it shall be made appear that the liquors lent or delivered as aforesaid, shall have had the duty paid upon them, or were purchased of any person or persons having licence or permit, the Liquors lent or delivered on the above consideration, to be deemed a sale.

person lending or delivering the same, as aforesaid, shall not be subject to the aforesaid pains and penalties.

Preamble.

And whereas divers other persons than those licenced to sell rum and other distilled spirits by retail, have heretofore supplied persons employed by them in the fishery, building vessel[l]s, and in other business, with rum and other liquors, without paying any excise thereon, and thereby have defrauded the government of the duty of excise, and have not been subject to the penalty provided by law against selling drink without licence, and the same practice will probably be continued, unless effectual care be taken to prevent the same,—

Be it therefore further enacted,

Persons not licensed supplying those employed by them in the fishery, &c., with spirituous liquors, to be deemed sellers.

[SECT. 10.] That all persons not licenced, as aforesaid, who hereafter shall, by themselves, or by any other person or persons under them, or by their order, allowance or connivance, supply any person or persons by them employed in the fishery, building of vessel[l]s, or in any other business or [i][e]mploy, with wine, rum or other distilled spirits, shall be deemed and taken to be sellers of such liquors, and be subjected to the aforesaid pains and penalties provided against persons selling any of the liquors aforesaid without licence, which shall be recovered in the like manner, unless they make it appear that such wine, rum or other distilled spirits, was purchased of a taverner, innholder or retailer, or other person or persons that had licence or permit to sell the same.

And be it further enacted,

One witness sufficient for conviction.

[SECT. 11.] That when any person shall be charged with selling strong drink without licence, one witness produced to the satisfaction of the court or justice before whom the trial is, shall be deemed sufficient for conviction. And when and so often as it shall be observed that there is a resort of persons to houses suspected of selling strong drink without licence, any justice of the peace in the same county, shall have full power to convene such persons before him, and examine them upon oath concerning the persons suspected of selling or retailing strong drink in such houses, outhouses or other dependencies thereof; and if upon examination of such witnesses, and hearing the defence of such suspected person, it shall appear to the justice there is sufficient proof of the violation of this act by selling strong drink without licence, judgment may thereupon be made up against such person, and he shall forf[ie][*ei*]t and pay in like manner as if process had been commenced by bill, plaint or information before the said justice; or otherwise such justice may bind over the person suspected, and the witnesses, to the next court of general sessions of the peace for the county where such person shall dwell.

And be it further enacted,

Penalty for selling strong drink to negroes, mulattoes, &c.

[SECT. 12.] That when and so often as any person shall be charged with selling strong drink without licence to any negro, Indian or mollat[t]o slave, or to any child or other person under the age of discretion, and other circumstances concurring, it shall appear to be highly probable in the judgment of the court or justice before whom the trial shall be, that the person complained of is guilty, then, and in every such case, unless the defendant shall acquit him- or herself upon oath (to be administred to him or her by the court or justice that shall try the cause), such defendant shall forf[ie][*ei*]t and pay four pounds to the farmer of excise, and costs of prosecution; but if the defendant shall acquit him- or herself upon oath as aforesaid, the court or justice may and shall enter up judgment for the defendant to recover costs.

And be it further enacted,

Penalty on persons refusing to give evidence.

[SECT. 13.] That if any person or persons shall be summoned to appear before a justice of the peace, or the grand jury, to give evidence relating to any person's selling strong drink without licence, or to appear before the court of general sessions of the peace, or other court proper to try the same, to give evidence on the trial of any person informed against, presented or indicted for selling strong drink without licence, and shall neglect or refuse to appear, or to give evidence in that behalf, every person so offending shall forf[ie][*ei*]t the sum of twenty pounds and cost of prosecution; the one half of the penalty aforesaid to be to his majesty for the use of the farmer, and the other half to and for the use of him or them who shall sue for the same as aforesaid. And when it shall so happen that witnesses are bound to sea before the sitting of the court where any person or persons informed against, for selling strong drink without licence, is or are to be prosecuted for the same, in every such case, the deposition of any witness or witnesses, in writing, taken before any two of his majesty's justices of the peace, *quorum unus*, and sealed up and delivered into court, the adverse party having first had a notification, in writing, sent to him or her of the time and place of caption, shall be esteemed as sufficient evidence, in law, to convict any person or persons offending against this act, as if such witness or witnesses had been present at the time of trial, and given his, her or their deposition *viva voce;* and every person or persons who shall be summoned to give evidence before two justices of the peace, in manner as aforesaid, and shall neglect or refuse to appear, or to give evidence relating to the facts he or she shall be enquired of, shall be liable and subject to the same penalty as he or she would have been by v[e][*i*]rtue of this act, for not appearing, or neglecting or refusing to give his or her evidence before the grand jury or court as aforesaid.

And be it further enacted,

[SECT. 14.] That all fines, forf[ie][*ei*]tures and penalties arising by this act shall and may be recovered by bill, plaint or information, before any court of record proper to try the same; and, where the sum forf[ie][*ei*]ted doth not exceed four pounds, by bill, plaint or information before any one of his majesty's justices of the peace in the respective counties where such offence shall be committed: which said justice is hereby impowered to try and determine the same. And said justice shall make a fair entry or record of all such proceedings: *saving always* to any person or persons who shall think him-, her- or themselves ag[*g*]r[ei][*ie*]ved by the sentence or determination of the said justice, liberty of appeal therefrom to the next court of general sessions of the peace to be holden in and for said county, at which court such offence shall be finally determined: *provided*, that in said appeal the same rules be observed as are already required, by law, in appeals from justices, to the court of general sessions of the peace: *saving, only*, that the recognizance for prosecuting the appeal shall be eight pounds. How fines are to be recovered.

Be it further enacted,

[SECT. 15.] That every farmer shall settle all accounts relating to said excise in the county where he is farmer, first giving seasonable and publick notice of the time and place or places where said business shall be transacted. Farmer to settle accounts.

Be it further enacted,

[SECT. 16.] That one or more person or persons, to be nominated and appointed by the general court, for and within the several counties within this province, publick notice being first given of the time and place and occasion of their meeting, shall have full power, and are hereby authorized, from time to time, to contract or agree with any person for or concerning the farming the duties in this act mentioned, upon rum and other the liquors and commodities aforesaid, in the respective counties for which they shall be appointed, as may be for the greatest profit and advantage of the publick, so as the same exceed not the term of one year after the commencement of this act; and every farmer, or his dep- Persons empowered to farm out the excise.

uty or deputies, of the duties of excise in any county, shall have power to inspect the houses of all such as are licenced, and of such as are suspected of selling without licence, [and] to demand, sue for, and receive the excise due from licenced persons or others by v[e][*i*]rtue of this act.

And be it further enacted,

Farmer to give bond that the sum agreed for be paid into the public treasury.

[SECT. 17.] That the farmer shall give bond with two sufficient sureties, to the province treasurer for the time being, and his successor in said office, in double the sum of money that shall be contracted for, with condition that the sum agreed on be paid into the province treasury, for the use of the province, at the expiration of one year from the commencement of this act; which bond the person or persons to be appointed a committee of such county are to take, and the same to lodge with the treasurer as aforesaid, within twenty days after such bond is executed; and the said treasurer, on failure or neglect of payment at the time therein limitted, may and is hereby impowered to issue out his execution, returnable in sixty days, against such farmer of excise and his sureties, or either of them, for the full sum expressed in the condition of their bonds, as they shall respectively become due, in the same manner as he is enabled by law to issue out his executions against def[f]ective constables, or to put such bond in suit; and the said committee shall render an account of their proceedings touching the farming this duty on rum, wine and other the liquors and species afore mentioned, in their respective counties, to the general court in the first week of the next sitting of this court, and shall receive such sum or sums for their trouble and expence in said affair as said court shall think fit to allow them. And every person farming the excise in any county may substitute and appoint one or more deputy or deputies under him, upon oath, to collect and receive the excise aforesaid, which shall become due in said county, and pay in the same to such farmer; which deputy and deputies shall have, use and exercise all such powers and authorities as in and by this act are given or committed to the farmer for the better collecting the duties aforesaid, or prosecuting offenders against this act.

Farmers may appoint deputies.

And be it further enacted,

Penalty for farmers' or deputies' offending.

[SECT. 18.] That in case any person farming the excise as aforesaid, or his deputy, shall, at any time during their continuance in said office, wittingly and willingly connive at, or allow, any person or persons within their respective divisions, not licenced by the court of general sessions of the peace, their selling any wines, rum or other liquors by this act forbidden, such farmer or deputy, for every such offence, shall forf[ie][*ei*]t the sum of fifty pounds and costs of prosecution; one half of the penalty aforesaid to be to his majesty for the use of this province, the other half to him or them that shall inform and sue for the same, and shall thenceforward be forever disabled for serving in said office: *saving*, that said farmer may give a permit to any person to sell wine, rum or spirits distilled, in quantity from twenty-five gallons and upward, agre[e]able to this act.

And be it further enacted,

Provision in case of death, &c.

[SECT. 19.] That in case of the death of the farmer of excise in any county, the executors or administrators of such farmer shall, upon their accepting of such trust of executor or administrator, have and enjoy all the powers, and be subject to all the duties, the farmer had or might enjoy or was subject to by force of this act.

Provided, always, and it is the true intent and meaning of this act,—

Proviso.

[SECT. 20.] That if any taverner or retailer shall sell to any other taverner or retailer any quantity of distilled liquors or wine, such taverner or retailer, selling as aforesaid, shall not be held to pay such duty, but the taverner or retailer who is the purchaser shall pay the same; and the seller as aforesaid, shall and is hereby required to deliver to the farmer of this duty, a true account of such liquors sold as aforesaid, and to whom sold.

And to the end that the revenue arising from the excise upon spirituous liquors may be increased and raised with more equal[l]ity,—

Be it enacted,

[SECT. 21.] That from and after the [26th] [*twenty-sixth*] day of March, one thousand seven hundred and fifty-six, to the twenty-sixth day of March, one thousand seven hundred and fifty-seven, upon all rum and other distilled spirits, and all wine, imported or manufactured, and sold for consumption within this province, there be laid and hereby is laid the duty or excise following; viz[t].,— Duties to be paid by private persons, for what liquors they expend.

For every gallon of rum and spirits distilled, fourpence;

For every gallon of wine of every sort, sixpence; to be paid to the farmer of excise, or his deputy, by every person having permit to sell the said liquors in each county, respectively.

And be it further enacted,

[SECT. 22.] That every person that shall import any of the liquors aforesaid, or to whom any of them shall or may be consigned, shall be and hereby is prohibited from selling the same, or any part thereof, without having a permit so to do from the farmer of excise, or his deputy; which permit shall be had and procured before the landing of such liquors. And every person distilling or manufacturing any of the said liquors, and every person owning or possessing any of them, excepting such as are or may be licenced by the court of general sessions of the peace, as aforesaid, shall be and hereby are prohibited from selling the same, or any part thereof, without having a permit so to do from the farmer of excise, or his deputy, on forf[ie][*ei*]ture of two hundred pounds, and of the value of the liquors so sold; and the said permit shall express the particular shop, house, warehouse, or distil[l]-house where the said liquors shall be permitted to be sold, and if any person who shall have such permit shall sell and deliver, or cause to be sold and delivered, any of the liquors aforesaid from any place or places not mentioned in such permit, he shall forf[ie][*ei*]t four pounds, to be paid to the farmer. Liquors not to be sold by the importer, &c., without a permit.

Provided, nevertheless,—

[SECT. 23.] That the impost officer, and his deputy, shall be and hereby are respectively impowered to grant a permit for selling the liquors aforesaid, or any of them, to any person applying for the same, until[l] the duty or excise aforesaid, in each county, respectively, shall be let or farmed, and until[l] the farmer shall give publick notice that said duty or excise is let or farmed to him as aforesaid. And said impost officer, and deputy, shall transmit to the farmer of each county an account of the permits by each of them respectively granted to persons living in such county. Proviso.

Be it further enacted,

[SECT. 24.] That if said farmer or his deputy, shall have information of any place where any of the liquors aforesaid shall have been sold by any person not having permit, as aforesaid, he may apply to any justice of the peace within the county, for a warrant to search such place, and said justice shall grant such warrant, directed to some proper officer, upon said farmer or deputy's making oath that he hath had information as aforesaid, and that he hath just cause to suspect that the liquors aforesaid, or some of them, have been sold at such place informed of as aforesaid, and having such warrant, and being attended by such officer, the said farmer, or his deputy, may, in the Farmer applying to a justice for a warrant, may search for liquors supposed to be concealed.

daytime, between sun-rising and sun-setting, demand admittance of the person owning or occupying such place, and upon refusal, shall have right to break open such place, and finding such liquors, may seize and take the same into his own custody; and the farmer aforesaid, or his deputy, shall be and hereby is impowered to command assistance and impress carriages necessary to secure the liquors seized as aforesaid, and any person refusing assistance or preventing said officers from executing their office, shall forf[ie][*ei*]t five pounds to the farmer; and the said farmer or deputy, shall make reasonable satisfaction for the assistance afforded, and carriages made use of, to secure the liquor seized as aforesaid; and the farmer, or his deputy, shall then file an information of such seizure in the inferior court of common pleas for the county wherein such seizure shall be made: which court shall summon the owner of such liquors, or the occupier of the shop, house, warehouse or distil[l]-house where the same were seized, to appear and shew cause, if any he has, why said liquors so seized should not be adjudged forf[ie][*ei*]ted; and if such owner or occupier shall not shew cause as aforesaid, or shall make default, the said liquors shall be adjudged forf[ie][*ei*]ted, and the said court shall order them to be sold at publick vendue, and the neet produce of such sale shall be paid, one half to the province treasurer, for the use of this province, and the other half to the farmer.

Provided,—

Proviso.

[SECT. 25.] That if the liquors seized as aforesaid be less in quantity than one hundred gallons, the farmer, or his deputy, shall file an information thereof with one of the justices of the peace within the county where the seizure shall be made, who shall summon the owner or occupier aforesaid in manner as aforesaid, and if such owner or occupier shall not shew cause, or shall make default as aforesaid, he shall adjudge such liquors forf[ie][*ei*]ted, and shall order them to be sold as aforesaid, and the neet produce of such sale to be disposed of as aforesaid: *saving* to the person convicted the liberty of an appeal, he entering into recognizance to the king, for the use of the farmer, in the sum of fifty pounds.

Provided, also,—

[SECT. 26.] That if such farmer or deputy shall not find any of the liquors aforesaid in the place informed of, and broken open, as aforesaid, he shall pay double damages.

Be it further enacted,

Persons having permit as aforesaid, to render an account to the farmer at the end of every half year: *saving*, &c.

[SECT. 27.] That every person having permit as aforesaid, shall, at the end of each half year, respectively, from the [26th] [*twenty-sixth*] day of March, one thousand seven hundred and fifty-six, be ready to render to the farmer aforesaid, or his deputy, an account, on oath, if required, of all the liquors aforesaid by him or her, and by any person or persons on his or her behalf, sold; and also of all of the aforesaid liquors by him or her imported, distilled or manufactured, or which have come into his or her possession since the [26] [*twenty-sixth*] of March afores[*ai*]d, except the same were bought of a licen[s][c]ed person in a quantity less than twenty-five gal[*l*]ons, which in his or her family have been consumed or expended within each half year, respectively: which account shall express the number of gallons of each kind of the liquors so sold and consumed, and shall pay therefor to the said farmer or his deputy the duty aforesaid, excepting for so much as shall have been sold to taverners, innholders or retailers having licence from the sessions as aforesaid, or to any other persons having permit as aforesaid; and so much as shall have been exported out of this province; and if any of said liquors shall have been sold to persons licenced by the sessions, or to persons having permit, said account shall exhibit the names of such licenced persons who purchased, and persons having permit, and the time when they purchased the same; and the person accounting shall exhibit a certificate under the hand of the licenced or permitted person purchasing, which shall express the number of gallons, and the kind of the liquors purchased, and the time when the same were purchased, and the name of the town and county wherein such licenced or permitted person lives, and shall lodge the said certificate with the said farmer or his deputy; and for the quantity of said liquors mentioned in such certificate, the said farmer or his deputy shall not demand any duty, but shall deliver said certificate to the farmer of the county wherein such licenced or permitted person, signing the same, lives: which last-mentioned farmer or his deputy shall settle with such licenced or permitted person for the duty aforesaid which may be due from him or her.

[SECT. 28.] And if any person having permit as aforesaid, shall ship or export any of the liquors aforesaid out of this province in a quantity not less than sixty gallons, and shall make entry thereof with the farmer aforesaid, or his deputy, and shall produce to such farmer or deputy, when he comes to settle his account of excise, one of the receipts or bills of lading given therefor by the master of the vessel on board which such liquors shall be shipped, expressing the quantity thereof and the time of their being ship[*p*]ed, and shall lodge such receipt or bill of lading with the farmer or his deputy aforesaid, and at the same time shall swear that such liquors are *bonâ fide* sent, or intended to be sent, out of this province, he or she shall not be held to pay thereon the duty aforesaid. Persons having a permit, as aforesaid, to give an account of liquors by them sent out of the province.

[SECT. 29.] And if any person not having permit shall purchase for exportation out of this province any of said liquors in a quantity not less than sixty gallons of a person having permit, the purchaser shall make entry thereof with the farmer or his deputy, and at the same time swear that such liquors are *bonâ fide* sent, or intended to be sent, out of the province, and shall within ten days after the purchase deliver one of the receipts or bills of lading given for such liquors, as aforesaid, to the person of whom he purchased the same, or be subject to pay the amount of the duty thereon to the person of whom he purchased as aforesaid, who shall pay such duty to the farmer or his deputy; but if the purchaser aforesaid shall deliver such receipt or bill of lading as aforesaid, and it be lodged with the farmer or his deputy, then, for the quantity of said liquors mentioned therein, the farmer or his deputy shall not demand any duty. Persons not having permit, to render an account, &c.

[SECT. 30.] And if the master of any vessel[l], or any other person, shall give such certificate, receipt or bill of lading, without receiving the liquors mentioned therein; or if any person shall procure such certificate, receipt or bill of lading, with design to defraud the farmer, and shall be thereof convicted, they and each of them shall forf[ie][*ei*]t and pay the sum of one hundred pounds; one half for the use of this government, and the other half for the use of the farmer. And if any such certificate, receipt or bill of lading shall be forged, counterfeited or altered, the person forging, counterfeiting or altering shall incur the penalty of one hundred pounds. Penalty for masters or others giving certificate without receiving the liquors.

Provided, nevertheless,—

[SECT. 31.] That the person having permit as aforesaid, shall not sell any of the liquors aforesaid in a quantity less than twenty-five gallons (to be sold and delivered to one person at one time), unless he or she hath licence from the court of general sessions of the peace, as aforesaid, on pain of incurring the several fines and penalties in the former part of this act laid upon those persons who sell the liquors aforesaid without licence. Proviso.

Be it further enacted,

Farmer to give certificate, on penalty.

[SECT. 32.] That the farmer aforesaid, or his deputy, when the exporter shall make an entry with him as aforesaid, or shall make an entry with him and swear as aforesaid, shall give to said exporter a certificate of such entry, or a certificate of such entry and oath, on penalty of one hundred pounds for the use of the exporter.

Provided, nevertheless,—

Proviso.

[SECT. 33.] That until[l] the duties aforesaid be let or farmed, the exporter aforesaid may make an entry as aforesaid with the impost officer or his deputy, or make such entry and swear as aforesaid; and of such entry, or of such entry and oath, the said impost officer or his deputy shall give the said exporter a certificate: and for the liquors mentioned in such certificate, when the same shall be exhibited, the farmer or his deputy shall not demand any duty.

And be it further enacted,

Persons applying for a permit, to give bond.

[SECT. 34.] That every person applying to the farmer or his deputy, or to the impost officer or his deputy, for a permit, shall give bond, if required, for the use of the farmer, with two sufficient sureties, in a sum not exceeding two hundred pounds, nor less than twenty pounds, at the discretion of the two next justices of the peace, conditioned for the payment of the excise that shall become due according to the account to be exhibited by such person taking such permit; and no person shall have such permit of the impost officer until[l] he hath given such bond.

Preamble.

And whereas the importer of any of the liquors aforesaid, or the person to whom they shall be consigned, may intend the same for his or her own private consumption, in which case such importer or consignee is not held by any preceeding part of this act to pay the duty or excise aforesaid; wherefore, in order to lay said duty or excise in as equal manner as may be,—

Be it enacted,

Persons importing liquors for private consumption, &c., to render account thereof to the farmer.

[SECT. 35.] That every person that shall bring or import into this province, either by land, or water, carriage, any of the liquors aforesaid for his own private consumption, and every person to whom any such liquors are consigned for his own private consumption, shall, at the end of each half year, respectively, make out an account expressing the kind and the full quantity of the liquors aforesaid, imported or consigned as aforesaid; which account such importer or consignee shall render to the farmer or his deputy, on oath, if required, and shall pay to the said farmer or his deputy, on the liquor or liquors mentioned in said account, the duty or excise aforesaid, deducting ten per cent for leakage, or pay treble duty or excise on the quantity so imported or consigned, to and for the use of the farmer.

Farmer may apply to a justice for a warrant, or citation, where he may suspect persons giving a false account, &c.

[SECT. 36.] And if said farmer or his deputy shall have reason to suspect any person of bringing or importing into this province, either by land, or water, carriage, any of the liquors aforesaid, or of being consignee as aforesaid, without having rendered account and paid the duty or excise as aforesaid, the said farmer may apply to any justice of the peace within the county where the person suspected lives, for a warrant or citation; and such justice is hereby impow[e]red and required to cite or apprehend such suspected person to appear before him within twenty-four hours on a complaint made against him or her by the farmer or his deputy touching the duty or excise aforesaid; which warrant or citation shall be served on or delivered to the suspected person himself or herself; and when the parties shall be before him, the said justice shall examine into the cause of complaint; and if it shall appear, either by the confession of the party, or by the evidence of one credible witness, that such suspected person has, by him- or herself, or by any one on his or her behalf, imported, or has had any of the liquors aforesaid consigned to him or her, without having render[e]'d an account thereof, and paid the duty or excise as aforesaid, such suspected person shall then render a full account, on oath, of the kinds and quantity of the liquors imported or consigned as aforesaid, and shall pay on such liquors treble duty or excise as aforesaid, and costs.

[SECT. 37.] And said justice is hereby impowered to make up judgment and award execution accordingly: *provided* the said treble duty exceed not four pounds; but if such duty exceed four pounds, then such justice shall bind the offender to answer his offence at the next court of general sessions of the peace for the county where the offence was committed, and such offender shall enter into recognizance, with two sufficient sureties, to answer for his offence, in the sum of fifty pounds; and any person or persons upon refusing to render such account and paying as aforesaid, shall forfict fifty pounds for the use of the farmer, in lieu of such treble duty, to be recovered as is hereafter provided in this act.

[SECT. 38.] And if no confession be made by such suspected person, and no evidence produced as aforesaid, he or she shall then clear him- or herself from the complaint aforesaid, by taking an oath in the form following; viz[t].,—

Form of the oath.

You, A. B., do swear that you have not, directly or indirectly, either by yourself, or any person on your behalf, imported into this province any wine, rum or spirits distilled, and that you have not had any of said liquors directly or indirectly consigned to you, but what you have paid the duty or excise upon, according to an act of said province, made in the twenty-ninth year of his majesty's reign, intitled "An Act for granting unto his majesty an excise upon spirits distilled, and wine, and upon limes, lemons and oranges." So help you God.

—which oath the said justice is hereby impowered and required to administer.

Penalty for refusing to take the oath.

[SECT. 39.] And if such suspected person shall refuse to take said oath, or shall neglect to appear upon the citation aforesaid, he or she shall pay the cost[s] of citation, and shall forf[ie] [*ei*]t, for the use of the farmer, the aforesaid sum of fifty pounds, and costs of prosecution; but if such suspected person shall take the said oath, the costs of citation or warrant shall be paid by the farmer or his deputy, respectively, who applied for such citation or warrant; who shall also pay to the person cited or apprehended, and taking said oath, the sum of twenty shillings.

Be it further enacted,

Farmer to grant a permit, on penalty.

[SECT. 40.] That the farmer aforesaid, or his deputy, shall be and hereby is obliged to grant a permit, under his hand, to every person applying for the same, on penalty of two hundred pounds, to and for the use of the person making application; which permit shall be in the form following; viz[t].,—

Form of the permit.

You, A. B. of C., in the county of D., are hereby permitted to sell rum and other distilled spirits, and wine, or any of said liquors, at , in C. aforesaid, until[l] the twenty-sixth day of March, one thousand seven hundred and fifty-seven, pursuant to an act of this province, made in the twenty-ninth year of his majesty's reign, intitled "An Act for granting unto his majesty an excise upon spirits distilled, and wine, and upon limes, lem[m]ons and oranges." Dated at C., this day of , 175 .

A. B., *Farmer (or deputy farmer) of excise for the county aforesaid.*

And for such permit the said farmer or his deputy shall be intitled to receive twopence, and no more; and the like sum for an entry made with him, and the like sum for a certificate given by him.

Be it further enacted,

Farmer to keep an office in each seaport town, &c.

[SECT. 41.] That the farmer aforesaid, either by himself or his deputy, shall keep an office in each seaport town within his county, where he or his deputy shall give his attendance on every Thursday, from nine of the clock in the morning to twelve at noon, to grant permits, receive entr[y][*ie*]s, give certificates, &c[a].

Provided,—

[SECT. 42.] That in the town of Boston such an office shall be kept, and attendance given on every Monday and Thursday, within the hours aforesaid, of each of said days, respectively.

Provided, also,—

[SECT. 43.] That said farmer or his deputy, on application made, shall at any other time grant permits, receive entries, and give certificates as aforesaid.

Preamble.

And whereas persons not belonging to this province may import the liquors aforesaid, and take permit to dispose of the same, and may go out of the province before the time comes about when persons selling said liquors are held to account with the farmer, and by that means may escape paying the duty upon what has been so disposed of; for preventing whereof,—

Be it enacted,

Persons importing liquors as aforesaid, to give bond.

[SECT. 44.] That every person importing the liquors aforesaid, and applying to the farmer or his deputy for a permit to sell the same, shall give bond to said farmer, if required, in a sum not exceeding two hundred pounds, nor less than twenty pounds, at the discretion of the two next justices of the peace, with sufficient surety or sureties, that he will render to said farmer or his deputy an account, on oath, if required, of the kind and full quantity of the liquors aforesaid sold by him, or by any person or persons on his behalf, and that he will pay thereon the duty or excise aforesaid before he leaves the province; and if such person shall refuse to give such bond, the said farmer or his deputy shall not be obliged to grant him a permit, anything in this act to the contrary notwithstanding; and if such person shall sell any of the liquors aforesaid without permit, he shall be subject to all the penalties that other persons selling without permit are subject to; or if such person shall give bond as aforesaid, and shall leave the province before such bond be discharged, the farmer may bring his action on said bond against the surety or sureties, for the recovery of the sum in such bond mentioned, which shall be for the use of the farmer.

Preamble.

And to the end that this government may know what monies shall be received by the farmer of each respective county; and his deputies, by v[e][*i*]rtue of this act,—

Be it enacted,

Farmer to give two receipts, &c.

[SECT. 45.] That to every person licenced by the sessions, and to every person having permit as aforesaid, the said farmer or his deputy, when said persons shall account with them, shall give two receipts, under their hand, for what each of them, respectively, have received, either as duty or as forf[ie][*ei*]ture, or in any other way; and the said receipts shall express the true and just sum received, and the consideration for which it was received; and one of the said receipts shall be lodged, within one month after the date thereof, by each person, respectively, to whom said receipt[s] shall be given, with the clerk of the sessions for the county wherein such person lives, on penalty of forty shillings, and of being rendered incapable of renewing his or her licence or permit for the future. And the clerk aforesaid shall transmit a true and fair copy of the receipts that shall be so lodged with him, to the secretary of this province, who shall lay the same before this court.

And be it further enacted,

[SECT. 46.] That the farmer of each respective county shall render an account, on oath, to the province treasurer, when he shall come to discharge his bond given for the farm of the duties aforesaid, of the sums and securities he and his deputy, or either of them, have in any way received by virtue of this act; and the said account shall express the name of each person of whom they, or either of them, have received any sum or security, how much that sum is, or security is for, and the time when the same were received; and it shall be part of the condition of the said farmer's said bond, that he will render such account as aforesaid, and if said farmer shall not have settled, when he comes to discharge the said bond, with every person obliged by this act to account and settle with him, his said bond shall not be discharged till he has so settled, and rendered an account, on oath, of such settlement to the province treasurer as aforesaid. Farmer to render an account, on oath, of sums received, to the province treasurer.

Provided, nevertheless,—

[SECT. 47.] That if said farmer shall, at the end of one month and of [three] [*ten*] months, respectively, from the time of payment expressed in said bond, [shall] render an account on oath as aforesaid, and shall swear that such account expresses the whole sum that he hath [paid and] received, either in money, or by securities, or by any other way whatsoever, then his said bond shall be discharged and be delivered up to him. Proviso.

Be it further enacted,

[SECT. 48.] That if any account of excise shall remain unpaid or not settled by bond or note for the space of ten months after the expiration of this act, unless the action is depending, the said farmer or his deputy shall not have right to bring any action against the person whose said account shall remain so unpaid or unsettled, but shall forf[ie][*ei*]t what might otherwise have been due from such person. Farmer limited for bringing his actions, &c.

Be it further enacted,

[SECT. 49.] That all fines, penalties and forf[ie][*ei*]tures, arising or accruing by any breach of this act, and not otherwise appropriated, shall be, one half to his majesty for the use of this province, and the other half for the use of the farmer; to be recovered by action, bill, plaint or information in any of his majesty's courts of record. [*Passed February* 28; *published March* 4, 1756. How fines, &c., arising by this act are to be disposed of.

CHAPTER 32.

AN ACT SUBJECTING THE INHABITANTS OF THE ISLAND OF NANTUCKET, AND THE PEOPLE CALLED QUAKERS, IN OTHER PARTS OF THE PROVINCE, TO AN ASSESSMENT TOWARDS THE CHARGE OF DEFENDING HIS MAJESTY'S TERRITORIES, IN LIEU OF THEIR PERSONAL SERVICE.

WHEREAS the impressing of the inhabitants of the Island of Nantucket, within this province, is attended with very great difficult[y][*ie*], by reason that the said island is situated at a considerable distance from any other part of the province, being an island at sea, more than thirty miles from the mainland, and the greatest part of the inhabitants being of the people called Quakers,— Preamble.

Be it therefore enacted by the Governo[u]r, Council and House of Representatives,

[SECT. 1.] That when and so often as it shall be found necessary that a number of men should be raised within the several towns in this Quakers to pay a sum in lieu of personal service. province, by impress, for the service of his majesty, and the quotas of such men assigned to the several towns, count[y][*ie*]s or regiments within the province, the inhabitants of the s[*ai*]d island of Nantucket shall pay into the publick treasury of th[e][*is*] province, the sum of thirteen pounds six shillings and eightpence, for each and every man that shall be assigned to them to raise as aforesaid; which mon[ey][*ie*]s shall be levied and collected on the polls and rateable estates of the inhabitants of said island, by the same rules of law, and in the same manner, as the province tax is levied and collected, and shall, from time to time, be added to their province tax in the then next tax after such impress or impresses.

Preamble. *And whereas* there are a number of the people called Quakers, inhabitants of many towns and districts within this province, besides those who live on the said island of Nantucket, who alledge a scruple of conscience to bear arms in war,—

Be it therefore enacted,

Colonels to return a list of Quakers, to the captain-general. [SECT. 2.] That the colonels of the several regiments of horse and foot within this province, the said island of Nantucket excepted, shall, between this and the last day of March, this present year, return to the captain-general a list of the names of the several persons belonging to their respective regiments, including and particularly setting forth the exact number of Quakers belonging to each of their said regiments, or that live within the districts of said regiments; and when and so often as it shall be found necessary that a number of men should be raised within the several towns and districts in this province, by impress, for the service of his majesty, then, and in that case, there shall be a computation made of what number in those regiments are Quakers, and those regiments shall have no more men impressed than their quota will be with other regiments, exclusive of Quakers.

And to the intent that Quakers may do their duty as to the necessary defence of the province,—

Be it enacted,

Captain of each company to lodge with the clerk of the town a list of the Quakers in such company. [SECT. 3.] That the captain of each military company, in which there are any of the people called Quakers, shall lodge with the clerk of the town to which such company belongs, a list of the Quakers in such company that have been exempted as aforesaid, and shall certify what number of men would have been liable to have been impressed, in proportion to the rest of the company, out of said list, if they had not been exempt as being Quakers; and shall also lodge a duplicate thereof in the secretary's office, and this within one month after receiving orders to make such impress; and for every of said Quakers who would have been liable to have been so impressed, thirteen pounds six shillings and eightpence shall be added to that town's proportion of the next province tax; and the assessors, in making their assessment, shall apportion such sum or sums among those persons, called Quakers, mentioned in such list or lists, and no others.

Rule for ascertaining who are Quakers. [SECT. 4.] And for the better ascertaining who are Quakers, the same rule shall be observed as is observed respecting the Quakers being
1737-38, chap. 6. freed from minister's rates, as by the laws of this province now in force,
1747-48, chap. 6. so far as is needful in this case: *provided*, that no persons shall be considered as Quakers for the purposes mentioned in this act, except such as professed themselves to be Quakers on or before the first day of March the present year.

[SECT. 5.] This act to continue and be in force from the twelfth of March, 1756 [*one thousand seven hundred and fifty-six*], for the space of three years, and no longer. [*Passed March* 8; *published March* 11, 1756.

CHAPTER 33.

AN ACT FOR REVIVING AND CONTINUING AN ACT MADE AND PASSED IN THE TWENTY-EIGHTH YEAR OF HIS PRESENT MAJESTY'S REIGN, INTITLED "AN ACT FOR GRANTING TO HIS MAJESTY SEVERAL RATES AND DUTIES OF IMPOST AND TONNAGE OF SHIPPING."

Be it enacted by the Governo[u]r, Council and House of Representatives,

That the act made and passed in the twenty-eighth year of his present majesty's reign, intitled "An Act for granting to his majesty several rates and duties of impost and tonnage of shipping," which expires the twenty-sixth of March, this present year, and every clause thereof, and every matter and thing therein contained: *saving, only*, so far as relates to the duties on liquors; be and hereby is and shall be revived and continued to the twenty-sixth day of April next following, and no longer. [*Passed March* 10; *published March* 11, 1756.

Last impost act continued. 1754-55, chap. 10. 1755-56, chap. 1.

CHAPTER 34.

AN ACT FOR PREVENTING CHARGE TO ANY PARTICULAR TOWN OR DISTRICT BY MEANS OF THE INHABITANTS OF NOVA SCOTIA THAT ARE OR MAY BE SENT TO THIS PROVINCE.

Preamble.

WHEREAS many towns and districts within this province have been compelled to receive the inhabitants of Nova Scotia which have been sent and are arrived here, and it may happen that in time to come some of said inhabitants by means of sickness, or from other causes, may be unable to support themselves, and it may be necessary that relief should be afforded to them,—

Be it therefore enacted by the Governour, Council and House of Represent[ati]ves,

Nova-Scotia inhabitants to be provided for, in case of sickness, &c.

That whensoever it shall so happen that any of said inhabitants of Nova Scotia shall, by sickness or otherwise, be rendered incapable of providing for their own support, the towns or districts where such inhabitants are or may be shall not be held to make provision for the support of such inhabitants at the charge of such towns or districts, but at the charge of the province; and if any time hereafter no special provision shall be made and in force for that purpose, then such of said inhabitants as shall be unable to provide for their own support shall be rel[ei][*ie*]ved and supported in like manner as sick and indigent persons who are not inhabitants of any town or district are by law to be relieved and supported; and the charge thereof shall be paid out of the province treasury. [*Passed March* 9;* *published March* 31.

* Signed March 6, according to the record.

CHAPTER 35.

AN ACT IN ADDITION TO AN ACT MADE IN THE PRESENT YEAR OF HIS MAJESTY'S REIGN, INTITLED "AN ACT MAKING PROVISION FOR THE INHABITANTS OF NOVA SCOTIA SENT HITHER FROM THAT GOVERNMENT AND LATELY ARRIVED IN THIS PROVINCE."

Preamble. 1755-56, chap. 23.

WHEREAS, since the passing an act made this present year of his majesty's reign, intitled "An Act making provision for the inhabitants of Nova Scotia sent hither from that government and lately arrived in this province," a further number of said inhabitants have been sent to and are arrived with this government, and no special provision has been made, by law, for their regulation and support, and the aforesaid act has in other respects been found insufficient,—

Be it therefore enacted by the Governour, Council and House of Represent[ati]ves,

Courts of general sessions, justices, selectmen, overseers of the poor; their power relating to said inhabitants.

[SECT. 1.] That the courts of general sessions of the peace, the justices of the peace in the several counties, the selectmen and the overseers of the poor in the several towns where said inhabitants may have been, or shall be disposed of, by virtue of any votes or orders of the general court, be and hereby are authorized and required to employ, bind out to service, or make provision for the support of the said inhabitants in like manner as the said courts of sessions, justices of the peace, selectmen or overseers, or any of them, would by law be authorized and impowered to do, were they, the said inhabitants of Nova Scotia, inhabitants of any town or towns within this province.

And be it further enacted,

Selectmen or overseers of the poor to provide implements of husbandry, &c., for said inhabitants.

[SECT. 2.] That the selectmen or overseers of the poor in the several towns where said inhabitants have been or may be disposed of as aforesaid, be and hereby are authorized and required to provide necessary implements of husbandry-work, weaving, spinning and other handicraft work, according to the capacity for labour and other circumstances of the several inhabitants aforesaid, not exceeding forty shillings for any one person, and also to provide an house or houses for any family or families, the heads whereof will undertake for the support of themselves and family, and also to afford rel[ei][*ie*]f and support to all such as are incapable of relieving and supporting themselves; and such selectmen or overseers shall keep an exact account of all charges in consequence of the act aforesaid, or of this additional act,—such account to be made up until[l] the first day of June next, and so until[l] the first day of June, annually, during the continuance of this act,—and shall transmit the same, from time to time, to the secretary's office, in order to be laid before the governour and council for allowance and payment, and in order to ascertain the sums advanced by this governm[*en*]t for the services aforesaid.

Accounts to be taken of charges in consequence of this act.

And be it further enacted,

Overseers' duty and charge.

[SECT. 3.] That in any town where overseers of the poor shall be chosen, it shall be part of their duty and charge to take care and provide for the inhabitants of Nova Scotia sent to such town; and in any town where there shall be no overseers of the poor, it shall be the duty and charge of the selectmen.

Limitation.

[SECT. 4.] This act to be in force until[l] the twentieth day of June, which will be in the year of our Lord one thousand seven hundred and fifty-seven, and no longer. [*Passed March* 6; *published March* 31.

CHAPTER 36.

AN ACT TO ENABLE THE COMMITTEE OF WAR MORE EFFECTUALLY TO PROVIDE NECESSAR[Y][*IE*]S FOR THE INTENDED EXPEDITION AGAINST CROWN POINT.

Preamble.

WHEREAS this court have agreed to join with the governments of Connecticut, New York, New Hampshire and Rhode Island, in carrying on an expedition against Crown Point, as soon as possible, and have chosen and appointed two committees, to transact the necessary affairs for the carrying on said expedition, so far as relates to this government, and as there will be occasion for the said committees to take up a considerable quantity of provisions, warlike stores, cloathing, &c., for that purpose; wherefore to prevent any impositions on this province by persons who are owners or possessors of such articles as are or shall be wanted for carrying said expedition into execution,—

Be it enacted by the Governour, Council and House of Representatives,

Application his majesty's justices of the peace, &c., in case provisions, &c., are withheld from said committee.

[SECT. 1.] That when and so often as any provisions, warlike stores, horses, carriages or any other kind of thing necessary for carrying into execution the designed expedition against Crown Point, shall be withheld from either of the said committees, or shall be denied them upon their offering a reasonable price or rate for the same; each and every of his majesty's justices of the peace is hereby authorized and required, upon application made in writing by either of the said committees, or by a major part of either of them, to issue a warrant within their respective counties, to the sher[r]iff of the said county, or his deputy, to impress the same, lying and being within their proper district, and if need be, to break open and enter, in the daytime, any shop, warehouse, storehouse or vessel, for that purpose, and take the same from thence; and all sher[r]iffs and deputy-sher[r]iffs, are directed and required to execute all such warrants accordingly.

Current price to be paid for commodities impressed or taken from the owners.

[SECT. 2.] And for all such commodities, horses, carriages or any other thing impressed or taken away by virtue of this act, the committee to whose order the same shall be delivered, shall pay, or cause to be paid to the owner thereof, or to his agent or factor, the then usual or current rates or prices; and in case of any dispute or disagreement between such committee and the owners of such articles concerning the rates or prices thereof, the same shall be fixed and determined by two meet persons, to be mutually chosen by them: and in case the owner, or his agent or factor, shall neglect or refuse to join in the choice of apprizers, it shall and may be lawful for the sher[r]iff or his deputy to choose one meet person in their behalf; and in either case the two persons so chosen or appointed, shall have power to ch[u][*oo*]se a third if they shall find it needful, and the rates or prices agreed upon and certified under the hands of the persons so chosen or appointed, or the major part of them, shall be as binding upon the committee, and upon the owner or owners of such articles so taken, as if they had been mutually agreed upon by them. [*Passed March* 10; *published March* 31.

Price of provisions, &c., to be fixed by persons mutually chosen, where there is any dispute.

CHAPTER 37.

AN ACT IN ADDITION TO, AND FOR RENDERING MORE EFFECTUAL, AN ACT MADE IN THE TWENTY-EIGHTH YEAR OF HIS PRESENT MAJESTY'S REIGN, INTITLED "AN ACT FOR GRANTING UNTO HIS MAJESTY AN EXCISE UPON SPIRITS DISTILLED, AND WINE, AND UPON LIMES, LEM[*M*]ONS AND ORANGES."

Preamble. 1754-55, chap. 16, § 1.

WHEREAS in and by the said act it is, among other things, provided, that from and after the twenty-sixth day of December, one thousand seven hundred and fifty-four, every person licen[s][*c*]ed for retailing rum or other spirits, or wine, shall pay the duties following, to the person or persons to whom the same shall be let or farmed; viz[t].,—

For every gallon of rum or spirits distilled, fourpence.

For every gallon of wine, of every sort, sixpence.

For every hundred of lemons or oranges, four shillings.

And for every hundred of limes, one shilling and sixpence.

—And so proportionably for any other quantity or number.

But the aforesaid duties of excise, arising between the twenty-sixth day of December, one thousand seven hundred and fifty-five, and the twenty-sixth day of March, one thousand seven hundred and fifty-six[th], are not farmed, nor is there any person or persons appointed to let or farm the same,—

Be it therefore enacted by the Governour, Council and House of Representatives,

Licensed persons to render an account from Dec. 26, 1755, to March 26, 1756.

[SECT. 1.] That every person licen[s][*c*]ed as afores[*ai*]d shall, on the twenty-seventh day of September next, pay the aforesaid duties of excise to the person or persons to whom the same shall be farm[*e*]'d, or to their respective deputies, on all distilled spirits, wine, lemons and oranges by him or her sold, used or consumed between the twenty-sixth day of December, one thousand seven hundred and fifty-five, and the twenty-sixth day of March, one thousand seven hundred and fifty-six; and for the ascertaining the amount of the same duties, every person licen[s][*c*]ed as aforesaid shall, on the said twenty-seventh day of September, render an account, in writing, of all the distilled spirits, wine, limes, lemons and oranges by him or her sold, used and consum[*e*]'d within that time, and shall, also, if required, make oath, before such farmer or farmers, or their respective deputies, who are hereby impowered to require and administer the same, in form following; viz[t].,—

Form of the oath.

"You, A. B., do swear that this account by you rend[*e*]red, is, according to the best of your knowledge, a just and true account of all the distilled spirits, wine, limes, lem[*m*]ons and oranges directly or indirectly sold, used or consumed by you, or any person or persons for or under you, by or with your order, consent, allowance or connivance, between the twenty-sixth day of Decem[*be*]r, one thousand seven hundred and fifty-five, and the twenty-sixth day of March, one thousand seven hundred and fifty-six. So help you God.

Licensed persons to render account, &c., on penalty, to be tried by the sessions.

[SECT. 2.] That every person licen[s][*c*]ed as aforesaid, who shall neglect or refuse to render such account, and pay the duties aforesaid to the person or persons to whom the same shall be let or farmed, or to their respective deputies, shall forf[ie][*ei*]t and pay to such farmer or farmers double the sum that the duties aforesaid in the judgm[*en*]t of the court of general sessions of the peace, held in the county where such licen[s][*c*]ed person dwelt, would have amounted unto, which court is hereby, upon the information of the said farmer or farmers, impowered to hear and determine the same, give judgm[*en*]t therein and award execution thereon.

And be it further enacted,

[SECT. 3.] That the committees respectively appointed in each county to contract and agree with any person or persons concerning the duties of excise arising by the act already pass[*e*]'d this session, shall and hereby are impowered, in like manner, and at such time as shall be agreed upon by the said committees, to sell the aforesaid duties of excise, arising between said twenty-sixth day of December, one thousand seven hundred and fifty-five, and the twenty-sixth day of March, one thousand seven hundred and fifty-six, to him or them that will purchase the same; the person or persons so purchasing the same duties, giving bond, with sufficient sureties, to the province treasurer, to pay into the treasury, by the twenty-sixth day of October next, the sum or sums for which the duties aforesaid are sold. **Former committees' power to contract with the farmers.**

Provided, always,—

[SECT. 4.] That the allowance for leakage and other wast[*e*] shall be the same as in and by the afores[*ai*]d act first mentioned is provided, and no other. [*Passed March* 10; *published March* 11,* 1756.

CHAPTER 38.

AN ACT TO PREVENT FARMERS AND COLLECTORS OF THE DUTIES OF EXCISE BEING MEMBERS OF THE GENERAL COURT OR ASSEMBLY OF THIS PROVINCE.

WHEREAS many inconveniencies may arise to this government by persons concerned in farming or collecting the duties of excise being members of the general court or assembly,— **Preamble.**

Be it enacted by the Governour, Council and House of Representatives,

That no person who shall, either directly or indirectly, be a purchaser or collector of the duties of excise laid by the act passed this present session of the gen[*era*]l court, or which shall be laid by any future act, or who shall, directly or indirectly, be a sharer w[*i*]th any such purchaser or collector in such duties, shall be allowed to be a member of the council or house of represent[*ati*]ves of this province during the t[*er*]m[e] of his being so concerned. [*Passed March* 9; † *published March* 31, 1756. **Purchasers or collectors of excise not to be members of the court.**

* According to the printed act the date of publication is March 31.

† Signed March 5, according to the record.

ACTS

PASSED AT THE SESSION BEGUN AND HELD AT BOSTON, ON THE THIRTIETH DAY OF MARCH, A. D. 1756.

CHAPTER 39.

AN ACT FOR PREVENTING PETITIONS TO THE GENERAL COURT RELATING TO LICENCES FOR RETAILING STRONG DRINK, AND KEEPING HOUSES OF PUBLICK ENTERTAINMENT.

Preamble.

WHEREAS petitions have often been preferr[*e*]d to the great and general court, for enabling the courts of general sessions of the peace to grant licences to innholders and retailers of strong drink, whereby the publick affairs of the province have been much interrupted, and the several sessions of this court protracted; therefore, for preventing such inconvenience for the future,—

Be it enacted by the Governo[u]r, Council and House of Representatives,

Court of sessions to grant licenses, if they think fit.

[SECT. 1.] That upon application made to the court of general sessions of the peace in any county within this province, at any of the terms by law appointed for holding the same in such county, for licence to keep an inn, tavern or other house of publick entertainment, or to retail strong liquors, the justices of such court are hereby authorized, at such term, to grant such licence, in case they shall judge it necessary or of publick convenience, and the person applying therefor be suitably qualified for such employment and recommended in manner as the law directs, and the house in which he is to exercise such licence be commodiously situated for the entertainment of travellers and other publick uses.

Provided,—

Time for granting licenses.

[SECT. 2.] That no such licence be firstly or originally granted at any time after the term by law appointed for granting of licences in such county, nor to any person who shall have applied for a licence at such term, and shall have been denied the same, unless it shall evidently appear that the cause of such denial be then removed; nor shall any licence be granted on any other day of the sitting of such court, but that whereon the justices of such county have been wont to give their more general attendance.

And whereas the granting of licences at any term of such court's sitting, frequently and indiscriminately, and the countenancing any unseasonable applications for them, may be attended with no small inconvenience,—

Be it therefore further enacted,

Persons not applying for licenses at the time appointed, to be excluded, unless.

[SECT. 3.] That no person applying for such licence at any other term of such court's sitting, than that by law assign[*e*]'d for granting licences, shall be admitted thereto, who shall not pay and deliver into the hands of the clerk of such court, besides the appointed fee, the sum of twelve shillings, to be by such clerk delivered to the treasurer of such county for the county's use, unless it shall appear to the satisfaction of the justices, that the nature of the case, or circumstances attending it, would not admit of an earlier application, or that the petitioner, by some providential and unavoidable lett or hindrance, was prevented doing it; in which case, no more shall be demanded than the appointed fee.

[SECT. 4.] This act to commence on and from the twentieth day of April instant, and to continue in force until[l] the first day of April, which will be in the year of our Lord one thousand seven hundred and fifty-nine, and no longer. [*Passed April* 3; *published April* 8, 1756. Limitation.

CHAPTER 40.

AN ACT FOR THE MORE SPEEDY LEVYING OF SOLDIERS FOR THE EXPEDITION AGAINST CROWN POINT.

WHEREAS this government, in conjunction with the other governments in New England and New York, have judged it necessary that there be a new expedition formed against Crown Point, and this government have determined to raise for said expedition three thousand five hundred men, including officers, to form an army, with what shall be raised by the other governments, under the command of Major General Winslow; wherefore, for the more speedy and effectual raising and levying of soldiers for the service aforesaid,— Preamble.

Be it enacted by the Governour, Council and House of Representatives,

[SECT. 1.] That there be and hereby is ordered to be a general muster of all the companies, both of horse and foot, in all the regiments within this province, on the twenty-second day of April instant; and if the number of three thousand five hundred men, including officers, shall not be [e][i]nlisted before that time, it shall and may be lawful to compleat the same by an impress; and upon due warning given, pursuant to the order of the captain or commanding officer of the several troops or companies, by one of the serjeants or corporals of the several troops and companies, to each person belonging to the same, either in person, or, in case of his absence from home, by leaving a notification, in writing, at the usual place of his abode, for mustering the said companies of horse and foot for the purposes before mentioned, every person, who by law is obliged to attend military musters, whether belonging to any troop or foot company, shall punctually attend and continue at such muster at the time and place that shall be appointed therefor, on pain of incurring the penalty of twenty pounds (unless it shall appear, on trial of the offence, that his attendance was necessarily and unavoidably prevented) to be recovered by action of debt, with full costs of suit, to be brought by the clerk of the respective troops or companies to which such person not appearing as aforesaid belongs, who is hereby impow[e]red to commence and prosecute such action; and if such delinquent person be a son under age or a servant, the said action to be brought against, and penalty recovered of, his parent or master; one third part of said penalty to be for the use of the clerk who shall sue for the same, and the remaining two thirds for the use of the town where the defendant lives.

Manner of notifying the muster of the several companies of militia, in order to raise volunteers, &c.

Fine in case of non-appearance.

[SECT. 2.] And every person who shall be impressed by the commanding officer of each company or troop, or such person as he shall appoint for the service aforesaid, shall duly attend the same, either by

Fine for not serving, when impressed.

himself or by some other effective able-bodied person in his stead, on penalty of the sum of ten pounds (unless he shall have had a discharge from such impress, in writing, under the hand of the captain or chief officer of such company, or troop, or regiment, or of the commander-in-chief of this province) to be recovered by warrant from the captain or chief officer of such company, directed to the clerk of such company or troop, to levy by distress and sale of the goods and chatt[e]l[e]s of such offender, or of the goods and chatt[e]l[e]s of his parent or master, in case such impressed person be a son under age or a servant; and the said clerk is hereby fully impowered and required to levy and collect the said sum in such manner as constables of towns and districts within this province are impow[e]red to levy town taxes; and for want of goods and chatt[e]l[e]s whereon to make distress, to commit[t] such offender to the common goal of the county, there to remain 'till such time as the same fine and charges are paid: which said fine of ten pounds, when received, shall be disposed of as fines are for persons impressed not attending the service, by virtue of an act of this province made and passed in the twenty-seventh year of his present majesty's reign, intitled "An Act for levying of soldiers, and to prevent soldiers and seamen in his majesty's service from being arrested for debt." [*Passed April* 13; *published April* 15, 1756.

Manner of recovery.

1753-54, chap. 41.

CHAPTER 41.

AN ACT IN ADDITION TO AN ACT, INTITLED "AN ACT FOR REGULATING OF THE MILITIA."

Preamble. 1693-94, chap. 3.

WHEREAS, by an act of this province made in the fifth year of the reign of their late majest[y][*ie*]s, William and Mary, intitled "An Act for regulating of the militia," several persons are excused from all trainings, military watches and wardings; and the government being oftentimes necessitated to borrow money for the public[k] service, and it may expedite the raising of money for that service, if the lenders were excused from the aforesaid duties; wherefore,—

Be it enacted by the Governour, Council and House of Representatives,

Persons lending the government £1,000, to be excused from military duties.

[SECT. 1.] That every person who shall at any one time lend the sum of one thousand pounds, or upwards, to the province treasurer, for the use of this government, shall be and hereby is exempted from all trainings, mil[l]itary watches and wardings, and from all impresses, during the continuance of this act.

And to the end it may be ascertained who the lender is, and that he may have evidence of his having lent the sum aforesaid for the use of this government,—

Be it enacted,

Method to ascertain who the lender is.

[SECT. 2.] That the person whose name shall be expressed in the receipt or obligation given by the treasurer for the sum lent (and not any other person, to whom such receipt or obligation may be made over or endorsed), shall be deemed the lender, and upon application made to him, the treasurer shall give a certificate to such lender, of his having lent the sum aforesaid for the use of this government; which certificate shall be a sufficient evidence of such lender's being intitled to the exemption aforesaid.

Limitation.

[SECT. 3.] This act to continue and be in force for the space of five years from the sixteenth day of April, one thousand seven hundred and fifty-six. [*Passed and published April* 16, 1756.

CHAPTER 42.

AN ACT IN ADDITION TO AN ACT, [E][I]NTITLED "AN ACT FOR SUPPLYING THE TREASURY WITH THE SUM OF SIXTY THOUSAND POUNDS."

WHEREAS, by an act made this present year of his majesty's reign, [e][i]ntitled "An Act for supplying the treasury with the sum of sixty thousand pounds," the province treasurer is [e][i]mpowered to borrow forty thousand pounds of his excellency the governour, and a further sum, not exceeding twenty thousand pounds, of such person or persons as shall be willing to lend the same; and for every sum borrowed of such person or persons, to make up the aforesaid sum of twenty thousand pounds, the said treasurer is directed to give a receipt and obligation, payable the second day of June, 1757. And in order to draw the said twenty thousand pounds into the treasury, so as to enable the treasurer effectually to discharge the receipts and obligations given therefor (with the interest that may be due thereon), it is in said act enacted, "That a tax of twenty-two thousand pounds be levied on polls, and estates both real and personal within this province, in manner following; that is to say, eleven thousand pounds, part thereof, according to such rules and in [such] proportions on the several towns and districts within this province as shall be agreed on and ordered by the general court or assembly, at their session in May, 1756, and to be paid into the publick treasury on or before the 31st of March next after; and the further sum of eleven thousand pounds, according to such rules and in such proportions on the several towns and districts aforesaid as shall be agreed on and ordered by the general court, at their session in May, 1757, and to be paid into the publick treasury on or before the 31st of March then next after"; whereby the receipts and obligations directed by said act to be given by the treasurer for one half of the said sum of twenty thousand pounds, to be borrowed as aforesaid, will become payable before the last-mentioned tax, which is one of the funds for the redemption of said receipts and obligations, will be payable into the treasury; wherefore, in order that the receipts and obligations aforesaid may be made payable in a suitable time after the said last-mentioned tax shall be payable into the treasury, and that no inconvenience may arise in consequence of the act aforesaid,— Preamble. 1755-56, chap. 27.

Be it enacted by the Governour, Council and House of Representatives,

That for one half of the said twenty thousand pounds which he is [e][i]mpowered to borrow by the act aforesaid, the treasurer shall give his receipts and obligations in the form following; viz[t].,—

Province of the Massachusetts Bay, the day of , 175 . Received of the sum of , for the use and service of the province of the Massachusetts Bay, and, in behalf of said province, I do hereby promise and oblige myself and successors in the office of treasurer to repay the said or order, on the second day of June, 1758, the aforesaid sum of , in coin[e]'d silver at six shillings and eightpence per ounce, or Spanish mill'd dollars, at six shillings each, with interest annually, at the rate of six per cent per annum. Witness my hand, H. G., Treasurer. Form of treasurer's receipt.

—anything in the act aforesaid to the contrary notwithstanding. [*Passed April* 20; *published April* 21, 1756.

CHAPTER 43.

AN ACT IN ADDITION TO THE SEVERAL ACTS AND LAWS OF THIS PROVINCE NOW IN FORCE RESPECTING POOR AND IDLE, DISORDERLY AND VAGRANT PERSONS.

Preamble.

WHEREAS some idle, dissolute and vagrant persons, having some estate and accordingly rateable, take no care of their families; nor improve their estates to the best advantage; which persons are not under the care and inspection of the overseers of the poor or [*the*] selectmen of the town where such idle persons dwell,—

Be it therefore enacted by the Governour, Council and House of Represent[ati]ves,

Overseers of the poor to take under, idle, dissolute persons who have estates.

[SECT. 1.] That where any idle, dissolute or vagrant persons, having a rateable estate, do neglect to take due care of themselves and their families, or to improve their estates, that in all such cases the overseers of the poor or the selectmen of the town shall be and hereby they are impow[e]red to take the like care and inspection of such person or persons who neglect the due care and improvem[en]t of their estates, and who mispend their time and money, and who live idle, vagrant and dissolute lives, as if they were poor, indigent and impotent persons, and accordingly, with the assent of two justices of the peace of the same county, *quorum unus*, put out into orderly families their children, if any they have, and improve their estates to the best advantage, and apply the produce and income thereof towards the support of them and their families.

Provided,—

Proviso.

[SECT. 2.] That any of the said idle persons thinking themselves aggr[ei][*ie*]ved, may make their application to, and have remedy from, the justices in the gen[*era*]l sessions of the peace in the same county, if they see cause, who are hereby impowered to rel[ei][*ie*]ve such aggr[ei][*ie*]ved person from the determination of the selectmen.

Preamble.

And whereas it is apprehended that many adult persons, both male and female, who by virtue of the laws of this governm[*en*]t are liable and lawfully may be sent and committed to the house of correction for the county, or workhouse for the town, in w[*hi*]ch such persons may respectively reside or be found, may be employed and kept to work with less inconvenience to the town or district from whence by law they may be sent, and with more advantage to them who by law are to take the effects and receive the benefit of their labours, by their being employed and kept to work by a master who should have power to direct, govern and employ them in and about such labour and business as they can best perform.

Be it enacted,

Persons liable to the house of correction, may be bound to service.

[SECT. 3.] That for the future it shall and may be lawful for the overseers of the poor of every town and district within this province, where any are specially chosen to that office, and for the selectmen of every town and district, where there are no persons specially chosen to the office of overseers of the poor, if they see meet (and such overseers and selectmen, respectively, are hereby authorized and impowered, by indenture, or by any other form of covenant, agreem[*en*]t or contract, valid and effectual in law), to put, place and bind out to service to such person or persons as they shall judge suitable, for a term not exceeding one year, at the longest, under one and the same contract, any adult person, whether male or female, residing and found in their respective towns or districts, whom they shall judge liable, by virtue of any law or laws of this governm[*en*]t, to be sent and committed to the house of correction or workhouse, from any county, town or district in this province; and the act[*s*] and doings of such overseers and selectmen, respectively, whereby any such person shall and may be put and bound out to service, pursuant to this act, shall be as valid and effectual, in law, to bind and hold the person so put to service, as if any such person, by his [or] her own act and consent, being of the age of twenty-one years, had bound and put out him- or herself a servant for the like term, by indenture, or by any other legal form or manner of covenant or contract.

Provided, always,—

[SECT. 4.] That it shall be in the power of the court of general session[s] of the peace for the county wherein any such person shall be put out to service as aforesaid by virtue of this act, upon application made to said court by any such person so put out to service, or any on his or her behalf, if they judge proper, to discharge and make void any act or doing of said overseers or selectmen, whereby any person shall be put to service as afores[*ai*]d, and by their order wholly to annul the same, and set such person so bound out, at liberty and free from his or her master, and also to allow costs to the person who shall be set at liberty by said court, against the town or district by whose overseers or selectmen such person so set at liberty shall have been bound out, and to award execution accordingly.

Proviso for applying to the court of general sessions of the peace.

[SECT. 5.] And in all cases wherein the said court of general sessions of the peace shall, by their order, discharge and set at liberty any person or persons bound to service by any overseers or selectmen as aforesaid, all indentures, covenants, contracts and agreem[*en*]ts, whereby and under which such person shall have been bound or put out as aforesaid, shall, from and after the time of such orders passing in sessions, be taken, held and adjudged absolutely void and of no effect, so far as such indentures, covenants, contracts or agreem[*en*]ts shall respect any time to come, after the time of such order's passing.

Upon their order, contracts may be dissolved.

And be it further enacted,

[SECT. 6.] That the proceeds of the labour and service of every person who by virtue of this act shall be bound out to service, over and above the necessary costs in and about the same, shall be taken by the overseers or selectmen, respectively, who shall bind out such person, to be improved and laid out for the support of the family or other poor and indigent kindred of the person bound out, with the maintenance of whom the person bound out shall by law be charg[*e*]able, if any such family or kindred such person shall have; but if the person bound out shall have no family or kindred with whose support he or she shall by law be chargeable, the proceeds of the labour of every such person, not having such family or kindred as afores[*ai*]d, shall be retained and kept by said overseers or selectmen, respectively, to be paid by them to such person bound out as aforesaid, or improved and laid out for his or her use, support and benefit by said overseers or selectmen, in such manner as to them shall appear most for the benefit and advantage of the person bound out as afores[*ai*]d; the said overseers or selectmen, respectively, to determine always whether to pay said proceeds in money directly to said person bound out as afores[*ai*]d, or themselves to dispose and lay out the same in some other manner to such person's use; and said overseers and selectmen are hereby required and obliged, annually, at the town or district meeting in March for the choice of town officers, to exhibit to their respective towns or districts a full and true account of their disposition of the earnings and proceeds of the labour of all persons w[*hi*]ch shall have been bound out by them, not having such family or kindred as afores[*ai*]d, during the whole last preceeding year, for such town's or district's examination and allowance.

Use of the earnings of the persons bound out.

[SECT. 7.] And for the proceeds of the labour and service of such person, having a family or kindred with whom he or she shall be chargeable as afores[*ai*]d, such overseers or selectmen shall be accountable to the town or district to w[*hi*]ch such family or kindred such person shall be chargeable with shall belong and are inhabitants; and said overseers and selectmen, respectively, shall pay all the earnings and proceeds of the labour of the person bound out as aforesaid, who shall have such family and kindred as afores[*ai*]d, to the town or district to which such family or kindred shall belong, or their order; always excepting a [a] reasonable allowance out of said proceeds to said overseers or selectmen for their care, trouble and cost in binding out such person and taking and recovering the proceeds afores[*ai*]d: which allowance s[*ai*]d overseers and selectmen are hereby impowered to retain in their hands, and in their account said overseers and selectmen shall be allowed all such reasonable charge and cost incurr[*e*]'d, and also a reasonable reward for their own care and trouble in and about the binding out of any such person, and taking and recovering the proceeds of his or her labour of the master to whom he or she shall be respectively bound and put out.

[SECT. 8.] This act to be in force for the space of three years from the thirtieth of April current, and no longer. [*Passed April* 20; *published April* 21, 1756.

CHAPTER 44.

AN ACT FOR ENQUIRING INTO THE RATEABLE ESTATES OF THE PROVINCE.

Preamble.

WHEREAS the rateable estates of the several towns and districts in this province may be very much altered since the last valuation taken by this court,—

Be it enacted by the Governour, Council and House of Representatives,

A new valuation to be taken of the ratable estates of the province.

[SECT. 1.] That the assessors of each town and district within this province, who shall have been chosen for the year one thousand seven hundred and fifty-six, shall, on oath, take and lodge in the secretary's office, by the last Wednesday in September, one thousand seven hundred and fifty-six, a true and perfect list, according to their best skill and understanding (and conformable to a list settled and agreed on by the general court and to be recorded in the secretary's office, a printed copy of which shall be, by the treasurer of the province, sent to the clerk of each town and district), therein setting forth an account of all male polls, of sixteen years old and upwards, whether at home or abroad, distinguishing such as are exempt from rates, through age or otherwise, and of all rateable estates both real and personal within their respective towns and districts; and all farms, parcel[l]s of land lying adjacent to and rated in such town or district, and by whom occupied; and what each person's real estate within the town or district, or adjoining as aforesaid, may rent for by the year; and of all Indian, negro and molatto servants, whether for life or for a term of years; and what number of vessels, and of what burthen, have sailed from their respective ports to any other port, in the year one thousand seven hundred and fifty-five. And the said assessors, in taking such valuation, shall distinguish the different improvements of the real estates into the following parts; viz[t]., houses, pasture and tillage lands; salt, fresh and English mowing land; with the number of acres of orchard, and what stock the pasture ordinarily is capable of feeding; and what quantity of produce

Directions for taking the same.

the said tillage, mowing and o[a]rchard land yearly affords, one year with another: excepting the governour, lieutenant-governo[u]r, president, fellows and tutors of Harvard College, settled ministers and grammar-school masters, with their families, who, for their polls, and estates in their own actual improvem[en]t, shall be exempted out of this act; and the said assessors, before they enter on this work, shall take the following oath; viz[t].,—

Form of the assessors' oath.

You, A. and B., being chosen assessors for the town of B., for the year one thousand seven hundred and fifty-six, do severally swear that you will faithfully and impartially, according to your best skill and judgment, do and perform the whole duty of an assessor, as directed and enjoined by an act of this province made the present year, [e][*i*]ntitled "An Act for [i][*e*]nquiring into the rateable estate[*s*] of the province," without favour or prejudice. So help you God.

—which oath, in such town or district where no justice dwells, may be administred by the town- or district-clerk; and every assessor who shall have been chosen by any town or district in the year one thousand seven hundred and fifty-six, accepting such choice, that shall refuse to take the said oath, or, taking the same, shall neglect or refuse to do the duty required by this act, or shall anyways prevaricate therein, shall, for each of these offences, forfeit and pay a fine of five pounds.

Fine for persons refusing to give the assessors an account of their ratable estates.

[SECT. 2.] And every person refusing or neglecting to give such assessor or assessors a true account of his rateable estate, improvem[*en*]ts or rents, agre[*e*]able to the true intent of this act, when thereunto required by the assessors, shall, for each offence, forfeit and pay the sum of twenty pounds. And in case any account given by any person in pursuance of this act, shall be, by the assessor or assessors taking the same, suspected of falshood, it shall be in the power of either of such assessors to administer an oath to the truth of such account, and if such suspected person shall refuse to swear to the truth of such acco[*un*]t, according to his best judgment, when thereunto required by any one of the assessors, such refusal shall be deemed a refusal to give an acco[*un*]t of his rateable estate; the person so refusing shall be subject to the fine in that case by this act provided, without further or other evidence for his conviction on trial, and every assessor shall be allowed out of the treasury of his respective town or district, the sum of three shillings, for every day he shall be necessarily employed in doing the duty enjoined by this act.

Assessor's pay.

And be it further enacted,

Copies of the last year's lists to be lodged in the secretary's office.

[SECT. 3.] That the assessors of each town and district in this province, who were chosen for the year one thousand seven hundred and fifty-five, shall, by the last Wednesday in May, [1756] [*one thousand seven hundred and fifty-six*] on oath, transmit to the secretary's office, a true and perfect copy of the list and valuation of estates, by which they made the taxes in their particular towns and districts for the year one thousand seven hundred and fifty-five, on penalty that each assessor neglecting his duty therein shall forfeit and pay the sum of five pounds.

Recovery of fines.

[SECT. 4.] All fines and forfeitures arising by this act may be recovered by bill, plaint or information, or by action of debt, in any of his maj[*es*]ty's courts within this province proper to try the same; and shall be applied, two thirds to him or them that shall inform or sue for the same, and the other third to his majesty to and for the use of this government. [*Passed April* 12; *published April* 21, 1756.

CHAPTER 45.

AN ACT FOR PREVENTING AND PUNISHING THE DESERTION OF SOLDIERS IN THE EXPEDITION AGAINST CROWN POINT, OR IN DEFENCE OF THE FRONTIERS OF THIS GOVERNMENT.

Preamble.

WHEREAS soldiers duly inlisted, or to be inlisted or impressed, for the present expedition against Crown Point, or for the defence of the frontiers of this province, have deserted, and may hereafter desert, and be found wandering, or otherwise absenting themselves illegally from his majesty's service,—

Be it therefore enacted by the Governour, Council and House of Representatives,

Sheriffs, constables, &c., may apprehend deserters, &c.

[SECT. 1.] That it shall and may be lawful for the sheriff of any county, or either of his deputies, or any constable or tythingman of the town or place, or any other person, where any person, who may be reasonably suspected to be such a deserter, shall be found, to apprehend or cause him to be apprehended, and to cause such person to be brought before any justice of the peace living in or near such town or place, who hath hereby power to examine such suspected person; and if, by his confession, or the testimony of one or more witness or witnesses, upon oath, or by the knowledge of such justice of the peace, or any other proof, it shall appear or be found that such suspected person is a listed or impressed soldier, as aforesaid, tho'[*ugh*] listed or impressed in any other government, and that he ought to be with the troop or company to which he belongs, such justice of the peace shall forthwith cause him to be conveyed to the goal of the county or place where he shall be found, and transmit an account thereof to the commander-in-chief or secretary of this province; and such deserter shall be returned to his service by the first opportunity, and the keeper of such goal shall receive the full subsistence of such deserter or deserters, during the time that he or they shall continue in his custody, for the maintenance of the said deserter or deserters, but shall not be intitled to any fee or reward on account of the imprisonment of such deserter or deserters.

And for the better encouragement of any person or persons to secure and apprehend such deserter or deserters,—

Be it further enacted,

Allowance for apprehending deserters.

[SECT. 2.] That upon the certificate of such justice of the peace to the province treasurer, there shall be paid by him to such persons as shall apprehend, or cause to be apprehended, any deserter from his majesty's said service, forty shillings and the costs of prosecution, to be deducted out of his wages, for every deserter that shall be so apprehended and committed. [*Passed April* 20; *published April* 21, 1756.

CHAPTER 46.

AN ACT IMPOWERING THE PROVINCE TREASURER TO BORROW THE SUM OF TEN THOUSAND POUNDS, AND FOR APPLYING THE SAME TO DEFR[A][*E*]Y THE CHARGES OF THE INTENDED EXPEDITION AGAINST CROWN POINT.

Be it enacted by the Governour, Council and House of Representatives,

Treasurer empowered to borrow £10,000.

[SECT. 1.] That the treasurer of the province be and he hereby is impowered and directed to borrow, of such persons as shall be willing to lend the same, a sum not exceeding ten thousand pounds, in Spanish mill'd dollars, at six shillings each, or in other coined silver of sterling alloy, at six shillings and eightpence per ounce; and the sum so borrowed shall be applied by the treasurer for the payment of such dra[f][*ugh*]ts as shall be drawn on him by the governour or commander-in-chief for the time being, by and with the advice of the council, for the service of the intended expedition against Crown Point, and for every sum so borrowed the treasurer shall give a rec[ie][*ei*]pt and obligation in the form following; viz[t].,—

Province of the Massachusetts, the day of , 175 . Rec[ie][*ei*]ved of the sum of , for the use and service of the province of the Massachusetts Bay, and, in behalf of said province, I do hereby promise and oblige myself and successors in the office of treasurer to repay the said or order, on or before the tenth day of June, 1758, the aforesaid sum of , in coined silver of sterling alloy, at six shillings and eightpence per ounce, or in Spanish mill'd dollars of full weight, at six shillings each, with interest annually, at the rate of six per cent per annum. Form of treasurer's receipt.

Witness my hand, A. B., Treasurer.

—*provided*, that no rec[ie][*ei*]pt shall be given for a less sum than six pounds.

And to enable the said treasurer to discharge the said obligations, and the interest that shall be due thereon,—

Be it further enacted,

[SECT. 2.] That there be and hereby there is granted to his most excellent majesty, a tax of eleven thousand five hundred pounds, to be levied upon the polls and estates within this province, according to such rules as shall be ordered by the general court of this province, at their sessions in May, one thousand seven hundred and fifty-seven. Tax of £11,500, in 1757.

And be it further enacted,

[SECT. 3.] That in case the general court shall not, by the twentieth day of June, one thousand seven hundred and fifty-seven, agree and conclude upon a tax act to draw into the treasury the aforesaid sum of eleven thousand five hundred pounds, by the thirty-first day of March then next following, that then the treasurer of the province for the time being, shall issue his warrants, directed to the selectmen or assessors of the several towns and districts within this province, requiring them, respectively, to assess, levy and pay in to the treasury, by the said thirty-first day of March, their respective proportions of said sum, according to the rates and proportions, rules and directions of the tax act then last preceeding. Tax for the money hereby emitted to be made according to the last tax act, in case.

And whereas humble trust and dependance is had by the general assembly on a reimbursement of the charges arising from the expeditions against Crown Point, and monies for that purpose are expected from Great Britain; wherefore, as a further fund to enable the treasurer to discharge the rec[ie][*ei*]pts and obligations aforesaid, by him given in pursuance of this act,— Preamble.

Be it further enacted,

[SECT. 4.] That the monies that shall be rec[ie][*ei*]ved from Great Britain, over and above what have been appropriated for the repayment of certain sums which the treasurer by divers acts has been directed to borrow, shall be applied by the said treasurer, or so much thereof as shall be needful[1], for the discharging said obligations (with the interest that may be due thereon), in pursuance of this act. Treasurer to apply the money that may be received from Great Britain, for the payment of the money borrowed.

Provided always, anything in this act to the contrary notwithstanding,—

[SECT. 5.] That in case the monies aforesaid shall arrive from Great Britain, and be rec[ie][*ei*]ved into the province treasury on or before the twentieth day of June, one thousand seven hundred and fifty-seven Tax not to go forth, in case.

(over and above what shall be sufficient to repay the sums borrowed by virtue of the acts aforesaid), and shall be sufficient for discharging the obligations given by the treasurer in pursuance of this act, then, and in such case, the tax, which otherwise by this act is ordered to go forth, shall be, and hereby is declared to be, null and void.

Provided, also,—

Proviso, in case of a surplusage.

[SECT. 6.] That the remainder of the sum that may be brought in by the tax ordered by this act to be assessed and levied, over and above what shall be sufficient to discharge the obligations aforesaid (with the interest that may be due thereon), shall be and remain as a stock in the treasury, and be appl[y][*i*]ed as the general court of this province shall hereafter order. [*Passed April* 20; *published April* 21, 1756.

CHAPTER 47.

AN ACT FOR GRANTING UNTO HIS MAJESTY SEVERAL RATES AND DUTIES OF IMPOST AND TUNNAGE OF SHIPPING.

WHEREAS, by an act made by this court at their session of May last, the province treasurer was impowered to borrow a sum not exceeding fifty thousand pounds, in mill'd dollars, at six shillings each, or in other silver at six shillings and eightpence per ounce, for a term not exceeding three years, for the discharge of the debts of this province, and by said act the treasurer was ordered to give his reciepts or obligations to the lenders to repay the money so borrowed; and as a further fund to enable the treasurer to discharge said reciepts or obligations, it is in said act enacted, "That the duties of impost, for the year one thousand seven hundred and fifty-six, shall be applied for that purpose, and for no other purpose whatsoever,"—

We, his majesty's most dutifull and loyal subjects, the representatives of the province of the Massachusetts Bay, in New England, being desirous of enabling the treasurer to discharge the reciepts and obligations aforesaid, have chearfully and unanimously given and granted and do hereby give and grant, to his most excellent majesty, to the end and use aforesaid, and to no other use, the several duties of impost upon all liquors, goods, wares and merchandise that shall be imported into this province, and tunnage of shipping, hereafter mentioned; and pray that it be enacted,—

And be it accordingly enacted by the Governour, Council and House of Representatives,

[SECT. 1.] That from and after the twenty-sixth day of April, one thousand seven hundred and fifty-six, to the twenty-sixth day of March, one thousand seven hundred and fifty-seven, there shall be paid by the importers of all wines, rum and other liquors, goods, wares and merchandizes that shall be imported into this province by any of the inhabitants thereof (except what is by this act hereafter exempted), the several rates and duties of impost following; vizt.,—

For every pipe of wine of every sort, ten shillings.

For every hogshead of rum, containing one hundred gallons, eight shillings.

For every hogshead of sugar, fourpence.

For every hogshead of molasses, fourpence.

For every hogshead of tobacco, ten shillings.

—And so, proportionably, for greater or less quantities.

And for all other commodities, goods or merchandizes not mentioned or not excepted, fourpence for every twenty shillings value, excepting such goods as are the product or manufacture of Great Britain.

[SECT. 2.] And for any of the above-mentioned liquors, goods, wares and merchandizes that shall be imported into this province by any of the inhabitants of the other provinces or colonies on this continent, or of the English West-India Islands, in any ship or vessell to them belonging, on the proper account of any of the said inhabitants of the said provinces, colonies or islands, there shall be paid by the importers double the impost laid by this act: *provided always*, that everything which is the growth or produce of the provinces or colonies aforesaid (tobacco and bar-iron excepted), and all provisions, salt, cotton-wool, pig-iron, mehogany, black-walnut, lignum-vitæ, red cedar, logwood, brazileto wood, hemp, raw skins and hides; and also all prize goods brought into and condemned in this province, are and shall be exempted from every the rates and duties aforesaid.

And be it further enacted,

[SECT. 3.] That all goods, wares and merchandize, the property of any of the inhabitants of any of the neighbouring provinces or colonies on this continent, that shall be imported into this province, and shall have paid, or secured to be paid, the duty of impost by this act provided to be paid, and afterwards shall be exported and landed in any of the said provinces or colonies on this continent, then, and in such case, the exporter, producing a certificate from some officer of his majesty's customs that the same have been landed in some of the provinces or colonies aforesaid, shall be allowed a drawback of the whole duty of impost by him paid, or secured to be paid, as by this act provided.

And be it further enacted,

[SECT. 4.] That the master of every ship or vessel coming into this province from any other place, shall, within twenty-four hours after his arrival in any port or harbour, and before bulk is broken, make report and deliver a manifest, in writing, under his hand, to the commissioner aforesaid, of the contents of the loading of such ship or vessel, therein particularly expressing the species, kind and quantities of all wines, liquors, goods, wares and merchandize imported in such ship or vessell, with the marks and numbers thereof, and to whom the same are consigned; and make oath before the commissioner that the same manifest contains a just and true account of all the lading taken on board and imported in such ship or vessell, so far as he knows or believes; and that if he knows of any more wines, liquors, goods, wares or merchandize laden on board such ship or vessel, and imported therein, he will forthwith make report thereof to the commissioner aforesaid, and cause the same to be added to his manifest.

And be it further enacted,

[SECT. 5.] That if the master of any ship or vessel shall break bulk, or suffer any of the wines, liquors, goods or wares and merchandize imported in such ship or vessell to be unloaden before report and entry thereof be made as aforesaid, he shall forfeit the sum of one hundred pounds.

And be it further enacted,

[SECT. 6.] That all merchants and other persons, being owners of any wines, liquors, goods, wares or merchandize imported into this province, for which any of the rates or duties aforesaid are payable, or having the same consigned to them, shall make an entry thereof with the commissioner aforesaid, and produce an invoice of all such goods as pay *ad valorem*, and make oath before him in form following; vizt.,—

You, A. B., do swear that the entry of the goods and merchandize by you now made, exhibits the sterling value of said goods, and that, *bonâ fide*, according to your best skill and judgment, it is not less than that value. So help you God.

—which oath the commissioner or reciever appointed in consequence of this act is hereby impowered and directed to administer; and the owners aforesaid shall pay to said commissioner, or give security to pay, the duty of impost by this act required, before such wines, liquors, goods, wares or merchandize be landed or taken out of the vessel in which the same shall be imported.

[SECT. 7.] And no wines, liquors, goods, wares or merchandize that by this act are liable to pay impost or duty, shall be landed on any wharfe, or in any warehouse or other place, but in the daytime only, and that after sunrise and before sunset, unless in the presence or with the consent of the commissioner or reciever, on pain of forfeiting all such wines, liquors, goods, wares and merchandize, and the lighter, boat or vessell out of which the same shall be landed or put into any warehouse or other place.

[SECT. 8.] And if any person or persons shall not have and produce an invoice of the quantities of rum or liquors to him or them consigned, then the cask wherein the same are, shall be gauged at the charge of the importer, that the contents thereof may be known.

Provided, nevertheless,—

[SECT. 9.] That the said commissioner shall be and he hereby is allowed to give credit to such person or persons whose duty of impost in one vessel shall exceed six pounds: which credit shall be so limitted as that he shall settle and ballance his accounts with every person, on or before the twenty-sixth day of March, one thousand seven hundred and fifty-seven, that the said accounts may be produced to this court as soon as may be after; and for all entries where the impost to be paid doth not exceed three shillings, the said commissioner shall not demand anything, and not more than sixpence for any other single entry to what value soever.

And be it further enacted,

[SECT. 10.] That the importer of all wines, liquors, goods, wares and merchandize, from and after the twenty-sixth day of April instant, and until the twenty-sixth of March next, by land-carriage, or in small vessells or boats, shall make report and deliver a manifest thereof to the commissioner aforesaid or his deputy, therein particularly expressing the species, kind and quantity of all such wines, liquors, goods, wares and merchandize so imported, with the marks and numbers thereof, when, how and by whom brought; and shall make oath, before the said commissioner or his deputy, to the truth of such report and manifest, and shall also pay, or secure to be paid, the several duties aforesaid by this act charg'd and chargeable upon such wines, liquors, goods, wares and merchandizes, before the same are landed, housed or put into any store or place whatsoever.

And be it further enacted,

[SECT. 11.] That every merchant or other person importing any wines in this province shall be allowed twelve per cent for leakage: *provided,* such wines shall not have been filled up on board; and that every hogshead, but or pipe of wine that hath two-thirds thereof leaked out, shall be accounted for outs, and the merchant or importer to pay no duty for the same. And no master of any ship or vessell shall suffer any wines to be filled up on board without giving a certificate of the quantity so filled up, under his hand, before the landing thereof, to the commissioner or reciever of impost for such port, on pain of forfeiting the sum of one hundred pounds.

[SECT. 12.] And if it may be made to appear that any wines imported in any ship or vessell be decayed at the time of unloading thereof, or in twenty days afterwards, oath being made before the commissioner or reciever that the same hath not been landed above that time, the duties and impost paid for such wines shall be repaid unto the importer thereof.

And be it further enacted,

[SECT. 13.] That the master of every ship or vessel importing any liquors, wines, goods, wares or merchandize, shall be liable to and pay the impost for such and so much thereof, contained in his manifest, as shall not be duly entered, and the duty paid for the same by the person or persons to whom such wines, liquors, goods, wares or merchandize are or shall be consigned. And it shall and may be lawful, to and for the master of every ship or other vessel, to secure and detain in his hands, at the owner's risque, all such wines, liquors, goods, wares and merchandize imported in any ship or vessel, until he recieves a certificate, from the commissioner or reciever of the impost, that the duty for the same is paid, and until he be repaid his necessary charges in securing the same; or such master may deliver such wines, liquors, goods, wares and merchandize as are not entred, unto the commissioner or reciever of the impost in such port, or his order, who is hereby impowered and directed to recieve and keep the same, at the owner's risque, until the impost thereof, with the charges, be paid or secured to be paid; and then to deliver such wines, liquors, goods, wares or merchandizes as such master shall direct.

And be it further enacted,

[SECT. 14.] That the commissioner or reciever of the impost in each port, shall be and hereby is empowered to sue the master of any ship or vessel, for the impost or duty of so much of the lading of any wines, liquors, goods, wares or merchandize imported therein, according to the manifest to be by him given upon oath, as aforesaid, as shall remain not entered and the duty of impost therefor not paid or secured to be paid. And where any goods, wares or merchandize are such that the value thereof is not known, whereby the impost to be recovered of the master, for the same, cannot be ascertained, the owner or person to whom such goods, wares or merchandize are or shall be consigned, shall be summoned to appear as an evidence at the court where such suit for the impost and the duty thereof shall be brought, and be there required to make oath to the value of such goods, wares or merchandize.

And be it further enacted,

[SECT. 15.] That the ship or vessel, with her tackle, apparrell and furniture, the master of which shall make default in anything by this act required to be performed by him, shall be liable to answer and make good the sum or sums forfeited by such master, according to this act, for any such default, as also to make good the impost or duty for all wines, liquors, goods, wares and merchandize not entered as aforesaid, or for which the duty of impost has not been paid; and, upon judgment recovered against such master, the said ship or vessel, with so much of the tackle or appurtenances thereof as shall be sufficient to satisfy said judgment, may be taken by execution for the same; and the commissioner or reciever of the impost is hereby impowered to make seizure of the said ship or vessell, and detain the same under seizure until judgment be given in any suit to be commenced and prosecuted for any of the said forfeitures or for the duty aforesaid; to the intent, that if judgment be rendered for the prosecutors or informer, such ship or vessel and appurtenances may be exposed to sale, for satisfaction thereof, as is before provided: *unless* the owners, or some on their behalf, for the releasing of such ship or vessel from under seizure or restraint, shall give sufficient security unto the commissioner or reciever of impost that seized the same, to respond and satisfy the sum or value of the forfeitures and duties, with charges, that shall be recovered against the master thereof, upon such suit to be brought for the same, as aforesaid; and the master occasioning such loss or damage unto his owners, through his default or neglect, shall be liable unto their action for the same.

And be it further enacted,

[SECT. 16.] That the naval officer within any of the ports of this province shall not clear or give passes to any master of any ship or vessel, outward bound, until he shall be certified, by the commissioner or reciever of the impost, that the duty and impost for the goods last imported in such ship or vessel are paid or secured to be paid.

[SECT. 17.] And the commissioner or reciever of the impost is hereby impowered to allow bills of store to the master of any ship or vessel importing any wines or liquors, for such private adventures as shall belong to the master or seamen of such ship or vessel, at the discretion of the commissioner or reciever, not exceeding three per cent of the lading; and the duties payable by this act for such wines or liquors, in such bills of stores mentioned and expressed, shall be abated.

And for the more effectual preventing any wines, rum or other distilled spirits being brought into the province from the neighbouring governments, by land, or in small boats or vessells, or any other way, and also to prevent wines, rum or other distilled spirits being first sent out of this province, and afterwards brought into the government again, to defraud the government of the duties of impost,—

Be it enacted,

[SECT. 18.] That the commissioner and reciever of the aforesaid duties of impost shall, and he is hereby impowered and enjoyned to, appoint one suitable person or persons as his deputy or deputys, in all such places of this province where it is likely that wine, rum or other distilled spirits will be brought out of other governments into this; which officers shall have power to seize the same, unless the owner shall make it appear that the duty of impost has been paid therefor since their being brought into or relanded in this government; and such officer or officers are also impowered to search, in all suspected places, for such wines, rum and distilled spirits brought or relanded in this government, where the duty is not paid as aforesaid, and to seize and secure the same for the ends and uses as in this act is hereafter provided.

And be it further enacted,

[SECT. 19.] That the commissioner or his deputys shall have full power to administer the several oaths aforesaid, and search in all suspected places for all such wines, rum, liquor, goods, wares and merchandize as are brought into this province, and landed contrary to the true intent and meaning of this act, and to seize the same for the use hereinafter mentioned.

And be it further enacted,

[SECT. 20.] That if the said commissioner, or his deputy, shall have information of any wines, rum or other distilled spirits being brought into and landed in any place in this province, for which the duties aforesaid shall not have been paid after their being brought into or relanded in this government, he may apply to any justice of the peace within the county, for a warrant to search such place; and said justice shall grant such warrant, directed to some proper officer, upon said commissioner or his deputy's making oath that he hath had information as aforesaid; and having such warrant, and being attended by such officer, the said commissioner or his deputy may, in the daytime, between sun-rising and sun-setting, demand admittance, of the person owning or occupying such place, and, upon refusal, shall have right to break open such place;

and, finding such liquors, may seize and take the same into his own custody; and the commissioner aforesaid, or his deputy, shall be and hereby is impowered to command assistance, and to impress carriages necessary to secure the liquors seized as aforesaid; and any persons refusing assistance, or preventing any of the said officers from executing their office, shall forfeit five pounds to the said commissioner; and he or his deputy shall make reasonable satisfaction for the assistance afforded, and carriages made use of, to secure the liquors seized as aforesaid; and the commissioner or his deputy shall then file an information of such seizure in the inferiour court of common pleas for the county wherein such seizure shall be made, which court shall summon the owner of such liquors, or the occupier of the shop, house or warehouse, or distill-house, where the same were seized, to appear and shew cause, if any he has, why said liquors so seized shall not be adjudged forfeited; and if such owner or occupier shall not shew cause as aforesaid, or shall make default, the said liquors shall be adjudged forfeited, and the said court shall order them to be sold at publick vendue; and the neet produce of such sale shall be paid, one half to the province treasurer for the use of this province, and the other half to the said commissioner.

And be it further enacted,

[SECT. 21.] That there shall be paid, by the master of every ship or other vessel, coming into any port or ports of this province, to trade or traffick, whereof all the owners are not belonging to this province (except such vessels as belong to Great Britain, the provinces or colonies of Pensilvania, West and East Jersey, Connecticutt, New York, New Hampshire and Rhode Island), every voyage such ship or vessel doth make, one pound of good pistol-powder for every ton such ship or vessel is in burthen: *saving* for that part which is owned in Great Britain, this province, or any of the aforesaid governments, which is hereby exempted; to be paid unto the commissioner or reciever of the duties of impost, and to be employed for the ends and uses aforesaid.

[SECT. 22.] And the said commissioner is hereby empowered to appoint a meet and suitable person, to repair unto and on board any ship or vessel, to take the exact measure and tunnage thereof, in case he shall suspect the register of such ship or vessel doth not express and set forth the full burthen of the same; the charge thereof to be paid by the master or owner of such ship or vessel, before she shall be cleared, in case she shall appear to be of a greater burthen: otherwise, to be paid by the commissioner out of the money recieved by him for impost, and shall be allowed him, accordingly, by the treasurer, in his accompts. And the naval officer shall not clear any vessel, until he be certified, also, by the commissioner, that the duty of tunnage for the same is paid, or that it is such a vessel for which none is payable according to this act.

And be it further enacted,

[SECT. 23.] That when and so often as any wine or rum imported into this province, the aforesaid duty of impost upon which shall have been paid agreeable to this act, shall be reshipped and exported from this government to any other part of the world, that then, and in every such case, the exporter of such wine or rum shall make oath, at the time of shipping, before the reciever of impost, or his deputy, that the whole of the wine or rum so shipped has, *bonâ fide*, had the aforesaid duty of impost paid on the same, and shall afterwards produce a certificate, from some officer of the customs, that the same has been landed out of this government,—or otherwise, in case such rum or wines shall be exported to any place where there is no officer of the customs, or to any foreign port, the master of the vessel in which the same shall be exported shall make oath that the same has been landed out of the government, and the exporter shall, upon producing such certificate, or upon such oath of the master, make oath that he verily believes no part of said wines or rum has been relanded in this province,—such exporter shall be allowed a drawback from the reciever of impost as follows; viz[t].,—

For every pipe of wine, eight shillings.

And for every hogshead of rum, six shillings.

Provided, always,—

That if, after the shipping of such wine or rum to be exported as aforesaid, and giving security as aforesaid, in order to obtain the drawback aforesaid, the wine or rum so shipped to be exported, or any part thereof, shall be relanded in this province, or brought into the same from any other province or colony, that then all such rum and wine so relanded and brought again into this province, shall be forfeited and may be seized by the commissioner aforesaid, or his deputy.

And be it further enacted,

[SECT. 24.] That there be one fit person, and no more, nominated and appointed by this court as a commissioner and reciever of the aforesaid duties of impost and tunnage of shipping, and for the inspection, care and management of the said office, and whatsoever relates thereto, to recieve commission for the same from the governour or commander-in-chief for the time being, with authority to substitute and appoint a deputy reciever in each port, or other places besides that in which he resides, and to grant warrants to such deputy-recievers for the said place, and to collect and recieve the impost and tunnage of shipping as aforesaid that shall become due within such port, and to render the account thereof, and to pay in the same, to the said commissioner and reciever: which said commissioner and reciever shall keep fair books of all entries and duties arising by virtue of this act; also, a particular account of every vessel, so that the duties of impost and tunnage arising on the said vessel may appear; and the same to lye open, at all seasonable times, to the view and perusal of the treasurer or reciever-general of this province (or any other person or persons whom this court shall appoint), with whom he shall accompt for all collections and payments, and pay all such monies as shall be in his hands, as the treasurer or reciever-general shall demand it. And the said commissioner or reciever and his deputy or deputys, before their entring upon the execution of their said office, shall be sworn to deal truly and faithfully therein, and shall attend in the said office from ten of the clock in the forenoon, until one in the afternoon.

[SECT. 25.] And the said commissioner or reciever, for his labour, care and expences in the said office, shall have and recieve, out of the province treasury, at the rate of sixty pounds per annum; and his deputy or deputies shall recieve for their service such sums as the said commissioner of impost, together with the province treasurer, shall judge necessary for whatever sums they shall recieve and pay; and the treasurer is hereby ordered, in passing and recieving the said commissioners accounts, accordingly, to allow the payment of such salary or salaries, as aforesaid, to himself and his deputies.

And be it further enacted,

[SECT. 26.] That all penalties, fines and forfeitures accruing and arising in consequence of any breach of this act, shall be one half to his majesty for the use of this province, and the other half to him or them that shall seize, inform and sue for the same, by action, bill, plaint or information, in any of his majesty's courts of record, wherein no essoign, protection or wager of law shall be allowed: the whole charge of the prosecution to be taken out of the half belonging to the informer.

And be it further enacted,

[SECT. 27.] That from and after the commencement of this act, in all causes where any claimer shall appear, and shall not make good the claim, the charges of prosecution shall be born and paid by the said claimer, and not by the informer. [*Passed April* 20; *published April* 21, 1756.

NOTES.—There were eight sessions of the General Court this year. The third session was convened, upon an extraordinary emergency, on the fifth of September, while the Assembly stood prorogued to September twenty-fourth. To remove any possible doubt as to the legality of the acts of the Assembly during this session, chapter 17 was enacted. See further on this subject, the note to chapter 17, *post.*

All the acts of this year were printed (chapters 15 and 47 separately) except the private acts, the titles of which are as follows:—

"An Act to dissolve the Marriage of Mary Parker with Phineas Parker, and to allow her to marry again." [*Passed and published June* 10, 1755.

"An Act to dissolve the Marriage of John Farnum jun^r with Elisabeth Farnum, and to allow him to marry again." [*Passed April* 20, 1756.

The engrossments of all these acts are preserved, except the private act last named, which has not been discovered.

The acts of the first and second sessions, including the private act first above named were certified for transmission, Nov. 25, 1755, and were delivered by the agent of the province, to the clerk of the Privy Council, in waiting, Feb. 24, 1756. On the second of March, they were read, in council, and referred to a committee. On the sixth of March they were referred, by this committee, to the Lords of Trade, and the latter, on the ninth of March, ordered them to be sent to Mr. Lamb for his opinion thereon in point of law.

The acts of the subsequent sessions were certified for transmission, in June, 1756, and were delivered to the clerk of the Privy Council, in waiting, August 12, 1756. On the thirteenth, they were referred to a committee, and on the eighteenth they were, in turn, referred by this committee, to the Lords of Trade, who, on the seventh of October, read this order of the committee and were thereupon informed by the secretary of the Board that the acts had been sent "in the usual manner, to Sir Matthew Lamb for his Opinion thereupon in point of Law."

Sir Matthew Lamb's report is dated Oct. 10, 1757, and contains no objection to either of the acts of this year, except to chapter 38, and the private act last above named.

All the acts of this year, with others, came up for consideration by the Board of Trade, in their meetings of May 12 and 30, 1758. At the former of these meetings, at which the late governor, Shirley, was present by invitation, the draught of a representation was ordered, and, at the latter, the draught was agreed to and ordered to be transcribed.

This representation sets forth that chapters 1, 2, 3, 4, 5, 6, 7, 8, 11, 12, 13, 14, 15, 16, 18, 19, 20, 22, 25, 28, 29, 30, 31, 33, 34, 36, 37, 40, 44, 45, and 47 "appear to have been passed for Temporary services, and are either expired by their own limitation or the purposes for which they were enacted have been completed"; that chapters 27, 42 and 46, "relative to the raising or borrowing monies for defraying the expences of Military and other public services have in great measure taken effect, but the execution of several provisions therein contained in which the public faith of the Province is greatly interested remains still to be completed, for this reason and as Sir Matthew Lamb, one of His Majesty's Counsel at Law, whose opinion has been taken on these Acts has no objection to any of them in point of law, We would humbly propose that they may receive His Majesty's Royal Confirmation"; and that chapters 9, 10, 17, 21, 23, 24, 26, 32, 35, 38, 39, and 43 "relate to the internal Œconomy of the Province and appear to have been enacted for it's private convenience, and We see no reason why His Majesty may not be graciously pleased to confirm them."

Accordingly, an order was passed, in Council, June 16, 1758, confirming chapters 9, 10, 17, 21, 23, 24, 26, 27, 32, 35, 38, 39, 42, 43 and 46.

It will be noticed that in neither the representation of the Board of Trade, nor the Order in Council, is mention made of chapter 41. Still another bill passed its several stages in both branches of the legislature, was signed by the Governor April 21, and, if the memorandum on the engrossment is correct, was actually published, April 22, 1756, but has not been found among the printed acts, nor was it included in the list transmitted to the Home Government. For this bill and other matters relating thereto, see note to chapter 40, *post.*

Chap. 1. "June 21, 1755. This Day the two Houses proceeded to the Election of a Commissioner or Receiver of the Duties of Impost & Tunnage of Shipping for the ensuing Year,

And Daniel Russel Esqr was elected to the said Office by the unanimous Vote of the Council, & House of Representatives;——To which the Governour signed his Consent." —*Council Records, vol.* XX., *p.* 501.

Chap. 3. "June 3^d 1755. A Petition of Ephraim Keith, Agent for the Precinct of Tetticut in the Town of Middleborô, setting forth the Necessity of erecting a Bridge over the River there, and the Difficulty of getting the Charge thereof defrayed, & praying that the same may be done by a Lottery, to be allowed by the Authority of this Court. In the House of Representatives; Whereas it appears *to this House* to this House that a Bridge over the River in Tetticut is necessary not only for the great Advantage of the Towns of Bridgwater & Middleborô, but also for several other Towns in the Counties of Bristol & Plymouth, as also for the great Advantage of the Southern Inhabitants travelling Westward; Therefore, Ordered that the Prayer of the Petition be so far granted as that the Petitioner have Liberty to bring in a Bill for the Purposes in the Petition mentioned;—— In Council, Read & Concur'd."—*Council Records, vol.* XX., *p.* 460.

"April 14, 1756. A Petition of Ephraim Keith for himself, and the other Managers of the Lottery for raising a Sum for Building a Bridge at Tetticut, shewing that they have proceeded therein in preparing for drawing the said Lottery so far as to dispose of near half the Tickets, but have been hindered by Sickness; and whereas the time for Drawing is at hand, Praying that this Court would consider & determine upon some proper way for their Releif——

In Council; Read & Ordered that George Leonard Esqr with such as the Honble House shall join be a Committee to consider of this Petition & report what they judge proper for this Court to do thereon.

In the House of Representatives; Read & Concur'd; And Mr Moorey * & Capt Howard are joined in the Affair "—*Ibid., vol. XXI, p.* 162.

"April 15, 1756. Report upon the Petition of Ephraim Keith, Entered yesterday—vizt——

The Committee appointed to take under Consideration the Petition of Ephraim Keith in behalf of the Managers of a Lottery for the Building a Bridge over Tetticut River, so called having met the said Managers & Considered of the Difficulties they labour under respecting the Disposal of the Tickets for said Lottery, report that the Scheme of said Lottery be altered in the following Manner in Order to finish & Compleat the same—vizt That there be,

One Prize of £125—£125.——Three ditto of £40. each £120
Three ditto of £25 each 75.——Seven ditto of £20. each £140
Eleven ditto of £10 each 110.——Twenty ditto of £5—each £100
Fifty ditto of £3. each 150.——Six Hundred & Thirty of £1. each £630—

In all £1450—And that the Number of Blanks be proportioned to the said Prizes as in the Scheme, published by said Managers, and the Deduction of Ten per Cent only be made from the above Prizes for the Charge of Building said Bridge: which is humbly Submitted—— By Order of the Committee——GEORGE LEONARD——

In Council; Read & Accepted, and Ordered that the said Scheme be and hereby is altered accordingly——In the House of Representatives; Read & Concur'd—Consented to by the Governour."—*Ibid., p.* 163.

Chap. 4. The votes and orders of the Assembly, and the speeches, messages, and proclamations of the Governor relative to the measures adopted to prevent the encroachments of the French, are too numerous and intricate to be given in full as notes to the acts of the Assembly, which they serve to illustrate.

It may, however, be proper to note, with regard to the first expedition against Crown Point, which drew so largely from the treasury of the province, and in which so many soldiers of the province enlisted, that, as soon as the expedition against Nova Scotia was well under way, Governor Shirley began to develop a plan of operations on the western frontiers, substantially identical with the plan successfully conducted on a larger scale by Major General Amherst in 1759.

In a speech to both branches of the Assembly, Feb. 13, 1755, the Governor represented that the projected expedition against Nova Scotia, by diverting the French from the exclusive pursuit of their operations in the south and west, afforded a most favorable opportunity for "building a fort upon the rocky eminence near Crown Point which may command the French fort there," and set forth the advantages of this position as the key to the reduction of Canada, and the expulsion of the French from he Continent in case of a rupture with France. He also declared that this expedition would require a considerable force, but, on the other hand, would perhaps save a long and expensive war; and that if he had neglected seasonably to point out this opportunity and to warn the people of their danger, he would have been guilty of a breach of vigilence which it was his duty to keep.

This speech was referred, the next day, to a committee of sixteen members of the house and twelve of the council, with instructions to sit forthwith. On the fifteenth, and while this committee were sitting, a message was received from the Governor containing intelligence which arrived the night before, from Brigadier Dwight, that the French were attempting to build a fort at the carrying-place beyond Crown Point, and declaring that it would be too late, if the French were allowed to complete this fort, to attempt the measures proposed in his speech of the 13th, and concluding, "I hope, Gentlemen, you will not lose an Hour's Time in considering and coming to a Determination upon what I have recommended to you."

The committee reported the same day, that, while they were aware that the country of which the Governor proposed to take possession lay beyond the bounds of the province as lately defined, and that there were other governments which would be more benefited by the expedition than would Massachusetts, still the measure seemed more likely to assist the movements at the south and east than the addition of an equal force to the expeditions already contemplated against Nova Scotia, and the French on the Ohio. The committee, however, could not, in view of the burdens already resting on the province, recommend any present appropriation, but expressed the hope that the inability of the province to defray the charges of this expedition would not discourage the Governor from its prosecution.

The Governor replied immediately in another message, ostensibly to remove the impression that he had authority to organize and conduct this expedition at the expense of the Crown, or even to give assurance that the Home Government would deem it reasonable to assume such an expense.

He reminded them, however, that the expenses of the capture of Louisbourg had been reimbursed without any previous arrangement or promise, and intimated that his own personal influence would be exercised in their behalf, whenever the opportunity was presented.

* Morey.

On the 17th, this last message was referred to the same committee, which on the 18th, submitted a report, an extract from which is hereunder given, together with the draught of a message to the Governor, which is given in full:—

"February 18, 1755. The Committee's Report on the Governour's Speech of the 13th & Message of the 15th Curt

The Committee to whom was refer'd the Consideration of his Excellency's Messages of the 13th & 15th Instant, having maturely deliberated thereon, report as their Opinion;——

That the attempting to erect a strong Fort upon the Eminence near to the French Fort at Crown Point, or upon some other Parts of his Majesty's Lands, not far distant from the said Fort, is a Measure highly necessary to be forthwith pursued, in order to secure his Majesty's Territories from any further Encroachments of the French, and remove such Encroachments as have been already made.

That in Order to erecting such a Fortress, and to repel any Force that may be brought to oppose the erecting of the same, and to revenge any Hostilities or Insults that may be offered, during the Execution of this Design, an Army of at least Five Thousand Men will be necessary,

That His Excellency the Governour be desired, forthwith to make the necessary Preparation for such an Expedition, to appoint & commissionate a General Officer to command the same; To advise his Majesty's other Governments hereafter mentioned of this Design, and in such Manner as he shall think most effectual to urge them to join therein, and to raise their respective Proportion of Men as follows; vizt New Hampshire Six hundred Men, Connecticut One Thousand, Rhode Island Four hundred, New York Eight hundred, or such larger Proportion as each Government shall think proper.

That His Excellency be desired to endeavour, that his own Regiment or Sir William Pepperills, or both, be employed in this Service.

That as soon as it shall appear that the said Number of Five Thousand Men, Including those from this Province, shall be agreed to be raised, His Excellency be desired to cause to be enlisted Twelve hundred Men, * * * *

That His Excellency be desired likewise to make Application to the Government of New Jersies to raise an additional Number of Men in Proportion to the Circumstances of that Government to be employed in the Service aforesd and also to the Government of Pensilvania, urging them to contribute a Quantity of Provision to be transported to Albany for the Service of the Army. By Order ℘ J. OSBORNE.

In the House of Representatives, Read & Accepted. In Council; Read & Concur'd." —*Council Records, vol.* XX., *p.* 401.

"February 18, 1755. Committee's Report of a Message to the Governour on the Affair of Crown Point,

May it please your Excellency,—

From a Sense of Duty & Loyalty to his Majesty, and of the indispensable Obligations we are under, by all Ways and Means in our Power to promote his Majesty's Interest, and to defeat the Designs of his Enemies, we have come into a Resolution to desire your Excellency to engage in an Attempt to erect a Fortress near to the French Fort at Crown Point, and to repel and revenge any Hostilities that may be offered to his Majesty's Forces while they are employed in this Service; And we have done this in humble Trust & Confidence, that his Majesty will be graciously pleased to relieve us from the Charge of this Undertaking; your Excellency very justly observes that our Case is distinguished from that of other Governments; For should we sit still, and those Governments take upon themselves the whole Burthen of this Attempt; Yet, even their Charge would fall far short of their Proportion to what we have already sustained since these last Commotions raised by the French,

And although your Excellency has been pleased to tell us that you have no Authority from his Majesty to defrey the Charge of the proposed Expedition, yet we depend upon your Excellency's humble Application to his Majesty in our behalf,

We assure your Excellency that, at all Events, we will not leave your Excellency to be a Sufferer by any Engagements made at our desire; But we are sensible that unless his Majesty shall be graciously pleased to enable us to defray our part of the Charge of this Expedition, we shall necessarily be involved in Difficulties so great, that we despair of being extricated from them for a long Course of Years to come.

In the House of Representatives; Read & Ordered that Mr Tyng, Colo Brattle, Colo Choat, Colo Otis, and Colo Laurence with such as the honble Board shall join be a Committee to present this Address to His Excellency the Governour. In Council; Read & Concur'd, And John Osborne, Jacob Wendell, Samuel Watts & Sylvanus Bourn Esqrs are joined in the Affair."—*Ibid., p.* 402.

On the 25th of March, the Governor, in a speech to the Assembly, reported the result of applications made by his order to other governments to secure their co-operation, and also other matters of importance relating to the expedition, and laid before them the letters and other papers relating thereto. This speech was immediately referred to a committee, and on the next day the committee made a partial report, asking leave to sit again. Among other things, they reported that the Governor be requested forthwith to issue his proclamation encouraging the enlistment of forces for the expedition, and also that he be requested to secure the co-operation of as many of the Indians of the Six Nations as practicable.

On the 27th, the following vote was passed:—

"March 26, 1755. In the House of Representatives; Voted that Mr Speaker, Mr Welles Colo Brattle, Mr James Bowdoin, Capt Williams and Mr James Russell with such as the Honble Board shall join, be a Committee on the part of this Government to provide for the intended Expedition to the Westward a sufficient Quantity of Provisions and Warlike Stores, and other Things necessary; and that the Committee in procuring the same give the Preference to the Inhabitants and the Produce of this Province:——In Council; Read & Concur'd; And John Osborne Jacob Wendell, Samuel Watts, Ezekiel Chever, John Wheelwright, and Thomas Hutchinson Esqrs are joined in the Affair.——Consented to by the Governour."—*Council Records, vol.* XX., *p.* 427.

On the 28th, the Governor sent another message to both houses, calling attention to the vote of the previous session authorizing him to issue his proclamation for raising the Massachusetts quota, exclusive of the forces to be raised in New York, as soon as he should be informed of the consent of the other New England Governments to the proposed expedition, and declaring that advices from New York gave him no encouragement to hope that any men would be raised there (although he had every reason to expect that province would bear its part of the expense of the expedition) and giving notice that he should give orders for raising enough more men than had been assigned to Massachusetts, to equal her proportion of the deficiency caused by this failure of New York.

The next day the Assembly passed an order granting an additional bounty to soldiers enlisted, and fixing the limits of their service, and requesting the Governor to issue his proclamation accordingly. At the same time an order was passed for advanced pay to non-commissioned officers and privates, and also the following vote:—

"March 29, 1755. In the House of Representatives, Voted that His Excellency the Captain General be desired to enlist three hundred able bodied, effective Men for the Expedition to Crown Point, in addition to the twelve hundred already granted; & that they have the same Bounty & Wages in all Respects, as those heretofore ordered:——In Council; Read & Concur'd;——Consented to by the Governour."—*Council Records, vol. XX., p.* 432.

These votes and orders were followed by the Governor's proclamation of March 29th, which offered all the inducements to volunteers that had been promised in the votes and orders of the General Court, and on the same day an act to empower the province treasurer to borrow £5,000 to defray the expenses of the expedition westward, was signed by the Governor. (1754-55, chap. 32.)

At the same time an address to His Majesty for reimbursement was ordered to be prepared, and this order was consented to by the Governor.

General Braddock having arrived in Virginia, as commander-in-chief of the American forces, Governor Shirley was summoned thither to a conference with him and Commodore Keppel in which the representatives of other colonies joined. The Governor had communicated to the Assembly, at the opening of the 4th session, his intention to attend this conference, and soon after its close he left the province, to which he did not return until the thirteenth of May.

Meanwhile the enlistments proceeded, additional bounties being granted by an order of the General Court which was promulgated in a proclamation by the Lieutenant-Governor, and an increase of pay and rations for both officers and men was agreed upon.

At the opening of the next session, in a speech to the Assembly, the Governor informed them that both the eastern and western expeditions had met with the entire approbation of the General, and that everything necessary on his part for forwarding them had been immediately done. He then proceeded to disclose the plans of Braddock's campaign, including, besides the attack of the forts on the Ohio, the reduction of those at Niagara, which last undertaking had been intrusted to Shirley, to be carried on with two regiments already enlisted as regulars by authority of the Crown, and under the respective commands of himself and Sir Wm. Pepperrel. The latter regiment was already in motion, and the former he expected to embark for Albany in a few days, and to follow it in person by the middle of June at furthest.

Finding that Pepperrel's regiment would not, from its incompleteness, and by reason of losses from details for other purposes, furnish an available force of over four hundred men, the Governor, on his return from the south, had applied for and received from the government of New Jersey a re-enforcement of five hundred men, and now asked the Assembly of his own province if it would not be wise to have his corps of nineteen hundred men increased. This he hoped might be done without weakening the movement against Crown Point; but, at all events, he should proceed against Niagara, whether his force were increased or not. He also submitted letters and other papers from General Johnson in command of the expedition against Crown Point, calling for immediate action, and asked that the pay for officers in command of the Indian allies should be fixed, that provision should be made for building proper storehouses between Albany and the carrying-place to Crown Point, also for building batteaux and other vessels and constructing a road nearly twenty miles in length, and made the following call on the house for an appropriation:—

"Gentlemen of the House of Represent^ves——I must recommend it to you, forthwith to make the needful Supplies; for which Purpose I shall order the Committee of War to lay an Estimate before you of what Sums will be wanting to defray the Expence of the Expedition, & the Treasurer to lay before you a State of the Treasury."—*Extract from the Governor's speech to both houses, May* 30, 1755.—*Council Records, vol. XX., p.* 456.

The speech containing this recommendation was immediately referred to two joint committees, one of which, charged with the consideration of that part of the speech which relates to the several expeditions against the French, was ordered to sit forthwith.

This committee reported May 31st, approving the expedition against Niagara, and recommending that as many of the forces raised for the Crown Point expedition as the Governor should deem necessary, be employed in the first-named service, during the term of their enlistment, provided the province should be free from the expense of their transportation and subsistence; that the other governments concerned in the expedition against Crown Point should raise no objection; that the soldiers should voluntarily enlist in this service; and that not less than thirty-seven hundred men, exclusive of the Indians, should be engaged in the expedition against Crown Point. This report was accepted by both branches, and consented to by the Governor.

On the second of June the Governor sent another Message to the Assembly, disclaiming any thought of reducing the force to be employed against Crown Point; but observing that affairs between the English and French in America, were in a different position from what they had been, inasmuch as the design of the enemy, now, was not to harass any particular colony, but to extirpate the whole, and that the plan communicated by him in his speech at the beginning of the session was calculated to frustrate the enemy's extensive operations. He therefore asked the Assembly to consider, whether it was not necessary to increase the New England forces in order to serve the general interest, without regard to their own particular situation, seeing that the Assembly had, in their vote of May 31st, agreed that the movement against Niagara was an important part of the proposed plan, but yet had made their support of that movement conditional upon the securing a full complement of men to be engaged against Crown Point, while it was uncertain whether the other colonies would contribute their full quotas towards that expedition,—which left it doubtful if, under that vote, the expedition to Niagara would receive any considerable addition.

A committee was immediately appointed to draught an answer to the Governor's message, but before they reported, a vote was passed by both branches, and received the Governor's signature, "that there shall be no augmentation of the Provincial forces raised for the expedition to Crown Point."

On the third of June the committee's report was presented and acted upon as follows:—

"The Committee appointed to prepare a proper Answer to His Excellency's Message of the second Instant, reported the following Draught; Vizt

May it please Your Excellency,

We have considered with Attention your Excellency's Message of Yesterday, We are fully sensible of the formidable Designs of the French against his Majesty's Territories upon this Continent, and we think that the Plan which your Excellency has communicated to us, if the several Parts of it can be properly supported, is well calculated to defeat them. The Expedition to Crown Point, now made a Part of this Plan, has been undertaken by the Governments in New England, & those of New York, & New Jersey, with a Contribution of Provisions from Pensylvania; and your Excellency cannot wonder if we think ourselves in some Measure, peculiarly obliged to make all necessary Provision for the Success of it. About one third of the Forces to be employed in it are in the Pay of this Province. This is undoubtedly more than our Proportion, whether we consider our Estates or the Number of our Inhabitants; & it is much more so, if any Regard be had to the very great Charges, to which we are exposed for our Defence. The Forces raised by New Jersies have since been destined for Niagara; and we have Consented that your Excellency on certain Conditions should employ part of the other Forces in the same Service, but we don't apprehend it will be safe to make any further Reduction. We agree with your Excellency that the Colonies have one common Interest at Stake; and that a Defeat of the Forces, wherever it may happen, may be of fatal Consequence. We wish the Governments to the Southward had contributed to this General Interest, in Proportion, as those to the Northward have done; If this had been the Case no Additional Force w^d now be wanting. As for this Province, It is the Opinion of the best Judges that at least an eighth part of the Males capable of bearing Arms, including every Rank & Order of Men, have enlisted into the Service, to act offensively against the Enemy; and the Defence of our Frontiers, which are already attacked, will require a large Number of those that remain. We have taken as many Men into our Pay as we can find either Money or Credit to Support; And it is utterly impossible for us to comply with your Excellency's Proposal; or to make any further Addition to the Forces to be employed in one or other of the Expeditions. At the same time we are sensible of the Necessity that the Expedition to Niagara should be well supported; and it is not only a Regard to your Excellency's Person, who has undertook in the Command of it but a real Concern for His Majesty's Service, wch makes us wish that your Excellency had it in your Power to strengthen it to any other Parts of the Plan, & to increase the Forces in some other Way than by the Assistance of this Government.

In Council; Read & Ordered that this Report be Accepted; & that Mr Danforth & Dr Pynchon, with such as the Honble House shall join be a Committee to wait on His Excellency therewith,—In the House of Representatives; Read & Concur'd, & Mr Cooper, Mr James Bowdoin & Mr Tyng are joined in the Affair."—*Council Records, vol.* XX , *p.* 460.

On the fifth of June, the Governor sent another message to the Assembly, calling attention to the latter part of his opening speech, in which he urged the necessity of providing supplies for carrying on the war, and on the next day sent still another message accompanied by an extract from a letter which he had received the night before from the Governor of Connecticut, containing proposals respecting the provisions contributed by Pennsylvania. On these proposals the Governor asked the immediate action of the Assembly, so that he might send an answer by the return of the express. He also intimated his wish to send by the same express an account of their doings upon the subjects contained in the letter of Maj. Gen. Johnson, and urged the necessity of immediate action thereupon, so "that he [Johnson] and the Colonies may know it."

The conclusion of this message, and the action of the Assembly thereupon, were as follows:—

"The Season is so far advanced, & the Forces destined to Crown Point should keep Pace with those designed for Niagara, in order to secure as much as may be the Success of both Expeditions. The first Division of the latter of these Forces will march on Monday next for Providence, in the Colony of Rhode Island where Transports are waiting for them, & they will be all imbarked in seven days from that Time, & sail for Albany, & from thence proceed directly for Oswego; Their Battoes for transporting them & their Stores being in such Forwardness as to be ready to receive them upon their arrival at Schenectady.

I would not mention to you how much General Johnson's Success in ingaging the Indians depends upon your making Provision for that Purpose.

In the House of Representatives; Read & Ordered that Col^o Lawrence, Col^o Williams, Capt Livermore, Mr Tyng & Mr Taylour with such as the Honble Board shall join, be a Committee to take the foregoing Message from His Excellency under Consideration, together with the Extracts from Governour Wentworths & Governour Fitch's Letters, & report thereon; & that the Committee be directed to sit forthwith;——In Council; Read & Concur'd, & John Otis, Thomas Hutchinson, Eleazer Porter & William Brattle Esq^rs are joined in the Affair."—*Extract from the Governor's Message to both houses.—Council Records, vol. XX, p.* 464.

On the ninth of June, the bill for supplying the treasury with fifty thousand pounds was passed to be engrossed, and was signed by the Governor two days later.

Chap. 6. "June 13, 1755. A Message was brought up from the House of Representatives, by Robert Hooper Esqr & others to acquaint his Excellency, that the House were informed, that there were divers Vessells, now loading at Newbury, with Provisions, (supposed to be designed for the French) under the Pretext of Carrying them to Newfoundland; and therefore desiring His Excellency, to give effectual Orders for preventing all Vessells, laden with Provisions or Warlike Stores from sailing out of any Place in this Province, untill further Order, and that he would write to the Governours of the other Colonies to do the same, & to the Commanding Officer at Newfoundland, to use his best Endeavours to prevent this Trade."—*Council Records, vol. XX., p.* 478.

"June 14, 1755. In Council; Voted that William Brattle Esqr with such as the Honble House shall join, be a Committee to wait on His Excellency, desiring him to acquaint the other Governments with what this Court hath done, respecting the transportation of Provisions, and Warlike Stores out of this Province, & to urge them to join in the same Measures;——In the House of Representatives; Read & Concur'd, and M^r. Cooper and M^r. Tyng are joined in the Affair."—*Ibid., p.* 484.

"August 16, 1755. In the House of Representatives, Whereas the House are informed that by the Acts of the Southern Governments Vessels are restrained from clearing out for this Province with Provisions; Which Prohibition may occasion a great Scarcity of Provisions among us, and thereby not only distress our own Inhabitants, but render it very difficult for the Government to supply our Forces; Therefore,

Voted that His Honour the Lieutenant Governour be desired to [write] to the Southern Governments, desiring of them that Liberty may be given to any Vessels bound to the Ports of Boston or Salem to clear out for those Ports with Provisions, sufficient Security being first given that the same shall be landed at one or the other of the said Ports; In Council; Read & Concur'd."—*Ibid., p.* 524.

Chap. 7. "June 18, 1755. In the House of Representatives; Ordered that Col^o Cotton, James Bowdoin Esqr & Mr James Russell with such as the Honble Board shall join, be a Committee to take under Consideration & project some more effectual Method to prevent Supplies of Provisions & Warlike Stores being carried to the French: In Council; Read & Concur'd, And Eleazer Porter & William Brattle Esq^rs are joined in the Affair."—*Council Records, vol. XX., p.* 492.

* * * *

"The Secretary delivered the following Message from his Excellency;

Gentlemen of the Council & House of Representatives,

By the French Vessels hovering upon our Coast, it seems highly probable, that they are very short of Provisions at Louisbourgh & other Northern Parts; and in these Circumstances there is nothing (under God) can have a greater Tendency to promote the Success of our Enterprizes, now on Foot, than effectually to prevent the French from receiving any Supplies from the English in these Parts. And as there are so many persons among us that are so false to the Interests of their Country, & so mad after this pernicious Trade, that no Laws will restrain them; and as there are divers small Harbours especially on our Eastern Coast, where these Traders may meet with the French Vessels & Carry on the Trade without Discovery, I must recommend it to you to provide for the Charge of a small, armed Vessel, sufficiently manned to cruize upon our Coast, in Parts most suspected; that they may intercept the Traders in this unlawful & mischievous Commerce: And whatsoever may be lawfully done for encouraging the Commander & Company of such armed Vessel out of the Captures & Seizures, made by them & legally condemned, I shall readily join with you in the proper Way of providing for it.

Gentlemen, This Affair requires the greatest Dispatch. In the House of Representatives; Read & Ordered that the foregoing Message be committed to the Committee appointed Yesterday to project some more effectual Method to prevent Supplies of Provisions & Warlike Stores being carried to the French; for Consideration, & that they report what they think proper for this Court to do thereon, & that the said Committee sit forthwith.—In Council; Read & Concur'd."—*Ibid., p.* 494.

"June 19, 1755. Report of the Committee on his Excellency's Message referring to a Guard Vessel for Preventing the carrying Provisions to the French. In the House of Representatives; Read & Ordered that this Report be recommitted; and that it be an Instruction to said Committee to take under Consideration a Conditional Embargo on Provisions & Warlike Stores for a limitted Time, the Committee to sit forthwith;—In Council; Read & Concur'd; And John Erving Esqr is appointed of the Committee in the Room of Eleazer Porter Esqr now absent."—*Ibid., p.* 496.

"June 21, 1755. Report for preventing Supplies going to the French. vizt The Committee to whom was referred his Excellency's Message of the 18th Cur^t with Respect to preventing the Supplying the French with Provisions &c^a beg leave to report vizt—That an Embargo be laid on all Vessels loaded with Provisions or Warlike Stores, unless what is necessary for the Voyage, (Fish excepted) for the Space of one Month, provided nevertheless that his Excellency the Governour or Commander in Chief, for the Time being, with the Advice of the Council may permit Supplies to be sent to the Army or Navy, with necessary Provisions within that time. And that His Excellency be desired to write forthwith to the other Governments, informing them of this Determination of this Government, desiring them immediately to come into the same Resolution, for three Months; Which if they should comply with, That the like Embargo be continued for three Months by this Government also.

The Committee beg Leave, further to report, That his Excellency be desired to write to Governour Lawrence, requesting him to send to Boston, one of the King's armed Vessels, to prevent any French Trade being carried on upon our Coasts, as well as to escort any Vessel or Vessels that may be sent to the Army or Navy with Provisions or Warlike Stores: All which is humbly submitted;— JOHN ERVING.

In the House of Representatives; Read & Ordered that this Report be accepted, and that a Bill be brought in accordingly. In Council; Read & Concur'd;——Consented to by the Governour."—*Ibid.*, *p.* 501.

* * * *

"In the House of Representatives; Voted that an Embargo be laid on all Vessels that have any Provisions or Warlike Stores on board except what may be necessary for their respective Voyages, till Wednesday next. In Council; Read & Concur'd;——Consented to by the Governour."—*Ibid.*, *p.* 501.

"June 25, 1755. The Bill for preventing the Exportation of Provision & Warlike Stores from any Part of this Province, was brought up from the House of Representatives, with their Concurrence, with Amendments as taken into a new Draught. Which were read and agreed to by the Council."—*Ibid.*, *p.* 505.

* * * *

"A Message was brought up from the House by Col° Rowland Cotton to propose unto the Board that the forementioned Act should be printed in To Morrow's News Paper, which was agreed to by the Council, and Orders were given for printing said Act accordingly."—*Ibid.*, *p.* 506.

August 12, 1755. A Petition of Joshua Winslow, Esqr of Boston Merch^t Praying that a Vessel belonging to him bound for Surinam, Duncan Ingraham Master may be permitted to proceed thither upon his giving Bond at the Impost Office.

In the House of Representatives; Read & Ordered that Thomas Foster Esqr Mr Tyng, and Col° Miller, with such as the hon^ble Board shall join be a Committee to take this Petition under Consideration; and report what they think proper for this Court to do thereon, ——In Council; Read & Concur'd, And Samuel Watts and John Erving Esq^rs are joined in the Affair.

On which Petition the Committee reported as follows; vizt

The Committee to whom was referred the above Pet^n beg Leave to report, That they are humbly of Opinion that the Prayer thereof be granted, and that the Commissioner of Impost be and hereby is impowered to take Bond of One Thousand Pounds Sterling, of the Petitioner, for the Landing the Provisions mentioned in the Petition, within the Port of Surinam; Provided the Quantity exceed not Eighty Barrells; and that the Chief Officer of said Vessel on his Return, make Oath that the said Provisions were actually landed within the Port aforesaid.

All which is humbly submitted,—— Per SAM^L WATTS per Order.

In Council; Read & Ordered that the Report on the other Side be Accepted.——In the House of Representatives; Read & Concur'd, Consented to by the Lieu^t Govern^r."—*Ibid.*, *p.* 515.

Chap. 8. "April 16, 1756. In the House of Representatives; Ordered that there be allowed & paid out of the Publick Treasury to Mr James Russell Commissioner of the Stamp Duties the Sum of One Hundred & Sixty Pounds in Consideration of his Services in said Trust the Year past. In Council; Read & Concur'd——Consented to by the Governour."—*Council Records, vol. XXI.*, *p.* 167.

"March 22, 1758. In the House of Representatives. Resolved That all Persons in this Province who purchased any stamped Papers or Blanks of the Commissioners of the Stamps during the continuance of the late Act for that Purpose, and who were possessed of the same or any part thereof unimproved at the expiration of said Act, shall upon application to the said Commissioner have the Value of said Stamps paid or remitted to him; the Accounts of such Stamps being presented under Oath to said Commissioner within six Months from this time.

In Council——Read and Nonconcurred."—*Ibid.*, *vol. XXII.*, *p.* 291.

Chap. 11. "September 8, 1755. A Memorial of William Cooper of Boston Merch^t Shewing that he has two Vessells bound for the Bay of Honduras, where it is necessary to carry more Provisions than is usual to be carried on Common Voyages, Therefore praying that he may be licenced to export the Provisions in the Memorial particularly mentioned, upon giv^g Bond according to Law.

In the House of Representatives; Read & Ordered that the Prayer of this Petition be granted, and that the Memorialist give Bond with two sufficient Sureties, in the Sum of One Thousand Pounds for the delivery of the said Provisions in the Bay, except so much as may be necessary for the Use of the People on board the said Vessells, (the Danger of the Seas excepted) And that the Petitioner make Oath before the Commiss^r of Impost, that the Provisions on board said Vessels are designed for no other Place than the Bay & for the Common Supplies of the said Vessell, & that the Masters of said Vessels, upon their Return, shall make Oath, (if required,) that they have delivered the same at the Bay aforesaid, except what was reserved for the Use of the said Vessel:—

In Council; Read & Concur'd;——Consented to by the Lieu^t Govern^r."—*Council Records, vol. XX.*, *p.* 530.

"September 8, 1755. A Memorial of Timothy Fitch & John Phillips jun^r of Boston Merchants, shewing that they are fitting out the Brigantines Neptune & Elizabeth for the Bay of Honduras, where it is necessary to carry more Provisions than is usual on common Voyages, Therefore Praying that they may be licenced to export the Provisions in the Memorial particularly mentioned, upon their giving Bond according to Law.

In Council; Read & Ordered that the Prayer of the Memorial be granted; & that the Petitioners give Bond with sufficient Sureties, in the Sum of One Thousand Pounds for each Vessel, for the delivery of the said Provisions in the Bay of Honduras, except so much as may be necessary for the Use of the People on board said Vessells (the Danger of the Seas excepted) and that the Petitioners make Oath before the Commissioner of Impost, that the Provisions on Board said Vessels are designed for no other Place than the said Bay, and the common Supplies of the Vessels, and that the Masters of said Vessels on their Return shall make Oath (if required) that they have delivered the same at the Bay aforesaid, excepting what was reserved for the Vessells Use.

In the House of Representves Read & Concur'd;—Consented to by the Lieut Govr."—*Ibid., p.* 531.

"September 8, 1755. A Petition of Thomas Boylstone of Boston Mercht shewing that he is fitting out the Brigantine Friendship for Surinam, Praying that he may be allowed to send thither, Fifty Barrells of Flour as part of her Cargo.

In Council; Read & Ordered that the Prayer of the Petition be granted; And that the Petitioner be allowed to ship the Fifty Barrells of Flour within mentioned, for the Port of Surinam, he giving Bond to the Commissioner of Impost, in One Thousand Pounds Sterling for the delivery of the said Flour at the Port aforesaid, and that the Chief Officer of said Vessel, on his Return, make Oath of the Delivery of said Flour accordingly—— In the House of Representatives; Read & Concur'd.

Consented to by the Lieutent Governr."—*Ibid.*

Chap. 12. "June 26, 1755. In the House of Representatives; Resolved that His Excellency the Captain General be desired to commission proper Officers for raising by Enlistment, not exceeding Five hundred Men, to march to Crown Point, to reinforce the Army destined there, if by Advice from the Army had in the Recess of this Court it shall be adjudged by the Commander in Chief for the Time being, with the Advice of the Council, That it is necessary that the Army should be so reinforced:—That each Man be paid a Dollar upon his Enlistment; and in Case of their being actually engaged in the Service, that they be allowed the same Bounty, (including the Dollar) Pay & Subsistence as the Forces already destined there, have; they finding their own good & sufficient Arms: The Pay and Subsistence to commence from the Time of their Marching; and that they be discharged as soon as the Place shall be reduced, or the Nature of the Case will admit of, or not exceeding the Time the other Forces are enlisted for; That the enlisting Officer be allowed half a Dollar for each Man so inlisted, and that his Excellency the Govr be desired to inform the other Governments of this Resolve, In Council; Read & Concur'd;——Consented to by the Governour."—*Council Records, vol. XX., p.* 507.

"August 6, 1755. But I must recommend to your first & immediate Consideration the Subject Matter of the last Letter received from the Governour, and especially that part of it which respects the Five hundred Men, ordered to be enlisted & kept in Readiness for the Service of the Expedition to Crown Point: His Excellency's Arguments for the Destination and immediate Employment of this additional Force are so weighty and Conclusive, that I need add nothing to induce you to express your Approbation of his Proposal; I have no certain Account what Proportion of those Men are enlisted, but I daily expect a Return from the several Officers."—*Extract from the Lieut. Governor's speech to the Assembly.—Ibid., p.* 510.

"August 7, 1755. In the House of Representatives; Ordered that Mr Speaker, Colo Otis, Mr Foster, Mr Cooper, & Capt Livermore with such as the Honble Board shall join, be a Committee to take under Consideration his Honour's Speech, with the Papers referr'd to therein, & report thereon as soon as may be. In Council; Read & Concur'd; And Ezekiel Chever, James Minot, Andrew Oliver & Thomas Hutchinson Esqrs are joined in the Affair."—*Ibid , p.* 511.

"August 8, 1755. On the Report of the Comtee on the Lieut Governours Speech, In the House of Representatives; Read & Accepted, And, Ordered that there be forthwith raised Three hundred Men to reinforce the Expedition to Crown Point, and that there be paid to each of said Three hundred Men, Twenty four Shillings by Way of Bounty, and Twelve Shillings more upon his producing sufficient Fire Arms at the first Muster, and that the Pay or Wages shall commence at the Time of Enlisting, and the Subsistence from the Time of marching from their Place of Dwelling to the Place of Rendezvouz; and that no Deduction shall be made of their Pay for any of the Bounty they so receive; And that there be allowed three Shillings to the Officer for each of the said Three hundred Men enlisted by him; And it is further Ordered that the like Bounty & Encouragement be allowed to each of the Five hundred Men, to whom this Court in their late Session allowed Six Shillings to hold himself in Readiness for the Service, Including the said Six Shillings; And His Honour the Lieutenant Governour is desired to give Orders for said Men to march in Companies as fast as they are compleated, to join the other Forces already gone, and to acquaint the other Governments concerned in this Expedition of these Resolutions, and urge them to raise a proportionable Number of Men for the said Service. In Council; Read & Concur'd;——Consented to by the Lt Governour."—*Ibid.*

"September 5, 1755. Mr Speaker and the House being accordingly come up, His Honour made the following Speech to both Houses, vizt

Gentlemen of the Council & House of Representatives, I have received late Advices from Major General Johnson which I shall order to be laid before you: And they are of such Importance, that I could by no Means think it proper to delay communicating them, to you untill the Time to which the General Court stood prorogued; And therefore I have called you together in a Manner somewhat extraordinary, but yet absolutely necessary for the publick Service

You will perceive, Gentlemen, That, not only the Provincial Forces fall Short of the proposed Number, but also that there is a probability of a much greater Forces prepared to resist them than we ever imagined that there would be; and athô our Troops appear to be animated with true Courage, and to be zealously bent to maintain the Honour of their King, and to remove and prevent all Encroachments upon his Majesty's Dominions, yet it will be Presumption to suffer them to engage with any great Inequality of Numbers, when we have it in our Power to prevent it.

I must therefore most earnestly recommend it to you to come into some vigorous & speedy Resolution, which may enable me to raise an additional Number of Men to join our other Forces without any Delay. I leave you to consider what Encouragement is proper & what Measures are necessary to be taken: But certainly something further must be done than has yet been done; for I have not been able to compleat the Eight hundred Men you desired me to raise in your last Session, notwithstanding my utmost Endeavours for that Purpose.

* * * *

The Secretary laid before the two Houses the Letters received from Major General Johnson, referred to in his Honour's Speech, with other publick Letters received in the Recess of the Court.

In the House of Representatives, Resolved that Two Thousand Men be raised as soon as may be, in addition to the Forces already ordered for the Crown Point Expedition; and that Mr Speaker, Mr Trowbridge, Judge Russell, Mr Tyng, Col^o^ Williams, Col^o^ Otis, & Mr Cooper with such as the Honble Board shall join, be a Committee to take under Consideration some suitable Method for raising the said Recruits, & report thereon, the said Committee to sit forthwith:—In Council; Read & Concur'd, and Benjamin Lynde, John Cushing, James Minot, Isaac Royal, Benjamin Lincoln & William Brattle Esq^rs^ are joined in the Affair."—*Ibid*, *pp*. 526, 527.

"September 6, 1755. In the House of Represent^ves^: Ordered that the Printers of the several News Papers be prohibited from publishing any Thing relating to the Expedition now carrying on against Crown Point without Permission of this Court, or of the Governour & Council in the Recess of the Court. In Council; Read & Concur'd;—Consented to by the Lieu^t^ Governour."—*Ibid.*, *p*. 527.

"September 6, 1755. Committee's Report about raising of Soldiers; vizt The Committee appointed to consider of some suitable Method of raising Two Thousand Men to reinforce the Army, destined to Crown Point, having attended that Service are humbly of Opinion that His Honour the Lieuten^t^ Governour be desired forthwith to give Orders for enlisting Two Thousand Men, to reinforce the said Army, under the Command of General Johnson upon the same Bounty, Pay & Subsistence that those already enlisted have received, or are entitled to, except that no Part of the Wages be advanced, as was to those who have hitherto enlisted. That His Honour be also desired forthwith to give Orders for Mustering the several Companies both of Horse and Foot in all the Regiments in this Province (except those in the County of York) on the fifteenth Instant; and if the two Thousand are not enlisted by that Time, that the Number be compleated by an Impress to be made as soon as may be: And that His Honour be desired in proportioning the present Levies, to order Five hundred Men to be raised out of the several Troops of Horse, either by their inlisting or Impresses out of them, the remaining Fifteen hundred Men out of the Foot Companies; Regard to be had to such Regiments as have done most in furnishing Men for his Majesty's Service, for the two Years last past.

The Committee further propose a Bill to be brought in to oblige all the Troopers & Foot Soldiers in the several Regiments, to appear on such Muster on the Penalty of Twenty Pounds, Lawful Money, and also such as are impressed to attend the Service aforesaid.

All wch is humbly submitted,—In the Name & by Order of the Com^tee^

BENJ^A^ LYNDE.

In the House of Representatives; Read & Ordered that this Report be accepted, And that Mr Trowbridge, Judge Russell & Mr Gridley with such as the Honble Board shall join, be a Committee to prepare & bring in a Bill accordingly. In Council; Read & Concurd; & Samuel Danforth & Stephen Sewall Esq^rs^ are joined in the Affair."—*Ibid.*

"September 9, 1755. In the House of Representatives; Whereas there is an absolute Need of a greater Number of Persons in the Expedition against Crown Point, that understand the Artillery.

Voted that Col^o^ Richard Gridley be desired, for the Necessity of the Service to assist there in that Part, and that he have the same Monthly pay for it, which he received for his Services in the Train of Artillery at the Seige of Louisbourgh; and further

Voted that His Honour the Lieuten^t^ Governour be desired to appoint him Colonel of one of the Regiments to be raised here for that Expedition, and that he receive his Pay in that Capacity too. And that an Express be immediately dispatched for his Answer.—In Council; Read & Concur'd."—*Ibid.*, *p*. 531.

"September 9, 1755. In the House of Representatives; Voted that His Honour the Lieu^t^ Govr be desired to issue a Proclamation, to encourage the Two Thousand Additional Troops to enlist for the Crown Point Expedition; promising to each able bodied effective Man who shall inlist on or before the fifteenth Instant, Four Dollars upon Enlistment, and two Dollars more to every Man who shall appear at the first Muster with a good Gun to carry with him, also promising a good Blanket to each Man, & Twenty Six Shillings & eight pence per Month Wages while in the Service, and that such who shall enlist as aforesaid shall be discharged preferably sooner than those who may be impressed, and as soon as the Men already enlisted shall be discharged, And that his Honour be requested to write to Major General Johnson, desiring him to dismiss a proportionable Number of the Troops of this Government, compared with the Troops of the other Governments as soon as the Service will admit of it; And that in discharging such Troops, he would prefer the Enlisted Men to those who may be impress'd:—In Council; Read & Concur'd."—*Ibid.*, *p*. 532.

"By the Honourable Spencer Phips Esqr Lieutenant Governour and Commander in Chief in and Over His Majesty's Province of the Massachusets Bay in New England.

A Proclamation.

Whereas upon Consideration of the great importance of the Expedition now carrying on against the French Fort at Crown Point and the great necessity of having a Force sufficient (by the divine Blessing) for the Execution of the said design; the Great and General Court or Assembly of this Province have made provision for Two thousand recruits of the Army under the Command of Major General Johnson, and have desired of Me, that I would issue Orders for raising the same accordingly; And have likewise voted the following encouragement to all such able bodied effective Men, as shall inlist in the said Service, Non Commission Officers as well as Soldiers. Viz

That each Man shall have a good Blanket or other warm Cloathing equivalent given him; and shall be allowed twenty six shillings ℔ month Wages, during the Service.

That there likewize shall be paid to every able bodied man who shall inlist on or before the 15 Instant, Four dollars upon inlistment and two dollars more to every such Man who shall appear at the first muster with a good Gun to carry with him.

And that whenever the Service will admit of any of the Troops being discharged the Voluntiers shall have the preference; and that such as shall now inlist, shall be discharged as soon as those who have already inlisted.

I do therefore hereby promise in behalf of his Majesty's said Province of the Massachusets Bay, that there shall be a full compliance with the Engagement made in each and every the Articles aforesaid.

Given at the Council Chamber in Boston the ninth day of September 1755. in the twenty-ninth Year of the Reign of Our Sovereign Lord George the Second, by the Grace of God of Great Britain, France and Ireland, King, Defender of the Faith &c^a^.

By Order of His Honour the
Lieutenant Governour with the S. PHIPS.
Advice of the Council
J. WILLARD Sec^ry^

God Save the King."—*Records of Civil Commissions; in Secretary's Office, vol.* 2., *p.* 279.

Chap. 14. "June 11, 1755. In the House of Representatives; Voted. that his Excellency the Captain General & Governour be desired immediately to declare War against the Arrasaguntacook Tribe of Indians, and all the Tribes of Indians Eastward and Northward of Piscataqua River, the Penobscot Tribe only excepted,

* * * *

That for the Defence of the Eastern Frontiers, a marching Army be raised by enlistment, consisting of three hundred Men exclusive of Officers, That they be continually employed in Scouting, & that their Destination be as follows;——That Fifty Men be employed in Scouting from Lebanon to Saco River; Sixty Men from Saco River to New Boston by the Way of Pearsons & Hobbs Town & New Glocester, Ninety Men from New Boston to Frankfort; One hundred Men from Frankfort to the Truckhouse on St Georges River;——

* * * *

That there be but Two Commission Officers, vizt a Captain & Lieutenant, to a Company of not less than Forty five Men, That the Establishment be for Five Months to commence from the twentieth day of June Instant & no longer, That the Pay & Subsistence of the Soldiers, that may be enlisted as aforesaid, commence upon the Day of their Enlistment; & that an Establishment be made accordingly,

Also Voted that Fort Halifax & the Store House at Cushnoc be garrisoned with Eighty Men & no more; Fort Brunswick, Five Men & no more;——Fort Frederick at Pemaquid, with Twenty Men & no more,——The Truck House at St Georges, with Forty three Men & no more;——The Truck House at Saco with Fifteen Men, & no more.

* * * *

And for an Additional Security to the Western Frontiers, Voted that there be four Men at Fort Dummer, & no more;——At Fort Massachusetts Forty Men & no more;——At Pontoosuck, Eleven Men & no more;——For the three Garrisons at Charlemont, Twenty four Men & no more;—At the two Garrisons at Colrain, Twenty four Men & no more;——At Northfield & Greenfield, Twenty Men & no more,

And that the Pay of the Officers & Soldiers in the several Forts & Garrisons be the same as was provided by the last Establishment made for said Forts & Garrisons.

And that if in the Judgment of the Captain General, He shall hereafter find it necessary, that there be a Number of Men employed in Scouting between the Rivers of Connecticut & Merrimack, that he be desired to raise Thirty Men by Inlistment, and destine them there for that Purpose, for the Time aforesaid; And that the same Pay & Subsistence & Bounty be allowed them, as are allowed to the Marching Forces proposed to be raised on the Eastern Frontiers; and that an Establishment be made accordingly In Council; Read & Concur'd;——Consented to by the Governour."—*Council Records, vol. XX., pp.* 475, 476.

"June 14, 1755. In the House of Representatives; Voted that there be an Addition of Fifteen Men for the Service of the Western Frontiers, to be employed as the Captain General shall order; And that, to prevent an Impress, there be a Bounty of Three Dollars per Man, allowed to each Man that finds his own Gun; The Money to be paid into the Hands of Israel Williams Esqr for that Service he to be accountable. In Council; Read & Concur'd;——Consented to by the Governour.

In the House of Representatives; Resolved that in Order to prevent an Impress of Men, there be a Bounty of Three Dollars per Man to Fifteen Men who shall inlist for Fort Massachusetts & find their own Gun, the said Fifteen Men to be part of the Forces already allowed on the Western Frontiers, the Money to be paid into the hands of Israel Williams Esqr for that Service, He to be accountable: In Council; Read & Concur'd;——Consented to by the Governour."—*Ibid., p* 484.

"August 14, 1755. In the House of Representatives; Voted that His Honour the Commander in Chief be desired to give Orders for the enlisting Ten Men, as an addition to the thirty Men already ordered to scout between Connecticut & Merrimack Rivers, the said Ten Men to be employed in said Service for a Term not exceeding Six Weeks. In Council; Read & Concur'd;——Consented to by the Lieu^t^ Governour."—*Ibid., p.* 519.

"August 15, 1755. A Petition of Nathan Willard Commander of Fort Dummer, shewing that the Number of the Garrison Soldiers there is so reduced, as renders it hazardous that upon the Appearance of any Body of the Enemy it will fall into their Hands, Praying that the said Garrison may be reinforced,

In the House of Representatives; Read & Voted that his Honour the Commander in Chief be desired to give Directions to the Memorialist Nathan Willard to enlist Six Men, for a Term not exceeding Six Weeks, as an Augmentation of the Forces already posted at Fort Dummer; None of the said Six Men being Inhabitants of that Place, or of the Lands round about the same except Daniel Sergeant, who is now there; And that each of the said Six Men be paid One Dollar, as a Bounty on their Enlistment as aforesaid. In Council; Read & Concur'd;——Consented to by the Lieu^t Governour."—*Ibid., p* 522.

"October 28th 1755. In the House of Representatives; Voted, That His Honor the Lieu^t Governor & Commander in Chief be desired to issue his Proclamation, remanding to their respective Posts all such persons belonging to this Government, and able of body, who were enlisted into his Majesties service in the expedition against Crown Point, and are now absent on Furlough;—Also, That his Honour be desired to give Orders that all Persons who are enlisted and receive the Province Bounty, or were impressed into the said service, and not afterwards excused, who did not actually proceed thereon, be forthwith sent to the Army; Also that he would give orders to the Colonels or Chief Officers of the several Regiments, to make enquiry who, belonging to their respective Regiments, are absent from their duty; and to take effectual care that they repair to the Army without delay. In Council; Read and Concurred."—*Ibid., vol. XXI., p.* 17.

"Province of the Massachusetts Bay By His Honour Spencer Phips Esqr Lieutenant Governour and Commander in Chief of the said Province.

A Proclamation.

For his Majesty's Service, and in pursuance of the Desire of his Majesty's Council, and the House of Representatives to me signified by their Vote of the 28th Instant I do hereby strictly require all Persons who have Inlisted into His Majesty's Service in the Expedition against Crown Point, and have receiv'd the Province Bounty, or that were impress'd into that Service, and have not actually proceeded thereon, nor been duly excused therefrom; as also, all such persons, belonging to this Government; and able of Body, who have been in his Majesty's Service in that Expedition, and are now absent on Furlough, that they forthwith repair to the Army under the command of Major General Johnson, and attend their duty there, as they would avoid being proceeded against, with the utmost Rigour of Law.——

Given at Boston the twenty ninth day of Octoberr 1755, and in the twenty ninth year of the Reign of our Sovereign Lord George the Second by the Grace of God of Great Britain, France, & Ireland, King Defender of the Faith &c.

By His Honour's Command

THO^S CLARKE Dp^ty Secr^y S. PHIPS.

God save the King."—*Records of Civil Commissions; in Secretary's Office, vol.* 2, *p.* 288.

Chap. 15. "February 18, 1756. In the House of Representatives; Voted that such Officers & Soldiers as shall go into his Majesty's Service in the proposed Expedition shall not be taxed for their Polls the present Year. And that the several towns which shall [exempt?] such Officers & Soldiers shall receive out of the Publick Treasury an equivalent thereto; and that publick Notice be given thereof accordingly——In Council Read & Concur'd——Consented to by the Governour."—*Council Records, vol. XXI., p.* 95.

Chap. 16. "Novr 4th 1755. A Petition of John Schollay, of Boston, praying for liberty from this Court to Ship off three barralls of Gun Powder in the Brigantine Peggy for North Carolina, where it is much wanted——In the House of Representatives; Read and Ordered, that the Prayer of the Petition be so far granted, as that the Pet^r be allowed to Ship off the Powder within mentioned in the said Vessell he giving Bond with sufficient sureties in the sum of One thousand Pounds for the delivery of the said Powder in North Carolina. In Council; Read and Concur'd.—Consented to by the Lt Govr."—*Council Records, vol. XXI., p.* 25.

"By the Honble Spencer Phips Esqr Lieutenant Governor & Comm^r in Chief of his Majesty's Province of the Massachusetts Bay in New England.

A Proclamation

Whereas An Act was made and passed by the Great & General Court or Assembly of the Province aforesaid at their Session held the twenty fourth day of September last, Entitled an Act for preventing the Exportation of Provisions and Warlike Stores out of this Province, Which Act was to continue untill the first day of December next; and therein it was also provided and enacted 'That if the Governor or Commander in Chief for the Time being shall see fit with the Advice & Consent of the Council to issue a Proclamation, prohibiting the Exportation of Provisions or Warlike Stores out of this Province for any time after the said first day of December next, not exceeding the first day of March next after, the Master & Owner & Owners Factor & Factors of any Vessel or Vessels on board of which such Provisions or Warlike Stores shall be exported contrary to such Proclamation, shall be respectively liable to the same Pains and Penalties as if the same had been exported before the said first day of Decem^r contrary to this Act.'

And whereas the said Great & General Court did at their Session held the twenty second of October following, pass an Act, entitled, An Act to prevent the Subjects of the French King being supplied with Provisions, Which Act was to continue during the Continuance of the Act first mentioned.

Upon due Consideration of the said Acts & the State of Affairs in relation to the Matters contained therein. I have thought fit with the Advice & Consent of his Majesty's Council of this Province to prohibit the Exportation of Provisions or Warlike Stores from any Port of this Province untill after the first day of January next and all persons concerned are required at their Peril to govern themselves accordingly, to order that the aforesaid Act entitled, An Act for preventing the Exportation of Provisions & Warlike Stores out of this Province & likewise the Act, entitled, An Act to prevent the Subjects of the French King being supplied with Provisions (herein before mentioned) shall be and hereby are Declared to be and remain in full Force & Virtue untill the first day of January next; and all Persons whatsoever are required strictly to conform themselves thereunto.

Given at the Council Chamber in Boston the twenty eight day of Novr 1755, and in the twenty ninth Year of the Reign of Our Sovereign Lord George the Second by the Grace of God of Great Britain France and Ireland King, Defender of the Faith &c.

By Order His Honour the Lieutenant Governor with the Advice and Consent of the Council S: PHIPS.

J. WILLARD Secry.

God Save the King."—*Records of Civil Commissions; in Secretary's Office, vol. 2, p. 291.*

"January 20, 1756. In the House of Representatives; Voted that the Lieut Governour & Commander in Chief be desired with the Advice & Consent of the Council to Issue a Proclamation forbidding the Exportation of Provisions or Warlike Stores out of this Province for a further time agreeable to the Power given by an Act passed this Court in September last—In Council Read & Concur'd."—*Council Records, vol. XXI, p. 57.*

"January 29, 1756. A Petition of Timothy Fitch of Boston Merchant Shewing that he is fitting out the Schooner Two Brothers, Thomas Stanley Master for the West Indies, Praying that he may be allowed to carry thither Fifty Barrells of Provisions for the use of the Inhabitants of the English Islands—In the House of Representatives; Read & Ordered that the Prayer of the Petn be granted, and that the Petitioner have Liberty to Export Fifty Barrells of Provisions on Board the Schooner Two Brothers, Thomas Stanley Master, to any of the English West India Islands, provided he give Bond to the Impost Officer in the Sum of Fifty Pounds Sterling to Land or dispose of the same at any one or more of the said Islands, and to Produce a Certificate from one of the Principal Officers of His Majestys Customs in such Place or Places respectively that said Provisions have been so landed or disposed of, & when such Certificate is produced to the said Impost Officer, the Bond aforesaid shall be Cancelled & delivered up In Council; Read & Concur'd—Consented to by the Lieutenant Governour."—*Ibid., p. 64.*

"A Petition of Samuel Sturges & Solomon Davis of Boston Merchts Praying for Liberty to Ship on Board a Sloop belonging to them for the Bay of Honduras Thirty Barrells of Beef, ten Barrells of Flour, Two Barrells of Mackarell & Three Quintals of Fish for the use of the English there—

In the House of Representatives; Read & Ordered That the Prayer of the Petition be so far granted as that the Petitioners have Liberty to Transport the Provisions therein mentioned to the Bay of Honduras, Provided they give Bond to the Impost Officer in the Sum of Five Hundred Pounds Sterling to carry the same to the Bay and there dispose of it: which Bond shall be Cancelled and delivered up when the Master of the Vessell on board which said Provisions shall be shipt, returns & makes Oath that said Provisions have been so disposed of—In Council; Read & Concur'd—Consented to by the Lieutenant Governour."—*Ibid, p. 65.*

"February 13, 1756. A Memorial of Nathaniel & George Bethune of Boston Merchants, Shewing that they are fitting out for Newfoundland the Brigantine Mermaid John Tozer Master, & praying that they may be allowed to Ship in her One hundred & Twenty Barrels of Provisions for the use of his Majestys Garrison there—

In the House of Representatives; Read & Ordered, That the Prayer of the Petition be granted, & that the Petitioners have liberty to Ship the Provisions mentioned on Board the Brigantine Mermaid, & that the Commissioners of Impost be & is hereby impowered & directed to take Bond of One thousand Pounds Sterling of the Petitioners for Landing the same at Newfoundland, and that the Chief Officer of the said Vessell at his return make Oath that the said Provisions were actually Landed there, & upon his taking the said Oath the said Bond to be Cancelled——In Council; Read & Concur'd—Consented to by the Governour."—*Ibid., p. 88.*

"February 14, 1756. A Memorial of John Phillips of Boston Merchant, shewing that he is fitting out the Brigantine Abigail John Atwood Master for the Bay of Honduras and praying that he may be allowed to transport in said Vessell Fifty Barrells of Beef and Thirty Barrells of Flour for the use of the Inhabitants there. In Council; Read & Ordered, That the Prayer of this Petition be so far granted as that the Petitioner be & hereby is allowed to Ship the above mentioned Provisions for the Bay of Honduras in the said Vessell, Provided he give Bond in One Thousand Pounds Sterling to Land the same there, And upon the Master or Chief Officer of said Vessell making Oath after her return, that the Provisions have been so Landed, the said Bonds shall be Cancelled. In the House of Representatives Read & Concur'd—Consented to by the Governour."—*Ibid., p. 90.*

Chap. 17. "The Massachusetts assembly stood prorogued to the 24th of September. The lieutenant-governor was advised to order a special session, by proclamation, on the 5th. There had been no precedent for this in the province. Recourse was had to precedents in parliamentary proceedings. When the Dutch threatened an invasion in 1667, King Charles II., having prorogued the parliament to October 10th, called, by proclamation, an intermediate session on the 25th of July. The Dutch did what mischief they could, and withdrew their ships. The parliament was again prorogued to the 10th of October, and, as no business was done, there was no room to call in question the validity of any proceedings.

The necessity of the case induced Mr. Phipps to comply with the advice given him, and the assembly, having sat every day, Sunday included, from the 5th to the 9th, and made provision for raising two thousand men as an additional force, were prorogued to the 10th of October;* when it was thought proper, by an act passed for that purpose, to establish all the proceedings of the intermediate session. Some of the council opposed this measure, lest it should be urged, in future time, as an objection to the proceedings of any intermediate session, and sufficient ground for a refusal to obey them, which might be of very bad consequence."—*Hutchinson's Hist. Mass., vol. 3, p.* 34.

Chap. 20. See note to chap. 16, *ante.*

Chap. 23. "Novr 6th 1755. In the House of Representatives; Ordered, that Mr Gridley, Mr Hooper & Colo Otis with such as the Honble Board shall join be a Committee to examine into the State of the French on Board Transports lying in the Harbour of Boston, and to report what they think proper for this Court to do thereon.——In Council; Read and Concurred, and Joseph Pynchon & William Brattle Esqrs are joined in the affair."—*Council Records, vol. XXI., p.* 28.

"Novr 7th 1755. Report on the Affair of the French People on board the Transports &c The Committee appointed to examine into the State of the French Nutrals in the several Transports, now lying in the harbour of Boston, having attended the affair are of opinion that liberty be given for landing so many of said Nutrals as will reduce those that may be left on board of any Transport, to the proportion of two Persons to a Ton, The Honble Benjamin Green Esqr of Halifax having assured the Committee that he will settle the affairs with the Masters of the Vessels.—Which is humbly submitted.

JOSEPH PYNCHON pr order.

In the House of Representatives, Read, and Ordered, that this report be accepted. In Council, Read, and Concurred. Consented to by the Lieut Governor.—

In the House of Representatives, Whereas, it appears to this House that it is not safe for the several transports with French People on board, now lying in the harbour of Boston to proceed on their respective Voyages under their present circumstance.—Therefore, Voted, That His Honour the Lieut Governor be desired to give Orders forthwith that they may not pass the Castle till further Orders. In Council, Read and Concurred."—*Ibid., p.* 29.

"December 12: 1755. In the House of Representatives; Ordered that Mr Gridley, Mr Witt, Mr James Russell, Mr Tyng, & Mr Wilder with such as the Honble Board shall join be a Committee to take under Consideration the Affair of the French Inhabitants of Nova Scotia who have lately been sent into this Province by Governour Lawrence & report thereon—In Council; Read & Concur'd & Samuel Watts, Andrew Oliver John Erving & Thos Hutchinson Esqrs are joined in the Affair."—*Ibid., p.* 32.

"Decemr 17, 1755. In Council; Voted that His Honour the Lieut Governour be desired to Write to Govr Lawrence to acquaint him that this Government have admitted a number of the Inhabitants of Nova Scotia, sent hither by his Order, who arrived when the Season was so far advanced that they could do but little for their own Support; That the Governmt have received them in expectation of being indemnified from all Charges that might arise on their Accounts; and therefore desire His Excellency will give Orders for defraying all such Charges; And further to acquaint him if any more should be sent hither, he would at the same time give the like Orders respecting them. In the House of Representatives; Read & Concur'd."—*Ibid., p.* 34.

"Decembr 20, 1755. A Bill entitled an Act making Provision for the Inhabitants of Nova Scotia sent hither from that Government and lately arrived in this Province (reported by the Committee)—In Council; Read a First & Second time & passed to be Engrossed with amendments as taken into a new Draught."—*Ibid., p.* 38.

Chap. 26. "September 12, 1753. A Petition of Thomas Berry Esqr and others Feeoffees of Ipswich Grammar School shewing that by Reason of their Omitting thrô a Mistake a Performance of some Conditions in their Constitution they are like to find Difficulty in recovering the Rents of the School Lands; Praying that this Court would by their Authority pass such Order as to secure the Estate of the said School

In Council; Read and Ordered that John Quincy and John Otis Esqrs with such as the Honble House shall join be a Committee to hear such of the Petitioners as are now attends, and Inspect the Records relating to Ipswich School, now brought to Town by the Town Clerk of Ipswich, and report what may be proper for this Court to do thereon

In the House of Representatives; Read and Concur'd; And Colo Buckminster Mr James Russell and Capt Livermore are joined in the Affair."—*Council Records, vol. XX., p.* 84.

"September 13, 1753. John Quincy Esqr from the Committee of both Houses on the Petition of the Feoffees of Ipswhich School, gave in the following Report; viz,

The Committee appointed to consider the within Petition having met & heard one of the Petitioners, and perused the Records relating to the School Lands in Ipswich, find the Principal Part of those Lands were formerly Leased to John Coggeshall Dec'd and his Heirs and Assigns, who are now in Possession of the same, are therefore of Opinion that the Petition be refer'd to the second Wednesday of the next Sitting of this Court, and that in the mean time the Petitioners serve the said Coggeshalls Heirs with a Copy of the Petition, that they may have an Opportunity to give in their Reasons, if they see Cause, why the Prayer thereof should not be granted. JOHN QUINCY ℘ Order

In Council; Read and Accepted, and Ordered that the Consideration of this Petition be refer'd to the next sitting of the Court, and that in the mean time the Petrs serve the within named Coggeshalls Heirs with a Copy of this Petition that so they may shew Cause, if any they have why the Prayer thereof should not be granted In the House of Representatives; Read and Concur'd."—*Ibid., p.* 86.

* The Assembly was prorogued to September 24. The historians here evidently confounded the date of the prorogation of Parliament with that of the Assembly.

"January 4, 1754. On the Petition of the Trustees of Ipswich School Lands In Council; Read again together with the Answer of the Heirs of John Coggshall and Ordered that the Petition be recommitted to the same Committee *to the same Committee* to hear the Parties and make Report to this Court as soon as may be, what they judge proper to be done thereon. In the House of Representatives; Read and Concur'd."—*Ibid., p.* 139.

"January 5, 1754. The Committee on the Petition of the Trustees of Ipswich School Lands gave in their Report

In Council; Read and Accepted, and Ordered that the Petitioners serve the Town of Ipswich with a Copy of this Petition, that they may shew Cause, if any they have, on the first Tuesday of the next Sitting of this Court, why the Prayer thereof should not be granted accordingly——In the House of Representatives; Read and Concur'd."—*Ibid., p.* 144.

"April 2d 1754. On the Petition of the Feoffees of Ipswich School, Enter'd

In Council; Read—again, together with the several Answers thereto, And Ordered that Benjamin Lynde & John Chandler Esqrs with such as the Honourable House of Representatives shall join be a Committee to take the same under Consideration, & make Report to this Court, what they judge proper to be done thereon, as soon as may be;——In the House of Representatives Read & Concur'd & Mr Lyman, Cpt Preble & Collo Bradford are joined in the Affair."—*Ibid., p.* 198.

"Att a Legall Meeting Of the Freeholder's & Others the Inhabitants of the Town of Ipswich Jany 12th 1756. * * *

Voted That The Selectmen be a Comtee to Confer with the Feoffees upon the Affair of the School Rents & See whether Can Come to any Agreement About the Management of said Rents and make Report att the Adjournt of the Meeting—

Attest SAMUEL ROGERS. Tn Cler."

—*Ipswich town-records, vol.* 4, *p.* 153.

"Att a Meeting Of the Inhabitants of the Town of Ipswich By Adjournt January 22d 1756. Collo John Choate Esq. Moderator of the Meeting

* * * *

The Comtee Appointed on the Twelfth Inst to Confer with the Feoffees of the Grammar School in Ipswich Respecting the Management of the School Rents Reported that they had Agreed thereon and then the Town Came into the Following Vote. Vizt——

Whereas the Town in Granting the School Farm att Chebbacco did not give those Persons to whose Trust they Committed the Improvement of Said Farm a power to Appoint Successors as the Private persons who Granted Lands in this Town for the Same use Did as Appears by Examining the Respective Grant by which Means those Grants being Differently Constituted and the Persons Intrusted by the Town as Aforesd being Long Since Dead Endless Disputes may Arise between the Town & Feoffees About the School (to the Support of which the whole Income if needed is to be Applyed) Unless Relief be had from the Generall Court and inasmuch as the Present Feoffees have Manifested there Agreement Thereto——

Voted That a joynt Application be made to the Great and Generall Court to Obtain an Act if they See meet Fully to Authorize and Impower the Present Four Feoffees and Such Successors as they shall from time to time Appoint in their Stead together with the Three Edest Selectmen of this Town for the time being other than Such Selectman or men as may att any time be of the Four Feeofees To be A Committee in Trust the Major Part of whom to Order the Affairs of the School Land & School Appoint the Schoolmaster from time Demand Recieve and Apply the Incomes Agreable to the True Intent of the Donors No Feoffee hereafter to be Appointed by the Present Feoffees or by their Successors Other than an Inhabitant of this Town and not to Act after he Removes his Dwelling out of it and to have no more than Four att one time And Least any Unforseen Inconvenience may happen in this Method it is Agreed that the Act be only made for Ten Years att First. * * *

Attest SAMUEL ROGERS T. Cler—."

—*Ibid.*

"Att an Aniversary or Genll Town Meeting of the Freeholders and others the Inhabitants of the Town of Ipswich Began and held March 3d 1761. and Continued by Adjournt to March 10th 1761. Ten Clock A. m.

* * * *

Voted That the School Rights in Birch Island bush Hill Bartholmew hill and Chebacco Woods and Laid out in Some other Estate that will be more Advantageous to the School and that the Feoffees with the Selectmen Appoint some Sutable persons to make Applica to the Great and Genl Court for Liberty of Selling the Lands aforesd.

* * * *

Pursuant to a Vote of the Town Relative to the Sale of the School Rights, Att a Meeting of the Feoffees of the School Lands in the Town of Ipswich together with the Selectmen Voted That Daniel Appleton Esq President of the Feoffees Sign the within petition to the Genl Court for the Sale of the Lands within mentioned as Appear by Said Petition on File and that Jno Choate Esq be Desired to Preferr the Same.

Attest. SAMUEL ROGERS T. Cler."

—*Ibid., p.* 189.

"April 17, 1761. A Petition of Daniel Appleton Esqr in the Name and behalf of the Feoffees in trust for the Grammer School in the Town of Ipswich Setting forth, That among other donations for the encouraging of Learning in said Town there was a Right of Commonage given them for that purpose, and when the Commons were divided this Right was laid out in five distinct pieces and some of them 4 or 5 miles distant from others, and one still lyes in Common with several other Rights, all which excepting one, at a place called Castle Neck Marshes rent but for six shillings a Year, and if obliged to be fenced must bring the Town in debt. And praying leave to sell the other four peices vizt that at Bush Hill, that at Bartholomew Hill, that at Birch Island and that at Chebacco amounting in the whole to twenty four Acres, and that the proceeds be laid out in other Lands for the use of said School.

In the House of Representatives; Voted that the Prayer of this Petition be so far granted that Capt Nathaniel Tredwell Treasurer of the said Feoffees be, and hereby is fully authorized and impowered to make Sale of the four first mentioned peices or parts of said Common Right in said Petition vizt those called Bush hill, Bartholomew Hill, Birch Island and Chebacco wood amounting in the whole to twenty four Acres for the most the same will fetch and to make and execute a good and sufficient Deed or Deeds of Conveyance thereof and to apply the Monies arising by the Sale thereof under the direction of said Feoffees for purchasing Land at a place called Jeffrys Neck in Ipswich for the use and benefit of the Grammar School in Ipswich forever, the said Nathaniel Treadwell to be accountable. In Council Read and Concurred- Consented to by the Governor."—*Council Records, vol. XXIII., p.* 743.

Chap. 27. "February 13, 1756. The Two Houses have reassumed the Consideration of further prosecuting an Expedition against the French Fort at Crown Point, & the other Encroachments made upon his Majestys Territories adjacent, and they are willing in conjunction with the other Governments to come into any reasonable measures for raising a Sufficient Force for this Province—They have tried every method they could conceive of to obtain an immediate Supply of Money for the Payment of the Wages of the Soldiers in the last Expedition, but all to no purpose—whilst those Troops remain unpaid, they think that any attempt for a new Enlistment would be altogether Fruitless: and indeed they are unable to raise money even for the Bounty for such Enlistment—

We have all imaginable reason to depend on a Reimbursement from His Majesty but untill it be actually granted & received we cannot apply it to the Payment of the Debts We have contracted, or to any future Service—Our dependence is upon your Excellency—If a sufficient Sum can be advanced for the Payment of the Soldiers employed last Year, & for a suitable Bounty to such Forces as it shall be found necessary to employ the ensuing year We will immediately proceed to the doing every thing requisite on our part towards the raising such Forces; but unless such Sum can be advanced, we are very sure that it will be in vain to attempt it."—*Message from both houses to the Governor, Council Records. vol. XXI., p.* 86.

"February 14, 1756. The Secretary delivered the following Message from His Excellency to both Houses. Vizt

Gentlemen of the Council & House of Representatives:

It is of the utmost Importance that the great Affair under your Consideration should be determined upon without delay, & prosecuted with the greatest Diligence & Vigour—That I may not be the means of losing a Minutes time. I send you an immediate Answer to your Message to me this Morning; and seeing Gentlemen that no other way can be found for the Payment of the Men employed the last Year, and for the Bounty that will be necessary upon a new Enlistment, except that of borrowing from me Moneys committed to my Trust, for the Service of his Majesty's Forces, rather than there should be a failure, or any further delay on the part of this Province I consent to Advance to you a Sum for the Purposes you desire; Provided it shall not exceed Thirty Thousand Pounds Sterling which is the most I am able to engage: I have no reason to think his Majesty ever expected any part of the Money sent over would be employed in this manner; And altho I doubt not when the necessity of this measure is properly represented that His Majesty will approve of my Conduct, yet I think it proper that you should by an Act of the Government secure to me the Repayment of the Sum advanced out of the first Moneys that shall be granted either by His Majesty or the Parliament of Great Britain for the use of this Province; And that in the same Act you make Provision for a Tax to be Levied in the Years 1757. & 1758, for the whole sum borrowed, such Tax to be a Collateral Security for the Repayment thereof, in case there should not be a Grant of Money, or that it should not arrive here before those Years; and that you enable the Province Treasurer to give me a proper Receipt for the Money to be advanced.

I intreat you Gentlemen to lay aside all private Business & let this most Weighty & interesting Affair take up your whole Attention."—*Ibid., p.* 89.

"February 25, 1756. The following Message was sent from the Board to the House of Representves by Sir William Pepperell Bart Jacob Wendell & Sylvanus Bourn Esqrs—

The Board are fully of Opinion that the Prospect of Success in the proposed Expedition very much depends on its being carried into Execution as early as possible; and that a few days delay of any necessary measures may be the occasion of a fatal Disappointment This Consideration has Caused the Board to give all the dispatch in their Power to every thing that has come before them relating to the Expedition; and in a particular manner the Bill for Supply of the Treasury was past on by the Board immediately on its being sent from the Honble House; And the House by a Message from the Board the 21st instant were informed that the said Bill was Engross'd, & only waited the Formality of being enacted, notwithstanding which it has not since been returned to the Board."—*Ibid., p.* 105.

"February 27, 1756. The following Message to the Board was sent from the House of Representatives The House are extreamly sensible of the Importance of the determined Expedition and of the necessity of Dispatch in the measures conducing to it, and of the immediate Payment of the Soldiers that served in the last Expedition, and early prepared Pass'd and sent to the Honble Board a Bill for the Supply of the Treasury for these Purposes;—But observing after the Engrossing of it, some material Omissions which in the Dispatch, had escaped them: and that the Enacting of it, was more than a Formality, they have therefore prepared and Passed to be Engrossed another Supply Bill, with an Additional Grant, which they now send to the Honourable Board, and earnestly pray their immediate Attention to it."—*Ibid, p.* 110.

"This objection he [Shirley] obviated too, by an offer to lend the province thirty thousand pounds sterling, out of the monies which had been remitted for the king's troops, and to repay himself out of the grant which it was expected parliament would make to the province for last year's charges; but with this caution, that an act of assembly should pass for levying a tax in the years 1757 and 1758, of thirty thousand pounds sterling, as a collateral security, the act to have no effect if the grant should be before made by parliament.

Declarations made to serve political purposes oftentimes will not bear a strict scrutiny." —*Hutchinson's Hist. Mass., vol.* 3, *p.* 45.

"July first 1756. * * *

During your Recess his Excellency the Governour has transmitted to me from Albany several Letters from the Right Hon[ble] Henry Fox Esq[r] one of his Majestys Principal Secretaries of State, containing divers Matters of great Importance which I am to lay before you.

I am in the first Place to inform you that his Majesty in his great Goodness was pleased to recommend to the consideration of the Parliament the Case of his Colonies in New England together with those of New York & New Jersey, & the Sum of £150,000 Sterling was thereupon granted, to be distributed in such Proportion as His Majesty shall think proper."—*Extract from speech of Lieutenant Governor Phips, to the Assembly.—Council Records, vol. XXI., p.* 221.

Chap. 28. "We hear that the Distemper among the Dogs prevails in many Places in this Province, as also to a great Degree in the Southern Colonies."—*Boston Weekly News-letter, March* 4, 1756.

Chap. 30. "April 1st 1756. A Petition of Samuel Grant of Boston Mercht Shewing that he is fitting out a Vessell for Newfoundland, Praying that he may be allowed to Export in her from hence Thirty Barrels of Beef In Council; Read & Ordered that the Prayer of the Petition be granted, and that the Petitioner have Liberty to Ship the Provisions within mentioned aboard the Sloop Eagle John Dobel Master and the Commissioner be & hereby is impowered & directed to take Bond of One Thousand Pounds Sterling of the Petitioner for Landing the same at Newfoundland; And that the Chief Officer of said Vessell at his Return make Oath that the said Provisions were actually Landed there, & on his taking the said Oath the said Bonds to be Cancelled ——In Council; Read & Concur'd——Consented to by the Governour."—*Council Records, vol. XXI., p.* 137.

"April 3, 1756. A Memorial of Joshua Winslow Esq[r] of Boston Merchant shewing that he is fitting out for a Voyage to Surinam the Brigantine Ordnance Packet Duncan Ingraham Master, Praying that he may be permitted to Ship on Board said Vessell Sixty Barrells of Flour, and Fifty Barrells of Beef——In the House of Representatives; Read & Ordered that the Prayer of the Petition be granted; And that the Petitioner have Liberty to Ship the Provisions mentioned on board the Ordnance Packet Duncan Ingraham Master, and that the Commissioner of Impost be and hereby is impowered & directed to take Bond of One Thousand Pounds Sterling of the Petitioner for Landing the same at the Port of Surinam and that the Chief Officer of the said Vessell at his Return make Oath that the said Provisions were actually Landed there & on his taking the said Oath s[d] Bond to be Cancelled In Council; Read & Concur'd—Consented to by the Governour."—*Ibid., p.* 143.

"April 9, 1756. A Petition of Henry Bromfield & Fortesque Vernon, Shewing that they are Loading the Brigantine Pursue, for the West Indies, Praying that they may be permitted to send a Quantity of Provisions as therein mentioned.——In Council; Read & Ordered that the Prayer of this Petition be granted & that the Petitioners have Liberty to Ship the Provisions mentioned on Board the Brigantine Pursue and that the Commissioner of Impost be and hereby is directed & impowered to take Bond of One Thousand Pounds Sterling of the Petitioners for Landing the same at the Port of Barbadoes and that the Chief Officer of the said Vessell at his return make Oath that the said Provisions were actually landed there, and on his taking the said Oath, the Bonds mentioned shall be Cancelled.——In the House of Representatives; Read & Concur'd——Consented to by the Governour."—*Ibid., p.* 154.

"April 16, 1756. A Petition of Samuel Welles jun[r] of Boston Merchant, shewing that he hath a Schooner now Loading for Surrinam, Praying that he may be permitted to send thither in said Vessell about One hundred Barrells of Provisions, he giving Bond at the Impost Office as usual—In the House of Representatives; Read & Ordered that the Prayer of the Petition be granted, and that the Petitioner be allowed to Ship the Provisions mentioned on Board the Schooner Neptune Thomas Harding Master, and that the Commissioner of Impost be and hereby is impowered & directed to take Bond of One Thousand Pounds Sterling for Landing the same at the Port of Surrinam, and that the Chief Officer of the said Vessell on his return make Oath that the said Provisions have been actually landed there, and thereupon that the said Bond be Cancell'd——In Council; read & Concur'd—Consented to by the Governour."—*Ibid., p.* 169.

"April 20, 1756. A Petition of Timothy Fitch of Boston Merchant Shewing that he is fitting out the Schooner Peggy Thomas Farrell Master, for a Voyage to the Bay of Honduras praying that he may be permitted to Ship upon her a Quantity of Provisions particularly mentioned, for the use of the English there——In the House of Representatives; Read & Ordered that the Prayer of this Petition be so far granted, as that the Petitioner be allowed to Ship the Provisions mention'd on Board the Schooner Peggy Thomas Farrell Master for the Bay of Honduras, and that the Commissioner of Impost be impowered & directed to take Bonds of One Thousand Pounds Sterling of the Petitioner for Landing the same at the said Bay, and that the Chief Commanding Officer of said Vessell at his return make Oath that the said Provisions were landed there, and that on his taking said Oath said Bonds to be cancelled——In Council; read & Concur'd.——Consented to by the Governour."—*Ibid., p.* 176.

"June 10, 1756. A Petition of John Avery of Boston Merchant Shewing that he is fitting out the Schooner Abigail Samuel Blunt Master on a Voyage for the Bay of Honduras, & Praying that he may be permitted to Load on Board said Vessell Seventy five Barrels of Provisions for the use of his Majesty's Subjects there In the House of Representatives; Read & Ordered that the Prayer of the Petition be so far granted as that the Petitioner be allowed to Ship the Seventy five Barrells of Provisions mentioned on Board the Schooner Abigail, Samuel Blunt Master & that the Commissioner of Impost be & hereby is impowered & directed to take Bond of the Petitioner in the Sum of One Thousand Pounds Sterling that the said Provisions be Landed at the Bay of Honduras & that the Chief Officer of the said Vessell at his Return make Oath that the same was bona fide landed there, and on his taking the said Oath the said Bonds to be Cancelled——In Council; Read & Concur'd——Consented to by the Lieut. Governour."

* * * *

A Petition of James Russell & John Noyes Merchants shewing that they are fitting out the Schooner Boscawen Caleb Symmes Master to the English West Indies, praying that they may be permitted to Load on Board said Vessell about Fifty Barrels of Pork, which is suitable only for that Market—In the House of Representatives; Read & Ordered that the Prayer of this Petition be so far granted as that the Petitioners be allowed to Ship Fifty Barrells of Provisions mentioned on Board the Schooner Boscawen Caleb Symmes Master, and that the Commiss^r of Impost be & hereby is impowered & Directed to take Bond of the Petitioners in the Sum of One Thousand Pounds Sterling for Landing the same at one or more of the English West India Islands, and that upon the Chief Officer of the said Vessell on his return producing a certificate from some officer of his Majesty's Customs in said Islands respectively that the said Provisions have been landed there, the said Bonds to be Cancelled——In Council; Read & Concur'd——Consented to by the Lieuten^t Govern^r."—*Ibid., pp.* 214, 215.

"By the Honourable Spencer Phips Esqr Lieutenant Governour & Commander in Chief, in & over His Majesty's Province of the Massachusetts Bay in New Eng^d

A Proclamation.

Whereas the Great & General Court or Assembly of this Province at their Sitting held by Adjournment the fourteenth Day of January last, pass'd an Act for preventing the Exportation of Provisions & Warlike Stores out of this Province, wherein (among other things) it is enacted, 'That if the Governour or Commander in Chief for the Time being shall see fit, with the Advice & Consent of the Council, to issue a Proclamation prohibiting the Exportation of Provisions or Warlike Stores out of the Province for any Time after the Twentieth day of June Instant; & not exceeding the Twentieth Day of November following in this present Year, the Master and Owner or Owners, Factor & Factors of any Vessel or Vessels on board of which such Provisions or Warlike Stores, contrary to such Proclamation, shall be respectively liable to the same Pains and Penalties as if the same had been exported before the said Twentieth Day of June contrary to the said Act.

I have thought fit, with the Advice & Consent of His Majesty's Council of this Province, further to prohibit the Exportation of Provisions or Warlike Stores from any part of this Province untill after the Twentieth Day of September next; And all Persons concerned are required to govern themselves accordingly.

Given at the Council Chamber in Boston, the Ninth Day of June 1756, In the Twenty ninth Year of the Reign of Our Sovereign Lord George the Second, by the Grace of God, of Great Britain, France & Ireland, King Defender of the Faith &c

By His Honour's Command with the
Advice & Consent of the Council S: PHIPS.
J. WILLARD Sec^ry.

God save the King."—*Records of Civil Commissions; in Secretary's Office, vol.* 2, *p.* 293.

"July 6, 1756. A Petition of Benjamin & Edward Davis of Boston Merch^ts Shewing that they are fitting out the Brigantine Middleburg Richard Humphreys Master for the Port of Esqueb near Surrinam; Praying that they may be permitted to send in the said Vessell a Quantity of Provisions to that Place. In the House of Representatives; Read & Ordered that the Prayer of the Petition be so far granted, and that the Petitioners have Liberty to Ship the Provisions mentioned on Board the Brigantine Middleburg Richard Humphreys Master & that the Commissioner of Impost be & he hereby is impowered & directed to take Bond of One Thousand Pounds Sterling of the Petitioners for Landing the same at the Port of Esqueb and that the Chief Officer of the said Vessell at his return make Oath that the said Provisions were Bona Fide landed there, & on his taking the said Oath the said Bond shall be Cancelled—In Council; Read & Concurd——Consented to by the Lieu^t Governour."—*Council Records, vol. XXI., p* 227.

"August 21, 1756. A Petition of Thomas Boylstone of Boston Merchant Praying for Liberty to Export in the Brigantine Dolphin Samuel Gallop Master, & the Brigantine Rebecca John Dorrington Master Provisions to Jamaica & the Bay of Honduras, upon his giving Bond according to Law.——In the House of Representatives; Read & Ordered that the Prayer of the Petition be granted, and that the Petitioner be allowed to Ship on Board each of the Vessells within mentioned Two Hundred Barrells of Provisions, and the Commissioner of Impost is hereby Impowered & directed to take Bonds of the Petitioner in the Sum of One Thousand Pounds Sterling for each Vessell, that the said Provisions shall be delivered at the Island of Jamaica or the Bay of Honduras, and that the Chief Officer of each of the said Vessells on their Return make Oath that the Provisions aforesaid were Bona Fide were landed & disposed of at one of the Ports of Jamaica or the Bay of Honduras; and upon their taking the said Oath the said Bonds shall be Cancelled. In Council; Read & Concur'd.—

* * * *

A Petition of Stephen Hall of Medford Esq[r] Praying for Liberty to Export on Board the Sloop a small Quantity of Provisions to Suranam, being Provisions most suitable for that Market——In Council; Read & Ordered that the Prayer of the Petition be granted & that the Petitioner be allowed to Ship on Board the said Sloop the Provisions within mentioned and the Commissioner of Impost is hereby Impowered & directed to take Bonds of the Petitioner in the Sum of One Thousand Pounds Sterling that the said Provisions shall be delivered at the Port of Suranam or in some English Island, and that the Chief Officer of the said Vessell on his return make Oath that the Provisions aforesaid were Bona Fide landed as aforesaid; & upon his taking the said Oath the said Bonds shall be Cancell'd——In the House of Representatives; Read & Concur'd."—*Ibid.*, *pp.* 250, 251.

"Septem[r] 7, 1756. A Memorial of Henry Bromfield of Boston Merchant, Praying for Liberty to Ship on Board the Schooner whereof Stephen Brown is Master bound for Newfoundland Forty Sheep for the particular Use of his Majesty's Garrison at St Johns at said Island In the House of Representatives; Read & Ordered that the Prayer of the Memorial be granted, and that the Memorialist be allowed to put on Board said Schooner the Forty Sheep mentioned, and that the Commissioner of Impost be & hereby is directed to take Bond of the Memorialist in the Sum of Five Hundred Pounds Sterling that the said Sheep shall be landed and delivered at Newfoundland, and that upon the Chief Officer of said Vessell his producing at his Return a Certificate from some Chief Officer of his Majestys Customs there, that the said Sheep were so landed & delivered the said Bond shall be Cancelled——In Council; Read & Concur'd—Consented to by the Governour."—*Ibid.*, *p.* 271.

"Septem[r] 8, 1756. A Petition of Richard Upham praying for Liberty to Export in the Schooner Merrimack now Loading for Halifax Twelve Head of Neat Cattle & Fifty Sheep, the Petitioner giving Bond at the Impost Office as usual. In the House of Representatives; Read & Ordered that the Prayer of the Petition be granted, and that the Petitioner be allowed to Ship on Board the Schooner Merrimack Enoch Howard Master the Twelve Head of Horned Cattle & Fifty Sheep mentioned in the Petition, and that the Commissioner of the Impost be and he hereby is impowered and directed to take Bond of the Petitioner in the Sum of Five Hundred Pounds Sterling that the Cattle & Sheep shall be landed & delivered at the Port of Halifax, and that upon the Chief Officer of the said Vessell (at his Return) his producing a Certificate from some Chief Officer of his Majestys Customs there, that the said Cattle and Sheep were Landed & delivered at the said Port of Halifax, the said Bond be Cancelled——In Council; Read & Concur'd——Consented to by the Governour."—*Ibid.*, *p.* 274.

"By His Excellency William Shirley Esq[r] Captain-General & Gover[r] in Chief in & over His Majesty's Province of the Massachusetts-Bay in New England, Vice-Admirall of the Same, &c.

A Proclamation.

Whereas the Greate & General Court or Assembly of this Province at their Setting held by Adjournment the Fourteenth day of January last, pass'd an Act entitled, An Act for preventing the Exportation of Provisions & warlike Stores out of this Province, wherein (among other things) it is enacted, That if the Governour or Commander in Chief for the Time being shall see fit, with the Advice & Consent of the Council, to issue a Proclamation prohibiting the Exportation of Provisions or Warlike Stores out of the Province, for any Time after the Twentieth day of June, and not exceeding the Twentieth day of November following in this present Year, the Master & Owner or Owners, Factor & Factors of any Vessel or Vessels on board of which such Provisions or Warlike Stores contrary to such Proclamation, shall be respectively liable to the same Pains & Penalties, as if the same had been exported before the said Twentieth day of June contrary to the said Act.

I have thought fit with the Advice & Consent of his Majesty's Council of this Province, further to prohibit the exportation of Provisions or Warlike Stores from any part of this Province, untill after the Twentieth Day of October next; And all persons conserned are required to govern themselves accordingly.

Given at the Council-Chamber in Boston the Seventeenth Day of Septem[r] 1756. In the Thirtieth Year of the Reign of our Sovereign Lord George the Second, by the Grace of God, of Great Britain, France, & Ireland, King, Defender of the Faith &c.

By his Excellency's Command with
the Advice & Consent of the Council W SHIRLEY.
J WILLARD Secry

God save the King."—*Records of Civil Commissions; in Secretary's Office*, *vol.* 2, *p.* 309.

"October 6, 1756. A Petition of Thomas Boylstone of Boston Merchant Shewing that he is fitting out the Ship Honduras Daniel Mc Carty Master on a Voyage for Jamaica & the Bay of Honduras Praying that he may be allowed to Ship on Board her a Quantity of Provisions for the last mentioned Place.——In Council; Read & Ordered that the Prayer of the Petition be so far granted as that the Petitioner be allowed to Ship the Provisions within mentioned aboard said Ship he giving Bond to the Commissioner of Impost of One Thousand Pounds Sterling to Land the said Provisions in the Island of Jamaica or the Bay of Honduras, & upon Return of the said Ship the Chief Officer making Oath that the said Provisions were bona fide Landed as abovesaid the said Bonds to be Cancelled.——In the House of Representatives, Read & Concur'd——Consented to by the Lieutenant Governour."—*Council Records*, *vol. XXI.*, *p.* 284.

"October 8, 1756. A Petition of John Hooton & Richard Hooton Praying to send to Surinam in the Schooner Mary whereof Thomas Tufton is Master a Quantity of Provisions particularly mentioned in the Petition. In Council; Read & Ordered that the Prayer of this Petition be so far granted, as that the Petitioners have Liberty to Ship the Provisions within mentioned aboard said Vessell, provided they give Bonds of One Thousand

Pounds Sterling to the Commissioner of Impost to Land the same in said Port of Surinam, And on the Return of the said Vessell if the Chief Officer shall make Oath that the said Provisions were bona fide Landed in said Port of Surinam then the Bonds shall be Cancelled—— In the House of Representatives Read & Concur'd——Consented to by the Lieuten^t Governour."—*Ibid., p.* 256.

"By the Honourable Spencer Phips Esqr Lieutenant Governour & Commander in Chief, in & over his Majesty's Province of the Massachusetts Bay in New England.

A Proclamation.

Whereas the Great & General Court or Assembly of this Province at their Sitting held by Adjournment the Fourteenth Day of January last, pass'd an Act entitled, An Act for preventing the Exportation of Provisions and Warlike Stores out of this Province; wherein (among other things) it is enacted, 'That if the Governour or Commander in Chief for the Time being shall see fit, with the Advice & Consent of the Council, to issue a Proclamation prohibiting the Exportation of Provisions or Warlike Stores out of the Province, for any Time after the Twentieth Day of June, and not exceeding the Twentieth Day of November following in this present Year, the Master and Owner or Owners, Factor & Factors of any Vessel or Vessels on board of which such Provisions or Warlike Stores, contrary to such Proclamation, shall be respectively liable to the same Pains & Penalties, as if the same had been exported before the said Twentieth Day of June contrary to the said Act.'

I have thought fit, with the Advice & Consent of his Majesty's Council of this Province, further to prohibit the Exportation of Provisions or Warlike Stores from any part of this Province untill after the Twentieth Day of November next; And all Persons concerned are required to govern themselves accordingly.

Given at the Council-Chamber in Boston, the Twentieth Day of October 1756, In the Thirtieth Year of the Reign of our Sovereign Lord George the Second, by the Grace of God of Great Britain, France & Ireland, King Defender of the Faith &c.

By His Honour's Command with the
Advice & Consent of the Council S: PHIPS.
J WILLARD Secry.

God save the King."—*Records of Civil Commissions; in Secretary's Office, vol.* 2, *p.* 310.

Chap. 31. "March 3, 1756. In the House of Representatives; Voted that John Quincy & Mr William Cooper with such as the Honble Board shall join be a Committee to Farm out the Excise on Spirituous Liquors for the County of Suffolk, In Council Read & Concur'd; And Samuel Watts Esqr is joined in the Affair.—Consented to by the Governour." —*Council Records, vol. XXI., p.* 114.

On the same day the following persons were chosen committees to farm out the excise for the respective counties hereafter named; viz.,—

Henry Gibbs and Daniel Epes, Esqs., on the part of the House, and Benjamin Lynde, Esq., on the part of the Council, for the county of Essex;—

Edmund Trowbridge and Samuel Livermore, Esqs., on the part of the House, and Ezekiel Chever, Esq., on the part of the part of the Council, for the county of Middlesex;—

Israel Williams and Elijah Williams, Esqs., on the part of the House, and Eleazer Porter, Esq , on the part of the Council, for the county of Hampshire;—

Thomas Steel and Timothy Payne, Esqs , on the part of the House, and Joseph Wilder, Esq., on the part of the Council, for the county of Worcester;—

Thomas Clap, Esq , and Mr. Israel Turner, on the part of the House, and John Cushing, Esq., on the part of the Council, for the county of Plymouth;—

James Otis and Rowland Cotton, Esqs , on the part of the House, and John Otis, Esq., on the part of the Council, for the county of Barnstable;—

Samuel ——, Esq., and Mr. Thomas Morey, on the part of the House, and George Leonard, Esq., on the part of the Council, for the county of Bristol;—

Mr. John Bradbury and Edward Milliken Esq , on the part of the House, and Richard Cutt, Esq , on the part of the Council, for the county of York;—

James Otis and Roland Cotton, Esqs., on the part of the House, and Sylvanus Bourn, Esq., on the part of the Council, for the county of Dukes county;—

Abishai Folger, Esq., and Mr. Richard Coffin, on the part of the House, and —— ——, on the part of the Council, for the county of Nantucket—*Ibid., pp.* 114, 115.

April 2, 1756. Thomas Greenwood, Esq., instead of Samuel Livermore, Esq., for the county of Middlesex, "who is absent in the Service of the Government."—*Ibid., p.* 142.

"April 16, 1756. The Committee for letting out to Farm the Excise on Spirituous Liquors for the County of Middlesex reported that they had let out the same to Braddyal Smith of Weston for the Sum of £811. 4 8 for which they have taken Bond of him with Sureties which they have Lodged in the Treasury, the Committees time & Expence amounting to £2. 15. 6—In the House of Representatives; Read & Ordered that this Report be accepted & that there be allowed and paid out of the Publick Treasury to the said Committee the Sum of Two Pounds Fifteen Shillings & Six Pence in discharge of their Accompt of time & Expences exhibited In Council; Read & Concur'd—Consented to by the Governour."—*Ibid., p.* 166.

The above report from the committee appointed to farm out the excise for Middlesex County, was followed by reports from the committees for the other counties, and the dates of these reports, together with the names of farmers of excise appointed by them, respectively, are as follows:—

April 16, 1756. Suffolk county; to William Coffin, for £32. 16.—*Ibid., p.* 168.
May 31, 1756. Plymouth county; to Josiah Keep, for £410.—*Ibid., p.* 190.
May 31, 1756. Worcester county; to Ezra Taylor, for £313. 12.—*Ibid., p.* 191.

May 31, 1756. Bristol county; to Joseph Joslyn, for £166. 13. 4.—*Ibid.*
June 1, 1756. Hampshire county; to Elisha Pomroy, for £165 —*Ibid., p.* 194.
June 1, 1756. Barnstable county; to Nathanael Little, for £204.—*Ibid , p.* 195.
June 1, 1756. Nantucket county; to Thomas Arthur, for £35. 14. 8.—*Ibid.*
June 8, 1756. Essex county; to Edward Harrington, for £1108 —*Ibid., p.* 205.
July 3, 1756. York county; to Capt. Ichabod Goodwin, for £200.—*Ibid. p.* 226.
August 21, 1756. Dukes County; to Nathaniel Little, for £35.—*Ibid., p.* 251.

Chap. 34. See note to chap. 35, *post.*

Chap. 35. "Decem^r^ 29, 1755. In the House of Representatives; Whereas a considerable Number of the Inhabitants of Nova Scotia arrived here the Twenty Sixth instant, being removed by the Governour & Council of that Province, for the Security thereof; & no Provision being made for their Support here, they are in great danger of Suffering during this rigorous Season without the Interposition of this Court——

Ordered, That Mr James Russell, Mr Cooper, & Mr Hill, with such as the Honble Board shall join be a Committee to provide for the Support of such Inhabitants of Nova Scotia, untill Advice may be had from Governour Lawrence, & his Orders concerning them, or untill there may be an Opportunity of Applying to His Excellency General Shirley Commander in Chief of His Majestys Forces in North America for his Directions concerning them, And the Comittee are to dispose of them in the mean time in such Towns in this Province, as they shall judge least inconvenient to the Publick, and the Select Men, or Overseers of the Poor of the several Towns to which they may be sent as aforesaid, are hereby authorized & required to recieve them & employ or Support them in such manner as shall incur the least Charge; And the said Inhabitants of Nova Scotia being so received & entertained in any Town shall not be Construed or understood to be an Admission of them as Town Inhabitants; The Court relying upon it that some other Provision will be made for them, without any Expence to this Government.

In Council; Read & Concur'd; And Samuel Watts, & William Brattle Esq^rs^ are joined in the Affair——Consented to by the Lieutenant Governour."—*Council Records, vol. XXI., p.* 51.

"January 16, 1756. A Message was sent down to the House by William Brattle Esqr to inform them that since the rising of the last Court two Vessells are arrived here with Inhabitants of Nova Scotia, that the Committee appointed for the disposing of the said Inhabitants, have been directed by His Honour the Lieutenant Governour with the Advice of His Majestys Council, to dispose of those Inhabitants on board one of the said Vessells, but they have recieved no Orders respecting those aboard the other Vessell, And therefore the Board desire the Honble House would take the Matter under Consideration." —*Ibid , p* 56.

"January 16, 1756. In the House of Representatives; Ordered that the Comittee appointed on the 27th of December last to provide for the Subsistence of the Inhabitants of Nova Scotia sent here by Govr Lawrence be directed to take necessary Care of such of the said Inhabitants as have since arrived here, until Govern^r^ Lawrences Orders, relating to them be had, or till Application may be made to His Excellency General Shirley for his Directions concerning them In Council Read & Concur'd—Consented to by the Lieutenant Governour."—*Ibid., p* 56.

"January 23, 1756. In the House of Representatives; Whereas a considerable Number of the Inhabitants of Nova Scotia arrived here since the 27th day of December last, being removed by the Governour & Council of that Province for the Security thereof, And no Provision being made for their Support they are in great danger of Suffering during the Winter Season, without the Interposition of this Court. Ordered, That the Committee already appointed on the 27th day of Decem^r^ do Provide for the Support of such Inhabitants of Nova Scotia, as have arrived since the 27th day of December last, untill Advice may be had from Col^o^ Lawrence & his Orders concerning them or untill there may be an Opportunity of applying to his Excellency Major General Shirley Commander in Chief of His Majestys Forces in North America for his direction concerning said Inhabitants; and the Committee are to dispose of them in the meantime (at their best discretion in such Towns within this Province as they shall judge least inconvenient to the Publick & at the least Charge; Regard to be had also as to the Taxes each Town pays, they are severally sent to and to the Numbers which any of the Towns have already recieved; And the Overseers of the Poor of the several Towns to which they are sent as aforesaid are hereby authorized and required to receive them, & employ & Support them in such manner as shall incur the least Charge; And the said Inhabitants of Nova Scotia being so recieved & entertained in any Town shall not be Construed or understood to be an Admission of them as Inhabitants, nor shall they be at the Charge of any of the Towns they are sent to; This Court relying upon it that some other Provision will be made for them without any Expence to this Government, And the Overseers of the Poor of the several Towns to whom the said Inhabitants have been or shall be sent by this & the aforementioned Order of the Court shall keep an exact Account of the necessary & unavoidable Charges they have been or may be at for their Support, until the Tenth day of April next, & shall transmit the same to the Secretarys Office for Payment in Order to ascertain the Sums advanced by this Government from time to time for the Service & Safety of Nova Scotia aforesaid ——In Council; Read & Concur'd—Consented to by the Lieut. Governour."—*Ibid., p* 61.

"February 4, 1756. In Council; Ordered That Sylvanus Bourn Joseph Pynchon, Benj^a^ Lincoln & William Brattle Esqr with such as the Honble House shall appoint be a Comittee to prepare a Message to His Excellency the Governour respecting the French Persons commonly called the French Newtrals, lately Inhabitants of Nova Scotia & sent hither by Order of His Majestys Governour of that Province; the Committee to Sit & report as soon as may be——In the House of Representatives; Read & Concurd; & Col^o^ Quincy, Col^o^ Clap, James Bowdoin, Col^o^ Miller, Col^o^ Lawrence & Col^o^ Buckminster are joined in the Affair."—*Ibid., p.* 73.

"February 7, 1756. * * *

We beg leave further to represent to Your Excellency that about three Months ago a Vessell arrived at Boston from Nova Scotia full Freighted with French Persons Inhabitants of that Province, whom the Governour & Council there in Concert with the Admirals of his Majestys Squadron then at Hallifax, judged necessary to be removed and distributed thro his Majestys several Colonies upon the Continent; His Honour the Lieu^{t} Governour with the Advice of the Council; soon after the Arrival of the said Vessell sent to Mr Green one of the Council of Nova Scotia then at Boston, & also the Agents employed in hiring & paying the Charge of the Vessells in which the said Inhabitants were transported, to enquire whether any Provision was made for their Subsistence: But the said Mr Green had received no Orders for that Purpose, and the Agents declined to continue the Subsistence after the Passengers landed, so that unless Provision had been made by this Government these unhappy People must have perished; And upon Information given that several other Vessells were designed hither the Lieutenant Governour acquainted Governour Lawrence by Letters with the desire of the Two Houses that no more of said Inhabitants should be sent to this Province; but it does not appear that the said Letter arrived seasonably; and the other Vessells came in soon after; and about One Thousand Persons in the whole have been Landed here; Application could not be made to your Excellency during your Absence; Therefore Orders were given to distribute the whole Number thro the several Towns, there to be supported untill your Excellencys Return to your Government—

The receiving among Us so great a Number of Persons whose gross Bigotry to the Roman Catholick Religion is notorious & whose Loyalty to his Majesty [Louis XV.] is a thing very disagreeable to Us, but as there seems to be a necessity for it We shall be ready to come into any reasonable Acts or Orders to enable & encourage them to provide for their own Maintenance; We humbly conceive that it will never be expected that in the meantime the Charge & Burthen of their Support should ly upon this Government—We must acquaint Your Excellency, that the Live Stock, Husbandry Tools & most of the Household Furniture of these People are left in the Province of Nova Scotia & that very few have brought with them any Goods or Estate of any kind soever—In the Southern Colonies where the Winters are more mild & Employments may be found so as to prevent any great Expence to the Governments; but here they are a dead weight, for many of our own Inhabitants are scarcely able to find Employ sufficient to support themselves during the Winter Season—

The Removal of the French Inhabitants from Nova Scotia seems to be as fully Connected with the Protection & Safety of that Province, as the removal of the Encroachments made by the Subjects of the French King; And We doubt not Your Excellency will think this matter comes under your immediate Care & direction in Consequence of the Commission you have lately received from his Majesty. Our other necessary & unavoidable Charges are as much as We can bear; We therefore earnestly Pray your Excellency to give such directions in this Affair as that this Government may be freed from any further Charge in Relation to it & reimbursed the Sums already advanced—

In Council; Read & Accepted & Ordered that Jacob Wendell, Isaac Royall & Richard Cutt Esq^{rs} with such as the Honble House shall appoint be a Committee to present the same to his Excellency accordingly.—In the House of Representatives Read & Concur'd, & Col^{o} Cotton, Col^{o} Clap, Col^{o} Miller & Col^{o} Dwight are joined with the Committee of the Board to present the same to his Excellency."—*Extract from Address to the Governor, ibid., p.* 80.

"February 14, 1756. * * *

With respect to the French Inhabitants sent hither from Nova Scotia which is the other part of the Subject of your Address: you seem to think yourselves that it was a necessary measure: I believe Governour Lawrence had no apprehensions that it would occasion any considerable Charge to this Province, or that it would be a disagreeable thing to have those People sent here: I am sorry it is likely to prove so burthensome: I have it not in my Power to Support them at the Charge of the Crown; you have a great deal of Encouragem^{t} to depend on it that his Majesty will not suffer any unreasonable Burthen to ly upon any of his Colonies: I will make a full Representation of the State of this Affair & in such a manner as that I hope you will receive a favourable Answer, and I shall be ready to join with you in proper measures to enable & induce those Persons to provide for their own Support & that of their Families."—*Extract from Governor's answer to the Address, ibid., p.* 90.

"February 16, 1756. A Bill entitled an Act in Addition to & for Amendment of an Act made the present Year of his Majestys Reign entitled an Act making Provision for the Inhabitants of Nova Scotia sent hither from that Government, lately arrived in this Province——In Council read a first & Second time and passed to be Engross'd."—*Ibid., p.* 92.

"February 25, 1756. In the House of Representatives; Ordered that Judge Russell, Col^{o} Otis and Capt Livermore with such as the Honble Board shall join be a Committee to take under Consideration the Bill pass'd this House, intitled an Act in Addition to an Act made in the Twenty Ninth Year of his present Majesty's Reign making provision for the Inhabitants of Nova Scotia &c^{a} and a Bill sent down from the Honble Board entitled an Act in Addition to & for Amendment of an Act made the present Year of his Majestys Reign, intitled an Act making Provision for the Inhabitants of Nova Scotia &c^{a}—In Council; Read & Concur'd, and Thomas Hutchinson & William Brattle Esq^{rs} are joined in the Affair—

In the House of Representatives; Ordered that the Committee appointed to Consider the Two Bills making Provision for the Inhabitants lately sent hither from Nova Scotia be directed to sit forthwith & report.—In Council; Read & Concur'd."—*Ibid., p.* 106.

"April 20, 1756. A Petition of Joseph Mitchel, one of the French Inhabitants of Nova Scotia now residing with his Family at Marshfield, complaining against John Little Esqr & Seth Bryant Select Men of said Town for using himself & Family very Ill, praying for Relief from this Court.—In Council; read & Ordered that Thomas Hutchinson & Benjamin Lincoln Esqrs with such as the Honble House shall join be a Committee to inquire into the matters of Fact mentioned in this Petition, and report as soon as may be what may be proper to be done by this Court thereon——In the House of Representatives; read & Concur'd; And Colo Quincy Mr Trowbridge and Mr Cooper are joined in the Affair."

* * * *

Report on the Petition of Joseph Mitchel Entered above—

The Committee appointed to take under Consideration the Petition of Joseph Mitchel are unable to make Inquiry into the Truth of the Facts mentioned before the Dissolution of the Court, by reason of the distance of Place where they are alledged to have been done, and therefore they are of Opinion that the Consideration of the Petition be referred to the next Session of the Court, the Committee are further humbly of Opinion that the Consideration of the Petition be referred to the next Session of the Court, the Committee are further humbly of Opinion, that it would be acting very different from the intention of the Legislature, if any of the Select Men of the Province should Cause any of the Children of the French from Nova Scotia to be disposed of for any Sum of Money or other Consideration except for the immediate Use and Benefit of such Child or Children, and that where any Child or Children are able and willing to Support themselves, or where their Parents or Friends, will undertake for their Support, such Child or Children ought not to be Separated from their Parents or Friends, and that the Select Men should as far as may be consult the Inclination of the Parents & Children in the Service for which any Children may be disposed of THOS HUTCHINSON per Order—

In Council; read & Accepted & Ordered that the Select Men of the several Towns where any French are placed govern themselves accordingly—In the House of Representatives; read & Concur'd—Consented to by the Governr."—*Ibid. pp.* 174, 175.

"April 21, 1756. In Council; Whereas this Government hath already recieved more than there Proportion of French Neutrals (so called) and besides the great Expence of their Support they are in other respects very Burthensome to the Inhabitants of this Province, and whereas there are some of his Majestys Colonies to which none of the French Neutrals have been sent therefore—Voted that no Master of a Vessell having any of said French Neutrals aboard presume to Land them in this Government without Leave of the Governour & Council and that only in Case of Distress; and all Persons whom it may concern are hereby strictly required to take Care that the Laws of this Province for preventing Strangers or other Persons who are like to be a Charge to this Government be put in Execution. In the House of Representatives; Read & Concur'd."—*Ibid*, *p* 178.

"May 28, 1756. The Committee appointed to consider & Report what is proper to be done by this Court in relation to the French Families last imported into this Province have attended that Service and would humbly propose that the said French Families be allowed to remain in this Province, and to be distributed into the several Sea Port Towns between Plymouth and Glocester, those Towns being included, and if any of those French People should hereafter be chargeable it should not be to the Towns where they reside, but to this Province—All which is humbly Submitted— By JOHN CUSHING per Order.

In the House of Representatives; Read & Ordered that this Report be Accepted—In Council; Read & Concur'd—Consented to by the Lieut Governr."—*Ibid., p.* 187.

"June 10, 1756. An Order was passed in Council, referring to the managing & employing of the French Inhabitants of Nova Scotia in the several Towns, Which being sent down was Non Concur'd by the House.

In the House of Representatives; It being found by Experience that the frequent Travelling & passing between Town & Town of many of the French People (lately dispersed thrô this Province by Order of the General Court) hath been attended with considerable Inconveniencies & may be productive of greater. Therefore Ordered & directed that the Select Men & Overseers of the Poor be very Carefull to keep the French People from Idling & Wandring about, and none of that People shall be permitted to travel from Town to Town without leave first obtained of Two of the Select Men or Overseers of the Poor where they respectively belong, of which such People shall produce Certificate or otherwise they shall be stopped & turned back by any Two English Householders who are hereby impowered to examine them & Stop or return them, if they have not Excuse as above In Council; Read & Concur'd—Consented to by the Lieutent Governr."—*Ibid., p.* 216.

"August 17, 1756. In the House of Representatives Whereas there is lately brought into this Town by John Gorham Esqr Sheriff of the County of Barnstable & Barnabas Gibbs, a Number of French People being Ninety Nine in the whole that were sent from Nova Scotia to Georgia, and some other Southern Governments who were in their way back to Nova Scotia, Therefore

Voted that said French People be committed to the Sheriff of the County of Suffolk untill the further Order of this Court, and that said Gorham & Gibbs be discharged from any further Care of them; And that also the said Sheriff of the County of Suffolk be directed to cause strict Search to be made after any Papers the said People may have in their Possession & to Secure the same in Order to their being delivered to a Committee of this Court——In Council; Read & Concur'd—Consented to by the Governour."—*Ibid., p.* 245.

"August 25, 1756. Report on the Affairs of the late French Inhabitants of Nova Scotia—vizt

The Committee appointed to consider what further may be necessary to be done with regard to the French Inhabitants of Nova Scotia who are now in the Province humbly Report as their Opinion, that those of them now in the Town of Boston, & under the Care of the Overseers of said Town amounting as We are informed to Eighty Four Persons, be forthwith moved from Boston, and distributed as near as may be among the Towns mentioned at the Foot of this Report; One or Two, more or less in each of said Towns, as shall best accommodate the French Families themselves, and that the Sheriffs of the County of Suffolk & Middlesex be directed to cause the said French Persons to be as soon as may be removed to said Towns respectively, and that the Select Men of said

Towns be directed to receive them accordingly; & in all Things concerning them to Govern themselves, by the Laws & Orders of this Court making Provision for the Inhabitants sent hither from that Government, and the Committee are further of Opinion that as Hanover has Nine & Pembrook but Five of the said Inhabitants, that Three of those at Hanover be removed to Pembrook——The Committee are further of Opinion that the Select Men of the several Towns where any of those French People are or may be placed be directed to assist them in procuring Employment at such Rates as they shall judge reasonable, and if thrô want of Employment or thrô want of Ability any of them cant Earn a Support for themselves & Families the Select Men be directed to afford them such Releif as may be necessary for their comfortable Subsistence, in the same manner as if they had been proper Inhabitants of this Province & exhibit their respective Accounts of Disbursement into the Secretarys Office as occasion shall require,

Which is Humbly Submitted— JOHN GREENLEAF.

Names of the Towns above referred to, with the Number of Persons respectively assigned to them, vizt Cambridge Ten, Walpole Five, Topsfield Five, Middleton Five, Westford Five, Sherburn Five, Littleton Five, Bedford Five, Tewksbury Four,—Brookfield Eight—Southborough Six—Grafton Six—Bellingham Four—Dunstable Four—Westborough Three—

In Council; Read & Accepted & Ordered that the French People therein mentioned be disposed of accordingly——In the House of Representatives; Read & Concur'd Consented to by the Governour."—*Ibid., p.* 255.

Chap. 36. "Febru^{a} 19, 1756. In the House of Representatives; Voted that there be a Committee consisting of Five Persons appointed to provide Provisions, Warlike Stores, and other Things requisite for carrying on the proposed Expedition against Crown Point, so far as may be necessary on the part of this Government——And that Mr Speaker, Mr James Russell, & Stephen Hall Esqr with such, as the Honble Board shall join be the said Committee, any three of whom to be a Quorum—In Council; Read & Concur'd; And John Osborne & Samuel Watts Esqr are joined in the Affair——Consented to by the Governour." —*Council Records, vol. XXI., p.* 95.

"February 24th 1756. In the House of Representatives; Voted that three Gentlemen be appointed as a Committee of War to reside at or near Albany, and to follow such Instructions as they shall receive from this Court, for the more effectual carrying into Execution the intended Expedition against Crown Point, the said Gentlemen to be chosen by joint Ballot with the hon^{ble} Board. In Council; Read & Concur'd."—*Ibid., p.* 105.

"February 25, 1756. The Two Houses according to agreement proceeded to the Election by joint Ballot, of three Gentlemen to be a Committee of War to reside at Albany, &^{ca}. And John Choat Josiah Dwight & John Murray Esq^{rs} were duly elected, to that Trust by the Major Vote of the Council & House of Representatives; To which the Governour Signed his Consent."—*Ibid., p.* 105.

"March 8, 1756. In the House of Representatives; Whereas two of the Gentlemen lately Chosen to reside at or near Albany for the more effectual carrying on the intended Expedition against Crown Point have declined that Service, and John Choat Esqr the other Gentleman then Chosen, having signified that he cannot attend thereon before the beginning of April, which it is apprehended will be too late—Therefore—Voted that Oliver Partridge, John Whetcomb, John Ashley, Elisha Williams & John Leach Esq^{rs} be a Committee to reside at Albany or Parts adjacent, and to repair thither as soon as may be, to take care of the Transportation of Provisions and other stores for the use of the Forces of this Province, proposed to be raised for the said intended Expedition, The said Committee to conform to such Instructions as they shall receive from this Court—In Council; Read & Non Concur'd."—*Ibid., p.* 121.

"March 8, 1756. Divers Messages passed between the Council & House of Representatives respecting the manner of Electing & appointing the Gentlemen to be a Committee of War to reside at or near Albany; but nothing agreed upon by both Houses in that Affair."—*Ibid., p* 123.

"March 9th 1756. Voted that John Whetcomb Esqr & Mr John Foye with such as the Honble House shall join be a Committee to reside at Albany or Parts adjacent & repair thither as soon as may be to take Care of the Transportation of the Provisions and other Stores for the Use of the Forces of this Province proposed to be raised for the said intended Expedition; the said Committee to Conform themselves to such Instructions as they shall receive from this Court. In the House of Representatives; Read & Concur'd; And Oliver Partridge John Ashley & John Leach Esq^{rs} are joined in the Affair—Consented to by the Governour."—*Ibid., p.* 124.

Chap. 37. "May 31, 1756. The Committee for Letting out to Farm the Excise on Spirituous Liquors in the County of Plymouth reported that they had agreed * * * for the Excise from the Twenty Sixth of December last to the Twenty Sixth of March last with Joseph Joslyn for £113. and taken Bonds * * with Sureties, which they have Lodged in the Treasury their Account amounting to £4. 13. 8—In the House of Representatives; Read & Ordered that this Report be accepted, & that there be allowed & paid out of the Publick Treasury, the Sum of Four Pounds thirteen Shillings & Eight Pence to the said Committee to discharge their Account of Time & Expence exhibited.—in Council; Read & Concur'd——Consented to by the Governour."—*Council Records, vol. XXI., p.* 190.

The above report from the committee appointed to farm out the excise for Plymouth county, was followed by reports from the committees for the other counties, and the dates of these reports together with the names of farmers of excise appointed by them, respectively, are as follows:—

May 31, 1756. Worcester county; to Ezra Taylor, for £78. 8.—*Ibid., p.* 191.

May 31, 1756. Bristol county; to Joseph Joslyn, for £33. 6. 1.—*Ibid.*
June 1, 1756. Hampshire county; to Elisha Pomroy, for £20.—*Ibid.*, *p.* 194.
June 1, 1756. Barnstable county; to Nathanael Little, for £57. 10.—*Ibid.*, *p.* 195.
June 1, 1756. Nantucket county; to Thomas Arthur, for £7. 9. 4.—*Ibid.*
June 8, 1756. Essex county; to Edward Harrington, for £300.—*Ibid*, *p.* 205.
July 3, 1756. York county; to Capt. Ichabod Goodwin, for £47. 10.—*Ibid.*, *p.* 226.

Chap. 38. "This Act is submitted to Your Lordshipps how far it is fitting to have this Exemption."—*Report of Sir Matthew Lamb: Mass. Bay, B. T., vol.* 75., *I. i.*, 5, *in Public-record Office.*

Chap. 40. "March 5th 1756. In the House of Representatives March 4th 1756 In Answer to His Excellencys Message of Yesterday—Voted, notwithstanding this Court are fully sensible that the Number of Three Thousand Men exclusive of officers already ordered by this Government to be employed on the intended Expedition against Crown Point is the full proportion of this Government considering the Numbers of this and the other Governments who it is depended on will join in said Expedition & much more than their proportion considering the very extended Frontiers of the Massachusetts Government, which said Government are obliged to defend at this time, without any Aid from any other Governments, who are Covered & defended by this Province, Yet considering of how great Importance it is to his Majesty's Governments that the proposed Expedition be carried into Execution; and being heartily desirous to Encourage the Service; agree— That the Number already Ordered by this Government to be raised for said Expedition be augmented to the Number of Thirty five hundred Men, inclusive of Officers; Provided always that the Governments of Rhode Island and New Hampshire who have not yet Certified this Government that they will join in the proposed Expedition shall agree to join the Forces of this & the Governments of Connecticut and New York with the Number of One Thousand each, and the same be made known & Certified from said Rhode Island & New Hampshire to this Government; And that no beating Orders be given nor Moneys granted out of the Treasury for raising the abovesaid Augmentation or any part of it, till the said Governments of Rhode Island & New Hampshire respectively shall have agreed to raise & send on the said Expedition the Number of One Thousand each, & the same be properly Certified to this Government.——The said Augmentation to be of Private Men, & when raised to be proportioned to the several Regiments & Companies already agreed to be raised In Council; Read & Concur'd——Consented to by the Governour."—*Council Records, vol. XXI.*, *p.* 118.

"April 19 1756. In the House of Representatives; Ordered that Mr Gridley Mr William Bowdoin & Colo Quincy with such as the Honble Board shall join be a Committee to consider what is proper to be done by this Court with regard to Articles of War, and a Court Martial in the Army now raising for the intended Expedition against Crown Point —In Council read & Concur'd; and John Cushing & Sylvanus Bourn Esqrs are joined in the Affair."—

* * * *

The Committee appointed to consider what is proper to be done with regard to the Government of the Army in the intended Expedition against Crown Point beg leave to report, that a Regimental & general Court Martial be appointed in the Army, and that for this purpose, It be Enacted by this Court that the Commission Officers of every Regiment may by the Appointment of their Colonel or Commanding Officer hold a Regimental Court Martial for Inflicting such Corporal Punishments as the Neglect of Duty, Disorders in Quarters, or other such Crimes may deserve, which Regimental Court shall not consist of less than Five Commission Officers of which Two to be Captains, and the Judgment to be by them given shall be according to the Plurality of Voices; and the Sentence shall not be put in Execution untill the Officer commanding the Regiment has confirmed and approved the same, And that it be likewise Enacted that there be a General Court Martial, which shall not consist of less than Thirteen Commission Officers under the Oath of Office, of which Seven to be field Officers, the President not to be under the degree of a Field Officer and the Sentence of this Court not to be put in Execution till Report be made of the whole Proceedings to the General Commanding in Chief, and his Directions signified thereon, and that a Bill be brought in accordingly & that the other Governments concerned in this Expedition be notified of this Act, and be desired to make like Provision for the Government of their several Forces in this Army
All which is humbly Submitted By John Cushing per Order

In Council—Read & Accepted—In the House of Representatives; Read & Concur'd; and Ordered that the said Committee prepare and bring in a Bill accordingly. In Council; Read & Concur'd."—*Ibid.*, *pp.* 172, 173.

"April 20, 1756. A Bill entitled an Act for the Government of the Forces in the Expedition intended against Crown Point—Having been read three times in the House of Representatives, and there passed to be Engrossed—In Council; read a First & Second time and passed a Concurrence."—*Ibid.*, *p.* 175.

The following is a copy of the engrossment of this Bill. As the province seal seems never to have been impressed upon the parchment as required by the charter, it is to be presumed that, for some reason, this act was purposely left incomplete, since it is hardly possible it could have been intentionally omitted from the list transmitted to the Privy Council, or have failed, either by accident or design, to have been included in any contemporary list or collection of the acts of the session in which it was passed. It is not unlikely that after signing the bill the Governor was convinced that this subject was properly within the exclusive province of the commander-in-chief whose forces were to be chiefly employed out of the provincial territory, and whose management of the army could not be controlled by regulations established by the legislatures of the respective colonies that had ordered levies for the army.

"Anno Regni Regis Georgii
Secundi vicesimo nono.

An Act for the Government of the Forces in the Expedition intended against Crown Point

Whereas this Government has levied & is now levying Forces for an Expedition against Crown Point, for the better Government of them therefore,

Be it Enacted by the Governour Council & House of Representatives, That the Commission Officers of every Regiment in said Forces may by the Appointm[t] of their Colonel or Commanding Officer hold a Regimental Court Martial for inflicting such Corporal Punishm[ts] as the Neglect of Duty, Disorders in Quarters or other such Crimes may deserve, which Regimental Court Martial shall not consist of less than five Commission Officers, two of whom shall not be under the Degree of Captains, and the Judgment to be by them given shall be according to the Plurality of Voices, & the Sentence shall not be put in Execution 'till the Officer commanding the Regiment has confirm'd & approved the same.

And be it further enacted, That there be a General Court Martial which shall not consist of less than thirteen Commiss[n] Officers in said Army under the Oath of Office, seven of whom shall be Field Officers and that the Sentence of this Court shall not be put in Execution 'till Report be made of the whole Proceedings to the General Commanding in Chief & his Directions be signified thereupon.

April 21st 1756 This Bill having been read three several times in the House of Represent[ves] Pass'd to be Enacted. T. HUBBARD Spk[r]

April 21st 1756 This Bill having been read three several times in Council.—Pass'd to be Enacted. J WILLARD Secry.

1756 By His Excellency the Governour I Consent to the Enacting of this Bill.
W: SHIRLEY.

Published 22 day April 1756."

ACTS,

Passed 1756–57.

ACTS

Passed at the Session begun and held at Boston, on the Twenty-sixth day of May, A. D. 1756.

CHAPTER 1.

AN ACT FOR THE SUPPLY OF THE TREASURY WITH THE SUM OF THREE THOUSAND AND SIX POUNDS THIRTEEN SHILLINGS AND FOURPENCE, AND FOR DRAWING THE SAME INTO THE TREASURY AGAIN; ALSO FOR APPORTIONING AND ASSESSING A TAX OF FIFTY-FIVE THOUSAND FIVE HUNDRED AND SIX POUNDS THIRTEEN SHILLINGS AND FOURPENCE, AND ALSO FOR APPORTIONING AND ASSESSING A FURTHER TAX OF THREE THOUSAND ONE HUNDRED AND NINETY-THREE POUNDS EIGHTEEN SHILLINGS, PAID THE REPRESENTATIVES FOR THEIR SERVICE AND ATTENDANCE IN THE GREAT AND GENERAL COURT, AND TRAVEL: WHICH SUMS AMOUNT, IN THE WHOLE, TO FIFTY-EIGHT THOUSAND SEVEN HUNDRED POUNDS ELEVEN SHILLINGS AND FOURPENCE.

Whereas the great and general court or assembly of this province did, at their session in March, one thousand seven hundred and fifty-five, pass an act for levying a tax of five thousand six hundred pounds; and in June following, another act for levying a further tax of thirty-six thousand pounds; and in October following, another act for levying a tax of five thousand six hundred pounds; and in March last another act for levying a tax of six thousand pounds; and by said acts provision was made that the general court, at this present session, might apportion the same on the several towns and districts within the province, if they thought fit; wherefore, for the ordering, directing and effectual drawing in the sum of fifty-eight thousand seven hundred pounds eleven shillings and fourpence, pursuant to the funds and grants aforesaid, into the treasury; we, his majesty's most loyal and dutiful subjects, the representatives in general court assembled, pray that it may be enacted,— 1754-55, chap. 32, § 2. 1755-56, chap. 4, § 7. 1755-56, chap. 18, § 2. 1755-56, chap. 29, § 4.

And be it accordingly enacted by the Lieutenant-Governour, Council and House of Representatives,

[Sect. 1.] That each town and district within this province be assessed and pay, as such town and district's proportion of the sum of fifty-five thousand five hundred and six pounds thirteen shillings and fourpence (and their representatives' pay, the sum of three thousand one hundred and ninety-three pounds eighteen shillings), the several sums following; that is to say,—

IN THE COUNTY OF SUFFOLK.

	[REPRESENTATIVES' PAY.]	[PROVINCE TAX.]	[SUM TOTAL.]	
Boston,	£117 4s. 0d.	£8,896 10s. 0d.	N[illegible]e [illegible] and thirteen pounds fourteen shillings,	£9,013 14s. 0d.
Roxbury,	29 16 0	499 10 0	Five [illegible] and twenty-nine pounds six shillings,	529 6 0
Dorchester,	28 8 0	494 6 6	Five [illegible] and [illegible]-two [illegible] fourteen shillings and sixpence,	522 14 6
Milton,	35 16 0	262 11 6	Two hundred and ninety-eight pounds [illegible] shill[in]gs and sixpence,	298 7 6
Braintree,	35 0 0	569 18 6	Six hundred and four pounds eighteen shillings and sixpence,	604 18 6
[illegible],	36 12 0	335 18 6	Three [illegible] and seventy-two pounds ten shillings and sixpence,	372 10 6
Hingham,	30 16 0	591 6 0	Six [illegible] and twenty-two pounds two shillings,	622 2 0
[illegible],	0 0 0	392 17 0	Three [illegible] and [illegible]-two [illegible] [illegible] shillings,	392 17 0
[illegible],	33 0 0	243 0 0	[illegible]o hundred and seventy-six pounds,	276 0 0
Wrentham,	0 0 0	415 10 0	Four [illegible] and [illegible] pounds ten shillings,	415 10 0
Brookl[y] [illegible],	26 8 0	151 4 0	One hundred and seventy-seven pounds [illegible] shillings,	177 12 0
[illegible],	36 12 0	199 7 0	Two hundred [and] [illegible]-five pounds [illegible] shillings,	235 19 0
[illegible],	36 16 0	339 0 0	Three [illegible] and [illegible]-five [illegible] [illegible] shillings,	375 16 0
Medway,	0 0 0	199 7 0	[illegible] [illegible] and [illegible] [illegible] seven shillings,	199 7 0
Bellingham,	0 0 0	77 8 0	[illegible] [illegible] pounds eight shillings,	77 8 0
Hull,	0 0 0	92 9 6	[illegible]-two [illegible] [illegible] shillings and sixpence,	92 9 6
Walpole,	0 0 0	148 4 0	One hundred and forty-eight pounds four shillings,	148 4 0
[illegible],	0 0 0	206 6 6	[illegible]o hundred and six pounds six [illegible] and [illegible],	206 6 6
	£446 8s. 0d.	£14,114 14s. 0d.		£14,561 2s. 0d.

IN THE COUNTY OF ESSEX.

Salem,	£36 16s. 0d.	£850 10s. 0d.	Eight hundred and eighty-[illegible] [illegible] six shill[in]gs,	£887 6s. 0d.
Danvers,	37 8 0	472 19 0	Five [illegible] and ten [illegible] [illegible] shillings,	510 7 0
Ipswich,	35 16 0	1,213 13 0	Twelve hundred and [illegible] [illegible] pounds [illegible] shillings,	1,249 9 0
Newbury,	31 12 0	1,562 3 6	Fifteen [illegible] and ninety-three [illegible] fifteen shill[in]gs and sixpence,	1,593 15 6
[illegible],	22 12 0	926 15 6	N[illegible] hundred and forty-nine [illegible] seven shill[in]gs and sixpence,	949 7 6
Lynn,	36 12 0	499 5 6	Five hundred and thir[illegible] pounds [illegible] shill[in]gs and sixpence,	535 17 6
[illegible]er,	38 0 0	685 2 6	Seven hundred and twenty-[illegible] pounds two shill[in]gs and sixp[illegible],	723 2 6
Beverly,	37 12 0	424 11 6	Four [illegible] and sixty-[three][*two*] [illegible] three shill[in]gs and [illegible],	462 3 6

Rowley,	£38 4s. 0d.	£432 0s. 0d.	Four hundred and seventy pounds four shillings,	£470 4s. 0d.
[illegible],	31 4 0	339 15 0	Three hundred and seventy pounds nineteen shillings,	370 19 0
Haverhill,	40 12 0	398 18 6	Four hundred and thirty-nine pounds ten shill[in]gs and sixpence,	439 10 6
[illegible],	26 4 0	706 [illegible] 6	Seven hundred and thirty-two pounds nine shillings and sixpence,	732 9 6
Topsfield,	0 0 0	189 0 0	One hundred and eighty-nine pounds,	189 0 0
Boxford,	38 4 0	249 19 6	Two hundred and eighty-eight pounds three shill[in]gs and sixpence,	288 3 6
Almsbury,	42 4 0	313 4 0	Three hundred and fifty-five pounds eight shillings,	355 8 0
Bradford,	36 8 0	280 7 0	Three hundred and sixteen pounds fifteen shillings,	316 15 0
Wenham,	0 0 0	158 17 0	One hundred and fifty-eight pounds seventeen shillings,	158 17 0
[illegible],	0 0 0	141 1 8	One hundred and forty-one pounds one shilling and sixpence,	141 1 6
[illegible],	0 0 0	113 12 8	One hundred and thirteen pounds twelve shill[in]gs and sixpence,	113 12 6
[illegible],	0 0 0	180 18 0	One hundred and eighty pounds eighteen shillings,	180 18 0
	£529 8s. 0d.	£10,138 19s. 0d.		£10,668 7s. 0d.

IN THE COUNTY OF MIDDLESEX.

Cambridge,	£0 0s. 0d.	£377 2s. 0d.	Three hundred and seventy-seven pounds two shill[in]gs,	£377 2s. 0d.
[illegible],	30 16 0	487 19 0	Five hundred and eighteen pounds fifteen shillings,	518 15 0
[illegible],	35 16 0	200 0 6	Two hundred and thirty-five pounds sixteen shill[in]gs and sixpence,	235 16 6
Woburn,	0 0 0	351 0 0	Three hundred and fifty-one pounds,	351 0 0
[illegible],	25 12 0	223 17 6	Two hundred and forty-nine pounds nine shill[in]gs and sixpence,	249 9 6
Newton,	35 16 0	351 0 0	Three hundred and eighty-six pounds sixteen shillings,	386 16 0
[illegible],	40 12 0	379 11 6	Four hundred and twenty pounds three shill[in]gs and sixpence,	420 3 6
Marlborough,	39 0 0	378 0 0	Four hundred and seventeen pounds,	417 0 0
Billerica,	34 8 0	221 8 0	Two hundred and fifty-five pounds sixteen shillings,	255 16 0
Framingham,	36 0 0	288 18 0	Three hundred and twenty-four pounds eighteen shillings,	324 18 0
Lexington,	34 16 0	241 11 4	Two hundred and seventy-six pounds seven shill[in]gs and four-pence,	276 7 4
[illegible],	0 0 0	216 0 0	Two hundred and sixteen pounds,	216 0 0
Sherburne,	0 0 0	149 3 6	One hundred and forty-nine pounds three shillings and sixpence,	149 3 6
Reading,	35 16 0	356 8 0	Three hundred and ninety-two pounds four shillings,	392 4 0
[illegible],	30 16 0	284 8 0	Three hundred and fifteen pounds four shillings,	315 4 0
[illegible],	37 8 0	159 12 6	One hundred and ninety-seven pounds and sixpence,	197 0 6
Medford,	30 16 0	279 13 6	Three hundred and ten pounds nine shill[in]gs and sixpence,	310 9 6
Littleton,	31 0 0	151 13 0	One hundred and eighty-two pounds thirteen shillings,	182 13 0
Hopkinston,	0 0 0	132 6 0	One hundred and thirty-two pounds six shillings,	132 6 0
Westford,	0 0 0	145 16 0	One hundred and forty-five pounds sixteen shillings,	145 16 0
[illegible],	3 11 0	37 2 6	Forty pounds thirteen shillings and sixpence,	40 13 6

IN THE COUNTY OF MIDDLESEX—*Continued.*

	[REPRESENTATIVES' PAY]	[PROVINCE TAX.]	[SUM TOTAL.]	
Waltham,	£30 8*s.* 0*d.*	£186 15*s.* 0*d.*	Two hundred and seventeen pounds three shillings,	217 3 0
Townshend,	0 0 0	82 11 6	Eighty-two pounds eleven shillings and sixpence,	82 11 6
Stow,	0 0 0	132 6 0	One hundred and thirty-two pounds six shillings,	132 6 0
Stoneham,	0 0 0	94 14 6	Ninety-four pounds fourteen shillings and sixpence,	94 14 6
Groton,	20 7 0	266 11 0	Two hundred and eighty-six pounds eighteen shillings,	286 18 0
Wilmington,	0 0 0	108 0 0	One hundred and eight pounds,	108 0 0
Natick,	0 0 0	75 3 0	Seventy-five pounds three shillings,	75 3 0
Dracut,	0 0 0	106 4 0	One hundred and six pounds four shillings,	106 4 0
Bedford,	0 0 0	123 19 6	One hundred and twenty-three pounds nineteen shill[in]gs and sixpence,	123 19 6
Holliston,	0 0 0	120 7 6	One hundred and twenty pounds seven shillings and sixpence,	120 7 6
Tewksbury,	0 0 0	106 4 0	One hundred and six pounds four shillings,	106 4 0
Acton,	0 0 0	78 6 0	Seventy-eight pounds six shillings,	78 6 0
Dunstable,	0 0 0	100 14 6	One hundred pounds fourteen shill[in]gs and sixpence,	100 14 6
Pepper[r]ell,	11 18 0	85 4 0	Ninety-seven pounds two shillings,	97 2 0
Lincoln,	24 16 0	149 4 8	One hundred and seventy-four pounds and eightpence,	174 0 8
Carlisle,	11 0 0	104 8 0	One hundred and fifteen pounds eight shill[in]gs,	115 8 0
	£580 12*s.* 0*d.*	£7,333 4*s.* 0*d.*		£7,913 16*s.* 0*d.*

IN THE COUNTY OF HAMPSHIRE.

Springfield,	£27 4*s.* 0*d.*	£525 12*s.* 0*d.*	Five hundred and fifty-two pounds sixteen shillings,	£552 16*s.* 0*d.*
Northampton,	20 4 0	299 11 6	Three hundred and nineteen pounds fifteen shill[in]gs and sixpence,	319 15 6
Hatfield,	16 16 0	161 15 6	One hundred and seventy-eight pounds eleven shill[in]gs and sixpence,	178 11 6
Westfield,	39 0 0	210 7 6	Two hundred and forty-nine pounds seven shill[in]gs and sixpence,	249 7 6
Enfield,	0 0 0	156 7 6	One hundred and fifty-six pounds seven shillings and sixpence,	156 7 6
Brimfield,	20 12 0	108 7 6	One hundred and twenty-eight pounds nineteen shill[in]gs and [6d.] [sixpence],	128 19 6
Sheffield,	20 0 0	233 6 6	Two hundred and fifty-three pounds six shill[in]gs and sixpence,	253 6 6
Northfield,	0 0 0	56 9 8	Fifty-six pounds nine shill[in]gs and sixpence,	56 9 6
Hadley,	21 10 0	180 16 0	Two hundred and two pounds six shillings,	202 6 0
Suffield,	0 0 0	290 5 0	Two hundred and ninety pounds five shillings,	290 5 0
Sunderland,	0 0 0	53 10 6	Fifty-three pounds ten shillings and sixpence,	53 10 6

[illegible]e,	£0 0s. 0d.	£39 3s. 6d.	Thirty-nine [illegible] three [illegible] and [illegible],	£39 3s. 6d.
[illegible]d,	0 0 0	177 15 0	[illegible] and [illegible] shill[in]gs,	177 15 0
[illegible]s,	0 0 0	111 12 0	[illegible] hundred and [illegible],	111 12 0
[illegible],	4 0 0	48 10 0	[illegible]-two [illegible],	52 10 0
[illegible] [illegible]y,	10 10 0	97 6 0	[illegible] and seven [illegible] shillings,	107 16 0
[illegible]r,	0 0 0	66 12 0	Sixty-six [illegible] twelve shillings,	66 12 0
[illegible]n,	0 0 0	56 14 0	Fifty-six [illegible] shillings,	56 14 0
Bedford,	0 0 0	37 16 0	[illegible],	37 16 0
Coldspring,	0 0 0	37 16 0	[illegible],	37 16 0
[illegible]h,	0 0 0	42 6 0	[illegible]-two [illegible] six shillings,	42 6 0
[illegible],	0 0 0	23 17 0	[illegible] shillings,	23 17 0
New Salem,	0 0 0	27 0 0	[illegible]-seven [illegible],	27 0 0
[illegible],	0 0 0	40 10 0	[illegible] shillings,	40 10 0
[illegible] (in [illegible]),	0 0 0	27 0 0	[illegible],	27 0 0
Ware [illegible],	0 0 0	27 0 0	[illegible],	27 0 0
[illegible]e,	0 0 0	54 0 0	[illegible],	54 0 0
[illegible]n,	0 0 0	22 10 0	[illegible]-two [pounds] ten shillings,	22 10 0
[illegible]d,	8 0 0	48 13 6	Fifty-six [illegible] and [illegible],	56 13 6
	£187 16s. 0d.	£3,262 10s. 0d.		£3,450 6s. 0d.

IN THE COUNTY OF WORCESTER.

[illegible]r,	£29 0s. 0d.	£[illegible]4 17s. 0d.	[illegible] shillings,	£314 7s. [illegible]
[illegible]r,	40 12 0	324 0 0	Three [illegible],	364 12 0
[illegible]n,	35 12 0	310 10 0	[illegible] forty-six [illegible] two [illegible],	346 2 0
Woodstock,	0 0 0	349 4 0	Three hundred [illegible] four shillings,	349 4 0
[illegible]d,	31 4 0	254 [illegible] 6	[illegible] two [illegible],	286 2 6
Oxford,	21 12 0	129* 7 0	[illegible] fifty [illegible] shillings,	150 19 0
[illegible]n,	7 0 0	43 0 0	Fifty pounds,	50 0 0
Sutton,	35 0 0	247 14 6	[illegible]-two [illegible] shill[in]gs [illegible],	282 14 6
[illegible]d,	31 18 5	178 13 0	[illegible] shillings [illegible],	210 11 5
[illegible],	0 0 0	15 0 0	[illegible],	15 0 0
[illegible] of [illegible],	7 9 7	25 10 0	[illegible] [teen] [illegible],	32 19‡ 7
[illegible]r,	13 16† 8	169 10 0†	[illegible] [and] eighty-[illegible] six [illegible],	183 6 8
[illegible] of [illegible]ncer,	6 13 4	84 15 0	[illegible] pounds [illegible],	91 8 4

* 120, in the parchment. † 6, in the parchment. ‡ 9, in the parchment.

IN THE COUNTY OF WORCESTER—*Continued.*

	[REPRESENTATIVES' PAY]	[PROVINCE TAX.]	[SUM TOTAL.]	
Southborough,	£0 [illegible]. [illegible].	£139 5s. 6d.	[illegible]e [illegible]d [and] thirty-nine [illegible]ds [illegible]e [illegible]gs [illegible]d sixpence,	£139 5s. 6d.
[illegible]h,	36 8 0	194 12 6	[illegible]o [illegible]d [[illegible]d] [illegible]e [illegible]s [illegible]d [illegible]e,	[illegible]31 0 6
[illegible],	28 18 0	226 16 0	Two [illegible]d [illegible]d fifty-[illegible]e [illegible]s [illegible]n [illegible] [illegible]s,	[illegible]35 14 0
[illegible]g,	39 0 0	190 2 6	[illegible]o [illegible]d [illegible]d [illegible]e [illegible]s [illegible]o [[illegible]]gs [illegible]d [illegible]e,	29 2 6
U[illegible]e,	38 4 0	172 2 6	[illegible]o [illegible]d [illegible]d [illegible]n [illegible]s [illegible]o] [*six*] [illegible]]gs [illegible]d [illegible]e,	[illegible]20 6* 6
[illegible],	0 0 0	156 3 0	[illegible]e [illegible]d [illegible]d fifty-six pounds [[illegible]d] three [illegible]il[illegible],	[illegible]56 3 0
[illegible]y,	0 0 0	102 12 0	[illegible]e [illegible]d [illegible]d [illegible]o [illegible]s [illegible]e [illegible]s,	[illegible]02 12 0
[illegible]n,	22 8 0	155 14 0	[illegible]e [illegible]d [illegible]d [illegible]t [illegible]s [illegible]o [illegible],	[illegible]78 2 0
[illegible],	0 0 0	85 19 0	[illegible]e [illegible]s [illegible]n [illegible],	85 19 0
[illegible]e,	21 12 0	67 5 6	[illegible]t [illegible]s e[illegible]n [illegible]s [illegible]d [illegible]e,	88 17 6
Leominster,	0 0 0	81 0 0	Eighty-one pounds,	81 0 0
[illegible]k,	33 4 0	99 18 0	[illegible]e [illegible]d [illegible]d [illegible]e [illegible]s two [illegible]s,	[illegible]33 2 0
[illegible]n,	0 0 0	51 6 0	[illegible]- [illegible]e [illegible]s six [illegible]s,	51 6 0
[illegible]n,	0 0 0	78 6 0	[illegible]t [illegible]s six [illegible]s,	78 6 0
[illegible]s,	0 0 0	22 10 0	[illegible]o [illegible]s [illegible]n [illegible].	22 10 0
Grafton,	0 0 0	131 8 0	[illegible]e [illegible]d [illegible]] t[illegible]-[illegible]e [illegible]s [illegible]t [illegible]ngs,	[illegible]31 8 0
[illegible]n,	0 0 0	58 10 0	[illegible]t [illegible]s [illegible]n [illegible],	58 10 0
	£480 2s. 0d.	£4,430 9s. 6d.		£4,910 11s. 6d.

IN THE COUNTY OF PLYMOUTH.

Plymouth,	[illegible]29 [illegible]s. [illegible].	£432 [illegible]. [illegible].	[illegible]r [illegible]d [illegible]d [illegible]-[illegible]e [illegible]s [illegible]e shillin[illegible]s,	£461 12s. 0d.
Scituate,	39 0 0	[illegible]94 0 0	S[illegible]x [illegible]d [illegible]d thirty-three pounds,	[illegible]63 0 0
Duxbury,	0 0 0	[illegible]95 15 0	[illegible]e [illegible]d [illegible]d [illegible]e [illegible]s [illegible]n [illegible]illin[illegible]s,	[illegible]95 15 0
Marshfield,	32 0 0	[illegible]03 13 0	Four [illegible]d [illegible]d thirty-five [illegible]s thirteen [illegible],	[illegible]35 13 0
Bridgwater,	34 4 0	[illegible]86 14 0	Seven [illegible]d [illegible]d twenty [illegible]s [illegible]r [illegible],	[illegible]20 18 0
Middleborough,	34 12 0	[illegible]02 19 6	Five hundred [illegible]d twenty-seven [illegible]s eleven shill[*in*]gs and six-p[illegible]e,	[illegible]37 11 6
Rochester,	33 14 0	[illegible]97 4 6	Three [illegible]d [illegible]d thirty [illegible]s [illegible]n [illegible]s [illegible]d [illegible]e,	30 18 6
Plympton,	36 8 0	[illegible]51 11 0	T[illegible]o [illegible]d [illegible]d eighty-seven [illegible]s [illegible]n [illegible].	[illegible]87 19 0
Pembrook,	36 12 0	[illegible]45 9 6	[illegible]o [illegible]d [illegible]d eighty-two pounds one shilling and sixpence,	[illegible]82 1 6
Kingston,	26 4 0	45 7 0	[illegible]e [illegible]d [illegible]d seventy-one pounds eleven shillings,	[illegible]71 11 0
Hanover,	0 0 0	74 12 0	[illegible]e [illegible]d [illegible]d seventy-four pounds twelve shillings,	74 12 0
Abbington,	0 0 0	[illegible]02 10 0	T[illegible]o [illegible]d [illegible]d two pounds ten shillings,	[illegible]02 10 0

Halifax,	£0 0s. 0d.	£119 14s. 0d.	One hundred and nineteen pounds fourteen shillings,	£119 14s. 0d.
Warham,	0 0 0	124 4 0	One hundred and twenty-four pounds four shillings,	124 4 0
	£302 6s. 0d.	£4,365 13s. 6d.		£4,667 19s.† 6d.

IN THE COUNTY OF BARNSTABLE.

Barnstable,	£41 16s. 0d.	£378 0s. 0d.	Four hundred and nineteen pounds sixteen shillings,	£419 16s. 0d.
Yarmouth,	0 0 0	247 10 0	Two hundred and forty-seven pounds ten shillings,	247 10 0
Sandwich,	44 4 0	270 0 0	Three hundred and fourteen pounds four shillings,	314 4 0
Eastham,	16 18 0	307 16 0	Three hundred and twenty-four pounds fourteen shill[in]gs,	324 14 0
Harwich,	24 12 0	238 19 0	Two hundred and sixty-three pounds eleven shillings,	263 11 0
Chatham,	0 0 0	135 13 6	One hundred and thirty-five pounds thirteen shillings and sixpence,	135 13 6
Truro,	0 0 0	145 11 6	One hundred and forty-five pounds eleven shillings and sixpence,	145 11 6
Falmouth,	0 0 0	167 8 0	One hundred and sixty-seven pounds eight shillings,	167 8 0
	£127 10s. 0d.	£1,890 18s. 0d.		£2,018 8s. 0d.

IN THE COUNTY OF BRISTOL.

Taunton,	£37 16s. 0d.	£521 6s. 6d.	Five [illegible]d ad fifty- [illegible]e [illegible]s two [illegible]d [illegible]e,	£559 2s. 6d.
Rehoboth,	34 12 0	747 4 6	[illegible]n [illegible]d ad [illegible]e [illegible]s [illegible]n [illegible]s ad [illegible]e,	781 16 6
Swanzey w[i]th Shawamet,	32 16 0	331 13 0	[illegible]e [illegible]d ad [illegible]r [illegible]s [illegible]e [illegible]s,	364 9 0
Dartmouth,	47 0 0	972 0 0	[illegible]e [illegible]d ad [illegible]n [illegible],	1,019 0 0
Norton,	38 4 0	326 0 6	[illegible]e [illegible]d ad [illegible]r [illegible]s [illegible]r [illegible][in]gs ad [illegible]e,	364 4 6
Attleborough,	35 4 0	355 19 0	[illegible]e [illegible]d [and] [illegible]s [illegible]e [illegible] [illegible],	391 3 0
Dighton,	0 0 0	229 19 0	[illegible]o [illegible]d ad [illegible]e [illegible]s [illegible]n [illegible],	229 19 0
Freetown,	0 0 0	212 8‡ 0	[illegible]o [illegible]d ad [illegible]e [illegible]s [illegible]t [illegible]s,	212 8 0
Raynham,	0 0 0	137 5 0	[illegible]e [illegible]d ad [illegible]n [illegible]s five [illegible],	137 5 0
Easton,	31 12 0	157 14 6	[illegible]e [illegible]d ad [illegible]e [illegible]s [illegible]x [illegible]s ad [illegible]e,	189 6 6
Berkley,	0 0 0	122 12 6	[illegible]e [illegible]d ad [illegible]o [illegible]s [illegible]e [illegible]s ad [illegible]e,	122 12 6
	£257 4s. 0d.	£4,114 2s. 6d.		£4,371 6s. 6d.

* 2, in the parchment.

† 9, in the parchment.

‡ 18, in the parchment.

IN THE COUNTY OF YORK.

	[REPRESENTATIVES' PAY.]	[PROVINCE TAX.]	[SUM TOTAL.]	
York,	[illegible]6 4. [illegible]	£528 15s. 0d.	Five [illegible]d ad [illegible]r [illegible]s [illegible]n [illegible]lings,	[illegible]4 19s. [illegible]
Kittery,	36 8 0	621 0 • 0	S[illegible] [illegible]d ad [illegible]n [illegible]s [illegible]t [illegible],	657 8 0
Wells,	36 12 0	237 12 0	Two [illegible]d ad [illegible]r [illegible]s four [illegible],	274 4 0
Berwick,	27 12 0	324 0 0	[illegible]e [illegible]d ad fifty- ne [illegible]s [illegible]e [illegible],	351 12 0
Falmouth,	15 8 0	513 0 0	Five [illegible]d ad twenty- [illegible]t [illegible]s [illegible]t [illegible],	528 8 0
Biddeford,	40 4 0	217 16 0	[illegible]o [illegible]d ad [illegible]y- [illegible]t [illegible],	258 0 0
Arundel,	26 0 0	121 1 0	[illegible]e [illegible]d ad [illegible]n [illegible]s ne shilling,	147 1 0
Scarborough,	29 8 0	185 12 6*	[illegible]o [illegible]red ad [illegible]n [illegible]s ad [illegible]e,	215 0 6
North Yarmouth,	0 0 0	80 15 6	[illegible]y [illegible]s [illegible]n [illegible]s ad [illegible],	80 15 6
George Town,	0 0 0	85 14 6	[illegible]e [illegible]s [illegible]n [illegible]s ad [illegible]e,	85 14 6
Brunswick,	0 0 0	77 3 6	[illegible]y-seven [illegible]s three [illegible]s ad [illegible]e,	77 3 6
Sheepscut,	0 0 0	54 0 0	[illegible]- for [illegible],	54 0 0
	£257 16s. 0d.	£3,046 10s. 0d.		£3,304 6s. 0d.

IN THE COUNTY OF DUKES COUNTY.

Edgartown,	£0 0s. 0d.	£208 16s. 0d.	Two hundred and eight pounds sixteen shillings,	£208 16s. 0d.
Chilmark,	0 0 0	187 8 6	One hundred and eighty-seven pounds eight shill[in]gs and sixpence,	187 8 6
Tisbury,	0 0 0	119 14 0	One hundred and nineteen pounds fourteen shillings,	119 14 0
	£0 0s. 0d.	£515 18s. 6d.		£515 18s. 6d.

IN NANTUCKET COUNTY.

	REPRESENTATIVES' PAY.	TAX FOR SOLDIERS.	PROVINCE TAX.		SUM TOTAL.
Sherburne,	£24 16s. 0d.	£1,506 13s. 4d.	£787 1s. 0d.	Two thousand three hundred and eighteen pounds ten shill[in]gs and fourpence,	£2,318 10s. 4d.

* 0, in the printed act.

	REPRESENT[ATI]V[E]S' PAY.	TAX FOR SOLDIERS.	PROVINCE TAX.		SUM TOTAL.
[illegible]k, . . .	£446 8s. [illegible].		£14,114 14s. 0d.	Fourteen [illegible] and [illegible] and [illegible]-ne [illegible] two [illegible] shilli[n]gs,	£14,561 2s. 0d.
[illegible]x, . . .	529 8 0		10,138 19 0	[illegible] [illegible] and sixty-eight [illegible] seven [illegible]ings, .	10,668 7 0
[illegible], . . .	580 12 0		7,333 4 0	Seven [illegible] hundred [illegible] [illegible] shillings, .	7,913 16 0
[illegible], . . .	187 16 0		3,262 10 0	Three [illegible] four [illegible] [illegible] shillings, . .	3,450 6 0
[illegible], . . .	480 2 0		4,430 9 6	Four [illegible] eleven shill[in]gs [illegible] sixpence, ...	4,910 11 6
[illegible]h, . . .	302 6 0		4,365 13 6	Four thousand six hundred [illegible] [illegible] shil-l[in]gs [illegible] [illegible]p[ence], ...	[illegible]67 19 6
[illegible], . . .	127 10 0		1,890 18 0	[illegible]th [illegible] eight [illegible], ...	2,018 8 0
Bristol, ...	257 4 0		4,114 2 6	Four [illegible] shillings [and [illegible]], ...	4,371 6 6*
York, ...	257 16 0		3,046 10 0	Three [illegible] three [illegible] [illegible], . .	3,304 6 0
[illegible]s [illegible]y, . .	0 0 0		515 18 6	Five [illegible] fifteen [illegible] eighteen [illegible]nce, .	[illegible]5 18 6
Nantucket, . . .	24 16 0	£1,506 13s. 4d. } †	787 1 0	Two thousand three hundred and eighteen pounds ten shillings and fourpence, ...	2,318 10 4
	£3,193 18 0	£1,506 13s. 4d. }	£54,000 0s. 0d.		£58,700 11s. 4d.

* 0, in the engrossment.

† In the engrossment, the figures included by the brace are in the third column.

And be it further enacted,

[SECT. 2.] That the treasurer do forthwith send out his warrants, directed to the selectmen or assessors of each town or district within this province, requiring them, respectively, to assess the sum hereby set upon such town or district, in manner following; that is to say, to assess all rateable polls above the age of sixteen years, within their respective towns or districts, or next adjo[y][*i*]ning to them, belonging to no other town, [at] nine shillings per poll, and proportionably in assessing the additional sum received out of the treasury for the payment of the representatives (excepting the governo[u]r, the lieutenant-governo[u]r and their families, the president, fellows, professors and students of Harvard College, settled ministers and grammar-school masters, who are hereby exempted as well from being taxed for their polls, as for their estates being in their own hands and under their actual management and improvement; as also all the estate pertaining to Harvard College); and other persons, if such there be, who, thro'[ugh] age, infirmity or extreme poverty, in the judgment of the assessors, are not able to pay towards publick charges, they may exempt their polls, and so much of their estates as in their prudence they shall think fit and judge meet.

Rules for assessment.

[SECT. 3.] And the justices in their general sessions, in the respective counties assembled, in granting a county tax or assessment, are hereby ordered and directed to apportion the same on the several towns and districts in such county in proportion to their province rate, exclusive of what hath been paid out of the publick treasury to the representatives of each town for his service; and the assessors of each town in the province are also directed, in making an assessment, to govern themselves by the same rule; and all estates, both real and personal, lying within the limits of such town or district, or next unto the same, not paying elsewhere, in whose hands, tenure, occupation or possession the same is or shall be found, and also the incomes or profits which any person or persons, except as before excepted, do or shall receive from any trade, faculty, business or employment whatsoever, and all profits which shall or may arise by money or other estate not particularly otherwise assessed, or commissions of profit in their improvement, according to their understanding or cunning, at one penny on the pound; and to abate or multiply the same, if need be, so as to make up the sum set and ordered hereby for such town or district to pay; and, in making their assessment, to estimate houses and lands at six years' income of the yearly rents whereat the same may be reasonably set or let for in the place where they lye: *saving* all contracts between landlord and tenant, and where no contract is, the landlord to reimburse one half of the tax set upon such houses and lands; and to estimate negro, Indian and molatto servants proportionably as other personal estate, according to their sound judgment and discretion; as also to estimate every ox of four years old and upwards, at forty shillings; every cow of three years old and upwards, at thirty shillings; every horse and mare [at] [*of*] three years old and upwards, at forty shillings; every swine of one year old and upwards, at eight shillings; goats and sheep of one year old, at three shillings each: likewise requiring the said assessors to make a fair list of the said assessment, setting forth, in distinct columns, against each particular person's name, how he or she is assessed at for polls, and how much for houses and lands, and how much for personal estate, and income by trade or faculty, and if as guardian, or for any estate in his or her improvement, in trust, to be distinctly expressed; and the list or lists, so perfected and signed by them, or the major part of them, to commit to the collectors, constable or constables of such town or district, and to return a certificate of the name or names of such collector, constable or constables, with the sum total to each of them committed, unto himself, some time before the last day of October next.

[Sect. 4.] And the treasurer for the time being, upon receipt of such certificate, is hereby impowered and ordered to issue forth his warrants to the collector, or constable or constables of such town or district, requiring him or them, respectively, to collect the whole of each respective sum assessed on each particular person, and to pay in their collection, and issue the acco[un][*mp*]ts of the whole, at or before the thirty-first day of March next, which will be in the year of our Lord one thousand seven hundred and fifty-seven.

And be it further enacted,

Inhabitants to bring in a true list of their polls, &c.

[Sect. 5.] That the assessors of each town or district, respectively, in convenient time before their making the assessment, shall give seasonable warning to the inhabitants, in a town meeting, or by posting up notifications in some place or places in such town or district, or notify the inhabitants some other way to give or bring in to the assessors true and perfect lists of their polls, rateable estate, and income by trade or faculty, and gain by money at interest, which they are to render to the assessors on oath, if required; and if they refuse to give in an account of the money at interest, on oath, the assessors are impowered to doom them; and if any person or persons shall neglect or refuse so to do, or bring in a false list, it shall be lawful to and for the assessors to assess such person or persons, according to their known ability in such town, in their sound judgment and discretion, their due proportion of this tax, as near as they can, agreable to the rules herein given, under the penalty of twenty shillings for each person that shall be convicted by legal proof, in the judgment of the said assessors, in bringing in a false list; the said fines to be for the use of the poor of such town or district where the delinquent lives, to be levied by warrant from the assessors, directed to the collectors or constables, in manner as is directed for gathering town assessments, to be paid in to the town treasurer or selectmen for the use aforesaid: *saving* to the party aggrieved at the judgment of the assessors in setting forth such fine, liberty of appeal therefrom to the court of general sessions of the peace within the county for relief as in case of being overrated. And if any person or persons shall not bring a list of their estates as aforesaid to the assessors, he or they so neglecting shall not be admitted to make application to the court of general sessions for any abatement of the assessment laid on him.

[Sect. 6.] And if the party be not convicted of any falseness in the list, by him presented, of the polls, rateable estate, or income by trade or faculty, business or employment, which he does or shall exercise, or in gain by money at interest or otherwise, or other estate not particularly assessed, such list shall be a rule for such person's proportion to the tax, which the assessors may not exceed.

And forasmuch as, oftentimes, sundry persons, not belonging to this province, bring considerable trade and merchandize, and by reason that the tax or rate of the town where they come to trade is finished and delivered to the constable or collectors, and, before the next year's assessment, are gone out of the province, and so pay nothing towards the support of the government, though, in the time of their residing here, they reaped considerable gain by trade, and had the protection of the government,—

Be it further enacted,

Transient traders to be rated.

[Sect. 7.] That when any such person or persons, shall come and reside in any town within this province, and bring any merchandize and trade to deal therewith, the assessors of such town are hereby impowered to rate and assess all such persons, according to their circumstances, pursuant to the rules and directions in this act provided, tho'[ugh] the former rate may have been finished, and the new one not perfected, as aforesaid.

And be it further enacted,

Merchants, &c., to be rated for carrying on trade in any other town beside where they dwell.

[SECT. 8.] That when any merchant, trader or factor, inhabitant of some one town within this province, or of any other province, shall traffic or carry on any trade or business, or set up a store in some other town in the province, the assessors of such town where such trade and business shall be carried on as aforesaid, be and hereby are impowered to rate and assess all such merchants, traders and factors, their goods and merchandize, for carrying on such trade and business and exercising their faculty in such town, pursuant to the rules and directions of this act: *provided* before any such assessors shall rate such persons as afore mentioned, the selectmen of the town where such trade is carried on, shall transmit a list of such persons as they shall judge may and ought to be rated, within the intent of this act, to the assessors of such town or district.

Selectmen to transmit a list of such persons before they are rated.

[SECT. 9.] And the constables or collectors are hereby enjoyned to levy and collect all such sums committed to them, and assessed on persons who are not of this province, or are residents in other towns than those where they carry on their trade, and pay the same.

And be it further enacted,

Supply of £3,006 13s. 4d. for future public debts.

[SECT. 10.] That the sum of three thousand and six pounds thirteen shillings and fourpence, part of the aforesaid tax, not appropriated in any supply bill for the payment of the publick debts, shall be and remain as a stock in the treasury, subject to the future orders of this court, and be employed for the payment of the public[k] debts, as this court shall hereafter direct.

And whereas it hath been the practice of some of the inhabitants of the town of Boston to remove to some other town in this province, and there reside for some months, to avoid paying their part of the taxes in the town of Boston, to which they really belong, to the great injury of said town,—

Be it therefore enacted,

Inhabitants of Boston removing to any other town, and returning again the same year, to pay the tax in Boston.

[SECT. 11.] That when any inhabitant[*s*] of the town of Boston shall remove to any other town in this province, and shall, in one year after, remove back to said Boston, and shall have been taxed in said town, he shall be subject to pay said taxes, in like manner as he would have been had he not removed from said Boston: *saving* so much as he shall be taxed in the town removed to, anything in this act to the contrary notwitstanding. [*Passed June* 8; *published June* 10.*

CHAPTER 2.

AN ACT IN ADDITION TO THE ACT FOR ENQUIRING INTO THE RATEABLE ESTATES OF THE PROVINCE.

Preamble. 1755-56, chap. 44.

WHEREAS in and by an act made in the present year of his maj[*es*]ty's reign, intitled "An Act for [i][*e*]nquiring into the rateable estates of the province," the assessors of each town and district in this province, that were chosen in the year one thousand seven hundred and fifty-

* On one sheet of the engrossment this date is given as June 17, 1756.

five, were required, on oath, to transmit into the secretary's office a copy of the list and valuation of estates, by the last Wednesday of May, one thousand seven hundred and fifty-six, on penalty of five pounds; but, by reason of the shortness of the time between the making and publishing said act and the said last Wednesday of May, the assessors in divers towns and districts of the province did not, as this court have been well informed, obtain the knowledge of said act, and have not been able to comply with the order and duty enjoyned, and yet are exposed to the penalty therein mentioned,—

Be it therefore enacted by the Lieutenant-Governour, Council and House of Representatives,

[Sect. 1.] That such assessors of the several towns and districts as have failed of returning a list by the said last Wednesday in May, as by said act required, shall not be subjected to the penalty of five pounds, or any part thereof; anything in the said act to the contrary notwithstanding.

Assessors not returning valuation lists, at time, indemnified.

And be it further enacted,

[Sect. 2.] That the assessors of the several towns and districts in this province, that were chosen in the year one thousand seven hundred and fifty-five, shall, by the last Wednesday of December, one thousand seven hundred and fifty-six, on oath, transmit into the secretary's office a true and perfect copy of the list and valuation of estates by which they made the province taxes in their particular towns and districts, for the year one thousand seven hundred and fifty-five, and also a true copy of the rate-bill of the province tax in the year one thousand seven hundred and fifty-five, on penalty that each assessor neglecting his duty therein shall forfeit and pay the sum of five pounds; such penalty to be recovered and applied as by said act was provided. [*Passed June 3;* published June* 10.†

Further time allowed.

CHAPTER 3.

AN ACT FOR SUPPLYING THE TREASURY WITH THE SUM OF FIFTY-EIGHT THOUSAND POUNDS, TO BE THENCE ISSUED FOR DISCHARGING THE PUBLIC[K] DEBTS, AND DRAWING THE SAME INTO THE TREASURY AGAIN.

Whereas no provision is made by this court to discharge the debts of the government for the ensuing year; *and whereas* the provision already made to defr[a][e]y the expence of the Crown-Point expedition will be insufficient,—

Preamble.

Be it enacted by the Lieutenant-Governour, Council and House of Represent[ati]ves,

[Sect. 1.] That the treasurer of the province be and he hereby is impowered and directed to borrow, from such person or persons as shall be willing to lend the same, a sum not exceeding fifty-eight thousand pounds, in mill'd dollars, at six shillings each, or in other silver at six shillings and eightpence per ounce; and the sum so borrowed shall be applied in manner as in this act is hereafter directed, and for twenty-nine thousand pounds of the sum so borrowed the treasurer shall give his receipt in the form following,—

Treasurer empowered to borrow £58,000.

Province of the Massachusetts Bay, the day of , 175 . Received of the sum of , for the use and service of the province of the Massachusetts Bay, and, in behalf of said prov-

Form of treasurer's receipt, for 1758.

* June 2, according to the record. † June 12, in the printed acts.

ince, I do hereby promise and oblige myself and successors in the office of treasurer to repay the said or order, the first day of June, 1758, the afores[*ai*]d sum of , in coined silver at six shillings and eightpence per ounce, or Spanish mill'd dollars, at six shillings each, with interest annually, at the rate of six per cent per annum.

Witness my hand, H. G., Treasurer.

[SECT. 2.] And for the remaining sum of twenty-nine thousand pounds the treasurer shall give his receipt in the form following,—

Form of treasurer's receipt, for 1759.

Province of the Massachusetts Bay, the day of 175 . Received of the sum of , for the use and service of the province of the Massachusetts Bay, and, in behalf of said province, I do hereby promise and oblige myself and successors in the office of treasurer to repay the said or order, the first day of June, 1759, the aforesaid sum of , in coined silver at six shillings and eightpence per ounce, or Spanish mill'd dollars, at six shillings each, with interest annually, at the rate of six per cent per annum.

Witness my hand, Treas[*ure*]r.

—and no receipt shall be given for less than six pounds.

And be it further enacted,

£20,000 to be applied for the expedition against Crown Point.

[SECT. 3.] That the aforesaid sum of fifty-eight thousand pounds, when receiv[*e*]'d into the treasury, shall be issued out in manner and for the purposes following; th[at] [*is*] is to say, twenty thousand pounds, part of the sum of fifty-eight thousand pounds, shall be applied for the service of the expedition against Crown Point, to pay off the soldiers, &c[a].; and the further sum of fourteen thousand pounds shall be applied for the service of the several forts and garrisons within this province, pursuant to such grants and orders as are or shall be made by this court for these purposes; and the further sum of nine thousand pounds, part of the aforesaid sum of fifty-eight thousand pounds, shall be applied for purchasing provisions, and the commissary's disbursments for the service of the several forts and garrisons within this province; and the further sum of eleven thousand five hundred pounds, part of the aforesaid sum of fifty-eight thousand pounds, shall be applied for the paym[*en*]t of such premiums and grants that now are or may hereafter be made by this court; and the further sum of three hundred and fifty pounds, part of the aforesaid sum of fifty-eight thousand pounds, shall be applied for the discharge of other debts owing from this province to persons that have served or shall serve them, by order of this court, in such matters and things where there is no establishm[*en*]t nor any certain sum assigned for that purpose; and for paper, writing and printing for this court; and the sum of three thousand pounds, part of the afores[*ai*]d sum of fifty-eight thousand pounds, shall be applied for the payment of his majesty's council and house of repres[*entati*]ves, serving in the great and general court during the several sessions for the present year; *and whereas* there are sometimes contingent and unforeseen charges that demand prompt pay,—

£14,000 for forts and garrisons.

£9,000 for provisions, commissary's disbursements, &c.

£11,500 for premiums, &c.

£350 for debts where there is no establishment, &c.

£3,000 for pay of councillors' and representatives' attendance.

Be it [*further*] *enacted*,

£150 for contingent charges.

[SECT. 4.] That the sum of one hundred and fifty pounds, being the remaining part of the afores[*ai*]d sum of fifty-eight thousand pounds, be applied to pay such contingent charges, and for no other purpose whatever.

And in order to draw the money into the treasury again, and enable the treasurer effectually to discharge the receipts and obligations (with the interest that may be due thereon), by him given in pursuance of this act,—

Be it enacted,

Tax of £66,000 granted in 1757 and 1758.

[SECT. 5.] That there be and hereby is granted to his most excellent majesty, a tax of sixty-six thousand pounds, to be levied on polls, and estates both real and personal within this province, in manner following; that is to say, thirty-two thousand pounds, part thereof, according to such rules and in such proportions on the several towns and districts within the province as shall be agreed on and ordered by the general court or assembly, at their session in May, one thousand seven hundred and fifty-seven, and to be paid into the public[k] treasury on or before the thirty-first day of March then next after; and the further sum of thirty-four thousand pounds, according to such rules and in such proportions on the several towns and districts aforesaid as shall be agreed on and ordered by the general court, at their session in May, one thousand seven hundred and fifty-eight, and to be paid into the treasury on or before the thirty-first of March then next after.

And be it further enacted,

[Sect. 6.] That if the general court, at their session in May, one thousand seven hundred and fifty-seven, and in May, one thousand seven hundred and fifty-eight, some time before the twentieth day of June in each year, shall not agree and conclude upon an act apportioning the sums which by this act are engaged to be, in each of said years, apportioned, assessed and levied, that then, and in such case, each town and district within this province shall pay, by a tax to be levyed on the polls, and estates both real and personal within their limits, the same proportion of the said sums as the said towns and districts were taxed by the general court in the tax act then last preceeding. **Rule for apportioning the tax, in case no tax act shall be agreed on.**

[Sect. 7.] And the province treasurer is hereby fully impowered and directed, some time in the month of June in each of the years aforesaid, to issue and send forth his warrants, directed to the selectmen or assessors of each town and district within this province, requiring them to assess the polls, and estates both real and personal within their several towns and districts, for their respective parts and proportions of the sums before directed and engaged to be assessed, to be paid into the treasury at the aforementioned time; and the assessors, as also persons assessed, shall observe, be governed by and subject to all such rules and directions as shall have been given in the last preceeding tax act.

And as a further fund to enable the treasurer to discharge said receipts and obligations, by him given in pursuance of this act,— **Further fund.**

Be it enacted,

[Sect. 8.] That the duties of excise upon spirituous liquors, for the year seventeen hundred and fifty-six, shall be applied for the payment and discharge of the principal and interest that shall become due on said notes, and to no other purpose.

And be it further enacted,

[Sect. 9.] That the treasurer is hereby directed and ordered to pay the sum of fifty-eight thousand pounds out of such appropriations as shall be directed by warrant, and no other; and the secretary, to whom it belongs to keep the muster-rolls and accompts of charge, shall lay before the house of represent[*ati*]ves, when they direct, such muster-rolls and accompts after paym[*en*]t thereof. **The treasurer to conform to the appropriations.**

Provided, always,—

[Sect. 10.] That the remainder of the sum which shall be brought into the treasury by the duties of excise before mentioned, and the tax of sixty-six thousand pounds, ordered by this act to be assessed and levied, over and above what shall be sufficient to discharge the notes and obligations afores[*ai*]d, shall be and remain as a stock in the treasury, to be applied as the general court of this province shall hereafter order, and to no other purpose whatsoever. [*Passed June* 4;* *published June* 10.†] **Proviso.**

* June 5, according to the record. † June 12, according to the printed act.

CHAPTER 4.

AN ACT TO PREVENT CHARGES ARISING BY SICK, LAME OR OTHERWISE INFIRM PERSONS, NOT BELONGING TO THIS PROVINCE, BEING LANDED AND LEFT WITHIN THE SAME.

Be it enacted by the Lieutenant-Governour, Council and House of Representatives,

Commanders and masters of ships, &c., not to land sick or lame persons without permission.

That from and after the first day of July next, no master or commander of any ship or vessel whatsoever, coming into, abiding in or going forth of any port, harbour or place within this province, shall cause or suffer to be landed or put on shoar within the same, any sick or otherwise impotent and infirm person, not being an inhabitant of this province, either belonging to or brought in such ship or vessel, unless the consent of the selectmen of the town where such sick or infirm person shall be landed be first had and obtained therefor, the same to be signified in writing, under their hands; nor unless security be first given, if demanded, to the satisfaction of such selectmen, for indemnifying and keeping such town free from any charge that may arise for the support or rel[ei][*ie*]f of the person so landed or left within the province; on pain of forfeiting, to the use of the poor of such town, the sum of one hundred pounds for every sick or infirm person so landed, to be recovered by the treasurer of such town, either by action, bill, plaint or information in any of his majesty's courts of record wherein no essoi[*g*]n, protection or wager of law shall be allowed. [*Passed June* 8; *published June* 10.*

Penalty.

CHAPTER 5.

AN ACT FOR [E][*I*]NLISTING THE INHABITANTS OF DORCHESTER, WEYMOUTH AND CHARLESTOWN INTO HIS MAJESTY'S SERVICE FOR THE DEFENCE OF CASTLE WILLIAM, AS OCCASION SHALL REQUIRE.

Preamble.

WHEREAS the safety of this province in a great measure depends on the strength of his majesty's Castle William, and it is necessary that a great number of men, skilful in the management of the great artillery, should be always ready to attend there,—

Be it enacted by the Lieutenant-Governo[u]r, Council and House of Representatives,

Inhabitants of Dorchester, Weymouth, and Charlestown, for military exercises at Castle William.

1748-49, chap. 7.

[SECT. 1.] That all the inhabitants of the town of Dorchester who are by law subject to common musters and military exercises, not exceeding sixty years of age, and such of the inhabitants of the towns of Weymouth and Charlestown as are willing to be [e][*i*]nlisted (not exceeding one hundred and twenty, in the whole, from the two last towns; viz[t]., sixty from Charlestown and sixty from Weymouth) shall be [e][*i*]nlisted under the present captains, or such other officers as the captain general or commander-in-chief shall commissionate, who shall repair to Castle William six days in each year; viz[t]., three days successively in the month of July next, and three days successively in the month of September next, and from thenceforward during the continuance of this act, three days successively in the month of May, and three days successively in the month of September, annually; and shall on the said days be, by the gunner and quarter-gunners, exercised

Their duty there.

* June 12, according to the printed act.

in the mounting, dismounting, levelling, traversing and firing the great guns, and shall be obliged hereunto, and to the observance of such orders as shall be given them in this exercise, under the like pains and penalties that soldiers are under to obey their officers in said castle in time of service.

And be it further enacted,

[Sect. 2.] That if any of the men [e][*i*]nlisted as aforesaid, shall not duly attend at time and place for the exercise of the great artillery as aforesaid, being thereof notified in person or by leaving a notification in writing at the usual place of his abode at least four days before the time he is to appear, for every such day's neglect of attendance such soldier shall pay to the clerk of the company, for the use of the company, ten shillings. Penalty for neglect of attendance.

And for the encouragement of the said men that shall be [e][*i*]nlisted and exercised as aforesaid,—

Be it further enacted,

[Sect. 3.] That every person so [e][*i*]nlisted shall be excused from all other military service, and from all impresses into other service, that other soldiers by law are liable to. Encouragement to enlist.

And be it further enacted,

[Sect. 4.] That upon any alarm at Castle William every man able of body, as well those [e][*i*]nlisted by virtue of this act, as also all others within the town of Dorchester, except such persons as are by law obliged to attend upon the governour for the time being, shall forthwith appear compleat with their arms and ammunition, according to law, at the said Castle William, there to attend and observe such commands as shall be given for his majesty's service, and that on the penalty of paying five pounds to the clerk of the said company, for the use of the province; the afores[*ai*]d fines to be recovered before any justice of the peace or court proper to hear and try the same. All Dorchester inhabitants to attend armed at the castle upon alarms.

[Sect. 5.] This act to be in force from the tenth day of June instant, to the tenth day of June, one thousand seven hundred and fifty-nine, and no longer. [*Passed June* 9;* *published June* 10.† Limitation.

CHAPTER 6.

AN ACT FOR CONTINUING THE ACT FOR ESTABLISHING AND REGULATING THE FEES OF THE SEVERAL OFFICERS WITHIN THIS PROVINCE.

Be it enacted by the Lieutenant-Governour, Council and House of Representatives,

That the act made and pass'd in the twenty-sixth year of his present majesty's reign, intitled "An Act for establishing and regulating fees of the several officers within this province," and every clause thereof, and every matter and thing therein contained, be and hereby is and shall be continued to the tenth day of December next, and from thence to the end of the then next session of the general court, and no longer. [*Passed June* 2; *published June* 10.† Fee-bill continued. 1752-53, chap. 28.

* Signed June 8, according to the record. † June 12, in the printed acts.

CHAPTER 7.

AN ACT FOR REVIVING AND CONTINUING SUNDRY LAWS, THAT ARE EXPIRED AND NEAR EXPIRING.

Preamble. Sundry laws, expired or near expiring, revived and continued.

WHEREAS the several acts hereinafter mentioned, which are now expired or near expiring, have been found useful and beneficial; viz[t]., one act made in the fourteenth year of his present majesty's reign, [e][*i*]ntitled "An Act to prevent damage being done to the harbour of
1740-41, chap. 15. Cape Cod by cattle and horse-kind feeding on Provincetown land"; another act made in the sixteenth year of said reign, [e][*i*]ntitled
1742-43, chap. 28. "An Act in further addition to and explanation of an act, [e][*i*]ntitled 'An Act for regulating townships, choice of town officers, &c[a]'"; three other acts made in the seventeenth year of said reign; viz[t].,
1743-44, chap. 14. one, [e][*i*]ntitled "An Act for preventing the destruction of white-pine trees within this province, and for encouraging the preservation
1743-44, chap. 16. of them for the use of the royal navy"; one other, [e][*i*]ntitled "An Act in addition to and for rend[*e*]ring more effectual an act made in the fourteenth year of his present majesty's reign, intitled 'An Act to prevent damage being done to the harbour of Cape Cod by cattle and horse-kind feeding on Provincetown land'"; and the other act, [e][*i*]n-
1743-44, chap. 21. titled "An Act to regulate the expence of private bridges"; an act
1744-45, chap. 27. made in the eighteenth year of said reign, [e][*i*]ntitled "An Act in addition to the act for preventing damage to the harbour of Cape Cod by cattle and horse-kind feeding on Provincetown land"; an act made
1748-49, chap. 12. in the twenty-second year of said reign, [e][*i*]ntitled "An Act for the more easy partition of lands"; and also two acts made in the twenty-
1750-51, chap. 21. fourth year of said reign: one, [e][*i*]ntitled "An Act providing for the support of ministers in new plantations"; and the other act, intitled
1750-51, chap. 22. "An Act in addition to an act for regulating fences, cattle, &c[a].,"—

Be it therefore enacted by the Lieutenant-Governour, Council and House of Representatives,

Their continuation for five years.

That such of the before-mentioned acts as are expired, with all and every article, clause, matter and thing therein respectively contained, be and hereby are revived, and shall be in force from the tenth day of June, one thousand seven hundred and fifty-six, to the tenth day of June, one thousand seven hundred and sixty-one; and such of said acts as are near expiring are hereby continued, and shall be in force till the said tenth day of June, one thousand seven hundred and sixty-one, and no longer. [*Passed June* 10; *published June* 12.

CHAPTER 8.

AN ACT IN ADDITION TO AND EXPLANATION OF AN ACT FOR GRANTING A TAX MADE AND PASS[*E*]'D IN THE PRESENT SESSION OF THIS COURT.

Preamble. 1756-57, chap. 1. § 11.

WHEREAS some doubt is made whether such persons as have removed out of the town of Boston before the passing the last tax act, and have returned, or shall return, within one year from the time of their removal, respectively, are or shall be obliged to pay taxes in such years in Boston,—

Be it enacted and declared by the Lieut[enan]t-Governour, Council and House of Repres[entati]ves,

That it was in said tax act intended, and shall be so understood, construed and take effect, that all persons who have removed, or shall remove, out of the town of Boston, and within one year have returned, or shall return, and have been taxed, or shall be taxed, respectively, for each or either of said years, in Boston, shall be liable and obliged to pay such tax or taxes, subducting only as in said act is provided. [*Passed June* 10; *published June* 12.

Persons returning to Boston after removal, liable to be taxed.

ACTS

PASSED AT THE SESSION BEGUN AND HELD AT BOSTON, ON THE ELEVENTH DAY OF AUGUST, A. D. 1756.

CHAPTER 9.

AN ACT FOR THE BETTER ORDERING THE LATE INHABITANTS OF NOVA SCOTIA, TRANSPORTED BY ORDER OF THE GOVERNMENT THERE.

Preamble. 1755-56, chaps. 23, 34 and 35.

WHEREAS many inconvenienc[*i*]es have arisen, and may still arise, from the liberty which the late French inhabitants of Nova Scotia have taken, and may, if not prevented, continue to take, of wandering from the several towns in which their residence has been assigned them, respectively, by this government,—

Be it therefore enacted by the Governour, Council and House of Representatives,

Penalty for French of Nova Scotia going beyond their limits, without license.

[SECT. 1.] That from and after the first day of October next, if any of the French inhabitants of Nova Scotia shall be found without the limits of the town or district in which he or she hath been or shall be ordered by this court to reside, without licen[s][c]e, first had, in writing, under the hands of at least two of the selectmen or overseers of the poor of such town or district; every such offender shall be imprisoned in close goal for the space of five days, without bail or mainprize, and kept on such diet only as is usually allowed to prisoners under close confinement; and it shall and may be lawful for any person of free condition, to apprehend such offender, and carry him or her before the next justice of the peace of the county, who is hereby authorized and required to give order for the imprisonment of such offender as aforesaid; and also for carrying him or her back, when discharged from imprisonment, to the town or district in which he or she has been or shall be placed by order of this government; the whole charge of the proceedings aforesaid to be born by the offender, if able; otherwise, by the province, such charge being first allowed and certified by the justice before whom the proceedings shall be had.

Power given to apprehend them.

And be it further enacted,

Penalty for selectmen, &c., giving license contrary to law.

[SECT. 2.] That no liceu[s][c]e shall be granted by the selectmen or overseers of the poor of any town or district, to any of the French aforesaid, for more than six days' absence at one time, from the place assign'd for their residence, nor to be absent from their several homes on the Lord's Day; and if any selectmen or overseers of the poor of any town or district, shall presume to give a licen[s][c]e for a longer absence, or upon the Lord's Day, they shall forfeit for every person so licen[s][c]ed, the sum of forty shillings, for the use of the poor of such town or district, to be recovered by the treasurer thereof, by action or information, to be brought before any one of his majesty's justices of the peace for the county where such offence shall be committed.

[SECT. 3.] This act to be in force [']till the first day of October, one thousand seven hundred and fifty-seven, and no longer. [*Passed September* 11. Limitation.

CHAPTER 10.

AN ACT FOR CONTINUING AN ACT, INTIT[U]LED "AN ACT TO IMPOWER THE PROPRIETORS OF THE MEETING-HOUSE IN THE FIRST PARISH IN SALEM, WHERE THE REVEREND MR DUDLEY LEAVITT NOW OFFICIATES, TO RAISE MONEY TO DEPREY MINISTERIAL AND OTHER NECESSARY CHARGES."

WHEREAS an act of this province made and pass[*e*]'d in the twenty-seventh year of his present majesty's reign, intit[u]led "An Act to impower the proprietors of the meeting-house in the first parish in Salem, where the Reverend Mr Dudley Leavitt now officiates, to raise money to defrey ministerial and other necessary charges," will expire on the twenty-second day of September next; which act has been found beneficial and necessary for the purposes for which it was pass'd,— Preamble. 1753-54, chap. 14.

Be it therefore enacted by the Governour, Council and House of Representatives,

That the said act, and every matter and clause therein contained, be and shall continue in force from the twenty-second day of September next, until[l] the twenty-second day of September, one thousand seven hundred and sixty-one, and from thence to the end of the then next session of the general court, and no longer. [*Passed August* 27.* Act continued until September, 1761.

* Signed August 16, according to the record.

ACTS

PASSED AT THE SESSION BEGUN AND HELD AT BOSTON, ON THE FIFTH DAY OF OCTOBER, A. D. 1756.

CHAPTER 11.

AN ACT IN ADDITION TO, AND FOR EXPLANATION OF, AN ACT MADE IN THE FOURTH YEAR OF HIS MAJESTY'S REIGN, INTIT[U]LED "AN ACT DIRECTING HOW RATES AND TAXES, TO BE GRANTED BY THE GENERAL ASSEMBLY, AS ALSO COUNTY, TOWN AND PRECINCT RATES, SHALL BE ASSESSED AND COLLECTED."

Preamble. 1730, chap. 1, § 13.

WHEREAS in and by an act made in the fourth year of his present majesty's reign, intit[u]led "An Act directing how rates and taxes to be granted by the general assembly, as also county, town and precinct rates shall be assessed and collected," it is, among other things, provided, That two or more assessors shall have power, by warrant under their hands and seals, to commit to the common goal such persons as, being duly assessed, shall refuse or neglect to pay the sums so assessed, by the space of twelve days after demand thereof, where no sufficient distress can or may be found, whereby the same may be levied: *and whereas* a doubt hath arisen, whether, by the assessors so impowered, be meant and intended the assessors for the time being, or the assessors by whom the persons to be committed were assessed,—

Be it therefore enacted by the Lieut[enant]-Governour, Council and House of Representatives,

Assessors for the time being intended.

[SECT. 1.] That by the assessors so impowered, in and by the act aforesaid, the assessors for the time being, and they only, are meant and intended; and that the said act shall be and always ought to have been so understood.

And be it further enacted,

Persons overrated unless relieved by the assessors, may apply to the general sessions of the peace. 1730, chap. 1, § 7.

[SECT. 2.] That any person apprehending himself overrated, and applying to the assessors for the time being for rel[ci][ie]f, shall, upon their refusal to ease him, have liberty to make application to the court of general sessions of the peace, to be held within and for the same county within which the assessment was made next after such refusal, the justices of which court are hereby authorized to grant him rel[ei][ie]f in such manner as is directed in and by the act afores[ai]d.

And be it further enacted,

[SECT. 3.] That the warrant for commitment to be granted by the assessors as aforesaid, shall be in the form following:—

Form of the warrant of commitment to be granted by assessors.

, ss. To A. B., one of the constables (collectors) of the town of C., in the county of S. Greeting:

Whereas application has been made to us the subscribers, assessors for the said town of C., by the said A. B., one of the constables (or collectors) of said town of C., in said county, that H. I., of said town of C., is assessed to the province tax in the rate-bill committed to him, the said A. B., to collect as constable (collector) for the year , the sum of ; and altho' the said tax has been demanded of the said H. I., yet he neglects and refuses to pay and satisfy the same, and there being no estate of the said H. I. to be found whereon to levy the same: these are therefore, in his majesty's name, to require you, the said A. B., to take into safe custody the body of the said H. I., and him commit to the common goal of the said county of S., there to remain until[l] he, the said H. I., shall pay and satisfy the above sums, with all necessary charges, or be discharged by due course of law.

Given under our hands and seals at C., this day of , in the year of his majesty's reign, *Annoque Domini* .

} Assessors of the Town of C.

[*Passed October* 14.*

CHAPTER 12.

AN ACT FOR PROVIDING AND MAINTAINING TWO ARMED VESSELS TO GUARD THE COAST, AND FOR SUPPLYING THE TREASURY WITH [7] SEVEN THOUSAND POUNDS FOR THAT END.

WHEREAS it appears necessary for his majesty's service, and for the preservation and defence of the trade and fishery of this province, that two armed vessels be provided for that purpose; and in order thereto that the treasury be supplyed with the sum of seven thousand pounds, which it appears most just and equal, considering the heavy burthen of the public[*k*] taxes, should be laid on the trade and fishery; wherefore,— Preamble.

Be it enacted by the Lieutenant-Governour, Council and House of Representatives,

[SECT. 1.] That from and after the first day of November next, during the continuance of the present war with France, and until[l] the first day of November then next following, there be and hereby is granted unto his most excellent majesty, a duty of sixpence per ton on all ships and other vessels, excepting common coasters, whaling and fishing vessels, entering into any port or harbour within this province, other than such as shall clear out of some other port or harbour within the same, and on all coasters trading from harbour to harbour within this province; and whaling and fishing vessels the like sum of sixpence per ton a year; and also a duty or excise of sixpence per pound upon tea, and twopence per pound upon coffee, and five per cent upon china-ware *ad valorem*, the income of which shall be applied to the providing and maintaining of two armed vessels ordered by this court to be provided and equipped for the guarding the coast[s] of this province against his majesty's enemies.

Duty of sixpence per ton, on all ships and other vessels, except coasters, &c., from Nov. 1, 1756, during the continuance of the present war with France; also a duty on tea, &c.,—for building two armed vessels.

And to render this act effectual,—

Be it further enacted,

[SECT. 2.] That the tonnage of all vessels, except whaling, fishing and coasting vessels, shall be measured and taken in manner as is directed in the act for building the light-house, passed in the first year of King George the First, chapter the sixth; and the commissioner of impost, or his deputy, is hereby directed and impowered, before he enters any ship or vessel, that is by law required to enter, to demand and receive the duty by this act intended to be paid, and shall certify

Manner of measuring Vessels.

1715-16, chap. 4, § 3.

Commissioner of impost to receive duty required by this act, &c.

* In the record, this act seems to have been signed during the previous session (Sept. 10). It appears again, however, under the above date. It probably failed to receive the Governor's assent before his departure, and the second enactment was deemed necessary at this session on account of the change in the gubernatorial office, since there was no intervening prorogation.

Naval officer directed.

the same to the naval officer, and the naval officer is hereby strictly forbidden to clear out any ship or other vessel until[l] the master or owner of such ship or vessel shall produce a certificate that he has paid the duty by this act designed to be paid; and in case the master of any ship or vessel refuse to enter at the custom-house office, as by law obliged, or to pay the duty by this act provided, any such delinquent or refusing master, over and above the penalty by law already provided, shall be liable to the action or actions of the impost officer for the time being, for the recovery of the duty by this act imposed in any of his majesty's courts of record, or before any justice of the peace, as the nature of the case shall require, to prosecute which action or actions the said impost officer or officers are hereby respectively impowered.

Penalty in case of refusal to pay the duties by this act required.

Be it further enacted,

Selectmen or assessors to tax whaling, fishing or coasting Vessels.

[SECT. 3.] That the selectmen or assessors of every town within this province, where any whaling, fishing or coasting vessels may belong, are hereby impowered and directed to assess and tax the vessels aforesaid according to the direction of this act hereinbefore expressed; the measure of the vessel, in case of doubt, to be taken at the cost of the respective owners or masters by the said assessors, unless the account of their measure first given in be just and true, in which case the charge to be born by the respective towns; and the said assessment and tax, when made, to commit to the constable or collectors of their towns, respectively, who are hereby impowered and obliged to collect the same of the master or other person having the principal care thereof, and pay it into the province treasury; and the said assessors are further required and directed to transmit to the province treasurer, yearly, a list of every vessel by them according to the tenor of this act assessed and taxed, together with [a] [*the*] certificate of the name or names of the constable or collectors to whom the said assessment shall have been by them committed to collect; and the province treasurer is hereby impowered and directed to issue out his warrants for the recovery of the said duty or tax assessed as aforesaid, on any whaling, coasting and fishing vessels, against any delinquent constables or collectors, as is by law in other cases made and provided. *Provided, nevertheless,* this act shall not be construed to exempt any vessels aforesaid from being taxed as vessels heretofore.

Manner of collecting the same.

Proviso.

And be it further enacted,

No person to sell tea, china-ware, or coffee, without license.

[SECT. 4.] That no person or persons whatsoever, from and after the first day of November next, other than such as shall obtain licences from the justices in general sessions to sell tea, china-ware and coffee, unless as is hereinafter provided, shall directly or indirectly, either by themselves or any under them, presume to sell the same; and every person shall, before such licence be granted, give bond, with sufficient sureties, for his, her or their well and truly paying the duties laid on those articles he, she or they shall be licenced to sell, and that he, she or they will use his, her or their licence in such house or houses as shall be therein named, and no other; and that he, she or they will render to the farmer or his deputy, on oath (which he is hereby impowered and directed to administer to the person exhibiting such account), a just and true account of all the aforesaid commodities by him, her or them taken in for sale, sold, used or consumed from time to time, and pay unto the farmer or his deputy, at the end of every half year, the sum or sums of excise that may arise pursuant to this law.

Licensed persons to give bond.

Provided, nevertheless,—

Proviso.

[SECT. 5.] It shall and may be lawful for any person, whether licenced or not, to dispose of any tea, coffee or china-ware in any quantity whatsoever, to any person licenced to sell the same, he or she complying with the terms of this act relating to a certificate.

Provided, always, and it is the true intent and meaning of this act,—

[SECT. 6.] That if any person, licenced to sell any of the aforesaid commodities, shall sell to any other such licenced person any quantity of the commodities aforesaid, such licenced person, selling as aforesaid, shall not be held to pay such duty, but the licenced person who is the purchaser shall pay the same; and the seller aforesaid shall and is hereby required to deliver to the farmer of this duty a true account of such commodities sold as aforesaid. **Proviso.**

And be it further enacted,

[SECT. 7.] That the said licence be renewed yearly, and bond given as aforesaid, and that the said licences be renewed to no person whatsoever, unless he or she, before their receiving the same, produce a certificate under the hand of the farmer, or his deputy, of his or her having paid the full of the excise due from them, respectively, as aforesaid. **Licenses to be renewed yearly.**

And be it further enacted,

[SECT. 8.] That if any person or persons, not licenced as aforesaid, unless as is herein provided, shall, from and after the first day of November next, presume, directly or indirectly, by themselves, or any under them, to sell any tea, china-ware or coffee, by any quantity, weight, number or measure, he, she or they shall for every such offence, on due conviction, forf[ie][*ei*]t and pay the sum of four pounds, one half to the informer and the other half to the farmer, the manner of conviction to be the same as of persons selling strong liquors without licence, as is by law already provided; and every person, licenced as aforesaid, who shall presume to sell any of the before-mentioned commodities, and shall refuse or neglect to account with the farmer, and pay the duties required by this act, or shall give a false account, shall be subject, for each offence, to the penalty of fifty pounds, and shall be rendered incapable of renewing his, her or their licence to sell the same for the future; the penalty to be recovered shall be to the farmer, and the manner of conviction shall be the same as of persons selling strong drink without licence, unless he, she or they who have thus rendered a false account shall, within twenty days after such account given to the farmer, *bonâ fide*, swear that there was an involuntary mistake made in such account, and within that time rectify the same. **Fine for selling without license.**

Provided, nevertheless,—

[SECT. 9.] That nothing in this act shall be construed to extend to any quantity of any of the commodities aforesaid which shall be sold for consumption out of this province to any person not belonging thereto; and the person selling shall produce a certificate from the purchaser, under oath, that he, *bonâ fide*, purchased the same with intent to carry it out of this government, and there to be consumed; and in case any person shall produce a false certificate, and be thereof convicted, he, she or they shall forf[ie][*ei*]t and pay to and for the use of the farmer, the sum of six pounds, to be recovered in any of his majesty's courts proper to try the same. **Proviso.**

And to the end the revenue arising from the aforesaid duties of excise may be advanced for the greater benefit and advantage of the public[*k*],—

Be it further enacted,

[SECT. 10.] That one or more persons, to be nominated and appointed annually during the continuance of this act by the general court for and within the several counties within this province, public[*k*] notice being first given of the time, place and occasion of their meeting, shall have full power, and are hereby authorized, from time to time, to contract and agree with any person for or concerning the farm- **Duty on tea, &c., to be farmed.**

ing the duties in this act mentioned, on tea, coffee and china-ware, in the respective counties for which they shall be appointed, as may be for the greatest profit and advantage of the public[*k*].

And be it further enacted,

Farmer to give bond.

[SECT. 11.] That the farmer shall give bond with two sufficient sureties, to the province treasurer for the time being, and his successors in said office, in double the sum of money that shall be contracted for, with condition that the sum agreed to, be paid into the province treasury, for the use of the province, at the expiration of one year from the date of such bond; which bond the person or persons to be appointed a com[*mit*]tee of such county are to take, and the same to lodge with the treasurer as aforesaid, within twenty days after such bond is executed; and the said treasurer, upon failure or neglect of payment at the time therein limitted, shall and is hereby impowered and directed to issue out his execution, returnable in sixty days, against such farmers of excise and their sureties, or either of them, for the full sum expressed in the condition of their bonds, as they shall respectively become due, in the same manner as he is enabled by law to issue out his executions against def[f]ective constables; and the said committee shall render an acco[mp][*un*]t of their proceedings touching the farming this duty on china-ware, tea and coffee aforementioned, in their respective counties, to the general court in the fall sessions, and shall receive such sum or sums of money for their trouble and expence in said affair as said court shall think fit to allow them. And every person farming the excise in any county may substitute and appoint one or more deputy or deputies under him, to collect and receive the excise aforesaid, which shall become due in such county, and pay the same to such farmer; which deputy or deputies shall have, use and exercise all such powers and authorities as in and by this act are given or com[*m*]itted to the farmers for the better collecting the duties aforesaid, or prosecuting the offenders against this act.

Treasurer to sue out the bond, in case.

Farmers may appoint deputies.

And be it further enacted,

Executors or administrators of deceased farmers to have their power, &c.

[SECT. 12.] That in case of the death of either of the farmers of excise in any counties, the executors or administrators of such farmers shall, upon taking such trust of executor or administrator upon them, have and enjoy all the powers, and be subject to all the duties, the farmer had or might enjoy or was subject to by force of this act.

And be it further enacted,

Court of sessions to give license,—

[SECT. 13.] That the justices in the several counties be and they hereby are impow[*e*]red, at their several sessions during the continuance of this act, to grant licences for selling and retailing any of the aforesaid articles to all such fit and proper persons as shall apply to them for the same, and all persons desiring licences are hereby directed to apply to the justices in sessions for said licence accordingly, they taking bonds, with sufficient sureties, to secure the full value of the excise on china-ware, tea and coffee, which it is probable may be sold by the persons petitioning for such licence, and the person receiving such licence shall pay no other or greater fee than two shillings in the whole (one shilling to the court, and one shilling to the clerk) for his or her licence and bond aforesaid.

And be it further enacted,

—or two justices, in case.

[SECT. 14.] That in such counties where the courts of general sessions shall not sit in thirty days after the said first day of November next, it shall be in the power of two of his majesty's justices of the peace in such county, *quorum unus*, to grant licences for selling the commodities aforesaid to all such persons as shall apply for the same, upon giving the security by this act required; and the justices granting such licence and returning a certificate thereof under their hands to the next court of general sessions of the peace shall be adjudged sufficient to entitle the person so licenced to sell said commodities from the date of such certificate until the expiration of one year from the return thereof as aforesaid.

And to the end that this government may know what monies shall be received by the farmer of each respective county and his deputies by virtue of this act,—

Be it enacted,

[SECT. 15.] That to every person licenced by the sessions, as aforesaid, the said farmer or his deputy, when said persons shall account with them, shall give two receipts under their hand for what each of them have respectively received, either as duty or forf[ie][*ei*]ture, or in any other way; and the said receipts shall express the true and just sum received, and the consideration for which it was received; and one of said receipts shall be lodged, within one month after the date thereof, by each person, respectively, to whom said receipt shall be given, with the clerk of the sessions for the county wherein such person lives, on penalty of forty shillings, and of being rendred incapable of renewing his or her licence for the future. And the clerk aforesaid shall transmit a fair and true copy of the receipts that shall be so lodged with him, to the secretary of this province, who shall lay the same before this court.

Farmer to give two receipts for what sums he receives.

And be it further enacted,

[SECT. 16.] That the farmer of each respective county shall render an acco[mp][*un*]t, on oath, to the province treasurer, when he shall come to discharge his bond given for the farm of the duties aforesaid, of the sums and securit[y][*ie*]s he or his deputy, or either of them, have in any way received by virtue of this act; and the said acco[mp][*un*]t shall express the name of each person of whom they, or either of them, have received any sum or security, how much that sum or security is for, and the time when the same were received; and it shall be part of the condition of the said farmer's said bond, that he will render such acco[mp][*un*]t, taken upon oath, as aforesaid, and if said farmer shall not have settled, when he comes to discharge the said bond, with every person obliged by this act to account and settle with him, his said bond shall not be discharged till he has so settled, and rendered an account, of such settlement to the province treasurer as aforesaid.

Farmer to render an account, on oath, to the treasurer, of what moneys or securities he or his deputies shall receive.

Provided, nevertheless,—

[SECT. 17.] That if said farmer shall, at the end of one month and of ten months, respectively, from the time of payment expressed in said bond, render an account on oath as aforesaid, and shall swear that such acco[mp][*un*]t expresses the whole sum that he hath received, either in money, or by securities, or by any other way whatsoever, then his bond shall be discharged and delivered up to him.

Proviso.

Be it further enacted,

[SECT. 18.] That if any acco[mp][*un*]t of excise shall remain unpaid and not settled by bond or note, for the space of ten months after the expiration of this act, unless the action is depending, the said farmer or his deputy shall not have right to bring any action against the person whose said account shall remain so unpaid or unsettled, but shall forfeit what might otherwise have been due from such person.

Farmer shall have no right to bring an action after ten months, except.

Be it further enacted,

[SECT. 19.] That all fines, penalties and forfeitures, arising and accruing by any breach of this act, and not otherwise appropriated, shall be, one half to his majesty for the use of this province, and the other half for the use of the farmer; to be recovered by action, bill, plaint or information in any of his majesty's courts of record.

How fines are to be disposed of.

And whereas it will be necessary that money should be advanced for the purchasing the vessels aforesaid before that a sufficiency will be brought into the treasury pursuant to this act; therefore,—

Be it enacted by the Lieutenant-Governour, Council and House of Representatives,

Treasurer empowered to borrow £7,000.

[SECT. 20.] That the treasurer of the province be and hereby is impow[*e*]red and directed to borrow from such person or persons as will be willing to lend the same, the said sum of seven thousand pounds in mill'd dollars, at six shillings each, or in other silver at six shillings and eightpence per ounce, for a term not exceeding two years; and the sum so borrowed shall be applied for purchasing the vessels aforesaid; and for every sum so borrowed, the treasurer shall give a receipt and obligation in form following:—

Form of treasurer's receipt.

Province of the Massachuset[*t*]s Bay, day of , 17 .
Received of the sum of , for the use and service of the province of the Massachuset[*t*]s Bay, and, in behalf of said province, I do hereby promise and oblige myself and successors in the office of treasurer to repay the said or order, the day of 17 , the aforesaid sum of , in coined silver of sterling alloy, at six shillings and eightpence per ounce, or Spanish mill'd dollars, at six shillings each, with interest annually at the rate of six per cent per annum.
Witness my hand.

—and no receipt shall be given for a sum less than six pounds.

And be it further enacted,

Proviso in case of deficiency.

[SECT. 21.] That if the sums that shall be brought into the treasury by virtue of this act, during the two years as aforesaid, be not sufficient to pay the seven thousand pounds aforesaid, and what interest shall become due for the same, the deficiency shall be made good by a tax upon all the polls and estates of the people in the province, according to such rules and in such proportion as shall be agreed on by the general court the next sessions after the s[*ai*]d two years shall determine.

And be it further enacted,

Rule for apportioning the tax, in case no tax act shall be agreed on.

[SECT. 22.] That in case the general court shall not, at their sessions in May, and before the twentieth day of June, one thousand seven hundred [*and*] fifty-nine, agree and conclude upon an act apportioning the sum which by this act is engaged to be, in said year, apportioned, assessed and levied, that then, and in such case, each town and district within this province shall pay a tax, to be levied upon the polls, and estates both real and personal within their districts, the same proportion of the same sum as the said towns and districts were taxed by the general court in the tax act then last preceeding, *saving* what relates to the pay of representatives, which shall be assessed on the several towns they represent; and the province treasurer is hereby fully impow[*e*]red and directed, some time in the month of June, one thousand seven hundred and fifty-nine, to issue and send forth his warrants, directed to the selectmen or assessors of each town and district within this province, requiring them to assess the polls, and estates both real and personal within their several towns and districts, for their respective part and proportion of the sum before directed and engaged to be assessed, and also for the fines upon the several towns for not sending a representative; and the assessors, as also persons assessed, shall observe, be governed by and subject to all such rules and directions as have been given in the last preceeding tax act. [*Passed and published October* 19.

CHAPTER 13.

AN ACT FOR THE BETTER REGULATING THE CHOICE OF PETIT JURORS.

Be it enacted by the L[e]ieut[*enant*]-*Governour, Council and House of Represent*[*ati*]*ves*,

[SECT. 1.] That the selectmen of each town within this province shall, within their respective towns, some time before the first of December next, take a list of the persons, liable by law, and which they shall judge able and well qualified, to serve on the petit juries, and lay the same before the town, at a meeting to be immediately called for that purpose; and the towns shall, respectively, at such meeting, select out of the list, such as they judge most suitable to serve as jurors, and put their names, written on seperate p[ei][*ie*]ces of paper, into a box, to be provided by the selectmen for that purpose, and deliver the same to the town clerk, to be by him kept under lock and key. 1748-49, chap. 19. Selectmen of each town to take a list of persons liable, &c., to serve as petit jurors, and lay the same before their towns.

And be it further enacted,

[SECT. 2.] That when, at any time after the first of December next, during the continuance of this act, any *v*[*e*][*i*]*n*[*i*][*e*]*re facias* shall issue forth for the choice of petit jurors, and the inhabitants of each town shall be assembled for that purpose, the town clerk, or one or more of the selectmen in case of his absence or sickness, shall carry into the meeting the box wherein the names of those persons are put who are designed to serve at the court from whence the *venire facias* issued, which shall be unlock'd in the meeting, and the major part of the selectmen (who are hereby enjo[y][*i*]ned to be present), and the constable who shall warn said meeting, shall particularly notify them and the town clerk for that purpose; and the town clerk, or, in his absence, one or more of the selectmen, shall draw out so many tickets as there are jurors required by the *venire*, who shall be the persons that shall be returned to serve as jurors: *saving*, that if any whose names are so drawn are sick, or otherwise unable to serve at that time, in the judgm[*en*]t of the town, their names shall be returned into the box and others drawn in their stead. Said list to be carried into the meeting called for that purpose, and as many names drawn out by the town clerk or selectmen as there shall be occasion for.

[SECT. 3.] And to the intent the same persons may not serve too often, the clerk or selectmen who shall draw the ticket or name of any person returned to serve as afores[*ai*]d, shall enter on the back thereof the date of such draft, and return the same into the box again, and said person or persons shall not be obliged (altho' drawn at any time), to serve as jurors oftner than once in three years; and no person who has served as a petit juror, within two years past, shall be obliged to serve again until[l] three years be compleated from the time of his last serving, notwithstanding his name's being drawn, as afores[*ai*]d. Persons to serve on juries but once in three years.

[SECT. 4.] And the selectmen shall, in the same manner, once in every year, during the continuance of this act, take a new list of such other persons as may become suitable and qualified, and lay the same before the town, whose names, being first by them allowed, shall be put into a box in manner as aforesaid; and, as well that all may do duty, as that the deficiency that may have happened by death, or otherwise, may be supplied at such time, the town may, if they think fit, make a new regulation of the list before received.

And whereas, it often happens that the persons returned to serve as petit jurors abscond, and the respective constables are put to great difficulty and frequently prevented from notifying them,— Preamble.

Be it further enacted,

[SECT. 5.] That, from and after the first of December next, and during the continuance of this act, the clerks of the respective courts in Rules for notification and issuing *venires*.

this province, shall, and hereby are obliged to, issue out their *venir[i]es* from their respective offices, thirty days, at least, before the return day; and the respective constables, upon the receipt of the said *venires*, are hereby obliged to notify their towns thereof, so that the sev[*era*]l meetings may be held six days, at least, before the sitting of the court from whence the *venire* issues; and the constables are hereby directed, in case they cannot personally notify those who are so drawn, upon their leaving a certificate of their being drawn, as aforesaid, with the time and place of their respective courts sitting, at the usual place of such person's abode, four days before the sitting thereof, [and] it shall be deemed a sufficient notification.

Penalty for persons not attending as jurors.

[SECT. 6.] And if any person, drawn and notified as aforesaid, shall neglect to attend and serve accordingly, unless reasonable excuse be made to the justices of the respective courts, he shall be fined in a sum not exceeding twenty shillings; and if such jurors belong to the town of Boston, they shall be fined in a sum not exceeding ten pounds, to be divided between the petit jurors, drawn as afores[*ai*]d serving at said courts.

And be it further enacted,

Method for preventing partial jurors.

[SECT. 7.] That the justices of the respective courts afores[*ai*]d, are hereby directed, upon motion from either party in any cause that shall be tried after the first of December next, and during the continuance of this act, to put any juror to answer upon oath (whether returned as afores[*ai*]d or a talisman) whether he doth expect to gain or loose by the issue of the cause then depending; whether he is any way related to either party; or directly or indirectly given his opinion, or is sensible of any prejudice in the cause. And if it shall then appear to said court that such juror doth not stand indifferent in said cause, he shall be set aside from the trial of that cause, and another appointed in his stead.

Preamble.

And whereas, it frequently happens that many of the jurors so chosen to serve in the several courts of judicature, within this province, fail of attendance, and, by reason of challenges made by parties to several of said jurors, the number of returned jurors are too few to serve at said courts; for remedy whereof,—

Be it enacted,

New *venires* to be issued, in case.

[SECT. 8.] That, from and after the first day [*of*] December next, and during the continuance of this act, it shall and may be lawful for the justices of the courts afores[*ai*]d, when sitting, and as they shall judge there is occasion, to cause new writts of *venire facias* to be forthwith issued out and directed to the constables of the sev[*era*]l towns in the county in which said court is held, for the appointm[*en*]t and return of so many good and lawful men, to serve upon the jury at said court, as shall be directed in the writ; w[*hi*]ch jurors shall be forthwith appointed, and, being notified and returned to the said court, shall be, and hereby are, obliged to give their immediate attendance accordingly, under the penalty by this act provided for non-appearance of jurors.

And be it further enacted,

Jurors' fees.

[SECT. 9.] That the fees of the petit jurors in the county of Suffolk, at the sup[*eriou*]r court, shall be twelve shillings and sixpence for every trial, the foreman to have eighteen pence, and the other jurors twelvepence each.

Limitation.

[SECT. 10.] This act to continue and be in force until[l] the first day of December, which shall be in the year of our Lord one thousand seven hundred and fifty-nine, and to the end of the session of the gen[*era*]l court next after, and no longer. [*Passed October* 13; *published October* 19.

CHAPTER 14.

AN ACT FOR PREVENTING ALL RIOTOUS, TUMULTUOUS AND DISORDERLY ASSEMBLIES OR COMPANIES OF PERSONS, AND FOR PREVENTING BONFIRES IN ANY OF THE STREETS OR LANES WITHIN ANY OF THE TOWNS OF THIS PROVINCE.

Preamble. 1752-53, chap. 18.

WHEREAS many and great disorders have of late years been committed by tumultuous companies of men, children and negroes, carrying about with them pageants or other shews through the streets and lanes of the town of Boston, and other towns within this province, abusing and insulting the inhabitants, and demanding and exacting money by menaces and abusive language; and besides the horrid profaneness, impiety and other gross immoralities usually found in such companies, it has been found by experience that such practices tend greatly to encourage and cultivate a turbulent temper and spirit in many of the inhabitants, and an opposition to all government and order,—

Be it therefore enacted by the Lieutenant-Governour, Council and House of Represent[ati]ves,

Persons disguised going about with pageants and armed with any weapons exacting money, &c.,

[SECT. 1.] That if any persons, being more than three in number, and being armed all or any of them with sticks, clubs or any kind of weapons, or disguised with vizards, so called, or painted or discoloured faces, or being in any other manner disguised, shall assemble together, having any kind of imagery or pageantry with them, as a publick shew, in any of the streets or lanes in the town of Boston or any other town within this province, or if any person or persons being of or belonging to any company having any imagery or pageantry for a publick shew, shall, by menaces or otherwise, exact, require, demand or ask any money or anything of value from any of the inhabitants or other persons, in the streets, lanes or houses of any town within this province, every person being of or assembled with such company, shall for each offence forfeit and pay the sum of forty shillings, or suffer imprisonment not exceeding one month; or if the offender shall be a negro servant, in lieu of the imprisonm[en]t, he may be whipped not exceeding ten stripes, at the discretion of the justice before whom the trial shall be.

—to be punished by fine or imprisonment.

Negroes, &c., may be punished by whipping.

And be it further enacted,

Persons carrying pageants, &c., in the night, though unarmed, to be punished.

[SECT. 2.] That if any person[s] to the number of three or more, between sun-setting and sun-rising, being assembled together in any of the streets or lanes of any town within this province, shall have any kind of imagery or pageantry for a publick shew, altho' none of the company so assembled shall be armed or disguised, or exact, demand or ask any money or thing of value, every person being of such company shall forfeit and pay the sum of forty shillings, or suffer imprisonm[en]t not exceeding one month; or if the offender shall be a negro servant, in lieu of the imprisonment, he may be whipped not exceeding ten stripes, at the discretion of the justice before whom the trial shall be.

And whereas bonfires have been sometimes kindled in the streets, lanes and other parts of several of the towns in this province, to the endangering the lives and estates of the inhabitants,—

Be it further enacted,

Bonfires in streets or lanes forbidden.

[SECT. 3.] That if any person or persons shall set fire to any pile, or any combustable stuff, or be any ways concerned in causing or making a bonfire in any street or lane, or any other part of any town within this province, such bonfire being within ten perches of any house or building, every person so offending shall for each offence forfeit the sum of forty shillings or suffer imprisonment not exceeding one month; or if

Penalty.

the offender shall be a negro servant, in lieu of the imprisonm[*en*]t, he may be whipped not exceeding ten stripes, at the discretion of the justice before whom the trial shall be.

Justice's power, &c.

[SECT. 4.] And for the better execution of all and every the foregoing orders, every justice of the peace, within his county, shall have power and authority to convent before him any person or persons who shall offend in any of the particulars before mentioned, and upon his own view, or other legal conviction of any such offence, to impose the penalties and fines aforesaid; and all the fines in this act, when recovered, shall be one half to the informer, and the other half to and for the use of the poor of the town where such offence shall be committed.

Masters and parents liable for their servants and children.

[SECT. 5.] And all masters are hereby made liable to the payment of the several fines as afores[*ai*]d, for the offences of their servants, and all parents for the offences of their children under age, not being servants.

Limitation.

[SECT. 6.] This act to continue and be in force for the space of five years from the twentieth of October, one thousand seven hundred and fifty-six, and no longer. [*Passed October* 15; *published October* 19.

CHAPTER 15.

AN ACT FOR CONTINUING "AN ACT FOR PREVENTING THE EXPORTATION OF PROVISIONS AND WARLIKE STORES, OUT OF THIS PROVINCE."

Preamble. 1755-56, chap. 11.

WHEREAS the act, [e][*i*]ntitled "An Act for preventing the exportation of provisions and warlike stores out of this province," passed in the twenty-ninth year of his present majesty's reign, is near expiring; which said act hath been found beneficial,—

Be it therefore enacted by the Lieutenant-Governour, Council and House of Representatives,

Continuance of the act.

That the before mentioned act, with all the articles, clauses and matters therein contained, be and hereby is continued from the time of the expiration thereof, to the twentieth day of December next, and no longer. [*Passed October* 21; * *published October* 19.

* According to the record, this act was signed October 22, 1756, and, again, February 26, 1757. The date of publication, which seems inconsistent with either of the dates of signing, is taken from the printed volume of acts,—the only place in which it has been found.

ACTS

PASSED AT THE SESSION BEGUN AND HELD AT BOSTON, ON THE SIXTH DAY OF JANUARY, A. D. 1757.

CHAPTER 16.

AN ACT FOR ALTERING THE TIMES APPOINTED FOR HOLDING THE SUPERIOUR COURT OF JUDICATURE, &c., IN THE COUNTIES OF PL[I][Y]MOUTH, BRISTOL AND BARNSTABLE.

Preamble. 1752-53, chap. 21, and see chap. 39, *post.*

WHEREAS the times appointed by law for holding the superiour court of judicature, court of assize and general goal delivery, within the counties of Pl[i][*y*]mouth, Bristol and Barnstable, are found to be inconvenient in regard of the extream heat of the season, as well as in other respects,—

Be it therefore enacted by the Lieutenant-Governo[*u*]*r, Council and House of Representatives,*

Times for holding superior courts in the counties of Plymouth, Barnstable, and Dukes county, and Bristol.

[SECT. 1.] That for the future, the time for holding the superiour court of judicature, court of assize and general goal delivery, at Pl[i][*y*]mouth, within and for the county of Pl[i][*y*]mouth, shall be the last Tuesday in April, annually; and that the time for holding the said court at Barnstable, for the counties of Barnstable and Dukes County, shall be the first Tuesday in May, annually; and that the time for holding the said court at Taunton, within and for the county of Bristol, shall be the second Tuesday in October, annually.

And be it further enacted,

All processes relating thereto, to be tried at said courts.

[SECT. 2.] That all writ[t]s and other processes already issued, returnable to the said court at the days heretofore appointed for holding the same in the several counties aforesaid, shall be returned, and all matters depending at said court, in either of said counties, shall be proceeded, on at the days respectively appointed by this act for holding the same. And all officers and other persons concerned, are required to conform themselves accordingly. [*Passed February* 25;* *published February* 28, 1757.†

* February 26, according to the record.

† On the engrossment, the date of publication is written February 23; but it is assumed that this is an error of the engrossing clerk.

CHAPTER 17.

AN ACT IN FURTHER ADDITION TO AN ACT, [E][I]NTITLED "AN ACT FOR REGULATING THE ASSIZE OF CASK, AND PREVENTING DECEIT IN PACKING FISH, &c[a]., FOR SALE," MADE IN THE FOURTH YEAR OF KING WILLIAM AND QUEEN MARY.

Preamble. 1692-93, chap. 17. Great complaints having been made of fraud in the cask, and manner of packing mackerel and other pickled fish, notwithstanding the provision heretofore made for preventing it; therefore,—

Be it enacted by the Lieutenant-Governo[u]r, Council and House of Representatives,

Assize of cask. [SECT. 1.] That all casks for pickled fish shall be made of staves, which shall be, [when] [*well*] worked, twenty-nine inches long, and the head shall be of the diameter of seventeen inches and an half; and the chine or part of the stave without each head, not more than an inch and an half; and the head not more than an inch thick; the cask to have the usual bilge, and to be tight and well made; or otherwise, shall hold thirty-one gallons and an half, and be marked, befor[*e*] packing, by a guager duly appointed and sworn.

And be it further enacted,

Manner of packing fish, &c. [SECT. 2.] That the mackerel and other pickled fish, shall be carefully pack[*e*]'d, well salted, and duly fill[*e*]'d by a packer chosen and sworn for the purpose, the whole of each barrel[l] to consist of the same kind of fish; and every packer shall brand each barrel[l] thus made and pack[*e*]'d, with the first letter of his Christian name, and his sirname at length, and with the first letter of the name of the town where the fish is pack[*e*]'d, for which he shall be paid by the owner of such fish, at the rate of eightpence by the ton, and no more.

And be it further enacted,

Forfeiture for showing or offering to sale fish not described as above. [SECT. 3.] That all and every person or persons who shall, after the first day of March, one thousand seven hundred and fifty-eight, offer or shew for sale any cask or casks of mackerel or other pickled fish not branded, or smaller than the barrel[l]s or casks described above, or where there shall be any fraud in packing the fish, the person or persons so offering them to sale, shall forfeit such cask of fish; and any justice of peace, on complaint made, may and shall issue his warrant for seizing and securing such forfeiture for trial.

And be it further enacted,

Penalty for fraudulent packing or branding. [SECT. 4.] That every packer who shall pack and brand any barrels or casks which are smaller than above directed, or fraudulently pack[*e*]'d, for every such offence, shall incur[r] the penalty of twenty shillings for each barrel[l] thus unjustly branded.

Preamble. *And inasmuch* as it is found very difficult for such persons as are appointed packers in sundry maritime towns, to repair, in order to be sworn, to the town where the court of general sessions of the peace is held, which is now requisite,—

Be it enacted and ordered,

Packers may be sworn before a justice. [SECT. 5.] That such packers may be sworn before any one justice of the peace for such county, in such town or place as may be nearest or most convenient, such justice certifying the caption to the clerk of the court of general sessions of the peace, at or before the next sitting of said court: *provided*, that this act shall not be construed or understood to prohibit the packing of oysters, or other kinds of fish, in kegs, which have heretofore usually been packed in such small casks.

And be it further enacted,

Disposal of fines. [SECT. 6.] That all fines and forfeitures by this act, shall be and belong, one half to his majesty for the use of this province, and the other half to him or them who shall inform and sue for the same. [*Passed February* 25; * *published February* 28, 1757.

CHAPTER 18.

AN ACT IN ADDITION TO AN ACT MADE AND PASSED IN THE FIFTH YEAR OF THE REIGN OF THEIR LATE MAJESTIES WILLIAM AND MARY, INTITLED "AN ACT FOR HIGHWAYS."

WHEREAS in and by an act made and passed in the fifth year of the reign of their late majesties King William and Queen Mary, intitled "An Act for highways," it is provided, that where highways or common roads are wanting, or where old ways may with more conveniency be turned or altered, upon application made to the justices in quarter-sessions in the county where they are wanted, they having first, by a committee, enquired into the necessity and conveniency thereof, the said justices are to order the same to be laid out or altered by a jury to be summoned by the sheriff for the said purpose; which method is found inconvenient, and causes great and needless charge to the respective counties in this province; for remedy whereof,— Preamble. 1693-94, chap. 6, § 3.

Be it enacted by the Lieutenant-Governour, Council and House of Representatives,

[SECT. 1.] That where a new highway or common road from town to town, or place to place, shall be wanting, or where an highway or common road already laid out, stated and established, may or can with greater convenience be turned or altered, upon application made to the justices of the court of general sessions of the peace, within the same county, and it being judged by them to be of common convenience or necessity, to have such new way laid out or old one altered, the said court be and hereby are impowered to appoint a committee of five disinterested, sufficient freeholders in the same county to view and lay out such highway or road; which committee shall give seasonable notice to all persons interested of the time and place of their meeting, and shall be under oath to perform the said service according to their best skill and judgment, with most convenience to the publick, and least prejudice or damage to private property; and shall also ascertain the place and course of said road in the best way and manner they can; which, having done, the said committee, or the major part of them, shall make return thereof to the next court of general sessions of the peace, to be held in the said county, after the said service is performed, under their hands and seals, to the end the same may be allowed and recorded, and after known for a publick highway. Court of sessions to appoint a committee to lay out or alter highways. Return to be made to said court.

Provided, nevertheless,—

[SECT. 2.] That if any person be damaged in his property, by the laying out or altering such highway, the town or district where the same is shall make such person or persons reasonable satisfaction according to the estimation of the committee, or major part of them, who laid out the same; which said committee are impowered and required, under oath, to estimate the same, and make return thereof as aforesaid; and if such person or persons so damaged find him- or themselves agrieved by any act or thing done by the said committee, in laying out said way or estimate of his or their damages, he or they may apply unto the court of general sessions of the peace, provided such applica- Proviso.

* February 26, according to the record.

tion be made to the court that shall be held in such county next after such return; and said court is hereby impowered to hear and determine the same, and shall and may enquire by a jury, under oath, to be summoned by the sheriff or his deputy for said purpose, if the person complaining desires the same; and if the jury shall not alter said way, or increase the damages, the person complaining shall be at all costs, to be taxed against him by said court, otherwise such cost shall be paid by the county; and the increase of damage found by the jury shall be p[*ai*]d by the town or district in which such way shall be laid.

And be it further enacted,

Jury's verdict to determine damage, and fix highways.

[SECT. 3.] That the verdict of such jury, return thereof being made, under their hands and seals, to said court, shall conclude the person or persons complaining [and] w[*i*]th regard to the damage, [*and*] also fix and determine the place of such road or highway, and re[c]cord shall be made thereof accordingly. [*Passed February* 19; * *published February* 28, 1757.

CHAPTER 19.

AN ACT FOR GRANTING UNTO HIS MAJESTY SEVERAL RATES AND DUTIES OF IMPOST AND TUNNAGE OF SHIPPING.

We, his majesty's most dutiful and loyal subjects, the representatives of the province of the Massachusets Bay, in New England, being desirous of lessening the public debts, have chearfully and unanimously given and granted, and do give and grant, to his most excellent majesty, for the service of this province, as they shall hereafter apply it, the several duties of impost upon all liquors, wines, goods and merchandize that shall be imported into this province, and tunnage of shipping, hereafter mentioned; and pray that it may be enacted,—

And be it accordingly enacted by the Lieutenant-Governour, Council and House of Representatives,

[SECT. 1.] That from and after the twenty-sixth day of March, one thousand seven hundred and fifty-seven, to the twenty-sixth day of March, one thousand seven hundred and fifty-eight, there shall be paid by the importers of all wines, rum and other liquors, goods, wares and merchandize, that shall be imported into this province by any of the inhabitants thereof (except what is by this act hereafter exempted), the several rates and duties of impost following; viz[t].,—

For every pipe of wine of every sort, ten shillings.

For every hogshead of rum, containing one hundred gallons, eight shillings.

For every hogshead of sugar, fourpence.

For every hogshead of molasses, fourpence.

For every hogshead of tobacco, ten shillings.

For every pound of tea that shall be imported from any of his majesty's plantations in America, one shilling.

—And so, proportionably, for greater or less quantities.

And for all other commodities, goods or merchandize not mentioned, or not excepted, fourpence for every twenty shillings value: excepting such goods as are the product or manufacture of Great Britain.

[SECT. 2.] And for any of the above-mentioned liquors, goods, wares and merchandize (excepting tea, which shall pay only one shilling), that shall be imported into this province by any of the inhabitants of the

* Signed February 26, according to the record.

other provinces or colonies on this continent, or of the English West-India Islands, in any ship or vessel to them belonging, on the proper account of any of the said inhabitants of the said provinces, colonies or islands, there shall be paid by the importers double the impost laid by this act: *provided always*, that every thing which is the growth or produce of the provinces or colonies aforesaid (tobacco and bar-iron excepted), and all provisions, salt, cotton-wool, pig-iron, mohogony, black-walnut, lignum-vitæ, red-cedar, log-wood, brazilletto-wood, hemp, raw skins and hides, and also all prize goods brought into and condemned in this province, are and shall be exempted from every the rates and duties aforesaid.

And be it further enacted,

[SECT. 3.] That all goods, wares and merchandize, the property of any of the inhabitants of any of the neighbouring provinces or colonies on this continent, that shall be imported into this province, and shall have paid, or for which there shall have been secured to be paid, the duty of impost, by this act provided to be paid, and afterwards shall be exported and landed in any of the said provinces or colonies on this continent, then, and in such case, the exporter producing a certificate from some officer of his majesty's customs, that the same have been landed in some of the provinces or colonies aforesaid, shall be allowed a drawback of the whole duty of impost by him paid, or secured to be paid, as by this act provided.

And be it further enacted,

[SECT. 4.] That the master of every ship or vessel coming into this province from any other place, shall, within twenty-four hours after his arrival in any port or harbour, and before bulk is broken, make report and deliver a manifest, in writing, under his hand, to the commissioner aforesaid, of the contents of the loading of such ship or vessel, therein particularly expressing the species, kind and quantities of all wines, liquors, goods, wares and merchandize imported in such ship or vessel, with the marks and numbers thereof, and to whom the same are consigned; and make oath before the commissioner that the same manifest contains a just and true account of all the lading taken on board and imported in such ship or vessel, so far as he knows or believes; and that if he knows of any more wines, liquors, goods, wares or merchandize laden on board such ship or vessel, and imported therein, he will forthwith make report thereof to the commissioner aforesaid, and cause the same to be added to his manifest.

And be it further enacted,

[SECT. 5.] That if the master of any ship or vessel shall break bulk, or suffer any of the wines, liquors, goods, or wares and merchandize imported in such ship or vessel to be unloaden before report and entry thereof be made as aforesaid, he shall forfiet the sum of one hundred pounds.

And be it further enacted,

[SECT. 6.] That all merchants and other persons, being owners of any wines, liquors, goods, wares or merchandize imported into this province, for which any of the rates or duties aforesaid are payable, or having the same consigned to them, shall make an entry thereof with the commissioner aforesaid, and produce an invoice of all such goods as pay *ad valorem*, and make oath before him in form following; vizt.,—

You, A. B., do swear that the entry of the goods and merchandize by you now made, exhibits the sterling value of said goods, and that, *bonâ fide*, according to your best skill and judgment, it is not less than that value. So help you God.

—which oath the commissioner or receiver appointed in consequence of this act is hereby impowered and directed to administer; and the owners aforesaid shall pay to said commissioner, or give security to pay, the duty of impost by this act required, before such wines, liquors, goods, wares or merchandize be landed or taken out of the vessel in which the same shall be imported.

[SECT. 7.] And no wines, liquors, goods, wares or merchandize that by this act are liable to pay impost or duty, shall be landed on any wharf, or in any warehouse or other place, but in the daytime only, and that after sunrise and before sunset, unless in the presence or with the consent of the commissioner or receiver, on pain of forficting all such wines, liquors, goods, wares and merchandize, and the lighter, boat or vessel out of which the same shall be landed or put into any warehouse or other place.

[SECT. 8.] And if any person or persons shall not have and produce an invoice of the quantities of rum or liquors to him or them consigned, then the cask wherein the same are, shall be gauged at the charge of the importer, that the contents thereof may be known.

Provided, nevertheless,—

[SECT. 9.] That the said commissioner shall be and he hereby is allowed to give credit to such person or persons whose duty of impost in one vessel shall not exceed six pounds; which credit shall be so limitted as that he shall settle and ballance his accounts with every person, on or before the twenty-sixth day of March, one thousand seven hundred and fifty-eight, that the said accounts may be produced to this court as soon as may be after; and for all entries where the impost to be paid doth not exceed three shillings the said commissioner shall not demand anything. and not more than sixpence for any other single entry, to what value soever.

And be it further enacted,

[SECT. 10.] That the importer of all wines, liquors, goods, wares and merchandize, from and after the twenty-sixth day of March next, and untill the twenty-sixth of March, one thousand seven hundred and fifty-eight, by land-carriage, or in small vessels or boats, shall make report and deliver a manifest thereof to the commissioner aforesaid or his deputy, therein particularly expressing the species, kind and quantity of all such wines, liquors, goods, wares and merchandize so imported, with the marks and numbers thereof, when, how and by whom brought; and shall make oath, before the said commissioner or his deputy, to the truth of such report and manifest, and shall also pay or secure to be paid the several duties aforesaid by this act charged and chargeable upon such wines, liquors, goods, wares and merchandize, before the same are landed, housed or put into any store or place whatsoever.

And be it further enacted,

[SECT. 11.] That every merchant or other person importing any wines in this province, shall be allowed twelve per cent for leakage: *provided*, such wines shall not have been filled up on board; and that every hogshead, butt or pipe of wine that hath two-thirds thereof leaked out, shall be accounted for outs, and the merchant or importer to pay no duty for the same. And no master of any ship or vessel shall suffer any wines to be filled up on board without giving a certificate of the quantity so filled up, under his hand, before the landing thereof, to the commissioner or receiver of impost for such port, on pain of forfieting the sum of one hundred pounds.

[SECT. 12.] And if it may be made to appear that any wines imported in any ship or vessel be decayed at the time of unloading thereof, or in twenty days afterwards, oath being made before the commissioner or receiver that the same hath not been landed above that time;

the duties and impost paid for such wines shall be repayed unto the importer thereof.

And be it further enacted,

[SECT. 13.] That the master of every ship or vessel importing any liquors, wines, goods, wares or merchandize, shall be liable to pay the impost for such and so much thereof, contained in his manifest, as shall not be duly entered, and the duty paid for the same by the person or persons to whom such wines, liquors, goods, wares or merchandize are or shall be consigned. And it shall and may be lawful, to and for the master of every ship or other vessel, to secure and detain in his hands, at the owner's risque, all such wines, liquors, goods, wares and merchandize imported in any ship or vessel, untill he receives a certificate, from the commissioner or receiver of impost, that the duty for the same is paid, and untill he be repaid his necessary charges in securing the same; or such master may deliver such wines, liquors, goods, wares and merchandize as are not entered, unto the commissioner or receiver of the impost in such port, or his order, who is hereby impowered and directed to receive and keep the same, at the owner's risque, untill the impost thereof, with the charges, be paid or secured to be paid; and then to deliver such wines, liquors, goods, wares or merchandize as such master shall direct.

And be it further enacted,

[SECT. 14.] That the commissioner or receiver of the impost in each port, shall be and hereby is impowered to sue the master of any ship or vessel, for the impost or duty of so much of the lading of any wines, liquors, goods, wares or merchandize imported therein, according to the manifest to be by him given upon oath, as aforesaid, as shall remain not entered and the duty of impost therefor not paid or secured to be paid. And where any goods, wares or merchandize are such that the value thereof is not known, whereby the impost to be recovered of the master, for the same, cannot be ascertained, the owner or person to whom such goods, wares or merchandize are or shall be consigned, shall be summoned to appear as an evidence at the court where such suit for the impost and the duty thereof shall be brought, and be there required to make oath to the value of such goods, wares or merchandize.

And be it further enacted,

[SECT. 15.] That the ship or vessel, with her tackle, apparel and furniture, the master of which shall make default in anything by this act required to be performed by him, shall be liable to answer and make good the sum or sums forfieted by such master, according to this act, for any such default, as also to make good the impost or duty for all wines, liquors, goods, wares and merchandize not entered as aforesaid, or for which the duty of impost has not been paid; and, upon judgment recovered against such master, the said ship or vessel, with so much of the tackle or appurtenances thereof as shall be sufficient to satisfy said judgment, may be taken by execution for the same; and the commissioner or receiver of the impost is hereby impowered to make seizure of the said ship or vessel, and detain the same under seizure untill judgment be given in any suit to be commenced and prosecuted for any of the said forfietures, or for the duty aforesaid; to the intent, that if judgment be rendered for the prosecutors or informer, such ship or vessel and appurtenances may be exposed to sale, for satisfaction thereof, as is before provided: *unless* the owners, or some on their behalf, for the releasing of such ship or vessel from under seizure or restraint, shall give sufficient security unto the commissioner or receiver of impost that seized the same, to respond or satisfy the sum or value of the forfietures and duties, with charges, that shall be recovered against the master thereof, upon such suit to be brought for the same, as aforesaid; and the master occasioning such loss or damage unto his owners, through his default or neglect, shall be liable to their action for the same.

And be it further enacted,

[SECT. 16.] That the naval officer within any of the ports of this province shall not clear or give passes to any master of any ship or vessel, outward bound, until he shall be certified, by the commissioner or receiver of the impost, that the duty and impost for the goods last imported in such ship or vessel are paid or secured to be paid.

[SECT. 17.] And the commissioner or receiver of the impost is hereby impowered to allow bills of store to the master of any ship or vessel importing any wines or liquors, for such private adventures as shall belong to the master or seamen of ship or vessel, at the discretion of the commissioner or receiver, not exceeding three per cent of the lading; and the duties payable by this act for such wines or liquors, in such bills of stores mentioned and expressed, shall be abated.

And for the more effectual preventing any wines, rum or other distilled spirits being brought into the province from the neighbouring governments, by land, or in small boats or vessels, or any other way, and also to prevent wines, rum or other distilled spirits being first sent out of this province, and afterwards brought into the government again, to defraud the government of the duties of impost,—

Be it enacted,

[SECT. 18.] That the commissioner and receiver of the aforesaid duties of impost shall, and he is hereby impowered and enjoined to, appoint one suitable person or persons as his deputy or deputies, in all such places of this province where it is likely that wine, rum or other distilled spirits will be brought out of other governments into this; which officers shall have power to seize the same, unless the owner shall make it appear that the duty of impost has been paid therefor since their being brought into or relanded in this government; and such officer or officers are also impowered to search, in all suspected places, for such wines, rum and distilled spirits or tea brought or relanded in this government, where the duty is not paid as aforesaid, and to seize and secure the same for the ends and uses as in this act is hereafter provided.

And be it further enacted,

[SECT. 19.] That the commissioner or his deputies shall have full power to administer the several oaths aforesaid, and search in all suspected places for all such wines, rum, liquors, tea, goods, wares and merchandize as are brought into this province, and landed contrary to the true intent and meaning of this act, and to seize the same for the uses hereinafter mentioned.

And be it further enacted,

[SECT. 20.] That if the said commissioner, or his deputy, shall have information of any wines, rum or other distilled spirits, or tea, being brought into and landed in any place in this province, for which the duties aforesaid shall not have been paid after their being brought into or relanded in this government, he may apply to any justice of the peace within the county, for a warrant to search such place; and said justice shall grant such warrant, directed to some proper officer, upon said commissioner or his deputy's making oath that he hath had information as aforesaid; and having such warrant, and being attended by such officer, the said commissioner or his deputy may, in the daytime, between sun-rising and sun-setting, demand admittance of the person owning or occupying such place, and, upon refusal, shall have right to break open such place; and, finding such liquors, or tea, may seize and take the same into his own custody; and the commissioner aforesaid, or his deputy, shall be and hereby is impowered to command assistance, and to impress carriages necessary to secure the liquors or tea seized as aforesaid; and any persons refusing assistance, or preventing any of the said officers from executing their office, shall forfeit five pounds to the said commissioner; and he or his deputy shall make reasonable satisfaction for the assistance afforded, and carriages made use of, to secure the liquors or tea seized as aforesaid; and the commissioner or his deputy shall then file an information of such seizure in the inferiour court of common pleas for the county wherein such seizure shall be made, which court shall summon the owner of such liquors or tea, or the occupier of such shop, house or warehouse, or distill-house, where the same were seized, to appear, and shew cause, if any he has, why said liquors or tea so seized shall not be adjudged forfeited; and if such owner or occupier shall not shew cause as aforesaid, or shall make default, the said liquors or tea shall be adjudged forfeited, and the said court shall order them to be sold at publick vendue; and the nett produce of such sale shall be paid, one half to the province treasurer for the use of this province, and the other half to the said commissioner.

And be it further enacted,

[Sect. 21.] That there shall be paid, by the master of every ship or other vessel, coming into any port or ports of this province, to trade or traffick, whereof all the owners are not belonging to this province (except such vessels as belong to Great Britain, the provinces or colonies of Pennsylvania, West and East Jersey, Connecticut, New York, New Hampshire and Rhode Island), every voyage such ship or vessel doth make, one pound of good pistol-powder for every ton such ship or vessel is in burthen: *saving* for that part which is owned in Great Britain, this province, or any of the aforesaid governments, which is hereby exempted; to be paid unto the commissioner or receiver of the duties of impost, and to be employed for the ends and uses aforesaid.

[Sect. 22.] And the said commissioner is hereby impowered to appoint a meet and suitable person, to repair unto and on board any ship or vessel, to take the exact measure and tunnage thereof, in case he shall suspect the register of such ship or vessel doth not express and set forth the full burthen of the same; the charge thereof to be paid by the master or owner of such ship or vessel, before she shall be cleared, in case she shall appear to be of a greater burthen: otherwise, to be paid by the commissioner out of the money received by him for impost, and shall be allowed him, accordingly, by the treasurer, in his accompts. And the naval officer shall not clear any vessel, until he be certified, also, by the commissioner, that the duty of tunnage for the same is paid, or that it is such a vessel for which none is payable according to this act.

And be it further enacted,

[Sect. 23.] That when and so often as any wine, rum or tea imported into this province, the aforesaid duty of impost upon which shall have been paid agreable to this act, shall be reshipped and exported from this government to any other part of the world, that then, and in every such case, the exporter of such wines or rum or tea shall make oath, at the time of shipping, before the receiver of impost, or his deputy, that the whole of the wine or rum or tea so shipped has, *bonâ fide*, had the aforesaid duty of impost paid on the same, and shall afterwards produce a certificate, from some officer of the customs, that the same has been landed out of this government,—or otherwise, in case such rum or wines or tea shall be exported to any place where there is no officer of the customs, or to any foreign port, the master of the vessel in which the same shall be exported shall make oath that the same has been landed out of the government, and the exporter shall, upon producing such certificate, or upon such oath of the master, make oath that he verily believes no part of said wines, rum or tea has been relanded in this province,—such exporter shall be allowed a drawback from the receiver of impost as follows; vizt.,—

For every pipe of wine, eight shillings.

For every hogshead of rum, six shillings.

And for every pound of tea, one shilling.

Provided, always,—

[SECT. 24.] That if, after the shipping of such wine or rum or tea, to be exported, as aforesaid, and giving security as aforesaid, in order to obtain the drawback aforesaid, the wine or rum or tea so shipped to be exported, or any part thereof, shall be relanded in this province, or brought into the same from any other province or colony, that then all such wine, rum and tea, so relanded and brought again into this province, shall be forfeited and may be seized by the commissioner aforesaid, or his deputy.

And be it further enacted,

[SECT. 25.] That there be one fit person, and no more, nominated and appointed by this court, as a commissioner and receiver of the aforesaid duties of impost and tunnage of shipping, and for the inspection, care and management of the said office, and whatsoever relates thereto, to receive commission for the same from the governour or commander-in-chief for the time being, with authority to substitute and appoint a deputy receiver in each port, or other places besides that in which he resides, and to grant warrants to such deputy receivers for the said place, and to collect and receive the impost and tunnage of shipping as aforesaid that shall become due within such port, and to render the account thereof, and to pay in the same, to the said commissioner and receiver: which said commissioner and receiver shall keep fair books of all entries and duties arising by virtue of this act; also, a particular account of every vessel, so that the duties of impost and tunnage arising on the said vessel may appear; and the same to lye open, at all seasonable times, to the view and perusal of the treasurer or receiver-general of this province (or any other person or persons whom this court shall appoint), with whom he shall account for all collections and payments, and pay all such monies as shall be in his hands, as the treasurer or receiver-general shall demand it. And the said commissioner or receiver and his deputy or deputies, before their entering upon the execution of their said office, shall be sworn to deal truly and faithfully therein, and shall attend in the said office from ten of the clock in the forenoon, until one in the afternoon.

[SECT. 26.] And the said commissioner or receiver, for his labour, care and expences in the said office, shall have and receive, out of the province treasury, at the rate of sixty pounds per annum; and his deputy or deputies shall receive for their service such sums as the said commissioner of impost, together with the province treasurer, shall judge necessary, for whatever sums they shall receive and pay; and the treasurer is hereby ordered, in passing and receiving the said commissioner's accounts, accordingly, to allow the payment of such salary or salaries, as aforesaid, to himself and his deputies.

And be it further enacted,

[SECT. 27.] That all penalties, fines and forfeitures accruing and arising in consequence of any breach of this act, shall be one half to his majesty for the use of this province, and the other half to him or them that shall seize, inform and sue for the same, by action, bill, plaint or information, in any of his majesty's courts of record, wherein no essoign, protection or wager of law shall be allowed: the whole charge of the prosecution to be taken out of the half belonging to the informer.

And be it further enacted,

[SECT. 28.] That from and after the commencement of this act, in all causes where any claimer shall appear, and shall not make good the claim, the charges of prosecution shall be born and paid by the said claimer, and not by the informer. [*Passed February* 25, 1757.*

CHAPTER 20.

AN ACT IN ADDITION TO AN ACT, INTIT[U]LED "AN ACT FOR THE BETTER REGULATING THE CHOICE OF PET[TY][*IT*] JURORS."

WHEREAS in and by an act made and pass[*e*]'d in the thirtieth year of his present majesty's reign, intitled "An Act for the better regulating the choice of petit jurors," it is, among other things, enacted, "that the selectmen of each town within this province shall, within their respective towns, some time before the first of December next, take a list of the persons, liable by law, and which they shall judge able and well qualified, to serve on the petit juries, and lay the same before the town, at a meeting to be immediately call[*e*]'d for that purpose; and the town shall, respectively, at such meeting, select out of the list, such as they judge most suitable to serve as jurors, and put their names, written on seperate p[ei][*ie*]ces of paper, into a box, to be provided by the selectmen for that purpose, and deliver the same to the town clerk, to be by him kept under lock and key." And it being represented to this court, that the town of Boston did not conform to the directions of said act, through inadvertence, before the first of December last, in taking a list of such inhabitants as were qualified to serve as petit jurors, but in said month of December, in the choice of petit jurors for the inferiour court of common pleas now sitting for the county of Suffolk, said town proceeded according to the act made in the thirteenth year of his present majesty's reign, relating to the choice of petit jurors, and have accordingly made return to said court of the persons then drawn to serve as petit jurors; *and whereas* it is very probable that many other towns in this province did not, before said first of December, take a list of the inhabitants qualified to serve in such towns as petit jurors and conform to said act, but have proceeded according to the act made in the thirteenth year of his present majesty's reign, whereby great disputes may arise as to the legality of the choice and return of such jurors, and the verdicts they may have given or shall give in all causes tryed and to them committed; for the remedy whereof, and to confirm the proceedings of such towns,—

Preamble. 1756-57, chap. 13, § 1.

1737-38, chap. 20. 1741-42, chap. 18.

Be it therefore enacted by the Lieutenant-Governour, Council and House of Representatives,

That the choice and return of the petit jurors made by the town of Boston to the said inferiour court now sitting, and of any other towns that have not conform'd to the act aforesaid, pass'd in October last, shall be and hereby is adjudged and held good and valid, and the verdicts given, or that shall be given in all causes committed to them, shall be effectual to all intents and purposes; and also that such towns as did not, before said first of December, take said list, are hereby allowed and directed to take said list some time on or before their annual meetings in March next, and then proceed in the same manner in all things as they are directed by said act; and until[l] said annual meeting said towns are impowered, in their choice of petit jurors, to

Choice of petit jurors in the town of Boston confirmed.

Selectmen to prepare lists for the choice of petit jurors before their annual meeting in March.

* February 26, according to the record.

proceed upon the lists given in the last year, and the choice to be made and returned shall be and hereby is deemed to be good and effectual in law, anything in the act pass[*e*]d in October last notwithstanding. [*Passed January* 10;* *published January* 11, 1757.

CHAPTER 21.

AN ACT FOR GRANTING UNTO HIS MAJESTY AN EXCISE UPON SPIRITS DISTILLED, AND WINE, AND UPON LIMES, LEMMONS AND ORANGES.

Preamble.

WE, his majesty's most loyal and dutiful subjects, the representatives of the province of the Massachuset[*t*]s Bay, in general court assembled, being desirous to lessen the present debt of the province, have chearfully and unanimously granted, and do hereby give and grant unto his most excellent majesty, for the end and use above mentioned, and for no other use, an excise upon all rum and other spirits distilled, and upon all wines whatsoever, and upon lemmons, limes and oranges, to be raised, levied, collected and paid in manner and form following:—

And be it accordingly enacted by the Lieutenant-Governour, Council and House of Representatives,

Time of this act's continuance.

[SECT. 1.] That from and after the twenty-sixth day of March, one thousand seven hundred and fifty-seven, and until[l] the twenty-sixth day of March, one thousand seven hundred and fifty-eight, every person al[l]ready licenced, or that shall be hereafter licenced, to retail rum or other spirits distilled, or wine, shall pay the duties following:—

For every gallon of rum and spirits distilled, fourpence.
For every gallon of wine of every sort, sixpence.
For every hundred of lemmons or oranges, four shillings.
For every hundred of limes, one shilling and sixpence.
—And so proportionably for any other quantity or number.

And be it further enacted,

Account to be taken.

[SECT. 2.] That every retailer of rum, wine or spirits distilled, taverner, innholder and common victualler, shall, on the said twenty-sixth day of March next, take a just and true account, in writing, of all wine, rum and spirits distilled, and of all limes, lemmons and oranges then by him or her, or in his or her possession; and that every person who shall be hereafter licenced to be taverner, innholder, common victualler or retailer of wine, rum or spirits distilled, shall take a like account of all wine, rum and other spirits distilled, and of all limes, lemmons and oranges by him or her, or in his or her possession, at the time of such licence granted; and that every taverner, innholder, common victualler and retailer of rum or other spirits distilled or wine, shall make a fair entry, in a book by them respectively to be kept for that purpose, of all such rum or other spirits distilled, or wine, as he or she, or any person or persons for him or her, shall buy, distil[l], take in or receive after such first account taken, and when and of whom the same was bought and taken in; and at the expiration of every half year shall take a just and true account how much thereof then remains by them; and shall, in writing, under their hands, render to him or them that shall farm the duties aforesaid, the whole of those several accounts, and shall also, if requested, make oath, in the form following, before such farmer or farmers, who are hereby impowered to administer the same:—

* Signed January 11, and, again, February 26, according to the record.

You, A. B., do swear that the account by you now rendered is, to the best of your knowledge, a just and true account of all the wines, rum and distilled spirits, limes, lemmons and oranges you had by you, or in your possession, on the twenty-sixth day of March, one thousand seven hundred and fifty-seven; and also of all the wine, rum and other distilled spirits bought, distilled, taken in or received by you, or by any person or persons for or under you, or by or with your knowledge, allowance, consent or connivance, and that there still remains thereof in your possession unsold, so much as is in this account said to remain by you unsold; and that you do not know or bel[ei][*ie*]ve that there hath been by you, or by any other person or persons for or under you, or by your or their order, allowance, consent or connivance, either directly or indirectly, sold, used or consumed any wine, or any liquor for, or as, wine; any rum or distilled spirits, or liquor for, or as, rum or distilled spirits; or that there hath been any limes, lemmons or oranges by you, or by any person or persons for or under you, or by your order, consent, allowance or connivance, used or consumed in making punch, or otherwise, since the said twenty-sixth day of March, besides what is contained in the account by you now rendered. So help you God. Form of the oath.

[SECT. 3.] And for every person that was not licenced on the said twenty-sixth day of March, the form of the oath shall be so varied, as that instead of expressing the day aforesaid, the time of taking and rendering their last account shall be inserted and used; and for every person rendering an account after the first, the oath shall be so varied, as that instead of expressing the day aforesaid, the time of taking and rendering their last account shall be inserted and used.

[SECT. 4.] And every such taverner, innholder, and common victualler and retailer shall pay the duties aforesaid to him or them that shall farm the same, or the whole of the several articles mentioned in such account rendered, save only for such part thereof as remains in their hands unsold: *provided, nevertheless*, that for leakage, &c[a]., ten per cent shall be allowed them on all liquors in such account mentioned, besides what remains in their hands unsold. Duties to be paid to the farmer. Ten per cent allowed for leakage.

And be it further enacted,

[SECT. 5.] That every person hereafter licenced to be a taverner, innholder, common victualler or retailer of wine, rum or spirits distilled shall, within thirty days after such licence granted, and before he or she sell by virtue of the same, not only become bound to keep good rule, &c[a]., as by law is already required, but shall also become bound, with sufficient sureties, by way of recognizance, to his majesty, for the use of him or them that have or shall farm the duties aforesaid, in a sufficient sum, to be ordered by the court that grants the licence, which sum shall not be less than fifty pounds, conditioned that they shall keep and render the accounts aforesaid, and pay the duties aforesaid, as in and by this act is required. Taverner, &c., to give bond.

And be it further enacted,

[SECT. 6.] That every such taverner, innholder, common victualler and retailer, who shall neglect or refuse to take, keep and render such accounts as by this act are required, or that shall neglect or refuse to take the oath aforesaid, if required, shall forf[ie][*ei*]t and pay, to him or them that shall farm the duties aforesaid, double the sum which the court of general sessions of the peace in that county shall adjudge that the duties of excise upon the liquors, limes, lemmons and oranges by such taverner, innholder, common victualler or retailer, or by any for or under him or them, sold, used or consumed would have amounted to; and no persons shall be licenced by the justices of the general sessions of the peace who hath not accounted with the farmer, and paid him the excise aforesaid, due from such person at the time of his or her taking or renewing such licence. Forfeiture for neglect in keeping and rendering account.

And whereas, notwithstanding the laws made against selling strong Preamble.

drink without licence, many persons, not regarding the penalties of said acts, do receive and entertain persons in their houses, and sell great quantities of spirits and other strong drink, without licence; by reason whereof great debaucheries are committed and kept secret, and such as take licences and pay the duties of excise therefor are greatly wronged, and the farmers unjustly deprived of their dues,—

Be it therefore enacted,

Forfeiture of £4 for selling without license.

[SECT. 7.] That if any distiller, importer or any other person whatsoever, after the said twenty-sixth day of March, shall presume, directly or indirectly, to sell any rum or other distilled spirits, or wine, in less quantity than twenty-five gallons, or any beer, ale, cyder, perry or other strong drink, in any quantity less than ten gallons, without licence first had and obtain[e]'d from the court of general sessions of the peace in that county, and recognizing in manner as aforesaid, shall forf[ie][*ei*]t and pay for each offence, the sum of four pounds, lawful money, and costs of prosecution, one half to the farmer of said duties and the other half to the informer; and all such as shall neglect or refuse to pay the fine aforesaid, shall stand closely committed in the common goal of the county, and not have the liberty of the goaler's house or yard, until[l] said sum of four pounds is paid, with costs; and any goaler giving liberty contrary to this act, shall forf[ie][*ei*]t and pay the said sum of four pounds, and costs of prosecution.

And whereas, in order to elude the design of this act, some persons may join together and buy wine, rum, brandy and other spirits distilled in quantities above twenty-five gallons, and afterwards divide the same among themselves in less quantities,—

Be it therefore enacted,

Persons not licensed joining together in purchasing liquors, and dividing the same, liable to a forfeiture.

[SECT. 8.] That where two or more persons, not licenced as aforesaid, shall join together, and purchase rum, brandy or other spirits distilled, or wine, or shall employ any other person not licenced as aforesaid to do it, and shall afterwards divide the same, or cause it to be divided among themselves, or otherwise, in less quantit[y][*ie*]s than twenty-five gallons, they shall be deemed and taken to be sellers of such rum, brandy and other distilled spirits and wine, and each and every of them shall be subject to the same pains, penalties and forf[ie][*ei*]tures as any person by this act is who shall sell rum or other spirits distilled, or wine, without licence first had and obtained.

And whereas some doubts have arisen whether the lending or delivering rum, brandy or other spirits distilled, or wine, to others for their use, upon agreement or in confidence of having the like liquors returned again, be a sale thereof; wherefore, for removing all such doubts,—

Be it enacted,

Liquors lent, or delivered, on the above consideration, to be deemed a sale.

[SECT. 9.] That all rum, brandy and other spirituous liquors and wine, lent or delivered to others for their use, upon such like consideration, is and shall be deemed and taken to be, an absolute sale thereof. And that every person not licenced as aforesaid, that shall order, allow, permit or connive at the selling rum, brandy or other distilled spirits, or wine, contrary to the true intent and meaning of this act, by his or their child or children, servant or servants, or any other person or persons in or belonging to his or her house or family, shall be deemed and taken to be the seller of such liquors, and be subject to the aforesaid pains and penalties provided against such offenders, and shall be recovered in like manner: *provided,* that if it shall be made appear that the liquors lent or delivered as aforesaid, shall have had the duty paid upon them, or were purchased of any person or persons having licence or permit, the person lending or delivering the same, aforesaid, shall not be subject to the aforesaid pains and penalties.

Preamble.

And whereas divers other persons than those licenced to sell rum and other distilled spirits by retail, have heretofore suppl[y][*i*]ed persons employed by them in the fishery, building vessels, and in other business, with rum and other liquors, without paying any excise thereon, and thereby have defrauded the government of the duty of excise, and have not been subject to the penalty provided by law against selling drink without licence, and the same practice will probably be continued, unless effectual care be taken to prevent the same,—

Be it therefore further enacted,

Persons not licenced supplying those employed by them, in the fishery, &c., with spirituous liquors, to be deemed sellers.

[SECT. 10.] That all persons not licenced, as aforesaid, who hereafter shall, by themselves, or by any other person or persons under them, or by their order, allowance or connivance, supply any person or persons employed by them in the fishery, building of vessels, or in any other business or employ, with rum or other distilled spirits, or wine, shall be deemed and taken to be sellers of such liquors, and be subject to the aforesaid pains and penalties provided against persons selling any of the liquors aforesaid without licence, which shall be recovered in the like manner, unless they make it appear that such wine, rum or other distilled spirits, was purchased of a taverner, innholder or retailer, or other person or persons that had licence or permit to sell the same.

And be it further enacted,

One witness sufficient for conviction.

[SECT. 11.] That when any person shall be charged with selling strong drink without licence, one witness produced to the satisfaction of the court or justice before whom the trial is, shall be deemed sufficient for conviction. And when and so often as it shall be observed that there is a resort of persons to houses suspected of selling strong drink without licence, any justice of the peace in the same county, shall have full power to convene such persons before him, and examine them upon oath concerning the persons suspected of selling or retailing strong drink in such houses, out-houses or other dependencies thereof; and if upon examining such witnesses, and hearing the defence of such suspected persons, it shall appear to the justice there is sufficient proof of the violation of this act by selling strong drink without licence, judgment may thereupon be made up against such person, and he shall forf[ie][*ei*]t and pay in like manner as if process had been commenced by bill, plaint or information before the said justice; or otherwise such justice may bind over the person suspected, and the witnesses, to the next court of general sessions of the peace for the county where such person shall dwell.

And be [it] *further enacted,*

Penalty for selling strong drink to negroes, mulattoes, &c.

[SECT. 12.] That when and so often as any person shall be charged with selling strong drink without licence to any negro, Indian or mollat[t]o slave, or to any child or other person under the age of discretion, and other circumstances concurring, it shall appear to be highly probable in the judgment of the court or justice before whom the trial shall be, that the person complained of is guilty, then, and in every such case, unless the defendant shall acquit him- or herself upon oath (to be administred to him or her by the court or justice that shall try the cause), such defendant shall forf[ie][*ei*]t and pay four pounds to the farmer of excise, and costs of prosecution; but if the defendant shall acquit him- or herself upon oath as aforesaid, the court or justice may and shall enter up judgment for the defendant to recover costs.

And be it further enacted,

Penalty on persons refusing to give evidence

[SECT. 13.] That if any person or persons shall be summoned to appear before a justice of the peace, or the grand jury, to give evidence relating to any person's selling strong drink without licence, or to appear before the court of general sessions of the peace, or other court proper to try the same, to give evidence on the tr[y][*i*]al of any person informed against, presented or indicted for selling strong drink without licence, and shall neglect or refuse to appear, or to give evidence in that behalf, every person so offending shall forf[ie][*ei*]t the sum of twenty pounds and cost of prosecution; the one half of the penalty aforesaid to be to his majesty for the use of the farmer, and the other half to and for the use of him or them who shall sue for the same as aforesaid. And when it shall so happen that witnesses are bound to sea before the sitting of the court where any person or persons informed against, for selling strong drink without licence, is or are to be prosecuted for the same, in every such case, the deposition of any witness or witnesses, in writing, taken before any two of his majesty's justices of the peace, *quorum unus*, and sealed up and delivered into court, the adverse party having first had a notification, in writing, sent to him or her of the time and place of caption, shall be esteemed as sufficient evidence, in the law, to convict any person or persons offending against this act, as if such witness or witnesses had been present at the time of tr[y][*i*]al, and given his, her or their deposition *viva voce;* and every person or persons who shall be summoned to give evidence before two justices of the peace, in manner as aforesaid, and shall neglect or refuse to appear, or to give evidence relating to the facts he or she shall be enquired of, shall be liable and subject to the same penalty as he or she would have been by virtue of this act, for not appearing, or neglecting or refusing to give his or her evidence before the grand jury or court as aforesaid.

And be it further enacted,

How fines are to be recovered.

[SECT. 14.] That all fines, forf[ie][*ei*]tures and penalties arising by this act shall and may be recovered by bill, plaint or information, before any court of record proper to try the same; and where the sum forf[ie][*ei*]ted doth not exceed four pounds, by bill, plaint or information before any one of his majesty's justices of the peace in the respective counties where such offence shall be committed: which said justice is hereby impowered to try and determine the same. And said justice shall make a fair entry or record of all such proceedings: *saving always* to any person or persons who shall think him-, her- or themselves aggrieved by the determination of the said justice, liberty of appeal therefrom to the next court of general sessions of the peace to be holden within and for said county, at which court such offence shall be finally determined: *provided,* that in the same appeal the same rules be observed as are already required, by law in appeals from justices, to the court of general sessions of the peace: *saving only,* that the recognizance for prosecuting the appeal[s] shall be eight pounds.

Be it further enacted,

Farmer to settle accounts.

[SECT. 15.] That every farmer shall settle all accounts relating to said excise in the several towns of the county where he is farmer, first giving seasonable and public[*k*] notice of the time and place or places where said business shall be transacted.

Be it further enacted,

Persons empowered to farm out the excise.

[SECT. 16.] That one or more person or persons, to be nominated and appointed by the general court, for and within the several counties in this province, public[*k*] notice being first given of the time and place and occasion of their meeting, shall have full power, and are hereby authorized, from time to time, to contract or agree with any person for or concerning the farming the duties in this act mentioned, upon rum and other the liquors and commodities aforesaid, in the respective counties for which they shall be appointed, as may be for the greatest profit and advantage of the public[*k*], so as the same exceed not the term of one year after the commencement of this act; and every farmer, or his deputy or deputies, of the duties of excise in any county, shall have power to inspect the houses of all such as are licenced, and of such as are suspected of selling without licence, to demand, sue for, and receive the excise due from licenced persons or others by virtue of this act.

And be it further enacted,

[SECT. 17.] That the farmer shall give bond with two sufficient sureties, to the province treasurer for the time being, and his successor in said office, in double the sum of money that shall be contracted for, with condition that the sum agreed on be paid into the province treasury, for the use of the province, at the expiration of one year from the commencement of this act; which bond the person or persons to be appointed a committee of such county are to take, and the same to lodge with the treasurer as aforesaid, within twenty days after such bond is executed; and the said treasurer, on failure or neglect of payment at the time therein limitted, may and is hereby impowered to issue out his execution, returnable in sixty days, against such farmer of excise and his sureties, or either of them, for the full sum expressed in the condition of their bonds, as they shall respectively become due, in the same manner as he is enabled by law to issue out his execution against defective constables, or to put such bond in suit; and the said committee shall render an account of their proceedings touching the farming this duty on rum, wine and other the liquors and species aforementioned, in their respective counties, to the general court in the first week of the next sitting of this court, and shall receive such sum or sums for their trouble and expence in said affair as said court shall think fit to allow them. Farmer to give bond that the sum agreed for be paid into the public treasury.

[SECT. 18.] And every person farming the excise in any county may substitute and appoint one or more deputy or deputies under him, upon oath, to collect and receive the excise aforesaid, which shall become due in said county, and pay in the same to such farmer; which deputy and deputies shall have, use and exercise all such powers and authorities as in and by this act are given or committed to the farmer for the better collecting the duties aforesaid, or prosecuting offenders against this act. Farmers may appoint deputies.

And be it further enacted,

[SECT. 19.] That in case any person farming the excise as aforesaid, or his deputy, shall, at any time during their continuance in said office, wittingly and willingly connive at, or allow, any person or persons within their respective divisions, not licenced by the court of general sessions of the peace, their selling any wines, rum or other liquors by this act forbidden, such farmer or deputy, for every such offence, shall forf[ie][*ei*]t the sum of fifty pounds and costs of prosecution; one half of the penalty aforesaid to be to his majesty for the use of this province, the other half to him or them that shall inform and sue for the same, and shall be thenceforward forever disabled for serving in said office: *saving* that said farmer may give a permit to any person to sell rum or other spirits distilled, or wine, in quantity from twenty-five gallons and upward[*s*], agreeable to this act. Penalty for farmers' or deputies' offending.

And be it further enacted,

[SECT. 20.] That in case of the death of the farmer of excise in any county, the executors or administrators of such farmer shall, upon their accepting of such trust of executor or administrator, have and enjoy all the powers, and be subject to all the duties, the farmer had or might enjoy and was subject to by force of this act. Provision in case of death, &c.

Provided, always, and it is the true intent and meaning of this act,—

[SECT. 21.] That if any taverner or retailer shall sell to any other taverner or retailer any quantity whatsoever of distilled liquors and wine, such taverner or retailer, selling as aforesaid, shall not be held to pay such duty, but the taverner or retailer who is the purchaser Proviso.

shall pay the same; and the seller as aforesaid, shall and is hereby required to deliver to the farmer of this duty, a true account of such liquors sold as aforesaid, and to whom sold.

And to the end that the revenue arising from the excise upon spirituous liquors may be increased and raised with more equality,—

Be it enacted,

Duties to be paid by private persons for what liquors they expend.

[SECT. 22.] That from and after the twenty-sixth day of March, one thousand seven hundred and fifty-seven, to the twenty-sixth day of March, one thousand seven hundred and fifty-eight, upon all rum and other distilled spirits, and all wine, imported or manufactured, and sold for consumption within this province, there be laid, and hereby is laid, the duty of excise following; viz[t].,—

For every gallon of rum and spirits distilled, fourpence.

For every gallon of wine of every sort, sixpence.

To be paid to the farmer of excise, or his deputy, by every person having permit to sell the said liquors in each county, respectively.

And be it further enacted,

Liquors not to be sold by the importer, &c., without a permit.

[SECT. 23.] That every person that shall import any of the liquors aforesaid, or to whom any of them shall or may be consigned, shall be and hereby is prohibited from selling the same, or any part thereof, without having a permit so to do from the farmer of excise, or his deputy; which permit shall be had and procured before the landing of such liquors. And every person distilling or manufacturing any of the said liquors, and every person owning or possessing any of them, excepting such as are or may be licenced by the court of general sessions of the peace, as aforesaid, shall be and hereby are prohibited from selling the same, or any part thereof, without having a permit so to do from the farmer of excise, or his deputy, on forf[ie][*ei*]ture of two hundred pounds, and of the value of the liquors so sold; and the said permit shall express the particular shop, house, warehouse, or distil[l]-house where the said liquors shall be permitted to be sold, and if any person who shall have such permit shall sell and deliver, or cause to be sold and delivered, any of the liquors aforesaid from any place or places not mentioned in such permit, he shall forf[ie][*ei*]t four pounds, to be paid to the farmer.

Provided, nevertheless,—

Proviso.

[SECT. 24.] That the impost officer, and his deputy, shall be and hereby are respectively impowered to grant a permit for selling the liquors aforesaid, or any of them, to any person applying for the same, until[l] the duty or excise aforesaid, in each county, respectively, shall be let or farmed, and until[l] the farmer shall give public[*k*] notice that said duty or excise is let or farmed to him as aforesaid. And said impost officer, and deputy, shall transmit to the farmer of each county an account of the permits by each of them respectively granted to persons living in such county.

And be it further enacted,

Farmer applying to a justice for a warrant may search for liquors supposed to be concealed.

[SECT. 25.] That if said farmer or his deputy, shall have information of any place where any of the liquors aforesaid shall have been sold by any person not having permit, as aforesaid, he may apply to any justice of the peace within the county, for a warrant to search such place, and said justice shall grant such warrant, directed to some proper officer, upon said farmer or deputies making oath that he hath had information as aforesaid, and that he hath just cause to suspect that the liquors aforesaid, or some of them, have been sold at such place informed of as aforesaid, and having such warrant, and being attended by such officer, the said farmer, or his deputy, may, in the day-time, between sun-rising and sun-setting, demand admittance of the person owning or occupying such place, and upon refusal, shall have right to break open said place, and finding such liquors, may seize and take the same into his own custody; and the farmer aforesaid, or his deputy, shall be and hereby is impowered to command assistance and impress carriages necessary to secure the liquors seized as aforesaid; and any person refusing assistance or preventing said officers from executing their office, shall forf[ie][*ei*]t five pounds to the farmer; and the said farmer, or his deputy, shall make reasonable satisfaction for the assistance afforded, and carriages made use of, to secure the liquors seized as aforesaid; and the farmer, or his deputy, shall then file an information of such seizure in the inferiour court of common pleas for the county wherein such seizure shall be made: which court shall summon the owner of such liquors, or the occupier of the shop, house, warehouse or distil[l]-house where the same were seized, to appear and shew cause, if any he has, why said liquors so seized should not be adjudged forf[ie][*ei*]ted; and if such owner or occupier shall not shew cause as aforesaid, or make default, the said liquors shall be adjudged forf[ie][*ei*]ted, and the said court shall order them to be sold at public[k] vendue, and the neet produce of such sale shall be paid, one half to the province treasurer, for the use of the province, and the other half to the farmer.

Provided,—

Proviso.

[SECT. 26.] That if the liquors seized as aforesaid be less in quantity than one hundred gallons, the farmer, or his deputy, shall file an information thereof with one of the justices of the peace within the county where the seizure shall be made, who shall summon the owner or occupier aforesaid in manner as aforesaid, and if such owner or occupier shall not shew cause, or shall make default as aforesaid, he shall adjudge such liquors forf[ie][*ei*]ted, and shall order them to be sold as aforesaid, and the neet produce of said sale to be disposed of as aforesaid: *saving* to the person convicted the liberty of an appeal, he ent[e]ring into recognizance to the king, for the use of the farmer, in the sum of fifty pounds.

Provided, also,—

[SECT. 27.] That if such farmer or deputy shall not find any of the liquors aforesaid in the place informed of, and broken open, as aforesaid, he shall pay double damages.

Be it further enacted,

Persons having permit as aforesaid, to render an account to the farmer, at the end of every half-year, saving, &c.

[SECT. 28.] That every person having permit as aforesaid, shall, at the end of each half year, respectively, from the twenty-sixth day of March, one thousand seven hundred and fifty-seven, be ready to render to the farmer aforesaid, or his deputy, an account, on oath, if required, of all the liquors aforesaid by him or her, and by any person or persons on his or her behalf, sold; and also of all the aforesaid liquors by him or her imported, distilled or manufactured, or which have come into his or her possession since the twenty-sixth of March aforesaid, except the same were bought of a licenced person in a quantity less than twenty-five gallons, which in his or her family have been consumed or expended within each half year, respectively: which account shall express the number of gallons of each kind of the liquors so sold and consumed, and shall pay therefor to the said farmer or his deputy the duty aforesaid, excepting for so much as shall have been sold to taverners, innholders or retailers having licence from the sessions as aforesaid, or to any other persons having permit as aforesaid; and so much as shall have been exported out of this province; and if any of said liquors shall have been sold to persons licenced by the sessions, or to persons having permit, said account shall exhibit the names of such licenced persons who purchased, and persons having permit, and the time when they purchased the same; and the person accounting shall exhibit a certificate under the hand of the licenced or permitted person purchasing, which shall express the number of gallons, and the kind of the liquors purchased, and the time when the same were purchased, and the name of the town and county wherein such licenced or permitted person lives, and shall lodge the said certificate with the said farmer or his deputy; and for the quantity of said liquors mentioned in such certificate, the said farmer or his deputy shall not demand any duty, but shall deliver said certificate to the farmer of the county wherein such licenced or permitted person, signing the same, lives: which last-mentioned farmer or his deputy shall settle with such licenced or permitted person for the duty aforesaid w[*hi*]ch may be due from him or her.

Persons having permit as aforesaid, to give an account of liquors by them sent out of the province.

[SECT. 29.] And if any person, having permit as aforesaid, shall ship or export any of the liquors aforesaid out of this province in a quantity not less than sixty gallons, and shall make a fair entry thereof with the farmer aforesaid, or his deputy, and shall produce to such farmer or deputy, when he comes to settle his account of excise, one of the receipts or bills of lading given therefor by the master of the vessel on board which such liquors shall be shipped, or if it shall be carried out of the province by land or in small boats, then of the person who is master of the land-carriage or boat, expressing the quantity thereof and the time of their being shipped, and shall lodge such receipt or bill of lading with the farmer or his deputy aforesaid, and at the same time shall swear that such liquors are *bonâ fide* sent, or intended to be sent, out of this province, he or she shall not be held to pay thereon the duty aforesaid.

Persons not having permit, to render an account, &c.

[SECT. 30.] And if any person not having permit shall purchase for exportation out of this province any of said liquors in a quantity not less than sixty gallons of a person having permit, the purchaser shall make entry thereof with the farmer or his deputy, and at the same time swear that such liquors are *bonâ fide* sent, or intended to be sent, out of this province, and shall within ten days after the purchase deliver one of the receipts or bills of lading given for such liquors, as aforesaid, to the person of whom he purchased the same, or be subject to pay the amount of the duty thereon to the person of whom he purchased as aforesaid, who shall pay such duty to the farmer or his deputy; but if the purchaser aforesaid shall deliver such receipt or bill of lading as aforesaid, and it be lodged with the farmer or his deputy, then, for the quantity of said liquors mentioned therein, the farmer or his deputy shall not demand any duty.

Penalty for masters' or others' giving certificate without receiving the liquors.

[SECT. 31.] And if the master of any vessel, or any other person, shall give such certificate, receipt or bill of lading, without receiving the liquors mentioned therein; or if any person shall procure such certificate, receipt or bill of lading, with design to defraud the farmer, and shall be thereof convicted, they and each of them shall forf[ie][*ei*]t and pay the sum of one hundred pounds; one half for the use of this government, and the other half for the use of the farmer. And if any such certificate, receipt or bill of lading shall be forged, counterf[ie][*ei*]ted or altered, the person forging, counterf[ie][*ei*]ting or altering shall incur the penalty of one hundred pounds.

Provided, nevertheless,—

Proviso.

[SECT. 32.] That the person having permit as aforesaid, shall not sell any of the liquors aforesaid in a quantity less than twenty-five gallons (to be sold and delivered to one person at one time), unless he or she hath licence from the court of general sessions of the peace, as aforesaid, on pain of incurring the several fines and penalties in the former part of this act laid upon those persons who sell the liquors aforesaid without licence.

Be it further enacted,

[SECT. 33.] That the farmer aforesaid, or his deputy, when the exporter shall make an entry with him as aforesaid, or shall make an entry with him and swear as aforesaid, shall give to said exporter a certificate of such entry, or a certificate of such entry and oath, on penalty of one hundred pounds for the use of the exporter. Farmer to give certificate, on penalty.

Provided, nevertheless,—

[SECT. 34.] That until[l] the duties aforesaid be let or farmed, the exporter aforesaid may make an entry as aforesaid with the impost officer or his deputy, or make such entry and swear as aforesaid; and of such entry, or of such entry and oath, the said impost officer or his deputy shall give the said exporter a certificate: and for the liquors mentioned in such certificate, when the same shall be exhibited, the farmer or his deputy shall not demand any duty. Proviso.

And be it further enacted,

[SECT. 35.] That every person applying to the farmer or his deputy, or to the impost officer or his deputy, for a permit, shall give bond, if required, for the use of the farmer, with two sufficient sureties, in a sum not exceeding two hundred pounds, nor less than twenty, at the discretion of the two next justices of the peace, conditioned for the payment of the excise that shall become due according to the account to be exhibited by such person taking such permit; and no person shall have such permit of the impost officer until[l] he hath given such bond. Persons applying for a permit, to give bond.

And whereas the importer of any of the liquors aforesaid, or the person to whom they shall be consigned, may intend the same for his or her own private consumption, in which case such importer or consignee is not held by any preceeding part of this act to pay the duty or excise aforesaid; wherefore, in order to lay said duty or excise in as equal manner as may be,— Preamble.

Be it enacted,

[SECT. 36.] That every person that shall bring or import into this province, either by land, or water, carriage, any of the liquors aforesaid for his own private consumption, shall, at the end of each half year, respectively, make out an account expressing the kind and the full quantity of the liquors aforesaid, imported or consigned as aforesaid; which account such importer or consignee shall render to the farmer or his deputy, on oath, if required, and shall pay to the said farmer or his deputy, on the liquor or liquors mentioned in said account, the duty or excise aforesaid, deducting ten per cent for leakage, or pay treble duty or excise on the quantity so imported or consigned, to and for the use of the farmer. Persons importing liquors for private consumption, &c., to render account thereof to the farmer.

[SECT. 37.] And if said farmer or his deputy shall have reason to suspect any person of bringing or importing into this province, either by land, or water, carriage, any of the liquors aforesaid, without having rend[e]red account and paid the duty or excise as aforesaid, the said farmer may apply to any justice of the peace within the county where the person suspected lives, for a warrant or citation; and such justice is hereby impowered and required to cite or apprehend such suspected person to appear before him within twenty-four hours on a complaint made against him or her by the farmer or his deputy touching the duty or excise aforesaid; which warrant or citation shall be served on or delivered to the suspected person himself or herself; and when the parties shall be before him the said justice shall examine into the cause of complaint; and if it shall appear, either by the confession of the party, or by the evidence of one credible witness, that such suspected person has, by him- or herself, or by any one on his or her behalf, imported, or has had any of the liquors aforesaid consigned to him or her, without having rendered an account thereof, or paid the duty or Farmer may apply to a justice for a warrant or citation, where he may suspect persons of giving a false account, &c.

excise as aforesaid, such suspected person shall then render a full account, on oath, of the kinds and quality of the liquors imported or consigned as aforesaid, and shall pay on such liquors treble duty or excise as aforesaid, and costs. And said justice is hereby impowered to make up judgment and award execution accordingly: *provided* the said treble duty exceed not four pounds; but if such duty exceed four pounds, then such justice shall bind the offender to answer his offence at the next court of general sessions of the peace for the county where the offence was committed, and such offender shall enter into recognizance, with two sufficient sureties, to answer for his offence, in the sum of fifty pounds; and any person or persons upon refusing to render such account and paying as aforesaid, shall forf[ie][*ei*]t fifty pounds for the use of the farmer, in lieu of such treble duty, to be recovered as is hereafter provided in this act.

[SECT. 38.] And if no confession be made by such suspected person, and no evidence produced as aforesaid, he or she shall then clear him- or herself from the complaint aforesaid, by taking an oath in the form following; viz[t].,—

Form of the oath.

You, A. B., do swear that you have not, directly or indirectly, either by yourself, or any person on your behalf, imported into this province any rum or spirits distilled, or wine, and that you have not had any of said liquors directly or indirectly consigned to you, but what you have paid the duty or excise upon, according to an act of said province, made in the thirtieth year of his majesty's reign, intitled "An Act for granting unto his majesty an excise upon spirits distilled, and wine, and upon limes, lem[m]ons and oranges." So help you God.

—which oath the said justice is hereby impowered and required to administer.

Penalty for refusing to take the oath.

[SECT. 39.] And if such suspected person shall refuse to take said oath, and shall neglect to appear upon the citation aforesaid, he or she shall pay the cost of citation, and shall forf[ie][*ei*]t, for the use of the farmer, the aforesaid sum of fifty pounds, and costs of prosecution; but if such suspected person shall take the said oath, the costs of citation or warrant shall be paid by the farmer or his deputy, respectively, who applied for such citation or warrant; who shall also pay to the person cited or apprehended, and taking said oath, the sum of twenty shillings.

And be it further enacted,

Farmer to grant a permit, on penalty.

[SECT. 40.] That the farmer aforesaid, or his deputy, shall be and hereby is obliged to grant a permit, under his hand, to every person applying for the same, on penalty of two hundred pounds, to and for the use of the person making application; which permit shall be in the form following; viz[t].,—

Form of the permit.

You, A. B. of C., in the county of D., are hereby permitted to sell rum and other distilled spirits, and wine, or any of said liquors, at , in C. aforesaid, until [1] the twenty-sixth day of March, one thousand seven hundred and fifty-eight, pursuant to an act of this province, made in the thirtieth year of his majesty's reign, intitled "An Act for granting unto his majesty an excise upon spirits distilled, and wine, and upon limes, lemmons and oranges." Dated at C., this day of , 175 .

A. B., *Farmer (or deputy farmer) of excise for the county aforesaid.*

And for such permit the said farmer or deputy shall be intitled to receive twopence, and no more; and the like sum for an entry made with him, and the like sum for a certificate given by him.

And be it further enacted,

Farmer to keep an office in each seaport town, &c.

[SECT. 41.] That the farmer aforesaid, either by himself or his deputy, shall keep an office in each seaport town within his county, where he or his deputy shall give his attendance on every Thursday, from nine of the clock in the morning to twelve at noon, to grant permits, receive entries, give certificates, &c[a].

Provided,—

[SECT. 42.] That in the town of Boston such an office shall be kept, and attendance given on every Monday and Thursday, within the hours aforesaid, of each of said days, respectively.

Provided, also,—

[SECT. 43.] That the said farmer or his deputy, on application made, shall at any other time grant permits, receive entries, and give certificates as afores[*ai*]d.

And whereas persons not belonging to this province may import the liquors aforesaid, and take permit to dispose of the same, and may go out of the province before the time comes about when persons selling said liquors are held to account with the farmer, and by that means may avoid paying the duty upon what has been so disposed of; for preventing whereof,— Preamble.

Be it enacted,

[SECT. 44.] That every person importing the liquors aforesaid, and applying to the farmer or his deputy for a permit to sell the same, shall give bond to said farmer, if required, in a sum not exceeding two hundred pounds, nor less than twenty pounds, at the discretion of the two next justices of the peace, with sufficient surety or sureties, that he will render to said farmer or his deputy an account, on oath, if required, of the kind and full quantity of the liquors aforesaid sold by him, or by any person or persons on his behalf, and that he will pay thereon the duty or excise aforesaid before he leaves the province; and if such person shall refuse to give such bond, the said farmer or his deputy shall not be obliged to grant him a permit, anything in this act to the contrary notwithstanding; and if such person shall sell any of the liquors aforesaid without permit, he shall be subject to all the penalties that other persons selling without permit are subject to; or if such person shall give bond as aforesaid, and shall leave the province before such bond be discharged, the farmer may bring his action on said bond against the surety or sureties, for the recovery of the sum in such bond mentioned, which shall be for the use of the farmer. Person importing liquors as afores[ai]d, to give bond.

And to the end that this government may know what monies shall be received by the farmers of each respective county, and his deputies, by virtue of this act,— Preamble.

Be it enacted,

[SECT. 45.] That to every person licenced by the sessions, and to every person having permit as aforesaid, the said farmer or his deputy, when said persons shall account with them, shall give two receipts, under their hand, for what each of them, respectively, have received, either as duty or as forf[ie][*ei*]ture, or in any other way; and the said receipts shall express the just and true sum received, and the consideration for which it was received; and one of the said receipts shall be lodged, within one month after the date thereof, by each person, respectively, to whom said receipt shall be given, with the clerk of the sessions for the county wherein such person lives, on penalty of forty shillings, one half to the poor of the town or district in which the person neglecting to lodge his receipt lives, and the other half to the person complaining or su[e]ing for the same, and of being rendered incapable of renewing his or her licence or permit for the future. And the clerk aforesaid shall transmit a true and fair copy of the receipts that shall be so lodged with him, to the secretary of this province, who shall lay the same before this court. Farmer to give two receipts, &c.

And be it further enacted,

Farmer to render an account, on oath, of sums received, to the province treasurer.

[SECT. 46.] That the farmer of each respective county shall render an account, on oath, to the province treasurer, when he shall come to discharge his bond given for the farm of the duties aforesaid, of the sums and securities he and his deputy, or either of them, have in any way received by virtue of this act; and the said account shall express the name of each person of [*whom*] they, or either of them, have received any sum or security, how much that sum or security is, and what it is for, and the time when the same were received; and it shall be part of the condition of the said farmer's said bond, that he will render such account as aforesaid; and if said farmer shall not have settled, when he comes to discharge said bond, with every person obliged by this act to account and settle with him, his said bond shall not be discharged [']till he has so settled, and rendered an account, on oath, of such settlement to the province treasurer as afores[*ai*]d. And if the account rendered by the farmer as aforesaid be a false one, he shall not only be liable to the pains and penalties to which a person convicted of perjury is liable, but also to pay a fine of fifty pounds, one half to the informer and the other half to his majesty for the use of the province; and in case the farmer shall neglect or refuse to render to the treasurer of the province, an account on oath as aforesaid, he shall forf[ie][*ei*]t and pay the sum of one thousand pounds to his majesty for the use of the province.

Provided, nevertheless,—

Proviso.

[SECT. 47.] That if said farmer shall, at the end of one month, and of ten months, respectively, from the time of payment expressed in said bond, render an account on oath as aforesaid, and shall swear that such account expresses the whole sum that he hath received, either in money or by securities, or by any other way whatsoever, then his said bond shall be discharged and be delivered up to him.

Be it further enacted,

Farmer limited for bringing his actions, &c.

[SECT. 48.] That if any account of excise shall remain unpaid or not settled by bond or note for the space of ten months after the expiration of this act, unless the action is depending, the said farmer or his deputy shall not have right to bring any action against the person whose said account shall remain so unpaid or unsettled, but shall forf[ie][*ei*]t what might otherwise have been due from such person.

Be it further enacted,

How fines, &c., arising by this act, are to be disposed of.

[SECT. 49.] That all fines, penalties and forf[ie][*ei*]tures, arising or accruing by any breach of this act, and not otherwise appropriated, shall be, one half to his majesty for the use of this province, and the other half for the use of the farmer; to be recovered by action, bill, plaint or information in any of his majesty's courts of record. [*Passed February* 4;* *published February* 5, 1757.

CHAPTER 22.

AN ACT FOR THE SUPPLY OF THE TREASURY WITH THE SUM OF THIRTY-FIVE THOUSAND POUNDS, AND FOR APPLYING THE SAME FOR THE PAYMENT OF THE FORCES RAISED FOR THE LATE EXPEDITION AGAINST CROWN POINT.

Preamble.

WHEREAS the provision, already made by this court at their session in June last for the above purpose, is insufficient to answer the ends proposed, and it being necessary that a further and an immediate supply should be made, that so the officers and private soldiers, who have served his majesty in the said expedition, may forthwith receive

* Signed February 26, according to the record.

their pay according to the several establishments, and that the committee of war may be enabled to discharge the debts they may have contracted for said expedition,—

Be it enacted by the Lieutenant-Governour, Council and House of Representatives,

[SECT. 1.] That the treasurer of the province be and he hereby is impowered and directed to borrow from such person or persons as shall be willing to lend the same, a sum not exceeding thirty-five thousand pounds in mill'd dollars, at six shillings each, or in other silver at six shillings and eightpence per ounce; and the sum so borrowed shall be applyed by the treasurer for the payment of all such draughts as shall from time to time be drawn on him by the governour and council, to be paid out of the appropriation for the forces in the late expedition, &c.; and for every sum so borrowed, the treasurer shall give a receipt and obligation in the form following:— Treasurer empowered to borrow £35,000.

Province of the Massachusetts Bay, the day of , 1757. Received of the sum of , for the use and service of the province of the Massachusetts Bay, and, in behalf of said province, I do hereby promise and oblige myself and successors in the office of treasurer to repay the said or order, the fifth day of June, 1759, the aforesaid sum of , in coined silver at six shillings and eightpence per ounce, or Spanish mill'd dollars, at six shillings each, with interest annually, at the rate of six per cent per annum. Form of treasurer's receipt.

Witness my hand, A. B., Treasurer.

—and that no receipt shall be given for a sum less than twenty pounds.

And as a fund to enable the treasurer effectually to discharge the receipts and obligations (with the interest that may be due thereon), by him given in pursuance of this act,— Fund.

Be it further enacted,

[SECT. 2.] That there be and hereby is granted unto his most excellent majesty a tax of thirty-nine thousand pounds, to be levied on polls, and estates real and personal within this province, according to such rules and in such proportion on the several towns and districts within the same as shall be agreed on and ordered by the general court of this province, at their session in May, seventeen hundred and fifty-eight, which sum shall be paid into the treasury on or before the thirty-first day of March next after. Tax of £39,000, in 1758.

And as a further fund to enable the treasurer to discharge the receipts and obligations (with the interest that may be due thereon), by him given in pursuance of this act,— Further fund.

Be it further enacted,

[SECT. 3.] That the duties of excise upon spirituous liquors, for the year seventeen hundred and fifty-seven, shall be applied for the payment and discharge of the principal and interest that shall become due on said notes, and to no other purpose whatsoever. Fund.

And be it further enacted,

[SECT. 4.] That in case the general court shall not at their session in May, and before the twentieth day of June, one thousand seven hundred and fifty-eight, agree and conclude upon an act apportioning the sum which by this act is engaged to be in said year apportioned, assessed and levied, that then, and in such case, each town and district within this province shall pay a tax, to be levied on the polls, and estates both real and personal within their limits, the same proportion of the said sum as the said towns and districts were taxed by the general court in the tax act then last preceeding: *saving* what relates to the pay of the representatives, which shall be assessed on the several towns they respectively represent; and the province treasurer is hereby fully Rule for apportioning the tax, in case no tax act shall be agreed on.

impowered and directed, some time in the month of June, one thousand seven hundred and fifty-eight, to issue and send forth his warrants, directed to the selectmen or assessor[r]s of each town and district within this province, requiring them to assess the polls, and estates both real and personal within their several towns and districts, and for their respective parts and proportions of the sum before directed and engaged to be assessed, to be paid into the treasury at the aforementioned time; and the assessors, as also persons assessed, shall observe, be governed by and subject to all such rules and directions as have been given in the then last preceeding tax act.

Provided, always,—

Proviso.

[SECT. 5.] That the remainder of the sum which shall be brought into the treasury by the duties of excise before mentioned, and the tax of thirty-nine thousand pounds ordered by this act to be assessed and levied, over and above what shall be sufficient to discharge the notes and obligations aforesaid, shall remain as a stock in the treasury, to be appl[y][*i*]ed as the general court of this province shall hereafter order, and to no other purpose whatsoever. [*Passed and published February* 9,* 1757.

CHAPTER 23.

AN ACT FOR THE MORE SPEEDY LEVYING EIGHTEEN HUNDRED MEN, INCLUSIVE OF OFFICERS, TO BE EMPLOYED IN HIS MAJESTY'S SERVICE.

Preamble.

WHEREAS, the general court of this province have determined that eighteen hundred men, including officers, should be raised by this government and employed in his majesty's service, for the defence of his majesty's colonies and for the annoyance of his majesty's enemies,—

Be it therefore enacted by the Lieutenant-Governour, Council and House of Representatives,

Eighteen hundred men to be raised, by enlistment or impress, from the several regiments of horse and foot.

[SECT. 1.] That eighteen hundred men, inclusive of officers, shall be raised by inlistment or impress from the several regiments of horse and foot, within this province, for a term not exceeding twelve months from the second day of February, instant, in such proportion from each regiment as the commander-in-chief of the province shall determine; said eighteen hundred men to be employed in his majesty's service under the command of his excellency, the right honourable the Earl of Loudoun, or of the general and commander-in-chief of his majesty's forces in North America for the time being.

And be it further enacted,

Time for paying the bounty limited, &c.

[SECT. 2.] That it shall and may be lawful for any person or persons that shall or may be employed for that purpose, to pay the bounty or encouragement promised by this government to any person or persons who shall [e][*i*]nlist into the service at any time on or before the twenty-first day of March next, and no longer; and no bounty shall be paid to any person until[l] he shall have been accepted by the muster-master.

And be it further enacted,

General muster to be on the 22d of March, 1757.

[SECT. 3.] That upon the twenty-second day of March next there shall be a general muster of all the companies of horse and foot within this province, at such place as the captain or commanding officer of each troop or company shall respectively determine; and every person

* Signed February 26, according to the record.

who by law is required to attend military musters shall, by one of the serjeants or corporals of the troop or company to which he shall belong, be duly warned, either in person or by a notification in writing to be left at the place of his usual abode, of the time and place of such muster; and every person belonging to such troop or company, who by law is obliged to attend military musters, shall punctually attend and continue at such muster at the time and place that shall be appointed therefor, and so, from time to time, as the commanding officer of such * company shall order, until[l] the whole number of men as aforesaid shall be raised, and until[l] such company shall be discharged from any further muster for said purpose, on pain of incurring the penalty of twenty pounds, unless it shall appear on the trial of the offence that his attendance was necessarily and unavoid[i][a]bly prevented; to be recovered by action of debt, with full costs of suit, to be brought by the clerk of the respective troops or companies to which such person not appearing as aforesaid belongs, who is hereby impowered and required to commence and prosecute such action to final judgment and execution; and if such delinquent person be a son under age, or a servant, the said action shall be brought against and penalty recovered of his parent or master; one third of the said penalty for the use of the clerk who shall sue for the same, the other two thirds for the purchasing arms for indigent persons who are not able to provide for themselves, living within the district of such company where such delinquent person dwells, as is hereafter provided.

Manner of notifying the muster of the several companies of militia, in order to raise volunteers, &c.

Fine for not attending.

How fines are to be disposed of.

And be it further enacted,

[SECT. 4.] That every person who shall be impressed or draughted by the commanding officer of such company or troop, or such person[s] as he shall appoint for the service aforesaid, on the said twenty-second day of March, or afterwards, shall be deemed duly entered in said service, and shall attend the said service, unless he shall, within twenty-four hours, pay to the commanding officer of the troop or company to which he belongs, or in which district he dwells, the sum of ten pounds, or within said time procure an able-bodied, effective person to serve in his stead, or that he shall have had a discharge from such impress or draught under the hand of the captain or chief officer of such company or troop, or regiment, or of the commander-in-chief of this province.

Fine for not serving when impressed, except.

Provided, nevertheless,—

[SECT. 5.] That if any person of the denomination called Quakers shall be impressed and commanded to attend the service aforesaid, and shall refuse to attend the same, or shall not within twenty-four hours pay the sum of ten pounds, it shall be in the power of the officer by whose command the said person was impressed, by a warrant directed to the clerk of the company where he dwells, to destrain the goods and chatt[el][*le*]s of such person sufficient for the payment of said sum and cost, to be sold at an outcry as soon as may be, and if such goods and chatt[el][*le*]s when sold shall be more than enough to pay the fine and cost; the overplus to be returned to such person in twenty-four hours, the said fine to be improved as is in this act hereafter provided.

Fine on Quakers for non-attendance, if impressed.

Manner of recovering the same.

And be it further enacted,

[SECT. 6.] That the monies paid by any person or persons impressed or draughted shall be improved, or so much thereof as shall be necessary, for the procuring one or more effective person or persons for said service, and the overplus, if any there be, shall be employed as there may and shall be occasion for the purchasing of arms for such persons living in the district of such company, as are unable to provide for themselves, and for no other purpose, and shall be paid by such officer accordingly into the hands of the town or district treasurer in which such company is; but if such company be not within a town or district,

How the money paid shall be improved.

* A blank in the parchment, but not in the print.

then such officer shall pay such monies into the hands of the colonel of the regiment to which such company belongs, taking his receipt for the same, to be by such colonel employed for the purchasing of arms for such persons as are unable to provide for themselves, as there may and shall be occasion.

And be it further enacted,

Every officer and clerk who receives any money by virtue of this act, to render an account, &c.

[SECT. 7.] That every officer and clerk of any company, who shall by virtue of this act receive any monies, shall within one month next after render an account thereof and pay in the same to the several persons respectively appointed to be the receivers thereof, upon pain of incurring the penalty of one hundred pounds to be recovered of such officer neglecting to render an account and pay the monies as aforesaid, by action of debt to be brought by the town or district treasurer, or colonel of such regiment respectively, who are hereby impowered and required to sue for the same: the said fine to be one third for the use of the prosecutor, the other two thirds for purchasing arms for such persons as are unable to provide for themselves, and shall remain as a stock in the hands of such receivers, to be employed for that purpose, and no other whatsoever.

And be it further enacted,

Power to colonels, &c., to issue warrants for impressing persons, in a certain case.

[SECT. 8.] That it shall and may be in the power of any colonel, captain or chief officer of any company to issue forth his or their warrants for the impressing persons belonging to their regiments or companies, who shall or may at any time remove from the district of the regiment or company to which he belongs into the district of any other regiment or company, until[l] the first day of April next, and such impress shall be as good and available in law as if the same had been made in the county, town or district whereto such person belonged.

And in order to prevent fraud in paying the bounty or encouragement promised by the general court, and also to prevent a deficiency in the number of men determined to be raised,—

Be it further enacted,

Colonel or chief officer of any regiment to transmit to the commander-in-chief a list of the names of enlisted or impressed men.

[SECT. 9.] That every colonel or chief officer of any regiment within this province shall, as soon as may be, after the fifteenth day of March next, and on or before the fifth day of April next, transmit to the commander-in-chief of the province a list of the names of the men belonging to such regiment who shall have enlisted as aforesaid, together with their places of abode, and also the number of men, their names and places of abode, who shall have been impressed or received in the room of any impressed men, agreable to the returns made to him by his several captains, in order to compleat the whole number that shall have been assigned as aforesaid. And every colonel or chief officer who shall neglect transmitting to the commander-in-chief the number of men, their names and place of abode, whether inlisted or impressed as aforesaid, shall forf[ie][*ei*]t and pay to his majesty the sum of twenty pounds for the use of this government, to be recovered by the province treasurer, who is hereby impowered and required to sue for the same in any of his majesty's courts of record within this province, and every captain or chief officer of any troop or company who shall not make return to his colonel or chief officer on or before the twenty-fifth day of March next, shall forf[ie][*ei*]t and pay the sum of twenty pounds to his majesty, to be recovered and applied in like manner with the penalty last mentioned; and if any officers are obliged to transmit their returns by an express, the charge thereof to be paid by the government. [*Passed February* 19;* *published February* 22,† 1757.

Penalty for their neglect.

Penalty for a captain or chief officer of any company not transmitting such a list to the colonel or chief officer.

* Signed February 26, according to the record.
† Published February 21, according to memorandum in the printed acts.

CHAPTER 24.

AN ACT FOR REVIVING AND CONTINUING SUNDRY LAWS THAT ARE EXPIRED AND NEAR EXPIRING.

WHEREAS, the several acts hereinafter mentioned, which are now expired or near expiring, have been found useful and beneficial; namely,— Preamble. Sundry laws, expired or near expiring, revived and continued.

One act made in the ninth and tenth year of his present majesty's reign, intitled "An Act to enable the overseers of the poor and selectmen to take care of idle and disorderly persons"; two acts made in the twenty-seventh year of said reign, one, intitled "An Act in addition to the several laws of this government made for the regulating of general fields," and the other act, intitled "An Act for preventing mischief by unruly dogs on the islands of Martha's Vineyard, Chebaquiduck, and also on the island of Nantucket." 1736-37, chap. 4. 1753-54, chap. 29. 1753-54, chap. 31.

Be it therefore enacted by the Lieutenant-Governour, Council and House of Representatives,

That such of the before mentioned acts as are expired, with all and every article, clause, matter and thing therein respectively contained, be and they hereby are revived; and such of said acts as are near expiring are continued, and shall be in force from the tenth day of February, instant, for the space of five years, and to the end of the next session of the general court, and no longer. [*Passed February* 8;* *published February* 28, 1757. Their continuation for five years, from the 10th of February, 1757.

CHAPTER 25.

AN ACT FOR PREVENTING THE EXPORTATION OF PROVISIONS AND WARLIKE STORES OUT OF THIS PROVINCE.

Be it enacted by the Lieutenant-Governour, Council and House of Representatives,

[SECT. 1.] That no warlike stores, or provisions of any kinds whatsoever, save such as shall be hereafter excepted, shall be exported or carried out of any port or harbour in this province, in any vessel whatsoever, during the continuance of this act: *saving* only such provisions and warlike stores as are necessary for the defence of each respective vessel outward bound, or for the victualling of the mariners on board the same, during their intended voyage, an account whereof, in writing, shall be given by the master of such vessel, on oath, to the impost officer, or his deputy; and when there is no impost officer or deputy, then to a justice of the peace of the county or town clerk of the town whence such vessel sails, on penalty of one thousand pounds, to be forfeited by the owner or freighter of every vessel of an hundred tons or under, and two thousand pounds to be forfeited by the owner or freighter of every vessel above one hundred tons. Exportation of warlike stores and provisions prohibited: saving. Penalty, &c., for breach of this act.

Provided, always,—

[SECT. 2.] And it shall be lawful for the master of any ship or [ort] other vessel to take on board and to transport fish in bulk, the owner, freighter or factor of such ship or other vessel, before she takes on board any part of her cargo, giving bond to the impost officer or his Fish, in bulk, may be taken on board, &c., owner or freighter giving bond for landing the same.

* Signed February 26, according to the record. † *Sic.*

deputy, with two sureties of known abilities, and residents in this province, in the sum of one thousand pounds for every vessel of a hundred ton[s] and under, and two thousand pounds for every one above one hundred tons (to be forfeited and recovered in manner as is hereafter expressed), that the fish to be laden on board is designed for, and shall be landed in, some part of Europe in amity with his majesty, and that he or they shall produce a certificate from the British consul or vice-consul, if any there be residing at the port of her deliveries, and if none, from some other proper authority, that said cargo has been there landed.

Provided, also.—

Bond to be given for provisions or warlike stores designed for any of His Majesty's colonies, &c.

[SECT. 3.] That it shall and may be lawful for the master of any ship or vessel, the owner or owners, factor or factors, freighter or freighters, first giving bond as aforesaid, to take on board and to transport any sort of provisions or warlike stores to any of his majesty's colonies, islands or settlements in North America, provided such bond be given before such warlike stores and provisions be put on board; the forfeiture to be sued for and recovered in any of his majesty's courts of record proper to try the same, and to be one moiety thereof to his majesty for the support of this governm[en]t, the other moiety to him or them who shall inform or sue for the same; and the master of such vessel transporting warlike stores or provisions, where no bond shall be given as aforesaid, shall, upon conviction, be liable to be sentenced to stand in the pillory and have one of his ears cut off; said bond[s] to be cancelled by a certificate of the officers of his maj[es]ty's customs in the respective ports where such provisions or warlike stores may be landed with consent of the commander-in-ch[ei][ie]f of this province for the time being; and without such certificate said bonds are to be in force and recovered in manner as afores[ai]d, danger[s] of the seas and captures by the enemy excepted.

Penalty for not giving bond as aforesaid.

And to prevent any fraud or collusion in the captures that may be made,—

Be it further enacted,

Same penalty, in case of collusive captures of cargoes.

[SECT. 4.] That if any masters or owners of any ships or vessels that may be clear'd out of this governm[en]t, laden with provisions for any of his majesty's other colonies or islands, shall be detected in causing any collusive captures of their cargo[e]s, they shall be subject to the same penalties as those are who shall export the same without first giving bond.

And be it further enacted,

Penalty for holding correspondence or communication with inhabitants of Louisbourg, &c.

[SECT. 5.] That it shall be unlawful for any of his majesty's subjects of this province, and they are hereby strictly forbidden to hold any correspondence or communication with any inhabitants of Louisbourg, or any other of the French settlements in North America, either by land or water; and if any person or persons belonging to this province shall presume to carry or send any vessel to Louisbourg, or any other French settlem[en]t in North America, during the continuance of this act, the ship, sloop or other vessel employed, with all her tackle, appurtenances and cargo, shall be forfeited, one half to his majesty for the use of this province, and the other half to him or them who shall inform and sue for the same in any of his majesty's courts within this province proper to try the same; and the master shall be liable to have one ear cut off, and be publickly whipp[e]'d thirty-nine lashes, and the owner or owners, freighter or freighters, and factor or factors of the owner or owners, or freighter, of such ship or other vessel, shall forfeit and pay, each, five hundred pounds, to be recovered and disposed of as above, and also be forever disabled to hold any place of honour or prof[f]it under this government.

[SECT. 6.] This act to continue and be in force until the first day of July, one thousand seven hundred and fifty-seven. [*Passed February 25; published February 28*, 1757. Limitation.

CHAPTER 26.

AN ACT IN FURTHER ADDITION TO AN ACT, INTITLED "AN ACT FOR REGULATING OF TOWNSHIPS, CHOICE OF TOWN OFFICERS, AND SETTING FORTH THEIR POWER."

WHEREAS in and by an act made in the fourth year of King William and Queen Mary, intitled "An Act for regulating of townships, choice of town officers, and setting forth their power," it is enacted, among other things, that every person duly chosen to serve in the office of constable, who shall refuse to take the oath to that office belonging, or pay the fine therein mentioned, shall be convened before the next sessions of the peace to be held for the county in which such town l[y][*i*]eth, to answer for his neglect and refusal; which, by experience, is found inconvenient, and, in some counties, impracticable,— Preamble. 1692-93, chap. 28, § 8. 1742-43, chap. 28.

Be it therefore enacted by the Lieutenant-Governour, Council and House of Representatives,

[SECT. 1.] That every person duly chosen to serve in the office of constable in any town or district in this province, who shall not, within six days after his being notified of his choice, take the oath to that office belonging, or pay his fine, such omission shall be judged a refusal. What shall be judged a refusal by a person chosen constable. And the court of general sessions of the peace for that county in which such town or district l[y][*i*]eth, are hereby directed and impowered, upon certificate under the hand of the town or district clerk, or two or more of the selectmen, that such person was legally chosen to the office of constable for such town or district, to convene before them such person at any of their sessions within the year for which he is chosen to serve, and to proceed with him in like manner as, by the act aforesaid, they are impowered. Court of sessions empowered to convene persons chosen to such office, at any of their sessions.

And whereas it is often found difficult personally to notify town, district and precinct officers to take the oaths to their respective offices belonging, within the time limit[*t*]ed by law,—

Be it enacted,

[SECT. 2.] That a notification under the hand of the town, district or precinct clerk, being left by the constable at the house or usual place of abode of any person duly chosen to serve in any office in any town, district or precinct, of whom an oath by law is required, shall be deemed a sufficient warning as if personally notified; What shall be deemed a sufficient warning of a person chosen constable, and the neglect of such person to take the oaths required by law within six days after leaving such notification, shall be deemed a refusal to serve in the office to which he is chosen, and be subject to the same penalties as if he had appeared and refused to serve. —as also a refusal, after such warning.

And be it further enacted,

[SECT. 3.] That in the absence of a justice of the peace, the clerk of any town, district or precinct in this province, be and he is hereby fully impowered to administer the oaths by law required to be administred, to any officer chosen in such town, district or precinct, of whom any oath is required by law; and the said clerk shall make record thereof in the town, district or precinct books. And when and so often as any town, district or precinct officers are sworn before a justice of By whom town, &c., officers may be sworn.

the peace, such justice shall transmit to the town, district or precinct clerk, respectively, a certificate of the officers by him sworn, which shall be registred in the town, district or precinct books by their respective clerks. [*Passed January* 29;* *published February* 28, 1757.

CHAPTER 27.

AN ACT FOR THE BETTER REGULATING THE FISHERY.

Preamble.

WHEREAS it has been found by long experience that great losses have arisen to the publick, and to many private persons, from fishing vessel[l]s departing too early on their voyages to the banks,—

Be it therefore enacted by the Lieutenant-Governo[u]r, Council and House of Representatives,

No fishing vessels to go on a fishing voyage for the banks of Newfoundland, &c., before the 25th of March, 1757,

[SECT. 1.] That no fishing vessel[l][*s*] shall depart out of any part of this province on a fishing voyage to the banks of Newfoundland, or any other of the banks, before the twenty-fifth day of March next.

—on penalty of £100.

[SECT. 2.] And the owner or owners of any vessel[l] that may depart contrary to the true intent and meaning of this act, shall forf[ie][*ei*]t and pay to his majesty, for the use of this government, the sum of one hundred pounds: *saving*, only such vessel[l]s and boats that are usually employed in catching fish for the support of the inhabitants and that shall not be absent more than four days at a time, extraordinary casualties excepted.

How the penalty shall be recovered.

[SECT. 3.] The penalty aforesaid to be sued for and recovered in any of the courts of record in this province by the treasurer thereof. [*Passed February* 14;* *published February* 28, 1757.

CHAPTER 28.

AN ACT FOR FURTHER REGULATING THE COURSE OF JUDICIAL PROCEEDINGS.

Preamble. 1753-54, chap. 42.

WHEREAS trials of civil actions, upon appeals and reviews, have been unnecessarily multiplied, to the great charge and gr[ei][*ie*]vance of many of his majesty's subjects within this province,—

Be it therefore enacted by the Lieutenant-Govern[ou]r, Council and House of Representatives,

[SECT. 1.] That no writ[t] of review shall hereafter be brought to any inferiour court of common pleas; and that whensoever in any action that now is depending, or shall hereafter be brought in any of the courts within this province, the party, whether plaintiff or defendant, which shall have recovered judgment on the first trial, shall likewise recover on a second trial, no review shall be allowed in such action.

Limitation.

[SECT. 2.] This act to continue and be in force for five years from the twenty-eighth day of January, one thousand seven hundred and fifty-seven, and no longer. [*Passed January* 27;* *published February* 28, 1757.

* Signed February 26, according to the record.

CHAPTER 29.

AN ACT FOR THE SUPPLY OF THE TREASURY WITH THE SUM OF THREE THOUSAND POUNDS.

WHEREAS this province, in conjunction with the governments of Connecticut, Rhode Island and New Hampshire, have agreed and concluded to levy four thousand men out of their several governments, under the command of his excellency the Earl of Loudoun, for his majesty's service in North America; *and whereas* the quota of men in this province to be levied is eighteen hundred, including officers; and as this government have voted a bounty for the encouragement of able-bodied men to inlist in said service,— Preamble.

Be it enacted by the Lieutenant-Governo[u]r, Council and House of Representatives,

[SECT. 1.] That the treasurer of the province be and he hereby is impowered and directed to borrow, of such persons as shall appear willing to lend, a sum not exceeding two thousand pounds; and for every sum so borrowed, he shall give his receipt or obligation in the form following:— Treasurer empowered to borrow £2,000.

Province of the Massachusetts Bay, the day of , 1757. Received of the sum of , for the use and service of the province of the Massachusetts Bay, and in behalf of said province, I do hereby promise and oblige myself and successors in the office of treasurer to repay the said or order, the fifteenth day of June, 1758, the aforesaid sum of , in coined silver at six shillings and eightpence per ounce, or mill'd dollars, at six shillings each, with interest at the rate of six per cent per annum until paid. Form of treasurer's receipt.

which money[s] shall be applied by the treasurer for the service aforesaid, to be drawn out of the treasury by warrant from the governo[u]r and council.

Provided, nevertheless,—

[SECT. 2.] That no draught shall be made on the treasury in favour of any of the colonels, majors, captains or any other persons, who shall be impowered to inlist men for the aforesaid service, until they have ascertained to the governo[u]r and council the number of men they have actually inlisted for the service aforesaid, and to whom they have either advanced or engaged to pay the bounty agreeable to the vote of this court. Proviso.

And as a fund to enable the treasurer to redeem the notes or obligations, with the interest that may be due thereon, by him given in pursuance of this act,—

Be it enacted,

[SECT. 3.] That the duties of impost for the year seventeen hundred and fifty-seven be and hereby is appropriated, and shall be applied for that purpose, and no other. Duties of impost appropriated.

And as a further fund and security,—

Be it enacted,

[SECT. 4.] That one thousand pounds, part of the surplusage that is or will shortly be in the treasury, be applied to answer such dra[f][*ugh*]ts as shall be made in pursuance of this act. [*Passed February* 23; * *published February* 28, 1757. Surplusage to be applied, &c.

* Signed February 26, according to the record.

CHAPTER 30.

AN ACT FOR ESTABLISHING AND REGULATING THE FEES OF THE SEVERAL OFFICERS, WITHIN THIS PROVINCE, HEREAFTER MENTIONED.

Be it enacted by the Lieutenant-Governour, Council and House of Representatives in General Court assembled,

Fees established. 1756-57, chap. 6. [SECT. 1.] That from and after the publication of this act, the establishment of the fees belonging to the several officers hereafter mentioned in this province, be as followeth; viz.,—

JUSTICES' FEES.

Justice's fees. For granting a writ and summons, or original summons, one shilling.
Subpœna, for each witness, one penny halfpenny.
Entring an action or filing a complaint in civil causes, two shillings.
Writ of execution, sixteen pence.
Filing papers, each, one penny halfpenny.
Taxing a bill of cost, threepence.
Entring up judgment in civil or criminal cases, ninepence.
Copy of every evidence, original papers or records, eightpence per page for each page of twenty-eight lines, eight words in a line: if less than a page, fourpence.
Each recognizance or bond of appeal, one shilling.
Taking affidavits out of their own courts in order for the trial for any cause, one shilling, and eighteen pence for his travel every ten miles, and so in proportion;—
in other cases, together with certificates, examining and entring, sixpence;—
in perpetuam, to each justice, one shilling.
Acknowledging an instrument with one or more seals, provided it be done at one and the same time, one shilling.
A warrant, one shilling.
Entring a complaint, making up judgment therein, the same as in civil causes.
For granting a warrant, swearing apprizers relating to strays, and entring the same, one shilling and sixpence.

CORONER'S FEES.

Coroner's fees. For serving a writ, summons or execution, and travelling fees, the same as by this act is hereafter allowed to sheriffs.
Bail bond, one shilling.
Every trial where the sheriff is concerned, eightpence.
Taking an inquisition, to be paid out of the deceased's estate, five shillings; if more than one at the same time, seven shillings and sixpence in the whole; if no estate, then, to be paid out of the county treasury, five shillings.
For travelling and expences for taking a inquisition, each day, four shillings.
The foreman of the jury, three shillings; and ten miles accounted a day's travel, one shilling per day;—
every other juror, two shillings and sixpence, and travel the same as the foreman.
The constable, for his expences, summoning the jury and attendance, four shillings per day.

JUDGE OF PROBATE'S AND REGISTER'S FEES.

Judge of probate's and register's fees.

For granting administration or guardianship,—
to the judge, three shillings.
To the register, for writing letter and bond of administration and guardianship, two shillings and sixpence.
For granting guardianship of divers minors to the same person and at the same time: to the judge, for each minor, one shilling and sixpence; to the register, for each letter of guardianship and bond, as before.
Proving a will or codicil; three shillings and sixpence to the judge, and two shillings and sixpence to the register.
Recording a will, letter of administration or guardianship, inventory or account, of one page, and filing the same, one shilling and threepence;—
for every page more, of twenty-eight lines, of eight words in a line, eightpence.
For copy of a will and inventory, for each page, eightpence.
Allowing accompts, three shillings to the judge.
Decree for settling of intestate estates: to the judge, three shillings;—
for examining such accompts, one shilling.
A citation, ninepence.
A *quietus:* to the judge, one shilling, to the register, one shilling.
Warrant or commission for apprizing or dividing estates; one shilling and sixpence to the judge; to the register, one shilling.
Making out commission to receive and examine the claims of creditors to insolvent estates; to the judge, one shilling, to the register, one shilling: for recording, eightpence each page.
Registering the commissioner's report, each page, eightpence.
Making out and entring an order upon the administrators for the distribution of the estate; to the judge, one shilling and sixpence, to the register, one shilling.
For proportioning such estate among the creditors, agreeable to the commissioner's return, when the estate exceeds not fifty pounds, three shillings; and, above that sum, four shillings.
For recording the same, eightpence per page.

And be it further enacted,

[SECT. 2.] That whensoever any fees shall be paid in the probate office for the probate of a will and letters testamentary, or for granting letters of administration or letters of guardianship or for any matter or thing from time to time arising in consequence of such letters testamentary or letters of administration or letters of guardianship, and until the estate upon which they are respectively granted shall be fully settled, a particular account of such fees before payment shall by the register or judge be set down in writing and given to the person paying the same. And any such fees, received without being thus ascertained in writing, shall be deemed illegal fees and the person receiving the same shall forfeit and suffer accordingly.

IN THE SUPERIOUR COURT.

JUSTICE'S FEES.

Justices of the superior court, fees.

Entring an action, six shillings and eightpence.
Taking special bail, one shilling and sixpence.
Allowing a writ of error, two shillings.
Allowing a *habeas corpus*, sixteen pence.
Taxing a bill of cost, eightpence.

Attorney's fee, to be allowed in the bill of cost taxed, where the case is tryed by a jury, twelve shillings; where it is otherwise, six shillings.
Granting liberty for the sale or partition of real estates, one shilling.
On receiving each petition, one shilling.
Allowance to the party for whom costs shall be taxed, and to witness in civil and criminal causes, one shilling and sixpence per day, ten miles' travel to be accounted a day; and the same allowance to be made to parties, as to witnesses at the inferiour courts, courts of sessions and before a justice of the peace.
Granting a writ of protection, one shilling.

CLERK'S FEES.

Clerk's fees.

A writ of review, three shillings.
A writ of *scire facias*, two shillings.
A writ of execution, one shilling and sixpence.
A writ of *facias habere possessionem*, two shillings and sixpence.
A writ of *habeas corpus*, two shillings.
Copies of all records, each page, of twenty-eight lines, eight words in a line, ninepence; less than a page, sixpence.
Entring each action for trial, four shillings.
Entring each complaint, two shillings.
Each petition entered and read, one shilling.
Order on each petition granted, one shilling.
Receiving and recording a verdict, one shilling.
Entring a rule of court, ninepence.
Confessing judgment or default, one shilling.
Every action withdrawn or nonsuit, one shilling.
Entring an appearance, sixpence.
Acknowledging satisfaction of a judgment, on record, eightpence.
Examining each bill of cost, eightpence.
Continuing each cause, and eutring the same next term, one shilling.
Filing each paper in each cause, one penny halfpenny.
Proving a deed in court, and certifying the same, one shilling.
Entring up judgment and recording the same at large, two shillings.
For each *venire*, to be paid out of the county treasuries, respectively, on the justice's certificates, threepence.
Every writ and seal other than before mentioned, two shillings.
Every subpœna, one penny halfpenny.
Each recognizance, one shilling.
A writ of protection, one shilling.

IN THE INFERIOUR COURT OF COMMON PLEAS.

JUSTICE'S FEES.

Justices of the inferior court, fees.

Entry of every action, five shillings and fourpence.
Taxing a bill of cost, sixpence.
Taking a recognizance on appeals, one shilling.
Proving a deed, one shilling.
Attorney's fee, to be allowed in the bill of cost taxed, six shillings.
Granting a writ of protection, one shilling.

IN THE COURT OF GENERAL SESSIONS OF THE PEACE.

For each day's attendance at the sessions, to be paid out of the fines, two shillings and eightpence.

For granting every licence to retailers and innholders, and taking their recognizance, six shillings in the whole, one third thereof to the clerk.

Court of general sessions of the peace.

Each recognizance in criminal causes, one shilling.

CLERK'S FEES.

Clerk's fees.

Every action entered, one shilling and fourpence.
Every writ and seal, sixpence.
Every appearance, fourpence.
Entring and recording a verdict, eightpence.
Recording a judgment, one shilling.
Copies of all records, each page, of twenty-eight lines, eight words in a line, eightpence.
Every action withdrawn or nonsuit, eightpence.
Every execution, one shilling and fourpence.
Confessing judgment or default, eightpence.
Acknowledging satisfaction of a judgment on record, eightpence.
A writ of *habeas corpus*, two shillings.
Continuing each cause, and entering at the next term, eightpence.
Each recognizance, one shilling.
Examining each bill of cost, sixpence.
Each *venire*, to be paid out of the county treasuries, respectively, by order of court, threepence.
Writ of *facias habere possessionem*, two shillings.
Filing each paper, one penny.
A writ of protection, one shilling.

GOVERNOUR AND SECRETARY'S FEES.

Governor and secretary's fees.

For registers: to the governour, three shillings; to the secretary, two shillings.
For certificates under the province seal: to the governour, three shillings; to the secretary, two shillings.
For warrants of apprizements, survey, &c.: to the governour, three shillings; to the secretary, three shillings.
To the governour, for a pass to the castle, for each vessel, one shilling: wood-sloops and other coasting vessels, for which passes have not been usually required, excepted.
For a certificate of naval stores, in the whole, three shillings.

SECRETARY'S FEES.

Secretary's fees.

For engrossing the acts or laws of the general assembly, six shillings each, to be paid out of the publick revenue.
Every commission for the justices of each county, and commission of oyer and terminer, six shillings and eightpence, to be paid out of the publick revenue.
Special warrant or mittimus by order of the governour and council, each, two shillings and sixpence.
Every commission under the great seal, for places of profit, six shillings and eightpence, to be paid by the person commissionated.
Every bond, three shillings.
Every order of council to the benefit of particular persons, two shillings.
Every writ for electing of assemblymen, directed to the sheriff or marshal under the province seal, five shillings, to be paid out of the publick revenue.
For transcribing the acts or laws passed by the general assembly into a book, eightpence per page,—each page to contain twenty-eight

lines, eight words in a line, and so proportionably,—to be paid out of the publick revenue.

Every commission for military officers, to be paid out of the publick treasury, two shillings.

CLERK-OF-THE-SESSIONS' FEES.

Clerk-of-the-sessions' fees.

Entring a complaint or indictment, one shilling and fourpence.

Discharging a recognizance, eightpence.

Each warrant for criminals, one shilling.

Every summons or subpœna, twopence.

Every recognizance for the peace or good behaviour, one shilling.

For every other recognizance, one shilling.

Entring up judgment, or entring satisfaction of judgment, on record.*

Warrant for county tax, one shilling.

For minuting the receipt of each petition, and order thereon, and recording, eightpence per page, as before.

Examining and casting the grand jury accounts, yearly, and order thereon, to be paid by the county treasurer by order of the court of sessions, one shilling and sixpence.

For copies of all records or original papers, eightpence per page, as before.

For filing each paper, one penny.

For transmitting to the selectmen of every town in the county a list of the names of the persons in such town licenced the year before, threepence, to be paid by each person licenced, and no more.

SHERIFF'S OR CONSTABLE'S FEES.

Sheriff's or constable's fees.

For serving an original summons, one shilling.

Every capeas or attachment in civil, or warrants in criminal, cases for trial, sixteen pence; and for travel out, one penny halfpenny per mile; and for the return of the writ (the travel to be inserted on the back of the writ or original summons), one penny halfpenny per mile.

Levying executions in personal actions, for the first twenty pounds or under, ninepence per pound; above that, not exceeding forty pounds, fourpence per pound; above that, not exceeding one hundred pounds, twopence per pound; for whatsoever it exceeds one hundred pounds, one penny per pound.

For travel out, one penny halfpenny per mile, and for the return of the execution, one penny halfpenny per mile; all travel in serving writs and executions, to be accounted from the officer's house who does the service, to the place of service, and from thence to the court-house or place of trial.

For giving livery and seisin of real estates, six shillings, travel as before: if of different parcels of land, four shillings each.

For serving an execution upon a judgment of court for partition of real estates, to the sheriff, five shillings per day; and for travel and expences, threepence per mile out from the place of his abode: and to each juror, two shillings per day; and for travel and expences, threepence per mile.

Every trial, eightpence.

Every default, fourpence.

A bail bond, eightpence.

For making out every precept for the choice of representatives, sending the same to the several towns, and returning it to the secretary's office, sixteen pence; to be paid out of the county treasuries, respectively.

To the officer attending the grand jury, each day, two shillings.

* *Sic.*

To the officer attending the petit jury, one shilling every cause.
For dispersing *venires* from the clerk of the superiour court, and the province treasurer's warrants, fourpence each.
For dispersing proclamations, sixpence each.
For the encouragement unto the sheriff to take and use all possible care and diligence for the safe keeping of the prisoners that shall be committed to his custody, he shall have such salary allowed him for the same as the justices of the court of general sessions of the peace within the same county shall think fit and order; not exceeding ten pounds per annum for the county of Suffolk, and not exceeding five pounds per annum apiece for the counties of Essex and Middlesex, and not exceeding three pounds per annum apiece in each of the other counties within the province: to be paid out of the treasury of such county.

CRYER'S FEES.

Crier's fees.

Calling the jury, fourpence.
A default or nonsuit, eightpence.
A judgment affirmed on a complaint, eightpence.
A verdict, eightpence.

TO THE CAPTAIN OF CASTLE WILLIAM.

Captain-of-the-castle's fees.

For every pass from the governour for outward-bound vessels (coasters, fishing and wood-vessels excepted), one shilling.

GOALER'S FEES.

Jailer's fees.

For turning the key on each prisoner committed, three shillings; viz., one shilling and sixpence in, and one shilling and sixpence out.
For dieting each person, for a week, three shillings.

MESSENGER-OF-THE-HOUSE-OF-REPRESENTATIVES' FEES.

Messenger-of-the-house-of-representatives' fees.

For serving every warrant from the house of representatives, which they may grant for arresting, imprisoning, or taking into custody any person, one shilling and sixpence.
For travel, each mile out, twopence per mile.
For keeping and providing food for such person, each day, one shilling and sixpence.
For his discharge or dismission, one shilling and sixpence.

GRAND JURORS' FEES.

Grand jurors' fees.

Foreman, per day, two shillings and sixpence.
Each other juror, two shillings.

PETIT JURORS' FEES.

Petit jurors' fees.

To the foreman, in every cause at the superiour and inferiour courts, or sessions, two shillings and sixpence.
To every other juror, one shilling and sixpence.

FOR MARRIAGES.

Fees for Marriages.

For each marriage, to the minister or justice officiating, four shillings.
For recording it: to the town clerk, to be paid by the minister or justice, fourpence; and to the clerk of the sessions, to be paid by the town clerk, twopence.
To the town clerk, for every publishment of the banns of matrimony, and entring thereof, one shilling.
Every certificate of such publishment, sixpence.
Recording births and deaths, each, twopence.
For a certificate of the birth or death of any person, threepence.

COUNTY REGISTER'S FEES.

County register's fees.

For entring or recording or copying any deed, conveyance or mortgage, for the first page, ninepence; and eightpence per page for so many pages more as it shall contain, accounting after the rate of twenty-eight lines, of eight words in a line, to each page; and proportionably for so much more as shall be under a page; and threepence for his attestation on the original, of the time, book and folio where it is recorded: the fees to be paid at the offering the instrument;—

and for a discharge of a mortgage, eightpence.

And be it further enacted,

Penalty for taking excessive fees.

[SECT. 3.] That if any person or persons shall demand or take any greater fee or fees, for any of the services aforesaid, than is by this law provided, he or they shall forfeit and pay to the person or persons injured, the sum of ten pounds for every offence, to be recovered in any court proper to hear and determine the same.

Limitation.

[SECT. 4.] This act to continue and be in force for the space of two years from the publication thereof, and from thence to the end of the next session of the general court, and no longer. [*Passed February* 25;* *published February* 28, 1757.

CHAPTER 31.

AN ACT TO PREVENT DAMAGE BEING DONE UNTO BILLINGSGATE BAY IN THE TOWN OF EASTHAM, BY CATTLE AND HORSE-KIND AND SHEEP FEEDING ON THE BEACH AND ISLANDS ADJOINING THERETO.

Preamble. 1742-43, chap. 11. 1746-47, chap. 22. 1749-50, chap. 25.

WHEREAS many persons frequently drive numbers of neat cattle, horse-kind and sheep to feed upon the beach and islands adjoining to Billingsgate Bay, whereby the ground is much broken and damnified, and the sand blown into the bay, to the great damage not only of private persons in their employment of getting oysters, but also to the publick, by filling up said bay, which is often used by seamen in stress of weather,—

Be it therefore enacted by the Lieutenant-Governo[u]r, Council and House of Representatives,

Horses, cattle, and sheep not to feed on Billingsgate beach, &c.

Penalty.

[SECT. 1.] That from and after the publication of this act, no person or persons shall presume to turn or drive any neat cattle, or horse-kind, or sheep, to or upon the islands or beach lying westerly of Billingsgate Bay and south of Griff[e][*i*]n's Island (so called) in the town of Eastham, to feed thereon, upon the penalty of ten shillings a head for all neat cattle, and for every horse or mare, and one shilling for each sheep that shall be turned or found feeding on said islands and beach which l[y][*i*]e south of Griff[e][*i*]n Island; which penalty shall be recovered by the selectmen or treasurer of the said town of Eastham, or any other person that shall inform and sue for the same, the one half of the said forfeiture to him or them who shall inform and sue for the same, and the other half to be to and for the use of the poor of said town.

And be it further enacted,

Cattle to be impounded if found feeding on the beach, &c.

[SECT. 2.] That if any neat cattle, or horse-kind, or sheep, shall at any time hereafter be found feeding on the said islands and beach south of Griff[e][*i*]n's Island, that it shall and may be lawful[l] for any

* Signed February 26, according to the record.

person to impound the same, immediately giving notice to the owners, if known, otherwise to give public[k] notice thereof in the said town of Eastham and the two next adjoining towns; and the impounder shall rel[ei][*ie*]ve the creatures with suitable meat and water while impounded; and if the owner thereof appear, he shall pay the sum of three shillings to the impounders for each neat beast and horse-kind, and fourpence for each sheep, and the reasonable cost of rel[ei][*ie*]ving them, besides the pound-keeper's fees. And if no owner appear within the space of six days to redeem the said cattle or horse-kind or sheep so impounded, and to pay the damages and costs occasioned by impounding the same, then and in every such case, the person or persons impounding such cattle, or horse-kind, or sheep, shall cause the same to be sold at publick vendue, to pay the cost and charges arising about the same (public[k] notice of the time and place of such sale to be given in the said town of Eastham and in the town of Truro forty-eight hours beforehand); and the overplus, if any there be, arising by such sale, to be returned to the owner of such cattle, or horse-kind, or sheep at any time within twelve months next after, upon his demanding the same; but if no owner appear within the said twelve months, then the said overplus shall be, one half to the party impounding, and the other half to the use of the poor of the said town of Eastham.

Rules referring to such impounded cattle.

And be it further enacted,

[SECT. 3.] That the said town of Eastham, at their meeting in March, annually, for the choice of town officers, be authorized and impowered to chuse one or more meet person or persons, whose duty it shall be to see that this act be observed, and prosecute the breakers thereof, who shall be sworn to the faithful discharge of their office; and in case any person [*or persons*] so chosen shall refuse to be sworn, he shall forfeit and pay three pounds to the poor of the said town of Eastham, and the said town of Eastham, at a town meeting warned for that purpose, may at any time before March next chuse such officers, who shall continue until their annual meeting in March next.

Officers to be chosen to put this act in execution.

And be it further enacted,

[SECT. 4.] That for and during the term of ten years, accounting from the first day of April, one thousand seven hundred and fifty-seven, it shall and may be lawful for Samuel Smith, Esq[r]., his heirs, executors and administrators, to feed, on the beach and islands aforesaid, twelve neat cattle, from the first day of April to the first day of June, and eighteen neat cattle, from [*the*] said first of June to the twentieth day of November, annually; and one cow, for the use of the family on said island, for and during the whole of the term before mentioned. And that the said Samuel Smith, be impowered to build, at his own expence, a pound on said island, for impounding such creatures as shall be found feeding on said island other than by this act is allowed; and that the pound-keeper or pound-keepers, who shall be chosen pursuant to this act, have the care and charge of the pound by this act allowed to be erected on said island as aforesaid; anything in this act to the contrary notwithstanding.

Samuel Smith, Esq., allowed to feed a number of cattle thereon.

Provided,—

[SECT. 5.] That the said Samuel Smith, his heirs, executors or administrators, shall and do make and maintain a good and sufficient fence across the north part of the said island, and into the sea; and keep a house and family on said island during the term aforesaid, and also make good all reasonable damage that shall accrue to the owners of the meadow lying between said island and Beach Hill.

Proviso.

And be it further enacted,

[SECT. 6.] That the said town of Eastham, at their meeting in March, annually, shall and may have liberty to chuse one or more per-

Town of Eastham empowered, &c.

son or persons to inspect said islands, and to add to or diminish said number of cattle feeding thereon, as they shall from time to time find necessary and most convenient for the benefit of said islands. [*Passed February* 11 ;* *published February* 28, 1757.

CHAPTER 32.

AN ACT FOR PREVENTING THE UNNECESSARY DESTRUCTION OF ALEWIVES IN THE TOWN OF SANDWICH.

Preamble. 1745-46, chap. 14. 1748-49, chap. 19.

WHEREAS the laws already provided against the destruction of the fish called alewives, do not in divers circumstances reach the case of Herring River, in the town of Sandwich, so that nevertheless great waste is made of them by ill-minded persons, to the great damage of the publick ; to prevent which,—

Be it enacted by the Lieutenant-Governour, Council and House of Representatives,

Regulation of the use of nets for taking alewives.

[SECT. 1.] That from and after the first day of April next, no person or persons whosoever shall, on any pretence, presume to stretch, set or draw any seine or drag-net, or set up any wares or other fishing-engines in any part of the river known by the name of Herring River, in the town of Sandwich, or ponds adjacent thereto, where the fish usually spawn, or use any other instrument for the catching alewives but dip-nets or scoop-nets, without first obtaining special licen[s][c]e therefor by a vote of the inhabitants of said Sandwich legally assembled at their anniversary meeting in March, nor in any manner whatever, at any time or place in said river or pond, but such as shall be determined and appointed at such meeting, on penalty of five pounds for each offence ; to be paid by every person concerned in taking said fish in either of the ways forbidden by this act, or in any other place than such as shall be assigned by the said town as aforesaid, and be recovered by action, bill, plaint or information in any court proper to try the same.

And be it further enacted,

Fish otherwise taken, to be forfeited.

[SECT. 2.] That all fish taken in said river or ponds, contrary to the true intent of this act, shall be liable to be forfeited to the overseers appointed by said town.

And be it further enacted,

Account to be taken of fish transported.

[SECT. 3.] That all coasters or boatmen shall give in upon oath, if required, to the town clerk of said Sandwich, what quantity of the said alewives they have taken on board, and who were the owners of said fish.

Disposal of fines.

[SECT. 4.] All fines and forfeitures arising by this act to be disposed of, one half for the benefit of the poor of said town, the other to him or them who shall inform and sue for the same.

Preamble.

And whereas a considerable part of the banks of said river is covered with thick woods, and thereby so obscured as that persons may frequently offend against this act without being discovered, and thereby the good design of it be defeated, unless special provision be made therefor,—

Be it therefore enacted,

Manner of prosecution. 1726-27, chap. 3.

[SECT. 5.] That the manner, rules and methods of conviction of offenders against this act be the same as are directed and provided in and by an act intitled "An Act in addition to and for rend[e]ring

* Signed February 26, according to the record.

more effectual an act made in the tenth year of the reign of King William the Third, intitled 'An Act for preventing of trespasses,'" made in the twelfth year of the reign of his late majesty, King George the First.

[SECT. 6.] This act to be in force for the space of three years from the first day of April next, and no longer. [*Passed February* 21; * *published February* 28, 1757. Limitation.

* Signed February 26, according to the record.

ACTS

PASSED AT THE SESSION BEGUN AND HELD AT BOSTON, ON THE THIRTIETH DAY OF MARCH, A. D. 1757.

CHAPTER 33.

AN ACT FOR REGULATING THE HOSPITAL ON RAINSFORD'S ISLAND, AND FURTHER PROVIDING IN CASE OF SICKNESS.

Preamble.

WHEREAS a good and convenient house hath been provided, at the charge of the province, on the island called Rainsford's Island, for the reception of such persons as shall be visited with any contagious sickness,—

Be it therefore enacted by the Council and House of Represent[ati]ves,

Inquiry to be made at the castle respecting infectious vessels. 1749-50, chap. 6.

[SECT. 1.] That [i][*e*]nquiry shall be made by the officer or other person on duty at Castle William, of every vessel coming from sea and passing by said castle, whether they are all well on board, and also whether any infectious sickness has been on board since they left the port from whence they last came; and if any vessel inquired of as aforesaid shall have any sickness on board, and upon further inquiry the same shall appear to be the plague, small-pox or any other malignant, infectious distemper, in such case order shall be given to the master or commander of such vessel forthwith to go down with his vessel, and anchor as near the hospital at Rainsford's Island as conveniently may be; or if any vessel [i][*e*]nquired of as afores[*ai*]d shall have had any infectious sickness on board since they left the port from whence they last came, in such case orders shall be given to the master or commander of such vessel immediately to anchor, and to remain at anchor until[l] a certificate shall be obtained from the major part of the selectmen of the town of Boston, that they are of opinion such vessel may come up to town without danger to the inhabitants, or until[l] the said master shall receive orders from the said selectmen to go with his vessel and anchor near the hospital aforesaid; and in case any master or commander shall, by himself or people on board, make false answer when hail'd by the castle, or, after orders given as aforesaid, shall neglect or refuse to anchor near the castle as afores[*ai*]d, or come on shore, or suffer any passengers or persons belonging to the vessel to come on shore, or any goods to be taken out before the vessel shall have anchor'd, or without liberty from the selectmen as aforesaid, or in case any master or commander, order'd to anchor near the hospital afores[*ai*]d, shall neglect or refuse so to do, in every such case every master or commander so offending shall forfeit and pay the sum of one hundred pounds, or suffer six months' imprisonment.

(Margin notes: Selectmen to certify the safety of vessels coming into the harbor. — Penalty for master's offence.)

And be it further enacted,

Leave to be had of the selectmen for landing passengers or goods.

[SECT. 2.] That upon application made to the selectmen of the town of Boston by any master or commander of any vessel at anchor near the hospital as afores[*ai*]d, the said selectmen are hereby impowered to permit such passengers, goods or lading, as they shall judge free from infection, to come on shore, or to be taken out and disposed of as the owners shall see meet; and such passengers and goods as shall not be permitted as afores[*ai*]d, shall remain on board, or be landed on said island.

Forfeiture for contempt by the master and others.

[SECT. 3.] Or if any master or immediate commander of any such vessel, for the time being, shall come on shoar, or suffer any of his people or passengers to come on shoar, or any boats to come on board, or suffer any goods to be taken out of his vessel, unless permitted as afores[*ai*]d, or shall come up with his vessel, until[l] by a certificate under the hands of the selectmen or major part of them as afores[*ai*]d, it shall appear to the capt[*ai*]n-general that said vessel, company and goods are clear of infection, and the orders for stopping and detaining the same be removed and taken off, he shall for every such offence forfeit the sum of fifty pounds; and in case he be not able to pay that sum, he shall suffer three months' imprisonm[*en*]t: and if any sailors or passengers coming in said vessel shall, without the knowledge or consent of the master, presume to come on shoar, or up above the said castle, or if any person from town or country shall, knowingly, presume to go on board such vessel, or go to the afores[*ai*]d house or island in time of infection there, without leave as afores[*ai*]d; or if any person put sick into the said house, or sent there on suspicion of being infected, shall presume to go off the island, without leave as afores[*ai*]d, —every person offending in any of the particulars above mentioned, shall forfeit the sum of forty pounds; and in case any person be not able to pay the said sum, he shall suffer two months' imprisonm[*en*]t: all the before-mentioned fines to be sued for and recovered by the selectmen of the town of Boston, for the time being; one moiety thereof to be to his majesty for the use of this government, the other moiety to the informer.

And be it further enacted,

Justices of the peace to order infectious vessels or persons to the hospital.

[SECT. 4.] That when and so often as any ship or other vessel, wherein any infection or infectious sickness hath lately been, shall come to any port or harbour within this province; or when and so often as any person or persons belonging to, or that may either by sea or land come into, any town or place near the publick hospital within this province, shall be visited, or who lately before may have been visited with any infectious sickness, two of the justices of the peace or selectmen of such place be and hereby are impowered immediately to order the said vessel and sick persons to the province hospital or house afores[*ai*]d, there to be taken care of according to the directions of this act; and where any such ship, vessel or persons cannot, without great inconvenience and damage, be ordered to the afores[*ai*]d house or hospital, in every such case the rules and directions are to be observed which are already made in and by an act pass'd in the 13th year of the reign of his late majesty King William the Third, intitled "An Act providing in case of sickness." 1701-2, chap. 9.

And be it further enacted,

Penalty for not answering, on oath, referring to infection.

[SECT. 5.] That if any master, seaman or passenger belonging to any ship, on board which any infection is or hath lately been, or is suspected to have lately been, or coming from any port where any infectious, mortal distemper prevails, shall refuse to make answer on oath to such questions as may be ask[*e*]'d him or them by the selectmen of the town, who are hereby impowered to administer the same, to which such ship shall come, relating to such infection, such master, seaman or passenger shall forfeit the sum of fifty pounds; and in case he be not able to pay said sum, he shall suffer six months' imprisonm[*en*]t; the above-mentioned fine to be sued for and recovered by the selectmen of the respective towns where the offence shall be committed: one moiety thereof to be to his majesty for the use of this governm[*en*]t, and the other moiety to the informer. And where any person shall be convicted of any offence against this act, and suffer the pains of imprisonm[*en*]t, and shall be unable to pay the costs of prosecution, such costs shall be paid by the several towns to which such persons respectively belong; or, if not inhabitants, shall be allowed and paid out of the province treasury.

Selectmen directed and empowered in providing nurses, attendance, &c.

[SECT. 6.] And the selectmen of Boston are directed and impowered to provide nurses, assistance and other necessaries for the comfort and rel[ei][*ie*]f of such sick persons sent to said hospital as afores[*ai*]d; the charge thereof to be born by the said persons themselves, if able; or, if poor and indigent, by the towns to which they respectively belong; or, if not inhabitants, then at the immediate charge of the province. [*Passed April* 13; *published April* 25, 1757.

CHAPTER 34.

AN ACT FOR THE EFFECTUAL PREVENTING THE CURRENCY OF THE BILLS OF CREDIT OF CONNECTICUT, NEW HAMPSHIRE AND RHODE ISLAND WITHIN THIS PROVINCE.

Preamble. 1753-54, chap. 23.

WHEREAS bills of credit still continue current within the governments of Connecticut, New Hampshire and Rhode Island, and have greatly depreciated in their value, and are liable to depreciate still further; and it is of great importance to the interest of the inhabitants of this province, and to the interest of such of his majesty's subjects in Great Britain and elsewhere as have trade and commerce here, that the currency of said bills should be effectually prevented throughout this government,—

Be it therefore enacted by the Lieutenant-Governour, Council and House of Representatives,

Bills of credit of Connecticut, New Hampshire or Rhode Island not to be received or paid.

[SECT. 1.] That every person within this province be and hereby is strictly forbidden to account, receive, take or pay any bill or bills of credit of either of the governments of Connecticut, New Hampshire or Rhode Island, in discharge of any contract or bargain, or for any valuable consideration whatsoever; and that every person who shall so account, receive, take or pay any of said bills within this province shall forf[ie][*ei*]t the sum of fifty pounds for every offence: one moiety thereof to his majesty, his heirs and successors, to and for the use of this government, the other moiety [to] [*of*] him or them that shall sue for the same, to be recovered with full costs of suit by action of debt in any of his majesty's courts of record within th[is][*e*] province, or by presentment of the grand jury.

And be it further enacted,

Persons chosen into any office, to take the following oath.

[SECT. 2.] That from and after the thirtieth day of March which will be in the year of our Lord one thousand seven hundred and fifty-seven, every person who shall be chose to serve in any office in any of the towns or districts or precincts of this province, shall, before his ent[e]rance upon such office, take the following oath, to be administred by a justice of the peace, or, where no justice of the peace shall be present, by the town, district, or precinct, clerk, who is hereby impowered to administer the same; viz[t].,—

Form of the oath.

You, A. B., do, in the presence of God, solemnly declare that you have not, since the thirtieth day of March, 1757, wittingly and willingly, directly or indirectly, either by yourself or any for or under you, been concerned in receiving or paying, within this government, any bill or bills of credit of either of the governments of Connecticut, New Hampshire or Rhode Island. So help you God.

[SECT. 3.] And where any person, chosen as aforesaid, shall refuse or neglect to take the oath aforesaid, on tendering the same, the town, district or precinct shall proceed to the choice of another person in his room; and where any person shall be elected by any town, district or precinct into any office, to the non-acceptance or refusal whereof a penalty is by law annexed, such person neglecting or refusing to take the oath aforesaid shall be liable to the same penalty as is by law provided for the non-acceptance or refusal of such office. Penalty in case of refusal to take said oath.

And be it further enacted,

[SECT. 4.] That when any person shall be chosen to represent any town within this province in the general court or assembly, such person so chosen shall take the oath aforesaid; and return shall be made by the selectmen, upon the back of the precept, that the person so chosen hath taken the oath required in the act made and passed in the thirtieth year of his majesty King George the Second, intitled "An Act for the effectual preventing the currency of the bills of credit of Connecticut, New Hampshire and Rhode Island within this province"; and if any person so chosen shall refuse or neglect to take the oath aforesaid, such refusal or neglect shall be deemed a refusal to serve as a representative; and the town shall proceed to the choice of another person in his room. Persons chosen representatives, to take the said oath. 1756-57, chap. 34.

And be it further enacted,

[SECT. 5.] That the oath aforesaid shall be administred to each of the members of his majesty's council, every year, at the same time when the usual oaths required to be taken by the said members of his majesty's council shall be administred; and all officers, civil and military, within this government, who shall be nominated or appointed, shall, before they receive their respective commissions, take the oath aforesaid, and their respective commissions shall be otherwise void; and all persons elected into any office by the general assembly shall be deemed not qualified to enter upon the execution of their respective offices until[1] they have taken the oath aforesaid. Councillors to take said oath,— and also all officers, civil and military.

And be it further enacted,

[SECT. 6.] That no execution shall be issued from the office of any clerk of any of the inferiour courts of common pleas, or of the superiour courts of judicature, for any sum whatsoever, unless the plaintiff or plaintiffs, suing in his or their own right, and dwelling within this province, shall first take the oath aforesaid, to be administred by a justice of the peace, or by the clerk of the court from which such execution shall issue; and certificate thereof shall be made on such execution; and if any execution shall issue or go forth without such certificate, the same shall be and is hereby declared to be void; and no licence shall be granted to, nor any recognizance taken from, any taverner, innholder or retailer, by the justices of any of the courts of sessions within this province, until[1] such taverner, innholder or retailer shall have taken said oath in presence of the court, or certificate of his having so done, from a justice of the peace, shall be presented to the court. The said oath to be taken upon issuing executions on judgment of courts.

And be it further enacted,

[SECT. 7.] That for every oath administred as aforesaid by the clerk of any court, he shall be allowed threepence, and for every certificate by him signed as aforesaid, threepence, and no more; and the cost and charge of such oath and certificate shall be added to the sum in the execution required to be levied accordingly. Clerk's fee.

Limitation.

[SECT. 8.] This act to continue and be in force until[1] the last day of March which will be in the year of our Lord one thousand seven hundred and sixty-two, and no longer. [*Passed and published March* 31, 1757.

CHAPTER 35.

AN ACT LAYING AN EMBARGO UPON SHIPS AND OTHER VESSELS IN THIS PROVINCE.

Preamble. 1754-55, chap. 27.

WHEREAS it is judged necessary for his majesty's service, that an embargo should be laid upon ships and other vessels within this province,—

Be it enacted by the Council and House of Representatives,

Embargo on all vessels until the 20th of April, on penalty.

[SECT. 1.] That no vessel[1] shall sail or depart from any port or other place of this province out of it, 'till the twentieth day of April instant, without leave first obtained from his majesty's council, or the major part of them; and if any vessel shall sail or depart to any port or place out of said province, without leave first had and obtained as aforesaid, the master of every vessel so departing shall forfeit and pay the sum of one hundred pounds, and the owner and owners of every vessel so departing shall forfeit and pay the sum of one hundred pounds, and the said last-mentioned forfeiture shall and may be recovered from any or either of the owners of such vessel where more than one person shall be interested.

And be it further enacted,

No fishing vessel to sail to the banks of Newfoundland until the said 20th of April:

[SECT. 2.] That no fishing vessel shall depart out of any port or place of this province to the banks of Newfoundland, or any other of the banks, before the said twentieth of April instant, without leave first had and obtained as afores[*ai*]d. And the owner or owners of any fishing vessel that may depart contrary to the true intent and meaning of this act, shall forfeit and pay the like sum of one hundred pounds: *saving*, only, such small vessels or boats as may be employed in catching of fish, and that shall not be absent more than four days at a time, extraordinary casualties excepted: the aforesaid penalties to be recovered by bill, plaint or information, before any of his majesty's courts of record within this province.

saving.

And be it further enacted,

Forfeitures, how to be disposed of.

[SECT. 3.] That all forfeitures by this act shall be, one half to his majesty, to be paid into the province treasury for the use of this province, the other half to him or them that shall inform and sue for the same.

And be it further enacted,

Power to take off or extend said embargo.

[SECT. 4.] That it shall and may be lawful for the commander-in-chief, or in his absence for the council, or the major part of them, at any time before the said twentieth [day] of April, to take off said embargo, or to extend it beyond said time not exceeding the first day of June, in the present year of his majesty's reign, under the same penalties, if in their judg[e]ment his majesty's service will permit the one or shall require the other. [*Passed and published April* 7, 1757.

CHAPTER 36.

AN ACT TO PREVENT THE DESERTION OF SOLDIERS DURING THE PRESENT WAR WITH FRANCE, AND THE LOSS OF ARMS, WHETHER LENT BY HIS MAJESTY, OR BELONGING TO THIS PROVINCE.

Whereas soldiers duly inlisted or impressed, or to be inlisted or impressed, have or may hereafter neglect or refuse attending at the time and place whereat they were or shall be ordered to muster, or may at other times absent themselves, without leave, from their duty, whence much disorder and injustice, as well as obstruction to his majesty's service, may happen,— Preamble. 1744-45, chap. 11. 1746-47, chap. 23.

Be it therefore enacted by His Majesty's Council and House of Representatives,

[Sect. 1.] That it shall and may be lawful for any person to apprehend any one who may be suspected to be such a deserter, if inlisted or impressed in this or either of the neighbouring governments, and bring him before any justice of the peace living in or near to the place where he shall be apprehended, who is hereby impowered to examine such suspected person; and if, by his confession, or the testimony of one or more witness or witnesses, upon oath, or by the knowledge of such justice of the peace, it shall appear or be found that such suspected person is an inlisted or impressed soldier, and ought to be with the troop or company to which he belongs, such justice of the peace shall forthwith cause him to be conveyed to the goal of the county in which he shall be found, and transmit an account thereof to the captain of the company, or colonel of the regiment, whereunto he belongs, or to the commander-in-chief of this province, to the end that such person be sent to the troop or company whereunto he belongs; and the keeper of such goal shall receive, out of such deserting soldier's wages, the same allowance as he would be intitled to by law if said soldier had been imprisoned for debt. Persons' power to apprehend deserters. Deserters to be committed to the jail of the county in which they shall be found.

And for the encouragement of any person or persons to apprehend and secure any deserting soldier,—

Be it further enacted,

[Sect. 2.] That upon certificate of such justice of the peace to the province treasurer, setting forth who the person was that apprehended and secured such deserter, there shall be paid him, out of the province treasury, forty shillings and the cost of prosecution, both to be deducted out of such deserter's wages, as also the charge of keeping him in goal, and of returning him to the troop or company whereunto he belongs. Reward for apprehending deserters.

And be it further enacted,

[Sect. 3.] That if any person shall harbour, conceal or assist any deserter from his majesty's service, knowing him to be such, the person so offending shall forf[ie][*ei*]t for every such offence the sum of five pounds; or if any person shall knowingly detain, buy or exchange, or otherwise receive any arms belonging to his majesty or to this province lent to the soldiers raised by this government, from any soldier or deserter, the person so offending shall forf[ie][*ei*]t for every such offence the like sum of five pounds; and in either case, upon conviction by the oath of one or more credible witness or witnesses, before two of his majesty's justices of the peace, *quorum unus*, who are hereby impowered and directed to try and determine the same, and to cause said penalties to be levied by distress and sale of the goods and chattels of the offender; one moiety thereof to be to and for the use of the informer, the other moiety to be paid into the province treasury for the use of the province, said penalties to be recovered by plaint or information. But Penalty for harboring or concealing said deserters. Penalty for detaining, exchanging, or buying arms from any soldier or deserter. Penalties, how to be levied and disposed of.

in case said offender doth not pay the same and the costs of prosecution, or shew of his goods or chattels whereon distress may be made to satisfy the same within four days after such conviction, then, and in such cases, said justices shall and may, by warrant under their hands and seals, either commit such offender to the common goal, there to remain, without bail or mainprize, for the space of two months, or cause such offender to be publickly whipped not exceeding twenty stripes, at the discretion of said justices: *saving*, always, to the party aggrieved at the sentence of said justices, a liberty of appeal to the court of general sessions of the peace.

And be it further enacted,

Justices' power to seize arms.

[SECT. 4.] That it shall and may be lawful for any justice of the peace, or military officer, to seize any such arms and send the same to the commissary-general of this province, and all reasonable charges shall be allowed therefor.

And be it further enacted,

Penalty for soldier's not returning arms.

[SECT. 5.] That whatsoever soldier shall receive of his captain arms belonging to his majesty or this province, and shall not return the same to his captain or the commanding officer, upon the expeditions being over, or his being dismissed, such soldier shall forf[ie][*ei*]t and pay three pounds ten shillings for each gun and bayonet, or three pounds for a gun and ten shillings for a bayonet not returned, to be deducted out of his wages. [*Passed and published April* 8, 1757.

CHAPTER 37.

AN ACT FOR SUPPLYING THE TREASURY WITH THE SUM OF TWELVE THOUSAND POUNDS.

Preamble.

WHEREAS the provision[s] already made to defray the expences of the late expedition against Crown Point are insufficient for that purpose,—

Be it therefore enacted by the Council and House of Representatives,

Treasurer empowered to borrow £12,000.

[SECT. 1.] That the treasurer of the province be and he hereby is impowered and directed to borrow from such person or persons as shall be willing to lend the same, said sum of twelve thousand pounds in mill'd dollars at six shillings each, or in other silver at six shillings and eightpence per ounce; and the sum so borrowed shall be applied in manner as in this act is hereafter directed: and for said sum of twelve thousand pounds, the treasurer shall give his receipt as in the form following; viz[t].,—

Form of treasurer's receipt.

Province of the Massachusetts Bay, the day of , 1757. Received of the sum of for the use and service of the province of the Massachusetts Bay; and, in behalf of said province, I do hereby promise and oblige myself and successors in the office of treasurer, to repay the said or order, the first day of June, 1758, the afores[*ai*]d sum of , in coined silver, at six shillings and eightpence per ounce, or Spanish mill'd dollars, at six shill[*in*]gs each, with interest annually, at the rate of six per cent per annum.

Witness my hand, H. G., Treasurer.

—and no receipt shall be given for less than twenty pounds.

And be it further enacted,

£6,000 for payment of officers and soldiers.

[SECT. 2.] That the afores[*ai*]d sum of twelve thousand pounds, when received into the treasury, shall be issued out in manner and for the purposes following; that is to say, six thousand pounds, part of said sum of twelve thous[*an*]d pounds, shall be applied for the paym[*en*]t and discharge of the officers and soldiers upon the expedition against Crown Point the [last] year [*last*]; and the further sum of one thous[*an*]d pounds, part of said sum of twelve thous[*an*]d pounds, shall be paid into the hands of the committee of war, for the service of this governm[*en*]t, towards defr[a][*e*]ying the charges of said expedition; and the further sum of three thousand pounds, part of said sum of twelve thousand pounds, shall be applied for the payment of such premiums and grants that now are or may hereafter be made by this court; and the further sum of two thousand pounds, being the remainder of s[*ai*]d sum of twelve thousand pounds, shall be applied for the paym[*en*]t of billeting the soldiers upon the present expedition.

£1,000 committee of war.

£3,000 for premiums and grants.

£2,000 for the present expedition.

And to enable the said treasurer to discharge the said obligations, and the interest that shall be due thereon,—

Be it further enacted,

[SECT. 3.] That there be and there hereby is granted to his most excellent majesty, a tax of thirteen thousand five hundred pounds, to be levied upon polls, and estates within this province, according to such rules and in such proportions as shall be ordered by the general court of this province at their sessions in May, one thousand seven hundred and fifty-seven.

Tax of £13,500 granted in 1757.

And be it further enacted,

[SECT. 4.] That in case the gen[*era*]l[l] court shall not, by the twentieth day of June, one thousand seven hundred and fifty-seven, agree and conclude upon a tax act to draw into the treasury the afores[*ai*]d sum of thirteen thous[*an*]d five hundred pounds, by the thirty-first day of March then next following, that then the treasurer of the province, for the time being, shall issue his warrants, directed to the selectmen or assessor[s] of the several towns and districts within this province, requiring them, respectively, to assess, levy and pay into the treasury, by the said thirty-first day of March, their respective proportions of s[*ai*]d sums according to the rates and proportions, rules and directions of the tax act then last preceeding.

Rule for apportioning the tax, in case no tax act shall be agreed on.

And whereas humble trust and depend[e][*a*]nce is had by the general assembly on a reimburs[*e*]m[*en*]t of the charges arising from the expeditions, and monies for that purpose are expected from Great Britain; wherefore, as a further fund to enable the treasurer to discharge the receipts and obligations afores[*ai*]d, by him given in pursuance of this act,—

Be it further enacted,

[SECT. 5.] That the monies that shall be received from Great Britain shall be applied by the said treas[*ure*]r, or so much thereof as shall be needful for the discharging such obligations, with the interest that may be due thereon, in pursuance of this act.

Parliamentary grant, when received, as a further fund.

Provided, always, anything in this act to the contrary notwithstand[*in*]g,—

[SECT. 6.] That in case the monies afores[*ai*]d shall arrive from Great Britain and be receiv[*e*]'d into the province treasury on or before the twentieth day of June, one thous[*an*]d seven hundred and fifty-seven, over and above what shall be sufficient to repay the sums borrowed by virtue of the act afores[*ai*]d, and shall be sufficient for discharging the obligations given by the treasurer in pursuance of this act, then and in such case the tax w[*hi*]ch otherwise by this act is ordered to go forth, shall be and hereby is declared to be null and void.

Proviso in case the money should be received on or before the 20th of June.

Provided, also,—

[SECT. 7.] That the remainder of the sum that may be brought in by the tax ordered by this act to be assessed and levied, over and above what shall be sufficient to discharge the obligations afores[*ai*]d, with

Further proviso.

the interest that may be due thereon, shall be and remain as a stock in the treasury, and be applied as the gen[era]l[l] court of this province shall hereafter order.

And be it further enacted,

Warrants to express the particular appropriation.

[SECT. 8.] That the treasurer is hereby directed and ordered to pay the said sum of twelve thous[an]d pounds out of such appropriations as shall be directed by warrant, and no other; and the secretary, to whom it belongs to keep the muster-rolls and acc[omp][un]ts of charge, shall lay before the house of repres[entati]ves, when they direct, such muster-rolls and acc[omp][un]ts, after paym[en]t thereof. [*Passed April* 15; *published April* 21, 1757.

Muster-rolls to be lodged with the secretary.

CHAPTER 38.

AN ACT APPOINTING THE TIMES FOR HOLDING THE SUPERIOUR COURT[S] OF JUDICATURE, &c., IN THE COUNTIES OF PLYMOUTH AND BARNSTABLE FOR THE PRESENT YEAR.

Preamble.

1756-57, chap. 16.

WHEREAS in and by a late act, intitled "An Act for altering the times appointed for holding the superiour court of judicature, &c[a]., in the counties of Pl[i][y]mouth, Bristol and Barnstable," it is provided, that his majesty's superiour court of judicature, court of assize and general goal delivery, shall, for the future, be held at Plymouth, within and for the county of Pl[i][y]mouth, on the last Tuesday of April, annually; and that the said court shall be held at Barnstable, for the counties of Barnstable and Dukes County, on the first Tuesday of May, annually; *and whereas*, since the passing said act, the administration of governm[en]t hath, by the death of the late lieutenant-governour, devolved on his majesty's council, whereby a general attendance of the members of said council, three of whom are justices of the said court, is rend[e]red more especially requisite at this time,—

Be it therefore enacted,

Times for holding Plymouth and Barnstable superior courts.

[SECT. 1.] That the said court, [shall] for the present year, [*shall*] be held at Plymouth, within and for the county of Pl[i][y]mouth, on the third Tuesday of July next; and at Barnstable, for the counties of Barnstable and Dukes County, on the fourth Tuesday of July next.

And be it further enacted,

Writs and other processes, &c.

[SECT. 2.] That all writ[t]s and other processes already issued, returnable to the said court, shall be returned, and all matters depending at the said court, in either of said counties, shall be proceeded on at the days respectively appointed by this act for holding the same. And all officers and other persons concerned are required to conform themselves accordingly. [*Passed April* 14; *published April* 25, 1757.

CHAPTER 39.

AN ACT FOR THE ENCOURAGEMENT OF SEAMEN TO ENLIST THEMSELVES IN SUCH VESSELS OF WAR AS ARE OR SHALL BE COMMISSION[*E*]'D AND FITTED OUT BY THE GOVERNMENT DURING THE PRESENT WAR WITH FRANCE.

Be it enacted by the Council and House of Representatives,

Distribution of prizes to be agreeable to

That the officers and ship's company of such vessels of war as are or shall be commission[e]'d by, and fitted out by, this government during the present war with the French, shall have the sole interest and property of and in all and every ship, vessel, goods and merchandize as they, or either of them, have or shall seize or take from the French king, his vassals or subjects, from the first of April instant, during the present war with the French; the said vessels, with the goods and merchandize so taken, to be divided amongst the captors in such proportions, and by such rules, as are establish[*e*]'d for the royal navy; and the captain, officers and ship's company shall appoint their respective agents for the receiving, management and distribution of their particular shares accordingly. [*Passed April* 23;* *published April* 25, 1757.

rules established for the royal navy.

CHAPTER 40.

AN ACT FOR ENQU[*I*]RING INTO THE RATEABLE ESTATES OF THE PROVINCE.

WHEREAS the rateable estates of the several towns and districts in this province may be very much altered since the last valuation taken by this court,—

Preamble.

1755-56, chap. 44. 1756-57, chap. 2.

Be it enacted by the Council and House of Representatives,

[SECT. 1.] That the assessors of each town and district within this province, who shall have been, or may be, chosen for the year one thousand seven hundred and fifty-seven, shall, on oath, take and lodge in the secretary's office, by the last Wednesday in November, one thousand seven hundred and fifty-seven, a true and perfect list, according to their best skill and understanding (and conformable to a list settled and agreed on by the general court), and to be recorded in the secretary's office, a printed copy of which shall be, by the treasurer of the province, sent to the clerk of each town and district, [t]herein setting forth an account of all male polls, of sixteen years old and upwards, whether at home or abroad, distinguishing such as are exempt from rates, thrô age or otherwise, and of all rateable estates both real and personal within their respective towns and districts; and all farms or parcels of land lying adjacent to and rated in such town or district, and by whom occupied; and what each person's real estate within the town or district, or adjoining as aforesaid, may rent for by the year, exclusive of taxes and necessary repairs of buildings and fences, and of all wharves, warehouses, grist-mills, fulling-mills, saw-mills, iron-works and furnaces, and what they may severally rent for by the year, exclusive of repairs; and of all Indian, negro and mollat[t]o servants, whether for life or for a term of years; and what number of tuns of open and deck'd vessels; trading stock abroad at the first cost; trading stock at home at the retail price wherever it is; money at interest, which any person has more than he pays interest for; value of rents of real estates not in their own improvement, and of annuities; value of debts due to, more than is due from, any person; and money in hand: *provided* it be so much as ten pounds; and of all horses, oxen, cows, goats, sheep and swine, at the respective ages set down in said list. And the said assessors, in taking such valuation, shall distinguish the different improvements of the real estates into the following parts; viz[t]., dwelling-houses; with the number of acres of pasture, tillage land, salt, fresh, and English mowing land and orchard; and what stock the pasture is ordinarily capable of feeding; and what quantity of produce the said

A valuation to be taken of the rateable estates of the province.

Directions for taking the same.

* Signed April 22, according to the record.

tillage, mowing and orchard land yearly affords, one year with another: excepting that the governour, lieutenant-governour, president, fellows, professors and tutors of Harvard College, settled ministers and grammar schoolmasters, with their families, for their polls, and for their estates in their own actual improvement, shall be exempted out of this act; and the said assessors, before they enter on this work, shall take the following oath; viz[t].,—

Form of the assessor's oath.

You, A. B., being chosen assessor for the town of B., for the year one thousand seven hundred and fifty-seven, do swear that you will faithfully and impartially, according to your best skill and judgment, do and perform the whole duty of an assessor, as directed and enjoined by an act of this province made the present year, intitled "An Act for enquiring into the rateable estates of the province," without favour or prejudice. So help you God.

Fine for assessor's neglect.

—which oath, in such town or district where no justice of the peace dwells, may be administred by the town- or district-clerk; and every assessor who shall have been or may be chosen by any town or district, in the year one thousand seven hundred and fifty-seven, accepting such choice, that shall refuse to take the said oath, or, taking the same, shall neglect or refuse to do the duty required by this act, or shall anyways prevaricate therein, shall, for each of these offences, forf[ie][*ei*]t and pay a fine of one hundred pounds.

Fine for refusing to give the assessors a true account.

[SECT. 2.] And every person refusing or neglecting to give such assessor or assessors, in writing and on oath (which the assessors respectively are required and impowered to administer), a true account of his rateable estate, improvements or rents, agreable to the true intent of this act, shall, for each offence, forf[ie][*ei*]t and pay the sum of one hundred pounds; which oath shall be in the following form; viz[t].,—

Form of the oath.

You, C, D., do swear that the account now exhibited by you, is, to the best of your knowledge and judgment, a full account of all your rateables, agreable to the list referred to in the act made in the thirtieth year of his present majesty's reign, intitled "An Act for [i][e]nquiring into the rateable estates of the province." So help you God.

Assessor's pay.

—and every assessor shall be allowed out of the treasury of his repective town or district, the sum of three shillings, for every day he shall be necessarily employed in doing the duty enjoined by this act.

And be it further enacted,

Copies of the last year's lists to be lodged in the secretary's office.

[SECT. 3.] That the assessors of each town and district in this province, who were chosen for the year one thousand seven hundred and fifty-six, shall, by the abovesaid last Wednesday in November, one thousand seven hundred and fifty-seven, transmit to the secretary's office, a true and perfect copy, on oath, of the list and valuation of estates, by which they made the taxes in their particular towns and districts for the year one thousand seven hundred and fifty-six, and also a true copy of the province tax made by such list and valuation, on penalty that each assessor neglecting his duty therein shall forf[ie][*ei*]t and pay the sum of twenty pounds.

Manner of recovery and disposal of fines.

[SECT. 4.] All fines and forf[ie][*ei*]tures arising by this act may be recovered by bill, plaint or information, or by action of debt, in any of his majesty's courts within this province proper to try the same; and shall be applied, one third to him or them that shall inform or sue for the same, and the other two thirds to his majesty to and for the use of this government. [*Passed April* 23; *published April* 25, 1757.

CHAPTER 41.

AN ACT FOR RAISING A SUM OF MONEY BY LOTTERY FOR THE ENCOURAGEMENT OF THE SETTLEMENT CALLED GERMANTOWN, IN THE TOWN OF BRAINTREE.

WHEREAS this court are willing to give all due encouragement to such foreign Protestants as are come over sea to reside within this province, those particularly who have settled together in a place called Germantown, within the township of Braintree, in the county of Suffolk, and for divers years past have carried on certain manufactures there, whereon they altogether depend for a livelihood; *and whereas* Joseph Palmer of said Germantown, gentleman, hath represented that certain of the said manufactures (particularly that of glass) wherein he is a principal adventurer are, by the consumption of some of the buildings by fire, and otherwise, declined and gone to decay, and hath thereupon prayed for the aid of this court,— Preamble. 1750-51, chap. 12, and note.

Be it therefore enacted by the Council and House of Representatives,

[SECT. 1.] That John Quincy, Josiah Quincy, Thomas Flucker and Isaac Winslow, Esqrs., with Mr. Edward Jackson, merchant, all of the county of Suffolk, or any three of them, be and hereby are allowed and impowered to set up and carry on one or more lottery or lotter[y][*ie*]s amounting in the whole to such a sum as by drawing or deducting ten per cent out of the same, or out of each prize or benefit ticket, may raise the sum of twelve hundred and fifteen pounds, and no more; and that the said sum be by them, or any three of them, applied within twelve months from and after drawing the first of the lotter[y][*ie*]s aforesaid, in the first place, to the payment of the charges of such lottery or lotter[y][*ie*]s, and then, the remainder to the erecting, on the said Joseph's lands there, such buildings and conveniencies for carrying on the manufactory aforesaid, as by the said Joseph shall be thought most suitable for that purpose, and for repairing such as remain unconsumed by fire. John Quincy, Josiah Quincy, Thomas Flucker and Isaac Winslow, Esqs., with Mr. Edward Jackson, allowed and empowered to set up and carry on a lottery in the town of Braintree, to enable Mr. Joseph Palmer to carry on certain manufactures.

[SECT. 2.] And that the said John Quincy, Josiah Quincy, Thomas Flucker, Isaac Winslow and Edward Jackson, or any three of them, be the managers of said lottery or lotteries and impowered to make all suitable and necessary rules for the managing thereof, and shall be sworn to the faithful discharge of their said trust; and, as well the said managers as the said Joseph, shall enter into bonds to the province treasurer, that the sum so raised shall be applied as soon as may be to the purposes designed, as aforesaid, and they shall be, and are hereby, declared answerable to the owners of the tickets in case of any deficiency or misconduct. Said persons, or any three of them, to be managers of said lottery.

And be it further enacted,

[SECT. 3.] That the said Joseph shall give bond, with sufficient sureties, of such tenor and form as a committee of this court (to be chosen for that purpose) shall direct, for the carrying on the manufactures heretofore begun there for the term of seven years next after the said buildings and convenienc[y][*ie*]s are finished, and that he, his heirs or assigns, will employ therein at least twenty manufacturers, a list of whose names shall be transmitted yearly by the said Joseph, his heirs or assigns, sometime in the month of February to the commander-in-chief for the time being, which said twenty manufacturers shall be exempted from impresses and all military duty so long as they continue in said manufactures. Said Palmer to give bond.

And be it further enacted,

[SECT. 4.] That if the said Joseph, his heirs or assigns, shall not carry on, or cause to be carried on, the said manufactures, for and dur- Privileges granted to said

Palmer, and duties enjoined.

ing the term of seven years as aforesaid, in such a manner that at least twenty manufacturers shall be therein employed, then, and in that case, the said buildings and conveniencies, together with the lands whereon they shall be erected, shall become the property of this province; and the said Joseph, his heirs or assigns, shall execute and deliver to the province treasurer for the time being, a sufficient deed of conveyance of such lands and premises for the use of the province, or otherwise shall pay into the province treasury the neat proceeds of such lottery or lotteries, at the election of the said Joseph, his heirs or assigns.

Provided,

[SECT. 5.] That the lottery or lotteries hereby allowed shall not be set up before the first day of September next. [*Passed April* 15; *published April* 25, 1757.

NOTES.—There were eight sessions of the General Court this year; but no acts were passed at the second, fifth and sixth sessions, and of the sixth session no record or prorogation appears. The engrossments of all the acts of this year are preserved, except of chapter 30, and all the public acts were printed with the sessions acts, except Chapters 1 and 19, which, being a tax-act and impost-act, respectively, were printed separately.

Chapters 35 to 41 inclusive, were signed by the major part of the Council, the Lieutenant-Governor having deceased the 4th day of April, 1757.

The following are the titles of two private acts passed, but no engrossments have been discovered, and they do not appear to have been printed:—

"An Act to dissolve the marriage of Lydia Kellog with Ephraim Kellog and to allow her to marry again."—[*Passed April* 18, 1757.

"An Act to dissolve the marriage of Jonah Galusha with Sarah Galusha and to allow him to marry again."—[*Passed April* 22, 1757.

All the acts of this year were duly certified to the Privy Council, by Governor Pownall, under the province seal, January 12 1758. They were received by the clerk of the Privy Council in waiting May 3, 1758, and on the eighth by his Majesty referred to the committee for Plantation Affairs, who in turn on the next day, referred them to the Board of Trade, by whom they were received and considered on the sixth day of June, and sent one week later to Sir Matthew Lamb for his opinion thereon in point of law.

On the thirty-first of July, 1759, the Lords of Trade signed their report to the Privy Council. In this report chapters 1, 2, 3, 5, 6, 8, 9, 15, 19, 21, 22, 23, 25, 29, 30, 35, 37, 38 and 40 are represented as "for temporary Services and are either expired by their own Limitations or the purposes for which they were enacted have been completed." Chapters 4, 7, 10, 11, 12, 13, 14, 16, 17, 18, 20, 24, 26, 27, 28, 31, 32, 33, 34, 36, 39 and 41 are represented as appearing to "relate to the internal Œconomy of the Province and appear to have been enacted for its private convenience, and we see no reason why His Majesty may not be graciously pleased to confirm them." No record of further action by the Home Government on these acts has been discovered.

Chap. 1. "July 7, 1756. A Petition of the Select Men of the Town of Dunstable setting forth that for want of proper Officers in the said Town for Collecting the Province & County Taxes for the Year 1754 and therefore Praying that the Province Treasurer & the Treasurer of the County of Middlesex may be impowered & directed to add said Taxes to the Taxes of the present Year & issue Warrants accordingly.

In the House of Representatives; Read & Ordered that the Prayer of the Petition be granted, and that the Province Treasurer be directed to add the Province Tax of the Town of Dunstable for the Year 1754 to the present Years Province Tax & to issue his Warrant accordingly; and that the Treasurer for the County of Middlesex add the said Towns County Tax for the said Year 1754 to their County Tax for this present Year, & Issue his Warrant to the Assessors of said Town accordingly—In Council; Read & Concur'd——Consented to by the Lieuten^t Govern^r"—*Council Records, vol. XXI., p.* 230.

"August 18, 1756. In the House of Representatives whereas by the Tax, which is this Year gone forth for £58,700. but £53,000. of said Sum is appropriated so that there will be a Surplusage of £5500 : 11 : 4 in the Treasury when the Taxes are paid in——Voted that the said Sum of Five thousand Five hundred Pounds Eleven Shillings & Four Pence when received into the Treasury be & hereby is applied for the use & Service of the Crown Point Expedition & that the Treasurer pay the same out of the Treasury to the Honble the Committee of War by Warrant from the Governour & Council——In Council; Read & Concurd——Consented to by the Governour."—*Ibid., p.* 246.

"Janu^a 7, 1757. A Petition of Daniel [Epes Junr*] in behalf and by order of the Assessors in the South Parish in Danvers shewing that the Sum of Two Hundred Pounds hath been Assessed on the Inhabitants of said Parish in the Year 1754 & 1755, but that the Warrants given to the Collectors to Collect the same being supposed insufficient many of the Inhabitants refuse to pay their Proportion of said Taxes, and Praying for Releif.

In the House of Representatives; Read & Ordered that the present Assessors of the South Precinct in the District of Danvers be and hereby are impowered and directed to Issue New Warrants in the Form of Law to the Collectors of said Precinct to whom the Taxes were Committed for the Years 1754. and 1755. to compleat their said Collections, and Pay in the same into the Precinct Treasury, and that the said Collectors Proceedings on their former Warrants are hereby confirmed any supposed Defects in said Warrants notwithstanding ——In Council; Read & Concurd——Consented to by the Lieuten^t Govern^r"—*Ibid., p.* 318.

* Missing in record; supplied from petition.

"January 17, 1757. A Petition of Jonathan Coffin in behalf of the Inhabitants of Nantucket shewing that in the Course of the last Year they have lost by the Enemy & Shipwrecks one fifth Part of all their Navigation, & upwards of One Hundred Men, or at least the benefit of their Service, and have many Widows & Fatherless Children thrown upon them for a Support by means of said Disasters. And inasmuch as the greater Part of the Inhabitants of said Place are Quakers they are by Law subject to the Payment of Thirteen Pounds Six Shillings & Eight Pence for each & every Man that must otherwise have gone into the Publick Service, the Payment of which would be very burdensome under their present distressing Circumstances, Therefore Praying for an Abatement.——

In the House of Representatives; Read & Ordered that the Prayer of this Memorial be so far granted as that the Assessors of said Island be and hereby are allowed in making their Assessments for their Province Tax for the Currant year to add thereto only the Sum of One Thousand Pounds for Deficiency of Soldiers instead of Fifteen Hundred & Six Pounds thirteen Shillings & four Pence, which was added to them by this Court for that reason in the last Tax Act, and that the Province Treasurer be, and hereby is directed on their Paying the said Sum of One Thousand Pounds into the Treasury to give a Discharge in full for their said Additional Tax.—In Council; Read & Concurr'd——Consented to by the Lieuten^t Govern^r"—*Ibid., p.* 338.

"April 7, 1757. A Petition of George Godfrey and John Adam Assessors of the Town of Taunton, Setting forth that they had assessed sundry Persons in said Town for their Polls, who were under the Age of Twenty One Years, some of which Persons although trading for themselves, & having no Parents, Masters or Guardians to pay said Tax yet refuse paying it themselves.——Therefore Praying that the said Taxes for the Year 1756. may be Confirmed or Established; which otherwise must produce great Confusion and sundry Law Suits.——

In the House of Representatives; Read & Ordered that the Prayer of this Petition be so far granted as that the Tax mentioned for the Year 1756 be and hereby is confirmed (any pretended Mistake therein mentioned notwithstanding) and that the Constables to whom the said Tax was Committed to Collect, be & they hereby are fully authorized and Impowered to Collect the same. In Council; Read & Concurred—Consented to by the Major Part of the Council."—*Ibid., p.* 432.

"April 16, 1757. A Petition of William Richardson Esqr for himself and the rest of the Select Men and Assessors of the Town of Lancaster Setting forth That in the Rate Bill for the Year 1756. which they Committed to Asahel Phelps, one of the Constables of said Town there were some Circumstantial Mistakes, but none as to the Sum to be Collected ——Therefore Praying Relief——

In the House of Representatives; Read & Ordered that the Tax for the Town & County Rate in the Town of Lancaster for the Year 1756. committed to Asahel Phelps to Collect be and hereby is confirmed and Established, and the said Phelps is hereby fully impowered to Collect the same, any supposed mistake in the Rate Bills to him committed notwithstanding——In Council; Read & Concurred——Consented to by a Major Part of the Council."—*Ibid., p.* 462.

"April 20, 1758. In the House of Representatives. Whereas it is represented to this House that the Assessors chosen for Sherburn on the Island of Nantucket for the year 1756 were not sworn or affirmed as prescribed by Law within seven days after they were chosen, although they were regularly chosen, and sworn or affirmed before said Taxes were made, from which great difficulties are like to arise, and many Law Suits by reason said Assessors were not sworn or affirmed within the time limited by Law.

Voted That the said Assessment made by the said Assessors for the year 1756 be, and are hereby declared good and valid in Law to all Intents and Purposes as it would have been, had the said Assessors been sworn or affirmed within seven days from their being chosen. In Council. Read and Concurred.

Consented to by the Governor."—*Ibid., vol. XXII., p.* 312.

Chap. 3. "I have endeavoured as far as lay in my Power that the several Votes of the Last Assembly relative to the Expedition which had not their designed Effect when His Excellency left the Province should be fully carried into Execution; And I have reason to think that We are forwarder than any other Government both in the Number of our Men & in the Provision made for them, but I find that the full Number proposed on the Part of this Province is not yet compleat. * * *

I recommend to you Gentlemen of the House of Representatives an Inquiry into the State of the Treasury, and proper measures for a further Supply not only for the Service of the Expedition, but for the other necessary Charges of the Government.

Gentlemen of the Council, & House of Representatives,

I shall be ready to concur with you in all necessary measures for the promoting His Majestys Service and the Interest of the Province, and I recommend to you as great dispatch as shall be consistent with the Importance of the Affairs which ly before you"—*Extract from the Lieutenant-Governor's speech to both Houses, May 27, 1756.—Council Records, vol. XXI., p.* 184.

Chap. 9. "May 28, 1756. In Council; Ordered that John Cushing Andrew Oliver & Stephen Sewall Esq^{rs} with such as the Honble House shall appoint be a Committee to Consider & Report what is proper to be done by this Court in relation to the French Families imported from Nova Scotia since the Dissolution of the last Assembly—In the House of Representatives; Read & Concur'd, and Col^o Cotton, Col^o Quincy Mr Flucker & Col^o Worthington are joined in the Affair"—*Council Records, vol. XXI., p.* 186.

"May 28, 1756. The Committees Report about the French Neutrals last arrived: vizt

The Committee appointed to consider & Report what is proper to be done by this Court in relation to the French Families last imported into this Province have attended that Service and would humbly propose that the said French Families be allowed to remain in this Province, and to be distributed into the several Sea Port Towns between Plymouth and Glocester, those Towns being included, and if any of those French People should hereafter be chargeable it should not be to the Towns where they reside, but to this Province—All which is humbly Submitted—

By John Cushing per Order.

In the House of Representatives; Read & Ordered that this Report be Accepted——In Council; Read & Concur'd—Consented to by the Lieut Governr "—*Ibid.*, *p.* 187.

"June 1, 1756 In Council; Ordered that Samuel Watts & William Brattle Esqrs with such as the Honble House shall join be a Committee to examine such Accounts of Charges as have been or may be offered to this Court for Supporting any of the French Inhabitants that have lately been brought from Nova Scotia into this Province; and that the Comittee project some method for easing the Province of such a Charge for the future & report as soon as may be——In the House of Representatives; Read & Concur'd; And Mr Welles Thomas Foster Esqr and Mr Payne are joined in the Affair "—*Ibid.*, *p.* 194.

"June 2, 1756. His Honour the Lieutenant Governour communicated to both Houses a Letter which he had received from Mr Handfield a Principal Officer in Nova Scotia relating to a Family of French Neutrals sent hither from thence

In the House of Representatives; Ordered that a Letter communicated by His Honour the Lieutenant Governour to this House from Mr Handfield to His Excellency Governour Shirley dated Annapolis Royal May 1756. be Committed to the Committee appointed to examine the Accounts offered to this Court of Charges for Supporting the Inhabitants of Nova Scotia, lately brought into this Province &ca to Consider the same and Report thereon——In Council; Read & Concur'd "—*Ibid.*, *p.* 196.

"June 8, 1756. On the Vote for a Committee referring to the French Neutrals entered May 31st——In the House of Representatives; Voted that Colo Gerrish & Colo Clap be of the Committee for the Purposes, within mentioned in the room of Thomas Foster Esqr and Mr Payne who are absent:——In Council; Read & Concur'd "—*Ibid.*, *p.* 204.

"June 9, 1756. In Council; Ordered That Andrew Oliver & Thomas Hutchinson Esqrs with such as the Honble House shall appoint be a Comittee to Write to Mr Agent Bollan directing him to make humble Representation to his Majesty of the great Burthen brought on the Province by means of the French Families sent hither from Nova Scotia & praying for a Reimbursement of the past Charge, and Relief from a further Burthen, and the Committee are to furnish the Agent with an Account of the past Charge, & with all necessary Facts relating to the Affair——In the House of Representatives; Read & Concur'd; and Mr Speaker, Mr Plucker & Mr Welles are joined in the Affair.

In the House of Representatives; Ordered that the Committee appointed to Consider the Affair of the French Neutrals (so called) be directed to sit forthwith & Report In Council; Read & Concur'd "—*Ibid.*, *p.* 207.

"June 9, 1756. Report on the Accounts of Charge for Supporting the French Neutrals.

The Committee appointed to Examine such Accounts of Charges as have been or may be offered to this Court for Supporting the French Inhabitants, that have been brought into this Province from Nova Scotia &ca having attended said Service report as their Opinion, That there are Accounts for the Support of said Inhabitants from sundry Towns in this Province, which are not brought in for Payment; Therefore that the Consideration of the whole be referred to the first Friday of the next Sitting of this Court, and that such Towns as have any demands on the Province for the Support & Maintenance of said French Inhabitants be directed to Lodge their Accounts by said time in the Secretarys Office——The Committee beg leave further to report that in their Opinion a Special & Effectual Provision is already made by an Act in Addition to an Act making Provision for the Inhabitants of Nova Scotia, sent hither from that Government, for the Support of said Inhabitants; & that if the Justices of the Peace, & Overseers of the Poor would but Conform to said Act, and Bind out to Service, or make Provision for the Support of said Inhabitants in the same Manner as by Law they are authorized and Impowered to do were said Inhabitants the Inhabitants of this Province——It would greatly lessen the Charge the Province otherwise will be at, & therefore that this Court give Notice that they expect a strict Observation of the same——which is humbly Submitted

Per Samuel Watts per Order

In Council; Read & not accepted——In the House of Representatives Read & Non Concur'd, and Ordered that this Report be accepted "—*Ibid.*, *p.* 208.

"June 10, 1756. An Order was passed in Council, referring to the managing & employing of the French Inhabitants of Nova Scotia in the several Towns, which being sent down was Non Concur'd by the House

In the House of Representatives; It being found by Experience that the frequent Travelling & passing between Town & Town of many of the French People (lately dispersed thrô this Province by Order of the General Court) hath been attended with considerable Inconveniencies & may be productive of greater.

Therefore Ordered & directed that the Select Men & Overseers of the Poor be very Carefull to keep the French People from Idling & wandring about, and none of that People shall be permitted to travel from Town to Town without leave first obtained of Two of the Select Men or Overseers of the Poor where they respectively belong, of which such People shall produce Certificate or otherwise they shall be stopped & turned back by any Two English House holders who are hereby impowered to examine them & Stop or return them, if they have not Excuse as above——In Council; Read & Concur'd—Consented to by the Lieutent Governr "—*Ibid.*, *p.* 216.

"August 14, 1756. In the House of Representatives; Ordered that Mr Tasker Capt Newhall Colo Cotton & Mr Morey with such as the Honble Board shall join be a Committee to take under Consideration what further may be necessary to be done with regard to the Inhabitants late of Nova Scotia who are now in the Province & report thereon—In Council; Read & Concur'd; And John Greenleaf, Andrew Oliver, Stephen Sewall & John Erving Esqrs are joined in the Affair "—*Ibid*, *p.* 239.

"August 16, 1756. The Deputy Secretary brought the following Message from His Excellency to both Houses,

Gentlemen of the Council & House of Representatives

This accompanies a Letter I receiv'd from his Excellency Govr Lawrence concerning the return of the French Inhabitants of Nova Scotia lately sent from thence & dispersed among the English Colonies, representing the pernicious Consequences of it, which are so clearly set forth in his Letter, that I need add nothing on that Subject, except that as I shall return to Great Britain nothing shall be wanting on my part to represent what you shall do for preventing this Evil, to his Majestys Ministers in such a Light as may I hope, induce his Majesty to have a favourable Consideration of it"—*Ibid.*, *p.* 240.

"August 17, 1756. John Greenleaf Esqr from the Committee appointed to consider the Affair of the French Families come in hither from Georgia reported thereon On which Report the following Vote was passed vizt

In the House of Representatives; Read & Ordered that the Report be recommitted, that the said Committee take under Consideration His Excellencys Message of Yesterday, the Letter from his Excellency Governour Lawrence accompanying the same & the Passports from the Governours of the several Southern Colonies; That they also consider the Affair of the Inhabitants of Nova Scotia lately arrived here from Georgia &^{ca} as also of those Inhabitants who were in the Province before the Arrival of those from Georgia and Report thereon as soon as may be—In Council; Read & Concur'd"—*Ibid.*, *p.* 241.

"August 17, 1756. In the House of Representatives Whereas there is lately brought into this Town by John Gorham Esqr Sheriff of the County of Barnstable & Barnabas Gibbs, a Number of French People being Ninety Nine in the whole that were sent from Nova Scotia to Georgia, and some other Southern Governments who were in their way back to Nova Scotia, Therefore Voted that said French People be committed to the Sheriff of the County of Suffolk untill the further Order of this Court, and that said Gorham & Gibbs be discharged from any further Care of them; And that also the said Sheriff of the County of Suffolk be directed to cause strict Search to be made after any Papers the said People may have in their Possession & to Secure the same in Order to their being delivered to a Committee of this Court——In Council; Read & Concur'd——Consented to by the Governour."—*Ibid.*, *p.* 245.

"August 20, 1756. A Petition of Francis Le Blanc, late Inhabitant of Nova Scotia, Praying that he & his Family may be removed to Point Shirley where he now dwells to the Town of York, for his more comfortable Subsistence among some Friends & Relations of his who dwell there.——In Council; Read & Ordered that James Minot Esqr with such as the Honourable House shall join be a Committee to Consider this Petition & Report what they judge proper to be done thereon.——In the House of Representatives; Read & Concur'd; & Thomas Foster & Major Stockbridge are joined in the Affair."—*Ibid.*, *p.* 249.

"August 23^d, 1756. A Petition of Eleanor Tibaudeau late an Inhabitant of Nova Scotia now resident in the Town of Malden shewing that her Husband is lately dead & has left her in a helpless Condition with Five small Children, Praying that her Niece now at Dorchester (a grown woman) may be allowed to Live with her. In Council; Read & Ordered that the Prayer of this Petition be granted In the House of Representatives; Read & Concur'd——Consented to by the Govern^r"—*Ibid.*, *p.* 252.

"August 25, 1756. Report on the Affairs of the late French Inhabitants of Nova Scotia——vizt

The Committee appointed to consider what further may be necessary to be done with regard to the French Inhabitants of Nova Scotia who are now in the Province humbly Report as their Opinion, that those of them now in the Town of Boston, & under the Care of the Overseers of said Town amounting as We are informed to Eighty Four Persons, be forthwith moved from Boston, and distributed as near as may be among the Towns mentioned at the Foot of this Report; One or Two, more or less in each of said Towns, as shall best accomodate the French Families themselves, and that the Sheriffs of the County of Suffolk & Middlesex be directed to cause the said French Persons to be as soon as may be removed to said Towns respectively, and that the Select Men of said Towns be directed to receive them accordingly; & in all Things concerning them to Govern themselves, by the Laws & Orders of this Court making Provision for the Inhabitants sent hither from that Government, and the Committee are further of Opinion that as Hanover has Nine & Pembrook but Five of the said Inhabitants, that Three of those at Hanover be removed to Pembrook——The Committee are further of Opinion that the Select Men of the several Towns where any of those French People are or may be placed be directed to assist them in procuring Employment at such Rates as they shall judge reasonable, and if thrô want of Employment or thrô want of Ability any of them cant Earn a Support for themselves & Families the Select Men be directed to afford them such Releif as may be necessary for their comfortable Subsistence, in the same Manner as if they had been proper Inhabitants of this Province & exhibit their respective Accounts of Disbursement into the Secretarys Office as occasion shall require,

Which is Humbly Submitted—— JOHN GREENLEAF

Names of the Towns above referred to, with the Number of Persons respectively assigned to them, vizt Cambridge Ten, Walpole Five, Topsfield Five, Middleton Five, Westford Five, Sherburn Five, Littleton Five, Bedford Five, Tewksbury Four,—Brookfield Eight—Southborough Six—Grafton Six—Bellingham Four—Dunstable Four—Westborough Three—In Council; Read & Accepted & Ordered that the French People therein mentioned be disposed of accordingly——In the House of Representatives; Read & Concur'd Consented to by the Governour"—*Ibid.*, *p.* 255.

"August 27th, 1756——Report on Francis Le Blancs Petition Entered August 20. 1756.

The Committee to whom was referr'd the Petition of Francis Le Blanc having met and considered the same, and finding the Petition so far true as that they cant get Labour at Point Shirley, so as to have any Hopes of Supporting them thro the ensuing Winter, therefore are of Opinion that they be removed to some other Place, where they may have better prospect of getting Labour for their better Support, all which is humbly Submitted—— JAMES MINOT per Order.

In Council; Read & Ordered that this Report be accepted—In the House of Representatives; Read & Concur'd—Consented to by the Governour "—*Ibid*, *p*. 259.

"August 28, 1756. A Bill entitled An Act relating to the Inhabitants of Nova Scotia transported hither by order of the Government there——Having been read three times in the House of Representatives & there passed to be Engrossed——In Council; Read a first time "—*Ibid*., *p* 263.

"August 30, 1756. A Bill entitled an Act relating to the Inhabitants of Nova Scotia transported hither by order of the Government there——In Council; Read a Second time, and passed a Concurrence with Amendments as taken into a new Draft "—*Ibid*., *p*. 264.

"September 1, 1756. In the House of Representatives; Ordered that Col° Hale, Col° Otis & Mr Welles be a Committee to Confer with a Committee of the Honourable Board on the Bill passed by the Honourable Board, and that pass'd by the House relating to the French Inhabitants of Nova Scotia lately sent hither from that Government. In Council; Read & Concur'd; And Benjamin Lynde Thomas Hutchinson & Stephen Sewell Esq^rs^ are appointed a Committee of the Board for said Conference."—*Ibid*., *p*. 266.

"September 2^d^, 1756. In the House of Representatives; Whereas sundry Persons a few Weeks since were stopp'd in this Province, late Inhabitants of Nova Scotia, and sent by the Government there to one of His Majestys Southern Colonies; which Inhabitants when Arrested were bound back to Nova Scotia, or to join some of His Majestys Enemies, and as it is reported that more are coming in the same manner and with the same design; and as such Practices must be of very dangerous Consequence——Therefore Voted that Col° White Col° Vassall & Mr Hunt with such as shall be joined by the Honble Board be a Committee in the Name of the Two Houses to Pray His Excellency the Governour to write to the several Commanders in Chief in the Southern Colonies representing the pernicious tendency of the Return or Wandering about of the said late Inhabitants of Nova Scotia, and how necessary it is that his Majestys Governours and all other his Majestys good Subjects should very carefully prevent the same——And the Committee are directed further to pray His Excellency to give Order by Proclamation or otherwise as may be thought best, that all those late Nova Scotia People which may be found returning from the Southern Governments within the Limits of this Province should be arrested & carefully prevented returning further——In Council; Read & Concur'd; and Sylvanus Bourn and John Otis Esq^rs^ are joined in the Affair "—*Ibid*., *p*. 267.

"September 2^d^, 1756. A Bill entitled an Act for the better ordering the late Inhabitants of Nova Scotia, transported by Order of the Government there——In Council; Read a first and Second time & passed to be Engrossed "—*Ibid*, *p*. 268.

"Septem^r^ 3, 1756. A Memorial of Thomas Hutchinson Esqr Praying that a French Family of the late Inhabitants of Nova Scotia (particularly named) now in Boston may be allowed to continue there, or be removed to Cambridge the Memorialist being willing (if required) to give Bond for their good behaviour——In Council; Read & Ordered that Ezekiel Chever & John Otis Esqr with such as the Honble Board shall join be a Committee to take this Memorial under consideration & report what they judge proper to be done thereon——In the House of Representatives Read & Non Concur'd & Ordered that the Memorial be dismissed "—*Ibid*, *p*. 269.

"Septem^r^ 4, 1756. The Bill intitled an Act for the better ordering the late Inhabitants of Nova Scotia transported by order of the Government there; being brought up with the Vote of the House of their Concurrence with Amendments; the said Amendments were considered & agreed to by the Council "—*Ibid*., *p*. 269.

"Septem^r^ 7, 1756. In the House of Representatives; It being represented to this Court that some of the Family of Magdaline Perlin, late Inhabitant of Nova Scotia are Sick, which renders it unsafe at present to remove them from the Town of Boston, where they now reside; Voted that Mr Sheriff Pollard be directed not to remove the said Family till the further Order of this Court ——In Council; Read & Concur'd "—*Ibid*., *p* 270.

"Septem^r^ 10, 1756. In the House of Representatives; Voted that Francis Le Blanc and his Family be removed from Point Shirley to Needham (the Vote of the 21st Ulto. notwithstanding) and that the Sheriff of the County of Suffolk be directed to remove them accordingly——In Council; Read & Concur'd——Consented to by the Governour——

In the House of Representatives; Voted that Thirteen of the French Inhabitants now residing at Glocester be removed to Wenham, and that the other Eleven now at said Town of Glocester be removed to Methuen, and that the Town of Glocester be at the Charge of their Removal. In Council; Read & Concur'd——Consented to by the Governour ——

A Petition of Margarett Dowcet one of the French Inhabitants of Nova Scotia, Shewing that She is now dangerously Sick in Boston, Praying that if She should recover She might be allowed to Live at Newbury with her Brother Dowcet, the only Friend & Relation She has in this Country. In the House of Representatives Read & thereupon Voted that the Prayer of this Petition be granted. In Council; Read & Concur'd——Consented to by the Governour "—*Ibid*., *p*. 277.

"Septem^r^ 10, 1756. In the House of Representatives; Voted that the French Family sent this Week to Littleton, be removed from thence to Harvard. In Council; Read and Concur'd——Consented to by the Governour "—*Ibid*, *p*. 279.

"October 13, 1756. In the House of Representatives; Voted that the late French Inhabitants of Nova Scotia now in the Towns of Charlestown & Marblehead being Forty Nine in all be forthwith removed from thence to the hereafter mentioned Towns in the following proportion viz. To Medway Six, to Bellingham Four, To Walpole Three, To Sherburn Five, To Natick Six, To Southborô Three, To Dudley Six, To Medfield Five, To Holliston Four, To Dracut Four, To Dunstable Three.——

Voted also that the Sheriffs of Essex & Middlesex Counties be directed to Cause the said French Persons to be Conveyed to said Towns respectively, and in all things concerning them to Govern themselves by the Laws & Orders of this Court making Provision for the Inhabitants of Nova Scotia sent here from that Government, and that said Laws & Orders be sent to the several Towns that they may be duly executed, especially those

Paragraphs relating to the keeping the said French Inhabitants in the several Towns. In Council; Read & Concur'd——Consented to by the Lieut Governr"—*Ibid.*, p. 290.

"Janua 21, 1757. In Council; Ordered that John Erving & William Brattle Esqrs with such as the Honourable House shall join be a Committee to Consider of some proper measures to free the Province from the Expence of Supporting a great Number of the French Inhabitants of Nova Scotia now in the Province, or to remove them from thence if it shall be judged Expedient and make Report——In the House of Representatives; Read & Concurr'd & Colo Williams, Thomas Foster Esqr and Mr Witt are joined in the Affair."—*Ibid.*, p. 343.

"Janua 21, 1757. In Council; Ordered that the Select Men or Overseers of the Poor of the several Towns wherein any of the French Inhabitants of Nova Scotia are placed be directed whenever they shall offer an Account of their Disbursements for the Support of them, to Annex thereto a List of the several French Persons in such Town with an Account of their Age and Sex, and the Circumstances of their Health & Capacity for Labour and that a Copy of this Vote be printed, and sent to the several Towns & Districts where any of said Inhabitants are placed——In the House of Representatives Read & Concurred Consented to by the Lieutenant Governour."—*Ibid*, p. 344.

"February 2, 1757. A Petition of Gludo Benway one of the French Inhabitants of Nova Scotia, Shewing that he and his Family were placed by the Government at Cambridge, and his Children were by the Select Men of said Town afterwards sent to Mr Campbell of Oxford whither the Petitioner and his Wife followed them that said Campbell dispersed their Five Children whereupon the Petitioner and his Family fled to Newtown that the Select Men of said Town refuse to do anything for them, and threaten to send them to Goal, Therefore Praying that the Court would Provide some comfortable Place for their Abode being willing to do all in their Power to Support themselves.

In the House of Representatives; Read & Ordered that the Select Men of the Town of Newtown be and hereby are allowed to remove the said Glude Benway & his Wife to the Town of Cambridge where they were originally placed by Order of this Court, and that the Select Men of said Cambridge be and hereby are directed to take Care of them agreeable to the Laws made respecting the Inhabitants of Nova Scotia now in the Province——In Council; Read and Concurr'd."—*Ibid*, p. 361.

"February 5, 1757. The Petition of Glude Benway as entered the 2d instant. Read again——In Council on a Motion made and Seconded Ordered that this Petition be reconsidered, & that the further Consideration thereof be referred to Tuesday next at 11. oClock"—*Ibid.*, p. 365.

"Februa 8, 1757. In Council; The Petition of Glude Benway Read & Non Concurr'd and inasmuch as it appears that there were but Ten of the French Neutrals Ordered by the Court to the Town of Cambridge in September last, that three of the French Neutrals were ordered to be sent to the Town of Dunstable, that the Select Men of the Town of Cambridge took Thirteen, the Three ordered to Dunstable being part of that Number and have Supported them ever since, Therefore Voted that the Select Men of the Town of Newtown have Liberty to send the said Glude Benway & Wife to the Town of Dunstable; and the Select Men of the Town of Dunstable are hereby directed to take Care of them agreeable to the Laws of the Government in that Case made and Provided.——In the House of Representatives; Read & Ordered that this Petition lye on the Table."—*Ibid.*, p. 367.

"February 9, 1757. A Petition of Charles Mius one of the late French Inhabitants of Nova Scotia complaining of the great hardships which he and his Family suffer at Plymouth where they now reside and of his being deprived of a Barrell of Beef and Six Bushels of Salt, his own Property brought from Cape Sables and Praying Relief——

In the House of Representatives; Read & Ordered That the Select Men of the Town of Plymouth be and hereby are directed to Assist the Petitioner in setling the Affair of the Beef and Salt mentioned with Mr Thompson; and that said Town have leave by their Select Men to remove the Petitioner and his Family to the Town of Wareham (who have not as yet received any of the Inhabitants of Nova Scotia) and that the Select Men of said Town of Wareham be and hereby are directed to provide for them as the Law directs——In Council; Read & Concurr'd——Consented to by the Lieutenant Governour."—*Ibid.*, p. 372.

"February 14, 1757. In the House of Representatives; Voted that Judge Russell Mr Gridley and Mr Bradbury with such as shall be joined by the Honourable Board be a Committee to Confer with his Excellency Governour Lawrence in Order to the obtaining a reimbursement of the Charges this Province have been at in Supporting the Inhabitants of Nova Scotia, as well those who were immediately ordered here by that Government as those who arrived here from some of his Majestys Southern Governments, and Report. In Council; Read & Concurr'd & John Erving & William Brattle Esqrs are joined in the Affair.——Consented to by the Lieutenant Governour."—*Ibid*, p. 378.

"Februa 1757. A Memorial of Benjamin Pickman Esqr by Order of the Overseers of the Poor of the Town of Salem—Shewing that Twelve of the French Nova Scotians, were at first placed in the Town of Salem & since that Twenty more who came from Cape Sables & being well acquainted with Boats & Vessells there is great hazard of their running away with some of them, and further representing that they are supported at a greater Expence at Salem than they would be in some other Towns of the Province—Therefore Praying that they may be removed.——

In the House of Representatives;——Read and Ordered that the Overseers of the Poor of the Town of Salem be and hereby are allowed and Impowered at the Charge of the Province to remove the late Inhabitants of Nova Scotia who have been placed there by order of this Court or of his Majestys Council from said Town to the Towns and in the Proportion following—vizt seven to Hopkington, five to Southborough & Eight to Tewksbury and that the Select Men of said Towns be and hereby are directed to Support the said Inhabitants late of Nova Scotia in the manner as is directed by the Laws in that Case made and Provided; And that the Twelve of said Inhabitants who were first Ordered to said Town of Salem be removed to the Town of Sturbridge to be under the Care and Direction of Moses Marcy Esq[r] who is hereby directed to provide for & Support them accordingly at as small Expence to the Publick as may be ——In Council; Read & Concurr'd——Consented to by the Lieutenant Governour."—*Ibid., p.* 386.

"Febru[a] 19, 1757. William Brattle Esq[r] from the Committee appointed to Confer with Governour Lawrence made the following Report——viz[t]

The Committee appointed to wait on his Excellency Govern[r] Lawrence to Confer with him upon the Charge of the French Neutrals &[ca] having attended said Service beg leave to Report. That it is the desire of Governour Lawrence that the Account of the French Neutrals which came from the Southern Governments into this Province be prepared and delivered to him, that he may lay the same before his Majestys Council at Hallifax for Payment. And further that his Excellency Gov[r] Lawrence is of Opinion that upon Applications made at home this Province will be reimbursed the necessary Charges it hath been at for the Support of the French Neutrals so called sent by the Government of Nova Scotia here, and that he will do every thing in his Power to assist this Government in obtaining the same ——By Order of the Committee——W. Brattle. In Council; Read and Concurred, and Ordered that this Report be accepted, and that the Committee who had the Disposal of the said French Neutrals with the Province Treasurer prepare the Accounts referred to accordingly.——In the House of Representatives; Read and Concurred——Consented to by the Lieutenant Governour."—*Ibid., p.* 394.

"Febru[a] 22, 1757. A Petition of Benoni Melancon one of the late Inhabitants of Nova Scotia Setting forth that He his Wife and Seven Children his Brother in Law & Wife and Four Children, were placed by the Government at Lancaster where they Lived Twelve Months enduring great hardships & Suffering Want till at length about Twenty Seven days since they left the Town, and went to Weymouth where he prays they may be allowed an House to Lodge in & Wood, and for the rest he will endeavour to maintain his Wife and Five Young Children, and place his Two Eldest Sons in some good Families. In Council; Read & Ordered that Sylvanus Bourn Esq[r] with such as the Honourable House shall join be a Committee to hear the Petitioner & any other Persons concerned, and report what they think proper to be done thereon. In the House of Representatives; Read & Concurr'd & Colonel Marcy & M[r] Turner are joined in the Affair."——*Ibid., p.* 400.

"Febru[a] 25, 1757. Sylvanus Bourn Esq[r] from the Committee on the Petition of Belloni Melancon made Report——That they had met and heard the Petitioner, and one of the Select Men of Lancaster relating the several matters therein complained of, and also heard the Representative of Weymouth where the French People mentioned in said Petition at present reside; and that it doth not appear that the Petitioner had any Grounds to Complain of the Select Men of Lancaster or either of them: relating the matters complained of and are therefore of Opinion that the said French People be ordered forthwith to return to Lancaster from whence they in a disorderly manner withdrew themselves

Which Report was read and accepted by both Houses & Ordered that the said French Neutrals so called be directed to return forthwith to the Town of Lancaster accordingly——Consented to by the Lieutent Governour."—*Ibid., p.* 412.

"Febru[a] 25, 1757. Col[o] Clap from the House of Representatives; came up to the Board with a Message to desire that the Committee for preparing the Account of the Charge of Maintaining the French Neutrals (so called) to be laid before Governour Lawrence may be directed to sit forthwith."—*Ibid., p.* 413.

"April 1, 1757. A Petition of Peter Boudreau one of the late French Inhabitants of Nova Scotia, Setting forth that He, his Wife and Family being Seven in all were placed at Scituate where they have endured Numberless Hardships being obliged to work hard, and when they have done their Work, that they are able to get little or nothing for it and that they are now threatned to have their Children taken from them, and therefore Praying Releif from this Court.——In Council; Read & Ordered that Samuel Watts & William Brattle Esq[rs] with such as the Honourable House shall appoint be a Committee to take this Petition under Consideration, and Report what they judge proper to be done thereon. In the House of Representatives; Read & Concurr'd, and Col[o] Cotton M[r] Prentice, and M[r] Humphrys are joined in the Affair."—*Ibid., p.* 420.

"April 8, 1757. A Petition of Samuel Livermore Esq[r] of Waltham in the County of Middlesex setting forth, that there have been a Number of the French Neutrals much greater than their proportion sent to the Town of Waltham, that they can be Supported much Cheaper in some other Towns of the Province and that many Towns are without any of the said French People.——Therefore praying that a part of them may be removed elsewhere

Read as also——A Petition of Daniel Henshaw and others the Select Men of the Town of Leicester, Praying that James Morris & Family, who were ordered there by this Court may be removed to some other Town where they may be more conveniently provided for, and at a Cheaper Rate than at Leicester.

In the House of Representatives——Ordered that M[r] Paine Major Noyes and Captain Taylor with such as the Honourable Board shall join be a Committee to Consider the Petitions of Samuel Livermore Esq[r] & Daniel Henshaw & others and Report thereon.——Also that the said Committee take under Consideration and Report what they judge proper to be done by this Court with regard to the Inhabitants late of Nova Scotia now within this Province——In Council Read & Concurr'd & John Erving & William Brattle Esq[rs] are joined in the Affair"—*Ibid., p.* 437.

"April 11, 1757. A Petition of Henry Gibbs Esq[r] of Newton—Praying the Order of this Court respecting Glude Benua his Wife and Five Children late Inhabitants of Nova Scotia, originally placed by this Government, and from thence sent to Oxford, but now resident in Newton, which Town having already the Care of Fourteen of said French People the said Gibbs prays in behalf of the Town of Newton that said Glude & his Family may be removed elsewhere.——which Petition being referred to the Committee of both Houses appointed on the Petition of Samuel Livermore Esq[r] said Committee reported that the said French Persons be removed to the Town of Dedham. In Council; Read &

Accepted and Ordered that the said French Inhabitants be removed from the Town of Newton to the Town of Dedham at the Charge of the Town of Newton, and that the Select Men of the Town of Dedham receive the said French Persons, and govern themselves with regard to them according to Law.——In the House of Representatives; Read & Concurr'd——Consented to by a Major Part of the Council "—*Ibid.*, *p* 444

"April 12, 1757. In the House of Representatives; Whereas there was a Vote or Order of this Court passed the 9th February last directing the Select Men of Plymouth to remove Charles Muis and Family some of the Neutral French from the Town of Plymouth to the Town of Wareham, but the said Charles Muis & Family being desirous of being removed to Marshfield and there appearing Mr Nathanael Ray Thomas ready to receive them & give Bond of Two Hundred Pounds Lawfull Money to save the Province from any Charge on said Charles & Family, and the Select Men of said Plymouth having removed them to Marshfield & took a Bond to the Province Treasurer for the Sum of Two Hundred Pounds to save the Province from Charges on Account of said Family.——Voted that said Charles Muis & Family be continued in said Town of Marshfield any Order or Resolve of this Court to the contrary notwithstanding, and that Thomas Foster Esqr be directed to deliver said Bond to the Province Treasurer.——In Council; Read & Concurr'd Consented to by a Major Part of the Council "—*Ibid.*, *p.* 451.

"April 16, 1757. In the House of Representatives; Voted that Thomas Flucker James Russell and Stephen Hall Esqrs with such as the Honourable Board shall join be a Committee to prepare an Account of the Charges this Province have been at in Supporting the late French Inhabitants of Nova Scotia, as well those who were immediately ordered here by that Government as those who arrived here from some of his Majestys Governments, that the last Account may be transmitted to Governour Lawrence as soon as may be and the other to Mr Bollan. In Council; Read & Concurred, and Samuel Watts & John Erving Esqrs are joined in the Affair——Consented to by a Major Part of the Council "—*Ibid.*, *p.* 466.

"April 19, 1757. In the House of Representatives; Whereas Charles Muis & Family some of the French Neutrals were ordered by a Vote of this Court of the 8th of February last to be removed from Plymouth to Wareham, but have been since removed to Marshfield which removal has been approved of by this Court, and there being still a considerable Number of said French Neutrals at Plymouth and none in the Town of Wareham——Voted that the Selectmen of Plymouth remove John Pelerine & Wife and Children, supposed to be Five in Number a Family of said French Neutrals to the Town of Wareham, and that the Select Men of the Town of Wareham be and hereby are directed to receive them, and provide for them as the Law directs. In Council; Read & Concurred Consented to by a Major Part of the Council "—*Ibid*, *p.* 478.

"April 20, 1757. A Petition of Thomas Foster Esqr of Plymouth—Setting forth that in June 1756. one Charles Muis and Family consisting of Nine Persons were permitted to go to Plymouth; that the Select Men refusing to take Care of them, the Petitioner undertook the Charge; that the said Family would have been able to have maintained themselves, had they continued in health, but so it fell out that they were all Sick, and one of the Number Died——Therefore Praying a Reimbursemt of his Expence upon them.——

In the House of Representatives; Read & Ordered that there be allowed and paid out of the Publick Treasury to the Petitioner the Sum of Eight Pounds Seven Shillings & ten Pence ¼ in full Discharge of his Account of Expences in Supporting Charles Muis & Family exhibited——In Council; Read & Concurred Consented to by a Major Part of the Council "—*Ibid.*, *p.* 486.

"April 22, 1757. A Petition of Henry Gibbs Esqr of Newton—Praying as Entered the 11th instant that the Town of Newtown may not be Burthened with the Support of Glude Benoni and Family lately Inhabitants of Nova Scotia, but that they may be removed to some other Town, together with the Report of the Committee thereupon——In Council; Read & accepted & Ordered that the said French Inhabitants be removed from the Town of Newtown to the Town of Dedham at the Charge of the Town of Newtown, and that the Selectmen of Dedham receive the said French Persons and govern themselves with regard to them according to Law. In the House of Representatives; Read and Concurred. Consented to by a Major Part of the Council——

A Petition of Samuel Livermore Esqr of Waltham——Praying that Seven of the French Inhabitants of Nova Scotia placed at Waltham may be removed elsewhere together with the Report of the Committee thereupon——In Council; Read and accepted and Ordered that the said French Inhabitants be removed from the Town of Waltham to the Town of Brookfield at the Charge of the Town of Waltham, and that the Selectmen of Brookfield receive the said French Persons and govern themselves with regard to them according to Law. In the House of Representatives; Read & Concurred Consented to by a Major Part of the Council "—*Ibid.*, *p.* 488.

"April 25, 1757. A Petition of Amos Fuller of Needham——Setting forth that there are Twelve of the French Inhabitants of Nova Scotia placed there, and as the Town is very small——Praying that they may be removed elsewhere——

In the House of Representatives; Read and Ordered that Five of the French Inhabitants late of Nova Scotia be removed from the Town of Needham to the Town of Wrentham at the Charge of the Town of Needham, and that the Selectmen of the Town of Wrentham receive the said French Persons, and govern themselves with regard to them according to Law.——In Council; Read and Concurred. Consented to by a Major Part of the Council "—*Ibid.*, *p.* 502.

Chap. 12. "May 28, 1756. The Secretary delivered the following Message from the Lieutenant Governour to both Houses——vizt

Gentlemen of the Council & House of Representatives,

The undoubted Accounts We have received of the Military Naval Preparations made in France, and the Appointment of a Gentleman of high Consideration there for his Knowledge in American Affairs to the chief Command of a Powerful Fleet, which in all probability is now at Sea, added to the repeated Accounts brought Us of some French Men of War having been lately seen on the Banks of Newfoundland are strong Intimations to Us to be upon our Guard, And I cannot upon this Occasion but recommend to your serious Consideration the Necessity of providing for the Defence of our Sea Coasts & more especially for putting both the Works & Stores of Castle William into such Order as that We may be prepared for any sudden Attack. and it appears to me that to this end it would be likewise requisite to provide a number of able & Skilful Gunners to direct in the Management of the great Artillery there——I shall give the proper Orders Gentlemen to see that the Militia are furnished with Arms & Ammunition according to Law; and shall chearfully Concur with you in every other measure, which the Safety of the Province may require."—*Council Records, vol. XXI, p.* 186.

"June 4, 1756. The Secretary carried down the following Message from his Honour the Lieutenant Governour to the House—viz[t]

Gentlemen of the House of Representatives,

I now send you Returns made to me of the Condition of the Fortifications in divers Maritime Towns in this Province, by Gentlemen I appointed to view the same, and as the whole Province may be much endangered by the Nakedness of those Places, & their disability to make Defence in Case of an Invasion by Sea of which We have no ground to Suppose ourselves free from danger. I must therefore desire you would give your speedy Attention to this important Affair, & make the necessary Provision for the Security of the Maritime Towns in the Province that may be exposed to the Enemy."—*Ibid*, *p.* 200.

"August 19, 1756. In the House of Representatives; Voted that the Sloop Massachusetts now in the Service & Pay of this Province, be as soon as may be equipped in manner following viz[t] with Six Guns that will carry Shot of Four Pounds, Two that will carry Shot of Six Pounds Twelve Swivel Guns, with Small Arms Powder & Ball equivalent, and that Sixty One able Bodied effective Men Officers included shall be put on Board said Sloop & Subsisted, whose Monthly Wages shall be as follows, viz[t] the Captain Six Pounds, Lieutenant Four Pounds, Master & Chirurgeon Three Pounds ten Shillings each, Boatswain & Carpenter Three Pounds each, Mate & Armourer Two Pounds ten Shillings each, Cook Steward & Cooper Two Pounds five Shillings each, & every Private Man Two Pounds; and whatever Prizes may be taken from the Enemy the following Distribution shall be made; viz[t] Three Sixteenth Parts to the Captain, Two to the Lieutenant Master & Chirurgeon, and Three to the Boatswain Carpenter Mate, Armourer, Cook, Steward & Cooper in equal Parts, And the remaining Eight Sixteenth Parts among the Private Men in equal Parts, and that the Duration of the Service be for Two Months & no longer.

And that His Excellency be desired to grant Commissions to a number of suitable Persons & to give all other necessary Directions accordingly. In Council; Read & Concur'd "—*Ibid*, *p.* 247.

"August 20, 1756. His Excellency sent the following Message to the House by the Deputy Secretary

Gentlemen of the House of Representatives,

War being now declared with France We may hourly expect that our Sea Coasts will be infested with Privateers, of that Nation, which will much Endanger our Trade from Europe and the West Indies, as als[o*] our Coasting Vessells which bring Us the most of our Bread Corn from the Southern Colonies:——Therefore I desire Gentlemen, you would make proper Provision for taking up some suitable vessell to be well Armed & Manned for the Defence of our Sea Coasts, which ought to be done without delay. In the Last War with France the Province maintained an Armed Snow & Brigantine, besides the Sloop Massachusetts for the service above mentioned "—*Ibid.*, *p* 249.

"Septem[r] 3, 1756. In the House of Representatives; Voted that Judge Russell M[r] Welles & Cap[t] White with such as the Hon[ble] Board shall join be a Committee to wait on his Excellency the Governour, requesting that he would use his interest with the Hon[ble] Washington Shirley Esq[r] Captain of his Majestys Ship Mermaid to make a short Cruise on our Coast more especially on the back of Cape Cod, there being certain Advice that one Privateer (if not more) is fitted out & gone from Louisbourgh & supposed (at Halifax) to be designed to visit our Coast in Quest of Provisions, The Sloop proposed for our Defence, being not yet prepared for that Service——In Council; Read & Non Concur'd "—*Ibid*, *p* 268.

"Septem[r] 10, 1756 In the House of Representatives; Voted that M[r] Speaker, M[r] Welles, M[r] Flucker M[r] Tasker & M[r] Gridley with such as the Hon[ble] Board shall join be a Committee in the Recess of the Court to Project some proper Method for the Security of the Sea Coast in this Time of Danger, and Report thereon at the next Sitting of this Court. In Council; Read & Concur'd and Jacob Wendell Ezekiel Chever, Andrew Oliver, and John Erving Esq[rs] are joined in the Affair."—*Ibid.*, *p.* 277.

"October 14, 1756. Report about Defending & Securing the Sea Coasts &[ca]

The Committee appointed to take under Consideration in the Recess of the Court, some proper Method for the Security of the Sea Coasts in this time of Danger, have attended that Service, and apprehending that the Governments of Connecticut and Rhode Island will provide themselves vessells for the Protection of their Trade & of their Coasters importing their Provisions &[ca] so far as the Island of Nantucket but no further; but after that our vessells will be greatly exposed to the Enemy, and our Fishery be intirely without Defence unless some Provision be made for their Protection.

They therefore beg leave to Report as their Opinion, that Two suitable Vessells be provided at the Charge of this Government, the one for the Protection of our Coasters from the Southward, and another for the Protection of the Fishery, and other inward Bound Vessells; and for which the Guns & other Warlike Stores which were reserved in the Sale of the Massachusetts Frigate now in the Commissarys Care, and of the Value of about Four Hundred Pounds Sterling may be well improved, & so far a saving to the Province and that a Committee be appointed for this Purpose: which is humbly Submitted——

By Order of the Committee Jacob Wendell.

* Missing from record.

In the House of Representatives; Read & Ordered that this Report be accepted and that Mr Speaker, Mr Welles & Mr Flucker with such as the Honble Board shall join be a Committee to Provide Two suitable Armed Vessells accordingly —— In Council; Read & Concur'd; and Thomas Hutchinson & John Erving Esqrs are joined in the Affair.—— Consented to by the Lieutenant Governour"—*Ibid*, p. 292.

"October 20, 1756. In the House of Representatives; Voted That John Quincy & Thomas Flucker Esqrs with such as the Honble Board shall join be a Committee to Farm out the Duties of Excise on Tea Coffee & China Ware in the County of Suffolk for one year from the 1st of November next. In Council; Read & Concur'd; and Samuel Watts Esqr is joined in the Affair Consented to by the Lieutenant Governour."——

On the same day the following persons were chosen committees to farm out the excise for the respective counties hereafter named; viz.,——

Henry Gibbs and Richard Reed, Esqs., on the part of the House, and Benjamin Lynde, Esq., on the part of the Council, for the county of Essex;—

James Russell and John Hunt, Esqs., on the part of the House, and Ezekiel Chever, Esq., on the part of the Council, for the county of Middlesex;—

Joseph Hawley, Esq., and Mr. Gideon Lyman, on the part of the House, and Eleazer Porter, Esq, on the part of the Council, for the county of Hampshire;—

Timothy Payne and William Richardson, Esqs., on the part of the House, and John Chandler, Esq., on the part of the Council, for the county of Worcester;—

David Stockbridge, Esq., and Capt. Ebenezer Sprout, on the part of the House, and John Cushing, Esq, on the part of the Council, for the county of Plymouth;—

James Otis and Rowland Cotton, Esqs., on the part of the House, and John Otis, Esq., on the part of the Council, for the county of Barnstable;—

Samuel White, Esq., and Mr. Thomas Morey, on the part of the House, and George Leonard, Esq, on the part of the Council, for the county of Bristol;—

John Bradbury, Esq, and Mr. James Gowen, on the part of the House, and John Hill, Esq., on the part of the Council, for the county of York;—

John Norton and Zaccheus Mayhew, Esqs., on the part of the House, and John Sumner, Esq, on the part of the Council, for the county of Dukes county;—

Abishai Folger, Esq, and Mr. Richard Coffin, on the part of the House, and Jonathan , Esq., on the part of the Council, for the county of Nantucket.—*Ibid.*, p. 299.

"Janua 28, 1757. In the House of Representatives; Ordered that John Murray Esqr be of the Committee appointed to Farm out the Duties of Excise on Tea Coffee & China Ware in the County of Worcester for One Year from the first of November last in the room of William Richardson Esqr who desires to be Excused from that Service——In Council; Read & Concur'd Consented to by the Lieutenant Governour"—*Ibid*, p. 354.

"January 13, 1757. The Report of the Committee for Letting out to Farm the Duties of Excise upon Tea, Coffee & China Ware in the County of Middlesex with their Account of Expence amounting to £3. 9. 6.——

In the House of Representatives; Read & Accepted & Ordered that there be allowed and paid out of the Publick Treasury to the said Committee the Sum of Forty Two Shillings & Six Pence in full discharge of their Account of time & Expences mentioned. In Council; Read & Concurr'd——Consented to by the Lieutenant Governour."—*Ibid.*, p. 331.

The above report from the committee appointed to farm out the excise for Middlesex county, was followed by reports from the committees for the other counties, and the dates of these reports, together with the names of farmers of excise appointed by them, respectively, are as follows.—

January 17, 1757. York county.—*Ibid.*, p. 337.
January 17, 1757. Nantucket county.—*Ibid*, p. 337.
January 18, 1757. Hampshire county—*Ibid*, p. 339.
January 21, 1757. Essex county.—*Ibid*, p 345.
January 25, 1757. Barnstable county.—*Ibid.*, p. 348.
February 12, 1757. Worcester county; to Caleb Richardson, for £7. 10*s*.—*Ibid.*, p. 377.
April 20, 1757. Bristol county.—*Ibid.*, p. 486.

"April 22, 1757. In the House of Representatives; Whereas the Committee for Farming the Excise on Tea &ca in the County of Suffolk have found it impracticable to dispose of it to the Value,

Therefore Voted that a Collector of said Duty be Chosen and Commissioned who shall be under Oath, have and Exercise the same Powers, as by Law the Farmers of said Excise in the other Counties have and Enjoy, and be accountable to this Court for his Collections, and receive Five ₩ Cent as a Reward for his Service——the Choice to be made by the Two Houses to morrow Morning at Ten a Clock ——In Council; Read & Concurred. Consented to by a Major Part of the Council"—*Ibid*, p. 492.

"April 23, 1757. John Chandler Esqr went down to the House of Representatives with a Message to inform them that the Board were now ready to proceed as was proposed to the Choice of a Person to Collect the Duty of Excise upon Tea Coffee, & China Ware for the County of Suffolk——

Accordingly the Two Houses proceeded to the Choice, and Mr John Cotton was elected by a Major Vote."—*Ibid*, p. 497.

"March 8, 1758. Gamaliel Bradford Esqr from the Committee for farming out the Excise on Coffee, Tea and China Ware in the County of Plymouth made report that they had sold the same to Mr John Russell of Plymouth for the Sum of Sixty one pounds six shillings and eight pence. And pray'd Allowance of their Expence, and for their time amounting to twenty eight shillings and eight pence.

In the House of Representatives. Read & Accepted; And Resolved That there be allowed and paid out of the Public Treasury the Sum of Twenty eight shillings and eight pence to the said Committee in discharge of their account of time and expences exhibited. In Council. Read and Concurred. Consented to by the Governor."—*Ibid.*, *vol. XXII.*, p. 254.

The above report from the committee appointed to farm out the excise for Plymouth county, was followed by reports from the committees for the other counties, and the dates of these reports, together with the names of farmers of excise appointed by them, respectively, are as follows:—

March 23, 1758. Suffolk county; to Mr. William Story, for £650.—*Ibid.*, *p.* 293.
March 23, 1758. York county; to Mr. James Sayward, for £40. 4*s.*—*Ibid.*, *p.* 293.
April 29, 1758. Essex county; to Mr. Jacob Ashton, for £378.—*Ibid.*, *p.* 349.
June 5, 1758. Worcester county; to Mr. Paul Crocker, for £11. 10*s.*—*Ibid.*, *p.* 371.
June 5, 1758. Barnstable county; to Mr. Isaac Hinckley, for £18. 13*s.* 4*d.*—*Ibid.*, *p.* 372.
October 7, 1758. Bristol county; to Mr. George Leonard, for £7. 1*s.*—*Ibid.*, *p* 417.
October 11, 1758. Nantucket county; to Mr. Thomas Arthur, for £9. 6*s.* 8*d.*—*Ibid*, *p.* 425.
January 10, 1759. Middlesex county; to Mr. John White, for £160—*Ibid.*, *p.* 472.

"January 11, 1759. In the House of Representatives. Voted That Thomas Flucker and Thomas Goldthwait Esq^rs with Such as the honourable Board shall join be a Committee to farm out the Duties of Excise on Tea Coffee and China Ware in the County of Suffolk the current Year. In Council Read and Concurred and Samuel Watts Esq is joined in the Affair. Consented to by the Governor."—*Ibid.*, *p.* 475.

On the same day the following persons were chosen committees to farm out the excise for the respective counties hereafter named; viz.,—

Joseph Gerrish, Esq., and Mr. Daniel Gidding, on the part of the House, and Benjamin Lynde, Esq, on the part of the Council, for the county of Essex;—

Andrew Bordman and James Russell, Esqs., on the part of the House, and William Brattle, Esq, on the part of the Council, for the county of Middlesex;—

Elijah Williams and Timothy Dwight, Esqs., on the part of the House, and Israel Williams, Esq, on the part of the Council, for the county of Hampshire;—

Timothy Ruggles and Edward Hartwell, Esqs., on the part of the House, and John Chandler, Esq, on the part of the Council, for the county of Worcester;—

George Watson, Esq., and Mr. John Brewster, on the part of the House, and Gamaliel Bradford, Esq, on the part of the Council, for the county of Plymouth;—

Rowland Cotton and Edward Bacon, Esqs, on the part of the House, and Silvanus Bourn, Esq., on the part of the Council, for the county of Barnstable;—

Samuel White, Esq, and Capt. Thomas Morey, on the part of the House, and George Leonard, Esq, on the part of the Council, for the county of Bristol;—

John Bradbury, Esq, and Mr. Benjamin Chadburn, on the part of the House, and Richard Cutt, Esq, on the part of the Council, for the county of York;—

John Norton, Esq, and Mr. Matthew Mayhew, on the part of the House, and John Sumner, Esq, on the part of the Council, for the county of Dukes county;—

Abishai Folger and Richard Coffin, Esqs, on the part of the House, and Josiah Cotton, Esq, on the part of the Council, for the county of Nantucket—*Ibid.*

"March 28, 1759. In the House of Representatives Voted That the several Comittees appointed to farm out the Excise upon Tea, Coffee &c be directed to suspend that Affair 'till the further Order of this Court. In Council. Read and Concurred. Consented to by the Governor."—*Ibid*, *p.* 640.

"Janu^a 7, 1757 In the House of Representatives; Ordered that Col^o Clap Mr Gibbs of Newton & Col^o Miller with such as the Honble Board shall join be a Committee to examine the Act lately passed this Court for providing and maintaining Two Armed Vessells to guard the Coast &^ca——Report what Defects they find therein, and what they judge proper to be done for remedying the same—In Council; Read and Concurr'd, and Ezekiel Chever and William Brattle Esq^rs are joined in the Affair."—*Ibid.*, *vol. XXI*, *p.* 318.

"Janu^a 18, 1757. In Council; Whereas in the Act lately passed this Court providing Two Armed Vessells &^ca it is not so fully expressed what Select Men or Assessors are impowered and directed to Assess & Tax the Vessells therein mentioned, Therefore Resolved That the Select Men or Assessors to be chosen next March be the Persons that shall Assess and Tax the Vessells aforesaid that have been liable to be Taxed from the First of last November to this time, and from this time to the first of November, and the Select Men or Assessors that after next March shall be chosen Annually during the Continuance of said Act shall be the Persons that shall Assess and Tax all the Vessells in their respective Towns liable to be taxed, the time to be reckoned from the First of November Annually; and the Treasurer of this Province is hereby directed to send to the Assessors of the Maritime Towns a Copy of said Act & this Resolve.——In the House of Representatives; Read & Concurr'd—Consented to by the Lieutenant Governour."—*Ibid.*, *p.* 339.

"Febru^a 18, 1757. In the House of Representatives; Voted that there be the following Establishment of Wages made for the Officers and Seamen to be employed in the Service of the Province on Board the Vessells now Building for Guarding the Coast.—vizt

	£	s.	
For a Captain	£8	0s.	ꝑ Month
For a Lieutenant	5	0	ditto
For a Master	4	0	ditto
For a Pilot	4	0	ditto
For a Doctor	3	10	ditto
For a Chaplain	3	10	ditto
For a Mate	3	0	ditto
For a Carpenter	3	0	ditto
For a Gunner	3	0	ditto
For a Boatswain	3	0	ꝑ Month
For a Cooper	2	10	ditto
For an Armourer	2	10	ditto
For a Coxswain	2	10	ditto
For a Boatswains Mate	2	5	ditto
For a Steward	2	5	ditto
For a Cook	2	5	ditto
For a Quarter Master	2	5	ditto
For each Seaman	2	0	ditto

In Council; Read & Concurr'd Consented to by the Lieutenant Governour."—*Ibid., p.* 392.

"April 5, 1757. In the House of Representatives; Ordered that Mr Tasker Mr Plucker and Richard Reed Esqr with such as the Honourable Board shall join be a Committee to take under Consideration some suitable method for Manning the Province Ship & Snow designed to Guard the Coast, and what Number of Men they judge proper the Establishment for each of said Vessells be made for and Report. In Council; Read & Concurr'd and Jacob Wendell and John Erving Esqrs are joined in the Affair.——

* * * *

In Council; Ordered that the Sherriff of the County of Suffolk be and hereby is impowered and directed to Impress Thirty Seamen for the Manning the Snow Prince of Wales Nathanael Dowse Commander in order to her Proceeding upon his intended Cruize as soon as may be.——In the House of Representatives; Read & Concurr'd Consented to by a Major Part of the Council"—*Ibid, p.* 425.

"April 8, 1757. The Committee appointed to Consider of suitable Method for Manning the Province Ship & Snow, and of the Number of Men needfull for that purpose

That there be One Hundred and Twenty five Men allowed for Manning the Ship Officers included.

And for the Snow Eighty Five Men Officers included——

And for Encouragement of able bodied Men to inlist in the above Service, that One Months Wages be advanced to each Private Man that shall inlist to be deducted out of his Pay. and that the Impost Officer be directed to pay into the Province Treasury what Sums he has Collected by virtue of the Act for Building the abovementioned Vessells to enable the Treasurer to pay the same in manner as aforesaid

JACOB WENDELL ₱ Order.

In the House of Representatives; Read & Ordered that this Report be accepted——In Council; Read & Concurr'd Consented to by a Major Part of the Council"—*Ibid., p.* 437.

"April 11, 1757. A Message from the House of Representatives; by Colo Cotton was brought up to the Board to inform them that one Henry Wilson an Inlisted Soldier in the present Expedition is impressed aboard the Province Snow Prince of Wales Captn Dowse therefore desiring the Board would give Orders for his Discharge, and that they would be pleased to give Orders to Captain Dowse not to Impress any Persons inlisted in the Land Service, nor any Persons out of Coasting Vessells."—*Ibid., p.* 445.

"April 15, 1757. Major Reed came up to the Board with a Message from the House of Representatives; to inquire whether the Council had appointed a Commander for the Province Ship destined for the Protection of the Fishery &ca——

John Chandler Esqr went down to the House of Representatives with a Message from the Council to inform the House that yesterday at a full Board it was agreed to defer the Appointment of a Commander for the Ship abovementioned untill Tuesday next."—*Ibid., p.* 460.

"April 15, 1757. In the House of Representatives; Voted that the following Message be sent to the Honourable his Majestys Council——vizt

May it please your Honours

It is with great Concern that the House are informed by your Message that the Consideration of the Affair of putting the Province Ship into Commission is again referred for several days to come, notwithstanding this House fully sensible of the necessity of her being speedily Commissioned signified their earnest desire thereof by Message to the honourable Council Six days ago, and being still of the same Opinion now beg leave to represent to your Honours that as there is now an Embargo on all our Navigation the Mariners sensible of this, and under necessity to get Employ as soon as possible would very readily in sufficient Numbers inlist themselves; whilst if there should be any further delay there is danger that an Impress would be necessary which might not only take up longer time to procure the Men, and force many against their Wills, who will doubtless embrace the first Opportunity to Desert, & so give continually fresh occasions to renew an Impress, a thing abhorrent to the English Constitution and peculiarly odious in this Countrey but also distress the Trade & Fishery; which this Ship at an immense Cost to the Province is designed to protect, by breaking up the Crews & Companies of many of the Vessells, & besides give occasion for horrid Murders a late Instance of which We have experienced with uncommon Aggravations——

We would but just mention that as it is necessary the Ship should be fit for the Sea as soon as the Embargo is over in order to answer the Purposes for which She was Built, so we think this can scarcely be done but by the Assistance of the Officers & Company; or at least neither so well nor by a great deal so Cheap; a Consideration of much Weight in a time of such a heavy Burthen of Charges on the Province. For these and divers other reasons that might be urged we earnestly move your Honours that Commissions may be made out as soon as possible to some suitable Person to Command and Officers to assist in Navigating the said Ship that so She may be with the greatest Dispatch Manned, and fitted for the Sea for his Majestys Service"—*Ibid., p.* 461.

"June 1, 1757. In the House of Representatives—Voted That the Treasurer be & hereby is directed to pay one Months Advance Wages to each of the Officers belonging to the Province Ship & Snow lately built and equipped by this Government to guard the Coast In Council——Read & Concurred. Consented to by a Major Part of the Council"—*Ibid., vol. XXII., p.* 15.

"June 15, 1757. In the House of Representatives. Voted That on the Ship King George, lately built and equip'd by this Province to guard the Coast, being furnished with two more nine pounders, the same Establishment of Wages and Subsistence be made for twenty five Seamen more with that made for those already allowed for that Service. In Council——Read and Concurred. Consented to by a Major Part of the Council."—*Ibid., p.* 57.

"November 26, 1757. In the House of Representatives. Voted That the following

Establishment be made for the Sloop Massachusetts, Thomas Sanders Master, employed in the Service of this Government, viz[t]

For the Sloop two shillings & eight pence ꝑ Tun ꝑ Month
For the Captain two Pounds thirteen shill[s] & four pence ꝑ Ditto
For the Mate two Pounds, six shillings & eight pence ꝑ Ditto
For four Sailors each, One pound six shill[s] & eight pence ꝑ Ditto

to be accounted from the date of the last Pay Roll and to continue till the further order of this Court. In Council. Read and Concurred. Consented to by the Governor."—*Ibid.*, *p.* 120.

"January 5, 1758. In the House of Representatives Voted That his Excellency the Governor with the Advice of his Majesty's Council be desired to issue his Warrant on the Treasury for Payment of the Officers and Seamen who have been employed in the Service on board the Province Ship King George, and also such Tradesmens and other Bills for the Province Ship and Snow as the Grants for building said Vessells are insufficient to discharge, out of the Appropriation for the eighteen hundred Men raised by this Government for his Majesty's Service under the Command of his Excellency the Earl of Loudoun. In Council. Read and Concurred. Consented to by the Governor."—*Ibid.*, *p.* 192.

"March 14, 1758. In the House of Representatives Voted That the following Establishment of Wages be made for One hundred and fifty Men (Officers included) for the Province Ship called the King George to continue until the first day of September next, provided the War with France shall continue so long viz[t]——

For a Captain	£8	0*s.*	ꝑ month
For a Leuitenant	5	0	ꝑ ditto
For a Master	4	0	ꝑ ditto
For a Pilot	4		ꝑ ditto
For a Surgeon	4		ꝑ ditto
For a Surgeon's Mate	2	1	ꝑ ditto
For a Chaplain	3	10	ꝑ ditto
For a Mate	3		ꝑ ditto
For a Carpenter	3		ꝑ ditto
For a Gunner	3		ꝑ ditto
For a Boatswain	3		ꝑ ditto
For a Sailmaker	2	1	ꝑ ditto
For an Armourer	2	1	ꝑ month
For a Coxswain	2	1	ꝑ ditto
For a Boatswain's Mate	2		ꝑ ditto
For a Steward	2		ꝑ ditto
For a Cook	2	0	ꝑ ditto
For a Quarter Master	2	0	ꝑ ditto
For each Seaman	2	0	ꝑ ditto

And that his Excellency be desired to give Orders for inlisting said Men accordingly. In Council. Read and Concurred. Consented to by the Governor."—*Ibid.*, *p.* 265.

"March 16, 1758. In the House of Representatives. Voted. That the following Allowance of Provisions be made to each Man in the Service on board the Province Ship of War King George viz[t]

Six Pounds of Bread
Four Pounds of Pork
Three Pounds of Beef
One and an half pound of Flour } ꝑ Week.
One Quart of Peas or Beans
Seven Jills of Rum——and
Three Galons of Beer.

In Council. Read and Concurred. Consented to by the Governor."—*Ibid.*, *p.* 271.

"June 2, 1758. In Council—Ordered That John Osborne, John Erving, William Brattle, Gamaliel Bradford and Thomas Hancock Esq with such as the honourable House shall appoint be a Committee to inquire into the Conduct of the Captain, Officers, and Seamen of the Province Snow Prince of Wales at the time she was taken by the Enemy, and into the Occasion of the Loss of said Snow

In the House of Representatives. Read and Concurred, and M[r] Goldthwait, M[r] Flucker, Col[o] White, Benjamin Prat Esq, M[r] Witt and Capt[n] Livermore are joined in the Affair."—*Ibid.*, *p.* 369.

"June 15, 1758. The Committee appointed to inquire into the Conduct of the Captain, Officers and Seamen of the Snow Prince of Wales at the time of her being taken, and respecting the Loss of said Snow made the following Report. viz[t]

That they had carefully examined the said Captain, and all the persons which were to be found that were taken in said Snow, and returned home viz[t] Marmaduke Masterman, Mate of said Snow, John Phillips jun[r] and Joseph Lovell Midshipmen, and after a full hearing of said Evidence and having taken the same in writing agreeable to the Interrogatories annexed—the Committee were of opinion That the said Captains Conduct in going so near to Louisbourgh was inconsistent with the Instructions which he had received from his Excellency the Governor. That the said Captain was to blame in lying to until the Enemy came up with him, and delivering up the said Snow without making any Resistance—Yet notwithstanding they do not apprehend that Captain Dowse did deliver up the said Vessell either through Cowardice or Treachery, but through Error of Judgment——And further that it appeared to the Committee that the other Officers and Seamen on board the said Snow were not blameable—

Signed—In the name of the Committee J. OSBORNE.

In Council. Read and thereupon Resolved That although there were no Marks of Cowardice or Treachery in Capt[n] Dowse's Behaviour, yet it appears that his going so near Louisbourgh in his passage to the Banks was extremely ill judged, and not warranted by his Instructions from his Excellency the Governor. And that hereby, as well as by suffering a Ship so much superior to come so near him when he was at no greater distance from an Enemy's Port before he endeavoured to avoid, or escape from her, the said Captⁿ Dowse unnecessarily exposed the Province Vessell, and that his Conduct herein has been unjustifiable and blame worthy. In the House of Representatives. Read and Concurred."—*Ibid.*, *p.* 402.

"October 7, 1758. The Secretary by Order of his Excellency the Governor delivered the following Message to the two Houses respectively vizᵗ

Gentlemen of the Council and House of Representatives

Hearing that the Snow Prince of Wales built and fitted out by the Government of this Province, and which was taken last Year by the Enemy was in Louisbourgh Harbour. I put in my Claim to her in the name of the Province. But before my Letters reached the Admiral, his Excellency of his own Motion acquainted me that he had retaken our Snow and would return her, For which I gave him the Thanks of the Province. His Excellency has since acquainted me, that She shall be delivered to Mʳ Clarke agreeable to my Claim.

I shall by no means think of fitting her out again, I would therefore advise with You what it were best to have done with her.

Province House Octʳ 7, 1758. T Pownall.

In the House of Representatives Ordered That Mʳ Russell, Mʳ Flucker and Mʳ Goldthwait with such as the honourable Board shall appoint be a Committee to take under consideration his Excellency's Message to the two Houses of this Forenoon, and report what they judge proper to be done thereon. In Council Read and Concurred and Sir William Pepperrell Barᵗ and John Erving Esqʳˢ are joined in the Affair."—*Ibid*, *p.* 418.

"October 14, 1758. The Committee appointed on his Excellency's Message of the 7ᵗʰ Instant relating to the Snow Prince of Wales made the following Report vizᵗ

Pursuant to the within Order We have considered of the Affair of the Snow Prince of Wales, and are humbly of opinion that his Excellency be desired to write to the Gentleman he appointed to Act as Agent relating to her, to take an Inventory of all the Stores that belong to her, and send Account of the state and condition of the Vessell and Stores by the first opportunity in order that she may be sold here to the highest Bidder.

Signed Wᵐ Pepperrell. ⅌ Order.

In Council. Read and Accepted. In the House of Representatives. Read and Concurred. Consented to by the Governor."—*Ibid*, *p.* 435.

"January 3, 1759. The Secretary by order of his Excellency the Governor delivered the following Message to the two Houses respectively.

Gentlemen of the Council and House of Representatives.

Conformable to a Vote of the General Court I ordered the Snow Prince of Wales to be sold, and appointed his Honor the Lieutenant Governor and the honourable Mʳ Erving to sell her. By their Report of their Doings to Me, You will see there is Two hundred and Fifty five Pounds, the Appropriation of which, You will please to consider.

Janʸ 3: 1759. T Pownall:—

In the House of Representatives. Ordered That the Committee appointed by his Excellency to sell the Province Snow Prince of Wales be directed to pay the Proceeds arising by the Sale of said Vessell into the Public Treasury for the further order of this Court. In Council. Read and Concurred. Consented to by the Governor"—*Ibid*, *p.* 449.

"March 15, 1759. In the House of Representatives. Voted That the following Establishment of Wages be made for One hundred and fifty Men (Officers included) for the Province Ship called the King George to continue until the first day of September next, provided the War with France shall continue so long vizᵗ

For a Captain	Eight pounds per Month
For a Lieutenant	Five pounds ditto
For a Master	Four pounds dᵒ
For a Pilot	Four pounds dᵒ
For a Surgeon	Four pounds dᵒ
For a Surgeon's Mate	Two pounds ten shillings dᵒ
For a Chaplain	Three pounds ten shillings dᵒ
For a Mate	Three pounds dᵒ
For a Carpenter	Three pounds dᵒ
For a Gunner	Three pounds dᵒ
For a Boatswain	Three pounds dᵒ
For a Sailmaker	Two pounds ten shillings dᵒ
For an Armourer	Two pounds ten shillings dᵒ
For a Coxswain	Two pounds ten shillings dᵒ
For a Boatswains Mate	Two pounds five shillings dᵒ
For a Steward	Two pounds five shillings dᵒ
For a Cook	Two pounds dᵒ
For a Quarter Master	Two pounds five shillings dᵒ
For each Seaman	Two pounds dᵒ

And that his Excellency be desired to give orders for inlisting said Men accordingly. In Council. Read and Concurred. Consented to by the Governor."—*Ibid.*, *p* 597.

"March 15, 1759. In the House of Representatives Voted That the following Allowance of Provisions be made to each man in the Service on board the Province Ship of War King George. vizᵗ

Six pounds of Bread
Four pounds of Pork
Four pounds of Beef
One pound and half of Flour } ⅌ week.
One quart of Peas or Beans
Seven Jills of Rum
Three Galons of Beer

In Council. Read and Concurred. Consented to by the Governor."—*Ibid.*

"March 28, 1759. A Memorial of Captⁿ Benjª Hallowell junʳ Commander of the Ship King George—Representing the difficulty he meets with in getting his Ship Manned occasioned by the great demand for Men for the Transport Service. And Praying that he may be impowered to impress out of inward bound Vessells a sufficient number of Men to make up his Complement.
In the House of Representatives Voted That the Captain General be desired to give Orders to Captⁿ Hallowell to impress out of the inward bound Vessells so many Seamen as to make up the Compliment of Men (with those he hath already inlisted) to compleat the number allowed by this Court to man the Ship King George of which said Hallowell is Commander. In Council. Read and Concurred. Consented to by the Governor."—*Ibid., p.* 639.

Chap. 15. "By the Honourable Spencer Phips Esqʳ Lieutenant Governour & Commander in Chief, in & over his Majesty's Province of the Massachusetts Bay in New England.

A Proclamation.

Whereas the Great & General Court or Assembly of this Province at their Setting held by Adjournment the Fourteenth Day of January last, pass'd an Act entitled, an Act for preventing the Exportation of Provisions & Warlike Stores out of this Province; wherein (among other Things) it is enacted, 'That if the Govʳ or Commander in Chief, for the Time being shall see fit, with the Advice & Consent of the Council, to issue a Proclamation prohibiting the Exportation of Provisions or Warlike Stores out of the Province, for any Time after the Twentieth Day of June, and not exceeding the Twentieth Day of November following in this present Year, the Master & Owner or Owners, Factor & Factors of any Vessel or Vessels on board of which such Provisions or Warlike Stores, contrary to such Proclamation, shall be respectively liable to the Pains & Penalties, as if the same had been exported before the said Twentieth Day of June, contrary to the said Act:'
And whereas the said Great & General Court at their Session in October last, did make & pass an Act for further continuing the said Act for preventing the Exportation of Provisions & Warlike Stores out of this Province, untill the Twentieth Day of December next.
I have thought fit, with the Advice & Consent of his Majesty's Council of this Province, further to prohibit the Exportation of Provisions or Warlike Stores from any part of this Province untill after the Twentieth Day of December next: And all Persons concerned are required to govern themselves accordingly.
Given at the Council-Chamber in Boston the Nineteenth Day of November 1756 In the Thirtieth Year of the Reign of our Sovereign Lord George the second, by the Grace of God, of Great Britain, France & Ireland, King, Defender of the Faith &c.
By Honour's Command, with the
Advice & Consent of the Council S. PHIPS
Thoˢ Clarke Depty Secry
God save the King."—*Records of Civil Commissions; in Secretary's Office, vol.* 2., *p.* 312.
"Januª 7, 1757. A Petition of Daniel Sergeant Praying Liberty to Export Two Hundred & Fifty Bushels of Corn to Barbadoes upon giving Bond to Land the same there.
In Council; Read & Ordered that the Prayer of this Petition be granted and that the Petitioner be allowed to Export the Two Hundred & Fifty Bushels of Corn above mentioned to the Island of Barbadoes aforesaid, and the Commissioner of Impost is hereby Impowered & directed to take the said Bond which shall be cancelled on the Petitioners producing a Certificate from the principal Officers of the Customs of the said Island that the said Corn was bona fide Landed and disposed of there.——In the House of Representatives; Read & Concur'd——Consented to by the Lieutenᵗ Governour."—*Council Records, vol. XXI., p.* 317.
"Januª 7, 1757. A Petition of Benjamin & Edward Davis Praying leave to Export Fifty Barrells of Beef to the Island of Antigua they being ready to enter into Bonds for the Delivery of them in said Port.——
In Council; Read & Ordered that the Prayer of this Petition be granted, and that the Petitioners be and hereby are impowered to transport the Beef above mentioned they giving Bond to the Commissioner of Impost in the Sum of One Thousand Pounds Sterling to Land the said Beef in the Island of Antigua aforesaid & upon producing a certificate from the Principal Officers of the Customs of the said Island of Antigua, that the said Beef has been bona fide Landed & disposed of there the said Bond to be Cancelled——In the House of Representatives; Read & Concur'd——Consented to by the Lieutenᵗ Governʳ"—*Ibid.*

GEORGE R. [L. S.] "Additional Instructions to Our Trusty and Wellbeloved William Shirley Esqʳ Our Captain General and Governor in Chief in and over Our Province and Territory of the Massachusetts Bay in New England in America; Given at Our Court at Kensington the Fifth day of July 1756, in the Thirtieth Year of Our Reign.

Whereas by Our Declaration dated the Seventeenth day of May last We have thought fit to declare War against the French King, his Subjects and Vassals; and whereas We have been inform'd, that heretofore in times of War Our Subjects in several of Our Colonies and Plantations in America, have corresponded with Our Enemies and supplied them with Provisions and Warlike-Stores, whereby Our Service has been greatly prejudiced and the safety of Our Dominions endanger'd.
It is therefore Our express Will and Pleasure, that you do, with the Advice of Our Council, take the most speedy and effectual Measures to hinder all Correspondance between any of Our Subjects Inhabiting Our Province of the Massachusetts Bay under Your

Government and the Subjects of the said French King, and to prevent any of the Colonies or Plantations belonging to Our Enemies or other Places possessed by them in America being supplied, either by Land or by Sea, from Our said Prov^ce under Your Government with Provisions or Warlike-Stores of any kind.

And in Case you shall find it necessary to have an Act passed for the Purposes abovementioned you are earnestly to recommend it in Our Name to Our Council and to the Representatives of Our said Province to prepare and pass such Act.

G. R."—*Records of Crown Commissions; in Secretary's Office, vol.* 1, *p.* 148.

"January 8, 1757. His Honour the Lieutenant Governour sent the following Message to the Two Houses—vizt

Gentlemen of the Council & House of Representatives,

Since your Last Session I had the Honour to receive his Majestys Additional Instruction signifying his Royal Pleasure that the most effectual Measures should be taken to prevent all Supplies of Provisions or Warlike Stores being sent from hence to the French and all Correspondence with them.——As the Force of your Act for these Purposes expired during your late Recess I have with the Advice & Consent of His Majestys Council given Orders to the Impost Officer to Clear no Vessells having on Board any of the foregoing Commodities without Special Licence untill the General Court should have Opportunity of resuming the Consideration of these Matters, the Force of this Order will expire likewise the 10th instant.—

I therefore earnestly recommend it to you Gentlemen to Frame a Law which shall effectually prevent the Enemy receiving Succours or Intelligence from Us."—*Council Records, vol. XXI., p.* 319.

"Janu^a 10, 1757. The Secretary by Order of His Honour the Lieutenant Governour communicated to the Two Houses a Letter dated the 9th October 1756. from the Right Honourable the Lords for Trade & Plantations Signifying his Majestys Pleasure that an Embargo be laid on all Vessells carrying Provisions to any other than his Majestys Colonies & Plantations."—*Ibid., p.* 321.

"Janu^a 10, 1757. Samuel Welles, Esqr came up from the House of Representatives with the following Message to His Honour the Lieutenant Governour——vizt

May it Please your Honour,

Pursuant to your Honours Message this Morning the House have appointed a Committee to bring in a Bill to prevent the Exportation of Provisions &^ca to the Enemy, but as We apprehend it is of great Importance that some effectual Provision be made for the same purpose through the Continent to accomplish which the Right Hono^ble the Earl of Loudouns Approbation & Influence will be the most likely means; the House therefore humbly apprehend that it will be proper to Suspend this Affair a few days till his Lordships Arrival, and humbly pray your Honour in the mean time with the Advice of his Majestys Council to give such Orders in this Affair as the Publick Interest & Safety may require"—*Ibid.*

"Letter from the Right Honourable Board of Trade, to Governor Shirley—

WHITEHALL October 9th 1756.

Sir.

It having been represented to His Majesty, that the several Islands and Colonies belonging to the French in America, have in Times of War been frequently supplyed with Provisions of various kinds, by means of the Trade carried on from His Majesty's Islands and Colonies to the Colonies and Settlements belonging to the Dutch, and other neutral Powers; it is His Majesty's Pleasure, that you do forthwith upon the receipt of this Order, give immediate Directions, that an Embargo be laid, during His Majesty's Pleasure, upon all Ships and Vessels clearing out with Provisions from any Port or Place within your Government, except those which shall be employed in carrying Provisions to any other of His Majesty's Colonies and Plantations, which Ships or Vessels are to be allowed to Sail from time to time, provided that the Masters or Owners do, before they are permitted to take any Provisions on board, enter into Bond (with two Sureties of known Residence there and Ability to answer the Penalty) with the chief Officers of the Customs of the Ports or Places from whence such Ships or Vessels shall set Sail, to the value of One Thousand Pounds, if the Ship be of less burthen than one hundred Tons, and of the Sum of two thousand Pounds, if above that burthen, that the Cargos of such Ships or Vessels, the particulars of which are to be expressed in the Bonds, shall not be landed in any other ports or places than such as belong to His Majesty, or are in possession of His Subjects, and that they will within twelve months after the Date thereof, the Danger of the Seas excepted, produce Certificates under the hands & seals of the principal officers of the Customs, at such Ports or Places, for which such Ships or Vessels cleared out, that the said Cargoes, expressing the particulars thereof, have actually been landed there, and when there shall be cause to suspect, that such Certificates are false and counterfeit, you shall take especial Care, that such Security be not cancelled or vacated, untill you shall have been informed from the said principal Officers of the Customs, that the Matter and Contents thereof are just and true, and in case the Masters or Owners of such Ships or Vessels shall not produce the said Certificates within the time limited, you are to attest the Copies of such Bonds, under your hand & seal, and to cause prosecution thereof, and you are also to give directions that no Person be admitted to be Security for another who has bonds standing out undischarged, unless he be esteemed responsible for more than the Value of such Bonds.

And in order the more fully to Answer His Majesty's Intention of distressing the Enemy and to render His Orders herein the more effectual, you are to take care in case the Masters or Owners of any Ships or Vessels having cleared out from the Colony under your Government, laden with Provisions for any of His Majesty's other Colonies or Islands, shall be detected in causing collusive Captures to be made of the Cargoes, that the severest Penalties be inflicted upon the Offenders, which the Laws will in such cases allow of

We are,
Sir
Your most Obedient
humble Servants
DUNK HALIFAX
ANDREW STONE
JAMES OSWALD "—*Records of*

WILLIAM SHIRLEY Esqr Governor of the Massachusetts Bay

Crown Commissions; in Secretary's Office, vol. 1, *p.* 144.

"A Proclamation Prohibiting the Exportation of Provisions, without Bonds being Given. By the Honourable Spencer Phips Esqr Lieutenant Govr and Commander in Chief, in & over his Majesty's Province of the Massachusetts Bay in New England.

A Proclamation.

It having been signified to Me by the Right Honourable the Lords Commissioners for Trade & Plantations, That it had been represented to his Majesty, that the several Islands & Colonies belonging to the French in America, have in Times of War been frequently supplied with Provisions of various Kinds, by Means of the Trade carried on from his Majesty's Islands & Colonies to the Colonies & Settlements belonging to the Dutch and other neutral Powers: And that it was his Majesty's Pleasure, that I should immediately give Directions that an Embargo be laid during his Pleasure, upon all Ships & Vessels clearing out with Provisions from any Port or Place within this Government, except those which shall be employed in carrying Provisions to any other of his Majesty's Colonies & Plantations: And that the Masters or Owners of all Vessels taking in Provisions as aforesaid, shall enter into Bonds (with Two Sureties of known Residence in the Province, and Ability to Answer the Penalty) with the chief Officers of the Customs of the Ports or Places from whence such Ships or Vessel shall set Sail, to the value of One Thousand Pounds if the Ship be of less Burthen than One Hundred Tons; and of the Sum of Two Thousand Pounds if above that Burthen, That the Cargoes of such Ships or Vessels, the Particulars of which shall be expressed in the Bonds, shall not be landed in any other Ports or Places than such as belong to his Majesty, or are in Possession of his Subjects; and that they will within twelve months after the Date thereof, the Danger of the Seas excepted, produce Certificates under the Hands & Seals of the principal Officers of the Customs at such Ports or Places for which such Ships or Vessels cleared out, That the said Cargoes, expressing the Particulars thereof, have actually been landed there: And that no Person be admitted as Security for another, who have Bonds standing out undischarged, unless he be esteemed Responsible for more than the Value of such Bonds.

I do therefore, in Obediance to said Order, and with Advice of his Majesty's Council, issue this Proclamation, hereby requiring all Officers of the Customs whom it may concern, as also all Masters & Owners of Ships or Vessels, strictly to conform to his Majestys Royall Will & Pleasure, signified as aforesaid: Saving that all Ships or Vessels laiding with Fish in Bulk for Europe (which appear not to be included in the Directions aforesaid) and with Provisions of no other kind, be permitted to take in their Cargoes & depart as usual, untill further Order.

And in order the more fully to answer his Majesty's Intention of distressing the Enemy, and to render his Orders herein the more effectual; I do hereby give Notice, That in Obediance to his Majesty's Command, I shall take especial Care, when there shall be cause to suspect any Certificate to be false or counterfeit, that no such Bond or Security shall be cancelled untill I have been informed from the said principal Officers of the Customs, that the matter & contents of such Certificate are just & true: And that in case the Masters or Owners of such Ships or Vessels shall produce the said Certificates within the Time limited, such Bonds will be prosecuted to effect. And further, That in case the Masters or Owners of such Ships or Vessels cleared out from this Government, laden with Provisions for any of his Majesty's other Colonies or Islands, shall be detected in causing collusive Captures to be made of the Cargoes, that the severest penalties shall be inflicted upon the Offenders, which the Laws will in such Cases allow of.

Given at Boston, the Eleventh Day of January, 1757, in the Thirtieth Year of the Reign of our Sovereign Lord George the Second, by the Grace of God, of Great Britain, France & Ireland, King, Defender of the Faith &c.

By His Honours Command
A Oliver Secry. S. PHIPS.

God Save the King."—*Records of Civil Commissions; in Secretary's Office, vol.* 2, *p.* 318.

"A Proclamation Prohibiting all Ships or Vessels to depart out of this Province, untill the tenth day of April next.

By the Honourable Spencer Phips Esqr Lieutenant Governour & Commander in Chief, in and over his Majesty's Province of the Massachusetts Bay in New England.

A Proclamation

His Majesty's Service requiring the utmost Precaution in all our Measures at this important & critical Conjuncture; and it being necessary, in order to facilitate and render more effectual the Operations of the ensuing Campain, that an Embargo should be laid on all Ships & Vessels within the several Ports of this Province;

I have therefore thought fit, with the Advice of his Majesty's Council, to issue this Proclamation, hereby strictly forbidding all Masters or Owners of any Ships or Vessels, within the Province, to suffer any such Ships or Vessels to depart out of the same untill the tenth Day of April next, unless this Prohibition or Embargo shall, before the Expiration of said Time, be publickly declared void & of no further Effect.

And I do hereby require all the Officers of his Majesty's Customs, & the Naval and Impost Officers, and their Deputies, to take especial Care that this Embargo be punctually observed & complied with: Strictly hereby forbidding them to give Certificates or Clearances for any Ships or Vessels whatsoever, within their respective Districts, to depart to any Port without the Province during the Continuance of this Prohibition or Embargo.

And all his Majesty's good Subjects who shall or may discover any Ship or Vessel privately or clandestinely loading within the Province, or departing out of the same, against the purport of this Proclamation & contrary to Law, are hereby requested to give immediate Information thereof to the Officers of his Majesty's Customs, that all Persons offending may be dealt with according to Law & the Nature of the Offence.

Given at the Council-Chamber in Boston the Ninth Day of March, 1757, in the Thirtieth Year of the Reign of our Sover^n Lord George the Second, by the Grace of God of Great Britain, France & Ireland King Def^r of the Faith &c.

By his Honours Command

And^w Oliver Secry. S. PHIPS.

God save the King."—*Ibid.*, *p.* 320.

Chap. 16. "June 26, 1755. In Council; Whereas the holding His Majesty's Superiour Court of Judicature Court of Assize, and General Goal delivery, at Taunton within & for the County of Bristol, on the second Tuesday of July next, which is the Time appointed by Law for holding the same would be Inconvenient by Reason of a late Order of this Court, for holding the said Superiour Court &c^a at Ipswich within & for the County of Essex on the first Tuesday of the same Month, Therefore,

Ordered that the said Superiour Court of Judicature &c^a which was by Law to have been holden at Taunton, within and for the County of Bristol on the second Tuesday of July next, shall be held there on the fifth Tuesday being the twenty ninth day of the said Month, and all Writs, and other Processes already issued and returnable to said Court at Taunton the second Tuesday, shall be returned on the said fifth Tuesday, and all matters whatsoever, continued or any Ways depending in said Court there, shall continue & be proceeded on by the Justices of the said Court, on the fifth Tuesday aforesaid, and all Officers & other Persons concerned are required to conform themselves accordingly.—In the House of Represent^ves Read & Concur'd;——Consented to by the Governour."—*Council Records, vol.* XX., *p.* 507.

Chap. 19. "June 4, 1757. A Petition of Joseph Jackson of Boston——Setting forth That in the month of December last He imported into this Province a Cask of Bever from Great Britain for which the Collector of Impost demands of him four pence for every twenty shillings value as the duty thereof by virtue of an Act of this Government intituled an Act for granting unto his Majesty several Rates & duties of Impost and Tunnage of Shipping. And further Setting forth That Although said Beaver was not the product of Great Britain, & so exempted from said duty; yet as it was the Product of America & reimported, he prays an Order of this Court to exempt him from paying the Duties on the aforesaid Cask of Beaver.

In the House of Representatives——Read & Ordered That the Prayer of this Petition be granted, & That the duty mentioned in the Petition be and hereby is remitted to the Petitioner, & the Impost Officer hereby is required not to demand the same. In Council——Read & Concurred. Consented to by a Major Part of the Council."—*Council Records, vol. XXII., p.* 28.

Chap. 21. "Febru^a 8, 1757. In the House of Representatives; Voted that Jeremy Gridley & Samuel White Esq^rs with such as the Honourable Board shall join be a Committee to Farm out the Duties of Excise on Spirituous Liquors in the County of Suffolk for the ensuing Year. In Council; Read and Concurred & John Erving is joined in the Affair Consented to by the Lieutenant Governour."—*Council Records, vol. XXI., p.* 370.

On the same day the following persons were chosen committees to farm out the excise for the respective counties hereafter named; viz.,—

John Tasker, Esq., and Mr. Daniel Staniford, on the part of the House, and Benjamin Lynde, Esq., on the part of the Council, for the county of Essex;—

Mr. Henry Prentice and James Russell, Esq., on the part of the House, and William Brattle, Esq., on the part of the Council, for the county of Middlesex;—

Israel Williams and Joseph Hawley, Esqs., on the part of the House, and Eleazer Porter, Esq., on the part of the Council, for the county of Hampshire;—

Timothy Paine and William Richardson, Esqs., on the part of the House, and John Chandler, Esq., on the part of the Council, for the county of Worcester;—

Thomas Foster and Gamaliel Bradford, Esqs., on the part of the House, and John Cushing, Esq., on the part of the Council, for the county of Plymouth;—

James Otis and Rowland Cotton, Esqs., on the part of the House, and Sylvanus Bourn, Esq., on the part of the Council, for the county of Barnstable;—

Samuel White, Esq., and Mr. Thomas Maxcy, on the part of the House, and George Leonard, Esq., on the part of the Council, for the county of Bristol;—

John Bradbury, Esq., and Mr. Benjamin Chadburn, on the part of the House, and Richard Cutt, Esq., on the part of the Council, for the county of York;—

John Norton, Esq., and Mr. Gershom Cathcart, on the part of the House, and Zaccheus Mayhew, Esq., on the part of the Council, for the county of Dukes county;—

Abishai Folger and Jonathan Coffin, Esqs., on the part of the House, and Josiah Coffin, on the part of the Council, for the county of Nantucket.—*Ibid.*

"Febru^a 25, 1757. A Petition of John Norton of Dukes County praying an Allowance of the Charges and Expences of sundry Committees in Farming the Excise in said County for our Years past, amounting as by an Account exhibited to Seven Pounds Sixteen Shillings ——

In the House of Representatives; Read & Ordered that the Sum of Seven Pounds Sixteen Shillings be allowed to be paid out of the Publick Treasury in full of the within

Account of the Charges of sundry Committees on Sale of the Duties of Excise in said County as mentioned, and that the said Sum be paid to John Norton Esqr for the several Persons concerned——In Council;——Read & Concurred——Consented to by the Lieu^t Governour"—*Ibid.*, *p.* 409.

"April 7, 1757. The Committee appointed the 8th February last to Farm out the Excise on Spirituous Liquors in the County of Middlesex made Report of their Doings therein having sold the same to William Storey of Boston for Nine Hundred & Three Pounds, and presented their Account of Expence amounting to Two Pounds four Shillings for which they prayed Allowance.——

In the House of Representatives; Read & Accepted & Ordered that there be allowed and paid out of the Publick Treasury to the said Committee the Sum of Two Pounds four Shillings in discharge of their Account of time & Expences exhibited——In Council; Read & Concurr'd——Consented to by a Major Part of the Council"—*Ibid*, *p.* 431.

The above report from the committee appointed to farm out the excise for Middlesex county, was followed by reports from the committees for the other counties, and the dates of these reports, together with the names of farmers of excise appointed by them, respectively, are as follows:—

April 7, 1757. Suffolk county; to Mr. William Coffin, for £3018.—*Ibid.*

April 22, 1757. Nantucket county.—*Ibid.*, *p.* 489.

May 28, 1757. Worcester county; to Capt. Edward Harrington, for £389.—*Ibid*, *vol. XXII.*, *p.* 9.

May 28, 1757. York county; to Capt. Ichabod Goodwin, for £210. 6*s.*—*Ibid.*

May 28, 1757. Bristol county; to Capt. Thomas Cobb, for £183.—*Ibid.*, *p* 10.

May 28, 1757. Plymouth county; to James Warren, Jr., Esq., for £445 6*s.* 8*d.*—*Ibid.*

August 20, 1757. Essex county; to Mr. Jacob Ashton, for £1637. 6*s.* 8*d*—*Ibid*, *p.* 81.

August 23, 1757. Barnstable county; to Mr. Nathanael Little, for £166. 13*s.* 4*d*—*Ibid.*, *p.* 84.

August 24, 1757. Dukes county; to Capt. Samuel Cobb, for £19. 6*s.* 8*d.*"—*Ibid*, *p.* 86.

"April 12, 1757. In the House of Representatives; Whereas in the Act intituled an Act for granting unto his Majesty an Excise upon Spirits distilled & Wine, and upon Limes, Lemmons & Oranges (which Commenced March 26. 1756) It is among other things Enacted——That to every Person Licensed by the Sessions, and to every Person having Permit as aforesaid the said Farmer or his Deputy (when said Persons shall account with them) shall give Two Receipts under their hands for what each of them respectively have received either as Duty or as Forfeiture, or in any other way, and said Receipts shall express the true and just Sums received, and the Consideration for which it was received, and one of the said Receipts shall be Lodged within one Month after the Date thereof by each Person respectively to whom said Receipts shall be given with the Clerk of the Sessions for the County wherein such Person lives on Penalty of Forty Shillings, and of being incapable of renewing his or her Licence or Permit for the future, and the Clerk aforesaid shall transmit a true & fair Copy of the Receipts that shall be Lodged with him to the Secretary of the Province who shall lay the same before this Court &^ca——

And it being represented to this Court that the time limited in the aforesaid Paragraph for the Lodging the said Receipts in the Office of the Clerk of the Sessions of the Peace within one Month from the Expiration of said Act (which was the 26th of March last) will be impracticable, Therefore Resolved that the several Persons obliged in the Act to Lodge such Receipts at that time shall be allowed till the 26th of May next to Lodge such Receipts, the time in said Paragraph mentioned notwithstanding——And that this Resolve be inserted in the Publick Prints——In Council; Read & Concurr'd——Consented to by a Major Part of the Council"—*Ibid.*, *vol. XXI.*, *p.* 452.

"January 11, 1758. A Memorial of Captn Jonas Fitch——Setting forth that the Excise Master for the County of York has demanded of him the duties of Excise upon the Rum by him delivered as Sub-commissary to the Soldiers of his Company and those of Captn Israel Herrick's Company in the Pay of the Province. And praying direction

In the House of Representatives Read and Voted That it appears to this Court That the Farmer of the Duties of Excise on spirituous Liquors for the County of York is not intitled by Law to the said duty on the Rum delivered to the Soldiers by the Memorialist as Sub-Commissary, And that the Memorialist be and hereby is directed to conform himself accordingly. In Council. Read and Nonconcurred."—*Ibid.*, *vol. XXII.*, *p.* 206.

Chap. 22. "Gentlemen of the Council & House of Representatives, The Forces which were raised in the Pay of the Government for the Service of the late Expedition being returned home, and many of them no doubt being in necessitous Circumstances, the first thing which I have to recommend to your Consideration in the present Session is a method of providing for a Speedy Payment of their Wages.

The Gentlemen sent by the Court to wait on his Excellency the Earl of Loudoun at Albany and to Sollicit his Lordship to Advance a Sum of Money for the Service of the Province are returned, and have made Report to me that although his Lordship treated them with great Condescension and Goodness, and as they were well assured was zealously disposed to promote the Interests of the Colonies, yet he gave them no Encouragement to expect the Advance of any Monies: but on the contrary was pleased to acquaint them that the Support of the Regular Forces would call for all the Publick Money that was then in the Treasury, and that his Compliance with the desire of the Provinces must therefore greatly Prejudice his Majestys Service——

There seems to be no way left in the present Emergency, but to make use of your Credit to the utmost in order to obtain such Supply as is requisite, and humbly to rely on his Majestys Favour to the Province, the Measures for obtaining whereof gone into by the Council in the Recess of the Court I shall order to be communicated to you.——

I must therefore recommend to you Gentlemen of the House of Representatives the immediate Consideration of this Affair, and must desire that you would let no other Business hinder you from compleating it, lest a Failure in your Engagements now should destroy that Confidence which is necessary in Order to Encourage our People to further Service——

The other Charges of Government must likewise in proper time be provided for in the best manner you can in Order to which the State of the Treasury, and an Estimate of the Sums necessary to be Supplyed shall be laid before you.

It has been much for the Honour of the Government that the several Assemblies since the Change of the Currency have been carefull to preserve the Publick Credit, & I have no reason to doubt of your being as well disposed as any of them."—*Extract from the Governor's speech to both houses, January* 6, 1757.—*Council Records, vol.* XXI., *p.* 315.

"January 8, 1757. The Commissioners appointed to wait on the Right Honourable the Earl of Loudoun at Albany made the following Report—vizt

To the Honourable Spencer Phips Esqr Lieutenant Governour & Commander in Chief, the Honble the Council, & House of Representatives—The Report of the Commissioners appointed by the Court to wait on the Right Honourable the Earl of Loudoun at Albany.——

Pursuant to Instructions received from his Honour We proceeded to Albany, and after having made the Compliments of the General Court to his Lordship We delivered the Copy of our Commission, and had repeated Conferences with him upon the Principal Business we were instructed upon, and represented the Inability of the Province to answer the present demand of Money for the Pay of the Forces returned from the Expedition in as strong a Light as it was in our Power to do—

His Lordship treated Us with great goodness, and at the same time with Plainess and Freedom, and was pleased to acquaint Us that being without any Instruction upon this Point, & the Circumstances of the Regular Forces requiring what Money was then in the Treasury it was not in his Power to make any Advance to Us, but his Lordship assured Us that he would recommend the Case of the Province in his Publick Letters and he was pleased to give Us his Advice, as to the Form of the Accounts & the Method of Application, and We are well assured that his Lordship is well disposed to promote the Interest of the Province——Having received this Answer from his Lordship We returned home without any delay, the Small Pox being in Albany prevented Sir William Pepperells going into the City—In Council; Read & Accepted.

In the House of Represen^{ves} Read & Concur'd——Consented to by the Lieutenant Governour."—*Ibid., p.* 320.

Chap. 23. "Janu^a 18, 1757. The Secretary delivered the following Message from the Lieutenant Governour to both Houses.——

Gentlemen of the Council & House of Representatives,

I have received a Letter from his Excellency the Right Honble the Earl of Loudoun informing me of his being now on his way to Boston.

As his Lordship expects that some Persons should be impowered by the Government to act in Concert with Commissioners from some of the Neighbouring Governments upon such Proposals as he shall be pleased to lay before them, I recommend it to you, Gentlemen, to make Choice of some suitable Persons without delay, who may be impowered to appear & Act in behalf of this Government at the Conferences which may be held by the Commissioners in Consequence of his Lordships Proposals.——S. PHIPS."—*Council Records, vol.* XXI., *p.* 340.

"January 19, 1757. In the House of Representatives; Voted that there be five Commissioners chosen on the Part of this Government to Confer with the Right Honourable the Earl of Loudoun the Governours of the Neighbouring Colonies and such Comissioners as may be appointed by their respective Governments on such Matters as his Lordship shall think proper to lay before them; and that Mr Speaker Col^o Otis, & Mr Welles with such as the Honourable Board shall appoint be the Commissioners for that Purpose, & that they report thereon from time to time——In Council; Read & Concur'd; and Thomas Hutchinson & William Brattle Esq^{rs} are joined in the Affair."—*Ibid., p* 341.

"Janu^a 21, 1757. In Council Voted that Thomas Hutchinson & William Brattle Esq^{rs} with such as shall be joined by the Honourable House be a Committee to receive any Proposals which the Right Honble the Earl of Loudoun may judge proper to lay before them, and to Confer upon such Proposals with Commissioners or Committees appointed by the Neighbouring Governments for the like Purpose——The said Committee to report from time to time as there shall be occasion.

In the House of Representatives; Read & Concurr'd & Mr Speaker Col^o Otis & Mr Welles are joined in the Affair.——Consented to by the Lieutenant Governour."—*Ibid., p.* 345.

"February 1, 1757. Thomas Hutchinson Esqr from the Committee appointed to Confer upon the Earl of Loudouns Proposals made the following Report

The Committee appointed to receive the Proposals of the Right Honble the Earl of Loudoun and to Confer with the Commissioners of the other Governments and from time to time to make report have so far attended the Service as to receive in conjunction with the other Governments Commissioners his Lordships Proposals to present certain Queries to his Lordship and to receive the Answers all which are herewith Humbly offered.

The Committee likewise Proceeded to Confer with the Commissioners from the other Governments and the said Commissioners for their respective Constituents have given their Voices that a Compliance with his Lordships Proposals is expedient and necessary.—

The Commissions from Connecticut & Rhode Island contained ample Powers from the Two Governments; that from New Hampshire was given by the Governour of the Province and not founded upon any Act of the Legislature—Your Committee did not apprehend themselves authorized to give their Voice to this general Question, but thought it their Duty to make this Report and to pray the further directions of the Honourable Court. THOMAS HUTCHINSON ℘ Order."—*Ibid., p.* 360.

"February 2, 1757. In the House of Representatives; Voted that the Committee appointed by this Court to receive any Proposals which the Right Honourable the Earl of Loudoun should judge Proper to lay before them, and to Confer with Commissioners from the Neighbouring Governments thereon be and hereby are fully Authorized & impowered to agree on the Part of this Government to his Lordships Requisition of Four Thousand Men so far as to Engage that this Government will raise their Proportion of the said Four Thousand Men to be employed in his Majestys Service in North America, subject to his Lordships Command under Officers Inhabitants of this Province, the said Men to be paid by this Government, and not to be held more than One Year from this time.——And the said Committee are hereby further impowered to Adjust and determine with said Commissioners this Governments Proportion of said Four Thousand Men.——In Council; Read & Concurr'd—Consented to by the Lieutenant Governour."—*Ibid.*, *p.* 361.

"February 4, 1757. The Committee appointed to receive the Proposals of the Right Honourable the Earl of Loudoun &ca reported further as follows—vizt—

The said Committee after divers Conferences with the Commissioners of the other Governments upon a just proportion of each Government to Four Thousand Men have not been able to Settle this Proportion so as to Compleat the Number among the whole and therefore the Committee determined to make a separate Answer to his Lordships Proposals which they have done this day in the following Words.

To His Excellency the Earl of Loudoun, General and Commander in Chief of all his Majestys Forces in North America &c &c.

The Commissioners on the Part of the Massachusetts Bay having spent much time without the desired Effect in Conference with the Commissioners from the other Governments of New England in order to Settle the Proportion of each Government to Four thousand Men are obliged to make this their Separate Answer to your Lordships Proposals, and by virtue of a Special Act or Vote of the General Assembly an Attested Copy whereof is herewith humbly presented to your Lordship——the said Commissioners Do agree that notwithstanding the said Province will have at least Eight Hundred Men in Pay for their immediate Protection and Defence, besides Three Hundred Men which must be Employed in Two Vessells of War, and if no regard be had to this Burthen 1750 Men will be this Provinces full proportion of 4000, yet that the aforesaid Number of 1750 Men shall be raised by this Government on the Terms and Conditions of the aforesaid Vote of the general Assembly——And the Commissioners do this from a sense of the great Importance of the proposed Service, and pray your Lordship that it may not be improved as a Precedent in any future proportions.

THOMAS HUTCHINSON
WILLIAM BRATTLE
THOMAS HUBBARD
JAMES OTIS

The Committee presented the aforesaid Answer to his Lordship who expressed his Concern at the Governments Reporting separately and was pleased to refer the Committee untill the Morning for his Lordships Answer,——

which is Humbly Submitted— THOs HUTCHINSON ℘ Order

In Council; Read & Sent down."—*Ibid.*, *p.* 364.

"February 7, 1757. The Committee appointed to receive Proposals from the Right Honble the Earl of Loudoun &c Reported further as follows—vizt

The said Committee having laid before his Lordship their determination that 1750 Men should be raised as this Provinces Proportion to Four Thousand Men, and the Commissioners from the Government of Connecticut having determined to raise 1250 only, those of Rhode Island 334, and New Hampshire but 220 it appeared that the whole Number Added together fell several Hundreds short of the proposed 4000, whereupon his Lordship recommended a further Consideration of the Affair to the Commissioners, but no Government seemed inclined to increase their Number,—His Lordship was then pleased to recommend to Connecticut the raising 1400 Men, to Rhode Island 450, and to New Hampshire 350, and to the Massachusetts 1800. The Commissioners from the other Governments did not absolutely agree to the respective Numbers, but engaged to recommend them to the several Assemblies and did not doubt a Compliance——your Committee likewise declined an absolute Engagement, but informed his Lordship they would make a Report to the Court, and were in hopes there would be no difficulty on the part of this Province.

The several Commissioners proposed to his Lordship several Circumstances relative to the raising the Men which he proposed to give his Answer to in Writing & when received by your Committee shall be laid before the Honourable Court——

which is Humbly Submitted—— THOMAS HUTCHINSON by Order

In Council; Read & Sent down."—*Ibid.*, *p.* 366.

"Febua 8, 1757. In the House of Representatives; Voted that the Committee appointed to receive Proposals from the Right Honourable the Earl of Loudoun &c be directed to Confer with his Lordship on the Subject Matter of the Message from the Honourable Board to the House of this Forenoon and Report. In Council; Read & Concurr'd——Consented to by the Lieutent Governour.

The Committee for receiving Proposals from Lord Loudoun &c having received this Morning his Lordships determination on certain Points proposed to his Lordship referred to in the Committees last Report, the same is herewith humbly presented.

Thomas Hutchinson ℘ Order.

In Council; Read and sent down with his Lordships Determination which is as follows—vizt

To the Governours and Commissioners of and from the several Governments of New England;

His Excellency the Earl of Loudouns Opinion and determination upon several Points proposed and conferred upon at his House the 5th instant relative to the Four Thousand Men agreed to be raised and employed under the Kings General & Commander in Chief in the Pay of said Governments.——

The first thing you proposed to me Gentlemen, was the time when I thought it would be necessary the Men should be at the place of Rendezvous; I think no time should be lost before you begin the raising your Men, much will depend upon an early or backward Spring—I should be glad that the whole Forces might be ready to be Mustered by the 25th of March at farthest.——

It is most agreeable to his Majestys Directions to me, and to my own Sentiments in the present Situation of our Affairs, that the Forces should be raised in Companies of One Hundred Men each (including Four Commission Officers) or as near to that Number as the whole that may be furnished by any particular Colony will admit——Besides the Officers to each Company I desire there may be one Officer to Command from each Colony who may Convey such Orders as he shall receive from me to all the Troops of such Colony.——

I desire particular Care may be taken that both Officers and Men may be such as are fit for the Service; and that none but able Bodied Men and such as can bear the Fatigue of a Campaign in this Country may be employed ——Unless the Muster Masters are faithful you will be in danger of having many insufficient Men sent out. I am afraid there was a great remissness in this respect the last year, and I hope there will be no Cause of Complaint for the future.——

It is of great Importance that in each Colony an exact Knowledge should be had from time to time of their Forces raised and actually Marched, that the whole number engaged may be Compleated, and any deficiency whether from desertion or any other cause may be made good.——After you have given me Assurances of a certain Number of Men, and I have Ordered my Plan & Measures with a dependance upon them it may be of extreme bad Consequence to disappoint me in any degree.

I find that it will be a very agreeable thing to your People that Courts Martial for the Trial of Offences should be Constituted from among their own Officers; and as I am willing they should be gratified in everything that may Consist with his Majestys Service I intend that all Offences in any of the Provincial Troops, that are not of the most heinous Nature shall be tried and determined by the Provincial Officers alone, and when any of the grossest Crimes shall make it necessary for me to appoint some of the Officers of his Majestys Regular Forces I intend even then to join some of your Provincial Officers to be assisting with them in trying & determining all such Cases.——

As I am very desirous the Forces should be raised and Engaged in the Service as soon as possible, I will allow at the Rate of Two Shillings Sterling ℔ Week in Lieu of Provisions to each Man from the time of their first Muster untill their Actual March or receiving the Kings Provisions, and this Allowance I make for the Sake of Forwarding this particular Service, and I do not intend it to serve as a Precedent for the future——That I may act with the greater Certainty with respect to this Allowance I expect that regular Returns be sent to me of the time and Place & Number of Men as often as any Muster shall be made."—*Ibid., p.* 367.

"February 15, 1757. The Committee appointed to receive the Proposals of the Right Honoble the Earl of Loudoun, and to Confer with the Commissioners from the other Governments of New England made their final Report as follows——vizt

The said Committee first Convened on Saturday the 29th of January together with Thomas Fitch Esqr Governour & Jonathan Trumbull Phineas Lyman Eliphalet Dyre & Elihu Hall Esqrs Commissioners from the Colony of Connecticut Theodore Atkinson Esqr Commissionated by the Governour of New Hampshire, and the following Commissioners from the General Assembly of Rhode Island——vizt Stephen Hopkins Esqr Governour & James Honeyman & George Brown Esqrs and having appointed William Brattle & Phineas Lyman Esqrs to acquaint his Lordship that they were met agreeable to his Lordships Proposals to the several Governments, he was pleased to desire that they would Attend him at his House which they immediately did, and his Lordship made the following Speech, and delivered a Copy thereof to Governour Fitch——vizt

Boston Saturday 29th January 1757.

Gentlemen

You must be very sensible that the Measures taken the last Year for the Preservation of his Majestys Dominions and Colonies upon this Continent and for the Annoyance of his Majestys Enemies have proved ineffectual and instead of removing the French from any of their Encroachments we have suffered them to make Considerable Advances upon Us.——

I will put you in Mind of some of the Proceedings to which I apprehend your Misfortunes may be in a great Measure attributed——

When I Left London which was the 17th of May the Ministry had received no Intelligence of the determination of any of the Governments to prosecute an Expedition against Crown Point, although this determination had been made by the Massachusetts the 16th of February. And I Cannot account for this Neglect in those whose Duty it was to have given the earliest Advice that might be. The want of this Advice rendered it impossible for me to receive any Orders with immediate Relation to your Resolutions.——

Upon my Arrival at Albany I found that your Forces fell very much short of the Number you had agreed to raise, and which you thought necessary for the Service, and from the best Information I Could get the Troops in general were not equal to those which you had always employed on former Occasions; I Could not therefore think it adviseable for them to proceed without the Assistance of Part of his Majestys Regular Troops.——

I met with unexpected Difficulties, and was much retarded in Setling the Connection between the Regulars and the Provincials, and before it could be fully effected, and any Proceeding had in Consequence of it, I received the News of the Surrender of the Forts & Garrisons at Oswego, and all his Majestys Possessions upon the Lakes to the French. The true State and Circumstances of these Forts & Garrisons were never represented to me by my Predecessor.

I had good reason to think that the Enemy flush'd with Success would make an Attack upon the Provincial Forces——I immediately wrote to the several Governours and demanded an Aid suitable to the State of their Affairs——What Success I had you very well know

——There was in some of you a Profession of Readiness to afford Assistance, and the Shew and Appearance of it in the Votes of the Assembly but it turned out in fact that the Attempts to carry those Votes into Execution were defeated and proved ineffectual.——

Sometime after I had applied to the several Governments for Aid it pleased God that the Recruits from London & the High Lands arrived, and I was able to Collect a greater Number of the Recruits raised for the Royal American Regiment than I had any hopes of being able to Collect at that Season of the Year all which I immediately joined to the Regular Troops, and as many of them as could be Spared I Marched for the Strengthning, & for the Security of the Provincial Forces——

I Have since received certain Intelligence that I was not mistaken in my Apprehensions of the designs of the French, and that it was the Account which they received from their Scouts & Spies of the Actual March of the Regulars the Number of which was reported to be greater than it really was which diverted them from the Resolutions which they had formed——What the Event of such an Attack would have been God only knows——I was extreamly anxious about it, and I have the greatest reason to think that if it had been made upon the Provincials alone it would have been followed with very fatal Consequences.

Your Forces after this by Sickness or Desertion or both were daily diminished, the Season was so far advanced that I had no further thought of any Offensive Measures against the Enemy and I determined that as soon as they withdrew the Provincials should be dismissed, and that the Charge which the several Governments were at for their Pay should Cease as soon as possible.

This has been the State & Progress of your Affairs the Year past I hope Gentlemen that under the Guidance & Blessing of Divine Providence the Plan of Operation for another year will be better prosecuted.

I Have desired a Meeting of your several Governments by their Governrs & Commissioners at this time in Order to their determining what Number of Men they will raise to be employed in Conjunction with his Majestys Regular Forces the ensuing Year.

Considering the vast Expence of Supporting so large a Number of Troops as are employed by his Majesty for the Protection of his Colonies, the Burthen whereof you bear no part in, you cannot think much of Contributing so small a proportion towards your own defence as I now require of you, for could I be assured of Four thousand good & Effective Men to be raised by the Four Governments of New England in such proportion as you shall settle among yourselves I would not urge you to go beyond that Number.——

I must recommend to you the giving better Encouragement to your Officers than you have formerly done which may be an Inducement to Persons who shall be equal to their Posts, and who will preserve Order & Discipline to engage in the Service and I think if some Part of your Mens Pay were Converted into a Fund to assist in giving them necessary Cloathing it would be of great Use.

The Particular Service in which I must Employ these Troops it is not in my Power to Communicate to you——I wait for Answers to my Letters gone to England before I can fully determine upon it myself, but if you were to wait untill I receive them before you proceed to raise the Men it would be too late to do it for the Service of this Year——Besides Gentlemen great Inconvenience must arise from making my design publick, and I know of no Advantage which can accrue from it——The Confining your Men to any particular Service appears to me to be a preposterous Measure Our Affairs are not in such a Situation as to make it reasonable for any Colony to be influenced by its particular interest——The Question is in what way & Manner the whole may be Secured and the Com mon Enemy of all most effectually annoyed——this is the Point I must keep in view and no Consideration will prevail on me to depart from it——

You may depend on my treating your Men with all that tenderness and Indulgence which will Consist with necessary Order and Discipline and that I will employ them whenever there shall be room for it in such Services as shall be most suitable to their Genius, and the way and Manner of Fighting to which they have been used, and that they shall be discharged at farthest at the Expiration of the Term for which they are raised, and as much sooner as the Service will admit, but to engage that I will employ them in this or that particular Place only is what I Cannot do upon any Terms for I think it would be more prejudicial to the Publick than the whole Benefit which We may expect from the Provincials would Countervail.

I Do not thus express myself to you Gentlemen because I think it a matter of but little Consequence, whether you Afford me Aid or not, no, I think it of such moment that you would never be able to Atone for a Refusal—I hope therefore you will spend no time upon this Point, but will without delay determine upon a Compliance with my Proposal to you that so We may begin our Preparations this Year earlier than We have ever done before.

LOUDOUN.——

The Commissioners having received the foregoing Speech went from Lord Loudouns House to the Council Chamber in Boston, and after a short Conference they agreed to meet on Monday the 31st at Mrs Ballards Great Room in King Street which had been provided for that Purpose.——

The Commissioners being met accordingly agreed upon the following Queries to be presented to his Lordship——

To His Excellency the Earl of Loudoun General & Commander in Chief of all his Majestys Forces in North America &c &c at Boston.

The Commissioners from the several Governments of New England Convened at Boston having received you Lordships Proposals for affording an Aid for the Service of the ensuing Year beg leave before they enter into a general Consideration of the Proposals humbly to pray your Lordship to Signify your Intention with regard to the following particulars.—

1st They pray your Lordship to inform them what Proportion or particular Parts of the Charge of the Provincial Forces your Lordship expects should be borne by the Colonies?

2d The Commissioners being apprehensive that it will be a great discouragement to the Inhabitants of the Northern Colonies from Inlisting unless Assurance can be given that they shall not March to the Southward of certain Limits, Therefore they humbly pray your Lordship to inform them whether it may Consist with the Publick Service that such Assurances should be given, and if it may Consist what Limits your Lordship will approve of?

3d The Commissioners humbly pray your Lordship to Signify for what Length of time it will be necessary that the Men be raised?

Signed at the desire of the Commissioners THOS FITCH.——

January 31. 1757.

The Commissioners being met the 1st February received the following Answer from the Earl of Loudoun.

To the Governours and Commissioners of & from the several Governments of New England.

His Excellency the Earl of Loudouns Answer to their Queries of Yesterday.——

1st When I had the Honour to be appointed to the Command of the Troops in North America the Plan for Supplying the necessary Expences of the War here was the same as when Major General Braddock came out—Vizt That the Provinces should not only bear the Expences of the Troops they raised for their own Defence, but should likewise Supply at their Expence the Regular Troops sent for their Protection with Provisions.——

It was afterwards agreed that a Contractor should be appointed to Supply the regular Troops with Provisions, and you will see by the Secretary of States Letter that the Troops raised by the several Provinces to Act in Conjunction with the regular Troops were to be provided likewise with Provisions. The Provincial Troops shall likewise be Provided with Ammunition.——The Artillery Stores will be provided by the King. and although I expect you should provide Surgeons & Medicines for the ordinary Service of your Troops I shall admit those into the Hospital whose Cases require it, & take the same Care of them as of the other Troops, and I Do not think myself intituled to go further.

2d As I am very unwilling that by anything that passes between you and me the Enemy should ever be informed that there was any part of his Majestys Dominions in North America that they could Invade and be safe from meeting with the Combined Forces of New England to drive them back, & Prescribe the Bounds they would permit them to come to, therefore hope you will not insist on a direct Answer to the Query——At the same time I do assure you that I neither now have nor ever had the smallest Intention of Marching the Troops raised by the New England Governments out of the Limits I know they will willingly go to, and that you will approve of their being Led into.

3d As to your Third Query I observe you have been formerly in the use of raising your Troops for a Year, and that Period will now Answer the Purposes of the Service: for although I see no reason to beleive I shall have occasion to detain them so long it will not prevent my sending them home as soon as the Service will permit, and if any unforeseen Accident should make it necessary for them to Continue longer in the Service it will leave time for a fresh Application to the several Governments for that Purpose.

Tuesday Morning 1st February 1757. LOUDOUN.

After reading the foregoing and Conference had between the Commissioners, and those on the Part of Connecticutt New Hampshire & Rhode Island having determined to Comply with his Lordships Proposals, and to raise each Governments Proportion of the 4000 Men the Massachusetts Committee made the following Report vizt as Entered the 1st

Whereupon the following Vote passed the Massachusetts Assembly——Vizt as Entered the 2d of February instant.

Pursuant whereunto the Committee made divers Proposals to the Commissioners of the other Governments as reported the 4th instant and made a Separate Answer to his Lordship as is likewise entered on said day——The Committee reported further as entered on the 7th——On the 8th his Lordship was pleased to Signify his Mind upon certain Points to the Commissioners in Writing——Vizt as Entered on said day.

The foregoing Account of the Proceedings of the Committee is humbly offered to the General Court——

THOMAS HUTCHINSON

Boston 10th February 1757—— In the Name of the Committee

In Council; Read and Ordered that this Report be accepted.

In the House of Representatives; Read & Concurr'd"—*Ibid.*, p. 379.

"Februa 16. 1757. In the House of Representatives; Voted that the following Establishment of Wages be made for Officers & Soldiers to be employed in his Majestys Service under the command of the Right Honourable the Earl of Loudoun Commander in Chief of His Majestys Forces in North America—vizt

	£	s	d	
For One Colonel	£18	0	0	℔ Month
For Two Lieutenant Colonels each	15	0	0	" ditto
For Two Majors each	12	0	0	" ditto
For Seventeen Captains each	8	0	0	" ditto
For Seventeen First / Seventeen Second } Lieutents each	5	0	0	" ditto
For Seventeen Ensigns each	3	10	0	" ditto
For Two Chaplains each	6	8	0	" ditto
For Two Surgeons each	10	0	0	" ditto
For Two Surgeons Mates each	5	6	8	" ditto
For each Sergeant	2	3	1	ditto
For each Corporal	1	18	7	ditto
For each Drummer	1	18	7	ditto
For each Private Soldier	1	16	0	ditto
For a Commissary	8	0	0	ditto

In Council; Read & Concurr'd——

Consented to by the Lieutent Governr"—*Ibid.*, p. 384.

"Februa 1757. In the House of Representatives; Voted that the Bounty Money for Inlisting Men into his Majestys Service shall be paid by the Treasurer to the Colonels or Chief Commanding Officers of each Regiment within this Province according to the Number of Men that shall be assigned them respectively to raise, at Six Dollars for each Man to be by them paid to such Persons as shall Inlist into said Service on or before the Twenty first day of March next, and pass Muster for effective by the Commissaries of the Musters that shall be appointed by his Honour the Lieutenant Govr for that purpose, the said Colonel or Chief Officer to Cause to be Lodged in the Secretarys Office an Account of the Disposition of such Moneys by them respectively received and to Pay the Ballances that may remain into the Province Treasury within One Month after the 22d of March next.——In Council; Read & Concurr'd——

Consented to by the Lieutenant Governour."—*Ibid., p.* 386.

"Februa 19, 1757. The Secretary delivered the following Message from his Honour the Lieut Governour to both Houses——vizt

Gentlemen of the Council & House of Representatives.

I Do not find that you have made any Provision for Arming the Eighteen Hundred Men proposed to be raised for the Service of the Current Year——You cannot but remember that by a Letter from Mr Secretary Fox dated the 13th of March last, his Majestys Pleasure was Signified for this Governments Arming as well as raising a Number of Troops to Act in Conjunction with his Majestys Forces.——His Excellency the Earl of Loudoun in the Proposals he has laid before you for raising Men for the Service of this Year goes upon the Plan of this Letter and expressly refers to it; and it appears very evident that his Lordship expects you to supply the Arms, as they are not included in the Articles which he has engaged to furnish the Troops withal at the Charge of the Crown.

I must therefore recommend it to you Gentlemen to make full Provision for Arming your Troops that no Disappointment or hindrance may arise for want of such Provision. And I recommend it to you likewise to come into such Resolutions as may be effectual to bring in such Arms when the Service is over.——There has been a very great Failure in this Respect the Year past, and I cannot but think if the arms were Estimated at something more than the Value, and the Men made accountable therefor they would be more Carefull to return them.

S. PHIPS.

Council Chamber
February 18th 1757

In the House of Representatives; Ordered that Colonel Williams Colonel Cotton & Mr Thomas with such as the Honourable Board shall join be a Committee to take under consideration his Honours Message dated the 18th instant relating to Supplying the Forces of the Province agreed to be raised for his Majestys Service with Arms, and Report what they judge proper for this Court to do thereon. In Council; Read & Concurr'd; and Thomas Hutchinson & William Brattle Esqrs are joined in the affair."—*Ibid., p.* 395.

"Februa 21, 1757. May it Please your Honour,

The Council and House of Representatives are sensible that it is of very great Importance that the Forces to be raised for the Service of the ensuing Year should be provided with good Arms. It had formerly been the Practice of the Government to require the Soldiers to furnish themselves with Arms, as far as they were capable of doing it, but this method was found inconvenient, and many times the Arms proved unfit for Service; and the Last Year Two Thousand of the Arms which had been sent over by his Majestys Orders were delivered for the Service of the Expedition to that Part of the Army which was raised by this Province, and the rest of our Men were furnished with such Arms as had been purchased by this Government Principally with a view to make up the Deficiency of Arms at Castle William——We wish that more effectual Provision had been made at the beginning of the Expedition to oblige the Soldiers to return their Arms We have in the present Session passed such Votes & Orders as appeared to Us the most likely to answer this Purpose, and we doubt not that by far the greatest part will be returned.

We can conceive no way of furnishing Arms for the present Service but by obliging the Men to bring such as they have, or by Impressing others from among the Inhabitants, many of which We have reason to fear will upon a Survey be deemed insufficient or else by making Application to his Majestys General that the Kings Arms which were made use of the Last Year may again be allowed for the Service of the present Year If there should not be a sufficient number of them returned for this Purpose what shall be wanting which we hope will not be many may be supplied from the Governments Arms.——

We are sensible that we have no right to demand the Kings Arms and that they are at the Disposal of his Majestys General, but We have no doubt that when a Representation is made that if all the Arms belonging to the Government and fit for Service should be delivered to the Soldiers there would still be a deficiency, that Castle William would be left in a manner destitute, and that it is not possible to purchase within the Province suitable Arms, his Lordship will allow the Arms which were used last Year to be again delivered—— But if after considering these Circumstances it shall appear to his Lordship to be necessary that the Kings Arms should be used in some other Service the Forces raised by this Province must bring the best that they have, and We think that untill his Lordships Pleasure be known, such Men as Inlist should be informed that it is expected that they furnish themselves with Arms, unless Orders shall hereafter be given to the Contrary.——

As the appointment of the Officers of these forces is with your Honour, such Security may be required from the Commander of each Company as shall oblige him to return any Arms that may be delivered for the use of the Men that are under him, and such Officer may take Receipts from the Men to be accountable on Penalty of a reasonable Deduction from their Wages, or other Satisfaction in case of Failure as shall be judged necessary.—— In Council; Read and Accepted and Ordered that Andrew Oliver Esqr with such as the Honourable House shall appoint be a Committee to present the same to his Honour the Lieutenant Governour Accordingly——In the House of Representves Read & Concurr'd & Colo Cotton & Judge Russell are joined in the Affair."—*Ibid., p.* 397.

"February 23, 1757. In the House of Representatives; Voted that the following Message be sent to His Honour the Lieutenant Governour.——viz[t]
The House considering that your Honour is now about to Issue your Orders to the Colonels of the several Regiments of Militia within the Province for the Levying their respective Proportions of the Eighteen Hundred Men agreed to be raised by this Government for his Majestys Service under the Right Honourable the Earl of Loudoun and apprehending that from the Nature of the thing and from past unhappy Experience there is great reason to fear a deficiency in the Number raised for that Service unless some more effectual Provision be made for speedy Collecting the Men inlisted and impressed than hath been made heretofore. And as Provision is made by the Assembly for the Subsistence of the Men from their first enteiing on the Service.——
The House therefore earnestly desire your Honour that in the Warrants to the Colonels for raising the said Men your Honour would be pleased to give them particular Orders to Collect together all the Men raised in their respective Regiments in some proper place within the same on or before the Thirty first day of March next in order to their being Mustered, and that they order the Men so Collected & Mustered to continue there ready to yield a punctual Obedience to your Honours further Orders.
The foregoing Message was accordingly delivered to his Honour the Lieutenant Governour in Council by a Committee of the House of Representatives "—*Ibid., p.* 406.
"Februa 24, 1757. In the House of Representatives Voted that his Honour the Lieuten[t] Governour be desired to give Orders to the Person he shall think proper to employ to repair to Albany to take Care of the Arms & Stores belonging to the Province: that he immediately Collect from the several Stores Forts & Officers hands, all the Kings Arms & Accoutrements that were left at Albany & Parts adjacent by the Forces raised by this Government the last Year on the Expedition against Crown Point & Ship them directly for Boston, unless his Excellency the Earl of Loudoun or some of his principal Officers give Orders to the contrary: and in that case that he see that a proper Certificate be taken and returned in order to Discharge the Commissary Generals Obligations (in behalf of this Government) to the Kings Store Keeper for the Arms & Accoutrements aforesaid In Council; Read & Concurr'd
Consented to by the Lieuten[t] Governour."—*Ibid., p.* 408.
"A Proclamation for the Encouragement of Persons to inlist into his Majesty's Service.
By the Honourable Spencer Phips Esq[r] Lieutenant Governour & Commander in Chief, in & over his Majesty's Province of the Massachusetts Bay in New England.

A Proclamation

For the Encouragement of Persons to inlist into his Majesty's Service in the Expedition under the Command of his Excellency the Right Honourable the Earl of Loudoun for the Defence of his Majesty's Colonies, and for the Annoyanc of his Majesty's Enemies in North America; the folloing Encouragement is given, & Bounties voted, by the Great & General Court or Assembly of this Province in their present Sessions: Viz.
To every Person who shall inlist into said Service on or before the 21st day of March next, over and above his Wages, which are one Pound sixteen Shillings per Month; a Blanket, Coat & Soldier's Hat, and Six Dollars; which Money is to be paid him upon his passing Muster, and his Poll to be freed from the Province-Tax for the Year 1757.
And as a further Encouragement
To such as have been upon either of the Crown Point Expeditions, the Expedit[ns] at Nova-Scotia, or Kennebeck, in the Year 1754. and to such as have been in the Batteau-Service, or have served as Pioneers, or in the independant ranging Companies under Captain Rogers, or that have been employed by this Government in Defence of the Frontiers of the Province within three Years last past, over & above the Bounty & Encouragement aforesaid, they shall be severally intitled upon their Inlistment as aforesaid, to four Dollars, to be paid them by their respective Colonels upon their passing muster: And that no Person shall be detained in said Service a Term exceeding twelve Months from the second Day of February Instant. And
That there be allowed to each Person who shall inlist as aforesaid for Subsistance Three Shillings per week from his passing Muster, untill he shall receive the Kings Allowance, over & above what his Lordship has been pleased to allow, which is two Shilling Sterling to each Man.
Given at Boston, the Twenty fifth Day of February 1757. In the Thirtieth Year of the Reign of our Sovereign Lord George the Second, by the Grace of God of Great Britain, France & Ireland, King, Defender of the Faith &c.
By his Honours Command. S. PHIPS
Andw Oliver Secry
God save the King."—*Records of Civil Commissions; in Secretary's Office, vol.* 2, *p.* 319.
"April 2d, 1757. In the House of Representatives; Ordered that the Committee of War be directed to furnish the Forces raised for the present Expedition with necessary Arms & Bayonets; and that they compleat Tents for Eighteen Hundred Men as soon as may be. ——In Council; Read & Concurr'd "—*Ibid., p.* 423.
"April 11, 1757. In the House of Representatives; Ordered that the several Gentlemen who were directed to receive and Transmit to the Commissary General the Arms belonging to this Province in their respective Counties by an Order passed this Court the 27th of January last, be also directed to prosecute all Persons within said Limits, that they may come to the knowledge of who are still possessed of any of said Arms or of those belonging to his Majesty, and to take Care that the Law passed in the 27th Year of His present Majestys Reign intituled an Act for Levying Soldiers &[c] so far as it respects the purchasing or Selling of Soldiers Arms be put in Execution——In Council; Read & Concurr'd——
Consented to by a Major Part of the Council."—*Ibid., p.* 448.
"April 16, 1757. In the House of Representatives; Voted that the Officers & Soldiers raised for the present Expedition be allowed and paid out of the Publick Treasury Five

Shillings and Eight Pence ℔ Week for their Billeting including the Allowance made them by Lord Loudoun; said Officers allowance to be from the 25th March Last, untill they receive the Kings Allowance; and that of the Soldiers from the time of their being Mustered till they receive said Allowance.——In Council; Read & Concurr'd——

Consented to by a Major Part of the Council"—*Ibid., p.* 464.

"April 18, 1757. In the House of Representatives; Voted that the following Message be sent to the Honourable Board——vizt

May it Please Your Honours

The House beg leave to express their Concern that notwithstanding they have made an Establishment for Wages for One Colonel, Two Lieutenant Colonels, and Two Majors to Command the 1800 Men raised by this Province to be under the General Command of his Excellency the Right Honourable the Earl of Loudoun, yet his Honor the late Lieutenant Governour has Commissioned only one General Officer to Command said Troops.——The House apprehend that from the nature of the Service, and the common dangers of War, the Life of that Officer is so precarious that it will be very inconvenient to have the Command solely in any one Gentleman without any Provision of some proper Person to Succeed him in that important Trust in Case of his Decease.——

They would therefore humbly propose to the Consideration of the Honoble his Majestys Council whether it might not be adviseable to make some further provision on this head, and that if they please, One Lieutenant Colonel & one Major may be appointed under the General Officer already in Commission——

T. HUBBARD Speakr."—*Ibid., p.* 469.

"April 19, 1757. In the House of Representatives; Ordered that the Committee of War be directed to procure and put into the hands of the Commissary of the Forces of this Province raised for his Majestys Service under the command of his Excellency the Earl of Loudoun such Articles as they shall apprehend will be for the Service and Comfort of the Soldiers and are not provided for by the Crown Point.* In Council; Read & Concurred

Consented to by a Major Part of the Council."—*Ibid., p.* 476.

"April 20, 1757. In the House of Representatives; Ordered that the following Establishment be made for the Officers hereafter mentioned of the Forces raised for his Majestys Service under the Command of the Earl of Loudoun—vizt

That there be allowed to a Surgeon General	£14	—	℔ Month.
To Three Surgeons Mates each	5	II	"
To the first Officer over the said Forces	18	0	"
To a Secretary to said officer who is to be Commissary of the Musters for the Army	8	0	"

In Council; Read & Concurred.

Consented to by a Major Part of the Council."—*Ibid., p.* 483.

"April 22, 1757. In the House of Representatives; Whereas a Soldiers Allowance in the Kings Service is 4lb of Pork or 7lb of Beef 7lb Bread 3 Pints of Peas 1lb of Flour or equivalent in Rice and 7 Jills of Molasses only——

Therefore Voted, that for the more comfortable Subsistence of the Forces raised by this Province for the present Campaign the Committee of War be directed to provide and put into the hands of the Commissary for said Forces a suitable Quantity of Cloaths, Chocolate, Sugar, Tobacco, Soap, & Ginger——In Council; April 22d. Read & Noncurred."—*Ibid., p.* 493.

"April 22, 1757. A Memorial of the Officers now in the Service of this Province for the intended Expedition to serve under the Right Honourable the Earl of Loudoun Setting forth that they have been at great Expence in Cloathing themselves and in Collecting the Troops &ca and praying that they may be allowed such Pay as will enable them to act with Credit and in Character as becomes the Officers of the Province——

In the House of Representatives; Ordered that the Prayer of this Memorial be so far granted as that the Province Treasurer be & hereby is directed to Advance one Months Wages to each of the Commission Officers going with the Forces raised by this Province to serve under the Right Honoble the Earl of Loudoun.——In Council; Read & Concurred.

Consented to by a Major Part of the Council."—*Ibid., p.* 494.

"April 25, 1757 In Council; Whereas this Court have directed the Committee of War to furnish the Commissary of the Forces of this Province under the Command of the Earl of Loudoun with such Articles as they shall apprehend will be for the Service and Comfort of the Soldiers——Ordered that the Committee of War be directed and impowered to agree for such Articles upon the best Terms they can, to be paid for out of the next Supply of the Treasury, and that such of the Soldiers who may be Supplyed with Cloathing or any other Articles shall be charged therewith by the Commissary at the Prime Cost with a reasonable Allowance for the charge of transportation; the amount of which shall when the Muster Rolls are made up be carried out in the Commissary Columns and be deducted from their Wages accordingly.

In the House of Representatives; Read & Concurred

Consented to by a Major Part of the Council—

In the House of Representatives; Whereas it has been represented to the House that some Persons that have been impressed, hired, or Voluntarily inlisted into his Majestys Service have since their entering therein given Notes of hand or other Securities to their Friends or others for Sums more than Ten Pounds in order to their bringing forward a Suit or Suits against them, to prevent their going in said Service which Conduct has a tendency to frustrate the good Intents of this Government Therefore Voted that Colonel Clap, Eldad Taylor & William Richardson Esqrs with such as the Honourable Board shall join be a Committee to take this matter into Consideration and report what is proper for this Court to do thereon. the Committee to sit forthwith——In Council; Read & Concurred & Benjamin Lynde & William Brattle Esqrs are joined in the Affair——In Council; Whereas it is of the utmost Importance that the Several Soldiers Impressed Inlisted or hired into his Majes-

* *Sic.*

tys Service for the intended Expedition under the Command of the Right Honourable the Earl of Loudoun be not detained or hindered in their proceeding on the same——

It is therefore Ordered That no Person be taken out of the Service by any Process (unless it be for some Criminal Matter) for any Debt that was not contracted before the Twenty Second day of February last, and in Case any Person in the Service aforesaid be Arrested for any such Debt and Service made on the Body: the Creditor shall before such Person is Committed make Oath before one of his Majestys Justices of the Peace in the County that the Debt was actually Contracted before the said Twenty Second day of February, and was for a true and valuable Consideration——It is also further Ordered that if any Soldier is already Committed for a Debt contracted since the said 22d day of February the Sherriff of the County where the Commitment is made shall forthwith discharge such Soldier

In the House of Representatives; Read & Concurred——

Consented to by a Major Part of the Council."—*Ibid., p.* 499.

"April 25, 1757. In the House of Representatives; Ordered that the Treasurer be & he is hereby directed to pay the one Months Advance Wages ordered to be paid each Commission Officer on the intended Expedition out of the appropriation for Grants——In Council; Read & Concurred——

Consented to by a Major Part of the Council"—*Ibid., p.* 501.

"The Right Honble Willm Pitt Esquire's Letter to the Governor of the Massachusetts Bay.

WHITEHAL 4 Febry 1757.

Sir

The King having nothing more at Heart than the Preservation of his good Subjects & Colonies of North America, has come to a Resolution of acting with the greatest vigour in those Parts, the ensuing Campaign, and all necessary Preparations are making for sending a considerable Reinforcement of Troops, together with a Strong Squadron of Ships, for that Purpose; and in order to Act offensively against the French in Canada.

It is His Majesty's Pleasure that you should forthwith call together your Council & Assembly, and press them in the Strongest Manner, to raise with the utmost Expedition, a Number of Provincial Troops at least equal to those raised the last Year, for the Service of the ensuing Campaign, over & above what they shall judge necessary for the immediate Defence of their own Province; and that the Troops, so raised, do act in such Parts, as the Earl of Loudoun, or the Commander in chief of His Majesty's Forces for the Time being, shall judge most conducive to the Service in general; And the King doubts not, but that the several Provinces, truly sensible of His paternal Care in sending so large a Force for their Security, will exert their utmost Endeavours to second & strengthen such offensive Operations against the French, as the Earl of Loudoun or the Commander in chief, for the Time being, shall judge expedient, and will not clogg the Enlistments of the Men, or the raising of the Money for their Pay, &ca with such Limitations, as have been hitherto found to render their Service difficult & ineffectual. And as a further Encouragement, I am to acquaint you, that the Raising of the Men, their Pay, Arms & Cloathing, will be all that will be required on the Part of the several Provinces, Measures having been already taken for laying up Magazines of Stores & Provisions of all kinds at the Expence of the Crown.

I cannot too Strongly recommend it to you, to use all your Influence with your Council and Assembly, for the punctual & immediate Execution of these His Majesty's Commands.

I am
Sir
Your most obedient
humble Servant

Govr of Massachusetts Bay. W PITT"—*Records of Crown Commissions; in Secretary's Office, vol.* I, *p.* 146.

"Letter from the Right Honoble William Pitt, Esqr to the Governor of the Massachusetts Bay.

WHITEHALL 19th Febry 1757.

Sir

Having in my Letter of the 4th Instant informed you, that it was the King's Intention to send a Strong Squadron of Ships of War to North America; I am now to acquaint you, that His Majesty has been pleased to appoint Rear Admiral Holburne to command the said Squadron; and it is the King's Pleasure, that in case any Naval Assistance shall be wanted for the Protection of your Government, you should apply for the same, to the said Rear Admiral, or to the Commander in Chief for the Time being, of His Majesty's Ships in those Seas, who will send you such Assistance as he may be able to do, consistently with the Service, with which he is charged by His Majesty's Instructions; and you will regularly communicate to the said Commander all such Intelligence as shall come to your Knowlege, concerning the Arrival of any Ships of War, or Vessels having Warlike-Stores on Board; and likewise all such Advices, as may concern their Motions & Destination, or may in any manner relate to that part of His Majesty's Service, with which the Commanders of the Kings Ships should be acquainted; and for better Execution of the Orders sent you in this Letter, you will be diligent in employing, proper Persons, & Vessels, not only to procure you the earliest Intelligence, but likewise to be dispatched, from Time to Time, to the said Commander of His Majesty's Ships, with such Accounts, as you shall have Occasion to communicate to him. It is also His Majesty's further Pleasure, that you should use all legal Methods, whenever the Commander in Chief, of His Majesty's Ships shall apply to you, to raise such a Number of Seamen, from Time to Time, as shall be wanted to recruit the Ships in North America.

I am, Sir, Your most obedient
humble Servant

Govr of Massachusetts Bay. W PITT."—*Ibid., p.* 147.

"March 16, 1759. A Memorial of Joseph Frye Esq——Setting forth That in the year 1757. He was appointed Colonel of Eighteen hundred men raised that year by the Prov-

ince and put under the Command of the Earl of Loudoun; that the whole care of this Body of Men, which it was thought at first required five Feild Officers, devolved on the Memorialist; That his Expence as well as care and trouble was hereby increased. That having the Misfortune to fall into the Enemy's hands at the Surrender of Fort William Henry, he suffered great hardships, was stript of his Arms, Cloathing and Camp Equipage, and by the Capitulation laid under Obligation not to take up Arms against the Enemy for the term of eighteen months. That having lost his Papers, and his men dispersed and skattered, his whole Attention was engaged from the time he came home to the latter end of February before he could get any tolerable State of the Regiment, and it was the 14 of April, before he had compleated the Rolls and other business of the Regiment. And Praying the consideration of the Court, and such Allowance as they shall judge meet.
In the House of Representatives. Read and Ordered That the Petitioner be allowed Wages from the time of his entering into the Service till the 14 April 1758, at eighteen pounds per Month deducting what he has already received out of the Treasury for that Service. In Council. Read and Concurred Consented to by the Governor."—*Council Records, vol. XXII., p.* 603.

Chap. 25. "May 31, 1757. In Council——Whereas in & by an Act intituled an Act for preventing the Exportation of Provisions & warlike Stores, it is among other things provided, That it shall be lawful for the Master of any Ship or Vessell, or the owner or Factor to transport any sort of Provisions or Warlike Stores to any of his Majesty's Colonies or Plantations in North America, or Fish in bulk to some place in Europe in Amity with his Majesty——first giving bond to the Impost Officer in the sum mentioned in the said Act to carry such Provisions & Stores to the Port for which they were design'd——And whereas by an Order from the honourable the Commissioners of his Majesty's Customs the several Collectors in the respective Ports are enjoined to take bonds for the same Purpose of all Masters who lade any Provisions or Warlike Stores, whereby the giving Bond at the Impost Office is become unnecessary. Wherefore Ordered that when it shall appear to the Impost Officer or his Deputies, that a Bond has been given at the Custom House for the purposes aforesaid, That then & in such case no bond shall be required at the Impost Office of any Master, Owner or Freighter loading as aforesaid. In the House of Representatives——Read & Concurred. Consented to by a Major Part of the Council."—*Council Records, vol. XXII., p.* 13.

Chap. 31. "June 8, 1756. A Petition of Samuel Smith for himself & the other Proprietors of the Island Beeches &^{ca} in Eastham lying West of Billingsgate & South of Griffiths Island, Setting forth the Benefit of the Act of this Court (now expired) for the Security of the said Beeches & Islands, and Praying that it may be revived, and forasmuch as the Petitioner is a Principal Proprietor here, and has been at great Cost to preserve them from Injury Praying for Liberty to keep a Number of Cattle (he making good any Damage they may do) as also to keep a Pound for Impounding Cattle & Horses that may be found Trespassing——
In the House of Representatives; Read & Ordered that the Petitioner Notify the Inhabitants of the Town of Eastham with this Petition by leaving an Attested Copy thereof with the Clerk of the said Town that they shew Cause if any they have on the Third Wednesday of the next Sitting of this Court why the Prayer thereof should not be granted——In Council; Read & Concur'd"—*Council Records, vol. XXI., p.* 206.
"December 13, 1757. A Petition of John Ralph and Others, Indians of the Town of Eastham and Harwich in the County of Barnstable——Setting forth That notwithstanding the Care of the Government the Town or Proprietors of Eastham have encroached on their property in a certain Neck of Beach and Thatch Ground or Island within or near the Town of Eastham called Billingsgate Point or Island, and have sold the same to Samuel Smith Esqr and Silvanus Snow, both of Eastham. That said place is the most convenient for the Whale Fishery of any within the County and hath ever since the memory of Man been improved for that purpose and no other; and as many of said Indians are Whalemen such an Alienation must prove very much to their prejudice, and praying for Releif.
In the House of Representatives. Read and Ordered That the Petitioners serve the Adverse Party with a Copy of this Petition, that they make answer thereto on the second Tuesday of the next Sitting of this Court——Also that the Guardians of the Potenumacutt Indians be duly notified thereof, that so they may give this Court the best Information they can relative to the matters complained of. In Council. Read and Concurred." —*Ibid., vol. XXII, p.* 150.
"March 14, 1758. A Petition of Thomas Ralph and Others, Indian Natives of the Towns of Eastham and Harwich——Setting forth That the English Inhabitants have encroached on their property, and that the Town of Eastham have sold to Samuel Smith Esq and Mr Silvanus Snow a certain Neck of Beach and Thatch Ground on one side of Billingsgate most commodiously situated for the whaling business, and which has from time immemorial been improved by them for that purpose, and praying Releif. In Council. Read again together with the Answer of Silvanus Snow, and other Papers accompanying the same and Ordered That James Minot and William Brattle Esq^{rs} with Such as the honourable House shall join be a Committee to take the same under consideration, to hear the Parties and report what they judge proper to be done thereon.
In the House of Representatives. Read and Concurred and Mr Bacon, Col^{o} White and Joseph Cushing Esq are joined in the Affair."—*Ibid , p.* 264.
"March 15, 1758. The Committee appointed the 14 Instant on the Petition of John Ralph and Others reported That they had heard the Parties who were desirous of a Committee to veiw the Premises. They therefore reported that a Committee be appointed for that purpose.
In the House of Representatives. Ordered That the Report be accepted, and that Mr Edward Bacon and Captn Joseph Robinson with such as the honourable Board shall

appoint be a Committee to view the Premises, hear the Parties and make Report. In Council. Read and Concurred and Gamaliel Bradford Esq is joined in the Affair. (17th) Consented to by the Governor."—*Ibid., p.* 269.

Chap. 32. "December 12, 1757. A Petition of Thomas Foster Esqr in behalf of the Town of Plymouth——Setting forth That the great Herring Pond (so called) lyeth in the Town of Plymouth from whence runneth a large Brook or River through the Town of Sandwich into the Sea, and that the Line between the two Towns runneth over the Neck of said Pond just above the place where the said Brook issues from it; That there are large Quantities of Alewives come up the Brook to cast their Spawn in the Pond, but as the Law now stands for regulating the taking of Alewives, the Town of Plymouth is deprived of all advantages of the Fishery, and the Town of Sandwich apprehending the sole right thereof to be in them refuse to treat with the Town of Plymouth about it. And praying that this Court, would interpose for their releif.

In the House of Representatives Read and Ordered That the Petitioner notify the Town of Sandwich of this Petition by leaving an attested copy thereof with the Clerk of said Town, that they shew cause (if any they have) on the second Thursday of the next Sitting of the Court why the Prayer thereof Should not be granted. In Council. Read and Concurred."—*Council Records, vol. XXII., p.* 148.

Chap. 35. "April 4th, 1757. In Council; Ordered that John Erving & William Brattle Esqrs with such as the Honourable House shall appoint be a Committee to Consider and Report what is further necessary to be done to restrain all Merchant Vessells, Fishing Vessells and others departing from any Ports in this Province agreeable to his Excellency. the Earl of Loudouns Letter desiring an Embargo, and the Committee are directed to sit forthwith.——

In the House of Representatives; Read & Concurr'd, and Colo White Colo Williams, and Major Epes are joined in the Affair.

The Committee aforesaid soon after reported—That an Embargo should be laid on all Ships & Vessells, (Fishing Vessells included) within the several Ports of this Province to the Twentieth day of April instant, and that a Bill be brought in accordingly——In Council; Read & Ordered that this Report be accepted "—*Council Records, vol. XXI., p.* 423.

"A Proclamation prohibiting the departure of any Ship or Vessel out of the Province untill the 20th day of April Instant.

By the Honourable His Majesty's Council for the Province of the Massachusetts Bay in New England.

A Proclamation.

Whereas the General Assembly have in their present Session passed an Act to prohibit the Departure of all Ships & Vessels from any Port or Place within the Province, and of all Fishing-Vessels, such only excepted as are not usually absent more than four Days at a Time, untill the Twentieth Day of April Instant, without special Permission from his Majesty's Council, or the major part of them, on Penalty of forfeiting One Hundred Pounds, to be paid by the Master; and the like Penalty of One Hundred Pounds to be paid by the Owner or Owners of every such Ship or Vessel departing as aforesaid: And Whereas Provision is made in said Act, that his Majesty's Council, or the major part of them, shall, if they see fit, lengthen out the said Embargo to the first Day of June next.

We have therefore thought fit, in Council to issue this Proclamation; hereby giving publick Notice of the aforesaid Act of Government; and strictly forbidding all Masters or Owners of any Ships or Vessels within the Province to suffer any such Ships or Vessels, without special Permission from his Majesty's Council or the major Part of them, to depart out of the same, or to proceed to any of the fishing-Banks untill the Twentieth Day of April Instant.

And we do hereby forbid all Officers concerned in the Clearing of Vessels to give Certificates or Clearances for any Ships or Vessels whatsoever within their respective Districts to depart out of the Province, during the Continuation of this Prohibition or Embargo, without permission as aforesaid.

And all his Majesty's good Subjects who shall or may discover any Ship or Vessel privately or clandestinely loading within the Province, or departing out the same contrary to Law, are hereby desired to give immediate Information thereof to his Majesty's Council, or to any of the Officers aforesaid, that all Persons offending may be prosecuted according to Law for any such Offence.

Given at the Council-Chamber in Boston the Seventh Day of April 1757. in the Thirtieth Year of the Reign of our Sovereign Lord George the Second, by the Grace of God, of Great Britain, France & Ireland, King, Defender of the Faith &c.

By Order of his Majesty's Council

A. Oliver Secry

	JOHN HILL	WM PEPPERRELL.
	JAMES MINOT	J. OSBORNE
JOHN ERVING	A OLIVER	JACOB WENDELL
RICHD CUTT	JOS: PYNCHON	BENJA LYNDE
WM BRATTLE	JOHN OTIS	S. DANFORTH
	THOS HUTCHINSON	SAML WATTS
	BENJA LINCOLN	GEORGE LEONARD "—

Records of Civil Commissions; in Secretary's Office, vol. 2, *p* 322.

"A Proclamation Prohibiting the Departure of any Ship or Vessel out of the Province untill the tenth Day of May next.

By the Honourable His Majesty's Council for the Province of the Massachusetts Bay in New England.

A Proclamation.

Whereas the General Assembly have in their present Session passed an Act to prohibit the Departure of all Ships & Vessels from any Port or Place within the Provce and of all fishing-Vessels, such only excepted as are not usually absent more than four Days at a Time, untill the Twentieth Day of April Instant without special Permission from His Majesty's Council, or the major part of them, on Penalty of forfeiting One Hundred Pounds, to be paid by the Master; and the like Penalty of One Hundred Pounds to be paid by the Owner or Owners of every such Ship or Vessel departing as aforesaid; And a Proclamation was issued by the Council on the Seventh Instant; giving publick Notice of the aforesaid Act, and forbidding the Departure of all Vessels accordingly; And Whereas Provision is made in said Act, that His Majesty's Council, or the Major Part of them, shall, if they see fit, lengthen out the said Embargo to the first Day of June next

We have therefore thought fit, in Council, to issue this Proclamation; hereby strictly forbidding all Masters or Owners of any Ships or Vessels within the Province to suffer any such Ships or Vessels, without special Permission from his Majesty's Council or the major Part of them, to depart out of the same, or to proceed to any of the fishing Banks untill the Tenth Day of May next; unless this Prohibition or Embargo shall before the said Tenth Day of May next, be decleared void and of no further Effect.

And we do hereby forbid all Officers concerned in the Clearing of Vessels to give Certificates or Clearances for any Ships or Vessels whatsoever within their respective Districts to depart out of the Province, during the continuation of this Prohibition or Embargo, without Permission as aforesaid.

And all his Majesty's good Subjects who shall or may discover any Ship or Vessel privately or clandestinely loading within the Province, or departing out of the same contrary to Law, are hereby desired to give immediate Information thereof to his Majesty's Council, or to any of the Officers aforesaid, that all Persons offending may be prosecuted according to Law for any such offence.

Given at the Council-Chamber in Boston the eighteen[th*] Day of April 1757. in the Thirtieth Year of the Reign of our Sovereign Lord George the Second, by the Grace of God, of Great Britain, France & Ireland King, Defender of the Faith &c.

By Order of his Majesty's Council
A Oliver Secry

	JOHN CHANDLER	W^M^ PEPPERRELL
	A OLIVER	J: OSBORNE
JOHN ERVING	JOSEPH PYNCHON	JACOB WENDELL
RICH^D^ CUTT	JOHN OTIS	JN^O^ CUSHING
W^M^ BRATTLE.	THO^S^ HUTCHINSON	DAN^L^ RUSSELL
	STEPHEN SEWALL	SAM^L^ WATTS
	ISAAC ROYALL	JOHN HILL

[God save the King*] "—*Ibid.*, *p.* 323.

"April 20, 1757. In Council; Whereas the Limitation of Four Days only for any Fishing Vessells to be out on their Voyage is found to be the means of Causing the Fishery intirely to Cease, and it being apprehended that no Inconvenience can arise from their being absent a longer time, provided they do not go beyond the Limits within which the Coasting Vessells which are allowed to depart from One Port to another usually pass—— Therefore Ordered That any Vessell employed in Fishing may have Liberty to be absent Twelve days from their respective departure; Provided always that if any Fishing Vessell shall go to the Eastward of Falmouth in Casco Bay or to the Southward of Cape Cod unless it shall be made to appear to have been absolutely unavoidable the Owners and Masters of such Vessells shall be liable to Forfeit and pay in like manner as if this Order had not been made and passed.——In the House of Representatives; Read and Nonconcurred "—*Council Records, vol. XXI., p.* 484.

"A Proclamation Prohibiting the departure of any Ships or Vessels from this Province untill the 20th day of May Instant.

By the Honourable His Majesty's Council for the Province of the Massachusetts Bay in New England.

A Proclamation.

Whereas the General Assembly have passed an Act to prohibit the Departure of all Ships & Vessels from any Port or Place within the Province, untill the Twentieth Day of April this present Year, without special Permission from His Majesty's Council or the major Part of them, on Penalty of forfeiting One Hundred Pounds, to be paid by the Master; and the like Penalty of One Hund[d] Pounds to be paid by the Owner or Owners of every such Ship or Vessel departing as aforesaid: And Whereas Provision is made in said Act, that His Majesty's Council, or the major Part of them, shall, if they see fit, lengthen out the said Embargo to the first day of June next.

We have therefore thought fit, in Council, to issue this Proclamation; hereby strictly forbidding all Masters or Owners of any Ships or Vessels within the Province to suffer any such Ships or Vessels to depart out of the same, (fishing Vessels and Vessels Bound to Nova-Scotia excepted, which are hereby permitted to depart as usual,) untill the Twentieth Day of May Instant.

And we do hereby forbid all Officers concerned in the Clearing of Vessels to give Certificates or Clearances for any Ships or Vessels whatsoever within their respective Districts (excepting as before excepted) to depart out of the Province during the Continuance of this Prohibition or Embargo, without Permission as aforesaid.

And all his Majesty's good Subjects who shall or may discover any Ship or Vessel privately or clandestinely loading within the Province, or departing out of the same contrary to Law, and to the Tenor of this Proclamation, are hereby desired to give immediate Information thereof to his Majesty's Council, or to any of the Officers aforesaid, that all Persons offending may be prosecuted according to Law for any such Offence.

Given at the Council-Chamber in Boston the Ninth Day of May 1757, in y[e] Thirtieth

* Not in the record; supplied from the original.

Year of the Reign of our Sovereign Lord George the Second, by the Grace of God, of Great Britain, France & Ireland, King, Defender of the Faith &c.

By Order of his Majesty's Council

Thos Clarke Depty Secry.

	SAML WATTS	J. OSBORNE
	GEORGE LEONARD	FRANS FOXCROFT
JOHN ERVING	JAMES MINOT	BENJA LYNDE
WM BRATTLE	A OLIVER	JNO CUSHING
	JOSEPH PYNCHON	DANL RUSSELL
	ISAAC ROYALL	S. DANFORTH.
	BENJA LINCOLN.	

God save the King."—*Records of Civil Commissions; in Secretary's Office, vol.* 2, *p.* 326.

"Letter from the Right Honorable Earl of Holdernesse, To the Governor of this Province

WHITEHALL 2d May 1757.

Sir.

The Crops of Corn having from the badness of the Season last Year, greatly failed in many Parts of Great Britain and Ireland, which makes a Supply thereof very much wanted, for which Reasons Orders have been sent to purchase large Quantities in America; and it being apprehended, that the Ships loaded therewith may not be able to Sail on Account of the Embargo laid in several Parts of America, by Lord Loudoun's Desire, on all Ships in general, by which means, His Majesty's Dominions in Europe may be greatly distressed: I am commanded to signify to you The King's Pleasure, that you do immediately, upon the Receipt of this Letter, cause any Embargo, that shall be then subsisting within your Government, either in Consequence of Lord Loudoun's application to you, or of any Directions, sent you by the Board of Trade, to be taken off from all Vessels loaded with Corn, or any other Species of Grain for Great Britain, and Ireland; and that you do take particular Care, that no future Embargo, which it may be thought expedient to lay, do extend to Vessels so loaded; but on the contrary you will give all proper Encouragement, and Assistance to Persons, who shall be employ'd, in the purchasing & shipping Corn, for the Supply of his Majesty's Dominions in Europe, taking Care, that they do give sufficient Security for landing the Cargoes at the Places for which they shall be designed, agreable to an Act of Parliament, passed this Session, Entitled, "An Act to prohibit, for a limited Time, the Exportation of Corn, Grain, Meal, Malt, &ca &ca" which Act has been transmitted to you, by the Lords Commissioners of Trade & Plantations.

I am
Sir
Your most Obedient
Humble Servant
HOLDERNESSE."—*Records of Crown Commissions; in Secretary's Office, vol.* 1, *p.* 148.

Govr of Massachusetts Bay

Chap. 36. The following additional Section appears on the engrossment apparently cancelled by pen lines.

"*And be it further enacted,*

That no person in his majestys service shall pawn, truck barter or sell his Arms, Ammunition or Cloathing on penalty of being punished by riding the Wooden Horse, runing the Gantlet, or other like Military Punishment, and the Person accepting & receiving the same, shall be compelled to restore and make good the same without Price or Redemption, and shall further (if in his Majesty's service) suffer Military Punishment as aforesaid."

Chap. 38. "April 6, 1757. In the House of Representatives; Ordered that Mr Gridley Colo Hale, Judge Russell, Colo Williams, Mr Paine Colo Clap, Colo Otis, Colo White and Mr Bradbury with such as the Honoble Board shall join be a Committee to take under Consideration what they judge the most suitable and Convenient times for the Sitting of the several Courts of Justice through the Province and Report——In Council; Read & Concurred; and Benjamin Lynde, Samuel Danforth Stephen Sewall, and Richard Cutt Esqr are joined in the Affair"—*Council Records, vol. XXI., p.* 427.

"April 7, 1757. In the House of Representatives; Ordered that the Committee of both Houses appointed to Consider of the most suitable & convenient times for holding the several Courts of Judicature within the Province be directed also to take under Consideration what alteration they judge proper should be made in the Places by Law assigned for holding said Courts & Report.——In Council; Read & Concurr'd"—*Ibid., p.* 430.

Chap. 40. "Septemr 7, 1756. In the House of Representatives; Resolved that the Valuation of the Estates of the Inhabitants thrô the Province be referred till the further Order of this Court, & that directions be sent to the Assessors of the several Towns to Suspend their Proceedings thereon accordingly——In Council; Read & Non Concur'd"—*Council Records, vol. XXI., p.* 270.

"Septemr 10, 1756. In the House of Representatives; Whereas an Act of the Province made & passed in the Twenty Ninth Year of his present Majestys Reign intitled an Act for inquiring into the Rateable Estates of the Province is apprehended to be imperfect both as to the Act itself the List thereby setled & agreed upon; And if the several Towns in the Province should by their Assessors conform thereto, that it would nevertheless be impracticable to make a just Valuation thereof——Therefore Voted that the Assessors of the several Towns within this Province be directed to suspend any further Proceedings as to taking the List of Valuation agreeable to said Act untill the further Order of this Court.——In Council; Read & Non Concur'd"—*Ibid., p.* 277.

"Septemr 11, 1756. On the Bill in Addition to an Act intitled an Act for Enquiring into the Rateable Estates of the Province.——

In the House of Representatives; Ordered that the Consideration of this Bill be referred to the next Sitting of this Court, and the Assessors of the several Towns are forbid any further Proceedings with respect to the Valuation in the mean time.—In Council; Read & Concur'd "—*Ibid.*, *p.* 280.

"June 11, 1757. In the House of Representatives. Ordered That the Secretary be directed to return to the several Towns the Lists of Valuation of Estates they sent into his Office the last Year in consequence of a late Act of the Government. In Council——Read and Concurred. Consented to by a Major Part of the Council."—*Ibid.*, *vol. XXII.*, *p.* 51.

"Augt 26, 1757. In the House of Representatives. Resolved That the valuation of Estates thro' the Province be putt off to another year And that directions be sent to the Assessors of the several Towns and Districts to stay their Proceedings therein accordingly. In Council—Read and Concurred Consented to by the Governor."—*Ibid.*, *p.* 94.

Chap. 41. "April 22, 1757. In the House of Representatives; Ordered that Samuel Welles & James Russell Esq^{rs} with such as the Honourable Board shall join be a Committee to take Bonds agreeable to an Act intituled an Act for raising a Sum of Money by Lottery for the Encouragement of the Settlement called Germantown in the Town of Braintree and lodge the same with the Province Treasurer.——In Council; Read & Concurred, and Samuel Danforth Esqr is joined in the Affair——Consented to by a Major Part of the Council "—*Council Records*, *vol. XXI.*, *p.* 490.

"January 24, 1758. In the House of Representatives Voted That the Managers of the German Town Lottery (so called) be and hereby are allowed to make use of the Representatives Room in the Recess of the Court to draw the several Classes of said Lottery, as also the Use of the Province Boxes, on condition of their making good any damage that shall ensue in consequence thereof to the said Room or Boxes. In Council. Read and Concurred. Consented to by the Governor."—*Ibid.*, *vol. XXII.*, *p.* 236.

TABLE

Showing the beginning and end of each year of the reign of George the Second, from the sixteenth to the thirtieth inclusive.

16th of George the Second, ...	from June 11, 1742,	to June	11, 1743.
17th of George the Second, ...	" 11, 1743,	"	11, 1744.
18th of George the Second, ...	" 11, 1744,	"	11, 1745.
19th of George the Second, ...	" 11, 1745,	"	11, 1746.
20th of George the Second, ...	" 11, 1746,	"	11, 1747.
21st of George the Second, ...	" 11, 1747,	"	11, 1748.
22d of George the Second, ...	" 11, 1748,	"	11, 1749.
23d of George the Second, ...	" 11, 1749,	"	11, 1750.
24th of George the Second, ...	" 11, 1750,	"	11, 1751.
25th of George the Second, ...	" 11, 1751,	"	11, 1752.
26th of George the Second, ...	" 11, 1752,	"	11, 1753.
27th of George the Second, ...	" 11, 1753,	"	11, 1754.
28th of George the Second, ...	" 11, 1754,	"	11, 1755.
29th of George the Second, ...	" 11, 1755,	"	11, 1756.
30th of George the Second, ...	" 11, 1756,	"	11, 1757.

Index of Names.

INDEX OF NAMES.

D.

G.

H.

* The Earl of Halifax after his marriage to Miss Annie Dunk in 1741, assumed the name of Dunk in addition to that of Montague. See Collins Peerage.

Q.

R.

List of the Acts and Resolves

CONTAINED IN THIS VOLUME.

130 [1105]

LIST OF THE PUBLIC ACTS.

Page.		TITLES.	Date of Passage.	Disallowed by Privy Council.	Expired or had its effect.
		1742-43.—First Session.	1742.		
5	Chapter 1.	An act for granting the sum of two thousand three hundred and fifty pounds for the support of his majesty's governour, .	June 4,	-	- -
6	Chapter 2.	An act for allowing necessary supplies to the Eastern and Western Indians, and for regulating trade w[*i*]th them [1737-38, chap. 7; 1740-41, chap. 11], . .	July 1,	-	June 25, 1743.
8	Chapter 3.	An act for supplying the treasury with the sum of fifteen thousand pounds, for discharging the publick debts, &c[a], and for drawing in the said bills into the treasury again, and for stating their value in discharging of publick and private debts, ...	July 1,	-	- -
12	Chapter 4.	An act in addition to and for rend[*e*]ring more effectual an act for regulating the assize of cask, and preventing deceit in packing of fish, beef and pork, for sale, made in the fourth year of the reign of King William and Queen Mary; and also for the preventing fraud and injustice in the measuring of grain [1692-3, chap. 17; 1718-19, chap. 16; 1722-23, chap. 4; 1730-31, chap. 5; 1737-38, chap. 12], .	July 1,	-	July 5, 1745.
13	Chapter 5.	An act for establishing and better regulating fees within this province [1692-3, chap. 37; 1701-2, chap. 7], ...	July 1,	-	1743.
18	Chapter 6.	An act for granting unto his majesty an excise upon wines, liquors and other strong drink sold by retail, and upon lemmons and limes, ...	July 1,	-	June 29, 1745.
22	Chapter 7.	An act for granting a sum for the pay of the members of the council and house of representatives in general court assembled, and for establishing the wages, &c., of sundry persons in the service of the province, ...	July 1,	-	- -
25	Chapter 8.	An act in addition to the several acts or laws of this province for the settlement and support of ministers [1692-3, chaps. 26 and 46; 1695-6, chap. 8; 1702, chap. 10; 1706, chap. 9; 1715-16, chap. 17; 1723-4, chap. 14; 1728-9, chap. 4; 1731-2, chap. 11; 1734-5, chap. 6; 1737-8, chap. 6; 1740-41, chap. 6], ...	July 1,	-	- -
25	Chapter 9.	An act for holding a court of oyer and terminer in and for the island of Nantucket,	July 1,	-	- -
26	Chapter 10.	An act for altering the time for holding the inferio[*u*]r court of common pleas in the county of Suffolk, and also the court of general sessions of the peace and inferior court of common pleas in the county of Hampshire [1740-41, chap. 13; 1699-1700, chap. 2, § 2], ...	July 1,	-	- -
26	Chapter 11.	An act to prevent dam[*m*]age being done unto Billingsgate Bay in the town of Eastham, by cattle and horse-kind, and sheep feeding on the beach and islands adjoining thereto, ...	July 1,	-	July 5, 1747.
		Third Session.	1742-43.		
28	Chapter 12.	An act to prevent encumbrances about the doors of the court-house in Boston, .	Jan. 6,	-	- -

List of the Public Acts—Continued.

Page.	TITLES.	Date of Passage.	Disallowed by Privy Council.	Expired or had its effect.
	1742-43.—THIRD SESSION—*Con.*	1742-43.		
28	Chapter 13. An act for preventing the unnecessary expense in the attendance of petit jurors of the several courts of justice within this province [1738-9, chap. 4], . . .	Jan. 15,	-	- -
29	Chapter 14. An act for supplying the treasury with the sum of twelve thousand pounds, for discharging the publick debts, &c., and for drawing in the said bills into the treasury again, and for stating their value in discharging of publick and private debts, ...	Jan. 12,	-	- -
33	Chapter 15. An act for apportioning and assessing a tax of eight thousand pounds in bills of the tenor and form last emitted, . . .	Jan. 15,	-	- -
34	Chapter 16. An act for making more effectual an act [e][i]ntitled, "An act for regulating the militia" [1693-94, chap. 3], . . .	Jan. 15,	-	Jan. 17, 1749-50.
35	Chapter 17. An act to prevent the spreading of the small-pox and other infectious sickness, and to prevent the concealing of the same [1739-40, chap. 1], ...	Jan. 15,	-	Jan. 17, 1749-50.
37	Chapter 18. An act in addition to the several laws of this province relating to the support of poor and indigent persons [1692-93, chap. 28, § 9; 1699-1700, chap. 8; 1735-36, chap. 4; 1740-41, chap. 20], . . .	Jan. 15,	-	Jan. 15, 1745-46.
38	Chapter 19. An act to prevent unnecessary law-suits [1734-35, chap. 4; 7 Mass., 143], . . .	Jan. 15,	-	Apr. 20, 1750.
39	Chapter 20. An act in addition to the several acts for regulating the assize of casks, and preventing deceit in the packing of fish, beef and pork for sale [1742-43, chap 4],	Jan. 15,	-	July 5, 1745.
39	Chapter 21. An act to enable the proprietors of Hassanamisco Lands in the township of Grafton to raise mon[ey][ie]s for supporting the ministry, and defraying the other charges arisen and arising there [1727-28, chap. 14; 1734-35, chap. 20],	Jan. 15,	-	- -
40	Chapter 22. An act to prevent firing the woods, . .	Jan. 15,	-	Jan. 17, 1745-46.
41	Chapter 23. An act for granting to Thomas Symmes, gentleman, and Grace Parker, widow, both of Charlestown, in the County of Middlesex, the sole privile[d]ge of making stone ware, ...	Jan. 15,	-	Jan. 17, 1758.
42	Chapter 24. An act for the more easy partition of lands,	Jan. 14,	-	Jan. 17, 1745-46.
43	Chapter 25. An act to prevent the multiplicity of law-suits, ...	Jan. 15,	-	Jan. 17, 1749-50.
44	Chapter 26. An act for inlisting the inhabitants of Dorchester into his majesty's service for the defence of Castle William, as occasion shall require, ...	Jan. 15,	-	Jan. 17, 1745-46.
45	Chapter 27. An act to prevent gaming for money or other gain [1736-37, chap. 17], . . .	Jan. 15,	-	Jan. 17, 1749-50.
47	Chapter 28. An act in further addition to and explanation of [the] [an] act [e][i]ntitled, an "Act for regulating townships, choice of town officers," &c. [1692-93, chap. 28; 1693-94, chap. 20, § 18; 1699-1700, chaps. 12, 26; 1710-11, chap. 7, § 1; 1713-14, chap. 16, § 1], ...	Jan. 15,	-	Jan. 15, 1746-7.
48	Chapter 29. An act for the more easy partition of lands or other real estate given by will, and held in common and undivided among the devisees, ...	Jan. 15,	-	Jan. 15, 1745-6.
49	Chapter 30. An act for erecting a tract of land commonly called New Lisborn, lying in the county of Hampshire, into a township by the name of Pelham, ...	Jan. 15,	-	- -

List of the Public Acts—Continued.

Page.	TITLES.	Date of Passage.	Disallowed by Privy Council.	Expired or had its effect.
	1742-43.—THIRD SESSION—*Con.*	1742-43.		
50	Chapter 31. An act for apportioning and assessing a tax of twenty thousand pounds in bills of credit of the tenor and form last emitted; and also for apportioning and assessing a further tax of one thousand six hundred and thirty-eight pounds and threepence one farthing, in bills of credit of said tenor and form paid the representatives for their service and attendance in general court, and travel [1741-42, chap. 11, § 15; 1741-42, chap. 11, § 26; 1742-43, chap. 3, § 6; 1742-43, chap. 3, § 7; 1741-42, chap. 11, § 29], .	Jan. 6,	-	- -
	FOURTH SESSION.	1743.		
64	Chapter 32. An act for fixing the times for holding the superio[*u*]r courts of judicature, courts of assize and general goal delivery, and courts of general sessions of the peace, and inferio[*u*]r courts of common pleas, within the several counties in this province [1699-1700, chap. 1; 1704-1705, chap. 1; 1708-1709, chap. 9; 1711-12, chap. 3, § 6; 1712-13, chap. 5; 1715-16, chap. 2; 1719-20, chaps. 4, 5; 1722-23, chap. 13; 1725-26, chap. 6; 1727-28, chap. 16; 1728-29, chap. 19; 1735-36, chap. 3; 1736-37, chap. 21; 1740-41, chap. 5; 1742-43, chap. 10; 1699-1700, chap. 3; 1703-1704, chap. 8; 1711-12, chap. 3; 1714, chap. 9, § 6; 1715-16, chap. 20; 1717-18, chap. 8; 1720-21, chaps. 1, 13; 1721, chap. 3; 1724-25, chap. 11; 1727-28, chap. 16; 1733-34, chap. 9; 1735-36, chap. 24; 1736-37, chap. 21; 1740-41, chap. 13; 1741-42, chap. 19], ...	Apr. 23,	-	- -
65	Chapter 33. An act in addition to the several acts for regulating fences [1693-94, chap. 7; 1698, chap. 12; 1718-19, chap. 3; 1727-28, chap. 13; 1740-41, chap. 19], . .	Apr. 23,	-	- -
66	Chapter 34. An act to enable the town of Weymouth to regulate and order the taking and disposing of the fish called shadd and alewives, within the limits of that town, .	Apr. 23,	-	Apr 30, 1746.
	1743-44.—FIRST SESSION.			
75	Chapter 1. An act for granting the sum of thirteen hundred and fifty pounds for the support of his majesty's governour, . . .	June 10,	-	- -
75	Chapter 2. An act for establishing the wages, &c[a], of sundry persons in the service of the province, ...	June 25,	-	- -
77	Chapter 3. An act to enable the surviving trustees, of the several towns within this province, of the sixty thousand pounds' loan, who have paid their towns' proportion thereof unto the province treasury, where there is not a majority of them living, to collect the several sums due from particular persons to such [trustees] [*towns*], . . .	June 17,	-	- -
78	Chapter 4. An act for holding a court of oyer and terminer in and for the island of Nantucket,	June 17,		- -

List of the Public Acts—Continued.

Page.	TITLES.	Date of Passage.	Disallowed by Privy Council.	Expired or had its effect.
	1743-44.—FIRST SESSION—*Con.*	1743.		
78	Chapter 5. An act for impowering the town of Boston, to impose and collect a tax or duty on coaches, chaises, &c[a]., for the use and service of said town, ...	June 25,	-	- -
79	Chapter 6. An act for preventing mich[ci][*ie*]f by unruly dogs on the island of Nantucket [100 Mass., 141], ...	June 25,	-	June 27, 1746.
80	Chapter 7. An act in addition to, and in explanation of sundry clauses of, an act, [e][*i*]ntit[*u*]led "An act to ascertain the value of money, and of the bills of publick credit of this province," &c[a], made and pass'd in the fifteenth year of his majesty's reign [1741-42, chap. 12, § 3], ...	June 25,	-	- -
81	Chapter 8. An act for granting unto his majesty several rates and duties of impost and tunnage of shipping, ...	June 25,	-	Aug. 18, 1744.
86	Chapter 9. An act for apportioning and assessing a tax of twenty thousand pounds, in bills of credit of the teno[u]r and form last emitted; and also for apportioning and assessing a further tax of three thousand seven hundred and thirty-eight pounds, four shillings and ninepence three farthings, in bills of credit of said tenor and form, paid the representatives for their service and attendance in general court, and travel, and to discharge a fine laid this present year on the towns of Medfield, Tiverton and Freetown, for not sending a representative [1741-42, chap. 11, § 27; 1742-43; chap. 14, § 5; 1741-42, chap. 11, § 29], ...	June 25,	-	- -
	SECOND SESSION.			
101	Chapter 10. An act for establishing and regulating fees within this province [1692-93, chap. 37; 1742-43, chap. 5], ...	Sept. 15,	-	Oct. 26, 1744.
107	Chapter 11. An act for securing the seasonable payment of town and precinct rates or assessments [1736-37, chap. 15], . .	Sept. 15,	-	Jan. 25, 1754.
108	Chapter 12. An act for erecting of workhouses for the reception and employment of the idle and indigent [1699-1700, chap 8; 1703-4, chap. 14; 1710-11, chap. 6; 1730-31, chap. 3; 1740-41, chap. 20; 1735-36, chap. 4], ...	Sept. 17,	-	- -
	THIRD SESSION.			
112	Chapter 13. An act for supplying the treasury with the sum of twenty thousand pounds for put[*t*]ing the province in a better posture of defence, for discharging the publick debts, &c., and for drawing in the said bills into the treasury again, and for stating their value in discharging publick and private debts, ...	Nov. 12,	-	- -
116	Chapter 14. An act for preventing the destruction of white pine trees within this province, and for encouraging the preservation of them, for the use of the royal navy, .	Nov. 11,	-	Nov. 12, 1746.
117	Chapter 15. An act to enable the proprietors of private ways to repair them in an equal manner,	Nov. 11,	-	Nov. 12, 1746.
117	Chapter 16. An act in addition to and for rendring more effectual an act made in the four-			

List of the Public Acts—Continued.

Page.	TITLES.		Date of Passage.	Disallowed by Privy Council.	Expired or had its effect.
	1743-44.—THIRD SESSION—*Con.*		1743.		
		teenth year of his present majesty's reign, [e][i]ntitled "An act to prevent dam[m]age being done to the harbour of Cape Cod by cattle and horse-kind feeding on Provincetown land" [1740-41, chap. 15], ...	Nov. 11,	-	- -
118	Chapter 17.	An act for the more speedy finishing of the land-bank or manufactory scheme, .	Nov. 10,	-	- -
	FOURTH SESSION.		1743-44.		
122	Chapter 18.	An act to prevent the great injury and injustice arising to the inhabitants of this province by the frequent and very large emissions of bills of public credit in the neighbouring governments [1738-39, chap. 14, § 1], ...	March 17,	-	Mar. 17, 1745-46.
124	Chapter 19.	An act for regulating the hospital on Rainsford['s] Island, and further providing in case of sickness [1738-39, chap. 8; 1701-2, chap. 9], . . .	March 5,	-	April 22, 1749.
126	Chapter 20.	An act providing that the solemn affirmation of the people called Quakers shall, in certain cases, be accepted instead of an oath in the usual form; and for preventing inconvenienc[i]es by means of their having heretofore acted in some town offices without taking the oaths by law required for such offices [1719-20, chap. 11], ...	March 1,	-	April 25, 1747.
127	Chapter 21.	An act to regulate the expence of private bridges, ...	March 21,	-	Mar. 24, 1746-47.
128	Chapter 22.	An act for rendring more effectual the laws already in being relating to the admeasurement of boards, plank and timber, and for preventing fraud and abuse in shingles, beef and pork exported from this province, and also for regulating the assize of staves and hoops [1695-6, chap. 5; 1710-11, chap. 7; 1727, chap. 7],	March 22,	-	Sept. 12, 1747.
131	Chapter 23.	An act to prevent unnecessary expence in suits at law, ...	March 22,	-	Mar. 24, 1746-47.
132	Chapter 24.	An act to impower justices of the peace to summon witnesses, ...	March 22,	-	- -
132	Chapter 25.	An act for the preservation of and to promote the growth of a certain parcel of wood and timber in the town-ship of Ipswich, in the county of Essex, . .	March 22,	-	- -
133	Chapter 26.	An act in addition to an act made in the fifteenth year of his present majesty's reign, intituled "An act in addition to an act made to prevent the destruction of the fish called alewives, and other fish" [1741-42, chap. 16], ...	Feb. 27,	-	- -
135	Chapter 27.	An act to confirm several votes of the proprietors of the westerly half of Leicester [1723-24, chap. 17], ...	Feb. 25,	-	- -
135	Chapter 28.	An act to explain a paragraph in an act of this province, made in the present year of his majesty's reign, for the more speedy finishing the land-bank or manufactory scheme [1743-44, chap. 17], .	Feb. 28,	-	- -
137	Chapter 29.	An act to enable justices of the peace and town clerks to administer an oath to sealers of weights and measures, &c [a]., and to establish their fees [1692-93, chap. 30, § 1], ...	March 5,	-	- -

List of the Public Acts—Continued.

Page.	TITLES.	Date of Passage.	Disallowed by Privy Council.	Expired or had its effect.
	1744-45.—FIRST SESSION.	1744.		
143	Chapter 1. An act for the more effectual guarding and securing our seacoasts, and for the encouragement of seamen to enlist themselves in the province Snow, or such vessels of war as shall be commissioned and fitted out by this or other of his majesty's governments during this present war with France, ...	June 19,	-	- -
144	Chapter 2. An act for levying soldiers, ...	June 18,	-	- -
147	Chapter 3. An act to prevent soldiers and seamen in his majesty's service being arrested for debt, ...	June 23,	-	June 23, 1746.
148	Chapter 4. An act for granting the sum of fourteen hundred and forty pounds for the support of his majesty's governour, . .	June 18,	-	- -
148	Chapter 5. An act for supplying the treasury with the sum of twenty-six thousand and thirty-seven pounds ten shillings in bills of credit, for putting the province in a better posture of defence, for discharging the publick debts, &c., and for drawing in the said bills into the treasury again, and for stating their value in discharging publick debts, ...	June 20,	-	- -
152	Chapter 6. An act to prevent all traiterous correspondence with his majesty's enemies [1706-7, chap. 8; 7 W. III., chap. 3], .	June 26,	-	June 27, 1746,
153	Chapter 7. An act for establishing the wages, &c., of sundry persons in the service of the province, ...	June 30,	-	- -
156	Chapter 8. An act to remove the trial of Jeremy Jude, so called, from the county of Nantucket to the county of Barnstable, ...	June 30,	-	- -
156	Chapter 9. An act for apportioning and assessing a tax of twenty-five thousand pounds, in bills of credit; and also for apportioning and assessing a further tax of eighteen hundred and seventy-one pounds fourteen shillings and eightpence, in bills of credit, paid the representatives for their service and attendance in general court, and travel; as also the sum of one hundred and thirty pounds, fines laid upon several towns for not sending a representative [1741-42, chap. 11, § 16; 1742-43, chap. 3, § 8; 1742-43, chap. 14, § 5; 1744-45, chap. 5, §§ 7 and 10], .	June 30,	-	- -
	SECOND SESSION.			
170	Chapter 10. An act for enlisting into his majesty's service a number of the inhabitants of the towns of Weymouth and Charlestown, so as to make two independent companies of sixty men each, exclusive of officers, for the defence of Castle William, as occasion shall require, . .	Aug. 18,	-	Jan. 17, 1745.
171	Chapter 11. An act for punishing of officers or soldiers who shall mutiny, or desert his majesty's service, ...	Aug. 18,	-	Aug. 30, 1746.
172	Chapter 12. An act in further addition to and explanation of the act for the more speedy finishing of the land-bank or manufactory scheme [1743-44, chap. 17], ...	Aug. 18,	-	- -
	THIRD SESSION.			
176	Chapter 13. An act for establishing and regulating fees within this province [1692-93, chap. 37; 1701-2, chap. 7; 1742-43, chap. 5], .	Oct. 26,	-	Apr. 26, 1746.

List of the Public Acts—Continued.

Page.		TITLES.	Date of Passage.	Disallowed by Privy Council.	Expired or had its effect.
		1744-45.—THIRD SESSION—*Con.*	1744.		
181	Chapter 14.	And act for reviving and continuing sundry laws of this province in this act mentioned, expired or near expiring [1738-39, chap. 25; 1739-40, chap. 3; 1739-40, chap. 8; 1739-40, chap. 12; 1741-42, chap. 6], ...	Oct. 26,	-	Jan. 30, 1752.
182	Chapter 15.	An act for appropriating a part of the island called Governour's Island, in the harbour of Boston, to the public use of this government, ...	Oct. 26,	-	- -
184	Chapter 16.	An act for granting unto his majesty several rates and duties of impost and tunnage of shipping, ...	Oct. 26,	-	Apr. 26, 1746.
		FOURTH SESSION.	1744-45.		
190	Chapter 17.	An act for the supplying the treasury with the sum of ten thousand pounds, for discharging the public[k] debts, &c[a]., and for drawing in the said bills into the treasury again, ...	Jan. 9,	-	- -
193	Chapter 18.	An act in addition to an act [e][i]ntitled "An act for the rel[ei][ie]f of poor prisoners for debt" [1741-42, chap. 6; 1744-45, chap. 14; 1741-42, chap. 12], .	1744. Dec. 26,	-	Jan. 30, 1752.
194	Chapter 19.	An act to encourage the [e][i]nlisting soldiers into his majesty's service, in the intended expedition against Cape Breton, ...	1744-45. Jan. 30,	-	- -
195	Chapter 20.	An act for raising, by a lottery, the sum of seven thousand five hundred pounds, for the service of this province in the present year, ...	Jan. 9,	-	- -
199	Chapter 21.	An act for supplying the treasury with the sum of fifty thousand pounds for putting the province in a better posture of defence, for discharging the public debts, &c., and for drawing in the said bills into the treasury again [1744-45, chap. 22], ...	Feb. 5,	-	- -
202	Chapter 22.	An act for granting to his majesty a duty of tonnage on shipping [1715-16, chap. 4],	1745. April 5,	-	April 6, 1752.
204	Chapter 23.	An act for supplying the treasury with the sum of fifty thousand pounds, for discharging the public[k] debts, &c., and for drawing in the said bills into the treasury again, ...	1744-45. March 9,	-	- -
206	Chapter 24.	An act for granting a sum for the pay of the members of the council and house of representatives, in general court assembled, and for establishing the wages, &c[a]., of sundry persons in the service of the province, ...	1745. April 5,	-	- -
208	Chapter 25.	An act to prevent mischief being done by unruly dogs [1737-38, chap. 10], . .	April 5,	-	June 26, 1755.
209	Chapter 26.	An act to prevent neat cattle and horses, running at large and feeding on the beaches adjoining to Eastern-Harbour Meadows, in the town of Truro [1738-39, chap. 16], ...	April 5,	-	July 3, 1750.
210	Chapter 27.	An act in addition to the act for preventing dam[m]age to the harbour of Cape Cod, by cattle and horse kind feeding on Provincetown lands [1740-41, chap. 15], ...	April 5,	-	- -
211	Chapter 28.	An act to regulate the pay of soldiers and mariners, and to prevent fraud therein [1744-45, chap. 7], ...	April 5,	-	April 6, 1747.

List of the Public Acts—Continued.

Page.	TITLES.	Date of Passage.	Disallowed by Privy Council.	Expired or had its effect.
	1744-45.—FOURTH SESSION—*Con.*	1744-45.		
212	Chapter 29. An act in further addition to an act ascertaining the value of money, and of the bills of public[k] credit of this province [1741-42, chap. 12], ...	Jan. 9,	-	- -
214	Chapter 30. An act for the more speedy extinguishment of fire, and preserving goods [e][i]ndangered by it [1711-12, chap. 5], ...	1745. April 5,	-	- -
215	Chapter 31. An act for ascertaining the bounds of the town of Dighton, and for the confirmation of their powers and privileges [1734-35, chap. 19], ...	1744-45. Jan. 8,	-	- -
	1745-46.—FIRST SESSION.	1745.		
223	Chapter 1. An act for apportioning and assessing a tax of thirty thousand pounds, in bills of credit; and also for apportioning and assessing a further tax of two thousand four hundred and twenty-one pounds eight shillings and sixpence, in bills of credit, paid the representatives for their service and attendance in general court, and travel; and also the sum of two hundred and thirty-five pounds, fines laid upon several towns for not sending a representative [1741-42, chap. 11, § 17; 1742-43, chap. 3, § 9; 1743-44, chap. 13, § 6; 1744-45, chap. 5, § 8; 1744-45, chap. 17, § 5], ...	June 28,	-	- -
236	Chapter 2. An act for granting unto his majesty an excise upon wines and spirits distilled, sold by retail, and upon limes and lemmons, ...	June 29,	-	June 29, 1748.
241	Chapter 3. An act for granting the sum of fifteen hundred pounds for the support of his majesty's governour, ...	June 25,	-	- -
241	Chapter 4. An act for granting a sum for the pay of the members of the council and house of representatives in general court assembled, and for establishing the wages, &c[a]., of sundry persons in the service of the province, ...	June 27,	-	- -
243	Chapter 5. An act for encouraging the killing of wolves, bears, wild cat[t]s and cattamounts, within this province [1741-42, chap. 23], ...	June 29,	-	July 9, 1750.
244	Chapter 6. An act for supplying the treasury with the sum of seventy thousand pounds, for discharging the public debts, &c[a]., and for drawing in the said bills into the treasury again, ...	July 2,	-	- -
248	Chapter 7. An act to prevent unnecessary cost being a[llowed] to parties and witnesses in the several courts of justice within this province, ...	June 29,	-	July 11, 1750.
	SECOND SESSION.			
249	Chapter 8. An act for supplying the treasury with the sum of seventy thousand pounds for the use and service of his majesty's garrison at Louisbourg, and for repairing the fortresses and other buildings there, and for drawing in the said bills into the treasury again, ...	Aug. 2,	-	- -

List of the Public Acts—Continued.

Page.	TITLES.		Date of Passage.	Disallowed by Privy Council.	Expired or had its effect.
	1745-46.—SECOND SESSION—*Con.*		1745.		
251	Chapter 9.	An act to subject the unimproved lands within this province to be sold for payment of taxes assessed on them by order of the great and general court and votes and agreements of the proprietors thereof, ...	July 26,	-	Aug. 7, 1752.
	FOURTH SESSION.				
253	Chapter 10.	An act for reviving an act [e][i]ntitled "An act for establishing and regulating fees within this province," made and pass'd in the eighteenth year of his present majesty's reign [1744-45, chap. 13], ...	Nov. 30,	-	Feb. 14, 1746-47.
	FIFTH SESSION.		1745-46.		
254	Chapter 11.	An act for the supplying the treasury with the sum of fifty thousand pounds, for discharging the publick debts, &c., and for drawing in the said bills into the treasury again, ...	Jan. 10,	-	- -
257	Chapter 12.	An act in addition to an act made and pass'd in the eighteenth and nineteenth year of his present majesty, [e][i]ntitled "An act for granting unto his majesty an excise upon wines and spirits distilled, sold by retail, and upon limes and lemmons" [1745-46, chap. 2], .	Jan. 31,	-	June 29, 1748.
258	Chapter 13.	An act for [e][i]nlisting the inhabitants of Dorchester, Weymouth and Charlestown into his majesty's service for the defence of Castle William, as occasion shall require [1742-43, chap. 26], . .	Jan. 25,	-	June 24, 1748.
259	Chapter 14.	An act for preventing the unnecessary destruction of alewives in the town of Sandwich [1743-44, chap. 26; 1726-27, chap. 3], ...	Jan. 29,	-	Mar. 11, 1748-49.
260	Chapter 15.	An act for supplying the treasury with the sum of twenty thousand pounds, .	Feb. 8,	-	- -
263	Chapter 16.	An act in addition to the act, [e][i]ntitled "An act for appointing commissioners of sewers" [1702, chap. 11; 1726-27, chap. 3], ...	Feb. 6,	-	Mar. 27, 1751.
264	Chapter 17.	An act for reviving and continuing sundry laws of this province in this act mentioned, expired, or near expiring [1740-41, chap. 19; 1742-43, chap. 18; 1742-43, chap. 22; 1742-43, chap. 29] . .	Jan. 29,	-	Apr. 13, 1753.
265	Chapter 18.	An act impowering the superio[u]r court of judicature, court of assize and general goal delivery, at their present term, to proceed to the trial of sundry prisoners now in his majesty's goal in the county of Suffolk, ...	1746. Apr. 24,	-	- -
265	Chapter 19.	An act in addition to an act, [e][i]ntitled "An act directing how rates and taxes to be granted by the general assembly, as also county, town, and precinct rates shall be assessed and collected," made and pass'd in the fourth year of his present majesty's reign [1730, chap. 1; 1743-44, chap. 11], ...	1745-46. Feb. 8.	-	- -
267	Chapter 20.	An aet in addition to, and for rendring more effectual, the laws already in being for preventing the destruction of the			

List of the Public Acts—Continued.

Page.		TITLES.	Date of Passage.	Disallowed by Privy Council.	Expired or had its effect.
		1745-46.—FIFTH SESSION—*Con.*	1745-46.		
		fish called alewives, and other fish [1741-42, chap. 16, § 1; 1743-44, chap. 26, § 1],	Mar. 22,	-	- -
269	Chapter 21.	An act for altering the times for holding the superiour court of judicature, court of assize, and general goal delivery within the counties of Essex and York [1742-43, chap. 32, § 2], ...	1746. Apr. 26,	-	- -
270	Chapter 22.	An act for the explanation and further enforcem[*en*]t of the laws made for the observation of the Lord's day [1741-42, chap. 7; 1692-3, chap. 22], . . .	Apr. 24,	-	- -
271	Chapter 23.	An act for granting unto his majesty several rates and duties of impost and tunnage of shipping, ...	1745-46. Jan. 10,	-	June 30, 1747.
		1746-47.—FIRST SESSION.	1746.		
279	Chapter 1.	An act for apportioning and assessing a tax of twenty-eight thousand four hundred and ninety-nine pounds seven shillings and sixpence, in bills of credit; and also for apportioning and assessing a further tax of two thousand four hundred and forty-two pounds three shillings and ninepence, in bills of credit, paid the representatives for their service and attendance in the general court, and travel; and also the sum of one hundred and twenty-seven pounds ten shillings, fines laid upon several towns for not sending a representative [1741-42, chap. 11, § 18; 1742-43, chap 15, § 1; 1743-44, chap. 13, § 7; 1744-45, chap. 17, § 6], ...	June 26,	-	- -
290	Chapter 2.	An act to prevent soldiers and seamen in his majesty's service from being arrested for debt [1744-45, chap. 3], . . .	June 28,	-	July 1, 1748.
292	Chapter 3.	An act for supplying the treasury with the sum of eighty-two thousand pounds, for carrying on the expedition proposed against Canada, and for discharging the publick debts, &c., and for drawing in the said bills into the treasury again, .	June 10,	-	- -
295	Chapter 4.	An act for granting a sum for the pay of the members of the council and house of representatives, in general court assembled, and for establishing the wages, &c., of sundry persons in the service of the province, ...	June 28,	-	- -
297	Chapter 5.	An act for supplying the treasury with the sum of twenty-five thousand pounds for the expedition against Canada, and for drawing in the said bills into the treasury again, ...	June 13,	-	- -
300	Chapter 6.	An act relating to views by a jury, in civil actions, ...	June 28,	-	Oct. 11, 1751.
300	Chapter 7.	An act for holding a court of oyer and terminer, in and for the island of Nantucket, ...	June 28,	-	- -
301	Chapter 8.	An act for reviving and continuing the laws of this province in this act mentioned, expired or near expiring [1743-44, chap. 6; 1744-45, chap. 6], ...	July 25,	-	Sept. 14, 1753.
		SECOND SESSION.			
302	Chapter 9.	An act for supplying the treasury with the sum of twenty thousand pounds for			

List of the Public Acts—Continued.

Page.		TITLES.	Date of Passage.	Disallowed by Privy Council.	Expired or had its effect.
		1746-47.—SECOND SESSION—*Con.*	1746.		
		the expedition against Canada, and for drawing in the said bills into the treasury again, ...	Aug. 15,	-	- -
		THIRD SESSION.			
305	Chapter 10.	An act in further addition to an act intitled, "An act for highways" [1713-14, chap. 8], ...	Sept. 13,	-	Jan. 27, 1750-51.
305	Chapter 11.	An act to prevent the firing of guns charged with shot[t] or ball in the town of Boston [1713-14, chap. 6], . . .	Sept. 13,	-	Sept. 13, 1749.
306	Chapter 12.	An act in addition to the several acts for the better regulating the Indians [1718-19, chap. 9], ...	Sept. 13,	-	Jan. 25, 1754.
307	Chapter 13.	An act to prevent the great injury and injustice arising to the inhabitants of this province by the frequent and very large emissions of bills of publick credit in the government of Rhode Island [1743-44, chap. 18], ...	Sept. 13,	-	Sept. 13, 1749.
310	Chapter 14.	An act for supplying the treasury with the sum of ten thousand pounds for the expedition against Canada, and for drawing in the said bills into the treasury again, ...	Sept. 13,	-	
		FIFTH SESSION.			
313	Chapter 15.	An act for making the town of Taunton the shire or county town of the county of Bristol, instead of the town of Bristol, and for removing the books of records, and papers, of the county of Bristol, that are in the town of Bristol, to the said town of Taunton, ...	Nov. 13,	-	- -
314	Chapter 16.	An act for supplying the treasury with the sum of twenty thousand two hundred pounds, for discharging the publick debts, &c[a]., and for drawing in the said bills into the treasury again, . .	Nov. 15,	-	- -
		SIXTH SESSION.	1746-47.		
318	Chapter 17.	An act more effectually to prevent profane cursing and swearing, ...	Feb. 10,	-	April 20, 1750.
321	Chapter 18.	An act to enable the proprietors of private ways to repair them in an equal manner, ...	Feb. 13,	-	Mar. 2, 1749-50.
322	Chapter 19.	An act for granting the sum of nineteen hundred pounds for the support of his majesty's governour, ...	Jan. 29,	-	- -
322	Chapter 20.	An act for supplying the treasury with the sum of eight thousand two hundred pounds, for defreying the charge of the late intended expedition against Canada, and for discharging the publick debts, &c[a], and for drawing in the said bills into the treasury again, ...	Jan. 29,	-	- -
324	Chapter 21.	An act to revive and amend an act made in the eighteenth year of his present majesty's reign, intitled "An act for levying soldiers" [1744-45, chap. 2; 1744-45, chap. 2, § 7; 1744-45, chap. 2, § 9; 1744-45, chap. 2, § 13], ...	Feb. 13,	-	Nov. 23, 1748.
326	Chapter 22.	An act for reviving and continuing sundry laws of this province expired or near			

List of the Public Acts—Continued.

Page.		TITLES.	Date of Passage.	Disallowed by Privy Council.	Expired or had its effect.
		1746-47.—SIXTH SESSION—*Con.*	1746-47.		
		expiring [1736-37, chap. 4; 1740-41, chap. 15; 1743-44, chap. 16; 1744-45, chap. 27; 1742-43, chap. 28; 1742-43, chap. 11; 1743-44, chap. 14; 1743-44, chap. 21], ...	Feb. 5,	-	April 20, 1756.
327	Chapter 23.	An act for reviving and continuing a law of this province, intitled "An act for punishing of officers or soldiers who shall mutiny or desert his majesty's service" [1744-45, chap. 11], . . .	Feb. 10,	-	Oct. 7/18, 1748.
		EIGHTH SESSION.	1747.		
328	Chapter 24.	An act for establishing and regulating fees within this province [1692-93, chap. 37; 1701-2, chap. 7; 1744-45, chap. 13; 1745-46, chap. 10], ...	April 25,	-	April 27, 1748.
334	Chapter 25.	An act for supplying the treasury with the sum of twenty thousand pounds, in bills of credit, for discharging the publick debts, and for drawing the said bills into the treasury again, ...	April 7,	-	- -
337	Chapter 26.	An act for the better regulating swine [1736-37, chap. 22], ...	April 25,	-	June 16, 1757.
338	Chapter 27.	An act to prevent dammage being done unto Nossett Meadow by cattle and horse-kind feeding on the beach adjoining thereto [1742-43, chap. 11], . . .	April 25,	-	April 27, 1752.
339	Chapter 28.	An act to prevent the destruction of the meadow[s] called Sandy-Neck Meadow, in Barnstable, and for the better preservation of the harbour there, . . .	April 25,		April 27, 1752.
		1747-48.—FIRST SESSION.			
345	Chapter 1.	An act for apportioning and assessing a tax of thirty-nine thousand one hundred and three pounds thirteen shillings and sevenpence; and also for apportioning and assessing a further tax of two thousand eight hundred and seventy-eight pounds eleven shillings and sixpence, paid the representatives for their service and attendance in the general court, and travel; amounting in the whole to forty-one thousand nine hundred and eighty-two pounds five shillings and [a] [*one*] penny [1744-45, chap. 21, § 4; 1746-47, chap. 4, § 2; 1746-47, chap. 14, § 5; 1746-47, chap. 20, § 5; 1746-47, chap. 25, § 4], . . .	June 29,	-	- -
357	Chapter 2.	An act for supplying the treasury with the sum of eight thousand pounds for defr[e][*a*]ying the charge of the late intended expedition against Canada, and for discharging the publick debts, &c., and for drawing in the said bills into the treasury again, ...	June 29,	-	- -
359	Chapter 3.	An act to prevent the destruction of wild-fowl [1737-38, chap. 16], ...	June 29,	-	July 2, 1752.
360	Chapter 4.	An act to prevent the disturbance given the general court, by coaches, chaises, chairs, carts, trucks, and other carriages, passing by the province court-house in the time of their sitting [1742-43, chap. 12], ...	June 29,	-	July 2, 1748.

List of the Public Acts—Continued.

Page.	TITLES.	Date of Passage.	Disallowed by Privy Council.	Expired or had its effect.
	1747-48.—FIRST SESSION—*Con.*	1747.		
361	Chapter 5. An act to prevent dam[*m*]age being done on the meadows and beaches lying in the township of Barnstable, on the south side of the harbour, contiguous to the [late] common fields in said town,	June 29,	-	July 2, 1752.
362	Chapter 6. An act for reviving and continuing sundry laws of this province, expired or near expiring [1737-38, chap. 6; 1737-38, chap. 8; 1740-41, chap. 6; 1743-44, chap. 20; 1743-44, chap. 22], . . .	June 29,	-	July 2, 1757.
363	Chapter 7. An act to prevent deceit in the gage of cask [1737-38, chap. 12], ...	June 29,	-	July 2, 1757.
363	Chapter 8. An act for granting unto his majesty several rates and duties of impost and tonnage of shipping, ...	June 29,	-	July 2, 1748.
	SECOND SESSION.			
370	Chapter 9. An act for granting a sum for the pay of the members of the council and house of representatives, in general court assembled, and for the establishing the wages, &c., of sundry persons in the service of this province, ...	Sept. 8,	-	- -
371	Chapter 10. An act for granting the sum of nineteen hundred pounds, for the support of his majesty's governour, ...	Aug. 12,	-	- -
372	Chapter 11. An act to enable the proprietors of Suncook to raise money for the support of their present minister, ...	Sept. 8,	-	Sept. 14, 1752.
373	Chapter 12. An act in further addition to and for explanation of certain clauses in three several acts hereinafter mention'd, made and pass'd in the [sixteenth] [*fifteenth*] seventeenth and eighteenth years of his present majesty's reign, for ascertaining the value of money, and of the bills of publick credit of this province [1741-42, chap. 12; 1744-45, chap. 29; 1743-44, chap. 7], ...	Sept. 12,	-	- -
	FOURTH SESSION.			
376	Chapter 13. An act for supplying the treasury with the sum of thirty-four thousand pounds, for discharging the publick debts, &c[a]., and for drawing the said bills into the treasury again, ...	Dec. 12,	-	- -
	FIFTH SESSION.	1747-48.		
380	Chapter 14. An act for supplying the treasury with the sum of twenty-five thousand pounds, for discharging the publick debts, &c[a]., and for drawing the said bills into the treasury again, ...	Feb. 24,	-	- -
382	Chapter 15. An act for altering the times appointed for holding the superiour court of judicature, court of assize and general goal delivery, within and for the counties of Essex and Bristol [1699-1700, chap. 3, § 2; 1742-43, chap. 32, § 2; 1745-46, chap. 21; 1746-47, chap. 15], . . .	Feb. 23,	-	- -
383	Chapter 16. An act for explaining an act, [e][*i*]ntit[*u*]led "An act to prevent and make void clandestine and illegal purchases			

List of the Public Acts—Continued.

Page.		TITLES.	Date of Passage.	Disallowed by Privy Council.	Expired or had its effect.
		1747-48.—FIFTH SESSION—*Con.*	1747-48.		
		of lands from [*the*] Indians," so far as relates to the devi[c][*s*]e or bequest of any real estate by the last will and testament of any Indians [1701-2, chap. 11], ...	March 3,	-	- -
		1748-49.—FIRST SESSION.	1748.		
389	Chapter 1.	An act for apportioning and assessing a tax of ninety-one thousand pounds; and also for apportioning and assessing a further tax of four thousand four hundred and eighteen pounds five shillings, paid the representatives for their service and attendance in the general court, and travel; and ninety pounds, sundry fines imposed on towns for not sending representatives, amounting in the whole to ninety-five thousand five hundred and eight pounds five shillings [1744-45, chap. 21, § 5; 1746-47, chap. 14, § 4; 1747-48, chap. 2, § 3; 1747-48, chap. 13, § 5; 1747-48, chap. 14, § 4; 1747-48, chap. 13, § 7; 1747-48, chap. 13, § 6], .	June 23,	-	- -
403	Chapter 2.	An act for granting unto his majesty several rates and duties of impost and tunnage of shipping, ...	June 23,	-	June 27, 1749.
408	Chapter 3.	An act for supplying the treasury with the sum of one hundred thousand pounds, for discharging the publick debts, &c[a]., and for drawing the said bills into the treasury again, ...	June 23,	-	- -
411	Chapter 4.	An act for granting unto his majesty an excise upon wines and spirits distilled, sold by retail, and upon limes, lemmons and oranges, ...	June 23,	-	June 29, 1751.
417	Chapter 5.	An act for levying soldiers [1744-45, chap. 2; 1746-47, chap. 21], ...	June 24,	-	July 3, 1750.
419	Chapter 6.	An act for continuing sundry laws of this province, expired or near expiring [1737-38, chap. 9; 1738-39, chap. 15; 1740-41, chap. 23; 1741-42, chap. 6], . . .	June 23,	-	June 27, 1758.
420	Chapter 7.	An act for enlisting the inhabitants of Dorchester, Weymouth and Charlestown into his majesty's service for the defence of castle William, as occasion shall require, ...	June 23,	-	Oct. 7/18, 1748.
		SECOND SESSION.			
422	Chapter 8.	An act for granting the sum of twenty-four hundred pounds, for the support of his majesty's governour, ...	Nov. 18,	-	- -
422	Chapter 9.	An act for the ease of prisoners for debt [1740-41, chap. 22], ...	Nov. 11,	-	Feb. 13, 1759.
423	Chapter 10.	An act appointing William Coffin, farmer of excise for the county of Suffolk, in the room of Jeffry Bedgood [1748-49, chap. 4, § 13], ...	Nov. 18,	-	- -
		THIRD SESSION.	1748-49.		
425	Chapter 11.	An act for inquiring into the rateable estate of the province [1741-42, chap. 9],	Jan. 28,	-	- -
426	Chapter 12.	An act for the more easy partition of lands [1742-43, chap. 24; 9 Mass., 374],	Feb. 1,	-	Feb. 2, 1756.
428	Chapter 13.	An act to prevent damage being done on the beach and meadows in Plymouth,			

List of the Public Acts—Continued.

Page.		TITLES.	Date of Passage.	Disallowed by Privy Council.	Expired or had its effect.
		1748-49.—THIRD SESSION—*Con.*	1748-49.		
		adjoining to said beach, commonly known by the name of Plymouth Beach,	Jan. 24,	-	Feb. 2, 1756.
429	Chapter 14.	An act to prevent damage by fire in the towns of Boston and Charlestown, .	Jan. 31,	-	Sept. 1, 1752.
430	Chapter 15.	An act for drawing in the bills of credit of the several denominations which have at any time been issued by this government and are still outstanding, and for ascertaining the rate of coin'd silver in this province for the future, ...	Jan. 26,	-	- -
442	Chapter 16.	An act in further addition to an act entitled "An act for the more speedy finishing the land-bank or manufactory scheme" [1744-45, chap. 12], ...	Jan. 3,	-	- -
444	Chapter 17.	An act in addition to, and for explanation of, an act entitled "An act for limitation of actions, and for avoiding suits at law, where the matter is of long standing" [1740-41, chap. 4, § 1], ...	Feb. 1,	-	- -
		FOURTH SESSION.	1749.		
446	Chapter 18.	An act to prevent damage being done on the beach in Biddeford, and meadows adjoining to said beach, commonly known by the name of Winter Harbour-Beach, ...	April 22,	-	April 27, 1752.
447	Chapter 19.	An act for continuing two laws of this province, in this act mentioned, which are near expiring [1741-42, chap. 18; 1745-46, chap. 14], ...	April 22,	-	April 27, 1754.
		1749-50.—FIRST SESSION.			
465	Chapter 1.	An act for granting the sum of twenty-two hundred pounds, for the support of his majesty's governour, ...	June 23,	-	- -
465	Chapter 2.	An act in addition to the several laws of this province made for regulating of the ferries betwixt Boston and Charlestown, and betwixt Boston and Winnisimet [1710-11, chap. 1; 1718-19, chap. 6; 1739-40, chap. 1], ...	June 29,	-	July 1, 1752.
467	Chapter 3.	An act to prevent the disturbance given the general court by the passing of coaches, chaises, carts, trucks and other carriages by the province court-house [1747-48, chap. 4], ...	June 23,	-	July 1, 1750.
467	Chapter 4.	An act for granting unto his majesty several rates and duties of impost and tunnage of shipping, ...	June 23,	-	July 1, 1750.
		SECOND SESSION.			
474	Chapter 5.	An act for the better regulating the choice of petit jurors [1741-42, chap. 18], .	Aug. 12,	-	Oct. 25, 1756.
476	Chapter 6.	An act for regulating the hospital on Rainsford Island, and further providing in case of sickness [1743-44, chap. 19, 1701-2, chap. 9], ...	Aug. 12,	-	Oct. 25, 1756.
479	Chapter 7.	An act for the punishing such offenders as shall be any ways concerned in contriving, writing or sending any incendiary or menacing letters in order to extort sums of money or other things of value from any of his majesty's good subjects,	Aug. 18,	-	Aug. 22, 1752.

List of the Public Acts—Continued.

Page.	TITLES.		Date of Passage.	Disallowed by Privy Council.	Expired or had its effect.
	1749-50.—THIRD SESSION.		1749-50.		
480	Chapter 8.	An act in addition to, and rendring more effectual, an act intitled "An act for drawing in the bills of credit of the several denominations which have at any time been issued by this government, and are still outstanding, and for ascertaining the rate of coined silver in this province for the future," made in the twenty-second year of his present majesty's reign [1748-49, chap. 15], .	Jan. 18,	-	- -
			1749.		
481	Chapter 9.	An act to prevent vexatious law-suits, .	Dec. 29,	-	- -
481	Chapter 10.	An act in addition to the act to enable two justices to adjourn a court upon special occasions [1694-95, chap. 21, § 2], .	1749-50. Jan. 22,	-	- -
482	Chapter 11.	An act to allow the town of Swanzey, in the county of Bristol, to set up and carry on a lottery for the rebuilding and keeping in repair Miles' Bridge, in said town [1719-20, chap. 8; 1732-33, chap. 14], ...	1749. Dec. 11,	-	- -
483	Chapter 12.	An act to prevent the unnecessary destruction of alewives in the town of Middleborough [1745-46, chap. 20; 1723-24, chap. 10], ...	Dec. 23,	-	Jan. 9, 1753.
485	Chapter 13.	An act to prevent any person's obstructing the fish in their passing up into Monatiquot River, within the town of Braintre[y][e], ...	Dec. 12,	-	Feb. 1, 1753.
485	Chapter 14.	An act to prevent damage being done on the beach, humocks and meadows belonging to the town of Scituate, lying between the southerly end of the Third Cliff, so called, and the mouth of the North River [1723-24, chap. 10], . .	Dec. 13,	-	Jan. 9, 1755.
486	Chapter 15.	An act to prevent damage being done on the meadows lying in the township of Yarmouth, called Nobscusset Meadow,	1749-50. Jan. 2,	-	Jan. 9, 1755.
488	Chapter 16.	An act for reviving and continuing of sundry laws that are expired or near expiring [1740-41, chap. 20; 1741-42, chap 1; 1741-42, chap. 4; 1741-42, chap. 14; 1742-43, chap. 34; 1743-44, chap. 23; 1746-47, chap. 27; 1742-43, chap. 16; 1742-43, chap. 4; 1742-43, chap. 20; 1742-43, chap. 19; 1742-43, chap. 25; 1746-47, chap. 10; 1746-47, chap. 11; 1746-47, chap. 17; 1746-47, chap. 18], ...	Jan. 11,	-	June 20, 1760.
489	Chapter 17.	An act for supplying the treasury with the sum of eighteen thousand four hundred pounds, lawful money, for discharging the publick debts, &c[a]., . . .	Jan. 22,	-	- -
	FOURTH SESSION.		1750.		
493	Chapter 18.	An act in addition to an act made and pass[e]'d in the twenty-second year of his maj[es]ty's reign, intit[u]led "An act for drawing in the bills of credit of the several denominations which have at any time been issued by this gover m[en]t and are still outstanding, and for ascertaining the rate of coined silver in this province for the future" [1748-49, chap. 15; 1749-50, chap. 8], . .	April 12,	-	- -
494	Chapter 19.	An act for ascertaining the rates at which coined silver and gold, and English half-			

List of the Public Acts—Continued.

Page.	TITLES.	Date of Passage.	Disallowed by Privy Council.	Expired or had its effect.
	1749-50.—FOURTH SESSION—*Con.*	1750.		
	pence and farthings, may pass within this government [1748-49, chap. 15, § 9],	March 31,	-	- -
495	Chapter 20. An act in further addition to the several acts of this province made for the distribution and settlement of the estates of intestates [1692-93, chap. 14, § 1; 1700-1701, chap. 4; 1710-11, chap. 2; 1719-20, chap. 10, §§ 3 and 4; 1723-24, chap. 3, § 2; 1730-31, chap. 2; 1733-34, chap. 5; 1734-35, chap. 16], ...	April 12,	-	- -
495	Chapter 21. An act for granting unto his majesty an excise upon sundry articles hereafter enumerated, for and towards the support of his majesty's governm[en]t, of this province [1748-49, chap. 4, § 8], .	April 20,	-	Aug. 1, 1753.
498	Chapter 22. An act against diminishing [and] [*or*] counterfeiting money [1700-1701, chap. 17; 1702-3, chap. 2], ...	April 18,	-	April 21, 1755.
499	Chapter 23. An act in addition to and for rendring more effectual an act for the restraining the taking excessive usury [1693, chap. 1], ...	April 11,	-	April 21, 1755.
500	Chapter 24. An act for preventing stage-plays and other theatrical entertainments, . .	April 11,	-	April 21, 1755.
501	Chapter 25. An act in addition to the act, intit[u]led "An act to prevent damage being done unto Billingsgate Bay, in the town of Eastham, by cattle and horse-kind, and sheep, feeding on the beach and islands adjoining thereto" [1742-43, chap. 11], .	April 17,	-	March 1, 1756.
502	Chapter 26. An act to prevent damage being done on the meadows and beaches lying in and adjoining on the north side of the town of Harwich, between Skeket Harbour, on the east, and Setucket Harbour, on the west, ...	April 18,	-	April 21, 1755.
503	Chapter 27. An act in addition to the act, intit[u]led "An act to encourage the increase of sheep and goats" [1740-41, chap. 23], .	April 12,	-	- -
	1750-51.—FIRST SESSION.			
513	Chapter 1. An act for impowering the province treasurer to borrow the sum of five thousand pounds, for applying the same to discharge the debts of the province, and defrey the charges of government, and for making provision for the repayment of the sum so borrowed, ...	June 21,	-	- -
515	Chapter 2. An act for granting the sum of three hundred pounds for the support of his honor the lieutenant-governour and commander-in-chief, ...	June 29,	-	- -
515	Chapter 3. An act in explanation of an act made and passed in the eighteenth year of his present majesty's reign, entituled "An act for granting to his majesty a duty of tonnage on shipping" [1744-45, chap. 22], ...	June 14,	-	- -
516	Chapter 4. An act for continuing several laws of this province, in this [*act*] mentioned, which are near expiring [1749-50, chap. 3; 1745-46, chap. 7; 1745-46, chap. 5], (1) [1744-45, chap. 26], (2)	June 28,	-	(1) Oct. 11, 1750. (2) July 3, 1750.
517	Chapter 5. An act in addition to the act for the bette[r] regulating swine [1746-47, chap. 26, §§ 1 and 2], ...	June 30,	-	June 16, 1757,

List of the Public Acts—Continued.

Page.		TITLES.	Date of Passage.	Disallowed by Privy Council.	Expired or had its effect.
		1750-51.—FIRST SESSION—*Con.*	1750.		
518	Chapter 6.	An act for granting to his majesty several rates and duties of impost and tonnage of shipping, ...	June 30,	-	June 30, 1751.
		SECOND SESSION.			
525	Chapter 7.	An act in explanation of an act made in the reign of King William the Third, intitled, "An act for review in civil causes" [1701-2, chap. 6], ...	Oct. 6,	-	- -
525	Chapter 8.	An act for establishing and regulating fees of the several officers, within this province, as are hereafter mentioned [1746-47, chap. 24], ...	Oct. 9,		Jan. 5, 1753.
531	Chapter 9.	An act for impowering the province treasurer to borrow the sum of four thousand pounds, for applying the same to discharge the debts of the province, and defrey the charges of government, and for making provision for the repayment of the sum so borrowed, ...	Oct. 10,	-	- -
533	Chapter 10.	An act in further addition to an act, intitled "An act for rendring more effectual the laws already in being, relating to the admeasurement of boards," &c., "and for preventing fraud and abuse in shingles" &c. [1743-44, chap. 22], . .	Oct. 10,	-	Oct. 12, 1755.
534	Chapter 11.	An act in addition to and explanation of an act made this present year, intitled "An act for granting unto his majesty several rates and duties of impost and tonnage of shipping" [1750-51, chap. 6],	Oct. 6,	-	- -
		THIRD SESSION.	1750-51.		
536	Chapter 12.	An act to regulate the importation of Germans and other passengers coming to settle in this province, ...	Feb. 6,		
537	Chapter 13.	An act for holding a superiour court of judicature, court of assize and general goal delivery at other times than those already appointed by law [1747-48, chap. 15], ...	Feb. 11,	-	- -
538	Chapter 14.	An act for raising the sum of twelve hundred pounds by lottery, for building and maintaining a bridge over the River Parker, in the town of Newbury, at the place called Old Town Ferry, . . .	Jan. 29,	-	- -
539	Chapter 15.	An act for supplying the treasury with twenty-six thousand seven hundred mill'd dollars, ...	Feb. 8,	-	- -
544	Chapter 16.	An act for granting the sum of three hundred pounds, for the support of his honor the lieutenant-governour and commander-in-chief, ...	Feb. 15,	-	- -
544	Chapter 17.	An act for preventing and suppressing of riots, routs and unlawful assemblies, .	Feb. 14,	-	Feb. 14, 1754.
546	Chapter 18.	An act in addition to an act, intitled "An act to prevent damage being done on the beach, humocks and meadows belonging to the town of Scituate, lying between the southerly end of the 'Third Clift,' so called, and the mouth of the North River" [1749-50, chap. 14], .	Feb. 8,	-	- -
546	Chapter 19.	An act for granting unto Benjamin Crabb the sole privile[*d*]ge of making candles of coarse spermacæti oyl, ...	Feb. 20,	-	May 31, 1761.

List of the Public Acts—Continued.

Page.		TITLES.	Date of Passage.	Disallowed by Privy Council.	Expired or had its effect.
		1750-51.—FOURTH SESSION.	1751.		
548	Chapter 20.	An act in addition to an act intitled "An act for supplying the treasury with twenty-six thousand seven hundred mill'd dollars" [1750-51, chap. 15, § 6],	April 18,	-	- -
549	Chapter 21.	An act providing for the support of ministers in new plantations [1715-16, chap. 17], ...	*	-	April 27, 1756.
550	Chapter 22.	An act in addition to an act for regulating fences, cattle, &c. [1693-94, chap. 7, § 9],	April 26,	-	April 27, 1756.
551	Chapter 23.	An act in addition to the several laws already in being for the more speedy finishing the land bank or manufactory scheme [1743-44, chap. 17; 1743-44, chap. 17, § 3], ...	April 24,	-	- -
554	Chapter 24.	An act in further addition to an act made and pass'd in the twenty-second year of his present majesty's reign, intitled "An act for drawing in the bills of credit of the several denominations which have at any time been issued by the government and are still outstanding, and for ascertaining the rate of coined silver in this province for the future" [1748-49, chap. 15], . . .	Apr. 26,	-	- -
		1751-52.—FIRST SESSION.			
555	Chapter 1.	An act to enable and impower the inhabitants of new plantations within this province, enjo[y][i]ned and subjected by law, or that may hereafter be enjo[y][i]ned and subjected, to pay province and county taxes, to assess, levy and collect the same, ...	June 21,	-	- -
557	Chapter 2.	An act in addition to an act made and pass[e]'d in the first year of the reign of his majesty King George the First, intitled "An act for building and maintaining a light-house upon the Great Brewster (called 'Beacon-Island'), at the entrance of the harbour of Boston" [1715-16, chap. 4], ...	June 22,	-	June 25, 1753.
557	Chapter 3.	An act for altering the time appointed for holding the court of general sessions of the peace and inferiour court of common pleas, at Concord, within and for the county of Middlesex [1742-43, chap. 32, § 1], ...	June 20,	-	- -
563	Chapter 4.	An act for altering the time for holding the court of general sessions of the peace and the inferiour court of common pleas for the county of Nantucket [1742-43, chap. 32, § 1], ...	June 18,	-	- -
563	Chapter 5.	An act for granting unto his majesty an excise upon wines and spirits distill[e]'d, sold by retail, and upon limes, lemmons and oranges, ...	June 18,	-	June 29, 1752.
573	Chapter 6.	An act for granting the sum of three hundred pounds for the support of his honour the lieutenant-governour and commander-in-chief, ...	June 21,	-	- -
574	Chapter 7.	An act for reviving and continuing sundry laws of this province, that are expired [and] [*or*] near expiring [1738-39, chap.			

* The date of the passage of this act has not been ascertained, owing to the imperfection of the records and the loss of the engrossment. The bill took its first reading, in the council, March 29, 1751.

List of the Public Acts—Continued.

Page.		TITLES.	Date of Passage.	Disallowed by Privy Council.	Expired or had its effect.
		1751-52.—FIRST SESSION—*Con.*	1751.		
		25; 1739-40, chap. 3; 1739-40, chap. 8; 1739-40, chap. 12; 1741-42, chap. 6; 1742-43, chap. 17; 1742-43, chap. 25; 1743-44, chap. 19; 1745-46, chap. 16; 1746-47, chap. 6; 1746-47, chap. 11], .	June 22,	-	July 1, 1754.
575	Chapter 8.	An act for continuing the time for drawing the lottery established by an act pass[e]'d in the twenty-fourth year of his present majesty, intit[u]led "An act for supplying the treasury with twenty-six thousand seven hundred mill'd dollars, and for making further provision relating to said lottery" [1750-51, chap. 15; 1750-51, chap. 20], . .	June 13,	-	- -
576	Chapter 9.	An act for granting to his majesty several rates and duties of impost and tunnage of shipping, ...	June 18,	-	June 18, 1752.
582	Chapter 10.	An act for apportioning and assessing a tax of thirty thousand three hundred and ninety-four pounds, eight shillings and eightpence; and also for apportioning and assessing a further tax of five thousand two hundred and ninety pounds eleven shillings and fourpence, paid the representatives for their service and attendance in the general court and travel[l], and for fines laid on several towns for not sending a representative; amounting in the whole to thirty-five thousand six hundred and eighty-five pounds [1749-50, chap. 17; 1750-51, chap. 1, § 5; 1750-51, chap. 9, § 5], .	June 21,	-	- -
		SECOND SESSION.			
595	Chapter 11.	An act for supplying the treasury with the sum of four thousand five hundred and forty-five pounds [1750-51, chap. 15],	Oct. 9,	-	- -
		THIRD SESSION.	1752.		
596	Chapter 12.	An act in addition to an act made and pass[e]'d in the thirteenth year of King William the Third, intitled "An act providing in case of sickness" [1701-2, chap. 9], ...	Jan. 30,	-	- -
597	Chapter 13.	An act in further addition to the act intitled "An act for review in civil causes" [1701-2, chap. 6; 1720-21, chap. 11; 1732-33, chap. 13; 1734-35, chap. 5; 1750-51, chap. 7], ...	Jan. 30,	-	- -
598	Chapter 14.	An act for erecting the village parish, and middle parish, so called, in the town of Salem, into a distinct and seperate district by the name of Danvers, . .	Jan. 28,	-	- -
599	Chapter 15.	An act for erecting the plantation called the Elbows, into a district by the name of Palmer, ...	Jan. 30,	-	- -
600	Chapter 16.	An act for supplying the treasury with the sum of eighteen thousand six hundred pounds, to be applied to discharge the debts of the province, and defrey the charges of the government, . . .	Jan. 23,	-	- -
603	Chapter 17.	An act for the better regulation of the course of judicial proceedings [1703-4, chap. 13, § 1], ...	Jan. 30,	-	Jan. 31, 1755.

List of the Public Acts—Continued.

Page.	TITLES.	Date of Passage.	Disallowed by Privy Council.	Expired or had its effect.
	1751-52.—THIRD SESSION—*Con.*	1752.		
604	Chapter 18. An act for granting the sum of three hundred pounds for the support of his hono[*u*]r the lieutenant-governo[*u*]r and commander-in-chief, ...	Jan. 30,	-	- -
604	Chapter 19. An act to impower the proprietors of the meeting-house in the first parish in Salem, where the reverend Mr. John Sparhawk now officiates, and also the proprietors of the meeting-house in the third parish in Newbury, where the reverend Mr. John Lowell officiates, to raise money for defr[a][*e*]ying ministerial and other necessary charges [1735-6, chap. 5, § 1], ...	Jan. 29,	-	Jan. 31, 1755.
	1752-53.—FIRST SESSION.			
609	Chapter 1. An act in further addition to the act for limitation of actions, and for avoiding suits at law, where the matter is of long standing [1748-49, chap. 17], . . .	June 5,	-	- -
609	Chapter 2. An act in addition to an act for the more speedy extinguishment of fire and preserving goods endangered by it [1744-45, chap. 30, § 1], ...	June 4,	-	- -
610	Chapter 3. An act for granting unto his majesty an excise upon wines and spirits distilled, sold by retail, and upon limes, lem[*m*]ons and oranges, ...	June 4,	-	June 29, 1753.
615	Chapter 4. An act for granting the sum of three hundred pounds for the support of his honour the lieutenant-governour and commander-in-chief, ...	June 4,	-	- -
616	Chapter 5. An act for altering the times for holding the superiour court of judicature, court of assize and general goal delivery, next to be holden within and for the count[y][*ie*]s of Worcester and Ham[*p*]shire [1742-43, chap. 32, § 2], . . .	June 5,	-	- -
616	Chapter 6. An act enabling the assessors of the town of Stoughton, for the year 1751, as also the assessors of the first and third parishes in said town, to assess the inhabitants of said town and parishes for the several taxes for said year; as also the constables or collectors for said year, to collect the same, ...	June 5,	-	- -
618	Chapter 7. An act for granting to his majesty several rates and duties of impost and tunnage of shipping, [1751-52, chap. 16], . .	June 4,	-	June 16, 1753.
625	Chapter 8. An act for the supply of the treasury with eight thousand one hundred and forty-two pounds four shillings, and for drawing the same again into the treasury; also for apportioning and assessing a tax of twenty-five thousand pounds; and also for apportioning and assessing a further tax of one thousand seven hundred and forty-two pounds four shillings, paid the representatives for their service and attendance in the general court, and travel, and for fines laid on several towns for not sending a representative: amounting in the whole to twenty-six thousand seven hundred forty-two pounds four shillings [1751-52, chap. 16], ...	June 5,	-	- -

List of the Public Acts—Continued.

Page.	TITLES.		Date of Passage.	Disallowed by Privy Council.	Expired or had its effect.
	1752-53.—SECOND SESSION.		1753.		
637	Chapter 9.	An act for dividing the town of Groton, and making a district by the name of Shirley, ...	Jan. 5,	-	- -
638	Chapter 10.	An act for erecting the second precinct, in the town of Northampton, into a seperate district, by the name of Southampton, ...	Jan. 5,	-	- -
639	Chapter 11.	An act for granting the sum of three hundred and fifty pounds, for the support of his honour the lieutenant-govern[*ou*]r, and commander-in-chief, . .	Jan. 5,	-	- -
639	Chapter 12.	An act for further regulating the proceedings of the courts of probate within this province [1692-3, chap. 46, § 2; 1703-4, chap. 12; 1719-20, chap. 10; 1738-9, chap. 23], ...	Jan. 5,	-	Jan. 6, 1756.
641	Chapter 13.	An act for the more easy partition of lands or other real estate given by will, and held in common and undivided among the devisees [1692-3, chap. 14; 1703-4, chap. 12; 1719-20, chap. 10], . . .	Jan. 5,	-	Jan. 6, 1763.
642	Chapter 14.	An act for allowing necessary supplies to the Eastern Indians, and for regulating trade with them, preventing abuses therein, and for the preventing persons hunting on the land to the eastward of Saco river, or trading with them, other than the truck-masters chosen by the general court [1742-43, chap. 2], . .	Jan. 5,	-	Jan. 6, 1756.
644	Chapter 15.	An act in addition to an act pass'd the thirteenth year of his present majesty's reign, [e][i]ntit[u]led "An act further to exempt persons commonly called An[n]abaptists within this province from being taxed for and towards the support of ministers" [1740-41, chap. 6], ...	Jan. 5,	-	Jan. 6, 1758.
645	Chapter 16.	An act to prevent the breaking or damnifying of lamps set up in or near streets, for enlightning the same, . . .	Jan. 5,	-	Jan. 6, 1758.
646	Chapter 17.	An act for reviving and continuing of sundry laws that are expired or near expiring [1745-46, chap. 9; 1746-47, chap. 27; 1746-47, chap. 28; 1747-48, chap. 3; 1748-49, chap. 14; 1748-49, chap. 18; 1749-50, chap. 7; 1740-41, chap. 19; 1742-43, chap. 18; 1742-43, chap. 22; 1749-50, chap. 12; 1749-50, chap. 13], .	Jan. 5,	-	July 11, 1761.
647	Chapter 18.	An act for further preventing all riotous, tumultuous and disorderly assemblies or companies of persons and for preventing bonfires in any of the streets or lanes within any of the towns of this province, ...	Jan. 5,	-	Mar. 10, 1756.
649	Chapter 19.	An act for confirming the proceedings of William Foye, Esq[r]., treasurer of this province, Daniel Russell, Esq[r]., commissioner of impost, and John Wheelwright, Esq[r]., commissary-general, in their respective capacities, ...	Jan. 5,	-	- -
649	Chapter 20.	An act for preventing damage by horses going at large, ...	Jan. 5,	-	Jan. 6, 1758.
	THIRD SESSION.				
651	Chapter 21.	An act for altering the times for holding the superiour court of judicature, court			

List of the Public Acts—Continued.

Page.		TITLES.	Date of Passage.		Disallowed by Privy Council.	Expired or had its effect.
		1752-53.—THIRD SESSION—*Con.*	1753.			
		of assize and general goal delivery, within the counties of Pl[i][*y*]mouth, Barnstable and Bristol [1742-43, chap. 32, § 2; 1747-48, chap. 15; 1746-47, chap. 15], ...	Apr.	12,	-	- -
652	Chapter 22,	An act in addition to the several acts or laws for the suppressing of lotteries [1719-20, chap. 8; 1732-33, chap. 14], .	Apr.	12,	-	- -
652	Chapter 23.	An act for erecting the second precinct in the town of Groton into a seperate district, ...	Apr.	12,	-	- -
653	Chapter 24.	An act for erecting the second precinct in the town of Leicester into a seperate district, ...	Apr.	12,	-	- -
654	Chapter 25.	An act for erecting the northwesterly part of the town of Rutland into a sep[a][*e*]-rate district, ...	Apr.	12,	-	- -
655	Chapter 26.	An act for erecting the second precinct in the town of Hadley, into a seperate district, ...	Apr.	12,	-	- -
656	Chapter 27.	An act for annexing certain lands within this province, to the counties of Hampshire, Worcester and York [1730-31, chap. 8], ...	Apr.	12,	-	- -
656	Chapter 28.	An act for establishing and regulating fees of the several officers within this province hereafter mentioned [1750-51, chap. 8], ...	Apr.	12,	-	June 11, 1756.
		1753-54.—FIRST SESSION.				
669	Chapter 1.	An act in addition to an act, intitled "An act directing how meetings of proprietors of lands lying in common may be called" [13 Allen, 543; 11 Mass., 175],	June	19,	-	- -
670	Chapter 2.	An act for erecting the township of New Salem, so called, in the county of Hampshire, into a district, ...	June	15,	-	- -
671	Chapter 3.	An act for erecting the north-easterly part of the town of Deerfield into a seperate district, ...	June	9,	-	- -
673	Chapter 4.	An act for erecting a place called Sheepscot, in the county of York, into a district by the name of Newcastle, . .	June	19,	-	- -
673	Chapter 5.	An act for granting unto his majesty an excise upon wines and spirits distill[*e*]'d, sold by retail, and upon limes, lemmons and oranges, ...	June	15,	-	July 9, 1754.
679	Chapter 6.	An act for reviving and continuing sundry laws of this province, expired or near expiring [1743-44, chap. 6; 1743-44, chap. 11; 1746-47, chap. 12; 1747-48, chap. 11; 1750-51, chap. 17], . .	June	15,	-	June 23, 1758.
679	Chapter 7.	An act for granting the sum of three hundred and forty pounds, for the support of his honour the lieutenant-govern[*ou*]r and commander-in-chief, . . .	June	11,	-	- -
680	Chapter 8.	An act for granting the sum of fifteen hundred pounds to encourage the manufact-[ory][*ure*] of linnen, ...	June	15,	-	Aug. 1, 1758.
682	Chapter 9.	An act to prevent firing the woods [1742-43, chap. 22; 1745-46, chap. 17], . .	June	19,	-	June 23, 1763.
684	Chapter 10.	An act for the supply of the treasury with nine thousand pounds, and for apportioning the same, and for drawing it into the treasury; and also for assessing a further tax of one thousand five hun-				

List of the Public Acts—Continued.

Page.		TITLES.	Date of Passage.	Disallowed by Privy Council.	Expired or had its effect.
		1753-54.—FIRST SESSION—*Con.*	1753.		
		dred and twenty-three pounds six shillings, paid the representatives for their service and attendance in the general court, and travel, and for fines laid on several towns, for not sending a representative; and the further sums hereafter mentioned, on the towns hereafter named, in the county of Suffolk, for the repairs of the town house; viz[t]., the town of Boston, fifteen hundred and sixteen pounds eighteen shillings and fourpence; the town of Braintree, thirty-six pounds ten shillings; the town of Brookline, nine pounds fifteen shillings; and the town of Chelsea, thirteen pounds six shillings: and also one other tax on the towns hereafter named, in the province, for former arrears now due; viz[t]., the town of Boston, twenty-two pounds eighteen shillings and fivepence; North Yarmouth, twenty-one pounds two shillings and ninepence; Georgetown, fifteen pounds six shillings and tenpence; Kittery, thirty-four pounds eleven shillings and sixpence; Berwick, thirteen shillings and sevenpence; Hopkinston, fifteen shillings and twopence; Cambridge, fourteen shillings and ninepence; Ipswich, sixty-eight pounds five shillings and fourpence; Marblehead, one hundred and eight pounds sixteen shillings and sevenpence; Boxford, thirteen shillings and fourpence; Leicester, five pounds thirteen shillings and fourpence; District of Spencer, two pounds sixteen shillings and eightpence; Bridgwater, fifteen pounds seven shillings and fivepence; Chatham, one pound nineteen shillings:—amounting in the whole to twelve thousand four hundred pounds, ...	June 21,	-	-
696	Chapter 11.	An act for granting to his majesty several rates and duties of impost and tunnage of shipping [1751-52, chap. 16], .	June 15,	-	June 26, 1754.
		SECOND SESSION.			
704	Chapter 12.	An act for setting off the inhabitants, as also estates of the proprietors, of that part of the precinct of Salem and Beverly, so called, which is part of Salem, to the town of Beverly, ...	Sept. 11,	-	- -
705	Chapter 13.	An act to appoint commissioners to examine into the boundary-line or lines between this government and New York, and to treat with the commissioners appointed by the colony of New York respecting the same, ...	Sept. 13,	-	- -
705	Chapter 14.	An act to impower the proprietors of the meeting-house in the first parish in Salem, where the Rev. Mr. Dudley Leavitt now officiates, to raise money to defrey ministerial and other necessary charges [1735-36, chap. 5, § 1], . .	Sept. 14,	-	Sept. 22, 1756.
706	Chapter 15.	An act in addition to an act, intitled "An act for encouraging the killing of wolves, bears, wild-cats and catamounts within this province" [1745-46, chap. 5; 1750-51, chap. 4], ...	Sept. 11,	-	Oct. 20, 1756.

List of the Public Acts—Continued.

Page.		TITLES.	Date of Passage.	Disallowed by Privy Council.	Expired or had its effect.
		1753-54.—THIRD SESSION.	**1754.**		
708	Chapter 16.	An act to incorporate William Starkey and others, by the name of the Marine Society, ...	Jan. 25,	-	- -
709	Chapter 17.	An act in addition to an act, [i][*e*]ntitled "An act impowering justices of the peace to decide differences not exceeding forty shillings" [1697, chap. 8; 1703-4, chap. 12, § 4], ...	Jan. 25,	-	- -
710	Chapter 18.	An act for the more easy recovering the charges that attend the partition and settlement of real estate[s], and to cause the persons interested in such estate[*s*] to be duly notified before partition be ordered, ...	Jan. 25,	-	- -
711	Chapter 19.	An act in addition to an act made in the fifth year of her late majesty Queen Anne, entitled "An act for a new choice of town officers on special occasions" [1706-7, chap. 3, § 2], ...	Jan. 25,	-	- -
711	Chapter 20.	An act in addition to an act, [i][*e*]ntitled "An act against diminishing or counterfeiting money" [1749-50, chap. 22], .	Jan. 25,	-	- -
712	Chapter 21.	An act for incorporating the plantation called Bedford, in the county of Hampshire, into a seperate district by the name of Granville, ...	Jan. 25,	-	- -
713	Chapter 22.	An act for erecting the north parish, in the town of Sunderland, into a seperate district, by the name of Montague, .	Jan. 25,	-	- -
714	Chapter 23.	An act for the effectual preventing the currency of the bills of credit of Connecticut, New Hampshire and Rhode Island, within this province [1748-49, chap. 15, § 11; 1753-54, chap. 23], .	1753. Dec. 27,	-	Mar. 31, 1757.
716	Chapter 24.	An act for supply of the treasury with ten thousand pounds, and applying the same for the discharge of the publick debts [1753-54, chap. 10, § 11; 1751-52, chap. 16], ...	Dec. 18.	-	- -
717	Chapter 25.	An act for granting the sum of fourteen hundred pounds, for the support of his majesty's governour, ...	Dec. 20,	-	- -
717	Chapter 26.	An act for impowering the province treasurer to borrow the sum of five thousand pounds, and for applying the same for the redemption of the bills of credit of this province that are still outstanding, and for making provision for the repayment of the sum so borrowed, .	1754. Jan. 25,	-	- -
719	Chapter 27.	An act to enable the proprietors of Stow, in the county of Middlesex, so often as it shall be thought necessary for them, to raise money for the use of said proprietors; and to tax and assess the original proprietors of said town, and their heirs, in equal proportion to their interest when the first lot[t]s were divided and drawn, ...	Jan. 25,	-	Jan. 26, 1759.
721	Chapter 28.	An act in addition to an act, entitled "An act to enable creditors to receive their just debts out of the effects of their absent or absconding debtors" [1738-39, chap. 15; 1748-49, chap. 6], . .	Jan. 25,	-	- -
721	Chapter 29.	An act in addition to the several laws of this government made for the regulating general fields [1741-42, chap. 3], . .	Jan. 25,	-	Feb. 1, 1757.
722	Chapter 30.	An act for preventing the unnecessary destruction of alewives in the town of			

List of the Public Acts—Continued.

Page.		TITLES.	Date of Passage.	Disallowed by Privy Council.	Expired or had its effect.
		1753-54.—THIRD SESSION—*Con.*	1754.		
		Sandwich [1745-46, chap. 14; 1748-49, chap. 19; 1726-27, chap. 3], . . .	Jan. 25,	-	April 1, 1757.
723	Chapter 31.	An act for preventing mischief by unruly dogs on the islands of Martha's Vineyard, Chebaqnid[o][*u*]ck, and also on the island of Nantucket, . . .	Jan. 11,	-	Mar. 1, 1757.
		FOURTH SESSION.			
725	Chapter 32.	An act for establishing and confirming divers writ[t]s and processes issued out of the office of the clerk of the inferiour court of common pleas for the county of Essex, since the twenty-fourth day of January last, so far as relates to the teste which such writ[t]s and processes bear, ...	March 27,	-	- -
726	Chapter 33.	An act for altering the times appointed for holding the superiour court of judicature, court of assize and general goal delivery, within and for the counties of Essex and York; and also for altering some of the courts of general sessions of the peace and inferiour court of common pleas, within and for the counties of Pl[i][*y*]mouth, Barnstable and York [1742-43, chap. 32; 1745-46, chap. 21], .	Apr. 19,	-	- -
727	Chapter 34.	An act in further addition to the act for limitation of actions, and for avoiding suits in law, where the matter is of long standing [1752-53, chap. 1; 1748-49, chap. 17], ...	Apr. 19,	-	Mar. 31, 1756.
728	Chapter 35.	An act for erecting a new town within the county of Middlesex, by the name of Lincoln, ...	Apr. 19,	-	- -
729	Chapter 36.	An act for dividing the town of Concord, and making a district of the northerly part thereof by the name of Carlisle, .	Apr. 19,	-	- -
730	Chapter 37.	An act for incorporating the plantation called Quabin, in the county of Hampshire, into a town by the name of Greenwich, ...	Apr. 20,	-	- -
731	Chapter 38.	An act for erecting a town in the county of Worcester, at a plantation called Nichewoag, by the name of Petersham,	Apr. 20,	-	- -
732	Chapter 39.	An act to enable the justices of the court of general sessions of the peace, at their several sessions in the county of Dukes County, more effectually to regulate and keep up a constant ferry from Dukes County to Falmouth, in the county of Barnstable [1729-30, chap. 7], . .	Apr. 19,	-	- -
732	Chapter 40.	An act impowering the province treasurer to borrow five thousand three hundred pounds, and for applying the same to defrey the charge of building a fort on Kennebeck River, and for sundry other purposes ordered by this court, . .	Apr. 18,	-	- -
734	Chapter 41.	An act for levying soldiers, and to prevent soldiers and seamen in his majesty's service from being arrested for debt [1748-49, chap. 5], ...	Apr. 20,	-	June 1, 1757.
738	Chapter 42.	An act for further regulating the course of judicial proceedings, ...	Apr. 23,	-	Jan. 25, 1757.
738	Chapter 43.	An act in addition to the act made and pass[*e*]'d in the eighth year of her late majesty Queen Ann[*e*], [e][*i*]ntit[u]led			

List of the Public Acts—Continued.

Page.		TITLES.	Date of Passage.	Disallowed by Privy Council.	Expired or had its effect.
		1753-54.—FOURTH SESSION—*Con.*	1754.		
		"An act for regulating of drains or common shores" [1709-10, chap. 5, § 3],	Apr. 17,	-	June 1, 1759.
739	Chapter 44.	An act to prevent neat-cattle and horses running at large and feeding on the beaches and meadows below the banks, in the town of Truro, from the house of Joshua Atkins to Bound Brook, and also on the common meadow at and about Pamit harbour and river, as far up as the wading-place by John Lumbart's [1750-51, chap. 4], . . .	Apr. 19,	-	June 1, 1757.
		1754-55.—FIRST SESSION.			
749	Chapter 1.	An act for impowering the corporation of Harvard College, in certain cases, to alienate lands or other real estate, and to make sale of a farm in Billerica, .	June 7,	-	- -
750	Chapter 2.	An act to enable John Payne of Boston, gentleman, to attest certain records in the probate office of the county of Suffolk, ...	June 11,	-	- -
750	Chapter 3.	An act for granting unto his majesty an excise upon sundry articles hereafter enumerated, for and towards the support of his maj[*es*]ty's governm[*en*]t of this province [1753-54, chap. 5, § 8], .	June 16,	-	July 1, 1756.
753	Chapter 4.	An act for punishing of officers or soldiers who shall mutiny, or desert his majesty's service, ...	June 19,	-	June 19, 1755.
755	Chapter 5.	An act for reviving and continuing sundry laws of this province, that are expired or near expiring [1738-39, chap. 25; 1739-40, chap. 8; 1739-40, chap. 12; 1741-42, chap. 6; 1742-43, chap. 17; 1742-43, chap. 25; 1743-44, chap. 19; 1745-46, chap. 16; 1746-47, chap. 6; 1746-47, chap. 11], ...	June 16,	-	July 1, 1759.
755	Chapter 6.	An act for granting the sum of thirteen hundred pounds, for the support of his majesty's governo[*u*]r, ...	June 7,	-	- -
756	Chapter 7.	An act for further continuing the act, [e][*i*]ntit[ut]led "An act in addition to an act, intitled 'An act for the better preservation and increase of deer within this province'" [1739-40, chap. 3], .	June 16,	-	July 1, 1764.
756	Chapter 8.	An act to prevent mischief being done by unruly dogs in the town of Beverly, .	June 6,	-	July 1, 1757.
757	Chapter 9.	An act for impowering the province treasurer to borrow the sum of twenty-one hundred and fourteen pounds, and applying the same towards the expence of sending three hundred men eastward [1751-52, chap. 16], ...	June 8,	-	- -
757	Chapter 10.	An act for granting unto his majesty several rates and duties of impost and tunnage of shipping, ...	June 16,	-	June 26, 1755.
764	Chapter 11.	An act for the supply of the treasury with the sum of nine thousand four hundred fifty-six pounds seven shillings and eightpence, and for drawing the same into the treasury again; also for apportioning and assessing a tax of eighteen thousand pounds; and also for apportioning and assessing a further tax of two thousand four hundred and twenty-three pounds one shilling, paid the rep-			

List of the Public Acts—Continued.

Page.		TITLES.	Date of Passage.	Disallowed by Privy Council.	Expired or had its effect.
		1754-55.—FIRST SESSION—*Con.*	1754.		
		resentatives for their service and attendance in the general court, and travel, and for fines laid on several towns for not sending a representative: both which sums amount, in the whole, to twenty thousand four hundred twenty-three pounds one shilling [1753-54, chap. 26, § 6; 1753-54, chap. 40, § 2], .	June 19,	-	- -
		SECOND SESSION.	1755.		
778	Chapter 12.	An act for the better securing and rendering more effectual grants and donations to pious and charitable uses, and for the better support and maintenance of ministers of the gospel, and defr[a][e]ying other charges relating to the publick worship [10 Mass., 97; 12 Mass., 545; 14 Mass., 336; 16 Mass., 493, 497, 501, 507; 10 Pick., 189, 451, 453; 12 Met., 255; 3 Gray, 38, 39, 146; 13 Allen, 505; 10 Allen, 6], ...	Jan. 10,	-	- -
780	Chapter 13.	An act for making an addition to the second precinct in the town of Brookfield, in the county of Worcester, and dividing the first precinct in said town into two precincts, ...	1754. Nov. 8,	-	- -
781	Chapter 14.	An act for setting off the inhabitants, as also the estates, of the westerly part of Oxford into a seperate district, by the name of Charlton, ...	Nov. 21,	-	- -
782	Chapter 15.	An act declaring in what manner the decrees and orders of the governour and council, in controversies concerning marriage and divorce, shall be carried into execution [1692-3, chap. 25, § 4], .	1755. Jan. 8,	-	- -
782	Chapter 16.	An act for granting unto his majesty an excise upon spirits distilled and wine, and upon limes, lemmons and oranges,	1754. Dec. 19,	-	Dec. 26, 1755.
790	Chapter 17.	An act for supplying the treasury with the sum of twenty-three thousand pounds for discharging the publick debts, and for drawing the same into the treasury,	1755. Jan. 8,	-	- -
793	Chapter 18.	An act for granting to his majesty several duties upon vellum, parchment and paper, for two years, towards defreying the charges of this government, . .	Jan. 8,	-	April 30, 1757.
796	Chapter 19.	An act in addition to an act, intit[u]led "An act for granting unto his majesty an excise upon sundry articles hereafter enumerated, for and towards the support of his majesty's government of this province" [1754-55, chap. 3; 1754-55, chap. 16, § 6], ...	Jan. 2,	-	July 1, 1756.
797	Chapter 20.	An act to prevent damage to English grain, arising from barberry-bushes, .	1754. Dec. 26,	-	June 10, 1764.
799	Chapter 21.	An act for the securing the growth and increase of a certain parcel of wood and timber in the townships of Ipswich and Wenham, in the county of Essex, . .	1755. Jan. 9,	-	Jan. 13, 1765.
800	Chapter 22.	An act for continuing an act of this province, intitled "An act to impower the proprietors of the meeting-house in the first parish in Salem, where the Rev[d] Mr. John Sparhawk now officiates, and also the proprietors of the meeting-house in the third parish in Newbury, where			

List of the Public Acts—Continued.

Page.		TITLES.	Date of Passage.	Disallowed by Privy Council.	Expired or had its effect.
		1754-55.—SECOND SESSION—*Con.*	1755.		
		the Rev[d] Mr. John Lowell officiates, to raise money for defreying ministerial and other necessary charges," . .	Jan. 10,	-	April 28, 1760.
800	Chapter 23.	An act for the supply of the treasury with the sum of six thousand pounds, and for applying the same for the payment of the forces raised for the late expedition at Kennebeck [1753-54, chap. 40; 1754-55, chap. 9], ...	1754. Nov. 23,	-	- -
		THIRD SESSION.	1755.		
802	Chapter 24.	An act in further addition to the several laws already in being for the more speedy finishing the land-bank or manufactory scheme [1748-49, chap. 16; 1750-51, chap. 23], ...	Feb. 27,	-	- -
803	Chapter 25.	An act in addition to an act made and pass[e]'d this present year of his majesty's reign, intitled "An act for supplying the treasury with the sum of twenty-three thousand pounds for discharging the publick debts, and for drawing the same into the treasury" [1754-55, chap. 17], ...	Feb. 18,	-	- -
804	Chapter 26.	An act for appointing assayers of potash and pearlash, ...	Feb. 21,	-	July 1, 1760.
806	Chapter 27.	An act for the more effectual carrying into execution such orders as shall, at any time, be given by his majesty's governour or commander-in-chief, at the desire of the two houses of assembly (or of the council, the general court not sitting), for restraining vessels from sailing out of any ports within this province, ...	Feb. 21,	-	Feb. 22, 1756.
807	Chapter 28.	An act in addition to and for rend[e]ring more effectual an act, [e][i]ntitled "An act for granting unto his majesty an excise upon spirits distilled, and wine, and upon limes, lemmons and oranges" [1754-55, chap. 16], ...	Feb. 22,	-	
808	Chapter 29.	An act for reviving a law of this province, made in the twenty-third year of his present majesty's reign, intitled "An act to prevent damage being done on the meadows lying in the township of Yarmouth, called Nobscusset Meadow" [1749-50, chap. 15], ...	Feb. 27,	-	Mar. 1, 1760.
808	Chapter 30.	An act in addition to an act made in the twenty-seventh year of his present majesty's reign, [e][i]ntitled "An act for levying soldiers, and to prevent soldiers and seamen in his majesty's service being arrested for debt" [1753-54, chap. 41], ...	Feb. 27,	-	June 1, 1759.
809	Chapter 31.	An act for preventing the unnecessary destruction of alewives, and other fish, within this province [1735-36, chap. 21; 1741-42, chap. 16, § 5; 1692-93, chap. 28, § 8; 1726-27, chap. 3; 1698, chap. 7], ...	Feb. 26,	-	Mar. 15, 1758.
		FOURTH SESSION.			
812	Chapter 32.	An act impowering the province treasurer to borrow the sum of five thousand			

List of the Public Acts—Continued.

Page.		TITLES.	Date of Passage.	Disallowed by Privy Council.	Expired or had its effect.
		1754-55.—FOURTH SESSION—*Con.*	1755.		
		pounds, and for applying the same to defr[a][e]y the charges of the intended expedition westward, ...	March 29,	-	- -
813	Chapter 33.	An act to impower the agent of this province at the court of Great Britain, to borrow money for the use of the province, ...	March 29,	-	- -
814	Chapter 34.	An act to encourage and facilitate the removal and prevention of French encroachments on his majesty's North American territories, ...	March 29,	-	July 31, 1755.
		1755-56.—FIRST SESSION.			
841	Chapter 1.	An act for granting unto his majesty several rates and duties of impost and tunnage of shipping, ...	June 21,	-	Feb. 26, 1756.
848	Chapter 2.	An act for the supply of the treasury with the sum of ten thousand one hundred and fifteen pounds fourteen shillings, and for drawing the same into the treasury again; also for apportioning and assessing a tax of thirty-six thousand pounds; and also for apportioning and assessing a further tax of three thousand one hundred and fifteen pounds fourteen shillings, paid the representatives for their service and attendance in the general court, and travel, and for fines laid upon towns that did not send a representative: which sums amount, in the whole, to thirty-nine thousand one hundred fifteen pounds fourteen shillings [1754-55, chap. 23, § 2; 1754-55, chap. 17, § 6], ...	June 24,	-	- -
861	Chapter 3.	An act to enable the precinct of Teticut, in the county of Pl[i][y]mouth, to raise a sum, by lottery, towards building a bridge over Teticut River, ...	June 10,	-	- -
861	Chapter 4.	An act for supplying the treasury with the sum of fifty thousand pounds, for discharging the publick debts, and for drawing the same into the treasury, .	June 11,	-	- -
864	Chapter 5.	An act for granting the sum of thirteen hundred pounds, for the support of his majesty's governour, ...	June 10,	-	- -
865	Chapter 6.	An act for the more effectual prevention of supplies of provisions and warlike stores to the French, from any parts of this province [1754-55, chap. 34], . .	June 14,	-	Sept. 12, 1755.
866	Chapter 7.	An act for preventing the exportation of provisions and warlike stores, out of this province, ...	June 25,	-	July 24, 1755.
867	Chapter 8.	An act in addition to an act, intit[u]led "An act for granting to his majesty several duties upon vellum, parchment and paper, for two years, towards defraying the charges of this government" [1754-55, chap. 18], ...	June 25,	-	- -
868	Chapter 9.	An act to prevent damage being done on the beach, humocks and meadows belonging to the town of Scituate, lying between the southerly end of the "Third Cliff," so called, and the mouth of the North River [1749-50, chap. 14; 1726-27, chap. 3], ...	June 25,	-	July 1, 1765.

List of the Public Acts—Continued.

Page.		TITLES.	Date of Passage.	Disallowed by Privy Council.	Expired or had its effect.
		1755-56.—FIRST SESSION—*Con.*	1755.		
869	Chapter 10.	An act for reviving and continuing sundry laws, that are expired and near expiring [1744-45, chap. 25; 1744-45, chap. 26; 1745-46, chap. 7; 1748-49, chap. 13; 1749-50, chap. 22; 1749-50, chap. 23; 1749-50, chap. 24; 1749-50, chap. 26; 1751-52, chap. 17; 1747-48, chap. 4],	June 25,	-	Aug. 15, 1760.
		SECOND SESSION.			
870	Chapter 11.	An act for preventing the exportation of provisions and warlike stores, out of this province, ...	Aug. 16,	-	Sept. 30, 1755.
		THIRD SESSION.			
872	Chapter 12.	An act for the more speedy levying of so[u]ldiers for the expedition against Crown Point [1693-94, chap. 3; 1753-54, chap. 41], ...	Sept. 8,	-	- -
873	Chapter 13.	An act for supplying the treasury with the sum of sixteen thousand pounds, for discharging the publick debts, and for drawing the same into the treasury, .	Sept. 8,	-	- -
874	Chapter 14.	An act for preventing and punishing the desertion of soldiers in the expedition against Crown Point, or in the defence of the frontiers of this government, .	Sept. 9,	-	- -
875	Chapter 15.	An act for apportioning and assessing a tax of eighteen thousand pounds, . .	Sept. 9,	-	- -
		FOURTH SESSION.			
880	Chapter 16.	An act for preventing the exportation of provisions and warlike stores out of this province, ...	Sept. 30,	-	Dec. 1, 1755.
882	Chapter 17.	An act for confirming the proceedings of the general assembly convened on the fifth of September, Anno Domini 1755,	Sept. 27,	-	- -
		FIFTH SESSION.			
883	Chapter 18.	An act impowering the province treasurer to borrow the sum of five thousand pounds, and for applying the same to defrey the charges of the intended expedition against Crown Point, . . .	Nov. 5,	-	- -
884	Chapter 19.	An act for granting the sum of three hundred pounds, for the support of his honour the lieutenant-governour and commander-in-chief, ...	Oct. 29,	-	- -
884	Chapter 20.	An act to prevent the subjects of the French king being supplyed with provisions, ...	Nov. 1,	-	Dec. 1, 1755.
885	Chapter 21.	An act for establishing certain recognizances entred into by persons heretofore licen[s][c]ed to be innholders, taverners and retailers, ...	Nov. 7,	-	- -
886	Chapter 22.	An act in further addition to the act for limitation of actions, and for avoiding suits in law where the matter is of long standing [1753-54, chap. 34; 1748-49, chap. 17], ...	Oct. 31,	-	Mar. 31, 1758.

List of the Public Acts—Continued.

Page.		TITLES.	Date of Passage.	Disallowed by Privy Council.	Expired or had its effect.
		1755-56.—SIXTH SESSION.	1755.		
887	Chapter 23.	An act making provision for the inhabitants of Nova Scotia, sent hither from that government, and lately arrived in this province, ...	Dec. 24,	-	- -
		SEVENTH SESSION.	1756.		
888	Chapter 24.	An act for raising a sum of money by a lottery or lotteries, for the paving and repairing the neck leading out of the town of Boston, called "Boston Neck,"	Jan. 23,	-	- -
891	Chapter 25.	An act for continuing an act made [*and passed*] in the twenty-eighth year of his majesty's reign, [e][i]ntitled "An act for granting unto his majesty several rates and duties of impost and t[u][*o*]nnage of shipping" [1754-55, chap. 10], .	Feb. 25,	-	Mar. 26, 1756.
891	Chapter 26.	An act for regulating the grammar school in Ipswich, and for incorporating certain persons to manage and direct the same, ...	Feb. 17,	-	Feb. 26, 1766.
893	Chapter 27.	An act for supplying the treasury with the sum of sixty thousand pounds, .	Feb. 28,	-	- -
898	Chapter 28.	An act for preventing any dangerous contagion that may be occasioned by dogs and other brute creatures, dying of the distemper prevalent among them, lying unburied, ...	March 3,	-	Oct. 1, 1757.
898	Chapter 29.	An act for the supply of the treasury with eleven thousand pounds, . . .	March 10,	-	- -
901	Chapter 30.	An act for preventing the exportation of provisions and warlike stores, out of this province, ...	Feb. 27,	-	June 20, 1756.
903	Chapter 31.	An act for granting unto his majesty an excise upon spirits distilled and wine, and upon limes, lem[*m*]ons and oranges, ...	Feb. 28,	-	Mar. 26, 1757.
915	Chapter 32.	An act subjecting the inhabitants of the island of Nantucket, and the people called Quakers, in other parts of the province, to an assessment towards the charge of defending his majesty's territories, in lieu of their personal service [1737-38, chap. 6; 1747-48, chap. 6], .	March 8,	-	Mar. 12, 1759.
917	Chapter 33.	An act for reviving and continuing an act made and passed in the twenty-eighth year of his present majesty's reign, intitled "An act for granting to his majesty several rates and duties of impost and tonnage of shipping" [1754-55, chap. 10; 1755-56, chap. 1], . . .	March 10,	-	April 26, 1756.
917	Chapter 34.	An act for preventing charge to any particular town or district by means of the inhabitants of Nova Scotia that are or may be sent to this province, . . .	March 9,	-	- -
918	Chapter 35.	An act in addition to an act made in the present year of his majesty's reign, intitled "An act making provision for the inhabitants of Nova Scotia sent hither from that government and lately arrived in this province" [1755-56, chap. 23], .	March 6,	-	June 20, 1757.
919	Chapter 36.	An act to enable the committee of war more effectually to provide necessar[y][*ie*]s for the intended expedition against Crown Point, ...	March 10,	-	- -
920	Chapter 37.	An act in addition to, and for rendering more effectual, an act made in the			

List of the Public Acts—Continued.

Page.		TITLES.	Date of Passage.	Disallowed by Privy Council.	Expired or had its effect.
		1755-56.—SEVENTH SESSION—*Con.*	1756.		
		twenty-eighth year of his present majesty's reign, intitled "An act for granting unto his majesty an excise upon spirits distilled, and wine, and upon limes, lem[*m*]ons and oranges" [1754-55, chap. 16, § 1], ...	March 10,	-	- -
921	Chapter 38.	An act to prevent farmers and collectors of the duties of excise being members of the general court or assembly of this province, ...	March 9,	-	- -
		EIGHTH SESSION.			
922	Chapter 39.	An act for preventing petitions to the general court relating to licences for retailing strong drink, and keeping houses of publick entertainment, ...	April 3,	-	April 1, 1759.
923	Chapter 40.	An act for the more speedy levying of soldiers for the expedition against Crown Point [1753-54, chap. 41], . .	April 13,	-	- -
924	Chapter 41.	An act in addition to an act, intitled "An act for regulating of the militia" [1693-94, chap. 3], ...	April 16,	-	April 16, 1761.
925	Chapter 42.	An act in addition to an act, [e][*i*]ntitled "An act for supplying the treasury with the sum of sixty thousand pounds" [1755-56, chap. 27], ...	April 20,	-	- -
926	Chapter 43.	An act in addition to the several acts and laws of this province now in force respecting poor and idle, disorderly and vagrant persons, ...	April 20,	-	April 30, 1759.
928	Chapter 44.	An act for enquiring into the rateable estates of the province, ...	April 12,	-	- -
930	Chapter 45.	An act for preventing and punishing the desertion of soldiers in the expedition against Crown Point, or in defence of the frontiers of this government, . .	April 20,	-	- -
930	Chapter 46.	An act impowering the province treasurer to borrow the sum of ten thousand pounds, and for applying the same to defr[a][*e*]y the charges of the intended expedition against Crown Point,	April 20,	-	- -
932	Chapter 47.	An act for granting unto his majesty several rates and duties of impost and tunnage of shipping, ...	April 20,	-	Mar. 26, 1757.
		1756-57.—FIRST SESSION.			
967	Chapter 1.	An act for the supply of the treasury with the sum of three thousand and six pounds thirteen shillings and fourpence, and for drawing the same into the treasury again; also for apportioning and assessing a tax of fifty-five thousand five hundred and six pounds thirteen shillings and fourpence, and also for apportioning and assessing a further tax of three thousand one hundred and ninety-three pounds eighteen shillings, paid the representatives for their service and attendance in the great and general court, and travel: which sums amount, in the whole, to fifty-eight thousand seven hundred pounds eleven shillings and fourpence [1754-55, chap. 32, § 2; 1755-56, chap. 4, § 7; 1755-56, chap. 18, § 2; 1755-56, chap. 29, § 4], . . .	June 8,	-	- -

List of the Public Acts—Continued.

Page.		TITLES.	Date of Passage.		Disallowed by Privy Council.	Expired or had its effect.
		1756-57.—FIRST SESSION—*Con.*	1756.			
978	Chapter 2.	An act in addition to the act for enquiring into the rateable estates of the province [1755-56, chap. 44],	June	3,	-	- -
979	Chapter 3.	An act for supplying the treasury with the sum of fifty-eight thousand pounds, to be thence issued for discharging the public[k] debts, and drawing the same into the treasury again,	June	4,	-	- -
982	Chapter 4.	An act to prevent charges arising by sick, lame or otherwise infirm persons, not belonging to this province, being landed and left within the same,	June	8,	-	- -
982	Chapter 5.	An act for [e][*i*]nlisting the inhabitants of Dorchester, Weymouth and Charlestown into his majesty's service for the defence of Castle William, as occasion shall require [1748-49, chap. 7],	June	9,	-	June 10, 1759.
983	Chapter 6.	An act for continuing the act for establishing and regulating the fees of the several officers within this province [1752-53, chap. 28],	June	2,	-	- -
984	Chapter 7.	An act for reviving and continuing sundry laws, that are expired and near expiring [1740-41, chap. 15; 1742-43, chap. 28; 1743-44, chap. 14; 1743-44, chap. 16; 1743-44, chap. 21; 1744-45, chap. 27; 1748-49, chap. 12; 1750-51, chap. 21; 1750-51, chap. 22],	June	10,	-	June 10, 1761.
984	Chapter 8.	An act in addition to and explanation of an act for granting a tax made and pass[*e*]'d in the present session of this court [1756-57, chap. 1, § 11],	June	10,	-	- -
		THIRD SESSION.				
986	Chapter 9.	An act for the better ordering the late inhabitants of Nova Scotia, transported by order of the government there [1755-56, chaps. 23, 34 and 35],	Sept.	11,	-	Oct. 1, 1757.
987	Chapter 10.	An act for continuing an act, intit[u]led "An act to impower the proprietors of the meeting-house in the first parish in Salem, where the Reverend Mr. Dudley Leavitt now officiates, to raise money to defrey ministerial and other necessary charges" [1753-54, chap. 14],	Aug.	27,	-	Nov. 28, 1761.
		FOURTH SESSION.				
988	Chapter 11.	An act in addition to, and for explanation of, an act made in the fourth year of his majesty's reign, intit[*u*]led "An act directing how rates and taxes, to be granted by the general assembly, as also county, town and precinct rates, shall be assessed and collected" [1730, chap. 1, § 13; 1730, chap. 1, § 7],	Oct.	14,	-	- -
989	Chapter 12.	An act for providing and maintaining two armed vessels to guard the coast, and for supplying the treasury with [7] seven thousand pounds for that end [1715-16, chap. 4, § 3],	Oct.	19,	-	Feb. 10, 1763.
995	Chapter 13.	An act for the better regulating the choice of petit jurors [1748-49, chap. 19],	Oct.	13,	-	Feb. 13, 1760.
997	Chapter 14.	An act for preventing all riotous, tumultuous and disorderly assemblies or com-				

List of the Public Acts—Continued.

Page.	TITLES.	Date of Passage.	Disallowed by Privy Council.	Expired or had its effect.
	1756-57.—FOURTH SESSION—*Con.*	1756.		
	panies of persons, and for preventing bonfires in any of the streets or lanes within any of the towns of this province [1752-53, chap. 18], ...	Oct. 15,	-	Oct. 20, 1761.
998	Chapter 15. An act for continuing "An act for preventing the exportation of provisions and warlike stores, out of this province" [1755-56, chap. 11], ...	Oct. 21,	-	Dec. 20, 1756.
	SEVENTH SESSION.	1757.		
999	Chapter 16. An act for altering the times appointed for holding the superiour court of judicature, &c., in the counties of Pl[i][y]mouth, Bristol and Barnstable [1752-53, chap. 21; and see chap. 38, *post*], . .	Feb. 28,	-	- -
1000	Chapter 17. An act in further addition to an act, [e][i]ntitled "An act for regulating the assize of cask, and preventing deceit in packing fish, &c[a], for sale," made in the fourth year of King William and Queen Mary [1692-93, chap. 17], . .	Feb. 25,	-	- -
1001	Chapter 18. An act in addition to an act made and passed in the fifth year of the reign of their late majesties William and Mary, intitled "An act for highways" [1693-94, chap. 6, § 3], ...	Feb. 19,	-	- -
1002	Chapter 19. An act for granting unto his majesty several rates and duties of impost and tunnage of shipping, ...	Feb. 25,	-	Mar. 26, 1758.
1009	Chapter 20. An act in addition to an act, intit[u]led "An act for the better regulating the choice of pet[ty][*it*] jurors" [1756-57, chap. 13, § 1; 1737-38, chap. 20; 1741-42, chap. 18], ...	Jan. 10,	-	- -
1010	Chapter 21. An act for granting unto his majesty an excise upon spirits distilled, and wine, and upon limes, lemmons and oranges,	Feb. 4,	-	Mar. 26, 1758.
1022	Chapter 22. An act for the supply of the treasury with the sum of thirty-five thousand pounds, and for applying the same for the payment of the forces raised for the late expedition against Crown Point, . .	Feb. 9,	-	- -
1024	Chapter 23. An act for the more speedy levying eighteen hundred men, inclusive of officers, to be employed in his majesty's service, ...	Feb. 19,	-	- -
1027	Chapter 24. An act for reviving and continuing sundry laws that are expired and near expiring [1736-37, chap. 4; 1753-54, chap. 29; 1753-54, chap. 31], ...	Feb. 8,	-	April 24, 1762.
1027	Chapter 25. An act for preventing the exportation of provisions and warlike stores out of this province, ...	Feb. 25,	-	July 1, 1757.
1029	Chapter 26. An act in further addition to an act, intitled "An act for regulating of townships, choice of town officers, and setting forth their powers" [1692-93, chap. 28, § 8; 1742-43, chap. 28], . . .	Jan. 29,	-	- -
1030	Chapter 27. An act for the better regulating the fishery, ...	Feb. 14,	-	Mar. 25, 1757.
1030	Chapter 28. An act for further regulating the course of judicial proceedings [1753-54, chap. 42],	Jan. 27,	-	Jan. 28, 1762.
1031	Chapter 29. An act for the supply of the treasury with the sum of three thousand pounds,	Feb. 23,	-	- -
1032	Chapter 30. An act for establishing and regulating the fees of the several officers, within this			

List of the Public Acts—Continued.

Page.		TITLES.	Date of Passage.	Disallowed by Privy Council.	Expired or had its effect.
		1756-57.—SEVENTH SESSION—*Con.*	1757.		
		province, hereafter mentioned [1756-57, chap. 6], ...	Feb. 25,	-	April 25, 1757.
1038	Chapter 31.	An act to prevent damage being done unto Billingsgate Bay, in the town of Eastham, by cattle and horse-kind and sheep feeding on the beach and islands adjoining thereto [1742-43, chap. 11; 1746-47, chap. 22; 1749-50, chap. 25], .	Feb. 11,	-	- -
1040	Chapter 32.	An act for preventing the unnecessary destruction of alewives in the town of Sandwich [1745-46, chap. 14; 1748-49, chap. 19; 1726-27, chap. 3], ...	Feb. 21,	-	April 1, 1760.
		EIGHTH SESSION.			
1042	Chapter 33.	An act for regulating the hospital on Rainsford's Island, and further providing in case of sickness [1749-50, chap. 6; 1701-2, chap. 9], ...	April 13,	-	- -
1044	Chapter 34.	An act for the effectual preventing the currency of the bills of credit of Connecticut, New Hampshire and Rhode Island within this province [1753-54, chap. 23; 1756-57, chap. 34], ...	March 31,	-	Mar. 31, 1762.
1046	Chapter 35.	An act laying an embargo upon ships and other vessels in this province [1754-55, chap. 27], ...	April 7,	-	April 20, 1757.
1047	Chapter 36.	An act to prevent the desertion of soldiers during the present war with France, and the loss of arms, whether lent by his majesty, or belonging to this province [1744-45, chap. 11; 1746-47, chap. 23], .	April 8,	-	- -
1048	Chapter 37.	An act for supplying the treasury with the sum of twelve thousand pounds, . .	April 15,	-	- -
1050	Chapter 38.	An act appointing the times for holding the superiour court[s] of judicature, &c., in the counties of Plymouth and Barnstable for the present year [1756-57, chap. 16], ...	April 14,	-	- -
1050	Chapter 39.	An act for the encouragement of seamen to enlist themselves in such vessels of war as are or shall be commission[e]'d and fitted out by the government during the present war with France, ...	April 23,	-	- -
1051	Chapter 40.	An act for enqu[i]ring into the rateable estates of the province [1755-56, chap. 44; 1756-57, chap. 2], ...	April 23,	-	- -
1053	Chapter 41.	An act for raising a sum of money by lottery for the encouragement of the settlement called Germantown, in the town of Braintree [1750-51, chap. 12, and note], ...	April 15,	-	- -

LIST OF THE TITLES OF PRIVATE ACTS.

Page.	TITLES.	Date of Passage.	Disallowed by Privy Council.
	1742-43.—FIRST SESSION.	1742.	1746.
67	An Act to take off the Entail from certain Lands in Ipswich in the County of Essex, late the Estate of John Wainwright, Esq[r], Deceased, & to enable Christain Wainwright, his Relict, Widow, to sell the same,	June 18,	May 28.
	1754-55.—SECOND SESSION.	1755.	
815	An Act to dissolve the Marriage of Mary Clapham with William Clapham, and to allow her to marry again,	Jan. 10,	-
	1755-56.—FIRST SESSION.	1755.	
939	An Act to dissolve the Marriage of Mary Parker with Phineas Parker, and to allow her to marry again,	June 10,	-
	EIGHTH SESSION.	1756.	
939	An Act to dissolve the Marriage of John Farnum jun[r] with Elisabeth Farnum, and to allow him to marry again,	April 20,	-
	1756-57.—EIGHTH SESSION.	1757.	
1054	An Act to dissolve the marriage of Lydia Kellog with Ephraim Kellog and to allow her to marry again,	April 18,	-
1054	An Act to dissolve the marriage of Jonah Galusha with Sarah Galusha and to allow him to marry again,	April. 22,	-

RESOLVES.

Page.	Acts relating to the general subject-matter. Year.	Chapter.	Subject of the Resolve.	Date.
68	1742-43,	3 and 14,	Resolve recommending to the justices of the Superior Court of Judicature to reconsider judgments upon bonds and mortgages; and as to the chancering the penalties thereof, . . .	June 8, 1743.
432	1748-49,	15, . .	Resolve that where assessments have not been made conformable to the directions of the treasurer, it be forthwith done; and declaring valid assessments so made, ...	Dec. 14, 1749.
449	1748-49,	4, . .	Resolve construing this act as to duties and penalties mentioned, ...	June 23, 1750.
818	1754-55,	11, . .	Resolve relating to the assessment of taxes in Groton, Shirley, Pepperell, Northampton and Southampton, ...	Nov. 5, 1754.
946	1755-56,	12, . .	Resolve for raising five hundred men for Crown Point, &c., ...	June 26, 1755.
947	1755-56,	12, . .	Resolve for raising two thousand men for Crown Point, &c., ...	Sept. 5, 1755.
948	1755-56,	14, . .	Resolve granting bounty for fifteen men for Fort Massachusetts, ...	June 14, 1755.
1064	1756-57,	12, . .	Resolve respecting the assessment of taxes on vessels under this act, ...	Jan. 18, 1757.
1066	1756-57,	12, . .	Resolve concerning the conduct of Capt. Dowse at the time of the capture of the Province Snow, .	June 15, 1758.
1072	1756-57,	21, . .	Resolve extending the time for lodging receipts under this act, ...	Apr. 12, 1757.

VOTES AND ORDERS.

Page.	Year.	Chapter.	Subject.	Date.
67	1742-43,	5, . .	Order that the several officers mentioned in said act take no other fees than what is directed in said act, &c., ...	June 23, 1743.
67	1742-43,	7, . .	Order that the pay of members of the General Court be drawn from the £6,500 appropriation for forts and garrisons, &c., ...	June 30, 1742.
68	1742-43,	9, . .	Order that £8 be granted for payment of Clerk of Court and Attorney for the King at the trial of Harry Jude at Nantucket, ...	Apr. 15, 1743.
68	1742-43,	3 and 14,	Vote directing alterations in the plates for public bills of credit, ...	Jan. 14, 1742-3.
68	1742-43,	3 and 14,	Order directing the printer to print the resolve relating to the equitable payment of debts, to be delivered in duplicate to each member, ...	June 17, 1743.
69	1742-43,	23, . .	Order that Isaac Parker of Charlestown receive for his encouragement in making stone-ware £125, he giving certain security, ...	Sept. 10, 1742.
69	1742-43,	23, . .	Order granting leave to Grace Parker, widow of Isaac Parker, and Thomas Symmes to bring in a bill for granting them the sole privilege of making stone-ware for fifteen years, . . .	Dec. 1, 1742.
69	1742-43,	23, . .	Order extending time for payment of the £125 loaned to Isaac Parker to the last of December, 1751, and allowing the payment of the same in three annual payments, ...	Mar. 10, 1747.
69	1742-43,	23, . .	Order renewing the order of March 10, 1747, . . .	Jan. 1, 1749.
69	1742-43,	23, . .	Order that the £300 old tenor said to be due from the estate of Isaac Parker, deceased, be remitted,	Mar. 9, 1756.
138	1743-44,	13, . .	Order appropriating £2,016 13*s.* 3*d.* 1*fg.*, taken from different appropriations, to "the payment of such grants as are or shall be made by this court," the said sums so taken to be made good to their respective appropriations by the next act for supply of the treasury, ...	Sept. 10, 1743.

Votes and Orders—Continued.

Page.	Acts relating to the general subject-matter. Year.	Chapter.	SUBJECT OF THE RESOLVE.	Date.
138	1743-44,	17, . .	Order that no private company or partnership proceed to the making or emitting of any bills of credit, as a medium of exchange in trade without the allowance and approbation of the general court, ...	Nov. 5, 1714.
140	1743-44,	26, . .	Order referring Timothy Sprague's petition relating to the Mill, &c., at Spot Pond, to the next session, and suspending proceedings, . . .	June 24, 1742.
140	1743-44,	27, . .	Order relating to the settlement of Leicester, in the county of Middlesex, ...	Feb. 15, 1713.
140	1743-44,	27, . .	Order appointing John Chandler, Esq., to lay out the land granted to the town of Leicester, . . .	Feb. 16, 1713.
218	1744-45,	2, . .	Vote establishing wages of the officers appointed for the defence of the frontiers, ...	Oct. 23, 1744.
218	1744-45,	2, . .	Vote granting a bounty for Indian scalps or captives, .	Oct. 25, 1744.
218	1744-45,	12, . .	Order for the burning of bills of the late Land-Bank or Manufactory scheme, ...	Aug. 18, 1744.
218	1744-45,	16, . .	Order freeing certain prize goods from duties of impost, and a further order exempting certain prize goods from duties, ...	Oct. 13, 1744.
218	1744-45,	19, . .	Vote establishing wages for the expedition against Cape Breton, ...	Feb. 8, 1744.
219	1744-45,	20, . .	Order directing the advertizement of the public-lottery act in all the weekly papers in Boston, . .	Jan. 10, 1744.
219	1744-45,	20, . .	Order forbidding delivery of lottery tickets to any Indian, negro or mulatto, &c., ...	Feb. 2, 1744.
219	1744-45,	27, . .	Order appointing a committee in relation to the preservation of Cape Cod harbor, ...	Mar. 20, 1743.
220	1744-45,	27, . .	Order accepting report of committee appointed March 20, 1743, upon Cape Cod harbor, and a committee appointed to bring in a bill, ...	Aug. 17, 1744.
220	1744-45,	31, . .	Order making the South Precinct of Taunton a township, to be named Dighton, ...	May 30, 1712.
220	1744-45,	31, . .	Order accepting report of a committee appointed to run the Dighton lines, and allowing charges, . .	Mar. 2, 1743.
341	1746-47,	1, . .	Vote authorizing assessment and collection of province and county tax in Natick, and the warrants therefor, ...	Oct. 4, 1746.
341	1746-47,	1, . .	Order remitting fine to town of Pembroke, . . .	June 11, 1747.
341	1746-47,	12, . .	Vote appointing time for the choice of guardians to the Indians in the several plantations, . . .	Jan. 3, 1746.
341	1746-47,	12, . .	Order substituting Capt. Thomas Wiswall as guardian over the Indians at Stoughton instead of Andrew Oliver, Esq., excused, ...	Jan. 9, 1746.
341	1746-47,	12, . .	Vote appointing guardians over the Freetown Indians and defining their powers and duties, . .	Jan. 26, 1749.
341	1746-47,	15, . .	Order of notice on petition that Dighton might be made the shire town of Bristol County, . . .	June 5, 1747.
342	1746-47,	15, . .	Order that the petition relating to Dighton, entered June 5, 1747, be dismissed, ...	Aug. 14, 1747.
342	1746-47,	17, . .	Order appointing committee to draft a bill against profane cursing and swearing, ...	Nov. 12, 1746.
342	1746-47,	20, . .	Vote increasing the bounty on Indian scalps and captives,	Apr. 23, 1747.
383	-	-	Order appointing a committee relating to the preservation of books, &c., saved at the burning of the court-house, ...	Dec. 9, 1747.
383	-	-	Order appointing a committee relating to the destruction of the court-house, &c., ...	Dec. 9, 1747.
384	-	-	Order accepting the report of the committee appointed December 9, 1747, ...	Dec. 11, 1747.
384	-	-	Order that the secretary employ clerks to make duplicates of the records of the General Court, . .	Dec. 11, 1747.
384	-	-	Order that the secretary employ some proper persons to put on file the papers saved from the flames, .	Dec. 1, 1749.
384	1747-48,	4, . .	Vote forbidding the beating of drums within ten rods of the court-house during the sessions, . .	June 13, 1746.
384	1747-48,	11, . .	Order that the petition of William Lovejoy and others of Suncook, set off to New Hampshire, be referred to the next May session, ...	Apr. 24, 1747.

Votes and Orders—Continued.

Page.	Acts relating to the general subject-matter.		Subject of the Resolve.	Date.
	Year.	Chapter.		
384	1747–48,	11, . .	Order appointing a committee to consider the petition of William Lovejoy and others of Suncook, .	May 30, 1747.
384	1747–48,	11, . .	Order recommitting report on petition of William Lovejoy and others, with directions to hear parties,	June 3, 1747.
385	1747–48,	15, . .	Order adjourning the Court of General Sessions of the Peace and Inferior Court of Common Pleas, .	Oct. 11, 1746.
448	1748–49,	4, . .	Vote appointing committees for farming out the excise on liquors for the several counties, ...	June 24, 1748.
450	1748–49,	7, . .	Order and vote as to the message of the Governor relating to a threatening letter, . . .	Apr. 21, 1749. Apr. 22, 1749.
454	1748–49,	15, . .	Orders and vote as to memorial of Thomas Hutchinson, Esq., referring to the medium of trade, .	Feb. 16, 1747–8. Feb. 26, 1747–8. Feb. 27, 1747–8.
455	1748–49,	15, . .	Vote dismissing Christopher Kilby, Esq., as the agent for the province, ...	Nov. 17, 1748.
455	1748–49,	15, . .	Order directing the Secretary to notify Mr. Kilby of his dismission from the agency, ...	Nov. 17, 1748.
455 456	1748–49,	15, . .	Votes and orders as to the reimbursement by Parliament for the charges at Cape Breton, .	Nov. 17, 1748. Nov. 18, 1748. Nov. 21, 1748. Nov. 22, 1748.
456	1748–49,	15, . .	Order appointing committee on the governor's message of November 21st, relating to rules in Superior Court, ...	Dec. 22, 1748.
456 457	1748–49,	15, . .	Orders and votes as to the parliamentary grant and the redemption of the bills of public credit, .	Jan. 6, 1748, to Apr. 21, 1759.
504	1749–50,	2, . .	Orders as to petition of Harvard College relating to Charles River Ferry, ...	Jan. 20, 1746. Feb. 13, 1746. June 2, 1747.
504	1749–50,	7, . .	Vote appointing a committee to consider a scandalous letter directed to the governor and council, .	Mar. 21, 1746.
505	1749–50,	7, . .	Order and vote as to threatening letters, ...	Apr. 21, 1749. Aug. 4, 1749.
507	1749–50,	19, . .	Vote relating to the currency of English halfpence, &c., and to the supply of small money for change, .	Jan. 6, 1749.
508	1749–50,	19, . .	Order directing the treasurer as to the payment of silver,	Jan. 30, 1751.
508	1749–50,	21, . .	Orders as to the encouragement of agriculture and the fisheries, and as to a duty upon imports not necessary, ...	June 6, 1749. Dec. 20, 1749.
557	1750–51,	2, . .	Vote that £200 be granted to the Lieut. Governor, . .	Apr. 7, 1750.
557 558	1750–51,	12, . .	Votes and orders concerning the use of the Ship Massachusetts Frigate for importing foreign protestants; and also concerning the sale thereof, &c.,	Jan. 26, 1749. Jan. 27, 1749. June 29, 1750. Apr. 3, 1752.
558 559 560	1750–51,	12, . .	Orders and votes relating to the importation of foreign protestants and the granting of townships for their encouragement, ...	Jan. 11, 1749, to Dec. 4, 1754.
560	1750–51,	14, . .	Order referring the petition of Daniel Farnum for a lottery for building a bridge at Newbury, to the next May session, ...	Apr. 9, 1750.
561	1750–51,	16, . .	Order granting £80 to the Lieut. Governor, . . .	Feb. 8, 1750–1.
561	1750–51,	21, . .	Order and vote relating to the support of ministers of the gospel, &c., ...	Feb. 4, 1747. Mar. 2, 1747.
606	1751–52,	10, . .	Vote relating to the time and manner of payment of taxes, ...	Jan. 3, 1752.
606	1751–52,	12, . .	Vote granting £600 for the relief of the poor of Boston,	June 5, 1752.
663	–	–	Order that the act of parliament, regulating the commencement of the year and correcting the calendar now in use, be printed and bound up with the laws of the province, &c., ...	Jan. 22, 1752.
663	1752–53,	3, . .	Vote appointing committees for each county, to farm out the excise under this act, ...	June 4, 1752.
664	1752–53,	18, . .	Vote appointing committee to draft bill for preventing pageants and shows, ...	Nov. 27, 1752.

Votes and Orders—Continued.

Page.	Acts relating to the general subject-matter. Year.	Chapter.	Subject of the Resolve.	Date.
664	1752-53,	21, . .	Order for adjournment of the Court of Sessions and Inferior Court for Bristol, ...	Dec. 1, 1752.
664 665	1752-53,	24, . .	Orders and vote relating to the erecting the westerly half of Leicester into a township, . .	Nov. 24, 1742. Apr. 2, 1743. July 18, 1744.
665	1752-53,	24, . .	Orders relating to the erecting the easterly part of Leicester and southerly part of Rutland into a new precinct, ...	Sept. 14, 1743. Mar. 22, 1743-4. June 19, 1744.
666	1752-53,	25, . .	Orders relating to the petition of Rutland district for power to levy tax on land, &c., . . .	June 6, 1754. Oct. 26, 1754. Nov. 2, 1754.
741	1753-54,	4, . .	Order setting off the plantation of Sheepscot into a district, ...	Apr. 11, 1753.
741	1753-54,	5, . .	Vote appointing committees for each county, to farm out the excise under this act, ...	June 19, 1753.
742	1753-54,	5, . .	Vote ordering the advertizing of the sale of the excise and fixing the commencement of the same, .	June 19, 1753.
742	1753-54,	5, . .	Orders accepting the reports of committees to farm out excise in the several counties, . . .	Sept. 14, 1753, to Jan. 21, 1754.
743	1753-54,	8, . .	Orders relating to the petition of Andrew Oliver and others for the encouragement of the manufacture of linen, ...	June 2, 1753. June 8, 1753.
744	1753-54,	16, . .	Order granting liberty to bring in a bill to incorporate the "Marine Society at Boston in New England,"	Dec. 26, 1753.
744	1753-54,	23, . .	Order relating to oath prescribed for town officers, . .	Apr. 15, 1754.
744	1753-54,	23, . .	Order as to collection of taxes in the town of Pelham, Order also as to the maintenance of highways in said town, ...	Oct. 25, 1754.
744 745	1753-54,	33, . .	Orders adjourning the Court of Sessions and Inferior Court of Barnstable, ...	Jan. 10, 1749. Jan. 27, 1749.
745	1753-54,	38, . .	Vote empowering John Murray, Esq., to issue a warrant for a meeting of the inhabitants of Petersham, to elect town officers, &c., ...	June 4, 1754.
746	1753-54,	40, . .	Vote relating to the governor's voyage to the Kennebeck, ...	Apr. 11, 1754.
816	1754-55,	1, . .	Order authorizing Harvard College to sell real estate in certain cases, ...	Apr. 19, 1754.
816 817	1754-55,	3, . .	Votes appointing committees for each county, to farm out the excise under this act, . . .	June 15, 1754. Jan. 10, 1755. Aug. 13, 1755.
816	1754-55,	3, . .	Vote ordering the advertizing of the sale of the excise and fixing the commencement of the same, .	June 17, 1754.
816 817	1754-55,	3, . .	Orders accepting reports of committees to farm out excise in the several counties, . . .	Nov. 25, 1754, to June 1, 1756.
817	1754-55,	8, . .	Vote requiring assessors of Beverly to omit taxing under this act for the years 1755 and 1756, . . .	Apr. 23, 1755.
818	1754-55,	9, . .	Vote for enlisting three hundred additional men for the expedition to the Eastward, ...	June 5, 1754.
818	1754-55,	11, . .	Order refunding Beverly £2 6*s.* 9*d.*, overpayment, . .	Nov. 14, 1754.
818 819	1754-55,	13, . .	Vote and orders on petitions of William Ayers and others, relating to the bounds, &c., of the precincts in Brookfield, ...	Apr. 10, 1754. Apr. 10, 1754. Nov. 1, 1754.
819	1754-55,	14, . .	Order of notice on town of Oxford, on petition of William Alton and others, ...	Apr. 9, 1754.
820	1754-55,	15, . .	Order assigning Mary Clapham certain personal estate belonging to William Clapham, ...	Feb. 26, 1755.
823	1754-55,	16, . .	Vote appointing committees for each county, to farm out the excise under this act, ...	Dec. 26, 1754.
823	1754-55,	16, . .	Vote ordering the advertizing of the sale of excise, with power to contract at private sale in certain eases, ...	Dec. 30, 1754.
823	1754-55,	16, . .	Order for committees to meet and agree on suitable times for farming excise, ...	Dec. 30, 1754.

Votes and Orders—Continued.

Page.	Acts relating to the general subject-matter.		Subject of the Resolve.	Date.
	Year.	Chapter.		
823	1754-55,	16, . .	Order appointing committee to prepare letter to Mr. Agent Bollan, concerning this act, ...	June 3, 1755.
824	1754-55,	16, . .	Orders accepting reports of committees to farm out excise in the several counties, ...	Feb. 22, 1755, to June 11, 1755.
834	1754-55,	18, . .	Vote electing a "Commissioner over the Duty of the Stamps," under this act, ...	Jan. 8, 1755.
835	1754-55,	21, . .	Order and vote upon petition of Thomas Brown and others, relating to "Wenham Great Swamp,"	Nov. 6, 1754. Nov. 25, 1754.
835	1754-55,	23, . .	Order as to equipment of officers and soldiers in the expedition to the eastward, ...	Dec. 5, 1754.
836	1754-55,	23, . .	Order allowing Maj. Gen. Winslow £130 for his services at the eastward, ...	Jan. 8, 1755.
836	1754-55,	23, . .	Order granting Gov. Shirley £250 for his services at the eastward, ...	Dec. 21, 1754.
836	1754-55,	26, . .	Vote granting John Franklin and company fifteen hundred acres of land, and exempting men in their employ, ...	Jan. 19, 1754.
836	1754-55,	26, . .	Order appointing committee to consider petition of Thomas Stevens, ...	Nov. 16, 1754.
837	1754-55,	26, . .	Order confirming the fifteen hundred acres of land to John Franklin and company, as laid out, .	Jan. 9, 1755.
837	1754-55,	27, . .	Vote instructing the impost officer and his deputies under this act; and desiring the governor to give orders, ...	Feb. 10, 1756.
837	1754-55,	27, . .	Order directing impost officer, in taking bonds under this act, to exempt codfish exported to Europe, ...	Feb. 12, 1755.
837	1754-55,	27, . .	Vote desiring the governor to lay a general embargo for one month, &c., ...	Feb. 15, 1755.
837	1754-55,	27, . .	Vote desiring the Captain General to extend the embargo on fishing-vessels until the fifteenth of March, ...	Feb. 15, 1755.
837	1754-55,	27, . .	Vote desiring the Governor to take off the embargo upon fishing vessels upon the first of March, . .	Feb. 21, 1755.
838	1754-55,	27, . .	Vote desiring the Governor to write to the commanders of his majesty's ships as to exportations to French settlements, ...	Mar. 26, 1755.
838	1754-55,	27, . .	Order granting leave to Samuel Hews and son to export provisions to Surinam, ...	Apr. 28, 1755.
838	1754-55,	31, . .	Vote exempting a certain cove in Danvers from the effect of this act, ...	Apr. 13, 1756.
838	1754-55,	34, . .	Vote desiring the Governor to give orders for the confinement of the French subjects, and to request the neighboring governments to do the same,	Feb. 15, 1755.
939	1755-56,	1, . .	Vote electing Daniel Russell, Esq., commissioner of impost, ...	June 21, 1755.
940	1755-56,	3, . .	Orders as to a lottery for erecting a bridge over Tetticut river, ...	June 3, 1755. Apr. 14, 1756. Apr. 15, 1756.
941	1755-56,	4, . .	Order appointing a committee to present an address to the Governor, as to Crown Point expedition, .	Feb. 18, 1755.
941	1755-56,	4, . .	Vote appointing a committee to provide provisions and warlike stores for the intended expedition westward, ...	Mar. 26, 1755.
942	1755-56,	4, . .	Order granting additional bounty to soldiers enlisted, and advance pay to non-commissioned officers and privates, ...	Mar. 20, 1755.
942	1755-56,	4, . .	Vote for enlisting three hundred men additional to the twelve hundred already granted, &c., . .	Mar. 29, 1755.
943	1755-56,	4, . .	Vote that there shall be no augmentation of the provincial forces raised for the expedition to Crown Point, ...	June 2, 1755.
943	1755-56,	4, . .	Orders appointing committees on the Governor's messages relating to the expedition to Crown Point, &c., ...	June 3, 1755. June 5, 1755.
944	1755-56,	6, . .	Vote for notifying the other governments of the passage of this act, and desiring them to join, . .	June 14, 1755.

Votes and Orders—Continued.

Page.	Acts relating to the general subject-matter.		Subject of the Resolve.	Date.
	Year.	Chapter.		
944	1755-56,	6, . .	Vote for desiring the southern governments to grant liberty for vessels with provisions to clear for Boston or Salem, ...	Aug. 16, 1755.
944 945	1755-56,	7, . .	Orders relating to the better preventing supplies to the French, ...	June 18, 1755, to June 21, 1755.
945	1755-56,	7, . .	Vote laying a temporary embargo, ...	June 21, 1755.
945	1755-56,	7, . .	Orders relating to the petition of Joshua Winslow for leave to export provisions to Surinam, .	Aug. 12, 1755. Aug. 12, 1755.
945	1755-56,	8, . .	Order allowing £160 to the commissioner of the stamp duties, ...	Apr. 16, 1756.
945 946	1755-56,	11, . .	Orders granting petitions for leave to export, &c., .	Sept. 8, 1755. Sept 8, 1755. Sept. 8, 1755.
946	1755-56,	12, . .	Orders respecting the raising of three hundred men for Crown Point, &c., ...	Aug. 7, 1755. Aug. 8, 1755.
947	1755-56,	12, . .	Order prohibiting the publishing of anything concerning the expedition against Crown Point, &c , .	Sept. 6, 1755.
947	1755-56,	12, . .	Order in relation to the raising of two thousand men for Crown Point, ...	Sept. 6, 1755.
947	1755-56,	12, . .	Votes desiring Col. Richard Gridley to assist in the artillery at Crown Point, and for appointing him a colonel of one of the regiments, .	Sept. 9, 1755. Sept. 9, 1755.
947	1755-56,	12, . .	Vote desiring the Lieut. Governor to issue a proclamation encouraging enlistments, &c , ...	Sept. 9, 1755.
948	1755-56,	14, . .	Vote for a declaration of war against the eastern Indians, except the Penobscot tribe; and that a marching army of three hundred men be enlisted, &c., ...	June 11, 1755.
948	1755-56,	14, . .	Vote providing for garrisons at the different forts, &c.; for additional security to the western frontiers; and for raising additional men by enlistment to scout between the rivers Connecticut and Merrimack, ...	June 11, 1755.
948	1755-56,	14, . .	Vote increasing the force on the western frontiers and offering bounty for enlistments, &c., . .	June 14, 1755.
948	1755-56,	14, . .	Vote for enlisting ten additional men to scout between the rivers Connecticut and Merrimack, &c , . .	Aug. 14, 1755.
949	1755-56,	14, . .	Vote relating to the reinforcement of Fort Dummer, .	Aug. 15, 1755.
949	1755-56,	14, . .	Vote remanding soldiers on furlough and persons absent from duty, &c., ...	Oct. 28, 1755.
949	1755-56,	15, . .	Vote exempting the polls of officers and soldiers in the proposed expedition, ...	Feb. 18, 1756.
949	1755-56,	16, . .	Order granting the petition of John Schollay for leave to export, &c., ...	Nov. 4, 1755.
950	1755-56,	16, . .	Vote for issuing a proclamation forbidding exportation of provisions, &c., ...	Jan. 20, 1756.
950	1755-56,	16, . .	Orders granting several petitions for leave to export, &c., ...	Jan. 29, 1756. Jan. 29, 1756. Feb. 13, 1756. Feb. 14, 1756.
951	1755-56,	23, . .	Orders and vote relating to the French neutrals on board transports in Boston harbor, ...	Nov. 6, 1755. Nov. 7, 1755. Nov. 7, 1755.
951	1755-56,	23, . .	Order and vote relating to the French inhabitants of Nova Scotia sent here by Gov. Lawrence,	Dec. 12, 1755. Dec. 17, 1755.
951 952 953	1755-56,	26, . .	Orders relating to the petitions of Feoffees of Ipswich Grammar School, ...	Sept. 12, 1753, to Apr. 17, 1761.
954 955 956	1755-56,	30, . .	Orders granting several petitions for leave to export, &c.,	Apr. 1, 1756, to Oct. 8, 1756.
957	1755-56,	31, . .	Vote appointing committees for each county, to farm out the excise under this act, ...	Mar. 3, 1756.
957 958	1755-56,	31, . .	Orders accepting reports of committees to farm out excise in the several counties, ...	Apr. 16, 1756, to Aug. 21, 1756.

Votes and Orders—Continued.

Page.	Acts relating to the general subject-matter. Year.	Chapter.	Subject of the Resolve.	Date.
958 959	1755-56,	35, . .	Orders relating to the support of the French neutrals, &c., ...	Dec. 29, 1755, to Feb. 25, 1756.
959 960	1755-56,	35, . .	Orders relating to the petition of Joseph Mitchel, a French neutral, ...	Apr. 20, 1756. Apr. 20, 1756.
960	1755-56,	35, . .	Vote prohibiting the landing of French neutrals, &c., .	Apr. 21, 1756.
960	1755-56,	35, . .	Order as to the disposition of the French families last imported, &c., ...	May 28, 1756.
960	1755-56,	35, . .	Order to prevent the French people from wandering from town to town, &c, ...	June 10, 1756.
960	1755-56,	35, . .	Vote committing to the sheriff of Suffolk the French people sent back from Georgia, &c., . . .	Aug. 17, 1756.
961	1755-56,	35, . .	Order for the distribution among the towns of certain Nova Scotians, ...	Aug. 25, 1756.
961	1755-56,	36, . .	Vote appointing committee to provide provisions, &c., for the expedition against Crown Point, . .	Feb. 19, 1756.
961	1755-56,	36, . .	Votes respecting committee of war to reside near Albany, &c., ...	Feb. 24, 1756. Feb. 25, 1756.
961	1755-56,	36, . .	Vote appointing committee to reside at Albany, to take care of the transportation of provisions, &c., .	Mar. 9, 1756.
961 962	1755-56,	37, . .	Orders accepting reports of committees to farm out excise in the several counties, ...	May 31, 1756, to July 3, 1756.
962	1755-56,	40, . .	Vote respecting the augmentation of the forces for the expedition against Crown Point, ...	Mar. 5, 1756.
962	1755-56,	40, . .	Orders respecting articles of war and court-martial in the army against Crown Point, . . .	Aug. 19, 1756. Aug. 19, 1756.
1054	1756-57,	1, . .	Order relating to the tax of Dunstable, &c., . . .	July 7, 1756.
1054	1756-57,	1, . .	Vote applying the surplusage brought in by this act, .	Aug. 18, 1756.
1054	1756-57,	1, . .	Order relating to the collection of the tax in south parish in Danvers, ...	Jan. 7, 1757.
1055	1756-57,	1, . .	Order for abatement in the tax of Nantucket, . . .	Jan. 17, 1757.
1055	1756-57,	1, . .	Order confirming certain assessments in Taunton, . .	Apr. 7, 1757.
1055	1756-57,	1, . .	Order confirming certain taxes in Lancaster, . . .	Apr. 16, 1757.
1055	1756-57,	1, . .	Vote confirming certain assessments to Sherburne, . .	Apr. 20, 1758.
1055 to 1061	1756-57,	9, . .	Orders and votes respecting the French neutrals, .	May 28, 1756, to Apr. 25, 1757.
1062	1756-57,	12, . .	Vote for equipping the sloop Massachusetts, &c., . .	Aug. 19, 1756.
1062 1063	1756-57,	12, . .	Vote and order respecting the defence of the sea-coast,	Sept. 10, 1756. Oct. 14, 1756.
1063	1756-57,	12, . .	Vote and order appointing committees for each county, to farm out the excise under this act, .	Oct. 20, 1756. Jan. 28, 1757.
1063 1064	1756-57,	12, . .	Orders accepting reports of committees to farm out excise in the several counties, ...	Jan. 13, 1757, to Jan. 10, 1759.
1063	1756-57,	12, . .	Votes relating to the appointment of a collector of excise in Suffolk County, ...	Apr. 22, 1757. Apr. 23, 1757.
1064	1756-57,	12, . .	Vote appointing committees for each county, to farm out the excise under this act, ...	Jan. 11, 1759.
1064	1756-57,	12, . .	Vote suspending action of committees for farming excise,	Mar. 28, 1759.
1064	1756-57,	12, . .	Order appointing committee to examine this act and report concerning defects, ...	Jan. 7, 1757.
1064 1065 1066	1756-57,	12, . .	Votes and orders respecting the equipment, &c., of the vessels for guarding the coast, ...	Feb. 18, 1757, to Mar. 16, 1758.
1066	1756-57,	12, . .	Order for an enquiry into the conduct of the officers and seamen of the Province Snow at the time of her capture, ...	June 2, 1758.
1067	1756-57,	12, . .	Orders relating to the sale of the Province Snow, captured in Louisburg Harbor, &c., . . .	Oct. 7, 1758. Jan. 3, 1759.
1067 1068	1756-57,	12, . .	Votes respecting an establishment, &c., for the province ship King George, ...	Mar. 15, 1759. Mar. 15, 1759. Mar. 28, 1759.
1068	1756-57,	15, . .	Orders granting petitions for leave to export, &c., .	Jan. 7, 1757. Jan. 7, 1757.

Votes and Orders—Concluded.

Page.	Acts relating to the general subject-matter. Year.	Chapter.	Subject of the Resolve.	Date.
1071	1756-57,	16, . .	Order for adjournment of the Superior Court of Judicature for Bristol, ...	June 26, 1755.
1071	1756-57,	19, . .	Order granting a petition for the exemption of certain goods from duty, ...	June 4, 1757.
1071	1756-57,	21, . .	Vote appointing committees for each county, to farm out the excise under this act, ...	Feb. 8, 1757.
1071	1756-57,	21, . .	Order allowing certain charges of sundry committees for farming excise, &c., ...	Feb. 25, 1757.
1072	1756-57,	21, . .	Orders accepting reports of committees to farm out excise in the several counties, ...	Apr. 7, 1757, to Aug. 24, 1757.
1073 to 1077	1756-57,	23, . .	Votes and order respecting the proposals by the Earl of Loudon, ...	Jan. 19, 1757, to Feb. 15, 1757.
1077 1078	1756-57,	23, . .	Votes respecting the wages, bounty, and supply of arms for the forces raised under this act, . .	Feb. 10, 1757, to Feb. 21, 1757.
1079	1756-57,	23, . .	Vote for a message to the Governor respecting the mustering the forces, ...	Feb. 23, 1757.
1079	1756-57,	23, . .	Vote for the appointment of an agent at Albany to take care of the arms, &c., ...	Feb. 24, 1757.
1079	1756-57,	23, . .	Order for furnishing the forces with arms, bayonets and tents, ...	Apr. 2, 1757.
1079	1756-57,	23, . .	Order directing the collectors of arms to prosecute delinquents, ...	Apr. 11, 1757.
1079 1080 1081	1756-57,	23, . .	Votes and orders respecting the billeting, supply and establishment of the forces, ...	Apr. 16, 1757, to Apr. 25, 1757.
1080	1756-57,	23, . .	Vote and order to prevent persons enlisted &c, from being taken out of the service by commitment for debts contracted since their enlistment, &c.,	Apr. 25, 1757. Apr. 25, 1757.
1082	1756-57,	23, . .	Order allowing Col. Joseph Frye certain wages, . .	Mar. 16, 1759.
1082	1756-57,	25, . .	Order respecting bonds at the impost office under this act,	May 31, 1757.
1082	1756-57,	31, . .	Orders relating to the use, &c., of certain beaches and islands in Eastham, ...	June 8, 1756, to Mar. 15, 1758.
1083	1756-57,	32, . .	Order of notice on petition of Plymouth respecting the alewive fishery, ...	Dec. 12, 1757.
1083	1756-57,	35, . .	Orders respecting an embargo on all vessels, . . .	Apr. 4, 1757.
1084	1756-57,	35, . .	Order granting liberty to fishing vessels to be absent twelve days, &c., ...	Apr. 20, 1757.
1085	1756-57,	38, . .	Orders respecting the time and place for holding the several courts, ...	Apr. 6, 1757. Apr. 7, 1757.
1085 1086	1756-57,	40, . .	Orders respecting the valuation of estates, . . .	Sept. 11, 1756. June 11, 1757. Aug. 26, 1757.
1086	1756-57,	41, . .	Order and vote respecting the Germantown lottery, .	Apr. 22, 1757. Jan. 24, 1758.

GENERAL INDEX.

INDEX.

A.

B.

C.

D.

E.

F.

G.

H.

I.

J.

K.

L.

M.

N.

O.

P.

Q.

R.

S.

T.

U.

V.

W.

Y.

Lightning Source UK Ltd.
Milton Keynes UK
UKHW022143201118
332601UK00014B/2150/P

9 780260 699695